Oxford Dictionary of
National Biography

Volume 4

Oxford Dictionary of National Biography

IN ASSOCIATION WITH

The British Academy

From the earliest times to the year 2000

Edited by
H. C. G. Matthew
and
Brian Harrison

Volume 4
Barney–Bellasis

OXFORD
UNIVERSITY PRESS

OXFORD
UNIVERSITY PRESS

Great Clarendon Street, Oxford OX2 6DP

Oxford University Press is a department of the University of Oxford.
It furthers the University's objective of excellence in research, scholarship,
and education by publishing worldwide in

Oxford New York

Auckland Bangkok Buenos Aires Cape Town
Chennai Dar es Salaam Delhi Hong Kong Istanbul Karachi
Kolkata Kuala Lumpur Madrid Melbourne Mexico City Mumbai Nairobi
São Paulo Shanghai Taipei Tokyo Toronto

Oxford is a registered trade mark of Oxford University Press
in the UK and in certain other countries

Published in the United States
by Oxford University Press Inc., New York

British Library Cataloguing in Publication Data
Data available

Library of Congress Cataloging in Publication Data
Data available: for details see volume 1, p. iv

ISBN 0-19-861354-7 (this volume)
ISBN 0-19-861411-X (set of sixty volumes)

Text captured by Alliance Phototypesetters, Pondicherry
Illustrations reproduced and archived by
Alliance Graphics Ltd, UK
Typeset in OUP Swift by Interactive Sciences Limited, Gloucester
Printed in Great Britain on acid-free paper by
Butler and Tanner Ltd,
Frome, Somerset

LIST OF ABBREVIATIONS

1 General abbreviations

AB	bachelor of arts
ABC	Australian Broadcasting Corporation
ABC TV	ABC Television
act.	active
A$	Australian dollar
AD	*anno domini*
AFC	Air Force Cross
AIDS	acquired immune deficiency syndrome
AK	Alaska
AL	Alabama
A level	advanced level [examination]
ALS	associate of the Linnean Society
AM	master of arts
AMICE	associate member of the Institution of Civil Engineers
ANZAC	Australian and New Zealand Army Corps
appx *pl.* appxs	appendix(es)
AR	Arkansas
ARA	associate of the Royal Academy
ARCA	associate of the Royal College of Art
ARCM	associate of the Royal College of Music
ARCO	associate of the Royal College of Organists
ARIBA	associate of the Royal Institute of British Architects
ARP	air-raid precautions
ARRC	associate of the Royal Red Cross
ARSA	associate of the Royal Scottish Academy
art.	article / item
ASC	Army Service Corps
Asch	Austrian Schilling
ASDIC	Antisubmarine Detection Investigation Committee
ATS	Auxiliary Territorial Service
ATV	Associated Television
Aug	August
AZ	Arizona
b.	born
BA	bachelor of arts
BA (Admin.)	bachelor of arts (administration)
BAFTA	British Academy of Film and Television Arts
BAO	bachelor of arts in obstetrics
bap.	baptized
BBC	British Broadcasting Corporation / Company
BC	before Christ
BCE	before the common (*or* Christian) era
BCE	bachelor of civil engineering
BCG	bacillus of Calmette and Guérin [inoculation against tuberculosis]
BCh	bachelor of surgery
BChir	bachelor of surgery
BCL	bachelor of civil law

BCnL	bachelor of canon law
BCom	bachelor of commerce
BD	bachelor of divinity
BEd	bachelor of education
BEng	bachelor of engineering
bk *pl.* bks	book(s)
BL	bachelor of law / letters / literature
BLitt	bachelor of letters
BM	bachelor of medicine
BMus	bachelor of music
BP	before present
BP	British Petroleum
Bros.	Brothers
BS	(1) bachelor of science; (2) bachelor of surgery; (3) British standard
BSc	bachelor of science
BSc (Econ.)	bachelor of science (economics)
BSc (Eng.)	bachelor of science (engineering)
bt	baronet
BTh	bachelor of theology
bur.	buried
C.	command [identifier for published parliamentary papers]
c.	*circa*
c.	*capitulum pl. capitula*: chapter(s)
CA	California
Cantab.	Cantabrigiensis
cap.	*capitulum pl. capitula*: chapter(s)
CB	companion of the Bath
CBE	commander of the Order of the British Empire
CBS	Columbia Broadcasting System
cc	cubic centimetres
C$	Canadian dollar
CD	compact disc
Cd	command [identifier for published parliamentary papers]
CE	Common (*or* Christian) Era
cent.	century
cf.	compare
CH	Companion of Honour
chap.	chapter
ChB	bachelor of surgery
CI	Imperial Order of the Crown of India
CIA	Central Intelligence Agency
CID	Criminal Investigation Department
CIE	companion of the Order of the Indian Empire
Cie	Compagnie
CLit	companion of literature
CM	master of surgery
cm	centimetre(s)

Cmd	command [identifier for published parliamentary papers]		edn	edition
CMG	companion of the Order of St Michael and St George		EEC	European Economic Community
			EFTA	European Free Trade Association
Cmnd	command [identifier for published parliamentary papers]		EICS	East India Company Service
			EMI	Electrical and Musical Industries (Ltd)
CO	Colorado		Eng.	English
Co.	company		enl.	enlarged
co.	county		ENSA	Entertainments National Service Association
col. *pl.* cols.	column(s)		ep. *pl.* epp.	*epistola(e)*
Corp.	corporation		ESP	extra-sensory perception
CSE	certificate of secondary education		esp.	especially
CSI	companion of the Order of the Star of India		esq.	esquire
CT	Connecticut		est.	estimate / estimated
CVO	commander of the Royal Victorian Order		EU	European Union
cwt	hundredweight		ex	sold by (*lit.* out of)
$	(American) dollar		excl.	excludes / excluding
d.	(1) penny (pence); (2) died		exh.	exhibited
DBE	dame commander of the Order of the British Empire		exh. cat.	exhibition catalogue
			f. *pl.* ff.	following [pages]
DCH	diploma in child health		FA	Football Association
DCh	doctor of surgery		FACP	fellow of the American College of Physicians
DCL	doctor of civil law		facs.	facsimile
DCnL	doctor of canon law		FANY	First Aid Nursing Yeomanry
DCVO	dame commander of the Royal Victorian Order		FBA	fellow of the British Academy
DD	doctor of divinity		FBI	Federation of British Industries
DE	Delaware		FCS	fellow of the Chemical Society
Dec	December		Feb	February
dem.	demolished		FEng	fellow of the Fellowship of Engineering
DEng	doctor of engineering		FFCM	fellow of the Faculty of Community Medicine
des.	destroyed		FGS	fellow of the Geological Society
DFC	Distinguished Flying Cross		fig.	figure
DipEd	diploma in education		FIMechE	fellow of the Institution of Mechanical Engineers
DipPsych	diploma in psychiatry			
diss.	dissertation		FL	Florida
DL	deputy lieutenant		*fl.*	*floruit*
DLitt	doctor of letters		FLS	fellow of the Linnean Society
DLittCelt	doctor of Celtic letters		FM	frequency modulation
DM	(1) Deutschmark; (2) doctor of medicine; (3) doctor of musical arts		fol. *pl.* fols.	folio(s)
			Fr	French francs
DMus	doctor of music		Fr.	French
DNA	dioxyribonucleic acid		FRAeS	fellow of the Royal Aeronautical Society
doc.	document		FRAI	fellow of the Royal Anthropological Institute
DOL	doctor of oriental learning		FRAM	fellow of the Royal Academy of Music
DPH	diploma in public health		FRAS	(1) fellow of the Royal Asiatic Society; (2) fellow of the Royal Astronomical Society
DPhil	doctor of philosophy			
DPM	diploma in psychological medicine		FRCM	fellow of the Royal College of Music
DSC	Distinguished Service Cross		FRCO	fellow of the Royal College of Organists
DSc	doctor of science		FRCOG	fellow of the Royal College of Obstetricians and Gynaecologists
DSc (Econ.)	doctor of science (economics)			
DSc (Eng.)	doctor of science (engineering)		FRCP(C)	fellow of the Royal College of Physicians of Canada
DSM	Distinguished Service Medal			
DSO	companion of the Distinguished Service Order		FRCP (Edin.)	fellow of the Royal College of Physicians of Edinburgh
DSocSc	doctor of social science			
DTech	doctor of technology		FRCP (Lond.)	fellow of the Royal College of Physicians of London
DTh	doctor of theology			
DTM	diploma in tropical medicine		FRCPath	fellow of the Royal College of Pathologists
DTMH	diploma in tropical medicine and hygiene		FRCPsych	fellow of the Royal College of Psychiatrists
DU	doctor of the university		FRCS	fellow of the Royal College of Surgeons
DUniv	doctor of the university		FRGS	fellow of the Royal Geographical Society
dwt	pennyweight		FRIBA	fellow of the Royal Institute of British Architects
EC	European Community		FRICS	fellow of the Royal Institute of Chartered Surveyors
ed. *pl.* eds.	edited / edited by / editor(s)			
Edin.	Edinburgh		FRS	fellow of the Royal Society
			FRSA	fellow of the Royal Society of Arts

FRSCM	fellow of the Royal School of Church Music	ISO	companion of the Imperial Service Order
FRSE	fellow of the Royal Society of Edinburgh	It.	Italian
FRSL	fellow of the Royal Society of Literature	ITA	Independent Television Authority
FSA	fellow of the Society of Antiquaries	ITV	Independent Television
ft	foot *pl.* feet	Jan	January
FTCL	fellow of Trinity College of Music, London	JP	justice of the peace
ft-lb per min.	foot-pounds per minute [unit of horsepower]	jun.	junior
FZS	fellow of the Zoological Society	KB	knight of the Order of the Bath
GA	Georgia	KBE	knight commander of the Order of the British Empire
GBE	knight or dame grand cross of the Order of the British Empire	KC	king's counsel
GCB	knight grand cross of the Order of the Bath	kcal	kilocalorie
GCE	general certificate of education	KCB	knight commander of the Order of the Bath
GCH	knight grand cross of the Royal Guelphic Order	KCH	knight commander of the Royal Guelphic Order
GCHQ	government communications headquarters	KCIE	knight commander of the Order of the Indian Empire
GCIE	knight grand commander of the Order of the Indian Empire	KCMG	knight commander of the Order of St Michael and St George
GCMG	knight or dame grand cross of the Order of St Michael and St George	KCSI	knight commander of the Order of the Star of India
GCSE	general certificate of secondary education	KCVO	knight commander of the Royal Victorian Order
GCSI	knight grand commander of the Order of the Star of India	keV	kilo-electron-volt
GCStJ	bailiff or dame grand cross of the order of St John of Jerusalem	KG	knight of the Order of the Garter
		KGB	[Soviet committee of state security]
GCVO	knight or dame grand cross of the Royal Victorian Order	KH	knight of the Royal Guelphic Order
		KLM	Koninklijke Luchtvaart Maatschappij (Royal Dutch Air Lines)
GEC	General Electric Company	km	kilometre(s)
Ger.	German	KP	knight of the Order of St Patrick
GI	government (*or* general) issue	KS	Kansas
GMT	Greenwich mean time	KT	knight of the Order of the Thistle
GP	general practitioner	kt	knight
GPU	[Soviet special police unit]	KY	Kentucky
GSO	general staff officer	£	pound(s) sterling
Heb.	Hebrew	£E	Egyptian pound
HEICS	Honourable East India Company Service	L	lira *pl.* lire
HI	Hawaii	l. *pl.* ll.	line(s)
HIV	human immunodeficiency virus	LA	Lousiana
HK$	Hong Kong dollar	LAA	light anti-aircraft
HM	his / her majesty('s)	LAH	licentiate of the Apothecaries' Hall, Dublin
HMAS	his / her majesty's Australian ship	Lat.	Latin
HMNZS	his / her majesty's New Zealand ship	lb	pound(s), unit of weight
HMS	his / her majesty's ship	LDS	licence in dental surgery
HMSO	His / Her Majesty's Stationery Office	*lit.*	literally
HMV	His Master's Voice	LittB	bachelor of letters
Hon.	Honourable	LittD	doctor of letters
hp	horsepower	LKQCPI	licentiate of the King and Queen's College of Physicians, Ireland
hr	hour(s)		
HRH	his / her royal highness	LLA	lady literate in arts
HTV	Harlech Television	LLB	bachelor of laws
IA	Iowa	LLD	doctor of laws
ibid.	*ibidem*: in the same place	LLM	master of laws
ICI	Imperial Chemical Industries (Ltd)	LM	licentiate in midwifery
ID	Idaho	LP	long-playing record
IL	Illinois	LRAM	licentiate of the Royal Academy of Music
illus.	illustration	LRCP	licentiate of the Royal College of Physicians
illustr.	illustrated	LRCPS (Glasgow)	licentiate of the Royal College of Physicians and Surgeons of Glasgow
IN	Indiana		
in.	inch(es)	LRCS	licentiate of the Royal College of Surgeons
Inc.	Incorporated	LSA	licentiate of the Society of Apothecaries
incl.	includes / including	LSD	lysergic acid diethylamide
IOU	I owe you	LVO	lieutenant of the Royal Victorian Order
IQ	intelligence quotient	M. *pl.* MM.	Monsieur *pl.* Messieurs
Ir£	Irish pound	m	metre(s)
IRA	Irish Republican Army		

m. *pl.* mm.	membrane(s)		ND	North Dakota
MA	(1) Massachusetts; (2) master of arts		n.d.	no date
MAI	master of engineering		NE	Nebraska
MB	bachelor of medicine		*nem. con.*	*nemine contradicente*: unanimously
MBA	master of business administration		new ser.	new series
MBE	member of the Order of the British Empire		NH	New Hampshire
MC	Military Cross		NHS	National Health Service
MCC	Marylebone Cricket Club		NJ	New Jersey
MCh	master of surgery		NKVD	[Soviet people's commissariat for internal affairs]
MChir	master of surgery		NM	New Mexico
MCom	master of commerce		nm	nanometre(s)
MD	(1) doctor of medicine; (2) Maryland		no. *pl.* nos.	number(s)
MDMA	methylenedioxymethamphetamine		Nov	November
ME	Maine		n.p.	no place [of publication]
MEd	master of education		NS	new style
MEng	master of engineering		NV	Nevada
MEP	member of the European parliament		NY	New York
MG	Morris Garages		NZBS	New Zealand Broadcasting Service
MGM	Metro-Goldwyn-Mayer		OBE	officer of the Order of the British Empire
Mgr	Monsignor		obit.	obituary
MI	(1) Michigan; (2) military intelligence		Oct	October
MI1c	[secret intelligence department]		OCTU	officer cadets training unit
MI5	[military intelligence department]		OECD	Organization for Economic Co-operation and Development
MI6	[secret intelligence department]		OEEC	Organization for European Economic Co-operation
MI9	[secret escape service]		OFM	order of Friars Minor [Franciscans]
MICE	member of the Institution of Civil Engineers		OFMCap	Ordine Frati Minori Cappucini: member of the Capuchin order
MIEE	member of the Institution of Electrical Engineers		OH	Ohio
min.	minute(s)		OK	Oklahoma
Mk	mark		O level	ordinary level [examination]
ML	(1) licentiate of medicine; (2) master of laws		OM	Order of Merit
MLitt	master of letters		OP	order of Preachers [Dominicans]
Mlle	Mademoiselle		op. *pl.* opp.	opus *pl.* opera
mm	millimetre(s)		OPEC	Organization of Petroleum Exporting Countries
Mme	Madame		OR	Oregon
MN	Minnesota		orig.	original
MO	Missouri		OS	old style
MOH	medical officer of health		OSB	Order of St Benedict
MP	member of parliament		OTC	Officers' Training Corps
m.p.h.	miles per hour		OWS	Old Watercolour Society
MPhil	master of philosophy		Oxon.	Oxoniensis
MRCP	member of the Royal College of Physicians		p. *pl.* pp.	page(s)
MRCS	member of the Royal College of Surgeons		PA	Pennsylvania
MRCVS	member of the Royal College of Veterinary Surgeons		p.a.	per annum
MRIA	member of the Royal Irish Academy		para.	paragraph
MS	(1) master of science; (2) Mississippi		PAYE	pay as you earn
MS *pl.* MSS	manuscript(s)		pbk *pl.* pbks	paperback(s)
MSc	master of science		*per.*	[during the] period
MSc (Econ.)	master of science (economics)		PhD	doctor of philosophy
MT	Montana		pl.	(1) plate(s); (2) plural
MusB	bachelor of music		priv. coll.	private collection
MusBac	bachelor of music		pt *pl.* pts	part(s)
MusD	doctor of music		pubd	published
MV	motor vessel		PVC	polyvinyl chloride
MVO	member of the Royal Victorian Order		q. *pl.* qq.	(1) question(s); (2) quire(s)
n. *pl.* nn.	note(s)		QC	queen's counsel
NAAFI	Navy, Army, and Air Force Institutes		R	rand
NASA	National Aeronautics and Space Administration		R.	Rex / Regina
NATO	North Atlantic Treaty Organization		*r*	recto
NBC	National Broadcasting Corporation		r.	reigned / ruled
NC	North Carolina		RA	Royal Academy / Royal Academician
NCO	non-commissioned officer			

RAC	Royal Automobile Club		Skr	Swedish krona
RAF	Royal Air Force		Span.	Spanish
RAFVR	Royal Air Force Volunteer Reserve		SPCK	Society for Promoting Christian Knowledge
RAM	[member of the] Royal Academy of Music		SS	(1) *Santissimi*; (2) *Schutzstaffel*; (3) steam ship
RAMC	Royal Army Medical Corps		STB	bachelor of theology
RCA	Royal College of Art		STD	doctor of theology
RCNC	Royal Corps of Naval Constructors		STM	master of theology
RCOG	Royal College of Obstetricians and Gynaecologists		STP	doctor of theology
			supp.	supposedly
RDI	royal designer for industry		suppl. *pl.* suppls.	supplement(s)
RE	Royal Engineers		*s.v.*	*sub verbo* / *sub voce*: under the word / heading
repr. *pl.* reprs.	reprint(s) / reprinted		SY	steam yacht
repro.	reproduced		TA	Territorial Army
rev.	revised / revised by / reviser / revision		TASS	[Soviet news agency]
Revd	Reverend		TB	tuberculosis (*lit.* tubercle bacillus)
RHA	Royal Hibernian Academy		TD	(1) *teachtaí dála* (member of the Dáil); (2) territorial decoration
RI	(1) Rhode Island; (2) Royal Institute of Painters in Water-Colours		TN	Tennessee
RIBA	Royal Institute of British Architects		TNT	trinitrotoluene
RIN	Royal Indian Navy		trans.	translated / translated by / translation / translator
RM	Reichsmark		TT	tourist trophy
RMS	Royal Mail steamer		TUC	Trades Union Congress
RN	Royal Navy		TX	Texas
RNA	ribonucleic acid		U-boat	*Unterseeboot*: submarine
RNAS	Royal Naval Air Service		Ufa	Universum-Film AG
RNR	Royal Naval Reserve		UMIST	University of Manchester Institute of Science and Technology
RNVR	Royal Naval Volunteer Reserve		UN	United Nations
RO	Record Office		UNESCO	United Nations Educational, Scientific, and Cultural Organization
r.p.m.	revolutions per minute		UNICEF	United Nations International Children's Emergency Fund
RRS	royal research ship		unpubd	unpublished
Rs	rupees		USS	United States ship
RSA	(1) Royal Scottish Academician; (2) Royal Society of Arts		UT	Utah
RSPCA	Royal Society for the Prevention of Cruelty to Animals		*v*	verso
			v.	versus
Rt Hon.	Right Honourable		VA	Virginia
Rt Revd	Right Reverend		VAD	Voluntary Aid Detachment
RUC	Royal Ulster Constabulary		VC	Victoria Cross
Russ.	Russian		VE-day	victory in Europe day
RWS	Royal Watercolour Society		Ven.	Venerable
S4C	Sianel Pedwar Cymru		VJ-day	victory over Japan day
s.	shilling(s)		vol. *pl.* vols.	volume(s)
s.a.	*sub anno*: under the year		VT	Vermont
SABC	South African Broadcasting Corporation		WA	Washington [state]
SAS	Special Air Service		WAAC	Women's Auxiliary Army Corps
SC	South Carolina		WAAF	Women's Auxiliary Air Force
ScD	doctor of science		WEA	Workers' Educational Association
S$	Singapore dollar		WHO	World Health Organization
SD	South Dakota		WI	Wisconsin
sec.	second(s)		WRAF	Women's Royal Air Force
sel.	selected		WRNS	Women's Royal Naval Service
sen.	senior		WV	West Virginia
Sept	September		WVS	Women's Voluntary Service
ser.	series		WY	Wyoming
SHAPE	supreme headquarters allied powers, Europe		¥	yen
SIDRO	Société Internationale d'Énergie Hydro-Électrique		YMCA	Young Men's Christian Association
sig. *pl.* sigs.	signature(s)		YWCA	Young Women's Christian Association
sing.	singular			
SIS	Secret Intelligence Service			
SJ	Society of Jesus			

2 Institution abbreviations

All Souls Oxf.	All Souls College, Oxford
AM Oxf.	Ashmolean Museum, Oxford
Balliol Oxf.	Balliol College, Oxford
BBC WAC	BBC Written Archives Centre, Reading
Beds. & Luton ARS	Bedfordshire and Luton Archives and Record Service, Bedford
Berks. RO	Berkshire Record Office, Reading
BFI	British Film Institute, London
BFI NFTVA	British Film Institute, London, National Film and Television Archive
BGS	British Geological Survey, Keyworth, Nottingham
Birm. CA	Birmingham Central Library, Birmingham City Archives
Birm. CL	Birmingham Central Library
BL	British Library, London
BL NSA	British Library, London, National Sound Archive
BL OIOC	British Library, London, Oriental and India Office Collections
BLPES	London School of Economics and Political Science, British Library of Political and Economic Science
BM	British Museum, London
Bodl. Oxf.	Bodleian Library, Oxford
Bodl. RH	Bodleian Library of Commonwealth and African Studies at Rhodes House, Oxford
Borth. Inst.	Borthwick Institute of Historical Research, University of York
Boston PL	Boston Public Library, Massachusetts
Bristol RO	Bristol Record Office
Bucks. RLSS	Buckinghamshire Records and Local Studies Service, Aylesbury
CAC Cam.	Churchill College, Cambridge, Churchill Archives Centre
Cambs. AS	Cambridgeshire Archive Service
CCC Cam.	Corpus Christi College, Cambridge
CCC Oxf.	Corpus Christi College, Oxford
Ches. & Chester ALSS	Cheshire and Chester Archives and Local Studies Service
Christ Church Oxf.	Christ Church, Oxford
Christies	Christies, London
City Westm. AC	City of Westminster Archives Centre, London
CKS	Centre for Kentish Studies, Maidstone
CLRO	Corporation of London Records Office
Coll. Arms	College of Arms, London
Col. U.	Columbia University, New York
Cornwall RO	Cornwall Record Office, Truro
Courtauld Inst.	Courtauld Institute of Art, London
CUL	Cambridge University Library
Cumbria AS	Cumbria Archive Service
Derbys. RO	Derbyshire Record Office, Matlock
Devon RO	Devon Record Office, Exeter
Dorset RO	Dorset Record Office, Dorchester
Duke U.	Duke University, Durham, North Carolina
Duke U., Perkins L.	Duke University, Durham, North Carolina, William R. Perkins Library
Durham Cath. CL	Durham Cathedral, chapter library
Durham RO	Durham Record Office
DWL	Dr Williams's Library, London
Essex RO	Essex Record Office
E. Sussex RO	East Sussex Record Office, Lewes
Eton	Eton College, Berkshire
FM Cam.	Fitzwilliam Museum, Cambridge
Folger	Folger Shakespeare Library, Washington, DC

Garr. Club	Garrick Club, London
Girton Cam.	Girton College, Cambridge
GL	Guildhall Library, London
Glos. RO	Gloucestershire Record Office, Gloucester
Gon. & Caius Cam.	Gonville and Caius College, Cambridge
Gov. Art Coll.	Government Art Collection
GS Lond.	Geological Society of London
Hants. RO	Hampshire Record Office, Winchester
Harris Man. Oxf.	Harris Manchester College, Oxford
Harvard TC	Harvard Theatre Collection, Harvard University, Cambridge, Massachusetts, Nathan Marsh Pusey Library
Harvard U.	Harvard University, Cambridge, Massachusetts
Harvard U., Houghton L.	Harvard University, Cambridge, Massachusetts, Houghton Library
Herefs. RO	Herefordshire Record Office, Hereford
Herts. ALS	Hertfordshire Archives and Local Studies, Hertford
Hist. Soc. Penn.	Historical Society of Pennsylvania, Philadelphia
HLRO	House of Lords Record Office, London
Hult. Arch.	Hulton Archive, London and New York
Hunt. L.	Huntington Library, San Marino, California
ICL	Imperial College, London
Inst. CE	Institution of Civil Engineers, London
Inst. EE	Institution of Electrical Engineers, London
IWM	Imperial War Museum, London
IWM FVA	Imperial War Museum, London, Film and Video Archive
IWM SA	Imperial War Museum, London, Sound Archive
JRL	John Rylands University Library of Manchester
King's AC Cam.	King's College Archives Centre, Cambridge
King's Cam.	King's College, Cambridge
King's Lond.	King's College, London
King's Lond., Liddell Hart C.	King's College, London, Liddell Hart Centre for Military Archives
Lancs. RO	Lancashire Record Office, Preston
L. Cong.	Library of Congress, Washington, DC
Leics. RO	Leicestershire, Leicester, and Rutland Record Office, Leicester
Lincs. Arch.	Lincolnshire Archives, Lincoln
Linn. Soc.	Linnean Society of London
LMA	London Metropolitan Archives
LPL	Lambeth Palace, London
Lpool RO	Liverpool Record Office and Local Studies Service
LUL	London University Library
Magd. Cam.	Magdalene College, Cambridge
Magd. Oxf.	Magdalen College, Oxford
Man. City Gall.	Manchester City Galleries
Man. CL	Manchester Central Library
Mass. Hist. Soc.	Massachusetts Historical Society, Boston
Merton Oxf.	Merton College, Oxford
MHS Oxf.	Museum of the History of Science, Oxford
Mitchell L., Glas.	Mitchell Library, Glasgow
Mitchell L., NSW	State Library of New South Wales, Sydney, Mitchell Library
Morgan L.	Pierpont Morgan Library, New York
NA Canada	National Archives of Canada, Ottawa
NA Ire.	National Archives of Ireland, Dublin
NAM	National Army Museum, London
NA Scot.	National Archives of Scotland, Edinburgh
News Int. RO	News International Record Office, London
NG Ire.	National Gallery of Ireland, Dublin

NG Scot.	National Gallery of Scotland, Edinburgh
NHM	Natural History Museum, London
NL Aus.	National Library of Australia, Canberra
NL Ire.	National Library of Ireland, Dublin
NL NZ	National Library of New Zealand, Wellington
NL NZ, Turnbull L.	National Library of New Zealand, Wellington, Alexander Turnbull Library
NL Scot.	National Library of Scotland, Edinburgh
NL Wales	National Library of Wales, Aberystwyth
NMG Wales	National Museum and Gallery of Wales, Cardiff
NMM	National Maritime Museum, London
Norfolk RO	Norfolk Record Office, Norwich
Northants. RO	Northamptonshire Record Office, Northampton
Northumbd RO	Northumberland Record Office
Notts. Arch.	Nottinghamshire Archives, Nottingham
NPG	National Portrait Gallery, London
NRA	National Archives, London, Historical Manuscripts Commission, National Register of Archives
Nuffield Oxf.	Nuffield College, Oxford
N. Yorks. CRO	North Yorkshire County Record Office, Northallerton
NYPL	New York Public Library
Oxf. UA	Oxford University Archives
Oxf. U. Mus. NH	Oxford University Museum of Natural History
Oxon. RO	Oxfordshire Record Office, Oxford
Pembroke Cam.	Pembroke College, Cambridge
PRO	National Archives, London, Public Record Office
PRO NIre.	Public Record Office for Northern Ireland, Belfast
Pusey Oxf.	Pusey House, Oxford
RA	Royal Academy of Arts, London
Ransom HRC	Harry Ransom Humanities Research Center, University of Texas, Austin
RAS	Royal Astronomical Society, London
RBG Kew	Royal Botanic Gardens, Kew, London
RCP Lond.	Royal College of Physicians of London
RCS Eng.	Royal College of Surgeons of England, London
RGS	Royal Geographical Society, London
RIBA	Royal Institute of British Architects, London
RIBA BAL	Royal Institute of British Architects, London, British Architectural Library
Royal Arch.	Royal Archives, Windsor Castle, Berkshire [by gracious permission of her majesty the queen]
Royal Irish Acad.	Royal Irish Academy, Dublin
Royal Scot. Acad.	Royal Scottish Academy, Edinburgh
RS	Royal Society, London
RSA	Royal Society of Arts, London
RS Friends, Lond.	Religious Society of Friends, London
St Ant. Oxf.	St Antony's College, Oxford
St John Cam.	St John's College, Cambridge
S. Antiquaries, Lond.	Society of Antiquaries of London
Sci. Mus.	Science Museum, London
Scot. NPG	Scottish National Portrait Gallery, Edinburgh
Scott Polar RI	University of Cambridge, Scott Polar Research Institute
Sheff. Arch.	Sheffield Archives
Shrops. RRC	Shropshire Records and Research Centre, Shrewsbury
SOAS	School of Oriental and African Studies, London
Som. ARS	Somerset Archive and Record Service, Taunton
Staffs. RO	Staffordshire Record Office, Stafford

Suffolk RO	Suffolk Record Office
Surrey HC	Surrey History Centre, Woking
TCD	Trinity College, Dublin
Trinity Cam.	Trinity College, Cambridge
U. Aberdeen	University of Aberdeen
U. Birm.	University of Birmingham
U. Birm. L.	University of Birmingham Library
U. Cal.	University of California
U. Cam.	University of Cambridge
UCL	University College, London
U. Durham	University of Durham
U. Durham L.	University of Durham Library
U. Edin.	University of Edinburgh
U. Edin., New Coll.	University of Edinburgh, New College
U. Edin., New Coll. L.	University of Edinburgh, New College Library
U. Edin. L.	University of Edinburgh Library
U. Glas.	University of Glasgow
U. Glas. L.	University of Glasgow Library
U. Hull	University of Hull
U. Hull, Brynmor Jones L.	University of Hull, Brynmor Jones Library
U. Leeds	University of Leeds
U. Leeds, Brotherton L.	University of Leeds, Brotherton Library
U. Lond.	University of London
U. Lpool	University of Liverpool
U. Lpool L.	University of Liverpool Library
U. Mich.	University of Michigan, Ann Arbor
U. Mich., Clements L.	University of Michigan, Ann Arbor, William L. Clements Library
U. Newcastle	University of Newcastle upon Tyne
U. Newcastle, Robinson L.	University of Newcastle upon Tyne, Robinson Library
U. Nott.	University of Nottingham
U. Nott. L.	University of Nottingham Library
U. Oxf.	University of Oxford
U. Reading	University of Reading
U. Reading L.	University of Reading Library
U. St Andr.	University of St Andrews
U. St Andr. L.	University of St Andrews Library
U. Southampton	University of Southampton
U. Southampton L.	University of Southampton Library
U. Sussex	University of Sussex, Brighton
U. Texas	University of Texas, Austin
U. Wales	University of Wales
U. Warwick Mod. RC	University of Warwick, Coventry, Modern Records Centre
V&A	Victoria and Albert Museum, London
V&A NAL	Victoria and Albert Museum, London, National Art Library
Warks. CRO	Warwickshire County Record Office, Warwick
Wellcome L.	Wellcome Library for the History and Understanding of Medicine, London
Westm. DA	Westminster Diocesan Archives, London
Wilts. & Swindon RO	Wiltshire and Swindon Record Office, Trowbridge
Worcs. RO	Worcestershire Record Office, Worcester
W. Sussex RO	West Sussex Record Office, Chichester
W. Yorks. AS	West Yorkshire Archive Service
Yale U.	Yale University, New Haven, Connecticut
Yale U., Beinecke L.	Yale University, New Haven, Connecticut, Beinecke Rare Book and Manuscript Library
Yale U. CBA	Yale University, New Haven, Connecticut, Yale Center for British Art

3 Bibliographic abbreviations

Adams, *Drama* — W. D. Adams, *A dictionary of the drama*, 1: *A–G* (1904); 2: *H–Z* (1956) [vol. 2 microfilm only]

AFM — J O'Donovan, ed. and trans., *Annala rioghachta Eireann / Annals of the kingdom of Ireland by the four masters*, 7 vols. (1848–51); 2nd edn (1856); 3rd edn (1990)

Allibone, *Dict.* — S. A. Allibone, *A critical dictionary of English literature and British and American authors*, 3 vols. (1859–71); suppl. by J. F. Kirk, 2 vols. (1891)

ANB — J. A. Garraty and M. C. Carnes, eds., *American national biography*, 24 vols. (1999)

Anderson, *Scot. nat.* — W. Anderson, *The Scottish nation, or, The surnames, families, literature, honours, and biographical history of the people of Scotland*, 3 vols. (1859–63)

Ann. mon. — H. R. Luard, ed., *Annales monastici*, 5 vols., Rolls Series, 36 (1864–9)

Ann. Ulster — S. Mac Airt and G. Mac Niocaill, eds., *Annals of Ulster (to AD 1131)* (1983)

APC — *Acts of the privy council of England*, new ser., 46 vols. (1890–1964)

APS — *The acts of the parliaments of Scotland*, 12 vols. in 13 (1814–75)

Arber, *Regs. Stationers* — F. Arber, ed., *A transcript of the registers of the Company of Stationers of London, 1554–1640 AD*, 5 vols. (1875–94)

ArchR — *Architectural Review*

ASC — D. Whitelock, D. C. Douglas, and S. I. Tucker, ed. and trans., *The Anglo-Saxon Chronicle: a revised translation* (1961)

AS chart. — P. H. Sawyer, *Anglo-Saxon charters: an annotated list and bibliography*, Royal Historical Society Guides and Handbooks (1968)

AusDB — D. Pike and others, eds., *Australian dictionary of biography*, 16 vols. (1966–2002)

Baker, *Serjeants* — J. H. Baker, *The order of serjeants at law*, SeldS, suppl. ser., 5 (1984)

Bale, *Cat.* — J. Bale, *Scriptorum illustrium Maioris Brytannie, quam nunc Angliam et Scotiam vocant: catalogus*, 2 vols. in 1 (Basel, 1557–9); facs. edn (1971)

Bale, *Index* — J. Bale, *Index Britanniae scriptorum*, ed. R. L. Poole and M. Bateson (1902); facs. edn (1990)

BBCS — *Bulletin of the Board of Celtic Studies*

BDMBR — J. O. Baylen and N. J. Gossman, eds., *Biographical dictionary of modern British radicals*, 3 vols. in 4 (1979–88)

Bede, *Hist. eccl.* — *Bede's Ecclesiastical history of the English people*, ed. and trans. B. Colgrave and R. A. B. Mynors, OMT (1969); repr. (1991)

Bénézit, *Dict.* — E. Bénézit, *Dictionnaire critique et documentaire des peintres, sculpteurs, dessinateurs et graveurs*, 3 vols. (Paris, 1911–23); new edn, 8 vols. (1948–66), repr. (1966); 3rd edn, rev. and enl., 10 vols. (1976); 4th edn, 14 vols. (1999)

BIHR — *Bulletin of the Institute of Historical Research*

Birch, *Seals* — W. de Birch, *Catalogue of seals in the department of manuscripts in the British Museum*, 6 vols. (1887–1900)

Bishop Burnet's History — *Bishop Burnet's History of his own time*, ed. M. J. Routh, 2nd edn, 6 vols. (1833)

Blackwood — *Blackwood's [Edinburgh] Magazine*, 328 vols. (1817–1980)

Blain, Clements & Grundy, *Feminist comp.* — V. Blain, P. Clements, and I. Grundy, eds., *The feminist companion to literature in English* (1990)

BL cat. — *The British Library general catalogue of printed books* [in 360 vols. with suppls., also CD-ROM and online]

BMJ — *British Medical Journal*

Boase & Courtney, *Bibl. Corn.* — G. C. Boase and W. P. Courtney, *Bibliotheca Cornubiensis: a catalogue of the writings … of Cornishmen*, 3 vols. (1874–82)

Boase, *Mod. Eng. biog.* — F. Boase, *Modern English biography: containing many thousand concise memoirs of persons who have died since the year 1850*, 6 vols. (privately printed, Truro, 1892–1921); repr. (1965)

Boswell, *Life* — *Boswell's Life of Johnson: together with Journal of a tour to the Hebrides and Johnson's Diary of a journey into north Wales*, ed. G. B. Hill, enl. edn, rev. L. F. Powell, 6 vols. (1934–50); 2nd edn (1964); repr. (1971)

Brown & Stratton, *Brit. mus.* — J. D. Brown and S. S. Stratton, *British musical biography* (1897)

Bryan, *Painters* — M. Bryan, *A biographical and critical dictionary of painters and engravers*, 2 vols. (1816); new edn, ed. G. Stanley (1849); new edn, ed. R. E. Graves and W. Armstrong, 2 vols. (1886–9); [4th edn], ed. G. C. Williamson, 5 vols. (1903–5) [various reprs.]

Burke, *Gen. GB* — J. Burke, *A genealogical and heraldic history of the commoners of Great Britain and Ireland*, 4 vols. (1833–8); new edn as *A genealogical and heraldic dictionary of the landed gentry of Great Britain and Ireland*, 3 vols. [1843–9] [many later edns]

Burke, *Gen. Ire.* — J. B. Burke, *A genealogical and heraldic history of the landed gentry of Ireland* (1899); 2nd edn (1904); 3rd edn (1912); 4th edn (1958); 5th edn as *Burke's Irish family records* (1976)

Burke, *Peerage* — J. Burke, *A general [later edns A genealogical] and heraldic dictionary of the peerage and baronetage of the United Kingdom [later edns the British empire]* (1829–)

Burney, *Hist. mus.* — C. Burney, *A general history of music, from the earliest ages to the present period*, 4 vols. (1776–89)

Burtchaell & Sadleir, *Alum. Dubl.* — G. D. Burtchaell and T. U. Sadleir, *Alumni Dublinenses: a register of the students, graduates, and provosts of Trinity College* (1924); [2nd edn], with suppl., in 2 pts (1935)

Calamy rev. — A. G. Matthews, *Calamy revised* (1934); repr. (1988)

CCI — *Calendar of confirmations and inventories granted and given up in the several commissariots of Scotland* (1876–)

CClR — *Calendar of the close rolls preserved in the Public Record Office*, 47 vols. (1892–1963)

CDS — J. Bain, ed., *Calendar of documents relating to Scotland*, 4 vols., PRO (1881–8); suppl. vol. 5, ed. G. G. Simpson and J. D. Galbraith [1986]

CEPR letters — W. H. Bliss, C. Johnson, and J. Twemlow, eds., *Calendar of entries in the papal registers relating to Great Britain and Ireland: papal letters* (1893–)

CGPLA — *Calendars of the grants of probate and letters of administration [in 4 ser.: England & Wales, Northern Ireland, Ireland, and Éire]*

Chambers, *Scots.* — R. Chambers, ed., *A biographical dictionary of eminent Scotsmen*, 4 vols. (1832–5)

Chancery records — chancery records pubd by the PRO

Chancery records (RC) — chancery records pubd by the Record Commissions

CIPM	*Calendar of inquisitions post mortem*, [20 vols.], PRO (1904–); also *Henry VII*, 3 vols. (1898–1955)
Clarendon, *Hist. rebellion*	E. Hyde, earl of Clarendon, *The history of the rebellion and civil wars in England*, 6 vols. (1888); repr. (1958) and (1992)
Cobbett, *Parl. hist.*	W. Cobbett and J. Wright, eds., *Cobbett's Parliamentary history of England*, 36 vols. (1806–1820)
Colvin, *Archs.*	H. Colvin, *A biographical dictionary of British architects, 1600–1840*, 3rd edn (1995)
Cooper, *Ath. Cantab.*	C. H. Cooper and T. Cooper, *Athenae Cantabrigienses*, 3 vols. (1858–1913); repr. (1967)
CPR	*Calendar of the patent rolls preserved in the Public Record Office* (1891–)
Crockford	*Crockford's Clerical Directory*
CS	Camden Society
CSP	*Calendar of state papers* [in 11 ser.: *domestic, Scotland, Scottish series, Ireland, colonial, Commonwealth, foreign, Spain* [at Simancas], *Rome, Milan,* and *Venice*]
CYS	Canterbury and York Society
DAB	*Dictionary of American biography*, 21 vols. (1928–36), repr. in 11 vols. (1964); 10 suppls. (1944–96)
DBB	D. J. Jeremy, ed., *Dictionary of business biography*, 5 vols. (1984–6)
DCB	G. W. Brown and others, *Dictionary of Canadian biography*, [14 vols.] (1966–)
Debrett's Peerage	*Debrett's Peerage* (1803–) [sometimes *Debrett's Illustrated peerage*]
Desmond, *Botanists*	R. Desmond, *Dictionary of British and Irish botanists and horticulturists* (1977); rev. edn (1994)
Dir. Brit. archs.	A. Felstead, J. Franklin, and L. Pinfield, eds., *Directory of British architects, 1834–1900* (1993); 2nd edn, ed. A. Brodie and others, 2 vols. (2001)
DLB	J. M. Bellamy and J. Saville, eds., *Dictionary of labour biography*, [10 vols.] (1972–)
DLitB	Dictionary of Literary Biography
DNB	*Dictionary of national biography*, 63 vols. (1885–1900), suppl., 3 vols. (1901); repr. in 22 vols. (1908–9); 10 further suppls. (1912–96); *Missing persons* (1993)
DNZB	W. H. Oliver and C. Orange, eds., *The dictionary of New Zealand biography*, 5 vols. (1990–2000)
DSAB	W. J. de Kock and others, eds., *Dictionary of South African biography*, 5 vols. (1968–87)
DSB	C. C. Gillispie and F. L. Holmes, eds., *Dictionary of scientific biography*, 16 vols. (1970–80); repr. in 8 vols. (1981); 2 vol. suppl. (1990)
DSBB	A. Slaven and S. Checkland, eds., *Dictionary of Scottish business biography, 1860–1960*, 2 vols. (1986–90)
DSCHT	N. M. de S. Cameron and others, eds., *Dictionary of Scottish church history and theology* (1993)
Dugdale, *Monasticon*	W. Dugdale, *Monasticon Anglicanum*, 3 vols. (1655–72); 2nd edn, 3 vols. (1661–82); new edn, ed. J. Caley, J. Ellis, and B. Bandinel, 6 vols. in 8 pts (1817–30); repr. (1846) and (1970)
DWB	J. E. Lloyd and others, eds., *Dictionary of Welsh biography down to 1940* (1959) [Eng. trans. of *Y bywgraffiadur Cymreig hyd 1940*, 2nd edn (1954)]
EdinR	*Edinburgh Review, or, Critical Journal*
EETS	Early English Text Society
Emden, *Cam.*	A. B. Emden, *A biographical register of the University of Cambridge to 1500* (1963)
Emden, *Oxf.*	A. B. Emden, *A biographical register of the University of Oxford to AD 1500*, 3 vols. (1957–9); also *A biographical register of the University of Oxford, AD 1501 to 1540* (1974)
EngHR	*English Historical Review*
Engraved Brit. ports.	F. M. O'Donoghue and H. M. Hake, *Catalogue of engraved British portraits preserved in the department of prints and drawings in the British Museum*, 6 vols. (1908–25)
ER	The English Reports, 178 vols. (1900–32)
ESTC	*English short title catalogue, 1475–1800* [CD-ROM and online]
Evelyn, *Diary*	*The diary of John Evelyn*, ed. E. S. De Beer, 6 vols. (1955); repr. (2000)
Farington, *Diary*	*The diary of Joseph Farington*, ed. K. Garlick and others, 17 vols. (1978–98)
Fasti Angl. (Hardy)	J. Le Neve, *Fasti ecclesiae Anglicanae*, ed. T. D. Hardy, 3 vols. (1854)
Fasti Angl., 1066–1300	[J. Le Neve], *Fasti ecclesiae Anglicanae, 1066–1300*, ed. D. E. Greenway and J. S. Barrow, [8 vols.] (1968–)
Fasti Angl., 1300–1541	[J. Le Neve], *Fasti ecclesiae Anglicanae, 1300–1541*, 12 vols. (1962–7)
Fasti Angl., 1541–1857	[J. Le Neve], *Fasti ecclesiae Anglicanae, 1541–1857*, ed. J. M. Horn, D. M. Smith, and D. S. Bailey, [9 vols.] (1969–)
Fasti Scot.	H. Scott, *Fasti ecclesiae Scoticanae*, 3 vols. in 6 (1871); new edn, [11 vols.] (1915–)
FO List	*Foreign Office List*
Fortescue, *Brit. army*	J. W. Fortescue, *A history of the British army*, 13 vols. (1899–1930)
Foss, *Judges*	E. Foss, *The judges of England*, 9 vols. (1848–64); repr. (1966)
Foster, *Alum. Oxon.*	J. Foster, ed., *Alumni Oxonienses: the members of the University of Oxford, 1715–1886*, 4 vols. (1887–8); later edn (1891); also *Alumni Oxonienses … 1500–1714*, 4 vols. (1891–2); 8 vol. repr. (1968) and (2000)
Fuller, *Worthies*	T. Fuller, *The history of the worthies of England*, 4 pts (1662); new edn, 2 vols., ed. J. Nichols (1811); new edn, 3 vols., ed. P. A. Nuttall (1840); repr. (1965)
GEC, *Baronetage*	G. E. Cokayne, *Complete baronetage*, 6 vols. (1900–09); repr. (1983) [microprint]
GEC, *Peerage*	G. E. C. [G. E. Cokayne], *The complete peerage of England, Scotland, Ireland, Great Britain, and the United Kingdom*, 8 vols. (1887–98); new edn, ed. V. Gibbs and others, 14 vols. in 15 (1910–98); microprint repr. (1982) and (1987)
Genest, *Eng. stage*	J. Genest, *Some account of the English stage from the Restoration in 1660 to 1830*, 10 vols. (1832); repr. [New York, 1965]
Gillow, *Lit. biog. hist.*	J. Gillow, *A literary and biographical history or bibliographical dictionary of the English Catholics, from the breach with Rome, in 1534, to the present time*, 5 vols. [1885–1902]; repr. (1961); repr. with preface by C. Gillow (1999)
Gir. Camb. opera	*Giraldi Cambrensis opera*, ed. J. S. Brewer, J. F. Dimock, and G. F. Warner, 8 vols., Rolls Series, 21 (1861–91)
GJ	*Geographical Journal*

Gladstone, *Diaries*	*The Gladstone diaries: with cabinet minutes and prime-ministerial correspondence*, ed. M. R. D. Foot and H. C. G. Matthew, 14 vols. (1968–94)
GM	*Gentleman's Magazine*
Graves, *Artists*	A. Graves, ed., *A dictionary of artists who have exhibited works in the principal London exhibitions of oil paintings from 1760 to 1880* (1884); new edn (1895); 3rd edn (1901); facs. edn (1969); repr. [1970], (1973), and (1984)
Graves, *Brit. Inst.*	A. Graves, *The British Institution, 1806–1867: a complete dictionary of contributors and their work from the foundation of the institution* (1875); facs. edn (1908); repr. (1969)
Graves, *RA exhibitors*	A. Graves, *The Royal Academy of Arts: a complete dictionary of contributors and their work from its foundation in 1769 to 1904*, 8 vols. (1905–6); repr. in 4 vols. (1970) and (1972)
Graves, *Soc. Artists*	A. Graves, *The Society of Artists of Great Britain, 1760–1791, the Free Society of Artists, 1761–1783: a complete dictionary* (1907); facs. edn (1969)
Greaves & Zaller, *BDBR*	R. L. Greaves and R. Zaller, eds., *Biographical dictionary of British radicals in the seventeenth century*, 3 vols. (1982–4)
Grove, *Dict. mus.*	G. Grove, ed., *A dictionary of music and musicians*, 5 vols. (1878–90); 2nd edn, ed. J. A. Fuller Maitland (1904–10); 3rd edn, ed. H. C. Colles (1927); 4th edn with suppl. (1940); 5th edn, ed. E. Blom, 9 vols. (1954); suppl. (1961) [see also *New Grove*]
Hall, *Dramatic ports.*	L. A. Hall, *Catalogue of dramatic portraits in the theatre collection of the Harvard College library*, 4 vols. (1930–34)
Hansard	*Hansard's parliamentary debates*, ser. 1–5 (1803–)
Highfill, Burnim & Langhans, *BDA*	P. H. Highfill, K. A. Burnim, and E. A. Langhans, *A biographical dictionary of actors, actresses, musicians, dancers, managers, and other stage personnel in London, 1660–1800*, 16 vols. (1973–93)
Hist. U. Oxf.	T. H. Aston, ed., *The history of the University of Oxford*, 8 vols. (1984–2000) [1: *The early Oxford schools*, ed. J. I. Catto (1984); 2: *Late medieval Oxford*, ed. J. I. Catto and R. Evans (1992); 3: *The collegiate university*, ed. J. McConica (1986); 4: *Seventeenth-century Oxford*, ed. N. Tyacke (1997); 5: *The eighteenth century*, ed. L. S. Sutherland and L. G. Mitchell (1986); 6–7: *Nineteenth-century Oxford*, ed. M. G. Brock and M. C. Curthoys (1997–2000); 8: *The twentieth century*, ed. B. Harrison (2000)]
HJ	*Historical Journal*
HMC	Historical Manuscripts Commission
Holdsworth, *Eng. law*	W. S. Holdsworth, *A history of English law*, ed. A. L. Goodhart and H. L. Hanbury, 17 vols. (1903–72)
HoP, *Commons*	*The history of parliament: the House of Commons* [1386–1421, ed. J. S. Roskell, L. Clark, and C. Rawcliffe, 4 vols. (1992); 1509–1558, ed. S. T. Bindoff, 3 vols. (1982); 1558–1603, ed. P. W. Hasler, 3 vols. (1981); 1660–1690, ed. B. D. Henning, 3 vols. (1983); 1690–1715, ed. D. W. Hayton, E. Cruickshanks, and S. Handley, 5 vols. (2002); 1715–1754, ed. R. Sedgwick, 2 vols. (1970); 1754–1790, ed. L. Namier and J. Brooke, 3 vols. (1964), repr. (1985); 1790–1820, ed. R. G. Thorne, 5 vols. (1986); in draft (used with permission): 1422–1504, 1604–1629, 1640–1660, and 1820–1832]
IGI	*International Genealogical Index*, Church of Jesus Christ of the Latterday Saints
ILN	*Illustrated London News*
IMC	Irish Manuscripts Commission
Irving, *Scots.*	J. Irving, ed., *The book of Scotsmen eminent for achievements in arms and arts, church and state, law, legislation and literature, commerce, science, travel and philanthropy* (1881)
JCS	*Journal of the Chemical Society*
JHC	*Journals of the House of Commons*
JHL	*Journals of the House of Lords*
John of Worcester, *Chron.*	*The chronicle of John of Worcester*, ed. R. R. Darlington and P. McGurk, trans. J. Bray and P. McGurk, 3 vols., OMT (1995–) [vol. 1 forthcoming]
Keeler, *Long Parliament*	M. F. Keeler, *The Long Parliament, 1640–1641: a biographical study of its members* (1954)
Kelly, *Handbk*	*The upper ten thousand: an alphabetical list of all members of noble families*, 3 vols. (1875–7); continued as *Kelly's handbook of the upper ten thousand for 1878* [1879], 2 vols. (1878–9); continued as *Kelly's handbook to the titled, landed and official classes*, 94 vols. (1880–1973)
LondG	*London Gazette*
LP Henry VIII	J. S. Brewer, J. Gairdner, and R. H. Brodie, eds., *Letters and papers, foreign and domestic, of the reign of Henry VIII*, 23 vols. in 38 (1862–1932); repr. (1965)
Mallalieu, *Watercolour artists*	H. L. Mallalieu, *The dictionary of British watercolour artists up to 1820*, 3 vols. (1976–90); vol. 1, 2nd edn (1986)
Memoirs FRS	*Biographical Memoirs of Fellows of the Royal Society*
MGH	Monumenta Germaniae Historica
MT	*Musical Times*
Munk, *Roll*	W. Munk, *The roll of the Royal College of Physicians of London*, 2 vols. (1861); 2nd edn, 3 vols. (1878)
N&Q	*Notes and Queries*
New Grove	S. Sadie, ed., *The new Grove dictionary of music and musicians*, 20 vols. (1980); 2nd edn, 29 vols. (2001) [also online edn; see also Grove, *Dict. mus.*]
Nichols, *Illustrations*	J. Nichols and J. B. Nichols, *Illustrations of the literary history of the eighteenth century*, 8 vols. (1817–58)
Nichols, *Lit. anecdotes*	J. Nichols, *Literary anecdotes of the eighteenth century*, 9 vols. (1812–16); facs. edn (1966)
Obits. FRS	*Obituary Notices of Fellows of the Royal Society*
O'Byrne, *Naval biog. dict.*	W. R. O'Byrne, *A naval biographical dictionary* (1849); repr. (1990); [2nd edn], 2 vols. (1861)
OHS	Oxford Historical Society
Old Westminsters	*The record of Old Westminsters*, 1–2, ed. G. F. R. Barker and A. H. Stenning (1928); suppl. 1, ed. J. B. Whitmore and G. R. Y. Radcliffe [1938]; 3, ed. J. B. Whitmore, G. R. Y. Radcliffe, and D. C. Simpson (1963); suppl. 2, ed. F. E. Pagan (1978); 4, ed. F. E. Pagan and H. E. Pagan (1992)
OMT	Oxford Medieval Texts
Ordericus Vitalis, *Eccl. hist.*	*The ecclesiastical history of Orderic Vitalis*, ed. and trans. M. Chibnall, 6 vols., OMT (1969–80); repr. (1990)
Paris, *Chron.*	*Matthaei Parisiensis, monachi sancti Albani, chronica majora*, ed. H. R. Luard, Rolls Series, 7 vols. (1872–83)
Parl. papers	*Parliamentary papers* (1801–)
PBA	*Proceedings of the British Academy*

Pepys, *Diary*	*The diary of Samuel Pepys*, ed. R. Latham and W. Matthews, 11 vols. (1970–83); repr. (1995) and (2000)
Pevsner	N. Pevsner and others, Buildings of England series
PICE	*Proceedings of the Institution of Civil Engineers*
Pipe rolls	*The great roll of the pipe for . . .*, PRSoc. (1884–)
PRO	Public Record Office
PRS	*Proceedings of the Royal Society of London*
PRSoc.	Pipe Roll Society
PTRS	*Philosophical Transactions of the Royal Society*
QR	*Quarterly Review*
RC	Record Commissions
Redgrave, *Artists*	S. Redgrave, *A dictionary of artists of the English school* (1874); rev. edn (1878); repr. (1970)
Reg. Oxf.	C. W. Boase and A. Clark, eds., *Register of the University of Oxford*, 5 vols., OHS, 1, 10–12, 14 (1885–9)
Reg. PCS	J. H. Burton and others, eds., *The register of the privy council of Scotland*, 1st ser., 14 vols. (1877–98); 2nd ser., 8 vols. (1899–1908); 3rd ser., [16 vols.] (1908–70)
Reg. RAN	H. W. C. Davis and others, eds., *Regesta regum Anglo-Normannorum, 1066–1154*, 4 vols. (1913–69)
RIBA Journal	*Journal of the Royal Institute of British Architects* [later *RIBA Journal*]
RotP	J. Strachey, ed., *Rotuli parliamentorum ut et petitiones, et placita in parliamento*, 6 vols. (1767–77)
RotS	D. Macpherson, J. Caley, and W. Illingworth, eds., *Rotuli Scotiae in Turri Londinensi et in domo capitulari Westmonasteriensi asservati*, 2 vols., RC, 14 (1814–19)
RS	Record(s) Society
Rymer, *Foedera*	T. Rymer and R. Sanderson, eds., *Foedera, conventiones, literae et cuiuscunque generis acta publica inter reges Angliae et alios quosvis imperatores, reges, pontifices, principes, vel communitates*, 20 vols. (1704–35); 2nd edn, 20 vols. (1726–35); 3rd edn, 10 vols. (1739–45), facs. edn (1967); new edn, ed. A. Clarke, J. Caley, and F. Holbrooke, 4 vols., RC, 50 (1816–30)
Sainty, *Judges*	J. Sainty, ed., *The judges of England, 1272–1990*, SeldS, suppl. ser., 10 (1993)
Sainty, *King's counsel*	J. Sainty, ed., *A list of English law officers and king's counsel*, SeldS, suppl. ser., 7 (1987)
SCH	Studies in Church History
Scots peerage	J. B. Paul, ed. *The Scots peerage, founded on Wood's edition of Sir Robert Douglas's Peerage of Scotland, containing an historical and genealogical account of the nobility of that kingdom*, 9 vols. (1904–14)
SeldS	Selden Society
SHR	*Scottish Historical Review*
State trials	T. B. Howell and T. J. Howell, eds., *Cobbett's Complete collection of state trials*, 34 vols. (1809–28)
STC, 1475–1640	A. W. Pollard, G. R. Redgrave, and others, eds., *A short-title catalogue of . . . English books . . . 1475–1640* (1926); 2nd edn, ed. W. A. Jackson, F. S. Ferguson, and K. F. Pantzer, 3 vols. (1976–91) [see also Wing, *STC*]
STS	Scottish Text Society
SurtS	Surtees Society
Symeon of Durham, *Opera*	*Symeonis monachi opera omnia*, ed. T. Arnold, 2 vols., Rolls Series, 75 (1882–5); repr. (1965)
Tanner, *Bibl. Brit.-Hib.*	T. Tanner, *Bibliotheca Britannico-Hibernica*, ed. D. Wilkins (1748); repr. (1963)
Thieme & Becker, *Allgemeines Lexikon*	U. Thieme, F. Becker, and H. Vollmer, eds., *Allgemeines Lexikon der bildenden Künstler von der Antike bis zur Gegenwart*, 37 vols. (Leipzig, 1907–50); repr. (1961–5), (1983), and (1992)
Thurloe, *State papers*	*A collection of the state papers of John Thurloe*, ed. T. Birch, 7 vols. (1742)
TLS	*Times Literary Supplement*
Tout, *Admin. hist.*	T. F. Tout, *Chapters in the administrative history of mediaeval England: the wardrobe, the chamber, and the small seals*, 6 vols. (1920–33); repr. (1967)
TRHS	*Transactions of the Royal Historical Society*
VCH	H. A. Doubleday and others, eds., *The Victoria history of the counties of England*, [88 vols.] (1900–)
Venn, *Alum. Cant.*	J. Venn and J. A. Venn, *Alumni Cantabrigienses: a biographical list of all known students, graduates, and holders of office at the University of Cambridge, from the earliest times to 1900*, 10 vols. (1922–54); repr. in 2 vols. (1974–8)
Vertue, *Note books*	[G. Vertue], *Note books*, ed. K. Esdaile, earl of Ilchester, and H. M. Hake, 6 vols., Walpole Society, 18, 20, 22, 24, 26, 30 (1930–55)
VF	*Vanity Fair*
Walford, *County families*	E. Walford, *The county families of the United Kingdom, or, Royal manual of the titled and untitled aristocracy of Great Britain and Ireland* (1860)
Walker rev.	A. G. Matthews, *Walker revised: being a revision of John Walker's Sufferings of the clergy during the grand rebellion, 1642–60* (1948); repr. (1988)
Walpole, *Corr.*	*The Yale edition of Horace Walpole's correspondence*, ed. W. S. Lewis, 48 vols. (1937–83)
Ward, *Men of the reign*	T. H. Ward, ed., *Men of the reign: a biographical dictionary of eminent persons of British and colonial birth who have died during the reign of Queen Victoria* (1885); repr. (Graz, 1968)
Waterhouse, *18c painters*	E. Waterhouse, *The dictionary of 18th century painters in oils and crayons* (1981); repr. as *British 18th century painters in oils and crayons* (1991), vol. 2 of *Dictionary of British art*
Watt, *Bibl. Brit.*	R. Watt, *Bibliotheca Britannica, or, A general index to British and foreign literature*, 4 vols. (1824) [many reprs.]
Wellesley index	W. E. Houghton, ed., *The Wellesley index to Victorian periodicals, 1824–1900*, 5 vols. (1966–89); new edn (1999) [CD-ROM]
Wing, *STC*	D. Wing, ed., *Short-title catalogue of . . . English books . . . 1641–1700*, 3 vols. (1945–51); 2nd edn (1972–88); rev. and enl. edn, ed. J. J. Morrison, C. W. Nelson, and M. Seccombe, 4 vols. (1994–8) [see also *STC, 1475–1640*]
Wisden	*John Wisden's Cricketer's Almanack*
Wood, *Ath. Oxon.*	A. Wood, *Athenae Oxonienses . . . to which are added the Fasti*, 2 vols. (1691–2); 2nd edn (1721); new edn, 4 vols., ed. P. Bliss (1813–20); repr. (1967) and (1969)
Wood, *Vic. painters*	C. Wood, *Dictionary of Victorian painters* (1971); 2nd edn (1978); 3rd edn as *Victorian painters*, 2 vols. (1995), vol. 4 of *Dictionary of British art*
WW	*Who's who* (1849–)
WWBMP	M. Stenton and S. Lees, eds., *Who's who of British members of parliament*, 4 vols. (1976–81)
WWW	*Who was who* (1929–)

Barney, Joseph (1753–1829?), painter, was born on 4 March 1753 in Wolverhampton and moved to London at the age of sixteen. He won a premium for a drawing of flowers at the Society of Artists in 1774, and studied under the Italian decorative painter Antonio Zucchi (1726–1795) and Angelica Kaufmann (1741–1807), exhibiting from their London address in 1777. His early work favoured the same neo-classical style of decorative and historical painting. Barney's one known major work, the compartmentalized ceiling in a room at Badger Hall, Shropshire, produced *c*.1781, is now installed on the staircase ceiling at Buscot Park, Faringdon, Oxfordshire, and is considered to be a 'very pretty work, clear and light in tone and wholly in the style of Angelica Kaufmann' (Waterhouse, 39). Barney assisted in finishing the 'mechanical paintings' of Matthew Boulton at Wolverhampton between 1778 and 1781, and was also concerned in the decoration of japanned trays for his own brother's business in the same town.

Barney exhibited paintings of various episodes from Shakespeare's plays together with biblical and other popular scenes at the Royal Academy between 1784 and 1827; similar works were exhibited at the British Institution between 1806 and 1829. In 1784 he used an address in Birmingham, but after 1786 he exhibited from numerous addresses in and around London. Barney exhibited a total of 143 works at the principal London exhibitions. He was appointed drawing-master at the Royal Military Academy, Woolwich, on 15 October 1793 and held the position for twenty-seven years, retiring on a yearly pension of 160*l*. 16*s*. In 1815, he became flower painter to the prince regent and exhibited many such subjects at the annual exhibitions. He also produced stipple engravings of decorative and sentimental subjects according to his own designs, or those of his contemporaries, for example, William Hamilton. Barney had married well before 1803 (a painting entitled *Mrs Barney* was shown at the Royal Academy that year) and his son Joseph W. Barney first exhibited at the Royal Academy and British Institution in 1815. He probably died in 1829, the last year he exhibited.

R. J. CLEEVELY

Sources Waterhouse, *18c painters* · I. Mackenzie, *British prints: dictionary and price guide* (1987) · Graves, *Artists* · Graves, *RA exhibitors* · Bénézit, *Dict.* · W. D. Jones, *Records of the Royal Military Academy (1741–1840)* (1851) · War Office, ordnance corresp., PRO, 44/686, no. 26
Archives Birm. CA, letters to Boulton family

Barnfield, Richard (*bap.* 1574, *d.* 1620), poet, was born at Norbury Manor House, Norbury, Shropshire, and was baptized at the parish church on 13 June 1574. He was the eldest son of Richard Barnfield (*c*.1544–1627), gentleman, and Mary Skrymsher (1552–1581), the daughter of the sheriff of Staffordshire, John Skrymsher. Mary died shortly after giving birth to her fourth child, Dorothea. Following her death in 1581 Barnfield, his younger sister, Dorothea, and his two brothers, Robert and John, were raised by their childless aunt, Elizabeth Collier, the wife of Mary's brother, James Skrymsher. 'Epitaph upon the Death of his Aunt' in Barnfield's *Poems: in Divers Humors* (in *The Encomion of Lady Pecunia*, 1598), is dedicated to Elizabeth.

Barnfield matriculated from Brasenose College, Oxford, on 27 November 1589 and graduated BA on 5 February 1592. After being rusticated for a time, Barnfield was readmitted on 19 March 1592, but appears not to have proceeded MA, as his name does not appear in the college register of congregation. Little is known about Barnfield following his graduation. It is possible that he studied law in London: *The Complaint of Poetrie* (1598) and *Poems: in Divers Humors* (1598) are dedicated to Edward Leigh and Nicholas Blackleach, both at Gray's Inn and former students of Brasenose College.

Barnfield's poetical works were published between 1594 and 1598. The attribution of the commemorative volume *Greenes Funeralls. By R. B. Gent* to Barnfield is uncertain; the work was printed by John Danter in 1594. Joseph Ritson first attributed this work to Barnfield in 1802. McKerrow reprinted it in 1911 as Barnfield's, but Summers excluded it from his edition of Barnfield's collected works in 1936. Also in 1594, Danter printed Barnfield's *The Affectionate Shepheard: Containing 'The Complaint of Daphnis for the Love of Ganymede'. The Affectionate Shepheard* consists of several parts. The poem's dedicatee, Lady Penelope Rich, and her lover, Charles Blount, accused Barnfield of using them as models for Queen Guendolena and Ganymede, two characters in the first part, 'The Tears of an Affectionate Shepheard Sick for Love, or, The Complaint of Daphnis for the Love of Ganymede'. The explicit nature of the homoerotic attraction between Daphnis and Ganymede in this part of the poem alienated eighteenth- and nineteenth-century readers. The final part, 'Helen's Rape, or, A Light Lantern for Light Ladies' is a witty contribution to the Gabriel Harvey–Thomas Nashe controversy over the intrinsic poetical qualities of the English hexameter. *The Affectionate Shepheard* was published anonymously, although Barnfield acknowledged its authorship in the prefatory material to *Cynthia: with Certaine Sonnets, and the Legend of Cassandra* (1595). The sonnets included in this collection resume the theme of the passionate love of Daphnis for Ganymede. It has been suggested that Barnfield's sonnet sequence is the only one apart from Shakespeare's to be addressed to a man, and it has been suggested that Barnfield might be considered as a candidate for the rival poet of Shakespeare's sequence (Clitheroe).

In the prefatory material to *Cynthia*, Barnfield rejects the attribution of two unnamed works, which might include *Greenes Funeralls*. In 1598 Jaggard published Barnfield's last volume of poems and pamphlets in verse, *Lady Pecunia*, which consists of four parts: 'The Encomion of Lady Pecunia, or, The Praise of Money', a tongue-in-cheek disquisition on wealth and the dangers of forgery; 'The Complaint of Poetry, for the Death of Liberality', a set piece that bewails the poverty of poets and the lack of generous patrons; 'The Combat between Conscience and Covetousness'; and 'Poems: in Divers Humors', which includes two poems long attributed to Shakespeare. Sonnet 8, 'If music and sweet poetry agree', and ode 20, 'As it fell upon a day, / In the merry month of May', were included in *The Passionate Pilgrime* (1599), but omitted by Edmund Malone in his 1790 edition of Shakespeare's *Complete Works*.

Barnfield's work started to enjoy increasing popularity in the second half of the 1590s. He is mentioned in Henry Chettle's *Piers Plainnes Seaven Yeres Prentiship* (1595), and associated with Spenser and Sidney in Francis Meres's *Palladis tamia* (1598). The inclusion of quotations from Barnfield in Samuel Nicholson's *Acolastus: his After-Witte* (1600) and in the anonymous *A Lovers Newest Curranto, or, The Lamentation of a Young Man's Folly* (c.1625) similarly confirms Barnfield's popularity among his contemporaries. Barnfield's poetic career was, however, short-lived: he died at Market Drayton, Shropshire, and was buried there on 6 February 1620, having been disinherited by his father twenty years earlier (Worrall). He was previously thought to have died in 1627, on the assumption that he was the Richard Barnfield whose will is preserved in the Lichfield Joint Record Office; however, the will is more likely to be that of his father.

Barnfield is mainly remembered in association with Shakespeare. There have, however, been noticeable exceptions. Edward Phillips ranks Barnfield alongside Lodge, Greene, and Breton in *Theatrum poetarum* (1675). Poet laureate Thomas Warton praised Barnfield's poetic achievements in *The History of English Poetry* (1774–81), but found his subject matter often objectionable and distasteful. J. O. Halliwell was a fairer critic of Barnfield's merits and he reprinted *The Affectionate Shepheard* in 1845. A. B. Grosart edited the complete poems in 1876, followed by E. Arber in 1882, M. Summers in 1936, and G. Klawitter in 1990.   SONIA MASSAI

Sources R. Tresswell and A. Vincent, *The visitation of Shropshire, taken in the year 1623*, ed. G. Grazebrook and J. P. Rylands, 2 vols., Harleian Society, 28–9 (1889) · *The complete poems of Richard Barnfield*, ed. A. B. Grosart (1876) · F. Clitheroe, *The life and selected writings of Richard Barnfield, 1574–1627* (1992) · A. Worrall, 'Richard Barnfield: a new biography', *N&Q*, 237 (1992), 370–71 · Wood, *Ath. Oxon.*, new edn, 1.683–4 · *STC, 1475–1640* · Arber, *Regs. Stationers*, vol. 2 · *Richard Barnfield: the complete poems*, ed. G. Klawitter (1990) · H. C. Morris, *Richard Barnfield, Colin's child* (1963) · J. Ritson, *Bibliographia poetica* (1802), 124–5 · R. B. McKerrow, ed., *Greenes funeralls* (1911) · W. Beloe, *Anecdotes of literature and scarce books*, 6 vols. (1807–12), vol. 2, p. 68 · E. Brydges, *Restituta, or, Titles, extracts, and characters of old books in English literature*, 4 vols. (1814–16), vol. 4, p. 499 · *Poems of Richard Barnfield*, ed. M. Summers (1936) · *Richard Barnfield of Darlaston, Staffordshire, esquire, poems 1594–1598*, ed. E. Arber (1882) · will, 7 April 1627, Lichfield Joint RO, B/C/11 [Richard Barnfield, sen.]

Barnham, Benedict (1558/9–1598), merchant and benefactor, was the fourth son of Francis Barnham (1514/15–1576), merchant, and his wife, Alice Bracebridge (Bradbridge; d. 1604) of Sussex. By 1573, the family was living at St Clement, Eastcheap, London. Barnham followed his eldest brother, Martin, to St Alban Hall, Oxford, and was a student there in 1572.

Barnham spent his adult life in London and, like his father, became a member of the Drapers' Company, alderman, and sheriff. In 1591 Barnham was third warden of the Drapers' Company, but surrendered this post on election as sheriff for 1591 and 1592. On 14 October 1591 he was elected and sworn alderman of Bread Street ward, a position he kept for the rest of his life. He was master of the Drapers' Company in 1592–3 and 1596–7, a member of parliament in 1588–9 for Minehead, and in 1597–8 for Yarmouth, Isle of Wight. He was a member of the Elizabethan Society of Antiquaries.

On 28 April 1583 Barnham married Dorothy (d. 1639), daughter of Ambrose Smith of Cheapside, silkman to the queen, at St Clement, Eastcheap. A son and three daughters died in infancy. Four daughters survived to marry: Elizabeth married Mervin *Touchet, second earl of Castlehaven; Alice, 'a little violent lady' (Spedding, 3.290), became the wife of Sir Francis *Bacon in 1606. Barnham was acquiring estates by 1575 and by his death on 3 April 1598 (aged thirty-nine) he held lands in Essex, Hampshire, Kent, and London. Under his will of 24 March 1597 and a codicil dated 31 March 1598 he left property valued at over £16,000 (gross), rising to over £20,100 in 1606 after further debts had been received. His principal beneficiaries were his wife and daughters. Legacies were made to, among others, Arthur Atye, principal of St Alban Hall, and his wife; the hall itself was left up to £250 to rebuild the front, and Barnham's arms were carved over the entrance in his memory. He was buried in St Clement, Eastcheap, on 27 April. An elaborate monument was erected to him, using £100 left for that purpose.   SARAH BENDALL

Sources A. B. Beaven, ed., *The aldermen of the City of London, temp. Henry III–[1912]*, 2 vols. (1908–13) · A. W. H. Clarke, ed., *The register of St Clement Eastcheap and St Martin Orgar* (1937) · *Reg. Oxf.*, vol. 2/2 · Merton College register, 1567–1603, Merton Oxf., 1.3, p. 191 · J. Stow, *A survey of the cities of London and Westminster and the borough of Southwark*, ed. J. Strype, new edn, 2 vols. (1720) · E. Hasted, *The history and topographical survey of the county of Kent*, 2–3 (1782–90) · A. H. Johnson, *The history of the Worshipful Company of the Drapers of London*, 5 vols. (1914–22), vols. 2 and 4 · will, PRO, PROB 11/91, fols. 304–9, 335 · introduction, *Archaeologia*, 1 (1770), i–xxxix, esp. xx · common serjeant's book, 1, CLRO, Probate inventories, fols. 98, 199v–200 · *The letters and life of Francis Bacon*, ed. J. Spedding, 7 vols. (1861–74), vol. 3 · F. Barnham, 'The character of Sir Martin Barnham Knight', 1696, Bodl. Oxf., MS Bodley 10 · I. Doolittle, 'Benedict Barnam: benefactor of Merton College', *Postmaster* (1981), 7 · *Analytical index, to the series of records known as Remembrancia, preserved among the archives of the City of London*, Corporation of London, ed. [W. H. Overall and H. C. Overall] (1878) · S. L. Lee, 'Sir Francis Barnham and a proposed academy of literature under James I: the family of Lady Bacon', *N&Q*, 6th ser., 9 (1884), 1–2 · B. B. Orridge, *Some account of the citizens of London and their rulers, from 1060 to 1867* (1867) · A. Wood, *The history and antiquities of the colleges and halls in the University of Oxford*, ed. J. Gutch (1786)
Wealth at death £16,106 11s. 9d. gross: inventory, CLRO, common serjeant's book 1, fols. 98, 199v–200

Barnham, Sir Francis (bap. 1576, d. 1646?), local politician and landowner, was baptized at Hollingbourne, Kent, on 20 October 1576, the eldest son of Martin Barnham of Hollingbourne (1547×50–1610) and his first wife, Ursula (d. 1579), daughter of Robert Rudston of Boughton Monchelsea in Kent. Martin Barnham had inherited a modest estate in Kent from his father, the London merchant and alderman Francis Barnham. Martin established himself firmly within local society through his own and his children's marriages, through his service in local government (he served as sheriff in 1598), and by adopting the role of benevolent landlord and mediator in disputes between neighbours.

Francis Barnham matriculated at Trinity College, Cambridge, as a fellow-commoner about 1592, without apparently graduating. On 8 November 1594 he was admitted as a student to Gray's Inn. On 3 January 1599 at Sevenoaks he married Elizabeth Lennard, daughter of Sampson Lennard and his wife, Margaret, Baroness Dacre. Barnham left an affectionate account of his father, which tells of his own life at this time:

> Within lesse than two yeares after my marriage I came to live in my fathers house, though I had then by covenant one yeeres beinge more with my father in lawe, whoe though he kept a very honorable house … yett the happinesse I promised my selfe in the daily comfort of my fathers kinde and familiar usage, and in his advise and instructions … made me hasten my cominge to live with him a yeare before my time. ('Manuscript', ed. Lennard, 204)

He wrote of this period that 'I can reckon noe part of my life, spent with more contentment', and this he ascribed principally to the 'goodnesse and sweetnesse of my fathers disposition' ('Manuscript', ed. Lennard, 204). He further recalled how when King James went to London a friend of his at court had offered to procure knighthoods for father and son for £80. Francis, though he 'doubted not to procure both our knighthoods without money by the power of some greater freinds I had in court' thought it worth taking up the offer for speed and certainty. His father vetoed the plan because, he said, 'yf I pay for my knighthood I shall never be called Sir Martin, but that I shall blush for shame to thinke how I came by it' (ibid., 205). Francis obtained a free knighthood for his father through the offices of the earl of Pembroke, and both he and his father were knighted on the king's coronation day, 23 July 1603. A few months later Sir Francis entered the House of Commons as MP for Grampound, Cornwall, in the parliaments of 1604 and 1614. He was admitted as a member of the Virginia Company in 1612. The estate that he inherited from his father in 1610, after due provision had been made by the latter for the children of his second marriage, were the two manors of Bilsington, 'a faire howse newly built at Hollingbourne, and an hundred pounds a yeere lands to it' (ibid., 197). Three years later he inherited from his mother's family the estate of Boughton Monchelsea. He later settled his heir there while himself continuing to keep house at Hollingbourne, and acquired a house in Maidstone.

By 1621 Barnham was a captain of the trained bands, and became a JP and deputy lieutenant. On 30 December 1624 he was named to a commission of martial law occasioned by disorders stemming from the English involvement of the troops of Mansfeld's expedition. His kinship to Sir Francis Bacon, who had married Barnham's cousin, may have given an early impetus to his career. In the early 1620s Barnham was proposed by Edmund Bolton as one of eighty-four members of a proposed royal academy for the study of public affairs, heraldry, and English history; Buckingham took up the idea and James I was apparently sympathetic, but the scheme died with the king. Barnham was MP for Maidstone in the parliament of 1621 and, apart from that of 1625 (when he did not stand), represented the town in all subsequent parliaments up to and including the Long Parliament. He acquired a house in town. He was not a distinguished parliamentarian, speaking rarely if at all in debates, but sat on several committees and was one of twenty-four members named on 3 May 1626 to assist in framing the articles of impeachment against the duke of Buckingham. In 1634 Barnham entertained at his Maidstone house Nathaniel Brent, Archbishop Laud's vicar-general, who acted in the case of John Miller, minister of the Walloon church at Maidstone, to direct his charges to worship in the parish church. On 24 August 1638 Sir Henry Wotton wrote that his 'chiefest friends', 'Sir Edmund Bacon, Sir Francis Barnham and Thomas Culpepper, all men of singular conversation', had stayed with him at Canterbury (*Life and Letters of Sir Henry Wotton*, 2.389–90).

Barnham's local influence and long service as MP for Maidstone made his an influential voice in the two elections for county members in 1640. He seems to have taken a neutral position in the acrimonious rivalry between Sir Roger Twysden and Sir Edward Dering, in which the first was the victor in March and the second in November. Barnham was described as a friend by Dering and as 'a right honest Gentleman, and a very noble friend of myne' by Twysden ('Sir Roger Twysden's journal', 2.195). At first he aligned himself with parliament, and was one of those selected by the Commons to counter royalist influence at the Kent assizes in June 1642. In September he advised the reluctant Twysden to give money on the propositions of the public faith. Barnham himself offered a free loan of £100, but his reservations were growing. In June 1643 parliament's attempt to have the covenant administered in Kent led to open rebellion in the county. When forces were sent to put it down, the Commons heard, Sir Francis Barham neither 'appeared nor assisted' (Everitt, 193). In early August he was purged from the county committee, and was soon afterwards threatened with sequestration and expulsion from the house. Sir Francis Barnham probably died in 1646, though an ambiguous report of Twysden set down in mid-1649 has been taken as evidence that he was still living at that time. He was succeeded by his son Robert (later first baronet), the eldest surviving son of a family of fifteen children of whom five died young.

STEPHEN WRIGHT

Sources Keeler, *Long Parliament* · 'A copy of an original manuscript of Sir Francis Barnham, formerly of Boughton Monchelsea knight', ed. T. B. Lennard, *The Ancestor*, 9 (1904), 191–209 · A. Everitt, *The community of Kent and the great rebellion, 1640–60* (1966) · 'Sir Roger Twysden's journal, from the Royden Hall MSS', ed. L. B. L. [L. B. Larking], *Archaeologia Cantiana*, 1 (1858), 186–214; 2 (1859), 175–220; 3 (1860), 145–76 · F. Jessup, 'The Kentish election of March 1640', *Archaeologia Cantiana*, 86 (1971), 1–10 · G. J. Armytage, ed., *A visitation of the county of Kent, begun … 1663, finished … 1668*, Harleian Society, 54 (1906) · W. B. Bannerman, ed., *The visitations of the county of Sussex … 1530 … and 1633–4*, Harleian Society, 53 (1905) · J. Foster, *The register of admissions to Gray's Inn, 1521–1889, together with the register of marriages in Gray's Inn chapel, 1695–1754* (privately printed, London, 1889) · Rymer, *Foedera*, 1st edn, 17.647 · *The life and letters of Sir Henry Wotton*, ed. L. P. Smith, 2 (1907), 389–90 · F. W. Jessup, *Sir Roger Twysden, 1597–1672* (1965) · J. Nichols, *The progresses, processions, and magnificent festivities of King James I, his royal consort, family and court*, 4 vols. (1828) · E. Portal, 'The Academy Royal of King James I', *PBA*, 16 (1930), 1–37 · D. R. Woolf, *The idea of history in early Stuart England* (1990), 191–2, 196 · T. K. Rabb, *Enterprise and empire: merchant and* *gentry investment in the expansion of England, 1575–1630* (1967) · P. Clark, *English provincial society from the Reformation to the revolution: religion, politics and society in Kent, 1500–1640* (1977), 119, 127, 261, 308, 331, 344, 477 · W. A. Shaw, *The knights of England*, 2 (1906), 120 · E. Hasted, *The history and topographical survey of the county of Kent*, 4–5 (1798) · GEC, *Baronetage*, 3.285

Barningham, John (*d.* 1449), prior of Ipswich and theologian, is of unknown origins. After joining the Carmelites in Ipswich he studied theology at Paris and Oxford, in both of which universities he was said to have incepted as a doctor. In 1448 he was appointed prior of Ipswich at the provincial chapter in Norwich, but died there the following year on 22 January 1449. In his theology Barningham was a defender of the doctrine of transubstantiation, but more probably as a theological exercise than as an attack against Lollards. His writings were collected and given to the Carmelites in Cambridge by David Boys (*d.* 1451). John Bale, who saw them there, recorded a commentary on *The Sentences* of Peter Lombard (seen also by John Leland in the London Carmelite house), two sets of theological disputations (one written while Barningham was lecturing at Oxford), a tract on the enormity of sin which began: 'There are three reasons for not sinning: it offends God, pleases the devil and harms ourselves', lectures on scripture, and collected sermons. RICHARD COPSEY

Sources J. Bale, Bodl. Oxf., MS Bodley 73 (SC 27635), fols. 1, 11v, 20, 36, 39v, 52v, 68, 108v · J. Bale, BL, Harley MS 1819, fols. 198v, 200v · Bale, *Cat.*, 1.589 · Emden, *Oxf.* · J. Bale, Bodl. Oxf., MS Selden supra 41, fols. 179, 374 · J. Bale, BL, MS Harley 3838, fols. 100v–101, 206v · J. Bale, *Illustrium Maioris Britannie scriptorum … summarium* (1548), fol. 199 · *Commentarii de scriptoribus Britannicis, auctore Joanne Lelando*, ed. A. Hall, 2 (1709), 453 · B. M. Xiberta, *De scriptoribus scholasticis saeculi XIV ex ordine Carmelitarum* (Louvain, 1931), 50, 112n.

Barns. For this title name *see* Seton, Sir John, Lord Barns (*c.*1553–1594).

Barnsley family (*per.* 1885–1987), architects, designers, and craftspeople, came to prominence with **(Arthur) Ernest Barnsley** (1863–1926), architect and designer, and **Sidney Howard Barnsley** (1865–1926), architect and furniture maker. Ernest Barnsley was born on 17 February 1863, the sixth child of Edward Barnsley (*d.* 1881), builder and manufacturer, of Birmingham and his wife, Amelia, *née* Heeley (?); Sidney Barnsley was the seventh and last child, born on 25 February 1865. Edward Barnsley was one of the partners in John Barnsley & Sons, one of the city's most successful building firms. Wesleyans in belief, prosperous, in touch with the city's intellectual élite, the Barnsley family shared in the progressive, civic culture of late Victorian Birmingham. It is not known exactly where Ernest and Sidney went to school, but in 1879 Ernest was articled to J. L. Ball, a young Birmingham architect, and Sidney may have joined him there later. They both attended classes at the city's School of Art.

In 1885 they both went to London, where Ernest Barnsley worked, first for W. H. Seth-Smith, and then for J. D. Sedding, while Sidney Barnsley joined the office of Richard Norman Shaw. Both Seddings and Shaws were leading architectural offices of the day, alive with the new ideas of the arts and crafts movement. Here the Barnsley brothers formed lasting allegiances: in Shaw's office with W. R. Lethaby and Robert Weir Schultz, and in Sedding's with Ernest Gimson who came, like them, from a background of industrial wealth and progressive thought in the midlands. Gimson would soon be inseparable from their lives. Ernest Barnsley left Sedding's office in 1887 and set up in practice on his own in Birmingham, marrying Alice Mary Townsley (*b. c.*1863) on 28 February 1888. Sidney Barnsley left Shaw early in 1888, and spent much of the next two and a half years in Greece with Schultz, studying Byzantine architecture at Lethaby's suggestion. (The fruits of his study can be seen in the beautiful little church of the Wisdom of God at Lower Kingswood in Surrey, which he designed on his return. His drawings for the church, together with relevant photographs, are in the possession of the Fine Art Society, London.) Gimson left Sedding's office at about the same time and spent two wandering years, sketching, looking for a cottage in the country, worrying about the prospect of working in an architectural office, and learning to make chairs and plasterwork with his own hands.

Late in 1890, or early in 1891, Gimson, Lethaby, the newly returned Sidney Barnsley, two slightly older architects, Mervyn Macartney and Reginald Blomfield, and Stephen Webb, a designer, set up a cabinet-making workshop in London, to make furniture to their designs, under the name Kenton & Co. It produced some fine furniture, but closed down some time in 1892, leaving Sidney Barnsley so shocked by the taste of the cabinet-makers when left to themselves that he decided never to employ craftsmen, and almost always made up his own designs. Later that year he and Gimson decided to leave London and settle in the country. There is little documentary evidence of the spirit in which this decision was taken, but it turned out to be the most important decision of their lives, a journey to be followed by no more journeys. Their purposes have usually, and perhaps not wrongly, been inferred from what followed.

Ernest and Sidney Barnsley in the Cotswolds Ernest Barnsley was persuaded to join them, against his wife's inclination, and in April 1893 they settled temporarily in the hamlet of Ewen, near Cirencester, in the Cotswolds. In 1894 they leased Pinbury Park, a sixteenth-century house standing by itself above the valley of the River Frome, 5 miles north-west of Cirencester. The property was repaired and altered for their occupation, an outbuilding was turned into a workshop, and they began to work, thinking of the countryside as the home of the crafts, hoping to gather others round them. The Barnsleys made heavy casefurniture (for example, cabinets and chests) in oak, with features borrowed from wagons and farm implements, while Gimson made light ladderback chairs and decorative plasterwork. Sidney Barnsley was the most focused of them. Lucy Morley (*d.* 1944), a relation of Gimson's who kept house for them and married Sidney Barnsley in 1895, would take over their elevenses and find Sidney working away and the other two standing by, whistling tunes from Gilbert and Sullivan. The Barnsley brothers were very different. Sidney was slight and shy; designing furniture and making it from start to finish seemed to be all in all to him. (Gimson came to have something of the same intensity.) Ernest was a big, jolly, expansive man, practical, easy-going and something of a bon vivant. All three must have seemed socially incongruous in the country, half-gentry half-workmen, but Ernest was the one on whom 'the county' left their cards.

By about 1900 Pinbury Park was getting too small for them. Ernest Barnsley now had four children and Sidney two. In 1900 Gimson married Emily Thompson. In the same year, Gimson and Ernest Barnsley went into partnership to produce furniture, but when they hired cabinet-makers from London and elsewhere they had to put them in a workshop in Cirencester. (Sidney Barnsley remained outside this project, working on his own.) In 1902, by agreement with their landlord, Lord Bathurst, they set up workshops in the outbuildings of the medieval and seventeenth-century Daneway House in the nearby village of Sapperton, using the house itself for showrooms, and built themselves houses in the village, paid for by Lord Bathurst in exchange for their unexpired lease. At Pinbury, Gimson had been unsure of his direction, cushioned (as they all were) by inherited wealth, and also occupied with his architectural work. Now he began to design furniture with energy and concentration. But within a few years a disagreement arose between him and Ernest Barnsley which destroyed their partnership and soured the country idyll. It is not clear whether it was a business or a domestic matter. But it drove a wedge between the three families, and from this time on Gimson and Sidney Barnsley, who were dear friends, were unable to meet in each other's homes.

After the disagreement Ernest Barnsley designed no more furniture. His later work is all architectural: mostly, small domestic buildings in the locality, designed in a reticent version of seventeenth-century Cotswold stone building, and one very large one. In 1909 the Hon. Claud Biddulph, a banker, commissioned Barnsley to build a house on his estate at Rodmarton, south of Cirencester. For Biddulph and his wife Margaret the house was not just a dwelling but an opportunity to provide employment on their estate, and Barnsley's design was built, so far as possible, from local materials by the estate workmen. The interior was furnished to designs by Ernest and Sidney Barnsley and others, and again, much of the work was carried out by local labour. The house took—as it was meant to take—a long time to build, and Rodmarton Manor was not finished until 1929, after Ernest Barnsley's death.

In Sapperton, Sidney Barnsley built a house for his family with big oak floorboards and whitewashed walls. In the garden he built a workshop with a wonderful view across the valley, where he worked each day by himself, producing tables and case-furniture. Some were simple oak pieces, others more sophisticated in making and materials, and none of them easily distinguishable from Gimson's work, except that Barnsley liked to set himself the challenge of difficult construction. As his work became known, there was no shortage of orders and in that sense the workshop paid for itself; but, like Gimson, he could

afford not to charge realistically for his own time and overheads. His two children, **(Emily) Grace Barnsley** (1896–1975), pottery decorator, and **(William) Edward Barnsley** (1900–1987), designer and craftsman, were born at Pinbury Park on 3 October 1896 and 17 February 1900 respectively. Family life was simple but sociable, despite the fact that their mother had been deaf since the age of nineteen. Looking back, Edward felt that he would have liked to have seen more of 'Big Uncle' as they called Gimson, but the feud made that difficult. As a girl Grace was taught to paint pottery by Alfred and Louise Powell who lived in Oakridge nearby, Alfred an architect in the Gimson–Barnsley mould, Louise a skilful embroiderer and calligrapher. Together, the Powells developed a graceful leafy style of painting on pottery and worked for many years in collaboration with Wedgwoods at Stoke-on-Trent. The young Edward, as one might expect, learned woodworking from his father.

Grace and Edward Barnsley In 1910 the children were sent to school at Bedales in Hampshire, whose progressive ethos matched that of the arts and crafts movement; Gimson and Alfred Powell both had connections with the school. In 1914 Grace attended Birmingham Municipal School of Art, and by 1916 she was decorating Wedgwood pottery with delicate patterns of flowers and foliage in the manner of the Powells. She worked in this way during the 1920s and 1930s, though she was never directly employed by the firm. Her brother was not so sure what he should do after school, partly because his father told him he could never earn a living as a furniture maker. In 1919 he was apprenticed to Geoffrey Lupton, an idealistic Old Bedalian who worked as a builder round Petersfield; with Lupton, Edward Barnsley spent about a year helping to build the new library at Bedales, which had been designed by Gimson. He learned more from this than he did from the year he then spent at the Central School of Arts and Crafts in London. In 1923 Lupton asked Edward to take over his joinery workshop at Froxfield, which he did; and in 1925 Lupton offered it for sale. Sidney Barnsley bought the property for his son and thus settled that Edward should, after all, do what his father had done. On 12 December the same year Edward married Tatiana Hedvig (Tania) Kellgren, and they left the church under an archway of hand-saws.

The Barnsley brothers were still working at Sapperton, though by 1924 the effort of woodworking had become too much for Sidney. Gimson had died in 1919, and his work was handsomely celebrated in a memorial volume, which made only passing mention of the Barnsleys. Sidney Barnsley was philosophical about the book, but in truth the record had been distorted. The whole Cotswold project had depended on the skills of sociable, business-like Ernest Barnsley, while in their ideals for architecture and the crafts, Gimson and Sidney Barnsley were twin spirits. Part of Gimson's achievement was the creation of a tradition of neo-rural designing and making, and that was also the Barnsleys' achievement. Ernest Barnsley died in Sapperton on 6 January 1926 and Sidney some months later, on 25 September. They were buried with Gimson in the churchyard at Sapperton. About 300 of Sidney Barnsley's drawings for architecture and furniture, together with a drawing by Edward Barnsley and photographs by Herbert Barnsley of the Barnsleys' homes and work, are at Cheltenham Art Gallery and Museum, Gloucestershire.

On 3 March 1926, between her uncle's and her father's death, Grace Barnsley married Oscar Caradock Davies (b. c.1894), son of the rector of Sapperton, who was an officer in the merchant navy. They were not ready to set up a home of their own, and Grace lived with her mother for some years at various addresses while working at her pottery. In the workshop at Froxfield, Edward Barnsley was doing joinery work for Geoffrey Lupton, and beginning to produce handmade furniture in the Gimson–Barnsley style. Like Gimson, he worked mainly as a designer, employing seven craftsmen; though he was a good craftsman himself, he was always anxious to acknowledge their skill. His life was not an idyll of rural craftsmanship, as his father's and Gimson's were supposed to be, for he had almost no money. It was a long struggle to earn his living as a furniture maker. Warm-hearted and a little naïve, Edward Barnsley was also insecure and prone to long bouts of depression. He believed in craftsmanship as a way of life, but was uneasy with his men in the workshop. He was happiest of all when walking alone in the Lake District. At home he preferred the solitary dialogue of writing letters, or working in the garden of the cottage where he and Tania lived, next to the workshop. They had two children, Karin (b. 1927) and Jon (b. 1930), who became an architect.

In 1934 Grace and Oscar Davies were finally able to settle at Rainham in Kent. They opened a café where they sold the products of the local Upchurch Pottery, and Wedgwood wares which Grace continued to decorate. In 1938 they took over Upchurch, renaming it the Roeginga Pottery, and here they produced sturdy earthenwares, some of which Grace decorated with floral patterns. These ventures were, however, cut short in 1939; the war brought Grace's career as a pottery decorator to an end.

In 1938 Edward Barnsley was appointed design adviser at the East Midlands Training College in Loughborough. Growing up in a little workshop world, he had not thought to look much beyond it; but now he went to Loughborough regularly to talk to the students about making and designing. This brought in a steady if small income. He felt at ease with the trainee teachers and over the next twenty-five years built up a tradition of craft skills at the college. Then, during the Second World War, he was drawn into craft politics and all the difficulties of creating a public face for the crafts. He was involved in the campaign which led, in 1950, to the establishment of the Crafts Centre of Great Britain with its London showroom in Hay Hill, Mayfair, and in attempts in the 1960s to create a craft quango, like the Arts Council and the Council of Industrial Design. It is hard to say whether all his letter-writing, the long committee meetings in London, and the late trains home advanced the cause, but he was driven to them by his belief in craftsmanship. And they were a

stretching of his abilities, an exercise of the middle years.

There were changes in the Edward Barnsley workshop after the war. Bert Upton, who had worked in aircraft production, was appointed foreman and was eager to use more woodworking machinery. Barnsley was unhappy with this development, but the savings made by machinery, especially in the preparation of wood, were too great to be resisted, especially after mains electricity reached Froxfield in the mid-1950s. And Barnsley himself introduced changes. In 1944 he had been struck by the wood-engraver John Farleigh saying that craftspeople had grown too severe and sad, that they should try to catch the temper of the times. His work never ceased to be, like his father's, a celebration of wood and workmanship, but his designs of the 1950s were lighter, looking more to eighteenth-century models.

Through all this Edward Barnsley held to the values of William Morris and the arts and crafts movement. He was delighted in the 1960s and 1970s with the growing historical interest in Gimson and the Barnsleys: more long letters, more working over the difficult and fruitful past. But, on the other hand, he was dismayed when craft began to be whimsical and think of itself as fine art. This trend became obvious at the 'Craftsman's Art' exhibition at the Victoria and Albert Museum in 1973; at the opening, Edward Barnsley could be found elsewhere in the museum, consoling himself with the eighteenth century.

Grace Davies (née Barnsley) died in Broxbourne, Hertfordshire, on 6 March 1975, and was buried in Petersfield, Hampshire. By that time it was becoming increasingly difficult for Edward Barnsley to run his workshop. His clients and admirers were concerned that the workshop might close down, and in 1980 the Edward Barnsley Educational Trust was established to run an apprenticeship scheme within the workshop; it now owns and runs the workshop as well. As he became more vague and forgetful, it distressed him to be where he had worked for so many years. He spent the last months of his life in a hospital in Portsmouth, the dogged, self-critical, generous, and always striving spirit cancelled out for much of the time by Alzheimer's disease. Edward Barnsley died on 2 December 1987 and his ashes were buried in his parents' grave in the churchyard at Sapperton. ALAN CRAWFORD

Sources M. Comino, *Gimson and the Barnsleys: 'Wonderful furniture of a commonplace kind'* (1980) · A. Carruthers, *Edward Barnsley and his workshop: arts and crafts in the twentieth century* (1992) · W. R. Lethaby, A. H. Powell, and F. L. Griggs, *Ernest Gimson: his life and work* (1924) · *'Good citizen's furniture': the work of Ernest and Sidney Barnsley* (1976) [exhibition catalogue, Cheltenham Art Gallery and Museum] · A. Carruthers, *Ernest Gimson and the Cotswold group of craftsmen: a catalogue of works by Ernest Gimson, Ernest and Sidney Barnsley and Peter Waals, in the collections of Leicestershire Museums* (1978) · *Edward Barnsley: sixty years of furniture design and cabinet making* (1982) [exhibition catalogue, Fine Art Society, London, Jan 25 – Feb 19 1982; Crafts Study Centre, Bath, April 3 – June 13 1982] · *Fitness for purpose and pleasure in use: furniture from the Edward Barnsley workshop, 1922 to the present day* (1985) [exhibition catalogue, Stockport Museums and Art Gallery] · M. Greensted, ed., *The arts and crafts movement in the Cotswolds* (1993) · A. Carruthers and M. Greensted, *Good citizen's furniture: the arts and crafts collections at Cheltenham* (1994) · J. Sarsby,

'Alfred Powell: idealism and realism in the Cotswolds', *Journal of Design History*, 10 (1997), 375–97 · T. Harrod, *The crafts in Britain in the 20th century* (1999) · *CGPLA Eng. & Wales* (1926) [Sidney Barnsley] · *CGPLA Eng. & Wales* (1926) [Ernest Barnsley] · d. cert. [Grace Barnsley] · m. cert. [Grace Barnsley]

Archives Edward Barnsley Educational Trust, Petersfield, Hampshire, designs, sketches, photographs, letters, and business records [Edward Barnsley] · Edward Barnsley Educational Trust, Petersfield, Hampshire, letters [Grace Barnsley] · Edward Barnsley Educational Trust, Peterfield, Hampshire, letters [Sidney Barnsley] · priv. coll., papers and photographs [Grace Barnsley] | BL, papers of Sidney Cockerell [Ernest Barnsley and Sidney Barnsley] · British School, Athens, notebooks, sketchbooks, and drawings [Sidney Barnsley] · Cheltenham Art Gallery and Museum, letters of Ernest Gimson [Ernest Barnsley and Sidney Barnsley] · Leics. RO, letters of Ernest Gimson [Ernest Barnsley and Sidney Barnsley] · PRO, board of trade file on Kenton & Co. Ltd, BT 31, box no. 5001, company no. 33484 [Ernest Barnsley and Sidney Barnsley]

Likenesses W. Rothenstein, lithograph, 1913 [Ernest Barnsley], Leicester Museum · photograph (Grace Barnsley, aged four), Edward Barnsley Educational Trust, Petersfield, Hampshire · photographs (Ernest Barnsley), Edward Barnsley Educational Trust, Petersfield, Hampshire · photographs (Ernest Barnsley), Cheltenham Art Gallery and Museum · photographs (Sidney Barnsley), Cheltenham Art Gallery and Museum · photographs (Sidney Barnsley), Edward Barnsley Educational Trust, Petersfield, Hampshire · photographs (Grace Barnsley), priv. coll.

Wealth at death £10,296 8s. 2d.—Sidney Barnsley: probate, 1926, *CGPLA Eng. & Wales* · £4317 5s. 5d.—Ernest Barnsley: probate, 1926, *CGPLA Eng. & Wales*

Barnsley, Alan Gabriel [*pseud.* Gabriel Fielding] (1916–1986), novelist and poet, was born on 25 March 1916 in Hexham, Northumberland, the fifth of the six children of George Barnsley (1875–1956), a clergyman in the Church of England, and his wife, Katherine Mary Fielding-Smith (1884–1974), who claimed descent from the eighteenth-century novelist and playwright Henry Fielding. Barnsley's father suffered from sleeping sickness, contracted in the First World War; his mother was a playwright and a breeder of whippets. Barnsley described his childhood as 'golden' until at the age of eight he was sent off to the Grange School, Eastbourne, Sussex, where he experienced hostility from masters and fellow pupils. Looking back as an adult on his time at the Grange, he thought that it probably 'was the beginning of the pain out of which I write' (Newquist, 196). He later attended St Edward's School, Oxford, and Llangefni county school, Anglesey, Wales. When his time came for university study, Barnsley enrolled at Trinity College, Dublin. His parents felt that Trinity would lead to a 'sympathetic career' in medicine and convinced Barnsley that his studies would also be a good preparation for writing (Newquist, 197). At Trinity Barnsley won prizes in anatomy, biology, and oratory and was a member of the Philosophical Society; but after earning his University of Dublin BA in May 1940, he was unable to gain admission to a local hospital for medical studies, probably because he was known to have written a satire on Dublin hospitals. Instead, he enrolled in May 1941 at St George's Hospital, London. He qualified MRCS LRCP in 1942.

In 1943 Barnsley married Edwina Eleanora Cook (*b.* 1923) of Storrington, Sussex, and joined the Royal Army Medical Corps, in which he served until 1946, leaving with the rank of captain. Barnsley entered in 1946 into general medical practice in Maidstone, Kent, a practice that continued until 1966. In time he also assumed the duty of deputy medical officer of Maidstone Prison. He and his wife were received into the Roman Catholic church on 8 September 1954. Barnsley's religious conversion also had literary links, which, along with illness and the stress of work, led him to take up writing in earnest. He had carefully read Graham Greene and Evelyn Waugh, both converts to Catholicism, and was a close friend of Muriel Spark, another convert. Spark dedicated her first novel, *The Comforters*, to the Barnsleys and was godmother to one of their children. Early on, Greene encouraged Barnsley's writing. For additional encouragement there had always been the example of his mother, of whom he wrote, 'it was her ardour and longing—not for me but for her own work—that contributed to my determination [to be a storyteller]' (Wakeman, 472).

Barnsley first tried poetry. *The Frog Prince and other Poems* came out in 1952. *Brotherly Love* (1954), his first novel, introduced John Blaydon, the character whose often disheartening experiences are at the centre of five novels. In *Brotherly Love* John Blaydon is troubled by a domineering mother and a lustful older brother, a misfit of a clergyman. A second volume of poetry, *XXVIII Poems*, appeared in 1955 and reflected the author's developing religious sensibility. In the second Blaydon novel, *In the Time of Greenbloom* (1956), the girl he loves is raped and murdered, he is treated cruelly at school, and he meets and is saved from despair by a fantastic Jew named Greenbloom, an Oxford student. In the novel *Eight Days* (1958), Barnsley temporarily departed from the world of the Blaydon family to enter Graham Greene country: a prison doctor, a recent convert to Roman Catholicism, on vacation in north Africa, becomes caught up in spy intrigue. Then with the publication of *Through Streets Broad and Narrow* (1960) Barnsley completed what at the time he considered a trilogy about John Blaydon, now a medical student in frequent distress in Dublin.

According to Barnsley, *The Birthday King* (1962) was an attempt to get away from the subjectivity of the trilogy (Wakeman, 472). The novel is about a family of part-Jewish Catholic industrialists in Nazi Germany. It won the W. H. Smith prize for literature as well as the St Thomas More gold medal in the USA in 1964. *Gentlemen in their Season* (1966), about a Catholic convert and an atheist working in the religious division of the BBC, followed. *New Queens for Old* (1972) consisted of a novella and nine short stories. It won the 1972 Governor's literary award in the state of Washington, USA. In *Pretty Doll Houses* (1979) Barnsley returned to the Blaydons with the usual echoes—in this case movement of the family from Sussex to Yorkshire to Anglesey—of Barnsley's own upbringing. Finally in 1986, the year of his death, he published *The Women of Guinea Lane*, in which John Blaydon, now a surgeon at Guinea Lane Hospital in Middlesex during the Second World War, observes the women around him.

J. K. L. Walker wrote in the *Times Literary Supplement* of

The Women of Guinea Lane: 'It is difficult not to admire Fielding's humanity, his sense that life, especially for women, is hard, that happiness is precarious and daily vulnerable to some unexplained assault on body or mind' (Walker). That humanity shows frequently in the novels in Barnsley's characters' search for love. To Barnsley 'it is not at all so lucky to *be* loved as it is to *love*' as the character Rachel says to John Blaydon in *Greenbloom* (p. 254). Barnsley himself told an interviewer that 'The most important part of living is loving' and that 'I have never seen a man make a success of his life without loving his fellow creatures' (Newquist, 203, 206).

As his writing took up more and more of his time and interest, Barnsley gradually cut back on his medical practice. In addition to his creative writing, he was publishing essays in literary journals, and from 1961 on he was doing occasional broadcasts for the BBC. For his journalism he received a Catholic Press Association award in 1965. Then in 1966 he accepted a one-year appointment as author-in-residence at Washington State University in Pullman, Washington. He never returned to medical practice. After his year as visiting artist ended, he accepted an appointment as professor at Washington State, where he taught until retiring in 1981. Barnsley had been made DLitt by Gonzaga University in Spokane, Washington, in 1967, and after his retirement Washington State named him professor emeritus.

Barnsley died on 27 November 1986 at 14625 NE 34th Street, apartment G 19, in Bellevue, Washington, having suffered for some months the effects of lung cancer. He was cremated on 2 December 1986 at Sunset crematory in Bellevue, Washington; later his ashes were interred in a churchyard near Aylesford, Kent. Inscribed on his headstone are the words 'Love is always more'. Barnsley was survived by his widow, three sons, and two daughters.

JOHN H. SCHWARZ

Sources A. Borrello, *Gabriel Fielding* (1974) · *WWW*, 1981–90 · *Who's who in America*, 43rd edn (1984–5) · R. Newquist, *Counterpoint* (1964) · d. cert. · will, 4 Jan 1984 · [J. Wakeman], ed., *World authors, 1950–70* (1975) · J. K. L. Walker, review of *The women of Guinea Lane*, *TLS* (29 Aug 1986) · F. Taliaferro, 'Who is Gabriel Fielding?', *New Criterion*, 2/3 (1983), 18–22 · private information (2004) [Edwina Barnsley; S. Nanji, Trinity College, Dublin; N. Thevakarrunai, St George's Hospital Medical School]
Archives Georgetown University, Washington, DC, papers · McMaster University, Hamilton, Ontario, corresp. and literary MSS | Washington State University, Pullman, Washington, DC, Borrello collection
Likenesses portrait (in old age), repro. in G. Fielding [A. G. Barnsley], *The women of Guinea Lane* (1986), jacket
Wealth at death bequests to widow and five children; left $10,000 to the Christian Children's Fund: will

Barnsley, (William) Edward (1900–1987). *See under* Barnsley family (*per.* 1885–1987).

Barnsley, (Arthur) Ernest (1863–1926). *See under* Barnsley family (*per.* 1885–1987).

Barnsley, (Emily) Grace (1896–1975). *See under* Barnsley family (*per.* 1885–1987).

Barnsley, Sidney Howard (1865–1926). *See under* Barnsley family (*per.* 1885–1987).

Barnston, John (1562/3–1645), Church of England clergyman, was of Cheshire gentry stock, the second son of William Barnston (*d.* 1620) of Churton and his wife, Elizabeth (*d.* 1606/7), daughter of Roger Massey of Coddington. William Barnston was a client of the Stanleys, earls of Derby, and a Restoration source describes John Barnston as 'Chaplain and Friend' to William, sixth earl of Derby, between 1620 and 1640 (Lloyd, 91). Barnston was educated at Brasenose College, Oxford, where he matriculated in 1581, aged eighteen, graduated BA in 1588, and proceeded MA in 1589; from 1588 to 1597 he was a fellow of his college. While fellow he also held the rectory of Begbroke, Oxfordshire, from which he resigned in August 1597. In 1615, when he was a chaplain to Lord Chancellor Ellesmere, he graduated BD and DD of the University of Oxford. This chaplaincy also suggests a Stanley connection, as Ellesmere was married to Alice, widow of Ferdinando, fifth earl of Derby.

In 1598 Barnston became rector of Everleigh in Wiltshire (to which he added the living of Winterslow in 1634). In 1601 he was collated to the prebend of Bishopstone at Salisbury Cathedral and from 1609 until his death he appears as a canon residentiary of the cathedral. In May 1634, when the cathedral was visited in Archbishop Laud's metropolitical visitation, Barnston was *locum tenens* dean. He was one of those canons most willing to break ranks with the chapter's general reply to the visitor, Dr Brent, by more vociferously condemning the negligent running of the cathedral and the faults of his colleagues (in part, perhaps, fighting old battles following a bitter dispute within the chapter five years earlier). Barnston was concerned with maintaining some order and decency within the cathedral: one colleague described him as one of those canons most active in getting up from their seats to try and impose decorum during service time, as men of all ranks walked through the church with their hats on and peered in on the chapter at prayer, as well as 'the ordinarie trudginge up and downe of youths, & clamours of children, to the great disturbance of the preachers in their sermons' (*Fourth Report*, HMC, appx, 135).

However, it is unknown how far Barnston was willing to align himself more positively with a ceremonialist and anti-puritan position, though such evidence as there is hints at a likely indifference to such preoccupations. Barnston's visitation articles for the parish of Bishopstone (where he had peculiar jurisdiction as prebendary) in 1624 prescribed that the church should possess the ornaments and books required by law, but were entirely silent as to the conduct and conformity of the minister. In 1645 Barnston's will ordained a sparse funeral—in private, at night, without sermon or mourning apparel.

Fuller says that Barnston was 'a bountiful housekeeper, of a cheerful spirit and peaceable disposition', and relates a story of his acting as a genial mediator in the consistory court (Fuller, 193). Tellingly, given the poisonous atmosphere of the chapter, colleagues praised him as unique in the conscientiousness with which he fulfilled the obligations of hospitality due from the residentiary canons of the cathedral, 'as well for the poorer as the richer sort', while he was the only canon who resided frequently enough at his benefice (*Fourth Report*, HMC, appx, 135). At Everleigh Barnston attempted as protestant pastor to fulfil his social obligations of neighbourliness while trying to reshape local custom. When he arrived in the parish he was faced with the long-established practice that the minister should offer bread, cheese, and beer at the parsonage after evening prayer on Christmas day. He countenanced this for a while, 'out of neighbourlie kindnesse, or out of weaknesses (for I misliked it)', but after the Gunpowder Plot, he attempted to divert the custom to the more respectably protestant 5 November 'in remembrance of the deliverance' (Whitlock, 75–6). However, Barnston's success was short-lived and by 1610 he had acquiesced in the return of the custom to Christmas day. In 1628 Barnston gave £100 to his old college to set up an annual lectureship in Hebrew. For £6 a year, the lecturer should read a lecture twice a week in term-time and once a week in vacation. Barnston is also known to have given in his lifetime a gift of £210 to the city of Salisbury.

Barnston died on 30 May 1645. He had lived to see himself 'outed of his spiritualities' by the parliamentary forces (Wood, *Ath. Oxon.: Fasti*, 1.363). His will vividly conveys the sense of an old man whose world had been overturned by war: 'considering how the tymes are, who knoweth what hee shalbe worth and how hee shall dye'. He left £5 for the poor of Everleigh (and a further £5 to the poor of Salisbury): 'I had intended better things for perpetuitye both for that and other places, butt all dasht by reason of my poverty and the tymes'. He gave a further £20 to the plundered of Everleigh, 'to bee divided amongst them Lovingly and Conscionablye'. Barnston attempted to preserve one piece of order after his death: a servant was to receive 20 shillings, 'To the intente hee helpe to place my bookes att the place whether they shalbe removed, in such order as they now stand as neare as hee cann' (PRO, PROB 11/199, fol. 491r). Barnston's wife, Mary, had died before him, in May 1625, and his will makes no mention of surviving children. He does single out among kin whom he recognized in the will, who included Masseys and Barnstons, his nephew William Barnston, who was to be his executor, urging him, 'Good cosen I desire yow for Christes sake to remember how God hath incresed mee, and yow by mee' (PRO, PROB 11/199, fol. 490v). John Barnston was buried in Salisbury Cathedral, where there are memorial tablets to his wife and to himself, the latter stating 'mutavit saecula, non obiit'.

RONALD BAYNE, *rev.* TIM WALES

Sources Foster, *Alum. Oxon.* • [C. B. Heberden], ed., *Brasenose College register, 1509–1909*, 1, OHS, 55 (1909), 61 • A. J. Butler, 'The benefactions bestowed on the college', *Brasenose College quatercentenary monographs*, ed. [F. Madan], 1, 23, OHS, 52 (1909) • *Fourth report*, HMC, 3 (1874), 127–36 • will, PRO, PROB 11/199, sig. 62 • *Fasti Angl., 1541–1857*, [Salisbury], 29, 97 • R. Whitlock, *The folklore of Wiltshire* (1976), 75–6 • K. Fincham, ed., *Visitation articles and injunctions of the early Stuart church*, 2 (1998), xv–xvi • Fuller, *Worthies* (1811), 193 • D. Lloyd, *Memoires of the lives … of those … personages that suffered …*

for the protestant religion (1668), 91–3 • Wood, *Ath. Oxon.: Fasti* (1815), 363 • A. Wood, *The history and antiquities of the colleges and halls in the University of Oxford*, ed. J. Gutch (1786), 364 • G. Ormerod, *The history of the county palatine and city of Chester*, 2nd edn, ed. T. Helsby, 2 (1882), 747 • R. Benson and H. Hatcher, *Old and New Sarum or Salisbury*, 2 vols. (1843), 448 • D. H. Robertson, *Sarum Close: a history of the life and education of the cathedral choristers for 700 years* (1938), 175–85 • *Wiltshire: the topographical collections of John Aubrey*, ed. J. E. Jackson, Wiltshire Archaeological and Natural History Society, 1 (1862), 366 n. • general register, 1579–1638, Oxon. RO, Oxf. dioc. papers, c. 265

Likenesses oils; recorded as owned by Salisbury corporation in 'The Salisbury corporationpictures', *Wiltshire Archaeological and Natural History Magazine*, 35 (1907–8), 148

Barnwell, John (*c*.1671–1724), colonial official and army officer in America, was born probably in Dublin, the son of Matthew Barnwell, alderman, and Margaret Carberry. Having lost his father, a captain in James II's Irish army, in the siege of Londonderry in 1690, Barnwell emigrated to South Carolina in 1701, at the age of approximately thirty. John Page, an alderman in Dublin who later became lord mayor, described Barnwell as an adventuresome sort, who emigrated 'out of a humor to goe to travel, but for no other Reasson' (Salley, 47). Barnwell settled on St Helena Island, the southernmost point of British colonization on the North American mainland. The area had been colonized earlier by Scottish Presbyterians, and Barnwell quickly established political, economic, and social ties in the community. Although a member of the Church of England, he became an outspoken defender of religious dissenter rights. In 1707 he led an angry crowd against Chief Justice Nicholas Trott, for his upholding of a Church Establishment Act that penalized dissenters. (The act was later overturned in the House of Lords.)

Barnwell was regularly elected to the Carolina general assembly, but it was in the colony's relations with Native Americans that he earned local fame. Barnwell, along with his ally and neighbour the Scot Thomas Nairne, led a political movement to improve intercultural relations with Carolina's American Indian neighbours, through government regulation of the Indian trade. Barnwell had developed an excellent rapport with the colony's most important allies, the Yamasee, whom he lived near, and he was selected by the assembly to be 'Commissioner of the Southern Indians'. He did not serve long in the position, but it led to his appointment as commander of an 'Indian army' to rescue neighbouring North Carolina, which was in the midst of war with a coalition of native peoples, the so-called 'Tuscarora War'.

Barnwell's army of 528 men travelled overland to North Carolina in January 1712. The force was almost entirely composed of Native Americans drawn from over a dozen different groups; he had difficulty keeping them and had many desertions. None the less, he succeeded in destroying several American Indian posts and earned the nickname Tuscarora Jack. After concluding a tenuous peace, he and his army returned by sea to South Carolina. The war resumed. Barnwell briefly lost favour in South Carolina because of a letter he wrote intimating that his colony would not have rescued North Carolina without his influence. Nevertheless, he regained favour during the Yamasee War in 1715, a conflict uniting many native peoples against South Carolina, and successfully led colonial troops against the colony's enemies.

With the colony's southern frontier exposed, Barnwell travelled secretly to Spanish Florida to negotiate with the Yamasee, to make peace and convince them to return to their lands along the Savannah River. When this effort failed, he travelled to Britain to promote the defence of South Carolina through the settlement of foreign protestants in a ring of fortified towns around the colony. He also called for extending British settlement south of the Savannah River into Spanish territory, which he and Sir Robert Montgomery promoted in their pamphlet *The most Delightful Golden Isles* (1717). Although Montgomery did not succeed in establishing a new colony, Barnwell led an expedition to build and man Fort King George (1721–7) on the Altamaha River in modern-day southern Georgia—a provocative threat by the British against Spanish Florida and an indicator of British intentions in the area. Barnwell's plans for settlement of poor protestants in heavily garrisoned communities were briefly adopted by South Carolina, but, more importantly, served as a rationale and blueprint for the settlement of a new colony, Georgia, in 1733.

Barnwell's last years included the production of several important maps of the American south, and a detailed census of southern Native Americans. He died at Beaufort, South Carolina, in 1724, and was buried in the Anglican church cemetery at Beaufort. He was survived by his wife, Anne Berners, and their eight children.

ALAN GALLAY

Sources J. W. Barnwell, 'The Tuscarora expedition: letters of Colonel John Barnwell', *South Carolina Historical and Genealogical Magazine*, 9 (1908), 28–54 · A. S. Salley, 'Barnwell of South Carolina', *South Carolina Historical and Genealogical Magazine*, 2 (1901), 46–57 · R. Montgomery and J. Barnwell, *The most delightful golden isles: being a proposal for the establishment of a colony to the south of Carolina* (1717) [repr. (1966)] · A. Gallay, *The Indian slave trade: the rise of the English empire in the American south, 1670–1717* (2001) · L. S. Rowland, 'Barnwell, John', *ANB*
Archives PRO, South Carolina records · South Carolina Archives and History Center, Columbia, South Carolina house of assembly journals

Baro, Peter (1534–1599), clergyman and university teacher, was born at Étampes (Seine-et-Oise), France, the son of Étienne Baron and his wife, Philippe Petit; in his autobiographical notes Peter says he was one of many children, first mentioning brothers Jean and Florent, so he was perhaps the third to survive. The family is believed to have belonged to the rich *bourgeoisie* or *petite noblesse*. Peter's first training was in the civil law. On 9 April 1556 he graduated BCL at the University of Bourges, and received the licenciate on the following day. In 1557 he was sworn advocate of the *parlement* of Paris. Having adopted the Reformed faith and intending to serve in its ministry, he went to Geneva where, at the age of twenty-six, in December 1560, he was ordained by Calvin himself. Having returned to France, he married (at Gien, on the Loire,

between 17 May and 7 June 1563) Guillemette, daughter of Étienne Burgoin, a merchant, and his wife, Lopza, *née* Dozival. Their first child, Marthe, was born at Orléans on 1 June 1564, followed by Pierre in January 1566 and a second son in 1567, both born at Orléans. The family moved to Sancerre, where further children were born in October 1568 and May 1569.

Baro was one of several Huguenot ministers who took refuge in England after the massacre of 24 August 1572 (in Baro's own laconic phrase, 'a cause des troubles de la France' (CUL, MS Mm.1.40, p. 185). Lord Burghley took him into his household and, as chancellor of Cambridge University, arranged for him to settle there. On 11 April 1573 Baro was admitted to Peterhouse as a fellow commoner, and by the end of August he was receiving an allowance reckoned at £6 10s. in a full year. At the same time he rented a small house from the college for 16s. a year. The master of Peterhouse, Andrew Perne, found him some college teaching. He was also engaged by the provost of King's, Roger Goad, to lecture on Hebrew 'privately' in the provost's lodge, and then on divinity 'publicly' in the college hall, for which a stipend of £20 was subscribed by the provost and the others attending. In 1574, through the efforts of Perne and Burghley, Baro was elected to the Lady Margaret professorship of divinity. His acceptance into Cambridge society seems evident in July 1574 when his son Andrew was baptized in Little St Mary's by the regius professor of Greek, Bartholomew Doddington. On 3 February 1575 Baro was admitted to the degree of LLB by incorporation. By a grace of 8 June he was authorized to incept DTh; he incorporated this degree at Oxford on 11 July. Twins Elizabeth and Catherine, born in August 1577, completed his family, for support of which his miscellaneous teaching fees were inadequate. On 18 March 1579 the university formally asked the secretaries of state to assist with some preferment; but it was not until 1605 that a living was annexed to the Lady Margaret chair, and Baro never held an English benefice.

In 1579 Baro was able to return to France to collect members of his family who had remained there. Back in England he had some hope of ministering at the French church in Threadneedle Street in association with Robert Le Maçon, and of succeeding Pierre de Villiers as lecturer. But he had already distanced himself from the strict Calvinism maintained by the London Huguenots. Views he had been developing in the Cambridge schools were this year published as *In Jonam prophetam prælectiones 30* (entered on 26 March). Although dedicated to the archbishop of Canterbury, Edmund Grindal, and including unexceptionable matter against the papacy and transubstantiation, the assertion that human will might refuse divine grace was a fundamental negation of the prevailing orthodoxy. To Baro's opponents this was an affront to the omnipotence of God. Letters patent of denization were granted to Baro, his wife, and their French-born children Peter and Mary on 15 April 1580; the fees were waived by the lord chancellor, Sir Christopher Hatton. In that year Baro published *De fide eiusque ortu & natura*, commenting on Romans 3: 28. By 1581 his lectures on Jonah and other interpretations of justifying faith were drawing sharp responses from the leading Cambridge theologians, principally the regius professor, William Whitaker, Walter Travers, and Laurence Chaderton. In spring 1583 his teachings were singled out for attack by a meeting of Kingsmen in London, a sign that his old patron Provost Goad had turned against him. On 21 October 1586 Baro dedicated to Grindal's successor, Archbishop John Whitgift, his *De præsentia & dignitate divinæ legis*. Some of his sermons and university disputations appeared in John Ludham's translation in Andrewas Gerardus, *A Speciall Treatise of Gods Providence*, entered on 30 August 1588; the entire work has sometimes been ascribed to Baro.

The Cambridge theological debate became a public issue in 1595, beginning on 27 February when Whitaker denounced his fellow professor's teachings before a high-profile congregation. The immediate rejoinder came not from Baro but from a junior figure, William Barrett of Gonville and Caius, whose university sermon of 29 April articulated Baro's opinions in an abrasive manner which particularly annoyed the seniors. In prosecuting Barrett, they also targeted Baro as his inspiration if not his direct mentor. In the effort to obtain condemnation of Barrett on disciplinary grounds, it was necessary to represent the anti-Calvinist theologians as a serious threat to the university's teaching authority, and therefore as perhaps a more substantial opposition than it actually was. On 7 June Baro was asked to give the university consistory his opinion of Barrett's sermon. Unlike Whitaker, Baro then observed the moratorium on further debate pending the meeting which Whitgift summoned to Lambeth. When the nine articles agreed there on 20 November were received in Cambridge, the Calvinists exulted in the endorsement of their beliefs. Goad (as vice-chancellor) instructed Baro to study the articles and to teach nothing contrary. By 8 December Baro's response had (according to Whitgift) displeased the queen; but Elizabeth had already objected to the mere making of the articles, and was upset by the continuing debate rather than by Baro's actual opinions. Baro at first maintained that the articles could be squared with his own theology; he defended his interpretation in writing to Whitgift on 13 December, and in two meetings with him at Lambeth in the same month. Then on 12 January 1596 he gave a university sermon in which he took the articles apart; central to his theme was the distinction between antecedent and consequent divine will. In this he followed Aquinas, and more recently sermons by Richard Hooker (1581) and Samuel Harsnett (1584) in maintaining that man might choose his own damnation. Goad and the two other heads who had been in Great St Mary's to hear Baro immediately decided to silence him; at the same time a group of puritan dons drew up their own protest. Whitgift rejected the vice-chancellor's suggestion of prosecution before the high commission; he thought Baro was being encouraged by rumours that the Lambeth articles were misliked at court. When Baro was interviewed informally by the vice-chancellor and others on 17 January, only the new regius professor, John Overall, supported him. On 22 January he appeared before the consistory,

where he continued to deny that he had condemned the articles. Burghley was asked to intervene, but responded by accusing the university of treating Baro 'as he were a theefe' (Cambridge, Trinity College, MS B.14.9, p. 129). In March the vice-chancellor and heads complained again to Burghley that Baro, 'busie and curious in alienâ republica', had for many years broached 'new and strange quæstions in religion' (ibid., p. 185) and the vice-chancellor took the issue to Whitgift personally. Their xenophobia echoed an earlier comment put into the queen's mouth by the archbishop. Nothing came directly of any of this, and on 22 March Baro felt able to thank Whitgift for protecting him. But to his friend Neils Hemmingsen in Copenhagen (a disciple of Philip Melancthon) he confided his distaste for the new spirit of intolerance he detected in England: 'we have hitheto been permitted to hold the same sentiments as yours on grace, but we are now scarcely allowed publicly to teach … much less to publish them' (Nichols, 1.92).

On 17 September 1596 Baro wrote to Burghley asking for support in his re-election to the Lady Margaret chair, the biennial tenure of which would expire in November. He took the opportunity to send a summary of his views on justification; it was probably this manuscript which Burghley passed to his chaplain Richard Neile for comment; the future Arminian archbishop could not at this stage accept Baro's belief in election 'on account of faith foreseen' (Tyacke, 111). Whitgift, however, intervened brutally in telling the new vice-chancellor, Thomas Jegon, that while he meant 'no impediment' to Baro's re-election, if the university was not minded to retain Baro, he would recommend Thomas Playfere. Jegon responded by recalling that he had himself been a pupil of 'that reverend old man' and 'paynfull teacher', and suggesting that, should he lose his chair, he might still scrape a living from college teaching (CUL, MS Mm.1.35, pp. 349, 356). In the event Whitgift's man was elected, and in November Baro left Cambridge to spend his final years in Dyers Yard, Crutched Friars, by the Tower of London. There he died in April 1599, and on 17 April was buried beneath the altar of St Olave, Hart Street. Bishop Bancroft ordered a full turnout of city clergy; the sermon was preached by the incumbent, John Sympson, and six divines carried the coffin.

By his will dated 1 March 1599 (when he gave his age as sixty-four) and proved on 27 April, Baro gave £100 to each of his twin daughters should they be unmarried at his death, and the rest of his goods in England and France to his surviving children, Peter, Andrew, Mary, and the twins. His wife seems to have died before the move to London and his sons were his executors. Peter had followed his father to Peterhouse as sizar (1576) and fellow (1585); he practised medicine at Boston, Lincolnshire, where through the continuing patronage of the Cecil family he became a freeman, mayor (1610), and a JP, dying in 1630. Andrew also lived at Boston until his death in 1658. Both sons established families which sustained contacts with Peterhouse and the profession of medicine.

Although Peter Baro's career ended in a second,

internal, exile, it was his views rather than those of Whitaker which eventually passed into mainstream Anglicanism. He was not the first to stand against the rigidities of Calvinism, but the events of 1595–6 made him the most prominent of those who have been called Arminians *avant la lettre*, and he helped to ensure that the church of his adoption would not be ruled by the dead hand of the man who had ordained him.

C. S. KNIGHTON

Sources Trinity Cam., MS B.14.9, pp. 83–185 · CUL, MSS Mm.1.35, pp. 349, 356; Mm.1.40, pp. 184–8; Mm.2.25, fols. 108v–109v (pp. 2–7-9) · Venn, *Alum. Cant.*, 1/1.95 · Cooper, *Ath. Cantab.*, 2.274–8 · J. Venn, ed., *Grace book Δ* (1910), 291, 294 · *ESTC*, 11760+ · T. A. Walker, *A biographical register of Peterhouse men*, 2 (1930), 297–8 · E. Haag and E. Haag, *La France protestante*, 2nd edn, 6 vols. (Paris, 1877–88), vol. 1, pp. 866–9 · F. de Schickler, *Les églises du refuge*, 2 vols. (Paris, 1892), 1.235–8 · 'The Huguenot families in England: 2, the Barons', *The Ancestor*, 3 (Oct 1902), 105–17 · J. Heywood and T. Wright, eds., *Cambridge University transactions during the puritan controversies of the 16th and 17th centuries*, 2 vols. (1854), 2.89–100 · W. B. Bannerman, ed., *The registers of St Olave, Hart Street, London, 1563–1700*, Harleian Society, register section, 46 (1916), 131 · *CPR, 1578–80*, 278 (no. 2189) · *Calendar of the manuscripts of the most hon. the marquis of Salisbury*, 13, HMC, 9 (1915), 204 · H. C. Porter, *Reformation and reaction in Tudor Cambridge* (1958), 376–90 and *passim* · P. G. Lake, 'Laurence Chaderton and the Cambridge moderate puritan tradition, 1570–1604', PhD diss., U. Cam., 1978, 160–261 · P. G. Lake, *Moderate puritans and the Elizabethan church* (1982), 227–41 and *passim* · N. Tyacke, *Anti-Calvinists: the rise of English Arminianism, c.1590–1640* (1987) · J. H. Hessels, ed., *Ecclesiae Londino-Batavae Archivum* (1887–97), 2, *Epistolae et Tractatus*, 648–56, 667–75 · E. S. Shuckburgh, trans., *Laurence Chaderton … from a Latin memoir of Dr Dillingham* (1884), 5–6 · J. Strype, *The life and acts of John Whitgift*, new edn, 3 vols. (1822), vol. 3, pp. 340–47 · will, PRO, PROB 11/93, fols. 214–15 · J. Nichols, ed., *The works of James Arminius*, 3 vols. (1825–8)
Archives BL, letters, Lansdowne MSS 80, no. 69; 82, no. 91 · CUL, treatise, MS Gg.1.29, no. 60 · Trinity Cam., letters, MS B.14.9, pp. 83–5, 87–8, 95–9
Wealth at death left £100 to each of his twin daughters, a small sum (10s.? each) to (50?) paupers and his Cambridge maid; residue of goods in England and France (unspecified) to be shared by his children: will, PRO, PROB 11/93, fols. 214–15

Baroda. *See* Gaikwar, Sayaji Rao, maharaja of Baroda (1863–1939).

Baron, (Joseph) Alexander (1917–1999), novelist and screenwriter, was born Joseph Alexander Bernstein on 4 December 1917 at 30 Penyston Road, Maidenhead, Berkshire, the son of Barnet Bernstein, later Baron (1894–1977), a Polish-born furrier, and his wife, Fanny, *née* Levinson (1895–1973). Once settled in England the family changed its name to Baron, which Alexander formally adopted in 1948. He was brought up with his younger sister, Ida, in a secular Jewish milieu in Stoke Newington and was educated at the Grocers' Company's School, Hackney (1929–35). Baron recalled that when seventeen 'I was driven by shame at not earning my own living to forgo a university scholarship I had won and to take a job as a municipal clerk' (Seymour-Smith and Kimmens, 134).

Already active in the anti-fascist struggle being waged in the East End, Baron soon became prominent in the national leadership of the Labour League of Youth. From 1938 to 1939 he was assistant editor of the left-wing weekly *Tribune*, and in 1939–40 he edited *Challenge*, the weekly journal of the Young Communist League. From this time Baron became increasingly disillusioned with communism, making his final break with radical politics soon after the war. In September 1939 Baron wished to join the RAF to fulfil his childhood passion for flying, but was rejected because of weak eyesight. Instead, he enlisted in the army and participated as an infantryman in the Sicilian and Italian campaigns, and, promoted to corporal, as a sapper in the D-day landing and in the fighting in north-western Europe. He was injured towards the end of the war. After a long convalescence he returned in 1946 to London, where he started work as editor of the journal *New Theatre*. After the success of *From the City, from the Plough* (1948), his first novel, he resigned to become a full-time writer.

Baron's life and work were both deeply touched by the conflicts and destiny of the twentieth century. *From the City, from the Plough*, a powerful, humane novel based on his own wartime experience, earned high critical acclaim, and became an instant best-seller of more than a million copies (it was compared by Randall Stevenson to the First World War classic *All Quiet on the Western Front*). *There's No Home* (1950, American title *The Wine of Etna*) tells the story of a love affair between a British soldier and an Italian girl during a brief interlude in the fighting, while *The Human Kind: a Sequence* (1953) narrates episodes in the infantry war as experienced by the ordinary soldier. In these simple tales Baron reveals profound truths about humanity *in extremis*. *The Human Kind* was filmed by Carl Foreman in 1963 under the title *The Victors*.

A second important group of Baron's novels shares an East End of London setting. *Rosie Hogarth* (1951) centres on the fortunes of an ex-soldier in a changed home landscape. *With Hope Farewell* (1952) is a novel of Jewish life in England and touches on the theme of antisemitism in post-war east London. After *The Golden Princess* (1954), a historical romance set at the time of the Spanish conquest of Mexico, and *Queen of the East* (1956), which retells a third-century love story based on an episode in Edward Gibbon's work, Baron returned to the contemporary London landscape in *Seeing Life* (1958), a tale of the television and mass entertainment industry.

On 4 August 1960 Baron married Delores Lopez-Salzedo (b. 1928), an advertising copywriter. They had one son. *The Lowlife* (1963), described by John Williams as 'a beautifully observed, understated study of an East End Jewish gambler', ranges from local racetracks to the middle-class suburbs, from seedy slums to swinging sixties Soho, and was one of the first British novels to include Caribbean immigrants among its characters (*The Guardian*, 8 Dec 1999). *Strip Jack Naked* (1966), a sequel to *The Lowlife*, follows the character of Harryboy Boas from his east London habitat to Paris and Venice. Baron's finest novel since the war trilogy was perhaps *King Dido* (1969), a finely structured, closely observed tragedy of poverty, violent tribalism, and social aspirations, set in the East End during 1911, the coronation year of George V.

In *The In-between Time* (1971) Baron moves his setting to north London and the lower middle-class milieu of the late 1930s. A novella, *Gentle Folk* (1976), describes a Fabian country house weekend in 1911 with a lyrical evocation of the social and intellectual landscape of late Edwardian England interspersed with brutal, premonitory visions of future loss and horror. Baron conceived both *King Dido* and *Gentle Folk* as representing 'the two nations at that time' (unpublished notes). Baron's last published novel, *Franco is Dying* (1977), is the story of an ageing former communist revisiting Spanish Civil War battlefields. Together with its sequel *The War Baby* (unpublished at the time of Baron's death), these represent, in the words of John Williams, 'Baron's darkest work, a requiem for the years of grand ideals and untold deaths'.

In addition to fourteen novels, Baron wrote original screenplays and radio scripts. From the 1960s to the end of the 1980s he adapted seventeen classics for BBC television productions including *Daniel Deronda*, *Oliver Twist*, *Jane Eyre*, *Sense and Sensibility*, *Poldark*, and *Vanity Fair*, and works by Dumas, Conrad, Tolstoy, Kipling, and Scott. Stocky in stature, he was described in a *Jewish Chronicle* obituary as 'quiet, self-effacing, thoughtful and kind, he masked his creative tension with a strongly reserved exterior.' Despite his private nature—he refused to give readings from his work or to attend launch parties—he enjoyed a wide circle of friends. He was deeply knowledgeable about literature, especially nineteenth-century English, French, and Russian novels, and widely read in the ancient classics and history. Baron left a memoir, *Chapter of Accidents*, unpublished at the time of his death and an unfinished personal history of the communist movement.

Baron was elected in 1992 to an honorary fellowship of Queen Mary and Westfield College, University of London. He died of cancer at the Royal Free Hospital, north London, on 6 December 1999, and was cremated three days later at Golders Green crematorium, north London. John Williams in his *Guardian* obituary referred to Baron as 'the great British novelist' of the Second World War 'and among the finest, most underrated, of the postwar period'.　　　　　　　　　　　　　　　WILLIAM BAKER

Sources M. Seymour-Smith and A. Kimmens, eds., *World authors, 1900–1950*, 4 vols. (1996) · *The Guardian* (8 Dec 1999) · *Jewish Chronicle* (31 Dec 1999), 17 · *The Times* (8 Dec 1999) · W. Baker, 'The world of Alexander Baron', *Jewish Quarterly*, 17 (winter 1969), 17–20 · E. Sicher, *Beyond marginality: Anglo-Jewish literature after the Holocaust* (1985), 179–80, 206–7 · R. Stevenson, *The British novel since the thirties* (1986), 74–75, 83, 119 · L. Metzger, ed., *Contemporary authors*, New Revision Series, 14 (1985), 37–8 · P. H. Newby, *The novel, 1945–1950* (1951), 13–14 · W. Allen, *Tradition and dream* (1964), 262 · private information (2004) [Nick Baron and Delores Baron] · d. cert.
Archives priv. coll. · U. Reading, record of contemporary writing
Likenesses J. Herman, oils, 1966–9, repro. in *Jewish Quarterly*, 21 (1973), facing p. 106; priv. coll. · photograph, 1976, repro. in *The Times* · photograph, repro. in Seymour-Smith and Kimmens, eds., *World authors*, rev. edn (1996), 134 · photograph (much older), repro. in *Jewish Chronicle*

Baron, Bartholomew [*name in religion* Bonaventure] (1610–1696), Franciscan theologian and writer, was born at Clonmel, co. Tipperary, on 24 July 1610, the second son of Lawrence Baron (*d.* 1622), a merchant of Clonmel, and his first

Bartholomew Baron (1610–1696), by Wolfgang Kilian, pubd 1668 (after Burkhard Schramann, 1662)

wife, Mary or Maria Butler (*d.* 1616), sister of Luke Wadding, the founder of St Isidore's College for Irish Franciscans at Rome. Both of his parents died when he was young, but Bartholomew's elder brother, Geoffrey *Baron, made sure he received a good education. By his own admission he frequently played the truant as a youth, but his remarkable intelligence was apparent to all. After being taught rhetoric in Clonmel he attended classes briefly at Waterford. In the summer of 1626 he went to the Franciscan noviciate at Timoleague, co. Cork, to study philosophy. There he surprised his friends by joining the Franciscans on 27 October 1626, disappointing the local Jesuits who had been trying to recruit him. In early 1629 the people of Clonmel chose him to compose and read an address in Latin to the lord deputy of Ireland, Henry Carey, Lord Falkland, who was visiting the town. Roger Boyle, earl of Cork, being in attendance for the reading, was sufficiently impressed to offer Baron employment. The mortified earl withdrew his offer when Baron revealed he was a Catholic.

Baron left Ireland about March 1629 to study philosophy at Louvain, before briefly studying at Salzburg and Augsburg. He was expected in Rome by September 1631, but Baron was a high-spirited youth and spent several years travelling Europe instead. On 8 January 1633, having finally arrived in Rome, he entered St Isidore's College there as a student of theology. He was ordained on 3 September 1634 and took the name Bonaventure. Upon completing his course he was appointed a lecturer at St Isidore's, on 4 September 1635, going on to become professor in theology and philosophy. Although he never returned to Ireland, he followed events there with interest, being a strong opponent of English rule. In 1642 he went to Rochelle to aid the embarkation of Irish soldiers who sailed with General Thomas Preston to fight for the Catholic confederation in Ireland. Baron's elder brother, Geoffrey, served in the Leinster army of the confederation and sent him a diary of the siege of Duncannon of 1644–5, which Bartholomew later published.

In 1651 Baron wrote somewhat guiltily about what he called his serene and apparently useless life in academia. He was offered the archbishopric of Cashel in 1668, but declined. He was a prolific writer and published a large number of works on theology, philosophy, science, and history, as well as collections of poetry. Some of his views on scientific matters were idiosyncratic to say the least, but his philosophical and theological writings were of a very high standard. As a theologian he specialized in the works of Duns Scotus, a medieval theologian widely championed by Irish scholars. However, Baron was most renowned in Rome for his Latin compositions, both in prose and in verse. His uncle Luke Wadding pointed to him as an example of learning supported by elegant expression. Certainly Baron was a very talented writer of Latin and he credited this skill to his Latin teachers in Ireland. In an essay in his *Panageryric*, published in Rome in 1643, he said that all writers should try to strike a balance between style and knowledge. He disliked theology, regarding it as a crude subject, and delighted in composing Latin verse during his vacations from lecturing. Certainly his early essays, poems, epigrams, and epistles, the bulk of which had been written by 1643, are more interesting and more personal than his more theologically oriented later works. In 1651 Baron complained that his writing style had deteriorated from his having to teach theology.

In 1653 Baron appears as guardian of the Franciscan province of Scotland, and he briefly left Rome in 1656 to act as commissary to the province of Bosnia-Croatia. He appears to have left Rome in 1661, possibly after a dispute with the master of the sacred palace. During the 1660s and 1670s he travelled widely and was always in demand as a lecturer or as a writer, although his precise movements are difficult to trace. He spent 1661–3 in Austria and Germany and, after stays in Würzburg and Paris, appears as lecturer of humanities at St Bonaventure's Friary in Lyon in 1669. By 1672 Baron was in Milan. Probably about 1674 he went to Florence, where he resided at the friary of San Francesco al Monte and was appointed historiographer

and theologian to Cosmo III, grand duke of Tuscany, on 15 September 1676. However, he made some powerful enemies, including Cardinal Ludovisi, who tried to have him removed from Florence and to prevent him from publishing anything in the future. About this time Baron began preparing a uniform twenty-two-volume edition of all his published materials. Two friars were commissioned on his behalf to travel around Europe to the many cities where books of his had been published. Probably about 1678–9, and no later than March 1683, he went back to Rome to resume his post as a lecturer of theology at St Isidore's until partial blindness forced him into retirement in 1686. During his final years creeping paralysis deprived him of his limbs and finally his sight. Baron died on 18 March 1696 at St Isidore's and was buried there.

TERRY CLAVIN

Sources B. Millet, 'Bonaventure Baron', *Tercentenary of the siege of Clonmel* (1950), 41–6 · G. Cleary, *Father Luke Wadding and St Isidore's College, Rome* (1925), 88–100 · B. Millet, *The Irish Franciscans, 1651–1666* (1964), 366, 469–73 · W. P. Burke, *History of Clonmel* (1907), 480–85 · T. Wall, 'A distinguished Irish humanist: Bonaventure Baron OFM of Clonmel', *Irish Ecclesiastical Record*, 67 (1946), 92–102 · C. P. Meehan, *Rise and fall of the Franciscans* (1872), 89–93, 271 · *Report on Franciscan manuscripts preserved at the convent, Merchants' Quay, Dublin*, HMC, 65 (1906), 10, 50, 98–9 · *Dictionary of Catholic biography*, vol. 2, pp. 303–4
Likenesses W. Kilian, line engraving (after B. Schramann, 1662), BM, NPG; repro. in *Works* (1668) [*see illus.*] · portrait, Franciscan House, Clonmel, co. Tipperary · portrait, Franciscan House, Merchant's Quay, Dublin

Baron, Bernard (1696–1762), engraver, was born in Paris, the son of Laurent Baron, an engraver, and his wife, Françoise Aveline. He studied under his stepfather, Nicolas-Henri Tardieu. Baron was one of a number of French artists who settled in London in the early eighteenth century and who played an enormous role in the development of the British school. He arrived in the winter of 1716–17 to work with Claude Dubosc on the engravings after Louis Laguerre's wall paintings of the duke of Marlborough's battles in Marlborough House. Work followed on other prints after important paintings, notably the Raphael cartoons then at Hampton Court, on which he assisted Dubosc and Nicolas Dorigny. Through Dorigny he would have been introduced to the Great Queen Street Academy, where he had the opportunity to draw from life.

Baron's reputation was based on large engravings after paintings, but he also produced prints in the less elevated genres of portraiture and book illustration. As early as 1720 he was publishing his own prints. He was identified by Hugh Howard as the subject of a drawing by Antoine Watteau (who was in London from 1719 to 1720) showing an engraver at work. About 1722 he married Grace Lafosse, a mantua maker who continued to take on apprentices until 1761. In November 1727 he gave his address as Change Court, over against Durham Yard, Strand.

At the end of 1729 Baron returned to Paris, and while there secured commissions for contributions to Pierre Crozat's collection of prints after Italian old masters and Jean de Julienne's collection of prints after Watteau. He also had his portrait painted by Jean-Baptiste Vanloo. He was back in London by June 1732, when he gave out his address as Orange Street, over against Orange Court, near Leicester Square. He was active in the London art world: in 1735 he gave evidence to the committee of the House of Commons that was to lead to the Engravers' Copyright Act, and in the same year he was one of the group of leading London artists portrayed by Gawen Hamilton in *A Conversation of Virtuosis … at the Kings Armes* (National Portrait Gallery). George Vertue listed him as a member of the Rose and Crown Club from 1742 to 1743.

Baron's most highly paid commission was for a large engraving of Holbein's painting of Henry VIII giving the patent to the Barber–Surgeons' Company, on which he spent two years and was paid, in 1736, the handsome sum of 150 guineas. Throughout the 1740s and 1750s he advertised prints after Titian, Van Dyck, Watteau, and other painters at prices up to 13*s*. 6*d*., which made them the most expensive prints on the market. In the 1740s he made a number of prints after paintings by William Hogarth, including plates 2 and 3 of *Marriage à la mode* (1745). At about this time he seems to have trained the engraver Luke Sullivan.

By 1745 Baron had moved to Panton Square, west of Leicester Square, where he remained for the rest of his life. He prospered through the sale both of his own prints and of imports from France and was one of the few printsellers in London who had a stock that was sufficiently valuable to merit fire insurance. In his will, made in 1752, he left his wife, Grace, his 'little estate situated at Torcy le grand', near Dieppe, and his 'small annuity on the town house in Paris'. On Grace's death the estate was to pass to their son, Bernard, and then, if he left no heir, to the engraver's brother Laurent Baron. Baron's debts were to be discharged by the sale of paintings, drawings, and prints 'by auction in my house, as they now hang up in their different rooms adding to them the drawings and prints of other masters which are in the press'. Baron died on 24 January 1762 in Panton Square. His plates passed to his son and were bought on the latter's death in 1770 by John Boydell.   SHEILA O'CONNELL

Sources T. Dodd, *The connoisseur's repertory* (1824), 481–4 · C. le Blanc, *Manuel de l'amateur d'estampes*, 1 (Paris, 1854), 150–51 · Vertue, *Note books*, 3.22, 27, 41; 6.213 · R. Portalis and H. Béraldi, *Les graveurs du dix-huitième siècle*, 1 (Paris, 1880), 96–7 · E. Croft-Murray, 'Catalogue of British drawings in the British Museum', vol. 2, BM, department of prints and drawings · J. E. Ruch, 'Bernard Baron: un graveur français en Angleterre', *Nouvelles de l'Estampe*, 12 (1973), 13–22 · T. Clayton, *The English print, 1688–1802* (1997) · J. Kerslake, *National Portrait Gallery: early Georgian portraits*, 1 (1977), 340–42 · Sun policy registers, GL, MS 11936 · *London Evening-Post* (21–3 Nov 1727) · *London Evening-Post* (21–4 Nov 1741) · *London Evening-Post* (24–7 Jan 1747) · *Daily Post* [London] (13 June 1732) · *Public Advertiser* (11 May 1759)
Likenesses A. Watteau, drawing, 1719–20, BM · G. Hamilton, oils, 1735 (*A conversation of virtuosis … at the Kings Armes*), NPG

Baron, Bernhard (1850–1929), tobacco manufacturer and philanthropist, was born on 5 December 1850 in the Russian town of Brest Litovsk. His parents were both Jewish and he was probably of French descent. In 1867 he emigrated to New York, where he worked in a tobacco factory, sleeping at night in the tobacco sheds; with tobacco lent to him by one of the foremen, he started to manufacture handmade cigarettes. He then moved to New Haven, Connecticut, where he found customers among the students of Yale University. After the failure in 1874 of a New York bank in which he had invested his savings, he was forced to find employment in the tobacco factory of Kinney Brothers of New York but, as soon as he had saved enough, moved to Baltimore, where he began manufacturing cigars. The business prospered and, according to Baron, became the largest undertaking of its kind south of Philadelphia. During this period, the mechanization of cigarette production was in its infancy, and in 1872 Baron took out his first patent for a machine for making cigarettes. In 1890 Baron was persuaded by a group of financiers to join a venture aimed at challenging the powerful tobacco trusts, and during 1890–95 was managing director of the National Cigarette Tobacco Company of New York.

In 1895 Baron visited England to sell the patent rights of his cigarette-making machine, but, attracted by the opportunities, decided to settle in London at St James' Place, Aldgate, where he established the Baron Cigarette Machine Company Limited (the patent was later sold to the United Cigarette Machine Company for £120,000). Subsequently, he decided to expand into the production of tobacco and cigarettes, and, at its incorporation in 1903, joined the board of Carreras Limited, a firm of tobacco retailers and blenders. The following year he became managing director and in 1905, chairman; he held both positions until his death. Carreras's cigarettes, notably their Black Cat and Craven A brands, which were backed by innovative marketing, including competitions and gift coupons, proved highly popular. In 1920 the business moved to new premises, the Arcadia Works, City Road, London, which in 1928 were replaced by a major new factory at Mornington Crescent.

Baron's business success brought him immense wealth, which was matched by the scale of his philanthropic ventures. The harshness of his early life fostered a deep sympathy with the poor and he gave liberally, regardless of religious creed. Among his major gifts were £65,000 to the St George's Jewish Settlement in east London, £35,000 to the London Hospital, and a new children's ward at the Middlesex Hospital. A caring employer, in 1926 he purchased Pennant Lodge at Brighton and set up a trust to manage the Bernhard Baron Convalescent Home for the use of his employees and others engaged in manual and domestic labour. Two years later he created a further trust of £575,000 to benefit hospitals and homes for disabled children, and in his will established a charities fund which supported organizations of many religious denominations. He celebrated his birthdays by making numerous gifts; to mark his seventy-seventh birthday he distributed £32,000, and that year alone donated a total of £180,000. During the course of his lifetime it is estimated that he gave at least £2 million to help the poor, but he was still able to leave almost £5 million at his death. An enthusiastic supporter of the Labour Party, he also gave generously to party funds.

While still living in the USA Baron had married Rachel Schwartz of Washington, who predeceased him in 1920. There were three daughters and one son, Louis Bernhard, who succeeded his father as chairman of Carreras and was created a baronet in 1930. Baron died at his home, 64 The Drive, Hove, Sussex, on 1 August 1929, and was buried on 6 August at the cemetery of the Liberal Jewish synagogue, Willesden, London.

A. E. WATKIN, *rev.* CHRISTINE CLARK

Sources C. Shaw, 'Baron, Bernhard', *DBB* · *The Times* (3 Aug 1929) · *CGPLA Eng. & Wales* (1929)
Likenesses W. Orpen, oils, 1927, Carreras Rothmans Ltd, Basildon, Essex · W. R. Dick, bust, Arcadia Works, Hampstead Road, London · W. Orpen, portrait, priv. coll.
Wealth at death £4,944,820: probate, 5 Sept 1929, *CGPLA Eng. & Wales*

Baron, Geoffrey (1606–1651), politician, was the eldest of the four sons of Lawrence Baron (d. 1622), wine merchant of Clonmel, co. Tipperary, and his first wife, Mary or Maria Butler, *née* Wadding (d. 1616), of Waterford. His brothers were Bartholomew *Baron, who became a Franciscan friar taking the name Bonaventure, Michael, and Luke, who died at the age of thirteen. He had a half-sister, Katherine Butler, from his mother's first marriage, and another, Bess, from his father's second marriage, to Katherine White. His maternal uncle, the Franciscan historian Luke Wadding, who lived in Rome for most of his life, was arguably the single most influential Irish Catholic cleric of the seventeenth century, acting as the chief source of advice to the curia on ecclesiastical appointments to Ireland for almost three decades. The sudden and untimely death of his father saddled Geoffrey at the age of sixteen with debts of £1900, and the need to provide £500 for other family members, in addition to his stepmother's jointure of £33 per annum and £10 per annum for his sister Bess. Within four years, however, he was optimistic that all debts would soon be discharged, a testimony not only to his own application but also to the support of his guardian, his great-uncle John White. Embroilment in commercial activities probably explains Baron's rather delayed entry into the Middle Temple inn of court on 10 December 1631 when he was already twenty-five, although it is evident that he had already been in London studying law from at least the previous year.

Baron was evidently a man of considerable talents who impressed those with whom he came in contact by his intelligence, urbanity, and courage. He is now recognized as a major political figure among the confederate Catholics of the 1640s. He was elected MP for Clonmel in the 1634 parliament, where he was evidently an active member of the disgruntled Catholic opposition in the second session, and was expelled from the house on 3 December of that year. He was not re-elected in 1640, probably because of his bad odour with the autocratic lord deputy, Thomas Wentworth, although this may also have been the result of local political manoeuvrings by the earl of Ormond in the previous year. After the outbreak of rebellion in October 1641, Baron swiftly became involved, together with other Catholic gentry in south Munster. He was a conduit between local leaders in counties Kilkenny, Tipperary, and Waterford and the city of Waterford in the winter of 1641–2 and was an important influence in undermining the mayor's attempts to keep the city aloof from the insurrection.

In 1642 Baron travelled to France as a confederate agent. He was imprisoned for a period on a ship in Dunkirk in 1643, and petitioned successfully for his recall to Ireland in that same year. On his return he served as a member of the confederate committee for public revenue. In early October 1645 he landed in La Rochelle, where he encountered the papal nuncio Rinuccini, on whom he made a strong positive impression, and proceeded to Paris, where he acted as the confederate resident. He was frustrated in his major objective, which was the acquisition of large scale French assistance, something he attributed to the triple combination of a lack of confederate military success, the influence of the exiled Bourbon queen of England, and French reluctance to antagonize the English parliament. During the winter of 1645–6 Baron became aware of the favourable religious terms for Irish Catholics which Sir Kenelm Digby, the queen of England's emissary to Rome, was prepared to offer to the pope. From this point on Baron, a fervent Catholic, evidently believed the confederates should accept nothing less than these terms. He evidently supported the clerical overthrow of the first Ormond peace in 1646 and returned to Ireland on 13 February 1647. Four days later he addressed the general assembly of the confederates and did much to counteract the resident French agent's support of the peace, by informing the assembled delegates that Mazarin's government did not disapprove of the rejection of the treaty. This was a critical intervention. Baron was probably somewhat economical with the truth although he seems to have realized correctly that the overwhelming French interest in Ireland at this juncture was not the issue of peace but the recruitment of soldiers. He then served as the representative of the clerical interest in a two-man delegation to Ormond in March 1647 which unsuccessfully negotiated for a new accommodation. He was selected for the supreme council in the second assembly of 1647 and was one of that body's representatives to discuss the crisis of the Inchiquin truce with Rinuccini in March and May of 1648. He was clearly identified at this stage as a strong partisan of the clergy. Nevertheless, on 27 June 1648 he subscribed to opposition to Rinuccini's censure of the truce and its supporters, although clerical apologists later explained this behaviour as an attempt to retain his position and voting rights on the supreme council.

With the success of the Cromwellian invasion of Ireland, in August 1650 Baron was one of eight commissioners proposed by the clerical convocation of Jamestown as acceptable candidates to whom Ormond should relinquish his authority. In September of that year he was an emissary to the commissioners of the clerical convocation seeking a suspension of all excommunications. In October 1651 he was specifically exempted from pardon in the articles governing the surrender of Limerick. With nine others Baron voluntarily gave himself up on 29 October and was sentenced to death by a court of officers under Ireton's presidency. He met his fate during the final days of October with impressive courage and was executed by hanging in Limerick. He was buried there in the same month.   TADHG Ó HANNRACHÁIN

Sources B. Jennings, ed., *Wadding papers* (1953), 238, 239, 365, 369, 438, 582 · B. O'Ferrall and D. O'Connell, *Commentarius Rinuccinianus de sedis apostolicae legatione ad foederatos Hiberniae Catholicos per annos 1645–1649*, ed. J. Kavanagh, 6 vols., IMC (1932–49), vol. 1, p. 724; vol. 2, pp. 278, 479, 509, 529, 575; vol. 3, pp. 80, 151, 174, 221, 452, 453; vol. 4, pp. 446, 449, 457, 645, 647 · *History of the Irish confederation and the war in Ireland … by Richard Bellings*, ed. J. T. Gilbert, 7 vols. (1882–91), vol. 1, p. 157; vol. 2, pp. 17–21, 67, 84, 103–7, 114–15, 127, 205–8, 314–17, 332–7; vol. 7, pp. 1–12 · TCD, MS 820, fol. 15v. · Bodl. Oxf., MS Carte 19, fol. 32 · B. McGrath, 'Parliament men and the confederate association', *Kingdoms in crisis: Ireland in the 1640s, essays in honour of Dónal Cregan*, ed. M. Ó Siochrú (2001), 103–4 · A. Clarke, '28 November 1634: a detail of Strafford's administration', *Journal of the Royal Society of Antiquaries of Ireland*, 93/2 (1963), 161–7 · D. Cregan, 'The confederate Catholics in Ireland: the personnel of the confederation, 1642–49', *Irish Historical Studies*, 29 (1994–5), 500–01 · M. Ó. Siochrú, *Confederate Ireland, 1642–1649: a constitutional and political analysis* (Dublin, 1999), 40, 42, 133, 138, 149, 165, 181, 224 · BL, Add. MSS 46920A, fol. 133; 46927, fol. 164 · NA Ire., SR 2/3/20, fols. 241, 270, 323 · BL, Add. MS 1941, fol. 162 · B. McGrath, 'A biographical dictionary of the membership of the Irish House of Commons, 1640–1641', PhD diss., University of Dublin, 1997, vol. 2, A55–A56
Archives Franciscan House of Studies, Killiney, co. Dublin, letters

Baron, John (1786–1851), physician, was born on 26 May 1786 at St Andrews, Fife, the third of the six children of William Barron (*d*. 1803), professor of logic and *belles-lettres* at the university, and Margaret Stark. Baron attended arts courses at St Andrews University from 1799 to 1801 and then studied medicine at Edinburgh University, graduating MD in 1805. During this time he was president of the student Royal Medical Society. After further study and a brief period in Lisbon attending a wealthy patient, he returned to Britain in 1808. In London he sought the patronage of Matthew Baillie, the distinguished anatomist, and Edward Jenner, the pioneer of smallpox vaccination. Both men lived in Gloucestershire, and with their support Baron set up in practice in Gloucester. He became a close friend to both his patrons as well as attending them in a professional capacity.

Baron is remembered as an expert on vaccination, but this reputation owes more to his role as Jenner's biographer rather than his own accomplishments in the practice: he took no part in the debates over vaccination beyond organizing a testimonial in 1811 in favour of the procedure from Gloucestershire medical practitioners, and he published no original work on the subject. He was given the task of preparing Jenner's biography by the Jenner family on the basis of his long friendship with him. Not surprisingly, the two-volume *Life of Edward Jenner*,

which appeared in 1823 and 1838, was deeply hagiographic. It charted the successful spread of vaccination across the world and established an image of Jenner as a heroic figure, an embattled defender of vaccination who never received due credit from his professional peers; but it skirted round the conflicts raised by Jenner's hypersensitivity to criticism. By the late 1830s Baron's continued unquestioning acceptance of Jenner's views on all aspects of vaccination had provoked increasing criticism from his fellow practitioners. His 1839 report for the Provincial Medical and Surgical Association—which prompted parliament to pass the 1840 act providing free vaccination for everyone in England and Wales—was attacked for reiterating Jenner's belief that the immunity conferred by vaccination was permanent, long after most practitioners accepted that it declined over time. Baron's use of statistics was also challenged by George Gregory, vaccinator at the London Smallpox Hospital and an acknowledged expert on the practice.

Baron's involvement in vaccination overshadowed his own research in pathological anatomy. In the late 1810s and 1820s he published a number of papers and a sequence of three books, of decreasing originality, on the structure and character of 'tubercles'—now recognized as various types of cysts and tumours—and their relationship to the lymphatic system. Baron's work illustrated the theory that solid tubercles developed from fluid-filled hydatids, and thus supported the views of John Hunter against those of the French pathologists G. L. Bayle, R. H. T. Laënnec, and F. J. V. Broussias. On the strength of this work, and the patronage of Baillie and Jenner, Baron was elected a fellow of the Royal Society in 1823.

Baron was active in many medical institutions. With Baillie's support he obtained the post of physician to the Gloucester Infirmary in 1809. Baron, an early advocate of the more humane treatment of lunatics, campaigned for the creation of the Gloucester Lunatic Asylum, which was opened in 1823, and he served as its first consulting physician. He was a fellow of the Royal Medico-Chirurgical Society from 1815 to his death, and he was a council member of and leading figure in the Provincial Medical and Surgical Association, which campaigned to protect the rights and interests of provincial doctors during the profound professional reforms of the mid-nineteenth century. Baron instigated the association's benevolent fund to support practitioners' widows and orphans, and he acted as its first president. In keeping with his strong religious faith he supported the work of the Medical Missionary Society. He also served on the local board of health set up to tackle the 1832 cholera epidemic. Baron himself contracted the disease, and though he survived his health did not recover; he was forced to retire in the following year. In the late 1840s he suffered a gradual paralysis, and he died on 2 October 1851 at 1 St Margaret's Terrace, Cheltenham, as the result of an attack of bronchitis.

DEBORAH BRUNTON

Sources T. J. Pettigrew, *Medical portrait gallery: biographical memoirs of the most celebrated physicians, surgeons … who have contributed to the advancement of medical science*, 4 vols. in 2 [1838–40] · *The Lancet* (1 Feb

1852), 258–9 · *London and Provincial Medical Directory* (1852), 657–8 · parish register (baptism), 8/6/1786, St Andrews, St Leonard's, NL Scot. · *Transactions of the Provincial Medical and Surgical Association* (1832–53), vols. 1–19 · *Medico-Chirurgical Transactions*, 1–34 (1815–51) **Likenesses** H. Room, oils, *c.*1838, RCP Lond. · W. Hall, engraving (after H. Room), Wellcome L. · chalk drawing, NPG

Baron, Richard (*d.* 1766), literary editor and political writer, was born at Leeds, and educated at Glasgow University between October 1737 and May 1740. He left with a testimonial signed by Francis Hutcheson and Robert Simpson. Baron became a friend of Thomas Gordon, author of the *Independent Whig*, and afterwards of Thomas Hollis, whom he helped in collecting works defending seventeenth-century republicanism. In 1751 he edited a collection of tracts by Gordon, *A Cordial for Low Spirits*, and in the following year he published a similar collection by Gordon and others, called *The Follies of Priestcraft and Orthodoxy Shaken*: an enlarged four-volume edition, including tracts by Benjamin Hoadly, Arthur Ashley Sykes, William Arnall, and Archdeacon Francis Blackburne, was prepared by him and published in 1767 for the benefit of his widow and three children, details of whom are unknown. In 1751 he also edited Algernon Sidney's *Discourse Concerning Government* and two years later, John Milton's prose works (for which he received £10 10s.). Baron afterwards found the second edition of Milton's *Eikonoklastes* and reprinted it in 1756. He also edited Edmund Ludlow's *Memoirs* in 1751, and Marchamont Nedham's *Excellencie of a Free State* (1757). In 1766 Thomas Hollis engaged him to superintend an edition of Andrew Marvell's works but the plan was dropped after Baron professed his inability to supply the necessary information; it was afterwards taken up by Captain Thompson in 1776. A man devoted to 'the cause of civil and religious liberty', Baron is described as an 'artless and undisguised' person, whose imprudence kept him poor. He died in 'miserable circumstances' in 1766 (*Protestant Dissenter's Magazine*, 167–8).

LESLIE STEPHEN, *rev.* PHILIP CARTER

Sources *Protestant Dissenter's Magazine*, 6 (1799), 166–8 · F. Blackburne, *Memoirs of Thomas Hollis*, 2 vols. (1780), 2.505, 573–4
Wealth at death miserable circumstances: *Protestant Dissenter's Magazine*, 168

Baron, Robert (*c.*1596–1639), Church of Scotland minister and writer on theology, was born at Kinnaird, Perthshire, the younger son of John Baron of Kinnaird (*fl.* 1550–1620) and brother of John Baron who in 1646 became principal of St Salvator's College, St Andrews. Both brothers were educated at St Andrews, where in 1613 Robert graduated MA. He remained there, teaching philosophy, until 1619 when he was ordained and moved to Keith, Banffshire, to succeed Patrick Forbes as minister of that parish.

Baron served as minister of Keith until 1624 and, during this time, met and married Jean Gibson who came from Strathisla. They had four children, John (*bap.* 1 Aug 1629); William (*bap.* 19 April 1631); James (*bap.* 31 Oct 1632); and Marie (*bap.* 16 Nov 1633). On 27 October 1624 Baron was translated to the parish of Greyfriars, Aberdeen, where he served until 1631 when, owing to his ill health, the town council relieved him of his preaching duties. He was

appointed on 21 December 1625 the first professor of divinity at Marischal College, Aberdeen—a post he held while continuing to serve as a minister at Greyfriars.

Baron received his DD degree in 1627. The publication of his thesis, 'Disputatio de authoritate sacrae scripturae, seu, De formali objecto fidei', resulted in a long-running dispute with the Scottish Jesuit George Turnbull. Baron's other publications dealt mainly with matters of philosophy and theology or were attacks on what he saw as doctrinal errors to be found in Roman Catholic theology. His first published work was *Philosophia theologiae ancillans* (1621) and among his last was an exploration of the distinction between mortal and venial sin, *Disputatio theologica, de vero discrimine peccati mortalis et venialis* (1633). Unpublished manuscripts include papers dealing with the principal rule of Christian faith and the extent of papal power and authority. His *Metaphysica generalis* was published posthumously in 1657. Baron's contemporaries spoke of him as an excellent scholar who was able to make even the most difficult subjects understood. Even his opponents recognized his worth—Robert Baillie refers to him as 'an ornament of our nation' whose only fault was to have been seduced by 'the Canterburian way' but who was none the less a 'meek and learned person' (Baillie, 1.195, 185).

Baron emerged as one of the six 'Aberdeen doctors', who, under the leadership of John Forbes of Corse, were supporters of the religious policies of both James VI and I and Charles I and were strongly resistant to the national covenant. It is probable that Baron co-authored with Forbes *The General Demands Concerning the Said Covenant, The Replies*, and *The Duplies* (1638), which were used to dispute the legality of the covenant with the covenanting commissioners. He was certainly involved in preaching against those who opposed the king—not least Samuel Rutherford.

Baron was nominated bishop of Orkney in 1638 but was never consecrated. On 28 March 1639 he sailed for London from Aberdeen to avoid being compelled to sign the covenant by the marquess of Montrose who, with his army, was advancing on the city. While returning to Scotland, Baron was taken ill at Berwick, 'heavilie diseased of his gravell' (Baillie, 1.185). He died there on 19 August 1639. Even death could not protect him from the scrutiny of the covenanters, however, for in August 1640 they brought his widow from Strathisla to Aberdeen and forced her to give them access to Baron's unpublished papers. They ruled that these contained evidence of Arminianism and collusion with Archbishop Laud. Had he been alive, Baron would have been deposed along with John Forbes and the other Aberdeen doctors. Following the Restoration £200 compensation was paid to Jean Gibson and her children in token of Baron's loyalty to Charles I.

IAN M. THOMPSON

Sources J. Gordon, *History of Scots affairs from 1637–1641*, ed. J. Robertson and G. Grub, 3, Spalding Club, 5 (1841) · *Fasti Scot.*, new edn · J. Spalding, *The history of the troubles and memorable transactions in Scotland, from 1624 to 1625*, 2 vols. (1792) · *Letters of Samuel Rutherford*, ed. A. A. Bonar, 2 vols. (1863), vol. 2 · R. Sibbald, *The history, ancient*

and modern, of the sheriffdoms of Fife and Kinross (1710) • R. Keith, *A large new catalogue of the bishops … within the kingdom of Scotland* (1755) • [R. Baillie], *Letters and journals*, ed. R. Aiken, 2 vols. (1775), vol. 1 • D. Macmillan, *The Aberdeen doctors* (1909) • *The funeral sermons, orations, epitaphs and other pieces on the death of Patrick Forbes*, Spottiswoode Society (1845) • M. Kitshoff, 'Aspects of Arminianism in Scotland', MTh diss., U. St Andr., 1967 • *APS*, 1124–1707
Archives U. Aberdeen, King's College, MSS • U. Edin., New Coll. L., papers

Baron, Robert (*bap.* 1630, *d.* 1658), poet and playwright, was baptized on 22 July 1630 in the parish of St Andrew, Norwich, the fourth child of Robert Baron (*d.* 1649) and his wife, Alice (*née* Carter). His father held numerous municipal posts in Norwich, including that of mayor, and bequeathed money to help found the Norwich Girls' Hospital. Robert was educated at a private school and at Norwich grammar school before being admitted to Gonville and Caius College, Cambridge, on 22 July 1645. He stayed there only a short time, for he was admitted to Gray's Inn on 23 October 1646, where he remained for the next several years.

In the spring of 1647 Baron published his first literary endeavour, *Erotopaignion, or, The Cyprian Academy*, dedicating it to the ardent royalist James Howell, then imprisoned in the Fleet. The volume has an engraved frontispiece with Baron's portrait and the inscription 'Aetat. suae 17', as well as commendatory verses by eleven friends from Norwich, Cambridge, and Gray's Inn. The work itself is a competent romance in prose and verse, containing two dramatic pieces: a masque entitled 'Deorum dona', based largely on Edmund Waller's poem 'To the King on his Navy', and a pastoral in three acts entitled 'Gripus and Hegio', based largely on John Webster's *Duchess of Malfi* and on Waller's poems, and containing a thinly veiled portrait of Cromwell as the rabble-rousing orator Lemuroc. However, the volume is chiefly notorious today for passages lifted wholesale from the works of other poets, notably Waller, Webster, Milton, Shakespeare, Suckling, and Lovelace. Baron has been harshly criticized by modern commentators for his plagiarism, but his contemporaries were fully aware of it, and in fact praised his skill in adapting the work of others.

By June 1647 Baron was in Paris, where Howell (still in the Fleet) wrote to him on 20 June to thank him for the gift of his book. Howell addressed Baron as 'my dear Nephew' (Moore Smith, 2), but this appears to be a general term of endearment, and does not imply a blood relationship. Knight, in the *Dictionary of National Biography*, assumed that several other letters published in Howell's *Epistolae Ho-elianae* were addressed to Baron, but Moore Smith shows that this is unlikely.

In 1649 Baron published a slight work called *An apologie for Paris. For rejecting of Juno and Pallas, and presenting of Ate's golden ball to Venus*. In his dedicatory letter to 'my Noble Lady, the Lady, E: R.', Baron says that the book arose from a private discussion at 'Sir John's' between Lady E. R.'s brother, Sir T. B., bt, and Baron. On 1 August of the same year, Baron's father died in office as mayor of Norwich, leaving Robert a house in Norwich and property in Bracon Ash and Mulbarton. The elder Baron was apparently a

strong parliamentarian, as Slagle (p. 255) notes, but he does not appear to have held his son's royalist views too strongly against him.

Baron's third book was *Pocula castalia*, published in 1650. It consists of five distinct parts: 'The Author's Motto', a poem prefaced with commendatory verses by James Howell and two others; 'Fortune's Tennis-Ball', a set of poems dedicated to Baron's friend John Wroth, and largely plagiarized from Suckling and Lovelace; 'Eliza', a series of love poems to a lady; a set of boldly royalist 'Poems', including one which obliquely expresses sympathy with Prince Charles; and a group of 'Epigrams' to various people, including Sir John Suckling and 'the Lady E. R.'

Baron's final work is an elaborately annotated play entitled *Mirza*, entered in the Stationers' register on 16 August 1655 and published later that year. The volume opens with a fawning dedicatory poem 'To his Majestie', followed by a half-dozen commendatory poems by others. The play itself tells the true story of King Abbas of Persia, who blinds his own son Mirza and kills his granddaughter Fatima at the urging of his favourite, Mahomet Ally-Beg, then kills himself when he realizes what he has done, leaving Mirza's son Soffie to ascend to the throne. Baron's chief source was Sir Thomas Herbert's *A Relation of some Yeares Travaile* (1634), but he also acknowledges Jonson's *Catiline* as his model, and mentions many other works in a hundred pages of dense notes. Henry Bold's poem 'To R. B. Esq.; Having Read his Mirza' (printed 1664), also notes Baron's debt to Jonson. John Denham's *Sophy* (1642) deals with the same subject matter, but in his preface Baron claims not to have seen Denham's play until he had written three acts of his own. Baron died in Norwich in 1658, leaving neither heirs nor a will.

DAVID KATHMAN

Sources G. C. Moore Smith, 'Robert Baron, author of *Mirza, a tragedie*', *N&Q*, 11th ser., 9 (1914), 1–3, 22–4, 43–4, 61–3 • K. C. Slagle, 'Robert Baron, cavalier poet', *N&Q*, 169 (1935), 254–6 • P. Loloi, 'Introduction', *Mirza: a tragedy, by Robert Baron* (1998) • *DNB* • J. F. Maule, 'Robert Baron's *Cyprian academy*', *N&Q*, 231 (1986), 393–4 • *IGI*
Likenesses W. Marshall, line engraving, BM, NPG; repro. in R. Baron, *Erotopaignion, or, The Cyprian academy* (1648)

Baron, Stephen (*fl.* 1508–1513), Franciscan friar and author, may have been French by birth—his collected sermons refer to him as 'the great glory of France' (S. Baron, *Sermones declamati*, sig. A1v). He was provincial of the English Observant Franciscans no later than 28 April 1508, an office he had relinquished by October 1513. He also became confessor to Henry VII, who in his will appointed 'our Confessour the provincial of the freres observan[tes]' as one of those to whom anyone with a grievance against that king should make application for restitution (PRO, E23/3). On 20 May 1504 Pope Julius II had given Henry permission either to continue with his current confessor, John Burnellus, also a Franciscan Observant, or to replace him on account of the king's concern over the soundness of his penitential injunctions. Baron may therefore have been the king's confessor who was incorporated at Cambridge in the following year.

Following the accession of Henry VIII, Baron continued for a while to serve as royal confessor, and he presented the new king with a brief treatise of moral instruction on the office of a prince, 'Tractatulus de regimine seu caritate principum'. Although he declared that he had 'neither gold nor gems, nor the desire to have them', the vellum manuscript's opening page is beautifully illuminated with royal symbols made jewel-like by their gold accents (BL, Royal MS 12.A.xvi, fol. 2r). At an unrecorded date Baron also gave at Cambridge a series of fifteen sermons on the last things, thereby gaining an abiding reputation as a preacher. In style all these writings are scholastic rather than humanist, eschewing rhetorical artifice and classical philology in favour of subdivisions in triplets. Their content is no less traditional. The sermons use a standard incipit for their topic (Deuteronomy 32: 28–9) and stress the time-honoured Catholic principles of divine grace and human choice. The treatise on kingship also follows a conventional medieval pattern by emphasizing the need for moral goodness in a ruler, rather than setting out principles for policy. These works were subsequently printed together as *Sermones declamati coram alma universitate Cantabrigiensi* and *De regimine principum*, first at London by Wynkyn de Worde (STC 1497, n.d.) and thereafter at least three times at Paris (n.d.). Nothing is known of Baron's later life, but he was remembered by John Fisher as a man of 'synguler wysdome, lernynge and vertue' (*English Works*, 1.271).   ASHLEY NULL

Sources *CPR, 1494–1509*, 567–8 • exchequer, treasury of receipt, royal wills, PRO, E23/3 [Henry VII's will] • *CEPR letters*, 18.120 • M. Bateson, ed., *Grace book B*, 1 (1903), 201 • G. F. Warner and J. P. Gilson, *Catalogue of Western manuscripts in the old Royal and King's collections*, 2 (1921) • J. R. H. Moorman, *The Grey friars in Cambridge, 1225–1538*, The Birkbeck Lectures (1952) • K. G. Rodgers, introduction to *The last things*, in St Thomas More, *The Yale edition of the complete works of St Thomas More*, 1, ed. A. S. G. Edwards, K. G. Rodgers, and C. H. Miller (1997), lx–cix • J. Pits, *Relationum historicarum de rebus Anglicis*, ed. [W. Bishop] (Paris, 1619) • A. G. Little, *Franciscan papers, lists, and documents* (1943) • L. Waddingus [L. Wadding], *Scriptores ordinis minorum* (1650) • J. W. Blench, *Preaching in England in the late fifteenth and sixteenth centuries* (1964) • Cooper, *Ath. Cantab.*, 1.23 • *The English works of John Fisher, bishop of Rochester ... part 1*, ed. J. E. B. Mayor, EETS, extra ser. 27 (1876), 271

Archives BL, 'Tractatulus de regimine seu caritate principum', Royal MS 12.A.xvi

Baroness, the. *See* Lindehleim, Joanna Maria (*d.* 1724).

Barons [Barnes], **William** (*d.* 1505), bishop of London, came from Hadleigh in Suffolk, where his father had property. He had at least two sisters, and an uncle who was a priest. He was a fellow of All Souls College, Oxford, from 1488, admitted as DCL by Bologna University on 1 February 1499, and was offered the chair of civil law at Oxford in 1501. On 2 February 1502 he was admitted as a fellow of Lincoln's Inn. During the vacancy of the see of Canterbury in 1500 Barons served as commissary of the prerogative court. He was now accounted a clerk and counsellor to the king, and owed at least some of a flurry of preferments to this. Between December 1500 and June 1502 he secured the rectories of Beaconsfield, Buckinghamshire, Gedney,

Lincolnshire, East Peckham, Kent, and Bosworth, Leicestershire, and in 1503 he became a prebendary of Wells and rector of Therfield, Hertfordshire. In 1501, at the wedding of Prince Arthur and Katherine of Aragon, when the banns were to be called in St Paul's, it was arranged that the king's secretary would 'object openly in Latin', alleging reasons why the marriage could not be lawful, but should be answered, also in Latin, by Barons's production of the papal dispensation; presumably this was played out.

On 1 February 1502 Barons became master of the rolls. His place in royal administration cannot be defined, but since the executors of his will included Christopher Bainbridge (*d.* 1514), the next master of the rolls, Thomas Ruthall (*d.* 1523), the king's secretary, and Christopher Urswick (*d.* 1522), the king's almoner, while as overseer of his will Barons appointed Sir Thomas Lovell (*d.* 1524), the treasurer of the royal household, it would appear that he had been moving in exalted circles. On 24 January he was present to assist Abbot Islip in laying the first stone for Henry VII's chapel in Westminster Abbey, and on 20 June following he was appointed a commissioner for the new treaty with Ferdinand of Aragon for Katherine's second match, after Arthur's death on 2 April. On 2 August Barons was papally provided to the see of London, at the personal request of the king. He received the temporalities on 13 November (resigning the mastership of the rolls that day) and was consecrated on 26 November. A reference in 1508 to the escape of two suspected Lollards, imprisoned by order of William 'of happy memory' bishop of London, suggests that he was active in the pursuit of heretics, but his death, on either 10 or 11 October 1505, prevented his making any impression as diocesan. It also prevented the completion of the manor house that Barons had been planning to build for himself in his home town of Hadleigh. He directed that his body be buried in St Paul's, without superfluous expense or worldly pomp.

JOHN FINES

Sources Emden, *Oxf.* • J. Gairdner, ed., *Letters and papers illustrative of the reigns of Richard III and Henry VII*, 1, Rolls Series, 24 (1861), 414 • will, PRO, PROB 11/14, sig. 40 • J. A. F. Thomson, *The later Lollards, 1414–1520* (1965), 189 • GL, MS 9531/8

Wealth at death see will, PRO, PROB 11/14, sig. 40

Baronsdale, William (*d.* 1608), physician, was born in Gloucestershire. He was educated at St John's College, Cambridge, being admitted a scholar on 5 November 1551, and graduated BA in 1555, became a fellow of his college in 1556, and proceeded MA in 1558 and MD in 1568. He was made a senior fellow and bursar of his college in January 1562, and twice held the Linacre lectureship in medicine, being elected to the office first on 5 September 1560, and again on 26 May 1564. After moving to London he was elected a fellow of the College of Physicians, though in what year is not recorded, and afterwards he held the offices of counsellor, in 1588, 1600, 1602, and 1604, censor from 1581 to 1585, and treasurer in 1583 (being the first fellow appointed to this newly founded office), 1604, 1605, and 1607. He was president of the college for eleven successive years, from 1589 to 1600. Baronsdale, who was married with a son and daughter, died in 1608, at some time before 17 June, when he was succeeded as elect by Thomas Moundeford.

J. F. PAYNE, rev. PATRICK WALLIS

Sources Venn, *Alum. Cant.* · Munk, *Roll* · Cooper, *Ath. Cantab.*, vols. 1–2 · G. Clark and A. M. Cooke, *A history of the Royal College of Physicians of London*, 3 vols. (1964–72) · will, PRO, PROB 11/111, fol. 409 **Wealth at death** property, including land in Southwark, London

Barowe [Barrow], **Thomas** (d. 1499), lawyer and administrator, was a native of north Lincolnshire, who became a scholar of Eton College in 1451, and was nominated by the provost for a scholarship at King's Hall, Cambridge, in 1456–7. Admitted as a bachelor of civil law in 1460, he incepted in civil law in 1469–70, and became a licentiate in 1475. Closely associated with Richard, duke of Gloucester, he may have come to Gloucester's attention through the latter's uncle, George Neville, archbishop of York (d. 1476), in whose diocese he held several valuable benefices in the early 1470s. Barowe retained close links with Cambridge, granting it £240, and being described in 1483 as 'to his mother the university a great and faithful lover' (Cambridge, St John's College, MS Baker xxvi 68). Rector of Cottingham in Yorkshire in December 1472, he became a canon of Beverley in 1475, and of York in 1478 (with the prebend of Langtoft). Although committed to administrative work on Gloucester's behalf at Middleham, he provided a personal link between the duke and the York Cathedral clergy, facilitating the former's grant of the advowson of Cottingham to the vicars-choral of York. In February 1482 he was appointed by Archbishop Thomas Rotherham (d. 1484) to serve as examiner of witnesses in the diocesan consistory court.

Barowe's loyal service to Gloucester is stressed in a grant of arms in January 1477, which claims Barowe 'hath many yerys vertuously and truly continued in the service of the high and mighty prince Richard' (BL, Add. MS 37687 C). In July of the same year Barowe was one of the feoffees licensed to grant the manor of Foulmire, Cambridgeshire, and its church to the president and fellows of Queens' College, Cambridge, so that they could celebrate for the souls of Richard, his wife, Anne, and others, including himself. In the following July, when the transfer was implemented, Barowe's name was included along with those of other 'gentlemen, servants and lovers of the duke' in the prayers of four priests at Queens' (Searle, 89–92). Described as Gloucester's counsellor in 1483, Barowe was rewarded for his loyalty when Richard usurped the throne. Three weeks before Buckingham's rebellion, on 22 September 1483, he replaced Robert Morton (d. 1497) as master of the rolls, the virtual head of chancery, and was assigned a tower within the Tower of London appointed for the custody of rolls and records.

Like many former fellows of King's, Barowe acted as a diplomat, being appointed an envoy to negotiate with Scotland in September 1484. On the dismissal of Chancellor John Russell (d. 1494) on 29 July 1485 the king appointed Barowe keeper of the great seal. Barowe's central executive and secretarial position in Richard III's regime inevitably ended at Bosworth. But though he resigned his position as master of the rolls, he retained a mastership of chancery granted by Richard III. He also acted as a receiver of petitions in the parliament of 1497. Barowe died two years later, between 23 June and 10 July 1499. In his will he requested burial within the precincts of St Stephen's Chapel, in Westminster Abbey, where he had been a canon since 16 July 1483.

JONATHAN HUGHES

Sources C. Ross, *Richard III* (1981) · R. B. Dobson, 'Richard III and the church of York', *Kings and nobles in the later middle ages*, ed. R. A. Griffiths and J. Sherbourne (1986), 130–54 · A. B. Cobham, *The King's Hall within the University of Cambridge in the later middle ages* (1969) · J. Hughes, '"True ornaments to know a holy man": northern religious life and the piety of Richard III', *The north of England in the age of Richard III*, ed. A. J. Pollard (1996), 149–90 · W. G. Searle, *The history of the Queens' College of St Margaret and St Bernard in the University of Cambridge*, 2 vols., Cambridge Antiquarian RS, 9, 13 (1867–71) · Emden, *Cam.*, 40–41

Barr [*née* Huddleston], **Amelia Edith** (1831–1919), novelist, was born on 29 March 1831 in Ulverston, Lancashire, the daughter of Mary Singleton (c.1806–c.1858) and William Henry Huddleston (d. c.1863), a Methodist minister. Her father's vocation required the family to move frequently; she spent her early childhood in Shipley, Yorkshire, began school at Penrith in Cumberland, moved to Ripon, Yorkshire, and then to Castletown, on the Isle of Man. It was while living in Castletown, she recalled in her autobiography, *All the Days of my Life* (1913), that 'I began to seriously try to write' (Barr, 58). At sixteen, when her father lost his independent fortune through a friend's fraud, she went as a teacher to a boarding-school in Downham Market, Norfolk. The family fortunes were partially restored a few months later by a gift of property from her mother's uncle, but upon seeing her father, not her mother, draw the first rents to cover his losses, she learned the lesson that a married woman's property was not her own.

Determined to support herself, Amelia Huddleston returned to teaching; when the school employing her failed, she entered the normal school at Glasgow, leaving after a few months to marry, on 11 July 1850, Robert Barr (d. 1866), a local businessman. When Barr's woollen mills failed, she urged him to emigrate, and they sailed for New York city, arriving in September 1853. They first established themselves in Chicago, Illinois, where she opened a school for girls; leaving hurriedly after her husband made enemies, they paused in Memphis, Tennessee, before moving on to Texas, finally settling in Austin. She moved to Galveston, Texas, in 1866 with her husband and five surviving children (she had already lost a daughter in Chicago and two more children in Austin), where almost immediately Robert Barr, her two sons, and another newborn boy died of yellow fever.

With three daughters to support, Amelia Barr returned to New York in 1868, where she at first made her living as a teacher. Encouraged by one of her employers, who told her 'If you can write, you can live' (Barr, 311), and by Henry Ward Beecher, whom she had met briefly years before in England, she began placing stories in magazines. She confined herself to essays and stories for more than a decade before publishing her first novel, *Jan Vedder's Wife* (1885), which firmly launched her career as a writer of popular historical romances set in England and the United States. Among her more than sixty other books were *The Bow of Orange Ribbon: a Romance of New York* (1886), *The Maid of Maiden Lane* (1900), and *Remember the Alamo* (1888), the latter surviving to inspire a film in the 1960s starring John Wayne. As a reviewer of *Bernicia* (1895) observed, she had found a formula and, 'standing always well within its clearly defined lines, continue[d] to give out the white bread and cream which a large public has learned to expect and to enjoy' (*The Bookman*, 167). The formula's steady proceeds allowed her to maintain a country house, Cherry Croft, at Cornwall-on-Hudson, New York. A heat stroke in July 1918 proved to be her final illness; Amelia Barr died on 10 March 1919 in Richmond Hill, Long Island, New York, and was buried on 13 March in Sleepy Hollow cemetery, near Tarrytown, New York.

MARY LOEFFELHOLZ

Sources A. E. Barr, *All the days of my life* (1913) · *New York Times* (12 March 1919) · 'Bernicia', *The Bookman* [New York] (3 April 1896), 167–8 [review] · A. Hinding, A. S. Bower, and C. A. Chambers, eds., *Women's history sources: a guide to archives and manuscript collections in the United States* (1979) · J. Sutherland, *The Longman companion to Victorian fiction* (1988) · m. reg. Scot.
Archives Ransom HRC · State Archives Library, Austin, Texas
Likenesses portrait, 1849, repro. in Barr, *All the days of my life* · two photographs, 1880–1909, repro. in Barr, *All the days of my life*

Barr, Andrew Greig (1872–1903), soft drinks manufacturer, was born on 5 May 1872 in Falkirk, the second of three sons of Robert Barr, cork cutter and aerated water manufacturer, and his wife, Jane Greig. He attended the Falkirk high school before completing his schooling at Daniel Stewart's College, Edinburgh. Although his father was already in business, the business was too small to absorb both Andrew and his elder brother, Robert, and Andrew began his business career as a clerk in the Clydesdale Bank in Falkirk. He was clearly adept at his work, for when the Clydesdale opened a small branch in nearby Larbert, Andrew Barr was put in charge of its business. Barr continued in the bank until 1887, when his father decided to open a branch of his business in Glasgow to exploit the expanding soft drinks market. Barr's elder brother went to manage the new development, and Andrew and his younger brother, William S. Barr, then joined their father in the Falkirk business.

Although Falkirk was the head office, Glasgow was the expanding market, and Robert Barr successfully established large new premises at 184 Great Eastern Road in the Parkhead district of Glasgow, producing lemonade, soda water, orangeade, sasparilla, and many other beverages. The business grew so quickly that Andrew Barr joined his brother in Glasgow in 1892. He worked aggressively to expand its activities, so much so that by 1897 he was sole proprietor, operating the Glasgow establishment as a separate concern from the family business in Falkirk.

Barr then embarked on a forceful strategy to capture the leading place in the Glasgow soft drinks market. A major new factory was constructed and twice extended in 1901 and 1902–3, fitted out with the latest plant and designed for efficient staging of production. The storeroom could cope with 30,000 crates, each containing a dozen bottles, and the works employed about 200 people, together with 150 horses to cope with deliveries. Advertising and brand image was important, and Barr had his vans designed with a distinctive white and gold livery carrying the company name prominently.

The heart of the new Parkhead works was the laboratory, where the syrups and essences were blended and combined according to formulae before adding to water. Barr personally supervised this activity, and in 1901 created what was later known as Barr's Irn Bru. When first introduced, his 'iron brew' was one of a number of similar competing products, but Barr's was the most successful, and the formula is still held exclusively by the senior members of the family. The phoneticized name, Irn Bru, was not introduced until 1946. Barr's new product was instantly popular and was to become the foundation of the Barr empire. He promoted it vigorously and also became heavily involved in the affairs of a number of trade associations. In particular he became treasurer of the Glasgow Bottle Exchange Association, set up to collect and recycle the expensive glass bottles to their appropriate owners. Barr had pioneered the use of the screw-on, replaceable bottle top, making it even more worthwhile to keep the bottles in circulation and prevent their use by others. Barr in fact regularly resorted to litigation to enforce his ownership of the expensive bottles and to prosecute those who tried to use them and fill them with their own products.

Andrew Barr's rise was meteoric, and by the age of thirty he was a major manufacturer in the soft drinks trade in Glasgow. With this successfully behind him, he married Isabel Margaret Gibb, at Dollar, on 25 April 1903. Tragically, his life was cut short eleven weeks later after a three-week battle with blood poisoning and a chill, which deteriorated into pneumonia. He died on 12 July 1903 at his home, 45 Roslea Drive, Dennistoun, Glasgow.

Knowing he would not recover, Andrew Barr had made provision in his will to enable his younger brother, William, to take over as manager of the Parkhead works for a period of eighteen months, with an option to purchase after twelve months. This was the outcome, and in 1904 the firm took the name of A. G. Barr & Co. as a private limited company with a share capital of £25,000. From 1904 to 1959 the Glasgow and Falkirk businesses grew steadily, though as separate operations; but in 1959 A. G. Barr & Co. purchased the Falkirk company to create a single company focused on Glasgow.

ANTHONY SLAVEN

Sources *The Scots Commercial Record* (10 Sept 1904) · *Glasgow and its environs* (1891) · *The Victualling Trades Review* (12 Feb 1890) · *The Victualling Trades Review* (1902) · *DSBB* · *Falkirk Mail* (18 July 1903) · b. cert. · d. cert. · m. cert.
Archives Barr & Co., Glasgow, company microfiche no. 5653
Wealth at death £18,409 7s. 7d.: confirmation, 19 Feb 1904, CCI

Barr, Archibald (1855–1931), engineer and manufacturer of range-finders, was born at Glenfield, near Paisley, Renfrewshire, on 18 November 1855, the third son of Archibald Barr, yarn merchant, and his wife, Jeanie Stirrat, of

Archibald Barr (1855–1931), by James Russell & Sons, 1930

Paisley. From Paisley grammar school he entered the local works of Messrs A. F. Craig & Co., manufacturers of spinning and weaving machinery, as an engineering apprentice under the Scottish 'sandwich' system, which enabled him to attend the winter sessions of Glasgow University, from which he graduated BSc in 1878.

In 1876 Barr was appointed as 'young assistant' to the regius professor of civil engineering and mechanics, James Thomson. In 1884 he was appointed professor of civil and mechanical engineering at the Yorkshire College of Science, later Leeds University. Glasgow University recalled him in 1889, to succeed Thomson in the oldest chair of engineering science in the United Kingdom; this gave him the freedom to continue his important consultative business. He graduated DSc in 1890.

At Leeds, Barr met William Stroud, the professor of physics. Stroud had a talent for applying scientific theory to practical problems, and Barr was highly accomplished in mechanical design. In 1888 they collaborated on an improved optical range-finder, which they patented that year. A version of the instrument was adopted by the Royal Navy in 1892, and in 1894 the professors set up a company, Barr and Stroud's Patents, to market the range-finder and other inventions. In 1895 they established a small workshop in Glasgow to assemble and test range-finders, expanding in 1904 into a large purpose-built factory at Anniesland on the outskirts of Glasgow. The firm supplied range-finders to nearly all of the world's navies, and manufactured smaller, portable instruments which were adopted by the British, French, and other European armies. In 1912, Barr and Stroud became a private limited company. Barr, who was the senior partner and the head of the design team at Anniesland, resigned his university chair at Glasgow in 1913, becoming emeritus professor. He remained chairman of Barr and Stroud until his death. Barr and Stroud remained the sole supplier of periscopes to the Royal Navy, and a leading supplier of optronics, including thermal imaging equipment, to the British army.

Although Barr published relatively little academic work during his university career, he was widely admired as a teacher. Like Lord Kelvin, with whom he had worked, he believed in fostering links between town and gown; he was able to raise £40,000 from local industrialists and charitable bodies to build Glasgow's James Watt engineering building in 1901 and to persuade companies to donate most of the £14,000 required for the purchase of the scientific equipment installed in its laboratories. When he returned to the university in 1889, there were only thirty-nine students in his field, but the number had risen to over 200 by the time of his retirement. His contribution to the university extended beyond the department of civil and mechanical engineering; he helped to organize a new faculty of science in 1893, and successfully campaigned for a lectureship in electrical engineering, which was established in 1898.

Barr married in 1885 Isabella (1862–1928), eldest daughter of John Young, a wood merchant, of Priory Park, Castlehead, Paisley; they had three sons, the second of whom was killed in action in France in 1915, and a daughter. He received the honorary degree of LLD from Glasgow University in 1914 and was elected FRS in 1923. He was president of several learned societies. A keen motorist, he was a member of the Scottish Automobile Club and an organizer of Scotland's first motor car reliability trials in 1901; he also helped to form the Scottish Aeronautical Club in 1909, becoming its president, and was a promoter of Scotland's first aviation meeting, held at Lanark in 1910. His charity manifested itself in his service as a governor of the Royal Scottish National Institution for the care of those with learning difficulties, in his gift of £8000 towards the cost of a new organ for Paisley Abbey, and in his bequest of his house for charitable purposes.

In 1913 Barr was presented with two portraits, painted by G. Fiddes Watt. They represent the professor in a mood of seriousness which was rarely evident to his students. Barr died at his home, Westerton of Mugdock, near Milngavie, near Glasgow, on 5 August 1931.

J. W. French, rev. Iain F. Russell

Sources M. Moss and I. Russell, *Range and vision: the first hundred years of Barr & Stroud* (1988) · C. A. Oakley, *A history of a faculty: engineering at Glasgow University* (1973) · J. W. French, *Proceedings of the Royal Philosophical Society of Glasgow*, 60 (1931–2), 78–84 · *Engineering* (14 Aug 1931), 205–6 · *Glasgow Herald* (6 Aug 1931) · [J. B. Neilson], ed., *Fortuna domus: a series of lectures delivered in the University of Glasgow in commemoration of the fifth centenary of its foundation* (1952) · WW

Archives U. Glas., business corresp. and papers, UGD 295 | CUL, corresp. with Lord Kelvin

Likenesses photograph, c.1911 (in court dress), U. Glas., Archives and Business Records Centre · G. F. Watt, oils, c.1913, U. Glas. · G. F. Watt, oils, 1913; whereabouts unknown · James Russell & Sons, photograph, 1930, NPG [see illus.]

Wealth at death £153,568 15s.: confirmation, 9 Nov 1931, CCI

Barr [formerly Babey], (**Albert William**) **Cleeve** (1910–2000), architect, was born on 5 October 1910 at 90 Woodland Road, Dulwich, London, the eldest of the four children of Sergeant Albert John Babey (1872–1918) of the Oxford and Buckinghamshire light infantry, and his wife, Ellen Cleeve (1877–1967). He and his surviving siblings took the surname Barr by deed poll in 1932. His father having died in the 1918 influenza epidemic, he was brought up by his mother in Marlow, where he attended Sir William Borlase's School. His first job was as a trainee manager in the Bank of England. Finding the class differences oppressive, Barr left to become an architect. After a spell (1934) at the Liverpool School of Architecture he went to work for Adams, Holden, and Pearson, where he was mainly employed on Charles Holden's Senate House, London.

On 7 September 1935 Barr married Edith Mary Edwards (1901–1965), a schoolteacher; they had three children. In the following year he became secretary of the Association of Architects, Surveyors, and Technical Assistants, a small trade union representing building professionals. His organizing and campaigning talents raised the association's profile and helped to radicalize British architecture in the run-up to the Second World War. Barr was among those socialists who opposed the 'capitalist war', but after the invasion of Russia rallied to the allied cause. After joining the RAF he helped deliver flying boats to the Russians and then acted as a liaison officer in Iran and Berlin, making use of the Russian which he had taught himself.

The post-war burgeoning of public practices chimed in with Barr's hopes for a reformed construction industry in which expert collaboration would bring the benefits of architecture to the mass of the British population. After finally qualifying as an architect in 1948 he joined the leading office of the moment, the in-house team building prefabricated primary schools for Hertfordshire county council. Templewood School, Welwyn Garden City, one of the most fetching of these schools, was built to Barr's designs and opened in 1950. In that year, hoping to spread the Hertfordshire methods of design to public housing, Barr along with Oliver Cox and others moved to the London county council (LCC). Their efforts to work out a standard 'language' for municipal housing were opposed by other strong personalities within the LCC's expanding but factious architects' department. But an enlarged group under Barr and Cox undertook the design of the Alton East section of the Roehampton estate, the grandest of the LCC's post-war housing ventures (1952–5). This pioneering 'mixed development' of high and low blocks, inspired by Scandinavian models, proved among the best council housing built in Britain.

As the pressure for housing completions grew in the 1950s, Barr's personal approach to design and production became more technocratic. His Picton Street estate, Camberwell, rationally laid out to suit the path of the travelling crane, lacked aesthetic merit. But his technical mastery of the subject, manifested in his book Public Authority Housing (1958), was unrivalled. It led after a short spell as architect to the Ministry of Education's development group (1957–9) to his appointment as chief architect to the Ministry of Housing and Local Government.

Here Barr set up a development group to influence the procurement of public housing by example. The value of this group's experimental projects was undermined by the ministry's policy of licensing privately owned building systems geared to profit and speed rather than need or quality, as a way of reducing the waiting lists for housing. The era of high-rise building was now reaching its peak. When an enlarged ministry of public buildings and works was created in 1964, Barr shifted across to become chief architect to the National Building Agency. The aim of this new body was to advise industry and local authorities on efficiency and productivity on building, while curbing the excesses of the new private building systems. The agency did useful work, but in the reaction against all systems of building and against public housing generally that followed the collapse of Ronan Point (1968), Barr grew increasingly isolated.

In the 1970s the National Building Agency took to nurturing housing associations. Barr stayed on as managing director, and took a personal interest in the growth of the unique UK Housing Association. Following the death of his first wife after a long illness, he had married the journalist Mary Wallace Harley, née Gibson (b. 1918/19), on 17 June 1966. He retired to Walton-on-Thames in 1975. In 1999 he moved to a residential home, New Park, at Trentham, Staffordshire; he died on 30 May 2000 in the City General Hospital, Stoke-on-Trent, and his body was cremated. He was survived by his second wife and by a son and daughter from his first marriage.

Among the British post-war architects who rose to influence in government, Barr stood out for the enthusiasm and rigour with which he promoted the idea that modern methods could revolutionize the whole process of procuring buildings, not just their appearance. His career ended in disappointment because of the incorrigibly political nature of public housing, and because his blend of technical and social idealism found scant favour with more artistic colleagues. Barr was a tough and persistent advocate of his views, but combined them with personal humility and dedication. ANDREW SAINT

Sources personal knowledge (2004) · private information (2004) [Michael Barr, son] · biographical file · Architects' Journal (15 Jan 1959), 187–8 · RIBA Journal, 83 (July 1976), 281–2 · b. cert. · m. certs. · d. cert. · The Guardian (8 June 2000)

Archives PRO, government papers of Ministry of Housing and National Building Agency

Barr, Elizabeth Brown (1905–1995), minister of the United Free Church of Scotland, was born on 2 October

1905 in Dennistoun, Glasgow, the youngest of five children of James *Barr (1862–1949) and his wife, Martha Wilson Stephen (1863–1959). Her father, a prominent minister of the Free (from 1900 United Free) Church and a committed Christian socialist, was also MP for Motherwell and Wishaw (1924–31) and later for Coatbridge and Airdrie (1935–45).

Educated at Bellahouston Academy, in 1925 Elizabeth Barr graduated MA from Glasgow University, where she was actively involved in the Student Christian Movement. In 1929 her father led the United Free Church minority that stayed out of the union with the Church of Scotland, and the 1930 general assembly of the United Free Church (Continuing) decided that, for the first time in Britain, the eldership and ministry of a Presbyterian church should be open to women.

Barr applied for acceptance as a candidate:

> Then came the temptation to look back … but I had a word … which confirmed my resolve. 'No man having put his hand to the plough and looking back is fit for (is well placed for) the Kingdom of God.' There was no doubt which plough was meant and, by the grace of God, I have not looked back. (Thomson, 3)

After earning a BD (with distinction in New Testament language and literature) at Glasgow University, she was licensed to preach (1933), and two years later she was ordained and inducted to the rural parish of Auchterarder. She then ministered in Clydebank after the ravages of wartime bombing (1943–55), in central Glasgow (1955–68), and at Miller Memorial United Free Church, Maryhill (1966–75).

Elizabeth Barr was known for her deep pastoral concern: her ability to relate to and make intimate friendships with all kinds of people. She was particularly interested in children, young people, and education, and in worship she was an imaginative communicator, using illustrations and visual aids to great effect. She was always meticulous in preparation and research—not least for the courts and committees of the church, where her excellent memory and attention to detail complemented the tenacious championing of causes dear to her heart. She was moderator of Perth United Free Church Presbytery in 1939, of Glasgow presbytery in 1950, and of the general assembly in 1960—a year commemorating the fourth centenary of the Scottish Reformation. 'No one was better equipped to capture the mood of that historic occasion and no one who was present in the Woodside Halls will readily forget the passion and conviction that permeated her Moderatorial address' (*Stedfast*, Sept 1995, 12).

Elizabeth Barr loved walking and cycling holidays in the highlands and islands, staying congenially in youth hostels and crofts. She also maintained a lifelong friendship with a Belgian refugee family who were given hospitality by the Barrs in the First World War. According to her church's magazine, she evinced 'a certain robustness of faith and evangelical commitment … combined with a breadth, an openness and a generosity of spirit towards those with whom she did not necessarily agree' (*Stedfast*, Sept 1995, 13). Her historical significance, however, is

mainly as a pioneer who broke with a 400-year Presbyterian tradition of exclusive male ministry. She was always aware that she was the object of interest and scrutiny, as a woman in what remained overwhelmingly a man's world. Yet she believed that none of the difficulties encountered during her ministry could be attributed to gender. Of her moderatorial year she wrote:

> It was an amazing honour, not because I was a woman, but because I was the woman I was. I like to think that the General Assembly was honouring the women folk of the Church … and we do wrong to separate them in describing the life, work and witness of the Church. (Thomson, 4)

After twenty years of active retirement she died in Gartnavel General Hospital, Glasgow, on 23 June 1995, and was buried five days later in the family plot at Fenwick cemetery, Ayrshire. She was unmarried.

LESLEY ORR MACDONALD

Sources A. D. Scrimgeour, 'Tribute to God's servant', *Stedfast* [magazine of the United Free Church of Scotland] (Sept 1995), 11–13 · *Stedfast* [magazine of the United Free Church of Scotland] (1960–61) · D. P. Thomson, ed., *Women in ministry* (1965), 3–5 · *United Free Church of Scotland jubilee handbook* (1989) · *West End News* [Glasgow] (21 Feb 1975), 6 · personal knowledge (2004) · private information (2004) · b. cert. · d. cert.
Likenesses photograph, 1960, priv. coll. · photographs, priv. coll.
Wealth at death £9434.69: confirmation, Scotland, 1995

Barr, James (1862–1949), minister of the United Free Church of Scotland and politician, was born on 26 July 1862 at Beanscroft Farm in the parish of Fenwick, Ayrshire, the eldest of eight children born to Allan Barr, farmer, and his wife, Elizabeth Brown. James, or Jimmy, was educated at the local subscription school at Waterside in Fenwick, and then at Kilmarnock Academy, where he was dux in 1879. That same year he entered Glasgow University, where he enjoyed a glittering period as an undergraduate winning numerous prizes and medals, and graduating MA in 1884 with a joint first in moral philosophy and logic.

After a year touring North America recuperating from a breakdown, Barr took up a scholarship at Trinity College, Glasgow, the college of the United Free Church, to study for the ministry. His first charge was at Johnstone and Wamphray Free Church in his native Ayrshire, which he took up in 1889 and where, a year later, he married Martha Wilson Stephen (1863–1959), a member of his old church in Kilmarnock and with whom he had five children. In 1896 he moved to Glasgow, first at Dennistoun Free Church and then, in 1907, he took charge of St Mary's in Govan, home of Clyde shipyards and other heavy industries, a position which he held until 1920, when he became secretary of the Home Mission Board of the United Free Church.

Barr brought an evangelical fervour and social commitment to his ministries. He introduced a more informal style to church services and was determined to reach those who did not attend regular worship; at St Mary's he established a 'Men's Own' society which was successful in attracting working men. He was active in the Liberal cause as early as the 1892 general election, seeing in Liberalism the vehicle for realizing disestablishment, temperance, home rule for Scotland, and the taxation of land values. A member of local school boards in Ayrshire, he was first elected to the Glasgow school board in 1903 and was returned in subsequent elections, topping the poll in 1910. His work in education and his general outlook brought him closer to the labour movement and in 1913 he was honoured by the boilermakers on Clydeside for his efforts on their behalf in the lock-out of 1910. Official recognition was bestowed on him in 1914 when he was invited onto the royal commission on the housing of the industrial population of Scotland, the *Report* of which (1917) was significant in promoting state involvement in the provision of housing.

In 1919 Barr was appointed to lead a national campaign by all temperance groups in support of prohibition, though the local veto poll of 1920 was a major disappointment as a clear majority voted for 'no change' rather than 'no licence'. However the issue brought him closer to the Independent Labour Party, which he joined in 1920. In 1924 he was elected Labour MP for Motherwell. He was not unique among Presbyterian ministers in embracing socialism, but he was certainly in a small minority, as most were strongly antagonistic to Labour. Moreover, he also spoke out clearly against the anti-Irish prejudices so noticeable in the protestant churches at this time; his victory at Motherwell had been against a sitting 'Orange and protestant' MP. A founder and past president of the Scottish Home Rule Association, he introduced in 1927 a Home Rule Bill for Scotland, the failure of which (and a similar bill in 1924) helped stimulate the formation of the nationalist movement in Scotland. As chairman of the Parliamentary Labour Party he loyally supported MacDonald and Snowden throughout the crisis of 1931, though he had misgivings that the government had sold out to the bankers. The formation of the National Government, however, proved the breaking point for him. He was defeated in the general election of October 1931, though he was returned in November 1935 for Coatbridge, which he held until his retirement in June 1945.

Barr controversially led the minority of the United Free Church against union with the Church of Scotland in 1929. He was in favour of unity but not at the price of the continuing establishment of church and state, and he became the first moderator of the United Free Church (Continuing), a position he held again in 1943. His writings on church questions included *The Scottish Church Question* (1920), *The United Free Church of Scotland* (1934), and *The Scottish Covenanters* (1946). One of his sons became professor of New Testament literature and exegesis, and his daughter Elizabeth Brown *Barr (1905–1995) became the first woman to be ordained as a Presbyterian minister in Scotland.

Barr remained committed to his principles throughout his life, a trait which sat uneasily with the compromises demanded of a parliamentary politician. But in his life and work he embodied much of Scottish history and society. His own family was steeped in the traditions of the covenanters, he was a great enthusiast for Burns, he was a

pacifist actively opposed to the Second South African War and the First World War, even though his three sons joined up and one died in the latter. He was an ardent supporter of home rule and prohibition, and just as ardently opposed to capital punishment. He believed in free education for all and, while a member of the Glasgow school board, supported the efforts which led in 1913 to the establishment of a chair in Scottish history and literature at Glasgow University. He opposed fascism and communism (see his book *Religious Liberty in Totalitarian States: the Challenge to the Church of Communism, Fascism, Nazism*, 1938). He supported Chamberlain over Munich and even in November 1939 was calling for a negotiated peace. He did not oppose the war but was not an enthusiastic supporter, and found his role in serving as convener of the committee on the position of conscientious objectors.

As befits the son of a 'bonnet laird', Barr has been described as looking like a farmer: a tall, brawny man and a powerful speaker. He died at 75 Clouston Street, Glasgow, on 24 February 1949 and was buried in his home parish of Fenwick.   JAMES J. SMYTH

Sources J. Barr, *Lang syne: memoirs of the Rev. James Barr, B.D.* (1949) · W. Knox, 'Barr, Rev James', *Scottish labour leaders, 1918–39: a biographical dictionary*, ed. W. Knox (1984) · A. Bogle, *Records of the Scottish Church History Society*, 21 (1981–3), 189–207 · T. Johnston, *Memories* (1952) · T. Gallagher, *Glasgow: the uneasy peace* (1987) · S. J. Brown, 'The social vision of Scottish Presbyterianism and the union of 1929', *Records of the Scottish Church History Society*, 24 (1990–92), 77–96 · *Glasgow Herald* (25 Feb 1949) · *Forward* (5 March 1949) · *Forward* (12 March 1949) · M. Keating and D. Bleiman, *Labour and Scottish nationalism* (1979) · I. Donnachie, C. Harvie, and I. S. Wood, *Forward! Labour politics in Scotland, 1888–1988* (1989) · J. Brand, *The national movement in Scotland* (1978) · *DSCHT*

Archives Bodl. RH, corresp. on Gold Coast | FILM BFI NFTVA, documentary footage

Likenesses photograph, repro. in Barr, *Lang syne*

Wealth at death £1378 13s. 0d.: confirmation, 13 April 1949, *CCI*

Barr [*née* Moyles], **(Sarah) Venie** (1875–1947), political activist and philanthropist, was born at Abbeyleix, Queen's county, on 3 October 1875, the daughter of James Moyles, a trader, and his wife, Eliza Jane Pratt. On 2 July 1901 she married Ainsworth Barr (d. 1935), son of James Barr. Her husband, a rugby international, who as part of the Irish fifteen won the triple crown in 1899, was a solicitor and later a prominent Belfast stockbroker. They had two sons, Bruce and James. Marriage brought Venie Barr to Belfast, where she embarked upon what was to prove a lifelong involvement in Unionist politics.

In 1910 Venie Barr was appointed honorary secretary of the South Belfast Women's Unionist Association, a post she held until 1918, when she became chair of the St Anne's Women's Unionist Association. She was active in anti-home rule agitation between 1910 and 1914, and was one of the founder members of the Ulster Women's Unionist Council (UWUC), formed on 23 January 1911. The UWUC was intended to act as an auxiliary to the all-male Ulster Unionist Council (UUC), formed in 1905. Largely content to remain in the shadow of the UUC, the women's organization was nevertheless active on a broad range of fronts, taking a vigorous role in social welfare, propaganda, and fund-raising, during and after the war. In 1912

Barr was prominent in the organization of the 'women's declaration' against home rule. This petition, the female counterpart to the male-only solemn league and covenant, collected 229,000 signatories in Ulster, an excess of 10,000 over the male petition. Barr was also a keen supporter of the Ulster Volunteer Force, a military organization formed in January 1913 to resist home rule. Although women were excluded from the ranks of the force, they were active as propagandists, clerks, fund-raisers, and nurses. She was appointed postmistress to the force, a position she held throughout the war years. These were among the busiest of her life, and she became deeply involved in charitable initiatives connected with the Ulster troops. She was one of the driving forces behind the Ulster women's gift fund, which sent parcels of food, clothing, and small gifts to prisoners of war and men at the front, and acted as the organization's honorary secretary from 1914 to 1918. She was appointed CBE (1920) in recognition of her work with the fund.

The post-war years brought no lessening of commitment to Unionist causes. In 1921 Barr became assistant honorary treasurer of the UWUC, and in 1923 she was elected vice-chair of the organization. In 1931 she became honorary treasurer, and she subsequently held both posts until her death. From 1919 she was a delegate to the UUC, presenting the Unionist women's perspective to the central male organization. Her addresses were noted for their confidence and fluidity. As a result of her war work Barr was concerned for those former servicemen and their families who suffered hardship after 1918, and she encouraged the co-operation of the UWUC with organizations such as the Soldiers' and Sailors' Families' Association during and after the war. She was also one of the Ulster representatives at the unveiling of the memorial to the 36th (Ulster) division at Thiepval on the Somme. She also acted as honorary secretary of the Belfast Council of Social Welfare, president of the Toc H Women Helpers (Belfast branch), and honorary treasurer of the Ulster Girl Guides. In the uncertain years following partition she assisted many young Ulster women to emigrate, mainly to Canada, and she travelled there in 1930 to both check on the progress of thirty-three women whom she had helped to move, and explore the possibilities for others.

The final years of Barr's life were dogged by ill health, although she continued her political work almost until the end, and resigned from the UWUC only a few months before her death. She died on 1 November 1947 at her home, Ravenna, 13 Malone Park, Belfast.

OONAGH WALSH

Sources minutes of the Ulster Women's Unionist Council, 1912–15, PRO NIre., D 1098/1/3 · N. Kingham, *United we stood: the official history of the Ulster Women's Unionist Council* (1975) · D. Urquhart, 'The female of the species is more deadlier than the male? The Ulster Women's Unionist Council, 1911–40', *Coming into the light: the work, politics and religion of women in Ulster, 1840–1940*, ed. J. Holmes and D. Urquhart (1994) · PRO NIre., Soldiers' and Sailors' Families' Association MSS, D 1071/J/H · Lady Londonderry, correspondence, PRO NIre., Londonderry (Lady) MSS, D 2846/1/1–8 · *Northern Whig and Belfast Post* (3 Nov 1947) · *Belfast News-Letter* (3 Nov 1947) · *Belfast Telegraph* (3 Nov 1947) · WWW · b. cert. · m. cert. · d. cert.

Archives PRO NIre., Soldiers' and Sailors' Families' Association MSS, D1071/J/H · PRO NIre., corresp. with Lady Londonderry, D2846/1/1–8
Likenesses photographs, PRO NIre., Ulster Women's Unionist Council MSS
Wealth at death £2431 8s. 4d.: probate, 10 March 1948, CGPLA NIre.

Barraclough, Geoffrey (1908–1984), historian, was born in Bradford, Yorkshire, on 10 May 1908, the eldest of three children (all sons) of Walter Barraclough, a prosperous wool merchant of that city, and his wife, Edith Mary Brayshaw. He was educated at Ackworth School (1917–19), Colwall (1919–21), 'which made a lifelong rebel of me', Bootham School in York (1921–4), and Bradford grammar school (1924–5). At seventeen he went to work in the family firm of O. S. Daniel & Co., selling essential oils in Europe. 'Whatever essential oils may have been', he wrote, 'I soon discovered that they were not essential to me.' In 1926 he won a scholarship to Oriel College, Oxford, where he developed an interest in medieval history, winning first-class honours in history in 1929. Graduate work followed at Munich (1929–31), where he took his new bride, Marjorie Gardiner; they had one son, Alan (b. 1930).

In 1931–3 Barraclough moved to the English School at Rome and did research on the papacy. His first books, *Public Notaries and the Papal Curia* (1934) and *Papal Provisions* (1935), were intended to correct what he regarded as the provincialism of English medievalists.

In 1934 Barraclough won a fellowship at Merton College, Oxford, and in 1936 moved to St John's College, Cambridge. He also published *Medieval Germany* (2 vols., 1938), and became editor of *Studies in Medieval History*, designed to introduce English readers to German scholarship. By the age of twenty-nine he was the leading authority on German medieval history in the English-speaking world.

When the Second World War began, Barraclough joined the Enigma project at Bletchley Park, first as an employee of the Foreign Office, and later as a squadron leader in the Royal Air Force. In Bletchley's Hut 3 he became 'first of the watch', presiding over the horseshoe table where Luftwaffe dispatches were read during the battle of Britain. In 1941 he was sent to the Mediterranean, and in 1944 was seconded to France. At the war's end he was in the Air Ministry at London.

During the war Barraclough wrote *The Origins of Modern Germany* (1946), which offered a historian's long view of the German problem. The book was widely read, and the policy it recommended was adopted by Britain and the United States.

In 1945 Barraclough became professor of medieval history at Liverpool. He divorced his first wife and married Diana Russell-Clarke; they had two sons, Nigel (b. 1947) and Giles (b. 1948). Diana was the daughter of Edward Russell-Clarke, barrister, of the Inner Temple. The new family moved to an Elizabethan house 18 miles from Liverpool, and lived there from 1945 to 1956, a decade of happiness and peace in Barraclough's life. At Liverpool he founded a programme in archival administration, where a generation of British archivists was trained. He published *The Mediaeval Empire* (1950), *Cheshire Charters* (1957), and *The Earldom and County Palatine of Chester* (1953). Barraclough also developed a new interest in applying history to present problems, and contributed to *The Listener*, the *New Statesman*, *The Observer*, and the *Manchester Guardian*. A collection of essays appeared as *History in a Changing World* (1955). He was also active in the Historical Association, of which he was president in 1964–7.

In 1956 Barraclough was offered the Stevenson research chair at the University of London formerly held by Arnold Toynbee, and the directorship of the Royal Institute of International Affairs. His task was to publish an annual *Survey of International Affairs*, a labour which he disliked. In 1962 he quit his job, and returned to St John's College, Cambridge, where he wrote his most successful book, *An Introduction to Contemporary History* (1964).

Increasingly restless, Barraclough took flight to America, teaching at Texas (1965) and San Diego (1965–8). He was married a third time, to Gwendolyn Lambert, and in 1968 moved to Brandeis. There he recovered stability in his life, publishing *The Medieval Papacy* (1968). There were no children of this marriage.

In 1970 Barraclough was called to Oxford as Chichele professor of modern history and a fellow of All Souls. There, things went badly again. Barraclough felt confined by the curriculum, oppressed by the ambience of All Souls, and disliked by colleagues who expected him to resume a narrow speciality in medieval history.

After two years of strife, Barraclough abruptly left Oxford and returned to Brandeis, remaining there from 1972 to 1981, his most prolific period. He published *The Crucible of Europe* (1976), a history of the ninth and tenth centuries; *Management in a Changing Economy* (1976), an application of history to economic planning; *Main Trends in History* (1976), a survey commissioned by UNESCO; 'The Times' Atlas of World History* (1978); *Turning Points in World History* (1979); *The Christian World* (1981); and *From Agadir to Armageddon* (1982). He wrote abundantly for *The Nation*, the *New Republic*, and the *New York Review of Books*.

Barraclough was lionized in Boston, and became a famous figure in American universities. He dressed in a wool tattersall shirt, an old tweed jacket, drab necktie, ancient Oxford bags, and gleaming British walking shoes. He walked rapidly with a curious rolling gait, his bald head cocked oddly to one side, and his round, ruddy face veiled by blue clouds of smoke from a battered pipe.

Honours cascaded upon Barraclough, from everywhere but Britain. 'His reputation in Europe and the United States … was enormous,' an English colleague wrote, but 'British colleagues, especially in his later years, tended to view his achievements rather more coolly.' His contribution was to enlarge the historian's territory beyond the boundaries of the nation state, and to expand the temporal context of history from the study of the past to the study of change. His work inspired young scholars throughout the world.

In 1981 Barraclough retired from Brandeis, and moved to Williams College, and in 1982 he taught at Munich.

There he fell severely ill of lung cancer. He returned to his second wife, Diana Barraclough, in Burford, Oxfordshire, and resumed a project on Cheshire charters which he had put aside thirty years before. As he neared the end of that last labour, he died at his home, Sylvester House, Witney Street, Burford, on 26 December 1984.

D. H. FISCHER, rev.

Sources G. Barraclough, 'Autobiography', priv. coll. · Brandeis University, Faculty Archives · A. J. P. Taylor, *A personal history* (1983) · *WWW* · personal knowledge (1990) · private information (1990) [Diana Barraclough] · *The Times* (31 Dec 1984) · *CGPLA Eng. & Wales* (1985)

Archives Ches. & Chester ALSS, papers | CUL, corresp. with Sir Herbert Butterfield · U. Reading L., corresp. with Sir Frank Stenton and Lady Stenton, papers

Wealth at death £548,553: probate, 1 Oct 1985, *CGPLA Eng. & Wales*

Barralet, John James (1747–1815), watercolour painter, was born in Dublin, and came of a French family. He was educated under James Mannin in the Dublin Society Schools, where he was awarded a premium in 1764. He specialized in landscapes, producing prosaic works with no hint of drama, although the trees are particularly well executed. However, his forte was undoubtedly the figures who people many of his works and give a lively immediacy to his watercolours. He worked in England between 1770 and 1779, setting up a drawing school in 1773 in James's Street, Golden Square, London, which he moved in 1777 to 24 St Alban's Street, Pall Mall. He exhibited in the Royal Academy between 1770 and 1776 and in the Society of Artists in London from 1773 to 1780, winning a gold palette in 1774 and becoming a fellow in 1777. In that year he showed six landscapes in chalk in the Exhibition, or Grand Museum, of Arts and Sciences in the Great Room, Royal Exchange, in the Strand.

In England, apart from landscapes, Barralet exhibited classical subjects, English historical subjects, and theatrical scenes, several of which were engraved, including *Samuel Foote in the Old Bachelor*. In 1772 he worked up sketches made by others during Captain Cook's journey round the world in the *Endeavour*.

In 1779 Barralet was back in Dublin to teach in place of Mannin during the latter's illness; he exhibited in the Society of Artists in Ireland in 1780. He did not succeed Mannin as a teacher in the Dublin Society Schools but became involved with antiquaries, doing much work for Francis Grose's *Antiquities of Ireland* (1791–5) and also for Thomas Milton's *Select Views from the Seats of the Nobility and Gentry of Ireland* (1783–93). He also essayed stained-glass painting, and on one occasion painted stage scenery for Crow Street Theatre. Four drawings (Ulster Museum) done near Glenarm Castle in 1787–9 show the improvement in his technique during his Dublin years. His portrait groups in watercolour include the Foster family at the Oriel Temple (priv. coll.) and a lively scene of the duchess of Rutland driving in the Phoenix Park in 1784 (priv. coll.).

In 1795 Barralet settled in Philadelphia, USA. Some of his best work dates from this period, including his *View of Philadelphia from the Great Elm Tree in Kensington* (1796) and the print of *The Apotheosis of George Washington*. A drawing of *America Welcoming Irish Immigrants Ashore c 1796* (Winterthur Museum) survives and his gouache of *Dunlap House, Philadelphia* (1807, Girard collection, Philadelphia) is a splendid view of a dignified American townscape. He was described in 1834 by William Dunlap as having had 'all the volatility of France united with Hibernian prodigality and eccentricity. He was a man of talent without discretion and any thing like common prudence; prodigally generous and graspingly poor' (Dunlap, 2.42–3). His American career included book illustrations, trade cards, and stock shares as well as landscapes. Towards the end of his life he appears to have used oils, painting in 1810 *The Bridge over the Schuylkill* (Historical Society of Pennsylvania, Philadelphia). In 1812 he was elected professor of the newly founded Society of Artists of the United States, which he had helped to found. Barralet died on 16 January 1815 in Philadelphia where, according to Strickland, 'he lived, as a widower, with two children', though nothing is known of his family. He died very impoverished. His brother, John Melchior Barralet (*c.*1750–*c.*1787), was also a landscape painter. He worked in Dublin before moving to London, where he became a drawing master.

ANNE CROOKSHANK

Sources W. G. Strickland, *A dictionary of Irish artists*, 1 (1913), 25–8 · A. Pasquin [J. Williams], *An authentic history of the professors of painting, sculpture, and architecture who have practiced in Ireland … to which are added, Memoirs of the royal academicians* [1796]; facs. edn as *An authentic history of painting in Ireland* with introduction by R. W. Lightbown (1970), 53 · A. Crookshank and the Knight of Glin [D. Fitzgerald], *The watercolours of Ireland: works on paper in pencil, pastel and paint, c.1600–1914* (1994), 53–8 · W. Dunlap, *History of the rise and progress of the arts of design in the United States*, 2 (New York, 1834), 42–3 · P. L. Jacobs, 'John James Barralet and the apotheosis of George Washington', *Winterthur Portfolio*, 12 (1977), 118

Barrallier, Francis Louis (1773–1853), army officer and surveyor, was the son of a French surveyor, who after the capture of Toulon in 1793 was employed by the British. Barrallier was permitted to go to New South Wales with the new governor, Captain P. G. King RN, and after their arrival at Sydney in April 1800 King employed him as an architect, appointing him ensign in the New South Wales Corps (afterwards the old 102nd foot) on 14 August 1800. He undertook the duties of aide-de-camp, engineer, and artillery officer in the settlement.

In December 1800 the *Lady Nelson*, an armed schooner, arrived from England under the command of Lieutenant James Grant RN. She was the first vessel to pass through the Bass Strait from the west. Grant was ordered to survey the strait, and in 1801 Ensign Barrallier accompanied him as surveyor, his task being to survey the southern coast, and map it between Wilson's promontory and Western Port. In July he went to Coal River (Newcastle) where he surveyed the harbour. In August 1801 King appointed him acting engineer and artillery officer; as such he improved Sydney's defences and designed the citadel, Fort Phillip. He also surveyed Hunter's River, which was discovered to be a natural harbour with three distinct rivers. While engaged on this task the explorers were surrounded by Aborigines, and narrowly escaped with their lives. Barrallier embarked upon another expedition in 1802:

with nine soldiers of his regiment and some Sydney Aborigines he attempted to cross the Blue Mountains. The party was absent for four months, and suffered many hardships, but was unsuccessful. Governor King recorded in his 'general orders' his appreciation of Barrallier's services, including those which had led to an advancement in knowledge of the natural history and geography of the settlement. Soon after his Blue Mountains expedition Barrallier quarrelled with King, and he returned to England in 1803.

Barrallier was promoted lieutenant in the 90th foot in 1805, which he joined at Antigua, where he was again employed in surveying. His conduct as an assistant engineer at the capture of Martinique in 1809 earned him promotion to a company in the 101st foot. He served on the staff of Lieutenant-General Sir George Beckwith at the capture of Guadeloupe in 1810, and was entrusted with the design and erection of a monument to the British who died there.

In 1812, Barrallier was ordered by the duke of York to undertake a very elaborate military survey of Barbados, a task which involved calculating the latitudes and longitudes of the chief points on the coast; he was engaged in this work for five years, with the exception of a short period in which he served with the quartermaster-general's department of the force that recaptured Guadeloupe in 1815. When the 101st regiment returned home to be disbanded at Chatham in 1817 Barrallier was placed on half pay; thereafter he had brief periods of full pay in other corps, finally retiring on the half-pay list of the rifle brigade in 1833. He became an honorary lieutenant-colonel in 1840, and died at his home, 24 Bedford Square, Commercial Road, London, on 11 June 1853, aged eighty.

H. M. CHICHESTER, rev. S. KINROSS

Sources V. Parsons, 'Barrallier, Francis Luis', *AusDB*, vol. 1 · *New South Wales general standing orders … 1791–1806*, 2 vols. (1802–6) · Boase, *Mod. Eng. biog.*

Barran family (*per. c.*1842–1952), clothing manufacturers, came to prominence with **Sir John Barran**, first baronet (1821–1905), who was born on 3 August 1821 at New Wandsworth, Surrey, the son of John Barran, a London gunmaker and his wife, Elizabeth Fletcher. He was educated privately. In 1842, for reasons which are not clear, he travelled by boat from London to Hull, and by railway to Leeds, where he found employment as an assistant in Thomas Gresham's small pawnbroking, jewellery, and clothing firm. As far as is known his family had no previous connection with Leeds. Within a few months he opened his own shop at 30 Bridge End South, Leeds, and began his career as a tailor. By 1851, when he referred to himself as a tailor and clothes dealer, he had moved to a more prestigious location at no. 1 Briggate, one of the major thoroughfares in Leeds. There he carried a stock of ready-made items and tailored made-to-measure garments. His business expanded rapidly. He was one of the first in Britain to use Singer's new sewing machine to manufacture clothes. He established a small factory in Alfred Street, Leeds, then moved to larger premises at 1 Boar Lane. By 1856 he had between twenty and thirty machines at work, sewing his ready-to-wear clothes.

In 1858 Barran saw a bandsaw used for cutting furniture veneers being demonstrated at a furniture exhibition in Leeds. He recognized its potential in his trade and had it modified for cutting cloth in quantity. This led to the real take-off of his business. In 1867 he moved to much larger premises in Park Row, Leeds, where his technical innovation continued. With his eldest son, also John, he patented a counterweight iron and a foot control for powered sewing machines. By the 1870s his business had become extensive: he had 2000 sewing machines at work in 1872, all driven from a gas engine through shafting. In 1877 a yet larger factory was opened at Park Square, Leeds, and, in the following decade, yet another huge factory, in Hanover Lane, and a warehouse in Somers Street were built. By 1904 the firm employed more than 3000 in Leeds. It was the pre-eminent business in the early years of the Leeds ready-made clothing industry, specializing in the ready-to-wear trade for boys' clothes. John Barran was known as the little boys' tailor, but also made men's ready-made clothing. He married his first wife, Ann (*d.* 1874), daughter of Major Hirst, a local woollen manufacturer, in 1842, soon after his arrival in Leeds. They had six sons. He married his second wife, Eliza (*née* Brown), the widow of John Bilton of Park Lea, Scarborough, in 1878.

The rise and early success of the Barran business was primarily the result of John Barran's personal endeavours. He was particularly perceptive and innovatory in his production techniques and organizational methods: he is recognized as one of the innovators of the 'divisional system' in the manufacture of clothing, by which different workers sewed different parts of the garment; he was instrumental in starting the transition from manufacture in small 'sweated workshops' to airy, purpose-built premises; and he was in the vanguard of improving employment conditions for women and children in the clothing trade, campaigning as early as 1864 for reductions in the working hours for girls in the trade and paying attention to the welfare provisions for his workers.

John Barran was a prominent Leeds Baptist and a resolute nonconformist. He acted as president of the local Young Men's Christian Association. He served Leeds in a variety of political and philanthropic roles. An obituary described him as having 'occupied well-nigh every important honorary position in Leeds' (*Yorkshire Evening Post*, 3 May 1905). He was involved in, and a benefactor for, the purchase of Roundhay Park for the town. He was its Liberal MP from 1876 to 1885, then served the Otley constituency from 1886 to 1895 as a Gladstonian Liberal. He was never an orator in parliament, where his main contribution was to look after local interests. He was mayor of Leeds from 1870 to 1871. He served as a member of the council of the Yorkshire College, the forerunner of Leeds University, chairing its finance committee. He also served as president of Leeds chamber of commerce from 1873 to 1876. He served a long term as JP for the West Riding of

Yorkshire and for Leeds. In February 1895 he was created a baronet for his public and political services. John Barran died at his London residence, 24 Queen's Gate, Kensington, on 3 May 1905.

His first son, John, died in tragic circumstances in 1886. His second son, Alfred, born on 29 June 1851, appears not to have been involved with the business, but three other sons, Charles, Henry, and Rowland [*see below*] were all closely connected with the firm. Charles was a partner from 1878 to 1888. Henry, born in Leeds in 1856, succeeded his father as chairman from 1903 to 1918 and floated the business as a public company in 1903. He remained a director to 1942. He was succeeded as chairman in 1918 by **Sir Rowland Hirst Barran** (1858–1949), who was the driving force in the company for much of the inter-war period. In 1887 he married Rose Cardew, daughter of the Revd Gilbert Bradley. They had one son and two daughters. His second marriage, in 1909, was to Louise (*d.* 1947), daughter of J. Stevenson Brown of Montreal, Canada. He was appointed a partner in the family business in 1882. He served as the Liberal MP for North Leeds from 1902 to 1918. In 1914 he undertook, with Sir Maurice Levy, the complete reorganization of war clothing contracts, for which work he was knighted in 1918. In the 1920s he took the firm into the women's ready-to-wear trade. He served as vice-chairman of the Federation of British Industries, and was a governor of Leeds grammar school and a life member of the court of Leeds University. He died at Bournemouth on 6 August 1949.

Sir John Nicholson Barran, second baronet (1872–1952), the eldest son of John Barran's first son, John, and Eliza Henrietta, daughter of Edward Nicholson of Wokingham, Berkshire, was the first of the third generation to enter the family firm. He was born on 16 August 1872 and educated at Winchester College and Trinity College, Cambridge. In 1902 he married Alice Margarita (*d.* 1939), daughter of the Revd Leighton Parks of New York city. They had three sons and two daughters. His second marriage was in 1946 to Esther, eldest daughter of the Hon. F. M. B. Fisher. He served as the Liberal MP for Hawick burghs from 1909 to 1918. Between 1909 and 1916 he was a parliamentary secretary to a number of government ministers including the postmaster-general, the president of the Local Government Board, the home secretary, and the foreign secretary. From 1916 to 1918 he was parliamentary secretary to H. H. Asquith. He was a director of the Barran business from 1903 to 1921. He was nominated one of the three sheriffs of Yorkshire in 1920. He died on 8 July 1952. The title passed to John Leighton Barran, third baronet (*d.* 1974), but the firm ceased to trade.   D. T. JENKINS

Sources D. Ryott, *John Barrans of Leeds, 1851–1951* (1951) • D. T. Jenkins, 'Barran, Sir John', *DBB* • *Yorkshire Post* (4 May 1905) [Sir John Barran] • *Yorkshire Evening Post* (3 May 1905) [Sir John Barran] • *Leeds Mercury* (4 May 1905) [Sir John Barran] • *Yorkshire Evening Post* (6 Aug 1949) [Sir Rowland Hirst Barran] • *Yorkshire who's who* (1912) • J. Thomas, 'A history of the Leeds clothing industry', *Yorkshire Bulletin of Economic and Social Research, occasional paper* (1955) • *The century's progress: Yorkshire* (1893) • *WWW, 1951–60* • m. cert. [Sir John Barran to Eliza Bilton] • m. cert. [Sir John Barran to Ann Hirst] • d.

cert. [Sir John Barran] · *CGPLA Eng. & Wales* (1952) [Sir John Nicholson Barran]

Archives W. Yorks. AS, Leeds, John Barran & Sons, business records

Wealth at death £408,048 5s. 10d.—Sir John Barran: Jenkins, 'Barran, Sir John' · £64,300 3s. 3d.—Sir John Nicholson Barran: probate, 1952, *CGPLA Eng. & Wales* · £107,577 4s. 11d.—Sir Rowland Hirst Barran: probate, 1949, *CGPLA Eng. & Wales*

Barran, Sir John, first baronet (1821–1905). *See under* Barran family (*per. c.*1842–1952).

Barran, Sir John Nicholson, second baronet (1872–1952). *See under* Barran family (*per. c.*1842–1952).

Barran, Sir Rowland Hirst (1858–1949). *See under* Barran family (*per. c.*1842–1952).

Barrasford, Thomas (1859–1910), variety theatre entrepreneur, was the son of a Newcastle publican, but nothing else is known about his early life. He followed his father into the licensed trade, taking a number of public houses in Jarrow in the 1880s and 1890s. He was also involved in boxing promotions and, for a period in the 1890s, he managed the black boxer Frank Craig, the so-called 'coffee house cooler' (Fairfax-Blakeborough, 161). His music-hall career began in the same decade when he purchased a circus building in Jarrow and re-opened it as the Jarrow Palace of Varieties. In 1899 he acquired the Leeds Tivoli and followed this with the rapid acquisition and refurbishment of a number of halls in the English provinces and Scotland, building up a syndicate of fourteen halls by the early 1900s. Barrasford formed his various interests into a limited company in 1903.

Barrasford placed particular emphasis on the interior design and furnishing of his properties which were among the most luxurious of all British variety theatres. The Liverpool Hippodrome, which he opened in 1902, was, indeed, regarded by many as Britain's best equipped variety theatre and was probably the first to offer tip-up plush seats at what contemporaries termed popular prices. Barrasford was also among the first to introduce the cinematograph into the variety theatre, eventually using his own projection device, the 'Barrascope', which he developed with photographer Owen Brooks and engineer Fred Borland in 1902.

The early twentieth-century variety industry was characterized by managements' use of so-called 'barring clauses', which prevented performers from taking engagements at theatres in close proximity to venues where they were already contracted for future appearances. Barrasford was especially assiduous in his recruitment of continental performers who were not usually bound by such restrictions and many leading European variety acts were introduced to Britain as a result. This also led to his developing considerable foreign interests and he eventually controlled variety theatres in Paris, Brussels, Barcelona, and Marseilles.

By 1904 Barrasford looked set to become Britain's leading variety entrepreneur, but he overstretched his resources in the course of intense competition with a rival syndicate headed by Oswald Stoll. There was some personal animosity between the two men, probably related to contractual disputes, and this translated into a battle over which company could be the first to open a major West End variety theatre. In fact, Stoll's Coliseum opened two days ahead of Barrasford's Lyceum, in December 1905. Barrasford was unable to gain a drink licence from the London county council and this proved a barrier to profitability. Barrasford was forced to sell the Lyceum in 1906 and he moved the headquarters of his now rather less ambitious company to the Brighton Hippodrome. He contracted Bright's disease about 1907 and in 1909 control of his variety chain passed to the London-based syndicate operated by Walter Gibbons.

Barrasford was married twice, his second wife being the music-hall singer Maud D'Almayne, who appears to have shared in some of his business enterprises in his final years. He had five children by the two marriages.

During his lifetime Barrasford developed a strong interest in horse-racing. He was a heavy gambler and he owned a small string of racehorses which were trained at Malton in the North Riding of Yorkshire. His most significant contribution to the race world was his development of a starting gate, once again the result of collaboration with the Leeds engineer Fred Borland. A device first used at Newmarket in 1897, the starting gate was prone to create movements and shadows which caused panic among the horses and Barrasford's model, which had an underground mechanism, was deemed far superior in this respect to most other early versions. It was used extensively in the north of England and on training grounds in Britain and the continent in the early years of the century. Barrasford died on 1 February 1910 from diabetes and pleurisy at The Hippodrome, 50 Skiddle Street, Brighton, and was buried in Brighton. He was survived by his second wife.   DAVE RUSSELL

Sources G. J. Mellor, *The northern music hall* (1970) · *The Era* (5 Feb 1910) · *Yorkshire Post* (2 Feb 1910) · W. H. Boardman, *Vaudeville days* (1935) · J. Fairfax-Blakeborough, *Paddock personalities* (1935) · d. cert. · *CGPLA Eng. & Wales* (1910)

Likenesses photograph, repro. in *The Era*

Wealth at death £17,337 10s.: probate, 25 April 1910, *CGPLA Eng. & Wales*

Barratt, Alfred (1844–1881), philosopher, was born at Heald Grove, Moss Side, Hulme, Manchester, on 12 July 1844, the eldest son of James Barratt, solicitor, of Heald Grove, and his wife, Ann, *née* Stewart. Extraordinarily precocious, he learned Hebrew as a child. Between the ages of eight and twelve he attended a small day school. From there he moved on to a grammar school at Sandbach, Cheshire, where he stayed for two years. From about 1858 he attended Rugby School, before proceeding in 1862 to Balliol College, Oxford. He took a double first in moderations and a first class in the classical, mathematical, and law and modern history schools in 1866. He obtained a fellowship at Brasenose College in 1867 and the Eldon law scholarship in 1870. He was called to the bar in 1872 but had no ambition to make his name there. In May 1876 he married Dorothea, the sister of an old schoolfriend, the Revd R. Hart Davis.

Deeply influenced by evolutionism, Barratt nevertheless showed little interest in the ideas of Charles Darwin. In content and in general broad scope his true mentor was Herbert Spencer, whom he regarded as the greatest philosopher of the time. Although he was critical of details, it was beneath Spencer's umbrella that Barratt wrote both on ethics and on ontology. The former is the subject of Barratt's first book, *Physical Ethics* (1869), as well as articles in *Mind*, and the latter the subject of the unfinished posthumously published *Physical Metempiric*. Thinking himself an egoist, a position he defended vigorously against Henry Sidgwick, Barratt argued that the highest good is pleasure, and that it is this which motivates all of our actions. This notion of motivation was crucial because, despite obvious affinities, Barratt was no utilitarian: he argued that, strictly speaking, utilitarianism, being concerned with ends, belongs to the realm of politics, whereas morality is always an internal psychological phenomenon, concerned only with motives and intentions.

Although he offered his claim about pleasure and morality as a formal proposition, Barratt clearly thought it something based in physical reality (hence the title of his book) and devoted much space to showing it to be a consequence of modern psychology. Despite this, it may be wondered to what extent Barratt thought that morality was justified by nature. Unlike some writing at his time, notably Spencer himself, he showed clear understanding that one cannot simply equate that which has evolved with that which is morally good.

> It is no doubt true that 'whatever is, is good,' because the course of the universe is a course of evolution, which is what we consider 'good,' because it has produced us and tends on the whole to our happiness; but it is not true that 'whatever is, is *right*,' (if by right is meant morally right), unless it be *assumed* that all natural facts are self-conscious to some mind which understands and follows the distinctions of Human Morality.   ('Ethics and politics', *Mind*, 2, 1877, 462–3)

Although he did not explore this point further, one assumes from remarks he made elsewhere that Barratt thought the Christian God to be such a mind.

Barratt's ontology produced a form of 'panpsychic monism', also being developed at that time by William Kingdom Clifford. He thought that mind and matter are one, and that corresponding to the smallest physical units we have the smallest mental units, which (following Leibniz) he labelled 'monads'. Important here was Spencer's upwardly progressive vision of life's history, with humans in some sense achieving the highest possible level of mind/matter integration and development here on earth:

> If mind be associated with ... the whole sphere of phenomena, a more thorough consciousness of the ultimate unity of our whole self is attained, and a considerable step made towards that final idea of human development in which mind becomes a perfect reproduction of nature, and its sequences completely assimilated to the laws of the outer world.   (*Physical Ethics*, 361)

Again though, this is fitted into a Christian (and unSpencerian) context, for it is made clear that God achieves some perfect fusion of mind and matter.

Barratt was popular among his colleagues, who described him as a man of modesty, simplicity, and friendliness. He had an extraordinarily retentive mind, a wide knowledge of languages, and a developed taste in music and art. He became secretary to the Oxford University commission in 1880 and collapsed from overwork in the spring of the next year, before dying at Munster House, Fulham, on 18 May 1881. He left his widow and an infant daughter. He was buried in Hendon churchyard.

Barratt died before he could truly make his mark. *Physical Ethics*—derivative, heavy in style, weighed down with footnotes and appendices, and littered with clever quotations (never translated from the original language)—reads like the work of a young person who has succeeded well in university examinations. His articles, however, have more force and style, and in his discussion of utilitarianism he brings his legal training to bear in an elegant fashion. Although panpsychic monism is hardly the philosophy of today, and any derivative of the philosophy of Herbert Spencer is even less so, had he lived longer Barratt might well have merited a paragraph rather than merely a footnote in a history of British philosophy.

MICHAEL RUSE

Sources D. Barratt, 'Biographical preface', in A. Barratt, *Physical metempiric* (1883) · b. cert. · *CGPLA Eng. & Wales* (1881) · *DNB*
Likenesses portrait (after drawing by D. Barratt), repro. in A. Barratt, *Physical metempiric* (1883), frontispiece
Wealth at death £11,171 13s. 11d.: probate, 1 July 1881, *CGPLA Eng. & Wales*

Barratt, Thomas James (1841–1914), soap manufacturer and pioneer of advertising, was born on 16 May 1841 at 25 Tottenham Place, St Pancras, London, the son of Thomas Barratt, a piano maker, and his wife, Emma Price. He was educated at a private day school, and at fifteen was apprenticed to a firm of London merchants, George and Frederick Evans. Merchant enterprise seems to have been in his nature, and through hard work and natural inclination he moved upward in another London establishment, Ellis and Hale, colonial brokers. In 1864 he joined the newly enlarged soap-making establishment of A. and F. Pears in Great Russell Street as a bookkeeper, shortly becoming a commercial traveller for the firm. Barratt's skill and dedication to the work were enhanced by a family connection with his marriage on 11 March 1865 to Mary Frances (d. 1916), eldest daughter of Francis Pears, after which he joined Francis and Andrew Pears as partner in the firm.

Leaving the soapworks to be overseen by his partners, Barratt began what would be his life's work: to expand the firm through increased advertising. The questionable value of advertising, along with its reputation of being the last resort of failures and frauds, made Barratt's task a difficult one. Francis Pears, uncertain of Barratt's vision and apparently unwilling to be a party to this endeavour, withdrew from the firm in 1875 leaving £4000 in capital. His son Andrew continued to manage the soapworks while Barratt handled advertising.

Barratt was an innovator, both in his use of advertising and his methods, as well as a great promoter of the advertising profession. By placing the name Pears repeatedly in a column of newspaper space, or filling several columns with a single PEARS spelt out in hundreds of iterations of the name in minute type, he contrived to get round newspaper restrictions against illustrated advertisements. Celebrity endorsements and comic, even self-parodying, advertisements became trade marks of Pears advertising. Regular daily advertising in the national and regional press made Pears one of the most recognized names in the English-speaking world, making, as Barratt claimed, as many as 2000 appearances before the average reader. Such was the coverage that W. E. Gladstone, speaking in the House of Commons, made a passing reference to amendments 'as thick as the leaves in Vallombrosa or as plentiful as the advertisements of Pears soap' (*DBB*, 189). Barratt continued personally to buy all the firm's advertising space until the end of his life.

Barratt was renowned in addition for his use of 'stunt' advertising. He imported 10 centime coins, accepted as pennies in England, which he had stamped 'Pears' and put into circulation at fourteen for the shilling. Buying works of art and then offering high-quality reproductions at a nominal price, Barratt created the Pears' Pictures for People plan which brought the name Pears into millions of homes. The most famous of these was the portrait of a child by Sir John Everett Millais, distributed by Barratt under the title *Bubbles*, which generated as much debate about the commercial use of art as it did simple enjoyment.

Under Barratt's hand the firm expanded, and Pears' soap became one of the most recognized products of the late nineteenth century. In 1892 A. and F. Pears became a public company with £810,000 in assets, continuing to pay a healthy 10 per cent dividend during Barratt's stewardship. Advertising expenditure, which had never exceeded £80 annually when Barratt joined the firm, stood at over £100,000 at the time of his death.

Barratt brought the same energy to his other interests that he brought to advertising. As a proponent of conservation, Barratt started a programme to buy open lands for preservation against development, a scheme which he urged others to emulate. He was also a historian, completing a multi-volume history of Hampstead. Notwithstanding the controversial commercial use of art in Pears' advertising, Barratt filled his estate, Bellmoor, with a substantial collection of British art. He was also passionately interested in microscopy, and was a fellow of the Royal Microscopical Society.

Barratt died at Queen's Highcliffe Hotel, Margate, on 26 April 1914 after a short illness, and was buried on 30 April at St Pancras cemetery, East Finchley. At some point Barratt had separated from his wife, and the principal beneficiaries of his estate were his two sons from a relationship with Florence Bell, daughter of a doctor, who lived with him and called herself Mrs Barratt. His collection of Nelson memorabilia, including a considerable amount of plate, was given to the Royal Naval Hospital, Greenwich.

Alfred Harmsworth, Lord Northcliffe, described Barratt as 'the father of Modern Advertising from whom I have learned so much' (*DBB*, 190), and he was popularly described as 'the man who washed the face of the world' (ibid.).   KELLEY GRAHAM

Sources C. H. W. Jackson, 'The great persuader', *Blackwood*, 317 (1975), 204–19 · *The Times* (7 Nov 1899) · *The Times* (21 Oct 1913) · *The Times* (27 April 1914) · *The Times* (30 April 1914) · H. H. Bassett, ed., *Men of note in finance and commerce* [1901] · T. R. Nevett, *Advertising in Britain: a history* (1982) · E. G. Garvey, *The adman in the parlour* (1996) · C. Wilson, *The history of Unilever: a study in economic growth and social change*, 1 (1954) · *CGPLA Eng. & Wales* (1914) · T. Nevett, 'Barratt, Thomas James', *DBB* · b. cert. · m. cert. · d. cert.
Likenesses S. J. Solomon, portrait, presented Oct 1913
Wealth at death £405,564 16s. 6d.: probate, 7 July 1914, *CGPLA Eng. & Wales*

Barratt, (Arthur) William (1877–1939), shoe manufacturer and retailer, was born on 8 October 1877 in Ethel Street, Northampton, the fourth of seven sons of John Barratt, a shoemaker, and Eleanor, *née* Yeomans. William Barratt, as he was always known, came from a working-class background, and after attending the local elementary school he worked as a shop assistant selling shoes in Northampton and London. The poor conditions he experienced encouraged his socialist convictions. In 1899 he married Alice Johnson, who survived him until 1958. They had two daughters by adoption. On return to Northampton he became a prominent member of the local Social Democratic Federation, which had growing influence in a town where the industry was subject to considerable technical change. As a local socialist council candidate he just failed to get elected.

In 1902 Barratt went into partnership with his brother to sell shoes in a local shop. Another brother made a chance purchase of a stock of boots which he then tried to sell by post. This alerted William Barratt to the potential of a mail-order business but financial difficulties led to the original partnership going bankrupt in 1906. However, the potential of the mail-order business was clear, exploiting as it did the possibility of selling in rural areas and more remote villages and towns. With the help of a Rushden shoe manufacturer, Barratt recommenced business and quickly began to make a more permanent mark in the shoe trade. W. Barratt & Co. was created as a limited liability company in 1907. In 1913 Barratt opened his large Footshape works in Northampton and in 1914 the first retail outlet in London of what was to become a major retailing chain. The rapid development of the firm was assisted by the boom conditions of government orders in the First World War, but continued into the post-war period through the combination of worldwide mail-order sales and urban retail outlets, of which there were 150 at the time of his death.

Barratt's standing in the shoe trade was founded on his general business acumen and a reputation for quality. The mail-order service gave the firm international renown, since wherever the post went so too could Barratt's shoes. Barratt pioneered his own personal advertising style in many different languages, marketing both the product and himself as the guarantee of quality. His motto was that he who has good goods to sell should shout, not whisper down a well. He believed that business organization should display 'the individual touch' and cultivated an image of himself as a man of the people. However, although Barratt played a decisive entrepreneurial role, a number of his brothers and others also made important contributions to the success of the company.

Barratt was an unsuccessful parliamentary candidate for Labour in the Bethnal Green constituency in 1931. In Northampton he succeeded in being elected to the town council between 1929 and 1934 as a Labour Party member, but then resigned in protest against what he saw as the unbusinesslike character of local government. This was typical of someone who was strong-willed and something of a loner. In 1933 he became president of the Northampton Town Boot and Shoe Manufacturers Association, but created controversy by urging a shorter working week for workers in the shoe industry.

Barratt's local interests involved the support of many sporting groups, including the Northampton 'Saints' rugby club. As a young man he participated enthusiastically in many sporting activities, including early motor cycle racing. With his wife he made a major contribution to Northampton by financing a modern maternity home to check maternal mortality and suffering, thus relieving some of the contradiction that he felt between his wealth and his political and social views. Together they spent between £50,000 and £60,000 on the home.

During his lifetime Barratt developed W. Barratt & Co. into one of the leading shoe manufacturing and retailing firms in inter-war Britain, with over 2000 employees. He died on 8 December 1939 at St Andrew's Hospital, Northampton, two weeks after having suffered a nervous breakdown. He was cremated, and his ashes scattered on his brother Richard's grave at Kingsthorpe cemetery, Northampton, on 12 December.   MICHAEL HAYNES

Sources *Northampton Chronicle and Echo* (8 Dec 1939) · *Northampton Chronicle and Echo* (12 Dec 1939) · *Northampton Independent* (15 Dec 1939) · *Mercury and Herald* (8 Dec 1939) · *Shoe and Leather News* (14 Dec 1939) · K. Brooker, 'Barratt, Arthur William', *DBB* · *The romance of Barratts* (c.1948) · A. V. Eason, 'Saint Crispin's men', a history of Northamptonshire's shoemakers (1994) · d. cert.
Likenesses E. Ager, photograph, repro. in *Northampton Independent*
Wealth at death £302,646: Brooker, 'Barratt, Arthur William'

Barraud, Henry (*bap.* 1811, *d.* 1874). *See under* Barraud, William (*bap.* 1810, *d.* 1850).

Barraud, William (*bap.* 1810, *d.* 1850), animal painter, was baptized on 4 April 1810 at St Mary's Church, Lambeth, London, one of the seventeen children of William Francis Barraud (*bap.* 1783, *d.* 1833), a clerk in the custom house, and his wife, Sophia, daughter of the miniature painter Thomas Hull. On his father's side he was descended from a French Huguenot family of watch- and clockmakers. Although it has been said that William Barraud initially worked in the custom house, there is no evidence that he was ever employed there. He was a pupil of the animal painter Abraham Cooper; his younger brother, **Henry**

Barraud (*bap.* 1811, *d.* 1874), baptized at St Mary's, Lambeth, on 16 May 1811, trained with the landscape painter J. J. Middleton.

Barraud's first exhibited work, *Study of an Ass*, was shown at the Royal Academy in 1829. This work won him a commission from John Turner of Clapham to paint a greyhound bitch; Barraud exhibited an equestrian portrait of his patron, accompanied by a brace of greyhounds, at the Royal Academy in 1830. He also painted an equestrian portrait of the famous fox-hunter John Warde, again accompanied by dogs; this was twice engraved. He appears to have collaborated on several works, including *Skirmish of Cavaliers and Roundheads* (1831, exh. RA) with W. Baily, a figure painter. Meanwhile, Henry Barraud first exhibited at the British Institution in 1831 and showed a wide range of works—including historical and architectural subjects and portraits—at the Royal Academy from 1833 to 1859.

Barraud's subsequent collaboration with his brother Henry seems to date from the mid-1830s, when they shared a studio in Soho and then at the Exchange Buildings in Cornhill; their first joint works to be exhibited (*The Last Resource* and *The Children of Thomas Keen, Esq. with their Favourite Pony*) appeared at the Royal Academy in 1836. This collaboration, as too the earlier one with Baily, may have been inspired by William's reluctance to paint figures. However, the exact nature of their collaboration is unknown, and it is difficult even to isolate their joint works from their individual ones, as at least some canvases signed simply 'Barraud' were the work of William alone. Their best joint works, exhibited at the Royal Academy from 1836 to 1849, are competent and highly finished equestrian and sporting paintings, clearly in the tradition of George Stubbs; William Shaw Sparrow has praised William somewhat vaguely for his 'genuine talent with a feeling for weight and a manly rhythm of line' (*British Sporting Artists*, 1965, 234).

In 1841 William Barraud married Mary, daughter of John Ratliff; their only child, Clement William, was born in 1843 and Mary died soon after. In 1850 he married Margaret, daughter of George Harrison. He died suddenly of dysentery and typhoid fever at 2 Campden House Road, Kensington, London, on 1 October 1850; there were no children. In 1842 Henry Barraud married Anna Maria (*d.* 1892), daughter of James Rose of St Clement Danes, London; they had nine children. About 1858 he converted to Roman Catholicism.

Henry's later work shows considerable range and an eye for the popular: *We Praise thee, O God*, a painting of infant choristers, was reproduced as an engraving which became a best-seller. He also painted romantic subjects, crowd scenes (including one of Lord's cricket ground), and large group portraits, including *Gladstone's First Cabinet* (1868, formerly in the National Liberal Club, London). Some of his portraits, including that of the prime minister, Lord Palmerston (1865), were painted from photographs; Henry Barraud was himself a keen photographer, and his son Herbert Rose Barraud (1845–1896) started a photographic firm. Another son, the painter Francis James Barraud (1856–1924), clearly inherited his father's ability to catch the public eye: he painted the image of a dog which became a celebrated advertisement, *His Master's Voice*, used on early HMV record labels. Henry Barraud died of kidney disease on 17 June 1874 at his home, 96 Gloucester Place, Portman Square, London.

ROSEMARY MITCHELL

Sources E. M. Barraud, *The story of a family* (1967) · F. G. Roe, 'The brothers Barraud: William Barraud (1810–50) and his brother Henry (1811–74) and the problem of their artistic partnership', *The British Racehorse*, 27 (1965), 284–91 · Wood, *Vic. painters*, 3rd edn · M. A. Wingfield, *A dictionary of sporting artists, 1650–1990* (1992) · *CGPLA Eng. & Wales* (1874) [Henry Barraud] · m. certs. · m. cert. [Henry Barraud]

Likenesses W. Barraud, self-portrait, oils, priv. coll. · miniature, priv. coll.

Wealth at death under £1500—Henry Barraud: administration, 1874

Barré, Isaac (1726–1802), army officer and politician, was born in Dublin on 15 October 1726, the only son of a merchant, Peter Barré (*d.* 1776), and his wife, Marie Madelaine, *née* Raboteau, both Huguenot refugees. He was educated at Trinity College, Dublin (1740–44), but preferred the army to the legal career intended for him by his parents. Early thespian skills suggest that he might have been a success at the bar; Horace Walpole recalled, on his entry into parliament in 1761, that 'in his younger days he had acted plays with so much applause that it was said [David] Garrick had offered him a thousand pounds a year to come upon the stage' (Walpole, *Memoirs*, 1.87).

Barré was commissioned in 1746 as an ensign in the 32nd foot, and was promoted in the same regiment to lieutenant in 1755 and captain in 1758. He served under James Wolfe on the Rochefort expedition of 1757 and afterwards in Canada, where Wolfe made him his adjutant-general, though he was merely a captain. Barré fought at Louisburg in 1758, and in 1759 at Quebec, where he lost an eye. Deprived by Wolfe's death there of his military patron, he returned to Britain in 1760, when he became a captain in the 28th foot and was promised but not given a colonelcy by Pitt. He renewed a friendship with Lord Shelburne, who had also been at Rochefort, and was then a political adherent of Lord Bute. Shelburne introduced him to the king's favourite as a potential politician: 'Barré … has parts which would certainly make a figure in a Parliamentary way, and, what is not always the case of great parts his are capable of a very great attachment' (Brown, 190–91). Shelburne was right on both counts. This fortunate political connection led to Barré's being made lieutenant-colonel in the 106th foot in 1761, and on 5 December Shelburne brought him into parliament for his borough of Chipping Wycombe. Barré represented it until 1774, then sat until 1790 for Calne, another Shelburne borough. He was that statesman's chief voice in the Commons and his close personal friend. His maiden speech on 10 December 1761 created a sensation as an abusive attack on the absent war minister William Pitt, motivated by his own patronage disappointment but also instigated by Pitt's great rival Henry Fox. Horace Walpole entered the house while he was speaking and saw:

Isaac Barré (1726–1802), by Sir Joshua Reynolds, 1766

a black, robust man, of a military figure, rather hard-favoured than not young, with a peculiar distortion on one side of his face, which it seems was owing to a bullet lodged loosely in his cheek, and which gave a savage glare to one eye. What I less expected from his appearance, was very classic and eloquent diction. (Walpole, *Memoirs*, 1.86)

Next day Barré repeated the attack to Pitt's face, mocking alike his political inconsistency and personal gestures. Such behaviour gained him a fearsome reputation, and throughout his parliamentary career he was noted for virulence and abuse, a terror to ministers. For most of his career was spent in opposition. When in 1763 Shelburne quitted Bute for Pitt, Barré followed him into opposition to the Grenville ministry, forfeiting various military appointments he had recently acquired, including that of adjutant-general, thereby losing £1500 a year altogether—a self-publicized political martyr. Ironically, in view of his parliamentary début, Barré was now, through Shelburne, an adherent of Pitt. For over two decades he was a prominent figure in the Commons, credited by Walpole with the best speech against general warrants on 29 January 1765:

The hero of the day was the famous Colonel Barré, a man, or I am mistaken, whose fame will not stop here. He spoke with infinite wit and humour, and with that first of merits to me, novelty: his manner is original. He spoke too with extreme bitterness. (*Letters of Horace Walpole*, 6.185–6)

Barré's knowledge of North America made him a champion of the colonists, whom he famously described as 'the sons of liberty' when opposing the intended Stamp Act on 6 February 1765. He challenged the taxation then on grounds of expediency not principle. But during the Stamp Act crisis of the following year Barré not only spoke for repeal but also took Pitt's line in opposing the complete right of taxation as stated in the Declaratory Act. His renown as a friend of America was commemorated in the founding of the Pennsylvania town of Wilkes-Barré in 1769. In 1766 Pitt, now head of the ministry as Lord Chatham, gave Barré the lucrative post of vice-treasurer of Ireland, one of several offers he had refused from Prime Minister Rockingham in 1765.

Barré spoke little as an office-holder, to the annoyance of George III, but did take the Chathamite line that British territories in India belonged to the state and not to the East India Company. His powers of invective were better suited to opposition, as Walpole noted after he resigned office with Chatham and Shelburne in October 1768. During the next fourteen years of parliamentary opposition to the Grafton and North ministries Barré was a leading personality in the Commons. India remained an interest of his. He served on the Burgoyne investigative committee of 1772, spoke for condemnation of Clive in 1773, and supported Lord North's Regulating Act of that year, being vainly offered by the prime minister, doubtless with mixed motives, a place on the Bengal council. Barré remained at Westminster to taunt government, though he surprised contemporaries, and set the Chathamite tone, by supporting the Boston Port Bill of 1774, calling for parliamentary unanimity after the outrage of the Boston Tea Party. But he believed that conciliation should accompany coercion, favouring repeal of the offending tea tax, and vigorously criticized the later 'Intolerable Acts' of 1774. His military experience led him to warn MPs that America would not be conquered easily, and that even then it would not be retained without colonial goodwill. During the American war he sometimes took his melodrama too far in accusing the ministers of being traitors, and especially when taunting Lord North himself.

When in 1782 the Rockingham and Shelburne parties took office on North's fall, Barré received the well-paid post of treasurer of the navy, with the promise of a pension of £3200 if he lost office, and in the Shelburne ministry the even better one of paymaster-general. Barré, so often the scourge of government corruption, brazenly defended these rewards by citing the forfeiture of his military career, whereby he might have become a general. He had been reinstated in his colonelcy on half pay in 1767, but had resigned his commission in 1773 on finding any prospect of promotion blocked by royal enmity; George III seemingly disliked him second only to Wilkes. The Younger Pitt, as soon as he became prime minister, gave Barré a lifetime sinecure as clerk of the pells, thereby removing the complaint about his pension. Barré had become totally blind by about this time, and took little further part in politics, but he had left his mark as a parliamentarian. The diarist Nathaniel Wraxall recalled that he was 'of an athletic frame and mould, endowed with extraordinary powers of voice'. The forceful oratory of Barré, who was well read and a good raconteur, kept the attention of MPs better than Edmund Burke, for he was alert 'not to fatigue the patience of the House' (Wraxall, 2.281–2). Barré was widely regarded as Shelburne's pensioner,

and not deemed to be of cabinet calibre. In 1790, having been loyal to Shelburne when his mentor was dropped by the Younger Pitt, he left parliament because he disagreed with Shelburne's support for the French Revolution. He died, unmarried, at his home in Stanhope Street, London, on 20 July 1802. PETER D. G. THOMAS

Sources P. Brown, *The Chathamites* (1967) • HoP, *Commons, 1754–90* • H. Walpole, *Memoirs of the reign of King George the Third*, ed. G. F. R. Barker, 4 vols. (1894) • *The letters of Horace Walpole, fourth earl of Orford*, ed. P. Toynbee, 16 vols. (1903–5); suppl., 3 vols. (1918–25) • N. W. Wraxall, *Historical memoirs of his own time*, new edn, 4 vols. (1836) • N. W. Wraxall, *Posthumous memoirs of his own time*, 2nd edn, 3 vols. (1836) • P. D. G. Thomas, *Tea party to independence: the third phase of the American Revolution, 1773–1776* (1991)
Archives Ches. & Chester ALSS, MS containing various versions of his life | CKS, letters to J. Amherst and W. Amherst • NRA, priv. coll., corresp. with Lord Lansdowne • NRA, priv. coll., Shelburne MSS • U. Mich., Shelburne MSS
Likenesses J. Reynolds, oils, 1766, priv. coll. [*see illus.*] • R. Houston, mezzotint, pubd 2 July 1771 (after pastel by H. D. Hamilton), BM, NPG, NG Ire. • J. Sayers, two caricatures, etchings, pubd 1782, NPG • G. Stuart, oils, 1785, Brooklyn Museum, New York • G. Stuart, oils, c.1785, NPG • J. Gillray, caricature, etching, pubd 1787, NPG • J. Hall, line engraving, pubd 5 April 1787 (after G. Stuart, c.1785), NG Ire. • W. T. Fry, stipple, pubd 1 Feb 1817 (after G. Stuart, c.1785), NG Ire.; repro. in *The British gallery of contemporary portraits*, 2 vols. (1822) • J. Reynolds, oils, Baynham Abbey, Lamberhurst, Kent; repro. in Brown, *Chathamites*, 113 • J. Ward, group portrait, mezzotint (after J. Reynolds), BM
Wealth at death £24,000: Brown, *The Chathamites*, 225

Barre, Richard (b. c.1130, d. in or after 1202), ecclesiastic and justice, was related to the Sifrewasts, Berkshire knights who also held land at their ancestral centre, Chiffrevast, in Normandy. Some time before 1150 he studied law at Bologna, where he was a fellow student of the canonist Étienne de Tournai. Barre acted as an envoy of Henry II to the papal court, both shortly before and after the murder of Thomas Becket. On the first occasion he was the bearer of a haughty and even minatory message from the king demanding that the pope should absolve all those who had been excommunicated by the archbishop of Canterbury. The mission, it need hardly be said, failed of its object. On the second occasion Barre was dispatched, in company with the archbishop of Rouen, the bishops of Évreux and Worcester, and others of the clergy, to express to the pope the king's horror and detestation of the murder. The archbishop of Rouen falling ill by the way, Barre was sent forward to Italy alone. On reaching Frascati he was refused audience by the pope; but when others of his party arrived, two who aroused less suspicion were admitted, and in the end the embassy was successful in averting the impending excommunication of the king.

Barre was entrusted with the great seal of Henry II's eldest son, Henry, after the latter's coronation in 1170, but on the revolt of the prince in 1173 he offered to surrender it to the king, disclaiming all allegiance to his son. In 1188 Barre undertook a mission to the courts of the king of Hungary and the German and Byzantine emperors, in preparation for Henry's projected crusade. He had become archdeacon of Lisieux some time after 1171, but left Normandy to become archdeacon of Ely in 1190, arriving in England with the new bishop of Ely, William de Longchamp, Richard I's chancellor and justiciar, 1190–91. In addition to his archdeaconries Barre held prebends at Hereford and Salisbury cathedrals. He sat at the bench occasionally in 1190 and rejoined the royal courts under the justiciar Hubert Walter; appointed a justice at Westminster in 1195, he was one of those before whom fines were most frequently levied until the beginning of the reign of King John. The new king's memory of Barre's association with Longchamp probably led to his dismissal from the judiciary. He died at Ely some time after 9 August 1202, when he witnessed a charter for Eye Priory. Barre was author of a *Compendium de veteri et novo testamento*, a compilation of passages from the Old and New testaments, in which he used marginal subject headings 'as do the experts in Roman law'; the work was dedicated to Longchamp (BL, Harley MS 3255; Lambeth Palace MS 105).

J. M. RIGG, rev. RALPH V. TURNER

Sources R. V. Turner, 'Richard Barre and Michael Belet: two Angevin civil servants', *Medieval Prosopography*, 6 (1985), 25–48 • *Fasti Angl., 1066–1300,* [Monastic cathedrals] • *Fasti Angl., 1066–1300,* [Salisbury] • L. Delisle and others, eds., *Recueil des actes de Henri II, roi d'Angleterre et duc de Normandie, concernant les provinces françaises et les affaires de France,* 1 (Paris, 1909) • D. M. Stenton, 'Development of the judiciary, 1100–1216', *Pleas before the king or his justices, 1198–1212,* ed. D. M. Stenton, 3, SeldS, 83 (1967), xlvii–ccxliv • *Pipe rolls* • J. C. Robertson and J. B. Sheppard, eds., *Materials for the history of Thomas Becket, archbishop of Canterbury,* 7 vols., Rolls Series, 67 (1875–85) • W. Stubbs, ed., *Gesta regis Henrici secundi Benedicti abbatis: the chronicle of the reigns of Henry II and Richard I, AD 1169–1192,* 2 vols., Rolls Series, 49 (1867) • *Chronica magistri Rogeri de Hovedene,* ed. W. Stubbs, 4 vols., Rolls Series, 51 (1868–71) • *Radulfi de Diceto … opera historica,* ed. W. Stubbs, 2 vols., Rolls Series, 68 (1876) • *Lettres d'Étienne de Tournai,* ed. J. de Silve (1893)

Archives BL, Harley MS 3255 • LPL, MS 105

Barré, William Vincent (*c.*1760–1829?), author, was born in Germany about 1760 of French protestant parents, who had left their native country on account of their religious opinions. He served first in the Russian navy, but returned to France when the Revolution broke out. He was a volunteer in the army during the Italian campaign of 1796 and was afterwards raised to the rank of captain for the bravery he had displayed on the field of battle. His knowledge of European languages brought him to the attention of Napoleon Bonaparte, who appointed him as his personal interpreter. However, he wrote some satirical verses about his employer, and was obliged to flee from France. Pursued by Fouché's police agents, he escaped in a small boat from Paris down the Seine as far as Le Havre, and went from there in an American vessel to England, where he appears to have arrived in 1803. The following year he published in London a *History of the French consulate under Napoleon Buonaparte: being an authentic narrative of his administration … including a sketch of his life,* in which he furiously attacked the first consul. Before this work appeared he had already translated into French Sir Robert Wilson's *History of the British Expedition to Egypt* (1802) and into English a pamphlet, *Answer from M. Mehée to M. Garat.* In 1805 he published in English *The Rise, Progress, Decline, and Fall of Buonaparte's Empire in France,* the second part of the earlier *History,* which was preceded by an advertisement of ten pages, in which he attacked the reviewers of his first book in the *Annual Review and History of Literature for 1803.* Barré left England for Ireland, where he appears to have had relatives, among them being the well-known orator, Isaac Barré. About the year 1806 he printed at Belfast, on a single sheet, some verses in French, entitled 'Monologue de l'Empereur Jaune, le nommé Napoléone Buonaparte, chrétien, athée, catholique et musulman, sur la destruction de son digne émule et rival l'Empereur Noir, le nommé Jacques Dessalines' with the motto, 'à ton tour, paillasse'. He seems to have published nothing more, and is believed to have committed suicide in Dublin in 1829.

H. VAN LAUN, rev. NILANJANA BANERJI

Sources E. Haag and E. Haag, *La France protestante,* 2nd edn, 6 vols. (Paris, 1877–88), vol. 1

Barret, George (1732?–1784), landscape painter, was born in Dublin, the son of a clothier. He was apprenticed to a stay maker and later attended the Dublin Society drawing schools under Robert West. While there he coloured prints for the publisher Silcock, and in 1747 he won a prize in the examination. He became a friend of Edmund Burke, then a student at Trinity College, Dublin. By tradition Burke introduced him to the wild scenery of the Dargle valley and the Powerscourt estate (notably its waterfall) in co. Wicklow and influenced him to paint in a remarkably Romantic style for the date.

Barret married Frances Percy in 1757. They had three sons who were painters: Joseph, James, and George *Barret (1767–1842). James and George specialized in watercolour, though James exhibited many oils at the Royal Academy in London. Barret also had a daughter, Mary, who worked as a miniaturist, and there were other children; Thomas Bodkin says he had nine in all. He was living at Hog Hill, Dublin, in 1761 and subsequently lived for many years in Orchard Street, Portman Square, London, but moved to Westbourne Green, Paddington, Middlesex, in 1772.

Although Barret's early works such as those for Russborough House, co. Wicklow (National Gallery of Ireland, Dublin), are of varied inspiration (mainly Dutch), before he left Ireland in 1763 he had developed a strong style of his own, seen at its best when painting wild nature. Of the thirty-one pictures he exhibited at the Royal Academy between 1769 and 1782, at least one-third are of mountainous, Romantic countryside. Writing to Burke in 1765, James Barry noted that:

> Barret presents you with such a glorious assemblage, as I have sometimes seen among high mountains rising into unusual agreeable appearances while the early beams of the sun sport themselves … through the vast arcades and sometimes glances on a great lake whose ascending vapours spread themselves like a veil over the distance. (*Works*, 1.16)

These comments are especially valid for his landscapes of Ireland, Llanberis in north Wales, and the Lake District. For a major patron, the duke of Buccleuch, he painted topographical views of Dalkeith and its park and a view of Melrose Abbey by moonlight (exh. RA, 1769). Even in his own day he was noted for his botanical accuracy. In his

Essay on Landscape Painting (1782) Joseph Pott observed that 'Every tree he [Barret] paints is distinctly characterised' and Burke acknowledged that he was 'a wonderful observer of the accidents of nature' (*Works*, 1.89). His gouaches and watercolours (held in priv. coll., the National Gallery of Ireland, Dublin, and the Victoria and Albert Museum, London) are very fine. He was a good painter of animals, one picture being titled *A Bull* (exh. RA, 1770) and another *Mares and Foals* (exh. RA, 1775), so that it is strange that he often collaborated with the animal painter Sawrey Gilpin. The best of his etchings is *A View of the Dargle* (British Museum, London).

Despite considerable success Barret's finances were always poor. He charged £168 for two views of Welbeck Park for the duke of Portland and for three works for Burton Constable he was paid £50 on account and £63 for expenses, but the final bill has been lost. In a letter dated 8 July 1775 he quotes for a 'half length 35 guineas' and he prices two works exhibited at the Royal Academy in the same year at 80 guineas each and another at 75 guineas. Apparently to save Barret from bankruptcy William Locke commissioned him about 1780 to paint a landscape mural (one of his best works) in Norbury Park, Surrey, and, according to Farington, paid his debts. Burke finally helped out when in 1782 he appointed Barret to the sinecure of master painter to the Chelsea Hospital, London (in which post his son James succeeded him). Barret died on 29 May 1784 at Westbourne Green and was buried in Paddington church. His family was given a pension of £30 by the Royal Academy in 1802.

W. C. MONKHOUSE, rev. ANNE CROOKSHANK

Sources W. G. Strickland, *A dictionary of Irish artists*, 2 vols. (1913) · A. Crookshank and the Knight of Glin [D. Fitzgerald], *The painters of Ireland, c.1660–1920* (1978), 112–20 · Farington, *Diary*, 1.214; 3.1068; 6.2074, 2244; 7.2597; 8.3056; 12.4219, 4374 · T. Bodkin, *Four Irish painters*, ed. J. Campbell, 2nd edn (1987), 1–16 · *The works of James Barry*, ed. E. Fryer, 1 (1809), 16, 89 · W. Carey, *Some memoirs of the patronage and progress of the fine arts in England and Ireland* (1826) · R. W. Goulding, *Catalogue of the pictures belonging to his grace the duke of Portland*, ed. C. K. Adams (1936), 428 · I. Hall, *An exhibition of paintings … collected … by William Constable* (1970) [exhibition catalogue, Ferens Art Gallery, Kingston upon Hull, 27 Jan – 22 Feb 1970] · letter, V&A, L 3532–1976 · L. Herrmann, *British landscape painting of the eighteenth century* (1973), 62

Archives U. Nott. L., letters to third duke of Portland, also account with memo of pictures painted for the duke

Likenesses G. Barret, self-portrait, pencil, Soane Museum, London · J. Greenwood, pen-and-pencil drawing, BM · J. Zoffany, group portrait, oils (*Royal Academicians*, 1772), Royal Collection

Barret, George (1767–1842), landscape painter, was born in Orchard Street, Oxford Street, London, in December 1767, the third son of George *Barret (1732?–1784) RA, the landscape painter, and his wife, Frances, *née* Percy, about four years after his father's arrival from Dublin. His eldest brother, Joseph, is known to have assisted their father at Norbury Park, Surrey; the second brother, James, also became a painter, occasionally exhibiting at the Royal Academy between 1785 and 1819; and a sister, Mary (*d.* 1836), was a talented miniature and still-life painter who studied with Mrs Mee and Romney and was elected to the Society of Painters in Water Colours in 1823. In the early 1770s in an unusual moment of prosperity, the family moved to the Manor House, Westbourne Grove, to relieve the father's asthma, and perhaps the son's also. Almost certainly taught by his father, the younger George exhibited at the Royal Academy from 1800 to 1803, and perhaps from 1795, although the earlier exhibits attributed to him, including collaborations with Sawrey Gilpin RA and Philip Reinagle RA, may actually have been his late father's. He showed occasional oil paintings thereafter, but concentrated on watercolours. Although not present at the meeting at the Stratford Coffee House, Oxford Street, on 30 November 1804, at which the Society of Painters in Water Colours was founded, he was one of six additional artists who joined before the first exhibition in April 1805. For thirty-eight years he did not miss an exhibition, and between 1812 and 1820, when oil paintings were admitted in an attempt to boost sales, he served on the committee. He lived in Paddington throughout his life, from 1805 to 1809 at 29 Lisson Grove, and thereafter at 17 and 162 Devonshire Place. His career was remarkably uneventful. He travelled little, although in 1804 he was recorded as taking views of the delightful scenery in the neighbourhood of Killarney with William Sawrey Gilpin, first president of the Society of Painters in Water Colours and the son of his father's collaborator. For the most part, though, his subjects were found in the Thames valley and home counties. Quiet rural scenes were his speciality, and although the execution is very English, there is often a Dutch inspiration to them: he excelled in painting light, and all his scenes, whether sunrise, sunset, or moonlight, are remarkable for their fine rendering of atmosphere, their diffusion and gradation of light, and their poetic feeling. In the opinion of Cosmo Monkhouse (*DNB*) he rivalled Turner in these respects, but while always pleasing, his work has little of Turner's strength or originality. Gradually he gave up topographical landscapes in favour of Claudian romantic compositions with titles such as *Retirement of the Weary Traveller*. When criticizing the work of others he would say, 'I like his art' or 'I do not like his art' and he also maintained that he 'gained more by studying in the *early morning*, and in the *evening* than at any other time' (anecdote by E. Dorrell transcribed by John Jenkins, 1853, Royal Watercolour Society archives). In 1823, his sister Mary joined him both as a member of the Society of Painters in Water Colours, and in his family home at Paddington, which she shared until her death. A number of his works were engraved for the fashionable annuals of the 1820s and 1830s, and in 1840 he published *The Theory and Practice of Water-Colour Painting*. However, although held in high regard by his colleagues, and greatly enjoyed by many later collectors and critics, he shared the family inability to make, or at least retain, money, and left his family destitute. His last years were saddened by the death of a son. He died of inflammation of the lungs on 19 March 1842, at 162 Devonshire Place, and was buried in the graveyard of St Mary's, Paddington, by the site of the Manor House in which he had lived as a youth. His colleagues, including his old friend the watercolourist Joshua Cristall subscribed to a tombstone and supported his widow and later his daughter, Catherine. A collection of his drawings is in the Victoria and Albert Museum, London.

HUON MALLALIEU

Sources J. L. Roget, *A history of the 'Old Water-Colour' Society*, 2 vols. (1891); repr. (1972) • *Old Water-Colour Society's Club*, 26 (1948), 41–5 • *Old Water-Colour Society's Club*, 52 (1977), 45–7 • Royal Watercolour Society archives, London, Barret MSS [incl. letters and exhibition catalogues] • d. cert. • A. Bury, 'George Barret junior, a classic water-colour painter', *The Connoisseur*, 105 (1940), 237–41 • I. O. Williams, *Early English watercolours and some cognate drawings by artists born not later than 1785* (1952) • M. Hardie, *Water-colour painting in Britain*, ed. D. Snelgrove, J. Mayne, and B. Taylor, 2nd edn, 3: *The Victorian period* [1968] • Mallalieu, *Watercolour artists* • L. Stainton, *British landscape watercolours, 1600–1860* (1985) [exhibition catalogue, BM]
Likenesses G. Barret, self-portrait, oils on panel, NG Ire.

Barret, John. *See* Barrett, John (*c*.1495–1563).

Barret, John (1631–1713), Presbyterian minister and religious writer, was admitted to Clare College, Cambridge, on 20 June 1646 and graduated BA in 1650. He was ordained at Wymeswold, Leicestershire, by the Wirksworth classis on 19 October 1652. Admitted as rector of St Peter's Church, Nottingham, in 1656, he was dismissed from the post in July 1662 for refusing to use the newly revised Book of Common Prayer or wear a surplice. By 1665 he had married Elizabeth, whose parentage is unknown; their son Joseph *Barrett was baptized in that year at Sandiacre, Derbyshire. They had at least two other children. In the 1660s and 1670s Barret often preached with the ejected ministers William Reynolds and John Whitlock, who were of similarly presbyterian persuasion, although by good fortune or 'a special providence' (*Nonconformist's Memorial*, 3.104), he did not suffer as much persecution by the authorities as they. He was licensed as a presbyterian teacher to preach at his house in Sandiacre and at Nottingham in 1672.

Barret was a prolific writer, a good deal of whose work is concerned with the day-to-day business of living the Christian life. Thus his publications included a 423-page practical treatise, *The Christian Temper, or, A Discourse Concerning the Nature and Properties of the Graces of Sanctification* (1678). His work *The Evil and Remedy of Scandal, a Practical Discourse on Psalm Cxix. Clxv.* (1711) similarly deals not so much with the more abstract questions of theology as with practical matters and the need for a love of God's law and repentance when that law is transgressed. This treatise is harsh, arguing for the full and proper obedience to God's law as the way to peace and happiness. It ends, however, on a reconciliatory note: those that have caused scandal, but who show proper repentance, should be restored to fellowship and admitted to communion. Other Christians should welcome them back wholeheartedly, eschewing severity in case it undermines their confidence. Barret was also heavily committed to the practice of infant baptism, upon which topic he entered into extended dispute with such individuals as Thomas Grantham (1634–1692), who wrote a major refutation of Barret's views in 1680. Barret's principal works in this area include *Fifty Queries Seriously Propounded to those that Question or Deny Infants Right*

to Baptism (1675) and *Much in a little, or, An abstract of Mr. Baxters plain scripture-proof for infants church-membership or baptism: with a few notes upon the anti-queries of T[homas] G[rantham]* (1678), in which works he makes his position plain: baptism is a child's birthright and those that deny it are not only in a state of doctrinal error by taking away the child's right to this blessing, but are guilty also of causing great distress to the church of Christ and even causing a breach within it. Some uncertainty has surrounded his authorship of two further rather polemical works—*A Reply to the Reverend Dean of St. Paul's Reflections on the Rector of Sutton, &c.* (1681) and *The Rector of Sutton Committed with the Dean of St. Paul's, or, A Defence of Dr. Stillingfleet's Irenicum* (1680)—both of which have also been attributed to Vincent Alsop (*d*. 1703). However, the title-page of the latter work indicates that it is 'by the author of the *Christian Temper*', which seems to suggest that it is indeed by Barret.

Barret died in Nottingham on 30 October 1713, and was buried on 2 November. His funeral sermon was preached by John Whitlock junior. His will of 1713 was proved on 2 April 1714 by his wife, Elizabeth.

KENNETH G. C. NEWPORT

Sources *Calamy rev.* • *The nonconformist's memorial … originally written by … Edmund Calamy*, ed. S. Palmer, [3rd edn], 3 vols. (1802–3) • *IGI* • *DNB* • J. Whitlock, *A short attempt for preserving the memory, and improving the death of three eminent, aged ministers of Christ … Mr. John Barret* (1714) • B. Carpenter, *Some account of the original introduction of Presbyterianism in Nottingham and neighbourhood* (1862) • Venn, *Alum. Cant.*
Archives DWL

Barret, Joseph. *See* Barrett, Joseph (1665–1699).

Barret, Patrick (*d*. 1415), bishop of Ferns and administrator, was a canon of the Augustinian abbey of Kells in the bishopric of Ossory. He was consecrated by the pope at Rome in December 1400 and was restored to the temporalities on 11 April 1401. From 1403 he was active in peace-keeping in Kilkenny, Carlow, and Waterford, as well as Wexford. In 1409 he began the building of Mountgarrett Castle in Wexford. He was absent, probably in England, from August 1409. He was appointed chancellor of Ireland on 18 March 1410 and held the office until 20 April 1413, partly by deputy from May 1412 as he was occupied by disturbances in Wexford. While he held the lordship of Wexford at farm, its lord, Reynold Grey of Ruthin, was exempted from the legislation which reserved absentee revenues to the king.

Barret died on 10 November 1415, and was buried in the abbey of Kells. As bishop, he compiled a catalogue of his predecessors in the see of Ferns. In 1402 he appropriated the church of Ardcolm to the abbey of St Peter and St Paul at Selsker in Wexford.   J. M. RIGG, *rev.* D. B. JOHNSTON

Sources *The whole works of Sir James Ware concerning Ireland*, ed. and trans. W. Harris, rev. edn, 2 vols. in 3 (1764) • E. Tresham, ed., *Rotulorum patentium et clausorum cancellariae Hiberniae calendarium*, Irish Record Commission (1828) • *Chancery records* • *CEPR letters*, 5.454; 6.64 • H. F. Hore and P. H. Hore, eds., *History of the town and county of Wexford*, 6 (1911)

Barret, Richard (*c*.1544–1599), Roman Catholic ecclesiastic, was born in Warwickshire. We know nothing of his parentage but he went to Oxford and was at Brasenose College; he graduated BA on 21 November 1565 and MA on 26 June 1570. He became a fellow of Oriel College before 1572 and was proctor of the university in 1574.

After conversion to Roman Catholicism Barret entered the English College at Douai, on 28 January 1576, and for the next three years lived partly at Douai and partly in Paris. His studies were in law, not theology, and because of his age he probably assisted in tutoring the younger students. He accompanied the college when it transferred to Rheims in 1578. In 1579, together with others, he visited Rome and eight of them asked for admittance to the English College, where the Jesuits had recently taken charge of the administration. He took the college oath on 23 April 1579 and began his theological studies. There is no record of his ordination. This indicates that it probably took place before October 1580 when the extant ordination registers begin. He was awarded the doctorate on 15 September 1582.

On the request of William Allen, Barret returned to Rheims and was made prefect of studies to succeed the recently deceased Gregory Martin. He entered into correspondence with the Jesuit Alfonso Agazzari, the rector of the English College in Rome, on matters concerning the two colleges. This was chiefly to do with the quality and the motives of those seeking admittance to the seminaries and the difficulties in discipline that had resulted in disturbances among the students. When Allen was made cardinal he was often absent from Rheims in Rome but it was not until 1588 that he gave up the presidency at Rheims and appointed Barret in his place. Barret's time as president was not an easy one. The political situation led to a return of the college to its original site in Douai in 1593 where it still retained possession of the house and garden. Allen was not an easy man to follow, and Barret's tightening up of discipline led to criticisms from such men as Nicholas Fitzherbert, whose views on Barret's temper and impetuosity were later written up and published in a short life of Allen. Barret's reputation has suffered as a result of this, although there were several who sought his counsel.

In 1596 Barret paid a visit to Rome to try to help in settling the troubles at the English College there. When Rome appointed George Blackwell as archpriest Barret was given charge of all the seminary priests in the Spanish Netherlands who were not directly under the nuncio there. He was also instructed to give all possible assistance to Blackwell and to deal with troublesome priests in England, including recommending their recall and even, if necessary, effecting it without waiting for instructions from Rome. Such powers would not promote his popularity. He died at Douai on 30 May 1599.

MICHAEL E. WILLIAMS

Sources The letters and memorials of William, Cardinal Allen (1532–1594), ed. T. F. Knox (1882), vol. 2 of Records of the English Catholics under the penal laws (1878–82) · T. F. Knox and others, eds., The first and second diaries of the English College, Douay (1878) · Letters of William Allen and Richard Barret, 1572–1598, ed. P. Renold, Catholic RS, 58 (1967) · G. Anstruther, The seminary priests 1: Elizabethan, 1558–1603 [1966], 24–5 · DNB · H. Foley, ed., Records of the English province of the Society of Jesus, 6 (1880), 568

Barret, Robert (fl. 1586?–1607), soldier and author, was the third and youngest son of Thomas Barrett (d. in or before 1591) of Kingswood, Wiltshire, 'Descended of the Barretts of [Pendine/Pen-tywyn]' in Carmarthenshire (Coll. Arms, Vincent MS 178 (als 157), fol. 478), and his wife, Edith Bridges of the Forest of Dean, Gloucestershire. He married Mary, daughter of David Hughs (probably on 14 February 1586, at St James's, Clerkenwell, Middlesex); two daughters, Jone and Mary, were born before 1591.

Barret confessed to 'having spent the most part of my time in the profession of Armes' in the preface to The Theorike and Practike of Moderne Warres (1598), his only published work, which counts, with those of William Garrard and Giles Clayton, among the most authoritative of the many military treatises issued in the period (Barret, Theorike, sig. ¶2r). Barret's work, 'Discoursed in dialogue wise' between a gentleman and a captain, exemplifies England's belated transition from knightly to professional principles of warfare. Detailing a wide range of military technique, it prescribes the 'severall duties' expected of 'the Officers in degrees' within the new hierarchy of military rank (ibid., title-page), and provides—in the influential manner of Leonard and Thomas Digges's Stratioticos (1579)—a practical grounding in the mathematical logistics of early modern war.

England had been isolated from the 'cosmopolitan stream of military science' (Jorgensen, 'Alien military doctrine', 49); Barret's work derives much of its authority from his service 'among forraine nations, as the French, the Dutch, the Italian, and Spaniard' (Barret, Theorike, sig. ¶2r), and includes a glossary 'shewing the signification of sundry forraine words, used in these discourses' (ibid., sig. Y3v). George Chalmers in 1799 shrewdly proposed that the downfall of Shakespeare's Parolles in All's Well that Ends Well ('the gallant militarist … that had the whole theoricke of warre in the knot of his scarfe, and the practise in the chape of his dagger' (IV. iii) was 'a continued sarcasm' on Barret's work (Chalmers, 379): contemporary dramatists indeed display a sustained engagement with the Elizabethan war-years, and the new discipline's 'Esperanto of war' (de Somogyi, 78). Barret's treatise, dedicated to Henry Herbert, earl of Pembroke, and his son William (later the co-dedicatee of the 1623 Shakespeare first folio), was very finely printed, in folio, with many diagrams and tables by William Ponsonby (Edmund Spenser's publisher), whose death in 1604 perhaps helps explain why 'The sacred warr', the enormous verse chronicle Barret began that year, remained unpublished (Bodl. Oxf., MS Add. C.281).

The 1200 pages of Barret's manuscript, subtitled 'An History Conteyning the Christian Conquest of the Holy-Land', demonstrate a Spenserian application, and its preface acknowledges Sallust and Du Bartas as the 'sweet patterne' (Bodl. Oxf., MS Add. C.281, p. xvii) of Barret's ambition. Its first 731 pages render the twenty-three books of the twelfth-century Historia Hierosolymitana of William, archbishop of Tyre, into alternately rhymed heroic couplets, 'inter-mixe[d] … with Poetical fictions, phrases, narrations, digressions, Reprizes, Ligations, descriptions, Representations, Similes, and poetical figures, with Epithetes, Motti, and names agreable' (ibid., p. xvii). Drawing on other sources Barret's remaining nine books continue the narrative 'untill our ages jarrs', via treatments of Tamburlaine and Lepanto. Barret's book 32 closes with a note that 'These trienniume historical-Martial toyles' were 'finished the 26. of March Anno 1606[/7]' (ibid., p. mcx), but the work further concludes with a verse 'Exhortation Elegiacall to all European Christians against the Turk' (ibid., p. mcxii); a prose account of 'the Military Offices of the Turkish Empery' (in the manner of his *Theorike and Practike*); and two detailed indexes 'of the most remarkable matters conteyned in this warrior Chronicle'.

The manuscript's title-page is dated 1613, and bears the signature of the poet Robert Southey ('1813', the year of his laureateship), who, according to its subsequent owner James Crossley, esteemed it 'the great poetical Manuscript treasure of his library' (manuscript left bound into Bodl. Oxf., MS Add. C.281). In 1885 the manuscript was sold to the bookseller Quaritch, who also purchased a copy of Barret's *Theorike*, 'with 10 sheets of MS. relating to Barret' (Sothebys sale catalogue 877, 35), since lost. Barret described himself in the preface to 'The sacred warr' as 'a rough-heawen Souldiar, retyred to a rustique Lyfe' (Bodl. Oxf., MS Add. C.281, p. xvii), probably to Wiltshire or Somerset, mentioned in his *Theorike* as 'these our Westerne parts' (Barret, *Theorike*, sig. ¶3r).   NICK DE SOMOGYI

Sources 'Old Grants 2', 6 Feb 1590/91, Coll. Arms, Vincent MS 178 (als 157), fol. 478 · R. Barret, *The theorike and practike of moderne warres* (1598) · P. A. Jorgensen, *Shakespeare's military world* (Los Angeles, 1956) · P. A. Jorgensen, 'Alien military doctrine in renaissance England', *Modern Language Quarterly*, 17 (1956), 43–9 · N. de Somogyi, *Shakespeare's theatre of war* (1998) · P. C. Bartrum, ed., *Welsh genealogies, AD 1400–1500*, 18 vols. (1983), vol. 1 · T. Corser, *Collectanea Anglo-poetica, or, A … catalogue of a … collection of early English poetry*, 1, Chetham Society, 52 (1860), 193–9 · M. P. Siddons, *The development of Welsh heraldry*, 3 vols. (1991–3), 2.16–17 · R. Barret, 'The sacred warr', Bodl. Oxf., MS Add. C. 281 · 'William (c. 1130–c.1190), archbishop of Tyre and chronicler', *Encyclopaedia Britannica*, 14th edn (1948) · sale catalogues (1884), 35 [Sothebys, 21 July 1884; BL, SCS 877]; (1885), 290 [Sothebys, 19 July 1885; BL, SCS 890] · G. Chalmers, *A supplemental apology for the believers in the Shakspeare-papers* (1799) · parish register, Clerkenwell, St James, LMA, 14 Feb 1586 [marriage]

Barret, William. *See* Barrett, William (*b. c.*1561, *d.* in or after 1630).

Barret, William (*d.* 1584), commercial agent and consul, is of obscure origins. The earliest mention of Barret concerns his assisting the merchant John Keele to load the Turkey Company's ship *Bark Reynolds* at Tripoli, Syria, with a cargo of galls, cottons, spices, and silk for its return journey to London departing on 29 March 1582. It is likely that Barret had arrived in Tripoli on the *Bark Reynolds* some three or four months earlier. After the ship sailed he remained in Tripoli responsible for trading its cargo of cloth, kerseys, and tin, and for remitting the profits to the

Turkey Company merchants in London via the ship *Emmanuel* which sailed from Tripoli in April 1583. In September 1583 a 'letter of directions' from the English ambassador in Constantinople, William Harborne, to Richard Forster, newly appointed English consul on the Syrian coast, refers to 'our friend William Barrat' as provider of spices there (Hakluyt, 5.260, 263). On 11 June 1584 he appears as 'M. William Barret our Consull' who welcomed the trader John Eldred and his companion William Shales on their return to Aleppo overland from Basrah. Eldred reports that Barret 'fell sicke immediately' and died eight days later, on 19 June. He was succeeded as consul by Anthony Bate (ibid., 6.8–9).

From his accumulated knowledge of the Levant spice trade Barret compiled detailed notes on 'The money and measures of Babylon, Balsara, and the Indies, with the customes, &c. written from Aleppo in Syria, An. 1584' (Hakluyt, 6.10–34). Given that terminology, measures, and prices for the same commodities differed markedly from one trading centre to another, notes such as these were essential information for any successful trader. Barret also noted the seasonal winds and monsoons and the usual resultant sailing dates. His notes conclude with mention of Portuguese routes to the Indies via the recently discovered island of St Helena. Rival claims by Venetian and English agents to the '70 ducats, & other merchandize' left by Barret on his death sparked a minor test case, resolved in May 1586 by a decree from the Ottoman sultan in favour of the English community on the basis of their new status as recognized traders.   CHRISTINE WOODHEAD

Sources R. Hakluyt, *The principal navigations, voyages, traffiques and discoveries of the English nation*, 2nd edn, 3 vols. (1598–1600); repr. 12 vols., Hakluyt Society, extra ser., 1–12 (1903–5), vols. 5, 6 · S. A. Skilliter, *William Harborne and the trade with Turkey, 1578–1582* (1977)
Wealth at death '70 ducats, & other merchandize': Hakluyt, *The principal navigations* vol. 5, pp. 290–91

Barreto, Don Marino [*real name* Marino Barreto y Casanova] (**1907–1995**), pianist and singer, was born on 11 June 1907 in Havana, Cuba, the eldest among the three sons of José Marino Barreto y Lopez, a doctor, dental surgeon, and politician, and his wife, whose maiden name was Casanova. Both parents were Cuban. Barreto studied piano as a child and accompanied his father, a gifted amateur violinist who had played with Ernesto Lecuona, whose band first brought Afro-Cuban rhythms to Europe. He began his career as an actor in Malaga, Spain, where the family moved in 1925 to escape the fascistic pre-Battista regime, and performed before King Alfonso XIII and Queen Victoria Eugénie. After appearing in *The Negro with a White Soul*, the first romantic film to feature a black artist opposite a European actress, he moved to Paris with his brother Emilio (1909–1997), a violinist, guitarist, bandleader, and much-recorded musician who remained in France and used the name Don Barreto. In 1926, as members of a band that included the clarinettist Sidney Bechet, they toured in the revue *Black People*, directed by the American dancer Louis Douglas, with music by Spencer Williams, before going their separate ways.

In 1928 Barreto travelled to London, where he accompanied a dance act at the Palladium and played in the band led by the American singer Noble Sissle at the Plaza. He also married, on 24 January 1929, Doris Colbert (*b. c.*1903), a dancer from Chicago who was then appearing in the London production of *Show Boat*, starring Paul Robeson. Barreto formed a double act with the African American singer Norris Smith, a long-time British resident, and in 1929 the pair went to France, becoming part of the sophisticated nightlife of Paris and performing on the Riviera. They recorded together before returning to London in 1935 to appear in cabaret at the Ritz. Augmented by a third voice, their Cuban Trio took part in a 1936 test transmission for BBC television.

The Second World War coincided with unprecedented interest in Afro-Cuban rhythms, many of which had previously remained unknown to the European public. Barreto got his big break when the Lecuona Cuban Boys, based in Paris, were offered a job at London's Embassy Club but then refused work permits by the Ministry of Labour. He stepped into the breach at the smart Bond Street venue, dropping his repertory of suave jazz and showtunes to provide authentic rumbas, congas, and *sons* for dancing. Throughout the 1940s he moved easily between Soho bottle parties and lengthy engagements at Ciro's, the society nightclub where he entertained Lord and Lady Mountbatten and the American generals Clarke, Patton, and Eisenhower, as well as the Woolworth heir Barbara Hutton and showbusiness figures. He also played troop concerts for the Entertainments National Service Association, including one for departing paratroopers on the eve of the Arnhem landings, with Ray Ellington on drums.

Barreto wrote several dance tunes with the African American composer Spencer Williams and others and continued to record, sometimes with Emilio Barreto and their younger brother, Sergio, a drummer. A retrospective reviewer wrote of the brothers' recordings: '[the] music sounds timeless to modern ears, while most of the highly-touted and highly orchestrated records of the same period sound as dated as Fletcher Henderson arrangements compared with vocal blues' (Borneman, 23). These historic titles enjoyed positive reassessment by a new generation of Latin enthusiasts when re-released on compact disc in the 1990s.

Barreto was a charismatic and handsome man who enjoyed an intense and involved private life. He is believed to have married a second time in Paris, to a Cuban, but music was his great love, and, despite close associations with the aristocracy, he cared for little other than playing his piano. In 1943 he began a long-standing intermittent relationship with Rita Evelyn Cann (1911–2001), a pianist and his former student, who played with him at the Embassy and Ciro's and whose own Havana Sextet he subsequently helped to promote. He was also involved with Lady Iris Mountbatten, the daughter of the marquess and marchioness of Carisbrooke (and great-granddaughter of Queen Victoria), and with other socialites, including Beatrice Helen Beckett, the first wife of Sir Anthony Eden. He had a son, born in London.

In 1950 Barreto moved back to Paris, then opened a nightclub in Madrid with his brothers. He spent further extended periods in Paris and Beirut before settling in 1962 in Stockholm, where he lived for fifteen years and helped bring up his nephew Juan Carlos Barreto, a singer and musician and the son of one of his two half-sisters. He continued to work in Italy, Germany, and Scandinavia, and in 1977 moved to Tenerife. With the exception of another short period in Sweden, he worked on the Canaries hotel circuit until shortly before his death. He was hospitalized with kidney problems in 1994 and, after a period on dialysis, died of kidney failure at Puerta della Cruz, Tenerife, on 3 August 1995.

By popularizing Afro-Cuban rhythms and dances in Britain, Barreto laid the groundwork for their wider acceptability. It was inevitable that in the pre- and post-war years what he played would be termed Latin-American—to note the music's 'African' origins would have been a little too radical for the day—and the term persists. Other exponents may have laid their claim to first expounding these rhythms in Britain, but it was the ebullient Cuban, with his dynamic piano playing and dramatic vocals, who introduced them via his recordings and broadcasts and in nightclubs, where he employed jazz musicians in his rumba bands. He is not to be confused with Aristide Barreto, his half-brother and the only son of the three children of his father's second marriage; as Marino Barreto jun. he was a popular and much-recorded singer, pianist, and percussionist who had a successful career in Italy.

VAL WILMER

Sources E. Borneman, 'Tropicana', *Melody Maker* (15 Dec 1956), 23 · R. E. Lotz, *Black people* (1997), 321–2 · personal knowledge (2004) · private information (2004) [Rita Cann] · m. cert.
Likenesses photograph, priv. coll.

Barrett, Eaton Stannard (1786–1820), poet and satirist, was born in Cork. Despite his contemporary success little is known of his life. With his younger brother Richard he attended a private school at Wandsworth Common, where he wrote a play which was successfully acted before the master and his family. He graduated from Trinity College, Dublin, and although he entered the Middle Temple, London, he was apparently never called to the bar.

In 1810 Barrett published *Woman and other Poems*. Written in the manner of Pope, 'Woman, a Poem' was, according to Reiman in his 1979 edition of it, 'more popular during Barrett's lifetime than any single work by a major or secondary poet then living, including Scott or Byron'. The volume ran into several editions, being reprinted as late as 1841.

Barrett's political satires opened with *The Rising Sun: a Serio-Comic Satiric Romance by Cervantes Hogg*, and *The Second Titan War Against Heaven* (both 1807). Most successful was *All the Talents: a Satirical Poem in Three Dialogues by Polypus* (1807; at least nineteen editions) ridiculing the whig ministry of the day, and providing the name by which that government is still known. Byron alludes to this work in *English Bards and Scotch Reviewers* (ll. 741–6). Further satires followed in quick succession.

Barrett's epistolary novel *The Heroine* (1813), parodying

Gothic and sentimental novels, evoked a comparison with *Tristram Shandy* and *Don Quixote* (*A Biographical Dictionary of the Living Authors of Great Britain and Ireland*), and Jane Austen read it with pleasure, but Crabb Robinson found it 'paltry in all respects' (*Diary*, 31 March 1816). It attracted some attention in the twentieth century. His comedy, *My Wife, what Wife?* (1815), was described by Hazlitt as 'altogether very amusing. The best part of it is a very unaccountable, easy, impudent, blundering Irish footman' (Hazlitt, 237–9).

In private Barrett's attractive manners and character won him many friends, but a letter in 1818 to John Cumming, a Dublin bookseller, shows him conscious of his ugliness and reveals his poverty. He died suddenly in Glamorgan, after bursting a blood vessel, on 20 March 1820, and was buried there. JOHN D. HAIGH

Sources DNB · *GM*, 1st ser., 90/1 (1820), 377 · *N&Q*, 8 (1853), 292, 350, 423 · *N&Q*, 9 (1854), 17 · *N&Q*, 11 (1855), 386 · *N&Q*, 2nd ser., 2 (1856), 36, 310 · E. S. Barrett, *Woman*, ed. D. H. Reiman (1979) · W. Hazlitt, 'A view of the English stage', in *The complete works of William Hazlitt*, ed. P. P. Howe, 5 (1930), 237–9 · H. C. Robinson, *Diary*, 31 March 1816 · *The complete poetical works: Lord Byron*, ed. J. J. McGann, 1 (1980) · J. C. Mendenhall, 'An old discovery', *University of Pennsylvania General Magazine*, 30 (1927), 10–14 [two letters from Barrett to John Cumming] · E. S. Barrett, *All the talents; The second Titan war, or, The talents buried under Portland-Isle; The talents run mad*, ed. D. H. Reiman (New York, 1979) [incl. introduction by D. H. Reiman] · W. Raleigh, introduction, in E. S. Barrett, *The heroine*, ed. W. Raleigh (1909), iii–xv · M. Sadleir, introduction, in E. S. Barrett, *The heroine*, ed. M. Sadleir (1927) [glossary explains satirical literary allusions] · R. Hogan, ed., *Dictionary of Irish literature*, rev. edn, 2 vols. (1996)

Barrett, Edward, Lord Barrett of Newburgh (1581–1644/5), politician and government official, born at Aveley, Essex, on 21 June 1581, was the elder son of Charles Barrett (1555/6–1584) and Christian Mildmay (1557–1627). The main estate at Belhus in Aveley had been held by the family since 1397, but there were also considerable properties in Berkshire and Hampshire. After the death of his father and grandfather Edward inherited, aged four, in 1585. He was ward first to his grandfather Sir Walter Mildmay, and then, on his death, to his mother's second husband, Sir John Leveson of Whorne's Place, Cuxton, Kent. Here, together with his brother and sister, he was brought up with the Leveson children of his mother's second marriage. He matriculated from Queen's College, Oxford, on 17 March 1598 and became a student of Lincoln's Inn in 1600.

In 1604 Barrett went on the grand tour, travelling to Florence. From there he may have been summoned to join the embassy of Lord Nottingham to Spain. He certainly sailed from Leghorn to Spain in February 1605, reaching the Spanish court at Valladolid by 24 May. He returned to England with the embassy. With his brother, Walter, he went on a second grand tour in 1607. The two tours cost the considerable sum of £1634 and gave Barrett a lasting interest in foreign languages and European affairs. On his return in 1608 he was knighted by James I. Barrett was married twice. On 22 April 1609 he married Jane Carey (c.1594–1633), and in August 1635 he married Catherine Perry, née Fenn (d. 1674).

Barrett sat for Whitchurch in the parliament of 1614, but most of the period 1608–18 was spent on estate matters. He assisted Sir John Leveson on behalf of Richard Leveson (Edward's half-brother) in a struggle over the inheritance of a substantial estate in the west midlands, and devoted much effort to improving the Barrett estates, where he made a park at Belhus in 1619. Barrett courted Buckingham and was noted as a coming man by Chamberlain. One benefit of this courtship was his nomination by the duchy of Cornwall for the seat of Newport in 1621. Although disappointed in his expectation of appointment as vice-chamberlain, he was appointed ambassador to France early in 1625. However, James I died before he could set out for Paris. Eventually Buckingham was appointed ambassador in December 1626, while Barrett was to go with him and remain in post, but again nothing came of the proposal. Instead, Barrett received a grant of £2000 and was created Lord Barrett of Newburgh in the Scottish peerage in 1627. In August 1628 he was granted a life patent to be chancellor of the exchequer. In this office he worked closely with his predecessor, Richard, Lord Weston, until Sir Francis Cottington replaced him in March 1629. Barrett was also created a baronet of Nova Scotia and obtained a patent to develop a settlement there but never acted on it. Finally, in April 1629, he was granted a life patent to be chancellor of the duchy of Lancaster. He was a conscientious manager of the duchy estates, and his correspondence with Lionel Cranfield, earl of Middlesex, and with his half-brother Sir Richard Leveson showed political shrewdness. Barrett was a pessimist about the political situation: he wrote in January 1636 that 'the Treasury is more empty of money than ever' and in August 1638 he wrote, 'of the business of Scotland I hear an ill sound from all parts' (*Fourth Report*, HMC, De La Warr MSS). He recorded his concerns about arms reaching Scotland and his fears about the independence being claimed by the Scottish general assembly. In the election for the Long Parliament, Barrett's active electioneering retained six of the seats normally controlled by the duchy of Lancaster for the king, but many more seats could not be held. In August 1642 his letters reveal that he still hoped for peace, although the king's attempt on Hull and the proclamation of Essex as a traitor made this unlikely. Barrett recognized that the actions of Lunsford and Prince Rupert made matters worse. Writing in November 1642, he complained of pillaging around Essex, while the sack of Brentford, he concluded, made war unavoidable. Life behind the parliamentary lines was hazardous, even for a passive royalist such as himself. In the course of 1643 his vulnerability increased. Since he had failed to lend money voluntarily to the parliamentarians, he was pursued in accordance with the ordinance for a mandatory fine equivalent to one-twentieth of his assets. In an attempt to stall this move, he presented a counter-petition stating that he had been forced to sell all his plate, that he had lost two-thirds of the income of his estate and the profits of his office, and that he was in debt. Barrett was buried at Aveley parish church on 2 January 1645. His will directed that his Berkshire and Hampshire estates should be sold to meet debts and legacies, with the surplus going to Catherine, his wife, and to Sir Richard Leveson. Both his marriages had been childless and his brother and sister, also childless, were dead. He left the reversion of the Belhus estate after his wife's death to his cousin Richard Lennard on condition that he took the name Barrett.   RICHARD WISKER

Sources T. Barrett-Lennard, *An account of the families of Lennard and Barrett* (1908), 356–403 · Essex RO, Chelmsford, Barrett-Lennard archive, D/DL/TI, 675–786 · W. Palin, *More about Stifford and its neighbourhood* (1872), 82–8 · Staffs. RO, Sutherland papers, D593 P/5/2/1–13, S/4/55/13, E3/6/5 · Leveson-Gower letter-books, Staffs. RO, Sutherland-Leveson-Gower family papers, D868, 1/54, 3/13v, 5/18, 25, 26, 27, 32 · *Fifth report*, HMC, 4 (1876), 118–19 [House of Lords] · *Fifth report*, HMC, 4 (1876), 140, 147, 161 [Sutherland MSS] · P. Morant, *The history and antiquities of the county of Essex*, 1 (1768), 79–82 · *Fourth report*, HMC, 3 (1874), 293–6, 307 [De La Warr MSS] · *VCH Essex*, 8.3, 6–9, 16 · *CSP dom.*, 1625–6, 178, 182, 485; 1628–99, 218, 528 · J. R. Gruenfelder, *Influence in early Stuart elections* (1981), 88, 185–8 · *APC*, 1627–8 · *Calendar of the manuscripts of the most hon. the marquess of Salisbury*, 17, HMC, 9 (1938), 39 · *VCH Berkshire*, 4.112 · *VCH Hampshire and the Isle of Wight*, 4.258, 271, 352 · S. E. Lehmberg, *Sir Walter Mildmay and Tudor government* (1964), 47 · 'Barrett', GEC, *Peerage*, new edn, 1.431 · 'Barrett', GEC, *Baronetage*, 2.382 · W. A. Shaw, *The knights of England*, 2 (1906); repr. (1971), 145 · Foster, *Alum. Oxon.* · parish register, Cuxton, Medway Archives and Local Studies Centre, Rochester, Kent

Archives Essex RO, Chelmsford, Barrett-Lennard Archive, D/DL/TI, 675–786 | Staffs. RO, Sutherland MSS, D593, P/5/2/1–13, S/4/55/13, E/3/6/5 · Staffs. RO, Leveson-Gower letter-books, D868 vols. 1, 3–5

Likenesses C. Johnson (Janssen), portrait, oils, c.1625; formerly at Belhus, Aveley, Essex

Wealth at death £46,600—£1080 Belhus rental 1651 x 20 = £21,600; £750 other estates rental x 20 = £15,000; wife's fortune £10,000: T. Barrett-Lennard, *An account of the families of Lennard and Barrett* (1908), 403; 1651 survey of Belhus quoted

Barrett, Francis (*fl.* 1780–1814), writer on magic and demonologist, described himself as a 'Professor of Chemistry, Natural and Occult Philosophy, the Cabala, etc.' (Barrett, *Magus*). His dates of birth and death, and his antecedents, are unknown. A dated manuscript translation of part of Georg von Welling's *Opus mago-cabalisticum* (1719) shows that Barrett was active in 1780, while a *Times* report of his inept attempts at ballooning in Greenwich and Swansea in 1802 refers to him as an apothecary who had once owned a shop in Walworth. He was married with one son.

In 1801 Barrett published *The Magus, or, Celestial Intelligencer*, in which he advertised private instruction on occult philosophy at 99 Norton Street, Marylebone. A frontispiece captioned FRC (*Frater rosae crucis*, Brother of the rosy cross), portrays a dark-haired, romantic-looking individual. Composed in the Christian tradition, *The Magus* was a farrago of Renaissance alchemy and natural and talismatic magic that fitted contemporary Gothic taste, and which was typical of the interests of late eighteenth-century Rosicrucian brotherhoods in Germany. The book's most startling feature was a set of gargoyle-like portraits of demons conjured up in ritual magic ceremonies. Barrett was almost certainly also the author of the anonymous *Lives of the Adepts in Alchymical*

Philosophy (1814) which John Ferguson dismissed as 'superficial and superstitious' (Ferguson, 41).

Rumours that Barrett founded a sodality in Cambridge appear unfounded and his one known pupil, John Parkins of Little Gonerby, Grantham, was the subject of criticism for dissolute behaviour. Interest in Barrett's ritual magic in the 1860s was due to the tea merchant and occultist Frederick Hockley (1808–1885), who reprinted *The Magus* in 1870. However, this did not succeed in rehabilitating Barrett's reputation in the eyes of late nineteenth-century writers on occultism who regarded him as a 'credulous amateur' (Barrett, *Lives*, 1888, 5).   W. H. BROCK

Sources R. Heisler, 'Behind The magus: Francis Barrett, magical balloonist', *The Pentacle*, 1 (1985), 53–7 · R. Cavendish, ed., *Man, myth and magic* (1983), 1.233 · *The Times* (13 Aug–22 Oct 1802) · F. Barrett, *The magus, or, Celestial intelligencer* (1801) · [F. Barrett], *Lives of alchemystical philosophers based on materials collected in 1815 and supplemented by recent researches*, rev. A. E. Waite, 2nd edn (1888) · J. Ferguson, ed., *Bibliotheca chemica*, 1 (1906), 75; 2 (1906), 41 · F. King, *Magic: the western tradition* (1975), 17 · *Ecce Homo, Critical remarks on the infamous publications of John Parkins* (1819)

Archives Wellcome L., holographs of his works | Yale U., Mellon MSS

Likenesses portrait, Wellcome L. · portrait, repro. in Barrett, *The magus*, frontispiece

Barrett, George (1752–1821), actuary, was the son of a farmer of Wheeler Street, a small hamlet in Surrey. At an early age he developed an aptitude for mathematics, taking a special interest in calculations relating to the duration of human life. Despite working as a schoolmaster, and subsequently as a land steward, he developed a series of life-assurance and annuity tables over a period of twenty-five years. In 1813 he was appointed actuary to the Hope Life Office in London, but retired just over two years later, at the age of sixty-four, to live with his sisters in Godalming.

Barrett's comprehensive series of life tables and the ingenious columnar method which he had devised for their construction won the ardent approval of Francis Baily, the astronomer and actuary, who endeavoured to get them published by subscription, and who in 1812 read a paper upon them before the Royal Society, which was then published as an appendix to the edition of 1813 of Baily's *Doctrine of Interest and Annuities*. There was subsequently some controversy as to the originality of Barrett's method, but his claims were defended by the mathematician Augustus De Morgan (*Assurance Magazine*, 4, 185; 12, 348). Barrett's method was later developed by Griffith Davies and others. Although his tables were never printed in full, they were purchased after his death by Charles Babbage and used by him in his *Comparative View of the Various Institutions for the Assurance of Lives* (1826). Barrett also published, in 1786, an *Essay towards a System of Police*. He died at Godalming in 1821.   ROBERT BROWN

Sources F. Baily, *Doctrine of interest and annuities*, appx (1813) · C. Babbage, *A comparative view of the various institutions for the assurance of lives* (1826) · C. Walford, *The insurance cyclopaedia*, 6 vols. (1871–80) · *Assurance Magazine*, 1 (1851), 1 · *Assurance Magazine and Journal of the Institute of Actuaries*, 4 (1853–4), 185–99 · *Assurance Magazine and Journal of the Institute of Actuaries*, 12 (1865–6), 348

Archives Institute of Actuaries, London, MSS

Barrett [Barret], **John** (*c*.1495–1563), Carmelite friar and protestant theologian, was born in Bishop's Lynn, where he joined the Carmelites. Later he studied at Cambridge and attended the lectures of Thomas Cranmer. Foxe records that Cranmer refused to allow Barrett to proceed because his theology was not sufficiently grounded in scripture: 'Among whom was Dr. Barret, a white friar, who afterwards dwelt in Norwich, was after that sort handled, giving him no less commendation for his happy rejecting of him for a better amendment' (Foxe, 8.5). He gained his BTh in 1528–9 and afterwards returned to Ipswich. He was back in Cambridge as prior in 1532–3 and should have determined for his doctorate in 1534 but was excused because of arduous and urgent business.

Barrett was early in adopting protestant beliefs, William Broman recording in 1535 that 'he has learned from the teaching of Dr. Barret, sometime a White Friar of Ipswich, about three or four years past, that the Sacrament of the Altar is but a figure and remembrance of the Passion of Christ' (*LP Henry VIII*, 9, no. 230). On 5 June 1535 Barrett was given permission to hold a benefice, and a further dispensation, on 9 June 1535, to wear the habit of his order beneath that of a secular priest. On 2 May 1541 he was appointed rector of Hetherset in Norfolk, which he resigned the following year, and in 1542 he was made divinity lecturer for Norwich Cathedral at a salary of £4. In July 1549 Barrett was one of the evangelicals who preached to Kett's rebels in their camp on Mousehold Heath outside Norwich. Then in 1550 he became rector of Cantley, Norfolk, and St Michael at Plea in Norwich.

Under Queen Mary, Barrett returned to his Catholic beliefs, causing John Bale, his near contemporary and a personal friend, to comment: 'led by what giddy spirit I do not know, like some mongrel dog, he has returned to his vomit' (Bale, *Cat.*, 2.112). On 22 March 1555 he wrote to Robert Watson, a fellow preacher on Mousehold Heath who was then in prison in Norwich for his protestant views, exhorting him to return to the Catholic faith (the letter is printed in Watson's *Aetiologia*, 1556). In 1558 he was appointed to the second prebend in Norwich Cathedral and made rector of Bishop's Thorpe, Norfolk.

Under Queen Elizabeth, Barrett adjusted his beliefs again and his acknowledgement of the queen's supremacy survives among the muniments of Corpus Christi College, Cambridge. He died on 12 July 1563 in Norwich and was buried in Norwich Cathedral, to which he left his books.

Bale preserves a list of Carmelite doctors at Paris which Barrett compiled about 1528 as a supplement to an earlier work by Jean Trisse. Three volumes of extracts from scripture, the church fathers, and protestant theologians, compiled by Barrett, are also in Corpus Christi College, Cambridge. Bale records two lost commentaries on the epistles of Paul and John and two collections of sermons, one to the clergy and the other homilies in English.

RICHARD COPSEY

Sources J. Bale, unpublished history of the province, BL, Harley MS 3838, fols. 110v–111v · Bale, *Cat.*, 2.112 · Venn, *Alum. Cant.*, 1/1.96 · Tanner, *Bibl. Brit.-Hib.*, 73–4 · Cooper, *Ath. Cantab.*, 1.224–5 · J. Foxe, *The acts and monuments of John Foxe*, ed. J. Pratt, [new edn], 8 vols. (1877); repr. (1903) · J. Barrett, acknowledgement of Queen Elizabeth's supremacy, [summer 1559], CCC Cam., MS 114 B, fol. 837 · *LP Henry VIII*, 9, no. 230 · R. Watson, *Aetiologia Roberti Watsoni Angli* (1556) · D. MacCulloch, *Thomas Cranmer: a life* (1996)

Barrett, John [Jacky] (1753/4–1821), classical scholar and eccentric, was born in Ballyroan, Queen's county, the son of Daniel Barrett (*d.* 1760), a Church of Ireland clergyman, and his wife, Rossamund Gofton (*d.* 1782). Although baptized John he was universally known as Jacky. His father died when he was six, which resulted in his mother's moving the family to Dublin. There Barrett was admitted to Trinity College on 9 July 1770, gained a scholarship in 1773, and graduated BA in 1775. In 1778 he was elected fellow of the college, and he proceeded BD in 1786 and DD in 1790. In 1791 he was co-opted as a senior fellow, and held several positions within the college, such as librarian, bursar, and registrar and, on several occasions, Archbishop King's lecturer. He was appointed professor of Hebrew in 1806 and elected vice-provost in 1807.

In 1800 Barrett published *An enquiry into the origins of the constellations that compose the zodiac, and the uses they were intended to promote*. Although it contained many fantastical theories regarding the origins of the zodiac it was innovative work in the area of comparative religion. In 1801 he published his most important work, *Evangelium secundum Mattaeum*, also known as *Codex Z Dublinensis rescriptus*. While examining a manuscript in the college library he noticed some earlier writings underneath the more recent Greek. The writings were identified as part of Isaiah, some orations of Gregory of Nazianzen, and a large portion of St Matthew's gospel. Barrett translated the portions of St Matthew, which he thought dated from the sixth century, demonstrating a fair degree of erudition in the process. His efforts were published at the expense of the college, and although they contained some errors they ably showed the significance of his discovery. In 1853, after the manuscript had been restored with the use of a chemical application, Samuel P. Tregelles was able to discover additional text, and published his findings in a supplement. In 1880 another edition of the work was published in which Thomas K. Abbott included additional material missed by both Barrett and Tregelles.

Barrett's contribution to both Trinity College and scholarship has been overshadowed to an extent by his reputation as an eccentric. A myriad stories concerning his eccentricity exist, many of which appear in Charles Lever's 1841 novel *Charles O'Malley: the Irish Dragoon*. Some historians of the University of Dublin have urged caution regarding these stories, since Barrett has 'attained the status of a character to whom stories are attributed when the narrator has forgotten to whom they originally referred' (McDowell and Webb, 82). It appears that Barrett had two chief passions in life, reading and the hoarding of money. He was a miser of extreme proportions, allowing himself no heat in his room and lighting candles only for reading.

His parsimony appears to have arisen from a frugal childhood that led to his being oblivious to the potential comforts afforded by money. Slovenly and paying no attention to his appearance, he was once removed by a porter who reckoned, from his state, that he had no business in the college. Though he was fluent in Greek and Latin he struggled with the English language and talked in a mixture of oaths and provincialisms acquired during his boyhood. Having been given the task of welcoming George IV to the college library in 1821 he addressed the king with a Latin oration, and although history failed to record what 'small talk, if any, then took place between the First Gentleman of Europe and the most dilapidated scholar of Europe' (ibid.) a newspaper did note that the king paid 'marked attention' (*Freeman's Journal*) to his proclamation.

Much of Barrett's eccentricity stemmed from his isolation from the outside world; he remained within the college environs for nearly all his life, save for occasional visits to the Bank of Ireland on the other side of College Green. There are only a handful of references to his venturing beyond. On a visit to Lord Charlemont's demesne he saw for the first time some sheep; having enquired what they were he declared that he had seen 'live mutton', and on viewing the sea he remarked that it was 'a broad flat superficies like Euclid's definition of a line expanding itself into a surface, and blue, like Xenophon's plain covered with wormwood' (*Dublin University Magazine*). Unmarried, he died in his room in Trinity on 15 November 1821, leaving £70,000 to charitable purposes, his will stating that he wanted to contribute 'towards the relief of the sick, indigent, poor and naked' (TCD, MS 2376). Several Dublin institutions, including Sir Patrick Dun's Hospital, the Rotunda Hospital, and various orphanages benefited from his bequest. Though the will awarded only token annuities to his surviving relatives additional moneys were later advanced to them, since the fund trustees deemed that, owing to their impoverished circumstances, they qualified under the main terms of the will. Barrett was buried on 19 November, possibly at Glasnevin, Dublin, as requested in his will. H. T. WELCH

Sources R. B. McDowell and D. A. Webb, *Trinity College, Dublin, 1592–1952: an academic history* (1982) • C. Maxwell, *A history of Trinity College Dublin, 1591–1892* (1946) • J. W. Stubbs, *The history of the University of Dublin, from its foundation to the end of the eighteenth century* (1889) • 'Notes regarding the life of John Barrett by T. T. Gray', TCD, MS 2377, misc. box III • will (certified copy), TCD, MS 2376, misc. box III • *Dublin University Magazine*, 18 (1841), 350–58 • C. Lever, *Charles O'Malley: the Irish dragoon* (1841) • Burtchaell & Sadleir, *Alum. Dubl.*, 2nd edn • A. J. Webb, *A compendium of Irish biography* (1878) • *Freeman's Journal* [Dublin] (31 Aug 1821) • A. Crookshank and D. Webb, *Paintings and sculptures in Trinity College, Dublin* (1990) • J. Barrett, speech to king (delivered in the library of Trinity College), Aug 1821, TCD, MUN 1498 • W. B. S. Taylor, *History of the University of Dublin* (1845) • *DNB*
Archives TCD, biblical and personal papers • TCD, corresp., MS 2373 • TCD, corresp. and sermons, MS portfolio, MS 2374 | CUL, historical collections on TCD, Add. MS 707 • NA Ire., deeds of trust relating to charitable bequest of John Barrett, D. 20, fols. 458–751
Likenesses J. Kirkwood, sketch, c.1810, TCD, MS 4726/5, misc. box III; repro. in *Dublin University Magazine* • G. F. Joseph, oils, 1820, TCD; repro. in Crookshank and Webb, *Painting and sculptures*

Wealth at death £70,000: 'certified copy of the will of John Barrett', TCD, MS 2376, misc. box III

Barrett, John (*bap.* 1764, *d.* 1810), naval officer, son of Patrick and Elizabeth Barrett, was baptized at St Peter's, Dublin, on 27 May 1764. After going to sea first on 15 January 1780 as captain's servant in the *Hannibal* he served as able seaman and midshipman on that ship and the *Agamemnon* until 10 June 1783. From 18 June 1790 he was again at sea as able seaman, midshipman, and then master's mate in the *Bellerophon*, *Vengeance*, and *Queen*, before passing his lieutenant's examination on 6 February 1793, and receiving his commission on 2 November 1793.

In command of the storeship *Experiment* Barrett distinguished himself in the evacuation of the British garrison from St Lucia, when the island was taken by the French on 19 June 1795; consequently, on 25 November, he was advanced to the rank of post captain.

In 1808 Barrett commanded the *Africa* (64 guns) in the fleet under Vice-Admiral Saumarez in the Baltic. On 20 October, while escorting a convoy, she was attacked in a dead calm by twenty-five Danish oared gun- and mortar-boats off the island of Amager near Copenhagen. The Danes poured in a heavy fire on the *Africa*'s bows and quarters, where her guns could not bear. Twice her flag was shot away, while her masts and yards were badly damaged, her rigging cut to pieces, and her hull shattered, with several large shot between wind and water. Nine of her men were killed and fifty-three wounded. The engagement lasted until the Danes withdrew at nightfall. 'Had the daylight and calm continued two hours longer, the *Africa* must either have sunk or surrendered' (James, 5.76).

Barrett was later again employed in convoying the Baltic trade. On 22 December 1810, a wild, stormy night, his ship, the *Minotaur* (74 guns), was driven on the Haak Sands off the Texel and lost, with nearly 500 of her crew. Captain Barrett was among the dead. Acting to the last with perfect coolness and composure, he is reported to have said: 'We all owe nature a debt; let us pay it like men of honour.' J. K. LAUGHTON, *rev.* RANDOLPH COCK

Sources lieutenants' passing certificates, PRO, ADM 6/92; ADM 107/17 • W. James, *The naval history of Great Britain, from the declaration of war by France in 1793, to the accession of George IV*, [5th edn], 6 vols. (1859–60) • E. P. Brenton, *The naval history of Great Britain, from the year 1783 to 1822*, 5 vols. (1823–5) • W. L. Clowes, *The Royal Navy: a history from the earliest times to the present*, 7 vols. (1897–1903)
Archives PRO, lieutenants' passing certificates, ADM 6/92, 107/17

Barrett [Barret], **Joseph** (1665–1699), religious writer, was born at Sandiacre, Derbyshire, on 2 August 1665 and was baptized there on 13 August, the son of the ejected minister John *Barret (1631–1713) and his wife, Elizabeth. In a short account of his life written when he was twenty Barrett noted that his first religious experience came when he was reading his primer, after which he begged his mother to teach him to pray and sing psalms. At school he developed a 'delight in holy duties: especially secret prayer, and singing of psalms', which led his fellow pupils to call him 'good man' ('Account', in Whitlock, *Funeral Sermon*, 35–6). During his childhood he also acquired a deep dislike of sabbath profanation and wrote how 'it hath saddened my heart to see or hear of others prophaning this day', noting that it was 'ordinary for boys in the summertime to bath themselves, and to go to get nuts upon it' (ibid., 37). Any profane behaviour such as 'cursing' or 'swearing' was abhorrent to him, and he also described his dislike of 'play' or 'needless (and consequently sinful) recreations' (ibid., 40, 43).

Barrett's father had intended him for the ministry, but owing to his son's poor eyesight thought it wiser for him to learn a trade. Though his parents wished him to be apprenticed in London he preferred to stay in Nottingham, where he married Millicent Reyner, daughter of John Reyner, formerly a fellow of Emmanuel College, Cambridge; they had five children. While an apprentice he apparently helped other servants with their catechism and kept up his religious duties.

A character testimony by John Whitlock jun., pastor of the Presbyterian congregation to which Barrett belonged, described him as 'that eminently holy, humble, active and zealous servant of Christ', who was a man 'given to prayer, and much in meditation, and self-examination' (Whitlock, *Funeral Sermon*, preface, no pagination). He described how Barrett earnestly went about setting up societies for the reformation of manners, as well as establishing a weekly hour of private prayer for the church and nation. In his funeral sermon Whitlock noted that he had aided a family of French protestants living in the locality on a monthly basis for several years, contributed to the education of young men for the ministry, and 'by his own purse encouraged and settled the preaching of the gospel among poor people that could not maintain it, and ignorant, careless people, that were unacquainted with the gospel' (ibid., 21). Barrett's own correspondence adds detail to Whitlock's portrait, demonstrating not only his active involvement in the campaign for the reformation of manners in Nottingham but the support he offered to societies in York, Chesterfield, and Hull, and his sponsorship of preaching and catechizing in the Derbyshire parishes of Middleton and Elton.

Included in *A Funeral Sermon* are some of Barrett's writings under the title 'Occasional meditations', in which he drew spiritual insights from everyday matters. One entitled 'Upon my candles going out suddenly', compared this with the sudden extinguishing of life. Other writings including his 'pious letters' are contained in *The Remains of Mr Joseph Barrett* (1700), edited by John Whitlock sen. and John Whitlock the younger, a volume which also included a memoir by his father. In both books he was held up as an exemplar of piety, not least to 'tradesmen that have much to do in the world'; his life showed how a man could be diligent in his worldly calling yet 'keep up much inward Communion with God, and be useful in his Place for the Good of others, both as to the Publick, and to the Souls and Body's of Particular Persons' (J. Whitlock sen., 'To the reader', in Whitlock, *Funeral Sermon*, unpaginated).

Barrett died at a relatively early age on 28 August 1699 of a 'violent fever', having several years previously suffered with 'nervous consumption' ('A brief character … by his father John Barret' in Whitlock, *Funeral Sermon*, 292), and was buried on 30 August.   CAROLINE L. LEACHMAN

Sources J. W. [J. Whitlock], *A funeral sermon upon the death of Mr Joseph Barrett* (1699) · *The remains of Mr Joseph Barrett*, ed. J. Whitlock and J. Whitlock (1700) · *Calamy rev.*

Barrett, Lucas (1837–1862), geologist and oceanographer, was born on 14 November 1837, the eldest son of George Barrett, a London iron-founder. In 1847 he was sent to Mr P. Ashton's school in Royston, Hertfordshire, where he collected fossils from the local chalk pits as a hobby. Four years later he transferred to University College School in Gower Street, where he remained until 1853. This was closer to the parental home and also the British Museum, where he took his fossils for identification. In 1853–4 he studied German and chemistry at Ebersdorf by Lobenstein, during which time he also undertook a geological walking tour in Bavaria.

Barrett was elected a fellow of the Geological Society of London in May 1855, the youngest to have been admitted up to that time. His first international field training came during that summer, when he accompanied a dredging expedition, led by Robert M'Andrew, from the Shetlands to Arctic Norway and Finnmark. On this voyage he made notable observations on the extant brachiopods which he presented in September at the annual meeting of the British Association for the Advancement of Science (BAAS) in Glasgow; this was his first paper. In the same year he was appointed curator of the Woodwardian Museum, Cambridge, as successor to Frederick McCoy.

Barrett's research on the deep-sea fauna continued during the spring of the following year, when he obtained a leave of absence from Cambridge to accompany J. W. Taylor on a dredging expedition to Greenland. During the period 1856–8 his duties at Cambridge included delivering most of the geological lectures for the aged Professor Adam Sedgwick, in addition to expanding considerably the collections of the Woodwardian Museum. A further dredging expedition during 1857, again led by M'Andrew, went to Vigo, on the north coast of Spain.

Barrett was admitted to Trinity College, Cambridge, in January 1859, but never graduated. In the same year he married Alice Maria, and was appointed—at the early age of twenty-one—director of the geological survey of the West Indies. He arrived in Jamaica in April, accompanied by his wife. The survey of Jamaica, undertaken in association with his assistant, J. G. Sawkins, was commenced in the eastern parishes of the island at a scale of one inch to a mile. Barrett's research in Jamaica was concerned with a number of important and varied facets of the island's geology, such as the copper and manganese ore deposits, and the dating, using fossil molluscs, of the Jamaican Cretaceous rocks, which had been incorrectly identified as Palaeozoic more than thirty years before by Sir H. T. De la Beche. He obtained use of a gunboat to dredge in 150–200 fathoms off the north coast of the island, as he hoped to date the late Cenozoic deposits of eastern Jamaica using Lyellian statistics by comparing the recent and fossil mollusc faunas. However, despite making good progress, the geological survey was not completely harmonious, as Sawkins seems to have been jealous of the position of his somewhat younger director.

In 1862 Barrett was granted six months' leave of absence and went to England in March as a commissioner for Jamaica at the International Exhibition, where his geological exhibits won a medal. June and July were spent in correcting the printed geological maps of the eastern parishes produced thus far by the survey. During October he acted as a local secretary at the annual meeting of the BAAS at Cambridge. He was also a member of several committees and led a field excursion to Hunstanton.

Returning to Jamaica in November, Barrett took a diving dress, pumps, and air-tubing for use in investigating the island's reefs, which could not be examined using conventional dredging. On 17 December he successfully descended for thirty minutes in shallow water, apparently among the Port Royal cays to the south of Kingston harbour. The next day he gave evidence before a committee in the house of assembly. On the following day, 19 December 1862, he made a longer descent in deeper water, but unexpectedly floated to the surface at some distance from his boat. His helmet was removed and he was taken ashore, but was found to be dead. His wife had remained behind in England and his only son, Arthur, was born in Cambridge the following January. Although the verdict at the inquest was death by drowning, this is at variance with the dry condition of Barrett's dress. Most probably, Barrett had purposely closed the principal valve of the diving dress, allowing it to inflate and float to the surface. This rapid ascent was presumably the cause of death due to a pulmonary air embolism, with nitrogen bubbles forming and blocking his blood vessels.

Despite dying so young, Barrett made a number of notable contributions to both geology and the study of deeper water faunas. Some of his more notable discoveries were documented only later by other authors (though he himself published eleven papers). Thus, although they were described subsequently by H. G. Seeley, in 1858 Barrett identified two bones from the Upper Cretaceous Cambridge Greensand as being of avian origin, then the earliest birds known. His investigations of deeper water faunas, based on observations made on a number of dredging expeditions in polar to tropical regions, led him to speculate that the sea bed below 100 fathoms constituted a single, nearly uniform, faunal province of global extent. In Jamaica he conclusively demonstrated that the so-called 'Submedial/Transition' (Lower Palaeozoic) rocks identified by De la Beche were actually Cretaceous. The overlying, supposedly Upper Palaeozoic deposits were thus concluded to be Eocene. Among the notable fossiliferous deposits discovered by Barrett was the Bowden shell bed and its exquisitely preserved molluscs. Barrett's attempts to date this and other late Cenozoic deposits led him to compare their included fossil molluscs with the island's extant fauna. It was his determination to investigate fully the recent molluscs that led to his untimely death.

STEPHEN K. DONOVAN

Sources L. J. Chubb, 'Lucas Barrett: a biography', *Geonotes* (*Quarterly Journal of the Geological Society of Jamaica*), 5/3–4 (1962), 2–34 · A. C. Ramsay, *Quarterly Journal of the Geological Society*, 20 (1864), xxxiii–xxxiv · S. P. Woodward, *The Geologist*, 6 (1863), 60–62 · L. J. Chubb, 'Centenary', *Geonotes* (*Quarterly Newsletter of the Jamica Group of the Geologists' Association*), 2 (1959), 145–6 · L. J. Chubb, 'Lucas Barrett, 1837–1862', *Geonotes* (*Quarterly Journal of the Geological Society of Jamaica*), 4/1–2 (1961), 12–14 · S. K. Donovan and S. J. Wood, 'Lucas Barrett's collection: Jamaican echinoids hiding amongst British immigrants', *Geological Curator*, 6 (1994–8), 133–5 · G. Draper, 'A note on the aquisition [*sic*] of Lucas Barrett's collection of rocks for the Geology Museum at the University of the West Indies', *Journal of the Geological Society of Jamaica*, 15 (1976), 33–6 · S. K. Donovan, 'An introduction to the Bowden shell bed, southeast Jamaica', *Contributions to Tertiary and Quaternary Geology*, 35 (1998), 3–8
Archives University of the West Indies, Mona, Jamaica, Geology Museum, rocks, minerals, fossils
Likenesses photograph, repro. in Donovan, 'An introduction to the Bowden shell bed', fig. 2 · wood-engraving, NPG; repro. in *ILN* (14 Feb 1863)
Wealth at death under £800: probate, 25 June 1863, *CGPLA Eng. & Wales*

Barrett, Rachel (1874–1953), suffragette and newspaper editor, was born on 12 November 1874 at 23 Union Street, Carmarthen, the daughter of Welsh-speaking parents, Rees Barrett, land and road surveyor, and Anne Barrett, *née* Jones. Educated at a private school in Stroud, she later won a scholarship to Aberystwyth College, gaining a BSc (London) in 1904, and taught in schools at Penarth and Carmarthen.

In 1906 Rachel Barrett joined the Women's Social and Political Union (WSPU), the women's suffrage organization founded by Emmeline Pankhurst, and helped Adela Pankhurst, the WSPU organizer in Cardiff. She spoke at many meetings on behalf of the cause and incurred the disapproval of her headmistress, especially, she said, when 'her science mistress was reported in the local papers as drenched with flour at an open air meeting at the Cardiff docks' (Barrett, 126–7). In July 1907 she resigned her teaching post and enrolled at the London School of Economics (LSE), intending to study for a DSc in economics. In 1908, however, Christabel Pankhurst asked her to become a full-time organizer for the WSPU. This meant giving up her studies at the LSE, but, 'it was a definite call', she said, 'and I obeyed' (ibid., 127). In 1910 she was appointed WSPU organizer for Wales and moved to Newport, Monmouthshire.

Rachel Barrett was recalled to London in the spring of 1912, following Christabel Pankhurst's flight to Paris, to help Annie Kenney run the national campaign. Later that year she was asked to become assistant editor of *The Suffragette*, the new weekly newspaper of the WSPU. Annie Kenney said that she had chosen Rachel for this task because she was 'an exceptionally clever and highly educated woman, she was a devoted worker and had tremendous admiration for Christabel' (Kenney, 179). Rachel Barrett's reaction to being asked to edit the paper was that it was 'an appalling task as I knew nothing whatever of journalism' (Barrett, 129), but she took it on and with it the risks which the increasingly militant tactics of the WSPU involved. When she went to Paris to consult with Christabel, she had to travel under cover, and whenever they talked on the telephone, she 'could always hear the click of Scotland Yard listening in' (ibid., 129). In April 1913 the WSPU offices were raided and the staff of the paper arrested on charges of conspiring to damage property. Rachel Barrett was sentenced to a month's imprisonment. She immediately went on hunger strike and was released five days later under the terms of the 'Cat and Mouse Act'. She was subsequently re-arrested and released twice more and while out on licence for the third time had herself smuggled into WSPU offices in Kingsway House where she carried on bringing out *The Suffragette*. She lived there in secret for five months, but while she was away in May 1914, the offices were raided once again. In consultation with Christabel, it was decided that she should go to Scotland, where newspaper law was different from England, in order to publish the paper from there. She lived in Edinburgh under an assumed name, calling herself Miss Ashworth, and brought out the paper each week until the last number appeared on the Friday after the First World War was declared.

Rachel Barrett never married. While working at *The Suffragette* she met Ida Alexa Ross Wylie (1885–1959) the Australian novelist, who was a contributor to the paper, and they are thought to have become lovers (Cline, 173). The couple figure in the 1920s as close friends of Radclyffe Hall and supporters over the trial of *The Well of Loneliness* in 1928. She died of a cerebral haemorrhage on 26 August 1953, at the age of seventy-eight at the Carylls Nursing Home in Faygate, Rusper, Sussex. Her death certificate describes her as a spinster and a teacher resident in Essex.   CAROLINE MORRELL

Sources R. Barrett, 'Autobiography', Museum of London, Suffragette Fellowship collection [on microfilm at the Fawcett Library, London] • A. Kenney, *Memories of a militant* (1924) • *Votes for Women* (1910–13) • A. Raeburn, *The militant suffragettes* (1973) • C. Pankhurst, *Unshackled: the story of how we won the vote* (1959) • *Annual Report* [Women's Social and Political Union], 8 (1913–14) • E. S. Pankhurst, *The suffragette movement: an intimate account of persons and ideals* (1931); repr. (1977) • D. Mitchell, *Queen Christabel: a biography of Christabel Pankhurst* (1977) • A. Rosen, *Rise up, women! The militant campaign of the Women's Social and Political Union, 1903–1914* (1974) • b. cert. • d. cert. • will • *CGPLA Eng. & Wales* (1953) • E. Crawford, *The women's suffrage movement: a reference guide, 1866–1928* (1999) • M. Baker, *Our three selves: a life of Radclyffe Hall* (1985) • S. Cline, *Radclyffe Hall: a woman called John* (1997)
Archives Museum of London, suffragette collection, autobiography [microfilm copy, Women's Library]
Likenesses photograph, repro. in *Votes for Women* (22 July 1910), 713–14 • photograph, repro. in *Votes for Women* (1 Dec 1911)
Wealth at death £6191 2s. 7d.: probate, 4 Nov 1953, *CGPLA Eng. & Wales*

Barrett, Rosa Mary (1855–1936), social reformer and feminist, was born in Jamaica, the youngest of the four surviving children of William Garland Barrett (1812–1865), Congregational minister and sometime missionary to Jamaica, and his wife, Martha, *née* Fletcher (1811?–1893).

One brother was the leading Congregationalist George Slatyer Barrett; another was the scientist and electrical engineer Sir William Fletcher *Barrett.

As a girl Rosa Barrett spent her pocket money on engaging a nurse to mind the children of charwomen who were out working, and in her early twenties she founded the first crèche in Dublin at Kingstown. It became the Cottage Home for Little Children, for which she acted as honorary secretary for fifty years and which is still in operation today. Most of its first hundred admissions of children up to eight years old resulted from a family crisis—usually the father's death, desertion, or drunkenness and violence—which necessitated the mother working outside the home and meant that she was unable to care for her children in the daytime. In a few cases the children were placed—with the surviving parent's permission—for adoption with approved families in Canada. But for the most part poor mothers were enabled, by payment of a penny a day or less, to go out to work without fearing for hungry infants left to the dangers of an unsupervised home or the street. Rosa Barrett aimed to ensure a head start of proper feeding and good care for the poorest children in the community. She publicized the work of such crèches and the social need for them in *Our Kingstown Nursery* (1880), *Guide to Dublin Charities* (1884), and *The Cottage Home for Little Children: a Retrospect* (c.1905).

Rosa Barrett went on to found the Irish section of the National Society for the Prevention of Cruelty to Children (NSPCC) in 1889, after having discovered badly treated pauper children in a so-called 'home' in Tuam. She called over an NSPCC inspector from London to investigate, and the persons responsible for the child neglect were imprisoned. Unfortunately the Catholic clergy were suspicious of the NSPCC on account of the number of protestants, including Rosa Barrett, on its Dublin committee. For her part, it is very possible that Rosa Barrett saw herself as something of a protestant mission worker and child rescuer in a benighted Catholic land.

In 1896 Rosa Barrett published a paper read before the Statistical and Social Inquiry Society of Ireland entitled *Foreign Legislation on Behalf of Destitute and Neglected Children* and in 1899 she published her pamphlet *The Rescue of the Young*. Her work *Juvenile Criminals* (1900) was awarded the medal of the Howard Penal Reform League. Rosa Barrett later became the hagiographic biographer of Ellice Hopkins, the rescuer of child prostitutes and campaigner for raising the age of legal consent for girls to sixteen. Ellice Hopkins's 'thrilling accounts of her public work' for the White Cross Men's Sexual Purity League constantly made Rosa Barrett feel ashamed (Barrett, *Ellice Hopkins*).

Rosa Barrett supported other causes, including temperance, women's suffrage, and peace. Prominent in the Irish Women's Temperance Association, Rosa Barrett was also a co-founder with Lady Aberdeen of the National Women's Health Association for Ireland in 1907, which organized a public education campaign to combat tuberculosis, and she was later chosen to represent the Irish Women's Suffrage Federation in London in 1912, lobbying Irish MPs regarding Asquith's Reform Bill. In 1915 Rosa Barrett gave her public support to the unpopular 'unpatriotic' Women's International Congress in The Hague, which called for women's participation in foreign affairs and an alternative to war for settling international disputes. She herself was a widely travelled woman, having visited Canada, South Africa, Norway, and Sweden, among many other countries, and for several years she was the compiler of Ward Lock's Irish Guides.

Towards the end of her life Rosa Barrett completed her brother William Fletcher Barrett's book on Christian Science, *The Religion of Health* (1925). Later still she seems to have become involved with spiritualism, publishing accounts by a medium—*The Seekers* (1928) and *Beyond* (1929). She died at her home, Cedarcot, 106 Handside Lane, Welwyn Garden City, on 28 August 1936. Although Rosa Barrett's practical work throughout her life was unremittingly serious and passionately altruistic, a correspondent in *The Times* (2 September 1936), who knew her personally, testified to her being a woman of keen humour and great charm.   SYBIL OLDFIELD

Sources M. Luddy, *Women and philanthropy in nineteenth-century Ireland* (1995) • R. M. Barrett, *Ellice Hopkins: a memoir*, ed. H. S. Holland (1907) • *The Times* (2 Sept 1936) • R. Barrett, *The rescue of the young* (1899) • census returns, Dublin, 1901 • d. cert.
Wealth at death £1059 18s. 11d.: probate, 28 Dec 1936, *CGPLA Eng. & Wales*

Barrett, Stephen (*bap.* 1719, *d.* 1801), schoolmaster and Church of England clergyman, was born at Bent, in the parish of Kildwick in Craven, Yorkshire, and was baptized there on 14 May 1719, the son of Peter Barrett of Sutton, Yorkshire, and his wife, Mary. He was educated at the grammar school in Skipton, where he excelled in poetry and classics. He matriculated from University College, Oxford, on 24 March 1738 and graduated BA in 1741 and MA in 1744. Having taken holy orders he became rector of the parishes of Purton and Ickleford, Hertfordshire, in 1744. Five years later, in 1749, he was appointed master of the free grammar school at Ashford, Kent, on the nomination of Sir Wyndham Knatchbull. He raised the school's academic reputation and attracted the patronage of the local gentry, who sent their sons to his school. Its success enabled Barrett to augment the master's salary of £30 to an income of 120 guineas per annum, presumably by charging fees for pupils who boarded. In 1751 he applied for the mastership of his old grammar school in Skipton; it seems that both he and the rival candidate, William West, offered bribes to some of the churchwardens who were electing to the post. Although at first Barrett disdained such means, in a letter dated 6 August 1751 he wrote that he would invest £100 in bribes to please his patron, Lord Thanet. He had secured a majority of votes when he suddenly pulled out of the competition, fearing a scandal, should details of his bribes leak out.

Barrett resigned from Ashford in 1764 but returned as headmaster two years later. By that time he had married Mary, daughter of Edward Jacob of Canterbury; their only child, Mary, was baptized at Ickleford, Hertfordshire, on 5 August 1764. Barrett resigned the mastership a second time, in 1773, when presented to the rectory of Hothfield,

Kent. He was a friend of Dr Johnson and Edward Cave, and a frequent contributor to the *Gentleman's Magazine*. He also published some verses, a Latin translation of Pope's 'Pastorals', and *Ovid's epistles translated into English verse, with critical essays and notes; being part of a poetical and oratorical lecture read to the grammar school of Ashford in the county of Kent, and calculated to initiate youth in the first principles of taste* (1759). Tobias Smollett gave a withering review of Barrett's works in the *Critical Review*: 'though he might be an excellent schoolmaster, he had, however, no pretensions to taste' (Nichols, *Lit. anecdotes*, 3.346n).

Barrett died at Church House, Northiam, Sussex, on 26 November 1801, and was buried at Hothfield on 3 December. He was survived by his daughter, who had married Edward Jeremiah Curteis, a barrister.

     A. H. BULLEN, *rev.* S. J. SKEDD

Sources Nichols, *Lit. anecdotes*, 3.346; 9.672 • *GM*, 1st ser., 71 (1801), 1152 • N. Carlisle, *A concise description of the endowed grammar schools in England and Wales*, 2 vols. (1818), 1.560–61 • A. J. Pearman, *Ashford: its church, vicars, college and grammar school*, 2nd edn (1886), 162 • *IGI* • Foster, *Alum. Oxon.* • A. M. Gibbon, *The ancient free grammar school of Skipton in Craven* (1947) • will, PRO, PROB 11/1366, sig. 781
Archives Yale U., Beinecke L., commonplace books

Barrett, Thomas Augustine [*pseuds.* Leslie Stuart, Lester Thomas] (1863?–1928), composer, was probably born on 15 March 1863 in Southport, Lancashire, the younger son of Thomas Barrett, cabinet-maker (*b. c.*1830), and his wife, Mary Ann Burke, *née* Lester (*b. c.*1832), both natives of western Ireland. He grew up in Liverpool, where he attended St Francis Xavier's School. His family then moved to Manchester, and there he first gained recognition as a keyboard player. He became church organist at St John's Roman Catholic Cathedral, Salford, under Bishop (later Cardinal) Herbert Vaughan, and later moved to the church of the Holy Name under the latter's brother Bernard Vaughan. He also made an impression with classical piano recitals, after which he formed his own choral society and, from 1889 to 1894, promoted a series of popular Saturday night concerts at St James's Hall, Manchester. Hugely successful, these introduced to Manchester many eminent performers of the time, including the pianist Paderewski and the opera singers Marie Roze and Zélie de Lussan. Two of the children of his marriage (on 9 March 1886) to Katharine Mary Fox (*b.* 1864) were named Bernard Vaughan and Marie Roze.

Through his father's work as property master at the Amphitheatre, Liverpool, Barrett acquired an early taste for the theatre. With his elder brother, Stephen (1855–1924), who became a music-hall performer under the name Lester Barrett, he was an *habitué* of The Ship inn, Manchester, a local bohemian haunt. Gradually the music he composed for local pantomimes, and especially his popular ballads under the name Leslie Stuart, and music-hall songs under the name Lester Thomas, began to eclipse his religious and other serious compositions.

Barrett's first major published successes were the ballad 'The Bandolero' (1894), introduced by the Irish baritone who called himself Signor Foli, and the music-hall songs 'Louisiana Lou' (1894) and 'Sweetheart May' (1895). In 1895 he moved to London to further his career, permanently adopting the pseudonym Leslie Stuart. He was almost immediately rewarded with the huge success of 'The Soldiers of the Queen' (1895). It became the hit song of Queen Victoria's diamond jubilee and remained much favoured during the Second South African War. Its success was augmented in the variety theatre by that of nostalgic, exotically rhythmic songs such as 'Little Dolly Daydream' (1897) and 'The Lily of Laguna' (1898), written for the American black-face minstrel Eugene Stratton.

The reputation of Leslie Stuart was further enhanced by the score for Owen Hall's musical play *Florodora* (1899). This proved a huge success at London's Lyric Theatre and across the Atlantic, most particularly for the double sextet 'Tell me, pretty maiden', in which six top-hatted gentlemen on bended knee paid court to six elegantly dressed young ladies. A further music-hall song hit was 'I may be crazy' (1902), and there were some fair stage successes in the songs he wrote for *The Silver Slipper* by Owen Hall (1901), *The School Girl* by Henry Hamilton and Paul M. Potter (1903), *The Belle of Mayfair* by Basil Hood and Charles H. E. Brookfield (1906), and *Havana* by George Grossmith and Graham Hill (1908). However, his individual musical style thereafter palled. *Captain Kidd* (which Seymour Hills adapted from an American farce; 1910) and *Peggy* by George Grossmith (1911), both given in London, failed to add to his reputation, as did *The Slim Princess* by Henry Blossom (1910), given in the USA.

By then Barrett's extravagant lifestyle was causing severe financial problems. On the back of his early successes he had built a luxurious home in Hampstead, where he entertained lavishly. He also had a taste for the racecourse, where his hot-headed and stubborn nature led to a break with his most loyal interpreter, Eugene Stratton. Further misfortune came from the pirating of popular sheet music, which was rife when his music was at its most popular at the beginning of the century and which made him a vigorous campaigner for composers' rights. In January 1913 he was declared bankrupt.

In 1915 Barrett's daughter May Leslie-Stuart appeared in a London revival of *Florodora*, and he also accompanied her in his songs on the variety stage. In 1920 he was discharged from bankruptcy. In 1926, now frail, he appeared to acclaim, performing a medley of his songs, which by then were evocative of a previous generation. He died at his daughter's home, Downe Lodge, Richmond, Surrey, on 27 March 1928 and was buried in Richmond cemetery three days later. His wife survived him.

ANDREW LAMB

Sources L. Stuart, 'My Bohemian life', *Empire News* (14 Aug–13 Nov 1927); repr. in L. Stuart, *My Bohemian life*, ed. A. Lamb (2003) · A. Lamb, *Leslie Stuart: composer of Florodora* (2002) · A. Lamb, 'Mr T. A. Barrett's Saturday concerts, 1889–1894', *Manchester Sounds* (2002) · T. Staveacre, *The songwriters* (1980) · T. Roberts, 'Stories of some successful songs', *Royal Magazine* (1900) · L. Stuart, 'Personal reminiscences', *Liverpool Review* (26 April 1902) · 'Popular composers: Mr Leslie Stuart', *The Era* (3 June 1899) · K. Gänzl, *The British musical theatre*, 2 vols. (1986) · *The Era* (28 March 1928) · *The Era* (4 April 1928) · W. Macqueen Pope, *The melodies linger on* (c.1950) · MT, 30–35 (1889–94) · *Manchester Guardian* (1889) · 'Vaughan, Bernard John', *DNB* · 'Vaughan, Herbert Alfred', *DNB* · will · m. cert. · census returns, 1881, 1901 · 'Mr Adrian Ross, musical comedy lyric laureate, discourses on "Havana"', *Play Pictorial*, 12/71 (1908), 31–2

Likenesses photograph, 1884, repro. in L. Stuart, 'My Bohemian life' · photograph, c.1891, repro. in *Spy* [Manchester] (1891) · photograph, c.1900 (repro. on postcard), priv. coll. · photographs, c.1900, repro. in *Royal Magazine* · photographs, c.1900–1916, repro. in A. Lamb, *Leslie Stuart: composer of Florodora* · photograph, c.1908 (repro. on postcard), priv. coll. · photographs, c.1915, repro. in Staveacre, *The songwriters* · photograph, 1916, repro. in S. Green, *The world of musical comedy* (1980)

Wealth at death £300: probate, 26 May 1928, *CGPLA Eng. & Wales*

Barrett, William (*b. c.*1561, *d.* in or after **1630**), theologian, is of unknown parentage. He matriculated as a pensioner at Trinity College, Cambridge, in 1580, graduating BA in 1585 and proceeding MA in 1588. He was appointed fellow and chaplain of Gonville and Caius College, Cambridge, from Michaelmas 1592 for three years. Apparently influenced by the views of Peter Baro, Lady Margaret professor of divinity, and in disagreement with the Calvinist regius professor William Whitaker's lectures attacking advocates of universal grace, on 29 April 1595 Barrett preached a sermon in the university church for his BD. He argued that sin was the primary cause of reprobation by God, not his will; that no one could be so strongly sustained by justifying faith that it could not fail, nor be sure of forgiveness of sins; and that it was proud and wicked to be certain of salvation. He bitterly attacked Calvin, saying, by report, 'he durst presume to lift himself up above the high and almighty God' (Fuller, 211).

This shocked and enraged the Calvinist dons, who were the majority, and when the vice-chancellor, Duport, found Barrett would not withdraw his statement, a consistory court made up entirely of Calvinist heads of house tried to change his views and ordered him to read a retraction in the university church. This he did, but the Calvinist party considered he was not reverent or sincere and organized a petition claiming the sermon savoured of popish doctrine. Barrett was threatened with expulsion. He appealed to Archbishop Whitgift, complaining of a smear campaign and asking for the archbishop's judgement of his views. Whitgift rebuked the heads of house for peremptory action, and exceeding their powers. He agreed with Barrett on reprobation, and thought the loss of justifying grace and faith debatable. Thus encouraged, Barrett revoked his recantation, which caused a renewed Cambridge outcry. Whitgift responded by preparing a questionnaire on which a panel of the university consistory court examined him, and urged the members to be satisfied if they were not seeking his overthrow and destruction.

As this failed to end the controversy, Whitgift summoned two Cambridge heads of house and Barrett to confer, and the latter made concessions, appearing more penitent. Though Whitgift allowed him to draw up a recantation in his own words, apparently he never read it publicly. The controversy led Whitgift to draw up the Lambeth articles of that year. Although intended as a private document, it stimulated discussion on the issues of pre-destination, free will, and the nature of grace. The Calvinist dons were right in thinking Barrett had 'kindled a fire like to grow to the disturbance of the whole church' (*Salisbury MSS*, 268).

Barrett remained at Cambridge until 1597. Then the ecclesiastical commissioners evidently suspected him of having become a Roman Catholic and perhaps planning to become a seminarist. He was ordered to give £100 surety against going abroad without licence; otherwise he would be put in custody. He chose to flee. Abroad, as a Roman Catholic, he may be the William Barret, Englishman, who in the course of his travels was lent books by a Louvain priest and the Franciscans for the writing of *Jus regis* (1612). This volume, dedicated to Louis XIII of France and available there and in England, argued that royal power is conferred by God alone, assisted, where a ruler is lacking, by the nobles and commons. Rulers hold power by an inalienable birthright, and popes have no power to depose them. Ecclesiastics, including the pope, are bound to civil obedience to kings. The pope has no secular power: Gregory VII initiated the claim to it, which has no basis in antiquity nor by authority of the church councils. This is clearly a contribution to the Roman Catholic debate on the extent of papal power, especially over power to depose, as relevant to England in the wake of the Gunpowder Plot as to France after the assassination of Henri IV. It displays a willingness to challenge the theological *status quo* similar to Barrett's stance at Cambridge, and his apologies for not being able to annotate it properly owing to his travels have a donnish note. Though the book purports to have been printed in Basel, its provenance is thought to be England, where Barrett lived as a layman after his continental sojourn. The views expressed in *Jus regis* were politically harmless, and may explain his return.

He may also have been the William Barret who edited and published an edition of the Jesuit Robert Southwell's *St Peters Complainte, Mary Magdal Teares, with other Workes* in London in 1620. This progresses from devotional poems acceptable to protestants at the beginning to *Short Rules of the Good Life* at the end, suggesting a somewhat furtive introduction of more Roman Catholic material. He was still alive in 1630, but the date of his death is unknown; he may have written *The Fables of Aesop with his Whole Life* (1639) in verse.   ELIZABETH ALLEN

Sources H. C. Porter, *Reformation and reaction in Tudor Cambridge* (1958), 345–62 · Venn, *Alum. Cant.* · N. Tyacke, *Anti-Calvinists: the rise of English Arminianism, c.1590–1640* (1987), 29–30 · T. Fuller and J. Nichols, *The history of the University of Cambridge, and of Waltham Abbey*, new edn (1840), 209–11 · C. H. Cooper, *Annals of Cambridge*, 2 (1843), 567–8 · *DNB* · J. Venn and others, eds., *Biographical history of Gonville and Caius College*, 1: 1349–1713 (1897), 145 · *Calendar of the manuscripts of the most hon. the marquis of Salisbury*, 5, HMC (1894), 268 · P. Lake, *Moderate puritans and the Elizabethan church* (1982), 201–18

Barrett, William (1727?–1789), surgeon and antiquary, was born at Notton in the parish of Lacock, Wiltshire, where he was baptized on 6 June 1729. Little is known of his parents except that they died while he was a child; his brother, Anthony Barrett, was still living at Notton in

1787. William Barrett inherited sufficient money from his parents to enable his guardians to send him to Winchester College. There he formed a close friendship with J. Mayo Tandy, the son of a wealthy sugar refiner from Bristol. Barrett spent most of his holidays in Bristol with the Tandy family and subsequently married his friend's sister, Maria.

In 1744 Barrett was apprenticed to a well-known apothecary and barber–surgeon named T. Rosewell, who had a shop in All Saints' Lane, Bristol. Soon after completing his apprenticeship Barrett married Maria Tandy (1730/31–1763); the marriage produced a son, William Tandy Barrett (b. 1758), and four daughters. Maria Barrett died on 8 May 1763, aged thirty-two, and was buried at St Mary Redcliffe, where a memorial was erected with a long Latin verse composed by her husband, praising her virtues. William Tandy Barrett was enrolled at Wadham College, Oxford, in 1776, and graduated BA in 1779. Soon afterwards he was ordained in the Church of England.

Barrett spent the whole of his medical career in Bristol. He practised as a surgeon and man-midwife, first from a house in Wine Street and later from his own house on St Augustine's Back. In 1755 he gained his certificate as a surgeon from the Company of Surgeons and in the same year he applied unsuccessfully for the post of surgeon to the Bristol Infirmary. He was, however, appointed surgeon to St Peter's Hospital, a workhouse for the poor of Bristol. His practice in the city evidently prospered, and he treated the families of some of the leading merchants as well as the Smyth family of Ashton Court. By the end of his career he had acquired various properties in Bristol, including his house on St Augustine's Back, and houses in Stokes Croft. He also purchased the advowson of High Ham in Somerset, where his son became rector.

Early in his career Barrett became interested in the antiquities of Bristol and began to collect materials for a history of the city. No history of Bristol existed, and Barrett determined to remedy this defect, spending a great deal of his time on the project. As early as 1758, when at the age of thirty-one his portrait was painted by John Rymsdick, he is described as 'William Barrett, surgeon and author of the History and Antiquities of Bristol'. In 1760 he applied to the mayor and corporation of Bristol for permission to examine their records. Although he was initially denied, his increasing reputation as a physician and surgeon soon enabled him to gain access to the city's store of historic documents. His position as a respected medical practitioner also gave him entry to the houses of many of the wealthy and most influential Bristol families, and access to their records. He was therefore able to amass a large collection of deeds and other historic documents; he also made use of the work of earlier antiquaries.

Barrett corresponded with numerous antiquaries and in 1775 was elected a fellow of the Society of Antiquaries. His thorough search for records of Bristol and his assiduous collection of material might have produced a valuable history of the city. Unfortunately he was completely duped by the historical fabrications of the young Thomas Chatterton (1752–1770). On the basis of a few genuine deeds, accounts, and other medieval records that he had acquired from St Mary Redcliffe, Chatterton persuaded Barrett to accept a mass of totally spurious 'evidence'. This included accounts of Bristol Castle, the topography of the city, the affairs of the fifteenth-century merchant William Canynges, and details of all the parish churches, including a totally fictitious church of St Andrew. Much of this material was supposedly based on the writings of an eleventh-century monk, Turgot, and a fifteenth-century priest, Thomas Rowley. In spite of initial misgivings about the authenticity of the material supplied by Chatterton, Barrett was convinced that he had found a hitherto unknown source for Bristol's history. Chatterton's elaborate hoax was therefore eagerly accepted by Barrett and the material incorporated into his *History*.

Barrett was not alone in his gullible acceptance of Chatterton's fabrications. Others who were misled and encouraged Barrett included Jeremiah Milles, dean of Exeter and president of the Society of Antiquaries; Robert Glynn, a physician and fellow of King's College, Cambridge; Andrew Coltée Ducarel, of Doctors' Commons; and Jacob Bryant, another prominent antiquary. Ranged against them in the fierce controversy over Chatterton's writings were numerous other scholars and critics. These included Horace Walpole and Samuel Johnson, both of whom had quickly come to realize that Chatterton's alleged medieval documents were in fact complete fiction. Barrett and his friends refused to believe that a lowly, young solicitor's clerk could have had either the incentive or the invention to have sustained such a lengthy deception. In 1772 Barrett wrote to Ducarel of his pleasure at the new information that Chatterton had produced: 'No one surely ever had such good fortune as myself in procuring manuscripts and ancient deeds to help me in investigating the history and antiquities of this city' (*GM*, 56.544).

By 1771–2 Barrett had made considerable progress with his research, and advertisements to announce imminent publication of the history were placed in *Farley's Bristol Journal*. But the work was still not complete when Barrett, troubled by gout, retired to his house at Wraxall with his three unmarried daughters. He had gathered an impressive list of subscribers for the book, and in his will written in September 1787 he asked his son and son-in-law to transcribe the book and oversee its publication. During the following year, encouraged by Dr Robert Glynn, he finally completed the work himself, and his *History and Antiquities of Bristol* was published in April 1789.

The work of just over 700 quarto pages was dedicated to the mayor, aldermen, and council of Bristol. Collection of the material had taken more than thirty years, and the book was well produced and illustrated. Barrett states on the title-page that it was compiled from 'original records and authentic manuscripts in public offices and private hands', and it does contain important material drawn from local records. But Barrett rarely quotes his authorities and gives few references for the sources he used. He does, however, provide useful information about churches, monuments, and secular buildings in the city. He writes vividly about the contemporary life of the city, the crowded shipping, and the docks, streets, and lanes. He also includes lively descriptions of the various weekly markets for fish, butter, poultry, corn, flour, fruit, and wool, as well as of cattle and sheep sent from Wales or arriving in 'trows' or barges from counties along the Severn. Unfortunately throughout the book he included the mass of erroneous material that he had received from Chatterton. This included the alleged work of the Saxon Turgot, which was supposed to have been translated by Rowley. Also included are descriptions, poems, plays, and plans from Rowley, and even a highly dubious specimen of Rowley's supposed handwriting. The potentially useful material in the *History* is therefore submerged beneath the spurious historical material that Barrett accepted from Chatterton. Barrett was aware of the misgivings that many people felt concerning Chatterton and his work. In his introduction he wrote:

> As to these manuscripts of Rowley, now first published; whatever judgement be formed about them, they are here faithfully transcribed, that by producing all the evidence the judicious reader may be enabled better to form his opinion concerning that controversy.   (Barrett, *History*, vii)

In spite of its many failings Barrett's work was the first complete history of Bristol to be published. His much younger friend Samuel Seyer, who in 1821–3 published a far more scholarly history of the city, paid tribute to Barrett's work and inspiration while regretting the way in which Barrett had been duped by Chatterton. Seyer called his work *Memoirs, Historical and Topographical, of Bristol* to avoid any conflict with Barrett's title. Soon after its publication Barrett's *History* was the subject of a long review by Richard Gough in the *Gentleman's Magazine*. Gough mercilessly attacked the numerous inaccuracies and historical fabrications that the book contained. He pointed to the absence of precise references to sources, to the fallacious etymology, the plans 'too fanciful, not to say absurd, to be admitted', and the lack of an index. Above all he poured scorn on the 'counterfeit dramatic compositions' derived from Chatterton, 'sufficient to blast the reputation of Rowlie as an original writer and the credit of Chatterton as an honest man' (*GM*, 59.921–4).

Barrett was already unwell, and this devastating critique of his life's work in such a prestigious publication must have been a dreadful blow. He died shortly afterwards, at the rectory in High Ham, Somerset, on 13 October 1789, while visiting his son, and was buried at High Ham.   J. H. BETTEY

Sources *GM*, 1st ser., 56 (1786), 361, 460–64, 544, 580; 59 (1789), 921–4, 1052, 1081–5 · W. Barrett, *History and antiquities of the city of Bristol* (1789) · will, PRO, PROB 11/1188/58 · W. Barrett, correspondence with the Smyth family of Ashton Court, 1765–88, Bristol RO, AC/F9/4; AC/C 118; 15266, 38459 (1), 04677 · G. Pryce, *History of Bristol* (1861), 362–3 · Foster, *Alum. Oxon.*, 1715–1886, 1.65 · W. Barrett, letter, Bristol Reference Library, Braikenridge collection, V, 1/17 · E. H. W. Meyerstein, *A life of Thomas Chatterton* (1930) · G. Munro Smith, *A history of the Bristol Royal Infirmary* (1917) · S. Seyer, *Memoirs historical and topographical of Bristol*, 2 vols. (1821–3) · parish register, Lacock, 6 June 1729 [baptism] · *DNB*

Archives BL, notes and corresp., Add. MS 5766 | Bristol RO, letters to Smyth family, incl. some relating to antiquarian subjects **Likenesses** W. Walker, engraving, 1758 (after J. Rymsdick, 1758), Bristol City Museum and Art Gallery; repro. in Barrett, *History*, frontispiece · W. Walker, stipple (after J. Rymsdick), NPG **Wealth at death** clearly well-to-do: will, PRO, PROB 11/1188/58

Barrett, Sir William Fletcher (1844–1925), physicist and psychical researcher, was born in Jamaica on 10 February 1844, the son of a Congregational minister, the Revd William Garland Barrett (1812–1865), missionary for the London Missionary Society, and his wife, Martha Barrett, *née* Fletcher (1811?–1893). His sister was the social reformer Rosa Mary *Barrett. The family returned to England in 1848 and in 1855 went to Manchester, where William attended Old Trafford grammar school. Subsequently he took classes in chemistry and physics at the Royal College of Chemistry, London. In 1863 he became assistant to John Tyndall at the Royal Institution, where he met and was much influenced by Michael Faraday. He was then successively science master at the International College, London (1867–9), lecturer on physics at the Royal School of Naval Architecture (1869–73), and professor of physics at the Royal College of Science, Dublin (1873–1910). An excellent lecturer at both a professional and a popular level, he fulfilled his duties as professor of physics with great conscientiousness.

Though not in the vanguard of physical research, Barrett was none the less a highly effective practical physicist and was especially known for two lines of research. The first was his early work on 'sensitive flames' and their uses in acoustic demonstrations. The second was a long line of studies of the electrical, magnetic, and thermal properties of metals, particularly iron and iron alloys. They included pioneering experiments (from 1873 onwards) on recalescence and on the discovery of the shortening of nickel through magnetization (1882); and a series of investigations (1896–1902), with W. Brown and R. A. Hadfield, of the electrical and magnetic behaviour of a large number of iron alloys. These led to the discovery of a silicon–iron alloy, later known under the trade name Stalloy, with high magnetic permeability and low hysteresis, which proved of great value in the construction of parts of electrical machinery subject to alternating magnetic fields, and of an iron–nickel alloy (Permalloy) with similar properties. Barrett was elected a fellow of the Royal Society of London in 1899 (he was also a fellow of the Royal Society of Edinburgh and the Royal Dublin Society) and was knighted in 1912.

In later years, following signs of incipient cataracts in his own eyes, Barrett became interested in various problems in the physics of vision. In 1905–8 he published the results of his experiments with a simple device of his own invention, the 'entoptiscope', which enabled him to work out the nature, location, and size of the causative agents within the eye of various visual phenomena, for example *muscae volitantes* ('floaters'), and Purkinje figures (the shadows of retinal blood vessels).

It is, however, for his leading part in the foundation of the Society for Psychical Research (SPR) that Barrett is now principally remembered. His interest in such matters arose from experiences with mesmerism dating back to the 1860s. He believed himself to have observed instances of thought transference and of 'community of sensation'; in the 1870s he was considerably impressed by rappings and object movements which he witnessed in good light with two unpaid mediums and he was also interested in a poltergeist which he investigated. In September 1876 he gave before the anthropological section of the British Association for the Advancement of Science a paper describing some of his experiences. It aroused a good deal of controversy, but he continued to collect materials and to experiment. On 7 July 1881 he published in *Nature* a preliminary account of his experiments on thought transference. Later that year, following a talk with E. Dawson Rogers, a prominent spiritualist, he took up the latter's suggestion that leading scientists and scholars might be drawn into a society for the scientific investigation of psychic phenomena. Between them they assembled a conference of interested persons in London on 5 and 6 January 1882 and the SPR was founded.

For the first year or two Barrett played a central role in the SPR's activities, and in 1884 he was instrumental in founding a similar society in the United States. Thereafter his involvement diminished, though he was a regular contributor of articles and case reports to the SPR's publications, and was president in 1904. He was sporadically at odds with the Cambridge group, centring on Henry Sidgwick, who largely ran the society and set its tone: Barrett was thought to be overly eager and too prone to accept evidence without sufficient scrutiny, and was often impatient with the group's slow and cautious approach. Friction was particularly acute over the case of the Creery sisters, young daughters of a Derbyshire clergyman, with whom Barrett had conducted ostensibly successful experiments in thought transference in 1881. Further successful experiments followed the foundation of the SPR, but the success rate declined, and in 1887 the two sisters were caught using a rather crude code, and the Sidgwick group responded by cutting the Creerys out of their case for telepathy (as it was now called). Barrett, who regarded his work with the Creerys as part of his justification for claiming to be the 'discoverer' of telepathy, was deeply displeased.

Barrett's most substantial contributions to psychical research were two book-length articles on water divining, published in the *Proceedings* of the SPR in 1897 and 1900. These contain an abundance of historical and anecdotal material, and various reports of experiments, including Barrett's own (the experiments are tests of individual dowsers). Barrett concludes that the movement of the divining rod is an involuntary muscular action instigated by subconscious knowledge, sometimes paranormally acquired, of the location of underground water.

Barrett was much influenced by F. W. H. Myers's theory of the 'subliminal self', which pervades his brief but very successful *Psychical Research* (1912). This work, though by no means deficient in critical spirit, makes it clear that recent developments—especially the 'cross-correspondences' between the automatic writings of different mediums—had completely convinced him of human survival of bodily death. Indeed, as can be seen from his larger and more speculative *On the Threshold of the Unseen* (1917), telepathy had become in his view not just a hidden or subliminal means of communication between incarnate minds, or even between incarnate and discarnate minds, but a sign of the underlying unity of all minds, and of all minds with the supreme mind or 'world-soul'. Although handicapped in later years by heart problems and increasing deafness, Barrett remained very active in psychical research until literally the day of his death. Three books were published posthumously: a large volume entitled *The Divining-Rod* (1926), co-authored by Theodore Besterman; *The Religion of Health* (1925), a sympathetic but not uncritical study of Christian Science; and a small, unfinished, but in its way pioneering work, *Death-Bed Visions* (1926).

Photographs of Barrett show a rather frail-looking individual whose long, thin face is made to seem longer and thinner by his pointed beard. He was a lively if probing conversationalist, with a wide curiosity and constant flow of ideas that some found inspiring and others rather taxing. Some hinted that he was prone to claim overmuch credit for discoveries or initiatives that were not wholly his, but others remarked on the transparent honesty and simplicity of a man who was never deterred by ridicule and opprobrium from publicly arguing for his beliefs. In private life Barrett was kind and courteous and liked to tell humorous stories. He had strong family ties—his sister Rosa [see Barrett, Rosa Mary] kept house for him for many years. In 1916 he married Dr Florence Elizabeth Willey (1867?–1945), a distinguished gynaecologist twenty-three years his junior, daughter of Benjamin Perry, and moved from Ireland to London to join her. Community of interests and mutual sympathy made this unusual marriage exceedingly happy. Barrett died suddenly of heart failure on 26 May 1925 at his home, 31 Devonshire Place, London, and was buried at Long Cross near Chertsey, Surrey, four days later.   ALAN GAULD

Sources J. Oppenheim, *The other world: spiritualism and psychical research in England, 1850–1914* (1985), 355–71 · W. F. Barrett, 'Some reminiscences of fifty years' psychical research', *Proceedings of the Society for Psychical Research*, 34 (1923–4), 275–97 · O. Lodge, 'Sir William Fletcher Barrett', *Nature*, 115 (1925), 880–81 · E. M. Sidgwick, 'In memory of Sir William Fletcher Barrett, FRS', *Proceedings of the Society for Psychical Research*, 35 (1924–5), 413–18 · R. A. Hadfield, *Journal of the Institution of Electrical Engineers*, 63 (1925), 1148–9 · *The Times* (28 May 1925) · D. Gow, 'The decease of Sir William Barrett, FRS', *Light*, 45 (1925), 268 · O. Lodge, A. C. Doyle, and E. Feilding, 'Tributes and appreciations', *Light*, 45 (1925), 280 · R. M. Barrett, letter, *Nature*, 116 (1925), 15 · R. J. Campbell, Foreword, *Personality survives death*, ed. F. E. Barrett (1937) · F. Nicol, 'The founders of the SPR', *Proceedings of the Society for Psychical Research*, 55 (1966–72), 341–67, esp. 341–7 · *WWW · WW*

Archives RS, corresp. and papers | CUL, letters to Sir George Stokes · CUL, Society for Psychical Research, corresp. with Sir Oliver Lodge · CUL, SPR archives · University of British Columbia, Woodward Biomedical Library, corresp. and papers

Likenesses photograph, Society for Psychical Research, London · photograph, College of Psychic Studies, London
Wealth at death £1771: *The Times* (1/8/1925)

Barrett, Wilson [*real name* William Henry Barrett] (1846–1904), actor and playwright, was born on 18 February 1846 at Manor House Farm, Chelmsford, Essex, the second child and eldest son of George Barrett, a farmer, and his wife, Charlotte Mary, *née* Wood. The failure of his father as a farmer drove the family in 1857 to London, where Barrett worked first as a labourer in a corn exchange and then with a firm of printers and engravers. He began his professional stage career as a 'general utility' actor at the Theatre Royal, Halifax, in 1864. After a series of temporary engagements at Nottingham and Liverpool he joined the company in Aberdeen, where he met Caroline Heath (1835–1887). She was an experienced performer and, despite her family's objections to the fact that she was more than ten years older than Barrett, they were married on 21 July 1866.

Early career The period to 1879 was marked by extended provincial engagements with occasional London visits. Barrett formed his own company in 1870 and began management of the Theatre Royal, Halifax, in 1869 and the Theatre Royal, Hull, in 1877. His first professional London engagement was at the Surrey, playing Tom Robinson in Charles Reade's *It's Never too Late to Mend* (26 June 1867); while employed at Drury Lane in 1868 he changed his forename to Wilson. He then formed his own combination company, which included his brothers George and Robert and his sister Mary, and which by 1875 comprised twenty-five actors touring a repertory of about twenty plays throughout northern England. Barrett was later to claim that he was the first manager to make the combination system a permanent fixture in England (*The Era*, 28 Aug 1886). He took the lease of the Leeds Amphitheatre in 1874, and opened in W. G. Wills's version of *Jane Shore* on 8 March 1875, when his wife played Jane and he himself took the part of Henry Shore. It was their first enduring success. After the theatre burnt down, destroying his entire stock of costumes and sets, Barrett was asked to advise on the building of a new theatre in Leeds. The Grand opened under his management on 16 November 1878, and he retained it for the next sixteen years.

While the Barretts were performing at the Princess's Theatre (June 1878–May 1879), Barrett decided to go into London management for the first time. He took over the Court Theatre, and opened with an adaptation of Sardou's *Fernande* on 10 October 1879; Henry Arthur Jones's first London play, *A Clerical Error*, was added to the programme on 13 October. Caroline Heath, however, returned to their home in Leeds to recuperate from a nervous breakdown, the symptoms of which had already been evident while she was on tour in 1877.

Barrett's tenancy of the Court introduced Helena Modjeska to the English stage in Mortimer's adaptation of *The Lady of the Camellias*, renamed *Heartsease* (1 May 1880). He demonstrated an acute awareness of the value of publicity by using Modjeska's aristocratic contacts. In 1881 he

Wilson Barrett (1846–1904), by W. & D. Downey, pubd 1891

produced the first in his career of three stagings of Shakespeare: *Romeo and Juliet*, with Modjeska as Juliet, Johnston Forbes-Robertson as Romeo, and himself as Mercutio (26 March). At the same time he started his management of a series of companies which toured his successes, while he settled in London at 21 North Bank, St John's Wood. Though critically less than successful, Barrett's production of W. G. Wills's sombre *Juana*, again with Modjeska (7 May 1881), began his collaboration with E. W. Godwin as his archaeological stage adviser.

Lessee of the Princess's Theatre Barrett decided to lease the ailing Princess's in 1881 and began his management with Comyns Carr's adaptation of Meilhac and Halevy's *Frou-Frou*, his last production with Modjeska (4 June). He augmented his company with Mary Eastlake, E. S. Willard, and his own brother George, and produced his first unqualified success, G. R. Sims's *Lights o' London* (10 September 1881). The play's combination of contemporary issues, detailed realism in staging (including supernumeraries drawn from among actual costermongers and street hawkers), and the manipulation of large crowd scenes doubtless influenced by the theatre practices of the Meiningen company, all contained within a populist melodramatic framework, became Barrett's house style for the remainder of his career. This was followed by a Dickensian crime drama, *The Romany Rye*, adapted by Sims from the novel by George Borrow (10 June 1882). Looking for a vehicle to crystallize his emerging artistic vision, Barrett collaborated with Henry Arthur Jones and Henry Herman on *The Silver King* (16 November 1882). The role of Wilfred Denver enabled him to develop a performance combining intense pathos, inner strength, and saintliness, which coloured most of his later roles. Critics unanimously proclaimed that Barrett had invested the melodramatic form with new meaning, which received even Matthew Arnold's approval (*Pall Mall Gazette*, 6 Dec 1882). The rights to the play were sold to American and Australian managers and Barrett made a profit of nearly £10,000.

Barrett's last great financial success at the Princess's came with Wills and Herman's *Claudian*, which was assisted by Godwin's archaeological reconstruction of Byzantium (6 December 1883). The scenery was much praised by John Ruskin, and the sensational act II earthquake scene made it a popular hit. There were those, however, who reacted against the play's religiosity and questioned the basis of Barrett's popularity. In 1883 Barrett's broker in Leeds absconded with the profits he had invested so that by the end of 1884 Barrett owed an accumulated debt of £32,000. Although he retained the Princess's until 1886, none of his remaining productions proved financially viable. He worked with Jones on three further plays: *Chatterton* (22 May 1884), *Hoodman Blind* (18 August 1885), and *Lord Harry* (18 February 1886), and with Sydney Grundy on a verse tragedy, *Clito* (1 May 1886). His most interesting production in the period, however, was of *Hamlet* (16 October 1884). Barrett seems to have attempted deliberately to flout prevailing performance orthodoxy by rejecting the reflective melancholy so much identified with Irving. Instead, audiences were challenged by an energetically youthful Hamlet who delivered his lines as though the play were a middle-class melodrama. The critical reaction was polarized, and there is evidence to suggest the beginnings of a deliberate campaign by critics with vested theatrical interests to discredit him. Pamphlets were circulated suggesting that Barrett was consciously manoeuvring to displace Irving, and ill feeling was exacerbated by public controversy about the exact extent to which Barrett could claim authorial contribution to *The Silver King* (Thomas, 85–6). The bad press and declining attendances were enough to have Barrett end his lease of the Princess's (23 July 1886). He had already mortgaged the rights to his plays and he now negotiated with his creditors for a licence to continue operating without being declared bankrupt. To recoup his losses, a preoccupation which remained with him for the next ten years, Barrett left with his company on his first visit to America on 21 September 1886, and opened at the Star Theatre, New York, with *Claudian* (11 October). A tour which included Boston, Chicago, Washington, and Philadelphia ended profitably, and the company returned to England in May 1887. Two months later Caroline Heath, who had never returned to the stage, died of a brain haemorrhage in London.

Career doldrums and triumph From December 1887 until mid-May 1888 Barrett managed the Globe Theatre, and his successes in revivals, particularly *The Lady of Lyons* (22 February 1888), and his collaborative work with Sims on *The Golden Ladder* (22 December 1887) enabled him to start repaying his creditors. Once again he returned to the Princess's, where he began work with Hall Caine on adapting *The Deemster*, renamed *Ben-my-chree* (17 May 1888). It was his only real success, and he added it to his repertory on his second American tour, which began in Boston on 14 October 1889, and this time took in St Louis and San Francisco. The costs of the company's transport and the general economic depression, however, exhausted his funds and Barrett returned to England in August 1890.

Over the next five years Barrett battled to retain his reputation both in London and in the provinces and to repay his creditors by further trips to America. These included a third tour, embracing Canada for the first time, from October 1892 to April 1893 and a fourth, which took in the southern states, including Texas, from November 1893 to June 1894. These years saw Barrett dogged by family tragedy: his daughters Ellen and Katherine died in 1892 and 1893 and his brothers Robert and George in 1893 and 1894 respectively. There were few successes by way of compensation. He relied principally on revivals, and added old triumphs of W. C. Macready such as Sheridan Knowles's *Virginius* to his stock. Even his staunchest admirers felt that his acting was showing 'mannered and mechanical methods' (*The Theatre*, December 1891). This was redressed somewhat by his performances as Othello at the Court Theatre, Liverpool (22 October 1891), and as Pete Quilliam in his own version of Hall Caine's *The Manxman* at Leeds (22 August 1894). But his absences on extended tours made his management of the theatres at Hull and Leeds untenable and he was forced to relinquish them both, in 1891 and 1894.

The turning point at this stage of Barrett's career came during his fifth American tour (November 1894–July 1895), with the opening at the Grand Opera House, St Louis, of his own *The Sign of the Cross* (27 March 1895). After a further tryout in Leeds (26 August 1895) it was staged at the Lyric (4 January 1896) and played for 435 performances, until 30 January 1897. The enormous popular success of the play enabled Barrett to pay off all his debts. However, it was his last major achievement.

The play itself aroused considerable critical hostility. Critics such as Shaw and William Archer saw it as a society drama clothed in a meretricious form of Christianity, while humanists, including G. W. Foote, found it prurient. On the other hand, religious journals took the play's message of conversion at face value, and Barrett's astute marketing ensured that audiences totally unfamiliar with theatregoing attended the production with the warm support of their clergy. Once again Barrett was able to send out touring companies to perform his own plays, and London audiences saw him as Virginius and Othello. Despite the antagonism of Archer and Shaw towards *The Sign of the Cross*, both men admired his revised version of *The Manxman*, which opened at the Lyric on 16 November 1896, and which Shaw described as 'a serious modern play' (*Saturday Review*, 5 Dec 1896).

There was much discussion about actors who might be considered for a knighthood during the diamond jubilee year, and Barrett's name was raised. In the event he was passed over. In December 1897 he began his first tour of Australia, and played his established repertory in Sydney, Melbourne, and Adelaide. He returned to England in July 1898 and after further provincial touring took over the management of Irving's Lyceum Theatre. Neither an original play, *Man and his Makers*, written with L. N. Parker (7 October 1899), nor revivals of *Hamlet* and *Othello* were sufficient to warrant extending his term beyond December. Moreover, declining audiences in the provinces suggested that his plays were suffering from overexposure.

Barrett went on his second Australian tour, beginning in August 1901, with Lillah McCarthy as his leading lady. This time he visited New Zealand and, on his return journey, South Africa, and arrived home in August 1902. Once again he alternated between the provinces and occasional London appearances. He tried out *The Christian King*, a sprawling epic about Alfred and the coming of Christianity to England, at the Prince's Theatre, Bristol (6 November 1902), before playing it at the Adelphi (18 December 1902). His last original play, *Lucky Durham*, opened at the Shakespeare Theatre, Liverpool (9 January 1904), and it was there that he gave his final performance, as Wilfred Denver. Although he had signed a lease for the Comedy Theatre in London on 15 June, he fell ill and was taken to a nursing home at 45 Devonshire Street, where he died from complications arising after a cancer operation, on 22 July 1904. He was buried at Hampstead cemetery on 25 July, leaving assets valued at more than £30,000.

Assessment Barrett's theatrical values were uncompromisingly Victorian. As such he looked back: his performances were modelled on those of Macready and his productions on the picturesque realizations of antiquity which both Macready and Charles Kean had pioneered. At the same time he saw his own role as pleasing and educating a popular audience. His personal attributes of a fine physique and voice made him an attractive stage personality, although his vanity inclined him to affectations which diminished his very considerable talents. His performances in Shakespeare's plays, for example, suggested a radically different approach to their interpretation. He chose, however, to devote his energies to revitalizing melodrama, a genre increasingly denigrated by his contemporaries. Conservative critics such as Clement Scott and William Winter admired Barrett's championing of traditional theatrical verities; Archer, Arthur Walkley, and Beerbohm were affronted by his failure to come to terms with the 'new drama' or were outraged particularly by what they took to be his conscious identification with his religious roles.

Nevertheless Barrett was an astute manager and entrepreneur who appreciated the value of publicity, which many of his fellow managers saw as vulgar and self-aggrandizing. He was devoted to the fellow actors in his companies, assisting them with their stagecraft and caring for their welfare with unflagging paternalism just as he diligently developed the dramatic talents of such writers as Jones and Caine. Though he may have been despised and rejected by many critics, his religious plays undoubtedly attracted new audiences to the theatre and provided enduring subject matter for the cinema.

VICTOR EMELJANOW

Sources DNB · *The Times* (23 July 1904) · *Daily Telegraph* (23 July 1904) · J. Thomas, *The art of the actor-manager: Wilson Barrett and the Victorian theatre* (1984) · F. W. Barrett, 'And give me yesterday', 1966 · 'Wilson Barrett's romantic career', *The Era* (11 Oct 1884), 7 · J. Coleman, 'Wilson Barrett and his work', *Longmans Magazine*, 7 (1885), 63–82 · A. Brereton, 'Wilson Barrett', *The Theatre*, 4th ser., 1 (1883), 33–41 · G. R. Sims, *My life* (1917) · L. McCarthy, *Myself and friends* (1933) · A. Goddard, *Players of the period* (1891) · D. Mayer, *Playing out the empire: Ben-Hur and other toga plays and films, 1883–1908: a critical anthology* (1994)
Archives GL · Ransom HRC | Theatre Museum, London, letters to the Lord Chamberlain's licensee · U. Leeds, Brotherton L., letters to Henry Arthur Jones
Likenesses M. Beerbohm, caricature, 1896, Indiana University, Bloomington, Indiana, Lilly Library · Barraud, photograph, photogravure (as Othello), NPG · W. & D. Downey, photograph, NPG; repro. in W. Downey and D. Downey, *The cabinet portrait gallery*, 2 (1891) [*see illus.*] · S. Hall, print, chromolithograph (as Wilfred Denver in *The Silver King*), NPG · photographs, Ransom HRC · photographs, priv. loc.
Wealth at death £30,862 16s. 9d.: probate, 24 Aug 1904, CGPLA Eng. & Wales

Sir James Matthew Barrie, baronet (1860–1937), by George Charles Beresford, 1902

Barrie, Sir James Matthew, baronet (1860–1937), playwright and novelist, was born in a small house in The Tenements, Brechin Road, Kirriemuir, Forfarshire, on 9 May 1860, the ninth child and third and youngest son of David Barrie (1814–1902), a handloom weaver in Kirriemuir, and his wife, Margaret (1820–1895), daughter of Alexander Ogilvy, a stonemason.

Early years and education, 1860–1884 The Barrie family had to endure not only poverty but a number of domestic tragedies, including the early death of two daughters. These events occurred before James was born, however. The first tragedy to involve him personally was the death in a skating accident of his thirteen-year-old brother David. In his autobiographical novel, *Margaret Ogilvy* (1896), Barrie tried to recapture his own childhood memories of this incident, especially as it affected his mother.

When David died in 1867 James was still at a local school. But a more ambitious academic route was planned for him. Taking advantage of the democratic Scottish university entrance system, Barrie's parents sent his eldest brother, Alexander, to Aberdeen University. Having graduated with honours in classics Alexander became a teacher at Glasgow Academy. James followed him as a pupil and studied there from 1868 until February 1871, when he transferred to Forfar Academy. When Alexander became one of the first school inspectors his younger brother again followed him, this time to Dumfries Academy. He later recorded in *The Greenwood Hat* (1930) that the years he spent there, from 1873 until 1878, were among the happiest of his life. The drama society in particular interested him, and for it he composed his first play, a melodrama in six scenes entitled *Bandalero the Bandit*.

Barrie was himself being prepared for higher education.

Edinburgh University was chosen, and he matriculated there in 1878. In *An Edinburgh Eleven* (1888) he paid tribute to the broad disciplinary base provided by this degree. His literary studies under Professor David Masson not only initiated a creative desire to imitate the dramatists of the English Renaissance; they also led Barrie to compose academic essays on Skelton ('The rector of Diss') and Nash for a projected academic work to be entitled *The Early Satirical Poetry of Great Britain*. In Professor Campbell Fraser's classes he studied one of the earliest psychology courses offered in Scotland. Fraser's views on perception and the fragility of personal identity had a lasting influence on a young man conscious of the many roles that he played in his own life. In an intensely competitive system Barrie graduated with an ordinary MA, in 1882.

It was journalism rather than academe that first welcomed Barrie. While still an undergraduate he had written articles for the *Edinburgh Courant*. An unexpected opportunity to become leader-writer at the *Nottingham Journal* then opened up, and he went south in January 1883. In Nottingham he learned techniques of writing and note-taking that remained with him for the rest of his life. His position also implied tackling a wide range of topics, from the Irish question to Darwinism. As Barrie also contributed fiction and reviews to the paper it is surprising that he found time to compose material for London magazines as well. Some of these were published, and so when the *Nottingham Journal* folded, in October 1884, he considered moving to the capital as a freelance writer. He wrote for advice to Frederick Greenwood, editor of the *St James's Gazette*, as he had shown particular interest in his 'Scotch' stories. When Greenwood sternly warned him against coming his young correspondent reacted by catching a train to London.

Literary apprenticeship, 1885–1900 Barrie arrived in the capital on 28 March 1885 and soon justified the bold move he had made. In the succeeding five years he published six books while contributing articles and reviews to fifteen major journals. The most immediately successful of these books were the story-collections *Auld Licht Idylls* (1888) and *A Window in Thrums* (1889). These were based largely on his mother's reminiscences of Kirriemuir. None the less the narrator clearly warns his readers not to interpret either village or characters realistically like 'a dull historian' (J. M. Barrie, *Auld Licht Idylls*, 10), but imaginatively. Seen in those terms Thrums represents those reinvented dreams of their rural past that its exiled inhabitants use to strengthen their identity in urban exile after the industrial revolution.

After the comparatively solitary life that he had led in Nottingham Barrie found London more congenial. The friends that he did make—notably Thomas Gilmour, secretary to Lord Rosebery, and Alexander Riach, a journalist on the *Daily Telegraph*—soon discovered their own lives appearing, lightly disguised, in their companion's other early prose works. For example the hero of *Better Dead* (1887) is called Riach, and Lord Rosebery becomes one of the leading figures that he considers killing in its highly melodramatic plot. Barrie's own romantic and sexual problems also figure in these works. Less than 5 feet tall, he was acutely conscious that women overlooked him in more ways than one. In his earliest fiction unprepossessing artisan writer-heroes recur with some regularity and have more sexual success than their creator had in the days when he shared a houseboat with Gilmour and the novelist Henry Marriott Watson. As outsider he had watched their romances unfold; in *When a Man's Single* (1888) Barrie turned the fictional tables on them. In that novel it is his own *alter ego*, the rustic journalist Rob Angus, who wins the beautiful, talented, and affluent heroine.

The 1890s saw Barrie firmly established as a leading novelist. Old Kirriemuir was revived in *The Little Minister* (1891) and this was followed by three novels on the topic of the artist as young man: *Sentimental Tommy* (1896), *Margaret Ogilvy* (1896), and *Tommy and Grizel* (1900). These produced initial sales of over 225,000 copies in Britain and the United States. Yet with the exception of works on the Peter Pan theme—*Peter Pan in Kensington Gardens* (1906), *Peter and Wendy* (1911)—they were also the last novels that he wrote. Instead he turned to and persevered with drama, although a mixed reception had greeted his early experiments in that mode. While *Ibsen's Ghost* (1891) and *Walker, London* (1892) proved him capable of writing farces in one-act and three-act form respectively, his attempt at a problem play, *The Wedding Guest* (1900), had failed to move its audiences. Even his dramatization in 1897 of *The Little Minister* did not match the popularity of its prose source. But Barrie was now under the spell of the theatre, attracted by its glamour and the artistic challenge of adapting to its visual dimension.

Social and sporting interests relieved Barrie's heavy work schedule. His love of cricket led him to found his own club, the Allahakbarries, in 1887; this group of media stars, explorers, and dignitaries remained active until 1913. His habit of invading the families of married friends and inventing dramatic games for their children also

dates from this period. Before the children of Arthur and Sylvia Du Maurier famously became the 'co-authors' of *Peter Pan*, Margaret, the daughter of W. E. Henley, and Bevil, the son of Arthur Quiller Couch, had enjoyed that role.

Romantically, however, Barrie was less successful. Attracted throughout his life to independent women who had gained that freedom on the stage or through noble birth, he found his powers of invention of more limited use in this area. In 1891 the object of his infatuation was Mary Ansell (*b.* 1862), the ambitious actress daughter of a licensed grocer. He demanded a major part for her in *Walker, London*. Three years later, when Barrie's mother became ill, this actress–playwright alliance was still in force, and Mary accompanied Barrie to Kirriemuir. Their engagement and marriage at his parents' house in July of that year were somewhat subdued, as Barrie himself had also fallen ill with pneumonia. That physical problems existed for the couple can be indirectly deduced from Sentimental Tommy's self-absorbed, role-playing inability to 'think himself' into sexual love (J. M. Barrie, *Tommy and Grizel*, 168, 380), but proof was as yet withheld.

The middle period, 1901–1916 Between 1901 and 1904 Barrie produced three major plays, all of which followed the pattern of those Shakespearian romances that Masson placed at the apex of literary achievement. In 1902 *Quality Street* and *The Admirable Crichton* used that form to explore different kinds of social imprisonment. In the former Phoebe Throssel's gender and gentility, in the latter Crichton's social position prevent their full potential flourishing in hierarchical, paternalistic, Victorian England. Once the central issue has been defined these plays test it out imaginatively in their equivalent of Prospero's island in *The Tempest*. The ball scenes in *Quality Street* and the island in *Crichton* allow them fantastically to prove those powers for greatness that are doomed to waste unseen in early twentieth-century England.

While *Quality Street* ran for eighteen months and *The Admirable Crichton* for ten it was the third 'romance'—*Peter Pan* (1904)—that broke all previous theatrical records and proved Barrie's most enduring success. Testing out the age-old questions of origin in a child's 'Never land', this strange adult pantomime uses the allegorical method described in 'The rector of Diss' to link the simplest kind of sensual appeal to a mythic exploration of the issues recently highlighted by Darwin. If Barrie prided himself on counterpointing light and serious messages in his art he was also intent on pushing the resources of the theatre to their absolute limits. *Peter Pan* was his most ambitious attempt at each. It should be remembered that only his most enthusiastic friend, the American impresario Charles Frohman, was willing to take a chance on producing a spectacle that, in its original form demanded a cast of over fifty, with five major scene changes and almost every dangerous piece of theatrical business known. It was this strange work that became the high point of every Christmas in the London theatre for three decades.

The fact that its central character was a little boy unable to face the facts of adulthood at a time when Barrie's own sexual inadequacies came under public scrutiny adds a sadder twist to the plot of the author's life. When he wrote *Peter Pan* he had found another 'distant' woman to adore. Sylvia Du Maurier, now wife of Arthur Llewelyn Davies, was a talented society lady. She also had a young family for Barrie to captivate in his accustomed role of playmate and storyteller. In his dedication to *Peter Pan* in 1928 he suggested that the games he played with the Llewelyn Davies boys in his newly acquired Surrey property, Black Lake Cottage, were part of the work's creation process. While he was enjoying the fruits of his theatrical fame and finding excuses to invade the Du Maurier family Mary Ansell found herself deprived of both a professional career and her husband's attention. In 1907 she began an affair with the young actor Gilbert Cannan. When Barrie's gardener blurted out the truth to him, and Mary refused his appeals to end the liaison, divorce proceedings became inevitable. The undefended case, on grounds of adultery, that the playwright brought before the court on 13 October 1909 was fully reported. As his own failure to consummate the marriage was part of the evidence his impotence became common knowledge.

In the light of this Barrie's continued dramatic interest in different kinds of female power is understandable. His basic thesis, as expressed in the dedication to *Peter Pan*, is that woman has a complex Russian-doll type of mind, superior to its simple male equivalent. This is played out in Wendy's clever manipulating of Peter. Before this it had been malevolently established in *Becky Sharp* (1893) and had been benevolently matched, ten years later, in *Little Mary* (1903). *Alice Sit by the Fire* (1905), *What every Woman Knows* (1908), *The Adored One* (1913), and *A Kiss for Cinderella* (1916) extend the survey. Unsurprisingly while London's West End found the benevolent side of heroine power easy to applaud it was not at all happy when the manipulative potential of the Machiavellian female was dramatized. The socially unthreatening cleverness of Maggie Shand in *What every Woman Knows* was acceptable. But when Leonora in *The Adored One* throws a man to his death from a railway carriage because his smoking annoys her baby, then fools a male judge and jury into acquitting her, the audiences booed. Barrie rewrote the conclusion, turning her crime (and the subversive power-play that accompanied it) into a dream. 'Reality' now became a rural idyll, with Leonora restored to Edwardian, paternalist views of woman's role in society.

Barrie's experiments with film techniques and the music hall also belong to this period. But it is the one-act form that dominates. The best of these—notably *The Twelve Pound Look* (1910) and *Rosalind* (1912)—continued his dual interest in heroine-ism and the split personality. Barrie admitted that personal problems were interrupting his work and causing him to tear up more plays than he completed. Before his divorce Barrie's agent, Addison Bright, was found guilty of embezzlement, and committed suicide in 1906. His friend and financier Charles Frohman sank with the *Lusitania* in 1912. First Arthur and then Sylvia Llewelyn Davies died, in 1906 and 1910 respectively, making Barrie the guardian of their 'lost boy' children. In

1913 his close friend the explorer Robert Scott wrote to him from the South Pole 'as a dying man', asking him to look after his wife and child (*Letters of J. M. Barrie*, 46, n. 3). Although Lady Scott maintained her independence Barrie was now at the head of a vastly expanded 'family'. That he took his duties very seriously is confirmed in the many thoughtful and loving letters he wrote to the Davies boys as they grew up.

Later years, 1917–1937 Barrie's melancholic moods were commented upon frequently by his friends during the period 1915–20. A more pessimistic view of life is also reflected in the two major fantasy plays, which appeared in 1917 and 1920. *Dear Brutus*, whose very title is drawn from *Julius Caesar*, is the most overtly Shakespearian of all Barrie's plays. There is, however, a melancholy wistfulness absent from its major source *A Midsummer Night's Dream*. The magic wood into which the Puck figure, Lob, sends his house guests on midsummer's eve is used to enact the sad truth that most people, if offered a second chance in life, would make the same mistakes all over again. *Mary Rose*, whose troubled ghost returns sadly from the world of faery to seek out her lost son, draws its storyline from a summer holiday spent in the Western Isles and from James Hogg's poem 'Kilmeny' rather than from Shakespeare; but it too is tragicomic in spirit.

In 1910 Barrie had been among those considered by the Liberal government for a peerage if a forced creation became necessary to get Lloyd George's budget through the House of Lords. Although this initiative proved unnecessary he was created a baronet by the king in 1913. In 1922 he was appointed to the Order of Merit. A year earlier Michael, one of the Llewelyn Davies boys, whom he had come to regard as his sons, died unexpectedly and in mysterious circumstances. Cynthia Asquith, who in 1918 had become the author's secretary at his Adelphi Terrace house, records 'What his death dealt Barrie in shock and in sorrow cannot—should not—be told' (Asquith, 135). Life and work continued, however, and in 1923 five of his plays were running contemporaneously in London. His powers as an orator were also regularly called upon at this time either to promote causes or to mark the honours being conferred upon him. His rectorial address at St Andrews University in 1922 wittily and pathetically discusses the need for 'courage', while his inauguration as Edinburgh University's chancellor, in 1930, produced an equally passionate speech, defending the right of all social classes to higher education. As he became president of the Society of Authors in 1928 and gained honorary doctorates from Oxford (1926) and Cambridge (1930) public opportunities to celebrate and brood upon his own life were not lacking.

The ghost story 'Farewell Miss Julie Logan' (1931) ended Barrie's prose fiction on a high note. Theatrically he was not so fortunate. The conclusion of his career saw him once more bewitched by a young actress, this time Elizabeth Bergner. It was at her suggestion that he began his last play, on the biblical theme of David and Jonathan. As *The Boy David* it had a successful trial run in Edinburgh towards the end of 1936. But the London opening was damned with faint praise, and it closed after seven weeks, on 21 January 1937. Barrie had been ill throughout this period. Cancer was suspected, bronchial pneumonia set in, and on 19 June at his home—3 Adelphi Terrace, London—the curtains closed on his own life. His body was buried in the family grave, on the hillside above Kirriemuir, on 24 June. At his request his name was inscribed on the stone 'with no embellishment of any kind' (Mackail, 718).

Posthumous reputation Barrie's literary epitaph is not so clearly established. That he was a genius was taken for granted in his own day. For William Archer 'no rational being doubts that Sir James is a humorist of original and delightful genius' (Archer, 231). Robert Louis Stevenson agreed: 'It looks to me as if you are a man of genius' (*Letters*, 273). But adulation turned to denigration shortly after Barrie's death. With the advent of Freudian criticism the temptation to turn 'this diminutive, dark-haired Scotsman' with the 'deep-hoarded sadness in his blue eyes' (Asquith, 2) into an Oedipal version of his own most famous creation proved irresistible. In 1971 Harry M. Geduld produced the most exhaustive of these analyses. While Geduld's *James Barrie* seeks evidence of a mother complex across a wide range of texts, later writers have advanced the same thesis from a much reduced canon, confined to *Margaret Ogilvy*, the Tommy novels, and *Peter Pan*.

While this movement withdrew Barrie's claim to genius on the grounds of authorial immaturity the Scottish literati were busy rejecting him on other grounds. As their interest was confined to treatments of Scotland another eclectic canon in which the prose works of his literary apprenticeship again dominate was erected. Critics like George Blake, whose own novels were resolutely realistic, serious, socialistic, and nationalistic, were unlikely to have much sympathy with a manneristic, right-wing, comic myth-maker offering Scottish stereotypes for the amusement of London audiences. Blake's book *Barrie and the Kailyard School* dismisses his countryman in literal and naturalistic terms, despite Barrie's consistent plea—from 'The rector of Diss' (1884) to *The Greenwood Hat* (1930)—that his art was essentially allegorical and artificial. Later a counter-movement, initiated by Jacqueline Rose and Leonee Ormond, paid attention to these claims. By redefining him on his own terms, as a man of many personalities whose finest dramas followed the seriously fantastic method of Shakespearian romance, they saw him not as a backward-looking sentimentalist but as one of the first modernists.

In the worlds beyond academe a more positive judgement had already been made. In the popular imagination Barrie's myths are retranslated for each age. Psychologically (the 'Wendy complex'), politically ('the boy David'), and commercially (Quality Street chocolates) his mythic prototypes outlive him. Andrew Birkin's BBC television trilogy *The Lost Boys* (1978), with its sensitive portrayal of Barrie's powerfully mysterious character, carried this legacy forward in another mode. Birkin's script and subsequent book also illustrated how Barrie's enthusiasms for the theatre and the media in general usually found support from those who shared these passions.

Later West End revivals of *The Admirable Crichton* and *Peter Pan* proved Barrie's continued power to please. More humbly his major full-length and one-act plays continued to attract amateur companies throughout Britain. The visual power of his dramas also made him an established cinematic favourite. From the earliest days of silent film, when Cecil B. de Mille produced *The Admirable Crichton* as *Man and Woman* (1919), to Disney's *Peter Pan* (1952), and Spielberg's *Hook* (1997), his thought-provoking images have given pleasure to audiences across the world.

The assessment emanating from stage and stalls was always of paramount importance to Barrie. His constant attendance at rehearsals, amending his text in consultation with actors and directors, proves the first contention; his absence from most first-night performances, in fear of audience rejection, the second. None the less James Barrie MA also sought academic approbation throughout his life. To this end he provided a far more detailed critical commentary on his own art than most authors do. Any academic assessment of his status as a writer must surely begin from those premises.   R. D. S. JACK

Sources D. G. Mackail, *The story of J.M.B.* (1941) · C. Asquith, *Portrait of Barrie* (1954) · L. Ormond, *J. M. Barrie* (1987) · J. Rose, *The case of Peter Pan* (1984) · W. Archer, *The old drama and the new* (1923) · J. M. Barrie, 'University notebooks', NL Scot., Adv. MSS 6648–51 · D. Masson, *Essays biographical and critical* (1856) · D. Masson, *Shakespeare personally* (1914) · *The letters of Robert Louis Stevenson*, ed. S. Colvin (1924), vol. 4 · H. Garland, *A bibliography of the writings of James Matthew Barrie* (1989) · A. Birkin, *J. M. Barrie & the lost boys* (1979) · R. D. S. Jack, *The road to the neverland* (1991) · R. L. Green, *Fifty years of Peter Pan* (1954) · R. D. S. Jack, 'Barrie and the extreme heroine', *Gendering the nation*, ed. C. Whyte (1995), 137–67 · J. Dunbar, *J. M. Barrie: the man behind the image* (1970) · *The letters of J. M. Barrie*, ed. V. Meynell (1942)

Archives Boston PL, letters · Harvard U., Houghton L., literary MSS and MSS · Indiana University, Bloomington, Lilly Library · NL Scot., corresp.; letters · NRA, corresp. and literary papers · NRA Scotland, priv. coll., corresp., literary MSS, and MSS · Princeton University, New Jersey, letters · Ransom HRC, MSS · Yale U., Beinecke L., corresp., literary MSS, and MSS · Yale U., Beinecke L., letters | BL, letters to William Archer, Add. MS 45290 · BL, corresp. with G. K. Chesterton and F. A. Chesterton, Add. MSS 73235, fols. 51–67; 73455 C, fol. 204; 73482 A, fol. 8 · BL, letters to G. L. Craik, Add. MS 61895 · BL, letters to Alfred Daniell, RP 2004 [copies] · BL, letters to Lady Juliet Duff, Add. MS 57853 · BL, Ashley collection, letters to Edmund Gosse · BL, letters to William Meredith, RP 2223 · BL, letters to George Bernard Shaw, Add. MS 50529 · BL, corresp. with Society of Authors, Add. MS 56660 · Bodl. Oxf., letters to Robert Bridges · Bodl. Oxf., corresp. with Geoffrey Dawson; letters to Lewis family; corresp. with Gilbert Murray; letters to A. A. W. Ponsonby · CAC Cam., letters to Duff Cooper · Cheltenham College, letters to Charles Turley · CUL, letters to Stanley Baldwin · CUL, letters to M. R. James · Dorset County Museum, Dorchester, letters to Florence Hardy; letters to Thomas Hardy · Ellen Terry Memorial Museum, Smallhythe, Kent, letters to Ellen Terry · GL, corresp. with Hodder and Stoughton · Harvard U., Houghton L., letters to Maude Adams · Harvard U., Houghton L., letters to Charles Frohman · Hunt. L., letters to R. Golding Bright · King's Cam., letters to Lady Keynes · Morgan L., letters to William Ernest Henley and literary MSS · NL Scot., letters to Sir Graham Balfour · NL Scot., letters to Haldane family; letters to Elizabeth Haldane; letters to Richard Burdon Haldane · NL Scot., letters to Seymour Hicks; letters to Sir William Nicholson; letters to Lilian

Norrie; letters to Katherine Oliver; letters to Lord Rosebery • NYPL, Berg collection • PRO NIre., letters to Lady Londonderry • Queen's University, Kingston, Ontario, letters to J. A. Roy • Richmond Local Studies Library, London, corresp. with Douglas Slader • Scott Polar RI, letters to Scott family • Shrops. RRC, letters to first Viscount Bridgeman • Theatre Museum, London, letters to Pauline Chase • U. Birm. L., corresp. with John Galsworthy • U. Leeds, Brotherton L., letters to Edmund Gosse • U. Leeds, Brotherton L., letters to Clement Shorter • U. Reading L., corresp. with Nancy Astor • Worcs. RO, letters to Sir Edward Elgar | FILM BFI NFTVA, documentary footage; home footage; news footage

Likenesses Barraud, photograph, c.1880–1889, NPG • two photographs, 1892–c.1904, V&A • H. Furniss, pen-and-ink drawing, c.1900–1910, NPG • G. C. Beresford, photograph, 1902, NPG [see illus.] • W. Nicholson, oils, 1904, Scot. NPG • A. L. Coburn, photogravure, 1909, NPG • M. Beerbohm, caricature, 1912, AM Oxf. • W. Stoneman, photographs, 1922, NPG • D. Low, caricature, 1927, NPG • J. Lavery, oils, 1930–39, Scot. NPG • W. T. Monnington, pencil drawing, 1932, NPG • G. C. Beresford, photographs, NPG • F. Hollyer, photograph, V&A • A. Lowe, caricature, Garr. Club • photograph (in his library), V&A • various photographs, Scot. NPG

Wealth at death £173,467 9s. 5d.: probate, 15 Sept 1937, CGPLA Eng. & Wales

Barrie [formerly Barry], **Michael Maltman** (1842–1909), journalist and tory-Marxist, was born in Glasgow, the son of Edward Barry, a shoemaker. Little is known of his early life except that he was educated at Glasgow grammar school. In 1864 he moved to London and became a journalist on *The Standard*, a newspaper with which he was to be associated throughout his life, although he also worked for other papers. Barry reported from the parliamentary gallery and lobby as well as covering labour matters. On 19 July 1869 he married, at the Bloomsbury chapel, Julia Charlotte, daughter of Robert London, cheesemonger.

In the later 1860s Barry entered radical circles in London and became a friend of Karl Marx, who provided him with information for newspaper articles and who was to become his patron on the left. Barry stood out among radicals because of his hostility to the Gladstonian sympathies of most contemporary labour leaders. Barry was converted to Marx's views and on Marx's death he told Eleanor Marx that 'he was more than my master, he was my political maker' (C. Tsuzuki, *The Life of Eleanor Marx, 1855–1898*, 1967, 71).

In October 1871 Barry became provisional chairman of the federal council of the International Working Men's Association (IWMA). His chairmanship was largely negative and the following year, after intriguing against other members, he was forced to leave amid accusations that he was a spy and an 'ultra moderate'. He published (1873) a report of the IWMA's fifth annual congress, held at The Hague in September 1872. Despite his acrimonious relationship with the IWMA, Barry became a notable figure in London's radical clubs of the 1870s both as an activist and as a speaker at meetings. In 1876 he edited *The People's Advocate*, a radical paper that advocated land nationalization, republicanism, and Irish nationalism but which lasted only five issues.

In the later 1870s Barry apparently began his shift towards the Conservative Party without relinquishing his Marxism. This was partly because of his hostility to Liberalism, partly because of the Conservatives' record on social reform, and partly because of his support for Beaconsfield's foreign policy during the Eastern crisis of 1875–8. Barry became an extreme Russophobe, and supported Turkish resistance to Russian intervention. He launched the small-scale radical anti-Russian movement that attempted to capitalize on the jingoism of these years. Barry actually claimed that Marx himself taught him to be a jingo. Barry became secretary of the National Society for the Resistance of Russian Aggression and the Protection of British Interests in the East and organized a series of meetings in 1876 and 1877, several of which ended in riot. He published *The Catechism of the Eastern Question* (1890).

In the early 1880s Barry became active in Conservative Party circles, and attended meetings of the National Union of Conservative Associations. At the same time he became an ally of Henry Hyde Champion in advocating the formation of an independent political party for working-class representation. The two were involved in the 'tory gold' scandal of November 1885, in which Barry received £340 from Conservative central office to fund two candidates of the Social Democratic Federation in the general election. The Conservatives hoped to split the Liberal–radical vote but the candidates polled badly. The ensuing crisis harmed the reputation of the Social Democratic Federation but also reinforced Barry's reputation for untrustworthiness.

Barry had by this time become involved in the politics of his native Scotland and changed his name to the Scottish spelling, Barrie. In 1888 he edited *The Labour Elector* (which lasted for two years) and, with Champion, attempted to launch an anti-Liberal alliance of labour based in Aberdeen. In August 1890 he addressed the Aberdeen Trades Council, advocating an eight-hour day and a halt to alien immigration (he was an antisemite). In July 1892 he unsuccessfully contested Banffshire as a Conservative Democrat. *The Labour Elector* was revived in January 1893 with a local supplement for Aberdeen. It was as short-lived as its predecessor, and lasted only until July 1894. The paper supported the newly formed Independent Labour Party. Standing as a Conservative, Barrie contested Morpeth in 1895 and 1900, in opposition to Thomas Burt, and North Aberdeen in 1906. On each occasion he was defeated. He died of pneumonia on 5 April 1909 at his home, Roseneath, 51 Beauval Road, East Dulwich, London, and was buried in Kensal Green cemetery. His wife, two sons, and two daughters survived him.

Barrie's tory-Marxism marks him out as an eccentric in the early labour movement, but he was not wholly unusual. Henry Hyndman among other early socialists also had strong tory leanings. Barrie is usually derided as an opportunist but his constant attachment to Marxism suggests he was more principled than his detractors allow. His main importance was as a journalist covering labour affairs and as an advocate of independent working-class representation.   ROHAN MCWILLIAM

Sources R. McWilliam, 'Barry, Michael Maltman', *BDMBR*, vol. 3, pt 1 · *Aberdeen Daily Journal* (9 April 1909) · R. D. Condon, 'The political career of Michael Maltman Barry, 1871–1905', BLitt diss., U. Oxf., 1972 · J. T. Ward, 'Tory-socialist: a preliminary note on Michael Maltman Barry, 1842–1909', *Scottish Labour History Society Journal*, 2 (1970), 25–37 · H. Cunningham, 'Michael Maltman Barry', *Scottish Labour History Society Journal* (1972), 17–22 · m. cert. · census returns, 1881
Archives Internationaal Instituut voor Sociale Geschiedenis, Marx-Engels archive, corresp. with Karl Marx
Wealth at death £16: probate, 19 May 1909, *CGPLA Eng. & Wales*

Barriffe, William (1599/1600–1643), military writer and parliamentarian army officer, was possibly the son of William Beriffe, a lawyer of Colchester and Lincoln's Inn. Nothing is certainly known of his family or early years. After being admitted to the artillery company of London on 13 March 1627 he quickly gained a reputation for military expertise, while the fame of his notes on practice led to the publication of *Military Discipline, or, The Yong Artillery Man* (1635). The latter was not a student of gunnery but a habitué of the artillery garden, where he learned how to become a competent infantry soldier. Barriffe's book, tailored to this clientele, eschewed '*fine phrases*' and historical and foreign examples; his prose was plain and clear, his diagrams numerous, and his instructions detailed as he 'set forth the *exact grounds* of this our *moderne discipline*, for the exercising of a *foot Company*' (Barriffe, *Military Discipline*, 1635, 'To … Sir Ralph Bosvile'). His aim was to help the young officer to educate himself in the practicalities of war, and help him to educate others.

In 1639 a second edition of *Military Discipline* added a chapter on 'the Swedish brigade' (title-page) which incorporated contemporary European practice in handling larger bodies of men. With it Barriffe published *Mars, his Triumph* (1639), a stirring account of a mock battle between Christians and Saracens involving eighty members of the artillery company, in which Christianity and the latest military practice ultimately triumphed. Here, as in *Military Discipline*, Barriffe expressed his belief that '*the* Souldier *and the* Citizen' should '*Make but* one man' (Barriffe, *Mars, his Triumph*, 7). Four more authorized editions of *Military Discipline* appeared between 1643 and 1661, as well as four pirated ones. A manual published in Boston in 1701 still saluted Barriffe as one of 'the Authors of best Note, upon this Subject … and … most in use among us' (N. Boone, *Military Discipline. The Compleat Souldier*).

Barriffe's military training, unlike that of many of his contemporaries, was entirely home grown. He was proudly the product of the artillery company, though he was also active from about 1628 in a secondary company at Cripplegate. With the outbreak of war he rose rapidly in the parliamentarian army. He was a major in Hampden's regiment in 1642, and by 1643 he was a lieutenant-colonel. He was probably dead, however, by August 1643, with his army pay still in arrears. His will was proved in February 1644.

Barriffe appears to have been gregarious, and the friendships represented by the laudatory verses prefacing *Military Discipline*, and the number of soldiers named in his work, reveal the degree of military interest in pre-civil war London. Later editions provide valuable evidence of the dispersal of these citizen officers into civil war armies. His personal life remains obscure. He left his property to his wife, Marie, and he is described variously as of Cripplegate and of Bythorn, Huntingdonshire. Above all he had, as the frontispiece to *Military Discipline* claimed, 'a Soldiers minde'.
BARBARA DONAGAN

Sources W. Barriffe, *Military discipline, or, The yong artillery man*, 2nd edn (1639) [see also later edns, esp. 3rd–6th, 1643–61] · W. Barriffe, *Mars, his triumph, or, The description of an exercise performed the xviii of October 1638* (1639) · M. A. E. Green, ed., *Calendar of the proceedings of the committee for advance of money, 1642–1656*, 1, PRO (1888), 224 · *CSP dom.*, 1641–3, 379, 398 · administration, 6, Feb 1643, PRO, PROB 6/119, fol. 10r · M. J. D. Cockle, *A bibliography of military books up to 1642*, 2nd edn (1957) · Venn, *Alum. Cant.*, 1/1.140 · G. A. Raikes, *The ancient vellum book of the Honourable Artillery Company … from 1611 to 1682* (1890), 40 · W. P. Baildon, ed., *The records of the Honorable Society of Lincoln's Inn: admissions*, 1 (1896), 111, 192 · W. P. Baildon, ed., *The records of the Honorable Society of Lincoln's Inn: the black books*, 2 (1898), 299 passim
Likenesses G. Glover, engraving, repro. in Barriffe, *Military discipline*, 2nd edn (1639), frontispiece · portrait, repro. in Barriffe, *Military discipline*, 4th edn (1643)
Wealth at death assesed at £50 for twentieth tax; received pay as sergeant major and later lieutenant-colonel (1642–3): Green, ed., *Calendar*, vol. 1, p. 224

Barrington, Daines (1727/8–1800), judge, antiquary, and naturalist, was born at Becket in the parish of Shrivenham in Berkshire, the fourth son and fourth of nine children of John Shute *Barrington, first Viscount Barrington (1678–1734), barrister and politician, and his wife, Anne (d. 1763), daughter of Sir William Daines of Bristol. A number of Barrington's siblings died young but four pursued careers of note. His eldest brother, William Wildman *Barrington, succeeded to the viscountcy and served as secretary at war, John *Barrington rose to major-general in the army, Samuel *Barrington was an admiral, and Shute *Barrington a bishop.

Barrington's early education is obscure. He matriculated at Queen's College, Oxford, on 4 July 1745, aged seventeen, but did not graduate and was admitted to the Inner Temple in the same year. He was called to the bar on 9 February 1750. He travelled briefly on the Oxford circuit and was junior counsel for the prosecution of Mary Blandy for the murder of her father in 1752. His brother William's position as a government minister from 1746 to 1778 helped him proceed through a number of offices: on 24 May 1751 he was appointed marshal of the high court of Admiralty, a position he resigned in 1753 when appointed secretary of Greenwich Hospital. He became a judge of great sessions for the counties of Merioneth, Caernarvonshire, and Anglesey in 1757, and recorder of Bristol in 1764 (when he was appointed king's counsel) and second justice of Chester in 1778. In the latter capacity he sat with Lloyd Kenyon to hear the adjournment application for the trial of William Davies Shipley, dean of St Asaph, in 1783. In 1785 Barrington resigned all his offices except the most valuable, that of commissary-general of the stores at Gibraltar which paid him over £500 a year until his death. Though Barrington participated in some important and celebrated legal cases, commentators are divided on his

Daines Barrington (1727/8–1800), by Charles Knight, 1795 (after Joseph Slater, 1770)

capacities as a lawyer. Some consider that only lack of ambition prevented further preferment, others, including Jeremy Bentham, saw him as an indifferent judge.

Barrington's first major published work was an important contribution to legal history, *Observations on the Statutes, Chiefly the More Ancient*, first published in 1766, which reached its fifth edition in 1796. It examined many of the major statutes from Magna Carta to the reign of James I, and was inspired by Barrington's interest in statute law reform. This, like many of his projects, followed concepts articulated in the early seventeenth century by Francis Bacon. He rejected 'a new arrangement and institute of the whole body of law, as in the time of Justinian, or a *Code Frederique*' (Lieberman, 189) nor did he wish parliament to interfere with the common law. He did expose several documents printed in the statute-book that were not acts of parliament and hence without legal authority, and also the number of statutes remaining in force whose provisions bore no relation to the requirements of eighteenth-century English society. They were of value in understanding the history of English life, but were of danger as, if unrepealed, they could be used in vindictive prosecutions. He argued that statute law should be made less prolix and rendered more intelligible to the general reader; the statute-book, he felt, could easily be reduced by half, under the supervision of a small committee of serjeants-at-law and barristers whose reports would then be acted on by parliament. Barrington's work complemented that of William Blackstone, particularly in its argument that much statute law was unnecessary and duplicated what was already common law.

Despite his progress in the law, Barrington's preoccupations were his antiquarian and natural historical pursuits. He was elected a fellow of the Society of Antiquaries and of the Royal Society in 1767. His paper on Welsh castles in the first volume of the Antiquaries' *Archaeologia* in 1770 was the first of some twenty-four communications published in that journal on topics as varied as the history of archery, gardening, and card-playing in England, Caesar's invasion of Britain, and the history of the Cornish language. Though some of this work had lasting value, Barrington's enthusiasm as an antiquary was not always matched by his skill and accuracy. Both Horace Walpole and Thomas James Mathias ridiculed his papers. Barrington was reported by Welbore Ellis to have accepted a seventeenth-century watch as having belonged to Robert Bruce. Barrington's edition and translation of King Alfred's *Orosius* published in 1773 attracted much criticism for its unreliability. He served as a vice-president of the Society of Antiquaries and exhibited numerous curious items at its meetings.

Barrington made a dozen contributions to the Royal Society's *Philosophical Transactions*, concerned mainly with natural history. One paper, published in 1770, reported his examination of Wolfgang Amadeus Mozart when the young prodigy was in London. Mozart was seen by Barrington and fellow virtuosi as a freak of nature. Their interest in him conformed to Francis Bacon's injunction to investigate not only the ordinary but the extraordinary course of nature. From this vantage point there was more coherence in Barrington's multifarious interests than at first might appear. Barrington's paper in the *Philosophical Transactions* on the singing of birds was appended to the third volume of his friend Thomas Pennant's *British Zoology*.

Barrington's most enduring contribution to science began with the publication of *The Naturalist's Journal* in 1767, initially anonymously. He inserted his name after the preface in later editions. This journal consisted primarily of a set of printed forms, each page covering one week, the days being ruled horizontally, while ten vertical columns were provided to record specific information such as wind and weather, plants flowering, and so on. The sort of methodical logging that these printed forms were designed to facilitate was again part of a Baconian project as interpreted by Benjamin Stillingfleet's *Miscellaneous Tracts* (1762). Barrington's *Naturalist's Journal* was intended as an aid to the widespread, systematic recording of natural phenomena over long time periods with a view eventually to the identification of the causal interrelations of those phenomena. Probably at Pennant's suggestion, soon after publication Barrington sent a copy of *The Naturalist's Journal* to Gilbert White at Selborne in Hampshire, who promptly adopted it and maintained it until his death with the sole exception of the year 1791. Barrington continued to encourage and cajole White. He and Pennant were the real-life correspondents to whom much of the material in White's *Natural History of Selborne* (1789) was addressed. He used White's journals to inform his own research and writing, and offered editorial comments and annotations on them. Barrington was thus much more than simply an initiator of White's work; the two usually met annually and Barrington hoped they would collaborate on a natural history work, but this never happened.

Arctic exploration, and in particular the search for a north-west passage as an alternative route to the East Indies, was another of Barrington's passions. While on the council of the Royal Society from 1769 to 1773, Barrington persuaded the society to approach his friend John Montagu, fourth earl of Sandwich, first lord of the Admiralty, with a proposal for an expedition that became Captain Constantine John Phipps's Arctic expedition of 1773. The failure of this expedition to find a passage or to get beyond lat. 80° N led Barrington in February 1774 to mobilize the Royal Society again to push for a voyage to the northern Pacific Ocean. This became the basis for James Cook's third and final Pacific expedition. Barrington collected a great deal of evidence concerning the possibility of reaching the north pole by sea and circumnavigating it. Following the arguments of the Swiss geographer Samuel Engel, with whom he corresponded, Barrington maintained that sea water did not freeze and therefore that ice blocking a passage could only come from rivers and so, at times, should be passable. Between 1774 and 1776 Barrington published several pamphlets on the possibility of reaching the north pole by sea. These, together with Barrington's translation of the journal of the Spaniard Francisco Antonio Maurelle's 1775 voyage in search of the passage, were included, with many of Barrington's other writings, in his *Miscellanies*, published in 1781. As in much of his other work, Barrington relied heavily—in his arguments favouring the prospect of a northern passage—on accumulating testimonies, in this case of seamen and other travellers making reports of ice-free waters in high latitudes. This approach underlies and unifies much of his legal, antiquarian, and natural historical work. It also laid him open to the accusations of credulity that dogged his reputation. An imaginary exchange between Sir Joseph Banks and the pseudonymous Peter Pindar in a jocular but barbed contribution to the debates in the Royal Society in the 1780s contained the following exchange:

> Sir Joseph: Pray then, what think ye of our famous Daines?
> Peter: Think, of a man denied by Nature brains!
> Whose trash so oft the Royal leaves disgraces;
> Who knows not jordens brown from Roman vases!
> About old pots his head for ever puzzling,
> And boring earth, like pigs for truffles muzzling.
> Who likewise from old urns to crotchets leaps,
> Delights in music, and at concerts sleeps.
> (P. Pindar, *Peter's Prophecy, or, The President and Poet*, 1788)

Barrington symbolized a form of intellectual life, the virtuoso or dilettante, that came under attack from some quarters in the later eighteenth century. Nevertheless Barrington's influence was real, and family connections placed him well to act as a patron. Among those who benefited was Johann Reinhold Forster, who owed his nomination to the Royal Society to Barrington and also his position as naturalist on Cook's second voyage. Forster assisted Barrington in return, though he later complained that Barrington published others' ideas as his own. For

example, when Forster suggested that the difficulty of distinguishing clearly between hares and rabbits might be dealt with by careful measurement of specimens, Barrington promptly dragged Forster around London measuring numerous specimens and then published the results as his own in the *Philosophical Transactions* of 1772. But these accusations may have been coloured by Forster's falling-out with Barrington during the disputes with Sandwich and the Admiralty about the collections gathered during Cook's second voyage. Forster named one tree *Barringtonia* after his patron.

Barrington, who never married, lived most of his life in his chambers in the King's Bench Walk in the Inner Temple. He was devoted to that institution and made numerous donations of books and manuscripts to its library. In his later years he did much to tend the Temple garden, as one of its superintendents from 1782. Barrington died in his chambers after a long illness on 14 March 1800. He was buried on 18 March in the vault of the Temple Church after a service attended by numerous legal dignitaries and those few family members and friends who survived him.   DAVID PHILIP MILLER

Sources DNB · Nichols, *Lit. anecdotes* · J. C. Davies, ed., *Catalogue of manuscripts in the library of the Honourable Society of the Inner Temple*, 3 vols. (1972) · J. Evans, *A history of the Society of Antiquaries* (1956) · P. Foster, 'The Hon. Daines Barrington FRS—annotations on two journals compiled by Gilbert White', *Notes and Records of the Royal Society*, 41 (1986–7), 77–93 · Nichols, *Illustrations* · G. Williams, *The British search for the northwest passage in the eighteenth century* (1962) · R. Mabey, *Gilbert White* (1986) · R. E. Cowgill, 'Mozart's music in London, 1764–1829: aspects of reception and canonicity', PhD diss., King's Lond., 2000 · J. Gascoigne, *Joseph Banks and the English Enlightenment* (1994) · D. Lieberman, *The province of legislation determined: legal theory in eighteenth-century Britain* (1989), 185–90 · Walpole, *Corr.* · GM, 1st ser., 70 (1800), 291–4 · GEC, *Peerage* · Foster, *Alum. Oxon.* · PRO, PROB 11/1338, sig. 175

Archives Inner Temple, London, papers · Queen's College, Oxford, letters · Yale U., Beinecke L., travel diary | BL, letters to T. Pennant, M/496 [microfilm] · NL Scot., letters to Lord Hailes · NL Wales, letters to J. Lloyd · NMM, letters to Lord Sandwich · Suffolk RO, Bury St Edmunds, letters to G. Ashby · Warks. CRO, letters to T. Pennant

Likenesses J. Slater, oils, 1770 · C. Knight, stipple, 1795 (after J. Slater, 1770), BM, NPG; repro. in D. Barrington, *Observations on the more ancient statutes*, 5th edn (1796) [*see illus.*] · W. Bromley, line engraving (after S. Drummond), BM, NPG; repro. in *European Magazine* (1795)

Wealth at death see will, PRO, PROB 11/1338, sig. 175

Barrington [*née* Wilson], **Emilie Isabel** (1841–1933), biographer and novelist, was born on 18 October 1841 at 15 Hertford Street, Mayfair, Westminster, the youngest of the six daughters of James *Wilson (1805–1860) and Elizabeth Preston (d. 1886). Her father was a merchant, an important figure in the Anti-Corn Law League, and the founder of *The Economist*. Although her early years were spent on the continent, in 1846 her father bought Fountainville near Westbury, of which town he soon afterwards became the MP. Like her sisters, Emilie Wilson received the normal education of an early Victorian upper middle-class girl, learning a range of languages and accomplishments from governesses. From 1855 to 1856, she attended a school in Cologne with her sister Zoe; in

1858 she went to a finishing school in Paris with Sophie Parnell, sister of the Irish politician C. S. Parnell.

In 1859 James Wilson was appointed financial member of the supreme council of India. Emilie and Julia Wilson remained with their recently married sister, Eliza, and her husband, Walter Bagehot, while their father, mother, and other sisters travelled to India. Following James Wilson's death in August 1860, the Wilson women returned to England and made their home with the Bagehots. In the early 1860s Emilie Wilson formed a close friendship with Emily Faithfull, a Langham Place member and the manager of the Victoria Press: both women were interested in expanding opportunities for women's employment. Still more, Wilson was committed to the improvement of the lower classes through art. She was an amateur artist herself, taking drawing lessons from Arthur Hughes, and an inveterate visitor to art exhibitions and artists' studios.

During a continental tour in 1867 Wilson became engaged to Russell Barrington (d. 1916), the eldest son of the Revd Lowther and Lady Catherine Barrington; they were married on 1 July 1868 at St Peter's, Eaton Square. A quiet, dull man, he tolerated her highly strung and dominant personality, and admired her artistic pretensions. Their first child, Guy, born in 1869, was mentally unstable; their second, Ivo, died in 1871, at the age of four months. In the same bitter year Barrington's submissions to the Royal Academy were rejected.

As a married woman Emilie Barrington aimed to become the hostess for a well-born and artistic London set: in this rather forlorn hope she became, as Wilfrid Blunt cruelly puts it, 'an indefatigable pursuer of artistic big game' (Blunt, 159). About the time of her marriage she met G. F. Watts at Rossetti's studio, and she became an intimate of the Little Holland House circle and a self-designated muse to the artist. After Walter Bagehot's death in 1877 she persuaded her husband and widowed sister to purchase a house on Melbury Road, next to Watts's studio, and she visited him daily, reading to him and playing music for him. Russell Barrington acted as a go-between for Watts and his buyers. This practice ended only after the artist's marriage in 1886: Emilie Barrington's failure to appreciate that she was no longer Watts's hostess and Mary Watts's jealousy led to such acrimony between the two women that the Wattses moved away in 1891. After the artist's death, Mrs Barrington's close friendship with the artist was memorialized in her *Reminiscences of G. F. Watts* (1905), a work criticized as unreliable by Watts's widow: in her own copy, she substituted 'a poisonous snake' for Mrs Barrington's name, and she published her own memoir in 1912 as a corrective. A later biographer of Watts, Ronald Chapman, disagreed with his widow's verdict, valuing Mrs Barrington's account for the light it shed on the artist's character.

After Watts's marriage Barrington soon transferred her allegiance to Frederic Leighton, forming a friendship with one of his sisters. Her *Life, Letters, and Works of Frederic Leighton* appeared in 1906. The first major biography of Leighton and based on family letters and the memories and papers of Leighton's friends, it is a moving and passionate analysis of Leighton's character and mentality. It remains an important source for Leighton's life and career, as the originals of many of the letters quoted in it have since been destroyed. After his death in 1896 Barrington was instrumental in ensuring that Leighton House became a museum, buying and donating several of his works to the museum. She was also a friend and admirer of the arts and crafts artist and designer Walter Crane. Another woman writer on art, Vernon Lee, was less impressed with Mrs Barrington herself: she described her as 'a rumpled, scrumpled little brown paper woman, of uncertain artistic pretensions, a sort of King Charles dog of the neighbouring studios' (Gunn, 87).

In 1881 Barrington played a role in the establishment of the Kyrle Society, the aim of which was to 'bring beauty home to the poor'; she painted a portrait of Octavia Hill, its leading figure, in 1889. Her increasing preoccupation with philanthropy—admittedly of a showy variety—was evidenced in the two novels she wrote in the 1890s, *Lena's Picture* (1892) and *Helen's Ordeal* (1894), where both heroines seek solace for their lovelorn states in helping others and triumph spiritually over material woes. Barrington and her sisters clearly held traditional views on women's role in society as providers of spiritual and material bounty, and three of them—including Emilie—signed the appeal against female suffrage which appeared in the June 1889 issue of the *Nineteenth Century*. In the same year she published a rather murky and mystical pamphlet, *The Reality of the Spiritual Life*. During the 1880s and 1890s she was also a contributor to periodicals and journals, writing for the *Fortnightly Review* and *The Spectator*.

In her later years Barrington lived mainly with her sister Eliza in her London home and at Herd's Hill in Langport, Somerset. A photograph of her, probably dating from the first years of the new century, shows a small and delicate-looking woman with a forceful expression. She edited the complete works of Walter Bagehot in nine volumes, the tenth (1915) being essentially a reissue of her life of Bagehot (1914). After the deaths of Russell Barrington and her much-loved daughter-in-law Ida in 1916, and of Eliza Bagehot in 1921, she embarked on *The Servant of All* (1927), a life of her father which drips with filial devotion; she also edited *The Love Letters of Walter Bagehot and Eliza Wilson* (1933). She died on 9 March 1933 at Herd's Hill. An autobiography, 'Memories of a long life', was probably destroyed after her death. Although energetic, passionate, and able, she found no true outlet for her ambitions in the role of an upper middle-class Victorian wife and mother, and her life has been described as 'a record of lost causes and lost confidants' (Westwater, 115).

ROSEMARY MITCHELL

Sources M. Westwater, *The Wilson sisters: a biographical study of upper middle-class Victorian life* (1984) · E. I. Barrington, *The servant of all: pages from the family, social, and political life of my father, James Wilson* (1927) · W. Blunt, *England's Michelangelo: a biography of George Frederic Watts* (1975); pbk edn (1989) · E. I. Barrington, *Reminiscences of G. F. Watts* (1905) · E. I. Barrington, *Life, letters, and works of Frederic Leighton* (1906) · L. Ormond and R. Ormond, *Lord Leighton* (1975) ·

P. Gunn, *Vernon Lee: Violet Paget, 1856–1935* (1964) • C. Dakers, *The Holland Park circle* (1999) • b. cert. • d. cert. • m. cert.

Likenesses photograph, 1900–04, repro. in Westwater, *Wilson sisters*, 114

Wealth at death £1234 16s. 2d.—except settled land: probate, 28 June 1933, *CGPLA Eng. & Wales* • £7180—settled land: probate, 5 Dec 1933, *CGPLA Eng. & Wales*

Barrington, Sir Francis, first baronet (*c.*1560–1628), politician, was the eldest son of Sir Thomas Barrington (1530–1581) of Barrington Hall in western Essex and his second wife, Winifred (*d.* 1602), coheir of Henry Pole, Lord Montagu, and widow of Sir Thomas Hastings of Stoke Poges in Buckinghamshire. Through his mother he was directly descended from George, duke of Clarence, and so enjoyed the right to quarter the royal arms of England. Barrington was educated at Trinity College, Cambridge, and about May 1579 married Joan [*see* Barrington, Joan (*c.*1558–1641)], daughter of Sir Henry Cromwell alias Williams of Hinchingbrooke, Huntingdonshire, who bore their ten children, two of whom probably predeceased him. Awarded the degree of MA in 1580, he travelled that summer to the Calvinistic city state of Geneva, but his sojourn abroad may have been cut short by the death of his father, whose will was proved on 2 May 1581. He inherited £800 in cash, the 1200-acre manor of Barrington Hall, and a lease of the adjacent property of Hatfield Broad Oak, and became an active county governor; he also served as an infantry captain in the Essex militia at the time of the Armada. He was elected to parliament in 1601 as junior knight of the shire for Essex, but played only a minor role in its proceedings.

Barrington acquired extensive estates in Yorkshire, Lincolnshire, Essex, and the Isle of Wight in 1602 on the death of his mother, whom he had converted to the protestant faith. He was knighted at Theobalds on 7 May 1603 by the new king, James I, and in March 1604 was re-elected to parliament as junior knight of the shire for Essex with the backing of his landlord, Robert Rich, third Lord Rich, the wealthiest landowner in Essex, who shared his puritan outlook. During the session of 1604 he belonged to the committee which drafted the apology of the Commons, and with other leading puritans he attempted, unsuccessfully, to secure legislation to improve the quality of the preaching ministry. In September, following parliament's prorogation, many puritan ministers were threatened with deprivation under newly promulgated canons which required all clergy to acknowledge that the prayer book contained nothing contrary to the word of God. As an enthusiastic patron of godly ministers, Barrington helped to organize the Essex petition opposing this requirement which was presented to James at Royston in November. Indeed, one of the petition's signatories was his kinsman and estate steward Richard Hildersham. However, neither Barrington nor his allies could prevent the ensuing deprivations, so when parliament reassembled he supported attempts to restore those ministers who had refused to subscribe. Furthermore, on 29 November 1606 he unsuccessfully preferred a bill which aimed to ensure that in future no ecclesiastical canons could be issued without first receiving parliamentary approval.

Barrington was granted honorary admission to Gray's Inn in London on 19 March 1606. He was removed from the Essex commission of the peace in August 1607 for opposing in parliament the proposed union with Scotland, though he was restored to the bench by 1610. He was among the first to purchase a baronetcy when the order was created in 1611. Following the marriage of his eldest son, Thomas *Barrington, in November 1611, he vacated Barrington Hall and settled at Priory House on the Hatfield Broad Oak estate. In May 1612 he purchased this manor from Lord Rich, paying £8000, and about the same time attempted, by means of intimidation, to acquire nearby Hatfield Forest, which was owned by the Roman Catholic Lord Monteagle. Barrington did not seek election to parliament in 1614, but resumed his parliamentary career in 1621, when he was elected senior knight of the shire for Essex. Religious matters continued to dominate his parliamentary agenda, but he also supported the suppression of the Virginia Company's lottery despite owning shares in the company. Following the dissolution of January 1622 he was summoned by the council to explain why he had failed to contribute to the palatine benevolence, and consequently he donated £50. Returned again as senior knight of the shire for Essex to the parliament of 1624, he expressed concern at the growing influence of Arminianism in the church through his appointment on 15 May to the committee to consider the charges against the bishop of Norwich, Samuel Harsnett. He also supported the growing clamour for war with Spain, being appointed to the joint conference on war preparations on 11 March and to the committee established on 12 April to draft the charges against the lord treasurer, the earl of Middlesex, who favoured a policy of peace.

Barrington secured his re-election to parliament as senior knight of the shire for Essex in 1625, and despite a severe outbreak of plague he attended both the Westminster and Oxford sittings. Following the dissolution he helped to prepare the defences of his home county against an anticipated Spanish invasion. He returned to the Commons in 1626, again as senior member for Essex, where he participated in the attempt to impeach Buckingham, thereby supporting his patron and ally Rich, by now the second earl of Warwick. On 5 April he helped to present the remonstrance which denied that the Commons, in exploiting the king's need of subsidies to attack the duke of Buckingham, had behaved in an unparliamentary fashion, and on 12 April he supported a proposal to strengthen the investigative powers of the twelve-strong committee for managing the impeachment proceedings. Consequently, after the dissolution he was struck off the commission of the peace and dismissed as a deputy lieutenant, which office he had held since 1603. Aggrieved at these blows to his local standing, he refused on 24 October to swear the oath of office as a commissioner for the forced loan, for which offence he was arrested and imprisoned in the Marshalsea, voluntarily accompanied by his wife of forty-seven years. The winter weather and damp conditions of his prison soon began to take a toll on his health, and by the spring it was clear that if he were not speedily released he would soon die of consumption. In desperation he appealed to the king, claiming that he had never had 'so much as a disloyal thought against your Majesty' (Lowndes, 2.23). As Charles did not want to make a martyr of him, he was transferred to a garden house in Southwark, where he remained until early January 1628, when all those held in connection with the forced loan were released.

Barrington, now regarded as a hero in his native Essex, was unanimously returned to the Commons as senior knight of the shire at the general election of March 1628. However, he probably fell ill during the session, as his name is not mentioned in the parliamentary records after 13 June. He died on 3 July. In his will, drafted on 26 October 1626, the day after his arrest, he requested burial in his private chapel at Hatfield Broad Oak and looked forward to a bodily resurrection and to joining 'the rest of God's saints'. He was succeeded by his eldest son, Sir Thomas Barrington, second baronet, who represented Essex in both the Short and Long parliaments.

ANDREW THRUSH

Sources Barrington, Sir Francis, HoP, *Commons, 1604–29* [draft] • HoP, *Commons, 1558–1603*, 1.399–401 • G. A. Lowndes, ed., 'The history of the Barrington family', *Transactions of the Essex Archaeological Society*, new ser., 1 (1878), 251–75, esp. 251–2; new ser., 2 (1879–83), 3–54, esp. 23–4 • *JHC*, 1 (1547–1628) • A. Searle, ed., *Barrington family letters, 1628–1632*, CS, 4th ser., 28 (1983) • M. Jansson and others, eds., *Proceedings in parliament, 1628*, 6 (1983), 146–8 • W. A. Shaw, *Knights of England*, 3 vols. (1906), 2.104 • GEC, *Baronetage*, 1.28 • will, PRO, PROB 11/154, fols. 50v–51 • PRO, C142/450/72 • marriage settlement, Essex RO, D/DHt T/26/23; D/DB L1/3/4–7 • Barrington MSS, BL, Egerton MS 2644 • copy of petition against silencing of ministers, 1604, BL, Add. MS 38492, fol. 6 • BL, Add. MS 11402, fol. 89v • *The manuscripts of the Right Honourable F. J. Savile Foljambe, of Osberton*, HMC, 41 (1897) • *Calendar of the manuscripts of the most hon. the marquess of Salisbury*, 16, HMC, 9 (1933), 138 • [T. Birch and R. F. Williams], eds., *The court and times of Charles the First*, 1 (1848), 161–2, 243, 329 • *APC, 1627–8*, 217 • *The letters of John Chamberlain*, ed. N. E. McClure, 1 (1939), 138 • Venn, *Alum. Cant.* • *The register of admissions to Gray's Inn, 1521–1889*, 2 vols. (1889), 1.112 • Bodl. Oxf., MS Tanner 309, fol. 123 • J. T. Cliffe, *The puritan gentry: the great puritan families of early Stuart England* (1984) • A. B. Brown, ed., *The genesis of the United States*, 2 vols. (1890), 543 • *Dudley Carleton to John Chamberlain, 1603–1624: Jacobean letters*, ed. M. Lee (1972), 98
Archives BL, corresp., Egerton MS 2644 • Essex RO, Chelmsford
Likenesses portrait, *c*.1605
Wealth at death wealthy in 1626: PRO, E401/2586, p. 461

Barrington [*formerly* Waldron], **George** (1755–1804), actor, pickpocket, and transported convict, was born in Maynooth, co. Kildare, Ireland. Some claim that his birth date was 14 May 1755 and that his father was Henry Waldron, a silversmith, and his mother a Miss Naish (Naith), a milliner. Others claim that his father was a Captain Barrington stationed at Rush, and that his mother's name was Waldron. Much about his early life has been romanticized. During his lifetime and after his death he was made a figure of fiction and legend, immortalized as the archetypal gentleman thief on canvas, in popular fiction, ballads, satires, and souvenirs, and in melodrama.

George Barrington (1755–1804), by Sir William Beechey, *c*.1785

First taught by John Donelly in a school in Maynooth, and then by a Dr Driscol, Waldron showed promise as a scholar. He was awarded a place at the Blue Coat Grammar School, Dublin, by a dignitary of the Irish church in the hope that he would enter university. Following a violent quarrel in 1771 he stabbed a schoolmate with a penknife and then absconded after a severe flogging, having stolen money and his headmaster's gold hunter watch. A tall, good-looking, and well-spoken youth, he soon found employment in Drogheda with a troupe of travelling players. John Price, a theatrical swindler and pickpocket, coached the absconder in the role of Jaffeir for Thomas Otway's play *Venice Preserv'd* and persuaded him to become his partner in crime. The young Waldron now changed his name to Barrington to suggest an aristocratic and theatrical background (John Barrington (1715–1773) was still renowned on the stages of London and Dublin), and he and Price successfully combined disguise with undetected thieving. By 1772, while Barrington's roguish reputation had spread, his fashionable clothes and impeccable manners protected him from arrest. The criminal partnership was terminated abruptly with Price's arrest in 1773, forcing Barrington to make a hasty escape to London.

Barrington's charm attracted friends in fashionable society in the metropolis, where picking the pockets of theatre patrons, racegoers, promenaders, and aristocrats proved profitable. His elegant thefts did not go unnoticed for long, and the press relished his daring exploits; his attempted snatch of the Russian Count Orlov's diamond snuff-box at Covent Garden in 1775 was widely reported, although he was not arrested. Indeed, he accused the press of besmirching his character and was bound over at

Tothill Fields Bridewell for uttering threats in 1776. The *London Chronicle* described him in 1777 as the 'genteelest thief ever remembered at the Old Bailey' (*London Chronicle*, 16–18 Jan 1777). Arrested again for stealing at the theatre in Drury Lane, he was sentenced to three years' hard labour on the prison hulk *Justicia*, but was conditionally pardoned. In March 1778 he was sentenced on another charge to five years' ballast-heaving. Through the intercession of an influential sponsor on grounds of good behaviour and illness he obtained a remission. He then travelled to Ireland and Scotland disguised variously as a clergyman, a quack doctor, and a rider for a manufacturing house in Birmingham, but he was rearrested in London in 1783 and forced to serve out the remainder of his first sentence at Newgate prison for failing to keep to parole conditions. He may have appeared in Glasgow in 1787 in a production of John Gay's *The Beggar's Opera*.

Such was Barrington's celebrity that about 1785 his portrait was painted by William Beechey. By this time he was London's 'Prince of Pickpockets'. His courtroom demeanour and oratory were also celebrated, and were so effective that he successfully evaded prosecution on seven occasions. *The famous speech of George Barrington esq., before the judge and jury at the Old Bailey, London, together with the learned recorder's answer* was published as a broadside in September 1788. His legendary pickpocketing skills were described in contemporary papers and magazines, often accompanied by engravings of his trial appearances. His image also adorned a commemorative Staffordshire mug about 1791.

In 1790 Barrington was arrested for stealing a gold watch and chain from Henry Hare Townsend at the Enfield racecourse. Tried at the Old Bailey on 17 September, he was sentenced to seven years' transportation; he sailed for New South Wales on the transport *Active*, one of the Third Fleet, and arrived at Port Jackson in September 1791. Captain Watkin Tench recorded his arrival: though dishevelled, his 'gait and manner bespeak liveliness and activity … his face is thoughtful and intelligent … his whole demeanour is humble, not servile' (Tench, 191).

Barrington was sent to the out-settlement at Toongabbie and was soon promoted to high constable. He was said to have undergone religious conversion and preached sermons twice on Sundays. In November 1792 he received a conditional pardon from Governor Phillip (making him free within the colony) and in 1796 Governor Hunter lifted all restrictions with an absolute pardon and appointed him superintendent of convicts at Parramatta, with a salary of £50 per annum. He received two small land grants and purchased 50 acres on the Hawkesbury River. A visiting naval officer remarked that his conduct 'not only acquires him protection but the friendship of everyone' (Captain Waterhouse to Captain Phillip, 24 Oct 1795, Banks MSS, Bradbourne collection, vol. 3, Australia 1786–1800, p. 178). His reform and diligence were mentioned frequently in colonial dispatches.

From the moment of his conviction in 1790 London and provincial publishers used Barrington's name without

scruple. The first attributed publication appeared in London in 1790 in the *Attick Miscellany*, entitled 'An heroic epistle from George Barrington to Major Semple on his sentence of transportation to the coast of New South Wales'. Barrington was later presented as the author of apparently authoritative accounts and histories of the colony which were in fact compilations from other sources. About 1793–4 *An Impartial and Circumstantial Narrative of the Present State of Botany Bay* appeared under his name; it was reissued in a more elaborate version in 1795, as *A Voyage to New South Wales* (sometimes *A Voyage to Botany Bay*). Another work, *The History of Botany Bay in New South Wales*, also carrying his name, was published in 1802. It had coloured illustrations, maps, and an account of crime in the colony. Versions of the *Voyage* and *History* appeared for more than twenty years, and there were translations into other languages, including French and Russian. While there is no evidence that Barrington had any part in these publications, he was nevertheless a man of fluent literacy. He had written to newspaper editors pleading his innocence, and his plea for mercy in 1776 was eloquent. His records as head constable were exemplary and written in a fine hand. His name was also associated with quelling a shipboard mutiny, and with a performance of the prologue of Edward Young's tragedy *The Revenge*; both events were figments of publishers' imaginations.

Lieutenant-Colonel David Collins, judge-advocate and secretary of the colony, had noted Barrington's 'asthmatic habit' in 1799, and in 1800 'infirmity' forced his retirement on a half pension. He died at Brush Farm, near Parramatta, on 27 December 1804, allegedly a lunatic. He left no will or known descendants and his properties were auctioned. He was buried at St John's Church, Parramatta, on 29 December. Such was Barrington's fame that it was suggested in 1827 that 'ninety-nine out of one hundred English people' would associate New South Wales with 'ropes, gibbets, arson, burglary, kangaroos, George Barrington and Governor Macquarie' (*Blackwood*, November 1827, 606).

SUZANNE L. G. RICKARD

Sources *DNB* · *AusDB* · *Australian encyclopaedia*, 1 (1965) · P. Serle, *Dictionary of Australian biography*, 2 vols. (1949) · J. A. Ferguson, *Bibliography of Australia*, 7 vols. (1941–69), vol. 1 · [F. Watson], ed., *Historical records of Australia*, 1st ser., 1–4 (1914–15) · R. S. Lambert, *The Prince of Pickpockets: a study of George Barrington who left his country for his country's good* (1930) · J. A. Ferguson, 'Studies in Australian bibliography [pt 4]', *Royal Australian Historical Society Journal and Proceedings*, 16 (1930–31), 51–80 · Bonwick transcripts, Mitchell L., NSW · A. W. Jose, 'The "Barrington" prologue', *Royal Australian Historical Society Journal and Proceedings*, 13 (1927), 292–4 · *London Chronicle* (16–18 Jan 1777) · *The famous speech of George Barrington esq., before the judge and jury at the Old Bailey* (1788) · gaol delivery rolls, 1756–1834, Old Bailey, PRO, S. Bk. 20 · convict indents, Archives Authority of New South Wales, Sydney · W. Tench, *A narrative of the expedition to Botany Bay, with an account of New South Wales* (1789) · *Monthly Review*, new ser., 18 (1795), 474 · *GM*, 1st ser., 65 (1795), 760 · D. Collins, *An account of the English colony in New South Wales*, 2 (1802), 221 · *Blackwood*, 22 (1827), 606 · S. Rickard, 'The enigma of George Barrington: a case study in history, legend and popular literature', thesis, Australian National University, 1989 · parish register, Parramatta, St John, 1805, Mitchell L., NSW, 101 · *The Athenaeum* (12 Feb 1898), 216 · *N&Q*, 9th ser., 2 (1898), 404 · S. Rickard, ed., *George Barrington's* *voyage to Botany Bay: retelling a convict's travel narrative of the 1790s* (2001)

Archives Mitchell L., NSW, Dixson collection · NL Aus., Rex Nan Kivell collection · NL Aus., Petherick collection
Likenesses W. Beechey, oils, c.1785, NL Aus., Rex Nan Kivell collection [*see illus.*] · Barlin, engraving, c.1790 (*George Barrington detected picking the pocket of Prince Orlow*), NL Aus., Rex Nan Kivell collection · Staffordshire mug, c.1790–1791 (*Barrington picking the pocket of J. Brown, esq*), National Gallery of Australia, Canberra · stipple, pubd 1803, BM · J. Chapman, stipple, pubd 1804, NPG · I. R. Cruikshank, two ink and watercolour drawings, V&A · several popular prints, BM, NPG
Wealth at death three blocks of farmland (totalling 90 acres): *Historical records of Australia*

Barrington [*née* Williams or Cromwell], **Joan**, **Lady Barrington** (c.1558–1641), godly matriarch and patron of clergy, was one of the eleven children of Sir Henry Williams (later Cromwell; c.1537–1604) of Hinchingbrooke, Huntingdonshire, and his wife, Joan (d. 1584), daughter of Sir Ralph *Warren (c.1483–1553), sometime lord mayor of London. In 1579 Joan married Sir Francis *Barrington (c.1560–1628) of Hatfield Broad Oak, Essex. Both held deep and sincere religious beliefs and played a pivotal role in the network of prominent godly families in early seventeenth-century Essex. They were also renowned for their patronage of the puritan ministry and intelligentsia. Arthur Hildersham, John Preston, Ezekiel Rogers, and Roger Williams were all at one time or another servants or beneficiaries of the Barringtons. 'Painful preachers' clearly appealed at times to their broad streak of self-hating introspection, but it was 'gentle professors' like John Harrison, their Hatfield chaplain, whom they preferred to keep within the bosom of their family. The common, unwavering object of their spiritual desires, however, was predestinarian Calvinism. A portrait of Theodore Beza, the sixteenth-century Calvinist scholar, hung in the upper gallery of their home in the old priory at Hatfield.

This was a time when the relationship between Calvinism and the Church of England was in crisis. None the less, Lady Barrington would have regarded her religious principles as entirely orthodox, and indeed as a reflection of her social pre-eminence. The Barrington family was no nest of puritan revolutionary vipers. Probably the greatest single beneficiary of their patronage was Leonard Mawe, the bishop of Bath and Wells, and master of Trinity College, Cambridge, from whom the Hatfield tithes were leased. But maintaining the value of the Barringtons' deep and substantial investments in the established order came increasingly to depend on intense political struggle, even personal sacrifice.

The marriage of Sir Francis (he was knighted in 1603 and received a baronetcy in 1611) and Lady Barrington has been called 'a cornerstone of the puritan connection in parliament in the 1620s' (Searle, 11). He was prominent among the opponents of the crown early in the reign of Charles I, while she was the aunt of John Hampden, Oliver St John, and Oliver Cromwell. In 1626–7 Joan shared her husband's short but uncomfortable incarceration in the Marshalsea prison for refusal to pay the forced loan. Sir Francis died on 3 July 1628, at least in part because of the conditions of his imprisonment. It would appear that Lady Barrington, now aged about seventy, underwent a 'crisis of faith' after the death of her husband, perhaps reflecting the deep personal and political trauma which helped accelerate his demise (ibid., 15). Certainly Roger Williams claimed to perceive a spiritual falling-off, his sense of which was doubtless sharpened by Lady Barrington's recent rebuttal of his suit for the hand of her niece. Not scrupling to take her to task, Williams succeeded only in deepening the agonies of a woman whose heart-burnings were of the most intense, often black, and melancholic variety. Some months after receiving the minister's reproofs, Lady Barrington's son-in-law Sir William Masham told her that her falling-out with Williams was bringing the godly into scandalous disrepute among their enemies, who were treating the whole affair as a source of derision. Williams never really recovered his favour with Lady Barrington, finding himself instead a few steps nearer to his departure for New England.

Lady Barrington's accounts for the period after her husband's death nevertheless reveal continuing regular and generous financial support for a large number of ministers, preachers, and authors. This was the time in which she came into her own as the archetypal clan matriarch. Her eldest son, Sir Thomas *Barrington (c.1585–1644), conspicuously deferred to her, and the greatest puritan patrons of the day, the earls of Warwick and Bedford, regularly conferred with her. Her legion of correspondents continued to testify to the warmth and generosity of which she was readily capable, as well as their respect for her opinions, and her continued commitment to the life of her own and others' eternal souls. Several young female relatives were brought up in her household, and she was active in arranging marriages within her wide circle.

Both Lady Barrington's piety and her many connections are evident in her will, drawn up on 17 October 1641. Within a few weeks she had died at the Priory, Hatfield, the will being proved on 14 December. She was probably buried in the Barrington chapel of Hatfield Broad Oak church, where her husband and children were also interred. The years which followed saw many of her former servants, clients, friends, and relations rise to prominence and the highest pinnacles of leadership in a struggle for the soul of a nation which almost certainly she would have found perplexing, but perhaps also unavoidable.

SEAN KELSEY

Sources GEC, *Baronetage*, 1.28 · A. Searle, ed., *Barrington family letters, 1628–1632*, CS, 4th ser., 28 (1983) · W. Hunt, *The puritan movement: the coming of revolution in an English county* (1983) · T. Webster, *Godly clergy in early Stuart England: the Caroline puritan movement, c.1620–1643* (1997) · will, PRO, PROB 11/187, sig. 151, fols. 360v–362r
Archives BL, letters, Egerton MS 2646, fols. 50, 62, 102 · Essex RO, Chelmsford, household accounts, D/DBa A15
Wealth at death over £2000: will, PRO, PROB 11/187, sig. 151, fols. 360v–362r

Barrington, John (*bap.* 1719, *d.* 1764), army officer, was baptized on 11 December 1719 at Little Baddow, Essex, the third son of John Shute *Barrington, first Viscount Barrington (1678–1734), and his wife, Anne (*d.* 1763), daughter and coheir of Sir William Daines (*c.*1656–1724), mayor and MP for Bristol. His brothers were William Wildman *Barrington, second Viscount Barrington, Daines *Barrington, Samuel *Barrington, and Shute *Barrington. He joined the 3rd regiment of guards (the Scots guards) in 1739 with the rank of lieutenant and it is likely that he served in Flanders during the War of the Austrian Succession. He transferred to the 2nd regiment of guards (the Coldstream Guards) on 17 September 1746 as captain-lieutenant and was made captain and lieutenant-colonel on 15 February 1748. He remained with this regiment and was a senior lieutenant-colonel in 1755 when his elder brother William was appointed secretary at war. Preferment now followed: on 12 June 1756 he was made an aide-de-camp to George II, a post which carried the brevet rank of colonel; and on 21 April 1758 he was appointed colonel of a new regiment, the 64th foot, formerly the 2nd battalion of the 11th regiment of foot.

In October 1758 the 64th, together with five other regiments of the line, was ordered to Portsmouth to join the expedition under Major-General Peregrine Thomas Hopson which was being sent against the French Leeward Islands of Martinique and Guadeloupe. Barrington, although a junior colonel, was appointed second in command, with a local field rank of major-general, despite the 'honourable protests of his brother, the Secretary-at-War' (Fortescue, *Brit. army*, 2.353). Owing to bad weather the transports did not reach Martinique until 15 January 1759. An attack by the French was successfully repulsed but it was decided that Guadeloupe would be an easier target. It was also the wealthiest of the French settlements and the focus of activity by French privateers.

The British arrived and took the southern fort of Basseterre on 23 January. A military stalemate ensued, with the French keeping up a series of raids on the ring of British defensive outposts. The physical condition of the British troops, who were mostly bottled up in the fort, deteriorated rapidly and Hopson himself became seriously ill. In the meantime Commodore John Moore, carrying on independent operations around the coast, attacked and captured Fort St Louis, which was situated at the eastern end of the narrow strait called the Salt River, which separated Guadeloupe proper (Basse-Terre) from the fertile agricultural part, known as Grand-Terre. The fort was left with a garrison of 300 highlanders and marines. Despite the entreaties of Barrington and other officers Hopson refused the opportunity thus presented to shift his base of operations, and died from his illness on 27 February.

The situation in which Barrington assumed command would have challenged the most senior and experienced of commanding officers. Out of an original force of 5000 only 2795 were still fit for active service. 600 invalids had been sent to Antigua and the sick list was growing rapidly. Nevertheless he moved rapidly to restore the initiative. Leaving the repaired Fort Basseterre with a garrison of the 63rd foot, Barrington re-embarked his troops and sailed to Fort St Louis. However, bad weather separated the fleet

and the first transports did not arrive until 11 March. This misfortune was compounded when news arrived the following day that a French squadron had been sighted off Barbados. This compelled Moore to sail away to counter the new threat, taking with him, with Barrington's consent, 600 troops to make up his crews.

The situation was now parlous in the extreme. The fleet was gone, Barrington's force was further weakened, and some of the transports had not yet arrived. Moreover it was soon realized that Fort St Louis offered no secure defence and the French were making preparations to lay siege. 'Yet with a resolution which stamps him as no common man, he resolved despite all difficulties to begin offensive operations at once' (Fortescue, *Brit. army*, 2.358). Using the transports, Barrington's plan was to concentrate his smaller force against the isolated French settlements along the coast and river valleys of Grande-Terre, to ravage the local economy through the ruthless destruction of property and crops. The strategy was successful. By 1 April the missing transports had all arrived and, having destroyed the main settlements on Grande-Terre, Barrington's intention was to extend the same tactics to Basse-Terre. He was now suffering from a severe attack of gout and while retaining command took no further part in the fighting.

Following a series of attacks between April 12 and 18 against French fortified positions along the coast, only the richest part of the island, Capesterre, remained to the French. The settlers, fearing further economic destruction, sued for peace. On 1 May their capitulation was granted on liberal terms, deterring a force of 600 regular French troops and 2000 buccaneers under General Beauharnais from attempting to relieve the island.

In the circumstances the capture of Guadeloupe was a remarkable achievement. Barrington was ably supported in the field by Brigadier John Clavering and Colonel Bryan Crump, but it was his assumption of command following Hopson's death which was critical to the eventual success of the expedition. During the fighting 59 officers and men were killed and 149 were wounded. Far more were to die from illness: 800 by the end of the year. Barrington's own constitution, sound before he went out, was ruined by the rigours of the local climate.

Barrington returned to England in June 1759. In July he transferred to the colonelcy of the 40th regiment of foot and in October to the 8th foot. In recognition of his services his field promotion to major-general was confirmed in September 1759. Later he was appointed deputy governor of Berwick upon Tweed, where his father and elder brother had been MPs. He died at Paris on 2 April 1764. He was survived by his wife, Elizabeth, daughter of Florentius Vassal of Jamaica, and four children, William, Richard, George, and Louisa. Some years later his elder brother, the second Viscount Barrington, wrote: 'He returned from Guadeloupe as poor as he went thither … left at his death a very bare subsistence for his widow; and his four children have since the year 1764 been educated and maintained by me' (*Secretary at War*, ed. Hayter, 328).

This was just as well since the second viscount died without children in 1793 and the title passed to John Barrington's three sons in turn. JONATHAN SPAIN

Sources GEC, *Peerage* · J. Lodge, *The peerage of Ireland*, rev. M. Archdall, rev. edn, 5 (1789) · *GM*, 1st ser., 26 (1756) · *GM*, 1st ser., 29 (1759) · *GM*, 1st ser., 34 (1764) · R. Cannon, ed., *Historical record of the eighth, or the king's regiment of foot* (1844) · F. Maurice, *The history of the Scots guards, from the creation of the regiment to the eve of the Great War*, 2 vols. (1934) · D. Mackinnon, *Origin and services of the Coldstream guards*, 2 vols. (1833) · *An eighteenth-century secretary at war: the papers of William Viscount Barrington*, ed. T. Hayter (1988) · Fortescue, *Brit. army*, 2nd edn, vol. 2 · R. Gardiner, *An account of the expedition to the West Indies, against Martinico, Guadeloupe, and the other Leeward Islands* (1759) · C. R. B. Knight, *Historical record of the Buffs, east Kent regiment (3rd foot): 1704–1914*, 1: 1704–1814 (1935) · L. I. Cowper, ed., *The King's Own: the story of a royal regiment*, 1 (1939) · A. C. Burns, *History of the British West Indies* (1994), 485–7 · Burke, *Peerage* (1999) · IGI
Archives BL, corresp. and papers, MSS Dep 9389

Barrington, John (1764–1824), businessman and philanthropist, was born on 9 October 1764 in Dublin, the first of three children of John Barrington (1723–1784) and his second wife, Mary Anne (*fl.* 1763–1789), daughter of William Plummer of Enniscorthy, co. Wexford. He was brought up in the Quaker faith to which the Barringtons had adhered since the seventeenth century. Following his father's death Barrington carried on the family business as a chandler in partnership with his mother. He later entered into a succession of other partnerships before he joined with his sons to form John Barrington & Sons, wholesale soap and candlemakers, a firm which endured through several generations.

In 1787 Barrington married Thomasina (*c*.1767–1788), daughter of Thomas and Eleanor Burton; she died on 15 July in the following year. His second wife, whom he married on 7 November 1792, was Margaret Manliffe (1773–1869) of Edenderry, King's county, and they had thirteen children, eleven of whom survived to adulthood. Over time, his business built up and the company moved to progressively larger premises. Barrington lived in a succession of houses—firstly alongside the factory at Bellview, by Dublin's Grand Canal Harbour, then in suburban locations outside the city at Rathfarnham and Blackrock. Finally, in 1808, he acquired about 150 acres at Glendruid, near Cabinteely, 9 miles south of Dublin, and built a substantial house with outhouses and a viewing tower.

As Barrington's fortunes increased he became involved with a number of charitable or philanthropic projects. The earliest of these was the fever hospital in Dublin's Cork Street, which opened in 1804 and for which he was active in fund-raising. Over its nearly one and a half centuries the hospital always had a number of Quakers, including John Barrington and his son Edward, on its board. In 1808 John Barrington was among those who established the Dublin Free School in School Street, close to his business premises in Bellview. This establishment was founded to give instruction to poor children of both sexes and was largely supported by subscriptions. Three years later, in a further attempt to foster the intellectual growth of the citizens of Dublin, Barrington and others established the Dublin Institution, operating from a house in Sackville Street, where there was a library and a lecture room. The aim of this foundation was to promote science, literature, and the arts, and it was funded by shares held by a group of individuals who also subscribed a small sum each year. Finally, at the close of his life, Barrington became a founder member of the Patriotic Assurance Company, a body which, like the others in which he was involved, included a substantial Quaker element among its promoters.

Though born and brought up as a member of the Religious Society of Friends, Barrington (according to the family biographer) left the society about 1801. However, he continued to attend the society's meetings, and his affiliations to organizations in which there was Quaker involvement show that he remained close to the society. Barrington's philanthropy also earned him an esteemed reputation beyond Quaker circles. According to his son Richard:

> my father, indeed, was no common man. I scarcely think I exaggerate when I give it as my opinion that he was very highly respected, not only by those in his own mercantile class, but also by those other classes with whom his activity in furthering objects for the common good brought him into contact. His well-known integrity and independence of opinion … were highly appreciated. (Barrington, 177)

John Barrington died of typhus fever on 2 April 1824 and was buried in the ancient churchyard of Tullagh, close to his home at Glendruid. In 1846 the Barrington family established a private burial-ground within the grounds of Glendruid, and Barrington's remains were exhumed from Tullagh and reburied in the family plot.

ROB GOODBODY

Sources A. Barrington, *The Barringtons: a family history* (1917) · T. H. Webb, 'Barrington', *Thomas Henry Webb pedigrees*, Friends Historical Library, Dublin · birth, marriage, and death records of Religious Society of Friends in Ireland, Friends' Historical Library, Dublin · S. Lewis, *A topographical dictionary of Ireland*, 2 vols. (1837) · R. S. Harrison, *Irish insurance: historical perspectives, 1650–1939* (1992)
Likenesses portrait, repro. in Barrington, *The Barringtons*, facing p. 174

Barrington, John Shute, first Viscount Barrington (1678–1734), politician and Christian apologist, born in Theobalds, Hertfordshire, was the third son of Benjamin Shute, a London merchant 'descended from Robert Shute of Hockington in the county of Cambridge, one of the twelve judges in the reign of Queen Elizabeth' (epitaph of the first Lord Barrington). His mother, Elizabeth, was the daughter of the Revd Joseph Caryl and sister to the first wife of Sir Thomas Abney. He was educated in Stoke Newington at the academy kept by Thomas Rowe, where Isaac Watts was at the time an older pupil, and at the age of sixteen was sent to the University of Utrecht where he took a doctorate and published several essays on philosophical and theological themes. In 1698 Shute returned to England and studied at the Inner Temple, and was in due course called to the bar. In 1701 he published anonymously *An essay upon the interest of England in respect to protestants dissenting from the established church*, which was reprinted two years later with the name of the author, and with corrections and additions, under the title *The Interest* *of England, &c., with some Thoughts about Occasional Conformity*. It was probably this publication that brought him the friendship of John Locke.

In 1704 Shute produced the first part of a work entitled *The Rights of Protestant Dissenters*, with an elaborate dedication to the queen. A corrected and enlarged edition of this first part was brought out the following year, together with the second part, *A vindication of their right to an absolute toleration from the objections of Sir H. Mackworth in his treatise intitled Peace at home* (1705). At the instance of Lord Somers, acting on behalf of the whig ministry, Shute was sent to Scotland in order to win Presbyterian support for the scheme of the union of the two kingdoms. His success there was rewarded in 1708 with a commissionership of the customs, from which he was removed by the tory administration in 1711. In a letter to Archbishop King of Dublin, dated 30 November 1708, just before Shute's appointment to the commissionership, Jonathan Swift describes him as 'a young man, but reckoned the shrewdest head in England, and the person in whom the presbyterians chiefly confide. … As to his principles he is truly a moderate man, frequenting the church and the meeting indifferently' (Swift, *Works*, 1824, 15.318).

Meanwhile Shute had inherited two considerable estates. The first, to which he succeeded in 1710, was that of John Wildman of Becket, Berkshire, who, although not a relative, had named Shute as his heir in 1706. Shute inherited his second estate, Tofts in Little Baddow, Essex, following the death of Francis Barrington, who had married Shute's first cousin. In accordance with his benefactor's will Shute assumed the name and arms of Barrington, a family of antiquity in Essex. On 23 June 1713, at St Benet Paul's Wharf, he married Anne (*d.* 1763), the daughter and coheir of Sir William Daines, a local whig leader of Bristol, where Daines was sheriff, mayor, and MP. The couple had six sons, including William Wildman *Barrington, Daines *Barrington, John *Barrington, Samuel *Barrington, and Shute *Barrington, and three daughters, Anne, Mary, and Sarah, mother of Sir Uvedale Price (1747–1829).

In the same year, 1713, Barrington published, separately, two parts of *A Dissuasive from Jacobitism*, the first 'showing in general what the nation is to expect from a popish king, and in particular from the Pretender', and the second considering more particularly 'the interest of the clergy and universities with relation to popery and the Pretender'. This treatise, which went through four editions in the first year of its publication, recommended the author to George I, who granted him an audience on the first day after his arrival in London. In the first parliament of the reign, which met on 17 March 1715, he represented Berwick, and he was returned by the same constituency in October 1722. In parliament he supported the Sunderland–Stanhope government and lived up to his reputation for religious moderation by submitting in 1718 a proposal for the relief of dissenters without causing offence to the Church of England.

On 11 June 1720 Barrington was created Baron Barrington of Newcastle in co. Limerick and Viscount Barrington of Ardglass in co. Down, in the Irish peerage. On account of his connection with the illegal Harburg lottery he was expelled from the Commons on 15 February 1723 after the house had voted that he was guilty of fraud. He was unsuccessful in his attempt to win back his seat at Berwick in 1727 and again in 1733, when he was defeated by four votes. Following his expulsion from parliament Barrington published two further works, *An Essay on the Several Dispensations of God to Mankind* (1725) and *Miscellanea sacra, or, A new method of considering so much of the history of the apostles as is contained in scripture* (2 vols., 1725); a second enlarged edition of this latter work (3 vols., 1770) was issued by his son Shute Barrington, then bishop of Llandaff. Barrington's chief works were later collected under the title *The Theological Works of the First Viscount Barrington, by the Rev. George Townsend, MA* (3 vols., 1828).

During the early 1730s Barrington was actively involved in the campaign to bring about the repeal of the Test and Corporation Acts. He died at Becket, Berkshire, on 14 December 1734, and was buried on 27 December in the parish church of Shrivenham, Oxfordshire. His wife, Anne, died on 8 February 1763.

ARTHUR H. GRANT, *rev.* PHILIP CARTER

Sources R. R. Sedgwick, 'Barrington, John', HoP, *Commons* • GEC, *Peerage*, new edn, vol. 1 • *GM*, 1st ser., 4 (1734), 703 • M. R. Watts, *The dissenters: from the Reformation to the French Revolution* (1978)
Likenesses stipple, pubd *c.*1802 (after J. Richardson), NPG

Barrington, Sir Jonah (1756/7–1834), judge and author, was born of impoverished protestant gentry stock, the third son of the thirteen children of John Barrington, of Knapton, near Abbeyleix, Queen's county (co. Laois), Ireland, and his wife, Sibella French, of Peterswell, co. Galway. Barrington was brought up by grandparents and schooled by them in Dublin. He entered Trinity College, Dublin, in 1773, at the age of sixteen. Leaving without a degree, he contemplated a career in the army, but the experience of recruiting for his prospective regiment changed his mind and he turned instead to the law.

After admission to the Irish bar in 1787, Barrington's rise within the profession was swift: the friendships which he cultivated, his own qualities, and the reputation which he gained as a *bon viveur* and wit all played their part. In 1789 he married Catherine, *née* Grogan, the daughter of Edward Grogan, a mercer of Dublin; they had seven children. In 1793 he secured a sinecure at the Dublin custom house and later the same year was made a king's counsel.

Barrington also sat as a member of the Irish House of Commons, representing Tuam, co. Galway, from 1790 to 1797 and Clogher, co. Tyrone, from 1798 to 1800. In parliament and outside he made no secret of his bitter opposition to the Act of Union of 1800. He was appointed judge of the Irish court of Admiralty in 1797 at a salary of £500 a year. Business was meagre, the jurisdiction of the court limited, and he had not qualified as an advocate (the LLD of 1798 was honorary), but it is likely that at some stage he received assurances that his remuneration would be increased up to the level enjoyed from 1805 by his Scottish counterpart. Nothing was done, however, and Barrington's knighthood, conferred in 1807, was no substitute for the ready cash which his increasingly extravagant tastes made it essential for him somehow to acquire. In 1806 and again in 1810 he instructed proceeds from the court-ordered sale of two derelicts, the *Nancy* and the *Redstrand*, to be paid into his personal bank account, a course of dealing that was later to catch up with him.

In 1810 or 1811 Barrington took his wife and family to England. He never returned to Ireland, where, controversially, his official duties in the Admiralty were left to be discharged by successive surrogates. He may have practised law for a short while in England, but in late 1814 or thereabouts he was on the move again, this time to France, where he spent all of his remaining years.

In exile, amid continuing anxieties over money, a daughter's inheritance, and publishers, Barrington pursued his true vocation as a writer, transforming his earlier work, *Historic Anecdotes, etc.* (1809–15), into a volume that appeared in 1833 under the titles of *Historic Memoirs, etc.* (London edn) and *Rise and Fall of the Irish Nation* (Paris edn). The volume deals with the emergence and eclipse of Grattan's parliament (1782–1800). The better-known and sociologically invaluable *Personal Sketches of his Own Times* (1827–32), written with panache and humour, takes the reader on his various peregrinations. The Irish passages breathe the lifestyle of the country's fire-eating 'half-mounted gentlemen'; the French narratives tell of Dorothy Jordan, of Napoleon, and of life in Paris before and after Waterloo.

In 1828 commissioners discovered the financial irregularities of 1806 and 1810. Pressed to explain, Barrington, by then in his seventies and in ill health, made a personal appearance in London and protested his innocence but did nothing to answer the damning documentary evidence the commissioners had found. Although the joint resolution of both houses of parliament, moved in 1830, to have Barrington removed from his judgeship—the first and only time that the procedure has been employed—proved a foregone conclusion, a later authority (Professor A. D. Gibb) in 1957 expressed the view that Barrington may have had a valid defence. It is more than probable that he did. Barrington died at Versailles, France, on 8 April 1834.

W. N. OSBOROUGH

Sources J. Barrington, *Personal sketches of his own times*, rev. T. Young, 3rd edn, 2 vols. (1869) · *The manuscripts of J. B. Fortescue*, 10 vols., HMC, 30 (1892–1927), vol. 9 · 'Commissioners of judicial inquiry in Ireland', *Parl. papers* (1829), 22.357, no. 85; vol. 4, no. 293; (1830), 4.749, no. 382 · J. Burke and J. B. Burke, *A genealogical and heraldic history of the extinct and dormant baronetcies of England, Ireland, and Scotland*, 2nd edn (1841) · Hansard 2 (1830), 24.1346; 25.1167, 1216–17, 1274–5, 1286 · *Annual Register* (1830) · *Annual Register* (1834) · A. D. Gibb, *Judicial corruption in the United Kingdom* (1957) · Burtchaell & Sadleir, *Alum. Dubl.* · E. Keane, P. Beryl Phair, and T. U. Sadleir, eds., *King's Inns admission papers, 1607–1867*, IMC (1982) · H. Farrar, *Irish marriages: being an index to the marriages in Walker's Hibernian Magazine, 1771–1812*, 2 vols. (1897) · *Index to Dublin grant books and wills down to 1800* (1895) · A. P. W. Malcomson, ed., *Eighteenth century Irish official papers in Great Britain*, 2 (1990)
Archives NL Ire. | Glos. RO, Redesdale MSS · Keele University, Harrowby MSS · NA Ire., Frazer collection · NL Ire., letters to Francis Moore
Likenesses J. Heath, stipple, pubd 1 Aug 1811 (after H. D. Hamilton), BM, NPG, NG Ire.; repro. in J. Barrington, *Historic anecdotes and secret memoirs of the legislative union, between Great Britain and Ireland* (1809–15) · cartoon (*The new Jonah B—ng—n*), BM · oils, TCD

Barrington [*née* Lytton], **Judith**, Lady Barrington (*d.* 1657), gentlewoman, was the daughter of the MP Sir Rowland Lytton (*d.* 1615) of Knebworth, Hertfordshire. Her family had puritan sympathies and was one in which daughters were encouraged to read. In 1612 she married Sir George Smith (*d.* 1620) of Annables, Harpenden, Hertfordshire; the couple had two sons, Rowland (1614–1639), and George (1619–1634).

Judith's interest in estate management is evident in her careful notes of purchases, rents, leases, details of acreage, farming practice, and tithes. When Sir George died in 1620 leaving debts on a mortgaged property, Judith obtained the wardship of her sons and secured the administration of the estate herself. Within two years she had cleared the debts and proved herself a knowledgeable and competent administrator. As a widow she made an impression in her neighbourhood and was considered a good match. Sir Thomas *Barrington (*c.*1585–1644), MP, a widower with five children who became her second husband in 1624, remarked that she had turned down other more eminent suitors than himself and that he thought himself very fortunate. He was obviously deeply smitten and wrote several times to his mother praising Judith; admitting 'I thinke tis a greate advantage to be a successor to a husband not superlatively good' (BL, Egerton MS 2644, fol. 209). The marriage appears to have provided both parties with happiness, although there were no children. Their letters show their mutual commitment to religious reform: both Sir Thomas and Judith supported puritan preachers and Benjamin King dedicated *The Marriage of the Lambe* to them in 1640.

After her marriage to Sir Thomas, which took her to Hatfield Broad Oak, Essex, Judith continued with the management of her jointure lands from her former marriage, mainly in Hertfordshire. When Sir Thomas inherited in 1628 the Barrington estates in Lincolnshire, Essex, and the Isle of Wight, she became closely involved in the management of these too. From 1629 her main residence would appear to have been Hatfield Priory. As well as documenting the family's domestic arrangements, extensive notes in her hand surviving for the period 1614 to the 1640s indicate a detailed understanding of different aspects of estate management. She commented knowledgeably on a number of topics including legal matters, forestry, and gardening. She understood, for example, the practical importance of different types of wood to an estate and the management of an effective programme for timber felling; she appreciated the properties of different varieties of fruit trees. She was not just concerned to maximize profits; she displayed a concern for poor tenants unable to pay rents and attempted to mitigate their financial problems. She explained her understanding of the nature of her role in management: 'I being the manager of all things and usually what he [the steward] did was by my command, as from my husband' (Essex RO, D/DBa L35). A closely written memorandum to the steward, John Kendall, in 1632 where she gave extensive instructions and advice confirms her interpretation of this relationship.

Once Sir Thomas became more frequently absent in London with the opening of the Long Parliament and subsequently with his attendance at the Westminster assembly, Lady Barrington sent him news about events in Essex. With the outbreak of civil war she purveyed military as well as other news, on several occasions offering Sir Thomas advice on matters such as selecting an assistant and calling out the trained bands in time to meet the royalist challenge.

On the death of Sir Thomas in 1644, Lady Barrington was left once more to manage her jointure lands. Almost immediately relations deteriorated between Lady Barrington and her stepson Sir John Barrington, who seems to have been determined to be precise about the exact entitlements of his stepmother. The dispute worsened until finally Sir John petitioned parliament, accusing her of denuding the estate of timber to her own advantage and to the long-term detriment of his heirs. Lady Barrington countered the accusations vigorously, refusing to give in to her litigious stepson. The very large number of his lawsuits and the evidence of her former competence lends support to her side of the argument.

Lady Barrington's relations with the rest of the family, moreover, had been and continued to be cordial and based on mutual affection. Judith had been a frequent and lively correspondent with her mother-in-law, Joan, Lady *Barrington, passing on news and gossip on a wide range of topics both domestic and foreign. She acted as a link in the extended family, placing some members in households, looking after their future, acting as an intermediary with holders of public office, and, for example, writing in 1631 to Viscount Dorchester to seek his help in preventing Sir Thomas's appointment to the unpopular position of sheriff. Later, in her will, codicils distributed bequests of silver and money to affectionately named relatives and servants.

Judith Barrington's extensive papers reveal a depth of knowledge of estate management unusual in the period among women. Her wide-ranging concerns show an understanding of planning for the long-term future of a family, without losing sight of obligations to tenants in difficulties. Her personal letters reveal a woman with real affection for her immediate family and concern for the welfare of the wider family kinship network. Although a few contemporaries and some historians concluded she was bossy and overbearing, the question needs to be raised as to whether this may owe more to her departure from the more acceptable feminine characteristics considered desirable by the contemporary writers, than to a fair analysis of her true character. When she died in 1657 Thomas Goodwin commented in his funeral sermon on her 'Affability mixt with much Gravity; Humility with great Eminency; Temperance and Moderation in midst of great abundance' (Goodwin, 63). She was buried at Knebworth.   CAROLINE M. K. BOWDEN

Sources A. Searle, ed., *Barrington family letters, 1628–1632*, CS, 4th ser., 28 (1983) · G. A. Lowndes, ed., 'The history of the Barrington family', *Transactions of the Essex Archaeological Society*, new ser., 1 (1878), 251–75; new ser., 2 (1879–83), 3–54 · J. T. Cliffe, *The puritan gentry: the great puritan families of early Stuart England* (1984) · F. W. Galpin, 'The household expenses of Sir T. Barrington', *Transactions of the Essex Archaeological Society*, new ser., 12 (1911–13), 203–24 · BL, Egerton MS 2644 · Essex RO, Barrington MSS, D/DBa · T. Goodwin, *A fair prospect* (1658) · will, PRO, PROB 11/268, sig. 362 · letter of J. Barrington to Secretary Dorchester, 1631, PRO, SP 16/205

Archives BL, Egerton MSS, 2644–2648, 2650–2651; Add. MS 46501 · Essex RO, MSS, D/DBa | PRO, J. Barrington to Secretary Dorchester, SP 16/205

Wealth at death see will, PRO, PROB 11/268, sig. 362

Barrington, Kenneth Frank [Ken] (1930–1981), cricketer, was born on 24 November 1930 in Reading, the eldest of the three sons and four daughters of Percy Barrington, a regular soldier, and his wife, Winifred Lambden. His early experience of poverty shaped his life, for cricket, his abiding passion, also became his passport to better times. After attending Wilson Central School and Katesgrove secondary school in Reading, he began his working life at fourteen as a motor mechanic. This was followed by two years as assistant groundsman at Reading cricket club. From there the stockily built Barrington joined Surrey in 1948 as a promising leg-spinner. Encouraged to concentrate on his batting, he worked his way up but did not make his first team début until 1953, having spent 1949–50 in Germany, doing his national service as a lance-corporal in the Royal Wiltshire regiment. On 6 March 1954 he married Ann Cozens (b. 1933), a secretary, the daughter of a butcher turned publican in Reading. She was an important source of strength to him. In the season following his marriage he scored his maiden century, becoming part of the great Surrey side of that vintage. In 1955 he won his first test cap against South Africa at Trent Bridge, but failed to score and was dropped after the next test. It was to be another four years before he returned. During this time he eliminated the risks within his game, and adopted an open-chested stance, which, although ungainly to the eye, proved highly effective in combating the surfeit of in-swing bowling then prevailing.

After a successful return against India in 1959 Barrington prospered on his first senior tour to the West Indies in 1959–60 and all subsequent ones, most notably in Australia (1962–3) and in South Africa (1964–5), where he averaged over 80 in the tests on both tours. Apart from the quickness of his eye and his strength on both front and back foot, the key to his success lay in his supreme concentration and determination never to surrender his wicket. At home he was nearly as dependable and at Old Trafford against Australia in 1964 he achieved his highest test score of 256, but the painstaking manner in which he accumulated his runs rarely made for compulsive viewing. In 1965 he was dropped for slow scoring after a turgid 137 against New Zealand at Edgbaston but celebrated his return at Headingley in style with a swashbuckling 163.

A drawback to this prodigious run scoring was the debilitating effect it had on Barrington's health. For in contrast to his easygoing approach off the field, batting was an emotionally taxing business and after an unhappy beginning to the 1966 series against the West Indies, Barrington, close to a nervous breakdown, felt compelled to withdraw. A year away from test cricket helped revive him, and in 1967 he was back to his best, heading the national averages and scoring centuries in three successive tests against Pakistan. He began the 1967–8 series against the West Indies with a courageous 143 at Port of Spain but once again the tension began to get to him. A serious heart attack in Australia later that year, when participating in a demanding double-wicket competition, brought his premature retirement and he acquired and ran a successful garage and motor dealership in Surrey. He returned to the game in 1975, first as a test selector (a position he held for the rest of his life), then as a manager and finally as assistant manager on five successive tours between 1976 and 1981. His technical expertise as a coach coupled with his benign charm and his devotion to his charges made him a universally revered figure.

Barrington almost cared too much, burdened himself with responsibility and obligations, and once again the strain began to take its toll. It was during a particularly traumatic tour to the West Indies, aggravated by political troubles, that Barrington collapsed and died of a heart attack in Bridgetown, Barbados, on 14 March 1981. His funeral was held at Randalls Park crematorium, Leatherhead, Surrey on 23 March. 'No cricketer was ever more widely mourned', declared *Wisden* (90). 'He set out to become an impregnable batsman and, changing his technique, made himself into one of the finest defensive players of cricket history', asserted John Arlott in *The Guardian* (15 March 1981). He was survived by his wife and their son Guy. His test record of 6806 runs, average 58.67, in a career of 31,714 runs with 76 centuries, average 45.63, ranks with the very best. He also took 273 wickets at an average of 32.63 and held 515 catches. Of medium height (5 foot 9 inches tall), he was a distinctive figure on the field with his neatly cut crinkling black hair, roman nose, and jutting jaw. His soldierly background was reflected in his immaculate dress and meticulous care of his cricket gear. He is commemorated by the Ken Barrington Cricket Centre, which was opened by Surrey at the Oval in 1990 to provide indoor nets and sporting facilities to encourage young cricketers. MARK PEEL

Sources M. Peel, *England expects: a biography of Ken Barrington* (1992) · B. Scovell, *Ken Barrington: a tribute* (1981) · C. Martin-Jenkins, *World cricketers: a biographical dictionary* (1996) · R. Marlar, *Wisden* (1982) · J. Arlott, *The Guardian* (15 March 1981) · J. Arlott, *The Guardian* (1 March 1990) · K. Barrington, *Running into hundreds* (1963) · K. Barrington, *Playing it straight* (1968)
Likenesses P. Eagar, photograph, c.1960, repro. in Marlar, *Wisden*
Wealth at death £190,229: probate, 14 May 1981, *CGPLA Eng. & Wales*

Barrington, Michael. *See* Tenison, Eva Mabel (1880–1961).

Barrington, Rutland [*real name* George Rutland Barrington Fleet] (1853–1922), actor and singer, was born at Penge, Surrey, on 15 January 1853. He was the fourth son of John George Fleet, a wholesale sugar dealer in Fenchurch Street, London, and his wife, Esther, the daughter of the Revd Ferdinand Faithfull, rector of Headley, near Epsom. He was educated at first by a private tutor, then at Headley rectory, and thereafter at Merchant Taylors' School, London, and, on leaving, entered business in the City, where he remained until he was twenty-one. His aunt, Emily *Faithfull, was a well-known dramatic reader, and she was instrumental in obtaining his first engagement with the actor Henry Neville. He made his first appearance on the stage at the Olympic Theatre on 1 September 1874 as Sir George Barclay in *Lady Clancarty* by Tom Taylor. In the following year he went on tour with Mrs Howard Paul, and he remained with her when she obtained an engagement with Richard D'Oyly Carte and insisted that Barrington should be engaged also.

Barrington made his début under D'Oyly Carte's management at the Opera Comique on 17 November 1877, when he took the part of Dr Daly in *The Sorcerer* by Gilbert and Sullivan, and had an immediate success. This first engagement with D'Oyly Carte lasted for eleven years, first at the Opera Comique and later at the Savoy, during which period he played many original parts in Gilbert and Sullivan operas, including Captain Corcoran in *HMS Pinafore* (May 1878), Archibald Grosvenor in *Patience* (April 1881), and King Hildebrand in *Princess Ida* (January 1884). Most important of his original roles was Pooh-Bah in *The Mikado* (March 1885), after which he was even given the affectionate nickname of Pooh-Bah by many of his admirers.

After quitting the Savoy, Barrington managed the St James's Theatre, and opened on 13 October 1888 with *The Dean's Daughter* by Sydney Grundy and F. C. Phillips, which was followed by Gilbert's *Brantinghame Hall*; but both plays proved unsuccessful, and Barrington was forced into bankruptcy.

For a short period Barrington played at the Comedy Theatre under Charles Hawtrey, but he returned to the Savoy, under D'Oyly Carte, in December 1889 in order to play the part of Giuseppe in Gilbert and Sullivan's *The Gondoliers*. This second engagement at the Savoy covered a period of four and a half years (1889–94); as the King in *Utopia Limited* (1893), Barrington performed in the last Gilbert and Sullivan opera. In 1894 he joined George Edwardes's company in order to play Dr Brierley in *A Gaiety Girl* on tour and at Daly's Theatre. After a few other engagements he became increasingly absorbed by musical comedy rather than comic opera and returned to Daly's, where he remained from 1896 to 1904, playing in *The Geisha*, *A Greek Slave*, *San Toy*, *A Country Girl*, and *The Cingalee*.

Thereafter, beyond appearing in *Amāsis* (1906), *The Girl in the Train* (1910), and in occasional revivals at Daly's and the Savoy, Barrington received only minor engagements at various theatres and music-halls. From 1916 to 1918 he was engaged with John Martin-Harvey. With that manager he played his last part, that of Claus in Maurice Maeterlinck's *The Burgomaster of Stilemonde* at the Lyceum Theatre, Edinburgh, in October 1918. In the following January he had a paralytic seizure, but he lingered on, in very straitened circumstances, for a few years. A benefit performance was given for him at the Savoy Theatre in February 1921, and in April 1922 he was elected an annuitant of King George's pension fund for actors. He died on 1 June 1922 at St James's Infirmary, Wandsworth Common.

Barrington was the author of a play, *Bartonmere Towers* (1893), a version of Kingsley's *The Water Babies*, and of two volumes of autobiography (1908, 1911). He also contributed to *Punch*, writing as Lady Gay. He had considerable skill as a watercolourist. In his time Barrington was a man of considerable importance in the theatre, with a fine figure, an abundant sense of humour, and a soft though penetrating voice. The tradition he left in the parts which he created at the Savoy and Daly's long survived him.

J. PARKER, *rev.* NILANJANA BANERJI

Sources *The Times* (2 June 1922) · B. Hunt, ed., *The green room book, or, Who's who on the stage* (1906), 19 · J. Parker, ed., *The green room book, or, Who's who on the stage* (1907), 20 · J. Parker, ed., *The green room book, or, Who's who on the stage* (1908), 25 · J. Parker, ed., *The green room book, or, Who's who on the stage* (1909), 28 · Adams, *Drama* · *Era Almanack and Annual* (1893–6) · E. Reid and H. Compton, eds., *The dramatic peerage* [1891] · R. Wilson and F. Lloyd, *The D'Oyly Carte years* (1984) · C. E. Pascoe, ed., *The dramatic list*, 2nd edn (1880) · *Who's who in the theatre* · Hall, *Dramatic ports.* · personal knowledge (1937)

Likenesses Elliott & Fry, photograph, 1881, NPG · photograph, repro. in *The Times* · photograph, postcard, NPG · portrait, repro. in *Illustrated Sporting and Dramatic News* (13 April 1878) · print (as Fleet), Harvard TC

Barrington, Samuel (1729–1800), naval officer, was the fifth son of John Shute *Barrington, first Viscount Barrington (1678–1734), barrister and MP, and his wife, Anne (*d.* 1763), daughter of Sir William Daines, mayor of and MP for Bristol. His brothers included William Wildman *Barrington, second Viscount Barrington, Daines *Barrington, John *Barrington, and Shute *Barrington. Barrington entered the *Lark* in 1740, under the care of Lord George Gordon. He passed his examination for the rank of lieutenant on 25 September 1745. Early in 1747 he had command of the sloop *Weasel*, and on 29 May he became captain of the frigate *Bellona*. In her he captured the French East Indiaman *Duc de Chartres* off Ushant on 18 August; he was shortly afterwards advanced to the *Romney*.

After the peace Barrington commanded the frigate *Seahorse* in the Mediterranean, and negotiated at Tetuan the release of Britons held by the Barbary corsairs. He next had command of the *Crown* (44 guns) on the coast of Guinea, and in 1754–5, in the *Norwich*, accompanied Commodore Keppel to North America. In 1757 he commanded the *Achilles* (60 guns) in Sir Edward Hawke's expedition to Basque Roads; on 29 May 1758 he assisted in the capture of the French ship of the line *Raisonnable*; and on 4 April 1759, while cruising off Cape Finisterre, he fell in with and captured the *Comte de Saint Florentin* (60 guns), a convoy escort commissioned by the city of Bordeaux.

Barrington afterwards joined Hawke off Brest, and from here he was detached as part of a squadron ordered, under Rear-Admiral Rodney, to destroy the flat-bottomed boats at Le Havre. Rodney hoisted his flag in the *Achilles*, and the objectives of the expedition were successfully carried out

Samuel Barrington (1729–1800), by Sir Joshua Reynolds, 1779

on 4 July. The *Achilles* then returned to the fleet off Brest, and in September, while with the detached squadron in Quiberon Bay, and attempting to cut out some French ships anchored inshore, she grounded heavily. The *Achilles* was got off, but was so badly damaged that she had to be sent home immediately. Barrington commanded the *Achilles* again in 1760 when she was one of the squadron sent out, under the Hon. John Byron, to destroy the fortifications of Louisbourg; and in 1761 he was with Commodore Keppel in the operations against Belle Île, before being sent home with dispatches announcing the successful landing.

In 1762 Barrington was transferred to the *Hero* (74 guns), but continued in the channel under Sir Edward Hawke, and afterwards under Sir Charles Hardy.

After the treaty of Paris (1763) he was unemployed until 1768, when he was appointed to the frigate *Venus* (36 guns), as the governor of the duke of Cumberland, who served with him as volunteer and midshipman. In October he nominally gave up the command, to which the prince was promoted, but resumed it again after a few days, when the prince was further advanced to rear-admiral, and hoisted his flag on the *Venus*, with Barrington as his flag captain. In 1771, on the dispute with Spain about the Falkland Islands, Barrington was appointed to the *Albion* (74 guns); he continued in her, attached to the Channel Fleet, for the next three years. In 1777 he commissioned the *Prince of Wales* (74 guns), and on 23 January 1778, after a few months' cruising in the channel and on the soundings, he was promoted rear-admiral of the white.

Barrington was appointed to command the Leeward Islands squadron after Admiral Shuldham had turned down the post. On 20 June 1778 Barrington arrived at Barbados in the *Prince of Wales*; he was soon joined by another ship of the line. Here Barrington awaited the arrival of an expeditionary force from New York with which he was to attack the French island of St Lucia. The force was to consist of five ships of the line under Commodore Hotham and 5000 troops under General James Grant. However, events in North America delayed the departure of the force and the French at Martinique were able to strike the first blow when news of France's entry into the war over the colonies reached the area at the end of August. On 7 September a French force seized the British island of Dominica and Barrington could do nothing to prevent it. Instead he took his few ships to Antigua to protect the naval dockyard there. Barrington then cruised off Martinique before returning to Barbados in mid-November. At the end of the month the expeditionary force from North America finally arrived and Barrington was able to prepare the attack on St Lucia.

On 12 December 1778 Barrington and Grant sailed from Barbados. The following day found them off St Lucia, and Hotham directed the landing of the troops. The resistance of the French defenders was weak and on 14 December their principal position on Morne Fortuné was captured. However, on the same day the British observed a fleet approaching the island. It was d'Estaing's French squadron which had come from North America and, having collected further forces from Martinique, was intent on preventing the British from completing their capture of St Lucia.

During the night of 14–15 December Barrington and Grant worked feverishly to get their forces into defensive positions on land and at sea. In the morning d'Estaing found the British squadron of seven ships of the line drawn up in line of battle across the entrance to the grand cul de sac. The troop transports were safe inside the bay, behind Barrington's line, while coastal batteries manned by Grant's troops gave further protection to the British ships. Ten French ships of the line attacked Barrington's squadron, but were driven off. A second attack, by twelve ships, took place in the afternoon, with a similar result. The bolder French captains, notably Suffren, wished to anchor their ships opposite the British line and engage in a close combat until their superior numbers eventually prevailed. D'Estaing, however, declined further combat at sea. Instead on 16 December he began to land his troops on St Lucia; they joined the remaining French defenders and forced Grant to withdraw his troops into fortified positions. On 18 December the French launched a major assault against British positions on the Vigie peninsula, but were bloodily repulsed.

Although defeated on sea and land d'Estaing was not, it seemed, willing to give up and he seemed ready to seek to starve the British into surrender. However, he now received word that Admiral Byron's squadron had followed him from North America and was coming to assist Barrington and Grant. On 29 December d'Estaing sailed away from St Lucia and on the following day the French governor of the island surrendered. On 6 January 1779 Byron's storm-battered fleet reached St Lucia. As Byron's squadron had orders to follow d'Estaing wherever he went, the admiral at first tried to preserve a distinction between his force and Barrington's Leeward Islands squadron. However, this policy quickly proved unworkable, so the two forces were merged and Barrington became Byron's second in command. On 19 March 1779 Barrington was advanced to vice-admiral of the blue. In the battle with d'Estaing off Grenada on 6 July 1779 Barrington commanded the van division of Byron's fleet and was hotly engaged, receiving a slight wound. On 22 July he was with Byron's fleet at St Kitts when, anchored in line of battle in Basseterre Roads, it successfully defied d'Estaing's fleet, which then left the area.

Like Byron, Barrington now returned to England. Both wished to justify their conduct in relation to the loss of Grenada, while Barrington felt aggrieved at what he took to be a lack of official appreciation of his capture and defence of St Lucia. He believed he had received only faint praise from the Admiralty, and Lord Sandwich, the first lord, feared that Barrington might join the group of disaffected naval officers led by Admiral Keppel. When Admiral Sir Charles Hardy, commander of the Channel Fleet, died in May 1780 Barrington was offered the post, but he declined it and seemed hostile to Lord North's government, despite the fact that his brother, William Wildman Barrington, second Viscount Barrington, had served as secretary of war until December 1778. Barrington did, however, agree to be second in command to Admiral Geary when he took over the Channel Fleet. In August 1780 Geary fell ill through exhaustion and Barrington was ordered to take the fleet to sea. He declined to do so and was dismissed, Admiral Darby taking over the Channel Fleet.

Barrington was promoted vice-admiral of the white on 16 September 1781, and with the fall of North's administration in early 1782 he was ready to return to active service. Flying his flag in the *Britannia* Barrington became second in command to Admiral Lord Howe in the Channel Fleet. For a time, while Howe was ill, Barrington commanded the fleet off Ushant. On 20 April 1782 Barrington's ships intercepted a French convoy and escort bound for the East Indies. The French ships of the line *Pégase* and *Actionnaire* were captured, along with most of the eighteen-ship convoy. Barrington took part in Lord Howe's relief of Gibraltar (16–19 October 1782) and commanded the van division of his fleet in the subsequent action with the French and Spanish fleets off Cape Spartel (20 October). After returning to England Barrington struck his flag on 20 February 1783 at the end of the war. On 24 September 1787 he was promoted admiral, and in the 1790 armament against Spain in the dispute for Nootka Sound, off Vancouver Island, he hoisted his flag in the *Royal George*, again as second in command to Lord Howe. Peace was preserved, but when war broke out with France in 1793 Barrington did not return to active service. He died, unmarried, on 16 August 1800.

Whatever his problems with politicians, Barrington was popular with both officers and men in the navy. One of his achievements in the West Indies was to obtain for his men a remission of the postage on their letters, which was a burden on them because they did not receive their pay while abroad. A brave and capable officer in action, Barrington's greatest achievement was the capture and defence of St Lucia in 1778. Amphibious operations were notoriously difficult to carry out smoothly and successfully, often being hindered by bad relations between the naval and military commanders. At St Lucia Barrington's good relations with General Grant were as important for success as his defiance of d'Estaing.

ALAN G. JAMIESON

Sources *The Barrington papers*, ed. D. Bonner-Smith, 2 vols., Navy RS, 77, 81 (1937–41) · J. Charnock, ed., *Biographia navalis*, 6 vols. (1794–8) · A. G. Jamieson, 'War in the Leeward Islands, 1775–1783', DPhil diss., U. Oxf., 1981 · N. A. M. Rodger, *The insatiable earl: a life of John Montagu, fourth earl of Sandwich* (1993) · J. H. Owen, 'Operations of the western squadron, 1781–82', *Naval Review*, 15 (1927), 33–53 · P. Mackesy, *The war for America, 1775–1783* (1964) · GEC, *Peerage*
Archives BL, MSS, Rep 9389 · PRO, dispatches, logs, etc., PRO 30/20 | NMM, letters to Lord Sandwich
Likenesses attrib. N. Dance, oils, *c*.1770, NMM · R. Earlom, mezzotint, pubd 1779 (after B. Wilson), BM, NPG · J. Reynolds, oils, 1779, NMM [*see illus.*] · R. Earlom, mezzotint, pubd 1780 (after J. Reynolds), BM, NPG · G. Stuart, oils, *c*.1786, Saltram, Devon · J. S. Copley, oils, 1787–95, NPG · J. Reynolds, oils, *c*.1788, Royal Collection · J. Collyer, line engraving, pubd 1790 (after P. Jean), BM, NPG · W. Sharp, line engraving, pubd 1810 (after J. S. Copley), BM · oils, NPG

Shute Barrington (1734–1826), by Sir Thomas Lawrence, *c*.1815

Barrington, Shute (1734–1826), bishop of Durham, was born on 26 May 1734 at the family seat of Becket, Berkshire, sixth and youngest son of the prominent protestant politician John Shute *Barrington, first Viscount Barrington in the Irish peerage (1678–1734), and of his wife, Anne (*d*. 1763), daughter and coheir of Sir William Daines, who served as MP, sheriff, and mayor of Bristol.

Education, marriages, and early career In December 1734, when Shute Barrington was six months old, his father died after being flung from a carriage. His eldest brother, William Wildman *Barrington, second Viscount Barrington (1717–1793), took over the paternal role of forwarding Shute's interests. His other brothers were John *Barrington, Samuel *Barrington, and Daines *Barrington. Shute was brought up at Becket until old enough for Eton College. He matriculated, on 10 April 1752, as a gentleman commoner at Merton College, Oxford, graduated BA on 21 January 1755, and became both a fellow of Merton and a student of Christ Church. Ordained in 1756 by Thomas Secker, then bishop of Oxford, he proceeded MA on 10 October 1757 and delivered an acclaimed public oration at the ceremonial presentation of the Pomfret marbles to Oxford University. As a young man Barrington underwent an operation for 'the stone', which left him with a lifetime caution about diet.

By 1759 William Barrington was secretary at war in the duke of Newcastle's administration and was urging Newcastle of Shute's merits: 'a most amiable and accomplished young man … who has never in his whole life done anything which I have not approved. … As we belong

to Berkshire a stall at Windsor would be peculiarly acceptable' (Barrington to Newcastle, 26 Dec 1759, BL, Add. MS 32896, fol. 333). At about the same time Shute Barrington gained another influential patron in George III, who took a liking to him and appointed him chaplain-in-ordinary shortly after he acceded to the throne in 1760.

On 2 February 1761 Barrington married Lady Diana Beauclerk (*d*. 1766), daughter of Charles, second duke of St Albans. William thought him bold to marry before his livelihood was secured but suggested him to Newcastle for dean of Bristol: an unlikely first preferment for a man under thirty, he conceded, but justified by his grandfather's connection with the city. Instead, on 12 September 1761, Barrington was awarded a Hereford prebend, which was exchanged for one of greater value on 22 May 1762. A Christ Church canonry was added on 10 October 1761 and he graduated DCL at Christ Church on 10 June 1762. About 1763 William Barrington secured Lord Grenville's assurance that Shute would be the next dean of Windsor. Unfortunately the Grenville administration fell in May 1765, four months before the deanery became vacant. Soon after this disappointment Shute suffered personal tragedy when, on 28 May 1766, Lady Diana died while bearing a stillborn child.

Barrington received the St Paul's prebend Consumpta per mare on 23 April 1768. In 1769, aged only thirty-five, he was nominated bishop of Llandaff; he kissed George III's hand on 14 July but a delay in the formalities meant that he was not consecrated until 1 October. He resigned his Hereford prebend but kept St Paul's. In 1770 Barrington published a second edition of his father's essays in biblical scholarship, *Miscellanea sacra*. He also contributed to the third edition (1782) of William Bowyer's *Critical Conjectures and Observations on the New Testament*.

On 20 June 1770 Barrington married, as his second wife, Jane (*d.* 1807), only daughter of Sir Berkeley William Guise bt, of Rendcombe, Gloucestershire; her dowry included extensive property. The marriage was childless except for an adopted daughter. Unfortunately Jane found the St Paul's residence intolerably confined and Barrington felt unable to keep the preferment without performing his full duties. On 5 December 1776 he exchanged it for the Windsor canonry of John Douglas, at a considerable loss of income.

Public controversies Barrington first experienced public controversy during the campaign against the constitutional requirement of subscription to the Thirty-Nine Articles, which climaxed in the Feathers tavern petition of February 1772. During the Lords debate on the 1771 abolition bill Barrington declared in favour of subscription, quoting the writings of Joseph Priestley as evidence of the abolitionists' subversive intentions. His stand caused outcry: not only had Shute ancestors been prominent parliamentarians in the civil war but his own father had been a leading defender of dissenters' interests, attacking subscription as a mistaken principle. Accused of breaking faith with his forebears, on 30 January 1772 Barrington aggravated matters by preaching the Westminster Abbey Lords sermon, commemorating the martyrdom of Charles I, in which he again uncompromisingly repudiated any need for constitutional reform.

In the spring of 1782 Lord Shelburne annoyed George III by manoeuvring William Barrington, now retired from active political service, out of his civil-list pension. The king received William amiably, assured him of his 'kind regards for him and his family' and reinstated the pension (Barrington, *Political Life*, 208). George III punished Shelburne by demanding the plum diocese of Salisbury for Shute Barrington rather than for Shelburne's candidate, Hinchcliffe of Peterborough.

At Salisbury, from 1782, Barrington won an immediate reputation for generosity and set up an endowed fund for the relief of necessitous clergy. He financed extensive repairs to the episcopal palace and boldly launched major restoration work on the cathedral, trusting to public subscription to cover the cost. An anonymous Berkshire gentleman toured the workings one day, signed the subscription book, and handed over a bank bill for £1000; he was George III. Barrington's 1783 charge declared his 'ardent wish of contributing to the general welfare' and being 'the general friend of all' (Barrington, *Sermons*, 76); to the end of his life he characteristically signed himself 'Your affectionate Friend and Brother'. The charge also, however, caused controversy by a sharp rebuke to Whitefield and to Calvinistic Methodism. Barrington enjoyed an uneasy theological relationship with the evangelicals; no enemy himself to inward religion, he was adamant that 'the extraordinary operations of the Holy Spirit' were

long over, and the spirit's ordinary working, on which he acknowledged reliance, was 'not manifested in fancied impulses or imaginary calls, but in the more certain evidence of it's fruits, a good life' (ibid., 89).

Barrington was much more at ease with the practical philanthropy of William Wilberforce. While most bishops regarded Wilberforce's circle warily Barrington worked closely with Wilberforce's friend Beilby Porteus, bishop of London, and after Porteus's death he himself became Wilberforce's principal episcopal patron. His high standing and influence, no less than his considerable wealth, were invaluable to Wilberforce, who described him to Hannah More as 'a very sun, the centre of an entire system' (Overton, 89). Barrington interested himself in Wilberforce's causes, denouncing the slave trade, in his 1775 sermon for the Society for the Propagation of the Gospel, as 'a traffic as inhuman in the mode of carrying it on, as it is unjustifiable in it's principle' (Barrington, *Sermons*, 45). In 1779 he sponsored a bill to uphold the sanctity of marriage by preventing divorced women from remarrying; passed by the Lords it was routed by Charles James Fox in the Commons. A response, entitled *The house of peeresses … containing the debates of several peeresses on the bishop of Llandaff's bill*, went to five editions.

Barrington's translation to Durham in 1791 greatly increased his scope for practical usefulness. As prince bishop of Durham he committed himself energetically to Wilberforce's agenda of philanthropy and moral reform. Already an active supporter of the 1788 Proclamation Society, he helped found the 1796 Society for Bettering the Condition and Improving the Comforts of the Poor, commending it repeatedly to his clergy and taking imaginative practical steps himself. Jane Barrington played a full part in her husband's charitable work; on one occasion she personally presented every cottager in a Durham village with a hive of bees. In due course Barrington joined at least forty-seven Wilberforce societies, becoming president of five, vice-president of twelve, governor of six, and patron of two.

In Salisbury, Barrington had given decisive support to the Sunday schools movement, commending to his clergy the work of Morton Pitt. Opponents of Sunday schooling blamed the French Revolution on mass education; Barrington dismissed that as fantasy. The experience of several parish Sunday schools, founded about 1784 with his encouragement, convinced him of their value as a means of eradicating vice among the rising generation of the lower social orders. In Durham, Barrington founded schools in the mining communities of Upper Weardale, financed by his shrewd uprating of the episcopal mining leases, and after the 1811 launch of the National Society he encouraged school building throughout the diocese. The Barrington School, established at Bishop Auckland in 1810, became the National Society's first model school and trained future teachers in the monitorial system of Andrew Bell, whom Barrington rewarded with the lucrative mastership of Sherburn Hospital. Another influence was Hannah More, praised in his 1797 charge. Near the end of his life a court action for unpaid lead-mining royalties won arrears of £70,000. With this were established both the Barrington Fund, to augment small benefices and help needy widows and orphans of diocesan clergy, and the Barrington Schools Fund, through which Barrington's educational work long outlasted his death.

Barrington was the most important ecclesiastical figure aligned with both the evangelical reformers and their high-church counterparts, known as the Hackney Phalanx. This entailed some delicate drawing of boundaries. The evangelicals often worked interdenominationally; Hackney worked only with professed churchmen. With Porteus, Barrington championed the 1799 interdenominational Religious Tract Society and its controversial offspring, the British and Foreign Bible Society, which was founded in March 1804 through evangelical impatience with the reluctance of the Society for Promoting Christian Knowledge (SPCK) to print bibles for Welsh Methodism. Porteus and Barrington's support 'was the most important thing that happened to the Bible Society for some years, perhaps decisive for its success, and there is no better sign of their closeness to Evangelicalism' (Brown, 246). Barrington appointed John Owen, the Bible Society's founding secretary, as one of his chaplains. In 1810, during the development of the National Society proposals, Barrington argued strongly against a rule requiring the society's schools to use only books from the SPCK catalogue, which excluded nonconformist authors. The rule stood, and Barrington's amendment, empowering a bishop to authorize additional books for use in his own diocese, was defeated. In consequence many Durham diocesan schools were unaffiliated to the National Society. Barrington none the less remained a valued supporter of the society, and of the SPCK. In the field of overseas mission he took a harder line. Both he and Porteus refused to lend their support to the Church Missionary Society, founded by John Venn and other evangelicals of the Clapham Sect. While the society protested its loyalty to the church and its bishops, Barrington and others feared that the Church of England's name would be used to support initiatives alien to its practices. In 1813 Barrington's continued refusal deterred his protégé Thomas Burgess, bishop of St David's, from accepting Church Missionary Society membership.

In 1794 the Roman Catholic historian John Lingard arrived in Barrington's diocese to tutor a small community of students who had been driven from Douai College by the French Revolution. The new college moved to Ushaw in 1808. Barrington gave generously to exiled French bishops and clergy, tactfully acting through his confidential lawyer, the prominent Catholic Charles Butler. Politically and ecclesiastically, however, he inherited his father's protestant convictions; his 1775 sermon for the Society for the Propagation of the Gospel urged the necessity of preserving 'untutored savages' from 'missionaries of the Romish Church', and proposed establishing an Indian hierarchy to check 'the encroachments of Popery' (Barrington, *Sermons*, 39–40). On 27 February

1799, decreed a general fast to strengthen the war effort against France, Barrington preached the official Lords sermon and caused major controversy by blaming Roman Catholicism for the French Revolution. Popish corruptions of the pure Catholic faith had, he claimed, crippled French Catholicism's ability to compel belief, leaving it helpless against rationalist scepticism. His 1801 Durham charge, while denying any wish to cause pain to the revolution's unhappy victims, re-emphasized this argument. Accused of preaching up a crusade against Catholics, Barrington, in his 1806 charge, restated 'the grounds of our separation from the Romish Church', identifying these chiefly as image worship, 'multiplying mediators and intercessors', and holding public services 'in an unknown tongue' (ibid., 328–40). In 1807 Lingard's published *Remarks*, criticizing Barrington's charge, caused an explosion of retaliatory pamphlets from clergy, including the evangelical G. S. Faber, Nathaniel Hollingsworth, and Thomas Le Mesurier. The most devastating of these, from Barrington's chaplain Henry Phillpotts, writing as 'a clergyman of the diocese', provoked Lingard's 1808 *General Vindication*, which Phillpotts immediately attacked in his *Second Letter*, thus drawing another counter-letter from Lingard. Barrington, whose wife died at Mongewell, near Wallingford, Berkshire, on 8 August 1807, made no response until April 1810, when he issued an *ad clerum* detailing the development of the controversy. Subtitled 'The grounds on which the Church of England separated from the Church of Rome reconsidered, in a view of the Romish doctrine of the Eucharist', this argued against transubstantiation, devotions focused on the host, and withholding the cup from the laity; it went through several impressions and was for some time regarded as a classic. Later in 1810 Barrington's last episcopal charge, entitled *Grounds of Union between the Churches of England and of Rome*, urged the Roman communion to reform and be reunited with 'the Catholics of the Church of England' (ibid., 443). The two charges and *ad clerum* were reissued, with Phillpotts's tracts, in 1813, and were influential in the debates on Catholic emancipation. Lingard, saddened by the 1809 typhus outbreak at Ushaw College, in which five students died, and by his failure to be appointed college president at the 1810 vacancy, left the diocese in 1811. Phillpotts was rewarded in 1808 with the wealthy rectory of Gateshead, adding a Durham prebend in 1809.

In exercising his valuable Durham patronage Barrington observed family piety by giving his nephew George the rich rectory of Sedgefield, but used the opulent incumbencies and canonries at his disposal principally to attract academically distinguished clergy into the diocese, among them William Paley, whose *Natural Theology* was written at Bishopwearmouth. Barrington hoped the influence of such clergy would raise standards generally. He paid great attention to clerical education; his 1789 Salisbury *ad clerum* laid down the high standards required of his ordinands, and his Durham examining chaplain Thomas Burgess gained a heroic reputation for strictness. Barrington had little success in countering the expansion of Methodism in his diocese. In the rapidly growing centres of population parish boundaries were unrealistic and church accommodation drastically inadequate, as an 1824 inquiry by Charles Thorp, acting archdeacon of Durham, made plain. Dividing Phillpotts's Gateshead parish required an act of parliament and took, in total, sixteen years; Barrington also licensed schoolrooms for worship in three hard-pressed parishes and built seven chapels of ease, but this had limited impact. While clergy with mining revenues were becoming rich and arousing deep resentments by their determination to improve lease values, tithe resistance imperilled the livelihood of poor clergy, and Barrington failed to enforce the statutory minimum curates' stipends laid down by parliament in 1796 and in 1813.

Relations between senior Durham clergy and the radical political establishment, never easy, deteriorated into open hostility after 1819. Phillpotts, with his singular gift for invective, was particularly hated. Barrington remained loyal, presenting Phillpotts to the lead-mining parish of Stanhope in 1820, and in 1821 giving his name to the libel suit against John Ambrose Williams, editor of the radical *Durham Chronicle*. Approaching ninety Barrington lived in increasing seclusion, keeping short Durham residences and dividing the rest of his time between Mongewell and Worthing. In 1826 he suffered a stroke, and five weeks later, on 25 March 1826, he died at his residence in Cavendish Square, London. He was buried in the family vault at Mongewell church on 31 March.

Barrington's attractive combination of personal piety and pastoral zeal won him many admirers. His life reflected his own definition of 'genuine Christianity' as 'the union of pure devotion with universal benevolence' (Barrington, *Sermons*, 244). He sustained an extraordinary level of public charity and unobtrusive private giving by a domestic regime of strict economy: 'No one … ever better understood the true value of money, or employed it more judiciously as the instrument of virtue' (*Durham County Advertiser*, 8 April 1826, 4, col. 1). His daily routine began and ended with more than an hour of devotional reading and private prayer, followed by corporate family worship. He believed religion to be inherently personal, necessitating self-reformation 'by the all-powerful aid of God's holy spirit … requiring, on our parts, earnest, painful, and laborious endeavours' (Barrington, *Sermons*, 74). Theologically he found common ground with both evangelicals and those of orthodox views, but he was not fully identified with any group. He combined a profound religious individualism, holding that a society could be reformed only by reforming the individuals who composed it, with a staunch defence of the Church of England's political establishment. While valuing discipline and order he thought formal and external religious observance worthless except as an expression of inward commitment. He is credited with having been the first bishop to discard the wig. E. A. VARLEY

Sources S. Barrington, *Sermons, charges and tracts* (1811) • W. Fordyce, *The history and antiquities of the county palatine of Durham*, 1 (1857) • *Durham County Advertiser* (1 April 1826) • *Durham County Advertiser* (8 April 1826) • *Durham County Advertiser* (22 April 1826) • *Durham County Advertiser* (29 April 1826) • F. K. Brown, *Fathers of the Victorians: the age of Wilberforce* (1961) • N. Sykes, *Church and state in England in the XVIII century* (1934) • S. H. Cassan, *Lives and memoirs of the bishops of Sherborne and Salisbury, from the year 705 to 1824*, 3 pts (1824) • W. B. Maynard, 'The ecclesiastical administration of the archdeaconry of Durham, 1774–1856', PhD diss., U. Durham, 1973 • S. Barrington, ed., *The political life of William Wildman Viscount Barrington* (1815) • G. F. A. Best, *Temporal pillars: Queen Anne's bounty, the ecclesiastical commissioners, and the Church of England* (1964) • E. A. Varley, *The last of the prince bishops: William Van Mildert and the high church movement of the early nineteenth century* (1992) • G. C. B. Davies, *Henry Phillpotts, bishop of Exeter* (1954) • *VCH Berkshire*, vol. 2 • R. Surtees, *The history and antiquities of the county palatine of Durham*, 1 (1816) • GEC, *Peerage*, new edn, vol. 1 • J. H. Overton, *The English church in the nineteenth century, 1800–1833* (1894) • *Fasti Angl.* (Hardy), vols. 1–2 • J. Walsh and others, eds., *The Church of England, c.1689–c.1833* (1993) • W. S. F. Pickering, *A social history of the diocese of Newcastle, 1882–1982* (1981) • J. C. D. Clark, *English society, 1688–1832: ideology, social structure and political practice during the ancien régime* (1985) • E. Hughes, *North country life in the eighteenth century*, 1 (1952) • D. Milburn, *A history of Ushaw College* (1964) • O. Chadwick, *The Victorian church*, 2 vols. (1966–70) • J. Murray, *Proclaim the good news: a short history of the Church Missionary Society* (1985)

Archives BL, corresp. and papers, DEP 9389 • LPL, corresp. • U. Durham L., corresp. and papers mainly relating to his translation to Durham • Wilts. & Swindon RO, corresp. and papers relating mainly to restoration of Salisbury Cathedral | BL, corresp. with first and second earls of Liverpool, Add. MSS 38197–38469 • BL, letters to Lord Auckland, Add. MSS 38197–38469 • Bodl. Oxf., corresp. with William Gilpin • Bodl. Oxf., letters to Thomas Burgess • LPL, corresp. with Sir James E. Smith

Likenesses G. Romney, oils, 1784–6, Christ Church Oxf. • attrib. J. Opie, oils, c.1800–1810, Bodl. Oxf. • W. Say, mezzotint, pubd 1812 (after W. Owen), NPG • T. Lawrence, oils, c.1815, Auckland Castle, co. Durham [see illus.] • E. Hastings, oils, 1821, Balliol Oxf. • F. Chantrey, marble statue, Durham Cathedral • F. Chantrey, pencil drawing, NPG • G. Hayter, group portrait, oils (*The trial of Queen Caroline*, 1820), NPG • W. Owen, oils, Balliol Oxf. • C. Picart, stipple (after H. Edridge), BM, NPG; repro. in *Contemporary portraits* (1810) • A. Robertson, miniature • C. Watson, engraving (after A. Robertson), repro. in Surtees, *History and antiquities of … Durham*, vol. 1, p. 124 • portrait, Salisbury episcopal palace

Wealth at death under £160,000: *Durham County Advertiser* (22 April 1826), 2, col. 5

Barrington, Sir Thomas, second baronet (c.1585–1644), politician, was the eldest son of Sir Francis *Barrington (c.1560–1628) and his wife, Joan (c.1558–1641) [see Barrington, Joan, Lady Barrington], daughter of Sir Henry Cromwell alias Williams of Hinchingbrooke, Huntingdonshire. Before he attended Cambridge University in 1601 Barrington was educated by his godly and forceful parents. In 1602 he was admitted to Gray's Inn. Although of a less than robust constitution and often subject to fits of melancholy and depression, throughout his life Barrington maintained an interest in both indoor and outdoor sports. In 1611 he married Frances Gobert, the daughter and coheir of John Gobert of Coventry. Although Frances brought £3000 to the marriage and together they produced six sons and two daughters, Barrington remained melancholic. The family chaplain, Ezekiel Rogers, commented that 'not only in the day but the night watching, and midnight raisings, I did much impair my health in accompanying of him' (BL, Egerton MS 2648, fol. 48). Frances died in 1623, and the following year Barrington married Judith (d. 1657) [see Barrington, Judith, Lady Barrington], daughter of Sir Rowland Lytton of Knebworth, Hertfordshire, and widow of Sir George Smith of Annables, Harpenden, in the same county. She shared his trenchant puritan beliefs and through her forceful personality gradually assumed the role of managing the Barrington estates. Barrington was knighted in 1613 and on his father's death in July 1628 inherited his baronetcy.

Barrington's depressive tendencies do not appear to have hindered his public activities. He was returned on his father's interest as an MP for Newtown, Isle of Wight, in 1621, 1624, 1625, 1626, and 1628. In his first parliament he kept an extensive diary of the proceedings of the Commons (published in Notestein, Relf, and Simpson, vol. 3). Barrington was an avid listener, and his notes provide a good representation of the tenor and mood of the house. He attempted to record the proceedings verbatim; included among his notes are important passages on the grievances relating to the East India Company, the fees of masters in chancery, and the attack on the notorious monopolist Sir Giles Mompesson. In the case of the latter, on 3 March 1621, in a rare speech in the house Barrington moved that Mompesson's papers should be seized.

Barrington did not play a leading role in parliament until 1626 when, although not recorded as speaking, he was named to numerous committees and was involved in the attempted impeachment of George Villiers, first duke of Buckingham. Shortly after the parliament ended Barrington was removed from the commission of the peace owing to his father's stern resistance to the forced loan. Although he was restored to the bench in 1628, this no doubt influenced his attitude towards the crown and in the 1628 parliament he was firmly identified as a defender of the Commons' privileges and liberties. Barrington's religious beliefs dominated his thinking and activities, and he concluded reluctantly that it was better for the parliament to salvage whatever it could in religion rather than oppose Charles outright. However, by the end of the 1629 session his disillusionment with the crown is clear:

Well, God of his mercy look on us; 'tis far more easy to speak bravely than to be magnanimous in suffering, yet he whose heart bleeds not at the threats of these times is too stupid. I pray God send us better grounds for comfort, and withal to be armed for the worst that can befall us. (Searle, 59–60)

In 1631 Barrington was admitted to the Providence Island Company. The company was primarily a puritan colonizing adventure, and Barrington found himself among not only those with similar religious views but many of the leading critics of Caroline policy, such as Robert, earl of Warwick, Viscount Saye and Sele, Robert, Lord Brooke, Benjamin Rudyerd, and John Pym. Barrington served as deputy governor in the early 1630s but his attendance at meetings tailed off later in the decade when, possibly, he did not wish to be too closely involved in the secret negotiations with the Scottish rebels. However, he successfully stood as an 'opposition' candidate for Essex in the elections to the Short Parliament with the full

support of the earl of Warwick and a puritan preaching campaign in the county. Shortly after the opening of parliament he delivered to the Commons an Essex petition which complained of Laudian innovations in religion and the harassment of godly ministers and asked for a parliament to be held annually. In the elections to the Long Parliament, Barrington secured a seat at Colchester, and he rapidly established himself as one of the leading opponents of Charles. He was heavily involved with the Commons financial administration concerning the collection and allocation of the 1641 subsidy, negotiations for a parliamentary loan from the City of London, and deliberations with the Scots for the payments due to them.

Predictably Barrington's main interest was in religion and moral reform. Included among the committees to which he was nominated were those for drafting the charges against Archbishop William Laud, for replacing scandalous clergy, and for impeaching bishops who had supported the canons of 1640. On 11 June 1641 he seconded the proposal that the house should discuss the 'root and branch' bill calling for the abolition of the episcopacy, stating that it was time to take an axe 'to the root of the tree … and cut it down' (BL, Egerton MS 2651, fol. 104). Throughout the Long Parliament he was closely connected with John Pym, whom he had known through the Providence Island adventure. It was Pym who moved that Barrington should be a witness at the trial of Strafford, and they both later presented to the upper house the Commons' bill of attainder against the earl. They also served together on the committee which drafted the protestation after the army plot of 3 May 1641 and on the important recess committee later the same year.

Barrington gradually came to believe that armed conflict was a distinct possibility and from mid-1641 became more and more involved with matters of defence. In January 1642 he was added to the militia committee, and he assisted in preparing the militia ordinance. Shortly afterwards, when his old friend the earl of Warwick was named lord lieutenant of Essex, Barrington was made one of the deputy lieutenants, and he helped organize the implementation of the ordinance in Essex. With Warwick fully occupied with his office of admiral of the fleet, Barrington quickly became the acknowledged leader of the parliamentarian party in Essex. In August 1642 he was dispatched by the Commons, along with his fellow MP for Colchester Sir Harbottle Grimston, to restore order in the county and appease the pro-parliamentarian crowds who had plundered the homes of Catholics and suspected royalists. From 1642 until his death in late 1644 Barrington shuttled between Westminster and Essex. In the Commons he was named to the committee for the defence of the kingdom, and he played a leading role in the formation of the eastern association. Despite initial reservations about the eastern association enterprise he carried the Commons' approval of it to the Lords. His puritanism made him a natural choice when he was named as a member of the Westminster assembly of divines. In Essex he was actively involved in the raising of troops and the collection of money—a task he seems to have performed exceedingly well despite the shortcomings of the association as an arrangement for collective defence. Barrington was usually based at the parliamentarian headquarters at Chelmsford but although a regimental colonel he is not known to have taken any active role in the fighting.

Barrington died at Hatfield Broad Oak, Essex, on 18 September 1644. His exertions on behalf of parliament and the Providence Island Company had left his son and heir, Sir John Barrington, £10,000 in debt and forced him to seek protection from his creditors by petitioning the Commons. After the Restoration the family was able to regain control of the vast Barrington estates, and Sir John enjoyed an annual income of about £4000.

CHRIS R. KYLE

Sources Essex RO, Barrington papers • A. Searle, ed., *Barrington family letters, 1628–1632*, CS, 4th ser., 28 (1983) • *JHC*, 1–4 (1547–1646) • W. Notestein, F. H. Relf, and H. Simpson, eds., *Commons debates, 1621*, 3 (1935) • BL, Egerton MS 2646 • colonial entry books, Bahamas, PRO, SP colonial, C.O. 124 • C. Holmes, *The eastern association in the English civil war* (1974) • J. T. Cliffe, *Puritans in conflict* (1988) • C. H. Firth and R. S. Rait, eds., *Acts and ordinances of the interregnum, 1642–1660*, 3 vols. (1911) • *The journal of Sir Simonds D'Ewes from the beginning of the Long Parliament to the opening of the trial of the earl of Strafford*, ed. W. Notestein (1923) • HoP, *Commons, 1604–29* [draft] • Keeler, *Long Parliament* • GEC, *Baronetage* • Rymer, *Foedera*, new edn, 2.8. • inquisition post mortem, PRO, C 142/777/100 • J. Foster, *The register of admissions to Gray's Inn, 1521–1889, together with the register of marriages in Gray's Inn chapel, 1695–1754* (privately printed, London, 1889) • J. Walter, *Understanding popular violence in the English revolution: the Colchester plunderers* (1999) • HoP, *Commons, 1640–60* [draft]
Archives BL, corresp. and papers, Egerton MSS 2643–2651 • Essex RO, Chelmsford, parliamentary diaries, family and estate papers
Wealth at death see PRO, C 142/777/100

Barrington, Sir Vincent Hunter Barrington Kennett-

(1844–1903), humanitarian worker and businessman, was born on 3 September 1844 at Bagna di Lucca, Italy, the eldest son of Vincent Frederick Kennett (*b.* 1799), a retired captain of the East India Company army, and his wife, Arabella Henrietta Barrington (formerly Hughes-Lee; *d.* 1884), daughter and coheir of Sir Jonah Barrington. Kennett added his mother's surname to his own on her death in 1884. Kennett was educated at Eton College and won a scholarship to Trinity College, Cambridge, in 1863 to read mathematics. He graduated in 1867, took a law degree in 1868, moved to the inns of court, and was called to the bar in 1872.

In 1867 Kennett became associated with the British league of the order of the hospital of St John of Jerusalem. This in turn led to his involvement with the Society for Aiding and Ameliorating the Condition of the Sick and Wounded in Time of War (known as the National Aid Society and, later, as the Red Cross). The British National Aid Society, which was established in 1868, offered humanitarian assistance to both sides during the Franco-Prussian War of 1870–71. Kennett became one of the convoy agents in charge of the distribution of funds and supplies and worked with the French republican armies in the Loire and later with the Prussians in Meaux. Following the armistice he became involved in further humanitarian work in eastern France. Kennett returned to England in

April 1871, but went on to provide help during the Carlist War in Spain (1873–5), the Serbo-Turkish War (1876–7), and the Turko-Russian War (1877–8). On 12 January 1878 he made a financially advantageous marriage to Alicia Georgette Sandeman, daughter of George Glas Sandeman, and a member of the Sandeman family of wine growers. Alicia Barrington was the author of *Bible History for Children* (1889). Kennett returned to Constantinople within a month of his wedding; the organizational role which he assumed during the conflict probably makes him one of the earliest instances of a 'professional', albeit unpaid, humanitarian administrator. After 1878 Kennett became involved in the St John Ambulance movement and served as an instructor.

Kennett was also a freelance business agent, serving on the commissions of universal exhibitions in Brussels, Melbourne, and Paris between 1876 and 1898. In 1883 he was elected to the London chamber of commerce, becoming its deputy chairman in 1889, and travelled to India on behalf of Edison Electrical Company. From 1883 he served on the Metropolitan Asylums Board. He worked with the Aid Society once again during the Sudan expedition and the Serbo-Bulgarian War in 1885. In the latter conflict he held a semi-official role, combining his humanitarian role with a diplomatic one. Kennett-Barrington was knighted in May 1886. He was an alderman of London county council in 1890–91. Despite his work with the chamber of commerce and at the Metropolitan Asylums Board becoming more demanding over the years, Kennett-Barrington nevertheless helped while on business trips to establish Red Cross branches in Buenos Aires in 1892 and in Venezuela in 1895.

Kennett-Barrington was an active man who participated in many sports, including fishing, shooting, and ballooning. He died at his home, 57 Albert Hall Mansions, Knightsbridge, on 13 July 1903 as the result of injuries received in a ballooning accident. He was survived by his wife. Kennett-Barrington is an example of the first generation of humanitarian administrators who undertook vital field work for the Red Cross. His letters provide an important record of an often poorly documented area of history. He won the silver and bronze medals of the Royal Humane Society (1873, 1885) and published *River Pollution* (1883), *Hospital and Ambulance Organisation of the Metropolitan Asylums Board* (1893), *Floating Hospitals for Infectious Cases* (1883), and *Ambulance Organisation of the Metropolis during Epidemics* (1884).

BERTRAND O. TAITHE

Sources A. L. Lascelles and J. M. Alberich, eds., *Letters from the Carlist wars, 1874–1876* (1987) • P. Morris, ed., *First aid to the battlefront: life and letters of Sir Kennett-Barrington (1844–1903)* (1992) • *Report of the English Society for Aiding and Ameliorating the Condition of the Sick and Wounded in Time of War on the Franco-German war of 1870–1871* (1872) • *Report to the Safford House Committee for the Relief of Sick and Wounded Turkish Soldiers* (1879) • m. cert. • d. cert. • *WWW* • *CGPLA Eng. & Wales* (1903)
Wealth at death £26,280 17s. 2d.: probate, 1 Dec 1903, *CGPLA Eng. & Wales*

Barrington, William Wildman, second Viscount Barrington

(1717–1793), politician, was born in Beckett, near Faringdon, Berkshire, on 15 January 1717, the eldest

**William Wildman Barrington, second Viscount Barrington
(1717–1793),** by Sir Thomas Lawrence, *c*.1791

son of John Shute *Barrington, first Viscount Barrington
(1678–1734), politician, and his wife, Anne Daines (*d*. 1763),
the daughter of Sir William Daines. He had five brothers,
including John *Barrington, who became a major-
general; Samuel *Barrington, later vice-admiral of the
white; Daines *Barrington, a judge and natural philosopher; and Shute *Barrington, bishop of Durham. There
were also three sisters: Sarah, mother of the writer and
rural improver Uvedale Price, Anne, and Mary. The
family's country seat at Beckett was a small house that had
been attacked and burnt during the civil war.

After having received his education under a Mr Graham,
the father of Sir Robert Graham, one of the barons of the
court of exchequer, Barrington succeeded to the peerage
on 14 December 1734. At the age of eighteen he went to
Geneva and proceeded from there on the grand tour. He
returned to England in 1738 and on 13 March 1740 was
elected as a member for Berwick upon Tweed. On 16 September 1740 he married Mary Grimston (*d*. 1764), the
daughter of Henry Lovell and Mary Cole, and the widow of
the Hon. Samuel Grimston. The couple had no children
and the marriage seems to have been an unhappy one:
there was a rumour, for example, that Barrington had a
liaison with Lady Harrington, the wife of the commander
of the Horse Grenadier Guards, until 1770. He had a very
ingratiating manner at times, with both political colleagues and acquaintances of the opposite sex. In 1771 the
Town and Country Magazine described him thus:

> He is in person genteel and well made, though under the
> middle size; his features rather delicate than masculine; his
> address gracious and engaging, particularly to the ladies; and

he possesses a spirit of liberality towards them that never
fails to please.   (*Town and Country Magazine*, 8, 1771, 10)

Barrington's political career was notorious because he
held continuous public office for over thirty years
throughout a whole series of ministerial changes. This
long tenure of office drew much contemporary criticism,
and for long the accepted verdict was that Barrington was
a sycophantic time-server. Modern reassessment is that he
was the quintessential politician–administrator in an age
when the civil service had not yet separated from politics,
and a man of principle who contributed much to the
development of the administration of government in
Britain. On entering parliament, Barrington, in contrast
with his later career, was associated with the opposition to
Walpole's government. His maiden speech on 2 March
1741 was against a bill which sought to revive a scheme
empowering justices of the peace to issue warrants in
search of seamen. He remained in opposition after Walpole's fall in 1742 until 1744, when, with the Cobham
group, he went over to government. In February 1746 he
was appointed a lord of the Admiralty and thus embarked
on a long and unbroken career in public service. As his
brother Shute noted, once the folly of opposition and the
rectitude of duty were 'offered to his mind, the force and
truth of them became irresistible' (Barrington, 11).

Barrington quickly gained a reputation as an effective
administrator and, at George II's request for a man of
economies, he was appointed to the office of the master of
the great wardrobe in 1754. He had applied to the duke of
Newcastle for a seat on the Treasury board, and got a better post instead. Thereafter he never asked for office,
always taking what he was given. Masters of the wardrobe
had political influence and could still progress to higher
office. Their duties involved providing the daily necessities of the king's court and creating the ceremonial
background of the king's life. While in office Barrington
continued with the process of economizing which had
been initiated by his predecessor Sir Thomas Robinson.
The year 1754 also saw him elected at Plymouth, which
remained his constituency until his retirement in May
1778. A year later, in 1755, he became secretary at war, a
post he held, in two spells, for nineteen years. If one added
the allowances he received in addition to his salary, the
secretary at war was paid only a little less than a secretary
of state. This was an opportune appointment, for up to
that time he had been relying heavily on his wife's
finances to bolster his own. By the 1760s Barrington was
enjoying more of the pleasures of life. His home in Cavendish Square, London, was the venue for parties, and opera
became a major interest of his. The dour image of him as
merely a punctilious administrator is a false one.

Barrington now settled into a long association with the
army which continued in the first instance until March
1761, and then from July 1765 until December 1778. During
the intervening years, much to his surprise, in March 1761
he was appointed chancellor of the exchequer as one of
the many personnel changes that accompanied the early
years of the succession of George III. When the duke of
Newcastle resigned and Lord Bute, the king's mentor,

became first lord of the Treasury, in May 1762 Barrington became treasurer of the navy, and served until 1765. The bulk of his career was thus involved in the administration of Britain's forces.

Animosity towards Barrington intensified during the 1760s. He was already unpopular as a result of his part in the Minorca disaster of 1756. Confusion had arisen as to whether Governor Fowke of Gibraltar should have relieved Minorca during a siege by offering military support. A series of letters sent by Barrington to Fowke became the centrepiece of the debate as to the propriety of Fowke's actions. Admiral Byng was shot for his part in the disaster, and Barrington had taken a firm line against him. However, when Governor Fowke was tried, Barrington was at pains to exonerate himself. Barrington was later taunted for this by Junius and others. In addition, during the 1760s he was castigated as the one who remained in office while others fell from grace. The personnel changes that came as a consequence of groups of politicians losing or gaining influence and office did not affect him. He was particularly attacked for staying in office when his patron the duke of Newcastle resigned in 1762. Barrington had been kept at the war office in 1756 by the duke, but he refused to join Newcastle in opposition in 1762, despite admitting his debt of gratitude to him. He further incurred the wrath of the satirical writers when he praised the conduct of the guards in dealing with the Wilkes riots in 1768. Barrington was eager to support his men, but his actions were attacked in the press and the use of the army in dealing with public unrest was debated in the house. Junius continued his attack on Barrington when the latter parted company with Christopher D'Oyly, his deputy secretary, in December 1771. Barrington was a particular target of Junius (namely Philip Francis) who as first clerk at the war office from 1763 to 1772 served under Barrington, and Barrington's historical reputation was coloured by these attacks. Junius announced in January 1772 in a private letter to the printer William Woodfall: 'Having nothing better to do, I propose to entertain myself and the public, with torturing that bloody wretch Barrington' (*Letters of Junius*, 386).

Barrington was highly regarded within government for his efficiency and integrity. While at the war office he gained the respect of officers and soldiers alike. Captain Alexander Mackintosh noted that 'such officers as have not interest at court, and nothing to plead but merit, or long services, have found in your Lordship an asserter of their rights' (A. Mackintosh to Lord Barrington, 7 Dec 1775, Suffolk RO, HA 174/1026/6a/4). George III held a good opinion of him, and trusted him to such an extent that he used him to sound out Lord North on his willingness to head the government in 1770. This good relationship with the king, which was such an integral and important part of the administration of the army, sustained Barrington into the 1770s. In 1760 Newcastle described him as 'the best Secretary at War that ever was' (Newcastle MSS, BL, Add. MS 32916, fols. 49–55). In 1763 he was informed by Lord Halifax that George III had stopped Pitt from removing him from the war office in the spring of that same year.

This high opinion arose out of Barrington's effective and reforming administration. During his first period at the war office he began to reform its procedures and regulations, but these reforms were not finally completed until his second tenure. The peacetime years were particularly important in this regard. George III was instrumental in supporting his initiatives. Careful management and frugality were given importance, as was the necessity of drawing up procedures to inform good conduct and practice. A brave and difficult attempt was also made to improve the way preferment was recommended and how commissions were bought and sold. Enemies were made within the political world as a result of these changes and because of his resistance to patronage pressure.

Although Barrington made his mark as an administrator rather than as a politician he was a frequent Commons speaker, and a more than competent debater. Horace Walpole named him in 1755 as one of the twenty-eight best speakers in the house, despite 'a lisp and a tedious precision' (Walpole, *Memoirs*, 2.115). He spoke mainly on military matters, but took a leading part in the Middlesex election case, moving the expulsion of John Wilkes on 3 February 1769. On America he was a hardliner, firm in his view that the king's subjects everywhere owed obedience to parliament. When the American war began he personally favoured withdrawal of the army and the use of the navy to reduce the colonies to submission. He therefore found his post increasingly disagreeable, and he had also grown tired of the constant applications for commissions. In March 1775 he described himself as 'a baker in a famine, his shop crowded with customers, and very little bread to give them' (Barrington, chap. 9). He first asked to resign that year, and the king finally permitted him to retire in December 1778, when he was given a pension of £2000 for his public service.

Apart from a brief period as postmaster-general from January to April 1782, Barrington found his public career had thus come to an end. There was, and has since been, disagreement about his motives. In a debate on the supply of the army, on 24 January 1770, he set out a justification of his career. To those who had witnessed his willingness to stay in office through numerous changes of administration such a justification struck them as an outrage. 'The very name of Barrington', exclaimed Junius in 1772, 'implies everything that is mean, cruel, false and contemptible' (*Letters of Junius*, 499). Criticisms were widespread among Barrington's contemporaries, but George III correctly perceived him as a faithful servant of the state. He was both forward- and backward-looking. His administrative role foreshadowed much of the work of the present day civil service, while he rejected the development of party discipline, which was in its infancy in the eighteenth century. Barrington was not out of step in claiming that it was the duty of politicians to serve the crown regardless of other affiliations. This was his justification to Newcastle in 1762. In essence it was those politicians, such as the Rockinghams, who tried to force themselves on the king who were breaking new ground.

Barrington believed that government was 'a duty whilst an honest man could support it' (Barrington to Sir Andrew Mitchell, 5 Dec 1762, Mitchell MSS, BL, Add. MS 6839, fol. 42). This did not mean blind duty, but a commitment as long as the administration was governing for the country's benefit. He claimed that the 'best and most moderate when formed into a party, may be carried lengths they never intended to go. I therefore stopped at the threshold' (ibid.). This was a clear reference to early abandonment of political opposition.

References to Barrington in available contemporary documentation tend to emphasize the low opinion in which he was held by many of the influential politicians of the age. He was not willing to be a pawn in their political machinations. Yet this dutiful servant had come to be respected by those who appreciated his skills of organization and attention to detail. Both he and others realized the significance of efficient administration in effective government. Barrington did not involve himself in the power struggles of the age, and thus became a thorn in many a side. Nevertheless, he inspired friendship and respect, not least among the less privileged he helped in the army. When he died, on 1 February 1793 in Cavendish Square, London, even Horace Walpole, his long-term enemy, realized that he would miss him. He was buried in Shrivenham church, Berkshire, and was succeeded as viscount by his nephew William Barrington, the son of John Barrington.   DYLAN E. JONES

Sources D. E. Jones, 'The career of Lord Barrington', PhD diss., U. Wales, 1990 · *An eighteenth-century secretary at war: the papers of William Viscount Barrington*, ed. T. Hayter (1988) · S. Barrington, *The political life of William Wildman, Viscount Barrington* (1814) · E. Channing and A. E. Coolidge, eds., *The Barrington–Bernard correspondence* (1912) · J. Shy, 'Confronting rebellion: private correspondence of Lord Barrington with General Gage', *Sources of American independence*, ed. H. H. Peckham (1978) · *The memoirs and papers of Sir Andrew Mitchell*, ed. A. Bisset, 2 vols. (1850) · *The letters of Junius*, ed. J. Cannon (1978) · BL, Mitchell MSS, Add. MSS 6804–6871, 11260–11262 · BL, Newcastle MSS, Add. MSS 32695–33201 · Suffolk RO, Barrington MSS, HA 174/1026 · Walpole, *Corr.*, 34.196–7 · H. Walpole, *Memoirs of the reign of King George the Second*, ed. Lord Holland, 2nd edn, 3 vols. (1847) · GEC, *Peerage*

Archives BL, corresp. and papers, Add. MSS 73546–73769 · Bucks. RLSS, roll of foreign accounts · NA Canada, memorandum on North America · priv. coll., foreign accounts · PRO, corresp., PRO 30/55 · Suffolk RO, HA 174/1026 | BL, corresp. with Sir Jeffrey Amherst and others, Add. MSS 21696–21697, 21708 · BL, letters to George Grenville, Add. MS 57810 · BL, corresp. with Lord Holdernesse, Egerton MS 3432 · BL, corresp. with Lord Holland, Add. MS 51387 · BL, corresp. with earl of Liverpool, Add. MSS 38209–38222, 38306–38309, 38471 · BL, corresp. with Lord London, Add. MSS 44068–44069 · BL, letters to Andrew Mitchell and Lord Bute, Add. MSS 5726–6834 · BL, corresp. with duke of Newcastle and others, Add. MSS 32708–33089, *passim* · BL, letters to Charles Yorke and earls of Hardwicke, Add. MSS 35430–35659 · BL OIOC, corresp. with Sir Philip Francis, MSS Eur. C 8, D 18, E 12–22, F 5–6 · CKS, corresp. with Sir Jeffrey Amherst · Hunt. L., letters to Hastings family · Hunt. L., letters to Lord London · JRL, letters to Samuel Bagshawe · NMM, letters to Lord Sandwich · NRA, priv. coll., letters to Lord Shelburne · PRO, War Office MSS, WO 1–5, 8, 10, 17–18, 24–26, 30–34, 36, 40, 49, 54–55, 64, 71–72 · PRO, letters to Lord Chatham, PRO 30/8 · U. Mich., Clements L., corresp. with Thomas Page

Likenesses T. Lawrence, oils, *c*.1791, priv. coll. [*see illus.*] · C. Knight, stipple (after T. Lawrence), BM, NPG · W. A. Rainger, mezzotint (after J. Reynolds), BM, NPG

Barriteau, Carl Aldric Stanley (1914–1998), clarinettist and bandleader, was born on 7 February 1914 in Port of Spain, Trinidad, the elder son and eldest of four children of Josiah Stanley Barriteau, stenographer and journalist, and his wife, May (*b. c*.1894). Both parents were Trinidadian. He spent his early childhood in Maracaibo, Venezuela, where his father worked for an oil company, and gained his initial musical inspiration through encountering the principal clarinettist with the Caracas symphony orchestra. His parents separated before he was twelve and his mother returned to Trinidad with her children, but with no financial support she was forced to place them in an orphanage. At Belmont Orphanage, an institution respected for the quality of its musical tuition, he learned to play music in the military band. His first instrument was the tenor horn, followed by the small E♭ clarinet.

By the time Barriteau was playing the more common B♭ clarinet he had taught himself to arrange music, and by the age of fourteen had written his first march. He joined the Trinidad constabulary band at seventeen and augmented his income by playing in dance bands. As a member of the Jazz Hounds he accompanied the Guyanese dancer Ken 'Snakehips' Johnson when he visited Trinidad in 1935. Johnson was impressed by Barriteau's playing and promised to arrange for the clarinettist to join him in England. In 1937, when Johnson's first band broke up, he kept his promise. Johnson's was an all-black swing band and the existence of such an organization at this date attracted a great deal of attention; it was a novelty with the public and, at the same time, a source of inspiration for local musicians. Barriteau played an invaluable part in Johnson's musical success. With his formal training and perfect pitch, he wrote some of the musical arrangements and became the band's musical director, often conducting at rehearsals. As a featured soloist, he developed a healthy personal following among undergraduates with an eye and ear for black jazz authenticity and was invited to play for Cambridge May balls.

The West Indian Dance Orchestra, as it became known, broadcast regularly during a long residency at the Café de Paris in London's West End and became a national favourite until March 1941, when a German bomb demolished the nightclub. Johnson and saxophonist Dave 'Baba' Williams were killed and Barriteau's right wrist was so badly broken he thought he might never play again. He recovered, however, and on 26 July 1941 married Rita Gabrielle Peggy Franklyn (*b*. 1920/21), a beautician, and daughter of Lewis George Franklyn, commercial traveller. She subsequently sang with his band as Rita Lynn.

Barriteau's wartime prestige as an instrumentalist was considerable. While primarily acknowledged as a clarinettist, he was greatly admired as an alto saxophonist by fellow musicians. He was employed as featured clarinet soloist by several of the top-ranking dance band leaders, including Lew Stone, Geraldo, Ambrose, and Joe Loss, but his rich lead alto was equally an important component of

Carl Aldric Stanley Barriteau (1914–1998), by Alan Duncan, 1942 [dedicated to George Roberts, saxophonist]

their bands' sound. In 1942 he attempted to reform Johnson's West Indian Dance Orchestra. They broadcast and their efforts were well received, but Barriteau was unable to raise the financial support necessary to lure his former colleagues away from London. He associated briefly with some of the emerging jazz 'modernists' before having another attempt at band-leading. In November 1947 he successfully organized a fifteen-piece band and moved to Scotland.

For several years Barriteau was consistently voted at or near the top of popularity polls on his instrument, yet this did not enable him to play as he pleased. His preference was for hard-swinging big band jazz, but appearing in dance halls he was forced to 'sweeten' his music in order to accommodate the public, even if there were some who liked to jive when he played (*Dance News Weekly*, 1947). Nevertheless, running a big band was an expensive undertaking and Barriteau, by his own admission, had no head for business. In 1952 he was declared bankrupt. He found work with Cyril Stapleton's orchestra, then toured Britain as a solo act. A short, balding man with a ready smile and impish sense of humour, he now sang rhythm and blues numbers in the style of the African-American bandleader Louis Jordan, and introduced a light-hearted comedy routine. He also formed a small touring group, and although rock and roll was anathema to him, became closely associated with the burgeoning beat generation through regular appearances on the BBC's prototype pop television programme *6-5 Special* in 1958. On 22 May 1959, following a divorce, he married Mary Shearer Kidd (*b*. 1921/2), a

singer and pianist who had previously performed with the Ivy Benson Orchestra and who, as Mae Cooper, had sung with him in Scotland; she was the daughter of Robert Kidd, film actor.

Barriteau was an outstanding technician—given exclusive permission by the American Artie Shaw to record Shaw's virtuoso *Concerto for Clarinet*—and immersed in the best dance music of his day. He became a nationally known musical figure during the era when big swing bands predominated, and was held in high esteem throughout the profession. He experienced frustration in the struggle for artistic expression, but to maintain a big band after the war as he did was a conspicuous achievement.

In 1960 Barriteau formed a double act with his wife, Mae Cooper, and they moved to Frankfurt, Germany, then in 1966 settled in Australia. They lived in the Sydney area where Barriteau continued to fulfil occasional jazz engagements while working mainly in cabaret. He featured the soprano and tenor saxophones in addition to his clarinet, but singing became increasingly part of his nightclub act. He travelled throughout the Far East and, despite moving into a retirement home in Queensland, never really stopped playing. He died in Australia on 24 August 1998. He was survived by his wife.

VAL WILMER

Sources *The Guardian* (1 Sept 1998) · *The Independent* (31 Aug 1998) · *The Times* (10 Sept 1998) · C. Hayes, 'Carl Barriteau', *Memory Lane*, 66 (1985), 12 · S. Henry, 'Young King Carl', *Band Wagon*, 3/6 (1945), 43 · K. Jones, 'The blitz and all that jazz', *Weekend Australian Review* (23/4 March 1991), 1–2 · R. Morton, 'He blew his way back to the top', *New Musical Express* (2 July 1954), 9 · *Dance News Weekly* (Nov 1947) · personal knowledge (2004) · private information (2004) · m. certs.
Likenesses A. Duncan, photograph, 1942, priv. coll. [*see illus.*] · photograph, 1943, repro. in *The Guardian* · H. Hammond, photographs, 1950–59, V&A · photographs, priv. coll.

Barritt, Mary. *See* Taft, Mary (1772–1851).

Barritt, Thomas (1743–1820), antiquary, was born at Hanging Ditch in Manchester, of a family which originated in Derbyshire but had latterly settled in south-east Lancashire. His father, John Barritt, was the first of the family to live in Manchester. Throughout his adult life Thomas Barritt worked as a saddler and kept a shop in Hanging Ditch until his death. On 25 February 1797 he married Ann Davis (*d*. after 1821) at Manchester collegiate church (now the cathedral) and they had two children—a son, Thomas, who emigrated to America and became a saddler at Poughkeepsie, New York, and a daughter, Emma.

No details of Barritt's education appear to have survived, but in his early adulthood he developed a passion for history and was one of Manchester's pioneering antiquaries. The low priority which he gave to his trade of saddlery is perhaps exemplified by a later nineteenth-century description of him as 'antiquary, herald, painter and saddler' (R. W. Proctor, *Memorials of Bygone Manchester*, 1880, 41). Because he was one of the first to investigate and record details of Manchester's past, his memory was revered by the influential group of local historians and antiquaries for which the city was noted in the mid-nineteenth century, although much of his work lacked permanent value when judged by the more rigorous standards of subsequent generations. He amassed a large and extremely diverse collection of archaeological objects and curiosities, many of them of local interest and origin but including others, of non-local relevance, which were bought from dealers. Perhaps the most celebrated item, and certainly the one of which he was most proud, was the supposed sword of Edward, the Black Prince.

Barritt was one of the early members of the Manchester Literary and Philosophical Society, founded in 1781, and he contributed several papers on antiquarian subjects to its *Memoirs*. He travelled incessantly about the Manchester district and filled several volumes with sketches, notes, and memoranda concerning buildings, archaeological sites, and people. It is these manuscript notebooks, now in Chetham's Library in Manchester, which represent his most valuable legacy—although they have been under-used by later historians because they remain unpublished. Barritt died on 29 October 1820 at Hanging Ditch and was buried at the collegiate church in Manchester.

ALAN G. CROSBY

Sources *DNB* · will, Lancs. RO, WCW March 1821, Thomas Barritt · private information (1885, 2004) · *IGI* · *Papers of the Manchester Literary Club*, 2 (1876), 156–9 · A. P. Stanley, *Historical memorials of Canterbury*, 10th edn (1883), 181–2
Archives Bodl. Oxf., history of heraldry · Chetham's Library, Manchester, MS collection of Lancashire pedigrees
Wealth at death see will, Lancs. RO, WCW March 1821, Thomas Barritt

Barro. For this title name *see* Hay, Sir John, Lord Barro (1578–1654).

Barron, Hugh (*c.*1747–1791), painter, was the son of John Barron, apothecary to the Westminster Dispensary, Soho, London, and elder brother of William Augustus *Barron (*b.* 1751, *d.* in or after 1806), painter. Barron's portraiture is notable for its early maturity and similarity to Reynolds's work. After attending a drawing school run by Daniel Fournier in 1764, Barron was a pupil of Joshua Reynolds (*c.*1764–6). He is listed as a member of the Society of Artists of Great Britain in 1765, and exhibited there annually from 1765 to 1772. By 1767 he had left Reynolds, and lived in Panton Street and Litchfield Street, Soho, before leaving for Italy between April 1770 and April 1771.

Barron was in Lisbon in April 1772, when the British envoy Robert Walpole gave him a letter of introduction (dated 28 April 1772) to William Hamilton in Naples, describing him as 'a Scholar of Sir Joshua Reynolds for Painting and of Giardini for Musick … Painting is his profession, and Musick is his Amusement' (Ingamells, 55). He was in Florence by August 1772, copying paintings in the Uffizi, and arrived in Rome later that year. A contemporary report notes that he obtained many commissions soon after his arrival in Rome, adding, 'Barron is a young man of very conspicuous merit, has the most of Sir Joshua's fine manner of any of his pupils, and … when he returns to England, he will cut a great figure in his way' (Ingamells, 55). 'In 1774 Barron had so pleased the Duke of Cumberland "with the fiddle" that the Duke "honoured

his abilities as a painter"' (ibid.). In May 1777 he was in Genoa and Turin; the painter James Northcote (1746–1831) received an introduction from him to Jacob More in Rome. He travelled in northern Italy in 1777–8, and is recorded in 1779 as working in Rome. In his absence, Barron was elected fellow of the Society of Artists in 1772, and a director in 1775, and exhibited at the society in 1775 and 1778. On his return to London he enjoyed some success, having two portraits engraved by Valentine Green, *Admiral George Brydges Rodney, First Baron*, in 1780, which was engraved again by Charles Knight in 1781, and *John Swan*, in 1782. In 1782, 1783, and 1786 he exhibited at the Royal Academy, and moved from King Street, Covent Garden, to Leicester Fields in 1783.

Critics have judged Barron harshly, arguing that he never fulfilled the promise of early pieces such as *The Bond Children* (1768, Tate collection) and *John, Second Earl of Egmont, and his Family* (1770, exh. Christies, 12 December 1930). His social and musical interests were recorded in his *Self-Portrait*, exhibited at the Society of Arts special exhibition of 1768 (Yale U. CBA). Barron died on 9 September 1791. His will, drawn up on 19 August, describes him as living in Fulham. He bequeathed property inherited from his father, and all his possessions, to 'my … honest friend' (Barron) Mrs Elizabeth Coudley, which suggests that he left neither wife nor children.   NICHOLAS GRINDLE

Sources J. Ingamells, ed., *A dictionary of British and Irish travellers in Italy, 1701–1800* (1997) · H. Barron, will and testament, Family History Centre, London, PROB II, 1208, 418 · Graves, *Soc. Artists* · Graves, *RA exhibitors* · *Engraved Brit. ports.* · C. F. Bell, 'Additions and corrections', in *The annals of Thomas Banks*, ed. C. F. Bell (1938) [esp. insert] · W. T. Whitley, *Artists and their friends in England, 1700–1799*, 2 vols. (1928) · E. Edwards, *Anecdotes of painters* (1808); facs. edn (1970) · archive material, Courtauld Inst., Witt Library · J. H. Plumb, *The pursuit of happiness: a view of life in Georgian England* (1977)
Archives Concoran Gallery, Washington, DC · Courtauld Inst., Witt Library · Tate collection
Likenesses H. Barron, self-portrait, oils, 1768, Yale U. CBA

Barron, (Arthur) Oswald (1868–1939), genealogist and heraldist, was born in West Ham, Essex, on 3 January 1868, the second of three sons (there were two daughters) of Henry Stracey Barron (1838–1918), consulting mechanical engineer and one-time chief engineer of the Imperial Ottoman Arsenal in Constantinople, and his wife, Harriet Marshall (1838–1918). He was of the sixth generation in descent from James Barron, gentleman, of late seventeenth-century London. His great-great-grandfather Francis was ironmonger to the king; his grandfather Francis William was master of the Ironmongers' Company in 1864; and his uncle Edward Jackson Barron, a distinguished antiquary. He was educated in London at the Merchant Taylors' School—the 'Blue Coat School' (1877–1883), but circumstances prevented him from going up to Oxford University.

After a few temporary appointments in private service, Barron took employment with the *Evening News* of London, and for some thirty years contributed a daily article to that newspaper under the byline 'The Londoner', and it is said that many bought the paper simply to read him. In his early twenties he became romantically involved with E. (Elizabeth) *Nesbit (1858–1924), the famous author of children's stories, and collaborated with her in several fields. Their joint book *The Butler in Bohemia* (1894) was dedicated to their mutual friend Rudyard Kipling. Barron's deep attachment to Nesbit ceased in 1899 when he married Hilda Leonora Florence Sanders, a member of an old Northamptonshire family, but his influence outlasted his departure and he is widely credited with having provided the plot for *The Railway Children*, which finally appeared in 1906.

His early interest in fiction aside, Barron's abiding passions were heraldry and genealogy. In time he was to be acknowledged as the chief living authority on these subjects. His first contribution of significance had, in fact, appeared in 1895 when his annotated edition of the parliamentary roll of c.1312 was published in *The Genealogist*. This was followed in 1898 by *Benolt's Visitation of Berkshire in 1532*, and in 1901 by *The St George's Kalendar*, several copies of which were ordered by the king.

However, it was with his editorship of and contributions to *The Ancestor* (1902–5) that Barron set his stamp upon his chosen subjects. Each issue of this quarterly review ran to some 300 pages, and in every one Barron's articles stripped away the pretensions of earlier writers—their 'well-springs of engaging nonsense'—and gradually put the study of heraldry and, indeed, genealogy, onto proper historical bases, shorn of myth, legend, snobbery, and mere whimsy. The last issue of *The Ancestor* appeared in January 1905, to enable Barron to concentrate on the demanding task (in addition to his daily *Evening News* column) of editing the genealogical and armorial sections of the Victoria county history; his own magisterial quartos, dealing with Northamptonshire county families, were published in 1906. His article on heraldry in the 1911 edition of the *Encyclopaedia Britannica* remains one of the best and most erudite introductions to the subject. From 1916 to 1919 he served in the Inns of Court reserve regiment with the rank of lieutenant, and in 1920 he was awarded the Médaille du Roi Albert for his services to Belgians in distress.

After the war Barron continued his heraldic studies in addition to writing for the *Evening News*, but he never produced the great comprehensive book on armory which might have been expected of him. In spite of his sometimes prickly relationship with the heraldic establishment—his earlier views that men could assume arms at will rather than having them properly granted had caused much controversy—his knowledge and deep sincerity won him respect and he was increasingly welcomed in official circles, particularly in the College of Arms. He had already been a gold staff officer (usher) at the coronation of King George V in 1911, but his final reward was to be appointed Maltravers herald-extraordinary in time for the coronation of King George VI in 1937 and thus to play a time-honoured role in the ceremony.

Barron's marriage to Hilda Sanders, which produced a daughter, Yolanda Wilmot Philipse Barron, lasted until his death at 22 Gay Street, Bath, on 24 September 1939. He

and his wife had been staying with relations in that city and his passing was sudden and unexpected. He was cremated at Arnos Vale crematorium in Bristol on 27 September, and his ashes taken to Hammersmith, London, where the couple lived. His papers were subsequently deposited with the Society of Antiquaries of London, of which he had been a fellow since 1901. He was a man held in affectionate respect by his peers, and his scholarship had brought new realism into the whole fields of heraldry and genealogy.   JOHN CAMPBELL-KEASE

Sources G. Andrews Moriarty, 'Oswald Barron', *New England Historical and Genealogical Register*, 94 (1940) • A. Wagner, 'An officer of arms', *The Times* (28 Sept 1939) • E. E. Dorling, *Antiquaries Journal*, 20 (1940), 124–5 • A. Wagner, *A herald's world* (1988) • R. Dennys, *The heraldic imagination* (1975) • J. Briggs, *A woman of passion: the life of E. Nesbit* (1987) • *WWW*, 1929–40 • census returns, 1881 [Henry Barron and Harriet Marshall]
Archives Hammersmith and Fulham Archives, London, corresp. and papers • S. Antiquaries, Lond., heraldic and genealogical corresp. and papers • W. Sussex RO, corresp. | BL, letters to Sir S. Cockerell, Add. MS 52704 • LUL, letters to J. H. Round
Likenesses G. Kruger [Gray], pencil sketch, 1911, S. Antiquaries, Lond. • photograph, Coll. Arms
Wealth at death £649 15s. 0d.: administration with will, 13 March 1940, CGPLA Eng. & Wales

Barron, (Mabel) Phyllis (1890–1964), designer and textile printer, was born on 19 March 1890 in Taplow, Buckinghamshire, the younger of two daughters of Walter Barron and his wife, Alice Maud Marguerite, formerly Clark, of Taplow House, Taplow. She was to describe her family as 'rich' and her father as 'something in the City' (Barron). Barron, as she was called by her friends, studied at the Slade School of Fine Art under Henry Tonks and Philip Wilson Steer before immersing herself in designing and printing textiles. Active between the two world wars, she produced furnishing and dress-stuffs together with her partner, Dorothy *Larcher (1882–1952), which were noted for their distinctive designs hand block-printed in subtle colours on quality materials. The major collection of their work is held by the Crafts Study Centre collection and archive at the Surrey Institute of Art and Design, University College, Farnham.

Barron had first become interested in textile printing having discovered some French printing blocks. Information was difficult to obtain but two dye books by Edward Bancroft and William Crookes respectively proved to be invaluable. In 1915 she cut her first block and experimented avidly—discharging patterns with nitric acid on indigo-dyed cloth, and printing with iron, rust, or cutch on linen and cotton.

In the early 1920s Dorothy Larcher joined Barron's workshop which moved shortly afterwards to 2 Parkhill Studios, Parkhill Road, Hampstead. Recalling his first meeting with both women in 1938 the etcher and educationist Robin Tanner referred to their partnership as 'a marriage of true minds' (Roscoe, 1993, 123–4). Describing Barron as 'a tall, large, handsome, commanding figure with fine eyes and brow, cropped silver hair, a beautiful outgoing expression and a warm lovely voice' he also remembered her *joie de vivre*, energy, fresh wit, and creative mind which combined with a high sense of standard made her an exuberant and forceful personality (ibid.).

Barron and Larcher moved to Hambutts House, Edge Road, Painswick, Gloucestershire, in 1930. It was a beautiful Georgian house with a stable block which they converted into a workshop with a large indigo vat. These were years of expansion and they experimented with overprinting and the use of synthetic dyes, employing women from the village to help with printing and sewing.

The Little Gallery run by Muriel Rose was Barron's and Larcher's main sales outlet in London following their move to the Cotswolds. They also exhibited regularly with the Red Rose Guild in Manchester and the Gloucestershire Guild of Craftsmen. The duke of Westminster had been an early and most influential patron commissioning all the materials for his yacht *The Flying Cloud* and introducing their work to a wealthy and discerning clientele. Other commissions included the new library and fellows' senior common room at Girton College, Cambridge, and curtaining for the choir stalls at Winchester Cathedral.

The outbreak of the Second World War ended production and Barron turned to local government work, parish affairs, and education. Her obituary recorded that:

> She took a leading—although never obtrusive—part in the life of Painswick, giving valued help as the chairman of the horticultural section of the Painswick show, as a member of the Painswick Food Production Society, as a member and for a while chairman of the Painswick Parish Council, as a member of the Gyde Home Committee and in other ways, while in a wider sphere she was for 22 years a member of the Stroud rural district council. She served for a considerable time as the chairman of the Council's Building Plans Committee and was the vice chairman of the Area Planning Committee. In addition she represented the Council on the Stroud Museum Committee, the Stroud Educational Foundation and other bodies. (*Gloucestershire Echo*, 25 Nov 1964)

Barron's death at Hambutts, Edge Road, Painswick, on 23 November 1964 followed a severe bout of influenza. She was cremated three days later at Cheltenham crematorium and her ashes scattered there in the rock and water garden. Examples of her textiles are in the Whitworth Art Gallery, Manchester; Cheltenham Museums and Art Gallery; and the Victoria and Albert Museum, London.   BARLEY ROSCOE

Sources B. Roscoe, 'Phyllis Barron and Dorothy Larcher', *The arts and crafts movement in the Cotswolds*, ed. M. Greensted (1993), 122–39 · B. Roscoe, 'Phyllis Barron and Dorothy Larcher', *Pioneers of modern craft*, ed. M. Coatts (1997), 61–70 · S. Bosence, *Hand block printing and resist dyeing* (1985), 40–49, 131 · *Gloucestershire Echo* (25 Nov 1964) · P. Barron, 'My life as a block printer', transcript of a talk given at Dartington Hall, Devon, 22 Feb 1964, Surrey Institute of Art and Design, Farnham, Crafts Study Centre collection and archive · R. Tanner, 'Phyllis Barron, 1890–1964', transcript of a talk given at the Holburne Museum and Crafts Study Centre, Bath, 1 June 1978, Surrey Institute of Art and Design, Farnham, Crafts Study Centre collection and archive · records, Cheltenham crematorium · b. cert. · d. cert. · private information (2004)
Archives Surrey Institute of Art and Design, Farnham, Crafts Study Centre, Barron and Larcher Archive, textiles, printing blocks, MSS, paper, and photographs | SOUND Surrey Institute of Art and Design, Farnham, Crafts Study Centre, Barron and Larcher Archive
Likenesses photographs, 1925–45 (with Dorothy Larcher), Surrey Institute of Art and Design, Farnham, Crafts Study Centre · photograph, *c*.1930, Surrey Institute of Art and Design, Farnham, Crafts Study Centre
Wealth at death £32,666: probate, 16 Feb 1965, *CGPLA Eng. & Wales*

Barron, William (*d*. 1803), historian, was the only son of John Barron of Glasgow. He was educated at the University of Glasgow, where he matriculated in 1757, but he appears not to have graduated. He was ordained as a Church of Scotland minister in 1762 and served in the parish of Wamphray until 1771 and thereafter at Whitburn in Linlithgowshire.

In 1774 appeared Barron's first publication, *An Essay on the Mechanical Principles of the Plough*. This was typical of the contemporary Scottish preoccupation with agricultural improvement to which men as varied as the politician George Dempster and the jurist Lord Kames had also contributed important technical treatises. Three years later followed Barron's most interesting work, a *History of the Colonization of the Free States of Antiquity* (1777). Here he sought to explain the principles of ancient imperialism and their applicability to a deeper understanding of the then current crisis in Britain's relationship with its American colonies.

Barron's conclusions included granting the Americans representation at Westminster on precisely the basis that the Scots had enjoyed since 1707. He also disdained anachronistic solutions to the problem of preserving liberty, arguing convincingly against the traditional view that citizen militias remained preferable to standing armies: in modern states, Barron observed, 'filled with manufacturers and mechanics, few of whom are bred to war, an army becomes in some measure necessary to protect those liberties, which cannot otherwise be successfully defended' (W. Barron, *History of the Colonization of the Free States of Antiquity*, 1777, 141). He also advised caution in matters constitutional, insisting that 'Men act from the dictates of their passions and their habits more frequently than from the direction of their reasons' (ibid., 113). Speculative models of political government ought in Barron's view to be approached with considerable scepticism.

In 1778 Barron was elected professor of logic, rhetoric, and metaphysics in the University of St Andrews in succession to Robert Watson. His historical interests soon bore further fruit in the *History of the political connection between England and Ireland from the reign of Henry II to the present time* (1780). His early expertise in the full economic exploitation of agricultural estates was also useful to his new academic colleagues, for Barron served as inspector of college and public works during the 1780s and was heavily involved in the oversight of the university's extensive properties.

Barron's final publication was more clearly related to his professorial responsibilities. Appearing posthumously, his *Lectures on Belles Lettres and Logic* (1806) reflects the reformulation of rhetorical studies in the Scottish universities which had been under way since the innovations introduced by Watson, Adam Smith, and George Campbell in mid-century. Assuming that the discipline should be primarily concerned not with the art of public oratory but with the study and critical evaluation of literature, this approach also promoted the adoption in Scotland of Anglicized literary norms, a cultural project to which Barron himself fully subscribed.

Barron died in St Andrews on 28 December 1803, leaving a widow, his second wife, Margaret Stark, whom he had married on 2 November 1782, and their four surviving children.   DAVID ALLAN

Sources *Fasti Scot.*, new edn, 1.235 · R. Crawford, ed., *Launch-site for English studies: three centuries of literary studies at the University of St Andrews* (1997), 6–7, 10, 12, 37, 40, 42, 49, 58 · united college minutes, U. St Andr. L., special collections department, muniments · W. I. Addison, ed., *The matriculation albums of the University of Glasgow from 1728 to 1858* (1913), 57 · W. I. Addison, *A roll of graduates of the University of Glasgow from 31st December 1727 to 31st December 1897* (1898) · R. G. Cant, *The University of St Andrews: a short history*, rev. edn (1970), 108n.
Archives BL, corresp. with earl of Liverpool, Add. MSS 38209–38225, 38306–38311 · U. St Andr. L.

Barron, William (1805–1891), landscape gardener, was born on 7 September 1805 in Eccles, Berwickshire, the son of John Barron, gardener, and his wife, Betty Johnston. (The year of his birth is usually cited as 1800, as a result of a mistake in his obituary in the *Gardeners' Chronicle*.) He served a three-year gardening apprenticeship at Blackadder, Berwickshire, before entering the Royal Botanic Garden, Edinburgh, where he was soon placed in charge of the glasshouses. From there he went to Syon House, Middlesex, where he helped to plant the new conservatory. On 1 March 1830 he was appointed gardener to Charles Stanhope, fourth earl of Harrington, at Elvaston Castle in Derbyshire, where he took up his post on 2 August, with instructions to create a new garden.

Early in 1831 Barron began transplanting mature trees; he became expert in their removal and he described his techniques in *The British Winter Garden* (1852). The gardens he created were seldom visited before 1851, when a series of articles in the *Gardeners' Chronicle* created a sensation by describing the transplanting operations, the grafted conifers, the avenues of multiple rows of different species, the architectural topiary, and the series of formal gardens enclosed by hedges. The revelation of Elvaston led to a topiary revival in the 1850s.

The fourth earl died in 1851 and his successor retrenched on expenditure, opened the gardens to the public, and instructed Barron to develop a commercial nursery at the garden. In 1862, on the death of Leicester Stanhope, fifth earl of Harrington, Barron bought 40 acres for a nursery site in nearby Borrowash, to which he moved from Elvaston in 1865. In addition to plant sales, Barron offered transplanting and landscape gardening. During Barron's life, among his firm's commissions were those undertaken at Stancliffe Hall, Matlock; Impney Hall, Droitwich; Locke Park, Barnsley; People's Park, Grimsby; and, his most famous work after Elvaston itself, Abbey Park, Leicester (between 1877 and 1882). In 1880 he successfully moved the Buckland yew, with a documented

William Barron (1805–1891), by unknown photographer

age of 800 years. One of his transplanting machines was preserved at Kew.

Barron retired in 1881 but came out of retirement for a commission for the ninth earl of Dysart, at Welbeck Abbey, in 1886. In 1887 he was the first witness called before the select commission on forestry. He was noted for his prodigious memory, he was deeply religious, and he was a staunch advocate of temperance.

Barron married Elizabeth Ashby, and their only child, John (born on 8 June 1844), having trained abroad in landscape gardening, became his father's partner by 1867. Barron died in Borrowash, Derbyshire, on 8 April 1891. The family continued the firm into the interwar years. Among the firm's later commissions were those at Queen's Park, Chesterfield (1893); the Bedford Embankment (1894); and Whitaker Park, Rawtenstall (1900).

                                                    BRENT ELLIOTT, *rev.*

Sources *Gardeners' Chronicle*, 3rd ser., 9 (1891), 522–4 · *Gardeners' Magazine* (25 April 1891), 242 · d. cert.
Likenesses photograph, Royal Horticultural Society, Lindley Library [*see illus.*]

Barron, William Augustus (*b.* 1751, *d.* in or after 1806), landscape painter and draughtsman, was born in London on 31 October 1751, the son of John Barron, apothecary to the Westminster Dispensary, Soho, London, and the younger brother of Hugh *Barron. A pupil of William Tomkins, in 1766 he gained a premium at the Society of Arts and entered the Royal Academy Schools in 1771. He practised as a landscape painter, and as a drawing-master. Only a moderately gifted painter, he was a skilled violinist. His musical ability gained him an introduction to Sir

Edward Walpole, who gave him a position in the exchequer, upon which he gave up painting. His view of Wanstead House was engraved by V. M. Picot in 1775; some of his views of Essex castles and landscapes have also been engraved. He exhibited views of the home counties at the Royal Academy from 1774 to 1777. In the print-room of the British Museum there is a large pen drawing by him of Richmond Bridge dated 1778. Citing Edwards, Waterhouse recorded that Barron was 'still alive 1806' (Waterhouse, *18c painters*, 1.40).

ERNEST RADFORD, *rev.* R. J. LAMBERT

Sources Waterhouse, *18c painters* · Bryan, *Painters* · M. H. Grant, *A dictionary of British landscape painters, from the 16th century to the early 20th century* (1952) · E. Edwards, *Anecdotes of painters* (1808); facs. edn (1970)

Barrow, Florence Mary (1876–1964), relief worker and promoter of improved housing, was born on 27 January 1876 in Birmingham, the only daughter of Richard Cadbury Barrow (1827–1894), Quaker businessman and mayor of Birmingham (1888–9), and his wife, Jane (b. 1831), daughter of the Quakers Hannah King and her husband, Benjamin Harrison. She was educated at Edgbaston high school and Mason College, Birmingham. At the age of eighteen, in 1894, she started a class in adult literacy for Birmingham women, thus pioneering the adult schools movement there. She went on in 1900 to train as a social worker at St Hilda's Settlement in Bethnal Green. August 1914 found her in Marseilles working in a quarantine department with Serbian refugees from the Balkan war of 1912.

In 1916 Florence Barrow was sent from Newcastle by sea to Murmansk in order to do Quaker relief work in Buzuluk, western Russia, helping what would later be termed 'displaced persons'—two and a half million Poles, Jews, and Belorussians who were in a desperate situation. She helped set up nurseries for abandoned children, feeding centres, co-operative craft workshops, pharmacies, even a circulating library. She witnessed the Russian Revolution of 1917 and noted: 'Men work for the common good but find it harder than they thought. Famine threatens; the rich are robbed of their spoils but selfishness appears under new forms. … New ideas and ideals seethe … who can prophesy what will emerge?' (Barrow, 'Stray memories', 4). She then crossed Russia by trans-Siberian railway, reached Japan, and then America, finally crossing the U-boat-infested Atlantic in a camouflaged vessel in order to report back to the Society of Friends in London.

In 1919 Florence Barrow was sent by the Friends' War Victims' Committee to distribute Quaker food relief in a starving Germany still punished by the allied blockade: '[German] feeling very bitter in Breslau, … and as [the doctor] showed us one tiny distorted form after another it was almost more than one could bear' (letter, 28 Sept 1919, Temp. MS 590/3). From 1921 to 1924 she was head of Quaker relief operations among Poles in Brest Litovsk: 'I think that she must be an ideal head; she is evidently very capable … and seems only to be head by reason of her extra care for everyone' (J. Fry, letter to Friends' House, 23

Florence Mary Barrow (1876–1964), by unknown photographer, c.1914

Jan 1922, Temp. MS 590/3). Her monument there was the orphanage she left behind.

On her return to Britain in 1924 Florence Barrow co-founded the Birmingham Conference on Politics, Economics and Citizenship (COPEC) House Improvement Society that pioneered municipal slum clearance and the regeneration of inner-city housing there. She was the driving force for over thirty-seven years behind 'practical schemes of reconditioning, reconstruction, conversion and rebuilding' (*The Friend*). At the age of fifty-six, in 1932, she left Birmingham for Syria, Salonika, and Egypt to work once more with refugees. During the later 1930s the Quakers sent her as a secret agent to Nazi Germany and Austria, taking messages to and from endangered Jews. She later said she had found it 'very trying to know that every conversation might be overheard' (*Birmingham Evening Mail*, 4 March 1964) and reported to the Gestapo.

Back in Birmingham at the start of the war, Florence Barrow continued to work on inner-city housing reform as honorary secretary of COPEC and to organize the reception of Jewish refugees into the city. In 1958 the city of Birmingham gave her its civic gold medal for services to its urban housing programme, including the provision of low-rented accommodation for single working women and 'sheltered housing' for the elderly and for handicapped people. The city regretted to report that her active days as a social worker were almost finished. She was eighty-two.

Quiet, gentle, almost timid in manner, and only 4 feet 6 inches tall, Florence Barrow's 'outward appearance gave little indication of the power within' ('Warwickshire Monthly Meeting', 14 Nov 1964, *London Yearly Meeting Proceedings*). She died at Bryony House, Selly Oak, Birmingham, on 3 March 1964. SYBIL OLDFIELD

Sources RS Friends, Lond., Temp. MS 590/3 · F. Barrow, 'Stray memories of Buzuluk, 1916–1918', RS Friends, Lond. · F. M. Fenter,

COPEC adventure: the story of Birmingham COPEC House Improvement Society (1960) • *The Friend* (13 March 1964) • *Birmingham Post and Birmingham Gazette* (3 Nov 1958) • *Birmingham Post and Birmingham Gazette* (4 March 1964) • *Birmingham Evening Mail and Despatch* (4 March 1964) • *Birmingham Evening Mail and Despatch* (7 March 1964) • Friends' House, London, *London Yearly Meeting Proceedings* (1965), 66–7 • *CGPLA Eng. & Wales* (1964)

Archives RS Friends, Lond., papers, MSS, and typescript **Likenesses** photograph, *c.*1914, priv. coll. [*see illus.*] • photograph, *c.*1925, priv. coll. • photograph, repro. in *Birmingham Post* (25 Feb 1932) • photograph, repro. in *Birmingham Post* (4 March 1964) **Wealth at death** £19,842: probate, 17 June 1964, *CGPLA Eng. & Wales*

Barrow, Sir George, second baronet (1806–1876), civil servant, was born in London on 22 October 1806, the eldest son of Sir John *Barrow, first baronet (1764–1848), promoter of exploration and author, and his wife, Anna Maria (1777–1857), daughter of Peter John Trüter of the Cape of Good Hope. Educated at Charterhouse School from 1819 to 1823 with his brother John *Barrow (1808–1898) [*see under* Barrow, Sir John], who became a noted travel writer, George Barrow gained a place in the Colonial Office in 1825, eventually becoming chief clerk (1870) in the African and Mediterranean department. On 23 July 1832 he married Rosamund Hester Elizabeth (*d.* 1906), daughter of William Pennell, consul-general in Brazil. A noted beauty, she was known as 'Nony' Croker, having been adopted by John Wilson Croker as his daughter after he married her eldest sister. Barrow's father had long been a friend and colleague of Croker at the Admiralty, and the marriage brought the two families close together. The Barrows, who had five daughters and three sons, spent much of their married life with the Crokers at West Molesey, Surrey.

Barrow succeeded to the baronetcy in 1848. In 1850 he inaugurated the Barrow monument at Ulverston, in his father's honour. His one published work, *Ceylon: Past and Present* (1857), presented an account of Robert Knox's captivity in Ceylon from 1659 to 1679, and used authentic sources to describe the island's current state. Barrow retired in 1872, having since 1870 been secretary of the Order of St Michael and St George. He was appointed CMG in 1874, and died at his London home, Ulverston Lodge, 24 Addison Road, Kensington, on 27 February 1876. He was buried in the churchyard at West Molesey, Surrey.

ANN MARGARET RIDLER

Sources Burke, *Peerage* • *ILN* (11 March 1876), 263 • *ILN* (22 April 1876), 407 • *Colonial Office List* • [R. L. Arrowsmith], ed., *Charterhouse register, June 1769–May 1872* (1964) • *The Times* (2 March 1876) [brief announcement of Sir George's death] • M. F. Brightfield, *John Wilson Croker* (1940) • C. Lloyd, *Mr Barrow of the admiralty: a life of Sir John Barrow, 1764–1848* (1970) • J. Barrow, *An auto-biographical memoir of Sir John Barrow* (1847) • G. T. Staunton, *Memoir of Sir John Barrow, bart.* (1852)

Likenesses portrait, repro. in *ILN* **Wealth at death** under £30,000: probate, 30 March 1876, *CGPLA Eng. & Wales*

Barrow, George (1853–1932), geologist, was born in London on 11 December 1853. He was the fifth child (and the third son) in the family of eight of John George Barrow (*b.* 1805/6), a general practitioner at the Royal College of Surgeons, and his wife, Eleanor (*b.* 1827/8). After study at the Philological School under Dr Abbott, Barrow matriculated at London University in 1871, holding a Turner scholarship. Admitted to King's College, he studied science, winning prizes in mathematics and geology. He then entered employment as secretary to the distinguished geologist and banker George Poulett Scrope, who, being aged, deaf, and blind, engaged him to read loudly for six hours a day. Presumably giving satisfaction in this, Barrow was recommended to Andrew Ramsay and was appointed to the geological survey on Scrope's death in 1876. Barrow gained much mineralogical knowledge from Allan Dick of the Royal School of Mines, and eventually advanced to district geologist for the London region in 1909. He retired in 1915.

Barrow's early survey work was carried out around Cleveland, Yorkshire, whence he moved to the southeastern highlands of Scotland, to south-west England, to the midlands, and, finally, to the London region. In the midlands, Barrow worked on the Staffordshire coalfields and around Cheadle. In the south-west, he studied the Isles of Scilly and granitic regions such as Bodmin, with their 'aureoles' of metamorphosed rocks. In the London area, he was active in economic geology, studying the water supply and advising on the construction of the underground system. It was, however, in Scotland, where he worked from 1884 to 1900, that Barrow made his most notable contributions, through his study of metamorphic rocks of the south-east Grampians, particularly in the lonely region between Glen Esk and Glen Clova in Forfarshire. Here he found it possible to analyse the region's schists according to their subsidiary minerals—biotite, garnet, staurolite, kyanite, and sillimanite. Barrow took these to indicate the degree of metamorphism of the original argillaceous rocks, resulting from the action of different intensities of heat and pressure. Thus Barrow found an invaluable tool (for which there were some less well-developed precedents) for subdividing and mapping metamorphic rocks, and the notion of such 'Barrovian zones' has become well established in geological theory.

However, though Barrow's originality was recognized and admired by his colleagues, his tenacity of views was not always appreciated. For example, extrapolating his zone concept, he held that the three main metamorphic regions of Scotland (later called Lewisian, Moinian, and Dalradian) were derived from the same source, being of Lewisian age but metamorphosed to different degrees. This notion was not accepted, and indeed was not formally published, apart from some comments to a paper by Cecil Tilley (1925). Eventually, Barrow's disagreements with his colleagues became such that it was thought best to move him from Scotland to the less controversial geology of the English midlands.

Barrow is recorded by his colleague Edward Greenly as having the demeanour of a schoolboy, but possessed of 'one of the most daring minds that modern geology has known' (Edward Greenly, *A Hand through Time*, 1938). He had the reputation of being a keen sportsman, a good shot and expert fisherman. He was awarded the Royal Geological Society of Cornwall's Bolitho medal (1912), and the Geological Society's Murchison medal (1913). He was president of the Geologists' Association for 1916–18 and led many of its field excursions in south-east England. Barrow died of angina at Clovelly, Haddon Road, Chorleywood, Hertfordshire on 23 July 1932.   DAVID OLDROYD

Sources H. H. Thomas, *Quarterly Journal of the Geological Society of London*, 89 (1933), lxxxvii–lxxxix · J. F. N. G. [J. F. N. Green] and S. W. W. [S. W. Wooldridge], *Proceedings of the Geologists' Association*, 44 (1933), 111–12 · J. S. F. [J. S. Flett], 'Mr George Barrow', *Nature*, 130 (1932), 267 · J. G. Murtaugh, 'Barrow, George (1853–1932)', *Biographies of geologists: materials for the study of the history of geology*, ed. A. La Rocque (The Ohio State University, Department of Geology, 1961), suppl. 2, pp. 2–3 · E. B. Bailey, *Geological survey of Great Britain* (1952) · M. Brown, 'P-T-t evolution of orogenic belts and the causes of regional metamorphism', *Milestones in geology: reviews to celebrate 150 volumes of the Journal of the Geological Society*, ed. M. J. Le Bas (1995), 67–81 · d. cert. · *CGPLA Eng. & Wales* (1932)
Likenesses photograph, 7 April 1920 (signed by George Barrow), GS Lond., archives, P57 · photograph, repro. in J. S. Flett, *The first hundred years of the Geological Survey of Great Britain* (1937), pl. X
Wealth at death £4947 3s. 9d.: probate, 8 Sept 1932, *CGPLA Eng. & Wales*

Barrow, Henry (*c*.1550–1593), religious separatist, was the third son of a Norfolk gentleman, Thomas Barrow of Shipdam, and his wife, Mary, daughter and coheir of Henry Bures of Acton, Suffolk. Through the Bures connection, Barrow was related to the family of Sir William Butts, Henry VIII's physician, and to Sir Nicholas Bacon, the eldest son of Lord Keeper Bacon, who married a Bures/Butts cousin. That made him a remote kinsman of the younger Bacon's uncle, William Cecil, Lord Burghley. Was Judith Bures, wife of Bishop John Aylmer of London, another relative? It may be significant that on trial, and asked to acknowledge the presence of the bishop, Barrow responded: 'His name is Elmar.' Barrow had no profession but never seems to have been in financial straits, thanks perhaps to an indulgent father. In 1566 he matriculated at Cambridge as a fellow-commoner of Clare College (he may have been also at Corpus Christi College) and he proceeded BA in 1569/70. Nothing more is known of Barrow until, in 1576, he entered Gray's Inn, where he remained, by his own testimony, 'some years'. Under interrogation by Archbishop Whitgift, Barrow admitted that he knew 'very little law', and there is a somewhat stereotypical tradition of a conversion from the dissolute life of a young man about town, and perhaps about court, which began when Barrow heard the stentorian voice of a preacher as he walked past a London church. Yet everything that Barrow uttered in his many court appearances and in his writings suggests that if he was not a barrister he was at least a formidable barrack-room lawyer.

Historians of congregationalism have debated how Barrow became one of its founding fathers, moving beyond puritanism into outright separatism. The influence of the original 'Brownist', Robert Browne, is often assumed, together with that of John Greenwood, who, unlike Barrow, was a minister and who may well have been drawn to separatism through Browne, or his writings. But in Archbishop Richard Bancroft's estimation, Greenwood was

without much account. Barrow was the man. And while Barrow and Greenwood were friends before their shared incarceration began, and probably knew each other in Norfolk, by 1585 Greenwood had renounced his orders and had gone to London, whereas Barrow remained in the country, to which he seems to have returned after his conversion. It must have been in Norfolk, only eighteen months after becoming 'a zealous professor', that he read Browne's writings with the intention of confuting them. But finding some passages 'too hard for him', he sought out a certain Thomas Wolsey, an ordained minister who evidently formed with Browne and Robert Harrison a kind of troika of early separatist leadership in East Anglia, and who was to spend the last thirty years of his life in a Norwich prison. The authority for this is a later pamphleteer, Stephen Offwood, who tells that Wolsey 'perverted' many zealous professors, twenty to be precise, of whom Barrow was one.

In November 1587 (not 1586 as older authorities state) Barrow began a long ordeal and martyrdom, self-consciously recapitulating the martyr experiences and narratives of John Foxe's *Acts and Monuments*. On 8 October Greenwood had been arrested, along with twenty other 'Brownists', as they gathered in a conventicle in the house of Henry Martin in the London parish of St Andrew by the Wardrobe. On 19 November Barrow went up to London to visit Greenwood 'and the other brethren' (Carlson, 3.91) in the Clink, a prison in Southwark, and was himself arrested. The pursuivant who conveyed him by boat to Lambeth told him that he had 'a long time sought me' (ibid., 92), and it emerged that Barrow had been shadowed and incriminating conversation recorded, even on his way down from Norfolk. If Barrow is to be trusted, and, in the tradition of the book of martyrs, all the accounts of successive trials and hearings are from his own pen, his first encounter with Archbishop Whitgift and other high commissioners began as he intended other proceedings should continue. He refused to acknowledge his letter of summons, claiming that it was 'without warrant, and against law' (ibid., 92), and would not take the oath *ex officio*. Having invoked the queen, he was asked: 'Doth she know yow then?' 'I know her' (ibid., 98). Committed to the Gatehouse at Westminster, Barrow appeared for a second time before the high commission on 27 November 1587, Whitgift presiding 'with a grimme and an angrie countenance' over a 'Vatican' of 'well-fed silken priests' (ibid., 102). Barrow again refused the oath, and the hearing ended with abuse from the archbishop: 'You shalnot prattle here. Away with him: clap him up close, close, let no man come at him: I wil make him tel an other tale, yet [ere] I have done with him' (ibid., 104).

This proved to be an idle boast, for Barrow would never yield an inch. His greatest moment came on 18 March 1589, the most likely, but by no means a certain, date for his fourth examination, when he faced an extraordinary tribunal composed of leading privy councillors and ecclesiastical commissioners, meeting in Lord Chancellor Hatton's rooms in Whitehall. Not only Barrow but 'twelve of the brethren' were arraigned on this occasion, but according to Barrow he was the only one who spoke, and now, before their honours, it was freely, and with literally fatal consequences. When Sir Christopher Hatton pointed to Whitgift and asked Barrow what he was, he answered: 'He is a monster, a miserable compound, I know not what to make him: he is neither ecclesiastical nor civil, even that second beast spoken of in the Revelation' (Carlson, 3.188). The ever enigmatic Burghley asked Barrow for the reference. Leland Carlson argues that yet another examination, conducted by a special commission composed of judges, bishops, and ecclesiastical lawyers, took place a week later, and not on 24 March 1588, the date proposed by the near-contemporary printed version of these trials. Although Barrow reverted to a strategy of refusing to take the oath, Whitgift decided to proceed without that formality, and elicited a fluent and fair statement of Barrow's separatist principles.

Barrow and Greenwood were imprisoned under the statute 23 Eliz. c. 1, for refusing to attend church, a statute which Barrow insisted was never intended for them. From the outset, he justified himself with 'four causes of separation', a kind of separatist quadrilateral. These were: false worship; the promiscuously inclusive nature of the established church; false and antichristian ministry; and false and antichristian church government. All of Barrow's voluminous prison writings, including the so-called *Brief Discoverie of the False Church* (419 closely printed pages, conveyed out of the Fleet prison sheet by sheet to an amanuensis and a printer in Dort) merely elaborated these basic principles. The second cause, 'the profane and ungodlie people received into and retayned in the bozom and bodie of their churches' (Carlson, 3.54), was fundamental, and John Robinson would later insist that even if there were no other cause for separation, this alone was sufficient. Barrow's sectarian ecclesiology was laced with a heady millenarianism. God was calling men 'forth out of Babilon', but would soon 'let fal the heavy milstone of his finall indignation upon them al, and grind them to dust' (ibid., 671).

Barrow and Greenwood spent years in the Fleet, in Barrow's case without any remission. With the open sewer of the Fleet River under their windows, conditions (to which more than a dozen of the separatists succumbed) were unhealthy, but lax. It was possible for weddings to be held on the premises, and the many conferences held with no fewer than forty-two clergy, in which Barrow mercilessly exposed the contradictions of the non-separating puritan position (material published at Dort in 1590), were well attended. Lancelot Andrewes was moved to say that their situation was 'most happie', a kind of perpetual sabbatical. 'It is the life I would chuse' (Carlson, 4.143). Barrow told the future bishop that he spoke philosophically but not Christianly. Fresh air and exercise were necessary for a natural body.

In the spring of 1593 legal proceedings against the London separatists intensified and the bishops undertook a parliamentary manoeuvre to include puritan sectaries in new anti-recusant legislation. This met with resistance in the House of Commons, and Whitgift retaliated by ending the long ordeal of Barrow and Greenwood on the scaffold. On 23 March they were condemned to death for the offence of writing and publishing seditious literature with malicious intent. This too was under the terms of a statute of 1581 originally aimed at Catholic recusants. The next day they were taken to the place of execution, only to be pardoned. A week later, they were carted again and had the nooses around their necks when there was another reprieve. They still had influential friends. But on 6 April, it was third time unlucky. The pair were duly hanged, 'so early and secretly as they well could in such a case' (Powicke, 79). Eyewitnesses reported that on the scaffold Barrow either recited the Lord's prayer or consented to its being said, which, if true, was inconsistent with the hard line he had always taken against it. There is evidence that not all in high places were satisfied that these proceedings were entirely safe, and a legend, first recorded in the mid-seventeenth century, grew up that the deaths of Barrow and Greenwood were regretted by the highest of all persons in the state. After years in prison, Barrow was still able to leave behind money to support the poor members of his church.

PATRICK COLLINSON

Sources H. Barrow, *A collection of certain letters and conferences lately passed betwixt certaine preachers and two prisoners in the Fleete* (1590) · L. H. Carlson, ed., *Elizabethan nonconformist texts*, 3–6 (1962–70) · P. Collinson, 'Separation in and out of the church: the consistency of Barrow and Greenwood', *Journal of the United Reformed Church History Society*, 5 (1992–7), 239–58 · F. J. Powicke, *Henry Barrow separatist (1550?–1593) and the exiled church of Amsterdam (1593–1622)* (1900) · S. Ofwod [S. Offwood], *An advertisement to Jhon Delecluse and Henry May the elder* [1632] · C. Burrage, *The early English dissenters in the light of recent research (1550–1641)*, 2 vols. (1912) · M. R. Watts, *The dissenters: from the Reformation to the French Revolution* (1978) · B. R. White, *The English separatist tradition* (1971) · BL, Harley MS 6848 · Masters' *History of the college of Corpus Christi and the Blessed Virgin Mary in the University of Cambridge*, ed. J. Lamb (1831) · J. R. Knott, *Discourses of martyrdom in English literature, 1563–1694* (1993) · G. Johnson, *A discourse of some troubles and excommunications in the banished English church at Amsterdam* (1603)

Barrow, Henry (*c*.1790–1870), maker of mathematical instruments, may have been born in Suffolk. Nothing is known of his education or apprenticeship, beyond his attendance at the London Mechanics' Institute. He married Elizabeth Mary Collins (1790–1834) in 1816 at Christ Church Greyfriars, London, producing six children by 1830, three of whom outlived him. The circumstances of Barrow's second marriage, between 1839 and 1868, remain obscure.

Barrow was an outworker for the mathematical instrument trade in London during the 1820s. He was well known to staff of the Royal Observatory at Greenwich, who in 1829 introduced him to Sir George Everest (1790–1863), surveyor-general of India, who was anxious to appoint a mathematical instrument maker to set up and run a new workshop for the survey based in Calcutta. Barrow was Everest's second choice for the post. He was taken on despite his age (about forty in 1830)—which might affect his ability to cope with the Indian climate—because of his good reputation, his steadiness, and his desire to make something of himself. Barrow accepted a five-year contract, uprooting his wife and family of six children, because it offered a chance to acquire the capital he needed to set up on his own account in London. Despite the deaths in Calcutta of his wife and six-year-old second son, William, he extended his contract for another four years in order to achieve this.

Barrow had to appoint and train a group of about nine people with few existing skills and no experience. Part of the work was to maintain and repair equipment for the revenue survey, which used simple surveying apparatus such as small theodolites and perambulators (measuring wheels), the latter lasting only about two years under normal field conditions. A more important task, in Everest's eyes, at least, was to repair the magnificent 3 foot theodolite and the zenith sector that were required for the measurement of a meridional arc extending from the tip of India to the foothills of the Himalayas. Everest had also purchased new equipment for the latter purpose while in England, and Barrow was needed to help set up the instruments for use.

Of the problems faced by Barrow, including professional isolation, inability to speak the languages, and living above the shop, by far the worst was his rapidly deteriorating relationship with Everest. Both men were strong-willed and independent. Everest, who could speak the native languages, was in the habit of dropping into the workshop several times a day when he was in Calcutta, and commenting on the work in hand. Some eighteen months after the start of his contract, Barrow lost his temper with Everest so severely that it triggered disciplinary procedures. (One consequence of this was that much information was disclosed about the instrument-making trade in London that would not otherwise have come to light.)

In 1837 Barrow was ordered up country to Kaliana to undertake the conversion of two field astronomy instruments to fixed-base observatory use. This involved recasting the metal supports for the telescopes and other complicated procedures that would not have been easy in a settled permanent workshop, let alone in the middle of the countryside with no facilities at all. Everest became ever more autocratic, Barrow's mood swings became more pronounced, and at the end of the job in 1839 Barrow was sacked and dispatched home to England.

Barrow's next appearance in the historical record shows him taking over the business of T. C. Robinson, a manufacturer of high-precision weighing balances and other special instruments. Barrow was well qualified to carry out such work and the business flourished quietly. Further orders arrived from the survey of India—Barrow's professional skills were well appreciated and no slur had been placed on his workmanship—and instruments under his signature went to Nepal with Joseph Dalton Hooker, to Spitsbergen with the Swedish ship *Eugenie*, and to the observatory at the Cape of Good Hope. Work on magnetic dip circles for expeditions formed a solid grounding for the future work on compasses that was to be the mainstay of the business after his retirement.

Barrow became a fellow of both the Royal Meteorological Society and the Royal Astronomical Society on his return to England, but does not appear to have played an active part in either. By the mid-1860s he was living at Belmont House, Westfield, near Hastings in Sussex, where he died on 2 April 1870 in his eightieth year. Examples of his work can be found in museum collections in England, India, and elsewhere. His son Henry, born in 1822, also became an instrument maker and took over his father's firm after his death. Another son, Francis, trained as a solicitor and became an appeal agent for the India privy council. A daughter Henrietta also survived him.

JANE INSLEY

Sources Letters from mathematical instrument maker to surveyor general, 1830–40, Dehra Dun, India, Survey of India Archives, vol. 307 · bonds and agreements, BL OIOC, o/1/351 no.7692 · trade directories, London, 1810–90 · will of Henry Barrow, 1868, Principal Registry of the Family Division, London [will drafted 1868, proved 23/4/1870] · Sci. Mus., scientific instrument collections · R. H. Phillimore, ed., *Historical records of the survey of India*, 4 (1958) · J. T. Stock, 'Precision balances—a chapter in their development', *Chemistry in Britain*, 7 (1971), 385–7 · J. E. Insley, 'Making mountains out of molehills? George Everest and Henry Barrow, 1830–1839', *Indian Journal of History of Science*, 30 (1995), 47–55 · d. cert.

Archives BL OIOC, bonds · Sci. Mus., scientific instruments · Survey of India, Dehra Dun, India, archives

Wealth at death under £5000

Barrow, Isaac (1612/13–1680), bishop of St Asaph, was the elder son of Isaac Barrow esquire (d. 1642) of Spinney Abbey, near Wicken, Cambridgeshire, and his wife, Katherine (d. 1647), daughter of Marlion Rythe of Twickenham, Middlesex. Isaac Barrow never married. He was admitted to Peterhouse, Cambridge, on 6 July 1629 and matriculated as a pensioner at Easter 1631. After graduating BA in 1632 he continued his education at Cambridge and proceeded MA in 1636. He was ordained at Peterborough in December 1641, becoming vicar of Cherry Hinton, Cambridgeshire, the same year. Elected a fellow of Peterhouse, he was ejected by parliament in January 1644 (thereby thwarting his procuring of a foundation scholarship for his nephew and namesake Isaac *Barrow, the future mathematician and theologian) and joined the king at Oxford where he served as chaplain of New College. After Oxford fell to parliament in 1646 Barrow was 'forc'd to shift from Place to Place' (Willis, 91) and lived an apparently quiet life during the interregnum. At the Restoration he recovered his fellowship and became a fellow of Eton College and rector of Downham, Cambridgeshire. His service to the royalist cause was furthermore acknowledged by the award of an honorary doctorate of divinity by royal mandate in 1660.

Barrow was nominated as bishop of Sodor and Man after the death of Samuel Rutter and was consecrated in Westminster Abbey on 5 July 1663. Like his patron, Charles Stanley, earl of Derby, hereditary lord of Man, Barrow was a high-churchman, 'a disciple in the school of Laud' (Keble, 1.133). He clearly found favour with the earl, for Derby appointed him governor of the Isle of Man in April 1664. Barrow took an active role in the government of the island as head of both the temporal and spiritual administration in the permanent absence of the earl of Derby. On the ecclesiastical side he found much to do, claiming that on his arrival he found the Manx 'without any true sense of religion' (Butler, 304–5). He attributed this to the ignorance of the clergy, the lack of books, and the extempore translation of the scriptures into Manx in church. Barrow determined to rectify the situation by setting up an English school in each parish and a grammar school. He placed renewed emphasis on the maintenance of parish schools, requiring the clergy themselves to teach rather than merely appoint often illiterate substitutes to perform the duty. Furthermore, the bishop made efforts to raise the educational standards of the Manx clergy and instituted three scholarships for native Manx students in Dublin. He also determined to increase the incomes of the clergy as part of his plan to improve clerical standards. £1000 was raised by subscription in England which Barrow used to purchase the impropriations of the island from the earl of Derby and these were thereafter employed for the augmentation of parish incomes and the maintenance of church schools. Barrow additionally managed to secure an annual royal bounty of £100 for the support of the poor clergy. Another indication of both his energy and his intention to supervise the Manx church closely came when he undertook the first episcopal visitation of the diocese since before the civil wars. He was also keen to encourage full and proper observance of the forms of worship in the island. Accordingly, he ordered new copies of the Book of Common Prayer for each of the island's seventeen parishes. Barrow was never seriously troubled by dissenters in the island, the numbers being very small, but he did order the handful of Quakers to attend church regularly and attempted to enforce regular church attendance with vigour.

Barrow was translated to the diocese of St Asaph in March 1670 but was permitted to retain Sodor and Man *in commendam* until 1671. Initially, he proved himself to be just as active as he had been in the Isle of Man. He supervised the restoration and repair of the fabric of the cathedral and his own residence at St Asaph. He also devoted considerable energies to securing through act of parliament the income from several sinecures to be directed towards the maintenance of the cathedral. Among his acts of charity he established and endowed an almshouse for widows at St Asaph and in his will bequeathed £200 towards a free school there. He found the situation concerning dissenters quite different from that in Man and took firm action against at least some of them, excommunicating John Evans, who rose to be the leader of the 'schismaticks many' in the Wrexham area (Richards, 41). By contrast, like his predecessors in the diocese, he took no action against the puritan schoolmaster Richard Jones, who lived unmolested at Denbigh until his death in 1673. Barrow's efforts to improve the standards of the clergy, vigorous though they may have been, do not necessarily seem to have borne fruit. In 1678 it was reported to Sancroft that the clergy in the diocese of St Asaph were mostly 'illiterate and Contemptible'. Barrow endeavoured to explain the perceived deficiencies in terms of the poverty of the inhabitants, the lack of books and 'all improvements' (Richards, 142). In the last two years of his life he spent much time at Park Hall, Shropshire, taking the cure, and left the running of episcopal affairs to his subordinates, who rarely troubled the bishop.

Barrow died, aged sixty-seven, on 24 June 1680 at Shrewsbury and was buried at St Asaph 'without the Cathedral West-Door' (Willis, 92–3).   J. R. DICKINSON

Sources Venn, *Alum. Cant.* · T. A. Walker, ed., *Admissions to Peterhouse or St Peter's College in the University of Cambridge* (1912) · A. W. Moore, *Sodor and Man* (1893) · B. Willis, *A survey of the cathedral church of St Asaph* (1720) · D. R. Thomas, *Esgobaeth Llanelwy: the history of the diocese of St Asaph*, rev. edn, 1 (1908) · T. Richards, *Wales under the penal code, 1662–1687* (1925) · W. Butler, *Memoirs of Mark Hildesley* (1799) · J. Keble, *The life of the right reverend father in God, Thomas Wilson*, 1 (1863) · W. Harrison, *An account of the diocese of Sodor and Man*, Manx Society, 29 (1879) · P. G. Clamp, 'English schooling in the Isle of Man, 1660–1700: the Barrovian design', *Journal of Educational Administration and History*, 20 (1988), 10–21 · J. W. Clay, ed., *The visitation of Cambridge … 1575 … 1619*, Harleian Society, 41 (1897) · G. J. Armytage, ed., *Middlesex pedigrees*, Harleian Society, 65 (1914) · N. K. Travers, ed., 'Transcript of Wicken parish registers', typescript, 1984, Cambs. AS · memorial, St Asaph Cathedral
Archives Bodl. Oxf., corresp.

Barrow, Isaac (1630–1677), mathematician and theologian, was born in London in October 1630, the son of Thomas Barrow, from a Cambridgeshire family, and his wife, Anne Buggin. Following the death of his mother in 1634 Isaac was sent to his grandfather's house where he remained until his father, already becoming a successful linen-draper, married Katherine Oxinden in 1636. Having baulked at his own father's attempt to make him a scholar, Thomas Barrow was nevertheless determined to make Isaac one, and to that end enrolled him at the Charterhouse, paying the master, Robert Brook, twice the going rate of £2 for his promise to supervise the boy's education. Two years later, to Thomas's chagrin, he learned that his son's education had been grossly neglected and that the lad distinguished himself only by 'being much given to fighting, and promoting it in others'. Isaac was quickly transferred to Felsted School in Essex, the renowned headmaster of which, Martin Holbeach, proved far more successful in discovering Barrow's precocity and instilling in him a love of learning.

The civil war years The coming of the civil war proved disastrous for Thomas Barrow. The Irish rising precipitated the collapse of his trade with Ireland and resulted in a loss of some £1000. At the same time his strong royalist sympathies, which recently had been rewarded by his appointment as linen-draper to the king, made his position in London increasingly untenable, so that by June 1642 he had removed his family to Cambridgeshire. As a consequence of these difficulties Thomas Barrow was forced to inform Holbeach that he could no longer afford to pay for Isaac's education. The good headmaster, however, was loath to lose his exceptional student, and in response removed Isaac to his own house and appointed him 'little Tutor' to William Fairfax, third Viscount Fairfax of Emley. A last ditch effort to secure Isaac's future was made on 15

Isaac Barrow (1630–1677), by David Loggan, 1676

December 1643, when he was admitted as a foundation scholar at Peterhouse, Cambridge, owing to the efforts of his uncle Isaac Barrow, a fellow of Peterhouse. However, within a few weeks the elder Isaac was ejected by the parliamentary visitors of the university, and the nephew remained in Felsted. There he became involved in the amorous affairs of Fairfax, who soon eloped with a local girl, taking along his young tutor to London. However, it did not take Fairfax long to exhaust his wife's dowry, and Barrow, not wishing to burden his friend, on the one hand, and refusing Holbeach's kind offer to return to Felsted and become his heir on the other, began wandering in England. At last he arrived at the Norfolk house of a former schoolfellow, Edward Walpole, and the latter, about to go up to Cambridge, resolved on taking Barrow along, promising to support him there.

Barrow was admitted a pensioner in Trinity College on 25 February 1646 with James Duport as tutor, but when, several months later, Walpole went down, Barrow was once again faced with uncertainty. By then Oxford had fallen and Thomas Barrow, who had been stranded at Oxford for the duration of the siege, sought out his son and pledged him £20 per annum toward his maintenance. Duport pitched in as well, offering his tuition gratis as well as providing his charge with free lodgings. Barrow's fortunes further improved the following year thanks to his election to a college scholarship. He graduated BA in March 1649 and shortly thereafter was elected fellow. Such academic success was based on merit alone, as Barrow never disguised his royalist and Anglican sympathies. Indeed, he put his fellowship on the line in October 1649 when he decided, after a momentary acquiescence, against subscribing to the Engagement (Charles I's treaty

with the Scots to allow presbyterianism to be established in England). Almost certainly he was spared expulsion thanks to the patronage of the master, Thomas Hill, who is reputed to have once laid his hands over Isaac's head and said: 'Thou art a good lad: 'tis pity thou art a Cavalier' (Pope, 140). Barrow would remain in need of further help from Hill as he became increasingly vocal in his religious and political convictions. Thus, on 5 November 1651, Barrow availed himself of the opportunity that arose with his appointment as the orator commemorating the anniversary of the Gunpowder Plot to articulate a forceful panegyric on the Stuart monarchy. Small wonder that several infuriated fellows conspired to effect Barrow's expulsion, but once again Hill intervened, this time by silencing the indignant fellows with the claim 'Barrow is a better man than any of us' (Pope, 140–41). Barrow's conflicts with some of his colleagues at Trinity, however, should not obscure the fact that his choice as the Gunpowder orator was indicative of the growing recognition of his exceptional literary skills and wit. Six months earlier, still a bachelor of arts, he had also been chosen moderator in the schools, an office which, as he himself remarked in an engaging Latin oration, required its occupant to excel at once in being serious and facetious.

Mastering the 'new philosophy' The exercises performed by Barrow to satisfy the MA requirements in the summer of 1652 also give first proof of his mastery of the 'new philosophy'. During the early 1650s Barrow devoted much time to the natural sciences, not only because they were part of the regular course of study but also because, like so many royalists at the time, he considered making medicine his profession. Accordingly his studies of astronomy and mathematics were supplemented by those of botany, anatomy, and chemistry, at least some of which were undertaken in the company of John Ray. That he ultimately did not persist in medicine can be attributed to Barrow's realization that 'that profession [was] not well consistent with the oath he had taken when admitted Fellow, to make Divinity the end of his studies' (Napier, l.xli). During this period Barrow also participated in the work of the lively scientific group that was formed in Trinity College and included, in addition to himself and Ray, Walter Needham, John Nidd, Alexander Akehurst, and Francis Willughby.

Barrow was enthusiastic about Cartesianism, though not without qualification. He approved of Descartes's mathematics and much of his physics, but he criticized him for neglecting experiments and was averse to the Frenchman's metaphysics. In time his early concern with the deleterious implications of Cartesianism for religion became increasingly pronounced, providing a development analogous in many ways to Henry More's own evolving reaction to Descartes. At no time, however, was Barrow's endorsement of the new science incompatible with his continued respect for Aristotle and other ancients. Truth, he believed, must be garnered from whatever source, and those in pursuit of truth should be careful to avoid all partisanship and dogmatism, whether ancient or modern. Likewise, he cautioned against permitting the rejection of an obsolete natural philosophy to lead to a rejection of classical literature; and it was with just such a concern that Barrow urged his Cambridge students to allow Aristotle to refine their language even if they rejected him as the source of all knowledge.

It was also during this period of the early 1650s that Barrow seriously embarked on his mathematical studies. The immediate results were the publication of compact editions of Euclid's *Elements* and *Data* in 1656 and 1657 respectively, and the composition of the equally compact editions of Apollonius, Archimedes, and Theodosius, published, however, only in 1675. More important still, it was during this same period that Barrow obtained his deep insights into higher mathematics, including the formulation of his method of tangents, which would form the more original part of his *Geometrical Lectures* a decade and a half later.

Barrow's studies were rudely interrupted in 1654. A new wave of anti-university propaganda—against which Barrow made an impassioned *Oratio ad academicos in commitiis*—produced a nervous mood at the university. It had already claimed as one of its victims James Duport, who was forced to forfeit his Greek professorship for persisting in his refusal to sign the Engagement. The ousted professor, however, nearly succeeded in arranging to have Barrow succeed him, ensuring to this end the support of Benjamin Whichcote, provost of King's College, and John Worthington, master of Jesus College. Indeed, Barrow may have actually been elected by the university, as he performed, with great success, the required probationary exercise. This time, however, his reputation as a scholar was insufficient to outweigh his politics. The ambitious and irascible Ralph Widdrington of Christ's College, brother of the speaker of the House of Commons, succeeded in obtaining in January 1655—in explicit violation of the statutes of the chair—an injunction from Cromwell himself to force his own induction. Heeding the handwriting on the wall, Barrow applied immediately for a Trinity travelling fellowship, and on 4 April 1655 was granted the necessary passport to travel abroad for three years.

Travel abroad After selling his books to supplement the £16 stipend attached to the fellowship, in June 1655 Barrow headed for Paris. There he met his father, whom he had not seen for almost a decade, and shared his meagre assets with him. Barrow's mocking description of the French capital, as both devoid of its former renown and inferior in every respect to Cambridge, should not obscure the fact that he much enjoyed his eight-month sojourn. He travelled next, in mid-February 1656, to Florence where he not only delighted in the city and in the company of many local scholars but also, owing to plague in Rome, remained for longer than he had intended. Through the instruction of one Fitton, the English curator of the Medicis' collection of coins and medals, Barrow also became proficient in numismatics.

At length, in November 1656, Barrow decided to travel east and embarked on a ship headed for Smyrna. On the way they were attacked by a Barbary corsair and Barrow distinguished himself in defending the ship. He stayed in Smyrna for seven months, enjoying the most generous hospitality of the English consul there, Spencer Bretton. At length he continued on to Constantinople where, again, his learning and engaging character recommended him to the English ambassador, Sir Thomas Bendish, as well as to the merchant Jonathan Dawes, future mayor of London. Barrow's animosity toward Islam was confirmed while in Constantinople, and despite his great linguistic skills—he was fluent in eight languages—he made little effort to master Arabic. Instead he studied the Greek fathers, especially Chrysostom, and served as agent to James Stock, a young merchant who supported Barrow and to whom the edition of Euclid's *Data* was dedicated, and Abraham Hill, both of whom were in the process of forming coin collections. Barrow left Constantinople in mid-December 1658, and, after taking a return route by way of Venice, Germany, and the Netherlands, arrived back at Trinity in September 1659 only to discover that a new master, John Wilkins, had just been installed. Although Wilkins would remain but briefly at Trinity, he would prove a valuable patron to Barrow in the coming years. Barrow's immediate concern, however, was to seek Anglican ordination, which he received from Bishop Ralph Brownrigg shortly before the latter's death in December 1659, mystifying Brownrigg's chaplain by 'rhyming answers to moral questions' (Feingold, 99).

Multiple professorships The Restoration catapulted Barrow into multiple academic positions. In 1660 Widdrington quickly vacated the Greek professorship into which he had been intruded five years earlier and Barrow was elected without competition. Within a year, the new professor obtained a royal patent that granted both himself and future incumbents the freedom to enjoy the income and privileges of a Trinity fellowship in addition to the meagre stipend attached to the chair. Barrow's first course was devoted to Sophocles but, as it attracted few students, he opted to proceed with a course on Aristotle's *Rhetoric*, which indeed proved far more successful. Unfortunately, the manuscript copy of these lectures was lent to a friend and never returned. At the same time Barrow made his first forays into the domain of theology. In 1661 he was granted the degree of BD *honoris causa* and invited to deliver the prestigious commencement sermon, which he did on 30 June 1661—his first public sermon. Two years later, on 5 July 1663, Barrow also preached at Westminster Abbey during his uncle's consecration sermon as bishop of Sodor and Man.

On 16 July 1662, on the recommendation of John Wilkins, Barrow was elected Gresham professor of geometry. His brief tenure also included substituting for the astronomy professor, Walter Pope, who went travelling on the continent. Barrow's lectures included a course on the projections of the sphere and another on perspectives. The text of the former was apparently prepared for publication, but alas it, too, was lent out and subsequently lost. On 17 September 1662 Barrow was elected fellow of the Royal Society but, with the exception of the odd meeting he attended while living in London, he never participated in its activities.

Following the foundation of the Lucasian professorship of mathematics at Cambridge in 1663 Barrow was elected its first incumbent, again on Wilkins's recommendation. Turning down an offer to become librarian of the Cottonian Library made at about the same time, Barrow returned to Cambridge and in 1664 resigned both the Greek and Gresham professorships he had held concurrently. He read three sets of lectures during his five years' tenure as Lucasian professor, and though they were subsequently published, their published form does not entirely reflect the order in which they were read. Delivery of the *Mathematical Lectures*, for example, was stretched over the period 1664–6, partly because Barrow injected what would become lectures one to five of the *Geometrical Lectures*—to which perhaps were added his lectures on Archimedes—during the winter and spring of 1665, and partly because the plague forced the university to close for several months thereafter. Barrow completed his delivery of the mathematical lectures in spring 1666 and, following another plague-related closure of the university, delivered the rest of the geometrical lectures either in the spring or autumn of 1667. He concluded his tenure as Lucasian professor by delivering the optical lectures in 1668–9, and these were the first to be published.

Having resigned his chair, however, Barrow would have nothing to do with the printing of his lectures, and were it not for the persistence of John Collins, the geometrical and optical lectures might have remained unpublished. The mathematical lectures languished until 1683, when the demand for Barrow's theological works must have led the publisher to believe they were saleable as well. Barrow displayed an even greater indifference toward the publication of Archimedes, Apollonius, and Theodosius. Although he consented to Collins's solicitation, he refused to revise them, thus leaving it to Collins and his associates to check the two-decade-old manuscripts and correct the proofs. As for his Gresham lectures on perspective, although Barrow agreed to allow Collins to publish them, he refused to attach his name to them and ultimately Collins gave up the idea.

Theological works Barrow's lack of concern with the fate of his mathematical works is puzzling until viewed as a consequence of his resolve to proceed at last with what had always been his intended vocation: divinity. Barrow claimed that he accepted the Greek professorship as a caretaker, and only until a qualified and more willing person came along. Likewise, he was induced to substitute the regius professorship of Greek with the Lucasian chair not only because he found the mathematical sciences more congenial but also because he was intent on securing the institutionalization of the mathematical sciences at Cambridge. Thus, having found a most worthy successor in Isaac Newton, Barrow resigned the professorship in 1669 and abandoned mathematics for good. His sentiments were expressed by his friend Abraham Hill: '[Barrow] had vowed in his ordination to serve God in the Gospel of his Son, and he could not make a bible out of his Euclid, or a pulpit out of his mathematical chair' (Feingold, 80–81). Thereafter Barrow remained a mere fellow of

Trinity, for though he intended to make theology his calling, he was reluctant to leave Cambridge, still less to become a church functionary. He did consent, however, to accept a small sinecure in Wales, bestowed on him by his uncle, now bishop of St Asaph, but the income was used solely for charity. On 16 May 1671 Barrow was also installed prebendary of Yetminster, a position he accepted, according to Walter Pope, simply because he needed to raise the sum of £500 for his half-sister Rebecca, 'for a portion, that would procure her a good husband' (Feingold, 82). Once the terms of the lease he had set out expired, however, Barrow resigned the prebend. As a consequence his friends conspired to obtain for Barrow—who had been in the meantime made DD and appointed in 1670 as royal chaplain—the one position he truly wished for: the mastership of Trinity College, then held by John Pearson.

Following John Wilkins's death in November 1672, the vacant bishopric of Chester was quickly secured for Pearson, and on 27 February 1673 Barrow was admitted as the new master of Trinity. His short tenure proved a happy one for both Barrow and Trinity. Admissions remained high, and little, if any, dissension plagued the society. Most important for the long-term prosperity of the college, however, was Barrow's contribution to the construction of the college's new library, which he did not live to see completed. According to Roger North, while serving as vice-chancellor (1675–6) Barrow attempted to press the Cambridge heads of house to contribute toward the building of a public theatre that would rival the Sheldonian Theatre in Oxford. His colleagues, however, proved too cautious and Barrow decided to build the library at Trinity instead, and to this end managed to secure, gratis, the good services of Sir Christopher Wren as architect. It was also Barrow who personally wrote numerous letters to potential benefactors, helping raise a not insignificant portion of the ultimate cost of over £16,000.

In April 1677, while in London for the annual election of Westminster scholars, Barrow contracted a 'malignant fever'. He tried to cure himself, as he had done once before, by fasting and taking opium, but this could well have aggravated his condition and he died on 4 May 1677. Three days later he was buried in Westminster Abbey where, some time later, his friends erected a monument to commemorate him.

Posthumous reputation Barrow's reputation has metamorphosed over the centuries. For the two centuries following his death it was chiefly as a consummate preacher and controversial theologian that he was remembered. Though the often unreliable Walter Pope claimed that certain urban congregations found Barrow's sermons too 'academic', the fact remains that they were highly regarded by many contemporaries. Indeed, Charles II jested that Barrow was an 'unfair' preacher because 'he exhausted every subject, and left no room for others to come after him'. A more serious threat to Barrow's reputation as a preacher arose from its essentially oral foundation, as only two of the sermons he delivered in London were published during his lifetime. However, as Barrow died intestate, his papers fell into the hands of his father, who was instrumental in ensuring the publication of his son's work. Thomas Barrow appointed John Tillotson and Abraham Hill as executors and the former published three volumes of Barrow's sermons between 1678 and 1680, followed in 1680 by an edition of *A Treatise of the Pope's Supremacy*, the only work which Barrow, on his deathbed, explicitly requested Tillotson to publish. In 1681 the publisher Brabazon Aylmer bought the copyright of all these works, as well as Barrow's manuscripts, from Thomas Barrow for the staggering price of £470, and proceeded to publish further editions. Thus was established Barrow's posthumous reputation, with collections of his sermons being published at regular intervals well into the nineteenth century. Not surprisingly, numerous readers, including Jean Leclerc, Henry Fielding, and the elder Pitt, expressed their great admiration of Barrow's eloquence no less than his power of reasoning.

As a mathematician Barrow was also highly regarded during the seventeenth and early eighteenth centuries. Henry Pemberton, in the preface to his *A View of Isaac Newton's Philosophy* (1728), wrote: 'he may be esteemed as having shewn a compass of invention equal, if not superior, to any of the moderns … [Newton] only excepted'. Late twentieth-century scholars, in contrast, have found it difficult to credit him with being more than just a well-read contemporary in mathematical literature and an elegant codifier. In part, this is due to the juxtaposition of Newton's and Barrow's careers, so that even while Barrow's lectures were being printed, their content was being rendered obsolete by his young protégé, Newton. Nor is there any allowance for the virtually unrevised publication of Barrow's university lectures, the assumption being that they represent both the sum total of his mathematical knowledge and the genesis of his mathematical ideas. Only when, and if, Barrow's one surviving manuscript notebook, once in the hands of William Jones—in all likelihood the very one into which, Barrow told Collins in early 1667, he 'used to cast some things that came into [his] head' (Rigaud, 2.47)—becomes available will it be possible to evaluate the scope and depth of his knowledge. Whatever the ultimate verdict on his originality, however, Barrow remains one of the last Renaissance universal scholars, capable of distinguishing himself as a theologian, classical scholar, and mathematician. He himself articulated the ideal to which he strived in one of his sermons when he wrote: 'he can hardly be a good scholar, who is not a general one'. MORDECHAI FEINGOLD

Sources M. Feingold, ed., *Before Newton: the life and times of Isaac Barrow* (1990) · *The theological works of Isaac Barrow*, ed. A. Napier, 9 vols. (1859) · *Brief lives, chiefly of contemporaries, set down by John Aubrey, between the years 1669 and 1696*, ed. A. Clark, 1 (1898), 87–93 · S. P. Rigaud and S. J. Rigaud, eds., *Correspondence of scientific men of the seventeenth century*, 2 vols. (1841) · P. H. Osmond, *Isaac Barrow, his life and times* (1944) · W. Pope, *The life of the right reverend father in God, Seth, lord bishop of Salisbury* (1697); repr. as *The life of Seth, Lord Bishop of Salisbury*, ed. J. B. Bamborough (1961) · D. T. Whiteside, 'Patterns of mathematical thought in the later seventeenth century', *Archive for History of Exact Sciences*, 1 (1960–62), 179–388
Archives RS, papers presented to the Royal Society · Trinity Cam. | BL, letters to John Collins, Add. MS 4293

Likenesses D. Loggan, drawing, 1676, NPG [*see illus.*] · L. F. Roubiliac, marble bust, 1756, Trinity Cam.; terracotta model, BM · R. Earlom, mezzotint, pubd 1811 (after D. Loggan), BM, NPG · B. Holl, line engraving (after portrait, Trinity Cam.), NPG · bust, Wesminster Abbey · oils, Trinity Cam. · print, NPG

Barrow, John (*fl.* **1735–1774**), teacher of mathematics and writer, is known solely through his publications. As a young man he taught mathematics and navigation to the 'young gentlemen' on Royal Navy ships. The status of the naval schoolmaster aboard was not high: he was for example excluded from the officers' mess, but Barrow was one of several able mathematicians who none the less served in this capacity, for which a certificate of competence was needed. He retired before 1750 and thereafter devoted himself to writing. He compiled dictionaries and other works which drew on his mathematical and scientific knowledge. Many of his works went through more than one edition and some were translated. His compilations included *Dictionarium polygraphicum* (1735), *Dictionarium medicum universale* (1749), a *Geographical Dictionary* (2 vols., 1759–60), and a *Dictionary of Arts and Sciences* (1764). The geographical dictionary included a dissertation on the figure and motion of the earth as well as the normal recitation of facts about dress and customs of various lands. His best-known work is *Navigatio Britannica* (1750) which was a useful practical handbook of navigation and chart making published by the eminent hydrographical publishers Mount and Page. It was still being advertised by them in 1787. It included a very thorough examination of nautical instruments and explained the use of the vernier, which was still something of a novelty. From his familiarity with various instruments it seems likely that Barrow kept in close contact with nautical instrument makers, as did other naval schoolmasters. The *Navigatio* was followed by *The Naval History of Great Britain* (4 vols., 1758) and *A Collection of Authentic, Useful, and Entertaining Voyages and Discoveries* (3 vols., 1765). Taylor gives a last known floruit date of 1774 (Taylor, 169). In the *Dictionary of National Biography* Barrow was described as a 'geographical compiler' and his identity with John Barrow, teacher of mathematics, was not realized. ELIZABETH BAIGENT

Sources E. G. R. Taylor, *The mathematical practitioners of Hanoverian England, 1714–1840* (1966) · *ESTC*

Barrow, Sir John, first baronet (**1764–1848**), promoter of exploration and author, was born on 19 June 1764 at Dragley Beck, Ulverston, Lancashire, the only child of Roger Barrow, journeyman tanner, and his wife, Mary. Educated at the local Town Bank grammar school, which he left at the age of thirteen, Barrow worked successively as a clerk in a Liverpool iron foundry, as a landsman on a Greenland whaler, and as a mathematics teacher in a Greenwich academy preparing young men for a naval career, until offered the position of comptroller of household to Lord Macartney's embassy to China (1792–4). He served with distinction during this embassy and Macartney's governorship of the Cape of Good Hope (1797–9), collecting much of the commercial and strategic intelligence about

Sir John Barrow, first baronet (1764–1848), attrib. John Jackson, c.1810

the eastern seas and southern Africa that Macartney forwarded to Henry Dundas, president of the Board of Control and secretary of state at war. Barrow was promoted to the post of auditor general to the Cape Colony in September 1798, and married Anna Maria Trüter (1777–1857) at Stellenbosch on 26 August 1799. His intention to settle at the Cape was frustrated by its return to the Dutch in 1803. He was offered the second secretaryship of the Admiralty by Dundas (by then Lord Melville) on 5 May 1804, and this he held, except for the period between 10 February 1806 and 7 April 1807, until 28 January 1845.

Barrow was elected to the Royal Society in 1805 and the Royal Society Club three years later. Through these he formed his close personal and professional relationship with Sir Joseph Banks, the president of the Royal Society. At Banks's suggestion, Barrow served on the council of the Royal Society for the first time in 1815 and over the next fifteen years alternated his council membership with his Admiralty colleague John Wilson Croker. He was appointed a vice-president several times thereafter. With Croker, assisted by Davies Gilbert, Thomas Young, and Thomas Amyot, Barrow attempted to have Robert Peel elected as president in 1826. The rift between amateur and professional scientists over the election of the duke of Somerset was a factor in his agreeing to assist Francis Beaufort and William Henry Smyth to form the Royal Geographical Society in 1830. He chaired early meetings of the new society, and secured royal patronage; he served as president between 1835 and 1837.

An ardent imperialist, Barrow entered the Admiralty convinced that Britain's security and future wealth depended on control of the world's sea lanes both for trade and for defence. He took an active interest in the development of naval dockyards and other facilities during the Napoleonic and American wars, and actively promoted the careers of promising young naval officers when peace was declared in 1815. His incomparable knowledge of naval traditions and organization was drawn upon by Sir James Graham in 1832 when the Navy Board and other civilian boards responsible for aspects of naval administration were replaced by departments answerable directly to the Board of Admiralty.

Even before hostilities ceased, Barrow, with Banks's assistance, initiated a series of expeditions to trace the course of the Niger, which culminated with Richard Lander's expedition of 1831. News of the melting of the north polar ice cap, conveyed to Banks by William Scoresby in 1817, prompted an equally sustained search for the northwest passage. Sir John Franklin's fatal voyage (1845) was the last of these planned attempts. Other parts of the world also claimed Barrow's attention. Australia was of particular interest, and he actively fostered the careers of the explorers Phillip Parker King, Allan Cunningham, and Charles Sturt, among others.

In 1837, when negotiating the details of George Grey's expedition to north-western Australia, Barrow convinced Lord Glenelg, then colonial secretary, to occupy Port Essington on Australia's north coast to safeguard the Australia–Asia trade route. This was the culmination of a string of strategic annexations which Barrow advocated publicly from 1804, when he argued that the Cape of Good Hope should have been retained after the treaty of Amiens. His successful arguments for the annexation of Fernando Po to control the west African slave trade, made in 1827, compelled the then colonial secretary, Lord Bathurst, to declare: 'if coveting islands is a breach of the Ten Commandments, then he [Barrow] is the greatest violator of the decalogue in the kingdom' (Eddy, 235). Barrow was an equally strenuous advocate of overseas settlement, publicizing both the Albany settlement in the Cape Colony (1820) and the foundation of Swan River Colony (Western Australia) in 1829, and emigration to southern Africa, southern and eastern Australia, and Upper Canada. He played a major role in the decision to send the Amherst embassy to China in 1815, having advocated such a mission as early as 1809.

As a writer Barrow is best known for his *Mutiny on the Bounty* (1831) but, during his lifetime, his accounts of his travels in eastern Asia and southern Africa, published between 1801 and 1807, were better known and more influential. These established new standards for travel writing. In all, he wrote or edited seventeen full length books (including biographies of his personal heroes Peter the Great and the admirals Howe and Anson) as well as half a dozen articles in both the *Edinburgh Review* and the *Geographical Journal*, more than twenty entries in the *Encyclopaedia Britannica*, and over two hundred articles in the *Quarterly Review*. His interests ranged widely, but the great bulk of his output had a geographical focus, usually with an underlying imperial theme and a belief in progress and the superiority of British civilization. He wrote extensively about Asia, the Americas, Australia and the Pacific, the eastern Mediterranean, and Africa, and used the *Quarterly* for his promotion of exploration and imperial expansion. Through his friendship with John Murray, the *Quarterly*'s publisher, he also secured the publication of a succession of travellers' accounts which generated the great public interest in exploration in the period after 1815. Collectively, these activities established his pre-eminence within British geography.

In 1835 Barrow was made a baronet for his contributions to science and literature. He died on 23 November 1848 at New Street, Spring Gardens, London, and was buried in the Pratt Street cemetery, Camden Town. His friends and admirers erected a memorial to him (modelled on the Eddystone lighthouse) on Hoad Hill at the head of Morecambe Bay and overlooking his birthplace, in 1851.

Of Barrow's children, the eldest son was George *Barrow (1806–1876), while the second son, **John Barrow** (1808–1898), most closely mirrored his father's career. He was born on 28 June 1808, educated at Charterhouse, and entered the Admiralty as a clerk in 1824 through Croker's influence. He was appointed head of the Admiralty record office in 1844 in recognition of his development of a system for recording naval correspondence and of his rescue of valuable Admiralty documents dating back to the Elizabethan period. Equally active in geographical and Royal Society circles, he was a founder member of the Hakluyt Society (1846) and the only civilian member of the Arctic Council established in 1851 to co-ordinate the search for Franklin. A minor, if fairly prolific, author, he published ten well reviewed volumes of his travels throughout Europe, as well as biographies of Drake (1843) and Sir William Sidney Smith (2 vols., 1848); he also edited several other works. Following his retirement from the Admiralty in 1855, he took an active interest in the militia, where he held the rank of lieutenant-colonel. He was a founder member of the Alpine Club in 1857. He died on 9 December 1898 at Monterosa, Kingham, near Chipping Norton, Oxfordshire, and was buried at Kensal Green cemetery.

J. M. R. CAMERON

Sources M. Boucher and N. Penn, *Britain at the Cape, 1795 to 1803* (1992) • V. S. Forbes, *Pioneer travellers in southern Africa* (1965) • C. Lloyd, *Mr Barrow of the admiralty* (1970) • G. T. Staunton, *Memoir of Sir John Barrow, bart.* (1852) • D. H. Varley, 'Mr. Chronometer', *Libraries and people*, ed. J. Keating, S. I. Malen, A. B. Smith, and L. E. Taylor (1970), 141–9 • J. Barrow, *An auto-biographical memoir of Sir John Barrow* (1847) • J. J. Eddy, *Britain and the Australian colonies, 1818–1831* (1969) • Boase, *Mod. Eng. biog.* • *The Times* (22 Dec 1898), 7 • *The Times* (24 Nov 1848), 5c • Allibone, *Dict.* • parish records, Ulverston parish, Cumbria AS, Barrow

Archives Beds. & Luton ARS, letters to Samuel Whitbread • BL, autobiographical and literary MSS, Add. MSS 35301–35309 • BL, Barrow bequest • BL, letters to Sir Joseph Banks, Add. MS 32439 • BL, letters to Sir Charles Napier, Add. MS 40028 • BL, letters to Macvey Napier, Add. MSS 34611–34625, *passim* • BL, letters to Charles Philip Yorke, Add. MSS 45042–45047 • BL, letters to Sir Joseph Yorke, Add. MS 35899 • Bodl. Oxf., MS account of the Cape of Good Hope • Derbys. RO, letters to Sir R. J. Wilmot-Horton • John Murray Archives, Barrow–Murray MSS • NL Scot., letters to Lord Stuart De Rothesay • NMM, 1812–17 letter-books • RGS, letters to Royal Geographical Society and papers • Scott Polar RI, corresp. with John Richardson | BL, corresp. with Sir Robert Peel, Add. MSS 40226–40608, *passim* • Brenthurst Library, Johannesburg, Macartney MSS • Kimberley public library, corresp. with Lord Macartney

Likenesses attrib. J. Jackson, oils, c.1810, NPG [*see illus.*] • J. Jackson, oils, 1825, John Murray Publishers, London • J. Lucas, oils, 1844, Ministry of Defence • T. Macdonald or J. Macdonald, watercolour and chalk drawing, 1844, RGS • J. Lucas, oils, 1846, Gov. Art Coll. • S. Pearce, group portrait, oils, 1851, NPG • T. Milnes, relief portrait on memorial tablet, Ulverston parish church, Cumbria • miniature, NPG

Wealth at death £23,105 16s. 6d.—John Barrow: will, 1899

Barrow, John (1808–1898). *See under* Barrow, Sir John, first baronet (1764–1848).

Barrow, John Henry (1796–1858), journalist and writer, was born on 4 January 1796 in Cheapside, London, the sixth of the ten children of Charles Barrow (1759–1826) of Bristol, a partner with his father-in-law in a firm of musical instrument makers, and his wife, Mary (1771–1851), daughter of Thomas Culliford and his wife, Mary. In 1801 Charles Barrow entered the navy pay office and rapidly became chief conductor of moneys in town, a position he systematically abused by embezzling over £5500. In 1810 he had to seek permanent refuge from English law in Douglas on the Isle of Man. Details of John Barrow's formal education have proved elusive, but Dickens was to describe him in November 1845 as 'an excellent scholar', capable of translating from both the French and Italian newspapers (*Letters of Charles Dickens*, 4.434). He built on the experiences of his youth in his two collections of poems and songs from the Manx tradition: *Manks Legends* (1818), of which no copy is known to survive, and *The Mona Melodies* (1820).

From his appointment in 1819 as reporter for *The Times* in the ecclesiastical and maritime courts at Doctors' Commons, J. H. Barrow became, in his own words, 'one of the most extensive contributors of my day to the Political and Literary Journals, Reviews and Periodicals of the Metropolis' (Royal Literary Fund archives). His reporting of the trial of Queen Caroline for that paper in 1820 increased his reputation as a shorthand writer. Admitted to Gray's Inn in 1823, Barrow was called to the bar in 1828 but never practised. On 16 August 1817 he had married Kitty Collins (1791/1794–1864) at St George's, Hanover Square. The marriage was childless, and Barrow left her in 1828 for Lucina Arabella Fidelia Pocock (1804/5–1851), daughter of Major Luke Pocock; they had ten children, six of whom survived their father.

Barrow founded and edited the *Mirror of Parliament* in 1828 as a rival to *Hansard*. It purported to provide a full record of the debates in both houses of parliament, and to this end he employed his nephew Charles Dickens as a gallery reporter and general assistant (1831–4), thereby considerably advancing Dickens's journalistic career. Barrow petitioned unsuccessfully for official recognition of the *Mirror of Parliament* in May 1834; the *Mirror* lost its fight with *Hansard* and ceased publication in 1841. Barrow estimated that he lost £5000 by the venture. Both he and his journal received a posthumous tribute from Gladstone who asserted, during a Commons debate in April 1877, that: 'I do not hesitate to say, that Barrow's *Mirror of Parliament* is the primary record, and not *Hansard's Debates*, because of the greater fullness which Barrow aimed at and obtained' (*Hansard 3*, 233, 1877, 1576–7).

Barrow was the leader writer for the *Morning Herald* (1839–42), *The Sun* (1842–5), and the *Hampshire Advertiser* (1848–55). He was appointed Indian correspondent for the *Daily News* (1846–7), and arrived in Calcutta in January 1846, shortly after the outbreak of the First Anglo-Sikh War. His first dispatch, printed in February, gave an account of the battles of Mudki and Ferozeshahr, and in March he reported the defeat of the Sikhs at Aliwal. Later dispatches were sent from Bombay and China. He had never restricted himself to journalism, however; he also wrote *Emir Malek, the Prince of Assassins* (1827), a historical novel of the thirteenth century, published anonymously, and the text to accompany Thomas Landseer's engravings in *Characteristic Sketches of Animals, Principally from the Zoological Gardens, Regent's Park* (1832).

In his final year Barrow experienced severe financial distress and on 2 March 1858 he applied for assistance from the Royal Literary Fund. In his submission he reported that in the previous year, while engaged on the preparation of a work to be entitled 'Memoirs of the professional life and times of the editor of the Mirror of Parliament', which sadly was never published if indeed it was ever completed, he had contracted:

> a combined Malady that has ever since disabled me from all possibility of completing my outstanding engagements or undertaking new ones. I can neither write, except at the cost of intolerable pain, with my own hand or read, owing to the position required for either pursuit. (Royal Literary Fund archives)

The general committee of the fund voted him £50 on 10 March, a bequest which 'shed a gleam of sunshine over the clouded and inauspicious end' to his career (Royal Literary Fund archives). Nevertheless Barrow died of liver disease on 29 March 1858 at his home, 18 Francis Street, Newington, London. He was buried on 3 April at Norwood cemetery in a common grave, near Lucina Pocock, who had been interred there in May 1851. After his death his widow, who had been ignorant of his whereabouts, herself appealed for aid from the fund and received an award of £25. She had previously been receiving financial assistance from friends, including Charles Dickens. She died in Clerkenwell on 9 March 1864.   PAUL GRAHAM

Sources CUL, Royal Literary Fund MSS · L. C. Staples, A. T. Butler, and A. Campling, 'The Dickens ancestry: some new discoveries', *The Dickensian*, 45 (1949), 179–82 · W. J. Carlton, 'Dickens's literary mentor', *Dickens Studies*, 1 (1965), 54–64 · W. J. Carlton, 'An echo of the Copperfield days', *The Dickensian*, 45 (1949), 149–52 · W. J. Carlton, 'Links with Dickens in the Isle of Man', *Journal of the Manx Museum*, 76 (1958), 42–5 · K. Fielding, 'John Henry Barrow and the Royal Literary Fund', *The Dickensian*, 48 (1952), 61–4 · *The letters of Charles Dickens*, ed. M. House, G. Storey, and others, 1 (1965), 33 · *The letters of Charles Dickens*, ed. M. House, G. Storey, and others, 4 (1977), 434; 5 (1981), 39 · W. J. Carlton, 'The Barrows of Bristol', *The Dickensian*, 46 (1950), 33–6 · *Hansard 3* (1877), 233.1576–7

Archives BM, submission to Drury Lane Theatre, Add. MS 27900, fol. 105 · BM, application for public office, Add. MS 40524, fol. 80 · PRO, application for diplomatic post, FO 63/516 · W. Sussex RO, letters to the duke of Richmond

Wealth at death sought Royal Literary Fund assistance in the last year of life: CUL, Royal Literary Fund MSS

Barrow, Philip (*d.* 1600), medical writer, was the son of John Barrow of Suffolk. He was licensed to practise surgery by the University of Cambridge in 1559, the record of which states that Barrow had studied seven years. Barrow describes himself in his will as a gentleman, originally of Bury St Edmunds, Suffolk. He had a younger brother, Izaak, and a sister, Joane, who married one Manninge of Hadley. Barrow married Katherine Netford of Linton, Cambridgeshire, and names two sons (Isack, his executor, and Thomas), six daughters (Elizabeth, Clarke, Sannderson, Watlinson, Chambers, and Chapman), and twenty-two grandchildren in his will.

Barrow was the author of *The Method of Phisicke: containing the causes, signes and cures of inward diseases in mans body, from the head to the foot. Whereunto is added, the form and rule of making remedies and medicines, which our physicians commonly use at this day; with the proportion, quantity, and names of each medicine* (1583). The *Method of Phisicke* went through seven editions by 1652 and was dedicated to 'the right honorable and his singular good lord and master the Lord Burghley'. It offers a straightforward example of the Elizabethan medical *practica*. The text follows the body, proceeding from the maladies of the head to those of the foot. Symptoms are described; prescriptions and the method of procuring and applying these prescriptions are offered. Barrow himself describes the work as a 'breviary or abridgement of physick', into which he 'interlaced experiments of mine own, which by long use & practise I have observed to be true' (Barrow, *Method*, 3rd edn, 1596, unpaginated preface). It is with the remedy, rather than with the cause, of disease that Barrow concerns himself. Defending the practicality of his approach, Barrow asserts that 'my reason was, because if my books should come to the hands of the unlearned a little would suffice (the former being more necessarie)' (ibid.).

The *Method* was written in the vernacular. Barrow's defence of this decision has led to some confusion over his place of residence. The author of the 'Alphabetical collections for an Athenae Cantab' suggests that Barrow 'seems to have been a London Physician by his talking of our Country Physitians', a statement based on Barrow's comments in the preface to his *Method of Phisicke* ('Alphabetical collections', BL, Add. MS 5863, fol. 78). In the passage to which the author refers, however, Barrow is in fact discussing his decision to publish in the vernacular,

> seeing that I shall runne into the babble of our countrey Physitians, who thinke thier Arte to be discredited, when it is published in a base tongue, and againe, are loth to have the secrets of their science revealed to everie man. (Barrow, *Method*, 3rd edn, 1596, unpaginated preface)

The authority of practice over art predominates in Barrow's assertion of the value of his work. In his dedication to Burghley, Barrow ascribes his expertise to his own practical experience of medicine, an arena 'in which some studie and industrie (besides many yeares) had made me in part able to judge' (Barrow, *Method*, 3rd edn, 1596, sig. A iii). The work should be viewed, he argues, as an endeavour undertaken in a spirit of 'honest zeale to benefite my countriemen, … and also that they might bring some commoditie unto the more ignorant sort of our common Practitioners and AEmperiques (if they were with diligence perused)' (ibid., sig. A iii r).

It is to his 'countriemen', the lay reader, that Barrow ostensibly writes. He saves, however, a few stern words for the student of medicine, venturing forth from 'the compasse of their little studie' into a commonwealth in which 'they shall meet diseases that Galen never dreamt of' (Barrow, *Method*, 3rd edn, 1596, unpaginated preface). Barrow's is an empirical medicine, one in which practice—and practical knowledge—serve to extend the boundaries of the art of medicine. 'Arte', argues Barrow, 'is weake without practise' (ibid.).

The popularity of Barrow's *Method*, with its seven editions, indicates that it found an audience which, in terms of disposable income, could not strictly be described as popular. A lawsuit of 1585 by Thomas Marshe, London printer and bookseller, cites the book's purchase, alongside several other popular medical works, by Edward Wingsfield of Kimbolton Castle, Huntingdonshire. The work sold for 5*s*., among the most expensive in a list which also included Andrew Boorde's *Breviare of Helthe*, 1*s*.; T. C.'s *Virtue of niter*, 6*d*.; *Approved Medicines*, 6*d*.; *Hospitall for the Diseased*, 1*s*.; and Bullein's *Bulwarkes of Defence Against Sicknes, Sornes and Woudnes*, 5*s*. 8*d*. (Plomer, 328).

Nothing is known of Barrow's death except that it took place in 1600. In his will, he states his desire to be buried with his late wife in the chancel of the parish church of Wicken, Cambridgeshire, leaving a bequest of £15 towards the building of a monument or tomb for his wife and himself. He also leaves £5 towards the building of a road from 'Spynney gate towardes the towne of Spinney'. Barrow's description of himself in the will as 'gent' is supported by his bequests of £16 in annuities and in excess of £360 plus 240*s*. in cash to his children, grandchildren, and the poor of Wicken parish.   K. A. JAMES

Sources will, PRO, PROB 11/96, sig. 43 • P. Barrow, *The method of phisicke* (1583); 3rd edn (1596) • T. P. Bart, ed., *The Cambridgeshire visitation by Henry St George* (1619) • J. Venn, ed., *Grace book Δ* (1910) • 'Alphabetical collections for an Athenae Cantab', BL, Add. MS 5863, fol. 78 • H. R. Plomer, 'Some Elizabethan book sales', *The Library*, 3rd ser., 7 (1916), 318–29, esp. 328 • Venn, *Alum. Cant.* • *STC, 1475–1640* • M. Pelling and C. Webster, 'Medical practitioners', *Health, medicine and mortality in the sixteenth century*, ed. C. Webster (1979), 165–235, esp. 195 • P. Slack, 'Mirrors of health and treasures of the poor men: the uses of vernacular medical literature of Tudor England', *Health, medicine and mortality in the sixteenth century*, ed. C. Webster (1979), 237–73, esp. 259 • A. Wear, 'Medicine in early modern England', *Health and healing in early modern England* (1998), 17–39, esp. 20, 27–9
Wealth at death £16 in annuities; £360, plus 240*s*., in cash bequests: will, PRO, PROB 11/96, sig. 43

Barrow, Samuel (1625?–1683), physician and lawyer of the army, was the eldest of the seven children of Samuel Barrow, a lawyer of Burwell, in Cambridgeshire, and his wife, Judith, daughter of George FitzGeffrey of Bedford.

Although the exact date and place of his birth are not known, the *Visitation of Essex* of 1634 states that he was then about nine years old. He may have attended school at Charterhouse. On 6 July 1639, at the age of about fourteen, Barrow entered Trinity College, Cambridge, as a pensioner, becoming a scholar in 1641, and BA in 1644. According to Sir Thomas Clarges, he was 'ejected out of Trinity Colledge in Cambridge for his affection to his Majesty' (Baker, 651). This may have taken place in 1644. It is not known where he studied medicine.

In February 1654 Barrow was appointed physician to the armies in Scotland and in December 1659 judge-advocate of the army. In the unstable period after the death of Cromwell in 1658 he became one of the closest advisers of General Monck; he was recommended to the general's brother, Nicholas, as 'a very discreet gentleman' (Baker, 651). When Monck marched south on 30 December 1659, Barrow rallied support for the general on the way. In London Monck was ordered by the Rump Parliament to take action against the hostile City, but Barrow was instrumental in persuading him to demand a full parliament with the recall of the secluded members, a decision which led inevitably to the restoration of the monarchy.

Barrow was sent to Breda with Clarges to negotiate with the king. Clarges was knighted on the spot, but, strangely, not Barrow. The reason may have lain in the rumour about the 'Doctor's relations with Cromwell' (Routledge, 5.27). In August 1660 Barrow was appointed physician-in-ordinary to the king, with a fee of £100 a year, and the next year judge-advocate-general to the first permanent establishment of guards. In June 1666 Barrow's old friend Sir William Clarke was mortally wounded in a battle at sea, and in July 1668 Barrow married the widow, Lady Dorothy (*d*. 1695), daughter of Thomas Hyliard of Hampshire and Elizabeth Kimpton.

Although Barrow wrote nothing of consequence, he was regarded as an authority on the events of the time. He was consulted by Thomas Skinner (or Skynner), a biographer of Monck, and encouraged Sir Thomas Morgan to write his *A true and just relation of Major-General Morgan's progress in France and Flanders with the 6,000 English in the years 1657 and 1658*. It was written in 1675 but not published until 1699. Barrow greatly admired John Milton, and his Latin verses in praise of *Paradise Lost*, signed 'S. B., M. D.', were prefixed to the second edition of 1674. He may have been of help to the poet after the Restoration, but there is no evidence of any close friendship between the two.

When Barrow became ill in 1681, he resigned the post of judge-advocate in favour of his stepson, George *Clarke (1661–1736). He died on 21 March 1683, and was buried in All Saints' Church, Fulham, Middlesex, on 25 March. In his will of 1676 he left all his property to his wife, apart from small gifts to brothers and sisters. No portrait of Barrow exists, but John Aubrey described him as a good-humoured man: 'He much resembled and spoke like Dr. Ezerel Tong' (*Brief Lives*, 1.94).   A. L. WYMAN

Sources R. Baker, *A chronicle of the kings of England*, rev. edn (1684), 651, 685 • T. Gumble, *The life of General Monck, duke of Albemarle*

(1671), 34, 85, 191 · *Calendar of the Clarendon state papers preserved in the Bodleian Library*, 5: *1660–1726*, ed. F. J. Routledge (1970), 13, 16, 24, 27 · *Report on the manuscripts of F. W. Leyborne-Popham*, HMC, 51 (1899), 211, 260–62 · A. L. Wyman, 'Samuel Barrow, physician to Charles II and admirer of John Milton', *Medical History*, 18 (1974), 335–48 · *Brief lives, chiefly of contemporaries, set down by John Aubrey, between the years 1669 and 1696*, ed. A. Clark, 1 (1898), 94 · F. J. Varley, *Cambridge during the civil war, 1642–1646* (1935) · will, PRO, PROB 11/373, sig. 54 · Hammersmith church register (marriage), Hammersmith Archives, 1668 · parish register (burials), All Saints' Church, Fulham, 25 March 1683

Archives BL, Egerton MS 2618 · PRO, SP 28/100/2, 28/85/3, 28/90 · Worcester College, Oxford, annotations by Barrow on T. Skynner, *Motum Nuperorium in Anglia*, 3 (1676)

Barrow, Thomas (1747–1814), Jesuit, was born at Eccleston, near Preston, on 17 September 1747, one of at least three sons of Thomas Barrow and his wife, Mary Crookall. He was educated at the English College at St Omer. Two of his brothers also became Jesuits. He entered the Society of Jesus at Watten in 1764. After the temporary suppression of the society in 1773 he rendered great services to the new English academy at Liège, and subsequently to Stonyhurst College. At the peace of Amiens he was sent to Liège to look after the property of his brethren, as well as the interests of the nuns of the Holy Sepulchre (who later settled at New Hall, Chelmsford). He died at Liège on 12 June 1814. Although described by one authority as 'a prodigy of learning' (Foley, 7.36), the only published specimens of his erudition were two sets of verses in Hebrew and Greek in honour, respectively, of the prince-bishop of Liège, Francis Charles de Velbruck (1772), and Francis Anthony de Mean, the last prince-bishop of Liège (1792).

THOMPSON COOPER, *rev.* ROBERT BROWN

Sources H. Foley, ed., *Records of the English province of the Society of Jesus*, 7 vols. in 8 (1875–83) · G. Oliver, *Collections towards illustrating the biography of the Scotch, English and Irish members of the Society of Jesus* (1835) · G. Holt, *The English Jesuits, 1650–1829: a biographical dictionary*, Catholic RS, 70 (1984)

Barrow [*alias* Waring, Harcourt], **William** (c.1609–1679), Jesuit, was born in Weeton-cum-Prees, Lancashire, the younger son of John Barrow, a yeoman and recusant, and Margaret (probably *née* Waring), also a recusant. In 1628 he entered the English College at St Omer where he was educated until he entered the Society of Jesus at Watten in 1632. He completed his studies at Liège and was ordained on 30 March 1641. He was prefect of morals at St Omer in 1642–3 and was sent on the English mission in 1644. He lived at the house of probation of St Ignatius (1644–9) and on 21 November 1646 he was professed of the four vows. He served as a missioner in London for thirty-five years. In 1671 he was procurator of the province in London, and in 1678 was declared rector of the College of St Ignatius, comprising the metropolis and the home counties. This rendered him conspicuous, and he was singled out as one of the victims in the aftermath of the Popish Plot. Opportunities were offered to him to escape to the continent but he remained in England to provide temporal and spiritual

William Barrow (*c*.1609–1679), by Martin Bouché, pubd 1683

comfort to his accused brethren. By constant change of dress and lodgings he eluded his pursuers until 7 May 1679, when he was betrayed by a servant and committed by the privy council to Newgate. He was tried at the Old Bailey session (13 June) with Father Whitbread (the provincial) and fathers Caldwell, Gavan, and Turner. Being condemned to death, he suffered with them at Tyburn on 20 June 1679. *The Tryals and Condemnation* of Barrow and the other martyrs was published as part of a series of state tracts in 1679 and their last protestations, *A Remonstrance of Piety and Innocence*, was published in 1683.

THOMPSON COOPER, *rev.* RUTH JORDAN

Sources G. Holt, *St Omers and Bruges colleges, 1593–1773: a biographical dictionary*, Catholic RS, 69 (1979), 28 · H. Chadwick, *St Omers to Stonyhurst* (1962), 189 · J. Warner, *The history of English persecution of Catholics and the presbyterian plot*, ed. T. A. Birrell, trans. J. Bligh, 1, Catholic RS, 47 (1953), 258–66 · Gillow, *Lit. biog. hist.*, 1.148–9 · J. Muddiman, 'The Venerable Wm. Harcourt SJ, vindicated', *The Month*, 145 (1925), 233–41 · R. Challoner, *Memoirs of missionary priests*, ed. J. H. Pollen, rev. edn (1924), 525–7, 530–31 · D. A. Bellenger, ed., *English and Welsh priests, 1558–1800* (1984) · 'St Omer's roll of honour, 5: Blessed Wm. Harcourt SJ', *Stonyhurst Magazine*, 28 (1945–7), 31–5 · L. Polgar, *Bibliographie sur l'histoire de la Compagnie de Jésus, 1901–1980*, 3 vols. in 6 (1981–90), 3/2.122 · *Engraved Brit. ports.*, 5.75

Archives Archivum Romanum Societis Iesu, Rome | Lancs. RO, newsletters by W. Harcourt, MSS DDCI/1151–1166 [alias of W. Waring]

Likenesses M. Bouché, line engraving, pubd 1683, NPG [*see illus.*] · group portrait, line engraving, after 1685 (*Titus Oates and Jesuits*),

BM · possibly by G. P. Harding, pen-and-ink and wash drawing, NPG

Barrow, William (*bap.* 1753, *d.* 1836), writer on theology, baptized on 3 February 1753 at Witherslack, Westmorland, was the son of John Barrow and his wife, Margaret. He was educated at Sedbergh School, Yorkshire, and entered Queen's College, Oxford, in 1774; he graduated BA in 1778 and proceeded MA in 1783. While at Oxford he developed an interest in educational theory, and from 1782 to 1799 he was master of the academy in Soho Square, London. His influential study *An essay on education; in which are particularly considered the merits and defects of the discipline and instruction in our academies* (2 vols., 1802) sold two large editions in a very few years. In this work Barrow drew heavily on his firsthand experience of schoolmastering, while taking full account of 'knowledge of the world' and the university system, in which he was a thoughtful defender of the status quo: 'Let not our universities be the only communities, which possess no lucrative appointments without laborious duties' (*An Essay on Education*, 2.336). For Barrow the focal point of any curriculum was theology, 'a subject … on which, above all others, the search after novelty should not be too earnestly pursued' (ibid., 361). He saw education as an essential means to counteract the effects of the French Revolution, which, in his opinion, had 'done an essential injury to the sentiments and principles of the populace of Britain, by propagating … notions … incompatible … with the stability and permanence of all social order' (ibid., 372).

In 1799, having been awarded the degree of DCL, Barrow delivered the Bampton lectures before the University of Oxford. These were published as *Sermons containing answers to some popular objections against the necessity or the credibility of the Christian revelation* (1799). In this work, which owed much to the methods of Archdeacon William Paley, Barrow rehearsed a comprehensive selection of well-established arguments for orthodox Christian belief against 'Lord Herbert, Tindal, and other advocates of natural religion' (*Sermons*, 47n.). He wrote not for expert theologians, but for undergraduates and general readers: 'men of some education, curiosity and reading … of integrity, candour and docility … [to whom] … we must probably owe, under Providence, whatever permanency we are to enjoy in our religious or our civil constitution' (ibid., ix). Later works, such as *Familiar Sermons* (3 vols., 1818–21) and *Familiar Dissertations on Theological and Moral Subjects* (1819), addressed a similar readership. Other publications by Barrow, who was an FSA, included a sermon, *The Right of Resisting Foreign Invasion*, preached at Southwell before the loyal volunteers of that place during the panic of 1803, and a treatise on *The expediency of translating our scriptures into several of the oriental languages and the means of rendering those translations useful* (1808).

In 1814 Barrow became prebendary of Eaton in the collegiate church at Southwell: this promotion was said to have been in recognition of his 'zeal and efficiency in support of the national religion' (*GM*, 100). From 1821 until 1829 he served as vicar-general of Southwell, and in April 1830 he was appointed archdeacon of Nottingham, a dignity still associated at that time with York Minster. Ill health forced him to resign this archdeaconry in 1832. He was married, but he and his wife, E. A. Williams (*d.* 1823), had no children. Barrow died on 19 April 1836 at Southwell, and was buried there. A tablet was raised to his memory in the collegiate church. RICHARD SHARP

Sources *GM*, 2nd ser., 6 (1836), 99–100 · Foster, *Alum. Oxon.* · W. Barrow, *Sermons containing answers to some popular objections against the necessity or the credibility of the Christian revelation* (1799) · W. Barrow, *An essay on education*, 2nd edn, 2 vols. (1804) · *DNB* · *IGI*

Barrowby, William (*bap.* 1682, *d.* 1758), physician, the son of John Barrowby, physician, and his wife, Abigail, was baptized at St Lawrence Jewry, London on 15 December 1682. After studying at Eton College he entered Trinity College, Oxford, on 6 November 1699 and graduated BA (1703), MA (1706), MB (1709), and MD (1713). He married Elizabeth while still at Oxford, but they eventually settled in London, where he practised in the City. The couple had many children. Barrowby became a licentiate of the Royal College of Physicians, London, in 1717, and a fellow in 1718. He served as censor at the college in 1721, 1730, and 1734. On 9 November 1721 he was elected a fellow of the Royal Society. He lived in London until 1746, when he apparently retired to the Isle of Wight, where he died on 17 October 1758.

Barrowby's son **William Barrowby** (*bap.* 1709, *d.* 1751), physician, was baptized in Oxford on 20 October 1709; he studied at Eton College from 1721 to 1728 and matriculated from Trinity College, Oxford, in 1728. On 10 January 1731 he transferred to Emmanuel College, Cambridge, where

William Barrowby (*bap.* 1682, *d.* 1758), by Johann Sebastian Müller (after Francis Hayman, 1740s)

he gained his MB in 1733. In 1736 he published his *Syllabus anatomicus praelectionibus annuatim habiendis adaptus*. He also translated two works of Jean Astruc: *De morbis veneris* (as *Treatise of the Venereal Diseases*, 2 vols., 1737; 2nd edn, 1754), and *Quæstio medico-chirurgica … an fistulis ani chirurgica sectio?* (as *Treatise on the Fistula in ano*, 1738). He may have been one of the authors, along with James Kilpatrick (later Kirkpatrick) and Isaac Schomberg of *A letter to the real and genuine Pierce Dod M.D., actual physician of St. Bartholomew's Hospital* (1746), an attack on Pierce Dod, then a physician at St Bartholomew's Hospital, London, and a fierce opponent of inoculation. William Wadd described Barrowby as high-spirited, but a humane and excellent physician. He was said to have been involved in the riots at the Drury Lane Theatre in 1743. Despite being 'a monster of lewdness and prophaneness', he was appointed physician to St Bartholomew's Hospital in 1750. He died very suddenly on 30 December 1751 of a 'dead palsy' (*GM*, 1752, 44).   KAYE BAGSHAW

Sources Foster, *Alum. Oxon.* · Venn, *Alum. Cant.* · R. A. Austen-Leigh, ed., *The Eton College register, 1698–1752* (1927) · *GM*, 1st ser., 22 (1752), 44 · Munk, *Roll* · W. Wadd, *Nugae chirurgicae, or, A biographical miscellany* (1824) · W. Wadd, *Mems. maxims and memoirs* (1827) · *GM*, 1st ser., 28 (1758), 504 · P. J. Wallis and R. V. Wallis, *Eighteenth century medics*, 2nd edn (1988) · *London Magazine*, 27 (1758), 540 · *London Magazine*, 20 (1751), 573 · letter, RCP Lond.
Likenesses J. S. Müller, engraving (after F. Hayman, 1740–49), BM, NPG, RCP Lond., Wellcome L. [*see illus.*]

Barrowby, William (*bap.* 1709, *d.* 1751). *See under* Barrowby, William (*bap.* 1682, *d.* 1758).

Barry, Alfred (1826–1910), Anglican bishop of Sydney and educationist, was born at Ely Place, Holborn, London, on 15 January 1826, the second son of Sir Charles *Barry (1795–1860), architect, whose *Life and Works* he published in 1867, and elder brother of Edward Middleton *Barry, whose Royal Academy lectures on architecture he edited with a memoir in 1881; his mother was Sarah (1798–1882), daughter of Samuel Rowsell. Educated at King's College, London, from 1841 to 1844, Barry proceeded in 1844 to Trinity College, Cambridge; in 1848 he was placed fourth among the wranglers and seventh in the first class of the classical tripos. He also won a Smith's prize. He was elected a fellow of Trinity in the same year. He graduated BA in 1848, and proceeded MA in 1851, BD in 1860, and DD in 1866. He was made a DCL of Oxford in 1870 and of Durham in 1888.

Ordained deacon in 1850 and priest in 1853, Barry became sub-warden of Trinity College, Glenalmond, the combined theological college and public school of the Scottish Episcopal church in 1849. On 13 August 1851 he married Louisa Victoria, daughter of Thomas Smart *Hughes, canon of Peterborough. In 1854 he became headmaster of Leeds grammar school, and from 1862 to 1868 he was principal of Cheltenham College. During his tenure of the latter office he extended the buildings of the school and raised its academic prestige.

In 1868 Barry was appointed principal of King's College, London (of which he had been a fellow since 1849), in succession to Richard William Jelf. Barry was an innovative

and energetic, even pushy, principal. He reorganized the administration of the college and relaxed the rules that demanded strict religious conformity. He brought its teaching up to date, especially in the fields of engineering and medicine, and extended the evening-class department to meet the needs of young working men keen to further their education. He arranged that students for the theological associateship could attend classes for two years without sacrificing their daytime employment, and devote their whole time to their college course only in their third year. A strong supporter of higher education for women, in 1871 he instituted 'lectures for ladies' at Richmond and Twickenham, and in 1881 he established at Kensington a women's department. From 1871 to 1877 he served on the London school board.

Of a fine presence and with a sonorous voice, Barry was an effective speaker and preacher. Gladstone made him a residentiary canon of Worcester in 1871, and in 1881 he transferred him to a similar office in Westminster Abbey. Appointed honorary chaplain to Queen Victoria in 1875, and chaplain-in-ordinary in 1879, Barry also held the Boyle lectureship from 1876 to 1878. He published the first series of lectures as *What is Natural Theology?* (1877) and the second as *The Manifold Witness for Christ* (1880).

Barry always had his aim set on high office in the church. However, his 'intense and notorious desire to secure a see' (Hearnshaw, 334) counted against him, and he was not appointed to an English bishopric. After refusing the see of Calcutta in 1876, in 1883 he accepted appointment to the diocese of Sydney, Australia. The bishop of Sydney was also primate of the Church of England in Australia and Tasmania, and was metropolitan of New South Wales. Barry was consecrated in Westminster Abbey on 1 January 1884. Misfortune attended his departure: he sent on to Australia his entire library, lectures, and manuscripts in a vessel which was lost in a shipwreck. Queen Victoria and others showed their sympathy by endeavouring to replace the books.

Barry was enthroned on 24 April 1884 in St Andrew's Cathedral, Sydney. Later that year he published a collection of sermons, *First Words in Australia*. Evangelicals, who were powerful in the diocese of Sydney, had not wanted Barry as bishop. He himself was a low-churchman of liberal sympathies, opposed to church parties and keen to promote Anglican comprehensiveness. In Sydney, where anti-Christian secularists were on the attack, he sought through lectures and writings to reinterpret Christian doctrines in the light of modern science and scholarship. For the sake of 'the higher life of the colony', he offered to co-operate with Christians of other denominations (Phillips, 14). Many protestants welcomed his leadership, but evangelicals were alarmed by his liberalism and his unwillingness to discourage the spread of moderate high-church practices in some Sydney churches. Barry emphasized the importance of the cathedral as the centre of diocesan life and introduced daily choral services, and he also overhauled the diocesan administration.

In the field of education Barry was likewise very active: he strengthened the existing church secondary schools, founded two more, and encouraged Anglicans to utilize the provisions for religious instruction in state schools. Elected in 1886 to the senate of the University of Sydney, he wanted to see closer links between theological and university education. To this end he arranged to move the diocesan theological college, Moore College, from the edge of Sydney to a new site adjacent to the university.

In 1886 he was the first bishop in Australia to 'set apart' a deaconess. As primate he successfully urged the Australian church to accept responsibility for missionary work in New Guinea. However, despite his vigorous leadership Barry was never at home in New South Wales. In colonial eyes his manner appeared distant and condescending. His two visits to England, involving long absences from Australia, seemed to indicate where his heart was. It was no surprise when in 1889 he resigned the see and returned permanently to England.

In England Barry once more failed in his quest for a see, and from 1889 to 1891 he was assistant to A. W. Thorold, bishop of Rochester. In 1891 he took charge of the diocese of Exeter during the absence in Japan of Bishop Edward Henry Bickersteth. Finally, from 1891 until his death, he was canon of St George's Chapel, Windsor, where he continued his literary activities. In 1892 he was Bampton lecturer at Oxford, taking as his subject 'Some lights of science on the faith'; in 1894–5 he gave the Hulsean lectures at Cambridge, entitled 'The ecclesiastical expansion of England in the growth of the Anglican communion'. From 1895 to 1900 he was rector of St James's, Piccadilly, rendering episcopal assistance in central London to the bishop, Frederick Temple. After 1900 he confined himself to his canonry at Windsor, representing the chapter in the lower house of convocation from 1893 until 1908. He died in his sleep at his residence in the cloisters, Windsor Castle, on 1 April 1910, and was buried on 6 April in the cloisters at Worcester Cathedral, beside his only daughter, Mary Louisa, who had died in 1880. His wife and two sons survived him.   E. H. PEARCE, rev. DAVID HILLIARD

Sources The Times (2 April 1910) · The Times (4 April 1910) · Guardian (8 April 1910) · S. Judd and K. Cable, Sydney Anglicans: a history of the diocese (1987) · F. J. C. Hearnshaw, The centenary history of King's College, London, 1828–1928 (1929) · E. D. Daw, 'Electing a primate: Alfred Barry and the diocese of Sydney, 1882–1883', Royal Australian Historical Society Journal and Proceedings, 66 (1980–81), 237–57 · R. Teale, 'Party or principle? The election to the Anglican see of Sydney in 1889–90', Royal Australian Historical Society Journal and Proceedings, 55 (1969–70), 141–58 · K. J. Cable, 'Barry, Alfred', AusDB, vol. 3 · Venn, Alum. Cant. · G. Sherington, Shore: a history of Sydney Church of England grammar school (1983) · W. Phillips, Defending 'a Christian country': churchmen and society in New South Wales in the 1880s and after (1981)
Archives LPL, papers | BL, letters to W. E. Gladstone, Add. MSS 44437–44785, passim · BL, letters to Lord Stanmore, Add. MSS 49215–49216 · Bodl. Oxf., corresp. with Sir Thomas Phillipps · Durham Cath. CL, letters to J. B. Lightfoot · LPL, corresp. with Edward Benson; corresp. with A. C. Tait
Likenesses T. C. Wageman, watercolour drawing, 1849, Trinity Cam. · portrait, watercolour, c.1870–1875, King's Lond. · E. Poynter, oils, 1883 · oils, c.1888, St Andrew's Cathedral, Sydney, Australia · oils, c.1888, University of Sydney, Sydney, Australia, St Paul's College · Lock & Whitfield, woodburytype photograph, NPG;

repro. in T. Cooper, Men of mark: a gallery of contemporary portraits (1883)
Wealth at death £20,070 18s. 6d.: resworn probate, 29 April 1910, CGPLA Eng. & Wales

Barry [née Street; other married names Dancer, Crawford], **Ann** [Anne] (bap. **1733**, d. **1801**), actress, was born in Bath, the daughter of James Street, a prominent apothecary, and baptized at Bath Abbey on 8 April 1733. Her father died while she was still attending a local boarding-school. Having been jilted at the age of seventeen, she was sent to York to stay with relatives, and there embarked on a career as an actress. In 1754 she returned briefly to act in her native city, and married (against her family's wishes) William Dancer, who had played Lear opposite her Cordelia. The couple performed in York and then Newcastle until 1757, and Ann was cast in roles in which her undoubted physical attractions helped smooth over the somewhat mixed responses to her capabilities as an actress. The list of parts is impressive, however, and included Jessica in The Merchant of Venice, Rosalind in As You Like It, Ophelia, Lady Macbeth, and the Queen in Richard III, as well as significant parts in other, non-Shakespearian, plays, among them Elizabeth in Jones's The Earl of Essex and Cleopatra in Dryden's All for Love. Family opposition to her chosen career continued, and when her mother died she was left a regular income with the proviso that she left the stage, a requirement she was able to circumvent.

By 1758 the Dancers were employed by Spranger *Barry (bap. **1717**, d. **1777**) at his Crow Street Theatre in Dublin, and it is from this point that Ann's career really gathered momentum. Given her original pairing with William Dancer, it was perhaps ominous that her first role in Dublin should have been as Cordelia, this time to Barry's Lear, for the actor–manager's encouragement of his young protégée soon extended beyond the confines of the theatre. When her husband died, on 27 December 1759, she was publicly acknowledged as Barry's mistress, and it was to be a further nine years before the pair married, probably in the summer of 1768. In 1766 she played in London for the first time, as Desdemona to Barry's Othello, at the King's Theatre. It was her most successfully realized role to date and, although she had already occasionally attempted non-tragic parts (most notably Polly Peachum in Gay's The Beggar's Opera, for instance), it was as a tragic heroine that the public knew her best. Her apparently slightly over-the-top delivery coupled with her striking good looks soon led to her being compared—sometimes favourably, and sometimes not—with Mrs Cibber, the actress who for a long time had been accustomed to playing Juliet to Barry's Romeo in the part that he had made particularly his own.

After a brief return to Dublin to play in Barry's ambitious Crow Street venture, Mrs Dancer returned to London, the plan to make a success of a new and large Dublin theatre in financial ruins, and at the end of 1767 she was engaged, with Barry, by David Garrick at Drury Lane. By 1768, when reprising Lady Macbeth, she had begun to be promoted as Mrs Barry. This association would have done little to hinder her career, but she was by now beginning to establish a very real reputation for herself. In March 1771, for instance, the *Gentleman's Magazine* reported that it was her efforts alone as the lead role in Mrs Celesia's *Almida* that had kept the production afloat: 'she rises like perfection out of Chaos' (*GM*, 1st ser., 41, 1771, 128). As a result of the professional rivalry between Barry and Garrick, the Barrys engaged themselves to Covent Garden for the 1774–5 season, where Ann played, among other roles, Beatrice in *Much Ado about Nothing* and Millamant in Congreve's *The Way of the World*; she was steadily adding comedy to her repertory. By now her husband was ill and increasingly unreliable. To her considerable sorrow, he died on 10 January 1777, leaving her the lease on their London house and his share of the Crow Street Theatre. However, it was her own efforts as an actress, and not the bequest, that saw her finances improve dramatically over the next few years.

Ann Barry continued at Covent Garden, with regular and much fêted trips to Dublin, and in 1778 she married for a third time; her new husband was Thomas Crawford (1750–1794), an Irish barrister who would later try his hand at acting to little avail. Not only was he openly dependent on his wife for financial support but, when he proved to be no actor, he followed her second husband's lead and failed to make a success of running the Crow Street Theatre. As Mrs Crawford, Ann reappeared in London at the Haymarket, playing Lady Randolph in John Home's *Douglas* in 1780. By 1783 she had separated herself from both the disastrous Crow Street venture and her third husband. Although she continued in regular employment as an actress, her best years were now behind her. In 1785 she played Calista in Nicholas Rowe's *The Fair Penitent*, and then toured the regional theatres, her career all but over. In 1797 she played a final London week, at Covent Garden, reprising her role as Lady Randolph; but she now lacked the ardent expression of her younger days, and the following year she performed for the last time. She then lived in a fairly comfortable retirement, dividing her time between Bath and London. When she died, on 29 November 1801, she was sixty-eight years old. She was buried alongside her second, and best-loved husband, Spranger Barry, in Westminster Abbey. Ann Barry is remembered as one of the finest actresses of her generation.   JOHN BULL

Sources Highfill, Burnim & Langhans, *BDA* · Genest, *Eng. stage* · *GM*, 1st ser., 21–68 (1751–98) · F. Gentleman, *The dramatic censor, or, Critical companion*, 2 vols. (1770) · R. Hitchcock, *An historical view of the Irish stage from the earliest period down to the close of the season 1788*, 2 vols. (1788–94) · J. Boaden, *Memoirs of Mrs Siddons*, 2 vols. (1827) · T. Gilliland, *The dramatic mirror, containing the history of the stage from the earliest period, to the present time*, 2 vols. (1808) · IGI
Likenesses attrib. J. Roberts, oils, *c.*1775 (as Gertrude), Garr. Club · J. Walker?, line and stipple, pubd 12 Feb 1780 (after D. Dodd?), NG Ire. · T. Bonner, engraving (as Almida in *Almida*), Harvard TC · S. De Wilde, mezzotint (after J. Watson, after T. Kettle, *c.*1765), NG Ire. · S. Paul, engraving (after T. Kettle), Harvard TC · S. W. Reynolds, engraving (after Reynolds), BM · J. Roberts, engraving (as Almeria in *The mourning bride*), Harvard TC · portraits, repro. in Highfill, Burnim & Langhans, *BDA* · prints, BM, NPG

Barry, Sir Charles (1795–1860), architect, was born on 23 May 1795 at 2 Bridge Street, Westminster, the ninth child and fourth surviving son of the eleven children of Walter Edward Barry (*d.* 1805), a well-to-do stationer and bookbinder to the government Stationery Office, and his first wife, Frances Maybank (1757–1798). He became Britain's leading architect.

Education in Britain and abroad Brought up by his stepmother, Sarah, *née* Routledge (1760–1846), Barry attended three local schools, but received little education beyond attaining 'a superficial knowledge of English, a good proficiency in arithmetic, and a remarkably beautiful handwriting' (A. Barry, *Life*, 5). Essentially he was self-educated. Having exhibited a marked taste for drawing—he made his bedroom a painting room and constantly drew on and repapered the walls—Barry was articled in 1810 to Middleton and Bailey, of Paradise Row, Lambeth, surveyors to the parish. In the ensuing six years he received a thorough grounding in professional skills, before eventually becoming manager of the practice, which conducted local building works, so acquiring 'a knowledge of business beyond the reach of an ordinary pupil', able to make 'his own working drawings, specifications and even estimates; and was a fair judge of materials and work' (Wolfe). From 1812 he was exhibiting regularly at the Royal Academy: he started with *A View of the Interior of Westminster Hall*, followed by original designs (*A Church*, 1813; *A Museum and Library, with an Observatory*, 1814; and *A Design for a Group of Buildings for a Nobleman's Park*, 1815) that nicely encapsulate themes of his subsequent practice.

On coming of age Barry received the inheritance that his father had left on trust for him—a freehold property at Glendon, Northamptonshire, and a share in his investments, said to amount to 'a few hundred pounds' (Wyatt, 120). Despite becoming engaged to his future wife, he decided to set out for Italy on an architectural tour. After leaving England on 28 June 1817 with John Soane's friend Edward Conduit, he spent nearly two months in Paris, living with families to learn French—when his skill on the flute proved a useful social accomplishment—and then concentrating on Italian. His architectural sympathies were strictly neo-classical: the glories of French Gothic architecture left him indifferent, and he condemned the 'wretched taste' of the Tuileries, and likewise that of the dome of the Pantheon; the Petit Trianon, however, he admired as 'a chef d'oeuvre of architecture' (C. Barry, travel diary, 7 and 19 July, 24 Aug 1817). His travel diaries already reveal his interest in engineering, praising the roof construction of the Halle aux Blés (1802) as 'far exceeding the complicated and expensive system adopted … in the Dome of St Paul's' (ibid., 10 July). Above all it was the gardens of Versailles that enraptured him, displaying 'to perfection the art of landscape gardening' (ibid., 24 August), an art that was to become one of the most significant elements of his practice. After an excursion to Normandy, he left Paris on 29 September for Italy by way of Lyons, Geneva, Bern, and the Simplon Pass. After travelling through Milan, Bologna (greatly interested in painting, with a young man's enthusiasm he declared

Sir Charles Barry (1795–1860), by John Prescott Knight, c.1851

Correggio's *Ascension* perhaps the finest picture in the world), and Florence, on 17 November he arrived in Rome, where he spent the winter, studying painting and sculpture as much as architecture, and indulging his great love of music; his way was eased by letters of recommendation from Benjamin West, president of the Royal Academy, and Joseph Gwilt.

In the new year, after consultations with home, Barry agreed to join a group of British artists, 'generally his superiors in education and knowledge both of books and men' (A. Barry, *Life*, 22)—including Charles Eastlake and William Kinnard (a London architect who was to edit a supplementary volume of *The Antiquities of Athens*, by J. Stuart and N. Revett, 1751)—who had decided to travel to Greece, the latest goal of English architects, and even to Constantinople. After setting off on 28 March 1818 they journeyed expeditiously via Naples—where the Toledo struck Barry as 'the finest street I ever saw, excepting the High Street in Oxford' (C. Barry, travel diary, 29 March 1818)—Bari, Corfu, and Patras to Delphi, where his drawings first began to impress his companions with 'that indescribable power of insight and imagination, which distinguishes the true artist from the mere draughtsman' (A. Barry, *Life*, 24). After passing through Corinth, they stayed in Athens for most of June. The Parthenon met Barry's conventional expectations as 'the finest model of grandeur, beauty and symmetry' (C. Barry, travel diary, 29 Nov 1818). He next crossed the Aegean to Delos and on to Smyrna, and then by land to Constantinople, where he agreed to accompany a Mr David Baillie to Egypt—almost

unknown to English architects—and Syria, as draughtsman at £200 p.a. and travelling expenses, with the crucial liberty to make copies of his drawings for himself. They visited Pergamos en route for Alexandria, and wintered in Egypt with Thomas Wyse (subsequently a member of the Fine Arts Commission), then travelled up the Nile as far as Aswan and Philae.

The ancient ruins, massive and entirely novel to his eyes, overwhelmed Barry, particularly Dendera's Great Temple, the Grand Portico at Karnak, which produced the most impressive effect he had ever experienced, Philae's enchanting long ranges of columns, and Abu Simbel's spirited sculpture. The unfloriated capitals of Egyptian columns left a lasting impression, confirming his idea that 'in large capitals, however enriched with foliage, the apparent capability of supporting their entablature should still be preserved' (Wolfe). In March 1819 they journeyed to Jerusalem, having in Sinai met the wealthy connoisseur William Bankes (for whom Barry was to work at Soughton, Flintshire, and Kingston Lacy, Dorset). Having made their way to Baalbek and Damascus in May, through Gerash and Acre, they were prevented from reaching Palmyra (famed by Robert Wood's noble book) by the rapacity of the local Bedouin.

Barry's engagement with Baillie terminated at Tripoli, and he promptly sailed for Smyrna, calling at Cyprus and Rhodes, and from Smyrna (after a visit to Ephesus) with Wyse to Malta. In the autumn they returned in a leisurely manner through Sicily and Naples to Rome, where Barry met a wealthy architectural student, John Lewis Wolfe (a pupil of Joseph Gwilt), who became his only close friend and his constant architectural adviser. They made a lengthy stay in Rome, where Barry's matured bold and masterly drawings won him celebrity and influential acquaintances, including Lord Lansdowne and Lord and Lady Holland. He made a close and critical study of the principal buildings: of all Rome he was most impressed by the Palazzo Farnese's vastness and unbroken entablature, but audaciously denounced Michelangelo's superimposed courtyard orders; he likewise criticized the admired Arch of Constantine for its broken entablature. The two friends moved to Florence in April 1820. Enthusiastic Greek that he was, and greatly as he had admired the Egyptian ruins, as Barry approached England ambitious to establish an architectural practice, he 'began to perceive that Italian was the style most capable of adaptation to modern requirements' though he favoured refining it *à la Grecque* (Wolfe). The Florentine palaces, such as the Strozzi, confirmed the impression already made by the Farnese; the austerity and extent of Michelozzi's Palazzo Riccardi commanded 'a silent admiration' (C. Barry, travel diary, 14–19 April 1820); and 'a grand cornice, without an order, became the prominent feature in his beau-ideal of a street-front' (Wolfe). Anticipating Ruskin, he regarded Giotto's campanile in its simplicity and distinctiveness of profile as 'the finest thing in its kind in Italy', wanting only a spire and a pedestal (C. Barry, travel diary, 14–19 April)—an indication of Barry's early appreciation of the vertical element in architectural design, which proved as significant a feature in his *œuvre* as his enthusiasm for Greek horizontality. Although not an admirer of Italian Gothic, which he regarded as a hybrid, a conviction that for towers the natural style was Gothic provided an inducement for him to study that style. After spending late May and early June with Wolfe in Venice, Barry drew Gothic as well as classical buildings; he scathingly dissected Vincenzo Scamozzi's Procuratie Nuove and Jacopo Sansovino's Libreria Vecchie, with their superimposed orders and multiplicity of details; but he shared Goethe's enthusiasm for the façades of the Villa Capra (Rotonda) by Palladio as unsurpassably beautiful. In July he returned through Milan (paying greater attention to the cathedral than on his first visit) and Turin to France, then via Nîmes and Avignon to Paris, where he passed August, before landing again in England on 1 September 1820.

Early career It was an England that offered much more inviting prospects to young architects than the country Barry had left three years earlier. The commercial prosperity just burgeoning promoted demand for exchanges, banks, newsrooms, and offices; an improving agriculture and land exploitation afforded new or enlarged houses for the rich; and outstandingly the government grant in 1818 of £1 million for church building created remunerative commissions. Barry acquired 39 Ely Place for home and office, and commenced as architect by designing a cast-iron church. At this period an architect's career was furthered by patronage or by success in competition: Barry benefited from both. Local committees chose architects for the new churches; that at Stand, Prestwich, near Manchester, applied to John Soane, who seems to have recommended Barry, with whom he had friends in common. Stand (1822–6) and neighbouring Campfield (1822–5) use effectively the same design (respectively without and with a spire) in contemporary Gothic, which Barry himself was later to deride, though they were more attractive compositions than many of the same period. The work enabled him to marry, and introduced him to a circle of influential Mancunians. He then won a notable competition for a new church at fashionable Brighton (August 1823), evincing the study of English medieval ecclesiastical architecture he had lately undertaken. This success opened up another circle of patrons, including Lord Egremont, owner of Petworth, and the influential Brighton solicitor Attree, for whom he built the Sussex Hospital (1826–8; since enlarged) and an Italianate villa (1829–30; dem. 1971) with a terraced garden that persuaded the duke and duchess of Sutherland to employ him at Trentham, their Staffordshire seat. An evangelical clergyman, the Revd Daniel Wilson, in 1826 engaged Barry to erect three Perpendicular Gothic churches in his large metropolitan parish of Islington, which again marked an advance in his Gothic work, though they were still, as the evangelicals required, traditional preaching-boxes. Much later, in 1843–5, he built a new parish church at Hurstpierpoint, Sussex, in the Early English style, with spire and raised chancel, cruciform in plan but 'admirably adapted' (A. Barry, *Life*, 136) for Anglican worship.

Meanwhile, the founders of the Manchester Institution, a cultural body, were seeking an architect. Having declined an initial invitation unsatisfactory in character, and warning against inviting leading architects who might give the work to their assistants, Barry contributed significantly to formulating the terms of their competition for designs. On the basis of the experience in competition that he had already acquired, Barry proposed instructions about the character of drawings and the means of ensuring anonymity very similar to those subsequently adopted in the Houses of Parliament competition. Of five architects finally invited (with Goodwin, John Foster junior, Lewis Wyatt, and J. B. Papworth) Barry proved the winner. It was in this building (1824–35; now Manchester City Galleries) that his accomplished planning skills were first recognized. Though Grecian, Barry's institution possesses a degree of bold modelling probably derived from his Egyptian experiences. It proved to be his only Greek revival public building—neither his Birmingham town hall competition entry (1831) nor his Lincoln's Inn Fields law courts design (1842) was executed. Similarly, a house, Buile Hill (1827; since altered), for Thomas Potter, later first mayor of Manchester, was his only Greek villa. Invited in 1836 to design the Manchester Athenaeum (1837–9; altered 1873), a *locus* for working-class education, Barry employed his Italianate *palazzo* style, first exhibited in his Travellers' Club (discussed below), but here modelled on the severer Roman Palazzo Farnese; extremely influential as a model for Manchester warehouses and banks, it served as a prototype for his Reform Club design (1837).

Major public commissions For years Barry had been an assiduous competitor, despite repeated failures for such important buildings as King's College (Greek, 1823, when he took part in an exhibition of rejected designs) and the Pitt Press (1831), both in Cambridge, the Law Institution, London (1828), Birmingham town hall (1830), Westminster Hospital (1831), and several churches. But 'sanguine hope, which gave zest to [his] hard work' (A. Barry, *Life*, 81) carried him forward. C. R. Cockerell apart, he was the most forward-looking of established architects. From 1829 Barry's career was marked by a series of brilliant competition successes: the Travellers' Club, Pall Mall (1829), the Birmingham grammar school (1833), the new Houses of Parliament (1836), and the Reform Club, Pall Mall (1837). The Travellers' clubhouse, designed in the austere palace style of the Florentine republic, hit London at the moment when connoisseurs were looking to Italian as the way forward from an exhausted Greek revival, and 'established Barry's reputation as the English leader of the international Renaissance Revival' simultaneously taking place in France and the German states (Hitchcock, 39). The trenchant contemporary critic W. H. Leeds hailed it as 'reconciling the seemingly antithetical qualities of richness and simplicity' (Leeds, 260), thanks to Barry's scrupulous care for detail as much as for general composition: the highly visible hipped roof, the great cornice or *cornicione* (scaled innovatively to the full height of the building) returning round the corners, together with the rusticated quoins, all emphasize the clubhouse's distinction as a cubic mass, rather than standing as a mere item in a succession of street façades; the rich balustrade elevated on a channelled socle which screens the area contributes also to this effect. A further horizontal emphasis is provided by the ornamental string course dividing the two floors and preparing the eye for the *cornicione*. In contrast to rival contemporary buildings, the windows of both lower and upper floors are ornamented, though the latter more richly. The garden front, invisible from Pall Mall, is of a more ornamental, even picturesque character. Contemporary accusations that the Travellers' plagiarized Raphael's Pandolfini Palace—and later, that the Reform Club copied the Palazzo Farnese—do not stand investigation: Barry's 'mind was teeming with the stores of memory ... [but] external influence was with him only suggestive' (A. Barry, *Life*, 85–6). And, as at Manchester, Barry's excellent planning, vital here on a confined site, commended his design to his clients.

Another London commission, enlarging the Royal College of Surgeons in Lincoln's Inn Fields (1833), established Barry's reputation for efficient remodelling of existing buildings—the basis of his country house practice. For the Reform Club (1838–41), accommodating the new type of 'Liberal' politician, and again won in limited competition (against Cockerell, Edward Blore, and Sydney Smirke), Barry modified his Manchester Athenaeum, based, as noted above, on Rome's Palazzo Farnese. Larger and more emphatic than the Travellers', the Reform confirmed the dominance of the *palazzo* model alike for major metropolitan commercial premises and domestic. Its notable innovation was an afterthought, the great hall created by roofing over the *cortile*; a feature repeated by Barry and so widely copied by his contemporaries as to become one of the two standard Victorian mansion plans.

Barry's Birmingham grammar school competition entry (1832) drew on his recent studies of English Perpendicular to provide well-lighted rooms and a highly ornamental façade with emphatic terminal features, which nevertheless in its economical repetition of identical bays simplified the mason's task, and also established characteristic elements of Barry's style. The design was again characterized by skilful planning. Barry had acquired some familiarity with a large school's needs in making Gothic additions and alterations at Dulwich College in 1831 (rebuilt c.1866); and his experience in planning the Travellers' clubhouse was also useful: organization around internal courts may have been a personal preference but it also suited urban requirements. For the central corridor connecting the two great schoolrooms (now reassembled at Edgbaston as the school's chapel) he designed exquisite fan vaulting. This commission (1833–7; dem. 1936) not only provided a preliminary run for the new Houses of Parliament, but also brought Barry into contact with A. W. N. Pugin, who designed some Gothic furniture and finishings, and with John Thomas, whose

facility in sculpture was likewise important at Westminster.

The new Houses of Parliament Almost immediately, Pugin's skill proved valuable in the urgent labour of drawing out designs for new Houses of Parliament to replace those gutted in the fire of 16 October 1834. An open competition was forced on the government by a press campaign led by Sir Edward Cust, a connoisseur with whom Barry had worked on a proposal for improving William Wilkins's National Gallery (1833). A parliamentary committee prescribed the 'national' styles of Gothic or Elizabethan, and laid down accommodation requirements. A serious attempt was made to establish rules of competition satisfactory to both profession and government. Premiums of £500 were offered for between three and five designs. Barry was obviously a leading competitor. In consideration of the lack of English secular models, he toured Belgium to study the famous town halls. Official incompetence in providing all the requisite details shortened the time available for preparing entries, and Barry turned to Pugin for the pen-and-ink drawings required for the competition; Barry himself was adept with the pencil rather than the pen. His masterly entry, widely spoken of beforehand with admiration, was declared the winner by the royal commissioners appointed to judge (Cust, Charles Hanbury Tracy, Thomas Liddell, and George Vivian). Despite savage contemporary criticisms of the competition, the designated styles, and the judges' award, alleging improper practices, there can be no doubt that the judgement was an honest one and that Barry's was the outstanding entry.

The actual orthography of Barry's competition drawings (now lost) was Pugin's, but the determining mind was Barry's. Unmistakably his were both the concept, essentially classical despite the Picturesque and characteristic vertical accents of the towers at either end—demanded by the lowness of the site, particularly seen from Westminster Bridge, if for no other reason—and the practical plan of the vast Gothic building; his experience in the Birmingham school of providing circulation space for large numbers, as well as his familiarity with the requirements of a gentlemen's club, proved invaluable. Similarly, the all-over ornamentation of the external elevations was characteristic of Barry's aesthetic views: ornament 'so limited in size as to increase the apparent scale of the building and ... so kept down by lowness of relief or marginal framing as not to interfere with profiles ... could never be overdone' (Wolfe).

Modifications in both plan and elevation (which brought further charges of impropriety), including a simplification of surface ornamentation, were made in the course of securing parliamentary approval. Pugin again proved an essential ally, providing quantities of Perpendicular Gothic detail for the urgent preparation of estimate drawings. Construction was authorized on an estimate of £707,104 and a building period of six years. But Barry's problems were unprecedented: no one had experience of constructing so vast a building, covering 8 acres, with a river front of some 800 feet. The site was riddled with quicksands, and had to be stabilized by an innovatory concrete raft. But much of it was still covered by buildings in use essential to the functioning of parliamentary government; so building had to be started on land that had to be reclaimed from the river, work that required the latest technology. Barry and experts searched the country to find the best building stone. The structure had to be fireproof, and Barry was again improving on the latest technology, for example by introducing iron roofs. The towers were so huge they required innovative engineering. And the client, the two houses of parliament as well as the executive government acting through the office of works, was a multi-headed monster.

Barry's masterminding of the whole enterprise was seen by a contemporary as 'the greatest combination of contrivance in planning, skill in construction, business management, and true art, that the world has seen' (*The Builder*, 19 May 1860, 305). The work exhausted even his vigorous body. 'No less than between 8,000 and 9,000 original drawings and models have been prepared for it, a large portion of which have emanated from my own hand', he declared in 1849, 'while the whole of the remainder have been made under my own immediate direction and supervision' (A. Barry, *Life*, 373–4). And this was only half way through the task. His only surviving daybook shows him engaged on drawings for the new houses almost every weekday of 1845, apart from a three-week French holiday in September, brief visits to Trentham, a week in the north in October, and a few days in mid-November and before Christmas given over to other commissions; even on his daughter's wedding day he was working on 'detailed drawings' for Westminster (C. Barry, work diary, 1 (a) 7, 16 July 1845).

The question of Barry's remuneration for this toil was a long-running dispute. Inadequately controlled expenditure on public works in the 1820s had produced demands to pay architects a fee instead of by commission; the crown architects of the 1820s had generally been paid a 3 per cent commission (rather than the traditional 5 per cent) on works executed, but also received an annual salary of £500. Barry's fee had, it seems, been calculated on the same basis of 3 per cent on the original estimate plus retainer, but the office of works refused to explain how they had arrived at their figure of £25,000; Barry, too far engaged to withdraw by the time a figure had been named, had politely protested, expressing a hope that he would be fairly reimbursed when a substantial part of the building had been completed. Apart from the first lump-sum contract for the river front, the successive contracts for the new houses were on the basis of prices agreed for materials and labour, so requiring measurement of work done. Who was to pay for mensuration was unclear, and bitterly contested between Barry, supported by the Institute of British Architects—for Barry here was fighting a battle that concerned the profession generally—on the one side, and on the other the government. The issue came to a head in 1854, when Barry, having already received £40,000 commission, requested another £5000.

Ultimately his remuneration was determined arbitrarily by government at 3 per cent on outlay, plus 1 per cent for measuring: 'the greatest injustice that has ever been the lot of architect employed for … a government' (*The Builder*, 19 May 1860, 305). Expenditure rose to some £2 million by the time of Barry's death, when, although the houses were substantially complete externally, much interior work remained to be done.

The appointment in 1841 of the Fine Arts Commission, chaired by the masterful Prince Albert, to arrange the embellishment of the palace interior with painting and free-standing sculpture, had complicated Barry's brief and added to the number of his masters. The exterior of the new houses Barry had conceived as England's history in stone, and he employed John Thomas to sculpt the succession of sovereigns, their heraldry, and appropriate symbols. An even more chafing complication, which seriously slowed work from 1843, had been the independent commission granted to the overweening D. B. Reid to construct a comprehensive heating and ventilation system, a concept that proved to be beyond the reach of contemporary technology, despite the addition of a central tower to act as a vast chimney. The delay, and alterations in the plan, some parliamentary in origin but in part the architect's own, provoked lengthy formal inquiries by both houses in 1843–4, during which Barry received vital support from Lord Lincoln, first commissioner of works in Peel's ministry (who in 1857 was to ask him to redesign his own country seat, Clumber House, Nottinghamshire). Barry's significant changes in the elevations, such as an emphasized horizontality in the river front design and the introduction of high roofs (1840), however, escaped criticism.

Subsequently Barry experienced much interference at Westminster. In 1846 controversy broke over the provision of a great clock, followed by an even more contentious one in 1855–9 over the great bell, in both of which Sir Edmund Beckett played a critical role. In 1849 a royal commission to control the work was instituted under the chairmanship of Lord De Grey, an amateur architect and president of the Royal Institute of British Architects; it merely added to the layers of confusion, and was wound up in December 1851, when the two chambers were essentially complete. A light-hearted session of the Commons in their new chamber provoked an attack on the acoustics, so that Barry was forced to lower the roof to meet the views of a select committee. To provide permanent interior lining for the structure, Barry established government wood-carving workshops at Thames Bank. Under heavy pressure to complete the House of Lords chamber, late in 1844 he again employed Pugin, who collected thousands of casts from medieval models, and thereafter as salaried superintendent of wood-carving was constantly inventing decoration until his final illness in 1851, though Barry exercised control even of detail. The demands for encaustic tiles, decorative metalwork, stained glass, and wallpapers gave a major boost to those manufactures.

'Such a work could not be carried out by the unaided

exertions of a single man' (A. Barry, *Life*, 194). Fundamental to his ability to carry through the great work was Barry's efficient office management; with already at least eight assistants as early as 1839, including John Gibson and R. R. Banks (and later his son Charles and G. Somers Clarke), he used the latest technology, and assisted by the engineer Alfred Meeson devised solutions for engineering the huge towers, unparalleled since the medieval cathedrals: the Victoria Tower was for decades 'the largest and highest square tower in the world' (E. N. Holmes, *Illustrations of the New Palace of Westminster*, 2nd ser., 1865). M. D. Wyatt remarked: 'It was given to him at once to know how and when to use men as tools and tools as men—never confounding their legitimate functions, but deriving every possible aid from each and all' (*The Builder*, 2 June 1860, 343). Although he was not good at delegating important work, and when he did delegate anything 'was impatient to have it finished', so that 'what Sir Charles expected to be done "in a couple of hours" became a proverb in his office' (A. Barry, *Life*, 327), and exercised his very determined will, he nevertheless established a strong *esprit de corps* and enthusiastic support in his office. His generosity to his assistants is indicated by the large collections of drawings and tracings that he allowed them to take away, to the present benefit of our national collections. Foremost among Barry's collaborators was Pugin.

Years after Barry's death, in 1867 Pugin's son published a pamphlet claiming that his own father was the 'art-architect' of the new houses. Controversy raged, but the weight of witnesses refuting the claim was generally held to have prevailed. As the detail of the Birmingham school showed, Barry himself had become proficient in Perpendicular Gothic before meeting Pugin. It was only in 1835–7 and again in 1844–52 that the two men worked closely together; and essential as Pugin's contribution had been to the progress of the works, Barry always maintained a detailed control. What however has never been satisfactorily explained was the disappearance not only of Barry's actual competition drawings (in Pugin's hand), but also of his letters to Pugin, which he had retrieved from Pugin's family shortly before his own death. Subsequent research has not shaken Barry's position.

Private commissions The Westminster project shortened Barry's life, and also cost him 'more than two-thirds of a lucrative practice' (A. Barry, *Life*, 377). He continued to work, however, for his early patrons the Sutherlands, for whom he had made improvements in York House, London, in the 1830s and again in the 1840s, and at their principal country seat, Trentham, Staffordshire, where he had begun in 1834 to enlarge the house, adding a new entrance block, an italianate belvedere tower (a concept perhaps borrowed from Wyatville's recent work at Chatsworth, but in a form that provided the popular model for imitation), and a second storey to the private wing (dem. 1910). Subsequently, in 1840–49, he rebuilt the stables and service quarters, adding an asymmetrical tower containing a water tank, while over many years from 1834, assisted by William Nesfield, he constructed gardens on a grand scale. Barry was a passionate architectural gardener. The

'architectural laying out and ornamentation of gardens' was 'a kind of work in which he took the greatest pleasure, and achieved very brilliant results ... His idea was that the definite artificial lines of a building should not be contrasted, but harmonized, with the free and careless grace of natural beauty' (A. Barry, *Life*, 113), by a gradual progression from architecturally formal terraces close to the house, through flower gardens and shrubberies decreasingly artificial that ultimately dissolved in the distant park. (His most perfect work of this character was at the smaller Shrubland Park, Suffolk, for Sir W. Middleton, from 1848.)

In 1844–50 Barry also worked on house and gardens at the Sutherlands' ancestral highland seat Dunrobin Castle: he supplied designs of a Scottish baronial or French character which proved unsuited to the site; after many changes of the ducal mind, new designs by W. Leslie, an Aberdeen architect, similar to Barry's, and to some extent modified by him at different times, were adopted; his proposals for the gardens were modified by the duke himself. At Cliveden (Buckinghamshire) he rebuilt the main house in 1850–51 after a disastrous fire, unusually employing an engaged giant order with unbroken entablature; the retention of the surviving wings required particular ingenuity in planning. But after Trentham, his principal work for the family was Bridgewater House, Pall Mall (1846–51), for the duke's brother Lord Francis Egerton (later earl of Ellesmere), who inherited the greater part of the estates of the third duke of Bridgewater. Even Alfred Barry commented that this building marked a change in his architecture, introducing his second manner. It is indeed treated more richly than the Reform Club, to which it bears a family resemblance, but that is not inappropriate in the town mansion of a great magnate. (It is sustained in later domestic works.) This treatment, however, largely contained in the window surrounds and the crowning balustrade, is neither as ostentatious as some critics have suggested nor as much of an innovation in Barry's manner. Much more elaborate was his 1834 design for the private wing at Trentham, with a Corinthian order over the ground-floor Ionic (itself on a rusticated base), crowned by a *cornicione* surmounted by balustrade and acroteria: a design that calls in question any chronological classification of Barry's work and suggests that a typological classification is more appropriate. The more restrained richness of Bridgewater House is anticipated in several earlier major works, most significantly the exterior faces of the Houses of Parliament, though the difference of style obscures that similarity, and also in Highclere Castle, Hampshire (considered below), but perhaps most obviously anticipated in the façade of his 1845 reconstruction of Soane's Whitehall government offices.

Working for magnates, Barry was extremely influential as a country house architect in establishing design models. But the very fact that his clientele lay largely among the greater landowners implied that his work was often one of improvement rather than design *ab initio*, and this has tended to obscure the significance of his country house practice. Those houses to which he gave 'finish, life, and variety' (A. Barry, *Life*, 117) in rebuilding include: Walton House (Mount Felix), Surrey (1835–9), which with Trentham marked the change of domestic taste from Greek revival to italianate, and in its planning based on a spinal corridor established the alternative form of the two basic Victorian mansion plans; Kingston Lacy, Dorset, for William Bankes (1835–41); Duncombe Park, Yorkshire (1843–51); Harewood House, Yorkshire, where he gave the wings of the mid-Georgian mansion greater importance, added a balustrade to the centre, and transformed the chimney stacks into architectural features, enlarged and decorated some of the principal rooms, and created a grand architectural garden adjoining the house (1843–50); Bowood, Wiltshire (tower, lodges, and garden works *c*.1830–57) for Lord Lansdowne; Canford Manor, Dorset (a Gothic revival house by Blore, recast in Houses of Parliament vein, with a huge entrance tower and great hall with elaborate timber roof, 1848–52); Shrubland Park, Suffolk, where Barry's additions to the house (1849–54) are a good example of his richer Italian manner; and Gawthorpe Hall, Lancashire ('Anglo-Italian', 1850–52). At Georgian Highclere, Hampshire (1838–49), although 'the whole constructional framework of the house was retained' (A. Barry, *Life*, 109), including the fenestration, the exterior was entirely reclad in a Jacobethan manner inspired by Wollaton that Barry termed 'Anglo-Italian'—defined by his son as 'Gothic principles [of] design, perpendicular lines prevailing, with pure Italian profiles and interior decoration' (C. Barry junior, diaries, 12 Jan 1846, RIBA drawings collection, BaFam 6(c)3)—in the enriched treatment of the window surrounds a precursor of his 'second manner'.

Public commissions Barry was employed by the government on a variety of projects in addition to the Houses of Parliament. In laying out Trafalgar Square in 1840, his choice of levels gave greater distinction to the long, low National Gallery, but the fountains were smaller than he wished. He designed a frontage for Pentonville model prison (1840), modified W. J. Smith's rendition of the Farnese for the embassy house at Constantinople (1842), was consulted on the proposed east front enlargement of Buckingham Palace (1845), gave architectural character to the vast Admiralty workshops for the steam fleet at Keyham, Plymouth, Devon (1848), and advised on the design of the new Westminster Bridge (1854). In 1845 he directed the widening of western Piccadilly. The enlargement of the council offices and Board of Trade in Whitehall (1845–6) incorporated the adjoining Home Office, a Tudor building, to create a symmetrical range with pronounced terminal accents; the reuse of Soane's columns to support a broken entablature crowned with acroteria transformed serene horizontality into dynamic verticality. Halifax town hall, the last building he designed (executed by E. M. Barry), although for local government, may be mentioned here; it was of an even further enriched character, with a notable asymmetrical tower and spire. A royal commissioner for the Great Exhibition of 1851, Barry succeeded in having Paxton's designs for the Crystal Palace modified so as to vault the transepts. When the palace was removed permanently to Sydenham, Kent, he vainly urged enlivening its skyline with domes, so that in sunshine it 'would have a fairy and transparent lightness of form characteristic of its construction and would have its outline traced out in dazzling stars of meteoric light which would not fail to excite the wonder and admiration of all who behold it' (C. Barry, draft letter to Francis Fuller, 29 Sept 1852).

Many, indeed, of Barry's official commissions proved abortive, including new courts of law (1840, 1845), and his huge domed recension of the Horse Guards (1846). Barry also devised several unofficial proposals for public buildings: he proposed revisions of Wilkins's National Gallery, and a remodelling of Green Park to embellish his widening of Piccadilly (*c*.1845); designs for a range of buildings around Westminster Hall and Old Palace Yard in harmony with the new Houses of Parliament were rejected in 1857. Nothing came of his admirable scheme to reuse the Marble Arch (removed from Buckingham Palace when the east front was built, 1851) as part of a grand terminal feature to Pall Mall. He was deeply involved in schemes of the 1850s for reorganizing the British Museum, and in 1859 designed premises for the Royal Academy to front Piccadilly, abandoned when Lord Derby's government resigned. In his last years he planned the improvement of Westminster, and consolidation of the government's offices into one gigantic palace of administration, of which his earlier Whitehall work would have formed a basic unit.

Marriage and family Before leaving for the continent in 1817 Barry had become engaged to Sarah Rowsell (1798–1882), daughter of a well-to-do stationer, whom he married on 7 December 1822. In 1827 they moved from Ely Place to 27 Foley Place, and in 1841 to 32 Great George Street, conveniently close to the new Houses of Parliament, where ten years later they and five children were modestly supported by three resident servants. Finally in 1853 they moved to The Elms, 29 North Side, Clapham Common, a large house standing in its own grounds. They had five sons and two daughters, of whom four sons are noticed separately, including Alfred *Barry, his father's biographer, Edward Middleton *Barry, who completed his work at Westminster, and the civil engineer John Wolfe Wolfe-*Barry; the eldest, Charles, is mentioned below. Barry seldom took a holiday but he continued to visit the continent with professional concern: in 1842 the Rhineland and Bavaria, with a particular eye to the Munich school of fresco painting, admired by the Fine Arts Commission; in September 1845 he toured northern France with his son Charles and fellow architect Ambrose Poynter; he returned to Italy in 1847; and in 1855, when he was a juror for the architectural section of the Paris Universal Exhibition, he made three visits there (one a family party), and also toured the Loire châteaux with Frederick Cockerell. September and October 1848 saw him in the highlands of Scotland staying with the ducal Sutherlands and Argylls. But essentially he was a Londoner: 'All his interests were in town' (A. Barry, *Life*, 324).

Barry's strong, determined-looking features, with prominent nose and firm mouth, expressed his inherent resolution 'to have his own way, good-humoured but determined' (A. Barry, *Life*, 333). He often rose at four, before working until breakfast at eight o'clock. After the day's business he dined at six or seven, had a brief nap, conversed or read until eight, drank tea, and worked until midnight. Good health sustained years of this regime, but from September 1844 he suffered attacks of ill health, and in early 1858 fell seriously ill. An 1845–6 journal of his eldest son, Charles, shows Barry as the devoted father of a united family, but beset by professional anxieties and in poor health; at this time he became a vegetarian, much to his family's concern. Particularly in his later years, his life was very much lived 'at home in the society of his wife and children' (A. Barry, *Life*, 328), the more so, perhaps, because four of his sons shared his professional interests. Though noted for his 'suavity of disposition' (Wyatt, 135) and sanguine in outlook, he was quick-tempered. Faced by parliamentary committees, Barry wasted no words: he was a practical man, who avoided abstract questions. Asked what style he would have chosen for the Whitehall offices had he made a *tabula rasa* of the existing buildings, he replied: 'that is a question which I can hardly answer, because I have never directed my attention to what would have been my course under such circumstances' ('Select committee on the foreign office reconstruction', q. 1397). He neither lectured nor wrote, and disliked publicity. But he was no recluse: 'frank, warm and genial' (Wolfe), Barry enjoyed society, and moved comfortably in aristocratic circles, a regular guest at Holland House dinners and of the Sutherlands, especially at their country seats (partly for professional reasons). But despite his whig intimates and attachment to the Liberals, he lacked political enthusiasm; for practical reasons he was gravely disturbed when the Conservative leader Peel tried to resign in December 1845. Barry retained his youthful enthusiasm for music, particularly opera, and in the early 1850s was a regular guest at Lady Hall's private concerts of Welsh music—some time before he became embroiled with her ministerial husband. But it was in his work that 'he found not only the occupation, but also most of the pleasures, of his life' (A. Barry, *Life*, 323). He was assiduous in attending architectural lectures, meetings of the Royal Society (of which he was a fellow), civil engineers, Society of Surveyors, the Royal Academy committee and club. He served as adviser to Leeds city council in their architectural competition for a town hall (1852) and argued strongly for the right of the victor (Cuthbert Brodrick) to carry out the work despite his youthfulness. Deeply concerned about architectural education, he with Cockerell and Hardwick in 1856 made recommendations for greatly improved facilities for students to the unresponsive Royal Academy. He was always closely associated with the Institute of British Architects from its beginnings and served as a vice-president, although he declined the presidency on Earl De Grey's death in 1859, the first professional to be so invited. As a trustee, he regularly attended Soane Museum committees, and as their surveyor likewise attended Dulwich College governors' meetings (1830–58). In 1857 he became a director of the Rock Life Insurance Company, assiduous in attendance. According to notes in his pocket diaries, his income in 1854 amounted to £8256, including £5000 from the Treasury, the remainder largely from commission; and in 1857, some £6900, of which nearly £3000 derived from the Houses of Parliament, and £1560 from railway company dividends.

Character and standing Barry's architecture sought instantaneously to impress: unity, mass, unbroken height, commanding cornices, all reached towards the sublime; but beauty resides in his detail, for which he had an exquisite feeling. He was continually studying his designs, though sometimes the original concept may be preferred to his incessant reworkings. His genius was widely admired during his lifetime: 'At a time when architecture ... [has] been flourishing in an unusual degree, he has long been its chief professor, and not only regarded so in England, but in Europe, where he was considered the most distinguished member of the greatest architectural societies' (*The Times*, 23 May 1860, 9f). Elected ARA in 1840 and RA in 1844, he received the Royal Institute of British Architects (RIBA) gold medal in 1850 and the gold medal for architecture at the Paris Universal Exhibition of 1855. He was knighted on 11 February 1852, after the completion of the House of Commons. Contemporaries had no doubts of his superiority: M. D. Wyatt, in his funerary oration delivered to the RIBA, ranked him with Jones and Wren (M. Hittorf placed him above both), hailing him as the greatest architect of at least the two previous centuries. Some mid-twentieth-century eyes have found his later work vulgar, thanks to 'an inherent insensitiveness'. A readiness 'to provide his clients with whatever "effects" they wanted', is said to discredit him: 'a man of great versatility, but questionable taste' (Fleetwood-Hesketh, 126–7). But to late Georgians the concept of the architect as hero was foreign, and Barry accepted the client's right to set out his brief. Nor was he a mid-Victorian zealot: 'not being a bigot to any particular style', Barry believed that 'any architect of talent' could 'make any style his own' ('Select committee on the foreign office reconstruction', qq. 1408, 1410); furthermore, he looked to the possibility that 'a new and effective style ... [might], with the aid of new materials and improved principles of construction, grow out of a fusion of styles' (ibid., q.1522). The leading early Victorian architect, he was exceptional in his artistic skill and integrity, asserting the supremacy of art over style.

Unmoved by contemporary passions, Barry has been accused of lacking personality and of emotional emptiness, but he was a designer on an imperial scale, who used stylistic differences for aesthetic effect: asked, in 1858 whether he would not wish the proposed government offices to be in Gothic to accord with the Houses of Parliament and Westminster Abbey, he remarked, 'I confess that for the sake of variety of effect I should have preferred any style whose sky line dealt in curvilinear or spherical forms of outline as a contrast to what is done at the Houses' ('Select committee on the foreign office reconstruction', q.1408). Even if, less revolutionary than his collaborator Pugin, Barry 'merely maintained long-established European standards, modulating them knowledgeably to meet new conditions and providing sufficient superficial novelty to hold contemporary attention' (Hitchcock, 219), his Italian paradigms and his planning proved the basis of Victorian secular architecture. Barry's work well bears comparison with that of his great European contemporaries. But his ultimate claim to fame is as the man who designed and carried through Britain's greatest national building, one which immediately acquired symbolic status and proved a magnet for artists: 'the work of a great man who expresses the great thought of a great nation' (*The Athenaeum*, 1856, 110).

Barry died suddenly at his Clapham home of a heart attack on 12 May 1860. He was buried in Westminster Abbey ten days later in the presence of nearly 500 representatives of the arts and sciences. His estate, sworn at under £80,000, was left to be divided equally among his children, subject to his wife's life interest (in fact, almost immediately she distributed £60,000 to them): less wealthy than the great contractors he employed, such as Thomas Grissell or Charles and Thomas Lucas, he made no attempt to establish a landed dynasty.

His eldest son, **Charles Barry** (1823–1900), architect, was born on 21 September 1823 at 39 Ely Place, Holborn, London. Educated at Sevenoaks grammar school, he entered his father's office in 1840. Although in 1845 he accepted his father's invitation to become his successor, delicate health compelled him to travel for some months, and on his return in 1847 he joined the elder Barry's principal assistant, Robert Richardson Banks (*c*.1812–1872), in independent practice, and became a fellow of the RIBA in 1854. While still in Barry's office, they appear to have designed 12, 18–19, and 20 Kensington Palace Gardens (1845–7) for the new Houses of Parliament contractors Grissell and Samuel Morton Peto. Charles junior succeeded his father as surveyor to the Dulwich College estate in 1858, was awarded the RIBA gold medal in 1877, and served very successfully as president of the institute in 1876–9. He was, however, acutely disappointed to discover that he 'had been utilised for an emergency' (*The Architect*, 8 June 1900, 362) and his influence did not persist. An obituary suggested that 'with him the artist was subservient to the man of business' (ibid.). His principal works include: Bylaugh Hall, Norfolk (1849–51; dem.); Dulwich College (1866–70)—the first Victorian large-scale use of terracotta, on which he gave a paper to the RIBA—and several churches and church halls in Dulwich, including Holy Trinity, Tulse Hill (1856), St Stephen's (1868–82), and St Peter's (1873), as well as the public library; Burlington House forecourt buildings for the learned societies, Piccadilly (1869–73); Stevenstone House, Devon (1869–74; ruined); the London board school in Winchester Street, Finsbury (1872); partly rebuilding Clumber House, Nottinghamshire, after a fire (1880; dem. 1938); the Great Eastern Hotel (1880–84; much enlarged); roofing the court of

the Royal Exchange (1884); the jubilee wing of the children's hospital, Great Ormond Street (1890; dem.); Shoreditch town hall extension (1892); and the Institution of Civil Engineers, Westminster (1896, £60,000; dem. 1910). Designs for the Foreign Office were awarded second prize in the government offices competition of 1857–8. He advised on the city extensions of Milan and Turin, and often acted as an arbitrator and competition assessor between 1874 and 1895. After Banks's death in 1872 he took his son Charles Edward Barry (1855–1937) into partnership. Aston Webb was a pupil. Charles Barry junior died at Worthing on 2 June 1900, and was buried four days later near by at Broadwater.   M. H. PORT

Sources A. Barry, *Life and works of Sir Charles Barry RA, FRS* (1867) · C. Barry, travel diaries and diaries, RIBA BAL, Drawings collection · C. Barry, jun., diaries, RIBA BAL, Drawings Collection · H. Wolfe, 'Memoir of Sir Charles Barry', RIBA BAL · M. D. Wyatt, 'On the architectural career of the late Sir Charles Barry', *Sessional Papers of the Royal Institute of British Architects* (1859–60), 118–37 · Man. CL, Manchester Royal Institution MSS · RIBA BAL, Sir Charles Barry MSS · M. Girouard, 'Charles Barry: a centenary assessment', *Country Life*, 128 (1960), 796–7 · C. L. Eastlake, *A history of the Gothic revival* (1872) · P. Fleetwood-Hesketh, 'Sir Charles Barry', *Victorian architecture*, ed. P. Ferriday (1963) · *The Builder*, 18 (1860), 305–7 · J. M. Crook and M. H. Port, eds., *The history of the king's works*, 6 (1973) · M. H. Port, ed., *The Houses of Parliament* (1976) · E. W. Pugin, *Who was the art architect of the Houses of Parliament: a statement of facts, founded on the letters of Sir Charles Barry and the diaries of Augustus Welby Pugin* (1867) · A. Barry, *The architect of the new palace at Westminster: a reply to a pamphlet by E. Pugin, esq*, 2nd edn (1868) · E. W. Pugin, *Notes on the reply of the Rev. Alfred Barry, DD* (1868) · E. M. Barry, *Correspondence with Mr J. R. Herbert RA* (1868) · *Catalogue of the drawings collection of the Royal Institute of British Architects: B* (1972) · Barry drawings, Potteries Museum and Art Gallery, Stoke-on-Trent · H. R. Hitchcock, *Early Victorian architecture in Britain*, 2 vols. (1954) · 'Select committee on the foreign office reconstruction', *Parl. papers* (1857–8), vol. 11, no. 417 · M. Whiffen, 'The architecture of Sir Charles Barry in Manchester and neighbourhood', *Art and architecture in Victorian Manchester*, ed. J. H. G. Archer (1985), 46–64 · R. Dell, *Burlington Magazine*, 8 (1906), 403–20 · J. Wolfe-Barry, *The architect of the new palace at Westminster: a memorandum* (1908) · A. Wedgwood, 'The throne in the House of Lords and its setting', *Architectural History*, 27 (1984), 59–73 · will of Walter Edward Barry, PRO, PROB 11/1426, fols. 393–400 · census returns, 1851, PRO, HO 107/1480 · marriage register, St Clement Eastcheap, GL [also in Guildhall RO] · W. H. Leeds, *The public buildings of London … by Pugin and Britton*, 2nd edn (1838), vol. 2 · *Rebuilding the Houses of Parliament*, HLRO, memorandum no. 69 (1984) · Sir Charles Barry's will, PPR · *The Times* (23 May 1860), 9f · *The parish of St James, Westminster*, 1/2, Survey of London, 30 (1960) · *The Athenaeum* (26 Jan 1856), 110 · parish register, 17 June 1795, St Margaret's, Westminster [baptism] · *The Builder*, 57 (1900), 78

Archives HLRO, corresp., notes, and drawings relating to Palace of Westminster · Lancs. RO, contract and working drawings for Gawthorpe Hall · RIBA, MSS · RIBA BAL, corresp. and papers incl. journals, notebooks, and sketchbooks · RIBA drawings collection, family papers, and architectural drawings | Dulwich College, London, corresp. as surveyor of Dulwich College · Highclere Castle, Highclere, letters and drawings relating to Highclere Castle · Lpool RO, letters to fourteenth earl of Derby · Man. CL, Manchester Archives and Local Studies, letters to Royal Manchester Institution · PRO, Office of Works MSS, Work 11 · W. Yorks. AS, Leeds, corresp. with Lord Canning and Fine Arts Commission MSS

Likenesses oils, *c*.1815, priv. coll. · oils, *c*.1833, priv. coll. · G. Hayter, oils, 1838, priv. coll. · J. Linnell, oils, 1839, repro. in Port, *Houses of Parliament*, p. 74 · P. Park, marble bust, 1848, Reform Club,

London · H. W. Pickersgill, oils, exh. RA 1849, Palace of Westminster, London · Lowes Dickinson, oils, c.1850, RIBA · J. P. Knight, oils, c.1851, NPG [see illus.] · engraving, c.1858 (after photograph), repro. in Barry, Life and works · J. H. Foley, statue, 1865, Palace of Westminster, London · J. B. Philip, relief, c.1870, Albert Memorial, Kensington Gardens, London · W. Behnes, bust · T. W. Harland, stipple and line engraving, NPG · J. Partridge, group portrait (The fine arts commissioners, 1846), NPG · H. W. Phillips, group portrait, oils (The Royal Commissioners for the Great Exhibition), V&A · J. Watkins, carte-de-visite, NPG; repro. in Album of Artists, vol. 1

Wealth at death under £80,000: probate, 4 June 1860, CGPLA Eng. & Wales

Barry, Charles (1823–1900). See under Barry, Sir Charles (1795–1860).

Barry, Sir David (1780–1835), army surgeon and physiologist, was born on 12 March 1780 in co. Roscommon, Ireland. After showing early talent in classics and mathematics, he eventually decided upon a career in medicine. He was examined for the army in the Royal College of Surgeons in Dublin in 1805, joined the 89th regiment as an assistant surgeon on 6 March 1806, and saw service in Portugal. After a brief spell as an ensign in 1809, he returned to the medical service in February 1810 with the 58th regiment of foot. When Field Marshal Beresford was wounded at Salamanca, Barry's attentive care won his abiding interest. From 1815 to 1820 Barry resided at Oporto as district surgeon. On his return to England in 1820 he was admitted extra-licentiate of the Royal College of Physicians, London, and was made an MD at King's College, Aberdeen.

In 1822 Barry travelled to Paris, where he came under the influence of François Magendie, who set him to work on the return of blood to the heart. He showed that movement of blood in the great veins is increased during inspiration when the sub-atmospheric pressure in the chest is further diminished. Georges Cuvier and André Duméril were appointed by the Académie des Sciences in 1825 to report on Barry's demonstrations. Their commendation was echoed in 1826 by René Laënnec. Barry's Experimental researches on the influence exercised by atmospheric pressure upon the progression of the blood in the veins, upon the function of absorption, and upon the prevention and cure of the symptoms caused by the bites of dogs and venomous animals was published in London in 1826, and won him a 'sudden, extensive, and high reputation' (Carson, 134). After graduating MD at Paris in 1827, Barry returned to London and was admitted a licentiate of the Royal College of Physicians on 1 October 1827. In 1828 he was sent with Nicolas Chervin, Pierre Louis, and Armand Trousseau to investigate an outbreak of yellow fever in Gibraltar. Asiatic cholera made its first appearance in Europe in 1830, and in June 1831 Barry, along with William Russell (1773–1839), an Edinburgh graduate recently returned from Calcutta, was dispatched to St Petersburg, where an epidemic was in progress. By the end of July Russell was in no doubt that the malady was the same as he had seen in India and Barry was convinced that it was new to Europe. On his return Barry was made deputy inspector of hospitals, and in November 1831, when the first cases of cholera appeared in Sunderland, he was empowered by the privy council to demand returns from all practitioners giving details of all the patients with 'autumnal diarrhoea', to allow for those physicians who resolutely refused to admit that Asiatic cholera had reached England. Their Official report made to government by Drs. Russell and Barry on the disease called cholera spasmodica as observed by them during their mission to Russia in 1831 (1831) won them knighthoods in 1832, when Barry was also elected FRS and honoured by Portugal and Russia.

In 1833 Barry was appointed one of the commissioners to inquire into the health of children working in factories, and in 1834 to inquire into the condition of the poorer classes and the medical charities in Ireland. He died suddenly on 4 November 1835 in Welbeck Street, London, from rupture of an aortic aneurysm, leaving a widow and children. His widow, who died in 1866, was the youngest daughter of Joseph Whately of Nonsuch Park, Surrey, prebendary of Bristol (1793–7), and sister of Richard Whately, archbishop of Dublin. When Barry's death was discussed at a meeting of the Westminster Medical Society, James Johnson (1777–1845) remarked that his witty, clubbable friend was 'inclined to be stout, a bon vivant though not irregular in his habits' (Johnson, 266).

C. S. BREATHNACH

Sources Munk, Roll · R. Drew, Commissioned officers in the medical services of the British army, 1660–1960, 2 (1968) · J. Johnson, 'Death of Sir David Barry', The Lancet (14 Nov 1835), 264–6 · Russell and Barry, letters and reports, Edinburgh Medical and Surgical Journal, 37 (1832), suppl., clv–clxxxiv · J. Carson, An inquiry into the causes of respiration; of the motion of the blood; animal heat; absorption and muscular motion: with practical inferences, 2nd edn (1833), 134, 208 · C. S. Breathnach, 'Sir David Barry's experiments on venous return', Medical History, 9 (1965), 133–41 · N. Longmate, King cholera (1966), 35–8 · GM, 2nd ser., 4 (1835), 663
Archives Royal College of Physicians of Edinburgh, papers

Barry, David fitz David, first earl of Barrymore (1605–1642), nobleman, was born on 10 March 1605, probably at Buttevant, co. Cork, a posthumous child of David fitz David Barry (d. 1604/5), son of David fitz James *Barry, de facto third Viscount Buttevant, and of Elizabeth, daughter of Richard Power, fourth Baron le Power. At the age of twelve he succeeded to the estates and title of his grandfather, and at sixteen, on 21 July 1621, he married Lady Alice (1608–1666), eldest daughter of Richard Boyle, first earl of Cork. The following year he inherited the estates of his great-uncle Richard, who, because he was deaf and mute, had been superseded in the title by his younger brother David. In May 1625 he was granted livery of all his lands by Charles I, without fine, and on 28 February 1628 was created earl of Barrymore. In 1634 Barrymore took his seat in parliament. In 1639 he was asked to raise 1000 men for service against the Scots in the first bishops' war. He landed in Lancashire in June of that year, but with only a small body of men as he had no money to pay them. He commanded a regiment again in 1640.

When the Irish rising of 1641 broke out Barrymore garrisoned his castle of Shandon and declined an offer from the insurgents to take the command of their army, replying 'I will first take an offer from my brother, Dungarvan, to be hangman-general at Youghal' (Lord Dungarvan was a son of the earl of Cork, who had stationed him with troops in Youghal to defend the town against the rebels). When Barrymore received a threat that his house of Castlelyons would be destroyed, he declared that he would defend it while one stone stood upon another, being resolved to live and die a faithful subject of the English crown. In May 1642 he and his brother-in-law pursued the Condons, took the castle of Ballymac-Patrick (now Careysville), and rescued some hundred women and children. This was the first successful attempt of the English in that part of the country, but the victory was marred by the execution on the spot of all the fifty-one rebels taken prisoner. An account of this expedition was published in the form of a letter (9 May 1642) from the earl of Cork at Dublin to his wife in London. Two months later Barrymore took Clogh-lea Castle, near Kilworth. After this he was joined with Lord Inchiquin in a commission for the civil government of Munster. On 3 September he headed troops which he maintained at his own expense at the battle of Liscarroll, in which his brother-in-law Lord Kinalmeaky was killed. Barrymore was, as is supposed, wounded, for he died later the same month, on 29 September. He was buried in the Boyle vault at Youghal. He left his wife and their two sons and two daughters ill provided for, and the earl of Cork appealed to the king on their behalf. Charles was in no position to help him at the time but he wrote from Oxford that the lord justice should grant his wardship and marriage to the mother without exacting any fine or rent for the crown.

ROBERT HARRISON, *rev.* JUDITH HUDSON BARRY

Sources GEC, *Peerage* · J. Lodge, *The peerage of Ireland*, rev. M. Archdall, rev. edn, 7 vols. (1789) · *CSP Ire.*, 1625–32 · J. Morrin, ed., *Calendar of the patent and close rolls of chancery in Ireland, of the reign of Charles I* (1863) · R. Bagwell, *Ireland under the Stuarts*, 2 (1909) · N. Canny, *The upstart earl: a study of the social and mental world of Richard Boyle, first earl of Cork, 1566–1643* (1982) · B. Burke, *A genealogical history of the dormant, abeyant, forfeited and extinct peerages of the British empire*, new edn (1883), 25

Barry, David fitz James, *de facto* third Viscount Buttevant (1550–1617), soldier, was the second son of James fitz Richard Barry Roe (*d.* 1581), lord of Ibawne, and Eileen, daughter of Cormac MacCarthy Reagh. James assumed possession of Barryscourt, near Cork, in 1558 and was summoned to parliament the following year as Viscount Buttevant. On his father's death as a prisoner in Dublin Castle on 10 April 1581 David succeeded to his lands and honours during the lifetime of his elder brother Richard, who was deaf and mute; he survived David by five years, dying on 24 April 1622. David's succession to his father's estates was unsuccessfully contested in a lifelong feud with Florence MacCarthy More. His lands and power were substantial not only in co. Cork but also in the province of Munster. In military terms, Barry lands could furnish 30 light horsemen and 200 pikemen in 1584, and Sir George Carew estimated the extent of Barry holdings in 1600 at 392 ploughlands. Buttevant Castle, formerly King John's Castle, situated on the River Awbeg and celebrated by Spenser as the 'Gentle Mulla' became their chief seat, so called from the Norman French *botavant* (or *botavaunt*), the outer works of a castle.

David Barry's loyalty had become suspect before the outbreak of the second Desmond rebellion in 1579. Lord Justice Sir William Pelham wanted him closely observed by Sir Warham St Leger. Though he had performed useful services 'done upon the traitors whose heads were sent to Cork' and was commended and guaranteed government protection by Pelham on 26 August 1580, later that same day he changed his opinion of Barry, ordering St Leger to arrest him and his brother William (*Carew Manuscripts*, 2.300–01). Before he handed the sword of office to Lord Grey of Wilton, Pelham had Barry's father incarcerated in Dublin Castle and referred to him as 'standing obstinately in his undutiful arrogancy' (ibid., 302). David duly became an active supporter of the rebel earl of Desmond. Sir Walter Ralegh wrote from Cork on 25 February 1581 that Barry had burnt all his castles and gone into rebellion. He was proclaimed traitor in May 1581, shortly after his father's death. Avaricious officials and captains anticipated land forfeitures following on the putting down of the rebellion; meanwhile, as an active rebel until 3 May 1582, Barry burnt, plundered, and slaughtered the enemy, destroying a detachment of troops under Captain William Apsley as they left their boats attempting to cross Bearhaven to get cover in Bantry Abbey. The ferocity of Lord Grey's suppression of the rebellion, and in particular the attack on Barry's forces on 2 May 1582 as they had camped in the woods of Dromfinnin during which thirty of his men were killed, persuaded Barry to plead for mercy the next day. Because of his influence and landed power in Cork and Munster, a pardon was granted and registered on 24 August 1582.

Henceforth it paid Lord Barry to remain loyal; his letters and gifts to Cecil in July 1597 were effusive and endorsed 'Lord Barry to my master' (*Salisbury MSS*, 7.304). During the Nine Years' War (1594–1603) O'Neill made many overtures to Barry to woo him onto the side of the Gaelic confederacy, arguing that their common Catholicism made the rising a religious crusade. In Barry's reply he claimed that Queen Elizabeth was indifferent to the exercise of their religion. With his brother John, sheriff of Liscarroll, and Sir George Thornton, provost-marshal in Munster, Barry played a notable part in the years 1599–1601 in helping the government's forces against O'Neill's Gaelic and Spanish allies. At the end of the war King James granted him the greater portion of the MacCarthy lands on 31-year leases. Although Lord Barry sat in Perrot's parliament in April 1585 without objection on grounds of precedence—a commonplace in the Irish house of peers—King James had to issue a special royal rescript for him to attend the Dublin parliament of 1613, ordering that 'if the question of his right to sit in parliament should be stirred by any person it should be silenced' (*DNB*). He also sat in parliament in 1615.

Barry married first Ellen, daughter of David Roche, fifth Viscount Roche of Fermoy. Their son David fitz David died in 1604–5, and his posthumously born son David fitz David *Barry (1605–1642) became first earl of Barrymore in 1628 through the influence of his father-in-law, Richard Boyle, earl of Cork. The marriage alliances of their five daughters were equally provident and prosperous. With his second wife, Sheelagh, daughter of Cormac MacCarthy of Muskerry, Lord Barry had three more sons and four daughters. He died at Barryscourt on 10 April 1617.

J. J. N. McGurk

Sources J. S. Brewer and W. Bullen, eds., *Calendar of the Carew manuscripts*, 2–4, PRO (1868–70) · *CSP Ire.*, 1574–85; 1588–92 · T. Stafford, *Pacata Hibernia*, 2 vols. (1633); repr. (1810) · *The Lismore papers, first series: autobiographical notes, remembrances and diaries of Sir Richard Boyle, first and 'great' earl of Cork*, ed. A. B. Grosart, 2 (privately printed, London, 1886) · *The Irish fiants of the Tudor sovereigns*, 4 vols. (1994) · *Calendar of the manuscripts of the most hon. the marquis of Salisbury*, 24 vols., HMC, 9 (1883–1976), vols. 4, 7, 10 · Burke, *Gen. Ire.* (1976), 66–73 · B. Burke, *A genealogical history of the dormant, abeyant, forfeited and extinct peerages of the British empire*, new edn (1883) · S. P. Johnston, ed., 'On a manuscript description of the city and county of Cork, c.1685', *Journal of the Royal Society of Antiquaries of Ireland*, 5th ser., 12 (1902), 353–76 · D. McCarthy, *Life and letters of Florence MacCarthy Mór* (1867) · S. Lewis, *A topographical dictionary of Ireland*, 1 (1837), under Cork · P. O'Flanagan and C. G. Buttimer, eds., *Cork: history and society—interdisciplinary essays on the history of an Irish county* (1993) · C. Smith, *The ancient and present state of the county and city of Cork*, new edn, 2 vols. (1815) · A. Thomas, *The walled towns of Ireland* (1992) [see under Cork] · E. Hogan, ed., *The description of Ireland … 1598* (1878) · S. G. Ellis, *Ireland in the age of the Tudors* (1998) · C. Brady, 'Faction and the origins of the Desmond rebellion of 1579', *Irish Historical Studies*, 22 (1980–81), 289–312 · N. P. Canny, *The Elizabethan conquest of Ireland: a pattern established, 1565–76* (1976) · N. MacCarthy-Morrough, *The Munster plantation … 1583–1641* (1986) · K. W. Nicholls, 'Some documents on Irish law and custom in the sixteenth century', *Analecta Hibernica*, 26 (1970), 105–29 · E. Barry, 'Barrymore [pts 1–2]', *Journal of the Cork Historical and Archaeological Society*, 2nd ser., 5 (1899), 1–17, 77–92 · E. Barry, 'Barrymore [pts 3–12]', *Journal of the Cork Historical and Archaeological Society*, 2nd ser., 6–8 (1900–02) · GEC, *Peerage*, new edn, 1.441–3 · *DNB*
Archives Ches. & Chester ALSS, title deeds, estate and family papers, Ref. Acc. 2802 | Chatsworth House, Derbyshire, Lismore papers, 6/120, 143 · NL Scot., papers, 6141
Wealth at death 392 ploughlands in 1600: Brewer and Bullen, eds., *Calendar*, 111, 513

Barry, Sir Edward, first baronet (1696–1776), physician, was born in Cork, co. Cork, Ireland, the son of Edward Barry, a medical practitioner, and his wife, Jane Barry. He was educated at Trinity College, Dublin (BA 1717, MD 1740), and at Leiden (MD 1719); he was elected FRS in 1733. He practised in Cork; he was married by 1725 and had four sons and two daughters. One daughter, Anne, married General Sir John Irwin, while the other daughter married the poet and dramatist Robert Jephson.

In 1739 Barry left Cork for Dublin. He was elected a fellow of the King and Queen's College of Physicians in Ireland (1740, president 1749). While continuing to practise medicine in Dublin, he was a member of the Irish House of Commons for Charleville, co. Cork, from about 1744 to 1760, being succeeded by his son Robert. His wife had died in childbed on 5 May 1741 and in December 1746 he married Jane Dopping (d. c.1777), daughter of the bishop of Ossory and granddaughter of Ralph Howard, professor of physic at Dublin. This marriage was childless. He was physician-general to the forces in Ireland, and professor of physic in the University of Dublin, 1745–61. His eldest son, Nathaniel, became a physician in Dublin.

In 1761 Barry left Ireland, was incorporated MD at Oxford, and was licensed to practise, which he did in London. Samuel Johnson said that Barry 'brought his reputation with him but had not great success' (Boswell 2.23). In 1762 he was made a fellow of the Royal College of Physicians, London.

Barry wrote on tuberculosis (1726, 1727), and on general medicine (1759). He is credited with puncturing tuberculous cavities to allow healing to take place. Barry wrote a well-produced history of wines (1775), largely devoted to classical times, though there is an appendix on modern wines. Alexander Henderson in his 1824 history of wines followed the plan of Barry's book but described him as having 'as antiquated notions in natural philosophy as in medicine' (Henderson, vi–vii).

In 1769 or 1770 Barry moved to Bath, Somerset. He was created a baronet in 1775, and died in Bath on 29 March 1776. His wife survived him by about a year.

Jean Loudon

Sources T. P. C. Kirkpatrick, 'Sir Edward Barry, MD, FRS', *Dublin Journal of Medical Science*, 128 (1909), 442–61 · Munk, *Roll* · *GM*, 1st ser., 46 (1776), 192 · J. Hastings, review of J. Hasting's *Pulmonary consumption*, *Edinburgh Medical and Surgical Journal*, 64 (1845), 458–77, esp. 477 · J. Boswell, *The life of Samuel Johnson*, 2 vols. (1791) · A. Henderson, *The history of ancient and modern wines* (1824) · Burtchaell & Sadleir, *Alum. Dubl.*, 2nd edn · R. W. Innes Smith, *English-speaking students of medicine at the University of Leyden* (1932)
Likenesses attrib. J. Reynolds, portrait, TCD; repro. in Kirkpatrick, 'Sir Edward Barry', facing p. 442

Barry, Edward (1759–1822), religious and medical writer, son of a physician of Bristol, was educated at Bristol School under Mr Lee, and studied medicine at St Andrews University, where he graduated MD. Preferring theology to medicine, he took orders in the Church of England, and was for several years curate of St Marylebone and one of the most popular preachers in London. It is said that the ordinary of Newgate, Mr Villette, often availed himself of Dr Barry's assistance in awakening the consciences of hardened criminals. Barry was grand chaplain to the freemasons, and on preaching before them on one occasion was presented with a gold medal and a request that they might be allowed to publish his sermon.

After moving to Reading, Barry employed himself in preparing some of his works for publication, the most noted being *The Friendly Call of Truth and Reason to a New Species of Dissenters* (1799; 4th edn, 1812). This work, which was not directed against regularly licensed dissenters but rather against Methodists and other church evangelicals inclined to secession, revealed Barry's sympathies as an old-fashioned high-churchman, who justified restrictive measures such as those taken in 1811 by Lord Sidmouth (whom he greatly admired) by appealing to familiar patristic texts from St Ignatius, St Cyprian, and St Augustine. Barry dedicated the book to Sir William Scott (afterwards Lord Stowell), whose approbation of Barry's services in the cause of the Church of England against the invasions of its discipline, and interest with his younger brother Lord Eldon, then lord chancellor, obtained for

Barry the two livings of St Mary and St Leonard, Wallingford. Barry was twice married: the surname of his second wife was Morrell.

Barry was popular at Wallingford, where his charitable giving was proverbial. His sermons continued to attract crowded audiences, and he started a successful evening lecture. His collected *Sermons Preached on Public Occasions* (enlarged edition, 1805) show that he had a clear and earnest style, well adapted to the service of charitable works and other appeals to higher feeling. A prolific author, he covered many subjects, ranging from *Theological, Philosophical and Moral Essays* (1791) to *A guide to the history of the human species, and the most important branches of medical philosophy* (1811), but he was most influential as a campaigner for animal welfare, and wrote and spoke passionately against bull-baiting and cock-fighting. He was also a noted critic of prize-fighting, and his *Letter on the Practice of Boxing* (1789) was particularly well known. Barry died at Wallingford on 16 January 1822 and was buried there. The immense concourse of persons at his funeral attested to the esteem in which he was held at Wallingford.   RICHARD SHARP

Sources GM, 1st ser., 92/1 (1822), 185–6 · DNB · E. Barry, *Sermons preached on public occasions*, 3rd edn (1805) · E. Barry, *The friendly call of truth and reason to a new species of dissenters*, 4th edn (1812)
Likenesses J. Jones, stipple engraving, pubd 1789 (after M. Brown), BM, NPG · A. Fogg, stipple engraving, 1805 (after J. Barry), repro. in Barry, *Sermons*, frontispiece

Barry, Edward Middleton (1830–1880), architect, was born on 7 June 1830 at 27 Foley Place, London, the third son of the seven children of Sir Charles *Barry (1795–1860), architect, and his wife, Sarah (1798–1882), daughter of Samuel Rowsell and his wife, Sarah Ellen (*née* Smith). Owing to frequent illness and a delicate constitution he was raised away from his family in London, in Blackheath, then a country village. Not as well educated as his brothers, he attended schools at Blackheath and Walthamstow, which to his later regret he left early. A solitary 'serious and thoughtful' child (Barry, 21), he occupied himself in thinking about his father's new palace at Westminster. Despite his elder brother Charles also being an architect, his father destined him, too, for a career in architecture and for a short time, when aged sixteen, he studied at University College, London, under the direction of Professor Donaldson. He was then for a year a pupil in the office of Thomas Henry Wyatt and David Brandon, following which he embarked on what should have been a formative tour of the continent. This was curtailed, however, by the opportunity to return and enter his father's office shortly after his elder brother Charles had left it, in 1847, along with Robert Richardson Banks—Sir Charles's chief assistant—to practise in partnership on their own account. In 1848 he entered the Royal Academy Schools. Given his parentage, background, and early signs of ability, Edward's expectations were not unreasonably considerable and, although he continued to work for his father, becoming his chief assistant, until the latter's death in 1860, he began now to establish an independent reputation in which his father greatly assisted.

Having come second in the competition for the Oxford University Museum (1854) Barry's first executed project was St Saviour's Church, Haverstock Hill (1855–6). Then, owing to the influence of his father, the Birmingham and Midland Institute appointed him their architect; for them he designed (1856–7) a noteworthy Ionic edifice with novel rounded ends very much in his father's manner. The years 1857–9 saw him design and execute the Gothic new Leeds grammar school. Also around this time (1857–8), following a fire which destroyed the existing theatre, in the short space of eight months and under his father's ever watchful eye, he reconstructed the theatre at Covent Garden. The erection of this regular (fireproofed) classic design and the adjoining Floral Hall, a glass and iron-frame structure, with highly enriched cast-iron decoration (1858–9), affords examples of his energy, constructive skill, and artistic promise. His confidence in his abilities was tested by his father's adverse reaction to his imaginative and well thought out five-storey Gothic design on a small corner site for St Giles's national schools, Endell Street (1859–60). He stood firm and was vindicated by the praise the schools elicited. It was due to the originality displayed in these works and chiefly at St Giles's schools, that he owed his election, in 1861, as an associate to the Royal Academy. Despite his growing reputation and work-load, he continued assisting his father, especially in completing the new palace at Westminster, in particular the Lords' Front and the upper parts of the clock and Victoria towers. When, in 1860, Sir Charles Barry died suddenly, upon Edward devolved the duty of completing his father's works: chiefly the new palace at Westminster, and Halifax town hall, where he faithfully carried out his father's wishes. He had also to safeguard his father's reputation, and assisted with the writing of *The Life and Works of Sir Charles Barry* by his cleric brother Alfred (1867) and in the pamphlet and press war of the Pugin–Barry controversy (1867–8), when it was asserted that credit for the design of the new palace at Westminster should go not to Sir Charles Barry but to A. W. N. Pugin. On 29 March 1862 Barry married Lucy (*c*.1839–*c*.1888), the daughter of Thomas Kettlewell.

Resuming independent practice, Barry undertook several distinguished works, including: the New Opera House, Malta (1861–4); Charing Cross Hotel and Eleanor Cross (1863–5), a work of reproduction rather than restoration; Cannon Street Hotel (1864–6); the arcade and enclosure to New Palace Yard at Westminster (fine railings to his design), and the restoration and decoration of the crypt of St Stephen's Chapel at the new palace (both 1866–8), the latter an admirable Gothic work he much enjoyed and a view of which was exhibited at the Paris Universal Exhibition of 1867, where it won the 'outspoken commendation of Viollet-le-Duc' (*RIBA Transactions*, 203–4); the rebuilding of Crewe Hall, Cheshire, his most pleasurable work (1866–71); the completion of the grand marble staircase and decoration of Fitzwilliam Museum, Cambridge (1871–4); and the renovation of the Reform Club (1878), the funds being available to replace much of the imitation marble his father had so abhorred with the actual material. From 1871 to 1876 he was architect of the Sick Children's Hospital, Great Ormond Street. Like his Charing Cross and Cannon Street hotels, this was in his version of the French Renaissance style, a predilection for which his father had nurtured. To the hospital he donated the design for the highly decorated chapel in memory of one of his three children who died in infancy. His last work of consequence was the quasi-Palladian Art Union building (1879).

Architectural practice brought Barry appointments and duties connected with his profession. In 1860 he was elected both as a fellow of the Royal Institute of British Architects and as an associate of the Institution of Civil Engineers; knowledgeable of construction and materials, he was keen for architects and engineers to work more closely together and thought that 'the London and North-Western Railway was as marvellous a work as the Great Pyramid of Gizeh' (*RIBA Transactions*, 202). He was elected a Royal Academician in 1869, and from 1873 to his death was the academy's professor of architecture, a responsibility he carried out with his usual vigour: his series of annual lectures was published in 1881. In 1874 he was appointed treasurer of the Royal Academy, where he earned the friendship and confidence of his colleagues in the council. He was elected one of the vice-presidents of the RIBA in 1878 and was expected to have served as president but for his untimely death.

Though well regarded by his professional colleagues and an able designer, and despite receiving recognition overseas in 1878 when the Paris Universal Exhibition awarded him the medal of honour, from his early years of practice Barry had more than his fair share of disappointments, which led him at times to question his taste and suitability for the profession. In 1862 he was one of nine architects selected to compete for the Albert Memorial, but was unsuccessful. In 1867 the competition for the new law courts took place, and if the report of the judges and professional referees had been followed, this work would have been entrusted (in partnership with A. E. Street) to Barry, who submitted a well-planned original Gothic design with a great dome and clock tower. At the time it was generally felt considerable injustice was done in passing him over in favour solely of Street. Nor did the consolation eventually offered by the government in the shape of entrusting him in 1868, after a competition in which he was unequivocally placed first, with the erection of a new national gallery prove effectual; for, eventually, he was limited to the task of constructing sizeable additional rooms without any alteration in the existing frontage. As galleries these Roman detailed rooms are admirably conceived. But, as originally designed, Barry's proposed building was a worthy conception with a great central dome and two smaller side domes, combining classical symmetry with picturesque effect which would have been 'one of the most universally admired buildings of this century' (*The Builder*, 149). It must therefore be regretted that he never had the opportunity of executing his best design.

So strongly did Barry feel the injury done him that in 1872 he published a pamphlet concerning both the new law courts and the national gallery competitions. But the harshest blow fell in 1870, when he was summarily and rudely dismissed by the new first commissioner Acton Ayrton from all further work at the new palace at Westminster as it was to be entrusted solely to the staff of the office of works, a move made on the grounds of economy and official control. To *The Builder* he wrote when smarting from the demand of the office of works to relinquish most of his and his father's drawings and papers connected with the new palace at Westminster—the only bequest to him in his father's will:

> What with the injustice I have suffered about the Law Courts, National Gallery, and this, it seems as if there was a dead-set made against me, and I am tempted to quit a profession where such things are possible. It would seem as if architects were outlawed and have no rights. (*The Builder*, 148)

Even his fellow Royal Academicians caused him pain. On the death of the architect Sydney Smirke (1877) the entrance to the new galleries at Burlington House remained unaltered, and therefore unsuited to Smirke's additions. The task of providing an adequate approach was, following the custom of appointing the treasurer as architect, honourably committed to Barry, and under his design the ornate doorway and easy stair of approach through the old building of Burlington House were substituted for the former steep staircase. Yet soon after his appointment the council passed a resolution, which he believed to be particularly directed against himself, prohibiting for the future the employment of their treasurer as architect.

A sensitive man by nature, Barry was embittered by these and other severe blows, which no doubt hastened his end; he felt himself to be 'worn out before his time' (Barry, 58). He sometimes regretted that he had not chosen the bar, and more than once declared that 'it sufficed for anything he would have liked to come in his way for it to end in failure' (*The Builder*, 148). Though full of energy and a seemingly indefatigable worker who left many unexecuted designs, he was never strong. An anxious man, for years he slept only three or four hours a night, and spent many wakeful hours reading, chiefly biography, modern histories, and books of travel. Continental travel—architecture and mountain scenery—afforded some respite. During his last years his health had been generally poor and he often envisaged a sudden death. On the morning of Tuesday 27 January 1880, however, he was cheerful about the future and left home, saying, 'I shall be back late to-night' (ibid.) as he had a meeting of council of the Royal Academy to attend. It was when about to move a series of resolutions at this meeting that he suddenly fell into the arms of his friend Pickersgill and, asking faintly 'Who is it?', expired from apoplexy and heart failure in the midst of his friends and colleagues. On 3 February 1880 he was buried in the Paddington old cemetery, Kilburn.

Simplicity, earnestness, amiability, and kindliness were

the prominent qualities which distinguished Barry in private life. His professional life was marred not only by disappointments but by his dogmatic intransigence that would allow for no view but his own. Though Barry devoted himself exclusively to no style he handled all with competence; 'he aimed at being a man of his day, neither a Greek nor a Goth, and ... strove to place the true principles of beauty above the mere question of form' (*The Builder*, 169); his methodical habit of mind and keen sense of proportion led no doubt to the preference for classic-based design in most of his compositions. He did not hesitate to declare his opinion that the prevalent taste for what was called 'pure Gothic' was no more than a passing fashion, unsuited to the real demands of the day, but he was no slavish 'classicist', and along with his best designs of this nature, such as the Birmingham and Midland Institute and the Covent Garden Opera House, are those which exhibit a degree of Gothic feeling which reveals he was not insensible to the charms of the style. Indeed, in street buildings his leaning was towards a French Renaissance blending of classic and Gothic, such as occurs in one of his most successful designs (made in association with St Aubyn), that for 'Temple Chambers' on the Thames Embankment (1875–9). It was in the freedom afforded by the French Renaissance, which allowed him fully to indulge his lifelong taste for high-quality sculpture resulting in more elaborately delicate ornament than is evident in his early works, that he found the happiest scope for the expression of his artistic ideas; most notably at Wykehurst Park, Sussex (1871–4), and in his two railway hotels and the Sick Children's Hospital, Great Ormond Street. Like his father, he was eminently practical in architecture. Yet his reputation never, and rightly so, rose to the heights of his father, partly because of his avowed eclecticism at a time when taste was more polarized, but more because, though talented, he did not inherit his father's genius. In planning he was admittedly a master. He was never satisfied with less than the very best arrangement and execution of practical detail in every building he undertook, and it is to his energy and conscientiousness in this department of his profession, as much perhaps as to his skill in artistic conception, that he owes the reputation he has left behind him of one of the foremost architects of his day who justly deserved more success than, through no fault of his own, came his way.

G. W. BURNET, *rev.* DAVID G. BLISSETT

Sources A. Barry, 'Introductory memoir', in E. M. Barry, *Lectures on architecture* (1881) · *The Builder*, 38 (1880), 147–50 · *Transactions of the Royal Institute of British Architects* (1879–80), 201–4 · *PICE*, 63 (1880–81), 322–6 · M. H. Port, ed., *The Houses of Parliament* (1976) · *CGPLA Eng. & Wales* (1880)
Archives BL, letters to Sir Austin Layard, Add. MSS 38995–38999, *passim* · RIBA BAL, Barry family file · RIBA BAL, drawings collection
Likenesses T. Woolner, marble bust, exh. RA 1882, RA · J. E. Mayall, photograph, repro. in E. M. Barry, *Lectures on Architecture* · W. Murden, group portrait, wood-engraving (*Associates of the Royal Academy in 1861*), BM, NPG; repro. in *ILN* (c.23 Feb 1861) · engraving, repro. in *The Builder*, 147 · photograph, RIBA BAL
Wealth at death under £70,000: probate, 20 Feb 1880, *CGPLA Eng. & Wales*

Barry, Elizabeth (1656×8–1713), actress and theatre manager, was the daughter of the barrister and royalist officer Colonel Robert Barry. As a child she became a member of the household of Sir William Davenant, the playwright and, until his death in 1668, manager of the Duke's Company. Sir William knew her father from his own royalist activities, and his wife, Henrietta Maria, Lady Davenant (according to the eighteenth-century actor and theatre historian Thomas Davies), gave Barry a genteel education and made her a constant companion. The Davenants kept a theatre 'nursery' for actresses in their home which was continued by Lady Davenant and their son Charles after William's death.

The development of the actress Barry is first listed in the Duke's Company for the 1673–4 season. At that time minor parts were not recorded, and her first known role is Draxilla in Thomas Otway's *Alcibiades* in September 1675 at the Dorset Garden Theatre. It is well known that she lacked promise, and her deficiencies seemed fatal—she could not speak lines adequately, sing, or dance. Although accounts vary and there are gaps in the evidence, it appears that John *Wilmot, earl of Rochester (1647–1680), and his friends noticed her from their seats in the pit, and he took a wager to make her 'the finest Player on the Stage' in under six months. In March 1676 she played Mrs Loveit in George Etherege's *Man of Mode*, perhaps because of a sudden incapacity of the usual performer. In July she played Leonora in Aphra Behn's *Abdelazer*, and she had an extraordinarily busy 1676–7 season; her parts included Hellena in Behn's *The Rover*, Lucia in Otway's *The Cheats of Scapin*, and Emilla in *The Fond Husband*. Robert D. Hume has hypothesized that her success as Mrs Loveit, not tutoring from Rochester, who was not known to be in London in the relevant months, accounts for the sudden blossoming of her career in the summer of 1676 (R. Hume, 'Elizabeth Barry's first roles and the cast of *The Man of Mode*', *Theatre History Studies*, 1985, 5.18). In fact, it is likely that Rochester took Barry to the country; among the first parts he taught her were the Little Gipsey in Behn's *The Rover* and Isabella in *Mustapha* (Betterton, 16–17). It was said that he made her rehearse these parts at least thirty times, twelve in costume, and she was a great hit as Isabella when she played it later. Rochester brought the king and duke and duchess of York to one of her performances, and Barry became a favourite; the duchess allowed Barry to act in her wedding and coronation clothes.

Barry, acknowledged in her time and this to have been the greatest actress of the Restoration, acted in repertory 142 named parts at the height of her career (1673–1708), and there may be more in cast lists that have not survived. In March 1677 she was a hit as Hellena in Behn's *The Rover* and the revival of the witty couple so successfully played by Nell Gwyn and Charles Hart a decade earlier was under way. By 1680 Barry was the leading lady for the Duke's Company and played opposite Thomas Betterton, then at the top of his profession. John Downes says that her performances in *The Orphan*, *Venice Preserv'd*, and *Fatal Marriage* 'gain'd her the Name of Famous Mrs. Barry, both at Court and City; for when ever She Acted any of [them], she forc'd

Tears from the Eyes of her Auditory' (Downes, 79). One of the most conscientious players of her time, she prepared carefully for every part. Her co-star Thomas Betterton wrote of her that:

> it has always been mine and Mrs. Barry's Practice to consult e'en the most indifferent Poet in any Part we have thought fit to accept of; and I may say it of her, she has often so exerted her self in an indifferent Part, that her Acting has given Success to such Plays, as to read would turn a Man's Stomach. (Gildon, 16)

Charles Gildon commented on the fact that she broke with the common practice of players, which was to ignore the play when they were not speaking. By continuing to act, she earned his compliment: 'This is to know her Part, this is to express the Passions in the Countenance and Gesture' (ibid., 40).

Not really a beauty, Barry mesmerized her audience with her commanding presence, expressive talent, and strong voice, which Cibber described as melodious. Anthony Aston said her facial expressions 'somewhat preceded her Action, as the latter did her Words, her Face ever expressing the Passions' (Aston, 302–3). She had dark hair and eyebrows, a striking rather than beautiful face with a sharply aquiline nose, and a physical abnormality: 'her mouth op'ning most on the Right Side, which she strove to draw t'other Way, and, at Times, composing her Face, as if sitting to have her Picture drawn' (ibid., 302). Unlike many of the tragic queens of the period she was not tall and was always heavy—in her mature years so heavy that Thomas Shadwell discussed costuming her in drapes and a mantle to disguise the size of her hips.

Rochester and Otway Barry and Rochester were lovers, and their daughter, Betty, was born in December 1677; their affair ended in 1678 with his blaming her sexual 'indiscretions'. Her affairs, real or reputed, with George Etherege, the earl of Dorset, and Sir Henry St John contributed to the establishment of the belief that actresses were usually of loose sexual morality. In the season of 1680–81 she was, according to William Chetwood, the object of 'a horse-laugh' from the audience when she spoke the lines of Nahum Tate's Cordelia in his *King Lear*—'Arm'd in my Virgin Innocence, I'll fly' (Chetwood, 28).

Rochester had helped Thomas Otway get his first play, *Alcibiades*, on the stage, and Barry played in it; she played Mrs Goodvile in *Friendship in Fashion* and Lady Dunce in *The Soldier's Fortune*. Otway created a series of parts for her that clinched her position at the top of her profession. She was Lavinia—the Juliet role—in his reworking of *Romeo and Juliet*, *Caius Marius*, but it was as Monimia in *The Orphan* (February 1680) that she made a sensation; Belvidera in *Venice Preserv'd* (February 1682) followed, and her reputation as a standard-setting tragic actress was made for the ages. If the letters published in *Familiar letters writ by … Rochester … with love-letters by the ingenious Mr. Thomas Otway, to … Mrs. Barry* (1697) can be believed, Otway fell in love with Barry and became obsessed with her. These letters, often printed in collected editions of Otway's works since 1712, have fed the legend, one doubted by the modern editor of his plays, J. C. Ghosh, that Barry treated Otway whimsically and cruelly. In one of these letters Otway wrote:

> I love you more than Health, or any Happiness, here or hereafter … though I have languished for seven long tedious Years of Desire, jealously and despairing, yet every Minute I see you I still discover something more bewitching … Remember Poor Otway.

In another he threatened to judge the entire sex by her treatment of him.

Tragedian and comic actress Today Barry's importance in the late seventeenth century's preference for pathetic and she-tragedies is recognized. John Dryden, Nahum Tate, John Banks, Thomas Otway, Nicholas Rowe, and Nathaniel Lee all wrote tragedies that depended upon her parts for their success. Like Sarah Siddons after her, she could rise to awe-inspiring majesty and also wring every ounce of pathos from a part. Edmund Curll, for instance, described a performance of Lee's *The Rival Queens* in which 'before our Eyes' the audience had seen Barry as Roxana 'murder an innocent Person' with unparalleled 'malice' and then in appealing to Alexander 'drew Tears from the greatest Part of the Audience' (Betterton, 22). In the 1680s as part of the United Company, she and Anne Bracegirdle were used to revive the tragedies with paired heroines, one strong, brave, and passionate and the other gentle with conservative feminine virtue, that Rebecca Marshall and Elizabeth Bowtell had played; plays such as William Congreve's *The Mourning Bride* (1697) and John Banks's *Cyrus the Great* (1696) were written with such parts.

Barry also became for her company the leading creator of witty, comic heroines, and in them she had the graceful, easy, genteel style that would make Anne Oldfield so admired in the next generation. At first Barry played a witty wife or virgin, but she soon added fallen women and adulterous wives, such as Mrs Goodvile in Otway's *Friendship in Fashion* (1678). In the 1690s she and Anne Bracegirdle were frequently paired as contrasting personality types, often as friends, collaborators, and even conspirators. Shadwell's bitter, innovative *The Wives' Excuse*, Thomas D'Urfey's revisionary *The Richmond Heiress*, and Congreve's dark *The Double-Dealer* and *The Way of the World* are important examples. In these plays Barry displayed her remarkable range of passions and ability to play complex personalities while Bracegirdle was usually required to exemplify feminine decorum.

Businesswoman and manager Managers and playwrights acknowledged Elizabeth Barry's power as a commanding presence in the theatre of her time and a sure hit-maker. Thomas Southerne said he wrote the long-popular *The Fatal Marriage* (1694) 'for her part, and her part has made the Play for me … by her power, and spirit of playing, she has breath'd a soul into it, that may keep it alive', and John Crowne wrote that adding her part to *Darius* was 'to the obvious benefit of the drama'. During the reign of James II Barry became the first actress, and perhaps the first player, to have a benefit, and the first to have benefits in her contract. She was also the usual assignee for benefits at the court between 1686 and 1694. Although the money remitted to her on royal warrants was in her name, it was payment for the whole company, which gave her some influence over the division of the money and some power over the other members of the company. Her wealth is clear from her financial dealings with Alexander Davenant, the son of Sir William. He had bought his brother Charles's share in Drury Lane in August 1687 and began swindling people almost immediately. Betterton, Christopher Rich, and his co-investor Sir Thomas Skipwith each lost money. In May 1692 Davenant borrowed £200 from Barry, and in April 1693 she gave him another £400 or £600 in the false belief that she had purchased a half share of profits.

In 1695 Barry was one of the three leaders of the secession from the United Company that brought the Lincoln's Inn Fields Company into existence. It is clear that until at least 1700, when Betterton gained sole management, she had the power of a co-manager. Vicious satires published during these years testify to the resentment such public role violation raised: 'To the most Virtuous and most Devoted Overkind, Notorious Madam Barry' (1689) begins, 'Retyre thou Miser from thy Shop the Stage' (Highfill, Burnim & Langhans, BDA, 1.319). Tom Brown accused Betterton and her of setting up as 'Sovereigns' and being niggardly towards 'the rest of the Cringing Fraternity' (T. Brown, The Works of Mr. Thomas Brown, 3 vols., 1707–8, 3.43). At least twenty-one epilogues were written for Barry; this important part of the performance often played the personality of the dramatic character against the reputation of the performer; in one, Barry spoke as 'herself' 'in a fret' after playing Madame de Vendosme in D'Urfey's The Intrigues at Versailles in 1697 (shortly after the actors' secession), that includes the lines:

How long, and oft, have I, in well wrought Scenes,
Dazled like Glittering Empresses and Queens
… The Play by Judges, has commended been,
And if it bring but the new Money in;
Money's a certain Medicine for my Spleen.
(Danchin, 6.402)

Congreve always cast Barry as a plotter, and her investment in Alexander Davenant and conduct during the actors' secession contributed to the portrait of a political Barry. Barry remained with the secession company through the time Vanbrugh took over management in 1704 and performed at his Queen's Theatre in the Haymarket. In addition, she performed numerous times at court and at venues such as the Inner Temple.

Assessment This same epilogue has Barry say:

How long, and oft, have I …
Acted all passions, love, grief, joy and shame,

and she did. In part after part she triumphed by portraying an exceptionally wide range of strong emotions. She was agonizingly repentant while remembering a range of other emotions as Calista in Nicholas Rowe's The Fair Penitent, passionate and jealous as Cassandra in Dryden's Cleomenes, wretched and noble in John Banks's plays about Jane Gray, Mary, Queen of Scots, and Anne Boleyn, and her mad scenes in such plays as The Fatal Marriage and Rowe's Jane Shore set a standard that generations of actresses tried to match. Contemporaries called her 'elegant', 'majestic',

and 'without rival'; after her performance in his Liberty Asserted, John Dennis wrote:

no Stage in Europe can boast of any thing that comes near to her Performance … That incomparable Actress changing like Nature which she represents, from Passion to Passion, from Extream to Extream, with piercing Force, and with easie Grace, changes the Hearts of all who see her with irresistible Pleasure. (Highfill, Burnim & Langhans, BDA, 1.322)

Colley Cibber said she had 'a power beyond all the actresses I have yet seen, or what your imagination can conceive' (ibid., 1.324). Elizabeth Howe, perhaps Barry's best modern critic, concludes that her 'powerful combination of pathos and eroticism in performance had its effect on comedy as well as tragedy' and argues that she created 'a striking series of wholly original heroines, prostitutes, and mistresses' in both forms (Howe, 129).

Cibber encapsulates her power—'Mrs. Barry, in Characters of Greatness, had a presence of elevated Dignity, her Mien and Motion superb, and gracefully majestick; her Voice full, clear, and strong, so that no Violence of Passion could be too much for her' (Fone, 92). Aphra Behn created the part of the suffering, wronged, fallen woman for her in The Revenge and a series of such plays by Behn, Mountfort, Southerne, and Crowne followed. In them such things as the double standard were problematized, and Barry could display the range of emotions common to tragedy. In the bitter or satirical comedies or in early examples of the English problem play, she displayed other modes of presentation and acting skills that looked towards Anne Oldfield and the elegant society women in troubled marriages.

After a brief retirement after performing the title role in Nathaniel Lee's Sophonisba on 17 June 1708 at Drury Lane, Barry returned to the stage as Mrs Frail on 7 April 1709 for William Congreve's Love for Love, a benefit for Thomas Betterton, and she and Bracegirdle supported him between them as Barry spoke the epilogue:

So we, to former leagues of friendship true
Have bid once more our peaceful Homes adieu …
In Peace and Ease Life's Remnant let him wear,
And hang his consecrated Buskin here.

She then acted the next season, and played many of her signature roles including Queen Elizabeth in The Unhappy Favourite, Isabella in The Fatal Marriage, Lady Easy in The Careless Husband, and Lady Cockwood in She Would if she Could. Her last recorded performance was as one of her most popular roles, Lady Easy in The Careless Husband, at Queen's on 13 June 1710. Barry retired to Acton in 1710; she was kept on the Queen's Theatre books at £100 per year with a guaranteed spring benefit to give her no less than £40. She died on 7 November 1713, perhaps after contracting rabies from her lapdog, and was buried in the Acton churchyard.   PAULA R. BACKSCHEIDER

Sources Highfill, Burnim & Langhans, BDA · W. Van Lennep and others, eds., The London stage, 1660–1800, 5 pts in 11 vols. (1960–68) · E. Howe, The first English actresses (1992) · C. Gildon, The life of Mr. Thomas Betterton (1710) · The works of Thomas Otway: plays, poems and love-letters, ed. J. C. Ghosh, 2 vols. (1932); repr. (1968) · W. R. Chetwood, A general history of the stage, from its origin in Greece to the *present time* (1749) • T. Davies, *Dramatic miscellanies*, 3 vols. (1784), vol. 3 • J. Downes, *Roscius Anglicanus*, ed. J. Milhous and R. D. Hume, new edn (1987) • C. Cibber, *An apology for the life of Colley Cibber*, new edn, ed. B. R. S. Fone (1968) • P. Holland, *The ornament of action: text and performance in Restoration comedy* (1979) • J. Powell, *Restoration theatre production* (1984) • J. D. Stewart, *Sir Godfrey Kneller and the English baroque portrait* (1983) • P. Danchin, ed., *The prologues and epilogues of the Restoration, 1660–1700*, 7 vols. (1981–8), vol. 6 • A. Aston, 'A brief supplement to Colley Cibber, esq.: his "Lives of the late famous actors and actresses" (1747)', in C. Cibber, *An apology for the life of Mr Colley Cibber*, new edn, ed. R. W. Lowe, 2 (1889), [297]–318; repr. (1966) • J. Milhous and R. D. Hume, eds., *A register of English theatrical documents, 1660–1737*, 1 (1991) • T. Betterton, [W. Oldys and others], *The history of the English stage* (1741) • GEC, *Peerage*

Likenesses G. Kneller, oils, 1700, priv. coll. • G. Kneller, oils, 1701, Hampton Court • M. Dahl, oils, City of New York Art Gallery • G. Kneller, oils, Strawberry Hill; portrait, Sothebys, 1972 • C. Knight, stipple (after Strawberry Hill portrait by G. Kneller), BM, NPG; repro. in F. G. Waldron, *The biographical mirrour* (1795) • engraving (as Gertrude), repro. in N. Rowe, ed., *The works of Mr William Shakespear* (1709), frontispiece • engraving, Hunt. L. • oils (after Strawberry Hill portrait by G. Kneller), Garr. Club • oils (after G. Kneller, 1701), Duke of Buccleuch's collection

Barry, Ernest James (1882–1968), sculler, was born on 13 February 1882 at 17 Hermit Road, Canning Town, London, the son of Henry Barry, lighterman, and his wife, Elizabeth Spall. While still an apprentice in 1902, he was entered for the Newcastle handicap, a sculling race on which considerable betting took place, and reached the final. He started favourite but lost by a length to Jack Dodds of Hexham, who, according to the local press, 'got five cuts at the water before Barry left the stakeboat'. There is little doubt that Barry was held back at the word 'go'. Coming out of his time, Barry won the 1903 Doggett's Coat and Badge 'pretty easily' but there are no further records until 1908. Then, still a virtual novice, he raced the Australian George Towns, who had already won the world championship four times and held the British championship since 1899. Towns led the lighter Barry as far as Chiswick church but was beaten by two lengths in 21 minutes 12.4 seconds, a time for the Putney to Mortlake course which was subsequently only once bettered in seventy years.

Barry challenged Dick Arnst of New Zealand for the world championship in August 1910 and the pair raced over 3¼ miles on the Zambezi River, 5 miles above Victoria Falls. Fearing the effects of the altitude, Barry delayed his effort until the last quarter-mile but both scullers stopped 300 yards from the finish. The huge New Zealander recovered first and paddled home alone. In 1911 and 1912 Barry successfully defended the *Sportsman* challenge cup for the British championship against W. Albany of Lea Bridge and W. H. Fogwell of Australia, and in July 1912, in appalling conditions, he took his revenge on Arnst over the Putney to Mortlake course to become the first English world champion for thirty-six years. After starting at odds of three to one on, Arnst led by two lengths at Harrods, where Barry closed the gap and with superior watermanship drew level above Hammersmith. The lead changed hands several times before Chiswick steps and at the crossing to Duke's Meadows, Barry, mastering the rough water better, gained two lengths within 150 yards.

Arnst was six lengths behind at Barnes Bridge but with a final effort closed to within two lengths. He could do no more, however, and stopped 80 yards from the post. The race was described as the finest professional sculling race ever seen in England.

Three months later Barry easily retained his title against the Canadian Edward Durnan over the same course, winning the *Sportsman* cup outright and £1000. In 1913 there followed a second defence of his world title for £500 a side against Harry Pearce of Australia, father of the 1928 Olympic winner and subsequent world champion Bob Pearce. Pearce led to Hammersmith but was six lengths down by Chiswick steps. One month after the outbreak of the First World War, in which he spent four years in the army, Barry beat another Australian, J. Paddon, and there were no further challengers until Felton in 1919.

The Zambezi River race of 1910 was Barry's sole defeat until, at the age of thirty-seven, in 1919, he lost to F. Felton of Australia, who was fitter and 2 stones heavier, when it was so rough at Putney it was possible to see under the bottom of the boats. This reverse was avenged by Barry a year later in 1920, before an estimated 150,000 spectators, on the Parramatta River, when he won by twelve lengths to gain his fifth world championship. He was, with some justice, known as the Incomparable. After his retirement as a sculler, Barry spent the rest of his working life as a professional coach in Denmark and Germany, enjoying such success that it is remarkable, and even sad, that he was never employed by British clubs. He was appointed king's bargemaster, a position from which he retired in 1952 because of ill health.

Over 6 feet in height, Barry still weighed no more than 11 stone 9 lb for his last race. Though a sufferer from asthma in old age, he retained full mental alertness and an upright, soldierly bearing. He married Lottie Hammerton, of Twickenham; there were two sons and three daughters of the marriage. Later in his life Barry had to sell all but two of his trophies to support himself and his daughter Thelma, who contracted poliomyelitis. He died at West Middlesex Hospital, Isleworth, on 21 July 1968.

DESMOND HILL, *rev.*

Sources *British Rowing Almanack* • H. Cleaver, *A history of rowing* (1957) • personal knowledge (1981) • private information (1981) • b. cert. • d. cert.

Wealth at death £5677: probate, 5 Sept 1968, *CGPLA Eng. & Wales*

Barry, George (1748–1805), topographical writer, was a native of Berwickshire. Educated at Edinburgh University, he was licensed to preach by the presbytery of Edinburgh. Initially he served as a tutor to the sons of gentlemen in Orkney, by whose patronage he became minister of second charge in Kirkwall, to which he was ordained on 18 September 1782. It was no doubt also advantageous that he married, on 12 August 1780, Sibella (*d.* 1812), daughter of John Yule, minister of first charge, Kirkwall. The couple had nine children.

Barry was translated and admitted to the nearby island and parish of Shapinsay on 12 September 1793. There is no evidence to support the view, stated in the *Dictionary of National Biography*, that Barry's unpopularity as a preacher was responsible for the establishment of a seceding congregation in Kirkwall, as this did not take place until 1796. Barry's interest in education led him to superintend the schools established in Orkney by the Society in Scotland for the Propagation of Christian Knowledge. He was also a contributor to Sir John Sinclair's *Statistical Account of Scotland* for the parishes of Kirkwall and St Ola, and of Shapinsay. His fame rests, however, on *The History of the Orkney Islands* (1805), which was published around the time of his death at Shapinsay on 11 May 1805. The work was well received and a second edition, with corrections and additions by the Revd James Headrick, appeared in 1808. Controversy arose over the extent to which Barry had used and acknowledged the still unpublished manuscripts of another Orkney minister and naturalist, George Low. William Elford Leach denounced Barry as a plagiarist in his preface to Low's *Fauna Orcadensis* (1813), although at least the manuscript of what was eventually published in 1879 as Low's, *A Tour through the Islands of Orkney and Schetland*, was cited as a source in the *History*. Samuel Hibbert, in acknowledging his own debt to Low in writing *A Description of the Shetland Islands* (1822), described the widespread circulation and free use of Low's manuscripts by other antiquaries. However culpable Barry may have been, he was therefore unfortunate to have been singled out for criticism. Barry received the degree of DD from Edinburgh University in 1804.

T. F. HENDERSON, *rev.* LIONEL ALEXANDER RITCHIE

Sources *GM*, 1st ser., 75 (1805), 879–80 · *Fasti Scot.*, new edn, 7.270–71 · J. Anderson, 'Introduction', in G. Low, *A tour through the islands of Orkney and Schetland* (1879), lxxii–lxxiii · Allibone, *Dict.* · S. Hibbert, *A description of the Shetland Islands* (1822), xii

Barry, Sir Gerald Reid (1898–1968), journalist and Festival of Britain administrator, was born at Fairfax, Berrylands Road, Surbiton, Surrey, on 20 November 1898, the fourth of six children of George Duncan Barry (*b.* 1864), who was then curate of St Mark's, Surbiton, and his wife, Edith Geraldine Reid. He was educated at Marlborough College, and in 1916 was elected to an exhibition at Corpus Christi College, Cambridge, where he planned to study history. But from 1917 to 1919 he served in the Royal Flying Corps and RAF, being demobilized with the rank of captain.

After the war Barry became a journalist, writing for the *Daily Express*. In 1921 he joined the *Saturday Review* as assistant editor, becoming its editor three years later at the age of twenty-six. The circumstances which led to his leaving that post in February 1930 caused a sensation and won him a great deal of sympathy and support. When its directors suddenly committed the *Saturday Review* to support Lord Beaverbrook's United Empire Party, without Barry's knowledge, he resigned, and his editorial staff went with him. The last issue of the *Saturday Review* edited by Barry strongly criticized the United Empire Party line; the next issue supported the Beaverbrook position. He and his editorial staff were applauded for their stand in defence of independent journalism.

Six days after his resignation the *Week-End Review* was created and Barry was announced as its editor. With his old editorial team, he produced the first number on 14

Sir Gerald Reid Barry (1898–1968), by Norman Parkinson, 1951

March 1930, which included messages of support from the prime minister, Baldwin, and public men from all parties. With a distinguished list of contributors, Barry made the *Week-End Review* a success, notably by running 'spreads' on subjects of topical interest. In 1932 he edited *A Week-End Calendar* and in 1933 he published *This England*, extracts from a *Week-End Review* column compiled from readers' submissions of absurdities from the English press. By late in 1933 the *Week-End Review* had lost its financial backing and in January 1934 it was merged into Kingsley Martin's *New Statesman*. Barry joined the board of directors of the *New Statesman* and the journal continued the famous 'This England' column and some other features from the *Week-End Review*.

In 1934 Barry became features editor of the popular, left-leaning daily, the *News Chronicle*, and its managing editor in February 1936. He brought to the paper his light touch and made it more readable. As editor through the challenging days of the abdication and Munich, and then throughout the Second World War, he enjoyed wittily attacking in his newspaper the blackshirts in Britain, Franco in Spain, Mussolini in Ethiopia, and the Japanese in Manchuria. He was also the founder of the celebrated *News Chronicle* schools competition. He resented the interference of the *New Chronicle's* chairman, Walter Layton, in editorial matters—most notably on the eve of the Munich agreement, when Layton prevented him from publishing evidence of Hitler's plans for further annexations. While Layton was a war civil servant, from 1940 to 1944, Barry had a freer hand to push the paper in a leftward direction, as he successfully excluded the acting chairman, Laurence

Cadbury, from editorial decisions. In 1947 he resigned as editor, but remained on the board.

Barry's next position was the one for which he is best remembered. On 10 March 1948 Herbert Morrison, lord president of the council, announced that Barry had accepted the job of director-general of the Festival of Britain, 1951. Barry was a founding member of the Labour think-tank PEP (Political and Economic Planning), along with Morrison's under-secretary, Max Nicholson, who helped Morrison select most of the festival committee. In addition, Barry had written an open letter to Stafford Cripps, as president of the Board of Trade, in the *News Chronicle* (14 September 1945) supporting the proposal of the Royal Society of Arts that the centenary of the 1851 exhibition should be marked by another international exhibition, focusing on trade and culture. In the end an international exhibition was deemed far too expensive and impractical in view of post-war shortages and the costs of reconstruction. In 1947 it was decided that a smaller, national exhibition should be funded by the government. Nicholson called Barry 'a great impresario', and Hugh Casson, who served as the 1951 South Bank site's chief architect, claimed that 'all architects knew him as a lover of architecture' (*The Times*, 25 Nov 1968). Barry saw the 1951 festival as a great opportunity for patronizing the arts, including poetry, music, painting, sculpture, architecture, design, and engineering. To work on the festival he picked a young team, most of whom had gained their experience in the war and were enthusiastic to display their designs and buildings to the public. Casson wrote upon Barry's death that 'he was marvellously equipped by his endless curiosity, seriousness of purpose, enthusiastic receptivity to ideas, personal courage and his capacity—amounting almost to genius—for getting the best out of everybody who worked for him' (ibid.). Barry bore three years of financial crises, opposition, bad press, and worse weather, guiding the festival to its completion and ultimate success. There were eight official government-funded exhibitions in England, Scotland, Northern Ireland, and Wales, twenty-two designated arts festivals, and a pleasure garden in Battersea. Eight and a half million people visited the London South Bank exhibition and the BBC aired 2700 festival-related broadcasts. On the local level, 2000 cities, towns, and villages across the UK organized and funded a festival event of some kind.

Barry, who famously described the festival as 'a tonic to the nation' after the privations of the war years, was determined that it should be 'a manifestation of gaiety and ordered imagination in a world that he knew to be short of both'. As well as restoring morale and raising aesthetic standards, he had a vision of the festival as 'a corporate act of national reassessment and of affirmation of our faith in the future', reflecting the national characteristics, ideals, and activities of an entire people (Leventhal, 449). In the event, the ideal of putting on a people's show was realized only to a limited extent, for instead of being staged by the people, the festival was devised mainly by professionals for them. Some of the values behind the festival have been criticized by later generations: 'radical, deep-felt, middle-

class, humorous, redolent to contemporary eyes of do-gooding and Hampstead, of petition-signing and Ealing films', as one of Barry's team recalled (*The Times*, 25 Nov 1968), but they were genuinely held. The organizers themselves were identified as typically 'the backbone of the BBC' (Frayn, 331). In 1951 Barry was knighted for his work on the festival and a plaque commemorating him was unveiled outside the Festival Hall in 1971.

Following his festival triumph and his wide-ranging interests, Barry served in a series of posts as consultant. These included working with the London county council on the redevelopment of the Crystal Palace site, advising the National Farmers' Union on public policy, and chairing the new Barbican committee. He also served on the government committee on the scope of town and country planning, the Cities Development Research Committee, and as deputy chairman of a committee on obscene libel laws. In 1959 Granada TV made him executive in charge of educational programming. He was made an honorary fellow of the Royal Institute of British Architects (1940) and a fellow of the Royal Society of Arts. In 1965 he edited, with J. Bronowski, James Fisher, and Julian Huxley, *Health and Wealth*.

Barry was married four times, and was three times divorced. In 1921 he married Gladwys Williams, daughter of G. Chishom Williams, a surgeon, and they had one son. In 1932 he married Mrs Helen Edith Selwyn Jepson, daughter of Richard Rigg, a barrister and former MP who later became mayor of the city of Westminster. His third marriage, in 1944, was to Mrs Vera Burton, daughter of Vladimir Poliakoff, and they also had one son. In 1959 he married Mrs Diana Wooton Schlumberger. He died in London on 21 November 1968.   BECKY E. CONEKIN

Sources *The Times* (22 Nov 1968), 12f · H. Casson, *The Times* (25 Nov 1968), 10f · K. Martin, *The Times* (28 Nov 1968), 10h · M. Banham and B. Hillier, *A tonic to the nation: the Festival of Britain, 1951* (1976) · B. Conekin, *The autobiography of a nation: the 1951 Festival of Britain, representing Britain in the post-war era* [forthcoming] · M. Frayn, 'Festival', *Age of austerity*, ed. M. Sissons and P. French (1963), 330–52 · B. Donoghue and G. W. Jones, *Herbert Morrison: portrait of a politician* (1973) · R. Hewison, *Culture and consensus: England, art and politics since 1940* (1995) · F. M. Leventhal, '"A tonic to the nation": the Festival of Britain, 1951', *Albion*, 27 (1995), 445–53 · b. cert. · *CGPLA Eng. & Wales* (1969)
Archives BLPES, corresp. and papers | PRO, MSS and statements relating to 1951 Festival of Britain, Work 25/21, Work 25/44 | FILM BFI NFTVA, news footage | SOUND BL NSA
Likenesses N. Parkinson, photograph, 1951, NPG [*see illus.*] · photograph, repro. in *The Times* · photographs, repro. in Banham and Hillier, eds., *A tonic to the nation* · photographs, Hult. Arch. · portraits, PRO, photographic records, work 25/224
Wealth at death £77,148: probate, 4 Feb 1969, *CGPLA Eng. & Wales*

Barry, Gerat (*d.* 1646), army officer in the Spanish service and military writer, was probably the individual of that name who embarked from Kinsale with the Spanish forces in March 1601 in the company of his father, David Fitz Garrot Barry of Rincorran (near Kinsale), his mother, and three brothers. He subsequently entered the Spanish service and was employed for a time in the fleet and later in the Netherlands and Germany. He distinguished himself as a private soldier at the siege of Rheinsberg in 1608 and was promoted through the ranks to ensign (1623) and captain (before 1627) in the regiment of Owen Roe O'Neill. He served at the siege of Breda of 1624–5, probably the most celebrated action of the Eighty Years' War between Spain and the United Provinces. Barry's *Siege of Breda* (1627) was actually a translation from the work of Hugo Hermannus published the previous year. The only significant change he made was to insert three pages on an action in which he participated, detailing how five Irish companies repulsed a sally. Barry was pensioned off in 1632 and was awarded the honorific 'councillor of war' in consideration of his long and distinguished service.

Barry's *Discourse of Military Discipline* (1634) is of particular interest because of the detailed examples of contemporaneous infantry battle formations. The fact that most of the examples were smaller and more linear than the traditional *tercio* would suggest that Spanish tactics were more modern than has usually been supposed. The book was a primer for would-be Irish mercenary officers in the Spanish service and was written at a time when Barry was involved in attempts to recruit from Ireland. In February 1634 he was commissioned major in the regiment of John Barry to be recruited in Ireland, though there is no evidence that the regiment actually materialized.

In 1641 Barry was one of the colonels authorized to raise regiments from the soldiers of Wentworth's disbanded army. In the event only one regiment was actually embarked before objections from the English parliament, and the rising of October 1641, put a halt to further shipments. Barry's regiment was awaiting embarkation at Kinsale in November 1641 when it was dispersed by order of the lords justices. The following month Barry was selected as general of the insurgent army in Munster. Like most of the Irish veterans of wars in the Netherlands, Barry was skilled in siegecraft but less assured in battle or campaigning. In June 1642 he managed to capture King John's Castle in Limerick by systematically erecting forts and a boom to deter relief shipping. He then undermined the main bastion and, not having sufficient gunpowder, fired a mine by burning the supports thereby collapsing a face of the bastion. In September 1642, however, Barry's army of some 6400 was routed by about one third that number of British forces at Liscarroll in north Cork. During a brief cavalry action Barry's ill-disciplined infantry fled across a nearby bog and escaped with the loss of some 600 men. While Barry retained nominal command of the Munster forces he was seen as 'old and unfortunate' (*Memoirs of James, Lord Audley*, 56) and James Touchet, earl of Castlehaven, assumed leadership from him during the 1643 campaigning season. Barry died in Limerick City in early March 1646.

The pen-picture of Barry by Richard Bellings, secretary to the Irish Confederation and its historian, is of an ageing plodder suddenly promoted beyond his level of competence to wage a type of warfare of which, for all his forty years' service, he had very little experience:

> … two things rendred him lesse capable of exercising soe great a charge. The one was … such a temper of abiletys and

parts as moved excellently by direction, but irregularly when they were the ballance upon which their owne motion depended. (*Irish Confederation*, ed. Gilbert, 1.74)

Barry's second handicap, according to Bellings, was that he was 'accustomed to the warre of Flanders, where all engines and all provisions attend almost inseparably upon the army', leaving him ill-prepared 'to follow the motions of an active warre, which … would call him now to the west, now to the east, and was not to relye for bread upon an infaillable providore, or expect a traine of artillery' (*Irish Confederation*, ed. Gilbert, 1.75). The picture is not entirely fair and Barry showed, in his capture of King John's Castle, that he could improvise in the absence of gunpowder. Despite his limitations, the Munster confederates might have done better to retain Barry than experiment with five different commanders over the period 1643 to 1647.   PÁDRAIG LENIHAN

Sources B. Jennings, ed., *Wild geese in Spanish Flanders, 1582–1700*, IMC (1964), 85, 103, 190, 264, 283, 287, 301, 580, 584 · *History of the Irish confederation and the war in Ireland … by Richard Bellings*, ed. J. T. Gilbert, 1 (1882), 74–5 · B. O'Ferrall and D. O'Connell, *Commentarius Rinuccinianus de sedis apostolicae legatione ad foederatos Hiberniae Catholicos per annos 1645–1649*, ed. J. Kavanagh, IMC, 1 (1932), 249 · B. O'Ferrall and D. O'Connell, *Commentarius Rinuccinianus de sedis apostolicae legatione ad foederatos Hiberniae Catholicos per annos 1645–1649*, ed. J. Kavanagh, IMC, 2 (1936), 488–9 · H. Gillman, ed., 'The rise and progress of the rebellion in Munster, 1642', *Journal of the Cork Historical and Archaeological Society*, 2nd ser., 2 (1896), 77–82 · J. Rastall, 'A relation of the rebellion in and about Limerick', 1642, TCD, MS 840, 91–6 · deposition of Richard Welsh, TCD, MS 829 (co. Limerick), 350 · *The memoirs of James, Lord Audley, earl of Castlehaven, his engagement and carriage in the wars of Ireland* (1680) · G. Carew, *Pacata Hibernia*, 238 · R. A. Stradling, *The Spanish monarchy and Irish mercenaries, the wild geese in Spain, 1618–68* (1994), 34, 38–9 · private information [D. Rankin]

Barry, Henry (1749/50–1822), army officer, of parents now unknown, was commissioned ensign in the 85th regiment on 22 February 1762. In 1768 he transferred to the 52nd regiment in Quebec, Canada, where he was promoted lieutenant on 23 September 1772. Two years later the 52nd moved to Boston, Massachusetts, and Barry presumably served with his regiment at the battle of Bunker Hill (17 June 1775), the capture of New York, and in skirmishes in New Jersey. He found time, nevertheless, to write two pamphlets (anonymously) stressing the advantage to America of the British connection, and the strength of the British army and navy. Having been promoted captain on 4 January 1777, he sailed for England with the 52nd a year later, but returned in 1780 as deputy to the adjutant-general of the forces in America, Lord Rawdon (later marquess of Hastings). Barry accompanied Rawdon to South Carolina and was credited with 'some of the best written despatches ever transmitted from an army on service to the British cabinet' (*GM*, 571). Captured at the battle of Cutaw Springs on 8 September 1781, he was exchanged the following March.

After a short period in England, Barry went to India with the local rank of lieutenant-colonel (13 June 1782). During the closing stages of the Second Anglo-Mysore War (1780–4), after 'filling with distinguished reputation the most confidential offices' (BL OIOC, H/612.437), he was sent with full powers to negotiate peace with Tipu Sultan, but found that a treaty had already been signed at Mangalore on 11 March 1784. He remained in south India, taking part (1785) in the return of Pondicherry to the French under the terms of the treaty of Versailles (1783), and serving in the Third Anglo-Mysore War (1790–92). His promotion to lieutenant-colonel of the 71st regiment (28 May 1790) and exchange into the 39th regiment (8 December 1790) were stigmatized by the war office as 'shameful jobs' (*Correspondence of … Cornwallis*, 2.142).

Barry returned to England in 1792, and after pleading with the East India Company for better field allowances for the king's regiments in India, retired on 31 March 1793. He was promoted colonel on 19 July 1793. His retirement was spent mainly in Bath, where his wide circle of friends included Mrs Hester Piozzi, and he acquired a reputation as both 'a great talker' and 'the greatest of adulators' (*Diaries*, ed. Bickley, 2.39, 327). Barry died aged seventy-two, in his lodgings at 19 Queen Square, Bath, on 2 November 1822, and was buried on 6 November at St Swithin's, Walcot, Bath. He left all his property, principally farms in Glamorgan, to his nephew, Robert Barry of Dublin.

R. J. BINGLE

Sources Army List · *GM*, 1st ser., 93/1 (1823), 571 · PRO, WO 25/30, 31 · will, PRO, PROB 11/564, fol. 111v · BL OIOC, H/91.85, H/612.437 · Madras military consultations, BL OIOC · *Report on American manuscripts in the Royal Institution of Great Britain*, 4 vols., HMC, 59 (1904–9) · *The papers of General Nathanael Greene*, ed. D. M. Conrad, others, and M. J. King, 9–10 (1997–8) · W. S. Moorsom, ed., *Historical record of the fifty-second regiment (Oxfordshire light infantry), from the year 1755 to the year 1858* (1860) · C. T. Atkinson, *The Dorsetshire regiment*, 2 vols. (1947) · *Correspondence of Charles, first Marquis Cornwallis*, ed. C. Ross, 3 vols. (1859) · *The diaries of Sylvester Douglas (Lord Glenbervie)*, ed. F. Bickley, 2 vols. (1928) · [E. Mangin], *Piozziana, or, Recollections of the late Mrs Piozzi* (1833)

Archives BL OIOC, Home Misc. series, H/91.85; H/612.437 · BL OIOC, Madras military consultations · PRO, WO 25/30, 31; PROB 11/564, fol. 111v

Likenesses H. D. Hamilton, oils, 1794–5, Castle Forbes, co. Longford · J. S. Copley, oils, exh. Leger Galleries 1992, priv. coll. · M. H. G. Jervis, pen-and-ink drawing, Bath Central Library, Hunt's scrapbook, 2.31 · E. Mangin, pen-and-ink silhouette, Bath Central Library, Chapman scrapbook, 2.139 · W. Nutter, stipple (after S. Shelley), BM, NPG

Wealth at death see will, PRO, PROB 11/564, fol. 111v

Barry, James, first Baron Barry of Santry (1603–1673), judge, was the eldest son of Richard Barry (*d.* in or after 1648), a merchant of Dublin, later mayor of Dublin and politician, and Anne (*d.* 1667), daughter of James Cusack, of Rathgar, Dublin. Barry was educated at Trinity College, Dublin, graduated BA in 1621, proceeded MA in 1624, and in 1627 was incorporated MA at both Oxford and Cambridge. He was called to the English bar at Lincoln's Inn in 1628 and to the Irish by King's Inns two years later. In 1629, remarkably for a man so young, he secured an appointment that presaged his meteoric rise—that of prime serjeant in Ireland. The circumstances were controversial. Charles I wished to nominate Maurice Eustace, by many years Barry's senior in age and experience, but the recently retired lord deputy, Henry Carey, Viscount Falkland, had already promised the post to Barry, and Eustace

was obliged to wait his turn. Barry was elected MP for Lismore, co. Waterford, in 1634, but barely a month later was made a baron of the exchequer, beating off yet another challenge, presented on this occasion by a protégé of Richard Boyle, earl of Cork. In 1637 Barry published *The Case of Tenures upon the Commission of Defective Titles*, in essence the advice of a split Irish judicial bench on a reference to them by Lord Deputy Wentworth on the question of the appropriate tenurial basis on which to make new grants of Irish land. There is a fulsome dedication of the work to Wentworth. *The Case of Tenures* prompted a celebrated rejoinder from Sir Henry Spelman.

Barry was knighted in 1640. He attended on the House of Lords in 1641, was absent from Ireland in 1642–4, and in 1648–50 was again in England, collecting, in collaboration with Sir Gerard Lowther, chief justice of the Irish common pleas, money for the Irish service. Of Barry's apparent conversion to the side of parliament it was later written: 'Spoiling the Saxon is an occupation that has ever united Irishmen, however widely divided in opinion, and in Barry's case it did not imply any diminution in his loyalty to the throne' (Ball, *Judges*, 1.265–6). Lowther regained judicial functions under the interregnum, but suspicions of Barry must have persisted, for although his claims to restoration were canvassed in 1654, he had for the moment to rest content with the permission granted him to resume legal practice. In 1659 Barry, representing co. Dublin, played a significant role in supporting Irish moves to secure the return of Charles II, and in the following year he chaired the convention in Dublin that represented protestant Ireland and which declared for Charles II in May. His reward was not long delayed: he was named chief justice of the Irish king's bench in November 1660, the accompanying salary increase citing Barry's 'faithful service to our dear father of glorious memory and eminent loyalty to us' (Lascelles).

In 1661 Barry was made Baron Barry of Santry. Two years later he presided at the trial of the conspirators involved in Colonel Blood's plot to seize Dublin Castle. Delivering sentence, Barry promised, with a wealth of biblical allusions, death and damnation for all rebels and traitors. Eustace, Barry's early rival, became Irish lord chancellor in 1660, and, when he died in 1665 and the following year when a further vacancy seemed likely, Barry was considered on both occasions for the job. James Butler, duke of Ormond, was enthusiastic but Edward Hyde, earl of Clarendon, was opposed, although considering him 'an extraordinarily able man and an excellent judge' (Ball, *Judges*, 1.336). Barry, in his estimation, was unpredictable and lazy and the bishops mistrusted him. Barry was closely involved throughout his career in the affairs of King's Inns, serving as treasurer in 1635–6 and again from 1661 to 1664.

Barry married Catharine, daughter of Sir William Parsons, Irish lord justice in 1640–43, and Elizabeth, daughter of John Lany, an alderman of Dublin. They had four sons and four daughters. Barry died in Dublin on 9 February 1673 and was buried on 14 February in St Mary's Chapel in Christ Church Cathedral. The barony became extinct in

1739 by forfeiture upon Barry's great-grandson, Henry, fourth Baron Barry (1710–1751), being convicted of the murder of a footman. Henry was reprieved (which has caused some experts to doubt the presumed fate of the barony), but not before a fresh axe had been acquired to carry out his planned beheading.   W. N. OSBOROUGH

Sources F. E. Ball, *The judges in Ireland, 1221–1921*, 1 (1926), 264–6, 335–6 · F. E. Ball, 'Some notes on the Irish judiciary in the reign of Charles II, 1660–1685', *Journal of Cork Historical and Archaeological Society*, ser. 2, 7 (1902), 90 · B. W. Adams, *History and description of Santry and Cloghran parishes co. Dublin* (1883) · E. Barry, 'Records of the Barrys', *Journal of Cork Historical and Archaeological Society*, ser. 2, 7 (1902), 1 · A. Clarke, *Prelude to restoration in Ireland* (1999) · C. Kenny, *King's Inns and the kingdom of Ireland* (1992) · R. Lascelles, ed., *Liber munerum publicorum Hiberniae … or, The establishments of Ireland*, later edn, 2 vols. in 7 pts (1852) · E. Keane, P. Beryl Phair, and T. U. Sadleir, eds., *King's Inns admission papers, 1607–1867*, IMC (1982) · GEC, *Peerage* · Burtchaell & Sadleir, *Alum. Dubl.*

Likenesses oils, King's Inns, Dublin; repro. in C. Kenny, *King's Inns*

Wealth at death land at Santry in 1641: details for 1641 and 1664 in Adams, *History and description of Santry and Cloghran parish*

Barry, James, fourth earl of Barrymore (1667–1748), politician and Jacobite conspirator, was the younger son of Richard Barry, second earl of Barrymore (*bap.* 1630, *d.* 1694), and his third wife, Dorothy Ferrar of Dromore, co. Down. He was also heir to one of the oldest baronies in Ireland, being descended from an Anglo-Norman dynasty settled there since the twelfth century. Evidence about his family's political allegiances during the political upheavals of the seventeenth century, however, is meagre and confusing. His father's second wife was the daughter of Henry Laurence, the president of Cromwell's council, but after the Restoration Richard quickly acquired a foot regiment, took his seat in the Irish House of Lords in May 1661, and appears to have sat in James II's Irish parliament in May 1689. By contrast, his elder son, Laurence, was attainted by that same parliament only to be fully restored following William III's victory at the battle of the Boyne. He took his seat in the Lords in August 1695 and signed the association in defence of the king on 2 December 1697, less than two years before his death.

James Barry succeeded his half-brother to the earldom on 17 April 1699, and immediately went to the trouble of securing a pardon for any treason that members of his family might be considered guilty of by virtue of their actions during and after the revolution. He himself had declared early against King James, being appointed a lieutenant-colonel in William of Orange's army on 31 December 1688. When the War of the Spanish Succession broke out in 1702, Barrymore again took up the profession of arms, bought himself the 13th regiment of foot for 1400 guineas from his brother-in-law, Sir John Jacob, and subsequently served with distinction in the Peninsula under Lord Galway, being taken prisoner in the English defeat at Almanza on 25 April 1707. At or about the time of his capture he achieved the rank of brigadier-general, and was subsequently promoted major-general in 1709 and lieutenant-general in 1711. He might even have gone on to pursue a professional military career had he not been

James Barry, fourth earl of Barrymore (1667–1748), attrib. John Riley

obliged to sell his regiment for party political reasons as part of the proscription of high-ranking tories which followed the abortive Jacobite rebellion of 1715.

Barrymore's first wife was Elizabeth Boyle (*bap.* 1662, *d.* 1703), a daughter of Charles Boyle, third Baron Clifford, and Lady Jane Seymour, and the granddaughter of the third duke of Somerset. Together they had a son and two daughters before her premature death in October 1703 brought him a fortune of £10,000. In June 1706 Barrymore eloped with Lady Elizabeth Savage (*d.* 1714), daughter of Richard *Savage, fourth Earl Rivers, and Penelope Downes, with whom he had one daughter. Following the deaths of his new father-in-law in 1712 and his wife two years later, by the summer of 1714 Barrymore was firmly installed at Rock Savage in Cheshire as heir both to the extensive Rivers estates in that and the neighbouring counties and to the influence that these exerted over the political life of north-west England. On 12 July 1716 he married again, this time Lady Anne Chichester (*d.* 1753), daughter of Arthur Chichester, third earl of Donegal, and Catharine Forbes; they had four sons and two daughters. Having taken his seat in the Irish House of Lords in February 1704, he first entered the English House of Commons in 1710 as tory member for the notoriously venal borough of Stockbridge in Hampshire. In 1713 he lost his seat there to Sir Richard Steele, only to be reinstated on petition the following April. At the general election of 1715 he was returned for the Lancashire borough of Wigan, which constituency, except for the parliament of 1727–34, he continued to represent for the next thirty-two years.

At Westminster, Barrymore's initial partisan affiliation

was to the earl of Nottingham's parliamentary connection; and though he attended the Commons with reasonable regularity, and even acted on occasion as a tory whip during the reigns of Queen Anne and George I, he rarely if ever spoke in the house. Following his dismissal from the army he did his best to avoid any factional associations at the national level that might further prejudice his personal interests; but with respect to the politics of his own locality he not only made strategic use of his extensive rental to influence county elections in Lancashire and Cheshire, but seems positively to have revelled in the complex partisan intrigues which bedevilled the boroughs of Chester, Liverpool, and Wigan during the first half of the eighteenth century. In 1727, though, his growing reputation for political duplicity led the tory hardliners then in the ascendant at Wigan to oust him from his parliamentary seat, following which he quit politics in England and withdrew to his estates in co. Cork. During the latter part of Lord Carteret's term of office as lord lieutenant, Barrymore seems to have played an active role in the Irish privy council, to which he was first appointed in January 1714, and of which he was to remain a member for the rest of his life. During this sojourn in Ireland he did make periodic visits to north-west England, helping promote the tory cause at Chester and Liverpool and successfully regaining his seat at Wigan in 1734.

However, it is Barrymore's seemingly impulsive espousal of the Pretender's cause late in life which not only merits his recognition as a figure of national importance, but begs some difficult questions with regard to his motivations. In the first place, despite several anecdotal suggestions to the contrary, there is no substantive evidence that Barrymore had ever shown conspicuous loyalty to or enthusiasm for the house of Stuart before the outbreak of war with Spain in 1739—or indeed that he was ever identified as a likely supporter of its restoration by the notoriously optimistic Jacobite agents and courtiers prior to that date. Nevertheless, a year later he was at the centre of efforts being made by the English Jacobites to secure French military backing for a projected rising and in May 1740, despite his seventy-three years, he travelled to Paris in person to persuade Cardinal Fleury of 'the feasibleness of the undertaking' (Cruickshanks, HoP, Commons, 1715–54, 1.440). Those associated with Barrymore in this enterprise baulked at providing a foreign government with written pledges of their commitment, however, and the plan came to nothing until, following Fleury's death in 1743, a new French ministry at last determined to give it their support. A force of 10,000 men was to land in Essex in February 1744 with sufficient weapons and ammunition to arm the English rebels expected to meet them there. As part of this agreement, 'Lord Barrymore, on whom the English nobles rely to carry out this great scheme, because of his unfailing zeal and his military experience, pledges himself … to be on the coast to welcome the French troops' (ibid., 441). Moreover, he not only engaged himself to provide £12,000 from his own pocket to help finance the rising, but even sent his own son Richard to France to accompany the invading force. By the time the fleet set sail, though, the British government had learned of the plot from a Jacobite agent and discovered evidence among his papers that implicated the aged earl. Taken up on 23 February, Barrymore was first examined by the lords of the council and then placed under house arrest until the end of March, when, with the French expedition abandoned, he was finally released on bail. His treasonable conversations continued unabated, but without a French force to engage the government's regular troops he was acutely aware that a domestic rising of artisans and tenant farmers would be tantamount to suicide. Even when Charles Edward Stuart crossed the border at the head of a Scottish army in November 1745, the English and Welsh Jacobites continued to procrastinate, and poor communications sealed the expedition's fate. A message from Lord Barrymore, promising to join the Young Pretender in London, was taken to Derby by his son Richard just two days after the rebels withdrew from the town.

Barrymore was saved from prosecution and probable execution only by his advanced age. So ill-concealed were his movements and correspondence during the years prior to the 'Forty-Five that the government rightly judged that a public humiliation of 'the Pretender's General', achieved in 1747 when Murray of Broughton turned king's evidence against Lord Lovat, would be of more value to the Hanoverian cause than another show trial. Barrymore died on 5 January 1748, probably in Dublin, and was buried at Castle Lyons, co. Cork.

STEPHEN W. BASKERVILLE

Sources E. Cruickshanks, 'Barry, James', HoP, Commons, 1715–54, 1.440–42 · L. Colley, In defiance of oligarchy: the tory party, 1714–60 (1982) · Royal Arch., Stuart papers · JRL, Crawford (Haigh) MSS · Puleston letters, NL Wales, MSS 3577–3583 · The manuscripts of the duke of Somerset, the marquis of Ailesbury, and the Rev. Sir T. H. G. Puleston, bart., HMC, 43 (1898) · J. R. Robinson, The last earls of Barrymore, 1769–1824 (1894) · B. Lenman and J. S. Gibson, The Jacobite threat—England, Scotland, Ireland, France: a source book (1990) · E. Cruickshanks, Political untouchables: the tories and the '45 (1979) · F. J. McLynn, France and the Jacobite rising of 1745 (1981) · P. K. Monod, Jacobitism and the English people, 1688–1788 (1989) · GEC, Peerage, new edn · J. Lodge, The peerage of Ireland, 1 (1754), 306–8

Archives JRL, Crawford (Haigh) MSS · NL Wales, letters to Francis Price · NL Wales, Puleston letters · Royal Arch., Stuart papers

Likenesses oils, c.1715, Tatton Park, Cheshire · attrib. J. Riley, portrait, priv. coll. [see illus.]

Barry, James (1741–1806), history painter, printmaker, and author, was born on 11 October 1741, in a modest cottage in Water Lane in Blackpool, a suburb of Cork, to John Barry and Juliana Reardon. He was the eldest child in a family that grew to include three more sons, Patrick, Redmond, and John, and a daughter, Mary Ann. His father, who worked as a builder or bricklayer, also apparently kept a tavern in Henry Street, Hamon's Marsh, but ended as a coasting trader between Ireland and England. While the father is said to have been a protestant, Juliana raised the children as Roman Catholics.

Formative years The little that is known about Barry's early years follows a script often encountered in the lives of artists. Demonstrating an aptitude for art at an early

James Barry (1741–1806), self-portrait, *c*.1786 [completed 1803]

age, he pursued his passion despite parental opposition. Cork, however, had few resources to offer, and after working with the landscape painter John Butts, Barry departed in 1763 for Dublin aged twenty-two. Here, upon exhibiting his picture *The Baptism of the King of Cashel by St. Patrick* (exh. 1763; Terenure College, Dublin) at the Dublin Society for the Encouragement of Arts, Manufactures, and Commerce, he met with instant acclaim, the society awarding him a special premium for history painting and three parliamentarians purchasing his work for the House of Commons. Barry studied in the society's drawing school under Jacob Ennis. At this time he also gained the support of an important mentor, the statesman and aesthetician Edmund Burke. In spring 1764 Burke arranged for him to travel to London to work for the painter and architect James 'Athenian' Stuart (1713–1788), and then, along with his kinsman William Burke, supported him for an extended period of study on the continent.

Departing from London in October 1765, Barry spent ten months in Paris before arriving in Rome in October the following year. A great deal of his correspondence has been published in *The Works of James Barry*, revealing a sharp critical intelligence as well as indications of the persecution mania that was to overshadow his career. Writing from Rome, Barry eloquently expressed his feelings on encountering the classical works about which he had heard so much:

> really and indeed I never before experienced any thing like that ardor, and I know not how to call it, that state of mind one gets on studying the antique.—A fairy land it is, in which one is apt to imagine he can gather treasures, which neither Raffael nor Michel Angelo were possessed of. (*Works*, 2.248)

Among the international artistic community his friends included the Scottish painters John and Alexander Runciman, the English sculptors James Paine jun., and Joseph Nollekens, the French artists Louis Gabriel Blanchet and Dominique Lefèvre, as well as the Savoyard John Francis Rigaud, who later became a Royal Academician in London.

Barry left Rome on 22 April 1770, having sent back to London his canvas *The Temptation of Adam* (NG Ire.), which was exhibited the following spring at the Royal Academy. He travelled for nine months through northern Italy, and while he was in Bologna the Accademia Clementina awarded him a diploma, for which honour he executed his picture *Philoctetes in the Island of Lemnos* (Pinacoteca Nazionale, Bologna), an essay in the Burkean sublime.

London career The Royal Academy, which had been created while Barry was in Rome, welcomed the artist on his return to England. In 1772, following the exhibition of *The Temptation of Adam* in the previous year, he exhibited three classical subjects, the most successful of which, judging by the number of prints made after it, was his *Venus Rising from the Sea* (Hugh Lane Municipal Gallery of Modern Art, Dublin), a work combining his study of classical sculpture with his understanding of Titian's handling of paint. His rise was rapid: he was elected an associate member of the academy on 2 November 1772 and full academician on 9 February 1773. From 1771 to 1776 he exhibited a total of fifteen works: eleven historical compositions, three portraits, and one historical portrait. He then ceased to exhibit, having received some unfavourable reviews and having embarked on a larger project.

In 1773 Barry was one of the Royal Academicians involved in a proposal to decorate St Paul's Cathedral with religious paintings, an attempt to gain for English artists the type of patronage so prevalent on the continent. Although ecclesiastical authorities frustrated this plan, the Society for the Encouragement of Arts, Manufactures, and Commerce, inspired by this offer, in 1774 approached ten artists, Barry among them, to decorate the Great Room of its new building in the Adelphi designed by Robert Adam. The artists, who were to divide the profits of an exhibition of their work once it was completed, declined, but in 1777 Barry submitted his own proposal to decorate the Great Room. His series of six paintings (four measure 12 ft x 15 ft and two 12 ft x 42 ft) have been called by Sir Ellis Waterhouse, 'the most considerable achievement in the true "grand style" by any British painter of the century' (Waterhouse, 199). Barry's subject was ambitious—undertaking, as his biographer, Edward Fryer, wrote, 'no less than the complete history of the human mind in its various stages from barbarity to refinement', ending in 'the final retribution awarded to all in a future world' (*Works*, 1.317). The first three paintings chart the progress of Greek civilization from a primitive to a civilized state, and these are followed by two canvases celebrating contemporary England. The final canvas, *Elysium and Tartarus*, contains Barry's selection of who belongs among God's elect.

After asserting that 'the principal merit of Painting as well as of Poetry, is its address to the mind' (*Works*, 2.318),

Barry warned the viewer that his works required close attention. In fact, what at first appears as another Enlightenment homage to pagan, classical culture as the basis of modern values contains a hidden religious allegory, hidden because it requires the viewer to engage in a dialogue with the works and hidden because it exalts the Roman Catholic church when such a message, had it been understood, would have proved intolerable. Indeed, while Barry was at work on his canvases, the anti-Catholic Gordon riots erupted in the streets of London. Barry's pictures were a critical success, with Samuel Johnson, who was notoriously non-visual, responding particularly to its appeal to the intellect: 'Whatever the hand may have done, the mind has done its part' (Boswell, *Life*, 224), but after eight years of labour Barry received only £503 12s., the total gross from two exhibitions held in 1783 and 1784, this at a time when Reynolds was paid 200 guineas for a full-length portrait.

Because the murals did not prove financially rewarding and did not engender future commissions, Barry completed few canvases after this monumental effort. He participated on a limited scale in John Boydell's Shakspeare Gallery, which, opening on 4 May 1789, included the work of most of Britain's finest painters, contributing two pictures, *King Lear Weeping over the Body of Cordelia* (1786–7; Tate collection) and *Iachimo Emerging from the Chest in Imogen's Chamber* (c.1788–92; Royal Dublin Society). In the early 1790s he also embarked on an ambitious scheme to illustrate John Milton's *Paradise Lost*, but little was ultimately accomplished, although the few prints that he executed before abandoning this plan are among his finest. He did, however, complete in 1804 his large canvas *The Birth of Pandora* (Manchester City Art Galleries), the culmination of a project he had conceived as a student in Rome. He was also to revisit his murals at the Society of Arts, frequently revising his master-work, and in acknowledgement of his achievement, the society voted him on 16 January 1799 a gold medal and 200 guineas, and made him a perpetual member not subject to contributions.

Printmaker In promoting his paintings Barry, like his colleagues, relied on the print trade, the reproductions of the works rather than the paintings themselves being the primary means of dissemination. As early as 1772 the engraver Valentine Green produced a mezzotint after Barry's painting *Venus Rising from the Sea*, which had been exhibited in that same year, but by 1776 the artist had taken over such tasks himself, becoming printmaker, publisher, and apparently sole distributor. In his prints reproducing his paintings, he often introduced creative variations on the original compositions. In addition, printmaking allowed him to expand the range of his subject matter, as he attempted more topical material than would be permitted in oils. Works such as *The Phoenix, or, The Resurrection of Freedom* (1776) and *William Pitt, Earl of Chatham* (1778) are political allegories with lengthy inscriptions, and even such prints as *Job Reproved by his Friends* (1777) and *The Conversion of Polemon* (1778), which on the surface appear to follow the standard repertory of academic art, being drawn from the Bible and classical history, contain pointed political messages more appropriate to the print medium.

Not only was Barry inventive in his subject matter, but he also experimented in a variety of media, including etching, engraving, aquatint, mezzotint, and lithography. Among painters of this period only George Stubbs and Thomas Gainsborough demonstrated a comparable inventiveness, with William Blake, a professional printmaker, occupying a niche of his own. Barry, who had his own press, produced multiple states of many of his prints, as he constantly tinkered with his plates, with each impression seemingly differing from the last. Professional engravers routinely issued proofs of their works, which, in addition to guaranteeing an early, rich impression, created an artificial rarity that increased the print's value. But Barry's production of multiple states has more to do with an obsessive engagement with the act of printing itself than with any concern about increasing market value. At a visceral level, he enjoyed exploring new aesthetic possibilities, and from 1776 until his death he executed a total of forty-six works; these included large, didactic, public performances as well as small, expressive, personal images, apparently created without an audience in mind.

Author From the beginning of his career, Barry sought to publish in an effort to educate the public on his views on art and also as a means of settling scores with his numerous enemies. His letters from France and Italy are filled with perceptive critical commentary. His first book, *An Inquiry into the Real and Imaginary Obstructions to the Acquisition of the Arts in England*, appeared in 1775, just four years after his return to London. This book passionately argues for the need to promote the exalted genre of history painting in England, a country that traditionally had produced ardent collectors of old-master canvases but few patrons of native talent beyond the commissioning of portraits.

In line with his desire to play a role in the public discourse on the arts in England, Barry stood for election as professor of painting at the Royal Academy, a position he won on 4 March 1782. In this capacity he delivered six lectures annually to the academy's students, lectures that he intended to rival Sir Joshua Reynolds's *Discourses* and that were published posthumously.

In 1783, to coincide with the first exhibition of his murals at the Society of Arts, Barry published *An Account of a Series of Pictures*, a book that provides an introduction to his paintings, but despite its length (221 pages), he was careful only to suggest rather than fully disclose the meaning of the series, forcing the viewer or reader to see beneath the surface. In 1784 he reissued this book with an addendum that focused on his disputes with those he felt had slighted or opposed him. After issuing prints reproducing in whole or in part his paintings in the Great Room, the artist published in 1793 a smaller book, *A Letter to the Society of Arts*, describing their content.

Barry's last major publication, *A Letter to the Dilettanti*

Society of 1798, appealed to the Society of Dilettanti to promote the arts to compensate for the Royal Academy's shameful performance. While Barry made a number of excellent observations concerning the role the arts should play in contemporary society, his paranoia led him into abusive tirades against his colleagues. For these and inflammatory remarks made in his lectures, he was expelled from the Royal Academy on 15 April 1799; he still remains the only artist to hold this distinction. In 1799 he quickly issued a second edition of his offending book, adding an appendix rehashing the events surrounding his expulsion.

Old age and death   From 1772 Barry lived in London at 29 Suffolk Street, but he left these premises about 1785, and after at least two more moves, in 1788 he settled into his permanent home at 36 Castle Street East. The appearance of the house declined along with that of its owner, and Henry Fuseli, a fellow academician who was originally from Zürich, made the inevitable analogy: 'Dat fellow looks like de door of his own house' (*New Monthly Magazine*, 5, March 1816, 135). Neither the door nor the artist presented a pretty picture. The Irish lawyer William Henry Curran has left an unsettling account of the ruinous condition of the house in 1804:

> The area was bestrewn with skeletons of cats and dogs, marrow-bones, waste-paper, fragments of boys' hoops, and other playthings, and with the many kinds of missiles, which the pious brats of the neighbourhood, had hurled against the unhallowed premises. A dead cat lay upon the projecting stone of the parlour window, immediately under a sort of appeal to the public, or a proclamation setting forth that a dark conspiracy existed for the wicked purpose of molesting the writer and injuring his reputation … This was in Barry's hand-writing, and occupied the place of one pane of glass. The rest of the framework was covered with what I had once imagined to be necromantic devices—some of his own etchings, but turned upside down, of his great paintings at the Adelphi.   (Curran, 171–2)

The poet Robert Southey, who visited Barry during his last years, commented on the artist's distressing condition:

> I knew Barry, and have been admitted into his den in his worst (that is to say, his maddest) days, when he was employed upon his Pandora. He wore at that time an old coat of green baize, but from which time had taken all the green that incrustations of paint and dirt had not covered. His wig was one which you might suppose he had borrowed from a scarecrow; all round it there projected a fringe of his own grey hair. He lived alone, in a house which was never cleaned; and he slept on a bedstead with no other furniture than a blanket nailed on the one side. I wanted him to visit me. 'No,' he said, 'he would not go out by day, because he could not spare time from his great picture; and if he went out in the evening the Academicians would waylay him and murder him'.   (*Life and Correspondence*, 54)

The assaults on the house became so pronounced that on 18 December 1804 the *Morning Chronicle* published the following report:

> A series of outrages have been recently committed upon the residence of that celebrated artist, Mr. Barry. This respectable Gentleman's house in Castle-Street, Cavendish-square, has been attacked in the dead of night several times within the last two months. His door has been battered, his windows broken, and the whole of the front of the house

covered with filth. The house is rendered in a great measure uninhabitable—not a pane of glass is to be seen unbroken.

Barry was forced to move into a small back room on the second floor, more convinced than ever that these assaults were part of a conspiracy to silence him.

To the end, Barry demonstrated a fierce independence. His circle of friends was not drawn so much from the artistic community as it was from the ranks of other professionals. He was particularly close to a group of medical men, among whom were Dr Edward Fryer, his biographer, as well as the brother of a Roman Catholic priest, Dr Anthony Carlisle, who at one point studied at the Royal Academy, and Dr John Cooke, who was a dissenting minister before he turned to medicine. Other close friends were General Francisco Miranda, the Venezuelan revolutionist, and Francis Douce, the collector who bequeathed a number of works by Barry to the Bodleian Library.

In his final years Barry's health was precarious. He suffered an illness in February 1799, but Robert Southey relates a near fatal collapse that apparently happened in January 1803, when the artist was carried to the home of his friend Dr Carlisle, who nursed him back to health. Finally, on 6 February 1806, while eating in a cook-shop in Wardour Street, as was his custom, Barry lost consciousness after having caught a severe cold. A friend could not return him to his home, as the keyhole of the door was again jammed with pebbles inserted by his neighbourhood tormentors. Eventually Barry was taken in by the architect Joseph Bonomi, dying, unmarried, in his home, 76 Great Titchfield Street, London, on 22 February from pleuritic fever after receiving the last rites from a priest. His body lay in state in the Great Room of the Society of Arts, and on 14 March, after an elaborate funeral procession, he was interred in the crypt of St Paul's Cathedral next to the grave of Sir Joshua Reynolds.

At the time of his death Barry had little money. On 21 December 1804 he had written to David Steuart Erskine, eleventh earl of Buchan, that he had an annual income of only £60 from funds in the American Bank and the English 5 per cent bank stock. The rent alone for his house came to £40, leaving little for subsistence. The earl, who had a history of supporting artists, was instrumental in seeing that an annuity was raised. On 28 November 1805 this annuity of £120 was purchased from Sir Robert Peel for £1200, the legal matters being handled by William Tooke and William George Tennant. Barry, however, died before the funds could be of use, and Sir Robert contributed £200 towards his funeral and a memorial tablet, after having 'sacked a cool 1000*l*. by his tight bargain' (Tooke to Britton, 10 Jan 1850).

Throughout his career, Barry had spurned his family. His father, with whom he did not get along, left what property he had to his wife with reversion to James as the eldest son. James, however, resigned this title, giving it to his uncle, John Reardon. Even when his niece, Margaret Bulkeley or Bulkley, travelled to London to knock on his door, Barry refused to see her. Having cut himself off from his relatives, he died intestate, but those who were still alive descended on London to salvage what they could from what remained.

Of Barry's three brothers, his favourite, John, had died young in 1769. In 1771 Patrick enlisted in the marines in Bristol, only to desert in the following year. Then, adopting his mother's maiden name, which he spelled Riordan, he entered the service of the East India Company. By 1789 he was back in London unsuccessfully attempting to beg money from James. Returning to the East Indies, he apparently died soon thereafter. The other brother, Redmond, served in the Royal Navy and was also in frequent legal and financial difficulties. He sold his claim to James's estate to his sister for approximately £400 but was soon reduced to beggary, dying in 1824 while being evicted from his lodgings.

His sister, Mary Ann, was the primary beneficiary of Barry's possessions. In 1804 she had written to him from Cork pleading for help after her husband, Jeremiah Bulkeley, had been confined to debtors' prison. To this and other pleas, James was again unresponsive. Once he died, however, Mrs Bulkeley moved aggressively to claim his estate. The artist had £41 14s. 9d. in cash on him at the time of his death; there were funds amounting to £163 in the banking house of Messrs Wright & Co.; and she sold the furniture at Christies in 1806, followed by the sale of her brother's art and library in 1807. From the plates reproducing the Society of Arts pictures, Mrs Bulkeley published 400 bound sets with text in 1808, and she also negotiated the sale of the 1809 two-volume edition of *The Works of James Barry*, prepared by Dr Fryer. But these few resources could sustain her and her daughter Margaret for only so long. The masterstroke came in 1809, the year in which Margaret seemingly entered Edinburgh University to study medicine after taking on a male persona and adopting the same name as her famous uncle. This James Barry eventually rose to the rank of inspector-general in the British army, the only one of the Barry family to enjoy a distinguished military career.

Self-image Barry's earliest surviving self-portrait (National Portrait Gallery, London) is an ambitious painting he executed as a student in Rome, where he shows himself at work on a canvas depicting two of his fellow artists confronting the Belvedere Torso. Throughout the remainder of his career he created a number of self-portraits in all media (oils, drawings, and prints) that demonstrate a continuing engagement with what it means to be an artist in a commercial society with little interest in promoting the grand style. His self-portrayals are far more rivetingly intense and hauntingly personal than the more public masks worn by his colleagues. One such example is a late drawing (c.1800–1805, Ashmolean Museum, Oxford), where the artist shows himself as deeply pensive and profoundly fatigued. It gives the appearance of a direct portrayal, transcribed from what he sees in the mirror. Although Barry was right-handed, the hand he lightly sketches holding the quill pen at the paper's bottom edge is his left, just as it would appear in a reversed mirror image. Most likely a drawing made by candlelight, the bold, expressive diagonal lines create a hallucinatory

intensity. The artist's disillusionment and the melancholy of which he frequently complained are tellingly portrayed.

W. H. Curran described Barry's appearance in his late years, a description that accords well with his self-presentation in the Ashmolean drawing:

> His face was striking. An Englishman would call it an Irish, an Irishman a Munster face; but Barry's had a character independent of national or provincial peculiarities. It had vulgar features, but no vulgar expression. It was rugged, austere, and passion-beaten; but the passions traced there were those of aspiring thought, and unconquerable energy, asserting itself to the last, and sullenly exulting in its resources. (Curran, 174)

In summer 1803 Barry completed the canvas he had used earlier as the model for his head in the self-portrait that he had introduced into *Crowning the Victors at Olympia*, his third mural at the Society of Arts, where he appears in the guise of Timanthes, the classical Greek painter. The resulting image (NG Ire.), his last public self-portrait, is complex and disturbing. He cradles his recreation of a lost painting by Timanthes, which, as described by Pliny, showed satyrs cautiously approaching a sleeping cyclops to measure the size of his thumb. The cyclops's chest is modelled on the Belvedere Torso, the sculpture he had featured so prominently in his early Roman self-portrait (c.1767; NPG). The cyclops's grand, muscular form testifies to Barry's mastery of a sublime, classical vocabulary, as he recasts the heroic past in a debased present. The powerful compression and radical cutting of this image also give it an unsettling power. Particularly disturbing is the painted sculpture, which shows the foot of Hercules trampling down the serpent of envy, with the serpent's open, fanged mouth hissing in the artist's ear. Barry's conception is taken from Horace, where Hercules conquers envy only by dying because his greatness then no longer poses a threat to the living. Barry's last public self-portrait bears witness to the dangerous situation in which his genius has placed him: his greatness has inflamed his colleagues, who continually hiss their poisonous invectives, from which only death can offer an escape.

Legacy Even after Barry died, the hostile rumblings against him did not cease. For almost 200 years his strong personality has overshadowed his achievement as an artist. His admirers have hailed him as a genius whom English society failed, a society that only paid lip-service to the concept that history painting deserved support. One of William Blake's annotations to his copy of *The Works of Sir Joshua Reynolds* expressed this sense of outrage:

> Who will Dare to Say that Polite Art is Encouraged or Either Wished or Tolerated in a Nation where The Society for the Encouragement of Art Suffer'd Barry to Give them his Labour for Nothing, A Society Composed of the Flower of the English Nobility & Gentry?—Suffering an Artist to Starve while he Supported Really what They, under Pretence of Encouraging, were Endeavouring to Depress.—Barry told me that while he Did that Work, he Lived on Bread & Apples. (*Complete Writings*, 446)

Barry's enshrinement in the pantheon of romantic geniuses martyred by a philistine society should not obscure his considerable achievements as an artist and author. The work, rather than the life, provides his greatest legacy. As John Barrell has ably demonstrated, Barry's writings establish him as an important figure in England's political discourse concerning art's role in promoting civic virtue in a society of divided interests. Barry's paintings, drawings, and prints often exhibit an intense, imaginative power and heroic monumentality found in the work of few of his contemporaries, and there is little comparable in Britain to his series of murals in the Great Room of the Society of Arts, which remain one of the art world's best-kept secrets.   WILLIAM L. PRESSLY

Sources *The works of James Barry*, ed. E. Fryer, 2 vols. (1809) · W. L. Pressly, *The life and art of James Barry* (1981) · W. L. Pressly, *James Barry: the artist as hero* (1983) · J. Barrell, *The political theory of painting from Reynolds to Hazlitt* (1986) · J. Barrell, *The birth of Pandora* (1992) · W. L. Pressly, 'A chapel of natural and revealed religion: James Barry's series for the Society's great room reinterpreted [pts 1–3]', *Journal of the Royal Society of Arts*, 132 (1983–4), 543–6, 634–7, 693–5 · W. L. Pressly, 'Portrait of a Cork family: the two James Barrys', *Journal of the Cork Historical and Archaeological Society*, 2nd ser., 90 (1985), 127–49 · W. Tooke, letter to J. Britton, 10 Jan 1850, Morgan L., MA2179 · E. Waterhouse, *Painting in Britain, 1530–1790* (1953) · W. H. Curran, *Sketches of the Irish bar*, 2 (1855) · Boswell, *Life*, vol. 4 · *The life and correspondence of Robert Southey*, ed. C. C. Southey, 6 vols. (1849–50), vol. 6 · *Complete writings of William Blake*, ed. G. Keynes (1957) · F. Cullen, *Visual politics: the representation of Ireland, 1750–1930* (1997) · *New Monthly Magazine*, 5 (1816), 133–5 · J. Barry, letter to the earl of Buchan, 21 Dec 1804, NPG, Heinz Archive and Library

Archives priv. coll., commonplace book · RSA, corresp. · Yale U., Farmington, Lewis Walpole Library, letters and papers | RSA, minutes and letters to the Society of Arts

Likenesses J. Barry, self-portrait, oils, *c*.1767, NPG · L. G. Blanchet, oils, *c*.1767, RSA · J. Barry, self-portrait, oils, *c*.1776 (with Edmund Burke), Crawford Art Gallery, Cork · J. Barry, self-portrait, oils, *c*.1780, V&A · J. Barry, self-portrait, oils, *c*.1780–1803, RSA · J. Barry, self-portrait, oils, *c*.1786 (completed 1803), NG Ire. [*see illus.*] · J. Barry, self-portrait, pen and brown ink over black chalk drawing, *c*.1800–1805, AM Oxf. · J. Barry, mezzotint, *c*.1802 · J. Barry, self-portrait, pen-and-ink drawing, *c*.1802, RSA · G. Dance, drawing, RA · N. Dance, pencil caricature, BM · W. Evans, chalk drawing, NPG · J. Northcote, pencil drawing, NG Ire. · J. Opie, oils, NG Ire. · H. Singleton, group portrait, oils (*Royal Academicians, 1793*), RA

Wealth at death £204 14*s*. 9*d*.—incl. cash, furniture, art, and library

Barry, James (*c*.1799–1865), army medical officer and transvestite, was probably born Margaret, the youngest daughter of Mrs Mary Ann Bulkley or Bulkeley, the sister of the artist James *Barry; her paternity is in doubt. From the age of ten she dressed and presented herself as a man, but the woman who laid out her corpse declared that she was female: 'The Devil, a General,' said the attendant. 'It's a woman. And a woman that has had a child' (Rose, 12).

The precocity and studiousness of the young Barry impressed several of the influential friends and supporters of her uncle, James Barry. These included the Latin American exile General Francisco de Miranda and David Steuart Erskine, eleventh earl of Buchan, to both of whom at various times Barry's paternity has been attributed. Miranda allowed Barry the free run of his extensive library. In December 1809 Mrs Bulkley settled in Edinburgh with 'James Barry', aged ten, who matriculated as a literary and medical student at the university. After a year Mrs

James Barry (*c*.1799–1865), by unknown photographer, *c*.1860 [left, with a servant]

Bulkley returned to London, leaving Barry under the protection of Lord Buchan. Barry was a figure of fun to the other students, being under 5 feet tall, slight, and 'apparently of delicate constitution … vain and … frivolous, yet was prompt to resent an offence' (*Medical Times and Gazette*, 1865). She invariably wore a long 'surtout' or overcoat. She not only took the mandatory courses but also studied midwifery under James Hamilton and anatomical dissection with Andrew Fyfe. The senate of the university sought to prevent her presenting her thesis 'De merocele, vel, Hernia crurati' (On hernia of the groin) on grounds of her youth, but Lord Buchan pointed out that the regulations did not specify any age limitations, and she was allowed to proceed. She was awarded her MD in 1812. The thesis was dedicated to Miranda and Buchan.

Thus Barry became not only the youngest but technically the first woman in Great Britain to graduate in medicine, an honour usually accorded to Elizabeth Garrett Anderson, who graduated in 1865, the year of Barry's death. In October 1812 Barry moved to London as a pupil dresser at St Thomas's Hospital, and was apprenticed to the surgeon Sir Astley Cooper. Having walked the wards, she decided to join the army, and on 15 July 1813 she was gazetted as a hospital assistant, the most junior medical commissioned rank, and was posted to the hospital of the

Plymouth garrison. She was promoted to assistant surgeon on 17 December 1815, and the following year was posted to Cape Town.

Barry arrived in the Cape in August 1816 with letters of introduction (including one from Lord Buchan) to the governor, Lord Charles Somerset. She quickly established herself as a family friend and confidante, and in 1817 was appointed physician to the governor's household. Lord Charles was a handsome widower, and there was later a scurrilous scandal—premised on the belief that Barry was a man—about their relationship. In 1818 she made a petulant remark, possibly motivated by jealousy, about the governor and a lady visitor, in the presence of Somerset's aide-de-camp, Captain Cloete. Cloete demanded a retraction, and when Barry refused they fought a duel in which neither was harmed. During the winter of 1819 Barry paid a largely undocumented visit to the island of Mauritius. It has been suggested that Somerset had discovered her sex and she had become pregnant, withdrawing to Mauritius to give birth in secret. There was at that time an epidemic of cholera on the island, but it is unlikely that news of it could have reached Cape Town before Barry's departure for Mauritius.

In March 1822 Barry was appointed colonial medical inspector by Somerset but she resisted his suggestion that she should leave the army, and remained on half pay. On 25 July 1826 she performed a caesarean section on the wife of Thomas Munick, a wealthy snuff merchant in Cape Town, and both mother and son flourished. The first recorded success of such an operation was in Zürich in 1818, and it was not until 1833 that the operation was performed in Great Britain with both mother and child surviving. James Hamilton, Barry's teacher in Edinburgh, had made two unsuccessful attempts at the operation in the first decade of the century and described the procedures to his students; Barry, as ever, kept detailed notes. Barry was promoted to staff surgeon in November 1827, and in October 1828 she took up an appointment in Mauritius.

Although Barry had spent the winter of 1819 in Mauritius, the governor, Sir Charles Colville, observed that she had no previous acquaintance with the island, demonstrating that her earlier visit had not become common knowledge. On 27 August 1829 she sailed for England, without leave, probably having received news that Lord Charles Somerset was seriously ill. Called to account for her unauthorized visit by the head of the army medical department, she apparently said, 'I was fed up with my hair and wanted a proper haircut' (Francis, 210). She attended on Lord Charles and he appeared to make a complete recovery, but died in February 1831. Barry attended the funeral before sailing for Jamaica, where she had been appointed staff surgeon. She arrived there on 13 June 1831, although her original orders had been dated 20 January 1830: it seems likely that Lord Fitzroy Somerset (later Lord Raglan), who was then military secretary, had secured the repeated delays in the interests of his brother.

Barry remained in Jamaica until 1836, and her next posting was to St Helena; she returned home under a cloud in

March 1838 and was court-martialled for 'conduct unbecoming'—she had criticized her fellow officers. She was exonerated and posted to the Windward and Leeward garrison, where she was appointed principal medical officer in 1842. After a bout of yellow fever she was invalided home for a year in December 1845 until being posted to Malta in November 1846. She served there for four and a half years, and then moved on to Corfu in 1851. In April 1851 she was promoted to deputy inspector-general of hospitals.

On the outbreak of the Crimean War she applied for a posting to the Crimea, but was rejected on grounds of her seniority. She appealed personally to Lord Raglan, and 462 wounded men from the Crimea were sent to Corfu for medical treatment; under her care they achieved a high recovery rate. In 1855 Barry spent her three-month leave with the 4th division before Sevastopol. There she met and chastised Florence Nightingale, who wrote after Barry's death to her sister, 'I never had such a blackguard rating in my life—I who have had more than any woman—than from Barry sitting on a horse … I should say she was the most hardened creature I ever met throughout the army' (Nightingale MSS, Wellcome L.).

In November 1857 Barry was posted to Canada with the local rank of inspector-general. She was confirmed in the rank of inspector-general of hospitals in 1858. After years in the tropics the Canadian climate led to chronic bronchitis, and, following a severe bout of influenza, she was invalided home in May 1859. She was retired on half pay shortly after her arrival in England.

Wherever Barry served there was immense respect for her medical skills, but her lack of diplomacy inevitably resulted in conflict with colleagues and authorities. She invariably championed the neglected and oppressed of any race or station in life. Prisons, leper colonies, and indigent patients always received her attention, and she never accepted fees for her private practice. Her appearance always attracted attention, for she was tiny, with small, soft hands, and a high squeaky voice; her flamboyant dress added to the impression of effeminacy. In every posting suspicion arose regarding either her gender or sexuality, but she behaved flirtatiously with attractive women, and at least one husband suspected her of paying improper attentions to his wife. Her querulousness and bizarre behaviour never detracted from her acceptance as a physician: Lord Charles Somerset described her as the 'most skilful of physicians and most wayward of men' (Albemarle, 2.96). Elsewhere, she is described as an infinitely generous and patient doctor, a passionate termagant, shrilling at authority and making enemies everywhere (Rose, 134).

Barry died on 25 July 1865 in lodgings at 14 Margaret Street, Cavendish Square, London. The death certificate gives Barry's sex as male, but it was signed by a Dr McKinnon, who had long known Barry and felt no need to carry out an intimate examination. Barry was buried as she had lived, as a man, in Kensal Green cemetery, after a service in St Paul's Cathedral. No London newspaper carried her obituary, but on 14 August 1865 a Dublin paper, *Saunder's*

News-Letter and Daily Advertiser, published an account entitled 'A female army combatant'; the *Manchester Guardian* carried the story on 21 August, and in Cumberland, where she had been a frequent visitor, the *Whitehaven News* gave a sympathetic account of the scandal on 24 August. The deputy inspector of hospitals, Edward Bradford, commented that: 'The stories which have circulated since [Barry's] death are too absurd to require serious refutation' ('The reputed female army surgeon', *Medical Times and Gazette*, 2 1865, 249), but the rumours persisted. The registrar-general requested clarification of the gender of the deceased, but Dr McKinnon replied that he had not examined the body 'as I could positively swear to the identity of the body as being that of a person whom I had been acquainted with as Inspector General of Hospitals for a period of eight or nine years'; moreover, he added 'whether Dr Barry was male, female or hermaphrodite I do not know' (Royal Army Medical College MSS, Wellcome L.).

Barry's origins and motives remain a mystery, but she was a passionate reformer and pioneer whose achievements in medicine have been obscured by her lifelong masquerade. Many years before such demands became commonplace, she not only demanded rigorous cleanliness and sound diet for the sick but also insisted on adequate living conditions and proper leisure for troops, prisoners, and others who came under her care. The Royal Army Medical College, Millbank, honoured her memory with the Barry room, containing a sketch of the doctor and other memorabilia, including a copy of her death certificate.   SYDNEY BRANDON

Sources I. Rae, *The strange story of Dr. James Barry* (1958) · J. Rose, *The perfect gentleman* (1977) · G. Thomas, earl of Albemarle, *Fifty years of my life*, 2 vols. (1876) · M. P. Russell, 'James Barry: 1792(?)–1865', *Edinburgh Medical Journal*, 3rd ser., 50 (1943), 558–67 · R. C. Francis, 'Can a woman do it better?', *Army Medical Services Magazine*, 44 (Oct 1990), 207– · d. cert.
Archives NL Scot. · Royal Army Medical Corps, Camberley, Surrey | PRO, WO 25/3899, 3910(G3), CO 48/97
Likenesses E. Lear, caricature, *c.*1856, Royal Army Medical College, Millbank, London · photograph, *c.*1860, Royal Army Medical College, Millbank, London [*see illus.*]

Barry, John (1745?–1803), naval officer in the American service, was born at Tacumshane, co. Wexford. Few details of his parents are known, other than that his mother's maiden name was Kelly; his father may have been a farmer. In 1755 Barry was apprenticed to a Wexford merchantman as a cabin boy. By 1760 he had settled in Philadelphia, where he worked as a successful shipmaster. On 31 October 1767, in Philadelphia, he married Mary Cleary, who died in 1774, and in 1777 he married Sarah Austin (*d.* in or before 1803). Neither marriage produced any children.

At the outbreak of the American War of Independence, Barry, a supporter of the revolutionaries, offered his services to congress, and in March 1776 he was made captain of the brig *Lexington* (16 guns). The *Lexington* met and engaged the British sloop *Edward* off the Virginia capes on 17 April. The *Lexington*'s capture of the *Edward* was the first American naval victory. Barry added to the success with

the capture of two additional sloops, and was rewarded with the command of the frigate *Effingham* (28 guns), which was then under construction at Philadelphia but was later burnt by the British before she was ready for sea. Shortly after his first victory in the *Lexington*, Barry was appointed to the *Raleigh* and sailed from Boston on a cruise on 25 September. He was almost immediately sighted by the *Experiment* (50 guns), commanded by Sir James Wallace, who put an end to the *Raleigh*'s cruise within two days of its commencement; Barry escaped on shore.

Barry then served with the army, raising an artillery battery comprised mostly of fellow seamen, and campaigning in New Jersey under George Washington until February 1777. In September 1780 his courage was recognized when he was placed in command of the frigate *Alliance* the revolutionaries' most formidable ship, which had just returned from a remarkable cruise around Britain as one of the squadron commanded by John Paul Jones. The *Alliance* sailed for France in February 1781, carrying Thomas Paine and Colonel John Laurens, the special envoy of the continental congress. On the return voyage Barry captured two British privateers, two merchant vessels, and later two small ships of war, the *Atalanta* and *Trepassy*. In the third engagement Barry was severely wounded in the shoulder by grapeshot. The capture of two British men-of-war was felt to be a great moral victory, and on his return Barry was widely praised. He later transported the marquis de Lafayette to France, served in the Caribbean, and was involved in the war's final naval engagement against HMS *Sybil* on 10 March 1783. When congress created the United States navy in March 1794, Barry was placed at the head of the list as senior captain, a distinction he kept for the rest of his life. In his flagship, the frigate *United States*, Barry spent the late 1790s defending American trading interests from pirates in the Caribbean. He died on 13 September 1803 in Philadelphia, where he was also buried.

J. K. LAUGHTON, *rev.* TROY O. BICKHAM

Sources R. G. Baker, 'Barry, John', *ANB* · W. B. Clark, *Gallant John Barry* (1938) · F. E. Benz, *Commodore Barry, naval hero* (1950) · J. Gurn, *Commodore Barry, father of the American navy* (1933) · L. Wibberley, *John Barry, father of the navy* (1957)
Archives Philadelphia Maritime Museum Library, Barry-Hayes MSS
Likenesses portraits, repro. in Gurn, *Commodore Barry* · portraits, repro. in Clark, *Gallant John Barry* · portraits, repro. in Wibberley, *John Barry* · portraits, repro. in Benz, *Commodore Barry*

Barry, John Milner (1768–1822), physician, was born at Kilgobbin, near Bandon, co. Cork, the eldest son of James Barry and his wife, Elizabeth Milner. He was educated at Bandon and at the University of Edinburgh, where he was awarded an MD degree in 1792 for a thesis on ascites. He then returned to Ireland and practised medicine in Cork.

Barry's professional life was marked by energy, enterprise, and innovation. He was among the first in Ireland to acknowledge the importance of smallpox vaccination, and he regarded Edward Jenner, the first scientific advocate of the procedure, as one of the great benefactors of mankind, an individual destined to enjoy an 'enviable species of immortality'. Barry obtained vaccine by post from a colleague in London and used it in Cork for the first time on 6 June 1800. He was not the first in Ireland to vaccinate, as has been generally claimed; the procedure had been carried out at the Dispensary for Infant Poor in Dublin since its establishment in March 1800. Barry published an article on smallpox in the *Medical and Physical Journal* (1800) and *An Account of the Nature and Effects of the Cow-Pock* (1801).

In 1801 Barry published *A Report on the Infectious Diseases of the City of Cork*, in which he described fever as an alarming and malignant disease, one which devoured its victims and terrified their relatives and friends. He called for the establishment of a fever hospital similar to those in Chester, Manchester, and Waterford. Subscriptions were raised and the Cork House of Recovery and Fever Hospital was opened on 8 November 1802, with Barry and Charles Daly as its first physicians. In 1803 Barry was one of the founders of the Cork Institution, where he lectured on agriculture and rural affairs until the demands of his medical practice forced his resignation in 1815.

On 3 September 1808, at Ballinvina church, co. Cork, Barry married Mary, eldest daughter of William Phair, a paper manufacturer of Mill View, co. Cork. They had at least eight children who survived to adulthood. Barry was an advocate of female education, inspired in part by a belief that middle- and upper-class women, including his own daughters, should instruct the poor. In Barry's opinion the education of the lower classes in Ireland had been neglected to such an extent that the majority were reduced to a state of ignorance bordering on barbarism. Their lack of literary, religious, and moral instruction made them unfit to discharge their duties properly and exposed many women to temptation and ruin. Barry also railed against drunkenness, not, it seems, from any moral standpoint, but because he regarded it as one of the primary agents in the propagation of disease.

Barry died on 16 May 1822, from apoplexy, at his home on Patrick's Hill, Cork. He was buried at Balinaltig cemetery, near Watergrasshill, co. Cork. On 1 May 1824 a cenotaph was erected 'in respectful and affectionate remembrance of Doctor John Milner Barry' in the grounds of the Cork Fever Hospital. According to the inscription, the institution had been 'the means of preventing the pernicious contagion of typhus fever from diffusing itself widely in the populous city of Cork'.

Barry's second son, **John O'Brien Milner Barry** (1815–1881), was born in Cork and studied medicine in Paris from 1833 to 1836. He was awarded an MD degree from the University of Edinburgh in 1837 for a thesis on endocarditis. He was licensed by the Royal College of Surgeons, Edinburgh, in the following year, and became a member of the Royal College of Physicians, London, in 1859, and a fellow in 1876. After practising in Laugharne and Totnes he settled in Tunbridge Wells in 1852 and practised there until his death from heart disease on 15 September 1881. He was buried in Rusthall cemetery. Twice married, he died childless.   LAURENCE M. GEARY

Sources J. Coleman, 'Biographical sketches, XVI', *Journal of the Cork Historical and Archaeological Society*, 2nd ser., 1 (1895), 305–12 · J. M. Barry, 'Some observations on the medical topography of Cork, as connected with the late epidemic fever', *An account of the rise, progress and decline of the fever lately epidemical in Ireland*, ed. F. Barker and J. Cheyne, 2 vols. (1821), 1.285–96 · U. Edin. L., special collections division, university archives · *Freeman's Journal* [Dublin] (9 Sept 1808) · *Cork Morning Intelligence* (18 May 1822) · *BMJ* (1 Oct 1881), 576 · Munk, *Roll* [John O'Brien Milner Barry]

Archives Wellcome L., papers, MS 5164

Wealth at death £21,992 18s. 3d.—John O'Brien Milner Barry: probate, 4 Nov 1881, *CGPLA Eng. & Wales*

Barry, John O'Brien Milner (1815–1881). *See under* Barry, John Milner (1768–1822).

Barry, Sir John Wolfe Wolfe- (1836–1918), civil engineer, was born on 7 December 1836 in London, the youngest son, in a family of five sons and two daughters, of Sir Charles *Barry (1795–1860), the architect of the houses of parliament, and his wife, Sarah Rowsell (1798–1882). He assumed the additional surname of Wolfe in 1898.

Educated at Trinity College, Glenalmond, and at King's College, London, he then became a pupil of Sir John Hawkshaw, under whom he subsequently acted as assistant resident engineer for the railway bridges and stations at Charing Cross and Cannon Street, London. In 1867 he began a long and distinguished career as a consulting civil engineer. In 1874 he married Rosalind Grace, youngest daughter of the Revd Evan Edward Rowsell, rector of Hambledon, Surrey; they had four sons and three daughters.

In the last quarter of the nineteenth century and the early years of the twentieth Wolfe-Barry and his firm were responsible for numerous engineering projects, especially railways, bridges, and docks. In 1884 he overcame the difficulties associated with linking London's shallow underground railways to form the Circle Line. His other works included the Caledonian Railway's shallow underground lines in Glasgow, and its branch line north of Oban, including the cantilever Connel Bridge across Loch Etive. He was employed on most of the railway bridges crossing the Thames east of Westminster, as well as the King Edward VII road bridge at Kew. Following the death in 1887 of the architect Sir Horace Jones he had sole responsibility for Tower Bridge, completed in 1894. Now an icon of London, its form was determined by the need to provide a low-level road crossing while letting large ships enter the upper Pool of London. He was also occupied with various docks in Britain, each of which was at the then limit of construction techniques, notably the Barry docks and railway; the Alexandra Dock, Newport; Immingham docks; and extensions to Grangemouth docks, Middlesbrough Dock, and the Surrey Commercial docks in London. With Sir Benjamin Baker and A. C. Hurtzig he was engineer for the Royal Edward Dock at Avonmouth.

Wolfe-Barry was also retained as a consulting engineer by many railway and harbour undertakings in India, China, and elsewhere. He was a member of many royal commissions, including that of the Port of London. He was one of the three members of the court of arbitration which in 1902 determined the price to be paid by the

Metropolitan Water Board to purchase the eight London water companies. From 1892 to 1906 Wolfe-Barry was one of two British representatives on the international Suez Canal commission. He was specially interested in the problems of town traffic and served on the royal commission on London traffic (1903–5), having expressed his views on the subject in both the inaugural addresses he gave as chairman to the Royal Society of Arts, in 1898 and 1899. He was knighted in 1897.

Wolfe-Barry took great interest in the Institution of Civil Engineers, of which he was a member for fifty-four years; he sat on its council for forty years, and was president in 1896–8. His final paper to the institution was 'Standardization … and its influence on the prosperity of the country' (1918). This chronicled his epoch-making initiative in 1901 in founding and championing the Engineering Standards Committee, which later developed into the independent British Standards Institution. He was chairman of the former body from 1905 until his death.

The establishment of industrial standards made mass production possible, and Wolfe-Barry saw that as the adoption of most industrial standards would be voluntary, co-operation was necessary in formulating them. His view was accepted by the council of the Institution of Civil Engineers, which appointed the main committee in 1901 and supported its subsequent development. Participants in the hierarchical structure of sectional committees, sub-committees, and panel committees included the other principal technical societies, representatives of manufacturing and commerce, and government and other agencies.

The initial advantage of standardization was that it simplified and lowered the cost of manufacturing processes. Early achievements by Wolfe-Barry's committees included reducing the number of patterns of tramway rail from seventy to nine and finding a uniform specification for portland cement which combined the best qualities of the many different specifications previously in use. The principle of standardization has subsequently been extended to a large variety of goods and services. The hierarchical committees, consensus-based decision-making, open participation, and regular reviewing advocated by Wolfe-Barry have been adopted worldwide by voluntary organizations concerned with developing industrial standards, including the International Organization for Standardization.

In addition to his professional achievements his colleagues attached 'almost equal importance to the genial atmosphere which Sir John diffused around him—an atmosphere of friendly sociability comparable to the mess-room of a good regiment' (Strain, 356). He was a fellow of the Royal Society and had many interests and activities outside his professional work, particularly in technical and scientific education. He introduced the requirement of a formal examination test of candidates for membership of the Institution of Civil Engineers. Wolfe-Barry was chairman of the City and Guilds Institute, and afterwards on the governing body of the Imperial College of Science and Technology. He was a member of the council of King's College, London, and the senate of the University of London. He took a prominent part in the establishment of the National Physical Laboratory, and held a number of civic offices in London.

Wolfe-Barry's wide experience, sound judgement, and untiring energy made him a leading figure in the engineering profession. He died at his home, Delahay House, 15 Chelsea Embankment, London, on 22 January 1918. His wife survived him.   ROBERT C. McWILLIAM

Sources [J. Strain], *PICE*, 206 (1917–18), 350–57 · J. Wolfe-Barry, 'The standardization of engineering materials, and its influence on the prosperity of the country: the "James Forrest" lecture, 1917', *PICE*, 204 (1916–17), 330–64 · W. H. White, 'Report of speeches at a complimentary dinner to Sir John Wolfe-Barry held in the Goldsmiths' Hall on 18 May 1911', 1911, British Standards Institution Archives, Engineering Standards Committee CL 1586 · minutes of the council, Inst. CE, book 16, 1901–3, 22 Jan 1901, item 25 · J. Wolfe-Barry, 'Standardization and its relation to the trade of the country', a lecture delivered before the Institution of Engineers and Shipbuilders in Scotland, at Glasgow, 11 Dec 1908, British Standards Institution Archives, Engineering Standards Committee CL 1104, 1908 · *CGPLA Eng. & Wales* (1918) · *DNB*
Likenesses H. von Herkomer, oils, 1900, priv. coll.; copy, 1912, Inst. CE · J. Russell & Sons, photograph, NPG · Spy [L. Ward], caricature, watercolour study, Athenaeum, London; repro. in *VF* (26 Jan 1905)
Wealth at death £278,362 12s. 11d.: probate, 28 March 1918, *CGPLA Eng. & Wales*

Barry, Lording (*bap.* 1580, *d.* 1629), playwright and pirate, was baptized on 17 April 1580 in St Laurence Pountney, St Laurence Pountney Lane, London, the fifth of eleven children of Nicholas Barry (*d.* 1607), citizen and fishmonger, and his second wife, Anne (*d.* 1631), daughter of George Lording, citizen and merchant taylor, and his wife, Alice. Both families were originally from Hertfordshire. There is no record of Barry's education, though his younger brother John attended Merchant Taylors' School, London, and received a BA and an MA at Cambridge.

In August 1607, a few months after his father's death, Barry and several co-investors, including William Trevell, Edward Sibthorpe, and Michael Drayton, borrowed nearly £120 from three different creditors to finance a new boys' theatre company in the Whitefriars district of London called the Children of the King's Revels, which had already begun operations earlier that year. Despite this capital infusion, business appears to have been slow, possibly because of a plague outbreak that autumn which probably closed the theatres. In order to finance the boys' room and board, Barry, Trevell, and Sibthorpe had to borrow a further £20 on 16 October from William Cooke, a haberdasher of St Laurence Pountney, for which Cooke received a one-sixth share in the venture.

Like several of his co-investors, Barry was a playwright. His only surviving play is *Ram-Alley, or, Merrie-Trickes*, set during a single day in and around the seedy Whitefriars district and modelled, sometimes closely, on the popular city comedies of Thomas Middleton. The main character, William Smallshanks, marries off his mistress, the 'honest whore' Frances, to a lawyer-usurer named Throte who has bankrupted him. William then proceeds to woo the lusty widow Taffata, who has been keeping two other lovers: honest Boucher, who has spurned the quick-witted and faithful Constantia, and William's father, Sir Oliver Smallshanks, a Falstaff-like foolish knight. Eventually William wins Taffata, and a climactic mock trial ends happily, with all the lovers paired off.

The play, probably written in 1607–8, was printed in two separate editions of 1611 and a third edition of 1636, all with an attribution to 'Lo: Barrey' and the Children of the King's Revels. Holdsworth demonstrated many similarities between *Ram-Alley* and Ben Jonson's *Epicene* (1609) and *The Alchemist* (1610), arguing that Barry's play was written in late 1610; however, this is extremely unlikely given Barry's activities at that time, described below, and Jonson almost certainly borrowed from Barry rather than vice versa. Lake argued that Middleton's *The Family of Love* was revised by Barry shortly before being registered for publication in 1607.

In February 1608 silk weaver George Andrews was persuaded to invest £70 in a share of the faltering Children of the King's Revels, and with this money veteran actor Martin Slater was hired as manager. However, in April 1608 an angry King James shut down the rival Blackfriars Boys, and apparently the other London playhouses as well; soon afterwards a plague outbreak kept the playhouses shut and they would remain closed for more than a year. Meanwhile, the loans of the previous summer were coming due. Barry and his partners were forced to default, resulting in a string of lawsuits and Barry's imprisonment in the Marshalsea prison for debt.

Under these dire circumstances Barry persuaded one of his creditors, John Keale, to bail him out of prison, whereupon he promptly fled London and took to the high seas as a pirate. In August he was one of a crew that kidnapped a waterman and captured two Flemish ships in the English Channel, killing one crew member. When dissension arose Barry and several others were put ashore on the Isle of Wight, whence Barry made his way to south-west Ireland by early 1609. There he joined the crew of the *Fly*, a pirate ship out of Cork that robbed two ships in a three-week period before being apprehended. Amazingly, Barry escaped serious consequences, but most of the *Fly*'s crew were sent back to London, where they were convicted in a sensational trial and hanged in December 1609. Barry became free of the Company of Fishmongers by patrimony through his father, and paid quarterage dues to the company from about 1611 to 1622.

After his close shave with the law Barry continued his seafaring life, including further piracy. In 1614–15 he was among English pirates who captured several ships in the Mediterranean, being described as 'Captaine Barrowe … who was a player in England' (Ewen, 14, n.1). In 1616 he gave a deposition before the admiralty court in London, and the following year he joined Sir Walter Ralegh's unsuccessful goldmining expedition to Guiana. Upon returning to England he bought an interest in a ship, the *Edward of London*, and he traded out of London until his death in 1629. His will, proved on 31 July that year, makes no mention of any wife or family. DAVID KATHMAN

Sources C. L. Ewen, *Lording Barry, poet and pirate* (1938) · W. Ingram, 'The playhouse as an investment, 1607–1614: Thomas Woodford and Whitefriars', *Medieval and Renaissance Drama in England*, 2 (1985), 209–30 · C. E. Jones, 'Introduction', *Ram-Alley, or, Merrie-tricks, a comedy by Lording Barry* (1952), vii–xxviii · R. V. Holdsworth, 'Ben Jonson and the date of *Ram Alley*', *N&Q*, 230 (1985), 482–6 · D. J. Lake, *The canon of Thomas Middleton's plays* (1975), 91–107 · Mrs E. P. Hart, ed., *Merchant Taylors' School register, 1561–1934*, 2 vols. (1936) · Fishmongers' quarterage book, 1610–42, GL, MS 5578 A/1

Wealth at death exact amount unknown; owned part of ship *Edward of London*: Ewen, *Lording Barry*

Barry, Martin (1802–1855), microscopist and embryologist, was born on 28 March 1802 at Fratton, Hampshire, one of three or more children whose father had a mercantile concern in Nova Scotia, with ships trading along the coast and with the West Indies. Barry received a liberal education and, following his father's death, which left him with independent means, he spent some time with a relative in the United States. He gained practical experience of commerce working in the family business under his brother J. T. Barry, but then changed direction and studied medicine at London, Edinburgh, Paris, Erlangen, and Berlin. He became a member of the Royal College of Surgeons, Edinburgh, and in 1833 obtained his MD (Edinburgh) and became a fellow of the Royal Society of Edinburgh.

Shortly after graduating Barry studied for a year (1834) with Friedrich Tiedemann at Heidelberg, under whom Theodor Ludwig Wilhelm Bischoff had also studied. He then spent time with Theodor Schwann and Rudolf Wagner. Barry became one of the very few British scientists who knew the German microscopic literature and practice of the 1830s and 1840s, which were greatly in advance of those in Great Britain.

Barry began reading the literature of embryology in 1835. He contributed two beautifully illustrated papers on the fertilization and development of the ovum in the rabbit and many other species, which were published in the *Philosophical Transactions* of the Royal Society of London (1838–9); he received their royal medal in 1839 and was elected a fellow in 1840. In 1842 Barry saw spermatozoa inside rabbit ova obtained from the fallopian tube (*Philosophical Transactions*, 1843, 33). This observation was challenged by Bischoff, who recognized its correctness nine years later. Barry also described thinning of the zona pellucida which surrounds the ovum at the point of penetration (*Philosophical Transactions*, 1840, 533 ff., para. 334), and observed early segmentation after fertilization. His idea that tissues arose from blood corpuscles may have been due to the use of dilute acetic acid, which dissolves the red cells (which lack nuclei) and leaves only the nucleated white cells.

In 1843 Barry delivered a course in physiology at St Thomas's Hospital, London. In 1844 he worked as house surgeon at the newly established Royal Maternity Hospital in Edinburgh, and was noted for his compassion towards his poor patients, who called him Barry Martin. James Y. Simpson acknowledged Barry's help and humanity in an article on the position of the foetal head during labour, which was based on Barry's observations in 335 cranial presentations at the Edinburgh Maternity Hospital (Simpson).

Barry left Edinburgh because of ill health and was in Arran in 1846, where he vaccinated the local children and founded a museum for birds' eggs. In 1848 he was seriously considered for the new chair in physiology at the Institutes of Medicine in Edinburgh University, but he withdrew his application at the last moment on the grounds that as a Quaker he could not subscribe to the Thirty-Nine Articles of the Church of England.

Barry spent much time on the continent between 1849 and 1853 and went to Giessen (where he met Justus von Liebig), Göttingen, Prague, and Breslau (where he worked with Johann Evangelista Purkinje). He then put forward the view, regarded as excessively speculative by some, that every part of the animal is directly descended from the nucleus of the germ cell.

Although Barry's health as a young man was good (he made an early ascent of Mont Blanc in 1834), he was ill in the late 1830s and again in 1845–6. In the early 1850s he developed a severe neuralgic affliction and in the autumn of 1853 he moved to Beccles, Suffolk, to be near his brother-in-law, Dr Robert Dashwood. He continued his microscopic studies until at least a month before his death at Newmarket, Beccles, on 27 April 1855. Barry died, unmarried, in the evangelical tradition, full of a Christian's hope.

Barry was an indefatigable worker, with a great wish to be regarded as an original discoverer. However, after his illness in the late 1830s he was painfully upset by criticism, and he could be considered dogmatic. Contemporaries regarded his later views as speculative, but he is remembered for his pioneering work on the entry of sperm into the interior of the ovum within hours after copulation, and the early segmentation of the ovum.

GEOFFREY L. ASHERSON

Sources *PRS*, 7 (1854–5), 577–82 [bibliography] · *Edinburgh Medical Journal*, 1 (1855–6), 81–91 · J. Farley, *Gametes and spores: ideas about sexual reproduction, 1750–1914* (1982) · A. Hirsch and others, eds., *Biographisches Lexikon der hervorragenden Aerzte aller Zeiten und Völker*, 2nd edn, ed. W. Haberling, F. Hübötter, and H. Vierordt, 6 vols. (Berlin and Vienna, 1929–35) [bibliography] · J. Y. Simpson, 'On head presentations with the forehead originally directed forwards or towards the pubis', in *The obstetric memoirs and contributions of James Y. Simpson*, ed. W. O. Priestley and H. R. Storer, 1 (1855), 454–81 · *DNB* · d. cert.

Likenesses C. C. Vogel, drawing, Staatliche Kunstsammlungen, Dresden, Germany; copy NPG

Barry, Michael Joseph (1817–1889), writer and lawyer, was born in Cork City, the eldest son of Michael Joseph Barry, a barrister and later professor of English law in the then Queen's College, Cork (now University College, Cork), and his wife, Anne England, sister of Dr England, the first Catholic bishop of Charleston, USA. Following his father to the law, Barry was called to the Irish bar in the Easter term 1839. In 1840, together with William (later Mr Justice) Keogh, he published a textbook, *A Treatise on the Practice of the High Court of Chancery of Ireland*, which was a success. He also had a great love for literature, and as Bouillon

de Garçon wrote a series of humorous poems entitled 'The Kishoge Papers' for the *Dublin University Magazine* in 1842–3. Barry joined Daniel O'Connell's Repeal Association in 1843, and began to write poetry for *The Nation*. His most famous songs from that time were 'The Green Flag' and 'Step together'. Only after 1845 did he also contribute political articles. He used the pseudonyms B., M. J. B., Beta, and Brutus; the latter, according to Charles Gavan Duffy, because the initials of Marcus Junius Brutus were the same as his own (Duffy, *Davis*, 112). He often spoke on behalf of Young Ireland in the Repeal Association, and was 'the most practical and persuasive of the young orators' (Duffy, *Young Ireland*, 2.54). Barry was also notorious for his sense of humour and dry wit. Duffy described him as a cautious character, who was not very spontaneous and rather predictable, but who possessed sound judgement (Duffy, *Young Ireland*, 1.113). In May 1845 Barry won the first prize of £100 in a Repeal essay competition with *Ireland, as she was, as she is, and as she shall be* (1845). He edited *The Songs of Ireland* (1845), which Thomas Davis had prepared. In 1846, he became editor and part-owner of the Cork *Southern Reporter*, but continued to work as a barrister, and defended Duffy in a government prosecution in 1846. He was on circuit when Young Ireland seceded from the Repeal Association in July 1846, but immediately resigned his membership and joined the seceders. He was a member of the council of the Irish Confederation, and regularly reported about the progress of the nationalist movement in Cork.

Barry was arrested on 2 August 1848 at his father's house in Blackrock Road, Cork, and sent to the county gaol, Cork, where he was for a long time the only prisoner. He was released after a couple of months' imprisonment. After that experience, he 'treated the experiment of '48 as final, and the cause of Irish nationality as lost' (Duffy, *Four Years*, 777). He denounced his earlier opinions, and accepted the union of Ireland and Great Britain. This sudden change of views surprised and enraged many nationalists. Barry recommended writing poetry, and in 1849 *Echoes from Parnassus* was published. He continued to edit the *Southern Reporter* until 1855, and afterwards resumed his work at the bar. In 1854 he published 'Waterloo Commemoration for 1854: a Poem'. In 1856 *Lays of the War* was published, and one of the poems was translated into French. Literary critics regarded these poems highly. He took a keen interest in the Crimean War, and became an active member of the committee that inaugurated and successfully carried through the great national banquet given the troops in Dublin on 22 October 1856. A Catholic all his life, he published *The Pope and the Romagna* in 1860 as a defence of his creed. In a pamphlet on emigration, *Irish Emigration Considered* (1863), he supported emigration as a healthy symptom and stated that its continuance was necessary and desirable for the emigrant, Ireland, and the empire. When he was appointed a divisional magistrate for Dublin in December 1871, it was seen as the final breach with his Young Ireland past, and he was heavily attacked by nationalists for accepting a government position (see, for instance, 'A Daniel come to judgment', *The*

Nation, 9 Dec 1871, 1261). Even as a police magistrate he was renowned for his dry humour. Duffy recounted that when a constable was giving evidence against an Irish American suspected of being in Ireland with seditious designs, he swore that the man wore a republican hat. 'A republican hat!' exclaimed the counsel for the prisoner, 'Does your worship know what that means?' 'I presume', said his worship (Barry), 'a republican hat is a hat without a crown' (Duffy, *Four Years*, 778). On his retirement a year later Barry moved to the continent, first to Paris, then to Heidelberg, where he lived with his wife and stepdaughter. His *The Kishoge Papers: Tales of Devilry and Drollery* were published as a book in 1875. *Heinrich and Leonore: an Alpine Story, and some Miscellaneous Verse* was published in 1886. After his wife's death, Barry returned to Cork, where he died at his home, 109 George's Street, on 23 January 1889.

BRIGITTE ANTON

Sources J. Coleman, 'Four former Cork celebrities: with two poems by Michael Joseph Barry', *Journal of the Cork Historical and Archaeological Society*, 2nd ser., 9 (1903), 240–61 • 'Gossip: on a verse written by Michael Joseph Barry, identified by Fr. Matthew Russell, with some stories of Barry and of the Russell family', *Irish Book Lover*, 3 (1911–12), 24–5 • J. Gilbert, 'A record of authors, artists and musical composers born in the co. Cork', *Journal of the Cork Historical and Archaeological Society*, ser., 19 (1913), 168–81 • 'Michael Joseph Barry (Bouillon de Garçon)', *Irish Book Lover*, 9 (1917–18), 25–7 • T. F. O'Sullivan, *The Young Irelanders*, 2nd edn (1945) • M. J. Barry, letter to W. S. O'Brien, 7 July 1847, NL Ire., O'Brien papers, item 1919, MS 438 • C. G. Duffy, *Young Ireland: a fragment of Irish history, 1840–1845*, rev. edn, 2 vols. (1896) • C. G. Duffy, *Four years of Irish history, 1845–1849: a sequel to 'Young Ireland'* (1883) • C. G. Duffy, *Thomas Davis: the memoirs of an Irish patriot, 1840–46* (1890) • C. G. Duffy, *My life in two hemispheres*, 2 vols. (1898); facs. edn (Shannon, 1969) • 'Prizes in the lottery of repeal', *Dublin University Magazine*, 27 (1846), 1–16 • Cork South Parish: baptisms, 21 June 1810–Dec 1834, NL Ire., P. 4778 [Mic] • M. J. Barry, ed., *The songs of Ireland* (1857) • M. J. Barry, *The pope and the Romagna* (1860) • *Dublin Gazette* (8 Dec 1871), 917, col. 1 • *Dublin Gazette* (10 Dec 1872), 881, col. 1 • 'A Daniel come to judgment', *The Nation* (9 Dec 1871), 1261–2 • *Morning News* [Belfast] (25 Jan 1889), 4, cols. 5–6 • *Freeman's Journal* [Dublin] (24 Jan 1889), 4 • *Irish Times* (25 Jan 1889), p. 4, col. 7 • *The Nation* (26 Jan 1889), 8–9 • *Cork Examiner* (24 Jan 1889), 1, col. 1

Archives NL Ire., William Smith O'Brien MSS, MS 438

Barry, Michael Maltman. *See* Barrie, Michael Maltman (1842–1909).

Barry, Philip of (*d. c*.1199), landholder, was a son of William of Barry, lord of Manorbier (Pembrokeshire), and Angharad, daughter of Gerald of Windsor, castellan of Pembroke, and *Nest, daughter of Rhys ap Tewdwr, king of Deheubarth (south Wales). Robert of *Barry, soldier, was his brother. Having received from his maternal uncle, *Robert fitz Stephen, a grant of three cantreds in Desmond, fitz Stephen's half-portion of the kingdom of Cork, consisting of the territory of Uí Liatháin plus two other cantreds to be chosen by lot, he crossed to Ireland at the end of February 1183, accompanied by his brother, Gerald of Barry (*Gerald of Wales), to take possession. From these lands he made grants to St Nicholas's Priory, Exeter, and to St Thomas's Abbey, Dublin. Barry's son Robert was killed at Lismore in 1185 and he himself died about 1199, during Gerald's first visit to Rome. His son William succeeded him, his Irish lands being confirmed by King John on 8

November 1207, from which the two additional cantreds can be identified as Muscraige Uí Donnacáin (or Muscraige Trí Maige, in co. Cork) and Cell Íte (Killeedy, co. Limerick). Philip of Barry had married a daughter of Richard fitz Tancred and a de Baskerville; according to his uncle, Gerald of Wales, it was from his mother's family that Philip's younger son, Gerald (who quarrelled with his uncle and namesake), inherited his wicked behaviour.

M. T. FLANAGAN

Sources Giraldus Cambrensis, *Expugnatio Hibernica / The conquest of Ireland*, ed. and trans. A. B. Scott and F. X. Martin (1978), 156–7, 188–9, 192–3, 234–5 • T. D. Hardy, ed., *Rotuli chartarum in Turri Londinensi asservati*, RC, 36 (1837) • *Gir. Camb. opera* • E. St J. Brooks, ed., 'Unpublished charters relating to Ireland, 1177–82, from the archives of the city of Exeter', *Proceedings of the Royal Irish Academy*, 43C (1935–7), 313–66 • J. T. Gilbert, ed., *Register of the abbey of St Thomas, Dublin*, Rolls Series, 94 (1889), 186 • J. Lodge, *The peerage of Ireland*, 1 (1754), 194 • J. Lodge, *The peerage of Ireland*, rev. M. Archdall, rev. edn, 1 (1789), 287 • Giraldus Cambrensis, *Speculum duorum, or, A mirror of two men*, ed. Y. Lefevre and R. B. C. Huygens, trans. B. Dawson (1974), 30, 38, 40, 58 • G. H. Orpen, *Ireland under the Normans*, 4 vols. (1911–20), vol. 2, p. 44

Barry, Sir Redmond (1813–1880), judge, was born on 7 June 1813 at Ballyclough, co. Cork, Ireland, fifth of the thirteen children of Major-General Henry Green Barry (*d.* 1838) and his wife, Phoebe, daughter of John Armstrong Drought of Lettybrook, King's county. After attending a private academy near Cork, Redmond spent four years at a school at Bexley, Kent, preparing for an army career; from 1833 he attended Trinity College, Dublin, (BA 1837) and he was called to the bar at King's Inns, Dublin, in November 1838.

Barry's failure to obtain a commission, and lack of opportunity at the Irish bar, led him to emigrate to New South Wales. He arrived at Sydney on 1 September 1839 and was admitted as a barrister of the supreme court on 19 October. He sailed for Melbourne in the District of Port Phillip (as Victoria was called before its separation from New South Wales) and arrived there on 13 November. Melbourne had been founded only five years before and, in the absence of a local superior court, its 5000 inhabitants provided little work for a barrister. However, a resident judge of the supreme court sat there from April 1841 and Barry began to establish a fair practice, though he was less successful than another Irishman, the more talented William Foster Stawell. In December 1841 he accepted the position of standing counsel for the Aborigines, at 3 guineas a brief, and from November he also held appointment as commissioner of the court of requests, dealing with small civil claims.

Upon the separation of Victoria from New South Wales in 1851, Barry was appointed its solicitor-general; and upon the establishment of the supreme court of Victoria in January 1852, he became its first puisne judge. When Sir William a'Beckett resigned as chief justice in February 1857, Barry expected to succeed him; but Stawell was preferred. Barry acted in Stawell's place for several extended periods and, in the absence of the governor also, administered the government of the colony for ten days in January 1875.

Sir Redmond Barry (1813–1880), by John Botterill

near his own and to whom he was devoted. Mrs Barrow and the children all survived him.

'Cheery, cultured, courteous Redmond Barry' was a handsome man with an imposing presence, though rather a high-pitched voice. He was courtly and somewhat pompous in manner, eloquent in speech, verbose and florid in his style of writing. He died unexpectedly, still in office, on 23 November 1880 at his home in Clarendon Street, East Melbourne, and was buried on 26 November in the Melbourne general cemetery.

PETER BALMFORD

Sources A. Galbally, *Redmond Barry: an Anglo-Irish Australian* (1995) · P. Ryan, *Redmond Barry: a colonial life, 1813–1880*, 2nd edn (1980) · Z. Cowen, *The Redmond Barry Centenary Oration* (1980) · F. B. Smith, *Journal of the Cork Historical and Archaeological Society*, 2nd ser., 93 (1988), 14–20 · *The Argus* [Melbourne] (24 Nov 1880), 4e, 5g, 6h · *The Argus* [Melbourne] (27 Nov 1880), 7c, 8a · A. Sutherland, 'Sir Redmond Barry', *Melbourne Review*, 7 (1882), 263–94 · H. G. Turner, *A history of the colony of Victoria*, 2 vols. (1904) · R. Boldrewood [T. A. Browne], *Old Melbourne memories* (1884) · Garryowen [E. Finn], *The chronicles of early Melbourne, 1835 to 1852*, new edn (1891) · J. M. Young, *Sir William Foster Stawell* (1989) · J. V. Barry, *The life and death of John Price* (1964) · L. Waller, 'Regina v. Edward Kelly', *Ned Kelly: man and myth*, ed. C. F. Cave, 2nd edn (1980), 105–53 · J. H. Phillips, *The trial of Ned Kelly* (1987) · *AusDB*
Archives Mitchell L., NSW · NL Aus., visitors' book · Public Record Office, Victoria, Australia · State Library of Victoria, Melbourne, Australia, corresp. and papers · Supreme Court of Victoria library, Melbourne, Australia
Likenesses J. Scurry, marble bust, after 1860, Supreme Court of Victoria library, Melbourne, Australia · C. Summers, marble bust, *c*.1860, State Library of Victoria, Melbourne, Australia · marble bust, after 1860, Trinity College, Melbourne, Australia · photograph, *c*.1860, State Library of Victoria, Melbourne, Australia · T. F. Chuck, two photographs, *c*.1865–*c*.1870, State Library of Victoria, Melbourne, Australia · portrait, *c*.1875, State Library of Victoria, Melbourne, Australia · G. F. Folingsby, oils, 1879, University of Melbourne, Australia · T. Woolner, bust, *c*.1879, Melbourne Public Library, Australia · J. Gilbert (completed by P. Ball), bronze statue, *c*.1885, State Library of Victoria, Melbourne, Australia · J. Botterill, oils, State Library of Victoria, Melbourne, Australia [*see illus.*] · caricature, repro. in *Weekly Times* (25 Oct 1873) · caricature, repro. in *Melbourne Punch* (12 Jan 1871) · caricature, repro. in *Melbourne Punch* (14 Dec 1871) · photograph, repro. in Galbally, *Redmond Barry*, facing p. 69; priv. coll.
Wealth at death died in poverty: *AusDB*

A competent though not outstanding judge, Barry is in that capacity remembered principally for the notoriety of some of those he tried: Eureka rebels, acquitted in March 1855 of treason; prisoners convicted in March 1857 of murdering John Price, the inspector-general of penal establishments; the bushranger Ned Kelly, convicted in October 1880 of murdering a constable. Modern analysis of the 1857 trials and Kelly's trial gives rise to some misgivings about Barry's conduct of them; but trials conducted more scrupulously would not necessarily have led to different verdicts.

Of greater significance is Barry's very substantial contribution to educational and cultural institutions in the growing colony, especially the University of Melbourne (of which he was foundation chancellor from 1853 until his death) and what are now the state library, the national gallery, and the museum of Victoria—all originally under one set of trustees of which he was chairman for the same period. His efforts for these bodies went far beyond the mere chairing of meetings or speaking on ceremonial occasions. He was the directing force: formulating principles, guiding staff, and conducting a heavy correspondence; selecting and ordering books and exhibits and sometimes even manhandling them.

Barry was knighted in 1860 and appointed KCMG in 1877. He published about twenty pamphlets: addresses on legal and educational subjects; lectures, catalogues, and biographical charts on artistic subjects. In his private life, he collected books, farmed near Melbourne, and enjoyed his club and dinners in society. He never married, though he acknowledged three sons and a daughter born to Louisa Bridget Barrow (1823–1889), for whom he built a house

Barry, Richard, seventh earl of Barrymore (1769–1793), rake and actor, was born on 14 August 1769, probably in London, the second child and eldest of three sons of Richard Barry, sixth earl of Barrymore (1745–1773), and Lady Emily Stanhope (1749–1780), daughter of William *Stanhope, second earl of Harrington [*see under* Stanhope, William, first earl of Harrington]. On his father's death on 1 August 1773 he succeeded to the title and 140,000 acres in co. Cork shortly before his fourth birthday and was orphaned at eleven. He was tutored from 1774 by the Revd John Tickell at Wargrave, Berkshire, before entering Eton College in 1784, where he developed pronouncedly spendthrift habits. He left Eton in 1786. He was introduced on the turf at Newmarket by Katharine Powlett (*née* Lowther), duchess of Bolton, in 1787, soon afterwards started buying horses, and began racing under his own colours in 1788. His considerable winnings on horses were lost by playing cards, and he borrowed heavily on the expectations of his majority.

Barrymore was tall, slender, and agile, with an aquiline nose, high forehead, and prominent chin. As a fencer, pugilist, cricketer, and gentleman jockey he excelled. Well read and often amusing, he showed many intuitive gifts, but was fickle, with a blackguard side. He became one of the Brighton cronies of George, prince of Wales (afterwards George IV), who bestowed on him the nickname of Hellgate in recognition of his harum-scarum antics. His brother Henry, who had a club foot, was known as Cripplegate, and his sister Caroline, whose language was notoriously uncultivated, as Billingsgate. Some of his exploits, such as going round the countryside at night exchanging the name-signs on village inns, were merely mischievous pranks. He enjoyed impersonating menial servants, or arranging elaborate jokes involving confused identities, but his countryside rampages with a hired mail coach by night were alarming, and other diversions were bullying or destructive. Barrymore relished watching seamy behaviour in slum districts such as St Giles's, and joined several bacchanalian clubs, but was not notably lecherous.

Barrymore had returned to live at Wargrave on leaving Eton, and in 1786 staged a performance of David Garrick's farce *Miss in her Teens* in a barn. Barrymore played Flash, his brothers, Henry and Augustus, were Puff and Fribble, and villagers took other parts. Shortly afterwards he rented a small house on a picturesque site near the banks of the Thames, and began transforming the environs of Wargrave into his pleasure grounds. He bought a pack of hounds, and organized balls and fêtes. Once he arrayed his hunting establishment in imitation of Louis XIV's at Fontainebleau with four superbly mounted black men decked in scarlet and silver, while a French horn player wafted the music of Handel through the woods.

At Wargrave in 1788 Barrymore built the most conspicuous private theatre of the eighteenth century. Earlier he had partly financed the Royal Circus theatre in St George's Fields, London, and despite its failure, Carlo Delpini, who wrote and produced its comic pantomimes, remained his collaborator. The cost of £60,000 given for the Wargrave playhouse may be exaggerated, but certainly it was a sumptuous and extravagant toy. Its inaugural performance on 26 January 1789 was of John Vanbrugh's comedy *The Confederacy*. A year later, after a successful season, Barrymore ordered his theatre's enlargement on the model of Vanbrugh's King's Theatre in the Haymarket, which could seat 400. The extended building was completed in time for Barrymore's coming-of-age celebrations, which lasted a week from 21 September 1790, and were attended by the prince of Wales. Among other performances at Wargrave he played Acres in Richard Brinsley Sheridan's *The Rivals* in April 1791.

Although Barrymore did not have a strong acting voice, he usually acquitted himself well. Probably his most successful rôle was as Scrub in George Farquhar's *The Beaux' Stratagem*. In March 1790 he bought Squib's auction rooms in Savile Row, which had lately been used as a puppet theatre, and converted them into another elegant playhouse. Barrymore, who was always open-handed, especially to actors and scene painters, did not confine his appearances to his own theatres. In 1788 he appeared on the Brighton boards as Bobadil in Ben Jonson's *Every Man in his Humour*, and in 1790 he performed 'a buffoon dance ... in a pantomime at Richmond' (Walpole, *Corr.*, 35.399). George Selwyn similarly witnessed 'that *étourdi* [scatterbrain] Lord Barrymore play the fool in three or four different characters upon our Richmond Theatre' (*Carlisle MSS*, 681).

By 1790 Barrymore needed a seat in the House of Commons to evade his creditors, and offered himself as candidate at Reading, where he held a banquet of which the centrepiece was a turtle weighing 150 pounds. He was defeated, but in March 1791 the twenty-six voters of the rotten borough of Heytesbury, Wiltshire, elected him as their MP; Barrymore had presumably paid the seat's patron, Sir William A'Court, bt. His debts accumulated until in June 1792 the Wargrave theatre, together with its costumes, decorations, and furnishings, was seized on his creditors' behalf. Christies raised only £1127 when the scenery, machinery, and other materials were auctioned in October. The private theatre was demolished, and stables erected on its site.

In the midst of these troubles Barrymore eloped on 6 June 1792 with Charlotte Goulding (*b.* 1774/5), daughter of a sedan chairman. It is accepted that they were married shortly afterwards. It was probably about this time that he sold the family estates, reserving £4000 a year for himself and £1000 a year for his widow for their lives. Barrymore had enlisted as an ensign in the Berkshire militia in 1789, and was promoted captain in 1793. On 6 March 1793, when escorting French prisoners, he was killed by the accidental discharge of his fowling-piece while riding in a gig near Folkestone, Kent. To avoid his corpse being seized by creditors, he was secretly buried at Wargrave on 17 March, in the chancel of the parish church. His widow, who was only eighteen at her husband's death, married Robert Williams, a captain in the 3rd foot guards, on 22 September 1794. On the death of his brother Henry, eighth earl of Barrymore, in 1823, the earldom become extinct.

RICHARD DAVENPORT-HINES

Sources J. R. Robinson, *The last earls of Barrymore, 1769–1824* (1894) · E. B. Chancellor, *Old Q and Barrymore* (1925) · A. Pasquin [J. Williams], *Life of the late earl of Barrymore* (1793) · *Truth opposed to fiction, or, An authentic and impartial review of the life of the late earl of Barrymore by a personal observer* (1793) · *The reminiscences of Henry Angelo*, ed. H. Lavers Smith, 2 vols. (1904) · S. Rosenfeld, *Temples of Thespis* (1978) · *Passages from the diaries of Mrs Lybbe Powys, 1756–1808*, ed. E. J. Climenson (1899) · J. Bernard, *Retrospections on the stage* (1830) · Walpole, *Corr.*, vols. 11, 31, 35, 43 · *The correspondence of George, prince of Wales, 1770–1812*, ed. A. Aspinall, 2: *1789–1794* (1964) · *The manuscripts of the earl of Carlisle*, HMC, 42 (1897), 681–2 · A. Aspinall, 'Barry, Richard', HoP, *Commons, 1790–1820* · R. A. Austen-Leigh, ed., *Eton College lists, 1678–1790* (1907)

Likenesses J. Jehner, engraving, 1778 (after portrait by R. Cosway), BM · W. Leney and P. Audinet, engraving, 1791 (after portrait by S. De Wilde; as Scrub in *The Beaux' stratagem*), BL; repro. in Rosenfeld, *Temples of Thespis*, facing p. 30 · engraving, 1791, BM · Gillray, group portrait (*Les trois magots*), repro. in Lavers Smith, ed.,

Reminiscences of Henry Angelo, vol. 2, facing p. 67 · T. Rowlandson, portrait, repro. in Lavers Smith, ed., *Reminiscences of Henry Angelo*, vol. 2, facing p. 60

Wealth at death under £5000: 26 March 1794, GEC, *Peerage*

Barry, Richard Hugh (1908–1999), army officer, was born on 9 November 1908 at 56 Cornwall Gardens, Kensington, London, the only son and elder of the two children of Lieutenant-Colonel Alfred Percival Barry, army officer, and his wife, Helen Charlotte, *née* Stephens. His great-grandfather was Sir Charles Barry, who rebuilt the houses of parliament. From childhood he looked to a military career. As a commoner at Winchester College, he won the school history prize in 1927; he went on that year to the Royal Military College, Sandhurst, and was commissioned in 1929 into his father's regiment, the Somerset light infantry.

Barry was a studious officer, and qualified early as an interpreter in French and German. He showed such gifts for training that in 1935 he was posted to the small arms school at Netheravon, where he became an expert instructor in the newly invented Bren light machine-gun and in light anti-tank weapons. He went, as a captain, to the Staff College in 1938, and was posted out in 1940 to the intelligence branch of the War Office. His fellow students, little appreciating the role intelligence was about to play in warfare, thereupon presented a pair of spectacles to 'Professor Barry, on his retirement from the Army' (*The Times*, 18 May 1999). He was determined to see some action, and secured a liaison post with the British expeditionary force, just in time to be hustled out safely from Dunkirk. He married, on 20 August 1940, Rosalind Joyce Evans (1913/14–1973), daughter of Benjamin Beardmore Evans, businessman. They had a son and two daughters.

After a short spell at the school of military intelligence at Minley Manor, Barry moved early in 1941 to the Special Operations Executive (SOE), where he was the first head of the operations department, under the eye of Colin Gubbins. His first effective task was to set up operation Savanna, a raid by Gaullist parachutists on an airfield in south Brittany; the raid failed in its object, but produced much useful information. He worked closely with de Gaulle's head of secret services, André Dewavrin (Colonel Passy), who long remembered his Mephistophelean laugh, and he became well known to several of the governments in exile in London, whom he helped to work back into their homelands. When General Eisenhower prepared the allied landing in north Africa which took place in November 1942, Barry joined his planning staff, and went forward to Algiers as a GSO1 (operations). Gubbins secured his recall to SOE in July 1943, and for the rest of the war Barry acted as his chief of staff, sitting on SOE's governing council. He was among the very few members of SOE who were privy to ultra-secret material, and helped the service make its distinguished mark on the war.

After the dissolution of SOE early in 1946, Barry was made military attaché in Stockholm. In 1948 he moved on to a four-year spell as deputy chief of staff, western Europe land forces, in Fontainebleau, and from 1952 to 1954 he was director of the standing group of NATO, in Washington. From 1954 to 1956 he supervised, as chief of staff, the withdrawal of British troops from Egypt, and had moved on to study at the Imperial Defence College before the Suez crisis. In 1958 he was promoted major-general and became British representative on the standing group. He retired from the army in 1962. He was appointed OBE in 1943, CBE in 1953, and CB in 1962.

Barry then had a chance to show his powers of command: settling at the Corridor House, Odiham, Hampshire, he became joint master and then chairman for many years of the Hampshire hunt. He was short, slight in build, always brisk in movement. He and his family were well known and liked in north Hampshire society. He continued to use his French and German as a translator, producing *Shadow War* (1972), an English version of Henri Michel's book, and *Inside Hitler's Headquarters* (1964), by Walter Warlimont, and other books.

Following the death of his wife, Rosalind, in a riding accident in 1973 Barry married, on 14 April 1975, a neighbour, Elizabeth Lucia Middleton (1919/20–1994), daughter of William Henry Middleton. Following her death in 1994 he moved to Little Place, a cottage in Farringdon, Hampshire. He died at Brendoncare, Anstey Road, Alton, Hampshire, on 30 April 1999, of bronchopneumonia. He was survived by the three children of his first marriage.

M. R. D. FOOT

Sources W. J. M. Mackenzie, *The secret history of SOE* (2000) · *The Times* (18 May 1999) · *Daily Telegraph* (14 June 1999) · M. R. D. Foot, *SOE in France: an account of the work of the British Special Operations Executive in France, 1940–1944*, 2nd edn (1968) · Colonel Passy [A. Dewavrin], *Memoirs* (Paris, 2000) · *WWW* · personal knowledge (2004) · private information (2004) · b. cert. · m. certs. · d. cert. · M. S. Leigh, ed., *Winchester College 1884–1934: a register* (1940)

Archives Foreign and Commonwealth Office, London | PRO, special operations executive archives, s.v. HS

Likenesses photograph, 1952, repro. in *The Times* · photograph, repro. in *Daily Telegraph*

Wealth at death £487,849: probate, 1 Feb 1999, CGPLA Eng. & Wales

Barry, Robert of (*d.* in or after 1185), soldier, was the younger son of William of Barry, lord of Manorbier (Pembrokeshire), and Angharad, daughter of Gerald of Windsor, castellan of Pembroke, and *Nest, daughter of Rhys ap Tewdwr, king of Deheubarth (south Wales). Philip of *Barry, landholder, was his brother. He accompanied his maternal uncle, *Robert fitz Stephen, to Ireland in May 1169, and took part at the siege of Wexford. His brother, Gerald of Barry (*Gerald of Wales), who indicated that Robert was still alive sixteen years later, extolled his military prowess in Ireland.

J. H. ROUND, *rev.* M. T. FLANAGAN

Sources Giraldus Cambrensis, *Expugnatio Hibernica | The conquest of Ireland*, ed. and trans. A. B. Scott and F. X. Martin (1978), 32–5, 36–7, 38–9, 156–7

Barry, Robert Raymond Smith- (1886–1949), air force officer, was born on 4 April 1886 at 2 Chapel Street, Mayfair, London, the only son of James Hugh Smith-Barry (1845–1927), of Foaty Island, Queenstown, co. Cork, and Stowell Park, Wiltshire, a JP for Wiltshire and formerly high sheriff for co. Louth, and his wife, Charlotte Jane (*d.* 1933), the daughter of William Willoughby Cole, third earl of Enniskillen. Arthur Hugh Smith Barry, first Baron Barrymore, a prominent Irish landlord and Conservative politician, was his uncle. He attended Eton College, where his housemaster described him as an awful boy with no aptitudes whatever, and entered Trinity College, Cambridge, in 1904 but left soon afterwards without taking a degree. For a time he was an honorary attaché in the diplomatic service. On 2 August 1913 he married Kathleen Beatrice Melita (Kitty), the fourth daughter of Colonel George William Cockburn, formerly of the 42nd highlanders. They had no children.

Despite the harsh judgement of his housemaster, or perhaps in response to it, Smith-Barry became a fine pianist, one of the most skilful and daring of pioneer pilots, and 'not only revolutionised flying instruction' in the Royal Flying Corps (RFC) and its successor, the Royal Air Force, 'but created it, for what we had been doing previously was a matter of the blind leading the blind' (Lee, 35). He had his first flying lessons at Larkhill on Salisbury Plain in September 1911, was commissioned in the special reserve of the newly formed Royal Flying Corps in August 1912, and by the following July was among its most experienced pilots. At Gosport, near Portsmouth, he joined 5 squadron, one of four sent to France with the British expeditionary force on 14 August 1914. Engine failure caused his BE 8 biplane to crash on the 18th, killing his passenger and putting Smith-Barry into hospital at St Quentin with two broken legs and other injuries. On learning of the imminent arrival of Germans, he had himself carried back to England, enduring severe pain throughout the long journey. Six months later, although still walking with a stick and limping badly (as he did for the rest of his life), he persuaded the authorities that he was fit enough for home flying and instructing at Northolt, Middlesex. There he proved, to himself and others, that the accident had neither impaired his skill nor undermined his self-confidence.

In April 1916 Smith-Barry—promoted captain—was one of three old Etonians appointed as flight commanders in 60 squadron, formed for service in France under another old Etonian, Ferdie Waldron. The squadron, based at Vert Galant (north of Amiens), took part in the Somme battle, beginning on 1 July. Waldron was killed on 3 July, and Smith-Barry, promoted major, took command for the rest of the year. One night in August he dealt with a massive accumulation of 'bumph' (as he regarded all official paper) by burning down the squadron office. But no commander defeats bumph, and Smith-Barry was soon reburied; moreover, he was strictly forbidden to escape it by flying on operations. This decision spared him an early death (only too likely, given his bold temperament) and allowed him time to consider the RFC's low level of flying skill. His solution saved countless lives, gave Britain a more competent air force during the last twenty months of the war, and provided a permanent framework for systematic tuition in many air forces.

As late as December 1916 'mystery still surrounded the less usual movements of an aeroplane' (Jones, 5.430). Consequently, numerous pilots were injured or killed in avoidable accidents and others suffered at the hands of better-trained German pilots. The situation appalled Smith-Barry, who demanded of General Trenchard (head of the RFC in France) a complete reorganization of training methods. Trenchard, well aware of Smith-Barry's merits, sent him back to England on 24 December 1916 to serve under General John Salmond, recently appointed to oversee just such a reorganization. Salmond, who also knew Smith-Barry of old, gave him a free hand in January 1917 to test his ideas in practice at Gosport.

More than twenty years later, at a dinner arranged in July 1938 to celebrate his Gosport achievement, Smith-Barry paid tribute to his colleagues there in a nicely mangled metaphor: 'I merely spelt out the alphabet', he said. 'They wrote the classical music' (Tredrey, 112). Others recognized the letters (or notes), but no one before Smith-Barry set them down in logical sequence. Pupil pilots, he insisted, must no longer sit in the passenger seat, looking over the instructor's shoulder and trying to learn by watching. Training aircraft must have a full set of controls in both cockpits—and the instructor not the pupil must occupy the passenger seat. He must not protect his pupil from dangerous situations. On the contrary, he must make him so familiar with sharp turns, stalls, spins, engine failure, wind gusts, bad weather, and other hazards that the pupil would instinctively take appropriate action. He must test himself (and the machine) to the limit by contour-chasing, hedge-hopping, diving into railway cuttings, circling church steeples, and examining at close range the cliffs of the Isle of Wight.

As for flying instructors, they could be drawn only from those pilots so lucky, or so naturally gifted, that they were still alive. They must now be taught to *understand* what luck, instinct, and experience had already given them, in order to help others reach their level of expertise more easily. A 'school of special flying' opened at Gosport in July 1917 where experienced pilots received two or three weeks of intensive tuition. Smith-Barry was promoted lieutenant-colonel and appointed commandant in August. The ablest of these pilots were required to serve a turn as instructors and urged to regard the work as of vital importance.

An instructor must be able to talk to his pupil while in the air, despite engine noise. Shouting, hand signals, blows on the head, and scribbled notes served little practical purpose. Smith-Barry therefore devised 'the Gosport tube': at one end it had two earpieces for the pupil and at the other a mouthpiece for the instructor. This tube made possible the famous 'Gosport patter', whereby instructors drilled into captive ears a methodical summary of essential procedures. In October 1917 the War Office published 500 copies of a pamphlet summarizing Smith-Barry's methods and distributed it to all units at home and abroad.

To implement his system, Smith-Barry found an ideal aircraft: the Avro 504 (J or K, depending on its engine). It was viceless, fully aerobatic, and fast enough to prepare pupils for the latest combat machines. With Salmond's support, Smith-Barry had it designated the RFC's sole trainer, and nearly 3000 were in service by the war's end. The Gosport system 'was brilliantly conceived, but so was the aeroplane which made it possible'; the Avro 504 shared with Smith-Barry and his colleagues 'the honour of having instituted and brought to perfection what remains today [1936] the finest school of advanced flying training there has ever been' (Stewart, 115).

Between the wars Smith-Barry became a country gentleman at his home, Conock Manor, near Upavon, Wiltshire. He remained an active pilot and joined the RAF volunteer reserve in May 1940, serving as a ferry pilot and ground instructor at several stations in England and India until his resignation in June 1943. He remained 'the Colonel' whatever rank the RAF awarded him, and both senior and junior officers regarded him with a mixture of veneration (for what he had achieved) and admiration (for his undiminished flying skill); they also found him difficult to deal with, except on his own terms.

After the death of his first wife, on 18 May 1941, Smith-Barry married Anne Garnier (d. 1969), the daughter of Canon Edward Southwell Garnier, in London in September 1945. They settled near Durban, South Africa, where Smith-Barry died on 2 May 1949, following an operation on the leg which had caused him pain ever since the BE 8 crash.

A small, slightly built man, strikingly handsome when young, with penetrating eyes in an unsmiling face, Smith-Barry had a forceful personality that could silence generals as readily as cadets. But he was usually charming, keen to emphasize his Irish origins, fluent in several languages (with a fund of unlikely tales in all of them), uninhibited in speech or dress, and increasingly eccentric in later life. He was a wealthy man, who spent freely on his own interests and pleasures, but secretly helped many others. VINCENT ORANGE

Sources F. D. Tredrey, Pioneer pilot: the great Smith Barry who taught the world how to fly (1976) · H. Penrose, British aviation: the Great War and armistice, 1915–1919 (1969) · H. A. Jones, The war in the air, 1914–1918 (1922–37), vol. 5 · A. G. Lee, Flypast: highlights from a flyer's life (1974) · O. Stewart, commentary, in L. Bridgman, The clouds remember: the aeroplanes of World War I (1936); repr. (1972) · P. H. Liddle, The airman's war, 1914–18 (1987) · G. Norris, The royal flying corps: a history (1965) · R. Barker, The royal flying corps in France: from Mons to the Somme (1994) · A. Boyle, Trenchard (1962) · S. F. Vincent, Flying fever (1972) · A. J. L. Scott, Sixty squadron, RAF, 1916–1919 (1920); repr. (1990) · W. Fry, Air of battle (1974) · Flight (5 May 1949), 541 · Burke, Peerage (1924) ['Barrymore'] · Walford, County families (1919) · Kelly, Handbk (1947) · b. cert.

Likenesses two photographs, 1918–42, repro. in Tredrey, Pioneer pilot · photograph, c.1940, repro. in Norris, Royal flying corps, 112 · P. Walbourn, portrait (after photographs, 1917), Central Flying School, Little Rissington, Gloucestershire

Barry, Spranger (bap. 1717, d. 1777), actor and impresario, was born in Skinner Row, Dublin, and baptized on 13 November 1717 at St Werburgh's, Dublin, the second of the two sons of William Barry and his wife, Catherine. Among the male acting fraternity of the third quarter of the eighteenth century, Barry was the only serious rival to David Garrick. He was brought up in Dublin, where his father was a successful silversmith, a trade to which he was apprenticed. Having been enabled to set up on his own with the assistance of a substantial dowry from his first wife, Anne, he turned to the theatre; however, in but one of the frequent financial disasters that he brought upon himself during his life, he was made bankrupt by the venture. Only in his mid-twenties, but apparently as impressive in his figure as in his voice, he was entrusted with the part of Othello as his very first role, at the Aungier Street Theatre, Dublin. He quickly established a reputation and acted there and then at Smock Alley for two seasons, working alongside the young Garrick, as well as Samuel Foote and Thomas Sheridan. Smock Alley had been where Robert Wilks and George Farquhar had started their theatre careers before heading for London and, when Garrick did likewise and the Dublin theatre proved reluctant to settle its debts to him, Barry followed their example and engaged himself to reprise the part of Shakespeare's Moor at Drury Lane.

Barry had hoped to renew his working relationship with Garrick, but discovered that the latter was already committed to Covent Garden, and thus a pattern was established that was to continue through both actors' careers, with periods of direct competition punctuated by increasingly uneasy attempts at collaboration. Thomas Gray wrote of Barry's Othello: 'I think he may make a better Player than any now on the Stage in a little while' (Highfill, Burnim & Langhans, BDA), and another contemporary, John Hill, wrote of his delivery of Othello's pronouncement to Desdemona in act 5: 'Had all his hairs been lives my great revenge had stomachs for them all', that the audience sees the actor physically change, 'his whole visage becomes inflamed, and he seems to raise himself above the ground while he pronounces it' (ibid.). Certainly, Garrick acknowledged his power in the part by never again attempting it himself. Barry then less successfully took the role of Macbeth before playing the first of the romantic lovers with which his career was to be most associated, Castalio in Thomas Otway's The Orphan. He continued at Drury Lane through the season of 1747–8 after the theatre had passed into the management of Garrick.

However, the initial collaboration between the two actors could not last. They frequently appeared alongside each other in productions and alternated roles, as, for instance, Hamlet and Macbeth, much to the delight of a public who welcomed the opportunity to make comparisons, and their mutual rivalry steadily increased. When, in 1748, Garrick allowed Barry to play Romeo, a part that he had made very much his own, the situation became intolerable. Complaining that Barry was too frequently 'indisposed' to perform, presumably as a result of the actor's very active social life, Garrick was clearly keen to see the back of him. At the end of the following season Barry left to join the Covent Garden company, which immediately set up the two actors against each other in simultaneous productions of Romeo and Juliet, Barry continuing his association with Mrs Cibber as Juliet. Mrs

Pritchard's distinction between the two is to the point: she found Garrick:

> so ardent and impassioned ... I should have expected he would have come up to me in the balcony; but had I been Juliet to Barry's Romeo—so tender, so eloquent, and so seductive was he, I should certainly have gone down to him. (Highfill, Burnim & Langhans, BDA)

Barry continued at Covent Garden until the end of the season in 1754. He played a variety of roles, including those of Essex in Jones's *The Earl of Essex* and Lothario in Nicholas Rowe's *The Fair Penitent*.

After his first wife died, leaving him a comfortable estate, Barry took up with Maria Isabella *Nossiter (1735–1759), who first appeared on stage in 1753 as Juliet to his Romeo. Following a disagreement over money with John Rich, the manager of Covent Garden, he returned briefly to Dublin and the Smock Alley Theatre with his young mistress; but he was back at Covent Garden for the 1755–6 season, when he had a great success with the part of Alexander in the revival of Cibber's *The Rival Queens* and a rather smaller one with his attempt once more to emulate Garrick, by this time taking on the role of King Lear, about which public opinion was very mixed. Barry, having once more left the Covent Garden company, had by now embarked on his involvement with the construction of a new house, the Crow Street Theatre in Dublin, which opened in 1758. The venture was to prove a financial disaster, and by 1766 Barry had returned to London under a generous profit-sharing agreement made with his old colleague, Samuel Foote, whose company was to occupy the King's Theatre. Maria Nossiter having died in 1759, he brought with him a recently widowed actress, Ann Dancer [see Barry, Ann], who had worked with him in Dublin and about 1768 became his second wife. Her first London engagement was to play Desdemona to Barry's Othello. Following his next reunion with Garrick, when he rejoined the Drury Lane company, in 1767, Barry and Mrs Dancer became a familiar partnership on stage; they had a long run together as Rhadamistus and Zenobia in Arthur Murphy's *Zenobia*.

It was not long, however, before the familiar pattern of hostility between Garrick and Barry resumed, this time fuelled by the increasing unreliability of both Barry and his wife. As a result either of theatrical politics or, possibly, of his exorbitant lifestyle, not only did announced performances fail to occur, but new productions had to be postponed and cancelled. By the early 1770s Garrick found himself forced to make new contractual arrangements with Barry, under which his salary was threatened if he did not perform as scheduled. Barry was also beginning to be neither young enough nor sprightly enough to continue to convince in the kinds of romantic leads with which he had made his reputation. He continued to work for Garrick at Drury Lane, although his increasingly unreliable presence was punctuated by brief returns to Dublin in vain attempts to sort out the troubled finances of the Crow Street venture. At the end of the 1773–4 season he broke with his rival for the last time and joined the Covent Garden company. Bowing to his increasing age and

infirmities, he now abandoned the romantic leads of his youth and took on such parts as Jaques in Shakespeare's *As You Like It*. On 28 November 1776 he made his final stage appearance, playing Evander opposite his wife as Euphrasia in Murphy's *The Grecian Daughter*, a collaboration they had first attempted at Drury Lane in 1772 and had just reprised in a triumphant short season at Edinburgh. On 10 January 1777 Barry died. He was buried in the north cloister of Westminster Abbey on 20 January, his wife having failed to persuade Garrick to provide an epitaph for the tomb. When Ann died, on 29 November 1801, she was buried alongside him in the abbey, the missing words of Garrick an entirely appropriate memorial of the tangled relationships between the two great male actors of their generation.   JOHN BULL

Sources Highfill, Burnim & Langhans, *BDA* · D. Pickering, ed., *Actors, directors and designers* (1996), vol. 3 of *International dictionary of theatre*, ed. M. Hawkins-Dady · P. Hartnoll, ed., *The Oxford companion to the theatre*, 4th edn (1983) · R. Hitchcock, *An historical view of the Irish stage from the earliest period down to the close of the season 1788*, 2 vols. (1788–94) · T. Wilkinson, *Memoirs of his own life*, 4 vols. (1790) · F. Gentleman, *The dramatic censor, or, Critical companion*, 2 vols. (1770) · T. Davies, *Dramatic miscellanies*, 3 vols. (1784) · Genest, *Eng. stage* · I. Wenman, *Mr Barry in the character of Othello* (1770) · A. Murphy, *The life of David Garrick*, 2 vols. (1801) · T. Gilliland, *The dramatic mirror, containing the history of the stage from the earliest period, to the present time*, 2 vols. (1808) · P. W. Montague-Smith, 'Ancestry of the actor, Spranger Barry', *N&Q*, 193 (1948), 432–3

Likenesses F. Hayman, double portrait, oils, c.1751–1754 (as Hamlet with Mrs Elmy as Gertrude), Garr. Club · W. Elliott, double portrait, engraving, 1753 (as Romeo with Mrs Nossiter as Juliet; after R. Pyle) · J. Reynolds, oils, c.1758 · J. Roberts, double portrait, oils, c.1775 (as Hamlet with Mrs Barry as Gertrude), Garr. Club · M. Jackson, engraving, 1777 (as Macbeth; after J. Gwinn) · engraving, 1777 (as Othello) · Terry, engraving, 1779 (as Varanes in *Theodosius*) · print, in or before 30 April 1806 · J. Collyer, double portrait, engraving (as Jaffeir in *Venice preserv'd* with Mrs Barry as Belvidera; after J. Roberts) · T. Cook, engraving (speaking the prologue to *The Earl of Essex*; after D. Dodd) · N. Dance, oils, Hunt. L. · E. Harding, engraving (after Reynolds), repro. in F. G. Waldron, *The biographical mirrour*, 3 vols. (1795–1810?) · J. Highmore, group portrait, oils (rehearsing Romeo with Miss and Mrs Pritchard, Fielding, Quin and Lavinia Fenton), priv. coll. · Taylor, engraving (as Timon; after D. Dodd) · Thornthwaite, double portrait, engraving (as Bajazet in *Tamerlane* with Mrs Barry as Selima; after J. Roberts), repro. in J. Bell, *Bell's British theatre* (1776) · W. Walker, engraving (as Timon in *Timon of Athens*; after J. Roberts), repro. in *Bell's edition of Shakespeare's plays* (1776) · double portrait, engraving (as King Lear with Mrs Barry as Cordelia), repro. in *Universal Museum* (Sept 1767) · engraving (as Alexander in *The rival queens*) · engraving (as Hotspur), Harvard TC · portrait, Garr. Club · theatrical prints, BM, NPG

Wealth at death left estate to widow, incl. leasehold house at Streatham, Surrey; also Theatre Royal, Crow Street, Dublin, and adjoining house with wardrobe and effects; £40 and £60 annuities to Ann and Julia Carter: will, 24 Jan 1770

Barry, Sir (Philip) Stuart Milner- (1906–1995), codebreaker and chess player, was born on 20 September 1906 in Hendon, London, the second youngest of six children (five sons and one daughter) of Edward Leopold Milner-Barry, a schoolteacher (later professor of modern languages at the University of Bangor) and his wife, Edith Mary, daughter of Dr William Besant, a renowned mathematical fellow of St John's College, Cambridge.

Milner-Barry was educated at Cheltenham College and Trinity College, Cambridge, where he obtained firsts in the classical tripos (part I) and the moral sciences tripos (part I). On coming down at the start of the great depression, he became a stockbroker, an occupation that did not suit his talents. He survived mentally through his devotion to chess. He had been boy champion of England in 1923 and played for England in the international chess olympiads of 1937, 1939, 1952, and 1956. He was chess correspondent of *The Times* from 1938 to 1945.

Milner-Barry was playing chess for England in Argentina, with his friends Hugh Alexander [*see* Alexander, (Conel) Hugh O'Donel] and Harry Golombek, when the United Kingdom declared war on Germany in September 1939. They immediately abandoned the tournament and sailed for England. Gordon Welchman, who had been in the same year as Milner-Barry at Trinity College, recruited him in early 1940 for the Government Code and Cypher School (GCCS). He joined Welchman in Hut 6, which was responsible for the attack on German army and air force Enigma, at Bletchley Park.

Despite his powerful intellect, Milner-Barry always claimed modestly that he was not clever enough to be a cryptanalyst: he described himself as almost innumerate, but breaking Enigma tended to require a mathematical brain. Initially he helped to find 'cribs' (the probable plain text of messages enciphered on Enigma), without which it was almost impossible to break Enigma keys quickly. Hut 6 'menus' (a form of program) for the 'bombes' (ultra-fast key-finding aids) depended entirely on accurate cribs. A single misplaced letter would almost certainly render a bombe run abortive, delaying the supply of vital intelligence.

Milner-Barry was a co-author, together with Alexander, Alan Turing, and Welchman, of a memorandum to Winston Churchill on 21 October (Trafalgar day) 1941. They explained that the lack of a small number of junior staff (probably about a hundred) was badly delaying the work of Huts 6 and 8 (naval Enigma). Stewart Menzies, the head of MI6, who also had overall responsibility for GCCS, had neglected to ensure that it was adequately staffed and managed, although it was then the only jewel in his crown. Milner-Barry was deputed to take the memorandum to Churchill, possibly because he was, in his own view, the most expendable member of the quartet. The following day Churchill issued an 'action this day' minute directing that they were to have everything they needed as a matter of the highest priority. On 18 November Menzies (who misguidedly thought that they had wasted the prime minister's time) reported that GCCS's needs were being rapidly met.

As Hut 6 expanded, Milner-Barry became its deputy head and the head of the cryptanalytical operational watch. His friendship with Alexander, together with his recognition of the critical importance of the battle of the Atlantic, enabled them to agree quickly on the allocation of scarce bombes between Huts 6 and 8, without delaying vital solutions by having to refer the issue upwards for decision.

After the BRUSA (Britain–United States of America) agreement of May 1943 between GCCS and the US war department on dividing signals intelligence work against Germany, Italy, and Japan, US army personnel were seconded to Hut 6 for training. Although Milner-Barry initially 'viewed the prospect with some consternation' because Hut 6 'was faced with technical problems which would make it difficult to find the time for training', the gifted American contingent made a real contribution to Hut 6's work. Milner-Barry later described their arrival as 'one of the luckiest things that happened to Hut 6' (letter, 10 May 1945, to William Bundy, 'Technical history of the 6813th signal security detachment', NARA, HCC Nr. 4685).

By September 1943, when Milner-Barry was promoted head of Hut 6, it comprised about 450 staff. His 'Hut 6 reports' were models of clarity and good sense, while his invaluable organizational skills helped Hut 6 to cope with a wide range of new Enigma problems in 1944, including a rewirable reflecting 'rotor' (D-Dora), a device called the '*Uhr*' which rendered Enigma's plugboard non-reciprocal (greatly reducing the power of the bombes), and encoded call-signs. Fortunately Hut 6 had begun to receive significant help from the US navy's fast and reliable four-rotor bombes and related equipment. Milner-Barry urged that the US navy should order more bombes specially for Hut 6 work. In the event the 100 or so US navy bombes available coped with the extra load, contributing almost half of Hut 6's equivalent bombe-time during the last quarter of 1944. Although he increasingly felt that Hut 6 was on the verge of losing the ability to decode Enigma, it held on until the end of the war, and this was due in no small part to his gifted leadership.

In 1947 Milner-Barry married Thelma Tennant Wells. They had one son and two daughters. After the war he joined the Treasury with the rank of principal. He was appointed an assistant secretary in 1947 and promoted to under-secretary in 1954. In 1966 he became the ceremonial officer in the Civil Service Department, with responsibility for administering the honours system, which he did with his usual tact and aplomb. He was aptly described by a head of the civil service as 'a wholly admirable person' (private information). He was appointed OBE in 1946 for his wartime work, and later CB in 1962, and KCVO in 1975. Sir Stuart Milner-Barry died on 25 March 1995 in Lewisham Hospital, London.   RALPH ERSKINE

Sources personal knowledge (2004) · private information (2004) · *The Times* (28 March 1995) · *WW* (1994) · F. H. Hinsley and others, *British intelligence in the Second World War*, 2 (1981) · P. S. Milner-Barry, '"Action this day": the letter from Bletchley Park cryptanalysts to the prime minister, 21 October 1941', *Intelligence and National Security*, 1/2 (1986), 272–6 · S. Milner-Barry, 'Hut 6: early days', *Codebreakers: the inside story of Bletchley Park*, ed. F. H. Hinsley and A. Stripp (1993), 89–99 · Capt. Walter J. Fried reports / SSA liaison with GCCS, National Archives and Records Administration, College Park, Maryland, Historic Cryptographic Collection, RG 457, no. 2612 · technical history of the 6813th signal security detachment, National Archives and Records Administration, College Park, Maryland, Historic Cryptographic Collection, no. 4685 · PRO, Government Code and Cypher School, directorate, Second World War policy papers, HW 14 files

Archives CAC Cam., papers relating to code-breaking at Bletchley Park

Barry, Thomas de (*fl.* 1560), poet, was a canon of Glasgow and chief magistrate of Bothwell. He wrote a poem on the battle of Otterburn, the greater part of which is quoted in the eighteenth-century editions of Fordun's *Scotichronicon*. According to Dempster he flourished in 1560, and he may be identical with the Thomas de Barry, presbyter, whose name appears as notary in a document preserved in the *Registrum episcopatus Glasguensis* in 1503.

[ANON.], *rev.* J. K. M^cGINLEY

Sources T. Dempster, *Historia ecclesiastica gentis Scotorum* (Bologna, 1627), 106–7 · Tanner, *Bibl. Brit.-Hib.*, 78 · C. Innes, ed., *Registrum episcopatus Glasguensis*, 2 vols., Bannatyne Club, 75 (1843), 294

Barry, Thomas (*c.*1810–1857), clown, was born in Ireland about 1810. He was noted with Samwell's circus in Swansea in 1842, and as a white-faced ring clown at Astley's circus for long periods between 1843 and 1856. In 1844 he sailed the Thames from Vauxhall to Westminster in a tub drawn by four geese, an illusion originated by Dicky Usher in 1809. Celebrated as a clown and at the zenith of his fame in 1847, he was found by Sam Wild to be as jovial and good-natured as he had been when performing with Wild's travelling circus ten years earlier. In 1850 he was charged before the Lambeth police court with having assaulted William Henry Harvey, the ballet master at Astley's.

In 1849 Barry was with Hengler's circus at Windsor, and his benefit at the end of the nine-week season was very profitable. At Astley's during the 1850s he was paid £10 per week. Perhaps his most famous turn was his comic imitation of a parliamentary candidate, with a speech from the hustings. A portrait shows that his make-up consisted of a white face, with small, delicately outlined red mouth, red triangles on his cheeks, greatly exaggerated black eyebrows, and a bald wig. He made guest appearances with other companies, being noted in 1853 at both Madame Macarte's circus in Wolverhampton and at E. T. Smith's Drury Lane circus in London. On one occasion, following a quarrel with the Shakespearian jester W. F. Wallett, he left Astley's in a huff to keep a public house: he was landlord of The Crown tavern, Lambeth, in 1848–50 and again in 1856–7. He finally left Astley's in 1856, when his right to choose his parts was withdrawn, but he died the following year, on 26 March, at Clapham, London. He was buried in Norwood cemetery. His widow, Elizabeth, an actress (formerly Mrs Hugh Campbell), lived until 1873, and his son, Tom Barry junior, followed his father's profession.

JOHN M. TURNER

Sources *The Era* (4 March 1849) · *The Era* (27 Oct 1850) · *The Era* (30 Oct 1853) · S. Wild, *Old Wild's* (1888) · G. Speaight, *A history of the circus* (1980) · G. C. D. Odell, *Annals of the New York stage*, 15 vols. (1927–49), vol. 9 · private information (2004) · burial register
Likenesses portrait, repro. in I. K. Fletcher, 'A portrait of Thomas Barry', *Theatre Notebook*, 17 (1963) · prints, Harvard TC

Barry, Thomas Bernardine (1897–1980), Irish revolutionary and folk hero, was born on 1 July 1897 in Killorglin, co. Kerry, the eldest son and second of eleven children of Thomas Barry, a policeman, and his wife, Margaret Donovan, both of co. Cork. After Tom was born his father turned to shopkeeping in their native county. He was educated in convent and national schools at Ross Carbery and Bandon in west co. Cork until 1911, when he spent a year as an apostolic student at Mungret College in co. Limerick. Eschewing the priesthood he became a clerk but stayed only until joining the Royal Artillery in 1915. He turned down the offer of a commission, saw action in France and Mesopotamia, and was both gassed and wounded.

Barry was demobilized in early 1919 and returned home to Bandon an active former serviceman. That September he enrolled in a business course in Cork city, but gave it up on joining the 3rd (West) Cork brigade of the Irish Republican Army in the summer of 1920. His lifelong conversion to revolutionary nationalism dates from this point.

Barry's position as training officer was effectively probationary until his command of the Kilmichael ambush of 28 November 1920. This action, which wiped out a patrol of auxiliary policemen, transformed him into a flying column leader and underground legend. The details of the ambush—why surviving auxiliaries were executed—have always been controversial, and became an obsession late in life.

After Kilmichael, Barry was involved in most of the major engagements with crown forces in west co. Cork, and in a parallel series of murders of suspected informers. He established a reputation as an aggressive, abrasive, and egotistical commander, attracting both loyalty and enmity.

Following the truce of 11 July 1921 Barry was appointed the chief liaison officer for Cork, a position requiring tact and which he quickly resigned. On 22 August he married Leslie Price (1897–1984), a teacher and Cumann na mBan activist from Dublin. Both were militantly opposed to the Anglo-Irish treaty of 6 December. Most of Cork's anti-treaty leaders sought compromise and unity; Barry sought confrontation. At IRA conventions in early 1922 he advocated using force to prevent the imminent general election, as well as the resumption of war with Britain. His proposals were defeated but his efforts helped divide republican forces.

When the Irish Civil War began on 28 June Barry was almost immediately captured by the national army in Dublin, but managed to escape in September. He then resumed his career as a flying column leader. His efforts were as self-directed and successful as before, but the IRA as a whole was losing the war by the onset of winter. Faced with defeat Barry became an advocate of peace negotiations. These were blocked by Liam Lynch, the IRA chief of staff, whom he despised. Once Lynch was killed in April 1923 Barry was promoted to the now-supreme army council and backed its unilateral ceasefire order.

Barry maintained his local influence and high rank in the IRA throughout the 1920s and 1930s, while working as a superintendent for the Cork harbour commissioners. He led numerous marches, demonstrations, and riots, and was jailed on several occasions in the 1930s. He was also involved in attacks on supposed enemies, including the murder of Admiral Henry Somerville in 1936. In the same year he was appointed chief of staff. His plan to launch a guerrilla war in Northern Ireland was a non-starter, owing as much to his own poor leadership as to flawed planning and organization. He resigned in 1938 rather than take part in the subsequent English bombing campaign. Apart from an unsuccessful foray into a Cork by-election in 1946, this ended his political career.

Barry published his memoirs of 1920–21, *Guerrilla Days in Ireland*, in 1949. These were a rapid and enduring success and augmented his popular reputation, which was frequently rehearsed at commemorations and in newspaper and radio interviews. General Tom Barry, as he was latterly known, died at his home, St Patrick's Street, Cork, on 2 July 1980, and was buried two days later at St Fin Barre's cemetery, Cork. He was mourned as a national hero.

PETER HART

Sources M. Ryan, *The Tom Barry story* (1982) · P. Hart, *The I.R.A. and its enemies* (1998) · M. Hopkinson, *Green against green: the Irish civil war* (1988) · T. Barry, *Guerrilla days in Ireland* (1949) · *Cork Examiner* (10 Nov 1915) · *Cork County Eagle* (22 Jan 1916) · *Irish Times* (3 July 1980) · *Cork Examiner* (3 July 1980) · census return for the Barry family household, 1911 · *Mungret Annual* (1911–12) · *Sunday Independent* (7 March 1976) · *Irish Press* (7 April 1980) · private information (2004) · *CGPLA Éire* (1980)
Archives PRO, British military intelligence file, WO 35/206 · University College, Dublin, Richard Mulcahy MSS · University College, Dublin, Ernie O'Malley MSS | SOUND Radio Telefís Éireann Sound Archives, Dublin
Likenesses group photograph, 22 Aug 1921, repro. in T. P. Coogan, *Michael Collins* (1990) · photograph, 1921, Crawford Municipal art gallery, Cork, Ireland
Wealth at death £16,361: probate, 19 Nov 1980, *CGPLA Éire*

Barrymore. For this title name *see* Barry, David fitz David, first earl of Barrymore (1605–1642); Barry, James, fourth earl of Barrymore (1667–1748); Barry, Richard, seventh earl of Barrymore (1769–1793).

Barrymore, Lionel [*real name* Lionel Blyth] (1878–1954), actor, was born on 28 April 1878 at 119 North Nine Street in Philadelphia, Pennsylvania, USA. His father was known as the actor Maurice Barrymore (1847–1905), but he had been born as Herbert Blyth to British parents who were living in India. Lionel Barrymore also had the surname Blyth, but he used the name Barrymore throughout his life. His mother was the American actress Georgina Drew Barrymore (1856–1892), who was descended from a noted British theatrical family; her parents were the actors John Drew and Louisa Lane Drew.

Lionel Barrymore was the eldest of his parents' three children. His sister, Ethel Barrymore (1879–1959), was one of the most respected stage actresses of her time. His brother, John Barrymore (1882–1942), was also a greatly admired actor whose performances as Richard III and Hamlet became legendary. The Barrymores were known as the 'royal family of Broadway', but Lionel's stage career was less successful than his siblings' acclaimed careers, and he left the stage altogether in 1925 and subsequently made his greatest impact as a film actor.

Barrymore was educated at Gilmore School, London, and in America at St Vincent's Academy, New York, and

Lionel Barrymore (1878–1954), by Clarence Sinclair Bull, c.1935

Seton Hall, New Jersey. He made his stage début in Kansas City at the age of sixteen, playing Thomas the coachman in a touring production of R. B. Sheridan's *The Rivals* which also featured his grandmother as Mrs Malaprop. Six years later, in 1900, he made his Broadway début in the play *Sag Harbor*. However, his primary interest during his younger years was painting rather than acting. He studied the visual arts at the Arts Students League in New York from 1895 to 1898 and at the Académie Julian in Paris from 1906 to 1910. Financial necessity prompted his return to the USA in 1910, and it also led him to work in film. In 1911 he made his film début in D. W. Griffith's *Friends*, and over the next few years he worked for Griffith as both an actor and a scenario writer at Biograph Studios. He also appeared in New York stage productions, including a poorly received *Macbeth* (1920) and the very popular civil war drama *The Copperhead* (1918). The latter gave him the opportunity to play a character who ages forty years by the final act, in which he makes a lengthy and climactic speech. Such aged and melodramatic roles soon became his speciality, particularly in films, even though his own years were not so advanced.

In June 1904 Barrymore had married Doris Rankin; they were divorced in 1923 and on 14 June that year he married the actress Irene Fenwick (1882–1936). From 1925 until his death he lived in Los Angeles, and for twenty years he was under contract to Hollywood's leading film studio, Metro-Goldwyn-Mayer. When 'talking pictures' were introduced his stage experience made him particularly valuable to MGM and he worked for several years as both a director and an actor. He claimed in later years that while directing the melodrama *Madame X* (1929) he invented the overhead boom, or moveable microphone, which enabled actors to move and speak more freely, but some have disputed this claim. His acting career finally hit its stride when he won the best actor Academy award for his part in the MGM melodrama *A Free Soul* (1930). Barrymore played a drunken lawyer who defends his daughter against a murder charge so passionately that he collapses and dies while summing-up to the jury. The ageing actor, then in his fifties and notable for his craggy profile, slightly hunched posture, and generally wizened appearance, was one of MGM's more unlikely stars, but he appeared in a succession of important films. Most notably he co-starred with both of his siblings in the epic *Rasputin and the Empress* (1932). This was the only occasion on which Ethel, John, and Lionel Barrymore worked together. The film was not a great success commercially or critically, but it does offer an appropriate showcase for each of the Barrymores: Lionel plays Rasputin with an oily and sinister gusto, his more handsome brother, John, is dashingly heroic, and Ethel regally plays the empress. The brothers also appeared together in the all-star production *Grand Hotel* (1932), with Lionel Barrymore memorable as Mr Kringelein, a dying and often overwrought clerk who tries to spend his entire life savings in his final days at the luxurious hotel.

Later in the decade Barrymore was increasingly seen only in smaller character roles but these included key parts in MGM's most important productions, including *David Copperfield* (1935), *Camille* (1936), and *Captains Courageous* (1937). He was said to be a personal favourite of the studio's top production executive, Louis B. Mayer, and Barrymore's acting style clearly fitted well with Mayer's taste for melodrama heavy with pathos. He was most often seen as a patriarch near to death and, whether his characters were benevolent or vicious, his performance was always forceful. In 1937 the studio planned a production of Dickens's *A Christmas Carol* which would feature Barrymore as Scrooge. Severe arthritis prevented him from taking this part (Reginald Owen was cast instead) and left him unable to walk and in a wheelchair, yet his career soon continued apace. He starred as Dr Gillespie in a series of fifteen medical dramas produced at MGM between 1938 and 1947, which centred on the kind-but-cranky Dr Gillespie and his younger associate, Dr Kildare. In one of his last films, Frank Capra's Christmas drama *It's a Wonderful Life* (1946), Barrymore clearly relished the role of Mr Potter, a character so bitter and miserly that, unlike Scrooge, he is given neither peace nor redemption in the ending. This may now be his best-known role, but it was only one of many intense performances in a long and remarkable career. He died of heart failure at Los Angeles on 15 November 1954 and was buried eight days later at Calvary cemetery, Los Angeles.　　　MARK GLANCY

Sources H. Alpert, *The Barrymores* (1965) · J. Kotsilibas-Davis, *The Barrymores: the royal family in Hollywood* (1981) · L. Barrymore and C. Shipp, *We Barrymores* (1951) · D. Thomson, *A biographical dictionary of film* (1975) · *The international dictionary of films and filmmakers*, 2nd edn, 3: *Actors and actresses*, ed. N. Thomas (1992)
Likenesses C. S. Bull, photograph, *c*.1935, Hult. Arch. [*see illus.*]
Wealth at death $25,000: Alpert, *The Barrymores*

Barstow, Sir George Lewis (1874–1966), civil servant and business executive, was born in India on 20 May 1874, the second son of Henry Clements Barstow (1838–1902) of the Indian Civil Service, and his wife, Cecilia Clementina, daughter of the Hon. and Revd John Baillie, canon of York. His grandfather was Thomas Barstow of Fulford Park and Garrow Hill, York; members of the family had been prominent merchant adventurers in York since the early seventeenth century. Barstow was a scholar of Clifton College, Bristol, and Emmanuel College, Cambridge, where he was in the first class in both parts of the classical tripos (1895–6). He entered the home civil service in the Local Government Board in 1896 and transferred to the Treasury in 1898.

In 1904 Barstow married Enid Lilian, only daughter of Sir Alfred Tristram *Lawrence (later first Baron Trevethin). They had a daughter and two sons, the elder of whom won the DSO, and the younger of whom was killed in action, in the Second World War. Barstow became a principal clerk at the Treasury in 1909 and was appointed companion of the Bath in 1913. During the First World War he was primarily involved in the problems of supply to the armed forces. In the unprecedented circumstances of a world war he earned the gratitude and respect of many chiefs of the services for being so positive and helpful when dealing with their requirements. But he was also a firm advocate of tight fiscal control and he questioned Winston Churchill's decision, as minister of munitions, to build four large-scale electricity generating plants, when smaller installations could be built at a reduced cost that would still provide the power necessary for munitions production. He suspected Churchill of seeking 'not to provide for war necessities but to equip the country for after-the-war trade', a form of 'State Capitalism' at the taxpayers' expense which his rigid Treasury outlook would not allow (Peden, 118).

In 1919 Barstow was appointed an assistant secretary in control of one of the major functions of the Treasury, the supply services, and served until 1927 in the post, where he was notable not only for his efficiency but also for the humour he brought to his job. It fell to him to approve on behalf of the Treasury the settlement of the numerous points, some trivial in terms of money but some serious, and many of them highly technical, arising out of the financial control of the railways during the war. It was not always easy to see where the Treasury might benefit from pressing against a particular company—and there were then over 100 of them covered by the agreement. But Barstow's acumen in discerning what to challenge and where to compromise impressed the highly skilled railway accountants with whom he dealt, and he showed an almost instinctive ability to combine a sense of equity with instant insistence on what was due to the public purse. He was promoted KCB in 1920.

During the British navy's transition from coal- to oil-firing before the war Barstow had been concerned in the Treasury with the negotiations whereby the British government took a substantial share in the Anglo-Persian Oil Company. When he left the Treasury in 1927 he was appointed to be the government director of the Anglo-Persian (later Anglo-Iranian) Oil Company in succession to Lord Bradbury and he so remained until 1946. By the time that he left the Treasury he had been in the civil service for nearly thirty years, but his resignation may have been hastened by a clash of personalities with Churchill, who was chancellor of the exchequer in 1924–9. Churchill was often impatient in his search for new ideas and methods, and Neville Chamberlain observed that he treated 'the older Treasury men like Barstow' with such 'marked discourtesy' that they 'eventually resigned' (Gilbert, 296).

Barstow was for many years also a director of the Midland Bank and other companies, but his most significant work after leaving the public service was on the board of the Prudential Assurance Company. He joined as a director in 1928, became deputy chairman in 1935, and was chairman from 1941 until his retirement from the board in 1953. He bore the heavy responsibility of chairman during the war years in London after 1941 and after the war he served the Prudential during a period of vigorous growth and reorganization. The board exchanged much of its earlier formal routine for a more lively and informed participation by all the directors who, under Barstow's chairmanship, learned to work in close intimacy with the management; the change had lasting effect.

As chairman Barstow regarded with trepidation the Attlee government's implementation of the insurance proposals in the Beveridge report. At the Prudential's annual general meeting in 1946 he hailed the 'humanitarian' instincts of the National Insurance Bill then before parliament, but also warned against undermining the spirit of free enterprise and voluntary thrift (Dennett, 293). And in May 1949 he went further, condemning the government's proposals to nationalize industrial assurance as 'an unmitigated disaster to the insurance industry and to the country' (The Times, 6 May 1949, 4f). He remained an active chairman until his retirement in 1953. At the Prudential, as in the civil service, Barstow was long remembered for his wit. He was a man of erudition and wide reading with catholic tastes both in literature and in the arts and a most retentive memory. A member of the Society of Dilettanti, he also possessed a marked talent for writing light verse which he employed for the pleasure of his family and friends. In the Confrères, a well-known dining club, he excelled most in the cut and thrust of conversation across the table rather than in the more formal statements of points of view which followed dinner.

While still at the Prudential, and after his retirement, Barstow reorganized the finances of the Church in Wales as chairman of the finance committee at an important time. He took a great interest in the University of Wales, and in particular University College, Swansea, of which he was president from 1929 to 1955. He was also deputy chairman of the court of the University of London and a governor of Christ College, Brecon. The Barstows were devoted to their home, Chapel House, Builth Wells, Brecknockshire, where Barstow died on 29 January 1966.

JOHN MELLOR, rev. MARK POTTLE

Sources personal knowledge (1981) • private information (1981) • The Times (6 May 1949), 4f, 8a–e • The Times (31 Jan 1966) • L. Dennett, A sense of security: 150 years of Prudential (1998) • G. C. Peden, The treasury and British public policy, 1906–1959 (2000) • M. Gilbert, Winston S. Churchill, 5: 1922–1939 (1976) • Venn, Alum. Cant.
Archives BL OIOC, corresp. with Sir B. Blackett
Likenesses Lady Caccia, portrait, Prudential Assurance Co. Collection, Holborn, London • A. Gwynne-Jones, portrait, U. Wales, Swansea
Wealth at death £32,758: probate, 15 April 1966, CGPLA Eng. & Wales

Bart [formerly **Begleiter**], **Lionel** (1930–1999), song-writer and composer of musicals, was born on 1 August 1930 at 24 Underwood Road in the East End of London to a Jewish family, the youngest of the eleven children of Morris Begleiter, a master tailor, and his wife, Yetta, née Darumstundler (1883/4–1970), both of whom had fled persecution in Polish Galicia. Bart's musical talent was noted as a child, although he did not receive any formal musical education and never learned to read music. As the youngest child, Bart considered himself an outsider, and his need to become a member of a 'gang' shaped his choice to enter the musical theatre. Bart also cited his father's gambling as an influence upon his profligate and later disastrous attitude to money. At the age of sixteen Bart went to St Martin's School of Art, London, to study painting. However, he felt uncomfortable with the solitude of a painter's life, and developed an interest in community theatre. His musical and theatrical sensibilities were shaped by his early involvement in the left-leaning International Youth Centre (IYC) and his membership of the Communist Party. From 1952 he staged cabarets for the IYC, wrote political songs, and gained his love for improvisation. His work was, and continued to be, steeped in the music-hall tradition and suffused with a strong sense of working-class identity.

Bart was talent-spotted by the actor Alfie Bass, who was running the Unity Theatre (a left-leaning theatre located near King's Cross), and heard a Bart song called 'Turn It Up'. For the Unity, Bart wrote Piecemeal—an agit-prop version of the Cinderella story—and his first real musical, a take-off of Ben Jonson's Volpone entitled Wally Pone, King of the Underworld. He changed his name from the Jewish Begleiter to the more anglophone Bart, taken from St Bartholomew's Hospital, which he passed on his journey from the East End to the Unity Theatre.

Bart's work brought him to the attention of Joan Littlewood, the director of the Theatre Royal, Stratford East, London. His collaboration with Littlewood brought him to prominence with the successful staging in 1959 of his first full-length musical, Fings ain't wot they used to be, based on the book by the former villain Frank Norman, which enjoyed a two-year run. Its storyline of aspiring Soho villains and teddy boys mirrored the changes within working-class culture during a period of dramatic reconstruction: 'They've changed our local palais into a bowling alley and fings ain't wot they used to be.'

In the mid-1950s Bart began a successful career as a song-writer with Tommy Steele, with whom his hits included 'Rock with the Caveman', 'A Handful of Songs', 'Water,

Water', and 'Little White Bull'. He also wrote a variety of hits for other artists such as 'Do you Mind?' for Anthony Newley, and won several Ivor Novello awards for song writing. His most famous pop song was 'Living Doll', written for Cliff Richard—the first million-selling single in Britain.

Bart's song-writing blended simple lyrics with catchy melodies. Following these successes he attracted the attention of Bernard Miles at the Mermaid Theatre, and wrote his second full-length musical, *Lock up your Daughters* (1959), a modern version of Henry Fielding's *Rape upon Rape*. His adaptation the following year of Charles Dickens's novel *Oliver Twist* into the musical *Oliver!* seamlessly combined his love of music-hall, Jewish folk themes, and lyrical style with his interest in social justice. Bart was unable initially to attract backers, who felt that the material was too dark, so he gambled with his own money to stage the show. Finally, the impresario Donald Albery took an option after hearing a tape of Bart's friends playing the parts.

The show was a spectacular success and enjoyed extensive West End and Broadway runs, making a star of Ron Moody in the role of Fagin. *Oliver!* proved to be Bart's greatest legacy, enjoying many professional and amateur revivals (it remains a particular favourite for schools), winning Tony awards, and spawning a multi-Oscar-winning film directed by Sir Carol Reed in 1968. The show featured many catchy anthems including 'Consider Yourself', 'Who will Buy', 'Pick a Pocket', 'Food Glorious Food', and 'As Long as He needs Me'.

The success of *Oliver!* led to Bart becoming one of the leading figures within the British entertainment world of the early 1960s. In his professional life he was sustained by the relative success of the follow-up musicals *Blitz!* and *Maggie May*. *Blitz!* was drawn from Bart's experiences as a child in the East End during the Second World War: Noël Coward, an unlikely mentor, suggested that the musical was twice as loud and long as the real thing (*The Guardian*). Bart further enhanced his reputation as a song-writer when he wrote the first James Bond theme tune—for the film *From Russia with Love*—which was an international hit for the singer Matt Monro.

Bart also became one of the pivotal figures of swinging London. He entered Princess Margaret's showbiz circle, befriended the Beatles and the Rolling Stones, and became as famous for his houses and castles, parties, drinking, and drug use as for writing music. He indulged in extensive largesse: a bowl containing £1000 in notes rested on the mantelpiece of his Fulham palace, from which anyone in need could help themselves. Many obliged. During this period, although openly homosexual within the theatrical world, he was proposed to by Judy Garland, and by Alma Cogan on national television.

Bart's professional fortunes declined in the second half of the 1960s. The musical *Twang!!* (1965) was a disastrous parody of the Robin Hood myth with a cast including Barbara Windsor as a nymphomaniac Maid Marian and Ronnie Corbett as one of the merry men. Joan Littlewood

was called to direct, but her decidedly anti-West End sensibilities proved unsuitable for the material and led to a falling out with Bart, whose belief in the show led him to gamble, as he had with *Oliver!*, by pouring in his own money. To facilitate this he made surely the most disastrous business decision in post-war British theatre by selling the rights to *Oliver!*, thereby losing—by his own later estimate—over £100 million in royalties on the show's subsequent revivals.

By the late 1960s Bart was a fallen idol. He wrote another show based on Federico Fellini's film *La strada* which played for only one night. *Quasimodo*, his adaptation of Victor Hugo's *The Hunchback of Notre Dame*—on which Noël Coward was heard to comment, 'Brilliant dear boy, but were you on drugs when you wrote it?' (*The Independent*, 5 April 1999)—was not staged at all. Subsequently Bart wrote the music for a film adaptation of *Black Beauty* and an American television film version of *Doctor Jekyll and Mr Hyde*.

After declaring bankruptcy in 1972, Bart was inactive and descended into alcoholism. His talent for self-destruction was apparent from his speech after the first night of a show entitled *Lionel*, written by Barry Fantoni and John Wells to showcase his hits. This might have revived his fortunes, but he damned the production and it closed within weeks. In the 1980s he developed a major liver complaint and diabetes, brought on by alcohol abuse. Subsequently he stopped drinking and moved to humbler surroundings in a small flat above a shop in Acton, west London.

In the mid- to late 1980s Bart enjoyed a revival which was orchestrated by the re-release of a comic version of 'Living Doll' by Cliff Richard and the Young Ones in 1986. In 1989 he was commissioned to write 'Happy Endings' for an award-winning Abbey National advertisement. In 1994 the theatrical impresario Sir Cameron Mackintosh successfully revived *Oliver!* with Bart's involvement. In a gesture of respect Mackintosh set aside a small amount of the show's profits for its writer. Following this there were smaller-scale revivals of *Maggie May*, *Blitz!*, and *Fings ain't wot they used to be*.

Lionel Bart was diagnosed with cancer, and died on 3 April 1999 at Hammersmith Hospital, London. Despite his apparently humble later lifestyle, he left £1,299,856 in his will to family and friends. During his later years Bart's reputation as the father of the modern British musical was re-established, and the revival of his shows had once again demonstrated his rare ability to combine memorable lyrics and melodies with potent concerns about people's lives.   MARK WHEELER

Sources D. Roper, *Bart! The unauthorised life and times, ins and outs, ups and downs of Lionel Bart* (1994) · *The Independent* (5 April 1999) · *The Independent* (9 April 1999) · *The Times* (5 April 1999) · *The Guardian* (10 Nov 1999) · *Sunday Telegraph* (4 April 1999) · members.aol.com/spiper007/MusicalStages/obit-bart.htm [*Musical Stages* online], 8 Oct 2000 · 'The knitting circle: popular culture', www.sbu.ac.uk/~stafflag/lionelbart.html, 5 April 1999 · b. cert. · d. cert.

Archives FILM BFI NFTVA, *Turning points*, 3 April 1999 · BFI NFTVA, documentary footage

Barter, Richard (1802–1870), physician and hydropath, was born at Cooldaniel, co. Cork, Ireland. The death of his father and the formative experience of the local Whiteboy insurrection, during which he 'often joined the peasantry in their midnight scampers through the country' (*Recollections of the Late Dr. Barter*, 5), both disrupted his early education and strengthened his populist sympathies. The extent of Barter's medical training is unclear but he became a dispensary doctor at Inniscarra, co. Cork, where he was a much-loved figure, travelling the district on his 'two-pound-ten' pony (ibid., 7), and establishing a lifelong habit of treating the poor gratis in the mornings and the gentry in the afternoons.

Barter's first experiment with water therapy was during the cholera epidemic of 1832. It resulted in a pamphlet, *On the Prevention and Cure of Cholera* (1832), on the curative powers of water-drinking. Soon after this he left Inniscarra, married a Miss Newman, and moved to a small estate in Blarney, co. Cork. St Anne's Hill was 'a modest residence … almost buried in an orchard and surrounded by wood' (*Recollections of the Late Dr. Barter*, 12), with the waters of St Anne's spring, a well-known holy well, running through the grounds. For some years he farmed enthusiastically, helping to establish the agricultural society of co. Cork. But after meeting the Priessnitz cold-water advocate, Captain Claridge, on tour in Cork, Barter became determined to introduce hydropathy into Ireland using the unrivalled opportunities at St Anne's.

The St Anne's Hill hydro, opened in 1842, consisted of a bath house with various douches, and a novelty 'vapour' bath based on the old Irish sweating houses. The early years of the hydro met with medical scepticism, social derision, and near financial disaster—the holy well ran dry soon after opening and had to be re-excavated. More than eighty regular boarders eventually came to be cured through the Priessnitz-style ascetic regime, which consisted of cold baths, exercise in rural surroundings, and Barter's uplifting philosophy of nature cure. Unlike many early hydropaths, Barter continually experimented with hot waters, finally opening in 1856 a luxurious Turkish bath, modelled on those described by the traveller David Urqhart in his *Pillars of Hercules* (1850). It was the first to be opened in Britain since the old medieval 'stews' disappeared in the seventeenth century. Urqhart and Barter collaborated in a popular and influential pamphlet, *The Turkish Bath, with a View to its Introduction into the British Dominions* (1856), though Urqhart later complained that Barter had vulgarized his ideas with his 'improved' hot-air system—reducing the optimum heat to 160 °F, without vapour. The new bath met with violent opposition, but this was gradually overcome by Barter's enthusiasm.

Barter suffered from a long-term stomach complaint and he died at St Anne's Hill, Blarney, on 3 October 1870. Barter had been an indefatigable promoter of public Turkish baths, travelling, lecturing, and opening Turkish baths throughout Ireland and the United Kingdom. He built his own free public Turkish bath at St Anne's, as well as designing the People's Bath opened in Cork in 1863 and two baths in Dublin; by 1868 there were fourteen Turkish baths in co. Cork alone. He steadfastly refused to allow access to 'these startling novelties' (*Recollections of the Late Dr. Barter*, 27) to be controlled by the medical profession, but insisted that they were perfectly safe to use by anyone with a degree of common sense. Barter undoubtedly introduced the use of warm and hot waters into British hydrotherapy and the public baths movement.

VIRGINIA SMITH

Sources *Recollections of the late Dr. Barter* (1875) · R. T. Claridge, *Hydropathy, or, The cold water cure* (1842) · J. Fife, ed., *Manual of the Turkish bath* (1865) · D. Urqhart, *The pillars of Hercules* (1850) · A. Campbell, *Report on public baths and washouses in the United Kingdom* (1918) · R. Metcalfe, *Sanitas sanitatum et omnia sanitas* (1877) · R. Metcalfe, *The rise and progress of hydrotherapy in England and Scotland* (1906)
Wealth at death under £9000: probate, 26 Oct 1870, CGPLA Ire.

Barthélémon [*married name* Henslow], **Cecilia Maria** (1767–1859), pianist and composer, was born on 1 September 1767, the daughter of the French-born violinist François Hippolyte *Barthélémon (1741–1808); her mother, Mary (Polly) *Young (1749–1799) [*see under* Young family (*per. c.*1700–1799)], 'also … a musician of no mean capacity' (Higham), was from a celebrated musical family, and a niece of Cecilia Arne, wife of Thomas. Cecilia Barthélémon accompanied her parents on their continental tour in 1776–7; she sang before King Ferdinand IV of Naples and Queen Marie-Antoinette of France. Her London début was on 3 March 1778 (some sources have 1779) at the Haymarket, singing a duet with her mother. She was taught by the leading pianist J. S. Schroeter and became 'not only a good organist and pianist but also a composer' (Landon, 168–9). During the 1780s the 'procession of new pianists' appearing on the London concert stage included Miss Parke, Miss Barthélémon, and Miss Reynolds, 'none of whom, at their débuts, would admit to more than fourteen years' (Plantinga, 118). Her talents as a keyboard virtuoso are attested to by her performance at a benefit concert for her father on 8 May 1783, when she played a 'Lesson [i.e. sonata] on the Piano Forte' by Clementi. She was listed in 1794 in Doane's *Musical Directory* as a resident of Kennington Lane (her parents' address was given as 8 Kennington Place) and as a soprano (singing at the Vauxhall Pleasure Gardens) and harpist. She took part in a charity concert at Brighton in August 1795 with her parents. Her performing career apparently ceased with her marriage to a captain in the 15th King's light dragoons, Edward Prentis (not W. H., as in some reference works) Henslow (d. 1857), later spelt Henslowe, at St Mary, Lambeth, on 12 January 1797; they had a daughter, Fanny. She also referred to herself by the name Hinchcliffe; her marriage to Henslow may have been her second. In 1791 she received a substantial inheritance from an aunt, but this was not Mrs Arne as claimed by Ehrlich. She produced four publications of instrumental music between 1791 and 1795, and a vocal piece, *The Capture of the Cape of Good Hope*, for soprano and piano or harpsichord (1795). The 300 or so subscribers to her op. 1, dedicated 'by Permission' to Princess Sophia

Matilda, included members of high society, as well as leading musicians. Her op. 2 was dedicated to Frederica, duchess of York. Her music, right from the start of her op. 1 no. 1, is confident, well paced, structurally assured, and stylistically accomplished.

During the 1790s, when Joseph Haydn visited England, he spent much time with the Barthélémon family 'at their retreat at Vauxhall' and 'gave music lessons to the daughter of the house' (Higham, 11). Cecilia dedicated her sonata op. 3 (1794) for piano or harpsichord to Haydn, and included in it effects reminiscent of his musical wit; she preserved relics including signed copies of his music, and wrote down her memories of her 'caro Maestro Haydn', with whom she often sat 'when he play'd' (Landon, 169); and she was a subscriber (as 'Mrs Ed. Henslow') to *The Creation* (1798). She is the source of the story of Haydn's replying, when she asked him 'Papa Haydn, Why do you cry?', 'Oh! *my dear Child*. I do not like to leave my English Friends, they are so kind to me' (ibid.). Her reminiscences also convey her affection for her 'Dear Father' and 'beloved mother'. She published a brief memoir of her father in 1827, prefaced to a selection from his oratorio *Jefte in Masfa*. Her third son, the Revd William Henry Henslow, said in *The Phonarthon*, published in 1840, that his mother, who had told him that their ancestor Anthony Young composed the music for 'God Save the King', was 'now living'. She died at Tottenhill, Norfolk, on 5 December 1859, of 'natural decay' (d. cert.)   SUSAN WOLLENBERG

Sources Highfill, Burnim & Langhans, *BDA* · C. Higham, *Francis Barthelemon* (1896) · H. C. Robbins Landon, *Haydn in England: 1791–1795* (1976), vol. 3 of *Haydn: chronicle and works* · *The collected correspondence and London notebooks of Joseph Haydn*, ed. H. C. Robbins Landon (1959) · L. Plantinga, *Clementi: his life and music* (1977) · C. Ehrlich, *The music profession in Britain since the eighteenth century: a social history* (1985) · D. Hayes, 'Some neglected women composers of the eighteenth century and their music', *Current Musicology*, 39 (1985), 42–65 · R. Fiske, *English theatre music in the eighteenth century*, 2nd edn (1986), 131 · J. Doane, ed., *A musical directory for the year 1794* [1794]; facs. edn (1993) · private information (2004) [O. Baldwin, T. Wilson] · d. cert.

Barthélémon, François Hippolyte (1741–1808), violinist and composer, was born at Bordeaux, France, on 27 July 1741. He was the eldest of sixteen children of the wig maker Emmanuel Barthélémon and Françoise Laroche. Charles Higham has said that he may have been an officer in the duke of Berwick's regiment in the Irish brigade, though other sources cast doubt on this suggestion. He spent time in Paris studying violin and composing music, and was violinist in the orchestra of the Comédie-Italienne (1755). In 1763 Thomas Alexander Erskine, sixth earl of Kellie, ensured his removal to London by securing him a post in the opera orchestra. One of his first appearances as violin soloist took place on 5 June 1764 at a benefit concert given for Mozart and his sister at the Great Room, Spring Garden, St James's Park; he later performed a violin concerto at Hickford's Room during the Mozarts' concert (13 May 1765). Barthélémon became an integral part of London's musical life as solo violinist and orchestral leader, viola d'amore player, and composer. He led the orchestras of the King's Theatre, Haymarket, Marylebone

Gardens, Covent Garden, Drury Lane, Sadler's Wells, the Academy of Ancient Music, the Society of French Emigrants, and the Salomon Concerts. In 1766 he married the well-known English singer Mary *Young (1749–1799) [*see under* Young family (*per.* c.1700–1799)]; they often performed together in concerts, oratorios, operas, and plays. Their daughter Cecilia Maria *Barthélémon (1767–1859), a singer, pianist, and composer, later performed with them and wrote a memoir of her father's life published in 1827.

Barthélémon's serious opera *Pelopida* (King's Theatre, 1766), while it was supported by Bach and Abel and considered by Charles Burney to demonstrate 'traits of genius' (Burney, 2.871), was not as successful as his burletta *Orpheus*, commissioned by David Garrick in 1767. The most repeated anecdote about Barthélémon concerns a song for Garrick's play *The Country Girl* (1766): it is said that he wrote the notes while looking over the author's shoulder as he produced the words. Dinner with Dr Johnson and the invitation to compose music for *Orpheus* followed. Later burlettas include *The Magic Girdle* (1770), *The Noble Pedlar* (1770), *The Wedding Day* (1773), and *La Zingara* (1773), all mounted at Marylebone Gardens, where he led the band and his wife sang. Barthélémon made several visits to Paris and performed at the Concert Spirituel between 1767 and 1769. In 1768 at the Comédie-Italienne his opera *La fleuve Scamandre* was not well received. The Barthélémons worked in Dublin (1771–2, 1783–4) and toured France, Germany, and Italy (1776–7). *Pelopida* was mounted in French in Bordeaux and Grand Duke Peter Leopold of Tuscany commissioned music for Semplici's oratorio *Jefte in Masfa*, which was performed in Florence (1776), Rome, and London (1782).

From the end of 1777 onwards Barthélémon was based in London, where he continued to perform and compose; he also invented a five-string instrument, the ipolito. His six published concertos and two solo concertos date from the 1770s. He became interested in the Swedenborg Society and wrote the morning hymn 'Awake my soul' (*c*.1780). In 1779 he gained an appointment for life as leader of the band at Vauxhall Gardens. His music for the ballet *Les petits riens* was given thirteen performances at the King's Theatre (1781), while *The amours of Alexander and Roxanna* gained one (1782). In 1783–4 Barthélémon composed ballet music for the King's Theatre, but he and his wife were among the musicians dismissed before the 1784–5 season. In 1785 he again led the orchestra for the ballets. As 'one of London's foremost virtuosi' (McVeigh, *Concert Life in London*, 99) he performed Corelli's violin sonatas in public concerts during the 1790s. In 1800 he sponsored a series of Lenten oratorios. Barthélémon was music master to George III's brother Henry Frederick, duke of Cumberland, and his brother-in-law Charles, duke of Brunswick, and also enjoyed the patronage of the prince of Wales, afterwards George IV. Among his non-royal pupils were General Christopher Ashley and George Bridgetower. His separately published tutors for the violin and the harpsichord include 'first principles' and 'rudiments' of music. Barthélémon's friendship with Haydn during the composer's two London visits in the 1790s continued through correspondence, and it is thought that he may have suggested the subject for *The Creation*; he boasted of a concerto written for him by Haydn which never materialized.

After his first wife's death in September 1799 Barthélémon married Sarah (whose background is unknown) and had two more children, George and Angelica Augusta. Ill health overshadowed his final years and he died at his house in Hatfield Street, Southwark, London, on 20 July 1808, having bequeathed his possessions to his wife.

FIONA M. PALMER

Sources S. McVeigh, *The violinist in London's concert life, 1750–1784: Felice Giardini and his contemporaries* (1989) · N. Zaslaw, 'Barthélémon, François-Hippolyte', *New Grove* · Highfill, Burnim & Langhans, *BDA*, 1.363–7 · [C. M. Henslowe], 'Memoir of the late F. H. Barthélémon, esq.', in F. H. Barthélémon, *Selections from the oratorio of Jefté in Masfa* (1827) · C. Higham, *Francis Barthelemon* (1896) · S. McVeigh, *Concert life in London from Mozart to Haydn* (1993) · T. B. Milligan, *The concerto and London's musical culture in the late 18th century* (1983) · C. Price, J. Milhous, and R. D. Hume, *Italian opera in late eighteenth-century London*, 1: *The King's Theatre, Haymarket, 1778–1791* (1995) · Burney, *Hist. mus.*, new edn · N. Temperley, *Haydn: 'The creation'*, Cambridge Music Handbook (1991) · R. R. Kidd, 'The sonata for keyboard with violin accompaniment in England (1750–1790)', PhD diss., Yale U., 1967 · J. Gribenski, 'François-Hippolyte Barthélémon', *Musik in Geschichte und Gegenwart*, 15, cols. 509–12 · H. C. Robbins Landon, *Haydn in England: 1791–1795* (1976), vol. 3 of *Haydn: chronicle and works* · C. Pierre, *Histoire du Concert Spirituel, 1725–1790* (Paris, 1975) · C. F. Pohl, *Mozart und Haydn in London*, 2 vols. (Vienna, 1867) · [J. S. Sainsbury], ed., *A dictionary of musicians*, 2 vols. (1825); repr. (New York, 1966) · H. D. Johnstone and R. Fiske, eds., *Music in Britain: the eighteenth century* (1990), vol. 4 of *The Blackwell history of music in Britain*, ed. I. Spink (1988–95) · W. T. Parke, *Musical memoirs*, 2 vols. (1830); repr. (New York, 1970) · A. M. Clarke, *Fiddlers ancient and modern* (1895) · M. Sands, 'Francis Barthelemon', *Musical Magazine and Review*, 71 (1941), 195–8

Wealth at death see will, Highfill, Burnim & Langhans, *BDA*

Barthlet, John. *See* Bartlett, John (*fl.* 1562–1567).

Bartholomaeus Anglicus (*b.* before 1203, *d.* 1272), Franciscan friar and encyclopaedist, is of unknown parentage, and there is no information about his early years. His association with the Suffolk Glanvilles, reported by John Leland, who identifies Bartholomaeus as Bartholomew de Glanville, depends upon a late fourteenth-century colophon in Cambridge, Peterhouse, MS 67. Bartholomew was a Glanville family name, but no such son is recorded in its genealogy *c.*1200 (Oxford, Queen's College, MS 71) and it is improbable that a Glanville would have chosen an academic career.

The first record of Bartholomaeus puts him in Paris in 1224. Before then he may have studied at Oxford (after 1214 when the university returned from its dispersion) when Grosseteste was master of the schools, and he certainly incepted at Paris as a regent master, the statutory age for teaching within the faculty of arts being twenty-one. Under the year 1224 Thomas Eccleston, in his *De adventu Fratrum Minorum in Anglia*, reports the Franciscan profession at Paris of Haymo of Faversham, Simon of Sandwich, and two others, probably Bartholomaeus and Johannes Anglicus; all ceased, by statute, to teach as regent masters after their profession. From 1224 to 1231 Bartholomaeus lectured on the whole Bible at the St Denis

Bartholomaeus Anglicus (*b.* before 1203, *d.* 1272), illuminated initial

Convent. In 1231 Bartholomaeus was sent as lector (and Johannes as minister) of the newly formed Franciscan province of Saxonia (northern and eastern Germany and north-eastern Europe). The academic year at Paris ended on 31 August, and on the feast of the Assumption (15 August) an unknown Franciscan preached a sermon that included a description of the camel similar to that of *De proprietatibus rerum* ('On the properties of things'), the Franciscan encyclopaedia compiled by Bartholomaeus. The preacher was possibly Bartholomaeus making a farewell gesture to the city he praised above all others.

In Saxonia the school at Magdeburg, established by Simon of Sandwich in 1228, became the provincial school, and there Bartholomaeus taught theology to all student friars and prepared some for higher studies at St Denis. Its library (of which only four books survive) was probably similar in size and content to the Dominican convent at Magdeburg (285 books) and was sufficient for Bartholomaeus to be able to compile his encyclopaedia there *c.*1245. The latest datable authority that he used was the first version of *Summa fratris Alexandri* (*c.*1242) and pointedly he did not incorporate the Franciscan records of Carpini's mission to the khans, available from 1247. The first attested use of the encyclopaedia is in Germany by the Franciscan Berthold von Regensburg *c.*1250.

Bartholomaeus clearly states in both prologue and epilogue his purpose in the encyclopaedia to provide for student friars and others a gloss on things and places mentioned in the Bible. These glosses are progressively arranged in nineteen books, based on the premise that a knowledge of the parts comprehends the whole and on the Augustinian belief that 'faith describes the universe insofar as it is useful to know it for salvation'. The primary references exceed 200 (from patristic and Neoplatonic writings to contemporary Parisian scholars, including much of the newly translated Aristotle), and many others are cited at second hand. Yet much of it was dated by 1245. Bartholomaeus never fully understood the science of his authorities (for instance, Ptolemy) or the higher speculations of his confrères (Blund on the soul, Grosseteste on light for example), and only in the geography of eastern Europe was he abreast of current knowledge. None the less, the encyclopaedic coverage and clear presentation of the work ensured its rapid and international circulation. It became a textbook at Paris in 1284, a source for preachers, and a very common reference in ecclesiastical libraries, and Bartholomaeus enjoyed a wide reputation as 'the Master of Properties'. The work was translated into French in 1372 and into English in 1398 by John Trevisa and was first printed at Cologne in 1472.

In 1247 Bartholomaeus was elected minister of Austria, split off from Saxonia between 1232 and 1237, and is recorded in that office in December 1249. Before 1255 (if the probable identification is certain) he was elected minister of Bohemia, which included the custody of Poland, and there he resolved a dispute between Duke Boleslaw and the cathedral chapter of Crakow. In 1256 he was succeeded by Brother Daniel and appointed papal legate north of the Carpathians by Alexander IV and directed to preach the cross in Bohemia, Moravia, Poland, and Austria. In February 1257, when he was in Rome, the bull *Dilectus filius nobis* established a cathedral at Lukow (165 miles north-east of Crakow) and Bartholomaeus as its bishop. It is unlikely that he was ever consecrated. In 1259 the Mongols sacked Sandomierz, Lublin, and Crakow, and devastated northern Poland, and the pope proclaimed a crusade against them. Bartholomaeus's whereabouts during these troubled years are unrecorded; possibly he remained at Rome.

In 1262, in his absence, Bartholomaeus was elected minister of Saxonia at the chapter held at Halberstadt (29 April), and returning to Magdeburg he remained in office until his death in 1272, holding nine provincial chapters. There survives from his ministry a copy of a letter of 16 October 1262 about the friars' rights to hear confession, and a copy of a letter sent in 1266 by Bonaventure as minister-general. His fame rightly rests on his encyclopaedia, which spread throughout Europe, but his service as teacher and administrator in the emerging Franciscan provinces of central Europe was perhaps at the time more important.   M. C. SEYMOUR

Sources M. C. Seymour, *Bartholomæus Anglicus and his encyclopedia* (1992)
Likenesses illuminated initial, Bodl. Oxf., MS Bodley 965B, fol. 1 [*see illus.*]

Bartholomew (d. 1184), bishop of Exeter, was a Norman, probably from Millières, a village between Lessay and Périers in the Cotentin; the obit of his brother (or father—the word is not clear) Peter de Melir, is entered in the Exeter martyrology under 26 April. Nothing is known of the rest of his family, except for two nephews, Jordan and Harold, who were with him at Exeter. As he was well educated in the arts, theology, and law, Bartholomew may have studied at Paris and other fashionable schools. It is possible that he is the Bartholomew listed among Paris masters

(c.1140) in the poem *Metamorphosis Goliae episcopi*, attributed to Walter Map, described as 'sharp of face, an orator and dialectician, clever in speech' (*Latin Poems*, 29). His other alma mater was Canterbury, presumably the household of Theobald, archbishop from 1138 to 1161, of which John of Salisbury, possibly a school friend, was a member from 1148. Bartholomew was archdeacon of Exeter throughout the episcopate of Robert of Chichester (1155–60?), but continued to perform services for Theobald and to remain in touch with John. And he certainly owed his promotion to the see after Robert's death to their combined efforts, aided by John's kinsmen and their other friends in the chapter. It is even possible that Henry II's chancellor, Thomas Becket, another Paris alumnus, who had custody of the vacant bishopric, had a hand in the matter. The king, however, had wanted to appoint Henry, dean of Mortain, as a reward to the Fitzharding family, and Bartholomew thought it advisable to give the archdeaconry he vacated as a sinecure to the disappointed dean. Bartholomew was consecrated bishop, after Theobald's death on 18 April 1161 and before the end of the year, by Walter, bishop of Rochester, Theobald's brother.

Almost the whole of the first decade of Bartholomew's episcopate was clouded by the quarrel between the king and Archbishop Thomas Becket. He had quickly obtained the king's favour, and was one of those sent from Normandy in April 1162 to secure the royal chancellor's election to Canterbury and to assist at his consecration on 3 June. In May 1163 he went with Thomas and the other bishops to Pope Alexander III's council at Tours. But by the autumn the king and Becket were no longer friends. Bartholomew was involved in all the stages of the quarrel's development, from the Council of Westminster in October, by way of the Council of Clarendon in January 1164, to Becket's trial for treason at Northampton in October, from which the archbishop fled in disguise to France. He was in the royal embassy to the pope, then at Sens, in November which failed to persuade Alexander to send legates to England with powers to determine the matter. After this he tried, with some success, to avoid trouble. There can be no doubt that he, like perhaps most of his fellows, sympathized in theory and in general with Becket's cause, the freedom of the church from royal tyranny. But he was also aware, as again were many others, of the personal ingredient in the quarrel, Becket's defects of character and education, and the unsoundness of the legal case he was developing on the subject of the proper treatment of criminous clerks. In his penitential (cap. 94), he expressed the traditional view that those who resist the just and reasonable orders of royal authority are anathema. He was kept informed, indirectly, of the exiles' fortunes by John of Salisbury from Rheims. But he also got on well with the king.

After Henry and Becket were reconciled at Fréteval in July 1170 and after the return of the exiles to England, Bartholomew, together both with all those who had sworn to observe the constitutions of Clarendon and with those who had taken part in the 'illegal' coronation of the young king on 14 June 1170, was suspended from office by papal bulls obtained by the archbishop before he returned to England. After the martyrdom, however, he was absolved by papal legates in time for him and the bishop of Chester to reconcile the polluted Canterbury Cathedral on 21 December 1171, when Bartholomew preached on the text, 'After the multitude of sorrows in my heart thy comforts have delighted my soul' (Psalms 93: 19, Vulgate).

The reconciliation of Henry II with the pope and church (Avranches, 21 May 1172) enabled Bartholomew to play once more a full part in both ecclesiastical and secular affairs, especially as a royal and papal judge; and in the latter capacity he acted often with Roger, bishop of Worcester (d. 1179), the king's cousin. Gerald of Wales quoted and elaborated Alexander III's view that they were the two greatest luminaries in the English church; and he thought that the pope delegated to them the hearing of almost all the English cases. One of these, a charge of illiteracy against the abbot of Malmesbury, provided Gerald with two amusing anecdotes for his *Gemma ecclesiastica*, which show that Bartholomew, although a high-principled prelate, could also be merciful. In addition, between 1171 and 1179 the bishop was often at the royal court, obviously well in the royal favour.

Basically, however, Bartholomew was an assiduous diocesan bishop. Although he had been close to his predecessor and proclaimed continuity by taking over Robert's classical intaglio as his own counter-seal, he made considerable changes in the episcopal household and entourage, possibly because his election to the see had caused a split in the cathedral chapter. Indeed, of the old order only Master Baldwin and Baldwin's successor as archdeacon of Totnes, Robert Fitzgille, were to flourish; and Baldwin, who became a Cistercian monk at Forde about 1170, went on to become archbishop of Canterbury. John of Salisbury, Robert's half-brother, a more detached old-timer, took refuge at Exeter after the martyrdom, and about May 1173 he was appointed cathedral treasurer. But he seems to have shared his time and legal expertise between Exeter and Canterbury until he was elected bishop of Chartres in 1176.

Bartholomew and Baldwin are said to have dedicated their theological writings to each other. The known works of the former are a treatise on free will and predestination (*De libero arbitrio* or *De fatalitate et fato*), a dialogue against the Jews (*Dialogus contra Judaeos*), a collection of a hundred sermons for all the Sundays and festivals of the year, and an extremely popular penitential. Only the last has been printed.

Bartholomew died on 14–15 December 1184 and was buried in Exeter Cathedral; but his tomb and effigy have not been identified. He impressed contemporaries by his learning and eloquence. He was remembered in the cathedral for his gifts of vestments and ornaments, and at large by a miraculous experience—during a visitation of his diocese he was said to have heard the voices of dead children lamenting the death of a man lavish in almsgiving for their souls. Some of his rather sharp remarks were recorded, and in his sermons to the laity a favourite topic was confession and penance. That Baldwin, an ascetic and difficult man, was one of his closest and lasting friends suggests that Bartholomew too did not suffer fools and sinners all that gladly.

FRANK BARLOW

Sources *Gir. Camb. opera*, vol. 7 · F. Barlow, ed., *Exeter, 1046–1184*, English Episcopal Acta, 11 (1995) · *The letters of John of Salisbury*, ed. and trans. H. E. Butler and W. J. Millor, rev. C. N. L. Brooke, 2 vols., OMT (1979–86) [Lat. orig. with parallel Eng. text] · J. C. Robertson and J. B. Sheppard, eds., *Materials for the history of Thomas Becket, archbishop of Canterbury*, 7 vols., Rolls Series, 67 (1875–85) · A. Morey, *Bartholomew of Exeter, bishop and canonist* (1937) · C. Duggan, *Twelfth century decretal collections and their importance in English history* (1963) · F. Barlow, *Thomas Becket* (1986) · *The Latin poems commonly attributed to Walter Mapes*, ed. T. Wright, CS, 16 (1841)

Bartholomew family (*per.* 1805–1986), map publishers, were Edinburgh geographers of international renown. The founder of the business was **George Bartholomew** (1784–1871), who was born on 9 January 1784, perhaps in Dunfermline, the eldest (natural) son of John Bartholomew (1754–1817) of Baldridge, Dunfermline, and Margaret Aitken (1758–1808). George, though as much a general engraver as a specialist map-engraver, was the direct ancestor of the Edinburgh family of map makers John Bartholomew & Son Ltd. He was brought up by his mother alone in humble circumstances on the south side of Edinburgh's Old Town (off Richmond Street).

George Bartholomew showed early promise by the neatness of his copperplate script, so that in 1797 he was apprenticed to the well-known engraver Daniel Lizars (1754–1812), at the Parliamentary Backstairs, and under whose watchful eye he succeeded to the tradition handed down from Andrew Bell (1726–1809), proprietor of the original *Encyclopaedia Britannica*, and before him from Richard Cooper, founder of the school of map engravers in Edinburgh. Bartholomew undertook a variety of engraving commissions, including business prospectuses, visiting cards, ornamental titling and the occasional presentation watch, all of which demonstrated his excellence in lettering.

In 1805 or 1806, a few years after the completion of his apprenticeship, Bartholomew set up on his own as an independent engraver, trading from East Richmond Street, though he continued to work for Lizars. After William Home Lizars (1788–1859) and his brother Daniel succeeded to the business on the death of their father in 1812, and moved to larger premises at 3 St James Square, Bartholomew widened his skills to take in map-engraving on both copper and steel plates.

On 15 May 1815 at St Cuthbert's Church, Edinburgh, Bartholomew married Anne McGregor (1791–1849) from Gladsmuir, a few miles to the east of Edinburgh. They had four sons and six daughters, of whom the eldest son, John [*see below*], was born on 26 April 1805, some ten years before the marriage. Following his marriage George continued to be listed in Edinburgh's trade directories as an independent engraver, usually based in East Richmond Street until the 1820s and then at 6 Leopold Place until the 1840s, as well as at addresses in Gayfield Place. He was identified with John Lothian's 'Plan of the City of Edinburgh' (1825, 1829), and Lothian's 'Plan of the Town of Leith and its Vicinity' (1826), which also appears in John Wood's *Atlas of Scottish Towns* (1828), which established his reputation with local publishers.

Since George's work was essentially carried out in the name of his employer, W. H. Lizars, it is hard to identify his contribution to the firm's output; however, enough evidence survives to show his involvement in county maps of Scotland and other general maps used for a sequence of atlases, such as Lothian's *County Atlas of Scotland* (1827), J. Thomson's *Atlas of Scotland* (1831), W. H. Lizars's *Edinburgh Geographical General Atlas* (1840), and Blackwood's *Atlas of Scotland* (1840). He continued to work, on occasion, for his son John, and indeed outlived the latter by a decade. He died of cancer of the cheek at 6 Salisbury Place, Edinburgh, on 23 October 1871. His family memorial is on the west wall of Warriston cemetery, Edinburgh.

About 1820 George's son **John Bartholomew** (1805–1861) was apprenticed to W. H. Lizars, where he developed his pictorial engraving skills. It is from this date that the family enterprise has traditionally taken its foundation. Bartholomew's work records demonstrate that he was probably trained in map-engraving by his father, by then Lizars's senior map-engraver. After completing his apprenticeship in 1826 John set up on his own account as an engraver, working during his early years from 4 East St James Street. Lizars continued to support him with orders for an increasing number of maps, his earliest being a 'Plan of Edinburgh for the General Post Office Directory' (1826). His brother William (1819–1881) followed a similar training, and worked for his father and in the Ordnance Survey office before succumbing to mental illness. From the mid-1850s he was permanently resident in the Crichton Royal Institute in Dumfries, then in the late 1870s was transferred to the Royal Edinburgh Asylum. Nevertheless, some remarkable full-size pen-and-ink drawings by him survive from the time that he was institutionalized which show patients suffering from a wide range of medical conditions.

On 25 May 1829 John Bartholomew married Margaret (1796–1864), the daughter of William McGregor (*d.* 1821), a farmer's servant of Gladsmuir. They had five children, of whom John (1831–1893) [*see below*] and Henry (1834–1899) became engravers; a daughter, Anne, survived him. John Bartholomew's first commercial premises were in 1859 at 4 North Bridge, which he shared with the publishers Adam and Charles Black, and which had the advantage of a printing works in an adjacent building, Spottiswood House. He prepared many maps for Black's publications, including travel guidebooks and also the eighth edition of the *Encyclopaedia Britannica*, in twenty-one volumes, which Adam Black had purchased from Constable in 1827. The close association between the two firms was to continue for more than forty years. John's work for Blacks and for atlases such as Lizars's *Edinburgh Geographical General Atlas* (1836) was of very high quality in the true tradition of Edinburgh engraving. In 1855 three generations of Bartholomews—John, his father, and his sons—shared the

work in premises at 59 York Place. John retired in 1859 and moved to Grangebank Cottage, Morningside, Edinburgh, where he died on 9 April 1861.

John and Margaret's son **John Bartholomew** (1831–1893) was born on 25 December 1831, probably at 4 East St James Street, Edinburgh. He was trained as a geographical draughtsman and engraver and spent two years with the noted German geographer Augustus Petermann in the London offices of Justus Perthes of Gotha. He travelled widely to obtain new work and introduced a programme of improvements, including the installation of lithographic printing, which brought considerable economies. On 5 July 1859 John married Annie (1836–1872), the daughter of John McGregor (1788–1863), a smith of Greenock. He moved into new premises in 1870 at 31 Chambers Street. Following his first wife's death, on 4 March 1874 he married Anne Cumming (1837–1908), the daughter of Primrose Nimmo, a master brassfounder of Edinburgh, and his wife, Anne Philip, who was related to George Philip, the founder of the Liverpool map makers, who in 1879 suggested the idea of a merger between the two companies. John rejected the idea, preferring to retain his independence and to continue working in his native Scotland.

The latter half of the nineteenth century was a time of exploration and colonial expansion, and maps were in demand to illustrate and exploit the changes that were taking place. John Bartholomew benefited from these opportunities by receiving requests for large numbers of maps and many new atlases, many from Edinburgh or Scottish publishers such as Fullarton, Nelson, Chambers, and Collins. In addition to regular work, he undertook special commissions such as engraving medical and botanical illustrations and the map of Treasure Island for Robert Louis Stevenson's famous novel. New quarter-inch maps of Scotland (1862) and England and Wales (1866) produced for A. and C. Black were followed by a set of thirty regional maps of Scotland (1875–86) at the half-inch to 1 mile scale. Land relief was shown by hachuring, a shading of short lines to imitate shadow cast by slopes: however, John experimented with the new technique of showing relief by layer colouring, where each height layer is represented in a different colour, graduating from light green through increasing shades of brown to white for mountain tops. This system was used for their now famous half-inch to 1 mile Reduced Ordnance Maps of Scotland (1890–95) and England and Wales (1897–1903), which, with their subsequent editions, have become a trademark for Bartholomew. John had a reserved nature, which made him unwilling to enter fully into public life, but he took great interest in the reformation of the Scottish Rights of Way and Recreation Society (1880) and was elected a fellow of the Royal Geographical Society in 1857. Among his sponsors were the publisher W. G. Blackie and the surveyor and geographer George Everest. John retired in 1888 and died in London on 30 March 1893.

John Bartholomew's elder son from his first marriage, **John George Bartholomew** (1860–1920), geographer and cartographer, was born on 22 March 1860 at 10 Comely

Green Place, Edinburgh. He was educated at the Royal High School and Edinburgh University but did not take his degree. About 1880 he started work at his father's firm, but in his early twenties he developed a severe tubercular condition, which, despite a recuperative eight-month sea voyage to Australia, troubled him throughout his life.

John George entered actively into the work of the business and perfected the intricate skills of map compilations and production under the guidance of his father. He saw through the press the first examples of contour layer coloured maps used for Baddeley's *Lake District Guide* in 1880, and showed a keen interest and sensitivity in developing the best colour gradations for the new half-inch maps. On his father's retirement John George, although only twenty-eight years old, took full control of the business. On 23 April 1889 he married Janet, known as Jennie (1857–1936), the daughter of Alexander Sinclair Macdonald, JP, of Sydera Hall, near Dornoch, Sutherland, with whom he had two daughters and three sons, including John (Ian) [*see below*], who succeeded him as head of the company.

In the year that he took control of the company, John George formed a partnership with the publisher Thomas Nelson, and in 1889 they moved into their new premises in Park Road, adjacent to Holyrood Park. After Nelson's death in 1892 he took as his partner his cousin Andrew G. Scott (1861–1938), and in 1911 he realized his ambitious plan for purpose-built offices and printing works at 12 Duncan Street, Newington.

It was as a result of John George's flair and energy that the business prospered. The company changed from producing maps solely for specific customers to the status of a fully fledged publishing house with its own list. John George introduced new popular titles that were revised at frequent intervals over the following years. They included the *Survey Gazetteer of the British Isles* (1887; eighteen editions to 1972), *Citizen's Atlas of the World* (1898; ten editions to 1952), and *Handy Reference Atlas of London* (1907; thirteen editions to 1968), plus commercial reference maps of the world and plans of major cities. Print runs increased; the firm produced half a million plans of London for the 1897 jubilee celebrations for Newnes, 60,000 cycling maps, 225,000 timetable maps for the London and North West Railway, and 40,000 road maps for the Automobile Association, as well as a plethora of individual maps and diagrams for books and encyclopaedias, and ephemera such as circular maps for the pottery of McIntyre of Burslem.

John George was reserved and studious, and his insistence on accuracy and quality in all his work made him a strict and exacting employer. He was also a benevolent one, however, who organized recreational activities and an innovatory company profit-sharing scheme for his staff. His friend Dr George Chisholm noted that, despite his ill health, he was 'singularly, though quietly, happy, a natural result of the qualities in him which inspired confidence and affection among those who came into intimate contact with him.' He was an elder at the United Free Church of St George, Edinburgh.

Throughout his life John George never lost his enthusiasm for accepting new challenges and furthering his interest in the geographical sciences. He enjoyed close acquaintance with many leading academics and travellers of the day, such as the explorers Sir Ernest Shackleton, Dr William Bruce, H. M. Stanley, and Cecil Rhodes. These friendships led him into collaboration with many of them to represent their work and discoveries in map form. To reflect the academic aspect of his work he gave his company premises the title of the Edinburgh Geographical Institute, the equal of the Perthes Geographical Institute in Gotha. The title proudly adorned the Palladian frontage of his new building, which had been taken from Falcon Hall in Morningside, where the family had lived from 1899 to 1907 before it was demolished.

John George's interest in the development of the geographical sciences led him with others to found in 1884 the Royal Scottish Geographical Society, of which he was honorary secretary until his death. He also compiled the detailed travellers' maps for the society's *Scottish Geographical Magazine* from its inception. He was elected a fellow of the Royal Society of Edinburgh (1887) and of the Royal Geographical Society of London (1888), receiving the latter institution's Victoria medal in 1905. In 1904 he was awarded the prestigious grand prix at the St Louis International Exhibition. He (unsuccessfully) championed the cause of a chair in geography at Edinburgh University, from which he received an honorary doctorate of laws in 1909, being described in his citation as 'a very Prince of Cartographers … [who] had done more than any other man to elevate and improve the standards and methods of cartographical workmanship'. His portrait by Edward Arthur Walton commemorating the event is now in the Scottish National Portrait Gallery. In 1910 he was honoured by appointment as geographer and cartographer to George V. He was an honorary member of various overseas geographical societies, including those of Paris, Portugal, Budapest, and Chicago, and in 1918 was awarded the Geographical Society of Chicago's Helen Carver medal.

John George's skill in depicting complex distributions clearly in map form was evident in a range of important maps and atlases, among them Sir Archibald Geikie's 'Geological Map of Scotland' (1892), 'The Naturalist's Map of Scotland' (1893), and 'Botanical Map of Scotland' (1907). The *Survey Atlas of Scotland* (1895) offered, in addition to thematic maps, complete coverage of Scotland on the half-inch to 1 mile scale. It was followed by the volume for England and Wales (1903), the *Climatological Atlas of India* (1906), and the *Atlas of World's Commerce* (1907). However, John George's grand scheme of representing the current state of knowledge of the natural sciences in a major five-volume physical atlas to rival the renowned *Physikalischer Atlas* by Berghaus foundered; the project was too large for a single publisher, and only the *Meteorology* (1899) and *Zoogeography* (1911) volumes were published. He successfully prepared Sir John Murray's 'Bathymetrical Survey of the Scottish Freshwater Lochs' (1910), using the newly developed layer colouring to great effect, and mapped the scientific findings of the *Challenger* oceanographic expedition of 1872–6, which included the newly discovered Bartholomew Deep, a 25,000 foot trench off Antofagasta in Chile, which Murray named in honour of his friend.

John George began working on *The Times Survey Atlas of the World* (1922), a very detailed portrayal of the world and Europe after the changes of the First World War, with a sequence of specially prepared thematic maps. He did not live to see it completed, however, since he had to travel to Estoril in Portugal with his wife and daughters to regain his health. Despite moving to the healthier hills around Sintra, he died on 14 April 1920, and his remains were buried there. The first and subsequent editions of *The Times* atlas made it one of the most important and respected atlases of the later twentieth century and a fitting memorial to John George's illustrious career.

John George's eldest son, **John** [*known as* Ian] **Bartholomew** (1890–1962), who took over the firm on his father's death, was born at 12 Blacket Place, Edinburgh, on 12 February 1890. He was educated at Merchiston Castle School in Edinburgh and studied cartography at the universities of Leipzig and Paris before taking an MA at Edinburgh University. In 1914 he was commissioned into the Gordon Highlanders and served in France and Flanders; he was awarded the MC in 1915 and later served on Haig's staff. His younger brother Hugh was killed in the war. On 22 May 1920 he married Marie Antoinette (1898–1972), the third daughter of Dr Georges Léon Hyacinthe Sarolea (1864–1928), a physician of Hasselt, Belgium, and his wife, Marie Félicité Goetsbloets (1871–1898). They had four sons and two daughters, one of whom died young. Also in 1920 he succeeded to the management of the family business. Ian continued many of his father's cartographic ventures, notably the association with *The Times*, and began new ones, such as the production of road maps to satisfy the demand of an expanding motoring market. He took an interest in the whole spectrum of the business from technical and cartographical aspects, including improvements to inks and papers and the introduction of rotary offset printing machines, to the design of new map projections for the age of global air travel. In 1921 he was appointed cartographer to George V. Ian Bartholomew was very active in geographical circles, being a member of the permanent committee of geographical names from 1926, a member of the national committee on geography based at the Royal Society from 1941, and honorary secretary of the Royal Scottish Geographical Society from 1920, acting as president in 1950–54; he was also instrumental in establishing the chair in geography at the University of Edinburgh, completing a project his father had begun. He was deeply attached to Scotland and was a trustee of the National Library of Scotland and active in the National Trust for Scotland. A shy man, he received various honours, notably the founder's medal of the Royal Geographical Society in 1961. That same year he was appointed CBE. He died in Edinburgh on 9 February 1962, having become severely disabled by arthritis in his later years, and was survived by his wife, who died on 14 January 1972.

Following service in the Second World War, three of Ian's sons joined the firm: John Christopher (*b.* 1923) became cartographic director in 1953, Robert Gordon (*b.* 1927) was production director from 1954 to 1986, and Peter Hugh (1924–1987) became chairman in 1956. John assisted his father in editing the plates of the mid-century edition of *The Times Atlas of the World* to reflect post-war changes and was later responsible for a number of new specialist atlases, among them the *Atlas of Europe* (1974) and *Family Atlas of the World* (1983).

In 1980 the company was sold to the Reader's Digest Corporation and in 1985 it passed to Rupert Murdoch's News International Corporation. It was then amalgamated with a sister News Corporation company, Harper Collins publishers in Glasgow, and continued to produce Bartholomew maps and atlases under the name Harper Collins Cartographic.

JOHN C. BARTHOLOMEW and K. L. WINCH

Sources L. Gardiner, *Bartholomew: 150 years* (1976) · R. G. Bartholomew, *Twelve generations of Bartholomew* (1990) [privately published] · D. A. Allan, 'John George Bartholomew: a centenary', *Scottish Geographical Magazine*, 76 (1960), 85–8 · *The Scotsman* (31 March 1893) · *The Times* (17 April 1920) · *Scottish Geographical Magazine* (15 Sept 1920) · H. R. M., 'Obituary of Dr J. G. Bartholomew', *GJ*, 55 (1920), 483–4 · *Proceedings of the Royal Society of Edinburgh*, 41 (1920–21) · *WWW* [John [Ian] Bartholomew] · *The Times* (12 Feb 1962) · *CCI* (1861); (1893); (1920); (1962) · Bartholomew company archive, NL Scot. · J. C. Bartholomew, 'The house of Bartholomew—mapmakers', *University of Edinburgh Journal*, 38 (1998), 169–73 · d. cert. [George Bartholomew] · D. H. J. Schenck, *Dictionary of the lithographic printers of Scotland* (1999) · private information (2004) [Bartholomew family; Mike Barfoot; D. H. J. Schenck] · W. T. Johnston, *Dictionary of Scottish artists*, pt 5: *Engravers* (1993) · *IGI* [George Bartholomew] · Post Office Directories · memorial stone, Warriston cemetery, Edinburgh [George Bartholomew] · T. Nicholson, 'Bartholomew and the half-inch layer coloured map, 1883–1903', *Cartographic Journal*, 37 (2000) · D. Smith, 'The business of the Bartholomew family firm, c.1826–1919', *International Map Collectors' Society Journal*, 75 (1998) · D. Smith, 'The cartography of the Bartholomew family firm, c.1826–1919', *International Map Collectors' Society Journal*, 76 (1999)

Archives NL Scot., papers [John George Bartholomew] · NL Scot., Bartholomew company archive | NL Scot., corresp., mainly with Sir Patrick Geddes [John George Bartholomew] · U. Edin. L., corresp. with Charles Sarolea [John George Bartholomew]

Likenesses E. A. Walton, oils, c.1910 (John George Bartholomew), Scot. NPG · E. A. Walton, study, c.1910 (John George Bartholomew), Royal Society of Edinburgh

Wealth at death £784 15s. 7d.—John Bartholomew: 9 April 1861, NA Scot., SC 70/1/110 pp. 310–4 · John George Bartholomew: confirmation, 1893 · £28,016 16s. 4d.—John George Bartholomew: confirmation, 9 June 1920, NA Scot. · £63,698 15s.—John [Ian] Bartholomew: 18 May 1962, NA Scot., SC 70/1/1502 p.95–102/

Bartholomew of Farne [St Bartholomew of Farne] (*d.* 1193), hermit, stands second in reputation only to Godric of Finchale among the hermits of northern England in the twelfth century. Just as Godric's fame depends on the life written by Reginald, a monk of Durham, so Bartholomew's rests very largely on the shorter life produced by another Durham monk, Geoffrey, who wrote within twenty years of his subject's death, and may well have been the author of the portion of the Durham chronicle attributed to Geoffrey of Coldingham.

This life provides all the concrete information that is available on Bartholomew. It recounts that he was born in the area (*provincia*) of Whitby and was given the Scandinavian name Tostius, changed in the face of juvenile mockery in favour of William. Prompted by a repeated vision of the Virgin Mary, in the company of Christ, St Peter, and St John, he abandoned youthful excesses. His travels took him to Norway for three years, where he accepted ordination as deacon and priest, but declined an offer of marriage. He returned to England, where he briefly had responsibility for a church in Northumberland, and then became a monk of Durham. In 1150, within a year of Bartholomew's admission, Prior Lawrence (*r.* 1149–54) acceded to his request, prompted by a vision of St Cuthbert, to embrace the life of a hermit on Farne, a small island just off the Northumberland coast, where Cuthbert himself had pursued the solitary life. Bartholomew apparently remained there for the rest of his life, apart from a brief return to Durham caused by dissension with Prior Thomas, who retired to Farne following his resignation, probably in 1162. Bartholomew's biographer records his care for the eider ducks for which Farne was famed, and which had been beloved of St Cuthbert.

Although Bartholomew was not the first Durham monk to reside on Farne, the long period that he spent there may well have contributed decisively to its taking on a permanent existence as one of the Durham monks' smallest dependent cells. During his last illness he was visited by monks from Durham's other cells in the vicinity, Holy Island and Coldingham. He died on 24 June 1193 on Farne and was buried in his oratory there, in the stone coffin that he himself had made for the purpose. He figures in a number of miracle stories, and, although not formally canonized, was taken into the canon of English saints through the work of the fourteenth-century northern hagiographer John of Tynemouth, which formed the basis for the *Nova legenda Anglie* printed by Wynkyn de Worde in 1516.   A. J. PIPER

Sources Geoffrey, 'Vita S. Bartholomei', Symeon of Durham, *Opera*, 1.295–325 · *Reginaldi monachi Dunelmensis libellus de admirandis beati Cuthberti virtutibus*, ed. [J. Raine], SurtS, 1 (1835) · E. Craster, 'The miracles of St Cuthbert at Farne', *Analecta Bollandiana*, 70 (1952), 9–19 · J. Raine, *The history and antiquities of north Durham* (1852) · C. Horstman, ed., *Nova legenda Anglie, as collected by John of Tynemouth, J. Capgrave, and others*, 1 (1901), introduction, 101–6

Bartholomew, Alfred (1801–1845), architect, was born on 28 March 1801 in Clerkenwell, London, the son of Josiah Bartholomew, a Clerkenwell watchmaker, and his wife, Betsy. He was the younger brother of Valentine *Bartholomew (1799–1879). He had a modest education before being articled to the church commissioners' architect J. H. Good, who had been a pupil of Sir John Soane. During his training Bartholomew studied the works of Soane, and devoted himself to measuring details of his masterpiece, the Bank of England. From that exemplar he absorbed an interest in the practicalities of building as well as a working knowledge of classical architecture. His first earnings

came from teaching perspective drawing, but his short professional career was devoted mainly to the study and practice of architecture. He designed an infants' school at Brixton, for which he exhibited a design at the Royal Academy in 1834, and a handsome Italianate building for the Finsbury Savings Bank in Clerkenwell (1840), which still survives. Just before his death he was elected to the post of district surveyor for Hornsey.

Bartholomew is chiefly remembered as an architectural writer, in particular as the author of *Specifications for Practical Architecture* (1840). At a time when architects were distancing themselves from the building trades, and the roles of architect and engineer were increasingly differentiated, he sought to maintain unity among members of the building community. The key to that unity, he believed, was that architectural styles, particularly the Gothic style, should be based on the mechanics of building. Therefore architects were just as obliged to understand the techniques of sound building as were building craftsmen. In *Specifications* he advocated the establishment of a great national college for the integrated training of architects and artificers. Though that institution did not materialize, in 1842 he succeeded in founding a society to fulfil the same aim, named the Freemasons of the Church in honour of the ideals which medieval masons were thought to have obeyed. He was also the author of *Hints Relative to the Construction of Fireproof Dwellings* (1839) and *Cyclopedia of the New Metropolitan Building Act* (1844). Previously he had devoted himself to a translation of the psalms, entitled *Sacred lyrics, being an attempt to render the psalms of David more applicable to parochial psalmody* (1831) but 'though warmly praised by nearly the whole bench of bishops, in complimentary letters to the author' (*The Builder*, 29) this was never adopted for general use. He was a fellow of the Society of Antiquaries.

In 1843 Bartholomew became editor of *The Builder* in succession to its first editor, J. A. Hansom. Like Hansom he saw the journal as a medium for creating a greater brotherhood in the building community, and during his time it began to secure the wide readership for which it was later famous. However, within a year an attack of rheumatic gout and fever forced him to resign, and he died, apparently unmarried, at his home, Warwick House, Gray's Inn, London, on 2 January 1845. He was followed at *The Builder* by George Godwin, its longest-serving and most influential editor.   ROBERT THORNE

Sources *DNB* · *The Builder*, 3 (1845), 29 · *GM*, 2nd ser., 23 (1845), 320–21 · G. G. Pace, 'Alfred Bartholomew: a pioneer of functional Gothic', *ArchR*, 92 (1942), 99–102 · M. Brooks, 'The Builder in the 1840s: the making of a magazine, the shaping of a profession', *Victorian Periodicals Review*, 14 (1981), 86–93

Bartholomew [*née* Fayermann; *other married name* Turnbull], **Anne Charlotte** (1800–1862), artist and writer, was born on 20 March 1800 in Loddon, Norfolk, the daughter of Arnall C. Fayermann, and was adopted at infancy by her grandfather George Thomas (1723/4–1806), the vicar of East Dereham, Norfolk, and brother of Dr John Thomas

(1712–1793), dean of Westminster and bishop of Rochester. Little else is known of her early life or education, but in 1826 and 1827 Anne Fayermann exhibited allegorical works and scenes of Swiss and French peasants at the British Institution. She continued her work as a figure painter and miniaturist after her marriage on 28 May 1827 to Walter Turnbull (d. 1838), musical composer. As Anne Turnbull she painted portrait miniatures, figure, and still-life subjects, which were exhibited at the Royal Academy (1829–44). Her sitters included actress Ellen Tree (RA, 1834), musician and singer Henry Phillips (RA, 1830), and the artist and caricaturist George Cruikshank (RA, 1840). She also published several written works: a collection of her poems, *The Song of Azrael, the Angel of Death: Recollections of a Village School and other Poems* (1840), and a domestic drama, *The Ring, or, The Farmer's Daughter* (1840), and a farce, *It's Only my Aunt* (1850). *It's Only my Aunt* was performed at the Theatre Royal, Marylebone, in May 1849.

On 30 July 1840 Anne Turnbull married Valentine *Bartholomew (1799–1879), flower painter in ordinary to the queen. Although it has been previously assumed that after her marriage Anne Bartholomew, like her husband, became a member of the Society of Painters in Water Colours, in fact she was not a member of the society. During the 1840s her name appeared in the society's catalogues as poet when Valentine Batholomew added quotations from her poems to his drawings. After her marriage she redirected her artistic career to include new subjects of still-life, in addition to the miniature portraits which she had painted before and, like her husband, she became a fruit and flower painter. Two watercolours of flowers by Anne Bartholomew are held in British national collections, both purchased after her death from the dealer Robert Jackson. *Study of a Garden Poppy* is held in the British Museum and *Pinks* is in the collection of the Victoria and Albert Museum. Exhibition records indicate, however, that her flower paintings were not exhibited publicly at the annual exhibitions at the Royal Academy or at the Society of British Artists. As Anne Bartholomew she exhibited twenty-nine miniature portraits, domestic and fruit subjects at the Royal Academy (1841–57) and thirty-nine paintings of similar subject-matter at the Society of British Artists (1841–62). She painted miniatures for brooches and bracelets, contributing nine examples to the Royal Academy from 1846 until 1854.

Anne Bartholomew was a member of the Society of Female Artists from its foundation in 1857, and exhibited there until 1862; in 1859 she had signed the women's petition to the Royal Academy of Arts requesting that the schools be opened to women. She herself also taught painting; one of her pupils was the still-life artist Anne Maria Fitzjames, whose portrait she exhibited at the Royal Academy in 1852. Another pupil was Anna Maria (Kenwell) Charrettie (1819–1875) who exhibited miniatures, watercolour flower pieces, and genre subjects at the Royal Academy and British Institution from 1842 until 1875. Anne Bartholomew moved with her husband to 23 Charlotte Street, Portland Place, from 16 Foley Place, in 1842. Their home was surrounded by friends doing similar work in central London, and the Bartholomews were active participants in the society of these artistic circles. Anne Bartholomew died at home in Charlotte Street on 18 August 1862, and was buried at Highgate cemetery.

MEAGHAN E. CLARKE

Sources E. C. Clayton, *English female artists*, 2 vols. (1876) · Graves, *Brit. Inst.* · Graves, *RA exhibitors*, vols. 1, 4 (1970) · J. Johnson, ed., *Works exhibited at the Royal Society of British Artists, 1824–1893, and the New English Art Club, 1888–1917*, 2 vols. (1975); repr. (1987) · J. L. Roget, *A history of the 'Old Water-Colour' Society*, 2 (1891) · D. Foskett, *Miniatures: dictionary and guide* (1987) · R. Ormond, *Early Victorian portraits*, 1 (1973) · *Art Journal*, 24 (1862), 206–7 · Foster, *Alum. Oxon.* · *IGI* · m. cert. [Valentine Bartholomew] · d. cert.
Wealth at death under £1500: probate, 22 Nov 1862, *CGPLA Eng. & Wales*

Bartholomew [*née* Mounsey], **Ann Shepherd** (1811–1891), composer, pianist, and organist, was born on 17 April 1811 at 21 Old Compton Street, Soho, London, the eldest child of Thomas Mounsey, a licensed victualler, and his wife, Mary, *née* Briggs. Her younger sister, **Elizabeth Mounsey** (1819–1905), was also a musician. The family, originally from Cumberland, settled at Shoreditch in 1824.

At the age of six Ann entered Jean-Bernard Logier's innovative piano academy and showed uncommon gifts; by 1819 she was touring with Logier, and her harmonic ability so astonished Louis Spohr on a visit to the school in 1820 that he illustrated it in his *Autobiography*. After instruction from Samuel Wesley and Thomas Attwood she narrowly missed appointment as organist at St Vedast's, Foster Lane, in 1828. She was engaged instead briefly at Clapton, then in 1829 at St Michael, Wood Street, Cheapside, where she worked good naturedly for nine years despite a cost-saving reduction in her salary; on 7 November 1837 she was appointed to St Vedast's, where she remained officially until her death. Elizabeth, wholly taught by Ann, played the piano and guitar in public from the age of thirteen and was organist at St Peter's, Cornhill, from 1834 until 1882. The Mounsey sisters were featured in the *Musical Keepsake* for 1834, in which year Ann became an associate of the Philharmonic Society. In 1840 she was a founder member of the Society of Female Musicians. Much in demand as a pianist, she was invited in 1843 to give a series of classical sacred concerts at Crosby Hall, Bishopsgate, and did so each season until 1848; Elizabeth, who had been elected to the Philharmonic Society in 1842, also performed in these concerts, and both sisters contributed works of their own.

Ann Mounsey had begun to compose in her teens, chiefly for the piano, but also for the violin and harp. Her varied output included waltzes, mazurkas, polonaises, variations, studies for a single hand, pieces for two and even three performers on the one piano, and keyboard reductions of works by Beethoven and others. She wrote numerous hymn tunes, often with Elizabeth, and produced such collections as *The Christian Month* (1842), *Hymns of Prayer and Praise* (1868), and *Thirty-Four Original Tunes* (1883). She became best-known, however, for her characterful songs, sometimes for two or more voices. Following her first ballad in 1832, she made many settings of classical and modern poets, including Goethe's 'Knowst thou the land' and 'The Erl King', and published pseudonymously at least one comic piece, *The Daguerreotype* (1839).

From the start of her career Ann Mounsey was closely associated with the poet and librettist **William Bartholomew** (1793–1867), who provided or translated texts for many of her songs as well as for her *Child's Vocal Album* (1840). Bartholomew (also a chemist, violinist, and painter of flowers) was noted for his skill in matching words to music; he collaborated with several composers including Mendelssohn, who through him also became friendly with the Mounsey sisters. Bartholomew asked Mendelssohn to compose something for Ann's concert series and offered him a paraphrase of Psalm 55, 'Hear my prayer' ('Oh, for the wings of a dove'), which Mendelssohn set for soprano and chorus with organ accompaniment for Ann to introduce on 8 January 1845. In the following year Bartholomew undertook the English adaptation of *Elijah*, keeping it remarkably scriptural despite unfortunate drafts such as 'I water my couch' (for the Widow). Ann assisted him in this and subsequent tasks, and they married at last on 28 March 1853. Their most important joint productions were a *Choral Ode* (1855), the cantata *Supplication and Thanksgiving* (1864), and especially *The Nativity*, an oratorio first performed under John Hullah in a crowded St Martin's Hall on 17 January 1855. The critic of *The Times* found this less a sacred drama than a sequence of proficient songs, but several numbers were encored and the composer was called to the platform for enthusiastic applause.

Living in Shoreditch, the Bartholomews mingled little in society. Moreover, William was paralysed from the waist down during the last years of his life and required constant care. After his death on 18 August 1867, Ann published less than before, but continued playing at St Vedast's, taught the organ and the piano, and contributed to the *City Press*. An arresting figure in her youth, she came to look outmoded, even rather stern, but she remained both generous and respected; even S. S. Wesley humbly sought her professional advice. The Mounsey sisters proved helpful to students of Mendelssohn, possessing as they did many letters from him, most of the original piano score of *Elijah*, and the autograph of 'Hear my prayer'. Ann donated this to the South Kensington Museum in 1871, and in 1880 gave other manuscripts to the Guildhall Library; she also supplied material for Lady Wallace's edition of Elise Polko's reminiscences of Mendelssohn (1869).

Ann Mounsey Bartholomew died at home at 58 Brunswick Place, City Road, Shoreditch, on 24 June 1891, after six years of mental instability. Elizabeth, who had nursed her despite increasing infirmity of her own, lived on until 3 October 1905.   PATRICK WADDINGTON

Sources Brown & Stratton, *Brit. mus.* · *Musical Keepsake* (1834), 35–40 · E. Polko, *Reminiscences of Felix Mendelssohn-Bartholdy: a social and artistic biography*, trans. Lady Wallace (1869) [with additional letters addressed to Eng. correspondents] · *Louis Spohr's autobiography: translated from the German* (1865) · *MT*, 32 (1891), 484 · L. Baillie and R. Balchin, eds., *The catalogue of printed music in the British Library to 1980*, 62 vols. (1981–7) · F. G. Edwards, *The history of Mendelssohn's 'Elijah'* (1896) · J. Bennett, *Forty years of music, 1865–1905* (1908) · C. E. Pearce, *Sims Reeves: fifty years of music in England* (1924) · *The Times* (18 Jan 1855), 10 · D. Dawe, *Organists of the City of London, 1666–1850* (1983) · B. Matthews, ed., *The Royal Society of Musicians of Great Britain: list of members, 1738–1984* (1985) · cert. of baptism, St Anne's, Soho

Archives BL, letters to F. G. Edwards [Ann Mounsey Bartholomew] · BL, memorandum on Mendelssohn's *Elijah* · Royal College of Music, London, corresp. with S. S. Wesley

Likenesses photograph, before 1891, BL · I. W. Slater, engraving (after sketch by J. Slater), repro. in *Musical Keepsake*, facing p. 35 · oils, repro. in J. D. Champlin, ed., *Cyclopedia of music and musicians*, 3 vols. (1888–90) · oils, repro. in B. Matthews, *The Royal Society of Musicians of Great Britain: a history, 1738–1988* (1988) · oils (William Bartholomew), repro. in Edwards, *History of Mendelssohn's 'Elijah'*, facing p. 48 · photograph (aged about sixty), Royal Society of Music, London

Wealth at death £9075 18s. 9d.: probate, 10 Sept 1891, *CGPLA Eng. & Wales* · under £4000—William Bartholomew: probate, 10 Sept 1867, *CGPLA Eng. & Wales* · £8868 10s. 2d.—Elizabeth Mounsey: probate, 3 Oct 1905, *CGPLA Eng. & Wales*

Bartholomew, David Ewen (d. 1821), naval officer, was a native of Linlithgowshire. An experienced merchant seaman, having sailed to the Baltic, the West Indies, and the Greenland whale fishery, he was pressed in London in 1795. He appears to have had a superior education relative to social status and was shortly after his impressment rated as a midshipman. He served in the West Indies, on the coast of Ireland, in the North Sea, and with Sir Home Popham in the *Romney* on the East India station. When the *Romney* was paid off in 1803 he found himself 'a passed midshipman adrift upon the wide world', and wrote to Lord St Vincent, then first lord of the Admiralty, stating his services and asking for advancement. Lord St Vincent was not likely to consider with favour the claims of anyone who might be supposed to be a protégé of Sir Home Popham, and ignored his letter. Bartholomew continued writing, and at the eighth letter St Vincent, wearied of his importunity, ordered him to be pressed. He was pressed inside the Admiralty building and sent down to the *Inflexible* at the Nore, but was soon afterwards again placed on the quarter-deck. The case was brought before parliament and was referred to a select committee which reported, by implication, that the impressment of Bartholomew was a violation of the usage of the navy, an arbitrary and violent act which must disgust all young men who have nothing but their merits to recommend them, and likely therefore to be injurious to the service.

It was probably in consequence of this report that Bartholomew was promoted lieutenant on 20 July 1805. In February 1812, while in command of the brig *Richmond*, on the south coast of Spain, he drove on shore and destroyed the French privateer *Intrépide*, for which he was made commander on 21 March 1812; after some little time on half pay he had command of the rocket-ship *Erebus* on the coast of North America. This formed one of the small squadron that, under Captain James Alexander Gordon, went up the Potomac, received the capitulation of Alexandria on 28 August, and forced its way back after an arduous and brilliant campaign of twenty-three days. He was next engaged on the coast of Georgia, and on 22 February 1815 in the boat expedition, under Captain Phillott, up the St Mary's River. For his conduct on these occasions he was promoted captain on 13 June, and made CB. In 1818 he was appointed to the *Leven*, a small frigate, for surveying service, in which he was engaged for nearly three years. He had surveyed the Azores, part of the west coast of Africa, and was employed in the Cape Verde Islands, when he sickened and died at Porto Praya in the island of St Iago on 19 February 1821. He was buried there.

Bartholomew was a brilliant officer and an apparent exception to any general statement about the lack of promotion prospects for men of humble origins in the Royal Navy.   J. K. LAUGHTON, *rev.* ANDREW LAMBERT

Sources M. Lewis, *A social history of the navy* (1960) • G. S. Ritchie, *The Admiralty chart: British naval hydrography in the nineteenth century* (1967) • H. J. Rose, *A new general biographical dictionary*, ed. H. J. Rose and T. Wright, 12 vols. (1853)

Bartholomew, Frederick Llewellyn [Freddie] (1924–1992), actor, was born on 28 March 1924 in Harlesden, London, the son of Cecil Llewellyn, a civil servant, and his wife, Lillie Mae. He was only three when he was sent to live in Warminster, Wiltshire, with his grandparents and aunt, Millicent (Cissie) Bartholomew. A year later his recitation of a poem at a church social in Islington convinced Aunt Cissie that he had genuine talent and she persuaded his parents to assign her sole guardianship. Freddie began appearing regularly in local variety shows, developing the habit of anticipating the audience by applauding his own act. He even made his screen début in *Fascination* (1930), prompting director Miles Mander to declare him 'a potential screen wonder' (*Film Weekly*, 8 March 1935).

Freddie's contribution to a second feature, *Lily Christine* (1932), failed to arouse interest among the agents of Wardour Street, as British regulations concerning minors in movies were somewhat strict. However, Italia Conti, founder of the renowned drama school, rallied to his cause and when Hollywood producer David O. Selznick arrived in London to cast MGM's adaptation of *David Copperfield* (1935) she helped prepare the boy for his audition. Despite seeing off 10,000 other applicants, Freddie seemed destined to lose the role after being denied a British work permit but, undeterred, Cissie smuggled him out of the country on a holiday trip and presented him at Selznick's office in full period costume (including a beaver hat). According to legend, the boy entered the room and announced, 'I am David Copperfield, sir', at which the mogul scooped him into his arms and declared, 'Right you are'.

More than holding his own against W. C. Fields as Micawber and Basil Rathbone as Murdstone, Freddie was a key reason for the film's success and MGM signed him to a seven-year contract at $250 a week. He impressed again opposite Greta Garbo in *Anna Karenina* (1935), but not everyone was charmed. Graham Greene wrote in his review of *Professional Soldier* (1936) that 'Master Freddie Bartholomew never begins to act. He has never begun as far as I know. He recites the words by rote in whatever part he plays, and his directors help him exercise a lustrous and repulsive charm' (*Spectator*, 22 May 1936). Greene continued the assault in his notice for *Kidnapped* (1938), in which he drew attention to Bartholomew's 'Fauntleroy

Frederick Llewellyn Bartholomew (1924–1992), by Rita Martin

features and Never-Never-Land voice' (*Spectator*, 5 Aug 1938). The latter was a reference to Selznick's production of *Little Lord Fauntleroy* (1936), which sparked a Freddie Bartholomew phenomenon in America, with parents curling their children's hair, dressing them in imitation costumes, and exhorting them to cultivate 'the Bartholomew presence'. Even the child superstar Jackie Cooper was impressed, telling *Photoplay* in November 1936, 'If I had Freddie's vocabulary I'd be the happiest boy in this town. About all us American kids ever say is "gee" and "darn"'.

Unsurprisingly all this acclaim (and the wealth that went with it) drew Freddie's parents to Hollywood. Lillie Mae accused Cissie of kidnapping her son and she vowed 'to fight all the way to Washington. I'm sure the president's wife will understand me because she's a mother, too' (Parish, 5). In all, twenty-seven lawsuits were exchanged, at a cost of some $83,000, before an uneasy truce awarded custody to Cissie and a percentage of Freddie's earnings to his parents. About the same time Cissie sued to have him released from his MGM contract, but her defeat only frittered away more of his fortune.

According to Anthony Powell in his autobiographical *To Keep the Ball Rolling*, Cissie was a splendidly sensible and unassuming English woman who, throughout the legal wranglings 'remained quiet, firm, unfussed, entirely dedicated to what she looked on as best—not solely with an eye to professional advancement—for her nephew; a lady of whose bearing in the circumstances any country might be proud' (*Daily Telegraph*, 25 Jan 1992). Despite being dubbed the 'George Arliss of child actors' by *Time* magazine (Parish, 1), Freddie was earning $2500 per week and stood second only to Shirley Temple in box-office popularity. His efforts in *Captains Courageous* (1937) helped Spencer Tracy to an Oscar, but his advancing years and Cissie's spat with Louis B. Mayer seriously damaged his prospects. He was increasingly loaned out for projects like *Lloyds of London* (1937) and *Spirit of Culver* (1939) and, following *Swiss Family Robinson* and *Tom Brown's Schooldays* (both 1940), he wound up his juvenile career with *A Yank at Eton* (1942) opposite America's first teenager, Mickey Rooney. In 1946

Bartholomew married Maely Daniels, his former press agent, who was twice married and eight years older, but they divorced seven years later.

Bartholomew took US citizenship in 1943 and served in the air corps during the Second World War, maintaining B-17 bombers. Attempts to reinvent himself as a vaudevillian, and cinematic comebacks in *Sepia Cinderella* (1947) and *St Benny the Dip* (1951), proved ignominious in the extreme and he found himself presenting a movie programme on a New York television station, WPIX. Gradually, he began directing shows like *New York Cooks* and *Second is Shenanigans*. In 1953 he married Aileen Paul, a television announcer; they had a son and two daughters. In 1954 Bartholomew joined the Fifth Avenue advertising agency Benton and Bowles. He produced dozens of commercials (many of them shot in the studios he'd graced as a boy) *en route* for becoming corporate vice-president in 1965. He died of emphysema in Sarasota, Florida, USA, on 23 January 1992. His second wife survived him.

DAVID PARKINSON

Sources J. R. Parish, *The great child stars* (USA, 1976) · R. Lamparski, *Whatever became of…?* (New York, 1967) · *The Times* (25 Jan 1992) · *Daily Telegraph* (25 Jan 1992) · D. Parkinson, ed., *Mornings in the dark: the Graham Greene film reader* (1993) · *Film Weekly* (8 March 1935) · *Film Weekly* (13 Sept 1935) · *Film Weekly* (9 May 1936) · *The Independent* (27 Jan 1992) · *Variety* (27 Jan 1992) · *Sunday Times* (8 Aug 1965) · press notes for *The devil is a sissy* (MGM, 1936), BFI [microfiche] · *Photoplay* (Nov 1936) · *Screen Movies* (Nov 1971) · home8.inet.tele.dk/aaaa/ Freddie.htm, 21 Aug 2002

Likenesses R. Martin, photograph, NPG [*see illus.*] · photographs, Ronald Grant Archive, London, Kobal collection · photographs, London, Kobal collection · photographs, Huntley Archive, London

Bartholomew, George (1784–1871). *See under* Bartholomew family (*per.* 1805–1986).

Bartholomew, (Harry) Guy (1884–1962), journalist and newspaper company chairman, was born on 17 October 1884 at 191 Belsize Road, Hampstead, London, the elder of two sons of Henry Bartholomew, a warehouseman, and his wife, Kate Shackall, who taught singing. Bart, as he later became known, was deliberately misleading about his origins and upbringing. Partly out of mischief and partly because he thought that it was commercially advantageous, he sometimes pretended to be Jewish. He never publicly dismissed the implausible suggestion that he was the illegitimate son of his first employer, the press baron Lord Northcliffe, whose features and mannerisms he shared. His education was 'elementary and perfunctory' (Edelman, 38). After leaving school at the age of fourteen, Bartholomew served his apprenticeship as an engraver on Alfred Harmsworth's *Illustrated Mail*. His technical expertise and fresh thinking were soon evident, and at nineteen he was asked to join the fledgeling *Daily Mirror*, two months after it was founded, starting at 30s. a week. Bart's talents were swiftly confirmed and he became assistant to Hannen Swaffer, himself a pioneering art editor. When eventually he succeeded Swaffer, Bartholomew continued to work in the field, as when he engraved blocks on a cross-channel ferry in order to publish the first

pictures of a royal visit to Paris. On 20 December 1906 Bartholomew married a widow from Scotland, Bertha Broome (*b.* 1876/7), daughter of John Shaxton. They had a son, Peter. Bartholomew's wife was seven years older than him.

Aged only twenty-eight, Bartholomew was appointed a director of the newspaper in 1913, by which time he had already played a key role in creating the *Daily Mirror* as a mass circulation title, well equipped to report the First World War in unusually graphic and striking fashion. A courageous battlefield photographer, an accomplished artist and cartoonist, and above all, a brilliant picture editor, Bartholomew had technical ability that extended to a key role in developing the Bartlane process of telephoto transmission.

Bart was as interested in content as layout, having a clear notion of how the *Daily Mirror* could emulate New York's sensationalist tabloid dailies without necessarily sacrificing its integrity and sense of purpose. Nevertheless, throughout the twenty years that Lord Rothermere owned the paper Bartholomew was rarely consulted upon anything other than pictorial content. Only when falling sales saw the *Daily Mirror* and the *Sunday Pictorial* sold off as linked companies in late 1933 did Bartholomew seize his opportunity. He was appointed editorial director, and a decade later became chairman of both companies (albeit ceding executive control of the *Pictorial* to Cecil Harmsworth *King, nephew of the first Viscount Rothermere).

In 1934, on the basis of advice from the advertising agency J. Walter Thompson, both King and Bartholomew agreed on a change in the ailing *Daily Mirror*'s market strategy. They aimed to attract fresh advertising revenue by targeting young working-class readers with disposable income, and set about transforming it into an American-style tabloid, staffed by a highly professional team of young editors, designers, and reporters (one of whom was Hugh Cudlipp). Market research was crucial to ensuring that the *Daily Mirror* pitched its sensationalist reporting and striking layout at just the right level. The paper consciously avoided going too far down-market. Similarly, any editorial move leftwards was very gradual, and it took the Second World War to ensure that, in A. J. P. Taylor's words, 'The English people at last found their voice.' (Edelman, 142). Wartime radicalism, with the *Daily Mirror* claiming to speak for ordinary servicemen and women, culminated in the advice 'Vote for them' (meaning Labour) in 1945. The general election in that year confirmed the paper's support for Labour, yet Bartholomew distanced himself from the Labour Party leadership, with the notable exception of Herbert Morrison. Ironically, it was Morrison who in March 1942 threatened to suppress the paper over a cartoon by the *Mirror*'s Philip Zec. This showed 'a torpedoed sailor with an oil-smeared face lying on a raft in a sinister, empty sea' (Edelman, 111). A caption read: 'The price of petrol has been increased by one penny—official'; and this was meant to emphasize that 'casualties as well as prices were rising' (ibid.). However, it created a furore: questions were asked in the House of Commons, and Morrison warned Bartholomew that the

Daily Mirror must in future refrain from publishing material which might depress public morale. The incident increased Churchill's loathing of the newspaper; and further injury was given to the Conservatives on the eve of the 1951 general election. On 23 October the paper carried eight letters under the heading 'Whose finger on the trigger?', implying that 'the country would be safer with Labour's finger on the atomic trigger' (ibid., 178).

Bartholomew's poor relations with both front benches may explain why there was no official recognition of his major contribution to the British newspaper industry. He was, however, appointed OBE in 1946 for producing *Good Morning*, a secret wartime newspaper for submarine crews modelled on the *Daily Mirror*, and with a now familiar mixture of striking headlines, racy stories, practical advice, punchy sports features, revealing and unusual photospreads, and addictive cartoon strips. The same formula had enabled King to relaunch the *Mirror*'s sister paper, the *Sunday Pictorial*, in 1937, with similar success.

Bartholomew was a very recognizable figure in Fleet Street in the later 1930s and 1940s: he was short and stocky with seemingly boundless energy, and possessed a great shock of white hair. Although he often seemed rather brusque and ill-mannered, he nevertheless retained the loyalty of his staff, who recognized that he had both the technical expertise, and also the drive necessary to persuade readers in large quantities to buy the *Daily Mirror*.

Although chairman of the *Sunday Pictorial*, Bartholomew saw it as an in-house rival; and his antipathy towards King, Cudlipp, and their team became increasingly irrational. Bartholomew's riposte to King's success was to purchase a rather grubby weekly, *Reveille*, and broaden its appeal. Wartime sales of about 100,000, mostly to servicemen, had leapt to 3 million by the end of 1951. However, the Mirror Group had invested heavily after 1945 in west Africa, Canada, and in particular Australia. Not all these initiatives succeeded, and each new enterprise required an enormous amount of time and effort to set up. Moreover, whenever Bartholomew travelled abroad on business he behaved in an increasingly eccentric fashion, while his performance back home was severely affected by heavy drinking: he had always adjourned every evening to Fleet Street's most famous wine bar, El Vino. In December 1951 King and Cudlipp orchestrated a board-room coup, with Bartholomew being replaced as chairman of the Mirror Group by Cecil King. The latter appointed Cudlipp as editorial director.

In 1952 King and Cudlipp nevertheless paid warm tribute to Bartholomew at the Mirror Group's annual general meeting, regaling shareholders with countless stories, some apocryphal and some true, of his relentless determination to score a scoop. Both men collected many of these anecdotes in their respective memoirs. Yet Bartholomew spent his last years in much reduced circumstances: he held no shares in the company he had built up, and had never made proper pension provision. He lived on a modest income established by Philip Zec once it became obvious that the outgoing chairman faced near penury. He retired to his Surrey home, Crawley Hill House, Crawley

Hill, Camberley, where he died on 4 May 1962. His son, Peter, a wartime commando and later a regional television executive, survived him. Hugh Cudlipp described Bartholomew as the 'godfather of the British tabloids', and he was undoubtedly one of the most important figures in the history of popular journalism in Britain.

ADRIAN SMITH

Sources H. Cudlipp, 'The godfather of the British tabloids', *British Journalism Review*, 8/2 (1997), 34–44 · H. Cudlipp, *Publish and be damned! The astonishing story of the 'Daily Mirror'* (1953) · *Strictly personal: some memoirs of Cecil H. King* (1969) · F. Williams, *Dangerous estate: the anatomy of newspapers* (1957) · M. Engel, *Tickle the public: one hundred years of the popular press* (1996) · M. Edelman, *'The Mirror': a political history* (1966) · A. C. H. Smith, *Paper voices: the popular press and social change, 1935–1965* (1975) · CGPLA Eng. & Wales (1962) · b. cert. · m. cert. · d. cert.

Likenesses photograph, Mirror Syndication International, London

Wealth at death £3200 10s. 0d.: probate, 28 June 1962, CGPLA Eng. & Wales

Bartholomew, John (1805–1861). *See under* Bartholomew family (*per.* 1805–1986).

Bartholomew, John (1831–1893). *See under* Bartholomew family (*per.* 1805–1986).

Bartholomew, John (1890–1962). *See under* Bartholomew family (*per.* 1805–1986).

Bartholomew, John George (1860–1920). *See under* Bartholomew family (*per.* 1805–1986).

Bartholomew, Valentine (1799–1879), flower painter, was born on 18 January 1799 in Red Lion Street, Clerkenwell, London, the son of Josiah Bartholomew, a watchmaker, and his wife, Betsy. Alfred *Bartholomew, the architect, was his younger brother. From 1821 to 1827 he worked for and resided with the lithographer Charles Joseph *Hullmandel (1789–1850), whose sister Evelina Adelaide Charlotte Hullmandel, he married on 22 December 1827. Like her father, Nicholas Hullmandel, Evelina was a good musician. She died in January 1839 and on 30 July 1840 at All Souls, St Marylebone, Bartholomew married the flower painter Anne Charlotte Turnbull [see Bartholomew, Anne Charlotte (1800–1862)], daughter of Arnall C. Fayermann and widow of Walter Turnbull, a composer. She also wrote plays and poems. After her marriage, Anne Bartholomew continued to exhibit miniature portraits and genre and fruit subjects under her married name. There seem to have been no children by either marriage.

Bartholomew exhibited from 1826 to 1854 at the Royal Academy and the Society of British Artists. From 1835 he was a member of the Old Watercolour Society, as the Society of Painters in Water Colours became known, the next year becoming himself an associate. He often exhibited there. Some of his watercolours of azaleas and camellias, drawn in 1840, are in the collections of the Victoria and Albert Museum, London. He published *Selection of Flowers* (1822) and other minor works; his pencil sketch of a novel South American orchid appeared as an engraving in *Curtis's Botanical Magazine* in 1836. In 1836 he became flower painter to the duchess of Kent and Princess Victoria; following the latter's coronation in 1837 he became flower painter in ordinary to her majesty. The last to hold this post, he was in office until his death. His work was noted in his lifetime for its grand scale yet careful execution. 'His models were reared in the conservatory, and his studio was supplied with orchids and rare exotics' (Roget, 246). In his prime his only rival in the genre was considered to be his second wife. With increasing age, his powers failed, such that others, particularly women, increasingly outshone him. A few of his exhibited watercolour drawings are of landscape subjects including two views of Windsor (exh. Old Watercolour Society, 1836), a view of Windsor, and another of Eton (exh. RA, 1836). His views of Luxembourg and Heidelberg, posthumously exhibited at the Old Watercolour Society, 1871–6, indicate some of the locations of his sketching trips abroad, one of which was with the landscape painter and lithographer J. D. Harding.

With a close friend who lived with him, Miss Charlotte Mary Davis, at his bedside, Bartholomew died on 21 March 1879 at his home, 23 Charlotte Street, Marylebone, London suffering from chronic bronchitis and partial paralysis. His will stipulated that he was to be buried at Highgate cemetery in the grave of his second wife.

D. J. MABBERLEY

Sources J. L. Roget, *A history of the 'Old Water-Colour' Society*, 2 vols. (1891) · *Art Journal*, 41 (1879), 109 · 'Fine art gossip', *The Athenaeum* (29 March 1879), 417 · 'Peristeria pendula', *Curtis's Botanical Magazine*, new ser., 10 (1836), 3479 · will, 1879, probate department of the principal registry of the family division, London · IGI · J. Raven, *Botanical drawings from the Broughton collection* (1974), 39 [exhibition catalogue, Fitzwilliam Museum, Cambridge, 28 June–29 Sept 1974] · m. cert. · d. cert. · *CGPLA Eng. & Wales* (1879) · Desmond, *Botanists* · Wood, *Vic. painters*, 3rd edn · Mallalieu, *Watercolour artists*
Likenesses E. Edwards, photograph, repro. in *Portraits of men of eminence*, 4 (1866), 89
Wealth at death under £14,000: probate, 7 May 1879, *CGPLA Eng. & Wales*

Bartholomew, William (1793–1867). *See under* Bartholomew, Ann Shepherd (1811–1891).

Bartleman, James (1769–1821), singer, born on 19 September 1769, was trained as a chorister at Westminster Abbey under Benjamin Cooke. He distinguished himself and became a great favourite both with his master and with Sir John Hawkins, whose daughter praised him for his sweetness of character and keen sense of humour; she also reported his persistent frail health, perhaps due to tuberculosis (Hawkins, 270–78). He sang glees at Covent Garden in 1784 and began in 1788 an almost lifelong connection with the Ancient Concerts. He also sang in oratorio at Covent Garden from 1791, appeared in Salomon's performance of Haydn's *Creation* (King's Theatre, 21 April 1800), and, from 1793, often sang with the Oxford Musical Society. Bartleman began as a tenor but from 1791 was billed as a bass. He seems to have been a bass-baritone, with a range of over two octaves, a fine, evenly produced voice (kept liquid by some distortion of vowels), and a 'chaste style'. He did much to revive Purcell's bass songs, and had a considerable musical library; the beautiful copy he made of

Marenzio's madrigals is in the British Library. He died unmarried at the Middlesex Hospital on 15 April 1821, and was buried on 21 April in the cloisters of Westminster Abbey.   J. A. F. MAITLAND, *rev.* JOHN ROSSELLI

Sources W. T. Parke, *Musical memoirs*, 1 (1830), 249 · L.-M. Hawkins, *Anecdotes, biographical sketches, and memoirs* (1822), 270–78 · *London Magazine*, 2 (1820), 660–5, esp. 661–3 · *London Magazine*, 3 (1821), 440–51, esp. 451 · J. L. Chester, ed., *The marriage, baptismal, and burial registers of the collegiate church or abbey of St Peter, Westminster*, Harleian Society, 10 (1876) · C. B. Hogan, ed., *The London stage, 1660–1800*, pt 5: *1776–1800* (1968) · Highfill, Burnim & Langhans, *BDA* · K. J. Kutsch and L. Riemens, eds., *Grosses Sängerlexicon* (1987–91)
Likenesses I. Thomson, engraving, 1830 (after oil painting by T. Hargreaves) · J. Thomson, stipple, pubd 1830 (after T. Hargreaves), BM, NPG · T. Hargreaves, miniature, V&A · W. H. Worthington, line print, NPG · W. H. Worthington, silhouette · prints, Harvard TC
Wealth at death under £5000: Chester, ed., *Registers of the … church or abbey of … Westminster* · his important musical library was sold after his death: Kutsch and Riemens, eds. *Grosses*

Bartlet, Benjamin (1714–1787), numismatist and topographer, was born on 1 September 1714 at Bradford, Yorkshire, the only son of Benjamin Bartlet (1678–1759), bookseller and apothecary, and his second wife, Elizabeth Green (1684–1751). The family were Quakers: his grandfather and father suffered the seizure of goods for absenting themselves from the parish church; and Benjamin junior in 1752 had 11s. 6d. taken for the Easter dues of the Revd Mr Kennet's widow. His father's house was in a prominent position in the town, opposite the market cross at the bottom of Westgate. The physician and botanist John Fothergill was apprenticed to his father and Bartlet also served an apprenticeship as apothecary there, and succeeded to the business. On 21 June 1744, at the Quakers' meeting-house in Chesterfield, he married Martha Heathcote (d. 1785), 'a most elegant woman' according to John Ludford (Noble, 2.185), eldest daughter of Cornelius Heathcote MD (1694–1730) and Elizabeth *née* Middlebrook (d. 1758); they had one child, Benjamin Newton Bartlet (1745–1788).

At Fothergill's suggestion Bartlet moved to London in 1766 to practise in Red Lion Street, a business he eventually relinquished on account of failing health to his partner, James Bogle French. He made a fortune sufficient for the purchase of an estate at Hartshill, in the Warwickshire parish of Mancetter, where he was friendly with John Ludford of nearby Ansley Hall. Ludford characterized Bartlet as 'not one of the Children of Thee and Thou … He frequently said to me, Though sincerely attached to his own persuasion, If he was to change Religion, he would join the Church, as the most liberal of all' (Noble, 2.184).

Bartlet had shown from an early age a great aptitude for antiquarian pursuits, and he formed a collection of coins and medals, bronzes, seals, books, manuscripts, prints, and drawings. His knowledge in various numismatic areas was extensive. On 7 January 1762 he was elected a fellow of the Society of Antiquaries, and at the time of his death was its treasurer. His only complete publication during his lifetime was 'The episcopal coins of Durham' (*Archaeologia*, 5, 1779, 335–9), in which his observations on the personal marks used on their coins by the bishops of Durham remain an important element in the dating of Edwardian pence. He had, however, prepared *Manduessedum Romanorum* on the history and antiquities of the parish of Mancetter, which, enlarged and corrected under the inspection of several local residents, principally Ludford, was printed posthumously in 1791 in Nichols's *Bibliotheca Topographica Britannica* and won praise: 'The materials are excellent; the plates are very valuable, especially the seals' (Noble, 2.186). He also contributed an account of the coins of Worcester to Treadway Russell Nash's *Collections for the History of Worcestershire* (1781–99), four of the coins illustrated on the plate being his own. Gough, in his advertisement prefixed to Martin's *History of the Town of Thetford* (1779) acknowledges 'that able master Mr B. Bartlet' for the arrangement of the coins.

Bartlet died at Hertford of 'a confirmed dropsy' (*GM*, 57/1, 1787, 276) on 3 March 1787, and was interred in the Quakers' burial-ground at Hartshill on 11 March; his wife had died in January 1785. He devised his property in trust to his nephew Bartlett Gurney of Norwich, who was to sell his personal effects and invest the profits for the benefit of his son, an alcoholic; the estates at Hartshill and other property were sold for more than £13,692. The first part of Bartlet's collection was auctioned by Gerard over six days from 25 April 1787, making more than £1447. A new edition of Bartlet's *Archaeologia* paper, with notes but without the illustrations, was published in 1817 by J. T. Brockett.

R. H. THOMPSON

Sources register of the Bradford Society of Friends, PRO, RG 6/1517 · *GM*, 1st ser., 55 (1785), 78 · *GM*, 1st ser., 57 (1787), 276 · *GM*, 1st ser., 58 (1788), 939 · will, PRO, PROB 11/1151, sig. 103 · M. Noble, 'The lives of the fellows of the Society of Antiquaries in London', 1818, Getty Research Institute, Research Library, Los Angeles, California, 870580, 2.184–6 · W. Scruton, 'The Bartlett family', *Bradford Antiquary*, 1 (1881–8), 187–91 · H. R. Hodgson, *The Society of Friends in Bradford* (1926) · D. M. Metcalf, 'A survey of numismatic research into the pennies of the first three Edwards (1279–1344)', *Edwardian monetary affairs*, ed. N. J. Mayhew (1977), 1–31 · P. J. Wallis and R. V. Wallis, *Eighteenth century medics*, 2nd edn (1988) · T. Nash, *Collections for the history of Worcestershire*, 2 vols. (1781–2); 2nd edn (1799) · T. Martin, *The history of the town of Thetford* (1779) · *DNB* · J. Burke and J. B. Burke, *A genealogical and heraldic history of the extinct and dormant baronetcies of England, Ireland, and Scotland*, 2nd edn (1841) · J. Hunter, *Familiae minorum gentium*, ed. J. W. Clay, 1, Harleian Society, 37 (1894), 325–6

Archives Getty Research Institute, Los Angeles, California, Research Library, Noble MSS, 870580

Wealth at death over £15,000; estates sold for more than £13,692: Scruton, 'Bartlett family' · coins sold for more than £1447: Gerard Sale 25 April – 1 May 1787, annotated copy in library of Royal and British Numismatic Societies

Bartlet, James Vernon (1863–1940), ecclesiastical historian, was born on 15 August 1863 in Scarborough, the only son of George Donald Bartlet (1823–1906), an English Presbyterian minister who was also a schoolmaster in Scarborough and in London, and his wife, Susan Robe McNellan, formerly of Alloa, near Stirling. He was educated at his father's private school in Highgate and at Highgate School, from where he proceeded in 1882 with a scholarship to Exeter College, Oxford. He obtained a first class in classical moderations (1883), a second class in *literae humaniores* (1886), and a first class in theology (1887). He won the senior Hall-Houghton Greek Testament prize in 1889. In that year he was appointed tutor and the first librarian at the newly established Mansfield College, Oxford, which he had entered in 1887 and where he studied under Andrew Martin Fairbairn. He remained at Mansfield until his retirement in 1928, being senior resident tutor from 1890 to 1900 and thereafter 'professor' of church history. He received the honorary degree of DD from St Andrews University in 1904.

Bartlet's upbringing was narrow and ultra-orthodox, but he was too good a scholar and had too great an integrity of intellect to be able to remain within its confines; not without personal struggle, he won through to a broader outlook. At Oxford he was greatly influenced by Edwin Hatch and by William Sanday, of whose New Testament seminar he was a valued member.

In 1900 Bartlet married Mary Elizabeth (c.1875–1904), daughter of Robert Edward Gibson, surgeon, of Norwich, with whom he had two sons. In 1904 Elizabeth Bartlet died, shortly preceded by her younger son. In 1906 Bartlet married Sarah, daughter of James Burgess, Congregational minister, of Little Baddow, Essex. She outlived her husband.

As a scholar, Bartlet's chief work was in New Testament studies, and early church history, and he was recognized as one of the leading Oxford scholars in these fields. In 1900 he published *The Apostolic Age: its Life, Doctrine, Worship and Polity*. This was followed by two commentaries, *The Acts* (1901) and *St Mark* (1922), in the Century Bible series. His Birkbeck lectures, delivered at Trinity College, Cambridge, in 1924, were edited by Cecil John Cadoux, his former student, and published posthumously (1943) as *Church-Life and Church-Order during the First Four Centuries*. He was a frequent contributor to symposia, encyclopaedias, and theological journals, his work always being marked by careful learning and a meticulous desire for accuracy. His presentation was strictly historical in its perspectives, never allowing finality to the terms or thought forms which they represented. This approach was developed through his membership of the Oxford Society of Historical Theology, of which he was secretary from 1894 to 1936, and found particular expression in the chapters which he contributed to *Christianity in History: a Study of Religious Development* (1917), a work produced in collaboration with Alexander James Carlyle.

Keenly interested in Christian reunion, and always eirenic in temper, Bartlet believed that the path to church unity lay through an 'objective' study of church history. He was a founder member of the Free Church Fellowship, and had a wide circle of friends in many denominations. He took a prominent part in the Conference on Christian Politics, Economics and Citizenship (COPEC) in 1924 and in the World Conference on Faith and Order held at Lausanne in 1927. Although never ordained, he was regarded as a leading figure in the Congregational churches. Tall and dignified in bearing, and delicate in health, he was a vehement teetotaller and non-smoker. His personal influence on generations of students was profound, despite strangely convoluted forms of speech and writing. His gentleness, sincerity, and deep devotion won the affection of all.

Bartlet died at his home, 35 Museum Road, Oxford, on 5 August 1940. His funeral service was held in Mansfield College chapel, and he was buried on 8 August in Wolvercote cemetery, Oxford, next to his parents and his first wife.

G. F. NUTTALL, rev. ELAINE KAYE

Sources C. J. Cadoux, 'Biographical memoir', in J. V. Bartlet, *Church-life and church-order during the first four centuries*, ed. C. J. Cadoux (1943) • *Mansfield College Magazine*, 118 (Jan 1941) • E. Kaye, *Mansfield College, Oxford: its origin, history and significance* (1996) • W. B. Selbie, 'James Vernon Bartlet', *Congregational Quarterly*, 18/4 (Oct 1940), 366–8 • A. J. Carlyle, 'James Vernon Bartlet', *Congregational Quarterly*, 19/1 (Jan 1941), 26–30 • W. T. P. Davies, *Mansfield College: its history, aims and achievements* (1947) • personal knowledge (1949) • *WWW*, 1929–40
Archives Mansfield College, Oxford, notebook | NL Scot., corresp. with publishers
Likenesses Elliott & Fry, photograph, c.1928, repro. in Cadoux, 'Biographical memoir' • F. Dodd, crayon drawing, 1934, Mansfield College, Oxford
Wealth at death £2232 16s. 1d.: probate, 16 Oct 1940, *CGPLA Eng. & Wales*

Bartlet, John (*bap.* 1599, *d.* 1680), clergyman and ejected minister, was baptized at St Mary Major, Exeter, on 22 April 1599, the son of William Bartlet of Exeter, goldsmith, and elder brother of another ejected minister, William *Bartlet of Bideford (1609/10–1682). He was educated at Magdalene College, Cambridge, where he was friends with the puritan Richard Sibbes. Matriculating in 1616, he graduated BA in 1620 and MA in 1623. Initially he was a student of anatomy but turned to divinity because of an aversion to food brought on by familiarity with the internal structure of the human gullet. Following three years as a fellow of Magdalene, in 1626 he obtained the curacy of Barnstaple, where in the same year on 29 August he married Joan Harwood (or Horwood), with whom he had a son, John, baptized in 1628.

On 3 September 1628 Bartlet obtained the suburban living of St Thomas the Martyr, Exeter, being then in high favour with Bishop Hall. Some years later in 1648 he became rector of St Mary Major, Exeter, where in the same year he signed the presbyterian *Joint Testimonie of the Ministers of Devon*. In 1654 he was assistant to the Devon triers and in the following year joined the presbyterian Devon Association of Ministers. Two years later on 15 July 1656, following the death of his first wife, he married Jane Shaw of St Sidwell at Exeter Cathedral; they had at least four children—John, Philip, and William and one daughter, later Mrs Robinson. On 23 September 1662 he was deprived of St Mary Major for nonconformity. In 1665 he was living at Exeter though apparently not preaching and on 2 April 1672 was licensed as a presbyterian preacher. With the withdrawal of the declaration of indulgence the persecution of dissent in Exeter began again, and on 25 June 1673 Bartlet was among forty-five dissenters arrested at a conventicle at the house of the merchant John Palmer, along with his fellow ministers the presbyterian Joseph Hallett, John Hopping, and George Trosse and the Independent Lewis Stucley and Thomas Powell.

Edmund Calamy described Bartlet as 'a very laborious constant preacher', who possessed 'an excellent copious gift in prayer', whose 'voice was low, but his matter very solid and acceptable' (cited in Palmer, 1.368). He wrote several works, the chief of which are *The Practical Christian*, published in 1670, and *Directions for Right Receiving the Lord's Supper* (1679), which was aimed at young people and examined the nature of communion and the preparation and knowledge required. Bartlet died in 1680 at Exeter and was buried at St Mary Major on 15 June 'in the grave of his former wives' (*Calamy rev.*, 32).

CAROLINE L. LEACHMAN

Sources Greaves & Zaller, *BDBR*, 45–6 • *Calamy rev.*, 31–2 • *The nonconformist's memorial … originally written by … Edmund Calamy*, ed. S. Palmer, 1 (1775), 368 • A. Gordon, ed., *Freedom after ejection: a review (1690–1692) of presbyterian and congregational nonconformity in England and Wales* (1917), 208 • *Walker rev.*, 108 • A. Brockett, *Nonconformity in Exeter, 1650–1875* (1962) • M. M. Rowe and A. M. Jackson, eds., *Exeter freemen, 1266–1967*, Devon and Cornwall RS, extra ser., 1 (1973) • W. G. Hoskins, ed., *Exeter in the seventeenth century: tax and rate assessments, 1602–1699*, Devon and Cornwall RS, new ser., 2 (1957), 11 • *IGI*
Wealth at death see *Calamy rev.*

Bartlet, William (1609/10–1682), clergyman and ejected minister, was the son of William Bartlet of Exeter, goldsmith. John *Bartlet (*bap.* 1599, *d.* 1680) was his elder brother. He matriculated at New Inn Hall, Oxford, on 4 November 1631 aged twenty-one and was ordained as a priest in the diocese of Exeter on 21 September 1634 as curate of All Saints in that city. He later served as curate of Bideford under Isaac Gifford and then Arthur Gifford, on whose ejection he was named to the rectory by an order of 25 July 1644. But on 23 June 1647 he was ordered by the committee for plundered ministers to explain his neglect of the cure, and he resigned by the 29th of the month.

The reason for Bartlet's absence, it seems, is that he had already become the minister to a congregation at Wapping in Middlesex; in that capacity, on 1 March 1647, he signed the preface to *A Model of the Primitive Congregational Way*. In 1649, probably just before the execution of Charles I, he issued *Eye Salve to Anoint the Eyes of the Ministers*, a violent attack on the efforts of the presbyterian clergy of London to oppose the king's trial, in which he pronounced Charles guilty of 'the abominations of tyranny, murder and oppression in his three kingdoms'; the army was 'instrumental from heaven to bring down that proud Nimrod, the King that hunted after not only the estates but the lives of the best of his subjects, and brake through the hedges and boundaries of all just laws' (*Eye Salve*, 2).

By 1 March 1649 Bartlet had returned to Bideford, signing as its lecturer a work directed against the growing rejection by the saints of church membership and formal ordinances, and the dangers of 'introducing a spirituall anarchy and confusion in the Kingdom of Christ' (*Soveraigne balsome*, 21); probably he had already gathered a congregational church in the town. In 1650 commissioners into the ministry in Devon reported that at Bideford 'Will Bartlot is curat, a constant preaching minister', and by February 1651 he was reappointed to the rectory (Hingeston, 7). Calamy and Walker exchanged fire over Bartlet's allegedly cruel treatment of Arthur Gifford, the sequestered rector. The truth may never be known, though it is possible that the authorities regarded Gifford with especial disfavour because his elder brother John was a royalist army colonel. In 1650 Bartlet was instrumental in the choice of Lewis Stuckley as pastor of a group at Exeter who had no minister, and attended the meeting at which the church there was formally constituted. According to a founder, Susannah Parr, 'Mr Bartlet came to the City with his church officers, he himself prayed and preached … afterwards seven or eight persons spake out the experiences they had of the change of their condition'. Later a confession of faith was read and 'subscribed by every one of us' (Parr, 3).

Bartlet's reputation stood high in the early 1650s. John Rogers referred to him in *Ohel* alongside William Ames and Henry Ainsworth as one of the 'champions of the church' (Nuttall, 42). His fame, and his considerable influence among Devon congregationalists, probably rested in large part on his *A Model*, an early manual of the congregational way, which antedated even John Owen's *Eschol … or, Rules of Direction for the Walking of Saints* (1648). For Bartlet, a:

> visible Church state, order and polity, which Jesus Christ only hath instituted and ordained under the New Testament is a free society or communion of visible saints, embodied and knit together by a voluntary consent to worship God according to his word, making up one ordinary congregation, with power of Government within itself only. (*A Model*, 30)

Many later works seemed merely to recycle this and other formulations, so that it has been remarked that 'the godly throughout the kingdom might almost have read his book' (Nuttall, 75). 'Compulsion in matters of religion', Bartlet thought, was not only 'to encroach upon the prerogative of God' but was 'against the very nature of the mind and conscience' (Nuttall, 104), and this toleration he extended in *A Model* even to Socinians and papists. He felt able in 1654 to take up a post as one of the commissioners for Devon and became, therefore, a part of the slightly less tolerant Cromwellian church establishment. The cause in the county was damaged during the protectorate by an acrimonious split in Stuckley's church, and it seems that the Bideford congregation also suffered. On 8 May 1658, despite or because of their 'many backslidings', Bartlet and fifty-two others renewed their earlier covenant, promising 'to walk up more closely and faithfully in the discharge of all our duties to the Lord and one another … yielding obedience to our pastor and governors over us in the Lord' (Nuttall, 81).

In May 1660 Bartlet and other Devon congregationalist ministers signed a loyal address to Charles II, but Bartlet was ejected from Bideford in 1662, and Gifford returned to the rectory. On 4 July 1662 it was reported that:

> Mr. Bartlet of Bidiford & his son were shipt for N[ew] E[ngland]: but an Oath upon them both afore they could get out of the harbor, & that stopt them, for they chused rather to dye in prison than take it. (Prince, 193)

Bartlet seems to have resumed his activities in the town, with assistance from his son John, who had himself been ejected in 1660 from the Devon rectory of Fremlingham.

In 1665 both were reported to be living at Bideford, and on 2 April 1672, William's house was licensed as a meeting-place. Calamy says of him that he was 'once imprisoned; and escaped at another time by a mistake of the officers, who seized another grave man in his stead. He was the chief object of the malice and fury of the haters of strict and serious godliness' (Calamy, *Continuation*, 265–6). John Bartlet, in a petition dated 30 October 1672 against his own imprisonment under the Five Mile Act, complained that his father had been forced into hiding to avoid arrest.

William Bartlet was buried, possibly at Bideford, on 28 January 1682. He was survived by his wife, Margaret (*d*. 1684), to whom he bequeathed a house, orchard, and garden, but little else. No sons are mentioned (John had died in 1679) but there were two surviving daughters, Mary, who in 1665 married Oliver Peard, the ejected minister of Barnstaple, and Elizabeth, who married Jeremiah, son of the dissenting preacher Richard Blinman, in 1670. The William Bartlett who wrote a preface to John Copplestone's *God's Works and Wonders in the Deep … Preached in Bideford* (1720) may well have been the grandson of William Bartlet, the congregationalist pioneer.

STEPHEN WRIGHT

Sources G. F. Nuttall, *Visible saints: the congregational way, 1640–1660* (1957) · *Calamy rev.* · W. Bartlet, *A model of the primitive congregational way* (1647) · E. Calamy, ed., *An abridgement of Mr. Baxter's history of his life and times, with an account of the ministers, &c., who were ejected after the Restauration of King Charles II*, 2nd edn, 2 vols. (1713) · E. Calamy, *A continuation of the account of the ministers … who were ejected and silenced after the Restoration in 1660*, 2 vols. (1727) · Foster, *Alum. Oxon.* · F. C. Hingeston, 'The rectors and patrons of Bideford in the deanery of Hartland', BL [printed at Exeter 1875, not published] · will, 1682/3, Devon RO, Moger abstracts · will, 1686/7, Devon RO, Moger abstracts [Elizabeth Bartlett] · *The nonconformist's memorial … originally written by … Edmund Calamy*, ed. S. Palmer, [3rd edn], 3 vols. (1802–3) · *Collections of the Massachusetts Historical Society*, 4th ser., 8 (1868) [*The Mather papers*, ed. T. Prince] · S. Parr, *Susannah's apologie against the elders* (1659) · W. Bartlet, *Kollorion, or, Eye salve to anoint the eyes of the ministers of the province of London that they may see their error (at least) in opposing the present proceedings of the parliament and army in the due execution of justice* (1649) · W. Bartlet, *Ba'al shemen, or, Soveraigne balsome, gently applied* (1649) · Wood, *Ath. Oxon.*, new edn · J. Watkin, *An essay toward a history of Bideford* (1792) · A. Gordon, ed., *Freedom after ejection: a review (1690–1692) of presbyterian and congregational nonconformity in England and Wales* (1917) · BL, Add. MS 15671, fols. 83, 91 · J. Copplestone, *God's works and wonders in the deep … preached in Bideford* (1720)

Wealth at death bequeathed 'house, orchard, and garden, but little else': will, 1682/3, Devon RO, Moger abstracts

Bartlett, Abraham Dee (1812–1897), taxidermist and zoo superintendent, was born in London on 27 October 1812, second son of John Bartlett, hairdresser and brush maker, and Jane Dunster. As a boy he was allowed to play in the beast room of the Royal Menagerie, Exeter 'Change, London, run by Edward Cross, his father's friend. His fondness for living animals led to an interest in taxidermy that was encouraged by Cross. At fourteen he was apprenticed to his father at his premises at 83 Drury Lane, London. He detested the hairdressing trade, and about 1834 became a taxidermist, trading at Little Russell Street, Covent Garden. He married Lydia Norvall, with whom he had four daughters, Clara (*b*. 1840), Emma (*b*. *c*.1844), Julia (*b*.

c.1848), and Ellen (b. c.1851), and two sons, Edward (1844–1908) and Clarence (c.1848–1903). His business proved successful, which permitted a move to a larger house in Camden (he owned three residences at his death).

Bartlett worked for leading naturalists, the British Museum, the Zoological Society of London (through the patronage of its secretary, David Mitchell), and the royal family; Queen Victoria gave him a gold watch for caring for her pet birds. His taxidermy display, including a reconstruction of the dodo, at the Great Exhibition of 1851 earned him a gold medal and an appointment as naturalist to the new Crystal Palace Company in 1852. He acted as London agent for the Calcutta-based curator Edward Blyth, and occasionally handled the latter's dealings in live animals with British purchasers. His association with the Zoological Society and familiarity with wild animals led to his being offered the superintendency of the zoological gardens in Regent's Park, London, in 1859, upon the death of John Thompson. He took up residence at the zoo and remained in post there until his death.

To the public, Bartlett *was* the zoo, a familiar figure in his long coat and top hat. Among notable zoo events with which he was associated was the controversial sale of the famous elephant Jumbo to P. T. Barnum. As a child he had seen an elephant run amok at the Exeter 'Change menagerie, and knew Jumbo had become too dangerous to remain in the zoo. He became an authority on the captive care of wild animals, and published nearly sixty papers and notes on the subject in the *Proceedings of the Zoological Society* and other journals. Among many honours he was awarded a silver medal by the Zoological Society in 1872, and made an associate of the Linnean Society in 1879.

Bartlett died at the zoological gardens on 7 May 1897, after a lingering illness. He was buried at St James's cemetery, Highgate, Middlesex, on 13 May. His younger son, Clarence, succeeded him in the post of superintendent of the zoo (having previously been assistant superintendent for twenty-four years), remaining there until a month before his death in 1903. Bartlett's elder son, Edward, a taxidermist, travelled as an animal collector to Peru. He became curator of the Maidstone Museum and later of Raja Brooke's museum, Kuching (Sarawak, Malaysia), and returned to England shortly before his father's death.

CHRISTINE BRANDON-JONES

Sources A. D. Bartlett, *Wild animals in captivity: being an account of the habits, food, management, and treatment of the beasts and birds at the 'Zoo' with reminiscences and anecdotes*, ed. E. Bartlett (1898) • E. Bartlett, 'Obituary: Abraham Dee Bartlett', *Zoologist*, 4 (1897), 267–8 • E. Blyth, letter to D. W. Mitchell, 4 May 1857, Zoological Society of London • H. Scherren, *The Zoological Society of London: a sketch of its foundation and development* (1905) • W. Blunt, *The ark in the park: the zoo in the nineteenth century* (1976) • W. P. Jolly, *Jumbo* (1976) • 'The late Mr Edward Bartlett', *The Field* (1 Feb 1908), 182 • *IGI* • b. cert. [Edward Bartlett] • *The Times* (May 1897) • d. cert.
Likenesses portrait, repro. in Blunt, *Ark in the park*, p. 97 • portrait, repro. in Jolly, *Jumbo*, p. 14
Wealth at death £5040 7s. 1d.: probate, 15 June 1897, *CGPLA Eng. & Wales*

Bartlett, Benjamin. See Bartlet, Benjamin (1714–1787).

Bartlett, Sir Charles John (1889–1955), motor vehicle manufacturer, was born on 12 December 1889 at Bibury, Gloucestershire, the son of George Bartlett, a miller journeyman, and Elizabeth, *née* Stevens. After attending the village school in Bibury he completed his formal education at Bath Technical College, studying business methods and specializing in accounting.

Having enlisted in the Devonshire and Dorsetshire regiment in 1914, Bartlett was severely wounded at the battle of Loos, and after recovery saw further service in France and the Middle East. He was demobilized in 1919 with the rank of sergeant and in the following year joined General Motors Ltd (the American car manufacturer) as an accounting clerk at its London branch in Hendon. His leadership qualities were soon recognized, and by rapid promotion he reached the post of managing director in 1926.

General Motors (GM) was anxious to acquire a British manufacturing base to circumvent import tariffs on foreign vehicles, and in 1926 the board recommended the purchase of the ailing Vauxhall Motor Company in Luton. Bartlett was considered an ideal person to oversee Vauxhall and transform it into a mass producer of vehicles. A story current at the time was that when J. D. Mooney, the director of General Motors' overseas operations, was told by Alfred P. Sloan, president and chairman of GM, to pick an Englishman to run Vauxhall, he replied: 'Well I guess it had better be Charlie Bartlett; he's about as English as they come' (Platt, 93).

Under Bartlett's control the first car to be produced in the recapitalized and reorganized Luton plant was the Vauxhall Cadet, which was followed by the much more popular Light Six in 1933, and later by the outstandingly successful Vauxhall Ten in 1937. The greatest success, however, was in the light truck market; 11,200 trucks were produced in 1931, and the figure rose to a commercial vehicle output of 60,800 Bedfords in 1954. According to Sir Reginald Pearson it was Bartlett who convinced Sloan that trucks would be very profitable for Vauxhall, and by the end of the 1930s Vauxhall was one of the 'Big Six' vehicle producers in Britain. CJB, as he was known, was summed up by a former colleague thus:

> He never lost his simple and sturdily democratic approach to industrial management. This robust attitude went well with a determined character, a strong stocky physique and a sense of humour leavened what could otherwise have been too paternal an outlook towards the Vauxhall workforce. (Platt, 93)

A number of policies were introduced under Bartlett's management to ensure good industrial relations and the loyalty of the workforce. Rates of pay were relatively high, a profit sharing scheme was introduced in 1935, he provided greater job security so that workers were not automatically laid off *en masse* when orders were low, and in 1941 he introduced a form of works council. He pursued an active policy of promoting shop floor workers to managerial positions, among the most notable being Sir Reginald Pearson. He also encouraged the development of welfare and leisure programmes. During the Bartlett era there were no serious industrial disputes at Vauxhall. Unionists in other car firms referred to it as 'the turnip patch' in recognition of its apparent rural tranquillity in industrial relations.

Despite his obvious success at managing Vauxhall, which included a huge reorganization to mass produce Churchill tanks and Bedford army trucks during the Second World War (for which he was knighted in 1944), Bartlett did not always see eye to eye with the top management of GM. These differences became more severe in the post-war years, particularly over future plans for the company. In April 1953 Bartlett was replaced by Walter Hill, a GM man, and he was offered the post of chairman without executive responsibility until his retirement in 1954.

Bartlett married Emily May, *née* Pincombe, on 24 October 1925. He was active in many associations, serving as president of the Luton chamber of commerce (1938–45), deputy lieutenant of Bedfordshire (1952), vice-president (1946–53) and president of the Royal Society for the Prevention of Accidents, and council member for the British Institute of Management. He retained a lifelong love of horticulture, was a keen cricketer and golfer, and had a passion for sport which led to the strong encouragement of recreational activities while managing director at Vauxhall. He died from heart failure at his home, Whitewalls, Kinsbourne Green, Harpenden, on 10 August 1955.

LEN HOLDEN

Sources C. J. Bartlett, *Some aspects of management co-ordination: to-day and to-morrow* (1948) · C. J. Bartlett, 'Management and productivity: the results to be achieved and the penalties of failure', *British Management Review* (1948) · L. T. Holden, 'A history of Vauxhall Motors to 1950', MPhil diss., Open University, 1983 · L. T. Holden, 'Think of me simply as the skipper: industrial relations at Vauxhall, 1920–1950', *Oral History*, 9 (1981), 18–32 · M. Platt, *An addiction to automobiles* (1980) · P. W. Copelin, 'Development and organisation of Vauxhall Motors Limited', *Studies in business organisation*, ed. R. S. Edwards and H. Townsend (1961), 78–92 · K. Ullyett, *The Vauxhall companion* (1971) · G. Turner, *The car makers* (1963) · W. J. Seymour, *An account of our stewardship: being a record of the wartime activities of Vauxhall Motors Ltd* (1946) · M. Sedgwick, *Vauxhall: a pictorial tribute* (National Motor Museum, Beaulieu, Hampshire, 1981) · L. C. Derbyshire, *The story of Vauxhall, 1857–1946* (1946) · L. T. Holden, 'Bartlett, Sir Charles John', *DBB* · *WWW* · *The Times* (11 Aug 1955) · *Luton News* (11 Aug 1955) · d. cert. · m. cert.
Archives U. Warwick Mod. RC, corresp. with A. P. Young
Likenesses photograph, Vauxhall Motors Ltd archive, Luton, Bedfordshire · photograph, repro. in Holden, 'Bartlett, Sir Charles John'
Wealth at death £42,485 16s. 1d.: probate, 29 Nov 1955, *CGPLA Eng. & Wales*

Bartlett, Sir Ellis Ashmead (1849–1902), politician, born in Brooklyn, New York, on 24 August 1849, was the eldest son of Ellis Bartlett of Plymouth, Massachusetts, a graduate of Amherst College and a good classical scholar, who died in 1852. His mother was Sophia, daughter of John King Ashmead of Philadelphia. On his father's side he was directly descended from Robert Bartlett or Bartelot, of Sussex, who landed on Plymouth Rock from the ship *Ann* in 1623 and married in 1628 Mary, daughter of Richard Warren, who had sailed in the *Mayflower* in 1620. On his mother's side he derived, through her father, from John Ashmead of Cheltenham, who settled in Philadelphia in

1682, and, through her mother, from Theodore Lehman, secretary to William Penn, first governor of Pennsylvania.

Ellis and his younger brother, William Lehman Ashmead (later married to Angela Burdett-Coutts), were brought to England in early boyhood by their widowed mother, and were educated at a private school, The Braddons, at Torquay. Ellis showed precocity in classics, but illness interrupted his studies, except in history, of which—aided by an admirable memory—he early gained a wide knowledge. On 16 February 1867 he matriculated from St Mary Hall, Oxford, but soon migrated to Christ Church. A taste for politics asserted itself at Oxford. Becoming the recognized leader of the Conservative Party in the Oxford Union, and an ardent champion of Disraeli, he was elected president of the union in Easter term 1873, defeating H. H. Asquith by a large majority. He was also prominent in athletics. After gaining a third class in moderations, he graduated BA at Christ Church in 1871 with first-class honours in law and history, and proceeded MA in 1874. After leaving Oxford he became an inspector of schools, 1874–7, and an examiner in the privy council office (education department), 1877–80. On 13 June 1877 he was called to the bar from the Inner Temple.

In 1874 Bartlett married Frances Christina, daughter of Henry Edward Walsh; they had five sons and three daughters. His liaison with Blanche Hozier, mother of Clementine Churchill, caused a public scandal in 1889.

Bartlett was initially influenced by H. P. Liddon, active in the campaign against the Turks' 'Bulgarian atrocities' of 1876, and helped to organize the London conference on them in December 1876. But in 1877–8 he visited Serbia, Bulgaria, and Roumelia and became strongly Russophobic. On his return to Britain he began a vigorous campaign against Russia. In 1880 Lord Beaconsfield assigned to him what was practically the 'pocket borough' of Eye, in Suffolk. He held the seat until it was disfranchised under the Redistribution Bill of 1884. In 1885 he was elected for the predominantly middle-class constituency of the Ecclesall division of Sheffield, for which he sat until his death. Energetic in his loyalty to the Conservative Party, he chiefly devoted himself both inside and outside the House of Commons to the interests of British imperialism as he conceived them. In the house he was untiring in his attacks on Liberal foreign policy and, notably in his first parliament, proved a constant torment to Gladstone. Strident even by the standards of that parliament, he became something of a caricature of a tory imperialist. At the time of the Hozier affair, W. S. Blunt thought him 'a rather absurd middle-aged Member of Parliament … with much underbred pretension … at whom the world generally laughs' (Longford, 272). Outside the house he quickly gained an exceptional reputation as a platform speaker, which he maintained throughout his public life. He was probably in greater demand among Conservative organizers of popular meetings than any other speaker, and invariably roused the enthusiasm of his audiences to the highest pitch. His organizing capacity was also of much service to his party. He was chairman of the National

Union of Conservative Associations for three years, 1886–8, and he carried on a ceaseless propaganda on behalf of his principles and his party by pamphlets, articles, and letters to the press; characteristic are *Shall England Keep India?* (1886) and *Union or Separation* (1893). In March 1880 he started *England*, the first Conservative penny weekly newspaper, which he maintained at considerable personal loss until 28 May 1898. The paper helped to involve him in financial embarrassments which clouded the closing years of his life.

Bartlett was civil lord of the Admiralty in Salisbury's minority government in 1885, and again in Salisbury's government of July 1886 to August 1892; he was knighted on the fall of the ministry. He published two pamphlets on South Africa, *British, Natives and Boers* (1894) and *The Transvaal Crisis* (1896). On the outbreak of war between Turkey and Greece in 1897 Sir Ellis went to Constantinople, where the sultan conferred on him the grand cordon of the Mejidiye, and he joined the Turkish army in the field. He was present at the defeat of the Greeks at Mati and was among the first non-combatants to enter Tyrnavo and Larissa (see his account in *The Battlefields of Thessaly*, 1897). He was afterwards taken prisoner by the commander of a Greek warship and carried to Athens, but was soon released. When the Second South African War broke out in South Africa in October 1899, Sir Ellis went to the front and witnessed some early stages of the campaign, in which two of his sons took part. He died, almost penniless, at 18 Langham Street, London, after an operation for appendicitis, on 18 January 1902, and was buried at Tunbridge Wells. His first son, also Ellis Ashmead Bartlett (1881–1931), was a prominent war correspondent and briefly a tory MP.

J. P. ANDERSON, rev. H. C. G. MATTHEW

Sources *The Times* (20 Jan 1902) · Gladstone, *Diaries* · E. Longford [E. H. Pakenham, countess of Longford], *A pilgrimage of passion: the life of Wilfrid Scawen Blunt* (1979)

Archives U. Lond., Institute of Commonwealth Studies, papers

Likenesses Russell & Sons, photograph, *c*.1892, NPG; repro. in R. Albery, *Our conservative statesmen* (1893), vol. 2 · E. Moore, portrait, 1895; formerly priv. coll. · B. Stone, photographs, 1897, NPG · G. C. Beresford, photographs, 1905–9, NPG · Spy [L. Ward], cartoon, chromolithograph, NPG; repro. in *VF*, 2 (21 Oct 1882) · lithograph, NPG

Wealth at death £100: administration, 24 Oct 1902, *CGPLA Eng. & Wales*

Bartlett, Sir Frederic Charles (1886–1969), psychologist, was born in Stow on the Wold, Gloucestershire, on 20 October 1886, the second son of William Bartlett, master bootmaker, and his wife, Temperance Matilda Howman. He was educated at home in his teens, his health being thought too poor, following an attack of pleurisy, for him to go away to school. This apparent handicap allowed him to read very widely, and to spend time walking in the Gloucestershire countryside. He preserved throughout his life a tendency to observe human everyday activity and to base psychological thought upon that observation, rather than upon academic thinking.

As an external student of London University, Bartlett obtained first-class honours in philosophy in 1909 and an

Sir Frederic Charles Bartlett (1886–1969), by Bassano, 1948

MA with special distinction in 1911. He moved next to Cambridge; he had by this time strong interests in sociological questions, and was attracted to St John's College, where W. H. R. Rivers was active. Rivers combined anthropological interests with a belief in the importance of experimental measurements of the performance of individual people and he encouraged Bartlett to work in the new laboratory of experimental psychology under C. S. Myers. Bartlett graduated in 1914, obtaining a first in part one of the moral sciences tripos, and then became assistant director of the laboratory. His health made him unfit for military service, whereas Myers and Rivers left Cambridge for the duration of the war, leaving Bartlett with the major responsibility for the laboratory. Even when they returned to Cambridge, Myers soon left again, and Rivers died; thus from 1922 Bartlett became director of the psychological laboratory and reader in experimental psychology. In 1920 he married Emily Mary (*d*. 1974), daughter of William Henry Smith JP, of Helmshore, Lancashire, herself a psychologist from the early days in Cambridge; they had two sons.

In 1931 Bartlett was made the first professor of experimental psychology in Cambridge, a post which he retained until he retired in 1952. During the thirty-year period of directing the laboratory he developed it from one assistant to over seventy staff and research workers, and trained many remarkable students. In the post-war years the chairs at Oxford, Cambridge, London, and numerous other universities were for a substantial time all occupied simultaneously by Bartlett's former students.

His achievements within the university were accompanied after 1939 by much public service. The war created a need for more information about people's performance under stress, their sensory abilities, and their ability to operate such devices as radar screens, target indicators, or tank gunnery controls. Bartlett served on the flying personnel research committee of the Air Ministry, and also on the Medical Research Council, and his laboratory in Cambridge became a centre for investigations of this kind. This work led to design improvements in the devices themselves and to changes in the models used to understand human behaviour.

Bartlett was assisted in his wartime research by K. J. W. Craik, who was one of the first to see the possible use in psychology of explanations derived from cybernetics and control engineering. Bartlett actively encouraged Craik's ideas, and following Craik's tragic accidental death in 1945, Bartlett fostered a group of research workers developing similar theories. Characteristically, Bartlett's own interest in control processes was stimulated not only by intellectual influences, but also by his keen interest in cricket and tennis. He would frequently discuss the ways in which the everyday behaviour of the player making a stroke required the psychologist to suppose that each action was controlled by a computed model of future events, a process far more complex than the simple theories of classical psychology.

After the war, Bartlett's research on human performance and machine design was extended to industrial problems: from 1944 the Medical Research Council maintained an applied psychology research unit within Bartlett's department, and after his retirement he continued to act as a consultant to it, as well as taking part energetically in committee work on the problem of improving the efficiency of individuals at work.

Bartlett's scientific thought was highly original and unconventional at the time, but was later widely accepted. Of the ten books which he wrote, or to which he contributed, the best-known is *Remembering* (1932), in which he reported a lengthy series of experiments on perception and on memory, which showed that human awareness of events was both selective and constructive: much which struck the eye was never seen or remembered, and conversely a great deal was thought to have been perceived or recalled which had not in fact occurred. This, as well as the choice of the items which were correctly reported, showed that perception and remembering were controlled by some process sensitive to the purposes and interests of the individual concerned. This line of thought departed from current orthodoxies, which, whether behaviourist or gestaltist, saw human awareness as passively determined by the pattern of present events or of past experience. Though they owed something to the work of Rivers, Myers, James Ward, whom he had known in Cambridge, and the neurologist Henry Head, Bartlett's ideas largely originated with his own observation of human behaviour, and *Remembering* is copiously illustrated with cases in which Africans had selectively remembered events of little importance to Britons or vice versa.

Bartlett was kindly, encouraging, and informal. He inspired enthusiasm, and could bring out the value in even the humblest contribution. His influence spread more through discussion classes and informal meetings than through his exciting lectures.

From 1924 to 1948, an unenviably long tour of office, Bartlett was editor of the *British Journal of Psychology*. He was president of section J (psychology) of the British Association for the Advancement of Science in 1929. He was elected FRS in 1932, the only psychologist so honoured for many years. He was created CBE in 1941 and knighted in 1948. He was president (1950) and honorary fellow (1954) of the British Psychological Society, and was an honorary member of the Experimental Psychology Society of the UK (1960). He was a foreign member or associate of the Société Française de Psychologie, of the American Philosophical Society of Philadelphia, of the US National Academy of Arts and Sciences, and of the American Academy of Arts and Sciences, and an honorary member of a number of foreign psychological societies. He received honorary degrees from Athens, Princeton, Louvain, London, Edinburgh, Oxford, and Padua. He also received the Baly and the Huxley medals (1943), the royal medal of the Royal Society (1952), the Longacre award of the Aero Medical Association (1952), and the gold medal of the International Academy of Aviation and Space Medicine (1964).

To the end of his life Bartlett took an active interest in new developments in psychology, which he discussed with a worldwide network of leading investigators who always found his comments worth seeking. He died in Cambridge on 30 September 1969; his wife survived him.

D. E. BROADBENT, *rev.* HUGH SERIES

Sources WWW, 1961–70 · D. E. Broadbent, *Memoirs FRS*, 16 (1970), 1–13 · *The Times* (1 Oct 1969) · personal knowledge (1981) · private information (1981) · b. cert. · *CGPLA Eng. & Wales* (1970)
Archives CUL, corresp. and papers
Likenesses Bassano, photograph, 1948, NPG [*see illus.*] · P. Graham, portrait, U. Cam., Psychological Laboratory · photograph, repro. in Broadbent, *Memoirs FRS*
Wealth at death £26,783: probate, 11 March 1970, *CGPLA Eng. & Wales*

Bartlett, Henry (*b.* 1617/18), Church of England clergyman and letter writer, was the son of John Bartlett of Maiden Newton, Dorset. He matriculated from Wadham College, Oxford, on 16 May 1634, aged sixteen, graduated BA on 16 February 1637, and proceeded MA on 7 July 1640. He became curate of Buttsbury, Essex, in 1645 and vicar of Fordingbridge, Hampshire, in 1647. From 1648 to 1651 he also held a fellowship at Wadham.

Bartlett left no published works of his own, but between 28 August 1652 and 4 April 1655 wrote letters to the eminent minister Richard Baxter of Kidderminster which reveal salient aspects of contemporary religious life, especially the consolidated and concerted effort of the godly clergy to create ministerial associations, modelled on Baxter's own Worcestershire association, and the controversy over the doctrine of justification in which Baxter and, indirectly, Bartlett were embroiled. In his first letter Bartlett spoke of his recent visit to Kidderminster in which the pressing agenda of propagating the gospel and of settling ecclesiological differences among ministers were discussed. Baxter's parish reforms and creation of a county-wide ministerial association were welcomed enthusiastically by Bartlett and his contacts in the west country, particularly Peter Ince, rector of Donhead St Mary, Wiltshire, and the latter's patron, Thomas Grove. Bartlett was one of the clerical leaders who sought to replicate Baxter's initiative seen in *The Humble Petition of many Thousands … in the County of Worcester* (1652). His letter to Baxter dated 22 March 1652 reported that 'we have in Hampshire subscribed one to the same effect with 8000 hands'; the counties of 'Dorset, Wilts, Somerset, they ar all going the same way but slowly' (Keeble and Nuttall, 1.95). The collected petitions were published as *The cryes of England to the parliament for the continuance of good entertainment to the Lord Jesus his embassadors* (1653), and emphasized the indispensable role of the established ministry.

Bartlett played a mediatorial role between Baxter and his critics. While he commended Baxter's achievement, beseeching him 'in the bowels of Christ hide not your talent' (Keeble and Nuttall, 1.86), and observing 'how much good your S[aints] rest … hath done in these parts' (ibid., 1.89), he also relayed the strong antipathy which some of his high Calvinist colleagues in the west country had to Baxter's *Aphorismes of Justification* (1649) and his *The Right Method for a Settled Peace of Conscience* (1653). The former work had been attacked as presenting a view virtually indistinguishable from the Roman Catholic position, while the latter offended high Calvinists in its espousal of the positions that Christ died for all and that once-convinced believers might fall away from their faith and irrevocably lose their salvation. Bartlett tried unsuccessfully to suppress publication of a virulent attack on Baxter's position by John Crandon, rector of Fawley, Hampshire, which appeared as *Mr Baxters Aphorisms Exorcised and Authorised* (1654). Crandon, as Bartlett had noted on 28 August 1652 was 'endevoring to prove you a flat papist' (ibid., 1.83), and he repeatedly urged Baxter to clear himself from such allegations.

None the less, Bartlett's letters testify to the high regard in which Baxter continued to be held by Bartlett himself and by his friends in the western association in Dorset. They also testify to the close contacts and frequent visiting between ministers in different parishes and areas. In his last surviving letter, of 4 April 1655, Bartlett revealed that he had hoped to call on Baxter in London, but had been prevented by the death of his mother. He reported positively on the recent meetings of ministers in Wiltshire or Dorset (which is not clear), rejoicing that proceedings were 'carried on with so much love, wisdome, & unity' and attended by a wide spectrum of clergy 'some Episcopall, but eminently holy, & watchful over their flockes, others Presbiteriall, others of the Congregationall way, all my very good friends' (Keeble and Nuttall, 1.171).

Little is known of Bartlett's later life. A letter of 28 June 1653 reveals the existence of his wife, but her name is unknown; there are also references to his 'family'. In August 1654 he was involved in sorting out trouble between the fellows of Wadham, where he maintained a link through Henry Dent, the son of a possible patron of the same name. The following year Bartlett succeeded Nathaniel Tucker as vicar of Portsmouth, Hampshire, but he no longer held the living by 27 November 1658, when his successor, Benjamin Burgess, was admitted. It is possible that he had died in the interim. PAUL C-H LIM

Sources DWL, Richard Baxter letters, MS 59 · M. Burrows, ed., *The register of the visitors of the University of Oxford, from AD 1647 to AD 1658*, CS, new ser., 29 (1881) · *Calamy rev.* · R. B. Gardiner, ed., *The registers of Wadham College, Oxford*, 1 (1889) · Foster, *Alum. Oxon.* · *Calendar of the correspondence of Richard Baxter*, ed. N. H. Keeble and G. F. Nuttall, 1 (1991)

Archives DWL, Richard Baxter letters, MS 59

Bartlett [Barthlet], **John** (*fl.* 1562–1567), Church of England clergyman and author, was perhaps one of the many evangelical laymen who entered the ministry late in life after the accession of Elizabeth I. It is not impossible that he was the John Bartelot who reported to Thomas Cromwell in 1535 that he and others had surprised the prior of Crutched Friars, London, in bed with a prostitute. Some time later Richard Layton informed Cromwell that he and 'your servant, Bartlett' had similarly surprised the abbot of Langdon.

One 'Barthlett' was in 1541 living in the London parish of St Dunstan-in-the-West, near the inns of court, and a John Bartlet received the degree of LLB at Cambridge in 1562 and was then briefly fellow of Jesus College (1562–3). The latter was almost certainly the nonconformist of 1566.

Soon after the establishment of a lectureship at St Giles Cripplegate in 1565 Bartlett was appointed to it, possibly by the vicar, Robert Crowley. When on 23 March 1566 Matthew Parker, archbishop of Canterbury, demanded unconditional conformity from the city clergy with regard to clerical vestments, Crowley and Bartlett were among the thirty-seven who upon refusal were summarily suspended. With John Philpot and John Gough they orchestrated the opposition to Parker during the following weeks.

Edmund Grindal, bishop of London, summoned Bartlett on 3 May for preaching while under suspension and ordered him to cease forthwith, 'seeming to offer impunity for the matter past, so he would promise silence for the time to come' (Nicholson, 288). Bartlett refused, claiming that it was his duty to instruct his flock. With two other ecclesiastical commissioners Grindal therefore placed him under house arrest. Next morning 'three-score' female parishioners of St Giles besieged Grindal's London residence. The celibate bishop shrank from the encounter, 'much misliking such kind of assembling', but sent a message that he was prepared to speak with 'half-a-dozen of their husbands'. Saved from further embarrassment by Philpot, who, hastily summoned by persons unknown, persuaded the women to depart, Grindal observed that 'his authority was greater with them than mine could have been' (ibid., 288–9).

It is not known when Bartlett was released from house

arrest, but during 1566 he published *The pedegrewe of heretiques, wherein is set out, the first roote of heretiques since the time of the gospell*. This was not a direct response to recent events but rather a reply to Richard Shacklock's translation of Cardinal Hosius's *De origine haeresium nostri temporis*, published in 1565 as *The Hatchet of Heresies*. Bartlett attempted to show that all Roman Catholic doctrine was tainted by heresies traceable to either Judas Iscariot or Simon Magus. The table of heretics he appended was of awesome length, including such peculiar sects as 'Visiblers' and 'Mice-feeders'. The title-page carried the emblem of Robert Dudley, earl of Leicester, to whom Bartlett dedicated the work, addressing him as 'a special Maecenas to every student' and 'so favourable and zealous a friend to the ministry'.

Bartlett's direct contribution to the vestiarian controversy, under the initials I. B., was *The fortresse of fathers, ernestlie defending the puritie of religion, and ceremonies … against such as wold bring in an abuse of idol stouff, and of thinges indifferent, and do appoinct th'aucthority of princes and prelates larger then the trueth is*. Four years before Thomas Cartwright officially launched the presbyterian campaigns of the 1570s and 1580s against the 'halfly reformed' religious settlement of 1559, Bartlett asserted that 'the lordship of bishops now exercised over both the rest of the clergy and over the lay people hath no ground in the word of God' (sig. A4).

Parker's opponents now appealed for support from Europe's protestant leaders. Following Percival Wiburn's unsuccessful visit to Geneva and Zürich in 1566 a second 'embassy' was dispatched in the summer of 1567 in the shape of Bartlett and George Withers, future archdeacon of Colchester. They 'conducted themselves like exiles' (Collinson, 81), eliciting sympathy from Theodore Beza in Geneva but managing to annoy and embarrass Heinrich Bullinger of Zürich, to whom Beza had dispatched them. Thereafter they concentrated their fire on the Elector Palatine Friedrich III. They asked him to write to Elizabeth, taking care not to criticize the queen herself but rather blaming her bishops for failing to offer her proper advice. Friedrich prudently ignored this invitation to interfere so flagrantly in England's internal affairs but had no objection to the continued presence of Withers and Bartlett in Heidelberg. Rudolf Gualter, Bullinger's colleague, later lamented that they were 'the chief authors of those changes' which had 'inflicted such a blow' upon churchmanship in the palatinate (Robinson, 1.364).

Withers matriculated at Heidelberg University and was subsequently granted a doctorate, but nothing further is heard of Bartlett, either abroad or in England. Presumably he died suddenly and unexpectedly.

A contemporary of the same name was vicar of Bishop's Stortford, Hertfordshire, from 1556 until deprived in 1561.

BRETT USHER

Sources Venn, *Alum. Cant.*, 1/1.99 · T. Wright, ed., *Three chapters of letters relating to the suppression of monasteries*, CS, 26 (1843), 59–60, 75–7 · R. G. Lang, ed., *Two Tudor subsidy assessment rolls for the city of London, 1541 and 1581*, London RS, 29 (1993), 77 · W. Nicholson, ed., *The remains of Edmund Grindal*, Parker Society, 9 (1843) · H. Robinson, ed. and trans., *The Zurich letters, comprising the correspondence of several English bishops and others with some of the Helvetian reformers, during the early part of the reign of Queen Elizabeth*, 2 vols., Parker Society, 7–8 (1842–5) · P. Collinson, *The Elizabethan puritan movement* (1967)

Bartlett, John (*fl.* 1605–1610), lutenist and composer, took a BMus degree at Oxford in 1610, four years after publishing a volume of lute songs whose full title is *A booke of ayres with a triplicitie of musicke, whereof the first part is for the lute or orpharion, and the viole de gambo, and 4. partes to sing, the second part is for 2. trebles to sing to the lute and viole, the third part is for the lute and one voyce, and the viole de gambo*. The metal-strung orpharion was a frequent alternative to the gut-strung lute, and the 'viole de gambo' (bass viol) was the usual (optional) reinforcement for the musical bass line. The 'triplicitie of musicke' followed a pattern established by Robert Jones in his *Ultimum vale* the previous year, with specific songs in each category. Jones and Bartlett were unusual in including duets for two treble voices, and Bartlett's 'Whither runneth my sweetheart?' is one of the best. His somewhat risqué solo song 'Of all the birds that I do know' finds a place in modern performance, but the rest of his songs are infrequently heard.

The *Booke of Ayres* is dedicated to Edward Seymour, earl of Hertford, addressing him as his 'singular good and Maister', and indeed Bartlett was one of several musicians who accompanied the earl on an embassy to Archduke Albert in Brussels in 1605. Bartlett would probably have been too young to have been already in Seymour's service when he famously entertained Queen Elizabeth I with lavish spectacle and music at Elvetham, Hampshire, in September 1591. Without more clues it is impossible to pick out the right John Bartlett from among the many recorded in the *International Genealogical Index* and to give any further detail of his birth, life, or death.

IAN HARWOOD

Sources J. Bartlett, *A booke of ayres, 1606*, ed. D. Greer, facs. edn (1967) · *New Grove* · Wood, *Ath. Oxon.: Fasti* (1815), 337

Bartlett, Josiah (1729–1795), physician and revolutionary politician in America, was born on 21 November 1729 in Amesbury, Massachusetts, the seventh and youngest child of Stephen Bartlett, a shoemaker, and his wife, Hannah Webster. Josiah had little schooling before being apprenticed to a relative, Dr Nehemiah Ordway, to study medicine in 1747. In 1750 Josiah started up his own medical practice in Kingston, New Hampshire, a frontier community. He established a reputation for skilful treatment of fevers, and his medical practice flourished. He augmented his medical income through land speculation, agricultural pursuits, and mercantile activities. On 15 January 1754 he married Mary (1730–1789), a cousin from Newton, New Hampshire, who was the daughter of Joseph and Sarah Hoyt Bartlett. Josiah and Mary had twelve children, of whom eight lived to maturity.

Bartlett's public service began with his election as selectman for Kingston in 1757. The number of important appointments he received is evidence of his growing influence; these included: proprietor in several new towns, justice of the peace, and lieutenant-colonel in the

Josiah Bartlett (1729–1795), by John Trumbull, 1790

New Hampshire militia. In 1765 Bartlett was elected to the colony's legislature; he was continuously re-elected until that body's dissolution in 1775. An early supporter of independence, he attended the extralegal New Hampshire provincial congress in 1774. Unable to attend the first continental congress, Bartlett helped draft instructions for the delegates. In 1775 he went as a delegate for New Hampshire to the second continental congress, where he served on a number of important committees, most notably the naval and marine committees.

During this time Bartlett remained very active in New Hampshire. In January 1776, for example, he was reappointed a delegate to its congress, elected a member of the executive council, reappointed colonel of the 7th New Hampshire militia regiment, and commissioned justice of the court of common pleas. Most of his time in 1776 was spent in congress, where Bartlett enthusiastically supported the independence movement and was probably the first delegate to vote in favour of independence.

In November 1776 Bartlett returned home, and in December he mustered his regiment, declined reappointment to the continental congress, and accompanied his militiamen to Rhode Island to serve with the American army there. In August 1777 he ministered to the wounded of the battle of Bennington. Early in 1778 he chaired the committee of the New Hampshire legislature appointed to consider the articles of confederation and thereafter reluctantly accepted reappointment to the continental congress, where he signed the newly approved articles. Bartlett's service to the state during this time continued to include seats on the executive council and the court of common pleas, as well as seats on the court of quarter sessions and the committee of safety. He also represented New Hampshire in interstate conferences on military policy, economic policy, and boundary questions.

In 1779 Bartlett again took a seat in the state legislature and was appointed a delegate to the convention to form a state constitution. In 1784, in recognition of his contributions to this process, he presided over the opening session of the state's new bicameral legislature. In 1781–2 he was appointed justice to the superior court, then the state's highest court. A supporter of the federal constitution, in 1788 he served as temporary president of the convention that considered its adoption. In 1790 he was chosen as chief executive of the state. He easily won re-election three times. In 1792 the state's constitution was revised and the title of governor reinstated, making Bartlett New Hampshire's first constitutional governor. In 1791 he signed an act incorporating the New Hampshire Medical Society and served as its first president. This organization grew out of meetings held in Bartlett's home and fulfilled his longstanding desire to fix standards to ensure good medical care for citizens of the state.

Josiah Bartlett's own health deteriorated steadily after the sudden death of his wife on 14 July 1789, and on 19 May 1795, within a year of leaving office as governor, he died in Kingston, following a stroke. He was buried four days later at the Congregationalist church, Kingston. B papers reveal his enormous involvement in all phases of the early public life of the state of New Hampshire, as well as his concern for both his patients and his family.

DENNIS M. CONRAD

Sources F. C. Mevers, ed., *The papers of Josiah Bartlett* (1979) • F. C. Meuers, 'Bartlett, Josiah', *ANB* • L. Bartlett, *Genealogical and biographical sketches of the Bartlett family in England and America* (1876) • J. F. Colby, 'Bartlett, Josiah', *DAB* • E. L. Page, 'Josiah Bartlett and the federation', *Historical New Hampshire*, 2 (1947), 1–6
Archives L. Cong. • New Hampshire Historical Society, Concord • New Hampshire State Library, Concord
Likenesses J. Trumbull, miniature, 1790, New Hampshire Historical Society, Concord [*see illus.*] • oils (after J. Trumbull), New Hampshire State House, Concord
Wealth at death moderate: will, Mevers, ed., *Papers of Josiah Bartlett*, 409–12

Bartlett, Thomas (1789–1872), theological writer, was the son of Thomas Bartlett, of Henley. He was educated at St Edmund Hall, Oxford, taking his BA degree in 1813, and proceeding MA in 1816. He took holy orders in 1812, and was rector of Kingstone, Kent, from 1816 to 1850, and of Chevening, Kent, from 1850 to 1854. He served as vicar of Luton from 1854 to 1857 and as rector of Burton Latimer, Northamptonshire, from 1857 to his death. From 1832 he was one of the six preachers of Canterbury Cathedral. Bartlett produced many evangelical publications, but his greatest achievements were his *Memoirs of the Life and Writings of Bishop Butler* (1839) and *Index to Butler's Analogy* (1842). Bartlett was married twice, first in 1814 to Catherine Sarah Cowper, a great-great-niece of Bishop Butler, and second to Lucinda Grace Hoare. Bartlett died at Burton Latimer on 28 May 1872, and was buried in the churchyard there.

ALFRED GOODWIN, rev. I. T. FOSTER

Sources *The Record* (3 June 1872) • *Church Times* (7 June 1872) • *Northampton Herald* (8 June 1872) • *Kettering Parish Magazine* (July 1872) • Boase, *Mod. Eng. biog.* • Foster, *Alum. Oxon.* • Crockford • *Men of the time* (1865)

Bartlett, (Charles) Vernon Oldfeld (1894–1983), journalist and broadcaster, was born on 30 April 1894 at Westbury, Wiltshire, the second of the three children and only son of Thomas Oldfeld Bartlett, bank manager, of Swanage, and his wife, Beatrice Mary Jecks. He was educated at Blundell's School at Tiverton but psoriasis forced him to leave early. He was sent to live abroad and acquired a fluent mastery of the main European languages that later stood him in good stead as a foreign correspondent.

In the First World War, Bartlett was in hospital recovering from a wound when his regiment (the Dorset) suffered an early poison gas attack. Later in 1915 he was the only man pulled out alive when his dugout received a direct hit. He was invalided out of the army with a burning conviction that further world wars must be prevented. He found work in Fleet Street, joining the *Daily Mail* as a general reporter. In 1917 he married Marguerite Eleonore (*d.* 1966), the Belgian refugee daughter of Henri van Bemden, a well-to-do food merchant of Antwerp. They had two sons, the younger of whom died in 1970.

Also in 1917 Bartlett joined Reuters which later sent him to cover the Paris peace conference, and in 1919 he became a foreign correspondent for *The Times*, reporting the turbulent post-war diplomatic developments from Geneva, Berlin, Rome, and Warsaw. With his international experience and his repugnance of war it was a natural step for him to become, in 1922, the director of the London office of the League of Nations, a post he held until 1932.

Bartlett was an early broadcaster, at first occasionally about the work of the league, and later analysing general international developments in a weekly series, *The Way of the World*. He became an outstanding communicator to whom a rising generation owed its interest in foreign affairs. The BBC *Yearbook* for 1931 noted: 'By his unobtrusive charm and his respect for truth and a certain quality of fair play which is inherent in his work, Mr Bartlett has made of international affairs a subject of general interest'.

That quality of fair play sometimes got Bartlett into trouble. In October 1933 Nazi Germany walked out of the disarmament conference at Geneva and left the League of Nations. Bartlett was far from pro-Nazi, but broadcasting on the BBC, which had employed him full time since October 1932, he made the immediate comment: 'I believe the British would have acted in much the same way as Germany has acted if they had been in the same position.'

This remark provoked an immediate political storm. There were violent protests from the prime minister, J. Ramsay MacDonald, and other MPs, as well as in the press. Bartlett himself said he received thousands of letters, the overwhelming majority in support. The BBC told him it would be easier for him to continue broadcasting if he were not on the staff, adding that the politics of any newspaper he joined might affect the frequency of his broadcast invitations. Bartlett therefore resigned, rejecting a lucrative offer from the Labour *Daily Herald* in favour of a smaller one from the more moderate *News Chronicle*. Yet, by what he regarded as cowardly treatment, it was several years before he was asked to broadcast again.

For the next two decades Bartlett travelled widely as the *News Chronicle's* diplomatic correspondent. In 1938, after Chamberlain at Munich yielded to Hitler's demands over Czechoslovakia, he stood as an Independent Progressive candidate opposed to the appeasement policy in the by-election at Bridgwater, then a safe Conservative seat. With no party machine to support him, though he had a number of keen volunteers, he won Bridgwater, and held it until 1950. He contributed usefully to debates on foreign affairs, but the role of an independent member was perhaps too lonely for one so gregarious by nature.

During the Second World War, Bartlett's broadcasting skill was put to good use. He spoke three times a week to America and often in French and German. His *Postscripts*, after the 9 o'clock home news, were wise, compassionate talks, often including touches of sardonic humour, and they did much to sustain domestic morale. For a time he served as British press attaché in Moscow. At one Kremlin dinner, emboldened by vodka, he responded to a toast to the press by declaring that without a free press there could not be a free people. Stalin commented: 'That young man talks too much.'

After retiring from the *News Chronicle* in 1954 Bartlett worked as a journalist in Singapore and in 1956 he was appointed CBE. In 1961 he moved to a farm in Tuscany where he produced wine and continued to write books—twenty-eight altogether. His first had been an autobiographical novel (1929) about calf love in pre-war Berlin. Others were about foreign affairs and his travels in southeast Asia, Africa, and Europe, and especially about his beloved Tuscany. An autobiography, written when he was forty-three, provides revealing insights into European diplomacy between the wars.

Bartlett's wife died in 1966 but three years later he made a happy second marriage, to Eleanor Needham (Jo), daughter of Lieutenant-Colonel Theodore Francis Ritchie DSO, Royal Army Medical Corps, and widow of Walter Menzel, of the International Committee of the Red Cross. Bartlett died at Yeovil, Somerset, on 18 January 1983.

LEONARD MIALL, *rev.*

Sources V. Bartlett, *Calf love* (1929) • V. Bartlett, *This is my life* (1937) • V. Bartlett, *I know what I liked* (1974) • *BBC Yearbook* (1931) • *Daily Telegraph* (17 Oct 1933) • A. Briggs, *Governing the BBC* (1979) • BBC WAC • personal knowledge (1990) • *CGPLA Eng. & Wales* (1983) **Archives** BL, corresp., Add. MSS 59500–59501 • News Int. RO, papers as *The Times* foreign correspondent • U. Reading L., corresp. and papers • U. Sussex, papers | Bodl. Oxf., corresp. with Gilbert Murray • Bodl. Oxf., corresp. as secretary of parliamentary committee on refugees • JRL, letters to the *Manchester Guardian* • King's Lond., Liddell Hart C., corresp. with Basil Liddell Hart | SOUND BL NSA, performance recording **Likenesses** photograph, 1941, Hult. Arch. **Wealth at death** £81,635: probate, 1 June 1983, *CGPLA Eng. & Wales*

Bartlett, William Henry (1809–1854), topographical artist, was born on 26 March 1809 at 5 Bartholomew Place, Kentish Town, London, the second child and elder son in the family of three children of William Bartlett and his wife, Ann. At the age of seven he was sent to a local boarding-school, where he was very miserable. He left school in 1821, and in 1822 was apprenticed to the antiquary John Britton (1771–1857) for seven years, and continued to work for him until 1831. Britton sent him all over England to make sketches and architectural drawings, and he did some of the illustrations for Britton's *Cathedral Antiquities of England* (1814–32), *Christian Architecture in England* (1826), and *Picturesque Antiquities of the English Cities* (1830). Bartlett thus became a minor but prolific figure among the topographical artists of the 1820s and 1830s, of whom the leading lights were R. P. Bonington, Samuel Prout, and J. M. W. Turner. He also exhibited at the Royal Academy in 1831 and 1833, and at the New Watercolour Society. On 6 July 1831 he married Susanna Moon (1811–1902), niece of Sir Francis Moon, fine art publisher, and lord mayor of London in 1854–5. They had three sons and two daughters.

For the next ten years Bartlett travelled all over Europe, the Middle East, and North America, fulfilling commissions for drawings for travel books, most of which were published by George Virtue (1793–1868). In 1832 he met Dr William Beattie (1793–1875), who asked him to do the illustrations for a book about Switzerland, *Switzerland Illustrated* (1836), and this was followed by a year in the Holy Land and Syria, making sketches for *Syria, the Holy Land, Asia Minor* (1836). Others of Beattie's books illustrated by Bartlett include *Scotland Illustrated* (1838), *The Waldenses* (1838), and *The Castles and Abbeys of England* (1844). Bartlett spent a year in North America in 1836–7, the first of four visits between 1836 and 1854, and illustrated *American Scenery* (1840) and *Canadian Scenery* (1842) for Nathaniel Parker Willis. He also did the drawings for Nicholas van Kampen's *The History and Topography of Holland and Belgium* (1837), and *The Beauties of the Bosphorus* (1839) for Julia Pardoe.

By the mid-1840s demand for travel book illustrations slackened, and Bartlett turned to writing his own books, illustrated with steel-engravings and woodcuts prepared from his drawings. *Walks about the City and Environs of Jerusalem* (1844) was followed by *Forty Days in the Desert on the Track of the Israelites* (1848) and *The Nile Boat* (1849). He also wrote and illustrated a history of early colonial America, *The Pilgrim Fathers* (1853), and published in three volumes *A History of the United States of America* (1856). He edited *Sharpe's London Magazine* from March 1849 to June 1852.

Bartlett died suddenly on 13 September 1854 on board the French steamer *Egypt*, on his way home from sketching the seven churches of Asia Minor, and was buried at sea. He had been in poor health for most of his life. His drawings were sold by auction by Messrs Southgate and Barrett in the following year.

R. E. GRAVES, *rev.* ANNE PIMLOTT BAKER

Sources A. M. Ross, *William Henry Bartlett: artist, author, and traveller* (1973) [incl. Beattie's *Brief memoirs*] • W. Beattie, *Brief memoirs of the late William Henry Bartlett* (1855) • P. Ferriday, 'A Victorian journeyman artist', *Country Life*, 143 (1968), 348–9 • J. Britton, *Art Journal*, 17 (1855), 24–6 • Graves, *RA exhibitors* • Boase, *Mod. Eng. biog.* • S. Houfe, *The dictionary of 19th century British book illustrators and caricaturists*, rev. edn (1996)
Archives AM Oxf., corresp. • U. Oxf., Griffith Institute, corresp.
Likenesses B. Holl, stipple, pubd 1839 (after H. Room), BM, NPG • C. J. Baselré, lithograph, repro. in Beattie, *Brief memoirs*, frontispiece

Bartley, George (1782?–1858), comedian, was born in Bath in or about 1782; one source states 1784. His father was box-keeper at the Bath theatre, and he thus had early opportunities of acquiring some stage experience, appearing in such characters as the page in Cross's musical drama *The Purse*. It is said that he was apprenticed to the cook at the York House Hotel, once a famous Bath hostelry; alternative sources say he was placed 'in the counting-house of a large mercantile concern'. Bartley appeared at Cheltenham in the summer of 1800 as Orlando in *As You Like It*, and is said to have reappeared in Bath before joining a travelling company. The course of his wanderings brought him to Guernsey, where he contracted his first marriage, his wife being a member of the company, possibly named Stanton, by whom he was nursed through an illness.

To the influence of Dorothy Jordan, who saw him in Margate in 1802, Bartley owed his engagement by Sheridan at Drury Lane. His London début is said to have taken place on 11 December 1802, but was most probably, as he himself stated, a week later. His opening character was Orlando. Dates of early performances are tentative. He is described as playing Colloony on 20 September 1803 in *The Irishman in Distress*, a forgotten farce of the elder Macready, and on 19 January 1803 had replaced Barrymore as Polydore in Otway's *The Orphan*. For some five years Bartley seems to have been employed principally as an understudy, replacing John Bannister, who then took serious characters, and occasionally attempting the roles vacated in consequence of the departure of Charles Kemble.

Dissatisfied with his remuneration, Bartley quitted London and played in the provinces. In 1809–11 he managed unsuccessfully the Glasgow theatre. Thereafter he acted with increasing reputation as a comedian in Manchester, Liverpool, and other towns. On 23 August 1814 he married his second wife, Sarah Smith [*see* Bartley, Sarah (1783?–1850)], a tragic actress, by whose reputation his own was overshadowed. On 13 October of the same year Mrs Bartley played Ophelia at Drury Lane, and on 12 April following Bartley reappeared at the same house as Falstaff, which was thenceforward his favourite character. A trip made by the couple to America, which followed in 1818, proved highly successful, with appearances at the Park Theatre, New York.

After his return Bartley accepted a winter engagement at Covent Garden, and played during the summer under Samuel James Arnold at the Lyceum. During Lent he was in the habit of giving a series of discourses on astronomy at the Lyceum. He also lectured on poetry. In 1829, when the management of Covent Garden collapsed, Bartley headed the actors who came forward with a proposal, which was accepted, to furnish funds and recommence performances. He became accordingly, in 1829–30, stage manager of the theatre, and, owing to the appearance of Fanny Kemble, the season was highly remunerative. Bartley retained this post during successive ownerships by Laporte, Bunn, Macready, and Madame Vestris.

The death, in 1843, of his only son, who was at Exeter College, Oxford, led to Bartley's retirement from the stage. His only remaining child, a daughter, died shortly afterwards, and Mrs Bartley followed her children in 1850. Bartley played Falstaff at Windsor Castle in the performance arranged by Charles Kean in 1850. He then appeared for a few nights at the Princess's Theatre, taking his farewell benefit on 18 December 1852, on which occasion, in his address to the public, he observed that the event marked the exact fiftieth anniversary of his London début.

On Saturday 17 July 1858 Bartley had an attack of paralysis, to which, five days later, on 22 July, he succumbed at his home, 11 Woburn Square. He is said to be buried in the churchyard of St Mary's, Oxford. Bartley was especially successful in playing comic older men, bluff uncles, and the like. He was for many years treasurer of the Covent Garden Theatrical Fund.

JOSEPH KNIGHT, *rev.* KATHARINE COCKIN

Sources Adams, *Drama* · T. A. Brown, *History of the American stage* (1870) · T. Gilliland, *The dramatic mirror, containing the history of the stage from the earliest period, to the present time*, 2 vols. (1808) · Hall, *Dramatic ports.* · Genest, *Eng. stage* · *Macready's reminiscences, and selections from his diaries and letters*, ed. F. Pollock, 2 vols. (1875) · *The biography of the British stage, being correct narratives of the lives of all the principal actors and actresses* (1824) · *The Era* (25 July 1858) · *Oxberry's Dramatic Biography*, 5/77 (1826) · CGPLA Eng. & Wales (1858)
Archives BL, letters to George Colman, Charles Kemble, and J. M. Kemble, Add. MSS 42893–42965
Likenesses S. Lane, oils, Dulwich Picture Gallery, London · I. Pocock, oils (as Hamlet), Garr. Club · prints, NPG · prints, Harvard TC
Wealth at death under £2000: probate, 9 Aug 1858, CGPLA Eng. & Wales

Bartley, Sir George Christopher Trout (1842–1910), banker and politician, was born at Rectory Place, Hackney, on 22 November 1842, the son of Robert Bartley, of the War Office and his second wife, Julia Anna, *née* Lucas. After early education at Blackheath, at Clapton, and at University College School, London, he became, in 1860, science examiner at the education branch of the Department of Science and Art in South Kensington, under Sir Henry *Cole. In 1864 he married Mary Charlotte, Cole's third daughter. They had four sons and one daughter. In 1866 he was made official examiner, and remained there until 1880 as assistant director of the science division, which was responsible for the establishment of science schools throughout the country.

Since 1870 Bartley had written several pamphlets on social questions, especially on thrift and poor law and on education. His first published work, *The Educational Condition and Requirements of one Square Mile in the East End of London* (1870) was quoted by William Edward Forster during the discussion of the Education Bill of 1870. In 1871 there

followed *Schools for the People*, which treated of the historical development and methods of schools for the working classes in England, and, with Emily Shirreff, he edited the journal of the Women's Educational Union, which aimed at the general improvement of women's education.

Poverty and the harsh effects of the existing poor law system also claimed his attention and in a series of pamphlets he urged its reform. In 1872 he read a paper before the Society of Arts on old-age pensions, urging that help should be given in old age to those who had made some provision for themselves. Twenty-one years later he laid before the House of Commons a bill for old-age pensions, which embodied his earlier principles. For the encouragement of thrift among the masses he published in 1872 twelve penny 'Provident Knowledge Papers', which he supplemented with other homilies on the same theme. In 1872 he started the instalment club at 77 Church Street, Edgware Road, London, which enabled workmen to buy tools or clothes by regular weekly payments. The foundation of the Middlesex Penny Bank at the same address followed the same year. In 1875, in conjunction with Sir Henry Cole, the duke of Devonshire, H. N. Hamilton Hoare and others, Bartley established the National Penny Bank, so-called because the minimum deposit was 1*d*. To encourage thrift, collectors were authorized to take deposits at many workplaces, such as the London docks and schools; other local branches were open in the evenings for the workmen's convenience. The scheme was a great success. By the year of Bartley's death over 2,800,000 accounts had been opened and some £25 million had passed through the bank.

In 1880 Bartley resigned his post at South Kensington to stand for parliament in the Conservative interest. He unsuccessfully opposed Henry Fawcett at Hackney in March of that year. From 1883 to 1885 he was chief agent to the Conservative Party. In 1885 he was returned for North Islington, and retained that seat until 1906. He was narrowly defeated in November 1907 at a by-election in West Hull. In the House of Commons Bartley, although a fluent speaker, strenuously advocated the curtailment of parliamentary speeches; in 1891 he voted against his party in opposition to the Free Education Bill brought in by the Salisbury government, and he played a prominent part in obstructing the chief measures of the Liberal government (1892–5). Bartley was created KCB in November 1902, and served as a JP for London and Middlesex.

He died at Henrietta House, 14 Henrietta Street, London, on 13 September 1910 after an operation, and was buried in Holtye churchyard, near Shovelstrode Manor, East Grinstead, his country house. He was survived by his wife and by his four sons and his daughter. His second son, Douglas Cole Bartley, barrister, succeeded him as managing director of the National Penny Bank.

W. B. OWEN, *rev.* ANITA MCCONNELL

Sources *The Penny Bank News* [ed. G. C. T. Bartley], 5 (15 Sept 1877) · *The Times* (15 Sept 1910), 13c · H. W. Lucy, *A diary of the Salisbury parliament, 1886–1892* (1892), 288–9 · H. W. Lucy, *A diary of the home rule parliament, 1892–1895* (1896), 259–61 · *Charity Organisation Review*, 8 (Sept 1892) · private information (1912) · d. cert.

Archives Lincs. Arch., Revesby Abbey MSS | CKS, letters to Aretas Akers-Douglas
Likenesses B. Stone, photographs, 1897–8, NPG · B. Gotto, bust; formerly in the possession of Lady Bartley, Shovelstrode Manor, East Grinstead, 1912; replica, formerly at National Penny Bank, 59 Victoria Street, Westminster, 1912
Wealth at death £92,813 3s. 1d.: probate, 3 Nov 1910, CGPLA Eng. & Wales

Bartley [*formerly* Smith], **Sarah** (1783?–1850), actress, was probably born in Liverpool on 23 October 1783. Accounts of her parentage are conflicting and hopelessly muddled; some accounts make her father an actor called Williamson and her mother a daughter of General Dillon of Galway, while others assert that her maiden name was O'Shaughnessy. On her mother's second marriage, apparently in 1793, she adopted the surname Smith; she had at this time already appeared on stage as Edward in Mrs Inchbald's comedy *Every One has his Fault* at Salisbury.

Sarah Smith's début in a serious character took place in Lancashire (probably at Liverpool), when, aged sixteen, she played Joanna in Thomas Holcroft's *The Deserted Daughter*. She then spent three years under Stephen Kemble at the Edinburgh Theatre Royal. Disillusioned by her experiences, she retired from the stage, but circumstances (including the need to assist her mother with the upkeep of her numerous family) drove her back into the profession. She obtained work on Tate Wikinson's York circuit, and remained there until his death in 1803. She then moved on to Birmingham and thence to Bath, where she enjoyed popular success and was hailed as the 'Siddons of Bath'. She was seen there by Thomas Harris, who engaged her for Covent Garden, where she appeared on 2 October 1805 as Lady Townly in Vanbrugh's *The Provoked Husband*. She had been reluctant to take part in comedy, but Sarah Siddons enjoyed the monopoly on characters which Sarah Smith wished to perform. She refused to play secondary parts to Mrs Siddons—Harris thought her 'unaccommodatingly fastidious'—but also refused to be bought out of her contract. On its expiry in 1808 she departed for Dublin, where she was warmly received. For her benefit she performed the melologue (part recitation, part song) on national music written for her by Thomas Moore.

Sarah Smith returned to London, where her reception was more cordial than formerly, and in 1811 migrated to Drury Lane. In January 1813 she created the character of Teresa in S. T. Coleridge's tragedy *Remorse*. On 23 August 1814 she married the widowed actor George *Bartley (1782?–1858); the happy relationship produced two children. Sarah Siddons's retirement in 1812 had left Sarah Bartley as the reigning tragedy queen of the London stage, but her position was soon usurped by Eliza O'Neill. In 1818 the Bartleys went to America, which secured her reputation and made a fortune. They returned to England in 1820, and undertook a provincial tour. She appeared at Covent Garden in November 1823 as Mrs Beverley in Edward Moore's *The Gamester*, but thereafter performed only infrequently, and instead she gave instruction to young women seeking a theatrical career. The death of

Sarah Bartley (1783?–1850), by Samuel De Wilde [reciting 'Ode on the Passions' by William Collins]

her son in 1843 and that of her daughter shortly afterwards greatly affected her. She was paralysed, and died from heart disease at her home, 11 Woburn Square, Bloomsbury, on 14 January 1850.

Sarah Bartley, a small woman with an expressive face and a melodious voice, was an actress of genuine talent, according to Leigh Hunt, for both tragedy and farce, exemplified in her portrayals of Belvidera in Otway's *Venice Preserv'd* and Estifania in Beaumont and Fletcher's *Rule a Wife and have a Wife*. Macready, by contrast, opined that 'Of the soul that goes to the making of an artist she had none' (*Reminiscences*, 1.61).   JOSEPH KNIGHT, *rev.* J. GILLILAND

Sources L. Hunt, *Critical essays on the performers of the London theatres* (1807) · *Macready's reminiscences, and selections from his diaries and letters*, ed. F. Pollock, 1 (1875) · *The biography of the British stage, being correct narratives of the lives of all the principal actors and actresses* (1824) · W. C. Russell, *Representative actors* (c.1875) · [J. Roach], *Authentic memoirs of the green-room* [1814] · T. Gilliland, *The dramatic mirror, containing the history of the stage from the earliest period, to the present time*, 2 vols. (1808) · Genest, *Eng. stage* · *Theatrical Inquisitor* · *The Era* (20 Jan 1850) · W. C. Lane and N. E. Browne, eds., *A. L. A. portrait index* (1906) · Hall, *Dramatic ports.* · A. Davies and E. Kilmurray, *Dictionary of British portraiture*, 4 vols. (1979–81) · Adams, *Drama* · *Drama, or, Theatrical Pocket Magazine*, 5 (1824), 190, 240, 246 · d. cert.
Archives NL Scot., corresp. with Sir Walter Scott
Likenesses S. De Wilde, watercolour drawing, Garr. Club [*see illus.*] · T. Hargreaves, miniature, engraving (after A. Cardon),

repro. in *La Belle Assemblée*, new ser., 5/115 • S. Lane, portrait, Dulwich Picture Gallery, London • portraits, Harvard TC • prints, BM, NPG

Bartlot, Richard (*d.* 1556), physician, was elected to a fellowship at All Souls College, Oxford, in 1495; he took the degree of MB at Oxford in 1503, and supplicated for that of MD on 3 November 1508, although it is not known whether he actually attained that degree. He was the first fellow admitted into the College of Physicians after its foundation in 1518, and he was president in 1527, 1528, 1531, and 1548.

Bartlot lived in Blackfriars, London, where it appears he had a garden of medicinal plants, and died towards the end of 1556. He was buried in the church of St Bartholomew-the-Great, Smithfield. The whole College of Physicians, including its president, John Caius, attended his funeral. Caius described him as a 'good and venerable old man, very famous for his learning, great knowledge, and experience in physic' (Munk).

Bartlot owned a considerable amount of property. He left his estate in Edgware to All Souls, on condition that daily masses would be celebrated in the college chapel for himself and his wife, Anne. He also left the college a silver basin and ewer. He left several considerable legacies to his brother Edmund, of Castle Moreton, Worcestershire, and to his brother's children.   SARAH BAKEWELL

Sources Munk, *Roll* • Foster, *Alum. Oxon.* • G. Lewis, 'The faculty of medicine', *Hist. U. Oxf.* 3: *Colleg. univ.*, 213–56, esp. 229, 248 • private information (2004) [J. S. G. Simmons]

Bartolozzi, Francesco (1728–1815), engraver, was born in Florence, Italy, on 25 September 1728, the son of Gaetano Pieri Bartolozzi, a goldsmith from Pistoia, and his wife, Maddalena Pieri. The boy's earliest work was carried out for his father, but he entered the Florentine academy at the age of fifteen, and with his lifelong friend Giovanni Battista Cipriani studied for three years under Ignazio Enrico Hugford and Giovanni Domenico Ferretti. His earliest bookplates were engraved in Florence, but after a brief spell at Bassano he moved to Venice, and on 24 August 1748 he was articled to Josef Wagner, an engraver and printseller, with whom he lived for six years. During this period he produced book illustrations and single prints, including some fine genre scenes after Pietro Longhi (1750–51). In 1754 he established his own workshop at Santa Maria Formosa, although much of his work was still published by Wagner. Among his later Venetian prints were a set of times of day after Giuseppe Zocchi (1760), four seasons after Giovanni Battista Piazzetta, and twelve months after Zocchi (1761). About 1755 he married Lúcia Ferro Domenico, the daughter of Francesco Domenico, a Venetian doctor. Their eldest son, Gaetano Stefano [*see below*], was born in Venice in 1757, before they accepted Cardinal Bottari's invitation to move to Rome. Their later children all died young.

In Rome in 1762 Bartolozzi worked for Piranesi, notably contributing to a book of prints after the Domenichinos in the chapel at Grotta Ferrata. He was already being

Francesco Bartolozzi (1728–1815), by Sir Joshua Reynolds, 1773?

hailed as the best engraver in Italy, and some of his interpretations of old master drawings were published in London by Thomas Bradford in 1763. In March of that year the British engraver Robert Strange met Bartolozzi at Bologna in company with Richard Dalton, art dealer and librarian to George III. Dalton was in Italy buying art and had engaged the Italian at an annual salary of £300. He invited Bartolozzi to London, promising him an appointment as engraver to the king.

Bartolozzi arrived in London in 1764, leaving his wife, who was in poor health, and young son behind. She remained in Italy and outlived him by many years. He worked in London for the next thirty-five years, lodging at first with Cipriani in Warwick Street, Soho. In Dalton's employ, he completed the collection of prints after Guercino's drawings, many of which were bought by the earl of Bute and given to George III, so that the series became a record of drawings in the Royal Collection. For Dalton, Bartolozzi also engraved a number of paintings that he had drawn in Italy. He exhibited with the Society of Artists from 1765 to 1768, but in the latter year he seceded to the Royal Academy with the rest of the artists who enjoyed court emoluments. Although engravers were theoretically excluded from membership of the new academy, an exception was made for Bartolozzi.

Together with Ryland, Bartolozzi established a vogue for dotted prints or 'stipples', and this became his characteristic manner. He collaborated with his friend Cipriani on a huge scale: they produced some 335 prints in total, including many tickets and invitation cards, notably for concerts featuring Felice de' Giardini and other Italian musical friends. Angelica Kauffman, Henry Bunbury, and

Joshua Reynolds also provided many designs, though Bartolozzi worked after a wide variety of artists. He published only a small proportion of his own work, but he kept control of some of his best prints after Cipriani and Reynolds and of some of those plates on which he had himself expended most effort. The vast bulk were commissioned by a variety of printsellers, among them James Birchall, William Dickinson, Emanuel Matthias Diemar, Thomas Macklin, William Palmer, Antonio de Poggi, Mary Ryland, Anthony Torre, Susan Vivares, and John Walker. While it went under the master's name, much of this work was executed by his numerous pupils. This was standard practice, but the size of Bartolozzi's studio and the shoddy quality of some of its products gave it a bad name in some circles. Redgrave remarked haughtily that it 'became a mere manufactory of this class of art' (Redgrave, *Artists*, 30). However, publishers wanted his distinguished name on their plates because it sold well—especially abroad, where unauthorized piracies appeared bearing such names as Bartolonii. Among those who worked for Bartolozzi were Pietro Bettelini, Thomas Cheesman, Jean Marie Delattre, Robert Marcuard, Giuseppe Antonio Minasi, John Ogborne, Benedetto Pastorini, Liugi and Nicolo Schiavonetti, John Keyes Sherwin, Gaetano Testolini, and Peltro William Tomkins.

In 1780 Bartolozzi took a house at North End, Fulham, where on 26 September 1786 the German diarist Sophie von la Roche visited him:

> To Fulham and Bartolozzi, the great engraver, whose works I had so often admired … We came upon the eminent artist with his worthy pupils at a nice house situated in the midst of a large flower garden, busts of his friends in the alleyways, and Apollo on a hill, overgrown with laurel, in front of his window. His rooms are charming and decorated with valuable drawings by Angelika and Cipriani … Mr. Bartolozzi showed us all the copperplates that he had engraved over a period of twenty years: the amount and beauty of the man's work is astonishing. He plucked me a bouquet from the feet of Apollo in friendly fashion. (Roche, 230–31)

Bartolozzi reverted to line engraving for serious projects, such as his 1782 portrait after Reynolds of Lord Chancellor Thurlow (in which only the flesh is stippled). This was one of the urgent commissions that delayed completion of *The Death of Chatham* (1788), a prestigious undertaking, but one that led to a court case with its painter and publisher, John Singleton Copley. Copley was aggrieved that the plate took almost a decade to finish, by which time several subscribers had died. He paid Bartolozzi 2000 guineas, of which Bartolozzi spent half hiring assistance, some of which proved unsatisfactory. Bartolozzi erased four years' endeavour by Testolini after they quarrelled, and this weakened the plate so that it would produce only 2500 impressions, a yield that Copley found very disappointing. A smaller duplicate plate had been engraved by Bartolozzi's principal assistant, Delattre, for £800. Copley considered this so poor that he refused to pay until he lost a court case.

Bartolozzi became very sensitive to criticism. In 1787 he exhibited proof impressions of his prints of Cipriani's drawings of Sir William Hamilton's vase in a printshop to answer allegations that they were not up to scratch. But he continued to attract top commissions and was the principal engraver employed by Thomas Macklin for his *Poets Gallery* series. Between 1792 and 1800 Bartolozzi engraved a total of 87 prints after Holbein drawings in the Royal Collection. In 1787 the German writer Michael Huber had estimated the cost of a complete collection of Bartolozzi's prints at 1000 guineas.

In 1801 Bartolozzi and his pupil Gregorio Francisco de Queiróz were invited to Lisbon to reform the royal printing press, established in 1768, with the aim of printing a magnificent edition of *The Lusiads*; they departed in November 1802. At Lisbon, Bartolozzi inherited the workshop that had been established along with the press to teach engraving on metal plates. The workshop operated from his own house in the Rua Quitéria, distant from the press, and as he was a foreigner, and already an old man, and left Queiróz in charge, matters were hardly satisfactory. Bartolozzi's own production in Portugal was disappointing, but in 1807 he was made a knight of the order of Christ, an honour awarded very readily at that time. The French invaded in that year, and Bartolozzi's income was seriously affected. He continued to work up to the instant of his death, in the workshop on 7 March 1815. He left two-thirds of his estate to his son and the remainder to Tereza de Almeida, who had cared for him. It seems that his affairs had not prospered, despite his salary of 600 reales, for his furniture, pictures, and silver were to be sold to pay his debts to Tereza's husband, Francisco Tomaz de Almeida, an engraver and Bartolozzi's executor. Whatever the outcome, Bartolozzi was buried in the common grave of his parish church of Santa Isabel, Lisbon.

Gaetano Stefano Bartolozzi (1757–1821), musician and printseller, inherited some of his father's talent but led a generally indolent and dissolute life. Following his arrival in London in 1774, his father established him as a print publisher in Great Titchfield Street, where he traded as F. Bartolozzi & Co. He made several visits to the continent as an agent for his father, taking consignments of his prints to Florence in 1778, Venice in 1787, 1793, and 1797, and Leipzig in 1802. He married in 1795 the pianist Teresa Jansen, the daughter of a dancing-master from Aix-la-Chapelle. He and his wife played frequently at London concerts and parties. A daughter, Lucia Elizabeth (1797–1856) [*see* Vestris, Lucia Elizabeth], was born in London; she later married and became Madame Vestris, a celebrated actress and singer. A second daughter, Josephine, was born in 1807; she married a singer named Anderson. In 1797 James Christie auctioned Gaetano's prints and plates, probably because he was seriously in debt, and in July 1808 he was again in debt, to the tune of £700, and was imprisoned in king's bench. William Beechey 'spoke highly of Him' to Farington '& sd. He had been ruined by His wife, a vain imprudent woman' (Farington, *Diary*, 3309–10). Another sale took place in 1811. Gaetano then spent two years in Paris, where his father sent prints for him to sell. He was passionately fond of music and while in Paris opened a musical and fencing academy, but this failed after a few years. He died in Paris on 25 February 1821.   TIMOTHY CLAYTON and ANITA McCONNELL

Sources E. Soares, *História da gravura artística em Portugal: os artistas e as suas obras* (1971), 101–21 · E. Soares, 'Francisco Bartolozzi e os seus discipulos em Portugal', *Estudos Nacionais, Instituto de Coimbra*, 3 (1930) [whole issue] · A. Petrucci, 'Bartolozzi, Francesco', *Dizionario biografico degli Italiani*, vol. 6, pp. 793–6 · J. de Castilho, *Lisboa antiga o Bairro Alto*, vol. 4 (1962), pp. 303–5 · R. Portalis and H. Béraldi, *Les graveurs du dix-huitième siècle*, 1 (Paris, 1880), 98–106 · S. Brinton, *Bartolozzi and his pupils in England* (1903) · J. T. H. Baily, *Francesco Bartolozzi: a biographical essay* (1907) · A. de Vesme and A. Calabi, *Francesco Bartolozzi* (1928) · A. Calabi, 'Francesco Bartolozzi', *Print Collector's Quarterly*, 14 (1927), 137–62 · G. Meissner, ed., *Allgemeines Künstlerlexikon: die bildenden Künstler aller Zeiten und Völker*, [new edn, 34 vols.] (Leipzig and Munich, 1983–) · Farington, *Diary* · A. W. Tuer, *Bartolozzi and his works*, 2 vols. (1881) · S. von la Roche, *Sophie in London, 1786* (1933), 230–31 · T. Dodd, 'Memoirs of English engravers, 1550–1800', BL, Add. MSS 33395 and 33396 · [K. H. von Heinecken], *Dictionnaire des artistes dont nous avons des estampes*, 2 (Leipzig, 1788), 175–201 · D. Mahon and N. Turner, *The drawings of Guercino in the collection of Her Majesty the Queen at Windsor* (1989), xxii–xxxiv · Royal Exchange Insurance, GL, MS 7253, policy 82851 · *A catalogue of the genuine and intire stock of capital and valuable prints, drawings and copper plates, some of which have never been published, and a few pleasing cabinet pictures, the property of Mr G. Bartolozzi, retiring from business* (1797) [sale catalogue, Christies, 23 June 1797] · A. Fremantle, ed., *The Wynne diaries*, 3 (1940)
Likenesses J. Zoffany, group portrait, oils, 1772 (*Royal Academicians*), Royal Collection · J. Reynolds, oils, 1773?, Saltram House, Devon [see illus.] · J. F. Rigaud, group portrait, oils, 1777, NPG · R. Menageot, stipple, pubd 1778, BM · J. Opie, oils, c.1785, NPG · H. Singleton, group portrait, oils, 1793 (*Royal Academicians*), RA · D. Pellegrini, oils, c.1795, Galleria dell' Academia, Venice · Pastorini and P. W. Tomkins, stipple with crayon, pubd 1803 (after W. Artaud), BM, NPG · T. Rowlandson, pen, watercolour, and pencil caricature, c.1815, Yale U. CBA · J. Romney, line engraving and etching, pubd 1817 (after F. Bartolozzi), NPG, BM · G. B. Cipriani, pencil drawing, Royal Collection · G. Dance, drawing, RA · H. Edridge, pencil drawing, BM · R. S. Marcuard, engraving (after J. Reynolds), BL, Add. MS 47790, fol. 92

Bartolozzi, Gaetano Stefano (1757–1821). *See under* Bartolozzi, Francesco (1728–1815).

Barton, Andrew (c.1470–1511), seaman and shipowner, was one of three brothers, Robert *Barton, John, and Andrew, sons of the seafaring merchant John Barton (d. in or before 1494). Like his brothers, Andrew was frequently employed as a naval commander by James IV, a role he combined with the more prosaic occupation of merchant seaman, carrying exports of Scottish wool and hides in his ship, the 120 ton *Lion*, from Leith to Bruges or Middelburg in the Low Countries.

All three Barton brothers were recipients of extensive favours from the king. Robert procured timber for shipbuilding, and skilled craftsmen from France, to work at the royal dockyards of Leith, Newhaven, and Pool of Airth; he carried a royal offering, a votive ship of silver, to the shrine of St James at Santiago de Compostela in Spain in 1508; and, following his return, he entertained the king in his Leith house. John Barton conveyed King James's illegitimate son, Alexander Stewart (d. 1513), archbishop of St Andrews, to France in September 1507 in a royal ship, the *Treasurer*, and by May 1512, if not before, he had been given command of one of the king's largest warships, the *Margaret*.

Andrew Barton's earliest recorded service to the crown occurs in July 1497, when he was one of those responsible for victualling the English pretender Perkin Warbeck's ship at Ayr. Thereafter he was the recipient of a number of small payments from James IV, and for a time he may have been captain of the royal warship *Margaret*, launched at Leith in 1505. Although on at least one occasion he played cards with the king, he is not described as a royal familiar in a major royal grant, made to him and his son Alexander on 16 October 1510, of lands in north-east Fife to the value of 222 merks; and his knighthood is the creation of a later age. Indeed his posthumous fame, which far exceeds that of his brothers, rests entirely on the description of his heroic last fight in a colourful sixteenth-century English ballad. Combining violence, chivalry, and inaccuracy in varying degrees, this work praises Andrew Barton's valour, but only in the context of eulogizing the Howards who defeated and killed him.

In 1507 James IV conferred on each of the Barton brothers letters of marque (reprisal) against the Portuguese in response to an act of piracy committed by certain Portuguese against their father, John, near Sluys in the 1470s. These letters authorized the Bartons to attack any Portuguese vessel which they encountered and to seize shipping and goods to the total value of their father's estimated loss—a staggering 50,000 French crowns (approximately £45,000 Scots). All three so blatantly misused the letters that in June 1510 James IV yielded to complaints by King Emanuel of Portugal and suspended the letters for a year.

Undeterred, Andrew Barton slipped away from Scotland to avoid answering a summons from the lords of council charging him with illegal seizure of a Breton ship carrying an Antwerp merchant's goods. On his arrival in Copenhagen, where his services had been requested by King Hans of Denmark, he took that king's pay and promptly sailed off again, without licence, in the *Lion*, purloining another ship, the *Jennet of Purwyn*, which had earlier been presented to King Hans by James IV. Barton is next to be found off the English east coast conducting indiscriminate attacks on every ship which he met and claiming that any goods which he seized were Portuguese. Late in June 1511 his two ships were overtaken in the Downs by two vessels—probably the *Barbara* and the *Mary Barking*—commanded by Lord Thomas Howard and his brother Sir Edward. Both Howards appear to have been on convoy duty and to have encountered Barton by chance. After a bloody fight Barton was killed and his ships taken by the English. James IV's formal protests to Henry VIII carry little conviction, and indeed the English king showed remarkable clemency in releasing Barton's captive crews. Privately King James may have been relieved: like his brother-in-law Henry VIII, the Scottish king knew that he had been sponsoring a pirate whose luck had run out.

NORMAN MACDOUGALL

Sources T. Dickson, ed., *Compota thesaurariorum regum Scotorum / Accounts of the lord high treasurer of Scotland*, 1 (1877) · J. B. Paul, ed.,

Compota thesaurariorum regum Scotorum / Accounts of the lord high treasurer of Scotland, 2–4 (1900–02) • *Ledger of Andrew Halyburton, 1492–1503,* ed. C. Innes (1867) • *The letters of James the fourth, 1505–13,* ed. R. K. Hannay and R. L. Mackie, Scottish History Society, 3rd ser., 45 (1953) • J. M. Thomson and others, eds., *Registrum magni sigilli regum Scotorum / The register of the great seal of Scotland,* 11 vols. (1882–1914), vol. 2, no. 3511 • *Hall's chronicle,* ed. H. Ellis (1809) • A. Spont, ed., *Letters and papers relating to the war with France, 1512–1513,* Navy RS, 10 (1897) • F. J. Child, ed., *The English and Scottish popular ballads,* 3 (1885), 342 • N. Macdougall, *James IV* (1989) • R. L. Mackie, *King James the fourth of Scotland: a brief survey of his life and times* (1958) • register of the great seal, treasurer's accounts, and exchequer rolls, NA Scot.

Barton, Bernard (1784–1849), poet, was born at Carlisle on 31 January 1784, the son of Quaker parents, John Barton (1755–1789) and his wife, Mary, *née* Done (1752–1784). His mother died a few days after his birth, and while he was still in his infancy, his father, a manufacturer, married another Quaker woman, Elizabeth Horne (1760–1833), moved to London, and finally engaged in the malting business at Hertford, where he died in the prime of life. To be near her family, his widow and children then made their home at Tottenham. Bernard was the brother of the educational writer Maria *Hack (1777–1844) and the half-brother of the economist John *Barton (1789–1852). He was sent to a Quaker school at Ipswich, and at the age of fourteen was apprenticed to a shopkeeper, Samuel Jesup, at Halstead in Essex. After eight years' service he moved to Woodbridge, married his employer's daughter, Lucy Jesup (1781–1808) on 6 August 1807, and entered into partnership with her brother Benjamin as coal and corn merchant. In the following year his wife died giving birth to a daughter, Lucy, whereupon Barton abandoned business and became tutor in the family of William Waterhouse, a Liverpool merchant. After staying a year in Liverpool, where he got to know the Roscoe family, he returned to Woodbridge, became a clerk in Messrs Alexander's Bank, and stayed there for forty years until within two days of his death.

Finding the work in the bank tiresome, Barton turned to his pen, eventually producing some eight volumes of verse, and numerous occasional pieces. In 1812 he published his first volume of poetry, *Metrical Effusions* and began a correspondence with Southey. Although Southey and Barton met only once (at Thomas Clarkson's home in Playford in 1824), Barton eventually felt that he knew Southey well enough to request help with the publication of a manuscript. Barton also hoped that Southey would arrange for favourable reviews in influential periodicals. About this time he addressed a copy of complimentary verses to James Hogg, who hastened to respond in grateful and flattering terms. Hogg had written a tragedy, which he wanted to see presented at a London theatre. Not knowing how to proceed, Hogg solicited Barton's assistance, who in turn sought counsel from Capel Lofft, on whose advice the scheme was dropped. Following *The Triumph of the Orwell* (1817), in 1818 appeared the *Convict's Appeal*, a protest in verse against capital punishment. The pamphlet bears no name on the title-page, but the dedication to

James Montgomery is signed 'B. B.'. In the same year Barton published by subscription *Poems by an Amateur,* which received little attention. Two years later, Harvey and Barton published *Poems,* favourably noticed in the *London Magazine,* the *Monthly Review,* and the *Edinburgh Review;* it reached a fourth edition in 1825. *Napoleon and other Poems* (dedicated to George IV), and *Verses on the Death of P. B. Shelley,* appeared in 1822.

It was at this time that Barton first wrote to Charles Lamb. The freedom with which the Quakers had been handled in the *Essays of Elia* induced Barton to remonstrate gently with the essayist. Charmed with his correspondent's homely earnestness and piety, Lamb carried on an extensive and intimate correspondence with Barton. The two men met first in 1822, perhaps at a contributors' dinner given by the proprietor of the *London Magazine.* Shortly after getting to know Lamb, Barton contemplated resigning his post at Woodbridge and living by his literary work. Lamb advised him strongly against such a course. 'Keep to your bank', wrote Lamb, 'and the bank will keep you' (*Letters of Charles Lamb,* 2.363). Southey gave similar advice.

After receiving some public notice and moderate praise, between 1822 and 1828 Barton published five volumes and some minor pieces, including *Poetic Vigils* (1824), *Devotional Verses* (1826), *A Missionary's Memorial* (1826), 'A Widow's Tale', *and other Poems* (1827), and 'A New Year's Eve', *and other Poems* (1828). His pursuit of literary fame may have taxed his health, for in his letters to Southey and Lamb he complained that he was suffering from low spirits and headache. Lamb attempted to encourage him with banter, while Southey advised him seriously never to write verses after supper. Clearly Barton wrote too hastily and too easily. 'The preparation of a book' says his biographer, Edward Fitzgerald:

> was amusement and excitement to one who had little
> enough of it in the ordinary course of daily life: treaties with
> publishers—arrangements of printing—correspondence
> with friends on the subject—and, when the little volume was
> at last afloat, watching it for a while somewhat as a boy
> watches a paper boat committed to the sea. (*Poems and
> Letters,* xvi)

In 1824 some Quakers, led by Joseph John Gurney, gave Barton tangible recognition and some financial relief by raising £1200 for his benefit. Barton hesitated to accept the money, but Charles Lamb's advice prevailed: 'Think that you are called to a poetical ministry—nothing worse—the minister is worthy of his hire' (Lucas, 2.421).

After an eight-year hiatus, during which Barton corresponded with numerous literary figures and friends including Robert Southey, William Jerdan, John Linnell, William Fitch, Edward Maxon, and Alan Cunningham, Barton, with his daughter, produced in 1836 *The Reliquary ... with a Prefatory Appeal for Poetry and Poets.* After another long period of silence, *Household Verses,* his last volume of poems, appeared in 1845. Dedicated to Queen Victoria, the volume attracted the attention of the prime minister, Robert Peel, who invited Barton to dinner at Whitehall.

After Peel left office, he procured Barton a pension of £100 a year.

During the next three years, Barton produced several additional minor works: *Sea-Weeds* (1844), *A Memorial of Joseph John Gurney* (1847), *Birthday Verses at Sixty-Four* (1848), *A Brief Memorial of Major Edward Mann* (1848), *Ichabod* (1848), and *On the Signs of the Times* (1848).

Preferring a sedentary life, Barton seldom left Woodbridge. He occasionally visited Charles Lamb, and once or twice went down into Hampshire to see his brother. Some holidays were spent with his friend W. Bodham Donne at Mattishall, Norfolk. Here he delighted in the conversation of Mrs Bodham, an old lady who in her youth had been the friend of Cowper. In later life Barton took less and less exercise. He liked to sit in his library and enjoy the view through the open window, or, if he started with any friends for a walk, he would soon stretch himself on the grass and wait for his friends' return. In 1846 he made a short visit to Aldborough for the benefit of his health. In later life, he complained of chest pains and shortness of breath, which his physician attributed to angina. Barton died at Thorsfare, Woodbridge, on 19 February 1849, after a short illness. In the same year his daughter, Lucy, published a selection of his letters and poems, to which Edward Fitzgerald contributed a biographical introduction. Concerned about his daughter's welfare, Barton had elicited from Fitzgerald a promise to look after Lucy. Lucy's subsequent marriage to Fitzgerald was not a success.

Bernard Barton is chiefly remembered as the friend of Lamb. His many volumes of verse are seldom read. Even the scanty book of selections published by his daughter contains much that might have been omitted. He never troubled to correct what he had written, but all his work is unaffected. As Fitzgerald recognized, Barton never thought his verse rose to great heights. His desire was 'to be a household poet with a large class of readers' (*Poems and Letters*, xxxv). Free from all tinge of bigotry, simple and sympathetic, Bernard Barton won the esteem and affection of a large circle of friends, young and old, orthodox and heterodox. His numerous letters are now valued above his poetry. More than 800 Barton letters survive, and include communications with many leading literary figures of his time. However, he treated his letters as he did his poetry, taking little care in producing them, and was unselfconscious about the art of letter-writing. Still, his comments on poets such as Hogg and Wordsworth, and on artists such as Colman and Blake, reveal a mind actively and eagerly engaged with the arts during his time.   A. H. BULLEN, rev. JAMES EDGAR BARCUS, JR.

Sources *Selections from the poems and letters of Bernard Barton*, ed. L. Barton (1849) [with a biographical notice by E. Fitzgerald] · *The literary correspondence of Bernard Barton*, ed. J. E. Barcus (1966) · E. V. Lucas, *Bernard Barton and his friends: a record of quiet lives* (1893) · *The letters of Charles Lamb: to which are added those of his sister, Mary Lamb*, ed. E. V. Lucas, 3 vols. (1935) · *Edward Fitzgerald and Bernard Barton*, ed. F. R. Barton (1924) · d. cert. · 'Dictionary of Quaker biography', RS Friends, Lond. [card index] · digest registers of births, marriages, and burials, RS Friends, Lond. [quarterly meetings for Cheshire and Staffordshire, London and Middlesex, Bedfordshire and Hertfordshire; microfilm]

Archives Harvard U., MSS · Haverford College, Philadelphia, MSS · RS Friends, Lond., MSS · Swarthmore College, Swarthmore, Pennsylvania, Friends Historical Library, papers · U. Leeds, Brotherton L., corresp., literary MSS, and papers · Yale U., MSS | BL, letters to George Crabbe, Add. MS 36756 · BL, corresp. with Sir Robert Peel, Add. MSS 40562–40600, *passim* · BL, letters to John Wooderspoon, Add. MSS 37032, 52524 · Bodl. Oxf., letters to James Montgomery; letters to G. Virtue · CUL, letters to Elizabeth Charlesworth and John Charlesworth; letters to Mrs E. S. Cowell · Lpool RO, corresp. with William Roscoe · RS Friends, Lond., letters to John Chandler and Lucy Chandler; letters to George Virtue and George Virtue junior · Trinity Cam., letters to Dawson Turner

Likenesses R. Cooper, print, BM, NPG · J. H. Lynch, print (after S. Laurence, 1847), NPG; repro. in *Edward Fitzgerald*, ed. Barton · R. Mendham, oils, Christchurch Mansion, Ipswich · print, BM

Barton, Charles (1767/8–1843), barrister and legal writer, was called to the bar on 20 November 1795 at the Inner Temple, and established a successful conveyancing practice. Among his clients was the Golden Lane Brewery, one of a number of joint-stock associations formed after the turn of the nineteenth century and whose deed he drew up. Barton edited and wrote a number of legal texts; in 1794 he produced an edition of William Noy's *The Grounds and Maxims* and also an *Analysis of English Laws* (2nd edn, 1817), and in 1796 he published *An Historical Treatise of a Suit in Equity*, whose title echoed that of Richard Boote's classic treatise on common law. This short work aimed to be a scientific deduction of the proceedings used on the equity side of the courts of exchequer and chancery, tracing each of the steps from the institution of a suit to a decree.

Barton was best known for writing two substantial books on conveyancing and land law. The first of these, *Elements of Conveyancing*, grew out of his lectures to his pupils, and was published in six volumes between 1802 and 1805, reaching a second edition (1810–22). This work was very well received, and the *Law Journal* commented that 'it is his merit that he has left little to be sought for in other works, by those who are possessed of his *Elements*'. Barton's second major work was his *Original Precedents in Conveyancing*, which was published in five volumes between 1807 and 1810 and which reached a third edition (published between 1821 and 1824). This work aimed to furnish the commonest forms in conveyancing to both pupils and solicitors in the most concise manner possible, progressing from the simplest to the most complicated. His son, Charles Barton the younger, published a supplement to his father's *Precedents*. Barton died of pneumonia, at 3 Great Norwood Street, Cheltenham on 18 November 1843.   MICHAEL LOBBAN

Sources *GM*, 2nd ser., 22 (1844), 215 · Holdsworth, *Eng. law*, 12.181–2; 13.469 · F. A. Inderwick and R. A. Roberts, eds., *A calendar of the Inner Temple records*, 5 (1936), 534, 593, 643 · 'Royal commision ... second report', *Parl. papers* (1830), 11.179, 575 [on the law of real property] · W. H. R. Brown, *Golden Lane Brewery* (1808) · d. cert. · C. Barton, *Elements of conveyancing* (1802–5), preface

Barton, Sir Derek Harold Richard (1918–1998), organic chemist, was born on 8 September 1918 at Grenfell, Sun Lane, Gravesend, Kent. His father, William Thomas

Sir Derek Harold Richard Barton (1918–1998), by Ron Case, 1969

Barton, was a carpenter, his mother was Maud Henrietta, formerly Lukes. He was educated at Tonbridge School, Kent, but he had to leave without any qualifications after his father's sudden death in 1935. For the next two years he worked in the family timber business but, convinced that there must be something more interesting in life, he attended Gillingham Technical College to pass the necessary examinations, including the Imperial College entrance examination. For financial reasons he had to choose London University, and he entered Imperial College in 1938. After only two years' study Barton obtained the top BSc with first-class honours in chemistry. Research in organic chemistry with Professor I. M. Heilbron followed. During the Second World War research on a topic of national interest was encouraged and Barton chose the synthesis of vinyl chloride, for which he received a research fellowship from the Distillers Company. In this he collaborated with a refugee German chemist named Mugdan who had spent his working life in industry. From him Barton learned how a practical industrial chemist would approach a problem.

Wide-ranging experience This early work involved the gas-phase pyrolysis of dichloroethanes. Barton studied this process using glass apparatus. At first the reaction was rapid but it slowed as the glass surface became contaminated. Barton later noticed that of two forms of dichloroethane one decomposed much faster than the other. Moreover the results varied from day to day. He traced these effects to differences in the method of preparation and to an uncontrolled factor—a leak in the apparatus which let in variable amounts of air. Small amounts of oxygen or chlorine, he found, had a spectacular effect on the rate of decomposition of 1,2 dichloroethane (CH_2Cl-CH_2Cl), but none at all on that of 1,1 dichloroethane ($CHCl_2$-CH_3) and he concluded that the reaction mechanisms must be different. He also found that in commercial 1,2 dichloroethane small quantities of an impurity, ethylene chlorohydrin (CH_2Cl-CH_2OH), acted as an inhibitor which he removed by treatment with aqueous potassium

permanganate or chromic acid. Barton completed his PhD in 1942, having laid the foundations for some important aspects of his later chemical researches.

About this time a medical examination revealed a cardiac weakness, and Barton was excused night-time fire-watch duties. The condition also precluded him from active service, and he remained at Imperial College working for two years in military intelligence developing secret inks for use on human skin behind enemy lines. On 20 December 1944 he married Jeanne Kate Wilkins (b. 1916/17), a clerk; they had one son. Barton then spent a year in chemical industry at Albright and Wilson in Birmingham. Here he was concerned with the synthesis of organo-phosphorus compounds. The work was routine but there was a good chemical library and his reading introduced him to the latest physical organic chemistry of E. D. Hughes and C. K. Ingold. Barton had become interested in the complex chemistry of the steroids as an undergraduate and he continued to pursue this subject in his spare time, preparing himself for the chance to investigate their reactions.

In 1945 Barton returned to Imperial College as an assistant lecturer, but as there was no vacancy in organic chemistry he spent four years teaching inorganic and physical chemistry. This forced him to take a far more mathematical approach to chemistry than he had formerly adopted. He was encouraged by E. R. H. Jones to attempt a correlation between optical rotation and molecular structure by analysing the literature on the triterpenoids. These are complex, cyclic hydrocarbons of general formula $C_{30}H_{48}$ which occur in nature. Many show optical activity based on stereoisomerism, a property of the three-dimensional carbon atom explained by J. H. Van't Hoff in 1874. Barton showed that, using Van't Hoff's principle of optical superposition, molecular structures could be correlated with optical activity. His approach was empirical with no theoretical basis and he called it the method of molecular rotational differences. It was useful in the period from 1940 to 1960 and can still be applied today. Barton later extended it to other natural compounds such as the bile acids, hormones, and steroids. This work contributed to his later researches in conformational analysis where preferred three-dimensional shapes of organic molecules are correlated with their chemical reactivities and physical properties.

In 1890 Hermann Sachse, an assistant at the Charlottenburg Institute in Germany, had pointed out that if the normal tetrahedral angle of 109° 28′ of the quadrivalent carbon atom was retained in the cyclohexane ring (C_6H_{12}) two conformations free from angle strain could exist. This observation was ignored until 1918 when Ernst Mohr, professor of chemistry at Heidelberg, reintroduced the theory of strain-free carbon rings. Mohr suggested two arrangements for cyclohexane which he called 'boat' and 'chair' structures. He found that the chair conformation in which three carbon atoms are above the plane of the molecule while the other three are below it was more stable than the boat arrangement in which the two carbon atoms at each end of the ring are raised above the rest. This was confirmed in 1943 by the Norwegian physical chemist Odd Hassel using electron diffraction techniques, and reconfirmed by K. S. Pitzer using statistical mechanics.

Conformational analysis Thus when Barton entered the field of conformational analysis some important groundwork had already been done, but it was Barton who first showed that conformational analysis could be applied to polycyclic systems with powerful effect. He realized the importance of the shape of the cyclohexane molecule to his studies of the steroids and showed that understanding the conformations of such complex molecules was essential to any study of their chemical reactivities. In 1948, as an ICI research fellow, he began to study the stereochemistry of abietic acid ($C_{20}H_{30}O_2$), a diterpene derivative which forms the chief constituent of rosin. When oxidized with nitric acid in the presence of a vanadium pentoxide catalyst a tri-carboxylic acid was obtained and using a mixture of organic chemistry and physical measurements Barton was able to determine the conformation of abietic acid. He also designed a set of molecular models that would accurately represent the geometry of the steroids and other complex molecules and allowed him to visualize the three-dimensional principles of conformational analysis. His application of these principles to the steroids enabled him to rationalize a large body of existing steroid chemistry which had proved incomprehensible using standard two-dimensional stereochemistry.

The reputation which Barton gained by these researches led to an invitation to spend a year as a visiting lecturer and associate professor at Harvard in 1949. He was required to stand in for R. B. Woodward during a sabbatical year, but as Woodward continued his research at Harvard he and Barton worked together and became firm friends. Barton disagreed with Louis Feiser's theory about steric effects in the steroids to account for their unusual reactivities. Having already begun to develop the concept of conformational analysis he analysed the observations in terms of the preferred conformation of the molecule. Heated discussions followed but Barton maintained his ideas which he announced in a short paper on 'The conformation of the steroid nucleus', published in the Swiss journal *Experientia* in 1950. In this paper Barton explained that 'conformation' referred to different spatial arrangements in molecular structures which allowed bonded atoms to remain combined without strain. He showed that the conformation of a complex molecule exerts an even greater influence on its chemical reactivity than the chemical groups it contains. Barton was in a unique position to do this, having acquired an excellent knowledge of steroid and terpinoid chemistry, while at the same time teaching and researching in the field of gas-phase chemical kinetics. He realized that there should be a relation between rates of reaction and the preferred conformations of the reacting molecules. The rates of reactivity of the same chemically active group in different isomers of

steroids could be predicted and even calculated from differences in spatial orientation. Conformational analysis was soon being applied to all types of compounds. The recognition that important differences in reactivity may come from small differences in spatial structures involving the same chemical groups introduced a new three-dimensional view of molecular structures that was widely utilized by practical organic chemists. Conformational analysis revolutionized organic chemistry and in recognition of his work Barton received many awards including the first Roger Adams award of the American Chemical Society, the Davy medal of the Royal Society and in 1969 the Nobel prize, shared with Odd Hassel.

Strain-free conformations can be found in five-membered rings and above, but in cyclic molecules containing 7 to 12 carbon atoms there are usually several conformations of similar energy. Since the 1960s experimental techniques such as X-ray and electron diffraction analyses and infrared, nuclear magnetic resonance, and microwave spectroscopies have been augmented by molecular mechanics, a computational method by which the total strain energies of various conformations can be calculated. The structure with the lowest energy is always found to be the most stable. By such calculations unstable conformations, difficult to study experimentally, can be examined and the quality of molecular mechanics calculations has become very high. However, Barton was always less interested in the quantitative aspects of conformational analysis than in applying its principles to experimental problems.

On his return to Britain, Barton was appointed reader and later, in 1953, professor of organic chemistry at Birkbeck College, London. Here he continued his research on conformational analysis by applying its principles to stereochemical problems in triterpenoid molecules. Lanosterol ($C_{29}H_{40}O$) was synthesized jointly by Barton and Woodward and Barton was able to correct the proposed structure for cycloartenol using his conformational principles. Both were later recognized as key compounds in biosynthesis. While at Birkbeck, Barton developed a synthesis of usnic acid, a main constituent of lichens. This involved free-radical coupling of phenols and led to a general theory of the biosynthesis of alkaloids through phenol coupling. He pursued this theory through classic laboratory syntheses and by isolating plant substances from plants fed with solutions containing radioactive atoms for labelling purposes. He also proposed the metabolic pathway by which morphine and other alkaloids are made in the poppy. In 1954 Barton was elected FRS and in the following year he was invited to become regius professor of chemistry at the University of Glasgow.

Professorships at Glasgow and London At Glasgow, Barton collaborated with Monteath Robertson, a leading X-ray crystallographer, attacking a variety of structural problems involving clerodin, limonin, and the sesquiterpene carophyllene on which Barton had begun work at Birkbeck. Barton's group used chemical degradation methods while Monteath studied the same compounds by crystallographic methods. At Glasgow, Barton also entered another field of research involving organic photochemistry. In particular he studied the effects of light on the molecular rearrangements of santonin. Arising from this work he published numerous papers on organic photochemistry in the early 1960s. During his vacations while at Glasgow, Barton returned to the United States to work at the Research Institute for Medicine and Chemistry in Cambridge, Massachusetts. Here he developed a photochemical procedure which became known as Barton's reaction. It brought together his interests in stereochemistry and photochemistry and was later used in the synthesis of the steroid hormone aldosterone. Barton was elected fellow of the Royal Society of Edinburgh in 1956, but his stay at Glasgow was ended abruptly in the following year when he was appointed professor of organic chemistry at Imperial College, London. Here he continued his work on organic syntheses and the development of new synthetic reactions for the next twenty years.

One of Barton's most important advances came early in his tenure at Imperial College. In 1958 he became associated with the newly established Research Institute for Medicine and Chemistry at Cambridge, England. The first objective of this group was to devise a viable synthesis of aldosterone, the hormone which controls the electrolyte balance in the body. Known methods involved unacceptably high temperatures, but Barton suggested a solution based on his photochemical work. He proposed a process in which the photolysis of corticosterone ($C_{21}H_{23}O_4$) would produce pure crystals of aldosterone acetate. The process revealed Barton's ingenuity in that he used light as the energy source, whereas most organic reactions used heat. It was also remarkable for the use of free radicals, but, most important, it provided a method for preparing the steroid aldosterone ($C_{21}H_{21}O_5$) at a time when the world supply was only a few milligrams. The power of his new synthesis was demonstrated at a lecture when he produced a bottle containing 60 grams of the steroid. Following this success Barton concentrated on the discovery of new chemical reactions which would provide economical and more efficient methods for the manufacture of complex organic compounds. He made many contributions to natural product research.

His first marriage was dissolved and Barton married his second wife, Christiane Cognet, in 1969. In the following year he was appointed Hofmann professor of organic chemistry and in 1972 he was awarded the royal medal of the Royal Society. In the same year he was knighted and also received the French Légion d'honneur (chevalier 1972; officer 1985). He was president of the Royal Society of Chemistry in 1973–4. Continuing his study of the applications of radical chemistry Barton developed a theory called phenolic oxidative coupling by which he could explain how complex structures such as morphine could be synthesized inside plants. In 1975 he invented a deoxygenation process to increase the biological activity of certain antibiotics by removing secondary hydroxyl radicals.

In the experimental development of this process Barton was assisted by S. W. McCombie and the resulting process became known as the Barton–McCombie reaction.

Move to France For some years Barton had been associated with the French Centre National de la Recherche Scientifique and in 1978, at sixty, he retired from Imperial College, having the previous year become director of the Institut de Chimie des Substances Naturelles, at Gif-sur-Yvette, France. The main reason for this move was his desire to avoid compulsory retirement at sixty-five. He spent eight years at Gif-sur-Yvette and settled easily into French life. His second wife, who was French, was naturally pleased to return to her native country. During this very creative period Barton worked on the invention of new reactions involving radicals which began a whole new approach to organic synthesis. It was in this field that he began to attack his last great scientific challenge, the oxidation of saturated hydrocarbons. His aim was to convert petroleum products into feedstocks for the fine chemicals industry. Drawing on his encyclopaedic knowledge of natural reactions and his imagination of primordial conditions on earth, he invented the successful Gif oxidation, using a combination of air, iron powder, hydrogen sulphide, vinegar, and a little pyridine. In 1980 he was awarded the Copley medal of the Royal Society. In 1983 he introduced radical reagents called Barton esters. He also made important contributions to fluorination, vitamin D chemistry, and the penicillins. In each case Barton made a major contribution which would have been the high point for most other organic chemists.

Last years and reputation Once more faced with the prospect of unwanted retirement in 1985 he looked for a new chance to continue his work on the discovery of new chemical reactions. He accepted an invitation to become distinguished professor of chemistry at Texas A and M University, USA, where he worked on novel reactions involving the oxidation of hydrocarbons. In 1992 his second wife died and a year later he married Judith Von-Leuenberger Cobb. He continued to travel the world as he had done for many years, attending international conferences, lecturing and acting as a consultant in industry and universities. In 1995 he became Dow professor of chemical invention, a post he held until his death at College Station, Texas A and M University, on 16 March 1998. He was survived by his third wife.

Derek Barton's personality was complex. The public persona he presented in scientific meetings was austere. With his scientific rigour he was prone to ask the most probing questions after a lecture and many of his scientific colleagues, finding it hard to live up to his demanding standards, were in awe of him. To those who knew him well, however, he revealed a sense of fun and a wealth of anecdotes. He also showed a surprisingly catholic range of interests including music and literature. Above all, he was intensely proud of the worldwide extent of his former colleagues with whom he maintained contact and always wished to help. Barton dominated organic chemistry for fifty years, changing the subject by his prodigious knowledge, vision, and insight. He produced a vast corpus of original work, even surpassing his personal target to publish a thousand papers before the age of eighty. During his long career he trained more than 300 students and postdoctoral fellows, many of whom went on to hold important chairs of chemistry. N. G. COLEY

Sources D. H. R. Barton, *Some recollections of gap jumping*, American Chemical Society (1991) · D. H. R. Barton, 'The principles of conformational analysis', *Nobel lectures: chemistry, 1963–1970* (1972), 298–311 · M. R. Feldman and D. H. R. Barton, 'Nobel laureate 1969', *Nobel laureates in chemistry 1901–1992*, ed. L. K. Jane, American Chemical Society and the Chemical Heritage Foundation (1993), 507–13 · W. A. Campbell and N. N. Greenwood, *Contemporary British chemists* (1971) · C. A. Russell, 'The origins of conformational analysis', *Van't Hoff–Le Bel centennial*, ed. O. B. Ramsay, American Chemical Society (1975), 159–78 · O. B. Ramsay, 'The early history and development of conformational analysis', *Essays on the history of organic chemistry*, ed. J. G. Trayukau (1987), 54–77 · W. B. Motherwell, *The Independent* (25 March 1998) · A. Tucker, *The Guardian* (6 April 1998) · *Daily Telegraph* (20 March 1998) · *The Times* (25 March 1998) · C. Rees, *Chemistry in Britain*, 34 (June 1998), 75–6 · b. cert. · m. cert. [Jeanne Kate Wilkins]

Archives Wellcome L., corresp. with Sir Ernst Chain

Likenesses R. Case, photograph, 1969, Hult. Arch. [*see illus.*] · photograph, repro. in Barton, *Some recollections*

Barton, Sir Edmund (1849–1920), prime minister of Australia, was born at Glebe, Sydney, New South Wales, on 18 January 1849, youngest son of William Barton, Australia's first stockbroker, and his wife, Mary Louisa (*née* Whydah), a schoolteacher. Known familiarly as Toby, he was educated at Sydney grammar school (1859–64), and after a brilliant career at Sydney University (BA 1868, MA 1870) was called to the bar in 1871. On 28 December 1877, he married Jean Mason Ross (1851–1938), daughter of David Ross, an engineer of Newcastle, New South Wales; they had four sons and two daughters. Barton proved himself a devoted family man.

Professional success came slowly, but, a keen cricketer, Barton caught the public eye by his tactful umpiring of a contentious game between New South Wales and a touring English eleven in 1879. Later that year he entered the New South Wales legislative assembly as member for Sydney University; he subsequently represented Wellington (1880–82), East Sydney (1882–7, 1891–4), and Hastings and Macleay (1898–1900). He was a member of the nominated legislative council in 1887–91 and 1897–8. A moderate Protectionist, he was speaker of the legislative assembly in 1883–7 and attorney-general for seven weeks in 1889 under George Richard Dibbs.

Previously seen as an amiable dilettante in politics, Barton found his energies roused by the first federal convention in Sydney in March–April 1891. He was one of the small committee who largely drafted the federal constitution, and his federalist credentials were endorsed by the veteran premier Sir Henry Parkes, who, although a political opponent, urged Barton to take on the leadership of the movement. Again attorney-general under the antifederalist Dibbs from October 1891 to December 1893, Barton accepted office only on the assurance of a free

Sir Edmund Barton (1849–1920), by unknown photographer, 1903

hand to promote the federal cause. Although the legislative assembly assented to the main principles of the Constitution Bill drafted at the Sydney convention, the movement stagnated in the face of a severe commercial depression and widespread industrial disputes. Barton, acting-premier for four months in 1892, incurred the mistrust of the labour movement through his handling of a bitter miners' strike at Broken Hill. Throughout the 1890s the labour movement was largely anti-federalist, fearing that a central government would favour employers.

Hoping to mobilize public opinion and thus to stimulate parliamentary action, Barton established the Federation League in Sydney in mid-1893. Working-class republicans attempted to take over the first meeting, but their influence soon dwindled; and on 31 July 1893 a conference of federalists at Corowa, on the border of New South Wales and Victoria, adopted the strategy of urging the popular election of delegates to a second federal convention to revise and adopt the draft constitution. From 1894 to 1897 Barton was out of parliament and in financial difficulties, and it was largely due to his rival George Houston Reid that a conference of premiers at Hobart in February 1895 agreed to the Corowa formula. When the New South Wales delegates were elected Barton was returned at the head of the poll; and at the meeting of the convention at Adelaide on 18 March 1897 he was chosen to draw up the preliminary resolutions and act as leader of the convention.

During this convention and its subsequent sessions at Sydney (September 1897) and Melbourne (January–March 1898) Barton was on top of his form. As chairman of both the constitutional and the drafting committees he was largely responsible for the revised Constitution Bill. A tactful manager of business and adroit lobbyist, he greatly facilitated the achievement of consensus, notably in securing an acceptable compromise over the respective powers of the senate, or states' house, and the popularly elected house of representatives. In New South Wales, which had most to lose as the only free-trade colony among protectionist neighbours, he was less successful. Nominated to the legislative council in 1897 as a spokesman for federation, he disliked the council's numerous and unwelcome amendments to the bill. During the referendum campaign in New South Wales in 1898 he stumped the country, coining the phrase: 'A nation for a continent and a continent for a nation'; but at the poll on 3 June a sufficient majority was not attained.

Considering Reid as premier too lukewarm for federation, Barton stood against him in the East Sydney seat at the July 1898 elections. He was defeated, but came into the legislative assembly at a by-election for a rural constituency in September 1898, and William Lyne relinquished the leadership of the Protectionist Party to him. Finding the partisanship required of a leader of the opposition incompatible with his role as spokesman for federation, Barton stood down in favour of Lyne, who in September 1899 managed to detach the Labor Party from its support of Reid and replace him as premier. Barton meanwhile led the 'Yes' campaign at a second federation referendum in 1899, this time successfully. He also campaigned in Queensland and took a prominent part in negotiations to bring in Western Australia.

In 1900 Barton went to London as leading member of the deputation which watched the passage of the Commonwealth of Australia Constitution Bill through the British parliament. He led the majority of the delegates in a bid to preserve section 74 of the constitution, making the future high court of Australia the final court of appeal on cases involving constitutional interpretation, but eventually accepted Joseph Chamberlain's compromise formula retaining the privy council in certain specified areas. Many saw Barton as the first prime minister of a federated Australia, but the governor-general, Lord Hopetoun, in December 1900 invited Lyne, as premier of the senior colony, to form a ministry. Unsupported by leading politicians elsewhere in Australia, Lyne failed and Barton was sworn in on 1 January 1901 as prime minister and minister for external affairs.

Tall, erect, clean-shaven, with iron-grey hair and remarkably expressive eyes, the new prime minister looked the part of 'Australia's noblest son', as his admirers called him. To the less reverent he was Tosspot Toby, whose love of food and drink was reflected in an 18-stone portliness. Yet he was capable of sustained hard work, and he was probably the only contemporary politician able to take command of a crew of captains who were accustomed to leadership in their respective states, and whose sympathies ranged from radical to conservative. The first federal elections in March 1901 left the Australian Labor Party holding the balance of power between Barton's Protectionists and the Free-Traders led by Reid. Labor supported Barton until his resignation in September 1903.

The new parliament was opened in Melbourne on 9 May 1901 by the duke of York (later George V). In its first session it legislated for a white Australia policy, excluding non-Europeans and political undesirables through a dictation test. The sugar industry was compensated for its loss of Pacific island labour by tariff protection. The racism behind these policies went with a concern to protect working-class living standards, then among the highest in the world. South-east Australia's manufacturing industries, hit by the 1890s' depression, were protected by a scale of tariffs, at first moderate out of deference to rural interests. The new Australian commonwealth saw itself as a laboratory for social reform. In 1902 women gained the right to vote and stand for parliament. In 1903 legislation was prepared for a system of industrial arbitration and conciliation.

In 1902 Barton visited Europe for Edward VII's coronation; he returned as a GCMG but was criticized by protestants for an audience with Pope Leo XIII at which both participants spoke Latin. Weary of office, in September 1903 he accepted doctor's orders to quit politics, taking a seat on the newly created high court, but with characteristic modesty assigning the post of chief justice to Sir Samuel Griffith. In his early years on the bench, Barton was sometimes criticized as being a mere echo of Griffith, with whom he shared a tendency to resist encroachment of the commonwealth government's powers on state rights. After serving as acting chief justice in 1913 he took a more cautiously evolutionary and independent line. On Griffith's retirement in October 1919 Barton hoped to succeed him, but was disappointed. Shortly afterwards his health broke down. While on vacation in the Blue Mountains he died suddenly on 7 January 1920 of cerebral embolism, at the Hydro Majestic Hotel, Medlow Bath. He was buried at South Head cemetery, Sydney, after a state funeral, on 9 January.

Possessing natural dignity and great charm, Barton won a respect and affection uncommon among Australian politicians. Although a less creative statesman than his friend and contemporary Alfred Deakin, he was more than once the indispensable architect of consensus when the Australian commonwealth was shaped.

GEOFFREY BOLTON

Sources J. Reynolds, *Edmund Barton* (1948) · J. A. La Nauze, *The making of the Australian constitution* (1972) · G. Sawer, *Australian federal politics and law, 1901–1929* (1956) · J. Quick and R. R. Garran, *The annotated constitution of the Australian commonwealth* (1901) · *AusDB* · B. R. Wise, *The making of the Australian Commonwealth* (1913) · *Sydney Morning Herald* (8 Jan 1920) · *The Times* (8 Jan 1920) · b. cert. · *Sydney Morning Herald* (10 Jan 1920) · d. cert. · Canberra *AusDB* files

Archives Mitchell L., NSW · NL Aus. | BL, corresp. with Sir E. T. H. Hutton, Add. MS 50084, *passim* · Mitchell L., NSW, Parkes

MSS · NL Aus., corresp. with Alfred Deakin, and second Baron Tennyson · NL Aus., corresp. with Viscount Novar | FILM Australian National Film Archive, news footage
Likenesses photograph, 1903, NL Aus. [*see illus.*] · Spy [L. Ward], caricature, chromolithograph, NPG; repro. in *VF* (16 Oct 1902) · portrait, Parliament House, Canberra, Australia · portrait, High Court, Canberra, Australia
Wealth at death £6565: probate, *AusDB*

Barton, Edward (1562/3–1598), diplomat, was born in 1562 or 1563, being thirty-five at his death in 1598. Armorial bearings on his tombstone suggest that he belonged to the family of Bartons of Smithhills Hall, Bolton, Lancashire. He had at least one elder brother, William, living in 1591 in the St Katharine's Dock area near the Tower of London, and a sister, Mary Lock.

Early life and career Barton had a small income from rented tenement property in St Katharine's Dock. It is probable that his branch of the family had settled in London, where as a young man he entered the service of the merchant William Harborne, under whose patronage he rose to become a major figure in early English–Ottoman diplomatic relations.

Barton served as assistant and secretary to Harborne during the latter's residence in Constantinople from 1583 to 1588 as, simultaneously, agent of the Turkey Company of Merchants and first English ambassador. He succeeded Harborne in both these posts and appears not to have returned to England. In July 1584 he was sent by Harborne to present to the Ottoman governors of Algiers, Tunis, and Tripoli Murad III's letters guaranteeing safe conduct for English traders on the north African coast, an important step in the establishment of the Barbary trade. By December 1584 Harborne already held him in high regard, as a man who despite his relative youth would be capable of deputizing as ambassador should Harborne be permitted to return to London. In particular, Barton's 'having the language' meant that he had an advantage over most other European agents in being able to converse directly with Ottoman officials and, as a result, potentially to be regarded more favourably by them (*CSP for.*, 19.168). His ability to speak Turkish remained one of Barton's major assets throughout his fifteen years in Constantinople. On Harborne's eventual departure in August 1588, Barton remained behind as official representative of the Turkey Company and Elizabeth I's agent in Constantinople, but was regarded in the Ottoman capital as having the equivalent of full ambassadorial status. He was formally granted the title by the queen only in October 1593, the delay being caused largely by the necessity to send a suitably expensive present (on this occasion mainly of garments and lengths of cloth) without which it was unlikely that his official credentials would be favourably received.

Commercial agent Under Harborne the work of the English embassy had been principally commercial, to establish the newly acquired trading privileges for English merchants in Ottoman lands, and to defend English claims against those of other western trading nations. Both Harborne and Barton were largely successful in these aims, maintaining the right of English merchants to trade independently under their own flag, as did the French and the Venetians. By 1589 Barton had acquired the right (previously disputed with France) to extend English protection to merchants from Christian countries without recognized commercial agreements trading in Cairo and Alexandria. In 1596 he temporarily won a major concession from the grand vizier Çigalazade to extend this protection to the Constantinople trade also. This latter privilege was rescinded within a few weeks due to Çigalazade's downfall and to French protests, but indicates the continuous commercial rivalry which constituted the everyday practical detail of Barton's work. Similarly, in 1589 a group of wealthy Florentine jewellers in Constantinople requested English commercial protection rather than French, considering the latter to have less influence with the sultan's government.

Like Harborne, and like his own successors at least until the middle of the seventeenth century, Barton's primary role in Constantinople was supposedly as representative of the Turkey Company (which became the Levant Company in 1592), by whom he was to be supported financially. Although the company claimed to allow Barton £1200 annually, he protested that they paid only his expenses in arrears. For the period August 1588 to October 1590 he calculated these as £2709 8s. 3d. This method of payment was clearly impractical and insufficient. Barton complained continually of being so seriously short of money in contrast to the representatives of other western countries that he could not maintain his household and wished to be recalled. In August 1591 an inquiry was begun by William Cecil, Lord Burghley, the lord treasurer, concerning 'what entertainment has been allowed to Mr. Barton in certainty, and whether he has been allowed the 4 per cent promised; what allowance he has had from the beginning of his service; when he last had any, and what it was for' (*CSP dom.*, 1591–4, 89). As a result, and probably connected with negotiations for its new charter of incorporation, the company was persuaded to allow Barton, in theory, from 1592 onwards, a regular salary of £1500 per annum. Despite this, his complaints of relative poverty, lack of credit, and enforced borrowing from friends continued unabated.

Barton's financial problems arose directly from the tension inherent in his dual role as agent both of the Levant Company and of Elizabeth. In contrast to Harborne, he quickly developed a prominent diplomatic role, evident in his fortnightly reports to Sir Francis Walsingham, principal secretary, and, from June 1590 onwards, to Burghley, via Sir Thomas Heneage, and later to Sir Robert Cecil. He readily admitted that the company's allowance sufficed for attending to the merchants' business, and that it was the negotiations and manoeuvring required to carry out the queen's instructions which incurred his extraordinary expenses. She, however, while expecting Barton to exert diplomatic influence in Constantinople, was uneasy about being seen in the West as too friendly with the Muslim sultan and was reluctant to underwrite her agent's essential expenses for hospitality and local present-giving. His requests for additional financial support from the queen generally came to nothing, despite his difficulties and the company's complaints. Due to his concentration on diplomacy, Barton experienced tension in his dealings with many of the company's merchants and factors in the Levant, from whom he was often unable to collect that part of his allowance due in consulage percentages.

Ambassador to the Porte Barton's principal instructions from Burghley were to influence the Ottoman government against Spain, and in favour of Henri IV against the Catholic League in France. Spanish envoys were to be eclipsed and the Ottomans motivated to send a fleet against Philip II. One of his first duties as Harborne's successor from 5 August 1588 was to announce to the sultan the defeat of the Spanish Armada, a fortunate beginning which gave extra impetus to the existing anti-Spanish stance of the English merchants in Constantinople. Barton also spent much effort trying to advance the claims of Don Antonio, prior of Crato, to the throne of Portugal and encouraging Ahmad al-Mansur, sultan of Morocco, to attack the Spanish coast in his support.

The image of Elizabeth as a moderate protestant sovereign and a bitter opponent of the sultan's Habsburg enemies chimed in favourably with Ottoman interests in the 1580s and 1590s. Both Harborne and Barton were referred to favourably as the 'Lutheran elshi [ambassador]' (*Shakespeare's Europe*, 28). Barton argued successfully for peace between the Ottoman empire and Poland in 1590–91 on the grounds partly that continuation of the war would prevent Polish raw materials being exported to England for use in naval campaigns against Philip and that the Ottomans would disadvantage their English ally. Although the Ottomans failed to support a naval war in the western Mediterranean, English–Ottoman diplomatic relations remained generally friendly. They survived Barton's less successful interventions in the appointment of a new Ottoman governor of Moldavia in 1591, who later rebelled, and his mediation with the sultan in 1594 on behalf of Sigismund Bathory of Transylvania, who subsequently joined forces with the emperor Rudolph II.

Although the French were the chief rivals of the English for commercial privileges in the Ottoman empire, the death of Henri III in 1589 and the growing support for Henri of Navarre left the French representatives in Constantinople openly divided. On instructions from Elizabeth, Barton promoted the sultan's recognition of Henri of Navarre as Henri IV, leaving Lancôme, the official ambassador appointed by the previous French regime and a sympathizer with the Catholic League, increasingly discredited and marginalized. In August 1592 Barton succeeded in having Lancôme imprisoned on suspicion of secretly working for Philip against both Ottoman and French interests. Shortly afterwards he had the satisfaction of having Lancôme released into his own charge to be sent by him as a prisoner to Henri IV. Protesting about his pay in January 1593, Barton cited his services to Henri, who was recognized as king in July, over the previous three years as contributing significantly to his extra expenses. He was next instructed to work closely with

Henri IV's new ambassador, the sieur de Brèves, in a combined anti-Habsburg lobby, attempting to influence the Ottoman government towards war in Hungary against the Austrian Habsburgs. However, a change of policy by Elizabeth resulted in new instructions in the summer of 1593 to try to preserve Ottoman–Habsburg peace. Unfortunately for Barton, by the time these contrary instructions arrived, war had already been declared and the grand vizier, Sinan Paşa, had left Constantinople on campaign. Barton's standing fell immediately with both sultan and grand vizier, to be restored only partially by the delivery of the much-delayed present to Murad in October 1593. His good understanding with de Brèves also collapsed, due to the differing policies of their respective governments regarding the Hungarian war and to the implications of Henri's reconversion to Catholicism in July 1593. De Brèves subsequently became Barton's main diplomatic rival in Constantinople.

The final years The most controversial period in Barton's career occurred in 1596, when he was obliged to remain in attendance on the new sultan, Mehmed III, by accompanying him on a military campaign into Hungary. The presence in the Ottoman army of the English ambassador, his suite of four gentlemen, twelve servants, an interpreter, and three janizary escorts, all provided at Ottoman expense with a coach, twenty-one horses, and thirty-six baggage camels and their handlers, and requisition slips for daily provision of food and wine, provided Barton's rivals and their masters in Europe with ample cause for adverse comment on the closeness of the heretical queen of England's relations with the Muslim sultan. In mitigation, Barton could argue, first, that he had been able to secure the release from prison of the household of the late Habsburg ambassador and to ensure their safe conduct home in the rear of the Ottoman army; second, that he would have been ideally situated to promote peace negotiations should circumstances have permitted; and third, that his presence was testimony to the high regard in which the English were held by the Ottomans. He also used the opportunity to compile for Cecil an eyewitness account of the Ottoman victory over the Archduke Maximilian's forces at Haçova (Mezo Keresztes) in October 1596. Barton's unease at being part of an anti-Christian army is reflected in Mehmed's victory letter to Elizabeth, in which the sultan assumes that although her ambassador had not had time to obtain her permission before leaving, she would approve of his action and of the good service which he had performed. English embarrassment over the episode continued beyond Barton's period of office and contributed to the further delay in sending another present to Constantinople, this time to mark Mehmed's accession, which had taken place in January 1595. The organ with its mechanical figures which was finally sent in 1599 served both to congratulate the sultan and to accompany the credentials of Barton's successor, Henry Lello.

Barton's greatest diplomatic successes came in the early 1590s, before Elizabeth's change of policy on the question of relations between the Ottomans and Rudolph. On a personal level, Barton preserved good relations with several important Ottoman officials, despite the deaths in 1591 and 1596 of the two most influential pro-English viziers, the admiral Hasan Paşa and the grand vizier Koca Sinan Paşa. His ability to speak Turkish, together with his prominence as the only non-Catholic representative, helped maintain his standing. On the other hand, he acquired certain jealous 'enemies' in the merchant and diplomatic communities who attempted to discredit him with Burghley. In 1591 he was obliged to defend himself against charges made by three disgruntled Englishmen of allowing counterfeit coins to be struck in his house, of favouring strangers, of unlawfully confiscating an English merchant's goods, of allowing his expenses to double for no good reason, and of wronging an influential Jew. With the aid of a detailed report from the traveller George Gifford who had stayed some time in his household, he was able to successfully rebut all these charges. The most difficult was that of the Jew, Don Solomon (also known as Alvaro Mendes). Don Solomon's enmity, Barton claimed, arose from his desire to speak for English interests in Constantinople himself: he had influential contacts in England. In 1594 Barton was again in difficulties due to Don Solomon's accusations that he had two Italianized Spaniards in his household who were both Spanish spies.

A genial host for English gentlemen visiting the city, Barton was described by Fynes Moryson, who stayed with him in 1597, as 'courteous and affable, of a good stature, corpulent, faire complexion and a free chearefull Countenance'. He was a man of 'great Worth', of 'good life and constant in the profession of the reformed religion' (*Shakespeare's Europe*, 27, 28, 30), who in 1591 had received a copy of Calvin's *Institutions of the Christian Religion* as a present from a friend in London, Thomas Humphreys. From 1588 to some time in 1594 or 1595 Barton continued to reside at Rapamat, the house first used by Harborne in 1583, at Findikli on the Bosphorus shore near the Ottoman arsenal at Tophane. However, accusations by local Muslims of excessive conviviality and of keeping a disorderly house (occasioned probably by his being the only non-Muslim household in the area) obliged him to move up the hill to Pera, to premises possibly on the site of the later British embassy building at Tepebaşi. In 1594 his regular household consisted of some eighteen to twenty people, mostly but not all English. Four janizaries were allocated to guard the premises and to escort Barton, his secretaries, or his guests when they journeyed in or beyond the city. Among those who served in Barton's household were Thomas Wilcocks, responsible for carrying important letters to and from the queen, mainly via the overland route through Poland; John Sanderson, attached to the embassy since the mid-1580s and who deputized for Barton during his absence on the 1596 campaign; Thomas Glover, Barton's secretary on the same campaign, who himself became ambassador in Constantinople from 1606 to 1611; the merchants William and Jonas Aldrich; and John Field, a physician.

Barton died, aged thirty-five, on 28 January 1598, of dysentery, on the island of Heybeli Ada in the Sea of Marmara and was buried there in a small Christian cemetery next to a monastery. He was unmarried and had no children. What remained of his estate was claimed in 1626 by his sister Mary Lock in a suit against the Levant Company.

CHRISTINE WOODHEAD

Sources S. A. Skilliter, 'The Turkish documents relating to Edward Barton's embassy to the Porte, 1588–1598', PhD diss., University of Manchester, 1965 · *CSP for., 1589–96* · *Shakespeare's Europe: unpublished chapters of Fynes Moryson's Itinerary*, ed. C. Hughes (1903) · S. Purchas, *Hakluytus posthumus, or, Purchas his pilgrimes*, 20 bks in 4 vols. (1625); repr. 20 vols., Hakluyt Society, extra ser., 14–33 (1905–7), vol. 6, pp. 94–104; vol. 8, pp. 304–20 · H. Ellis, ed., *Original letters illustrative of English history*, 3rd ser., 4 (1846), 138–47 · CSP dom., vol. 3

Archives BL, Cotton MSS, corresp. and accounts, Nero B. XI–XII · Newnham College, Cambridge, MSS and notes relating to him [copies] · PRO, state papers, SP 97/2 Turkey

Barton [*née* Stockton], **Eleanor** (1872/3–1960), socialist and co-operative movement activist, was born in the Manchester area, but the exact date and place are uncertain. Her father, William Stockton, was variously described as a porter, a prison warder, and a Chelsea pensioner. Her mother was Julia, *née* Farrar or Farrell. Members of her family were said to have been actively associated with the early socialist movement in Manchester. Little is known of her early life. At Chorlton upon Medlock in 1894 she married Alfred Barton (d. 1933), a librarian and an active anarchist (later a Labour Party stalwart). They had a son and a daughter, Linda (later Mrs Bennett).

In 1897 Eleanor Barton and her husband moved to Sheffield, where they began a long association with local socialist and co-operative movements; and eventually (in 1901) she joined the Women's Co-operative Guild. This organization, founded in 1883 by Alice Acland and Mary Lawrenson, was more than a co-operative retail store users' group (although it is difficult to overestimate the importance of shopping at the Co-op, with its accompanying 'dividend', to the average working-class or lower-middle-class family in the early and middle years of the twentieth century). The impetus behind its inception was the perceived inferior position of women within the co-operative movement, and from the outset the guild was a virtually autonomous, mainly working-class, women's organization. Despite the fact that the guild's activities reflected the broader social and political aspects of the movement, its independent and sometimes controversial line occasionally complicated relations, particularly with the Co-operative Union. However, this strengthened its appeal to Eleanor, who soon became the secretary of the Hillsborough branch, and rapidly rose to membership first of the Yorkshire area committee, then of the guild's central committee in 1912–1914 and again in 1920. Even before this, she had been prominent in preparing the guild's evidence to the royal commission on divorce, which reported in 1912. In 1913 she became the guild's national treasurer, and in 1914 its president.

In 1919 Eleanor Barton was active in the Hands Off Russia movement, and also toured America on the invitation of the Labor Party of America, speaking on maternal and child welfare, issues which played a considerable part in her political life. From 1919 to 1922 she served on Sheffield city council for the Attercliffe ward, and during this time she also became a justice of the peace. While her husband maintained his connection with the council to the extent of becoming an alderman, Eleanor had her sights set on a parliamentary seat. In 1922 and 1923 she stood for King's Norton, Birmingham, as a Labour candidate, being narrowly defeated on both occasions, and in 1929 she stood for Central Nottingham, where, although again defeated, she reduced the Conservative majority by 5000.

Eleanor Barton's greatest influence was exerted through the Women's Co-operative Guild, of which she became assistant secretary in 1921, and general secretary from 1925 to 1937. In the latter position, especially, she played an important part in forming the radical policies of the guild on such controversial issues as birth control and abortion (the guild passed a resolution in favour of relaxing the law on abortion in 1934, one year before the formation of the Abortion Law Reform Association). She was also, as a confirmed pacifist, a strong proponent of the guild's international connections, especially through the League of Nations. She drafted the guild's pledge card, and it was during her time as secretary that the guild initiated the wearing of white, rather than red, poppies on Armistice Day as an anti-militarist gesture from 1933 onwards. In addition she served on numerous government committees, especially the royal commission on licensing of 1931, and was for many years a guild representative on the Standing Joint Committee of Industrial Women's Organizations. She was the first woman to be a director of the Co-operative Newspaper Publishing Society. On a more apparently mundane level, she was a strong supporter of co-operative shopping, and in 1921 prepared a leaflet entitled *Co-Operative Women, Support your Own Stores*.

Eleanor Barton is also remembered for her 'strictness' (a later general secretary, Kathleen Kempton, thought that she could even be rather dictatorial). Certainly during her tenure as secretary she was noted for her dominance over the central committee, which, on her retirement in 1937, issued strict guidelines on the duties and responsibilities of the general secretary. This seems to have had limited immediate effect, since Eleanor Barton was immediately succeeded as general secretary by her niece, Rose Simpson, whose controversial period in office ended with her virtual removal by the central committee in 1939–1940.

In retirement Eleanor Barton kept up her co-operative connections (she was president of the South Yorkshire Federation of Co-operative Societies in 1947–1948), but after the deaths of her husband and son she went in 1949 to live with her daughter in New Zealand. There she still wrote regularly to the guild, her letters being read at the annual conference and printed in guild publications. She died at 6 Wilmay Avenue, Papatoetoe, New Zealand, on 9 March 1960. She was cremated at Purewa on 11 March 1960.   DAVID DOUGHAN

Sources J. Gaffin and D. Thoms, *Caring and sharing: the centenary history of the Co-operative Women's Guild* (1983) · 'Barton, Eleanor', *DLB*, vol. 1 · 'Barton, Alfred', *DLB*, vol. 6 · 'Death of guild stalwart', *Co-operative News* (19 March 1960) · d. cert. · census returns, 1881
Archives BLPES, Women's Co-operative Guild MSS · Co-operative Union, Manchester, Women's Co-operative Guild MSS · U. Hull, Brynmor Jones L., Women's Co-operative Guild MSS
Likenesses photograph, repro. in Gaffin and Thoms, *Caring and Sharing*, p. 25
Wealth at death £1253 16s. 11d. in England: New Zealand probate sealed in England, 4 Oct 1960, CGPLA Eng. & Wales

Barton, Elizabeth [called the Holy Maid of Kent, the Nun of Kent] (c.1506–1534), Benedictine nun and visionary, is of obscure origins. Nothing is known about her early life or family. Barton is unlikely to have received any sort of formal education during her childhood, and she was almost certainly illiterate. By the time she first entered the public arena, at the age of nineteen, she was working as a servant in the household of a certain Thomas Cobb, farm manager to Archbishop Warham, at Goldwell House in the village of Aldington, some 20 miles from Canterbury, near the Kent coast.

Prophetic calling Barton's early religious experiences are similar to those of other unlearned holy maids of late medieval England who became renowned, and sometimes notorious, for their miraculous fasts, visionary illnesses, and prophetic raptures. In 1525 Barton was afflicted by a disease which lasted for several months and which prevented her from eating and drinking; it was described some years later as 'an impostume in her stomach, which divers times redounded upwards to her throat and was like to stop her breath' (Whatmore, 464). In the course of this period of sickness and delirium she began to demonstrate supernatural abilities, predicting the death of a child being nursed in a neighbouring bed. In the following weeks and months the condition from which she suffered, which may have been a form of epilepsy, manifested itself in seizures (both her body and her face became contorted), alternating with periods of paralysis. During her death-like trances she made various pronouncements on matters of religion, such as the seven deadly sins, the ten commandments, and the nature of heaven, hell, and purgatory. She spoke about the importance of the mass, pilgrimage, confession to priests, and prayer to the Virgin and the saints; had revelations concerning the souls of the dead; and saw visions of heaven, 'where S. Michael wayed soules, [and] where Sainct Peter carried the keyes' (Lambarde, 150). All of her revelations appear to have been perfectly orthodox and some, which were in verse form, can be identified as traditional charms or Marian prayers.

As Barton's fame spread her parish priest, Richard Master, rode to Canterbury to inform Archbishop Warham of Barton's activities. Warham responded by saying that 'if she had any more such speeches, he should be at them as nigh as he could and mark them well' (Whatmore, 465). In the meantime he sent an ecclesiastical commission to conduct an investigation. The commissioners, who included Edward Bocking, a monk from the Benedictine house of Christ Church, Canterbury, questioned Barton and found her orthodox on the points of faith. The later accounts of her life, many of which claim to be based on contemporary tracts, differ as to what happened next. According to some versions Barton predicted that she would be healed of her disease at the chapel of Our Lady in the neighbouring village of Court-at-Street, and this miracle, which occurred during Lent 1526, was witnessed by not only the commissioners but also some two or three thousand people. However, in one important source the narrative takes another turn. This is a printed pamphlet entitled 'A marveilous woorke of late done at Courte of Streete in Kent', which has not survived, but which was summarized in detail by William Lambarde in his *A Perambulation of Kent*. Here we are told that Barton frequently visited the chapel, and that her cure—although promised by God—was delayed. This text also states that Barton's illness and trances continued in the years to come. None the less, the various sources do tend to agree on two points: that Barton claimed that it was divine will both that she should be professed as a nun and that Bocking should become her spiritual father.

The convent of St Sepulchre Immediately after the events at Court-at-Street, Barton entered the Benedictine priory of St Sepulchre, Canterbury, as a postulant, and it appears that after consultation with his advisers Warham agreed that she should be admitted to the noviciate. By the summer of 1527 she had taken her vows. Warham also authorized Bocking's appointment as her confessor, and sent an account of her revelations directly to Henry VIII. The king passed the document to Thomas More, demanding his opinion of its contents. The latter replied 'that in good faithe I founde nothinge in these wordes that I coulde eny thinge regarde or esteme, For savinge that some parte fell in rime, and that, God wotte, full rude, els for any reason, God wott, that I saw therin, a righte simple woman mighte, in my mynde, speake it of her owne witt well ynoughe' (*Correspondence*, 481). Under the guidance of her confessor she learned about the lives and revelations of St Bridget of Sweden and St Catherine of Siena, and from the nature of some of her subsequent mystical experiences and visions (and in particular her intervention in matters of national politics) it is clear that she began to model herself on them.

Barton's life in the convent was by no means an isolated one. As her reputation for sanctity grew people travelled from far and wide to consult her about their lives and sins, to ask her to discern spirits, or to seek her intercession for the sick, the dying, and the dead. Warham himself met her several times, and praised her warmly to John Fisher, bishop of Rochester, with whom, by his own admission, Warham discussed her revelations on three occasions. In a letter dated 1 October 1528 Warham wrote to Cardinal Wolsey explaining that she had requested to speak with him and recommending her to him as 'a very well disposyd and vertuouse woman' (PRO, SP 1/50, fol. 163). Wolsey interviewed her at least twice, and it was probably the cardinal who gained Barton admittance to the king. She told Henry about her revelations in person on a number of different occasions, including once when, accompanied by the prioress of her convent, she visited the royal manor of Hanworth. According to an anonymous source Barton enjoyed royal favour for a time (PRO, SP 1/80, fol. 138). If this were the case it might well reflect the king's continuing sympathies with the old order up to the early 1530s; but if Henry sought to control Barton through his patronage the plan evidently failed.

Political involvement and opposition to the divorce In the years between 1526 and 1534 Barton's prophecies became increasingly concerned with affairs of church and state. As early as 1528 William Tyndale wrote critically about her in *The Obedience of a Christian Man*. By 1530, when it was becoming apparent that Henry VIII's religious allegiances were shifting somewhat, Barton opposed his policies in relation to the church, asserting that the rights, estates, and revenues of the pope should be protected, and that heretics should be condemned and their books destroyed. However, it was her intervention in the matter of the king's divorce from Katherine of Aragon which was to bring about Barton's downfall. She made various prognostications about the state of the country, foretelling wars and plagues and other forms of disaster, and in her most contentious prophecy she stated

> that in case hys Highnes proceded to thaccomplishment of the seid devorce and maried another, that then hys Majestie shulde not be kynge of this Realme by the space of one moneth after, And in the reputacion of God shuld not be kynge one day nor one houre.   (25 Henry VIII, c. 12, *Statutes of the Realm*, 446)

Interpretations of this revelation varied: it is unclear whether Barton actually intended to encourage insurrection within the realm or simply to try and persuade Henry to change his course of action, or indeed whether she envisaged his spiritual or actual death. She also issued Warham and Wolsey with threats of the divine punishment which would follow if they continued to support the king in his plan to remarry, and some time later, in October 1532, at the time of Henry's attempted reconciliation with the French king, Barton predicted his excommunication in a seditious eucharistic vision. By the end of 1532 More was becoming anxious about the rumours which were circulating concerning her prophecies, and decided to talk with her. Some time in 1533 they spoke together in a chapel at Syon, and he formed 'a greate good opinion of her' (*Correspondence*, 485), but shortly thereafter he wrote to her warning her 'frome talkinge with any persons speciallye with ley persons, of eny suche maner thinges as perteyne to princes' affeirs, or the state of the realme' (ibid., 466).

Barton's authority should not be underestimated. Thomas Cranmer noted that

> many learned men, but specially divers and many religious men, had great confidence in her, and often resorted unto her and communed with her, to the intent they might by her know the will of God; and chiefly concerning the king's marriage, the great heresies and schisms within the realms, and the taking away the liberties of the church.
> (*Miscellaneous Writings*, 273)

Barton's influence extended to the monks at the charterhouses of Sheen and London, the friars at Canterbury, Greenwich, and Richmond, and the nuns at Syon Abbey, but she also held sway over 'divers and many as well great men of the realm as mean men' (ibid.). Her extensive network of lay supporters included courtiers, priests, merchants, servants, and a large number of women of various ranks in society. Although Katherine of Aragon refused to grant her an audience Barton sent letters to Pope Clement VII, encouraging him in his stand against the English king, and communicated through translators with his ambassadors Silvestro Dario and Antonio de Pulleo. The subsequent inquiries carried out by Thomas Cromwell and Thomas Cranmer revealed links between Barton and some of the most powerful of the king's critics, such as Gertrude Courtenay, marchioness of Exeter. While Barton seems to have relied largely on word of mouth for the dissemination of her prophecies, and plans were afoot to preach them from the pulpit, the act of attainder against her states that Master, Bocking, and John Dering (another monk of Christ Church, Canterbury) 'made wryte and caused to be wrytyn sondry bokes, bothe greate and small both prynted and wrytyn' concerning her miracles and revelations (25 Henry VIII, c. 12, *Statutes of the Realm*, 448). One of these works—probably authored by Bocking—was seized at the press. It provided her persecutors with considerable evidence against her.

Condemnation and execution   In the summer of 1533 Cranmer (possibly working on the instructions of the king himself) wrote to the prioress of St Sepulchre's asking her to bring Barton to his manor at Otford. On 11 August she was questioned, but was released without charge. Thomas Cromwell then questioned her and, towards the end of September, Bocking was arrested along with one of his brethren, and his premises were searched. Shortly afterwards Cromwell sent for Master. By early November, following a full scale investigation, Barton was imprisoned in the Tower. She was examined by the council and on 16 November, John Salcot, bishop of Bangor and abbot of Hyde, wrote to Lady Lisle, 'our holy Nun of Kent hath confessed her treason against God and the King—that is to say, she hath confessed herself not only a traitress but also an heretic. And she with her complices are like to suffer death' (Byrne, 1.617). Shortly thereafter she was denounced by the lord chancellor before a special assembly made up of the king's councillors, judges, prelates, and the nobility. On 23 November 1533 Barton was forced to do penance at Paul's Cross in London, alongside her chief followers, Bocking, Master, Dering, Thomas Lawrence (register to the archdeacon of Canterbury), Hugh Rich (warden of Richmond Priory), Henry Risby (warden of Greyfriars, Canterbury), Henry Gold (parson of St Mary Aldermary in London and former chaplain to Warham), and two laymen, Edward Thwaites and Thomas Gold (brother to Henry). The sermon was preached by Salcot and described in detail the crimes which had been committed. Barton was then required to make her confession. The Spanish ambassador described this as a comedy staged 'to blot out from people's minds the impression they have that the Nun is a saint and a prophet' (*CSP Spain*, 1531–3, no. 1154). A fortnight later the proceedings were repeated at Canterbury. Barton had secretly sent messages to her adherents

that she had retracted only at the command of God, but when she was made to recant publicly, her supporters quickly began to lose faith in her. On 25 November, the marchioness of Exeter wrote to the king asking for forgiveness for giving credence to the nun. It is only one of a number of such letters.

In March 1534 Barton, Bocking, Master, Dering, Rich, Risby, and Henry Gold were indicted of high treason by act of attainder. Thomas More succeeded in defending his relations with Barton and his name was dropped from the bill; John Fisher did not and he was attainted of misprision and concealment of treason along with Thomas Gold, Lawrence, Thwaites, and two others, Fisher's chaplain, John Addison, and Queen Katherine's chaplain, Thomas Abell. The act of attainder called upon the public to surrender any books, scrolls or other writings about the revelations and miracles attributed to Barton and her adherents, on pain of imprisonment and the imposition of a fine. On 20 April 1534 Barton was executed by hanging and beheading alongside the others convicted of treason, with the exception of Master, who received a reprieve. On the same day the citizens of London were required to make the oath of succession, as John Husee noted:

> This day the Nun of Kent, with ii Friars Observants, ii monks, and one secular priest, were drawn from the Tower to Tyburn, and there hanged and headed. God, if it be his pleasure, have mercy on their souls. Also this day the most part of this City are sworn to the King and his legitimate issue by the Queen's Grace now had and hereafter to come, and so shall all the realm over be sworn in like manner. (Byrne, 2.130)

The executions were clearly intended as a warning to those who opposed the king's policies and reforms. Barton's head was impaled on London Bridge, while the heads of her associates were placed on the gates of the city. Her body was buried the same day along with those of Rich and Risby at Greyfriars Church in Newgate Street. Even before her condemnation an inventory was made of her possessions, the most valuable and useful of which had been already sold or distributed among the nuns of her convent. They included two plates, four dishes, two saucers, and a basin for which the prioress of St Sepulchre paid 4s.; a counterpane, for which she paid 12d.; a coat sold for 5s.; an Irish mantle, a collar, two chests, two stoles, and a candlestick, which the prioress kept; and two new cushions given to the church.

Character and appearance   Barton has been variously characterized as a charlatan, an impresario, a puppet, a hysteric, and a naïve and innocent victim. Those who were responsible for the suppression of her prophecies and for her condemnation and death represented her as a cunning, greedy, and sexually immoral hypocrite. Salcot, for example, in the sermon he preached at the public penance, declared that she would have her followers 'fast so much, that the sharpness of their bones had almost worn through their body' while she remained 'fat and ruddy' (Whatmore, 469). This description of Barton's physical appearance seems unlikely, given her illnesses and inedia, but Salcot intended to undermine his audience's credence in every aspect of her story. More significantly Salcot depicts Barton as a tool of Bocking and the conservative clergy, a view reiterated not only in the act of attainder and other contemporary texts but also by modern historians. On the basis of the evidence it is impossible to ascertain the truth of such representations. What is manifest, however, is that she was an intelligent, courageous, and extremely charismatic woman, who was able to gain the confidence of even the most sceptical individuals. More, for example, approached her with caution, but was impressed by her humility, and many of her supporters had absolute faith in her virtue and chastity.

Significance Barton's greatest significance lies in the related fields of religion and politics, and in particular her opposition to Henry VIII's divorce and to his policies regarding the church. While most nineteenth- and twentieth-century accounts of this crucial period in English history tend to downplay or dismiss out of hand Barton's role as a figure-head of the conservative resistance to the Reformation, and to deny her political agency, recent studies have demanded that the evidence be reassessed. Almost all the first-hand evidence concerning Barton's life and revelations was destroyed following her arrest, and the surviving image of her is a profoundly hostile one derived from the protestant propaganda which circulated widely at the time of her condemnation and in the century after her death. It is impossible to do more than speculate about whether, had the events of Henry's reign followed another course, she would have been hailed as a genuine saint. Alternative views which represent Barton as a genuine holy woman and as one of the first Catholic martyrs in the reign of Henry can be found in the recusant writings of the sixteenth century, but even these accounts tend to be somewhat contradictory and confused. What is clear, however, is that Barton was an English woman visionary who consciously sought to emulate St Bridget of Sweden and St Catherine of Siena, and whose career might also usefully be compared with that of Joan of Arc.

DIANE WATT

Sources W. Lambarde, 'Courtopstrete, commonly: but truly Court at Strete', *A perambulation of Kent* (1576), 148–53 • L. E. Whatmore, ed., 'The sermon against the Holy Maid of Kent and her adherents … 1533', *EngHR*, 58 (1943), 463–75 • A. Luders and others, eds., *Statutes of the realm*, 11 vols. in 12, RC (1810–28), vol. 3, pp. 446–51 • *The correspondence of Sir Thomas More*, ed. E. F. Rogers (1947), letters 192, 464–66; 195, 469–70; 197, 480–88; 198, 488–91; 199, 491–501; 200, 501–7 • R. Morison, *Apomaxis calumniarum* (1537), fols. 73–78v • *Miscellaneous writings and letters of Thomas Cranmer*, ed. J. E. Cox, Parker Society, [18] (1846), 272–4 • T. Wright, ed., *Three chapters of letters relating to the suppression of the monasteries* (1843), nos. 6–11, 14–34 • M. St C. Byrne, ed., *The Lisle letters*, 6 vols. (1981), vol. 1, no. 77; vol. 2, nos. 152, 171 • D. Watt, 'Of the seed of Abraham: Elizabeth Barton, the "Holy Maid of Kent"', *Secretaries of God: women prophets in late medieval and early modern England* (1997), 51–80 • E. J. Devereux, 'Elizabeth Barton and Tudor censorship', *Bulletin of the John Rylands University Library*, 49 (1966–7), 91–106 • R. Rex, 'The execution of the Holy Maid of Kent', *Historical Research*, 64 (1991), 216–20 • S. L. Jansen, 'Elizabeth Barton: "the Holy Maid of Kent"', *Dangerous talk and strange behavior: women and popular resistance to the reforms of Henry VIII* (1996), 41–56 • S. L. Jansen, 'Elizabeth Barton and political prophecy', *Dangerous talk and strange behavior: women and popular resistance to the reforms of Henry VIII* (1996), 57–75 • A. Neame, *The*

Holy Maid of Kent (1971) • private information (2004) [Ethan Shagan] • *Doctrinal treatises and introductions to different portions of the holy scriptures: by William Tyndale, martyr 1536*, ed. H. Walter, Parker Society, 42 (1848), 325–7 • J. Stow, *A summarie of Englyshe chronicles* (1565), fol. 187 • J. G. Nichols, ed., *The chronicle of the grey friars of London*, CS, 53 (1852), 37 • PRO, SP 1/50, fols. 138, 163

Archives BL, inventory of Barton's goods, Cotton MS Cleopatra E.iv, fol. 84 | BL, Harley MS 4990 • PRO, MSS, SP 1/50, 1/73, 1/77, 1/79, 1/80, 1/82, 1/138, 1/139, 1/140, 1/143

Wealth at death clothing, furniture, and eating utensils • 10s.—price of articles already sold: BL, Cotton MS Cleopatra E.iv, fol. 84

Barton, Frances. *See* Abington, Frances (1737–1815).

Barton, Hob a. *See* Barton, Robert (d. 1540).

Barton, Sir John (d. in or before **1335**), administrator, was a Yorkshireman. His father's name was probably Adam, and in the light of John's own association with Fryton in Ryedale, in the North Riding, it is likely that his family took its name from Barton-le-Street, a few miles east of Fryton. It is not always possible to distinguish the Fryton John Barton from others bearing the same, common, name, particularly in the early stages of his career; he could have been identical with the attorney John Barton who was active in king's bench between 1290 and 1307, but this seems unlikely, and more probably he owed his early advancement to a tenurial connection with the locally powerful Mowbrays, of whom he held land at Fryton and nearby Howthorpe. In June 1300 he obtained a grant of free warren on his demesne at both places, and in the following month was styled knight, apparently for the first time, in a commission to raise troops for Scotland. He received a similar commission in April 1303, while on 23 November 1304 he was one of four trailbaston justices appointed for Yorkshire, a commission repeated the following April.

Barton's trailbaston commission was an early and experimental one, of a kind superseded by arrangements made later in 1305. But he continued to be active in the administration of Yorkshire. He received numerous commissions of oyer and terminer. He was a knight of the shire at the parliaments of August 1312, September 1313, and October 1318. One of the knights summoned to Doncaster in April 1315 for a council to concert measures against the Scots, in 1316 he was a commissioner of array, and in 1318 he was ordered to raise men to resist Scottish attack. He was an assessor and collector of taxes in 1316, 1319, and 1322. In 1322 he was exempted from service in Scotland and elsewhere, in consequence of his having been appointed to administer the affairs of Alice Lacy, dowager countess of Lancaster; the fact that he witnessed three of her charters later that year suggests that this was no sinecure, and in May 1324 he was summoned to attend a great council at Westminster. In the spring of 1326 he was inquiring into defects in York Castle.

A number of deeds show Barton adding to his holdings at Howthorpe, and also at Newsham, near Kirby Wiske, a few miles from Thirsk. In 1328 he sold the manor of Howthorpe to Warter Priory, in the East Riding, but since he is recorded in the same year as making over common rights at Fryton and Howthorpe to his son Thomas, both transactions probably represent efforts to put his affairs in order, in terms both spiritual and secular. Barton married twice. His first marriage, which had taken place by 1300, was to a woman named Lucy, who is likely to have been the mother of Barton's known children, his sons Thomas and Adam. This marriage probably foundered as a result of Lucy's liaison in 1313 with Peter Wakefield, a runaway monk from St Mary's Abbey, York. The fact that on 29 June 1335 Barton's widow was named as Agnes, with dower lands at Fryton, Howthorpe, and other places in the North Riding, shows that he had married again, as well as that he was dead by then.   HENRY SUMMERSON

Sources Chancery records · VCH Yorkshire North Riding, 1.507 · The register of William Greenfield, lord archbishop of York, 1306–1315, ed. W. Brown and A. H. Thompson, 1, SurtS, 145 (1931) · The register of William Greenfield, lord archbishop of York, 1306–1315, ed. W. Brown and A. H. Thompson, 3, SurtS, 151 (1936) · F. Palgrave, ed., The parliamentary writs and writs of military summons, 2/3 (1834), 488 · RotS, 1.146, 190 · Dugdale, Monasticon, new edn, 6/1.299 · CIPM, 7, nos. 81, 250 · F. H. Slingsby, ed., Feet of fines for the county of York from 1272 to 1300, Yorkshire Archaeological Society, 121 (1956) · W. Brown, ed., Yorkshire deeds, 2, Yorkshire Archaeological Society, 50 (1914) · G. O. Sayles, ed., Select cases in the court of king's bench, 1, SeldS, 55 (1936) · CCIR, 1337–9, 499 · CPR, 1292–1301, 529

Barton, John (fl. 1417), physician and alleged heretic, was the subject of a testimonial issued at Reading on 11 May 1417 by Archbishop Chichele, stating that John Barton, described as a doctor of the city of London, had purged himself in a provincial council held at St Paul's of the crime of 'heresy and Lollardy', which he had been accused of committing in the capital and elsewhere. Either as a penance, or as proof of his innocence, Barton then wrote a short Confutatio Lollardorum, dedicated to Henry V, and preserved in a single copy in the library of All Souls College, Oxford (MS 42, fols. 308–14). Nothing further is known for certain about him. It is possible that he was the John Barton who suffered poverty as a chaplain in the London parish of St Peter-le-Poer in 1379–81, but John Barton is a common name. Tanner (Coxe, Catalogus, 2.13) explained All Souls' possession of the manuscript of the Confutatio by making him an Oxford master who died at Ludgate in 1439 and produced other writings, but offers no evidence for this. It is equally likely that there is a connection with the two London lawyers, brothers both called John Barton (d. 1431 and 1434), whose property Chichele arranged should be acquired by All Souls, but this suggestion too lacks proof.   MICHAEL WILKS

Sources E. F. Jacob, ed., The register of Henry Chichele, archbishop of Canterbury, 1414–1443, 4, CYS, 47 (1947), 168–9 · A. Hudson, The premature reformation: Wycliffite texts and Lollard history (1988) · A. K. McHardy, ed., The church in London, 1375–1392, London RS, 13 (1977), no. 100, p. 14 · Hist. U. Oxf. 2: Late med. Oxf., 651–3 · H. O. Coxe, ed., Catalogus codicum MSS qui in collegiis aulisque Oxoniensibus hodie adservantur, 2 vols. (1852)
Archives All Souls Oxf., MS 42, fols. 308–14

Barton, John (c.1605–1675), schoolmaster, is of uncertain origin. He may be the John Barton of Northamptonshire who matriculated as a sizar of Peterhouse, Cambridge, in 1622, studied under Philip Poulett, son of Sir Anthony Poulett of Hinton St George, Somerset, graduated BA in 1624, proceeded MA in 1636, and was ordained priest in 1627. Thomas Walker's identification of this Barton's parents as Richard Barton of Estcott, Northamptonshire, and his wife, Anne Bayly, in unlikely. The author of The Art of Rhetorick (1634) is identified on the title-page as 'J. B. Master of the free-school in Kinfare in Staffordshire'; both the dedication and the address to the reader are signed 'John Barton'. While in Kinver, Barton married Jane (b. c.1610), daughter of Edward Moseley of Whittington, on 17 October 1633. Their son Edward was baptized on 24 August 1634.

Barton's first book, The Art of Rhetorick Concisely and Compleatly Handled, Exemplified out of Holy Writ, comprises a 35-page treatise in English and a 14-page version in Latin. Barton follows the Ramist practice of dividing rhetoric into elocutio (stylistic ornamentation) and pronuntiatio (oratorical delivery). However, he uses the English terms 'adornation' for style and 'action' for delivery. Each of the book's eight chapters includes definitions, illustrations, and commentary; the commentary appears to be Barton's own, as do many of the English names for the tropes and figures. Metaphor is called 'comparation', synecdoche is 'comprehension', and irony is 'simulation'. The book is dedicated to John Poulett, baron of Hinton St George, Somerset. In his address to the reader Barton criticizes the former Oxford schoolmaster Charles Butler, whose popular Latin edition of Talon's Rhetorica, printed at least seven times before 1630, may have been viewed as competition.

In 1639 Barton was hired to replace Richard Billingsley as the headmaster of King Edward's School in Birmingham. The school tenants, outraged that so few of Billingsley's pupils were being sent up to the universities, had agreed to double their rents so long as 'an able and sufficient' replacement could be found (Izon, xiv). School records show that Barton was paid £40 per year, exactly twice as much as Billingsley had been paid. In Birmingham a daughter, Jane, was baptized on 25 November 1641. Barton seems to have played a role in the founding of the first library in Birmingham before he was replaced as chief master in 1645. Moreover, Joseph Hill credits Barton with writing Prince Rupert's Burning Love to England (1643), an anonymous war tract describing the destruction of Birmingham during the civil war. It was printed for Thomas Underhill and is 'written in a scholarly manner' (Hill, 14).

Barton's last book, The Latine Grammar Composed in the English Tongue (1652), printed for Thomas Underhill, is a 66-page textbook for children, treating orthography, 'merologie' (the study of the parts of speech), syntax, and prosody. The title-page identifies the author as 'J. B. Mr of Arts, and not long since Master of the Free School of Birmingham in Warwickshire'. The epistle to the reader is signed 'John Barton'. Barton's plan was to compose a dual-language grammar book, with Latin and Greek rules juxtaposed on each page, but instead he relegated the Greek grammar to a brief appendix. In his introductory epistle he acknowledges his debt to Thomas Farnaby, author of *Systema grammaticum* (1641): 'Learned Farnaby ... whom I have been most ingaged unto of all others'.

John Barton may have been a relative of the author William Barton (1598?–1678), who was a native of Northamptonshire, a graduate of Cambridge (though not Peterhouse), and a minister in Staffordshire. His *Book of Psalms in Metre* (1645), printed for Thomas Underhill, contains liminary verses by 'Jo. Barton'. At some point Barton must have returned to Kinver. He died in July 1675 and was buried in Kinver church on 26 July. In the parish register he is referred to as 'Mr. John Barton'; that he was buried in the middle chancel is a sign of his importance in the community.   EDWARD A. MALONE

Sources J. Hill, *The book makers of old Birmingham: authors, printers and book sellers* (1907) · *The records of King Edward's School, Birmingham*, 6, ed. J. Izon, Dugdale Society, 30 (1974) · K. Narveson, 'John Barton (c.1610–1675)', *British rhetoricians and logicians, 1500–1660: first series*, ed. E. A. Malone, DLitB, 236 (2001), 40–46 · private information (2004) [V. Morgan, Kinver Historical Society; D. Hopwood, Birmingham Central Library] · T. A. Walker, ed., *Admissions to Peterhouse or St Peter's College in the University of Cambridge* (1912) · Staffs. RO, F1197/1/1, fol. 3/3 and F1197/1/2, fol. 1/2 · Venn, *Alum. Cant.* · M. W. Greenslade, ed., *A history of the county of Stafford*, 20: *Seisdon hundred (part)* (1984) · *IGI* · *DNB* [William Barton] · parish register, St Martin's, Birmingham, 1641–6, Birm. CL · T. Hutton, *King Edward's School, Birmingham, 1552–1952* (1952)

Barton, John (1789–1852), political economist and botanist, was born on 11 June 1789 in Southwark, London, the son of John Barton (1755–1789) and his second wife, Elizabeth, *née* Horne (1760–1833). He was the half-brother of Maria *Hack, children's writer, and Bernard *Barton, poet. The elder John Barton, a manufacturer, was a member of the first committee formed for the abolition of the slave trade in 1787. Towards the end of his life he was engaged in the malting business in Hertford. After his death in 1789, the children were brought up by Mrs Barton and her family in Tottenham, Middlesex. A man of independent means, Barton travelled widely, visiting France and Italy and possibly venturing as far afield as Poland and Russia, and pursued interests in economics and botany. In 1827 he left the Society of Friends and joined the Church of England. Throughout his life he was a staunch supporter of mechanics' institutes and schools, and he helped to establish the Chichester savings bank. His *A Lecture on the Geography of Plants* (1827) shows Barton to have been well read in German scientific literature, notably in A. Humboldt's work on the geographical distribution of plants.

Although he never published the systematic economic treatise which might have established his reputation, Barton's closely argued pamphlets were influential. His *Observations on the Circumstances which Influence the Condition of the Labouring Classes* (1817) questioned the linkage by Thomas Malthus of population growth to increasing wage rates, arguing that the likely age of first marriage and thus birth rates were influenced, not by wage rates or poor-relief practices, but by perceived employment prospects which, paradoxically, were best when wages were low. A rise in wage levels, Barton argued, encouraged employers to invest in labour-saving technology. In opposition to David Ricardo, he maintained that only when circulating capital increased did employment rise: any increase in fixed capital was unlikely to stimulate, and might significantly diminish, the demand for labour.

Barton's pamphlets influenced both Ricardo and Malthus. In the third edition of his *The Principles of Political Economy* (1821) Ricardo added a chapter on machinery, conceding that Barton 'had taken a correct view of some of the effects of an increasing amount of fixed capital on the condition of the labouring classes', but maintaining that there was a, perhaps imperfect, positive relationship between increases in capital and the demand for labour. Malthus accepted Barton's contention that any increase in poor relief should be measured, not in nominal terms, but in real monetary terms.

Later Barton became increasingly preoccupied with the effects of overpopulation. In his *An inquiry into the causes of the progressive depreciation of agricultural labour in modern times* (1820) and *A Statement of the Consequences Likely to Ensue from our Growing Excess of Population* (1830) Barton argued that only where land was cheap and plentiful would economic growth be maximized and accordingly favoured emigration schemes and colonization of Canada and other territories. He dismissed claims that free trade and cheap food could transform the economy, perceiving instead a tendency to overstock the labour market in industrial areas. The expansion of capital and population beyond a certain point was 'a national evil', creating social problems which could be offset by greater prosperity. Accordingly Barton favoured the maintenance of agricultural protection. By 1846 he was deeply worried by the likely effects of free trade on monetary policy, and in two letters to *The Standard* he argued that, by increasing the demand for imports, free trade would precipitate an outflow of gold and thereby provoke a monetary crisis. His last pamphlet, *The Monetary Crisis of 1847* (1847), offered a brief vindication of this analysis.

In 1811 Barton married Ann Woodrouffe Smith (*d.* 1822). With his second wife, Frances (Fanny) Rickman (*d.* 1842), daughter of James Rickman, he had six surviving children, one of whom, John *Barton (1836–1908), became a missionary in India. Barton died in Chichester on 10 March 1852. His *Economic Writings* were edited by G. Sotiroff (2 vols., 1962).   DAVID EASTWOOD, *rev.*

Sources J. Barton, *Observations on the circumstances which influence the condition of the labouring classes* (1817); repr. (1934) · G. Sotiroff, 'John Barton (1789–1852)', *Economic Journal*, 62 (1952), 87–102 · 'Barton, Bernard', *DNB* · C. E. Barton, *John Barton: a memoir* (1910) · private information (2004) [Robert Barton]
Archives BLPES, corresp. and papers

Barton, John (1836–1908), missionary, was born at East Leigh, Havant, Hampshire, on 31 December 1836, sixth of the nine children of John *Barton (1789–1852) and his wife, Fanny (*d.* 1842), daughter of James Rickman. After schooling at Bishop Waltham and at Cholmondeley School, Highgate, Middlesex, he entered Christ's College,

Cambridge, in 1855, to read mathematics. He was a hard-working and laconic but sociable giant of a man, and an avid botanist, mountaineer, and hillwalker; he was also an invigorating secretary of the university's Church Missionary Union, none of which left much time for his studies. In 1859, after last-minute cramming, he graduated with honours in mathematics and natural science. In the same year he was accepted as a missionary by the Church Missionary Society (CMS), in March, and on 5 May he married Catherine Frances, daughter of Edward Wigram and sister of Frederic Wigram honorary secretary of the CMS. Of frail health, she died in May 1860, followed soon afterwards by their two-month-old daughter.

In December 1860 Barton arrived in Calcutta. He was ordained priest in the following February and posted up-country to superintend the CMS college at Agra and the nearby orphanage at Sikandra. In May 1863 he was transferred to the mission school at Amritsar. Here he met Emily Eugenia, second daughter of the Revd Charles Boileau Elliott; they married at Ludhiana on 12 October 1863. In March 1865, after a year's furlough, Barton became principal of the CMS's new university college at Calcutta. He had originally doubted the worth of missionary colleges but was now convinced that the prestige and respect they generated were crucial in persuading Indians to listen to what missionaries had to say.

Barton was plagued by dysentery and every hot season he left Calcutta for southern India, the foothills, or Burma. He returned to Britain in 1869 to recoup his health, and he worked as secretary under Henry Venn at Church Missionary House before returning to India in the autumn of 1871 as secretary of the CMS's Madras mission. Barton was neither doctrinaire nor conservative in matters of ritual and his two tours of the Madras missions, combined with his earlier travels, convinced him that church union was the only way forward for India's Christian community.

Barton left Madras in 1876. In 1877, with six sons and two daughters all in need of an education, he accepted the living of Holy Trinity, Cambridge, where he remained until 1893, with the exceptions of a four-month deputation to Ceylon in 1884 and a year as acting bishop at Tinnevelly in Madras in 1889. At Cambridge he was a founder council member of Ridley Hall Theological College, and a hugely successful popularizer of missionary endeavour; ninety-seven undergraduates were accepted as missionaries during his time in Cambridge.

Barton turned down the bishoprics of Travancore (in 1889), Tinnevelly (in 1889), and Japan (in 1893). In 1893 he became chief secretary of the Church Pastoral Aid Society, a body which handed out grants-in-aid to clergy needing extra curates and lay preachers. The job bristled with the politics of personality, and additionally Barton was too liberal for many of the evangelicals on his committee. He resigned in 1899. His active retirement was curtailed by a stroke in 1905 and he died at his home, Moorcroft, Weybridge, Surrey, on 26 November 1908, and was buried in the Weybridge parish churchyard on 1 December. A tablet and memorial window to him were placed in Holy Trinity Church, Cambridge.

Barton was survived by his second wife and eight children, one of whom, Cecil Edward Barton (1870–1909), missionary in the Punjab, wrote—but did not live to see published—a memoir of his father (1910).

CHARLOTTE FELL-SMITH, *rev.* KATHERINE PRIOR

Sources C. E. Barton, *John Barton: a memoir* (1910) · Venn, *Alum. Cant.* · W. M. Young, 'John Barton—an appreciation', *Church Missionary Review*, 60 (1909), 84–90 · ecclesiastical records, BL OIOC · *The Times* (12 March 1852), 1 · *The Times* (7 May 1859), 1 · *The Times* (19 May 1860), 1 · *The Times* (28 Nov 1908), 1 · *The Times* (1 Dec 1908), 13 · E. Stock, *The history of the Church Missionary Society: its environment, its men and its work*, 4 vols. (1899–1916)
Archives U. Birm. L., family papers | U. Birm. L., Church Missionary Society archive
Likenesses Mason & Basevi, photograph, 1885, repro. in Barton, *John Barton*, facing p. 114 · photographs, repro. in Barton, *John Barton*
Wealth at death £14,581 0s. 7d.: probate, 10 Feb 1909, *CGPLA Eng. & Wales*

Barton, Matthew (1714/15–1795), naval officer, entered the navy in 1730, on the *Fox*, under the command of Captain Arnold, and served with him on the coast of South Carolina. Afterwards he served in the Mediterranean under captains John Byng, Vanbrugh, and Lord Augustus Fitzroy. In March 1739, being then a midshipman of the *Somerset*, he was made acting lieutenant in the prize *St Joseph* (probably the *San Josef*) by Admiral Nicholas Haddock. On 2 January 1740 Barton passed his lieutenant's examination and was commissioned lieutenant of the sloop *Swift*. On 27 September he was appointed fourth lieutenant of the *Princess Caroline* (80 guns), commanded by Captain Thomas Griffin, forming part of the fleet which sailed with Sir Chaloner Ogle for the West Indies. On arriving at Jamaica, Admiral Edward Vernon selected the *Princess Caroline* for his flag, and Captain Griffin was removed to the *Burford*, taking Barton with him. After the failure at Cartagena the *Burford* came home and paid off.

Barton was appointed second lieutenant of the *Nonsuch* (50 guns) in which ship he went to the Mediterranean and continued until after the battle off Toulon (11 February 1744), when, in September, he was appointed first lieutenant of the *Marlborough*, and in March 1745 fourth lieutenant of the *Neptune*, carrying the flag of Vice-Admiral William Rowley, the commander-in-chief, by whom, in May, he was promoted to the command of the fireship *Duke*. Rowley's successor, Vice-Admiral Henry Medley, promoted Barton captain of the frigate *Antelope* on 2 February 1746. In that ship and afterwards in the xebec *Postilion*, he remained in the Mediterranean until the peace, when the *Postilion* was paid off at Port Mahon, and Barton returned to Britain in the flagship with Vice-Admiral George Byng. He had no further employment at sea until the recommencement of war with France, when he was appointed to the *Litchfield* (50 guns), one of the fleet which went to North America with Edward Boscawen in the summer of 1755. In June 1756, off Louisbourg, the *Litchfield* and the *Norwich* met with and captured the French ship *Arc-en-Ciel* (50 guns), armed *en flûte*, and carrying stores. Back in Britain in 1757 Barton was ordered to take an emissary to Morocco, but the venture was abandoned and Barton was ordered to cruise down to Guinea to intercept French warships said to be operating off that coast. He was ordered to proceed from there to the West Indies. By the time Barton reached Sierre Leone the French had gone. Barton sailed on to St Kitts and escorted the homeward bound convoys to Britain in the summer of 1758. No sooner had Barton returned than he was ordered back to Africa under the orders of Commodore Augustus Keppel, as part of the squadron destined for Goree. The squadron sailed on 11 November. On 28 November a heavy gale scattered the fleet; at night the *Litchfield* by her reckoning was twenty-five leagues from the African shore. At six o'clock on the following morning she struck on the coast near Masagan. The *Litchfield* went over on her beam ends and could not be righted. The high seas continued all night and though two strong swimmers got a line ashore they could not secure a larger rope. Attempts to launch a raft were defeated and when, the next morning, a raft was launched it was smashed on the rocky shore. Fortunately the hull held together until the gale moderated, when those (some 220 of a crew of 350) who had not been washed overboard or drowned managed to reach the land only about 400 yards away. These survivors were made prisoners by the emperor of Morocco, who considered himself at war with Britain. After a tedious negotiation they were at last ransomed by the British government, and arrived at Gibraltar on 27 June 1760.

Barton arrived in Britain on 7 August, was tried for the loss of his ship, was fully acquitted, and in October was appointed to a fine ship, the *Téméraire* (74 guns), captured from the French only the year before. In this ship he served, under Keppel, in the expedition against Belle-Isle in April 1761, had especial charge of the landing, and was sent home with dispatches. He afterwards convoyed a number of transports to Barbados, and served under Sir George Rodney at the reduction of Martinique in January 1762. In the following March he was detached, under Commodore Sir James Douglas, to Jamaica, and in June and July he formed part of the expedition against Havana, for much of the time commanding the naval brigade on shore. Under the stress of fatigue and climate his health gave way, and he was compelled to exchange into the *Devonshire* for a passage to England, which was not, however, put out of commission until the peace in 1763. Barton became rear-admiral of the blue on 28 April 1777, and vice-admiral on 19 March 1779. On 26 September 1780 he advanced to vice-admiral of the white. On 24 September 1787 he became admiral of the blue and on 1 February 1793 admiral of the white. However, after his return from Havana and the peace of Paris in 1763, Barton did not serve again on account of his poor health. He died at Hampstead on 30 December 1795 aged eighty years, and was buried on 6 January at St Andrew's, Holborn. It would appear from his will, proved on 5 January 1796, that Barton was survived by his wife, Rachel, about whom no further details are known.   J. K. LAUGHTON, *rev.* RICHARD HARDING

Sources 1756–8, PRO, ADM 1/1487; ADM 1/1488; ADM 1/1489 · 1762–3, PRO, ADM 1/1493 · J. Charnock, ed., *Biographia navalis*, 6 (1798), 17–27 · journal of Hon Augustus Keppell, 16 Feb–4 Oct 1762, PRO, ADM 50/12 · journal of Admiral George Pocock, 19 Feb 1762–18 Jan 1763, PRO, ADM 50/21 · PRO, ADM 6/15 (commissions warrants), 243; 337; ADM 6/16, 38; ADM 6/17, 337, 393, 411, 252; ADM 107/3 (passing certificates) p. 357, 2 Jan 1739; ADM 8/20 (fleet disposition lists); ADM 8/21 · [J. Sutherland], *An authentic narrative of the loss of HM ship Litchfield, Capt. Barton, on the coast of Africa: with some account of the sufferings of the capt. and the surviving part of the crew, in a journal kept by a lieutenant* [1760] · *GM*, 1st ser., 66 (1796), 81 · LMA, Microfilm XO92/179

Wealth at death approx. £10,000 in liquid assets: will, PRO, PROB 11/1270, sig. 3

Barton, Pamela Espeut (1917–1943), golfer, was born on 4 March 1917 at 118 Castelnau, Barnes, Surrey, the daughter of Henry Charles Johnston Barton, a tea buyer, and his wife, Ethel Maude Espeut. She began playing golf at the age of twelve, with her elder sister Mervyn (later Sutherland-Pilch), who also became an international golfer. The sisters had lessons from J. H. Taylor at their home course of Royal Mid-Surrey, but afterwards went to Archie Compston at Coombe Hill, where their lessons were paid for by a golfing uncle. Compston was 'a forthright, unconventional teacher' and much sought after in the game (Lucas, 131). He had a profound influence on Pamela Barton, shortening her backswing and transforming her from a good but erratic player into one who could consistently challenge the best. Without his help it is unlikely that she would have climbed so high, so quickly in the years ahead. Nevertheless Barton's one great defining attribute, apart from natural talent and enormous competitive enthusiasm, was her sheer physical strength, which set her apart from almost all her female contemporaries.

The Barton sisters cut their competitive teeth in the girls' championship, but their first major success was in winning the *Bystander* foursomes at Ranelagh in the autumn of 1933: they had thirty-four years and a combined handicap of eleven between them. Soon after leaving school, Pamela played at Porthcawl in her first ladies' championship and reached the final, losing to Helen Holm. This made her reputation, and at seventeen she was picked to play for Great Britain against France at Chantilly. Her England début came the following year, and she played in all of the international matches from 1935 to 1939. She won the French championship at Le Touquet in 1934 and was then sent with the British team to contest the second Curtis cup match at Chevy Chase, Maryland, which the Americans won fairly comfortably.

In 1935 the Barton sisters met in the semi-final of the ladies' championship at Newcastle, co. Down, and Pam (as she was always called) emerged victorious, only to lose in the final once again, this time to Wanda Morgan. She was selected for a lengthy tour of Australia and New Zealand, an experience which stood her in excellent stead for what was to become her *annus mirabilis*, the season of 1936. In that year she at last won the ladies' title, defeating Bridget Newell in the final at Southport and Ainsdale, and then played for Britain and Ireland in the team that drew the third Curtis cup match over the King's course, Gleneagles. In the autumn she travelled to America, and at Canoe Brook, New Jersey, became only the second lady to have

Pamela Espeut Barton (1917–1943), by unknown photographer, 1937

won both British and American ladies' championships in the same year, defeating Maureen Orcutt 4 and 3 in the thirty-six-hole final. Only Dorothy Campbell had ever done this before, in 1909, and it was to be another thirty-three years before the great French player Catherine Lacoste was to repeat the feat.

Barton did not defend her American title in 1937, which was by her own standards rather a lean year, although she did publish a golf book, *A Stroke a Hole*, but retained her amateur status by making no money from it. In 1938 she was runner-up in the French championship and in 1939 she won the British title for the second time, at Portrush, a course well suited to the 'pugnacious and powerful golfer' that she had become (Wilson, 92). This effectively ended her brief but brilliant career.

Barton worked as an ambulance driver during the worst phases of the London blitz, and in the summer of 1941 she joined the Women's Auxiliary Air Force as a radio operator. She was commissioned within the year and was afterwards based at RAF Manston in Kent. She was killed in a flying accident at RAF Detling on 13 November 1943. She had flown there from Manston with a pilot friend to attend a dance and the accident happened in the early hours of the morning, as they were taking off to return home. She was buried in St John's cemetery, Margate.

With Pam Barton's death British women's golf lost its leading personality, somebody who, in the words of Henry Cotton 'had the proportions of life right and did not make herself a slave to golf. *She loved golf but she loved life*

more' (Cotton, 174). As Laddie Lucas wrote many years later,

> Relatively short of stature and well built, Pam possessed, beneath a head of reddish hair, an engaging freckled face which mostly wore a smile. A warm friendliness, and a modesty which brushed success easily aside, drew people to her. A totally unaffected personality allowed her to devote her days to golf without people saying she had surrendered herself unreasonably to the game. It camouflaged an intense ambition to get to the top. And stay there.   (Lucas, 134)

It was a saying of hers that 'Gentility never pays in bunkers' (Barton, *A Stroke a Hole*, 55). Her example of cheerful, hard hitting was much missed after the war, as British women struggled to compete on the international stage. In America a Pam Barton Fund was established to raise money for the visiting Curtis cup side of 1950, and supported by clubs all over America, but few in Britain were aware of this act of kindness in memory of their former champion.   MARK POTTLE

Sources *Golfer's Handbook* (1940) · L. Lucas, *The sport of Prince's: reflections of a golfer* (1980) · *The Times* (15 Nov 1943) · L. Mair, *One hundred years of women's golf* (1992) · E. Wilson, *A gallery of women golfers* (1961) · R. Green, *The illustrated encyclopedia of golf* (1994) · H. Cotton, *This game of golf* (1948) · B. Darwin, *Golf between two wars* (1944) · R. Stockman, *The history of RAF Manston* (1987) · R. Cossey, *Golfing ladies: five centuries of golf in Great Britain and Ireland* (1984) · b. cert. · d. cert.
Archives FILM BFI NFTVA, sports footage
Likenesses photograph, 1937, Empire Sports Photo Agency, Nottingham [*see illus.*] · photographs, repro. in Cossey, *Golfing ladies*
Wealth at death £4841 4s. 0d.: administration, 28 Feb 1944, CGPLA Eng. & Wales

Barton, Richard. *See* Bradshaigh, Richard (1601/2–1669).

Barton, Richard (1706–1759), topographer and religious writer, was born in Painstown, co. Meath, Ireland, the third son of the Revd John Barton (*fl.* 1675–1735), dean of Ardagh, and Elinor Jenney, daughter of the Revd Henry Jenney, archdeacon of Dromore diocese, and granddaughter of Sir William Brownlow, a leading protestant in co. Armagh in the 1620s. He was first educated privately by the leading pedagogue Dr Thomas Sheridan, and he matriculated on 9 February 1722 at Trinity College, Dublin. There he became a scholar in 1724 and graduated BA in the spring of 1726, proceeding MA in 1731. Like his two elder brothers, he followed his father into the Church of Ireland; he became a deacon in 1728 and was ordained the following year. He never married, and followed his clerical career with great dedication. He was curate of Donaghcloney, co. Down, in the diocese of Dromore, between 1728 and 1742 and then rector of Shankhill, near Lurgan, co. Armagh, between 1742 and 1759.

Barton's duties as a Church of Ireland clergyman were taken seriously by him and went hand in hand with his topographical and natural history work. He later recorded his work, in his first curacy in Donaghcloney, of evangelizing among Catholics in the area, though he eschewed the use of the Irish language as it was a sign of barbarity and preferred to use English to erode the 'lairs of the wild beasts'. He also interested himself in the theological controversies of the time and in 1751 published *The Analogy of*

Divine Wisdom, an attack on those Arian ideas on the Trinity held not only in England but in the Irish episcopacy by Bishop Clayton of Clogher. He was praised by John Wesley on his tour through co. Armagh in 1756 as a clergyman who had forgone likely preferment to concentrate on his mission around Lurgan and his evangelical preaching in a town described earlier by Jonathan Swift as a pleasant place in which to live 'if it had not been for the Quakers, Presbyterians and Papists then beginning to inhabit it' (Lodge MS, G. IV. 5, fol. 82).

Wesley also recorded something of Barton's eccentricity on his visit in 1756, pointing out that he lived in a house near Lough Neagh with no doors and few windows. Barton's other source of fame was his concentration for nearly twenty years from the early 1730s on the topography and natural history of Lough Neagh and its hinterland. In 1738 he was already in touch with the noted historian and topographer Walter Harris, who later founded the Physico-Historical Society and recorded Barton's name as the natural history 'inquirer' or collector of information for co. Armagh for the society. Barton joined Harris's society, and there are several letters from him in 1745 recording his work on a dictionary of place names for the county (which has been lost) and his continuing experiments on the petrifying qualities of Lough Neagh, a topic which fascinated many eighteenth-century natural historians.

In connection with this work Barton published in 1751 *Lectures in Natural Philosophy*, which looked at current knowledge in that field and added findings from his local lough on geology and both medicinal and mechanical properties of the waters, and *A Dialogue Concerning Something of Importance to Ireland, Particularly to the County of Armagh*, which was intended to encourage funding and support for a full civil and topographical survey of that county in the wake of the Physico-Historical Society's collapse. Although these appeals proved unsuccessful all of Barton's books were well subscribed, particularly the first, which had more than 550 subscriptions. Barton remained in Lurgan throughout these years; he died and was buried there on 6 August 1759.   EOIN MAGENNIS

Sources Burtchaell & Sadleir, *Alum. Dubl.* · Allibone, *Dict.* · J. McMinn, ed., *Jonathan Swift's travels* (1996) · Armagh County Museum, T. G. F. Paterson MSS · Armagh Public Library, Physico-Historial Society MSS · Armagh Public Library, John Lodge MSS **Archives** Armagh Public Library, Physico-Historical Society MSS | Armagh County Museum, T. G. F. Paterson MSS

Barton, Robert [*called* Hob a Barton] (*d.* 1540), sea captain and administrator, known to the English as the pirate Hob a Barton, was one of three sons of John Barton, sea captain in Leith, the port of Edinburgh. Some time prior to 1476 his father's ship and goods were captured by Portuguese ships. John senior was dead by 1494, when James IV granted Robert and his brother John letters of marque against the Portuguese while not authorizing their use. In 1497 James employed Robert to escort Perkin Warbeck on his departure from Scotland. Over the next ten years he undertook various commissions for the king in France

and Flanders, including purchase of ships and naval supplies. He was also involved in James's shipbuilding schemes in Scotland. His trading ventures brought him considerable wealth which he invested in property, notably the lands of Over Barnton, acquired from the crown in 1508.

In July 1507 James renewed the letters of marque in favour of Robert and John and their brother Andrew *Barton. In 1508 Robert, having captured a Portuguese ship, was arrested in the Scottish staple port of Veere and was released only after strong protests by James. Although the letters of marque were suspended in June 1510, the Bartons continued their depredations, including seizure of goods belonging to English merchants. After Andrew's death in 1511 Robert took service under the French flag and renewed his attacks on English shipping. He was still involved with James IV's navy and in May 1513 took command of a new Scottish ship, the *Lion*, at Honfleur. His surviving brother, John, who sailed with the Scottish fleet to France in July 1513, died later that year.

Early in 1514 the *Lion* had to take refuge in Corunna, where Barton and an envoy sent by the Scottish council to John Stewart, duke of Albany, were taken prisoner, though they were released when France and Spain agreed a truce. In the following year Barton returned to France to escort Albany to Scotland. On 12 October 1516 Albany, as governor of Scotland, appointed Barton comptroller, responsible for collecting revenues from the property (crown lands and customs) and defraying the cost of the king's and governor's households. Though Gavin Douglas denounced the appointment of 'ane very pyrett and seyrevare' as comptroller (BL, Cotton MS Caligula B.iii, fol. 311), Barton's acumen and private resources enabled him to hold the office far longer than any of his predecessors. In 1519 he earned the gratitude of the queen mother, Margaret Tudor, by lending her his own money when she was on the point of pawning her jewels and unable to pay her household expenses. Nevertheless, internal unrest and intermittent hostilities with England depressed crown revenues, while expenditure on the king, governor, and queen mother was difficult to contain. Following James V's assumption of personal rule in July 1524 his household expenditure outstripped Barton's ability to fund it. On 30 July 1525 Barton warned that the crown's property could not sustain the burden and protested that whatever might happen in future should not be laid to his charge since 'he has done his exact diligence, spendit his awn geire and may sustene na forrare' (*APS*, *1424–1567*, 296). On 17 August 1525 James Colville replaced him as comptroller.

Approached by the deposed Christian II to assist him in recovering the throne of Denmark, Barton had agreed to provide a small fleet of ships. Though this does not appear to have materialized, his heirs were to claim he had spent money that had not been repaid. In 1527 he procured the release of some of Christian's sailors arrested in Scotland, receiving arms and munitions from Christian's chancellor as security for his expenditure. His plans for assisting Christian were frustrated by James V's seizure of the munitions for use against the earl of Angus and his own return to office on Colville's resignation.

On 6 March 1529 James appointed Barton treasurer, comptroller, great custumar, master of the coin, master of the artillery, and conservator of the mines of Scotland, to which he added custumar of Edinburgh and chamberlain-depute of Galloway. Though these were the most extensive financial powers held by any subject since the 1420s, they were undermined by the priority given to repaying Colville and a previous treasurer, Sir John Campbell. Moreover, James had embarked on an expensive building programme for the royal palaces. By August 1530 Barton's deficit as comptroller had risen to £7467 Scots, equivalent to a year's net income from the property. On 9 September Barton was again replaced by Colville as comptroller and soon afterwards by William Stewart as treasurer. By December 1530 Barton was in serious difficulties with his creditors, especially royal officers and servants who were distraining his lands and goods for payment of sums that had been allowed in his accounts. Because these were really the king's debts, the council gave Barton protection until he was repaid. Although repayment in annual instalments was promised, these came only intermittently. In July 1536 James granted protection to Barton, who was 'of gret age, febill and vaik in persoun' (Hannay, Acts, 456), probably so that he could accompany the king to France. Nevertheless, in June 1538 the lords of council ruled that this protection was invalid. They found Barton guilty of deforcing a royal officer acting for one of his creditors, though their sentence of escheat and imprisonment was not carried out. Barton is recorded as still living on 27 February 1540, but he had died by 23 March following, when James V replied to a demand by Christian II's daughter, the countess palatine of the Rhine, for the goods entrusted to Barton. Professing ignorance of the matter, James claimed he would have seen to restitution, had it not been that Barton was dead and had her envoy been willing to wait to sue his heirs. In 1541 Barton's widow and his eldest son John renounced sums still due to him from James V in return for a pension for two of his younger sons. About that time John Barton obtained renewal of the letters of marque against the Portuguese. They were suspended by the privy council in 1561 and finally revoked by parliament in 1563.

Barton's first wife, Elizabeth Jameson, died possibly before 1507 and certainly by 1509, the probable year of his second marriage, to Elizabeth Crawford, daughter of Thomas Crawford of Bonnington and widow of Gilbert Edmonston, sea captain, of Leith. From his first marriage Barton had three sons, John Barton of Duddingston, Henry, and James; and a daughter, Margaret, who married James Sandilands of Calder. In 1511 he had granted all his lands to Robert, his son from his second marriage, who married his ward, Barbara Mowbray, the heiress of Barn-bougle, and took the name of Mowbray.

ATHOL MURRAY

Sources W. S. Reid, *Skipper from Leith, the history of Robert Barton of Over Barnton* (1962) · A. L. Murray, 'Financing the royal household: James V and his comptrollers', *The Renaissance and Reformation in Scotland: essays in honour of Gordon Donaldson*, ed. I. B. Cowan and D. Shaw (1983), 41–59 · R. K. Hannay, ed., *Acts of the lords of council in public affairs, 1501–1554* (1932) · *LP Henry VIII* · *The letters of James the fourth, 1505–13*, ed. R. K. Hannay and R. L. Mackie, Scottish History Society, 3rd ser., 45 (1953) · *The letters of James V*, ed. R. K. Hannay and D. Hay (1954) · S. Mowat, *The port of Leith, its history and its people* (1994) · *APS, 1424–1567* · M. Livingstone, D. Hay Fleming, and others, eds., *Registrum secreti sigilli regum Scotorum / The register of the privy seal of Scotland*, 1–2 (1908–21) · J. D. Marwick, ed., *Extracts from the records of the burgh of Edinburgh, AD 1403–1528*, [1], Scottish Burgh RS, 2 (1869) · BL, Cotton MS Caligula B.iii, fol. 311 · MS Acta dominorum concilii et sessionis, 1540, NA Scot., CS6/12

Barton, Sir Robert (1770–1853), army officer, fifth son of William Barton, esquire, of the Grove, co. Tipperary, and his wife, Grace, eldest daughter of the Very Revd Charles Massy, dean of Limerick, was born at Fethard, co. Tipperary. Barton was in the south of France in 1790 and, like other Englishmen there, enrolled as a volunteer in the national guard; he received the thanks of the National Convention (France) for his conduct at Moissac during the disorders at Montauban. Having returned to England, he obtained a commission in the 11th light dragoons, with which he served under the duke of York in 1795, and again in the Netherlands in 1799, receiving the thanks of Sir Ralph Abercromby for his services on 8 September at Oude Carspel. He was major, 2nd Life Guards, from June 1805 to April 1814, and commanded the regiment at the time of the Burdett riots in April 1810, its role in which led to its great unpopularity. He also commanded the two squadrons of the regiment subsequently sent to the Peninsula, where he served for a time. He was major, 60th foot, from April 1814 to March 1816, when he was placed on half pay. He was promoted major-general in 1819, lieutenant-general in 1837, and general in November 1851, having been knighted (KCH) in March 1837. His first wife, Maria, was the daughter of John Painter (of the Navy Office, Somerset House) and niece of Lady Northcote; they had a son and two daughters. His second wife, Marian Colette (d. 1844), was the widow of Colonel McPherson and daughter of John Addison; they had one daughter. He died at 2 Montague Place, Montague Square, London on 17 March 1853.   H. M. CHICHESTER, rev. DAVID GATES

Sources *GM*, 2nd ser., 39 (1853), 544 · *Army List* (1791–1838) · Boase, *Mod. Eng. biog.*

Barton, Robert Childers (1881–1975), Irish nationalist and politician, was born on 14 March 1881 at Glendalough House, Annamoe, co. Wicklow, son of Charles William Barton (1836–1890), a landowner, and his wife, Agnes Alexandra Frances, *née* Childers (d. 1918). The family owned a large estate in Wicklow and was staunchly Church of Ireland and Unionist. Robert Barton was educated at Rugby, Christ Church, Oxford (matriculated 1905; distinction awarded in diploma in economics, 1908), and the Royal Agricultural College at Cirencester. Having inherited the estate when his father died in 1890 he returned from college eager to reform and modernize production and improve conditions for his staff and tenants. His cousin, (Robert) Erskine *Childers, orphaned in childhood and having grown up in the Barton household, was like an elder brother to Bob Barton, as he was known. In 1908, while Barton and Childers were on a motoring holiday in the midlands and west of Ireland inspecting agricultural co-operatives, both became converted to home rule. Barton joined the Irish National Volunteers in 1913, rising to the rank of commandant, and acted for a time as secretary to the inspector-general, Colonel Maurice Moore, brother of the author George Moore.

In 1915 Barton volunteered for service in the First World War; he joined the Inns of Court Officers' Training Corps on 4 October and was given a commission in the Irish battalion of the Royal Dublin Fusiliers (24 April 1916). Sent to Dublin in the final days of the Easter rising he was horrified at the treatment meted out to the defeated rebels and subsequently resigned his commission. He soon joined Sinn Féin and the IRA and in the general election of 1918 was returned for West Wicklow for Sinn Féin. As such he did not take his seat at Westminster. On the establishment of the underground republican cabinet he was appointed director of agriculture (equivalent to a minister of agriculture). Despite the facts that his department consisted of a few rooms over a warehouse in North Earl Street in Dublin and that he was on the run, Barton succeeded in organizing a national land bank, which collaborated with the Irish co-operative movement to provide loans enabling land-hungry small farmers and potential farmers to acquire land. It also set up land courts to settle disputes over land. These measures had an important effect in calming conflict in the countryside at the time.

Barton had been arrested in February 1919 for seditious speeches and made a sensational escape on 16 March, leaving a sawn bar, a dummy in his bed, and a note to the governor to say that the occupant had had to leave, owing to the discomfort of the place. Rearrested in January 1920 he was sentenced to three years' penal servitude, of which he served nineteen months, being released in time to sign the truce with General Sir Neville Macready at the Mansion House in Dublin on 11 July 1921. Two days later he accompanied De Valera, Griffith, Stack, and Childers to London to negotiate terms. Following the truce De Valera reorganized the executive, appointing Barton minister for economic affairs.

Barton was one of the plenipotentiaries who travelled to London in October 1921 on behalf of the Irish government to negotiate the terms of a treaty to end the Anglo-Irish War. The talks lasted for two months. Although he had opposed signing the Anglo-Irish treaty on the terms offered, he ultimately did so, on the basis that the alternative would be to condemn Ireland to a continuation of the war. It was, in his words to the Dáil, 'the lesser of alternative outrages forced upon me and between which I had to choose' (Boylan, 15). Yet he remained a supporter of De Valera, and, when the government split, took the anti-treaty side. He was elected to the Dáil for Kildare-Wicklow in the general election of June 1922, but followed De Valera's lead in declining to take his seat. In 1922 he published a pamphlet, *The Truth about the Treaty and Document No 2: a Reply to Michael Collins*, reprinted from an article in *The Republic of Ireland*. The same year he was appointed to the republican council of state. He narrowly failed to

secure election for Wicklow at the general election of August 1923. Afterwards he served as chairman of the Wicklow county council, to which he had been elected in 1920, and continued to farm. He headed the Agricultural Credit Corporation from 1934 to 1954 and was appointed the first chairman of Bord na Móna, the turf development board by Todd Andrews, its managing director, in 1946. Barton also served on the Hospitals Trust Board from its foundation in the 1930s to 1953, and was a director of the *Irish Press* newspaper.

On 21 July 1950 Barton married Rachel Warren, a niece of Molly Childers, the widow of Erskine Childers. He died at Glendalough House on 10 August 1975 and was buried in a private service.   CARLA KING

Sources *Irish Times* (11 Aug 1975), 13 • *Irish Press* (11 Aug 1975), 3 • J. N. Young, *Erskine H. Childers, president of Ireland* (1985) • A. Boyle, *The riddle of Erskine Childers: a biography* (1977) • T. Cox, *Damned Englishman: a study of Erskine Childers, 1870–1922* (New York, 1975) • A. Mitchell, *Revolutionary government in Ireland: Dáil Éireann, 1919-22* (Dublin, 1995) • P. Ó Farrell, *Who's who in the Irish war of independence and civil war, 1916–1923* (Dublin, 1997) • *Irish Independent* (11 Aug 1975), 6 • D. Hoctor, *The department's story: a history of the department of agriculture* (Dublin, 1971) • H. Boylan, *A dictionary of Irish biography*, 3rd edn (1998) • *Thom's Irish who's who* (1923), 13 • C. S. Andrews, *Man of no property* (Dublin and Cork, 1982) • Burke, *Gen. Ire.* (1958) • T. Jones, *Whitehall diary*, ed. K. Middlemass, vol. 3: *Ireland, 1918–1925* (1971) • M. Laffan, *The resurrection of Ireland: the Sinn Féin party, 1916–1923* (1999) • T. Ryle Dwyer, *De Valera: the man and the myths* (Dublin, 1991) • T. P. Coogan, *De Valera: long fellow, long shadow* (1993)

Archives NA Ire., papers relating to Anglo-Irish treaty • NL Ire., scrapbooks, MSS 5637–5638, 5650 • TCD, corresp. and papers | NL Ire., Dulcibella Barton MSS, letters, circulars, etc., relating to Sinn Féin, MS 8786 • NL Ire., Seán T. O'Kelly papers • NL Ire., Éamonn Kent papers • NL Ire., Maurice Moore papers • TCD, Erskine Childers papers | SOUND BBC Radio 4 interview with Barton and Erskine Childers, June 1970

Likenesses J. Lavery, oils, 1921, Hugh Lane Gallery of Modern Art, Dublin • group portrait, photograph, 1921 (*Treaty delegation*), Hult. Arch.

Barton, Rose (1856–1929), watercolour painter, was born at Rochestown, co. Tipperary, on 21 April 1856, the second daughter of Augustine Barton (*d.* 1874), solicitor. She was of the Anglo-Irish gentry, educated privately, and presented at Dublin Castle in 1872. She first exhibited in Dublin in 1878, at the Royal Hibernian Academy, and in London in 1880, at the Dudley Gallery and the Society of Lady Artists. She divided her time between Dublin and London.

In 1880, with her friend Mildred Anne Butler, Barton studied in Paris at the studio of the French artist Henri Gervex. This made her aware of impressionism, although one commentator has noted:

> she could not be described strictly as an 'Impressionist', like Claude Monet she was sensitive to the mysterious effect of the famous London fog and she liked to sketch the same views at different times of the day, under changing weather conditions. (Murray, 12)

In the same exhibition catalogue it was noted that it was from impressionism that Barton acquired most of the traits that characterize her work: 'a fondness for *plein air* sketching and commonplace subjects, a certain impressionistic woolliness of outline, and a preference for the brighter colours' (ibid., 9). Both Butler and Barton also studied in London under Paul Jacob Naftel.

Barton exhibited in Cork in 1883 and 1884. She exhibited with several societies but primarily with the Royal Society of Painters in Water Colours and the Society of Women Artists. In 1904 her book *Familiar London* was published, with sixty-one colour illustrations and accompanying text. While the text verged on the sentimental and was badly organized it does give a sense of Barton's favourite haunts for sketching, which included Chelsea, and some idea of her philosophy. She noted:

> so many pictures seem to be painted to satisfy some fashion or eccentricity rather than to follow the great principles without which art becomes debased … 'painting for the pot' has ruined the work of many … there is much painting which seems to be photographic, so to speak; and interpretation, the true object of Art, often gives way to mere imitation.   (Murray, 10)

It has been observed that one of her greatest achievements was the depiction of changing weather conditions, and she loved to capture the reflections of objects in the rain and the atmosphere of fog. The area around Trinity College in Dublin was another of her favourite painting locations. She painted a number of topographical views of Irish houses, including Mount Juliet and Lismore Castle, at each of which she often stayed. She was also noted for her portrayal of children. Among her best known works are *Ha'Penny Bridge* (1892), *Hop Pickers in Kent Returning Home* (1894), and *Going to the Levée at Dublin Castle* (1897).

Barton was elected an associate of the Royal Watercolour Society in 1893 and became a member in 1911. Having suffered recurring attacks of asthma throughout the last years of her life she died, unmarried, at her home, 79 Park Mansions, Knightsbridge, London, on 10 October 1929. Examples of her works are held by the Ulster Museum in Belfast, the Hugh Lane Municipal Gallery of Modern Art, and the National Gallery in Dublin.   MARIA LUDDY

Sources P. Murray and others, *Rose Barton RWS (1856–1929): exhibition of watercolours and drawings* (1987) [exhibition catalogue, Crawford Municipal Art Gallery, Cork, 7–30 Jan 1987] • T. Snoddy, *Dictionary of Irish artists: 20th century* (1996) • *Irish women artists: from the eighteenth century to the present day* (1987) [exhibition catalogue, NG Ire., the Douglas Hyde Gallery, TCD, and the Hugh Lane Municipal Gallery of Modern Art, Dublin, July–Aug 1987] • *Irish Independent* (15 May 1999) [on prices for Barton's paintings]
Archives priv. coll., sketchbooks and some letters

Barton, Sir Sidney (1876–1946), diplomatist, was born at Devonshire Place, Union Road, Exeter, on 26 November 1876, the youngest son in a family of four sons and four daughters of James Barton (1834–1919), captain in the Royal Artillery, and his wife, Mary Barbara (*d.* 1929), youngest of four daughters of Sir David William Barclay, tenth baronet, of Pierston, Ayrshire, and his first wife, Lise Josephe de Rune, youngest daughter of Charles Malo de Rune, of Mauritius. James Barton had resigned his army commission on becoming a member of the Plymouth Brethren during the wave of religious feeling that swept Britain after the Crimean War and from him Barton inherited the religious feeling that dominated his life.

Barton was a foundation scholar of St Paul's School but there was no question of his proceeding to higher education since his father, who had 'peculiar views on education … objected to universities' (*The Times*, 22 Jan 1946). Instead, in September 1895, Barton went straight from school to Peking (Beijing) as a student interpreter in the consular service. The Boxer uprising found him absent on special service at Weihaiwei, but he contrived, as ever, to reach the centre of things by joining as interpreter and then assistant political officer the China field force which stormed Tientsin (Tianjin) and subsequently took part in the relief of the legations. For his services he was awarded the China medal with clasp and was mentioned in dispatches.

Barton passed with distinction through the various grades in the consular service and in November 1910 was called to the bar by the Middle Temple. In May the following year he was promoted to the responsible post of Chinese secretary in Peking and in March 1922 he became consul-general in Shanghai, a post which at that time came next to New York in importance. He was able to render most valuable services to British interests which he defended to the limits of his great vitality and nervous energy. This naturally made him very popular with the British community, while he was respected but cordially disliked by the Chinese officials with whom he had to deal. Although temperamentally inclined to forceful measures he was by no means a 'gunboat consul'. In a period when central government, indeed any government at all, had broken down, strong measures were frequently deemed necessary to protect British interests. Barton was never afraid to advocate such measures or to take them on his own responsibility, but he was careful not to overstep the line between the defensive and the aggressive. His qualities of strength, resourcefulness, courage, and good temper under strain were exactly right in the circumstances of the time and he played a leading part in keeping alive British trade and influence through long years of storms.

In May 1929 Barton was promoted to the diplomatic rank of British minister in Addis Ababa. His methods were characteristically blunt and he proved himself, as in China, to be quite fearless and at his best in dangerous situations. He won the confidence of the emperor to an exceptional degree and was making a great success of his post when Italy invaded Abyssinia (Ethiopia) in 1935. He was horrified and deeply upset that the League of Nations and Britain in particular did not take a tougher line to prevent 'an international crime' (telegram, 18 Feb 1935, PRO, FO 371/20166 J643/1/1). He also spoke forcefully of Italy's 'criminal frightfulness' in using mustard gas and inflicting 'appalling' suffering on the Ethiopian people (telegram, 20 March 1936, PRO, FO 371/20166 J2458/45/1). Meanwhile, with his usual energy he organized security for British and foreign nationals and made ready to receive refugees at the British legation. According to a contemporary source, Barton was distressed by the 'thinly disguised portrait' Evelyn Waugh had drawn of him and his daughter Esme in *Black Mischief* (written after Waugh attended the emperor's coronation in 1930 (W. F. Deedes,

Dear Bill: W. F. Deedes Reports, 1998, 32). He returned to England after Italy captured Addis Ababa in May 1936 and he retired in May 1937. He maintained his keen interest in Abyssinian affairs and was partly instrumental in securing the secret return of the emperor to his capital.

Barton was appointed CMG in 1913, KBE in 1926, KCVO in 1931, and GBE in 1936. On 23 July 1904 he married Mary Ethel Winifred (*d.* 1945), eldest daughter of Alexander Palmer MacEwen, a director of Jardine, Matheson & Co. She shared her husband's ideals and vigorously pursued complementary activities which were rewarded with appointment as an OBE in 1928 and, in 1937, a CBE (for welfare work in Addis Ababa). They had two sons and two daughters, one of whom married, in 1933, Baron Filippo Muzi Falconi, Italian minister at Sofia. His wife died in April 1945 and on 20 January 1946 Barton died of cancer of the lung and larynx, at his home, 19 Neville Street, South Kensington, London. He was survived by one son and two daughters. EDWARD CROWE, *rev.* LORNA LLOYD

Sources *DNB* · *The Times* (22 Jan 1946) · *WWW* · Burke, *Peerage* · W. N. Medlicott, D. Dakin, and M. E. Lambert, eds., *Documents on British foreign policy, 1919–1939*, 2nd ser., 14–16 (1976–7) · PRO, FO 371 J1 Abyssinia, 1935–6 · *FO List* (1935) · *FO List* (1938) · *FO List* (1947) · b. cert. · d. cert. · *CGPLA Eng. & Wales* (1946)
Archives SOUND BL NSA, documentary recording
Likenesses W. Stoneman, photograph, 1939, NPG · photograph, repro. in *The Times*
Wealth at death £4726 7s. 3d.: probate, 1 May 1946, *CGPLA Eng. & Wales*

Barton, Thomas (1599/1600–1682), Church of England clergyman, of unknown parentage, was a resident of Kent when, on 21 June 1616 at the age of sixteen, he matriculated from Magdalen Hall, Oxford. He graduated BA on 27 January 1619, proceeding MA on 12 June 1621. He was ordained deacon on 23 September 1621 by Bishop Buckeridge of Rochester, and priest on 19 September 1624 by Bishop Carleton of Chichester. It was presumably in the early 1620s that he married Benedict Dobell (*bap.* 1607): in 1624 her father, Walter Dobell of Streat Place, Sussex, presented him to the rectory of Streat. He resigned this living within two years and on 25 April 1626, also on Dobell's presentation, he was instituted as rector of another Sussex parish, Westmeston. On 20 November 1629 he was presented by Charles I to the rectory of Eynesbury, Huntingdonshire, a living served consistently by its vicar, Edmund Marmion, from 1615 to 1644. In 1629 Barton was involved in a suit in chancery about his wife's dowry. On 23 March 1633 Barton buried a daughter, Mary, at Westmeston.

In 1642 Barton went into print to defend the practice of bowing at the name of Jesus, against the objections of a neighbouring minister, Mascal Gyles, vicar of Ditchling. The two men may be seen as clerical exemplars of royalist / Anglican and parliamentarian / puritan outlooks. Barton's *Antiteixisma, or, A Counterscarfe*, was written against Gyles in August 1642 in response to a request from Barton's brother-in-law, Walter Dobell the younger. His opening epistle to Charles I stressed that 'no clouds of horror shall frighten my obedience before God and the King' and recognized 'your majesties supremacy, next under Christ', and the writer signed himself 'Most loyal to Your majesty and obedient to the church' (sig. A2). His distaste for parliamentarian puritanism is reflected in references to 'confessor Prynne' and 'father Burton' in a second contribution to the controversy (Barton, *Tryall*, 7). Barton later claimed to have been sequestrated in 1642, but on 2 June 1643, when Barton was 'yet rector of Westmeston in Sussex', he signed *A Sermon of the Christian Race*, preached before the king at Oxford on 9 May, a work dedicated to Thomas Covert, lieutenant-colonel of horse at the royal headquarters. After the Restoration it was claimed that Barton had been chaplain to Prince Rupert throughout the war. He was certainly an active royalist, and complained of his unpopularity as a result. He was 'despised … for his fidelity to the king, and obedience to the church' by most of his countrymen, 'misled, and therefore disaffected to the royal cause' (Barton, *Sermon*, 24).

On 25 July 1646 the Wiltshire county committee was told that about Christmas 1644 Barton came to West Tytherley, Hampshire, and demanded the tithes. When it was objected that parishioners had paid already to a Mr Langley, he responded 'that there was a proclamation to forbid them to pay their tythes to [Langley] for that he was a rebel' (*Walker rev.*). 'Not long after there came a party of souldiers in his name and did fetch away five of the parish, whereof this deponent was one, and carried them to Winchester, and kept them prisoners till they had paid £25' (ibid.) in lieu of the tithes. On 13 April 1647 the committee for plundered ministers granted a fifth of the tithes of Westmeston to Barton's children. Barton himself appears to have gone to London, but remained firmly royalist. In the preface to his *King David's Church-Prayer*, the published version of a sermon preached at St Margaret Pattens on 24 June 1649, he called on God to 'destroy the brain sick monster, subdue the rebels, and return the deceived people obedient subjects'. Even more notably he explicitly urged allegiance to Charles II, newly proclaimed in Edinburgh, praying for the prince's welfare and that of other members of the royal family in exile or captivity.

On 25 August 1660 Barton was restored to his rectory of Westmeston. On 21 March 1663 he was created DD at Oxford by virtue of a letter from the earl of Clarendon, chancellor of the university. He was buried at Westmeston on 25 March 1682. STEPHEN WRIGHT

Sources *Walker rev.* · W. Renshaw, 'Some clergy of the archdeaconry of Lewes and South Malling deanery', *Sussex Archaeological Collections*, 55 (1912), 220–77 · Foster, *Alum. Oxon.* · J. Rix, note, *N&Q*, 4th ser., 1 (1868) · Wood, *Ath. Oxon.: Fasti* (1820) · G. Hennessy, *Chichester diocese clergy lists* (1900) · *CSP dom.*, 1629 · T. Barton, *A tryall of the counter-scarfe* (1643) · J. Comber, *Sussex genealogies: Lewes centre* (1933) · T. Barton, *A sermon of the Christian race, preached before his Majesty at Christ Church in Oxford, 9 May 1643* · T. Barton, *King David's church-prayer; set forth in a sermon preached at S. Margaret Pattens, alias Rood-Church, London, on St John Baptists day in the afternoon, being Sunday 24 June 1649* · *Calamy rev.*

Barton, Thomas (1729/30–1780), missionary and Church of England clergyman, was born in Ireland, descended from an English family that settled there in the reign of Charles I. After graduating at Dublin University he emigrated to America, and in 1751 opened a school at Norriston, Pennsylvania. He was a tutor at the academy (now university) at Philadelphia. In 1753 he married Esther Rittenhouse, the daughter of a neighbouring farmer, and sister of David Rittenhouse, the distinguished mathematician, astronomer, and president of the American Philosophical Society, whose close friendship Barton enjoyed until his death. Thomas and Esther had at least two children: William Barton, the biographer of David Rittenhouse, and Benjamin Smith Barton, the American physician and naturalist.

In 1754 Barton went to England, where he received episcopal orders. He returned to America as a missionary of the Society for the Propagation of the Gospel in Foreign Parts, with which he remained connected until 1759. In July 1755 he accompanied, as chaplain, the expedition to remove the French from Fort Duquesne (later Pittsburgh), which ended in the defeat and death of the expedition's leader, General Edward Braddock. On leaving York county, Pennsylvania, Barton settled at Lancaster as rector of St James's Church. He remained there for nearly twenty years, dividing his time between the duties of his office and the pursuit of natural history. During the American War of Independence he remained loyal to Britain and was compelled to quit his post. He moved to New York where he died on 25 May 1780, aged fifty. His wife survived him.   A. R. BUCKLAND, *rev.* TROY O. BICKHAM

Sources W. Barton, *Memoirs of the life of David Rittenhouse* (1813)

Barton [Berton], **William** (*d.* after **1382**), theologian and university principal, originated in the diocese of Canterbury, and must have read the arts course at Oxford in the early 1350s. First recorded in 1356 as a fellow of Merton College, he vacated his fellowship in 1361, although he acted as a feoffee for the college as late as 1380. He was bachelor of theology by 1376 and doctor by 1380. He was admitted rector of Lanteglos by Camelford, Cornwall, on 18 February 1360, but evidently failed, in spite of a recommendation on Oxford's roll for papal graces in 1362, to be provided to a canonry and prebend in the collegiate church of Wingham, Kent, which he was enabled to hold in plurality with Lanteglos. From 1372 he held a succession of livings in Heckfield and Houghton, Hampshire, and Cooling, Kent, to the last of which he was admitted in February 1382.

During this time Barton probably resided at Oxford, where he exercised numerous responsibilities, representing the theology faculty in a dispute with the law faculties in 1376, and before 1379, according to John Wyclif (*d.* 1384), forcing a Franciscan friar who had preached on the poverty of the primitive church to recant; presumably Barton was acting as a commissary of the chancellor. He was elected chancellor probably in Michaelmas term 1379, and held office until Whitsuntide (2 June) 1381. He was one of the commissioners appointed by the crown to inquire into the dissensions at Queen's College on 7 February 1380. But much of his energy was taken up in refuting and finally condemning the opinions of John Wyclif, his former colleague as a fellow of Merton, on ecclesiastical property and the eucharist. According to Wyclif, who described him as one whom he had believed a special

friend and conspicuous defender of Catholic truth, Barton had argued in a determination in several parts that Wyclif's views were heretical, and had made a protestation to Rome about them. This work, which is not extant, is known only from Wyclif's riposte in *De veritate sacrae scripturae*, where he is not named; but the author's identity is given in a marginal note in the Peterhouse manuscript of Wyclif's tract (Cambridge, MS Peterhouse 223, fol. 230*r*). On becoming chancellor Barton convoked a body of doctors to examine Wyclif's writings, evidently in 1380 or 1381; this body condemned Wyclif's views (though it did not name him) on the eucharist and the civil dominion of the clergy, but evidently only by a small majority. Its conclusions were challenged by Wyclif in a public lecture, his *Confessio*, on 10 May 1381. Barton was present at the Canterbury session of the Blackfriars Council in which the English hierarchy definitively condemned Lollard doctrine on 1 July 1382, but is not mentioned thereafter.

Three tracts, determinations against Wyclif, articles against him, and a work on his condemnation, are mentioned by Bale without incipit. These entries are probably deduced from Wyclif's writings and proceedings against him; none are extant.   JEREMY CATTO

Sources Merton College records, Merton Oxf., 291, 360, 370, 374, 428, 3690–3691, 3694–3695, *Catalogus vetus*, 8 • Peterhouse, Cambridge, MS 223, fol. 230 • F. C. Hingeston-Randolph, ed., *The register of Thomas de Brantyngham, bishop of Exeter*, 2 vols. (1901–6), vol. 1, p. 21 • T. F. Kirby, ed., *Wykeham's register*, 1, Hampshire RS, 11 (1896), 43, 123, 126 • J. R. Magrath, *The Queen's College*, 1 (1921), 110 • *CPR, 1374–7*, 291 • *CClR, 1377–81*, 493 • *Snappe's formulary and other records*, ed. H. E. Salter, OHS, 80 (1924), 331 • J. Wyclif, *De veritate sacrae scripturae*, ed. R. Buddensieg, 1 (1905), 345 • Bale, *Cat.*, 1.500–01 • J. A. Robson, *Wyclif and the Oxford schools* (1961), 223 • Emden, *Oxf.*, 1.123–4 • J. I. Catto, 'Wyclif and Wycliffism at Oxford, 1356–1430', *Hist. U. Oxf.* 2: *Late med. Oxf.*, 175–261

Barton, William (**1597/8–1678**), translator and hymnologist, matriculated as a sizar at Trinity College, Cambridge, in Lent 1619; he graduated BA in 1622 and proceeded MA in 1625. He was ordained priest on 21 September 1623. He is probably to be identified with the William Barton who was vicar of Mayfield, Staffordshire, at the opening of the civil wars, and who is described in a certificate presented to the House of Lords on 19 June 1643 as 'a man of godly life, and able and orthodox in his ministry', and as 'having been forced to desert his flock and family by the plundering cavaliers of Staffordshire' (*Fifth Report*, HMC, 92). Barton became minister of St John Zachary, London, in 1646; from 1656, he served as vicar of St Martin's, Leicester, probably until his death.

Barton's verse-translation of the Psalms was first published in 1644; it was reprinted and altered in 1645, 1646, 1651, 1654, and later. The text having been revised for 'the last time' by its author, it was posthumously republished in 1682. In the preface, Barton says: 'I have (in this my last Translation) corrected all the harsh passages, and added a great number of second Metres'. He continues:

> The *Scots* of late have put forth a Psalm-Book, most what Composed out of mine and Mr. *Rous* his, but it did not give full satisfaction, for somebody hath been at Charge to put forth a new Edition of mine, and printed some Thousands of

mine, in *Holland*, as it is reported. But whether they were Printed there or no, I am in doubt, for I am sure that *1,500* of my Books were heretofore Printed by stealth in *England* and carried over into Ireland. (Barton, *The Book of Psalms in Metre*, 1691, sig. A5r)

In 1655 he had prepared the way for his enlarged and improved Psalms by publishing *A view of the many errors and som gross absurdities in the old translations of the Psalms in English metre*. In 1659 he published *A Century of Select Hymns*, which was enlarged in 1668 to *Four Centuries*, and in 1688 to *Six Centuries*, the last being edited by his son, Edward Barton, minister of Welford in Northamptonshire. The *Four Centuries* open with Justin Martyr on the use and excellency of spiritual songs, followed by Barton's letter to 'Reverend and Religious Ministers of England', 'especially in and about the City of London': 'These Hymns are plainer than Psalms and more suitable to our condition' (sigs. A3r, A4r). The first hymn is a good example of Barton's simple, forthright style:

> Now *Babylon* is fallen and sunk
> that City great in state:
> Because she made the Nations drunk
> with wine adulterate.
> (p. 1)

Hymn 31 returns to the drunkard's calamities:

> Strange women shall thine eyes behold,
> strange words thou shalt rehearse,
> and lust shall make thy heart full bold,
> to utter things perverse.
> (p. 142)

Barton's *Centuries* were dedicated to Sir Matthew Hale. His work prompted Richard Baxter to suggest that Barton should specially translate and versify the Te Deum.

Barton died in May 1678, aged eighty.

A. B. GROSART, *rev.* D. K. MONEY

Sources Venn, *Alum. Cant.* · Wing, *STC* · *Fifth report*, HMC, 4 (1876), 92 · private information (1885) [W. T. Brooke]

Bartram, John (1699–1777), botanist and explorer in America, was born on 23 May 1699 on a farm at Marple, Pennsylvania, near Darby, the elder of two sons of William Bartram (*d.* 1711), farmer, and his first wife, Elizabeth (*d.* 1701), daughter of James Chambers Hunt and his wife, Elizabeth. His parents were Quakers, and his father had emigrated as a child in 1681 with his parents from Derbyshire. John received a limited education in the Darby Quaker school for about four years. After remarrying in 1707, Bartram's father took his second wife and their children in 1711 to live in eastern North Carolina, where he died in an American Indian attack. John and his brother James had been left behind in Pennsylvania with his grandmother. John's un-Quaker-like hostility toward American Indians might have arisen because of his father's fate.

On 25 April 1723 Bartram married Mary Maris (*d.* 1727), a Quaker. Bartram's grandmother died on 14 July 1723 and he inherited her 200 acre farm at Kingsessing, near Philadelphia, with buildings, livestock, orchards, equipment, and almost £100. In 1728 he bought additional land. He and Mary had two sons, one of whom died at the age of

four. After Mary's death, he married on 10 October 1729 Ann Mendenhall (1696/7–1784). With his own hands he built their stone house. They had five sons and four daughters. His sons Isaac and Moses became apothecaries, John inherited the farm, and William *Bartram (1739–1823) followed in his father's footsteps as botanical explorer and author.

As a child Bartram was interested in science, and by the age of twelve he focused on medical botany. While a farmer he developed America's first botanical garden. He became acquainted with Joseph Breintnell in Philadelphia, whose hobby was making ink impressions of leaves. Bartram helped him collect and identify them. Breintnall sent a set of leaf impressions to his London correspondent, Peter Collinson, a fellow Quaker and leading figure in the Royal Society. However, Collinson was interested in more than leaves. He wanted to locate an American who would collect live plants or seeds for him, and Breintnall recommended Bartram. They began corresponding in 1733, and they exchanged several letters per year until Collinson died in 1768. They were the best of friends, but never met, as neither ever travelled abroad.

In exchange for botanical specimens and letters Collinson sent Bartram books, advice, and various other kinds of assistance, including introductions to other British collectors and American naturalists. Collinson published seven of Bartram's letters in the *Philosophical Transactions of the Royal Society* between 1734 and 1757, six being zoological observations and the seventh on the aurora borealis seen in Philadelphia. Collinson also published another of Bartram's letters, on plant experiments, in the *Gentleman's Magazine* of September 1755.

As Bartram's acquaintances increased, he began making botanical journeys to different parts of British America, supported by British patrons and sometimes staying with other American naturalists. In 1736 he journeyed to the sources of the Schuylkill River in Pennsylvania; and in 1738 he travelled for five weeks in Virginia, including into the Blue Ridge Mountains, covering 1000 miles and spending only one night in each town. He also made shorter trips into the pine barrens of New Jersey, the cedar swamps of Delaware, and the Catskill Mountains of New York state. In 1742 Benjamin Franklin and some other Philadelphians solicited subscriptions to enable Bartram to collect plants full time. However, James Logan, a powerful Quaker in Pennsylvania politics and agent of the Penns, who on other occasions was a helpful patron to Bartram, opposed the project and it failed. In 1743 Bartram accompanied Conrad Weiser, Indian agent, and Lewis Evans, cartographer, on an expedition into Iroquois lands. Weiser's protection allowed them to penetrate much further west than earlier travellers and provided Bartram with much new material for observation and collection. They left Philadelphia on 3 July and Bartram returned to his farm on 19 August. He kept a journal on 'the inhabitants, climate, soil, rivers, productions, and other matters worthy of notice', which Collinson published in London in 1751. Bartram's handwriting was unclear and the publisher was careless; the published version contains misspelt names and other errors. In September 1753 he returned to the Catskills, this time taking his son William (Billy), aged fourteen. He was the one child who fully shared his father's enthusiasms for nature and exploration. Billy added a new dimension to these trips with drawings of plants, animals, and scenes they encountered. Two years later Bartram also took Billy on a trip to Connecticut. The Seven Years' War inhibited travel for several years, but in the spring of 1761 he sailed alone to Charles Town (Charleston), where he visited Dr Alexander Garden and collected South Carolina plants. On the return voyage he was able to stop and visit relatives near Wilmington, North Carolina. In autumn 1761 he decided it was safe to visit western Pennsylvania. In spring 1765 Collinson had Bartram appointed botanist to George III, with an annual stipend of £50. This enabled him to plan a collecting trip with Billy through the Carolinas, Georgia, and Florida, lasting from July 1765 until April 1766. It was his longest and last journey, a daring wilderness exploration at the age of sixty-six, and he contracted malaria. He kept a lengthy journal that was partially published in 1767 and completely in 1942.

Bartram was a close observer and an independent thinker. In 1739 he suggested organizing a society for the study of nature and arts, and in 1743 Benjamin Franklin organized the American Philosophical Society, which lasted a few years. Bartram was a founder member both then and when it was revived in 1769. Although loyal to his Quaker congregation, he was critical of Quaker ideas on pacifism and on the divinity of Jesus. The Society of Friends disowned him in 1757; yet he continued attending Quaker meetings and was buried in the Darby Friends burial-ground. In 1770 he carved above a window of his house his belief: ''Tis God alone, Almighty Lord, The Holy One, by me ador'd.'

Bartram's achievements were widely recognized not only by prominent British and American naturalists but also by his election in 1769 to the Swedish Vetenskaps-akademien (Royal Academy of Sciences). (He had provided much assistance to the Swedish naturalist Peter Kalm on his visit to North America between 1749 and 1751.) In 1772 he received a gold medal from the Society of Gentlemen in Edinburgh. A number of the items he collected and sent to his associates in the Royal Society, including several American Indian artefacts, can still be seen at the British Museum. He died at his home, Kingsessing Farm, on 22 September 1777.   FRANK N. EGERTON

Sources E. Berkeley and D. S. Berkeley, *The life and travels of John Bartram: from Lake Ontario to the River St John* (1982) · *The correspondence of John Bartram, 1734–1777*, ed. E. Berkeley and D. S. Berkeley (1992) · T. P. Slaughter, *The natures of John and William Bartram* (1996) · J. Bartram, *Diary of a journey through the Carolinas, Georgia, and Florida from July 1, 1765, to April 10, 1766*, ed. F. Harper (1942) · J. Bartram, *Observations on the inhabitants, climate, soil, rivers, productions, animals, and other matters … from Pennsylvania to Lake Ontario* (1751) · R. P. Stearns, *Science in the British colonies of America* (1970) · *Chain of friendship: selected letters of Dr. John Fothergill of London, 1735–1780*, ed. B. C. Corner and C. C. Booth (1971) · W. Bartram, 'Some account of the late Mr John Bartram, of Pennsylvania', in 'John and William Bartram's America', ed. H. G. Cruickshank (1957) [repr. in *John and William Bartram's America: selections from the writings of the Philadelphia naturalists*, ed. H. G. Cruickshank (1957), 21–7] · J. Ewan, introduction, in W. Darlington, *Memorials of John Bartram and Humphry Marshall*, facs. edn (1967), v–lii · R. M. Cutting, ed., *John and William Bartram, William Byrd II, and St John de Crevecoeur: a reference guide* (1976)

Archives Academy of Natural Sciences, Philadelphia, papers · American Philosophical Society, Philadelphia, collections · Hist. Soc. Penn., papers, etc. · NHM, lists of plants | NHM, letters to John Fothergill · RS, letters to Royal Society

Wealth at death left a prosperous farm and a library

Bartram, William (1739–1823), botanist and ornithologist, was born on 9 April 1739 at Kingsessing, Pennsylvania, the third son of naturalist John *Bartram (1699–1777) and his second wife, Ann Mendenhall (1696/7–1784), both Quakers. William's great-grandfather had moved from Derbyshire to America in the early 1680s. William's formal education included Latin and French studies from 1752 to 1755 at the Academy of Philadelphia, later known as the University of Pennsylvania. His early talent for botany and drawing was encouraged by his father, although the family hoped that he would eventually pursue a practical career, such as medicine, engraving, or surveying. During Bartram's years at the Academy of Philadelphia his father took him on botanical trips to Connecticut and to the Catskill Mountains and further promoted his natural history interests by allowing him to work on natural history illustrations on Saturdays and Sundays, instead of attending Quaker meetings. As early as 1756 Bartram was sending his drawings to George Edwards, librarian of the Royal College of Physicians and a leading British ornithologist, who incorporated them and Bartram's descriptions of Pennsylvania birds into the *Gleanings of Natural History* (1758–64). Bartram also sent preserved bird specimens to Edwards and provided illustrations of oaks to Johann F. Gronovius in the Netherlands. Other material was sent to the Bartrams' London correspondent, Peter Collinson, a Quaker merchant, who had two of William's turtle drawings printed in the *Gentleman's Magazine* in 1758. Bartram was apprenticed to a Pennsylvania merchant in 1757 and subsequently moved in 1761 to the Cape Fear River area of North Carolina, where his uncle, Colonel William Bartram, owned a large plantation at Ashwood. There Bartram opened a trading store, the first in a series of business ventures that all ended in failure. During his initial sojourn on the Cape Fear he spent much of his time exploring eastern North Carolina and drawing the flora and fauna of the region, activities that probably contributed to the failure of his business.

In 1765 and 1766 Bartram accompanied his father, recently appointed royal botanist to George III, through coastal South Carolina, Georgia, and East Florida, the experience gained forming the basis for his subsequent travels through the region. At the conclusion of their trip the younger Bartram remained in Florida, where he tried to establish a rice and indigo plantation in a remote area along the St Johns River. After the failure of this venture he returned to Pennsylvania, where from 1767 to 1770 he engaged in agriculture and a mercantile business while continuing to pursue his natural history interests. In 1768 Collinson obtained commissions for William Bartram to draw molluscs for the duchess of Portland and turtles and molluscs for John Fothergill, a London Quaker physician who became the Bartrams' patron following Collinson's death. Bartram's talent was recognized by his election in 1768 as a corresponding member of the American Society for Promoting Useful Knowledge and in 1769 as a member of the American Philosophical Society. By 1770 he had again suffered business failures, leaving him almost bankrupt. Largely to escape his debtors, he fled precipitously to Ashwood, where he resumed his natural history exploration and sent more drawings to Fothergill.

In October 1772 Fothergill offered financial support for Bartram to collect plants and seeds suitable for introduction into England and to provide illustrations of birds, reptiles, insects, and plants from North America. Fothergill wished him to explore Canada in order to obtain species most likely to endure the English climate, but Bartram insisted on a trip through the American south-east, and from 1773 to 1778 he journeyed through North and South Carolina, Georgia, Florida, Alabama, Louisiana, and portions of the lower Mississippi river valley. Often travelling alone through remote wilderness areas, he made extensive notes on the flora, fauna, geography, geology, weather, and Native Americans of the region and sent plant specimens, drawings, and two manuscript volumes of the trip to Fothergill.

Upon returning to the family home at Kingsessing in January 1778, Bartram began work on an account of his discoveries and observations. By 1786 a prospectus announced the forthcoming volume, but publication was delayed in part due to the disruptive effects of the American War of Independence and to a severe leg fracture that he suffered about 1787. Bartram's *Travels through North & South Carolina, Georgia, East & West Florida* was published in Philadelphia late in 1791 or early 1792, with reprints and editions following quickly in London (1792, 1794), Dublin (1793), Vienna (1793), Berlin (1793), the Netherlands (1794), and Paris (1799). This classic of American writing established his reputation both as a literary figure and as a naturalist, but the publication delays cost him priority recognition for describing species he had discovered in the 1760s and 1770s; in the interval many had been published, in Humphry Marshall's *Arbustum Americanum* (1785), Thomas Walter's *Flora Caroliniana* (1788), William Aiton's *Hortus Kewensis* (1789), Jean Baptiste Lamarck's *Encyclopédie methodique* (1783–97), Charles Louis l'Heritier's *Stirpes novae* (1785–91), and Johann Friedrich Gmelin's *Systema naturae* (1788–93). Bartram used more than 350 Latin binomial names for plants, of which more than 120 represented new scientific names, but his terminology has not been generally accepted by botanists. The *Travels* also presented considerable zoological material, particularly in ornithology, where some 215 species of American birds were listed, along with information on migration dates and behaviour for many species. Witmer Stone described the book as a 'landmark in the progress of American ornithology'

(Stone, 21), but unfortunately Bartram apparently never saw its proof sheets so that a number of uncorrected typographical errors and inconsistencies became the target of critics and detractors. Beyond its scientific importance, the *Travels* exerted a profound influence on travel literature and on the Romantic movement: Fagin described the work as 'the first genuine and artistic interpretation of the American landscape' (Fagin, 10). Its florid, luxuriant style and vivid imagery caught the attention of Samuel Taylor Coleridge, William Wordsworth, and François-August Chateaubriand, who extracted portions into their notebooks. Figures and images from the *Travels* are readily recognized in Wordsworth's *Ruth*, in Coleridge's 'Kubla Khan' and 'Rime of the Ancient Mariner', and in Chateaubriand's *Atala* and *Les Natchez*. Other writers, such as Robert Southey and Henry David Thoreau, read and quoted extensively from the book.

In the years following publication of the *Travels* Bartram remained one of the central figures in American natural history, both through the data he provided to various authors and by his influence and support for other naturalists. Teachers from the University of Pennsylvania, including Benjamin Smith Barton, often took their botany and natural history students to the garden, which provided access to an extensive collection of American plants and to Bartram's expertise and tutelage. As a mentor Bartram strongly influenced the careers of Thomas Nuttall, botanist and ornithologist, and of Thomas Say, who was later known as the 'father of American entomology'. In 1802 the Philadelphia artists Charles Willson Peale and Rubens Peale introduced Bartram to Alexander Wilson, a Scottish emigrant who, under Bartram's guidance and support, produced the *American Ornithology* (1808–13), a landmark document in the development of an independent scientific community in the United States.

Bartram provided material on reptiles to François Marie Daudin for the *Histoire naturelle générale des reptiles* (1801–4), and Thomas Pennant quoted both John and William Bartram for information on North American mammals in the *Arctic Zoology* (1784–7). Although most authors who relied on Bartram readily acknowledged their source, others, including Barton, took advantage of their relationship with him by not properly crediting his contributions. Bartram's considerable knowledge of Creek and Cherokee Indian culture and linguistics was particularly important to Barton's *New Views of the Origin of the Tribes and Nations of America* (1797), and Bartram was a key contributor to Barton's *Fragments of the Natural History of Pennsylvania* (1799), especially in the field of ornithology. Bartram drew most of the thirty plant illustrations for Barton's *Elements of Botany* (1803) and a few of Bartram's papers were published in Barton's *Philadelphia Medical and Physical Journal*.

Bartram was described by his contemporaries as modest, simple, pious, genial, and idealistic, but he was also a tough and courageous explorer, hardened by years of solitary travel in the wilderness. A Quaker deist, Bartram expounded the belief that all nature revealed the perfection of the creator. His intense curiosity and eclectic interests spanned an array of subjects, and his writing typically exemplified a distinctive blend of careful science with romantic prose. He never married. Physically and mentally active until the end, he died suddenly at his home at Kingsessing on 22 July 1823.

MARCUS B. SIMPSON JUN.

Sources F. Harper, *The travels of William Bartram* (1958) · N. B. Fagin, *William Bartram: interpreter of the American landscape* (1933) · E. Berkeley and D. S. Berkeley, *The correspondence of John Bartram* (1992) · J. L. Lowes, *The road to Xanadu* (1927) · W. Darlington, *Memorials of John Bartram and Humphry Marshall: with notices of their botanical contemporaries* (1849) · *William Bartram: botanical and zoological drawings, 1756–1788*, ed. J. Ewan (1968) · E. Earnest, *John and William Bartram: botanists and explorers* (1940) · T. P. Slaughter, *The natures of John and William Bartram* (1996) · T. P. Slaughter, *William Bartram: travels and other writings* (1996) · E. O. Merrill, *Bartonia*, 23 (1944–5), 10–35 · W. Stone, *Bartonia*, 12 (1932), 20–32 · E. Coues, *Proceedings of the Academy of Natural Sciences of Philadelphia*, 27 (1875), 338–58

Archives Harvard U., Arnold Arboretum, MSS · Hist. Soc. Penn., John and William Bartram MSS · NHM, papers relating to travels in southern United States | Boston PL, Benjamin Smith Barton MSS · NHM, department of botany, John Fothergill collection

Likenesses C. W. Peale, oils, 1808, Independence National Historic Park, Philadelphia, Pennsylvania

Barttelot, Edmund Musgrave (1859–1888), army officer, was born on 28 March 1859 at Hilliers, near Petworth, Sussex, the second son of Sir Walter *Barttelot, first baronet (1820–1893), Conservative MP, and his wife, Harriet (*d.* July 1863), fourth daughter of the Revd Sir Christopher Musgrave, ninth baronet, of Edenhall, Cumberland. He was educated at Rugby School and the Royal Military College, Sandhurst. Barttelot was commissioned second-lieutenant in the 7th fusiliers on 22 January 1879, joining the 2nd battalion. He served in the Second Anglo-Afghan War, including the defence of Kandahar (lieutenant, Royal Fusiliers, January 1881). On his return to England in 1882, he volunteered for the Egyptian expedition and became adjutant of the mounted infantry, serving at Qassasin and Tell al-Kebir. He returned home in October 1882, but joined the reconstituted, British officered Egyptian army in February 1883, serving as staff officer at Suakin. He was on special service, mainly transport duties, during the Gordon relief expedition (1884–5). He was mentioned in dispatches and received a brevet majority in September 1886, when he was promoted captain.

Barttelot came home on leave in the autumn of 1886, but in January 1887 received a year's extension in order to join the expedition to be led by Henry Morton Stanley in relief of Emin Pasha, an Austrian doctor who had become Gordon's governor of Equatoria in the southern Sudan. Emin had been isolated by the fall of Khartoum, and the expedition was mounted as a private commercial venture by the Imperial British East Africa Company acting through the Emin Pasha Relief Committee. Barttelot was one of seven successful applicants and was intended to command sixty-one Sudanese soldiers recruited for the expedition. He joined the expedition at Aden in February 1887, reaching Yambuya in June by way of Zanzibar, the Cape, and the Congo.

Tensions arose between Stanley and Barttelot, and he was left at Yambuya to command the rear column while Stanley pushed ahead to meet Emin. Contact was lost with

Edmund Musgrave Barttelot (1859–1888), by unknown engraver, pubd 1890

Stanley, and Barttelot found it increasingly difficult to supply his force without resorting to coercion of the local population. Morale was affected by disease and by Barttelot's authoritarian manner, which alienated both his white subordinates and carriers recruited from Zanzibaris and the local Manyema. Barttelot regarded Africans with contempt, and maintained discipline by flogging and execution. Barttelot also failed to persuade Tippu Tip, an influential Arab slave dealer engaged by Stanley for the purpose, to provide more carriers. In June 1888 Barttelot set out to find Stanley, but many carriers deserted. Barttelot returned to negotiate with Tippu Tip, rejoining his party at Banalya on 17 July. The highly strung Barttelot had suffered repeated bouts of fever, leaving him suspicious of others and, conceivably, temporarily unbalanced. Barttelot's arrival at Banalya coincided with a noisy Manyema celebration, which exasperated him. On the morning of 19 July 1888 he went to remonstrate with a woman beating a drum. In the act of striking her, he was shot through the head by her husband. He was buried at Banalya on the same day.

When he finally returned from locating Emin, Stanley found the rear column in disarray. Subsequently, Stanley rejoined Emin and marched to the east coast, making various discoveries *en route*. All was overshadowed, however, by the controversy over the rear column ignited by Stanley's account, which blamed Barttelot. Memorials were erected to Barttelot in Stopham and Storrington churches and at Sandhurst.

IAN F. W. BECKETT

Sources I. R. Smith, *The Emin Pasha relief expedition, 1886–1890* (1972) · T. Gould, *In limbo: the story of Stanley's rear column* (1979) · W. G. Barttelot, *The life of Edmund Musgrave Barttelot, captain and brevet major, royal fusiliers, commander of the rear column of the Emin Pasha relief expedition, being an account of his services for the relief of Kandahar, of Gordon, and of Emin* (1890) · J. M. Jadot, 'Edmund Barttelot, 1859–1888', in *Biographie coloniale belge*, Académie Royale des Sciences Coloniales, 5 (1958), 37–42 · H. M. Stanley, *In darkest Africa*, 2 vols. (1890) · J. R. Troup, *With Stanley's rear column* (1890) · H. Ward, *My life with Stanley's rear column* (1891) · J. S. Jameson, *The story of the rear column of the Emin Pasha relief expedition*, ed. Mrs J. S. Jameson (1890) · J. R. Werner, *A visit to Stanley's rear guard* (1889) · T. Pakenham, *The scramble for Africa* (1991) · H. Keown-Boyd, *Soldiers of the*

Nile: a biographical history of the British officers of the Egyptian army, 1882–1925 (1996) • Boase, *Mod. Eng. biog.* • Burke, *Peerage* (1967)
Archives priv. coll. | SOAS, Mackinnon MSS, includes letters from the officers of the rear column, F.2
Likenesses engraving, pubd 1890, NPG [*see illus.*] • photographs, repro. in Barttelot, *Life of Edmund Musgrave Barttelot* • photographs, repro. in Jameson, *Story of the rear column* • photographs, repro. in Troup, *With Stanley's rear column* • photographs, repro. in Ward, *My life with Stanley's rear column*
Wealth at death £363 7s. 1d.: administration, 26 Nov 1888, CGPLA Eng. & Wales

Barttelot, Sir Walter Barttelot, first baronet (1820–1893), politician, born on 10 October 1820 at Richmond, Surrey, was the eldest son of George Barttelot (1788–1872), of Stopham House, Pulborough, Sussex, and his wife, Emma, youngest daughter of James Woodbridge of Richmond. The Barttelots were an old Sussex family. The father served with distinction in the Royal Horse Artillery during the Peninsular War.

Walter Barttelot was educated at Rugby School, and served in the 1st (Royal) Dragoons from 1839 to 1853, when he retired with the rank of captain. He was afterwards honorary colonel of the 2nd battalion the Royal Sussex regiment. From December 1860 to 1885 he was one of the Conservative members for West Sussex. Then he was returned for the newly constituted Horsham division, and held the seat until his death.

Barttelot was a frequent speaker in the House of Commons and became known as a specialist on the malt tax. He failed, despite Cobden's support, to amend Gladstone's 1864 budget so as to reduce the malt duty, but in May 1867 he obtained the appointment of a select committee to examine it, on which he served. He gradually came to be considered the chief spokesman of the agricultural interest in the house, while he also interested himself in church matters and military questions. In 1870 he moved the rejection of Osborne Morgan's Burials Bill, which he continued to oppose until it became law in 1880. In the same year he tried to lengthen the number of years' service under the new Army Enlistment Bill from three to five years. He was one of the most determined opponents of the Irish Land Bill of 1881, and he accepted with great misgivings the act carried in 1889 by his own party creating county councils. His last important parliamentary appearance was in June 1892, when he offered a searching criticism of the War Office in connection with the report of Lord Wantage's committee. 'There was not a more rigid conservative in the United Kingdom or a more generous opponent' was the verdict of the leading Liberal paper on his parliamentary career (*Daily News*, 3 Feb 1893). H. W. Lucy's view was that he 'is, perhaps, one of the most impressive speakers in the House of Commons, and it is a pity he has so little to say that is worth hearing' (Lucy, 145).

Barttelot was created a baronet by Disraeli in June 1875, was named a CB in 1880, and sworn of the privy council in 1892. He was twice married: first, in April 1852, to Harriet, fourth daughter and coheir of Sir Christopher Musgrave, baronet, of Edenhall, Cumberland (she died on 29 July 1863); and secondly, in April 1868, to Margaret, only child of Henry Boldero, of South Lodge, St Leonards (she died on 28 January 1893). With his first wife he had two sons and one daughter. The elder son, Sir Walter George Barttelot, second baronet (1855–1900), having formerly served in the 5th dragoon guards, was killed during the Second South African War at Retief's Nek, Orange Free State, on 23 July 1900, being then major in the 1st Devon yeomanry; the younger son was Edmund Musgrave *Barttelot. With his wife, Georgiana Mary (d. 6 Feb 1946), daughter of George Edmond Balfour of The Manor, Sidmouth, Sir Walter George Barttelot was father of Sir Walter Balfour Barttelot (1880–1918), his successor as baronet. Sir Walter Barttelot died at Stopham House on 2 February 1893, the day of his second wife's funeral.

G. LE G. NORGATE, *rev.* H. C. G. MATTHEW

Sources *The Times* (3 Feb 1893) • *Sussex Daily News* (3 Feb 1893) • H. W. Lucy, *Men and manner in parliament* (1919) • Burke, *Peerage*
Archives W. Sussex RO, Richard MSS • W. Sussex RO, letters to duke of Richmond
Likenesses Spy [L. Ward], lithograph, repro. in VF (1886), pl. 504
Wealth at death £105,227 5s. 4d.: probate, 29 March 1893, CGPLA Eng. & Wales

Barvitus. *See* Barinthus (*supp. fl.* 6th cent.).

Barwell [*née* Bacon], **Louisa Mary** (1800–1885), writer on education, was born in the parish of St Peter Mancroft, Norwich, on 4 March 1800, the eldest daughter of Richard Mackenzie *Bacon (1776–1844), journalist, inventor, and writer on music, and his wife, Jane Louisa, *née* Noverre (1768–1808). At the age of eighteen she was associated with her father in the editorship of the *Quarterly Musical Magazine and Review* (1818–30). She is said to have been a very talented musician with an exquisite voice and the ability to score-read.

After her marriage to John Barwell (1798–1876), a wine merchant in Norwich, Louisa devoted much of her time to the composition of educational works. She frequently contributed to the *Quarterly Journal of Education* (from about 1831) and the *New Monthly Magazine*, and pre-empted some of the later views and plans of education. Her writings on this subject, which relate music to general education, include *The Schoolmaster: Essays on Practical Education* (1836) and *Letters from Hofwyl by a Parent, on the Educational Institutions of Von Fellenberg* (1842). (The Barwells formed a close friendship with Von Fellenberg, in whose school at Hofwyl all their sons were placed.) One of her books for children, *Childhood's Hours* (1851), was used in the royal nursery by Queen Victoria's children, and her *Little Lessons for Little Learners* (1833) appeared in numerous editions. Her husband, who shared her interest in education, was largely responsible for securing the success of a scheme by which a charity day school for girls in Norwich was converted into an industrial training school for girls. Louisa Barwell's closest friend was perhaps Lady Byron, with whom she corresponded on a regular basis and whose papers she arranged in 1842. She survived her friend by nearly a quarter of a century, and died on 2 February 1885 at 33 Surrey Street, Norwich, leaving four sons and a daughter (also Louisa Mary).

ALEXANDER GORDON, *rev.* DAVID J. GOLBY

Sources J. C. Kassler, 'Bacon (2)', *New Grove* · *Norfolk News* (7 Feb 1885) · *The Times* (13 Feb 1885) · d. cert. · *CGPLA Eng. & Wales* (1885) · private information (1885)
Archives Bodl. Oxf., corresp. with Lady Byron, Lord and Lady Lovelace · Bodl. Oxf., Noel MSS · NL Scot., corresp. with George Combe
Wealth at death £1452 15s. 10d.: probate, 27 April 1885, *CGPLA Eng. & Wales*

Barwell, Richard (1741–1804), East India Company servant, was born in Calcutta on 8 October 1741, the second of the four sons of William Barwell (1705–1769), governor of Fort William, Bengal (1748–9), afterwards a director of the East India Company, and his third wife, Elizabeth Peirce (1722–1771). Barwell also had a half-brother and two half-sisters (one of whom died in infancy) from his father's second marriage. He went to Westminster School in January 1750 and was last listed in the records as a pupil in 1754. Strong family connections with the East India Company facilitated his nomination as a writer and he arrived back in Calcutta in 1758. He held a variety of junior appointments until in 1768 he was appointed second in council at Cossimbazar. From there he moved back to Calcutta in 1770 as military paymaster-general and mint-master with a seat on the council of Fort William. Retaining his place in council and edging up in seniority, he became chief at Patna in 1771 and at Dacca in 1773, where he accumulated a large part of his fortune.

Immense fortunes could be made by officials profiting from the privileged position occupied by the company in Bengal in the 1760s and early 1770s following Clive's assertion of British control of administration and of revenue collection. Barwell was energetic in forwarding his own interests. He engaged in corrupt dealings in timber and salt, and in multifarious financial transactions as principal and as agent. As his administrative experience expanded, so did his personal fortune. In February 1772 Warren Hastings returned to Calcutta as governor, appointed by the company to regenerate the failing administration and economy of Bengal. At first, Hastings took exception to Barwell's prolixity in council, but in time he came to appreciate his resourcefulness, while Barwell, for his part, came to acknowledge Hastings's patience and resolution.

In 1773 the government of Bengal was completely remodelled by the East India Regulating Act. Hastings was appointed governor-general and chaired a supreme council consisting of four councillors. Barwell's nomination as one of the councillors was unexpected. He had few friends or admirers in England. He could claim to his credit continuity with the previous council and a length of service in India, but little else. The other councillors, new to India, came out from London zealous to expose corruption. Barwell was the one councillor on whom Hastings could rely for steady support, but his was not a reassuring name with which to be linked. References in Barwell's correspondence and elsewhere illustrate his trust in the powers of bribery and the expense that he was prepared to incur to secure any object on which he had set his mind, whether public business, private business, or some amatory

Richard Barwell (1741–1804), by Sir Joshua Reynolds, 1780–81 [with his son Richard Barwell]

arrangement. He also gambled heavily, more often than not unsuccessfully.

In the early part of 1775 Barwell displayed matrimonial ambitions towards one of the daughters of General Clavering, the senior protagonist in the opposition to Hastings, but this design was aborted after Clavering accused Barwell of peculation and a bloodless duel took place. On 13 September 1776 Barwell married Elizabeth Jane (c.1753–1778), daughter of Robert Sanderson, a company official, but she died after barely two years of marriage. There were two sons. Barwell entertained lavishly at his mansion, Kidderpore House, Calcutta, and played for high stakes at his lodge at Barasat. He also owned other valuable properties in Calcutta.

In December 1778 Barwell informed Hastings that he intended to leave India. His wife had just died, and his formidable half-sister Mary, who managed his affairs at home, believed that his interests would be better served by his presence in England. Hastings, appalled by the prospect of losing his principal ally, persuaded him to stay. A year later pressure on Barwell to return was as strong as ever. Furthermore, he was facing accusations of revenue frauds from the East India Company directors and any chance that he might have had of succeeding Hastings as governor-general had vanished. Following a truce cobbled together between Hastings and Philip Francis, the core of the opposition since Clavering's death in 1777, Hastings acquiesced in Barwell's departure and he sailed for home on 3 March 1780.

Contemporary rumours that Barwell's wealth amounted to £400,000 were probably an exaggeration, although it was certainly substantial, and he behaved as a classic 'nabob'. He bought Stansted House in west Sussex from the earl of Halifax for £102,500 in 1781. He had it largely reconstructed by Joseph Bonomi and James Wyatt, and the grounds 'improved' by Capability Brown. He also purchased large areas of land and property in the surrounding countryside as well as a house in St James's Square, London, which he kept until 1796. He quickly acquired a parliamentary seat at Helston in 1781, moving to St Ives in 1784 and Winchelsea in 1790, from which seat he resigned in December 1796. He also attempted to acquire parliamentary influence through the purchase of two seats at Tregony: he supported Pitt, but was not recorded as speaking in the Commons after 1790. Barwell married Catherine (1769–1847), the daughter of Nathaniel Coffin, a customs official from Boston, Massachusetts, and his wife, Elizabeth, on 24 June 1785. There were at least ten children of this second marriage, and, additionally, one or more natural children were born in England. A picture of Barwell in his library with a son of his first marriage, painted by Sir Joshua Reynolds in 1780–81, portrays a slightly built, rather commonplace man in early middle age.

Barwell died at Stansted House on 2 September 1804. He was commemorated by a monument, by Nollekens, in the chancel of the church of St John the Baptist at Westbourne, Sussex, where he was buried. His extravagant way of life and his numerous family left his estates heavily encumbered. Shortly after his death Stansted House and his other Sussex estates were sold by his trustees.

T. H. BOWYER

Sources 'The letters of Richard Barwell', *Bengal Past and Present*, 8–18 (1914–19) • L. S. Sutherland, 'Two letter-books of Richard Barwell, 1769–1773', *Indian Archives*, 7 (1953), 115–45; 8 (1954), 14–42 • Bengal civilians, BL OIOC, O/6/21, fol. 98 • K. Feiling, *Warren Hastings* (1954) • S. Weitzman, *Warren Hastings and Philip Francis* (1929) • H. E. Busteed, *Echoes from old Calcutta*, 4th edn (1908) • J. Parkes and H. Merivale, *Memoirs of Sir Philip Francis*, 2 vols. (1867) • 'The Barwell family', *Bengal Past and Present*, 26 (1923), 184–7 • W. Foster, 'William Barwell, governor of Fort William, 1748–1749', *Bengal Past and Present*, 27 (1924), 35–43 • E. Cotton, 'Mr. Barwell of Stansted Park', *Bengal Past and Present*, 49 (1935), 1–4 • F. H. Arnold, 'Memoirs of Mrs. Oldfield', *Sussex Archaeological Collections*, 38 (1892), 96–8 • J. H. Sperling, 'Westbourne monumental inscriptions', *Sussex Archaeological Collections*, 22 (1870), 210–13, esp. 201, 203 • HoP, *Commons* • *Old Westminsters*, vol. 1

Archives BL OIOC, corresp. and minutes as member of the Bengal council, home misc. series; letter-books, MS Eur. D 535 • Calcutta Historical Society | BL, letters to Warren Hastings, Add. MSS 29135–29192, *passim*

Likenesses J. Reynolds, oils, 1780–81; Christies, 17 April 1964, lot 48 [*see illus.*] • W. Dickinson, mezzotint (after J. Reynolds), BM • G. Stuart, oils, Luton Hoo, Bedfordshire

Wealth at death substantial; est. at £400,000 (probably exaggerated): *Memoirs of William Hickey*, ed. A. Spencer (1913–25), 2.299

Barwick, John (*fl.* 1290–1300), Franciscan friar and theologian, was probably born *c.*1260, perhaps in the north of England. He entered the Franciscans' Oxford convent as a young man, and had become twenty-second lector there by 6 January 1291, when he is recorded as preaching to the community. He completed his doctorate of theology about this time, and probably later lectured at Paris. He had certainly left Oxford by 1300, when he is recorded as a member of the convent at Stamford, where he was licensed to hear confessions on 27 August 1300. Nothing further is known of his career, but he died at Stamford, probably in the second or third decade of the fourteenth century, and may be buried there.

In his work as a theologian Barwick has been associated with his fellow Franciscans, Duns Scotus (*d.* 1308) and William Ockham (*d.* 1349). Scotus must have been his contemporary at Oxford, because he is known to have entered the convent there in 1290, but Barwick had left for Stamford long before Ockham arrived in Oxford. No work by Barwick survives, although at least one early fourteenth-century French theologian cites him in his own work. According to Bale, Barwick was the author of a treatise *De formis*, a collection of astrological predictions, and a commentary on the *Sentences* of Peter Lombard, titles which, in themselves, give few indications of his philosophical interests. The library catalogue of St Augustine's Abbey, Canterbury, records a *Quodlibet Egidii et Berwyle*, an entry that probably suggests a text by the theologian and political theorist Giles of Rome, presented to the abbey by Barwick.

JAMES G. CLARK

Sources Emden, *Oxf.*, 1.180–81 • Bale, *Cat.*, 1.413 • Tanner, *Bibl. Brit.-Hib.*, 79 • A. G. Little and F. Pelster, *Oxford theology and theologians*, OHS, 96 (1934)

Barwick, John (1612–1664), dean of St Paul's, was born in Witherslack, Westmorland, on 20 April 1612, the third of five sons of George Barwick, a husbandman, and his wife, Jane. From an early age John and his brother Peter *Barwick (1619–1705) demonstrated an aptitude for academic study. They attended a number of 'obscure mean Schools' before they were placed in Sedbergh School in Yorkshire, where, under the guidance of Gilbert Nelson, they attained 'a greater Proficiency in learning' (P. Barwick, 6). John matriculated as a sizar from St John's College, Cambridge, on 14 May 1631, and graduated BA early in 1635. He successfully presented to the king and the privy council the position of the college in a dispute between two contenders for the mastership of the college, and, on 5 April 1636, was elected a fellow of the college. He proceeded MA in 1638. Widely perceived to be an Arminian and a Laudian, he was ordained deacon in Lincoln Cathedral on 20 December 1640. In the following year he was made canon of Durham Cathedral and chaplain to Thomas Morton, bishop of Durham.

In July 1642 Barwick was involved in a plot to transfer a large sum of money and silver plate from Cambridge to the king, who was then at Nottingham. Oliver Cromwell received information about the plan and lay in wait with a number of soldiers for the shipment at Lower Hedges, between Cambridge and Huntingdon. The conspirators became aware of Cromwell's plans and formed a party of horse, including Barwick, who conveyed the consignment by the back roads to Nottingham. In conjunction with the

Cambridge royalists William Lacy, Isaac Barrow, Seth Ward, William Quarles, and Peter Gunning, Barwick was also involved in the writing and publication of *Certain Disquisitions and Considerations Representing … the Unlawfulness of the Oath, Entituled, a Solemn League and Covenant*. Each of the authors brought their part of the manuscript to Gunning's chamber where they 'conferr'd and agreed upon the whole' (P. Barwick, 39–40). The first edition of this title was seized on the press and burnt, but a second edition was printed at Oxford in 1644. Barwick was also implicated in the publication of *Querela Cantabrigiensis, or, A remonstrance by way of apologie, for the banished members of the late flourishing University of Cambridge* (1647).

Ejected from his fellowship in 1644, Barwick went to London, where he acted as chaplain to the bishop of Durham, Thomas Morton, who was then living at Durham House in the Strand. While in London

> he had the management of the King's Affairs, and as a secret Spy, carried on a private Correspondence betwixt London and Oxford, where the King's Head Quarters were; on the one Hand communicating to his Majesty all the Designs and Endeavours of the Rebels, and conveying his Royal Orders and Commands on the other. (P. Barwick, 46–7)

Barwick communicated with Oxford via a network of 'adventurous Women' employed by the bookseller Richard Royston to disperse royalist material throughout England. Much of his information about the activities of parliament and its armies was provided by Sir Thomas Middleton, Colonel Roger Pope MP, and Francis Cresset, 'a gentleman of a Shropshire family who was in great credit with the Earl of Pembroke' (ibid., 62–3, 57–8). Barwick's reward came in 1646 in the shape of an Oxford BD.

Following the fall of Oxford in June 1646 Cresset got himself appointed as a servant to Charles I, who was then in the custody of the Scots, and was instrumental in smuggling letters between the king and Barwick. When Charles came under the control of the army in summer 1647 'his Servants and Friends were allowed the Liberty of coming to him' and Barwick made 'frequent Journeys' to the king (P. Barwick, 85–6). In August 1648 Barwick was apparently involved in a plot to organize a royalist revolt in London, and towards the end of the year he played a significant part in the negotiations concerning the treaty of the Isle of Wight.

In the weeks after the regicide Barwick fell ill but he continued to communicate with the king's ministers in exile through his brother Edward. It was Edward's job to collect letters from the Post Office addressed to a fictional Dutch merchant named James van Delft. He was, however, betrayed by an employee of the Post Office named Mr Bostocke who had previously been 'esteemed very hearty in the King's Interest' (P. Barwick, 115–18). John was able to burn all his letters and ciphers before he was arrested, and on 9 April he and Edward were committed to the Gatehouse prison. Edward was released after a few weeks and died soon afterwards, but, on 12 April, John was committed to the Tower of London on a charge of high treason. On 2 June 1651 the council of state referred a petition from Barwick, presumably for his release, to the committee for

examinations. He was finally freed in August 1652 after lodging bail of £400 with two sureties of £200, which were provided by Thomas Wharton and Richard Royston.

After his release from custody Barwick stayed with his old friend and patron Bishop Morton before visiting Lady Savile. He then stayed for several months at the home of Sir Thomas Eversfield in Suffolk, and when his host died he moved with Eversfield's widow to stay with her sister in Denbigh in north Wales; there he renewed his friendship with Lady Eversfield's brother-in-law Sir Thomas Middleton. He finally settled at his brother Peter's house in St Paul's Churchyard, and resumed his correspondence with the royalists in exile. Barwick's principal contact was with Edward Hyde, and much of his correspondence during the 1650s was concerned with finding money for the king and trying to maintain the structures of the Church of England, particularly the continuance of the episcopal succession.

In June 1658 Barwick ministered on the scaffold to Dr John Hewitt, who was executed for conspiring against Oliver Cromwell. In 1659 he preached the funeral sermon of Bishop Thomas Morton, which he later published, with a biography of his friend, as *Hieronikēs, or, The Fight, Victory, and Triumph of S. Paul* (1660). In late 1659 and early 1660 he negotiated with 'many Citizens of London of principal note' (P. Barwick, 189) about the likely terms for a restoration of the monarchy, and repeatedly tried to induce General George Monck to declare for the king. Shortly before the Restoration Barwick was sent to the court at Breda by the bishops in England in order to ascertain the likely status of the Church of England after the king's return from exile. He was warmly received by Charles and his ministers; he preached before the king at Breda, and was afterwards made one of Charles's chaplains.

In 1660 Barwick received a DD by royal mandate, but did not resume his fellowship at St John's College. He was appointed dean of Durham Cathedral on 1 November 1660, and enjoyed and two 'very rich Benefices' close by, the rectories of Wolsingham and Houghton-le-Spring. He resigned both of these parishes when he was made dean of St Paul's in 1661. At St Paul's 'His first Care … was … to restore the Celebration of Divine Service by the sacred Musick of a Choir' (P. Barwick, 311). He and John Dolben visited the regicide Hugh Peters shortly before his execution in an attempt to persuade him to admit that his actions had been evil. He was one of the nine assistants to the bishops at the Savoy conference, and on 18 February 1661 he was elected prolocutor of the lower house of convocation of the province of Canterbury. About the end of November 1662 'he began to be very ill, and was some Months confined to his Chamber' (P. Barwick, 329). He wanted to retire to the rectory at Therfield in Hertfordshire, to which he had recently been presented, but he was too weak for this journey and instead went to Chiswick, only 5 miles from London, where he stayed with a certain Thomas Elborow, formerly a pupil of his at Cambridge. The following spring he returned to London, where he died from consumption on 22 October 1664. He was unmarried. His friend Peter Gunning preached his funeral sermon at St Paul's, and the bishop of London read the service.

Barwick's will, dated 21 October 1664, bequeathed a significant sum of money and plate to his three surviving brothers and their families. He also left rings and various smaller sums of money to more than thirty named individuals, and gave £100 towards the cost of repairing St Paul's Cathedral. His will also reveals Barwick to have been a bibliophile. He left his copy of 'Historia Bizantina' to Gilbert Sheldon 'as an acknowledgement of my gratitude for those many favours I have allwaies received from his Grace'; presented a folio edition of the works of Charles I to his 'good freind' John Ottway; and gave £10 to a Mr Thomas Cooke to buy a book 'to be kept in remembra[nce] of me'. In addition he directed that 'Fortie pounds in good usefull Schoole bookes' should be sent to his old school at Sedbergh, and bequeathed £300 to St John's College, Cambridge, 'to be imployed for buying bookes to their library' (PRO, PROB 11/315, fols. 89r, 90r).

JASON Mᶜ ELLIGOTT

Sources P. Barwick, *The life of … Dr John Barwick*, ed. and trans. H. Bedford (1724) · *Walker rev.* · Venn, *Alum. Cant.* · *CSP dom.*, 1635–64 · R. Newcourt, *Repertorium ecclesiasticum parochiale Londinense*, 2 vols. (1708–10) · R. S. Bosher, *The making of the Restoration settlement: the influence of the Laudians, 1649–1662* (1951) · J. Spurr, *The Restoration Church of England, 1646–1689* (1991) · J. Barwick, *Hieronikēs, or, The fight, victory, and triumph of S. Paul* (1660) · will, PRO, PROB 11/315, fols. 88–90

Archives Glos. RO, misc. papers · St John Cam., corresp. and papers | BL, Nicholas MSS, letters to E. Nicholas · Bodl. Oxf., MSS Clarendon, letters to E. Hyde

Likenesses G. Vertue, line engraving, BM, NPG; repro. in Barwick, *Life*

Wealth at death £2100 cash bequeathed to friends and relatives; silver; goods; some land: will, PRO, PROB 11/315, fols. 88–90

Barwick, Peter (1619–1705), physician, was born at Witherslack, Westmorland, the son of George Barwick, husbandman, and his wife, Jane. Like his elder brother, John *Barwick (1612–1664), later dean of St Paul's, he was educated at Sedbergh School under Gilbert Nelson, and at St John's College, Cambridge, where he was admitted as a sizar on 12 October 1638 and proceeded BA on 3 December 1642. Two years later he was appointed by Bishop Matthew Wren to a fellowship at St John's, but adverse political circumstances meant that he was not admitted. Leaving Cambridge, he became tutor to Ferdinando Sacheverell of Old Hayes, Leicestershire, but returned to his alma mater in 1647 to take his MA, and then applied himself to the study of medicine. In 1651 he attended Charles II at Worcester, and throughout the interregnum he persisted, along with his brother John, in supporting the royalist and Anglican cause. On 3 July 1655 he received his MD from Cambridge and five months later was admitted a candidate for membership of the College of Physicians in London. He was not elected a fellow, however, until 26 June 1665. In the later 1650s he was living in London with his brother, John, when both men were active in promoting Anglican rites in the church according to the proscribed Book of Common Prayer. At about the same time

he married Anne Sayon, a merchant's widow, and kinswoman of Archbishop William Laud.

At the Restoration in 1660 Barwick was rewarded for his loyalty to the Stuart cause by being consulted by the king on medical matters. Little is known of his specific medical practice or philosophy, though he did attain some eminence in the City of London, for his treatment of smallpox and fevers as well as for his defence of the Harveian doctrine of the circulation of the blood. He is said to have written a treatise on the latter, though this is no longer extant. In 1665 he achieved further fame through his heroic efforts in ministering to the sick in the time of the last great epidemic of bubonic plague. An extremely pious man, Barwick was a constant attender at nearby St Paul's Cathedral throughout the year of the plague (his house was adjacent to the cathedral), and he corresponded with many of the leading Anglican divines of the day, including his close friend William Sancroft, dean of St Paul's. In one letter Barwick graphically described the destruction wrought in London by the great fire of 1666 in which his own home was destroyed. He subsequently moved to the precincts of Westminster Abbey. Some indication of Barwick's charitable and pious disposition can be gleaned from his biographer, Helkiah Bedford, who describes how he began every day with prayers at six o'clock, after which he attended on the medical needs of the local poor, prescribing for them gratis, as well as relieving many others of their financial needs and wants. Increasingly active in the day-to-day running of the College of Physicians, he held the office of censor in 1674, 1684, and 1687, and was an elect from 26 March 1685 to 6 November 1691, a position which he may have resigned through lack of sympathy with the growing dominance of the whig element in the college. At the same time failing health and impaired eyesight may have hastened his withdrawal from the politics of college life, and in 1694 he retired altogether from medical practice.

Barwick is now chiefly remembered for writing the biography of his more celebrated brother, John Barwick; it was finally published in Latin in 1721, and an English translation by the non-juror Helkiah Bedford appeared in 1724. Bedford annexed to this work a brief biography of Peter Barwick, which is the chief source for his life. The *Vita Joannis Barwick*, begun in 1671, was clearly intended as more than simply a memoir of Barwick's brother; it is perhaps better understood as a statement of his own commitment and lifelong zeal for the restored Anglican church and its royal head. Appended to the *Vita*, for example, was an appendix vindicating Charles I as the author of the *Eikon basiliké*. The manuscript remains of the original work are to be found in the library of Barwick's old college, St John's, Cambridge (MS H.9A). Barwick died in Westminster on 4 September 1705, and was buried in the church of St Faith, under St Paul's Cathedral. Of his four children (three daughters and one son), only one daughter, Anne (b. 1662), survived him. She married Sir Ralph Dutton of Sherborne in Gloucestershire in 1679. Barwick made at least three wills, of which two survive. That of 1671 makes reference to Barwick's sickness at the time of the 1665 plague and pays tribute to his friend, Dr Buck, who administered communion to Barwick at that time. It also refers to his wish to endow a lectureship at St John's, the purpose of which was to instruct the scholars in the just authority and true antiquity of the Church of England. Interestingly, in his later will of 1702 Barwick rescinded this clause, being now convinced 'that such Lectures have little benefit in them besides the salary to the Reader'. Among his executors he named Dr Hans Sloane, and as overseer he appointed Ralph, earl of Montagu, whom he had approached to act as his grandsons' patron and protector.   PETER ELMER

Sources [H. Bedford], preface, in P. Barwick, *The life of … Dr John Barwick*, ed. and trans. H. Bedford (1724) · Munk, *Roll* · Bodl. Oxf., MSS Tanner 40, fol. 128; 41, fol. 167; 45, fols. 32, 37, 44, 60, 93, 99, 100, 109; 447, fols. 14–19 [will of *c*.1671] · annals, RCP Lond., 4.72–3 · will, 22 July 1702, PRO, PROB 11/484/176 · H. J. Cook, *The decline of the old medical regime in Stuart London* (1986), 202, 223 · Bodl. Oxf., MS Rawl. 100, fols. 43–5 · Venn, *Alum. Cant.*
Archives Glos. RO, papers · St John Cam. | BL, Sloane MSS, letters to Sir Hans Sloane, etc.
Likenesses G. Vertue, line engraving, 1721, Wellcome L.; version, BM, NPG · engraving, repro. in Bedford, preface, in Barwick, *Life*, facing frontispiece
Wealth at death see will, PRO, PROB 11/484/176

Barwis, Richard (1602–1649), politician, was the only son of Anthony Barwis (*d.* 1616), gentleman landowner of Ilekirk Grange, Cumberland, and his wife, Grace (*d.* 1616), daughter of William Fleming of Rydal, Westmorland. His family had figured prominently in Cumberland and Westmorland affairs since the thirteenth century, and had settled at Ilekirk Grange, in the parish of Westward, near Carlisle, in the early Tudor period. Orphaned at the age of fourteen, Barwis became the *de facto* ward of his uncle, John Fleming, who neglected the upkeep of his estate and married him to Frances (*d.* 1670), daughter of a prominent recusant, Sir Edward Musgrave of Hayton Castle. They had no children. After coming of age Barwis set about improving his patrimony, and there appears little substance to a later allegation that having inherited a 'fair estate' he 'trifled it away' (E. Sandford, *A Cursory Relation of All the Antiquities and Familyes in Cumberland*, ed. R. S. Ferguson, Cumberland and Westmorland Antiquarian and Archaeological Society, tract ser., 4, 1890, 27).

Known as the Great Barwis or Great Richard on account of his formidable stature and strength (MacDonald, 117–18), Barwis cut a large figure in early Stuart Cumberland. He was appointed a JP for the county in 1626, served as a forced loan commissioner the following year, and was generally one of the most trusted and conscientious of the county's governors. He became a freeman of Carlisle and member of its merchant guild in 1624, and was returned for the city to the 1628 parliament. Appointed sheriff of Cumberland in 1634, he sympathized with the city's efforts to be removed from the first writ for ship money but was nevertheless diligent in collecting the levy. In 1635 he played a leading role in obtaining a royal charter of incorporation for Carlisle, in which he was named as the city's mayor. He was returned for Carlisle to the Short Parliament, and again to the Long Parliament, but his only

significant parliamentary appointment before the outbreak of civil war was in August 1641, when he was made a commissioner for disarming Cumberland's recusants.

Although Barwis would emerge as a committed opponent of the royal cause, he confined himself in the summer of 1642 to pledging £50 for the defence of parliament. He probably spent the second half of 1642 in the north, endeavouring to preserve his estate against the king's party, but by January 1643 he had returned to Westminster, where he was named to committees for sequestering the property of royalist MPs and other 'malignants'. These appointments suggest that he was broadly aligned with the parliamentary 'war party', as does his nomination in October 1643 as an additional commissioner to implement the terms of the solemn league and covenant. He evidently supported John Pym's policy of a military alliance with the Scots. Indeed, he and his brother-in-law, Sir Wilfrid Lawson, were behind an unsuccessful attempt to seize Carlisle for parliament in the spring of 1643, which may well have been timed to coincide with a projected Scottish invasion.

Barwis spent most of 1644 and 1645 in the northern counties working alongside Sir William Armyne and the other parliamentary commissioners in their efforts to maintain General Leven's army. He seems to have been on friendly terms with the covenanters until at least September 1644, when he encouraged the Scottish commander David Leslie to invade Cumberland and Westmorland. But soon thereafter he became involved in an acrimonious dispute with Leslie and his countrymen over military command in the region, particularly in relation to the siege of Carlisle. The quarrel escalated in the spring of 1645 when the Scots became convinced that Barwis's friends and kinsmen had been behind an insurrection in the north against their army. In a lengthy paper presented to parliament in June 1645, the Scots commissioners accused Barwis and his faction of protecting 'delinquents', corresponding with the enemy, and starving the Scottish forces of supplies. The Commons set up a committee to investigate these charges, but its only achievement was to interrogate and then imprison the Scots' principal informant, John Musgrave. In a series of pamphlets written during his imprisonment Musgrave reiterated the allegation that Barwis and his friends were in league with the royalists. He also claimed that Barwis pretended to be an Independent at Westminster, but back in Cumberland 'held up and countenanced the booke of common prayer (that English masse)' (Musgrave, *Another Word to the Wise*, sig. B). In fact, Barwis was one of the few Cumberland gentlemen who were keen to promote a godly ministry in the northern counties. However, there is ample evidence that several of his friends had collaborated with royalists, and Musgrave was right to identify him as the lynchpin of a loose alliance of northern anti-Scots (among them former royalists) and Westminster Independents that was keen to eradicate Scottish influence in English affairs. Barwis and his friends certainly received protection from some of Westminster's most radical politicians, including Philip, Lord Wharton, and Sir Arthur Hesilrige. Barwis may also have been on friendly terms with another Independent grandee, Algernon Percy, tenth earl of Northumberland. Barwis's family had been tenants of the Percys since Tudor times, and Barwis was apparently a regular correspondent of the earl's steward, Hugh Potter.

Barwis was a key player in the Independents' propaganda campaign against the Scottish army, and was rewarded in December 1645 with appointment as a deputy lieutenant for Cumberland. He began his second term as mayor of Carlisle in February 1648 following a purge of the city's royalist office-holders. But when Carlisle was seized by the royalists in April 1648 he was imprisoned, and probably remained in custody until the city fell to parliament in October. Perhaps as a result of his imprisonment Barwis had fallen ill by January 1649; he died on 13 February and was buried in Westward church. He was described on his memorial as 'excellently accomplished' and of 'saintly soul'; Carlisle's 'wise guide'; and his county's 'chief ornament' (MacDonald, 119). He left the bulk of his estate—all of which lay in Cumberland, and included Ilekirk Grange, two manors, tithes, coalmines, quarries, and salt pans—to his widow.　　DAVID SCOTT

Sources HoP, *Commons, 1690–1715* [draft] · D. Scott, 'The Barwis affair: political allegiance and the Scots during the British civil wars', *EngHR*, 115 (2000), 843–63 · A. MacDonald, 'The family of Barwis', *Transactions of the Cumberland and Westmorland Antiquarian and Archaeological Society*, new ser., 37 (1936–7), 106–29 · F. B. Swift, 'Barwis of Cumberland, pt 2', *Transactions of the Cumberland and Westmorland Antiquarian and Archaeological Society*, new ser., 51 (1952), 117–22 · [J. Musgrave], *A word to the wise* (1646) · [J. Musgrave], *Another word to the wise* (1646) · [J. Musgrave], *Yet another word to the wise* (1646) · [J. Musgrave], *A fourth word to the wise* (1647) · *JHC*, 2–5 (1640–48) · *CSP dom.*, 1635–48 · C. B. Phillips, 'The gentry in Cumberland and Westmorland, 1600–1665', PhD diss., University of Lancaster, 1974 · *JHL*, 4–8 (1628–46) · municipal records, Cumbria AS, Carlisle, Ca/2 [unfol.] · H. W. Meikle, ed., *Correspondence of the Scots commissioners in London, 1644–1646*, Roxburghe Club, 160 (1917) · will, PRO, PROB 11/207, fol. 264 · inquisition post mortem, PRO, C142/354/101 [Anthony Barwis] · court of wards, PRO, 9/205, fol. 10v · Bodl. Oxf., MS Nalson XIX, fols. 265–7 · Bodl. Oxf., MS Nalson IV, fol. 35
Likenesses portrait, repro. in MacDonald, 'The family of Barwis'
Wealth at death see will, PRO, PROB 11/207, fol. 264

Barzilai, Ishac. *See* Robles, Antonio Rodrigues (d. 1688).

Baseley, (Cyril) Godfrey (1904–1997), radio broadcaster and writer, was born on 2 October 1904 at The Square, Alvechurch, Worcestershire, the second of the three children of Walter Ernest Baseley, master butcher, and his wife, Mary Ellen, *née* Court. His parents were members of the Society of Friends, and he was sent to Quaker boarding-schools, Sibford in Oxfordshire and Bootham in York. More athletic than academic, he left school without passing matriculation examinations, and worked in the family butchery business.

In adult life Baseley professed no formal religion: at his request there was no religious ceremony at his cremation; but when he married his wife, Bessie Hartwright (always known as Betty; b. 1912/13), on 6 August 1934 it was according to the rites and ceremonies of the Church of England. They had two daughters.

Apart from competitive motorcycling, Baseley's main hobby was amateur dramatics: he studied elocution and drama at night school (where he eventually taught), and was soon playing small parts in the professional theatre in Birmingham. From Birmingham too he began to broadcast with increasing regularity from 1929 until 1939 as actor, narrator, and poetry reader.

At the outbreak of the Second World War, all BBC contracts were cancelled, and so Baseley found work first in civil defence, then in an aircraft factory, and finally with the Ministry of Information. He travelled the midlands with a loudspeaker van, writing and delivering (and at times improvising, at which he excelled) morale-boosting talks on the theme 'Dig for victory'.

Baseley's country background and his knowledge of farming and gardening (in which, though, he had no formal training), together with his resonant baritone voice, led to his being engaged on a full-time BBC staff contract. From 1 May 1943 he was attached to the outside broadcasts department in London; but after three months he willingly returned to Birmingham, where, apart from a brief spell in television in London, he was based for the rest of his professional life.

As a BBC staff producer, Baseley commissioned, or wrote, scripts; he engaged performers, whom he directed at the microphone; he learned how to manage BBC budgets, how to work with technical staff, and (sometimes with difficulty) to comply with the strictures of his superiors. He had enormous flair for invention, and energetically defended his suggested programmes. He was formidable in argument, but fair-minded enough to modify apparently fixed views in the face of persuasive reasoning.

Baseley originated many programmes, mainly on farming and the countryside. At a farmers' advisory council meeting to discuss such broadcasts, one Lincolnshire farmer, Henry Burtt, suggested that what was wanted was 'a farming Dick Barton' (*Dick Barton* being an immensely popular adventure radio serial in short episodes). At what seemed an absurd suggestion most people present laughed. Baseley did not. He developed the idea, and against initial opposition persuaded the BBC to give *The Archers*, as it was called, a week's trial from 29 May 1950. Well received when broadcast in the midland region in 1950, it began regular broadcasts on the national Home Service from 1 January 1951, and became one of the BBC's most successful programmes. It won plaudits and prizes and, for some of its participants—but oddly not for Baseley himself—national honours. For more than twenty-one years it became almost an obsession: he believed it to have social significance above mere entertainment.

Fearing that BBC plans in the document *Broadcasting in the Seventies* might threaten the programme, Baseley published in 1971 'The Archers': a Slice of my Life. Ten of its twelve chapters recounted the origin and growth of the programme and his part in it. In 1972 he was, without warning and for debatable reasons, dismissed by letter. He was to have no further contact with the programme. He turned to lecturing and writing, producing several books on country themes. He made no great fortune but, through an otherwise quiet retirement, his name continued to be linked with *The Archers*.

Not always an easy man to work with, Baseley could be overbearing, blunt, and bluff. In private, though, as host, husband, and father, he was genial and surprisingly benign. He relished the fact that he was known by the first syllable of his second name (he never used his first name); and the title 'creator' pleased him. On his death certificate he is described as 'Broadcaster and Writer. Creator of "The Archers" (retired)'.

Baseley was undeniably the programme's prime mover, advocate, defender, and apologist. Undoubtedly he depended on the contribution of the talented writers, actors, directors, and technicians who worked under his editorial control. Yet without Baseley *The Archers* would almost certainly never have existed. He died on 2 February 1997 at the Princess of Wales Community Hospital, Bromsgrove, and his remains were afterwards cremated.

NORMAN PAINTING

Sources b. cert. · m. cert. · d. cert. · archives, BBC WAC · personal knowledge (2004) · G. Baseley, *'The Archers': a slice of my life* (1971) · *Radio Times* (1930–79) · N. Painting, *Forever Ambridge: thirty years of 'The Archers'*, rev. edn (1980) · private information (2004) [J. Brodie] · *CGPLA Eng. & Wales* (1997) · *The Times* (3 Feb 1997) · *Daily Telegraph* (3 Feb 1997) · *The Independent* (4 Feb 1997)
Archives BBC WAC | SOUND BBC Sound Archives
Likenesses P. Rasmussen, pastels, repro. in Baseley, *'The Archers'*, frontispiece; priv. coll. · photographs, BBC Archives, London · photographs, BBC Archives, Birmingham
Wealth at death under £180,000: probate, 20 Feb 1997, *CGPLA Eng. & Wales*

Basevi, George (1794–1845), architect, was born on 1 April 1794 in London, the younger son of George Basevi senior, a City merchant. His father's sister, Maria, was married to Isaac D'Israeli and was the mother of Benjamin Disraeli, earl of Beaconsfield. Basevi attended Dr Charles Burney's school in Greenwich before becoming a pupil of John Soane in December 1810. During his articles he also studied at the Royal Academy Schools, where Soane had recently been appointed professor of architecture. In 1815 he visited Paris with his brother, and on completion of his architectural training in 1816 he embarked on a three-year study tour of Italy and Greece, staying the longest in Rome and Athens, but also travelling extensively elsewhere in Italy and even visiting Constantinople. In 1820, the year after his return to London, he exhibited a drawing of the temple of Hephaestos (the so-called Theseum) at the Royal Academy and opened his own practice in Albany. He was appointed surveyor to the Guardian Assurance Company on its formation in 1821, and soon afterwards he designed the church of St Thomas, Stockport, Cheshire (1822–5), for the commissioners of the Church Building Act (1818). This handsome and expensive structure (it cost £25,632 2s. 1d.) boasted an impressive free-standing portico of six Greek Ionic columns at the east end of the building and a clock tower 118 feet tall surmounted by an open stone monopteros at the west end. This commission was rapidly followed by a similar one for the church of St Mary, Greenwich, Kent (1823–4; des.).

George Basevi (1794–1845), by Waller Brothers, c.1845

Many of Basevi's projects came to him through his extensive family connections. These included work at country houses such as Titness Park, near Sunninghill, Berkshire, for Sampson Ricardo; Gatcombe Park, Gloucestershire (c.1820), for David Ricardo; and Painswick House, Gloucestershire (1827–32), for W. H. Hyett, his brother-in-law. Even more substantial, however, was the commission that came to him through his relatives William and George Haldimand, the financiers whose syndicate took over the development of Belgrave Square from Thomas Cubitt in 1825 and immediately appointed Basevi their surveyor. Basevi designed and handled the construction of the terraced houses making up the four sides of the square (1825–40), though not the four detached villas at the corners. He treated the stuccoed terraces of eleven or twelve houses on each side as single palatial façades, giving each a central columnar portico and end pavilions in a similar manner to John Nash's terraces in Regent's Park. His pride in the project may be indicated by the fact that he signed his name at the side of the portico of no. 31, a house which was to be occupied by George Haldimand. The financial success of this speculative development during an economically depressed period was due in large part to Basevi's precise and scholarly attention to detail, not just in the design of the individual houses but also in the paving, street furniture, and composition of the square as a whole.

The high esteem in which Belgrave Square was held led to Basevi's being given opportunities to design a number of other substantial London developments. One, as surveyor for the Thurloe estate in South Kensington of John Alexander and his son H. B. Alexander, included both Alexander Square (1827–30) and Thurloe Square (c.1839–45). Another, for the Henry Smith's charity estate in South Kensington, resulted in the construction from 1833 onwards of Pelham Crescent, Pelham Place, New Brompton (now Egerton) Crescent, and Walton Place. These appointments also brought forth commissions for two churches in Chelsea: St Saviour, Walton Place (1839–40), and St Jude (1843–4, des. 1933). Both of these were Gothic, an idiom which Basevi employed competently if rather uninspiringly on a number of occasions where it lent an appropriately pious character, such as at Truesdale's Hospital and Dr Fryer's almshouses, Stamford, Lincolnshire (1832); Parson's almshouses, St Mary Street, Ely, Cambridgeshire (1844–5); Holy Trinity, Twickenham, Middlesex (1840–41); and Coulsdon rectory, Surrey (1841–3). At Balliol College, Oxford, where his brother Nathaniel had been an undergraduate, Basevi designed a building on the west side of the garden quadrangle (1826–7) and a Gothic plaster ceiling for the chapel (1841, des. 1856). His designs for the rebuilding of the main front of the college (1841) were, however, rejected.

In 1834 Basevi's proposals for the Fitzwilliam Museum, Cambridge, were selected in an open competition from a field of thirty-six different designs by twenty-seven architects. While he did not live to see the museum completed, it is his best-known and most successful work, in many ways realizing Soane's own ideal of a public architecture based on the fullest interpretation of the ruins of imperial Rome. For his model, Basevi chose a building which had only recently been excavated, the Capitolium at Brescia, where the main portico jutted forward from a continuous flanking colonnade. Basevi adopted this same device for the museum, so that the free-standing columns of the octastyle portico were continued on either side to link to the two terminal pavilions. The whole composition, decked out in a fully elaborated Corinthian order of unparalleled richness, was thus given a sculptural dynamism by the prominent projections of the portico and pavilions from the colonnade. The result was that the museum, despite facing an extremely narrow street with no possibility of an axial vista, possessed a monumental presence through the dramatic views which were created along the length of the street. Work began on the

museum in 1837, and in 1845, following Basevi's death, C. R. Cockerell was appointed his successor. He faithfully followed Basevi's intentions in the exquisite plasterwork of the gallery interiors, but in the ambitious toplit staircase hall, where Basevi himself had changed his mind several times, Cockerell modified his designs. However, funds ran out before the hall was finished, so that it was left to E. M. Barry in the 1870s to complete the staircase with a riot of high Victorian polychromy and sculpture, which unexpectedly complements the imposing grandeur of Basevi's exterior.

Basevi's last major work was the Conservative Club, St James's Street, London (1843–5), on which he worked with Sidney Smirke. For this shared commission the two men collaborated on the exterior, though Basevi alone was responsible for the interiors of the ground floor. His premature death prevented him from taking up a second joint appointment with Smirke to rebuild the Carlton Club in Pall Mall.

Basevi and his wife, Frances Agneta Biscoe, had eight children; his son James Palladio Basevi (1832–1871) was an officer in the Royal Engineers. A plaster bust of Basevi by [T. I.?] Mazzotti after an unknown original is in the Fitzwilliam Museum. He was described by a contemporary as 'cold and somewhat haughty', though in professional matters he was acknowledged as being 'scrupulously just'. He was a member of the Royal Institute of British Architects and a fellow of the Society of Antiquaries and the Royal Society. He died on 16 October 1845, aged fifty-one, after falling through an opening in the floor of the old bell chamber of the west tower of Ely Cathedral while inspecting repairs. His remains were buried in Bishop Alcock's chapel at the east end of the cathedral.

RICHARD JOHN

Sources W. H. F. Basevi, 'The grand tour of an architect', *The Architect*, 108 (1922), 43, 70, 117, 156 • A. T. Bolton, ed., *The portrait of Sir John Soane* (1927), 271–8 • Colvin, *Archs.* • H. R. Hitchcock, *Early Victorian architecture in Britain*, 1 (1954), 168–9, 172–3, 304–5 • M. Jordan, 'The life and work of George Basevi (1794–1845)', PhD diss., Courtauld Inst., 1979 • M. H. Port, *Six hundred new churches* (1961), 80 • S. Smirke, 'George Basevi', *The dictionary of architecture*, ed. [W. Papworth] (1853–92) • D. Stroud, *The Thurloe estate* (1959) • D. Stroud, *The South Kensington estate of Henry Smith's charity* (1975), 21–8 • D. Watkin, ed., *The triumph of the classical: Cambridge architecture* (1977), 49–54 [exhibition catalogue, Fitzwilliam Museum, Cambridge, 1977] • R. Willis, *The architectural history of the University of Cambridge, and of the colleges of Cambridge and Eton*, ed. J. W. Clark, 3 (1886), 204–10, 212–14, 217–18 • F. H. W. Sheppard, ed., *The parish of southern Kensington*, Survey of London, 41 (1983) • 'Memoir of George Basevi, Esq.', *The Builder*, 3 (1845), 510–11 • d. cert. • will, PRO, PROB 11/2026, fols. 157–8

Likenesses Waller Brothers, memorial brass, c.1845, Ely Cathedral [*see illus.*] • T. I. (?) Mazzotti, plaster bust, FM Cam.

Wealth at death owned properties in Savile Row, Westminster, and Highgate, Middlesex: will, PRO, PROB 11/2026, fols. 157–8

Basham, William Richard (1807–1877), physician, was born at Diss, Norfolk, on 4 July 1807, the son of William Basham and his wife, Mary, formerly Holton. His early years were spent at Leiston in Suffolk. He was of a robust physique, being described in later life as having 'a portly frame, with a massive well-balanced head and clear brown eye' (*The Lancet*, 27 Oct 1877). Originally it was decided that he should follow a career in business and he began work in a banker's office. He then took up the study of chemistry and it is assumed that this provided his introduction to medicine. He entered Westminster Hospital, London, as a student on 5 January 1831 under the tutelage of such prominent practitioners as John Bright, Anthony Carlisle, George Guthrie, and Anthony White. In 1833 he went to Edinburgh to complete his studies, and presented his MD thesis, 'On the agency of the atmosphere on vegetable and animal life', in the following year. Basham then returned to the Westminster Hospital to serve as house physician from 1834 to 1835. He then joined the East India Company and made a tour of duty to India and China sailing in *The Hythe*. During a skirmish on the Canton River he sustained a serious, suppurating leg wound which he was forced to incise.

After his return to England in 1838 Basham became a member of the Royal College of Physicians. He was appointed physician to the Westminster Hospital in 1843. With the development of the Westminster Hospital medical school in 1849 he was appointed lecturer in materia medica and botany, and joint lecturer in medicine with Hamilton Roe. On the latter's retirement in 1855 Basham was made sole lecturer, a post which he held until 1871. In 1850 he was elected fellow of the Royal College of Physicians of which he was twice censor, first between 1864 and 1866 and again in 1873. He was also the examiner in medicine for 1870–71. The Croonian lecture which he delivered in 1864 reflected his deep interest in dropsy and renal disease and his belief in the value of the microscope. The lecture was incorporated into the third edition, which appeared in 1866, of Basham's *On dropsy connected with disease of the kidneys (morbus Brightii) and some other diseases of these organs associated with albuminous and purulent urine: illustrated by numerous drawings from the microscope* (1858). Basham was a fine draughtsman and put this skill to good use in the illustration of his works, as in the several plates which illustrate his *Aids to the Diagnosis of Diseases of the Kidneys* (1872). The bulk of his published work related to dropsy and renal disease but his *Introductory Lecture Addressed to Students of the Westminster Hospital at the Commencement of the Session 1871–72* (1871), subtitled *The Relationship Existing between Medicine and the other Arts and Sciences*, provides interesting material pertaining to the history of medicine. A further area of Basham's professional life worthy of mention is his involvement in the treatment of cholera. His career at the Westminster Hospital coincided with major outbreaks of the disease in 1832, 1848, and 1853. He believed that he could effect a cure by following Thomas Sydenham's methods of dealing with fever: that is, by the administration of calomel and opium. Basham was slow to accept the correct cause of the disease as defined by the epidemiologist John Snow.

Basham was in every respect a dedicated 'Westminster man', devoting his working life to the hospital and the medical school and using his skills as chemist, botanist,

and microscopist to good account. Aside from his professional interests he was an accomplished watercolourist and a genial host and conversationalist, who was also interested in topics such as geology, ethnology, and folklore. He was also a keen gardener at his country house at Halliford, near Shepperton, and he bathed in the Serpentine in Hyde Park, London, in all seasons. On 13 February 1877 Basham suffered a stroke while attending a board meeting at the hospital. He was cared for during his illness by his friends Sir George Burrows and Dr Radcliffe and, albeit in ailing health, he survived a further eight months until his rather unexpected death at his home, 17 Chester Street, Belgrave Square, London, on 16 October 1877.

DIANA BERRY

Sources *The Lancet* (27 Oct 1877) · *BMJ* (27 Oct 1877), 609 · J. Langdon-Davies, *Westminster Hospital, 1719–1948: two centuries of voluntary service* (1952) · J. G. Humble and P. Hansell, *Westminster Hospital, 1716–1974* (1974) · *DNB* · Munk, *Roll*
Likenesses G. Hayter, oils, 1858, Westminster Hospital, London · L. Caldesi & Co., photograph, RCP Lond. · photograph (after copy of a portrait), RCP Lond.
Wealth at death under £4000: probate, 19 Nov 1877, *CGPLA Eng. & Wales*

Bashford, Ernest Francis (1873–1923), oncologist, was born on 21 November 1873 at High Lawn, Bowdon, Cheshire, the eldest son of William Taylor Bashford, photographer, and his wife, Elizabeth, *née* Booth. He was educated at George Heriot's School before entering the University of Edinburgh where he had a distinguished academic career. He was Whitman prizeman in clinical medicine, Patterson prizeman in clinical surgery, and appointed to the Houldsworth research scholarship in experimental pharmacology and the Stark scholarship in clinical medicine and pathology. He graduated MB ChB in 1899. Bashford was awarded the M'Cosh graduate scholarship for study and research in the medical schools of Europe. He travelled to Germany where he worked with Paul Ehrlich at the Royal Prussian Institute for Experimental Therapeutics in Frankfurt am Main, and then with Oscar Liebreich in the Pharmacological Institute, Berlin. On his return to Edinburgh he became assistant to Thomas Richard Fraser, professor of materia medica, pharmacology, and clinical medicine.

In 1902 Bashford married Elisabeth, the eldest daughter of Felix Alfermann of Frankfurt am Main; they had one daughter. In the same year he was awarded the MD with gold medal and was appointed general superintendent of research to the newly established Imperial Cancer Research Fund. A year later he became director of the laboratories of the fund which were situated in the Examinations Hall, Victoria Embankment, London, and operated under the direction of the Royal College of Physicians and the Royal College of Surgeons of England. During his time as director Bashford established the modern experimental investigation of cancer in Britain. At the time of his appointment there was much speculation concerning the cause of cancer which many believed to be an infectious disease. As a consequence studies of the disease were misdirected and the lack of progress induced considerable pessimism concerning the successful outcome of cancer research. Bashford believed the elucidation of the cause and nature of cancer to be a biological problem and not one confined to human pathology. His approach was to employ a combination of comparative, statistical, and experimental methods to the study of the incidence and growth of malignant tumours. Bashford and his colleague James Alexander Murray made statistical investigations of the zoological distribution of cancer and an ethnological study based on reports received from all parts of the British empire. Their experimental work on animals involved the investigation of the transplantability of animal tumours based on the work of C. O. Jensen of Copenhagen. They developed techniques that enabled them to study growth, immunity, and resistance to implantation of tumours. In the *Scientific Report of the Investigations of the Cancer Research Fund* (1905) Bashford wrote, 'The comparative study [of the incidence of the disease] and the experimental propagation of cancer have revealed properties of cancer cells incompatible with all the hypotheses which have been advanced in explanation of the process'.

During the twelve years that he directed the laboratory Bashford established the Imperial Cancer Research Fund as an experimental research institution of international status. He also gained for himself an international reputation with his reports for the fund and contributions to the medical literature on pharmacology, immunity, and biochemistry. He was president of the first international cancer congress held in Heidelberg in 1906 and delegate of the British government to the international conference on cancer research in Paris in 1910.

Bashford was described by a contemporary as having a forceful, brilliant, and wayward character. He threw himself with enthusiasm into the controversies that raged around topics of cancer research and he claimed that he personally and successfully opposed the efforts of the German cancer committee to gather all cancer research under its control. After ten years in the post of director the brilliance and resource that characterized his work began to fade and in 1914, at the age of forty-one, he resigned from the Cancer Research Fund on the grounds of ill health. He was succeeded as director by J. A. Murray, who held the post until 1935.

From 1915 Bashford served with the Royal Army Medical Corps, first with the Mediterranean expeditionary force and later in France. After the war he held the post of adviser in pathology for the army of occupation. He was mentioned in dispatches and was appointed OBE in 1919. He died from heart failure at Manderscheid, Eifel, Germany, on 23 August 1923. He was survived by his wife.

M. P. EARLES

Sources *WWW*, 1916–28 · *BMJ* (18 Sept 1923), 440–41 · *The Lancet* (8 Sept 1923), 536 · E. F. Bashford, *Scientific report of the investigations of the Cancer Research Fund* (1905) · b. cert. · *CGPLA Eng. & Wales* (1923)
Archives Wellcome L.
Likenesses photograph, repro. in J. Austoker, *A history of the Imperial Cancer Research Fund, 1902–1986* (1988)
Wealth at death £796 6s. 4d.: probate, 26 Oct 1923, *CGPLA Eng. & Wales*

Bashforth, Francis (1819–1912), mathematician, was born at Thurnscoe, near Doncaster, on 8 January 1819, the eldest son of John Bashforth, who farmed the glebe at Thurnscoe. He was educated at Brampton Bierlow and afterwards at Doncaster grammar school, going on to enter St John's College, Cambridge, as a sizar, in 1840. An entirely different account of Bashforth's parentage and early life, which was published in *The Times* (14 February 1912, 11d) and repeated in the *Yorkshire Weekly Post* (17 February 1912, 24a), was corrected by Bashforth's son in a letter to *The Times* (23 February 1912, 11c) to the version given here. Bashforth was second wrangler in 1843, when John Couch Adams was senior wrangler. Although not intimate as undergraduates, the two mathematicians later became firm friends. Bashforth was elected a fellow of his college in 1843, and was ordained deacon in 1850 and priest in 1851. In 1857 he accepted the college living of Minting, near Horncastle, Lincolnshire, of which he remained rector until 1908. In 1905 he was made an honorary fellow of his college.

After taking his degree Bashforth spent three years in practical civil engineering, working partly in London and partly with one of the new railway companies which were then being formed throughout the country. He was engaged on the survey of projected lines, and in this way gained that practical experience in careful measurement which afterwards proved so valuable to him in his experiments in gunnery. Bashforth was anxious to obtain a post as professor of mathematics in the provinces, but such appointments were rare in those days. In 1864, however, he was appointed professor of applied mathematics to the advanced class of artillery officers at Woolwich, which afterwards developed into the Artillery College.

Bashforth's main interest lay in the science of ballistics, and he initiated a series of experiments between 1864 and 1880 which led to an understanding of the effects of air resistance on projectiles. Great Britain entered the Crimean War with obsolete military equipment. The muzzle-loading musket, 'Brown Bess', and the cast-iron smooth-bore cannon, firing a spherical solid shot, were still employed. The ineffectiveness of such artillery in the Crimea in general, and the exigencies of the siege of Sevastopol in particular, called for more powerful weapons. In the preface to his *Mathematical Treatise on the Motion of Projectiles* (1873) Bashforth wrote: 'Feeling that the satisfactory solution of any question in gunnery depends upon the construction of a trustworthy chronograph, it therefore became my duty to recommend that a proper instrument should be procured, and that a systematic course of experiments should be undertaken to determine, in the first instance, the resistance of the air to the motion of projectiles.' He accordingly set to work to construct the chronograph, first tried in November 1865, which bears his name; under his direction the military authorities carried out at Shoeburyness, Essex, experiments to determine the air resistance, in which projectiles were fired through a series of screens whose ruptures were electrically timed by the chronograph. His results are set out in his 1873 treatise, and he described his experiments in his

Report on the Experiments Made with the Bashforth Chronograph (1865–1870), published by the government in 1870, and republished with revisions and supplements in 1879, 1890, 1895, and 1900. On 14 September 1869 Bashforth married Elizabeth Jane, daughter of the Revd Samuel Rotton Piggott, vicar of Bredgar, Kent. They had one son.

Bashforth's ballistic experiments and the theory based upon them required continual amplification, and he received much assistance from his pupils. In 1872 a new scheme of army reorganization reduced the scope and importance of his post, and he resigned his position at Woolwich, receiving a government award of £500 for improvements to the chronograph. Thereafter he resumed his clerical duties at Minting, the living of which he had been allowed, by the indulgence of his bishop, to retain. Nevertheless, in 1873 he was appointed adviser to the War Office on questions relating to the science of artillery, and in 1878 he was requested by the government to lend his chronograph and to help in a new series of experiments to be carried out with both very high and very low velocities. The invitation gave Bashforth much satisfaction, and he superintended the working out of the results of a large number of experiments made in the years 1878 to 1880. His *Final Report* was published in 1880, and in 1885 he received from the government a grant of £2000 for his work. He utilized his leisure by preparing, in conjunction with Professor Adams, a treatise entitled *Capillary Action* (1883), and he also published *The Bashforth Chronograph* (1890). In 1908 he retired to Torunnan, Woodhall Spa, Lincolnshire, where he died on 13 February 1912. Bashforth was a worthy successor to Benjamin Robins (1707–1751); they are the two principal English authorities on the science of ballistics.

GEORGE GREENHILL, rev. ANITA MCCONNELL

Sources *The Times* (14 Feb 1912), 11d · *The Times* (23 Feb 1912), 11c · *Yorkshire Weekly Post* (17 Feb 1912), 24a · 'Return showing the amount expended on experiments', *Parl. papers* (1878), 47.495, no. 233 [awards to inventors; ships of war and weapons] · 'Statement of the sums expended on experiments', *Parl. papers* (1886), session 2, 40.807, no. 39 [awards to inventors; ordnance and small arms] · *Encyclopaedia Britannica*, 9th edn (1875–89), vol. 11, p. 298 [description and illustration of Bashforth's chronograph] · *BL cat.* · J. H. Hardcastle, 'Bashforth, 1819–1912', *Arms and Explosives*, 20 (1912), 108–11 · *The Eagle*, 33 (1911–12), 215–16 · G. Greenhill, *The Eagle*, 34 (1912–13), 109–11 · *The Eagle*, 34 (1912–13), 257–60 · Venn, *Alum. Cant.* · m. cert. · d. cert.

Wealth at death £24,368 11s. 7d.: probate, 3 May 1912, *CGPLA Eng. & Wales*

Basing. For this title name *see* Booth, George Sclater-, first Baron Basing (1826–1894).

Basing, Adam of (*d.* 1262x6), draper, is believed to have been the son of the aldermanic landowner Peter of Basing; he was the grandson of Solomon of Basing, alderman of London and mayor in 1217. Adam became a draper and city merchant, achieving eminence as a supplier to the royal household while at the same time pursuing a successful civic career. Little detail is known of his political activity in London, but the fact that he was elected an alderman of Cheap ward in 1247–60, was sheriff 1243–4, and mayor 1251–2 is evidence of his high standing.

The full range of Basing's mercantile activities is not known, and it is as the supplier of large quantities of cloths of gold, fine silks, embroideries, and ecclesiastical vestments to Henry III between 1238 and 1260 that he is best-known. Some were for domestic use, either for the king himself or for his family: in 1238, for example, he provided rich silk cloths for a quilt and mattress for the king's sister Eleanor, and in 1251 vestments for the chapel of the king's daughter Margaret on her marriage to Alexander III, king of Scots. However, a large part of the goods supplied by Basing were silk vestments—chasubles, copes, and mitres—or the decorative elements to adorn them, destined to be presented by the king to esteemed clerics visiting his court or to churches visited by the king. Not surprisingly Henry bestowed many upon St Peter's, Westminster, the church that he favoured above all others.

Because so much of Basing's trade was in vestments or embroideries it has been suggested that he ran his own tailoring and embroidery workshops. There is no evidence to support this conjecture and it is equally possible that he purchased or commissioned such goods directly from city craftsmen. The circumstances under which medieval embroideries were worked are unknown and may have been more domestic in nature; the embroideries that Basing traded in were often orphreys, the jewel-enriched or embroidered bands used to adorn vestments, which could be worked in frames in limited accommodation.

Adam of Basing's marriage to Desiderata, the daughter of Arnulf fitz Alulf and Dyonisia Viel, further strengthened his family's links within the London aldermanic class. His son Thomas, like a nephew also named Thomas, became an important woolmonger; he died young, however, and the fortunes of the family were advanced by Adam's grandson Peter, who married into the Frowicks, another wealthy aldermanic family. In 1247 Adam of Basing had acquired the soke of Aldermanbury, within the northern boundary of the city, which included six shops and the advowsons of three churches. To this he gradually added further property in the locality, in Cheap and in Wood Street, as well as land in more distant parishes such as St Giles and St Pancras. The imposing mansion he built in Aldermanbury in the 1250s was destroyed by irate Londoners during the troubles of 1263. The family name is commemorated in that ward in Basinghall Street, Basing Lane, and Bassishaw. Basing was alive in 1262, but had died by August 1266, when the king granted the wardship of his son and heir, Thomas, to a member of another aldermanic family.

KAY STANILAND

Sources A. B. Beaven, ed., *The aldermen of the City of London, temp. Henry III–[1912]*, 1 (1908) · G. A. Williams, *Medieval London: from commune to capital* (1963) · R. K. Lancaster, 'Artists, suppliers and clerks: the human factors in the art patronage of King Henry III', *Journal of the Warburg and Courtauld Institutes*, 35 (1972), 81–107 · *Calendar of the liberate rolls*, 6 vols., PRO (1916–64) · *CCIR* · K. Staniland, 'The nuptials of Alexander III of Scotland and Margaret Plantagenet', *Nottingham Medieval Studies*, 31 (1986), 20–45 · E. Williams, *Early Holborn and the legal quarter of London* (1927)

Basingstoke, John of [John Basing] (*d.* 1252), scholar and ecclesiastic, takes his name from the town of Basingstoke in Hampshire. Two contemporary sources speak of him: the chronicler Matthew Paris, and Robert Grosseteste, bishop of Lincoln (*d.* 1253). Basingstoke was closely associated with Grosseteste, and was a friend of Simon de Montfort and an acquaintance of Paris. According to John Leland (*d.* 1552) he studied at Oxford. Matthew Paris notes that he both studied and taught at Paris, without specifying whether he taught the arts or theology there. The only dates known for him concern his appointment as archdeacon of Leicester (1236) and his death (1252).

Basingstoke spent a period of unknown length in the Byzantine territories, which the capture of Constantinople had opened up to soldiers, colonists, and clerics from western Europe. He became proficient in the Greek language and sojourned at Athens. Matthew Paris, who admired him, recounts that Basingstoke spoke of a girl, Constantina, who at nineteen was learned in the trivium and quadrivium and whose knowledge exceeded that which Basingstoke himself had from the University of Paris. Paris refers to Constantina as the daughter of the archbishop of Athens. In a letter (*Roberti Grosseteste … epistolae*, ep. 17), Grosseteste invokes Basingstoke as a witness, along with the Dominican Roger Bacon, the Franciscan Adam Marsh, Robert Marsh, and Thomas Wallensis. This reference, to be dated near the beginning of Grosseteste's episcopate (*c.*1236) thus places Basingstoke within the bishop's inner circle. About 1242, according to Paris, Grosseteste acquired from the Byzantine area a codex containing the 'Testaments of the twelve patriarchs', a work of whose existence Basingstoke had learned at Athens and reported to Grosseteste. The codex, which Grosseteste sent for, survives in Cambridge University Library as MS Ff. 1.24. It is the oldest witness (late tenth-century) to the text of the 'Testaments'. It may have been in the library of Michael Choniates, archbishop of Athens, up to the Latin invasion of 1204. Grosseteste translated it into Latin, with the help (according to Paris) of Nicolas the Greek of St Albans. The version was widely read (seventy-nine known copies survive), and was to be frequently translated into the vernacular languages and published in early modern times.

Matthew Paris attributes several works to Basingstoke, none of which has been identified: the Latin version of a Greek writing on the order of the gospels; *Templum domini*, a piece of scholastic analysis; and a compendium of Greek grammar which Basingstoke himself apparently referred to as 'the Donatus of the Greeks' (Paris, *Chron.*, 5.286). It is tempting to think that the latter work may have constituted at least part of the basis of Grosseteste's knowledge of Greek, which was to result in numerous translations and retranslations of Greek and Byzantine writings. Grosseteste certainly had a source in England who illustrated for him the Byzantine pronunciation of Greek and instructed him in the use of accents. He named Basingstoke acting archdeacon of Leicester for the first year of his episcopate (he was consecrated on 7 June 1235), and appointed him permanently, giving him the prebend of St

Margaret's, Leicester, which he himself had retained up to his election to Lincoln diocese. Basingstoke's knowledge of the Byzantine world and of the Greek language formed the basis of their relationship.

Matthew Paris credited Basingstoke with the knowledge of a Greek system of representing numbers by the employment of a system of strokes. He records his death in the year 1252.   JAMES MCEVOY

Sources Paris, *Chron.* · *Roberti Grosseteste episcopi quondam Lincolniensis epistolae*, ed. H. R. Luard, Rolls Series, 25 (1861) · *Commentarii de scriptoribus Britannicis, auctore Joanne Lelando*, ed. A. Hall, 2 (1709), 266 · Bale, *Cat.*, 1.302 · M. de Jonge, *Studies in the 'Testaments of the twelve patriarchs'* (1975) · R. W. Southern, *Robert Grosseteste: the growth of an English mind in medieval Europe*, 2nd edn (1992) · M. de Jonge, 'Robert Grosseteste and the *Testaments of the twelve patriarchs*', *Journal of Theological Studies*, new ser., 42 (1991), 115–25

Basire, Isaac, de Preaumont (*bap.* 1608, *d.* 1676), Church of England clergyman and traveller, the son of Jean Basire, advocate and minor noble, and his wife, Judith le Macherier (*d.* 1626), was baptized at the Huguenot church in Rouen, France, in 1608. Little is known of his early years, but he was a student at the School of Erasmus in Rotterdam from October 1623. He enrolled at Leiden University in 1625, eventually graduating MA. In 1627 he published *De purgatorio et indulgentiis*, a disputation, and studied in The Hague, while an entry in the register of the Queen Elizabeth College, Guernsey, about this time lists him as a master there.

By 1629 Basire was firmly established in England, in order, he claimed, to further his studies, but there would seem to be more to it than that. His time at Leiden coincided with the rise of Arminianism, favoured in the university by two of his teachers, Gerard Vossius and Johannes Polyander. Since both were admirers of the Church of England and of the emphasis placed by English Arminians on the sacraments and the liturgy it is likely that they influenced his choice. Basire was not, however, a full-blooded Arminian. Polyander himself supported the canons of Dort, and in England Basire worked closely with the Calvinist Bishop Thomas Morton of Coventry and Lichfield. On 31 May 1629 Basire was ordained deacon by Bishop Morton and ordained priest the following day. In 1631 he became Morton's domestic chaplain and accompanied him to Durham when he was translated there in 1632.

In 1635 Basire spent three months at St John's College, Cambridge, graduating BD in July 1635. Probably later that year or in 1636 he married Frances Corbett (*d.* 1676), a member of an old Shropshire family. The couple had seven children in the 1640s, of whom five survived infancy. Mary, the eldest (*b.* 1642), in 1671 married one of her father's curates, Jeremy Nelson, later a canon of Carlisle. Isaac (*b.* 1643) after the Restoration became a barrister and the official of his father's archdeaconry of Northumberland, working closely with him. Charles (1645–1691) was later rector of Boldon in the diocese of Durham. John was born in 1647, and Peter, the youngest, spent some time in France as a little boy under the care of various tutors, and became a Roman Catholic. He reconverted on his return to England and went to St John's College, Cambridge.

After his marriage promotion came quickly to Basire. In 1636 he became rector of Eaglescliffe; he was made DD in 1640 and in 1641 he was appointed a chaplain to the king. In 1643 Morton collated him to the seventh stall in Durham Cathedral, and in 1644 he became archdeacon of Northumberland with the rectory of Howick annexed. However, that year Basire was sequestered. When in 1645 the rich living of Stanhope, in the gift of the bishop of Durham, fell vacant, the king instructed the reluctant Morton to present Basire, but the appointment was purely nominal.

Basire's movements during the next three years are very uncertain. There is evidence that he was imprisoned briefly in Stockton Castle because of his loyalty to the king and that he visited Carlisle while it was under siege in 1645. Wood records that he was in attendance on the king and preached before him in 1646 during the siege of Oxford. He was also one of the chaplains licensed under the seal of the university 'to preach the Word of God throughout England' (Wood, *Ath. Oxon.: Fasti*, 2.57). In February or March 1647 he went into exile, leaving his wife at Eaglescliffe to look after their children and live upon the so-called 'fifths' of her husband's income, the unreliable parliamentary provision for the families of sequestered ministers. Basire went to live in Rouen on the patrimony of Preaumont left to him by his father. He hoped to be joined there by a number of pupils, whose fees would help maintain him and also enable him to send regular amounts to his wife. In the event only three pupils joined him, on 25 June 1647, and he had difficulty in getting any fees paid at all. All three came from families who supported the royal cause: Thomas Lambton, whose father had been killed at Marston Moor in 1644; John Ashburnham, whose father had been a gentleman-in-waiting on the king and who had accompanied Charles when he had escaped from Oxford during the siege; and one Andrews, of whom nothing is known.

Basire took them to Paris, where they stayed until March 1648 when they left for Italy. Basire took the precaution of obtaining letters of commendation from the exiled Queen Henrietta Maria: one was to a cardinal in Rome, 'for fear of the Inquisition', and another was to Sir Kenelm Digby, the king's representative there (Hunter MSS, fol. 9, nos. 61 and 63). They made leisurely progress, passing through Pisa, where they saw a stately tower of marble, 'built so strangely that a man would think it falling' (Hunter MSS, fol. 134, p. 120). Arriving in Rome they rested before setting out in October on a journey through the kingdom of Naples, then through Sicily to Malta where they were received so hospitably by the grand master of the order of St John that 'we were never in more danger of a religious knighthood' (Hunter MSS, fol. 94). They finally reached Rome again in February 1649, having travelled 1800 miles in four months. By this time his pupils had begun to return home, the last to leave being John Ashburnham, who left in May 1650.

Now alone Basire began to plan a long considered journey through the Near East. His purpose was to make known to the Greek Orthodox church the excellence of the Church of England and, as he wrote to Sir Richard Browne, the king's representative in Paris, to 'incline the Greek church to a communion with the Church of England together with a canonical reformation of some grosser errors' (*Correspondence*, 118). He had hoped that the exiled Charles II would have empowered him to take the first steps towards union. Basire believed that the essential teaching of the Church of England was contained in the prayer book catechism, so wherever he went he translated it, or had it translated, into the local language, leaving it behind that it might influence people to accept the Church of England as part of the true church. On one occasion he arranged for a Turkish translation to be sent to Mesopotamia.

From 1650 to 1654 Basire travelled the Near East in his self-appointed apostolate. He first went to Zante (Zátynthos) where he preached so effectively that he was persecuted by the Roman Catholics and had to escape to the mainland, where the metropolitan asked him to preach in Greek to the bishops and clergy, being 'well taken', as he modestly put it. After a brief visit to Italy, where he took a course in medicine at Padua University, Basire spent Easter 1652 at Aleppo, taking the opportunity of discussions with the leaders of the Greek church there. In the summer he visited the sacred sites in the Holy Land, being delighted to be given a certificate of pilgrimage by the 'Pope's Vicar' in which he was styled 'Sacerdotem Ecclesiae Anglicanae', at which titles, he said, 'many marvelled, especially the French ambassador there' (*Correspondence*, 117ff). He spent the winter of 1652 to 1653 in Aleppo and in the spring of 1653 made a remarkable journey of 600 miles to Constantinople, travelling with twenty Turkish merchants with whom he talked in Arabic and to whom he acted as medical adviser, using the knowledge he had gained at Padua University. In Constantinople he acted as chaplain to the British embassy and also to the French community there, on condition that with them he would use his own translation of the Book of Common Prayer.

In 1654 all Basire's plans for his tour were upset when he accepted an invitation from George Racoczi II, prince of Transylvania, to be professor of theology at the University of Alba Julia believing that it was a further opportunity to stress the position of the Church of England as a bridge to unity. While the prince welcomed him and Charles II wrote an endorsement of him in November 1655, there was opposition from the radical Calvinist members of the staff. Nicholas Bethlen, future chancellor of Transylvania, then a student there, liked Basire personally but was critical of his teaching and beliefs. Basire aimed to reorganize the Transylvanian church on Anglican lines and to improve the education provided by the college, preparing a detailed plan of reform. However, this was forestalled by a Turkish invasion in which the country was devastated and the University of Alba Julia destroyed. Forced to flee, Basire acted as secretary to Racoczi, corresponding on his behalf with countries from which the prince hoped for assistance and drafting proclamations, the most notable being *Tuba Transylvanica*, of which no copy seems to have survived. A number of letters have survived in which Basire tells Racoczi that he must act more firmly to care for the people of his kingdom who were suffering terribly, even urging him to abdicate if he could do nothing to help them.

In 1660, when Racoczi was killed at the battle of Gyala, Basire stayed to perform his obsequies and to act as tutor to the young prince, Ferenc, but finally began his long journey home and landed at Hull in June 1661, where he found his wife and their five children in perfect health. On 26 November John Evelyn records hearing at Westminster Abbey

> Dr Basire, that great traveller or rather French apostle who had been planting the Church of England in divers parts of the Levant and Asia. He showed that the Church of England was, for purity of doctrine, substance, decency and beauty, the most perfect under heaven. (*Diary*, 3.303)

It is doubtful, however, whether Basire's efforts had had any success. Certainly he established friendly relations with local patriarchs and bishops and presented them with catechisms, but there is no evidence that they modified their views because of him. Perhaps on occasions the orthodox leaders found in Basire and his Anglicanism simply an encouragement in their continual struggle against the Latins. At least Basire and the others had made the Greeks aware of Anglicanism and their fellow Anglicans aware of the Orthodox, and so anticipated the contacts which would take place in the nineteenth century.

Between the death of Racoczi and Basire's return to England new editions of two of his books were published. In *The History of the English and Scottish Presbyteries* (1650; 2nd edn, 1660) Basire roundly condemned the presbyterians for their betrayal of king and church and urged the Huguenots to recognize the Church of England as the one true protestant church in England, with which they could enter into union, since he and like-minded clergy such as Jean Durel and Samuel Brevint regarded the Huguenot lack of bishops as an accident of history. In *The Ancient Liberty of the Brittanick Church* (1661) Basire made his contribution to the classical definition of Anglicanism in the seventeenth century, a definition which was part of the conservative protestant counter-reformation against the Calvinist reformed inheritance. He argued that the Church of England was neither a reformed section of the Roman church nor a conservative branch of the reformed church. It had its own identity, going back to the earliest days of Christianity in Britain; it was part of the true Catholic church, based on the scripture, the creeds, the threefold ministry, and the first four general councils of the church; and free of the corruptions of Rome.

By January 1662 Basire was established again in Durham, contemplating the restoration of the church and its liturgy in the north, a task which 'will take up the whole man; 1st to reform the persons; 2nd to repair the churches' (Hunter MSS, fol. 137), and demanding, given his other commitments as prebendary and as royal chaplain,

a year of 475 days. For the next twenty years he co-operated with the bishop in the restoration. Often asked to write accounts of his travels and of the various churches he had encountered, he always pleaded pressure of work and lack of time. He did, however, produce two books. *Sacrilege Arraigned* (1668) originated in a sermon preached before Charles I at Oxford in 1646 and printed by royal command. His theme was that sacrilege is 'the abuse of things sacred, or belonging to the service of God, whether the Abuse be committed by way of violation, through profaneness or usurpation, through fraud or covetousness' (p. 13). This sacrilege was seen in many ways: the stealing of tithes by laymen; impropriations; the usurpation by others of the place of the clergy. *Dead Man's Real Speech* (1673) contained both the sermon he preached at Bishop John Cosin's funeral in 1672 on Hebrews 11:4, 'and by it he being dead yet speaketh', and a detailed account of Cosin's life. In the latter Basire showed how the dead man spoke to them by the example of his actions, interspersed with notes about his own life and beliefs, especially in the excellence of the Church of England: 'I dare pronounce of the Church of England what David said of Goliath's sword, There is none like it, both for Primitive Doctrine, Worship, Discipline and Government, Episcopal Hierarchy, the most moderate and regular' (p. 41).

In the last three years of his life Basire was often in poor health. In September 1676 he was suffering from jaundice, scurvy, and 'stone-griping in his belly' (Bodl. Oxf., MS Rawl. lett. 101, fol. 39). He died in Durham on 13 October 1676 and was buried the following day in the cathedral churchyard, 'decently and frugally' at his own request, but alongside the grave of a servant who had served him for many years rather than alongside his wife of forty years, who had predeceased him by only a few months.

COLIN BRENNEN

Sources Durham Cath. CL, Hunter MSS · *The correspondence of Isaac Basire*, ed. W. N. Darnell (1831) · *DNB* · Wood, *Ath. Oxon.: Fasti* (1820), 57 · *An excellent letter from John Basire*, trans. I. Basire (1670) · *Diary and correspondence of John Evelyn*, ed. W. Bray, rev. edn, ed. [J. Forster], 4 vols. (1859–62) · Bodl. Oxf., MSS Rawl. · I. Basire, *The history of the English and Scottish presbyteries* (1660) · I. Basire, *The ancient liberty of the Brittanick church* (1661) · I. Basire, *Dead man's real speech* (1673) · G. du Rieu, ed., *Album studiosorum academiae Lugduno Batavae, MDLXXV–MDCCCLXXV: accedunt nomina curatorum et professorum per eadem secula* (The Hague, 1875) · admission register, St John Cam. · register, Durham Cathedral
Archives Durham Cath. CL, corresp. and papers
Wealth at death reasonably well off: will

Basire, Isaac (1704–1768), printmaker and draughtsman, was the son of James Basire of St James's, Westminster, who was thought to have been of Huguenot origin. Isaac was the progenitor of four generations of the Basire family to be noted as printmakers from the early eighteenth century to 1869. He was apprenticed to the silver-engraver Lewis Cuney of London on 26 April 1717 and to Samuel David Jallason of St James's, Westminster, in 1721. There is little information on his career and personal life except that he was 'a fine chubby-faced man' (Nichols, *Lit. anecdotes*, 3.717). In George Vertue's list of 'London engravers for 1744', he is described as 'Basire-etching' (Vertue, *Note* *books*, 6.198). Though his output is of a modest calibre various publication lines on his prints reveal that he lived and worked in St John's Gate, Clerkenwell, from where he specialized in cartography, engraving several notable maps including John Rocque's 1749 map of London (with Richard William Seale). He also produced ornamental designs and title-pages such as one for Bailey's *Dictionary* in 1755. In 1760 he was also engraver to the Royal Society for whom he worked until his death.

Like many other printmakers in the first third of the eighteenth century, Isaac Basire regularly plagiarized, and undercut, the more lucrative designs of his competitors. In 1733 he copied and then published a set of flower prints at half the price of that of his commercial rival, Henry Fletcher, who had originally produced and published the same designs. As a result of this venture, Basire was one of the engravers invited to give evidence before the House of Commons committee reviewing the so-called Hogarth Act which resulted in the establishment of copyright protection for engravers in 1733. The passing of this important legislation served to stabilize and improve the position of British printmakers and was one of the fundamental reasons behind the flourishing of that art during the ensuing generations.

Isaac Basire married Sarah Flavill on 24 August 1728 at St John, Clerkenwell, London, and they had three children before Isaac's death in Islington on 24 August 1768 in the house to which his modest success had allowed him to retire. He was buried on 27 August 1768 at the church of St John, Clerkenwell.

Isaac Basire's eldest son, **James Basire** (*bap.* 1730, *d.* 1802), engraver, was baptized at St John, Clerkenwell, on 6 October 1730. His younger brothers were Isaac, who was apprenticed to the printer William Griffin in 1759, and John (*c*.1734–*c*.1802), who was apprenticed to James Gibbs, a watch-finisher, and made free of the Clockmakers' Company in 1756 before turning to engraving and taking over his father's publishing company at 16 St John's Gate, Clerkenwell. Although John's career was evidently solid, his older brother James was by far the most successful and acclaimed of the entire Basire family and was renowned for his 'correct drawing and firm lines' (Eaves, xxiii). Bound on 3 September 1745, he received his first training under apprenticeship to the engraver Richard William Seale of St Andrew's, Holborn. He then continued his education under the guidance of the artist, engraver, and antiquarian Richard Dalton who took the young Basire to Italy in 1749. At Easter 1750 'Giacomo Bessier'—as he there rather presumptuously signed himself—is recorded as residing at the Palazzo Zuccari in Rome, in a small community comprising Dalton, Thomas Patch, Joseph Wilton, and Matthew Brettingham. Inspired by this artistic company, Basire spent much time training his eye and hand by making chalk drawings after Raphael and Guercino, and several of these sketches were later worked up into copperplates and published by John Boydell in 1765. Under the auspices of his master, Dalton, it is also likely that Basire mixed freely with the many English gentlemen and artists, including Sir Joshua Reynolds, who were in Rome

at that time. He certainly made one important contact in the architect James 'Athenian' Stuart who later employed him to engrave some of the plates for his and Nicholas Revett's luxury publication *The Antiquities of Athens, Measured and Delineated* (1762–1816). Stuart and Revett's confidence in Basire's skill is suggested by the fact that he was responsible for producing some of the crucial first plates in this expensive volume where the need to please the subscribers and secure their continuing support was essential.

It is not clear when Basire returned from Rome but it was probably by the time he was made free of the Stationers' Company on 5 December 1752 and by the 1760s his career as a reproductive etcher and engraver had really begun to flourish. At premises in Fetter Lane, and later in Great Queen Street, in 1760 he also took on the first in a long line of apprentices. During the 1760s his name is associated with a diverse range of genres including engraved portraits, cartography, a few etchings after Hogarth, notably *The Farmer's Return* (n.d.), and numerous title-page vignettes such as the delicate classical design that he etched for George Keate's *The Alps: a Poem* (1763). It was in 1761 that he sent the first of many plates for exhibition at the Free Society of Artists. Most of these were classical antiquities and architectural subjects but the wide range of patrons Basire served as well as the diversity of his talents can be usefully assessed from Algernon Graves's *A dictionary of artists who have exhibited works in the principal London exhibitions from 1760 to 1893* (1969) which lists over eighty-five exhibition pieces by Basire between 1761 and 1783.

Having already familiarized himself with the techniques of drawing and the work of the Italian old masters Basire became involved in the connoisseur Charles Rogers's publication of his *Collection of Prints in Imitation of Drawings* (1778) and with William Wynne Ryland was responsible for developing 'various dotted techniques' (Clayton, 176) which, when combined with soft-ground etching, served to produce effective facsimiles of many important old master chalk drawings. Most importantly, however, following George Vertue's death in 1755 he was appointed engraver to the Society of Antiquaries on 8 March 1759 and after that time documentary or pictorial antiquarian engraving, for both the society and more commercial publishers, formed the mainstay of Basire's career. Over the next twenty years, this institutional position afforded Basire constant employment and exposure, and a much enhanced reputation as well as introductions to a number of potential patrons who needed the services of a specialist antiquarian engraver; one such was Charles Cordiner who later employed Basire among a group of engravers to produce the plates for his *Antiquities and Scenery of the North of Scotland* (1780). Nearly all of the society's engraved publications were executed by Basire during this period and he was solely responsible for providing some unity to the often scrappy appearance of the volumes of *Archaeologia* and *Vetusta monumenta* where engravings such as *A View of Richmond Palace … as Built by King Henry VII* (1765) typify what Richard Gough would later commend as Basire's 'accurate drawings of monuments' (*GM*, 1st ser., 79/1, 1809, 319). Furthermore, it was under the auspices of the Society of Antiquaries that Basire embarked upon one of the most extravagant print ventures of the whole eighteenth century. This began in 1770 when he was commissioned to engrave the first of a suite of spectacular and enormous historical paintings: *The Field of the Cloth of Gold* (*c*.1550–1580), which depicts the festivities following the meeting of Henry VIII with the French king Francis I within the pale of Calais in 1520. Initially the society charged Edward Edwards to make a reduced watercolour copy of this painting but the shape and size of the original painting were such that it was impossible to reduce it to an engraving of an ordinary format. Consequently, after consultation with Basire, they were forced to commission James Whatman to produce a new size of paper especially for the publication; his 'antiquarian' paper at 31 by 53 inches remained the largest paper available for more than a century. Evidently, then, the fame of this work, which was proclaimed as the largest single plate ever to be engraved, was ensured before Basire ever set burin to copper. His work on this single plate, measuring 4 feet 1 inch by 2 feet 3 inches, was intricate, minutely detailed, and finely executed and took Basire over two years to complete. It was also highly prized by the society who, with the help of a contribution from Lord Hardwicke, paid Basire £200 for his labour and printed only 400 copies, some of which were sold to the public at 2 guineas each.

It appears that Basire earned a reputation as a reliable and diplomatic man who was able to answer the needs of the many demands of such a diffuse institution. This is confirmed by a note from Richard Gough in 1782, which recorded that 'Mr James Basire['s] … burin will do credit to every individual or body of men who employ it' (Nichols, *Lit. anecdotes*, 2.586). Consequently he must have been an obvious choice when, following in his father's footsteps, he was appointed engraver to the Royal Society in 1770. He also worked closely with many of the leading artists of the day. He was a friend of Benjamin Woolett and was employed to engrave several individually published works after Benjamin Wilson and Benjamin West, including West's *Pylades and Orestes* in 1766, one of the first prints of a contemporary painting to be published by John Boydell. By the beginning of the 1770s Basire's workload was onerous but he was helped by several apprentices including his two sons, James Basire [*see below*] and Richard Woolett Basire, and, most famously, William Blake who worked in the Great Queen Street workshop between 1773 and 1778 and is said to have thought Basire to be 'a superior, liberal-minded man, ingenious and upright; and a kind master' (Gilchrist, 1.14).

Although Basire's use of engraved outline and cross-hatching was typical of a painstaking and methodical style that was already going out of fashion, Blake was attracted to Basire's studio by his knowledge of Italian art and his connections with contemporary artists. While bound apprentice, Blake was sent to draw the monuments and buildings that Basire later engraved for patrons such as Richard Gough, and, though Blake soon sought other training, he 'always retained a loyal feeling towards his old master; and would stoutly defend him and his style against that of more attractive and famous engravers' (ibid., 20).

James Basire the elder was married twice: first to Anne Beaupuy and second to Isabella Turner, and from his second marriage had two sons. He died on 6 September 1802 at 34 Great Queen Street, Lincoln's Inn Fields, and was buried in Pentonville Chapel. He was survived by his elder son, **James Basire** (1769–1822), engraver, who was born on 12 November 1769. Having been bound apprentice to his father on 3 September 1784, the younger James Basire continued in the family tradition as an engraver. Though his career followed his father's closely, he never attained his father's celebrity. He was bequeathed £500 in Richard Gough's will of 1809 as a mark of respect to his father rather than to himself. Like his father he was made free of the Stationers' Company (1 March 1791) and succeeded him as engraver to the Royal Society. Much of his best line engraving of natural history subjects can be found in the pages of the society's *Philosophical Transactions*. He continued the family firm's interest in cartography, producing maps for Thomas Telford and John Rennie, and for Hansard. Given the overlap in their subjects, style, and institutional involvement, as well as the rather unhelpful signature Js. Basire which appears on both men's prints, the work of the father and the son has often been confused.

It is probable James Basire's passage in the art world was enhanced by his father's reputation and this is evinced by the number of plates that he too executed for the Society of Antiquaries. Nevertheless, he was not formally appointed engraver to the society and the changing relationship between the society and its engravers is demonstrated in Joseph Farington's record of the competition that the younger Basire faced when submitting his sketches of the Townley Helmet, for publication in *Vetusta monumenta*, in 1799. In this instance he did win the commission but during the first decades of the nineteenth century the society employed a variety of engravers to work on its publications. Typically, James Basire worked in the very simple linear style of outline engraving that had been made popular by John Flaxman and his followers. Its clarity and apparent authority answered the needs of John Carter, an antiquarian and architectural draughtsman, who had previously worked with the elder James and continued to employ the younger James to produce the diagrammatic plates for his treatises on English cathedrals, such as *Some Account of the Collegiate Chapel of Saint Stephen, Westminster* (1795–1806), which were sponsored by the Society of Antiquaries. Like his father, James augmented his income by taking on apprentices and by working for commercial publishers producing illustrations for popular topographical publications; he also engraved the *Oxford Almanack* for the years 1797 to 1809 and 1811 to 1814. The most important work of the latter part of his career was a set of seventeen plates of the Bayeux tapestry on which he worked in 1819–22.

James Basire married Mary Cox on 1 May 1795 and they had three children. James died on 13 May 1822 at Chigwell Wells, Essex. His eldest son was **James Basire** (1796–1869). Though he continued in the family business as a line engraver, by the 1830s he had branched out into the new, fashionable, and cost-effective medium of lithography. This he used to great effect in the diagrams and illustrations he was regularly employed to produce to accompany the published reports of parliamentary committees. Examples of his work can be found in the appendices to *Report from the Select Committee on the National Gallery* (1853) and *The Report from the Select Committee on the South Kensington Museum* (1860). Despite the frequent division of labour in the lithographic process, James Basire was not only a skilled printmaker and cartographer (he produced railway, canal, and sewerage maps as well as maps for Hansard), he was also a professional lithographic printer and the publication lines on his prints reveal that he ran a lithographic printshop, first at 7 Quality Court, Chancery Lane, from 1822 to 1840, and then at 4 Red Lion Square from 1846 to 1850. He is not known to have married and was the last of the Basire family of printmakers and engravers. He died on 17 May 1869 at his home, 66 Huntingdon Street, Barnsbury Park, Islington, London.

LUCY PELTZ

Sources B. Adams, *London illustrated, 1604–1851* (1983) · D. Bindman, *William Blake: his art and times* (1982) · J. Britton, *The autobiography of John Britton*, 3 vols. in 2 (privately printed, London, 1849–50) · Bryan, *Painters* (1903–5) · T. Clayton, *The English print, 1688–1802* (1997) · M. Eaves, *The counter-arts conspiracy: art and industry in the age of Blake* (1992) · A. Gilchrist, *Life of William Blake, 'Pictor ignotus'*, 2 vols. (1863) · Graves, *Artists*, 3rd edn · J. Ingamells, ed., *A dictionary of British and Irish travellers in Italy, 1701–1800* (1997) · Nichols, *Lit. anecdotes* · R. Paulson, *Hogarth*, 2 (1992) · F. Tatham, *The letters of William Blake, together with a life*, ed. A. G. B. Russell (1906) · G. Meissner, ed., *Allgemeines Künstlerlexikon: die bildenden Künstler aller Zeiten und Völker*, [new edn, 34 vols.] (Leipzig and Munich, 1983–) · Thieme & Becker, *Allgemeines Lexikon* · D. Alexander, 'Basire', *The dictionary of art*, ed. J. Turner (1996) · M. Twyman, *A directory of London lithographic printers, 1800–1850* (1976) · Vertue, *Note books* · CGPLA Eng. & Wales (1869) · private information (2004) [D. Alexander, B. Nurse, L. Worms]
Likenesses J. Basire, engraving (James Basire, d. 1802), repro. in Nichols, *Lit. anecdotes* · line engraving (James Basire, d. 1802), BM, NPG; repro. in Nichols, *Lit. anecdotes* · oils (James Basire, d. 1802)
Wealth at death under £8000—James Basire (d. 1869): probate, 18 June 1869, CGPLA Eng. & Wales

Basire, James (*bap.* 1730, *d.* 1802). *See under* Basire, Isaac (1704–1768).

Basire, James (1769–1822). *See under* Basire, Isaac (1704–1768).

Basire, James (1796–1869). *See under* Basire, Isaac (1704–1768).

Baskervile [*née* Shawe], **Susan** (*bap.* 1573, *d.* 1649), theatre company associate, was baptized at St Botolph's, Aldgate, London, on 15 April 1573, the daughter of Edmonde Shawe. A younger brother, John, was also baptized there on 12 February 1575. On 4 January 1592, aged eighteen, Susan married Robert Browne (*d.* 1603) of St Saviour's,

Southwark. They had five children, Robert, William, Susanna, Elizabeth, and Anne.

Browne was an actor with the Earl of Derby's Men in 1599 while they played at the Boar's Head playhouse in Whitechapel. By 1600 he had become the actor-lessee of the theatre, where Oliver Woodliffe, a haberdasher, and Francis Langley, were co-landlords. Woodliffe and Langley seriously impeded the running of the theatre, hiring men to stop performances, taking money from the gatherers (who collected entrance money), and enforcing payments from the companies. When trouble of this kind led the Worcester's Men to curtail their season in the theatre in 1601, Browne took them to court and the company counter-sued. Browne won the case, but when he died in 1603 Joan, wife of the famous actor Edward Alleyn, wrote to her husband that he died 'very pore' (R. A. Foakes and R. T. Rickert, eds., *Henslowe's Diary*, 1961, 297).

Some time after this Susan Browne married Thomas *Greene (*bap.* 1573, *d.* 1612), the leader and clown of the Worcester's Men, who after the accession of James I were known as the Servants of Queen Anne. These actors now played at their own theatre, the Red Bull in Clerkenwell. The Greenes had one daughter, Honor, who was baptized at St James's, Clerkenwell, on 17 April 1609. Greene died in 1612 and that August was buried in the chancel at St James's; Honor was buried with her father in 1618.

Susan was now a widow with prospects. She was the owner of at least part of the Boar's Head playhouse from her marriage to Browne, and also held considerable shares in the Red Bull. Apart from inheriting shares in these buildings, she also felt she was entitled to Greene's company share along with some money she claimed the actors owed him. The company disagreed, but Robert Sidney, Viscount Lisle, the chamberlain to Queen Anne, upheld her claim, and eventually the company came to terms with her, allowing her a half-share of their profits until the debt was cleared. Subsequent disputes over payments led to the negotiation of a number of further agreements.

In June 1613 Susan married James Baskervile; they had one son, Francis, who died in 1616. Both Baskerviles involved themselves in the theatre company's finances until their expectations accrued to the value of 3s. 8d. per day, a sum that the company found it difficult to find. In the end the hold Mistress Baskervile had over the company, which following the queen's death in 1619 was renamed the Players of the Revels, became intolerable for them; in 1623 three of the actors took her to court. There was a long and tortuous battle, involving former members of the old Queen's Servants, until the actors lost their suit in 1626. By this time Susan's third husband, who seems to have married her bigamously, had deserted her. None the less, despite both the novelty of share-ownership in the developing economically centred theatre world and the ambiguous situation regarding widows' rights after the deaths of their player-husbands, Susan stands as an example of a 'theatre widow' able to survive and even flourish. As well as owning shares in the Boar's Head and the Red Bull, there is also evidence that she owned a twenty-fourth part of the Fortune Theatre. As executor and beneficiary to the will of her son, the actor William Browne, drawn up in 1634, she also showed herself a sharp financial dealer, coming to blows with her daughter-in-law about her son's assets. Nothing is known of her later life. She must have died in late January 1649 at St James's, Clerkenwell, where she was buried on 1 February.

EVA GRIFFITH

Sources GL, MS 9220 · memoranda book, LMA, St Botolph Aldgate MS 9234/2 · H. Berry, *The Boar's Head playhouse* (Washington, 1986) · R. Hoyenden, ed., *Registers of St James Clerkenwell*, Harleian Society (1884–91) · PRO, C24/500/103 and 9 · C. J. Sisson, 'The Red Bull company and the importunate widow', *Shakespeare Survey*, 7 (1954), 57–68 · C. J. Sisson, 'Notes on early Stuart stage history', *Modern Language Review*, 37 (1942), 25–36 · M. Eccles, 'Elizabethan actors, I: A–D', *N&Q*, 236 (1991), 38–49, esp. 41 · M. Eccles, 'Elizabethan actors, II: E–J', *N&Q*, 236 (1991), 454–61, esp. 456–7 · LMA, DLC/2.7 [photocopy R1098] · F. G. Fleay, *A chronicle history of the London stage, 1559–1642* (1890) · E. A. J. Honigmann and S. Brock, eds., *Playhouse wills, 1558–1642: an edition of wills by Shakespeare and his contemporaries in the London theatre* (1993) · PRO, REQ2/709
Archives Hunt. L., The Wallace Collection
Wealth at death 1/24 share of Fortune Theatre plus shares in tiring-house and yard of the Red Bull?: Sisson, 'Notes on early Stuart stage history'; PRO, REQ2/709

Baskerville, Hannibal (1597–1668), antiquarian dilettante, was born at St Valéry in Picardy on 5 April 1597, the only son of Sir Thomas *Baskerville (d. 1597), commander of the English army in France, and his wife, Mary (d. 1632), daughter of Sir Thomas Throgmorton or Throckmorton of Tortworth, Gloucestershire. His father died in France when he was only nine weeks old. He was educated by Henry Peacham, author of *The Compleat Gentleman*, and on 12 May 1612 was admitted to Brasenose College, Oxford. Later he travelled on the continent with an English ambassador. In 1599 his mother had married, second, Sir James Scudamore. In 1619 her servant Thomas Clerkson wrote to Baskerville passing on his mother's advice to take his 'adversaries' to court (MS Rawl. lett. 41). The adversary in this case was her husband, who claimed the wardship of Baskerville and the dower of his mother. By November 1621 the case had been settled in Baskerville's favour and he was from then on able to enjoy his inheritance, namely the manors of Sunningwell and Bayworth in Berkshire which his father had purchased. Soon afterwards he married his cousin Mary (1602–1644), widow of John Morgan and daughter of his uncle Nicholas Baskerville. They had six sons and two daughters, including Thomas *Baskerville, topographer.

On the strength of Anthony Wood's description of a visit to his house in February 1659, Baskerville has been regarded as an antiquary. While his papers show an interest in recent historical events there is no substantial body of work which would qualify Baskerville as a scholar. His antiquarian activities apparently amounted to little more than dabblings, predominantly relating to his own family. His surviving papers include only brief memoranda, such as his notes on church monuments observed on his travels, details about Oxford colleges, a memorandum on the Royal Mint, lists of ambassadors and soldiers, and a few transcribed poems.

In 1619, at the same time as he took action against Scudamore, Baskerville made a vow to give a certain proportion of his estate to pious uses. Forty years later Wood, who thought him a 'melancholy and retird man', was told that he then gave:

> the third or fourth part of his estate to the poor. He was so great a cherisher of wandering beggars that he built for them a larg place like a barne to receive them, and hung up a little bell at his back-dore for them to ring when they wanted anything. (Wood, *Ath. Oxon.*, xxxiii)

This resulted in him being indicted for harbouring beggars on more than one occasion. He died in 1668, perhaps on 16 March. Nearly the whole value of his moveable goods was spent on his lavish funeral at Sunningwell church on 18 March. His heir was his son Thomas (d. 1700).

IAN MORTIMER

Sources Wood, *Ath. Oxon.*, new edn, 1.xxxiii–xxxiv · Bodl. Oxf., MS Rawl. D, vol. 859 · *VCH Berkshire*, 4.424, 426 · Bodl. Oxf., MS Rawl. letters, 41 · E. Ashmole, *The visitation of Berkshire, 1664–6*, ed. W. C. Metcalfe (1882), 10 · *DNB* · catalogue entry, PRO, C115/62/5482–92 [*Baskerville v. Scudamore*] · [C. B. Heberden], ed., *Brasenose College register, 1509–1909*, 1, OHS, 55 (1909), 119
Archives BL, passports for foreign travel, Harley MS 4762
Wealth at death £118 in moveable possessions; also two manors: probate inventory, Berks. RO

Baskerville, John (1706–1775), printer and typefounder, was born at Sion Hill, Wolverley, near Kidderminster, Worcestershire, the son of John Baskervile (d. 1738) and his wife, Sara or Sarah; he was baptized at Wolverley on 28 January 1707. It is likely that the family were landowners and farmers in a small way. In later life Baskerville (who occasionally spelt the name Baskervill) was accustomed to allow his parents the sole benefits, amounting to £75 a year, from a small inheritance.

Early years and marriage According to a story gathered at second hand after his death, Baskerville was a footman to 'a clergyman of King's Norton, near Birmingham, who used to instruct the poor youths of his parish in writing', a task in which Baskerville assisted him (Noble, 362). In 1726 he moved to Birmingham, where he became a writing-master in a little court near the upper part of High Street. He was also a letter-cutter and about 1730 cut the following text on a slab of slate, 22 by 27 cm, in five lines of roman, italic, and Gothic lettering: 'Grave stones cut in any of the hands by John Baskervill writing-master' (the slate is now held by the Central Library, Birmingham). Some lines are ornamented with professionally executed flourishes in the manner of contemporary writing-masters, and one is cut in a letter that closely resembles the style that he later adopted for his printing type. Although anecdotes were published during the nineteenth century of two unsigned gravestones that were said to have been cut by Baskerville, no known surviving example can be attributed to him.

In 1728 Baskerville and his father jointly mortgaged their estate at Wolverley, probably in order to provide capital for the son's enterprises. In 1742, describing his occupation as 'Japanner' and referring to essays that he had already made for several years, Baskerville submitted a

John Baskerville (1706–1775), by James Millar, 1774

petition for a patent for 'Machinery for Rolling and Grinding Metal Plates or Veneers'; the making of 'japanned' or varnished goods which imitated imported lacquer work from Japan or China was already being carried on successfully in Birmingham, notably by John Taylor. Baskerville had taken a house in Moor Street, Birmingham, in 1740, and it served as his warehouse and workshop until 1749. Samuel Derrick, in a letter describing a visit to Baskerville in 1760, noted the large scale of the japanning business and Baskerville's talent for recruiting the skilled workmen that gave the enterprise its reputation. He carried on this profitable business throughout the greater part of his life, constantly introducing technical improvements.

In 1748 Baskerville secured a lease on 8 acres to the north-east of Birmingham. He named the estate Easy Hill, and built himself the house, with extensive gardens, in which he lived for the rest of his life. At some point before 1757 and possibly even before 1750, he was joined here by Sarah Eaves, *née* Ruston (*d.* 1788), married with a son and two daughters, whose husband, guilty of fraud, had deserted her and fled the country. He lived with Mrs Eaves, who was nominally his housekeeper, until the death of her husband in 1764 enabled them to marry at St Martin's, Birmingham, on 1 June—a disregard of contemporary ideas of morality that prompted ill-natured remarks in more than one memoir, although a more tolerant visitor, G. C. Lichtenberg, found her in 1775 to be 'an excellent woman' (*Lichtenberg's Visits to England*, 94).

Printer and typefounder Judging by a letter written in 1757 in which Baskerville recalled that he had 'pursued the Scheme of printing and Letter founding for Seven Years', it was about 1750 that he began his career as a printer and typefounder (Jay, 9). The earliest surviving news of his

preparation for printing is given in his letter dated 2 October 1752 to the London publisher and bookseller Robert Dodsley, sending impressions of some punches for new types 'to remove in some Measure y[ou]r Impatience'. It has been suggested that Baskerville's close link with Dodsley may have been established by an author already published by the latter, the poet William Shenstone, who was a close acquaintance of Baskerville's. In his letter Baskerville adds an assurance that 'the press is creeping slowly towards Perfection' and concludes with a request, relating to the examples of types: 'Pray put it in no One's Power to let Mr [William] Caslon see them' (Straus and Dent, 94). It is clear from this letter that Dodsley was already in agreement with Baskerville for the distribution of his first production, and that the novelty of its appearance was designed to make an impact on the public.

Although details of many of his improvements would be given in his letters to Dodsley and to other correspondents, Baskerville's only public explanation for his move at this time into this new activity is contained in the preface to his edition of Milton's *Paradise Lost* (1758):

> Amongst the several mechanic Arts that have engaged my attention, there is no one which I have pursued with so much steadiness and pleasure, as that of *Letter-Founding*. Having been an early admirer of the beauty of Letters, I became insensibly desirous of contributing to the perfection of them. I formed to my self Ideas of greater accuracy than had yet appeared, and have endeavoured to produce a *Sett of Types* according to what I conceived to be their true proportion.   (sig. A3r)

In the same passage there is a further reference to Caslon who, having served an apprenticeship in Birmingham as a metalworker and set up in business in London, had turned to punch-cutting and typefounding about 1720 in order to supply a consortium of London printers with types modelled largely on those that were available to them from typefounders in London or abroad. By 1730 the familiar design of his types and the high quality of their manufacture had enabled Caslon's typefoundry to dominate the market for types in Britain. His unceasing industry had also enabled him to make types for Arabic, Greek, Hebrew, Coptic, and other non-Latin scripts, as well as blackletter and ornaments. For all the superficial politeness of the phrasing, it is with evidently ironic intention that in his preface Baskerville offered the observation that by attempting to do too much Caslon had left 'room for improvement' in his roman and italic type (ibid.).

The letters of which Baskerville claimed to have been an early admirer were probably those of the published work of writing-masters. During the second half of the sixteenth century a new calligraphic style was developed in Italy. Smoother curves and a greater contrast between thick and thin strokes resulted from the use of a finer, more flexible pen. This effect was enhanced in printed writing manuals by the use of copperplate engraving. On the other hand printing types in use in the first half of the eighteenth century often repeated styles that had been introduced almost two centuries before. A contrast had thus developed in England, as in other countries, between the style of the letters used by printers and those of a new generation of writing-masters. Among the latter, the names of John Ayres, Charles Snell, and George Shelley were prominent, and they gained a wide reputation with their manuals during the years of Baskerville's youth.

Although his own references to the progress of the new type in correspondence with Dodsley imply that he was solely responsible for it, Baskerville appears to have had his punches made for him by a professional craftsman who worked under his close guidance. An obituary notice of John Handy in 1793 calls him 'the artist who executed the admired types of the late celebrated Mr. Baskerville', and it is not difficult to identify Handy as the unnamed person who was still in the service of Sarah Baskerville in 1775 after her husband's death and who was described as a:

> very honest man which performed all the manual opperations both in respect of filing the punchions, making the letter moulds and every other improvement which Mr Baskerville made in printing … This man can manage both the making of original punchions the foundry the paper and everything. (*GM*, 91; Pardoe, 140)

Further innovations Baskerville's innovations in printing went far beyond the making of new printing types. He had new presses made in which, although he maintained that no new principle was introduced, great attention was paid to accuracy of construction. The platen, or plate which made the impression on the type, was of brass instead of wood, and the 'stone' or bed on which the type rested was also of brass, features that had long been common in the Netherlands. Ink also received attention. Long after Baskerville's death, the printer T. C. Hansard claimed to have Baskerville's recipe, which he described in his technical manual *Typographia* (1825). After the basic varnish for the ink had been made in the conventional manner by boiling linseed oil, a quantity of amber and rosin was dissolved in it after it had cooled, an addition that (according to C. H. Bloy) would give an added sheen to ink after it had dried. The quality of the ink also depended on taking great care in the selection of the finest old linseed oil as a basis, on the careful preparation of the lampblack that was used as a pigment (which according to a French report was made by burning colza oil), and on the maturing of the varnish for some months before the pigment was added to it.

The characteristics of Baskerville's paper and its treatment after printing were no less novel than his typography. However, the source of his paper stock remains largely undocumented. He dealt in writing paper, which was advertised in the press and also in the prospectus for his edition of *Paradise Lost*, and Gaskell, remarking that there was no evidence that Baskerville ever owned a paper mill, observed that references in these advertisements to the special treatment applied to Baskerville's writing papers as 'manufacture' may account for occasional contemporary statements that he was a paper maker. Several sheets of Baskerville's edition of Virgil (1757) were printed on a 'wove' paper without a watermark, and this remains the first known use of such paper. Prized by fine printers for its smoothness, wove paper was made with a mould covered with a fabric of uniformly woven fine brass wires in place of the traditional use of single parallel 'laid' wires stitched at intervals; its invention was subsequently sometimes attributed to Baskerville, but it was probably invented by James Whatman of Kent. Similar paper is used in Baskerville's quarto edition of Milton (1759) and his edition of Dodsley's *Select Fables* (1761) but, although these are the only three titles for which he used wove paper, Baskerville's laid papers were often made in moulds of a fineness that makes their characteristic ribbing far less obtrusive than it is in most contemporary laid papers. The features of Baskerville's printing papers suggest that they were also the fruit of experimentation by Whatman, but there is some slight evidence that Baskerville may have had paper made to his own specification: in a letter of 7 April 1759 Dodsley asked Baskerville for 'twenty reams of Post made from your own moldes' (Hanson, review, 141).

Among the best-known of Baskerville's innovations, and the source of severe criticism of his books by some contemporaries, was his treatment of the printed sheets by 'glazing' or pressing them. Details of the process were guarded by him as a secret and as a result accounts are both sketchy and contradictory. According to information given by the manager of the printing office of Beaumarchais, which bought Baskerville's equipment after his death, the process involved two big brass cylinders between which the printed sheets were passed under pressure, while Hansard was told by an unnamed informant that Baskerville's method was to have 'a continued succession of hot plates of copper ready, between which as soon as they were printed … the wet plates were inserted. The wet was thus expelled, the ink set, and the trim, glossy surface put on all simultaneously' (Hansard, 331). It is possible that both sources give an incomplete account of Baskerville's technique, or that it changed over time. Several commentators observed that, with their glossy finish, the products of his printing office echoed the characteristics of his japanned wares. More relevantly, two visitors to Birmingham in 1765 found his printing 'so much resembling Copper Plate engraving as not to be distinguished' (Pardoe, 98). Baskerville inserted a minimum of packing in the tympans of his presses (the pair of frames that intervened between the solid platen and the type in order to cushion the impression) so that his new type was sharply impressed on the smooth paper with a thin film of ink, and the sheet received an additional gloss from the pressing that was applied after printing. The result was an effect that had hitherto been obtainable by the infinitely more laborious and expensive technique of printing from engraved copperplates.

Although Baskerville's books were priced in sheets (that is, unbound) and he is not known to have had a bindery of his own, a group of surviving bindings with similar tools and using his types for their labels indicate that one may have been closely associated with his printing office.

There is also evidence that he was concerned in the production of marbled paper.

Printing Virgil, Milton, and the Bible In 1754 Baskerville issued a specimen of his type incorporating a prospectus for his first printed work, a collection of Virgil's works, with additional specimen settings for the title-page and a page of the text. Publication was to be by subscription, with a price of 1 guinea in sheets. The correspondence with Dodsley dating from this time continues to give an account of Baskerville's progress of the different sizes of his type and the perfection of his printing press. The edition was announced for the beginning of 1757, and the continued delay in its completion caused Dodsley some anxiety until its appearance early in May. *Publii Virgilii Maronis Bucolica, Georgica, et Aeneis*, a quarto of nearly 450 pages, is regarded by many critics as the most accomplished of all Baskerville's printed books. Its startlingly novel and calligraphic type, the density of the ink, the excellence of the presswork, the smoothness and gloss of the paper—all these elements work in harmony in a design that was unusually sober for a relatively expensive book, since there are no copperplates or ornaments of any kind. Baskerville's biographers Straus and Dent rightly named the simplicity of the work of Robert and Andrew Foulis, university printers in Glasgow, among the influences on his book design. Before the completion of the Virgil edition Baskerville had been inclined to follow it with what he called a 'pocket classic'. In the event the second work from his press, and the most successful and often reprinted, was an octavo edition of Milton's *Paradise Lost* and *Paradise Regained*. Issued for reasons of copyright under the names of J. and R. Tonson and published with the date 1758 (it appeared in January 1759), it was oversubscribed, the greatest success of all Baskerville's productions in terms of sales.

In January 1758 Baskerville made an application to the University of Cambridge for leave to print an octavo prayer book (the university held the sole rights for this title jointly with the king's printer in London) and proposed to send two presses and workmen to Cambridge as soon as a place could be found for them. He was appointed university printer in December 1758, with permission to print two octavo prayer books, and—a project that he had described as his highest ambition—a folio Bible, for which he issued a prospectus in 1759. These projects were far from remunerative. Baskerville paid the university £20 for every 1000 copies of the octavo prayer book. Moreover in granting him his title, which he had leave to use only on these two projects, the university did not restrict the output of their existing university printer, Joseph Bentham, who continued to print prayer books and a folio Bible with the Cambridge imprint. Three editions of Baskerville's octavo prayer book were printed, the first of which was in big type (the Great Primer size used for the Virgil), 'calculated for people who begin to want Spectacles but are ashamed to use them at Church', and each appeared in two different versions, with and without a border of type ornaments to each page (Straus and Dent, 97). An initial prospectus for the Bible showed the same border but

offered subscribers the opportunity of expressing a choice of border or 'plain lines', and a revised prospectus of 1761 acknowledged that '[a]s many Gentlemen have objected to every Kind of Ornament round the Page, the work will be printed quite plain, with the marginal notes all at the bottom' (*The Holy Bible*, specimen, 1759; *The Holy Bible*, specimen, 1761). The resulting work, the folio Bible of 1763, has been judged as coming close to the Virgil, and the little duodecimo edition of Horace—a 'pocket classic' issued in 1762—as an example of Baskerville's mastery of his new style of book production, thus justifying his choice of the simpler design.

Shortly after the appearance of the Virgil in 1757 Baskerville approached the University of Oxford, offering to make a Greek type for its exclusive use. The offer was accepted and plans were laid for the production of a Greek New Testament as soon as the type should be ready. However, the resulting type was a disappointment both to printers and to classical scholars, and although the New Testament was printed in 1763, in quarto and octavo, the type was put aside by the university press and hardly ever used again.

Frustrations The 'tragedy' of Baskerville's professional life as a printer—the term is L. W. Hanson's—is that the high hopes of recognition for his unique contribution to his new profession, which were encouraged by Dodsley and by an initially friendly reception in the press, turned quickly to bitter disappointment (Hanson, review, 135). Writing to Horace Walpole in 1762, Baskerville complained already that 'the Booksellers do not chuse to encourage me, tho' I have offered them as low terms as I could possibly live by'. His work at Cambridge was done 'under such Shackles as greatly hurt me', and he complained of the expense of carriage to and from Cambridge and of maintaining a second printing house there:

> It is surely a particular hardship that I should not get Bread in my own Country (and it is too late to go abroad) after having acquired the Reputation of excelling in the Most useful Art known to Mankind, while everyone who excels as a Players, Fidler, Dancer &c. not only lives in Affluence, but has it in their power to save a Fortune.

He had sent specimens to the courts of Russia and Denmark, and would do the same to the other courts of Europe, offering to sell them 'the whole scheme', unless Walpole would save it for his own country. Its loss, a friend had said, would be 'a national Reproach' (Jay, 19–20). It was no doubt with the imminent disposal of his materials in mind that Baskerville prepared a first complete specimen of his types about this date.

One problem was the cost of Baskerville's printing, the result of methods of production which could not fail to be greater than those of the trade printers. There was also the matter of the text. Quite early in his correspondence with Dodsley, Baskerville outlined a scheme of proof correction which made it 'scarcely possible for the least difference, even of a point, to escape notice' (Straus and Dent, 96). 'Would that he had used it himself', wrote Gaskell, 'for his books are extraordinary as a group for their textual inaccuracy' (Gaskell, xxi). The make-up of

Baskerville's books is hugely complicated by the innumerable cancels (inserted reprinted leaves with textual corrections) that they contain—such practices added greatly to the cost of each title. It is not that Baskerville did not find any patronage at all among the London booksellers: the list of works with his imprint runs to over fifty items. But 'a closer look at the books which Baskerville printed for others suggests ... that he resembled Oscar Wilde's acquaintance who had dined *once* in every great house in London. Very few publishers asked Baskerville to print for them twice' (Hanson, review, 142).

A sense of wounded provincial pride is evident in Baskerville's reactions. In 1760, shortly after a visit to Birmingham where he called on both Matthew Boulton and Baskerville, Benjamin Franklin wrote intended words of comfort to the printer:

> Let me give you a pleasant instance of the prejudice some have entertained against your work. Soon after I returned, discoursing with a gentleman concerning the artists of Birmingham, he said you would be a means of blinding all the readers in the nation; for the strokes of your letters, being too thin and narrow, hurt the eye, and he could never read a line of them without pain. 'I thought,' said I, 'you were going to complain of the gloss on the paper some object to.' 'No, no,' said he, 'I have heard that mentioned, but it is not that; it is in the form and cut of the letters themselves; they have not that height and thickness of stroke which make the common printing [type] so much more comfortable to the eye.' (Jay, 17)

The conclusion of Franklin's letter, in which he tells how he got his gentleman to denounce a specimen of Caslon's type by tearing off the heading and passing it off as Baskerville's, can only have served to confirm Baskerville in his sense that the jealousy and prejudice now directed against him was personal and irrational.

Later activities From 1764 to 1768 Baskerville seems almost to have withdrawn from book printing, and in 1767–8 his assistant, Robert Martin, printed works under his own name with Baskerville's types. However, Baskerville was aroused again to activity by a Birmingham printer, Orion Adams, who in 1768 advertised a family Bible to be printed by Robert Martin, of which the title would be 'much more beautifully and methodically displayed than in Mr. Baskerville's'. A vituperative public argument ensued with Adams's partner Nicholas Boden, prompting Baskerville to print another folio Bible. He also began to print a new series of quarto classical texts under his own imprint: Lucretius's *De rerum natura*, the works of Catullus, Tibullus, and Propertius, and the comedies of Terence, a three-volume edition of Shaftesbury's *Characteristics*, and a four-volume edition of Ariosto's *Orlando Furioso*, for the Molini brothers in Paris.

The printing of the *Orlando Furioso* is significant, since it demonstrates that Baskerville's reputation was growing in continental Europe. Voltaire, to whom Baskerville had sent copies of his Virgil and Milton, had permitted the printer to set specimen pages of his own works in 1771. Fournier the younger praised his types in the second volume of his *Manuel typographique* (Paris, 1766). When the young Giambattista Bodoni left Rome in 1768 bound for England, it was presumably the reputation of Baskerville that had attracted him. In the preface to his first type specimen of 1771 Bodoni noted the praise that Baskerville's types had attracted and although at that date, as a printer in the Bourbon state of Parma, Bodoni prudently expressed a preference for those of Fournier, his mature style clearly shows Baskerville's influence. Among Bodoni's types of 1771 there is already a close copy of Baskerville's Greek.

Reaction to Baskerville's types was grudging in England, especially in London. The materials of a new typefoundry, established in Bristol by Joseph Fry and brought to London in 1768, were based on Baskerville's, but finding that the reception from the English trade was lukewarm, the foundry added types imitating closely the more traditional forms of those of the Caslon foundry. Nevertheless, the new style gradually became more acceptable. In the 1770s the Glasgow typefoundry of Alexander Wilson introduced types that were strongly influenced by Baskerville's.

Baskerville's failure to impose his style on the English book trade, centred as it still largely was on London, must have been all the more galling to an entrepreneur whose success in Birmingham, among a population renowned for its vigorous activity, was conspicuous. In 1761, the coronation year of George III, he was appointed high bailiff of Birmingham, a civic office with largely ceremonial duties. He was also a member of the Lunar Society, the club of scientific and industrial figures of the midlands founded by Matthew Boulton and including Erasmus Darwin, Josiah Wedgwood, Sir Joseph Banks, Sir William Herschel, and Joseph Priestley among its members. But although he had risen to become one of the major entrepreneurs of the city, Baskerville was not immune from local jealousies. As early as January 1749 he had found it necessary to place a notice in the *Birmingham Gazette* denying a malicious allegation that he had been arrested some time previously for debt. Contemporary accounts of his gorgeous coach, with painted panels 'got up in the japanware fashion', and of his showy clothes, display unconcealed dislike and derision: '[h]is favourite dress was green, edged with narrow gold lace; a scarlet waistcoat, with a very broad gold lace; and a small round hat, likewise edged with gold lace' (Noble, 361–2).

Death and reputation Baskerville died at his house at Easy Hill in January 1775. Most sources date the death 8 January although the *Birmingham Gazette* of 23 January gives the date as 'Monday last', that is, 16 January (Pardoe, 132). Baskerville's will left legacies to his own relatives and those of his wife, but she was the chief beneficiary, with provision for her daughters should she marry again, 'which If She Chuse I wish her happy Equal to her merit' (Straus and Dent, 116). Some bequests were explicitly curtailed on account of the 'Malice & Spleen' shown by the recipients. Baskerville left directions that his body was to be buried:

> in a Conical Building in my own premises Hearetofore used as a mill which I have lately Raised Higher and painted and in a vault which I have prepared for It. This Doubtless to

many may appear a Whim perhaps It is so—But it is a whim for many years Resolve'd upon, as I have a Hearty Contempt for all Superstition the Farce of a Consecrated Ground the Irish Barbarism of Sure and Certain Hopes &c I also consider Revelation as it is call'd Exclusive of the Scraps of Morality casually Intermixt with It to be the most Impudent Abuse of Common Sense which Ever was Invented to Befool Mankind.

He also attached to the will the text to be used for his epitaph:

Stranger—Beneath this Cone in Uncons[e]crated Ground
A Friend to the Liberties of mankind Directed his Body to be
    Inhum'd
May the Example Contribute to Emancipate thy mind
From the Idle Fears of Superstition
And the wicked arts of priesthood.
(Straus and Dent, 117)

The house at Easy Hill was burnt during riots in 1791. Baskerville's body was disinterred in 1820 and, having remained in a plumber's shop for some years, was placed without ceremony in a vault in Christ Church, Birmingham, in 1829. When this church was demolished in 1898 it was removed and buried beneath the chapel of the Church of England cemetery, Warstone Lane, Birmingham. This building in turn was later demolished and the vaults were bricked up.

One of the most balanced views of Baskerville, published anonymously in the *European Magazine* in 1785, was the work of the historian William Hutton:

In private life he was a humourist, idle in the extreme, but his invention was of the true Birmingham mould, active. He could well design, but procured others to execute; wherever he found merit, he caressed it: he was remarkably polite to the stranger, fond of shew: a figure rather of the smaller size, and delighted to adorn that figure with gold lace.— Although constructed with the light timbers of a frigate, his movement was as solemn as a ship of the line.

During the twenty-five years I knew him, though in the decline of life, he retained the traces of a handsome man. If he exhibited a peevish temper we may consider good nature and intense thinking are not always found together.

Taste accompanied him through the different walks of agriculture, architecture and the fine arts. Whatever passed through his fingers, bore the lively marks of John Baskerville.   (Hutton, 356–7)

Legacy After Baskerville's death his widow offered his printing office with the typefoundry and its materials for sale for £4000. In December 1779, negotiations having brought the price down to £3700, a sale was concluded with Pierre Augustin Caron de Beaumarchais. He was a principal actor in the Société Typographique et Littéraire which was established in order to produce the complete works of Voltaire at a printing office set up for this purpose at Kehl on the right bank of the Rhine in the principality of Baden-Durlach. To the edition of Voltaire in eighty-five volumes (issued in 1784–9) was added one of the works of Rousseau, and of the comedy *Le mariage de Figaro* by Beaumarchais himself. Pierre Didot, son of François-Ambroise, whose new types of about 1781 are recognized as among the earliest manifestations of a new

and more austere style in European typography, praised Baskerville as having shown the way by eliminating excessive ornament from printing:

Il sembloit que le Goût marchât à ses côtés;
Et de tous ces fleurons il a banni l'usage:
Le simple est du vrai beau la plus parfaite image.
('It seemed that Taste walked by his side. He banished the use of all these ornaments. Simplicity is the most perfect image of true beauty.' Didot, 4)

The knowledge that Baskerville's types were being used at Kehl attracted the attention of Vittorio Alfieri, who ordered the printing of several of his own plays, including *L'America libera*, from Beaumarchais, placing false dates on some that he judged too radical for immediate publication. The attraction of Baskerville's association with the rationalist and politically radical stream of British thought is nowhere better demonstrated than in the use of his types during the revolution in France in the official journal, the *Gazette Nationale, ou, Le Moniteur Universel*, following Beaumarchais's move to Paris in 1790; for some years the journal's imprint read, 'imprimé … avec les caractères de Baskerville'. Explicit copies of Baskerville's types were also made by the foundries of De Boubers, Brussels, and by the brothers Levrault in Strasbourg, who in 1797 included 'caractères dans le genre de Baskerville' in their specimen, the work of Claude Jacob, a self-styled pupil of Baskerville who on behalf of Beaumarchais had worked briefly with his punch-cutter in Birmingham.

Baskerville's original materials disappeared from view during the nineteenth century, only for the punches and matrices to be rediscovered in the possession of a Parisian typefoundry in the early twentieth century, and to be employed again for fine printing. Versions of 'Baskerville' types were made for the typesetting systems Monotype and Linotype, and for a German typefoundry. The surviving original matrices remain in France, on deposit at the Imprimerie Nationale, Paris; the punches were presented by their current owners, the Parisian typefoundry of Deberny et Peignot, to Cambridge University Press in 1953, and are now at the Cambridge University Library.

JAMES MOSLEY

Sources J. Balston, *The Whatmans and wove paper: its invention and development in the West; research into the origins of genuine loom-woven wire-cloth* (1998) • L. Jay, *Letters of the famous 18th century printer, John Baskerville of Birmingham, together with a bibliography of works printed by him at Birmingham* (1932) • W. Bennett, *John Baskerville, the Birmingham printer: his press, relations, and friends*, 2 vols. (1937–9) • C. H. Bloy, *A history of printing ink, balls and rollers, 1440–1850* (1967) • T. Cave, *John Baskerville, 1706–1775: the printer, his ancestry* (1936) • S. Derrick, *Letters written from Leverpoole, Chester, Corke, the Lake of Kilarney, Dublin, Tunbridge-Wells, and Bath*, 2 vols. (1767) • P. Didot, *Épître sur les progrès de l'imprimerie* (Paris, 1784) • J. Dreyfus, 'The Baskerville punches, 1750–1950', *The Library*, 5th ser., 5 (1950), 26–48 • J. Dreyfus, 'Baskerville's methods of printing', *Signature*, new ser., 12 (1951), 44–9 • P. Gaskell, *A bibliography of John Baskerville* (1959); 2nd edn (1973) • T. C. Hansard, *Typographia: an historical sketch of the origin and progress of the art of printing* (1825) • L. W. Hanson, review of *John Baskerville: a bibliography*, *The Library*, 5th ser., 15 (1960), 135–43 • L. W. Hanson, '*John Baskerville: a bibliography*: further notes', *The Library*, 5th ser., 15 (1960), 201–6 • [W. Hutton], 'An account of John

Baskerville, printer', *European Magazine* (Nov 1785), 356–7 · J. Kerslake, *National Portrait Gallery: early Georgian portraits*, 2 vols. (1977), 11–12 · *Lichtenberg's visits to England*, ed. and trans. W. H. Quarrell and M. L. Mare (1938) · *A biographical history of England, from the revolution to the end of George I's reign: being a continuation of the Rev. J. Granger's work*, ed. M. Noble, 2 (1806), 362 · F. Pardoe, *John Baskerville of Birmingham: letter-founder and printer* (1975) · D. Patterson, 'John Baskerville, marbler', *The Library*, 6th ser., 12 (1990), 212–21 · T. B. Reed, *A history of the old English letter foundries*, ed. A. F. Johnson (1952) · R. Straus and R. K. Dent, *John Baskerville: a memoir* (1907) · B. Walker, *The resting places of the remains of John Baskerville, the thrice-buried printer* · J. Wardrop, 'Mr Whatman, paper-maker', *Signature*, 9 (1938), 1–18 · *The letters of William Shenstone*, ed. M. Williams (1939) · *GM*, 1st ser., 63 (1793), 91 · *IGI*

Archives Bibliothèque Nationale, Paris, Étienne Alexandre Jacques Anisson-Duperron, 'Notes recueillies à l'Imprimerie du Fort de Kehl sur cet Établissement', MSS nouv. acq. fr. 6149–6150 · Birm. CA, letters to Matthew Boulton

Likenesses J. Millar, oils, 1774, Birmingham Museum and Art Gallery [*see illus.*] · J. Millar, oils, 1774 (copy), NPG · S. Raven, miniature (after Millar), Birmingham Museum and Art Gallery

Baskerville, Sir Simon (*bap.* 1574, *d.* 1641), physician, the son of Thomas Baskervile or Baskerville, apothecary, and sometime one of the stewards of Exeter, who was descended from the ancient family of the Baskerviles in Herefordshire, was born in Exeter and baptized at the church of St Mary Major, Exeter, on 27 October 1574. He was sent to Oxford, and matriculated on 10 March 1592 as a member of Exeter College, where he was placed under the care of the learned and pious William Helm. On the first vacancy he was elected a fellow of the college before he had graduated BA, and he did not take that degree until 8 July 1596. On 24 April 1599 he proceeded MA. Baskerville remained a fellow until 1609. He was licensed by the university to practise medicine on 29 November 1605.

When King James I visited the university, Baskerville debated natural philosophy before the king and won his respect. Serving as proctor of the university in 1606, Baskerville wrote some verses commemorating the visit of King Christian IV of Denmark. Baskerville left Oxford in 1608 in order to travel and is known to have been living in France during 1609.

Baskerville graduated MB at Oxford on 20 June 1611, and was afterwards created doctor in that faculty. He seems to have practised at Oxford for some years with considerable success. He then moved to London, where he was admitted a candidate in the College of Physicians on 18 April 1614 and a fellow on 20 March 1615. He was censor of the college in 1615 and several subsequent years, anatomy reader in 1626, and consiliarius in 1640. Baskerville was admitted to Lincoln's Inn in 1625. He attained great eminence in the medical profession, and was appointed physician to James I and afterwards to Charles I, who knighted him at Oxford on 30 August 1636. Described as a physician of Fleet Street, he had no fewer than a hundred patients a week, and became so wealthy that he acquired the nickname of Sir Simon Baskerville the rich.

Like many of the royal physicians, Baskerville supported the king's cause during the civil wars, and refused to take a fee from an orthodox clergyman, or from a royalist of less than £100 a year. There were rumours that he

was a Roman Catholic, but these were probably false. Baskerville, who was married, died on 5 July 1641, and was buried in St Paul's Cathedral, where a mural monument with a Latin epitaph was erected to his memory.

THOMPSON COOPER, *rev.* BRIAN NANCE

Sources B. Hamey, 'Bustorum aliquot reliquiae', BL, Sloane MS 2149, fol. 9 · D. Lloyd, *Memoires of the lives … of those … personages that suffered … for the protestant religion* (1668), 635 · S. Baskerville, Verses to Christian IV of Denmark, 1606, BL, Royal MS 12A LXIV, fol. 15b · annals, RCP Lond. · Fuller, *Worthies* (1662) · *CSP dom.*, 1581–1638 · Foster, *Alum. Oxon.* · S. Baskerville, BL, Add. MS 34102, fol. 204 · W. J. Birkin, 'The fellows of the Royal College of Physicians of London, 1603–1643: a social study', PhD diss., University of North Carolina at Chapel Hill, 1977 · Wood, *Ath. Oxon.* · C. W. Boase, ed., *Registrum Collegii Exoniensis*, new edn, OHS, 27 (1894) · will, 1641, PRO, PROB 11/186, fol. 297

Wealth at death property and bequests: will, PRO, PROB 11/186, fol. 297

Baskerville, Sir Thomas (*d.* 1597), soldier, was the younger son of Henry Baskerville, esquire, of Hereford, and Anne, daughter of John Ratford of Gloucester. In his early career Baskerville was active in local government: he apparently served as a JP for Herefordshire from about 1569 to 1585, and was an escheator for the same county in 1580–81. Some members of the Baskerville family were included in a list of 'supposed adherents' of Mary, queen of Scots, drawn up in 1572, but he was not among them. He later resided at Goodrest in Warwickshire.

As a soldier, Baskerville enjoyed a distinguished career fighting in the protestant cause. Between 1585 and 1588 he served as a captain in the Netherlands under both Robert Dudley, earl of Leicester, and Peregrine Bertie, Baron Willoughby de Eresby; the latter knighted him after the capture of Bergen op Zoom in 1588, and praised his 'valour' during the campaign in a letter to William Cecil, Baron Burghley, lord treasurer, (*CSP for.*, 22.209). It is also likely that even before 1585 Baskerville had fought as a mercenary in the Netherlands under Sir John Norris, with whom he later quarrelled. The quarrel was viewed seriously enough to prompt intervention from the privy council. Baskerville accompanied Burghley's son Robert Cecil to Bergen in March 1588. During this time Robert wrote to his father that Baskerville was 'a proper gentleman …. There is not a more serviceable gentleman in all the garrison' (Cecil, 34–5). Baskerville continued to serve under Willoughby in France throughout 1589 and 1590, fighting on behalf of Henri IV. During this period he was promoted to sergeant-major-general. He was appointed governor of Rammekens Castle, near Flushing, in August 1591 by the nomination of Sir Robert Sidney, a post he attempted, but failed, to have transferred to his brother Nicholas in October 1596. He received a commission to serve as sergeant-major of foot under Robert Devereux, earl of Essex, in France on 28 July 1591 and was present at the siege of Rouen in November of the same year. Much of the period between 1592 and 1594 he spent engaged in military duties in Brittany, under Norris, with whom he appears to have resolved his differences, and the Netherlands, returning to England briefly in March 1594 suffering from an ague.

In 1593 Baskerville was elected MP for Carmarthen Boroughs, through the support of Essex, and in opposition to the candidate of Sir John Puckering, the lord keeper. Baskerville attended the parliamentary session of 19 February to 10 April, sitting on committees dealing with the poor law on 12 March and the relief of maimed soldiers and mariners on 30 March. He was re-elected for the parliament of 1597, but died before he could attend. Baskerville's intimacy with Essex stemmed from their close military companionship. He lent Essex £400 in 1595 and the earl was godfather to his son, the antiquary Hannibal *Baskerville (1597–1668), in 1597. However, he was also associated with the Cecils through a connection with the Cecils of Allt yr Ynys, Herefordshire, from whom Burghley was descended.

In 1595 Baskerville was appointed colonel-general in command of the land forces accompanying Sir Francis Drake and Sir John Hawkins on their last expedition to the Indies. On the death of Drake it was Baskerville who the next day, 'caried him a league of, and buried him in the sea' (Maynarde, 20). He succeeded to the command and brought the expedition home. A partial account of the journey, Henry Savile's *Libell of Spanish Lies* (1596), included 'an approbation of this discourse, by Sir Thomas Baskervile, then generall of the English fleete'. A manuscript account apparently penned by Baskerville also survives: 'Sir Thomas Baskerville's account of his voyage after the great treasure of Portrica &c when he was generall of her ma[jes]ties Indian Armada' (BL, Harley MS 4762, fols. 69–74). During 1596 and 1597 he was colonel-general of English forces in Picardy in command of 2000 men. In addition to the role of leading troops in the field, what emerges from Baskerville's surviving papers is an overwhelming sense of the vast amount of his time and energy that was consumed by logistical matters: his continual efforts to ensure that his men were paid and that adequate munitions and supplies were requisitioned dominate his numerous letters and reports. However, it was said that he was unkind to his men and diverted their pay to himself, though this may be an ill-founded rumour.

Baskerville married Mary (*d.* 1632), daughter of Sir Thomas Throckmorton (1538/9–1607) of Tortworth, Gloucestershire, and Ellen, daughter of Sir Richard Berkeley, at some point before 1597. A substantial number of love letters survive from Baskerville to his wife, whom he addressed as 'swete mall', 'best beloved', and 'dearest frend'; however, none of her replies are extant (BL, Harley MS 4762). On one occasion, before departing from Plymouth, he wrote with his customary passion:

> swette malle, I send to acompanye the my soule w[hi]ch I praye the lodg in thy bosom, for I protest I cary nothing w[i]t[h] me butt my bodye w[hi]ch wer nott my Honnor and reputacion so much engaged in this jorney as itt is I would lykwise wishe itt w[i]th thee. (BL, Harley MS 4762, fol. 109r)

His wife appears to have accompanied him on his last expedition to France in 1597. Baskerville died of a fever at Picquency, in Picardy, on 4 June, barely two months after the birth of his son, Hannibal, at St Valéry. News of his death was widely reported: Edward Wilton informed Essex that 'he lay sick not past 5 or 6 days, and died raving' (*Salisbury MSS*, 7.242). He was buried in the new choir of St Paul's, beneath a monument destroyed by the fire of London in 1666. The inscription on Baskerville's tomb recorded his exploits in 'Netherlands, Seas, India's, Spain and France' and praised his 'noble virtues', expressing the belief:

> That valour should not perish void of fame
> Nor noble Deeds, but leave a noble Name.
> (Dugdale, 72)

His nuncupative will, which was drawn up on his deathbed, survives in several variant copies, including a two-line version seemingly penned in his own hand, which is endorsed: 'The will S[i]r Th[omas] begann to wryte' (BL, Harley MS 4762, fol. 62r). Among the beneficiaries of Baskerville's will were his servant James Collins, a preacher, Thomas Man, and a relation, John Tomkins: 'for thee Jacke I am most sorrye that I cannot doe as I would for I meant to make thee as my childe, But I hope my wiefe will have a care of thee'. His wife, Mary, was made his sole executor. She was to enjoy the estate 'duringe her naturall liefe' and was charged with the 'bringinge upp' of their 'child' Hannibal, to whom the lands would pass on her death. Baskerville trusted that Essex would also have 'a care of' his 'young son' (PRO, PROB 11/90, sig. 71). On 28 June 1599 Baskerville's widow, Mary, entered a disastrous marriage with Sir James Scudamore (1568–1619). She died and was buried at Sunningwell, Berkshire, on 17 October 1632.

JAMES DAYBELL

Sources APC, *1581–2*, 192, 193; *1589–90*, 118, 119, 171; *1590*, 183; *1590–91*, 329; *1591*, 233, 242, 467; *1592*, 37, 38; *1592–3*, 62, 65, 66, 160; *1596–7*, 17, 194, 220, 229, 244, 291, 298, 324, 496; *1597*, 203 · VCH *Warwickshire* · K. R. Andrews, *Drake's voyages: a re-assessment of their place in Elizabethan maritime expansion* (1967), 158–79 · CPR, *1569–72*, 1893, 2537; *1575–8*, 1860, 1870; *1580–82*, 947, 981 · CSP dom., *1547–80*, 374, 383; *1581–90*, 259, 582; *1591–4*, 57, 74, 252, 315, 332, 497, 513, 529, 541; *1595–7*, 13, 43, 73–4, 80, 88–93, 209–10, 219, 221–3, 291–2, 296, 365, 380, 392, 396, 403, 406, 412, 414, 434–5, 446, 559; *1598–1601*, 222; *1580–1625, addenda*, 282, 285 · CSP for., *1584–5*, 635; *1585–6*, 25, 129; *June 1586–June 1588*, 109, 376; *June 1586–March 1587*, 3, 343, 440, 498; *April–Dec 1587*, 290; *1588*, 137, 209, 229, 261–3, 291, 347, 410; *1589*, 52, 71, 138, 176 · A. Cecil, *A life of Robert Cecil first earl of Salisbury* (1915), 34–5 · W. Dugdale, *The history of St Paul's Cathedral in London*, new edn, ed. H. Ellis (1818), 72 · P. E. J. Hammer, *The polarisation of Elizabethan politics: the political career of Robert Devereux, 2nd earl of Essex, 1585–1597* (1999), 147, 186, 218, 222 · HoP, *Commons, 1558–1603*, 1.312–14, 402; 3.501–2 · *Calendar of the manuscripts of the most hon. the marquis of Salisbury*, 24 vols., HMC, 9 (1883–1976), vol. 4, pp. 167, 169, 293, 295, 534, 550, 563; vol. 5, pp. 178, 240, 297, 318–20, 358; vol. 6, pp. 141, 152, 164, 172, 173, 196, 204, 213, 215, 256, 315, 393, 400–02, 408, 433–4, 441, 468, 502, 523, 554; vol. 7, pp. 30, 40, 44, 76, 88, 184, 200, 232, 237, 242, 245, 256, 286; vol. 8, pp. 288, 553 · T. Maynarde, 'Sir Francis Drake's voyage, 1595', *Hakluyt Society* [ed. W. D. Cooley], 1st ser., 4 (1849), 20, 25, 48 · H. Savile, *A libell of Spanish lies* (1596) · R. B. Wernham, *After the Armada: Elizabethan England and the struggle for western Europe, 1588–1595* (1984), 152, 311–13, 32–3, 326, 467, 506, 529–36, 542–3, 546 · R. B. Wernham, ed., *The expedition of Sir John Norris and Sir Francis Drake to Spain and Portugal, 1589*, Navy Records Society, 127 (1988), 70–71, 190 · PRO, PROB 11/90, sig. 71 · PRO, PROB 11/94, sig. 59

Archives BL, Cotton MS Otho, E. xi. 224, fols. 230–231v · BL, Hungerford family pedigrees, Add. MS 14284, fol. 66 · BL, Add. MS 38091, fol. 1 · BL, papers, Harley MS 4762 · BL, Lansdowne MS 121, fol. 67v · BL, Sloane MS 33, fols. 9b–10b · Bodl. Oxf., Hungerford family pedigrees, MSS Ashmole 851, p. 64; 852, p. 257 · Hatfield House, Hertfordshire, Cecil MSS 143, fol. 6; 204, fol. 87

Wealth at death £60 bequeathed to James Collins; £40 in debts; estate of Goodrest, Warwickshire; left gratuity to Thomas Man: will, PRO, PROB 11/90, sig. 71; BL, Harley MS 4762, fol. 52

Baskerville, Thomas (1630/31–1700), topographer, was born, probably at Bayworth House, Sunningwell, Berkshire, in 1630 or early 1631, the eldest surviving son of the eccentric antiquary Hannibal *Baskerville (1597–1668) and his second wife and cousin, Mary (1602–1644)—daughter of Nicholas Baskerville and widow of John Morgan—and grandson of Sir Thomas *Baskerville (d. 1597), the Elizabethan sea captain and the original purchaser of the Sunningwell estate, which Thomas 'mightily improved' (Buchanan-Brown, 232). Baskerville had five brothers and two sisters, though one source makes him one of eighteen children. Nothing is known of his personal life; he was recorded as being aged thirty-four in 1665, and he fathered his only son, Matthew Thomas (1688/9–1721), at an advanced age.

In 1649 Baskerville witnessed Leveller troops massing near his house before their encounter with Cromwell at Burford. However, he had no great interest in state affairs. He spent much of his life after 1649 travelling and left behind two large manuscripts about the journeys he made in the Restoration period. These had been copied up years later from rough notes and are not always coherent, but it is clear that he made at least the following journeys: through Essex in 1662; from London to Dover via Rochester and Canterbury after 1667; around Buckinghamshire and Hertfordshire in 1671 and again, in part, in 1682; to Gloucester via Buckingham, Warwick, Worcester, and Hereford in 1674 and again, in part, in 1682–3; to Tewkesbury and Evesham in 1678; from Abingdon to Southampton via Winchester in 1679; from Oxford to Cambridge and on to East Anglia in 1681; around Burford, Winchcombe, and Cheltenham, and from Faringdon via the Cotswolds to Bristol, both in 1682; and, at an unknown date, north to York and Hull via Towcester, Northampton, Leicester, and Nottingham. The attribution to him by the *Dictionary of National Biography* of a journey into parts of Wiltshire, Gloucestershire, and Oxfordshire, which, from internal evidence, was made in 1692 or later, is less certain. The account in question (BL, Harleian MS 4716) is not in Baskerville's hand, and although there seems little doubt that the volume in which it appears belonged to his son, Matthew Thomas was of neither an age nor temperament to have been likely to undertake the journey. It may be that this was one of the two books left to him by his father that Matthew Thomas refused to show to the antiquary Thomas Hearne.

Unusually for his time, Baskerville was more interested in the contemporary world than in antiquities or classical learning. His writing is not of great quality but it is lively and packed with detail about local sights, crafts, and markets. He also highlights the sheer diversity of foreign and inland trade at that time with lists of the exotic goods to be found at ordinary markets. Baskerville had a keen critical eye—Leicester he thought 'an old stinking town',

Nottingham 'paradise restored'. There are also flashes of a savage sense of humour when he writes of the women of Harrogate importuning rich visitors to the spa that 'their faces did shine like bacon rind. And for beauty may vie with an old Bath guide's ass, the sulphur waters had so soiled their pristine complexions' (Portland MSS, pt 2, 308, 314). Hearne—who thought Baskerville 'not capable of writing any thing tolerable' (Remains, 7.265)—records that he 'was so whimsical a Man as to call himself King of Jerusalem, and he would ramble about all the Country and pick up all strange, odd Things, good and bad' (Buchanan-Brown, 229). Baskerville contracted to have his writings printed, together with an engraving of himself and some of his verses, but died before this could proceed. He was buried at Sunningwell on 16 November 1700. By the time Matthew Thomas died on 9 February 1721 the Sunningwell estate was already lost, thanks entirely to his debauched, spendthrift ways.

ANDREW WARMINGTON

Sources *The manuscripts of his grace the duke of Portland*, 10 vols., HMC, 29 (1891–1931), vol. 2 [BL, Add. MS 70523] · *Remarks and collections of Thomas Hearne*, ed. C. E. Doble and others, 11 vols., OHS, 2, 7, 13, 34, 42–3, 48, 50, 65, 67, 72 (1885–1921), vols. 3, 7 · *The remains of Thomas Hearne: Reliquiae Hearnianae*, ed. J. Bliss, rev. edn, rev. J. Buchanan-Brown (1966) · BL, Harleian MS 4716 · E. Ashmole, *The visitation of Berkshire, 1664–6*, ed. W. C. Metcalfe (1882) · Wood, *Ath. Oxon.*, new edn, 1.xxxiii–xxxiv · *DNB*

Archives BL, account of his travels, Add. MS 70523 · BL, collection of epitaphs and topographical information, Harleian MS 4716

Likenesses etching, pubd 1819 (after G. Cruikshank), BM, NPG

Baskerville, Thomas (1812–1840), surgeon and writer on botany, was born on 26 April 1812, and served a four-year medical apprenticeship to Mr Soulby, of Ash near Sandwich in Kent. From 1 December 1829 to 9 April 1834 he seems to have attended University College, London, taking courses in botany delivered by John Lindley and attending lectures on anatomy under Jones Quain, dissection under Richard Quain, and surgery under Samuel Cooper. In November 1834 he attended the North London Hospital (later University College Hospital). He obtained the membership of the Royal College of Surgeons on 22 December 1835 and settled in medical practice at Canterbury.

The little prominence Baskerville acquired, however, was in botany. He was the author of *Affinities of Plants, with some Observations upon Progressive Development* (1839). This work reveals Baskerville's great interest in plant morphology and French ideas of transmutation and embryology. It was dedicated to John Lindley and intended to develop some of Lindley's ideas on affinity; but it was forestalled by Lindley's own *Nixus plantarum* (1833). Baskerville rejected Lamarckian transmutation while proposing a universal connection and gradation of beings. His scheme of using affinities for classification led him to express plant relationships graphically, as if laid out on the surface of a sphere. The system received no publicity and was no doubt too metaphysical to be workable. Only the French dictionary compiler M. H. Baillon makes any mention of it, in 1876. Baskerville died from erysipelas on 3

March 1840, at his home, 12 Great Chapel Street, Westminster, London. John Lindley named a genus of plants after him. JANET BROWNE

Sources records, RCS Eng. · d. cert.

Baskett, John (1664/5–1742), stationer and printer, was the son of Roger Baskett, gentleman of Salisbury. On 4 December 1682 he was apprenticed to the London stationer Edward Darrell or Dorrell, who supplied stationery to various government offices; he was released from his indentures on 5 May 1690, after which he appears to have worked as a stationer with his former master and another stationer, Godfrey Richards. On 15 June 1691, aged twenty-six, Baskett married Sarah Briscoe (b. 1669/70), of Mortlake, Surrey, at St Faith's under St Paul's Church, London. He was noted as supplying paper to the university press at Oxford from 1693. About 1694 he petitioned the Admiralty, offering to save several thousand pounds by supplying the navy with parchment cartridges, following the imposition of paper duty, and from 1695 until 1717 he appears frequently in the Treasury books as John Baskett of Paternoster Row, a supplier of paper. He even applied for the post of commissioner for collecting paper duty. By 1700 Baskett was in partnership with Richards to supply stationery to the customs, and from 1702 (the year of Richards's death), he was also active in the printing trade with Oliver Elliston, a former fellow apprentice under Darrell, and Thomas Simpson, who had married Sarah Bacott, probably Baskett's sister, on 23 December 1693. Elliston's death in late 1706 or early 1707 resulted in the formation in 1708 of a new lucrative ten-year partnership with Simpson and Samuel Ashurst, a former Elliston apprentice who married Baskett's daughter Sarah on 7 December 1710. In 1706–7 Baskett financed the printing of a folio edition of Clarendon's *History* at Oxford.

As R. J. Goulden has noted, 'the year 1710 divides Baskett's career neatly', as it was on 10 January 1710 that the old patent for the office of king's printer expired (Goulden, 'John Baskett', 20). The old patentees owed Baskett and his partners at least £8000; in resolving the debt Baskett was able to acquire a half-share in the new thirty-year patent (which covered the printing of bibles and official publications), and from 1711 his name began to appear on the imprints of books printed under the patent at the printing house in Blackfriars. About April 1712 he was formally appointed as queen's printer, a position confirmed by George I about November 1714. (From 1719 he exercised the right as king's printer to publish colonial acts in London, printing the Acts of the Assembly of New York that year, of Maryland in 1723, and of Massachusetts in 1724.) In 1711 Baskett also gained a third-share in Robert Freebairn's new patent as queen's printer in Scotland, and on 2 January 1712, Oxford University agreed to allow Baskett, Ashurst, and John Williams (who managed the king's printing house in London) a twenty-one-year monopoly (from 1713) on the printing of books at the university from the following year, much to the surprise of the Stationers' Company, which had been in dispute with the university over the printing of psalters and almanacs. Little wonder that Baskett was described in a 1712 petition by 'poor paper-makers and printers' as

> one particular man, who, having the press at Oxford in his hands, the Queen's printing-house in London, the patent for printing Bibles, &c. in England, and being now by a new grant made Her Majesty's printer in Scotland, is making a monopoly of the greatest and best part of the printing trade in Britain. (ibid., 21)

In 1716 Baskett also bought the reversionary interest of Benjamin Tooke and John Barber as queen's printers, thereby extending the life of his share in the patent to sixty years. However, in that same year he received a setback concerning his share as queen's printer in Scotland, as the right of one of the other two partners, James Watson, to print bibles in Scotland and sell them throughout Britain was confirmed by the Scottish courts. Watson duly printed bibles in 1715, 1716, 1719, and 1722. Finally Lord Mansfield in London ruled in favour of Baskett, and in 1725 Baskett, who had not previously published in Scotland, set up a printing house in Edinburgh in partnership with Freebairn and published four editions of the Bible between 1725 and 1729; from 1734 Edinburgh bibles were published with only Freebairn's name in their imprints. The extent of Baskett's printing privileges required a prodigious vigilance but he nevertheless managed to bring almost forty law cases against infringements, such as when he prosecuted William Dicey, the printer of the *Northampton Mercury*, in 1721 for including accounts of the king's speech.

In 1714 and 1715 Baskett served as master of the Stationers' Company, and over his working life he bound twenty-seven apprentices with the company, including the typefounder William Caslon the younger. He also employed William Norris as corrector to his press. In 1713 he published the Book of Common Prayer in three different formats, and two years later published four editions of the Bible. A condition of his lease of the university press at Oxford was the contribution of £2000 towards the building of a new university printing house; the move into Clarendon House took place in October 1713, from where, during 1716 and 1717, he printed an ambitious two-volume imperial folio bible decorated with engravings by Hoffman, Du Bosc, and Vendergulcht, later described by the bibliophile Thomas Dibdin as a magnificent work. However, it contained numerous errors and was nicknamed the Vinegar Bible from a mistranscription of the parable of the vineyard. Three special luxurious vellum copies were made, of which two remain in the British Library and the Bodleian Library. Even loose sheets of this work, described as 'shining examples of paper and print' by Daniel Price, were much sought (Nichols, *Illustrations*, 708). Baskett published a total of twelve distinct editions of the Bible during his tenure at Oxford.

Baskett had faced a cash-flow problem as soon as he took up his share of the queen's printing office, and in January 1713 had borrowed £2000 from a London fishmonger, offering his share as security. The Vinegar Bible also overextended his resources. Between then and 1718 he borrowed further sums from James Brooks, a stationer, and

John Eyre, a kinsman and London grocer. In the latter year he mortgaged his leasehold of the Oxford University Press for £4500. In 1720 he received a loan of £2000 from Ashurst, while in January 1722 Eyre agreed to take over Baskett's 1713 debt in exchange for whatever profit and goods Baskett could produce as king's printer. Nevertheless at this time Baskett's printing house contained the largest fount of double pica in England. Eyre also repaid the remaining part of the Ashurst loan, gaining further rights in the printing office as a result. In April 1723 Baskett leased out his share of the Oxford patent in return for two-thirds of the profits; however, by December, Eyre was the direct recipient for this sum. In the same month Baskett formally acknowledged a debt of nearly £25,000 to Eyre. In 1724 he sold his reversion of the office of king's printer to Eyre for £10,000. However, on 22 June 1726 Baskett sued Eyre, claiming that Eyre had misrepresented the extent of the debt. Eyre responded by seizing as many of Baskett's assets as he could, prompting a series of law cases over Baskett's privileges. In 1727 Baskett was insolvent, and within two years had gone bankrupt. He stopped attending meetings of the Stationers' Company governing body. His estate was assigned to three trustees in November 1728 while the courts continued to decide on the extent of his debts to Eyre and Ashurst. The eventual sum, almost £12,000, was repaid in June 1731 by an attorney in exchange for interest on the capital, and rights to the king's printing house. In the same year the University of Cambridge press syndics leased their right to print bibles to William Ged, the first printer in Britain to use stereotypes. Baskett challenged Ged's right to bible printing; the suit was long and protracted, reaching a conclusion only some sixteen years after Baskett's own death when king's bench found for the university, but it did succeed in restricting Ged's publication of the Bible. In 1732 he secured the renewal of the lease for the Oxford press upon its expiry in 1734. By April 1736 Baskett was able to discharge his bankruptcy and to recover some of his original assets, including the printing house itself. He was still in the process of paying off other sizeable creditors (he offered to sell the Oxford lease to the Stationers' Company in September 1737) when, on 13 January 1738, the printing office was destroyed by fire. All that survived were leaves of the Bible currently being printed; the damage was estimated at £5000. However, Baskett's business survived, owing to insurance and the loan of presses from fellow printers. Soon after, Baskett petitioned the king and was granted a forty-year monopoly for the supply of stationery to parliament.

Baskett's last publication was a duodecimo New Testament, published before he died at Blackfriars, London on 22 June 1742. His will was proved a day later, and he was buried in St Anne's Blackfriars, London. He left legacies totalling £5000, including that of his printing house to his son **Thomas Baskett** (bap. 1701, d. 1761), an annuity to his sons Robert and John (the latter predeceased Baskett by a month), 10s. each to his compositors and pressmen, and 5s. to each boy he employed. He also went to some lengths

in his will to ensure that his remaining patents stayed in the family.

Of John's and Sarah's surviving children, Thomas and Robert followed their father's profession. Thomas was baptized in the parish of St Faith's under St Paul's on 3 July 1701; he was freed by patrimony as a member of the Stationers' Company by his father on 4 July 1732. He married Elizabeth, with whom he had a son, Mark, who was baptized in St Anne's Blackfriars on 20 October 1737. Thomas and Robert (who had served an apprenticeship with the Oxford printer Charles Combes) succeeded to the office of king's printer and the lease of the press at Oxford following their father's death, publishing bibles under their names from 1743 to 1745. In 1743 they instigated a court case against the university press at Cambridge over the right to print statutes. From 1745 only Thomas's name appears in imprints as Robert retired to Epsom in 1744, where he died at some point between 2 August 1766 when he made his will and 15 July 1767 when the will was proved. Following Robert's sale of his interest in the Oxford press in 1744, Thomas secured a new twenty-one-year lease, and it was at Oxford that, during 1756–61, he printed the important second edition of Edmund Gibson's *Codex juris ecclesiae Anglicane* (1761), which coincided with the reform of the university press under William Blackstone.

Thomas Baskett died on 30 March 1761, leaving Mark as his sole heir to the office of king's printer and the university press at Oxford. Mark printed bibles in 1761, 1763, and 1768 and a prayer book in 1766, but he was not interested in printing and allowed his premises to become, in one contemporary view, 'more like an Ale House than a Printing Room', with drunken and idle employees (Carter, 353). In 1766 he relinquished his lease of the Oxford press, and in 1784 sold the Blackfriars printing house to John Walters. WILLIAM GIBSON

Sources Nichols, *Illustrations*, vol. 3 · J. Lee, *Memorial for the bible societies in Scotland* (1824) · BL, Add. MSS 6, 880 · D. F. McKenzie, ed., *Stationers' Company apprentices*, [3]: *1701–1800* (1978) · PRO, C11/1425/5 [*Baskett v. Dicey*] · *The Charlemagne Tower collection of American colonial laws* (Philadelphia, 1890) · W. Gibson, 'Bishop Gibson's *Codex* and the reform of the Oxford University Press', *N&Q*, 240 (1995), 47–52 · *The correspondence of the Reverend Francis Blomefield, 1705–52*, ed. D. Stoker, Norfolk RS, 55 (1992) · *The autobiography of Benjamin Franklin*, ed. L. W. Labaree and others (1964); repr. (1976) · will, PRO, PROB 11/718, sig. 176 · R. J. Goulden, 'John Baskett', *Factotum: Newsletter of the XVIIIth-Century Short Title Catalogue*, 7 (Dec 1979), 19–24 · R. J. Goulden, *Some chancery lawsuits, 1714–1758: an analytical list* (privately printed, Croydon, 1983) · private information (2004) [M. Treadwell, Trent University, Canada] · R. L. Haig, 'New light on the king's printing office, 1680–1730', *Studies in Bibliography*, 8 (1956), 157–67 · H. R. Plomer and others, *A dictionary of the printers and booksellers who were at work in England, Scotland, and Ireland from 1726 to 1775* (1932) · H. Carter, *A history of the Oxford University Press*, 1: *To the year 1780* (1975) · D. McKitterick, *A history of Cambridge University Press*, 2 (1998) · *The Bowyer ledgers: the printing accounts of William Bowyer, father and son, reproduced on microfiche with a checklist of Bowyer printing 1699–1777, a commentary, indexes and appendixes*, ed. K. Maslen and J. Lancaster (1991) · G. Offor and C. W. Bingham, 'Leese: lancers', *N&Q*, 2nd ser., 8 (1859), 229

Wealth at death modest; printing works and patents; £5000 in legacies comprising income from printing and stationery: will, PRO, PROB 11/718, sig. 176

Baskett, Thomas (*bap.* 1701, *d.* 1761). *See under* Baskett, John (1664/5–1742).

Basnett, David, Baron Basnett (1924–1989), trade unionist, was born on 9 February 1924 at 1 Ivy Leigh, Liverpool, the son of Andrew Basnett, a collector with a gas company and regional secretary of the General and Municipal Workers' Union (GMWU), and his wife, (Mary) Charlotte Kerr. His mother died when he was six. After attending a local elementary school he won a scholarship to Quarry Bank high school in Liverpool. His first job after leaving school was as a bank clerk. During the Second World War he served as a pilot in the Royal Air Force, in Sunderland flying boats involved in reconnaissance missions over the Atlantic.

Basnett joined the GMWU as a regional official for Liverpool in 1948 and was appointed as the union's first national education officer in 1955. Five years later he was promoted to the post of national industrial officer, with responsibility for negotiations in the chemicals and glass industries. He gained a reputation as one of the most intelligent and progressive of the new generation of union officials, not least through his active participation in the innovative phase of productivity bargaining at ICI and elsewhere in the chemicals industry. He was a tall, thin, and quietly spoken man, whose demeanour was more like that of an academic or civil servant than of a manual workers' trade union official. In 1956 he married Kathleen Joan Molyneaux, the daughter of John Joseph Molyneaux, general practitioner.

Basnett achieved wider public recognition during the dramatic seven-week strike at the Pilkington Glass Company in St Helens, Lancashire, in 1970. The dispute exposed chronic weaknesses in union organization and in union–management relations. The closed-shop agreement covering nearly 8000 workers had produced complacency on the part of local union officials and management, the virtual collapse of union membership participation, and the absence of effective joint procedures. Within a few days the strike became a national *cause célèbre*, and Basnett was subjected to intense public scrutiny as he struggled to defeat a putative 'breakaway union', to negotiate an end to the bitter dispute, and thereafter to reconstruct the credibility of the GMWU in St Helens.

The courage and expertise shown by Basnett at Pilkington undoubtedly contributed to his success in the election for the post of GMWU general secretary in 1973. The dispute confirmed also that the union required substantial reorganization and improved services in order to encourage growth and effective membership participation. Basnett was not wholly successful in his attempts to reform the GMWU. In the thirteen years before he retired in 1986, he was able to conclude mergers with several unions, most notably with the Boilermakers to form the General, Municipal, Boilermakers, and Allied Trades Unions in 1982. The tradition and practices of regional autonomy, however, impeded the implementation of other reforms

David Basnett, Baron Basnett (1924–1989), by unknown photographer

that might have allowed the union to benefit more from the growth of overall union membership in the 1970s and strengthen it for the more difficult challenges of the 1980s.

Basnett was appointed to the general council of the Trades Union Congress (TUC) in 1966 and became one of its most prominent members during the following twenty years. He served as chairman of the finance and general purposes committee and the economic committee. He represented the TUC on the National Economic Development Council from 1973 to 1986, as a founder member of the National Enterprise Board (1975–9) and as a member of several committees of inquiry and three royal commissions—most notably the 1974–7 royal commission on the press, for which he co-authored a minority report.

Basnett's contribution to the trade union movement can be divided into two distinct periods, separated by the year in which he was chairman of the TUC (1977–8). Throughout the 1970s he worked closely with Jack Jones of the Transport and General Workers' Union in the 'inner cabinet' of the TUC, negotiating with the Heath, Wilson, and Callaghan governments on a wide range of economic, industrial, and social policies. In his 1978 presidential address to the congress, Basnett outlined his strong commitment to the view that union leaders had a right and a duty to participate with government in developing policies designed to improve economic performance and reduce social inequality. A few days later, Callaghan astonished the TUC by his decision to delay the expected general election. Over the following six months the widespread industrial disruption of the 'winter of discontent' buried what was left of the 'social contract' with the Labour government, contributed to its electoral defeat in the spring of 1979, and ended the first, most successful, phase of Basnett's career.

The Conservative governments of the 1980s were determined to weaken the power of trade unions and to exclude their leaders from any involvement in policy making. The focus of Basnett's activity therefore shifted to the relationship between unions and the Labour Party; he helped to create a new organization in 1979, Trade Unionists for a Labour Victory, promoted conferences between union and Labour Party leaders, and pressed for reforms in the party's structure and organization. The failure of many of these initiatives and the weakness of trade unions throughout the 1980s may have contributed to his decision to retire early in 1986. More important, one of his two sons, Ian, a doctor, had suffered serious neck and spinal injuries on a rugby field in 1984. Basnett chose to strengthen further the close family life that he shared with his wife, Kathleen, Ian, and his other son, Paul. Basnett was made a life peer in 1987 and derived considerable satisfaction from his contributions to the House of Lords. He died of cancer at his home, Windrush, St John's Avenue, Leatherhead, Surrey, on 25 January 1989.

DAVID WINCHESTER, rev.

Sources Annual Report [Trades Union Congress] (1978) · Annual Report [Trades Union Congress] (1989) · The Independent (27 Jan 1989) · b. cert. · CGPLA Eng. & Wales (1989) · personal knowledge (1996)
Likenesses photograph, 1980, Hult. Arch. · photograph, News International Syndication, London [see illus.]
Wealth at death £37,670: probate, 20 March 1989, CGPLA Eng. & Wales

Bass, Alfred [Alfie; *formerly* Abraham Basalinsky] (1916–1987), actor, was born on 10 April 1916 at 7 Gibraltar Walk, Bethnal Green, London, the youngest among the ten children of Jacob Basalinsky, a cabinet-maker, and his wife, Ada Miller. After an elementary school education he followed his father's trade, but was also engaged in local boys' club dramatics. He was early on active in supporting the labour movement, often attended union meetings, and took part in the battle of Cable Street against Oswald Mosley's fascists. Alfie Bass's first professional engagement was in 1939 at the Unity Theatre, St Pancras, noted for its social dramas; he played Izzie in *Plant in the Sun* with Paul Robeson. In the same year he made his television début. At the outbreak of war he was rejected by the RAF but worked in an engineering factory and continued to appear at the Unity. It was at the Arts Theatre, though, in 1943, that he scored a success in Ted Willis's *Buster*, following which he took over the role of Cohen in James Bridie's *Mr Bolfry* at the Playhouse. He was called up to the Middlesex regiment as a dispatch rider, but an accident returned

him to acting—in concert parties and in Ministry of Information and army film unit documentaries. Bass married (Margaret) Beryl Bryson, a dressmaker, in Liverpool on 26 January 1946. They had a son and a daughter.

After the war Bass resumed theatre work, at the Old Vic; at the Liverpool Playhouse, as Abel Drugger in Ben Jonson's *The Alchemist* (1945); and at the Palace Theatre in London, as the leprechaun Og in the musical *Finian's Rainbow* (1947). He was also popular in various Shakespearian parts (Launcelot Gobbo, Grumio, Autolycus) at Stratford upon Avon during Barry Jackson's final year as administrator (1948). In 1953 he played his favourite role, in Wolf Mankowitz's *The Bespoke Overcoat* at the Arts, as the Ghost returning to get an overcoat from the tailor who had 'sweated' him to death (in 1955 he appeared in a short BBC version). In 1955 Bass was in the *Punch Revue* at the Duke of York's Theatre. His biggest stage success came in 1968: he took over the difficult role of the milkman, Tevye, in the internationally successful musical *Fiddler on the Roof*, to which 'he brought an added touch of sympathy and wistfulness' (*The Independent*, 20 July 1987). A later success was as Eccles, the father, in a revival of Tom Robertson's *Caste* at Greenwich (1972). He was also popularly received in pantomimes at the London Palladium, including *Jack and the Beanstalk*.

Bass also had a busy film career, specializing in 'little man' roles, often cheerful cockney Jews, later in cameos. He made his first appearance, uncredited, in *The Bells Go Down* (1943). He was also uncredited in David Lean's *Brief Encounter* (1945), but sandwiched it between two Ealing films, *Johnny Frenchman* (1945) and *It always Rains on Sunday* (1948). He was extremely busy throughout the 1950s, appearing in more than thirty films, notably Hitchcock's *Stage Fright* (1950), *The Lavender Hill Mob* (1951), as Shorty, one of the gang, and *A Tale of Two Cities* (1958), as Jerry Cruncher. In the 1960s he was in the Beatles' *Help!* (1965), as well as *Alfie* (1966) and *Up the Junction* (1967). He also delivered, as a Jewish vampire in Roman Polanski's *The Fearless Vampire Killers* (1967), a memorable riposte when threatened with a crucifix: 'Boy, have you got the wrong vampire!' His last film appearance was in the James Bond film *Moonraker* (1979), as a consumptive Italian.

It was, though, television which made Bass a household name. He appeared in four series (1957–60) of *The Army Game*, as Private 'Excused Boots' Bisley, one of a group of national service conscripts at a surplus ordnance depot in pursuit of easy money and ways of outwitting the fiery sergeant-major; his nickname came from his being allowed to wear plimsolls. Bass also took part in the film spin-off, *I Only Arsked!* (1958). With Bill Fraser, who had played sergeant-major Claude Snudge in the series, he then enjoyed the long-running series *Bootsie and Snudge* (1960–63), where the two were transplanted into a decrepit London gentlemen's club, The Imperial, as shoeshine boy and major-domo. The duo reappeared in the diplomatic service in the sitcom *Foreign Affairs* (1964), set in the British embassy in Bosnik, and played similar characters in the series *Vacant Lot* (1967), but this was short-lived, as was a final series of *Bootsie and Snudge* (1974), with Bootsie winning a fortune on the pools and Snudge appointing himself 'financial advisor'. Among Bass's other television series were *Are you being Served?* (1979), as Mr Goldberg, and *Dick Turpin* (1979–80), as Isaac Rag. An earlier notable television appearance of a different kind was as Flute in *A Midsummer Night's Dream* (1964).

Short of stature, Alfie Bass was a very popular, hard-working, reliable, and respected actor, appreciative of finding something positive in all roles. Ever concerned with political and social issues, he also did much work for boys' clubs and disabled children. He died on 16 July 1987 in Barnet General Hospital, north London, following a heart attack. He was survived by his wife and their son and daughter.   ROBERT SHARP

Sources *The Times* (18 July 1987) · *The Independent* (20 July 1987) · www.uk.imdb.com, 17 Sept 2001 · www.phill.co.uk/comedy, 5 Sept 2001 · private information (2004) · d. cert.

Wealth at death £85,000: probate, 13 May 1988, *CGPLA Eng. & Wales*

Bass, George (*b.* 1771, *d.* in or after 1803), explorer, was born in Aswarby, Lincolnshire, on 30 January 1771, the only child of George Bass (1739–1777), a tenant farmer, and his wife, Sarah, *née* Newman (1736–1828). Following his father's death George and his mother moved to Boston. Here he attended the grammar school and in 1787 was apprenticed to a surgeon apothecary. By 1789 he had been admitted to the Company of Surgeons. Tall, good-looking, and energetic, he probably chose the navy because it offered variety and adventure and in 1789 he passed the qualifying examination for naval surgeons. During the next four years he was surgeon on board the *Shark* and the *Druid* with responsibility for ship's hygiene as well as treatment of the sick and injured. In 1794 he transferred to the *Reliance*, whose captain was Henry Waterhouse, which was bound for New South Wales, carrying Governor John Hunter to the colony. Bass was fortunate that Matthew Flinders, the famous hydrographer and a fellow native of Lincolnshire, was a fellow officer and could assist him in his aim of acquiring navigational and sea-manship skills. With truth he could later write to his mother: 'I have two professions—I am a sailor as well as a surgeon' (Bowden, 'George Bass, surgeon and sailor', 44). Well-read, with a talent for languages, he mastered the dialect of the Port Jackson (Sydney) Aboriginal people from Bennelong, who had been taken to England and was returning on board the *Reliance*. Bass arrived in Australia in 1795, intent upon seeing 'more of the country than any of my predecessors' (Bowden, *George Bass*, 82).

That year, accompanied by Flinders and sailing in the *Tom Thumb*, Bass commenced exploring the George's River, which flows into Botany Bay. On their next journey in 1796 they discovered Port Hacking and Lake Illawarra. Bass's land exploration led to the discovery of coal and included an unsuccessful attempt to cross the Blue Mount-ains. At this time he also ventured into commerce: when Governor Hunter sent the *Reliance* and the *Supply* to Cape Horn to purchase livestock, Bass obtained a cow and nine-teen sheep. In December 1797, Hunter, who judged the surgeon to have 'a well-informed mind and an active dis-position' (Bowden, 'George Bass, surgeon and sailor', 41), gave Bass permission to recruit six volunteer seamen and draw rations for six weeks to undertake further explor-ation. In early 1798 in a whaleboat Bass explored Twofold Bay, the Shoalhaven River, Wilson's Promontory, and Western Port Bay, and saw what he inferred from the strong westerly seas and swell to be a strait between Van Diemen's Land (Tasmania) and the Australian mainland (the two were at the time thought to be connected). In all, he covered 600 miles of coastline in eleven weeks. The fol-lowing year he set out in the *Norfolk*, under the command of Matthew Flinders, to verify the existence of the strait which Governor King, acting on Flinders's suggestion, was to name in Bass's honour. They circumnavigated Van Diemen's Land, producing its first map and the first chart of Bass Strait. It was Bass's report on the Derwent River that was decisive in establishing a settlement there in 1803. He also collected plants and birds, and became the first person to give a precise description of a wombat. Flin-ders noted that Bass's 'ardour for discovery was not to be repressed by any obstacles nor deterred by any danger' (Bowden, 'George Bass, surgeon and sailor', 38).

By 1799, however, Bass's health had deteriorated and he was judged unfit for duty and returned to England with Charles Bishop, a sea captain and Sydney merchant. *En route* he charted and named Pacific islands, including the Bass Islands, and the Strait of Singapore from Maca to Bombay. In England he met Elizabeth (1768–1824), sister of Henry Waterhouse, and daughter of William Waterhouse and Susanna Brewer. They married on 8 October 1800, at St James's Church, Piccadilly, London. Faced with poor health, a low salary, and doubtful career prospects, he obtained twelve months' leave in order to pursue com-mercial interests: importing goods to Sydney with Charles Bishop. He bought a ship, the *Venus*, and in it he and Bishop sailed to Port Jackson but were unable to sell their cargo because of an excess of speculators. Bass then reached an agreement with Governor King to import a cargo of salted pork. In February 1803 he left Port Jackson for South America in the *Venus* but nothing more was heard of him. He probably died in the Pacific Ocean. Bass's journal of the *Norfolk* voyage is included in the account of the colony of New South Wales by David Collins. The fate of the ori-ginal, like that of its author, is unknown. In 1998 the State Library of New South Wales acquired the important col-lection of letters between Bass, his mother, and his wife.

GILLIAN WINTER

Sources D. Collins, *An account of the English colony in New South Wales*, 2 (1802) · [F. Watson], ed., *Historical records of Australia*, 1st ser., 2–5 (1914–15) · K. M. Bowden, *George Bass, 1771–1803* (Melbourne, 1952) · K. M. Bowden, 'George Bass, surgeon and sailor', *Bulletin of the Post-Graduate Committee in Medicine* [University of Sydney], 17/2 (1961), 33–56 · K. M. Bowden, 'Bass, George', *AusDB*, vol. 1 · V. Cole, 'George Bass and the whaleboat voyage', *Victorian Historical Journal*, 69/2 (Nov 1998), 77–97

Archives State Library of New South Wales, Sydney, papers
Likenesses portrait, repro. in Bowden, *George Bass, 1771–1803*; formerly in possession of Major Twickenham

Bass, Michael Arthur, first Baron Burton (1837–1909), brewer and benefactor, was born at Brewery House, High Street, Burton upon Trent, on 12 November 1837, the elder son of Michael Thomas *Bass (1799–1884), brewer, and his wife, Eliza Jane (*d.* 1897), daughter of Major Samuel Arden of Longcroft Hall, Staffordshire. He was educated at Harrow School and Trinity College, Cambridge, where he graduated BA in 1860, MA in 1864. On leaving university, he entered the flourishing brewing business of Bass, Ratcliff, and Gretton. He married on 28 October 1869 Harriet Georgiana, daughter of Edward Thornewill of Dove Cliff, Staffordshire; they had a daughter, Nellie Lisa, born on 27 December 1873, who married in 1894 James Evan Bruce Baillie, formerly MP for Inverness-shire.

Already in 1860 Bass, as the firm was invariably known, was one of Britain's leading breweries, with an annual output of 340,000 barrels. By 1876 Bass's production was close on a million barrels. Three years later an article in the *British Mercury* (6 June 1879) thought the firm 'a mercantile colossus that has o'erstrided every similar institution in England, if not the world … a monument to the energy of men'. Bass's pre-eminence as a market leader was undoubtedly the achievement of M. T. Bass, but his son was a capable and loyal deputy until his father's death in 1884. Then, for the next quarter of a century, in more difficult times for brewers, he kept the firm on course.

While other brewers stumbled, caught out by a decelerating demand for beer, increasing competition among brewers, the headlong, expensive acquisition of public houses after the mid-1880s, and the temperance movement storm, Michael Bass ensured that Bass retained its supreme reputation for a quality product and sound management (only Guinness—an Irish firm—came to equal its standing in the brewing industry). This was a notable achievement for a third-generation businessman who was a prime exemplar of the richest type of late Victorian plutocrat. Michael Bass's business qualities were numerous: he possessed a sound understanding of brewing (especially of the hop trade); he was proud of his calling; he was genial, a respected manager of his departmental heads; even towards the end of his life he put in a six-hour day at the firm's offices in Burton.

Bass entered parliament in 1865 as Liberal member for Stafford before representing East Staffordshire between 1868 and 1885, and the Burton division of Staffordshire in 1885–6. He proved a popular member of the house, and was a personal friend of W. E. Gladstone. His father having refused both a baronetcy and a peerage, Bass was made a baronet *in vita patris* in 1882, with remainder to his brother, Hamar Alfred Bass, and his heirs male; Hamar Bass died in 1898, leaving his son, William Arthur Hamar Bass, heir to the baronetcy. Bass was opposed to Gladstone's home-rule policy in 1886, but on other great questions he remained for some time a consistent Liberal. He

Michael Arthur Bass, first Baron Burton (1837–1909), by C. Keene, pubd 1907

was raised to the peerage on Gladstone's recommendation on 13 August 1886 as Baron Burton of Rangemore and of Burton upon Trent, both in Staffordshire.

The growing hostility of the Liberal Party to the brewing interest, as shown in their licensing policy, and the widening of the breach on the Irish question, led Lord Burton to a final secession from the Liberals in 1894, and he became a Liberal Unionist under Lord Hartington and Joseph Chamberlain. After 1903 he warmly supported Chamberlain's policy of tariff-reform, and, although in poor health, he initially led the opposition to Herbert Asquith's licensing bill in 1908, which was rejected by the House of Lords.

Always outspoken and good-humoured, Burton was a personal friend of Edward VII, both before and after his accession. The king frequently visited him at his London residence, Chesterfield House, Mayfair, at his Scottish seat, Glen Quoich Lodge, and at Rangemore, his vast house near Burton. The king conferred upon him the decoration of KCVO when he visited Balmoral in 1904. He was a deputy lieutenant and a JP for Staffordshire, and a director of the South Eastern Railway Company. In his younger days he was an active freemason and remained a liberal contributor to masonic charities. An excellent shot and an expert deerstalker, he was long in command of the

2nd volunteer battalion of the North Staffordshire regiment, retiring in August 1881 with the rank of honorary colonel. He built and presented to the regiment the spacious drill hall at Burton, and gave for competition at Bisley the Bass charity vase and a cup for ambulance work.

Burton's gifts and benefactions to the town of Burton were, like those of his father, munificent. Contemporaries compared them with George Peabody and Baroness Burdett-Coutts. When Burton died the *Brewers' Gazette* (4 February 1909) reckoned the practical form of his munificence saved the ratepayers of Burton upon Trent 2*s.* in the pound over many years. He and his father presented Burton with a town hall and municipal offices at a cost of over £65,000. Lord Burton gave club buildings to both the Liberal and Conservative parties in succession; he constructed, at a cost of about £20,000, the ferry bridge which spans the valley at the south end of Burton, and afterwards freed the bridge from tolls at a cost of £12,950, and in 1890 added an approach to it over the marshy ground, known as the Fleet Green Viaduct. As a loyal churchman, he generously contributed towards diocesan funds, but was most notably a builder of churches. St Paul's Church at Burton, built by him and his father, is a miniature late Victorian cathedral. It cost £120,000, with a further £40,000 provided for its endowment. Large sums in addition were given for improvements and embellishments, including £30,000 for a church institute. In addition, father and son built St Margaret's, Burton, and the church at Rangemore, and Lord Burton was in the middle of financing St Chad's, Burton, and the restoration of the old parish church, St Modwen's (at a cost of £20,000), when he died. Since both the Ratcliff and Gretton partners were also church builders in the Burton neighbourhoods, the brewery's patronage of church building—beer and God in harness—is a remarkable example of late Victorian philanthropy.

Burton had a cultivated taste as an art collector, and Chesterfield House, his residence in Mayfair, was furnished in the style of the eighteenth century and contained a choice collection of pictures by English artists of that period which became widely known owing to his generosity in lending them to public exhibitions. Gainsborough, Reynolds, and Romney were especially well represented. His more modern pictures were at Rangemore, and included some of the best work of Stanfield, Creswick, and their contemporaries. At Rangemore he was reckoned to have spent as much as £200,000 on its improvement.

Burton died at his London home, Chesterfield House, Mayfair, on 1 February 1909 after an operation for a kidney affliction and was buried on 5 February at Rangemore church. He was survived by his wife. The grand pallbearers at his funeral were good testimony to his popularity among the aristocracy and his standing in the brewing industry. In default of male heirs, the peerage, by a second patent of 29 November 1897, descended to his daughter and her heirs male. By his will he strictly entailed the bulk of his property to his wife for life, then to his daughter, then to her descendants; and Burton stipulated that every person and the husband of every person in the entail should assume the surname and arms of Bass, and reside at Rangemore for at least four months in every year.

CHARLES WELCH, *rev.* R. G. WILSON

Sources Bass Museum, Burton upon Trent, Bass archives · GEC, *Peerage* · *Brewers' Gazette* (4 Feb 1909) · *Burton Evening Gazette* (2 Feb 1909), 36–50 · *Brewers' Journal* (15 Feb 1909) · *CGPLA Eng. & Wales* (1909) · *British Mercury* (6 June 1879) · C. C. Owen, 'The greatest brewery in the world': a history of Bass, Ratcliff & Gretton, Derbyshire RS, 29 (1992) · *Brewing Trade Review* (Feb 1909)
Archives Bass Museum, Burton upon Trent
Likenesses H. von Herkomer, painting, 1883, priv. coll. · H. von Herkomer, painting, 1896, Burton town hall, Burton upon Trent; replica, priv. coll. · C. Keene, photograph, pubd 1907, NPG [*see illus.*] · F. W. Pomeroy, statue, 1911, King Edward Place, Burton upon Trent · H. J. Brooks, group portrait, oils (*Private view of the Old Masters Exhibition, Royal Academy, 1888*), NPG · F. W. Pomeroy, bust, priv. coll. · Spy [L. Ward], caricature, Hentschel-colourtype, NPG; repro. in *VF* (25 Nov 1908)
Wealth at death £1,000,000: probate, 11 March 1909, *CGPLA Eng. & Wales*

Bass, Michael Thomas (1799–1884), brewer and politician, was born on 6 July 1799 at Burton upon Trent, the eldest son of Michael Thomas Bass (1759–1827), brewer, and his wife, Sarah, *née* Hoskins (1763–1837). He was educated at the grammar school in Burton and afterwards at Nottingham, entering the family brewery (founded in 1777 by his grandfather) when he was eighteen years old. When Bass served his apprenticeship there in the late 1810s the firm was not in a particularly flourishing state.

The sale of Burton ales, long celebrated in England and the Baltic, was badly dislocated by the Napoleonic wars (1793–1815). The once buoyant export trade with Russia never fully recovered, and the number of breweries in the town contracted from thirteen in 1780 to five by the mid-1820s. Salvation came from an unexpected quarter. After 1822 a rapid switch was made from the Russian to the Indian export trade. The beer sold in the East Indies was a bright, pale ale—East India pale ale or IPA—a beer quite different from the high-coloured, sweet, strong beer that had comforted the Russians during their long winters. Sales burgeoned. By 1832–3 Bass, the market leader, sold over 5000 barrels a year there, around 40 per cent of the firm's total output. In comparison with the production of the great London breweries this barrelage was minute. But no British brewing firm made more rapid strides than Bass in the next forty years. It became the largest brewery in the world, propelling Burton to become the great brewing centre of Victorian Britain. At the heart of these extraordinary developments was M. T. Bass, who took over the firm's direction on his father's death in 1827.

Market conditions became increasingly favourable. The coming of the railways to Burton in 1839 meant that the delays, pilferage, and expense in transporting beer by canal boat could be avoided. Bright Burton beer, by the late 1830s the most fashionable beer in Britain, could be sent by rail to London at a quarter of the cost, with journey

Michael Thomas
Bass (1799–1884),
by W. W. Winter

times slashed from over a week to half a day. It was never a cheap beer, but demand by a growing lower middle class gave it premium status for half a century.

M. T. Bass grasped his opportunities firmly. It is difficult to trace in detail the precise qualities of his entrepreneurship: few of his papers survive, in contrast to the abundance of statistics compiled in vast ledgers for the firm by an army of clerks. The figures reveal headlong expansion. Victorian commentators loved statistics to reveal progress: no firm provided a more dazzling series than Bass. Production rose from a mere 8480 barrels in 1830 to 340,000 in 1860 (placing the firm alongside the biggest London breweries), then soared in the booming beer market of the 1860s and 1870s to reach almost a million barrels by the late 1870s. In 1881 the firm's three breweries in Burton (powered by thirty-two steam engines) and twenty-six malthouses covered 145 acres. They consumed 100,000 tons of brewing materials a year; the firm's turnover was £2.5m a year, producing a revenue of £1000 a day for the government; the capital of the company was £3.2m. It was simply Britain's biggest brewery and best-known firm.

Michael Bass's achievement, shared with two generations of his highly competent Ratcliff and Gretton partners, was based on an extraordinary vision and superb management skills. This is evident both in the construction and expansion of his great brewery, his early use of science in brewing, and the way he exploited the free trade (Bass owned a mere handful of public houses at this stage). In fact Bass had opened four agencies (in London, Liverpool, Stoke-on-Trent, and Birmingham) before the railway came to Burton. Their number then expanded rapidly. In 1880 there were twenty-one in the United Kingdom with a branch in Paris. From these bases beer was distributed across Britain and Ireland and, from London and Liverpool, around the world. Bass's pale ales, imitated (not with total success before the late 1870s) everywhere in Britain, maintained their superb reputation. Their sale

was aided by modest advertising and branding: the famous red triangle used on pale ale labels (the first registered trade mark) was recognized worldwide.

M. T. Bass's reputation as the leading Victorian brewer was not only dependent on the creation of his great brewery, but also on his advocacy of the brewing trade generally. While the Ratcliffs and Grettons took on the detailed management of barley purchases, malting, brewing, sales, and finance, M. T. Bass, although not relaxing for a moment his hand on the tiller (he was tough in dealing with his partners), took on the role of spokesman not only for his own firm but for brewers in Burton and Britain as well at a time when hostility to the trade by temperance reformers and Liberal nonconformists was mounting. His public relations and political skills were considerable.

In 1835 Bass married Eliza Jane, eldest daughter of Major Samuel Arden of Longcroft Hall, a member of an old Staffordshire landed family; they had two sons and two daughters. In 1847 Bass was first returned as MP for Derby in the Liberal interest, a connection he was to maintain until the year before his death, although according to the *Brewers' Guardian* of 6 May 1884 'in the House of Commons he was better known for his regular attendance than for any feats of oratory'. His assiduity was reflected in the series of statistics he engaged Professor Leone Levi to collect on living standards and the liquor trade in the early 1870s, and his role in tempering Liberal anti-drink legislation after 1868. Unlike his son Michael Arthur *Bass, first Baron Burton, he remained a committed Liberal, advocating free trade, low taxation, and improved working-class living standards. He was active in the promotion of legislation to abolish imprisonment for small debtors; he brought in a bill (which caused some ridicule in Derby) to suppress organ-grinders as street nuisances. W. E. Gladstone offered him a peerage, but he did not wish to join the House of Lords.

Bass's enormous popularity in Derby, only checked by his opposition to the Ground Game Act of 1881, was due principally to his magnificent benefactions to the town. Matching gifts he made in Burton, his donations amounted according to his obituarists to £80,000, and had given Derby a new library, art gallery, recreation ground, and swimming-baths. One critic remained unimpressed, commenting that his charity was merely 'some feathers being given back by the man who had taken the goose' (*Licensed Victuallers' Gazette*, 2 May 1874). Besides these gifts, he was generous in his support of the Licensed Victuallers' asylum and schools (the association's annual dinner providing the great set piece for the defence of the brewing industry), the United Commercial Travellers Association schools, and the formation of the Amalgamated Society of Railway Servants in 1870. The latter interest clearly stemmed from his representation of a railway town, his investment in and advocacy of the railways since the 1830s, and a genuine concern about the long hours worked by railway employees. As a result of his charitable efforts, Liberal stance, and standing with the party's leaders, and his position as a highly successful brewer, his reputation stood supreme in the Victorian brewing industry.

A man of enormous activity and energy, Bass did not confine his interests to business and politics. Brewers enjoyed ample incomes (the Bass, Ratcliff, and Gretton families had all produced millionaire members by 1900); day-to-day management could be delegated to other partners and departmental managers. Bass was a keen sportsman, enjoying regular fox-hunting in the midland counties until a few years before his death. He was an early convert to the growing practice among the Victorian rich of enjoying holidays and recreations in Scotland. From the 1840s onwards he made an annual pilgrimage of between four and six weeks there to shoot grouse, stalk deer, and catch salmon. In later years he leased Tulchan Lodge, Strathspey. Earlier in his life, he had been an officer in the Derbyshire yeoman cavalry, assisting in quelling the local riots before the passage of the Reform Act of 1832. More domestically, he enjoyed a game of whist and billiards each evening with his family.

In 1852 Bass became a magistrate and deputy lieutenant for the counties of Staffordshire and Derbyshire. He also eventually became a landowner on some scale, although his landholdings in no sense matched his immense wealth. As early as 1848 he leased Byrkley Lodge and in 1853 Rangemore House from the Sneyd family (lessees in turn of the duchy of Lancaster). At Rangemore, Bass brought two large houses, village, church, and estate up to model standards. Rangemore Hall was much extended; Sir Joseph Paxton 'made of the … gardens and conservatories a veritable paradise' (Barnard, 17). By 1883 Bass owned 2283 acres in five counties.

Bass died on 29 April 1884 at Rangemore House, Staffordshire, and was buried in Rangemore churchyard on 5 May. Both his sons became members of parliament. Michael Arthur Bass succeeded him as head of the brewery, was MP for East Staffordshire, and became a baronet in 1882 during his father's lifetime. His other son, Hamar Bass, MP for Tamworth, was addicted to the turf and was effectively excluded from the brewery's management.

R. G. WILSON

Sources C. C. Owen, 'The greatest brewery in the world': a history of Bass, Ratcliff & Gretton, Derbyshire RS, 29 (1992) · T. R. Gourvish and R. G. Wilson, The British brewing industry, 1830–1980 (1994) · Brewers' Guardian (6 May 1884) · Brewers' Journal (15 May 1884) · A. Barnard, Noted breweries of Great Britain and Ireland, 1 (1889) · 'A glass of pale ale' and 'A visit to Burton' (1880) · [J. Hogg], ed., Fortunes made in business: a series of original sketches, 3 vols. (1884–7) · Licensed Victuallers' Gazette and Hotel Courier (4 Nov 1874) · CGPLA Eng. & Wales (1884)
Archives Bass Museum, Burton upon Trent
Likenesses Ape [C. Pellegrini], chromolithograph, NPG; repro. in VF (20 May 1871) · J. E. Boehm, bronze statue, The Wardwick, Derby · W. W. Winter, photograph, NPG [see illus.] · photographs, Bass Museum, Burton upon Trent
Wealth at death £1,830,291 10s. 5d. in UK: probate, 27 May 1884, CGPLA Eng. & Wales

Bassandyne [Bassendyne], **Thomas** (d. 1577), printer and bookseller, was a native of Scotland, although his place of birth, parents, and details of his early life and education are unknown. He is believed to have learned the art of printing abroad, possibly at Paris and Leiden, but he first emerges in Edinburgh in 1564. In March of that year, the printing type of the imprisoned printer John Scot, confiscated in 1563 on account of his printing the work by the Catholic Ninian Winzet, was placed in the hands of Bassandyne by the magistrates of Edinburgh. By 1568 the type was back with Scot but in the intervening period there is no evidence that Bassandyne printed himself. That year Bassandyne was also in trouble with clerical and secular authority. In July the general assembly of the Church of Scotland ordered him to withdraw all copies of The Fall of the Roman Kirk in which the king was offensively proclaimed 'supreme head of the primitive kirk', and, similarly, copies of a psalm book which had printed at the back a 'baudie' song called 'Welcome fortune'. The assembly appointed the divine Alexander Arbuthnet (not to be confused with the printer of the same name) to revise the obnoxious books and henceforth Bassandyne was instructed to print nothing 'without licence of the magistrate, or reviseing of the Kirk' (Thomson, 1.125–6). The offending works were probably printed for Bassandyne by Scot and it is not until 1571–2 that the former certainly began to print in his own right. By now he was working from his place of business at the Nether Bow on the south side of the High Street where he had lived since about 1567. For a device he adopted Jean Crespin's anchor with the initials 'TB'.

The tumultuous period of the Marian civil war (1568–73) saw Bassandyne participate in a propaganda war as he printed for the queen's men in opposition to the incumbent royal printer Robert Lekpreuik, who printed for the king. While the reformed church gave financial support to Lekpreuik, the victorious king's men convicted Bassandyne of treason in January 1572 and his property was forfeited. He was denounced a rebel for his part in the treasonable withholding of Edinburgh Castle, though his specific involvement with the castilians is unknown. However, he soon recovered his position and in February 1573 the regent, the earl of Morton, granted a remission for payment of just over £66 Scots. Subsequently, although Bassandyne was never appointed king's printer, his career seems ironically to have eclipsed that of Lekpreuik who himself was imprisoned in 1574. But the two rivals were much more closely connected than presbyterian historians such as David Calderwood have suggested, and on his death Bassandyne left a small legacy and pension to Lekpreuik. Bassandyne's own church politics were episcopalian (in line with the Erastianism of The Fall of the Roman Kirk), not Catholic.

From 1573 Bassandyne's press delivered some high quality productions—though few survive—including a fine edition of the works of Sir David Lindsay (1574), a psalms of David in metre (1575), and most famously his accurate New Testament (1576, but published 1579), which was part of Scotland's first domestic Bible printing, produced in partnership with the Edinburgh merchant Alexander *Arbuthnet. The partners struck a production agreement in December 1574 and the following March they submitted to the general assembly their proposal to print the

Geneva Bible in English. The church adopted a pragmatic approach in spite of Bassandyne's episcopalian record and accepted the proposal, delivering an authorized text to the printers the following month. The privy council provided a supporting licence in July requiring copies to be delivered within nine months, and a subscription scheme was initiated, the first in British book history. Initially Bassandyne seems to have taken the initiative in printing yet progressed fitfully, employing the Flemish compositor Solomon Kirkemar (or Kirknett) to improve accuracy, and in January 1577 he was forced by the privy council to give up his printed sheets to Arbuthnet. Bassandyne's tardiness, perhaps due to ill health or an unrealistic schedule, had led to a breach in his agreement with Arbuthnet to hand over all existing materials should he fail to deliver finished copies in 1576. This occurred even though the latter obtained an official extension to the delivery schedule in July 1576 only a month after they were jointly granted a ten year copyright for the Bible. Therefore in January 1577 Bassandyne's printed but unbound New Testament, along with his types and materials, passed to Arbuthnet along with responsibility for completing the project.

Bassandyne married Katherine Norvell (or Norwell; d. 1593), and they had a daughter, Alesoun, but no sons. After Bassandyne's death on 14 October 1577, a sympathetic town council allowed the widow to remain at the Nether Bow rent-free, and perhaps the printing but certainly the bookselling side of the business continued under Katherine before she married the printer and bookseller Robert Smyth. On Katherine's death in 1593 her testament shows she still possessed a considerable quantity of book stock. Bassandyne's own will and testament also survive and his inventory proves he was a major bookseller as well as a printer. The listing of over 300 titles provides one of the most interesting sources for stock holding in the period and indicates he was supplied by London and the continent, including the printer Christopher Plantin at Antwerp. At his death, Bassandyne's estate was valued at over £2000 Scots. A. J. MANN

Sources W. Scott and D. Laing, eds., *The Bannatyne miscellany*, 3 vols., Bannatyne Club, 19–19b (1827–55), vol. 2, pp. 191–204 • NA Scot., commissary court records, Edinburgh, cc8/2/8 • *Reg. PCS*, 1st ser., 2.544–6, 582–3 • D. Calderwood, *The history of the Kirk of Scotland*, ed. T. Thomson and D. Laing, 8 vols., Wodrow Society, 7 (1842–9), vol. 1, pp. 125, 134; vol. 2, p. 423; vol. 3, pp. 246, 452 • J. Lee, *Memorial for the Bible societies in Scotland* (1824), 32–4, 116–17, appx 6–7 • Burgh council minute books, Edinburgh city archives, Edinburgh council papers, v.4, 79; v.5, 182 • T. Thomson, ed., *Acts and proceedings of the general assemblies of the Kirk of Scotland*, 3 pts, Bannatyne Club, 81 (1839–45), pt 1, pp. 125, 164, 327–9 • M. Livingstone, D. Hay Fleming, and others, eds., *Registrum secreti sigilli regum Scotorum / The register of the privy seal of Scotland*, 7 (1966), p. 94, no. 642 • NA Scot., Registrum secreti sigilli regum Scotorum, manuscript registers, NAS.PS.1.43, 103R • R. Wodrow, *Collections upon the lives of the reformers and most eminent ministers of the Church of Scotland*, ed. W. J. Duncan, 1, Maitland Club, 32 (1834), vol. 1, pp. 214, 217, 509, 521 • R. Dickson and J. P. Edmond, *Annals of Scottish printing from the introduction of the art in 1507 to the beginning of the seventeenth century* (1890); facs. edn (1975) • W. T. Dobson, *History of the Bassandyne Bible* (1887)

Wealth at death £2009 Scots: Scott and Laing, eds., *The Bannatyne miscellany*

Bassano, Alvise (d. 1554), musician and instrument maker, was presumably born in Bassano, near Venice, in the late fifteenth century, the second son of Maestro Jeronimo (d. 1539?), known as Piva ('bagpipe'). By 1515 he was playing in Venice, and he served in Bologna from 1519 to 1521. In 1531 he and three of his younger brothers, Anthony (d. 1574), Jasper (d. 1577), and John (d. 1570), using the surname de Jeronimo, briefly joined the sackbut consort at the English court and then returned to Venice. Anthony came back to court in 1538 as 'maker of divers instruments of music'. The eldest brother, Jacopo (d. 1559x66), seems to have accompanied him but soon went back to Venice. Alvise, Jasper, and John and their youngest brother, **Baptista Bassano** (d. 1576), hurriedly journeyed to England in 1539, leaving Venice without the doge's permission. Henry VIII's Venetian agent Edmund Harvel claimed that as musicians they were 'all excellent and esteemed above all other in this city in their virtue' (Lasocki and Prior, 9). They and Anthony, dubbed 'brothers in the science or art of music' (ibid., 10), received their official appointment to the court in 1540, now using the surname Bassani, which eventually settled down as Bassano. Baptista was buried at St Botolph without Bishopsgate, London, on 11 April 1576. The Bassanos made up a consort of five recorders, being joined in 1550 by **Augustine Bassano** (d. 1604), Alvise's eldest son, to form a six-member consort that was staffed largely by their descendants until the amalgamation of the wind consorts into one group in the 1630s. It is the only permanent recorder consort known before the twentieth century. The consort's initial repertory has not survived, but probably consisted of dances and arrangements of vocal pieces such as *frottole* and *canzonette*. Augustine was buried at St Olave, Hart Street, London, on 24 October 1604.

By 1544 Alvise and his brothers were given housing in the former monks' quarters of the dissolved monastery of the Charterhouse, just outside the city of London, complete with gardens and a unique water supply and sewage system. They were forced out by Sir Edward North about 1552, after an unsuccessful legal battle; he turned the property into a mansion. Alvise died between 15 and 31 August 1554. Anthony, Jasper, and John meanwhile moved to the east of the city, the area in which most of the Italians in London lived. In 1552 they jointly bought a messuage on Mark Lane, where they set up an instrument making shop; Anthony's descendants owned the property into the eighteenth century. Baptista moved to the liberty of Norton Folgate, just outside the city of London to the north-east. In addition to playing in the recorder consort he seems to have acted as lute and Italian instructor to Princess Elizabeth between 1545 and 1552. With Margaret Johnson (d. 1587), whom he termed 'my reputed wieff' in his will, he had a daughter, Emilia *Lanier, the main candidate for identification as the 'dark lady' of Shakespeare's sonnets.

The second and third generations in England also served as wind musicians at court. Alvise Bassano's second son,

Lodovico Bassano (d. 1593), took over his place in the recorder consort; Anthony's sons Mark Anthony (1546/7–1599) and Andrea (1554–1626) served in the sackbut consort; and Arthur (1547–1624), Edward (1551–1615), and **Jeronimo Bassano** (1559–1635), born on 11 March 1559, served in the recorder consort. Arthur's son Anthony (1579–1658) took over his father's place in the recorder consort; Thomas (1589?–1617), probably Andrea's son, served in the flute consort; and Jeronimo's sons filled a variety of places: Scipio (1586–1613) in the viol consort; Edward (1588–1638) in the sackbut consort; and Henry (1597–1665) in the recorder and sackbut consorts. Andrea, Anthony, Arthur, Jeronimo, and perhaps others continued to work as instrument makers and repairers. Augustine, Lodovico, and Jeronimo were composers of lute and woodwind music, Jeronimo's fantasias being the most important recorder consort music written before the twentieth century. Lodovico was buried at St Botolph, Aldgate, on 18 July 1593; Jeronimo was buried at Waltham Abbey in Essex on 22 August 1635. The later repertory of the court recorder consort, some of which is preserved in the so-called Fitzwilliam wind manuscript, consisted of such fantasias as well as dances (allemandes, courantes, pavanes, and galliards) and arrangements of vocal pieces (motets, madrigals, and *canzonette*). The consort, as Augustine stated in a legal case in 1564, was 'bounden to give daily attendance upon the Queen's Majesty' (Lasocki and Prior, 152), presumably to supply music for dances and to entertain courtiers and guests in the presence chamber.

The Bassanos prospered in England. Their instruments (particularly recorders but also cornetts, crumhorns, curtals, flutes, shawms, lutes, and viols) were well known and prized in France, Germany, and Spain as well as in England. The second and third generations largely married into the gentry: Lodovico married Elizabeth Daman on 13 November 1592, and Jeronimo married Dorothy Symonds on 4 February 1584. Three members of the second generation, Arthur, Edward, and Jeronimo, held enough property (in Hoxton, Middlesex, and Waltham Abbey and Walthamstow, Essex) to merit calling themselves 'esquire', the social rank above gentleman. As inflation degraded the monetary value of a court place, later generations moved into more lucrative professions, such as the law and civil service. Circumstantial evidence strongly suggests that the family were of Jewish origin; they were outwardly Catholic in Venice, but in England attended their parish churches (Jeronimo, for instance, was baptized at All Hallows Barking), and later generations gave evidence of their Christian piety.

DAVID LASOCKI

Sources A. Ashbee and D. Lasocki, eds., *A biographical dictionary of English court musicians, 1485–1714*, 2 vols. (1998) · D. Lasocki and R. Prior, *The Bassanos: Venetian musicians and instrument makers in England, 1531–1665* (1995) · A. Ruffatti, 'La famiglia Piva-Bassano nei documenti degli archivi di Bassano del Grappa', *Musica e Storia*, 6 (1998), 349–67 · parish register, London, All Hallows Barking [baptism: Jeronimo Bassano], 20 March 1559 · parish register, Waltham Abbey, Essex [burial: Jeronimo Bassano], 22 Aug 1635 · parish register, London, St Botolph, Aldgate [marriage: Lodovico Bassano], 13 Nov 1592 · parish register, London, St Botolph, Aldgate [burial: Lodovico Bassano], 18 July 1593

Bassano, Augustine (d. 1604). *See under* Bassano, Alvise (d. 1554).

Bassano, Baptista (d. 1576). *See under* Bassano, Alvise (d. 1554).

Bassano, Jeronimo (1559–1635). *See under* Bassano, Alvise (d. 1554).

Bassano, Lodovico (d. 1593). *See under* Bassano, Alvise (d. 1554).

Bassantin [Bassendyne], **James** (d. 1568), astronomer and astrologer, was the son of the laird of Bassendean in the Merse, Berwickshire, and was born in the reign of James IV (r. 1488–1513). He entered the University of Glasgow at an early age, and, after finishing his studies in the humanities, devoted himself to mathematics and its related sciences, in which he acquired remarkable proficiency. To improve further in these subjects he travelled in the Low Countries, Switzerland, France, Italy, and Germany, before finally settling in France, first in Lyons and later in Paris, as a teacher of mathematics. His success there may have been because he was able to introduce new ideas and materials that he had learned in Germany and Italy exactly at the moment that a lack of modern methods in practical mathematics was felt in France. His major work, the *Astronomique discours*, first published in Lyons in 1557 (Latin trans. Lyons 1559, Geneva 1599), is an elaborately illustrated book with movable diagrams which describes the basic elements of astronomy and planetary motion based on the monumental *Astronomicum Caesaream* of Peter Apian (1540). Further evidence for the influence of German protestant astronomers on Bassantin is provided by his appeal to the authority of Melanchthon to justify his predictions to Sir Robert Melville.

Slightly earlier, for the same publisher in Lyons in 1555, Bassantin had produced a revised and enlarged edition of the *Paraphrase de l'astrolabe* by Jacques Focard (1546) to which was added his 'Amplification de l'usage de l'astrolabe'. The same text was also added to Guillaume Cavellat's 1558 Paris edition of Dominique Jacquinot's *L'vsage de l'astrolabe* (repr. 1559, 1573, 1598). Bassantin indeed may have been one of the two mutual friends of Jacquinot and Cavellat who revised the whole work. His 'Amplification' concerned first the finding of the positions in ecliptic latitude of the moon, the planets, and the fixed stars, which even Stoefler said could not be found with the astrolabe, and second the use of the shadow square.

In 1562 Bassantin returned to Scotland. On the way there, according to Sir James Melville (*Memoirs of His Own Life*, 203), he met Sir Robert Melville (Sir James's brother), and predicted to him that there would be 'at length captivity and utter wreck' for Mary, queen of Scots, at the hands of Elizabeth of England, and also that the kingdom of England would at length fall of right to the crown of Scotland, but at the cost of many bloody battles, in which the Spaniards would take part. Bassantin was a convinced protestant and in politics a supporter of the regent Murray. He was said by Gerard Jan Vossius not to have been skilled in any language except his mother tongue, French, and a little Latin. He wrote his books in French, which he spoke with difficulty and wrote ungrammatically. Although many traditional Latin, Greek, and Arabic sources of astronomy were closed to him, and he depended for his knowledge in a great degree on his own observation, he had a high reputation in his time. His planetary system was that of Ptolemy. He died in 1568.

Works by Bassantin under the titles 'Super mathematica genethliaca, or, Calculs des horoscops', 'Arithmetica', 'Musique selon Platon', and 'De Mathesi in genere' were probably never published.

A. J. Turner

Sources *Thomae Dempsteri Historia ecclesiastica gentis Scotorum, sive, De scriptoribus Scotis*, ed. D. Irving, rev. edn, 2 vols., Bannatyne Club, 21 (1829) · *Biographia Britannica, or, The lives of the most eminent persons who have flourished in Great Britain and Ireland*, 7 vols. (1747–66) · *Memoirs of his own life by Sir James Melville of Halhill*, ed. T. Thomson, Bannatyne Club, 18 (1827) · I. Pantin, ed., *Imprimeurs et libraires Parisiens du XVIe siècle: fascicule Cavellat, Marnef et Cavellat* (1986)

Basse, William (*c*.1583–1653?), poet, was described by Anthony Wood as 'of Moreton near Thame in Oxfordshire, sometime a retainer to the lord Wenman of Thame Park' (Wood, *Ath. Oxon.*, 4.222). Based on references in Basse's poetry, Bond suggested that he originally came to Thame from Northamptonshire, possibly as a page in the service of Sir Richard (from 1628 Lord) Wenman's first wife, Agnes, daughter of Sir George Fermor of Easton Neston, Northamptonshire. There is no evidence that Basse attended either university but his proximity to Oxford led to numerous friendships with poets who studied there, including Francis Beaumont, William Browne, and George Wither.

In 1602 Basse published his first literary work, a poem of seventy-five six-line stanzas entitled *Sword and Buckler, or, The Serving-Mans Defence*. It opens with a prefatory poem 'To the honest and faithful brotherhood of true-hearts, all the old and young serving-men of England health and happines', followed by a short poem 'To the reader' in which Basse calls this work 'first that ere I writ' (*Poetical Works*, 7). The latter was reprinted by Michael Baret before the third book of *Hipponomie, or, The Vineyard of Horsemanship* (1618). The main body of *Sword and Buckler* is a vigorous defence of servants against accusations of idleness and immorality, containing distinct echoes of Spenser. In stanza 73 Basse emphasizes his youth and says that he 'live[s] in the place and manner of a Page' (ibid., 28), but the poem's numerous classical allusions suggest that he had received a good education in Wenman's household.

Basse's second published work, *Three Pastoral Elegies of Anander, Anetor, and Muridella* (1602), is a pleasant example of Spenserian pastoral love poetry, with a digression in the third elegy to pay tribute to Spenser as 'Collin'. Basse dedicated the volume to Jane, Lady Tasburgh, the mother (through her first husband) of his patron Sir Richard Wenman. In the dedication he once again stresses his 'young invention' and promises a greater work:

> when encrease of Age and Learning sets
> My Minde in wealthi'r state then now it is.
> (*Poetical Works*, 35)

An eight-line verse preface attributes the following elegies to a 'Shepheards youth' who has 'Beene nursed up in Colins lore' (ibid., 36).

Basse is probably the 'W. B.' who wrote commendatory verses for his contemporary Francis Beaumont's Ovidian poem *Salmacis and Hermaphrodite* in 1602. Within the next decade Basse wrote an Ovidian narrative poem of his own: 'Urania, or, The Woman in the Moon'. This light-hearted satire tells how two gods sent to earth from Mount Olympus fall in love with the title character, who then flies up to Olympus and wreaks havoc before being sentenced to live on the moon for ever. Its four cantos correspond to the four quarters of the lunar cycle, and it is heavily influenced by both Ovid and Spenser. Basse dedicated the poem to Prince Henry, but it was never published, perhaps owing to Henry's death in November 1612. Basse wrote an elegy for Henry, *Great Brittaines Sunnes-Set*, which was published at Oxford in 1613 with a dedication 'To his honourable master, Sir Richard Wenman, knight' (*Poetical Works*, 91).

Bond argues convincingly that Basse is the 'W. B.' who wrote a commendatory poem for the second book of William Browne's *Britannia's Pastorals* (1616), grouped with verses by Ben Jonson and George Wither. Browne, Jonson, and Wither all demonstrably knew Basse's work and were probably his friends; Wither called him 'the noblest Nymph of Thame' in eclogue two of *The Shepherd's Hunting* (1615). Ault persuasively argues that Basse wrote 'A Memento for Mortalitie', a poem printed in the popular miscellany *A Helpe to Discourse* (1619), though his authorship of the entire volume (attributed to 'W. B. and E. P.') is less certain. He may have written a commendatory poem, signed 'W. B.', for Philip Massinger's play *The Bondsman* (1624). Basse signed his complete name to a poem celebrating the Cotswold athletic games, addressed to 'my right generous friend, Master Robert Dover' (p. 107), printed in *Annalia Dubrensia* (1636) but probably written in 1618.

Basse's most famous occasional poem is his enormously popular sixteen-line elegy on Shakespeare, written between 1616 (when Shakespeare died) and 1623 (when Jonson responded to Basse in his own tribute to Shakespeare in the First Folio). Wells and Taylor list twenty-seven different seventeenth-century manuscript versions of the poem, ten of which attribute it to Basse, including one (British Library, Lansdowne MS 777, fol. 67v) in the handwriting of Basse's friend William Browne. It first reached print in the 1633 edition of John Donne's poems, but was dropped from the 1635 edition, and was next printed in the 1640 edition of Shakespeare's poems, with a correct attribution to 'W. B.' and the title 'On the Death of William Shakespeare, who Died in Aprill, Anno. Dom. 1616' (sig. K8v). The same year it was also printed anonymously in *Wits Recreation*.

Basse also wrote numerous songs, of which at least

three survive. *Maister Basse his Careere, or, The New Hunting of the Hare* was printed as a broadside about 1620 by Edward Allde, and, under the title 'The Hunter's Song', was first published with music (possibly by Basse) in *Wit and Drollery* (1682). 'Tom of Bedlam', written about the same time, was eventually published with music by John Cooper in *Choice Ayres, Songs, and Dialogues* (1676) and several later collections. Izaak Walton, in *The Compleat Angler* (1653), gives the words to 'The Angler's Song', 'lately made at my request by Mr. *William Basse*, one that has made the choice Songs of the *Hunter in his Carrere*, and of *Tom of Bedlam*, and many others of note' (p. 89).

Despite his wide-ranging literary friendships, Basse remained in Oxfordshire, connected with the Wenman household, for his entire adult life. His daughter Jane was buried at Thame in 1634, and his wife, Eleanor, was buried there on 23 September 1637; Elizabeth Basse (baptized 1625) and Dorothy Basse (married 1637) may also have been his daughters. Basse's poetry collection *Polyhymnia*, only fragments of which survive, included numerous verses written for the Wenmans and their kinsmen the Norreys of nearby Rycote. It was dedicated to Bridget, countess of Lindsey, and contained poems for Francis, Lord Norreys (Bridget's grandfather); Elizabeth Cary, Viscountess Falkland (born at Burford Priory, Oxfordshire); and the aunt, first wife, and two eldest daughters of Sir Richard Wenman. It also included a poem on the consecration of Wadham College, Oxford (dated 1613), and 'Elegy on a Bullfinch' (dated 19 June 1648), indicating that it was written over many years. Two distinct manuscripts of *Polyhymnia* were described in the nineteenth century, but both are now lost.

The crowning achievement of Basse's career was *The Pastorals and other Workes*, also written over a period of decades. The centrepiece of the volume is 'Clio, Nine Eclogues in Honour of Nine Virtues', a patent imitation of Spenser's *Shepheard's Calendar*. Unlike the politically tinged pastorals of Spenser and Browne, this work is primarily personal. Basse introduces himself into the narrative as the shepherd Colliden, lovingly describes the countryside around Thame and in the Cotswolds, and inserts a superfluous acrostic on Sir Richard Wenman's name. He also presents a thinly veiled portrait of Mary Herbert, countess of Pembroke, as 'Poemenarcha', friend of poets and sister of 'Philisiden'. Rounding out the volume are Basse's early poem 'Urania', with the original dedication to Prince Henry supplemented with one to Lord Wenman's eldest daughter, Lady Penelope Dynham, and 'The Metamorphosis of the Walnut-Tree of Boarstall', written after 1646.

Basse originally dedicated *The Pastorals* to Lord Wenman, who died in 1640, but it was not prepared for publication until the early 1650s. Warton published a commendatory poem by Richard Bathurst of Oxford, 'To Mr William Basse upon the intended publication of his poems, Jan. 13th, 1651' (Warton, 288–9), which compares Basse to 'an aged oake' (ibid.) with a 'gray Muse' (ibid.) and says that 'our deceased Grandsires lisp'd thy Rhymes' (ibid.). This poem

(without the date) also appears in an illustrated manuscript of *The Pastorals* which Basse personally prepared for the press in 1653; however, the volume was never published, probably because of Basse's death. This manuscript was used by Bond for his edition of 1893, and is now in the Folger Shakespeare Library, Washington (MS V.b. 235). DAVID KATHMAN

Sources *The poetical works of William Basse*, ed. R. W. Bond (1893) · B. Blackley, 'William Basse', *Seventeenth-century British nondramatic poets: first series*, ed. M. Thomas Hester, DLitB, 121 (1992), 17–25 · J. Hunter, 'Chorus vatum Anglicanorum', BL, Add. MSS 24487–24492 (*c*.1842) · Wood, *Ath. Oxon.*, new edn, 4.222 · S. Wells and G. Taylor, *William Shakespeare: a textual companion* (1987), 163–4 · W. Shakespeare, *Poems* (1640) · I. Walton, *The compleat angler, or, The contemplative man's recreation* (1653) · T. Warton, *The life and literary remains of Ralph Bathurst, dean of Wells* (1761) · N. Ault, 'A memento for mortalitie', *TLS* (12 Jan 1933), 24

Bassendyne, Thomas. *See* Bassandyne, Thomas (*d*. 1577).

Basset family (*per. c*.**1275–1835**). For members of this family *see* individual entries under Basset and related entries; for information on the family *see* Bassett, James (*c*.1526–1558).

Basset, Adeliza (*d*. in or after **1210**). *See under* Dunstanville, de, family (*per. c*.1090–*c*.1292).

Basset, Alan (*d*. **1232**), administrator, was one of the three sons (probably the youngest) of Thomas *Basset (*d*. *c*.1182). He founded the Bassets of Wycombe, and was a noted servant of Richard I, John, and Henry III. In 1197 Richard I sent him on a diplomatic mission with William (I) Marshal to the counts of Flanders and Boulogne to detach them from their allegiance to King Philip of France, and shortly afterwards, with his elder brother Thomas, he attested as surety for Richard in France concerning the king's treaty with the count of Flanders against Philip. Between 1197 and 1199 he witnessed six more of Richard's documents in France. Following Richard's death, he was soon in attendance upon John; Alan, Thomas, and Gilbert Basset were all described as barons when they witnessed the homage of the king of Scots to John at Lincoln on 22 November 1200. In 1202 and 1203 Alan witnessed ten of John's charters in France, and, between 1200 and 1215, twenty-five royal charters in England. Remaining loyal to John, he is often recorded in that king's service, and received such rewards as numerous quittances of scutage. In 1215 he was named in Magna Carta as one of the 'noblemen' whose counsel the king relied upon, and he was among the royalist barons who attended John at Runnymede. He appears to have accompanied John on his expedition to the north of England in the winter of 1215–16. He was in Henry III's service by 14 December 1216. In 1217 he fought at the battle of Lincoln, and helped to pacify the kingdom afterwards, and in 1220 he was one of three ambassadors sent to France to arrange a four-year truce. He was still in royal service in 1228, but died late in 1232.

Basset and his brothers each held only enough knights' fees in chief to constitute a very small barony. Richard I granted Alan the manor of Woking in Surrey and the vill of Mapledurwell in Hampshire as one half fee each, while

John granted him part of the manor of Wycombe, on highly favourable terms, to hold in chief as one fee of the honour of Wallingford. He held five fees of that honour, two being in Wootton Bassett and Broad Town (both in Wiltshire) which he held of the inheritance of his wife, Alina de Gai, together with the manor of Compton Bassett, also in Wiltshire. John also granted him the manors of Berwick Bassett in Wiltshire and Greywell in Hampshire.

Basset and Aline had a daughter, Aline, and another daughter, whose name is unknown. With his likely first wife, Alice de Gray (the similarity of their names is such that the possibility that Alan had only one wife cannot be excluded), he had seven children—Thomas, Gilbert, Alice, Fulk, David, Warin, and Philip. Gilbert *Basset, Fulk *Basset, and Philip *Basset are the subjects of separate notices. Thomas (d. 1230) was a crown servant, and David was in royal service in Ireland.   W. T. REEDY

Sources W. T. Reedy, ed., *Basset charters, c.1120–1250*, PRSoc., new ser., 50 (1995) · GEC, *Peerage* · E. B. Fryde and others, eds., *Handbook of British chronology*, 3rd edn, Royal Historical Society Guides and Handbooks, 2 (1986) · PRSoc. · court of common pleas, feet of fines, PRO, CP 25/1 · A. Hughes, *List of sheriffs for England and Wales: from the earliest times to AD 1831*, PRO (1898) · *Chancery records* (RC) · D. A. Carpenter, *The minority of Henry III* (1990) · J. C. Holt, *Magna Carta*, 2nd edn (1992) · Paris, *Chron.*, vol. 2 · *Chronica magistri Rogeri de Hovedene*, ed. W. Stubbs, 4, Rolls Series, 51 (1871) · H. E. Salter and A. H. Cooke, eds., *The Boarstall cartulary*, OHS, 88 (1930), appx 2 · I. J. Sanders, *English baronies: a study of their origin and descent, 1086–1327* (1960) · 'Basset, Philip', *DNB* · R. C. Stacey, *Politics, policy and finance under Henry III, 1216–1245* (1987) · *Curia regis rolls preserved in the Public Record Office* (1922–) · C. Roberts, ed., *Excerpta è rotulis finium in Turri Londinensi asservatis, Henrico Tertio rege*, AD 1216–1272, 1, RC, 32 (1835), 231

Basset, Sir Francis. *See* Bassett, Sir Francis (1593?–1645).

Basset, Francis, Baron de Dunstanville and Baron Basset (1757–1835), politician and landowner, was born at Walcot, Oxfordshire, on 9 August 1757, first-born of two sons and five daughters of Francis Basset (1715–1769), MP and landowner, of Tehidy, Cornwall, and his wife, Margaret, daughter of Sir John *St Aubyn, third baronet, politician, of Clowance. Educated at Harrow School (1770–71), Eton College (1771–4), and King's College, Cambridge (1775), he proceeded without graduating to France and Italy, ciceroned by the Revd William Sandys. He took an MA in 1786.

Basset was created baronet on 24 November 1779 for patriotic services, as lieutenant-colonel of the North Devon militia, for his part in countering a Franco-Spanish armada by marching the Cornish miners to Plymouth, strengthening its defences, and fortifying Portreath. Appointed recorder of Penryn in 1778, he was thence, like his father, returned to parliament for the borough in 1780. He married on 16 May 1780 Frances Susanna Hippisley Coxe (1761–1823), daughter of John Hippisley Coxe of Ston Easton, Somerset: they had one daughter. In parliament he supported North's ministry, he spoke against motions to dismantle crown patronage in 1781, and he opposed peace with the American colonies, witness his speech

Francis Basset, Baron de Dunstanville and Baron Basset (1757–1835), by Thomas Gainsborough, c.1786

seconding the address in 1782. Critical of parliamentary reform, he published anonymously his *Thoughts on Equal Representation* (1783). He joined North in opposition, voting against peace preliminaries. Promised a peerage by the duke of Portland later that year, to steady him after dissension over Cornish patronage, he attached himself to the Foxite whigs and Fox sponsored his membership of Brooks's Club in 1785. He criticized Pitt's commercial entente in debate in 1787 as well as in his pamphlet *Observations on a Treaty with France*.

Basset was a catch rather for electoral clout than political potential. In 1784 and 1790 he contested a clutch of Cornish boroughs, harassing Pittite patrons, and in addition supporting his brother-in-law's unsuccessful county candidature in 1790. James Boswell, who met this 'genteel, smart little man, well-informed and lively' in 1792, found Basset's 'high Tory talk' incongruous with his Foxite dress (*Papers of Boswell*, 18.151). He seldom debated yet he deplored parliamentary reform, on 30 April 1792, and vigilantly opposed it in Cornwall. He joined those 'third party' opposition deserters who were attaching themselves to the government during hostilities with revolutionary France, and supported war on 18 February 1793, albeit with a parting compliment to Fox. Not then averse to piecemeal reform, as shown by his defence of the Stockbridge election bill, he further voted against aspects of Pitt's repressive domestic measures. The junction of the Portland whigs with Pitt's administration in July 1794 ended the last vestiges of his opposition, as his pamphlet *The Theory and Practice of the French Constitution* proved. He became a major in the Cornish yeoman cavalry and commandant of the Penryn Volunteers in 1794, and again in 1803.

Basset solicited Portland for his promised peerage at this juncture, but was kept waiting. Claiming Cornish preoccupations and threatening to abandon his seat and electoral patronage, he was still denied. On 26 January 1795 he explained his absence from the division on the address by objection to its bellicosity; he also disliked the opposition amendment; so he voted against Grey's peace motion, but on 5 February and 10 June he voted against the loan to allied Austria. On domestic issues he reliably supported the administration. He suppressed riots in Cornwall in 1795 and advocated measures against sedition late that year, presenting two like-minded Cornish petitions on the issue. He was to claim later, in 1810, that this legislation had saved the country, though he argued that Pitt, unlike Edmund Burke, had been slow to see the French threat, which he had exposed in his pamphlet *The Crimes of Democracy* (1798). At the dissolution of parliament he obtained the barony of de Dunstanville, on 17 June 1796, which was supplemented by that of Basset, granted on 30 November 1797, with a special remainder to his daughter.

De Dunstanville was thus able to pursue Cornish interests, although now that his borough interests mattered less, he discarded several of them nonchalantly. He was a partner in the Cornish Bank (1779–1801), and chaired the Cornish Metal Company (1785–92). His mines, especially Cook's Kitchen and Dolcoath, were profitable, although he misfired in supporting Jonathan Hornblower against James Watt, both of whom were competitors for a steam engine patent in the early 1790s, simply because he wished to disoblige Watt's Pittite patron, Lord Falmouth. In 1809 he inaugurated a tramway connecting Portreath to the south Cornish coast. The fall in copper and tin prices after 1815 reduced his income, which had peaked at £24,000 a year, to about £8000. He was also an agriculturist and contributed successive articles to Arthur Young's *Annals* over the period 1794 to 1805 on experiments, oxen, crops and prices, and mildew. He pursued parliamentary regulation for corn mills in 1794–6. Owning a fine collection of pictures, he patronized the artist John Opie, and took part in his funeral. Joseph Farington's *Diary* records his artistic interests. He edited Richard Carew's *Survey of Cornwall* in 1811, and became FRS in 1829.

De Dunstanville, professing diminished interest in politics, transferred his allegiance from Pitt to Addington in 1801 and adhered to the latter, although he was averse to his allying with Fox in government, in 1806. He periodically attended the Lords, opposing the acquittal of Lord Melville in 1805, and in 1807 was exonerated by private act after sitting without swearing the oath. Having visited Rome in 1817, he made startling and cogent speeches in support of Catholic relief (1819–29), but still opposed parliamentary reform. He married second on 13 July 1824 Harriet (1777–1864), fourth daughter of Sir William Lemon, first baronet, of Carclew, and Jane Buller; they had no children. After 1832 he confined himself to presenting Cornish petitions in the Lords. *En route* there he was smitten by a paralytic seizure, and he died at his London residence, Stratheden House, Knightsbridge, on 14 February 1835; he was buried at Illogan church on 26 February after a twelve-day funeral procession. His daughter, Frances, Baroness Basset (1781–1855), was unmarried. His entailed estates passed to his nephew and heir, John Basset.

ROLAND THORNE

Sources L. B. Namier, 'Basset, Sir Francis', HoP, *Commons, 1754–90* · R. G. Thorne, 'Basset, Sir Francis', HoP, *Commons, 1790–1820* · *GM*, 2nd ser., 3 (1835), 655 · Boase & Courtney, *Bibl. Corn.*, 1.112–13 · W. Cobbett and T. C. Hansard, eds., *Parliamentary debates* (1780–1833) · *Hansard 1* · *Hansard 2* · U. Nott. L., Portland MSS · Farington, *Diary* · Devon RO, Sidmouth papers · *The journal of James Boswell, 1789–1794*, ed. G. Scott and F. A. Pottle (New York, 1934), vol. 18 of *Private papers of James Boswell from Malahide Castle* (1928–34), 151–2 · A. C. Todd, *Beyond the blaze: a biography of Davies Gilbert* (1967) · *DNB* · GEC, *Peerage* · I. Fitzroy Jones, *Some notes on the Hippisley family* (1952), 119
Archives BL, corresp. with first and second earls of Liverpool, Add. MSS 38216–38421, *passim* · BL, letters to Lord Grenville, Add. MS 58991 · Devon RO, Sidmouth MSS, corresp. · priv. coll., letters to Reginald Pole Carew · U. Nott. L., Portland MSS, corresp., PWF 279, PWV 107
Likenesses J. Reynolds, oils, *c*.1775, Eton · L. F. Abbott, oils, 1780–89, King's Cam. · T. Gainsborough, oils, *c*.1786, Corcoran Gallery of Art, Washington, DC [*see illus.*] · attrib. G. Dupont, oils, Norton Simon Foundation, Los Angeles · G. H. Every, mezzotint (after T. Gainsborough), BM, NPG · R. Westmacott, medallion bust, St Illogan church, Cornwall · oils, Royal Cornwall Institution, Truro
Wealth at death see Todd, *Beyond the blaze*

Basset, Fulk (*d.* 1259), bishop of London, was the second son of Alan *Basset of Wycombe (*d.* 1232), one of the baronial allies of King John. His aristocratic connections were important throughout his career, and were enhanced in 1241 when the deaths in quick succession of his elder brother, Gilbert, and then of Gilbert's only son and heir, left Fulk as the head of this branch of the Basset family. But even before then they had clearly helped him in his ascent of the ladder of ecclesiastical preferment, starting *c*.1223, when he was presented to the wealthy living of Howden in Yorkshire. And by 1227 he had acquired another lucrative benefice, becoming provost of Beverley—a papal dispensation in that year licensed him to hold that office with Howden. As provost, he received letters from the crown in 1234 requesting his knights and free tenants to provide him with an aid to acquit his debts. These latter may well have stemmed from the events of the previous year, when Basset's brothers, Gilbert *Basset (*d.* 1241) and Philip *Basset (*d.* 1271), had been in conflict with the king as a result of their support for Hubert de Burgh (*d.* 1243). There is no sign that Basset gave them any active assistance, but his family's troubles may well have involved him in expense. He became dean of York in 1239, and in December 1241 was elected bishop of London by the canons of St Paul's. According to Matthew Paris, they acted against the will of Henry III, who had besought them to elect Peter d'Aigueblanche, bishop of Hereford (*d.* 1268). However, the king evidently took this reverse with good grace, for letters patent giving royal assent to the election were issued on 28 January 1242, and he was later

Fulk Basset
(d. 1259), seal

The London example, attributed to Basset, contains lists of the churches in the diocese, arranged by archdeaconry, with information about their patronage and value, as well as information about religious houses. Its compilation was probably begun before Basset became bishop, and may well have continued after his death. But there is every likelihood that the attribution to him does reflect a genuine concern with this *matricula*, and, by extension, with the fiscal potential of the diocese. He also issued two sets of episcopal canons, the second a very comprehensive one.

Fulk Basset's pursuit of the rights of his diocese and of the province of Canterbury occasionally led him into conflict with the crown. In 1249 he and the bishop of Lincoln were warned not to take any steps to execute a papal mandate for the induction of Master Robert of Gloucester to the church of Enford, Wiltshire, the advowson of which was claimed by the crown, on pain of being proceeded against by way of their baronies. In 1256 he was similarly warned not to proceed to the excommunication and deposition of Roger, abbot of Gloucester, because litigation concerning Roger was pending in the royal courts and the court of the archbishop of Canterbury. However, on this occasion Basset's potential misdemeanour was explicitly ascribed to ignorance of the situation, and the king expressed his intention to discuss the matter with him. More seriously, however, Basset was one of the bishops arraigned in 1259 for attempts to extract money from John Mansel (d. 1265) and Henry of Wingham (d. 1262), the royal collectors of the papal tenth for the crusade and the 'Sicilian business', and ordered to desist. But these squabbles with the crown did not affect the favour shown him by Henry III. All though his tenure of the see Basset received a succession of gifts of venison, timber, and wine, exemptions from attendance at shire courts, or deferrals of suits with which he was concerned. On his behalf a distraint of knighthood was delayed in 1256, and he was granted wardships in 1244 and 1247.

Many of these favours were clearly in recognition of Basset's continuing service to the crown. In 1244 he was one of those commissioned to escort the king of Scots to Newcastle for negotiations with Henry III. In 1245 he received letters of protection for a journey overseas. This was to the Council of Lyons, where, in 1246, Basset was one of the six bishops who promised to collect a subsidy of 6000 marks for the papacy. Matthew Paris says that he should be blamed for this less than the others, since he was the last to seal the document, and did so unwillingly. Certainly, later in 1246, he appears to have supported the clergy of the diocese of London in their opposition to the papal demand for a third of the income of all beneficed clergy in England for three years, and a half of that of non-residents. Shortly after these problems with the papacy Basset clashed with Archbishop Boniface of Canterbury. He advised the canons of St Paul's to appeal to the king against the archbishop's attempt to subject them to visitation in 1250, and was excommunicated by Boniface for his pains. He seems to have contemplated organizing resistance to archiepiscopal claims—he wrote to the

to make a substantial gift of venison for Basset's consecration feast. But the temporalities were not restored until 16 March 1244, and he was consecrated only on 9 October following, because the archbishopric of Canterbury was vacant from 1240 to 1245, and it proved difficult to make arrangements that did not infringe rights claimed by Canterbury Cathedral priory. This delay was, of course, profitable to the crown, but the keeper of the bishopric from 1242 to 1244, Ralph Dayrell, was not an especially harsh administrator.

Although Fulk Basset might not have been Henry's first choice, Matthew Paris clearly regarded him as being suitable for his new position—'a discreet and careful man, of good moral character and distinguished lineage' (Paris, *Chron.*, 4.171). He was not a scholar–bishop, but he was one of the correspondents of the Franciscan Adam Marsh (d. 1259), a noted doctor in the schools. Before his consecration Basset had been a subject of the papal campaign to ensure that candidates for bishoprics were adequately learned: Boniface, the archbishop-elect of Canterbury (d. 1270), had received orders from the pope to examine him. But although there is no reason to regard Basset as a reformer of the type of Robert Grosseteste (d. 1253), even before he became bishop of London he had scruples about his own pluralism; in 1238 he appeared before Gregory IX (r. 1227–41) and remorsefully offered to resign into his hands the two benefices with cure of souls that he held without dispensation.

As bishop, Fulk Basset was an active diocesan administrator. He was not one of the first thirteenth-century bishops to keep a full record of his *acta*, but there does survive, in a late fourteenth-century copy, a document entitled *Registrum Fulconis Basset quondam London episcopi*. This is, in fact, a *matricula*, a systematic survey of a diocese which was doubtless of great service to the bishop's clerks in the business of litigation and ecclesiastical discipline.

abbot of St Albans asking for support, and later met with other bishops at Dunstable to discuss the matter—but clearly thought better of it. In 1251 he submitted and was absolved, possibly because he feared that Henry III, who was supporting Boniface, would take vengeance not only on himself but on other members of his family. It was in the same year, 1251, that his relative by marriage, the justice Henry of Bath (d. 1260), was accused of corruption, and fell out of favour with the king to such an extent that Henry was said to have been contemplating his murder, only to be warned that Basset was prepared to respond with spiritual sanctions, while the other Basset relatives would apply secular ones.

In 1252 Basset was one of the bishops who opposed the grant of a crusading tenth to the crown, and infuriated Henry by agreeing to it only on condition of royal confirmation of the charters. However, he was once again present when Henry was reconciled with the episcopate at a meeting in London in 1253. At this point in his career Basset was clearly aligned more with the reforming clergy than with the crown, a position that perhaps lies behind the story that he heard bells in the air on the night of Grosseteste's death in October 1253. Two years later, however, he is again found resisting papal exactions, saying, according to Matthew Paris, that he would prefer decapitation to submission to such oppression. Once again the king was angered by his attitude, but once again there was no complete break between the two, for in June 1255 Basset was excused attendance at the eyre in Surrey because he had been detained by the king at Woodstock on most urgent and difficult royal business.

In 1257 Basset performed further services for the crown. He was one of the guardians of the lands of Richard, earl of Cornwall (d. 1272) on the latter's departure to the continent to seek the imperial title, and in the same year became a member of the king's council. Even so there seems to have been an expectation in 1258 that Basset would take the side of the barons in their dispute with the king. But in the event he was one of the royal nominees to the reforming committee of twenty-four, and was seriously criticized by Matthew Paris for his attitude. However, he did not become a member of the new council of fifteen elected to oversee the administration of the realm, and it is not possible to form a view of his political standpoint from his later actions, since he died before the consequences of the baronial reform movement had developed. He was one of the victims of a plague that struck London early in 1259, and died on 21 May. He was buried in St Paul's Cathedral four days later. Basset was possibly the father of Fulk of *Sandford, archbishop of Dublin.

It is hard to avoid the conclusion that Basset's career ended on a subdued note. The sources, unsurprisingly, do not permit of any real assessment of his personality, but his actions point to both conscientiousness and independence of judgement.   R. M. FRANKLIN

Sources Paris, *Chron.* · *Chancery records* · F. M. Powicke and C. R. Cheney, eds., *Councils and synods with other documents relating to the English church, 1205–1313*, 2 vols. (1964) · M. Gibbs and J. Lang, *Bishops and reform, 1215–1272* (1934) · C. R. Cheney, *English bishops' chanceries, 1100–1250* (1950) · F. Barlow, ed., *Durham annals and documents of the thirteenth century*, SurtS, 155 (1945) · D. M. Smith, *Guide to bishops' registers of England and Wales: a survey from the middle ages to the abolition of the episcopacy in 1646*, Royal Historical Society Guides and Handbooks, 11 (1981) · W. R. Matthews and W. M. Atkins, eds., *A history of St Paul's Cathedral and the men associated with it* (1957) · S. L. Waugh, *The lordship of England: royal wardships and marriages in English society and politics, 1217–1327* (1988) · *Matthaei Parisiensis, monachi Sancti Albani, Historia Anglorum, sive … Historia minor*, ed. F. Madden, 3 vols., Rolls Series, 44 (1886–9) · N. Denholm-Young, *Richard of Cornwall* (1947) · B. Harvey, *Westminster Abbey and its estates in the middle ages* (1977)
Likenesses seal, BL; Birch, *Seals*, 1909 [*see illus.*]

Basset, Fulk. *See* Sandford, Fulk of (d. 1271).

Basset, Gilbert (d. 1241), knight and rebel, was the son and heir of Alan *Basset (d. 1232) and his wife, Alice or Alina de Gai (d. 1230), or possibly an earlier wife, Alice de Gray. Alan was probably the youngest of the three sons of Thomas *Basset (d. c.1182) and Adeliza *Basset, née de Dunstanville [*see under* Dunstanville, de, family]. His elder brothers, Gilbert (d. 1205) and Thomas *Basset (d. 1220), lord of Headington, were both active in royal service, Gilbert being heir to a major landholding within the honour of Wallingford, established at the beginning of the twelfth century by his grandfather, an earlier Gilbert Basset, probably a close kinsman of Ralph (d. 1127?) and Richard Basset (d. in or before 1144), justiciars under Henry I. Alan was granted Compton Bassett in Wiltshire by his father before 1180, and he later acquired the manors of Mapledurwell and Woking from Richard I, High Wycombe and Berwick Bassett from John, Winterbourne in Wiltshire from his grandfather Walter de Dunstanville, and Wootton Bassett by right of his wife. Alan was active in the household of the future king, John, from at least 1193, and a regular witness to royal charters both in Normandy and England from 1197 onwards, but his closest contacts appear to have lain with the household of William (I) Marshal, earl of Pembroke (d. 1219), whom he served from at least 1197 until the time of the earl's death—a connection perhaps established through the Dunstanvilles, Alan's maternal kin, native to Dénestanville within the Marshal's Norman lordship of Longueville. Alan's younger sons, Thomas and Warin, are both to be found in the household of William (II) Marshal (d. 1231).

Gilbert Basset followed his father and brothers into royal service, and eventually into the Marshal household. He may well have been the son who discharged Alan's service on the king's Poitevin expedition of 1214, and makes his first certain appearance during the civil war after 1215, when he was granted custody of land at Sutton in Surrey by John. For much of the next decade he was retained as a royal household knight. He was appointed constable of Devizes Castle in 1229, served on the expedition to Brittany in 1230, and in the following year received custody of St Briavels Castle and the Forest of Dean. He was also granted the income and long-term custody of various royal escheats, including Marden and Upavon in Wiltshire, this last a valuable manor formerly held by the disgraced alien courtier, Peter de Mauley.

Basset succeeded to his family lands following the death

of his father in 1232. In addition, from the estate of his brother Thomas Basset, he obtained custody of Kirtlington in Oxfordshire, Speen in Berkshire, held of the Marshal earls of Pembroke, and property at Leeds in Yorkshire, held of the Lacy family and transferred by Basset in 1230 or 1231 to his younger brother Philip. In 1232 Basset's career at court suffered an eclipse following the downfall of the justiciar Hubert de Burgh, and the accession to power of Peter des Roches, bishop of Winchester. Basset was dismissed as keeper of the castles of Devizes and St Briavels in October 1232, and in February 1233 was deprived of the manor of Upavon following a suit in the king's court brought by Peter de Mauley (d. 1241), the manor's former custodian and a close associate of Peter des Roches, who claimed that he had relinquished custody of Upavon only after threats to his life by Hubert de Burgh. Rather than warrant the royal charter by which Basset held the manor, Henry III restored custody to Mauley in what he afterwards admitted was an unlawful, arbitrary exercise of royal will. The Upavon case was followed in June 1233 by the seizure of Basset's other estates, and the issue of orders for Basset's arrest and the destruction of his property. Basset had meanwhile gone into rebellion against the king, taking with him a large number of his kinsmen, including his brothers Warin and Philip, and his cousin Richard Siward (d. 1248). They were joined in rebellion by their immediate overlord, Richard Marshal, earl of Pembroke, so that between the summer of 1233 and the following April, England and the Welsh marches were plunged into civil war. It was at Basset's manor of High Wycombe in August 1233 that the rebel alliance was confirmed, and thereafter, in company with Richard Siward, Basset led a series of daring attacks against the king and his ministers. In October 1233 he was involved in a dramatic raid upon Devizes in which Hubert de Burgh, the disgraced justiciar, was plucked from captivity. Following the death in Ireland of Richard Marshal and the dismissal of Peter des Roches, Basset's outlawry was revoked and he was readmitted to court, from May 1234 serving as a regular witness to royal charters. At the same time he was restored to custody of Upavon and his other estates held of the crown. Between 1234 and 1241 he received numerous gifts of game and timber to restock his parks and rebuild his houses ravaged during the late disturbances.

In the summer of 1234 Basset married Isabella, daughter of William de Ferrers, earl of Derby, a close kinswoman of the Marshal earls of Pembroke, and received the manor of Greywell in Hampshire as a marriage portion. From 1234 to the time of his death he served as a regular witness to the charters of Hubert de Burgh and Gilbert Marshal (d. 1241), Richard Marshal's brother and heir. He died as the result of a hunting accident in July or August 1241. He had at some time previously bestowed property on Blackmore Priory in Essex and the Basset family foundation of an Augustinian priory at Bicester in Oxfordshire where he had chosen to be buried. His wife, Isabella, outlived him; she married Reginald de Mohun of Dunster (d. 1258) and died c.1260. Basset's infant son died within a few weeks of

his father, on 22 August 1241, so that the family estate passed to Basset's younger brother Fulk *Basset, future bishop of London, and after Fulk's death in 1259 to their brother Philip *Basset (d. 1271), justiciar of England. Basset's coat of arms, barry wavy of six pieces or and gules, confirms, or asserts, his descent from the first Ralph *Basset (d. 1127?), justiciar under Henry I. It is possible that he was the father of Fulk of *Sandford, archbishop of Dublin.   NICHOLAS VINCENT

Sources Chancery records · Pipe rolls · Paris, *Chron.* · N. Vincent, *Peter des Roches: an alien in English politics, 1205–38*, Cambridge Studies in Medieval Life and Thought, 4th ser., 31 (1996) · H. E. Salter and A. H. Cooke, eds., *The Boarstall cartulary*, OHS, 88 (1930) · V. C. M. London, ed., *The cartulary of Bradenstoke Priory*, Wilts RS, 35 (1979) · *A descriptive catalogue of ancient deeds in the Public Record Office*, 3 (1900) · L. Landon, *The itinerary of King Richard I*, PRSoc., new ser., 13 (1935) · Coll. Arms, Glover MSS [A fols. 99r–110v] · Additional Charter, BL, 10613 · T. D. Tremlett, H. Stanford London, and A. Wagner, eds., *Rolls of arms, Henry III*, Harleian Society, 113–14 (1967) · W. Kennett, *Parochial antiquities attempted in the history of Ambrosden, Burcester and other adjacent parts*, new edn, 2 vols. (1818)

Basset, John (1791–1843), writer on Cornish mining, was born on 17 November 1791 at Illogan, Cornwall, the son of the Revd John Basset (d. 1816), rector of Illogan and Camborne, and Mary Wingfield of Durham, his wife. He was baptized at Illogan church on 28 November 1791. On 26 June 1830 he married Elizabeth Mary (b. 1805), the eldest daughter of Sir Rose Price of Trengwainton, one-time high sheriff of Cornwall. Their eldest son, John Francis Basset, was born on 15 July 1831 and succeeded to Tehidy, the property of his cousin Frances, Baroness Basset, in 1855. Their third son, Gustavas Lambart Basset, was born in 1833, and in 1877 built a chemical laboratory at Camborne for the use of the Miners' Association of Cornwall and Devon.

John Basset was deeply interested in Cornish mining and the welfare of the miner. In 1836 he engaged in the debate surrounding the proposed reform of the stannary (mining) courts of the duchy of Cornwall, and in the same year he published *Remarks and Suggestions as to the Re-establishment of the Mining Courts of the Duchy of Cornwall*. His *Origin and History of the Bounding Custom* appeared in 1839, and his *Observations on Cornish Mining* was published during 1842. This pamphlet was an attempt to allay the fears of those who considered that the reduction on tariffs on foreign ores proposed by Sir Robert Peel posed a threat to the Cornish copper-mining industry. Basset believed that the key to preserving Cornish interests was in maintaining the monopoly of copper smelting in Great Britain and (in a decade that was to witness the discovery of massive copper deposits in North America, South Australia, and elsewhere) he welcomed the expansion of overseas production of copper ore.

Basset's most valuable contribution to Cornish mining literature was, perhaps, his treatise, 'On the machinery used for raising miners in the Harz', published in 1840 in that year's *Report of the Royal Cornwall Polytechnic Society* (pp. 59–62). This work drew attention to the so-called 'man engines' that had been installed in several Harz mines in Germany, contraptions which allowed miners to descend or to return to the surface by riding what were essentially pump-rods adapted (through the fitting of steps) for use as lifts. The up-and-down motion of the man engine allowed a miner to step on and off from one level to another, enabling him to make his way in stages down the shaft or back to the surface. Following the publication of Basset's paper, the Royal Cornwall Polytechnic Society in 1841 offered a prize for the successful construction of a model of a man engine suitable for installation in the Cornish mines. The prize was won by Michael Loam, who shortly afterwards installed a full-size man engine at the Tresavean mine, near Redruth. The invention won the praise of W. Francis, the Gwennap poet, who in 1845 wrote with feeling:

> The engine by which he is raised from below
> Now supersedes climbing, health's deadliest foe—
> This miners know well and their gratitude show.
> (Jenkin, 184)

Thereafter, man engines progressively replaced the traditional ladder-ways at the larger Cornish mines, though progress was slow: by 1862 only eight had been installed in Cornwall. However, Basset's 1840 article had also drawn attention to the use in the Harz district of the 'fils de fer', iron wire used in the manufacture of iron ropes. Although used originally to haul buckets up a shaft, iron rope had been employed lately, according to Basset, to haul ascending and descending machines (gigs or cages); this observation also was noted carefully in Cornwall—so much so that by the end of the nineteenth century most Cornish mines were using such rope to haul miners to the surface.

Basset was high sheriff of Cornwall in 1837, and MP for Helston in 1840–41. His London home was in Upper Brook Street, but he died at Boppart am Rhein, Germany, on 4 July 1843. W. H. TREGELLAS, *rev.* PHILIP PAYTON

Sources Boase & Courtney, *Bibl. Corn.* · A. K. H. Jenkin, *The Cornish miner* (1927) · R. R. Pennington, *Stannary law: a history of the mining law of Cornwall and Devon* (1973) · *GM*, 2nd ser., 20 (1843), 323
Archives Cornish Studies Library, Cornish Centre, Redruth, pamphlets

Basset, Joshua (*bap.* 1641, *d.* in or after 1714), college head, was baptized at St Margaret's, King's Lynn, on 4 April 1641, the fifth child of John Basset (*d.* 1660), merchant and alderman of King's Lynn, and Elizabeth, daughter of John Greene of King's Lynn. His eldest brother was William Basset (1630–1693), who studied at Pembroke College, Cambridge, and graduated MD in 1687. After studying at Lynn grammar school, Joshua was admitted as a sizar at Gonville and Caius College, Cambridge, on 13 October 1657. He was elected to a scholarship in Michaelmas term 1657, graduated BA in 1661–2, and proceeded MA in 1665, in which year he became a junior fellow of Caius. In 1669, with the support of the master and nine fellows of Caius, he petitioned the king for a mandate to be admitted to the next senior fellowship, on the grounds that as soon as he had obtained the junior fellowship his friends had withheld the allowance they formerly paid him, leaving him with not enough to maintain himself. Basset became a

senior fellow at midsummer 1673. He was ordained deacon in 1663 and priest in 1666. Among the college posts he held was that of dean, from 1674 to 1681.

Like many other Cambridge academics, Basset contributed to volumes of occasional verse. His first effort, in *Musarum Cantabrigiensium threnodia in obitum … Georgii Ducis Albaemarlae* (Cambridge, 1670), is conventional in its contents, but the three poems he contributed to a volume of verses published to mark the death of Charles II and the accession of James II (*Moestissimae ac laetissimae academiae Cantabrigiensis affectus*, Cambridge, 1685) are more revealing. In the first he rejoices that James has survived the attacks of Titus Oates so that he may serve the one apostolic and catholic faith. The tenor of these lines suggests that Basset may have converted to Catholicism as early as 1685. In *Reason and Authority, or, The Motives of a Late Protestants Reconciliation to the Catholic Church*, which appeared anonymously in 1687, Basset gave a lively account of his own theological development. He had attempted to construct a scheme of divinity on rational grounds, which he found resulted in a 'confused Babel of Religion'. The Church of England did not constitute a lawful authority sufficient to oblige his reason and conscience. Only the Church of Rome provided 'fundamental doctrines, authoritatively imposed, and universally received throughout the whole Christian world'. To the protestant allegation that the Catholic church was corrupt in faith and morals Basset replied that, if that were the case, then 'Christ failed of his promise, and so good night to Christianity'. His decision to convert seems to be have been taken after the publication of John Tillotson's *Discourse Against Transubstantiation* in 1684. A large part of *Reason and Authority* is devoted to a refutation of Tillotson's arguments and to demonstrating that some Anglican writers, such as Herbert Thorndike, had professed a Catholic eucharistic theology.

On the death of Richard Minshull, master of Sidney Sussex College, Cambridge, on 31 December 1686, Basset was appointed his successor by a royal mandate dated 3 January 1687. The speed with which James II acted suggests that Basset had already been marked out for preferment. Basset had been instrumental in securing the recantation of Edward Spence, who had attacked the Catholic church in a university sermon on 5 November 1686. He may have been known at court before then, however; in *Reason and Authority* he alludes to attending a sermon at Whitehall in Charles II's reign. Familiarity with court circles is also implied in his reported claim that he had been granted free liberty to come to London and Westminster to wait on the king, the queen consort, or the queen dowager.

When the fellows of Sidney requested that their new master should take the anti-Catholic oath required by the college statutes, a second royal mandate was issued on 12 January dispensing Basset from taking the oaths of allegiance and supremacy. This was followed on 25 February by a royal warrant again exempting Basset and other Cambridge converts from the oaths. Basset was finally admitted as master on 7 March 1687.

Much of the information about the impact of Joshua

Basset on the college is derived from letters written in 1725–6 by Joseph Craven, a fellow at the time, to the bishops of Lincoln and Norwich. These reveal that the first mandate was brought by Alban Placid Francis, a Benedictine monk of Lambspring, who functioned as Basset's chaplain. At first Francis took his meals with the master, at the king's expense, but after the alteration of the college statutes in June 1687 he was made a fellow-commoner and came to meals in his habit. An attempt was made to award Francis an MA degree, but this foundered in the face of concerted opposition by the university. From Caius, Basset brought two pupils, at least one of them a Catholic, who were admitted in November 1687.

The college chapel continued to be used for Anglican services, although Basset objected to its use for the customary Gunpowder day service on 5 November 1687:

> He locked the door of the Chappel against us, having the night before taken the key from the scholar who kept it; and so forcibly hindered us from divine service that morning, as we had resolved not to omit it. (Sidney Sussex College, MR 108/1/4)

Basset had one of the rooms in the Master's Lodge fitted as a chapel, which was used by members of the Catholic community in Cambridge.

On the birth of the prince of Wales on 10 June 1688, Basset contributed two poems to the *Genethliacon*, published by the university. Others were not so loyal, and the prospect of a Catholic succession set in train the events that led to the invasion of William of Orange. In mid-November, shortly after William's landing, Basset left the college. On 1 December James II, in a desperate attempt to placate his Anglican critics in Cambridge, rescinded the alterations to the statutes of Sidney Sussex College, and authorized the fellows to elect a new master. In December 1688, following the king's flight from London, the mob attacked local Catholics and their property in Cambridge: Basset's chapel was despoiled, and the college subsequently spent 11s. on 'mending the chamber broken by the rabble' (Sidney Sussex College, MR 32, p. 486).

Following his departure from Cambridge, Basset first went to King's Lynn, from which he soon moved to avoid the mob, and apparently settled in London. Craven reports that 'he solicited causes sometimes for a maintenance' (Sidney Sussex College, MR 108/1). Cole records, on the authority of Charles Ashton, master of Jesus College, that Basset approached his successor, James Johnson, when the latter was in London, in an attempt to recover his property from Sidney, 'but was roughly made to understand that if he did not desist he would be informed against as a Popish Priest' (BL, Add. MS 5821, fol. 120). In the archives at Sidney is a list submitted by Basset of goods left in the lodge, with valuations.

The eirenic tract *An Essay towards a Proposal for Catholick Communion* (1704) has been sometimes attributed to Basset. This has some importance in the history of ecumenism, but it is doubtful whether it is by Basset, as it is somewhat different in style from his other writings.

There is no certain evidence as to when or where Basset died. According to Cole he lived to a great age and died in London 'in no very affluent circumstances' (BL, Add. MS 5821). Basset was still alive at the beginning of 1714, when he presented Sidney with a copy of *Ecclesiae theoria nova Dodwelliana exposita* (1713), a detailed critique of the ecclesiology of Henry Dodwell. On the title-page he was styled 'Suo Tempore, Collegii Sidneiani Magister'. Craven, writing in 1726, paid a grudging tribute to his predecessor:

> As to his government, we found him a passionate, proud and insolent man, whenever he was opposed, which made us very cautious in conversing with him, who saw he waited for and catched at all occasions to do us mischief in what concerned our religion. I don't deny, that he had learning and other abilities to have done us good, but his interest lay the contrary way. (Sidney Sussex College, MR 108/1/2)

NICHOLAS ROGERS

Sources correspondence of Joseph Craven with Richard Reynolds, bishop of Lincoln, and John Leng, bishop of Norwich, 1725–6, Sidney Sussex College, Cambridge, MR 108/1 · William Cole's papers, vol. 20, BL, Add. MS 5821, fols. 118v–120 · J. Venn and others, eds., *Biographical history of Gonville and Caius College*, 1: 1349–1713 (1897), 400 · M. Goldie, 'Joshua Basset, popery and revolution', *Sidney Sussex College, Cambridge: historical essays in commemoration of the quatercentenary*, ed. D. E. D. Beales and H. B. Nisbet (1996), 111–30 · parish register, King's Lynn, St Margaret, 4 April 1641 [baptism] · B. Mackerell, *The history and antiquities … of King's Lynn* (1738), 57, 78 · documents relating to the revision of the college statutes, Sidney Sussex College, Cambridge, MR 19/4, 7, 8 · J. Twigg, *The University of Cambridge and the English Revolution, 1625–1688* (1990), 275–87

Basset, Peter (*fl.* 1415–1437), soldier and historian, was co-author of an incomplete account in French of English activities in France between the capture of Harfleur in 1415 and the raising of the siege of Orléans in May 1429. Only one manuscript of this work is known, in London, College of Arms, MS 9, folios xxxir–lxvv, written in an early fifteenth-century hand but bound up with papers of a later date. According to a Latin preface inserted by William Worcester, the work was compiled for Sir John Fastolf in the year of his death (1459) by three men, Peter Basset, Christopher Hanson *de patria almayn*, who had served under Thomas Beaufort, duke of Exeter (*d.* 1427), and Luke Nanton, native of 'Pekyant', one of Sir John Fastolf's clerks, 'by the diligence' of Worcester himself. Worcester's hand can be seen in corrections and glosses. The exact contribution of each author is unknown, but the chronicle is a bare narrative embodying extensive lists, both for the English and French, of those present, taken prisoner or killed in engagements, or appointed to captaincies. Edward Hall (*d.* 1547) drew extensively on the text and lists for his own chronicle. In his preface Hall names a Ihon Basset as one of the English writers he had consulted, but in his account of the death of Henry V states that Peter Basset 'which at the time of his death was his chamberlain' was the source of the information that the king had died of 'a plurisis' (*Hall's Chronicle*, 113). In 1557 John Bale ascribed to Peter Basset a work in English entitled *Acta regis Henrici quinti*; he also claimed that Basset had been Henry's chamberlain, and noted the same statement concerning the cause of death, a statement that Bale seems to have Basset as making in 1430. There is no contemporary corroboration that Basset was Henry V's chamberlain, nor has any such English work been identified.

Basset is described in Worcester's preface to the chronicle in College of Arms, MS 9, as an esquire of the English nation who had served in arms in France for thirty-five years under Henry V, John, duke of Bedford (d. 1435), and several other royal lieutenants. Several Peter Bassets occur in the records of English armies in France in the years after 1415. But given the link with Fastolf, it seems highly likely that the historian was the Peter Basset who stood bail in 1426 for the *procureur* of Pirmil when the latter had been flung into prison by the captain of Isle-sous-Brûlon in Maine, which lay near to Hanson's garrison of Ste Suzanne, and who was one of the men sent to reinforce Fastolf's garrison of Alençon in October 1429. He is later found among reinforcements at Essay (March 1431), and served at the siege of St Celerin in 1432, rejoining the garrison of Alençon in January 1434 and remaining there until at least December 1437. No record has been found of his service in Fastolf's English administration, whereas Hanson and Nanton were certainly in Sir John's employ until the latter's death.   ANNE CURRY

Sources Coll. Arms, MS 9 · B. J. H. Rowe, 'A contemporary account of the Hundred Years' War from 1415 to 1429', *EngHR*, 41 (1926), 504–13 · *Hall's chronicle*, ed. H. Ellis (1809) · K. B. McFarlane, 'William Worcester: a preliminary survey', *Studies presented to Sir Hilary Jenkinson*, ed. J. C. Davies (1957), 196–221 · A. Gransden, *Historical writing in England*, 2 (1982) · J. G. Nichols, *N&Q*, 2nd ser., 9 (1860), 424 · W. D. Macray, *N&Q*, 2nd ser., 9 (1860), 512 · manuscrits français, Bibliothèque Nationale, Paris, 25766/713; 25766/794; 25768/239; 25769/579; 25771/831; 25771/864; 25774/1279 · accounts various, PRO, E101/51/2 · additional charters, BL, 11833 · Bale, *Cat.*
Archives Coll. Arms, MS 9

Basset, Philip (d. 1271), justiciar and royalist nobleman, was a younger son and eventually—on the death of his brother, Fulk *Basset, bishop of London, in 1259—heir of Alan *Basset, lord of Wycombe, Buckinghamshire. Despite a strong family tradition of royal service, which Basset continued by his presumably youthful participation in Henry III's expedition to Brittany and Poitou in 1230, Philip Basset and several of his brothers (he had at least four) were at the heart of the rebellion of 1233–4 against the Poitevin faction, for Henry had seized a Basset manor in favour of a foreigner and had disgraced the justiciar Hubert de Burgh, for whom the Basset family had worked during Henry's minority. However, on the death in 1234 of the rebellion's head, the earl marshal, Henry granted the rebels peace and restoration. Basset went on crusade in 1240 with the king's brother, Richard of Cornwall, henceforth a lifelong associate. In the 1240s and 1250s he served the king in many matters, military, administrative, and judicial. Evidently often at court, he witnessed many charters and received frequent gifts from the king. No great interruption occurred as a result of his support of Fulk in the latter's clash with the king in 1251 over the disgrace of Henry of Bath, senior justice *coram rege* and a Basset relation.

When the greatest crisis of the reign broke in 1258, Basset's omission from the twelve chosen by the king for the twenty-four to formulate a plan of reform probably does not denote that he had deserted Henry. Rather, he was not quite important enough to be included; Fulk, the head of his family, was in the king's twelve however. Yet if it is correct to classify Basset as a royalist at this date, he must be considered a moderate royalist—a characterization applying to the rest of his life. His name was evidently acceptable to the barons when they were choosing the twelve to act on their behalf in parliaments. He was also named in the twenty-four chosen to arrange taxation. After Fulk's death in May 1259 Basset became an arbitrator on the demands of Simon de Montfort and his wife against Henry, and he filled a vacancy on the most important body, the Council of Fifteen, which was a mixture of royalists and reformers. The council had to split in the king's forthcoming absence, and Basset was designated in October among those who should remain in England, with the justiciar Hugh Bigod. He was active in the justiciar's administration, and Henry's letters from France show an increasing reliance on Bigod and Basset at the expense of the radical reformers. After Henry's return in April 1260 Basset's involvement in administration continued, and he was prominent in the group who advised the king now that Henry had largely freed himself from the Council of Fifteen. Basset was also entrusted with castles from November 1259 onwards. When Henry reasserted his authority at Whitsuntide 1261, although he dared not abolish the justiciarship, he hoped to turn it to his advantage by appointing his henchman to it. There are hints that Basset chafed at Henry's restriction of the judicial role of the office to little more than the presidency of the court *coram rege*, by contrast with the wide-ranging eyres envisaged in the 1258 scheme of reform and partly implemented by the previous holders of the resurrected office. However, though rarely mentioned in royal records, Basset loyally dispatched much judicial business and many kinds of administrative business. His function as the head of government, under the king, is signalled by his employment as the leading member of the regency council when Henry went abroad in July 1262 and by Henry's frequent letters from abroad ordering him to act in matters great and small. This monitoring by the king, together with disturbances in the Welsh marches and a visit of Simon de Montfort to encourage his supporters, may, however, have weakened the justiciar's authority, and the royalist position was crumbling by the time of Henry's return in December.

By July 1263 Basset was probably one of the few accompanying Henry at the Tower of London, and the capitulation to their opponents entailed Basset's loss of the justiciarship (between about 15 and 18 July) to its previous occupant, Hugh Despenser. While justiciar, Basset was also, for various periods, sheriff of four shires and constable of at least five castles, and he was sufficiently trusted by the new regime to be kept in such positions. But he worked against the constraints imposed on the king, and incurred destruction of property (probably in March 1264) for his stance. Basset was prominent at the royalist capture of Northampton on 5 April, which seemed a decisive defeat for the Montfortians. There is a hint that he expected Henry to reappoint him as justiciar. Even if disappointed by Henry's policy of merely ignoring Despenser, Basset fought courageously for Henry at Lewes on 14 May, suffering wounds and imprisonment—eventually at Dover. After the battle of Evesham (4 August 1265) he moderated Henry's desire for revenge, protesting against the decree disinheriting the rebels and, as one of the arbitrators who drew up the dictum of Kenilworth (31 October 1266), securing a more lenient policy. He helped to construct Henry's reconciliation with the earl of Gloucester after the earl seized London in 1267, and, despite such blocking of the king's desires, Basset remained frequently at court.

Basset's first wife was Helewisa de Lovaine, and their daughter, Alina, was Basset's sole heir. Alina married first Hugh Despenser, and second, after his death, Hugh Bigod's son, Roger (d. 1306), who became earl of Norfolk. Basset married as his second wife, in 1254 or 1255, Ela, the daughter of William *Longespée, earl of Salisbury, and widow of Thomas, earl of Warwick. An impression of respect for Basset from all sides arises from the chroniclers' epitaphs noting his death on 29 October 1271. This occurred at North Weald Bassett, one of his Essex properties, but he was buried at Stanley, near his Wiltshire properties. His widow long outlived him.

R. MALCOLM HOGG

Sources PRO · *Chancery records* · H. T. Riley, ed. and trans., *Chronicles of the mayors and sheriffs of London, AD 1188 to AD 1274 … The French chronicle of London, AD 1259 to AD 1343* (1863) · *Ann. mon.*, 4.247 · Paris, *Chron.* · CIPM, vol. 1, no. 807, 272–3 · A. Gransden, ed. and trans., *The chronicle of Bury St Edmunds, 1212–1301* [1964], 50 · W. Stubbs, ed., *Chronicles of the reigns of Edward I and Edward II*, 1, Rolls Series, 76 (1882), 82

Basset, Philippa, countess of Warwick (d. 1265), magnate, was the eldest of three daughters and coheirs of Thomas *Basset, lord of Colyton and Whitford, Devon, and Headington, Oxfordshire. When he died in 1220 she took Headington as her third of his estate. Meanwhile, however, Philippa had become the second wife of Henry de Newburgh, fifth earl of Warwick, whose wardship and marriage Thomas Basset had purchased for 500 marks in 1205. It was not an exalted marriage for a man of Newburgh's rank and it may well have been considered disparaging. When he died, on 10 October 1229, she was assigned a third of the Newburgh estate in dower. She was one of several dowagers whose longevity was a major factor in curtailing the resources of successive earls of Warwick during the thirteenth century, which is thought to have reduced their influence in national politics.

On Newburgh's death Philippa paid 100 marks to the king to be allowed to remain unmarried or to marry a man of her own choosing. By 4 November 1229, however, she had married the warlike Sir Richard *Siward (d. 1248), probably on the urging of her cousin, Gilbert Basset. Siward, in company with Gilbert and his brothers, rebelled in 1233. As a consequence, Philippa's lands became vulnerable. In January 1234 the sheriff of Oxford

was ordered to carry their houses at Headington to Beckley where they were to provide the material for the rebuilding of the house belonging to Richard, earl of Cornwall, which Richard Siward had fired. Meanwhile, however, Philippa had been allowed to retain her dower lands and was given free passage to join her rebellious husband in the Welsh marches. Their marriage was annulled in 1242, perhaps because she had married under duress. Before the annulment Philippa made an agreement with Siward for the equal sharing of their goods. When it came to carrying this out, however, discord arose between them, most particularly over the matter of Siward's debts. It was finally agreed, on 19 September 1242, that Philippa would pay him £75 for his share of their goods minus the sum that he owed the merchants, which she would satisfy. In 1246 she was at law, defending her tenure of the double hundred of Bullingdon, which had traditionally been attached to the manor of Headington.

Philippa remained unmarried and died shortly before 29 November 1265. She was buried at Bicester Priory, which had been founded by Gilbert Basset and endowed by members of the family. She had given the canons 7s. rent at Horton for a light to burn before the altar of St John the Baptist in their conventual church, which benefaction was made for her soul and those of her ancestors and children. She appears to have been the mother of the younger Richard Siward, who was brought up in Scotland. Her heirs, however, were found to be Margery, Ela, and Isabel, the daughters of Philippa's sister, Alice, and her husband, John Bisset.

PETER COSS

Sources GEC, *Peerage* · I. J. Sanders, *English baronies: a study of their origin and descent, 1086–1327* (1960), 51–2 · *VCH Oxfordshire*, 5.5; 6.30–31 · *Close rolls of the reign of Henry III*, 4, PRO (1911), 493–4 · E. Mason, 'The resources of the earldom of Warwick in the thirteenth century', *Midland History*, 3 (1975–6), 67–75 · D. Crouch, 'The last adventure of Richard Siward', *Morgannwg*, 35 (1991), 7–30

Basset, Ralph (d. 1127?), justice, was included by the chronicler Orderic Vitalis in his list of new men raised from the dust by Henry I, men allegedly of obscure birth who rose by their service to Henry and acquired great wealth in the process. He came from Montreuil-au-Houlme near Argentan in Normandy, not far from the abbey of St Évroul where Orderic was a monk and to which Ralph was a benefactor. In England either Ralph Basset the justice or an earlier namesake was in 1086 an under-tenant of Robert (I) d'Oilly at Marsworth in Buckinghamshire and Tiscot in Hertfordshire. He could also have been connected with Robert d'Oilly in Normandy, given that Robert may have come from Ouilly-le-Basset. Basset first appears as a witness to a royal document in 1101 or 1102. In 1106 he was appointed by the king to a judicial commission empowered to hear a complaint against Osbert, the sheriff of Yorkshire. About 1110 he was a member of another group set up to investigate the king's rights in Winchester, a city which had been omitted from the Domesday Book, and in the same or the following year was present when a lawsuit involving the abbey of Abingdon was heard before the Empress Matilda in the king's court meeting 'in the treasury of Winchester', possibly at a meeting of the court of the exchequer.

Between 1110 and 1127 Basset was one of the most prominent of Henry I's justices, and was described by the chronicler Henry of Huntingdon as one of the 'justices of all England', a description which indicates the geographical scope of his authority, as opposed to those who acted for the king only in their own locality. As such he was an early example of a royal justice who conducted local visitations to investigate the administration of the king's rights, setting a precedent for the later general eyres. Two sessions where he presided have become well known. The first took place at Huntingdon, where a man named Bricstan was brought to trial for concealment of treasure, a case reported by Orderic Vitalis. At the second, according to the Anglo-Saxon Chronicle, Basset was responsible for hanging forty-four thieves in 1124 at 'Hundehoge', probably Huncote in Leicestershire. In 1130, by which date he was dead, his earlier activities as a justice were mentioned in the accounts of ten counties, including Yorkshire, Norfolk and Suffolk, and Middlesex. He had also heard forest pleas in Surrey, and, judging from a charter reference to his 'gelds and assizes', he had also been active in Devon. Basset evidently spent most of his career in England. Only once did he attest a royal document issued in Normandy; otherwise his attestations show him to have been at Henry I's court, at such preferred royal residences as Woodstock, Westminster, and Winchester.

Basset fell terminally ill at Northampton, and instructed that he be clothed in the habit of a monk, for he had entered the fraternity of Abingdon Abbey, a house he was said to love with a special affection. The year of his death is most likely to have been 1127; it antedated that of Abbot Vincent of Abingdon in the spring of 1130. One of his sons, Richard *Basset, was also a justice of Henry I; two others, Nicholas and Turstin, later held land of the honour of Wallingford, at least some of which they inherited from their father, who bequeathed the churches of his demesne manors to his fourth son, Ralph, an ecclesiastic. Although Basset acquired land in the course of his career, most of his estates seem to have been held as undertenancies. The most important estate which he held in chief of the crown was the manor of Mixbury in Oxfordshire, held by Roger d'Ivry in 1086. Only the initial—A—of his wife's name is known, and the names of his daughters not at all.   JUDITH A. GREEN

Sources W. T. Reedy, 'The first two Bassets of Weldon', *Northamptonshire Past and Present*, 4 (1966–72), 241–5, 295–8 · Ordericus Vitalis, *Eccl. hist.*, 6 · Henry, archdeacon of Huntingdon, *Historia Anglorum*, ed. D. E. Greenway, OMT (1996) · *ASC* · J. Stevenson, ed., *Chronicon monasterii de Abingdon*, 2 vols., Rolls Series, 2 (1858), 170 · *Reg. RAN*, vol. 2 · *Pipe rolls, 31 Henry I* · A. Farley, ed., *Domesday Book*, 2 vols. (1783) · H. E. Salter, ed., *Eynsham cartulary*, 1, OHS, 49 (1907), 91 · W. T. Reedy, 'The origins of the general eyre in the reign of Henry I', *Speculum*, 41 (1966), 688–724 · H. E. Salter and A. H. Cooke, eds., *The Boarstall cartulary*, OHS, 88 (1930), 319, 327 · A. Saltman, *Theobald, archbishop of Canterbury* (1956), 414 · R. C. van Caenegem, ed., *English lawsuits from William I to Richard I*, SeldS, 1, 106 (1990), nos. 172, 189, 204, 219, 221, 237 · W. T. Reedy, ed., *Basset charters, c.1120–1250*, PRSoc., new ser., 50 (1995)

Basset, Sir Ralph [Basset of Drayton] (*d.* 1265), baronial leader, was a rich knight from a well-connected midlands family. His date of birth is unknown, but it was probably no later than 1230, since his son was active politically in 1265. He succeeded his father, Ralph, on the latter's death between 1255 and 1257, inheriting five manors in Staffordshire (including Drayton, by which name he is usually distinguished), Leicestershire, Nottinghamshire, and Dorset, worth something over £100 p.a. The impressive aisled hall at Drayton Basset may well date from his era. He married, presumably before *c.*1245, Margaret, daughter of Roger de Somery of Dudley, Worcestershire, an heiress in her own right through her mother, Nichola d'Aubigny. Although Basset is normally described as a baronial leader, there is no evidence linking him as such with Simon de Montfort until after the battle of Lewes. Between 1257 and 1262 he answered several military summons of the king, but in the early summer of 1263 he joined the anarchic rebellion of Roger Leyburn, Roger Clifford, Hamo L'Estrange, and other knights expelled from the Lord Edward's household. They attacked the lands of their enemies at court, including those of the archbishop of Canterbury and the bishop of Hereford, for which they were all excommunicated by the archbishop at Boulogne on 3 October, but subsequently pardoned by the first Montfortian government. On 18 August these knights, including Basset, began secret negotiations with Edward.

However, Basset did not defect to the king, despite Henry III's invitation of 28 October, and after the battle of Lewes—where he is not known to have fought—he was appointed on 7 June 1264 as the Montfortian keeper of the peace in Shropshire and Staffordshire. Early in 1265 he was summoned to Montfort's Model Parliament, which he attended, and was appointed in December 1264 'at pleasure' constable of Shrewsbury and Bridgnorth castles, with repeated mandates over the next six months to harass royalists and arrest his predecessor, Hamo L'Estrange. His reasons for supporting Simon de Montfort are unclear. Montfort's ascendancy in the midlands after Lewes and his rhetoric against foreigners are possible explanations, but Basset also had disputes with local royalists, especially his father-in-law (in 1263 his predecessor as keeper of Shropshire and Staffordshire), Roger de Somery, to whom he was now in debt, and who retained the manor of Barrow upon Soar, due to Basset's wife as coheir of the d'Aubigny earls of Arundel. Basset also detested his cousin Robert of Tattershall, another coheir. He occupied Tattershall's Leicestershire manors to the tune of £70 p.a. after his capture at Lewes. Another royalist neighbour with whom he clashed was Phillip Marmion, lord of Tamworth. Basset received no rewards from Montfort but it was claimed in 1266 that before Evesham he had been given Tattershall's manor of Breedon in Leicestershire, worth £40 p.a., by Robert de Ferrers, earl of Derby. Basset was killed at the battle of Evesham on 4 August 1265; his death (as a knight-banneret) was noted by several chroniclers, but Rishanger's story that Basset, Hugh Despenser, and others refused Montfort's offer to escape before the battle seems apocryphal. Although, after Evesham, Basset's manors were granted to royalists—Roger Clifford, Robert de Tibetot, Robert of Tattershall, and William Bagot—they were quickly restored to his widow, Margaret, and his heir, Ralph, as a reward for Roger de Somery's services to the king. Margaret remarried about 1270; her new husband was another midlands knight, Ralph of Cromwell (d. 1289); she became a nun in 1293.

H. W. RIDGEWAY

Sources Chancery records · GEC, Peerage · Rymer, Foedera, 3rd edn, 1/1.430, 442 · Bodl. Oxf., MS Bodley 91, fols. 136r–136v · Calendar of inquisitions miscellaneous (chancery), PRO, 1 (1916), 769, 771, 848, 929–30, 936 · Willelmi Rishanger … chronica et annales, ed. H. T. Riley, pt 2 of Chronica monasterii S. Albani, Rolls Series, 28 (1865), 26–8 · Ann. mon., 2.365; 4.171, 174, 454 · J. Nichols, The history and antiquities of the county of Leicester, 2/1 (1795), 17; 3/2 (1804), 685 · P. R. Coss, Lordship, knighthood and locality, c.1180–1280 (1991), 292–3 · J. Hunt, 'Families at war: royalists and Montfortians in the west midlands', Midland History, 22 (1997), 1–34

Basset, Ralph [Ralph Basset of Sapcote] (c.1220–1279?), baron, belonged to a family with several branches, which was important in central and local government and well established in the midlands. Basset was a rich landholder, worth over £120 p.a., holding his principal manor of Sapcote, Leicestershire, and at least two others: Cheadle, Staffordshire, and Langwith, Derbyshire. Basset was born at the latest in the early 1220s since his public career began in 1240, when he was a member of a royal forest eyre touring Northamptonshire, Oxfordshire, and Buckinghamshire. His main significance, however, was as a retainer of his overlord, Simon de Montfort, earl of Leicester; Sapcote itself is only 10 miles from Leicester. He joined Montfort's affinity in 1239 or 1240, and was one of the earl's leading retainers and one of the most frequent witnesses of Montfort's charters. He does not seem to have gone on crusade with Montfort in 1240–42, but served with him in the king's army in Wales in the summer of 1245 and in Gascony between late 1248 and 1251, when Montfort was the king's lieutenant in the duchy. His main rewards from Henry III during those years—a charter of free warren in 1245 and a life-licence in 1255 to hunt in the royal forest in Nottinghamshire and Derbyshire—were probably obtained through Montfort's influence. Nevertheless, Basset's pilgrimage to Santiago de Compostela in February 1248 may imply that he did not intend to follow Montfort on the proposed crusade to which the earl pledged himself late in 1247.

Basset's career during the baronial movement indicates Montfort's power and interests. In June 1258, probably on the latter's recommendation, he was appointed under the provisions of Oxford constable of Northampton Castle, a strategic position, but he was dismissed on 19 May 1260 on the failure of Montfort and the Lord Edward's brief rebellion against the baronial council. From 29 September 1261 until about 13 January 1262 Basset was rebel sheriff of Leicestershire during the opposition to the king's overthrow of the provisions of Oxford, but his appointment 'by letters of the barons' (not by election of the county) probably stemmed from Montfort; in Easter 1262 he was summoned before the exchequer to account for a quarter

of a year's farm of the shire. In 1263 Basset was again useful during Montfort's renewed rebellion against the king; in July he was reappointed constable of Northampton 'by counsel of the magnates' and again served as rebel sheriff of Leicestershire, from 29 September until, allegedly, 25 July 1264, undermining the rule of the royal incumbent, William Bagot. Basset was one of the rebel barons appealing to Louis IX late in 1263, and in April 1264 he was captured by the king at the battle of Northampton. Released after the battle of Lewes, Basset was appointed by the Montfortian regime on 4 June, not surprisingly, as keeper of the peace in Leicestershire. Otherwise, his role and rewards during this period are obscure; all we know of him was that he was summoned to Montfort's Model Parliament of early 1265, and was joint custodian of the lands late of the earl of Winchester in March of that year.

It is not certain that Basset fought for Montfort at Evesham. The pardon he obtained in July 1266, through the good offices of midland royalists, states unconvincingly that he assisted the king during the Evesham campaign, but this must be set alongside the Lord Edward's order of 14 October 1265 to release him upon payment of ransom. Perhaps Basset was captured during Edward's surprise raid on Kenilworth, and then tried to change sides. A Warwickshire jury of the period merely declared that Basset was 'with the earl of Leicester under arms'. But if Basset tried to distance himself from Montfort towards the end, he did not escape punishment in 1266. His lands were confiscated by the king and granted to John de Verdon, and in September 1267 he contracted to ransom them under the dictum of Kenilworth for 1000 marks, repayable over two years. He seems after that to have retired from public life.

Other details of Basset's career are unclear. It is curious that he had nothing to do with the recorded events of Montfort's posthumous miracle cult. According to Nichols he married before 1258 Milicent, the younger daughter and coheir of Robert of Chalcombe, of Northamptonshire, a union which linked him to other retainers of Montfort, the Despensers and Segraves. The date of his death cannot be established, but Nichols noted that by 1279 he had been succeeded at Sapcote by his son Simon. The Complete Peerage suggests that he died 'about 1282'.

H. W. RIDGEWAY

Sources Chancery records · J. R. Maddicott, Simon de Montfort (1994) · Calendar of inquisitions miscellaneous (chancery), PRO, 1 (1916), 929 · R. F. Treharne and I. J. Sanders, eds., Documents of the baronial movement of reform and rebellion, 1258–1267 (1973), 112, 284 · PRO, E 159/36 m.10; SC 1/8/22 · Rymer, Foedera, new edn, vol. 1, pt 1, p. 442 · W. Stubbs, ed., Chronicles of the reigns of Edward I and Edward II, 1, Rolls Series, 76 (1882), 61 · J. Nichols, The history and antiquities of the county of Leicester, 4/2 (1811), 890 · GEC, Peerage

Basset, Richard (d. in or before 1144), justice, was the son of Ralph *Basset (d. 1127?), another of Henry I's justices. His official career began in the third decade of Henry's reign, his name first appearing in royal documents in the king's confirmation of the settlement whereby he married Matilda, daughter of Geoffrey *Ridel, another justice, who had drowned in the White Ship in 1120. The marriage took place some time between November 1120 and April

1123. Basset was given custody of Geoffrey's land and the wardship of his children, including Robert Ridel. At some stage, presumably after the death of Robert Ridel, his marriage brought him into possession of the barony of Great Weldon in Northamptonshire, in addition to his share of his father's lands, and others he evidently acquired in the course of his career.

In 1125 Basset and a colleague were sent to Peterborough Abbey to take charge of the revenues for the king after the abbot's death, and he is recorded as sole witness to a royal writ issued in 1126 or 1127. In the years before 1129 he also acted as a royal justice in Hertfordshire, Norfolk, and Suffolk, while in the fiscal year 1129/30 he appears as a key figure in royal administration, for he and Aubrey de Vere were jointly appointed sheriffs of no fewer than eleven English counties, on special terms by which they paid to the king a large surplus over and above the shire revenues they held at farm. Their assignment, which may not have lasted longer than one year, was evidently intended to improve the yield of revenues received from the sheriffs, and was arranged in the aftermath of an audit of the treasury in the preceding year. In the same year Basset also heard pleas in Sussex, Leicestershire, Suffolk, and Lincolnshire, and the range of his judicial activities indicates that his authority, like his father's, was not confined to a single county. He was one of several justices whose local visitations are referred to in the pipe roll of 1130, and which set precedents for the later general eyre. The Leicestershire survey of 1130 contains a reference to a tenant of Richard's, who held his land by the service 'of finding for the justiciar a messenger to go through the whole of England' (*Leicestershire Survey*, 15); but as the tenant's name was Warin Ridel, the reference may in fact relate to the period when Geoffrey Ridel was lord of the estate in question. A number of royal documents issued in and around 1130 provide further illustration of his work at that time, including the royal precept addressed to him and 'all the royal justices and ministers of Surrey' which declared that Battle Abbey was to be free of various customs and obligations, particularly work on London Bridge. The frequency with which he attested documents issued in Henry I's name before the king's final departure from England in 1133 suggests that Basset was often at court between 1131 and 1133, notably at the councils held at Northampton in 1131 and at Westminster in the following year.

Basset is not known to have been employed as a justice or sheriff by King Stephen—although his name occurs as a witness to a charter of Stephen's of 1136, the document may not be authentic. He built a stone castle in Normandy at Montreuil-au-Houlme on his patrimonial estates. This was taken over by William de Montpinçon, who held it against the Angevins in 1136. Basset died in or before 1144, when the Empress Matilda restored to his son Geoffrey Ridel all his father's lands in England and Normandy. Richard and his wife founded an Augustinian priory at Launde in Leicestershire, probably in the early 1120s, and are known to have had at least three sons, Geoffrey Ridel of Great Weldon (named after his maternal grandfather),

Ralph Basset of Drayton, Staffordshire, and William *Basset of Sapcote, who became a sheriff and justice. An impression and a drawing of Richard's seal survive, showing a knight in full armour striking a monster which has a figure in its mouth; it was presumably intended to represent Richard Basset as the upholder of justice.

JUDITH A. GREEN

Sources W. T. Reedy, 'The first two Bassets of Weldon', *Northamptonshire Past and Present*, 4 (1966–72), 241–5, 295–8 · J. A. Green, *The government of England under Henry I* (1986), 231–2 · *Pipe rolls*, 31 Henry I · *Reg. RAN*, vols. 2–3 · Ordericus Vitalis, *Eccl. hist.*, 6 · T. A. Heslop, 'Seals', *English romanesque art, 1066–1200*, ed. G. Zarnecki, J. Holt, and T. Holland (1984), 298–319, esp. 318 [exhibition catalogue, Hayward Gallery, London, 5 April – 8 July 1984] · C. F. Slade, ed., *The Leicestershire survey, c. AD 1130*, new edn (1956), 15 · W. T. Reedy, 'The origins of the general eyre in the reign of Henry I', *Speculum*, 41 (1966), 688–724 · W. T. Reedy, ed., *Basset charters, c.1120–1250*, PRSoc., new ser., 50 (1995)
Likenesses seal, repro. in *English romanesque art*

Basset, Thomas (*d. c.*1182), justice, belonged to a distinguished family of royal servants which began with Ralph Basset (*d.* 1127?), the brother of Thomas's father, Gilbert (*d.* in or before 1154). Thomas Basset had entered Henry II's service by 1163. His first known post in the royal administration was as sheriff of Oxfordshire (1163–4). A baron of the exchequer from 1169 to *c.*1181, he was an itinerant justice in the south and west in 1175, and again in 1179; in December 1180 he joined the justiciar Ranulf de Glanville and other royal justices at Lincoln in approving a final concord. He was custodian of the honour of Wallingford for the king from 1172 to 1179. He witnessed royal documents in England fourteen times between 1174 and 1179, and he was with the king in Normandy, *c.*1181, attesting at Barfleur. He died shortly afterwards, perhaps in 1182.

In 1166 Thomas Basset held seven knights' fees of the king, representing estates of the honour of Wallingford in Middlesex, Berkshire, Buckinghamshire, and Oxfordshire. He still held the fees in 1172, when he was pardoned scutage on them.

Basset married Adeliza de Dunstanville [see Basset, Adeliza, *under* Dunstanville, de, family], who survived him, dying in or after 1210, and they had three sons and a daughter, Isabel, who married Albert (III) de Grelley, lord of Manchester. When Albert died in late September 1180, Basset, by the king's order, took custody of Isabel, of his son-in-law's land, and of their son and heir, Robert de Grelley, holding the custody until his death. All three of Basset's sons followed him into the king's service: the eldest, Gilbert (*d.* 1205); Thomas *Basset (*d.* 1220), to whom King John granted the barony of Headington, Oxfordshire, in 1203; and Alan *Basset of Wycombe (*d.* 1232), apparently the youngest, founder of the line of Bassets of Wycombe, Buckinghamshire. In 1194 the two younger sons were both serving in Richard I's army in Normandy; and they continued to serve John and Henry III.

RALPH V. TURNER

Sources W. T. Reedy, ed., *Basset charters, c.1120–1250*, PRSoc., new ser., 50 (1995) · *Pipe rolls*, 4, 11–12, 16, 18, 25–6, 28 Henry II · J. H. Round, ed., *Rotuli de dominabus et pueris et puellis de XII comitatibus (1185)*, PRSoc., 35 (1913) · H. Hall, ed., *The Red Book of the Exchequer*, 3 vols., Rolls Series, 99 (1896) · D. M. Stenton, ed., *Pleas before the king or his justices, 1198–1212*, 3, SeldS, 83 (1967) · A. Hughes, *List of sheriffs for England and Wales: from the earliest times to AD 1831*, PRO (1898); repr. (New York, 1963) · R. W. Eyton, *Court, household, and itinerary of King Henry II* (1878) · J. H. Round, ed., *Calendar of documents preserved in France, illustrative of the history of Great Britain and Ireland* (1899) · I. J. Sanders, *English baronies: a study of their origin and descent, 1086–1327* (1960) · VCH *Oxfordshire*, vol. 6 · VCH *Hampshire and the Isle of Wight*, vol. 4 · VCH *Berkshire*, vol. 4

Wealth at death held seven knights' fees at least: Reedy, ed., *Basset Charters*

Basset, Thomas (*d.* 1220), soldier and courtier, was a younger son of Thomas *Basset (*d. c.*1182) of Headington and Adeliza *Basset [*see under* Dunstanville, de, family], daughter of Walter de Dunstanville, lord of Castle Combe in Wiltshire. First recorded before *c.*1180, the younger Thomas Basset had by 1190 been granted custody of land in Oxfordshire through the favour of Richard I, and over the next few years he was maintained in royal service, briefly holding land in Hereford and Shropshire. As a counsellor of the king's brother John, count of Mortain, in 1191 he was excommunicated by the chancellor, William de Longchamp (*d.* 1197), John's rival for the government of England during the absence of King Richard on crusade. In 1192 Basset served briefly as John's deputy keeper for the Berkshire manors of Cookham and Bray. However, he seems to have held aloof from John's rebellion against King Richard, and therefore retained his place at court. In 1194 the king granted him the Devon manor of Colyton in fee, to which the neighbouring manor of Whitford was added in 1198. These grants probably represent the reward for his service in the royal household, where he makes numerous appearances between 1197 and 1199, both in England and in Normandy; he witnessed a large number of the charters of King Richard, and was one of the few royal servants to attend the king's deathbed at Châlus near Limoges.

Under King John, before 1202 Basset served as constable of Dover, and between 1202 and 1214 as sheriff and constable of Oxford, an office previously held by his father and his elder brother, Gilbert Basset. In 1202 John granted him custody of the Oxfordshire barony of Headington, confirmed to him in perpetuity in 1203, to be held thereafter as a single knight's fee rendering £20 a year to the exchequer. In 1204 he received temporary custody of several manors seized from Norman landholders who had defected to the French, and in 1205 fined 500 marks with the crown, for custody of the lands and heir of Waleran, late earl of Warwick. The heir, Henry de Newburgh, was in due course married to Basset's daughter Philippa *Basset. A year later Basset fined 200 marks to have custody of the lands of his uncle, Walter de Dunstanville, previously held by Thomas's brother, Gilbert. Thomas Basset also inherited the manor of North Stoke in Oxfordshire, which he held from 1206 onwards. He served on the king's expedition to Ireland in 1210, and during the civil war of 1215–17 remained loyal to the king, taking custody of Warwick Castle and of the estates of several rebel knights. Roger of Wendover names him as one of John's evil counsellors, and his prominence as a royal *familiaris* is underlined by

his having been one of the men on whose advice Magna Carta was said to have been granted. In May 1217 he fought on the royalist side at the battle of Lincoln. He married Philippa Maubanc, probably a Norman, and when he died, shortly before 1 May 1220, his lands were divided among their three daughters, Joan (who married Reginald de *Vautort (*d.* 1245) [*see under* Vautort family], Alice, and Philippa, and their husbands. Philippa and Joan died without children, and their lands descended to the daughters and heirs of Alice, the children of her second marriage, to John Biset.   NICHOLAS VINCENT

Sources *Chancery records* · *Pipe rolls* · I. J. Sanders, *English baronies: a study of their origin and descent, 1086–1327* (1960) · *Chronica magistri Rogeri de Hovedene*, ed. W. Stubbs, 4 vols., Rolls Series, 51 (1868–71) · Paris, *Chron.* · L. Landon, *The itinerary of King Richard I*, PRSoc., new ser., 13 (1935) · W. T. Reedy, ed., *Basset charters, c.1120–1250*, PRSoc., new ser., 50 (1995) · Otterton Cartulary, Devon RO, MS TD51, 150–55

Basset, William (*d.* in or after **1185**), justice and sheriff, was a younger son of Richard *Basset (*d.* in or before 1144) and grandson of Ralph *Basset (*d.* 1127?), who were among the new men staffing Henry I's government. His mother was Matilda, daughter of Geoffrey *Ridel (*d.* 1120), another royal officer. He entered the royal administration as under-sheriff of Warwickshire and Leicestershire in 1163, and was then sheriff until 1170, when he was displaced by the inquest of sheriffs. He was subsequently sheriff of Lincolnshire from 1177 to 1185. William rarely witnessed royal charters, but served mainly as an associate of the justiciar. He held pleas on eyre and in the *curia regis* between 1168 and 1184, and sat at the exchequer from autumn 1169 to 31 May 1185, after which he appears no longer. He is one of only seven justices whose opinions are cited in early texts of the law book *Glanvill*. He probably settled at Sapcote, Leicestershire, and also held land in Warwickshire, Buckinghamshire, and other counties. He was father of Simon Basset (*d.* 1205) who was an assessor of tallage upon Nottinghamshire and Derbyshire in 1197, and who married Elizabeth, heir of Richard de Vernon. William gave a mill to Launde Priory, Leicestershire, a house of Austin canons founded by his parents.   RALPH V. TURNER

Sources R. V. Turner, *The English judiciary in the age of Glanvill and Bracton, c.1176–1239* (1985) · R. W. Eyton, *Court, household, and itinerary of King Henry II* (1878) · *Pipe rolls* · A. Hughes, *List of sheriffs for England and Wales: from the earliest times to AD 1831*, PRO (1898); repr. (New York, 1963) · D. M. Stenton, 'Development of the judiciary, 1100–1216', *Pleas before the king or his justices, 1198–1212*, ed. D. M. Stenton, 3, SeldS, 83 (1967), xlvii–ccxliv · W. T. Reedy, 'The first two Bassets of Weldon [pt 2]', *Northamptonshire Past and Present*, 4 (1966–72), 295–8

Basset, William (*d.* 1249), justice, was a justice in eyre on the 1226–8 circuit (Nottinghamshire and Derbyshire, Northamptonshire, Buckinghamshire, Bedfordshire, Huntingdonshire, Cambridgeshire) and the 1232 circuit (Nottinghamshire and Derbyshire, Cambridgeshire, Huntingdonshire). Round believed that this William Basset may have been the son of Simon Basset of Sapcote, Leicestershire, who was a royal servant in 1197–8 and a royal justice in 1199, and who died in 1205. Simon was the son and heir of the distinguished justice William *Basset of Sapcote (*d.* in or after 1185). It was very probably the justice

William Basset (d. 1249) who was responsible with others in 1230 for the assize of arms in Leicestershire and who in 1232 was a collector of a fortieth and an escheator there. Because of his association with Leicestershire this William is very probably identifiable with William Basset of Sapcote, and with the itinerant justice who died in 1249. William the justice was in royal service by 1223, when he was a justice to take an assize *utrum*. He was a justice of gaol delivery between 1227 and 1232. In 1225 he helped to collect a fifteenth in Nottinghamshire and Derbyshire, and was also a justice for taking an assize of mort d'ancestor. In 1228–9 he was a justice to take assizes of novel disseisin. He again held assizes in the following year, and at Stafford he was a justice to take various assizes plus pleas of dower. In 1237 he helped to collect a thirtieth. He died shortly before 2 July 1249.   W. T. REEDY

Sources W. T. Reedy, ed., *Basset charters, c.1120–1250*, PRSoc., new ser., 50 (1995) • PRSoc. • A. Hughes, *List of sheriffs for England and Wales: from the earliest times to AD 1831*, PRO (1898); repr. (New York, 1963) • D. Crook, *Records of the general eyre*, Public Record Office Handbooks, 20 (1982) • R. R. Darlington, ed., *The cartulary of Darley Abbey*, 2 (1945) • R. W. Eyton, *Court, household, and itinerary of King Henry II* (1878) • J. E. Lally, 'Court and household of Henry II', PhD diss., U. Lpool, 1969 • *DNB* • GEC, *Peerage* • *Chancery records* (RC)

Basset, Sir William (d. 1356/7), justice, was a Yorkshireman, probably from the neighbourhood of Selby—a grant of free warren in 1340 described him as holding land at Barlow, South Duffield, and Brayton, all in that region. He may have been the son of the Walter Basset recorded at Brayton in 1302. William is first recorded in 1322, when he was appointed a commissioner to inspect the embankments of the River Ouse east and south of Selby. Nothing can be said about his education, though he is once reported as quoting a Latin maxim in court. He became a serjeant-at-law in 1324. Recorded as an advocate in the bench in 1335, he had been knighted by 1336, while at Easter 1337 he was appointed a justice in the common bench. In 1340 he was one of only two such justices to survive Edward III's judicial purge of that year, and in October 1341 was appointed a justice of king's bench, although in the event his transfer to that court only took effect at the following Easter. From the late 1320s he had been increasingly frequently employed by the crown to hold inquests and as a commissioner of oyer and terminer, particularly in Yorkshire and Lincolnshire; in 1338, for instance, he was a commissioner to establish the boundary between Westmorland and Yorkshire, and in 1339 to settle a long-running dispute between the master and brethren of the hospital of St Leonard, York. Regularly associated in Yorkshire peace commissions from 1339 onwards, in 1340 he was one of the two commissioners appointed to supervise the assessment and collection of the ninth in that county, while in 1342 and 1346 he was one of the king's proctors at the northern convocation. In 1343 and 1347 he was a trier of petitions in parliament. During the 1340s and early 1350s he regularly headed the justices of assize and gaol delivery in the northern counties, and in April 1345 was one of the justices named for an

eyre in the bishopric of Durham, though this never took place.

Basset remained a justice of king's bench until Michaelmas term 1353, being given cloth for his robes on 24 October that year. But his health may have been failing, for on 14 February 1354 he was instructed to hand over his assize records to Thomas Seton and others, and Seton also replaced him in king's bench. Basset's retirement was certainly not due to any misdemeanour, for on 2 February he was granted an annuity of £40 'for long service in the office of a justice and in subvention of the maintenance of his estate in the order of knighthood' (*CPR, 1354–8*, 8). He was included in the Yorkshire commission of the peace for July 1354, and was still alive in May 1356, when he was appointed to inquire into obstructions in Yorkshire rivers, but a reference to his heirs holding land at Brayton in 1357 suggests that he was dead by then. The name of his wife is uncertain (she may have been the Margaret Basset referred to at South Duffield in 1361); he had at least three sons—John, William, and Thomas.

HENRY SUMMERSON

Sources *Chancery records* • Assize rolls, PRO, JUST/1/1146/12 • Baker, *Serjeants*, 498 • *RotP*, vol. 2 • G. O. Sayles, ed., *Select cases in the court of king's bench*, 7 vols., SeldS, 55, 57–8, 74, 76, 82, 88 (1936–71), vols. 5–6 • M. S. Arnold, ed., *Select cases of trespass from the king's courts, 1307–1399*, 1 (1985) • J. T. Fowler, ed., *The coucher book of Selby*, Yorkshire Archaeological Society, 10 (1891) • W. P. Baildon, ed., *Feet of fines for the county of York, from 1327 to 1347, 1–20 Edward III*, 1, Yorkshire Archaeological Society, 42 (1910) • W. P. Baildon, ed., *Feet of fines for the county of York, from 1347 to 1377, 21–51 Edward III*, 2, Yorkshire Archaeological Society, 52 (1915) • B. H. Putnam, ed., *Yorkshire sessions of the peace, 1361–1364*, Yorkshire Archaeological Society, 100 (1939) • *Inquisitions and assessments relating to feudal aids*, 6, PRO (1921) • *CPR, 1354–8*

Basset, William (bap. 1644, d. 1696), Church of England clergyman, and religious controversialist, was baptized on 22 October 1644 at Great Harborough in Warwickshire, the son of Thomas Basset (b. 1601/2), minister of that parish. His mother was called Susanna. He matriculated at Magdalen College, Oxford, in 1662, graduated BA in 1664, and proceeded MA on 7 March 1667. He was ordained, became rector of Brinklow, Warwickshire, in 1671 and was presented to St Swithin London Stone in London by the Salters' Company in 1683. He remained in this last parish until his death in 1696, and so must have sworn the oaths of loyalty to William III, despite an earlier enthusiasm for Stuart legitimacy which was expressed in quite dreadful verse as well as from the pulpit (*Panegyrick on the Coronation*, 1685).

Basset was chiefly remarkable for his vigorous Anglican apologetic. Four sermons published between 1670 and 1684 denounced nonconformists for schism and political subversion; opposed the Exclusion Parliaments' schemes to reunite English protestants; defended the form and theory of Anglican communion; attacked occasional conformity; and—a minor obsession—promoted 'corporal worship', or kneeling and bowing in church services, as decent and ancient ceremonies which helped congregations achieve a spiritual state. Similarly orthodox was his *Answer to the Brief History of the Unitarians* (1693). This was an exhaustive, point-by-point refutation of the work of the Socinian Stephen Nye, which accused his adversary of ignoring key passages of scripture as he denied the divinity of Christ. Interestingly, Basset dedicated this work to Archbishop John Tillotson. It is possible that he felt it appropriate to offer his defence of Jesus's place within the Trinity to his primate, but it is also possible that the dedication was an ironic rebuke to a cleric whose willingness to consider liturgical compromises with dissenters would have enraged a person of Basset's views and who was, moreover, widely suspected of Socianism himself. The combative tone of all Basset's work certainly suggests he did not shy from controversy.

Besides his zeal for the established church, Basset also demonstrated considerable local patriotism. In 1679 he preached to a group of Warwickshire men based in London, who had set up a trust to apprentice the poor of their native county. The sermon praised the scheme as an example to other shires and included a brief panegyric to his locality, lauding its antiquities, noble families, piety, and charities. This performance gained Basset a place in Colvile's *Worthies of Warwickshire* (1870).

TONY CLAYDON

Sources Foster, *Alum. Oxon.* · R. Newcourt, *Repertorium ecclesiasticum parochiale Londinense*, 1 (1708), 544 · Wing, *STC* · F. L. Colvile, *The worthies of Warwickshire who lived between 1500 and 1800* [1870]

Bassett [Basset], **Sir Francis** (1593?–1645), royalist army officer, was the eldest son of James Bassett (1566–1603), esquire, of Tehidy, Cornwall, and his wife, Jane, daughter of Sir Francis *Godolphin [*see under* Godolphin, Sir William] of Godolphin in the same county. James died in February 1603, when his son was ten. Francis Bassett matriculated, aged sixteen, at Exeter College, Oxford, in December 1610; in July 1613 he was admitted to Lincoln's Inn, where he completed his education. On 31 August 1620 he married Ann, daughter of Sir Jonathan Trelawny of Trelawne, Cornwall. By 1624, when he was named to the Cornish commission for piracy, Bassett had been appointed vice-admiral for north Cornwall. On 18 March 1625 he was named to the commission for impressing mariners in Cornwall in preparation for the expedition to Cadiz, and the following year he was appointed a Cornish forced loan commissioner.

As vice-admiral Bassett was deeply concerned by the escalating problem of Turkish pirates from the Barbary coast seizing Cornish fishing and merchant boats and raiding the coast, taking their captives to slavery. In May 1626 a Turkish man-of-war with forty pirates on board was captured by Cornishmen and taken into St Ives, in Bassett's vice-admiralty. Bassett's hatred of the Turks is clear from the tone of his request for a commission of oyer and terminer to try them: he complained that 'the waching of these doggs' (PRO, SP 16/27/54) cost him 10s. a day and, as the ship was of little value, he desired to be free of both as soon as possible. By June Bassett had received the commission, but the additional instructions not to execute the Turks irritated him, as 'they are a great charge for their diet and guard' (PRO, SP 16/27/54).

Bassett made a financial contribution towards the king's journey north in the first bishops' war of 1639, but he was less enthusiastic about preparations for the second bishops' war the following year. Writing to Secretary Nicholas, Bassett proposed that the 1600 impressed Cornishmen should be discharged, leaving 'those few of us for the preservation of this poor part, the Turks having lately infested us, and most obvious we are to all other enemies'. Concerned about the labour shortage in agriculture and anxious to prevent the tin mines flooding, Bassett pressed particularly for the discharge of the 300 men from the far west of the county, offering in return to guarantee full payment of coat and conduct money from that area. This, he claimed, would enable him 'to serve with power our Royal master, which shall be ever my passionate desire' (CSP dom., 1640, 456–9).

On 21 July 1642 Lord Mohun wrote to Bassett:

> to give you notice that the Commissioners of Array doe meet at Lostwithiell Wednesday next, Pray doe mee the honor: to meet your friends Sir Nich: Slanning, Sir Bevill Grenvile & Mr Arundle of Trerise heer a Tuesday, where we shall conferre about some busines concerning setling of this County. (Cornwall RO, B 35/44)

A week later, Bassett also received a personal appeal from the king evoking his duty of loyalty as vice-admiral. He became an active commissioner of array from early August and sheriff of Cornwall in September.

Bassett played a crucial role in Cornish royalist organization. He shared responsibility with Sir Nicholas Slanning for the distribution of imported arms and ammunition to the various Cornish regiments and garrisons, and was in charge of supplying the Cornish army with money. Between October 1642 and June 1643 Bassett paid Sir Ralph Hopton £1598 9s. 8d., including, in January 1643, £204 to equip and pay his men before the battle of Braddock Down. In April 1643 Bassett went to great lengths to raise over £900 to equip additional troops for the regrouped Cornish royalist army which went on to victory at Stratton the following month. More than half the money was borrowed from a French merchant. Bassett's other sources of revenue included the weekly rate, the profits of prizes seized by royalist privateers, and, from 1643, the sequestration of Cornish parliamentarians' estates. Bassett's accounts record payments made to him by the sequestrators, and the value of tin seized from parliamentarians.

Bassett also repaired and equipped St Michael's Mount, which he owned, at great personal expense. This included the construction of new gun platforms and a new gate, provision of fourteen new guns at £10 each, twenty-one new pairs of wheels and gun carriages, as well as powder and match, muskets, and bullets. Between 1642 and 1644 Bassett paid twelve men and a gunner at the Mount and, in 1645, when the garrison increased to fifty soldiers by the king's command, Bassett met the additional cost from his own resources.

In July 1644, while at Launceston trying to raise the *posse comitatus* for the king, Bassett saw Queen Henrietta Maria pass by, en route for Falmouth and into exile. Bassett wrote to his wife: 'Here is the woefullest spectacle my eyes yet ever lookt on, the most worn and weakest pittiful creature in the world, the poore Queene shifting for an houres life longer' (Cornwall RO, B35/6). The following month Bassett joined the army led by the king, which defeated Essex's army at Lostwithiel. After the parliamentarian surrender on 2 September, Bassett wrote to his wife, 'The King in hearing of thousands as soon as he saw me this morninge cryd to me "Now Mr Sheriffe, I leve Cornwall to yu safe and sound"' (Cornwall RO, B35/7). Two days later, before crossing the Tamar, the king rewarded Bassett with a knighthood.

Bassett died on 19 September 1645. His widow petitioned the king that through fortifying and equipping the Mount and lending money to the royalist cause her husband had 'contracted diverse great debts to satisfie w[hi]ch a good part of his estate hath bin sold since, to the almost ruine of his family' (Cornwall RO, B35/59). She estimated his total expenditure on the Mount alone since 1642 to be £1620. 5s. 8d. Bassett's brother Arthur succeeded him as governor of the Mount, surrendering it to Thomas Fairfax in April 1646. In 1657 Sir Francis's son and heir, John, impoverished by his father's losses during the war and by his own composition fine, was obliged to sell the Mount to Colonel John St Aubyn, whose descendants still live there. ANNE DUFFIN

Sources A. Duffin, *Faction and faith: politics and religion of the Cornish gentry before the civil war* (1996) · M. Coate, *Cornwall in the great civil war and interregnum, 1642–1660* (1933) · Cornwall RO, Bassett papers · Foster, *Alum. Oxon.* · J. L. Vivian, ed., *The visitations of Cornwall, comprising the herald's visitations of 1530, 1573, and 1620* (1887)

Archives Cornwall RO, letters and papers · Cornwall RO, papers relating to civil war

Likenesses oils, exh. Royal Cornwall Museum, River Street, Truro 1992, priv. coll.

Bassett, James (c.1526–1558), courtier, was described as being about twenty-four in January 1551. He was the third son of Sir John Bassett (1462–1528), landowner, of Umberleigh in Devon, and his second wife, Honor Grenville (1493×5–1566), daughter of Sir Thomas Grenville of Stowe, Cornwall [see Plantagenet, Honor, *under* Plantagenet, Arthur]. His siblings were Philippa (1516–1582), Katherine (b. 1517), John (1518–1541), Anne (1521–1557), Mary (c.1522×5–1598), and George (c.1522×5–c.1580). He came from the Cornish gentry family of Bassett, which had established itself at Tehidy, near Redruth, by the late thirteenth century. In 1330–31 Sir Ralph Bassett was licensed to embattle the manor house at Tehidy and during the fourteenth and fifteenth centuries a substantial landed estate was created, concentrated in the parishes of Illogan, Redruth, and Camborne. By the early sixteenth century a cadet branch was established at Umberleigh. After the death of Sir John Bassett in 1528, Honor married Arthur *Plantagenet, Viscount Lisle (b. before 1472, d. 1542), soon to be made deputy of Calais. The preservation of the Lisle papers accounts for the detailed knowledge of James Bassett's early life and education. During 1534 he was sent to study under Hugh Cook, alias Faringdon, abbot of Reading, who thought the boy a 'very

towardly child' (*LP Henry VIII*, 7, no. 1452). In order to begin studying French, thought useful for entry into a diplomatic career, Bassett was sent in 1535–6 to the Collège de Calvi in Paris. However, the boy was neglected by Guilliame Poyet, the president of the *parlement* of Paris, who had promised to look after him. Lady Lisle withdrew Bassett from his care and sent him to a crammer in St Omer.

When he returned to Paris in December 1536, Bassett was placed with a merchant friend of the Lisles, Guillaume le Gras. There he had his every whim catered for, even managing to secure a bed all to himself, an almost unheard-of luxury for such a young child. He began dancing lessons and was frequently brought clothes of velvet, taffeta, and silk by Lisle's secretary John Husee. Perhaps indicative of Bassett's demanding nature is the fact that the family correspondence features him ten times more often than his elder brother George. The Wallop family saw him as thoroughly charming, Sir John Wallop imagining him as 'the jolliest and wisest child … my wife and I take great pleasure in hearing him speak' (*LP Henry VIII*, 11, no. 1342). However, Bassett's words were not always so honeyed, especially when it came to eating the fish he loathed during Lent.

As early as 1537, Lisle attempted to procure a living for his stepson but was put off by the refusal of Thomas Cranmer, archbishop of Canterbury, to allow cure of souls to children. Bassett wrote to his mother in September that he would like to learn Latin, 'a thing which I specially desire in order to associate with foreigners' (*LP Henry VIII*, 12, no. 788). To accomplish this, however, he felt it necessary to attend the Collège de Navarre in Paris, where he could rub shoulders with members of the French aristocracy, like Claude de Lorraine, first duc de Guise. Despite his parents' objections on the grounds of cost and his previous unhappy experience, he managed to persuade them by writing to their friends to enlist their help. John Bekynsaw told how Stephen Gardiner, bishop of Winchester, was approached by him in order to gain his support in the matter.

Bassett went to the college in November 1537, taking with him his cassock, and, true to character, a velvet bonnet decorated with gold buttons. Despite being a diligent student, according to his *maître de chambre*, Pierre du Val, Bassett wrote to his mother in February 1538 that his correspondence was monitored and his replies dictated, which worried him in case he should become unwell and not be able to tell anybody. He seems to have exaggerated his mistreatment, complaining that he was forced to share a bed with two other boys of a lower social status. Lady Lisle did not allow him to stay long at the college, despite advice from Bekynsaw, who asked that she be not moved by everything written by a twelve-year-old boy. By September 1538 Bassett was leaving France and Calais to begin a new life serving Stephen Gardiner, at that time the most influential member of Henry VIII's council. Husee wryly commented that the priesthood would not have suited Bassett anyway, as he was 'meeter to serve the temporal powers than the spiritual dignities' (*LP Henry VIII*, 13, no. 446).

Bassett became involved in conservative Catholic circles as a result of his mother's influence on his religion and of service in Gardiner's household. He proved himself a loyal and trustworthy servant to Gardiner and referred to his place 'ever about the bishop and one of the chiefest about him, and one that knew the most part of things that were done' (*Acts and Monuments*, 6.235). When in June 1548 Gardiner was imprisoned for giving his St Peter's day sermon, which was regarded by Edward Seymour, duke of Somerset and lord protector, as against the recent reformation in religion, Bassett was among those who sought his release. His persistent nature is evident in his suits to privy councillors and MPs on Gardiner's behalf, but he gained nothing except 'fair words and promises' (ibid.). Bassett appeared as a witness at Gardiner's trial in 1551. He defended his master by detailing how Gardiner's speeches exhorted obedience from the people, and claiming that it did not occur to the bishop that the St Peter's day sermon was in any way offensive; indeed, Gardiner was never more merry than at the feast afterwards. Bassett also visited Gardiner in prison and briefly joined him in the Tower of London in October 1551, before going over to Flanders.

Gardiner was released on Mary I's accession in July 1553 and promoted to lord chancellor on 23 August. Bassett returned to England and was appointed to the privy chamber in 1553 and then to the privy chamber of Philip of Spain in 1554. He was trusted by the king and queen, acted as a private secretary to Mary, and was used frequently as a go-between. The Venetian ambassador, Federico Badoer, reported in January 1558 that Bassett was the man sent by the queen to inform Philip of 'the sure advice of her being pregnant' (*CSP Venice, 1557–8*, no. 1146). Bassett reinforced his Catholic credentials by marrying, in or before June 1556, Mary (d. 1572) [see Bassett, Mary], the second of five children of William *Roper (1495×8–1578) and his wife, Margaret *Roper (1505–1544). The couple had two sons. When their first son was born he was named after the king, who attended the christening and gave presents. For his loyal service James Bassett was awarded with grants of land from the former estate of Sir Peter Carew in March 1555 and given a pension of 1300 crowns. He also enjoyed the income from his late brother's estate at Umberleigh, having the wardship of his nephew Arthur Bassett (1541–1586). Bassett purchased property in Devon, where he was returned as knight of the shire in November 1554, 1555, and 1558. He had already represented Taunton in parliament in October 1553, a borough that Gardiner controlled, and was MP for Downton in April 1554, but was not an active MP, preferring instead to observe the proceedings.

Edward Courtenay, earl of Devonshire, was chief among Bassett's other correspondents during Mary's reign; Bassett looked after the earl's interests at court while he was in exile. Devonshire wrote from Louvain that Bassett and James Wingfield were men he had always 'reposed trust in … to accomplish his affairs … there is none to whom I could write with more hope of remedy' (*CSP dom., 1553–8*, no. 285). Bassett advised the earl about

how best to regain the favour of the king and queen and put in a good word with them on his behalf.

Bassett did not neglect Gardiner, despite his other duties. In November 1555 he wrote to Devonshire about Gardiner's last hours, when he 'could think upon nothing else, but spent day and night altogether with him, until he died'. He was named as an executor of Gardiner's will, in which he received £20. Bassett did not long survive his master. He made his will in September 1558, leaving to his wife jewels and half his goods. He remembered other family members and servants with small sums of money and personal effects such as a gilt cup given to him by Gomez Suárez de Figueroa, fifth count of Feria. He lamented that he was unable to offer more, as he was 'at this present tyme endebted unto soundrie persons in certayne greate somes'. His will also records his continued adherence to the Catholic faith; he bequeathed to 'suche good Religious ffolks' £40 to say masses for his soul and the souls of all Christians (PRO, PROB 11/42A, sig. 19). Bassett died on 21 November 1558 and was buried five days later at Blackfriars, London. At the time his wife was pregnant with their son Charles, who went into exile with his brother during Elizabeth I's reign. A precocious child, Bassett matured over his seventeen years' service to Gardiner, proving his loyalty at his trial and sensitivity at his death, and rising to become a steadfast confidant to nobles and monarchs alike.

SARAH CLAYTON

Sources HoP, *Commons, 1509–58*, 1.394–5 · *LP Henry VIII*, vols. 5–14 · M. St C. Byrne, ed., *The Lisle letters: an abridgement* (1983) · *CSP dom.*, rev. edn, 1553–8 · *CSP Venice, 1555–8* · *CSP Spain, 1554–8* · *The acts and monuments of John Foxe*, ed. S. R. Cattley, 8 vols. (1837–41), vols. 5–6 · will, PRO, PROB 11/42A, sig. 19 · J. A. Muller, *Stephen Gardiner and the Tudor reaction* (1926); repr. (1970) · *The letters of Stephen Gardiner*, ed. J. A. Muller (1933) · G. Redmond, *In defence of the church Catholic: the life of Stephen Gardiner* (1990)

Archives PRO, SP 1 · PRO, SP 3

Wealth at death land, cash, and personal estate to family, friends, servants, and 'good religious folkes': will, PRO, PROB 11/42A, sig. 19

Bassett [*née* Roper], **Mary** (d. 1572), translator, was the second of five children of Margaret *Roper (1505–1544), favourite daughter of Sir Thomas *More, and her husband, William *Roper (1495×8–1578). Herself a fine classicist, Margaret Roper was determined that her daughter should be taught Latin and Greek by the most distinguished scholars and approached Roger Ascham. In a letter written to Mary in 1554 Ascham explained his failure to take up the invitation, saying that at the time nothing would induce him to leave Cambridge University. However other tutors were found, including John Morwen of Corpus Christi College, Oxford, who taught her Greek and Latin. Her education was praised by Ascham, and Nicholas Harpsfield in his *Life … of Sir Thomas More* described her as a person of rare learning and an expert in Greek and Latin.

There is little evidence regarding the detail of Mary's personal life. She married first Stephen Clarke, but there were no children of the marriage; and second, by June 1556, James *Bassett (c.1526–1558), Stephen Gardiner's secretary, who, like Mary, became a part of the royal household. This was a short marriage, since Bassett died on 21 November 1558, but they had two sons, Philip and Charles, the latter still unborn when his father made his will in September 1558. A devout Catholic to the end of her life, Mary Bassett attended Queen Mary's court as a gentlewoman of the privy chamber. Ascham's letter of 1554 in search of friendly contacts at court praised her intellectual capabilities, particularly in view of the innumerable distractions for ladies of the court. In fact Mary made excellent use of her opportunities, gaining a reputation for her skill in translation. She dedicated to the queen a presentation copy in a velvet binding of five books of Eusebius's *Ecclesiastical History*, which she had translated from Greek into English. In her preface Bassett elaborated on her aims in translation, explaining that she tried to reflect as clearly as possible the aims and intentions of the author of the original text. She considered the *Ecclesiastical History* to be an important work which ought to be read by all Christians, both men and women. Her linguistic skills enabled her to judge the existing Greek edition as being full of mistakes. She expressed conventional authorial reluctance to make the translation available publicly, claiming that she had been pressed by friends to make this fine copy. Mary explained that she could not bear to disappoint them and she feared lest refusal be interpreted as pride or sloth.

Mary Bassett's second extant translation is the later part of her grandfather's *History of the Passion*, the original of which had been given to the family together with some other manuscripts at the time of More's execution. Her translation from the Latin appeared under her own name in the volume of More's collected works in English published by More's nephew William Rastell in 1557. Rastell himself praised the quality of the work and Harpsfield described Bassett's translation as being of such elegance that the reader might think that it was the original written by Sir Thomas himself in English. Harpsfield refers to other translations by Mary Bassett including the *History* of Socrates, Theodoretus, Sozomenus, and Evagrius, but he adds that out of modesty she suppressed them. No trace of these has yet been found.

Mary Bassett's will drawn up in 1566 is a clear indication of the strength of her Catholic faith. She committed her soul to the blessed lady St Mary and any beneficiaries who were heretics were to be excluded. Her bequest to her younger son, Charles, hinted at purchases of land which she negotiated on his behalf partly by using her own resources. The will also contains interesting links with her grandfather Thomas More and she passed on to her elder son, Philip, the gold cross that had belonged to him, as well as a gold ring with a ruby that King Philip had given her. Mary Bassett died in London on 20 March 1572.

CAROLINE M. K. BOWDEN

Sources E. E. Reynolds, *Margaret Roper: eldest daughter of St Thomas More* (1960) · P. E. Hallett, ed., *St Thomas More's 'History of the passion'* (1941) · N. Harpsfield, *The life and death of Sr Thomas Moore, knight*, ed. E. V. Hitchcock, EETS, original ser., 186 (1932) · HoP, *Commons, 1509–58*, 1.392–4 · will, PRO, PROB 11/54, fols. 82v–83r
Wealth at death wealthy; bequeathed lands and jewels

Bassey, Okon Asuguo [*known as* Hogan Bassey, Hogan Kid Bassey] (1932–1998), boxer and sports administrator, was born in Creek Town, Calabar, Nigeria, on 3 June 1932, the eldest of five sons of Chief Asuquo Bassey. He was educated at Creek Town School, Calabar, and Ahmaddiya School, Olowogbowo, Lagos, and it was during this time that he first took up boxing. He turned professional at the age of sixteen and won his country's flyweight title in 1949 by outpointing Dick Turpin (not to be confused with the English boxer of the same name). He lost a rematch but outpointed Steve Jeffra in 1951 to win the bantamweight title.

Aided by Douglas Collister and Jack Fransworth, two Nigerian-based Englishmen with boxing contacts at home, Bassey left for Liverpool in 1952. Managed by Peter Banasko, a local former boxer and one of the few black British managers active at the time, Bassey made his British début in January 1952: a fourth-round knock-out of Ray Hillyard at Liverpool Stadium. Eighteen contests followed (with fourteen wins) in the year. Stocky and powerfully built, Bassey packed a knock-out punch in either hand but was also a technically gifted boxer. These skills, together with his pleasant demeanour, professionalism, and humility outside the ring, quickly endeared him to the British boxing public.

In February 1953 Bassey took a significant step up in class by meeting the former European bantamweight champion Luis Romero in Manchester. Bassey won by an eighth-round knock-out. Next was the highly rated Londoner Sammy McCarthy. Again Bassey won. A rare defeat followed, however, to Belfast's Billy 'Spider' Kelly, in London. Seven wins from eight contests in 1954 were followed by five victories in 1955. In November 1955 Bassey was matched with Kelly for the empire featherweight title. Bassey was not expected to win the contest but, in a superlative display of skill and strength, he stopped Kelly in the eighth round. He left Peter Banasko for George Biddles after this contest. On 3 December 1955 he married Maria Williams (*b.* 1934/5), machinist, of Liverpool; she was the daughter of Benjamin Peter Williams.

After successfully defending his empire title in April 1957 Bassey next visited America, where he surprised many by his conclusive points victory over the world-class Puerto Rican Miguel Berrios. Two months later he was matched with the European champion, the French Algerian Cherif Hamia, for the vacant world featherweight title in Paris. Although he was knocked down in the second round, his non-stop style bewildered Hamia, and in the tenth round the referee stopped the contest in Bassey's favour. Bassey, the first Nigerian to hold a world boxing title, was duly made MBE, and in the process became the first Nigerian to hold such an honour.

Having relinquished the empire title to concentrate on his world crown, Bassey's first defence came in April 1958. Few expected him to beat the upcoming Mexican Ricardo Moreno in Los Angeles. Again, however, Bassey stunned the 20,000 partisan crowd, by knocking Moreno out in the third round. He also beat former world champion Willie Pep in a non-title bout in Boston. His second and last

Okon Asuguo Bassey (1932–1998), by Bernard Zimmerman, 1958 [left, with Jules Touan]

defence of his world featherweight title came against the talented American Davey Moore, and their clash in March 1959 in Los Angeles proved to be the toughest of his career. After a fierce contest lasting thirteen rounds, Biddles refused to send his fighter out for the fourteenth round; he explained later that owing to cuts Bassey could not see. The return match, in August 1959, ended in similar fashion at the end of the tenth round. Aged only twenty-seven, but knowing that his best years were behind him, Bassey sensibly chose to retire.

On his return to Nigeria, Bassey was appointed director of physical education and was given the job of coaching the Olympic boxing team. He wrote an instructional book, *Hogan on Boxing* (1963), before producing two Olympic medallists: Nojeem Mayegun (1964) and Isaac Ikhouria (1972). He was awarded the (Senegalese) Lion of Africa award in 1973, and Nigeria's highest honour, membership of the order of the Niger, in 1979. Meanwhile, his first marriage having ended in divorce, in 1977 he married Mary Magdalene. There were eight children of his two marriages.

As the first black African boxing champion since Battling Siki (Baye Phal) in the 1920s, Bassey enabled Nigerian boxing and sport to expand beyond both their own and Africa's borders at a time of increasing Western awareness of African culture. His influence long remained a force in his country of birth and he was at the end of the twentieth century voted the greatest Nigerian athlete of the century, above fellow boxer Dick Tiger (also Liverpool-

based for a time), basketball player Hakeem Olajuwon, and footballer Christian Okoye. He died in the early hours of 26 January 1998 at his home in Apapa, Lagos.

GARY SHAW

Sources G. Odd, *Boxing: the great champions* (1978) · S. Andre and N. Fleischer, *A pictorial history of boxing* (1975) · H. Bassey, *Hogan on boxing* (1963) · M. Mulcahey, 'Forgotten champs: Hogan Bassey', www.maxboxing.com, 10 June 2002 · P. Demeyin, 'Hogan "Kid" Bassey', www.nigerdeltacongress.com, 10 June 2002 · *The Times* (23 Feb 1998) · m. cert. [Maria Williams]
Likenesses B. Zimmerman, photograph, 1958 (with Jules Touan), News International Syndication, London [*see illus.*] · photograph, repro. in *The Times*

Bassingbourn, Humphrey of (*d.* 1238×41), ecclesiastic and justice, was a native of Bassingbourn in Cambridgeshire, related to the local lords of the manor, including Warin of Bassingbourn, a prominent counsellor of King John. In 1206 Humphrey was presented by the king to Bassingbourn church, and by 1225 was rector of the nearby church of Wendy. As a landowner in his own right he held property at Biggleswade in Bedfordshire, and possibly also at Gravenhurst. He makes his first recorded appearance as a canon of Salisbury, prebendary of Netherbury, and archdeacon of Wiltshire, appointed some time between 1179 and 1193. In 1193 he was promoted to the archdeaconry of Salisbury, an office which he held until his death or resignation at a date between 1238 and 1241. He also held a prebend at Lincoln Cathedral from before 1219. In all probability he is to be identified with a namesake, rector of a moiety of the church of Leverton in Lincolnshire, who was dead by 1239 and who gave relics to Waltham Abbey, the patron of Leverton church.

In 1200 Bassingbourn witnessed a pair of royal charters, issued by the king in France, and in 1206 he served briefly as a royal justice, sent to hear pleas and to levy the king's tallage in East Anglia and the counties of the east midlands. Following the imposition of the papal interdict upon England in 1208, he was restored through royal favour to various rents that he held in Yorkshire and elsewhere, but in 1216, during the civil war, he may have joined the rebel barons, since he was fined 100 marks and a palfrey to have the king's grace, and was issued with royal letters of protection shortly afterwards. Despite his contacts with the royal court, his career appears to have been spent mostly at Salisbury. His time as archdeacon there coincided with the removal of the site of the cathedral from Old Sarum to Salisbury and the imposition of reform upon the morals and learning of the parish clergy.

NICHOLAS VINCENT

Sources *Chancery records* · *Pipe rolls* · G. H. Fowler, ed., *The cartulary of the Cistercian Abbey of Old Wardon, Bedfordshire: from the manuscript (Latin 223) in the John Rylands Library, Manchester* (1931) · J. Godber, ed., *The cartulary of Newnham Priory*, 1 vol. in 2 pts, Bedfordshire Historical RS, 43 (1963–4) · R. Ransford, ed., *The early charters of the Augustinian canons of Waltham Abbey, Essex, 1062–1230* (1989) · F. N. Davis, ed., *Rotuli Roberti Grosseteste, episcopi Lincolniensis*, CYS, 10 (1913)

Bassnett, Christopher (1677–1744), Presbyterian minister, was born at Chester on 30 January 1677, the son of an apothecary, Nathaniel Bassnett, and perhaps related to Samuel Bassnett of Coventry, one of the ejected ministers of 1662. He was trained for the ministry at the Revd Richard Frankland's academy at Rathmell, which he entered on 1 April 1696. In September 1709, upon the recommendation of his close friend Matthew Henry, Bassnett was appointed minister to the Presbyterian congregation at Kaye or Key Street Chapel, Liverpool. Here he remained, apart from a period (March 1711 – January 1712) when a bout of depression obliged him to relinquish his duties, until his death in 1744.

Bassnett married, at Northowram and Colney dissenting chapel on 9 February 1714, Anne Cheney (*d.* 1737), the widow of John Cheney and daughter of the Revd Samuel Eaton of Stand. They had a daughter, Frances, who was born in 1715. Bassnett assisted in establishing a school in 1716 for the free education of poor children in Liverpool, and from 1728 or 1729 he was assisted in the ministry by John Brekell. He was the author of several religious treatises, which included *The Seaman's Character* (1712), *Zebulan's Blessing* (1714), and *Church Officers and their Mission* (1717). Bassnett died in Liverpool on 22 July 1744 and was buried in Toxteth Park Chapel. He was a homely, useful preacher, who preserved the old puritan habit of preaching extemporaneously.

ALEXANDER GORDON, *rev.* M. J. MERCER

Sources C. Surman, index, DWL · B. Nightingale, *Lancashire nonconformity*, 6 vols. [1890–93], vol. 6 · R. Halley, *Lancashire: its puritanism and nonconformity*, 2 vols. (1869), vol. 2 · F. Nicholson and E. Axon, *The older nonconformity in Kendal* (1915) · J. Toulmin, *An historical view of the state of the protestant dissenters in England* (1814) · J. H. Turner, T. Dickenson, and O. Heywood, eds., *The nonconformist register of baptisms, marriages, and deaths* (1881) · G. E. Evans, *Vestiges of protestant dissent* (1897) · 'Various protestant dissenting congregations', DWL, Wilson MSS · *IGI*

Archives Somerset House, Bassnett's register of baptisms at Key Street Chapel

Bastable, Charles Francis (1855–1945), economist, was born at Charleville, co. Cork, the only son of the Revd Robert Bastable (1800–1889), rector of Knocktemple and Kilbolane. His mother was a daughter of Dr Little of Sligo. He was educated at Fermoy College, Fermoy, co. Cork, and in 1873 entered the University of Dublin, Trinity College, where he graduated BA in 1878 with a senior moderatorship (first-class honours) in history and political science, a course which then included political economy. He proceeded to the degrees of MA in 1882 and LLD in 1890.

At first Bastable thought of practising law as a career, and he was called to the Irish bar in 1881; but in 1882 an opportunity of developing his interest in economic studies arose. The Whately professorship of political economy in Trinity College, Dublin, had been filled quinquennially by examination since its establishment in 1832; Bastable was the successful candidate at the examination which took place in 1882 and was appointed to the chair. At the end of his term of office in 1887 the regulations governing the post were altered; he was elected for a second term and went on to hold the position as a non-fellow professor for another forty-five years until his retirement in 1932. Thus although he had ten predecessors in the Whately chair, Bastable was the first to retain it as a professional academic economist and he became well known to other

Charles Francis Bastable (1855–1945), by Chancellor

such economists throughout Europe in his time. Yet initially at least the duties of the post were not such as to occupy all the time of an established academic and the salary reflected this. Hence Bastable was compelled to seek other posts; he held the chair of jurisprudence and political economy at Queen's College, Galway, from 1883 until 1903, was appointed professor of jurisprudence and international law in Trinity College, Dublin, in 1902, and became regius professor of laws in 1908, a post which he also held until his retirement in 1932. In 1905 he was George Rae lecturer at the University College of North Wales and he was Warburton lecturer at the University of Manchester in the academic year 1909/10.

A founder member of the Royal Economic Society, Bastable served on its first council and contributed a total of twenty-six articles to its *Economic Journal* between 1891 and 1920. At the Oxford meeting of the British Association in 1894 he was president of section F, economics and statistics. He was an honorary secretary of the Statistical and Social Inquiry Society of Ireland from 1886 until 1895 and one of its vice-presidents until 1915. In 1921 he was elected a fellow of the British Academy. After the formation of the Irish Free State he was a member of its fiscal inquiry committee of 1923.

Although throughout his long teaching career Bastable always gave courses on legal subjects, his main research interest was in economics, especially in international trade, money, and public finance. In the theory of international trade he followed the broad lines of the analysis of comparative costs and reciprocal demand as first set out by David Ricardo and developed by J. S. Mill, but made significant improvements within them. These were incorporated into the successive editions of his *Theory of International Trade* (1st edn, 1887), a work which he described as 'specially intended for serious students of economic theory'. It reached a wide audience of such students, being translated into French and Italian. *The Commerce of Nations* (1891) was a more popular book, in which

Bastable, who was sympathetic to the historical method in economics as developed by his compatriots J. K. Ingram and T. E. Cliffe Leslie, took the approach 'that existing commercial policy and the doctrines respecting it are best explained by reference to their history'. In a succinct review of the development of world trade from the seventeenth century up to his own day he did not attempt to conceal his own belief in the merits of free trade, but the conclusion which he reached was realistic and prescient:

> though we cannot expect any speedy abandonment of the protective system, which will doubtless continue for a long time, we may look for breaches in it and at intervals steady and sustained reforms, leading finally, though by slow degrees, to the adoption of complete free trade. (3rd edn, 1903, 211)

Bastable's contributions to the classical theory of international trade gained him a more lasting, if limited, reputation than his work in public finance, to which he devoted as much, if not more, attention. In the United Kingdom in the late Victorian era, when the public sector was small and taxation low, it was a subject which was not the focus of much attention. There had been no comprehensive treatment of it since the time of J. R. McCulloch and, although he published many articles on aspects of the subject, Bastable's major contribution was that he provided just such a survey at an appropriate time. His *Public Finance* (1892) drew on his extensive knowledge of European and American as well as British writings in that field to provide a clear statement of accepted principles and practices. The book became a definitive text, a handbook for civil servants as well as academic students, which was not superseded until the 1930s, when the principles of fiscal policy which Bastable and his contemporaries regarded as fundamental were being challenged, most notably by J. M. Keynes and his followers.

The heavy teaching load which Bastable always carried limited his ability to produce original work in his later years. With characteristic modesty he decided against revising his *Public Finance* thoroughly, on the ground that it was a task for which a younger man, who could take a more radical approach, would be better suited. Held in high regard by his many pupils, Bastable was a reserved and very private man, who lived a secluded life after his retirement. Survived by his wife, Josephine Anna, and son, he died at his home, 52 Brighton Road, Rathgar, co. Dublin, on 3 January 1945. R. D. COLLISON BLACK

Sources G. A. Duncan, 'Charles Francis Bastable, 1855–1945', *PBA*, 31 (1945), 241–4 · J. G. Smith, *Economic Journal*, 55 (1945), 127–30 · J. A. Bristow, 'Bastable, Charles Francis', *The new Palgrave: a dictionary of economics*, ed. J. Eatwell, M. Milgate, and P. Newman (1987) · *WWW* · R. D. C. Black, 'Select bibliography of economic writings by members of Trinity College, Dublin', *Hermathena*, 66 (1945), 55–68 · R. D. C. Black, *The Statistical and Social Inquiry Society of Ireland centenary volume, 1847–1947* (1947) · R. B. McDowell and D. A. Webb, *Trinity College, Dublin, 1592–1952: an academic history* (1982) · J. W. Angell, *The theory of international prices* (1926) · J. Viner, *Studies in the theory of international trade* (1938) · A. I. Bloomfield, 'Impact of growth and technology on trade in nineteenth-century British thought', *History of Political Economy*, 10 (1978), 608–35 · *CGPLA Éire* (1945) · d. cert.

Archives TCD, letters | BLPES, Cannan collection, letters · BLPES, Giffen collection, letters · Col. U., letters to Edwin Seligman · Lausanne, Fonds Walras, letters
Likenesses Chancellor, photograph, repro. in Duncan, *PBA* · Chancellor, photograph, British Academy, London [*see illus.*] · photograph, repro. in Black, *Statistical and Social Inquiry Society*, facing p. 80
Wealth at death £11,279 19s. 10d. (in England): probate, 24 July 1945, *CGPLA Eng. & Wales* · £4015 15s. 2d.: probate, 3 July 1945, *CGPLA Éire*

Bastard of Fauconberg, the. *See* Neville, Thomas (d. 1471).

Bastard, John Pollexfen (1756–1816), member of parliament and militia officer, was born on 18 September 1756 at Kitley, near Plymouth, Devon, the eldest son of William Bastard (1727–1782), landowner, of Kitley, and his second wife, Anne (d. 1765), daughter of Thomas Worsley of Hovingham, Yorkshire. His family, settled in Devon since the Norman conquest, had acquired Kitley when his great-grandfather William Bastard (1667–1703) of Gerston married the heiress Anne Pollexfen (d. 1723). He was educated at Eton College (1766–74) and was admitted a student of the Middle Temple in 1771. He married first, about 1780, Sarah (d. 1808), widow of Charles Wymondesold of East Lockinge, Berkshire, and second, on 2 July 1809, Judith Anne (1772/3–1848), daughter of Henry Martin (1733–1794), naval officer and MP for Southampton; they had no children.

Having succeeded to the family estates following his father's death Bastard was MP (on Sir Francis Basset's interest) for the corporation borough of Truro from 1783 to 1784, and for Devon from 1784 until his death. He prided himself on his independence from party but his dislike of government waste and his championship of the militia meant that he increasingly voted with the opposition. On 1 August 1783 he was appointed lieutenant-colonel of the East Devonshire militia, and on 9 November 1798 colonel. In 1801 he quelled a revolt by dockyard workers at Plymouth, an action reminiscent of his father, who in August 1779 had rallied the local gentry to escort French prisoners of war away from Plymouth arsenal when a Franco-Spanish fleet was threatening the coast. William Bastard had been rewarded in September 1779 with a baronetcy, which neither he nor his heirs ever assumed; his son contented himself with the thanks of king and government.

On 22 August 1803 Bastard was appointed colonel-in-chief of the South Devonshire Volunteers. He went to Italy for his health, and died at Leghorn on 4 April 1816. His remains were interred in the family vault at Yealmpton church, near Kitley, on 17 June 1816. His brother Edmund Bastard (1758–1816), MP for Dartmouth (1787–1812), succeeded to the Kitley estate. ALASTAIR W. MASSIE

Sources H. Walrond, *Historical records of the 1st Devon militia* (1897) · HoP, *Commons, 1754–90* · HoP, *Commons, 1790–1820* · *Généalogie de la maison de Bastard* (1847) · *Report and Transactions of the Devonshire Association*, 18 (1886), 299–300 · Burke, *Gen. GB* (1952) · *Annual Register* (1779), 245 · *GM*, 1st ser., 86/1 (1816), 474, 635 · R. A. Austen-Leigh, ed., *The Eton College register, 1753–1790* (1921) · H. A. C. Sturgess, ed., *Register of admissions to the Honourable Society of the Middle Temple, from the fifteenth century to the year 1944*, 1 (1949) · memorial tablet, Yealmpton church, Devon

Likenesses S. W. Reynolds, double portrait, mezzotint, pubd 1795 (with his brother, Edmund; after J. Northcote), repro. in Walrond, *Historical records*, facing p. 194 · W. Raddon, line engraving, pubd 1817, NPG

Bastard, Thomas (1565/6–1618), epigrammatist and Church of England clergyman, was born at Blandford, Dorset. He went to Winchester College and then as scholar on 27 August 1586 to New College, Oxford. There it was quickly realized that he was, in Wood's words, 'endowed with many rare gifts, was an excellent Grecian, Latinist and poet' (Wood, *Ath. Oxon.*, 2.227). He was one of the contributors to a memorial volume for Sir Philip Sidney, 'Peplus illustrissimi viri D. Philippi Sidnaei. Supremis honoribus dicatus, Oxonii, 1587', and to the volume of Latin, Greek, and Hebrew elegies, written on the death of Ann, countess of Oxford, daughter of Lord Burghley (BL, Lansdowne MS 104, no. 78). In 1588 he was admitted perpetual fellow of New College, proceeding BA in 1590 and MA in 1606.

The year 1591 marked a disastrous turn in Bastard's career. In Wood's eccentric formulation, Bastard was 'guilty of the vices belonging to poets and given to libelling … [and] forced to leave his fellowship' (Wood, *Ath. Oxon.*, 2.227). These 'libels' described in shocking detail the pecadilloes of some prominent Oxford clergymen and academics. Fortunately Bastard and his 'little family' (including a wife whom he described as 'no great helpmeet'; *Chrestoleros*, 1, no. 30) received assistance from two prominent courtiers. First, Sir Charles Blount, Lord Mountjoy, made him one of his chaplains, for which Bastard registered his gratitude throughout his poems. Later, in 1592, Thomas Howard, earl of Suffolk, presented him livings as vicar of Bere Regis, and in 1606, rector of Almer in his native Dorset. However the livings were small and poor, and Bastard was never able to obtain a more lucrative benefice. (See Atkins, 768, for an itemization of Bastard's pathetically small estate.)

Bastard published some of his sermons in 1615, but his literary reputation is based on a volume of 285 epigrams published in 1598 called *Chrestoleros* (a coinage suggesting 'useful' and 'trifling'). At Winchester College the writing of Latin epigrams using the model of Martial was a central exercise in the curriculum, and the most important epigrammatists of the 1590s—John Owen, John Hoskins, Sir John Davies, Bastard—were trained there. At the time of the publication of *Chrestoleros* in 1598, Bastard had, according to Dudley Carleton, 'the name of a lively wit', but his poems were unimpressive: he 'botches up his verse with variations, and his conceits so run upon his poverty that his wit is rather to be pitied than commended' (*CSP dom.*, 1580–1625, *addenda*, 385) As Sir John Harington said in a painfully frank poem to Bastard, the

> dusty wits of this ungratefull time,
> Carpe at thy booke of Epigrams, and scoffe it.
> (Harington, *Letters and Epigrams*, ed. N. E. McClure, 1930, no. 160)

Perhaps the high point in Bastard's literary reputation occurred when the fashionable playwright John Marston quoted a couplet from one of Bastard's epigrams

(*Chrestoleros*, 4, no. 32) at a climactic moment in the very popular play *The Malcontent* (1604), the author being described as an 'honest priest' (act v, scene iv).

According to Wood, Bastard was a valued social companion: 'His discourses were always pleasant and facete, which made his company desired by all ingenious men' (Wood, *Ath. Oxon.*, 2.227); he was included in the circle of sophisticates (including Donne) who produced the volume of burlesque poetical tributes to Thomas Coryat called *The Odcombian Banquet* (1611). However most of Bastard's life was lived in poverty and far from the stimulation of London. In Dorset, he said, his wit became 'keycold' (*Chrestoleros*, 1, no. 2), and in his last days he fell to pieces:

> This poet and preacher being towards his latter end crazed, and thereupon brought into debt, was at length committed to the prison in Allhallows parish, in Dorchester, where dying very obscurely and in a mean condition, was buried in the churchyard belonging to the parish on 19 April 1618, leaving behind him many memorials of his wit and drollery. (Wood, *Ath. Oxon.*, 2.228)

P. J. FINKELPEARL

Sources DNB · *The poems English and Latin of the Rev. Thomas Bastard, M. A. (1566–1618)*, ed. A. Grosart (1880) · Wood, *Ath. Oxon.*, new edn · S. H. Atkins, 'Thomas Bastard', *TLS* (26 Sept 1936), 768 · A. G. Chester, 'Thomas Bastard's "lost" satire', *N&Q*, 195 (1950), 533–4 · R. Nemser, introduction, in *The poems of Sir John Davies*, ed. R. Krueger (1975) · D. Nicholls, 'Thomas Bastard 1566–1618: "Chrestoleros" (1598)', *Zeitschrift für Anglistik und Amerikanistik* (Leipzig), 31.326–42

Wealth at death none: *TLS*, 768

Bastian, (Henry) Charlton (1837–1915), physician and neurologist, was born on 26 April 1837 in Truro, Cornwall, the third son in a family of four sons and one daughter of James Bastian, merchant, and his wife, Charlotte Eliza Bullmore. After attending school in Falmouth he entered University College, London, in 1856, and graduated BA (1859), MA (1861), MB (1863), and MD (1866). He became MRCS (1860), MRCP (1865), and FRCP (1870). In 1866 he married Julia Augusta, third daughter of Charles Orme, brewer, of 81 Avenue Road, Regent's Park, London; they were to have three sons and one daughter.

Charlton Bastian first worked in London at St Mary's Hospital, Paddington, as assistant physician and lecturer in pathology. He returned to University College as professor of pathological anatomy in 1867, and became a physician to University College Hospital in 1878. He also held another senior post, as physician in nervous diseases at the National Hospital, Queen Square, from 1868 to 1902. He held the chair of medicine at University College Hospital from 1887 to 1898. Bastian served as a censor of the Royal College of Physicians of London (1897–8) and later received an honorary fellowship of the Royal College of Physicians of Ireland and an honorary MD degree from the Royal University of Ireland.

As a child Bastian was fascinated by natural history, and among his early publications was a complete flora of Falmouth and a collection of the ferns of Great Britain. He was an authority on free nematode worms and named 100 new species in his monograph *The Anguillulidae* in 1864. He was elected FRS for this work in 1868, at the age of thirty-one, but had to abandon this interest when he developed an allergy to the worms. He was a strong supporter of the theory of evolution and numbered Herbert Spencer among his lifelong friends. His reputation in medicine was made in the late 1860s by his neurological studies of aphasias and other speech disorders. His standing in medicine was not harmed when he became the British champion of 'spontaneous generation of life' and a leading opponent of the germ theory of disease. However, as support for spontaneous generation faded and germ theory gained more supporters in the medical profession, Bastian's star waned. He found himself confronting many of the leading scientists and clinicians of the day, including Thomas Huxley, John Tyndall, Joseph Lister, and Louis Pasteur. One of the great paradoxes of Bastian's work is that in neurology his views were highly conventional, while in biology, and what became bacteriology, they became unorthodox and eventually eccentric. However, Bastian would maintain that he followed the evidence as he saw it and avoided metaphysics.

Bastian's first major publication in neurology was about the identification of a degenerated tract in the spinal cord, which was later named after Sir William Gowers (whose investigation was more definitive). In 1869 he published a seminal paper on various forms of speech loss and their relation to cerebral disease. Wernicke's sensory aphasia—a form of word deafness which was again later identified with another doctor—was initially described by Bastian. His approach to the understanding of aphasias was based on the idea that independent centres in the brain controlled speech and vision. His views on localization in mental functioning were set out in *The Brain as an Organ of Mind* (1880), *On Paralyses: Cerebral, Bulbar and Spinal* (1886), and *On Various Forms of Hysterical or Functional Paralysis* (1893). His classic *Treatise on Aphasia and other Speech Disorders* (1898) was based on his Lumleian lectures and was translated into Italian and German.

Bastian regarded his true life's work and achievement as the studies he made on the origins of life, despite the opprobrium this brought him. His views on this subject first came to light in the late 1860s when he defended the doctrine of spontaneous generation by both logic and experiment. Mainstream biological opinion assumed that life always came from life—*omne vivum ex ovo*—and that the actual origins of life, if not the creation of life, occurred at some distant time. Darwin, despite choosing the title *On the Origin of Species* for his main work on evolution, avoided consideration of the first origin of life and only sought to explain how existing species transmute into other species. None the less, both Darwin and Wallace found Bastian's ideas interesting, for if scientists accepted that life had originated once from non-living matter, then it was illogical to deny that this process might still be occurring. All the more so, when no one knew in what conditions life had first appeared. However, Huxley and other leading Darwinians regarded Bastian's views as unnecessarily contentious and he was ostracized for damaging the cause of evolution.

In the 1870s the British debate about spontaneous generation was fought in public over the experimental demonstrations of the phenomenon and the standing of the germ theory of disease. Bastian's main opponent was John Tyndall, who gathered increasing support across the scientific community and in the late 1870s enlisted none other than Pasteur in the cause. Bastian mostly fought alone, though he enjoyed the tacit support of many doctors who thought that germs were the result rather than the cause of infectious and septic diseases. With hindsight, it is clear that Bastian's challenges to what became a consensus on the continuity of life and the bacterial causes of disease helped to shape the new orthodoxy. His work led others to the recognition that certain bacteria could survive boiling and to improved sterilization procedures in bacteriological research. Bastian regularly defended his unfashionable views at scientific and medical meetings, and he published extensively. He completed three books on the subject in the 1870s: *The Modes of Origin of Lowest Organisms* (1871), *The Beginnings of Life* (1872), and *Evolution and the Origin of Life* (1874). Quite suddenly, in 1878, Bastian gave up his fight. The main reason was the pressure of his clinical work, though few would have enjoyed the lonely pursuit of what had quickly become unfashionable views.

Bastian had not, however, altered his convictions, and on his retirement in 1900 he returned to the question of the origin of life with undiminished energy. He published four further monographs: *Studies in Heterogenesis* (1901–4), *The Nature and Origin of Living Matter* (1905), *The Evolution of Life* (1907), and *The Origin of Life* (1911). By this time his views were quite heterodox and he found it difficult to publish his work in mainstream journals. Bastian died at his home, Fairfield, Chesham Bois, Buckinghamshire, on 17 November 1915. He was survived by his wife. He was cremated and his ashes buried, probably at Kensal Green, London.   MICHAEL WORBOYS

Sources G. Clarke, 'Bastian, Henry Charlton', *DSB* · M. Rang, 'The life and work of Henry Charlton Bastian', 1954, UCL, department of medicine · F. W. M. [F. W. Mott], *PRS*, 89B (1915–17), xxi–xxiv · *The Lancet* (27 Nov 1915), 1222–4 · J. E. Strick, 'The British spontaneous generation debates of 1860–1880: Medicine, evolution and laboratory science in the Victorian context', PhD diss., Princeton University, 1997 · J. E. Strick, *Sparks of life: Darwinism and the Victorian debates over spontaneous generation* (2000) · *DNB* · *CGPLA Eng. & Wales* (1916)

Archives RS · Wellcome L., corresp.

Likenesses Maull and Fox, photograph, 1868, RS · photograph, repro. in *The Lancet*, 1223 · photomechanical print (*Side view of the Brain*; after etching, 1809), Wellcome L.

Wealth at death £3833 11s. 1d.: resworn probate, 26 Feb 1916, *CGPLA Eng. & Wales*

Bastin, Clifford Sidney [Cliff] (1912–1991), footballer, was born on 14 March 1912 at 40 New North Road, Exeter, the son of Sidney Henry Bastin, dairyman, and his wife, Maud, née Butt. He was educated at Ladysmith Road elementary school, where he showed a precocious talent for football. He was soon playing for Exeter Boys, and was capped for England Schoolboys against Wales when he was fourteen.

After turning out for local recreational teams St Mark's and St James's, and starting training as an electrician, he was signed for Exeter City, then in the third division south; he made his first team début on 14 April 1928, at the remarkably early age of sixteen years and one month.

Not long after his professional début, Bastin was spotted playing against Watford by the Arsenal manager Herbert Chapman. Chapman had gone to look at Tommy Barnett, a member of the Watford team, but was more impressed by the neat, stocky young man with fair hair and the fashionable down-the-middle parting who was playing inside left for Exeter. It was not so much what 'Boy' Bastin did as the cool, mature way in which he did it that persuaded Chapman to sign him in May 1929. The fee was £2000. Alex James was also signed from Preston a few weeks later and though eleven years older than Bastin formed a left-wing partnership with him which became a major attacking feature of the Arsenal side that dominated English football in the 1930s. At first it seemed that both would be competing for the inside left position but at the end of 1929 Chapman persuaded Bastin that he was really an outside left and in the early months of 1930 the partnership was born.

Bastin made his Arsenal début away at Everton on 5 October 1929 and scored his first goal for the team in a home match against Sheffield Wednesday at the beginning of January 1930. Later that month he scored his first goal in an FA cup fixture by converting a cross from Joe Hulme on the right in a match against Chelsea. It was the first of the 26 he scored in the FA cup; his total of 178 goals for the club in 396 games remained an Arsenal record until 1997 and was a remarkable total for a winger. Cool and intelligent, he could shoot well with either foot and was always looking for goalmouth opportunities. In 1930 he was the youngest player to date to appear in the cup final (only Howard Kendall was younger, in 1964), and he supplied the pass for James to score the crucial first goal. When Arsenal won the first division championship for the first time in 1930–31, Bastin scored 28 goals; he scored 33 when they repeated the feat two seasons later. He played twenty-one times for England between 1931 and 1938, and scored the goal which gave them a draw against Italy in Rome in 1933; on this occasion the home crowd chanted 'Basta Bastin' ('enough of Bastin').

Not surprisingly, Bastin greatly admired the management skills of Herbert Chapman, whom he thought might have been prime minister if circumstances had been different. Chapman reciprocated, seeing Bastin as a model professional, modest, loyal, and respectable. Alex James, on the other hand, was more independent and argumentative. Bastin was devastated when Chapman died suddenly in January 1934.

Bastin's form declined in the late 1930s as he suffered increasingly from deafness after a bout of influenza led to an infection of the middle ear in 1936. By the early 1940s he could not hear the roar of the crowd. He was still able to play 241 wartime games and score 70 wartime goals but he later admitted that his loss of hearing had undermined his footballing effectiveness. During the war he was declared unfit for military service and managed an ARP post on the top of the main stand at Highbury.

Bastin retired from football in September 1946, his last appearance for Arsenal being against Manchester United. He and his wife, Joan Lilian, née Shaul (b. 1915/16)—she was the daughter of Stanley George Shaul, provision merchant, and they had married on 24 June 1939—ran a café on the North Circular Road for a time. He also wrote a football column for the *Sunday Pictorial*. In 1950 he was one of the first footballers to publish a ghosted autobiography. *Cliff Bastin Remembers* was the first book by the young Brian Glanville, some of whose comments provoked contemporary controversy in football circles. Later Bastin returned to Exeter, where he became landlord of the Horse and Groom pub, from which he retired in 1977. He died in the Royal Devon and Exeter Hospital, Wonford, Exeter, on 3 December 1991, of myelofibrosis and renal failure; he was survived by his wife. TONY MASON

Sources C. Bastin and B. Glanville, *Cliff Bastin remembers* (1950) · *The Times* (6 Dec 1991) · *The Independent* (11 Dec 1991) · S. Studd, *Herbert Chapman: football emperor* (1998) · P. Soar and M. Tyler, *Arsenal, 1886–1986: the official centenary history* (1986) · F. Ollier, *Arsenal: a complete record, 1886–1992* (1992) · J. Harris and T. Hogg, *Arsenal who's who* (1996) · b. cert. · m. cert. · d. cert.
Likenesses photograph, 1936 (with Bob Johns), Hult. Arch. · photograph, repro. in *The Times* · photograph (with Alex James), repro. in *The Independent*

Bastin, (Alfred) Harold (1875–1962), entomologist and photographer, was born at 48 Lower Union Street, Torquay, on 7 July 1875, the son of Richard Bastin (1849–1917), an ironmonger, and his wife, Priscilla Barter (1850–1933), originally from Reading. He had a Quaker upbringing and the family (of two sons and two daughters) moved between Alton and Reading in the decade 1878–88 before finally settling in his mother's home town (although his restless father continued to reside elsewhere for long periods). Schooled in Alton and in Reading, Bastin's interest in insects was developed through visits to the department of entomology at the British Museum (Natural History), London. By 1903 he had established an entomology business in Reading with his younger brother, Leonard (1880–1947). On 4 July 1905 Bastin married, at Altrincham in Cheshire, Ellen Mary (1873–1971), daughter of Alfred Taylor, a clergyman, and a sister of Alfred Edward Taylor (1869–1965), professor of moral philosophy at the universities of St Andrews and Edinburgh. Bastin's brother, Leonard, left Reading around this time, and by 1909 Bastin had moved to 7 Upper Redlands Road. A son and daughter were both born in Reading and for a period of over forty years Bastin made a living from model making, photography, and writing.

Bastin's models illustrated the life history of insects and the damage caused by insect pests and plant diseases, and he developed a technique for reproducing artificial flowers and leaves from wax-filled moulds. He supplied models to various museums, schools, and other institutions, including Reading and Bristol museums, the British Museum (Natural History), Charterhouse School, the

Royal Horticultural Society, and Sutton's Seeds of Reading. A notable example of his skill was the cabinet of economic insects commissioned by Professor F. J. Cole for the department of zoology at the University of Reading (later displayed in the Cole Museum of Zoology). Bastin also became a professional photographer and assembled an extensive commercial negative library covering all aspects of natural history, among which entomology continued to occupy a prime place. His range of subjects also extended to scenes of farming, rural industries, and town and country life in the southern counties of England. His photographs of woodland industries taken before the 1920s are of a remarkable quality and provide a valuable record of trades now extinct in their traditional form.

Bastin employed his photographs to illustrate his books, the products of a writing career of over forty years. His first work, *Insects: their Life-Histories and Habits* (1913) set out the aim he was to follow in all his writing on insects: 'An attempt is made to set forth in simple terms the salient facts on entomology'. This was followed by *British Insects, and How to Know them* (1917), *Introducing British Butterflies* (1937), and three final volumes published in Hutchinson's Nature Library, *Freaks and Marvels of Insect Life* (1954), *Plants without Flowers* (1955), and *Insect Communities* (1956). Several of his books were translated into other European languages, including German, and appeared in American editions; he also contributed to other works.

Bastin died of heart failure on 22 March 1962 at 36 St Catherine's Road, Southbourne and was cremated at Bournemouth crematorium on 27 March. He had always been a retiring man and his death away from his adopted home of Reading, where he had lived for over seventy years, passed virtually unnoticed. Nevertheless, he impressed his contemporaries, and Richard Ford of Yarmouth, Isle of Wight, described him as 'a wonderful naturalist and observer of entomology' (private information). He began his career in an era of widespread popular enthusiasm for the practice of natural history, before entomology became a more specialized pursuit and before the practice of collecting and selling specimens from the wild had lost favour. Bastin's principal achievement was that of a popularizer of natural history through his books, photographs, and models, which ensured that his meticulous craftsmanship and powers of observation were recorded and transmitted to the benefit of others.

JOHN S. CREASEY

Sources J. S. Creasey, 'Harold Bastin of Reading: photographer and entomologist', *Berks and Bucks Countryside*, 19/139 (March 1979), 12–13 • private information (2004) • NHM, Bastin MSS, 1941–4 • City Museum and Art Gallery, Bristol, history files, Bastin MSS, 1912–44, 11, 11a, 1128, 1415, 1535 • General Register Office for England • census returns, 1891 • 'Society of Friends, monthly meetings', 1898, Berks. RO, D/F 2B3/32, 251–2 • *CGPLA Eng. & Wales* (1962) • b. cert. • m. cert. • d. cert.
Archives City Museum and Art Gallery, Bristol, history files, corresp.; reserve collection, models, 11, 11a, 1128, 1415, 1535 • NHM, corresp.; natural history photograph collection • NMG Wales, papers • priv. coll., files, incl. corresp. • RBG Kew, corresp. • Reading Museum Service, reserve collection, models • Topham Picturepoint, Edenbridge, Kent, social history negatives • U. Reading, Cole Museum of Zoology, cabinet of insects
Likenesses photographs, before 1920 (with Leonard Bastin), Topham Picturepoint, Edenbridge, Kent • photograph (in later life), priv. coll.; copy, Rural History Centre, U. Reading • photographs, repro. in J. S. Creasey, 'Photographer and entomologist Harold Bastin', *British Journal of Photography* (12 May 1978), 408–10 • photographs, repro. in Creasey, 'Harold Bastin of Reading'
Wealth at death £4330 19s.: probate, 22 June 1962, *CGPLA Eng. & Wales*

Baston, Philip (*d.* after 1327), Carmelite friar, was born near Nottingham and, like his brother, the poet Robert *Baston, joined the Carmelites there. He studied first at the Carmelite house, Lincoln, where he was ordained deacon on 19 May 1296 and priest on 22 September 1296, and then continued his studies at Oxford. By 1312 he was a member of the king's chapel, and on 18 August 1313 an order was issued for several law texts in the exchequer to be given to him to deliver to the king in Windsor. He was confessor to Edward II by June 1318, and still held that post in 1327, when an order was given to provide him for life with a suitable habit from the royal wardrobe. He was the king's almoner in the years 1319–21. On 1 February 1319, soon after the Carmelites had taken up residence in Beaumont Palace, Oxford, Baston and the prior received royal alms on behalf of the community. Bale claims that Baston was prior of the Carmelite friary at Scarborough at some period, but there is no confirmation of this. He died some time after 1327 and was buried in the Carmelite house, Nottingham. Bale records the titles of two lost works, without incipits, attributing to Baston a collection of letters and the usual sermons. However, the collection of letters was attributed to his brother Robert in John Bale's *Anglorum Heliades* (1536), and to both brothers in Bale's later printed *Catalogus*.   RICHARD COPSEY

Sources J. Bale, BL, MS Harley 3838, fol. 59v • Bale, *Cat.*, 2.45 • Emden, *Oxf.* • B. Zimmerman, 'De Roberto Baston, poeta, eiusque fratre germano Philippo', *Analecta Ordinis Carmelitarum Discalceatorum*, 3 (1928–9), 104–11 • *Commentarii de scriptoribus Britannicis, auctore Joanne Lelando*, ed. A. Hall, 2 (1709), 338 • J. Pits, *Relationum historicarum de rebus Anglicis*, ed. [W. Bishop] (Paris, 1619), 411 • J. Bale, Bodl. Oxf., MS Selden supra 41, fol. 163v

Baston, Robert (*d.* in or before 1348), Carmelite friar and poet, was born near Nottingham, and, like his brother Philip *Baston, joined the Carmelites there. According to Bale he studied in Oxford. His fame as a poet led to his being selected to accompany Edward II to Scotland in 1314, when he was present at the battle of Bannockburn. Evidently Edward hoped that Baston would write a poem commemorating an English triumph but, in the event, Baston was captured by the Scots and forced instead to compose a work recording their victory. This poem has been preserved in chapter 23 of Bower's *Scotichronicon*, with Baston's authorship revealed in the final verse.

> I am a Carmelite, surnamed Baston.
> I grieve that I am left to outlive such carnage.
> If I have sinned by omitting what ought to be recounted,
> Let the gap be filled by others whose pronouncements are
>   free from bias.
> (Bower, 6.375)

Anthony Wood preserves a story that, in the rout after the

battle, Baston assured King Edward that, if he prayed to the Virgin Mary, he would be saved. Edward did so, promising that, if he escaped, he would found a house for the Carmelites in thanksgiving. Following his safe return to England the king gave the Carmelites his mansion of Beaumont in Oxford with an annual subsidy. This story has been discounted by some, but contemporary documents approving the foundation in 1318 specifically refer to 'a vow made by the king when in danger' (*CPR*, 1317–21, 75, 237).

Baston himself was back in England by 7 October 1318, when he was given a licence to hear confessions in the diocese of Lincoln. Bale claims that he became prior of the Carmelite house in Scarborough, which, if true, must have happened shortly after its foundation in 1319. Baston, though, certainly returned to Nottingham later, as his licence to hear confessions in Lincoln diocese was confirmed in September 1335. He died there some time before February 1348.

Baston's reputation as a poet rests on his one surviving work and, in general, comments on its literary quality have been less than complimentary. The poem, in irregular rhymed hexameters (174 lines), is incomplete, although a further 43 lines were discovered in 1904. Nevertheless, it remains valuable as a unique eyewitness account of the battle of Bannockburn, containing such small details as the presence of four German volunteers in the English army, and the revelry in the English camp the night before the battle, which are unrecorded elsewhere. However, Baston's aim is clearly to write a lament rather than a descriptive record: as he says, 'Why should I beat about the bush? What can I sing about so vast a slaughter?' True to his brief he praises the Scottish king, Robert I, who 'heartens the Scottish nobles', 'exhorts and encourages the multitude of his followers', and 'scoffed and jeered at the English and their treaties'. However, Baston's true feelings are perhaps best revealed early in the poem:

> Weeping in my tent, I lament the battles joined
> not knowing (God be my witness!) which king is to blame for them.
> (Bower, 6.366–75)

Although not great poetry, the work is a memorable achievement, given the circumstances of its composition.

Other compositions have been attributed to Baston but, as Rigg has shown, these are, for the most part, poems found in BL, MS Cotton Titus A.xx, many of which could not be by him. Their attribution is due to later marginal notes by John Bale. Two other poems in this collection, on Bannockburn and the English victory at Falkirk in 1298, could be by Baston, but there is no direct evidence of his authorship. A lost collection of letters mentioned by Bale is also doubtful, as these were originally attributed by Bale to Robert's brother Philip, and only later to Robert.

RICHARD COPSEY

Sources W. Bower, *Scotichronicon*, ed. D. E. R. Watt and others, new edn, 9 vols. (1987–98), vol. 6, pp. 366–75, 458–61 • B. Zimmerman, 'De Roberto Baston, poeta, eiusque fratre germano Philippo', *Analecta Ordinis Carmelitarum Discalceatorum*, 3 (1928–9), 104–15, 164–86 • A. G. Rigg, 'Antiquaries and authors: the supposed works of Robert Baston, O. Carm', *Medieval scribes, manuscripts and libraries: essays presented to N. R. Ker*, ed. M. B. Parkes and A. G. Watson (1978), 317–31 • W. D. Macray, 'Robert Baston's poem on the battle of Bannockburn', *EngHR*, 19 (1904), 507–8 • J. Bale, BL, MS Harley 3838, fols. 59–59v • Bale, *Cat.*, 1.369 • Emden, *Oxf.* • *Commentarii de scriptoribus Britannicis, auctore Joanne Lelando*, ed. A. Hall, 2 (1709), 338 • J. Pits, *Relationum historicarum de rebus Anglicis*, ed. [W. Bishop] (Paris, 1619), 399–400 • Tanner, *Bibl. Brit.-Hib.*, 79 • N. Trevet, *Annales sex regum Angliae, 1135–1307*, ed. T. Hog, EHS, 6 (1845), 403

Bastwick, John

Bastwick, John (1595?–1654), religious controversialist and pamphleteer, was born probably in Writtle, near Chelmsford, Essex, fourth child and only son of John Bastwick (*c*.1540–1596), yeoman, and his second wife, Sara Lovet (*c*.1570–1625). His father seems to have been the first Bastwick to have achieved some wealth and status; how he did so is unclear. At his death he had properties in Writtle, Burnham, and North Fambridge, Essex, as well as a profitable ferry across the Crouch River. Five months later, his widow married Robert Cotton, gentleman, of Frating, near Colchester, who reared John and his sister Joan (the only other child to survive infancy) as his own. Bastwick learned swordplay and dancing, and 'gentlemanly deportment'. He wrote, 'I was bred in as great a hatred of Puritans as my tender years were capable of'. In 1611, however, as Robert Cotton lay dying, he appointed his cousin Robert Cotton of West Bergholt, rather than his brother, as his executor. Bastwick claimed this was because his stepfather had come to believe that puritans like his cousin 'were the true servants of the Lord' (Bastwick, *Answer*, 4–5).

Early career Bastwick was sent to study with Richard Rogers, puritan lecturer at Wethersfield, Essex, who was not only 'one of the best Latinists in the kingdom' but also taught him 'all the principles of the true Protestant religion' (Bastwick, *Second Part*, preface, sig. a3v). In 1614 Bastwick went to Emmanuel College, Cambridge. In 1616, on coming of age and acquiring control of his inheritance, he immediately applied to the privy council for a pass to leave the country—'being unwilling to content myself with home comparing of men and domestical experience'—in a search for 'the right way to find blessedness' (Bastwick, *Answer*, 5). He may also have been influenced by the good reputation of continental medical schools. Most of his medical training was probably acquired at Leiden University, where he arrived in January 1617.

Among the English exiles Bastwick met in Leiden were Thomas Brewer, John Robinson, John Dury, and William Ames, but the warmest relationship he formed was with Alexander Leighton, a Scot who was also studying medicine, of whom Bastwick wrote 'his jests and drolleries quite won my heart' (Bastwick, *Flagellum*, 70), although Leighton's religious views were already radical. In late 1621 Bastwick departed for the University of Padua, Italy. 'Many English gentlemen prize the physicians of Padua,' the traveller Fynes Moryson noted, 'but that hinders not ignorant men corruptly to procure the doctor's degree, which … may easily be obtained' (*Shakespeare's Europe: Unpublished Chapters from Fynes Moryson's Itinerary*, ed. C. Hughes, 1903, 433–4). Bastwick was awarded his degree

D. Baſtwick, for writing a Booke againſt Po-
piſh-Biſhops was firſt fined 1000# and Committed Cloſe-priſoner in the Gatehouſe, by the high
Commiſsion. After that for writing of the Party of Miniſters &c, was cenſured in the Starr-
Chamber to be depriued of his practiſe in Phy-
ſick, to looſe both his Eares in the pillorie, was
fined 5000#, baniſhed into the Iſle of Sillyes,
and there Committed to perpetuall cloſe impriſonment, where hee was most cruelly u-
ſed, and no freinds, no not ſo much as his
wife or Children once permitted to ſee him
on pain of impriſonment, as afore ſaid.

John Bastwick (1595?–1654), by Wenceslaus Hollar, 1640s

in January 1622, perhaps on the basis of his Leiden experience.

Bastwick's whereabouts are unknown until 1624: he may have seen military service. In March he re-registered at Leiden, where his first publication appeared. This was *Elenchus religionis papisticae* ('A refutation of the religion of the papists'), intended for young protestant gentlemen travellers whose faith was attacked by Catholic proselytizers. 'How can he esteem or reverence his homeland, who is trained to believe the native religion is to be detested?' (Bastwick, *Elenchus*, 222). Written in Latin, using the formal structure of a university disputation, it was intended for an educated and intellectual audience.

Late in 1624 Bastwick returned to England and visited his sister at Colchester, where he encountered Richard Daniel, a former schoolfellow, now an apothecary, who had fallen on hard times. Bastwick offered to work with him, each recommending the other, a common practice at the time. Daniel wanted to make the arrangement permanent, but Bastwick left for London, 'the queen of cities' (Bastwick, *Flagellum*, 68).

In 1625 Bastwick became an extra-licentiate of the College of Physicians, and in 1627 a full licentiate. In theory all London physicians needed this licence: in practice many unlicensed ones flourished, such as the wealthy Leonard Poe, physician to two kings and many courtiers, whose daughter Susanna (*d*. in or after 1657) [*see below*] had married the unknown John Bastwick by 1626 when their twin girls were born. It is somewhat surprising that Poe consented: perhaps, unqualified himself, he was impressed by a university education.

The Bastwicks settled in Warwick Lane, near St Paul's Cathedral. Bastwick's letters from this period mainly relate to the client–patron relationship. 'Cultivate modesty and humility,' he advised. 'Believe me, there is no great house that will not spew you out, if you wear out your patron's patience' (MS Rawl. D377/14). However, the fourth earl of Dorset is the only person who can be identified with certainty as one of Bastwick's patrons. Bastwick was also seeking intellectual success. In 1627 an expanded version of *Elenchus religionis papisticae* appeared, licensed by Thomas Worrall, the bishop of London's chaplain. Bastwick sent it to theologians and Cambridge heads of colleges, asking for their comments. Although occasionally begged by Daniel the apothecary to return to Colchester, Bastwick always refused: 'I would not leave London' (Bastwick, *Flagellum*, 68).

The reappearance of Alexander Leighton, however, would transform Bastwick's life. By now Leighton had published several unlicensed works. The latest, *Sion's Plea Against the Prelacy*, described Buckingham's murder as an act of God, and criticized the Catholic queen, Henrietta Maria. While this work was at press, Leighton took a post in Utrecht, leaving his wife to sell their house. Just as she had done so, he wrote to say he had changed his mind. Suddenly homeless, she remembered that Leighton had pointed out Bastwick's home. In June 1629 she appeared on his doorstep, asking for shelter for a few days. 'I was happy … to be able to offer an opportunity of kindness … for the sake of a man once familiar and loved', Bastwick wrote.

Bastwick also sent Leighton to Colchester to work with Richard Daniel, but the two fell out. Leighton returned to London and gave Bastwick a copy of *Sion's Plea*. Bastwick was not completely ignorant of his friend's views, but had not realized just how radical he was. 'Forseeing then the danger from the Court … I rebuked his irreverent scribbling and fled his society.' He did more: when Leighton was arrested in February 1630 Bastwick left London and 'sought the security of a hiding place in a rural town [Colchester]' (Bastwick, *Flagellum*, 70–74). Further disaster followed. A quarrel with Dr Poe seems to have led to a complete rupture. When Poe died in 1631, the Bastwicks were cut out of his will.

Bastwick in court: chancery, king's bench, and high commission Bastwick accepted Daniel's offer to house him. However, as Daniel realized that Bastwick intended to return to London as soon as he could, 'gradually he became aggressive … seeking to provoke my wife with insults, my family with injuries'. Bastwick's decision to leave provoked an ominous response from Daniel: '"The removing of your ears is in my power. It is for you as with your friend

Leighton", (for he had now suffered that terrible punishment)' (Bastwick, *Flagellum*, 71). Daniel immediately sued Bastwick through the court of chancery for unpaid rent. One of the questions put to witnesses was 'what was the cause … of his coming from London to Colchester to live with the defendant?' (PRO, C21/D20/15). Clearly it was intended to reveal his connection with Leighton: but Bastwick got the question expunged.

Instantly two more lawsuits were filed, one in king's bench and one in the ecclesiastical court of high commission. A long list of charges was submitted against Bastwick in the latter: however, it is worth noting that *Elenchus* was not mentioned. According to Bastwick, it was claimed that he had helped to produce Leighton's book and had frequented conventicles, but both these charges were dropped, presumably for lack of evidence. Three further charges exemplify the sort of private criticisms which Bastwick had made of the church: that he had affirmed a double-beneficed minister could not be an honest man (a dig at the pluralist Thomas Newcomen, another Colchester enemy); and that he had asserted it was unlawful to bow at the name of Jesus and to kneel at communion. Bastwick admitted that he had private doubts about these ceremonies, but stated firmly that he had always carried them out. 'I carried out the rite itself without hesitation. Indeed, by my example I encouraged hesitant brethren to go forward … that by my example they might escape danger' (Bastwick, *Apologeticus*, 17).

Bastwick was further charged with using the word 'grolls' (a Dutch term meaning 'idiots') of bishops. 'This word … grew upon me during my wanderings … I make use of [it] often against family, friends and neighbours … If however there be sin in this, I beg pardon.' The most serious charges related to his relationship with Leighton. Bastwick's account of these reflects the Elizabethan tradition in which Richard Rogers and others had trained him. 'I liked Leighton once and till now heard of nothing criminal about him: but I rebuked his irreverence and fled his society.' He described *Sion's Plea* as part 'horrible scandal', part 'deserving of praise' (Bastwick, *Apologeticus*, 20–21). He admitted his doubts about certain aspects of the established church, and his friendship with Leighton, but believed that because he had outwardly conformed to the ceremonies, kept his criticisms for the ears of close friends, and distanced himself from Leighton when the latter's extremism became clear, he had committed no offence. 'At dining tables, amongst trusted friends, one may say things not meant for public ears' (ibid., 17). In the climate of the times, this superficial conformity was no longer acceptable (as it would have been fifty years earlier). Indeed, for Laudians it was perhaps as offensive as outright defiance.

On 12 May 1634 the chancery case was dismissed: the judges commented that 'malice' had set the plaintiffs to work, and that it was 'a bill of scandal and vexation' (PRO, C33/165, fol. 539). For the rest of his life, Bastwick repeatedly pointed out that while his enemies were dismissed by one court, they were believed in another: but his own actions made disaster certain. In June a new edition of

Elenchus appeared, with a new appendix written in response to a Catholic critic who had claimed that the early Christian church was 'monarchical' rather than 'aristocratical' in government, and that therefore all bishops were subject to the pope. Bastwick denied the pope's primacy, but also claimed that all bishops were subject to the civil power in their kingdom—an argument again reflecting his upbringing by Elizabethan puritans. As with the previous edition of *Elenchus*, Bastwick dispatched copies to various notables. This time, however, they were confiscated—by order of Thomas Worrall, who had originally licensed *Elenchus*. The publication and distribution of the book was added to the charges against him. 'It was held to be a chief fault in me, which to our forefathers was a chief honour and glory', he wrote (Bastwick, *Apologeticus*, sig. A4). Significantly, he began to abandon his conciliatory approach, refusing to declare himself guilty and throw himself on the court's mercy, as his lawyer begged him. 'I was not conscious to myself of any delinquency … and resolved to die rather than by baseness of submission make myself an offender' (Bastwick, *A More Full Answer*, 5). On 12 February 1635 Bastwick appeared before the high commission, in his own eyes a defender of the king's prerogative and traditional puritanism. To the court he was an accomplice of Leighton, an opponent of episcopacy who refused to admit his guilt and submit to their authority. Its response was ferocious. Bastwick was excommunicated, suspended from the practice of medicine, and fined £1000. He would be held in the Gatehouse Prison, Westminster, until he should recant.

Trial in Star Chamber Unfortunately, Bastwick quarrelled with the keeper of the Gatehouse, Aquila Wykes, notoriously lenient towards Catholics and hostile to puritans. Most prisoners were permitted to take exercise in the courtyard: Bastwick was not, and his visitors were carefully monitored, perhaps because of his publishing activities. An appeal to the earl of Dorset for help appeared as an appendix to yet another edition of *Elenchus*, retitled *Flagellum pontificis et episcoporum Latialium* ('The flail of the Latin pontiff and bishops'). He also wrote an account of his trial, *Apologeticus ad praesules Anglicanos* ('A narrative to the Anglican bishops'). By early 1636, Bastwick was thus openly critical of the Laudian hierarchy, but was little known, because he still wrote in Latin for an élite audience.

In April 1636 plague broke out in London, and in May gaolers were given leave to escort prisoners into the country. Either through spite or oversight, Bastwick was left locked in his cell. In this terrifying situation, he had an experience which he believed was a vision from God. It inspired him to write *The Letany of John Bastwicke*, which took its name from a parody of the litany, 'from bishops, priests and deacons, good God deliver us'. Written in English, peppered with lavatorial humour, it had echoes of the Elizabethan Marprelate tracts, and also foreshadowed the radical religious writings of the civil war. He now believed himself destined to martyrdom—and that this would hasten the second coming. The *Letany* was actually written as a series, of which only four parts survive. Bastwick circulated handwritten copies and gave readings to visitors. One of these was a young apprentice, John Lilburne, who came both for religious instruction and because, according to Bastwick, 'he could neither make a leg with grace, nor put off his hat seemly, until I ... taught him' (Bastwick, *Just Defence*, 11). He asked Bastwick to let him get the *Letany* printed. He managed it, but was betrayed, whipped, and imprisoned.

At the time Lilburne's fate was little noticed. Bastwick, and two companions with much longer histories of opposition, occupied national attention in 1637. Of these, William Prynne, a lawyer, was as opposed to long-haired men as to religious 'innovations'. Imprisoned since 1634, his production of pamphlets continued. Henry Burton, himself a cleric, claimed Anglican bishops were popish agents in his outspoken works. Archbishop Laud decided to silence the three together.

In the Bill of Information, published on 10 March 1637, three works were charged against all three defendants. These were Bastwick's *Apologeticus* (published under his own name over a year previously); *Newes from Ipswiche*, an anonymous work possibly written by Prynne; and *A Divine Tragedy*, another anonymous work almost certainly jointly written by Burton and Prynne, which was probably printed, and definitely circulated, in tandem with the second work. Bastwick was charged individually with the *Letany*, and Burton with *An Apologie of an Appeale*, both works having been published under their authors' names. Prynne had no works charged against him individually. Fifteen other persons were also named in the bill as being involved in 'printing, publishing and circulating various libels', but they do not seem to have actually come to trial. After a trial remarkable for the defendants' outspoken defiance, on 14 June 1637 the Star Chamber judges found all three guilty of seditious libel. They were each to lose their ears after pillorying, to be fined £5000, and to be sentenced to life imprisonment.

The earlopping took place on 30 June in Westminster Palace Yard, in front of a vast and sympathetic crowd. Bastwick's path to the pillory was strewn with flowers, and he bowed gracefully to the applauding audience. All three men spoke eloquently of their joy in martyrdom. When the moment came to lose his ears, Bastwick produced his own scalpel for the deed. The blood spurted out 'so much as his doublet (of white damask) was all bestreamed with it'. 'As I have now lost some of my blood, so am I ready and willing to spill every drop that is in my veins ... for maintaining the truth of God, and the honour of the King', he cried (Prynne, 62–4).

The government had not realized that the journeys of the three to their remote prisons meant that hundreds outside London would see and pity them. Bastwick was taken to Lostwithiel Castle: Susanna smuggled messages in, but their discovery led to his removal to Star Castle in the Isles of Scilly. There he 'lived a living death and a dying life', confined alone in a windowless dungeon, with no books, writing, or visitors. Even gaolers were forbidden to speak to him (Bastwick, *Flagellum*, 1641 edn, preface, 8–9).

The struggle against Independency   In November 1640 the three 'holy Christian martyrs' were recalled from exile by the Long Parliament. Their return was received ecstatically: but although parliament discussed the payment of damages, nothing was decided. Bastwick reprinted *Flagellum pontificis*, with a new preface in which he thanked the 'King, Parliament and People of England' for his freedom. In early 1642, Bastwick volunteered to help train soldiers for parliament, and was sent to Leicester. In July he was captured by the royalists, one of the earliest prisoners taken. He was sent to York Castle, where he was beaten up and partially lost his hearing, then sent to Helmsley, and finally to Knaresborough. John Lilburne, now well known as a radical leader and daring soldier, never forgot Bastwick, and sent him 10s. Bastwick tipped Lilburne's messenger 11s.

In October 1644 Bastwick was finally released and returned to London, where both presbyterians and Independents sought his support. He chose presbyterianism, disappointing many Independents who 'had given him money and assistance when he had suffered under Laud'. Money was a problem: Prynne, Burton, Lilburne, and Bastwick all spent years trying to get parliament to pay them some damages. 'At this day,' Bastwick wrote, 'I have not in the world by some hundreds of pounds, what my father left me' (Bastwick, *Second Part*, 58–62).

In 1645 Bastwick published a massive new work, *Independency not Gods Ordinance*, which depicted Independency as new popery. He was also involved in the tortuous attempts of the presbyterians to discredit leading Independents. Driven by jealous resentment of his former pupil, Bastwick denounced Lilburne, who was arrested, but the charges were plainly false and soon dropped. Bastwick's attempts to justify himself (in *A Just Defence of John Bastwicke*) made matters worse. '[Lilburne's] acquaintance with me ... was the cause that he became so in favour', he wrote crossly, 'and now he is become a very gallant fellow, and hath commenced Lieutenant-Colonel; and who but *John* among the controlleresses of dripping-pannes, the Independent sisters?' (Bastwick, *Just Defence*, 15–16). It was a disappointing year: he also failed to obtain a seat in the new parliament (partly because Lilburne worked to prevent it), and former friends, such as Henry Burton, criticized him in print.

It is significant that Bastwick's next publication was a debate with the Catholic Wat Montagu (*The Church of England a True Church*): appearing at a time when many were discarding the very concept of a single church, it illustrates that Bastwick was out of touch with current issues. An expanded version of *Independency not Gods Ordinance*, under the title *The Utter Routing of the Whole Army of the Independents and Sectaries* (1646), aroused little interest. His last work, *The Storming of the Anabaptists Garrisons* (1647), seems to have gone unnoticed. Perhaps Bastwick could no longer afford printing costs: he repeatedly petitioned parliament for financial assistance, without success. His last years are obscure: the last item in his handwriting is a note, 'Patientia omnia vincit' ('patience conquers all'), dated

1650 (Sloane MS 2035B). In 1651 he was questioned in connection with the 'presbyterian plot', but not charged. His old fellow sufferer William Prynne noted his death on 28 September 1654; his burial, in an unknown grave, took place on 6 October.

Susanna Bastwick [*née* Poe] (*d.* in or after 1657), petitioner and possibly poet, was the third daughter of Dr Leonard Poe (*c.*1570–1631) and his wife, Dionise Boone (*fl.* 1600–1630). Twin girls (Judith and Dionise) were born to the Bastwicks in 1626. A son, John the elder, was born in 1633; John the younger in 1636; and Susanna, the last child, after her parents' reunion in 1640. Susanna's dedication to her husband was total: she broke off contact with her family when Bastwick quarrelled with her father; she lived with him in the Gatehouse Prison; and she accompanied him to the scaffold in 1637. Before the earlopping she kissed each ear; afterwards, she picked them up and put them in her bosom, an act which aroused the enthusiasm of Thomas Carlyle: 'Brave Dame Bastwick, worthy to be a mother of men!' (T. Carlyle, *Historical Sketches of Notable Persons and Events in the Reigns of James I and Charles I*, 1898, 273). Whenever Bastwick was in prison, she campaigned tirelessly for his relief. John Lilburne also affectionately remembered her visiting him in gaol. She published several petitions she made to parliament, and may also have been the author of three admiring poems, signed S. B., appended to Bastwick's *Independency not God's Ordinance* (1646).

> To set forth all thy parts, learning and skill
> It were a work too hard for Homer's quill

one began. A work appeared in 1647, by B. S., solely to praise Bastwick: its author had 'known him for more than 20 years' and 'had more experience of his conversation than anyone in England' (B. S., 8). After Bastwick's death Susanna petitioned Cromwell for aid, describing herself as 'a woman of sorrows' (S. Bastwick), and in 1657 Irish lands were settled on her and her children. However, in 1661 they were confiscated by Charles II. Her death date is unknown.   FRANCES CONDICK

Sources F. M. Condick, 'The life and works of Dr John Bastwick, 1595–1654', PhD diss., U. Lond., 1983 · J. Bastwick, *The answer … to the exceptions made against his 'Letany'* (1637) · J. Bastwick, *The second part of that book … called 'Independency not Gods ordinance'* (1646) · J. Bastwick, *Flagellum pontificis et episcoporum Latialium* (1635); preface (1641) · J. Bastwick, *The utter routing of the whole army of Independents and sectaries* (1646) · J. Bastwick, *Apologeticus ad praesules Anglicanos* (1636) · J. Bastwick, *The letany of John Bastwicke* (1637) · J. Bastwick, *A just defence of John Bastwicke* (1645) · *State trials*, 3.711–55 · *A brief relation of certain speciall and most materiall passages … at the censure of … Dr Bastwicke, Mr Burton and Mr Prynne* (1638) · W. Prynne, *A new discovery of the prelates tyranny* (1641) · P. Gregg, *Free-born John: a biography of John Lilburne* (1961) · S. Bastwick, *The remonstrance of Susanna Bastwicke* (1654) · Bodl. Oxf., MS Tanner 299; 72/232; 72/237, fols. 143v–146v · Bodl. Oxf., MS Rawl. C. 827; D. 377/14 · E. Bewlay, *The family of Poe or Pöe* (1906) · B. S., *Innocency cleared, true worth predicated … in the case of Dr. Bastwicke* (1646) · chancery suit: *Daniel v. Bastwick*, PRO, C21/D20/15; C2/CHAS 1/D6/5; C33/163, fol. 738; C33/165, fols. 36, 38, 114, 539 · records of trial in high commission, PRO, SP 16/261, fols. 81b, 87, 97, 178–178v; SP 16/276/42; SP 16/277/71; SP 16/282/22 · Essex RO, Chelmsford, D/AER/4/184; D/ABW/6/50, 3/560; D/DU/253/2–12; DP/206/1/1, 59/1/1;

D/DP/M549 · J. Bastwick, *A more full answer of John Bastwick … to follow the 'Letany' as the fourth part of it* (1637) · *JHC*, 7–8 (1651–67) · BL, Sloane MSS 2035B, 2131 · BL, Stowe MS 190 · 11 Aug 1642, 16 March 1646, HLRO, main papers collection

Archives BL, MS versions of letter to fourth earl of Dorset describing events in Colchester and reappearance of Leighton, Sloane MS 2131 · BL, Stowe MS 190 · BL, Sloane MS 2035B · BL, Star Chamber sentence and speech from the pillory, Add. MS 5540 · Bodl. Oxf., only surviving copy letter-book to Sir Roger Manners, Isaac Basire, Thomas Goad, and anonymous recipients, MS Rawl. D. 377 · Bodl. Oxf., MS Rawl. C. 827 · Bodl. Oxf., MS Tanner 299, 72/232; 72/237 · Essex RO, Chelmsford, D/AER/4/184; D/ABW/6/50, 3/560; D/DU/253/2–12; DP/206/1/1, 59/1/1; D/DP/M549 · HLRO, main papers, 11 Aug 1642, 16 March 1646 · PRO, C21/D20/15; C2/CHAS 1/D6/5; C33/163; C33/165; PROB 11/116/7; 159/37; SP 16/261; SP 16/276/42; SP 16/277/71; SP 16/282/22; SP 18/100/36; SP 18/97/78; SP 18/100/36; SP 18/15

Likenesses W. Hollar, engraving, 1640–49, BM, NPG [*see illus.*] · print, after 1642, CUL, Add. MS 4139 · T. Cross, line engraving, BM, NPG; repro. in Bastwick, *Utter routing*, frontispiece · line engraving, BM, NPG; repro. in Pryne, *New discovery*

Wealth at death lands worth at least £400 at his death, plus other items, perhaps the 'jewels, plate, ready money' inherited from his father, together with earnings made as physician

Bastwick, Susanna (*d.* in or after **1657**). *See under* Bastwick, John (1595?–1654).

Batchelor, George Keith (1920–2000), fluid dynamicist, was born on 8 March 1920 in Melbourne, Australia, the elder child of George Conybere Batchelor (*b.* 1897), an electrician and warehouseman, and Ivy Constance Berneye (1899–1943). He had one sister, Doris Ivy (*b.* 1928), and a stepsister Anne, from the second marriage of his father in 1946. Batchelor's great-grandfather David Scott Batchelor had emigrated from Broughty Ferry, Scotland, in 1852 to work on the construction of the Catholic cathedral in Melbourne. His grandfather George Batchelor was a wholesale distributor of books and magazines.

The Batchelor family settled in 1929 at 107 Eglinton Street, Moonee Ponds, in the northern suburbs of Melbourne, where George lived throughout his teenage and university years until his departure for England in 1945. He attended Moonee Ponds West state school (1929–30), Essendon high school (1931–4), and Melbourne high school (1935–6). He developed an early love of physics and mathematics, and a fierce ambition to succeed. His father, recognizing his son's talents, was prepared to make the necessary financial sacrifices to support his subsequent university career; with the additional aid of prizes and scholarships, Batchelor was able to study physics and mathematics at Melbourne University (1937–40). He was then drawn to work in aerodynamics at the Council for Scientific and Industrial Research's division of aeronautics (later the Aeronautical Research Laboratory) in Melbourne, as a result of which he gained his MSc degree in 1941.

Batchelor's aim had for some time been to travel to England on graduation to pursue research for a PhD. During the Second World War this was impossible, and he therefore remained at the division of aeronautics in Melbourne, working on practical problems in aerodynamics related to the war effort. His interest in fundamental problems of fluid dynamics developed during these years. In particular, he recognized the phenomenon of turbulence as the greatest challenge in fluid dynamics, and resolved to devote his energies to this field of research as soon as the war ended. He wrote to Geoffrey Ingram Taylor, the great British authority on turbulence, who agreed to take him on as a research student.

On 27 January 1944 Batchelor married Wilma Maud Rätz (1918–1997), who had trained as a social worker at the University of Melbourne. In January 1945, the end of the war being then in sight, he and Wilma embarked for England on a cargo ship, the *Umgeni*, on a voyage that lasted ten weeks, travelling via New Zealand, the Panama Canal, Jamaica, and New York and then in convoy across the Atlantic. On arrival in Cambridge, Batchelor settled immediately to work on turbulence as a research student at Trinity College and in close partnership with A. A. Townsend, a fellow Australian based at the Cavendish laboratory, skilled in the experimental techniques required for the study of wind-tunnel turbulence. Taylor was himself engaged on other problems, and was evidently happy to give Batchelor and Townsend free rein in their research.

Batchelor rapidly made his mark in the subject through his brilliant interpretation of the papers of the great Soviet mathematician A. N. Kolmogorov. Batchelor presented his critique of this work, and of parallel lines of enquiry by Onsager, Heisenberg, and von Weizsäcker, at the sixth International Congress for Applied Mechanics held in Paris in 1946; this was his début on the international scientific stage, and marked him as a rising star of the subject. Over the next fifteen years he published a succession of profound studies of turbulence and its applications not only to aerodynamics, but also to chemical engineering, the dynamics of ocean and atmosphere, and the magneto-hydrodynamics of interstellar gas clouds.

In 1947 Batchelor became a fellow of Trinity College; he resisted the temptation to become deeply involved in college teaching, jealously guarding his time for research and for the development of a research group of outstanding young fluid dynamicists. He and Wilma designed their own house, Cobbers, in Conduit Head Road, Cambridge, and here raised a family of three daughters, Adrienne (*b.* 1947), Clare (*b.* 1950), and Bryony (*b.* 1953).

Batchelor's monograph *The Theory of Homogeneous Turbulence* (1953; repr. 1960, 1970) provided the definitive account of the subject as then understood, and was for several decades an indispensable reference work. On the basis of his research in turbulence, Batchelor was elected a fellow of the Royal Society in 1957. In the previous year he had founded the *Journal of Fluid Mechanics*, which soon established itself under his firm editorship as the leading international medium of publication of papers in all aspects of fluid mechanics, theoretical and experimental.

By this time Batchelor was firmly established as a lecturer in the mathematics faculty in Cambridge. He recognized the need for a more coherent framework for research activity than was provided by the Cambridge colleges, and was instrumental in establishing in 1959 the department of applied mathematics and theoretical physics, which initially occupied rooms in the new museums site but which in 1964 moved to buildings in Silver Street vacated by Cambridge University Press. Batchelor was appointed head of department in 1959, a position for which he was so naturally inclined and qualified that he held it until his retirement in 1983. This tenure was challenged by Professor Fred Hoyle in 1964, but Batchelor secured a majority in a vote within the department which led to his reappointment as head and to Hoyle's dramatic, not to say tempestuous, departure from the department to found the new institute of theoretical astronomy on Madingley Road. Batchelor had been promoted to a readership in 1959, and was elected to the newly founded professorship of applied mathematics in 1964.

Batchelor's *Introduction to Fluid Dynamics* (1967), a textbook of great depth and authority, rapidly became the standard text for advanced university courses. The book is characterized both by its exceptional thoroughness and lucidity, and by the emphasis that Batchelor places on the physical interpretation of mathematical results, important for the development of physical intuition as a vital ingredient of any attack on problems involving complex physical processes.

In the course of writing this book Batchelor recognized that the techniques of turbulence theory could equally be applied to problems involving the dynamics of fluids in which small particles, drops, or bubbles are suspended. He developed these ideas in a powerful series of papers in the early 1970s, and coined the term 'microhydrodynamics' to describe this new field of study, which was largely created by his efforts and by those of the new group of research students and senior visitors drawn to work with him in this area.

Batchelor did everything he could to develop links with scientists in the former Soviet Union and eastern Europe throughout the 1960s and 1970s, when travel and exchanges were still severely restricted. He provided great moral support for colleagues in Poland, and was a regular participant at the biennial meetings in fluid mechanics held during these years in Poland, one of the few locations where fluid dynamicists from East and West could meet for free discussion of scientific problems. Perceiving a need for more active European co-operation in scientific research, he helped to establish in 1964 the European Mechanics Committee (later renamed the European Society for Mechanics), which he chaired until 1987. This committee was responsible for stimulating the great series of Euromech colloquia, which were run with an informality of style and an economy of resource that Batchelor was always at great pains to preserve.

Batchelor set little store by honours, yet received many: he was elected to foreign membership of the academies of Sweden, France, Poland, USA, and Australia, the land of his birth, and he won several medals and prizes. It was perhaps the G. I. Taylor medal of the American Society of Engineering Science, awarded in 1997, that he cherished most, for he held his mentor in deep esteem; he edited the four volumes of Taylor's *Collected Papers* (1958–1971), and wrote his biography, *The Life and Legacy of G. I. Taylor* (1997). Batchelor himself devoted his life to promoting the great Cambridge tradition of fundamental research in fluid mechanics of which Taylor had been a prime exemplar.

Batchelor was a man of intense vision, and of strongly held views that were frequently orthogonal to accepted wisdom. In his major initiatives, he faced considerable initial opposition, but his record as founder editor of the *Journal of Fluid Mechanics*, as founding head of the University of Cambridge department of applied mathematics and theoretical physics, and as co-founder of Euromech speaks for itself, and firmly establishes him as a leading figure of twentieth-century science. A man of meticulous and painstaking standards, he was an unfailing source of support and sound advice for his many research students over four decades. Batchelor suffered symptoms of Parkinson's disease from about 1995 onwards, and the sudden death of his wife, Wilma, came as a cruel blow in 1997. He moved into rooms in Trinity College in 1999 with a view to writing his memoirs, but his health continued to decline, and he died at Midfield Lodge Nursing Home, Cambridge Road, Oakington, Cambridge, on 30 March 2000, shortly after his eightieth birthday. He was cremated at Cambridge crematorium on 10 April 2000.   H. K. MOFFATT

Sources H. K. Moffatt, 'G. K. Batchelor and the homogenisation of turbulence', *Annual Review of Fluid Dynamics*, 34 (2002), 19–35 • H. K. Moffatt, memorial address, Trinity College, Cambridge, 4 July 2000, *Annual Record, Trinity College, Cambridge* (2000) • G. Batchelor, 'Research as a life style', *Applied Mechanics Review*, 50/8 (Aug 1997) • personal knowledge (2004) • private information (2004) • *The Times* (12 April 2000) • *Daily Telegraph* (18 April 2000) • T. J. Pedley, *The Guardian* (12 April 2000) • J. R. C. Hout, *The Independent* (17 April 2000) • d. cert.
Archives RS | U. Glas., Archives and Business Records Centre, corresp. with Sir E. C. Ballard
Likenesses R. Shepherd, oils, 1984, U. Cam., department of applied mathematics and theoretical physics

Batchelor, Joy Ethel (1914–1991). *See under* Halas, John (1912–1995).

Batchelor, Thomas (1775–1838), farmer and writer on language, was born on 25 September 1775 at Marston Moretaine, Bedfordshire, the fifth child of Joseph Batchelor (1741–1804) and Ann Brandon (d. 1792), farmers. He was baptized in 1785 at Ampthill where, from the age of ten to thirteen, he went to school. At this time, spelling book fables were the only texts he could read with any real sense of enjoyment, his particular favourite being *Robinson Crusoe*. After he left school, Quarle's *Emblems* became his favourite, and this, in conjunction with Isaac Watts's hymns, nourished his interest in rhyme. These were subsequently complemented by *Paradise Lost*, Edward Young's *Night Thoughts*, and Daniel Fenning's *The Royal English Dictionary, or, A Treasury of the English Language* (1761).

In 1792 the family moved to Boughton End, half a mile south of Lidlington, where they were tenant farmers of the duke of Bedford. Although Batchelor initially had difficulty in reading without the help of a dictionary, by the age of nineteen he had written about 1500 lines of verse

mainly dealing with local news. He continued to compose short pieces while working in the fields, and one of his poems was published in the *Monthly Mirror* in 1801. A journey through his native village of Marston in 1799 provided material and the inspiration for his *Village Scenes: the Progress of Agriculture, and other Poems* which was eventually published in 1804, the year of his father's death. The draft with its numerous corrections was eventually deposited in Bedfordshire Record Office.

In conjunction with his brothers Batchelor continued to run the farm, but his precarious financial position compelled him to look for other forms of income. In 1806, while employed by the board of agriculture, he embarked on an extensive survey of his native county. His *General View of the Agriculture of the County of Bedford*, one of a series edited by Arthur Young, was published two years later. On 6 August 1807 he married Elizabeth Franklin; their only child, Elizabeth, was born in 1809. The same year his texts *An Orthoepical Analysis of the English Language* and *An Orthoepical Analysis of the Dialect of Bedfordshire* were published in one volume. The former focused on explaining the provincial variations in pronouncing various words in different languages and dialects. Batchelor invented an orthoepical alphabet of his own consisting of thirty characters all designated by new names. One of the key aims of the latter was to provide a means of 'explaining the diversity of dialect among civilised nations' (Zettersten, xi). Batchelor's interest in orthography also encompassed several other fields of linguistics but principally phonetics and phonology. His research into dialects led him to study vocabulary and syntax, and he was responsible for pioneering a detailed investigation of the Bedfordshire dialect.

The long-term aim of Batchelor's research was to enhance the quality of pronunciation in the provincial schools of Bedfordshire. Shortly after its publication, however, his work was criticized in the *Monthly Review* (63, 1810) and, following the bankruptcy of his publishers in the same year, his interest in the topic virtually ceased. According to Zettersten, Batchelor occupies a distinguished place in the history of English phonology, being the first scholar to appreciate the dipthongizations of two of the most significant sound changes in the English language. His area of research remained virtually untouched until the completion of D. H. Shaw's PhD thesis in the 1960s and the publication of the first volumes of the *Surveys of English Dialects* (Zettersten, x).

After 1810 Batchelor devoted his energies to devising numerous series of shorthand based on the phonetic principle. His interest in this topic was prompted by Thomas Gurney, brother of his grandmother, who had been appointed the first shorthand writer to the House of Commons in the 1750s. While Batchelor's efforts in this sphere proved too cumbersome to be used commercially, the subsequent transcription of his manuscripts provides a valuable insight into the language used by the contemporary middle class in Batchelor's locality.

After 1809 Batchelor focused primarily on agricultural

interests and was commissioned by the board of agriculture to undertake a survey of Dorset, a task which he finished in the following year. Much to his annoyance, however, it was published in 1814 under the name of William Stevenson, who had revised Batchelor's work and incorporated some additional material. In addition to his farming activities he was a prolific agricultural writer of articles on a wide variety of rural issues. Many of his contributions were published in the *Farmers' Journal* under the name of Bedfordshire. It is also highly likely that he was the editor of the Bedfordshire *Monthly Review* after 1823. He also invented the lever drill (an improvement to the seed drill) which was of limited commercial success.

Batchelor died at Lidlington on 23 February 1838 and was buried alongside his wife and other relatives in the old graveyard near the church of St Margaret, which rapidly fell into disuse and was pulled down (*VCH*, 3.307). Despite his lowly social position, living an isolated life in a country village, and being almost completely self-educated, Batchelor achieved a modest level of distinction in linguistics, agriculture, and poetry which was only recognized after his death. He was a perceptive observer who did not accept the evidence of other orthoepists in an uncritical way. Batchelor was an enterprising and enthusiastic pioneer whose potential had been inhibited by family, farming, and financial troubles.   JOHN MARTIN

Sources A. Zettersten, *A critical facsimile edition of Thomas Batchelor* (1974), pt 1 · Beds. & Luton ARS, Batchelor papers · D. H. Shaw, 'A comparative study (descriptive and historical) of the dialect of Bedfordshire, based upon a survey conducted in the widely spread areas of the county', PhD diss., King's Lond., 1968 · 'review', *Monthly Review*, new ser., 63 (1810), 331–2 · T. Batchelor, *General view of the agriculture of the county of Bedford* (1808) · *VCH Bedfordshire*, 3.307 · N. E. Agar, *The Bedfordshire farm worker in the nineteenth century*, Bedfordshire Historical RS, 60 (1981) · *A bibliographical dictionary of the living authors of Great Britain and Ireland* (1816) · J. Dugdale, *British traveller* (1819) · A. F. Cirket, 'Thomas Batchelor', *Bedfordshire Magazine*, 15 (1975–7), 45–55
Archives Beds. & Luton ARS, papers
Wealth at death bequeathed all Galvanic equipment and relevant books to nephew: Cirket, 'Thomas Batchelor', 54–5

Bate, Charles Spence (1819–1889), dental surgeon and zoologist, was born on 16 March 1819 at Trenick House, in the parish of St Clement near Truro, Cornwall, the eldest son of Charles Bate (1789–1872), a Truro dentist, and his wife, Harriet Spence (1788–1879). After his education at Truro grammar school (1829–37), Bate spent two years in the surgery of Mr Blewett, before training in dentistry under his father's instruction. When qualified, he established himself at Swansea in 1841. On 17 June 1847 at Little Hempston church near Totnes he married Emily Amelia (*d*. 4 April 1884), daughter of John Hele, and sister of the Revd Henry Hele, the rector there; they had two sons and one daughter. In 1851 Bate moved to 8 Mulgrave Place, Lockyer Street, Plymouth, where he succeeded to his father's dental practice. He rose to be the leading member of the profession outside London, receiving the licence in dental surgery of the Royal College of Surgeons in 1860. He was elected a member of the Odontological Society in 1856, and acted as its vice-president from 1860 to 1862. In

1885 he became the first provincial dentist to fill the office of president of that society. Furthermore, some four years earlier, he served as vice-president to the dental section of the international medical congress in London.

In 1879 Bate founded the Western Counties Dental Association (WCDA), and was elected its first president. At the Bath meeting of the British Dental Association (BDA) on 2 August 1880, Bate proposed that the WCDA should be 'amalgamated as a branch of the British Dental Association'. After some deliberation his proposal was accepted and, early in 1881, the Western Counties became the second branch of the British Dental Association. In 1883 Bate served as president of the BDA. During July of the same year, he gave the presidential address at the third annual meeting of the BDA (in Plymouth), where he presented *A Review of the Scientific Progress of Dental Surgery from 1771 to 1883*. He also contributed many papers on dentistry to the *British Journal of Dental Science*, the *Transactions of the Odontological Society*, and the *Medical Gazette*. His work *The Pathology of Dental Caries* was published in 1864.

While at Swansea, Bate had made the acquaintance of many scientific students, and took up the study of natural history. On the occasion of the British Association (BA) visit to Swansea in 1848, he became a member of the society and during the 1869 meeting (in Exeter), acted as vice-president of the biological section. He played an important role in bringing the 1877 BA meeting (of which he was vice-president) to Plymouth.

Bate was elected a member of the Plymouth Institution in 1852, was a member of the council from 1853 to 1883, served as secretary from 1854 to 1860, and acted as president in 1861–2 and 1869–70. He was a curator of the museum and the editor of the *Transactions* of the society from 1869 to 1883, and in nearly every year from 1853 to 1882 he lectured before its members.

Bate was also a founder of the Devonshire Association, and senior general secretary in 1862 and president in 1863. He contributed many papers to its *Transactions*, especially on the antiquities of Dartmoor—a district very familiar to him. About 1875 he published *On some Roman-British Remains found near Plymouth*.

Bate is known to have corresponded with a number of contemporary scientists including the zoologist the Revd George Gordon, and the naturalist Charles Darwin (with whom he exchanged a range of material, information, and ideas). In 1856, a correspondence was also struck up between Bate and the naturalist Thomas Edward (1814–1886), who was 'engaged in collecting marine objects along the sea-coast of Banff' (Smiles). Between 1861 and 1865, Bate received 'multitudes of bottles' from Edward, which contained specimens. Of the numerous specimens described in *A History of the British Sessile-Eyed Crustacea* (2 vols., 1863–8), by Bate and John Obadiah Westwood, Edward provided 127 samples from the Moray Firth. Of these samples, 21 were new species.

Bate drew up a *Catalogue of the specimens of the amphipodous Crustacea in the collection at the British Museum* (1862) for the trustees of the museum. He also examined the typical specimens at the Jardin des Plantes in Paris, at the Royal College of Surgeons, and in many private collections, in order to ensure accuracy in the latter work. In 1888 his *Report on the Crustacea Macrura Dredged by HMS Challenger during the Years 1873 and 1876* (vol. 24) was published. This work took over ten years to complete, and included the examination of about 2000 specimens. Elected fellow of the Linnean Society in 1854, Bate also made contributions both to the second volume of the society's *Proceedings*, and to the third volume (zoology) of the *Journal*, but afterwards resigned from the society. On 6 June 1861 he was elected a fellow of the Royal Society.

Bate partly withdrew from practice as a dentist about 1887; on 8 September that year, at Upper Norwood, Surrey, he married his second wife, Eugenie, daughter of General Charles Payne. On 9 July 1889, he was seized with illness at his house in Lockyer Street, Plymouth. He died as a result of cancer on 29 July 1889 at his other home, The Rock, South Brent, Devon, and was buried (near his first wife) in Plymouth cemetery.   YOLANDA FOOTE

Sources Boase & Courtney, *Bibl. Corn.*, 1.15–17, 3.1056–7 • G. C. Boase, *Collectanea Cornubiensia: a collection of biographical and topographical notes relating to the county of Cornwall* (1890), 57, 846, 1467 • *Western Morning News* (30 July 1889), 5 • *Western Morning News* (1 Aug 1889), 5 • *Report and Transactions of the Devonshire Association*, 21 (1889), 60–64 • *Dental Record* (1889), 428 • S. Smiles, *Life of a Scotch naturalist: Thomas Edward* (1876) • *The advance of the dental profession: a centenary history, 1880–1980*, British Dental Association (privately printed, London, 1979) • L. C. Sanders, *Celebrities of the century: being a dictionary of men and women of the nineteenth century* (1887) • Z. Cope, *The Royal College of Surgeons of England: a history* (1959) • F. Burkhardt and S. Smith, eds., *A calendar of the correspondence of Charles Darwin, 1821–1882* (1985) • *DNB* • m. certs. • d. cert.
Archives NHM, papers • RCS Eng., notebooks | CUL, letters to Charles Darwin • NHM, letters to Albert Gunther relating to zoological record • Oxf. U. Mus. NH, corresp. with J. O. Westwood
Wealth at death £4668 9s. 2d.: probate, 28 Oct 1889, *CGPLA Eng. & Wales*

Bate, Dorothea Minola Alice (1878–1951), palaeontologist, was born on 8 November 1878 at Napier House, Spilman Street, Carmarthen, the younger of two daughters and second child in the family of three of Henry Reginald Bate (d. 1921), a police superintendent and honorary army major, and Elizabeth Fraser Whitehill (d. 1929). Her education, she was heard to remark, was only briefly interrupted by school. She seems to have acquired her love of natural history from her childhood in the Carmarthen countryside. With very little formal education of any description, her obituaries recount how, at the age of seventeen, she arrived at the Natural History Museum in South Kensington and talked her way into a job sorting bird skins in the bird room at a time when there were no women employed by the museum. It was here and in the field that she learned ornithology and anatomy and, as her interests in fossil mammals and birds grew, palaeontology and geology.

Dorothea Bate was a woman of great charm and energy and over the next fifty years she became one of the outstanding personalities and scientists in the museum. For much of that time she was a volunteer, an unofficial scientific worker, paid piece-work according to the number of fossils she prepared, and often having to rely on public

grants and the sale of her own fossils to fund her explorations abroad. Her maxims were long remembered in the Natural History Museum: remain very civil to people whom you do not like, never refuse a letter of introduction, and the Lord helps those who help themselves! A portrait of Dorothea Bate by her sister shows an authoritative looking young woman, dark hair swept up, wearing a gown of black with white lace trim and a large pink rose pinned to her splendid bosom. Her face is tilted up, the gaze direct, the chin expressing utter determination.

In 1901 Dorothea Bate published in the *Geological Magazine* her first scientific paper: 'A short account of a bone cave in the Carboniferous limestone of the Wye valley', in which she discussed her discovery of fossil bones of small mammals from the Pleistocene period. Her writing already showed her characteristic lucidity and command of her subject, and the piece also recorded her considerable physical courage: the cave discussed was half-way up a cliff face and so low inside that she was forced to crawl about it on hands and knees.

Even before her first article appeared, Dorothea Bate had left England to explore (on her own) bone caves in Cyprus which until then had not been systematically searched. She discovered twelve ossiferous cave deposits, five at Cape Pyla and seven on the southern slopes of the Kyrenia hills. She found first, in considerable quantity, fossil bones of dwarf hippopotami (*H. minutus*), but she was convinced there was a second 'beast'. In a letter of 4 February 1902 she desperately—and successfully—pleaded with the museum to secure her a grant from the Royal Society to enable her to continue her excavations. What she then found in a single cave deposit in the Kyrenia hills was her second beast. It was in fact a new species of dwarf elephant which she named *Elephas cypriotes*. She described these important finds in detailed papers which were subsequently presented to the Royal Society.

Dorothea Bate was in Cyprus for eighteen months, staying with the family of Clarence Wodehouse, commissioner for the district of Papho. There she led a life of contrast. One day she might be attending a ball at Government House, playing croquet and tennis, and taking tea with other members of the British community, the next she could be sleeping rough in a derelict shepherd's hut while out on a dig and being bitten to distraction by fleas. She travelled in remote areas, sometimes accompanied by only a guide and a man to dig, sometimes quite alone. On 21 November 1902 she wrote in her work diary, 'When I got back this evening heard that the old abbot of Chrysostomo had been murdered at 9am this morning—in the hummocks between Miamilia and the monastery—where I pass nearly every day' (Bate, Cyprus work diary, vol. 3). The entry for the following day is a laconic 'Did not like to go to Chrysostomo today' (ibid.).

Bate also spent her time on the island observing and collecting mammals and birds, writing and publishing papers on her return. She left Cyprus in November 1902 when the Royal Society grant ran out, travelling deck class to economize, and was rescued from a night among sheep and pigs only by the kindness of the chief officer, who gave her his cabin. Her passion for mammalian palaeontology later took her to Crete, the Balearic Islands (where she discovered *Myotragus*, a unique species of antelope), Corsica, Sardinia, Malta, and Palestine, publishing numerous reports on their Pleistocene faunas. In the 1920s she was first consulted by the archaeologist Professor Dorothy Garrod and later joined her excavations in Palestine at Mount Carmel, publishing in 1937 her classic work, *The Stone Age of Mount Carmel*, volume 1, part 2: *Palaeontology, the Fossil Fauna of the Wady el-Mughara Caves*.

Dorothea Bate's interests extended from fossil ostriches in China, on which she collaborated with Percy R. Lowe, to the fossil fauna of the Sudan. Her unique breadth and depth of knowledge led to an almost insurmountable workload, for it was said that if sufficient quantities of fossil bones were sent to her she could identify, date, and source them, and tell the enquirer about the climate and environment as well. That was the heart of her approach. Her recognition of the importance of these studies made her a pioneer of the science of archaeozoology. Among the many archaeologists and anthropologists who found her expertise indispensable were John Desmond Clark, Gertrude Caton Thomson, Louis Leakey, and Charles McBurney. In 1940 she was awarded the Wollaston fund of the Geological Society for her work on mammalian palaeontology and made a fellow of the society.

In the early 1940s Dorothea Bate was transferred to the Natural History Museum's zoological branch at Tring in Hertfordshire and in 1948, at the age of sixty-nine, she was taken on to the permanent staff of the museum and appointed officer-in-charge at Tring (despite an official retirement age for staff of sixty). Her workload by now was such that she knew there was no longer time to do all she wanted, and her health was not good. Lying on her desk after she had left it for the last time was a scrap of paper headed 'Papers to write', the final one of which was to have been 'on Pleistocene Mammals of the Mediterranean Islands' which she had discovered so many years ago. In the margin by this heading she had written simply 'Swan Song'. She suffered from cancer but died on 13 January 1951 at 31 Ailsa Road, Essex, Westcliff-on-Sea, of a coronary thrombosis. She was a Christian Scientist and her wish was to be cremated. KAROLYN SHINDLER

Sources W. N. Edwards, *Quarterly Journal of the Geological Society of London*, 106 (1950), lvi–lviii · *The Times* (23 Jan 1951) · D. Bate, 'Cyprus work diary', 1901–2, vols. 1–3, NHM, earth sciences library, palaeontology MSS · D. M. A. Bate, 'Preliminary note on the discovery of a pigmy elephant in the Pleistocene of Cyprus', *PRS*, 71 (1902–3), 498–501 · D. M. A. Bate, 'Further note on the remains of *Elephas cypriotes* from a cave-deposit in Cyprus', *PTRS*, 197B (1905), 347–60 · geology department account book, NHM, archives, DF 102/9 · minutes of trustees of the British Museum (natural history), 1934–51, NHM, archives, DF 900 · D. M. A. Bate, 'A short account of a bone cave in the Carboniferous limestone of the Wye valley', *Geological Magazine*, new ser., 4th decade, 8 (1901), 101–6 · D. M. A. Bate to Henry Woodward, 4 Feb 1902, NHM, archives, DF 100/34/77 · letters from Dorothy Garrod to Dorothea Bate from 1926, NHM, archives, DF 100/120 · D. A. E. Garrod and D. M. A. Bate, *The Stone Age of Mount Carmel*, 1 (1937) · *Quarterly Journal of the Geological Society of London*, 96 (1940), lvi–lvii · memorandum to Miss D. M. A. Bate from T. Woodisse, 25 Aug 1948, NHM, archives, zoological museum at Tring file, DF 1004 · D. M. A. Bate, MS notes, Syria and Palestine, NHM, earth sciences library · private information (2004) · b. cert. · b. cert. [Thomas Bate] · d. cert. · church history, First Church of Christ, Scientist, Boston, Massachusetts

Archives NHM, archives, corresp. and museum administrative papers · NHM, earth sciences library

Likenesses L. Luddington, portrait, NHM, earth sciences library, palaeontology MSS · photographs, NHM, earth sciences library, palaeontology MSS

Wealth at death £15,369 6s. 1d.: probate, 5 April 1951, *CGPLA Eng. & Wales*

Bate, George [*pseud.* Theodorus Veridicus] (1608–1668), physician and author, was born in Maids Moreton, Buckinghamshire, in 1608, the son of John Bate of Burton. On 20 February 1624, aged fifteen, he matriculated at New College, Oxford, where he was one of the college clerks. Migrating to Queen's College and then to St Edmund's, Bate graduated BA in 1626 and MA and BA in 1629, the latter giving him licence to practise around Oxford, and DM in 1637. Early observers may have labelled him a puritan, but when Charles I established the court in Oxford Bate became a member of the royal party, and was made physician to the king.

Settling in London by 1639 Bate became a fellow of the College of Physicians in 1640 and served as censor in 1645, 1646, and 1648, and was named an elect in 1657. In 1656 he was part of the board of physicians which recommended the establishment of college of physicians in Edinburgh. However, Bate is best known for his published defence of Charles I in his confrontation with parliament. *The Regall Apology, or, The Declaration of the Commons*, written in English, was first published in Paris and London in 1648. Using the pseudonym Theodorus Veridicus, Bate turned his original account into an expanded Latin work, *Elenchus motuum nuperorum in Anglia*; the first part, dealing with the king's relationship with parliament, was published in Paris in 1649, and in Frankfurt and Edinburgh in 1650. Another English version, *A Compendious Narrative of the Late Troubles in England*, was printed in London in 1652. A second part of *Elenchus motuum* in Latin, covering the years 1649–59, appeared in London in 1661 and Amsterdam in 1662. A later edition in English followed. All renditions purport to be based on documentary sources, but Bate's contemporary, Baldwin Hamey, threw doubt on Bate's authorship of *Elenchus motuum* (Munk, 1.228); another credited Edward Hyde, earl of Clarendon, with providing materials used in the second part of the work (Wood, *Ath. Oxon.*, 1817, 3.827–31). None the less, Robert Pugh, a captain in the king's army, certainly thought Bate was the writer, and named him in an attack on the book, *Elenchus elenchi, sive, Animadversiones in Georgii Batei*, published in Paris in 1664.

Despite his association with Charles I, Bate became physician to the Charterhouse in 1643 and to Oliver Cromwell as general of the parliamentary army. In 1651 Bate and Lawrence Wright, physician-in-ordinary and Bate's senior by twenty years, ministered to Cromwell, who was dangerously ill in Edinburgh; Cromwell named Bate his chief physician in 1653. For the next five years Bate attended the lord protector and his family, including Cromwell's beloved daughter, Elizabeth Claypole, on her deathbed in August 1658. Just a few weeks later, when Cromwell developed fever and back pain, Bate and the other state physicians diagnosed a 'bastard tertian ague' (Bruce-Chwatt, 144); the protector died on 3 September 1658. Bate apparently unsuccessfully treated the duke of Gloucester before his death in 1660, possibly as a result of smallpox.

With the restoration of the monarchy, on 20 June 1660, Bate was named first physician. Rumours circulated that Bate had somehow hastened Cromwell's death with a lethal medication. However, Bate personally evaded responsibility by detailing the symptoms of the protector's fatal illness and the results of the autopsy. In the next year he published *The lives, actions, and execution of the prime actors, and principall contrivers of that horrid murder of our late pious and sacred soveraigne King Charles I*. Bate worked with Francis Glisson and Assuerus Regimorter on rickets, resulting in the 1650 publication of *De rachitide*. He lectured on anatomy in London at the College of Physicians in 1666 and was an original fellow of the Royal Society. Bate left a posthumous collection of his prescriptions, *Pharmacopoeia Bateana*, edited by his long-time apothecary, Jack Shipton, and published in 1688. Bate's remedies encompassed medicinal waters, spirits, oils, salts, electuaries, and infusions like *rosa solis*, which Bate vouched was good for the heart and liver. William Salmon published a second edition in 1691, dedicated to William III, which was 1000 pages in length and contained some of the recipes of Jonathan Goddard, including his eponymous drops for apoplexy.

Bate died on 19 April 1668 at his home in Hatton Garden, London, and was buried at the church of All Saints at Kingston upon Thames, Surrey, alongside his wife, Elizabeth (*b.* 1626/7), who predeceased him by a year. His will was proved on 21 April 1668. He bequeathed a sizable estate, including property in Maids Moreton and tenements in London, to his three children, Edward and Robert Bate and Dame Anne James, wife of Sir Demetrius James, and provided generously in his will for many grandchildren, nieces, nephews, in-laws, and the parish poor.   ELIZABETH LANE FURDELL

Sources DNB • Munk, *Roll* • L. J. Bruce-Chwatt, 'George Bate: Cromwell's devious physician', *Journal of the Royal College of Physicians of London*, 17 (1983), 144–6 • G. C. Peachey, 'Thomas Trapham … and others', *Proceedings of the Royal Society of Medicine*, 24 (1930–31), 1441–9 • J. C. Sainty and R. Bucholz, eds., *Officials of the royal household, 1660–1837*, 1: *Department of the lord chamberlain and associated offices* (1997) • will, PRO, PROB 11/326, sig. 39 • letter, BL, Sloane MS 123, fol. 26 • Foster, *Alum. Oxon.*

Archives RCP Lond., medical diary • Wellcome L., medical recipe book

Wealth at death see will, PRO, PROB 11/326, sig. 39

Bate, James (1703–1775), Church of England clergyman and writer on religion, was born at Boughton Malherbe in Kent, the eldest of the three sons of the Revd Richard Bate (*d.* 1737), vicar of Chilham and rector of Wareham, and his wife, Elizabeth Stanhope (*d.* 1751). His youngest brother was Julius *Bate (1710–1771), an Anglican priest.

After attending King's School, Canterbury, Bate entered Corpus Christi College, Cambridge, on 4 July 1720. He passed BA in 1723, and was elected fellow shortly afterwards, but he accepted later from the bishop of Ely a fellowship in St John's College, Cambridge. He commenced MA in 1727. Ordained deacon on 18 December 1726, he became an Anglican priest on 1 June 1729. In 1730 he became moderator of the university, and in 1731 one of the taxers.

Bate accompanied Horace Walpole as chaplain when the latter went to Paris as ambassador. He was evidently not impressed by what he saw in France. Indeed the sojourn seemed only to reinforce in Bate's mind the superiority of English government, religion, and life since he commented at the time of the Jacobite rising of 1745 that anyone who has travelled knows of 'the advantages of *such* a Constitution in Church and State' (Bate, *A Parochial Letter*, 5). On his return home he was presented to the good living of St Paul's, Deptford, on 23 June 1731, which remained his parish until his death.

Bate gained a reputation as an able scholar, an attentive pastor, and a zealous champion of protestantism and orthodox Anglicanism; it is the last of these which is most evident from his writings. He did not shrink from intellectual debate or controversy; in fact he seemed to revel in it. Unlike his brother Julius he does not seem to have been attracted to Hutchinsonianism with its promise of a comprehensive solution to the dangers facing religion; this despite the fact that he was Julius's Hebrew tutor at St John's College, Cambridge. He wrote against catholicism, evangelicalism, and heterodoxy using traditional Anglican rhetoric. Though there is little novelty in his arguments the power of his writing and preaching remains evident. He was able to grasp the core of an argument, quickly dispose of secondary considerations, and then argue logically and forcefully against the principal ideas. He could be quite witty as well. When he wrote against Thomas Chubb he observed that 'the real undisguised *Logic* of this writer seems fairly reduciable [*sic*] to this one syllogism: "That which is wrong, can never come from God; Mr *Chubb* thinks *this* wrong; therefore *this* can never come from God"' (*Infidelity Scourged*, 2). Along with the bishop of London, Bate wrote against George Whitefield in 1739. He had little new to add to the debate, but because he had a personal acquaintance with the evangelist he was able to catch the latter in some apparent inconsistencies. And, again, his reasoning is clear and concise, and his arguments cogent in *Methodism displayed, or, Remarks upon Mr. Whitefield's answer, to the bishop of London's last pastoral letter* (1739). He published many sermons, but his *magnum opus*—or what he seemed to regard as such—was *An Essay towards a Rationale of the Literal Doctrine of Original Sin* (1752; revised, 1766), in which he challenged Conyers Middleton's views. Bate's reputation as a staunch defender of the faith was still intact when he died in 1775; and Colin Milne, who preached the funeral sermon, was able to say that the parish and nation were by his death deprived of 'a burning and shining light, who, for upwards of forty years, taught ..., undaunted, the whole Counsel of God' (Milne, 24).   A. B. GROSART, rev. J. S. CHAMBERLAIN

Sources Nichols, *Lit. anecdotes*, 2.52; 3.56–7 · C. Milne, *The boldness and freedom of an apostolical eloquence recommended to the imitation of ministers* (1775) · BL, Add. MS 32326, vol. 6, fol. 937 · Venn, *Alum. Cant.* · A. Chalmers, ed., *The general biographical dictionary*, new edn, 32 vols. (1812–17) · J. Bate, *A parochial letter to the inhabitants of St Paul's, Deptford* (1745) · J. Bate, *Infidelity scourged, or, Christianity vindicated* (1746)
Archives CUL, treatise

Bate, John (*d.* 1430), logician and theologian, was, according to Leland, born west of the Severn (perhaps in the Welsh marches), but educated at the Carmelite convent in York. As a Carmelite friar he was a member of the London convent when he was ordained deacon by Bishop Richard Clifford (*d.* 1421) in 1415. Prior of the York Carmelite convent before his death of a 'violent disease', he was buried in the choir of the convent where Bale apparently saw his tomb, for he quotes one line from the epitaph inscribed on it: 'Bati doctoris haec condita petra cadaver'. Bate obtained a doctorate in theology at Oxford where he had probably been sent by the society of the York convent. Sixteenth-century antiquarians report that he had some knowledge of Greek. They also note many treatises written by him, some with incipits; these include commentaries on Aristotelian logic and on other logical texts used in the medieval faculties of arts, an introduction to the *Sentences* of Peter Lombard, and various sermon collections. None of these works is known to have survived. Bate died on 26 January 1430.   JOHN M. FLETCHER

Sources Emden, *Oxf.* · Bale, *Cat.*, 1.567–8 · *Commentarii de scriptoribus Britannicis, auctore Joanne Lelando*, ed. A. Hall, 2 (1709), 334

Bate, John (*fl.* 1626–1635), writer on mechanics, is an obscure figure; his birth and death dates, parentage, and virtually all personal details remain unknown. Bate's *The Mysteries of Nature and Art* (1634) is the first comprehensive illustrated English book on waterworks and hydraulic machinery. It also includes sections on drawing, painting, recipes, and folk remedies, as well as one on fireworks and incendiary devices largely derivative of earlier English and continental works on the subject. A second, greatly expanded edition in 1635 was followed by a third edition, printed in 1654, which has few changes from the second edition.

Judging from the engraved portrait by George Gifford in the second edition, Bate was probably born in the first decade of the century, and probably died before the third edition, possibly as an Irish colonist (a John Bate died there before 1653, leaving four daughters in London, which may explain the third edition the following year). Beyond his book, the only possible hint to his career is John Smith's recommendation of a gunner's scale made by 'John Bates', an instrument maker on Tower Hill (*Seaman's Grammar*, 1626). This supposition is strengthened by Bate's dedicatory poem to his 'worthy friend', the gunner John Babbington, in the latter's book on fireworks (*Pyrotechnia*, 1635). Both this book and Bate's first and second editions

were printed by the same printer, Ralph Mabb. Bate's influence extended to the young Isaac Newton, who owned a copy of *Mysteries*, copied extracts from Bate's section on drawing, and was probably inspired by his section on waterworks.   STEVEN A. WALTON

Sources J. Bate, *The mysteries of nature and art* (1634); 2nd edn (1635); 3rd edn (1654) · E. G. R. Taylor, *The mathematical practitioners of Tudor and Stuart England* (1954) · J. Babbington, *Pyrotechnia* (1635) · F. E. Manuel, *A portrait of Isaac Newton* (1968)
Likenesses G. Gifford, engraving, 1635, repro. in J. Bate, *The mysteries of nature and art*, 2nd edn (1635), frontispiece

Bate, Julius (1710–1771), Church of England clergyman and theological writer, was born and baptized on 13 March 1710 at Boughton Malherbe, Kent, the twin brother of John Bate and one of ten children of the Revd Richard Bate (*c.*1674–1737), rector of Wareham and vicar of Chilham, Kent, and his wife, Elizabeth (1676/7–1751), daughter of the Revd Michael Stanhope and his wife, Catherine Musgrave. His sister Catherine (1704–1770) was the mother of the hymn writer Augustus Montague Toplady (1740–1778).

Bate attended school locally, at Sutton Valence, and was admitted as a sizar at St John's College, Cambridge, on 3 July 1727, aged seventeen; he took his BA degree in 1731 and his MA in 1742. Like his elder brothers James *Bate (1703–1775) and John he took holy orders; he was ordained deacon in London on 9 June 1734 and priest at St David's on 2 November 1735. He became an early follower of the physico-theologian John Hutchinson and worked hard throughout his life to foster the latter's influence. He was patronized by the chancellor of Oxford University, Charles Seymour, sixth duke of Somerset, who on Hutchinson's recommendation gave him immediate preferment in the shape of the rectory of Sutton, Sussex (held from 1735 until his death), near the ducal seat of Petworth. He was also rector of Clapham, in the same county, from 1742, and chaplain to William Stanhope, first earl of Harrington. On 27 January 1740 he married Mary (*b.* 1722), daughter of the Revd Christopher Tillier, vicar of Climping, Sussex, and his wife, Anne.

Bate had read Hutchinson's writings and studied Hebrew for several years before the two eventually met. Bate attended Hutchinson in his last illness, in 1737, and thereafter became an inveterate apologist for his late teacher. Indeed there is a strong case for arguing that Bate fashioned 'Hutchinsonianism' as a distinct ideology as a result of co-editing Hutchinson's collected works and writing numerous pamphlets in defence of his master's mystical theology and his distinctive interpretation of the Hebrew text of the Bible. He thereby brought Hutchinson to the notice of far more people than had been the case in Hutchinson's lifetime. An arch-exponent of a typological approach to scripture, Bate had some unsurprisingly bruising pamphlet exchanges in the early 1740s with William Warburton, on a correct understanding of Genesis and the teachings of Moses, after publication of Warburton's *The Divine Legation of Moses*. Warburton made a personal criticism of Bate and William Romaine in the preface to volume 2 and elsewhere called Bate 'Zany to a mountebank' (that is, Hutchinson himself; Warburton, 12.58), while Bate damned Warburton as 'that Puff of Vanity' (J. Bate, *The Faith of the Ancient Jews in the Law of Moses, and the Evidence of the Types Vindicated*, 1757, 2).

Bate was suspicious of any theologian who was too dependent on natural religion rather than revelation. For, as he put it, 'Natural Religion is a Phantom, a Mist or Cloud the Infidel marches in, covered from our sight' (J. Bate, *The Use and Intent of Prophecy, and History of the Fall*, 1750, 4). He took a strong line against Isaac Newton, whom he dubbed 'the Dagon of Modern Philosophers' (J. Bate, *The Philosophical Principles of Moses Asserted; and Defended from the Misrepresentations*, 1744, 2), and started from the assumption that Moses's philosophical principles were true and revealed from God. He also became involved in the exchanges between Thomas Sherlock, bishop of London, and Conyers Middleton over the veracity of miracles. Bate's *The Use and Intent of Prophecy, and History of the Fall* (1750) was a wide-ranging attempt to vindicate Sherlock's chain of prophecies stretching from Adam to Christ. His mature understanding of the Hutchinsonian system was contained in his *Enquiry into the occasional and standing similitudes of the Lord God, in the Old and New Testament* (1756), which *inter alia* looked at key words like angel, glory, and cherubim, criticized those 'who now-a-days mistake rabbinism for Hebrew' (p. 14), and insisted that Abraham entertained 'the Lord in Trinity' (p. 16). There were also controversial exchanges with Archdeacon John Sharp and Benjamin Kennicott.

Apart from his own writings Bate's energies went towards producing an edition of Hutchinson's collected works jointly with Robert Spearman; this appeared in twelve volumes in 1748. His last book was the culmination of his life's mission, the *Critica Hebraea, or, A Hebrew-English Dictionary without Points* (1767), 'points' being a practice castigated as the 'hydra of pointing' (preface). For Bate as for Hutchinson there was a precise correspondence between the words of the Hebrew language of the Bible and reality, but this harmonious meaning was lost when Hebrew words were given 'pointed' consonants by many modern Hebraists. Bate died at Arundel on 20 January 1771 and was buried in the parish church; he was survived by his wife. His faith in Hutchinson never wavered, and if at his life's end his uncritical preference had few imitators, his efforts were respected. He was 'as a writer', opined one obituarist, 'warm, strenuous and undaunted in asserting the truth' (*GM*).   NIGEL ASTON

Sources *GM*, 1st ser., 41 (1771), 192 • Venn, *Alum. Cant.*, 2/1.105 • Nichols, *Lit. anecdotes*, 3.52–6 • Nichols, *Illustrations*, 2.126 • *Monthly Review*, 36 (1767), 355–61 • R. Spearman, *Life of John Hutchinson* (1748) • W. Warburton, *Works*, new edn, 12 vols. (1811–41), vol. 12 • B. W. Young, *Religion and Enlightenment in eighteenth-century England: theological debate from Locke to Burke* (1998) • C. D. A. Leighton, 'Hutchinsonianism: a counter-Enlightenment reform movement', *Journal of Religious History*, 23 (1999), 168–84 • A. J. Kuhn, 'Glory or gravity: Hutchinson vs. Newton', *Journal of the History of Ideas*, 22 (1961), 303–22 • *DNB* • *IGI* • parish register, Kent, Boughton Malherbe, 13 March 1710, CKS [baptism] • parish register, Arundel, W. Sussex RO [burial] • parish register, W. Sussex RO, Par 8 1/1/2 • memorial inscription, Chilham church, Kent

Archives Bristol Central Library, Catcott corresp., B 26063

Bate, Philip Argall Turner (1909–1999), musicologist and collector of musical instruments, was born in Glasgow on 26 March 1909, the only child of English parents, Percy Herbert Bate (1868–1913), secretary to the Glasgow Museum of Arts, and Mary Turner (1872–1963). His father became curator of the Municipal Art Gallery and Museum in Aberdeen, and died when Philip was four. He had not liked hearing music in the house, although he allowed Philip to sing nursery rhymes accompanied by his mother at the piano. The mother, a keen musician, was a pianist and violinist who also sang in Charles Sanford Terry's Aberdeen Bach Choir.

Bate attended Aberdeen grammar school, where, hearing a schools concert by the Scottish Orchestra, he was inspired to learn the clarinet. He won a Carnegie award to study at Aberdeen University, and took an honours degree in pure science in 1932. He intended to pursue postgraduate work in geology. However, he had been a keen member of the university dramatic societies, and when the new drama department of the Aberdeen station of the BBC sought amateur cast members for broadcasts, Bate was frequently chosen, not least for his English accent. Through this contact with the BBC, Bate applied for and was appointed to a post with the corporation in London. He spent most of the rest of his career working for the BBC's music department—initially as a balance control assistant (1934–7), then as a studio manager (1937–9). After a brief wartime period in military censorship, he was recalled by the BBC, and produced the famous recording of James Blades playing the drumbeat used as the symbol of the European resistance. After the war he worked in television as a producer for the Empire Music Service (1946–56).

Bate produced some of the first live broadcasts of Edinburgh Festival performances and pioneered many live interview programmes, such as *The Conductor Speaks*, with Sir Henry Wood, Sir Malcolm Sargent, Sir Thomas Beecham, and Leopold Stokowsky. Later, realizing the potential of ballet on television, he produced Margot Fonteyn's first television appearance and encouraged groups such as the ballet of the Paris Opéra to come to Britain for the first time. From 1956 until 1967 he was employed in senior training positions for the BBC. His last working year he spent as the first head of training at the new communications centre in Dublin. He was married twice, first on 21 July 1936, to Sheila Glassford Begg (b. 1905/6), from whom he was divorced, and second, on 23 May 1959, to Yvonne Mary Leigh-Pollitt (b. 1921).

Throughout his life, Bate collected and studied musical instruments. He started while still at school, haunting junk shops and markets: one clarinet from a market stall cost him a week's pocket money. His first flute, by William Henry Potter, was given to him by friends, and the next he inherited from his flautist grandfather. When working in London he was a regular visitor to the Caledonian Road, Portobello, and Bermondsey markets, as well as to the salerooms. He made many friendships with those who shared his interests, notably Canon Francis Galpin, who encouraged Bate to turn his scientific training to the study of instruments. Bate was able to use his woodworking skills to make instruments as well as restoring those in his collection. Later, after mastering metalworking techniques, he made reproductions of draw-trumpets which were used by David Munrow in his concerts and recordings with the Early Music Consort of London.

In 1946 Bate and a group of friends founded the Galpin Society, the first society to specialize in the history and study of musical instruments. Bate was its first chairman, and then its president from 1977 until his death. He published extensively, writing books including *The Oboe* (1956), *The Trumpet and Trombone* (1966), and *The Flute: a Study of its History, Development and Construction* (1969) as well as many articles for the Grove dictionaries of music. By the mid-1960s his collection of instruments had grown to cover the history of woodwind from 1680 onwards as well as including some brass instruments and an important collection of printed instrument tutors. He felt convinced that his collection was of value to those concerned with the interpretation of music, and the instruments could be used so long as they were properly maintained. So in 1968 he presented the Bate Collection of Musical Instruments to the University of Oxford. The gift was conditional upon the collection being used for teaching and being provided with a specialist curator to care for it and lecture on it. In the following years Bate continued to add to the collection, and saw it grow further through the acquisition of collections made by many of his friends and colleagues in the Galpin Society. His generous support for the curators was a strength to them, and his continued enjoyment of the instruments inspired the students and scholars who met him. He was made an honorary MA by Oxford University in 1973. Philip Bate died, survived by his wife, in the Whittington Hospital, Islington, London, on 3 November 1999. He was cremated and his ashes were interred in the music faculty garden next to the Bate Collection in Oxford.　　　　　　　　　　　HÉLÈNE LA RUE

Sources P. Bate and H. La Rue, recorded interview, 3 Sept 1995, priv. coll. · *The Times* (8 Nov 1999) · *The Independent* (5 Nov 1999) · *The Scotsman* (27 Nov 1999) · m. certs. · private information (2004) [Yvonne Bate, widow]
Archives U. Oxf., faculty of music, Bate Collection of Musical Instruments, library and archives | U. Oxf., faculty of music, Bate Collection of Musical Instruments
Likenesses L. Fox, oils, U. Oxf., faculty of music, Bate Collection of Musical Instruments
Wealth at death £144,758—gross; £143,058—net: probate, 28 April 2000, *CGPLA Eng. & Wales*

Bate, Robert Brettell (1782–1847), maker of scientific instruments, was born in Old Swinford, Worcestershire, on 27 February 1782, the third of four sons of Overs Bate, mercer and banker of Old Swinford, and his wife, Susannah Brettell. Both his parents came from prosperous merchant and landowning families. No record of his schooling or any apprenticeship has been found, but by 1804 he was in London, living with his uncle, a haberdasher. On 11 February 1804 he married his cousin Anna Maria, daughter of Benjamin Sikes, a collector of excise living in Clerkenwell. They had five children: Mary, Bartholomew (apprenticed to his father in 1822), Anna Maria, John, and Ann, who in 1843 married Richard Thomas Staples-Brown. Shortly before Sikes's death in 1803 his improved hydrometer had been adopted by the government excise department for revenue purposes. The right to supply this instrument passed to his family, and thus Bate, as nephew and son-in-law, was appointed mathematical instrument maker to HM excise, a privilege later extended to his widow.

In 1813 the Clockmakers' Company, having observed that Bate had opened a shop where he was selling sundials and other mathematical instruments, summoned him to take up his freedom within that company. Bate's response was to enrol in the Spectaclemakers' Company, an action which became the subject of the test case in the notorious dispute between these two companies, as to which should control the makers and the retailers of mathematical instruments. When judgment was finally delivered in November 1817, Bate was described as a maker of spectacles, but a retailer of other mathematical instruments. He continued this profitable line of business and examples of virtually all types of optical, mathematical, and philosophical instruments bearing his signature are known.

Bate was admitted to the Spectaclemakers' livery in 1822, moving up through the ranks to become master in 1828–30, thereafter sitting in the court of assistants. He was appointed optician in ordinary to King George IV, this post being renewed on the accessions of William IV and Queen Victoria. Helped by eminent scientists, Bate worked continually to improve the hydrometers and his skills were acknowledged when he was asked to make the models for the new standard weights and measures of capacity enacted by parliament in 1825 to replace existing ancient local measures. Bate and Henry Kater worked on these models in 1825–6, and subsequently Bate supplied hundreds of sets of standards to government and municipal offices throughout the United Kingdom and overseas. He also made bullion balances for the Bank of England, the East India Company, and other establishments. John Bate stood in for his father during his frequent absences—he suffered from chronic bronchitis—giving evidence to several parliamentary commissions on weights and measures before his own early death from consumption in 1840.

Appointed sole Admiralty chart agent in 1830, Bate was co-publisher of the *Nautical Magazine* during its early years, and he wrote and/or published navigation books and some dozen handbooks concerning apparatus which he sold. He retailed mathematical, scientific, and optical instruments, collaborating with David Brewster on the kaleidoscope (1816), and took out patents for hydrometers and spectacle frames. The firm traded from 17 Poultry, in the City of London, from 1807, moving to larger premises at 20–21 in 1820 where a workforce of some twenty people was employed. In later years Bate also rented a house in Hampstead, where he died on 27 December 1847. His widow ran the firm until 1850, closing it down shortly before her own death in 1851. Bate and his wife were buried at St John, Clerkenwell, as were several members of their families.

Bate and his family had various properties and business interests in the west midlands. He was a partner in his brother John Henzey Bate's unsuccessful Eagle Furnace Company of Dudley, and he maintained an interest in the family bank, which traded as Hill, Hill, Bate and Robins, later as Bate and Robins. It was purchased by Midland Bank in 1851.   ANITA McCONNELL

Sources A. McConnell, *R. B. Bate of the Poultry, 1782–1847* (1993) · d. cert. · parish register, Old Swinford, 27 Feb 1782 [birth] · parish register, Old Swinford [baptism]
Archives Hydrographic Office, Taunton, letters in, etc. · PRO, CUST and DSIR classes, letters and invoices
Wealth at death £14,000

Batecombe [Batecumbe], **William** (*fl.* **1348**), astronomer, was probably connected with one of the villages named Batcombe in Dorset and Somerset. Nothing is known of his personal circumstances beyond his association with the University of Oxford, and the fact that he is described as magister. Most of his extensive writings on astronomy are lost, but an influential collection of astronomical (Alfonsine) tables dated 1348, for which he seems to have been responsible, is still extant.

Works ascribed to Batecombe by John Bale in the sixteenth century include *De sphaera solida* ('On the solid sphere') and *De sphaerae concavae fabrica et usu* ('On the manufacture and use of the hollow sphere'), seen in the library of Robert Recorde. These were perhaps the same work, relating to a three-dimensional celestial sphere, or armillary. An anonymous manuscript copy of a work opening in the same way as the one Bale saw is still extant in the Bibliothèque Nationale, Paris. Another work, now lost, had the title *De conclusione sophiae* ('On the end of wisdom') and might have provided justification for Bale's claim that Batecombe studied natural philosophy before turning to mathematics. We must assume that Bale read the word *sophiae* correctly, and that it was not *sapheae*, since *saphea* (from the Arabic for plate) was a name commonly applied by astronomers to a certain type of universal astrolabe. Bale ascribed a work on the astrolabe to him, with no other details, and M. R. James lists a work formerly in the library of the Austin Friars, York, and going under the title *Equatorium abbreviatum cum canonibus Badcomb* ('A concise equatorium, with Batecombe's canons'). This might have been a treatise on the equatorium (an instrument for calculating planetary positions more rapidly than could be done using astronomical tables), but 'equatorium' might conceivably have been a description of Batecombe's tables, since they too 'equate' the planets in a certain technical sense. On the whole it seems more probable that the work did concern an instrument.

The 1348 tables were described as a 'perpetual almanac', for technical reasons associated with their main purpose, which was that of lightening the heavy task of computing daily almanacs (ephemerides). They were an advance on fourteenth-century Parisian versions of the Alfonsine tables, by which the positions and motions of the heavenly bodies were calculated, tables first produced under the aegis of Alfonso X of León and Castile about 1271. There are at least six extant English manuscripts of the 1348 work with tables, or canons for their use, or both, and others in European libraries. The canons say merely that they were written in Oxford. A mid-fifteenth-century copyist—Thomas Cory, monk of Muchelney—begins by ascribing the tables to either 'Battecombe' or [Simon] Bredon or [Thomas] Bradwardine, but the known careers of Bredon and Bradwardine do not fit well with the idea of their authorship. Among John Dee's manuscripts was one with a table of 'latitudes' according to 'Bachecombe'. This is very probably a reference to a subsidiary part of the 1348 tables, dealing with planetary latitudes rather than the geographical latitudes of places, and strengthens the Batecombe ascriptions.

The 1348 tables, which followed close on the heels of those of William Rede, were an important staging post on the way to still greater Oxford achievements, notably by John Killingworth. They became widely known. A Hebrew translation was made by the fifteenth-century Mordecai Finzi of Mantua, who mentions that he was assisted by a Christian scholar—who remains unnamed. Pico della Mirandola's notorious polemic of the 1490s against astrology also mentions the 1348 tables, and when other European writers of the time, such as Henry Arnaut of Zwolle, refer to 'English tables' (*tabulae anglicanae*), they are likely to have the same in mind.

Nothing is known of Batecombe's death. A remark by Thomas Tanner in 1748 has led some scholars to confuse him with William Bathcombe, a Cambridge bachelor of canon law who died in 1487.   J. D. NORTH

Sources J. D. North, 'The Alfonsine tables in England', *Stars, minds and fate: essays in ancient and medieval cosmology* (1989), 327–59 · Emden, *Oxf.* · Bale, *Cat.* · M. R. James, ed., 'The catalogue of the library of the Augustinian friars at York', *Fasciculus Joanni Willis Clark dicatus* (1909), 2–96, esp. 56 · Emden, *Cam.* · Tanner, *Bibl. Brit.-Hib.*

Bateman, Ellen Douglass (1844–1936). *See under* Bateman, Hezekiah Linthicum (1812–1875).

Bateman, Henry Mayo (1887–1970), cartoonist, was born on 15 February 1887, of English parents, at Moss Vale, Sutton Forest, New South Wales, Australia, the only son and the elder of two children of Henry Charles Bateman (1857–1940), then a farmer and later an export packager, and his wife, (Amelia) Rose Mayo, formerly Brooks (1865–1956). The family returned to England in 1888.

Nicknamed Binks, Bateman was educated at Forest Hill House, which he left at the age of sixteen to study drawing and painting at Westminster School of Art, London, and then at Goldsmiths' College at New Cross, and for two or

Henry Mayo Bateman (1887–1970), by Howard Coster, 1933

three years in the London studio of Charles van Haven-maet. In 1903 his first published drawing appeared in *Scraps* and the tentative beginnings of his long association with *The Tatler* magazine occurred the following year. He found it unusually difficult to choose between a career as a fine artist and one as a cartoonist but on his twenty-first birthday he decided to fulfil a childhood ambition 'to make people laugh', which correct choice of métier was nevertheless followed by a prolonged nervous break-down.

In 1909 the diffident, moody young Bateman, in his own words, 'went mad on paper' (*H. M. Bateman by Himself*, 61). He began drawing people not as they looked but as they felt—then an unusual concept. Among his earliest influences were Phil May and Tom Browne, but especially two artists of comic genius—Henry Ospovat and, particularly, Emmanuel Poiré (Caran d'Ache). In his introduction to *Caran d'Ache the Supreme* (1933) Bateman described him as 'the greatest master of the art of telling a story in pictures'. Both artists provided the impetus towards Bateman's refreshing and occasionally disconcerting freedom of expression. The humour of his line was an intrinsic part of the cartoon. According to P. V. Bradshaw, 'If he seldom saw beauty in his subjects he always supplied it in his line' (Bradshaw, pt 16, p. 7). There was youthful cynicism in his humour and 'a certain suspicion of virulence' (ibid., 5). This was partly based on an awareness of convention and the grudging acceptance of its constraints rather

than a rebellion against it. Bateman neither looked nor acted the part of the bohemian artist. He dressed conventionally, as many artists dressed in those days, even at the drawing-board.

For the (glossy) *Sketch*, and billed as 'Our Untamed Artist', Bateman caricatured theatre personalities from life. He also sketched imaginary (and hilarious) but totally convincing pianists, singers, and music-hall performers, but above all he drew suburbia—viewed at first hand from his home, Parkstone, 40 Nightingale Lane, Clapham, London. According to one contemporary observer, cited by Anderson, 'It is fair and reasonable to call Clapham the capital of Suburbia' (Anderson, 51). In his pre-First World War cartoons for *London Opinion*, *The Sketch*, and *The Bystander* every nuance of gentility was noted and later brought together in his first collection of cartoons, *Burlesques* (1916); others appeared in *Suburbia* (1922).

Bateman attempted to overcome shyness and to release pent-up energies by taking lessons in boxing and, incongruously, tap-dancing. After volunteering for military service in 1915 the far from robust cartoonist was hastily returned to civilian life where the ignominy of rejection accentuated a tendency towards depression which was partly assuaged by numerous fishing expeditions in the company of his closest friend, the author and gourmet William Caine. Until his sudden death in 1925, Caine was also the subject of many Bateman cartoons. *Punch* began publishing his work in 1915, at a time when an increasing melancholy somehow transmogrified into an even livelier humour. He brought to perfection the strip without words, of which 'The Boy who Breathed on the Glass in the British Museum' (British Museum, London) is a classic example. Many of his best cartoons in this genre were reprinted in *A Book of Drawings* (1921), with an introduction by G. K. Chesterton. His output was prodigious and highly paid.

Bateman was an active if reserved member of the Chelsea Arts Club and the London Sketch Club, but even these amiable islands of male *bonhomie* in a male-oriented world could not altogether cheer him up. After the First World War he moved from London to Reigate, Surrey, where for fourteen years he lived quietly but industriously. He was not entirely a recluse. On 29 September 1926, at St Mark's Church in Hamilton Terrace, Maida Vale, London, he married Brenda Mary Collison Weir (1903?–1988), the daughter of Octavius Weir, a country gentleman from Stratford St Mary, Suffolk; the couple had two daughters. Bateman and his wife were like chalk and cheese: at first the novelty of their differences wore well but not for long. He was at the height of his fame, yet his wife—who adored his cartoons—wistfully observed, 'I thought he'd be more funny than he was' (interview, 'The Man who Went Mad on Paper'). This lament lasted throughout their marriage.

The genesis of a series which would in time bring Bateman worldwide fame began in 1912 with 'The Missed Putt', which he considered to be the first of The Man Who ... cartoons which illustrated social gaffes and clangers based on middle- and upper-middle-class aspirations, snobbery, manners, and etiquette. The first of the full-colour, double-page spreads in *The Tatler* appeared in 1922 with 'The Guardsman who Dropped It' (Cavalry and Guards Club, London), soon followed by many more in similar vein, such as 'The Man who Lit his Cigar before the Royal Toast' and 'The Man who Asked for a Double Scotch in the Grand Pump Room at Bath' (Grand Pump Room, Bath). In most drawings, with humour strengthened by accurate observation, a serenely innocent figure, or someone crushed with embarrassment, is surrounded by a writhing assembly ululating with outrage.

Further collections of Bateman's work appeared: *Rebound* (1927), *Brought Forward* (1931), and *Considered Trifles* (1934). One-man exhibitions were held, beginning with one at the Brook Street Gallery, London, in 1911, followed by two at the Leicester Galleries, London, in 1919 and 1921, and another in Sydney, Australia, in 1938. As the Second World War began, a luxury edition of the best of The Man Who ... had to be abandoned when a bomb destroyed the plates. The Man Who ... was essentially formulaic and in time Bateman grew bored with the repetition; his style became 'tricksy' (his own word) and lost the zest of earlier works. Cartooning also took its toll of his 'straight' draughtsmanship, though his little volume *The Art of Drawing* (1926) was and remains a classic exposition of basic skills. Apart from his autobiography (*H. M. Bateman by Himself*, 1937) he wrote and illustrated several books, including *The Evening Rise* (1960), and illustrated many more. Among his authors were Lewis Carroll, George Robey, William Caine, and A. P. Herbert. Advertisers bid for The Man Who ... to promote Shell, Colman's mustard, Guinness, the *News Chronicle*, and Kensitas, Lucky Strike, and Bar-One cigarettes, among many (perhaps too many) others.

Shortly after the outbreak of the Second World War, as a highly paid cartoonist Bateman decided he could afford the luxury of semi-retirement. With advancing years his moroseness and some surprising meannesses increased and in 1947 he separated from his family, moving to Brook Cottage, Sampford Courtenay, Devon, where he lived from 1953 and indulged in and wrote about his lifelong recreation of trout fishing with the fly. The Inland Revenue, which had once provided him with some of his funniest cartoons, became the object of a sad, paranoiac obsession, resulting in (mostly unpublished) cartoons containing his virulence but not the beauty of line nor much of the humour of his earlier work. That bee-in-a-bonnet apart, he was in old age an upright figure, as clipped, neat, and peppery as the 'Colonels' (1924) he drew with relish and affection, and, when he chose, he could be an amiable host. An exhibition of his work was held at the Fine Art Society, London, in 1962.

In the late 1960s, tired of a post-war Britain in which he felt totally alien, Bateman moved to the Maltese island of Gozo where, with the Royal Lady Hotel at Mgarr as his base, he painted landscape watercolours which failed to achieve the high standards he set himself. Humour was his forte. Thanks to the ubiquity of embarrassment his best cartoons, and there are many, will ring comically true as long as human nature persists.

H. M. Bateman died of heart failure on 11 February 1970 while taking his usual solitary morning walk. He was buried in the English church on Malta. Posthumous exhibitions of his work were held at the Leicester Galleries, London, in 1974, and the Langton Gallery, London, in 1978, 1980, and 1981. Some of his drawings are in the collection of the Cartoon Art Trust. JOHN JENSEN

Sources H. M. Bateman, *H. M. Bateman by himself* (1937) • A. Anderson, *The man who was H. M. Bateman* (1982) • *H. M. Bateman, The Man Who ... and other drawings*, ed. J. Jensen (1975) • P. V. Bradshaw, *The art of the illustrator* (1917) • H. M. Bateman, 'Humour in art', *Journal of the Royal Society of Arts*, 97 (1948–9), 629–39 • *H. M. Bateman, 1887–1970* (1987) [exhibition catalogue, Royal Festival Hall and National Theatre, London] • M. Boxer, 'Foreword', in *The best of H. M. Bateman: 'The Tatler' cartoons, 1922–26* (1987) • personal knowledge (2004) • private information (1981, 2004) • b. cert. • 'The man who went mad on paper', television documentary, Television South-West (TSW), 1988 • m. cert. [H. C. Bateman and (Amelia) Rose Mayo] • b. cert. [H. C. Bateman]

Archives FILM TSW, 'The man who went mad on paper', documentary, 1988

Likenesses B. Park, photograph, 1916, repro. in Bradshaw, *Art of the illustrator* • H. L. Oakley, silhouette, 1929, NPG • two photographs, 1931, Hult. Arch. • H. Coster, photograph, 1933, NPG [*see illus.*] • two self-portraits, caricatures, 1933–64, NPG • H. Coster, photograph, repro. in Anderson, *The man who was H. M. Bateman* • self-portrait, caricature, repro. in *H. M. Bateman*, ed. Jensen • self-portrait, caricature, repro. in Bateman, *H. M. Bateman*

Wealth at death £61,865: administration with will, 9 July 1970, *CGPLA Eng. & Wales*

Bateman [*née* Neden, Needham]**, Hester** (*bap.* 1708, *d.* 1794), silversmith, was baptized on 7 October 1708 at St Michael-le-Querne, Paternoster Row, in the City of London, the daughter of John Neden or Needham. Little is known of her early life, but as she was unable to sign her name it must be assumed that any education she received was rudimentary. She was living in the parish of St Botolph, Aldersgate, at the time of her marriage on 20 May 1732 to John Bateman (1704–1760), wiredrawer and gold chain maker, of St Bartholomew-the-Less. They had five children, Letitia (*b.* 1733), Ann (*b.* 1736), Peter (*b.* 1740), John, and Jonathan (1747–1791).

It is reasonable to assume that Hester Bateman may have been involved with the business for some time before her husband died of consumption in 1760. In his will Bateman left his tools to his wife, which suggests that he expected her to continue the business. As a wiredrawer and gold chain maker he had not needed to register a mark at Goldsmiths' Hall. It is significant that Hester Bateman should have done so after her husband's death: by registering her first mark in April 1761 she signalled to the silversmithing trade that she intended to continue her husband's work.

Although by then in her early fifties Hester Bateman began building on the established business with the help of her workmen and apprentices, and her sons Jonathan and Peter, who were both apprenticed to their sister Letitia's husband, Richard Clarke. Given the understanding that we now possess of the complex organization of the gold and silver trades it cannot be assumed that she made the silver that bears her mark. Any manufacturing silversmith of the time relied upon a system of in-house specialists and outworkers to complete the product successfully. What is more certain is that Hester Bateman was the driving force behind the enterprise. She gradually expanded the range of goods and the quantity to supply a largely middle-class market using the latest, most cost-efficient manufacturing processes. The firm's deliberate use of new ideas and technology allowed it to compete with the cheap silver and Sheffield plate from Birmingham and Sheffield. Hester Bateman must be credited with the energy and foresight to pursue this strategy which enabled her to turn a small family business into one of the most successful medium-sized manufactories of its day. Her son Jonathan was a liveryman of the Goldsmiths' Company in 1784 when his own son Jonathan was apprenticed to him. Peter Bateman worked with his sister Ann after his elder brother's death.

The type of products produced in the earliest years of Hester Bateman's business were small silver articles such as spoons, wine labels, buttons, and seals. On registering her third (1774), fifth (1776), sixth (1778), and seventh (1781) marks she called herself a spoon maker although as early as 1774 she had used the more general title of plateworker. Surviving examples of her workshops' production before the late 1770s are comparatively rare and it has been suggested that she was supplying other goldsmiths who marked the silver as their own before sale. Pieces stamped for Hester Bateman from the last two decades of the century are much more common, which suggests increasing output and range of product.

Largely in the neo-classical style, the silver is almost exclusively for domestic use and includes coffee pots, tea urns, cruets, teapots, and salvers among the larger items, along with the smaller objects such as snuffer trays, goblets, salts, mustards, and sugar tongs. At its best the workmanship combined simple manufacturing and decorating techniques to form an elegant if repetitious effect. It used easily worked sheet silver and a repertoire of bright-cut, pierced, or beaded ornament that could be repeated or recombined in unlimited variations. The Bateman style was not high fashion but it was fashionable. In particular, the middle class appreciated the cost-effectiveness of using thin-gauge metal and less time-consuming manufacturing methods.

Hester Bateman retired when John and Peter entered their mark in 1790. At the time of her death on 16 September 1794, she was living in the parish of St Andrew, Holborn. She was buried at St Luke's, Old Street, on 26 September. The firm continued to invest in new technology to increase the competitive pricing of its own production. A flatting mill for the working of sheet metal was introduced in 1791, enabling the Batemans to dispense with the need to buy in sheet and perhaps recoup their investment by supplying other workshops. A steam engine to power the manufacturing processes had been added by 1802, ten years ahead of the most prestigious business of the time,

Rundell, Bridge, and Rundell, the royal goldsmiths. The willingness to exploit the latest technology to produce good quality silver of a standardized design, which had been the foundation of Hester Bateman's success, ensured the survival of the firm into the mid-nineteenth century.　　ANN EATWELL

Sources D. S. Shure, *Hester Bateman, queen of English silversmiths* (1959) · A. G. Grimwade, *London goldsmiths, 1697–1837: their marks and lives, from the original registers at Goldsmiths' Hall*, 3rd edn (1990) · P. Glanville and J. F. Goldsborough, *Women silversmiths, 1685–1845* (1990) · E. J. G. Smith, 'Women silversmiths I', *Collectors Guide* (May 1969), 67–81 · E. J. G. Smith, 'Women silversmiths II', *Collectors Guide* (Sept 1969), 81–7 · H. E. Gillingham, 'Concerning Hester Bateman', *Antiques*, 39 (Feb 1941), 76–7 · W. Walter, 'New light on Hester Bateman', *Antiques*, 63 (Jan 1953), 36–40 · G. B. Hughes, 'An eighteenth-century woman silversmith', *Country Life*, 128 (1960), 508–10
Archives Goldsmiths' Hall, London, artefacts · V&A, artefacts

Bateman, Hezekiah Linthicum (1812–1875), actor and theatre manager, was born in Baltimore, Maryland, USA, on 6 December 1812, the fourth child and second son of Amzi Bateman (c.1777–1816) and his wife, Catherine Schaeffer Evans Bateman (c.1784–1870). Amzi Bateman, a fisherman by trade, was a member of the 6th regiment of the Maryland militia and actively participated in the defence of Baltimore against the invasion of British troops during the Anglo-American War. Following Amzi's death his widow, Catherine, tutored students to support her young family.

Hezekiah, unwillingly apprenticed as a young man to a firm of Baltimore engineers, left that position in the winter of 1832–3 with the intention of becoming an actor. He played juvenile roles with a neighbour, Junius Brutus Booth the elder, and with Ellen Tree (later Mrs Charles Kean). In 1839 he was employed by the theatrical management team of Noah M. Ludlow and Sol S. Smith for their stock company, and made his début at their St Louis Theatre on 8 April 1839. Smith thought Bateman 'a good actor for the experience he then had' (Smith, 140).

At the time Bateman was employed, Ludlow and Smith also took on the comedian Joseph Leathley (Joe) *Cowell and his daughter Sidney Frances Cowell (1823–1881) [see Bateman, Sidney Frances]. Bateman and the sixteen-year-old Sidney were married in St Louis on 10 November 1839. Of their eight children, four would be remembered for careers on the stage: **Kate Josephine Bateman** (1842–1917), **Ellen Douglass Bateman** (1844–1936), **Virginia Frances Bateman** (1853–1940), the mother of Fay *Compton (1894–1978) and Edward Montague Compton *Mackenzie (1883–1972), and **Isabel Emilie Bateman** (1854–1934).

When the Ludlow and Smith company experienced financial difficulties at the end of the 1840 summer season in St Louis, the Batemans returned to Baltimore, where Hezekiah entered into a grocery business. This commercial enterprise was short-lived, however, and after several appearances at local Baltimore theatres the family sailed for England. Hezekiah made his début on a British stage at

Hezekiah Linthicum Bateman (1812–1875), by unknown photographer, *c.*1870

Osbaldiston's Victoria Theatre, Surrey, on 16 September 1846. Badly received, he was hissed off the stage and returned to America, penniless and in steerage.

Hezekiah and Sidney next joined James Bates's theatrical company at the Louisville Theatre in Louisville, Kentucky, in October 1847. On 17 December 1847 *Children of the Wood* was announced, but, it was said, the two children scheduled to play were suddenly taken ill, and in their place the two Bateman daughters—Kate, aged five, and Ellen, aged three—were quickly taught the roles and went on. The local newspaper reported that they 'performed their parts most sweetly' (*Louisville Daily Journal*, 18 Dec 1847). The two little girls earned laurels in subsequent performances in Cincinnati, followed by another season in Louisville. In May 1848 the elder Batemans left the Bates company and became managers of their small daughters.

Between August and October of 1851 the 'Bateman Children' played London's St James's Theatre during the Great Exhibition, and then toured the British Isles; they returned to America in August 1852. For the next three years Hezekiah Bateman toured with the children throughout the United States, until November 1855, when he briefly assumed management of the St Louis Theatre. Between 1856 and 1859 he managed, toured with, and occasionally acted in Sidney's two plays *Self* and *Geraldine*.

In 1859 the Bateman family settled in Brooklyn, New York. In 1860 Ellen, with no further interest in the theatre, married a French-born silk manufacturer, Claude Greppo,

and settled in Paterson, New Jersey. Kate, in the meantime, embarked on a stage career as an adult star. She made her New York début in her mother's adaptation of *Evangeline* at New York's Winter Garden.

Hezekiah Bateman managed Kate's successful tour following her New York appearance, culminating in May 1863 at New York's Niblo's Garden with the wildly popular *Leah, the Forsaken*, an adaptation by Augustin Daly of Mosenthal's *Deborah*. During the summer of 1863, now with some financial means owing to the success of *Leah*, the family could afford to enjoy a European vacation. Before returning to America, however, Bateman secured an engagement for Kate at London's Adelphi Theatre. *Leah, the Forsaken*, now in an adaptation by John Oxenford, ran for a West End record-breaking 211 nights.

With America in the throes of civil war, theatrical prospects in the British Isles were more promising than those in the United States. In January 1864 Bateman took Sidney and the two younger girls, Virginia and Isabel, to England, where they settled permanently. Following Kate's Adelphi engagement, Bateman managed her tour of the British Isles and, in 1866, returned with her to America for a tour of the USA. Simultaneously he managed a tour of concert artists, including Mme Parepa and Carl Rosa. Kate's marriage to George Crowe on 13 October 1866 permitted Bateman to turn management duties over to Crowe, and he was free, between 1867 and 1869, to manage the tour of a troupe of French artistes who were introducing the operettas of Jacques Offenbach to America. In January 1869 he sold his interest in the troupe to the American railroad financier Jim Fisk.

Bateman then returned to England and, on 22 February 1871, assumed management of London's Lyceum Theatre. His plan, initially, was to use the theatre as a showcase for Kate and the younger daughters, Virginia and Isabel, who were then embarking on their own theatrical careers. In April 1871 he saw a young actor named Henry Irving in *The Dream of Eugene Aram*. Upon his return he announced to his family: 'I have found the greatest actor of the century' (*Black and White*, 25 April 1896, 523).

Fanchette and *Pickwick*, the first two Lyceum productions under Bateman's management, fell far short of financial success. On 25 November 1871, however, the future prospects for Bateman's finances improved radically with the presentation of *The Bells*, an English translation and adaptation by Leopold Lewis of the Erckmann–Chatrain tale *Le Juif polonais*. Irving's weird and wonderful power in the leading role made an indelible mark on the history of British theatre and solidified both Irving's reputation and the financial position of Bateman's Lyceum.

Bateman and Irving followed the 151 night run of *The Bells* with *Charles I*, *The Dream of Eugene Aram*, *Richelieu*, *Philip*, and then *Hamlet*. *Hamlet*, which opened on 31 October 1874, was, from the first night, an unqualified success and a triumph for both the manager and the actor. Five months later, with *Hamlet* still on the boards, Irving organized a dinner party at a Pall Mall restaurant for Bateman, after which the group repaired to the Westminster Club for further socializing. There may have been sharp words exchanged between Bateman and the management when he was asked to leave the club at the required closing time. Upon rising the following morning, 22 March 1875, Bateman was suddenly seized by sharp chest pains, and he died within hours at his home, Rutland Lodge, Rutland Gardens, Knightsbridge, London. *The Times*, in eulogizing him, stated that 'he stood gallantly forward as the promoter of an intellectual and morally irreproachable drama at a day when the theatrical world was threatened with a deluge of vice and frivolity' (*The Times*, 24 March 1875, 8). He was buried in Kensal Green cemetery, London, on 27 March.

Following his demise his widow and three of his daughters, Kate, Virginia, and Isabel, attempted to keep the Lyceum going, but conflicts between Irving and Sidney Bateman finally made a parting of the ways inevitable. Irving took over the Lyceum in 1878, while the Batemans took possession of Sadler's Wells. Debts mounted at the Wells, and when Sidney died in 1881 the daughters were left to deal with the debt.

Kate continued to tour the British provinces before retiring in 1892, and thereafter ran a stage school in London. Virginia married the actor Edward *Compton (1854–1918) on 12 June 1882, and afterwards acted in and co-managed the Compton Comedy Company. Isabel, after paying off the last penny of the debt, left the theatre in 1898 and entered the Anglican sisterhood of St Mary the Virgin in Wantage, Berkshire, in time becoming mother superior of the order.   GAYLE T. HARRIS

Sources W. G. B. Carson, *The theatre on the frontier* (1932); 2nd edn (1965) · L. Irving, *Henry Irving: the actor and his world* [1951] · N. M. Ludlow, *Dramatic life as I found it* (1880); repr. (1966) · C. Mackenzie, *My life and times*, 10 vols. (1963–71), vol. 1 · E. Matchett, *The Baltimore directory and register* (1816) · *Matchett's Baltimore city directories* (1829) · *Matchett's Baltimore city directories* (1844–5) · S. Smith, *Theatrical management in the west and south for thirty years* (1868) · *Baltimore American* (25 May 1816) · *Black and White* (25 April 1896) · *Daily Telegraph* (27 March 1875) · *The Era* (28 March 1857) · *Louisville Daily Democrat* (1839–59) · *Louisville Daily Journal* (18 Dec 1847) · *Louisville Daily Journal* (1839–59) · *New York Spirit of the Times* (18 May 1839) · *New York Spirit of the Times* (27 March 1875) · *New York Tribune* (14 Jan 1869) · *Theatrical Journal* (22 Feb 1871) · *The Times* (24 March 1875) · *The Times* (1846–75) · P. Hartnoll, ed., *The Oxford companion to the theatre*, 3rd edn (1967) · *DNB* · office records, Baltimore (Maryland) cemetery · Baltimore County (Maryland), wills, 10:196–7 · Sol Smith to Noah Ludlow, 6 May 1839, Missouri Historical Society, St Louis, Missouri, Smith–Ludlow collection · marriage licence, 10 Nov 1839, Recorder of Deeds, St Louis, Missouri · marriage licence, Brooklyn, New York, 13 Oct 1866 · playbill for Victoria Theatre, Surrey, 16 Sept 1846, priv. coll. · playbill for Victoria Theatre, Surrey, 18 Sept 1846, priv. coll.
Archives Louisiana State University, Baton Rouge, Louisiana, E. C. Wharton collection · Missouri Historical Society, St Louis, Missouri, Smith–Ludlow collection
Likenesses photograph, *c*.1870, Theatre Museum, London [*see illus.*] · A. Bryant, sketch, *c*.1873, Harvard TC · photograph, Howard University, Washington, DC · photograph, priv. coll.
Wealth at death under £8000: resworn administration, April 1876, *CGPLA Eng. & Wales*

Bateman, Isabel Emilie (1854–1934). *See under* Bateman, Hezekiah Linthicum (1812–1875).

Bateman, James (1812–1897), horticulturist and botanist, was born on 18 July 1812 at Redivals, near Bury in Lancashire, the only child of John Bateman (1782–1858), banker, ironfounder, and manufacturer, of Knypersley Hall in Staffordshire and Tolson Hall in Westmorland, and his wife, Elizabeth (*d.* 1857), second daughter of George Holt of Redivals. He matriculated from Lincoln College, Oxford, on 2 April 1829, graduating BA from Magdalen College in 1834, and MA in 1845.

Bateman early became interested in growing tropical plants, notably orchids. In 1833, while a student at Oxford, he sent at his own expense an Oxford gardener, Thomas Colley, to collect orchids in British Guiana. Of the sixty species Colley brought back about a third were new, among them a new genus which John Lindley (1799–1865) named *Batemannia colleyi* in 1834. Bateman's concise account of Colley's travels in Loudon's *Gardener's Magazine* (11, 1835, 1–7) was his first publication. Shortly afterwards he induced an English merchant in Guatemala, George Ure Skinner (1804–1867), to send him orchids. Bateman's interest in these Central American plants resulted in the largest book ever devoted to orchids, *The Orchidaceae of Mexico and Guatemala* (1837–43), published in ten parts, with forty life-size hand-coloured lithograph plates and some amusing vignettes by George Cruikshank; only 125 copies were printed. His other costly publications, both with hand-coloured lithograph plates by Walter Fitch (1817–1892), were *A Monograph of Odontoglossum* (1864–1874), with thirty plates, and *A Second Century of Orchidaceous Plants* (1867), with 100 plates. In 1864 he published a *Guide to Cool Orchid-Growing*. He was elected a fellow of the Linnean Society in 1833 and of the Royal Society in 1838.

On 24 April 1838 Bateman married Maria Sybilla Egerton, third daughter of Rowland Egerton Warburton and sister of Peter Egerton Warburton; they had three sons, John *Bateman, Rowland, and Robert, and a daughter, Katherine, who married Ulrick Ralph Burke. In 1840 Bateman moved from Knypersley Hall, where he grew a large collection of orchids, to Biddulph Grange, Staffordshire. There, assisted by the landscape painter and garden designer Edward W. Cooke (1811–1880), Bateman created a fantastic garden, complete with 'Chinese' and 'Egyptian' sections, a costly undertaking made possible by wealth from his father's business activities. In 1863 he laid out the Oxford University Museum Parks.

Bateman left Biddulph Grange in 1869 and rented a house at Hyde Park Gate, London; he often gave popular lectures to the Royal Horticultural Society. In 1884 he and his wife, who suffered from bronchitis, moved to Worthing, Sussex. His articles on orchids appeared in the *Gardeners' Chronicle* under the pseudonym Serapias, and he also published some theological pamphlets. His orchidological publications and the generic name *Batemannia* (the *n* deliberately doubled, in accordance with Renaissance Latinization tradition) are his memorials. He died at his home, Springbank, Victoria Road, Worthing, on 27 November 1897 and was buried on 2 December in Worthing cemetery. He was survived by his wife.

E. I. CARLYLE, *rev.* WILLIAM T. STEARN

Sources *Gardeners' Chronicle*, 3rd ser., 22 (1897), 400–02 • *Orchid Review*, 6 (1898), 10–14 • *Proceedings of the Linnean Society of London*, 120 (1897–8), 33–5 • Burke, *Gen. GB* • P. Hayden, *Biddulph Grange: a Victorian garden rediscovered* (1989) • W. Blunt and W. T. Stearn, *The art of botanical illustration*, new edn (1994), 249, 251, 255 • *CGPLA Eng. & Wales* (1898)
Likenesses Maull & Co., photograph, RS • engraving, repro. in E. Nelmes and W. Cuthberton, *Curtis' Botanical Magazine dedications* (1932), 42 • engraving, repro. in *Gardeners' Chronicle*, 403 • photograph, repro. in Hayden, *Biddulph Grange*, 49
Wealth at death £273 18s. 11d.: probate, 23 Feb 1898, *CGPLA Eng. & Wales*

Bateman, John (1839–1910), landowner and author, was born on 19 March 1839, the eldest of the four children of James *Bateman (1812–1897), landowner, of Knypersley Hall, Staffordshire, and his wife, Maria Sybilla Egerton Warburton, daughter of the Revd Rowland Egerton Warburton of Norley, Cheshire. Bateman's father was a distinguished botanist and horticulturist who wrote on orchids. Bateman attended Trinity College, Cambridge, but without graduating. He married on 4 October 1865 Jessy Caroline (d. 1925), daughter of the Hon. Richard Bootle Wilbraham MP, and sister of Edward, first earl of Lathom; they had one daughter, Agnes Mary.

In 1871, with the probable assistance of his wealthy father, Bateman purchased Brightlingsea Hall, near Colchester, an estate of 1400 acres. In 1875 he purchased a property, 3000 acres in size but of insignificant income, in co. Mayo, Ireland, probably as a hunting preserve. In flight from Staffordshire industrialism, Bateman became in Essex an agricultural improver, experimenting in forestry and tobacco growing, and advocating efficient methods of ensilage. He was known as a doer of good works, assisting his nonconformist dependants equally with his Anglican co-religionists. Like others of his class, he was obsessed by the mania for shooting wild and semi-wild animals that overtook English landed society in the late nineteenth century. In 1882 he celebrated through eight issues of the *Essex County Standard* a shooting expedition he had undertaken to the River Plate in Argentina. He held various public offices: head of the local Conservative Party, member of the Essex county council and of the Brightlingsea urban district council, and chairman of the local bench, a post he held until his death.

Bateman's claim to fame rests upon the book that has become known to historians simply as 'Bateman', a compilation of statistical material about the landowners of Great Britain and Ireland. The book went through four editions. The first, entitled *The Acre-ocracy of England*, appeared in 1876. The later editions (1878, 1879, and 1883), which were expanded to cover the British Isles, were retitled *The Great Landowners of Great Britain and Ireland*. No other European nation has so detailed a record of its landed élite of the nineteenth century, or probably of any century, as Bateman provided.

The book had its origin in the political debate over the distribution of land in England. After the repeal of the corn laws, critics of aristocracy, such as John Bright, turned their attention to the concentration of land ownership, and to what they saw as the aristocratic monopoly of

land. The census of 1861 apparently proved their point, for it estimated the number of landowners to be only 30,000, in a population of more than 30 million. The earl of Derby challenged the figure as grotesquely low, and caused parliament to undertake a census of landowners. Published in instalments between 1874 and 1876, the vast parliamentary *Return of Owners of Land* listed all owners, giving their acreage and income (except for land held in London).

The *Return*, however, was not readily usable. It arranged its data by county, and much labour was required to discover the total acreage or income of any landowner—and they were many—who held land in several counties. Moreover, discrepancies of various kinds were to be found from county to county. Bateman not only undertook the task of arranging the data into a national whole, but also, by enquiries to owners, sought to correct the *Return* so far as was possible. He thus transformed the raw data of the *Return* into a handbook of all owners of estates of 2000 acres and above. For estates of 3000 acres and above he provided prosopographical information, which the government had not asked for, on the owner's education, clubs, and military and political service. Finally, he worked up tables showing the distribution of land among various classes of landowner.

Bateman's work has served historians well. Whether it served as well the cause he had at heart is another matter. He seems to have thought that his work supported the established system of landholding against its critics. In fact it made clear—clearer than the official *Return* could—how great was the concentration of landholding in Great Britain. It strengthened rather than refuted the charge of an aristocratic monopoly, and was thus a somewhat misguided work for a tory politician. This may explain why Bateman's obituary in *The Times* made no mention of his book, and also perhaps why the *Morning Post*, the country gentleman's daily paper, left his death, on 12 October 1910, as well as his book, unmentioned.　　　DAVID SPRING

Sources D. Spring, introduction, in J. Bateman, *The great landowners of Great Britain and Ireland*, 4th edn (1883), 7–22; repr. with introduction by D. Spring (1971) • *The Times* (13 Oct 1910) • *Essex County Chronicle* (14 Oct 1910) • B. L. James, 'The "great landowners" of Wales', *National Library of Wales Journal*, 14 (1965–6), 301–19 • Burke, *Gen. GB* • *WWW* • Venn, *Alum. Cant.* • *Essex County Standard* (Sept–Dec 1882) • 'Return … of names of owners of one acre and upwards', *Parl. papers* (1874), vol. 72, C. 1097, C. 899 • 'Summary of returns of owners of land', *Parl. papers* (1876), vol. 80, no. 335 • Burke, *Peerage*
Wealth at death £10,848 10s. 5d.: probate, 24 Nov 1910, *CGPLA Eng. & Wales*

Bateman, John Frederic La Trobe (1810–1889), civil engineer, was born at Lower Wyke, near Halifax, on 30 May 1810, the eldest son of John Bateman (1772–1851), an unsuccessful inventor, and his wife, Mary Agnes, daughter of Benjamin La Trobe, a Moravian missionary at Fairfield, near Ashton under Lyne. He had three brothers and two sisters. In 1817, because of an unhappy family situation, Bateman was sent away to Moravian schools first at Fairfield, then at Ockbrook, Derby, and then back to Fairfield, where he again became part of the family of his uncle-in-law, Frederic William Foster. The influence of the

La Trobe family and the Moravians' enlightened view of education played a large part in determining Bateman's profession; in 1825 he was apprenticed to a Mr Dunn, a surveyor and mining engineer in Oldham.

One of Bateman's first tasks involved the enlargement of a canal reservoir and this work, coupled with an investigation into the flooding of the River Medlock, laid the foundation of a career that was to span over fifty years and whose output forms the basis of the modern UK water supply industry. In 1835 he became involved with William *Fairbairn in designing and constructing reservoirs for the millowners on the River Bann in Ireland. On 1 September 1841 he married Fairbairn's only daughter, Anne (d. 1894); they had three sons and four daughters.

After the work in Ireland Bateman was almost continuously employed in the construction of reservoirs and waterworks, the greatest of which was the system that supplied Manchester with much of its water during the nineteenth century. His first involvement was in 1844 when he was consulted about the supply of water to Manchester and Salford. In 1846, despite the current theory that rainfall decreased with altitude, the idea was proposed of obtaining water from the Pennines. The works in Longdendale were started in 1848 and were finished in the spring of 1877, with the Woodhead Reservoir being one of the first to be started but the last to be finished: the scheme was then the largest in Europe. As the Longdendale scheme approached completion it became clear that additional sources of supply must be obtained because demand for water had risen due to increased population and consumption per head. At Bateman's suggestion, the corporation decided to construct new works at Lake Thirlmere. A bill was introduced into parliament in 1878, and, despite the formation of the Thirlmere Defence Association to fight the proposal, the act was passed in 1879. (The association played some part in the subsequent foundation of the National Trust.) Bateman superintended the start of the project but most of the work was under the control of George Hill, who established a long-lasting civil engineering firm, G. H. Hill & Sons.

In 1852 Bateman was asked to advise the town council of Glasgow about the supply of water to the city. On his advice in the parliamentary session of 1854–5 an act was passed to allow the supply of water from Loch Katrine. The works were started in the spring of 1856 and completed by March 1860. They were described as worthy to 'bear comparison with the most extensive aqueducts in the world, not excluding those of ancient Rome' (Gale). Bateman carried out extensive water supply works in the UK. These include the systems for Aberdâr, Accrington, Ashton, Belfast, Birkenhead, Blackburn, Bolton, Cheltenham, Chester, Chorley, Colne and Marsden, Colne valley, Darwen, Dewsbury, Dublin, Forfar, Gloucester, Halifax, Kendal, Macclesfield, Newcastle upon Tyne, Oldham, Perth, Stockport, St Helens, Warrington, and Wolverhampton. In addition, he was consulted over the feasibility of schemes for supply of water to Barnsley, Edinburgh, and Liverpool. In 1869, as a result of being involved with Glasgow water supply, Bateman and J. W. Bazalgette combined to propose a scheme to dispose of Glasgow sewage by gravitation. Bateman was also connected with various harbour and dock trusts throughout the British Isles, acted as consulting engineer to the Clyde Navigation Trust, and was employed by the government in 1863 on the Shannon navigation inquiry.

In addition to these activities, Bateman carried out several works abroad. In 1869 he proposed, in a pamphlet entitled Channel Railway, written with Julian John Revy, to construct a submarine railway between France and England in a cast-iron tube. In the same year he went out as representative of the Royal Society, on the invitation of the khedive, to attend the opening of the Suez Canal, and wrote a long report of his visit, which was read to the society on 6 January 1870 and published in the Proceedings. In the winter of 1870–71 he visited Buenos Aires at the request of the Argentine government, for the purpose of designing harbour works. His plans were not adopted, but he was afterwards employed to design and carry out the drainage and water supply of the city. In 1874 he prepared water schemes for Naples and Constantinople, and he was also engineer for reclamation schemes in Spain and Majorca. The crown agents to the colonies employed him in Ceylon to design and carry out works for supplying Colombo with water.

In all his undertakings Bateman advocated soft water in preference to hard, and favoured gravitation schemes where they were practicable to avoid the necessity of pumping. In 1855 he prepared an important paper for the British Association on the state of knowledge on the supply of water to towns, defining the nature of the problem, giving an outline of previous measures, enumerating the sources from which towns could be supplied, and comparing their merits. To supplement the activities of amateur meteorologists he devoted a great deal of time to methods of quantifying rainfall, mainly by setting up collection stations near the reservoirs that he constructed; these stations became part of G. J. Symonds's national system, as reported to the British Association in 1865. In the same year, he published a pamphlet, On the Supply of Water to London from the Sources of the River Severn, which created considerable discussion. He designed and surveyed the scheme at his own expense, at the cost of about £5000. A royal commission was held, and in 1868 it reported very much in favour of the project, which was purely a gravitation scheme, designed at an estimated outlay of £11.4 million to convey 230 million gallons of water a day to London. In 1883 Bateman assumed by royal licence the prefix, surname, and arms of La Trobe, as a compliment to his grandfather.

From 1833 to 1881 Bateman directed his business alone but used the apprenticeship system extensively, one of his more famous protégés being Alexander Richardson Binnie. From 1881 to 1885 George Hill was his partner, but in 1888 he took as partners his son-in-law, Richard Clere Parsons, and his son, Lee La Trobe Bateman. He was elected a member of the Institution of Civil Engineers on 23 June 1840 and fellow of the Royal Society of London on 7 June

1860, and was president of the institution in 1878 and 1879. He was a fellow of the Royal Society of Edinburgh, the Royal Geographical Society, the Geological Society, the Society of Arts, and the Royal Institution. La Trobe Bateman died on 10 June 1889 at his home, Moor Park, Farnham, an estate he had purchased in 1859, where his coat of arms may still be seen.   PETER RUSSELL

Sources PICE, 97 (1888–9), 392–8 · J. F. Bateman, *History and description of Manchester waterworks* (1884) · P. E. Russell, 'John Frederic La Trobe-Bateman, FRS, water engineer, 1810–1889', MSc diss., University of Manchester, 1980 [incl. bibliography of Bateman's works, chap. 3] · private information (2004) · P. E. Russell, 'John Frederic La Trobe-Bateman (1810–1889): water engineer', *Transactions* [Newcomen Society], 52 (1980–81), 119–38 · G. J. M. Gale, 'On Glasgow waterworks', *Transactions of the Institution of Engineers in Scotland*, 2 (1863–4) · baptismal register of Brethrens' congregation, Lower Wyke, Halifax, Yorkshire, 1810 · d. cert.
Archives Inst. CE, papers relating to Newcastle waterworks
Likenesses C. Wilkinson, oils (after photograph), Inst. CE
Wealth at death £43,227 19s. 3d.: probate, 6 Aug 1889, CGPLA Eng. & Wales

Bateman, Kate Josephine (1842–1917). *See under* Bateman, Hezekiah Linthicum (1812–1875).

Bateman [*née* Harker], **Mary** (1768–1809), thief and poisoner, was born in Asenby, Yorkshire, the daughter of a small farmer named Harker. She evidently received a good education for one of her class, and could read and write proficiently. At the age of thirteen her father sent her into service in Thirsk. Seven years later she removed to York, where she learned the rudiments of dressmaking, and it was here that her life of crime began in earnest. After only one year she had to flee to Leeds after being caught in the act of robbery. During the next four years she worked as a mantua maker, and began to practise as a wise woman, telling fortunes and pretending to remove spells. In 1792 she married a wheelwright named John Bateman.

Although her magical activities undoubtedly brought in a healthy income, Bateman displayed what may have been a pathological need to steal. She was, moreover, none too discreet in the manner of her robberies. Caught several times by lodgers and neighbours, she seems to have avoided prosecution by buying off her victims. There is no evidence that John Bateman was an accomplice in his wife's various frauds and thefts. Indeed in 1796 he was apparently motivated by shame to join the army, bringing Mary with him. They returned to Leeds within a year, however, and Mary resumed her criminal career.

In 1806 Bateman hit upon a new scam that brought her to the attention of a wider public. Encouraged by the local popularity of the millenarian prophet Joanna Southcott, she joined and attended meetings of the Southcottians, a group of people she presumably saw as possible victims for her magical frauds. To seal her reputation among them, and also to exploit them, she publicly claimed that one of her hens had laid three miraculous eggs bearing the inscription 'Christ is coming'. Hundreds came to see these unusual vehicles of divine communication, with visitors having to pay a penny each to satisfy their curiosity.

Considering her lack of discretion and tendency to take her frauds too far, it was perhaps inevitable that Bateman would eventually find herself before a criminal court. That day came in October 1808 after a Leeds clothier named William Perigo accused her of murdering his wife, Rebecca, by poisoning. Mrs Perigo had consulted Bateman about a pain she felt in her breast, and was informed that she was suffering from the effects of an 'evil wish'. Bateman commenced to extract large sums of money from the couple under the pretence of effecting a cure.

Bateman was tried at the York assizes in March 1809, and found guilty of murder and fraud. She was hanged at noon on Monday 20 March. Her body was taken to Leeds General Infirmary for dissection, but, with an opportunism worthy of the woman herself, the infirmary publicly exhibited her corpse, charging 3d. per person and thereby raised more than £30.   OWEN DAVIES

Sources *Extraordinary life and character of Mary Bateman, the Yorkshire witch* (1809) · *Leeds Mercury* (25 March 1809) · *York Herald* (25 March 1809) · *Yorkshire Notes and Queries*, 1 (1905), 64

Bateman [*née* Cowell], **Sidney Frances** (1823–1881), actress and playwright, was born in New York on 29 March 1823. Her father was Joseph Leathley *Cowell (1792–1863), an English-born low comedian, who settled in the United States in 1821 and there enjoyed success as an actor and circus manager. Her mother, *née* Frances Sheppard, was an actress who died in New Orleans about 1838. Sidney spent her early years on a farm north of Cincinnati, Ohio. A special friend of her childhood was Junius Brutus Booth the elder, a long-time friend of her father's. While appearing at the St Louis (Missouri) Theatre, she married, on 10 November 1839, a fellow actor, Hezekiah Linthicum *Bateman (1812–1875). They became the parents of eight children, notably Kate Josephine Bateman (later Mrs Crowe), Ellen Douglass Bateman (later Mrs Greppo), Virginia Frances Bateman (later Mrs Compton), and Isabel Emilie Bateman, all of whom are noticed in Hezekiah's article. From the earliest years, both parents dedicated themselves to their children's dramatic education and careers.

In addition to numerous shorter dramatic pieces written for and acted by her young daughters Kate and Ellen, Mrs Bateman wrote several popular plays, chiefly a comedy entitled *Self*, first produced at Bateman's St Louis Theatre on 18 June 1856, and a tragedy in blank verse entitled *Geraldine, or, The Master Passion*, introduced at Wallack's Theatre, New York, on 22 August 1859. Both were played for many years by leading artists of the day.

In 1871 Hezekiah Linthicum Bateman took the lease on the Lyceum Theatre, London, and, in concert with Henry Irving, raised it to a pre-eminent position among London theatres. After Bateman's death in 1875 his widow continued in its management, but in August 1878, following some disagreement over Isabel Bateman's position as leading lady, she surrendered the Lyceum lease as well as its costumes and props to Irving. She later purchased the lease of Sadler's Wells Theatre, virtually rebuilt it to meet the fire code requirements, and opened on 9 October 1879 with a revival of a dramatic version of *Rob Roy*, featuring her daughter Kate as Helen Macgregor. Mrs Bateman's management of Sadler's Wells continued until her death in 1881. During this time she presented a variety of dramatic entertainments: *Romeo and Juliet*, *Macbeth*, *The School for Scandal*, an American production of *The Danites* by Joaquin Miller, revivals of *The Hunchback* and *Mary Warner*, and Christmas pantomimes.

Sidney Bateman died at 7 Taviton Street, Gordon Square, London, on 13 January 1881 and was buried in the old Hendon churchyard, on 17 January.   GAYLE T. HARRIS

Sources C. Mackenzie, *My life and times*, 10 vols. (1963–71), vol. 1 · V. F. B. Compton, 'Mother', [n.d.], Ransom HRC, Sir Compton Mackenzie MSS · J. Cowell, *Thirty years passed among the players in England and America*, 2 pts (1844) · *DAB* · J. J. Weisert, *The curtain rose* (1958) · letters of administration, 8 April 1881, Principal Registry of the Family Division, London · *New Orleans Courier* (19 April 1838) · *New Orleans Courier* (14 Dec 1838) · *Daily Argus* (12 Aug 1838–14 Sept 1839) · *Daily Pennant* (6 Dec 1839) · m. cert. · *Daily Telegraph* (18 Jan 1881) · 'Stage notes', *The Academy* (15 Jan 1881), 52 · various playbills for Sadler's Wells Theatre, 1879–81, Theatre Museum, Covent Garden, London · playbill for Victoria Theatre, Surrey, 16 and 18 Sept 1846, priv. coll. · d. cert.

Archives priv. coll. | Folger, Augustin Daly MSS · Lincoln Central Library, letters to Hallam Tennyson and Alfred, Lord Tennyson · Ransom HRC, Sir Compton Mackenzie MSS

Likenesses photograph, Howard University, Washington, DC

Wealth at death under £2000: administration, 8 April 1881, *CGPLA Eng. & Wales*

Bateman, Thomas (1778–1821), physician and dermatologist, was born on 29 April 1778 at Whitby, Yorkshire, the only son of a surgeon with a medical practice in the town. Educated there by a dissenting minister, at the age of eleven Bateman attended a private school at Thornton, 20 miles away. His father died when he was fifteen and the next year he attended a local apothecary's shop to learn pharmacy. He also studied French, and was taught mineralogy by Andrew Crawford, a local medical practitioner. Three years later Bateman moved to London and studied at the Great Windmill Street school of medicine. He also attended Matthew Baillie's medical practice at St George's Hospital (1797–8). He moved to Edinburgh in 1798, and was clinical clerk to Professor Andrew Duncan during the winter of 1800–01. He became a member of the Royal Medical Society and took his MD in 1801 with an inaugural dissertation, 'De haemorrhoea petechiali'.

On Bateman's return to London the same year, he became a pupil of Robert Willan at the Public Dispensary, Carey Street. Bateman was made a temporary assistant, perhaps to favour his election as a physician in 1804. In the same year he was appointed to the London Fever Hospital, where he studied and, in 1819, published a book on the relation between epidemic disease in London and the weather. He also noted that debility in the course of a fever might be due to excessive stimulatory treatment. In 1805 Bateman was admitted a licentiate of the Royal College of Physicians.

With Henry Reeve, Bateman helped to found the *Edinburgh Medical and Surgical Journal* in 1805. Bateman contributed medical intelligence and regular articles. In particular, he wrote quarterly reports on the diagnosis of patients seen at the Carey Street dispensary. Bateman wrote rapidly and accurately, so that it was his first copy which went to press. The journal continued as the *Edinburgh Medical Journal* and later became the *Scottish Medical Journal*.

Bateman's greatest contribution followed from his association with Robert Willan. Willan was a key figure in the development of modern dermatology, a pioneer, who divided skin diseases into eight orders based on their appearance rather than any theoretical system. When ill health forced Willan to retire in 1811, Bateman became the principal authority in London on dermatology, and acquired a large and successful practice. In 1813 he published *A Practical Synopsis of Cutaneous Diseases According to the Arrangement of Dr. Willan*. The book, in particular the fifth edition (1819), was the most influential dermatological work of the nineteenth century.

Willan was responsible for all the eight orders, but covered only the first four in his classic book; the elaboration of the last four—pustulae, vesiculae, tubercula, and maculae—was due to Bateman. Bateman's *Delineation of Cutaneous Diseases* (1817), which was also a continuation of Willan's work, was augmented by Talbot Fox as the *Atlas of Skin Diseases* (1877). The synopsis had a great success and was translated into French, German, Italian, Portuguese, and Swedish, and reached the attention of the tsar.

Bateman also wrote nearly all the medical articles in Abraham Rees's *Cyclopaedia* from the letter C onwards, except that dealing with history of medicine. He was the first librarian of the Royal Medical and Chirurgical Society, which later became the Royal Society of Medicine, and he compiled its first catalogue.

Bateman's health had begun to fail in 1815 and he lost the sight of one eye. In 1817 treatment with mercury caused toxicity, although many of the symptoms may have been due to cardiac arrhythmia and heart failure as part of an underlying disease. He returned to the Fever Hospital during a severe fever epidemic in London in 1817, and wrote *A Succinct Account of the Contagious Fever of this Country* (1818). He resigned because of illness in 1818 and retired from the Public Dispensary in 1819. Bateman shortly afterwards moved first to Bishop Burton, near Beverley, and then to his native town, Whitby, where he died, unmarried, on 9 April 1821. He had returned to religion a year before his death.   GEOFFREY L. ASHERSON

Sources [J. Rumsey], *Some account of the life and character of the late Thomas Bateman, MD, FLS* (1826) · [T. Bateman], 'Biographical memoir of the late Dr Willan', *Edinburgh Medical and Surgical Journal*, 8 (1812), 502–12 · [T. Bateman], 'Biographical memoir of the late Henry Reeve', *Edinburgh Medical and Surgical Journal*, 11 (1815), 249–63 · T. Bateman, 'Notes of a case of mercurial erethism', *Medico-Chirurgical Transactions*, 9 (1818), 220–33 · J. T. Crissey and L. C. Parish, *The dermatology and syphilology of the nineteenth century* (1981) · 'Bateman: literary executor of Willan', *Journal of the American Medical Association*, 187 (1964), 612–13 · H. MacCormac, 'At the public dispensary with Willan and Bateman', *British Journal of Dermatology and Syphilis*, 45 (1933), 385–95 · Munk, *Roll* · W. A. Pusey, *The history of dermatology* (1933) · J. D. Rolleston, 'Willan and Bateman on fevers', *British Journal of Dermatology and Syphilis*, 45 (1933), 396–405 · *GM*, 1st ser., 91/1 (1821), 381

Archives RCP Lond., papers · Wellcome L., commonplace book

Bateman, Thomas (*bap.* **1821**, *d.* **1861**), archaeologist and antiquary, was baptized on 8 November 1821 at Rowsley, Derbyshire, the only child of **William Bateman** (1787–1835), antiquary, of Middleton by Youlgreave, Derbyshire, and his wife, Mary (*d.* 1822), daughter of James Crompton of Brightmet, Lancashire. Grandson of a prosperous Manchester cotton merchant who purchased the Middleton estate on his retirement, Thomas devoted his time and wealth to antiquarian and ethnological pursuits. After a long liaison with a local married woman, Mary Ann Mason, which caused his grandfather to threaten to disinherit him, Bateman married, on 2 August 1847, Sarah Parker (*b.* 1825), daughter of William and Margaret Parker, also of Middleton by Youlgreave. Sarah was the sister of his bailiff and companion on archaeological excavations, William Parker. Between 1848 and 1858 Thomas and Sarah Bateman had four daughters and one son, Thomas William, born in 1852.

Bateman inherited his learned and antiquarian tastes from his grandfather Thomas (*d.* 1847) and his father, William, who established the basis of a fine library and museum, which he later extended. At first taught at home by his tutor Joseph Wall, Bateman was sent by his grandfather (after his father's death on 11 June 1835) to a private academy in Bootle. He was one of the early fellows of the Ethnological Society and acted as local secretary for Derbyshire for the British Archaeological Association and from 1854 to 1860 for the Society of Antiquaries. After William Bateman's premature death, Thomas published his father's antiquarian and barrow-digging notes and from 1843 himself undertook a very extensive series of excavations in the tumuli of Yorkshire, Staffordshire, and, especially, Derbyshire. These culminated in 1845, when Bateman dug at least thirty-seven barrows in one season in the Derbyshire and Staffordshire moorlands. From 1848 to 1849 he continued numerous excavations in this area with Samuel Carrington, a schoolmaster from Wetton in north Staffordshire, while in north Yorkshire James Ruddock of Pickering opened barrows under Bateman's direction. Archaeological finds were transferred to Bateman's residence, Lomberdale House, near Middleton, built in 1844 to Bateman's design as an appropriate home for the Bateman Museum. By 1855 he was able to publish the first volume of a descriptive catalogue of his *Antiquities and Miscellaneous Objects*.

Highly regarded in his lifetime, Bateman's reputation rests largely on his publications relating to barrow-digging. Himself a follower of such pioneers as Richard Colt Hoare and William Cunnington, Bateman influenced later archaeologists such as William Boyd Dawkins and J. Wilfrid Jackson in Derbyshire. Disillusioned with Stephen Glover, who handled the subscriptions for his first book, *Vestiges of the Antiquities of Derbyshire* (1847), he financed all his later publications himself. As well as many articles in learned journals such as the *Archaeological Journal*, the *Journal of the British Archaeological Association*, and *The Reliquary*, edited by Llewellynn Jewitt, Bateman produced *Ten Years' Digging in Celtic and Saxon Gravehills* in 1861. This was to be his last work: he died of a severe internal haemorrhage a fortnight afterwards on 28 August 1861 at Lomberdale House and was buried, as he had instructed, in unconsecrated ground but in an impressive tomb on a hillside in Middleton.

Despite his wishes, Bateman's very large and important antiquarian and archaeological collections were dispersed within a generation. Sheffield Museum eventually purchased archaeological material on loan there from 1876; other artefacts were auctioned by Sothebys in 1893, and the remainder is said to have been sold in 1895 after the death of his son and heir, Thomas William Bateman.

MARGARET O'SULLIVAN

Sources B. M. Marsden, 'Thomas Bateman, 1821–1861', in T. Bateman, *Ten years' digging in Celtic and Saxon gravehills*, reprint (1978) · parish registers, Youlgreave, Derbyshire, Derbys. RO · parish register (birth), Rowsley, Derbyshire, 8 Nov 1821 · *DNB* · B. M. Marsden, *The barrow knight* (1988)
Archives Bodl. Oxf., collections for a history of the family · Chatsworth House, Derbyshire, Derbyshire collections · Derby Local Studies Library, collection of Derbyshire ballads · Derbys. RO, corresp. · priv. coll. · Sheff. Arch., antiquarian papers · Sheffield City Museum, antiquarian corresp. and notes; archaeological notebook
Likenesses H. Adlard, stipple (after P. W. Justyne), BM, NPG
Wealth at death £70,000: probate, 23 Nov 1861, *CGPLA Eng. & Wales*

Bateman, Virginia Frances (1853–1940). *See under* Bateman, Hezekiah Linthicum (1812–1875).

Bateman [Norwich], **William** (*c.*1298–1355), diplomat, founder of Trinity Hall, Cambridge, and bishop of Norwich, was probably born in Norwich (from which he was sometimes named), the third son of William and Margery Bateman. His father was many times bailiff of the city, and in 1326–7 its member of parliament. William's eldest brother, Bartholomew, was knighted by Edward III, and William, Lord Kerdeston, a Norfolk baron, was one of several nephews. Bateman studied at Cambridge and was made a doctor of civil law as early as 1328, when he was collated to the archdeaconry of Norwich by Bishop William Airmyn (*d.* 1336). Although claims that he was also doctor of canon law seem to be unfounded, Bateman clearly became expert in both disciplines.

Bateman's reputation at the curia led to his appointment as papal chaplain (by 1330) and auditor of the sacred palace (by 1332). In the 1340s he was acting as resident royal proctor at Avignon. Pope Benedict XII (*r.* 1334–42) provided him to the deanery of Lincoln in 1340, and in August sent him to persuade Edward III, then at Ghent, to abandon hostilities with France. In November of that year he returned to the curia with the king's response. In March 1341 royal envoys brought him instructions to condemn the conduct of Archbishop John Stratford (*d.* 1348) before pope and cardinals, and to object to the election of William Zouche (*d.* 1352) as archbishop of York. As dean he was engaged in a long-standing dispute with his chapter about their respective jurisdictions, and appeared in person before Stratford's court at Otford when the archbishop published his award on 23 August 1343. In the interests of his cathedral church he sought to promote the canonization process of Bishop John Dalderby (*d.* 1320).

On the death of Antony (II) Bek, bishop of Norwich, in 1343, the king issued his *congé d'élire*. Bateman was elected by 'divine inspiration', but on 23 January 1344 Pope Clement VI (r. 1342–52), claiming prior reservation, provided him to the see. The chronicler Adam Murimuth cynically observed that Bateman preferred that method of appointment to election. From Avignon he returned with orders to discuss Clement's concern about the 'novelties' being practised in England—such as the measures against alien holders of benefices—and to examine the possible involvement of Archbishop Stratford. In London he appeared before the royal council, where he promised his services at the curia. His temporalities were restored on 2 March, and he re-embarked with royal letters. Back in Avignon he secured a bull authorizing the defraying of his expenses to and from the curia (as papal nuncio) by means of a tax on the clergy, to be raised by the archbishop and the dean of St Paul's. Such self-interest was condemned by Murimuth. Bateman was consecrated on 23 May by the pope, and was probably instrumental in securing the now vacant deanery of Lincoln for John Offord (d. 1349).

Early in 1345, while at Avignon, Bateman was among those appointed to procure dispensations for the marriages of the prince of Wales with a daughter of the duke of Brabant and of Richard (II) Fitzalan, earl of Arundel (d. 1376), with Isabella Despenser. On 16 October he was present at Westminster with the king, archbishop, and others of the king's privy council, to consider Pope Clement's lengthy letter advocating peace with France and urging a crusade. The pope, Murimuth alleged, exhibited partiality by putting the blame for breaking the truce on the English. In November Bateman was one of those deputed to meet the papal nuncio Nicolino Canali, archbishop of Ravenna. He continued to be employed on diplomatic missions to Avignon and elsewhere, particularly in association with Michael Northburgh (d. 1361). In 1348, for instance, he was seeking an accommodation with the Flemings—part of Edward's plan to build continental alliances—while between 1351 and his death he was preoccupied, both abroad and in councils and parliaments at home, with the negotiation of truces or with attempts to procure a permanent peace with France. In return for his services to the royal council he was granted an annuity in 1352. In the meantime he attended the Westminster parliaments of September 1346 and January 1348, at both of which he was appointed to hear and try Gascon petitions. His itinerary shows him to have been in London or his convenient manor of Terling, Essex, at the appropriate times, but it does not record his presence at St Paul's for Stratford's provincial council (1 October 1347), although Blomefield cites a rousing defence of ecclesiastical liberties against secular encroachment which Bateman allegedly delivered there.

Bateman was intermittently absent for some five out of his nine years and eight months as diocesan. He visited the cathedral priory in 1345, subsequently issuing injunctions, and there are indications of his primary visitation among the parishes. The black death brought heavy clerical mortality during the spring and summer months of 1349, during much of which time the bishop was in his diocese. He proved a vigorous defender of the rights of his see. He forced Robert, Lord Morley (d. 1360), to undergo solemn penance for damage done to the temporalities of his see, despite the fact that they had been in the king's hand when the damage was inflicted. Following disputes with the priory he acquired papal bulls that confirmed to the diocesan the right to first fruits of all vacant benefices—including those belonging to the chapter. However, his attempt to curb the exemption of the abbey of Bury St Edmunds by holding a visitation was unsuccessful, despite actions in the papal and royal courts over six years. Finally, in 1351, the king himself asked the bishop to settle the dispute, but not before the bishop had been condemned in the court of king's bench to pay an immense sum as damages—later rescinded.

Bateman's conflict with the townsmen of the bishop's borough of Lynn was even more damaging. The burgesses brought an action in the court of king's bench. The issues in dispute concerned the bishop's right to exercise secular jurisdiction (view of frankpledge, court of hustings, and overall cognizance of pleas), and the demand of the burgesses to elect their mayor. The dispute dragged on until August 1346, when the king, his patience exhausted, confiscated the Norwich temporalities. On their restoration just over a year later the cognizance of pleas in Lynn was deliberately reserved. The royal council was divided over the matter and no decision was reached about the Lynn franchises until May 1350, when they were restored to the bishop, but only as an act of the king's special grace. The contending parties eventually sealed an indenture, dated 13 May 1352, under which the burgesses acquired the right to choose a mayor, but the elect was to be presented to the bishop and to take an oath to preserve the liberties of the church of Norwich.

A generous benefactor of Norwich Cathedral priory, Bateman appropriated the church of Fring, Norfolk, to the priorate for the support of a perpetual chantry there. A monk was to celebrate daily for the bishop's soul at the principal altar in the choir. The weekly celebrant was to receive 2s., and every monk 4s., in two instalments, as well as further sums from the priory of St Leonard, Norwich. To the high altar of the cathedral he gave a large silver and gilt representation of the Holy Trinity, of great value, as well as a smaller image, together with relics, of 20 pounds' weight.

Bateman's household included some notable clerks, including Robert Hereward, John Offord, and Simon Sudbury (d. 1381). As eminent a lawyer as Master Thomas Astley sought the bishop's advice and considered him to be in matters concerning benefices the best authority in the realm. Bateman added a pertinent gloss to the synodal statute (1255) of Walter Suffield (d. 1257), one of his predecessors. The late fourteenth-century legist John Lydford (d. 1407) copied two of his opinions into his precedent book, and at his death there were seven canonists in his *familia*. He was responsible for the foundation of Trinity Hall in Cambridge and for the completion of Edmund Gonville's hall, renamed in honour of the Annunciation of Our Lady (now Gonville and Caius). This 'refoundation'—Bateman acted as Gonville's executor—is dated 21 December 1351 and was confirmed by Bishop Thomas Lisle (*d.* 1361) on 1 January of the following year. Bateman's remodelled statutes were issued in 1353. There was provision for legal studies and no restriction on the number of legists.

At Trinity Hall, founded in 1350 (when he granted the fruits of Blofield church to the college *ad tempus*), Bateman had unfettered scope for his own ideas. It was to be a college of scholars of canon and civil law, with some seven to ten canonists and ten to thirteen civilians. The college was appropriately equipped by the founder with thirty books devoted to civil law, and thirty-five to canon law. In September 1353 he was responsible for a 'treaty of amity' between the two colleges, Trinity Hall being regarded as the 'elder sister'. It is likely that his former diocesan chancellor and vicar-general, Master Walter Everdon, played a part in the final arrangements.

Bateman's final diplomatic mission was as a member of an unsuccessful embassy to Avignon, charged with explaining in the presence of the French envoys the nature of Edward's policy for peace. While engaged in this business he unexpectedly fell ill in December 1354, and on the 23rd was licensed to choose a confessor. He died at Avignon on 6 January following. A biased source alleges that his last words were 'Buri, Buri, St Edmond, St Edmond'. According to Lawrence Leck, prior of Norwich, Bateman was buried in the cathedral church of Avignon before the high altar, although in 1740 no record of his burial could be found. By an indenture dated the day of the bishop's death his executors agreed to leave £261 to the monks of his cathedral priory as compensation for injuries he had inflicted upon them, in return for which the latter agreed to withdraw any actions for debt and not to withhold any of his chattels.   ROY MARTIN HAINES

Sources CUL, UA Luard 39 · opinions from foreign divines about the marriage, CUL, Cambridge MS Ii v 3, fols. 1–96 · Lincs. Arch., D/ii/60/2 [Stratford's decision in dean and chapter dispute], 14, 16 · Dalderby's projected canonization, Lincs. Arch., Di/20/2/B, 1–3 · Norfolk RO, Reg./2/4 · calendar of institutions, period of black death, Norfolk RO, MS 21509/60 · Norfolk RO, D & C Reg. 10 · *Chancery records* · *Documents relating to the university and colleges of Cambridge*, Cambridge University Commission, 3 vols. (1852) · T. Arnold, ed., *Memorials of St Edmund's Abbey*, 3 vols., Rolls Series, 96 (1890–96) · G. O. Sayles, ed., *Select cases in the court of king's bench*, 7 vols., SeldS, 55, 57–8, 74, 76, 82, 88 (1936–71), vol. 2, pp. cxxvii–cxxviii; vol. 5, pp. clii–cliii · Laurence, 'De vita et morte reverendi admodum Willielmi Bateman', *Desiderata curiosa*, ed. F. Peck, 2 (1735), bk 7, 1–4 · [H. Wharton], *Anglia sacra*, 1 (1691) · A. W. W. Dale, ed., *Warren's book* (1911) · F. Blomefield and C. Parkin, *An essay towards a topographical history of the county of Norfolk*, 5 vols. (1739–75), vol. 2, pp. 359–64 · C. Crawley, *Trinity Hall: the history of a Cambridge college, 1350–1975* (1976) · G. E. Corrie, 'A catalogue of the books given to Trinity Hall, Cambridge, by the founder', *Proceedings of the Cambridge Antiquarian Society*, 2 (1860–64), 73–8 · A. H. Thompson, 'William Bateman, bishop of Norwich', *Norfolk Archaeology*, 25 (1933–5), 102–37 · C. Given-Wilson, *The royal household and the king's affinity: service, politics and finance in England, 1360–1413* (1986) · D. M. Owen, *The medieval canon law: teaching, literature and transmission* (1990) · C. N. L. Brooke, *A history of Gonville and Caius College* (1985) · H. Rashdall, *The universities of Europe in the middle ages*, ed. F. M. Powicke and A. B. Emden, new edn, 3 (1936) · I. J. Churchill, *Canterbury administration: the administrative machinery of the archbishopric of Canterbury*, 2 vols. (1933) · R. M. Haines, *Archbishop John Stratford: political revolutionary and champion of the liberties of the English church*, Pontifical Institute of Medieval Studies: Texts and Studies, 76 (1986) · W. M. Ormrod, *The reign of Edward III* (1990) · *Hemingby's register*, ed. H. M. Chew, Wiltshire Archaeological and Natural History Society, Records Branch, 18 (1963) · Emden, *Cam.* · *Fasti Angl., 1300–1541*, [Lincoln, Mon. cath. (SP), Introduction] · *Fasti Angl., 1300–1541*, [Introduction] · *Fasti Angl., 1300–1541*, [Monastic cathedrals] · *John Lydford's book*, ed. D. M. Owen, Devon and Cornwall RS, new ser., 20 (1974) · J. W. Clark, 'Bishop Bateman', *Proceedings of the Cambridge Antiquarian Society*, 9 (1894–8), 297–336 · RotP
Archives CUL, UA Luard 39 · Norfolk RO, D & C Reg. 10 · Norfolk RO, MS 21509/60 · Norfolk RO, Reg./2/4 | Lincs. Arch., Di /20/2/B, 1–3
Likenesses J. Faber, mezzotint, 1714 (after an unknown artist), BM, NPG · W. Robins, *c.*1781 (after Bateman's episcopal seal)

Bateman, William (1787–1835). *See under* Bateman, Thomas (*bap.* 1821, *d.* 1861).

Bates, Cadwallader John (1853–1902), antiquary, was born at Kensington Gate, London, on 14 January 1853, the eldest son of Thomas Bates (1810–1882) and his first wife, Emily (*d.* 1853), daughter of John Batten of Thorn Falcon, Somerset. His father, of Aydon White House and Heddon, Northumberland, was a barrister who had been a fellow of Jesus College, Cambridge, from 1834 to 1849. The Bates family had been established in Northumberland since the fourteenth century, but through his mother Bates was a kinsman of Cadwallader, twelfth Lord Blayney of Gregynog (extinct 1874), after whom he was named. He was at Eton College from 1866 but left after two years because of weak eyesight, which was to trouble him throughout his life. In 1869 he proceeded to Jesus College, Cambridge, but poor sight led to his being awarded an *aegrotat* in the moral sciences tripos of 1871. He proceeded MA in 1875. Between 1871 and 1882 he travelled much abroad, especially in Germany and Poland, where two of his uncles had lived for many years, in particular Edward Bates, who lived at Schloss Clöden, Brandenburg, Prussia. In 1882, having inherited this Prussian property, he succeeded to the family estates in Northumberland, to the family interest in the Heddon colliery, and to Kirklevington, near Yarm, Yorkshire. He invested in land in Silesia and had family interests in Wittenberg. Although his interests were mainly scholarly, he had a practical knowledge of farming and mastered the intricacies of the herd-book to rebuild partially the celebrated Kirklevington shorthorn herd, dispersed in 1850, of his great-uncle Thomas Bates, whose biography he published in 1897.

In 1882 Cadwallader Bates bought Langley Castle, near Haydon Bridge, from the commissioners of the Greenwich Hospital estates and spent large sums on restoring it, using the Durham architect C. Hodgson Fowler. As magistrate and deputy lieutenant, Bates took his full share of county business in Northumberland, and was high sheriff in 1890. His enduring contribution to county life lay, however, in his historical work, especially on the medieval history of Northumbria. In *Border Holds* (1891), the first but only volume published of a detailed study of Northumberland castles, he showed keen observation and documentary accuracy on a subject much burdened with legend. Twenty-seven castles and towers were discussed, but no sequel was published. A concise *History of Northumberland* (1895), more popular in tone, raised standards in his day. Bates was active as a promoter of the collaborative *History of Northumberland*, and made contributions to its first six volumes (1893–1902). He was a vice-president of the Society of Antiquaries of Newcastle upon Tyne and, from 1880, a frequent contributor to *Archaeologia Aeliana*. He was deeply read in Christian origins and medieval hagiography, and left some unfinished studies of St Patrick and St Gildas. Attracted by its difficulty, he took up the history of the Paschal controversy and likewise left several studies on the subject.

In 1893, while on a visit to Austrian Poland, Bates was received into the Uniate Church. On 3 September 1895 he married Josephine (*d.* 1933), second daughter of François Jacob d'Echarvine, of Tailloires, Savoy; there were no children. Bates's indefatigable historical labours told on his health, and he died at his home at Langley Castle of heart failure on 18 March 1902; he was buried in the castle grounds. A collection of his letters, spirited in expression and displaying wide learning in local antiquities, was published in 1906.   G. S. WOODS, *rev.* ALAN BELL

Sources *The Times* (20 March 1902) · *Letters of C. J. Bates*, ed. M. Culley (1906) · T. Hodgkin, *Archaeologia Aeliana*, new ser., 24 (1903), 178–83 · 'Biographies of contributors to the society's literature', *Archaeologia Aeliana*, 3rd ser., 10 (1913), 292–6 · Burke, *Gen. GB* (1952)

Archives BL, diary, Add. MS 65380

Likenesses photograph, repro. in *Archaeologia Aeliana*, 3rd ser., 10

Wealth at death £93,789 6s. 6d.: probate, 11 Aug 1902, CGPLA Eng. & Wales

Bates [*née* Dwyer], **Daisy May** (1859–1951), anthropologist and social worker among Aboriginal Australians, was born around 16 October 1859, at Roscrea, co. Tipperary, Ireland, the third of four children of Edward Dwyer, shopkeeper and small farmer, and his wife Bridget, *née* Hunt. Both parents died within five years and relatives cared for the children. Daisy received a secondary education which added linguistic facility to her characteristic lifetime oral fluency, selective memory, and aristocratic values. Born a Roman Catholic she claimed Anglicanism and the O'Dwyer surname.

Bates alleged that her migration to Australia was necessitated by tuberculosis, but her longevity under harsh conditions suggests that this was part of her increasingly fictitious persona. She sailed on the *Almora* for Queensland, disembarking at Townsville in January 1883. While a governess on Fanning Downs station near Charters Towers, on 13 March 1884 she married according to Anglican rites Edwin Henry Murrant (1864–1902), a stockman who became notorious in the Second South African War as Breaker Morant [*see* Morant, Harry Harbord]. They soon separated, and their union remained unknown until 1978.

On 17 February 1885 Daisy bigamously married John

Bates (1856–1935), drover, in the Anglican church, Nowra, New South Wales. Their son, Arnold Hamilton Bates, was born at Bathurst on 26 August 1886. Sporadic family relationships virtually ceased from 1902.

In 1894 Daisy Bates returned to England, gaining journalistic experience that would later sustain her when she contributed 270 newspaper articles on Aborigines. She arrived in Perth in 1899 to investigate claims in *The Times* of atrocities against Kimberley Aborigines. After visiting the north-west with her husband, she accepted an invitation from Perth's Catholic bishop M. Gibney to spend three months at the Trappist Beagle Bay mission, which enabled her to gain first-hand knowledge of the position of Aborigines.

Yet, when *The Times* published further allegations during May 1904, Bates surprisingly wrote defending pastoralist and government Aboriginal relations. Possibly these opinions recommended her for official employment, because she was appointed by the government of Western Australia to collect ethnographic and linguistic data. Across five years she visited Aboriginal communities, amassing data for a government-sponsored book, for which she sought advice from Andrew Lang.

Bates's project became diverted in 1910, when she was assigned to A. R. (Radcliffe-)Brown's Western Australian anthropological expedition. Their friction is legendary; the distressing conditions among exiled diseased Aborigines on Dorré and Bernier islands influenced her towards welfare activities. Insight into antipathy between Bates and Brown was provided by a fellow expeditioner, Grant Watson, and by later anthropological evaluations of White and Needham.

The interlude in Bates's official work proved disastrous, because the incoming government terminated her appointment in 1912, reneging on publishing her book. So commenced her self-imposed years of tented isolation and penury at Eucla and Ooldea, a bizarre attraction for train passengers, including whistle-stop visits by royalty.

From 1932 Bates was befriended by a journalist, Ernestine Hill, who popularized her seclusion and affectionate grandmotherly Aboriginal title, Kabbarli. Bates was appointed CBE in 1934, and from 1936 she received a meagre government weekly allowance of £2, later £5 5s., to prepare her papers for the National Library of Australia (fifty-two boxes eventuated).

Bates is judged harshly from her later newspaper notes and *The Passing of the Aborigines* (1938), but her Ooldea years belong to her old age when both she and her writings approached mythology. Her ill-fated memoir, *The Native Tribes of Western Australia* (1985), based upon participant observation, only needed careful editing to establish its significance. Her work remains controversial, although championed by feminist writers. Bates shared the contemporary opinion that the Aboriginal peoples were doomed; she was contemptuous of people of mixed heritage and preferred male informants; she camped distant from 'her' people. She later publicized Aboriginal cannibalism, which provided fuel for racists, but which was a travesty of reality.

Blue-eyed and slightly built, Bates was 5 feet 3 inches tall, a grand eccentric, aptly described in her bush setting, equipped with umbrella, 'gloved, veiled, tailored, sailor-hatted, cravatted, shirt-waisted, voluminously skirted' (Hill, 3). She passed her final years in mock gentility in Adelaide, where she died at the Hydro Sanatorium, Prospect, on 18 April 1951 from myocardial degeneration and senility, leaving £66. She was buried on 20 April 1951 at North Road cemetery, Nailsworth, Adelaide.

D. J. MULVANEY

Sources D. Bates, *The native tribes of Western Australia*, ed. I. White (1985) · I. White, 'Daisy Bates: legend and reality', *First in their field*, ed. J. Marcus (1993), 47–65 · E. Hill, *Kabbarli: a personal memoir of Daisy Bates* (1973) · *AusDB*, 7.208–9 · E. Salter, *Daisy Bates: 'the great white queen of the never never'* (1971) · E. L. Grant Watson, *But to what purpose* (1946) · E. L. Grant Watson, *Journey under southern stars* (1968) · R. Needham, *Remarks and inventions: skeptical essays about kinship* (1974) · R. Needham, 'Kinship refutations', *Oceania*, 53 (1982), 123–38 · I. White, 'Reply to Rodney Needham', *Oceania*, 52 (1982), 139–40 · I. White, 'Mrs Bates and Mr Brown', *Oceania*, 52 (1981), 193–210 · private information (2004)
Archives Adelaide University, Barr Smith Library · Battye Library of Western Australia, Perth, MSS · Mitchell L., NSW, corresp. and MSS · NL Aus., MS 365 · State Library of South Australia, Adelaide · State Library of Victoria, Melbourne, La Trobe manuscript collection, corresp. and MSS · University of Queensland, Brisbane, Fryer Library, corresp. and MSS | FILM Screen Sound Australia, Canberra
Likenesses photographs, University of Adelaide, Barr Smith Library · photographs, Battye Library of Western Australia, Perth · photographs, NL Aus.
Wealth at death £66 9s. 6d.: probate, with will, South Australia

Bates, Sir David Robert (1916–1994), theoretical physicist, was born on 18 November 1916 in Omagh, co. Tyrone, the younger of two surviving children of Walter Vivian Bates and his wife, Mary Olive, *née* Shera. Walter Bates came from Mountrath, Queen's county, and had set up a pharmacist's shop in Omagh. His wife's father was land agent for Lord Justice Ross near Omagh. Bates first went to a private school in Omagh but, to obtain a better education for him and his sister Margaret, his mother moved with them to Belfast, while the father travelled between there and Omagh. Bates attended a preparatory school, Inchmarlo, and the Royal Belfast Academical Institution, 1929–34, of which he was later a governor. He won a scholarship to the Queen's University of Belfast and graduated with first-class honours in mathematical and experimental physics in 1937. His professors were George Eméleus and Sir Harrie Massey. Under Massey he obtained the MSc degree for calculations on atomic recombination in the upper atmosphere, the beginning of a lifelong pursuit.

In 1939 Massey went to University College, London, as Goldschmidt professor of applied mathematics. Bates went with him and began work for a PhD degree, but did not complete it because of the Second World War. During the war he worked first at the Admiralty research laboratory with Massey and others on countermeasures to the magnetic mine, and then at the mine design department at Havant.

After the war Bates became a lecturer at University College, London, and with his research students Michael Seaton and Agnete Damgaard of Denmark began a programme of quantum mechanical calculations of atomic and molecular processes, especially those of importance in the upper atmosphere. For much of 1950 he was in Pasadena, California, and collaborated with Marcel Nicolet from Belgium. He also went to Princeton where he wrote an important paper with Lyman Spitzer on the formation of interstellar molecules. Bates received the DSc degree in 1951 and was appointed reader in physics, but the same year he was elected professor of applied mathematics in the Queen's University of Belfast, and appointed head of the department. He was elected to the fellowship of the Royal Society in 1955 and met his wife, Barbara Bailey Morris, a medical social worker, while in London for the admission ceremony. They were married on 20 March 1956. There were two children, Katherine Mary and Adam.

Bates worked almost entirely on the rates of atomic and molecular processes, especially in the presence of free electrons, and on the interpretation of the properties of natural plasmas in terms of those rates. His earliest investigations concerned ionized oxygen in the upper atmosphere, and he continued to study the atmosphere and ionosphere throughout his career. He developed procedures for quantum mechanical calculations of rates of ionization by collision with electrons, of recombination of ions with electrons with the emission of radiation, of rates of emission of radiation by excited atoms (oscillator strengths), and of recombination of electrons with ionized molecules, followed by dissociation. He and Agnete Damgaard developed the powerful Bates–Damgaard method for the calculation of oscillator strengths, used by himself and others to generate a large body of reliable values. After 1960 Bates had a powerful electronic computer (DEUCE) in Belfast for his calculations.

Through his fundamental work Bates accounted for the main layered structure of the ionosphere. With Marcel Nicolet he demonstrated the importance of oxygen and other molecules in the upper atmosphere and identified radiation from them in the light from the night sky and the dayglow.

Bates built up in Belfast an impressive group of theoretical physicists working on calculations of atomic processes. In his later years he worked particularly on collisions between atoms and molecules. He also studied clouds of interstellar molecules and laboratory plasmas. Widely admired and respected, his co-operation was sought by other groups, in particular the Harvard–Smithsonian Center for Astrophysics, which he visited a number of times.

Bates was deeply attached to Belfast and Ulster and refused many invitations to move to larger and more renowned institutions. By his devotion to his chosen field his own group and department won renown. Not surprisingly he was very distressed by the sectarian troubles in Ulster and the way in which they intensified over the years. He was one of the founders of the Alliance Party and served as vice-president.

Bates published more than 330 articles in scientific journals, a third of them after he suffered a serious heart attack in 1973. He edited books on atomic and molecular physics, and was editor for twenty-eight years of the annual series Advances in Atomic, Molecular and Optical Physics and for thirty-one years of the journal *Planetary and Space Sciences*.

Bates's work was recognized by many honours besides his fellowship of the Royal Society. He was a member of the Royal Irish Academy (1952, vice-president 1976); he was elected to the International Academy of Aeronautics (1961) and to the International Academy of Quantum Molecular Science (1985); and he was a foreign member of the American Academy of Arts and Sciences (1974), of the Royal Academy of Belgium (1979), and of the National Academy of Science (1984). The National University of Ireland, the universities of Ulster, Dublin, Glasgow, Stirling, Essex, York (England and Canada), and the Queen's University of Belfast conferred honorary degrees upon him. He received the Hughes medal of the Royal Society (1970), the Charles Chree medal of the Institute of Physics (1978), the gold medal of the Royal Astronomical Society (1979), and the Fleming medal of the American Geophysical Union (1987). He was made a knight bachelor in 1978 for services to science and education. The European Geophysical Society instituted the Sir David Bates medal in his honour, of which he was the first recipient.

Bates died in Belfast of heart failure on 5 January 1994. He was survived by his wife and two children.

ALAN COOK

Sources A. Dalgarno, *Memoirs FRS*, 43 (1997), 47–71 · *The Times* (18 Jan 1994) · *The Independent* (10 Jan 1994) · *WWW*, 1991–5 · Burke, *Peerage*
Likenesses B. Blackshaw, oils, 1981, Queen's University, Belfast · photograph, repro. in *The Times*
Wealth at death £145,943: probate, 23 May 1994, *CGPLA NIre*.

Bates, Sir (Richard) Dawson, first baronet (1876–1949), politician, was born at Strandtown, Belfast, on 23 November 1876, the only son of Richard Dawson Bates, solicitor and clerk of the crown and peace for Belfast, and Mary, daughter of Professor R. F. Dill MD of Queen's College, Belfast. His grandfather John Bates (d. 1855) ran the Conservative political machine in Belfast for many years, serving as town clerk from 1842 until he was disgraced by a chancery court ruling of maladministration in 1855. Dawson Bates attended Coleraine Academical Institution and was admitted as a solicitor in 1900. He was apprenticed to his uncle Edward, with whom he founded E. and R. D. Bates, in 1908. Relatively late in life, in 1920, he married Jessie Muriel Cleland (d. 1972), daughter of Sir Charles Cleland, a leading figure in Glasgow Unionist circles. A son, John, was born in 1921 (d. 1998). Bates was knighted in 1921 and became a baronet in 1937. He was a deputy lieutenant of Belfast, a JP for co. Down and, briefly, a Belfast harbour commissioner.

Like his grandfather, Dawson Bates preferred politics to the law. In a career spanning almost forty years he held only two main positions. When the Ulster Unionist Council was formed in 1905, creating a separate voice for Ulster Unionism for the first time, he became part-time secretary at £100 p.a., a position which he held until his appointment as minister of home affairs in the first Northern Ireland cabinet in June 1921. In 1912 he organized with great efficiency the Balmoral and Craigavon anti-home rule demonstrations and the Ulster covenant, where Andrew Bonar Law and Sir Edward Carson laid the foundation for Ulster Unionism's successful opposition to the third Home Rule Bill. He played a vital role at this time in uniting the local Unionist associations and the political leadership behind an uncomplicated and uncompromising policy of defence of the union. He was active in the Ulster Volunteer Force (UVF), and took a leading part in the Larne gun-running in April 1914. Being delicate in health Bates did not see service in the First World War, but he later was appointed OBE for his fund-raising work with UVF charities. Throughout his period as a Unionist organizer he collaborated with southern unionist bodies, though admitting in 1918 that he believed in fighting home rule from a purely Ulster point of view, adding—disingenuously or naïvely—'as a means of saving the south' (Buckland, *Irish Unionism*, 254). In fact Bates epitomized the new breed of middle-class, Belfast oriented Ulster Unionist, for whom the concerns of southern landed unionism were remote. He was more concerned with retaining the support of the Ulster protestant working class. This is reflected in both his early organizational work and in the populist approach that later characterized his ministerial career. During the Belfast general strike of January 1919 he railed to Sir James Craig that 'the leaders are practically Sinn Féiners', and he strongly promoted the anti-socialist Ulster Unionist Labour Association (ibid., 431). In 1920 he played a prominent part in the creation of the Ulster special constabulary, a protestant paramilitary force which grew from the ruins of the UVF.

During the first half of his career Bates showed no interest in representative office. In 1921, however, he was pressed by Craig to stand for the newly established Northern Ireland parliament. He was returned for the proportional representation constituency of East Belfast, continuing in the single seat successor constituency of Victoria until his retirement in 1945. When Craig formed his cabinet Bates was in many ways an obvious choice as minister for home affairs, and he held the position for twenty-two years. Faced with a serious challenge to the security of the newly partitioned territory he responded harshly: he did not co-operate with the conciliation committee established under the Craig–Collins pact of 30 March 1922; in the same year he introduced the Civil Authorities (Special Powers) Act, a draconian piece of emergency legislation which he subsequently made permanent; and he continued the internment of republican suspects until 1924. He showed courage in drawing the teeth of the extremist Ulster Protestant Association in 1922, but this movement represented a direct challenge to his own Unionist Party. In other cases, such as the attacks on Catholics returning from the Eucharistic Congress in 1932, he caused the law officers to intervene with magistrates so that prison sentences were not imposed.

Bates's non-conciliatory approach to communal relations did not cease with the restoration of peace in 1923. In 1924–5 he took a more alarmist view than his colleagues over the likely outcome of the Irish boundary commission, and planned resistance. In 1922 and 1929 he discontinued proportional representation, in first local and then regional elections. During the 1930s he promoted schemes relating to various local councils where Unionist and nationalist voters were closely balanced. Derry's ward boundaries, for instance, were redrawn in 1936 so that, notwithstanding a large Catholic majority in the adult population, the city council retained a strong Unionist majority until 1973. Bates was unenthusiastic about his inspector-general's wish to increase Catholic recruitment into the Royal Ulster Constabulary, and in 1934 he declined to use his office telephone for important business while a Catholic continued to be employed as a telephonist at Stormont. He once told an audience

> so long as we live there will always be the danger of … merging into the Free State. We will never get rid of it. One only has to go to England to see the extraordinary apathy towards us of people who should be our friends.   (*Irish News*, 30 March 1938)

Bates was well attuned to the voice of popular protestantism. Conversely, he was much resented by nationalists. As early as 1922 the Irish Free State leader Michael Collins told Winston Churchill that Bates was 'notorious for his antipathy to our [Ulster Catholic] people' (Farrell, 99). But what in some contexts appeared to be simply hardline Unionism in other contexts seemed more like weakness. When pervasive corruption was uncovered in the Belfast corporation housing department in 1927 Bates refused to suspend the body. Again, when an inquiry by his own department in 1941 revealed more widespread corruption in the corporation, creating what he himself told the cabinet was an extremely serious state of affairs, he proposed only a weak compromise because he feared the power of the corporation to destroy the government through its influence over the Belfast Unionist Party. In June 1935 he placed a ban on all processions in the city, but lifted it ten days later, after ignoring an illegal loyalist march. The parade on 12 July that followed shortly afterwards occasioned the only major outbreak of lethal rioting in the city between 1922 and 1969.

Bates was also widely criticized by his own side. Stephen Tallents, later the province's imperial secretary, reported to Whitehall in 1922 that 'Bates has the most difficult task in Northern Ireland, and appears to be the least competent of all the present ministers to rise to the occasion' (Hepburn, 240). In 1925 the newspaper editor J. R. Fisher, Northern Ireland's unofficial representative on the boundary commission, described him as an 'ass' whose 'not an inch' rhetoric was most unhelpful (Jackson, 343). In later years indifferent health exacerbated his inaction and indecision. Sir Wilfrid Spender, long serving head of the Northern Ireland civil service, held a low opinion of his ministerial qualities from the beginning, and by 1938 thought him 'incapable of giving his responsible officials coherent directions on policy' (Buckland, *Factory*, 18).

Bates's parliamentary private secretary (and successor) Edmond Warnock resigned in 1940, regarding his superior as incapable of performing his duties. Another of Bates's aides, William Lowry, referred to him as 'our great unconscious humorist' (Barton, 214). Bates's conduct of wartime domestic defence preparations came under particular scrutiny, and in the autumn of 1942 he survived a parliamentary vote of censure by 20 to 4 with several considered abstentions. He should have retired when James Craig, first Viscount Craigavon, died in 1940, but he continued to serve in J. M. Andrews's government, partly it seems because of personal financial needs. He was not appointed to the new government of Sir Basil Brooke in May 1943.

In later years Bates lived in some style at Magherabuoy House, Portrush, but although he remained senior partner in his firm until his death, and was also a director of the Brookvale Linen Company, he is said to have been in straitened financial circumstances in later life. One of his civil servants remembers him as 'small, white-haired, slightly stooped, always looking preoccupied' (Shea, 116). After 1921 he could travel nowhere in Northern Ireland without a police escort. In 1947 the family moved for health—and possibly also security—reasons to rented accommodation at Butleigh House, near Glastonbury, Somerset, where he died on 10 June 1949. His body was flown back to Ulster a few days later for burial in Ballywillan cemetery, Portrush, following a Church of Ireland ceremony. He was a freemason and member of the Orange Order. His son succeeded to the baronetcy.

A. C. HEPBURN

Sources P. Buckland, *The factory of grievances* (1979) · B. Barton, *Brookeborough: the making of a prime minister* (1988) · P. Buckland, *Irish unionism*, 2 vols. (1972–3) · *Belfast News-Letter* (11 June 1949) · *Belfast News-Letter* (15 June 1949) · *Northern Whig and Belfast Post* (11 June 1949) · *Northern Whig and Belfast Post* (15 June 1949) · J. F. Harbinson, *The Ulster unionist party, 1882–1973* (1973) · M. Farrell, *Arming the protestants* (1983) · P. Bew, P. Gibbon, and H. Patterson, *Northern Ireland, 1921–94* (1995) · *The Times* (11 June 1949) · *WW* (1949) · A. Jackson, *Ireland, 1798–1998* (1999) · *Irish News and Belfast Morning News* (11 June 1949) · *CGPLA NIre.* (1950) · d. cert. · P. Shea, *Voices and the sound of drums* (1981) · A. C. Hepburn, *Ireland, 1905–25* (1998), vol. 2 · family gravestone

Archives PRO NIre., Lord Carson papers, D1507 · PRO NIre., Viscount Craigavon papers, D1415 · PRO NIre., Northern Ireland cabinet papers · PRO NIre., Ulster Unionist Council papers, D989

Likenesses photograph, repro. in *Belfast News-Letter* (11 June 1949)

Wealth at death £14,802 6s. 7d.: probate, 24 July 1950, *CGPLA NIre.*

Bates, Harry (1850–1899), sculptor, was born in Stevenage, Hertfordshire, on 26 April 1850, the fifth of eight children of Joseph and Anne Bates. After brief training as an architect's clerk, he served as an apprentice (*c.*1866) and then as an employee (1869–79) of Farmer and Brindley, a London-based architectural stone-carving firm. As his peripatetic work involved either the copying of existing carvings or executing the designs of others, he had little personal scope for development as an artist. In 1879 he settled in London, where he briefly studied at the South London Technical Art School at Lambeth under Jules Dalou before transferring to the Royal Academy Schools in 1881. His student career culminated in 1883 with a gold medal travelling scholarship for his relief *Socrates Teaching the People in the Agora* (1886; marble version, University of Manchester). Edmund Gosse claimed that the work created 'a great sensation' (Gosse, 278) and praised it for being 'founded on the best traditions of Greek relief … yet … instinct with the vitality of modern feeling' (ibid., 280).

Following his award Bates worked in Paris (1883–5), where he rented a studio and, on Dalou's advice, received tuition from Auguste Rodin, the most advanced figure in Parisian sculpture. Rodin's influence on him was limited: there is a linear delicacy, personal to Bates, found throughout his work, and he remained more obviously classical than Rodin both in style and in subject matter. The *Aeneid Triptych* (1885, Glasgow Art Gallery and Museum) possesses, nevertheless, an emotional depth, an unearthly symbolism, and a fluidity of modelling which are all reminiscent of Rodin's *Gates of Hell*.

Bates's all-too-brief career following his return to London distinguished him as a major figure within the New Sculpture, the movement which saw British sculpture reaching unprecedented technical and imaginative heights. If anything, he was stylistically closer to the lyrical realism of Hamo Thornycroft than he was to the decorative fantasy of Alfred Gilbert. He worked in collaboration with Thornycroft on the carved decorations (1888–93) of the Institute of Chartered Accountants' building in the City of London, a highly successful essay in Genoese baroque. Distinctive of Bates was his classical idealism. This represented a major advance on the often dry, didactic neo-classicism which had dominated earlier nineteenth-century sculpture. Bates believed that students should be inspired by 'the wonderful drapery, clothing yet revealing the superb forms' of the Elgin marbles (Johnson, 586).

Bates was nothing if not versatile, having benefited from his earlier grounding as a carver. His work ranges from door knockers and church furnishings to portraiture, architectural decoration, public monuments, and imaginative sculptures. He sympathized with the ideals of the Arts and Crafts movement which stressed the unity of carving and sculpture, and was elected a member of the Art Workers' Guild (1886). He did not, however, neglect his academic career. From 1884 to 1899 he regularly attracted critical acclaim at the Royal Academy and was elected to associate membership in January 1892. Among his major exhibits were *Hounds in Leash* (1891; plaster version, Tate collection), a life-sized portrayal of two leaping Great Danes and a nude, restraining huntsman; *Pandora* (1891, Tate collection), a crouching marble figure holding an ivory and bronze casket, conveying a convincing mood of melancholy and reverie; and *Mors januae vitae* ('Death the gateway of life'; 1899, Sudley Art Gallery, Liverpool). The last work, which has affinities with mixed-media sculpture by Alfred Gilbert and George Frampton, shows an ivory figure of a nude adolescent female, crowned by a sinister, bronze personification of Death, with a parade of souls on the elaborate base. Poignantly, *Mors januae vitae* was exhibited posthumously.

Harry Bates died at his home, 10 Hall Road, St John's Wood, London, on 30 January 1899, aged forty-eight, and was buried on 4 February at his birthplace, Stevenage, Hertfordshire. His estate was valued for probate at £387 1s. 6d. and his widow, Nancie (whom he had married at some time before 1887) was left destitute. His poverty came about through his insistence on producing, at his own expense, the elaborate, large-scale bronze pedestal statuary and reliefs for his equestrian statue in Calcutta of Frederick, first Earl Roberts (1894–7). This work was executed in replica in Kelvingrove Park, Glasgow, and as a later bronze reduction (1924) in Horse Guards Parade, London. Described by G. F. Watts as 'the finest equestrian statue of modern times' (Beattie, 220), it testifies not only to Bates's vivid observation of nature but also to his intense artistic idealism. MARK STOCKER

Sources S. Beattie, *The New Sculpture* (1983) · F. Pearson, 'Bates, Harry', *The dictionary of art*, ed. J. Turner (1996) · W. Armstrong, 'Mr Harry Bates', *The Portfolio*, 19 (1888), 170–74 · T. Friedman and others, eds., *The alliance of sculpture and architecture: Hamo Thornycroft, John Belcher, and the Institute of Chartered Accountants building* (1993) [exhibition catalogue, Heinz Gallery, RIBA, London, 14 Jan – 20 Feb 1993] · E. J. W. Johnson, 'Mr Harry Bates ARA', *The Artist*, 17 (1897), 579–88 · *DNB* · B. Read, *Victorian sculpture* (1982) · E. Gosse, 'The new sculpture, 1879–1894 [pt 3]', *Art Journal*, new ser., 14 (1894), 277–82, esp. 278–80 · J. Glaves-Smith, ed., *Reverie, myth, sensuality: sculpture in Britain, 1880–1910* (1992) [exhibition catalogue, Stoke-on-Trent City Museum and Art Gallery, 26 Sept–29 Nov 1992, and Cartwright Hall, Bradford, 12 Dec 1992–7 March 1993] · *Magazine of Art*, 23 (1898–9), 240 · J. Blackwood, *London's immortals: the complete outdoor commemorative statues* (1989) · *CGPLA Eng. & Wales* (1899) · G. Popp and H. Valentine, *Royal Academy of Arts directory of membership: from the foundation in 1768 to 1995, including honorary members* (1996) · Graves, *RA exhibitors*, 1 (1905), 141 · J. Crichton-Browne, *Victorian jottings from an old commonplace book* (1926)

Archives Mitchell L., NSW, Tom Roberts papers, ref. ML 2480 · PRO, information on Bates's *Lord Roberts* statue and poverty at time of death, Works MS 20/136

Likenesses T. Roberts, oils, 1885 (*The sculptor's studio*), Australian National Gallery, Canberra · M. Loudan, painting (oils), 1894, priv. coll. · Ball, photograph, c.1895, repro. in *Magazine of Art*

Wealth at death £387 1s. 6d.: probate, 17 April 1899, *CGPLA Eng. & Wales*

Bates, Henry Walter (1825–1892), naturalist, was born at Leicester on 8 February 1825, the eldest of the four sons of Henry (1794–1870), a hosiery manufacturer, and Sarah, *née* Gill (1803–1860). He was educated at Creaton's academy at Billesdon, a village 10 miles east of Leicester. He left school in 1838, but continued his education at evening classes at the Leicester Mechanics' Institute, while apprentice to another Leicester hosier, Alderman Gregory. On Gregory's death he briefly managed the business before becoming a clerk at Allsopp's brewery in Burton upon Trent. A number of his fellow students were interested in nature and he became a self-taught naturalist, spending his free time in the careful observation and collection of insect life in the Leicestershire countryside and later around Burton upon Trent. He published his first paper, a 'Note on coleopterous insects frequenting damp places' in 1843, in the first

Henry Walter Bates (1825–1892), by John Thomson

number of *The Zoologist*, which subsequently carried several of his early articles on local entomology.

In 1844 Bates met Alfred Russel Wallace, then a master at Leicester collegiate school. They collected insects together and found a common interest in the writings of Darwin and, more unusually, in those of von Humboldt and Lyell. After Wallace returned to south Wales in 1846 they corresponded, and at Wallace's suggestion decided upon an expedition to the Amazon, to study the region's wildlife—collecting duplicate specimens for sale to defray their expenses—in the hope of contributing ideas to the debate about the origin of species. After rapid preparations at the British Museum and Kew Gardens, they sailed from Liverpool in the trading vessel *Mischief* on 26 April 1848, and arrived in Belém (then known as Pará) on 28 May. Their initial base was Belém, from where they collected locally, on the island of Marajó, and on expeditions up the River Tocantins in 1848 and 1849; they separated in 1849.

Wallace returned to England in 1852, but Bates was to remain in Amazonia for eleven years, collecting around bases at Belém, Ega (1850–51 and 1855–9), and Santarém and Villa Nova (1851–5); along the Amazon; and on expeditions up the Tapajos (1852) and as far west as São Paulo on the Solimões in 1857. He worked alone, using local river craft, and, after their introduction in 1853, steamboats. Although his main interest was in insects, particularly butterflies and beetles, he also collected animals, birds, reptiles, plants, shells, and Indian artefacts. These were

sold by his London agent, Samuel Stevens, to museums and private collectors, but he also sought specific items for public and private collections. In total he dispatched some 14,700 species back to England, 8000 of them new to science.

During 1858 Bates's health deteriorated and he left the upper Amazon in February 1859 and spent two months in Belém before embarking for England on 2 June 1859. He settled in Leicester, describing himself in 1863 as a worsted hosier. However, he had begun to write up the collections he had made, and produced a series of major papers, published in the *Transactions* of the Linnean and Entomological societies, and the *Annals and Magazine of Natural History* between 1859 and 1862. The most significant was the 'Contributions to an insect fauna of the Amazon valley: Lepidoptera Heliconidae' (*Transactions of the Linnean Society*, 1862) which described resemblances between two families of butterflies, of which the similarity of one to the other served as protection against predators. Such protection, or mimicry, could be an aid to survival and thus to natural selection, and has come to be known as Batesian mimicry. The phenomenon offered supporting evidence to the arguments on natural selection expounded by Charles Darwin in *The Origin of Species* (1859). In a letter to Bates in November 1862, Darwin described the paper as one of the most 'remarkable and admirable' he had ever read (Stecher, 36), and Bates became an advocate of Darwinian ideas, making early reference to them at meetings of the Entomological and Linnean societies. In 1860 the two men had begun a correspondence which lasted until Darwin's death in 1882. Darwin frequently asked Bates for information on the insects and other wildlife of Amazonia, and it was at his suggestion that Bates wrote an account of his travel experiences, Darwin recommending Bates to his own publisher, John Murray.

The Naturalist on the River Amazons (2 vols., 1863) was a major contribution to the knowledge and literature of Amazonia. Bates had spent longer on the Amazon than any of his European predecessors, and the book was an immediate success and has become a travel classic. It remained in print through the nineteenth century, in eight editions, and was also published in Russian, German, and Swedish in 1865, 1866, and 1872 respectively. It is a curiously structured book, part detailed diary, part general account of the region, and part precise description of particular fauna, but it provides a fascinating record of the natural environment and wildlife of Amazonia before the major impact of the rubber boom. There are also detailed descriptions of the way of life and customs of Amerindian groups Bates encountered on his travels. The book's enduring appeal lies in its elegant yet scientific pen-portraits of places, people, and wildlife, as in his description of the wings of the varied and beautiful butterflies he observed around Ega: 'on these expanded membranes nature writes, as on a tablet, the story of the modification of species, so truly do all changes of the organisation register themselves thereon' (Bates, 353).

Bates sought employment in science and in 1862 applied

for a post in the zoology department of the British Museum, which went, as a result of patronage, to the poet Arthur O'Shaughnessy. In 1864, with the support of Darwin and Murray, Bates became the assistant secretary of the Royal Geographical Society, effectively its principal full-time official. He was responsible for the administration of its affairs, organization of its meetings, oversight of its office and global correspondence. He edited its *Proceedings* and *Journal*, and frequently drafted the annual review of the state of geography, as promulgated in the presidential address. He was also involved in the society's move in 1870 from Whitehall Place to Savile Row. His duties included serving as secretary of section E (geography) of the British Association for the Advancement of Science, and he was involved in planning the section's programme between 1864 and 1881, and served as its vice-president in 1887–8. He was also a member of a number of the association's commissions, including those on geographical education, Morocco, and New Guinea.

With his Amazon experience, Bates was well qualified to sustain the activities of the Royal Geographical Society in exploration. During his tenure the society gave direct support to eighteen major expeditions, including those of Livingstone and Stanley in Africa, Chandless in Brazil, Trotter in the Pamirs, and Nares to the Arctic. It was said of Bates that he knew all of the great and most of the lesser travellers of this heyday of Victorian exploration. Besides practical advice to such travellers, he was a skilled editor of their tales for the society's journals. He also edited a number of travel books, including Belt's *The Naturalist in Nicaragua* (1874), Humbert's *Japan and the Japanese* (1874), and Koldeway's *The German Arctic Expedition of 1869–70* (1874), as well as a six-volume compendium of *Illustrated Travels* (1869).

Bates's twenty-seven-year tenure at the Royal Geographical Society coincided with a crucial period in the development of geography in Britain, a transition from its essentially explorer tradition to its establishment as an academic discipline in schools and universities. There was debate within the society concerning the relative importance of exploration and education and, despite his explorer background, Bates allied himself with the innovators, becoming involved in efforts to make the subject more scientific and academic. He encouraged explorers to investigate the geology, climate, and biology of the countries they visited, and contributed advice on natural history collecting to the 1871 edition of the society's essential *Handbook to Travellers*. He was invited to edit the sixth and seventh editions of Mary Somerville's *Physical Geography* (1870 and 1877). He was a somewhat unlikely choice, since he was a well-known evolutionist and Mrs Somerville was opposed to Darwinian ideas. Bates was also involved in the society's effort to foster geography in schools by means of a series of prize examinations between 1869 and 1884, and in its programme of scientific lectures on physical geography in 1877–9. In the 1880s he supported the activities of members of the society seeking to establish geography at Oxford and Cambridge. He was responsible for inviting H. J. Mackinder to set down his ideas on the subject, which

were delivered as a lecture on 'The scope and methods of geography' to the society in January 1887. In July of that year Mackinder was appointed to a readership in geography at Oxford University, partly funded by the society, and he later acknowledged Bates's contributions to his thinking, particularly on the content of physical geography. Bates was also among those who campaigned for the release of the Russian geographer and anarchist Peter Kropotkin from imprisonment in France in 1886, and they became acquainted during Kropotkin's exile in England. The latter records in his *Memoirs of a Revolutionist* that Bates had supported his view that 'true Darwinism' involved 'mutual aid' rather than the 'mutual struggle' advocated by Thomas Huxley (Kropotkin, 300), and urged him to publish these ideas, which Kropotkin did in his *Mutual Aid* (1902).

Bates was credited, with Roderick Murchison and Clements Markham, with building up the prosperity of the Royal Geographical Society, and with contributing to securing for geography its proper place in English education. A. R. Wallace and others claimed that Bates's duties at the RGS were to the detriment of his activities as a naturalist, but throughout the period after his return from Brazil he sustained an impressive stream of entomological publications, initially from his own collections, and later on insects sent to him by travellers from around the world, but particularly from the tropics. These were published in the *Transactions of the Entomological Society*, the *Entomologist's Monthly Magazine*, the *Annals and Magazine of Natural History*, and other journals. He also made a major entomological contribution to the *Biologia Centrali Americana* of F. D. Godman and O. Salvin (1880–1911). However, after his mimicry papers he wrote little on Darwinism or on the geographical distributions of species which had so engaged him in Amazonia. His scientific contributions were acknowledged by his election to honorary fellowships of the Zoological (1863), Entomological (1871), and Linnean societies (1872), and he served as president of the Entomological Society in 1868–9 and 1878. He was elected fellow of the Royal Society in 1881.

On 15 January 1863 Bates married Sarah Ann Mason (1840–1897), of Leicester. The *Dictionary of National Biography* followed Bates's friend and memorialist Edward Clodd in giving the marriage date as January 1861, presumably to hide the fact that their first child, Alice, was born out of wedlock, in February 1862. In a letter to Darwin of April 1863, Bates described his wife as 'a plain domesticated woman' (Stecher, 43), and there is circumstantial evidence that she was illiterate; however, the marriage appears to have been a happy one. There were two daughters and three sons of the marriage, and Bates was reported to have been deeply grieved by the early death of Alice, at the age of twenty-nine. He had moved to London early in 1863, and for the remainder of his life the family lived at addresses in Harmood Street, Bartholomew Road, and Carleton Road in the Kentish Town district of London, and kept a seaside home at Folkestone.

Bates was described as a good-looking man of rugged

appearance, with a large head and a high, deeply furrowed forehead. He suffered from gastric trouble as a youth, and there are suggestions in several newspaper obituaries that he returned from Amazonia broken in health. His diet there was certainly meagre, and he caught yellow fever in 1851, and an attack of 'ague' (malaria) while at São Paulo in 1857 was responsible for the decline in health which prompted his decision to leave Brazil. In England, however, he lived for a further three decades, dying of influenza complicated by bronchitis at 11 Carleton Road, Tufnell Park, London, on 16 February 1892. He was buried in Marylebone cemetery in north London. The obelisk marking his grave (where his wife, Sarah, is also buried), is topped by a globe which has South America to the fore, and records him as 'Author of the Naturalist on the River Amazons. For twenty-seven years secretary of the Royal Geographical Society. Erected by his many friends.' Bates's circle of friends in late Victorian exploration, science, and geography included Livingstone, Stanley, Edward Whymper, Darwin, Joseph Hooker, Wallace, Huxley, Murchison, Markham, Francis Galton, and Mackinder. He contributed in differing ways to their activities, facilitating and publishing the activities of explorers, contributing to the ideas of the evolutionists, and providing support for the innovators in geography. His estate went to the support of his wife and family. Because of the commercial nature of his activities in Amazonia, many of the specimens collected by Bates had been dispersed to museums and private collectors. Some of his own material went to the British Museum before or on his death, or to a French collector, M. René Oberthür.

Bates was a modest and unassuming man, but he was a traveller of original mind, a writer of original style, and a man of letters in his own prose and in the editing of the work of others. He was a skilled field scientist in the collection, classification, and description of insects, and he made major contributions to entomology and natural history, and to the explorer and academic traditions in geography. JOHN DICKENSON

Sources H. P. Moon, *Henry Walter Bates, FRS, 1825–1892: explorer, scientist and Darwinian* (1976) · H. W. Bates, *The naturalist on the River Amazons*, xviii–lxxxix [with memoir by E. Clodd] · J. Dickenson, 'The naturalist on the River Amazon, and a wider world: reflections on the centenary of Henry Walter Bates', *GJ*, 158 (1992), 207–14 · E. G. Linsley, ed., *The principal contributions of Henry Walter Bates to a knowledge of the butterflies and longhorn beetles of the Amazon valley* (1978) · R. M. Stecher, 'The Darwin–Bates letters: correspondence between two nineteenth-century travellers and naturalists', *Annals of Science*, 25 (1969), 1–47, 95–125 · P. Kropotkin, *Memoirs of a revolutionist*, ed. J. A. Rogers (1962) · Leics. RO, Bates papers
Archives BL, pocket book, Add. MS 42138 · Leics. RO · NHM, notebooks · RGS · Royal Entomological Society of London, corresp. and unpublished MS on the classification of carabidae | CUL, letters to Charles Darwin · NHM, corresp. with Thomas Belt · Oxf. U. Mus. NH, letters to J. O. Westwood and notes · U. Edin. L., corresp. with Sir Charles Lyell · U. Newcastle, Robinson L., letters to Sir Walter Trevelyan
Likenesses T. Simms, portrait, RGS · J. Thomson, photograph, RGS · J. Thomson, photogravure, NPG [see illus.]
Wealth at death £7974 7s. 3d.: resworn probate, May 1892, CGPLA Eng. & Wales

Bates, Herbert Ernest (1905–1974), writer, was born on 16 May 1905 at 51 Grove Road, Rushden, Northamptonshire, the eldest of the three children (two sons and a daughter) of Albert Ernest Bates (*b.* 1878) and his wife, Lucy Elizabeth, *née* Lucas (1878–1972). He came from a family of shoemakers; his maternal grandfather's craftsmanship was renowned, and his parents also followed the trade. As he was to write later, he:

> grew up in an atmosphere of intense respectability ... My parents were never a farthing in debt; great was the pride they took, as my grandparents did, in paying their way ... My father pursued his passion for nature and the countryside, and incidentally fostered my own.

Rushden, which became Evensford in his fiction, was to carry much imaginative weight, and a love of nature was to become, next to writing, the absorption of his own life. After his death it was written that 'as he wrote he gardened and as he gardened he wrote'.

From a local school Bates failed his public-school entrance examination but won a free place at Kettering grammar school, where he stayed until he was just over sixteen. Here he was inspired to be a writer by his English master, Edmund Kirby, to whom he later dedicated two books. He achieved a third class in the joint Oxford and Cambridge university certificate but was dissuaded from a university education by his father. This decision influenced his later literary output as a 'self-made' writer of character, rather than of ideas (Baldwin, 44). He was thenceforth always outside literary circles and untouched by modernism.

At sixteen Bates became a reporter for the Wellingborough branch of the Northampton *Chronicle*, and then a warehouse clerk for a leather merchant in Rushden. It was here that he began to write in earnest. Although he rejected his parents' Methodism and indeed all organized religious beliefs in his early twenties, he had poetry on a religious theme published in *The Kettering Reminder*, and indeed he first saw himself as a poet. His early verse is imbued with a Romantic sensibility typical of Georgian poetry. This exposure led to a weekly column written under the name Boy Blue called 'At the Sign of the Rainbow' which lasted for four months. During this time he was reading Chekhov, Maupassant, Flaubert, and Turgenev, and writing his first novel, *The Two Sisters* (1926), which after being rejected nine times was accepted by Edward Garnett at Jonathan Cape, who mistook Bates, writing as H. E. Bates, for a woman. This novel was experimental in its narrative of 'emotion states punctuated by moments of crisis' (Baldwin, 65). Garnett came to act as his chief reader and literary adviser, and Bates was to continue under his tutelage until Garnett's death in 1937. Bates was later to pay his own touching and memorable tribute in his *Edward Garnett: a Personal Portrait*, published in 1950. For some twenty years, and for about as many books, Cape was to be Bates's publisher. His sales, however, claimed Cape, never earned fully the advances he paid against them.

Bates followed his first success to London and worked

Herbert Ernest Bates (1905–1974), by Mark Gerson, 1953

briefly, at Garnett's instigation, in the children's department of John and Edward Bumpus, booksellers. His book *The Seekers*, a children's fantasy, was promoted by the Bumpus brothers in their Christmas catalogue. This job was his last formal employment. From now on he devoted himself entirely to writing. Short stories, the work for which he will be remembered and revered, were appearing in the *New Statesman* and the *Manchester Guardian*. During these early years Bates lacked confidence and struggled for inspiration. A collection of short stories, *Day's End*, was published in 1928; and in 1929, more traditional than *Two Sisters*, came *Catherine Foster*, the plot of which is borrowed from *Madame Bovary*. Only with *Charlotte's Row* (1931) did Bates begin to find his own voice, drawing on his father's past and his Northamptonshire upbringing.

On 18 July 1931 Bates married Marjorie Helen (*b*. 1908/9), known as Madge, the daughter of a soldier, Herbert Henry Cox, whom he had met in Rushden. Madge provided Bates with the security he craved as a writer. They settled in Little Chart, Ashford, Kent, which was to provide much inspiration for books on gardening. They had two sons and two daughters. One son, Richard, was later to make for himself a distinguished career in television and was to adapt for that medium many of his father's most successful novels and short stories.

Bates displayed a new confidence in his work in the 1930s, such as *The Fallow Land* (1932), a tale of rural life. Marriage acted as a stabilizing force, and Bates began to solidify his position within the tradition of rural fiction with *The Poacher* (1935), and proved an unsentimental and yet lyrical chronicler of the country. Occasionally relegating character to scene, he was at his best when the mood

of character and nature were symbolically fused. His stories about Uncle Silas (1940), a Rabelaisian nonagenarian peasant farmer, based on his uncle Joseph Betts, were very popular. Bates also published nature essays in *Through the Woods* (1936) and *Down the River* (1937), both of which expressed early environmentalist opinions. *Spella Ho* (1938) was the industrial counterpart to the rural novels. Finances were tight, so Bates also wrote a regular column, 'Country life', for *The Spectator*, and reviews for the *New Clarion* and *John O'London's Weekly*. His collection of short stories *The Woman who had Imagination* (1934) brought him critical acclaim, and with the further collection, *Cut and Come Again* (1935), Bates was firmly established as one of the most gifted short story writers. The latter volume remains his greatest achievement in the genre. He wrote about technique in *The Modern English Short Story: a Critical Survey* (1950).

The Second World War was for Bates the turning point of his career. During 1941 he was recruited, without precedent, to the Royal Air Force as a morale-boosting short story writer—officially a flight lieutenant to public relations, Air Ministry. He was granted unusual freedom of movement at Oakington near Cambridge and a year later had become squadron leader and, under the pseudonym Flying Officer X, author of *The Greatest People in the World* (1942). These stories immortalized battle of Britain pilots. The eventual publishing success was enormous and Cape at last had a financially rewarding H. E. Bates in his list. But after a wrangle with Cape over royalties (Cape maintained that as a civil servant Bates should receive very little), Bates transferred allegiance to Michael Joseph, who remained his publishers for the rest of his life. His first book for them was *Fair Stood the Wind for France* (1945), hailed as a masterpiece in America, but lacking the depth of his other work.

In addition to the Flying Officer X stories, Bates's output during the war was prolific, including *The Bride Comes to Evensford* (1943). Under the impetus of war and the sudden flowering of popular success Bates was now to write a long series of best-sellers. Chosen by book clubs, reissued by Penguin, translated throughout the world, made often into films, titles still famous after a generation came from him in extraordinary succession. *The Purple Plain* (1947), *The Jacaranda Tree* (1952), and *The Scarlet Sword* (1950) derived from his travels in India and Burma with the Royal Air Force. He returned again to Northamptonshire for *The Sleepless Moon* (1956) and *Love for Lydia* (1952), a historical novel and perhaps his most accomplished. In *The Face of England* (1953) he showed concern for the direction of change in Britain after the devastation of war, and he revised *O More than Happy Countryman* (1943) and *In the Heart of the Country* (1942) as *The Country Heart* (1949), setting out his love for rural England.

Bates scaled the heights of popularity and success with *The Darling Buds of May* (1958), which began an earthy series of rusticity for which he may be best remembered. *Darling Buds* was Bates's response to what he called the 'bony, steely, wiry, unbending time' of the welfare state years, and to the critics who had 'ignored or slighted' his work

(Baldwin, 198). The critics despised the carnivalesque Larkin family, but in his autobiography Bates rose in their defence: 'the books are as English as puns, steak and kidney pudding and Canterbury Tales of Chaucer'. The novels were filmed as an enormously popular television series in 1991.

Great affluence came to Bates late in life, but illness and overwork gradually took their toll. There was a sense that final, popular, works such as *A Moment in Time* (1964) and *A Crown of Wild Myrtle* (1962) were artistically weak; and *The Wedding Party* (1965) was 'one of the least happy of his collections of stories' (Baldwin, 214). In February 1966 he suffered two heart attacks and a bout of pneumonia. He continued to write, producing the experimental *The Distant Horns of Summer* (1967) and *The White Admiral* (1968), the best of his children's books, which dramatized warfare among wasps, moths, and bees in Flying Officer X style. He also produced three volumes of memoirs, two books on gardening, and a handful of magazine articles. He was made CBE in 1973. After being admitted to the Kent and Canterbury Hospital in January 1974, Bates died on 28 January of kidney failure and related complications. He was cremated in a private ceremony. His poetry was finally collected in *Give them their Life* in 1990.

Critics place Bates's reputation as lying firmly with his short story collections. Descending from both the Romantic and the naturalistic literary traditions, Bates fused these sensibilities in an original and commanding way. Remaining detached from moral, philosophical, political, and religious preoccupations of the twentieth century, Bates was always more concerned with individuals rather than with movements, with established techniques rather than with experiment. Often neglected, Bates contributed to a vital tradition in twentieth-century literature. ROBERT LUSTY, *rev.* CLARE L. TAYLOR

Sources D. R. Baldwin, *H. E. Bates: a literary life* (1987) · P. Eades, *The life and times of H. E. Bates* (1995) · H. E. Bates, *The vanished world: an autobiography of childhood and youth* (1969) · H. E. Bates, *The ripening world: a writer's autobiography containing 'The blossoming world' and 'The world in ripeness'* (1971–2) · *The Times* (30 Jan 1974) · G. M. Johnson, ed., *British novelists between the wars*, DLitB, 191 (1998), 162 · b. cert. · m. cert. · d. cert. · *CGPLA Eng. & Wales* (1974) · personal knowledge (1986) · private information (1986)

Archives Hunt. L., letters, literary papers · NRA, corresp. and literary papers · Ransom HRC, corresp. and papers · Rushden Library, Northamptonshire, collection · U. Reading L., corresp. · Yale U., Beinecke L., papers | BL, corresp. with Society of Authors, Add. MS 63211 · Georgetown University, Washington, DC, corresp. with Bruce Marshall · JRL, corresp. with Basil Dean · LUL, letters to Charles Lahr, literary papers · Northampton Central Library, letters to Joe Braddock · Northants. RO, letters to Reginald Underwood · U. Aberdeen, letters to J. B. Chapman · W. Yorks. AS, Bradford, letters to Malachi Whitaker

Likenesses M. Gerson, photograph, 1953, NPG [*see illus.*] · photograph, Hult. Arch. · photographs, repro. in Baldwin, *H. E. Bates: a literary life*

Wealth at death £67,309: probate, 7 Aug 1974, *CGPLA Eng. & Wales*

Bates, Joah (*bap.* 1741, *d.* 1799), musician, was baptized at Halifax on 8 March 1741, the son of Henry Bates, a former woolcomber, turned innkeeper and parish clerk, and his wife, Susan Lister. He received his early education at Dr Ogden's school, and learned music from Hartley, organist at Rochdale. He went afterwards to Manchester grammar school, when William Purnell was high master, and while there he was much struck by the organ playing of Robert Wainwright, organist of the collegiate church. He was subsequently sent to Eton College, where, on 2 August 1756, he obtained a scholarship. While he was at Eton he did not have access to a keyboard instrument, but he kept up his practice by playing on imaginary keys on the table. One of the masters, George Graham, discovered his passion for music, and, being himself an enthusiastic amateur, gave him much encouragement. On 31 July 1758 he was nominated for a scholarship at King's College, Cambridge. He matriculated at Christ's College on 30 November 1759 and was awarded a scholarship before the end of the year; but on 4 May 1760 he was granted a scholarship at King's, and was raised to a fellowship in 1763. He took the degrees of BA in 1764 and MA in 1767. During his term of residence in Cambridge he organized and himself conducted a performance of *Messiah* in his native town, that occasion allegedly being the first on which an oratorio had been performed north of the Trent. In his orchestra Herschel the astronomer was said to have played first violin.

John Montagu, fourth earl of Sandwich, first lord of the Admiralty, whose second son was a pupil of Bates, was at this time attracted to his wonderful musical and general talents; Sandwich made Bates his private secretary and procured for him a small post in the Post Office worth £100 per annum. He was a commissioner of the sixpenny office from 1772 to 1776 and of Greenwich Hospital from 1775 until his death. In March 1776 he obtained the more lucrative post of commissioner of the victualling office through the same interest, and in the same year he became conductor to the Concerts of Ancient Music, which had just started. By this time he had written a *Treatise on Harmony*, which was translated into German. On 21 December 1780 he married his pupil the singer Sarah Harrop (*c.*1755–1811) [*see* Bates, Sarah]. In 1783, in conjunction with the second Earl Fitzwilliam and Sir Watkin Williams Wynn, he organized the first Handel commemoration concerts, which took place in Westminster Abbey in May and June 1784. At these performances he held the post of conductor. In 1785 the king appointed him a commissioner of the customs, and about the same time his name appears as vice-president of Westminster Hospital. He subsequently invested all his own and his wife's fortune in the unfortunate project of the Albion mills at Blackfriars Bridge, and when these were destroyed by fire on 2 March 1791, he was nearly ruined. According to Charles Burney the vexation and trouble resulting from this misfortune brought on a complaint in his chest which finally proved fatal. In 1793 he resigned the conductorship of the Ancient Concerts, and he died on 8 June 1799 at his home, 14 John Street, King's Road, London. EVA ZÖLLNER

Sources Highfill, Burnim & Langhans, *BDA* · W. Weber, *The rise of musical classics in eighteenth-century England* (1992) · S. McVeigh, *Concert life in London from Mozart to Haydn* (1993) · *New Grove* · [A. H.

Mann], 'Mr and Mrs Joah Bates, a distinguished amateur and a notable singer', *MT*, 46 (1905), 13–20, 99–100 · *GM*, 1st ser., 61 (1791), 274 · *GM*, 1st ser., 69 (1799), 532–3 · Venn, *Alum. Cant.* · R. A. Austen-Leigh, ed., *The Eton College register, 1753–1790* (1921), 31 · J. A. Graham and B. A. Phythian, eds., *The Manchester grammar school, 1515–1965* (1965), 24

Archives NMM, letters to Lord Sandwich
Likenesses J. Gillray, caricature, etching, pubd 1787, NPG · W. Daniell, etching, pubd 1809 (after G. Dance, 1794), BM, NPG
Wealth at death see will, 21 July 1799, Highfill, Burnim & Langhans, *BDA*

Bates, Joshua (1788–1864), merchant and banker, was born on 10 October 1788 at Weymouth, Massachusetts, United States, the youngest of three children and only son of Colonel Joshua Bates (*d.* 1804), a leading local businessman, and his wife, Tirzah, *née* Pratt. He was educated at public schools and by the Revd Jacob Norton of the First Church at Weymouth. In 1813 he married Lucretia Augustus Sturgis (*d.* 1863), a cousin of William Sturgis of Bryant and Sturgis, leading Boston merchants, and they had two children, William and Elizabeth. In 1839 Elizabeth married Jean Sylvain van de Weyer, Belgian ambassador in London; William died in a shooting accident in December 1834, a loss from which Bates never fully recovered. He acquired British citizenship in 1842.

In December 1803 Bates started work as a clerk with the Boston merchant, William R. Gray, the eldest son of William Gray senior, New England's leading merchant, for whom Bates worked subsequently. About 1809 he formed Beckford and Bates, with a Captain Beckford, also formerly in Gray's service, but the business failed in 1812. He rejoined the Grays, by then owners of one of the United States' largest shipowning concerns, and in 1816 he was sent to Europe as their confidential agent.

Bates may then have lived in France, as at some stage he became fluent in French, but from 1821, perhaps from 1818, he was resident in London. Peter C. Labouchère, a banker and son-in-law of Sir Francis Baring, whom Bates met in 1817 and who became his 'staunch friend and a father' (J. Bates, diaries, Barings archives, DEP 74, 3.75) introduced him to John Baring. The latter was a grandson of Sir Francis and in January 1826 the two formed Bates and Baring, merchants specializing in the American trade. Bates provided £10,000 of capital and Baring £20,000, but they divided the profits equally. In 1828 their business was merged with that of Baring Brothers, London's most prestigious, but no longer most prosperous, merchant bankers. The merger was effected to strengthen Barings' management; the firm's fortunes were flagging and Alexander Baring, the senior partner, appointed Bates and John Baring, along with John's brother Thomas, to revive the business. As a measure of his importance, Bates was assigned a five-eighths interest in the profits for him to distribute between himself, Thomas, and John, 'as I tho't it proper' (ibid.). He divided them equally, 'altho I was entitled to much more' (ibid.). Throughout his time at Barings, Bates's share of the profits was roughly a quarter, though his contribution to the firm's capital was enormous and reached £500,000, or one-third, about 1863.

Following Alexander Baring's retirement in 1830 and

Joshua Bates (1788–1864), by unknown artist

John's virtual withdrawal, Bates and Thomas Baring were, in practice, joint senior partners, though Thomas, being the junior in both age and experience, deferred to Bates in the early years. Although temperamentally different, they worked in almost perfect harmony and formed the greatest partnership in Barings' history. Baring, an establishment figure, led the bond-issuing business while Bates managed trade finance, merchanting, and London agency work for overseas merchants. In 1853 an agent described them as 'warmly attached' but with qualities 'strikingly different, Mr Baring being a man of brilliant and active mind and keen perceptions while Mr Bates was the thoroughly trained merchant, with a steadiness of mind that made him the balance wheel of the concern' (Ward, 6).

At Barings, Bates was a force for change and modernization. Of particular importance was the company's refocus on the rapidly growing international trade of North America and, to a lesser extent, of the Far East. United States representation was improved through the appointment of a local agent, and north Atlantic business was boosted through the establishment of a Liverpool house. The speculative profits of merchanting were steadily replaced by safer commissions earned from trade finance and agency work. Bates overhauled internal procedures, in particular the recording and organization of information. He dominated the counting house, read all the letters and 'had the knack of seeing everything without appearing to take any trouble to do so' (Rathbone, 124). The depth and detail of his knowledge and the soundness of his judgement were legion throughout London.

When Bates wrote in 1859 that 'Baring Brothers & Co.

now is beyond doubt the first commercial house in the world' (25 Jan 1859, Barings archives, DEP 74), equally little doubt existed that the achievement was his. Profits rose from £50,000 in 1828 to almost £200,000 in 1864 and were accompanied by an increase in the balance sheet from £2.25 million to £10.5 million. An analytical approach and attention to commercial intelligence enabled Bates to make accurate predictions of the financial panics of 1837 and 1847. Barings emerged almost unscathed from these which, at least in 1837, left them with no serious competitors in the American trade. The firm ended up by giving 'much and rather patronizing advice through their American specialist Mr Joshua Bates' to the Bank of England in its search for a resolution to the 1837 panic (Clapham, 2.152). Bates was, however, prepared to take a risk, as when in 1844 he led Barings into the utterly uncharted territory of financing the pioneering Weardale Iron and Coal Company, the projections for which 'are so very extraordinary that we cannot believe them to be true' (Barings archives, DEP 74, 3.79). By 1863 his personal investment totalled a staggering £250,000 but he valued it at only half as much.

Bates's position at Barings, coupled with his great wealth, meant that by the 1850s he vied with George Peabody (1795–1869) as the leading American merchant in London. He made friends in high places, not only among the American political and business elite, but also among some of Europe's leading families, though his unexciting personality meant he was courted more for his wealth than for himself. He was close to Napoleon III, to whom he advanced money, and to King Leopold I in Belgium.

Bates's undue deference to wealth and rank resulted in 'pain and mortification ... in consequence of my social position' (Barings archives, DEP 74, 3.73). In the early days of his partnership, he agonized over his social ostracism by the Barings, particularly by Alexander Baring, but which was as much due to his wife, an 'audaciously vulgar old woman' (*Journal of Benjamin Moran*, 308), as to his own social clumsiness. His daughter and son-in-law were close to Queen Victoria and Prince Albert, who were godparents to their children, and from this Bates derived immense satisfaction. Bates himself was 'pawky, dour, charmless; with little imagination and less humour', according to the official Barings historian (Ziegler, 123); 'I never saw a more busy, calm and dry man. His tone was dry, his words few', commented the bank's American agent (Elliott, 141). Another compatriot, with no axe to grind, described him as 'illiterate and ignorant but possessed [of] a strong mind and much business ability' (*Journal of Benjamin Moran*, 308).

Bates's lifestyle was opulent if not showy. By 1830 he was living at 50 Portland Place, London, and he moved to no. 46 in 1838. In 1851 he acquired and refurbished 21 Arlington Street, a mansion adjacent to London's Green Park, at a cost of £20,000. From 1834 he had a second home at Wimbledon and in 1842 he purchased, for £8400, Sheen House, a country retreat at East Sheen, Surrey, where he spent as much again on refurbishment. 'The house is a large & noble one', wrote a visitor, 'the rooms immense,

the decorations brilliant' (*Letters of Henry Adams*, 1.465). He entertained lavishly; the guest list at a 'good and gay dinner' one night in March 1858 included a royal princess, a duke, three duchesses, Earl Grey, and the bishop of Oxford. In 1859 he built for his daughter's family a great mansion at New Lodge, Windsor Forest, at a cost of £25,000.

Bates seemed to float above politics but, like his partners, he was a protectionist, regarding Peel's free-trade reforms as 'wrong, not only in the abstract but in reference to the condition of the country, its debt, poor laws, etc.' (Barings archives, HC1.20.8). British governments frequently called upon him for informal advice and he gave expert evidence to committees of the House of Commons.

Bates also maintained his American connections. In particular he sponsored the establishment of the Boston Public Library through a gift in 1853 of $50,000 for the purchase of books; in 1856–59 he gave a further 27,000 volumes, worth $50,000. Part of the new building was named Bates Hall. In 1854, following a convention made in the previous year between the British and United States governments for the appointment of commissioners to settle long-standing claims by one country against the other, Bates was appointed 'umpire'. He decided on '32 or 33' cases but regretted that 'more time was not given me to perfect my decisions' which, he reckoned, 'would cut a poor figure alongside the more elaborate opinions of the learned commissioners' (3 Feb 1855, Barings archives, DEP 74, vol. 5).

In the mid-1850s Bates estimated his personal fortune at £0.75 million; he wanted to retire but believed that his junior partners had insufficient ability and capital to be effective successors. His withdrawal, he thought, probably correctly, would cause Barings' liquidation, so great were his contributions of capital and management. Certainly his fears for the capabilities of his juniors proved well-founded when, under their management, Barings collapsed in 1890. With Thomas Baring, Joshua Bates soldiered on at Barings until his death at New Lodge on 24 September 1864. He was buried at Kensal Green cemetery alongside his wife, who had died a year earlier.

JOHN ORBELL

Sources P. Ziegler, *The sixth great power: Barings, 1762–1929* (1988) · R. W. Hidy, *The house of Baring in American trade and finance: English merchant bankers at work, 1763–1861* (1949) · D. Kynaston, *The City of London*, 1 (1994) · J. Orbell, *Baring Brothers & Co. Limited: a history to 1939* (privately printed, London, 1939) · *A memorial of Joshua Bates from the city of Boston*, Boston, MA, City Council (1865) · H. U. Faulkner, 'Bates, Joshua', *DAB* · W. Rathbone, *A sketch of family history during four generations* (privately printed, Liverpool, 1894) · S. G. Ward, *Ward family papers* (1900), 6 · ING Barings, London, Barings archives, DEP 74 · J. Clapham, *The Bank of England: a history*, 2 (1944), 152 · *The journal of Benjamin Moran*, ed. S. Wallace and F. Gillespie, 2 (1949), 308 · M. H. Elliott, *Uncle Sam Ward and his circle* (1938), 141 · *The letters of Henry Adams*, ed. J. C. Levenson (1982), 1.465 · d. cert.
Archives ING Barings, London, Barings archives, corresp. as a partner in ING Barings · NA Canada, MSS | ING Barings, London, Barings archives, letters to Thomas Baring
Likenesses W. Behnes, bust, Boston PL · portraits, ING Barings, London [*see illus.*]

Wealth at death under £700,000: resworn probate, March 1864, *CGPLA Eng. & Wales*

Bates, Sir Percy Elly, fourth baronet (1879–1946), merchant and shipowner, was born at Beechenhurst, Wavertree, Liverpool, on 12 May 1879, the second of seven sons of Edward Percy Bates (1845–1899), who became second baronet, and his wife, Constance Elisabeth, daughter of Samuel Robert Graves, a former mayor of and member of parliament for Liverpool.

Educated at Winchester College (1892–7), Bates then studied in Germany for a year. Apprenticeship with William Johnston & Co., shipowners, of Liverpool followed, but after his father's death Bates joined the family business of Edward Bates & Sons, merchants and shipowners, long established in Liverpool and India. In 1903 he succeeded his brother in the baronetcy and in 1910 began his connection with the Cunard Steam-Ship Company of which he became deputy chairman in 1922. In 1924 Bates became a director of the *Morning Post*, then in 1930 chairman. He held that position until the sale of the paper in 1937, and became a friend of fellow director, Rudyard Kipling, whom he greatly admired and often quoted.

In the First World War, Bates joined the transport department of the Admiralty. When the Ministry of Shipping was created, he continued as director of commercial services, being concerned with the shipment of civilian supplies to Britain and her allies. In recognition of his war service Bates was appointed GBE in 1920. Nevertheless, he, in general, disliked government interference in commerce. During the Second World War he was a member both of the advisory council and of the liner committee of the Ministry of War Transport.

In 1930 Bates became chairman of Cunard in succession to Sir Thomas Royden. He and his predecessor had together masterminded a scheme to provide a weekly transatlantic passenger service using two large, fast modern liners instead of the current three vessels. Before the end of 1930 Cunard had placed the order for the first of the 'big ships' with shipbuilders John Brown at Clydebank where the new vessel was given the yard number 534. The year 1930 also witnessed the collapse of the Royal Mail group, one of the biggest British shipping groups, and Cunard put in a bid for the transatlantic White Star Line which was one of the group's companies. The initial bid by Bates was unsuccessful, but attempts to obtain White Star were to become closely linked to the fortunes of the 'big ships' project over the next few years.

The economic crisis of 1931 forced Cunard to suspend construction of no. 534 at the end of that year. Bates now sought government financial support to complete the 'big ships' project. The government was unenthusiastic, but suggested assistance might be available if Cunard merged with White Star on terms acceptable to the creditors of the latter company. Bates still wanted White Star, but intended to absorb it rather than agree to a merger. Eventually the government decided to provide financial support, confirmed by the North Atlantic Shipping Act of 1934, and Bates accepted a merger with White Star. The

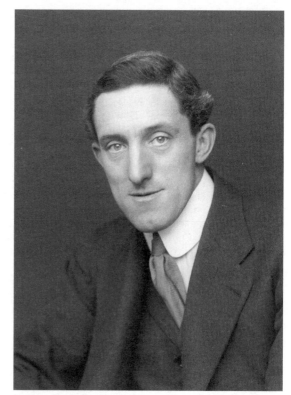

Sir Percy Elly Bates, fourth baronet (1879–1946), by George Charles Beresford, 1913

new Cunard-White Star company was formed in 1934 with Bates as chairman.

Work recommenced on no. 534 in 1934 and the ship was launched later in the year as the *Queen Mary*, entering transatlantic service in 1936. The second 'big ship', the *Queen Elizabeth*, was launched by John Brown in 1938, but did not enter commercial service before the outbreak of the Second World War.

Although deeply committed to the 'big ships' project, Bates was not unaware of the beginnings of transatlantic air travel during the 1930s. He mistakenly believed that the aeroplane would not compete with the ocean liner, but would cater for a small and select passenger market. Between 1934 and his death, Bates made various efforts, all unsuccessful, to obtain a share for Cunard in transatlantic air travel.

During the Second World War, the two *Queens* served as troopships, initially east of Suez from 1940 to 1942, then on the north Atlantic run from 1942 to 1944. On the latter service they brought across many of the American troops who took part in the Normandy landings in 1944. Bates took great pride in the work of these ships and liked to believe that they shortened the war in Europe by a whole year. These great ships had unexpected ends: the *Queen Elizabeth* was destroyed by fire in Hong Kong harbour in 1971 while being converted into a floating university; the *Queen Mary* became a floating museum, berthed at Long Beach, California, from 1967.

Bates was terse in speech and judgement: he never encumbered his talk with platitudes, or troubled to obscure the directness of his thought. Such characteristics, allied with a determined jaw, and, on occasion, an emphatic manner, made him formidable to those who did not know him well. However, he was always scrupulous in the use of power, ready for interchange of ideas and considerate and sensitive in personal relationships. He regarded himself as fortunate in having a group of brothers and other colleagues who looked to him for leadership and on whose support he relied. During his career he gave due time to those offices which fall to a leading shipowner; he was a member of the Mersey Docks and Harbour Board (1908–10), chairman of the Liverpool Steamship Owners' Association (1911, 1945), president of the Institute of Marine Engineers (1939), and chairman of the General Council of British Shipping (1945). He was also high sheriff of Cheshire (1920–21), and a justice of the peace for the county.

On 20 June 1907 Bates married Mary Ann (1880–1973), daughter of William Lefroy, dean of Norwich. They had one son, Edward Percy, a pilot officer in the Royal Air Force whose death in action over Germany in 1945, borne by his father with outward stoicism, was a deep wound. He found relaxation in golf and shooting, was enthusiastic about curling, and was a keen fisherman. Annual fishing trips to Ireland, Scotland, and Scandinavia were occasions when Bates and his brothers could all get together.

Having presided as host on a short preliminary run of the *Queen Elizabeth*, Bates suffered a heart attack at his office in Liverpool on 14 October 1946. He died at his home, Hinderton Hall, Neston, Wirral, Cheshire, on 16 October 1946, on the very morning when he should have sailed on the *Queen Elizabeth*'s first voyage as an Atlantic passenger ship. He was buried at Childwall church, Wavertree, Liverpool, and was survived by his wife.

Bates was succeeded as chairman of the Cunard Steam-Ship Company and Cunard-White Star by two younger brothers, first Frederic Alan Bates (1884–1957) and then Colonel Denis Haughton Bates (1886–1959). Born on 25 August 1886, the latter served with the duke of Lancaster's own yeomanry during the First World War and was mentioned in dispatches. On 12 December 1922 he married Aline Mary Crook (d. 1974), daughter of Edward Tipping Crook of Woodlands Hall, Bridgnorth; they had a son and a daughter. He died on 13 September 1959. His only son, **Philip Edward Bates** (1925–2000), shipping executive, was born on 19 July 1925 and educated at Shrewsbury School. In 1943 he was commissioned into the Royal Marines and began service with the 3rd commando brigade in the Far East. He was demobilized in 1946 but continued to serve in the Royal Marine Forces Volunteer Reserve, and was commanding officer of its Merseyside unit. Having joined the freight shipping line T. & J. Brocklebank, part of the Cunard group, he became a director in 1952, managing director in 1959, and deputy chairman in 1962. He was made a member of Cunard's board in 1957, and in 1965 became managing director of Cunard Line, presiding over the shift of Cunard's management base from Liverpool to Southampton. Though he had been closely involved from the beginning in the decision to build the *Queen Elizabeth II* (popularly known as QE2), his main interest remained in freight transportation. In 1968 he negotiated Cunard's entry into Atlantic Container Line, a freight-shipping consortium formed by Swedish, Dutch, and French companies in 1965 which was prominent in the growing container trade. He was seconded by Cunard as temporary chairman of the consortium later in 1968, but remained as chairman until his retirement in 1983. He had married, on 22 April 1952, Mary Patricia Carol Moberly Bell, an assistant purser on the *Queen Mary*, and younger daughter of Lieutenant-Colonel Clive Vincent Moberly Bell, army officer; they had two sons and two daughters. He died on 29 February 2000. His wife survived him.

ALAN G. JAMIESON

Sources P. E. Bates, ed., *Bates of Bellefield, Gyrn Castle and Manydown* (privately printed, 1994) · F. E. Hyde, *Cunard and the north Atlantic, 1840–1973: a history of shipping and financial management* (1975) · E. Green and M. Moss, *A business of national importance: the Royal Mail shipping group, 1902–1937* (1982) · private information (1959) · CGPLA Eng. & Wales (2000) · *The Times* (23 March 2000) · *Daily Telegraph* (14 April 2000) · Burke, *Peerage*
Archives NMM, corresp. and papers · U. Lpool, papers and ephemera belonging to or of particular interest to him | U. Lpool, letters to Frederick Bates
Likenesses G. C. Beresford, photograph, 1913, NPG [*see illus.*] · W. Stoneman, photograph, 1921, NPG · G. Kelly, oils, 1947, Liverpool Maritime Museum · A. T. Nowell, portrait, Gyrn Castle, Denbighshire
Wealth at death £486,085 13s. 5d.: probate, 4 Feb 1947, CGPLA Eng. & Wales · Philip Edward Bates: £608,125 gross, £587,305 net: probate, 29 June 2000, CGPLA Eng. & Wales

Bates, Philip Edward (1925–2000). *See under* Bates, Sir Percy Elly, fourth baronet (1879–1946).

Bates [*née* Harrop], **Sarah** (*c.*1755–1811), singer, was born somewhere in Lancashire, traditionally of poor parents, although a connection with a Manchester music publisher named Harrop was suggested by Weber. She is said to have been educated in Halifax, the birthplace of her husband, Joah *Bates (*bap.* 1741, *d.* 1799), and to have worked for some time in a factory in that town. On one occasion she sang in public there and was heard by a Dr Howard, of Leicester, who prophesied that 'she would one day throw all the English, nay even the Italian, female singers far behind her'. While she resumed her ordinary occupations, Dr Howard sounded her praises in London, until at last the Sandwich Catch Club deputed him to bring her to London, where she met with very great success. There she studied Italian music under Sacchini and the compositions of Handel and the older masters under her future husband. She was a successful concert singer, both before and after her marriage to Joah Bates, which took place on 21 December 1780. Her chief success was in sacred music, which she delivered impressively. Among her secular songs the most famous was Purcell's 'Mad Bess'. She is said to have brought her husband £6000 or £7000 as a dowry, the tangible results of her popularity as an artist. Her success, it is said, gave a great impetus to the cultivation of music among the factory girls in the north of England. Sarah Bates died at her home at Foley Place in Marylebone on 11 December 1811.

J. A. F. Maitland, rev. Eva Zöllner

Sources Highfill, Burnim & Langhans, *BDA* · W. Weber, *The rise of the musical classics in eighteenth-century England* (1992) · S. McVeigh, *Concert life in London from Mozart to Haydn* (1993) · [A. H. Mann], 'Mr and Mrs Joah Bates, a distinguished amateur and a notable singer', *MT*, 46 (1905), 13–20, 99–100 · *New Grove* · *GM*, 1st ser., 81/2 (1811), 597

Likenesses Delaltré, stipple (after A. Kauffman?), NPG · O. Humphry, pastel drawing, Knole, Kent

Bates, Thomas (*fl.* 1704–1745), surgeon, is known to have served for five years as a naval surgeon in the Mediterranean. In 1709 he published *An enchridion of fevers, incident to sea-men during the summer—in the Mediterranean; explicating their causes … and method of cure*, which was based on his observations while in service. After leaving the navy he practised medicine in London and was a surgeon to the royal household.

Bates is remembered for his contribution to the extermination of the cattle plague epidemic which threatened England in 1714. This epidemic, which is said to have destroyed 1.5 million cattle in western Europe between 1711 and 1714, first appeared in herds on three farms in Islington, Middlesex, in July 1714. At the request of the privy council Bates enquired into the nature of the plague. In the summer of 1714 he recommended the implementation of radical measures to curb the spread of the disease; to the surprise of continental nations these measures proved highly effective. Bates recommended the immediate isolation of infected herds and the destruction of all cows affected by the disease. He also recommended that compensation of 40s. per cow destroyed be paid to the owners in order to encourage recognition of the presence of the disease. By the end of 1714 cattle plague had been stamped out, with the sacrifice of some 6000 cattle.

In 1718, in the *Philosophical Transactions of the Royal Society*, Bates published 'A brief account of the contagious disease which raged among the milch cowes near London'. On the strength of his work he was elected a fellow of the Royal Society in December 1718.

In 1745, when the disease again threatened Britain, Bates wrote to the *Gentleman's Magazine*, reiterating some precautions which might be taken against the disease. Bates was then in retirement in Hampshire. The date of his death is uncertain.

Claire E. J. Herrick

Sources L. Wilkinson, *Animals and disease: an introduction to the history of comparative medicine* (1992), 51–3, 228 · G. Fleming, *Animal plagues*, 1 (1871), 257–324 · J. Redington, ed., *Calendar of Treasury papers*, 6 vols., PRO (1868–89), 1709–16 · J.-F. Beugnot and others, eds., *Dictionnaire usuel de chirurgie et de médecine vétérinaires*, new edn, 2 vols. (Paris, 1859), 362

Bates, Thomas (1775–1849), stockbreeder, was born on 21 June 1775 at Matfen, Northumberland, the younger of the two sons of George Bates of Aydon Castle, near Corbridge, Northumberland, and his wife, Diana (*d.* 1822), daughter of Thomas Moore of Bishop's Castle, Shropshire. He was descended from a family long settled in the district. Bates was educated at the grammar school at Haydon Bridge,

and afterwards at Witton-le-Wear School, where 'he never joined in his schoolfellows' games, but would sit for hours in the churchyard with a book' (Bell, 110). He then studied at the University of Edinburgh, hoping to enter the church, but at the age of fifteen he was called home to help manage his father's farms. Before he was eighteen he became tenant of his father's farm at Aydon White House, and in 1794 he bought his first shorthorn cattle.

Disappointed in the expectation of inheriting £300,000 from his godfather in 1795, in 1796 Bates became tenant of his father's small estate of Wark Eals, on the North Tyne River. He became friendly with George Culley (1735–1813) and Matthew Culley, through a family marriage, and was introduced to a large circle of agricultural acquaintances from the Tees region, including Charles Colling (1751–1836) and Robert Colling (1749–1820). In 1800 Bates took a twenty-one years' lease of two large farms at Halton Castle, near Corbridge, at a high rent, and began to breed cattle. He bought his first shorthorn cows from Charles Colling, paying 100 guineas for one of them. It was this sale which first made Colling's stock famous. Bates then quickly became renowned as a cattle breeder of taste and judgement, and at Charles Colling's famous Ketton sale in 1810 he bought a cow called Duchess, the founder animal of his well-known herd of shorthorns. Bates crossed Colling's animals with west highland cattle. He exhibited his cattle at the local shows from 1804 to 1812.

Wishing to follow up Culley's principles with regard to experiments and trials, Bates set out his views in December 1807 in an elaborate letter, which he styled 'An address to the board of agriculture and to the other agricultural societies of the kingdom on the importance of an institution for ascertaining the merits of different breeds of livestock, pointing out the advantages that will accrue therefrom to the landed interest and the kingdom in general'. From 1809 to 1811 he spent his winters at the University of Edinburgh in order to study chemistry as applied to the principles of manuring. In 1811 he was sufficiently well off to buy half of the manor of Kirklevington, about 1000 acres, near Yarm, in Cleveland, for £30,000, £20,000 of which he paid in cash. He was anxious to own a freehold so that he could make his own improvements. At Kirklevington he experimented in crop rotation and manuring, and built up his stock of shorthorns. In 1818, when his lease of Halton ran out, he bought the Ridley Hall estate on the South Tyne. At one point, in the 1820s, during the agricultural depression, he contemplated emigrating to Ohio, in the United States, but moved to Kirklevington instead, in 1828, and lived there for the rest of his life. He corresponded with most of the leading agriculturists of the day and wrote frequently to the newspapers, mainly on agricultural politics.

Bates was a man of remarkable force of character, but his love of argument, his combativeness, and his plain speaking did not make him a universal favourite. Because of his disagreement with the way the awards were made at the Tyneside Society's show in 1812, he gave up showing cattle at agricultural meetings for twenty-six years, and did not exhibit again until the first show of the Yorkshire

Agricultural Society, held at York in 1838, when he won five prizes with seven animals. A year later he caused a great sensation at the first show of the then newly established English Agricultural Society (from 1840 the Royal Agricultural Society of England), held at Oxford in 1839, with his four shorthorns, all of which won prizes, and one of which, called Duke of Northumberland, was said to be one of the finest bulls ever bred. Bates continued showing and winning prizes at subsequent meetings of the Royal Agricultural Society of England until 1848.

Bates was unmarried, though he had been engaged at one time to a young woman who died of consumption. Up to 1849 he enjoyed good health, preferring to live in the open air, and very simply, but he became ill and died of kidney disease on 25 July 1849; a stained-glass window was erected in his memory at Kirklevington church. Only one of Bates's five nephews was a farmer, and he had emigrated to Prussia; so the Kirklevington herd was sold on 9 May 1850. More than 5000 people came to the sale, from as far away as the United States and Europe, and the sixty-eight animals were sold for £4558 1s.

By the early 1860s more than two-thirds of the cattle brought to Smithfield market were shorthorns, which became unrivalled as dual-purpose animals, suitable for both beef and milk production. The supremacy of the shorthorn lasted until after the First World War, when the Friesian, with its superior milk yield, overtook it.

ERNEST CLARKE, rev. ANNE PIMLOTT BAKER

Sources 'Memoir of Thomas Bates', *Farmer's Magazine*, 2nd ser., 21 (1850), 1–8 · C. J. Bates, *Thomas Bates and the Kirklevington shorthorns* (1897) · T. Bell, *The history of improved shorthorn or Durham cattle and of the Kirklevington herd from the notes of the late Thomas Bates* (1871), 102–357 · The Druid [H. H. Dixon], *Saddle and sirloin, or, English farm and sporting worthies* (1870), 148–9 · J. Thirsk, ed., *The agrarian history of England and Wales*, 6, ed. G. E. Mingay (1989)
Likenesses W. Ross, engraving, repro. in *Farmer's Magazine* (1850) · E. Wilson, black wash drawing, NPG
Wealth at death sale of herd in May 1850 brought £4558 1s.

Bates, William (1625–1699), clergyman and ejected minister, was born in November 1625, the son of William Bates, gentleman, of St Mary Magdalene parish, Bermondsey, Surrey. He matriculated on 9 July 1641 at New Inn Hall, Oxford, but moved to Cambridge after the occupation of Oxford by the king's forces. Admitted as a pensioner at Emmanuel College in 1643, he graduated BA from Queens' in 1645 and proceeded MA in 1648. In 1649 he was admitted as vicar of Tottenham, Middlesex, where he was in receipt of £100 out of the sale of bishops' lands for that calendar year.

After succeeding William Strong as vicar of St Dunstan-in-the-West, Bates was named as an assistant to the Middlesex commission into the ministry under the ordinance of August 1654. On 19 March 1658 Abraham Pinchbecke (d. 1681/2) conveyed to Richard Baxter from Covent Garden the respects of his friend William Bates, and gave news that Bates's first wife had miscarried and that his daughter had died. On 14 March 1660 Bates was named by the Rump Parliament as a commissioner for approbation of ministers. As Baxter records, he was among the leading ministers who helped turn opinion in the City of London

in favour of the restoration of Charles II. In June 1660 he was appointed a chaplain-in-ordinary to the king, but he never preached at court; following a request of Charles II dated from Whitehall 9 November, he was created doctor of divinity by the University of Cambridge. Baxter, Bates's friend, who had preached once a week with him at St Dunstan's, wrote that Bates was also offered the deanery of Lichfield.

On 19 March 1661 it was reported that Sheldon, bishop of London, had sent for Bates and Thomas Jacomb (1622–1687), rector of St Martin Ludgate, and told them that if they would not read the Book of Common Prayer, nor order their curates to do so, he would send those who would. Bates ordered the Psalms, two lessons, the ten commandments, and the creed to be read; his curate vowed to resist by all legal means any attempt to oust him. Bates and his co-thinkers were still part of the religious establishment, but their outlook did not fit well with the current fashion. On 23 May 1661 Samuel Pepys attended the lord mayor's banquet, and noted Bates's puritan dislike of the practice of drinking toasts. On 10 August 1662 Pepys:

> walked to St Dunstans, the church being now finished and is a very fine church; and here I heard Dr Bates, who made a most eloquent sermon. And I am sorry I have hitherto had so low an opinion of the man. (Pepys, 1.105, 3.161)

The following week he returned for Bates's farewell sermon; the church was crowded, but if his hearers expected loud denunciation of the coming ejections, they were disappointed. At the end of his sermon Bates remarked:

> I know you expect I should say something as to my nonconformity. I shall only say thus much. It is neither fancy, faction nor humour that makes me not to comply, but merely for fear of offending God. And … if it be my unhappiness to be in an error, surely men will have no reason to be angry with me in this world, and I hope God will pardon me in the next. (Bates, *Peacemaker*, 32)

By licence of 1 July 1664, on 12 July Bates, then described as a widower of the parish of Hackney aged thirty-six, married Margaret (d. 1721), a spinster aged twenty-one, daughter of Edward Gravenor, gentleman of St Giles Cripplegate.

Bates had been centrally involved in negotiations around the various schemes for comprehension within the Anglican church, and for toleration of other churches. A commissioner at the Savoy conference in 1661, he 'spake very solidly, judiciously and pertinently when he spake' (Keeble and Nuttall, 1.305). After the rejection of the Uniformity Bill on 19 May 1662, the king signalled his willingness to grant individual indulgences; in response Edmund Calamy, Bates, Manton, and others drew up petition to him. Charles promised a bill which would return many to their livings, but the bill of 23 February did not allow the king sufficient dispensing power to effect this, and anyway, it was rejected. Bates continued to entertain high hopes, delivering a speech on behalf of the dissenting ministers of London in the king's presence on 22 November 1667. He besought Charles to suppress 'prophaneness in manners and pernicious doctrines in religion', 'degenerate wickedness', and 'the licentiousness of the press'

(Scott, 8.11–12). In January 1668 Bates was involved, with Manton and Baxter, in discussions with Dr John Wilkins (1614–1672), bishop of Chester, and Hezekiah Burton (d. 1681) over a plan for a broad comprehension. A division had evolved between senior presbyterians like Bates, conservative in outlook, with friends in aristocratic circles (known as the Dons), and a group of younger men, based chiefly among the urban middle class, who thought comprehension a lost cause and agreed with Independents and Baptists in seeking toleration (the Ducklings). In February 1668 bills for both comprehension and toleration were lost. In September, encouraged by the court, the presbyterians drew up an address, presented by Bates and others, thanking the king for his clemency. Charles 'promised us that he would do his utmost to get us comprehended within the public establishment', but in the meantime they should have fewer meetings, which 'gave occasion to clamorous people to come with complaints to him' (Sylvester, 36–7). Nothing came of this.

For more than a decade, therefore, Bates and the other dissenting ministers remained in the cold. After ejection from St Dunstan's, Bates continued to preach in the area, at the house of the countess of Exeter and elsewhere, and was said to hold a regular conventicle in a room over Temple Bar Gate, next to his old church. In February 1664 he and Manton were reported to have preached at an all-day fast in Whitefriars at which the countess was joined by other eminent figures including Lord Wharton, Sir William Waller, Lady Mary Armyne, and Richard Hampden. But pressure on the dissenters increased. In 1666 they were required by the 'Oxford oath' to promise not to engage in any attempt to alter religion and the state. In a letter to Baxter of 22 February 1666 Bates recounted that Sir Orlando Bridgeman had 'professed to me that the sense of the oath was only to exclude *seditious and tumultuous* endeavours'. Bridgeman, chief justice of the common pleas, gave further assurances that Judge Keeling 'was of his mind, and would be there and be kind to us.' By this means twenty ministers were persuaded to take the oath; but Bates claimed that Keeling, having silently acquiesced in their subscription in the limited sense expounded by Bridgeman, then declared that they had:

> renounced the Covenant ... which sticks in the teeth of so many. And he hoped, that as there was one King, and one faith, so there would be one government. And if we did not conform, it would be judged we did this to save a stake ... It was not possible for us to recollect ourselves from the confusion which this caused, so as to make any reply. We retired with sadness. (Sylvester, 3.14–15)

In 1669 Bates was reported to be one of the combination lecturers at Hackney. On 28 March 1672, following the king's declaration of indulgence, he was one of four men to attend Charles at the house of Lord Arlington, in order to present their thanks. Licensed as a presbyterian teacher on 8 May 1672, he was also in that year one of the six men appointed to the joint presbyterian–congregational lecture at Pinners' Hall, later known as the Ancient Merchants' lecture. At Middlesex sessions on 2 November 1682 it was certified that Bates had been fined for preaching three times in October at the Hackney house of George Hockenhull, £20 for the first offence and £40 for each of the other two. Yet, if Calamy is to be believed, there was little in his preaching to arouse the suspicion of the authorities. His orthodox high Calvinist exegeses, and pious exhortations to a quiet and holy life, were delivered in quiet and reasonable tones, a style very far from that of the angry radicals. Despite brushes with the authorities Bates won a reputation as a sober, serious, and respectable scholar, and maintained it in high circles far from nonconformity. Calamy reported that he was respected by Lord Chancellor Finch and his son the earl of Nottingham, and that Archbishop Tillotson 'highly valued him and would often even after his Advancement to that high station, converse privately with him, with great freedom and openness' (Calamy, *Abridgement*, 2.49).

King James's political about-turn in spring 1687 brought religious toleration back to the political agenda. Bates was one of those who opposed all addresses to the king. In a discussion with Dyckfeld, the emissary of William, prince of Orange, Bates was told that although 'the Prince would give them some liberty by a law ... it was his opinion that if ever the Prince came to the throne, he would fall for all intents and purposes with the Prelatists' (Lacey, 186); this conflicted with assurances Dyckfeld had given to Roger Morrice and contributed to the dissenters' uncertainty as to what might be expected of the future King William.

But Bates and other moderate dissenters were more immediately preoccupied by the present incumbent. By November they were convinced of the need to build bridges with Anglicans concerned at the drift of royal policy. A meeting was arranged by Dr Nicholas Stratford between Dr William Lloyd, the bishop of St Asaph, and Bates, which recognized the need for 'the absolute necessity of a good understanding or coalition' (Lacey, 193). But there was much bitterness still to be overcome. Bates remarked that:

> considering how falsely they had been dealt with at first about [16]60, and how violently they had been dealt with afterwards, few of them escaping prisons and almost none of them distresses and fines, it was reasonable and proper for him to say only this, that now there could be only a concord in desire and affection. (ibid.)

He and his friends would co-operate only for the narrow purpose of defending the anti-Catholic Test Acts. He rejected Lloyd's suggestion that nonconformists should cease to meet during Church of England services. In October 1688 James called before him the leading nonconformist ministers, including Bates, on three occasions, but they promised him only their prayers and their obedience. Events shortly made these discussions irrelevant. By January 1689 Bates was conferring with Baxter and John Howe over plans for a religious settlement appropriate to the new political dispensation.

In early 1690 Bates and Mr Woodcock were reported to have 'competent supply' (Gordon, 72) at Hackney; that year he became an original manager of the common fund of presbyterians and congregationalists, subscribing £50 to the fund on 5 May 1690. In 1694, on the expulsion of

Daniel Williams from his lectureship at Pinners' Hall, Bates also withdrew, and founded the Salters' Hall lecture. In July 1694, he was certified as preacher of a meeting-house in Mare Street, Hackney. Bates died in Hackney on 14 July 1699, and was buried in the chancel of St John-at-Hackney, on 21 July. The administration of his property was granted on 14 September 1699 to his widow, Margaret. His collection of books was bought for over £500 by Daniel Williams and provided the nucleus of Dr Williams's Library now at Gordon Square, London.

STEPHEN WRIGHT

Sources *Calamy rev.* · D. Lacey, *Dissent and parliamentary politics in England, 1660–89* (1969) · W. Bates, *Works* (1723) · *Calendar of the correspondence of Richard Baxter*, ed. N. H. Keeble and G. F. Nuttall, 2 vols. (1991) · E. Calamy, ed., *An abridgement of Mr. Baxter's history of his life and times, with an account of the ministers, &c., who were ejected after the Restauration of King Charles II*, 2nd edn, 2 vols. (1713) · *Reliquiae Baxterianae, or, Mr Richard Baxter's narrative of the most memorable passages of his life and times*, ed. M. Sylvester, 1 vol. in 3 pts (1696) · A. Gordon, ed., *Freedom after ejection: a review (1690–1692) of presbyterian and congregational nonconformity in England and Wales* (1917) · *Venn, Alum. Cant.* · N. Keeble, *The literary culture of nonconformity* (1987) · W. A. Shaw, *A history of the English church during the civil wars and under the Commonwealth, 1640–1660*, 2 vols. (1900) · J. Jeaffreson, ed., *Middlesex county records* (1886), 4 · *CSP dom., 1671–2* · Pepys, *Diary* · C. Whiting, *Studies in English puritanism* (1931) · J. T. Cliffe, *The puritan gentry besieged, 1650–1700* (1993) · W. Bates, *The peacemaker* (1663) · W. Harris, *Some memoirs of the life and character of T. Manton, D.D.* (1725) · *The diary of Ralph Thoresby*, ed. J. Hunter (1830) · W. Scott, ed., *A collection of scarce and valuable tracts … Lord Somers*, 2nd edn, 13 vols. (1809–15) · J. L. Chester and G. J. Armytage, eds., *Allegations for marriage licences issued from the faculty office of the archbishop of Canterbury at London, 1543 to 1869*, Harleian Society, 24 (1886)

Likenesses W. Faithorne, line engraving, BM, NPG; repro. in W. Bates, *The harmony of the divine attributes* (1674) · attrib. G. Kneller, oils, DWL · J. Sturt, line engraving, BM, NPG; repro. in *Sermons* (1687) · R. White, line engraving (after G. Kneller), BM, NPG; repro. in *The works of William Bates* (1700)

Batesford, John (*d.* 1319), justice, is first referred to in 1273 as a former clerk of the exchequer of the Jews. Although his surname suggests a Suffolk origin, there is no other evidence to connect him with that county, and his property acquisitions and dealings suggest that he may have come from Bentworth in Hampshire. A series of appointments he received to act as the attorney of Edmund, earl of Cornwall, suggest that he may have been in the earl's service between 1273 and 1293. He was steward of Westminster Abbey in 1292–5. Full-time assize justices were appointed for the first time in 1293, and between 1293 and 1297 Batesford and William Howard were the assize justices for the seven northern counties. From 1297 to 1303 he acted as regular assize justice with a number of different partners in a circuit covering ten counties in the south and south-west. In 1301 Batesford was commissioned with others to treat with the men of Hampshire, Surrey, and Sussex on the king's behalf for a loan of grain required for the army in Scotland. He was replaced as an assize justice in 1303 because of other, unspecified, business he was then undertaking for the king. In 1307 he was appointed as one of the justices of a trailbaston circuit of eleven counties in eastern England and the south midlands.

Batesford again acted as a regular assize justice between 1307 and 1311, mainly with Roger Beaufou and John Foxley, in an eight-county circuit covering the south and south-west. In 1310 he was placed on a commission for the trial of offenders indicted before the keepers of the peace in Warwickshire and Leicestershire. Between 1295 and 1318 he was regularly summoned to parliament among the royal justices, and, from the fact that his name does not occur in the writ issued to summon the parliament of 1319, it may be inferred that he was then dead. He was certainly dead by 1320 when his executors were ordered to cause the records of the proceedings before him as justice of assize or otherwise to be transmitted to the exchequer. Batesford was in clerical orders and in 1294 held the living of Leire in Leicestershire. The Philip Batesford who was assaulted in 1295 while acting as usher at an assize session before him was probably a relative and may have been his brother.

PAUL BRAND

Sources *Chancery records* · PRO, CP 25/1 · PRO, CP 40 · PRO, JUST 1 · PRO, C 66

Bateson, Sir Alexander Dingwall (1866–1935), judge, was born at Allerton, Liverpool, on 30 April 1866, the youngest of the six sons of William Gandy Bateson, a partner in a well-known firm of shipping solicitors in Liverpool, and his wife, Agnes Dingwall, daughter of Sir Thomas Blaikie, of Aberdeen. Like his elder brother Harold Dingwall Bateson, he was educated at Rugby School and at Trinity College, Oxford, where he took a third in classical moderations (1887) and graduated with a pass BA degree in 1888. He played rugby for the college but, unlike Harold, did not obtain a blue; as a cricketer he was an adventurous batsman and sound wicket-keeper.

Having been called to the bar by the Inner Temple in 1891, Bateson began his professional career in the chambers of Joseph Walton. With such backing and under such a mentor, as well as his family connections, he had conspicuous advantages: he quickly specialized in shipping work, mainly in salvage and collision cases in the Admiralty division, occasionally in the commercial court. His progress was steady, his practice substantial. With a pleasing voice, incisive in manner and speech, he was both a lucid and a businesslike advocate. In 1893 he married Isabel Mary (*d.* 1919), fourth daughter of William Latham QC; they had four sons and two daughters.

In 1909 Bateson was appointed junior counsel to the Admiralty for Admiralty division work, but did not hold that office for long: in 1910, with his friend, and principal rival in the Admiralty court, (Edward) Maurice Hill, he took silk, and thereafter there were few shipping cases in the Admiralty division, House of Lords, or privy council in which he was not on one side or the other. He secured the confidence of the maritime business community more by his attention to detail and capacity for decision than through any profound legal learning, such as his same rival who preceded him to the bench enjoyed. He was elected a bencher of his inn in 1920.

Under the Administration of Justice Act (1925) power was given to appoint an additional judge of the Probate,

Divorce, and Admiralty Division, which had become congested: divorce-law reform increased divorce cases, while depression in shipping had not yet decreased shipping cases. With the universal approbation of the bar—and in accordance with its universal expectation—the lord chancellor (Viscount Cave) in May 1925 selected Bateson for appointment to the new post. He received the customary knighthood. The division in which he sat brought together in a single court quite disparate legal disciplines, and indeed from 1970 no longer survived in that form, the subjects being dispersed between the Queen's Bench (Admiralty), Chancery (Probate), and Family (Divorce) divisions. Bateson was entirely conversant with maritime law and practice; in the probate and matrimonial jurisdiction he lacked any previous expertise. Although he never wholly assimilated all the historical principles of the earlier ecclesiastical law, his sound common sense and humanity stood him in good stead. He appreciated that the duty of a judge in family matters is to give judgments, not to deliver sermons. He disliked anything which attracted public attention to himself, and made no gratuitous comments on manners or morals. Dignified, courteous, careful, and diligent, Bateson was a master of fact, not of law. He seldom reserved a judgment, yet his judgments were rarely reversed. He continued to show that supreme judicial qualification, the ability to reach a conclusion. As a result he gave full satisfaction not only to the shipping community but also to other litigants and the bar.

During the First World War, Bateson had been a regular worker at the Kensington Red Cross depot, where he helped to make thousands of 'Thomas splints', rings of mild steel shaped to fit round the thigh. Bateson said to a colleague of this experience, 'the noise of the hammering prevents my hearing the bombs' (*The Times*, 16 Jan 1935, 12). He had the English quality best captured by the French word 'sangfroid'. His outside interests included agriculture, forestry, and shooting, and for many years he farmed at Lotus, Beeswing by Dumfries, Kirkcudbrightshire, where he usually spent his vacations. He died at his home, 30 Phillimore Gardens, London, on 11 January 1935. His obituary in *The Times* (12 January 1935) commented that 'the premature close of his judicial career must be regarded as a serious public loss'. Today a judge of his age would be compelled to retire.

NOEL MIDDLETON, rev. MICHAEL BELOFF

Sources *The Times* (12 Jan 1935), 14 · *The Times* (15 Jan 1935), 4, 14 · *The Times* (16 Jan 1935), 12 · private information (1949)
Wealth at death £45,245 2s. 6d.: probate, 25 Feb 1935, *CGPLA Eng. & Wales*

Bateson, Gregory (1904–1980), anthropologist and communications theorist, was born on 9 May 1904 at Grantchester, Cambridgeshire, the youngest of three sons of William *Bateson (1861–1926), zoologist and geneticist, and his wife, (Caroline) Beatrice (1870?–1941), daughter of Arthur Durham and his wife, Mary Ellis; his parents were both English. Bateson attended Warden House (1913–17) and Charterhouse (1917–21) schools, and then Cambridge University (BA, 1926; MA, 1930).

Bateson's father, also a Cambridge man, was renowned for championing the work of Gregor Mendel on genetic mutation, at a time when work on the evolution of species focused in narrowly Darwinian terms on natural selection. Gregory Bateson became equally innovative (and idiosyncratic) in rediscovering for anthropology an aesthetic holism which he associated with the poet William Blake. In efforts to elucidate a pervading unity underlying all the world's phenomena, he made incisive contributions to communication theory, family therapy, dolphin studies, and ecology—and was recognized in these fields sometimes with more alacrity and respect than in his 'native' discipline and land. Only a non-specialist, interdisciplinary anthropology, he contended, could expect to treat the vast intricacies of social milieux.

Bateson studied anthropology at Cambridge with A. C. Haddon (having switched from part one of the natural sciences tripos). He first undertook fieldwork in New Britain, among the Baining and Sulka, and New Guinea, among the Iatmul (1927–30); there he met Margaret Mead, also fieldworking, with her then husband Reo Fortune. Bateson's fieldwork resulted in an unconventional ethnography, *Naven: a survey of problems suggested by the composite picture of the culture of a New Guinea tribe drawn from three points of view* (1936; 2nd edn 1958). *Naven* concerned cultural style and form, village formation, initiation, and gender relations; it was also a disquisition on the perspectivalism or context which underlies scientists' supposedly objective inductions. In language somewhat reminiscent of the work of Ruth Benedict, Bateson spoke of the 'ethos' (emotional tone) and 'eidos' (intellectual patterning) of Iatmul culture. He distinguished between 'centripetal' and 'peripheral' mechanisms of social organization. The first was based on a complementarity of members' behaviour, different and yet compatible; and the second was based on a symmetricality—the same and hence equivalent. He described how 'schismogenesis' ('complementary' or 'symmetrical') could occur if the cumulative reactions of people or groups to one another's behaviour was not counteracted. 'Schismogenesis' was his own term, which he used to define 'the origin of differentiation between groups and cultures caused by the reciprocal exaggeration of behaviour patterns and responses that may result in the destruction of the social balance' (*Oxford English Dictionary*).

The exponential curve of schismogenesis, and that of its opposite, mutual love, Bateson extrapolated, pertained not just to the Iatmul but universally, and is evidenced in class war, the arms race, megalomania, and true love. Indeed, the universality of feedback mechanisms, of circular or 'recursive' causal systems, in both biology and society, was advocated by Bateson throughout his life. In advance of Habermas, Giddens, or Bourdieu, he emphasized how (in the words of his biographer, Peter Harries-Jones, *A Recursive Vision*, Toronto, 1995, 3) informations 'continually enter into, become entangled with, and then re-enter the universe they describe'. So analysis must acknowledge the cumulative effects of interaction between entities and at the same time recognize the importance of homeostatic or steady-state systems. Preaching this at the famous Macy conferences of 1946–8, together with Norbert Wiener, Bateson became one of the founders of the new science of cybernetics.

Bateson married Margaret Mead (1901–1978), on 13 March 1936, and set out with her for an ethnographic field trip to Bali (1936–8). Researching into posture, gesture, painting, childhood relationships, play, and the 'schizophrenia' of trance, Bateson took some 25,000 photographs, some of which appeared in their joint publication, *Balinese Character: A Photographic Analysis* (1942). Bateson and Mead separated in 1948 and were divorced two years later; their daughter, Mary Catherine Bateson, wrote an insightful narrative of their lives together, *With a Daughter's Eye* (1984). Bateson had by then also exchanged St John's College, Cambridge, for the New School for Social Research, New York (1946), and then Harvard University (1947); soon he moved to the Langley Porter Clinic, University of California medical school, in San Francisco.

At Langley Porter (1948–9) Bateson worked with psychiatrist Jurgen Ruesch and produced *Communication: the Social Matrix of Psychiatry* (1951), a book which developed Norbert Wiener's insight that 'information' was synonymous with 'negative entropy' or order. In other words, patterns of social interaction—the habitual communication of information—lie beneath life in society: its structure and order, its sense of value and propriety, and its aesthetics and cosmology. The what and the how of reiterative communication provided the vital context within which 'behaviour' came to be learned. Indeed, learning to learn ('deutero-learning') was a matter of coming to know oneself in a habitual context.

In 1950 Bateson married Elizabeth Sumner; they had a son, John, in 1951 and subsequently divorced. He then married Lois Cammack in 1961 and they had a daughter, Nora, in 1969. From 1949 to 1963 Bateson headed a research team at Veterans Administration Hospital, Palo Alto, California, further exploring communicative practices among dogs, otters, monkeys, and wolves, and among human alcoholics; also the place that paradox seemed to assume in the communication of play, humour, and jokes. Between 1954 and 1959 this came together in a psychotherapeutic project on schizophrenic communication which Bateson directed. Schizophrenics, it was surmised, display abnormal communicative behaviour which derives from their experiencing a repetitive pattern of paradoxical injunctions at some stage in their lives (the 'double-bind' theory).

From Palo Alto, Bateson moved to be associate director of the Communications Institute at St Thomas, in the Virgin Islands (1963–4), followed by an associate directorship at the Oceanic Institute, Waimanalo, Hawaii (1965–72). Over nine years he worked with John Lilly on various projects exploring dolphin communication. This culminated in perhaps his most influential work, *Steps to an ecology of mind: collected essays in anthropology, psychiatry, evolution and epistemology* (1972). In this series of papers spanning his career Bateson worked to disclose the patterns connecting different points of view in an ecological field. All living organisms contributed to the patterning within an ecosystem and to its regeneration, he argued. Indeed, organism-plus-environment made a single recursive system of ongoing life, with parts and whole continuously modifying one another.

In 1976 Bateson was appointed to the board of regents of the University of California, a mark of the estimation in which he was now held within the American academy; but he resigned three years later in protest over the 'evil' of nuclear weapons. His final work, *Mind and Nature: a Necessary Unity* (1979), was a Blakean reflection on the patterns—complex and beautiful—which connect human consciousness to much of the natural world. He died of cancer on 4 July 1980 at the Zen Center, San Francisco, California, and was cremated three days later at Marin county; his ashes were scattered at Esalen Institute cliffs, San Francisco.

It was said of Bateson by the celebrated psychiatrist, R. D. Laing (echoing a comment of Erving Goffman's), that he possessed 'the most distinctive perceptual capacities of anyone I've met' (R. Evans, *R. D. Laing*, New York, 1976, 75). Claude Lévi-Strauss, meanwhile, lauded his culture theory and Konrad Lorenz his theoretical ethology. In combining insights into culture and character formation, into the logic and paradoxes of perception and learning, into the recursive effects of messages in communicative circuits, and into the mathematics of progression and stability, Bateson was a most distinctive anthropologist. He anticipated some innovative trends in late twentieth-century anthropology, such as exploration of the culturally viable relations between 'nature' and 'culture', of environmentalism, and the application of anthropology to the study of natural science. His diverse writings will continue to be mined for stimulating ideas.

NIGEL RAPPORT

Sources D. Lipset, *Gregory Bateson* (Englewood Cliffs, New Jersey, 1980) · P. Harries-Jones, *A recursive vision* (Toronto, 1995) · M. C. Bateson, *With a daughter's eye* (New York, 1984) · J. Brockman, ed., *About Bateson* (New York, 1977) · R. Donaldson, *Gregory Bateson archive: a guide/catalog*, 4 vols. (Ann Arbor, 1987) · C. Wilder and J. Weakland, eds., *Rigor and imagination* (New York, 1981) · E. Leach, *Royal Anthropological Institute News*, 40 (1980) · R. May, 'About Gregory Bateson', *Journal of Humanistic Psychology*, 16/4 (1976), 33–51 · R. Donaldson, ed., *Sacred unity* (New York, 1991) · J. Howard, *Margaret Mead* (1984)
Archives U. Cal., Santa Cruz, corresp., book and article MSS, notebooks, and tapes
Likenesses photographs, repro. in Bateson, *With a daughter's eye* · photographs, repro. in Lipset, *Gregory Bateson*

Bateson, Margaret. *See* Heitland, Margaret (1860–1938).

Bateson, Mary (1865–1906), historian and suffragist, was born on 12 September 1865 at Ings House, Robin Hood's Bay, Yorkshire, the daughter of William Henry *Bateson (1812–1881), master of St John's College, Cambridge, and his wife, Anna Aikin (1829–1918), a promoter of women's rights and liberal causes in Cambridge. William *Bateson, the biologist, was her elder brother, and Margaret *Heitland, the journalist and women's suffragist, was her elder sister. She attended the Misses Thornton's school in Cambridge in the mid-1870s before spending a year at the Institut Friedländer in Baden, Germany. Her command of German was substantial enough for her to be engaged as the German teacher at the Perse School for Girls at the same time as she was a pupil there (1881–4), preparing to enter Newnham College, Cambridge, of which her parents had been among the founders in 1871. She attended Newnham from 1884 to 1887, taking a first class in the historical tripos at Cambridge in 1887 and winning the historical essay prize at Newnham for a dissertation, 'Monastic civilisation in the fens'.

Bateson remained a member of the Newnham community for the rest of her life as an associate, lecturer, and fellow of the college. She lectured in English constitutional history, served on the college council, and shared in the unsuccessful effort of 1895–7 to have women admitted to full membership of Cambridge University. Eleanor Sidgwick, second principal of Newnham, described Bateson, who recognized the connection between financial security and scholarly production, as the prime mover behind the foundation of Newnham's research fellowships. Bateson was awarded one of the first of these fellowships in 1903 from a fund to which she had contributed £250. Upon the expiry of her fellowship she gave the money back to the fund to assist other scholars.

It is primarily for her medieval scholarship that Bateson is remembered outside Newnham. Under the mentorship of Cambridge colleagues Mandell Creighton and, later, F. W. Maitland, Bateson continued her studies of medieval culture, editing texts and publishing both scholarly and popular history. Her earlier work focused on monastic and religious history; her *editio princeps* of Ælfric's *Letter to the Monks of Eynsham*, which was published as appendix 7 in G. W. Kitchin (ed.), *Compotus Rolls of the Obedientiaries of St. Swithun's Priory, Winchester* (1892), remained the only available text of this important Benedictine reform document until 1984. Her essay 'Origin and early history of double monasteries' (*Transactions of the Royal Historical Society*, new ser., 13, 1899, 137–98), is a foundational text in the history of women's religious communities. Using a wide range of primary sources, Bateson established a history and a precedent for 'double monasteries'—houses for monks and nuns ruled by an abbess, usually of royal birth.

In almost every year from 1890 to 1906 Bateson contributed an article or short edited text to the *English Historical Review*; she collaborated with its editors (Maitland and R. L. Poole) to prepare *The Charters of the Borough of Cambridge* (1901) and the *Index Britanniae scriptorum* (1902). She also contributed 108 biographical articles to the original edition of the *DNB*. The subjects of all these entries are men; they include saints, monks, and noblemen. Some date to the Anglo-Saxon or early modern periods; most cluster in the Anglo-Norman and high middle ages.

By the mid-1890s Bateson's focus had changed from monasteries and cathedrals to boroughs and towns, and her later work tends to address the medieval history of municipal customs and laws. She edited the *Records of the Borough of Leicester* (3 vols., 1899, 1901, and 1905) as well as

the *Cambridge Gild Records* (Cambridge Antiquarian Society, 1903). Her final and probably most important editorial work was the mammoth two-volume *Borough Customs* (Selden Society, 1904 and 1906) that brought together tenth- to seventeenth-century texts such as charters, law codes, custumals, letters patent, patent rolls, council orders, and ordinance rolls to 'set out the rules which obtained in the borough-moots', as she notes in the introduction to volume 1.

Bateson's essay 'The laws of Bréteuil' (*English Historical Review*, 15, 1900, 73–8, 302–18, 496–523, 754–7; and 16, 1901, 92–110, 332–45) is still an important text in the field of legal history, as it illustrates that the Norman town of Bréteuil, not the English town of Bristol (as was previously believed), is the origin of many English borough laws and customs. Her substantial scholarly reputation was such that she was asked to be the prestigious Warburton lecturer at the University of Manchester in 1905; her two lectures were entitled 'Survivals of ancient customs in English borough law'.

Bateson also wrote a large quantity of popular history. Her only book that is not a scholarly edition of a historical text, *Mediaeval England*, appeared in the popular Unwin history series The Story of the Nations (1903). She contributed 'The French in America' to the 1903 edition of the *Cambridge Modern History*, and a number of social history essays to H. D. Traill's monumental historical encyclopaedia *Social England* (1901–4), as well as a chapter, 'The borough of Peterborough', for the *Victoria County History of Northampton* (1906). Bateson's skills as a writer for the general public were acknowledged when she was asked by Cambridge University Press to act as a general editor of the *Cambridge Medieval History*, a post which she was unable to take up before her untimely death at forty-one.

Mary Bateson the historian was also Mary Bateson the suffragist and women's rights crusader, despite the disapproval of Creighton, her Newnham colleague Alice Gardner, and others. She served the Cambridge Women's Suffrage Association (an affiliate of the National Union of Women's Suffrage Societies, the NUWSS) in a variety of capacities throughout the 1880s and 1890s: in a paid position as meeting organizer (1888), as executive committee member (1889), secretary of the association (1892–8), secretary to the special appeal (1894), and national conference delegate (1896).

Bateson spoke as part of a suffrage deputation to the prime minister, Sir Henry Campbell-Bannerman, on 19 May 1906, representing women graduates of universities in a group of 350 representatives from twenty-five different NUWSS affiliates. She made a brief speech and presented a petition signed by 1530 women university graduates 'who believe the disenfranchisement of one sex to be injurious to both, and a national wrong in a country which pretends to be governed on a representative system' (NUWSS, 11).

Bateson also took the socially unusual step of moving out of her mother's house and into a home of her own on Huntingdon Road. It seems that she valued her peace and quiet over the custom of an adult, unmarried daughter living with her parents. She was remembered in obituaries as a gracious, compassionate woman with a sense of humour and a keen intellect. Gardner noted that any party was sure to succeed if Mary Bateson were on the guest list, and mentions Bateson's 'unexpected sallies of wit' at college meetings (Gardner, 'In memoriam', 34). Thomas Frederick Tout, the historian, stated that she 'was popular socially in circles that cared little for her personal [academic] distinction' and referred to her 'rare sense of humour … her deep, hearty laugh … [her] downright breezy good-fellowship' (Tout, 6). Bateson's Girton colleague Ellen A. McArthur recalled her as 'absolutely honest, independent, and fearless, full of commonsense, and endowed with a sense of humour' (McArthur, 1033).

Bateson's death from a brain haemorrhage, at the Nursing Hostel, Thompsons Lane, Cambridge, on 30 November 1906 shocked all the communities of which she was a part. Bertrand Russell, for one, found her death 'very sad—she will be a terrible loss to Newnham and to Cambridge … I respected and admired her very much indeed. She was the last person one would have thought of as likely to die' (Bertrand Russell to M. Llewellyn-Davies, 4 Dec 1906, McMaster University). She was buried in the Histon Road cemetery in Cambridge. She left her library and about £2500 to Newnham College, where she is commemorated by a named research fellowship. All the memorials refer to her good nature, her firm work ethic, and her enormous scholarly production. A bust of her, sculpted by her sister Edith Bateson, still stands at the old entrance to the Newnham College Library; it presents her, appropriately, reading a book.   MARY DOCKRAY-MILLER

Sources A. Gardner, *A short history of Newnham College* (1921) • E. A. McArthur, 'In memoriam: Mary Bateson, 1865–1906', *The Queen* (8 Dec 1906) • E. B. Sidgwick, 'Report of the principal', 1907', *Records of Newnham College* • NUWSS, *Women's suffrage deputation* (1906) • E. Crawford, *The women's suffrage movement: a reference guide, 1866–1928* (1999) • T. F. Tout, 'Mary Bateson', *Manchester Guardian* (3 Dec 1906) • A. Gardner, 'In memoriam: Mary Bateson', *Newnham College Letter* (1906), 34–9 • letters to Margaret Llewellyn-Davies, McMaster University, Hamilton, Ontario, Bertrand Russell archive VI, I • d. cert.
Likenesses photograph, *c*.1900, Newnham College Archives, Cambridge • photograph, *c*.1900, repro. in McArthur, 'In memoriam' • E. Bateson, bust, 1907, Newnham College Library
Wealth at death £8788 19*s*. 5*d*.: probate, 8 March 1907, *CGPLA Eng. & Wales*

Bateson, Thomas (*d.* 1630), composer and organist, first appears as the father of a son baptized in 1592; he may have been born in the Wirral, Cheshire, but the identity of both his parents and his wife is unknown. In 1599 he was appointed organist of Chester Cathedral, where he remained ten years. It seems that Bateson was also an organ technician, for among the various payments he received during this time was one for 'mending the organs'. In 1604 he began publication with *The First Set of English Madrigals to 3, 4, 5 and 6 Voices*, dedicated to Sir William Norres, to whom Bateson (as he noted in his preface) had 'sent them … ever as they were composed in loose

papers'. Norres appears to have been more than a merely nominal patron.

By 24 March 1609 Bateson had moved to Ireland, where he had been appointed organist and a vicar-choral of Christ Church, Dublin. In 1612 (some sources record 1615) he became, it seems, the first person to be granted a BMus degree by Trinity College, Dublin, and in 1622 he was admitted MA. Meanwhile in 1618 he had issued *The Second Set of Madrigals to 3, 4, 5 and 6 Parts: Apt for Viols and Voices*, which, like his first collection, was published in London. The volume's dedicatee was Arthur, Lord Chichester, lord high treasurer of Ireland, and again it was evidently the patron who had prompted its contents, Bateson stating in his preface that these had been 'solely intended for your honour's private recreation'.

It is curious that only one anthem ('Holy, lord God almighty', for seven voices) should have survived from the work of a lifelong church musician—though a service by Bateson, now lost, was still sung at Chester into the early nineteenth century. Thus his reputation rests solely on the fifty-nine compositions contained in his two publications. One madrigal, 'When Oriana walked', had been intended for *The Triumphs of Oriana*, that collection published in 1601 in praise of the aged Queen Elizabeth, but it had arrived too late for inclusion, and three years later it was slipped into Bateson's own first set, which also contains a second madrigal called 'Oriana's Farewell' (ending 'In heaven lives Oriana'), which was a posthumous tribute to the Virgin Queen.

Like all English madrigalists Bateson owed a fundamental debt to the light canzonet style naturalized into English music by Thomas Morley in his five madrigal volumes of the 1590s, though he seems to have been more generally impressed by this style as enriched in John Wilbye's first volume (1598), and especially by certain of the madrigals in the first of Thomas Weelkes's first three collections (1597–1600). To instance only the most obvious evidence: Bateson's 'Those sweet delightful lilies' (1604) is audibly indebted to Weelkes's setting of the same text in his 1597 volume, while at the openings of 'If love be blind' and the second part of 'Sweet Gemma' (both 1604) he employed Weelkes's special device of using a melodic idea which, while being worked imitatively in the upper voices, also provided the bass, though now presented in an augmentation which controlled the harmonic course.

Marks of such direct influence are less marked in Bateson's 1618 volume than in its predecessor, though two pieces do also borrow from other composers. The case of 'If floods of tears' is curious. This text had already been used by John Dowland in his second book of lute songs (1600), and Bateson took not only the poem but Dowland's first two musical phrases—yet for some unknown reason he cast his setting as an archaic viol-accompanied song more typical of a mid-sixteenth century tradition. Another borrowing, though a belated one, was clearly personal in nature. Francis Pilkington, another important madrigalist, had been a lay clerk in the cathedral choir during the whole of Bateson's Chester period, and Bateson ghosted the opening section of his former colleague's

'Have I found her?' (published 1613) to make his own setting of the same text issued five years later.

Bateson proved generally at his best when using five and six voices in a serious vein, and his ability to produce an effect of high pathos, sometimes heightened by bold dissonance, is impressive; nevertheless, some of his liveliest pieces, for instance 'Cupid in a bed of roses' and 'Camilla fair' (both 1618), are splendidly accomplished. He was clearly a man of taste, and his choice of verse showed much discrimination. Though his technique was not flawless, and in creative stature he was the equal neither of Weelkes nor Wilbye, Bateson remains one of the most impressive of the English madrigalists.

Bateson made his will on 2 March 1630 and died, in Dublin, a fortnight before his quarterly rent was due (which would have been, presumably, on 25 March); his widow was allowed a new lease on 30 April. He may have been buried in Christ Church Cathedral.   DAVID BROWN

Sources *New Grove* · E. H. Fellowes, *The English madrigal composers*, 2nd edn (1950) · J. C. Bridge, 'The organists of Chester Cathedral', *Journal of the Architectural, Archaeological, and Historic Society of the County and City of Chester and North Wales*, new ser., 19 (1913), 63–124 · H. W. Shaw, *The succession of organists of the Chapel Royal and the cathedrals of England and Wales from c.1538* (1991)

Bateson, William (1861–1926), biologist, was born on 8 August 1861 in St Hilda's Terrace, Ruswarp, near Whitby, Yorkshire, the second of six children of William Henry *Bateson (1812–1881), master of St John's College, Cambridge, and his wife, Anna Aikin (1829–1918), daughter of James Aikin (1792–1878), Liverpool shipping merchant. As the reformist master of St John's College, William Henry Bateson had achieved a reputation both in national educational circles and more especially in the politics of Cambridge University. There, freed from the rule of celibacy by his promotion from fellow to master, he had married the beautiful and spirited Anna Aikin, fond of the arts and a strong advocate for the rights of women.

Both families owed their financial success to the previous generation of self-made vigorous men (Bateson's paternal grandfather, Richard Bateson (b. 1770), was a successful Liverpool cotton merchant). Their traditions were alike, Liberal, and the marriage of Bateson's parents in 1858 strengthened this political stance and perpetuated feminist aspirations. In the span of eight years William, his four sisters, and his brother Edward were born. Surrounded by these sisters William enjoyed much attention. Naturally he was affected by their feminist persuasion, and he was to take pride in the academic successes of his sisters Anna and Mary at Newnham College, Cambridge. Mary *Bateson (1865–1906), went on to become a widely respected medievalist. Another sister, Margaret [see Heitland, Margaret] became a journalist and social activist.

Education, early research, and marriage William Bateson was a disappointment at school at Rugby (1875–9), but he redeemed the family reputation by winning a first in the natural sciences tripos at Cambridge, part one in 1882 and part two in 1883. There, at his father's college and as a member of the circle of enthusiasts who gathered around

William Bateson (1861–1926), by Vernon Henry Mottram, 1909

the zoologists Francis Maitland Balfour and Adam Sedgwick, Bateson imbibed the heady wine of comparative embryology—the window through which to glimpse the evolutionary ancestry of animal species. This study of the lines of descent known as phylogeny was founded on the assumption that the embryo recapitulates in its development the evolutionary history of the species. Bateson's first success in research was his study of the acorn worm, *Balanoglossus*, carried out in the recapitulationist tradition. The fruit of two summers spent in Hampton, Virginia, under the zoologist W. K. Brooks, supported by funds from the Royal Society, was the first accurate account of the worm's embryology and anatomy. Bateson claimed it as an example of a primitive chordate, and thus an indicator of the line of descent of the vertebrates from the invertebrates. The implications of this research and the influence of Brooks led Bateson to make a radical shift, turning from embryology to the study of variation, first in the wild and in museum collections and subsequently in the experimental tradition of hybridization. This took him in 1886 to the salt lakes of the Russian steppes and in 1887 to the brackish water of Egypt before he settled down in Cambridge to make a systematic collection of examples of variation in the animal kingdom. The resulting book, *Materials for the Study of Variation* (1894), attacked the recapitulationist research tradition of the British evolutionists but failed to impress them. Instead it increased its author's growing alienation from those who held power in Cambridge zoology. Consequently Bateson, who was especially attached to Cambridge, continued on college support—he was elected a fellow of St John's College in 1885 on the strength of his *Balanoglossus* work. To the stipend of his college fellowship he was able to add (in 1892) that of college steward in charge of the wine cellar, kitchen garden, and kitchens. These two sources constituted his salary for the next fifteen years. Support for his research came from the Balfour studentship in 1887 and a succession of annual grants (from 1900 to 1906) from the Royal Society, to which he had been elected fellow in 1894.

In 1889 Bateson met (Caroline) Beatrice Durham (1870?–

1941), the daughter of a senior surgeon at Guy's Hospital, Arthur Edward Durham (1834–1895). Their subsequent engagement was broken off and all correspondence intercepted due to disapproval of Bateson by Beatrice's mother. Seven years later, Beatrice's parents having died, they renewed their acquaintance and in 1896 they married. Of their three sons John was killed in the First World War in 1918, Martin committed suicide in 1922, but Gregory *Bateson (1904–1980) had a distinguished career in social anthropology and psychology. The marriage thus had its deep sadnesses—like that of many others whose sons were lost in the war—but it was a good partnership. Bateson was aggressive, demanding, and at times domineering, but enthusiastic and playful. He would mock, tease, and humiliate Beatrice. She was reserved and unlike her formidable sisters she tended to belittle herself; her strength was her devotion to Bateson. Until 1903 she performed most of the menial tasks associated with her husband's experiments. After his death she gathered together his correspondence and published extracts in her 160-page memoir alongside a collection of his public lectures in *William Bateson, F.R.S., Naturalist: his Essays and Addresses* (1928). The latter displays Bateson's oratorical powers and underlines his popularity as a lecturer. Published separately as *Problems of Genetics* (1913) were his Silliman lectures of 1907. The memoir concentrates on the Cambridge years and makes only brief references to her husband's later career at the John Innes Horticultural Institute of which he became the architect and first director in 1910. These were years of dedication, frustration, and a feeling of exile from Cambridge, added to which came the sad events of the First World War. Peace established, leadership in genetics passed from England to the United States of America where T. H. Morgan was building a reputation with the chromosome theory of heredity, a theory opposed by Bateson until 1921.

Discontinuity in evolution There were four concerns that prompted Bateson to question the Darwinian orthodoxy of continuity—the view that evolution results from the cumulative action of natural selection upon slight variations in such fashion that over a long period of time progeny diverge significantly from their originating species. His first concern was his adherence to the belief that specific differences are real, not mere products of the taxonomist, in short that there are natural kinds among living organisms. Species were for Bateson more than mere populations with certain frequencies of characters. Second, the view of variation as continuous relied heavily on the principle of utility. Slight variations were preserved and accumulated only because each one which was preserved offered its possessor some advantage in the struggle for life. Despite his family background in liberal politics and trade, he was vehemently opposed to arguments from utility. Indeed, he seems to have turned against the commercial world to which both his and his wife's family owed the advantages they enjoyed. By a process of gentrification he came to identify with the aims and to admire the institutions of the academic élite. Thus he tried to discourage his sister Anna from entering the trade of market gardening. At the same time he opposed positive eugenics because he rejected the simplistic utilitarian basis upon which decisions would be made regarding who should breed with whom. Third, he came increasingly to admire those sciences that had achieved reliable knowledge based on the experimental method, where predictions could be tested and causal chains established. Those most relevant to biology, he judged, were chemistry and physiology. Thus he emphasized the aim of his genetic research as the study of the physiology of heredity. This alignment suggested the need for experiment rather than the mere descriptions and phylogenetic speculations of the morphological tradition, and it invited the search for discontinuities in biology analogous to those in chemistry that mark the chemical elements.

The fourth source of Bateson's changed view was the influence of the Johns Hopkins professor, W. K. Brooks. When Bateson came to work with him in 1883 Brooks was just finishing his book *The Law of Heredity: a Study of the Cause of Variation, and the Origin of Living Organisms* (1883), in which he stressed the inadequacy of natural selection acting on purely fortuitous small variations, the suggestion to explore the nature of variation as a phenomenon of the whole organism, and the need for a large programme of experimental hybridization. Brooks's rhetorical, aphoristic style of speech and writing appealed to the 22-year-old Cambridge student, fresh from his graduation. Nearly forty years later Bateson recalled that the 'notion on which [Brooks] used to expiate, that there was a special physiology of heredity capable of independent study, came as a new idea' (cited in Bateson, *William Bateson*, 390).

Bateson's attention to variation was first aroused by his study of *Balanoglossus*. It concerned the origin of the vertebrates: had they derived from a worm-like creature with segmentation and bilateral symmetry, a flatworm lacking segmentation, or a jellyfish-like radially symmetrical progenitor? All three choices presented problems involving major organizational features. Bateson suggested that some of these—such as the presence or extent of segmentation and the type of symmetry—did occur spontaneously in evolution and thus could overcome these problems. Thus *Balanoglossus*, with scarcely any evidence of segmentation, could have derived from a radially symmetrical progenitor. This proposal had the advantage that it obviated the need for a radical reorganization of the major organs, such as would be needed for a worm-like progenitor. He found such variations in symmetry, and in the number of parts, from the study of the symmetry changes in plants and from data he collected on the multiplication of like parts in animals.

Bateson's first step had been to probe the relation between organisms and environment where environmental change was under way in the wild. Abandoning embryology he journeyed to the salt lakes of the steppes looking for changes in molluscs that showed adaptation to the increasing salt content of these waters. Both in Russia and in Egypt he did not find a continuity of variation in the molluscs paralleling the continuity of change in the environment. When he had returned to Cambridge he set about accumulating data on variation using as his model the approach Charles Darwin used in the material for his great work *The Variation of Animals and Plants under Domestication* (1868). Like Darwin, Bateson began accumulating a mountain of empirical evidence for variation, but unlike the former he concentrated on monstrosities, sports of nature, objects usually assigned to the subject of teratology. They spoke to him of a discontinuous form of variation which came from within the organism—variations ready made which natural selection had either to reject or accept. Hence to answer the question 'What is the origin of species?' Bateson turned to these sports of nature. They were of two kinds: those involving the reproduction of parts and changes of symmetry he termed meristic and those in which there was a qualitative change as in the presence or absence of a chemical substance (albino forms) which he called substantive.

Experimental hybridization Bateson's hybridization experiments date from 1895. They were aimed at demonstrating that discontinuous variations are not swamped by breeding with the normal type. At the Royal Horticultural Society's first international conference on plant hybridization held in London in 1899 both he and the Dutch botanist Huge De Vries described their experiments without drawing any Mendelian-like conclusions. The following spring Bateson read a paper by De Vries (the first paper in the series marking the rediscovery of Mendel's law) as he travelled to London to address the society. This paper contained no reference to the Moravian monk Gregor Mendel, whose account of what became known as the Mendelian theory had been published in 1866. Subsequent rediscovery papers gave credit to Mendel, and Bateson promptly turned to Mendel's text 'Versüche über Pflanzenhybriden' and recognized its significance. It was the key he needed. It gave a causal explanation for the production of variation which was independent of the environment; it showed how hereditary differences were separated from hybrid mixture because of the purity of the germ cells. The theory offered an algorithm with which to predict the outcome of experiments in crossing. Eagerly he persuaded the society to have the paper translated into English and published in its *Journal*. Aided by his contacts in the Royal Horticultural Society and his friends in the Royal Society, Bateson gained support for the programme of Mendelian experiments upon which he now embarked.

In Cambridge University he continued the outsider to the biological community. Apart from serving as deputy to the ageing zoology professor and expert ornithologist, Alfred Newton, he received no university teaching appointment until the readership of zoology in the winter of 1907–8. Shortly thereafter he was offered the directorship of the new John Innes Horticultural Institute at Merton, close to London. The institution of the first chair of genetics in Britain at Cambridge University in 1912 came too late for him. By that time he had become deeply involved in the establishment of what was to become and has remained a research centre for genetics, the John Innes.

Public opposition to the new experimental tradition came not from Cambridge but from the school of biometricians led by the statistician Karl Pearson and Bateson's former close friend at Cambridge W. F. R. Weldon. Weldon had begun to fall out with Bateson in 1890 following the latter's attacks on orthodox Darwinism. Then, too, they were rivals for academic appointments, and when Bateson joined the Royal Society's evolution committee he proceeded to take it over and soon after to appropriate its funds, which hitherto had supported Weldon's biometric research. The ensuing controversy between biometricians and Mendelians is notorious. Bateson heaped all the scorn and sarcasm he could muster on his opponents, who continued to support the ancestral theory of inheritance proposed by Francis Galton. At first Bateson allowed that heredity might be of two kinds—ancestral for continuously varying characters but Mendelian for discontinuously varying ones. Later he inferred that the ancestral theory was just a special case of the fundamental theory, which was Mendelian. Weldon, on the other hand, attacked the Mendelian theory, but when he became convinced that it should have a place he modified it in order to accommodate it within the ancestral theory which he considered fundamental.

Genetics Bateson was not just Mendel's apostle to the English speaking world. Nor was he merely 'defender of the faith'. His research with the devoted circle of supporters around him in Cambridge led to the discovery of what he called partial gametic coupling (since renamed linkage), of the interactions known as epistasis and hypostasis between hereditary determinants, of the Mendelian character of sex limited inheritance differences, and of Mendelian heredity in man. He also made a major contribution to the terminology of genetics—allelomorph (now allele), homozygote, heterozygote, F_1, F_2, F_3 generation—and last but not least he coined the word genetics, defining it as

the elucidation of the phenomena of heredity and variation: in other words, to the physiology of descent, with implied bearings on the theoretical problems of the evolutionist and systematist, and applications to the practical problems of breeders, whether of animals or plants. (W. Bateson, 'The progress of genetic research', *Report of the Third International Conference 1906 on Genetics*, 1907, 91)

This passage occurs in his inaugural address to the third international conference on hybridization and plant breeding, which like the first of 1899 was held in London under the auspices of the Royal Horticultural Society.

Bateson's persistent efforts to attract funding for establishing genetic research on a long-term basis at Cambridge eventually led to the endowment of the first chair in the subject. Bateson's vitriolic attack on the critics of Mendelism in his *Mendel's Principles of Heredity: a Defence* (1902) was softened in the much expanded major text *Mendel's Principles of Heredity* (1909), a work which quickly became the classic of the first phase of genetics. His campaign for the subject also played a part in the decision of the Lloyd George administration to include plant and animal breeding among the collection of research institutes to be established under the Development Act of 1909. The John Innes Horticultural Institute was the result of a private benefaction which in Bateson's hands became the instrument for the continuation of most of his Cambridge research. Of the other lines of work which he instituted the most successful was the study of fruit. The resulting knowledge of the compatibility and incompatibility among varieties of apples, pears, cherries, and plums was perhaps the most valuable achievement of Bateson's years at the John Innes.

Bateson is a striking example of the trend from descriptive to experimental tradition in biology which took place about the beginning of the twentieth century. Embryology had already established an experimental tradition in Germany. But the study of heredity had been largely in terms of pedigrees. The growing band of cytologists had also begun to speculate about heredity, but they did not produce a successful theory, and Bateson was particularly scornful of the leading cytological theory—that of August Weismann. Nor was he attracted to statistical theories like those of the biometricians. They were actuarial: giving statements of probability. Was it not better, opined Bateson, to determine by experiment the hereditary constitution of organisms? The historiography of the controversy between Mendelians and biometricians which used to portray the former as right and the latter as wrong has been superseded by a more even-handed treatment. The use of this episode as a case history for the sociology of knowledge approach has led to a fruitful debate from which it is clear that there were deep-seated differences between the two sides not of a kind easily settled by experimental investigation. Inevitably the resolution of the controversy was the work not of the leaders but of their successors. Meanwhile Bateson had risen to a position of world fame despite his sceptical attitude to Darwinian evolution. In 1922 he accepted the request to become a trustee of the British Museum, but he declined the offer of a knighthood. The Royal Society had honoured him twice, with the Darwinian medal in 1904 and the Royal medal in 1920. In 1910 he received an honorary DSc from Sheffield University, and St John's College made him an honorary fellow.

Bateson remained director of the John Innes Horticultural Institute until his death from heart failure at his home, Manor House, Watery Lane, Merton, Surrey, on 8 February 1926. He was cremated at Golders Green four days later. He was survived by his wife. ROBERT OLBY

Sources B. Bateson, William Bateson, F.R.S., naturalist (1928) · Scientific papers of William Bateson, ed. R. C. Punnett, 2 vols. (1928); repr. (1971) · D. Lipset, Gregory Bateson: the legacy of a scientist (1980) · W. Bateson, Mendel's principles of heredity (1909) · W. Bateson, Materials for the study of variation treated with especial regard to discontinuity in the origin of species (1894); repr. (1992) · B. Barnes and D. Mackenzie, 'Scientific judgement: the biometry–Mendelism controversy', Natural order: historical studies of scientific culture, ed. S. B. Barnes and D. Mackenzie (1979), 191–210 · R. Olby, 'The dimensions of scientific controversy: the biometric–Mendelian debate', British Journal for the History of Science, 22 (1989), 299–320 · W. Coleman, 'Bateson and chromosomes: conservative thought in science', Centaurus, 15 (1970), 228–314 · R. Olby, 'William Bateson's introduction of Mendelism to England: a reassessment', British Journal for the History of Science, 20 (1987), 399–420 · A. G. Cock, 'William Bateson's rejection and eventual acceptance of chromosome theory', Annals of Science, 40 (1983), 19–59 · R. Olby, 'Scientists and bureaucrats in the establishment of the John Innes Horticultural Institute under William Bateson', Annals of Science, 46 (1989), 497–510 · G. Webster, 'William Bateson and the science of form', in W. Bateson, Materials for the study of variation treated with especial regard to discontinuity in the origin of species (1992), xxix–lix · R. Olby, 'Das Experiment nach Mendel', Die Experimentalisierung des Lebens, ed. H.-J. Rheinberger and M. Hagner (1993), 135–49 · b. cert. · d. cert.

Archives American Philosophical Society, Philadelphia, MSS · CUL, corresp. and papers; record books of experimental work · John Innes Centre and Sainsbury Laboratory, Norwich, John Innes archives, corresp. and papers · U. Oxf., department of plant sciences, notebooks | BL, corresp. with Sir Sydney Cockerell, Add. MS 52704 · Bodl. Oxf., corresp. with Edmund Brisco Ford · CUL, corresp. with Charles C. Hurst · Oxf. U. Mus. NH, letters and postcards to Sir E. B. Poulton · Rice University, Houston, Texas, Woodson Research Center, letters to Sir Julian Huxley · St John Cam., letters to Sir Joseph Larmor · UCL, corresp. with Karl Pearson · UCL, corresp. with Sir Francis Galton

Likenesses photograph, 1907 (with R. C. Punnett), John Innes Centre and Sainsbury Laboratory, Norwich, John Innes archives; repro. in Lipset, Gregory Bateson · D. G. Lillie, watercolour caricature, 1909?, NPG · V. H. Mottram, photograph, 1909, NPG [see illus.] · Osterstock, photograph, 1910?, NPG · W. Strang, chalk drawing, 1910, U. Cam., Zoology Department · E. Wells, chalk drawing, 1914, John Innes Centre and Sainsbury Laboratory, Norwich · W. Rothenstein, chalk drawing, 1917, NPG · W. A. Forster, chalk drawing, 1923, NPG · W. A. Forster, pencil drawing, 1923, John Innes Centre and Sainsbury Laboratory, Norwich, John Innes archives; repro. in Bateson, William Bateson · photograph, 1923 (with Wilhelm Johannsen), John Innes Centre and Sainsbury Laboratory, Norwich, John Innes archives; repro. in Lipset, Gregory Bateson · C. A. Jørgensen, 1924 (with Wilhelm Johannsen), John Innes Centre and Sainsbury Laboratory, Norwich, John Innes archives; repro. in C. D. Darlington, The facts of life (1953) · photograph, John Innes Centre and Sainsbury Laboratory, Norwich, John Innes archives; repro. in Lipset, Gregory Bateson

Wealth at death £25,298 12s. 7d.: probate, 1 May 1926, CGPLA Eng. & Wales

Bateson, William Henry (1812–1881), college head, was born in Everton, Liverpool, on 3 June 1812, the fifth son of Richard Bateson, Liverpool merchant, and his wife, Lucy Wheeler Gordon. Educated at Shrewsbury School, under Dr Samuel Butler, Bateson failed to gain an expected Oxford scholarship and entered St John's, Cambridge, in 1831. Weakened by typhus, he eventually graduated in 1836, senior optime in mathematics and third in the first class of the classical tripos (BA, 1836; MA, 1839; BD, 1846; DD, 1857). He was elected to fellowship of St John's in 1837 and became second master at Leicester collegiate school. He read briefly for the bar, before taking holy orders; he was ordained deacon in December 1839, and priest c.1840. Between 1840 and 1843 he was attached to the Cambridgeshire parishes of Horningsea and Madingley, where he established elementary schools.

A tripos examiner at Cambridge and a successful private classics tutor (one of his pupils was Charles Kingsley) Bateson became St John's College preacher in 1843, then steward, and, in 1846, senior bursar. With astute business acumen and shrewd judgement, he eradicated long-standing debts, restoring financial security to St John's. Following a contest with Dr Rowland Williams of King's College, Bateson was elected public orator of the university in 1848, commended by Dr Whewell, master of Trinity College, for his Latin prose. Bateson was secretary to both the innovative 1849 revising syndicate established to modify university statutes, and the 1852 royal commission on Cambridge, chaired by John Graham, which recommended general university improvements, and became the crucial link between the two committees.

Credited for outstanding achievements as senior bursar, Bateson was elected master of St John's in 1857. In that year, on 11 June, he married Anna Aikin (1829–1918), daughter of James Aikin (1792–1878), Liverpool shipping merchant; they had six children. She shared his interest in education and was a strong advocate of women's rights. Whereas his liberal academic and political views had earlier prevented him from becoming either tutor or lecturer, as master he now created a new moral tone, skilfully controlling the vociferous senior colleagues with whom he shared authority. His name became synonymous with sweeping reforms: he advocated the admission to Cambridge of students unattached to a college, providing convincing evidence to the 1867 Oxford and Cambridge education select committee; sought life tenure for fellows; and led other Cambridge clergy in a successful campaign to abolish religious tests. As bursar and master his influence was paramount in liberalizing St John's College statutes in 1848 and 1857. A leading member of the council of senate, Bateson was vice-chancellor of Cambridge University in 1858. In 1872 he was one of several academics appointed to the second royal commission on Oxford and Cambridge universities, which investigated the extent of their property and income. In 1880 he succeeded Chief Justice Cockburn on the 1877 statutory commission and was influential in framing new college statutes for St John's, which were effected in 1882, a year after his death.

Behind a dignified coldness, Bateson was patient and kind-hearted with a logical, creative intellect. A first-rate chairman and astute debater, there were few important syndicates and trusts of which he was not a member. Indispensable on the Cambridge improvement board, he was a school governor at Shrewsbury and Rugby, and the inaugural chairman of the Perse Girls' School, Cambridge, where he was highly regarded as an enthusiastic promoter of higher education for women. Though renowned for his sermons and elegant prose, Bateson produced few publications. He was revered as an exceptional university administrator, and ultimately a wise elder statesman rather than as a researcher. Bateson was responsible for the construction in 1865–9 of the new chapel and lodge at St John's. He personally financed the chapel's wooden panelled ceilings and in the final weeks of his life donated £500 anonymously to college funds. Still working, William Bateson died at the master's lodge from a sudden spasmodic bronchial attack on 27 March 1881, and was buried on 31 March in Madingley churchyard, Cambridge. Bateson founded an academic dynasty

in Cambridge. His children included Margaret *Heitland (1860–1938), journalist and suffragist; William *Bateson (1861–1926), geneticist; and Mary *Bateson (1865–1906), medieval and municipal historian.   JANET SHEPHERD

Sources DNB · The Times (29 March 1881) · J. E. Sandys, The Eagle, 11 (1881), 458–78 · Cambridge University Reporter (1857–81) · 'Select committee on the Oxford and Cambridge Universities Education bill: special report', Parl. papers (1867), 13.31–46, no. 497 · St John Cam., Bateson MSS · Cambridge Review (30 March 1881) · D. Winstanley, Later Victorian Cambridge (1947) · H. F. Howard, An account of the finances of the College of St John the Evangelist in the University of Cambridge, 1511–1926 (1935) · E. Miller, Portrait of a college: a history of the College of Saint John the Evangelist, Cambridge (1961) · P. Searby, A history of the University of Cambridge, 3: 1750–1870, ed. C. N. L. Brooke and others (1997) · Boase, Mod. Eng. biog. · Venn, Alum. Cant.

Archives St John Cam., archives, MSS · St John Cam., MSS | Ransom HRC, letters to Sir John Frederick William Herschel

Likenesses J. Robertson, oils, 1864–5, St John Cam., master's lodge · E. H. Palmer, watercolour portrait, St John Cam.

Wealth at death under £30,000: probate, 23 May 1881, CGPLA Eng. & Wales

Batey, John Thomas (1862–1951), shipbuilder, was born in Newcastle upon Tyne on 28 July 1862, one of the eleven children of the tug boat operator Francis Batey (1842–1915) and Margaret, née Nicholls (1842–1912). Batey was educated at the Royal Grammar School, Newcastle, and in 1880 began an apprenticeship at Andrew Leslie's shipyard at Hebburn. In 1886 the shipyard amalgamated with the engine builders R. and W. Hawthorn to form R. and W. Hawthorn, Leslie & Co. Ltd. While still an apprentice, Batey took evening classes and obtained a bronze medal in naval architecture and a first class honours degree, a rare qualification on Tyneside at that time. Later he lectured part-time in naval architecture at Rutherford College in Newcastle. Batey married Adelaide Frederick Sewell (1861–1946). They had two daughters and two sons.

Batey became chief draughtsman at William Dobson's Low Walker shipyard in 1889 and remained there for twelve years. In 1901 he rejoined the Hebburn shipyard of Hawthorn Leslie as chief draughtsman, but soon became general manager under Herbert (later Sir Herbert) Rowell. In 1907 Batey became a director of the company. In this period Hawthorn Leslie had a series of Admiralty contracts to build torpedo boat destroyers, turning out more than thirty by 1914. Nevertheless, a number of merchant ships were also built, including several specialist iron-ore carriers. One of these, the Sir Ernest Cassel (10,800 deadweight tons) built in 1910, was the largest single-decked vessel engaged in ocean trade at that time. Rowell and Batey carried through a shipyard modernization programme shortly before the First World War, with capital investment including cranage and pneumatic tools.

During the First World War the yard built two light cruisers, twenty-one destroyers, and twelve merchant ships. In 1916 Rowell became company chairman and Batey took on increased responsibility for running the shipyard. On Rowell's death in 1921 Batey was appointed managing director. During the 1920s Hawthorn Leslie built several passenger liners, such as the Andania (14,000 gross tons) of 1922 for Cunard, a type of large merchant ship the management had long wanted to build. Close production control and bold sales policy led to the shipyard being more successful than many of its rivals in the depressed inter-war years. After a small loss in 1932–3, increasing naval orders improved the yard's performance. Batey retired from the company in 1935.

In 1934 Batey had become president of the North East Coast Institution of Engineers and Shipbuilders, a body he had first joined in 1885, soon after its foundation. Similarly, after many years of membership, Batey became president of the Institution of Naval Architects in 1938. He was awarded an honorary DSc by Durham University in 1935 and in the following year he was honoured with presidency of the international conference of naval architects held in New York. An early supporter of standardization in shipbuilding and engineering, Batey served as a member of the British Engineering Standards Association, which later became the British Standards Institution. Batey was active in various employers' organizations, being chairman of the Tyne Shipbuilders Association for four years and later serving on the central board of the Shipbuilding Employers' Federation.

Early acquaintance with inadequate responses to accidents at work led Batey to take a keen interest in the St John Ambulance Brigade, an activity he pursued right up until his death. In recognition of his work he was made a knight grace of the venerable order of St John of Jerusalem. Batey was president of the Hebburn Nursing Association and chairman of the chest hospital in the west end of Newcastle. Batey died of cancer on 23 July 1951 at Egypt End, Farnham Common, Farnham Royal, Buckinghamshire.   ALAN G. JAMIESON

Sources J. F. Clarke, *Power on land and sea: … a history of R. & W. Hawthorn Leslie & Co. Ltd* (1979) · D. Dougan, *The history of north east shipbuilding* (1968) · J. F. Clarke, *A century of service to engineering and shipbuilding: a centenary history of the North East Coast Institution of Engineers and Shipbuilders, 1884–1984* (1984) · J. F. Clarke, 'Batey, John Thomas', *DBB* · d. cert.

Archives Tyne and Wear Archives Service, Newcastle upon Tyne, R. and W. Hawthorn, Leslie & Co. Ltd archives

Wealth at death £88,441: Clarke, 'Batey, John Thomas'

Bath. For this title name *see* Bourchier, Margaret, countess of Bath (1510–1562) [*see under* Kitson family (*per. c.*1520–*c.*1660)]; Bourchier, Henry, fifth earl of Bath (*c.*1587–1654); Grenville, John, first earl of Bath (1628–1701); Pulteney, William, earl of Bath (1684–1764); Thynne, Thomas, third Viscount Weymouth and first marquess of Bath (1734–1796); Pulteney, (Henrietta) Laura, *suo jure* countess of Bath (1766–1808); Thynne, John Alexander, fourth marquess of Bath (1831–1896); Thynne, Henry Frederick, sixth marquess of Bath (1905–1992).

Bath, Adelard of (*b.* in or before **1080**?, *d.* in or after **1150**), scientist and translator, was a pioneer in introducing Arabic mathematics into England.

Evidence for his career Although absolute confidence cannot be placed in the autobiographical details included within the fictitious context of his literary works, Adelard's connection with Bath is assured by a self-reference in his *Quaestiones naturales* and the reference to

Bath in three of his other works—the astronomical tables, the *Liber prestigiorum*, and the *De opere astrolapsus*—in technical examples, which could mean that they were composed in Bath (though not adapted for the meridian of Bath) or that Adelard used the example of Bath simply because it was his place of origin. Independent evidence is provided by the cartulary of Bath Priory, in which the name Aðelardus appears four times, though these may not all refer to the same person. One document of 1106 describes Aðelardus as *filius Fastradi*: Fastrad was one of the principal tenants of Giso, bishop of Wells (*d.* 1088). If this Aðelardus is the scholar Adelard of Bath, his birth must be placed in 1080 or before. Giso's successor, John of Tours (*d.* 1122), moved the seat of his bishopric from Wells to Bath, where the Roman spa was being redeveloped and would have attracted doctors and scholars. John may have encouraged Adelard to go to Tours, the bishop's native city. Adelard's *De eodem et diverso* suggests that he went to Tours in the company of his 'nephew', and applied himself to 'Gallic studies': he met a famous, but unnamed, wise man, who elucidated the science of astronomy for him, and he learnt music there, playing the harp in front of a queen. Adelard's style and interests are remarkably close to those of another alumnus of Tours, Hildebert de Lavardin, who returned to Tours as bishop in 1125. In his *Quaestiones naturales* Adelard takes his 'nephew' and other students to Laon where his 'nephew' promises to pursue 'Gallic studies'. Laon was the natural place to go to, since the sons and nephews of several of Henry I's key administrators were students there, including the two nephews of Roger, bishop of Salisbury (*d.* 1139), Henry's viceroy. Having dismissed his students outside Laon, Adelard departed for a seven-year period of travel devoted to the 'studies of the Arabs'. Where Adelard spent these seven years, which resulted in the *Quaestiones naturales*, is not stated, but there is dependable evidence for an Italian phase of Adelard's career, perhaps also inspired by John of Tours, in the dedication of the *De eodem et diverso* to William, bishop of Syracuse in Sicily, whose bishopric falls between 1105 and 1124. The questions to which Adelard provides answers in the *Quaestiones naturales* are associated with Salerno, from where, according to the *De eodem et diverso*, Adelard was travelling when he met a Greek philosopher in Magna Graecia (Puglia, southern Italy), who was an expert in medicine and the nature of things. Adelard should probably be believed when he says that he also visited the Norman kingdom of Antioch, and Mamistra (Misis) in Cilicia, where the earthquake that he experienced could have been the severe one that affected the area in 1114.

The dedication of the *Quaestiones naturales* mentions Adelard's recent return to England after a long absence during the reign of Henry I—that is, before 1135—after which it is likely, but not certain, that he resided in Bath. At first he may have supported King Stephen, who held the city of Bath. By 1150, however, he seems to have followed the tide and at least sought the patronage of the young Henry Plantagenet, son of the Empress Matilda, and the future Henry II. Adelard's *De opere astrolapsus* is dedicated to a Henry *regis nepos*, who, Adelard continues, had reached 'the age of discretion'. This is most likely to have been the young Henry, who was the grandson (*nepos*) of Henry I and was formally declared by his father to have come of age early in 1150. At the same time he was invested with the duchy of Normandy and his succession to the English throne looked probable. Hence the appropriateness of addressing him as 'grandson of the king'. Adelard may have changed his allegiance earlier, for the earliest apparent knowledge of his *Quaestiones naturales* is in the *Dragmaticon* (1144–9) of William de Conches, who was tutor to Henry and the other sons of Geoffrey Plantagenet after Geoffrey had become duke of Normandy in April 1144. If this is so, the Richard, bishop of Bayeux, to whom the *Quaestiones naturales* is dedicated in most manuscripts is Richard of Kent, bishop from 1135 to 1142, the son of Matilda's principal supporter Robert, earl of Gloucester, rather than Richard fitz Samson, bishop from 1107 to 1133. One family of manuscripts dedicates the work to *presul G*, who may be William (Guillelmus in Latin), bishop of Syracuse. Adelard's astronomical tables probably also date from around this time, since they give the date 26 January 1126 in an example, and appear already in a manuscript copy written before 1140 (Bodl. Oxf., MS Auct. F.1.9). Some modern scholars have ascribed to Adelard a set of horoscopes drawn up evidently by a partisan of King Stephen on several dates between 1150 and 1151. These horoscopes show the use of the tables of al-Khwarizmi, which Adelard had translated; it is equally possible, however, that they were drawn up by Robert of Chester (*fl.* 1144–1150), who revised Adelard's translation and was in London (Stephen's centre of operations) in 1147 and 1150.

Philosophical works Adelard's writings fall into two internally coherent groups: his original more literary works, intended for a wide audience; and the translation of a curriculum of mathematical works written presumably for fellow scientists.

The *De eodem et diverso* is a work in the tradition of the protrepticon—or exhortation to the study of philosophy—of which Boethius's *De consolatione philosophiae* was Adelard's principal model. It takes the form of a dramatic dialogue between Philocosmia, who advocates worldly pleasures, and Philosophia, whose defence of scholarship leads into a summary of the contents of each of the seven liberal arts. While Adelard adopts a highly literate and entertaining style, his serious aim is to show how the epistemology of Plato and Aristotle can be reconciled in a theory of universals which is very similar to what was later called the indifference theory: that is, that the terms (*voces*) 'individual', 'species', and 'genus' can be applied to the one thing (*res*) and differ only according to the different levels at which that thing is considered. Adelard's intention is to rescue such *voces*, as reaching 'the causes and beginnings [*initia*] of the causes of things', in the face of an Epicurean attitude in which only the sensible things (*res*) are regarded as of any relevance.

The *Quaestiones naturales* refers to a future discussion of 'beginning or beginnings [*initia*]', and complements the *De eodem et diverso* by concentrating on things themselves and their rational causes, rather than on *voces* and the epistemological order of knowing things. In fact, the approach taken in the *De eodem et diverso* is characteristic of what Adelard calls 'Gallic studies', which he contrasts to the method of 'the studies of the Arabs' followed in the *Quaestiones naturales*. The extent to which it is Arabic has been much debated. The dialogue is built on a framework of apparently pre-existing 'natural questions', which have Arabic parallels, and which probably formed the basis of debate in the school of Salerno, with which Adelard was familiar. The subject matter is summed up in a motto which Adelard inserted between the list of questions and the beginning of the text: *Sic faciunt causae rerum* ('This is how the causes of things work'), and, if the heart of the *De eodem et diverso* can be considered to be logic, that of the *Quaestiones naturales* is natural science. While some of the questions may appear frivolous (such as 'Why is the nose above the mouth?', 'Why are the fingers unequal in length?'), the answers apply consistent physical principles—such as that similars derive from similars—in a way that presages the arrival of Aristotle's *libri naturales* in the West.

The *Quaestiones naturales* itself is complemented by Adelard's *De opere astrolapsus*, which deals with cosmology: the first half of the work describes the cosmos itself, whereas the second half describes the visible model of the cosmos—the astrolabe—and gives instructions in how to use the instrument, some of which refer back to the section on geometry in the *De eodem et diverso*. In this, it is similar to another instructional work—on the abacus—which Adelard probably wrote early in his life. Finally, a little work on hawking—*De avibus*—is introduced as a diversion from the serious matter of the *Quaestiones naturales*, and gives advice, in dialogue form, on how to rear hawks and cure the diseases to which they are prone.

All these works except the *De opere astrolapsus* include a 'nephew' as participant in a dialogue with Adelard (*Quaestiones naturales* and *De avibus*), or as the silent auditor (in the *De eodem et diverso*). They are written in the highest quality humanistic Latin, are full of wit and verbal artifice, with many-layered allusions to classical literature, and (in the *De eodem et diverso*) the inclusion of verse. Thus they were as much models of style and learned discourse as instructional manuals, comparable to and perhaps influenced by the work of Hildebert de Lavardin. Their aim was evidently to provide a good humanistic education to the young noblemen that Adelard had in his charge.

Translations from Arabic This broadly didactic purpose contrasts with the second group of works which Adelard probably wrote for himself and his fellow scientists. Here, he seems to have been following a programme set out by 'Arabic masters': this could well have been in the west midlands where the astronomer Petrus Alfonsi was instructing Walcher, prior of Great Malvern, in Arabic astronomy. This programme began with the study of Euclid's *Elements*, of which there is one translation (known as Adelard I) clearly in Adelard's style, and continued through the study of spherical geometry (Adelard may have worked on Theodosius's *Spherics*) to that of astronomy. Adelard expresses his debt to his Arabic masters for information on the cosmos in his *De opere astrolapsus*, but his own contribution to the field is a translation of the canons (rules) and tables of al-Khwarizmi. With these tables, from which one could work out the positions of the planets, the sun, and the moon, at any time, an astronomer could then apply himself to the practical aspect of his art—astrology. Adelard translated a convenient handbook on the subject (Abu Maʿshar's *Abbreviation of the Introduction to Astrology*), a set of astrological aphorisms (Pseudo-Ptolemy's *Centiloquium*), and a text on how to make astrological talismans (Thabit ibn Qurra, *Liber prestigiorum*). None of these translations has a preface or a dedication. They were apparently translated with the help of Arabic speakers and for the purpose of making advances in the knowledge of mathematics (including astrology).

Reputation as teacher and scholar The evidence for his teaching in these subjects is provided in notes referring to Adelard's opinions in glosses both to Boethius's *De musica* and to another version of Euclid's *Elements*, known as Adelard II. The latter might well have been written by a pupil of Adelard (Robert of Chester has been suggested), as was the introduction to *Helcep Saracenicum* ('Saracen calculation')—written calculations with numerals having place value—composed for 'his master Adelard' by a certain Ocreatus. Adelard's reputation in geometry in particular is attested by his name appearing in a list of three 'modern' geometers in an introduction to arithmetic in Cambridge, Trinity College, MS R.15.16. While the precise place (or places) of his teaching activity is uncertain, he was evidently the key figure at the beginning of a scientific movement that developed in England throughout the twelfth century and culminated in the work of Robert Grosseteste (d. 1253) in the early thirteenth century.

Adelard's reputation as a mathematician was assured by the translation of Euclid. His name was attached to several versions of Euclid's *Elements*, works of chiromancy and geomancy and other texts on divination and magic. Although he was probably not the author of the texts on the algorism (pen-reckoning; the *Dixit algorismi*), the whole quadrivium (*Liber ysagogarum Alchorismi*), and glosses to Boethius's *De arithmetica* which have been attributed to him, it is very likely that mathematical texts were written by his pupils and associates, or under his influence.

Adelard's models are the Latin classics and, beyond them, Greek science and philosophy. He wished to rely on reason rather than on revelation; his God was the God of Aristotle rather than of St Paul. His works too were evidently appreciated as classics. His *Quaestiones naturales* were frequently copied alongside the classical text on natural questions by Seneca, and the *De eodem et diverso*, in the one manuscript that contains it, accompanies an entertaining retelling of the case histories in Pseudo-Quintilian's *Declamationes XIX*, for which Adelard may have been responsible. As a scholar he occupies a place on the European stage, and his work must rank alongside

that of scholars in Paris, Chartres, and Orléans (with whom he must have had contacts) who showed a renewed interest in the Latin and Greek classics, and a new confidence in human reason. But in addition to the sources recovered by other scholars Adelard turned to Arabic texts; and in this respect he was unique for his time.

CHARLES BURNETT

Sources C. Burnett, ed., *Adelard of Bath: an English scientist and Arabist of the early twelfth century* (1987) · *Adelard of Bath: conversations with his nephew*, ed. and trans. C. Burnett and others (1998) · C. H. Haskins, *Studies in the history of mediaeval science*, 2nd edn (1927), 20–42 · L. Cochrane, *Adelard of Bath: the first English scientist* (1994) · B. G. Dickey, 'Adelard of Bath: an examination based on heretofore unexamined manuscripts', PhD diss., University of Toronto, 1982 · C. Burnett, '*Algorismi vel helcep decentior est diligentia*: the arithmetic of Adelard of Bath and his circle', *Mathematische Probleme im Mittelalter: der lateinische und arabische Sprachbereich*, ed. M. Folkerts (1996), 221–331 · C. Burnett, 'Adelard of Bath's doctrine on universals and the *Consolatio philosophiae* of Boethius', *Didascalia*, 1 (1995), 1–14 · W. Hunt, ed., *Two chartularies of the priory of St Peter at Bath*, Somerset RS, 7 (1893), pt 1, nos. 34, 41, 53, 54 · *Pipe rolls*, 31 Henry I · Reg. RAN, 3.282 (no. 764) · horoscopes, BL, Royal MS App. 85, fols. 1–2 · Robert of Chester's (?) redaction of Euclid's '*Elements*', the so-called Adelard II version, ed. H. L. L. Busard and M. Folkerts, 1 (1992), 1–31 [the versions of Euclid's *Elements* attributed to Adelard]

Archives BL, Royal MS App. 85, fols. 1–2 · Bodl. Oxf., MS Auct F. 1.9

Bath, Henry of (d. 1260), justice and administrator, began his career as an administrator under his kinsman Hugh of Bath, whose chattels came to Henry when he died in 1236. Hugh was a cleric who was keeper of the honour of Berkhamsted until about 1222, and was successively undersheriff of Bedfordshire and Buckinghamshire, and then Berkshire, and finally a justice of the Jews. Henry's relationship to Hugh is not known, but he was almost certainly not his son. Henry first appears in 1221, apparently working as a bailiff of the honour of Berkhamsted under Hugh, whom he succeeded as under-sheriff of Berkshire from 1228 to 1229; his career was afterwards independent of Hugh's. He then served as under-sheriff of Hampshire from 1229 to 1232, and as sheriff of Gloucestershire from 1232 to 1234, when the county was the chief base for the marcher war of 1233–4. He held that office as an agent of the regime of Peter de Rivaux, and as such he needed a pardon when the regime fell in 1234. Nevertheless he immediately became sheriff of Northamptonshire, remaining in that office until 1240, except for two months as sheriff of Surrey and Sussex in 1236. In 1238 he became a junior justice of the bench, continuing to administer Northamptonshire through deputies, and in 1240–41 he was the second most senior justice on the eyre circuit of William of York, holding the Hampshire eyre of January 1241 himself as senior justice.

In the summer of 1241 Bath went on a mission to Ireland, before becoming a justice *coram rege* for two terms in 1241 and 1242, after which he became sheriff of Yorkshire on the king's departure for Gascony. He held that office until 1248, but acted through deputies after January 1245, when he became chief justice of the bench in succession to Robert of Lexinton. He had been an occasional commissioner of assize from 1235 onwards, and after 1243 he was one of the leading assize commissioners, at first dealing with business mainly in Yorkshire and the north, and then in many counties, but especially those in which he held estates. He remained as chief justice of the bench until 1249, but was chief justice of an eyre circuit from 1247 to 1249, when the bench did not sit. He was promoted to become chief justice of the court *coram rege* in October 1249, for which he was granted a salary of £100 a year in 1250. He was absent for much of the time as head of an eyre circuit between April 1250 and February 1251, when an accusation of perversion of justice against him led to the loss of his judicial office and of his keepership of Gloucester Castle, as well as a fine of 2000 marks, part of which was still unpaid on his death. The accusation took the form of an appeal of trespass, felony, and false judgment, made by Sir Philip d'Arcy, whom Bath had offended by winning a case during the previous year's Lincolnshire eyre at which he had been the chief justice. It was made at a council meeting at Woodstock, and Bath was allowed to defend himself at a full council or parliament at Windsor shortly afterwards. The accusation led to more general charges of corruption and perversion of justice, including an accusation that he had been bribed to allow a convicted and imprisoned felon to escape justice. The king seems to have turned against him, probably as a result of Bath's vigorous efforts to muster support, so the matter was only settled by the fine.

Bath was temporarily out of favour for two years, until he was recalled in the summer of 1253, just before the king's departure for Gascony, as chief justice *coram rege*, and thereby to an even higher place in the king's counsels. He served in this office until his death. His concurrent service as chief justice of the bench from July 1256 to April 1258 may have been a move by the king to satisfy the demand for the appointment of a justiciar; much of the routine business must have been carried out by his puisne justices. During that period he was one of the most important members of the king's council dealing with English affairs, and he continued to be active in the period of baronial control between 1258 and his death; for example, he was on a committee for the appointment of sheriffs.

Bath had estates mainly in Gloucestershire in the Forest of Dean, at Lydney, Newent, and Westbury-on-Severn; in Berkshire at Upper Lambourn, where he seems mostly to have lived until about 1251, and where he had a private chapel from 1240; and in the Holland area of Lincolnshire around Whaplode, Pinchbeck, and Boston, where he seems to have lived during the period of his disgrace. He probably originated from one of those counties. He had other interests in Devon, Norfolk, Suffolk, Sussex, Yorkshire, and near London. Bath died in November 1260; his widow, Alina, whom he had married between about 1230 and 1235, and who was said by Matthew Paris to be descended from the Sandfords and Bassets, married Nicholas of Yattendon, a Berkshire knight in the service of the Lord Edward; when she died in 1274 her main executor was Queen Eleanor. Bath's property descended to his son John, who had married Philippa, daughter and heir of Geoffrey

of Benniworth, a leading Lincolnshire knight. John of Bath was a rebel against the king who was captured at Northampton in 1264. DAVID CROOK

Sources C. A. F. Meekings, *King's bench justices, 1239–58* [forthcoming] · C. A. F. Meekings, ed., *Crown pleas of the Wiltshire eyre, 1249*, Wiltshire Archaeological and Natural History Society, Records Branch, 16 (1961) · Paris, *Chron.*, vols. 4, 5 · D. Crook, *Records of the general eyre*, Public Record Office Handbooks, 20 (1982) · H. R. Luard, ed., *Flores historiarum*, 3 vols., Rolls Series, 95 (1890), vol. 2 · *Ann. mon.*, vol. 4 · *CIPM*, 2, nos. 45, 811 · *Chancery records* · court of common pleas, feet of fines, PRO, CP 25/1 · PRO, Plea rolls, KB 26; JUST 1 · Pipe rolls, E 372 · PRO, Queen's Remembrancer's and Lord Treasurer's Remembrancer's Memoranda rolls, E 159, E 368 · PRO, C 60/58, m 19 · PRO, C 66/74, m 2d

Bath [Bathe], **Sir John** (1569/70–1630), politician, was the youngest of the four children of John Bath (*d.* 1586), chancellor of the Irish exchequer, and his first wife, Eleanor (*d. c.*1575), daughter of Jenico Preston, third Viscount Gormanston, and his first wife, Katherine, daughter of Gerald Fitzgerald, ninth earl of Kildare. He was admitted to the Middle Temple in 1595 and about the same time married Janet (*d.* in or after 1605), daughter of Thomas Dillon, chief justice of Connaught. In 1599, when his eldest surviving brother, William *Bathe, entered the Jesuit order, he received a conveyance of Drumcondra Castle and the family estates in north co. Dublin subject to the life interest of his stepmother, Janet Finglas, whose second marriage, to William Warren, exercised a profound influence on Bath's life. It was at Drumcondra Castle that the notorious third marriage of Hugh O'Neill, earl of Tyrone, to Mabel Bagenal took place in 1591 and Warren played an ambiguous role as intermediary during the Nine Years' War.

In December 1605 Bath signed a petition against the government's use of 'mandates' to compel attendance at divine service. By 1610 he was in Madrid and in receipt of a pension from the Spanish crown. O'Neill, writing from exile in Rome on 29 July 1610 to request Philip III's permission to negotiate a reconciliation with James I, nominated Bath to represent him in London. The request was not granted and Bath remained in the Spanish service in Madrid where his brother William died in 1614. He visited Ireland in 1617, apparently in connection with his stepmother's death, and was granted both confirmation of his estate at Balgriffin in co. Dublin and a lease of assorted properties in Leinster (10 March, 24 April). The suspicions of the exile community in Spain were aroused by reports of his ease of access to government officials and others in Ireland, and when he returned to Madrid the Spanish council of state decided on 19 May 1618 that he should no longer be trusted or admitted to court. On 16 June following Bath killed Donal O'Sullivan Beare in a confused affray. He appears to have been imprisoned for some years and his banishment was mooted, but the circumstances in which he left Spain are unrecorded. His reception in England lends credence to Spanish suspicions, for he was knighted by James I on 19 August 1623 and admitted as a gentleman of the privy chamber before April 1624, when he was awarded a gift of £300 under the privy seal.

Bath retained his privy chamber place when Charles I succeeded and became involved in representations on behalf of his fellow Old English landholders in the pale counties in Ireland. War with Spain gave them an opportunity to demonstrate their loyalty and Bath persuaded them to offer to assist in the defence of Ireland by raising trained bands at their own expense. He presented the case for trusting the Old English cogently and successfully to the English privy council, tracing their alienation and proposing the removal of their disabilities through the substitution of an oath of allegiance for the oath of supremacy. Later he was dispatched to Ireland where he secured a goodwill subvention for the standing army in November 1625 and was rewarded with a grant of £2100. When the Irish administration vetoed the trained bands scheme, Bath and the earl of Westmeath negotiated an alternative plan which was adopted in September 1626. Charles offered concessions, including the replacement of the oath of supremacy, in return for financial support for the enlargement of the professional army. The change of emphasis from a policy founded upon trust to one redolent of distrust was resented in Ireland and Bath played no further part in the negotiations that led in May 1628 to the 'graces' relating to the renunciation of crown title to certain lands.

In April 1627 Bath offered to take Irish soldiers into the service of Venice and in April 1630, in return for relinquishing £1300 remaining from his 1625 grant, he received ecclesiastical property in Ireland worth some £300 a year. This was contested by Archbishop Ussher and Bath agreed to accept a sum of £3500 instead. In December 1630 the property was surrendered by his heirs, James, the eldest of the five children of his first marriage, and Luke, the eldest of the three sons of his second marriage, to Barbara (d. 1642), the daughter of a Dublin alderman, Patrick Gough. Bath died before 17 October 1630, when arrangements were made to settle his debts. He was buried in St Margaret's Church, Clonturk, co. Dublin.

AIDAN CLARKE

Sources M. K. Walsh, *Destruction by peace* (1986) · A. Clarke, *The Old English in Ireland, 1625–42* (Dublin, 1966); repr. (2000) · F. E. Ball, *A history of the county Dublin*, 6 vols. (1902–20) · *CSP Ire.*, 1603–6; 1625–32; 1647–60 · *CSP dom.*, 1623–6 · *CSP Venice*, 1629–32 · *Calendar of the Irish patent rolls of James I* (before 1830) · J. Morrin, ed., *Calendar of the patent and close rolls of chancery in Ireland*, 3 vols. (1861–3) · M. C. Griffith, ed., *Calendar of inquisitions formerly in the office of the chief remembrancer of the exchequer*, IMC (1991) · 'Some funeral entries of Ireland', *Journal of the Association for the Preservation of the Memorials of the Dead, Ireland*, 7 (1907–9), 39 · B. Jennings, ed., *Wild geese in Spanish Flanders, 1582–1700*, IMC (1964) · F. X. Nugent, *Friar Nugent* (Rome and London, 1962) · S. P. O Mathuna, *William Bathe S.J., 1564–1614* (Amsterdam, 1986) · W. A. Shaw, *The knights of England*, 2 (1906), 182 · GEC, *Peerage*, 6. 22 · H. A. C. Sturgess, ed., *Register of admissions to the Honourable Society of the Middle Temple, from the fifteenth century to the year 1944*, 1 (1949), 69
Archives PRO, SP Ire., memorial, 63/268. 62 · PRO, SP Ire., notes presented to the privy council, 63/176. 112

Bathe, John (1612–1649), Jesuit, was born on 23 June 1612 at Drogheda, co. Louth, the son of Christopher Bathe, merchant and alderman of Drogheda, and his wife, Catherine Warren, a member of a prominent Navan family. He received his early education from a diocesan priest, Father William Meagher, and later at the Jesuit college or school in Drogheda, where he studied humanities and philosophy. In 1630 he entered the Irish College of Seville, and over the next seven years studied theology and philosophy at the Jesuit college of San Hermenegildo. Despite being under the canonical age he was ordained in September 1635, most probably for the archdiocese of Armagh, as he returned to Drogheda two years later as a secular priest. Towards the end of 1638 he applied to the superior of the Irish Jesuit mission, Father Robert Nugent, to be admitted to the Society of Jesus. His request was successful and he subsequently entered the Jesuit noviciate at Malines in the Spanish Netherlands on 17 May 1639. On the completion of his noviceship two years later he was recalled to Drogheda in May 1641.

Bathe remained in Drogheda throughout the period of the confederate wars. In a 1642 report on the state of the Irish mission to the Jesuit general, Muzio Vitelleschi, Robert Nugent initially claimed that Bathe, his uncle and fellow Jesuit Robert Bathe, and the priest John Moore had been imprisoned by the puritans. However, he later corrected this story stating that Moore had in fact fled Drogheda and that both Bathes were being sheltered by Catholic families in the town. By 1646 John Bathe was the only remaining Jesuit in Drogheda, his uncle having moved to Kilkenny.

On the fall of Drogheda to the Cromwellian forces on 11 September 1649 Bathe and his brother Thomas, a secular priest, went into hiding in the town. A manuscript history written by one of the Jesuits on the Irish mission, preserved in the archives of the Irish College in Rome, recorded the proceeding events as follows:

> On the following day [12 September], when the soldiers were searching through the ruins of the city, they discovered one of our Fathers, named John Bathe, with his brother, a secular priest. Suspecting that they were religious, they examined them, and finding that they were priests, and one of them, moreover, a Jesuit, they led them off in triumph, and, accompanied by a tumultuous crowd, conducted them to the market-place, and there … they tied them both to stakes fixed in the ground, and pierced their bodies with shots till they expired. (Murphy, *Cromwell in Ireland*, 107–8)

Both the actual date and the nature of the Bathes' deaths have been disputed, though the most recent research supports the details of the preceding account. The two Bathe brothers were among five men, all Catholic priests, who were executed in Drogheda on grounds of their faith in the days following the town's fall. The names of John Bathe, Thomas Bathe, Peter Taaffe, Dominic Dillon, and Richard Overton are included in the list of those whose cause for beatification has been submitted to the Holy See.

THOMAS J. MORRISSEY

Sources F. Finnegan, 'Biographical dictionary of Irish Jesuits, 1598–1773', Irish Jesuit Archives, Dublin · G. Rice, 'The five martyrs of Drogheda', *Ríocht na Midhe: Records of Meath Archaeological and Historical Society*, 9/3 (1997), 102–27 · 'Memorials of the Irish province, S. J.', Irish Jesuit Archives, Dublin, vol. 1, pp. 320–22 · D. Murphy, *Cromwell in Ireland: a history of Cromwell's Irish campaign* (1883), 107–8 · D. Murphy, *Our martyrs* (1896), 312 · G. Oliver, *Collections towards illustrating the biography of the Scotch, English and Irish members, SJ* (1838)

Archives Archives of the Irish Province of the Society of Jesus, Dublin

Bathe, William (1564–1614), Jesuit and linguistic scholar, was born on Easter Sunday, 2 April 1564, the eldest son of John Bathe (or Bath, *d.* 1586), of Drumcondra on the outskirts of Dublin, and his wife, Eleanor (*d. c.*1575), daughter of Jenico Preston, third Viscount Gormanston, and his first wife, Katherine, daughter of Gerald Fitzgerald, ninth earl of Kildare. John Bathe became chancellor of the exchequer in Ireland in 1577. The Bathes were a Norman family who had been settled for more than three centuries in co. Dublin and were connected by marriage with the Norman houses of Netterville of Slane, Howth, and Roscommon, and on the Gaelic side with O'Connor of Offaly, O'Carroll of Ely, and O'Donnell of Tirconnail. William Bathe studied humanities in Ireland, presumably with a private tutor, and then entered St John's College, Oxford, to study philosophy. He did not take his degree as this would have entailed taking the oath of supremacy. While at Oxford, when he was still only twenty, he published *A Brief Introduction to the True Art of Music* (1584). An adaptation of this work entitled *A Briefe Introduction to the Skill of Song* appeared a few years later. These manuals are said to have been the earliest of their kind to be published in English. To these publications, as well as to his family's friendship with Sir John Perrot, lord deputy in Ireland, he owed his reception at the court of Elizabeth I. The queen's esteem for the young man took a tangible form. In 1587–9 she made three grants of lands to the owner of the manor of Drumcondra. One confirmed to him the succession to all his father's properties held on lease from the crown; the others were new grants bearing lucrative rentals.

Early in the 1590s Bathe renounced his inheritance in favour of his younger brother Sir John *Bath and went to Louvain to study theology. Some three years later, on 15 August 1596, he entered the Jesuit noviciate at Tournai. On completing his noviciate he spent a year studying moral theology at St Omer, and in 1599 was sent to Padua to complete his studies. There he was ordained, probably in the summer of 1602. He was then named as secretary to Luigi Mansoni, papal envoy to Ireland, and journeyed to Spain, but the Irish defeat at Kinsale and a change in Spanish foreign policy rendered Mansoni's embassy superfluous. From early spring 1603 until his death Bathe remained in Spain. He was appointed spiritual director at the Irish College, Salamanca, became noted as a man of prayer and mortification, and was in much demand as a preacher and spiritual guide. While at the college, and in collaboration with Stephen White, a noted linguist, and others, he published in 1611 his *Janua linguarum, seu, Modus maxime accomodatus quo patefit ad omnes linguas intelligendas*. In this the efficient methodology he had applied to teaching music was applied to teaching languages. Twenty years before Comenius's celebrated graded series of Latin primers Bathe had used a similar bilingual approach. The *Janua linguarum* went into many editions in various European languages including English. The English version, in turn, went into many editions, but without any reference to the book's Catholic and Irish authorship.

Holywood, superior of the Jesuit mission in Ireland, sought Bathe's return to Ireland. Bathe also sought permission to return, but always it was claimed that his services were needed in Spain. After 1610 the father general of the Jesuits sought his presence in Rome as his adviser on the Irish mission in the post of procurator, but each time Bathe's Spanish superiors stressed his importance to their work in Spain. The general was still negotiating when Bathe died in 1614. Different dates are given for Bathe's death. Ó Mathúna gives the date as 24 March 1614, which would suggest Salamanca as the likely place of death, but the account in the Irish Jesuit Archives states that he died at Madrid on 17 June 1614, while conducting a retreat at the Spanish court. He was buried in Spain.

In addition to Bathe's *Brief Introduction to the True Art of Music* and *Janua linguarum* he wrote a treatise on the sacrament of penance, *Appareois para administrar el sacramento de la penitencia*, which was published in Milan by Joseph Creswell under the name of Peter Manrique in 1614. He also wrote *A Methodical Institution Concerning the Chief Mysteries of Christian Religion* in English and Latin.

THOMAS J. MORRISSEY

Sources Irish Jesuit Archives, Dublin · S. P. Ó Mathúna, *William Bathe, S.J., 1564–1614: a pioneer in linguistics* (1986) · E. Hogan, 'Father William Bathe', *Distinguished Irishmen of the sixteenth century* (1894) · G. Oliver, *Collections towards illustrating the biography of the Scotch, English and Irish members, SJ* (1838), 215 · 'Irish ecclesiastical colleges since the Reformation', *Irish Ecclesiastical Record*, [new ser.], 10 (1873–4), 519–32, esp. 523–7

Archives Archives of the Irish Province of the Society of Jesus, Dublin

Bather, Edward (1779–1847), Church of England clergyman, was the eldest son of the Revd John Bather, vicar of Meole Brace, Shrewsbury, and Martha Hannah, daughter of the Revd James Hallifax, rector of Whitchurch, Shropshire. He was educated at the Royal Free Grammar School, Shrewsbury, at Rugby School, and at Oriel College, Oxford (BA 1803, MA 1808). In 1804 he was presented to the vicarage of Meole Brace by his mother, an executrix of his father, and in 1828 he was collated to the archdeaconry of Shropshire and the prebend of Ufton in the church of Lichfield. He married, first, in 1805, Emma (*d.* 1825), daughter of the Revd Robert Hallifax of Standish, Gloucestershire, and, secondly, in 1828, Mary, eldest daughter of Samuel *Butler, headmaster of Shrewsbury School, and afterwards bishop of Lichfield. He had no issue by either of these marriages.

Bather had a high reputation as a preacher, and published *Sermons, Chiefly Practical* (3 vols., 1827–40) and many miscellaneous discourses, including a funeral sermon on the death of Bishop Butler, his father-in-law, and fourteen charges delivered to the clergy of the archdeaconry of Shrewsbury. A posthumous work by him, *Hints on the Art of Catechizing*, was published by his widow in 1848 (3rd edn, 1852). A collection of *Sermons on Old Testament Histories*, selected from his parochial discourses, appeared in 1850, and a selection from his charges, *On some Ministerial Duties: Catechizing, Preaching …*, was edited, with a preface, by Charles John Vaughan (1876). Bather may be regarded as an evangelical. In later life he was blind, and kept aloof from party strife, tending his parish. He died at Meole Brace on 3 October 1847.

THOMPSON COOPER, *rev.* H. C. G. MATTHEW

Sources Foster, *Alum. Oxon.* · *GM*, 2nd ser., 28 (1847), 542 · J. S. Reynolds, *The evangelicals at Oxford, 1735–1871: a record of an unchronicled movement* (1953)
Archives BL, corresp. with Samuel Butler, Add. MSS 34586, 34589–34592
Likenesses S. Cousins, mezzotint, pubd 1838 (after W. Etty), BM, NPG

Bather, Elizabeth Constance (1904–1988), police officer, was born on 11 October 1904 in Winchester, Hampshire, the daughter of the Revd Arthur George Bather, a housemaster at Winchester College, Hampshire, and his wife, Lilian Dundas Firth. She was educated at St Swithun's School, Winchester. From 1937 to 1946 she was a JP in Winchester, where she gained experience of young offenders, and she was also a member of Hampshire county council. She joined the Women's Auxiliary Air Force at the beginning of the Second World War, and became a senior officer at Bomber Command before being posted to Canada to help set up the Canadian Women's Auxiliary Air Force. She reached the rank of group officer in 1944, and was appointed OBE in 1946 for her services to the force.

Despite her lack of police experience and her height (she was only 5 feet 4 inches tall), Elizabeth Bather was appointed in 1945 the first woman chief inspector in the Metropolitan Police Force of London, and after a year she succeeded Dorothy Peto as chief superintendent of the Metropolitan women police. She was promoted chief superintendent in 1949. The women police had grown out of the women patrols during the First World War, and had been started as an experimental force of 100 in 1919 with Sophia Stanley as the first superintendent, but in 1922 the government had decided to disband the whole force, and it was only as a result of Mrs Stanley's efforts, backed by the MPs Lady Astor and Margaret Wintringham, that a nucleus of twenty-five was retained, from which a new force could be built, and Dorothy Peto, appointed in 1930, could broaden the work of the force. Elizabeth Bather stressed the need for policewomen to be feminine, and was determined to recruit 'women of charm; women who can bring the gentle touch to a rough world'. She had the uniform redesigned, and allowed policewomen to wear make-up on duty and in summer to go on duty without their tunics. She also encouraged women police to concentrate on juvenile crime and welfare matters, which continued to be the main focus of policewomen until the early 1970s. She gave evidence to the Wolfenden committee on homosexual offences and prostitution, which reported in 1957.

After her retirement in 1960 Elizabeth Bather served on the Hartley Wintney and Hart district councils in Hampshire from 1967 to 1976. A keen sportswoman, she rode, hunted, fished, and shot. Bather died on 8 January 1988 at Heathersides, Nately Scures, Hook, Hampshire. She was unmarried.

ANNE PIMLOTT BAKER

Sources *The Times* (11 Jan 1988) · L. Wyles, *A woman at Scotland Yard* (1952) · *WW* · E. Tancred, *Women police, 1914–1950* (1951) · *CGPLA Eng. & Wales* (1988)
Likenesses photograph, repro. in *The Times*
Wealth at death £316,110: probate, 2 March 1988, *CGPLA Eng. & Wales*

Bather [*née* Blomfield], **Lucy Elizabeth** [*pseud.* Aunt Lucy] (1829×36–1864), children's writer, was the fourth daughter, from his second marriage, of Charles James *Blomfield (1786–1857), bishop of London, and his wife, Dorothy, *née* Cox (1795–1870), widow of Thomas Kent. Lucy Bather was born at the bishop's palace in Fulham, Middlesex, in 1829 or 1830 (according to her death certificate, which recorded her age as thirty-four) or on 31 March 1836 (according to the account of her death in the *Gentleman's Magazine*). She grew up on the episcopal estate in Fulham where her education, like that of her brothers and sisters, was supervised by her father. By the age of six she already knew something of the classical languages (Blomfield, *Memoir*, 2.225, 373). On 29 August 1861 Lucy Blomfield married Arthur Henry Bather, of Meole Brace, near Shrewsbury, Shropshire, fourth son of John Bather, recorder of Shrewsbury.

Both before and after her marriage Lucy Bather wrote a number of stories for juvenile readers, generally of morally improving content, imparted in an attractive and sprightly style. Her most notable work, *Footprints on the Sands of Time: Biographies for Young People* (1860), is dedicated to her nephews and nieces by L. E. B., and addressed to 'My dear Young Friends' from Aunt Lucy, the pseudonym by which she was best known.

Lucy Bather also translated some religious works from the French. She died at The Hall, Meole Brace, near Shrewsbury, after complications resulting from a premature labour, on 5 September 1864.

ARTHUR H. GRANT, *rev.* VICTORIA MILLAR

Sources *GM*, 3rd ser., 17 (1864), 533 · A. Blomfield, *A memoir of Charles James Blomfield, with selections from his correspondence*, 2 (1863), 225, 357, 373 · *Morning Post* (2 Sept 1861) · *The Record* (9 Sept 1864) · L. E. Blomfield, *Footprints in the sands of time: biographies for young people* (1860) · d. cert.

Bathilda. See Balthild (d. c.680).

Bathurst, Allen, first Earl Bathurst (1684–1775), politician, was born at St James's Square, Westminster, London, on 16 November 1684. He was the eldest son of Frances Apsley (d. 1727), the second daughter of Sir Allen Apsley of Apsley, Sussex, and Sir Benjamin Bathurst (d. 1704), governor of the East India Company in 1688–9, treasurer to Princess Anne of Denmark on the establishment of her household, and cofferer from her accession until her death. Sir Benjamin died on 27 April 1704, his widow in August 1727; both were buried at Paulerspury, Northamptonshire. Allen Bathurst was educated at Trinity College, Oxford, where his uncle Dean Bathurst was president, but his degree is not recorded. On 6 July 1704 he married his cousin Catherine (*bap.* 1688, *d.* 1768), the daughter of Sir Peter Apsley; the couple had four sons and five daughters, including Henry *Bathurst, second Earl Bathurst (1714–1794). He represented Cirencester in parliament from May

1705 until January 1712, when he was created Baron Bathurst, being one of the twelve tory gentlemen who were raised to the peerage at the same time.

Bathurst was always an ardent supporter of the principles of his party, and he became conspicuous while in the upper house for his support of Bishop Atterbury and for his keen criticisms of Sir Robert Walpole. On the latter's fall from office Bathurst was made a privy councillor and captain of the band of pensioners, an office which he retained from the summer of 1742 to the end of 1744. Shortly after the accession of George III he was granted a pension of £2000 a year on the Irish revenues, and on 12 August 1772 he received a further mark of royal favour with his elevation to an earldom. Throughout his long life Bathurst sought the company of prominent literary figures. Alexander Pope, as well as being a correspondent, addressed to him the third of his *Moral Essays*, that on the use of riches. He was friends with Congreve, Prior, and Swift, and later Sterne, who included a character sketch of Bathurst in the third of his *Letters to Eliza* (1775). He was also cited in an address by Edmund Burke (22 March 1775). Burke's call for conciliation with America drew attention to the fact that during Bathurst's lifetime England had achieved prosperity as an imperial power. Bathurst's name and his letters appear frequently in J. J. Cartwright's selections from the *Wentworth Papers, 1705–1739* (1883), and the letters which passed between him and Pope are in the first three volumes of the latter's correspondence. Many of the references reveal Bathurst's love of gardening. He died at Cirencester on 16 September 1775 in his ninety-first year, and was buried at St John the Baptist Church, Cirencester, alongside his wife, who had died on 8 June 1768.
                              W. P. COURTNEY, rev. PHILIP CARTER

Sources GEC, *Peerage*, new edn, vol. 2 · *Annual Register* (1775) · *GM*, 1st ser., 45 (1775), 455 · Foster, *Alum. Oxon.* · *The correspondence of Alexander Pope*, ed. G. Sherburn, 1–3 (1956) · Burke, *Peerage*
Archives BL, letters to Lord Strafford, Add. MSS 31141–31142 · Royal Arch., accounts as comptroller of household to George, Prince of Wales
Likenesses C. Bestland, stipple, pubd 1803, BM, NPG · J. Nollekens, marble bust on monument, St John the Baptist Church, Cirencester, Gloucestershire

Bathurst, Ann (b. c.1638, d. in or before 1704), diarist and prophet, is of unknown parentage. What little is known of her origins is found in the eight-page autobiography that begins her two-volume diary, 'Rhapsodical Meditations and Visions', a manuscript that covers the period 17 March 1679 to 21 October 1696 (Bodl. Oxf., MS Rawl. D 1262, 1263). Her parents were pious and taught their daughter by 'their precept and example' to cultivate a religious disposition (Bathurst, 'Meditations', 1.2). As a girl she enjoyed listening to sermons, reading the Bible, and praying with her sister Elizabeth, but she also developed an acute sense of her own sinfulness. About 1659, when she was eighteen, she fell into a dangerous illness and for six months suffered from extreme religious turmoil, out of which began her lifelong regime of spiritual enquiry.

It is not known when Bathurst began to associate with the prophet Jane Lead and her circle, but like Lead's diary *Fountain of Gardens* (1697), Bathurst's diary resonates with ideas, adapted from Jakob Boehme, regarding the transformative role which the Virgin Wisdom was to play in the coming of the New Jerusalem. On 26 May 1684, Bathurst writes: 'This morning I found such a sweet overshadowing from sweet Sophia, the Virgin Spouse of the Soul, as if she were come to cohabite with me' (Bathurst, 'Meditations', 1.216). By 1697, when the Philadelphian Society was founded by Jane Lead and her spiritual son Francis Lee, Bathurst was considered one of its prophets, and its meetings were first held every Sunday at Bathurst's house in Baldwins Gardens, London. The Philadelphians developed millennial prophecies based on the promise in Revelation 12 that a woman clothed with the sun would appear as a great wonder in the heavens, labouring to be delivered of a child. Bathurst's diary documents her daily study of the great mystery of spiritual impregnation and her ongoing labour to give birth to a new reality. On 3 July 1693, she writes typically:

> I am as if some strange thing had happened unto me to be held many hours in that travel [travail] since the inconceivable conception that has been upon me twelve hours, first as I said in the womb, then in the heart, then in the head. I have felt for some time since some moving of travel between my breasts as some new manifestation. (Bathurst, 'Another volume')

For Bathurst, the production of a glorified body was to be a collective, as well as an individual, labour. She meditated with a small community of spiritual sisters, identified in the diary only by initials and feminine pronouns, but who certainly included Mrs Joanna Openbridge with whom Bathurst lived at Baldwins Gardens. The women not only enjoyed singing and praying together, but on occasion, collaborated in vision production. That Bathurst's visions served to inspire others is indicated by the fact that entries from her diaries, dating from 11 June to 19 September 1679, were copied by several hands, into a large journal, still extant in the Bodleian Library (MS Rawl. D 1338).

During the period 1697–1700, as the Philadelphian movement expanded, its meetings became crowded and were frequently disrupted by disagreements. Owing to Mrs Bathurst's frail health, the meeting at Baldwins Gardens was the first to revert to being a small gathering of the spiritually initiated. The Philadelphian movement eventually petered out after Jane Lead's death in 1704. In a vision recorded by Richard Roach at the time, Lead descends from heaven to tell him that he should take her place as the leader of the Philadelphian movement, 'that upon the death of Mrs. Bathurst it being needful somebody should strike in her Place for the Support of the Meeting at B.G. [Baldwins Gardens]' (Roach, 2.117; Thune, 136). Roach's vision suggests that Lead may have considered Bathurst as her successor, and that Bathurst may have died just before or about the same time as Lead.
                                            SYLVIA BOWERBANK

Sources A. Bathurst, 'Rhapsodical meditations and visions by Mrs Ann Bathurst, from 17 March, 1679 to 29 June, 1693', Bodl. Oxf., MS Rawl. D 1262 · A. Bathurst, 'Another volume of Ann Bathurst's rhapsodies, 30 June, 1693 to 21 October, 1696', Bodl. Oxf., MS Rawl.

D 1263 • R. Roach, miscellaneous papers, Bodl. Oxf., MSS Rawlinson D. 832–833, esp. D. 833 • A. Bathurst, 'A book of daily rhapsodical visions and trances from 11 June to 19 Sept. 1679, written by several hands, more or less clumsy, and copied from another and original MS', Bodl. Oxf., MS Rawl. D. 1338 • N. Thune, *The Behmenists and the Philadelphians: a contribution to the study of English mysticism in the 17th and 18th centuries* (1948) • J. Lead, *A fountain of gardens: watered by the rivers of divine pleasure*, 3 vols. (1697–1701) • J. Lead, *A message to the Philadelphian society, whithersoever dispersed over the whole earth* (1696) • D. Hirst, *Hidden riches: traditional symbolism from the Renaissance to Blake* (1964)

Wealth at death voluntary simplicity and poverty: Bathurst, 'Rhapsodical meditations'

Bathurst, Benjamin (1784–1809), diplomatist, born in London on 14 May 1784, was the third son of Henry *Bathurst (*bap.* 1744, *d.* 1837), bishop of Norwich, and his wife, Grace (*c.*1756–1823), daughter of Charles Coote, dean of Kilfenora. He was educated at Winchester College and at New College, Oxford, where he took his BA (1803) and was a fellow until November 1805. On 25 May 1805 he married Phillida (Philadelphia; *c.*1774–1855), daughter of Sir John Call, bt; she died at Lucca on 17 September 1855. They had two daughters and a son.

Through the influence of his relative, Lord Bathurst, Bathurst was first appointed to a minor post in the embassy at Vienna in 1804, and then in the following year was made secretary to the legation at Stockholm. In 1808 he returned to England, passing the summer and autumn in Devon and Cornwall, as he told a friend the following spring, 'to recover my health which was much shattered by long illness, and various disappointments,' presumably at not getting a better diplomatic appointment (*Memoirs and Correspondence of Dr Henry Bathurst*, 550–51). When he had recovered sufficiently, he returned to London seeking fresh employment. He had great success in March 1809 when the foreign secretary, George Canning, appointed him envoy-extraordinary to Austria, for which he had to leave at a few days' notice. This appointment was also influenced by his connection with Lord Bathurst, whom Canning wanted to enlist in his plot to force Lord Castlereagh out of the cabinet; but the choice of such a junior diplomat, even one who had served at Vienna, indicates Canning's scepticism about Austria's revolt against Napoleon, which he refused to support by an alliance or regular subsidy.

Following Austria's defeat by France, it was required by the treaty of Schönbrunn (14 October 1809) to break off relations with Britain. Bathurst left for home from Buda, in a fearful state of mind, carrying a passport in the name of a German merchant, though he spoke little German and his slim, 6 foot bearing, luxurious clothes, and four-horse carriage suggested a rich foreign aristocrat. Along with his servant and the embassy messenger he arrived in the Prussian town of Perleberg, half way between Berlin and his destination of the port of Hamburg, on the afternoon of 25 November. At his request, the military governor provided two troopers for his protection, whom Bathurst dismissed at about 8 p.m. When his companions looked for him at the departure time of 9 p.m., he could not be found. Despite an extensive search, no trace was ever discovered, though three weeks later a pair of trousers, obviously recently left where it would be sure to be seen, was found with an incomplete letter to his wife in a pocket. In 1852 a skeleton with a hatchet mark on the skull came to light in a house that was being demolished. Mrs Tryphena Thistlethwayte, who arrived four months later, confidently pronounced that it could not be her brother's; but such a judgement can hardly be conclusive.

Napoleon provided passports for Bathurst's wife, who spent four months in 1810 at Berlin, Perleberg, and Paris with her brother, George Call, investigating in vain the fate of her husband. At the time she thought that her husband had been driven to commit suicide in some remote place by the mental strain of his hazardous journey through French-occupied territory, but she later came to believe that he had been murdered for political reasons. The general assumption was that he was killed by the French or their agents for the papers he was carrying, but he had already destroyed them. One plausible explanation, proposed by Sir John Hall in *Four Famous Mysteries* (1922), is that Bathurst was murdered by a secret military association working with British aid against the French occupation, which feared that his mental state would lead him to disclose their activities. But it is far more likely that he fled from the messenger, believing that he would betray him to the French, and was killed while trying to make his way back to England via the Baltic and Sweden. The British government, unable to discover Bathurst's fate and receiving embarrassing reports of his derangement, declined the propaganda opportunity of charging Napoleon with his murder, and also refused to risk offending its allies by pursuing the matter at the Congress of Vienna.

NEVILLE THOMPSON

Sources J. Hall, *Four famous mysteries* (1922) • *Memoirs and correspondence of Dr Henry Bathurst, lord bishop of Norwich*, ed. T. Thistlethwayte (1853) • W. M. W. Call, 'The search for the lost Mr Bathurst', *Westminster Review*, 134 (1890), 396–414 • Mrs. Benjamin Bathurst's journal, BL, Bathurst MSS, Loan 57, vol. 79 • Burke, *Gen. GB* • O. W. Johnston, 'Bathurst and Lutze: perceptions of British consular service in Northern Germany under Napoleon', *The Consortium on Revolutionary Europe, 1750–1850* [Baton Rouge, LA] (1997) • N. Thompson, 'The continental system as a sieve: the disappearance of Benjamin Bathurst in 1809', *International History Review*, 24/3 (Sept 2002), 528–57

Archives PRO, letter-book of corresp. with Foreign Office, FO 7/88 | BL, Bathurst MSS, Mrs Bathurst's journal

Bathurst, Catherine Anne [*name in religion* Mary Catherine Philip] (1825–1907), Roman Catholic nun, was born at Summerleaze, Wookey, Somerset, on 14 July 1825, the youngest of the three daughters and six sons of General Sir James Bathurst (1782–1850) and Lady Caroline Stuart (*d.* 1864), daughter of Andrew Thomas, Earl Castle Stuart. Her father had served as aide-de-camp to the duke of Wellington, and the Wellingtons not only stood as godparents but also provided their godchild with an income. She was an intelligent and lively child. Her early education was received at home under governesses and concluded at York Place School, London (1837–9), where Mendelssohn was among her music masters.

In 1850 Bathurst's brother Stuart, who held the living of Kibworth Beauchamp in Leicestershire, was received into the Roman Catholic church. Within a few months Bathurst herself followed him, being baptized *sub conditione* by Father Brownbill SJ at Farm Street. On joining her brother in Birmingham she was introduced to J. H. Newman, who was to remain her guide and friend until his death. More than eighty of Newman's letters to Bathurst are extant and reveal her gradual development from scrupulous young convert to confident religious superior.

It was to take Bathurst several years and a number of false starts to determine her place in life. In 1852 she joined a small community of Sisters of Charity of the Precious Blood founded at Greenwich by a fellow convert, Elizabeth Lockhart. A year later she was trying her vocation with the Sisters of Providence in Loughborough, but remained there little more than a year, returning to live as a visitor at Greenwich. In 1856, when Lockhart's community was affiliated to the Franciscans and moved to Bayswater, Bathurst returned to Birmingham. With several other women she took charge of the Oratory poor schools and orphanage and conducted them successfully for three years.

Through her brother, now mission priest at Stone, Staffordshire, Bathurst learned of Mother Margaret Hallahan's community of Dominican sisters. She entered as a postulant on 30 May 1861 and was clothed in the habit on 7 November the same year, receiving the name Sister Mary Catherine Philip. In April 1862 the suicide of Bathurst's surviving sister precipitated a complete breakdown and she returned once again to Birmingham. From there she went to work with the Dominican friars at Kentish Town. Some years later, during a visit to Belgium, the Dominicans in Ghent persuaded her to begin a foundation of third order sisters. The community was established in 1868, and two years later imposing conventual and school buildings were opened at Meirelbeke, just outside the city. The convent school attracted both local and English girls, and there was also a day school for working-class children and an orphanage.

Relations with Bishop Bracq of Ghent were not always easy, and in 1878 Bathurst accepted the invitation of Cardinal Manning to open a similar establishment at Harrow, where she hoped the presence of the sisters would exercise a discreet Catholic influence on his alma mater. Two years later the mother house was transferred there, and the Belgian house was closed in 1883. Several branch houses were founded in which the sisters were engaged in the teaching or care of destitute children.

Bathurst had obtained her teaching certificate at Liverpool in June 1857 and continued to teach both school children or novices until the week of her death. In the estimation of her early examiners she was unusually gifted and adapted for this work. In the 1890s she managed to persuade Manning of the necessity of allowing girls at St Dominic's, Harrow on the Hill, to sit for the Oxford and Cambridge local examinations. Her efforts were rewarded when the first two girls presented passed first and second in England in modern languages and Latin. Increasing age

and infirmity caused Bathurst to resign as prioress-general in 1906, though she maintained a lively interest in the school and community. She died on 14 December 1907 at the convent in Harrow, where she was buried. She left a community of fifty sisters, with convents at Harrow, Kilburn, Watford, and Bognor. The order remained at the building in Harrow until about 1980; it subsequently became St Dominic's Sixth-Form College.

ANSELM NYE

Sources St Dominic's convent, Stone, Harrow generalate collection · *The conventual third order of St Dominic and its development in England, by a Dominican of Stone* (1923) · J. Sugg, *Ever yours affly: John Henry Newman and his female circle* (1996) · Burke, *Gen. GB* (1914)
Likenesses photographs, St Dominic's convent, Stone

Bathurst, Charles, first Viscount Bledisloe (1867–1958), agriculturist and politician, was born in London on 21 September 1867, the second but first surviving son of the barrister Charles Bathurst (1836–1907), of Lydney Park, Gloucestershire, where he owned 4000 acres of land, and his wife, Mary Elizabeth (d. 1885), only daughter of Lieutenant-Colonel Thomas Pasley Hay. He was educated at Sherborne School, at Eton College, and at University College, Oxford, where he obtained third classes in classical honour moderations in 1888 and in jurisprudence in 1890. In 1892 he was called to the bar by the Inner Temple, and for a time practised in the Chancery Division as a conveyancing barrister. As heir to the family estate after the death of his elder brother in 1883 Bathurst attended the Royal Agricultural College, Cirencester, from 1893 to 1896 to equip himself for his inheritance and, as it turned out, for his career. At Cirencester he edited the college magazine, won the Ducie gold medal, and as one of the college's most famous old students was later chairman of its board of governors from 1919 to 1925; it became customary for estate management students to visit his Lydney estate to study its management and its farming. It is likely that while at Cirencester he formed the view that the one hope for the future of agriculture in Britain was for the landowners to become professional, businesslike, and efficient managers. This became his persistent message. On 17 December 1898 he married Bertha Susan (d. 1926), fifth daughter of Henry Charles *Lopes, first Baron Ludlow, himself the third son of a Devonshire landed magnate and a prominent judge; this marriage reflected Bathurst's alignment with the professional wing of the landed class. They had two sons and one daughter.

Rather unexpectedly the crushing defeat of the Unionists in the 1906 election created the opening for Bathurst to enter politics. Walter Long, the Unionists' leading country gentleman, decided that one way of containing the anti-landlord effects of that defeat was to mobilize the landowners in an effective organization, and in 1907 he took the lead in forming the Central Land Association (CLA); he seems to have been responsible for recruiting Bathurst as the first honorary secretary of the CLA. He was very successful in this post, and steered membership of the new association to over 1000 by 1909, when he resigned. It also provided him with close contacts with leading tories, which helped him become MP for the Wilton division of Wiltshire in the January 1910 election. He wished to make the CLA into a non-party pressure group representing landowners of every political colour, but was frustrated by its domination by tories and by the hysterical anti-Liberalism of the CLA's allies in the Land Union.

Enjoying the patronage of Milner and Steel-Maitland, Bathurst quickly established himself in alliance with Christopher Turnor as one of the Conservatives' leading agricultural reformers in the Commons and a key contributor to mounting a defence against Lloyd George's land campaign of 1912–14. He and Turnor, together with B. Peto and C. Mills, formed a group of radical agricultural reformers, at times acting as a private inquiry committee and at times as an agricultural policy subcommittee of the Unionist Social Reform Committee. They attempted, with no great success, to formulate a Conservative counter to the land campaign, which was perceived as threatening to undermine the Conservatives' rural vote. Unable to agree on any convincing riposte to the Liberals' promise of a minimum wage for agricultural labourers, the reform group did strongly advocate a grant-aided scheme for assisting tenant farmers to become owners. Although this did not find favour with either the old guard of tory landed grandees who regarded it as a recipe for dismantling the great estates, or with the traditional gentry who denied that their workers were badly paid, it did lead Henry Chaplin to hail Bathurst as the 'most promising ally of the agricultural interest that we have had in Parliament now for some time' (Fforde, 64).

By 1914 Bathurst had achieved a high reputation, and some enemies, within the Conservative Party, but little in the way of agricultural advance. By 1915, as chairman of the central chamber of agriculture, he was recording his 'conviction that upon the well-being of Great Britain's oldest industry depend the ultimate economic welfare of her people, their physical and mental virility', and virtually welcoming the war, on the grounds that:

> the Great European War may—and God grant that it will— cause the nation at large to realise the wisdom, and the ultimate economy, if not the necessity, of making Britain more self-contained in the matter of food production for her teeming population. (A. H. H. Matthews, 'Preface' to *Fifty Years of Agricultural Politics: the History of the Central Chamber of Agriculture*, 1915, vii, x)

How far the war was good for British agriculture, as distinct from the incomes of British farmers, may be questionable, but it definitely helped Bathurst's career. In 1916 he became the spokesman in the Commons for the new Ministry of Food when he was appointed parliamentary secretary to the food controller, Lord Devenport, whom he succeeded as chairman of the royal commission on sugar supply in 1917, when he was also appointed KBE. He was director of sugar distribution from 1918 to 1919, and confirmed his position as a leading member alongside R. E. Prothero (Lord Ernle) of the official agricultural interest by serving from 1917 to 1920 as chairman of the federation

of county war agricultural executive committees, the bodies which induced or cajoled farmers into applying agricultural policies at the farm level.

In October 1918 Bathurst was rewarded for his war services with a peerage and took the title of Baron Bledisloe from the hundred in which the family seat of Lydney lies. With his experience and public standing he seemed an excellent choice for a post-war president in 1921–2 of the CLA (by then called the Central Landowners' Association), but raised hackles among the grandees by publicly calling, in 1922, for the larger landowners to renounce their passive and unenterprising attitudes of the previous sixty years, abandon their ineffective attachment to a property defence league which merely stimulated revolutionary propaganda, and place themselves at the head of the agricultural industry as professional managers of the resources of the land, co-operating with the farmers and farm workers. From the conventional landowner's point of view this was only slightly less subversive than the position of his friend and fellow landowner Turnor, who spoke at this time of sixty years of failure by government to grasp the importance of agriculture and of neglect by rich and complacent landowners who did not understand their own business. It was a precursor of Bledisloe's call in 1929 for permanent regulation of farm rents by compulsory valuation as the only alternative to land nationalization. He saw this as a way of removing the fundamental objection to all government aid to agriculture, that the benefits of such aid would ultimately go to the landlords who were not the wealth producers or employers. This radical outburst earned him a formal rebuke from the CLA. In politics also he steered an idiosyncratic and radical course. Initially, with his peerage, a Lloyd George adherent, he was reconciled to the Conservatives to the extent of becoming a member of the government's agricultural advisory committee in 1922, but did not fully rejoin the party until accepting office as parliamentary secretary to the Ministry of Agriculture in Baldwin's second administration, 1924–8. In 1927 he served as chairman of the royal commission on land drainage, which recommended drastic rationalization of the 365 separate drainage authorities then responsible for the management of rivers in England and Wales. In the interval it had not been implausible for Ramsay MacDonald to consider inviting him to become minister of agriculture in the first Labour government, although in the event the approach was not made.

In June 1929, however, Bledisloe accepted from MacDonald appointment as governor-general of New Zealand; he subsequently 'proved to be perhaps the most popular representative of the Crown who has ever been appointed to the Dominion' (*The Times*, 4 July 1958, 12). Aristocratic affability, seriously knowledgeable enthusiasm for farming, and a keen interest in livestock—and his purchase and restoration of the neglected site of the signing of the Waitangi treaty in 1840, which he subsequently gave to the nation—combined to this end. His first wife having died in 1926, on 16 April 1928 Bledisloe married Alina Kate Elaine (d. 1956), younger daughter of John Jones

Jenkins, the first Baron Glantawe, a south Wales tinplate manufacturer, and widow of Thomas Cooper Cooper-Smith. The charm of his second wife made an essential contribution to the success of his governorship. On its conclusion in June 1935 he received a step in the peerage, becoming Viscount Bledisloe. The concluding official activity of Bledisloe's career was to serve as chairman of the royal commission on the closer union of the two Rhodesias and Nyasaland, which reported in March 1939 in favour of a union. The report circumspectly added the qualification that, as the natives of Northern Rhodesia and Nyasaland had good reason to fear the application of the Southern Rhodesian pass laws, it was for the present impossible to contemplate 68,000 white people governing 4 million natives; the government which enacted the federation in 1953 was not so cautious. Bledisloe's sympathies, although he had gone out of his way to encourage Maori farmers during his time in New Zealand, were clearly with the white population, as he showed in his two goodwill tours in 1947 and 1948 of Australasia and of South Africa and Southern Rhodesia, which he made on behalf of the Royal Agricultural Society of England, of which he had been president in 1946.

Bledisloe was also president or chairman of the British Dairy Farmers' Association, the Bath and West of England Agricultural Society, the Farmers' Club, and the Lawes Agricultural Trust, Rothamsted, but perhaps his strongest loyalty, after his attachment to the Lydney estate, was to the Forest of Dean, of which he was verderer from 1897 until his death on 3 July 1958, at Lydney Park; he was buried four days later at St Mary's, Lydney. He was succeeded by his elder son, Benjamin Ludlow (1899–1979).

F. M. L. THOMPSON

Sources *The Times* (13 Sept 1922), 12 • *The Times* (4 July 1958), 12 • *DNB* • Burke, *Peerage* • GEC, *Peerage* • M. Fforde, *Conservatism and collectivism, 1886–1914* (1990) • E. H. H. Green, *The crisis of conservatism: the politics, economics and ideology of the Conservative Party, 1880–1914* (1995) • A. F. Cooper, *British agricultural policy, 1912–36* (1989) • A. H. H. Matthews, *Fifty years of agricultural politics* (1915) • minutes of Central Landowners' Association Executive Committee, 1923, U. Reading, Rural History Centre, Country Landowners' Association MSS • minutes of Central Landowners' Association Executive Committee, 1929, U. Reading, Rural History Centre, Country Landowners' Association MSS • T. Jones, *Whitehall diary*, ed. K. Middlemas, 3 vols. (1969–71) • *Real old tory politics: the political diaries of Robert Sanders, Lord Bayford, 1910–35*, ed. J. Ramsden (1984)
Archives priv. coll., corresp. • U. Reading, Rural History Centre, Country Landowners' Association MSS | Bodl. Oxf., Attlee MSS, letters to Clement Attlee • Bodl. RH, corresp. with Lord Lugard and related papers • HLRO, Bonar Law MSS, corresp. with Andrew Bonar Law • HLRO, letters to David Lloyd George • U. Newcastle, Robinson L., Runciman MSS, corresp. with Walter Runciman • U. Reading L., letters to Sir E. J. Russell
Likenesses photograph, 1915, repro. in Matthews, *Fifty years of agricultural politics*, frontispiece • oils, c.1919–1925, Royal Agricultural College, Cirencester
Wealth at death £107,624 15s. 11d.: probate, 19 Nov 1958, CGPLA Eng. & Wales

Bathurst, Charles Bragge (*bap.* 1754, *d.* 1831), politician, was baptized Charles Bragge on 28 February 1754, elder son among three children of Charles Bragge (*d.* in or after 1780), landowner, of Cleve Hill, Mangotsfield, Gloucestershire, whose father, from Essex, had married into that estate, and his wife, Anne (1718–1793), daughter of Benjamin Bathurst, politician, of Lydney, Gloucestershire. Educated as founder's kin at Winchester College (from in or before 1770), and at New College, Oxford (from in or before 1772), he entered Lincoln's Inn in 1772, from where he was called to the bar in 1778. He served as bankruptcy commissioner (1778–1800) and secretary to the commissioners of peace (1779–91); his cousin Henry Bathurst was lord chancellor. After practising at Gloucester quarter sessions, he graduated BCL in 1785 and retained his fellowship until he married, on 1 August 1788, Charlotte (1762–1839), daughter of Anthony *Addington, physician, and Mary Hiley (*d.* 1778), of Fringford, Oxfordshire; two sons and two daughters of their nine children survived infancy. This match with the sister of his schoolfellow, Henry Addington, promoted a political career already started under other auspices.

Bragge had been newly appointed recorder of Monmouth through the influence of the duke of Beaufort, whose interest had returned his Bathurst grandfather as MP there, and Bragge too became its member, gratis, on 28 December 1790. He first spoke in parliament against delaying prorogation on 2 June 1791; a contemporary pamphlet upholding impeachments after dissolutions was probably his. Beaufort secured his return in 1796 for Bristol, which he represented until 1812, and he gave strong support to the ministry, championing Pitt against Fox in debate on 14 December 1796. Through the influence of his brother-in-law, Addington, who was speaker, he became counsel to the Board of Control for India in September 1797, and in November chaired the bank committee. Pitt was certain that he would decline his offer of honorary office as queen's solicitor in 1798 as Bragge had opposed Pitt's measure to levy income tax even on taxpayers with large families, such as Bragge's own. He opposed trade unions in 1799, and published a bill to make colliery thefts felonious in 1800. As the first paid chairman of supply, he received £1200 per session from 1799 to 1801.

Addington, who became premier in 1801, wanted Bragge as speaker, but the king apparently objected, despite Bragge's obvious preference for business, electoral, and procedural matters. He was sworn of the privy council on 18 November 1801, and became treasurer of the navy, which brought him an income of £4000 plus a house. Addington, claiming he followed the king's advice, did not consult him on public affairs, and the speakership was again mooted in 1802. Mocked by Pitt's friends, Bragge rebuked Canning for accentuating policy differences between Addington and Pitt on 24 November. In June 1803 he sacrificed his office for a seat on the Board of Trade and, in August, the secretaryship at war, after having declined the India board.

Even though the king praised his business ability, Bragge was often harassed in debate; he refused the Irish chief secretaryship, in January 1804. When Pitt had replaced Addington and Bragge had resigned from office,

Bragge questioned his military measures, thereby ignoring Addington's advice to abstain from criticism for reasons of self-interest. He had just acquired his uncle Poole Bathurst's encumbered Lydney estate worth £2500, and taken his surname of Bathurst (on 11 May 1804), and was thus in need of a lucrative office to pay his debts and support his family. He none the less deprecated Addington's action in soliciting for him in negotiations to rejoin Pitt, but he did accept the chairmanship of Gloucestershire quarter sessions. He was plainly embarrassed when Pitt and Addington, now Lord Sidmouth, disagreed over Lord Melville's naval administration, for it was his veto on banking navy funds at Coutts that had triggered the malversation by Melville; Sidmouth was then requesting the duchy of Lancaster on his behalf. Bathurst resumed attendance on the naval committee to investigate Melville's alleged embezzlements and advocated criminal prosecution of Melville. He regretted his divergence from Pitt, and did not, as alleged, pen the pamphlet *A Plain Reply*, occasioned by the split between Pitt and Sidmouth.

Bathurst, as Sidmouth discovered after successfully soliciting a cabinet office for him in Grenville's ministry in 1806, would have accepted the War Office, had it been available. Grenville was well disposed towards him, for he backed ministers, particularly over military reorganization, and eventually Bathurst was appointed to the Royal Mint, although he did not take office until the dissolution of parliament, thereby avoiding the costs of a by-election necessitated by his assumption of office. His allegiance to the Grenville administration wavered although he continued to support it: he preferred gradual to immediate slave trade abolition and approved of royal hostility to measures of Catholic relief, as did Sidmouth, who prompted his vocal defence in April 1807 of the king's dismissal of Grenville.

Bathurst was offered the surveyorship of woods and forests in the duke of Portland's ministry, but he declined to take office without Sidmouth. He shone in voicing his opposition to military reformation and to the Copenhagen and Peninsular operations. A ministerial ruse to banish him to India with Vansittart, another staunch supporter of Sidmouth, as commissioners, misfired. His proposed censure of the duke of York for allowing his mistress to dispense military patronage was negatived on 20 March 1809. In May 1809 he supported modest parliamentary reform, but denied the charge of ministerial corruption levelled by William Madocks. When Perceval, as premier, proposed a merger with the Sidmouthites in October 1809, he was tempted with the promise of the War Office and a seat in cabinet, but he advised Sidmouth against parleying without consulting other opposition leaders. Following Sidmouth, he voted for the address in 1810, but supported the Walcheren inquiry, favouring censure. Though guardedly critical of the house's handling of the reformer Sir Francis Burdett, he voted against parliamentary reform on 21 May, and opposed piecemeal abolition of sinecures on 1 June. He discouraged Sidmouth from negotiating office for him, dreading the costs of the ensuing by-election. Yet he stood by Perceval over the

regency, and abandoned his motion vetoing the queen's interference. Report then assigned him the exchequer or speakership. Courted on his own by Perceval in January 1812, he preferred to wait for Sidmouth to conclude a deal; he anticipated high office. He eventually attained a cabinet post and the duchy of Lancaster in June 1812, when Lord Liverpool, as premier, included Sidmouthites in his government. To avoid the expenses of a Bristol by-election, Sidmouth procured him Bodmin.

Bathurst subsequently defended ministers on multifarious topics, some beyond his range. He regularly decried Catholic relief and opposed legal and parliamentary reform. A select committeeman on India, he voted for Christian missions in 1813. His championship of the Anglican clergy suggested a wish to represent his university, which created him DCL in 1814. A commissioner for building new churches (1818), he also sat on poor law committees. The chairmanship of secret committees awarded him a new brief denouncing popular radicalism, which he resumed in his last two parliaments, when he represented Harwich. He attributed unrest to abeyant royal authority and foreign example. In 1819 his resignation was rumoured. With additional, unwanted, and unremunerated office as president of the India board from January 1821, he left office and parliament for health reasons in January 1823, having obtained civil-list pensions for himself and his wife that were divisible among their children. Bathurst died at Lydney Park on 13 August 1831 and was buried in Lydney.   ROLAND THORNE

Sources R. G. Thorne, 'Bragge (afterwards, Bragge Bathurst), Charles', HoP, *Commons, 1790–1820* · Glos. RO, Bragge Bathurst MSS, D 421 X/17 · *GM*, 1st ser., 63 (1793), 576 · *GM*, 1st ser., 101/2 (1831), 269–70, 653 · Devon RO, Sidmouth papers · Cobbett, *Parl. hist.* · Hansard 1 · Hansard 2 · LondG (19–22 May 1804), 639–40 · *Boyle's Court Guide* (1792–1819) · Foster, *Alum. Oxon.* · Winchester College register

Archives BL, verses and translations; corresp., Add. MS 61910 · Glos. RO, corresp. and papers, D 421 [esp. X/17] | Devon RO, Sidmouth MSS

Bathurst, Henry, second Earl Bathurst (1714–1794), lord chancellor, was born on 20 May 1714, the second son of Allen *Bathurst, first Earl Bathurst (1684–1775), and his wife, Catherine (*bap.* 1688, *d.* 1768), daughter of Sir Peter Apsley of Apsley, Sussex, and his wife, Catherine. Educated at Eton College, Bathurst matriculated at Balliol College, Oxford, on 14 May 1730. He was admitted to the Inner Temple, probably in the same year, and was called to the bar in 1736. Admitted to Lincoln's Inn on 22 June 1743, he was appointed king's counsel on 20 January 1746 and became a bencher of the Inner Temple on 25 April of the same year. Returned to parliament for the family seat at Cirencester, Gloucestershire, on 14 April 1735, he voted consistently against the government until Sir Robert Walpole's fall in 1742. Following the change of ministry and his father's receipt of minor office, Bathurst supported the government. Upon his father's dismissal in 1744, he attached himself to Frederick, prince of Wales, becoming his solicitor-general in 1745 and his attorney-general in 1748. After Frederick's death in 1751, Bathurst went over to the government and was continued in office as attorney-general to George, prince of Wales. He was put up for Cirencester at the general election of 1754, but withdrew in favour of his elder brother, Benjamin.

Following the death of Mr Justice Gundry in 1754, Bathurst's father applied to the lord chancellor on his son's behalf for the vacancy in the court of common pleas. Lord Hardwicke undertook to do no more than mention Bathurst's name to the king and do justice to his character, but Bathurst was nevertheless appointed, taking office on 2 May 1754. On 19 September 1754 he married Anne James (d. 1758), widow of Charles Philipps. They had no children. On 14 June 1759 he married Tryphena Scawen (1723–1807), daughter of Thomas Scawen of Carshalton, Surrey, and Maidwell, Northamptonshire, formerly MP for Surrey, and his wife, Tryphena Russell. They had four daughters and two sons, including Henry *Bathurst (1762–1834), politician.

As a judge sitting alone Bathurst tended to avoid deciding points of law, and in banco usually deferred to the chief justice. Charles Yorke, the lord chancellor, died suddenly early in 1770, and on 20 January 1770 the great seal was put into commission, Bathurst becoming the second of three commissioners. As the commissioners were thought incompetent, there was considerable surprise when on 23 January 1771 Bathurst, regarded as the least competent, was appointed lord chancellor and raised to the peerage as Baron Apsley. Bathurst's judgments as lord chancellor are not memorable, though it was conceded that he made few mistakes, relying on the judges and the master of the rolls, Sir Thomas Sewell, in equity cases, and on Lord Mansfield in the House of Lords.

Bathurst succeeded to the earldom of Bathurst upon his father's death in 1775. In December 1777, shortly after the surrender at Saratoga, he expressed himself privately to be in favour of peace and negotiation with the Americans, though in the following February he strenuously urged the House of Lords not to acknowledge American independence or to withdraw the British forces. In the same month he wrote to Lord North offering his resignation, supposing himself deliberately slighted over the acceptance of General Howe's resignation of the command in America. The offer was refused, but in April 1778 the king explained to Bathurst the impossibility of continuing him in office, given the assistance from the lord chancellor required by the cabinet, and Edward Thurlow became lord chancellor on 3 June 1778. On 24 November 1779 Bathurst became lord president of the council, holding office until Lord North's fall in 1782. The offer of his services as lord chancellor in 1783—upon the formation of the coalition between Charles James Fox and Lord North—was refused on the grounds that Lord Thurlow had no intention of resigning.

Bathurst is supposed to have been the original author of a practice book on trials at nisi prius, known from subsequent editions by his nephew Francis Buller as Buller's Nisi prius, published in 1767 and said to be based upon an earlier work published in 1760, which reached a seventh edition in 1817. A work on the theory of evidence published in 1761 and also supposed to have been by Bathurst was subsequently incorporated into the work on nisi prius. Bathurst was also author of The Case of the Unfortunate Martha Sophia Swordfeager (1771), an attempt to demonstrate the validity of Miss Swordfeager's marriage to the supposed husband who had deserted her.

Honourable and good humoured, Bathurst was responsible for the building of Apsley House, London, and received the dedication of the translation of the speeches of Isaeus by William Jones, whom he had appointed a commissioner in bankruptcy. His abilities were mediocre and unsuited to the high offices which he came to fill, but even his critic Lord Campbell admitted that his career had been without reproach and that, so far as the public could observe, he had performed his duties decently. He died on 6 August 1794 at his home, Oakley Grove, Gloucestershire, and was buried in the family vault there.　　N. G. JONES

Sources HoP, Commons, 1715–54 · J. Campbell, Lives of the lord chancellors, 5th edn, 10 vols. (1868), vol. 7, pp. 118–52 · E. Foss, Biographia juridica: a biographical dictionary of the judges of England … 1066–1870 (1870) · GM, 1st ser., 64 (1794), 770 · J. S. A. [J. S. Anderson], 'Bathurst, Henry', Biographical dictionary of the common law, ed. A. W. B. Simpson (1984) · Report on the manuscripts of Earl Bathurst, preserved at Cirencester Park, HMC, 76 (1923), v–ix, 12–21 · GEC, Peerage, new edn, vol. 2 · The correspondence of King George the Third with Lord North from 1768 to 1783, ed. W. B. Donne, 2 (1867), 173 · F. A. Inderwick and R. A. Roberts, eds., A calendar of the Inner Temple records, 4 (1933), 231, 315, 502 · J. E. Doyle, The official baronage of England, 1 (1886), 119–20 · Foster, Alum. Oxon. · Sainty, Judges, 81 · R. A. Austen-Leigh, ed., The Eton College register, 1698–1752 (1927) · IGI

Archives BL, corresp., loan 57 · HLRO, notebooks | BL, letters to Lord Hardwicke, etc., Add. MSS 35609–35681, passim · BL, corresp. with earl of Liverpool, Add. MSS 38208–38580, passim · BL, letters to earl of Liverpool, loan 72 · BL, letters to Sir John Eardley Wilmot, Add. MS 9828 · U. Nott. L., letters to duke of Portland

Likenesses R. Houston, mezzotint, 1773, BM · J. Nollekens, bust, 1776, Palace of Westminster, London · T. Watson, engraving, 1776 · R. van Bleeck, portrait engraving, 1782? · C. J. Sayer, etching, 1782, NPG · W. H. Brown, line drawing, repro. in J. E. Doyle, The official baronage of England, 1 (1886), 120 · N. Dance, portrait, oils, Lincoln's Inn · D. Martin, portrait, Balliol Oxf. · bust, marble, Cirencester Parish Church

Bathurst, Henry (bap. 1744, d. 1837), bishop of Norwich, was born at Westminster, London, and baptized on 15 October 1744, the seventh son of Benjamin Bathurst of Lydney Park (1688–1767), and the third of his fourteen children with his second wife, Catherine Whitfield, daughter of Laurence Brodrick DD, chaplain to the House of Commons; Benjamin Bathurst was the father of thirty-six children from his two marriages. Bathurst was educated at Winchester College between 1756 and 1761 and he matriculated at New College, Oxford, on 21 April 1761 as founder's kin. He graduated BCL on 21 October 1768, receiving the DCL degree on 5 June 1776 after having moved to Christ Church.

Bathurst took holy orders (ordained priest on 24 December 1769 in the Oxford diocese), and was vicar of Sapperton from 1773 to 1775, and again from 1785 to 1833, on the presentation of his cousin, Allen, first Earl Bathurst. He subsequently received the New College livings of St Mary with St Faith's, Witchingham, Norfolk, and of St John Maddermarket, Norwich, on 29 June 1775 (resigned in

Henry Bathurst (*bap.* 1744, *d.* 1837), by Sir Martin Archer Shee, 1818

1786), where he was non-resident. He married on 15 August 1780 Grace (*c*.1756–1823), daughter of Charles Coote DD, dean of Kilfenora, co. Clare. They had eight sons and three daughters, including Benjamin *Bathurst, diplomatist. Bathurst was installed canon of the seventh prebend at Christ Church on 13 May 1775, and he exchanged it for the second prebendal stall in Durham Cathedral on 6 April 1795. Thereafter he concentrated his efforts on receiving further preferment, claiming that from the Durham prebend he had 'never been able (literally speaking) to lay by sixpence for a family of eight children' (Bathurst to Lord Grenville, 18 June 1800, BL, Add. MS 59002, fol. 63). He also enlisted the influence of his cousin and former pupil, the third Earl Bathurst, with William Pitt. Bathurst's opportunity arose in 1805 when Charles Manners-Sutton was translated to Canterbury and Bathurst received the vacant see of Norwich.

Bathurst remained in Norwich for the next thirty-two years. Always friendly to protestant dissenters, he became best-known for his whiggish sympathies (he was a long-standing friend of Thomas Coke of Holkham) and especially for his support of Roman Catholic emancipation. The latter originated in his wife's family background and in his own visits to Ireland; he made several speeches in the upper house on the subject. After arguing in favour of Lord Grenville's motion for Catholic relief on 27 May 1808 he observed 'I have lost Winchester, my dear Sir, but I have satisfied my conscience' (*GM*, new ser., 7, 1837, 653). The bishop even laid before parliament a petition for emancipation from the Roman Catholics of Tuam in 1826. His

stance was not popular with many clergy in the Norwich diocese. Bathurst, who uniquely on the episcopal bench voted for the 1832 Reform Act, welcomed the arrival in power of the whig governments of lords Grey and Melbourne and was disappointed not to be offered promotion to a wealthier English see than Norwich (he refused the archbishopric of Dublin in 1831). He died in Hereford Street, London, on 5 April 1837, and was buried in Great Malvern Abbey on 14 April. His wife had died on 16 April 1823.

Bathurst was widely read but published little himself apart from a few sermons, his visitation charges of 1806 and 1813, and *A letter to the late Mr. Wilberforce on Christianity and politics, how far they are reconcilable* (1818). He was an expert whist player, with many opportunities for the game during his annual winter sojourns in Bath, Cheltenham, or Malvern. Bathurst was not an energetic pastor and old age increased his inertia (he made his last Norwich visitation in 1820), making him what his latest biographer has called 'perhaps the worst diocesan administrator the diocese had ever had' (Hanekamp, 261): in his time Norwich had a reputation as 'the Dead See'. In fairness, Bathurst urged the appointment of a coadjutor for any bishop over seventy years of age, but the suggestion was not acted on in his lifetime. He delegated many episcopal duties and relied increasingly on his eldest son, Henry Bathurst, archdeacon of Norwich from November 1814, to guide affairs on his behalf.

A fellow of New College (BCL, 1804), **Henry Bathurst** (1781–1844) received his father's ceaseless patronage: he was chancellor of the diocese (1805–9), rector of Ashby and Oby with Thirne (1806–29), then rector of North Creake (1809), and he finally received the living of Hollesley in Suffolk in 1828. He produced the *Memoirs* of his father in 1837, which included a charge (1815) and a sermon (1816) by himself. A supplement of 1842 entitled *An Easter Offering for the Whigs* gave vent to frustration on his father's behalf for not receiving a wealthier English see and to his own for not being offered the succession to Norwich by Lord Melbourne. Archdeacon Bathurst died on 10 September 1844 leaving two sons and four daughters.

NIGEL ASTON

Sources *GM*, 2nd ser., 7 (1837), 653–4 · *GM*, 2nd ser., 12 (1839), 652 · A. B. Bathurst, *History of the Apsley and Bathurst families* (1903) · H. Bathurst, *Memoirs of the late Dr Henry Bathurst*, 2 vols. (1837) · *Memoirs and correspondence of Dr Henry Bathurst, lord bishop of Norwich*, ed. T. Thistlethwayte (1853) · J. C. Hanekamp, *An appeal for justice: the life of Dr. Henry Bathurst, lord bishop of Norwich, 1744–1837* (1992) · Foster, *Alum. Oxon.* · *Woodforde at Oxford, 1759–1776*, ed. W. N. Hargreaves-Mawdsley, OHS, new ser., 21 (1969) · D. Turner, *List of Norfolk benefices* (1847), 8, 21, 26, 37 · *Fasti Angl.* (Hardy), 3.310 · *Fasti Angl., 1541–1857*, [Bristol], 104 · C. Mackie, *Norfolk annals: a chronological record of remarkable events in the nineteenth century*, 1: *1801–1850* (1901), 359 · 'Reminiscences of the late bishop of Norwich, by one of his daughters', *Bentley's Miscellany*, 21 (1847), 194–203 · 'The late bishop of Norwich, and his contemporaries, by one of his daughters', *Bentley's Miscellany*, 21 (1847), 311–18 · R. Hale, 'The Church of England in Norwich during the century', *Norwich in the nineteenth century*, ed. C. Barringer (1984), 160–75 · R. G. Wilson, 'The cathedral in the Georgian period, 1720–1840', *Norwich Cathedral: church, city and diocese, 1096–1996*, ed. I. Atherton and others (1996), 578–611, esp. 581–3 · *DNB* · corresp. with Lord Grenville, BL, Add. MS 59002, fols. 45–

80 · Winchester College records · D. L. Scott, 'Henry Bathurst, a latitudinarian bishop of Norwich', *Theology*, 62 (1959), 461–4 · A. Burns, *The diocesan revival in the Church of England, c.1800–1870* (1999)
Archives Norfolk RO, MS 4257; MC271/10–12; 738/7–11; 1203/1–2 | BL, corresp. with Lord Grenville, Add. MS 59002, fols. 45–80 · U. Durham L., corresp. with Earl Grey
Likenesses W. C. Edwards, line engraving, pubd 1816 (after G. Hayter), BM, NPG · G. Hayter, pencil drawing, c.1816, NPG · G. Hayter, portrait, c.1816, priv. coll. · M. A. Shee, oils, 1818, bishop's palace, Norwich [*see illus.*] · P. Turnerelli, bust, exh. RA 1819 · C. Turner, engraving, 1820 (after M. A. Shee) · J. Lonsdale, portrait, c.1822, priv. coll. · C. Moore, model, exh. RA 1825 · T. Kirkby, oils, 1826, New College, Oxford · A. Edouart, silhouette, 1829, Castle Museum, Norwich · H. B. Burlowe, bust, exh. RA 1833 · E. Scriven, engraving, 1834 (after T. Wageman) · T. Wageman, portrait, 1834 · F. Chantrey, marble statue, 1841, Norwich Cathedral · J. Brown, portrait (after miniature, 1853) · T. A. Dean, engraving (after M. Sharp, 1830) · T. A. Dean, stipple (after M. Sharp), BM, NPG; repro. in W. Jerdan, *National portrait gallery of illustrious and eminent personages* (1830) · J. Herbert, wax bust, bishop's house, Norwich · portrait (after G. Hayter), Rye Library, Norwich
Wealth at death 2650 bottles of wine and 2000 books were sold between 26 June and 5 July 1837: Mackie, *Norfolk annals*, 1.359

Bathurst, Henry, third Earl Bathurst (1762–1834), politician, was born on 22 May 1762, the second of six children of Henry *Bathurst, second Earl Bathurst (1714–1794), lord chancellor, and his second wife, Tryphena, daughter of Thomas Scawen of Maidwell, Northamptonshire. He had one brother and four sisters. He was educated at Eton College from 1773 to 1778. In April 1779 he matriculated at Christ Church, Oxford, where his close friends were his second cousin and former tutor, Canon Henry Bathurst (whom he persuaded Pitt to appoint bishop of Norwich in 1805), William Wyndham Grenville, and Richard Wellesley. Bathurst did not take his degree but on 16 June 1814 was awarded a DCL at the university's encaenia honouring the duke of Wellington, the rulers of Russia and Prussia, and other victors in the war against Napoleon. In 1781–3 he travelled in France and Germany, the only time that Bathurst—who was to have long-term responsibility for foreign and colonial affairs—ever left his own country. On 1 April 1789 he married Georgina Lennox (d. 20 Jan 1841), daughter of Lord George Henry *Lennox and sister of Charles, fourth duke of Richmond. They had five sons, one of whom died in infancy, and four daughters.

In 1783, as Lord Apsley, Bathurst became MP for the family borough of Cirencester, which he represented until he succeeded to the peerage in 1794. On the formation of William Pitt's ministry at the end of 1783 he was appointed a lord of the Admiralty, leaving that board in 1789 to become a lord of the Treasury. In 1791 he asked to resign, probably to concentrate on family matters since his father was in failing health. In 1793 he returned as a commissioner of the Board of Control (and was consequently sworn of the privy council), where he remained to the end of Pitt's government in 1801. From 1790 to his death he was a teller of the exchequer and from 1800 clerk of the crown in chancery (jointly with his brother Apsley Bathurst until the latter's death in 1816).

After the fragmentation of Pitt's overwhelming political combination in 1801 Bathurst began to take a more prominent part in politics, trying to reconcile the factions to act again under his mentor and friend on the basis of opposing France until it was reduced to its pre-war borders and leaving Catholic emancipation alone. He had accepted the necessity of Catholic relief to reconcile Ireland to the union of 1801 but soon concluded that the attitude of the king and parliament made it a dangerous and divisive issue. He also encouraged Pitt to criticize the peace of Amiens. When Pitt formed his second government in 1804 he insisted that Bathurst become master of the Royal Mint. During his interrupted tenure, the mint moved from the Tower of London to the new building designed by Robert Smirke, whom Bathurst appointed surveyor. Bathurst was not, however, able to win Grenville's support for the ministry. At the formation of the 'ministry of all the talents' by Grenville after Pitt's death in January 1806, Bathurst refused to continue in office. But he remained hopeful, particularly after the death of Charles James Fox in September, that his friend's government would be the foundation for reuniting Pitt's followers. In 1807 he warned Grenville against the proposed Catholic concessions that destroyed his ministry.

In the governments of the duke of Portland in 1807–9 and Spencer Perceval in 1809–12 Bathurst was in cabinet as president of the Board of Trade, as Britain countered Napoleon's Continental System with orders in council regulating shipping to the continent. Since this was unpaid, he was again master of the mint. For six weeks in October–November 1809 he was also foreign secretary until Lord Wellesley could be summoned from his diplomatic mission to Spain. Both prime ministers depended on Bathurst's moderation, conciliatory manner, and commitment to preserving the administration in dealing with more fractious and ambitious colleagues.

On the formation of Lord Liverpool's government in June 1812 Bathurst was appointed secretary of state for war and the colonies when William Wellesley-Pole refused. For the next ten years he, Liverpool, and the foreign secretary, Lord Castlereagh, were effectively an inner cabinet that decided foreign, military, and colonial policy. Bathurst did not spare himself in supporting the war in the Peninsula, though he could never supply all that the duke of Wellington wanted. They exchanged over 500 letters between 1812 and 1814 and, despite Wellington's frequently sharp tone, developed great mutual respect and confidence. This relationship was important again in the desperate Waterloo campaign of 1815 and in politics after 1818. Two of Bathurst's sons served at Waterloo and sent interesting accounts to their parents. Bathurst also had to provide resources for the war against the United States in 1812–14, but this had to take second place to the conflict in Europe until Napoleon's first abdication. As the minister responsible for Napoleon's confinement at St Helena, he was criticized by Napoleon's admirers in Britain for the restrictions placed on him, though Lady Holland thanked Bathurst for allowing her to send small gifts to her hero. In 1817 he was made KG at the express wish of the prince regent for his part in the victorious wars.

After 1815, and increasingly after 1822 when George

Canning succeeded Castlereagh and consulted Bathurst less, Bathurst could devote more attention to the colonies. The most pressing concerns were the protectorate of the Ionian Islands, particularly after the Greek revolt in 1821, and from 1823 the amelioration of slavery. Bathurst pressed the colonial governors hard but the West Indies legislatures refused to adopt a programme to improve conditions and gradually emancipate the slaves. He was concerned with religious instruction to prepare for freedom and, although no evangelical himself, favoured such ministers in all colonies. In an age of military governors he upheld the authority of the crown and its agents but privately urged governors to use their powers with restraint. In 1824–5, principally in response to the anti-slavery campaign, the Colonial Office was enlarged and reorganized, and the post of second under-secretary, abolished in 1816, was restored.

In 1827, when Canning formed his ministry after Liverpool's stroke, he asked Bathurst, the most moderate of those associated with Wellington, to remain but to move from the Colonial to the Home office. Bathurst, however, resigned with his friends. He ended his long political career as lord president of the council in Wellington's government from 1828 to 1830. Like the duke he opposed the first Reform Bill in 1831–2, believing that it would destroy rather than improve the constitution. He died at his London home, 16 Arlington Street, after a short illness on 27 July 1834 and was buried in the abbey church at Cirencester. Charles Greville, a family friend and Bathurst's (ungrateful) secretary from 1812 to 1821, summed him up fairly, if rather harshly, as:

> a very amiable man with a good understanding, though his talents were far from brilliant, a High Churchman and a High Tory, but a cool Politician, a bad speaker, a good writer, greatly averse to changes, but acquiescing in many. He was nervous and reserved, with a good deal of humour, and habitually a jester. (*Greville Memoirs*, 3.65)

NEVILLE THOMPSON

Sources *Report on the manuscripts of Earl Bathurst, preserved at Cirencester Park*, HMC, 76 (1923) · *Supplementary despatches* (correspondence) *and memoranda of Field Marshal Arthur, duke of Wellington*, ed. A. R. Wellesley, second duke of Wellington, 15 vols. (1858–72) · *Despatches, correspondence, and memoranda of Field Marshal Arthur, duke of Wellington*, ed. A. R. Wellesley, second duke of Wellington, 8 vols. (1867–80) · N. D. McLachlan, 'Bathurst at the colonial office, 1812–27: a reconnaissance', *Historical Studies* [University of Melbourne], 13 (1967–9), 477–502 · N. Thompson, *Earl Bathurst and the British empire* (1999) · GEC, *Peerage* · HoP, *Commons* · *The Greville memoirs, 1814–1860*, ed. L. Strachey and R. Fulford, 8 vols. (1938) · *The Times* (29 July 1834)
Archives BL, corresp. and papers, loan 57 · Glos. RO, Cirencester MSS · NL Scot., dispatches and papers received · Surrey HC, secret service accounts | BL, corresp. with Lord Aberdeen, Add. MSS 43074–43260 · BL, corresp. with Sir William A'Court, Add. MSS 41511–41523 · BL, corresp. with Lord Grenville, Add. MS 58944 · BL, corresp. with Lord Liverpool, Add. MSS 38247–38575 · BL, corresp. with Sir Hudson Lowe, Add. MSS 20111–20233, *passim* · BL, corresp. with Sir H. Lowe, Add. MS 49508, *passim* · BL, corresp. with Sir Robert Peel, Add. MSS 40226–40398 · BL, corresp. with comte de Puisaye, Add. MS 7981 · BL, corresp. with George Rose, Add. MS 42773 · BL, corresp. with Lord Wellesley, Add. MSS 37288–37314, *passim* · BL OIOC, corresp. with Mary Skelton, MS Eur. E 334 · CKS, corresp. with Lord Camden · Cumbria AS, Carlisle, letters to Lord

Lonsdale · Derbys. RO, corresp. with Sir R. J. Wilmot-Horton · LPL, corresp. with Bishop Howley · Mitchell L., NSW, letters to Sir Robert Wilmot Horton · Mount Stuart Trust Archive, Mount Stuart, Rothesay, letters to Lord Hastings · NA Scot., corresp. with Lord Dalhousie · NA Scot., letters to Sir Alexander Hope · NL Scot., corresp. with Sir Alexander Cochrane and Thomas Cochrane · NL Scot., corresp. with Sir Francis Graham · NL Scot., corresp. with Lord Melville · NL Scot., dispatches and letters to Lord Stuart De Rothesay · PRO, letters to William Pitt, PRO 30/8 · PRO NIre., corresp. with Lord Castlereagh · Sandon Hall, Staffordshire, Harrowby Manuscript Trust, corresp. with Lord Harrowby · U. Nott. L., letters to Lord William Bentinck · U. Nott. L., letters to fourth duke of Newcastle · U. Southampton L., letters to duke of Wellington [copies]
Likenesses N. Dance, portrait, 1776 (with his brother), Cirencester, Gloucestershire · T. Watson, mezzotint, pubd 1776 (with his brother; after N. Dance), BM · T. Phillips, portrait, 1809, Cirencester, Gloucestershire · T. Lawrence, oils, c.1818, Wellington Museum, London · T. Lawrence, oils, c.1820–1823, Royal Collection · T. Lawrence, portrait, 1820–23, Windsor Castle · W. Salter, oils, 1834, NPG · F. Chantrey, marble bust, Cirencester, Gloucestershire · G. Hayter, group portrait, oils (*The trial of Queen Caroline, 1820*), NPG · G. Jones, group portrait, oils (*Catholic Emancipation Act, 1829*), Palace of Westminster, London; on loan · H. Meyer, stipple (after T. Phillips), BM, NPG; repro. in *The British gallery of contemporary portraits* (1810)

Bathurst, Henry (1781–1844). *See under* Bathurst, Henry (bap. 1744, d. 1837).

Bathurst, John (d. 1659), physician, was born in Sussex, the second son of Dr John Bathurst of Goudhurst, Kent, and Dorothy Maplisden, of Marden, Kent, daughter of Captain Edward Maplisden, a mariner. The Bathursts and Maplisdens were minor gentry families of long standing in Kent. The year of Bathurst's birth is unknown. At his death in 1659 he was said by his colleague Baldwin Hamey to be fifty-two years of age. Yet this date does not tally with Bathurst's educational history. He matriculated from Pembroke College, Cambridge, as a sizar in 1614: received his BA in 1618 and his MA in 1621, but did not receive his MD until 1637. In the interim he was headmaster at Richmond grammar school in the North Riding of Yorkshire. He was connected with Yorkshire and London for the rest of his life. His years as headmaster ended in 1631; presumably he practised medicine, probably in the North Riding, for at least four years between 1631 and 1637, a term required of every fellow by the College of Physicians, London. On 27 January 1636 he married Elizabeth Willance, coheir of Brian Willance, of Clints, Yorkshire. With the marriage the lordship of Clints manor passed to Bathurst and his wife, and remained in the Bathurst family until 1761.

Immediately after taking his MD in 1637 Bathurst moved to London, where on 13 January 1637 he was first mentioned in the annals of the Royal College of Physicians. He may have been waiting for the formal granting of his degree. On 22 December 1637 he asked that he might be tested on 'questions relating to the method of treating a deep and unclean ulcer accompanied by inflammation: to which he fully and appositely gave satisfaction' (annals, RCP Lond., 3.469). After a few more questions by Dr Argent, Bathurst was elected both candidate and fellow on the same day, 22 December 1637. Bathurst appears to have come to the college in the company of Thomas Sheafe, who received his own MD from Pembroke in 1636.

Bathurst had a distinguished career in the college. He was chosen as a censor in 1641 and again in 1650. In 1657 he was elevated to the honoured office of elect, a position left vacant by the death of William Harvey in that year. Though a fellow in good standing, Bathurst was not regular in his attendance at the college. Some of his time may have been spent in handling his affairs in Yorkshire. On 23 November 1643 he was assessed at £200 by the parliamentary committee empowered to raise money for the war effort against Charles I. This was an average assessment for a college physician and allowance was made for Bathurst because he had already paid some of his assessment in Yorkshire. His residence in the City was in the ward of Farringdon Without, at least for the years 1643 to 1645. He was steadily acquiring wealth and enough fame for a young physician, Thomas Wharton, to be practising under his tutelage during 1645, if not longer. Wharton went on to a distinguished career as an anatomist, and made discoveries in the structure and functioning of human glands.

In 1649 Bathurst was visited by Samuel Hartlib, who wrote that Bathurst:

> told me his whole design for founding a College for making and training up of schoolmasters by constituting of a master, fellows, candidates and classes. The revenue to be 4 thousand a year by the State, who should lay a tax upon every person for this purpose. This College to be an inspector and seminary of all schoolmasters of all free-schools throughout the kingdom who are to furnish all places by their approbation. (Turnbull, 64)

Bathurst's plan did not come to fruition, but he continued to do all that he could, leaving an additional £20 in his will for the maintenance of two more impoverished scholars at the 'new University or College at Durham so long as it continues'. The Cromwellian college did not long survive the protectorate. Bathurst had but one requirement for all his poor scholars: that they be 'pious, virtuous and competently learned'.

Bathurst may be best known as Oliver Cromwell's physician. He also did service in 1653 tending the sick seamen of Cromwell's navy, engaged in a naval trade war with the Dutch. He was mentioned with approval by George Starkey as one of the physicians to the Ely House and Savoy hospitals who were 'chymically given' (Webster, 296). Bathurst's growing wealth and importance in Yorkshire secured his election as MP for Richmond in 1656, and again in 1658, and he is remembered as one of those parliamentarians who unsuccessfully urged Cromwell to accept the English crown. Yet, despite these ties, he numbered prominent royalists such as Philip Warwick and Sir Orlando Bridgeman among his closest friends. He was also physician to the family of Sir Richard and Lady Fanshawe, and intervened with Cromwell in 1651 to secure Fanshawe's release from prison on the grounds of poor health. Along with Thomas Ridgley he again successfully treated Fanshawe in 1656. A fashionable practice and shrewd investments in Yorkshire lands and mines, where

he dealt harshly with customary tenants, made Bathurst a very wealthy man. His income was said to be £2000 a year at the time of his death in 1659: this despite his giving all fees earned on Sunday to the poor. After his purchase of the nearby lordship of Arkengarthdale in 1656, he settled money on a schoolmaster to teach freely all children of tenants of the manor in elementary subjects and the rudiments of Latin. He made a similar provision for the Helwith School at New Forest, another manor which he had purchased. Bathurst, John Clarke, and Edmund Trench were held up by a puritan preacher in the Restoration as proof to his flock that piety and worldly success were not incompatible.

Bathurst's own success is evident from his will which runs to some fourteen pages. His family was large, and he provided well for all, including his wife, Elizabeth; seven sons, Christopher, Philip, Moses, John, Theodore, Charles, and Francis; and three daughters, Dorothy, Elizabeth, and Constance. His eldest son, Christopher, followed his father into the medical profession, took an MD at Padua in 1653, and practised in Lincolnshire, though the money and lands bequeathed to him probably obviated the need to work. Philip also had a trust fund, and was left a house in the Strand-without-Temple, London. Moses became a wealthy City merchant. To John, along with the usual generous allowance, went a house in Redriff, Surrey, and Bathurst's own London dwelling in the parish of St Ann Blackfriars. Theodore Bathurst became a barrister, and, like his father, MP for Richmond from 1690 to 1695; Charles Bathurst's management of the family lands in Yorkshire was the envy of the neighbouring landlords. Sizeable bequests of cash went in 1660 to Bathurst's married daughter, Dorothy, and handsome dowries to his unmarried daughters, Elizabeth and Constance. His own experience of struggling through Cambridge as a poor sizar made him especially sensitive to the needs of other poor scholars and schoolmasters. By his will of 1659 he established two exhibitions at Cambridge for poor Richmond grammar school boys. He also left £100 to the College of Physicians. His judgement and prudence in nearly everything he touched laid the foundation of his family's continued prosperity well on into the next century.

Bathurst died on 26 April 1659, probably in the parish of St Ann Blackfriars, and may have been buried in St Ann's Church, or its environs, although direct evidence is lacking: the church was completely destroyed in the great fire of 1666.   WILLIAM BIRKEN

Sources Munk, *Roll* · annals, RCP Lond., 3.469 · Venn, *Alum. Cant.* · *VCH Yorkshire* · Foster, *Alum. Oxon.* · Wood, *Ath. Oxon.* · G. H. Turnbull, *Hartlib, Dury and Comenius: gleanings from Hartlib's papers* (1947) · A. Fanshawe, *Memoirs of Lady Fanshawe* (1905) · W. Berry, *County genealogies: pedigrees of the families in the county of Kent* (1830) · *CSP dom.*, 1653–4 · R. B. Shatter, *The social ideas of religious leaders, 1660–1688* (1940) · G. J. Armytage, ed., *A visitation of the county of Surrey, begun … 1662, finished … 1668*, Harleian Society, 60 (1910) · R. Fieldhouse, *A history of Richmond and Swaledale* (1978) · A. M. Everitt, *The county committee of Kent in the Civil War* (1957) · D. C. Coleman, *Sir John Banks, baronet and businessman* (1963) · M. A. E. Green, ed., *Calendar of the proceedings of the committee for advance of money, 1642–1656*, 3 vols., PRO (1888) · C. Webster, *The great instauration: science,* *medicine and reform, 1626–1660* (1975) • will, PRO, PROB 11/301, sig. 237

Bathurst, Katherine (1862–1933), inspector of schools, was born on 10 May 1862 at Diddington, Huntingdonshire, daughter of the Revd Frederick Bathurst (1826/7–1910), who was vicar of the parish and later archdeacon of Bedford, and his first wife, Catherine Georgiana Moore (*d.* 1902). She was educated at home and at a private school in Brighton, received further tuition in Dresden, and then travelled through Italy and Switzerland. Miss Bathurst taught with some success at Morley College for Working Men and Women, London, 1894–5, and though she never undertook a formal course of study leading to a qualification, she attended classes and lectures at the recently formed London School of Economics for two years, 1895–7.

During the last quarter of the nineteenth century there was an expansion of women inspectorates in various government departments. In 1896 the education department had appointed its first two women sub-inspectors to supervise schools with girls' and infant departments. A year later, in September 1897, Miss Bathurst became the third sub-inspector. Sent to work in the East End of London under the supervision of a chief inspector, she was, by her own admission, soon in trouble with the teachers on account of being 'unjudiciously plain spoken'. She was transferred to another chief inspector in the Lambeth district, the Revd Charles D. Dupont, who soon reported to Sir John Gorst, vice-president of the committee of the privy council on education, that she was 'a very clever woman and capable of becoming a very dangerous one' (*Reminiscences*, March–April 1932, Bathurst MSS), and was unsuitable as an inspector.

Presumably, she heard this comment from Gorst himself (his wife was Miss Bathurst's mother's cousin), as they corresponded privately on departmental and political matters. She was posted to Cardiff and Barry districts in February 1899, where her outspokenness in the infant schools she visited alarmed Gorst. Miss Bathurst also concerned herself with the improvement of conditions of service of the sub-inspectors, especially on the issue of the burden of marking teachers' certificate papers, complaining directly to the secretary of the department, Sir George Kekewich. In April 1901 Miss Bathurst, along with the other women sub-inspectors, was given the new title of junior inspector. She requested a transfer at the end of 1901 and was posted to Oxfordshire under Edmond Holmes, where she was once more officially reprimanded for her conduct.

In 1904 Robert Morant, permanent secretary of the Board of Education, proposed a separate section of the inspectorate for women, each member to be entitled woman inspector. They were to be based in towns on the staff of the divisional inspector. As a result of this reorganization, Miss Bathurst moved to Manchester in March 1904 to work under E. M. Sneyd-Kynnersley, an aloof and autocratic divisional inspector. Morant suggested that the first inquiry which the women inspectors should undertake was an investigation into the instruction given to children between three and five years in public elementary schools.

During the survey Miss Bathurst was greatly disturbed by the conditions in which the infants were taught and by the teaching methods used. Her criticisms echoed many of the concerns earlier voiced by women members of school boards about the brutality with which young children were treated in elementary schools. She found that the premises were often ill-ventilated, overcrowded, and unhygienic. Given the inadequate home conditions of many of the town children, the existing school system for the younger ones needed to be replaced by nurseries with playrooms at their centre and which also contained hammocks. Miss Bathurst deplored the overemphasis on the three Rs and the attainment of high standards at an early age. Blackboards and books were to be banished and their places to be taken by 'occupations' and play. She noted that needlework, for up to an hour a day, was begun at the four- and five-year-old stage: 'little children sitting on seats without backs, whose feet cannot reach the floor, are kept in the constrained position necessary for needlework for no object whatever except to satisfy the requirements of the inspector' (Board of Education, *Reports on Children under Five Years of Age in Public Elementary Schools*, 1905, 43).

Urged on by Gorst, who had been manoeuvred out of office by Morant, Miss Bathurst voiced many criticisms in her report, including the shortcomings of some of her superiors. After reading it the lord president, Londonderry, who had consulted Morant, ordered that she must resign from the service in February 1905. For her part, Miss Bathurst produced a supplementary report on the day of her resignation, attacking the existing system of inspection. Morant wished to suppress the supplementary report, but she insisted that it was published together with her initial report. When the *Reports on Children under Five Years of Age in Public Elementary Schools* appeared in 1905 Miss Bathurst's two reports carried numerous footnotes, written by Morant, contradicting many of the statements she made, a unique example of an official document in which differences between a ministry and one of its servants were aired publicly. The report's publication resulted in widespread sympathy for Miss Bathurst, and some of her criticisms were acknowledged by the board in the 1905 code, which encouraged a more humane attitude to the teaching of infants.

It does not appear that Miss Bathurst gained further employment, though she applied for many posts. In articles published in the *Nineteenth Century and After* (1905–7) she continued her campaign to improve the condition of the young, emphasizing the need for nurseries and drawing attention to the lack of educational opportunities for girls as compared with boys. She died at her home, Highfield, Queens Road, Ryde, Isle of Wight, on 12 March 1933.   PETER GORDON

Sources P. Gordon, 'Katherine Bathurst: a controversial woman inspector', *History of Education*, 17 (1988), 193–207 • priv. coll., Bathurst MSS • H. E. Boothroyd, *A history of the inspectorate* (1923) • b. cert. • d. cert.

Archives priv. coll.
Wealth at death £2697 16*s*. 1*d*.: probate, 10 May 1933, *CGPLA Eng. & Wales*

Bathurst [*née* Borthwick], **Lilias Margaret Frances**, Countess Bathurst (1871–1965), newspaper publisher, was born on 12 October 1871 at 60 Eaton Place, London, the elder child and only daughter of Algernon *Borthwick, Baron Glenesk (1830–1908), journalist, newspaper publisher, and politician, and his wife, Alice Beatrice (1841–1898), daughter of Thomas *Lister, author. On 15 November 1893 she married Seymour Henry, seventh Earl Bathurst (1864–1943), who had succeeded his father the previous year. They had three sons and a daughter. Her husband was an aristocratic landowner whose estates amounted to 12,000 acres, mainly centred on Cirencester Park, Gloucestershire, and whose principal publication was *The Breeding of Foxhounds* (1926), but Lady Bathurst is chiefly notable as the proprietor of the *Morning Post* from the death of her father in 1908 until 1924. Algernon Borthwick, when editor, had bought the paper in 1876 and restored its fortunes. His son Oliver predeceased him, so Lady Bathurst found herself inheriting, late in 1908, the oldest surviving London daily paper (founded in 1772), with which she was the third generation of her family to be involved.

Lady Bathurst, who found politics absorbingly interesting, inherited also her father's Conservative convictions. These did not necessarily match official party policies, nor was the party concerned in the paper's business. Rather, her guiding principle, like her father's, was 'independence'—of thought and of ownership. In later years she described her principles as loyalty to the crown, to the church, and to every cause which was honourable and right. In practice this meant that the *Morning Post* was imperialist, protectionist, intransigent about Irish nationalism, strong on military matters, against female suffrage, and in general die-hard. It was also somewhat aristocratic, a fact reflected in its social columns and in the long-standing appeal of its classified advertisements to persons seeking or offering employment in domestic service.

Lady Bathurst argued her points with her editors but she rarely wrote in the paper. Her first editor, already in post, was Fabian Ware. The two did not see sufficiently eye to eye, and Ware may have been too unbusinesslike and too liberal in his choice of contributors. In July 1911 Lady Bathurst replaced him with H. A. Gwynne, who had just parted company with *The Standard* and was urged on her by Rudyard Kipling. The appointment proved critical, for Gwynne remained editor right up to the paper's amalgamation with the *Daily Telegraph* in 1937. Proprietor and editor enjoyed a harmonious relationship: Lady Bathurst insisted that she be kept informed of matters involving policy or large expense; while Gwynne thought a proprietor, editor, and manager should ideally resemble a cabinet, airing differences of opinion but showing a united front to the outside world. Lady Bathurst of course got her way when she wanted. She backed up Gwynne in political rows, such as when the paper was prosecuted in 1918 for flouting the wartime censorship, and accepted Gwynne's ceaseless politicking among the Unionist Party leaders.

Lilias Margaret Frances Bathurst, Countess Bathurst (1871–1965), by Philip A. de Laszlo, 1919

However, she had enthusiasms of her own, including Zeppelins. 'It is like a glove on a hand' exclaimed Lord Roberts as the *Morning Post* airship slid into its hangar (Simonis, 37). There followed a ripping sound, and the airship collapsed. During the First World War, Lady Bathurst worked for a time as a nurse in France.

Lady Bathurst dismissed attempts to make her extend her newspaper interests. As early as 1914, and again in 1918, she considered disposing of the *Morning Post* itself. After the war the paper's finances worsened steadily, but Lady Bathurst was not the type to seek improvement by a change of editor. In December 1922, with circulation down to about 50,000 from its profitable peak of nearly 90,000, she instructed her son, Lord Apsley, to look for a purchaser. Negotiations with the Conservative directors of the *Yorkshire Post* and with a separate group of Conservative Party financiers stalled. On 14 April 1924 a paragraph in the *Morning Post* announced the sale instead to 'a body of influential Conservatives with whom the Duke of Northumberland is associated'. Although the new owners intended to continue the paper's traditions 'by more modern methods', Lord Apsley remained a director. In what *The Times* (14 April 1924) called an announcement 'issued officially', Lady Bathurst blamed heavy taxation.

Lady Bathurst enjoyed helping advance Lord Apsley's political career. He was a Conservative MP for most of the twenty years from 1922 until his death in a flying accident in 1942. Her husband died in September 1943. Lady Bathurst lived on until 30 December 1965, dying of senile decay at her home, The Cranhams, Chesterton, Cirencester, Gloucestershire.   COLIN SEYMOUR-URE

Sources *The rasp of war: the letters of H. A. Gwynne to the Countess Bathurst, 1914–1918*, ed. K. Wilson (1988) · W. Hindle, *The Morning Post, 1772–1937: portrait of a newspaper* (1937) · H. Simonis, *The street of ink* (1917) · *The Times* (25 Nov 1908) · *The Times* (27 Sept 1943) · *The Times* (29 April 1949) · *The Times* (27 June 1950) · *The Times* (1 Jan 1966) · 'The *Morning Post*', *The Times* (14 April 1924) · S. E. Koss, *The rise and fall of the political press in Britain*, 2 (1984) · K. M. Wilson, 'The *Yorkshire Post*, Conservative Central Office, and the negotiations for the purchase of the *Morning Post*, 1923–24', *Publishing History*, 33 (1993), 89–94 · G. Boyce, 'The fourth estate: the reappraisal of a concept', *Newspaper history: from the seventeenth century to the present day*, ed. J. Curran, P. Wingate, and G. Boyce (1978), 19–40 · C. À Court Repington, *The First World War*, 2 (1920) · GEC, *Peerage*, new edn, vol. 6 · Burke, *Peerage* (1970) · 'Ware, Sir Fabian Arthur Goulstone', *DNB* · 'Borthwick, Sir Algernon, first Baron Glenesk', *DNB* · 'Gwynne, Howell Arthur', *DNB* · *CGPLA Eng. & Wales* (1966) · b. cert. · m. cert. · d. cert.
Archives U. Leeds, Brotherton L., corresp. and papers incl. MSS relating to the British League of Help and Morning Post business | Bodl. Oxf., H. A. Gwynne MSS
Likenesses P. A. de Laszlo, portrait, 1919, priv. coll. [*see illus.*]
Wealth at death £17,029: probate, 14 April 1966, *CGPLA Eng. & Wales*

Bathurst, Ralph (1619/20–1704), dean of Wells and college head, was born at Hothorpe, Northamptonshire, the fifth of thirteen sons and four daughters of George Bathurst (*c*.1579–1656) and his wife, Elizabeth Villiers. He was educated at Coventry Free School, and matriculated at Gloucester Hall, Oxford, at the age of fourteen on 10 November 1634. Within a few days, however, he migrated to the college his father had attended, Trinity, to which he would be attached in one capacity or another for the next seventy years. Trinity's president was Ralph Kettell, whose marriage to Bathurst's widowed grandmother made him effectively Bathurst's grandfather. On 5 June 1637 he was elected scholar. He graduated BA in 1638, and was elected fellow on 5 July 1640.

The civil war years that followed were personally disastrous to Bathurst on several counts. Six of his twelve brothers were killed fighting for the royalists. Bathurst himself felt compelled to abandon his studies towards the degree of BD in favour of the more practical and less controversial art of medicine, and he seems to have left the university for a time for this purpose. On 2 March 1644 he was ordained priest by Robert Skinner, bishop of Oxford, and in the following years he is said to have assisted Skinner with clandestine ordinations, although there is no firm evidence of this.

Bathurst's close friends included Dr Thomas Willis, and in 1650 these two doctors and others assisted Dr William Petty in the resuscitation of Anne Greene, who had been hanged at Oxford for murdering her child. The pamphlet published to describe this event, *Newes from the Dead* (1651), includes several epigrams by Bathurst, not all under his name, which display an aptitude for occasional verse in English and Latin. Other poetry of his that survives includes prefatory verses to Hobbes's *Human Nature* (1650) and panegyrics to Charles I, Cromwell, and Charles II. In

Ralph Bathurst (1619/20–1704), by David Loggan

1654 Bathurst was awarded the degree of doctor of medicine on the strength of work he seems to have undertaken caring for the sick and wounded of the navy. He remained a fellow of Trinity and was instrumental in the election of his friend Seth Ward as president in 1659, though Ward was ejected after the Restoration.

In 1662 Bathurst was involved in the foundation of the Royal Society, a project which grew out of the scientific circle that met at Wadham College and whose members included Bathurst, Willis, Petty, John Wilkins, Robert Boyle, and Christopher Wren. His connection with the Royal Society continued for many years, in the form of active membership of the Oxford branch and of benefactions. In 1663 Bathurst was made a chaplain to Charles II. On 10 September 1664 he succeeded Hannibal Potter as president of Trinity, and took advantage of the opportunity to marry the accomplished Mary Tristram (1617–1690), widow of John Palmer, president of All Souls, on 31 December of the same year. Her tomb notes her expertise in 'most of the chiefe languages, both antient and moderne' (Warton, 216) as well as her three children by her previous marriage: the marriage with Bathurst was childless.

At Trinity, Bathurst embarked upon a vigorous programme of fund-raising and building, and started by commissioning his friend Wren to design a new building (1665). Although chafing at Bathurst's shrewd insistence that it had to form part of a quadrangle—quadrangles were better for fund-raising—Wren complied. This was the first of a number of building projects at Trinity, part of a concerted campaign to attract 'persons of Quality' to the college (Blakiston, 157).

From 1673 to 1676 Bathurst served as vice-chancellor of the university, in which capacity he repaired the university church, endeavoured to improve the quality of the sermons, and defended the privileges of the university with regard to wine licences. He permitted the king's players to perform at Oxford in the summer term, which earned him a panegyric from John Dryden. He had also taken up the post of dean of Wells in 1670—a commitment which required a little bending of Trinity's statutes—and spent two months a year in residence there, applying his talent for organization. However, when offered the bishopric of Bristol in 1691 he refused it, preferring to concentrate on discharging the duties he already had.

Bathurst's wife died on 14 April 1690, and was buried at Bishop's Lydiard in Somerset. At Trinity his building campaign was crowned by the magnificent baroque chapel (begun in 1691, consecrated on 12 April 1694), designed probably by Henry Aldrich with input from Wren, and featuring wood carvings probably by Grinling Gibbons. Bathurst put up £2000 of his own money for this project as well as engaging in a vigorous and witty fund-raising campaign. A sample of his style can be seen in the following condolence with one unwilling donor who uses gout as an excuse:

> I am sorry ... that your [ladyship] hath been so severely handled with That Malady which is usually accounted the Companion of the Rich: and that my letter should have the Ill Fortune to come when it was in your Right hand, which the Scripture makes to be the Giving Hand. But since I find it so well recovered as to write with your wonted Accuratenesse, I hope it will also ere long be able to extend it selfe.   (Trinity College, MSS misc. vol. 1, 93d/158)

The success of this strategy manifested itself in the opulence of Trinity chapel and, less tangibly, in a rise in the status of the college within the university.

Still president of the college into his eighties, Bathurst was 'stark blind, deaf, and memory lost' (Blakiston, 159) in his final years, and fell while walking in Trinity's garden. His refusal to have the broken thigh bone set—he is said to have argued that an old man's bones had no marrow in them—may have hastened his death, which took place on 14 June 1704. He was buried, not in Garsington churchyard alongside his mentor Kettell, as he had requested, but in the college chapel he had built.

Bathurst's own gifts as a preacher, physician, administrator, and wit were considerable, but overshadowed by his unselfish encouragement of others. Writers including John Aubrey, Anthony Wood, William Derham, and Robert Plot had cause to be grateful for his provision of information and practical assistance: other protégés included Arthur Charlett and his own nephew Allen Bathurst. He corresponded with many of the leading intellectual figures of the day, and sought in his dealings with the university and the Royal Society to provide an environment in which learning could flourish. His best epitaph, perhaps,

is from his own will: 'It hath been my endeavour ... by an honest calling to do some good in my generation' (Warton, 193).   MATTHEW STEGGLE

Sources T. Warton, *The life and literary remains of Ralph Bathurst* (1761) • H. E. D. Blakiston, *Trinity College* (1898), 154–83 • R. T. Gunther, *Early science in Oxford*, 4: *The Philosophical Society* (1925) • H. Lyons, *The Royal Society, 1660–1940: a history of its administration under its charters* (1944) • L. S. Colchester, ed., *Wells Cathedral: a history* (1982) • Trinity College, Oxford, MSS Misc. vol. 1
Archives Trinity College, Oxford, papers
Likenesses G. Kneller, oils, 1694, Trinity College, Oxford • W. Sonman, oils, 1698 (after D. Loggan), Trinity College, Oxford • bust, 1704? (after death mask), Trinity College, Oxford • A. Walker, engraving, 1761 (after D. Loggan, 1676), repro. in Warton, *Life and literary remains of Ralph Bathurst*, frontispiece • D. Loggan, line engraving, BM, NPG [*see illus.*]
Wealth at death considerable; total specific legacies over £300: will

Bathurst, Richard (1722/3–1762), physician and writer, was born in Jamaica, the son of Colonel Richard Bathurst (*d. c.*1755), proprietor of the Orange River estate. His father retired to Lincoln in 1750, having left his hereditary holdings in disarray. He brought with him Francis Barber, an eight-year-old Jamaican slave to whom he willed his freedom in 1754. Barber was passed from the service of his son to Samuel Johnson in 1752. '"My dear friend Dr. Bathurst", (said Johnson with a warmth of approbation,) "declared he was glad that his father ... had left his affairs in total ruin, because having no estate, he was not under the temptation of having slaves"' (Boswell, *Life*, 4.28).

Bathurst was in London in the late 1730s, attending the lectures of Dr Frank Nicholls at St Thomas's Hospital. In February 1739 he was admitted pensioner of Peterhouse, Cambridge, aged sixteen. He took the degree of MB in 1745, and was a physician at the Middlesex Hospital, London, from September 1754 to 1756. On 13 January 1757 he wrote to Samuel Johnson from Barbados and again from Jamaica on 18 March. His letters suggest that he left England because of poverty, and Hawkins reports that Bathurst told Johnson 'that in the course of ten years' exercise of his faculty, he had never opened his hand to more than one guinea' (Hawkins, 209).

While in London, Bathurst was a member of the Ivy Lane Club and Samuel Johnson's dearest friend. On 22 March 1753 Johnson wrote to the publisher George Strahan proposing a 'Geographical Dictionary' to be compiled by Bathurst. The work never materialized, nor did Bathurst make any contributions to *The Adventurer*, the periodical edited by Johnson's friend John Hawkesworth from 1752 to 1754, although he has long been associated with the project (Fairer, 139–41). While Johnson was the editor of the *Literary Magazine* in 1756 Bathurst contributed an article, 'Strait lacing in stays' (1.14–16) and (probably) a review of *Physiological Essays* by Robert Whytt (1.86–9). What else he may have written is unknown.

Bathurst joined the British expedition against Havana in 1762 and died there of a fever some time before its conclusion on 12 August. Johnson wrote to a friend that the 'conquest [had been] too dearly obtained; for Bathurst died before it. "*Vix Priamus tanti totaque Troja fuit*" ('scarcely were Priam and all Troy of such great value'; *Letters of Samuel Johnson*, 1.211).   ROBERT DEMARIA, JUN.

Sources T. Lawrence, *GM*, 1st ser., 57 (1787), 192 • Boswell, *Life* • J. Boswell, *The life of Samuel Johnson*, ed. J. W. Croker, rev. J. Wright, [another edn], 10 vols. (1835) • J. Wiltshire, *Samuel Johnson in the medical world* (1991) • D. Fairer, 'Authorship problems in *The Adventurer*', *Review of English Studies*, new ser., 25 (1974), 137–51 • J. Hawkins, *The life of Samuel Johnson, LL.D.*, 2nd edn (1787) • D. D. Eddy, ed., *Literary Magazine*, 3 vols. (1978) • A. L. Reade, *Johnsonian gleanings*, 2: *Francis Barber: the doctor's negro servant* (privately printed, London, 1912) • *The letters of Samuel Johnson*, ed. B. Redford, 5 vols. (1992–4) • Venn, *Alum. Cant.* • *DNB*

Bathurst, Theodore (*c*.1587–1652), Latin poet and Church of England clergyman, is said to have descended from an ancient family of Hothorpe in Northamptonshire (*DNB*), though a later holder of the name is found in a family of Kentish origin (Armytage, 8). The premature death of his father is mentioned in some dedicatory verses that he addressed to Thomas Neville, master of Trinity College, Cambridge, whence he matriculated as sizar in June 1602. He was soon after encouraged to migrate to Pembroke College by the master, Lancelot Andrewes, and graduated BA there in 1606; he was elected fellow in July 1608 and took his MA degree in 1609.

Early in his Cambridge career Bathurst embarked on a translation of Edmund Spenser's *The Shepheardes Calender* (1579) into Latin verse. A surviving manuscript of the January and February eclogues (BL, Add. MS 33586, fols. 75–81*v*) was dedicated to Neville, who like Andrewes had been a contemporary of Spenser's at Pembroke. In the full version, essentially complete by 1616, the main body of the poem is rendered in hexameters, with a variety of mixed metres adopted or devised for the songs. After his death two manuscripts said to bear autograph revisions came to the hands of William Dillingham, master of Emmanuel College, whose parallel-text edition appeared at London on 1 November 1653. In the same month John Hacket, acknowledging the receipt of a complimentary copy, offered some information on the genesis and text of the poem (BL, Sloane MS 1710, fol. 188). By 27 December, Sir Richard Fanshawe informed John Evelyn that the poem would 'where it's true origine shall be unknowne, passe for a Native of ould Rome, and that as farr, as the utmost bounds extend of the Commonwealth of Learning' (BL, Add. MS 28104, fol. 6*v*). Dillingham's text was included in the 1679 folio of Spenser's *Works*, and reissued in 1732 by John Ball in a handsomely illustrated edition in which the arguments to each month omitted by Bathurst are Latinized from the versions of John Hughes (1715).

Bathurst's full translation survives in variant texts of uncertain chronology. A manuscript version interleaved in a copy of the 1579 edition of Spenser's poem now in Pembroke College Library includes an autograph draft dedication to Samuel Harsnet, successor to Andrewes as master of Pembroke. Another, transcribed in two hands and differing in many readings from the version published by Dillingham, is found in a copy that once belonged to Ben Jonson (BL, C.117.b.10).

Following Lancelot Andrewes's promotion to the see of Ely (1609–19) Bathurst obtained successive livings in the diocese. In March 1616 he was presented to the college living of Thriplow, but resigned it by April 1618 on obtaining the Huntingdonshire rectory of Orton Waterville, worth £80 a year. In the following June he proceeded BD, and in February 1619 surrendered his Pembroke fellowship during a dispute over the election of a new master (BL, Harley MS 7034, fols. 158–76). His later professional standing may be gathered from his nomination by parliament, as Theophilus Bathurst, to the Westminster assembly of divines on 12 June 1643. A survey drawn up during the interregnum describes him as 'a constant preaching minister' (BL, Lansdowne MS 459, fol. 93*v*). He was buried at Orton on 17 May 1652.   W. H. KELLIHER

Sources G. J. Armytage, ed., *A visitation of the county of Surrey, begun … 1662, finished … 1668*, Harleian Society, 60 (1910) • Venn, *Alum. Cant.*, 1/1 • J. Rushworth, *Historical collections*, new edn, 8 vols. (1721–2) • L. Bradner, 'The Latin translations of Spenser's *Shepheardes calendar*', *Modern Philology*, 33 (1935), 21–6 • F. R. Johnson, *A critical bibliography of … Edmund Spenser* (1933) • T. A. Birrell, *The library of John Morris* (1976) • W. Cole's collections, BL, Add. MS 5798–6402 • T. Baker's collections, BL, Harley MSS 7028–7050; CUL, MSS Mm.1.35.–Mm.2.35
Archives BL, Lansdowne MS 459; Sloane MS 1710

Bathurst [*née* Meeking], **Violet Emily Mildred, Lady Apsley** (1895–1966), politician, was born at 3 Cavendish Square, London, on 29 April 1895, the elder of two daughters of Lieutenant Bertram Charles Christopher Spencer Meeking (1864–1900) of the Royal Hussars, and his wife, Violet Charlotte Fletcher (*d.* 1921). Her father died of enteric fever at Bloemfontein, during the Second South African War, when she was not yet five; in 1912 her mother married Herbert Johnson. On the death of her grandfather Charles Meeking in 1912, she succeeded to the family estate, Richings Park, Colnbrook, Buckinghamshire, which she sold in 1922. During the First World War she served with a voluntary aid detachment.

Violet Meeking was active in Conservative politics from the 1920s, an involvement which was reinforced by her marriage on 27 February 1924 to Allen Algernon Bathurst, Lord Apsley (1895–1942); they had two sons. Her husband was the elder son of Seymour Henry Bathurst, seventh Earl Bathurst, and his wife, Lilias Margaret Frances *Bathurst, Countess Bathurst, who, as daughter of Algernon Borthwick, Baron Glenesk, had inherited the proprietorship of the *Morning Post*. Lord Apsley was Unionist MP for Southampton (1922–9) and National Conservative MP for Bristol Central (1931–42); Lady Apsley, as she was now known, served as president of the women's Conservative associations in his constituencies (1924–9 and 1932–52). When, as parliamentary private secretary to the department of overseas trade, Lord Apsley was sent to Australia to investigate complaints about the treatment of emigrant settlers, Lady Apsley convinced him that she should accompany him to investigate the women's point of view. They published their experiences in the jointly written *Amateur Settlers* (1926).

Lady Apsley was a lifelong participant in equestrian sports, and rode with hounds. She wrote three books on the subject: *To whom the Goddess* (1932), on hunting and riding for women, written with Lady Diana Shedden; *Bridleways through History* (1936), a history of hunting from prehistoric times, written with her husband; and *The Fox-Hunter's Bedside Book* (1949), a compilation of stories about the sport. From 1946 to 1956 she was joint master of Earl Bathurst's hunt. Inspired by her husband, who was a keen aviator and had commercial interests in airlines, she obtained her aircraft pilot's licence in 1930.

Lady Apsley was county commandant for the Auxiliary Territorial Service for Gloucestershire, where the Apsleys lived, in 1938–9, and group commander in 1939–40. She was ATS welfare officer for the county from 1940 to 1943. After the outbreak of war she became increasingly involved in local politics, serving on Sudbury rural district council (1941–3). On her husband's death, on 17 December 1942, on active service on Malta, she was nominated to succeed him as Conservative candidate for the Bristol Central parliamentary constituency. Because of the wartime electoral truce between the parties, no official Labour candidate stood against her, but there were three independents, including Jennie Lee. As a result she had to undertake a great deal of campaigning, despite being confined to a wheelchair following a hunting accident. She won the seat (18 February 1943) with a slightly larger majority than her husband had enjoyed.

Lady Apsley made a profound impact on the House of Commons when she appeared in her wheelchair, dressed in mourning. Her maiden speech (23 March 1943), in a debate on war pensions and disablement, drew upon both her personal experience and her position as national chair, since 1942, of the women's section of the British Legion. Her parliamentary career was, however, short, for she lost the Bristol seat in the 1945 general election. She subsequently contested Bristol North-East as Conservative and National Liberal candidate, but without success. She died on 19 January 1966.　　　G. E. MAGUIRE

Sources *The Times* (21 Jan 1966) · b. cert. · *WWW* · P. Brookes, *Women at Westminster: an account of women in the British parliament, 1918–1966* (1967) · G. E. Maguire, *Conservative women* (1998) · S. McCowan, *Widening horizons: women and the conservative party* (1975) · Burke, *Gen. GB* (1937) [Meeking, late of Richings Park] · Burke, *Peerage* (1967) [Bathurst] · *CGPLA Eng. & Wales* (1967)
Wealth at death £88,256: probate, 24 April 1967, *CGPLA Eng. & Wales*

Bathurst, Walter (1764?–1827), naval officer, was a nephew of Dr Henry *Bathurst, bishop of Norwich, and son of another of the thirty-six children of Benjamin, younger brother of Allen, first Earl Bathurst. After being on the books of the guardship at Plymouth for more than a year, he was, on 5 October 1781, appointed to the *Yarmouth* which, in the beginning of 1782, accompanied Sir George Rodney to the West Indies, and participated in the victory to leeward of Dominica on 12 April. He served in the frigate *Perseus*, was made lieutenant on 15 November 1790, and in April 1791 was appointed to the brig *Ferret* on the home station. He continued in her for nearly three years, and on 30 December 1793 was appointed to the frigate *Andromache*, in which he served on the Newfoundland

station, and afterwards with the fleet off Cadiz under Lord St Vincent. In May 1797 he was transferred to the *Ville de Paris*, and on 3 July 1798 was appointed her captain by St Vincent. His promotion was not confirmed until 24 October 1799, having to be promoted commander from 22 August 1798 in the interval, but he continued to command the *Ville de Paris* until May 1800, mostly with Lord St Vincent's flag. He afterwards commanded the frigate *Eurydice*, the *Terpsichore*, and the *Pitt*, in the East Indies, in all of which he took several rich prizes. Having brought home the first Bombay-built frigate, the *Pitt*, rechristened *Salsette*, he still commanded her up the Baltic in 1808. In 1808 he married Marianne Wood of Manchester Street, Manchester Square, London; they had five surviving children, and she survived her husband.

In July 1809 Bathurst escorted part of Lord Chatham's army to Walcheren. In 1810 he was appointed to the *Fame* (74 guns) in which he went out to the Mediterranean; he stayed there until the end of the war. He had no further service until 1824, when he commissioned the *Genoa* (74 guns) which on 20 October 1827 formed part of the fleet commanded by Sir Edward Codrington at Navarino. Being badly out of position, the *Genoa*'s loss was very heavy; her dead considerably exceeded those of any other ship. Bathurst was killed on the quarter-deck shortly after the beginning of the action. The lord high admiral wrote with his own hand a letter of condolence to Bathurst's widow. Bathurst's son John Oldenshaw Bathurst (*b.* 1817) became commander, RN, and died relatively young. Bathurst was a brave and kindly captain, beloved of his entire crew.

J. K. LAUGHTON, *rev.* ANDREW LAMBERT

Sources C. M. Wodehouse, *Navarino* (1965) · D. Syrett and R. L. DiNardo, *The commissioned sea officers of the Royal Navy, 1660–1815*, rev. edn, Occasional Publications of the Navy RS, 1 (1994) · PRO, official MSS · *GM*, 1st ser., 97/2 (1827) · O'Byrne, *Naval biog. dict.*
Archives BL, corresp. with Shawe, Add. MS 13753

Batman, John (1801–1839), pioneer in Australia, was born at Parramatta, New South Wales, on 21 January 1801, the second son of William Bateman, a Middlesex cutler, transported in 1796 after being convicted of receiving stolen saltpetre worth £48, and his wife, Mary, who travelled out with him as a free woman. He was educated at John Tull's elementary school at Parramatta and in 1810, the year his father's sentence expired, was baptized, together with his sister and four brothers, at the parish church. In 1816 he was apprenticed as a blacksmith, but soon took up farming and on 29 November 1821 (by then a strong, sociable, and handsome man) sailed for Launceston in Van Diemen's Land. Here he leased land for grazing, supplying meat to the government in 1823; in the next year he was granted 600 acres at Kingston, near Ben Lomond. He was joined by Elizabeth Thompson (1804–1852), also known as Elizabeth Callaghan, a convict absconder, transported for passing counterfeit money. They were married at St John's, Launceston, on 29 March 1828 and in 1833 she was officially pardoned; by then they had six daughters—another daughter and, finally, a son (who was drowned as a boy) were to follow.

Meanwhile Batman had actively assisted Governor

Arthur in suppressing bushranging and in the protracted struggles with the Aborigines; in a dispatch in November 1830 Arthur described him as 'one of the few who supposed they might be influenced by kindness', but a recent historian, Lloyd Robson, in his *History of Tasmania*, has argued that Batman's proceedings showed him to be 'a liar as well as a murderer' (Robson, 1.213). He extended his grazing activities, owning 7000 acres in 1835, but the land was in rugged country, so he was interested in seeking more. He thought of possibilities on the mainland, and at the time of the short-lived penal settlement at Western Port (1826–7) he and Joseph Gellibrand applied for a grant, promising to ship there sheep and cattle worth about £3500; but the settlement was soon closed. In 1834, with surveyor John Helder Wedge, he proposed an exploring expedition on the mainland, but did not proceed with it; however, the next year, after the Hentys had gone to Portland, Batman, Gellibrand, Swanston, and Wedge formed an association for colonizing Port Phillip and sent over Batman to report on the capabilities of the district. He sailed in May 1835 with a small party, and on 6 June, on a creek about 6 miles north-east of the site of the future Melbourne, made a so-called treaty with a group of Aborigines, by which (in consideration of some small gifts and a promised annual tribute of knives, scissors, axes, and clothing) they agreed to make over to him two tracts of land totalling 600,000 acres. Since no one can sell Aboriginal land, it can be presumed that they did not understand the nature of the transaction which Batman believed to have taken place; and Batman's later assertion that they walked around the boundaries of the land they had 'bought' is, of course, absurd. He wrote in his diary on 7 June that before he left the spot, two chiefs:

> came and laid their cloaks or royal mantles at my feet, wishing me to accept the same. On my consenting to take them, they placed them on my neck and over my shoulders, and seemed quite pleased to see me walk about with them on.

Batman then asked one of them to make his mark, and after 'hesitating for a few minutes, he took the tomahawk and cut out in the bark of the tree his mark, which is attached to this deed, and is the signature of the country and tribe.'

Batman then returned to the Maribyrnong (Saltwater) River, which he had gone up, and was surprised to strike the (freshwater) Yarra further down. He sent a boat up it and its crew reported a 'site for a village', soon to be the site of Melbourne. Batman's diary, though slightly ambiguous, suggests that he was not on the boat, and on the map drawn on his return he marked the township's site on the south bank—a place so unsuitable as to confirm the belief that he had not seen it. He set sail next day, leaving a small party to establish headquarters at Indented Head; by 13 June he had returned to announce his success to his colleagues in Van Diemen's Land. No government recognized the 'treaty': the governor of Van Diemen's Land had no authority on the mainland; in Sydney, Governor Bourke knew that all land in Australia was vested in the British crown, and that 'sales' by native chiefs could not be recognized (which was the policy of the Colonial Office in London). So at first all settlers at Port Phillip were regarded as trespassers without rights, though after the settlement was officially recognized in 1836, Batman's association succeeded in obtaining a sum of £7000 from the government 'in consideration of the expenses incurred in the first settlement'.

By this time Batman had sold his Kingston property for £10,000 and in April had settled permanently with his family on 20 acres of land just outside Melbourne's official limits. He grazed his flocks as a squatter nearby and appeared a prosperous merchant, storekeeper, shipping agent, and banker. He bought three allotments for £158 at the first Melbourne land sale in July 1837, and five more at the second in November for £292; but by this time his excessive drinking (as early as 1835 his partner James Simpson spoke of 'his cups getting the better of his reason') and his inexorably progressing syphilis were crippling him. He had had to abandon his sheep; he borrowed too much in buying, building, and trading; he lent money without good security; and he suffered losses owing to the incompetence of some of his agents. When he died on 6 May 1839 at Melbourne he was almost penniless, but he was respected enough for seventy settlers and a group of Aborigines to attend his funeral in Melbourne's old cemetery on 8 May. Backed by his associates he had acted in establishing a settlement on Port Phillip when most others had only talked. Then he lost everything; but his name has long been well remembered in Melbourne.

A. G. L. SHAW

Sources C. P. Billot, *John Batman: the story of John Batman and the founding of Melbourne* (1979) • P. L. Brown, 'Batman, John', *AusDB*, vol. 1 • J. S. Duncan, 'John Batman's walkabout', *Journal of the Royal Historical Society of Victoria*, 57/2 (1986), 1–12 • R. Harcourt, 'Batman's treaties', *Victorian Historical Journal*, 62 (1991–2), 85–97 • J. Bonwick, *Port Phillip settlement* (1883) • J. Bonwick, *John Batman: the founder of Victoria* (1867) • F. P. Labillière, *Early history of the colony of Victoria* (1878) • L. Robson, *A history of Tasmania*, 1: *Van Diemen's Land from the earliest times to 1855* (1983) • A. S. Kenyon, 'The Port Phillip Association', *Victorian History Magazine*, 16/pt 3 (1937), 102–4 • P. Jones, ed., *Beginnings of permanent government* (1981), vol. 1 of *Historical records of Victoria*, ed. M. Cannon • *The early development of Melbourne* (1984), vol. 3 of *Historical records of Victoria*, ed. M. Cannon • J. Batman, diary, State Library of Victoria, Melbourne, La Trobe Library, Batman MSS • Public Records Office, Victoria, Australia, Batman Boxes

Archives Mitchell L., NSW, Port Phillip MSS • State Library of Tasmania, Hobart • State Library of Victoria, Melbourne • State Library of Victoria, Melbourne, Port Phillip Association MSS | State Library of Victoria, Melbourne, A. S. Kenyon, 'Notes on Batman' • University of Tasmania, Hobart, Royal Society of Tasmania collection, Swanston MSS

Likenesses J. Flett, photograph (of pencil sketch), State Library of Victoria, Melbourne, La Trobe picture collection • C. Nuttall, pencil drawing, priv. coll. • photograph, State Library of Victoria, Melbourne, La Trobe picture collection • photoprint (of watercolour), State Library of Victoria, Melbourne, La Trobe picture collection

Wealth at death almost penniless; owned land, but legal expenses had exceeded its value at death: Billot, *John Batman*

Batman [Bateman], **Stephan** [Stephen] (*c*.1543–1584), Church of England clergyman and author, was born at Bruton, Somerset, the eldest son of Henry Batman or

Bruer (d. 1571), who came to England from Zwolle in the Netherlands, in 1540 or 1541, and Elizabeth, daughter of Henry Whithorne. Stephan had seven brothers and three younger sisters. Their grandfather, Albertus Bruer, had fought for the emperor Charles V.

Batman is not credited with a university degree in surviving records. His eclectic learning and skills as a limner suggest that he may have been educated while apprenticed or employed by a scholar. He married Sybil, daughter of John Baker of Middlesex; not long after his twenty-first birthday Batman was living at Leeds, Kent, where his eldest son, Arthur, was baptized in November 1564, suggesting a date of birth for the father not later than 1543. By 1566 Batman was probably in London and was known to have antiquarian interests, since a merchant in Aldermanbury gave him an ancient bone. Batman's *The Travayled Pylgrime* (1569) is dedicated to Sir William Damsell, one of the leading parishioners of St Mary Aldermanbury (who paid for their own minister), in gratitude for 'so many benefits received'. In September 1567 and January 1570, when Batman's children Jane and Nathaniel were baptized there, the father was described in the parish register as the current minister.

Batman was instituted to the rectory of St Mary, Newington Butts, on 12 January 1570; the parish, a peculiar jurisdiction of the archbishop of Canterbury, was within walking distance of Lambeth Palace. Batman was a member of Archbishop Parker's household, described as chaplain to the archbishop in the dispensation for him to hold the living of Merstham, Surrey, in plurality, granted in February 1571. He revered the memory of Matthew Parker, whom he described as 'a great preferrour and daylye chearisher of those in whome he espyed anye towardnesse in learning and qualitie' (*The Doome*, 399). There is no evidence for the statement in the *Dictionary of National Biography* that Batman was chaplain to Henry Carey, first Lord Hunsdon, but dedications of books to Hunsdon (who owned the manor of Paris Garden, close to Newington rectory) in 1577 and 1582 suggest that he was offering his services after Parker's death. The Newington registers for 1571 record the burials of a daughter, Susan (in March), of fifteen-month-old Nathaniel (in April), as well as 'Harry Batman Father of Stephan Batman parson' (21 June), and the baptism of another son, Mathei (in November). Batman's handwriting appears sporadically in the Newington parish registers from 1570 until 1584. His last entries were made in February 1584, and the next incumbents of both livings were instituted in December. No will survives.

Batman claimed to have collected 6700 books for Parker, who subsequently gave some of them to Corpus Christi College, Cambridge; the majority must have been printed titles. Batman also collected and annotated some twenty-three medieval manuscripts for himself, including texts by Chaucer and Middle English religious literature; his interest seems to have derived from personal piety, his respect for the past, and practical concerns as a protestant minister. His comments frequently urge other readers not to disregard the spiritual value of 'papisticall'

texts, whose contents he tried to accommodate to his beliefs, substituting in one, for example, 'troble of conscience' for 'purgatori' (Bodl. Oxf., MS Bodley 416, fol. 130 r), while endeavouring to preserve them from destruction by protestant zealots. He illustrated some of these manuscripts; his drawings and interest in iconography are also evident from his own works. A short description of colours added to *Batman uppon Bartholome* (1582) may be part of a lost work on limning, listed as belonging to Parker's son John: '4° Bateman of the Art of Lymning'.

Batman's interest in recovering the past for the sake of the present characterizes his manuscript commonplace books preserved at Harvard (Harvard U., Houghton L., MS English f 1015) and at Oxford (Bodl. Oxf., MS Douce 363). The latter includes George Cavendish's *Life of Wolsey* in Batman's hand (with drawings), and has fine coloured and gilded historiated initials in other texts.

Batman's publications also demonstrate his virtuoso range, emblematic cast of mind, and moral impulse towards protestant edification. In *A Christall Glasse of Christian Reformation* (1569), woodcuts accompanying expositions of the perils of sin and benefits of virtue provide entertaining insights into Elizabethan life. *The Travayled Pylgrime* (an allegorical ages-of-man poem, adapted from Olivier de la Marche, via Hernando de Acuña) depicted 'the fonde devise of man, and the straunge Combats that he is daylie forced unto' to exhort 'every faythfull Christian'. (He gave the 'Author', or pilgrim figure, the heraldic arms of his own family.) Batman's pastoral concerns to provide all classes of readers with moral and religious comfort are as unmistakable as Langland's or Bunyan's; and *Travayled Pylgrime* has been recognized as an important precedent for Edmund Spenser's *Faerie Queene*, book 1 (1590).

Batman's condemnation of the 'erroneous trumperies' in which pagan 'Antiquitie hath bene nozzeled' did not interfere with his scholarly task of describing and identifying the symbols of ancient art in the first handbook of iconography printed in English: his *Golden Booke of the Leaden Goddes* (1577; no illustrations). In 1574 Batman had obtained a tenth-century manuscript of one of his principal sources, Isidore of Seville's *Etymologiae*. Nor did the rector of Newington stint his criticisms of contemporary England, whether inveighing against the Anabaptist Family of Love or complaining how the abuse of clerical livings by patrons forced their parsons to take second jobs: 'when worldly extremities shall thus hinder divine study: & when the shepherds perish for want of knowledge, what shal the sheepe doo?' (*New Arival of the Three Gracis*, 1580?, sig. D1r).

Batman's later translations include substantial additions. *The Doome Warning All Men to the Judgemente … in Maner of a Generall Chronicle* (1581) translates *Prodigiorum ac ostentorum chronicon Conradus Lycosthenes* (1557), while adding 'newly received prodigies' (to 1580) from named English sources, and from his friends' and his own observations. *Batman uppon Bartholome, his booke De proprietatibus rerum, newly corrected, enlarged and amended* (1582),

Batman's most influential learned work, advertises itself as a source for the signification of similitudes found in pagan and biblical texts. The thirteenth-century source text (by Bartholomaeus Anglicus), a standard repertory of ancient and medieval learning, became widely used in the sixteenth century as a popular encyclopaedia.

Joyfull newes out of Helvetia, from Theophr. Paracelsum, declaring the ruinate fall of the papall dignitie, also a treatise against usury (1575), attributed to Batman in Andrew Maunsell's *Catalogue* (1595), cannot be traced and is presumed not to survive.

Spenser (certainly) and Shakespeare (probably) used *Batman uppon Bartholome*. Batman's learning and imagination influenced late Elizabethan literature by demonstrating how to use images and concepts derived from the literature of either medieval piety or pagan antiquity without compromising protestant teaching. Latin prefatory verses to his works by James Sandford, Christopher Carlile, and Thomas Newton attest to Batman's contemporary reputation among scholars. The inventor Sir Hugh Platt (1594) and the antiquary Francis Thynne (1598) knew him as a limner and a connoisseur of manuscripts, and Batman was able to claim the respect and friendship of his patron, Matthew Parker, and William Camden, among others.

RIVKAH ZIM

Sources BL, Add. MS 24487, 272 [cf. copy of Batman pedigree in London, College of Arms, MS Vincent 351] • *The doome warning all men to the judgemente, wherein are contayned for the most parte all the straunge prodigies hapned in the worlde, with divers secrete figures of revelations tending to mannes stayed conversion towardes God, in maner of a generall chronicle, gathered out of sundrie approved authors* (1581), 357, 399–400, 410 • M. B. Parkes, 'Stephan Batman's manuscripts', *Medieval heritage essays in honour of Tadahiro Ikegami*, ed. M. Kanno and others (1997), 125–56 • *STC, 1475–1640* • E. J. Brockhurst, 'The life and works of Stephen Batman, 15-?–1584', MA diss., U. Lond., 1947 • parish register, St Mary Aldermanbury, GL, MS 3572/1, fols. 30v and 33v • faculty office muniment book, LPL, F1/B, fol. 40v • registers, St Mary Newington, LMA, P92/MRY 1 and 2 • *The travayled pylgrime, bringing newes from all partes of the worlde* (1569) • *El cavallero determinado traduzido de lengua francesa en castellana por Don Hernando de Acuña, y dirigido al emperador Don Carlos quinto maximo rey de España nuestro señor* (1555) • *Registrum Matthei Parker, diocesis Cantuariensis, AD 1559–1575*, ed. W. H. Frere and E. M. Thompson, 3 vols., CYS, 35–6, 39 (1928–33), 859, 874, 1026 • Bodl. Oxf., MS Douce 363 • *The new arival of the three Gracis, into Anglia, lamenting the abusis of this present age* (1580?) • *The displaying of an horrible secte of … heretiques … the familie of love, with the lives of their authours* [i.e. D. Joris and H. Niclas] … *newely set foorth by J. R[ogers]*, ed. J. Rogers and S. Bateman (1578), sigs. A7v–B1r [Batman's epistle] • A. Maunsell, *The first part of the catalogue of English printed bookes* (1595), 7, col. b • A. L. Prescott, 'Spenser's chivalric restoration: from Bateman's *Travayled pylgrime* to the Redcrosse Knight', *Studies in Philology*, 86 (1989), 166–97 • LPL, Register Whitgift I, fol. 427v

Batmanson, John (d. 1531), religious controversialist and prior of the London Charterhouse, has in the past been identified with the lawyer of that name who was sent to Scotland in 1509 to negotiate with James IV. However, the monastic historian David Knowles suggests that the lawyer and the prior were two different people, probably father and son. John Batmanson the elder (d. 1518) was a

graduate of Oxford, and his first wife, Margaret (*fl.* 1511), was probably the future prior's mother. Apparently John senior remarried, for a second wife, Joan, asked to be buried in the London Charterhouse when she herself died in 1518.

There is no evidence that John Batmanson the younger went to university. He was ordained deacon in 1510 and joined the strictly enclosed Carthusian order, probably at the London Charterhouse. While there, according to Erasmus in a letter of 1520, he was induced by Dr Edward Lee (later archbishop of York) to attack Erasmus's edition of the New Testament. The humanist describes his opponent as 'a young man, as appears from his writings, altogether ignorant but vain-glorious to madness' (Thompson, 342). Erasmus's comments about Batmanson are mild, however, compared with those of Thomas More. Knowles shows that More's 'Letter to a monk' of 1519 is addressed to Batmanson, although the latter is not identified by name. Presented as a response 'to a certain monk's ignorant and virulent letter, a senseless invective' against Erasmus's edition, More in this letter describes Batmanson as arrogant and 'an unlearned, obscure little monk', and his letter as 'replete with reproach, abuse, slander, and mockery' and a 'shockingly heated attack, in which you so intemperately vomit abuse by the wagonload onto a man who has done you no wrong' (More, 15.199, 263, 271, 265, 203).

More knew the London Charterhouse well: in his youth he spent four years living at or near the priory, joining the monks' devotions. His 'Letter to a monk' suggests that he had known Batmanson for many years: 'My old, dear friend, tell me, what sly, crafty demon has managed to plant so much guile and insidious subterfuge in a heart as sincere and as candid as yours was while you were still a layman' (More, 15.203). It also describes Batmanson as 'a self-tutored young man', which confirms that he had not attended university (ibid., 15.271).

Batmanson's attack on Erasmus's translation does not survive, and its contents have to be surmised from More's response, although More may not be entirely fair in his presentation of his opponent's arguments. Apparently Batmanson wrote that Erasmus's teaching was new and unorthodox, described him as a vagrant, pseudo-theologian, and slanderer, and implied that he was a heretic, a schismatic, and a 'herald of Antichrist' (More, 15.203). He criticized the way Erasmus had translated certain words, and believing that older is better, may well have had reservations about the very idea of a new translation, being concerned about its potential for arousing discord, and shocked by Erasmus's assertion that the church fathers were occasionally wrong. Batmanson's own theological position seems to have been old-fashioned and traditional.

Bale, Pits, and Petreius list other works that Batmanson supposedly wrote, including treatises against the work of Luther and Lefèvre d'Étaples, works on scriptural subjects, and some instructions for novices, but none of these appears to be extant. He apparently retracted his writings about Luther and Erasmus. Bale thought him arrogant, audacious, and quarrelsome, but Pits and Petreius describe him as very learned, pious, and zealous. Even More contrasts his attack upon Erasmus with 'the goodness and holiness of the rest of your character' (More, 15.267).

Batmanson became prior of Hinton Charterhouse, Somerset, in 1523, and held that office until 1529 when he was made prior of the London Charterhouse. Little is known of his priorate at either house, apart from the fact that while prior of London he obtained dispensation for two monks, George Norton and Andrew Boorde, to leave the monastic life.

Batmanson died on 16 November 1531 at the London Charterhouse, after only two years as prior there, and was buried in its cemetery. At the time of his death, the sexton of the house claimed to have had a vision in which Batmanson and his predecessor said that some of the monks' observances should be made even stricter. He was succeeded as prior by John Houghton who was executed in 1535, the first of eighteen Carthusians martyred for refusing to swear the oath of supremacy. The remaining monks were expelled from the London Charterhouse, but about 1545, when the foundations for a new mansion were being laid in the cemetery, the workmen discovered the body of John Batmanson, still intact with all his garments, and reinterred it elsewhere.   C. B. ROWNTREE

Sources St Thomas More, 'Letter to a monk', *The Yale edition of the complete works of St Thomas More*, ed. D. Kinney, 15 (1986), xli–xlv, 198–311 · D. Knowles [M. C. Knowles], *The religious orders in England*, 3 (1959), 153–4, 224, 469 · E. M. Thompson, *The Carthusian order in England* (1930), 342–3, 390, 494–5 · *Opus epistolarum Des. Erasmi Roterdami*, ed. P. S. Allen and H. M. Allen, 4: *1519–1521* (1922), 258–9, 287 · R. Marius, *Thomas More: a biography* (1984), 257–60 · P. G. Bietenholz and T. B. Deutscher, eds., *Contemporaries of Erasmus: a biographical register*, 1 (1985), 99–100 · Bale, *Cat.*, 1.709; 2.75 · T. Petreius, *Bibliotheca Cartusiana, sive, Illustrium sacri Cartusiensis ordinis scriptorum catalogus* (1609), 157 · J. Pits, *Relationum historicarum de rebus Anglicis*, ed. [W. Bishop] (Paris, 1619), 710–11 · Emden, *Cam.*, 44–5 · Emden, *Oxf.*, 1.131–2 · R. Sharpe, *A handlist of the Latin writers of Great Britain and Ireland before 1540* (1997), 214 · A. Gruys, ed., *Cartusiana: un instrument heuristique*, 3 vols. (Paris, 1976–8), vol 1, p. 47; vol. 3, p. 443 · L. Le Vasseur, *Ephemerides ordinis cartusiensis*, 4 (1892), 137 · L. Hendriks, *The London Charterhouse: its monks and its martyrs* (1889), 74–5 · Tanner, *Bibl. Brit.-Hib.*, 80–81 · J. Clark, ed., *The chartae of the Carthusian general chapter: MS Paris Bibliothèque Nationale Latin 10890*, 3 vols., Analecta Cartusiana, 100/23 (Salzburg, 1996–7), vol. 2, p. 66 · *LP Henry VIII*, 7, no. 1047 · C. Smedt and others, eds., 'Catalogus codicum hagiographicorum qui vindobonae asservantur in bibliotheca privata serenissimi Caesaris Austriaci', *Analecta Bollandiana*, 14 (1895), 231–83 · J. Hogg, ed., 'Dom Palémon Bastin's extracts from the Acta of the Carthusian general chapter for the Provincia Angliae: Parkminster MS B.77', *The chartae of the Carthusian general chapter*, Analecta Cartusiana, 100/21 (Salzburg, 1989), 33–102, esp. 68, 72

Batoni, Pompeo Girolamo (1708–1787), painter and draughtsman, was born on 25 January 1708 in Lucca, Italy, and baptized in San Frediano, Lucca, on 5 February, the son of Paolino Batoni, goldsmith, and his wife, Chiara Sesti. For nearly half a century he recorded the visits to Rome of British travellers on the grand tour in portraits

Pompeo Girolamo Batoni (1708–1787), self-portrait, 1773–4

which remain among the most memorable artistic accomplishments of the eighteenth century. He was equally gifted as a history painter, and his religious and mythological paintings were sought by patrons from the United Kingdom and Europe.

Batoni trained in the Lucchese goldsmith's shop of his father, but in 1727 left his native city to study painting in Rome. There in 1727–30 he engaged in the usual activities of newly arrived artists, copying the antique sculptures in the Vatican and the frescoes of Raphael and Annibale Carracci and drawing from the models in the private academies of local artists. His drawings came to the attention of British antiquaries and collectors in Rome and provided him with both a source of income and the beginnings of a reputation. The most important of these clients was Richard Topham, who owned fifty-three drawings by Batoni (Eton College Library, Windsor). These drawings, nine of which are signed, are among the most beautiful surviving reproductions of antique sculpture in Roman collections of the time. In November 1729 he married Caterina Setti (1711–1742). Following her death, Batoni married secondly, on 21 December 1747, Lucia Fattori. From 1750 they lived in the via della Croce, Rome, moving in 1759 to via Bocca di Leone 25.

Beginning in the 1730s, Batoni painted altarpieces for Roman churches in a strongly classicizing style which proved immediately popular and anticipated the neoclassicism of the later eighteenth century. By 1740 the artist's reputation was firmly established as a history painter, both for private patrons and the church. His colossal altarpiece for St Peter's, the *Fall of Simon Magus* (1746–55;

S. Maria degli Angeli, Rome), represents the climax of his development as a history painter. Enormous and complex, rich in varied attitudes, gestures, and expressions, the painting was exhibited in St Peter's in 1755, but within a year the project to translate it into mosaic was abandoned, and in 1757 the rejected canvas was transferred to S. Maria degli Angeli. Batoni did not give up history painting thereafter, but he never again produced a major altarpiece for a Roman church nor did he pursue private commissions for subject pictures with anything like his previous vigour.

During the 1740s Batoni forged his connections with British (primarily Irish) visitors to Rome with dramatic consequences for his career. He began slowly, producing only half a dozen portraits during the decade, notably *Joseph Leeson, 1st Earl of Milltown* (1744; National Gallery of Ireland, Dublin). Between 1750 and 1760 he produced nearly sixty portraits of British sitters alone, including nine of Sir Matthew Featherstonhaugh and his family (1751–2; Uppark, Sussex) and such sensitive and beguiling images as *John, Lord Brudenell, Later Marquess of Monthermer* (1758; priv. coll.). During this decade Batoni painted only about twenty subject paintings, and he maintained a similar ratio over the following two decades, continuing to concentrate on portraits.

Batoni's fame as a portrait painter was quickly established as firmly on the continent as in Britain, and a great number of royal and sovereign sitters visited his studio. But his major output remained his portraits of British gentlemen on the grand tour. He did not invent the grand tour portrait: nearly all the features associated with his portraiture had been anticipated in the preceding decades by the Italian painters Francesco Trevisani, Giorgio Domenico Dupra, Marco Benefial, and Agostino Masucci. But Batoni surpassed them in the freshness of his colouring, the precision of his draughtsmanship, and the polish of his handling. No contemporary painter could draw more incisively than Batoni, and few could match his ability to produce an accurate likeness. He valued his ability for making a striking likeness of everyone he painted, and his sitters were almost always pleased with this aspect of their portraits. Accurate likenesses were highly valued in the eighteenth century, but Batoni's were more than accurate; they were vivid and powerfully compelling. His likeness of Stephen Beckingham (priv. coll.), painted in Rome in 1752 but thought to have been lost in transit, was so accurate and memorable that several years later a stranger, meeting Beckingham in London, recognized him as the sitter in a portrait languishing in an Italian customs house, providentially then recovered (and the story recorded) on a stretcher.

A striking feature of Batoni's portraits was the emblematic use of antiquities and views of Rome to establish both the sitter's presence in the city and his status as a learned, cultivated, yet leisured aristocrat. Batoni popularized the portrait type of a casually posed sitter in an open-air setting, surrounded by classical statuary and antique fragments and often set against the backdrop of a classical building. These portrait accessories included the most famous antique marbles admired in eighteenth-century Rome and a host of lesser-known antiquities included presumably at the sitter's request.

One sitter, Thomas Dundas, later first Baron Dundas, commissioned from Batoni in 1764 an enormous canvas (Aske Hall, Yorkshire) depicting him before a group of fictitiously arranged antique marbles which included the *Apollo Belvedere*, *Belvedere Antinous*, *Laocoon*, and the Vatican *Ariadne* (or *Cleopatra*) from the Museo Pio-Clementino in the Vatican. The sculptures were among the most famous of all antiquity, and there can be no doubt that they were included at the sitter's request; presumably Dundas was not content with the more general allusions to the taste for the antique which appear in most of Batoni's British portraits. The Colosseum was another favourite portrait accessory of Batoni's sitters, before which monument they often chose to be shown. Colonel William Gordon in a portrait of 1766 (Fyvie Castle, Aberdeenshire) which epitomizes both the Scot in Italy, proud of his national identity, and the sophisticated traveller keenly interested in the splendours of ancient Rome, is shown wearing the plaid before a view of the Colosseum beside a marble statue of *Roma*.

Batoni's British sitters may have occasionally invested the marbles of ancient Rome with more topical and personal meanings. An inscription on the portrait of Thomas William Coke, later first earl of Leicester, of 1774 at Holkham Hall, Norfolk, records the contemporary belief that as a token of the impression Coke had made upon Louisa Stolberg, countess of Albany, wife of Charles Edward Stuart, the Young Pretender, she afterwards gave him the life-size portrait of himself that she had commissioned from Batoni. Behind the sitter is the Vatican *Ariadne*, known in the eighteenth century as *Cleopatra*, whose fame among contemporary writers, artists, and connoisseurs was immense. Batoni capitalized upon the current enthusiasm for the sculpture and employed it in various ways in several portraits. In Lord Coke's portrait he may have intended an explicit reference to the countess of Albany, whose features were said to have been recognized in the *Ariadne*. The head of the reclining marble figure has been repositioned slightly to reveal more of the facial features and the bust is discreetly draped, in contrast to his other representations of the statue. The fact of so suggestive a figure being introduced into the picture with such marked prominence, presumably at the countess's express command, gave rise to much comment. Horace Walpole remarked how 'The young Mr Coke is returned from his travels in love with the Pretender's queen, who has permitted him to have her picture' (Walpole, *Corr.*, 39.178).

For many visitors on the grand tour to be portrayed in Rome was a significant record of their travels and its result eagerly awaited by relatives at home: 'If Lord Cholmondeley goes to Rome, pray tell him I wish he would bring me a head of himself by Pompeio Battoni', Horace Walpole wrote to Sir Horace Mann in 1771 (Walpole, *Corr.*,

13.349). Batoni's reputation among the international travellers who visited Rome in the second half of the eighteenth century was highest among the British, and for nearly half a century they offered Batoni sustained and fruitful patronage. His virtuosity in depicting British gentlemen on the grand tour was highly admired, and James Bruce's acclamation that he was 'the best painter in Italy' (James L. Caw, *Scottish Portraits*, 1903, 2.42, quoting letter of August 1762), and Lady Anna Riggs Miller's declaration that he was 'esteemed the best portrait painter in the world' (*Letters from Italy*, 2nd edn, 1776, 2.283, letter of 14 May 1771), are typical of contemporary estimations of his talent.

The importance of British patronage to Batoni's career as a portrait painter is shown by a survey of his *œuvre* as it exists today. Of approximately 275 surviving portraits, including autograph replicas and variant portraits of the same sitter, 200, or about 75 per cent, depict British and Irish sitters. The majority, about 170, are English, followed by Irish, Scottish, and Welsh sitters. Of the remaining portraits, about thirty represent Italians, and the rest of Batoni's sitters are more or less evenly divided among several nationalities, with Poles, Russians, Germans, and Austrians predominating.

In spite of the considerable patronage Batoni had received from British travellers to Rome, after his death there on 4 February 1787 his reputation diminished. His portraits, on which such a substantial part of his fame had depended, had been shipped on completion to England, Scotland, and Ireland to hang in the homes of the sitter or a relative, where most of them have remained ever since, unseen except by the occasional privileged visitor. Only one painting, *A Portrait of a Nobleman, Whole Length* (exh. Society of Artists, 1778), seems to have been shown publicly in London in the artist's lifetime, and none was exhibited in Great Britain in the late eighteenth century or the nineteenth.

Batoni's critical fortunes began to revive in the twentieth century with the increasing general and scholarly interest in Italian painting of the seventeenth and eighteenth centuries. A monographic exhibition was devoted to the artist in Lucca in 1967; a second, focusing on his patronage by the British, was held in London in 1982; and a monograph and *catalogue raisonné* of his art was published in 1985.   EDGAR PETERS BOWRON

Sources I. B. Barsali, 'Batoni, Pompeo Girolamo', *Dizionario biografico degli Italiani*, ed. A. M. Ghisalberti, 7 (Rome, 1965) · F. Benaglio, 'Abbozzo della vita di Pompeo Batoni pittore', *Vita e prose scelte di Francesco Benaglio*, ed. A. Marchesan (1894), 15–66 · O. Boni, *Elogio di Pompeo Girolamo Batoni* (1787) · A. M. Clark, *Pompeo Batoni: a complete catalogue of his works with an introductory text*, ed. E. P. Bowron (1985) · J. Ingamells, ed., *A dictionary of British and Irish travellers in Italy, 1701–1800* (1997) · I. B. Barsali, ed., *Mostra di Pompeo Batoni* (1967) [exhibition catalogue, Palazzo Ducale, Lucca] · E. P. Bowron, *Pompeo Batoni (1708–87) and his British patrons* (1982) [exhibition catalogue, Iveagh Bequest, Kenwood House, London] · J. G. Puhlmann, *Ein Potsdamer Maler in Rom: Briefe des Batonie-Schülers Johann Gottlieb Puhlmann aus den Jahren 1774 bis 1787*, ed. G. Eckardt (1979) · E. Lazzareschi, *Rassegna Nazionale*, 191 (1913), 228 n. 1

Likenesses P. G. Batoni, self-portrait, 1765, Bayerische Staatsgemäldesammlungen, Munich · P. G. Batoni, self-portrait, 1773–4, Galleria degli Uffizi, Florence [*see illus.*]

Batsford, Bradley Thomas (1821–1904), bookseller and publisher, was born in Hertford, the fifth of the nine children of James Batsford (1791–1835), a tailor, and his wife, Mary, *née* Bradley. When his father died he left for London, where he lived with his cousins above their Leicester Square bookshop and bindery. In 1837 he was apprenticed to one of those cousins, the bookseller Henry Bickers. When he came of age in 1842 he inherited £325 from his grandfather, Roger Bradley, which enabled him to set up his own business. On 2 April 1843 he married Letitia Josephine (1821/2–1906), daughter of Raphael Turner, carver and gilder, and opened a bookshop at 30 High Holborn. The shop moved a few years later to 52 High Holborn, then to 94 High Holborn in 1893.

Batsford's sons Bradley Batsford (1846–1906), Henry George Batsford (1851–1882), and Herbert Batsford (1861–1917) all followed him into the business. During the manpower shortage of the First World War, his youngest daughter Florence worked briefly for the firm as a travelling saleswoman—perhaps the first in the British book trade, though she found the job distasteful.

B. T. Batsford began as a medical and general bookseller. In 1862 the death of a competitor, John Weale, who specialized in architectural and engineering books, allowed Batsford to move into that market and out of general bookselling. With his son Bradley taking the initiative,

Bradley Thomas Batsford (1821–1904), by unknown photographer, 1880s

the firm then ventured into publishing. Their first known title was J. K. Colling's *Examples of English Medieval Foliage and Coloured Decoration* (1874).

By the end of the century, Batsford had built up an international clientele and a reputation for publishing finely illustrated volumes on architectural history and the decorative arts. In the early 1890s he pioneered the use of photographs in architecture books. He also produced practical handbooks for builders, notably Charles F. Mitchell's *Building Construction and Drawing*: first published in 1888, it went through numerous editions and was still selling briskly more than a century later. The firm and its authors were remarkably loyal to each other: J. Alfred Gotch published with Batsford for fifty-six years, including his magisterial *Architecture of the Renaissance in England* (1891–4) and *Early Renaissance Architecture in England* (1901).

A fire in 1874 destroyed most of the early records of the firm and much of the stock. B. T. Batsford handed the business over to his sons Bradley and Herbert in 1902. He died at his home, 128 Abbey Road, St John's Wood, London, on 3 November 1904. He had published mainly for professional architects, but Herbert would appeal to general readers with beautifully illustrated books on English villages and country houses.   JONATHAN ROSE

Sources H. Bolitho, *A Batsford century* (1943) · J. Richardson, 'Batsford: a tradition of arts and crafts publishing', *British Book News* (Feb 1990), 80–83 · J. Rose, 'B. T. Batsford', *British literary publishing houses, 1820–1880*, ed. P. J. Anderson and J. Rose, DLitB, 106 (1991), 15–18 · *CGPLA Eng. & Wales* (1904) · m. cert. · d. cert.
Likenesses photograph, 1880–89, repro. in Bolitho, *Batsford century*, facing p. 24 [*see illus.*]
Wealth at death £2954 13s. 4d.: probate, 9 Dec 1904, *CGPLA Eng. & Wales*

Batsford, Henry George [Harry] (1880–1951), publisher and author, was born at 37 Cold Harbour Lane, London, on 18 April 1880, the only son of Henry George Batsford (*b.* 1851), publisher and bookseller, who died two years later, and his wife, Matilda, daughter of William Ward. He was educated at Henley House School, Kilburn, London, where his science master was H. G. Wells, and at the City of London School. In 1897, after studying briefly in Germany, he entered the family bookselling and publishing business which had been founded fifty-four years earlier by his grandfather, Bradley Thomas *Batsford. In 1917 he succeeded his uncle, Herbert Batsford, as chairman and managing director of B. T. Batsford Ltd, and he remained in that position until his death.

In 1926 Harry Batsford's work as a publisher of books on the technique and history of architecture was recognized by his election as an honorary associate of the Royal Institute of British Architects. In the early thirties, responding to economic pressure and changing taste, Batsford widened the scope of his firm's activities: he initiated more than one series of books, fully illustrated by photographs, on the architecture and topography of Britain, which gave the term 'a Batsford book' a recognized significance. These series, of which the best-known were the British Heritage and the Face of Britain, introduced to a

Henry George Batsford (1880–1951), by unknown photographer

new and wider public the beauties of Britain's landscape and ancient buildings and were not without influence in helping to preserve both from destruction. Batsford himself wrote, sometimes pseudonymously, or in collaboration with Charles Daniel Fry, a number of works, among them *Homes and Gardens of England* (1932), *The Landscape of England* (as Charles Bradley Ford, 1933), *The Cathedrals of England* (1934), and *The English Cottage* (1938). One of his authors, John Russell, recorded that of Batsford's 'passion for architecture there could never be any doubt; and in this, as in everything else, his inclination was always to put aside what was notorious and large in favour of what was plain, inviolate and true' (*Architectural Review*, April 1952).

Batsford published Gertrude Stein, Cecil Beaton, Sacheverell Sitwell, A. E. Richardson, and the popular series of social histories by Marjorie and C. H. B. Quennell. One Batsford book, James Pope-Hennessy's *London Fabric*, won the Hawthornden prize. In 1930 the firm moved from 94 High Holborn to an elegant Mayfair town house at 15 North Audley Street. During the Second World War, Batsford and some of his staff relocated to Malvern Wells.

In 1928 Batsford married Rose Verene (*d.* 1930), daughter of François André Sennwald, of Chaux de Milieux, Neuchâtel, Switzerland; there were no children. In himself Batsford was vital, generous, and individualistic. He loved England and knew the country and its antiquities with exceptional intimacy, but he also felt himself a citizen of the world and had travelled enthusiastically in Europe and America. Apart from architecture, he had a keen amateur's knowledge of subjects as diverse as astronomy, natural history, geology, railway locomotives, and watches. He had a great fondness for animals, particularly for cats, for whose welfare he left a special legacy in his will. Batsford died at Paddington Hospital, London, on 20 December 1951, of barbiturate acid poisoning (self-administered); the coroner returned an open verdict on the circumstances of his death.

SAMUEL CARR, rev. JONATHAN ROSE

Sources *The Times* (21 Dec 1951) · H. Bolitho, *A Batsford century* (1943) · J. Richardson, 'Batsford: a tradition of arts and crafts publishing', *British Book News* (Feb 1990), 80–83 · J. Rose, 'B. T. Batsford', *British literary publishing houses, 1820–1880*, ed. P. J. Anderson and J. Rose, DLitB, 106 (1991), 15–18 · personal knowledge (1971) · CGPLA *Eng. & Wales* (1952) · b. cert. · d. cert.
Archives BL, corresp. with Society of Authors, Add. MS 63211
Likenesses P. Evans, drawing, 1926–9, NPG · J. Berry, oils, *c.*1951, B. T. Batsford & Co., London · photographs, repro. in Bolitho, *Batsford century*, facing pp. 59, 90 [*see illus.*] · photographs, B. T. Batsford & Co., London
Wealth at death £15,188 8*s.* 4*d.*: probate, 15 Aug 1952, CGPLA *Eng. & Wales*

Batt, Antony (*d.* 1651), Benedictine monk, first appears making his religious profession at the Benedictine house of St Laurence at Dieulouard in Lorraine in 1616. Nothing is known of his early life and he cannot be identified with the secular priest William Batt of Wiltshire, ordained in 1604 who, unlike him, spent many years working in England, although some of the dedications in Antony Batt's books suggest west-country associations. He spent most of his life resident in the community at Dieulouard, and was made secretary of the English Benedictine congregation in 1629 at its third general chapter held at St Gregory's, Douai. In 1633 he was appointed first titular cathedral prior of Peterborough, a title he resigned in 1642. By about 1640 he was resident at St Edmund's, Paris, and in the years 1641–2 he acted as superior and novice master at the English priory at La Celle-en-Brie, near Meaux, probably returning to Dieulouard for his final years of 'study and the practice of religious duties' (Allanson, 1.125) although some authorities say he remained at Paris. His writings, mainly translated selections from the Bible and from established spiritual authors, show no knowledge of the new spirituality of his time and were intended principally for English readers. The 1640 French version of his *Thesaurus absconditus in Agro Dominico inventus*, dedicated to the abbess of Faremoutiers, allowed him, unusually among the English exiles in France, to reach an audience of French *dévotes* who might not have found his Latin work accessible. An unpublished translation by Batt, 'A spirituall looking-glass', survives as Ampleforth Abbey MS 86. He died on 12 January 1651.

DOMINIC AIDAN BELLENGER

Sources D. Rogers, 'Antony Batt: a forgotten Benedictine translator', *Studies in seventeenth-century English literature, history and bibliography*, ed. G. A. M. Janssens and F. G. A. M. Aaarts (1984), 179–93 · A. Allanson, 'Biography of the English Benedictines', 2 vols., vol. 1, 1850, Downside Abbey · D. Lunn, *The English Benedictines, 1540–1688* (1980) · G. Anstruther, *The seminary priests*, 2 (1975) · Y. Chaussy, *Les bénédictins anglais réfugiés en France au XVIIᵉ siècle (1611–1669)* (Paris, 1967) · DNB · A. F. Allison and D. M. Rogers, eds., *The contemporary printed literature of the English Counter-Reformation between 1558 and 1640*, 2 vols. (1989–94)

Batt, William (1744–1812), physician and chemist, was born at Collingbourne, Wiltshire, on 18 June 1744, and is said to have been a student at Oxford University. He then studied medicine in London, after which he went to Montpellier, where he took his MD in 1770. In 1771 he continued his studies at Leiden, and after completing them he returned to England. Owing to his poor health he subsequently moved to Genoa, where he built up an extensive medical practice and in 1774 was appointed professor of chemistry at the university there. Before this the study of chemistry at the University of Genoa had been neglected, but soon after his appointment the lectures became well attended. Batt also made a special study of botany and gathered an extensive collection of rare plants. He resigned his professorship in 1787 on account of a prolonged visit to England.

Batt's wide range of interests and public spirit won him the admiration of his fellow citizens, which was greatly increased by his work in Genoa during the severe epidemic of 1800. He was the author of a considerable number of treatises on medical subjects, the principal of which are: *Pharmacopea* (1787); *Storia della epidemia che fece strage in Genova all epoca del blocco* (1800); *Reflessioni sulla febbre degli spedali* (1800); *Considerazioni sull'innesto della vaccina* (1801); *Alcuni dettagli sulla febbre gialla* (1804); *Memoria sulla scarlattina perniciosa* (1807); and *Storia di una epidemia che regnò in Genova nel 1808* (1809). Many of his papers appeared in the *Transactions of the Medical Society of Genoa*. Batt died on 9 February 1812 at Genoa.

[ANON.], *rev.* CLAIRE E. J. HERRICK

Sources R. W. Innes Smith, *English-speaking students of medicine at the University of Leyden* (1932) · L. Isnardi, *Storia della università di Genova: continuata fino a' di nostri per E. Celesia*, 2 vols. (Genova, 1861–7), vol. 2, pp. 19–22 · Foster, *Alum. Oxon.*
Archives Wilts. & Swindon RO, family papers, letters mostly to his uncle Oliver Calley

Battel, Andrew (*b.* 1560s?, *d.* in or after 1613), traveller and trader, was probably born in Leigh, Essex; his parents are unknown. According to Samuel Purchas, a former neighbour in Essex, who published an account of his experiences, Battel sailed from Plymouth on 7 May 1589 on a voyage under the direction of Abraham Cocke, a veteran captain who had travelled earlier to South America and who commanded two 50 ton pinnaces, the *May-Morning* and the *Dolphin*. Having travelled, via Santa Cruz de Tenerife in the Canary Islands and the Guinea coast, across the Atlantic, they arrived first at Ilhe Grande on the coast of Brazil, and then at the Isla de Lobos Marinos (Seal Island) in the mouth of the River Plate. A plan to go to Buenos Aires was thwarted by a storm which drove them back to the Isla Verda (probably Flores). Seeking fresh supplies, the group then sailed to the island of St Sebastian, where Battel and four companions were captured by Indians and deposited with local Portuguese authorities; Cocke left the captives behind and Battel never saw him again.

The Portuguese shipped Battel to their settlement of St Paul-de-Luanda in Angola, where he spent four months as a prisoner before they took him a further 130 miles up the River Quansa to a garrisoned town. The Portuguese pilot who had taken Battel to the fort died there, and Battel then took a commission to lead the pinnace down the river. Though he became sick and languished in Luanda, complaining that the locals hated him because he was an Englishman, Governor João Furtado de Mendonça hired him to lead a trading mission down the Congo River to acquire ivory, maize, and palm oil. Successful as a trader, Battel none the less tried to escape on a Dutch ship in 1591, but the Portuguese caught him and sent him to languish at their fort at Massanganu. His second escape attempt failed in 1596, and he remained in the service of the Portuguese, who forced him to fight for them in campaigns in Sowonso, Namba Calamba, Sollancango, and Combrecaianga (possibly Kumba ria Kaiangu). Shot in the leg near Ingombe, Battel sailed on a Portuguese frigate, along with sixty soldiers, and began to trade along the coast. But the Portuguese left Battel among the Jagas, an interior nation which Battel later claimed practised infanticide and human sacrifices. After twenty-one months among the Jagas, Battel rejoined the Portuguese at Massangano. When he heard of the death of Elizabeth I he petitioned for his release from the Portuguese, but an outgoing governor never fulfilled his promise to allow Battel to leave and he remained with the Portuguese in Loango until 1610, when he apparently went to London.

Battel's narrative, as published by Purchas in *Purchas his Pilgrimage* (1613) and amplified in a 1625 edition, concludes with remarks about the cultures of various African nations, including detailed comment about the appearance of Loango's capital city at Mani Longo and the rituals practised there by the king. This amateur ethnography also includes information about the customs of various African groups, observations on fauna such as zebras, crocodiles, gorillas, and chimpanzees, and a description of various flora, including the baobab tree—information which retained its currency because Battel journeyed along routes that were not traversed again by Europeans for at least 300 years. Purchas refers to Battel as still living in 1613, but no further details are known of his later life or of his death.

ALFRED GOODWIN, *rev.* PETER C. MANCALL

Sources S. Purchas, *Purchas his pilgrimage* (1613), bk 7, chap. 9 · S. Purchas, *Purchas his pilgrimes*, 4 vols. (1625), vol. 2, bk 7, chap. 3 · *Strange adventures of Andrew Battel of Leigh, in Angola and the adjoining regions*, ed. E. G. Ravenstein, Hakluyt Society, 2nd ser., 6 (1901) · J. Pinkerton, ed., *A general collection of the best and most interesting voyages and travels in all parts of the world*, 17 vols. (1808–14)

Batteley, John (*bap.* 1646, *d.* 1708), Church of England clergyman and antiquary, was the eldest son of Nicholas Batteley (*d.* 1681), apothecary, of Bury St Edmunds, and his wife, Anne. He was baptized in St James's Church there on 18 November 1646, and attended King Edward VI Grammar School, Bury, under Thomas Stephens and Edward Leedes. He was followed there by his brother Nicholas *Batteley (*bap.* 1648, *d.* 1704), whose career he advanced along with his own, and by several others of the family. On 3 April 1662 he was admitted to Trinity College, Cambridge, as a sub-sizar; his tutor was Benjamin Pulleyne, future regius professor of Greek. Batteley matriculated on

5 July. In October he was awarded an annual exhibition of £5 from his old school. In 1664 he became a scholar of Trinity, and in 1668 a fellow. He graduated BA in 1666, MA in 1669, and DD in 1684. On 2 October 1675 he was ordained priest in the diocese of Ely. He was appointed domestic chaplain to Archbishop Sancroft, himself an old boy of Bury School, and was collated by him to the rectories of Hunton and Adisham, Kent, in 1684. He is said to have become chancellor of Brecon in the same year. He was still chaplain to Sancroft in October 1686 when, during the consecration of bishops Samuel Parker and Thomas Cartwright at Lambeth, he had to pick his master up from the floor on which he had measured his length. Batteley later served as chaplain to Archbishop Tillotson. He viewed James II's policies with disfavour, and in particular opposed toleration for recusant boys at his old school.

On 1 October 1687 Batteley was collated to the archdeaconry of Suffolk, which he relinquished on receiving the superior archdeaconry of Canterbury, to which he was collated on 22 March 1688. On 1 September following he was inducted as master of King's Bridge alias Eastbridge Hospital, Canterbury, of which he became a conscientious custodian and generous benefactor. In the same year his Canterbury preferments were completed with a canonry of the cathedral, in which he was installed on 14 November.

On 6 May 1694 Batteley preached in the cathedral in the presence of Queen Mary. The country was at war, and Batteley's tone was martial: 'A man's faith … teaches him to set the battle regularly in array' (Batteley, 23). But it was the devil, not the French, that he had in his sights. This was to be the only work that Batteley published in his lifetime, though he followed his brother Nicholas in making extensive study of the history of his adopted county. His *Antiquitates Rutupinae*, concerning the Roman stations of Thanet, was cast as a dialogue between Henry Wharton and Henry Maurice, Batteley's fellow chaplains at Lambeth. It was published posthumously by Thomas Terry in 1711. Batteley corresponded extensively with other scholars. In January 1708 he was nominated a fellow of the Society of Antiquaries, the revival of which he had assisted.

Batteley died at his prebendal house on 10 October 1708 and was buried in the south cross of the cathedral. He had married twice; his second wife, Mary, youngest daughter of Sir Henry Oxenden of Deane, Kent, died at Canterbury on Christmas day 1741, aged eighty-five. Batteley had no children. His nephew Oliver *Batteley (1697–1762) [*see under* Batteley, Nicholas] appears to have been his literary executor, as he republished *Antiquitates Rutupinae* in 1745, along with Batteley's hitherto unprinted history of Bury St Edmunds to the year 1272. Batteley had, along with his colleague in the Canterbury chapter John Mill, been concerned to demonstrate the Anglo-Saxon roots of the Anglican church. Although his own religion was untainted by superstition on the one side, or enthusiasm on the other, it is of interest that he was the owner of a thirteenth-century reliquary of Thomas Becket, now in the Burrell Collection.

C. S. KNIGHTON

Sources *Bury St Edmunds, St James parish registers*, Suffolk Green Books, 17, 3 pts (1915–16), 'Baptisms 1558–1800', 133; 'Burials 1562–1800', 157 [Nicholas Batteley: father] · S. H. A. H. [S. H. A. Hervey], *Biographical list of boys educated at King Edward VI Free Grammar School, Bury St Edmunds, from 1550 to 1900* (1908), 19 · Venn, *Alum. Cant.*, 1/1.109 · W. W. Rouse Ball and J. A. Venn, eds., *Admissions to Trinity College, Cambridge*, 2 (1913), 459 · E. Hasted, *The history and topographical survey of the county of Kent*, 2nd edn, 12 vols. (1797–1801) · Nichols, *Illustrations*, 4.85–91, 95–102 · *Fasti Angl.*, *1541–1857*, [Canterbury], 16, 18 · *Fasti Angl.*, *1541–1857*, [Ely], 48 · P. Collinson, P. N. Ramsay, and M. Sparks, eds., *A history of Canterbury Cathedral* (1995), 221, pl. 15 · H. Ellis, ed., *Original letters of eminent literary men of the sixteenth, seventeenth, and eighteenth centuries*, CS, 23 (1843), 101 · *The diary of Thomas Cartwright, bishop of Chester*, ed. J. Hunter, CS, 22 (1843), 6 · R. W. Elliott, *The story of King Edward VI School, Bury St Edmunds* (1963), 65–6, 71 · BL, Add. MS 5863, fol. 102v (old fol. 84v) · J. Batteley, *A sermon preach'd before the queen, in Christ's-Church, Canterbury; May vi. 1694* (1694) · J. Strype, *The life and acts of John Whitgift*, new edn, 3 vols. (1822), vol. 3, p. 358

Archives CUL, copy of *Antiquitates Rutupinae* with MS inscription, Bury 28.1

Likenesses attrib. J. B. Buckshorn, oils, Trinity Cam. · oils, Trinity Cam.

Batteley, Nicholas (*bap.* 1648, *d.* 1704), antiquary, was baptized on 14 June 1648, at St James's Church, Bury St Edmunds, Suffolk, the second son of Nicholas Batteley (*d.* 1681), apothecary, of Bury St Edmunds and his wife, Anne, and was thus the younger brother of John *Batteley (*bap.* 1646, *d.* 1708), antiquary. He attended King Edward VI Grammar School in Bury, and on 30 March 1665 entered Trinity College, Cambridge, as a pensioner, where his tutor was Benjamin Pulleyn. In July his old school granted him an annual exhibition of £5. In Lent 1667 he matriculated, and in 1669 he graduated BA. In 1672 he migrated to Peterhouse, being admitted pensioner there on 27 February; by the week of 15 March he had been advanced to a Parke fellowship, which he held for life. He proceeded MA as a member of Peterhouse in 1672, and was ordained priest in the diocese of Ely on 18 September 1675. On 15 October 1680 he was instituted to the rectory of Nowton, Suffolk, on the presentation of the earl of St Albans. In 1681 he acquired additionally the rectory of Creeting St Mary, Suffolk.

Batteley married on 20 September 1683 Anne Pocklington of Brington, Huntingdonshire; a daughter, Anne, was born in the following year. In August 1685 Archbishop Sancroft collated him to the vicarage of Bekesbourne, near Canterbury, and in the same month to the rectory of Ivychurch, also in Kent. These preferments were owed to John Batteley's association with the archbishop. His brother's subsequent positions at Canterbury encouraged Nicholas to take an interest in the history of the city and cathedral. In 1690 or 1691, following the death of a child, Nicholas and his family stayed with his brother, and there was opportunity for prolonged study in the cathedral archives. Batteley sent a mass of material, especially relating to Archbishop Parker, to the antiquary John Strype, unnecessarily apologizing for his own relentless scholarship: 'If you imploye me in concerns of this nature, you must arm yourselfe with patience' (CUL, Add. MS 3, fol. 65).

The culmination of Batteley's work was the publication of a second edition of William Somner's *Antiquities of Canterbury* in 1703. Batteley used the author's manuscript corrections and addenda to the original (1640) edition, and contributed a second part of his own, *Cantuaria sacra*, treating the history of the see, cathedral, and the other religious foundations of the city. Shortly after publication he received a not untypical letter from another scholar, Thomas Brett, praising his erudition and pointing out at some length 'those … very few and very slight errors' which 'have not lessened [his] esteem of the work, but rather increased it' (Nichols, *Illustrations*, 4.103, 105). Batteley also left much useful work unpublished, including a history of Eastbridge Hospital (where his brother was master), eventually printed by John Duncombe in 1785.

Batteley's first wife must have died by 1696, as in the following year a son, Oliver, was born to his second wife, the daughter of Dr John Oliver. Batteley himself died at Bekesbourne on 19 May 1704 and was buried in the parish church, where his widow raised a memorial: 'viro docto, prudenti, pio' ('to a learned, wise, and devout man'; BL, Add. MS 5863, fol. 103). The only son of Batteley's first marriage, also Nicholas (*d.* 1741), followed his father to Bury grammar school and Trinity, and became a Suffolk clergyman.

Oliver Batteley (1697–1762), the only son of Nicholas senior's second marriage, was elected scholar of Westminster School in 1712, and proceeded to Christ Church, Oxford, where he matriculated on 8 June 1716. He graduated BA in 1720, and proceeded MA in 1723, BD in 1734. In 1731–2 he served as junior proctor. In 1736 he became rector of Iron Acton, Gloucestershire. On 28 June 1757 he was collated to the prebend of Fairwell in Llandaff Cathedral. He died, without family, between 23 July and 4 December 1762. He is said to have found a country rectory a poor exchange for the civilities of the Christ Church common room.

C. S. KNIGHTON

Sources *Bury St Edmunds, St James parish registers*, Suffolk Green Books, 17, 3 pts (1915–16), *Baptisms*, 136 · S. H. A. H. [S. H. A. Hervey], *Biographical list of boys educated at King Edward VI Free Grammar School, Bury St Edmunds, from 1550 to 1900* (1908), 19–20 · Venn, *Alum. Cant.*, 1/1.109 · W. W. Rouse Ball and J. A. Venn, eds., *Admissions to Trinity College, Cambridge*, 5 vols. (1911–16), 2.472 · T. A. Walker, ed., *Admissions to Peterhouse or St Peter's College in the University of Cambridge* (1912), 147 · private information (2004) [Perne Librarian, Peterhouse, Cambridge] · J. Gage, *The history and antiquities of Suffolk: Thingoe hundred* (1838), 496, 501 · E. Hasted, *The history and topographical survey of the county of Kent*, 2nd edn, 12 vols. (1797–1801); facs. edn (1972), vol. 8, p. 405; vol. 9, pp. 273, 275; vol. 11, pp. 305 (note c to 304), 351 note n, 384; vol. 12, p.654 · Nichols, *Illustrations*, 4.92–3, 93–4, 103–5 · CUL, Add. MS 3, fols. 65–66v · BL, Add. MS 5863, fol. 103 (old fol. 85) · *Old Westminsters*, 1.62 · Foster, *Alum. Oxon., 1500–1714* [Oliver Batteley] · *Fasti Angl., 1541–1857*, [Chichester], 265 · *Fasti Angl., 1541–1857*, [Canterbury], 498 · codicil of 23 July 1762 to will of Oliver Batteley, PRO, PROB 11/882, fols. 26–9

Archives Bodl. Oxf., collections relating to Kent · LPL, antiquarian collections | BL, letters to John Strype, Add. MS 5853 · CUL, letters to John Strype

Wealth at death lands in Iron Acton and elsewhere; Oliver Batteley: will, PRO, PROB 11/882, fols. 26–9

Batteley, Oliver (1697–1762). *See under* Batteley, Nicholas (*bap.* 1648, *d.* 1704).

Battell, Ralph (1649–1713), Church of England clergyman, was born in Church Street, Hertford, on 11 April 1649, the son of Ralph Battell (1619–1701) and his wife, Elizabeth. His father was vicar of All Saints', Hertford, from 1662 and of Letchworth, Hertfordshire, from 1676, both livings that he held until his death; he was also master of Hertford Free School. At Hertford the elder Ralph Battell erected the first post-Restoration organ to replace the one removed under the 1644 ordinance requiring the speedy demolition of all organs. Of his four other sons and three daughters, Mary (1671–1699) and her brother Affabell (1660–1734) were successively organists at All Saints'.

Ralph Battell was admitted pensioner at Peterhouse, Cambridge, on 26 July 1665 and matriculated there in 1669. He graduated BA in 1670, proceeded MA in 1673, and was created DD by royal mandate in 1705. Ordained deacon at Ely on 3 March 1672 and priest at London in September 1673, he was appointed vicar of Edworth in Bedfordshire. On 10 June 1682 he married Elizabeth Dod (d. 1728) at Stapleford, Hertfordshire. In 1683 he published *Vulgar Errors in Divinity Removed* (a work alleged to contain Pelagian errors by the Calvinist William Howarth in his *Absolute Elections of Persons* [1694]) and in 1684 *A Sermon on Matthew vii.12*. About 1679 he journeyed to Rome, Venice, and Loreto, which he observed was 'remarkable for mud' (Gander). In November 1680, on the death of Joseph Glanvill, he was installed as a prebendary of Worcester Cathedral.

Battell was appointed subdean of the Chapel Royal at the time of the coronation of William III and Mary II on 11 April 1689, in succession to William Holder. On 10 December 1691 he admitted one William Battell, presumably his brother, a Chapel Royal 'officiating' priest, as a gentleman-extraordinary of the chapel. On 10 July 1699 Ralph succeeded Jonathan Blagrave as sub-almoner, in which post he survived the dismissal of the high almoner, William Lloyd, in 1702. He promoted church music, despite the 'notorious neglect of the duty in the Chappell, at which the Queen was offended' in 1693, to which he responded by ordering '(besides the bare penalty of the mulct) public admonitions … suspension or deprivation' (MS 'Old cheque book', fol. 54v). In 1694 he published *The Lawfulness and Expediency of Church-Musick Asserted*, a sermon on Psalm 100: 1–2. In 1699 he oversaw 'a new establishment of a composers place' for John Blow. In 1712 he authorized the publication of *Divine Harmony, or, A New Collection of Select Anthems Us'd at her Majesty's chapells Royal*, generally attributed to John Church, but by J. Hawkins to William Croft. He had admitted both men to the Chapel Royal in 1696 and 1700, respectively, and had officiated at the marriage of the latter to Mary George on 7 February 1705 in the Chapel Royal at St James's Palace.

Battell continued to serve as subdean until his death on 20 March 1713. He was survived by his wife, who died in 1728, and two sons, Nathaniel and Affabell, and two daughters, Elizabeth and Bridget. Battell and his widow were buried at All Saints', Hertford.   DAVID BALDWIN

Sources MS 'Old cheque book' of the Chapel Royal, 1558–1744, St James's Palace, Archive of Her Majesty's Chapel Royal · A. Ashbee

Ralph Battell (1649–1713), by John Simon (after Michael Dahl)

and J. Harley, eds., *The cheque books of the Chapel Royal*, 2 vols. (2000) · will, PRO, PROB 11/532, sig. 52 · certificate books of admission for members of the Chapel Royal, 1672–1714, PRO, LS13/197, 198, 199 · *IGI* · Venn, *Alum. Cant.* · *Fasti Angl., 1541–1857*, [Ely] · register of births, marriages, baptisms, and deaths, 1647–1709, chapels royal, St James, Whitehall, and Windsor, PRO, RG8/110 · private information (2004) [transcript of churchyard inscriptions at All Saints', Hertford, re Ralph Battell, father and son, recorded before destruction of headstone in 1880 and to Mary Battell inside church before loss in fire, 1891] · BL, Nicholas papers, Egerton MS 2543 · marriage licences, Chapel Royal, 1687–1728, PRO, RG8/76 · E. Chamberlayne, *Angliae notitiae*, 17th edn (1692) · assignments, lord chamberlain's department: Elizabeth and Ralph Battell as witnesses to will of Morgan Harris, 1690 · R. Gander, 'Hertford grammar school', unpublished MS · *DNB* · W. Dickinson, notebook, Bodl. Oxf., MS Gough Misc. Antiq. 17 · G. Sheldrick, *Three centuries of music at All Saints' Church, Hertford* (1987)

Likenesses J. Simon, mezzotint (after M. Dahl), BM, NPG [*see illus.*]

Wealth at death investment with brothers and father in the Cock Inn, Chelmsford, 1700; property in Hertfordshire: will, PRO, PROB 11/532, sig. 52

Batten, Adrian (*bap.* 1591, *d.* 1637), composer, was baptized at Salisbury, Wiltshire, on 1 March 1591, one of the seven children of Richard Batten (*d.* in or before 1619), a joiner, and Elizabeth Nowell. He had at least three brothers, Edward, John, and William. His parents had apparently lived at Salisbury for some years—they had married there at St Thomas's Church in 1573—but Adrian's musical education began at Winchester, where he was probably a cathedral chorister and where, according to later evidence, he studied under John Holmes, the organist. Batten's son Adrian was baptized at St Swithun upon Kingsgate, Winchester, in 1614.

Later in 1614 Batten left Winchester to become a lay vicar at Westminster Abbey, where he stayed for the next twelve years. His sons Thomas and Richard were baptized at St Margaret's, Westminster, in 1616 and 1621 respectively, but they both died young, within weeks of each other, in the summer of 1625. A daughter, Susan, died in 1623. Little is known of Batten's activities during his time at the abbey. As a singer he was present in 1625 at the funeral service for James I. Probably in 1626 he moved to St Paul's Cathedral, as a vicar-choral, in which capacity he is first recorded in December 1628; William Boyce wrote that Batten was also an organist there.

Batten seems to have had a relatively uneventful church career, and he is not known to have been involved with secular music. He supplemented his regular income with work as a music copyist. Westminster Abbey records of 1622 attest to his copying services by Thomas Weelkes, Thomas Tallis, and Thomas Tomkins, and his name is associated with a major source of church music known as the Batten organ book (c.1630; Bodl. Oxf.), although the attribution of its compilation to Batten is doubtful. His reputation rests solely on the church music he composed. His surviving output is extensive—several services and more than fifty anthems—but although he was a competent enough composer he never achieved the heights of his greater contemporaries such as Orlando Gibbons and Tomkins. Firmly placing Batten among composers of the second rank, the eighteenth-century historian Charles Burney wrote that he was:

> merely a good harmonist of the old school, without adding any thing to the common stock of ideas in melody or modulation with which the art was furnished long before he was born. Nor did he correct any of the errors in accent with which former times abounded. So that his imitations of anterior composers were entire. He seems to have jogged on in the plain, safe, and beaten track, without looking much about him, nor if he had, does he seem likely to have penetrated far into the musical *terra incognita*. (Burney, *Hist. mus.*, 2.290)

Later studies of Batten's music have suggested that it suffers not so much from a short-sighted conservatism—after all, Batten was not alone in being conservative and can hardly be criticized simply for failing to test stylistic boundaries—as from his inability to capitalize on those techniques that were already well established. His attempts at word-painting, though potentially capable of enlivening even the dullest texture, sometimes border on the ridiculous in their overstatement (for example the phrase 'is cast down' in the anthem 'I heard a voice'). And his tendency to cadence frequently, combined with his unwillingness to wander far from the tonic key, can cause a monotony that makes some of his large-scale pieces hard-going and unrewarding. It is generally agreed that his simple, less substantial works are his best, but among his more ambitious pieces the five-part full anthem 'Hear the prayers' is particularly fine, and the eight-part 'O clap your hands', though inevitably runner-up to Gibbons's setting of the text, demonstrates an imaginative management of chordal and polyphonic resources.

At the end of his life Batten was living in the parish of St Sepulchre, Newgate Street. He must have died, presumably in London, about May 1637, when he was not listed among the vicars-choral at St Paul's, and at any rate by 22 July 1637, when administration of his estate was granted to John Gilbert, a Salisbury clothier.   PETER LYNAN

Sources Burney, *Hist. mus.*, new edn • P. Le Huray, *Music and the Reformation in England, 1549–1660* (1967); repr. with corrections (1978) • *IGI* • *New Grove*, 2nd edn

Batten, Edith Mary [Mollie] (1905–1985), welfare worker and educationist, was born in London on 8 February 1905, the third of the four children and elder daughter of Charles William Batten, general draper, of High Street, Wandsworth, London, and his wife, Edith Wallis, daughter of Robert Black, of Chelsea, London. The family moved to Southport in 1916, where Mollie Batten was educated at the Southport High School for Girls. In 1925 she gained a BSc in chemistry at the University of Liverpool.

Returning in 1925 to London, where her father died, Mollie Batten had to find work and took a clerical job in an office in Piccadilly, later moving to McVitie and Price's Hendon factory, where she became an assistant to the personnel officer. From here she was dismissed owing to a disagreement with management over the treatment of a worker. In 1928 she became secretary of the Invalid Children's Aid Association branch in West Ham. Residing in the St Helen's Settlement, Stratford, she became a member of the Church of England, being prepared for confirmation by the vicar of Barnet, the Revd Leslie Hunter. During this time she attended evening classes at the London School of Economics and gained a BSc (Econ) degree in 1932.

Mollie Batten was appointed warden of the Birmingham settlement in 1933 and soon became a nationally recognized pioneer in the training of social workers and youth workers. She helped to rebuild and expand the settlement's premises and was responsible for changes in its constitution, which brought the warden and staff representation on to its council. In 1937–8 she was a JP for the city of Birmingham.

In 1938 Mollie Batten became organizing secretary of the British Association of Residential Settlements. The Hire Purchase Act (1938) owed much to evidence she had collected. She became a member of the Ministry of Labour's Factory and Welfare Advisory Board in 1938, and in 1940 she joined the ministry itself. She had a particular concern for the welfare of workers outside working hours. In 1942 she was appointed to the Manpower Services Board and was involved in the call-up of women in the London area. Offered a permanent civil service appointment, she nevertheless resigned in 1947 and went to St Anne's College, Oxford, where she read for a theology degree, gaining a second-class honours BA in 1949 (MA, 1953).

This and her past experience splendidly equipped Mollie Batten to become principal of William Temple College in 1950. The college, which she moved from Hawarden, Flintshire, to Rugby in 1954, was a memorial to the archbishop and was initially to be a theological college for women. Under Mollie Batten's imaginative guidance, and with the unflagging support of her old friend Leslie Hunter, now bishop of Sheffield and chairman of governors, it became a unique centre for the study of the secular realities of modern society in the light of Christian faith. There were resident students on two- and three-year courses for the Cambridge diploma and certificate in religious knowledge. But large numbers of men and women came on short courses from industry, social work, education, administration, and the civil service. Mollie Batten's wide field of contacts in these areas enabled her to bring in a steady flow of distinguished speakers to stimulate penetrating yet practical thought on the topics in hand. To avoid a tendency to heavy cigarette smoking she took to smoking a small pipe while listening to lectures. Sadly, the churches failed to perceive the value of the college or to support it in any way, although the growing number of industrial chaplains found in it and in its principal an important resource. Engagements with the World Council of Churches, with the church in Canada and in Hong Kong, and contacts in Germany nevertheless demonstrate an impressive reputation outside Britain.

Mollie Batten retired to London in 1966 but continued in part-time research work for the church assembly's board for social responsibility. After moving to Midhurst, Sussex, in 1969 she played an active part in the diocese of Chichester and the neighbouring diocese of Portsmouth, presiding in the latter over a working party on the south Hampshire development plan. She was sometime chairman of the Chichester constituency Labour Party.

Mollie Batten was a lifelong supporter of the Anglican Group for the Ordination of Women. Her vigorous intellect, innovative spirit, warmth of character, and infectious enjoyment of life evoked exceptional responses of loyalty and affection. She was appointed OBE in 1948. She died at the Cottage Hospital, Midhurst, on 27 January 1985. She was unmarried.   S. W. PHIPPS, *rev.*

Sources personal knowledge (1990) · *WWW* · *CGPLA Eng. & Wales* (1985)

Wealth at death £55,615: probate, 1 May 1985, *CGPLA Eng. & Wales*

Batten, Jean (1909–1982), aviator, was born on 15 September 1909 in Rotorua, New Zealand, the youngest child and only daughter of Frederick Batten, a dentist, and his wife, Ellen Blackmore (1876/7–1966). Frederick was the son of an English immigrant surveyor, James William Batten, from Reading; Ellen's father, John Blackmore, from Devon, was an ex-British army sergeant-major drill instructor who went to New Zealand in 1869.

From the moment of Batten's birth, her mother, a formidable and ambitious woman with unusually emphatic feminist views for her day, determined that her daughter would be encouraged to achieve and compete in a masculine world. After Blériot flew across the English Channel, she pinned a newspaper picture of the French pilot on the wall beside the cot. When, in 1913, the Battens moved to Auckland, where Jean, at the age of five, was sent to Melmerley Ladies' School, Ellen began regularly to take her down to the harbour to watch the flying boats at a pilot training base. When Batten was eleven, in 1920, her parents permanently separated. She lived thereafter with her mother, with whom she formed an excessively close lifelong bond. At the Ladies' College in Auckland she excelled academically but gained a reputation as a loner—an intelligent, solitary person who made few friends.

In 1924, aged fifteen, Jean Batten went to secretarial school in Auckland and began to study the piano and ballet, hoping to make a career in both. However, the news of Charles Lindbergh's non-stop flight from New York to Paris in May 1927 led her to change her mind. The exploit inspired her to learn to fly. Early in 1930, having sold her piano to pay the fares, she and her mother went to England. At the London Aeroplane Club, Batten obtained first her private and then her commercial flying licences. To pay for the flying she borrowed from Fred Truman, a young New Zealand pilot about to leave the RAF. Anxious to marry her, he gave her his entire gratuity of £500. When it was spent she dropped him for another benefactor, Victor Dorée, who also wanted to marry her, and bought her a Gipsy Moth whose previous owner was the prince of Wales. In this aircraft (G-AALG) she set off in April 1933 to try to fly to Australia faster than Amy Johnson's 1930 time of nineteen and a half days. She got only as far as Karachi, where she suffered catastrophic engine failure and crashed, wrecking the aeroplane, but escaping uninjured.

Back in England, Batten turned to Lord Wakefield, head of the Castrol Oil Company. Impressed by her pluck and beauty, he agreed to provide her with another second-hand Moth. In this aircraft (G-AARB) Batten, now engaged to a London stockbroker, Edward Walter, set out in April 1934 to fly to Australia. This flight also ended in disaster. Running out of fuel on the outskirts of Rome she flew into a cluster of radio masts, crash-landing among them in the dark and almost severing her lip.

On her third attempt, made in the repaired Moth, now fitted with replacement lower wings borrowed from Edward Walter's own aeroplane, Batten finally made it to Australia. Her flight of fourteen days and twenty-two and a half hours shattered Amy Johnson's 1930 time to Darwin by more than four days. The feat made her an overnight international celebrity. In Australia and New Zealand she was lionized. Lecture tours brought her prosperity. She revelled in the adulation, impressing the crowds with her glamour and charm and carefully prepared speeches—in all of which she heaped extravagant praise, for her support, upon her mother.

In Sydney, Batten fell in love with an Australian airline pilot, Beverley Shepherd, and broke off her engagement to Edward Walter; he was so angry he sent her a bill for his aeroplane wings. Secretly engaged to Shepherd, she flew the Moth back to England in April 1935, becoming the first woman to fly from England to Australia and back. In search of new records, she was now able to afford a Percival Gull cabin plane (G-ADPR), in which, in November 1935, she flew from England to Brazil, crossing the south Atlantic in a brilliantly accurate feat of navigation aided only by a watch and a compass. Her England–South America and Atlantic crossings were world records. In Buenos Aires she received a cabled offer from Charles Lindbergh to fly up and make a coast-to-coast lecture tour of the

United States. It would greatly have increased her celebrity and prosperity, but she was persuaded by her mother to refuse and returned to England. The two women retired to a Hertfordshire cottage.

In October 1936 Batten emerged from seclusion to make the longest of all her great journeys—the first-ever direct flight from England to New Zealand. But the flight and the stress of fame took its toll. In New Zealand she suffered a nervous breakdown. After her recovery she went to Sydney by sea to marry Beverley Shepherd. However, on the day of her arrival he was killed in an air crash. Stricken with grief, she dropped out of public view again. In October 1937 Batten flew the Gull back to England. The flight of five days and eighteen hours established a solo Australia–England absolute record. It was her last long-distance flight: her brief years of fame had lasted only from 1933 to 1937. During the Second World War she worked first as an ambulance driver, then in a munitions factory, and finally as a fund-raising lecturer with the National Savings Committee. She fell in love again, this time with an RAF bomber pilot whom she identified in her unpublished memoirs only as Richard; he was killed on operations over Europe.

In 1946 Batten and her mother moved, first to Jamaica, then to Spain, before going to Tenerife. Aged eighty-nine, her mother died in Tenerife in 1966. At the end of 1969 Batten made a dramatic return to public life, following face-lift surgery and having dyed her hair jet black. From her small apartment in Puerto de la Cruz, Tenerife, she travelled the world during the 1970s, persuading the airlines to give her free first-class tickets and offering herself for radio and television interviews.

However, despite her return to the limelight, Jean Batten was now a sad, lonely, and increasingly eccentric figure, self-absorbed with her fame of forty years earlier. In 1982, disillusioned, she sold her Tenerife apartment and flew to Majorca, intending to buy a new home there. It was not until September 1987 that a New Zealand documentary film maker, researching her life, discovered that she had died in Palma on 22 November 1982—less than six weeks after arriving on the island. Infection from a dog bite had caused a fatal pulmonary abscess. Through a bureaucratic blunder the New Zealand government and her relatives had not been notified. In January 1983 she had been buried in an unmarked paupers' mass grave in Palma cemetery. Although she had appeared to live her last years in poverty, she left an estate valued at nearly £100,000. A memorial plaque now identifies her grave. A bronze statue stands beside Auckland airport's international terminal, which now bears her name and in which her Gull is on permanent display.

A stunningly attractive brunette of film-star glamour and poise, Jean Batten used her seductive charm to persuade a series of men to fund her flying ambitions. She was ruthless, determined, and, in the air, seemingly fearless, taking huge and unnecessary risks on many of her flights. Behind her daring lay the powerful driving force of her mother. As a record-seeking long-distance pilot she

was spectacularly successful, openly competing with men and becoming one of the most remarkable woman aviators of the 1930s. IAN MACKERSEY

Sources J. Batten, *Solo flight* (1938) · I. Mackersey, *Jean Batten: the Garbo of the skies* (1990) · private information (2004)
Archives FILM BFI NFTVA, documentary footage | SOUND BL NSA, oral history interviews
Likenesses photographs, 1934–7, Hult. Arch.
Wealth at death approx. £100,000

Batten, Sir William (1600/01–1667), naval officer, was the second son of Andrew Batten, mariner, of Easton in Gordano, Somerset, where he was born. He became a freeman of the Merchant Taylors in 1623 and in 1625, by a licence of 23 September, aged twenty-four, he married Margaret, daughter of Thomas Browne, a London cordwainer. By the following year he had adopted his father's profession, taking out letters of marque for the *Salutation* of London in August 1626. In 1629 he was engaged in whaling, and remained in the merchant service until 1638 when he commanded the *Confident*, hired by the king. On 6 September 1638, through the patronage of Lord Admiral Northumberland, and for payment of about £1500, he acquired the surveyorship of the navy. His connections with the London mercantile community and his enthusiasm for 'new fancies in religion' (Clarendon, *Hist. rebellion*, 2.225) secured his nomination as second in command to the earl of Warwick when parliament vetted appointments to the summer guard for 1642. Batten was temporarily in command of the fleet when the king's agents tried to secure control on 1 July. The same day Warwick was declared admiral by parliament, Batten becoming vice-admiral and treasurer. Warwick thought his deputy 'a very able and good man' (Powell and Timings, 18). On 15 September Batten became one of the professional members of the new navy commission, with responsibility for rigging and stores. But his chief service would be afloat. Because there was no royalist fleet for him to engage, his functions were to maintain supplies and communications for parliamentary forces while denying them to the king, and in operations against coastal towns. His first mission was to seize privateers serving the royalists at Newcastle. On 11 October, when Warwick was needed in parliament, Batten was made acting commander-in-chief.

Early in 1643 Batten was sent north to intercept the queen's return from the Netherlands. The queen landed, with a neutral Dutch escort, at Bridlington on 23 February, and at dawn the next day the parliamentary ships bombarded the village. The queen (with her dog) was obliged to shelter in a ditch while Batten shot at them, until he was warned to cease fire by the Dutch admiral. In June 1644 he gave support at the siege of Lyme. On 10 July he resumed his duel with the queen as she sailed from Falmouth. Batten gave chase but was outrun by the queen's lighter ships, which delivered her safely to Brest. In the winter of 1644–5 he assisted at the defence of Plymouth, building a blockhouse there which came to be called Mount Batten. In February 1645 he helped to repel the royalists from Weymouth, leaving once he had seen the streets 'well strawed with their dead bodies' (Powell and

Timings, 190). Following Warwick's enforced resignation under the self-denying ordinance Batten was made commander at sea on 22 May 1645, his commission subject to periodic renewal. He was involved in the assault on Haverfordwest in July and August. In February 1646 he was at the siege of Dartmouth and in April he took the surrender of Portland. He then sailed to the Isles of Scilly to capture the prince of Wales, whom on 12 April he had surrounded on St Mary's. But a storm dispersed his ships, and once again Batten missed a major prize. In July he was at the siege of Pendennis; in September he was able to secure the Scillies, though the prince had escaped.

On 21 December 1646 Batten was sent to Newcastle to investigate a Dutch man-of-war which was correctly thought to be waiting to spirit the king away from his Scottish keepers. During this operation Batten established a rapport with the Scots; as well as a common religious persuasion there was a shared feeling that their contributions to the war were undervalued by the parliamentary leadership. Batten's chaplain, Samuel Kem, preached before the king advocating reconciliation, and it is possible that Batten himself expected Charles to compromise in the presbyterian interest. From this point Batten began a secret correspondence with the Scots. In February 1647 he returned to the Downs in the *Constant Warwick* (a privateer in which he had a share, and to which he had transferred to enter the Tyne). He moved to the *St Andrew* for the summer guard. In May he arrested some Swedish ships that had refused to salute. In June, unaware of Batten's own untrustworthiness, the army command warned him against possible mutiny in the fleet. His hand was forced when presbyterian members were ejected from the Commons and several attempted to escape by sea. Batten's ships intercepted them, but on 17 August he allowed them to proceed. Batten was now watched, and was reported to have forecast that the army meant to have the king executed: this was not yet actually in prospect, and Batten's alleged remark was considered inflammatory. The navy commission was reinforced with radicals and, on 17 September, Batten was made to resign his vice-admiralty. Since he remained a commissioner, the extent of his collusion with the Scots cannot have been known.

By April 1648 Batten's attempts to subvert seamen had been observed in a Leadenhall Street tavern, and on 23 May he was given positive vetting by a royalist agent. At the same time the city hierarchy petitioned for his return to sea command. Warwick arranged to meet him at Portsmouth in June but could not find him; Batten had been there shortly before, conspiring with the seamen and hoping to hire additional ships abroad before any coup was attempted. The actual revolt in the Downs, though assisted by Samuel Kem, pre-empted Batten's larger schemes, and instead of leading the mutiny he was obliged to follow in its wake. On 10 June the Derby House committee finally realized that Batten had defected (though supposing it to be to aid royalist land forces in Essex) and repeatedly ordered him to appear before them. Probably between 14 and 18 July, Batten, with Captain Elias Jordan, boarded the *Constant Warwick* at Leigh Road in

the Thames and took her over to the Netherlands. The prince of Wales was already at sea with his new fleet, and on 28 July he ordered Batten back to the Downs. There, on 10 August, Batten was welcomed by the prince, knighted, and made rear-admiral (the highest post available). Batten publicly justified his action by recounting his personal grievances against those whom he had previously served, together with his belief in a constitutional settlement under the crown: 'we fought all this time to bring the King to his Parliament, and yet now it is made treason to offer to bring him thither' (Powell and Timings, 366). His conversion to royalism was distrusted by many about the prince, but he was at first welcomed by the seamen. He lost their affection, however, by striking deals with the owners of captured ships, thereby denying the men their prize-money. When on 29–30 August there was some prospect of a general action against the parliamentary fleet, Batten was seen, according to Charles II's later recollection, mopping his sweat with a large white napkin. Prince Rupert affected to believe this was a signal to the enemy, and proposed to shoot him at the first sign of trouble.

As the royalists retreated Batten chose neither to fight nor to attempt to win over another detachment of parliamentary ships they chanced to meet. Despite his dubious conduct he was advanced to vice-admiral in September when the royalists had returned to the Netherlands; but he was removed from effective command by the appointment of Rupert as admiral in October. Batten was reluctant to return to the fleet, suspecting Rupert of inciting the men against him, and he decided to accept an amnesty offered by parliament. As part of the deal the *Constant Warwick* was returned on 5 November. On the 18th Batten and Jordan resigned their commissions, and were then given the prince's leave to return to England. It appears this permission was subsequently revoked, but the two men were seemingly home by December.

Astonishingly it was not until the creation of a new navy committee on 16 January 1649 that Batten was automatically excluded from his commissionership. He had been declared a delinquent in September 1648, but his property appears to have escaped sequestration, and he continued as a commercial shipowner. Militarily he was no longer employable. His only friends seem to have been the Dutch: in April 1649 the Dutch admiral Tromp advised Charles II to recall him, and at the start of the First Dutch War in 1652 it was rumoured that he would fight for the Hollanders. An attempt to obtain compensation for his share in the *Constant Warwick* was predictably dismissed in November 1654. He appears to have remained in England and been commercially active until the Restoration. At some point in the 1650s his wife, Margaret (with whom he had two sons and two daughters), died, and on 3 February 1659 he married his second wife, Elizabeth, *née* Turner, widow of William Woodstocke of Westminster.

On 28 March 1660 Batten wrote to the king offering to arrange transport when the Restoration should occur, and in hope of some future employment. On 20 June he was rewarded with his old place of surveyor of the navy. The final phase of his life is vividly portrayed by his junior colleague at the Navy Board, Samuel Pepys, in whose pages Batten appears as a corrupt, idle, and foul-mouthed incompetent. Pepys grew to detest Batten and supposed the feeling to be reciprocated. Batten was certainly infuriated by Pepys telling him his business, not least because the younger man was so often right. Within a year or so Pepys was able to defeat Batten in technical arguments over cordage and timber. Their greatest disagreement was over a contract for masts which Pepys negotiated, in Batten's absence, with Sir William Warren in September 1663. Batten, who favoured the rival firm of Wood and Castle (Castle being Batten's son-in-law), reproached Pepys 'most passionately' when he found he had been outmanoeuvred (Pool, 27). Pepys's diary and the navy white book are full of the rogueries and knaveries of the surveyor. That Batten took bribes from contractors is undoubted and unremarkable. That he was a poor bookkeeper is confirmed by his successor, Thomas Middleton, who could find precious little evidence for Batten 'ever to have been Surveyor' (Latham, 184). The only serious allegation against Batten in these years, however, is that he withheld sums—perhaps more than £1000—from the Chatham chest for seamen's welfare. Of Batten's conduct in general Sir William Coventry judged that 'only his heaviness and unaptness for business' made him act 'without advice and rashly and to gratify people that do eat and drink and play with him' (Pepys, *Diary*, 4.194–5).

In 1661 Batten was elected MP for Rochester. As surveyor he was also a JP for the counties in which the naval dockyards stood. In 1663–4 he was master of Trinity House and in that capacity built almshouses for the corporation. In December 1664 he had a patent to erect two lighthouses in Harwich, the dues from which were his principal resource. From his first wife he acquired a pleasant house at Walthamstow, Essex, which he filled with fine objects and where he cultivated a garden and a vineyard. Pepys's first impression that he lived there 'like a prince' (Pepys, *Diary*, 1.280) was naïve, but Batten certainly lived comfortably beyond his means. At his death he owed more than £4000, including £666 to Pepys for a share of the privateer they had fitted out during the Second Dutch War. By the start of the war in 1665 Batten's health had declined, and he was consequently absent at critical times. He lived long enough to see the Dutch strike more boldly into the Thames than he had dared to do in 1648. He died in London on 5 October 1667 and was buried at Walthamstow on the 12th. He had fallen out with his eldest son, William, a barrister, and left him only £10. To his second surviving son, Benjamin, a naval lieutenant, he left the modest landholding in Somerset which he had inherited from his own father. To his black servant, Mingo, he entrusted the keeping of the Harwich lighthouses, with a stipend of £20 a year. The lighthouse dues were all he could leave his wife. She resolved her financial difficulties by marrying the Swedish resident in London, Baron Leijonbergh. Batten also left two married daughters, Martha Castle and Mary Leming. All the children were from his first marriage.

Batten was of displeasing appearance but (as Pepys allowed) could be an amiable companion, with a simple sense of humour and a fund of good stories. His inadequacies as an administrator in his last years are familiar only because of the chance that made him a principal character in Pepys's diary. It is for his conduct in the 1640s that he must principally be judged, and it was no friend who acknowledged his 'unquestionable courage and industry' in those times (Clarendon, *Hist. rebellion*, 4.374).

C. S. KNIGHTON

Sources HoP, *Commons, 1660–90*, 1.607 · *CSP dom.*, 1627–67 · J. R. Powell, *The navy in the English civil war* (1962) · J. R. Powell and E. K. Timings, eds., *Documents relating to the civil war, 1642–1648*, Navy RS, 105 (1963) · *Report on the Pepys manuscripts*, HMC, 70 (1911), 220, 235, 279, 285, 292, 294–5 · Clarendon, *Hist. rebellion*, 2.23, 225, 467–8; 4.331–2, 341, 373–4, 416–17 · D. E. Kennedy, 'The English naval revolt of 1648', *EngHR*, 77 (1962), 247–56, esp. 247–9, 251–2, 255 · M. L. Baumber, 'Parliamentary naval politics, 1641–49', *Mariner's Mirror*, 82 (1996), 403–6 · K. R. Andrews, *Ships, money, and politics: seafaring and naval enterprise in the reign of Charles I* (1991), 37, 44, 81–2 · B. Capp, *Cromwell's navy: the fleet and the English revolution, 1648–1660* (1989), 3, 15–16, 20–21, 23, 26–8, 31, 33–6, 38–9, 48, 60 · B. Pool, *Navy board contracts, 1660–1832* (1966), 26–7 · Pepys, *Diary*, vols. 1–8; 10.21–2 · *Samuel Pepys and the Second Dutch War: Pepys's navy white book and Brooke House papers*, ed. R. Latham, Navy RS, 133 (1995) [transcribed by W. Matthews and C. Knighton] · *Calendar of the Clarendon state papers preserved in the Bodleian Library*, 4: 1657–1660, ed. F. J. Routledge (1932), 374, 621

Likenesses T. Athow, wash drawing, AM Oxf. · oils (after portrait at Hengrave Hall), NMM · portrait, Hengrave Hall, Suffolk

Wealth at death left £800 in cash to family; £30 p.a. from land at Easton Gordano alias St George's, Somerset; also dues from Harwich lighthouses: Pepys, *Diary*, vol. 8, pp. 476–7; will, PRO, PROB 11/325, fols. 217v–219 · debts over £4000: HoP, *Commons, 1660–90*

Batten, William (1889–1959), rugby player, was born on 26 May 1889 at 9 Gorton Terrace, Kinsley, Hemsworth, Yorkshire, the son of James Batten (1848–1910), a coalminer, and his wife, Ann, *née* Hughes. He played rugby as a junior with Kinsley and Ackworth United before joining Hunslet in the Northern Union. His signing-on fee was a new suit. He made his début on 9 February 1907 in a 15–0 win against Barrow. In his second season, aged only eighteen, he helped Hunslet to become the first team to win all four cups. In the 1911–12 season Batten broke the club record by scoring twenty-five tries. He became Hunslet's captain in 1911 but was transferred to Hull on 5 April 1913 for £600, double the previous world record fee. His transfer came about because Batten felt he should be paid as much as contemporary colonial players in England and top association footballers were receiving. Ultimately Hull were reported to have paid Batten an unprecedented £14 a match.

Billy Batten became the most outstanding and controversial personality in Northern Union (later rugby league) football. A centre three-quarter, weighing over 13 stone, he was regarded as the most thrustful player of his generation and the hardest-tackling back in the game. Many of his tries were scored by hurdling his opponents, a dangerous practice which was eventually outlawed. His style of play and swarthy, muscular appearance fascinated fans and made him a huge crowd-puller. His effect on the attendances at Hull was such that his £600 transfer fee was recouped by the club within a few games. He scored three tries on his Hull début against Keighley on 12 April 1913. He became such an idol on Humberside that his absence from the team in any fixture was reckoned to cost the club £100 in lost gate money. He flourished in a team strengthened by Australian imports. In 1914 he starred as Hull won the challenge cup for the first time after beating Wakefield Trinity 6–0 in the final at Halifax.

In 1920 Batten scored the only try of the game when Hull beat Huddersfield 3–2 at Headingley to lift their first rugby league championship. Hull retained the trophy in 1921 after defeating Hull Kingston Rovers in the final. In 1922 he was a try-scorer in Hull's 9–10 challenge cup final defeat by Rochdale Hornets and was again a scorer when the club won its first Yorkshire challenge cup in 1923 by defeating Huddersfield 10–4 in the final. Batten also helped Hull to win the Yorkshire league championship twice. In April 1920 Batten became the first player to receive a benefit of over £1000 (£1079), a mark of the enormous respect afforded him by the sport. He played his last game for Hull at Bramley on 5 April 1924. He was transferred to Wakefield Trinity for £350, helped them to Yorkshire cup finals in 1924 (when they won) and 1926 (when they were runners-up), and finished his professional career with Castleford in 1927 before returning to the amateur ranks.

Batten won nineteen Yorkshire caps (1908–26) and played in twenty-seven international and test matches (1908–23). Despite being a centre, he played most of his games at representative level as a winger, where his damaging running was a sore trial to opponents. He made only one tour of Australasia—the inaugural Lions tour of 1910, when he played in all the test matches. He declined to tour in 1914 for personal reasons and in 1920 refused to play in any tour trials, declaring that the selectors should have known enough about him after thirteen years at the pinnacle of the game.

Batten was a generous man, who did not forget his roots. In 1921 when the mining villages of Kinsley and Fitzwilliam were in severe hardship, he gave much of his Hull benefit proceeds to suffering villagers. On 11 January 1909 he married Ann Glover (b. 1887/8), a domestic servant, with whom he had eight children: William, Sydney Melbourne, Mary, Eric, Florence, Emily, Ann, and Robert. Three sons, William, Eric, and Robert, became professional rugby league players, and Eric emulated his father in playing for Yorkshire, England, and Great Britain. Two of Batten's brothers, Edward and James, were also professional players.

For most of his working life Batten was a colliery corporal, although he did briefly in the 1920s become the licensee of the Old King's Arms, Kirkgate, Wakefield. He served throughout the Second World War in the fire service. He died on 26 January 1959 of cardiovascular degeneration at Stanley Royd Hospital, Wakefield, and was buried four days later at Hemsworth parish church. He was survived by his wife. ROBERT GATE

Sources G. G. Wilkinson, 'Billy Batten', *Rugby League Review*, 110 (1950), 166–7 · [Knightrider], 'Billy Batten', *Rugby League Magazine*, 7 (1964), 20–21 · souvenir programme of W. Batten's benefit, Hull *v.* York, 3 April 1920 · b. cert. · m. cert. · d. cert. · *Yorkshire Evening News* (29 Jan 1959) · private information (2004) [grandson]
Likenesses photograph, 1913, repro. in J. Huntington-Whiteley, ed., *The book of British sporting heroes* (1995) [exhibition catalogue, National Portrait Gallery, London, 16 Oct 1998–24 Jan 1999]; priv. coll.

Battersea. For this title name *see* Flower, Cyril, Baron Battersea (1843–1907); Flower, Constance, Lady Battersea (1843–1931).

Battie, William (*bap.* **1703**, *d.* **1776**), physician, the son of the Revd Edward Battie (1664?–1714), rector of Modbury, Devon, and his wife, Catherine, was baptized in Modbury on 1 September 1703. He was educated, as his father had been, at Eton College, from 1717, where he was a king's scholar, and at King's College, Cambridge, from 1722. In 1724 he applied for, and was eventually awarded, the Craven scholarship at King's College, and in 1725 he was elected to a fellowship of the college. He remained a fellow until 1739. Battie graduated BA in 1727, and his interest in the classics is apparent from two of his early publications, scholarly editions of Aristotle's *Rhetoric* (1728) and Isocrates's *Orations* (1729). After obtaining his MA in 1730 he studied law and for a short time was a student at the Middle Temple, in 1732, before having to withdraw because of lack of money. He then chose medicine and made steady progress. By about 1735 he was practising medicine and delivering anatomical lectures in Cambridge. After leaving Cambridge he established a large medical practice in Uxbridge, Middlesex, where his success owed a great deal to his cousins, who were prosperous tradesmen in the town. He also seems to have benefited from the patronage of Henry Godolphin (1648–1733), provost of Eton.

Battie's life seems to have entered a new phase between 1737 and 1738. Around this time he received a legacy of over £20,000 from one of his cousins. He graduated MD in 1737, at Cambridge, and subsequently moved to London. He became a fellow of the Royal College of Physicians in 1738. In the same year he married a daughter of Barnham Goode, under-master at Eton, a native of Maldon in Surrey, and an alumnus both of Eton and of King's College, Cambridge. They had three daughters: Anne (*d.* 1830), who married Sir George Young; and Catherine and Philadelphia, who both married gentlemen.

Battie played a prominent role in the Royal College of Physicians. He acted as a censor in 1743, 1747, and 1749, and in 1746 he delivered the Harveian oration, which was published in the same year. In 1750 he took part in a dispute between the college and Isaac Schomberg, who wanted to practise medicine in London without possessing the required MD from either Oxford or Cambridge universities. This led to Battie's being attacked by Moses Mendes in a pamphlet, *The Battiad* (1751). Battie was also Lumleian orator from 1749 to 1754; his lectures, published in 1751 and 1757 as *De principiis animalibus*, show that he was familiar with contemporary developments in physiological experimentation.

Battie is best remembered as a pioneer in the treatment

William Battie (*bap.* 1703, *d.* 1776), by unknown artist

of the insane, a branch of medicine which was then emerging in somewhat specialized form. In 1742 he was elected a governor of the Bethlem Hospital, and for the rest of his life he took an active part in effecting reforms at the hospital. Battie was elected as the first physician to St Luke's Hospital for Lunaticks when it opened in 1751; this institution was a major addition to the public provision for the insane in London. In 1758 Battie published his best-known work, *A Treatise on Madness*. In it he expressed ideas which were to become influential in the treatment of the insane during the eighteenth century. Battie was optimistic about the curability of madness, though he believed that idiopathic madness ('original madness') was incurable. He also stressed the need to provide clinical education to medical students studying in institutions for the insane, and apparently he tried to implement a plan for this at St Luke's. The idea does not, however, seem to have been successful and was soon abandoned. Most importantly, Battie emphasized the curative effect of a well-designed and judiciously managed hospital in the treatment of madness, instead of the traditional purges, blood-letting, and medications, arguing that the disease was more likely to be cured by careful arrangement of the patient's physical and psychological environment. Battie thus firmly anchored the treatment of the insane within the medical institution, which he argued should become the focal point in the treatment of madness.

Battie's *Treatise on Madness* prompted John Monro, physician to the Bethlem Hospital, to publish *Remarks on Dr Battie's Treatise on Madness* in 1758. In this work Monro offered thorough examination and criticism of Battie's work, particularly over the definition of madness. Closely following the contemporary medical concept of madness,

Battie maintained that madness consisted in 'deluded imagination', caused by stimuli on the nervous system ('delusive sensation'). Monro, on the other hand, argued that not all cases of madness were accompanied by illusory perception, and he emphasized the role played by judgement. Despite their differences on the definition of madness, it would be wrong to paint the Battie–Monro debate as one between the progressive St Luke's and the traditional Bethlem. They agreed at least as often as they differed, especially over the primacy of management in the hospital. The dispute itself, which was probably the first debate in psychiatry, indicates a growing interest in the question of the treatment of madness. This was exemplified in 1763, when an anonymous author writing to *Gentleman's Magazine* criticized Battie's definition of madness, which he expressed in another of his works, *Aphorismi de cognoscendi & curandis morbis* (1760).

Battie was practising at a time when some of those treating the insane were beginning to be called upon to give expert advice to non-medical bodies. In 1763, for example, Battie gave evidence before a parliamentary committee to enquire into private madhouses, and the findings were incorporated into the 1774 act to regulate madhouses. Battie also gave a successful performance in 1763 in the court case *Wood* v. *Monro*, which established the legal opinion that insanity could be detected only by expert interviewing. Battie also had an extensive private practice in the treatment of the insane. About 1750 he acquired premises in Islington for private patients, and in 1754 he took over a long-established madhouse. The private practice was extremely lucrative: in one case the bill to the patient amounted to about £750. Battie owned a large house in Great Russell Street, London, as well as country houses at Twickenham and Marlow.

In 1764 Battie retired from the office of physician at St Luke's. In the same year he was elected president of the College of Physicians. He was still active in 1773, when he attended the third earl of Orford, who showed symptoms of mental illness. Battie himself was 'of eccentric habits, sometimes appearing like a labourer, and doing strange things' (Munk, 143).

Battie died a widower on 13 June 1776, at his house in London, and was buried on 19 June at Kingston, Surrey. Horace Walpole reported that Battie died worth £100,000, though the *London Chronicle* put the figure at £200,000. In 1747 Battie had founded a scholarship at Cambridge worth £20 a year, and he nominated the scholars during his lifetime.

Although Battie's influence on later psychiatric practice was limited, he was often cited favourably in medical textbooks and treatises on madness during the late-eighteenth and early-nineteenth centuries. Even after the mid-nineteenth century, when many of his ideas became either commonplace or outdated, some psychiatrists acknowledged that Battie had anticipated some of their own concerns. Battie's clearly articulated, optimistic, and progressive views on the treatment of the insane were typical of much Enlightenment thought.

AKIHITO SUZUKI

Sources W. Battie, *Treatise on madness*, in *A treatise on madness, by William Battie, M.D., and Remarks on Dr. Battie's Treatise on madness, by John Monro*, ed. R. Hunter and I. Macalpine (1962) · R. A. Austen-Leigh, ed., *The Eton College register, 1698–1752* (1927) · Nichols, *Lit. anecdotes* · J. H. Jesse, *Memoirs of celebrated Etonians* (1875) · Venn, *Alum. Cant.* · Burke, *Peerage* · Munk, *Roll* · A. Suzuki, 'Mind and its disease in Enlightenment British medicine', PhD diss., U. Lond., 1992 · DNB · *London Magazine*, 45 (1776), 392
Likenesses oils, RCP Lond. [*see illus.*]
Wealth at death £100,000 or £200,000

Battier [*née* Fleming], **Henrietta** (*c.*1751–1813), poet and satirist, was the daughter of John Fleming of Staholmock, co. Meath, Ireland. She later wrote that 'strangers possess my paternal acres' (Battier, preface). By the age of eleven she was writing poetry; she thought well enough of a poem written that year (for Good Friday) to publish it in her collected volume. Her husband was the son of a Dublin banker of Huguenot extraction; they had at least four children. Although called Battier he was not Major John Gaspard Battier as has previously been thought.

Battier was probably the 'Polly Pindar, half-sister to Peter Pindar', whose *The Mousiad: an Heroic-Comic Poem* was published at Dublin in 1787 by P. Byrne. The poem and its typography closely resemble *The Lousiad: an Heroi-Comic Poem* by John Wolcot ('Peter Pindar'), whose first canto Byrne published in 1785. The pseudonym and general style even more closely resemble those of Battier's later satires. If this work is hers, she was at Ipswich in Suffolk on 21 May 1787: the *Mousiad's* preface 'To the reviewers' is so dated.

Meanwhile, on a visit to London with her husband in 1783–4, Battier had put together a volume of manuscript poems which she hoped to get published. She approached Samuel Johnson, who gave her his name to head her subscription list, together with warm encouragement and practical help towards securing more subscribers. Her hopes of publishing were dashed by Johnson's death, and further delayed by serious illness and the death of a child. Not until 1791 did her volume appear: *The protected fugitives: a collection of miscellaneous poems, the genuine products of a lady, never before published.* The poems (both personal and public, sentimental and sharply topical) show a remarkable talent, but little resemblance to her even more remarkable satire.

While in London, Battier appeared on stage at Drury Lane theatre, playing Lady Rachel Russell in three performances of Thomas Stratford's tragedy on the death of the protestant hero Lord Russell, a role she mentions in *The Protected Fugitives* (Battier, 120–33). She developed friendly relations with the clientele at the Shakespeare tavern, for whom she celebrated the duchess of Devonshire's famous electioneering of 1784 (ibid., 158–62). She then, however, fell seriously ill. Her husband was ill too; her son died in September 1789; a daughter was probably already dead.

The same year as her collection, Battier published in Dublin her first known satire as 'Patt. Pindar': *The Kirwanade, or, Poetical Epistle. Humbly Addressed to the Modern Apostle*, in two separate parts, periodical-style. It opens magnificently:

Unknowing either, and to both unknown,
An individual, fearless and alone,
I lift the Gauntlet, in full Chapter thrown
By THEE, O! K[irwa]n, with satanic grace …

Her target, Walter Blake Kirwan, dean of Killala, a convert to the Church of Ireland from Catholicism, had subscribed to *The Protected Fugitives*. Battier threw down another gauntlet in *The Gibbonade, or, Political Reviewer* (three numbers, 1 May 1793–12 September 1794). This attacked Lord Fitzgibbon (later earl of Clare) and praised the United Irishmen and the spirit of Swift ('friend of Ierne'). Battier had to struggle to keep afloat financially; she sold her own works from her poor lodgings at 17 Fade Street, Dublin, where undergraduates from Trinity College regularly dropped in. Thomas Moore the poet later remembered her as 'odd, acute, warm-hearted, and intrepid'. His then boundless admiration for Battier's work cooled with time to the condescension he felt due to an old woman.

Battier's political lampoons probably sold well. In 1795 she published as 'Pat. T. Pindar', in Dublin and London, an exuberant *Marriage Ode Royal after the Manner of Dryden*, on the marriage of the prince of Wales. 'Royal' in the title appears upside down. In 1797 came *The Lemon*, another trenchant reading of Irish politics, in 1799 *An Address on … the Projected Union*. This work, addressed to 'the Illustrious Stephen III, King of Dalkey, Emperor of the Mugglins, Grand Master of the Noble, Illustrious and Ancient Orders of the Lobster, Crab, Scallop', was written in Battier's capacity as poet laureate to a club of radicals for its annual festal day (a politicized festival of misrule) on the island of Dalkey near Dublin, as recounted in Moore's *Memoirs*. Battier died at Sandymount, Dublin, between September and November 1813. ISOBEL GRUNDY

Sources [H. Battier], *The protected fugitives: a collection of miscellaneous poems* (Dublin, 1791) · *Memoirs, journal and correspondence of Thomas Moore*, ed. J. Russell, 8 vols. (1853–6) · A. Carpenter, ed., *Verse in English from eighteenth-century Ireland* (1998) · D. J. O'Donoghue, *The poets of Ireland: a biographical dictionary with bibliographical particulars*, 1 vol. in 3 pts (1892–3) · A. H. Scouten, ed., *The London stage, 1660–1800*, pt 3: *1729–1747* (1961)

Battine, William (1765–1836), lawyer and poet, was born at East Marden, Sussex, on 25 January 1765, the only son of William Battine. Through his mother's family he was one of the coheirs of the dormant barony of Bray, but he never publicly urged his claim. He was educated at Eton College and Trinity Hall, Cambridge, where he took the degree of LLB in 1780, and that of LLD in 1785. He became a fellow of Trinity Hall in 1788.

Admitted as a student to the Middle Temple as early as 1773, Battine was admitted fellow of the College of Doctors of Law in London on 3 November 1785, and soon secured a large practice in the ecclesiastical and admiralty courts.

During the 1790s Battine became a close friend of the prince of Wales, the future George IV, and was later credited with having settled a quarrel between the prince and his father, George III. From 1812 until 1827 he was one of the gentlemen of the privy chamber in ordinary.

For many years Battine was advocate-general in the high

court of Admiralty, and chancellor of the diocese of Lincoln; he also held several other minor legal offices. He was elected a fellow of the Royal Society on 1 June 1797.

In 1822 Battine published a dramatic poem, entitled *Another Cain: a Mystery*, written, he claimed, 'to correct the blasphemy' in Lord Byron's *Cain*. He was also the author of a pamphlet which argued that gentlemen of the privy chamber were exempt from arrest in civil suits, an indignity to which Battine had himself apparently been subjected.

In his later years Battine became increasingly eccentric and, having squandered the wealth he had acquired in his profession, lived in great poverty. He died on 5 September 1836 at Fitzroy Place, Surrey, and was, according to his own wish, buried privately five days later in the church of St George the Martyr, Southwark.

SIDNEY LEE, *rev.* JONATHAN HARRIS

Sources GM, 2nd ser., 6 (1836), 545–6 · Venn, *Alum. Cant.* · J. Hutchinson, ed., *A catalogue of notable Middle Templars: with brief biographical notices* (1902), 14 · T. Thomson, *History of the Royal Society from its institution to the end of the eighteenth century* (1812), appx 4, p. lxv

Battishill, Jonathan (1738–1801), composer and organist, was born in London in May 1738, the son of Jonathan Battishill, a solicitor, and Mary Leverton, his wife, and grandson of Jonathan Battishill, rector of Sheepwash, Devon. At the age of nine he became a chorister of St Paul's Cathedral, and was, after his voice broke, articled pupil to the famously strict choirmaster William Savage. His scientific knowledge of music and manual execution advanced rapidly, and when his term of apprenticeship expired he was already known as one of the best extemporizers on the organ in the country. At this time he composed some very successful songs for Sadler's Wells Theatre. Possessed of a fine tenor voice, he was also a frequent soloist in London concerts, including Handel's *Alexander's Feast* at the Little Theatre in the Haymarket on 16 March 1756. He was then associated with William Boyce at the Chapel Royal as his deputy organist, and about the same time was engaged to conduct the band from the harpsichord at Covent Garden Theatre. He composed theatrical music for performance there and at the Drury Lane Theatre. On 11 June 1758 he was elected a member of the Madrigal Society, and on 2 August 1761 became a member of the Society of Musicians. From about 1762 he was a 'priviledged member' of the Noblemen's and Gentlemen's Catch Club. He became acquainted with Elizabeth Davies, a singing actress at Covent Garden (the original Madge in *Love in a Village*), and married her on 19 December 1765 at St George's, Bloomsbury. In 1764 he was appointed organist of the united London parishes of St Clement, Eastcheap, and St Martin Orgar, and in 1767 also of Christ Church Greyfriars. These appointments, which he held until his death, forced him to sever his connection with Boyce. About the same time he gave up his post at Covent Garden, and his wife retired from public life. He remained active as a teacher, and in 1764 composed the cantata *The Shepherd and Shepherdess*, and most of the music—all the choruses and some of the airs—for the opera *Almena* (2 November 1764, Drury Lane), of which the overture and the rest of the airs were written

by Michael Arne. The music was apparently let down by Richard Rolt's libretto, and so the work was performed only five times. In spite of this failure Battishill persevered with theatrical composition, which had previously included the music to a pantomime called *The Rites of Hecate* (26 December 1763, Drury Lane), which was a success. Soon after this he set to music a collection of hymns by Charles Wesley, and wrote a number of songs and a set of sonatas for harpsichord. The *Collection of Songs for Three or Four Voices*, from around 1770, was 'one of the first published collections of glees to contain fragments of keyboard accompaniment cued into the vocal parts' (*Recollections of R. J. S. Stevens*, 288). About 1771 he received a gold medal from the Catch Club for his cheerful glee 'Come bind my hair, ye wood nymphs fair'. About 1776 he composed several choruses for Lee and Baildon's entertainments at the Crown and Anchor tavern. His propensity for liquor became more pronounced after 1777, when 'his wife eloped with the actor Webster to Dublin' (Jones). The subsequent decline in his fortunes and health was a definite factor in his failure to be appointed organist of St Paul's in 1796, on the death of John Jones, despite being an obvious candidate. His love of literature (he had collected six to seven thousand volumes) occupied him during his later years. After a long illness he died at Islington, London, on 10 December 1801, and was buried, in accordance with his wishes, in the vaults of St Paul's, near the remains of Boyce. The funeral service was composed by Busby, and Battishill's own widely admired and effective seven-part anthem 'Call to remembrance' (1767, revised 1797; it remains in the cathedral repertory to the present day) was sung, and accompanied by Attwood. His works are mostly from the period 1760–75, and have been thought similar to those of Purcell. The songs are often energetic and vigorous and the part-writing is highly accomplished. His playing of the organ and harpsichord and extempore performance were considered dignified and tasteful, and he rejected mere dexterity and rapidity of execution. His playing of Handel's keyboard works was particularly praised. He was blessed with an exceptional memory, as exemplified by the oft-cited occasion when he played and sang several airs by Samuel Arnold from memory, which he had not heard for at least twenty years.

Besides the collection of his works published during his lifetime, including the popular song 'May-Eve, or, Kate of Aberdeen' and the catch 'I loved thee beautiful and kind', several anthems, chants, psalm tunes, hymns, and pieces for organ or piano were published after his death by Page in 1804. The British Library has a copy of *Two Anthems as they are Sung in St Paul's Cathedral* (1767). These are the aforementioned 'Call to remembrance' and 'How long wilt thou forget me?' (five parts with organ).

J. A. F. MAITLAND, *rev.* DAVID J. GOLBY

Sources P. W. Jones, 'Battishill, Jonathan', *New Grove* · Brown & Stratton, *Brit. mus.*, 35 · *Recollections of R. J. S. Stevens: an organist in Georgian London*, ed. M. Argent (1992) · W. Bingley, *Musical biography*, 2nd edn, 2 (1834), 222–5 · J. B. Trend, 'Jonathan Battishill', *Music and Letters*, 13 (1932), 264–71 · Highfill, Burnim & Langhans, *BDA*

Likenesses S. Harding, stipple, pubd 1803 (after miniature by L. Sullivan, 1765), BM, NPG • J. Chapman, stipple, pubd 1805 (after Drummond), NPG

Battley, Richard (*bap.* **1772**, *d.* **1856**), apothecary and manufacturing chemist, was baptized on 26 September 1772 at Wakefield, Yorkshire, the second son of John Battley, an architect of local repute, and his wife, Ruth Gledhill. After attending Wakefield grammar school, he was privately trained for medicine by a doctor in the town. He then moved to Newcastle upon Tyne, where he gained experience as a medical attendant in the neighbouring collieries.

In 1795 Battley became a student at St Thomas's and Guy's hospitals in London, where he made friends with the ophthalmic surgeon John Cunningham Saunders. He then served in the Royal Navy as an assistant surgeon, and was present at several engagements under Admiral Sir William Sidney Smith. Having returned to London, he acquired the practice of an apothecary in St Paul's Churchyard. Together with Saunders and with John Richard Farre he was co-founder of the London Ophthalmic Infirmary, later Moorfields Eye Hospital, which opened in 1805. Battley acted as honorary secretary until 1818, for some years supplying medicines free of charge. About 1812 he established a pharmaceutical chemist's business in Cripplegate, and also lectured on pharmacology.

Battley's efforts to set up and maintain Moorfields Hospital encountered difficulties and impediments which were compounded by persistent attacks in *The Lancet* by the editor, Thomas Wakley. However, Battley possessed formidable energy and perseverance, and he often lingered over experiments with noxious substances until driven away by severe headaches and feeble pulse; several times he nearly died. These characteristics made him irascible and sometimes over-hasty in his remarks, but many acknowledged his wide generosity. He introduced a number of pharmaceutical innovations and in 1827 he started up a laboratory to analyse the vegetable substances of materia medica; later he added a museum, which was open to all medical students.

Battley married twice. His first wife left no surviving children. On 4 August 1829 he married Elinor, daughter of the Norwich surgeon William Dalrymple and his wife, Marianne Bertram. They had two daughters, one of whom married Reginald Palgrave, clerk to the House of Commons. Shortly after retiring and selling his business, Battley died at Reigate, on 4 March 1856, leaving £75,665.

[ANON.], *rev.* T. A. B. CORLEY

Sources GM, 2nd ser., 45 (1856), 534–6 • Boase, *Mod. Eng. biog.* • E. T. Collins, *The history and traditions of the Moorfields Eye Hospital: one hundred years of ophthalmic discovery and development* (1929) • IGI • will
Wealth at death £75,665: will, PRO

Batty, Robert (**1762/3–1849**), obstetric physician, was born at Kirkby Lonsdale, Westmorland. After receiving his medical education in London and Edinburgh, he graduated MD at the University of St Andrews on 30 August 1797, shortly after which he settled in London as an obstetric physician. He is probably the Dr Batty who gave lectures on midwifery at Great Marlborough Street, London, in 1799. On 30 September 1800 he was admitted by the Royal College of Physicians a licentiate in midwifery, and on 22 December 1804 a licentiate of the college. He was physician to the maternity hospital, Brownlow Street, and for some years was editor of the *Medical and Physical Journal*. Like his son, Colonel Robert *Batty (1788/9–1848), he was known as an amateur artist but did not achieve his son's eminence in that field. None the less he exhibited at the Royal Academy, 1788–97. He spent his last years at Fairlight Lodge, Hastings, where he died on 16 November 1849 at the age of eighty-six.

[ANON.], *rev.* ELIZABETH BAIGENT

Sources GM, 2nd ser., 34 (1850), 293 • Munk, *Roll* • Venn, *Alum. Cant.* • Bénézit, *Dict.* • S. C. Lawrence, *Charitable knowledge: hospital pupils and practitioners in eighteenth-century London* (1996)
Likenesses attrib. G. Dance, pencil drawing, 1799, RCP Lond. • W. Daniell, soft-ground etching, pubd 1810 (after pencil drawing attrib. G. Dance, 1799), BM, Wellcome L. • W. H. Clift, pencil and watercolour • photograph (after pencil drawing attrib. G. Dance, 1799), Wellcome L.

Batty, Robert (**1788/9–1848**), army officer and artist, was born in London, son of the obstetric physician, medical journal editor, and amateur artist Dr Robert *Batty (1762/3–1849). After attending school in Kirkby Lonsdale, Westmorland, and in London, at the age of fifteen he travelled to Italy with his cousin, Henry Bickersteth (later Lord Langdale), where he 'had the opportunity of cultivating a taste for art, which belonged to his family' (Redgrave, 31). He studied at Caius College, Cambridge (admitted March 1808), obtaining an MB in 1813, but did not practise medicine. Instead, having become an ensign in the 1st (Grenadier) guards on 14 January 1813, Batty served with its 1st battalion towards the end of the Peninsular War, notably at the blockade of Bayonne, before embarking for England from Bordeaux on 23 July 1814. During the duke of Wellington's 1815 campaign in the Netherlands, he fought with the 3rd battalion at Quatre Bras on 16 June. Approaching Bossu Wood, from which the French could outflank the main British position at the nearby crossroads, the guards fixed bayonets and attacked. Thick trees dispersed the men and the enemy 'contested every bush … but [they] could not resist us', despite 'tremendous' losses inflicted by their cavalry, as the British emerged from cover (Brett-James, 56–7). Two days later, at Waterloo (where he was slightly wounded in the thigh), Batty's battalion attacked enemy skirmishers after the fall of La Haye-Sainte and advanced decisively against the imperial guard in the evening. Following Wellington's victory, Batty entered Paris with the 3rd battalion on 7 July, having *en route* been at the storming of the fortress of Péronne on 26 June. Three days later, he became a lieutenant and captain in the first guards. He served in the army of occupation in France. In 1821 he married Johanna Maria, eldest daughter of Sir John Barrow, bt (1764–1848), of Ulverston, secretary of the Admiralty; they had children and she survived her husband. On 28 February 1822 he was elected

FRS. Batty acted as Lieutenant-General Sir William Clinton's aide-de-camp with the 1826–7 expedition to Portugal in support of the young Portuguese queen against Spanish-backed rebels. Without becoming major, he went on half-pay as lieutenant-colonel on 30 December 1828, and sold his commission on 1 November 1839.

Batty compiled, and illustrated with plates etched by himself, accounts of his active service, *The campaign of the left wing of the allied army in the western Pyrenees and south of France, 1813–4* (1823) and *A Sketch of the Campaign of 1815*. He wrote, too, illustrated topographical books about the scenery of France (1822); Germany (1823); Wales (1823); Hanover, Saxony, and Denmark (1828); and India; and *Select Views of the Principal Cities of Europe* (1830–33), which suggests that he spent little time with his regiment after its return from France in 1818. Numerous other watercolours of Spanish and Portuguese scenes were unpublished, but he did illustrate John Barrow's account *A Family Tour through South Holland, up the Rhine and across the Netherlands* (1831). Between 1825 and 1832 he occasionally exhibited at the Royal Academy. He suffered from paralysis, but painted until within a few weeks of his death. Acknowledged as 'an amateur artist of considerable merit' (Bryan, *Painters*, 11), he died at Ridgemount Place, Ampthill Square, London, on 20 November 1848, aged fifty-nine. Among artists of the English school, Samuel Redgrave concluded that 'his industry was great, his works carefully and truthfully drawn, his architecture correct in its proportions and outlines, and his merits as a topographical draughtsman deserve recognition' (Redgrave, 31). His sister, Mrs Philip Martineau, 'the fair daughter' of Dr Batty, enjoyed a reputation for 'eminent … topographical taste' after publishing in 1820 a collection of illustrations of Italian scenery (Bryan, *Painters*, 11). Batty's son Robert Braithwaite Batty (1828/9–1861) was educated at Emmanuel College, Cambridge (BA, second wrangler, 1853; MA 1856), and was a fellow and lecturer in mathematics at Emmanuel. Ordained (deacon 1854, priest 1855) in 1860, he went to India as a missionary with the Church Missionary Society. He died of dysentery, aged thirty-two, on 22 June 1861 at the mission house, Amritsar. JOHN SWEETMAN

Sources *Army List* · *GM*, 2nd ser., 31 (1849), 207–8 · F. W. Hamilton, *The origin and history of the first or grenadier guards*, 2–3 (1874) · H. L. Aubrey-Fletcher, *A history of the foot guards* (1927) · E. Longford [E. H. Pakenham, countess of Longford], *Wellington*, 1: *The years of the sword* (1969); pbk edn (1971) · E. A. Brett-James, *The hundred days* (1964) · Redgrave, *Artists* · Bryan, *Painters* (1866) · C. Dalton, *The Waterloo roll call*, 2nd edn (1904); repr. (1971) · W. Siborne, *The Waterloo campaign, 1815* (1895) · Venn, *Alum. Cant.* · *The record of the Royal Society of London*, 4th edn (1940) · Boase, *Mod. Eng. biog.* · *DNB* · H. Ottley, *A biographical and critical dictionary of recent and living painters and engravers* (1866)

Batty, Thomas (*c.*1832–1903), animal trainer and circus proprietor, was a nephew of William Batty, the lessee of Astley's Amphitheatre, London. Celebrated as a lion tamer, he is also said to have been the first to train an elephant to stand on its head. He had many life-threatening struggles with the lions he 'tamed': he had so many scars on one side of his body that, it was said, a half-crown could not be placed between them. He would enter the ring, clad in Lincoln green and long leather boots, with a short whip in his hand. The lions would spring at the bars of their cage with fierce snarls, and he would strike at their paws with his whip, provoking their fury. Someone in the audience would always entreat him not to enter the cage, but he would slip in and have a lively ten minutes or so. From about 1859 he performed on the continent. On one occasion, in Hamburg, he entered the cage wearing a glittering spangled costume, whereupon one of the lions mauled him badly, tearing off the costume and scoring his back. He escaped by using the butt of the gun which he carried at that time; another tamer, Lucas, was killed by the same lions in Paris in 1869. Batty returned to Britain in 1874 and began a provincial tour with his own circus, which enjoyed a reputation for grandeur and excellence. He claimed to pay more in wages to his performers than any two other travelling circuses.

Batty and his first wife (whose name is unknown) had ten children who were brought up in the circus. Their son George became a famous jockey act rider and proprietor. Mrs Batty died in 1875 and Batty later married Sarah Footit, *née* Crockett (*c.*1836–1923). His fortunes declined in his later years, and he entered the workhouse at Newcastle upon Tyne. He died in the Newcastle City Lunatic Asylum, Gosforth, on 22 September 1903.

JOHN M. TURNER

Sources C. Keith, *Circus life and amusements* (1879) · *World's Fair* (6 Oct 1923), 8b · *World's Fair* (13 Oct 1928), 42b · 'ABC of the show', *World's Fair* (1938–9) · *Era Almanack and Annual* (1876) · R. Wood, *Victorian delights* (1967) · H. Thétard, *La merveilleuse histoire du cirque* (1978) · d. cert.
Archives Circus Friends Association archive, Blackburn, cuttings in scrapbooks
Likenesses portrait, Harvard TC

Baty, Richard (*bap.* 1696, *d.* 1758), Church of England clergyman, was born at Arthuret, Cumberland, and baptized there on 27 December 1696. He was educated at Glasgow University, where he received an MA in 1725. He returned to Cumberland to become curate of Kirkandrew upon Esk, a position he held until 1732, when he was presented by the patron of the living, Viscount Preston, to be rector of the parish. Baty built a rectory for himself at his own expense, and provided a ferry for the use of his parishioners—the first ferry across the River Esk, which ran through the town and across which there was no bridge. He insisted on the importance of education, and promoted the erection of a schoolhouse in the neighbourhood. His genial temper made him popular with all his neighbours, and with the noblemen and gentlemen on both sides of the border; but he was held by some to be too profuse in his hospitality. He studied the eye and its diseases, and won local fame as a skilful oculist.

Baty published a number of works at Newcastle, including *A Sermon on the Sacrament, with Prayers for the Use of Persons in Private* (1751), *Seasonable Advice to a Careless World* (1756), and *The Young Clergyman's Companion in Visiting the Sick*. He died in 1758. [ANON.], rev. ROBERT BROWN

Sources W. Hutchinson, *The history of the county of Cumberland*, 2 vols. (1794) · A. Chalmers, ed., *The general biographical dictionary*, new edn, 32 vols. (1812–17) · *IGI*

Baude [Bawd, Bawood], **Peter** (d. 1546), gun-founder, is thought to have been born in France, but nothing is known of his origins or family circumstances. It is said he came to Britain as early as 1509 but the first official reference to him is as a 'gunner' at the Tower of London in 1528 with a pension of 16d. a day.

By 1531 Baude was established at a foundry in Houndsditch, where he was joined by the three Owen brothers, John, Robert, and Thomas, to whom Baude doubtless imparted his skills. Three of Baude's bronze guns from this time have survived. A cannon and a culverin were recovered from the *Mary Rose*, while at the Tower there has survived, though badly damaged, a three-barrelled gun enclosed in a square casing which illustrates Baude's decorative skills. Over the next twelve years official records list substantial sums earned by Baude and his Owen associates for casting bronze, but not as yet iron, guns. A change, however, was on the way.

Threatened by the combined forces of Spain and France, by 1539 Henry VIII had begun an ambitious fortification of the southern coastline. Naval construction also increased. In consequence, Henry was in need of quantities of ordnance which, if cast in bronze, were beyond the resources of his depleted treasury. This must have prompted what Holinshed later described as the making at Buxted in Sussex in 1543 by 'Rafe Hoge and Peter Bawd' (*Holinshed's Chronicles*, 3.832) of the first pieces cast of iron ever made in England. In fact iron guns had been cast in the early 1500s, but with detachable breach and barrel. These presumably proved unsatisfactory and were not continued. What was needed was an iron gun cast in one piece like a bronze gun.

Baude was the obvious choice for this undertaking. He was at the peak of his career, and on 10 October 1542 he had been granted his denization papers in the name of Bawood. Others involved in the same enterprise were Ralph Hogge and William Levett. Hogge was then a skilled furnace master and employed by Levett, rector of Buxted and holder of the post of king's 'gunstonemaker'. Although attracting no contemporary notice, success must have attended the work of this trio. Iron guns made by Levett were sent in 1544 to the defence of Portsmouth and the Isle of Wight against the French. Furnaces casting iron guns started up in the Weald. Baude too turned to casting iron guns: a demi-culverin of his at Portsmouth was included in the 1547 inventory of Henry VIII's possessions.

Baude died in 1546. In July of that year John and Thomas Owen were appointed king's gun-founders in his place. An eminent gun-founder even without taking account of his contribution to the re-emergence of cast-iron ordnance, Baude occupies a pivotal position in the history of English ordnance. He was one of a small group of outstanding foreign craftsmen recruited from the continent in the first half of the sixteenth century to enhance Henry VIII's ordnance capability and avoid dependence on imported guns.   EDMUND TEESDALE

Sources *LP Henry VIII*, vols. 5–21 · *APC*, 1542–99 · H. L. Blackmore, *The armouries of the Tower of London* (1976) · C. Ffoulkes, *Gunfounders of England* (1937) · *Holinshed's chronicles of England, Scotland and Ireland*, ed. H. Ellis, 6 vols. (1807–8) · H. Schubert, 'The first cast-iron cannon made in England', *Journal of the Iron and Steel Institute*, 146/2 (1942), 131–40 · R. Jenkins, 'Iron founding in England, 1490–1603', *Transactions* [Newcomen Society], 19 (1938–9), 35–49 · A. D. Saunders, 'The coastal defences in the south-east', *Archaeological Journal*, 126 (1969), 201–11 · J. R. Kenyon, 'Ordnance and the king's fortifications in 1547–48, Society of Antiquaries MS 129 folios 250–374', *Archaeologia*, 107 (1982), 165–213 · private information (2004)
Archives Mary Rose Trust, Portsmouth, bronze guns · Tower of London, gun in casing

Baudouin, Nicolas (1525/6–1613), Reformed minister, was a native of Rouen, Normandy. Like many of his Huguenot compatriots, he fled to Geneva, signing the *Livre des habitants* on 14 April 1559. He moved on within the year, when the Company of Pastors sent him to Guernsey to participate in the establishment of an *église dressée*—a Reformed church on the Genevan model. This was at the request of an islander, Guillaume Beauvoir, deacon at the English church in Geneva, 1556–8. A letter of Calvin's dated 16 December 1559, which Baudouin carried to Beauvoir, called him pure in doctrine. Another of the same date, from Remond Chauvet, minister of St Gervais, described him to Beauvoir as 'éloquent et orné de bonne Grâce' (Schickler, 2.368).

Baudouin was later stated to have set about assembling his flock on 14 February 1560. Though he was then or later appointed to Guernsey's principal church, St Peter Port, generally he met an unenthusiastic response in Guernsey, where the population and administration were hostile to Reformed ideas. In 1562 François de St-Paul, believing he wished to leave, wrote to Calvin that the Huguenot church at Dieppe, which Baudouin knew well, had written to him requesting his presence there.

The following year matters improved with the arrival in Guernsey of English royal commissioners, who noted that Baudouin was a godly preacher who, with the support of a few well-disposed people, had taken continual pains in advancing the Reformation: preaching thrice weekly, upholding royal interests, and catechizing young and old. A consistory having been set up on 17 May 1563, he was granted an income. Protestants were advanced to secular power in 1565 and a *Discipline* was introduced for the Channel Islands in 1567. Baudouin also preached at the first service of the French-speaking Reformed church at Southampton on 28 October 1567 and it has been suggested that he may have played a role in the establishment of that church as well.

Baudouin married Louise Morise, daughter of Guillaume Morise (d. 1584), seigneur de la Ripaudière, minister in Jersey. If they first met in the Channel Islands, as seems likely, this marriage may not have been his first, since a son, Adrian, is noted as godfather to a daughter, Marthe, born in 1570. Baudouin's other recorded children were Samuel (d. 1568), Timothee (b. 1564), and Simon (1572–1573). Louise died in 1573, and Baudouin later married Clemence Baucher (d. 1607).

The bishop of Winchester's appointment of a commissary in Guernsey in 1581 led to a bitter dispute between the secular and spiritual powers. About that time the clergy were petitioning for the right to small tithes, and Baudouin also fell out with the island authorities over his excommunication of a *jurat* (a permanent juryman and legislator). He fled to London, and in 1584, bearing a testimonial from Sir Francis Walsingham, he was appointed to his late father-in-law's parish of Ste Marie, Jersey. Baudouin was followed to Jersey by several colleagues, and a thirteen-year rift between the islands' churches resulted.

In 1599, following the death of the incumbent of St Peter Port, the parishioners requested the return of their 'pere en Christ', and Baudouin resumed that living ('Papier ou livre des colloques', fol. 55v). From 1606 he was frequently incapacitated by illness and infirmity, requiring assistance in administering the Lord's supper. Last recorded as attending a colloquy meeting in April 1611, he died on 16 April 1613. The record of his burial the following day notes he had been 'ministre de nostre Eglize de St pierre port lespace de cinquante trois ans' (St Peter Port parish register). While this was not strictly correct, it is not surprising that the church chose to claim wholly for itself this important figure in Guernsey's Reformation.

D. M. OGIER

Sources F. de Schickler, *Les églises du réfuge en Angleterre*, 3 vols. (Paris, 1892) · D. M. Ogier, *Reformation and society in Guernsey* (1996) · parish registers, St Peter Port, Guernsey, Priaulx Library, Guernsey, SR · G. Syvret, ed., *Chroniques des îles de Jersey, Guernesey, Auregny et Serk* (1832) · report of the Royal Commission of 1563, Hatfield House, Hertfordshire, Salisbury papers, Cecil papers, 207/12 · 'Papier ou livre des colloques des églises de Guernezey', Priaulx Library, Guernsey, SR · a notebook of Pierre le Roy, Island Archives Service, Guernsey, AQ 83/25 · P. F. Geisendorf, ed., *Livre des habitants de Genève*, 1: *1549–1560* (Geneva, 1957) · A. Maulvault, 'La réforme à Guernesey: observation sur une des *Lettres françaises de Calvin* publiées par M. Jules Bonnet', *Bulletin Historique et Littéraire* [Société de l'Histoire du Protestantisme Français], 17 (1868), 254–6 · G. Daval and J. Daval, *Histoire de la Réformation à Dieppe, 1557–1657*, ed. E. Lesens, 2 vols. (Rouen, 1878–9) · A. Spicer, *The French-speaking Reformed community and their church in Southampton, 1567–c.1620* (1997)

Bauer, Ferdinand Lukas (1760–1826), botanical artist, was born on 20 January 1760 at Feldsberg, Austria, the son of Lukas Bauer or Baur (1706/7–1762), court painter to the prince of Liechtenstein, and his wife, Theresia, *née* Hirsch. Three sons—Joseph (1756–1831), Franz Andreas *Bauer (1758–1840), and Ferdinand—showed a talent for drawing and in their formative years were influenced by Prior Norbert Boccius (1729–1806). About 1780 Franz and Ferdinand moved to Vienna and there met Baron Nickolaus von Jacquin (1727–1817). Because of Ferdinand's talent, Jacquin set him to help prepare his *Icones plantarum rariorum* (1781–93). Through Jacquin he met John Sibthorp and was subsequently taken on as illustrator for his *Flora Graeca* (1806–40). In 1786 Bauer accompanied Sibthorp to Italy, the Aegean, Turkey, Greece, and Cyprus. Late that year he returned to England with Sibthorp to continue illustrating the *Flora Graeca*. In London in the 1790s he also illustrated papers for the *Transactions of the Linnean Society* and through this his work became known to Sir Joseph Banks, who was then looking for a botanical artist to go on a voyage of exploration to Australia. Bauer was recruited for HMS *Investigator*, commanded by Lieutenant Matthew Flinders RN. His salary for the voyage was paid by the Admiralty, he was under the orders of the naturalist to the expedition, Robert Brown, and he shared the artwork with William Westall.

Investigator sailed from Spithead in July 1801 and after calling at Madeira and the Cape of Good Hope crossed the Southern Ocean to Western Australia. The vessel then sailed eastwards, touching various points and making natural history collections, along the southern coast and passing through Bass Strait to anchor at Port Jackson. More plants were collected in the neighbourhood of Sydney while *Investigator* was refitted, and in late July 1802 she sailed up the Queensland coast, passing into the Gulf of Carpentaria in early November. In this remote place, with the hurricane season approaching, she was found to be unseaworthy; the survey was terminated shortly after and *Investigator* sailed to Timor and thence back to Sydney where the vessel was declared irreparable and in June 1804 downgraded to the status of a hulk.

Bauer remained in Australia collecting and drawing plants while (abortive) attempts were made to obtain a new survey ship. He resided in the settlement of Sydney but made a short trip during March and April 1804 to the Hunter River where he drew plants and collected herbarium specimens. He also sailed for Norfolk Island on *Albion* on 21 August 1804, returning to Sydney on 11 March 1805 for the sea trial of the hastily refitted *Investigator*. Bauer and Brown finally left Sydney on 23 May 1805 in the still-leaking *Investigator* and arrived at Liverpool on 13 October.

Bauer prepared well over 2000 plant and animal field drawings during the voyage of *Investigator*. He remained in London from 1806 to 1814, during which time he completed some 234 watercolours from his original field sketches. The work was paid for by the Admiralty and most drawings passed to it. The British Museum acquired the Admiralty drawings in 1843. At his death Ferdinand Bauer's original pencil sketches of landscapes from Norfolk Island and some of his botanical drawings were bought by his brother Franz, who was by this time a plant illustrator at Kew. When Franz died in 1840 they were auctioned at Christies and bought by Robert Brown, now keeper of botany in the British Museum, and given to the museum. James Britten, writing in 1909, confirmed that the museum received botanical drawings from the Admiralty and others from Brown. Consequently Ferdinand Bauer's completed watercolours of Australian plants and animals and Norfolk Island field sketches are to be found today in the botany and zoology libraries of the Natural History Museum, London.

Fifteen of his plates (seventeen drawings) appeared in Bauer's only publication, *Illustrationes florae Novae Hollandiae* (1813–16), for which he engraved the copper plates himself. This work was originally conceived as illustrating Robert Brown's *Prodromus* of 1810 but, because of cost, and the labour involved, this intention was not realized. A further ten illustrations prepared from Bauer's originals were engraved by other artists as uncoloured plates and published in the atlas accompanying Flinders's narrative of the *Investigator* voyage (1814) and published along with William Westall's Australian coastal profiles. However, the post-Napoleonic war period was a time of depression and *Illustrationes florae Novae Hollandiae* was not a commercial success. Consequently, with Europe now relatively peaceful, in 1814 he returned to Vienna, taking his original Australian field drawings with him. Bauer visited England only once more, in 1819, and died at Hietzing, Vienna, on 17 March 1826. At the subsequent auction, held in March 1827, many of these drawings were bought by Emperor Franz I. The majority of the surviving original field sketches, both coloured and pencil drawings, are now in the Natürhistorisches Museum, Vienna; many of them are dated, located, and colour-coded. They also include both plants and animals seen at *Investigator* landing places—that is from Madeira, South Africa, the various Australian collecting sites, Norfolk Island, and Timor—and numerous orchids from New South Wales. The copper plates made for *Illustrationes florae Novae Hollandiae* survive in London and an edition was printed from them in 1989.

Some authorities feel that Bauer was the most accomplished botanical artist ever but he is little known because so few of his drawings were published. His watercolours are superb and the animal drawings in particular have a most lifelike quality. Accounts were published of these beautiful drawings from the 1960s onwards, but it was not until the 1990s that catalogues of the Bauer animal and plant watercolours in the Natural History Museum were prepared. The Bauer brothers are commemorated in the Australian plant genus *Bauera* (Cunnoniaceae).

D. T. MOORE

Sources J. Lhotsky, 'A biographical sketch of Ferdinand Bauer, natural history painter to the expedition under Captain Flinders', *Proceedings of the Linnean Society of London*, 1 (1838–48), 39–40 • J. Lhotsky, 'Biographical sketch of Ferdinand Bauer, natural history painter', *Journal of Botany*, 2 (1843), 106–13 • J. Britten, 'Ferdinand Bauer's drawings of Australian plants', *Journal of Botany, British and Foreign*, 47 (1909), 140–46 • M. Flinders, *A voyage to Terra Australis*, 2 vols. (1814) • D. T. Moore, 'The pencil landscape drawings made by Ferdinand Bauer in Norfolk Island from August 1804 to February 1805, in the Natural History Museum, London', *Archives of Natural History*, 25 (1998), 213–20 • M. J. Norst, *Ferdinand Bauer: the Australian natural history drawings* (1989) • D. J. Mabberley and D. T. Moore, 'Catalogue of the holdings in the Natural History Museum (London) of the Australian botanical drawings of Ferdinand Bauer (1760–1826) and cognate materials relating to the *Investigator* voyage of 1801–1805', *Bulletin of the Natural History Museum, London* [Botany Series], 29 (1999), 81–226 • A. Wheeler and D. T. Moore, 'The animal drawings of Ferdinand Bauer in the Natural History Museum, London', *Archives of Natural History*, 21 (1994), 309–44 • W. Blunt and W. T. Stearn, *The art of botanical illustration*, new edn (1994) • W. Lack, 'The Sibthorpian herbarium at Oxford', *Taxon*, 46 (1997), 253–63 • W. Lack and V. Ibáñez, 'Recording colour in late eighteenth century botanical drawings: Sydney Parkinson, Ferdinand Bauer and Thaddäus Haenke', *Curtis's Botanical Magazine*, [6th ser.], 14 (1997), 87–100 • will, PRO, PROB 11/1715, sig. 420 • P. Watts, A. Pomfrett, and D. J. Mabberley, *An exquisite eye: the Australian flora and fauna drawing, 1801–1820, of Ferdinand Bauer* (Historic Houses Trust of New South Wales, 1997)
Archives Linn. Soc., letters from Australia • Natürhistorisches Museum, Vienna, original field drawings of Australian botanical and zoological subjects • NHM, botany library, completed botanical and zoological watercolours and pencil sketches of Norfolk Island
Wealth at death see will extract, Norst, *Ferdinand Bauer*, 112

Bauer, Franz Andreas (1758–1840), microscopist and botanical artist, was born on 4 October 1758 in Feldsberg, Austria (now Valtice, Czech Republic). He was the second of the four sons of Lukas Bauer or Baur (1706/7–1762), a religious and court painter to the prince of Liechtenstein. After his father's death he was trained by his mother, Theresia, *née* Hirsch, and encouraged by Dr Norbert Boccius, prior of Feldsberg monastery. His first published drawing, at the age of thirteen, was of *Anemone pratensis* (unsigned) in a work by von Störck (1771). On moving to Vienna about 1780, Franz and his brother Ferdinand Lukas *Bauer (1760–1826) met Baron Nikolaus Joseph von Jacquin (1727–1817), director of the Schönbrunn Imperial Gardens, and improved their botanical techniques by working on his *Icones plantarum rariorum* (1781–93). During the spring of 1786 Ferdinand Bauer was engaged by John Sibthorp (1758–1796) for a botanical tour of the Near East and returned with him to England. Two years later, Franz Bauer began a European tour with his friend Joseph Franz von Jacquin. On visiting London, after seeing his brother (then working for Sibthorp at Oxford), to use the library and herbarium of Sir Joseph Banks, Bauer was persuaded to work at Kew as a resident draughtsman to draw newly discovered plants. He took up the position in 1790, and was occupied in such work over the next eighteen years; all his drawings became the property of Banks. In addition he drew specimens for Robert Brown and Banks's other friends. For a short period Bauer acted as unpaid drawing-master to Queen Charlotte and the princesses and also had other pupils including T. C. Holland and William Hooker (1779–1832). After 1816 he worked for Sir Everard Home (1756–1832), Banks's physician, using his talent for microscopical detail to produce accurate drawings of animal and human organs for various papers, subsequently reprinted as Home's *Lectures on Comparative Anatomy* (1814–28). Bauer became a fellow of the Linnean Society in 1804 and of the Royal Society in 1821.

Although unofficially identified as 'Botanick painter to His Majesty' when working at Kew, Bauer's salary was paid by Banks, and ceased with his death in 1820. Banks bequeathed his library and herbarium to the British Museum and at one time it was intended that all the botanical books were to be sent to Kew with Bauer filling the post of librarian. That scheme failed but Bauer received a life annuity of £300 under Banks's will on condition that he continue to work at Kew, while various codicils and conditions caused further difficulties that halted other provisions for Bauer's future (Meynell, 'Francis Bauer', 211–12; Desmond, *Kew*, 409–10). With Robert Brown, Bauer was involved in implementing the provisions of Banks's will.

Bauer remained at Kew throughout his life and produced drawings, including those for Lindley's *Illustrations of Orchidaceous Plants* (1830–38) and William Hooker's *Genera filicum* (1842), and even produced popular articles on

Franz Andreas Bauer (1758–1840), by William Brockedon, 1834

the diseases of corn under his own name (*Penny Magazine*, 2, 1833). Apparently Bauer simply followed his own bent, satisfying a curiosity and fascination with the floral mechanisms of the Orchidaceae and of micro-organisms. His sketchbooks of 1805 and 1813 reflect this continued interest in palynology and plant pathology, while a paper (*Transactions of the Linnean Society*, 18, 1840, 475–82) demonstrated a concern to establish the priority of his research. Meynell ('Francis Bauer', 214) emphasized that a feature of Bauer's work was its continuity, with some projects taking several decades, although on occasion he produced single drawings for particular papers.

Everyone for whom he worked valued Bauer's opinion on scientific questions, realizing that in order to achieve such detailed drawings he thoroughly understood the material. Baker established that Bauer had recognized in his drawings numerous microscopic features of pollen 'that were not cleared up until … half a century later' and concluded that, had his work been known, the science of palynology would have advanced much earlier. This contradicts the contention of Olby (*DSB*, 1.520–21) that Bauer's microscopical paintings had little scientific worth since they were made without the benefit of modern laboratory techniques. It was during the studies of pollen that Bauer published his lithographs of *Strelitzia depicta* (1818) that are virtually original watercolours. His knowledge, together with a general affability and modesty, encouraged his medical and botanical acquaintances to meet regularly at Kew as a discussion circle, while most scientists visiting London endeavoured to meet him.

Bauer died at his home, Eglantine Cottage, 20 Waterloo Place, Kew Green, on 11 December 1840 at the age of eighty-two; he was buried on 16 December at St Anne's Church, Kew Green. The epitaph on a memorial tablet recognized that 'In microscopical drawing he was altogether unrivalled'; not surprisingly it was found that he had sixteen microscopes. Shortly before his death, Bauer had adopted Elizabeth Baker, his maid for the past twenty-five years, as his daughter. To the end of his life he is said to have retained his German accent and had difficulty in writing polished English (Haverfield).

Together with his brother Ferdinand, Franz Bauer created a standard of botanical artistry combined with critical observation that has never been equalled. Banks had considered that any description of the plants portrayed in the *Delineations of Exotic Plants* (1796–1803) was superfluous as the figures displayed every aspect. Bauer has since been regarded as one of the outstanding artists in the 'golden age' of flower painting (Desmond, *Kew*, 434); Blunt (Blunt and Stearn, 199), when deciding 'the greatest botanical artist of all time', stated 'I myself unhesitatingly give first place to Franz Bauer', believing he was 'the more perfect craftsman' when compared with his brother. Stearn (*Endeavour*, 27, 35), however, felt that the two brothers had to be honoured together, as they stood 'unrivalled … as supreme masters of their craft which came nearer to perfection than that of any other artist before or since'.

R. J. CLEEVELY

Sources W. T. Stearn, 'Franz and Ferdinand Bauer, masters of botanical illustration', *Endeavour*, 19 (1960), 27–35 · R. Desmond, *Kew: the history of the Royal Botanic Gardens* (1995), 108–12, 409, 412–13, 434 · G. Meynell, 'Francis Bauer, Joseph Banks, Everard Home and others', *Archives of Natural History*, 11 (1983), 209–21 · *Proceedings of the Linnean Society of London*, 1 (1838–48), 101–4 · W. Blunt and W. T. Stearn, *The art of botanical illustration* (1950), 195–202 · G. Meynell, 'Banks papers in the Kent Archives Office, including notebooks by Joseph Banks and Francis Bauer', *Archives of Natural History*, 10 (1981–2), 77–88 · H. G. Baker, 'A palynological treasure-house', *Nature*, 167 (1951), 457–60 · R. Olby, 'Bauer, Franz Andreas', *DSB* · *The Athenaeum* (26 Dec 1840), 1025–6 · J. Stewart and W. T. Stearn, *Orchid paintings of Franz Bauer* (1993) · F. A. Stafleu and R. S. Cowan, *Taxonomic literature: a selective guide*, 2nd edn, 5, Regnum Vegetabile, 112 (1985), 7146–7 · Desmond, *Botanists*, 47–8 · W. T. Thistleton-Dyer, 'Historical account of Kew to 1841', *Bulletin of Miscellaneous Information* [RBG Kew] (1891), 279–327 · R. Wittmack, 'Zwei österreichische Pflanzenmaler in England: Franz und Ferdinand Bauer', *Beiträge z. landwirtschaftlichen Pflanzenbau inbesondere Getreidebau* (1924), 37–42 · T. T. Haverfield, 'Notes on Kew and Kew Gardens', *Leisure Hour*, 11 (1862), 767–8 · F. Scheer, *Kew and its gardens* (1840) · H. W. Lack, *The Flora Graeca story: Sibthorp, Bauer, and Hawkins in the Levant* (1999)

Archives FM Cam., watercolour · Linn. Soc., drawings · NHM, botanical notes and drawings · RBG Kew, memoranda and papers relating to diseases in corn · RS, drawings · University of Göttingen Library, drawings; MSS | CKS, Banks MSS · Cornwall RO, Hawkins archive, letters, J3/2/132, 138 · UCL, letters to N. J. von Jacquin

Likenesses W. Brockedon, pencil-and-chalk drawing, 1834, NPG [see illus.] · R. Westmacott, memorial tablet, St Anne's Church, Kew Green · oils, RBG Kew; repro. in Stearn, 'Franz and Ferdinand Bauer', 27 · oils, Carnegie Mellon University, Pennsylvania, Hunt Botanical Library

Wealth at death exact sum unknown: will, PRO, PROB 11/1937, fol. 149v; Meynell, 'Francis Bauer', 219

Bauerman, Hilary (1835–1909), mineralogist and geologist, was born in London on 16 March 1835, the younger son in the family of two sons and one daughter of Hilary John Bauerman and his wife, Anna Hudina Rosetta, daughter of Dr Wychers. His parents migrated from Emden, in Hesse, to London in August 1829. On 6 November 1851 Bauerman was entered as one of the seven original students of the Government School of Mines, later the Royal School of Mines, in Jermyn Street. At the change of name in 1862 the degree of associate of the Royal School of Mines was conferred on him. In 1853 he went to the *Bergakademie* at Freiberg in Saxony to complete his studies, and on his return to England in 1855 he was appointed an assistant geologist to the Geological Survey of Great Britain. In 1858 he went to Canada as geologist to the North American boundary commission; from 1863, when this task was completed, he was intermittently engaged for many years in searching for mineral deposits and surveying mining properties in various parts of Europe, Asia, and America, mostly by private persons or by companies, but also by the Indian and Egyptian governments (1867–9).

Apart from this fieldwork, Bauerman contributed to technical and scientific literature. His *Treatise on the Metallurgy of Iron* (1868) reached its sixth and last edition in 1890, and was followed by his *Text-Book of Systematic Mineralogy* (1881) and *Text-Book of Descriptive Mineralogy* (1884). Lastly, in 1887, he assisted J. A. Phillips to revise and enlarge the latter's *Elements of Metallurgy*, which was originally published in 1874.

In his later years Bauerman devoted himself mainly to teaching: in 1874 he first acted as an examiner for the Department of Science and Art; in 1883 he was lecturer in metallurgy at Firth College, Sheffield; and in 1888 he succeeded John Percy as professor of metallurgy at the Ordnance College, Woolwich. He retired from the post in 1906 but maintained until his death a keen interest in the developments of metallurgy and mining. He was a fellow, and for some time a vice-president, of the Geological Society; an associate member of the Institution of Civil Engineers, by which he was awarded the Howard prize in 1897; an honorary member of the Iron and Steel Institute, and also of the Institution of Mining and Metallurgy, which awarded him its gold medal in 1906 in recognition of his many services in the advancement of metallurgical science.

Despite partial deafness, which increased with his years, Bauerman's prodigious memory and his genial manner made him a highly successful teacher. He was an indefatigable and versatile worker, his favourite hobbies in later years being crystallography and geometry. He died, unmarried, at his home, 142 Cavendish Road, Balham, London, on 5 December 1909, and was cremated at Brookwood. He left a bequest to encourage the study of mineralogical science in connection with the Royal School of Mines.   T. K. ROSE, *rev.* ANITA MCCONNELL

Sources 'Hilary Bauerman, 1835–1909', *Mineralogical Magazine*, 15 (1908–10), 443–4 · *Geological Magazine*, new ser., 5th decade, 7 (1910), 46–8 · W. J. Sollas, *Quarterly Journal of the Geological Society*, 66 (1910),

l–li · F. G. Stanley, *Mapping the frontier: Charles Wilson's diary of the survey of the 49th parallel* (1970) · *The Engineer* (10 Dec 1909), 604 · *Mining Journal* (18 Dec 1909) · *Journal of the Iron and Steel Institute*, 80 (1909), 305–7 · *Nature*, 82 (1909–10), 195–6 · *The Times* (10 Dec 1909) · private information (1912) · CGPLA Eng. & Wales (1910)

Wealth at death £15,323 6s. 3d.: probate, 9 Feb 1910, CGPLA Eng. & Wales

Baukwell [Bankwell], **Roger** (d. in or after 1350), justice, derived his name from Bakewell in Derbyshire, where he appears to have held property. His parentage is unknown. He is first recorded in Michaelmas term 1314, acting as an attorney in the court of common pleas. During the 1320s he became a pleader in that court, and was created a serjeant at Michaelmas 1329, serving in that capacity at the Northamptonshire eyre of 1329–30. No sooner had he begun to receive commissions of oyer and terminer, and to take assizes, than on 27 February 1331 he was appointed a justice of the bench in Dublin. He may have gone to Ireland—there is a break in the flow of commissions in this year—but the appointment does not seem to have taken effect, and he was certainly back in England by 25 June 1332, when he was made an assessor of tallage in Derbyshire and Nottinghamshire. On 2 October 1333 he was appointed chief justice of the Dublin bench, but again seems to have failed to establish himself there, and from 1334 his career was restricted to England, and particularly to the north midlands.

As well as being a regular assize justice on the midland circuit, Baukwell received numerous separate commissions. Thus in July 1335 he was appointed to investigate the behaviour of tax collectors in Northamptonshire, Warwickshire, and Rutland. In April 1338 he was ordered to define the boundaries of Sherwood Forest. In April 1340 he was made an assessor and collector of the ninth of wool, sheaves, and lambs in Derbyshire. On 8 January 1341, following Edward III's dismissal of much of the judiciary, Baukwell was made a justice of king's bench, and ten days later was appointed a justice for an abortive London eyre. Later in the same year he was a justice on a commission investigating official misconduct in Lincolnshire, Derbyshire, and Nottinghamshire. A trier of petitions in the parliaments of Easter 1341, Easter 1343, and Hilary 1347, in May 1345 he was added to the panel of justices appointed to hold an eyre (which never took place) in the bishopric of Durham.

In 1346 Baukwell received an increment of 20 marks to his annual salary, and in the same year was one of fourteen justices whom the keeper of the great wardrobe was ordered to provide with cloth and fur for robes. He served in king's bench until Michaelmas 1348, but continued to take assizes and to act as a commissioner after that date—his last commission was issued on 25 June 1350, suggesting that he had survived the black death, but died shortly after the epidemic. Unusually for a professional justice by this date, Baukwell was an ecclesiastic—hence his acting as an assize justice at Lincoln on 18 February 1333, but not as a gaol delivery justice on the following day. His rewards in terms of benefices were fairly modest. In 1339 he was presented to a prebend in the royal free chapel of Penkridge, Staffordshire, where in 1349 he became sacrist; in 1341 he was recorded as parson of Dronfield in north-east Derbyshire. HENRY SUMMERSON

Sources Chancery records · Baker, Serjeants, 155, 499 · Sainty, Judges · G. O. Sayles, ed., Select cases in the court of king's bench, 7 vols., SeldS, 55, 57–8, 74, 76, 82, 88 (1936–71), vol. 6, p. xxi · RotP, 2.126, 135, 164 · W. C. Bolland, ed., Year books of Edward II, 18: 8 Edward II, SeldS, 37 (1920), 131 · D. W. Sutherland, ed., The eyre of Northamptonshire: 3–4 Edward III, AD 1329–1330, 2 vols., SeldS, 97–8 (1983) · B. W. McLane, ed., The 1341 royal inquest in Lincolnshire, Lincoln RS, 78 (1988) · J. P. Yeatman, The feudal history of the county of Derby, 4, section 8 (1905), 381 · H. G. Richardson and G. O. Sayles, The administration of Ireland, 1172–1377 (1963) · A. Musson, Public order and law enforcement: the local administration of criminal justice, 1294–1350 (1996)

Baum, John David (1940–1999), paediatrician, was born at 28 Loveday Street, Birmingham, on 23 July 1940 to Isidor Baum (d. 1980), a gown manufacturer's traveller, and his wife, Mary, née Rosenberg (d. 1974), both immigrants from eastern Europe. He had three elder brothers and one younger sister, all of whom developed medical or scientific careers. Baum was educated at George Dixon's Grammar School and Birmingham University medical school, where he qualified MB ChB in 1963. After gaining the MRCP (London) in 1966, he began his paediatric training, mainly at the Royal Postgraduate Medical School, Hammersmith Hospital. That paediatric department, led by Professor Peter Tizard, was in the forefront of developing clinical neonatology in the United Kingdom. On 5 January 1967 he married Angela Rose Goschalk (b. 1945/6), artist and painter. When Tizard was appointed to the new academic department of paediatrics at Oxford in 1972 Baum moved with him, progressing from lecturer to clinical reader, then to an appointment as professorial fellow at St Catherine's College. His clinical work was mainly at the new John Radcliffe Hospital. His research, initially into retinopathy of prematurity (which he studied further during a year at the University of Colorado, Denver), included temperature conservation and the scientific aspects of breast milk feeding, developing a human milk pasteurizer, and methods for measuring breast milk flow. He gained his MD (Birmingham) in 1973, and the Guthrie medal of the British Paediatric Association (BPA) for his research.

Baum's training in London included an MSc in biochemistry and collaboration with many laboratory scientists, but his interests extended to the psychological and social aspects of child health. That expressed itself in the creation of an outstanding service for children with diabetes in Oxford, where he combined the best scientific care with that from other disciplines. His approach was described in his 1985 book, Care of the Child with Diabetes. He was a successful networker more than two decades before that term became current. His failure to succeed Tizard to the Oxford chair was a major disappointment, though his appointment as professor of child health in the University of Bristol in 1985 offered Baum a broader canvas on which to thrive. He was founding director of the Bristol Institute of Child Health. Baum had the skill, enthusiasm, charisma, and concern to cajole others to work together for the benefit of children. He was involved in founding Helen House, Oxford, the first children's hospice in the UK, as well as many projects for disadvantaged children. He relished contacts with other countries, and was a popular secretary of the European Society of Paediatric Research from 1983 to 1987.

Baum's organizational skills and energy were seen at their best in his work for the BPA, notably organizing its scientific meetings (he was never afraid to mix fireworks, celebration, and fun with the science) as well as directing the research unit. The BPA was a 70-year-old organization comprising all British paediatricians, but its political influence for children was limited because it did not have a royal charter as a medical college, and because most consultant paediatricians belonged to the London or Scottish colleges of physicians. The 400-year-old London college did not wish the paediatricians to break away and erode its influence. Many paediatricians wished the BPA to become an independent college; a few were prepared to campaign forcefully. Baum was one of the group who funded and fought that long campaign, though he saw himself as a facilitator rather than as a front-line warrior, for by nature he avoided confrontation. When the battle for paediatric independence was over, and in 1996 a royal charter for the College of Paediatrics and Child Health had been granted, he was elected, in 1997, its second president.

It was the ideal role for Baum: the strife was over, and he could be the first peacetime president for paediatricians. He revelled in it, and was as happy choosing the appropriate blue for the new presidential robe as he was at establishing clinical and training standards, or links with children's organizations in other countries. The position gave scope to the part of his character that loved ceremony with its pomp and ritual, as well as the part that loved eccentricity, the offbeat, and the bizarre.

A short man with the distinctive features for which portrait painters pine—expressive eyes and a jumble of thick curling hair—Baum favoured a flamboyant, rather dandified dress with waistcoat and bow-tie. His family and religion were important: he had four sons, and was a pivotal figure in Bristol's small Orthodox Hebrew congregation. While taking part in a charity bicycle ride from London to Sandringham he died of a heart attack in Harlow on 5 September 1999. That venture by the Royal College of Paediatrics and Child Health had been in aid of children in Bosnia and Kosova. Baum was buried at Rosh Pina near the Sea of Galilee in Israel; his wife survived him.

ROY MEADOW

Sources B. Valman, ed., The Royal College of Paediatrics and Child Health at the millennium (2000) · J. Forfar, A. Jackson, and B. Laurance, eds., The British Paediatric Association, 1928–1988 · Debrett's People of today (1998) · WW (1998) · personal knowledge (2004) · private information (2004) · A. Wilkinson, 'Professor David Baum', The Independent (17 Sept 1999) · The Times (29 Sept 1999) · L. Joffe, 'David Baum', The Guardian (15 Sept 1999) · b. cert. · m. cert. · d. cert. · CGPLA Eng. & Wales (1999)

Likenesses photograph, repro. in *The Times* · photograph, repro. in Forfar, Jackson, and Laurance, eds., *The British Paediatric Association*

Wealth at death £82,202—gross; £79,202—net: probate, 15 Nov 1999, *CGPLA Eng. & Wales*

Baumburgh, Thomas (*d.* 1340), administrator, probably derived his name not, as is often suggested, from Bamburgh in Northumberland but from Baumber in Lincolnshire. He was in royal service by 1322 and was a senior clerk of chancery from 1332, in which year, as also in 1340, he was receiver of petitions from England in parliament. Between 1 April and 23 June 1332 he was one of the keepers of the great seal, and again between 13 January and 17 February 1334; John Stratford, bishop of Winchester, was chancellor on both occasions. Baumburgh again held this important office between 6 and 19 July 1338, during the chancellorship of Richard Bynteworth, bishop of London; after Bynteworth's death he assumed it once more between 8 December 1339 and 16 February 1340, during which period the chancellorship was vacant. Baumburgh died in 1340; by his will, proved on 8 May, he left property in Holborn to the hospital of St Bartholomew, Smithfield.

J. M. RIGG, *rev.* W. M. ORMROD

Sources B. Wilkinson, *The chancery under Edward III* (1929) · Tout, *Admin. hist.* · *Chancery records* · R. R. Sharpe, ed., *Calendar of wills proved and enrolled in the court of husting, London, AD 1258 – AD 1688*, 2 vols. (1889–90)

Wealth at death left property in Holborn to the hospital of St Bartholomew, Smithfield: will, Sharpe, ed., *Calendar of wills*

Baume, Pierre Henri Joseph (1797–1875), radical activist and eccentric, was born at Marseilles on 17 October 1797, the son of Henri Joseph Baume (1770–1831) and Marie Claire Antoinette Merlat (1780–1837). His parents ran a wig-making shop and were inclined both to anti-clericalism and adultery. When he was still young his father moved to Naples, and Baume was placed in a military college in that city. A fortunate encounter there with the mathematician John Lewis Guillemard (1765–1844) resulted in his visiting London in 1816 where he taught French and Italian, and, shortly thereafter, to gaining employment as secretary to Prince Castelcicala, the Neapolitan ambassador in Paris. Baume frequently returned to England on business and for pleasure. By the late 1820s he was closely associated with the advocates of infidelism and social reform in London. In 1832 he became a naturalized citizen. He was, respectively, a preacher of the doctrine of 'reforming optimism' at his own atheist 'chapels', a publisher and vendor of cheap free-thought literature, the proprietor of an experimental cottage community near Holloway, Islington, a theatre manager, and a promoter in Manchester of teetotal public houses. Baume published many polemical notes in the radical press, but he produced nothing more sustained than an eight-page lecture of 1829 in which he strongly endorsed Warburton's 'Dead Bodies Bill', for the legalization of the use of the corpses of paupers for anatomical dissection.

For many years Baume hoped to establish an educational institute on communist principles, but the project was never realized. During the course of the Owenite socialist agitation his distinctive appearance, considerable knowledge, ready speech, and ability to devise striking placards and proclamations made him a notable character. Many regarded him as dangerously mad, however. When his unmarried half-sister Charlotte died in childbirth in December 1832, Baume delivered her body and that of her child to University College for dissection, and was then arrested on suspicion of their murder. Partly as a result of this act, and partly because he was also suspected of being the father of the child, he was dubbed the 'Islington Monster'. It was further alleged that a boy he had adopted and whom he had publicly 'named' by Robert Owen was in fact his and Charlotte's first-born. He certainly had liaisons with Sophie Cornelie de Loigerot (1799–1824), who bore him a son, H. Charles Loigerot (1819–1866), and with Sophie Marguerite Montelli (1816–1840), with whom he had a daughter, Sophie (*b.* 1839).

In May 1837 Baume was committed to Fleet prison for one year for refusing to meet certain financial demands. Believed to have amassed a fortune as a foreign spy, he was as renowned for his promises of financial support to radical causes as he was for never fulfilling the promises. Abstemious in the extreme, he lived at one time chiefly upon dried peas, which he carried in his pocket, and at another time upon a mixture of garden snails and cabbage. He was always obsessed by the belief that he was surrounded by government spies, and he hoarded his extensive correspondence as he hoarded his money.

For several years Baume resided in Manchester, where he organized Sunday lectures on radical social and educational topics, but in 1857 he paid a visit to the Isle of Man, and subsequently took up his residence there, purchasing various properties. After his death, at Duke Street, Douglas, on 28 October 1875, his estate was found to be worth over £50,000, and included, besides many American and foreign investments, a property at Colney Hatch, Southgate, Middlesex, and another at Dibden Hill, Chalfont St Giles, Buckinghamshire, estimated to be worth £4000. Except for the Buckinghamshire property, which was given to an heir apparent in whom lineal descent was facially observed, the rest of the estate was left in trust for philanthropic purposes in the Isle of Man. Baume was buried on 2 November at St George's, Douglas.

ROGER COOTER

Sources DNB · P. H. J. Baume, diary, WI, 1108 [723 pp] · G. J. Holyoake, *The history of co-operation*, 2 vols. (1875–9) · R. Richardson, *Death, dissection and the destitute* (1987) · *Manchester Guardian* (30 Oct 1875), 9 · R. Cooter, *Phrenology in the British Isles: an annotated historical biobibliography and index* (1989) · J. Cowin, 'Old Baume's' bequests of over £30,000 to the Isle of Man' (1894) · 'Baume's Money', *The Manx Quarterly*, 12 (June 1913), 1227–9 · PRO, MH 74 [material on the death of Charlotte Baume] · PRO, HO 64/16 [police spy reports] · The estate of P. H. Baume, an account of the receipts and expenditure of the trustees and executors of his will to the 2nd day of November 1989 [printed; Isle of Man] · Last will and testament of P. H. Baume, 10 Sept 1875, Manx Museum [copy also with National Trust] · personal knowledge (2004) · Manx National Heritage Library, Douglas, Isle of Man, Baume MSS

Archives Manx National Heritage Library, Douglas, Isle of Man · PRO, MH 74, HO 64/16 · Wellcome L., MS diary

Likenesses E. E. Geflowski, bust, after 1875 · portrait, Manx National Heritage Library, Douglas, Isle of Man, Baume MSS
Wealth at death under £600: probate, 3 Feb 1876, *CGPLA Eng. & Wales* · approx. £50,000: *DNB*; Cowin 'Old Baume's' Bequests; estate of P. H. Baume, an account

Bauthumley, Jacob. *See* Bothumley, Jacob (1613–1692).

Bauwens, Lieven (1769–1822). *See under* Industrial spies (*act. c.*1700–*c.*1800).

Bauzá, Felipe (1764–1834), hydrographer, was born in Palma, Majorca, in the Spanish Balearic Islands. He entered the Spanish navy at the age of fifteen, and experienced active service as he rose through the ranks. His career as a hydrographer began under Tofiño y Varela, surveying for the maritime atlas of Spain, and continued on the circumnavigation under Alessandro Malaspina, 1789–94, when he took charge of the charts and plans made during the voyage. On the way back, Bauzá and his shipmate Espinosa y Tello travelled overland from Valparaiso to Buenos Aires, making geophysical, magnetic, and surveying observations. After further active service, he was posted in May 1797 to the hydrographic office in Madrid. In the war of independence against Napoleon's troops in 1810, Bauzá found himself fighting alongside British troops at Cadiz. He subsequently returned to Madrid and in 1815 succeeded Espinosa y Tello as director of the Depósito Hidrográfico. Honours accrued to Bauzá: in 1807 membership of the Spanish Academy of History; in 1816 membership of the Royal Bavarian Academy and award of a Russian order; in 1821 membership of the Academy of Sciences of Turin; and in Britain, election to the Royal Society in 1819, in recognition of his skills in astronomy and hydrography.

Bauzá was elected in 1822 as a liberal member of the Spanish Cortes, representing his home district of Palma, during the troubled years of civil strife. In 1823 Ferdinand VII exiled those who opposed him and Bauzá found himself condemned and with a price on his head. With financial assistance from Henry Richard Vassall Fox, third Baron Holland, one of many English sympathizers, he joined the flood of refugees making for Gibraltar. He had married Teresa Ravera of Madrid, and they had a son, Felipe (1802–1875), later a prominent geologist, and two daughters, Ana and Amélie. He parted company with them at Gibraltar in October, having made a British will in which he stated that he was worth less than his wife had brought to the marriage, and that she and their children should be his sole inheritors. Then, with as many hydrographical charts and documents as he could take with him, Bauzá made his way to London, where he at first stayed at Holland House and took English lessons.

After a few months Bauzá found a permanent home in Johnson Street, Somers Town, in north London, in the heart of the Spanish exile community, which included over a thousand families. A cultured man, he was welcomed into London literary and scientific society, especially among hydrographers and astronomers to whom he was already known. He corresponded with Fernandez de Navarrete, his locum tenens in Madrid, and responded to British requests for information on matters of navigation in those parts of South America which he had visited and charted, and which, as the Spanish empire decayed, were of growing interest to the Admiralty. The hydrographer of the navy, Captain W. E. Parry, introduced him into the Royal Society, where he regularly attended meetings, and he became a member of the Athenaeum. Captains Philip King, John Purdy, F. W. Beechey, and John Franklin often sought his help, but Bauzá's closest associations were with Captain Basil Hall, concerning the Pacific coast of the Americas in 1826, and with Captain W. H. Smythe, at whose house he found a warm welcome. Together they checked Smythe's chart of the Strait of Gibraltar and Bauzá offered data on a shoal at Tarifa which had escaped Smythe's notice. The British hydrographers were also eager to learn about the organization at the admired Madrid office. Bauzá visited William Herschel's observatory at Slough. In 1826 he spent three months in Paris and was invited to meet Alexander von Humboldt. The Spanish naval ministry instructed him to send plans and descriptions of the instruments at the Royal Greenwich Observatory, and he assisted with the order put on the London instrument maker Thomas Jones for similar apparatus for the San Fernando observatory; when Jones dallied over the order, Bauzá was called on to investigate the delay. In August 1826 the death sentence on Bauzá was confirmed, ending hope of return. However, in the early 1830s he was corresponding with Trinity House over the cost and procurement of lighthouses for Spanish ports. The new hydrographer, Francis Beaufort, introduced Bauzá as a member of the Royal Geographical Society in 1831, and consulted him on the prospective voyage of the *Beagle* under Fitzroy.

On 25 October 1832 Queen Christine, the Spanish regent, declared an amnesty for the exiles but Bauzá was unable to take advantage of it. He died at his home from a massive cerebral haemorrhage on 3 March 1834 and was buried on 8 March 1834 in a vault at the Catholic chapel in Moorfields, in the City of London. His obituarist in *Nautical Magazine* commented on Bauzá's excellent qualities, and his kind and affectionate disposition. His wife appeared in Gibraltar on 10 March 1835 to prove his will. His son studied in Madrid, then spent a considerable time in Paris and in Freiburg, but it is not known if he was able to meet his father in France. Some of the papers which Bauzá brought from Spain are now in the British Library.

ANITA McCONNELL

Sources U. Lamb, 'The London years of Felipe Bauzá: Spanish hydrographer in exile, 1823–34', *Journal of Navigation*, 34 (1981), 319–40 · C. Gobbi, 'The Spanish quarter of Somers Town', *Camden Historical Review*, 6 (1978), 6–9 · copy of Gibraltar probate, PRO, PROB 11/1843, sig. 142 · BL, Add. MS 17636, fol. 258 · serie 'Real observatorio', Asuntos particulares, Archivo general da Marina, Madrid, file 4868 · V. Llorens Castillo, *Liberales y romanticos* (1954), 26, 37, 147 · *The Times* (11 March 1834), 3b · 'El illustrissimo señor D. Felipe Bauzá, 1802–1875', *Boletín de la Comisión del Mapa Geológico de España*, 3 (1876), 97–114 · *Nautical Magazine*, 3 (1834), 245 · will, proved, Gibraltar, 10 March 1835

Likenesses portrait, Museo Naval, Madrid; repro. in Lamb, 'London years of Felipe Bauzá'
Wealth at death see will, PRO, PROB 11/1843, sig. 142

Bauzan, Sir Stephen (*b.* after **1210**, *d.* **1257**), knight, came from a prominent knightly family of Devon, who were tenants of the honour of Trematon in Cornwall. He was almost certainly a younger son—his brother, Richard, was holding by 1242–3 what appear to have been the family estates—and it is probable that he was born shortly after 1210. Bauzan's career offers a good example of a thirteenth-century professional household knight and colonial administrator, whose fortunes derived entirely from the service of three great lords, the Marshals, the Clares, and, latterly, Henry III. He first appears in March 1234 as a retainer of Richard Marshal, earl of Pembroke, and continued in the service in Wales of the next earl, Gilbert Marshal, who granted him land in Cardiganshire. In 1242–3 Bauzan served in the royal army in Poitou in the retinue of Philip Basset, kinsman of the Marshals. After this campaign, he joined the retinue of Richard de Clare, earl of Gloucester; he served as his sheriff in Glamorgan from about 1243–6 and was granted land by him at Hellidon, Northamptonshire. His marriage to Agnes (ancestry unknown) was perhaps contracted not much before 1257.

Bauzan again changed masters, and was retained as a knight of the king's household on 17 July 1249. He was a justice in Worcestershire, London, and Dorset from July 1249 to February 1252. At Christmas 1251, gaining favour in the inner circles of the royal household, he arranged provisions for the marriage at York of Henry III's daughter Margaret to the king of Scots, and Matthew Paris noted that he subsequently accompanied Margaret to Scotland. This indicates that Bauzan was now in the service of Henry III's queen, Eleanor of Provence, who had much influence over the composition of the early households of the royal children. In January 1253 Bauzan was styled on the queen's jewel roll knight of the Lord Edward, Henry III's heir, and in July 1253 he was an attorney for Eleanor's uncle, Peter of Savoy. In July 1253, he remained in England with the queen and Edward, sailing with them to join the king in Gascony in May 1254. He became Edward's constable of Carmarthen and Cardigan castles when the prince was given them, and on 27 August he was appointed Edward's first seneschal of Gascony. After the king's departure he remained with Edward in Gascony until autumn 1255, but their administration aroused opposition, and the king may have forced Edward to dismiss Bauzan on 30 September before they returned to England. Nevertheless he remained in Edward's household, witnessing a charter at Southwark on 24 March 1257, and in April went on Edward's service to Wales to defend Carmarthen against Llywelyn ap Gruffudd. Bauzan was killed on 2 June, leading a large force in a mistaken sortie from Carmarthen; the men fell into a Welsh ambush outside Dynefwr and suffered 'one of the most devastating defeats inflicted on an English army in Wales in the thirteenth century' (Davies, 310).

For his services to Henry III, Bauzan received part of the Hastings wardship (replacing his £20 p.a. fee), 1251–6, the farm of Wootton, Oxfordshire, 1251–7, and £20 p.a. land in Cork granted in 1253; between 1255 and 1257 Edward made him constable of Totnes Castle, Devon, part of the prince's wardship. Matthew Paris noted that Bauzan was 'most dear to the king' and 'an excellent knight' (Paris, 5.646); Henry III allowed Bauzan's widow, as a favour, to enjoy all his offices for five years after his death. In January 1258 the king also confirmed Bauzan's will 'sealed by the bishop of Worcester and others' (*CPR, 1247–58*, 615), made before going to war in Wales. In October 1259 Queen Eleanor obtained royal confirmation of Richard Bauzan's endowment to Buckfastleigh Abbey, Devon, commemorating his brother, Stephen, slain in royal service in Wales. Even Edward I, many years later, in May 1290, remembered Stephen Bauzan when establishing a daily mass at Carmarthen 'for the souls of faithful men slain in those parts in the service of the king and his ancestors' (*Calendar of the Charter Rolls, 1257–1300*, 345). Bauzan left no heirs; his widow remarried late in 1264. Her new husband was the prosperous midlands knight, Anschetil de Martinwast (*d.* 1274), seneschal of Simon de Montfort, earl of Leicester.

H. W. Ridgeway

Sources *Chancery records* · H. C. M. Lyte, ed., *Liber feodorum: the book of fees*, 2 (1923), 2.757, 771, 776, 777, 795, 933, 1288 · J. G. Edwards, ed., *Littere Wallie* (1940), 38–9 · G. Williams, ed., *Glamorgan county history*, 3: *The middle ages*, ed. T. B. Pugh (1971), 69 · Paris, *Chron.*, 5.272, 646 · Paris, *Chron.*, 6.373 · PRO, E 101/349/12, m. 1; E 159/36, m. 5d; JUST 1/1187, m. 2 · J. P. Trabut-Cussac, *L'Administration anglaise en Gascogne sous Henry III et Édouard I de 1254 à 1307* (Geneva, 1972), 3–15, 372–3 · J. R. Studd, 'A catalogue of the acts of the Lord Edward', PhD diss., U. Leeds, 1971 · J. E. Lloyd, *A history of Wales from the earliest times to the Edwardian conquest*, 3rd edn, 2 (1939), 720 · R. R. Davies, *Conquest, coexistence, and change: Wales, 1063–1415*, History of Wales, 2 (1987), 310 · Dugdale, *Monasticon*, new edn, 5.385 · *Ann. mon.*, 1.158

Bavand, William (*fl.* **1559**), translator, whose origins are obscure, after leaving Oxford University became a student at Middle Temple. In 1559 he published *A Work Touching the Good Ordering of a Common Weale*, a faithful translation of Joannes Ferrarius Montanus's *De republica bene instituenda*. Its nine books of turgid prose are dedicated to the new Queen Elizabeth because, since God has called her to rule over England, 'it behoveth your grace to be vigilant and careful, that the weighty administration thereof be by your good government throughly executed and discharged'. Large tracts of it take the form of lists of prescriptions and proscriptions, by adherence to which a monarch might improve his or her reign. A curious collection of ordinances, they range from the banal—'wealth ought not to be put before godly laws and good orders'; 'naughty courtiers do corrupt a good prince and make him to forsake the way of righteousness'—to the legislative—'loiterers and vagabonds should be forced to work for a living or else banished from the country'. Other passages touch on perils of civilization such as the dangers of sea travel. Although it does not make for light reading, the work is occasionally seasoned with anecdotal stories and some satisfactory verse translations from passages of classical authors, mainly Latin, that appear in the original text. Illustrating, for example, the idea (vital, according to the book, for a good society) that a 'child should not receive any milke but of his own mother', is Dido's speech from the fourth book (ll. 366–7) of Virgil's *Aeneid*, in which she venomously denies that Aeneas was born of a goddess:

> But on the mount of Caucasus,
> thou wast begote and bred:
> And in the ragged rockes thereof,
> the Tygres wilde thee fedde.

In the prologue to his translation of Seneca's *Thyestes* (1560), Jasper Heywood makes a short list of translators and other writers working in the inns of court. Along with Blandville, Googe, and North, Bavand is mentioned thus:

> There Bavande bides that turned his toil
> A common wealth to frame,
> And greater grace in English gives
> To worthy authors name.

Ross Kennedy

Sources Tanner, *Bibl. Brit.-Hib.* · Wood, *Ath. Oxon.*, new edn, 1.310 · J. Heywood, *The second tragedie of Seneca entitled Thyestes* (1560)

Bavant, John (*fl.* 1550–1598), Roman Catholic priest, was a native of Cheshire, but the identity of his parents is unknown. He received his education at Christ Church, Oxford, where he graduated BA in 1550 and MA in 1552. He was one of the original three fellows of St John's College, Oxford, named in 1558, and the first Greek reader there. During his residence at Oxford he was tutor to Edmund Campion and Gregory Martin. Wages for lecturers at the new college were meagre, however, and by 1563 Bavant had left St John's to accept a living. However, he left England soon after and went to France. He pursued his theological studies at Rheims and Rome, and was ordained and created DTh. In 1581 he was sent from Rheims to England as a missionary priest.

In 1585 Bavant was apprehended in London, and kept in the Counter in Wood Street, before being sent as a prisoner to Wisbech Castle in Cambridgeshire. On 13 June 1586, Dr Robert Gray of Wisbech addressed to Sir Francis Walsingham, principal secretary, a petition praying for Bavant's release, on grounds of his old age, which was eventually granted. Yet Bavant lived for many more years and became active in recusant leadership. Although not a Jesuit, he was part of a national Catholic network organized by the society, in which he was in charge of East Anglia. In January 1595 he went back to Wisbech Castle to resolve a dispute among Jesuits incarcerated there, concerning whether they should observe communal rules of order while in prison. In 1598, when a recusant hierarchy was set up among priests who did not belong to one of the orders, Bavant became one of twelve assistants to the 'archpriest' George Blackwell; he was made responsible for Norfolk. He is presumed to have died by 1600.

THOMPSON COOPER, *rev.* SARAH ELIZABETH WALL

Sources J. Bossy, *The English Catholic community, 1570–1850* (1975) · W. H. Stevenson and H. E. Salter, *The early history of St John's College, Oxford*, OHS, new ser., 1 (1939) · *Dodd's Church history of England*, ed. M. A. Tierney, 5 vols. (1839–43), vol. 1 · Wood, *Ath. Oxon.*, 1st edn · J. Morris, ed., *The troubles of our Catholic forefathers related by themselves*, 1–2 (1872–5) · T. F. Knox and others, eds., *The first and second diaries of the English College, Douay* (1878) · M. C. Questier, *Newsletters*

from the archpresbyterate of George Birkhead, CS, 5th ser., 12 (1998) · G. Anstruther, *The seminary priests*, 1 (1969)

Baverstock, Donald Leighton (1924–1995), television producer and executive, was born on 18 January 1924 at the maternity home in Glossop Terrace, Cardiff, the only son in the family of three children of Thomas Baverstock (1896–1979), colliery clerk and later grocer, and his wife, Sarahann, *née* Thomas (1898–1979), teacher. He attended Canton high school, Cardiff, from 1935 to 1941, and in 1942 went to Christ Church, Oxford, as an undergraduate cadet. Commissioned in the RAF between 1943 and 1946, he flew numerous operations with Bomber Command as a navigator. He returned to Oxford in 1946, graduating with a second-class degree in modern history in 1948. Of medium height, stocky, with dark wavy hair, his intensity, directness, and preoccupation with current matters characterized him as 'ebullient, pugnacious and unpredictable' (Briggs, 387). He smoked heavily and, later, drank.

In 1949, following spells teaching and with a shipping agent, Baverstock joined the BBC's general overseas service as a producer, making political and current affairs radio programmes. His ambition, though, lay in television, achieved in 1954 by appointment as a talks producer. His successes included an acclaimed eightieth birthday tribute to Sir Winston Churchill in the same year. The start of ITV in 1955 gave BBC television its first competition—and additional permitted broadcasting hours. To exploit the extra time and aided by production assistant Alasdair Milne (a future BBC director-general), Baverstock produced an innovative topical interview programme, *Highlight* (1955–7). On 17 August 1957 he married Gillian Mary Darrell Waters, then working as a publishing assistant. She was the daughter of Kenneth Darrell Waters, surgeon, and his wife, Enid Blyton, children's writer. They had two sons and two daughters.

In 1957 the government allowed the BBC and ITV flexibility in allocating their hours. This ended the 'toddlers' truce', the 6 p.m. to 7 p.m. period when screens were blank, supposedly so that mothers could put children to bed without the distraction of television. Baverstock and Milne filled the gap by developing *Highlight* into a weeknightly magazine, *Tonight* (1957–65). The programme established a new style. '[It] had a scepticism towards authority and received opinion that was very refreshing … It was helping to shape the mood and attitude of the country, while … the mood and attitude of the country were helping to shape *Tonight*' (Bernard Levin, on *25 Years Ago—Tonight*). Presented by the avuncular Cliff Michelmore, it made household names of its reporters (including Fyfe Robertson and Alan Whicker) and a trademark of its specially written topical songs. *Tonight*'s success depended also on the diversity of its stories. They ranged, for example, from a film about life on rubbish tips in Lima, to an interview with the teenage spokesman for the society for the prevention of cruelty to long-haired men. 'We were people questioning what was going on in the world … We didn't really have anything to say to the audience; we had questions to ask … Every so often we had a laugh' (Baverstock, on *25 Years Ago—Tonight*). But he was tough.

'He would ... dissect each item ... with merciless criticism. His team respected his creative vision despite what was often intolerably rude behaviour' (*The Independent*).

In April 1961 Baverstock became assistant controller of programmes. 'I ... decided to remove all kinds of programmes which ... were losing audiences ... There were endless pictures of birds ... and the audience was showing its ennui'. He recognized, too, the need, 'to force ... BBC television to realise they had to schedule programmes after the [mid-evening] news as well as before' (Baverstock). He also led the search for original Saturday-night entertainment. The result—*That Was The Week That Was* (1962–3)—set new standards for television satire. His masterly handling of the programme's coverage of President Kennedy's assassination in November 1963 captured the national mood. His managerial style, though, led to his BBC decline. 'His ill-considered over-promotion damaged both the television service and his own career' (Miall, 167). '[He] had little talent for man-management, but plenty for interference and within a few months all four departmental heads had left' (ibid., 39–40). In 1964 BBC2 opened with Baverstock and Michael Peacock, former editor of television news, respectively chiefs of programmes, BBC1 and BBC2. Their boss, Huw Wheldon, a future managing director, wanted them to switch jobs. Baverstock resisted and in 1965 he, Milne, and another *Tonight* producer, Tony Jay, resigned becoming, briefly, independent producers.

In 1967 the new ITV franchise holder Yorkshire Television appointed Baverstock its director of programmes, thus beginning another period of significant achievement. He founded the soap opera *Emmerdale Farm* and secured considerable space for Yorkshire Television programmes on national television. A former Yorkshire Television managing director John Fairley said, 'He was the nearest thing to a genius I ever came across in television ... He built from scratch the best documentary department in British TV at that time and it lasted to the ... mid 90s' (private information).

Baverstock's drinking led to his leaving Yorkshire in 1973 to head Granada Video Ltd (1974–5). He rejoined the BBC (1975–7) as a programme editor, but by then his creativity was ebbing. Retirement followed. In 1994 he and his wife, Gillian, were divorced. He died on 17 March 1995 at Airedale General Hospital, Steeton, Keighley, Yorkshire. He was buried on 24 March at Ilkley cemetery.

NICHOLAS MOSS

Sources staff files, BBC WAC, L 2/22 • *The Independent* (18 March 1995) • *The Times* (18 March 1995) • *Daily Telegraph* (18 March 1995) • D. Baverstock, interview, 22 Oct 1985, BBC WAC [unpubd] • *25 years ago—Tonight*, BBC TV programme, 18 Feb 1982 • G. W. Goldie, *Facing the nation: television and politics, 1936–1976* (1977) • A. Briggs, *The history of broadcasting in the United Kingdom*, rev. edn, 5 (1995) • L. Miall, *Inside the BBC: British broadcasting characters* (1994) • A. Milne, *DG: the memoirs of a British broadcaster* (1988) • B. Sendall, *Expansion and change, 1958–68* (1983), vol. 2 of *Independent television in Britain* (1982–90) • A. Whicker, *In the 'Whicker's World'* (1982) • personal knowledge (2004) • private information (2004) [Gillian Baverstock, wife; Brenda Grogan, sister; Sir Roger Cary; Sir Paul Fox; John Fairley; Leonard Miall; Colin Shaw; Alan Whicker] • *WWW*, 1991–5 • b. cert. • m. cert. • d. cert.

Archives BBC WAC | FILM BFI NFTVA

Likenesses photograph, repro. in *The Times* • photograph, repro. in *The Independent* • photograph, repro. in *Daily Telegraph*
Wealth at death £389,487: administration with will, 20 April 1995, CGPLA Eng. & Wales

Baverstock, James B. (1741–1815), brewer and radical, was born on 10 June 1741 at Alton, Hampshire, the son of James Baverstock, brewer. Nothing is known of Baverstock's upbringing, but in 1763 he joined his father in business in a brewhouse that the family had built that year in Turk Street, Alton, later to become known as the Alton Brewery. Baverstock soon distinguished himself by making 'a valuable contribution to the scientific approach to brewing in its earliest days' (Janes, 23), and he is generally regarded as the first person to make use of a hydrometer in the brewing process. After reading Michael Combrune's *Theory and Practice of Brewing* (1762), Baverstock purchased a thermometer but was forced to use the instrument in secret after his father discouraged him from such 'experimental innovations' (*Treatises*, xiii). About 1768 he became acquainted with Benjamin Martin of Fleet Street, who was then advertising a hydrometer as an instrument 'useful in discovering the strength of beer, ale, wine and worts' (ibid., xiii–xiv), but it was a further two years before Baverstock's experiments with a hydrometer achieved anything conclusive. In the meantime he married in 1769 Jane Hinton, daughter of the Revd John Hinton of Chawton, near Alton; the couple reputedly had a large family including two sons, Thomas Baverstock and James Hinton Baverstock. In January 1770 Baverstock presented a manuscript to Martin outlining the findings of his tests with a hydrometer, but ironically Martin, the instrument's inventor, rejected the practical benefits Baverstock proposed. Baverstock then reported his findings to Samuel Whitbread, founder of a brewery in Chiswell Street, London, but his experiments were again discounted, with Whitbread allegedly retorting: 'Go home, young man, attend to your business and do not engage in such visionary pursuits' (ibid., xiv–xv). Soon thereafter Baverstock was introduced to Henry Thrale, MP for Southwark and proprietor of the Anchor brewery, who was himself being encouraged by Samuel Johnson to pursue innovations in brewing. Thrale showed an unmatched enthusiasm for Baverstock's experiments with a hydrometer, declaring such 'an instrument of great use to the brewer in various parts of his business' (ibid., xvii). Gradually the hydrometer was adopted by most notable brewers, including Whitbread, a development which James Hinton Baverstock described as an 'indisputable testimony in favour of [his father's] ... judgement in this particular, and of his scientific and practical knowledge in the art of brewing' (ibid., xv).

In 1773 Baverstock entered a partnership with John Dowden at Alton; they traded as Baverstock and Dowden until 1786, when Baverstock moved to Windsor, Berkshire, and there entered into a partnership with John and Richard Ramsbottom, brewers and bankers, at the Windsor brewery in Thames Street. During his time at Windsor the brewery was regarded as producing 'the best Windsor ale in flavour and transparency' (*Treatises*, xix), and in 1796 it began sending beer to London. It produced some 11,000 barrels per annum, progressively increasing to 30,000 barrels a year in 1801, when Baverstock chose his eldest son, Thomas, to succeed him at Windsor. He then returned to Alton to take control of his brewery there, which he had leased to the widow of his former partner, Dowden. In his trade, Baverstock had earned the respect of his colleagues and was 'highly and very justly celebrated as a practical brewer' (ibid., xix). His innovations, first presented in manuscript to Martin in 1770, were published in honour of the Society of Arts as *Hydrometrical Observations and Experiments in the Brewery* (1785), as a result of which Baverstock was engulfed by enquiries from brewers and some West Indian planters seeking further information. Baverstock also wrote a *Short Address to the Public on the Prejudices Against the Brewery* (1807) and *Observations on the Prejudices Against the Brewery* (1811), and in 1808, writing as 'a Hampshire Brewer', he was engaged in a brief controversy with 'Candidus' in the pages of William Cobbett's *Political Register* over 'the production of *uniformly* good beer' (Cobbett's *Political Register*, 12 Nov 1808, 768). His final work, 'Observations on the state of the brewery and on the saccharine quality of malt', was published in the fourth number of John Abraham Valpy's *The Pamphleteer* in 1813, and his writings were edited and reissued in 1824 by his son James Hinton as *Treatises on Brewing with Notes and an Introduction* (1824).

It was probably through Whitbread and Cobbett that Baverstock was introduced to Timothy Brown, a prosperous banker and freethinker. In the early regency years he was part of a circle of radicals and freethinkers, including Cobbett, who met regularly at Brown's Peckham Lodge, Camberwell, Surrey, and in 1813 he was embroiled in the controversial publication by Daniel Isaac Eaton of Baron d'Holbach's *Ecce homo*. Baverstock's failing health, however, brought an abrupt end to his radical and brewing activities. In 1815 he moved to Southampton for the benefit of his health, but he died there on 26 December 1815 at the age of seventy-four. MICHAEL T. DAVIS

Sources H. H. Janes, *The red barrel: a history of Watney Mann* [1963] · L. Richmond and A. Turton, *The brewing industry: a guide to historical records* (1990) · I. McCalman, *Radical underworld: prophets, revolutionaries, and pornographers in London, 1795–1840* (1988) · *Treatises on brewing*, ed. J. H. Baverstock (1824) · *Cobbett's Weekly Political Register* (12 Nov 1808), 768–73 · *Cobbett's Weekly Political Register* (26 Nov 1808), 855–8 · *Cobbett's Weekly Political Register* (10 Dec 1808), 910–15 · *Cobbett's Weekly Political Register* (24 Dec 1808), 973–7 · *GM*, 1st ser., 86/1 (1816), 88 · P. Mathias, *The brewing industry in England, 1700–1830* (1959)

Bawden, Edward (1903–1989), painter and designer, was born on 10 March 1903 in Braintree, Essex, the only child of Edward Bawden, a Braintree ironmonger of Cornish stock, and his wife, Eleanor Game, the daughter of a Suffolk gamekeeper. He went to Braintree high school, to the Friends' school in Saffron Walden, Essex, and to the Cambridge Art School, and then—on a royal exhibition—to the Royal College of Art (RCA) in London. Here he studied writing and illumination, but took his diploma in book illustration. His design tutor was the painter Paul Nash; other contemporaries at the RCA were Barnett Freedman,

Edward Bawden (1903–1989), by Howard Coster, 1946

Henry Moore, and Douglas Percy Bliss, his future biographer. But his closest student friendship, and the most fruitful artistically, was with someone who was in many ways his opposite—Eric Ravilious.

Nash helped Bawden to get his earliest commissions—posters for London Transport and designs for the Curwen Press. In 1928 Bawden and Ravilious worked together on a large mural in Morley College, London—the first of many mural designs; while Bawden's line drawings of English place names for petrol advertisements—'Stow on the Wold but Shell on the road'—made him familiar to a wider audience.

In 1932 Bawden married his contemporary at the RCA, Charlotte Epton, the daughter of Robert Epton, solicitor, of Lincoln. They had a son and a daughter, both of whom became artists. In the same year the Bawdens and Eric and Eileen (Tirzah) Ravilious moved to Brick House in Great Bardfield, Essex, which they had previously visited at weekends. Here Bawden began painting the local Essex landscapes; and in 1933 he held his first one-man show at the Zwemmer Gallery in London.

In 1940 Bawden was appointed an official war artist. He went to France, where he drew scenes of the evacuation from Dunkirk; he was among the last to leave. He then went to the Middle East and Africa: Egypt, Sudan, Ethiopia, Eritrea, and Libya. He made many fine watercolours both of the fighting and of the historic background—landscape and architectural—against which it took place. He returned by sea from Africa in 1942 and was torpedoed;

after five days in an open boat he was rescued by a French warship of the Vichy government and interned for two months in Casablanca in Morocco. But he returned to the war—to Arabia, Egypt, Iraq, Persia, and Italy. Much of his war work is in the Imperial War Museum in London.

After the war Bawden lived in Great Bardfield and taught part-time at the RCA under Robin Darwin; he was known as an excellent teacher. Although in the post-war climate his work now seemed less fashionable than it had before the war, he was always busy. His dexterity was not impaired by an operation he had in 1946 to remove the poisoned top joint of his index finger. He worked industriously on book illustrations—for *Life in an English Village* (1949); *The Arabs* (1947) by Richard B. Serjeant, published by Penguin; and for Faber and Faber, the Kynock Press, the Nonesuch Press, and the Limited Editions Club of New York—and linocutting, of which seemingly humble yet intractable craft he was a master. Among his many fine prints, *Liverpool Street Station* and *Brighton Pier* are outstandingly original. He also made several mural designs—that for the Lion and Unicorn Press pavilion in the Festival of Britain in London in 1951 was perhaps the most notable, and a striking example was executed for Blackwell's bookshop in Oxford. But it was his landscape watercolours—technically adventurous and highly individual—that he always considered his central activity. Photographs, self-portraits, and the early portrait by Ravilious at the RCA show him as tall, spare, and serious, and with a sharp-eyed, ironic, and humorous expression. In character, he was paradoxical: not strong as a child, but a tenacious survivor as an adult; shy and diffident, but unstoppable; insecure and highly self-critical, yet self-reliant; imaginative, yet very organized; possessing curious blind spots—such as his inability to drive or enjoy music—yet extraordinarily versatile and capable of learning anything he set his hand to—from engraving on copper to designing a cast-iron garden seat. He was not an easy man to get on with, and his ruthless determination to work bore heavily on his family. Shyness sometimes made him seem dry, mocking, and contrary, and he hated sentimentality.

Bawden's style was individual, clear, and economical; people, landscapes, and buildings were simply and unambiguously delineated. He drew animate and inanimate subjects with equal ease, simplifying complicated subject matter and making epigrammatic or decorative images out of seemingly unlikely material, and he was as skilful with a fine pen as with the thick, solid technique of linocutting. Although he abhorred influences, he has been likened to Edward Lear, whose work he admired and who in some respects—in terms of shyness, solitariness, and precision—he resembled. He was a skilful and resourceful designer, a brilliant creator of pattern when this skill was out of fashion, and a draughtsman of wit and individuality. His life's work reveals him also as a serious artist whose vision of the world around him was personal and comprehensive. Bawden's clarity may have been for him a mixed blessing, for by removing ambivalence and leaving the observer with little to puzzle over, it made him seem simpler and less profound than other artists whose work

is harder to fathom. That, and the fact that he did many different things, meant that his work was accorded respect and admiration rather than the renown it merited.

Bawden became a CBE in 1946, an ARA in 1947, an RDI in 1949, and an RA in 1956, and he received honorary doctorates from the RCA and Essex University. From 1951 to 1958 he was a trustee of the Tate Gallery, London. He was given a retrospective exhibition of his work at the Victoria and Albert Museum in 1989. When his wife died in 1970 he moved to Saffron Walden, where he worked steadily and fruitfully to the end of his life. On 21 November 1989, after a morning spent working on a linocut, he had a stroke and died later that day at his home, 2 Park Lane, Saffron Walden.　　　　　　　　　DAVID GENTLEMAN, *rev.*

Sources J. M. Richards, *Edward Bawden*, Penguin Modern Painters (1946) · D. P. Bliss, *Edward Bawden* (1980) · R. Harling, *Edward Bawden* (1950) · J. Howes, *Edward Bawden: a retrospective survey* (1988) · *CGPLA Eng. & Wales* (1990) · personal knowledge (1996)
Archives IWM, letters as official war artist | BL, letters to Rauri McLean, deposit 9349 · Tate collection, corresp. with John Nash · Tate collection, corresp. with Lady Sempill
Likenesses H. Coster, photograph, 1946, NPG [*see illus.*] · E. Bawden, two self-portraits, pencil and watercolour, 1986, NPG · G. Deutsch, photograph, Hult. Arch. · E. Ravilious, portrait, Royal College of Art, London
Wealth at death £366,302: probate limited to literary estate, 6 Dec 1990, *CGPLA Eng. & Wales* · £117,570: probate save and except literary estate, 6 June 1990, *CGPLA Eng. & Wales*

Bawden, Sir Frederick Charles (1908–1972), virologist and plant pathologist, was born on 18 August 1908 in North Tawton, Devon, the younger son and youngest of the three children of George Bawden, relieving officer and registrar of births and deaths, and his wife, Ellen Balment. In 1911 his parents became master and matron of the Okehampton poor-law institution—the workhouse. Early observation of poverty there probably helped to establish Bawden's sympathetic social outlook, while the large institutional garden, mainly devoted to potatoes, may have led to his subsequent interest in agriculture.

Bawden was educated at Okehampton grammar school and Queen Elizabeth School in Crediton. With help from a Ministry of Agriculture and Fisheries scholarship he went to Emmanuel College, Cambridge, and studied botany, chemistry, and physiology. He obtained a first class in part one of the natural sciences tripos in 1928, and the diploma in agricultural science in 1930. In the latter year, having already worked for two years on cereal rusts, he started work at the Potato Virus Research Station (Cambridge) as assistant to R. N. Salaman. That apprenticeship led logically to his subsequent posts: virus physiologist at Rothamsted Experimental Station, Harpenden, in 1936, head of the department of plant pathology in 1940, its deputy director in 1950, and its director in 1958.

Bawden was known primarily as a virus worker; he isolated one of the first virus preparations for which reasonable claims of purity could be made, and wrote *Plant Viruses and Virus Diseases* (1939). However, although he did no research on fungus infections other than his early work on rusts, he had a lifelong interest in them. They occupied as much space as virus infections in his *Plant Diseases* (1948). He discussed them in several articles and condemned the tendency to segregate specialists on different infective agents into different departments or institutes. Bawden's approach to viruses was broad-minded. He published papers on their chemical, physical, and serological properties, and on their classification, multiplication, and physiological effects. He knew more chemistry than most plant pathologists, but recognized that much of what passed for knowledge in the 1930s about nucleic acids and proteins was baseless.

After the end of the Second World War many students from the less economically developed countries went to Rothamsted for training in plant pathology. Although Bawden welcomed them enthusiastically, he was critical that many were not given jobs in their speciality when they returned home. During frequent visits to India, the Caribbean, and some African countries he gained experience of tropical agriculture; he demonstrated that tropical crops were not as healthy as farmers and governments thought and that when a diseased state was recognized its cause was often wrongly attributed. He disliked formal visits or demonstrations of elaborate equipment: he preferred to get into the field to see crops and discuss them with farmers. He served, often as chairman, on several committees concerned with tropical agriculture.

Bawden was a pragmatist. He argued that researchers who understood that the primary object of farming was to produce food knew more about needs and possibilities than anyone else. He criticized aspects of British agricultural research policy—especially the customer–contractor principle which was introduced in the 1970s. He was delighted that projects which he supported in spite of criticism, such as freeing the King Edward potato clone from paracrinkle virus, and the synthesis of pyrethrin analogues, were ultimately extremely profitable. During his directorship Rothamsted grew beyond its previous bounds in size and staff. He realized, however, that getting research applied was often harder than doing it, and in this respect he contrasted agriculture unfavourably with medicine.

Bawden took a keen interest in the manner of the presentation of research. He had a sharp eye for ambiguity, prolixity, and illegitimately general statements. In spite of a humorous, cheerful, and friendly manner, he could be blunt. Apart from the routine of ensuring that there was a supply of test plants he made little use of assistance and insisted on doing all virus assays himself. As a rule that meant doing them out of normal working hours. He was elected a fellow of the Royal Society in 1949, served on many of its committees, and was treasurer from 1968 to 1972. He was knighted in 1967, had honorary degrees from Hull, Bath, Reading, and Brunel universities, and was a member of several foreign academies.

On 6 September 1934 Bawden married Marjorie Elizabeth, a childhood friend and also a botanist, the daughter of Alfred Alderman Cudmore, agricultural engineer. They had two sons. He died in Luton and Dunstable Hospital on 8 February 1972.　　　　　　　　　　N. W. PIRIE, *rev.*

Sources N. W. Pirie, *Memoirs FRS*, 19 (1973), 19–63 · personal knowledge (1986) · B. D. Harrison, 'Bawden, F. C.: plant pathologist and pioneer in plant virus research', *Annual Review of Phytopathology*, 32 (1994), 39–47 · WWW, 1971–80
Archives RS, corresp. and papers
Wealth at death £40,499: probate, 13 April 1972, *CGPLA Eng. & Wales*

Bawdwen, William (1762–1816), antiquary, was born on 9 March 1762, the son and heir of William Bawdwen JP, of Stone Gap, Craven, Yorkshire, and his wife, Grace, daughter of Samuel Mortimer of Swaffham and widow of Henry Horsfall of Malsis Hall. He was admitted to Manchester School on 31 January 1775. He subsequently took holy orders and was curate of Wakefield for some years. He married Ann, daughter of William Shackleton of Wakefield, on 20 December 1793. From autumn 1797 until his death on 14 September 1816 he was vicar of Hooton Pagnell, Yorkshire, where he died and was buried, and curate of its daughter church at Frickley-cum-Clayton. He was survived by his wife and twelve children, of whom the eldest sons were William, land agent to Earl Manvers of Thoresby Park, Nottinghamshire, and Walter (1808–1867), chaplain to the Manchester Royal Infirmary.

Bawdwen began a translation of the Domesday Book from the edition published by the record commission in 1783. While only the first two volumes were published, his obituary in the *Gentleman's Magazine* claimed the other eight volumes were 'completely ready' before Bawdwen's death in 1816. Bawdwen's published translations cover the Domesday surveys of Yorkshire, Derbyshire, Nottinghamshire, Rutland, Lincolnshire, Hertfordshire, Middlesex, Buckinghamshire, Oxfordshire, Gloucestershire, and Dorset. His declared intention was to provide as literal a translation as possible. This in part defeated his other aim, of making Domesday more accessible, since the resulting text is often turgid. His work contains many minor errors, and does not compare favourably with those of contemporaries who concentrated on single counties. On the other hand, Bawdwen deserves credit for the sheer scale of the task he attempted and for the vast amount of work completed, and his introductory notes suggest he was thoroughly versed in the Domesday literature then available.

　　　　　　　　　　　　　　　　RICHARD DENNIS

Sources *GM*, 1st ser., 86/2 (1816), 286 · J. F. Smith, ed., *The admission register of the Manchester School, with some notes of the more distinguished scholars*, 3 vols. in 4 pts, Chetham Society, 69, 73, 93, 94 (1866–74), vol. 1, p. 212; vol. 2, 285 · J. Hunter, *South Yorkshire: the history and topography of the deanery of Doncaster*, 2 (1831), 146–50 · J. H. Lupton, *Wakefield worthies* (1864), 9 · W. Bawdwen, ed. and trans., *Domesday Book, for the county of Dorset* (1815)

Bax, Sir Arnold Edward Trevor (1883–1953), composer, was born on 8 November 1883 in Heath Villa, Angles Road, Streatham, London, the eldest son of Alfred Ridley Bax (1844–1918) and his wife, Charlotte Ellen Lea (1860–1940). His father was a barrister of the Middle Temple, though having a private income he never practised. His youngest brother, Clifford Lea Bax (1886–1962), in his day was a celebrated playwright and essaist. In 1896 the family moved to a Hampstead mansion, Ivy Bank, whose gardens and

Sir Arnold Edward Trevor Bax (1883–1953), by Herbert Lambert, pubd 1923

ambience coloured the teens and early twenties of the children.

Early music In his autobiography, *Farewell, my Youth* (1943), Bax could not remember the time when he was not able to read music at the piano, and he showed an easy musical facility from an early age, encouraged by his mother. He attended the Hampstead Conservatoire (from 1898), and in September 1900 entered the Royal Academy of Music, where he remained until the summer of 1905. At the academy he was a composition pupil of Frederick Corder and a piano pupil of Tobias Matthay. He won the Battison Haynes prize (1902) and a Macfarren scholarship (1902). Later he won the Charles Lucas medal with his *Variations for Orchestra* (1904), rehearsed at the Royal College of Music under the Patron's Fund scheme, in May 1905, an occasion vividly described in Bax's autobiography. The work was otherwise never performed, but survives. Later he was elected an associate of the Royal Academy of Music (1911) and a fellow (1927).

In 1902 Bax discovered the poetry of W. B. Yeats, and under its influence explored the west of Ireland, where the remote Donegal coastal village of Glencolumcille became a constant refuge from the world. Here he learned the Irish language and wrote 'Celtic twilight' poetry, short stories, and plays, influenced by Yeats, J. M. Synge and A. E. (George Russell). Bax used a variety of Irish pseudonyms which evolved into 'Dermot O'Byrne', under which name he published such work from 1909 (and in the *Irish Review* in 1913).

Bax's financial independence freed him from ever taking a paid position, and he was able to travel. Soon he visited Germany, and at Dresden in 1906 attended an early performance of Richard Strauss's *Salome*. His early travels, vividly evoked in his autobiography, ended when he visited St Petersburg and the Ukraine in the spring of 1910 in pursuit of a Ukrainian girl. But on 28 January 1911 he married Elsa Luisa Sobrino (*b.* 1885/6), daughter of a pianist, Carlos Sobrino, and his wife, Luisa, a well-known singer of the day; they set up house in a suburb of Dublin. They had two children, Dermot (1912–1976) and Maeve Astrid (later Rosenberg; 1913–1987). Here Bax became well known in literary circles, publishing vivid stories, verse, and a Synge-like play, all reflecting a first-hand knowledge of the language, customs, legends, and history of the west of Ireland. His particular friends were Padraig and Mary Colum, who had started the *Irish Review* in 1912.

Bax made his reputation with a succession of vivid orchestral tone poems, largely on Irish and nature themes, which first came to general notice when Sir Henry Wood conducted *In the Faery Hills* at the Promenade Concerts in 1910. This had been preceded by a number of other similar orchestral scores. The first of these was *Cathaleen-ni-Hoolihan*, a student work first written as the slow movement of an early quartet in E, later reworked as a tone poem for two violins and piano, and then revised as an orchestral tone poem. It remained unperformed until 1970, but is now revealed as already exhibiting many of the elements of his later works in the form.

In an autobiographical radio talk (recorded on 6 May 1949) Bax described the influence of Ireland in finding his style: he began 'using figures of a definitely Celtic curve, an idiom which in the end was … second nature to me' (*Farewell*, 165). In his mid-twenties Bax tended to be a musical magpie, celebrating his latest discoveries in new compositions, in which his musical personality was so strong that any influences instantly became his own. Thus he assimilated Wagner, Strauss, the Russian 'Five' (Balakirev, Borodin, Cui, Mussorgsky, Rimsky-Korsakov), Glazunov, Debussy and Ravel, Sibelius and early Stravinsky. Many of these influences were probably first encountered at the keyboard: Bax was so commanding a pianist, fluently reading full scores on the keyboard at sight, that he was called in for piano rehearsals of all manner of new works, which were instantly grist to his mill. Along with many others, Bax was dazzled by the brilliance of the Diaghilev ballet, first seen in the summer of 1911. By the outbreak of war in August 1914 the music of Debussy, Ravel, and the young Stravinsky had provided the examples for a significant development of his musical language, first seen in the five-movement tone poem *Spring Fire* (1913).

In 1911, emulating what he had seen during Diaghilev's first London season, Bax had written his own Russian ballet, 'a little-Russian fairy tale in action and dance' which he called *Tamara*. It survives only in piano score, and its thirty numbers would have run for about two hours. It was never orchestrated or produced, for when the summer ballet season of 1912 was announced, the appearance of

Balakirev's *Thamar* made all competitors redundant. However, the music was to inform other later scores, and a suite, orchestrated by Graham Parlett, demonstrates how at the time Bax had swallowed his Russian models whole. When after the war he wrote spoof Russian ballet music for J. M. Barrie's whimsical play *The Truth about the Russian Dancers*, as a vehicle for the ballerina Tamara Karsavina, he used some of the music of *Tamara*, including its most romantic tune.

The First World War and the Easter rising During the First World War, Bax was a non-combatant. A heart condition, which troubled him intermittently all his life, kept him from the trenches. This meant that at a time when many of his contemporaries were serving overseas, he was able to produce a remarkable body of music as he found his technical and artistic maturity in his early thirties. In addition to piano music, this included his large-scale piano quintet, two violin sonatas, songs, and orchestral tone poems such as *The Garden of Fand*, *Nympholept*, *November Woods*, *Tintagel*, and the fifty-minute *Symphonic Variations* for piano and orchestra.

While living in Dublin, Bax had many republican friends, and although he returned to England in August 1914, the Easter rising in April 1916 and the execution of the leaders on 3 May came as a tremendous shock. This event was reflected in a variety of Bax's music, most notably in the orchestral *In Memoriam* ('In memoriam Padraig Pearse'), which remained largely unknown until recorded by Vernon Handley in 1998. More love song than elegy, this is a remarkably passionate piece, dominated by a tune which Bax later reused in his music for the 1948 film of *Oliver Twist*; but this was not his only elegy for Irish friends. Various chamber works, such as the *Elegiac Trio* for flute, viola, and harp (1916), the harp quintet (1919), and the sextet for cor anglais, harp, and strings called *In Memoriam* (1917), were also elegiac. Other pieces which contemporary commentators viewed as 'war' works, such as the stormy first symphony, first performed in 1922, and the second, given four years later, should also appear in this category.

As well as music reflecting the Irish tragedy, there was a pamphlet of verse written under the pseudonym Dermot O'Byrne, *A Dublin Ballad and other Poems*, that was banned by the British censor in Ireland. The middle verse of the poem 'Shells at Oranmore', dated April 1916, was later chosen by the Irish department of external affairs as the motto for the issue of its weekly bulletin marking the fiftieth anniversary of the Easter rising in 1966.

Creative maturity After the First World War, Bax was able to write new works in rapid succession. He produced two piano sonatas; starting work on a third in 1921, he found he had conceived a symphony, and the work was orchestrated, and first performed in December 1922. The fiery character of the music seems to suggest conflict, and while contemporary commentators associated it with the First World War, it is now generally felt to reflect events in Ireland. A similarly epic second symphony followed and was in short score by October 1924, though not completed

in full score until 1926. It was first performed in Boston in December 1929, but was not heard in London until May 1930, two months after the première of the third symphony. The fact that at one point it alludes to *In Memoriam* of 1916 suggests that it too may have had an Irish genesis.

Bax was at his musical peak for a comparatively short time, and his fame as a symphonist really dates from the 1930s, when his reputation was soon overtaken by Vaughan Williams and Walton. But in the 1920s he was widely considered the leading British composer of his generation, and between the wars he produced most of his mature works. In a magazine interview in 1928 he described himself as a 'brazen romantic'. Strangely enough he did not take the opportunity in the 1930s to bring forward what subsequently became known to be his large number of pre-war works, and they remained unperformed until after his death.

Bax's third symphony was completed in 1929 and after its first performance in 1930 was championed as one of his most frequently heard major works; it was his first symphony to be recorded (1943). Four more symphonies followed: the fourth (1931, first performed in San Francisco in 1932), the fifth (1932, first performed in 1934), the sixth (1935), and the seventh (1939, but not performed in England until a broadcast in 1941 and a Promenade Concert in 1943). Other works written in the 1930s include the popular *Overture to a Picaresque Comedy*, a variety of chamber works for larger groups, including a nonet, a string quintet (1933), the third string quartet, and an octet for horn, piano, and strings. Bax's violin concerto was completed in 1938 but not performed until 1943, when Eda Kersey played the solo part.

Bax was always indifferent to formal honours, but during the 1930s he received the gold medal of the Royal Philharmonic Society (1931), the Cobbett medal for chamber music (1931), and honorary doctorates from the universities of Oxford (1934) and Durham (1935) and the National University of Ireland (1947). He was knighted (June 1937) and appointed KCVO (1953). After the death of Walford Davies, he was appointed master of the king's music in 1942.

During the First World War, Bax developed an increasingly passionate affair with the pianist Harriet Pearl Alice *Cohen (1895–1967), and in 1918 he left his wife and children and found rooms at Swiss Cottage, London, where he lived until the onset of the Second World War. His relationship with Harriet Cohen cooled, though he wrote many works for her; her name remained coupled with his, and she became identified with his piano music during his lifetime. In 1926 Bax met Mary Gleaves (1904–1995), who although unmusical formed another emotional thread for the rest of his life; it was she who accompanied Bax in the 1930s to his winter retreat in Morar, Inverness-shire, where he orchestrated works written in London. Bax kept Mary's existence from Harriet Cohen, who found out only in 1948.

Neglect and revival At the outset of the Second World War, Bax stopped composing, moved to Sussex, and produced his autobiography, which presents his life only to the age of thirty. During the war he was persuaded to turn to film music and wrote the score for *Malta, GC*, from which extracts were promoted on the radio and in the concert hall. After the war he wrote a number of further works, including the popular music for David Lean's film *Oliver Twist* (1948) and the short *Morning Song* and concertante for piano (left hand) and orchestra, all three for Harriet Cohen. It was at this time that he wrote the concertante for three winds and orchestra, consisting of three movements that feature successively cor anglais, clarinet, and French horn, followed by a finale combining all three.

Bax died on 3 October 1953 at Glen House, Ballyvolane, Cork, Ireland; he was there as a visiting examiner at the University of Cork. He was buried at St Finbarr's cemetery, Cork. After his death his reputation was kept alive by just one work, the orchestral tone poem *Tintagel*. This neglect was compounded when his publisher, Chappell & Co., suffered a disastrous fire in 1964, which destroyed the printed stocks of most of his music. The gradual revival of Bax's music started with Vernon Handley's performances of the fourth symphony and other works at Guildford, and with the pioneering recordings by Lyrita Recorded Edition of the first, second, fifth, sixth, and seventh symphonies. This movement was developed with the exploration of the unknown and early orchestral works by the conductor Leslie Head in the 1970s and by the monographs by Colin Scott-Sutherland (1973) and Lewis Foreman (1983). The Bax centenary in 1983 was celebrated by twelve BBC programmes, which revealed to a wide audience the richness of the less well-known scores, and with the establishment of the Sir Arnold Bax Trust in 1985 the mechanism was in place for promoting the Chandos Records cycle of Bax's music conducted by Bryden Thomson, Vernon Handley, and Martyn Brabbins, which has promoted Bax to a world audience.   LEWIS FOREMAN

Sources *'Farewell, my youth' and other writings by Arnold Bax*, ed. L. Foreman (1992) · *Ideala poems and some early love letters by Arnold Bax*, ed. C. Scott-Sutherland (2001) · L. Foreman, *Bax: a composer and his times*, 2nd edn (1987) · G. Parlett, *A catalogue of the works of Sir Arnold Bax* (1999) · C. Scott-Sutherland, *Arnold Bax* (1973) · BL, Bax Collection, Add. MSS 54724–54781 · Harriet Cohen papers, BL, Deposit 1999/10 · b. cert. · m. cert. · *CGPLA Eng. & Wales* (1954) · A. Payne, 'Bax, Sir Arnold (Edward)', *New Grove* · priv. coll. · personal knowledge (2004) · private information (2004)
Archives BL, Add. MSS 50173–50181, 54724–54781, 57523 · LUL · Royal Academy of Music, London, manuscripts · University of Strathclyde, Glasgow, manuscripts | BL, corresp. with Society of Authors, Add. MS 63211 · BL, letters to J. F. Stainer, Add. MS 62121 · BL, letters to Sir Henry Wood, Add. MS 56419
Likenesses H. Lambert, photogravure, pubd 1923, NPG [*see illus.*] · P. Evans, pen-and-ink drawing, c.1925–1929, NPG · H. Coster, photographs, c.1930–1939, NPG · V. Bax, oils, 1933, Royal Academy of Music, London · W. Stoneman, photograph, 1947, NPG · S. Murphy, death mask, c.1953, University College, Cork, Boole Library
Wealth at death £11,935 19s. 11d.: probate, 6 Aug 1954, *CGPLA Eng. & Wales*

Bax, Ernest Belfort (1854–1926), Marxist theoretician and activist, was born at his parents' home, 27 Clarendon Square, Leamington Spa, Warwickshire, on 23 July 1854, the last of four children of Daniel Bax (*d.* 1882), a manufacturer, and his wife, Eleanor, daughter of John Carter of

Greenwich. His parents were strict nonconformists who followed evangelical and sabbatarian principles. The family moved to Brighton shortly after his birth, and remained there until 1864, when they moved to Hampstead. Educated mainly by private tutors, Bax began to rebel against his comfortable and pious bourgeois background early. At the age of sixteen he identified himself with the 'Communards' in Paris as they struggled to erect a new social order amid the military collapse of France. This sympathy drew him to the London positivists, one of the few groups in England to favour the revolutionaries in Paris. Although he did not join the positivists, their vision of a new religion centring on the ideal of humanity, derived from Auguste Comte, strongly influenced Bax.

In 1875 Bax travelled to Germany to study musical composition at the Stuttgart conservatory. After a year he abandoned the plan, although he remained sufficiently conversant with musical forms to serve as a music critic for the London *Star* in the 1880s, a position he passed on to his close friend George Bernard Shaw. The hope of becoming a composer would be realized by his nephew Arnold *Bax. During the 1880s and early 1890s he earned his living by journalism, supplemented after 1882 by his father's inheritance. But in 1894 he was called to the bar by the Middle Temple and commenced practice as a barrister. He did not abandon journalism, editing the socialist journals *Time* and *Today* and continuing to write copiously on philosophy and socialism.

In 1879, while he was working as a correspondent for the *London Standard* in Berlin, Bax's acquaintance with the German philosopher Edward von Hartmann had led to a lifelong interest in philosophical questions. A decisive turn to his thought came when he read Marx's *Kapital*. His short piece on Marxist theory, published in 1881, won Bax the praise and gratitude of Marx. Bax did not, however, adopt the orthodox Marxist standpoint, fixed in the years just ahead by the strictly materialistic and deterministic version of Engels. Marxism, according to Bax, still required philosophy, which he defined as 'the final pronouncements of thought on the great problems of life' (E. B. Bax, *Outlooks from the New Standpoint*, 1891, 196). Over the next two decades he attempted to develop the ethical, religious, and metaphysical meaning of socialism by drawing on the German philosophical tradition. From Kant he drew insight into man's ethical life, while Hegel provided a dialectical logic which swept away 'all accepted habits of thought' and disclosed the dynamic nature of reality. But Bax rejected Hegel's rationalism in favour of a notion found in Schopenhauer and von Hartmann, of a non-rational impulse beneath consciousness. Bax called this impulse the 'alogical'. It remained fundamental to his thought.

Bax accepted Marx's analysis of capitalism. But he was occupied mainly with changes in human consciousness and denied that moral and aesthetic principles evolved in subordination to economic causes. By means of his metaphysical augmentation of Marxist materialism Bax developed a view of history according to which humankind was moving from the unconscious social solidarity of primitive societies, through a period of private property, individualism, and the class struggle, toward the future solidarity consciousness of communism. Scattered through his writings were speculations that humanity was developing a 'super organic' consciousness in which the tension-ridden personality characteristic of history would be overcome. Although Bax never produced a general interpretation of history, he wrote three books dealing with the French Revolution and published three studies of the Reformation era in Germany.

Bax attempted to instruct his socialist colleagues in the larger meaning of their cause. In 1882 he joined the Democratic Federation (later Social Democratic Federation), founded a year earlier by Henry Mayers Hyndman, and moving toward a Marxist political programme. Two years later Bax joined William Morris in breaking with Hyndman to form the Socialist League. Both men rejected Hyndman's utilitarian-oriented Marxism in favour of a conception of socialism which emphasized ethical and aesthetic values. Bax and Morris worked closely together, editing the league's journal, *The Commonweal*, and collaborating on a book, *Socialism and the Ground up*, which combined a straightforward account of Marxist economic theory with the utopian vision of the authors. The daughter of Morris described their relationship:

> A strange pair they made, Bax with his fine, regular features and bushy moustache … tall and thin, in his black coat … smoking with perhaps a glass at his elbow; my father … sitting at the writing table … with perhaps a dry grin on his face at a vagary of Bax's. (M. Morris, *William Morris*, 2, 1936, 173)

In 1889 Bax left the Socialist League, now the scene of a bitter conflict between those, including Bax, who favoured political action, and a quasi-anarchist wing. He returned to Hyndman's Social Democratic Federation, convinced that it offered the best hope of holding the practical and ideal sides of the movement together. In the years ahead Bax served on the federation's executive, edited its journal, *Justice*, for a short time, and remained one of Hyndman's closest associates. He devoted himself to what he saw as the higher meaning of Marxism, firmly committed to its international mission, and battling against those social democrats who played down the revolutionary goal in order to enhance their appeal to the workers. Toward those socialists who developed, in the Independent Labour Party, a popular ethically inspired form of socialism, Bax had only contempt. Their sentimental socialism was a 'bastard enthusiasm … born of the morbid self consciousness of our Christian and middle class civilization run to seed' (*The Religion of Socialism*, 1885, 100). He strongly opposed the tendency among some socialists to assert the compatibility of Christianity and socialism. Although he became less active in the movement after the turn of the century, Bax continued to be seen by Hyndman as the 'only original thinker now in any country' (H. M. Hyndman to George Bernard Shaw, 2 Jan 1914, BL, Shaw MSS) capable of formulating a new philosophical synthesis.

Bax's role in the early British socialist movement was, however, idiosyncratic. This was most evident in the social criticism to which he devoted much of his journalistic activity. He attacked many features of British life—imperialism, the legal system, and particularly the middle-class family, 'the most perfect specimen of the complete sham that history has presented' (*The Religion of Socialism*, 1885, 141). In contrast to nearly all of his socialist colleagues, Bax was convinced that prevailing moral and legal conventions permitted the female to dominate the male. He fiercely opposed the contemporary feminist movement. Although Bax looked to the working class as the bearer of the 'religion of socialism', his manner—abstract and impractical—foreclosed any popular appeal. A young Glasgow socialist, Edwin Muir, recalled hearing him 'mumble his way through a long and intricate paper on some aspect of historical determinism, never raising his eyes from the bundle of papers he held before him' (E. Muir, *Autobiography*, 1954, 112).

Even so, Bax was an interesting figure in the development of modern socialism. His attempt to do justice to the complexities of human consciousness anticipated later Marxists who broke with the rigid materialism and determinism of orthodoxy. He remained, however, a late Victorian; his socialist faith was a solution to the crisis of religious belief which occupied so many of his contemporaries.

Bax was married twice. His first wife, Emily Gordon Wright, whom he married in 1877, died at the age of thirty-six after bearing seven children. In 1897 he married a German woman, Maria Johanna Cecelia Henneberg. He died within hours of his second wife at 204 Bedford Hill, Balham, London, on 26 November 1926.

STANLEY PIERSON

Sources E. B. Bax, *Reminiscences and reflexions of a mid and late Victorian* (New York, 1920) · R. Arch, *Ernest Belfort Bax, thinker and pioneer* (1927) · A. Bax, *Farewell, my youth* (1943) · E. P. Thompson, *William Morris: romantic to revolutionary* (1955) · S. Pierson, 'Ernest Belfort Bax: the encounter of Marxism and late Victorian culture', *Journal of British Studies*, 12/1 (1972–3), 39–60 · J. Cowley, *The Victorian encounter with Marx: a study of Ernest Belfort Bax* (1992) · b. cert. · d. cert.
Archives Internationaal Instituut voor Sociale Geschiedenis, Amsterdam, corresp.
Likenesses photograph, repro. in Cowley, *Victorian encounter with Marx* · photographs, repro. in Bax, *Reminiscences and reflexions of a mid and late Victorian*, frontispiece
Wealth at death £3760 8s. 7d.: probate, 12 March 1927, CGPLA Eng. & Wales

Baxendale, Joseph (1785–1872), transport entrepreneur, was born at Lancaster on 28 September 1785, the eldest child in a family of two sons and two daughters of Josiah Baxendale (1761–1835) of Castle Hill, Lancaster, surgeon, and his wife, Mabella (1756–1829), daughter of Thomas Salisbury of Marshfield House, Settle. His father carried on a prosperous practice in Lancaster for some forty years and was a leading citizen. His mother was descended from a family of minor gentry from Newton in Bowland on the Lancashire–Yorkshire border.

Baxendale was educated at Lancaster but left in 1804 for Preston, and afterwards London, where in 1806 he was with Samuel Croughton, wholesale linen draper, of 33 St Paul's Churchyard, the agent for Bannister, Hall & Co., calico-printers of Preston. In 1809 Baxendale returned to Lancashire and became a one-fifth partner in Bannister Hall with Charles Swainson, his cousin through the Salisbury family. The £4000 needed to purchase this share in the partnership Baxendale borrowed from his father and uncle. During these years he travelled much between London and Preston and resided at Darwen Cottage, Walton-le-Dale, near Preston. In 1816 he married Mary (1789–1862), the youngest daughter of Richard Birley (1743–1812) of Blackburn, a wealthy cotton mill owner and co-founder of the firm of Birley, Cardwell & Co., cotton spinners of Blackburn. They had four sons and three daughters.

Retiring from Bannister Hall in December 1816 with some £6000 in net profit, Baxendale purchased in April 1817 a one-sixth share in the old established but ailing business of T. and M. Pickford & Co., carriers of Manchester. The £8000 Baxendale needed for this purpose was mostly borrowed from the trustees of his wife's marriage settlement. Two other new partners contributed similar capital at the same time, but the poor condition of the firm's affairs (culminating in the bankruptcy of Thomas and Matthew *Pickford in 1820) increased Baxendale's active role in the business. By 1824 he was appointed the salaried managing partner.

During the next twenty years Baxendale's energetic and far-sighted management turned the firm's fortunes from bankruptcy to great prosperity and expanded it to become the largest carrying business in the United Kingdom, giving a comprehensive service to all major towns and cities in England and Scotland, and a household name in nineteenth-century Britain. Baxendale's leadership and personality became a legend with his employees, whose welfare was his constant concern.

In the 1820s and 1830s the firm relied on canals and roads for the transport of goods, but Baxendale early appreciated the advantages of railways and that Pickford & Co. should go with them rather than against them. His dealings with the Liverpool and Manchester Railway commenced in 1829, even before that line was opened. In 1838 he accepted appointment as general superintendent of the new London and Birmingham Railway, and in 1837 became a director of the South Eastern Railway. From 1841 to 1845 he was chairman of that company and as such instrumental in the construction of the line to Paris via Folkestone and Boulogne. Initially unable to persuade his co-directors of the desirability of using Folkestone harbour, he purchased and developed the site personally in association with his friend Sir William Cubitt, but afterwards sold it to his company at no profit. He was, in the 1840s, a director of the Compagnie du Chemin de Fer du Nord and of the Amiens and Boulogne Railway, and was received by King Louis Philippe. In 1852 he suggested driving a tunnel under the channel to provide a direct rail route. In the late 1830s Baxendale acted as consultant for the construction of the Belgian state railway system. He was also a director of the Regent's Canal Company from 1836, and of the East India Railway Company in the 1840s.

Having, in 1823, moved the headquarters of Pickfords from Manchester to London, Baxendale moved his own residence from Eccles to Woodside, a spacious Georgian villa at Whetstone, near Finchley, on the Great North Road. From there he travelled continuously in his specially constructed fly carriage to check on the activities of his drivers, as he likewise did in his canal boat, the *Joseph*, on his firm's canal traffic. By degrees he bought out the remaining interests of the Pickford family and of his two other partners, Langton and Inman, so that by 1847 ownership of the business was entirely in the hands of Baxendale and his three elder sons, Joseph Hornby, Lloyd, and Richard Birley, who had become partners in 1843. Baxendale resigned active management of the firm to his sons in 1847 following a period of illness spent abroad. He also resigned his railway directorships.

The last twenty-five years of his life were spent in retirement at Woodside attending to his locally celebrated garden, his increasing investments, and his charitable interests, while keeping a watchful eye on the fortunes of the firm. He was a JP and deputy lieutenant for Middlesex and Hertfordshire and a magistrate for the liberty of St Albans, as well as visitor of the Jesus Hospital Charity, Barnet (which named Baxendale Street on its Bethnal Green estate after him). He was made associate member of the Institution of Civil Engineers in 1837.

A tory in politics and a staunch member of the established church, Baxendale built St John's Church, Whetstone, on part of his estate there in 1832, and during fifty years' residence at Woodside purchased considerable property in the area as well as two agricultural estates at Henham in Essex and Little Dartmouth in Devon. Another investment was a block of houses in Park Village West, Regent's Park, sub-leased from his friend the architect John Nash. Baxendale occupied no. 16 as his London residence from 1838.

Baxendale died at Woodside on 24 March 1872, aged eighty-six, and was buried on 30 March with others of his family in the vault beneath St John's Church. His personal estate at death amounted to £700,000 in investments, in addition to his freehold estates and the business of Pickford & Co., by then entirely made over to his sons. A lifetime's endeavours brought rich rewards and gained him the admiration of Samuel Smiles, who named him 'the Franklin of Business' (Smiles, 172) and praised him for his enlightened treatment of his employees.

By the time of Baxendale's death the firm of Pickford & Co., with its headquarters at 57 Gresham Street in the City of London, employed some 1800 horses and a huge staff of clerks, messengers, and porters. Its fortunes were directed by Baxendale's three elder sons, and in turn by three of his grandsons. Prosperity remained with the firm and its partners until 1901, in which year it became a private limited company and embarked on long-drawn-out litigation with the London and North Western Railway, for whom the firm had acted as cartage agents since 1847. Unsuccessful in the courts and badly affected by the loss of the agency, the partners quarrelled and Joseph's grandson Joseph William Baxendale left the firm in 1908. Thereafter undercapitalized, Pickfords was forced into amalgamation with its rival Carter Paterson in 1912, was bought up by Hay's Wharf Cartage Company in 1920 and finally lost all independence when, with Hay's Wharf Cartage and Carter Paterson, it was acquired by the four railway companies jointly (that is, the London, Midland and Scottish Railway, the London and North-Eastern Railway, the Great Western Railway, and the Southern Railway) in 1934.

T. D. BAXENDALE

Sources S. Smiles, *Thrift* (1875) · C. G. Harper, *Stage-coach and mail in days of yore*, 2 (1903) · G. L. Turnbull, *Traffic and transport: an economic history of Pickfords* (1979) · d. cert. · CGPLA Eng. & Wales (1872) · D. Stevenson, *Fifty years on the London and North Western Railway* (1891) · parish register (birth), 28 Sept 1785, Lancaster, Lancashire, St Mary · parish register (baptism), 28 Oct 1785, Lancaster, Lancashire, St Mary · parish register (baptism), 1761, Liverpool, Lancashire, St George · parish register (baptism), 1756, Giggleswick, Yorkshire · parish register (burial), 30 March 1872, Whetstone, Middlesex, St John · private information (2004)

Likenesses H. W. Pickersgill, oils, 1847, priv. coll. · C. Turner, mezzotint, pubd 1848 (after portrait by H. W. Pickersgill), BM, NPG; repro. in Harper, *Stage-coach and mail in days of yore* · J. S. Westmacott, marble statuette, 1849, priv. coll. · J. S. Westmacott, marble statuette, 1851, priv. coll. · oils, priv. coll.

Wealth at death under £700,000—in UK: probate, 16 May 1872, CGPLA Eng. & Wales · realty—Henham, Essex, 1660 acres valued at £40,000; Little Dartmouth, Devon, 780 acres valued at £15,000; Whetstone, Middlesex, 84 acres valued at £31,000: Family MSS, conveyancing deeds reciting 1883 realty valuations

Baxendale, Lloyd Henry (1858–1937), road transport entrepreneur, was born on 3 February 1858 at Totteridge, Hertfordshire, the eldest son of Lloyd Baxendale, gentleman, and his wife, Ellen, *née* Turner. Although born into an active transport dynasty, his education was that of a member of the upper class, Eton College being followed by Christ Church, Oxford. He married Constance Louisa, daughter of Charles Raymond Pelly, and they had one daughter.

Baxendale's grandfather Joseph *Baxendale, son of a Lancaster physician, had become a partner of Pickfords' road- and canal-carrying business in 1817. Harry Baxendale, as he was usually known, whose father was Joseph's second son, was one of three members of the third generation of Baxendales to join the Pickfords' business: he entered the firm in 1879, and was preceded by his older cousin, Joseph William (1871), the only son of Joseph's eldest son, and followed by his younger brother, Frank (1884). By a partnership agreement of 1894, eight shares were allocated to Joseph William as senior partner, six to Harry, and three to Frank. Capital was distributed in similar proportions in 1901 when the firm converted to limited liability.

Joseph William's tenure as chairman of the limited company was short. The firm's link to the London and North Western Railway (LNWR) as its cartage agents was broken in 1901, apparently as the result of Pickfords' resentment of what was seen as the restrictive and ungenerous attitude of the railway company. However, this adversely affected Pickfords' position and, following a family row, Joseph William resigned and withdrew his capital. A cartage agreement with the new Great Central Railway Company did not provide an adequate alternative, especially at a time when capital for conversion to mechanical transport was required by Pickfords.

On succeeding as chairman, Harry Baxendale presided over this difficult transitional period of the establishment of mechanical transport in the company's service. Steam vehicles were Pickfords' first choice. They purchased eleven Hindley wagons (made in Bourton, Dorset) in 1905, and brought in, as engineer, William Elliott, who remained with Pickfords to become manager of the heavy haulage department, chief engineer, and, finally, general manager of Pickfords and Hay's Wharf Cartage Company.

Motorization was expensive and Pickfords were financially weak, following their break with the LNWR and J. W. Baxendale's retirement and withdrawal of his capital. In these circumstances, amalgamation with their major cartage rival, Carter Paterson & Co., came about in 1912. Harry Baxendale became chairman of the joint company, but 'although face was saved to some extent … the real power lay with the Patersons' (Turnbull, *Traffic and Transport*, 156). Some progress with rationalization was made before the First World War intervened; Carter Paterson and the former Beans Express (another road carrying company) took over London and suburban parcels traffic, but Pickfords retained their provincial strength and heavy haulage specialism.

This aspect of Pickfords' operations prospered with the increased demand for the transport of heavy war *matériel*, whereas Carter Paterson's parcels trade collapsed. In 1920 the Pickfords' side of the combine's operation attracted a successful bid from the Hay's Wharf Cartage Company. Baxendale ceded the chairmanship of Pickfords to Major O. C. Magniac of Hay's Wharf, but, together with James Paterson, remained a director and joined the board of Hay's Wharf Cartage. After lengthy negotiations, on 1 July 1933 Hay's Wharf Cartage, Pickfords, and Carter Paterson were acquired by the four main-line railway companies. Although James Paterson remained in power at Carter Paterson, and W. J. Elliott of Pickfords became general manager of Pickfords and Hay's Wharf Cartage, Baxendale, who was by then seventy-five, resigned in December 1933.

Baxendale's Berkshire home, Greenham Lodge, near Newbury, provided the focus for quite different business interests. In addition to his other interests, Baxendale served as chairman of the Newbury Racecourse Company, formed in 1905; the grandstands of the course were built on former Greenham Lodge estate land, and when George V and Queen Mary visited the Newbury races he personally received them. Local affairs also occupied Baxendale, as JP, a Conservative county councillor for six years from 1889, and churchwarden of his local church. Baxendale died on 21 May 1937 at his home; the funeral took place at Greenham church, where he was buried, and he was survived by his wife.

RICHARD A. STOREY

Sources G. Turnbull, 'Baxendale, Lloyd Henry', *DBB* · G. L. Turnbull, *Traffic and transport: an economic history of Pickfords* (1979) · *Transport Saga, 1646–1947* (privately printed, London, 1947) [Hay's Wharf Cartage Company Ltd] · A. Ingram, *The story of Pickfords* (1994) · *CGPLA Eng. & Wales* (1937) · d. cert.
Wealth at death £309,042 2s. 8d.: probate, 28 June 1937, *CGPLA Eng. & Wales*

Baxendell, Joseph (1815–1887), meteorologist and astronomer, was born on 19 April 1815 at Bank Top, Manchester, the son of Thomas Baxendell and his wife, Mary Shepley. One of a family of six sons and two daughters, he was described by contemporaries as largely self-educated, but he attended Thomas Whalley's school, Cheetham Hill, Manchester. He left school and, when he was about fourteen, shipped as an ordinary hand on the *Mary Scott*, a ship engaged in South American trade, and spent six years at sea. He continued to study and to develop his powers of observation, witnessing, for instance, the wonderful shower of meteors in the Pacific in November 1833. When he abandoned seafaring life in 1835 he returned to Manchester, and assisted his father, who was a land steward. He afterwards had a business of his own as an estate agent. On 10 April 1865, he married Mary Anne, sister of Norman Robert Pogson, government astronomer for Madras, whose three eldest sons she was raising. With her Baxendell had one son, named after himself, who succeeded him as meteorologist to the corporation of Southport.

Baxendell figured a 13 inch speculum metal mirror for a reflecting telescope, at the observatory of his friend Robert Worthington at Crumpsall Hall, near Manchester, who also had a 5 inch refractor. His first of twelve contributions to the Royal Astronomical Society, on observations on a variable star, was made in 1849, and he was elected a fellow in 1858. In February 1859 he succeeded Henry Halford Jones as astronomer to the Manchester corporation. He superintended the erection of the Fernley Meteorological Observatory in Hesketh Park, Southport, and was appointed meteorologist to the corporation of that town in 1871. In 1877, he built a private astronomical observatory at his home, 14 Liverpool Road, Birkdale, near Southport, where he continued to observe until his death.

Baxendell's fifty-five other papers are in the Royal Society's *Proceedings*, the Liverpool Astronomical Society's *Journal*, and a number of other publications, but his more important work was contributed to the Manchester Literary and Philosophical Society, which he joined in January 1858. In the following year he was placed on the council, and in 1861 became joint secretary as well as editor of its *Memoirs*. The former post he retained until 1885, and the latter until his death. He was one of the founders of the physical and mathematical section of the society in 1859, and his enthusiasm for meteorology helped give the science a prominent place. From 1873 to 1877 he was a member of the Crumpsall local board, his only venture into public life.

After the co-operation between 1781 and 1786 of Edward Piggott (1753–1825) and John Goodricke (1764–1786) who observed two known variable stars, Baxendell was the first British systematic observer of variable stars, followed by Norman Pogson after 1853 and George Knott after 1859. Commencing in 1836 at Manchester, and continuing from 1877 to 1888 at his Southport home with a 6 inch Cooke refractor lent and installed by Thomas S. Bazley (1829–1919), Baxendell discovered eighteen variables, including the nova T. Bootes in 1860. His mass of fifty-two years' observations were passed to H. H. Turner, Savilian professor at Oxford, who considered them of such value that he enlisted Mary Blagg (1858–1944) to edit, analyse, and extract from them twenty-three long-period variables. These were published in ten papers in the *Monthly Notices of the Royal Astronomical Society* between 1907 and 1918, with a discussion by Turner. Balfour Stewart credited Baxendell's 1871 paper as making him the pioneer in connecting terrestrial atmospheric forces with sun-spot cycles. He predicted the long drought of 1868 and advised the Manchester corporation in the regulation of the water supply. He later predicted the outbreak of an epidemic at Southport. Usually a retiring figure, he entered the limelight in 1867 with a vehement critique of the behaviour of the government and the Royal Society in cancelling the storm warning system. This early form of official weather prediction had been established by the meteorological department of the Board of Trade in 1860. When the Royal Society took over the supervision of the department six years later it refused to deal with forecasts, despite their popularity. Baxendell's role in the controversy probably explained his late election to the Royal Society (in 1884).

In religion Baxendell was a churchman and he supported, in the Victorian imperial tradition, Jewish resettlement of Palestine. In his later years, his scientific, religious, and political interests converged in his premillennialist calculations of the prophetic meaning of the Great Pyramid—he concluded, for instance, that Gladstone's accession to power marked the troubles that would precede the second coming of Christ. Baxendell died at Birkdale on 7 October 1887. His wife survived him.

C. W. SUTTON, *rev.* KATHARINE ANDERSON

Sources *Monthly Notices of the Royal Astronomical Society*, 48 (1887–8), 157–60 · B. S. [B. Stewart], *PRS*, 43 (1887–8), iv · B. Stewart, *Nature*, 36 (1887), 585 · J. Bottomley, *Memoirs of the Literary and Philosophical Society of Manchester*, 4th ser., 1 (1888), 28–58 · *Manchester Guardian* (10 Oct 1887) · private information (1901) · *CGPLA Eng. & Wales* (1887) · Royal Observatory of Scotland, Edinburgh, C. P. Smyth Archives, Baxendell–C. P. Smyth correspondence · *The Observatory*, 10 (1887), 399–400 · H. H. Turner, 'Baxendell's observations of U Geminorum', *Monthly Notices of the Royal Astronomical Society*, 67 (1906–7), 316–29
Archives RAS, letters and observations · RS
Likenesses C. Turner, mezzotint, pubd 1848 (after H. W. Pickersgill), BM, NPG
Wealth at death £2949 18s. 10d.: probate, 9 Dec 1887, *CGPLA Eng. & Wales*

Baxter, Andrew (1686/7–1750), natural philosopher and metaphysician, was born at Old Aberdeen, the son of a merchant and his wife, Elizabeth Frazer. Baxter studied at King's College, Aberdeen, from 1699 to 1703, and in 1719 was employed by the Hays of Drumelzier, whom he subsequently served in various capacities. While residing with the Hays at Duns Castle in 1723, he corresponded with

Henry Home (later Lord Kames) on the conceptual foundations of Newton's laws of motion. In the following year Baxter married a clergyman's daughter, Alice Mabon (d. 1760), and they had a son and three daughters. In 1732 he launched his public career as a metaphysician, penning an anonymous pamphlet attacking the heterodox thinker William Dudgeon; writing to his friend William Warburton in 1740, Baxter noted that he had written a further lengthy polemic against Dudgeon, which remained in manuscript.

In October 1733 Baxter published the first edition of the work which established his reputation as one of Britain's leading exponents of Newtonian metaphysics, *An Enquiry into the Nature of the Human Soul*; he issued a second enlarged edition in 1737, and a third in 1745. Echoing the writings of Samuel Clarke, Baxter's basic thesis in the *Enquiry* was that matter is essentially inert and that all natural phenomena imply the constant action of an immaterial principle as well as the universal superintendence of a divine power. Like Clarke, Baxter was anxious to refute the views of atheists, deists, and materialists such as Lucretius, Thomas Hobbes, and Spinoza, who had all implied that matter is intrinsically active. Baxter also criticized John Locke's analysis of the soul, and warned against the sceptical consequences of George Berkeley's immaterialism. His critique of Berkeley was one of the first to appear in Britain, and it left its mark on Scottish metaphysicians like Thomas Reid. Along with his refutation of Berkeley, Baxter included a lengthy essay arguing that dreams were caused by the action of spiritual beings and, according to Warburton, Baxter's speculations on the subject undermined the credibility of the book as a whole.

Baxter's Latin dialogue on the rudiments of astronomy, *Matho, sive, Cosmotheoria puerilis*, of 1738, grew out of his work as a private tutor, and he went on to tutor sons of the nobility, including John, the future twelfth Lord Gray. Baxter supplemented his teaching income through his publications, for he produced an expanded English translation of *Matho* in two volumes in 1740, which appeared in a second edition in 1745 and a third, in which a new dialogue was substituted for an erroneous one, in 1765. Leaving his family in Berwick upon Tweed, in the spring of 1741 he went with his pupil William Hay to Utrecht, where he also took on the care of Walter Stuart, the eighth Lord Blantyre. They remained in Utrecht, making occasional excursions to Spa, Cleves, and other watering holes on the grand tour, until 1747, when Baxter returned to his wife and family in Northumberland. He spent the remainder of his life at Whittingehame in Haddingtonshire, where he helped to look after the affairs of the Hays. On one of his visits to Spa, Baxter met John *Wilkes (1725–1797), then travelling with a tutor, and was infatuated by the young man. They had an intense relationship while in Holland, and a correspondence between them was maintained during the rest of Baxter's life. 'My first desire', he says in a letter to his 'dearest Mr. Wilkes' of April 1749, 'is to serve virtue and religion; my second and ardent wish to testify my respect to Mr. Wilkes' (BL, Add. MS 30867). In the

mid-1740s Baxter composed a dialogue on the *vis viva* controversy; it was called 'Histor' after the chief interlocutor, who was intended to represent Wilkes, and whom Baxter laboured to make a worthy representative of the original in wit and vivacity. This dialogue defended Newton and Clarke against Leibniz, and was offered to Andrew Millar in 1747 for publication, but it was rejected because three independent readers judged that the discussion had lost its interest.

Baxter's health deteriorated in the summer of 1749, and on 29 January 1750 he wrote a touching letter to Wilkes announcing the hopelessness of his case. Wilkes printed this letter in 1753 and distributed copies among his friends. Baxter died on 23 April 1750, and was buried at Whittingehame in the Hay family vault. His last completed book, *An Appendix to the First Part of the Enquiry* (1750), appeared shortly after his death. Dedicated to Wilkes, the *Appendix* attacked the presentation of Newton's speculations regarding the existence of an ethereal medium in Colin Maclaurin's *An Account of Sir Isaac Newton's Philosophical Discoveries* (1748) and replied to Maclaurin's criticism of a passage in Baxter's *Matho*. His widow died in 1760, and was buried in Linlithgow. In 1779 a posthumous work, *The Evidence of Reason in Proof of the Immortality of the Soul*, was published from manuscripts in the possession of Baxter's son, Alexander, by John Duncan, who also appended the text of Baxter's letter to Wilkes of January 1750. In addition, Alexander gave information for the life of Baxter printed in the second edition of *Biographia Britannica* (1778–1793), where Baxter was described as very studious, often reading through the night, a cheerful and modest companion, very popular with young men, and elegant, though severely economical. Offers of preferment failed to induce him to take orders in the Church of England.

PAUL WOOD

Sources A. Baxter, 'Histor', U. Aberdeen, MS 204 · Baxter–Kames correspondence, NA Scot., GD 24/1/546 · P. Russell, 'Wishart, Baxter and Hume's *Letter from a gentleman*', *Hume Studies*, 28 (1997), 245–76 · H. Klemme, 'Anmerkungen zur schottischen Aufklärung (in Aberdeen): neue Briefe von Baxter, Beattie, Fordyce, Reid und Stewart', *Archiv für Geschichte der Philosophie*, 74 (1992), 247–71 · H. M. Bracken, *The early reception of Berkeley's immaterialism, 1710–1733*, rev. edn (1965) · [W. Warburton], *Letters from a late eminent prelate to one of his friends*, ed. R. Hurd, 3rd edn (1809) · A. Baxter to J. Wilkes, April 1749, BL, Add. MS 30687 · A. Kippis and others, eds., *Biographia Britannica, or, The lives of the most eminent persons who have flourished in Great Britain and Ireland*, 2nd edn, 5 vols. (1778–93) · G. S. Rousseau, 'In the house of Madam Vander Tasse, on the Long Bridge: a homosexual university club in early modern Europe', *Journal of Homosexuality*, 16 (1988), 311–47

Archives U. Aberdeen L., MS 204 · U. Edin. L., MS La III. 807/1–2 | BL, Add. MS 30687 · NA Scot., corresp. with W. Lord Kames, GD 24/1/546

Baxter, Charles (1809–1879), portrait and subject painter, was born in Little Britain, London, on 9 March 1809, the son of a book-clasp maker. As a boy he was drawn to art, though his father and friends tried to discourage him from this, 'stigmatising an artist's life as "an idle kind of employment and a beggarly profession"' (*Art Journal*, 1864, 146). He was urged to pursue a trade instead and was accordingly apprenticed to a bookbinder. His impulse towards art, though, was so strong that he soon gave up his business, and commenced a career as a painter, chiefly of miniatures and portraits. In 1834, while working on a miniature portrait of the actress Mrs Charles Jones, he met George Clint, to whom Jones was also sitting. They became friends and Baxter subsequently received valuable guidance from Clint. He exhibited for the first time at the Royal Academy in 1834 and in 1839 he joined the Clipstone Street Artists' Society, studying alongside Paul Falconer Poole, William Müller, Joseph Jenkins, Francis (Frank) Topham, and others. Baxter became a member of the Society of British Artists in 1842, and contributed to its exhibitions many of the poetical and rustic subjects and fancy portraits upon which his reputation chiefly rests. He was 'essentially a painter of female beauty' (Art Journal, 1864, 147), his female heads 'especially characterised by refinement of expression and purity of colour' (Art Journal, 1879, 73).

Among Baxter's best works were The Orphan (1843), which was exhibited at the Suffolk Street gallery; The Wanderers (1847); L'allegro (1852) and Love me, Love my Dog (1854), both exhibited at the Royal Academy—the latter, depicting a young boy with a small King Charles spaniel, was considered in its day 'a gem of its kind, admirably drawn and exquisitely painted' (Art Journal, 1864, 147); Sunshine and The Bouquet (1855); The Dream of Love (1857), which was in the collection of the Huth family, among the chief patrons of the artist; Little Red Riding Hood (1859); Olivia and Sophia (1862), from the Vicar of Wakefield, which was admired for 'the brilliancy of its tones' (ibid.); The Ballad (1863); Peasant Girl of Chioggia (1869); and Rich and rare were the gems she wore (1872).

Baxter lived at 6 Lidlington Place, Hampstead Road, London, until a few months before his death. He died, apparently unmarried, on 10 January 1879, at Snowden Villa, Hither Green Lane, in south London. His work was often reproduced and much collected and he is represented in the Victoria and Albert Museum. His studio sale was held at Christies on 15 March 1879. MARK POTTLE

Sources Art Journal (1864), 145-7 · Art Journal (1879), 73 · B. Stewart and M. Cutten, The dictionary of portrait painters in Britain up to 1920 (1997) · Wood, Vic. painters, 2nd edn · D. Foskett, A dictionary of British miniature painters, 1 (1972), 156 · The exhibition of the Royal Academy (1834-72) [exhibition catalogues] · exhibition catalogues (1842-79) [Society of British Artists] · CGPLA Eng. & Wales (1879)
Archives NL Scot., corresp. with Robert Louis Stevenson
Likenesses J. & C. Watkins, carte-de-visite, NPG · photograph, BM
Wealth at death under £3000: probate, 24 Feb 1879, CGPLA Eng. & Wales

Baxter, Sir David, baronet (bap. 1793, d. 1872), linen manufacturer and benefactor, was born in Dundee and baptized there on 24 March 1793, the second son of William Baxter (1767–1854), linen merchant, of Balgavies, and his wife, Elisabeth (Betty) Gorell (d. 1804). He was educated at a local school and, entering business, became, while still young, manager of the Dundee Sugar Refining Company. The concern was never prosperous and, notwithstanding his prudent and energetic management, it collapsed in 1826. Thereupon, he became partner in the linen-manufacturing firm of Baxter Brothers, which included his father and his two younger brothers—Edward, his elder brother, having left it in the previous year to commence the business of a general merchant. From the time he joined the firm he was, in practice, its head and, on the death of his two brothers and his father within a few years afterwards, he and the former manager of the works remained the sole partners. In 1828 an attempt had been made by him to introduce power-loom weaving, but after a short trial it was abandoned until 1836, when its revival was followed by complete and extraordinary success. Through the mechanical skill of the junior partner in perfecting the machinery, and the business capacity and tact of David Baxter, the firm speedily became one of the largest manufacturing houses in the world; and to its remarkable success may be in a large degree ascribed the position which Dundee has attained as the chief seat of linen manufacture in Britain.

Although much immersed in the cares of business, Baxter took an active, if not very prominent, share in public affairs. In 1825 he was chosen as police commissioner, and in 1828 a guild councillor and member of the harbour board. In 1833 he married Elizabeth Montgomery of Barrahill, Ayrshire. They had no children. A Liberal in politics, he took a lively interest in parliamentary elections, both in Dundee and in the county of Fife, where in 1856 he purchased the estate of Kilmaron. His enlightened regard for the welfare of his native town was, however, manifested chiefly in noble and generous benefactions which have given his name one of the highest places of honour in its annals. The most notable of these was perhaps his and his sisters' presentation of 38 acres of land to Dundee as a pleasure garden and recreation ground, which, under the name of Baxter Park, was opened by Earl Russell in September 1863. On 1 January 1863 he was made a baronet. The foundation of the Albert Institute of Literature, Science, and Art was due also chiefly to his liberality and that of his relatives; and in connection with the Dundee Infirmary he erected a convalescent home at Broughty Ferry at a cost of £30,000. More important was his support of higher education in Scotland. Besides building and endowing a girls' school at Cupar, Fife, he established at Edinburgh University scholarships in the mathematical, philosophical, physical, and natural sciences, and endowed a chair of engineering. Before his last illness he was concerned with a scheme to link Dundee with the neighbouring University of St Andrews, and this was subsequently brought to fruition by his sister Mary Ann *Baxter and other relatives, whose generous benefactions enabled the creation of University College, Dundee.

He died on 13 October 1872 at his home, Kilmaron Castle, near Cupar, Fife, survived by his wife. Of his heritable and personal property, valued at £1,200,000, one half was divided among near relatives, and the other among distant relatives and public institutions, the largest legacies being £50,000 to the Free Church of Scotland, £40,000 to Edinburgh University, and £20,000 towards the foundation of a mechanics' institute in Dundee.

T. F. HENDERSON, rev. ANITA MCCONNELL

Sources J. Thompson, *The history of Dundee*, ed. J. Maclaren, rev. edn (1874) · W. Norrie, *Dundee celebrities of the nineteenth century* (1873) · *The Times* (20 Dec 1884) · parish register, Dundee, Forfarshire [birth and baptism], March 1793 · d. cert. · *CGPLA Eng. & Wales* (1872) · D. Southgate, *University education in Dundee: a centenary history* (1982)

Likenesses J. Steell, statue, 1873, Dundee · J. Watson-Gordon, oils, U. Edin.

Wealth at death £1,200,000

Baxter [*née* Foster], **Elizabeth** [Lizzie] (1837–1926), evangelist, was born on 16 December 1837 at 81 High Street, Evesham, the third daughter of eight children born to Thomas Nelson Foster (1799–1858), a Quaker manufacturer of agricultural fertilizers, and his second wife, Elizabeth Gibbs. Elizabeth (Lizzie) Foster was privately educated and then attended a boarding-school in Worcester. She experienced an evangelical conversion in 1858 and became involved with the mid-century religious revival. In 1866 she was invited by William Pennefather, vicar of St Jude's, Mildmay Park, Islington, London, to become the superintendent of his deaconesses' training home. She led the work for two years, during which time she designed the distinctive bonnet and dress of the Mildmay deaconesses.

In 1868 Elizabeth Foster married Michael Paget Baxter (1834–1910), thus entering a family already involved in prophetic speculation. Her father-in-law was Robert Baxter (1802–1889), a parliamentary lawyer who in his early years had joined the Catholic Apostolic church, but who had left after forty-three of his prophecies remained unfulfilled. Elizabeth's husband was active in evangelistic work; he had been ordained deacon in 1860 and had ministered for seven months at Onondaga, Ontario, Canada, but was not ordained priest. He had returned to England and become an itinerant preacher; his message, centred on the imminent return of Jesus Christ, earned him the nickname Prophet Baxter. In 1866 he had become the founder–proprietor of the *Christian Herald*, a popular nondenominational evangelical journal. He and Elizabeth had two children, one of whom died in infancy.

Both Michael and Elizabeth Baxter were involved in evangelistic crusades throughout England, in campaigns on the continent (where they distributed thousands of gospels and tracts), and in the Moody and Sankey missions. In 1883 Elizabeth founded Bethshan, a home in Islington for promoting holiness and divine healing. Her interpretation of divine healing, which she viewed—as did other contemporaries—as available to all who trusted in Christ's atonement, was later widely influential, especially among Pentecostalists. Bethshan seeded a number of similar holiness and healing centres: a missionary training home, opened in an adjoining house in 1886, which prepared men and women to work at home and overseas (by 1900, 336 students had trained there); the international convention on holiness and divine healing, which met in the Royal Agricultural Hall, Islington; and the Kurku and Central Indian Hill Mission, which worked among the poor hill tribes of northern India. In 1894 Elizabeth undertook a world tour, during which she spoke on divine healing (and visited her Indian mission); in 1899–1900 she made a second visit to India.

Elizabeth Baxter was an Anglican but had far wider sympathies, which led to her involvement in many evangelical organizations. She was prominent in the Holiness Movement, led the women's meetings at the Keswick Convention, and had close friends in the Salvation Army. Her commitment to premillennialism provided an incentive for her missionary work and philanthropic activity. Small and frail in appearance, she was known for her simple faith and radiant spirit, for her Sunday school lessons which appeared in the *Christian Herald*, and for her devotional tracts on scripture passages. Elizabeth died of a stroke at Hove on 19 December 1926, and was buried in the family grave at Marylebone cemetery, East Finchley, Middlesex.   A. F. MUNDEN

Sources N. Wiseman, *Elizabeth Baxter* (1928) · E. Miller, *The history and doctrine of Irvingism, or of the so-called Catholic and Apostolic church*, 2 vols. (1878) · A. L. Drummond, *Edward Irving and his circle* [1937] · Venn, *Alum. Cant.* · *The Times* (8 Jan 1910) · *The Times* (22 Dec 1926) · N. Wiseman, *Michael Paget Baxter* (1923)

Baxter, Ethelreda (1883–1963). *See under* Baxter, William Alexander (1877–1973).

Baxter, Evan Buchanan (1844–1885), physician, was born at St Petersburg, Russia, where his father, James Baxter (d. 1863/4), had resided for some years as a high official in the education department of the Russian government service. His father also directed the English school at St Petersburg during his residence there, and it was here that Evan began his education. Soon afterwards, on being appointed government inspector of schools in the province of Podolsk, Russian Poland, his father took up his residence at Kamenets, where Evan was brought up and educated until he was sixteen, under the care of his father and an old French tutor; Evan's mother, whose maiden name was Ross, had died while he was very young.

In 1861 Baxter came to England and entered the general literature and science department of King's College, London. The next year he obtained an open scholarship in classics at Lincoln College, Oxford, and stayed there for three terms. His university career, however, was interrupted by his father's illness. He returned to Russia to nurse and attend him, and remained there for about a year until his father's death. On coming back he resolved not to return to Oxford. He had become a positivist. 'The only profession', he said, 'which attracted me was that of medicine, holding out, as it did, an opportunity for the study of physical science and a hope of comparative intellectual freedom'.

In October 1864 Baxter entered the medical department of King's College, London, with the first Warneford scholarship. In 1865 he was elected a junior scholar, and in the same year he won the Dasent prize with his essay, 'The minor poems of Milton'. In 1868 he was appointed assistant house physician to King's College Hospital; in 1868–9 he filled the office of house physician, and in 1869 he gained the first Warneford prize. In 1870 and 1871 he became Sambrooke medical registrar to King's College

Hospital. It was at this time that he began to be appreciated not only as someone of high intellectual calibre, but also as a great teacher and a careful clinical observer. In 1865 he matriculated in honours at the University of London, and he graduated MB in 1869 and MD in 1870, with high honours. In 1871 he was appointed medical tutor at King's College, and he held this post until 1874, when he was chosen as the successor to Professor Alfred Garrod in the chair of materia medica and therapeutics, and as an assistant physician to King's College Hospital; these offices he was to hold until a month or two before his death. On 14 September 1874 he married Sophie Caroline Mason, a widow, daughter of George Edward Du Bocket; she had been a nursing sister in the Franco-Prussian War and at King's College Hospital.

In 1872 Baxter became a member of the Royal College of Physicians, and in 1877 he was elected a fellow. Subsequently he was appointed an examiner in materia medica and therapeutics, and he also filled for five years the corresponding office in the University of London. In 1881 Baxter was appointed physician to the Royal Free Hospital, where he was an advocate of medical education for women. He was also physician to the Blackfriars Hospital for Skin Diseases. He served on the council of the Pathological Society and worked at the Evelina Hospital for Sick Children for many years.

Baxter translated G. E. Van Rindfleisch's work of 1866 under the title *Pathological Histology* (2 vols., 1872) for the New Sydenham Society; he prepared the fourth edition of Alfred Garrod's *Essentials of Materia medica* (1874); and he made some valuable experiments which were described in the paper 'The action of the chinchona alkaloids and their congeners on bacteria and colourless blood corpuscles', published in *The Practitioner* in 1873. He also drew up the able *Report on the Experimental Study of Certain Disinfectants*, printed in the Privy Council Reports (new series, 1875); and he contributed a remarkable article to the *British and Foreign Medico-Chirurgical Review* in 1877 on the vasomotor nervous system. His minor writings include a series of physiological notes which he contributed to *The Academy* over many years.

Baxter died at his home in 28 Weymouth Street, Portland Place, London, on 14 January 1885. He was survived by his wife.   THOMPSON COOPER, *rev.* KAYE BAGSHAW

Sources Munk, *Roll* · *BMJ* (24 Jan 1885), 204 · *The Lancet* (24 Jan 1885), 181–3 · m. cert. · *CGPLA Eng. & Wales* (1885)
Wealth at death £9265 5s. 5d.: probate, 4 Feb 1885, *CGPLA Eng. & Wales*

Baxter, George (1804–1867), colour printer, was born at 37 High Street, Lewes, Sussex, on 31 July 1804, the second son and second child in the family of three sons and three daughters of John *Baxter (1781–1858), printer and bookseller, and his wife, Charlotte, *née* Warner. He spent his childhood in Lewes, attending the Cliffe House Academy and then high school. After school he was apprenticed to a wood-engraver. In 1825 he moved to London and in 1827 settled in Islington. On 23 August 1827 he married his cousin Mary, daughter of Robert Harrild, manufacturer of

printing machinery. They had one son and two daughters.

Over the next eight years Baxter applied himself to developing and perfecting the colour printing process which brought him international fame. In 1829 he produced his first coloured print, *Butterflies*, and achieved popular acclaim in 1834 with the coloured plates for *Feathered Tribes of the British Islands* by Robert Mudie. Baxter enjoyed a fruitful collaboration with Mudie and had illustrated thirteen of his books by 1844.

In 1836 Baxter received a royal patent for his printing process. His technique was innovatory, combining an engraved metal plate with as many as twenty engraved wooden blocks, each printed in a separate colour. The prints combined quality and cheapness and were produced in vast numbers. For the next twenty-five years Baxter dominated colour printing, branching out into a variety of publishing areas, including decorated music sheets, notepaper, pocket-books, and his famous needle cases. He claimed to have produced 20 million prints by the end of his career. Baxter's subjects were remarkably varied and included sentimental treatments of religious and romantic themes, prints of typical London figures, and newsworthy events. His piety led him to produce some of his most powerful work for the immensely influential and prosperous missionary societies. In collaboration with John Snow, Baxter worked for the London Missionary Society from 1837 to 1843, and in 1844–5 with the Baptist and Wesleyan missionary societies. His most celebrated missionary print was *The Massacre of the Lamented Missionary, the Rev. J. Williams and Mr. Harris at Erromanga* (1841).

Had he restricted his output to such enterprises, Baxter would undoubtedly have become very wealthy; yet he suffered commercially throughout his career because of his perfectionism and over-ambition. It is ironic that his greatest financial disasters were projects which resulted from the interest which both Queen Victoria and Prince Albert showed in his work. The large prints which he brought out by royal command to commemorate the coronation and opening of the House of Commons in 1838 and the prints he produced, after Lord Brougham had arranged an interview with Albert, to commemorate the Great Exhibition of 1851, were hopelessly delayed and proved very expensive failures. Nevertheless, Baxter's work and his royal connections made him famous during the years directly following the Great Exhibition, and he gained public recognition for his achievements: he was awarded the great gold medal of Austria (1852), and medals for his exhibits at the Great Exhibitions in New York (1853) and Paris (1855), was elected a member of the Royal Society of Arts (1855), and received the grand gold medal of Sweden (1857). The years 1850–55 were also those of his greatest commercial success. A single print, *The Madonna*, sold in excess of 700,000 copies.

By 1856, however, Baxter was in financial difficulties as a result of competition from rival companies, and because of photography's growing appeal. His markets were poached, and his temperament appeared to decline with his financial fortunes. He became increasingly embittered, alienating both his family and personal friends. In 1859 he produced his last print, *Dogs of St. Bernard*, and in 1865 he was declared bankrupt. After unsuccessful attempts to sell his enormous stock of prints through public auctions, he retired to his wife's house, suitably named The Retreat, at Peak Hill, Sydenham, London. In 1866 Baxter suffered a blow to the head in an omnibus accident; he never properly recovered, and he died at home on 11 January 1867. He was buried at Christ Church, Forest Hill, Sydenham, and was survived by his wife.

MARCUS M. G. WOOD

Sources M. E. Mitzman, *George Baxter and the Baxter prints* (1978) · C. T. C. Lewis, *George Baxter, colour printer: his life and work* (1908) · H. G. Clarke, *The centenary Baxter book* (1936) · C. F. Bullock, *The life of George Baxter, engraver, artist, and colour printer* (1901) · d. cert. · *CGPLA Eng. & Wales* (1868)
Archives New Baxter Society, St Albans, Hertfordshire, MSS · St Bride's Printing Library, London, MSS · V&A, MSS | Bodl. Oxf., John Johnson MSS
Likenesses daguerreotype photograph, repro. in Lewis, *George Baxter, colour printer*
Wealth at death under £100: probate, 5 Dec 1868, *CGPLA Eng. & Wales*

Baxter, James Keir (1926–1972), poet and publicist, was born on 29 June 1926 at 97 Elm Row, Dunedin, Otago, New Zealand, the son of Archibald McColl Learmond Baxter (1881–1970), a small farmer descended from immigrant Scottish highlanders, and his wife, Millicent Amiel Macmillan Brown (1888–1984), the daughter of the Scottish foundation professor of English at Canterbury College. James was named Keir after the socialist Keir Hardie; his elder brother and only sibling, Terence, had been named after the Irish nationalist Terence McSweeney. During the First World War, Archibald Baxter had suffered brutal punishment for his refusal to enlist. Both parents exerted a powerful influence on the young James Baxter, though to his mind his father's was the more benign. Like him, James was an autodidact, although he could play the academic game and, in adulthood, was seldom found far from a university. From the stories of his father's forerunners he constructed the ideal of a close-knit tribal society; he later discovered it among the Maori and tried to re-create it in a community.

The land and seascapes of Baxter's Otago childhood yielded images which permeate his writings. He was often unhappy at school, most acutely so when boarding at Sibford School in England, when the family visited Europe, and in wartime at King's High School in Dunedin, as the son of prominent pacifists. In 1944 he enrolled at Otago University. A shortish, thick-set figure with a large head and a long pale face, a slow smile and a mellifluous voice, he at once became a celebrity, for his drinking as well as for his writing. He fell unhappily in love; the memory of this event tormented him for years.

As a child Baxter began to fill notebooks with poems. His first collection, *Beyond the Palisade* (1944), was widely acclaimed. Both this and *Blow, Wind of Fruitfulness* (1948) show the eloquence and fluency, and the formal discipline and control, which characterize the best of his output.

James Keir Baxter (1926–1972), by unknown photographer [detail]

Thus began a prodigal flood of volumes, pamphlets, broadsheets, polemics, and sermons; much remains unpublished.

In 1948 Baxter moved to Christchurch. He hung around the university college, consulted a Jungian psychoanalyst, and was baptized into the Anglican church. On 9 December he married Jacqueline Cecilia Sturm (*b.* 1927), a student he had known in Dunedin. It proved a troubled but persistent marriage. The couple moved to Wellington, where two children were born—Hilary Anne in 1949 and John McColl in 1952, but they separated informally in 1957. In 1954 James had joined Alcoholics Anonymous.

Distracted by the demands of family life, university studies, teacher training, and employment, Baxter wrote less well but published voluminously. He wrote plays—*Jack Winter's Dream* (1958) and *The Wide Open Cage* (1959). He was received into the Roman Catholic church in January 1958 and left for Asia on a UNESCO fellowship in September. *Howrah Bridge and other Poems* (1961) memorably records that journey. His emphatic but ambiguous adherence to Roman Catholicism and his experience of Indian spirituality led him to the communitarian experiments of his closing years.

The Baxters were reunited in India. After their return James lived the life of a breadwinner, a family man, a total abstainer, and a devout Catholic. The tensions show clearly in his writing: *Pig Island Letters* (1966) exhibits a renewed intensity. He played some part in literary politics and wrote polemics against participation in the Vietnam War.

In 1966 Baxter returned to Otago University as Burns literary fellow. The family man and the devout churchman now reconstructed his life as child, young poet, drunk, and tormented lover. Out of this contradiction he wrote a great number of powerful poems, eminent among them the sequence 'Words to Lay a Strong Ghost', in which he relived, in undiminished grief and anger, his first love affair. He wrote plays for a Dunedin theatre, including many adaptations of Greek tragedy; literary criticism, notably the semi-autobiographical *Man on the Horse* (1967); polemics in verse and prose; and devotional pieces, collected as *The Flowering Cross* (1969). He also gave lectures and seminars, talked to students, and gathered a following around him in his office at the Catholic Education Centre, where he worked in 1968.

At the end of that year Baxter went north to a remote, largely Catholic, Maori community on the Whanganui River called Jerusalem or Hiruharama. He explained this as a call from God; he also said that he could no longer manage domesticity. There, and in Wellington and Auckland, he championed young people alienated from an inhuman society and attempted to establish a community. With a sure sense of theatre, he transformed his image into that of an unkempt bearded prophet in cast-off clothes and rosary beads. Now calling himself Hemi, he became a public figure, the subject of feature articles in newspapers. He extolled the communal values of Maori society. His Catholicism acquired a new emphasis upon the love and friendship of God, which contended with his readiness to despair.

From Jerusalem, Baxter sent off the collection *Runes* (1973), a volume which looks back to the sophisticated rhetoric of the 1960s and forward to the relaxed conversational tone of *Jerusalem Sonnets* (1970), *Jerusalem Daybook* (1971), and *Autumn Testament* (1972). These sequences of unrhymed sonnets, sometimes with prose notes, were as carefully composed as ever, with an art more complete than any Baxter had displayed before. They provide the main basis for his later reputation. All this time he had seriously neglected himself. He had intended to do something about some mild heart attacks, but he suffered a massive attack on 22 October 1972 and died in an Auckland suburban house, 544 Glenfield Road, where he had asked for help. He was buried at Jerusalem three days later, following a requiem mass on the marae. His *Collected Poems* were published in 1979.　　　　　W. H. OLIVER

Sources F. McKay, *The life of James K. Baxter* (1990) • W. H. Oliver, *James K. Baxter: a portrait* (1983) • J. K. Baxter, *The man on the horse* (1967) • L. Jones, ed., 'James K. Baxter: poet and prophet', *New Zealand Journal of Literature*, 13 (1995) • V. O'Sullivan, *James K. Baxter* (1976) • C. K. Stead, 'Towards Jerusalem: the later poetry of James K. Baxter', *Islands*, 2/1 (1973), 7–18 • J. E. Weir and B. A. Lyon, *A preliminary bibliography of works by and works about James K. Baxter* (1979) • C. Brasch, 'Phrases and poems', *New Zealand Monthly Review* (Dec 1966), 12–13 • J. E. Weir, *The poetry of James K. Baxter* (1970) • C. Doyle, *James K. Baxter* (1976) • P. Lawlor, *The two Baxters: diary notes with an essay by Vincent O'Sullivan* (1979)
Archives NL NZ, Turnbull L. • University of Otago, Dunedin, MSS • Victoria University, Wellington, New Zealand, MSS |FILM Archives New Zealand, Wellington • BFI NFTVA, 'Images of James K. Baxter', B6053/01 • BFI NFTVA, 'In memoriam: James K. Baxter', B5535/06 • BFI NFTVA, performance recordings • New Zealand Film Archive, Wellington • TVNZ (Television New Zealand), Wellington |SOUND Radio New Zealand Sound Archive, Christchurch
Likenesses T. Schoon, photograph, 1940–49, priv. coll. • portraits, 1940–72, repro. in Oliver, *James K. Baxter* • M. Friedlander, photograph, c.1966–1967, priv. coll. • E. Noordhof, crayon?, 1967, priv. coll. • A. Westra, photograph, c.1970, priv. coll. • M. de Hamel, photograph, c.1971–1972, priv. coll. • A. Thornton, oils?, priv. coll. • photograph, *Otago Daily Times* offices • photograph, NL NZ, Turnbull L. [*see illus.*]

Baxter, John (*fl.* 1794–1816). *See under* London Corresponding Society (*act.* 1792–1799).

Baxter, John (1781–1858), printer, was born at Rickhurst, Surrey, on 20 October 1781, the son of John Baxter. In early life he was employed in the Strand, London, in the publishing office of James Mathews, the father of the comedian Charles Mathews. On 22 November 1801 he married Charlotte Warner at St Martin-in-the-Fields, London; they had three sons and three daughters.

While he was still a young man, Baxter's health began to fail and he went to Brighton, but soon afterwards settled in Lewes as a bookseller and printer. He was the first printer to use the inking roller, a cylindrical device used to ink type evenly on the forme. It was made under his superintendence by a saddler at Lewes, and the printer Robert Harrild (1780–1853), who assisted him in his experiments, afterwards took out a patent for the composition roller, and realized by it a handsome fortune. Among the earliest of Baxter's enterprises was the publication of a large quarto Bible, annotated by the Revd John Styles DD, and illustrated with wood-engravings. This work, known as Baxter's Bible, had immense sales, especially in America. His other publications include several important works on the topography of Sussex, and *The Library of Agricultural and Horticultural Knowledge* (1830; 2nd edn, 1832), which had a very extensive circulation. Along with his youngest son, William Edwin Baxter, he started the *Sussex Agricultural Express*. He was an enthusiastic cricketer, and the joint, if not the sole, author of the book of rules for that sport, the first ever published, named *Lambert's Cricketer's Guide*, after the celebrated professional of that name. Successful in his business, Baxter retired about 1850. He died on 12 November 1858 at Lewes. Baxter's second son, George *Baxter (1804–1867), was the inventor of the process of printing in oil colours.

T. F. HENDERSON, *rev.* M. CLARE LOUGHLIN-CHOW

Sources M. A. Lower, *The worthies of Sussex* (1865) • C. T. C. Lewis, *George Baxter, colour printer: his life and work* (1908) • CGPLA Eng. & Wales (1858) • IGI
Wealth at death under £7000: probate, 16 Dec 1858, CGPLA Eng. & Wales

Baxter, John (1896–1975), film director and producer, is a figure about whose origins and upbringing little is known. He was probably born in Sidcup, Kent, a cousin of the Baxters of Fochabers, Scotland, famous purveyors of soups and jams. In the First World War he served with the Honourable Artillery Company and was stationed for eighteen months in the Passchendaele sector of the Ypres salient. In 1921 he married Margaret Mack, known as Greta, a performer with the Carla Rosa Opera Company. Baxter derived great personal pleasure from gardening and classical music, which he enjoyed at his home, Aldahvu, Elstree, and later at his house in Selsey. A Christian Scientist, he was a regular attender at church.

Baxter came to the cinema in the early 1930s, following a decade working in variety and theatre as a singer, union

John Baxter (1896–1975), by Kurt Hutton, 1948 [with director Mary Field at the Pump Room, Bath, during the Festival of All the Arts]

representative, and, ultimately, manager; throughout his career he remained devoted to the world of the music-hall and its artistes. He joined the small film production company Sound City in 1932 to help in casting its first important talkie, *Reunion*, a drama involving former servicemen. Baxter's military experience and knowledge led to his acting as associate director on the production, and his first solo directorial credit came only two films later with the striking *Doss House* (1933). Uncommonly for British cinema at the time, the film constructed a stark realism of setting for its slice of life drama; the much praised authenticity of detail, it was claimed, derived from Baxter's pre-production visits to lodging-houses for the destitute. A number of themes characteristic of the director emerged in this modest drama about a group of dispossessed who gather one night in a local hostel: a dignified treatment of ordinary people, a strong belief in the virtues of loyalty and comradeship, and a humanistic concern and sympathy for the poor and neglected in society. Baxter virtually remade the film on several occasions, most notably in his wartime drama *The Common Touch* (1941), which readily conformed to the contemporary theme of social reconstruction. Such material has inevitably led to comparisons with the great Hollywood director Frank Capra. In 1935

Baxter took the plunge into independent production and formed his own company with John Barter, a colleague from the theatre. Always nostalgic for the good old days of music-hall, Baxter's films invariably featured variety turns and his generosity towards artistes who had fallen on hard times was legendary, with places found for unfortunates in crowd scenes in films such as *Music Hall* (1934), *Sunshine Ahead* (1936), and *Talking Feet* (1937).

Early in 1939 Baxter moved to another company, British National, where he set up an independent production unit (he was later to join the board) and commenced a series of medium-budget features which constitute his most accomplished and acknowledged pictures. Although he continued to work with music-hall performers, such as the immensely popular Arthur Lucan and Kitty McShane, and Flanagan and Allen, it was with an adaptation of Walter Greenwood's *Love on the Dole* (1941) that the director produced a masterpiece. This frank tale of the depression had been refused sanction by the British Board of Film Censors on several occasions in the 1930s, but the new social consensus surrounding the 'people's war' considerably relaxed their views. Baxter's moving and honest treatment faithfully captured the spirit of the original, and in Deborah Kerr he discovered a genuine film star. Further wartime films such as *The Common Touch*, *Let the People Sing* (1942), and *The Shipbuilders* (1943) eloquently expressed his most persistent themes: the pride and common decency of working people, and the human waste of unemployment, both derived from a Christian commitment to fellowship and social justice. Baxter's modest social dramas of ordinary folk attracted favourable comment from critics who were exasperated with the conventionally flimsy and frothy commercial cinema. Interestingly, film-makers connected with the celebrated documentary film movement found particular significance in the director's evocative social themes, although they shied from his somewhat overt and cloying sentimentality and curious lyricism.

John Baxter reached the height of his film-making during the war, and with the advent of peace he settled back into modest production. A series of children's films were produced for the Rank Organisation, but of greater significance was Baxter's appointment in 1951 as production controller for Group 3, a state-sponsored initiative to aid independent film producers and to foster new talent. In particular, the films provided opportunities for a number of young actors, including Peter Finch, Peter Sellers, Kenneth More, Robert Shaw, Joan Collins, and Diane Cilento; directors who had their careers advanced through employment at the group included Lewis Gilbert, John Guillermin, Cyril Frankel, and Philip Leacock. In the four years of the group, twenty-two feature-length films were produced, of which John Baxter personally contributed *Judgement Deferred* (1951), the inaugural project. In 1952 Baxter assumed greater authority within Group 3 and became managing director on the resignation of John Grierson. The kindly and experienced veteran film-maker was the perfect steward for the production group with its co-operative structures and ideals.

John Baxter's film career came to its conclusion in 1959 with *Make mine a Million*, an Arthur Askey vehicle he produced for Jack Hylton Productions. His association with the impresario and former band leader led to his move into television with the independent company Television Wales and the West. He joined as executive controller in 1960 and was later appointed managing director. Baxter retired in 1968, when the company lost its franchise.

John Baxter died late in January 1975, followed eleven days later by his wife, Greta. He was a virtually forgotten film-maker, and former colleagues were impelled to redress the numerous inaccuracies in the short obituaries which appeared. Slowly, film historians have begun to reassess the merits of this compassionate and dedicated film-maker, who, over nearly three decades, created a unique body of work which brought to British screens a genuine concern for the downtrodden of society. In 1989 the film-maker was honoured with a retrospective at the National Film Theatre.   ALAN BURTON

Sources G. Brown and A. Aldgate, *The common touch: the films of John Baxter* (1989) · S. C. Shafer, *British popular films, 1929–1939* (1997), 182–93 · J. Montgomery, *Comedy films* (1954), 204–12 · R. D. MacCann, 'Subsidy for the screen: Grierson and Group 3, 1951–55', *Sight and Sound*, 46 (1976–7), 168–73
Archives BFI | SOUND BL NSA, performance recording
Likenesses K. Hutton, photograph, 1948, Hult. Arch. [*see illus.*]

Baxter [*née* Young], (**Mary**) **Kathleen** (1901–1988), advocate of women's rights, was born on 30 May 1901 to a Roman Catholic family in Bradford, Yorkshire, the eighth child in the family of three daughters and five sons (one of whom died in infancy) of Richard Aloysius Young, woollen manufacturer, and his wife, (Mary) Ann Barker. Her father died during her infancy. She was educated at St Joseph's College, Bradford, and won an open scholarship to the Society of Oxford Home Students (later St Anne's College), Oxford, where she obtained a third class in modern history in 1922 and a second in philosophy, politics, and economics in 1923.

Kathleen Young entered the Inland Revenue and was inspector of taxes in Bradford and Leeds until her marriage in Westminster Cathedral, London, on 12 September 1931 to Herbert James (H. J.) Baxter, a barrister who later became a county court judge. He was the son of James Baxter, whose career was in the army and civil service. There were two daughters of the marriage, and a son, who became a Roman Catholic priest. When she married she was obliged by the Income Tax Act to resign from the Inland Revenue. She became a tax consultant to a London firm of chartered accountants. During the Second World War she worked in the Ministry of Supply at the wool control in Ilkley, Yorkshire.

After the war the family moved from London to a house in Bessel's Green, Kent, which remained their home for forty years. Kathleen Baxter used her intellectual and analytical abilities to further causes she believed in. In her career she had experienced discrimination against women. She worked for equal rights, better education, and better job opportunities for women, to enable them to take their

place in decision making and become an effective voice for the improvement of society.

In 1951 Kathleen Baxter joined the National Council of Women, founded in 1895, a non-party-political organization affiliated to the International Council of Women. She held high office on many of the council's specialist committees. In the 1950s she led a campaign, with their education committee, which achieved improvement in the university grants system. She also founded the council's science and technology committee, which pressed for better education in science and mathematics for girls, and inaugurated a status-of-women committee, which submitted important points for incorporation into the Sex Equality Act of 1975. She was elected vice-president (1961–4), and subsequently, as president (1964–6), she was involved with national and international issues. In 1966, as vice-chair of the European Centre of the International Council of Women, she led the British women's delegation to the international conference in Tehran, at which Britain's resolution on slavery was passed unanimously. She served on the United Kingdom human rights year national executive in 1968. As a governor of the British Institute of Human Rights she was asked by the United Nations' secretary-general to write a background paper on the advancement of women's rights for the 1968 international conference on human rights, and she gave evidence to the UN session on human rights in Geneva. At the time of Britain's application for membership of the European Economic Community, she successfully pressed the government to consult the major women's organizations and was largely responsible for the establishment of the Women's Consultative Council (renamed in 1969 the Women's National Commission): its first co-chairs were herself and a government minister. In late middle age she studied law, from both interest in her husband's profession and knowledge that it would further her own work; she was called to the bar (Inner Temple) in 1971 but ceased taking cases when her husband became gravely ill in 1974. After his death in that year, she was appointed honorary legal adviser to the National Council of Women, while still continuing to serve on the executive of the Women's National Commission. In her dual capacity she chaired working parties commenting on documents from the Law Commission and the Criminal Law Revision Committee relating to women, children, and the family.

In 1978 Kathleen Baxter was awarded the papal cross *pro ecclesia et pontifice* for outstanding service to the church. She was president of the National Board of Catholic Women (1974–7), a founder member of the Catholic bishops' conference legislation committee, and a member of their bioethical advisory committee on artificial insemination, *in vitro* fertilization, and genetic engineering, helping to foster a broad social concern in these Catholic circles. In Kent she served on the hospital, maternity wing, and old people's home committees, and as a governor of four schools. She was devoted to her family and four grandsons, and greatly enjoyed music and tennis.

Kathleen Baxter combined high intelligence with an affectionate nature. She was a good-looking woman with an appearance of natural dignity and authority; silver hair framed a broad forehead, beneath which strikingly blue eyes claimed attention, and a smile of warmth and charm promised interest and encouragement. She died on 25 October 1988 in hospital in Bromley, Kent.

DIANA GRANTHAM REID, *rev.*

Sources National Council of Women headquarters, London, National Council of Women Archives · personal knowledge (1996) · private information (1996)

Baxter [*née* fforde], **Kathleen Mary Carver** [Kay] (1904–1994), careers adviser and playwright, was born in Bulandshahar, India, on 16 September 1904, the eldest daughter of Arthur Brownlow fforde, an Indian Civil Service judge, and his wife, Mary Alice Branson. Arthur Frederic Brownlow *fforde was her elder brother. A peripatetic childhood meant that she attended seven schools before settling at St Albans High School; her grandmother, who lived at 59 Gordon Square, London, acted as a welcome anchor. She went to Newnham College, Cambridge, in 1923; she took part 1 of the English tripos in 1925 and part 2 of the modern and medieval languages tripos in 1927. There followed two years at the Royal Academy of Dramatic Art and two with Birmingham Repertory Theatre. On 5 November 1931 she married a fellow actor and stage director, Major (Frank) Godfrey Baxter RE MC. In 1943 his plane, returning home, crashed on the runway. She grieved for him for the rest of her life.

Earning a living in the 1930s called for resilience and adaptability. From 1931 to 1940 Kay Baxter taught English at the Cone School, Oxford Street, London, during the day and at evening classes in the London County Council Institute. To these tasks she added her own school for small children, from 1932 to 1937. In 1940–41 she was a housemistress at Cheltenham Ladies' College. She spent two years (1941–3) with the Amalgamated Press as journalist and sub-editor, and another two (1942–4) as secretary to the Joint Agency for Women Teachers. In 1944 she settled in Cambridge as secretary of the Cambridge University Women's Appointments Board, and remained there until February 1966. This agency had been established only just before the Second World War, to help university-educated women find employment matching their intelligence and qualifications. Her work in advancing this cause, inspired by her own experience, is recognized as one of her major achievements. She put energy and understanding into each individual's circumstances, and persuaded employers who had hitherto employed only men to increase opportunities for women.

In 1958 a sabbatical enabled Kay Baxter to spend six months as resident guest lecturer at Union Theological College, New York. The connection led to annual lecture tours in the United States for ten years after her retirement, held under the auspices of the Association of American Colleges. They included spells as Du Pont guest lecturer, Delaware (1970–71 and 1972), and at the Roman Catholic Corpus Christi College for Missionary Teachers (1969, 1970, and 1971). She preached the sermon in the cathedral of St John the Divine in New York in 1973.

From 1957 and for the next twenty years Kay Baxter was in much demand as a member of a number of public bodies. Educational institutions included the Girls' Schools Association, St Albans High School, Cheltenham Ladies' College, Lord Mayor Treloar's School for Handicapped Children, and Westcott House Theological College, Cambridge (1966–70), on whose council she was the first woman member. She served for ten years as a member of the Women's Employment Federation (1956–66) and for two (1957–9) on the royal commission on doctors' and dentists' remuneration.

Kay Baxter's most challenging roles were as a member of the archbishop's committee on women in holy orders (1963–6), of the Central Religious Advisory Council of the BBC/ITV (1965–9), and of the general synod Church of England commission on broadcasting (1971–3). She was patient with the objection to women's ordination that was held by a hard core of synod. On one occasion her sense of humour was too much for her. 'Give me a double gin with my tonic', she said one evening, after a gruelling session, 'they're down to genes now' (personal knowledge). Her contacts led to her being the first woman to preach the sermon in Westminster Abbey, in 1970, and to conduct the Good Friday three-hour service, in 1971. She also preached during this time at Coventry Cathedral.

In 1963 Kay Baxter was elected a fellow of Newnham College, and returned there as resident tutor and director of studies in theology. The total load proved too much even for her abundant energy. She gradually withdrew from all her Cambridge work, and in 1966 moved to Hampshire to live with her sister Phyllis, who had suffered chronic illness throughout her life and now lived alone. After her sister's death, in 1987, she returned to East Anglia, where she died peacefully at Addison House, a nursing home at 18 Sand Street, Soham, Cambridgeshire, on 3 January 1994. She was cremated seven days later in Cambridge.

Kay Baxter's main interest was religious drama. She wrote three successful plays: *Pull Devil, Pull Baker* (1947), a verse mime with music; *Gerald of Wales* (1951); and the Southwark Cathedral Festival of Britain pageant, *Play your Trumpets Angels* (1951). Both the latter were commissioned by the Arts Council. Her books were *Speak what we Feel: a Christian Looks at the Contemporary Theatre* (published by the SPCK in the USA in 1964); *And I look for the resurrection* (Tennessee, 1968); and, with C. Le Fleming, *The Silver Dove* (SPCK, 1970). In *Speak what we Feel* she reveals much of what inspired her. She saw that the decline in religious faith posed the theatre with a problem that neither the Greek nor medieval writer had to face. The challenge, she said, could refresh dramatic energy: 'the findings of astronomers, anthropologists, psychiatrists, neurologists, biochemists, economists and politicians are all relevant to the Psalmist's question "What is man that thou art mindful of him?" … We must affirm valid images and new ones' (K. Baxter, *Speak what we Feel*).

Kay Baxter moved in several worlds: schools, the University of Cambridge, journalism, the theatre, government commissions, the Church of England, and the BBC. She was not an aggressive feminist but she was one of the first to work on the subject of women's employment after leaving university. Newnham College—by statute without a chapel—held an informal celebration of her life on 4 September 1994. Speakers from each of her worlds spoke of her intelligence, charm, wit, energy, and deep Christian faith. She was a good-looking woman with a beautiful speaking voice. It was this irresistible combination that enabled her to notch up a number of firsts for women without fuss.   PHYLLIS HETZEL

Sources manuscript questionnaires completed by K. Baxter, Newnham College, Cambridge, archive · P. Hetzel, *The Independent* (15 Feb 1994) · P. Hetzel, *Newnham College Roll Letter* (1995) · historical register supplements, CUL, department of manuscripts and university archives · staff file, Newnham College, Cambridge · P. Walker, funeral address, 10 Jan 1994, Newnham College, Cambridge, archive · personal knowledge (2004) · private information (2004) [family]
Archives Newnham College, Cambridge, archive
Likenesses photograph, 1923–7, Newnham College, Cambridge, archive
Wealth at death £171,441: probate, 1994, *CGPLA Eng. & Wales*

Baxter [*née* Barnes], **Lucy** [*pseud.* Leader Scott] (**1837–1902**), writer on art, was born at Dorchester on 21 January 1837, the third daughter of William *Barnes (1801–1886), the Dorset poet and philologist, and his wife, Julia, *née* Miles (1805–1852). Her childhood seems to have been a happy one, despite the family's straitened finances and her mother's death in 1852. Barnes was an affectionate father who believed in persuasion rather than punishment, and his multifarious literary, linguistic, antiquarian, and artistic interests no doubt influenced Lucy's tastes. He rescued old paintings from junk shops, cleaned them, and used them in the education of his children; in her 1887 biography of her father—still the standard quarry for the Barnes scholar, despite the inadequacy of its treatment of his early life—Lucy Baxter claimed that he had thus acquired a Ribera and a Gainsborough.

From an early age, Lucy Barnes determined to pursue a literary career and, according to the *Dictionary of National Biography*, it was by writing stories and magazine articles that she earned enough money to visit Italy in the 1860s. Another account suggests that she went there as a governess to a family who were travelling on the continent. While in Italy, Lucy Barnes met and in 1867 married Samuel Thomas Baxter, whose family had long been established in Florence; they settled at Villa Bianca, at the foot of the hills near Vincigliata and Settignano. Mrs Baxter became a prominent figure in Anglo-Florentine and Italian literary and artistic circles in the city, and the Accademia della Belle Arti elected her an honorary member in 1882.

Lucy Baxter's many publications appeared under the pseudonym of Leader Scott—a combination of the maiden names of her grandmothers. She collaborated with John Temple *Leader, probably a relative and also resident in Florence. Her works consisted of popularizations of scholarly work on Florentine art and artists, including *Luca della Robbia* (1883), *The Renaissance of Art in Italy* (1883), and *Correggio* (1902), and more lightweight essays, which were often later collected and republished.

The best-known of these collections was *Echoes of Old Florence* (1894), but a typical example was *Tuscan Studies and Sketches* (1887): half of this work was devoted to studies of Florentine art and architecture, derived from her researches in the Magliabecchiana and other Florentine libraries and archives, while the other half consisted of travel essays (describing, among others, visits to the seaside at Pisa and to the medieval town of San Gimignano) and accounts of Italian customs such as the festival of the dead. Her *magnum opus* was *The Cathedral Builders* (1899), a monumental work examining Romanesque architecture and the role of *magistri comacini* in its creation. Although largely based on *I maestri comacini* (1893), Giuseppe Merzario's work on the same subject, which she had originally hoped to translate into English, *The Cathedral Builders*—which was beautifully illustrated with both photographs and fine drawings—did show her keen eye for architectural detail and involved some archival research. Her main arguments, however, were advanced with a boldness not justified by the evidence, which was scanty at best in the early medieval period. Her presentation of the *magistri* as a fully organized and all-enveloping masonic guild from the sixth or seventh centuries AD is decidedly speculative; although her work was no doubt a useful introduction to the subject for the English-speaking reader, it was entirely ignored by twentieth-century scholars of Romanesque architecture.

Lucy Baxter was much distressed by the death of a daughter in 1900; her grief seems to have damaged her health and she died at the Villa Bianca on 10 November 1902, survived by her husband, two daughters, and a son. Although the reigning matriarch of Anglo-Florentine society for many years (her place was now taken by the less erudite but more imposing Janet Ross), she had governed with a gentle hand; one contemporary recalled with affection the 'serene gentleness of [her] old-fashioned feminine presence' (*The Athenaeum*).

ROSEMARY MITCHELL

Sources *DNB* · *The Athenaeum* (22 Nov 1902), 684 · *The Athenaeum* (29 Nov 1902), 723 [correction] · L. Baxter, *The life of William Barnes, poet and philologist* (1887) · G. Dugdale, *William Barnes of Dorset* (1953) · J. Pemble, *The Mediterranean passion: Victorians and Edwardians in the south* (1987)

Baxter, Margaret (*bap.* 1636, *d.* 1681). *See under* Baxter, Richard (1615–1691).

Baxter, Margery (*fl.* 1428–1429). *See under* Lollard women (*act. c.*1390–*c.*1520).

Baxter, Mary Ann (1801–1884), benefactor, was born on 4 May 1801 at Dundee, the seventh child of eight surviving children of William Baxter (1767–1854), linen merchant and manufacturer, and his wife, Betty or Elisabeth Gorell (*d.* 1804), daughter of Edward Gorell of Hazle Hall, near Clapham, Yorkshire. Her father, a member of a leading Dundee business dynasty, developed the firm of Baxter Brothers & Co. into one of the largest linen manufacturing and exporting businesses in Britain, especially renowned for its canvas and sail cloth. Her elder brother, Sir David

Mary Ann Baxter (1801–1884), by Edward Hughes, 1883

*Baxter, first baronet, was a partner in the firm and a major benefactor of the city.

Little is known of Mary Ann Baxter's early years. After her mother's death, her father was left to bring up the young family, moving in the early 1820s to Ellangowan, on the eastern side of Dundee, where Mary Ann Baxter, who never married, spent most of her life. On her father's death she inherited the house at Ellangowan in life-rent, and she and her older sister Eleanor were bequeathed the country estate of Balgavies, Forfarshire, which their father had purchased about 1849, in their own right. She also received a significant inheritance on the death of her brother Sir David Baxter in 1872.

From the late 1850s Mary Ann Baxter developed a more public role, conducted in a quiet, retired manner. It is likely that her religious devotion and piety did not sit well with her inherited wealth and the poor social conditions in Dundee. She viewed her wealth, as one obituarist later noted, as 'the stewardship which had been committed to her' (Obituary Book 1, 16). One of the strongest influences upon her life was her devotion and deep commitment to the Congregational church. Her father had been a member of Ward Chapel, Dundee, since its opening in 1833. In 1853 some of the family, including Mary Ann Baxter and her two sisters, Eleanor and Elisa (Mrs Francis Molison), left Ward Chapel and moved to Panmure Street Church. Encouraged by David Russell, the minister of Ward

Chapel until 1848 and a director of the London Missionary Society, she gave considerable financial support to missionary work overseas. The undenominational and evangelical character of the society appealed to her. She also provided money to purchase a steamer in 1874, named the *Ellangowan*, to explore areas in New Guinea, where the Baxter River was named after her. In 1869 she provided more than £16,000 as an endowment to Theological Hall, a central college for the training of Congregational ministers in Edinburgh.

Mary Ann Baxter followed the tradition of gifts and bequests made by members of the family, in particular by her brothers Edward and David. The best-known was the gift in 1863 of Baxter Park to the city of Dundee, given jointly by Mary Ann and her sister Eleanor and brother David. Often her benevolence was a response to the many applications for financial help which she received. Many causes and local institutions benefited, including the local hospitals, the sailors' home, the 'Mars' training shop for homeless boys, churches, and schools. She and Eleanor also set up three scholarships in the high school of Dundee to create a connection with Edinburgh University.

However, the most outstanding of all Mary Ann Baxter's contributions was the founding of University College in Dundee. From the time of the visit of the British Association for the Advancement of Science to Dundee in 1867, there had been a growing public discussion of the need to improve Dundee's public institutions. Mary Ann Baxter's distant cousin, John Boyd Baxter (1796–1882), a procurator fiscal of Forfar, was one of the first to raise publicly in the 1870s the idea of setting up a college, and at a meeting of the directors of the high school of Dundee in December 1880 he announced that, should a college be set up, Miss Baxter would lead the subscribers with a substantial donation. Despite her advancing years, Mary Ann Baxter became involved in this cause in a way which revealed her own definite views about higher education. She was indeed well versed in social and political questions of the day. As the main provider of funds she insisted that the college be founded with a constitution satisfactory to the main benefactors. John Boyd Baxter was her public spokesman, though he did not always seem to express her views as she would have liked. At one point, when the negotiations seemed to flounder, her exasperation was evident in her correspondence with him. The key clause in the deed of endowment and trust which was signed by Mary Ann Baxter and John Boyd Baxter on 30 and 31 December 1881 was the 'Founding, establishing, endowing, maintaining and conducting a college for promoting the education of persons of both sexes and the study of science, literature and fine arts' (Shafe, 11). Opening the college to both men and women was a progressive idea at that period, though unlike some of her contemporaries in the Ladies' Educational associations in Edinburgh, Glasgow, and elsewhere, from whom she was separated both by her age and private nature, she appears not to have had any previous involvement in women's educational movements. A further clause in the foundation deed established the non-denominational character of the college.

As main benefactor, Mary Ann Baxter was directly involved in the choice of location of the college in the Nethergate area of Dundee and provided funds to build a new chemistry department. The scale of her gifts, which amounted to £140,000, with £10,000 from John Boyd Baxter, enabled the originally modest plans for a college of adult or higher education in Dundee to result in the foundation of a university college on the lines of Owens College, Manchester. University College, Dundee, opened on 5 October 1883 without the presence of its co-founders. Mary Ann Baxter was unable to attend as her sister Elisa died a few days before the opening. John Boyd Baxter had died in 1882. Mary Ann's portrait by E. Hughes was presented at the ceremony to the college in acknowledgement of her generosity and commitment to the ideal of a college in Dundee. The Dundee poet William McGonagall celebrated her munificence in his characteristic doggerel, 'The inauguration of the University College, Dundee' (1883):

> Now since Miss Baxter has lived to see it erected,
> I hope by the students she will long be respected
> For establishing a College in Bonnie Dundee,
> Where learning can be got of a very high degree.

Mary Ann Baxter died on 19 December 1884 at Ellangowan, Dundee, and was buried at Roodyards burial-ground, Dundee. Her will reflected the breadth of her philanthropic interests, including bequests for missionary work overseas, and to local hospitals, members of her extended family network, and long-serving domestic servants. Inherited wealth achieved through a successful family business was reflected in the gross value of her estate, a sum of £283,586, which was in addition to her lifetime of benevolence.   SHEILA HAMILTON

Sources Dundee Central Library, Dundee Local Studies Department, Dundee obituary book 1, 1869–94, 15–18 · Dundee Central Library, The Lamb Collection, MS, 215/26 · *Dundee Yearbook* (1882–4) · D. Southgate, *University education in Dundee: a centenary history* (1982) · M. Shafe, *University education in Dundee* (1982) · T. Y. Miller, ed., *Dundee, past and present* (1909) · S. J. Jones, ed., *Dundee and district* (1968) · H. Escott, *A history of Scottish Congregationalism* (1960) · A. J. Cooke, ed., *Baxter's of Dundee* (1980) · Jubilee manual of the Congregational church meeting in Ward Chapel, Dundee, including a history of the church since 1810, 1883, NL Scot., 5. 4042 · W. Norrie, *Dundee and Dundonians seventy years ago* (1892) · W. Norrie, *Dundee celebrities of the nineteenth century* (1873) · will and inventory, NA Scot., SC 45/31/35 · census, 1841, General Register House, 282 (book 3) · census, 1851, General Register House, 282 vol. 202 (3) · A. Mitchell, ed., *Pre-1855 gravestone inscriptions in Angus*, 4 (1984) · W. D. McNaughton, *The Scottish Congregational ministry, 1794–1993* (1993) · *Dundee directories* · parish records (baptism), OPR 282/8
Likenesses E. Hughes, portrait, 1883, University of Dundee [*see illus.*]
Wealth at death £283,586 2s. 6½d.: confirmation, 30 June 1885, CCI · £318 6s. 10d.: eik additional estate, 3 Feb 1887, CCI

Baxter, Nathaniel (*fl.* 1569–1611), Church of England clergyman and author, probably matriculated from Magdalen College, Oxford, in 1569 and was incepted MA in 1577. He was one of ten radical protestants who on 25 May 1577 signed a second letter censuring Thomas Cartwright, the Lady Margaret professor of divinity at Cambridge, for his compromise in accepting that ministers might conform in matters of dress and ceremony in order to preach the gospel. He subsequently held a series of minor ecclesiastical positions, becoming in rapid succession vicar of Redbourne, Hertfordshire, in 1577, vicar of Finedon, Northamptonshire, on 23 April 1578 (resigned 1579); rector of Titchmarsh on 16 January 1579, and of Leire, Leicestershire, in 1582, and, on the presentation of the queen, vicar of St Margaret, Lothbury, London, on 2 July 1588 (resigned April 1589) and rector of St Giles-in-the-Fields on 15 August 1590 (resigned 1591).

Baxter wrote and translated a number of religious works, establishing himself as a vociferous Calvinist, critical of the established church. In 1578 he published a translation, dedicated to Sir John Brockett, *The lectures or daily sermons of that Reverend Divine, D. John Calvine … upon the prophet Jonas*, which also contained a translation entitled 'Exposition on 2 last epistles of S. John by Augustine Marlorat'. A later edition of *The Lectures* was dedicated to Sir Francis Walsingham. It contained a long prefatory letter which declared the translator's sympathy for the protestant principles of Walsingham and warned readers not to waste their time reading profane and frivolous books such as the Arthurian legends. There was also a complaint to the reader written in rhyming fourteeners which attempted to reconcile Christian and pagan culture. The latter work was dedicated to Ursula, Lady Walsingham, suggesting that Baxter saw the Leicester–Sidney circle as a source of patronage and preferment. Whether his hopes were answered is unclear. In 1585 Baxter published two works in Latin, *D. Nathanaelis Baxteri Colcestrensis quaestiones et responsa in P. Rami dialecticam* and *Eusebii Pagetti catechismus Latine aeditus Magistro Nath. Baxter Colcestrense*. The inference from the first title that he had a doctorate, and that he was either a native of or a resident in Colchester, remains unexplained.

In 1592 Baxter became warden of St Mary's College, Youghal, being inducted on 23 May by William Lyon, bishop of Cork and Cloyne. In the next five years Baxter was involved in two rather unpleasant financial scandals. On 17 February 1593 he was accused of appropriating goods from a Mrs Jane Shelley, whose husband was held prisoner in the Gatehouse and who was anxious to have them returned. More seriously still, on 25 August 1597 Baxter appears to have been suspected of financial mismanagement of the college. He was forced to agree to give a bond of 1000 marks as a pledge that he would resign his position within forty days after a demand to see the revenues of the college had been made. On 26 April 1598 a complaint was made to the court of revenue exchequer that he had obstructed the officer of the court when he had tried to sequester the revenues of the college. On 30 June Baxter passed a letter of attorney on to three men so that the financial affairs of the college could be investigated. They passed matters over to Sir Thomas Norris, and Baxter resigned, leaving Ireland in 1599 without the return of his bond because the college's finances had disappeared.

Baxter next appears as a preacher in Bristol, where he became involved in a dispute with the prominent divine

John Downe. On 5 November 1601 Baxter publicly attacked Downe's argument that faith did not entail assurance of salvation but granted the believer what he termed 'affiance', a promise which was not absolutely binding, when the latter preached a sermon. For Baxter, the one necessitated the other. After considerable delay a public dispute was organized on 27 July 1602. In 1635, four years after Downe's death, and undoubtedly some years after Baxter's, Downe's supporters published the arguments of both men as *A Treatise of the True Nature and Definition of Justifying Faith together with a Defence of the same Against the Answere of N. Baxter*. Downe, a skilful and persuasive theologian, portrays Baxter as underhand and truculent.

Baxter's last living was the vicarage of Micheltroy, Monmouthshire, which he held from 1602. He wrote two more works, *Praefatio in commentarios D. N. Baxteri in epistolam ad Colossenses* (1605?) and the long poem *Sir Philip Sydneys Ouránia, that is Endimions Song and Tragedie* (1606). This ambitious last work, sometimes attributed to Nicholas Breton, has met with almost universal disapproval from critics. Heavily influenced by Chaucer, Spenser, and Sidney, Baxter casts himself as the shepherd-poet Endymion, who describes the mysteries of the world to Cynthia (Mary Herbert, countess of Pembroke) and her retinue. Sir Philip Sidney appears, recognizes Baxter as his old Greek tutor Tergaster, and listens sympathetically to his complaint that the once respected academic is now 'stripped, and naked, destitute alone'. No external evidence links Baxter to Sidney, but his dedicatory epistle to Sidney's father-in-law, Walsingham, which must have been penned twenty years earlier, suggests that there he was probably speaking the truth. The poem is clearly an appeal for patronage from the Sidney family, whom it flatters at length, and to whom the numerous letters of dedication are addressed. It is also an exposition of Baxter's attempt to merge Christian doctrine with Greek philosophy. Baxter had evidently fallen on hard times, undoubtedly as a result of the recorded experiences of the previous decade. The poem ends with Baxter claiming that his misfortune is a result of 'envies sophistication' and suggesting that he cannot write his tragedy during his lifetime because it has a bloody end. Nothing is known of Baxter after 1611.

ANDREW HADFIELD

Sources N. Baxter, *Sir Philip Sydneys Ouránia* (1606) · M. Brennan, *Literary patronage in the English Renaissance: the Pembroke family* (1988) · *DNB* · *CSP dom.*, 1591–4 · Foster, *Alum. Oxon.* · A. F. S. Pearson, *Thomas Cartwright and Elizabethan puritanism, 1535–1603* (1925) · K. Duncan Jones, *Sir Philip Sidney: courtier poet* (1991) · M. W. Wallace, *The life of Sir Philip Sidney* (1915) · C. W. Field, *Index ecclesiasticas, A–M: Reformation period* (1989) · J. Downe, *A treatise of the true nature and definition of justifying faith* (1635) · H. I. Longden, *Northamptonshire and Rutland clergy from 1500*, ed. P. I. King and others, 16 vols. in 6, Northamptonshire RS (1938–52), vol. 2, p. 21 · G. Hennessy, *Novum repertorium ecclesiasticum parochiale Londinense, or, London diocesan clergy succession from the earliest time to the year 1898* (1898), 173, 279

Baxter, Richard (1615–1691), ejected minister and religious writer, was born in the village of Rowton, Shropshire, on 12 November 1615, the son of Richard Baxter (d.

Richard Baxter (1615–1691), attrib. John Riley

1663) of Eaton Constantine, Shropshire, and his wife, Beatrice Adeney (d. 1635). He was baptized in the parish church at High Ercall the following Sunday, 19 November.

Early years and education Baxter described his father as 'a mean Freeholder (called a Gentleman for his Ancestors sake, but of small Estate)' and 'entangled by Debts' as a result, at least in part, of his 'having been addicted to Gaming in his Youth, and his Father [also Richard] before him' (Baxter, *Breviate*, 1; *Reliquiae Baxterianae*, 1.1). These impoverished circumstances may help to explain why Baxter was brought up until the age of ten or eleven not at Eaton Constantine but by his maternal grandparents in their home at Rowton. 'The bare reading of the Scriptures in private', however, led his father to reform his manner of life so thoroughly that he came to be 'reviled commonly by the Name of *Puritan*, *Precisian* and *Hypocrite*'. Even before he moved to his parents' home, Baxter was deeply affected by his father's 'serious speeches of God and the Life to come'. He afterwards acknowledged his father as 'the Instrument of my first Convictions, and Approbation of a Holy Life'. That his father, who 'never scrupled Common-Prayer or Ceremonies, nor spake against Bishops', was reviled merely 'for reading Scripture … and for praying … in his House, and for reproving Drunkards and Swearers, and for talking sometimes a few words of Scripture and the Life to come', persuaded the young Baxter that hostility to puritanism was bred of 'mere Malice' and that 'Godly People were the best' (*Reliquiae Baxterianae*, 1.2–3).

Baxter gives a dismal account of his education. At Rowton, each of a succession of four 'readers' at the chapel was ignorant, and two led immoral lives. At Eaton Constantine the school was taught by ill-educated, dissolute, and uninterested curates, one of them holding forged orders. However, when Baxter transferred to Wroxeter (afterwards Donnington) grammar school, then only recently founded in 1627, he at last received some regular tuition from the schoolmaster John Owen. His fellow pupils included Richard Allestree, afterwards regius professor of divinity at Oxford and provost of Eton College, and Francis and Andrew Newport, sons of the school's patron Sir Richard Newport, afterwards first Baron Newport of Eyton-on-Severn, Shropshire. At the age of sixteen Baxter was persuaded by Owen not to pursue his studies at university but instead to put himself under the instruction of Owen's friend Richard Wickstead at Ludlow, where Wickstead was chaplain to the council of Wales and the marches. The arrangement was not a success. Baxter found Wickstead negligent and ill-equipped for advanced tuition, and he did not care for the town, 'full of Temptations, through the multitude of Persons, (Counsellors, Attorneys, Officers, and Clerks), and much given to tipling and excess' (*Reliquiae Baxterianae*, 1.4). When after eighteen months Baxter returned home, he for three months supplied as schoolmaster the place of Wickstead, sick with what proved to be a fatal consumption, and then, perhaps at Sir Richard Newport's suggestion, he journeyed to London and was introduced to society and to court life by Sir Henry Herbert, the *de facto* master of the revels, a first cousin of Newport. Baxter found London no more congenial than Ludlow and returned to the midlands after only a month to attend his mother during the winter of 1634–5 in what proved to be her final illness. She died on 10 May 1635.

After the death of Baxter's mother his father married in 1636 Mary Huncks, daughter of Sir Thomas Huncks and sister of Sir Fulke and Sir Henry Huncks, respectively royalist governors of Shrewsbury and of Banbury during the civil war, and a first cousin of Edward, second Viscount Conway (*d.* 1655), and his sister, Brilliana Harley. Baxter regarded his stepmother with great affection and admiration, speaking of her as 'a Special Blessing to our Family' and a woman of 'extraordinary holiness' who lived 'in the greatest Mortification, Austerity to her Body, and constancy of Prayer and all Devotion, of any one that ever I knew' (*Reliquiae Baxterianae*, 1.12, 3.189). In the later 1650s she and his father lived with Baxter for a time at Kidderminster when the house at Eaton Constantine was let to a tenant. As a widow she lived in the house at Eaton Constantine, and then, in the 1670s, with Baxter in Totteridge and in London; she died of cancer in August 1680 at the age of ninety-six.

Baxter's own 'vehement desires' had been to proceed from school to university to achieve 'Academick Glory', and throughout his life he regretted his lack of a university education and pointed to his 'wanting Academical Honours' as a mark of his insufficiency as a minister (Baxter, *Poetical Fragments*, 42; *Reliquiae Baxterianae*, 1.85). In 1681 he wrote in reply to an enquiry from Anthony Wood that his 'faults are no disgrace to any University; for I was

of none, & have little but what I had out of books, & inconsiderable helpes of Country tutors' (Keeble and Nuttall, 2.225). Nevertheless, though lacking in formal qualifications and without the benefit of educational supervision, through omnivorous reading Baxter became one of the most learned of seventeenth-century divines. As a youth it was through books that he realized his vocation. Baxter underwent no single life-transforming moment of spiritual regeneration. In such later writings as *The Right Method for a Settled Peace of Conscience* (1653) he was to caution against depending for evidence of election upon a profound conversion experience, such as many contemporary guides to godliness held to be an essential mark of grace. As a young man he was himself troubled that he could not 'distinctly trace the Workings of the Spirit upon my heart in that method which Mr. [Robert] *Bolton*, Mr. [Thomas] *Hooker*, Mr. [John] *Rogers*, and other Divines describe nor knew the Time of my Conversion, being wrought on by … Degrees'. This experience convinced him that '*Education* is God's ordinary way for the Conveyance of his Grace' (*Reliquiae Baxterianae*, 1.6–7). For Baxter, reading was the means of conveyance. His father encouraged him as a child to read the historical books of the Bible, and, when at school, it was through 'an old torn' copy of Edmund Bunny's protestant revision of the Jesuit Robert Parsons's *A Booke of Christian Exercise Appertayning to Resolution* (1584), which was lent to his father by 'a poor Day-Labourer', through *The Bruised Reede and Smoaking Flax* (1630) by Richard Sibbes, which his father purchased from 'a poor Pedlar', and through a servant's copy of 'a little Piece of Mr. [William] *Perkins's* Works' that 'without any means but Books' God was 'pleased to resolve me for himself' (ibid., 1.3–4). Subsequently Ezekiel Culverwell's *Treatise of Faith* (1623):

> did me much good, and many other excellent Books, were made my Teachers and Comforters: And the use that God made of Books, above Ministers, to the benefit of my Soul, made me somewhat excessively in love with good Books. (ibid., 1.5)

The excitement of reading and of intellectual discovery led Baxter to engross himself in the medieval schoolmen and in contemporary doctrinal debate: 'I was quickly past my Fundamentals, and was running up into a multitude of Controversies, and greatly delighted with metaphysical and scholastick Writings' because 'I thought they narrowly searched after Truth, and brought Things out of the darkness of Confusion'. Subsequently, however, he came to lay 'smaller stress … upon these Controversies and Curiosities' and to value most highly 'the fundamental Doctrines of the Catechism' (*Reliquiae Baxterianae*, 1.126). He always afterwards maintained that a person of true devotion and practical faith who 'yet never heard of most of the Questions in *Scotus*, or *Ockham* or *Aquinas*'s sums, is far richer in knowledg, and a much wiser man, than he that hath those Controversies at his fingers ends' (Baxter, *Directions*, 1.106–7). And yet, though he felt himself 'much better in [George] *Herberts* Temple: Or in a heavenly Treatise of *faith* and *Love*' than engaged in controversial divinity, he was repeatedly drawn into disputation and he retained all his life a good deal of the schoolman's fondness for nice distinctions and multiplying subdivisions: 'I could never from my first Studies endure Confusion!', he wrote (Baxter, *Knowledge and Love Compared*, 9). One side of him remained inveterately bookish. His recommendations of particular titles often developed into extended reading lists. In *A Christian Directory* (1673) he lists somewhere in the region of 1000 authors and works to make up 'The *Poor mans Library*, which … cometh short of a Rich and Sumptuous Library' (Baxter, *Christian Directory*, bk 3, question 174, pp. 921–8). As might be expected, he himself assembled an extensive and dearly prized collection which, even after losses due to removals and distraints, still numbered more than 1400 volumes at his death.

Though books played such a large part in his early life, Baxter does acknowledge also the influence upon him in these formative years of four local Shropshire ministers: Humphrey Barnet, curate of Uppington; George Baxter (no relation), rector of Little Wenlock; Francis Garbett, vicar of Wroxeter; and 'especially old Mr. *Samuel Smith*', curate of Cressage (*Reliquiae Baxterianae*, 1.9). The churchmanship of these men was subsequently of a presbyterian temper, but, with the exception of Barnet, they conformed in the 1630s to the ceremonies of the established episcopal church. At Shrewsbury, however, Baxter, now in his early twenties, encountered men far less willing to tolerate the Book of Common Prayer: they included Walter Cradock; George Fawler, in 1643 appointed chaplain of Bridewell Hospital, London; Michael Old, whose house at Sheriffhales, on the Shropshire–Staffordshire border, was licensed for nonconformist worship in 1672; and the schoolmaster Richard Symonds. Baxter was not convinced by their arguments against conformity, and he came to disapprove strongly of enthusiasm such as Cradock's ('a gross Antinomian', he afterwards called him), but the 'fervent Prayers and savoury Conference and Holy Lives' of these 'very zealous godly Nonconformists' greatly inspired him (Baxter, *Catholick Communion Defended*, 'Account', 28; *Reliquiae Baxterianae*, 1.13), and his confidence in episcopal authority was shaken by its opposition to such Christian commitment and its determination to pursue, and to silence, such devout men. He was struck, too, by the fact that, like himself, both Fawler and Old had been first 'awakened … to a serious resolved care of their Salvation' by reading Bunny (Baxter, *Against the Revolt*, 540).

Having, then, 'no Scruple at all against Subscription' and thinking 'the Conformists had the better Cause' (*Reliquiae Baxterianae*, 1.13), Baxter was ordained deacon at Worcester on 23 December 1638 by John Thornborough, the elderly bishop of the diocese. (That, by the late 1630s, it was highly unusual to be ordained without a university training in part explains Baxter's sensitivity on this point.) There is no record of a subsequent ordination, though the probability is that Baxter did proceed to the priesthood. It was, by Baxter's own account, his friend James Berry, afterwards one of Cromwell's major-generals, who persuaded him to enter the ministry. Baxter came to disapprove strongly of Berry's Cromwellian sympathies and of

his patronage of sectaries and Quakers, but in the late 1630s the two men were very close: Berry lived with Baxter, he may have been one of the Shrewsbury nonconformists who so impressed him, and he secured Baxter's appointment as master of the school founded at Dudley, Worcestershire, by the ironmaster Richard Foley (d. 1657) of Stourbridge. Though Baxter held this position only briefly, he lived with Richard Foley and his wife, 'a Gentlewoman of … extraordinary Meekness and Patience, with sincere Piety', who was to die two years later (ibid., 1.14), and thereafter he enjoyed a lifelong connection with the Foley family: he had a high regard for all three of Foley's sons, and was in particular to enjoy the friendship and patronage of Thomas Foley until his death in 1677.

Civil war years Baxter was nine months at Dudley, during which he preached his first public sermon at the parish church of St Edmund, before moving in the autumn of 1639 to Bridgnorth, Shropshire, where he lived in the house of the schoolmaster, Richard Swaine, and served as assistant to the vicar, William Madstard, 'very honest and conscionable, and an excellent Preacher'. He found the parishioners there 'a very ignorant, dead-hearted People', unlike the 'poor Tractable people' of Dudley, and he was to leave deeply disappointed by his inability to penetrate their 'obdurateness' (*Reliquiae Baxterianae*, 1.15). By then Baxter's churchmanship had assumed a distinctively puritan character, but, because Bridgnorth was exempt from episcopal jurisdiction as a royal peculiar, this led to no confrontation with ecclesiastical authority. At Dudley he had begun 'a serious impartial Trial of the whole Cause' of nonconformity by undertaking a sustained course of reading. His conclusion was that a prescribed liturgy was lawful and that, though the Book of Common Prayer had 'much *disorder* and *defectiveness* in it', it might be used. However, to subscribe that it contained nothing contrary to the word of God 'was that, which if it had been to do again, I durst not do'. Though he did not object to the use of a ring in marriage, nor to kneeling to receive the sacrament, he never wore a surplice, or made the sign of the cross in baptism. At this time he had grave misgivings about the sacrament of baptism itself, only resolved (in favour of paedobaptism) five or six years later. Above all, he regretted the lack of church discipline and was opposed to the '*promiscuous giving of the Lord's Supper to all Drunkards, Swearers, Fornicators, Scorners at Godliness &c.*' (ibid., 1.13). His resolution, and his sympathies, were sufficiently declared when in 1639 he refused to pray against the invading Scots. And it was at Bridgnorth that he made his first public stand on a matter of ecclesiastical policy when, at a meeting of ministers in 1640, he spoke against the 'et cetera' oath. Its notoriously loose wording and apparently limitless applicability hardened opposition to episcopacy, and to the ecclesiastical policy of William Laud, archbishop of Canterbury, in Baxter, as it did in many throughout the country. At Dudley he had read books on ecclesiology lent to him by 'godly honest' nonconformists and he continued to be troubled by the 'Sufferings from the Bishops' which they endured. He pursued his reading at Bridgnorth, and his growing disquiet at 'the English Diocesan frame' was further sharpened by what appeared to him to be this act of ecclesiastical tyranny (ibid., 1.13–14, 1.15–16).

In March 1641 Baxter was invited to Kidderminster, Worcestershire, as a preacher or 'lecturer'. Having grown deeply dissatisfied with the conduct and ministry of their vicar, George Dance, and his curates, the parishioners of Kidderminster had resolved to report them to the committee for scandalous ministers, to prevent which Dance agreed to allow £60 p.a. from his stipend to provide for a preacher (formally his assistant or curate), chosen by fourteen representatives of the parishioners, in the place of one of his curates, John Dide. This arrangement, reached through the mediation of Sir Henry Herbert, now MP for neighbouring Bewdley, was sealed with a bond for £500 signed by Dance on 26 February 1641. The fourteen feoffees first approached Anthony Lapthorne, afterwards rector of Sedgefield, co. Durham, but they were dissatisfied with his preaching. They then invited Baxter to visit Kidderminster to deliver a sermon, which he did on Sunday 4 April 1641. A certificate electing him to the position was signed the next day and Baxter moved shortly thereafter.

There is no doubt that Baxter was relieved to leave Bridgnorth, but his initial experiences at Kidderminster were not wholly encouraging. Many were offended by the forcefulness of his preaching and by his insistence on the need for church discipline and controlled admission to the Lord's supper. When in 1642 the churchwarden sought to implement a parliamentary order for the destruction of any remaining images of the persons of the Trinity or of the Virgin Mary, Baxter, whom they supposed responsible, became the target of 'a Crew of the drunken riotous Party of the Town', putting him in fear for his life (*Reliquiae Baxterianae*, 1.40). The tensions and hostilities surrounding the outbreak of civil war further heightened feelings: 'a violent Country Gentleman' passing Baxter in the street 'stopt and said, *There goeth a Traitor*'; 'if a Stranger past … that had short Hair and a Civil Habit, the Rabble presently cried, [*Down with the Round-heads*]' (ibid.). In these circumstances Baxter decided it would be prudent to withdraw from Kidderminster for a while. He went for a month in early 1642 to Gloucester, where he stayed with 'Mr. *Darney* the Town Clark' and first met his lifelong friend John Corbet. After his return to Kidderminster 'the Fury of the Rabble was so hot' that he withdrew again, and, being 'with one Mr. *Hunt* near Inkborough' (Inkberrow, Worcestershire), he witnessed the first engagement of the war, at Powick Bridge, near Worcester, on 23 September 1642. During a sermon he was delivering the next Sunday at the parish church of Alcester for the rector, his friend Samuel Clarke, 'the People heard the Cannon play' at the battle of Edgehill, the scene of which he and Clarke visited the next day (ibid., 1.42–3). With the outbreak of hostilities, Baxter, with no close friends in Kidderminster and feeling still more vulnerable, decided to stay with his friend Simon King, Swaine's successor as schoolmaster at Bridgnorth in 1640–41 but now curate at Trinity Church, Coventry.

Baxter expected the war to end within a few weeks, but he did not in fact return to Kidderminster until 1647. Coventry was a parliamentarian garrison, and there he was joined by 'the Religious part of my Neighbours … that would fain have lived quietly at home' but who were 'forced … to be gone' from Kidderminster and by those he describes as 'the most religious Men of the Parts round about' more generally. A number of puritan ministers from the central counties of England also sought safety in the town. These included men already known to Baxter, such as Cradock; men who would become his firm friends, such as Obadiah Grew, Richard Vines, and 'my special Friend' Robert Morton, curate of Bewdley, the father of Richard Morton; and men whom he admired but with whom he afterwards engaged in theological controversy, such as Anthony Burgess (*Reliquiae Baxterianae*, 1.44, 1.45). After a month with King, Baxter, though he did not become chaplain to the garrison regiment, accepted an invitation to lodge in the house of the governor, John Barker, and to preach weekly to the soldiers of the garrison and once every Sunday to the people at large, 'not taking of any of them a Penny for either, save my Diet only'. He found there 'a very Judicious Auditory' containing 'many very godly … Gentlemen', including Sir Richard Skeffington, fourth baronet, 'a most noble, holy Man', and the writer George Abbot (ibid., 1.44).

In autumn 1643 Baxter accompanied a party to establish a parliamentarian garrison at Wem, Shropshire, in order that he might visit his father, who had been plundered by royalist soldiers and imprisoned at Lilleshall Abbey. Baxter succeeded in securing his father's release. When Shrewsbury was captured by the royalists, Baxter's father enjoyed the protection of the new governor, his brother-in-law Sir Fulke Huncks, though he was again to be imprisoned before the town was recaptured by the parliamentarians. When Sir Fulke left upon the appointment of Sir Francis Ottley as governor in 1643, his mother remained behind, living with Baxter's father and her daughter, Mary, Baxter's stepmother, in whose house she died in 1645 or 1646, aged between eighty and 100 years. (Her bequest to Baxter's stepmother of £50 led to a protracted dispute between the Baxters and her executor, Edward, second Viscount Conway, and his successor, Edward, third viscount, afterwards first earl of Conway; it was still occasioning correspondence in 1680.) Baxter himself continued undisturbed at Coventry until summer 1645, living 'in safety in a City of defence … seeing no enemy while the Kingdom was in Wars and Flames' (Baxter, *Dying Thoughts*, 224–5). However, when after the battle of Naseby he visited the parliamentarian army quarters at Leicester, he was appalled to discover 'a new face of things which I never dreamt of'. While 'We that lived quietly in *Coventry* did keep to our old Principles, and … were unfeignedly for King and Parliament', anticipating that the king would be brought to a reconciliation with his parliament and to consent to a reformation of the national church, Baxter now encountered in the New Model Army a body of men among whom radical and enthusiastic ideas were eagerly embraced and officers among whom 'hot-headed Sectaries had got into the highest places' and were Cromwell's 'chief Favourites'. Their intentions Baxter took to be no less than 'to subvert both Church and State': they 'were far from thinking of … any healing way between the Episcopal and the Presbyterians'; 'they took the King for a Tyrant and an Enemy, and really intended absolutely to master him, or ruine him'. Baxter's puritanism valued order, tradition, and authority; the revolutionary and radical wing of the movement, as represented by Anabaptists and, later, Quakers, disclosed to him a prospect of anarchy. Though he had encountered Anabaptists at Coventry, disputing with Benjamin Cox, he had given no credence to the reports that there were 'Swarms of Anabaptists' in the army. He now realized how far prevailing opinion had moved during his secure residence at Coventry and he reproached himself for having in 1642 or 1643 declined an invitation from Cromwell to act as chaplain 'with that famous Troop which he began his Army with', an invitation perhaps initiated by Berry:

These very men that then invited me to be their Pastor, were the Men that afterwards headed much of the Army … which made me wish that I had gone among them … for then all the Fire was in one Spark. (*Reliquiae Baxterianae*, 1.50–51)

Realizing his mistake, Baxter now agreed to act as chaplain in the regiment commanded by Edward Whalley, but with the express intention of countering the spread of radical ideas among the troops, which, not surprisingly, drew upon him 'the discountenance of *Cromwell* and the chief Officers of his Mind' (*Reliquiae Baxterianae*, 1.56). Baxter deplored the influence of such Independent ministers as Hugh Peters and, among Cromwell's officers, of sectaries and enthusiasts such as Thomas Rainborow. Levellers and Diggers he regarded as the tools of 'Anabaptists', a term by which he encompassed all shades of enthusiastic opinion. It was, it may be supposed, his experiences in the army which resolved those early doubts about the sacrament of baptism. Similarly, his army experiences gave to Baxter's theology its characteristic emphasis upon continuing moral commitment, growth in grace, and the conditionality of justification. He became convinced that the antinomian emphasis which resulted from the exclusive stress upon free grace characteristic of Ranters and other radicals, and which Baxter detected also in the Calvinist theology of such Independents as John Owen, far from exalting divine mercy or constituting Christian liberation, was antithetical to the moral life. In his first publication, *Aphorismes of Justification* (1649), Baxter argued for a process of justification involving human co-operation with grace. This apparent retreat from predestinarian orthodoxy embroiled Baxter in prolonged controversy, with Owen among others, but he would maintain his position throughout his life, repeatedly drawing upon himself charges of Arminianism, popery, and even Pelagianism.

With Whalley's regiment Baxter followed the New Model Army westwards as it successively reduced the royalist strongholds of Bridgwater, Sherborne, Bristol, and Exeter, and then, in 1646, Banbury and Worcester. On the advice of the physician Sir Theodore Mayerne, whom he consulted in London, Baxter took the waters at Tunbridge Wells for three weeks in the later summer of 1646, but later that year his health declined until, in February 1647, having caught a chill riding in snowy weather, and having suffered for a week from constant bleeding from the nose, he was compelled to remain in his quarters with Sir John Coke of Melbourne Hall, Derbyshire. He then went for three weeks to the house of Verney Noel of Kirkby Mallory, Leicestershire, and then for three months to Rous Lench Court, the Worcestershire home of Sir Thomas and Lady Rous. It was at Kirkby Mallory that he began the composition of perhaps his most famous book, *The Saints Everlasting Rest* (1650), and he continued it at Rous Lench.

Poor health was a permanent feature of Baxter's life. As a child he suffered from catarrh, colds, and a prolonged cough. In the early 1630s he was 'in expectation of Death, by a violent Cough, with Spitting of Blood, &c. of two years continuance'; 'From the Age of 21 till near 23, my Weakness was so great, that I expected not to live above a year' (*Reliquiae Baxterianae*, 1.5, 1.12). He did not expect to survive the publication of *Aphorismes of Justification* long enough to produce another book; when *The Saints Everlasting Rest* appeared, it was addressed to its reader as the legacy of a dying man. The thirty or more different physicians Baxter was to consult during his life were unable to prescribe any sustained relief from 'the same Symptoms as most men have about Fourscore years of Age'. Baxter suffered chronically from flatulency and gastric problems, 'incredible Inflammations of Stomach, Bowels, Back, Sides, Head, Thighs, as if I had been daily fill'd with Wind'; from scurvy and from repeated haemorrhaging from 'Eyes, and Teeth, and Jaws, and Joynts, so that I had scarce rest night or day'; he was prone to catch colds and chills, and he suffered regularly from headaches, from 'terrible Toothach', and from gallstones, in later life the severity of the pain leaving 'scarce any part or hour … free' (ibid., 1.9–10, 1.80–83, 3.173–4, where he also details the various remedies he tried). If there was something of the hypochondriac in his disposition (one diagnosis he was given was 'that my Disease was the Hypocondriack Melancholy', another that it was 'nothing but Hypochondriack Flatulency, and somewhat of a Scorbutical Malady'), he had good cause anxiously to attend to his bodily condition: physical indisposition at best, pain at worst, were his constant experience. This, coupled with his lifelong expectation that death was imminent, led him to value time intensely and to expatiate on the traditional puritan theme of the sinfulness of time-wasting with particular forcefulness; as he wrote in the autobiographical poem 'Love Breathing Thanks and Praise':

A Life still near to Death, did me possess
With a deep sense of Time's great Preciousness.

To this preoccupation with the efficient management of time may be attributed Baxter's quite extraordinary industry and voluminous literary output:

The frequent sight of Death's most awful face,
Rebuk'd my sloth, and bid me mend my pace.

'Expecting to be so quickly in another World' also lent

urgency to Baxter's evangelistic and pastoral ministry: as he aphoristically put it:

I Preach'd, as never sure to Preach again
And as a dying man to dying men!
(Baxter, *Poetical Fragments*, 38–40; *Reliquiae Baxterianae*, 1.86)

Kidderminster years It was five months before Baxter was sufficiently recovered to visit Kidderminster in the summer of 1647. In May, while still at Rous Lench Court, he had received an invitation to return to Kidderminster. Its 265 signatories (including a number who had fought for parliament) are evidence that, despite the hostility Baxter had experienced in 1641–2, he had made his mark with many of the parishioners. While with the army Baxter had considered himself committed to his position at Kidderminster and had not entertained any other pastoral appointment. During his absence, however, the parish had reinstituted its proceedings against Dance and the living had been sequestered by the committee for plundered ministers. What Baxter was now offered was consequently the position of vicar. This he declined, agreeing only to take up his old lectureship for a salary of £80–90 per annum. The parishioners then offered the position to Oliver Bromskill, curate at Sheriffhales, whom Baxter had known at Coventry, but he declined the invitation, as did Baxter again when, soon after his return to Kidderminster, he was 'vehemently urged … to take the Vicaridge' (*Reliquiae Baxterianae*, 1.79). However, unbeknown to Baxter, in March 1648 the parishioners proceeded to secure his appointment as vicar. Only in 1651 did they disclose what they had done. Baxter nevertheless allowed Dance to continue living in the vicarage, on an allowance of £40 per annum from the parish revenue, while he himself lodged in rooms on the upper floor of a house in the High Street; and he raised no objection to Dance conducting prayer book services for the lord of the manor, Sir Ralph Clare. He similarly took no steps to prevent the remaining curate from reading the common prayer to adherents of the episcopal church at the chapelry at Mitton.

Many of those who had opposed Baxter in 1641 and 1642 had fought and died for the royalist cause, which, together with the changed political situation, prevented any recurrence of the earlier hostility upon his return. It was during the ensuing years at Kidderminster that Baxter became a figure of national renown and it is upon his pastorate there that his enduring reputation in part rests. During the 1650s he effected a remarkable transformation: 'When I came thither first, there was about one Family in a Street that worshipped God and called on his name', but 'when I came away there were some Streets where there was not past one Family in the Side of a Street that did not so'; 'on the Lord's Day … you might hear an hundred Families singing Psalms and repeating Sermons, as you passed through the Streets'. The parish of Kidderminster then comprised the market town and twenty surrounding villages, some 800 families in all, or 3000–4000 inhabitants, of whom rather more than 1800 were adults. Of these, about 600 were full communicants under Baxter's ministry, 'of whom there was not twelve that I had

not good hopes of, as to their sincerity'. Those who were not full church members, among whom Baxter believed were many of sincere faith 'kept off by Husbands, by Parents, by Masters, and some dissuaded by Men that differed from us', did not oppose or obstruct Baxter's ministry (*Reliquiae Baxterianae*, 1.84–5).

The church order and worship at Kidderminster followed a moderate line between the enthusiasm of radical puritanism and the prescriptiveness of both strict presbyterianism and prayer book worship. Baxter was not opposed to a written liturgy or to forms of prayer, though he himself used extempore prayers. He administered the sacrament to seated communicants, but would refuse it to none who wished to kneel. He administered infant baptism (though with parents, not godparents, taking the vows), and engaged in oral and written disputation with the famed Baptist John Tombes, curate at neighbouring Bewdley, Worcestershire. *Plain Scripture Proof of Infants Church Membership and Baptism* (1651) arose out of these debates and was the first of several titles on this subject. Baxter did not observe Christmas, regarding it as a spurious festival of late institution, but he was far from the (false) stereotype of the puritan killjoy. He delighted in the singing of psalms, and, himself the author of poems which have since become such well-known hymns as 'Ye holy angels bright' (from 'A Psalm of Praise' in *Poetical Fragments*, 84–8), he advocated the composition of hymns for congregational singing at a time when praise in worship was limited to the words of the psalms. He was similarly a keen advocate of aesthetic and sensory aids to devotion: 'God would not have given us, either our Senses themselves, or their usual objects, if they might not have been serviceable to his own praise'; hence, it is 'a point of our Spiritual Prudence, and a singular help to the furthering of the work of Faith, to call in our Sense to its assistance' (Baxter, *Saints Everlasting Rest*, 757).

Baxter held that church discipline and controlled admission to the Lord's supper were fundamental to the being of a true church, but he did not conceive of this in rigid or mechanistic terms. His own conditions for church membership were liberal. In *Certain Disputations of Right to Sacraments* (1657) he argued that a credible 'Profession of a Saving Faith', with which the quality of their lives is consistent, is a sufficient condition 'of Mens title to Church-Communion' (*Reliquiae Baxterianae*, 1.113). Recognizing that 'God breaketh not all Mens hearts alike', Baxter did not ask potential church members for a rehearsal of spiritual experience such as was required by many Independent and separatist churches. He was hostile to their prescriptiveness and, as one committed to a parochially organized national church, to their exclusivity. However, although he rejected the Independents' strictness (he would not 'with Independants, un-church the Parish-Church, and gather a Church out of them anew'), Baxter was equally dissatisfied with episcopal laxity and its 'meer Mock-shew of Discipline'; the outward holiness of church society must be maintained if it is to be recognizable as a church (ibid., 1.91, 1.7). Full communicants were therefore required to submit to church discipline, accepting admonishment for sins in private or, in extreme cases, public confession of wrongdoing and resolution to reform at a parish meeting for discipline held every first Wednesday of the month. Excommunication was the ultimate sanction. Baxter recognized that such discipline is mere tyranny unless it is accompanied by a commitment to instruction and pastoral oversight. Parishioners were given the opportunity to understand Christian duties and obligations, and encouragement to fulfil them. It was Baxter's promotion of catechetical instruction which was the truly distinctive feature of his Kidderminster ministry and at the root of his success. He devoted the afternoons of every Monday and Tuesday, and his assistant the mornings, to an hour's 'private Catechising and Conference (he going through the Parish, and the Town coming to me)' with fourteen families each week until they had seen every family in the town and its environs. The rota then began again. (Baxter's assistants in this work, of whose 'honesty and diligence' he speaks very highly, included Thomas Baldwin, Joseph Read, Richard Sargeant, and Humphrey Waldron, all of them nonconformist ministers following the Restoration.) Only a half-dozen families refused to participate; 'And few Families went from us without some tears, or seemingly serious promises for a Godly Life' (ibid., 1.83, 1.85, 1.88).

In *Gildas Salvianus: the Reformed Pastor* (1656), a book which, either as a full text or in abridged form, has been available ever since its first publication, Baxter gave impassioned expression to both his pastoral ideals and his pastoral zeal. *The Reformed Pastor* arose out of Baxter's dismay at, and determination to rectify, pastoral neglect in the west midlands such as he had experienced as a young man. It is a permanent contribution to the literature of pastoral theology and perhaps the finest product of the practical concern of puritanism for the well-being of souls. Despite its emphasis on catechizing, the book is instinct with the awesome seriousness of the preacher's office. Baxter himself was a powerful and committed evangelistic preacher, with a puritan's characteristically clear-sighted grasp of the needs of his hearers. He set himself firmly in the line of puritan plain preaching addressed to the needs of a 'popular auditory': he had no patience with such preaching as that of Lancelot Andrewes, which 'did but play with holy things'; 'it was the plain and pressing downright Preacher, that onely seemed to me to be in good sadness, and to make somewhat of it, and to speak with life, and light, and weight' (R. Baxter, *Treatise of Conversion*, 1657, epistle to the reader; Keeble and Nuttall, 1.255). His preaching enjoyed great success, both in Kidderminster, where five extra galleries had to be added to the parish church, St Mary's, and during a visit to London in the winter of 1654–5, when, on the occasion of his preaching at St Lawrence Jewry the sermon published as *Making Light of Christ and Salvation* (1655), Roger Boyle, Lord Broghill, afterwards earl of Orrery, with whom Baxter lodged during his visit, and James Howard, earl of Suffolk, who had taken Baxter by coach, could not gain entrance to the church such was the crush, and the vicar, Richard Vines, Baxter's friend from Coventry days, 'was fain to get up into the Pulpit, and sit behind me, and I to stand between his Legs' (*Reliquiae Baxterianae*, 1.112).

Baxter was in London in the winter of 1654–5 at Broghill's instigation to serve as one of the divines charged to draw up a statement of religious fundamentals which the subcommittee set up to advise Cromwell and the grand committee on religion could put forward as a definition of tolerable religious orthodoxy under the 'Instrument of government', the protectorate's constitution. Broghill, a member of the committee, first nominated Archbishop James Ussher; when, because of advanced age, he declined to serve, Broghill named Baxter in his place. It was during this visit that Baxter met Ussher, the man whom, of all his contemporaries, he perhaps most admired. Ussher's *Reduction of Episcopacie unto the Form of Synodicall Government used in the Antient Church*, published anonymously in 1656 but circulating in the 1640s, shaped Baxter's thinking on episcopacy and church government throughout his life. In his *Five Disputations of Church-Government and Worship* (1659) Baxter argued that 'the English Diocesane Prelacy is intollerable' (*Reliquiae Baxterianae*, 1.117) and proposed a scheme of modified episcopacy, consisting essentially of parochial bishops, which, he maintained, was consistent with, and preserved the best aspects of, the church polities of presbyterians, Independents, and moderate episcopalians alike.

Baxter's growing national reputation derived in part from the establishment during these years of the Worcestershire Voluntary Association of Ministers, a genuinely innovative movement initiated in 1652 which by 1659 had come to be imitated in many other counties. Its seventy or so members (from Staffordshire, Shropshire, Gloucestershire, and Oxfordshire, as well as Worcestershire) included some of Independent and episcopalian persuasion, but its membership was predominantly presbyterian, though not in a sense which implied commitment to the details of that church polity. Baxter consistently maintained that the term 'presbyterian' was in common usage merely a synonym for 'puritan' and that, while 'Presbytery generally took in *Scotland*, yet it was but a stranger here'; those in England known as presbyterians in fact 'addicted themselves to no Sect or Party at all'. He claimed to know only one presbyterian strictly so-called in all Worcestershire (Thomas Hall, curate of King's Norton). The members of the association he characterized as 'meer Catholicks; Men of no Faction, nor siding with any Party, but owning that which was good in all' (*Reliquiae Baxterianae*, 1.97, 2.146). Just over half would conform at the Restoration.

The association adopted the confession of faith published in *Christian Concord, or, The Agreement of the Associated Pastors and Churches of Worcestershire* (1653). Its members agreed to pursue a regular programme of catechizing within their cures: *The Reformed Pastor* was originally written to encourage members in this work and the association published its *Agreement for Catechizing* in 1656. And they undertook to meet monthly, at Bromsgrove, Evesham, Kidderminster, Upton-on-Severn, and Worcester, with quarterly meetings at Worcester. The monthly meetings at Evesham and Kidderminster were regularly held, on the first Thursday of every month at Kidderminster, where, after a meal, there was a disputation on a previously agreed topic, and on occasion discussion of cases of discipline. (Some members also attended Baxter's weekly Thursday lecture, joining him afterwards in his home.) A number of these disputations appeared in Baxter's publications, some are among extant Baxter papers, and correspondence on behalf of the association is among Baxter's surviving letters. These 'comfortable' meetings Baxter held among the most rewarding and enjoyable experiences of his life, and the work of the association in uniting men in pastoral commitment he regarded as a shining example of true Christian fellowship and charity. In 1660, when its day was done, *Universal Concord* published to 'the World … what our Religion and our Terms of Communion were' (*Reliquiae Baxterianae*, 1.85, 1.119).

In the creation of the Worcestershire Association, Baxter's commitment to pastoral service combined with his passionate desire for unity among Christians of differing persuasions. 'God hath possessed my heart with such a burning desire after the peace & unity of the Churches that I cannot forget it, or lay it by. I feele a supernaturall power forceing my zeale, & thoughts that way', Baxter wrote in a letter of February 1652 (Keeble and Nuttall, 1.92). In addition to the formation of the association, throughout the 1650s this zeal inspired a number of attempts to secure national church unity. In 1652–4 Baxter was in correspondence with the international ecumenist John Dury, an admirer of the association project, seeking to convene, with parliamentary support, a conference of representatives from the main ecclesiastical parties to reach an agreement upon a comprehensive national church settlement. It was a scheme which, Dury reported, enjoyed the support of the lord protector, who was 'forward in the worke'. Baxter himself remarked that the protector 'is noted as a man of a Catholike spiritt, desirous of the unity & Peace of all the servants of Christ', and in April 1658 his friend John Howe, then Cromwell's chaplain, reported that the lord protector 'expressed great willingnesse' to promote the association movement throughout England (Keeble and Nuttall, 1.128, 300, 302). In 1652 Baxter was responsible for the publication of *The Humble Petition of many Thousands … of the County of Worcester*, presented to the Rump Parliament on 22 December 1652 by John Bridges, patron of the Kidderminster living, and Thomas Foley. It asked that 'godly, prudent, peaceable Divines of each party' might be summoned to a national conference to determine 'a meet way for accommodation and unity', as well as for financial support for the ministry and a university education for all ministers. Baxter's *The Worcestershire-Petition Defended* (1653), written against the published objections of the Quaker Benjamin Nicholson to these petitions, was handed out to MPs at the door of the house, but the next day the Rump was turned out. In 1655, in the preface to *True Christianity*, Baxter urged the

first protectorate parliament to pursue church unity. One of the sermons he preached during his visit to London in 1654–5 was published as *Catholick Unity* (1660) and during that same visit, through the good offices of Broghill and Robert Rich, second earl of Warwick, he preached to Cromwell 'on I. Cor. i.10 against the Divisions and Distractions of the Church'. Cromwell afterwards twice sent for Baxter for several hours' discussion, but to little avail: 'I saw that what he learned must be from himself; being more disposed to speak many hours, than to hear one', was Baxter's assessment (*Reliquiae Baxterianae*, 2.205).

Baxter's experience at the 1654–5 London conference was itself equally disappointing. Owen, a leading member of the group, had been responsible for drawing up and publishing fifteen fundamentals of belief (*Proposals for the Furtherance and Propagation of the Gospel in this Nation*, 1653). In contrast, Baxter, who 'knew how ticklish a Business the Enumeration of Fundamentals was', 'would have had the Brethren to have offered the Parliament the *Creed*, *Lord's Prayer*, and *Decalogue* alone as our Essentials or Fundamentals', responding to the objection that papists or Socinians might subscribe these with the startling words 'So much the better, and so much the fitter it is to be the Matter of our Concord'. For Owen and the 'over-Orthodox Doctors' this was an unacceptably broad and loose formulation (*Reliquiae Baxterianae*, 2.197–9). Baxter's meetings with Ussher, however, were an inspiration: the two agreed 'in halfe an Hour' on a form of modified episcopacy sufficient for 'Concord … in matters of Church-Government' among 'moderate Men' of all ecclesiastical persuasions (ibid., 2.217). In 1655 Baxter reported this to Ralph Brownrig, deprived bishop of Exeter, when commending to him terms of reconciliation between episcopalians and presbyterians. In September 1656, when asked by Edward Harley, newly elected to the second protectorate parliament, how best to serve the interests of the 'distressed Church', Baxter, again referring to the ease with which he and Ussher had 'agreed in halfe an Hour', advised him, first, to 'take heed of being too forward in imposing on others' and to confine any required profession of faith to Scripture fundamentals, else it would merely exclude and divide; 'In a doubtful case, I had rather erre in grantinge too much liberty, than too little'. Second, he urged the calling of a conference of 'two of the most moderate & best esteemed' representatives of the episcopal, presbyterian, and Independent traditions. And third, he recommended that one version of the psalms should be authorized nationally for use in churches (Keeble and Nuttall, 1.222–6). In 1657 Baxter was recommending to the New England evangelist John Eliot as 'an excellent worke' a proposal that the Congregational New England churches should propound terms of reconciliation between Independents and presbyterian churches in England (ibid., 1.240). On this same business he corresponded also with such episcopalians as Thomas Good and Henry Hammond, with Independents such as Philip Nye, and, during the last years of the interregnum, with two former Independents, now Baptists, Thomas Lambe (or Lamb) and William Allen, whom he so effectively convinced of the lamentable consequences of disunity that after the Restoration he was to find them as hostile to nonconformity as once they had been committed to separatism.

The Restoration Looking back after the Restoration, Baxter was to acknowledge that, under 'an Usurper whom I opposed' he had enjoyed 'Liberty and Advantage to preach [the] Gospel with Success, which I cannot have under a King to whom I have sworn and performed true Subjection and Obedience'. He never modified his political opposition to Cromwell, and regretted what he took to be the corrupting effect of power upon him (his famous summary characterization is in *Reliquiae Baxterianae*, 1.98–100). During the 1650s 'I did seasonably and moderately by Preaching and Printing condemn the Usurpation, and … in open Conference declare *Cromwell* and his Adherents to be Guilty of Treason and Rebellion, aggravated with Perfidiousness and Hypocrisie'. Nevertheless, 'I perceived that it was his design to do good in the main, and to promote the Gospel and the Interest of Godliness, more than any had done before him', and, on the basis of his experience of that 'incredible Age', Baxter passionately rebutted the Restoration opinion that 'all Religion was then trodden down, and Heresy and Schism were the only Piety' (*Reliquiae Baxterianae*, 1.71, 1.86–7). Baxter especially admired, and commended, the work of the Triers in approving ministers.

Of Cromwell's son, Baxter had great hopes as a man who, having 'never had any hand in the War', nor having sought power, and who seemed 'to own the Sober Party', might 'be used in the healing of the Land'. Here was a godly magistrate under whom a national reformed church might flourish. In October and November 1658 Baxter dedicated to Richard Cromwell *A Key for Catholicks* (1659) and *Five Disputations of Church Government and Worship* (1659), in the second expressing the hope that the new protector might 'be the happy instrument of *taking away* the divisions of the *Godly*' (*Reliquiae Baxterianae*, 1.100; Keeble and Nuttall, 1.358). Early in 1659 Baxter wrote his most controversial book, *A Holy Commonwealth* (1659), a retort to the model of a '*Heathenish Commonwealth*' given in James Harrington's *Oceana* (1659), broken off in despair when the army ousted the protector in April (*Reliquiae Baxterianae*, 1.118). It contains as an appendix Baxter's understanding of the issues which led to civil war and a justificatory account of his own actions and allegiance at that time. Following the Restoration, charges that Baxter (and nonconformists generally) were seditious repeatedly cited this text as evidence that, as a man who would not rule out resistance to the supreme governor, Baxter was a potential traitor and threat to the safety of the state. After ten years of this, in a statement dated 15 April 1670 published in the second edition of *The Life of Faith* (1670, sigs. b3–b3v), Baxter withdrew the book and repented of having published it, though 'without recanting any particular Doctrine in it' (*Reliquiae Baxterianae*, 3.71–2). In 1683 it was one of the books publicly burnt as seditious by a decree of 21 July of the University of Oxford.

In the last years of the interregnum Baxter had had increasing contacts with men of royalist persuasion, including, rather unexpectedly, John Maitland, earl (afterwards duke) of Lauderdale, with whom he was in correspondence. In the summer of 1659 he was informed by Sir Ralph Clare of the impending rising of George Booth. Clare, who, through Hammond, claimed to know the mind of the king, assured Baxter that 'all Moderation was intended' were the monarchy to be restored (*Reliquiae Baxterianae*, 2.208). In March 1660 Baxter was invited by Lauderdale to London, where he arrived on 13 April, to receive from Lauderdale expressions of the king's 'Favour and Acceptance' (Baxter, *Penitent Confession*, 43). Having been identified as an opinion-maker whom it was well to secure for the cause of monarchy's restoration, Baxter was visited also by Sir William Morice, newly appointed secretary of state, and by James Sharpe, afterwards archbishop of St Andrews. Baxter's disappointment at the overthrow of Richard Cromwell, his bitterness at the peremptory actions of the army, and his dismay at the constitutional instability of 1659 all combined with his innate respect for tradition and order to confirm his support for the royalist cause. Though he was far from thinking Charles I a martyr, he certainly did not approve of the regicide and he had served with parliament not with a view to redrafting the constitution but in order to secure true religion.

On 30 April Baxter preached before the Convention at St Margaret's, Westminster, *A Sermon of Repentance* (1660), and, following the Convention's vote to recall Charles II on 1 May, on 10 May he preached at St Paul's before the lord mayor a sermon, *Right Rejoycing* (1660). On 25 June he (with other presbyterians) was appointed a chaplain to the king, and on 22 July he preached before Charles *The Life of Faith* (1660). His standing, and the anxiety of the restored regime to secure his unqualified allegiance, was evidenced further by the offer to him of the bishopric of Hereford made in October by Edward Hyde, earl of Clarendon. This offer Baxter declined in a letter of 1 November, for the characteristic reason that to accept would inhibit him from promoting church unity. As this indicates, in the ecclesiastical negotiations which accompanied the Restoration, his aim remained what it had been during the interregnum. In his *Sermon of Repentance* he had spoken of church unity and had again mentioned his agreement with Ussher. This prompted 'many moderate Episcopal Divines' to request further details from him and had led to a series of meetings. Reconciliation was the theme not only of *Universal Concord* but, in that same year, 1660, also of both *Catholick Unity* and *The True Catholick and Catholic Church Described*, written:

> for Catholicism against all *Sects*; to shew the Sin and Folly and Mischief of all Sects that would appropriate the Church to themselves, and trouble the World with the Question, Which of all these Parties is the Church? as if they knew not that the Catholick Church is that which containeth all the Parts, though some more pure, and some less. (*Reliquiae Baxterianae*, 2.218, 1.112)

It was, he affirmed, never the intention of the so-called presbyterians to argue for a presbyterian system: rather, their aim was as comprehensive a national church settlement as possible.

This Baxter and other presbyterian delegates, including Simeon Ashe, Edmund Calamy, Thomas Manton, Edward Reynolds, William Spurstowe, and John Wallis, pursued in the late summer at a meeting (or perhaps meetings) with the king at the London lodgings of Edward Montagu, second earl of Manchester, who, with Broghill, had been instrumental in securing Charles's participation. The king, professing 'his gladness to hear our Inclinations to Agreement, and his Resolution to do his part to bring us together', invited a written submission of the presbyterians' preferred terms. Drawn up chiefly by Calamy and Reynolds, this included Ussher's *Reduction* as grounds for agreement. The presbyterians had hoped to discuss these terms with episcopalian divines but instead were advised that the king 'would put all that he thought meet to grant us' in a royal declaration (*Reliquiae Baxterianae*, 2.231, 2.259). When on 4 September the presbyterians received from Clarendon a draft *Declaration on Ecclesiastical Affairs* they were disappointed to find that it 'would not serve to heal our Differences'. Consultation with Manchester, 'our sure Friend', Denzil, Lord Holles, and Arthur Annesley, first earl of Anglesey, persuaded Baxter to moderate the paper of criticisms he drew up, which was then submitted to Clarendon (ibid., 2.265), but at a meeting between, on the one side, Reynolds, Baxter, and Calamy, and, on the other, George Morley, John Cosin, and Humphrey Henchman, then all bishops elect, it nevertheless proved impossible to reach agreement. However, a further conference between presbyterian and episcopal representatives, held on 22 October at Worcester House, Clarendon's residence, in the presence of the king, led, three days later, to a far more conciliatory final *Declaration* than Baxter had anticipated, 'such as any sober honest Ministers might submit to', as he gratefully told Clarendon. He told Clarendon also of his resolution to do all that he could to persuade all 'to Conform according to the Terms of this Declaration' and to 'promote our happy Concord', looking forward to 'the Day that Factions and Parties may all be swallowed up in Unity' (though he was not a named subscriber to the published address of thanks *To the King's most Excellent Majesty*, 1660). Unhappily, however, Baxter's fear that the *Declaration* 'was but for present use, and that shortly it would be revok'd or nullified' was realized when, in a vote on 28 November, the Commons failed to pass the *Declaration* into law (ibid., 2.279, 2.281).

On 24 March of the following year, 1661, a conference was convened at Savoy House, in accordance with an undertaking in the *Declaration*, to discuss revisions of the prayer book. Baxter took a leading part in the proceedings. His position was that, though he himself could readily admit as lawful such practices as kneeling to receive the sacrament, he could not accept as lawful the imposition of such indifferent matters upon those who conscientiously judged them inadmissible; still less could acceptance of them be elevated into a condition of communion. He hence argued strenuously for extensive revision of the prayer book and for sufficient latitude to accommodate those who on conscientious grounds could not conform to some of its rites. Baxter's determination to debate every point in detail clearly exasperated episcopalian delegates. Izaak Walton reports that Robert Sanderson, bishop of Lincoln, exclaimed in exasperation that '*he had never met with a man of more pertinacious confidence, and less abilities in all his conversation*' (Walton, 404). Clarendon reproved Baxter for being 'severe and strict, like a Melancholy Man' (*Reliquiae Baxterianae*, 2.365). Despite his tenacity, however, Baxter was in his own mind convinced that the case was now hopeless and that sincere intentions to accommodate tender consciences were wanting: 'we spoke to the Deaf', was his judgement; 'I perceived that they intended no Abatements' (ibid., 2.336, 2.345). Even so, he was determined that presbyterian arguments and aspirations should not go by default, and he was especially anxious that they should be available for the subsequent judgement of history. This led him to assemble a collection of papers presented to the conference, which, with his own proposed reformed liturgy, was published without his authorization as *A Petition for Peace: with the Reformation of the Liturgy* (1661). It led him also to compile a detailed record of the conference's proceedings in the *Reliquiae*, with full documentation (ibid., 2.303–72).

Baxter claimed that at the Savoy he 'foreknew and foretold them what they were about to do' (*Reliquiae Baxterianae*, 2.345). This would not have required exceptional prescience. A bill for religious uniformity was making its way through the Commons even as the conference was in session. Ever since the Restoration, the episcopal church of England had been re-establishing itself at parochial level, and, from late 1660, its bench of bishops began to be replenished. And as its liturgy and practices were reintroduced, so the reaction against puritanism gathered apace. As a leading figure, Baxter attracted the hostile attention of such partisan episcopalians as Thomas Pierce and Thomas Tomkins and of such vitriolic royalist pamphleteers as Sir Roger L'Estrange. Informers attended his sermons and, so he believed, misreported them: 'I scarce ever preached a Sermon in the City, but I had News from *Westminster* that I had preached seditiously, or against the Government'; 'the daily Clamours of Accusers even wearied me' (ibid., 2.301, 2.302). It was even rumoured that he was to lead a rebellion in the north. By the Act of Confirming and Restoring of Ministers he was in the autumn of 1660 deprived of his Kidderminster living in favour of Dance, and George Morley, then bishop of Worcester, took strenuous measures to ensure that Baxter would neither return to the parish nor preach within his diocese, even as an unpaid lecturer, which he offered to do. Clare, whom Baxter saw as the chief opponent of his return to Kidderminster, stood ready to support Morley, with 'his Troop to apprehend me' if need be (ibid., 2.374). So far was he from reciprocating Baxter's consideration towards him that Dance would not tolerate Baxter's returning even to preach a farewell sermon at Kidderminster. (What he would have preached was published years later as *Richard Baxter's Farewel Sermon*, 1683). Baxter gave an account of these dealings in an epistle of 11 November 1661 to his Kidderminster people prefaced to *The Mischiefs of Self-Ignorance* (1662), which led to a retort from Morley in *The Bishop of Worcester's Letter to a Friend* (1662) and to a controversy involving, on Baxter's side though without his approval, Edward Bagshaw and, among others in defence of the bishop, L'Estrange. The increasing hostility Baxter experienced led him in 1662 to consider, as it did others, emigration 'to live and end my days in quietness, out of the noise of a Peace-hating Generation'. His want of languages, his ill health, and the possibility of future service in England, urged by friends, combined to dissuade him (ibid., 2.383).

During these two years Baxter preached at several locations in London. For a year he preached as invited, his sermons including a series delivered at Westminster Abbey (*The Vain Religion of the Formal Hypocrite*, 1660). He then joined with William Bates at St Dunstan-in-the-West, Fleet Street, preaching once a week, delivering there between May and August 1661 the sermons published as *The Mischiefs of Self-Ignorance* (1662). He preached also at St Bride's, Fleet Street, and at St Anne Blackfriars, where John Herring and John Gibbons, both ejected in 1662, were respectively vicar and rector. The sermons published as *A Saint or a Brute* (1662) and *Now or Never* (1662), and in parts of *The Divine Life* (1664), were preached at St Anne's. Concurrently, at St Mary Magdalen, Milk Street, where Thomas Vincent was rector, he gave a lecture on weekdays, sponsored by his friend Henry Ashurst. On 19 May 1662 the Act of Uniformity received the royal assent, and it became effective on St Bartholomew's day, 24 August 1662. From that date, only ministers who had received episcopal ordination, who had published their unfeigned assent and consent to all in the Book of Common Prayer, and who repudiated the solemn league and covenant, could hold benefices in the Church of England. None of these prescriptions necessarily excluded Baxter: he was episcopally ordained, he accepted the lawfulness of set forms of prayer, and he had never subscribed the solemn league and covenant. Nevertheless, the exclusivity of these terms was abhorrent to him. A church which insists upon compliance with a particular liturgical or ecclesiological form has elevated incidental matters of external performance above the essentials of Christian faith. Any church—even the national church—which demands the suppression of conscientious scruples as the price of membership is, he argued, sectarian: he would not subscribe to a church established on such divisive principles. He delivered his farewell sermon on Colossians 2: 6–7 at St Anne Blackfriars on 25 May, well before the last Sunday before 24 August, in order to 'let all Ministers in *England* understand in time, whether I intended to Conform or not' (*Reliquiae Baxterianae*, 2.384). It was included in the various collections of farewell sermons published in 1662 and 1663, but without Baxter's authorization and in an imperfect text, 'mangled so both [in] Matter and Style, that I could not

own it' (ibid., 2.303); Baxter himself published an authorized text in *Directions for Weak Distempered Christians* (1669).

Nonconformity During the years 1660–62 Baxter lodged first, for about a year, at Thomas Foley's house in Austin Friars, and then for another year in the house of Dr John Micklethwaite in Little Britain. Following his marriage on 10 September 1662 to Margaret Charlton [*see below*] he and his wife lived in a house in Moorfields until, 'All Publick Service being at an end', they moved on 14 July 1663 to a house in the country, at Acton, Middlesex, 'that I might set my self to writing, and do what Service I could for Posterity, and live as much as possibly I could out of the World' (*Reliquiae Baxterianae*, 2.440). Among the works written during these years was the first part of the autobiographical narrative posthumously published by Matthew Sylvester as *Reliquiae Baxterianae* (1696), and much of the massive work of casuistical divinity, *A Christian Directory* (1673). At Acton he developed a close friendship with his neighbour, Sir Matthew Hale, afterwards lord chief justice, with whom he enjoyed long conversations on metaphysical divinity. Baxter's great admiration for this 'Pillar of Justice, the Refuge of the subject who feared Oppression, and one of the greatest Honours of His Majestie's Government' (ibid., 3.47) informs his *Additional Notes on the Life and Death of Sir Matthew Hale* (1682), a companion piece to the biography of Hale by Gilbert Burnet. When the plague broke out in London, Baxter went to stay with his friend Richard Hampden, in Great Hampden, Buckinghamshire, where he completed the second part of the *Reliquiae* (dated 28 September 1665).

At Acton it was Baxter's habit, after joining in common prayer at the parish church on a Sunday, to preach in his home to his household and some neighbours. When the first Conventicle Act expired on 1 March 1669, the numbers of those attending greatly increased until, at the instigation of the rector, Bruno Ryves, Baxter was arrested on 12 June 1669 under the Five Mile Act of 1665 and imprisoned in Clerkenwell, though he was released within a few days on an error in the warrant. It is characteristic of Baxter to have continued his ministry despite the prescriptions of the Clarendon code, but equally characteristic was his determination to do so without disturbing parish worship. During the years 1660–63 he had attended parish churches in London, particularly those where John Wilkins and John Tillotson preached, and he regularly attended the parish church at Acton. Baxter was always a reluctant nonconformist, seeking ways to bridge the gulf between nonconformist and conformist and aspiring to the creation of a more liberally established national church which could comprehend within it a much broader range of ecclesiological and theological opinion. To this end he continued to argue for church unity in such books as *The Cure of Church-Divisions* (1670) and *The True and Only Way of Concord* (1680), to discountenance separatism in such works as the series of tracts against Edward Bagshaw beginning with *A Defence of the Principles of Love* (1671), and to advocate occasional conformity to the Church of England in, for example, the series of tracts beginning with *Catholick Communion Defended*

(1684). He was also concerned in negotiations with latitu-dinarian episcopal divines aimed at effecting comprehension. In 1668 the lord keeper, Sir Orlando Bridgeman, instigated meetings between Baxter, William Bates, and Thomas Manton on the one side (Baxter also informally consulted Owen), and John Wilkins, now bishop of Chester, and his chaplain, Humphrey Burton, on the other. These discussions led to Hale's drawing up a comprehension bill which, however, the Commons refused to entertain. In 1670 Baxter had discussions with Lauderdale, who offered him, with the king's consent, whatever ecclesiastical or academic position in Scotland he might desire, even a bishopric. At the invitation of Broghill, now earl of Orrery, in December 1673 Baxter drew up a paper summarizing what would unite all English protestants against the papists, but the draft was much criticized by George Morley, now bishop of Winchester, to whom Orrery passed it. In 1675 there was a new round of negotiations between Baxter, Manton, Bates, and Matthew Poole and the episcopalians Tillotson and Edward Stillingfleet, encouraged, so it was reported, by Morley, Seth Ward, bishop of Salisbury, Charles Howard, first earl of Carlisle, and George Savile, then Viscount Halifax. These negotiations again came to nothing.

After his brief imprisonment in 1669, Baxter and his wife moved to Totteridge, near Barnet in Hertfordshire. It was there, 'in a troublesome, poor, smoaky, suffocating Room, in the midst of daily pains of the Sciatica', that Baxter wrote his Latin work of systematic divinity, *Methodus theologiae Christianae* (1681), intended to make up with *A Christian Directory* 'one Compleat Body of *Theologie*, The *Latin* one the Theory, and the *English* one the Practical part' (*Reliquiae Baxterianae*, 3.70, 3.190). There he enjoyed the companionship of John Corbet, his friend from the 1640s, who, with his wife, in the summer of 1670 went to live in the Baxters' house. When, in March 1672, Charles II's declaration of indulgence was issued, Baxter hesitated before applying for a licence to preach. In common with many, he suspected that the papists were the beneficiaries chiefly intended; he had misgivings about the legality of the indulgence and doubted it would be confirmed by parliament; he was chary of any expedient as arbitrary as the exercise of the royal prerogative; but above all, toleration of dissenting religious opinion and practice as a national policy would spell the end of his hopes of a comprehension which could accommodate that diversity within a national church: it would institute nonconformity within the religious life of the nation. Nevertheless, on 25 October Baxter did eventually apply for a licence, provided that it were issued to him as 'a mere Nonconformist', rather than in the name of a particular sect or denomination. The licence was issued to him as 'a Nonconforming Minister' on 27 October, and, unusually, it authorized him to preach 'in any licensed or allowed Place' (Turner, 1.575). He preached publicly for the first time since 1662 on 19 November 1672.

Although parliament compelled the king to withdraw the indulgence on 7 March 1673 Baxter's period of retirement was over. For the rest of his life he preached and ministered as and where he could (though never gathering a congregation of his own and always with respect to parishioners' obligation to their parish church). He was first invited to become one of the Merchants' lecturers at Pinners' Hall, though after delivering four lectures claims that he opposed congregationalism and that he 'Preached up *Arminianism*, and Free-Will, and *Man's Power*' led him to withdraw (*Reliquiae Baxterianae*, 3.103). At Easter 1673 he and his wife moved to a house in Southampton Square (now Bloomsbury Square). With her active and resourceful encouragement, rooms were hired over St James's market house in the parish of St Martin-in-the-Fields where Baxter preached each morning. He preached also, with the assistance of Joseph Read, in a meeting-house built at his wife's instigation in Dyott Street, Bloomsbury. On Thursdays he preached at a meeting-house in Fetter Lane, off Fleet Street in Holborn. These activities led to prosecutions under the second Conventicle Act, which were ineffective, but in June 1675 he had to submit to a warrant for the distraint of £50 worth of goods. He and his wife then moved from Southampton Square to a house in Oxendon Street, running parallel to Haymarket, where his wife built a meeting-house, but after Baxter had preached there only one day, Sir Henry Coventry, secretary of state, whose house was adjoining in what became Coventry Street, had a warrant issued for Baxter's arrest. Baxter eluded the officers and retired to the house of his friend Richard Beresford at Rickmansworth, Hertfordshire. During this visit in the second half of 1675 he engaged in a seven-hour public debate with the leading Quaker William Penn, followed by an exchange of letters. When he returned to London, Baxter refrained from public preaching, such was the closeness of the watch kept upon him by the authorities. On 16 April 1676 he began to preach again at a meeting-house hired by his wife in Swallow Street, off Piccadilly. On 9 November 1676, however, he had to desist since constables with a warrant set guard upon the door to the meeting-house. When, after this incident, Baxter, on the recommendation of Lauderdale, spoke to Henry Compton, bishop of London, about his situation, there was an outcry that the bishop, who 'spake very fairly, with peaceable words', 'was Treating of a Peace with the Presbyterians' (ibid., 3.178). Margaret Baxter then recommended that Baxter should preach each Sunday to a congregation in Globe Alley, Southwark, whose minister, Thomas Wadsworth, had died on 26 October 1676, which he was able to do throughout 1677 without disturbance by law officers.

Last years and death During the 1680s Baxter sustained a series of trials and adversities. The decade opened with a succession of bereavements, including, in 1680, the deaths of his friends John Corbet and Henry Ashurst, for both of whom Baxter preached and published funeral sermons (1681), and, most grievously, on 14 June 1681 of his wife, of whose life he published *A Breviate* (1681). It was under the emotional pressure of his grief at her death that he published his *Poetical Fragments* (1681). In October 1682 constables executed warrants to distrain goods to the value of £195 in fines for preaching, taking all his possessions, 'even the bed that I lay sick on', and 'threatned to com upon me again', so that Baxter had 'utterly to forsake my House and Goods and all, and take secret Lodgings distant in a stranger's House' (*Reliquiae Baxterianae*, 3.191). In November 1684 he was again arrested, and bound over to good behaviour in the sum of £400. And then, at the instigation of L'Estrange, so Baxter believed, he was arrested on 28 February 1685 and imprisoned in the king's bench prison, Southwark, to be brought before Judge George Jeffreys to answer the charge that passages in his *Paraphrase on the New Testament* (1685) were seditious. (To the second edition of 1695 is appended Baxter's own account of the cause of his imprisonment, with the accused passages (see Keeble and Nuttall, 2.283–4).) Even within the records of proceedings conducted by that intemperate and partisan judge, Jeffreys's behaviour towards Baxter was a scandal and a disgrace to his profession. Among the extant Baxter letters there is an eyewitness account, written ten years later, of Baxter being supported at the bar by Henry Ashurst (1645–1711), the son of Baxter's old friend, created a baronet in 1688, while Jeffreys was 'driveing on furiously, like that Great Hanebal, makeing his way over the alps with fire and vinegar, pouring all the contempt and scorn upon him, as if he had ben a link boy or rak kennel' (a rake-kennel was a scavenger) (ibid., 2.331). Baxter's bearing under this onslaught so impressed Tillotson that he later wrote to Sylvester 'Nothing more honourable than when the Reverend Baxter stood at bay, berogued, abused, despised—Never more great than then' (ibid., 2.330). Baxter was found guilty, fined 500 marks, and imprisoned until it was paid. He returned to prison, though he passed at least some of his term of confinement in a nearby private house. During these eighteen months he devoted himself to sustained study of the book of Revelation, engaging in a correspondence with the millenarian Thomas Beverley, with whose confident predictions of the apocalypse he was to disagree in *The Glorious Kingdom of Christ* (1691) and *A Reply to Mr. Tho. Beverley's Answer* (1691).

Through the good offices of William Herbert, then marquess of Powis, Baxter's fine was remitted on 24 November 1686 and he moved to a house in Charterhouse Yard (now Charterhouse Square) in Finsbury. There he assisted Sylvester to minister to his congregation in Rutland House, preaching, when his health allowed, every Sunday morning and alternate Thursdays. He welcomed the revolution of 1688 and the accession of William in an unpublished paper, 'King James his abdication of the crown plainly proved' (Thomas, 24b), and in *R. Baxters Sence of the Subscribed Articles of Religion* (1689) gratefully accepted the provisions of the Act of Toleration. He had not, however, abandoned his old hopes: in *An End of Doctrinal Controversies* (1691) he published 'a Summary of *Catholick* reconciling *Theology*' (*Reliquiae Baxterianae*, 3.182); in *Church Concord* (1691) he supported the Happy Union of Presbyterians and Independents; and he looked still towards a comprehensive national protestant church, whose reformed character he defended *Against the Revolt to a Foreign Jurisdiction* (1691), that is, of Rome. Still, too, he sought to safeguard

protestant doctrine from antinomianism in *The Scripture Gospel Defended* (1690), a piece provoked by the republication of the sermons of Tobias Crisp, though by so doing he exacerbated the doctrinal differences within nonconformity which were to lead to the breakup of the Happy Union in 1692.

Baxter died on 8 December 1691, in Charterhouse Yard, after a steady decline during the previous months. He was buried, like his wife, in Christ Church Greyfriars. The funeral sermon was preached by William Bates and published in 1692. By his will of 27 July 1689, proved on 23 December 1691, Baxter left property in Eaton Constantine to William *Baxter, his first cousin once removed. He left to Sylvester his books, with directions that they should be distributed among young students, and his manuscripts, with instructions that they were to be published only with the approval of William Lorimer, Thomas Doelittle, Roger Morrice, or Daniel Williams. Five works were posthumously published (most notably the autobiographical *Reliquiae Baxterianae*, 1696, edited by Sylvester), but a great mass of papers remains unpublished—held, with Baxter's letters, in Dr Williams's Library, London.

Literary career Even in the Kidderminster years, amid association and parochial business, Baxter's 'Writings were my chiefest daily Labour' (*Reliquiae Baxterianae*, 1.84). He was a quite exceptionally prolific writer, the author of more than 130 books (the exact figure depends upon how works published in a variety of forms are counted), several of them folios over 1 million words in length, as well as of hundreds of letters and unpublished papers and treatises. The majority of his published works are exercises in homiletic, catechetical, practical, or controversial divinity, but he essayed also meditative works, biblical commentary and paraphrase, poetry, historiography, biography and autobiography, and, in *The Poor Mans Family Book* (1674), a dialogic fiction in the manner of Arthur Dent. These works enjoyed an unprecedented popularity, many titles—notably *The Saints Everlasting Rest* and *A Call to the Unconverted* (1658)—going through repeated printings. Puritanism had always utilized the press, but there had never been a literary career like this, either in scale or in success: Baxter was the first author of a string of bestsellers in British literary history.

Baxter received nothing for his publications. It was his custom to receive from his publisher copies of the published text in lieu of a fee; these he gave away (see Keeble and Nuttall, 2.287–8, for an account of these arrangements). Until 1681 his publisher was the Kidderminster bookseller Nevill Simmons; he was succeeded by B. Simmons, probably his widow, who had perhaps to give up the business as a consequence of having published the *Paraphrase on the New Testament*, her last known imprint. Thereafter Baxter used booksellers such as Thomas Parkhurst who specialized in nonconformist writing. After the Restoration he had the provisions of the Licensing Act with which to contend. It was his rule not to evade the law by surreptitious printing without licence, but in order to procure licences he had several times to excise passages which offended the censor. Marvell's antagonist, Samuel

Parker, refused to license the manuscript of *The Cure of Church Divisions*. What was withheld as unpublishable became evident when, with the lapse of the act in 1679, Baxter published within two years a succession of defences of nonconformity, beginning with *The Nonconformists Plea for Peace* (1679). There followed its *Second Part* (1680), its *Defence* (1680), *An Apology for the Nonconformists Ministry* (1681), *A Second True Defence of the Meer Nonconformists* (1681), and *A Third Defence of the Cause of Peace* (1681).

This literary career was not planned or premeditated. Baxter himself maintained that every one of his titles was '*extorted*' from him by '*sudden unexpected occasion*' and written 'by the unexpected conduct of Gods urgent Providence' (*Right Method for a Settled Peace of Conscience*, 1653, prefatory epistle, sig. b2v, and *Paraphrase on the New Testament*, 1685, sig. A3; Keeble and Nuttall, 1.97, 2.267), and many were addressed to a pressing need; but Baxter was ready with his pen upon even slight occasion. He wrote with extraordinary facility and at great speed. Tillotson 'oft pressed him to let his books lie by him some time, & to review them again & again, but could never prevail with him, who said, they must come forth so, or not at all' (Keeble and Nuttall, 2.329). Baxter's wife was of a similar mind, believing he would have 'done better to have written fewer Books, and to have done those few better' (Baxter, *Breviate*, 9), and privately Baxter himself came to agree 'that fewer well studied and polished had been better'. Written 'in the crowd of my other Imployments, which would allow me no great Leisure for Polishing and Exactness, or any Ornament', they had no literary pretensions (*Reliquiae Baxterianae*, 1.124). Their business was pastoral: 'the Writings of Divines are nothing else but a preaching the Gospel to the eye, as the *voice* preacheth it to the ear' (Baxter, *Christian Directory*, 1.2.60). Nevertheless, though he published too much, and can be both prolix and repetitive, Baxter is a very considerable writer, remarkable for the unaffected directness of his style, the intimacy of his address to the reader, the interest of his autobiographical and anecdotal digressions, the range of his curiosity, his gift for effective imagery, and his frequently moving homiletic rhetoric.

Five works stand out from the mass of his publications: *The Saints Everlasting Rest* has a permanent place within the canon of devotional literature; readers continue to be inspired by the pastoral fervour of *The Reformed Pastor*; the *Call to the Unconverted* (1658) is a classic of puritan evangelism; the *Breviate* is one of the most affecting of seventeenth-century biographies, unique in its intimate record of a marital relationship; and, above all, the *Reliquiae*, which, despite the muddle of its organization, the inaccuracies of its text, and its omission of passages from Baxter's manuscript (much of which is still extant in Dr Williams's Library), is one of the outstanding achievements of early autobiographical writing and an indispensable historical source for the later seventeenth century. Although Sylvester's inadequacies as an editor have been frequently lamented, no one has yet undertaken a full scholarly edition of this work. It is known chiefly through the abridgement first published by J. M. Lloyd Thomas in

1925 which presents a coherent text but at the expense of the extraordinarily compendious character of the original, its comprehensive account of current affairs, its wide-ranging curiosity, and its vital engagement with contemporary controversies, political and ecclesiastical. It is both a greater and more idiosyncratic work than any abridgement could represent.

Both that curiosity and that disputatiousness are much in evidence in Baxter's correspondence. He was an indefatigable and voluminous letter-writer, as willing to answer the least query from a troubled parishioner as to argue a theological case with a university professor, or to respond to an unsolicited enquiry from a reader of one of his books as to approaches from peers and politicians. The 1200 or so extant letters exchanged with some 350 correspondents afford a richly varied insight not only into Baxter's own thinking and relationships, but also into the culture of the times as it was lived and experienced at every level (or, at least, every literate level) of society. The largest single group among Baxter's correspondents consists of some seventy men who became nonconformist ministers at the Restoration, but the interest of the letters is not confined to the history of nonconformity, ecclesiastical affairs, or theological controversy. Baxter was an acute enquirer into matters arcane and mundane, inveterately interested in both public affairs and individuals' experience, encyclopaedically industrious in establishing the grounds for the opinions which, for over half a century, he freely discussed in letters with persons of every walk of life, from peers, the gentry, and members of the professions, to merchants, apprentices, farmers, and seamen. The result is not merely a rich historical archive: the range of this correspondence, the vitality of its engagement with a great variety of topics, the immediacy of its expression, and the unpredictabilities of its mood and tone make this collection a record of felt experience unique among early epistolary archives.

Baxterianism Though he was very chary of prophetic radicalism, Baxter could respond to intimations of the divine as enthusiastically, even mystically, as any Quaker. He was equally sensitive to more disturbing supernatural phenomena, believing in witchcraft and in ghosts: one of his last works was a collection of evidences of *The Certainty of the Worlds of Spirits* (1691). Nevertheless, and despite his inveterate disputatiousness and a temperament which could be impatient, irritated, and severe, Baxter valued reasonableness, good sense, and moderation. Works such as *The Unreasonableness of Infidelity* (1655) and *The Reasons of the Christian Religion* (1667) demonstrate affinities with the Cambridge Platonists and set Baxter in the line of developing rationalism which was to lead to John Locke and the deists. In all the century's ecclesiological and doctrinal disputes, he sought a middle way. On church order, 'You could not (except a Catholick Christian) have trulier called me, than an *Episcopal-Presbyterian-Independent*' (Baxter, *Third Defence*, 'Answer to Hinckley', 110). In doctrine he followed Amyraldus (Moïse Amyraut) in developing a mean between Calvinism and Arminianism which maintained the decree of election but rejected predestined reprobation and a limited atonement. *Richard Baxter's Catholick Theologie* (1675) sought to reconcile the opposed doctrinal camps. Similarly, as a nonconformist Baxter refused to separate wholly from the established church and practised occasional conformity.

This repeated transgression of partisan boundaries makes Baxter a subtle and elusive figure; but it also testifies to an almost visionary consistency and simplicity (in the best sense) in his thought. He declined to accept any denominational label, always describing himself as a 'meer Christian' (a term later taken up by C. S. Lewis), 'catholick Christian', or 'mere Catholick':

> the Church that I am of is the Christian Church, and hath been visible wherever the Christian Religion and Church hath been visible: But must you know what Sect or Party I am of? I am against all Sects and dividing Parties: But if any will call *Meer Christians* by the name of a *Party* … I am of that Party which is so against Parties: If the Name of CHRISTIAN be not enough, call me a CATHOLICK CHRISTIAN. (Baxter, *Church-History*, 'What history is credible', sig. b1)

To his application for a licence under the 1672 indulgence he appended a statement of 'My Case' which began:

> My Religion is meerly Christian … The Church which I am a member of is the universality of Christians; in conjunction with all particular Churches of Christians in England or elsewhere in the world, whose communion according to my capacity I desire. (Keeble and Nuttall, 2.140)

When asked to define this 'mere Christianity' he referred to the creed, decalogue, and Lord's prayer, refusing further elaboration. To his mind, confessions of faith were invariably divisive because invariably troubling to some sincere consciences. In any case, words are never adequate to express the divine will and nature. With remarkable boldness, at the meetings in London in 1654–5 he had argued that 'no particular Words in the World are *Essentials* of our Religion' (*Reliquiae Baxterianae*, 2.198). Such liberalism was at once infuriating in its vagueness and intolerable in its laxity to more doctrinaire contemporaries, be they Independent or episcopalian.

Baxter might allow only that he adhered to the belief and practice of the primitive church, but within his own lifetime the emphases of his thought and ministry were recognized as constituting a distinctively Baxterian position. Baxter records having heard the adjective 'Baxterian' in 1680, but as early as 1653 it was used by John Crandon in the prefatory epistle of his *Mr. Baxters Aphorismes Exorcized* and in 1659 by the Fifth Monarchist John Rogers (J. Rogers, *A Christian Concertation with Mr. Prin*, 1659, 6). For Baxter's critics the term denoted confused thinking: 'Baxterianism … is a meer Gallimophery, Hodgpodg Divinity' ([S. Young], *Vindiciae anti-Baxterianae*, 1696, 111). By the end of the century, however, those sympathetic to Baxter's desire to moderate differences constituted a recognizable strand in dissent to which belonged, for example, Manton, Bates, Howe, and, in the next generation, Daniel Williams and Edmund Calamy. It was Calamy who, in his 1702 abridgement of the *Reliquiae* and its successive enlargements, transformed Baxter's autobiographical papers into a history of nonconformity and a comprehensive record of the lives of ejected ministers; and in his *Defence of Moderate Nonconformity* (1703–5) he passed the Baxterian tradition to the eighteenth century.

Baxter was especially admired by Philip Doddridge and by John Wesley and he continued to be revered by nineteenth-century dissent for his combination of commitment with catholicity, of zeal with reasonableness, qualities which commended him to Church of England clergy quite as strongly as to nonconformists. The list of those who have written admiringly of him crosses all shades of ecclesiastical and theological opinion: William Blaikie, John Brown, Coleridge, Alexander Gordon, Hensley Henson, William Magee, Geoffrey F. Nuttall, John Ryle, Arthur Stanley, John Stoughton, Richard Trench, John Tulloch. In its interdenominational character this list (which could easily be extended) is a fine and fitting testimony to the genius of Baxterianism.

Margaret Baxter [*née* Charlton] (*bap.* 1636, *d.* 1681), religious nonconformist and wife of Richard Baxter, was born in Apley Castle, near Wellington, Shropshire, the second daughter of Francis Charlton (*d.* 1642) and his wife, Mary (*d.* 1661). She was baptized in Wellington parish church on 18 September 1636. The Charltons were long established gentry, 'one of the Chief Families in the county' (Baxter, *Breviate*, 1). After her husband's death on 22 November 1642, Mary Charlton married Thomas Hanmer, to protect her family in time of war and to prevent the estate's heir, Margaret's younger brother Francis (1639–1698), from becoming the ward of his uncle Robert Charlton, the 'next heir', whom she distrusted (ibid., 2). Hanmer was a royalist and in March 1643 he agreed to a demand from the lord lieutenant of Shropshire, Arthur Capel, first Baron Capel, that Apley Castle should be fortified and garrisoned, but in 1644 it was won by parliamentarian forces, plundered, and Hanmer taken prisoner. The children, including Margaret, witnessed this engagement. It appears that Robert Charlton then took charge of the children, but that some time later Mary Hanmer, 'by great wisdom and diligence, surprised them' and conveyed them 'to one Mr. *Bernards* in *Essex*' (ibid.). She then managed the estate until the marriage in 1655 or 1656 of Francis to Dorothy, daughter of Oliver St John.

In 1655 or 1656 Mary Hanmer rented a house in Kidderminster and moved there in order, it appears, to be under Richard Baxter's ministry. Her son Francis Charlton believed that Baxter exerted an undue influence over his mother, turning her against him. Margaret Charlton stayed for a time in Oxford with her sister, Mary (*b.* 1631), wife of Ambrose Upton, canon of Christ Church, where a sermon by Henry Hickman 'much moved her' and induced 'serious thoughts on her present state, and her salvation' (Baxter, *Breviate*, 4). By early 1658 she had joined her mother in Kidderminster. The next year she endured a prolonged spiritual crisis and also a period of serious ill health. Passages she extracted from letters of counsel received from Baxter during this period, together with extracts from her own papers of self-analysis and meditation, which Baxter saw only after her death, were printed by him in the *Breviate*. Her recovery of good health she attributed to Baxter's prayers, and of faith to his ministerial care. On 10 April 1660 a service of thanksgiving was held for her. The preceding night she reaffirmed her covenant with God in a paper (ibid., 10–21) which in *Poetical Fragments* Baxter versified in a poem from which derives the hymn 'Lord, it belongs not to my care' (Baxter, *Poetical Fragments*, 81–3).

Two days later Baxter set out for London, and, probably in the summer, Margaret Charlton and her mother followed, taking rooms in Sweetings Alley (now Aldersgate Street), off Threadneedle Street, close to Baxter's accommodation with his friend Thomas Foley in Austin Friars. In January 1661 Mary Hanmer died. Baxter preached her funeral sermon at St Mary Magdalen, Milk Street, and, though no copy is known, apparently published it, since in 1682 it was 'reprinted at the desire of her Daughter, before her death' as *The Last Work of a Believer*. A relationship between Baxter and Margaret Charlton was rumoured in London in 1661. On 29 April 1662 a licence was granted for their marriage, which took place on 10 September at St Benet Fink, performed by Baxter's old friend Samuel Clarke. The difference in bride and groom's ages and social status occasioned much comment (she brought a dowry of £1650). For the remainder of her life Margaret Baxter was to sustain her husband with emotional, spiritual, and material support without which, it may fairly be conjectured, he could hardly have survived the adversities of the years ahead. To his deep affection for her, and indebtedness to her, he gives moving testimony in the *Breviate of the Life of Margaret Baxter* (1681).

From the *Breviate* it appears that Margaret Baxter, though a truly devout woman, remained prone to misgivings and doubts about her own sincerity. Her 'too timerous and tender a nature' and her vulnerability to 'a diseased fearfulness' her husband attributed in part to her childhood experience of the war (Baxter, *Breviate*, 9, 76). She was, nevertheless, of resolute character, full of initiative and resourcefulness, which, with her willingness to expend her estate on his behalf, enabled her repeatedly to secure London properties for her husband to preach in. She accompanied him to Clerkenwell prison in 1669 and 'was never so chearful a Companion' as then, having brought with her 'so many Necessaries, that we kept House as contentedly and comfortably as at home' (*Reliquiae Baxterianae*, 3.50–51). He 'never knew her equal' in practical divinity: she was, in her husband's view, '*better at resolving a case of conscience than most Divines that ever I knew in all my life*', so that he came 'to put all, save secret cases, to her' (Baxter, *Breviate*, 67, 68); it may be conjectured that in its directions and resolutions *A Christian Directory* preserves something of Margaret Baxter's advice.

John Corbet's wife, Frances, who had returned to live with the Baxters after the death of her husband in December 1680, was with Margaret Baxter when she died on 14 June 1681. Margaret was buried on 17 June in her mother's grave in the chancel of Christ Church Greyfriars. John Howe, her husband's friend since the 1650s, preached and published the funeral sermon. From her will of 10 February 1670 it appears that prior to her marriage Thomas

Foley, Richard Hampden, and John Swinfen had been appointed trustees of her estate; they were required after her death to disburse the (unspecified) remainder of her estate as she had signified to her husband.

N. H. KEEBLE

Sources R. Baxter, *Against the revolt to a foreign jurisdiction* (1691) · R. Baxter, *A breviate of the life of Margaret Baxter* (1681) · R. Baxter, *Catholick communion defended*, 2 vols. (1684) · R. Baxter, *Church-history of the government of bishops and their councils* (1680) · R. Baxter, *Poetical fragments* (1681) · *Reliquiae Baxterianae, or, Mr Richard Baxter's narrative of the most memorable passages of his life and times*, ed. M. Sylvester, 1 vol. in 3 pts (1696) · R. Baxter, *Richard Baxter's dying thoughts* (1683) · R. Baxter, *Richard Baxter's penitent confession* (1691) · R. Baxter, *The saints everlasting rest* (1650) · R. Baxter, *A third defence of the cause of peace* (1681) · R. Baxter, *A treatise of knowledge and love compared* (1689) · R. Baxter, *A Christian directory* (1673) · I. Walton, *The lives of John Donne, Sir Henry Wotton, Richard Hooker, George Herbert, and Robert Sanderson*, [new edn] (1927); repr. (1966) · R. Baxter, *Directions for weak distempered Christians* (1669) · *Calendar of the correspondence of Richard Baxter*, ed. N. H. Keeble and G. F. Nuttall, 2 vols. (1991) · *A subject index to the Calendar of the correspondence of Richard Baxter: with another Baxter letter*, ed. N. H. Keeble (1994) · A. G. Matthews, *The works of Richard Baxter: an annotated list* (1932) · R. Thomas, *The Baxter treatises: a catalogue of the Richard Baxter papers (other than the letters) in Dr. Williams's Library* (1959) · G. L. Turner, ed., *Original records of early nonconformity under persecution and indulgence*, 3 vols. (1911–14) · *The autobiography of Richard Baxter*, ed. N. H. Keeble and J. M. Lloyd Thomas, [new edn] (1974) · *A holy commonwealth*, ed. W. Lamont (1994) · W. Orme, ed., *The practical works of Richard Baxter, with a life of the author*, 23 vols. (1830) · R. B. Schlatter, ed., *Richard Baxter and puritan politics* (New Brunswick, 1957) · J. T. Wilkinson, ed., *Richard Baxter and Margaret Charlton: a puritan love story. Being the breviate of the life of Margaret Baxter* (1928) · C. G. Bolam and others, *The English presbyterians: from Elizabethan puritanism to modern Unitarianism* (1968) · R. S. Bosher, *The making of the Restoration settlement: the influence of the Laudians, 1649–1662*, rev. edn (1957) · W. M. Lamont, *Richard Baxter and the millennium: protestant imperialism and the English revolution* (1979) · N. H. Keeble, *Richard Baxter: Puritan man of letters* (1982) · N. H. Keeble, *The literary culture of nonconformity in later seventeenth-century England* (1987) · *Calamy rev.* · G. F. Nuttall, *Richard Baxter* (1965) · G. F. Nuttall and O. Chadwick, eds., *From uniformity to unity* (1962) · G. F. Nuttall and others, *The beginnings of nonconformity* (1964) · F. J. Powicke, *A life of the Reverend Richard Baxter, 1615–1691* (1924) · F. J. Powicke, *The Reverend Richard Baxter under the cross, 1662–1691* (1927) · N. H. Keeble, 'Richard Baxter's preaching ministry: its history and texts', *Journal of Ecclesiastical History*, 35 (1984), 539–59 · G. F. Nuttall, 'The MS of *Reliquiae Baxterianae* (1696)', *Journal of Ecclesiastical History*, 6 (1955), 72–9 · A. A. Rollason, 'Extract from the will of Richard Baxter referring to Sylvester and Morrice', *Transactions of the Congregational Historical Society*, 5 (1911–12), 370–71 · 'A transcript of Richard Baxter's library catalogue', ed. G. F. Nuttall, *Journal of Ecclesiastical History*, 2 (1951), 207–21; 3 (1952), 74–100 · G. F. Nuttall, 'The Worcestershire Association: its membership', *Journal of Ecclesiastical History*, 1 (1950), 197–206 · G. F. Nuttall, 'Richard Baxter's correspondence: a preliminary survey', *Journal of Ecclesiastical History*, 1 (1950), 85–95 · will of Richard Baxter, PRO, PROB 11/407, fols. 121r–123v (sig. 205) · parish register, Wellington parish church, Shropshire [Margaret Baxter], 18 Sept 1636 [baptism]

Archives BL, autobiography and papers, Egerton MS 2570 · DWL, corresp. and papers | Bedford estate office, London, Woburn Abbey MSS · BL, Add. MSS 4229, 3209; Harley MS 6621; Portland Loan 29/73/2 (Harley papers) · LPL, Fairhurst MSS; Ginson MSS · RS, Boyle letters

Likenesses miniature, 1670 (after R. White), NPG · oils, 1670 (after R. White), NPG · T. Trotter, line engraving, 1783 (after J. Riley, BM, NPG; repro. in J. Middleton, *Biographica Evangelica* (1779–86) · attrib. J. Riley, oils, DWL [*see illus.*] · R. White, line engraving, BM, NPG; repro. in R. Baxter, *Life of faith* (1670)

Baxter, Robert Dudley (1827–1875), political writer and statistician, was born on 3 February 1827 at Doncaster, the son of Robert Baxter, of Stoke Golding, Leicestershire, and of the firm of Baxter & Co., parliamentary lawyers, of Westminster. He was a collateral descendant of Richard Baxter, the seventeenth-century presbyterian divine, and of Sir Dudley Ryder, lord chief justice of England and ancestor of the earls of Harrowby. His mother was Joanna Maria Nona, youngest daughter of Thomas Paget, of Comberford Hall, near Tamworth, Staffordshire, and aunt of Henry Alford, dean of Canterbury. Baxter was educated privately, and entered Trinity College, Cambridge, in 1845, graduating in 1849 in mathematics and classics. He also had a great love of literature. He then studied for the legal profession. On 15 July 1856 he married Mary, youngest daughter of Robert Taylor, of Broomland and Dumfriesshire; they had four children, of whom two survived. He entered his father's firm in 1860. Partners in the firm, Philip Rose and Markham Spofforth, acted as central agents for the Conservative Party, and Rose as Disraeli's personal lawyer, confidant, and executor. Baxter became assistant to Spofforth in this work.

A Conservative from his earliest years, Baxter wrote pamphlets on political, economic, and statistical issues, for example on the volunteer movement and on the budget and income tax, both published in 1860. He became particularly influential when franchise reform was debated in parliament in 1866 and 1867. His statistical competence and intimate knowledge of the electoral system and registration laws gave him authority across party divisions. In March 1866 he published a pamphlet on the Liberal Reform Bill, which showed that the proportion of working-class electors in boroughs would be much higher than Gladstone had claimed in presenting the bill, and that there would be a majority of working-class voters in the electorate as a whole. This pamphlet made a strong impression, not only in the Conservative Party but among the Adullamite dissidents in the Liberal Party. Sir Edward Bulwer-Lytton made a direct reference to it in the Commons in April 1866. Another of Baxter's pamphlets, on the Liberal Redistribution Bill, showed that under its proposals there would be a further aggravation of the bias of the electoral system against the rural and in favour of the urban voter. In a letter to *The Times*, published on 18 June 1866, he argued that a rating qualification was a safer basis for the franchise than one based on rental. On that day the Russell government was defeated on an amendment, moved by an Adullamite, substituting rating for the rental qualification in the bill.

In addition to his public statements Baxter furnished the Conservative leaders with private memoranda. These assumed great importance in 1867 when the divided Conservative cabinet put forward its own reform proposals. He supplied Disraeli with essential information and worked, often under great pressure, on the various proposals under discussion. Some of the figures given by him on the extent of working-class enfranchisement were so alarming that they had to be kept from the dissident members of the cabinet, Cranborne, Carnarvon, and Peel.

Baxter's preferred solution would have been a £5 rating franchise in the boroughs, with the compounding provisions—under which many householders included their rates with the payment of rent to their landlords—lowered to that point. He fully accepted the final outcome of household suffrage in the boroughs.

In an analysis of the 1868 general election Baxter showed that, in spite of their numerical inferiority in the Commons, the Conservatives represented a larger number of voters than the Liberals and that the future of the party was therefore, contrary to widely held views, fully assured. In 1868 he had worked hard to secure the election of Lord George Hamilton for Middlesex, a victory which showed the growing strength of Conservatism in middle-class suburban areas. In the early 1870s he influenced the debate on local taxation, when there was strong support among Conservatives for a reduction of the rates. He argued that the burden on real property was higher than often claimed and that a report on the subject, prepared by Goschen for the Liberal government, was misleading. He also wrote on the effects of railway extension and on the national debt. In 1873 he declined an invitation to stand with W. H. Smith at Westminster. His health, never robust, deteriorated and he died at Oakhill, Hampstead, London, on 20 May 1875.   E. J. FEUCHTWANGER

Sources M. Baxter, *In memoriam R. Dudley Baxter* (privately printed, 1878) · H. J. Hanham, *Elections and party management: politics in the time of Disraeli and Gladstone* (1959) · R. Blake, *Disraeli* (1966) · E. J. Feuchtwanger, *Disraeli, democracy and the tory party: conservative leadership and organization after the second Reform Bill* (1968) · DNB · Venn, *Alum. Cant.* · Boase, *Mod. Eng. biog.*

Archives Bodl. Oxf., Hughenden MSS, letters | Bodl. Oxf., papers and corresp. with Benjamin Disraeli

Wealth at death under £6000: probate, 29 June 1875, CGPLA Eng. & Wales

Baxter, Roger (1784?–1827), missionary, was a native of Walton-le-Dale, near Preston, in Lancashire. He finished his studies at Stonyhurst College, and entered the Society of Jesus in 1810. He published a history of the reformation in England, in 1814, and several controversial tracts, including the often reprinted *The most Important Tenets of Roman Catholicism* (1819). He went to the University of George Town, Columbia, where he became professor of rhetoric. After rendering great services to the missions of Maryland and Pennsylvania, he returned sick to England in 1826, and led a controversial mission to Enfield. He then went back to Philadelphia, but died there on 24 May 1827.

THOMPSON COOPER, *rev.* H. C. G. MATTHEW

Sources Gillow, *Lit. biog. hist.* · G. Oliver, *Collections towards illustrating the biographies of the Scotch, English and Irish members of the Society of Jesus*, 2nd edn (1845) · A. de Backer, *Bibliothèque des écrivains de la Compagnie de Jésus*, 7 vols. (1853)

Baxter, Thomas (*fl.* 1732), schoolteacher, is known only for his booklet *The Circle Squared* (1732), published when he was master of a private school at Crathorne, in the North Riding of Yorkshire. By worked examples he sought to relate the diameter and circumference of the circle, also of the cone and ellipse. The book was dismissed by Augustus De Morgan as an absurdity.

F. Y. EDGEWORTH, *rev.* ANITA MCCONNELL

Sources A. De Morgan, *A budget of paradoxes* (1872), 87

Baxter, Thomas (1782–1821), china painter, was born in Worcester on 18 February 1782. His father had workshops at 1 Goldsmith Street, Gough Square, Fleet Street, London, connected with Worcester, for painting and gilding china; Baxter received his first instruction from him. He also painted on enamel, and his usual subjects were shells. He was a fellow student of B. R. Haydon at the Royal Academy Schools, which he entered on 23 October 1800 at the age of nineteen (Hutchison, 159). He exhibited studies of fruit and flowers in the Royal Academy exhibitions from 1802 to 1821, and stood, unsuccessfully, as a candidate for election as an associate of the Royal Academy in 1811. He was patronized by Lord Nelson, and was often employed by him in making sketches at Merton, Surrey. He also painted for him a rich dessert service. In his paintings upon plaques of porcelain he introduced figures from the works of Sir Joshua Reynolds, Benjamin West, and other well-known painters.

In 1810 he published *An Illustration of the Egyptian, Grecian and Roman Costume*. In 1814 he left Worcester and established an art school in London, and had pupils who were afterwards distinguished in their special line. In 1816 he connected himself with Dillwyn's factory at Swansea, and was there three years. His great work at that place, which from the description of it must have been remarkable rather for ingenuity than for good taste, was a 'Shakespeare cup'. In 1819 he returned to Worcester, and was again employed at Messrs Flight and Barrs, and afterwards at Messrs Chamberlain's factory. In addition to studies of fruit, Baxter also painted portraits (of which one, a watercolour attributed to Baxter of the actor J. P. Kemble in the role of Coriolanus, is mentioned by Walker in *Regency Portraits*, 1.293), made some drawings for John Britton's *The history and antiquities of the cathedral church of Salisbury* (1814), and contributed a plate to S. Curtis, *Beauties of Flora* (1806–20). He made two 'very clever' copies of the 'Portland vase', and occasionally produced engravings. Baxter died in London on 18 April 1821. Examples of his work are in the British Museum and the Victoria and Albert Museum, London, and the Worcester Art Gallery.

ERNEST RADFORD, rev. ANNETTE PEACH

Sources R. W. Binns, *A century of potting in the city of Worcester*, 2nd edn (1877) • Desmond, *Botanists* • Mallalieu, *Watercolour artists* • S. C. Hutchison, 'The Royal Academy Schools, 1768–1830', *Walpole Society*, 38 (1960–62), 123–91, esp. 159 • R. Walker, *National Portrait Gallery: Regency portraits*, 1 (1985), 293 • Farington, *Diary*, 9.4025

Baxter, William (1650–1723), classicist and antiquary, was born in 1650 in Llanllugan in Montgomeryshire, the eldest son of John Baxter (d. 1681) and Catherine, *née* Bolliver. Richard *Baxter, the divine, was the cousin of William's father, and upon Richard's death in 1691 William became his heir, inheriting property in Eaton Constantine, Shropshire.

Little is known about Baxter's parents, but he benefited as a youth from the assistance and guidance of Richard Baxter and his wife, Margaret. He received little formal education before he entered Harrow School at age eighteen, where he studied for some five years, choosing not to proceed to Oxford or Cambridge. Instead he became, in 1673, a private tutor at Brampton, near Huntingdon. From 1676 to 1679 he was schoolmaster in Hitchin, during which time he published a Latin grammar, *De analogia* (1679). Returning to London, Baxter studied as a physician; he also provided nine translations from Plutarch's *Moralia* for the edition that appeared between 1684 and 1690, and contributed to a translation of Diogenes Laertius in 1688.

As a young man, Baxter was politically active, and published in 1684 *Anti-Dodwellisme*, a translation of Hugo Grotius's *Dissertatio de coenae*. *The Observator* singled him out in 1682 and 1683 as a coffee-house wit of whiggish sympathies. Baxter eventually abandoned nonconformity, although some thought his later orthodoxy suspect.

In 1689 Baxter became schoolmaster at Stoke Newington; in this same year, on 16 July, he married Sarah Carturit (or Cartwright) of Hillingdon in Middlesex, a decision he later characterized as ill-judged. A son was born in 1689; an infant daughter died in 1694, but three more children followed between 1695 and 1701. In 1694 he taught at Tottenham High Cross, and in 1710 became headmaster of the Mercers' School in London, where he remained until 1721.

In 1695 Baxter published an annotated edition of Anacreon which was followed, in 1701, by one of Horace. A second edition of his Anacreon, published in 1710, achieved greater notice, and two later editions. A revised edition of his Horace published posthumously in 1725 was lauded throughout the eighteenth century.

Baxter contributed three letters on antiquarian subjects to *Philosophical Transactions*, and another to the first issue of *Archaeologia*; however, he was best known for his *Glossarium antiquitatum Britannicarum*. Although he had begun the *Glossarium* as early as 1702, an ailing Baxter required the aid of Moses Williams to see it through the press in 1719. It was greeted with some hostility: Thomas Hearne, for one, opined that Baxter built 'wholly upon Fancy, without Authority' (*Remarks*, 7.37). A second edition was published, with some additions of material from William Stukeley and Edward Lhuyd, in 1733.

At his death Baxter left an unfinished Welsh dictionary, and notes on Juvenal, Persius, and Ovid; Moses Williams published a proposal for the Juvenal in 1732. In 1726 was published, again under the editorship of Williams, *Reliquiae Baxterianae*, which contained his unfinished 'Glossary of Roman antiquities' (which runs through the letter A only), his 'Autoris vitae fragmentum', and four letters: praised for its 'grammatical and philological erudition' (*New Memoirs of Literature*, 54), it was reissued in 1731 as *Glossarium antiquitatum Romanarum*.

Baxter's etymological speculations were sometimes derided; even Lhuyd, a friend and admirer, feared that he was 'too apt to indulge fancy' (Gunther, 14.476), while William Nicolson wrote that Baxter's etymologies often seemed 'too Bold' (Nicolson, 8). Hearne thought Baxter himself a 'learned, but whimsical, Man', and tells us that the earl of Oxford looked upon him 'as a Mad Man' (*Remarks*, 8.88; 7.62); another contemporary noted that 'To talk as well as live in a manner peculiar to himself, was a privilege Will Baxter always claimed' (Nichols, *Lit. anecdotes*, 1.360). He was prone to academic disputes, and fell out with Richard Bentley over the latter's Horace. He similarly quarrelled with Joshua Barnes, a rival editor of the Anacreontea.

William Baxter died in some penury at Hillingdon, where he had been living since about 1721, following an extended period of ill health, on 31 May 1723, and was buried there on 4 June.   MARK MCDAYTER

Sources *Reliquiae Baxterianae, sive, Willielmi Baxteri opera posthuma*, ed. [M. Williams] (1726) · A. Percival, *Transactions of the Honourable Society of Cymmrodorion* (1957), 58–86 · P. Bayle and others, *A general dictionary, historical and critical*, 3 (1735) · J. Nichols, *Biographical and literary anecdotes of William Bowyer, printer, FSA, and of many of his learned friends* (privately printed, London, 1782) · *Remarks and collections of Thomas Hearne*, ed. C. E. Doble and others, 11 vols., OHS, 2, 7, 13, 34, 42–3, 48, 50, 65, 67, 72 (1885–1921) · W. Nicolson, *The Irish historical library* (1724) · *The family memoirs of the Rev. William Stukeley*, ed. W. C. Lukis, 3 vols., SurtS, 73, 76, 80 (1882–7) · R. T. Gunther, *Early science in Oxford*, 14: *Life and letters of Edward Lhwyd* (1945) · *New Memoirs of Literature*, 4 (July 1726), 54–7 · A. Kippis and others, eds., *Biographia Britannica, or, The lives of the most eminent persons who have flourished in Great Britain and Ireland*, 2nd edn, 5 vols. (1778–93) · Nichols, *Lit. anecdotes*, vol. 1 · J. T. Wilkinson, *Richard Baxter and Margaret Charlton: a puritan love story* (1928)
Archives BL, Sloane MS 3986 · Bodl. Oxf., letters to Edward Lhuyd
Likenesses W. Stukeley, two watercolour sketches, 1723, Bodl. Oxf., MS Eng. e. 136, fols. 22 and 23 · W. Stukeley, watercolour sketch, 1726, BL, Add. MS 35057, fol. 20 · G. Vertue, line engraving (after Highmore, *c*.1719), BM, NPG; repro. in W. Baxter, *Glossarium antiquitatum Britannicarum* (1719)
Wealth at death seemingly quite poor; pension from Mercers' School; had just received money from Lord Winchilsea: *Family memoirs of William Stukeley*, ed. Lukis; Percival, 'William Baxter'

Baxter, William (1787–1871), botanist, was born at Rugby on 15 January 1787. Nothing is known of his parents or early life, except that his mother was said to have been born in Hill Morton near Rugby. In 1813 he was appointed curator of the Oxford Physic Garden. At the time of his appointment botany in Oxford had, it is widely reported, sunk to a low level and the then professor, George Williams (1762–1834), was generally more highly regarded as a scholar than for his practical contributions to botanic science or to the teaching of undergraduates—a responsibility that was passed down to Baxter along with the practical management of the garden. During Williams's time Baxter made many improvements to the garden, not least of which was the raising of its whole level by 10 inches so that it was no longer subject to regular flooding. However, it was after Williams's death in 1834 and the appointment of Charles Daubeny (1795–1867) to the professorship that most progress was made, with the garden being completely rearranged according to a new scheme.

Not unexpectedly perhaps, given the state in which he first encountered the garden, Baxter's chief interest was in cryptogamic botany, and in 1825 and 1828 he issued his 'Stirpes cryptogamae Oxonienses' which consisted of some 160 dried specimens of ferns, mosses, lichens, and microscopical leaf fungi found in the neighbourhood of Oxford. His efforts were not restricted to these plants,

however. He undertook much fieldwork in and around Oxford, recording the discovery of many new plants in the area, and in 1831 he visited Rugby with his son for the same purposes. As well as contributing to regional natural histories by other authors with whom he was in correspondence—*Midland Flora* by Thomas Purton (1768–1833) and *Flora of Oxfordshire* by Richard Walker (1791–1870) among them—Baxter published his own work under the title *Phaenogamous Botany, or, Figures and Descriptions of the Genera of British Flowering Plants*, in six volumes between 1834 and 1843. It was a handsome work, containing over 500 hand-coloured plates and including many verses.

Baxter was made an associate of the Linnean Society of London on 6 May 1825 and was a member of the Botanical Society of London. He was also a chief mover in the founding of the Oxford Botanical and Natural History Society, which was formerly established under the presidency of Daubeny on 31 August 1831 with Baxter as its secretary. No record remains of Baxter's marriage, but in 1851 when he retired from active management of the botanic garden a son, William Hart Baxter (1816?–1890), who had previously held the position of curator of the botanic gardens in Bath, took over. For the remainder of his life, Baxter did little which brought him into public notice and at the time of his death, at his home, 7 Longwall Street, Oxford, on 1 November 1871, he was almost unknown to contemporaneous horticulturists. He was, however, despite reportedly being susceptible to periodic attacks of mental depression, remembered as a man for his 'amiable disposition, his great knowledge, his extraordinary memory, and his willingness to oblige' (*Gardeners' Chronicle*), not to mention the extensive botanical library which he left and which during his lifetime was regarded as the most complete of any British gardener.   GILES HUDSON

Sources G. C. Druce, 'William Baxter', *Ashmolean Natural History Society of Oxfordshire report for 1903* (1904), 22–5 · *Journal of Botany, British and Foreign*, 9 (1871), 380–1 · J. A. Schultes, 'Schultes's botanical visit to England', *Botanical Miscellany*, 1 (1830), 58–9 · *Gardener's Magazine*, 14 (1838), 110–13 · H. M. Clokie, *An account of the herbaria of the department of botany in the University of Oxford* (1964), lx–lxi · *Journal of Horticulture, Cottage Gardener and Country Gentleman*, 21 (1871), 362 · *Gardeners' Chronicle* (4 Nov 1871), 1426–7 · D. A. Cadbury, *Computer-mapped flora of Warwickshire* (1971), 54–5 · *Scottish Naturalist*, 98 (1986), 90–91 · Desmond, *Botanists*, rev. edn, 56 · G. C. Druce, 'William Baxter, curator of the Oxford Botanic Gardens and his correspondence', *Gardeners' Chronicle*, 3rd ser., 75 (1924), 106, 120–21 · CGPLA Eng. & Wales (1871)
Archives Bodl. Oxf., notes on customs and superstitions · U. Cam., department of plant sciences, flora aquatica Oxoniensis · U. Oxf., department of plant sciences, herbarium and papers · U. Oxf., Taylor Institution, copy of J. Ray's synopsis
Likenesses Whessell, engraving (after A. Burt), RBG Kew, Hope collection · portrait, Carnegie Mellon University, Pennsylvania, Hunt Botanical Library
Wealth at death under £200: administration with will, 27 Dec 1871, CGPLA Eng. & Wales

Baxter, William Alexander (1877–1973), food manufacturer, was born on 25 September 1877 at George Lane, Fochabers, Moray, the eldest son of George Baxter (*d.* 1925), master grocer, and his wife, Margaret Duncan. He

William Alexander Baxter (1877–1973), by unknown photographer

made his reputation by supplying relatively simple foods of high quality to a wide clientele, including the royal household.

Baxter's formal education at Alexander Milne's Free School, Fochabers, ended at the age of thirteen, when he joined his father in the family's Spey Street grocery business in Fochabers. His training in business had begun much earlier, however: when he was six his father wrapped him in the shop foreman's apron and set him to work weighing tea and sugar. Later, when he graduated to collecting orders after school on Friday afternoons, George Baxter greeted his son's return with the same question, 'Well, did ye get any *new* customers today?'. This paternal dictum guided his business life.

The Spey Street shop was already established as a supplier of groceries to local great houses, in large part because Baxter's father had been a gardener to the duke of Richmond and Gordon at nearby Gordon Castle before setting up shop in 1868. The duke encouraged the venture by lending his custom, and the local gentry soon followed. George Baxter supplied Gordon Castle with continental wines, cheeses, and other delicacies. He visited Speyside distilleries to select fine malt whiskies for the ducal table, and also blended them under the trade name of Baxter's Pure Malt Scotch Whisky. Baxter's mother, Margaret, also employed a small staff to produce preserves made from local soft fruits taken as part payment for groceries from village women. These preserves sold well, and were appreciated by Gordon Castle visitors, who sent orders from London. The duke provided the Baxters with a recipe for marmalade used at the castle since 1837, which they marketed as Castle Marmalade.

Baxter, who was often known as WAB, was the family's travelling salesman, whose sales technique was enhanced by a genial disposition and a flair for marketing. With his sample-laden bicycle he would board the train for Wick, and cycle back to Fochabers, taking orders on the way.

There were also, later, buying trips to London and Europe. When Baxter fell ill in 1914, he was nursed back to health at the family home, Highfield House, by a nursing sister, Ethelreda (Ethel) Adam [**Ethelreda Baxter** (1883–1963)], the daughter of Andrew Adam, a farm manager. She and William Baxter were married at Aberdeen on 11 November 1914; they had two sons.

Ethel Baxter subsequently took charge of the firm's preserve making, but her strong, independent views resulted in the newly married couple's embarking on a bold venture as preserve manufacturers in their own right, leaving the grocery business to William's younger brother, George. Family tradition records that Baxter met the duke of Richmond and Gordon one Sunday morning after church, and together they paced out Baxters' original half-acre site by the River Spey.

William and Ethel Baxter were partners in every sense of the word. Ethel ran the factory, bought the fruit, hired local labour, supervised production, and experimented with new recipes. William's forte was in securing new customers—for example, Harrods in 1919. Fortnum and Mason's formidable buyer, Mr Reilly, failed to understand Baxter's Scottish accent, but bought his products on taste alone. The comptroller of the royal household bought several cases of Ethel's Little Scarlet Strawberry Jam, thus beginning the firm's long association with the royal household.

In the 1920s and 1930s, the Baxters identified market opportunities for the abundant local produce surrounding them in the rich Laich of Moray. Their product range extended into meat processing. Moray chickens weighing precisely 2¼ lb were used for one of their new products—jars of whole chicken in natural jelly. Royal Game Soup—probably Baxters' best-known product—came into being when Baxter recognized that venison, then unpopular, could be utilized in soup making. Ethel mixed venison with pheasant, game, and seasoning, and canned soup became part of their range. Many other entrepreneurial examples followed. Expansion provided greater factory employment opportunities in the Fochabers area. In 1916 Ethel Baxter and a small group of women began full-time jam manufacture. In the 1930s employment increased gradually. Restrictions during the Second World War reduced staff and production to the minimum, but by the 1950s a steady payroll of 120 was achieved, rising to 500 during the fresh fruit season. By 1960 staffing levels rose to 300 and 900 respectively.

In 1945 the Baxter family formed a private limited company, W. A. Baxter & Sons Ltd, with £4000 capital in £1 shares. By 1956 share capital had increased to £26,000. William and Ethel's two sons, Gordon and Ian, and their wives, joined the firm; the business expanded overseas, opening offices in Chicago and Brussels. Ethel Baxter died at Dr Gray's Hospital, Elgin, on 15 August 1963. Her public role was largely taken on by Gordon Baxter's wife, Ena Baxter, whose kitchen and gourmet canned soups, their tins girdled with Gordon tartan, became the premier product of the firm. Shortly before his own death in 1973,

William Baxter proudly claimed in his memoirs 'there has been a Mrs Baxter right at the heart of our family business for the last 105 years' (Baxter, 2).

Baxter lived at Highfield House, Fochabers, from 1904 until shortly before his death. He died at Dr Gray's Hospital, Elgin, aged ninety-six, on 15 October 1973. As president of W. A. Baxter & Sons Ltd, he saw Baxters' share capital expand from £70,000 in 1967 to £500,000 in 1970. During his lifetime all shares were held in family hands and at the time of his death he himself held only 1400 ordinary shares. He was buried beside his wife in Bellie kirkyard, Fochabers, after a funeral service in the Gordon Chapel of the Scottish Episcopal Church, Fochabers, where he had been a long-standing lay elector and benefactor.

BRENDA M. WHITE

Sources W. A. Baxter, 'The Baxter story', *Speyside Courier* [Baxter & Sons magazine] (1973–4) · private information (2004) · W. A. Baxter & Sons Ltd, Fochabers · *Banffshire Herald* (20 Oct 1973) · *Elgin Courant* (27 Oct 1925) · *Glasgow Herald* (17 Oct 1973) · *Northern Scot* (20 Oct 1973) · *Northern Scot* (27 Oct 1973) · *The Scotsman* (17 Oct 1973) · 'A visit to a modern factory', *Elgin Courant and Courier* (10 Aug 1934), 1 · J. Watson, *Morayshire described* (1983), 308 · Inventory of W. A. Baxter, Elgin Sheriff Court, 160215ODG, SC 26 · Testamentary disposition and settlement of W. A. Baxter, Elgin Sheriff Court, SC 26 · company registration file, W. A. Baxter & Sons Ltd, no. 23572 · b. cert. · m. cert. · d. cert. · d. cert. [Ethelreda Baxter]
Archives priv. coll.
Likenesses photograph, Mitchell L., Glas. [*see illus.*] · photographs, priv. coll.
Wealth at death £13,334.22: confirmation, 1 Feb 1974, CCI

Baxter, William Edward (1825–1890), politician and author, born on 24 June 1825 at Dundee, was the eldest son of Edward Baxter, a Dundee merchant, of Kincaldrum in Forfarshire, and his first wife, Euphemia, daughter of William Wilson, a wool merchant of Dundee. Sir David *Baxter was his uncle. He was educated at Dundee high school and at Edinburgh University. On leaving the university he entered his father's counting-house, and some years afterwards became partner in the firm of Edward Baxter & Co. In 1870 that firm was dissolved, and he became senior partner in the new firm of W. E. Baxter & Co. In November 1847 he married Janet, eldest daughter of J. Home Scott, a solicitor of Dundee; with her he had a family of two sons and five daughters. He found time for much foreign travel and interested himself in politics. He published many lectures and several travel books, notably *Impressions of Central and Southern Europe* (1850), *The Tagus and the Tiber* (2 vols., 1852), and *America and the Americans* (1855); he also published *Hints to Thinkers* (1860).

In March 1855 Baxter was returned to parliament for the Montrose burghs as a Liberal, in succession to Joseph Hume, holding the seat until 1885. After refusing office several times he became secretary to the Admiralty in December 1868, in Gladstone's first administration, and distinguished himself by his reforms and retrenchments. In 1871 he resigned this office, on becoming joint secretary of the Treasury, a post which he resigned in August 1873 because of differences between him and the chancellor of the exchequer, Robert Lowe. He was sworn of the privy council on 24 March 1873. Baxter continued to carry on business as a foreign merchant in Dundee until his death. He died on 10 August 1890 at Kincaldrum, Forfarshire.

E. I. CARLYLE, rev. H. C. G. MATTHEW

Sources Boase, *Mod. Eng. biog.* · 'Our portrait gallery, second series no. 35', *Dublin University Magazine*, 88 (1876), 652–64 · *Dundee Advertiser* (11 Aug 1890) · Burke, *Gen. GB*
Archives NL Scot., travel journals | BL, corresp. with W. E. Gladstone, Add. MSS 44411–44787, *passim* · W. Sussex RO, corresp. with Richard Cobden and John Morley
Likenesses Lock and Whitfield, photograph, repro. in *Dublin University Magazine*, 653 · Spy [L. Ward], lithograph, repro. in *VF* (25 April 1885), 462 · portrait, repro. in *ILN* (23 Aug 1890) · portrait, repro. in *ILN* (6 Dec 1890)
Wealth at death £128,903 11s. 5d.: confirmation, 18 Nov 1890, CCI

Baxter, William Giles (1856–1888). *See under* Ally Sloper group (*act.* 1867–1923).

Bayard, Nicholas. *See* Byard, Nicholas de (*fl. c.*1300).

Bayes, Gilbert (1872–1953), sculptor, was born on 4 April 1872 at 6 Oval Road, Gloucester Road, St John's Wood, London, the third of four children of Alfred Walter Bayes (1832–1909), a painter and etcher, and his wife, Emily Ann (*née* Fielden; *fl. c.*1840–*c.*1910). He was the brother of the painters Walter Bayes (1869–1956) and Jessie Bayes (1878–1970). He studied at Finsbury Technical College (1891–6) and at the Royal Academy Schools (1896–9). In 1899 he won the Royal Academy gold medal and travelling scholarship. Most of his overseas study was spent in Paris, where his bronze relief *Jason Ploughing the Acre of Mars* (1900; Robert McDougall Art Gallery, Christchurch, New Zealand) won an honourable mention at the Universal Exposition (1900). In 1906 he married the artist Gertrude Smith (*c.*1875–1952); they had two children.

Bayes's early works are mainly reliefs and statuettes, often equestrian, inspired by classical, medieval, and Nordic mythology (for example, the bronze *Sigurd*, 1910; Tate collection). From the outset, he showed remarkable versatility, designing such objects as chessmen, caskets, cabinets, mirrors, medals, statuettes, trophies, and portrait busts. Before 1914 his work formed part of the New Sculpture movement, and reflected the influence of George Frampton and Alfred Gilbert. Like Frampton, Bayes experimented with the decorative and expressive potential of colour, and frequently applied mosaics, enamels, and glazes to his sculpture. In the earliest major article on Bayes (1902), Walter Shaw Sparrow admired his 'artistic gaiety and lightness of touch', adding that his work 'is certainly never dull, it never bores you' (Sparrow, 11–12).

In both his versatility and his careful craftsmanship, Bayes upheld the ideals of the arts and crafts movement and he also had a strong social conscience, without adopting socialism like many of its proponents. In 1945 he declared, 'It is up to the artist to serve the community and deserve well of it, not to make feeble things that won't function' (Irvine and Atterbury, 18). At the same time, he deplored the increasing divergence between the crafts and fine arts. He was elected a member of the Art Workers' Guild in 1896 and master in 1925. His performances at the guild's theatrical masques and revels won widespread praise.

Bayes began to enjoy national prominence as a sculptor with his First World War memorials. These revealed a tendency towards elegantly stylized, geometrical art deco forms (for example, Hythe war memorial, Kent, 1921), which developed further in the reliefs for the Pavilion of Concrete Utilities Bureau at the 1924 British Empire Exhibition, Wembley (Portmeirion, Wales). His success in the art deco style was reflected in the gold medal he received at the 1925 Exposition International des Arts Décoratifs et Industriels Modernes, Paris. The simplified, archaic qualities of his distinctive, double-sided reliefs (for example, *The Lure of the Pipes of Pan*, 1932; artificial stone, Birmingham Museum and Art Gallery) have affinities with works by his younger contemporaries, such as Ivan Meštrović and Paul Manship. Like them, Bayes never rejected his academic training and his work continued to make historical references, evident in the early Renaissance flavour of the Royal Doulton stoneware panel *Madonna and Child* (1924). His two large outdoor equestrian bronzes, *Offerings of War* and *Offerings of Peace* (1918–26; Art Gallery of New South Wales, Sydney), owe much to the French nineteenth-century sculptor Emmanuel Fremiet.

During the inter-war years Bayes eagerly experimented with modern materials. These included Doulton's polychrome stoneware, which was used for many garden sculptures. The most important and ambitious work in this medium was *History of Pottery through the Ages* (1939), the frieze for Doulton House, Lambeth Embankment, London, subsequently acquired by the Victoria and Albert Museum when the building was demolished. Bayes also used 'artificial stone' or pre-cast concrete, in the large-scale relief *History of Drama through the Ages* for the Saville Theatre (now MGM cinema), Shaftesbury Avenue, London (1930). His architectural collaboration with T. P. Bennett in this work and, elsewhere, with John James Burnet and Thomas Tait, maintained an important aspect of the New Sculpture movement, adapting it to updated stylistic demands.

Probably Bayes's best-known landmark is the *Queen of Time* clock at Selfridges, London (1930), one of many works commissioned for the department store by Gordon Selfridge, his admiring patron. Bayes's work catered for 'high life' in the *Unicorns in Battle* decorative panel, executed with Alfred Oakley for the RMS *Queen Mary* (1936), but he also believed in bringing colour to council estates administered by the St Pancras housing association. The *Four Seasons* clock and fairytale lunette panels (1937; Sidney Street estate) still survive *in situ*. A further area of his practice was as a medallist (for example, *Country Life Marksmanship Medal*, 1912; *Queen Mary Medal*, 1935). These mirror in miniature his stylistic progress from the New Sculpture to art deco, although their design and modelling are sometimes compromised by poor lettering. A commission in a related genre, the great seal and counterseal of George V (1912), is elegant and intricate but literally failed to make a successful impression.

Bayes's awards and offices culminated with a gold medal at the Salon de la Société des Artistes Français (1939) and election as president of the Royal Society of British Sculptors (1939–44). Although he regularly exhibited at the Royal Academy between 1889 and 1952, he was not elected to it, perhaps because he was a victim of his sheer versatility as a 'sculptor–craftsman' at a time when the role of fine art became increasingly important.

Bayes died in the Hospital of St John and St Elizabeth, Marylebone, London, on 10 July 1953. He was liked by his fellow artists, from his mentor, Frampton, to contemporaries such as William Reid Dick and Kathleen Scott. His chief interests were his enormous output of work and the garden at his residence from 1930 in Greville Place, Maida Vale, London, which contained examples of his sculpture. Bayes's last years were saddened by his wife's ill health and, at another level, by what he perceived as the aesthetic narrowness of modern art, which overlooked his craftsmanship and humanism. As a result of the exhibitions 'The Doulton story' held at the Victoria and Albert Museum in 1979 and 'Gilbert Bayes' at the Fine Art Society, London, and Henry Moore Centre, Leeds, in 1998, his place in twentieth-century British sculpture and ceramics has been favourably reappraised. Examples of Bayes's work may be seen in the Tate collection, the British Museum and Victoria and Albert Museum, London, and the Birmingham Museum and Art Gallery.　　MARK STOCKER

Sources L. Irvine and P. Atterbury, eds., *Gilbert Bayes, sculptor, 1872–1953* (1998) · R. Dirks, 'Mr Gilbert Bayes', *Art Journal*, new ser., 28 (1908), 193–9 · W. S. Sparrow, 'A young English sculptor: Gilbert Bayes', *The Studio*, 25 (1902), 102–10 · P. Ward-Jackson, *Gilbert Bayes: from arts and crafts to light monumental* (1998) · G. Bayes, *Modelling for sculpture: a book for the beginner* (1930) · C. Marriott, 'The recent work of Gilbert Bayes', *The Studio*, 72 (1917–18), 100–13 · P. Atterbury and L. Irvine, *The Doulton story* (1979) [exhibition catalogue, V&A, 30 May – 12 August 1979] · M. H. Spielmann, *British sculpture and sculptors of to-day* (1901) · T. P. Bennett, 'Recent work by Mr Gilbert Bayes', *The Studio*, 89 (1925), 197–202 · P. Attwood, 'Bayes, Gilbert', *The dictionary of art*, ed. J. Turner (1996) · B. Read, *Victorian sculpture* (1982) · CGPLA Eng. & Wales (1953)

Archives Henry Moore Institute, Leeds, papers and photographs · priv. coll.

Likenesses M. Frampton, oils, *c*.1925, Art Workers' Guild, London · B. Cundy, photograph, *c*.1929, repro. in Irvine and Atterbury, eds., *Gilbert Bayes*, 16 · two photographs, 1930–34, repro. in Irvine and Atterbury, eds., *Gilbert Bayes*

Wealth at death £9976 3*s*. 9*d*.: probate, 6 Oct 1953, CGPLA Eng. & Wales

Bayes, Joshua (*bap.* 1671, *d.* 1746), Presbyterian minister, was born in Sheffield and baptized on 10 February 1671 at St Peter's, the son of Joshua Bayes and nephew of the Revd Samuel Bayes (*d.* 1681), who was ejected from his living in Northamptonshire by the Act of Uniformity (1662). Bayes probably received his early education in Sheffield before being admitted on 15 November 1686 to Richard Frankland's academy at Attercliffe, where he received his ministerial training. On leaving the academy he moved to London. There on 22 June 1694 he was ordained, together with six others including Edmund Calamy, at Dr Annesley's Meeting-House, Bishopsgate Within. This was the first public ordination of dissenters in London since the Act of Uniformity.

Bayes's first ministerial appointment seems to have been at the Presbyterian meeting-house in Box Lane near Hemel Hempstead, Hertfordshire, where he remained from 1694 to 1706 before becoming morning preacher and assistant to John Sheffield at St Thomas's Meeting-House, Southwark. In the afternoons he assisted Christopher Taylor at Leather Lane, Hatton Garden. While engaged in these services he was chosen, with several other notable dissenting ministers in London, including Daniel Mayo and Jeremiah Smith, to complete Matthew Henry's *Exposition of the Old and New Testaments*. Bayes's assignment was the epistle to the Galatians. About 1700 Bayes married Ann Carpenter, with whom he had four sons and three daughters including Thomas *Bayes (1701?–1761), mathematician and Presbyterian minister, and Anne (d. 1789), who married Thomas West, a glover of Fenchurch Street.

On the death of Taylor in 1723 Bayes succeeded him as pastor at Leather Lane and resigned his morning duties at St Thomas's. He was assisted first by John Cornish (d. 1727) and afterwards by his own son, Thomas. Though his congregation was not large it consisted mainly of persons of substance who contributed largely to his support and collected a considerable sum annually for the Presbyterian Fund. In 1732 he succeeded Calamy as merchants lecturer at Salters' Hall. It was here in 1735 that he preached his acclaimed sermon, later to be published, against popery and the worship of God in an unknown tongue. Among his other published works were sermons occasioned by the deaths of his colleagues Christopher Taylor (1723) and John Cornish (1728) and *A Sermon Preached to the Society for the Reformation of Manners* (1723).

Bayes was a man of considerable learning and ability. As a minister he was much admired, and Wilson described him as 'a judicious, serious and exact preacher' (Wilson, 4.399). In his religious sentiments he was a moderate Calvinist who, though firmly orthodox, was prepared to tolerate opinions which differed from his own. He died in London on 24 April 1746 and was buried in Bunhill Fields.

A. B. GROSART, rev. M. J. MERCER

Sources W. Wilson, *The history and antiquities of the dissenting churches and meeting houses in London, Westminster and Southwark*, 4 vols. (1808–14), vol. 4, pp. 312, 396 · Surman, index of nonconformist ministers, DWL · J. Toulmin, *An historical view of the state of the protestant dissenters in England* (1814) · Calamy rev., 40 · F. Nicholson and E. Axon, *The older nonconformity in Kendal* (1915) · J. A. Jones, ed., *Bunhill memorials* (1849) · W. D. Jeremy, *The Presbyterian Fund and Dr Daniel Williams's Trust* (1885) · GM, 1st ser., 59 (1789), 85 · H. J. Rose, *A new general biographical dictionary*, ed. H. J. Rose and T. Wright, 12 vols. (1853) · W. Urwick, *Nonconformity in Hertfordshire* (1884), 390 · J. Hunter, *Familiae minorum gentium*, ed. J. W. Clay, 3, Harleian Society, 39 (1895), 833 · IGI

Likenesses Hopwood, stipple, NPG · oils, DWL; repro. in Wilson, *History ... of the dissenting churches*

Bayes, Thomas (1701?–1761), mathematician and Presbyterian minister, was probably born in Hertfordshire, the eldest in the family of four sons and three daughters of the Revd Joshua *Bayes and his wife, Ann Carpenter. He entered Edinburgh University in 1719 and studied for three years, though without taking a degree. He was licensed to preach while in Edinburgh, ordained by 1727,

and began his ministry as an assistant to his father, at the time minister of the Presbyterian meeting-house at Leather Lane, Hatton Garden, London. In 1731 he was appointed to minister in Tunbridge Wells at the meeting-house in Little Mount Sion, and in that year a tract attributed to him—*Divine benevolence, or, An attempt to prove that the principal end of the divine providence and government is the happiness of his creatures*—was published by John Noon.

In 1736 Noon published another anonymous tract which has always been attributed to Bayes—*An introduction to the doctrine of fluxions, and a defence of the mathematicians against the objections of the author of The analyst*. The author of *The Analyst, or, A Discourse Addressed to an Infidel Mathematician* (1734), George Berkeley (1685–1753), had attacked the practitioners of the Newtonian calculus, and impugned their piety; among the replies in defence of the mathematicians, that of Bayes was considered the most acute. Perhaps on this account he was elected a fellow of the Royal Society in 1742.

Bayes's fame rests on his posthumous paper, 'An essay towards solving a problem in the doctrine of chances', which was published in 1764 in the *Philosophical Transactions of the Royal Society* for the year 1763, having been 'found among [his] papers' by his friend the Revd Richard Price, who wrote an introduction for it. It contains a solution to the problem (in Bayes's words): '*Given* the number of times in which an unknown event has happened and failed: *Required* the chance that the probability of its happening in a single trial lies somewhere between any two degrees of probability that can be named' (*Philosophical Transactions*, 53, 1764, 370–418).

The problem is fundamental to statistical inference. It owes its origin to the *Ars conjectandi* of James Bernoulli (1713), and was extensively treated by Abraham de Moivre. Possibly Bayes learned of it directly from de Moivre, although he may equally well have encountered it first in his writings, or in *Observations on Man, his Frame, his Duty, and his Expectations* (1749) by David Hartley.

Bayes's tentative solution to the problem involves assuming that the lack of knowledge of the probability about which an inference is to be made may be represented by a uniform probability distribution, for which he gives an ingenious argument which has often been overlooked. The resulting type of statistical methodology is referred to as Bayesian and involves assigning a probability distribution to every unknown. Commonly rejected for much of the twentieth century, the use of such arguments has become more popular recently, though they remain controversial. Bayes's paper also includes a result which is a special case of a more general theorem in conditional probability which, anachronistically, has therefore become known as Bayes's theorem. In addition it contains some interesting contributions to the evaluation of the beta probability integral. Bayes's only other known published work is a short letter to John Canton on Stirling's approximation which was also printed in the *Philosophical Transactions* for 1763.

In 1752 Bayes retired from his ministry, but continued to live in Tunbridge Wells until his death. He died on 7 April

1761, and was buried in the Bayes and Cotton family vault in Bunhill Fields, the nonconformist burial-ground at Moorgate, London. He was unmarried. His will, executed on 12 December 1760, shows him to have been a man of substance. Richard Price described Bayes as the most ingenious man he ever knew, and William Whiston wrote that he was a very good mathematician. He is also said to have been a good Greek scholar and a poor preacher, and it is clear that he was retiring and modest.

A. W. F. EDWARDS

Sources A. I. Dale, *A history of inverse probability from Thomas Bayes to Karl Pearson* (1991) · G. A. Barnard, 'Thomas Bayes—a biographical note', *Biometrika*, 45 (1958), 293–5; repr. in E. S. Pearson and M. G. Kendall, eds., *Studies in the history of probability and statistics*, 1 (1970) · J. D. Holland, 'The Reverend Thomas Bayes, FRS, 1702–61', *Journal of the Royal Statistical Society: series A*, 125 (1962), 451–61 · S. M. Stigler, *The history of statistics* (1986) · D. R. Bellhouse, 'Tidbits on Thomas', *Institute of Mathematical Statistics Bulletin*, 19 (1990), 478–9 · A. Hald, 'Evaluations of the beta probability integral by Bayes and Price', *Archive for History of Exact Sciences*, 41 (1990–91), 139–56 · private information, 1995 · burial register, 15 April 1761, Bunhill Fields burial-ground, Moorgate, London
Archives Equitable Life Assurance Society, notebook
Wealth at death approx. £2000–£3000: will, PRO

Bayes, Walter John (1869–1956). *See under* Camden Town Group (act. 1911–1913).

Bayeux, John de (c.1190–1249), baron, was the heir of Hugh de Bayeux, lord of the Lincolnshire barony of Thoresway, who died in 1196, but exactly how he was related to Hugh is obscure. He may have been Hugh's son, but his mother is unlikely to have been the Eleanor who as Hugh's widow paid 100 marks in 1197 for freedom to remarry as she chose (she subsequently remarried twice, and in 1219 was charged, though acquitted, with the murder of her third husband). John was a minor when Hugh died, and the Lincolnshire estates passed to Hugh's daughter, Maud, and to her husband, Richard of Sandford; the latter was described in 1204 as having the custody of Hugh's heir, and only when Richard died, early in 1219, did John inherit Thoresway. But John had probably come of age in around 1212, when he paid for the enrolment on that year's pipe roll of the conveyance to him of estates in Dorset—perhaps this formed part of a settlement devised by Hugh before his death. And he also appears to have come into lands in Lincolnshire—he took part in the baronial revolt against King John, and in September 1217 the sheriff of Lincolnshire was one of those instructed to restore John's estates to him. Less than two years later John de Bayeux was employed as a justice itinerant, replacing William of Whitfield in Somerset and Devon. In 1228 he again served as a justice itinerant in Devon, and his links with the south-west, and particularly with Dorset, were clearly important to him; he several times took assizes at Dorchester in the 1220s and early 1230s, in 1224 he was instructed to release a Bordeaux ship that had been arrested at Exeter, and by 1227 he had become constable of Plympton Castle, an office he still held in 1236.

But John de Bayeux was also active in Lincolnshire, where in 1229 he was instructed to arrest ships and arrange for their going to Portsmouth. This was in advance of Henry III's expedition to Brittany, which eventually took place in the following year; Bayeux received a protection to cover his absence, and presumably accompanied the army. Four years later he was serving in Wales, since he was ordered to bring the men of the town of Montgomery back into the king's allegiance. But although he was summoned to take part in Henry III's campaign in Poitou in 1242, in the end he paid a fine of 100 marks instead. Bayeux may have had some difficulty in establishing himself in his Lincolnshire estates when he came into his full inheritance, since in 1223 he was convicted of disseisin at Thoresway itself. Three years later a fine with some of his tenants at Cadeby numbered among the latter's duties summoning the knights of Bayeux's barony to sessions of his court. And once established he may have proved a difficult neighbour; in 1234 he paid 400 marks for licence to settle an appeal of homicide in Lincolnshire, in which he and four members of his household were charged with killing Roger de Mowbray of Welbourn (a manor of which Bayeux was lord). Three years later he was alleged to have forbidden the men of Lindsey's west riding wapentake to make suit to the public courts more than twice a year, following a public reading of Magna Carta. Bayeux's stand was fully in accordance with clause 35 of the 1225 reissue of Magna Carta, itself confirmed early in 1237. But it infuriated the sheriff, and may help to explain why Bayeux does not appear to have been employed by the crown after the mid-1230s. He died early in 1249. He had been married to a woman named Matilda, who was still alive in 1241, and they had a son named Robert, who in 1238 or 1239 was charged with abducting a royal ward in Dorset. But Robert must have predeceased his father, since John's heir was his brother Stephen, who was said in 1249 to be aged over sixty, and who died in the following year.

HENRY SUMMERSON

Sources *Chancery records* (RC) · *Curia regis rolls preserved in the Public Record Office* (1922–), vols. 5, 8, 11, 16 · *Pipe rolls* · D. M. Stenton, ed., *Rolls of the justices in eyre … Lincolnshire, 1218–1219, and Worcestershire, 1221*, SeldS, 53 (1934) · W. O. Massingberd, ed., *Lincolnshire records: abstracts of final concords* (privately printed, London, 1896), 217–18 · I. J. Sanders, *English baronies: a study of their origin and descent, 1086–1327* (1960), 88–9 · D. Crook, *Records of the general eyre*, Public Record Office Handbooks, 20 (1982), 1 · J. C. Holt, *Magna Carta* (1965) · *CIPM*, 1, no. 159

Bayeux, Osbert de (*fl.* 1120–1184), ecclesiastic and suspected murderer, was a nephew of Archbishop *Thurstan of York (d. 1140). An archdeacon named Osbert occurs in the 1120s; if this was Osbert de Bayeux then he must have been promoted as archdeacon, presumably by his uncle, at an early age. As Osbert the archdeacon, nephew of Thurstan, he was mentioned in a charter of 1137–40, his archdeaconry probably being that of Richmond. In 1140–41, after Thurstan's death, along with Archdeacon Walter of London he opposed the election of William Fitzherbert, treasurer of York, as archbishop. In the years which followed, between 1142 and 1154, he witnessed several charters issued by lay persons, and after 1147 he attested *acta* of Fitzherbert's successful rival, Archbishop Henry Murdac. But in 1153 he secured first the deposition of

Abbot Germanus of Selby, whose appointment had been obtained by Murdac, and then the reinstallation of Abbot Elias Paynel, who had resigned at Murdac's command. Shortly afterwards, however, Elias Paynel was deposed again, this time by Archbishop Theobald of Canterbury (d. 1161); Germanus was restored and Osbert was rebuked by the archbishop. The motives for his intervention at Selby are obscure, but they indicate that, despite his opposition to William Fitzherbert, Osbert did not feel any loyalty towards Murdac's candidate.

After the death of Henry Murdac, Osbert tried, unsuccessfully, to prevent Archbishop Fitzherbert's return, and, when the archbishop died after only a week in the city of York there were rumours of a poisoned chalice, and Osbert was accused of his murder. Charges were brought against the archdeacon by a chaplain of Archbishop Fitzherbert's named Symphorian, at a council presided over by King Stephen, probably at Michaelmas 1154. Osbert maintained that he was innocent and demanded trial by an ecclesiastical court. The death of Stephen prevented any immediate action, and after the accession of Henry II, Archbishop Theobald struggled to withdraw the case from royal into ecclesiastical jurisdiction. When the trial began in 1156 Symphorian failed to produce witnesses, but Osbert was not able to prove his innocence, and so the case was referred to the papal court. Osbert evidently appeared before both Adrian IV and Alexander III, but there is no record of any formal judgment. By 1158, however, Osbert had been replaced as archdeacon, and this suggests that in 1157 he was degraded and removed from office. In late 1154 Osbert had supported the election of Archbishop Roger de Pont l'Évêque (d. 1181), and evidence from a papal decretal of about 1175–80 suggests that Pont l'Évêque had offered to grant the revenues of the precentorship of York to Osbert's son; this was a promise which, Osbert later claimed, the archbishop failed to fulfil.

After 1158 Osbert continued to style himself archdeacon, though now a minor secular lord. In 1166, as Osbert de Bayeux, archdeacon, he held half a knight's fee of the honour of Lacy, and lands by knight service of the honour of Skipton. Some time between 1159 and 1170 he was acting as steward of Hugh de Tilly, and over the years after his retirement he was a benefactor of various religious houses, Drax, Pontefract, and Guisborough, as well as of the knights templar and hospitaller. He may have married, and he had two sons who appear in the written records: William de Bayeux, son of Osbert the archdeacon, is located in Yorkshire in 1191 as one owing £15 to Aaron the Jew of Lincoln; and Turstin de Baius, son of Osbert the archdeacon, attested a charter of Fountains Abbey dating from between about 1160 and 1180, which raises the possibility that he was born when Osbert still held the office of archdeacon. Osbert was still alive in 1184 when he witnessed a final concord at York. He is mentioned on an escheat roll of 1194, when Hugh Bardolf answered for 42s. 8d. from the farm of Osbert the archdeacon in Bingley, but whether he was then still living is not clear. Osbert belonged in one sense to the world of the late eleventh and early twelfth centuries, to the era of the married, worldly cleric, and he contrasts sharply with a number of his colleagues in the York chapter who were drawn to and influenced by the wave of spirituality ushered in by the great age of the new monasticism.

JANET BURTON

Sources C. T. Clay, 'Notes on the early archdeacons in the church of York', Yorkshire Archaeological Journal, 36 (1944–7), 269–87 · J. E. Burton, ed., York, 1070–1154, English Episcopal Acta, 5 (1988) · J. Raine, ed., The historians of the church of York and its archbishops, 3 vols., Rolls Series, 71 (1879–94) · The letters of John of Salisbury, ed. and trans. H. E. Butler and W. J. Millor, rev. C. N. L. Brooke, 2 vols., OMT (1979–86) [Lat. orig. with parallel Eng. text] · D. Nicholl, Thurstan: archbishop of York, 1114–1140 (1964) · R. M. T. Hill and C. N. L. Brooke, 'From 627 until the early thirteenth century', A history of York Minster, ed. G. E. Aylmer and R. Cant (1977), 1–43 · Letters and charters of Gilbert Foliot, ed. A. Morey and others (1967) · D. Knowles, 'The case of St William of York', in D. Knowles, The historian and character and other essays, ed. C. N. L. Brooke and G. Constable (1963), 76–97 · C. H. Talbot, 'New documents in the case of St William of York', Cambridge Historical Journal, 10 (1950–52), 1–15 · A. Morey, 'Canonist evidence in the case of St William of York', Cambridge Historical Journal, 10 (1950–52), 352–3 · R. Howlett, ed., Chronicles of the reigns of Stephen, Henry II, and Richard I, 1, Rolls Series, 82 (1884) · W. Farrer and others, eds., Early Yorkshire charters, 12 vols. (1914–65)

Bayeux, Serlo of (c.1050–1113×22), poet, was born about the middle of the eleventh century as the son of an unknown married priest, possibly at Bretteville-sur-Odon in Normandy. He should not be confused with his contemporary, Serlo, abbot of Gloucester (d. 1104). The little that is known about Serlo of Bayeux's career comes primarily from his poems. He was a canon of Bayeux Cathedral who lost his paternal possessions on account of the fact that he was the son of a priest. Six of his eight known poems are concerned with his predicament as a priest's son, his fight to regain his lost property, and his appeal to Odo, bishop of Bayeux. They are (in chronological order): two invectives against anonymous knights, written probably before 1079 or 1080; two invectives against St Étienne at Caen (one to the monks and one to Abbot Gilbert) composed in 1079 or 1080; an encomium to his patron, Bishop Odo, written after 1087; and his sixth poem 'On the Defence of the Sons of Priests' dated to 1095 or 1096. A seventh poem is addressed to the English poet Muriel, a nun of Wilton, whose own work has not survived; it is one of a series of poems dedicated to her by Serlo, Baudri of Bourgueil, and Hildebert de Lavardin. Serlo's eighth poem is historically the most interesting, for it contains his eyewitness account of the English conquest of Bayeux by Henry I in 1105, which led to the defeat in the following year of the king's brother, Duke Robert Curthose, at Tinchebray. Apart from the horror and destruction inflicted by the Anglo-Norman assault, Serlo, as a ducal supporter, describes the city as having eleven churches (the cathedral being the largest), Bishop Odo's beautifully decorated court, and the house of the rich burgher Conan, as well as the precious chapter house and the ducal castle. The main occupation of the inhabitants was trade, a statement which leads Serlo to reproach his fellow citizens for crimes like robbery, false moneying, and oppressing widows and orphans. He ends his poem with an apostrophe to his new benefactor, an unidentified member of the ruling family who had given him a mantle.

Serlo does not appear in the mortuary roll of Matilda, abbess of La Trinité at Caen, compiled in 1113, and was therefore probably still alive at that date. He had died by 1122, however, since his name appears in the mortuary roll of Vital, abbot of Savigny, compiled in that year. The position of his name there in third place, after Bishop Odo and the burgher Conan, indicates that he was a prominent inhabitant of Bayeux.   ELISABETH VAN HOUTS

Sources H. Böhmer, 'Der sogennante Serlo von Bayeux und die ihm zugeschriebenen Gedichte', *Neues Archiv der Gesellschaft für Ältere Deutsche Geschichtskunde*, 22 (1897), 703–38 · A. Boutemy, 'Deux poèmes inconnus de Serlon de Bayeux et une copie nouvelle de son poème contre les moines de Caen', *Le Moyen Age*, 48 (1938), 244–57 · E. M. C. van Houts, 'Latin poetry and the Anglo-Norman court, 1066–1135: the *Carmen de Hastingae proelio*', *Journal of Medieval History*, 15 (1989), 39–62, esp. 44–5 · L. Delisle, ed., *Rouleaux des morts du IXe au XVe siècle* (1866), no. 36, 185; no. 38, 286–7 · T. Wright, ed., *The Anglo-Latin satirical poets and epigrammatists of the twelfth century*, 2, Rolls Series, 59 (1872), 2.241–51, 254 · 'Defensio pro filiis presbyterorum', *Libelli de lite imperatorum et pontificum saeculis XI et XII conscripti*, ed. E. Dümmler and others, MGH, 3 (Hanover, 1897), 579–83

Bayfield [*alias* Somersam], **Richard** (*d.* 1531), Benedictine monk and protestant martyr, was born at Hadleigh in Suffolk of unknown parentage. His alias, presumably a locative surname, suggests that his family originated at Somersham, a few miles north-east of Hadleigh. He was professed at Bury St Edmunds Abbey in 1514, and ordained priest in 1518. In the early 1520s, having responsibility for the abbey's hospitality, he came to know Robert Barnes, who visited to see a former colleague from their Louvain University days, Edmund Rougham. Barnes was at the time at Cambridge and one of the leaders of those interested in the new Lutheran theology. Bayfield came under the influence both of Barnes (who provided him with Erasmus's new Latin translation of the New Testament), and of two London Lollards, Lawrence Maxwell and John Stacy, who seem also to have been visiting the abbey to hold talks with Barnes. The outcome was that Bayfield was incarcerated in the abbot's prison, from which Barnes was able to free him only with difficulty. Barnes took Bayfield back with him to Cambridge, where Bayfield developed an admiration for Thomas Bilney and Thomas Arthur. When Barnes was convicted of heresy in early 1526, Bayfield was offered shelter in London by Maxwell and Stacy.

For Bayfield's movements in the years which followed the major source is John Foxe's *Acts and Monuments*, which is not without its difficulties. According to Foxe, Maxwell and Stacy arranged for Bayfield to go overseas soon after his arrival in London. If so, he was back in England, probably the following year, and there is evidence that he was beginning to traffic in prohibited books. Early in 1528 he was arrested and convicted of heresy before Cuthbert Tunstall, the bishop of London, for asserting that praise was only to be given to God and not to anything created, and that a priest needed no licence to preach. According to Foxe, Bayfield performed only part of his penance before absconding abroad again, and then, thinking better of it, reappearing before Tunstall two months later. He was exiled from the diocese of London and told to return to Bury and wear his monk's habit. He returned to Bury but ignored the other provisions. He then left Bury and fled abroad again.

Bayfield now took on the role of the main supplier of prohibited reformation books to the English market, a role vacant since the arrest of Thomas Garrett in 1528. The major source of such books was the Low Countries and in particular Antwerp. There is a stray reference to Bayfield also supplying the French market. He is known to have sent three major consignments to England, the first via Colchester in mid-1530, the second via St Katharine by the Tower, London, in late 1530, and the third via Norfolk about Easter 1531. The second consignment was wholly intercepted by Lord Chancellor Sir Thomas More, and the third probably partially so. A list of books recovered from Bayfield gives over fifty titles, of which he said he was bringing in multiple copies. Many were Lutheran but many also were by writers such as Oecolampadius, Lambert, and Zwingli who represented a more anti-sacramental theology.

Bayfield showed signs of not always appreciating the extreme danger he was in. He had indiscreet conversations with people who did not share his views. He was arrested at a London bookbinder's, possibly in October 1531, imprisoned, and interrogated by More. The authorities seem to have been alarmed that Bayfield was a source of anti-sacramental ideas, and even moved him out of a cell which he shared with another suspect, Thomas Patmere. His trial by the new bishop of London, John Stokesley, opened at St Paul's on 10 November. He was convicted as a relapsed heretic, degraded, and burnt with excruciating slowness at Smithfield, probably on 27 November, although some authorities give 4 December.

Thomas More maintained that Bayfield was a bigamous monk, having one wife in England and another in Brabant, but this would appear to be no more than one of More's fantasies. John Foxe, who seems to have been able to supplement the documentary record with somebody's personal reminiscences, described Bayfield in his first Latin martyrology as 'natura formidolosus, gratia autem fortissimus [by nature fearful, by grace on the other hand, most strong]' (Foxe, 4.767n.).   ANDREW HOPE

Sources J. Foxe, *Acts and monuments*, 4 (1858) · St Thomas More, *The confutation of Tyndale's answer*, ed. L. A. Schuster and others, 3 vols. (1973), vol. 8 of *The Yale edition of the complete works of St Thomas More* · St Thomas More, *The apology*, ed. J. B. Trapp (1979), vol. 9 of *The Yale edition of the complete works of St Thomas More* · J. Strype, *Ecclesiastical memorials*, 3 vols. (1822), vol. 1

Bayfield, Robert (*bap.* 1629), physician, the son of Robert Bayfield, was baptized at St Stephen's, Norwich, on 16 February 1629. Other than this, all that is known of Bayfield's life is that he was the author of five works: *Enchiridion medicum, containing the causes, signs, and cures of all those diseases that do chiefly affect the body of man. … Whereunto is added a treatise, De facultatibus medicamentorum compositorum et dosibus* (1655); *Exercitationes anatomicae* (2nd edn, 1668); *Tēs*

Robert Bayfield (*bap.* 1629), by William Faithorne the elder, 1654

October 1828. In 1832 he married Matilda, daughter of Major E. Colls of Limerick; they had at least two sons. He graduated BA in 1834, MA in 1848, and BD and DD in 1852. Having been ordained, he was from 1842 to 1864 the first incumbent of Holy Trinity, Birkenhead. Many of his parishioners were Welsh labourers, attracted to what was then a boom town, and Baylee, who had a facility for languages, taught himself Welsh in order to conduct services in that language. His proselytizing among the Roman Catholic Irish dock labourers in Birkenhead and his associations with the Orange order provoked riots in his parish; in October 1862 1000 police and volunteers guarded his church when he provocatively held a debate entitled 'Sympathy with Garibaldi'.

A well-known champion of the evangelical party, Baylee was a zealous theological controversialist. Accounts were published of his disputes with T. J. Brown on papal infallibility (1852), with Edward Miall on church establishments (1864), and with the secularist Charles Bradlaugh (1867). His other writings included an assertion of the divine origin of the Church of England (1838), a refutation of Unitarianism (1852), and a statement of the harmony of Genesis and geology (1857). His *Introduction to the Study of the Bible* (3 vols.) went through a second edition in 1870. In later years he adopted extreme millenarian views, publishing an account of Old Testament prophecies (1871) and a commentary on the Apocalypse (1876).

Baylee is chiefly remembered as the founder and first principal of St Aidan's Theological College, Birkenhead, which opened in 1856, and where he prepared many students for ordination. The college grew out of Baylee's experience of the Liverpool Parochial Assistant Association, founded in 1846 to supply lay visitors to assist the clergy, and of a private theological class which he conducted under the sanction of J. B. Sumner, bishop of Chester. These encouraged the idea of combining pastoral work and theological education in the training of ordinands. One of his sons, Joseph Tyrrell Baylee, assisted him in the teaching. Although supported by an influential body of subscribers, the college never paid its way and was continually subject to allegations, notably in 1863 by John Allen, archdeacon of Shropshire, about the low academic and social standing of its entrants. The college was accused of 'sheep-stealing' after a clumsy attempt in 1860 to recruit Methodist ministers. Amid mounting complaints about Baylee's administration, and concern about his unorthodox eschatological teaching, the college's governing council decided to close the institution in 1868 (it was reconstituted in 1869 under closer diocesan control). Baylee was presented to the vicarage of Shepscombe, Gloucestershire, in 1871, where he died on 7 July 1883. He had married again, and was survived by his second wife, Jane.   THOMPSON COOPER, *rev.* M. C. CURTHOYS

iatrikēs Karpos, or, A treatise de morborum capitis essentiis et prognosticis: adorned with above three hundred choice and rare observations (1663); *Hē Probolētēs alētheias, or, The bulwark of truth, being a treatise of God, of Jesus Christ, of the Holy-Ghost, and the Trinity in unity, against atheists and hereticks* (1657), bearing Edmund Calamy's imprimatur (republished at Glasgow in 1772); and *Tractatus de tumoribus praeter naturam, or, A Treatise of Preternatural Tumors* (1662); the second part of this book is dedicated to Sir Thomas Browne.

[ANON.], *rev.* MICHAEL BEVAN

Sources J. Granger, *A biographical history of England, from Egbert the Great to the revolution*, 2 vols. (1769); suppl. (1774) · *IGI* · BL cat.
Likenesses W. Faithorne the elder, line engraving, 1654, BM, NPG [*see illus.*] · W. Faithorne the elder, line engraving, 1657, Wellcome L.; repro. in R. Bayfield, *Bulwark of truth* (1657) · W. Faithorne the elder, line print, BM, NPG; repro. in R. Bayfield, *Enchiridion Medicum* (1655) · W. Faithorne the elder, print, repro. in R. Bayfield, *Tractatus de tumoribus praeter naturam* (1662)

Bayford. For this title name *see* Sanders, Robert Arthur, Baron Bayford (1867–1940).

Baylee, Joseph (1807–1883), theological teacher and writer, was born on 23 July 1807, at Limerick, the fifth son of John Tyrrell Baylee, a Quaker schoolmaster, and his wife, Jane, granddaughter of Lord Dunboyne and widow of Henry Bennis. Initially self-educated, by his own account, Baylee entered Trinity College, Dublin, on 20

Sources *The Record* (13 July 1883) · *Liverpool Daily Post* (11 July 1883) · F. B. Heiser, *The story of Saint Aidan's College Birkenhead* (1947) · Burtchaell & Sadleir, *Alum. Dubl.* · B. Heeney, *A different kind of gentleman: parish clergy as professional men in early and mid-Victorian England* (1976) · A. Haig, *The Victorian clergy* (1984) · S. Gilley, 'The Garibaldi riots of 1862', *HJ*, 16 (1973), 697–732 · *CGPLA Eng. & Wales* (1883)

Bayley, (William) Butterworth (1781–1860), administrator in India, twelfth child of Thomas Butterworth *Bayley (1744–1802) of Hope Hall, Eccles, Lancashire, and his wife, Mary Leggatt, was born on 30 November 1781. Butterworth Bayley was educated at Eton College and in 1798 had just gone up to Trinity College, Cambridge, when his father obtained for him a writership in the East India Company's service in Bengal. He arrived at Calcutta in November 1799 in time to join the first intake at Fort William College, Lord Wellesley's ambitious experiment in equipping civil servants for the governance of empire. At the college Bayley came under the influence of the Revd William Carey, the Baptist missionary of Serampore fame, whom Wellesley had hired to teach Bengali to the young civilians; from him Bayley acquired a lifelong interest in missionary work and Indian education. Bayley proved himself a talented linguist at Fort William, winning prizes in Hindustani and Persian, and in 1803 he became an assistant in the governor-general's office and in the office of the Persian translator. Like many of his contemporaries he was inspired by Wellesley's vision of a strong and rigorously governed Indian empire, and instead of the brilliance promised by prestigious diplomatic appointments he opted for a life of administrative service at the very heart of government.

Although Bayley's career included some judicial appointments outside Calcutta he was rarely long absent from the scene of official decision making. In 1807 he became registrar to the *sadr diwani adalat* and the *sadr nizamat adalat*. In 1810 he was made judge and magistrate of Burdwan, a post he held until 1814, when he was appointed secretary to the revenue and judicial departments of the government of Bengal. In July 1817 he officiated as chief secretary to government, in which position he was confirmed in 1819. Bayley worked happily under Lord Hastings, not least because of the governor-general's favourable attitude towards missionary activities and the encouragement he offered to experiments in elementary education. In 1823 Bayley temporarily sat on the supreme council and in November 1825 became a permanent member of the council. In 1828 he was acting governor-general in the five months between the departure of Lord Amherst and the arrival of Lord Bentinck. In July 1828 he became president of the Board of Trade. He returned to England on furlough in 1830 and resigned the company's service in 1834. He had married on 18 February 1809 Anne Augusta, daughter of William Jackson, registrar of the supreme court of Calcutta.

Bayley was a conservative administrator and believed that expediency alone and not new philosophies of government justified tampering with the system. Thus he was out of step with the radicalizing tendencies of Bentinck's administration. He had been trained in the principles laid down by Cornwallis in 1793, in particular the supremacy of the rule of law and the separation of the executive and judicial functions of government, and only reluctantly accepted the reforms of 1831, which, by uniting the offices of collector and magistrate, created the archetypal district officer of British India. Bayley was also slow to accept the principle of employing Indians at subordinate levels of the administration, having imbibed in the Cornwallis era the stricture that government agents must be aloof from the temptations (financial and otherwise) offered by relations with Indians.

Throughout his years in India, Bayley ardently supported the cause of missionary schools, almost to the point of official indiscretion, and missionaries of all denominations saw in his departure the loss of an ally in office. Bayley served on the general committee of public instruction (founded in 1823) and the council of Fort William College, of which he was president in 1823 and again in 1825. He was also appointed to supervise the progress of the Chinsura schools which received a government subsidy. As a private individual he was president of the Calcutta School Book Society from 1817 until 1830, a member of the Calcutta diocesan committee of the Society for the Propagation of Christian Knowledge, and a regular subscriber to the Baptist missionary schools at Serampore.

In 1833 Bayley was elected to the court of directors of the East India Company; in 1839 he became deputy chairman and in 1840 chairman. In 1854 he was recommended for permanent membership of the newly reconstituted court, but his long-standing wariness of change led him to reject the place. Similarly he refused a seat in the new Council of India, established in 1859 on the abolition of the East India Company. Bayley was not long to witness the changes produced by the uprising of 1857. He died on 29 May 1860 at St Leonards in Sussex. His youngest son, Steuart Colvin *Bayley, followed him into the Bengal civil service.   KATHERINE PRIOR

Sources M. A. Laird, *Missionaries and education in Bengal, 1793–1837* (1972) · H. T. Prinsep and R. Doss, eds., *A general register of the Hon'ble East India Company's civil servants of the Bengal establishment from 1790 to 1842* (1844) · E. Axon, 'The Bayley family', BL OIOC · E. Stokes, *The English utilitarians and India* (1959) · BL OIOC, Haileybury MSS · ecclesiastical records, East India Company, BL OIOC · H. E. C. Stapylton, *The Eton school lists, from 1791 to 1850*, 2nd edn (1864) · *CGPLA Eng. & Wales* (1860)
Archives BL OIOC, Home misc. series, corresp. and minutes | BL OIOC, letters to Lord Amherst, MS Eur. F 140
Likenesses M. Gauci, lithograph (after T. George), BM
Wealth at death under £40,000: probate, 21 June 1860, *CGPLA Eng. & Wales*

Bayley, Cornelius (1751–1812), Church of England clergyman, was born at Ashe, near Whitchurch, Shropshire, and baptized on 27 November 1751 at the Presbyterian chapel at Dodington by Whitchurch. His father, Thomas Bayley, reportedly a Methodist, was a leather-breeches maker in Manchester who claimed to have been deprived of an estate of which he was the lawful heir. His mother, an Anglican, was noted for her piety. Bayley was a notably pious child, of whom a 'very careless and wicked man' who occupied the room next to that in which he prayed was heard to say, 'That child's prayers will make my hell sevenfold the hotter' (*Christian Observer*, 477). Bayley was educated at Whitchurch grammar school, where he later, aged seventeen, acted as master for a short time. He became a Methodist preacher, and taught English from 1773 at Kingswood School before his ordination as a priest in the Church of England in 1781, serving his time as a curate under John Fletcher in Madeley, Shropshire, between 1781 and 1782, and then under Richard Conyers at Deptford. He preached for the Methodists as late as 1784, but relations were becoming strained, and they finally broke in the 1790s. He had defended episcopacy in *Questions for Children on the Ministerial Office* (1795), which led to a reply by an anonymous Methodist layman, *The Primitive Gospel Ministry*, a highly personal attack to which Bayley responded in *A Reply to the Personal Reflections in a Pamphlet Lately Published* (1796).

Bayley was the first incumbent of St James's Church, Manchester, a 'proprietary church' which he built on land obtained from Sir John Parker Mosley, a local Methodist, in 1787, obtaining the presentation to it for sixty years. The church was consecrated by the bishop of Chester on 18 August 1788, and it rapidly became a centre of Anglican evangelicalism, attracting Charles Simeon and likeminded preachers. Bayley was a good preacher, and his church acquired a large and fashionable congregation. His proficiency in Hebrew was widely admired, and the publication of his Hebrew grammar, *An Entrance into the Sacred Tongue* (1778), led to the award of the honorary degree of doctor of divinity by the University of Aberdeen. He was admitted as a 'ten-year' man at Trinity College, Cambridge, where he gained the degree of BD in 1792, and was made DD in 1800. A second edition of the Hebrew grammar appeared after his death. He produced notes and a preface to the Elizabethan *Homilies* in 1811, noting its value as a 'bulwark against the united efforts of papists and dissenters' (C. Bayley, 'Preface', *Homilies*, 1811, i). He defended his scripture-based account of the Trinity from a Swedenborgian criticism in a long pamphlet entitled *The Swedenborgian Doctrine of the Trinity Considered* (1785), in which he was also critical of 'rational' Christianity. He was active in the Sunday school movement in Manchester, producing *An Address to the Public on Sunday Schools* in 1784.

Bayley was an exemplary parish priest whose diligence in visiting the sick and distributing charity took its toll on his health. He was seriously ill for two years before his death, which occurred at Manchester on 12 April 1812. He had married Rachel Norton of Manchester on 24 May 1783; the wedding was conducted at Buxton by John Wesley. On Bayley's death in 1812 the living of St James was bought by his clergyman son-in-law. B. W. YOUNG

Sources *Christian Observer*, 11 (1812), 477–9 · H. D. Rack, 'The providential moment: church building, Methodism and evangelical entryism in Manchester, 1788–1825', *Transactions of the Historic Society of Lancashire and Cheshire*, 141 (1991), 235–60 · C. Hulbert, *Memoirs of seventy years of an eventful life* (privately printed, Providence Grove, 1852) · E. A. Rose, 'Cornelius Bayley and the Manchester Methodists', *Proceedings of the Wesley Historical Society*, 34 (1963–4), 153–8 · IGI

Archives Man. CL

Bayley, Sir Edward Clive (1821–1884), administrator in India and antiquary, son of Edward Clive Bayley, of the Bayleys of Hope Hall, Eccles, Lancashire, and his wife, Margaret, daughter of James Fenton, was born in St Petersburg on 17 October 1821. His father's younger brother, (William) Butterworth *Bayley, was a director of the East India Company and in 1839 Edward obtained through him a place at the East India College, Haileybury, and a career in the Bengal civil service.

Bayley arrived in India in 1842 and until 1849 served principally at Meerut. On 6 March 1850 he married Emily Metcalfe [see Bayley, Emily Anne Theophila (1830–1911), under Metcalfe, Sir Thomas Theophilus], eldest daughter of Sir Thomas Theophilus Metcalfe, the resident of Delhi. They had thirteen children—including Georgiana Charlotte Clive *Chapman—of whom two died in infancy. His promotion was rapid, something which the satirical *Charivari's Album* of 1875 attributed in part to his uncle's high office in the company. In April 1849 he was appointed deputy commissioner of Gujarat in the newly annexed state of the Punjab. The following November he became undersecretary to the government of India in the foreign department, where he served under Sir Henry Elliot, the orientalist and archaeologist, who warmly encouraged his antiquarian pursuits. Two years later he returned to the Punjab as deputy commissioner of Kangra, but in 1854 he was compelled by ill health to take furlough. In England he studied law and was called to the bar at the Middle Temple in 1857. He returned to India on the outbreak of the uprising and in September 1857 was ordered to Allahabad to assist John Peter Grant in his provisional government of the Central Provinces. Thereafter he served in a judicial capacity in Benares, Azamgarh, Allahabad, and Agra. In 1862, after a short stint as foreign secretary, he became home secretary, an office he held for the next ten years. From 1873 until his retirement in 1878 he was a member of the supreme council. He was made CSI in 1875, KCSI in 1877, and CIE in 1878; he was vice-chancellor of Calcutta University for five years from 1870.

Bayley was a respected antiquarian and the foremost authority on Indian numismatics. He also dabbled in Indian architecture and, in a gesture typical of his sentimental regard for India's faded Muslim élite, designed and built at Allahabad a court waiting-room in traditional Mughal style. Five times president of the Asiatic Society of Bengal, he published in the society's journal some fifteen papers on Indian sculpture, inscriptions, and coins. Two further papers 'On the genealogy of modern numerals' appeared in the *Journal of the Royal Asiatic Society* (1882–3) and another on the coins of the Hindu kings of Kabul in the *Numismatic Chronicle* (1882). In retirement he edited the ninth volume, on the local Muslim dynasties of Gujarat, of Elliot's *History of India as Told by its Own Historians* (1886), and served for three years as vice-president of the Royal Asiatic Society. He died at Wilmington Lodge, Keymer, Sussex, on 30 April 1884.

STANLEY LANE-POOLE, *rev.* KATHERINE PRIOR

Sources *Journal of the Royal Asiatic Society of Great Britain and Ireland*, new ser., 16 (1884), iii–viii · E. C. Bayley, *The history of India as told by its own historians: the local Muhammadan dynasties* (1886) · *East-India Register and Directory* (1842–60) · *Indian Army and Civil Service List* (1861–2) · E. Axon, 'The Bayley family', BL OIOC · *Charivari's album* (1875) · F. C. Danvers and others, *Memorials of old Haileybury College* (1894) · H. T. Prinsep and R. Doss, eds., *A general register of the Hon'ble East India Company's civil servants of the Bengal establishment from 1790 to 1842* (1844) · *The Times* (5 May 1884), 10 · BL OIOC, Haileybury MSS · M. M. Kaye, *The golden calm* (1980) · *Bengal and Agra Directory and Annual Register* (1847–57) · *Bengal Directory* (1873–9) · *CGPLA Eng. & Wales* (1884)
Archives BL OIOC, Indian letters and papers of the Metcalfe, Bayley, and Ricketts families [microfilm] · NRA, priv. coll., letters and papers | CUL, corresp. with Lord Mayo
Likenesses Bourne & Shepherd?, albumen print photograph, *c.*1860, NPG · photograph, 1861, BL OIOC · group portrait, photograph, 1864–5 (with Lord Lawrence and his council), BL OIOC; repro. in C. A. Bayly, *The raj: India and the British, 1600–1947* (1900) · Isca, coloured lithograph, repro. in *Charivari's Album*
Wealth at death £7398 19s. 2d.: probate, 29 July 1884, *CGPLA Eng. & Wales*

Bayley, Emily Anne Theophila, Lady Bayley (1830–1911). *See under* Metcalfe, Sir Thomas Theophilus, fourth baronet (1795–1853).

Bayley, Frederick William Naylor (1808–1852), newspaper editor and author, was born in Ireland. In 1825 he accompanied his father, who was in the army, to Barbados, a period described in his *Four Years in Residence in the West Indies* (1830). About the time of his return to England in 1829 he began to publish verses—and throughout his life published them in newspapers—and volumes such as *Six Sketches of Taglioni* (1831) and *Gems for the Drawing Room* (1852). He also wrote popular songs, such as 'The Newfoundland Dog', and a novel, *Scenes and Stories by a Clergyman in Debt* (3 vols., 1835). About 1831 he was music critic for the *Morning Post*. He started and edited *National Omnibus*, a penny weekly, and from May 1842 until 1848 was first editor of the *Illustrated London News*, owned by Herbert Ingram; his first number set a style and format that lasted the century. Known as Alphabet (or sometimes Omnibus) Bayley, in the 1840s he was one of London's most innovative editors. However, he was improvident and became an alcoholic. He died from delirium tremens at the New Bull's Head inn, Digbeth, Birmingham, on 1 December 1852, and was buried in Birmingham cemetery.

H. C. G. MATTHEW

Sources Boase, *Mod. Eng. biog.* · d. cert. · *DNB* · *GM*, 2nd ser., 39 (1853), 324
Likenesses R. J. Hammerton, lithograph, NPG

Bayley, Henry Vincent (1777–1844), Church of England clergyman, was the seventh son of Thomas Butterworth *Bayley (1744–1802), of Hope Hall, near Manchester, where he was born on 6 December 1777. His mother was Mary, only child of Vincent Leggatt. Bayley was educated at Winwick grammar school, Lancashire, and at Eton College, which he entered in May 1789 and left on 9 December 1795. At Eton he was the associate of Sir William Pepys, Henry Hallam, William Frere, William Herbert, and

others, who were known as the literati, and he contributed to *Musae Etonenses*. He went to Trinity College, Cambridge, in April 1796. In February 1798 he became Battie scholar, and in April he was elected a scholar of Trinity College. He took his BA degree in 1800, and won the bachelor's prizes in 1801 and 1802. Richard Porson pronounced him the first Greek scholar of his standing in England, and in 1802 he was elected a fellow of his college. In 1803 he was ordained by Bishop Majendie of Chester, who appointed him his chaplain. On 25 September 1803 he published *A Sermon Preached at an Ordination Held in the Cathedral Church of Chester*, his only published sermon. Not long afterwards he accepted the tutorship of Bishop G. P. Tomline's eldest son, and became examining chaplain to the bishop, by whom he was preferred to the rectory of Stilton, in Huntingdonshire (1804–6), and to the subdeanery of Lincoln in May 1805, which post he held until 1828. On 17 June 1807 he married Hannah (d. 1839), daughter of James Touchet of Broomhouse, near Manchester.

The beautification and renovation of Lincoln Cathedral became Bayley's chief preoccupation. He opened the cathedral library to the public, and helped to establish a public library in Lincoln. Though a high-churchman—'a most leading man among the Church party', William Palmer called him (Best, 292)—Bayley recognized the need for church reform, and he was counted among the Hackney Phalanx group. At Lincoln, however, he found himself in periodic disagreement over reform with John Kaye, his bishop. Moreover, his recognition of a general need for reform did not inhibit him from enthusiastically accumulating pluralities. In 1810 he was presented to the united vicarages of Messingham and Bottesford, where he renovated the parish church, chiefly at his own expense; in 1812 he was presented to the valuable vicarage of Great Carlton, near Louth, which he rarely visited, although he retained the benefice until his death. Later he was preferred to the archdeaconry of Stow with the prebend of Liddington (29 September 1823); to the rectory of West Meon with Privett, in Hampshire (1826); and to the twelfth stall in Westminster Abbey (1828), when he resigned his subdeanery and canonry at Lincoln.

In 1824 Bayley took the degree of DD at Cambridge. In 1827 he declined to stand for the regius professorship of divinity at Cambridge, owing probably to his growing infirmities. His last days were passed chiefly at West Meon, his Hampshire rectory. He repaired the church at Privett, and the rebuilding of the church of West Meon was begun on 9 August 1843. In that year his deteriorating eyesight prevented him reading or writing. When blind he recited the prayers from memory. He died on 12 August 1844. He was buried in the same vault as his wife, who had died at West Meon on 17 June 1839. The new church was consecrated by the bishop of Winchester on 5 May 1846.

ARTHUR H. GRANT, *rev.* H. C. G. MATTHEW

Sources *Lincolnshire Chronicle* (23 Aug 1844) · *Hampshire Chronicle* (9 May 1846) · *GM*, 2nd ser., 22 (1844), 325 · *A memoir of Henry Vincent Bayley* (privately printed, London, 1846) · W. Herbert, ed., *Musae Etonenses: seu carminum delectus nunc primum in lucem editus*, 3 vols. in

2 (1795) · G. F. A. Best, *Temporal pillars: Queen Anne's bounty, the ecclesiastical commissioners, and the Church of England* (1964) · W. B. Stonehouse, *A Stow visitation*, ed. N. S. Harding (1940) · Venn, *Alum. Cant.* **Archives** LPL, letters to Wordsworth family

Bayley, Sir John, first baronet (1763–1841), judge and legal writer, was born on 3 August 1763, at Elton, Huntingdonshire, the second son of John Bayley (*d.* 1790) of Abbots Ripton, whose ancestors had emigrated from Spanish Flanders in the seventeenth century, and his wife, Sarah (*d.* 1801), the daughter of the prebend of Peterborough, White Kennett. Bayley was educated at Eton College, and intended to go on to King's College, Cambridge, and into the church. However, he never matriculated and instead began a career in law. He was admitted in November 1783 into Gray's Inn, having spent a year in the office of the attorneys William and Joseph Lyon of Coney Court. After two years in the office of the special pleader William Lamb, Bayley began to practise himself in that branch of the law, with considerable success. His reputation was aided by the publication, in 1789, of his *Treatise on the Law of Bills of Exchange*, one of a number of pioneering late eighteenth-century systematic treatises of law. By 1836 the book had gone through five English and two American editions. In 1790 Bayley brought out a new edition of Lord Raymond's law reports. At this time he also compiled a manuscript digest of the law of evidence, which was widely used by later pupils.

Bayley was called to the bar in June 1792, and rapidly acquired a large practice on the home circuit. As a lawyer Bayley was notable less for his eloquence as an advocate than for his mastery of case law and the technicalities of legal practice; his work therefore consisted chiefly of legal arguments. In 1799 he was made a serjeant-at-law, and appointed to the recordership of Maidstone. At a time when many judges were appointed late in life, Bayley advanced to the bench at an unusually early age. In 1808 he was made a puisne judge of the king's bench, when Justice Laurence moved to the common pleas to fill the place left vacant by the death of Justice Rooke. Bayley received a knighthood at the same time.

Bayley remained on the king's bench until November 1830, when he moved at his own request into the exchequer, taking advantage of the statute which authorized the appointment of a fifth judge in each court. As a judge he was extremely popular with the bar, as was clearly manifested in 1823 when Bayley, wanting a lighter burden of work, first sought a place on the exchequer bench: 11 silks and 101 barristers practising in the king's bench presented two memorials to Bayley, which persuaded him to stay. When he finally left the court in 1830 an address by Henry Brougham again reaffirmed the fondness the bar had for this judge. He retired from the bench in February 1834, and in the following month was created a baronet and sworn of the privy council.

Bayley was distinguished by his particular mastery of the common law. He was described by the *Legal Observer* as one of a kind of case lawyers, 'who has a clue to the labyrinth' of the common law, 'who, trusting neither to digest or treatise, can out boldly out to the wide ocean of reports

Sir John Bayley, first baronet (1763–1841), by William Russell, *c.*1808

and steer his client safely to harbour' (23, 1842, 177). Bayley always carried with him seven little red manuscript books, 'which are said to contain every case that ever was or ever will be decided in Westminster Hall' (Napier). The pleasure which he derived from sitting on the bench was reflected in Cotte's comment that 'il s'amuse à juger' (Campbell, 2.397n). His manner of giving judgments was praised by Joseph Chitty as 'the model which should be invariably adopted' (Chitty, 2.43), though the fact that as a judge he was more wedded to precedent than principle may help explain why he never reached the highest judicial office. Bayley was one of the judges who tried James Watson for high treason in 1817, summing up the evidence when his friend Lord Ellenborough was too tired to proceed. Along with the other judges of the king's bench he also advised Peel in the 1820s on the reform of the criminal law.

He remained throughout his life a very devout man, producing in 1816 an edition of the Book of Common Prayer, as well as *The Prophecies of Christ and Christian Times, Selected from the Old and New Testament* (ed. H. Clissold, 1828). The dean of Gloucester wrote to Bayley on 12 February 1813, complimenting him on his new edition of the prayer book, and adding 'Law and Divinity thrive equally under your protection'. Indeed, Bayley always believed that he would have risen higher in the church than he did in the law.

Bayley married Elizabeth (*d.* 1837), the youngest daughter of John Markett of Meopham Court, on 20 May 1790, and they had six children. Two of their sons became barristers: one, Francis, brought out an edition of his father's book on bills, and became judge in the Westminster county court. Bayley died on 10 October 1841 at his country home, Vine House, near Sevenoaks, Kent.

MICHAEL LOBBAN

Sources *Law Times* (29 March 1845), 506–7 · 'A memoir of the late Mr Baron Bayley', *Legal Observer*, 23 (1841–2), 177–9 · Foss, *Judges*, vol. 9 · John, Lord Campbell, *The lives of the chief justices of England*, 3 vols. (1849–57), vols. 2–3 · *The Times* (18 Oct 1841) · *The Times* (1 Feb 1834) · 'Judicial characters, no. XIII: Mr Baron Bayley', *Legal Observer*, 7 (1833–4), 305–6 · *Legal Observer*, 2 (1831), 97 · Burke, *Peerage* (1970) · J. Foster, *The register of admissions to Gray's Inn, 1521–1889, together with the register of marriages in Gray's Inn chapel, 1695–1754* (privately printed, London, 1889) · *N&Q*, 3rd ser., 1 (1862), 474 · J. Napier, *Manual of improved precedents* (1831) · J. Chitty, *The practice of the law in all its departments*, 2 (1836), 43 · Baker, *Serjeants* · Sainty, *Judges* · DNB · private information (2004)

Archives BL, corresp. with Robert Peel · Durham RO, corresp. with Edward Pease

Likenesses W. Russell, oils, *c*.1808, NPG [*see illus.*] · E. B. Stephens, marble bust, exh. RA 1849, St John's Church, Meopham, Kent · E. B. Stephens, marble bust, 1850, Eton · S. Topham, line engraving (after W. Robinson), NPG

Bayley, John Whitcomb (*d.* 1869), antiquary, second son of John Bayley (*d.* 1811), a farmer, of Hempsted, Gloucestershire, became, at an early age, a junior clerk in the Tower Record Office. In or about 1819 he was appointed chief clerk, and afterwards a subcommissioner on the public records. In the latter capacity he edited *Calendars of the Proceedings in Chancery in the Reign of Queen Elizabeth* (1827–32), for which work he was paid £2739, but claimed further remuneration. His exorbitant charges and editorial methods were vigorously attacked by Charles Purton Cooper, then secretary to the record commission, Sir N. H. Nicolas, and others during a campaign principally directed at Francis Palgrave. Frederic Madden described Bayley in 1832 as 'one of the greatest knaves breathing'. A committee was appointed in 1832 to inquire into the matter, and, after meeting no fewer than seventeen times, issued a report, of which twenty-five copies were printed for the private use of the board. The committee concluded that he had claimed fees for work done by others and his charges were excessive. Bayley's demands upon the corporation of Liverpool, whom he had charged between £3000 and £4000 for record searches, became the subject of a separate inquiry.

Owing to his long absence, Bayley's office at the Tower was declared vacant in May 1834. He had been admitted to the Inner Temple in August 1815, but was never called to the bar. He married Sophia Anne (*d.* 1854), daughter of the Rt Hon. Colonel Robert Ward, of Bangor Castle, co. Down, in September 1824; they had one daughter. During the rest of his life he lived mainly in Cheltenham, but in his last years moved to Paris.

As an antiquary, Bayley's chief work was his *History and Antiquities of the Tower of London* (1821–5). He also worked on a parliamentary history of England, for which he obtained copious abstracts of the returns to parliament from 1702 to 1710, from the original records in the Rolls chapel. The manuscript of this work, together with a valuable collection of charters, letters patent, and other documents illustrative of local history, is now in the British Library (Add.

MSS 15661–15665). Bayley was a fellow of the Society of Antiquaries and of the Royal Society. He was elected to the former in 1819, but expelled in 1845 for being sixteen years in arrears; he was elected to the latter in 1823. He died on 25 March 1869 at 85 boulevard de Mont Rouge in Paris.

GORDON GOODWIN, rev. BERNARD NURSE

Sources C. P. Cooper, *Observations on the calendar of proceedings in chancery*, ed. F. Palgrave (1832) · N. H. Nicolas, *Letter to Lord Brougham* (1832) · 'Select committee on … the record commission: minutes of evidence and appendix', *Parl. papers* (1836), 16.1–937, no. 565 · *Report of the committee … to inquire into … Mr Bayley's publication of the calendars of the proceedings in chancery* (1833) · *The bill of John Bayley esq.* … (1833) · *GM*, 1st ser., 81/1 (1811), 192 · *GM*, 1st ser., 94/2 (1824), 272 · *GM*, 1st ser., 95/2 (1825), 256 · *GM*, 2nd ser., 42 (1854), 202 · J. D. Cantwell, *The Public Record Office, 1838–1958* (1991) · Burke, *Peerage* (1884) · admissions register, 1815, Inner Temple, London · CGPLA Eng. & Wales (1870)

Archives BL, local history notes, Add. MSS 15661–15665 · Lpool RO, transcripts of documents relating to Liverpool | Bodl. Oxf., corresp. with Sir Thomas Phillipps · Duke U., Perkins L., corresp. with Thomas Cadell · Hounslow Reference Library, London, letters

Wealth at death under £300: administration, 8 Feb 1870, CGPLA Eng. & Wales

Bayley, Mary (*b.* 1816, *d.* in or after 1892), temperance activist and writer, was born in Market Lavington, Wiltshire. Nothing is known of her early life. Her husband, George Bayley (1807–1888), was born in Rotherhithe, served in the merchant navy between the ages of sixteen and forty-four, and was an elder brother of the Trinity House for thirty-one years. Presumably influenced by his wife, who was already active in the temperance movement, Bayley became an abstainer at the age of fifty-three. Mary and George Bayley had five daughters, the first of whom was born in 1846; only one, the novelist and writer Elizabeth Boyd Bayley, outlived her parents. After a period abroad (the eldest Bayley daughter was born in Calcutta), the family settled in London, first at 8 Lansdowne Crescent in Kensington. They moved to Barnet in 1864, for the sake of the children's health, and latterly lived in Kempshott Road, Streatham Common. Mary Bayley also suffered from poor health: in the autumn of 1860 she suffered a long and severe illness which struck her again in 1882, and from about 1887 until her death she regarded herself as an invalid.

An Anglican hostile to Roman Catholicism, Mrs Bayley's principal concern was the effect of alcohol abuse on the working classes. She believed that 'this dreadful vice' was responsible for filling England with 'moral wrecks' and caused the deaths of 60,000 people a year. Her aim was to eliminate male drunkenness through the domestic influence of wives and mothers, explaining that 'long experience had taught me that all real, healthy, permanent, domestic reform must begin with the mother' (M. Bayley, *Mended Homes and what Repaired Them*, 1861, 26, 5). In 1853 Mary Bayley began her mothers' meetings in the notorious Kensington potteries area, offering working-class women religious and domestic education, and bringing women of different social classes together so that the rich could exercise a good influence over the poor.

Mary Bayley doubted that it was wise for poor women to

be employed outside the home. In her pamphlets she argued that if poor women went out to work, they would have less time to make their homes attractive to their husbands and sons; if their homes were uncomfortable, the men would go to the public house and waste their money on drink. This would mean that the household needed more money to survive, thus driving women out to work and producing a vicious circle of drinking and decline. Mrs Bayley particularly attacked laundry work for women—an occupation much associated with female drunkenness—arguing in *Mended Homes* that washing machines operated by men should be introduced to allow poor women to go back to their proper places by the domestic fireside.

Having concentrated at first on the failings of working-class wives and mothers, Mary Bayley turned her attention in 1860 to the position of the men themselves. With her husband and other sympathizers she established a model Workmen's Temperance Hall in Portland Road, Notting Hill. The hall was opened on 12 March 1861 by Samuel Gurney before a large ecumenical gathering attended by the bishop of London. The object of the hall was to provide working men with a place to meet which would be a real alternative both to the warmth and congeniality of the public house and to their impoverished homes: it was to be a self-financing coffee house, offering working men non-alcoholic refreshments and bathing facilities in pleasant surroundings. The attached Bible mission provided non-sectarian religious teaching to reinforce the temperance message. The Bayleys had great plans for the hall and the temperance society which supported it, but their experiment was short-lived. They moved away from the area in 1864, and without their constant support the hall's fortunes declined. In 1866 a problem arose over the title to the hall and it closed its doors. However, Elizabeth Boyd Bayley later claimed that the hall had been of considerable significance as an influence on the work of Ellice Hopkins, the purity campaigner, and Louisa Daniells, the founder of the Soldiers' Homes.

Mary Bayley was a prolific writer of pamphlets championing temperance and female domesticity, including *Ragged Homes and how to Mend them* (1860), *Danger Signals: how to Use them Wisely* (1887), and *Home Weal and Home Woe* (1892), which was written in collaboration with her daughter Elizabeth. She died in or after 1892.

MICHELLE CALE

Sources M. Bayley and E. Bayley, *Home weal and home woe* (1892) · census returns for Kensington, 1861, PRO, RG 9/19; for Streatham, 1891, RG 12/458 · F. H. W. Sheppard, ed., *Northern Kensington*, Survey of London, 37 (1973) · *Kelly's directory of Surrey* (1891) · Trinity House Lighthouse Service archives

Bayley, Peter (*bap.* 1778, *d.* 1823), poet, was baptized on 1 September 1778 in Nantwich, the second, but first surviving, of the five children of Peter Bayley (1742–1803), attorney, and his wife, Sarah (1758–1832), the daughter of Martin Tomkinson of Bucknall-cum-Bagnall, Stoke-on-Trent. Educated at Rugby School from 1790 to 1795 and at Merton College, Oxford, from 1796 to 1798, Bayley was admitted to

Lincoln's Inn on 19 January 1799. Hoping to pursue one of the arts, he refused to devote himself to legal studies; this led to a breach with his father, financial difficulties, and imprisonment for debt. In 1803 he published *Poems*, a collection which reflects a profound and early admiration of Wordsworth and Coleridge's *Lyrical Ballads*; unwilling to be publicly associated with those writers, however (Francis Jeffrey had just commenced his attacks on the 'Lake school'), Bayley presented an imitation of Wordsworth's 'Idiot Boy' as a burlesque. Wordsworth and Coleridge responded by assisting Robert Southey in writing a ferocious review of the volume for the *Annual Review*. Bayley had written other poetry, but this review, along with financial security on his father's death, subdued his literary ambitions.

Having returned to Nantwich in 1803, Bayley married his cousin Mary Wright (1774?–1830) on 1 October 1807; they had three children, Charlotte Maria (1808–1844), Mary Anne (1810–1844), and William Peter (1813–1881). Bayley spent the years after his marriage living in rural Staffordshire, but moved back to London later in life. He appears to have published nothing more of substance until 1817, when 'Gryphiadæa', a burlesque Greek poem, appeared in the *Classical Journal*. In 1820 he published two English poems, *Sketches from St George's Fields* and *A Queen's Appeal*, the former drawing on his experiences of prison life, the latter supporting Queen Caroline. In 1822 Bayley began editing a new literary periodical, the *London Museum*, which supplies evidence of his continuing love of Wordsworth's poetry. He died in London on 25 January 1823, leaving many literary works in manuscript. *Idwal*, a Spenserian poem, and *Orestes in Argos*, a tragedy, were published posthumously in 1824 and 1825 respectively.

DAVID CHANDLER

Sources *London Museum*, 2 (1823), 77–8 · C. Stretton, 'The pedigree of the Bayleys of Willaston, count Chester', Bodl. Oxf., MS 32210 · D. Chandler, '"Twisted in persecution's loving ways": Peter Bayley reviewed by Southey, Wordsworth and Coleridge', *Wordsworth Circle*, 24 (1993), 256–61 · W. P. Baildon, ed., *The records of the Honorable Society of Lincoln's Inn: admissions*, 2 vols. (1896) · Bayley, published works · *IGI* · will of Peter Bayley (1742–1803), PRO

Bayley, Robert Slater (1800/01–1859), Congregational minister, was educated at Highbury College, and took up his first pastorate at Louth, in Lincolnshire, concerning which place he published *Notitiae Ludae, or, Notices of Louth* in 1834. The following year he took charge of the Howard Street congregation in Sheffield. During this time he was active in the establishment of the People's College, where he also lectured on a variety of subjects. In 1846 he started a monthly periodical, the *People's College Journal*, which was printed at the college and intended to further the interests of popular education, but it folded in May 1847. His engagement with popular politics at this time is revealed by a pamphlet of 1841, *Chartism v. whigism: a letter to the Rev. R. S. Bayley, FSA, in reply to his charges against the Chartists*.

In the late 1840s Bayley moved to London to serve the Ratcliffe Highway congregation; he continued to publish a variety of sermons and lectures, including *A Course of Lectures on the Inspiration of the Scriptures* (1852). In 1857 he moved to Hereford, where he remained until his death from 'apoplexy with epilepsy' at Eight Gate, in the parish of All Saints, on 15 November 1859.

J. M. RIGG, *rev.* J. M. V. QUINN

Sources GM, 3rd ser., 8 (1860), 186 · d. cert.

Bayley, Sir Steuart Colvin (1836–1925), administrator in India, youngest son of (William) Butterworth *Bayley (1781–1860) of the Bengal civil service and his wife, Anne Augusta, daughter of William Jackson, registrar of the Calcutta supreme court, was born in London on 26 November 1836. He was educated at Eton College and the East India College, Haileybury, and arrived in India to take up a post in the Bengal civil service in March 1856. On 21 November 1860 he married, at Patna, Anna (d. 1924), daughter of Robert Nesham Farquharson of the Indian Civil Service; they had thirteen children.

Bayley spent most of his career in the provinces of Bengal and Bihar. From 1862 until 1867 he was attached to the secretariat of the government of Bengal, officiating while still relatively junior as chief secretary for short periods in 1865 and again in 1867. In January 1871 he was appointed commissioner of Chittagong and in March 1872 commissioner of Patna. For his efforts in coping with the famine of 1873–4 in that division he was made CSI. In 1877 he accompanied the viceroy, Lord Lytton, on his tour of southern India as his private secretary for famine affairs. Promoted KCSI in 1878, he was appointed in the same year chief commissioner of Assam. In 1881 he was made CIE and transferred to Hyderabad as resident, and in the following year he was appointed home member of the executive council.

In April 1887 Bayley was appointed lieutenant-governor of Bengal. His administration was an unspectacular one in which he concentrated on damping down the racial animosity roused by the controversy over the Ilbert Bill in 1883–4. He tried in a quiet, uninflammatory way to increase the participation of Indians in low-level public affairs by extending both the system of honorary magistrates and the application of the elective principle in local self-government. He also attempted to facilitate the advancement of Indians in government service, but again in a muted and gradual fashion. He was considered an accessible governor and a hard worker, but by his own admission he had aimed, internally at least, for a 'colourless', calming administration. Discontent on the margins of Bengal was not, however, treated in such a conciliatory fashion and in 1889–90 Bayley sent a punitive expedition to the frontier hill tracts of Chittagong to suppress uprisings and raids by the indigenous peoples there. In December 1890 he resigned as lieutenant-governor, having been appointed political secretary to the India Office. A statue was subsequently erected by the citizens of Calcutta in his memory. In 1895 Bayley became a member of the Council of India. He retired finally from the service in 1905, on the eve of Curzon's partition of Bengal, a radical step which he viewed with considerable misgiving. In 1911 he was promoted GCSI.

Bayley served on the committee of the Athenaeum from 1900 to 1920 and was its chairman for five years. He was also chairman of the Royal Society of Arts from 1906 to 1908. He was a widely read man and an insightful and often humorous literary critic. By inclination a conservative, he was nevertheless realist enough to appreciate the growth of nationalist sentiment in India and to try to accommodate it, albeit in a limited and cautious way. He died at his home at 2 Cathcart Road, Kensington, London, on 3 June 1925 and was buried in Brompton cemetery. His wife had predeceased him, after sixty-four years of marriage, by only six months.

P. C. LYON, *rev.* KATHERINE PRIOR

Sources C. E. Buckland, *Bengal under the lieutenant-governors*, 2 vols. (1901) · *The Times* (4 June 1925), 14 · BL OIOC, Haileybury MSS · F. C. Danvers and others, *Memorials of old Haileybury College* (1894) · H. E. C. Stapylton, *The Eton school lists, from 1791 to 1850*, 2nd edn (1864) · CGPLA Eng. & Wales (1925)

Archives priv. coll. | BL, corresp. with Lord Ripon, Add. MS 43612 · BL OIOC, letters to Claude Clerk, MS Eur. D 538 · Bodl. Oxf., corresp. with Lord Kimberley

Likenesses H. Thornycroft, statue, *c.*1896, near treasury buildings, Calcutta · photograph, *c.*1911, BL OIOC · W. Stoneman, photograph, 1917, NPG · Messrs Bourne & Shepherd, photograph, repro. in Buckland, *Bengal under the lieutenant-governors*, vol. 2

Wealth at death £3840 13s. 7d.: probate, 24 July 1925, CGPLA Eng. & Wales

Bayley, Thomas Butterworth (1744–1802), penal reformer, was born at Manchester to one of the town's well-established nonconformist families. His father, Daniel Bayley, was deputy lieutenant for Lancashire and served, along with his father-in-law Thomas Butterworth, as a trustee of Manchester's Cross Street Chapel. Thomas Butterworth Bayley studied at Edinburgh University, where he was schooled in the radical ideas of John Wilkes, with whom he corresponded and to whose daughter he (unsuccessfully) proposed. On his return to Manchester he was chosen as a justice of the peace for Lancashire, joined the bench, and several years later was appointed permanent chairman of the quarter sessions. A judge in the Unitarian whig tradition, Bayley had already criticized aspects of the existing penal policy, including overcrowding and the fee system in prisons when, in the wake of the 1782 Gilbert's Act, he was asked to investigate the condition of correction houses at Manchester, Lancaster, and Preston. His report, co-authored with Samuel Clowes, called for better standards of convict welfare, recommending the separation of categories of inmates, improved hygiene, and new prisoner work regimes. On the basis of their suggestions, and bolstered by fears of further outbreaks of gaol fever, the Manchester sessions took the decision to rebuild the town's prison in late 1785. Work on the New Bailey house of correction began in 1787 and that of Preston in the following year. In addition to his advisory role in regional and later nationwide prison improvement, Bayley also took an active interest in welfare and sanitary reform, influencing legislation to regulate factory work for children, calling for a minimum wage, and founding and chairing Manchester's board of health in 1796. Several of the board's co-founders, including his closest friend, the physician Thomas Percival, had also been involved with him in the establishment of the Manchester Literary and Philosophical Society. Like many of the city's Unitarian reformers, Bayley maintained a life-long belief in the benefits of education. He was a trustee of the Warrington Academy, promoted the establishment of Sunday schools in the region, and was behind the unsuccessful scheme to set up a Manchester college of arts and sciences. Much influenced by the economic theories of Adam Smith, Bayley also undertook reforms in the management of his estate at Hope, near Manchester, for which he was elected a fellow of the Royal Society. On this subject he published, among other pamphlets, *On a Cheap and Expeditious Method of Draining Land* (1772). He was married to Mary Leggatt, the only child of Vincent Leggatt of London, and their children included the Indian administrator (William) Butterworth *Bayley (1781–1860) and Henry Vincent *Bayley (1777–1844), Church of England clergyman. Bayley died of 'a disorder of the bowels' at his home in Buxton on 24 June 1802.   PHILIP CARTER

Sources DNB · T. Percival, *Biographical memoirs of the late Thomas Butterworth Bayley* (1802) · GM, 1st ser., 72 (1802), 689, 777 · M. De Lacy, *Prison reform in Lancashire, 1700–1850* (1986) · T. Baker, *Memorials of a dissenting chapel* (1884)
Archives BL, corresp. with earl of Liverpool, Add. MSS 38222–38471, *passim* · Man. CL, Manchester Archives and Local Studies, letters to J. L. Philips, etc. · NA Scot., corresp. with Henry Dundas

Bayley, Walter (1529–1593), physician, was born in Portisham, Dorset, the fifth and youngest son of Henry Bayley of Warnewall. His mother's maiden name was Samways. He attended Winchester College before, in 1548, entering New College, Oxford, where he became a fellow in 1550. He graduated BA on 24 October 1552 and MA on 6 July 1556, then obtained his MB and was admitted to medical practice on 21 February 1559. In 1561 he became regius professor of medicine at Oxford, and he continued as such until 1582. He was awarded his MD on 26 July 1563, and was elected a fellow of the College of Physicians in 1581. Queen Elizabeth I made him one of her physicians, and he was in the service of the earl of Leicester. As well as pursuing such a successful medical and academic career, he was a canon of Wells, Somerset, from 1573 to 1579. About 1566 Bayley married Anne, *née* Evans, the daughter of Arman or Harman Evans, citizen of Oxford, but formerly of Randerout in Gulickland.

Bayley published several works, all privately and anonymously, as gifts for his friends. The first appeared in 1586: *A Brief Treatise Touching the Preservation of the Eyesight*. It is mainly derivative, but contains one observation of his own, recording how a man named Hoorde preserved his sight until he was more than eighty-four years of age by using 'eye-bright in ale'. In 1587 he published *A Brief Discourse of Certain Bathes of Medicinal Waters in the County of Warwick*, and in 1588, *A Short Discourse of the Three Kinds of Pepper in Common Use*.

Bayley was a resident of London, living in Salisbury Court, near Fleet Street. He died on 3 March 1593 and was buried in the chapel of New College, Oxford, where his eldest son William had a tablet engraved to his memory.

By the time of his death, his wife Anne was an invalid, possibly mentally ill. He left two sons, William and Walter, and four daughters, one of whom married Anthony Ailworth, who had succeeded Bayley as regius professor of medicine.   SARAH BAKEWELL

Sources D. Power, *Dr Walter Bayley and his works, 1529–1592* (1907) [incl. repr. of will] · L. G. H. Horton-Smith, *Dr Walter Baily (or Bayley), c.1529–1592: physician to Queen Elizabeth I…* (1952) · Foster, *Alum. Oxon.* · Munk, *Roll* · L. G. H. Horton-Smith, 'Dr Walter Baily and Sir John Wolley: two Elizabethans', *N&Q*, 185 (1943), 18–19 · C. A. Wood, 'The first English monograph on ophthalmology', *Bulletin of the Society of Medical History of Chicago*, 2 (1917–22), 146–57 · will, 4 Jan 1591 [proved 25 March 1592]

Baylie, Richard (1585–1667), college head and dean of Salisbury, was born either at Coventry, Warwickshire, or Lichfield, Staffordshire, in 1585, probably in July. He was elected from Coventry School to a scholarship at St John's College about midsummer 1601. He matriculated on 3 July 1601, graduated BA on 3 July 1605, proceeded MA on 27 June 1609, and obtained a fellowship probably about the latter date. At the troubled election of William Laud to the college presidency on 10 May 1611 he was expelled for destroying ballot papers but, after restoration by the visitor, was won over by Laud. Baylie was ordained priest on 19 September 1613, and elected proctor with Laud's support in 1615. He proceeded BD on 18 July 1616, and was vice-president of St John's in the year 1621 to 1622.

After Laud became bishop of St David's in 1621 Baylie became his chaplain and from 1622 chancellor of the diocese, with a canonry. He resigned his Oxford fellowship on 24 July 1623. His patron's *An answere to Mr. Fishers relation of a third conference between a certaine B. (as he stiles him) and himselfe* was published by R. B. as chaplain in 1624. Laud ceded him the rectory of Ibstock, Leicestershire, on 6 March 1626 and on 3 April Baylie married Elizabeth (d. 1668), daughter of Laud's half-brother, William Robinson, rector of Long Whatton in the same county. The couple had at least three sons and three daughters, including Richard, created BCL at Oxford in 1661; John, who graduated BCL at Oxford in 1663 and was later chancellor of the diocese of Bath and Wells; and Samuel (d. 1658), a sailor.

Baylie resigned his Welsh preferment in September 1626 after Laud's translation to Bath and Wells. Already a royal chaplain, on 7 January 1628 he was presented by the king to the archdeaconry of Nottingham and a canonry of York. In the 1629 parliament Baylie's Arminianism was cited to attack Laud, and the following year he warned clergy off current disputes in reformed churches. After Laud moved to London, Baylie received a canonry of St Paul's on 2 May 1631 and the vicarage of Northall, Middlesex, on 24 April 1632.

Elected president of St John's College on 12 January 1633, Baylie proceeded DD on 16 July. He was often attacked in Oxford as an Arminian, and a hostile senior fellow, John Lufton, gave him much trouble in college. Through Laud's agency Lufton was bought off by 1636, with Ibstock rectory and a lucrative Welsh sinecure, but finally removed from Oxford only by Sir John Lambe's insistence that he reside at his living. Baylie continued

William Juxon's work on Laud's new quadrangle at St John's, completed in 1636. In late 1634 he tried to reconcile Bulstrode Whitelocke, a St John's man, with Archbishop Laud. The archbishop, probably desiring a friend in a chapter where Bishop John Williams of Lincoln had influence and in which John Prideaux was a canon, placed his nephew by marriage in the deanery of Salisbury on 22 April 1635. On 8 May Baylie resigned his archdeaconry to his father-in-law.

Soon after returning to St John's, Baylie became a delegate for the university press, a special concern for Laud. Printing linked the two, and it was probably Baylie who introduced Laud to the man who became his privileged printer, Richard Badger (who repeatedly stood surety for first fruits in the younger man's preferments from 1623). Laud, as chancellor of Oxford, nominated Baylie vice-chancellor for the years 1636/7 and 1637/8. His protégé was in place for the visit of the king and queen to Oxford in late August 1636. Laud's definitive statutes had been given to the university just before Baylie's vice-chancellorship and their implementation fell to him. His mandate saw the building of a convocation house and an extension to the Bodleian Library, projects dear to the chancellor. However, Baylie encountered many difficulties with the city following the grant of an enlarged charter to the university by Laud's influence and the chancellor was not always pleased with him. When Baylie allowed an imprudent question supporting the new Scottish liturgy for the university Act of 1638, Laud insisted on withdrawal.

The previous year Baylie had obtained Bradfield rectory in Berkshire, on 22 October, and resigned Northall on 30 December. In 1638 the archbishop appointed him one of his commissioners for visitation of Merton College. Perhaps mindful of his own troubles with a recalcitrant fellow, Baylie, unlike Bishop John Bancroft of Oxford and other commissioners, hesitated to condemn the warden, Sir Nathaniel Brent. Peter Turner, the archbishop's confidant at Merton, complained about Baylie's attitude but none the less his stance may have contributed to Laud's reluctance to proceed vigorously.

On the break between king and parliament Baylie subscribed to the 1642 protestation only with reservations. He welcomed royal troopers to Oxford and never wavered in loyalty. When St John's surrendered its plate to the king after first paying for the privilege of not doing so, Baylie's initials, R. B., appeared on coinage minted from it. By Laud's will his kinsman became his sole executor after his execution on 10 January 1645. Baylie was to be recipient of all the archbishop's papers and sermons and it was left to his judgement to burn anything harmful to Laud's reputation.

Baylie was a university commissioner in negotiating Oxford's surrender in May and June 1646, and pressed for safeguards. He compounded for delinquency in December 1646 and was fined £257. Prominently recalcitrant, on 20 January 1648 he was formally removed from the presidency of St John's by the parliament for contempt of its authority. Still he resisted, and, following a stay of removal granted Elizabeth Baylie on 13 April owing to her children's illness, he was finally ejected from his lodgings on 2 June.

Thereafter Baylie lived quietly at Oxford on the proceeds of a lease, in the names of three of his children, which he had acquired during his Welsh preferment. He attended John Fell's semi-clandestine episcopal services in the city and on 28 April 1660 was signatory to an Oxfordshire royalists' manifesto disavowing revenge on their enemies.

Restored to St John's by a commission of visitation on 31 July 1660, Baylie strove to keep discipline in those heady days and within a few months restored Anglican ritual. He led an academic delegation to London in April 1661 when the mayor and burgesses refused to swear an oath to the university. In the same year, Baylie refused the see of Lichfield, according to Wood because it had been 'skim'd' by the previous bishop, Accepted Frewen, who had reaped lucrative post-Restoration renewals of leases (Wood, *Ath. Oxon.*, 4.822). He was nominated vice-chancellor for the year 1661/2 by the new chancellor, the earl of Clarendon, whom he entertained in September 1661, and in office took a tough line with religious dissent. In 1662 he began work on a side-chapel which he added to the north of the main altar at St John's, and with a gift from a former fellow in 1663 he paved the sanctuary in marble. In the latter year he welcomed the king and queen with the duke and duchess of York to the college. In 1665 he received the St John's rectory of Hanborough, Oxfordshire.

Baylie was diligent in sifting and preserving Laud's papers in these years. In 1667 he edited for the press *A Summarie of Devotions, Compiled and used by Dr William Laud*. The archbishop's marginal responses to William Prynne's calumnies were kept by him and after his death, by the agency of Anthony Wood, were eventually published in 1695 by Henry Wharton. He published nothing of his own other than poems contributed to collective university volumes between 1633 and 1662.

Baylie died on 27 July 1667 at Salisbury, where he had restored cathedral furnishings after 1660 with help from members of the Hyde family. He was buried in the chapel of St John's College. His widow, Elizabeth, died the following year on 29 September. Baylie was succeeded at St John's by his daughter Mary's husband, Peter *Mews (1619–1706).   A. J. HEGARTY

Sources Wood, *Ath. Oxon.*, new edn • Wood, *Ath. Oxon.: Fasti*, new edn • Foster, *Alum. Oxon.* • St John's College, Oxford, MS 272 • *The life and times of Anthony Wood*, ed. A. Clark, 5 vols., OHS, 19, 21, 26, 30, 40 (1891–1900) • copy of Laud's will, Bodl. Oxf., MS Add. C. 304b, fols. 20r–29r • W. C. Costin, *The history of St John's College, Oxford, 1598–1860*, OHS, new ser., 12 (1958) • *Fasti Angl., 1541–1857*, [St Paul's, London; York; Salisbury], vols. 1, 4, 6 • office of first fruits and tenths, composition books, PRO, E 334/16, E 334/17, E 334/19 • PRO, SO 3/9 • A. Milton, *Catholic and Reformed: the Roman and protestant churches in English protestant thought, 1600–1640* (1995), 433 • P. E. McCullough, 'Making dead men speak', *HJ*, 41 (1998), 401–24 • R. A. Beddard, 'Restoration Oxford and the making of the protestant establishment', *Hist. U. Oxf.* 4: 17th-cent. Oxf., 803–62

Archives Bodl. Oxf., corresp., notes, and orations; two sermons and other sermon notes in Richard Baylie's hand, MS Rawl. E. 28

Likenesses J. Latham?, alabaster effigy on a monument, after 1676, St John's College chapel, Oxford, Baylie Chapel; repro. in

R. A. Adams, ed., *Memorial inscriptions in St John's College Oxford* (1996)

Baylie, Thomas (1581/2–1663), ejected minister, was born in Wiltshire; his parents are unknown. He matriculated from St Alban Hall, Oxford, on 31 October 1600, aged eighteen, and was elected a demy of Magdalen College from 1602. Having graduated BA on 12 December 1604 he proceeded MA on 8 July 1607, and was a fellow of Magdalen from 1610 to 1615.

Having resigned his fellowship Baylie married Sarah (*bap.* 1593?, *d.* 1660), daughter of Robert *Parker (*c.*1564–1614), minister in the Netherlands, and his wife, Dorothy, and sister of Thomas *Parker (1595–1677); their son Robert was born in 1615 or 1616. Baylie proceeded BD on 11 May 1621, was licensed to preach on 18 May, and that year became rector of Manningford Bruce in his native county. His BD thesis, *De merito mortis Christi et modo conversionis*, and a sermon given at St Mary's, Oxford, on 5 July 1622, were published in 1626 with a dedication to the attorney-general, Sir Thomas Coventry.

On 25 April 1642 Baylie was nominated as a Wiltshire representative to the Westminster assembly. He was rector of Beckenham, Kent, in 1647, and by that year had also succeeded the sequestered George Morley in the rich rectory of Mildenhall, Wiltshire. According to Anthony Wood he preached there 'the tenets held up by the fifth monarchy men, he being by that time one himself' (Wood, *Ath. Oxon.*), and subsequently joined the county's commission of triers and ejectors, but the latter claim at least is erroneous.

Baylie's wife, Sarah, died in 1660 and was buried at Mildenhall on 3 May. Six weeks later Morley petitioned the House of Lords for the return of his living but, following Morley's elevation to the see of Worcester, another rector was installed in Baylie's place on 1 September. Once ejected Baylie set up a conventicle at Marlborough, where in 1663 he died, and was buried on 27 March in St Peter's Church. His son William, a graduate of New Inn Hall, Oxford, who was vicar of Mere, Wiltshire, in November 1661, seems to have retained his living.

THOMPSON COOPER, *rev.* VIVIENNE LARMINIE

Sources Foster, *Alum. Oxon.* · *Calamy rev.* · Wood, *Ath. Oxon.*, new edn, 3.633 · *DNB*

Baylies, William (*bap.* 1722, *d.* 1787), physician, was baptized at All Saints' Church, Evesham, Worcestershire, on 25 March 1722, the only son of a prosperous apothecary, William Baylies (1683–1760), and his wife, Ann, *née* Fletcher (1688–1732). In his youth he was trained as an apothecary. On 12 July 1745 he married by licence Elizabeth (1727–1754), the eldest child of Robert Cookes, an attorney, and a substantial heir on the death of her brother in 1750. Their only child died as an infant in November 1749.

Baylies gained his MD at Aberdeen in 1748 and was elected a fellow of the College of Physicians in Edinburgh on 7 August 1759. He was a supporter of Worcester Infirmary and in 1751, with Dr John Wall, was one of the largest shareholders in the new Worcester Porcelain Company.

His house in Evesham, built by his father-in-law in 1692, with important garden features, was admired by Bishop Pococke in 1757. Baylies became a Worcestershire magistrate on 5 October 1755. He had moved to Bath by May 1757, but did not gain a hospital appointment, having clashed with the established medical figures there. As a result of the quarrel he published *A narrative of facts demonstrating the existence and course of a physical confederacy, made known in the printed letters of Dr Lucas and Dr Oliver* (1757). In 1758 he failed to be elected FRS. Wealthy after his father's death, in 1761 he contested Evesham as a tory in the parliamentary election; he lost to Sir John Rushout and his son, and unsuccessfully attempted to challenge the result.

In 1764 Baylies moved to a post at the Middlesex Hospital, London, becoming a licentiate of the London Royal College of Physicians in 1765. He lived in Great George Street, Westminster, and was known for his opulent lifestyle. However, on 4 April 1766 he asked for leave of absence from the hospital to attend to business out of town. He never returned and was dismissed in the following August. His Worcestershire estate was auctioned in May 1766 and Baylies fled to Dresden, apparently to escape his creditors. There were also rumours that in 1750 he had poisoned his wife's brother, who was about to come of age and inherit a fortune. This had then been settled on Baylies's wife. In 1774 Baylies moved to Berlin and was appointed as Frederick the Great's physician. Baylies died in Berlin, a bankrupt, on 2 March 1787. Although he had wished to be interred in Evesham, he was buried on 7 March in a vault of the Dorotheen Städtische Kirche, Berlin, and a substantial monument was erected in his memory by Prince Ferdinand, the king's brother. All Baylies's goods were sold in Berlin, including medical books, instruments, paintings, and his late wife's jewels.

Baylies also published *Remarks on Dr Perry's Analysis of the Stratford Mineral Waters* (1745), *Practical Reflections on the Uses and Abuses of Bath Waters* (1757), *A History of the General Hospital at Bath* (1758), *Aphorisms on the Smallpox* (1768; German edn, 1775), and *Facts and Observations Relative to Inoculation at Berlin* (1781; French edn, 1776).

JOAN LANE

Sources E. A. B. Barnard, 'An 18th century Worcestershire doctor: William Baylies of Evesham, 1724–87', *Transactions of the Worcestershire Archaeological Society*, 22 (1945), 35–54 · J. Chambers, *Biographical illustrations of Worcestershire* (1820) · H. W. McMenemey, *A history of the Royal Worcester Infirmary* (1947) · G. May, *History of Evesham* (1845) · *Worcestershire*, Pevsner (1968) · H. St G. Saunders, *The Middlesex Hospital, 1745–1948* (1949) · Munk, *Roll* · *Berrow's Worcester Journal* · Worcs. RO, Foley III, 203 · quarter sessions order book, Worcs. RO, BA6/3 · parish register, All Saints, Evesham, Worcs. RO · parish register, St Lawrence, Evesham, Worcs. RO · Governors' minutes, Middlesex Hospital

Archives BL, letters to Sir R. M. Keith, Add. MSS 35504–35509 · NL Scot., corresp. with Hugh Elliot · NL Scot., Elliot-Murray-Kynynm MSS

Likenesses H. Schmid, oils?, 1779 · D. Berger, engraving, 1783 (after H. Schmid, 1779), repro. in Barnard, '18th century Worcestershire doctor', facing p. 51

Wealth at death bankrupt: Barnard, '18th century Worcestershire doctor'

Baylis, Edward (1791–1861), insurance company manager, about whose early life nothing is known, began his career as a clerk in the Alliance insurance office. He was an enthusiast for the cause of life insurance, and during the years between 1838 and 1854 he founded a number of life offices: the Victoria, 1838, the English and Scottish Law, 1839, the Anchor, 1842, the Candidate, 1843, the Professional, 1847, the Trafalgar, 1851, the Waterloo, 1852, and the British Nation, 1854. In all these schemes there was, according to a later commentator, 'a curious mixing up of philanthropy with business' (Walford, 258). Baylis acted as both manager and actuary in most of his offices, and granted loans in connection with life insurance. Although his expectations were quite unrealistic there was no suggestion his practices were fraudulent. Shareholders and policyholders were promised extravagant advantages which never materialized and, in consequence, all Baylis's offices were short-lived, except for the English and Scottish Law. Baylis wrote in 1844 a skilful textbook, *The Arithmetic of Annuities and Life Assurance*. With his wife, Ellen Maria, he had at least five sons and a daughter between 1820 and 1834. He died on 12 September 1861, aged seventy, at the Retreat Hotel, Bas Harms Kraal, in the Cape of Good Hope, where he had settled in his old age. His son Thomas Hutchinson *Baylis joined the same profession, also without great success.

CORNELIUS WALFORD, rev. ROBERT BROWN

Sources C. Walford, *The insurance cyclopaedia*, 6 vols. (1871–80) · Boase, *Mod. Eng. biog.* · CGPLA Eng. & Wales (1862)
Wealth at death £800: probate, 19 May 1862, CGPLA Eng. & Wales

Baylis, George (1846–1936), farmer, was born on 7 January 1846, the son of George Baylis, a farmer, and his wife, Caroline (*née* Bomford), at Prospect House Farm, Bengeworth, near Evesham. The family moved to Woodley Farm, Reading, in 1849. Baylis was celebrated in the late nineteenth century—a period of general agricultural depression—for making money out of farming when so many others could barely make a living. His success derived from two key traits. First, he was an innovator with the ability to work from first principles and to institute a farming system suited to the prevailing economic conditions. Second, he was a businessman with the managerial flair necessary to make full use of the competitive advantage that his style of operation created. Such was the potency of this combination that, from a very ordinary beginning, Baylis rose to become one of the largest farmers in England.

Baylis initially chose law for a career, but not far into his training as a solicitor he changed his mind and, at the age of twenty-one, he took on the tenancy of a 240 acre farm at nearby Bradfield. This he worked in the normal way, following a four-course rotation and keeping livestock for the purpose of converting fodder crops into manure that then went back onto the land to maintain its fertility. Year by year he consistently lost money in the process. In 1875, still under thirty, he moved to a larger farm, the 400 acre Wyfield Manor on the Berkshire downs at Boxford, near Newbury, which he bought with £15,000 of borrowed capital. By virtue of the mortgage if nothing else, he had to make his farming pay. The result was a new system which was profitable and which furthermore laid the foundations for subsequent expansion.

At the heart of this departure was the removal of livestock from the whole farming equation. Under existing practice, the cultivation of root crops, the raising, feeding, and housing of animals, and the carting of manure out to the fields was a very laborious and costly way of keeping the land in a fertile state for corn production. In the harsh agricultural environment of the last quarter of the nineteenth century, with corn prices falling, it was for many the road to ruin. On the other hand the pioneer agricultural scientists Sir John Bennet Lawes and Sir Joseph Henry Gilbert had been conducting cropping experiments at Rothamsted in Hertfordshire since 1843. These were showing that even over a period of thirty years corn could be grown continuously on the same plot of land without any assistance from livestock, provided that fertility levels were sustained through the application of artificial manures.

Baylis studied the findings and organized his own practice accordingly. He settled upon a six-course rotation in which corn was grown in alternate years separated by bare fallow, clover, and bare fallow. Fertilizer, in the form of superphosphate, kainit, and nitrate of soda, was applied to the corn crops; cultivation of the bare fallow kept the soil clean, and the ploughing in of straw stubble and clover provided a rich humus base for plant growth. All the products of the system were sold straight off the farm: grain and clover hay went to market while the now surplus straw found buyers among the local racehorse stables and Hampshire strawberry growers. Moreover, the labour requirements of the different operations dovetailed throughout the year to provide a steady round of work for the farm staff.

Knowing that there were gains to be made from economies of scale, for example in the bulk purchase of fertilizer, Baylis soon set out on a programme of further expansion. Taking advantage of the ruinous position many tenant farmers and their landlords were finding themselves in, he was able to rent farms at little or no cost and to turn them round into profitable concerns. Between 1885 and 1900 he added a little over 3000 acres to his operation in this way, much of which was rented initially but then purchased later out of accumulated profits. By 1930 the total land under his control had risen to 12,140 acres, three-quarters of it in Berkshire and the rest in Hampshire. About half of the total he owned outright, to the value of £100,000.

Baylis married Maria Ferguson in 1870 and they had four sons, who followed him into farming, and five daughters. He died at his home, Wyfield Manor, Boxford, Newbury, on 21 May 1936 and was buried in Winterbourne churchyard, Berkshire. ROY BRIGDEN

Sources C. S. Orwin, *A specialist in arable farming*, in C. S. Orwin, *Progress in English farming systems*, 3 (1930) · H. G. Robinson, 'Notable farming enterprises', *Journal of the Royal Agricultural Society of England*, 91 (1930), 20–38 · private information (2004) · b. cert. · d. cert.
Wealth at death £245,596 0s. 10d.: probate, 7 Aug 1936, CGPLA Eng. & Wales

Baylis, Lilian Mary (1874–1937), theatre manager, was born at 19 Nottingham Street, Marylebone, London, on 9 May 1874, the eldest daughter of Edward William Baylis, an employee of Gillows furniture store in Oxford Street and a baritone singer (known as Newton Baylis), and his wife, Elizabeth Cons, a contralto singer and pianist. The eldest of ten children (five of whom survived infancy), Lilian was educated at home and later attended a convent school, St Augustine's in Kilburn, on alternate weeks. She also received tuition from the violinist and composer John Tiplady Carrodus. When Lilian was seventeen the family emigrated to south Africa, where they toured musical acts under the name of the Gipsy Revellers. After settling in Johannesburg, Lilian spent a five-year period managing an orchestra for women.

In 1898, following a period of ill health in south Africa, Lilian returned to London for a visit. Rather than going back to her family, she stayed on in London to assist her aunt Emma *Cons in running the Victoria Theatre, Waterloo Road, Lambeth, familiarly known as the Old Vic. As a pioneer of housing reform and many other social improvements to working-class lives, especially women's lives, Emma Cons had acquired the Victoria in 1880 with the specific purpose of transforming it from a rather unsavoury, run-down venue into an alcohol-free site of family entertainment. Running the Old Vic as a temperance hall, aunt and niece had always to find forms of entertainment that would compensate for the absence of alcohol. Their programme relied heavily on costume recitals and ballad concerts, and, in the interests of variety, they explored the possibilities of cinema, symphony concerts, military bands, and, like many of the music-halls, the performance of sketches and scenes from theatre. Their endeavours benefited at the turn of the century from the appointment of Charles Corri to the position of music director. Nevertheless, their hall ran into increasing financial difficulties—not least because of the constant demands made by the London county council for improvements to health and safety aspects of the building.

A major change came after Emma's death in July 1912, as Lilian succeeded her in management and began to steer the theatre on a different course. She obtained a theatre licence from the lord chamberlain so that she could start staging Shakespeare. The first two attempts to introduce Shakespeare to the Old Vic—by the actress Rosina Filippi, who wanted to launch a people's theatre, and by the actor Shakespeare Stewart—met with failure. Lilian herself pursued both the idea of a people's theatre and Shakespeare, and managed to succeed where the others had failed. Her success was due in part to the actor–manager Ben Greet, who, having recently returned from America, joined her as director in 1914. The first season of combined opera and Shakespeare ran from October 1914 until April 1915 and included sixteen operas and sixteen plays. Working to an extremely low budget, Greet's productions were plain, rather than spectacular, cut to suit the tastes of an ordinary audience and Lilian's demand for a curtain down at 10.30 p.m. Initially the box-office receipts from the

Lilian Mary Baylis (1874–1937), by Charles Ernest Butler, 1926

opera had to subsidize the Shakespeare, but gradually Lilian's determination paid off: Shakespeare found an audience at the Old Vic—an audience, moreover, that included schoolchildren for the new Shakespearian matinées.

Through Greet came other contacts beneficial to the Old Vic, most notably the actress Sybil Thorndike, who joined the Vic in 1915 and, like Greet, stayed throughout the wartime years. 1915 also saw the inauguration of a new tradition at the Vic: the morality play *Everyman*, which remained in the repertory as an annual event at Lent. For Lilian, with her deeply religious outlook and her faith in God, whom she believed guided her in her work for the theatre (as did her lifelong spiritual adviser, Father Andrew, superior of a neo-Franciscan order), *Everyman* held a special interest. As Sybil Thorndike explained, this was 'one of the few plays she watched through from start to finish' (Thorndike and Thorndike, 40–41).

Lilian's theatrical management was always tempestuous. She was iron-willed and determined to put the theatre before all else. Her dedication to the theatre's survival meant that she offered permanently low wages and delayed costly improvements to the building. During wartime she insisted that the performers carry on, even through bombing raids. Because of her fierce temper, she was constantly rowing with (and, in consequence, losing) staff. Tired of his stormy relationship with Lilian, Greet left the Old Vic in 1918. She waited for the former member of the company Robert Aitkins to come back from the war to take his place. Aitkins overhauled the Shakespeare repertory in the interests of quality and stayed on as director until 1925. He was succeeded by Andrew Leigh (1925–9), Harcourt Williams (1929–33), and, thereafter, Tyrone Guthrie.

Lilian's 1925–6 Shakespeare season at the Old Vic was very successful, not least because the West End star Edith Evans joined the theatre. Other West End performers were to follow over the years—most notably John Gielgud and Laurence Olivier. The 1920s also brought Lilian personal success: in 1924 she was made an honorary MA of Oxford University in recognition for her work at the Old Vic, and in 1929 she was granted admission to the Order of the Companions of Honour (the only theatrical manager to be admitted at that time, and one of just a very few women to join the order).

However, the 1920s also brought a major problem for her theatre. Under Emma Cons's management, the Old Vic had established an educational branch for its activities, Morley College, which for twenty-five years had operated out of the theatre. As both institutions grew, so it became necessary to separate them, and, in consequence, to rehouse the college and refurbish the Old Vic. Lilian had the exhausting task of raising funds to ensure a future for both ventures. As testimony to her enterprise, she not only played a key role in the reorganization of the theatre and the college, but she also undertook to raise funds to renovate a second venue, Sadler's Wells. Sadler's Wells opened on 6 January 1931 to become the venue for opera and ballet companies, with the ballet overseen by Ninette de Valois. Lilian kept up managerial involvement in both venues until her death. She died of a heart attack on 25 November 1937 at her home, 27 Stockwell Park Road, London, and was cremated at the end of the month.

Lilian Baylis is chiefly remembered for her work in making the Old Vic the home of Shakespeare. The theatre teems with stories about her. Her bluntness was legendary, as when she brusquely explained why a singer, the daughter of a potential benefactor of Sadler's Wells, had never been offered a part: 'She hasn't got any voice' (Dent, 40). Sybil Thorndike, arriving at the last minute for a performance at the Old Vic during the First World War after crossing London during an air raid, found her fretting and fuming at the pit door, and not inclined to accept the explanation for her lateness: '"Raid", she snorted, "What's a raid when my curtain's up"' (Thorndike and Thorndike, 58–9). Theatrical biographies variously describe her as 'a cockney cinderella who achieved a throne without a prince' (Findlater, 65) and as 'the most courageous woman that was ever associated with the Theatre' (Thorndike and Thorndike, 7).   ELAINE ASTON

Sources R. Findlater [K. B. F. Bain], *Lilian Baylis: the lady of the Old Vic* (1975) · S. Thorndike and R. Thorndike, *Lilian Baylis: as I knew her* (1938) · E. G. H. Williams, ed., *Vic-Wells: the work of Lilian Baylis* (1938) · L. Baylis and C. Hamilton, *The Old Vic* (1926) · P. Roberts, ed., *Lilian Baylis festival: souvenir programme* (1974) · E. Fagg, *The old 'Old Vic': a glimpse of the old theatre from its origin as 'the Royal Coburg', first managed by William Barrymore, to its revival under Lilian Baylis* (1936) · E. J. Dent, *A theatre for everybody: the story of the Old Vic and Sadler's Wells* (1946) · J. Parker, ed., *Who's who in the theatre*, 5th edn (1925) · *DNB*

Archives University of Bristol, theatre collection, Old Vic archive, corresp. and MSS | University of Bristol, theatre collection, corresp. with Emma Cons | FILM BFI NFTVA, documentary footage | SOUND BL NSA, 'Tribute to the lady', 6 May 1974, T2811 BW · BL NSA, 'A centenary celebration of Lilian Baylis', 14 Jan 1988, C125/315 BD1 · BL NSA, documentary recordings · BL NSA, performance recordings

Likenesses W. Rothenstein, chalk drawing, 1916, Old Vic Theatre, London · C. E. Butler, oils, 1926, Old Vic Theatre, London [*see illus.*] · A. Dalston, oils, *c*.1930, Old Vic Theatre, London · C. Leslie, oils, 1931, NPG; version, *Vic-Wells Association*, on loan to Old Vic Theatre · E. Gabain, oils, Sadler's Wells Theatre, London · photograph, Mander and Mitchenson collection · photographs, Old Vic Theatre, London · portraits, Sadler's Wells Theatre, London · portraits, Old Vic Theatre, London

Wealth at death £10,037 11s. 2d.: probate, 7 April 1938

Baylis, Thomas Henry (1817–1908), lawyer and author, was born in London on 22 June 1817, the second son of Edward Baylis, deputy lieutenant and JP for Middlesex. He was educated at Harrow School (1825–34) before matriculating in 1835 as a scholar at Brasenose College, Oxford, where he graduated BA in 1838 and MA in 1841. Although he entered as a student of the Inner Temple in 1834, he practised for some time as a special pleader. He was called to the bar in 1856, when he joined the northern circuit. He became QC in 1875, and two years later a bencher of the Inner Temple. From 1876 to 1903 he was judge of the court of passage at Liverpool, an ancient court of record with local jurisdiction wider than that of a county court.

On 14 August 1841 Baylis married Louisa Lord (d. 1900), the youngest daughter of John Ingle, deputy lieutenant and JP for Devon. They had several children, and their third son, Thomas Erskine, was called to the bar in 1874.

Baylis was an officer in the Army Volunteer Reserve, retiring in 1882 with the volunteer decoration as lieutenant-colonel of the 18th Middlesex rifles. He was a vice-president of the Royal United Services Institution to which he presented an autograph letter from the signal officer on board the flagship *Victory* at Trafalgar, explaining the substitution of 'expects' for 'confides' in Nelson's famous signal: 'England expects every man to do his duty.' In his pamphlet, *The True Account of Nelson's Famous Signal* (1905), he discussed whether Nelson had permanently lost the sight of one eye. He was also one of the founders of the Egypt Exploration Fund, drafting the original articles of association.

As a lawyer, Baylis was chiefly known for a treatise on domestic servants, *The Rights, Duties, and Relations of Domestic Servants and their Masters and Mistresses* (1857). Other works included *Fire Hints* (1884), *Introductory Address on the Office of Reader or Lector and Lecture on Treasure Trove*, delivered in the Inner Temple Hall, Michaelmas 1898 (1901), and *Workmen's Compensation Act* (1902). Baylis also published *The Temple Church and Chapel of St Anne*, a guidebook to the Inner Temple Church (1893). He died on 4 October 1908 at Lucknow, Wellington Road, Bournemouth, and was buried in Bournemouth cemetery.

J. S. COTTON, *rev.* HUGH MOONEY

Sources *Law Journal* (10 Oct 1908), 616 · *BL cat.* · personal knowledge (1912) · *CGPLA Eng. & Wales* (1908)
Wealth at death £38,578 17s. 3d.: probate, 17 Dec 1908, *CGPLA Eng. & Wales*

Baylis, Thomas Hutchinson (1823–1876), insurance company manager, was the son of Edward *Baylis (1791–1861), also an insurance company manager, and his wife, Ellen Maria. Little is known about his early life, but he began as a clerk in the Anchor insurance office, one of his father's companies. In 1850 he became manager of the Trafalgar office, also founded by his father. About 1852 he founded the United General Life insurance office and the Unity Bank. Baylis became embroiled in controversy with fellow directors of Unity General, and at a general meeting of shareholders on 21 October 1856 it was resolved that 'Mr Thomas H. Baylis, the late Managing Director, be no longer an officer of this association' (Walford). A suggestion of malpractice lingers, but no firm evidence survives.

Baylis sailed to Australia early in January 1857, and tried to organize insurance companies there, but, achieving no success, he returned to England in July of that year. He then founded and became managing director of the British, Foreign, and Colonial Insurance Association, which soon went into liquidation, and of the Consols Life Association, which lasted from 1858 to 1862. Into these insurance offices Baylis introduced new features, including a scheme for obtaining paid-up policies by way of the lottery. This ran counter to the lottery acts, and was declared illegal. His project for linking insurance premiums to investments in government consols was more successful, and was copied by other offices. In 1869 Baylis introduced 'positive life assurance', an ingenious form of life policy, which was adopted in 1870 by at least one other company. Under such policies, lives exposed to tropical climates were insured at something nearly approaching ordinary rates. Baylis died on 17 November 1876 at 9 Vere Street, off Oxford Street, London; he was survived by his wife, Harriet Laura Baylis.

CORNELIUS WALFORD, *rev.* ROBERT BROWN

Sources C. Walford, *The insurance cyclopaedia*, 6 vols. (1871–80) · Boase, *Mod. Eng. biog.* · *CGPLA Eng. & Wales* (1876) · d. cert.
Archives Herts. ALS, corresp. with Lord Lytton
Wealth at death under £2000: probate, 12 Dec 1876, *CGPLA Eng. & Wales*

Bayliss, Sir William Maddock (1860–1924), physiologist, was born at Wolverhampton on 2 May 1860, the only son of Moses Bayliss, manufacturer of ironware, and his wife, Jane Maddock. After education at Mowbray House School, Wolverhampton, he had the opportunity of entering his father's business, but his interests lay in the direction of science and medicine. Nevertheless, he maintained a lifelong connection with the family business, of which he was a director.

With the object of pursuing a career in medicine, Bayliss was apprenticed at the Wolverhampton Hospital, but he never finished his medical training. In 1880 he entered University College, London, gaining a medical entrance scholarship the following year, and coming under the influence of Edwin Ray Lankester and, especially, John Scott Burdon-Sanderson. In 1883 Burdon-Sanderson went to Oxford, as the first Waynflete professor of physiology. Bayliss, who took a BSc in physics and zoology, but failed the second MB examination at University College, followed him, entering Wadham College in 1885 with the intention of developing his career in physiology. He obtained a first-class degree in natural science (physiology) in 1888.

For a time Bayliss participated in the teaching of physiology at Oxford, but in 1888 returned to University College, where a professorship of general physiology was created for him in 1912. Bayliss was elected to membership of the Physiological Society in 1890; he served as secretary from 1900 to 1922 and then as treasurer until 1924. He regularly attended the society's meetings, and in 1922, when summoned to Buckingham Palace to receive his knighthood, he refused the invitation because it coincided with a society meeting.

Bayliss's scientific researches had begun before going to Oxford with a study of the electric currents developed in the salivary glands, done in collaboration with John Rose Bradford. In 1890 Bayliss met his future brother-in-law, Ernest Henry *Starling, and the two men began a collaboration that lasted until Bayliss's death. In 1893 Bayliss married Gertrude Ellen Starling, daughter of Matthew Henry Starling, clerk of the crown, Bombay; they had three sons and one daughter.

Bayliss's association with E. H. Starling produced several great advances in the knowledge of physiology. One of their earliest papers was on the electric currents of the mammalian heart, and their classic account of venous and capillary pressures appeared in 1894. In 1898–9 they published papers on the innervation of the intestine, which held the field until the use of X-ray methods shed new light on the subject. A particularly significant contribution came in 1902, when they discovered that the presence of acid in the duodenum stimulated pancreatic secretion. They showed that this was due to the release from the duodenum of a blood-borne factor, which they called secretin; and they coined the word 'hormone' to describe such chemical messengers.

Throughout those years Bayliss pursued other investigations, mostly concerned with the vascular system, including studies on the circulation through the brain and on vasomotor reflexes. Much of this work was later summarized in *The Vasomotor System* (1923). In 1903 Bayliss sued Stephen Coleridge, secretary of the National Anti-Vivisection Society, for libel, after allegations of cruelty to an experimental animal. Bayliss won the 'Brown Dog' case and £2000 in damages, which he donated to University College for the support of physiological research.

Bayliss became particularly interested in the chemistry and physics of physiology. He was a founder member of the Biochemical Society, and chairman in 1914–15, and in 1919–20. He worked on enzyme action, and the properties of colloidal systems; his lectures on the subject formed the basis of *The Nature of Enzyme Action* (1908). The most important form in which the interest was expressed was his *Principles of General Physiology* (1915), which quickly became a standard authority. It was a monument of erudition and clear statement, and was a major contribution to twentieth-century physiology. Such was its popularity and influence that Bayliss also wrote *An Introduction to General Physiology* (1919), and several American universities formed Bayliss Clubs to discuss his work. The *Principles* went through four editions, and was revised after Bayliss's death by his son Leonard and A. V. Hill, the fifth edition appearing in 1959–60.

During the First World War, Bayliss's principal contribution was his work on wound shock, which resulted in the use of gum-saline solutions to replace lost blood, a treatment which met with considerable success. In the summer of 1918 over 50,000 litres of gum-saline were sent out to the British forces in France.

Bayliss was elected FRS in 1903 and knighted in 1922, and held many honorary degrees from British and foreign universities and academies. He was a member of the council of the Royal Society (1913–15), Croonian lecturer (1904), royal medallist (1911), and Copley medallist (1919). He received the Baly medal of the Royal College of Physicians (1917), and delivered the Oliver-Sharpey lectures (1918), the Sylvanus Thompson lectures (1919), and the Herter lectures (1922). Wadham College made him an honorary fellow in 1922.

Bayliss, who entertained regularly, delighted in the society of other scientific men: not least that of young physiologists, many of whom gravitated to University College to work with Starling and himself. Bayliss possessed an honesty and a generosity of outlook, and a faculty of getting to the bottom of problems, which was coupled with great erudition. He died at his Hampstead home, St Cuthberts, West Heath Road, on 27 August 1924.

E. M. TANSEY

Sources C. L. Evans, *Reminiscences of Bayliss and Starling* (1964) [for the Physiological Society] · C. L. Evans, 'Bayliss, William Maddock', *DSB* · L. Bayliss, 'William Maddock Bayliss, 1860–1924: life and scientific work', *Perspectives in Biologic and Medicine*, 4 (1961), 460–79 · J. B. [J. Barcroft], *PRS*, 99B (1925–6), xxvii–xxxii · *Nature*, 114 (1924), 474–6 · W. M. Bayliss, *An introduction to general physiology* (1919) · *The Times* (28 Aug 1924) · T. W. Goodwin, *History of the Biochemical Society, 1911–1986* (1987), 15–17, 23, 27 · private information (1937) · *CGPLA Eng. & Wales* (1924)

Archives UCL, corresp. and papers · Wellcome L., corresp. and papers | CAC Cam., corresp. with A. V. Hill · Wellcome L., Physiological Society, Scharpey-Schafer MSS

Likenesses W. Stoneman, photograph, 1917, NPG · Maull & Fox, photograph, Wellcome L. · photographs, Wellcome L.; repro. in Evans, *Reminiscences*; copies, Wellcome L.; Physiological Society archives · photographs, UCL · photogravure (after J. Russell & Sons), Wellcome L.

Wealth at death £102,387 12s. 2d.: probate, 30 Oct 1924, *CGPLA Eng. & Wales*

Bayliss, Sir Wyke (1835–1906), painter and writer, was born at Madeley, Shropshire, on 21 October 1835, the second son of John Cox Bayliss of Prior's Leigh and Anne Wyke. His father was a railway engineer and a successful teacher of military and mathematical drawing. At an early age Bayliss showed an aptitude for drawing, and studied under his father, from whom he obtained the sound knowledge of perspective and architecture which influenced his later career as a painter. He was educated at Marlborough House, London, and later attended the Royal Academy Schools and the School of Design at Somerset House.

On 30 June 1858 Bayliss married Elizabeth Letitia (*b.* 1835/6), daughter of a French protestant minister, Isaac Broade of Longton, Staffordshire; they had no children. From the first Bayliss's interest lay entirely in depicting architecture, and his whole life as an artist was spent in painting, in oil and watercolour, the interiors of cathedrals and churches. A very competent draughtsman and colourist, he defended himself against those who attacked his choice of subjects by saying that it is in the 'infinite variety of the aspect of a Cathedral interior that I find its infinite charm' (Bayliss, 18). He exhibited twice at the Royal Academy, sending *La Sainte-Chapelle* in 1865 and *Treves Cathedral* and *Strasbourg Cathedral* in 1879. His best work was given to the Society (later Royal Society) of British Artists, of which he was elected a member in 1865. In 1888 he became president of the society in succession to James Abbott McNeill Whistler (with whom he had his disagreements) and until the close of his life he held this office, for which his geniality, ability as an orator, wide artistic sympathies, and energy were well adapted. He was notably supportive of women as professional artists, and believed that exhibitions of the Royal Society of British Artists should always 'include something new and strange', so as to avoid 'conventionalism, and smug contentment with past achievements' (ibid., 158).

Bayliss was also renowned as an author. For his contemporaries the best-known of his books was *Rex regum* (1898; rev. edn, 1902), an elaborate study of the traditional likenesses of Christ. The most enduring of his works, however, has proved to be *Five Great Painters of the Victorian Era* (1902), in which he wrote on Frederic Leighton, John Everett Millais, Edward Burne-Jones, George Frederick Watts, and William Holman Hunt. In his *Seven Angels of the Renascence* (1905), a blending of fact and sentiment, he gave his views upon seven selected great masters and their influence upon the art of the middle ages. Among his other publications were *The Elements of Aerial Perspective* (1885); *The Witness of Art* (1876; 2nd edn, 1878); and *The Higher Life in Art* (1879; 2nd edn, 1888). Bayliss also published a short volume of poems entitled *Saecula tria: an Allegory of Life* (1857); on occasion he wrote poetry to accompany his paintings. Before his death he completed *Olives: the Reminiscences of a President*, which was edited by his wife and published, with a preface by Frederick Wedmore, in 1906.

Bayliss, who was elected fellow of the Society of Antiquaries in 1870, was knighted by Queen Victoria in 1897. He was an accomplished chess player and keen cyclist. He died at his home, 7 North Road, Clapham Park, London, on 5 April 1906, and was buried at Streatham cemetery; his wife survived him. A memorial was placed in the church of Madeley, Shropshire, his birthplace.

MARTIN HARDIE, rev. KATE FLINT

Sources W. Bayliss, *Olives: the reminiscences of a president* (1906) · *The Times* (7 April 1906) · *WW* (1906) · Graves, *RA exhibitors* · Allibone, *Dict.*, suppl. · *Men and women of the time* (1899) · *Our contemporaries* (1897) · *Contemporary Review*, 74 (Sept 1898) · m. cert. · d. cert. · private information (1912)
Archives U. Glas.
Likenesses J. M. Whistler?, two caricatures, 1888, U. Glas. L., special collections · W. Hodgson, black chalk and grey wash, 1891, NPG · Richards, pink, white, and black chalk on brown paper, NPG · photograph, repro. in Bayliss, *Olives*, frontispiece
Wealth at death £2640 5*s*.: probate, 26 June 1906, *CGPLA Eng. & Wales*

Bayly, Ada Ellen [*pseud.* Edna Lyall] (1857–1903), novelist, born at 5 Montpelier Villas, Brighton, Sussex, on 25 March 1857, was the youngest of the three daughters and a son of Robert Bayly, barrister of the Inner Temple, and his wife, Mary Winter. Her father died when she was eleven, and her mother three years later. A delicate child, she was first educated at home, then in the house of her uncle and guardian, T. B. Winter of Caterham, Surrey, and finally at private schools at Brighton. After leaving school Bayly lived successively with her two married sisters. Until 1880 she lived at Lincoln with her eldest sister, who had married John Henchman Crowfoot, canon of the cathedral. From 1880 until her death her home was with her second sister, wife of the Revd Humphrey Gurney Jameson—in London until 1881, in Lincoln from 1881 to 1884, and after 1884 at Eastbourne, where she devoted much time and money to charitable and religious causes. Bayly combined throughout her life strong religious feeling with an earnest faith in political and social liberalism. She was secretary of the Eastbourne branch of the Women's Liberal Association, and a warm supporter of women's suffrage.

Under the pseudonym of Edna Lyall, which she formed by transposing nine letters of her three names, in 1879 Bayly published her first book, *Won by Waiting*, a juvenile story of a girl's life, which initially attracted no attention, but was reissued, to her annoyance, in 1886, after she became known, and by 1894 was in a thirteenth edition. In 1882 her second novel, *Donovan, a Modern Englishman*, was published. It dealt with her religious beliefs and spiritual experiences, and had a redeemed agnostic, Donovan Farrant, as its hero. Although only 320 copies were sold, the book won the admiration of Gladstone, who wrote to Bayly in 1883 describing its first volume as 'a very delicate and refined work of art'. An intelligent review in the *National Reformer* led to a correspondence with the freethinker Charles Bradlaugh, many of whose political convictions she shared. In spite of their religious differences, her liberal sentiments resented his exclusion on religious grounds from the House of Commons (1880–85). She subscribed three times to the fund for defraying his electoral expenses. After his death on 30 January 1891 she published an appeal for a memorial fund, and subscribed to it her royalties for the half-year, amounting to £200. With Bradlaugh's daughter, Hypatia Bradlaugh Bonner, she formed a lasting friendship. Bayly based her novel *We Two* (1884), a sequel to *Donovan*, on some notes supplied by Bradlaugh. The secularist hero, Luke Raeburn, resembles Bradlaugh, although the novel centres on the conversion of his

daughter to Christianity. With *We Two* Bayly's reputation was established, although for the copyright of these two books she received no more than £50. But with the publication in 1885 of *In the Golden Days*, an able historical novel of the seventeenth century, her profits became substantial. *In the Golden Days* was the last book read to Ruskin on his deathbed (W. G. Collingwood, *Life of John Ruskin*, 1900, 403). Contemporary opinion held *Donovan*, *We Two*, and *In the Golden Days* to be Bayly's best books.

In 1886 a stranger falsely claimed in public to be Edna Lyall, and a report also circulated that the author was in a lunatic asylum. Bayly met the falsehood by announcing her identity, and the experience suggested her *Autobiography of a Slander* (1887), which enjoyed an immense vogue and was translated into French, German, and Norwegian. This was followed in 1889 by *Derrick Vaughan: Novelist*, which is partly autobiographical.

Bayly's next novels primarily displayed her political convictions. An ardent home ruler, in *Doreen* (1894) she presented the Irish revolutionary leader Michael Davitt in the guise of her hero, Donal Moore. Gladstone, writing to her on 25 November 1894, commended 'the singular courage with which you stake your wide public reputation upon the Irish cause'. She supported the Armenian cause in *The Autobiography of a Truth* (1896), the profits of which she gave to the Armenian Relief Fund. Strongly opposed to the Second South African War, she spoke out with customary frankness in her last novel, *The Hinderers* (1902). Also in 1902, Bayly published *The Burges Letters*, her autobiography.

Slight in build and of medium height, with dark brown hair and dark grey-blue eyes, Bayly was fond of music and of travelling, and described her tours in vivacious letters. Contemporaries felt that her earnest political purpose prevented her mastery of the whole art of fiction, and her apolitical romances such as *Wayfaring Men* (1897) and *In Spite of All* (1901) were more to their taste.

An attack of pericarditis in 1889 left permanent ill effects. Ada Ellen Bayly died on 8 February 1903 at her home, 6 College Road, Eastbourne. Following cremation, her ashes were buried at the foot of the old cross in Bosbury churchyard, near Bosbury Hill, Herefordshire, a place which figures in her novel *In Spite of All*, and of which her brother, the Revd R. Burges Bayly, was vicar.

In 1906 a memorial window by Kempe was placed in St Peter's Church, Eastbourne (built 1896), where Bayly had worshipped and to which she had presented the seats. She had given to St Saviour's Church in 1887 a peal of three bells named Donovan, Erica, and Hugo, after leading characters in her three chief books.

ELIZABETH LEE, *rev.* ANNETTE PEACH

Sources J. M. Escreet, *The life of Edna Lyall* (1904) · G. A. Payne, *Edna Lyall: an appreciation* (1903) [preface incl. list of articles and portrait illustrations appearing in periodicals and magazines between 1886 and 1901] · H. C. Black, *Notable women authors of the day* (1893) [incl. portraits] · A. E. Bayly, *The Burges letters* (1902) · J. Sutherland, *The Longman companion to Victorian fiction* (1988) · *Gallery of Celebrities*, 1 (21 March 1891), 8–9 · *The Times* (10 Feb 1903) · Allibone, *Dict.*, suppl. · A. T. C. Pratt, ed., *People of the period: being a collection of the biographies of upwards of six thousand living celebrities*, 2 vols. (1897) ·

The Athenaeum (14 Feb 1903), 210 · Gladstone, *Diaries* · private information (1912)
Likenesses G. P. Abraham, photograph, repro. in Escreet, *Life of Edna Lyall*, frontispiece · Elliott & Fry, photograph (in later years), repro. in *Gallery of Celebrities*, 8–9 · E. Whymper, print, BM · photograph (aged twenty-two), repro. in Escreet, *Life of Edna Lyall*, facing p. 32
Wealth at death £25,966 10s. 2d.: probate, 2 April 1903, *CGPLA Eng. & Wales*

Bayly, Anselm (1718/19–1794), Church of England clergyman and writer, was born in Gloucestershire, the son of Anselm Bayly of Haresfield, in the same county. He matriculated, aged twenty-one, from Exeter College, Oxford, in November 1740 but he graduated BCL from Christ Church on 12 June 1749, and DCL on 10 July 1764. In January 1741 he was made a lay vicar of Westminster Abbey and a gentleman of the Chapel Royal. He went on to become a minor canon of Westminster and St Paul's and, in 1764, subdean of the Chapel Royal. On 15 January 1751 he was presented by the chapter of St Paul's to the vicarage of Tottenham, Middlesex, and he held this living until his death in November 1794. Bayly was married to Elizabeth Ridley and they had one daughter, Rebecca. Both women survived him.

Bayly published several philological pieces, including an English grammar (1772), a Hebrew grammar (1773), *An Introduction Literary and Philosophical to Language* (1755; expanded, 1758), and an essay on English accidence (1771). He believed oratory was the active form of poetry and music, and he dedicated his *Alliance of Musick, Poetry and Oratory* (1789) to William Pitt the elder, claiming in the preface that Pitt's oratory had saved both church and state. With regard to prosody Bayly was an anti-contractionist, believing in the articulation of every syllable; he has been criticized subsequently by Paul Fussell for neglecting metrical forms. Bayly brought out two other tracts on singing, in 1771, and edited a collection of anthems for the Chapel Royal in 1769. In addition to publishing sermons and an annotated Bible he contributed a pamphlet to the Conyers Middleton debate on prophecy in 1751 and wrote, under the name of Antisocinus, against Joseph Priestley in 1787. In the same year he patented (no. 1615) an elastic girdle for the prevention and relief of ruptures, fractures, and swellings.

J. M. RIGG, *rev.* EMMA MAJOR

Sources Foster, *Alum. Oxon.*, 1715–1886 · *ESTC* · A. Bayly, admon., PRO, PROB 6/171, fols. 192v–196r · A. Bayly, *Alliance of musick, poetry and oratory* (1789) · *New Grove* · P. Fussell, *Theory of prosody in the 18th century* (1954), 85–6, 146 · W. F. Hook, *An ecclesiastical biography*, 8 vols. (1845–52) · Watt, *Bibl. Brit.* · Brown & Stratton, *Brit. mus.* · *European Magazine and London Review*, 26 (1794), 381

Bayly, Benjamin (1671–1720), Church of England clergyman, matriculated at St Edmund Hall, Oxford, on 20 March 1688, and graduated BA of Wadham College on 15 October 1692. He took his MA on 30 October 1695. He was rector of St James's, Bristol, from 1697 until his death. For some time he was also vicar of Olveston, Gloucestershire. Bayly was the author of *An Essay on Inspiration*, first published anonymously in London in 1707. A second edition

appeared in 1708. In addition two volumes of collected sermons, many of which were issued repeatedly in the author's lifetime, were published in 1721. He died in London on 25 April 1720.

A. R. BUCKLAND, *rev.* ROBERT BROWN

Sources W. Barrett, *The history and antiquities of the city of Bristol* (1789) · Watt, *Bibl. Brit.*
Likenesses G. Vertue, line engraving, BM, NPG

Bayly, John (1595/6–1633), scholar and Church of England clergyman, was born in Herefordshire, the eldest son of Lewis *Bayly (c.1575–1631), later bishop of Bangor, and of his first wife, probably called Judith Appleton, and brother of Thomas *Bayly (d. c.1657), also later a clergyman. By 1611 he was an undergraduate at Exeter College, Oxford, of which he was elected fellow in 1612. Under the tutelage of John Prideaux (1578–1650), he graduated BA in May 1615 and proceeded MA in June 1617. Ordained by his father (later accused of inappropriate ordinations) in September 1617, he remained at Exeter College until his resignation from the fellowship in June 1619, but from 1618 onwards—in one of the rare Jacobean cases of nepotism, according to Fincham—was presented through the patronage of Bishop Bayly to several benefices in Anglesey and Denbighshire, together with the precentorship of Bangor in 1620. At a later date he also became guardian of Christ's Hospital, Ruthyn, and a chaplain to Charles I.

By October 1630 Bayly was back at Exeter College, where, in the course of his lectures and disputations preparatory to the degrees of BD and DD, he earned the disapprobation of the newly elected chancellor, William Laud. Defended by Prideaux, he took both degrees in December, having in the interim published together in Oxford two short but learned sermons. The first, *The Angell Guardian*, on ministering angels ordained for the comfort of the elect (a reference which perhaps marked him out as resistant to Laudian innovations), was dedicated to his father, who was still under investigation for misconduct; the second, *The Light Enlightning*, on the revelation of God above all through scripture in Jesus but also through nature, was dedicated to Prideaux.

In accordance with the views expressed in his *The Practise of Pietie* that parents should provide for their children principally during their lifetime, Bishop Bayly, having helped his son to so much preferment, left him only £5 in his will of September 1631. He bequeathed the same sum to Bayly's daughter Jane, in the only reference that has yet come to light to Bayly's having a family of his own. John Bayly died, according to Bishop Humphreys, as quoted in Wood, in the summer of 1633.

T. F. TOUT, *rev.* VIVIENNE LARMINIE

Sources C. W. Boase, ed., *Registrum Collegii Exoniensis*, new edn, OHS, 27 (1894), 95 · Wood, *Ath. Oxon.*, new edn, 2.499–500 · A. H. Dodd, 'Bishop Lewes Bayly, c.1575–1631', *Transactions of the Caernarvonshire Historical Society*, 28 (1967), 19–33 · Foster, *Alum. Oxon.* · *CSP dom.*, Jan 1619–June 1623, 1629–31 · J. Bayly, *Two sermons: 'The angell guardian', 'The light enlightning'* (1630) · K. Fincham, *Prelate as pastor: the episcopate of James I* (1990), 191, 195 · N. Tyacke, *Anti-Calvinists: the rise of English Arminianism, c.1590–1640* (1987), 81 · will of Bishop Bayly, PRO, PROB 11/161, fol. 420

Bayly, Lewis (*c*.1575–1631), bishop of Bangor and devotional writer, was probably born in Carmarthen, according to his own later statement; his parents are unknown but Thomas Bayly, curate of Carmarthen at that date, may have been his father. Apart from the fact that he acquired significant learning in the Bible and in classical languages, evidence of his education is lacking, but at some point he entered the household of the Jones family of Abermarlais. By late 1595 or early 1596 when his eldest son John *Bayly (1595/6–1633) was born, he had married his first wife, probably called Judith Appleton, and seems to have been living in Herefordshire; the couple had four further children, Mary, Theophilus (who predeceased his father), Theodore (sometimes confused with his brother), and Thomas *Bayly (*d. c.*1657). It may have been through the Jones family that Bayly secured in 1597 the living of Shipston-on-Stour, then in Worcestershire but within the jurisdiction of the president of the council of the marches, the earl of Pembroke. In 1600 Bayly was presented to the crown living of Evesham, in the same county; there he became headmaster of the grammar school and assisted in procuring a royal charter of incorporation for the town.

Bayly became renowned for his preaching and within a few years of the accession of King James he was appointed a chaplain to Prince Henry. In 1606 Bayly was presented to the rectory of Llanedi, Carmarthenshire, which was in the young prince's gift; like the vicarage of Weaverham, Cheshire, which he acquired the following year, it seems to have been a sinecure, and he remained largely at Evesham, where his wife died on 26 March 1608. Apart from his royal duties he was engaged in turning sermons preached there into what was to become a protestant classic, *The Practise of Pietie*. The date of the first edition is unknown, but the second appeared in 1612. The widespread and enduring popularity of this substantial work, which in subsequent editions usually ran to about 800 pages, seems to have derived from its practical tone and from the variety of its content. In addition to offering prayers and meditations, this manual of godly life included advice on bible reading and on preparation for communion and for death, instruction in some of the fundamentals of the faith, and polemic against Roman Catholic errors. The dedications reveal that Bayly wrote from a conviction that 'wee are fallen into the dregs of Time, which being the last, must needs be the worst dayes', in which so-called Christians 'are now reputed the most discreet, who make the least profession of their Faith': 'never was there more neede of plaine and unfained Admonitions' ('To the high and mighty Prince Charles', *The Practise of Pietie*, 1619 edn). His standpoint was that of a conformist Calvinist, having emphases in common with puritanism, but also a respect for the authority of the church. While believing firmly in predestination to salvation and to damnation, he produced many biblical instances of God's mercy to the repentant. A strict sabbatarian, he commended almsgiving and condemned time wasted at stage plays and the bad examples set by some of the greatest in society, but he also supported private confession and conformity to outward rites and ceremonies.

Bayly gained a high profile and more royal favour, but his later career was several times undermined by his strong opinions and quarrelsome nature. On 7 February 1611 he became treasurer of St Paul's Cathedral and on 25 June that year gained a BD at Oxford; he became DD on 21 June 1613. Although in 1612 he was reprimanded by the privy council for bringing accusations of popery against its members, including the earl of Northampton, and for disputing with the king on the sabbath, probably early in 1613 he was presented by John King, bishop of London, to succeed Henry Mason (instituted on 12 December 1612 but given another living in February) in the rectory of St Matthew's Friday Street. On 7 February 1614 he became a prebendary of Lichfield and on 2 July 1615 he was admitted to Lincoln's Inn at the request of John Jeffreys. The following year he became a chaplain to the king and, in the face of opposition from Archbishop George Abbot, the marquess of Buckingham secured his election on 28 August to the bishopric of Bangor; he was consecrated on 8 December.

Bangor was a poor diocese and from the outset Bishop Bayly enhanced his income by retaining his positions at St Paul's and Lichfield and by holding *in commendam* rectories including Llanbeulan, Llanddeusant and Trefdraeth, Anglesey, and Llanfihangel-y-traethau, Merioneth. Embroiled in local politics, his episcopate proved controversial in Bangor and beyond. Between 1617 and 1619 he had a disagreement with the powerful Sir John Wynn of Gwydir over church lands and tithes at Llanfair Dyffyn Clwyd, presented by Bayly to his son John. However, having realized that this also made an enemy of Wynn's kinsman John Williams (dean of Salisbury and from 1621 bishop of Lincoln and lord keeper), Bayly made up the quarrel. In the Caernarvonshire county election of 1620 he supported the Wynn candidate, Sir Richard Wynn, against John Griffith II of Cefnamwlch, Llŷn; Griffith won, but became an arch-enemy. In 1622 Griffith's uncle, Edmund Griffith, dean of Bangor, together with the chapter, brought proceedings against Bayly in the court of chancery to recover £100 for the maintenance of four scholars or choristers at the cathedral and Friars School, Bangor. The previous summer Bayly had been committed to the Fleet for a spell of imprisonment, as a result of his expressed opposition to the Book of Sports, and this had led to his losing the treasurership at St Paul's. In 1623 Bayly sought Sir John Wynn's assistance in a dispute with Sir John Bodfel concerning the removal of the incumbent of Beddgelert parish, of which Bodfel was patron. An active member of the bench from his appointment in 1622, Bayly was also accused of receiving bribes in his capacity as a justice of the peace. It was also complained that he had paid a £600 bribe for his see, funded by imposing a double benevolence on the clergy, but his stiffest test occurred in 1626, when Sir Eubule Thelwall, MP for Denbighshire, accused him in parliament of embezzlement, of sexual misdemeanours, and of appointing inappropriate, unqualified or non-Welsh speaking candidates to benefices, including Bayly's own sons. John Griffith II, again MP for Caernarvonshire, urged that proceedings be taken against the bishop, but the dissolution of parliament saved him. In 1628, as vice-admiral of north Wales, Griffith complained that Bayly had interfered in matters regarding the defence of the coasts.

Bayly strongly defended himself against the many accusations, often malicious, made against him. When accused of maladministration he maintained that he had appointed learned preachers and encouraged preaching, supervised his clergy, catechized, given hospitality beyond his means, and spent £600 repairing the cathedral. In 1626 he sought aid from Sir John and others for the repairs. In 1629 he supported as an aid to preachers the printing of the Latin–Welsh and Welsh–Latin dictionary which appeared in 1632 by John Davies, rector of Mallwyd, assuring the printer, John Beale of Aldersgate Street, London, that he would purchase 100 copies for their use. He also proved vigilant in the face of the perceived threat from Roman Catholic recusants like Hugh Owen of Gwenynog, Anglesey.

Bayly married a second wife, Ann, daughter of Sir Henry Bagenal of Newry Castle, Ireland, and Plas Newydd, Anglesey. Probably because she had brought him substantial property, when he came to make his will on 8 September 1631, he left the bulk of his estate to their young son Nicholas, with the reversion to their daughter Ellinor. He died on 26 October and was buried in Bangor Cathedral on the south side of the communion rails. *The Practise of Pietie* continued to be popular, deeply influencing, among others, John Bunyan; new editions appeared frequently over the next century, often cheaply produced and with an eye-catching frontispiece. Translated into French (1625), Welsh (by Rowland Vaughan of Caer-gai, 1629), German (1629), Polish (1647), a Native American language in New England (1665), and Romansch (1668), it was sometimes bound with Charles Drelincourt's *Les consolations contre les frayeurs de la mort*; both joined the Bible as core texts of European protestant devotion and have been credited as fundamental influences in the rise of pietism.

J. GWYNFOR JONES and VIVIENNE LARMINIE

Sources BL, Lansdowne MS 984, fols. 99, 116 · Foster, *Alum. Oxon.* · *Fasti Angl.* (Hardy), 1.106, 592; 2.357 · *CSP dom.*, 1611–18, 156, 279; 1625–6, 172; 1628–9, 364; 1636, 230 · J. Ballinger, ed., *Calendar of Wynn of Gwydir papers, 1515–1690* (1926), nos. 797, 802, 827, 829, 831, 834, 846, 863–4, 954–5, 966, 968, 999, 1050, 1094, 1166, 1440, 1445, 1542 · J. E. Griffith, *Pedigrees of Anglesey and Carnarvonshire families* (privately printed, Horncastle, 1914), 57 · Wood, *Ath. Oxon.*, new edn, 2.525–31 · B. Willis, *A survey of the cathedral church of Bangor* (1721), 110–11 · *JHC*, 1 (1547–1628), 831, 837, 845, 850–51, 855, 863, 865, 877 · *JHL*, 3 (1620–28), 546, 553–4, 572, 676 · will, PRO, PROB 11/161, sig. 53 · *DWB*, 28–9 · K. Fincham, *Prelate as pastor: the episcopate of James I* (1990), 23–4, 32, 81–2, 84, 125, 145, 181–2, 183, 188, 211, 221, 250, 273 · *The letters of John Chamberlain*, ed. N. E. McClure, 2 (1939), 29–30 · H. Barber and H. Lewis, *The history of Friars School, Bangor* (1901), 33 · E. A. B. Bernard, 'Lewis Bayly, bishop of Bangor (d.1631) and Thomas Bayly (d.1657) his son', *Transactions of the Honourable Society of Cymmrodorion* (1928–9), 99–132 · A. H. Dodd, 'Bishop Lewes Bayly, c.1575–1631', *Transactions of the Caernarvonshire Historical Society*, 28 (1967), 19–33 · J. G. Jones, 'Bishop Lewis Bayly and the Wynns of Gwydir, 1616–27', *Welsh History Review / Cylchgrawn Hanes Cymru*, 6/2 (1972–3), 404–23 · I. Green, *Print and protestantism in early modern England* (2000) · *STC, 1475–1640* · Wing, *STC* · W. B. Bidwell and M. Jansson, eds., *Proceedings in parliament, 1626*, 4 vols. (1991–6), vols. 1–2
Wealth at death approx. £500: will, PRO, PROB 11/161, sig. 53

Bayly, Sir Lewis (1857–1938), naval officer, was born at Woolwich on 28 September 1857, the third son of Captain Neville Bayly, Royal Horse Artillery, and his wife, Henrietta Charlotte, daughter of General Charles George Gordon, Royal Artillery, and great-great-nephew of Admiral Sir Richard Keats. He was educated in the *Britannia*, passing out in 1872 as a navigating cadet, but he was promoted sub-lieutenant for navigating duties in 1876, when the navigating branch was abolished, and changed over to the executive branch; he became lieutenant in 1881. He served in the Second Anglo-Asante War (1873–4) and in the Congo expedition (1875) in the *Encounter*, and in the 1882 Egyptian campaign. In 1883 he specialized in the use of torpedoes. He married in 1892 Yves Henrietta Stella, daughter of Henry Annesley Voysey; they had no children. Bayly was promoted commander in June 1894, and captain in December 1899. His first important appointment was as naval attaché to the USA in June 1900; in the two years there he gained experience that was to stand him in good stead in his last appointment.

In 1907, after commanding the cruiser *Talbot* on the China station and the battleship *Queen* in the Mediterranean, Bayly was selected to command the destroyer flotillas in the Home Fleet, with the rank of commodore, in the *Attentive*. In Bayly's own words, 'destroyers were then a comparatively new arm, and their capabilities when working in flotillas were not very well understood' (Bayly, 120). A fine seaman and a hard taskmaster, he completed an immense programme of exercises during the next two years and laid solid foundations for the future handling and administration of flotillas. In 1908 he was appointed president of the War College, Portsmouth, and promoted to flag rank; he held the presidency until 1911 when he was given command of the 1st battle-cruiser squadron (flag in the *Indomitable* and later in the *Lion*), followed by the command of the 3rd battle squadron (1913–14, flag in the *King Edward VII*), and, in 1914, by that of the 1st battle squadron (flag in the *Marlborough*). This squadron was part of the Grand Fleet assembled at Scapa Flow on the outbreak of war in August 1914. In September Bayly was promoted vice-admiral. In December he was appointed to command the recently strengthened Channel Fleet (flag in the *Lord Nelson*), in preparation for offensive operations on the Belgian coast, but a few days later was relieved of his command because, during exercises, one of his battleships, the *Formidable*, was sunk by torpedo submarine with the loss of 547 lives. Bayly had ignored the threat of submarines and failed to take even the elementary precautions then in force, especially that of steaming a zigzag course. He was informed that he had lost their lordships' confidence. He asked for a court martial, but this was refused, and he was appointed president of the Royal Naval College, Greenwich. With that appointment his active career appeared to have ended, but his greatest work still lay ahead of him. In July 1915 he was appointed to command the western approaches with base at Queenstown and in the beginning of 1916 was raised to the position of commander-in-chief. The German U-boat campaign was at its height and the frequent sinkings in the western approaches could only be checked by extremely vigorous defence measures and by exploiting new methods of attacking the submarines. Bayly had all the qualities for conducting the anti-submarine campaign, but for the first two years he never had sufficient ships for the large area for which he was responsible, until, in 1917, welcome reinforcements from the USA began to arrive.

Bayly, who had been promoted admiral in 1917, proved the ideal commander of a mixed Anglo-American force. He made the senior American officer (Captain Joel Roberts Poinsett Pringle, afterwards vice-admiral) his chief of staff, the first foreign naval officer to hold such an appointment, and he mixed the ships of the two navies in his flotillas and squadrons so that after a few months they were all one navy. Although in his own service his reputation was that of a hard taskmaster with a brusque, intolerant manner, the American navy discovered a human side which led him to be known to most American sailors as Uncle Lewis. By the end of the war, he was as well known in the USA as in Britain. It was the joint practice of naval warfare that broadened and deepened into a sympathetic understanding between Bayly and Pringle and those who served under them, and this understanding spread further and helped increase friendship between the two English-speaking countries.

In 1921 Bayly, who had retired in July 1919, visited the USA as the guest of the Queenstown Association, a club formed by officers who had served under him from 1915 to 1918, and of which he was vice-president. In 1934 he was again the guest of the American navy when, at the naval academy at Annapolis, he unveiled a memorial, which the secretary of the navy had granted him permission to erect, to his American chief of staff, Vice-Admiral Pringle.

Bayly was appointed CVO in 1907, CB in 1912, KCB in 1914, and KCMG in 1918. He received the grand cross of the Dannebrog in 1912 and the American DSO. He died at his home, 68 Arlington House, St James's, London, on 16 May 1938. His volume of memoirs, *Pull Together!*, was published in 1939. A hard taskmaster, Bayly drove himself even harder than he drove his subordinates. His work with the Americans at Queenstown was an outstanding example of allied command in war, revealing the human side of a man the Americans referred to as 'Old Frozen Face' (Marder, 5.121–2).

W. M. JAMES, *rev.* ANDREW LAMBERT

Sources L. Bayly, *Pull together!* (1939) · A. J. Marder, *From the Dreadnought to Scapa Flow: the Royal Navy in the Fisher era, 1904–1919*, 5 vols. (1961–70) · *WWW*, 1929–40 · *CGPLA Eng. & Wales* (1938)
Archives BL, Jellicoe MSS
Likenesses photographs, repro. in Bayly, *Pull together!*, frontispiece, 130, 232
Wealth at death £345 15s. 5d.: probate, 6 July 1938, *CGPLA Eng. & Wales*

Bayly, Nathaniel Thomas Haynes (1797–1839), poet and playwright, was born in Bath on 13 October 1797, the only

Nathaniel Thomas Haynes Bayly (1797–1839), by Frederick Richard Say, in or before 1831

child of Nathaniel Bayly of Mount Beacon House, Walcot, Bath, a wealthy attorney and land agent. Eminently well connected, being cousin to the earl of Stamford and Warrington and on his mother's side related to Sir George Thomas, bt, and the Thomases of Ratton Park, Sussex, Bayly was reared with every comfort. He began writing verse and plays at the age of seven, and was subsequently entered as a commoner at Winchester College, where his name appears on the long roll for 1812–14. The claim (*Songs*, 1.2) that he conducted there a weekly school newspaper is probably fanciful.

Rejecting the law as 'too dull for one of his versatile genius' (*Songs*, 1.5), Bayly went up to Oxford intent on the church. He matriculated at St Mary Hall (a dependency of Oriel) on 9 December 1818, but did not settle academically. Although in residence for three years, he tended to prefer 'an idle life in Bath' (Hunter) or, during vacations, when ostensibly being supervised by a private tutor, yachting in the Solent with his cousin Sir George Thomas. Out of the blue, he was written to by a young woman anxious about the health of her brother Thomas (son of Colonel Darby of Bath), a pensioner at St John's College, Cambridge. Bayly gallantly responded and spent several weeks at the brother's bedside until his death, aged eighteen, in November 1819. He visited the Darby household in Bath and fell in love with his correspondent. Marriage was however opposed by both families on financial grounds and Bayly's pain is expressed in a poem entitled 'Anne', signed 'Thomas' (*Bath Herald*, April 1822). As the rejected romantic hero, Bayly moved to Scotland and later to Dublin to recover his equilibrium but more practically to mix in literary circles in furtherance of his poetical career: *Outlines of Edinburgh, and other Poems* and *Erin and other Poems* appeared in 1822. At Dublin he also indulged in private theatricals (in which 'he shone conspicuously' (*Songs*, 1.13)) and wrote a few early songs.

Bayly's literary career originated in Bath with satirical verse epistles, first printed pseudonymously as 'Q in the Corner' in the *Bath Herald* and collected under various titles between 1817 and 1819. In *Rough Sketches of Bath* (1817; 1818; 1819) 'Q' sang his native city's praises:

> I seize my pen, determined to rehearse
> The sports of Bladud in heroic verse;
> To sing of those who walk in fashion's path,
> And thus immortalize the charms of Bath!
> (*Songs*, 2.277)

By contrast his other poems at this time were more Romantic in spirit, moody and melancholic, coloured by his experience of unseasonable death, as in 'The Tribute of a Friend' (on Darby, 1819) and *Mournful Recollections* (1820).

Bayly returned to Bath in January 1824 and found his reputation as lyric poet and songwriter made him sought after at soirées. At one of these he met an admirer of his work, his future wife, Helena Beecher Hayes, only daughter of the late Benjamin Hayes of Marble Hill, co. Cork. Being less impressed with his person than expected, she absented herself in Paris for over a year, anticipating their drifting apart, but she missed his wit and conversation and they were eventually married at Cheltenham on 11 July 1826. Soon afterwards, on their wedding journey, at Lord Ashtown's villa near Southampton, in a summer house in the grounds, Bayly composed one of the best-known of his numerous songs, 'I'd be a butterfly born in a bower'. Although comfortably off, Bayly had expensive tastes. He entertained beyond his means at their large house in Catharine Place, attracting the nobility to fashionable parties. His first novel, *The Aylmers* (1827), published anonymously and much praised by Theodore Hook (who became a loyal friend), generated local resentment when it was found to satirize some of his Bath friends. The character of Edward Robinson is in part a self-portrait.

Keen to make his name as a playwright, Bayly left Bath in 1829 to settle in London, where it is said that his first staged play, *The Witness*, was performed some time that year at the English Opera House (*Songs*, 1.44). His first recorded piece, however (entirely written, he contended, on a stagecoach between his uncle's place in Sussex and London), was *Perfection, or, The Lady of Munster* (Drury Lane, 1830), with Madame Vestris as the Irish heiress Kate O'Brien. Though slight, the piece was arguably Bayly's most successful farce ('very favourably received', said *The Times*) and was acted eighteen times. Financial difficulties came in 1831 with the simultaneous collapse of the Baylys' coalmining investments and a serious loss of revenue from their extensive Irish property through their agents' incompetence. Their income never fully recovered and Bayly was compelled to write for his living. Fortunately Vestris recognized his worth and staged many of his pieces at the Olympic during the 1830s. In the process Bayly acquired some reputation as a *farceur*; he also wrote for the St James's and, during 1838, popular farces such as *Tom Noddy's Secret*, for the Haymarket. A number were printed by Lacy, Webster, and others, including a short series by William Strange, published about 1836–7 as Bayly's Farces (with well-known Olympic hits such as *The Barrack Room* and *The Ladder of Love*). His last recorded play was *Friends and Neighbours* (St James's, February 1839).

After 1831 Bayly was totally dependent on his writings and the burden of family responsibility preyed on his mind. He spent extended periods abroad to restore his physical and mental well-being: *Musings and Prosings* (1833), a subscription edition which contained some of his dramatic writing including *Perfection*, was published at Boulogne. Of his later work, his volume of poems *Weeds of Witchery* (1835), dedicated to Hook, was generally much admired. He also composed the 'poetical illustrations' to a folio art book showing women emblematized as flowers (1837); and he was 'liberally paid' (*Songs*, 1.46) by Richard Bentley for two novels combined under the title *Kindness in Women* (1837), but its completion was temporarily threatened by 'brain-fever'. Although he recovered sufficiently to spend 1837–8 with his family in Boulogne (and to visit Macready in London in June 1838), Bayly deteriorated again during the following autumn. His move to Cheltenham for the spa waters brought no improvement and he died there of jaundice complicated by dropsy on 22 April 1839, aged forty-one. He was buried in the new cemetery and a tablet to his memory with a simple epitaph by Hook was placed by his mother in St James's Church.

Bayly was about 5 feet 7 inches tall and endowed with romantic good looks. His early demise was a severe shock to the literary and theatrical world and a benefit for his necessitous family was organized by Charles Dance at Drury Lane. Dickens gave £5 and persuaded the Literary Fund to add another £50 to the original £50 grant bestowed immediately before Bayly's death. Bayly had never managed money well and his estate was assumed to be worthless. In fact the copyrights on his hundreds of songs, published throughout his career (many of which won acclaim in North America), like 'The Soldier's Tear', 'We met—'twas in a crowd', and perhaps the best-known 'She wore a wreath of roses', were far from negligible. This was realized nineteen years later, when, having rediscovered his will, Helena Bayly finally applied for probate in May 1858. First collected in Philadelphia (as *Poems*, ed. Grisewold, 1843), Mrs Bayly's 1844 edition of the poems and songs is more complete. A modern selection, with music (much by Sir Henry Bishop), appeared as *Songs of the Affections* (1932).   JOHN RUSSELL STEPHENS

Sources *Songs, ballads, and other poems by the late T. H. Bayly*, ed. [H. B. Bayly], 2 vols. (1844) [incl. memoir] · J. Hunter, 'Biographical notices of some of my contemporaries who have gained some celebrity', BL, Add. MS 36527, fol. 145 · A. Nicoll, *Early nineteenth century drama, 1800–1850*, 2nd edn (1955), vol. 4 of *A history of English drama, 1660–1900* (1952–9) · *Wellesley index* · BL, Loan MSS, Royal Literary Fund archive, case no. 955 · *The diaries of William Charles Macready, 1833–1851*, ed. W. Toynbee, 2 vols. (1912) · J. R. Planché, *Recollections and reflections*, rev. edn (1901) · Foster, *Alum. Oxon.* · *The Times*

(19 May 1858) [grant of probate] · R. S. Neale, *Bath, 1680–1850: a social history, or, A valley of pleasure, yet a sink of iniquity* (1981)

Archives Boston PL, letters · Boston University, corresp. · Bristol RO, corresp. and papers | BL, agreements with R. Bentley, Add. MS 46612, fols. 335–6; Add. MS 46613, fols. 36–7, 207; Add. MS 46649, fol. 137 · NL Scot., letters to William Blackwood & Sons · Som. ARS, letters to John Braham

Likenesses F. R. Say, chalk drawing, in or before 1831, NPG [*see illus.*] · portrait, 1844, repro. in Bayly, *Songs, ballads, and other poems*, vol. 1, frontispiece · C. Cook, sculpture · R. Cooper, stipple and line engraving (after miniature by S. Lover), NPG · H. P. Riviere, lithograph (after C. Jagger), BM · J. Sands, stipple (after T. Sampson), NPG

Bayly, Sir Patrick Uniacke (1914–1998), naval officer, was born on 4 August 1914 at Bayly Farm, Nenagh, co. Tipperary, the second of three sons of Lancelot Francis Sanderson Bayly (1869–1952), artist, and his wife and cousin, Eileen Maude Bayly (1886–1961). He was educated at Aravon, Bray, co. Wicklow, and at the Royal Naval College, Dartmouth (1928–31). The family had an association with the navy dating back to Trafalgar, when Midshipman James Bayly was on board HMS *Euryalus*. Following his sub-lieutenants' courses and time in the cruiser *Amphion* and the sloop *Penzance*, Bayly was appointed first lieutenant in the river gunboat *Cicala*, joining her at Canton (Guangzhou) during a Japanese air raid on the city in 1938.

From November 1939 to July 1941, although he lacked the specialist qualification, Bayly was gunnery officer aboard the First World War cruiser *Durban*. Reports written on him in later years frequently mention his initiative, a quality apparent during his time in *Durban*. In Singapore during a refit Bayly learned to fly when some Gypsy Moth float-planes in a hangar set him thinking. The three D class cruisers, whose role was to patrol the 4000 miles between Colombo and Formosa (Taiwan) looking for enemy raiders, were hopelessly obsolete. Bayly's suggestion was to remove the midships turret and torpedo tubes and replace them with a Gypsy Moth and a crane, thus vastly increasing their range of observation. This novel and quite practical idea was not taken up.

Sent to Scotland to train beach landing parties in 1942, Bayly was flown to north Africa in June 1943 as an emergency replacement for a sick principal beachmaster. He was promoted acting lieutenant-commander and appointed commanding officer of M beach commando (as it was now called). His astute choice of beaches and coolness under fire gained him a DSC and bar in successive landings in Sicily and at Salerno. In the former, Bayly and his team brought the 51st division safely ashore in roughly half of the programmed time. At Salerno the opposition was much stiffer in the face of a well-camouflaged battery of the particularly effective 88 mm. guns. The landing proceeded on schedule.

Despite the decorations that Bayly won in the summer of 1942, it was perhaps his last such operation, the crossing of the River Volturno under fire that October, that gave him the most satisfaction. Summoned at about twelve hours' notice to prepare a landing for tanks at dawn, the team arrived at the river, which was in spate, with the assault phase in trouble: barely a company was across, instead of a battalion. The army refused them a boat, but they found one abandoned with a rent in the canvas bow. The hole was stuffed with clothing, and with the bow lifted clear of the water by positioning themselves and the equipment in the stern, they paddled across. Uncertain as to the state of the front, Bayly split his team, sending four along the bank while with the other three he swept downstream to the sea before paddling back close to the north shore. Just after they landed on the only suitable beach the other four arrived. Accompanied by a runner, Bayly returned to the brigade headquarters to report, after which he and his group crossed again to the beach. They were under fire both ways from multi-barrelled mortars. The tanks landed at dawn.

To his surprise Bayly had a virtually untroubled view of the D-day landings from the bridge of the cruiser *Mauritius*, to which he had been appointed first lieutenant in 1944. He left the *Mauritius* early in 1945 and, having married Third Officer Moira Gourlay (Moy) Jardine (*b.* 1922), of the WRNS, on 4 April, was delighted to be on the Royal Naval Staff College course at Greenwich. Another enjoyable period ashore followed, appropriately enough at the Staff College, Camberley, before Bayly's next appointment saw him in the Mediterranean as staff officer (operations) first in *Orion* and later in the modernized *Mauritius*, the flagships successively of the 1st cruiser squadron. Frequently involved in the anti-immigration patrols off Palestine, with others of the ship's company he often witnessed harrowing scenes, which he described at some length in an unpublished memoir.

Promoted commander, in mid-July 1948 Bayly joined the directorate of training and staff duties. His 68-page booklet *Notes on the Royal Navy* became the 'bible' for the Joint Services Staff College. Other navies also sought it, and by 1954 some 17,000 copies had been printed. Bayly took command in November 1951 of the sloop *Alacrity*, and later of the destroyer *Constance*. Both saw action in the Korean War, from which he emerged with a second bar to his DSC, together with appointment to the American Legion of Merit.

On his promotion to captain in 1954 Bayly went to the joint planning staff in the newly created Ministry of Defence. During the Suez crisis of 1956 his paper 'The control of the Nile' demonstrated the futility of a proposed scheme to influence Egyptian policy by controlling the headwaters of the river. To his surprise it was significant enough to be quoted by the prime minister. In the following year, after a truncated spell at the Imperial Defence College, he was appointed to command HMS *Cavendish* as captain (D), 6th destroyer squadron. This was followed by a more relaxed two years in the NATO headquarters in Norfolk, Virginia, and an equally happy period as commodore, chief of staff, to the commander-in-chief of the Mediterranean Fleet.

Bayly then got what he said was the best job in the navy: that of flag officer, sea training, with the rank of rear-admiral. On the wall behind his desk was an appropriate quotation from Nelson's letter to St Vincent before the battle of Copenhagen: 'I am brushing these fellows up, they do not have that activity that my mind carries with it'. He was appointed CB in 1965, and his next post was that of admiral president of the Royal Naval College, Greenwich. Bayly's last post, on promotion to vice-admiral, was in NATO as chief of staff to the commander of naval forces in southern Europe. Appointed KBE in 1968, he retired in 1970. Bayly was the director of the Maritime Trust from 1971 to 1988. He was a trustee of the British Korean Veterans' Association and patron of the Royal Naval Commando Association. For twelve years he was chairman of the governors of the girls' Royal Naval School at Haslemere.

Pat Bayly was a gentleman of the old school. Although invariably courteous, he was barely tolerant of fools or incompetents. He disclaimed any intellectual pretensions, but was an accomplished watercolourist and could dash off competent verse. He also researched at length the site of St Paul's shipwreck on Malta. His description in his unpublished memoir of the passage down the Volturno under fire, the four men lying back in the stern of the boat to lift its damaged bow clear of the water, 'floating down like the Lady of Shallot', was typical. He had no doubts about the role of luck in a successful career, one of his after-dinner speech topics being called, with typical humility, 'Right place, right time'.

Sir Patrick Bayly died in Forest Brow residential home for the elderly, 63 Forest Road, Liss, Hampshire, on 1 May 1998, survived by his wife and two daughters. His ashes were buried at sea, off the Nab tower in the Solent, on 28 May 1998.   ALAN McGOWAN

Sources P. Bayly, memoir, priv. coll. · family papers, priv. coll. · *Navy List* · P. Bayly, journals, 1933–4, priv. coll. · R. H. Mackenzie, *The Trafalgar roll* (1913) · *The story of the 46th division, 1939–1945* [n.d.] · *Daily Telegraph* (15 May 1998) · *The Times* (12 May 1998) · b. cert. · m. cert. · d. cert. · private information (2004) [family]
Archives priv. coll., family papers
Likenesses photograph, repro. in *The Times* · photograph, repro. in *Daily Telegraph*
Wealth at death under £180,000: probate, 8 June 1998, *CGPLA Eng. & Wales*

Bayly, Thomas (d. *c*.1657), Church of England clergyman and Roman Catholic controversialist, was the fourth son of Dr Lewis *Bayly (*c*.1575–1631), bishop of Bangor, and his first wife, probably named Judith Appleton. His brother was John *Bayly (1595/6–1633), scholar and clergyman. He was educated at Magdalene College, Cambridge, where he matriculated as a fellow-commoner at Michaelmas 1627; he graduated BA in 1627–8, MA in 1631. On 23 August 1629 he was ordained deacon, and on 23 May 1630 priest in his father's diocese of Bangor. On 29 August 1629 he was instituted to the vicarage of Llanwynno, on 24 May 1630 to that of Llandinam and on 29 August 1631 to the rectory of Llaniestyn. At the time of the visitation of Bishop Dolben in 1632 he was rector of Llandyrnog and comportioner of Llandinam. In 1634 he was instituted to the rectory of Holgate, Shropshire, and on 29 May 1638 was instituted subdean of Wells. For the next few years nothing is known of him.

On 7 August 1644 Bayly was incorporated in the degree of MA at Oxford, and graduated DD in the same year. He became an officer in the royal army under the earl of Worcester. Bayly tells us that he first met the earl by accident in the Welsh mountains, and helped find shelter for him at Bala. In *Certamen religiosum* (1649) he described a conference between the earl and Charles I held at Raglan Castle about January 1646. Papers purporting to have been issued by the earl and the king were appended to the account. In it Bayly claimed that the earl, a Roman Catholic, made strenuous efforts to convert the king, who nevertheless remained 'constant to his religion' and that Charles told him that Worcester had not been admitted into his counsel of war because it would be said he was advised by Jesuits. Bayly's account was disputed by many, notably Hamon Lestrange. Its propaganda purpose was to disprove the common view 'that the late king was a papist in his heart; and that he intended to bring in popery' (Bayly, *Certamen*, sig. A4). Nevertheless, it may strike the later reader as plausible. Bayly was present at the fall of Raglan Castle on 19 August 1646. He was named by the earl of Worcester as one of six commissioners who negotiated with Fairfax, and it was reported that the articles of surrender were chiefly framed by him.

In summer 1649, following the execution of the king, Bayly published *The Royal Charter Granted unto Kings by God Himself*, noting in a bitter preface that 'the two houses gave out that they fought in defence of the King's person, crown and dignity', and blaming the course of events largely on London, 'thou great city, the pantapolis of all miseries: the seminary of rebellion'. Perhaps it was as a result of this work that he was imprisoned in Newgate, but on 19 February 1650 he was ordered to be released on bond of £1000 that he would not undertake actions likely to undermine the government.

Not long afterwards Bayly went abroad and toured in Flanders and France. In *Certamen religiosum* (about September 1649) he had styled himself 'sub dean of Wells'. But by 1654, when his *An End to Controversy between the Roman Catholique and the Protestant Religions Justified* was printed at Douai, he had converted to Roman Catholicism. It may be that closer acquaintance with the churches there may have been influential in this, but as a long prefatory account shows he had been much affected by the collapse of the established church in England, a punishment, as he thought, for its schism. He was especially outraged that the execution of Charles I, the head of state and of church, had not inspired more protest from the dispossessed higher clergy.

The Life and Death of the Renowned John Fisher, issued under Bayly's name in 1655, was in fact written by Richard Hall (*d*. 1604). Dodd was told that a manuscript copy had found its way into the possession of Sir Wingfield Bodenham, who lent it to Bayly. He made a copy and sold it to a bookseller, who in turn issued it under Bayly's name, and apparently with his knowledge, for he contributed an epistle but omitted any attribution to Hall. On 3 May 1655 Marmaduke Langdale reported from Brussels that Bayly was *en route* for Rome, there to act as Cromwell's ambassador to the pope, though evidence for the claim is lacking. Indeed, the rest of Bayly's life is obscure. He had dedicated *An End to Controversy* to an earlier Catholic convert, Walter Mountague, son of Henry, first earl of Manchester, and then Lord Abbot of Nanteul. The epistle to the *Life of Fisher* was addressed to John Questall, a merchant in Antwerp. Perhaps these were both earlier ports of call.

The probability that Bayly did not return from his journey to Italy finds corroboration in reports received by Wood that he had been welcomed into the household of Cardinal Ottoboni, then papal nuncio at Ferrara, and also in contradictory reports that he had died in poverty in that country. The former version is preferred by historians of English Catholicism. The two accounts are not necessarily quite opposed, for there is evidence from both sets of Wood's reporters that he died in Italy not long before the restoration of King Charles and this is accepted by Dodd.

THOMPSON COOPER, rev. STEPHEN WRIGHT

Sources Walker rev. · T. Bayly, *Worcesters apophthegme, or, Witty sayings of the right honourable Henry (late) marquess and earl of Worcester* (1650) · Wood, *Ath. Oxon.*, new edn · *CSP dom.*, 1649–50 · Gillow, *Lit. biog. hist.* · C. Dodd [H. Tootell], *The church history of England, from the year 1500, to the year 1688*, 3 vols. (1737–42) · T. Bayly, *Certamen religiosum, or, A conference between his late majestie … and Henry late marquis of Worcester* (1649) [E1355 (1)] · T. Bayly, *The royal charter granted unto kings by God himself* (1649) [E1356 (1)] · T. Bayly, *An end to controversy between the Roman Catholique and the protestant religions justified* (1654)

Bayly, William (*bap.* 1738, *d.* 1810), astronomer, was born at Bishops Cannings, near Devizes, Wiltshire, the son of a small farmer. He was probably the child whose parents were John and Elizabeth Baily (not Bayly), recorded as being baptized in Bishops Cannings on 8 October 1738. Much of his boyhood was spent at the plough, but he took advantage of the offer of an exciseman from a neighbouring village to teach him the elements of mathematics, and was also helped later by a Mr Kingston of Bath. He became an usher at a school at Stoke, near Bristol, and to another nearby.

On 14 November 1766 Bayly was appointed assistant to the astronomer royal Nevil Maskelyne at the Royal Observatory, Greenwich. Already well versed in mathematics, he now acquired the skills of observational astronomy so well that Maskelyne recommended that he should be one of the Royal Society's observers of the forthcoming transit of Venus. On 13 April 1769 he and Jeremiah Dixon sailed together for Nordkapp in Norway in HMS *Emerald*, and Bayly successfully observed the transit on 3 June at Nordkapp. He returned to Greenwich, where the Revd Malachy Hitchins had temporarily taken his place since April, and remained there as Maskelyne's assistant until 25 March 1771. He was married, but his wife's name is not known.

Why Bayly left Greenwich when he did is not clear, but he did not have long to wait for a new job. Captain Cook arrived home after his first Pacific voyage on 13 July 1771, and soon plans were being made for a second voyage of discovery in the southern hemisphere, this time with two vessels. On 14 December, on Maskelyne's recommendation, the board of longitude appointed William Wales and

Bayly to go as astronomers in the *Resolution* (Captain Cook) and *Adventure* (Captain Furneaux), respectively, 'to make Nautical & Astronomical Observations, and to perform other Services tending to the Improvement of Geography & Navigation' (*Journals*, 2.724). One of the important secondary objects of the voyage was the trying out of the new longitude timekeepers, Wales having a chronometer by Larcum Kendall and one by John Arnold, and Bayly two by Arnold. The two sloops sailed together from Plymouth on 13 July 1772, and remained in company until February 1773, when they lost touch with each other in dense fog in the southern Indian Ocean. They met again in New Zealand in May, but five months later, in gales off New Zealand, they lost touch once more, not to meet again. *Adventure* sailed home independently via Cape Horn, and reached Spithead on 14 July 1774. Of Bayly's Arnold chronometers, one stopped at the Cape outward bound, the other performed reasonably well throughout.

After returning to England, Bayly began preparing for submission to the board of longitude the observations he had made on the voyage. (They were eventually published in 1777, edited by Wales.) Then, when Cook reached England in *Resolution*, a little over a year after *Adventure*, plans were made for a third voyage, to explore the north Pacific Ocean. The ships were to be Cook's *Resolution* once again and the smaller *Discovery* (Captain Charles Clerke). Bayly was appointed astronomer for the *Discovery*. He joined the ship on 6 June 1776 and sailed a month later.

After Cook was killed in Hawaii on 14 February 1779 Clerke took command of the expedition, but died himself on 22 August. James King, who had been second lieutenant in *Resolution* and its astronomer, then took command of the *Discovery*, and Bayly transferred to the *Resolution*. He finally left her at Stromness, Orkney, on 8 September 1780. He was commissioned by the board to prepare the observations of Cook, King, and himself for the press, and they were published in 1782.

Bayly was appointed headmaster of the Royal Naval Academy in Portsmouth Dockyard on 18 February 1785, and kept his post, despite disciplinary and other troubles, until the academy was transformed into the Royal Naval College in 1807, when he was pensioned. His final years were sad, as he lost in rapid succession his wife and seven children, all by consumption, except for a son, a midshipman, killed in action in the frigate *Amelia* off Belle Isle on 9 April 1799. He died at Portsea, Hampshire, on 21 December 1810.

DEREK HOWSE

Sources *GM*, 1st ser., 81/1 (1811), 184 · *Naval Chronicle*, 24 (1810), 516 · board of longitude papers, CUL, RGO 14, vols. 5, 6 · *The journals of Captain James Cook*, ed. J. C. Beaglehole, 2, Hakluyt Society, 35 (1961); repr. (1969) · *The journals of Captain James Cook*, ed. J. C. Beaglehole, 3/1–2, Hakluyt Society, 36a–b (1967) · council minutes, 1768, RS · *Letters and papers of Admiral of the Fleet Sir Thos. Byam Martin, GCB*, ed. R. V. Hamilton, 3 vols., Navy RS, 12, 19, 24 (1898–1903) · W. James, *The naval history of Great Britain, from the declaration of war by France in 1793, to the accession of George IV*, [5th edn], 6 vols. (1859–60), vol. 2 · private information (2004) · F. B. Sullivan, 'The Royal Academy at Portsmouth, 1729–1806', *Mariner's Mirror*, 63 (1977), 311–26 · *DNB*

Archives CUL · NL NZ, Turnbull L. · PRO · Sci. Mus., MS relating to navigational and astronomical problems

Baynard, Ann (1672/3–1697), exemplar of godly life, was born at Preston, Lancashire, the only child of Edward *Baynard (1641?–1717), physician and poet, and his wife, who was probably Anne, daughter of Robert Rawlinson of Carke, Lancashire. At some point during the following decade the family moved to London, where Ann's father became a fellow of the Royal College of Physicians. As a child she was educated by her father in science, mathematics, philosophy, and classical languages and literature. According to John Prude she had mastered these subjects by her early twenties and had become a 'subtle disputant' in the 'hard and knotty Arguments of Metaphysical Learning' (Prude, 24). She perfected her knowledge of Greek through her study of the New Testament, and wrote a number of Latin compositions which have not survived. As Prude concluded, she had a 'vast and comprehensive Knowledge, a large and exalted Mind, a strong and capacious Memory, still coveting more and more Knowledge' (ibid., 25).

Baynard declared, however, that secular learning was worthless unless it led to the knowledge of God. She reportedly remarked that it was useless to be 'so Skilful in Arithmetick, as that we can divide, and subdivide, to the smallest Fractions; if … We do not so learn to number our days, that we may apply our hearts unto Wisdom' (Prude, 26). She was a diligent churchgoer, never missing daily services unless prevented by illness, and spent much of her time in solitary meditation and other pious exercises. Generous to the poor, she set aside a fixed portion of her income for charity. Baynard was active in her attempts to persuade others to lead a religious life, with frequent offers of 'friendly Reproof, good Counsel, or some learned or pious Discourse' to friends and acquaintances (Prude, 29).

Two years before her death, while meditating in the churchyard at Barnes, Surrey, Baynard felt a 'strong Impulse' break in upon her mind that in a short time 'she should die, and be buried in this very Church-yard'. She lived in Barnes during these final years and was frequently ill; she died there, unmarried, on 12 June 1697, in her twenty-fifth year. On her deathbed she urged all young people to study philosophy and especially 'to read the great Book of Nature, wherein they may see the Wisdom and Power of the Great Creator, in the Order of the Universe, and in the Production, and Preservation of things' (Prude, 30). She concluded her deathbed advice to her contemporaries with a particular appeal to her own sex to make an effort to educate themselves:

> That Women … are capable of such improvements, which will better their Judgments and Understandings, is past all doubt; would they but set to't in earnest, and spend but half of that time in study and thinking, which they do in Visits, Vanity, and Toys. 'Twould introduce a composure of Mind, and lay a sound Basis, and Ground-work for Wisdom and Knowledge; by which they would be better enabled to serve God, and help their Neighbours. (Prude, 30–31)

Ann Baynard was buried on 26 June 1697 in Barnes churchyard, where a small monument was erected to her memory. Her funeral sermon was preached by John Prude, curate of St Clement Danes, London, and was published in 1697. Although Baynard composed a number of works in Latin as well as English, none has survived.

SARA H. MENDELSON

Sources J. Prude, *A sermon at the funeral of the learned and ingenious Mrs. Ann Baynard* (1697) · G. Ballard, *Memoirs of several ladies of Great Britain* (1752) · DNB · G. Ballard, *Memoirs of several ladies of Great Britain*, ed. R. Perry (1985)

Baynard, Edward (1641?–1717), physician and poet, was probably born in 1641, possibly in Preston, Lancashire. His parentage and schooling are somewhat obscure, but Jeremy Collier states that he was the second son of one Edward Baynard. Collier traced the family line back to the Norman conquest, and Baynard himself seems to have emphasized his status as a gentleman. He received an MA from King's College, Aberdeen, in 1670, matriculated into the medical school at the University of Leiden in May 1671, and received an MD from Aberdeen in or before 1672. Thereafter he settled in Preston and married. The identity of his wife is uncertain. Jeremy Collier wrote in Baynard's lifetime that she was Anne, daughter of Robert Rawlinson of Carke in Lancashire. However, Baynard's will indicates that his 'dear wife' (she is not named) was connected with the Lloyd family of Flintshire. His daughter, Ann *Baynard (d. 1697), was born in Preston in 1672 or 1673.

During the next decade Baynard moved to London. He became an honorary fellow of the Royal College of Physicians in March 1684 and a full fellow in 1687. By that date he had established cordial relations with his future collaborator, Sir John Floyer. In the preface to *Pharmako-basanos, or, The Touch-Stone of Medicines* (1687) the latter mentions how they had tasted plants together in Chelsea Physic Garden. Baynard's relations with other physicians were much stormier. Although one should distinguish him from Francis Bernard, satirized as Horoscope in Samuel Garth's *The Dispensary*, Baynard was involved in the acrimonious disputes that racked the College of Physicians during the 1690s. In 1693 his name was omitted from the printed list of college members. His protests were so vociferous that he was summoned before the college. When kept waiting he stormed off, declaring that he was 'a gentleman' and would not wait beyond the appointed hour (Cook, 226). The following month he was admonished for having called the president of the college 'the son of A Whore' (annals, RCP Lond., 6.63). In 1695–6 Baynard was one of the minority of college members who refused to support its attempts to establish a dispensary for medicines in the City of London, a measure which was designed to reduce the influence of the Society of Apothecaries and of empirical physicians.

In view of Baynard's irascibility it is not surprising that like a number of other learned London physicians he cultivated a reputation for wit and for verses. He was a friend and correspondent of the satirical writer Tom Brown, and is thought to have contributed to *Commendatory Verses, on the Author of the Two Arthurs*, a collection of verses satirizing the literary output of Sir Richard Blackmore, published in March 1700 and probably edited by Brown.

Although responses to this verse in *Discommendatory*

Verses, on those which are Truly Commendatory (1700) suggested that Baynard 'prattles like ... a F[oo]l' and 'neither Cures nor Kills' (Boys, 98–100), Baynard established a national therapeutic reputation and a lucrative practice which was split between London and Bath. In 1694 he was resident in Surrey Street, London (J. Houghton, *A Collection for Improvement of Husbandry and Trade*, no. 106, 10 Aug 1694) and in 1701 was in Ludgate Hill, London. In 1695 and 1698 he contributed short pieces to the *Philosophical Transactions* describing the cure of retention of urine by chemical means and giving an account of what happened to a child on swallowing two copper farthings, and how his subsequent symptoms were relieved by the bath.

Baynard was a strong advocate of balneology, and in particular of cold baths. In 1702 the Lichfield physician Sir John Floyer published *The Ancient Psychrolousia Revived*; the second half of this work was a long letter by Baynard, describing and advocating cures by cold bathing. Whereas Floyer was interested in the relationship between bathing and baptism, Baynard couched his opinions in a vigorous and almost satirically secular and down-to-earth style, larding his accounts of cures by cold baths with saws and verses. His contributions were expanded in the third and subsequent editions. His comments attacking the pernicious effects of high living, wet-nursing, and excessive swaddling anticipated the advocacy of 'natural' regimens advocated by many later eighteenth-century doctors. The same antipathy to excessive indulgence permeates his verse *Advice to Claret-Drinkers*, published in 1709, which begins 'Pass by a Tavern-Door, my son'. In 1716 *Health, a poem shewing how to procure, preserve and restore it, to which is annex'd the doctor's decade* was published pseudonymously as by Dabry Dawne. Baynard's name appeared on the title page of a Dublin edition the following year and there were twenty editions up to 1789. Written in crude verse, and incorporating the *Advice to Claret-Drinkers*, it eulogized the benefits of a moderate diet and abstinence from drink and luxurious living.

Baynard made his will on 18 July 1717, leaving bequests to servants, nephews, and cousins and setting aside money for a tombstone at the east end of the churchyard of Barnes in Surrey, where his daughter Ann had been buried. He revised the will on 27 August, but died in the next three weeks, for the will was proved on 17 September 1717. The large sale catalogue published for the auction of his library in June 1721 bears testimony to his wide learning, but as it contains works published after his death it is unclear exactly how many lots came from his collection.

MARK S. R. JENNER

Sources will, PRO, PROB 11/559, sig. 165 · J. Prude, *A sermon at the funeral of the learned and ingenious Mrs. Ann Baynard* (1697) · R. C. Boys, *Sir Richard Blackmore and the wits* (1949) [incl. critical edn of *Commendatory verses, on the author of the Two Arthurs*, 1700, and *Discommendatory verses, on those which are truly commendatory*, 1700] · J. Collier, *The great historical ... dictionary* (1701) · 'Dr John Floyer and Dr Edward Baynard on cold bathing', *Palatine Note-Book*, 2 (1882), 207–12 · *A catalogue of the libraries of Edward Baynard MD* (1721) · BL, Sloane MS 4037, fol. 97 · BL, Stowe MS 305, fols. 216–18 · G. Ballard, *Memoirs of several ladies of Great Britain* (1752) · J. Houghton, *A collection for improvement of husbandry and trade*, 20 vols. (1692–1703) · H. J. Cook, *The decline of the old medical regime in Stuart London* (1986) · Munk, *Roll* · R. W. Innes Smith, *English-speaking students of medicine at the University of Leyden* (1932) · P. J. Anderson, ed., *Officers and graduates of University and King's College, Aberdeen, MVD–MDCCCLX*, New Spalding Club, 11 (1893) · annals, RCP Lond.

Wealth at death relatively affluent; bequeathed land and lottery tickets: will, PRO, PROB 11/559, sig. 165

Baynard, Fulk. *See* Bainard, Fulk (*b.* in or before 1167, *d.* in or after 1243).

Baynard [Banyard], **Robert** (*d.* 1329/30), administrator and justice, was the son of Robert Baynard and his wife, Joan, and the grandson of Fulk *Bainard. The family was one of Norfolk gentry, with their principal residence at Great Hautbois. Robert Baynard senior appears to have been still alive in 1302, raising the possibility of confusion between father and son, but as the former had been of age by about 1230, it was probably the younger Robert who begins to appear in government records from the late 1280s, as a justice of gaol delivery in 1287 and 1288, and as knight of the shire for Norfolk at the parliament of July 1290. It was certainly Robert Baynard junior who was summoned to perform military service in Scotland in May 1298. He also seems to have had connections with men in government service, since he later complained to the treasurer and barons of the exchequer that William Gerberge, clerk to Hugh Cressingham during the latter's northern eyres of 1292–4, had left his judicial records at Baynard's house at Chedgrave in Norfolk and persistently failed to remove them. Under Edward II Baynard himself was frequently active in the service of the crown. In February 1310 he was appointed a keeper of the vacant see of Ely. He was sheriff of Norfolk and Suffolk from April 1311 to March 1312, and again in October and November 1312. He was summoned to perform military service against the Scots in 1314, 1316, and 1319. Between 1309 and 1326 he was ten times a knight of the shire for Norfolk, while in 1313 he three times received an individual summons to parliament (the fact that he is not recorded as having sat prevents his being styled a peer). He was also frequently an assessor and collector of taxes, a commissioner of array, and a justice of oyer and terminer; in March 1314 he was ordered to prepare himself for an embassy overseas, but there is no evidence that he went. His rewards included a licence to crenellate at Great Hautbois in 1312, and two weekly markets at Wheatacre in 1318.

Edward II's regime clearly felt able to rely on Baynard's loyalty in the crisis of 1326, since he was commissioned to disperse seditious assemblies in February, and empowered to compel ships in Norfolk ports to join the king's fleet in August. Nevertheless he attended the parliament of 1326–7 at which Edward II was deposed, and on 9 March 1327 was appointed a justice in the court of king's bench. He may have thrown in his lot with Queen Isabella and Roger Mortimer to save his estates from devastation by their invading forces, but he may also have become disaffected towards the existing regime. He had at least some links with the king's opponents, since in 1314 he had witnessed a deed of Humphrey (VII) de Bohun, earl of Hereford, while the fact that on 20 July 1327 his debts to the exchequer were pardoned may indicate that he had come under financial pressure from Edward II's government. Baynard was paid as a justice of king's bench only until Easter 1329, but he was active as a justice of assize and gaol delivery in the home counties during much of that year, holding assizes for Buckinghamshire on 2 October; however, he was dead by 22 February 1330. At the time of his death his wife was named as Maud; the fact that she long outlived Robert, being still alive in 1346, and that her husband's eldest son, Thomas, was said to be twenty-six when his father died, raises the possibility that she was the latter's second wife. Robert Baynard also had a second son, another Robert, who was old enough to be married by 1330.　　　　　　　　　　　　　　HENRY SUMMERSON

Sources Chancery records · F. Palgrave, ed., *The parliamentary writs and writs of military summons*, 2/3 (1834), 470–71 · P. Vinogradoff and L. Ehrlich, eds., *Year books of Edward II*, 14: *6 Edward II*, SeldS, 38 (1921), 49–58 · G. O. Sayles, ed., *Select cases in the court of king's bench*, 7 vols., SeldS, 55, 57–8, 74, 76, 82, 88 (1936–71); vol. 1, pp. 16–17; vol. 4, pp. 37–8 · *Inquisitions and assessments relating to feudal aids*, 3, PRO (1904) · [R. E. Latham], ed., *Calendar of memoranda rolls (exchequer) …: Michaelmas 1326 – Michaelmas 1327*, PRO (1968), 773 · PRO, Assize rolls, JUST/1/1402 · GEC, *Peerage* · *CIPM*, 7, no. 290
Wealth at death property: *CIPM*

Bayne, Alexander, of Rires (*c*.1684–1737), advocate and jurist, was the eldest son of John Bayne of Logie (*d*. in or before 1700), sheriff-clerk of Fife, and his wife, Cecilia Gibson (*fl*. 1670–1705), daughter of John Gibson of Durie and Elizabeth (widow of Sir Thomas Hope of Craighall and daughter of Sir John Aytoun of that ilk). After university education at St Leonard's College, St Andrews, Bayne studied law with John Spottiswoode in Edinburgh in 1704, before matriculating as a law student in Leiden on 14 June 1706 (when he gave his age as twenty-two). On 17 November 1707 he was admitted to Lincoln's Inn in London, though he does not seem to have been called to the English bar.

Logie had at one time belonged to the Wemyss family, and Bayne became a protégé of and secretary to David, fourth earl of Wemyss, whose English affairs he managed at this time. He also participated in London society; described as 'the particular friend' (Bond, 2.32 n. 1) of Richard Steele, he was involved in the group around Steele and Joseph Addison. It has been conjectured that he was sometimes the A. B. occasionally referred to in *The Spectator* and *The Tatler*. As well as these links with the London literati and wits, Bayne had a strong interest in music.

By 1713 Bayne had returned to Scotland and he married, probably in 1714, Mary Carstairs (1695?–1759), third and youngest daughter of Sir John Carstairs of Kilconquhar in Fife, for whom he interceded with the government after the Jacobite rising in 1715, Sir John having been attained for high treason. Bayne's own principles were doubted by some, and he was alleged not to favour the current establishment in the kirk. Of the children born to the marriage, Alexander, Bayne's heir (*d*. 1758), graduated MD from the University of Edinburgh in 1749 and practised as a physician in Perth; William (1730–1782) became a distinguished naval captain, and died of fatal wounds sustained in a battle off Dominica—he was commemorated by a memorial by Nollekens in Westminster Abbey; and Anne (*d*. 1743) married the famous portrait painter Allan Ramsay and was his subject in two portraits. Bayne maintained his and his wife's family interests in Fife, purchasing the estate of Rires in 1719. He continued to assist the Wemyss family in a number of ways into the 1720s.

Bayne was admitted advocate on 10 July 1714. He may have been the author of *An Introduction to the Knowledge and Practice of the Thoro' Bass*, published in Edinburgh in 1717; more certainly he helped establish the harpsichord maker Thomas Fenton in Edinburgh at the end of 1718. Some of Bayne's own musical compositions have survived but are not judged to be of high quality. He was a central and enthusiastic member of the Edinburgh Musical Society, as it promoted concerts and developed the taste for music in early eighteenth-century Edinburgh. He was also an amateur painter.

On 26 November 1722 Bayne offered private classes in Scots law, perhaps in place of those formerly given by John Spottiswoode; within a day he gained the endorsement of most of the lords of session for his petition to the town council to be made a professor in the university and, on 28 November, the town council elected him professor of Scots law. Bayne was a successful teacher, and student manuscripts of his lectures are relatively common. He used Sir George Mackenzie's *Institutions of the Law of Scotland* as his textbook, publishing his own edition in 1730; in the same year he published *Institutions of the Criminal Law of Scotland*, based on special classes on criminal law he had given. In 1731 Bayne published his *Notes for the Use of the Students of the Municipal Law*, drawn from his lectures to his classes. In 1726 he had published an edition of Sir Thomas Hope's *Minor Practicks*, to which he appended *A Discourse on the Rise and Progress of the Law of Scotland and the Method of Studying it*, based on a (Latin) *lectio inauguralis* of 1723.

Bayne's manners, 'English' accent, and harpsichord playing were subjected to the malicious criticism of Lord Kames. Lord Braxfield, however, told James Boswell that he taught himself Scots law by reading Mackenzie's *Institutions* along with Bayne's notes, and Braxfield 'thought well' of Bayne (Reed and Pottle, 239). Bayne's interests were varied. As well as music and the arts generally, they included the natural sciences, and his account of an eclipse was included in volume 40 of the *Philosophical Transactions* of the Royal Society. Concerned with the growing ideals of politeness, elegance, and decorum that were to be such a feature of Scottish society in the eighteenth century, these varied interests are all reflected in the library Bayne collected. His health started to break down in 1735, and by January 1737 he was seriously ill. He died on 22 April 1737, at Alnwick, Northumberland (where he was buried), on his way to Bath to recuperate.

JOHN W. CAIRNS

Sources registers of deeds; commensary records; services of heirs, NA Scot. · *Edinburgh Evening Courant* (1723–32) · *Caledonian Mercury* (1722–36) · D. F. Bond, ed., *The Tatler*, 3 vols. (1987) · OPR index · A. Smart, *Allan Ramsay: painter, essayist, and man of the Enlightenment* (1992) · C. MacLaurin, 'An observation of the eclipse of the sun', *PTRS*, 40 (1737–8), 177–95, esp. 182 · minutes of Edinburgh town council, Edinburgh City archives · *Boswell in extremes, 1776–*

1778, ed. C. M. Weis and F. A. Pottle (1971), vol. 10 of *The Yale editions of the private papers of James Boswell*, trade edn (1950–89) • *Boswell, laird of Auchinleck, 1778–1782*, ed. J. W. Reed and F. A. Pottle (1977), vol. 11 of *The Yale editions of the private papers of James Boswell*, trade edn (1950–89) • J. Duncombe, *Letters by several eminent persons deceased … with notes explanatory and historical*, 2 vols. (1772) • W. Menzies, 'Alexander Bayne of Rires, advocate', *Juridical Review*, 36 (1924), 60–70 • lecture notes, U. Edin.

Archives NL Scot., lectures • priv. coll., family MSS • U. Edin. L., lecture notes and remarks on Scots law

Bayne, Peter [*pseud.* Ellis Brandt] (1830–1896), journalist and author, second son of Charles John Bayne (*d.* 11 Oct 1832), minister of Fodderty, Ross-shire, and his wife, Isabella Jane Duguid, was born at the manse, Fodderty, on 19 October 1830. He was educated at Inverness Academy, Aberdeen grammar school, Bellevue Academy, and Marischal College, Aberdeen, where he graduated MA in 1850. While an undergraduate at Aberdeen he won the prize for an English poem, and in 1854 was awarded the Blackwell prize for a prose essay. From Aberdeen he went to Edinburgh, and entered theological classes at New College in preparation for the ministry. But bronchial weakness and asthma made preaching an impossibility, and he turned to journalistic and literary work as a profession. As early as 1850 Bayne began to write for Edinburgh magazines, and in the years that followed much of his work appeared in Hogg's *Weekly Magazine* and Tait's *Edinburgh Magazine*. He was for a short time editor of *The Glasgow Commonwealth*, and in 1856, on the death of his friend Hugh Miller, whose life he wrote in two volumes (1871), succeeded him in Edinburgh as editor of *The Witness*. A visit to Germany to learn German led to his marriage in 1858 to Clotilda (*d.* 1865), daughter of General J. P. Gerwien.

Up to this point Bayne's career had been uniformly successful, and his collected essays had made him known in Scotland and also in America; but in 1860 he took up the post of editor of *The Dial*, a weekly newspaper planned by the National Newspaper League Company on an ambitious scale in London. *The Dial* proved a financial failure; Bayne not only struggled heroically to save the situation by editorial ability, but lost all his own property in the venture, and burdened himself with debts that crippled him for many years. In April 1862 he retired from *The Dial*, and became editor of the *Weekly Review*, the paper of the English Presbyterian church. He resigned in 1865, because his views on inspiration were held to be unsound, and he declined any further editorial responsibilities. But he became a regular leader writer for the *Christian World*, under the editorship of James Clarke. For more than twenty years his unusual combination of broad-minded progressive liberalism with earnest and eager evangelicalism gave a distinct colour to the religious, social, political, and literary teaching of this influential paper. He found here the main work of his life, but he also wrote independently—sometimes as Ellis Brandt—on the history of England in the seventeenth century (notably *The Chief Actors in the Puritan Revolution* (1878)), many essays in literary criticism, and a biography of Martin Luther. He contributed occasionally to *The Nonconformist*, *The Spectator*, and other weekly papers, as well as to the leading reviews, notably the *Contemporary Review*, *The Fortnightly*, the *British Quarterly*, the *London Quarterly*, and *Fraser's Magazine*. Some of his essays were collected in *The Christian Life* (1855), *Essays, Biographical, Critical, and Miscellaneous* (1859), and *Lessons from my Masters* (1879). In 1879 the degree of LLD was conferred on him by Aberdeen University.

Bayne was thrice married, but had children only with his first wife, who died in childbirth in 1865, leaving him with three sons and two daughters. His second wife, Anna Katharine, daughter of Herbert Mayo of Oakhill, Hampstead, whom he married in 1869, cared devotedly for his children; she died in 1882. His third wife, Marie Josephine Meuret, daughter of Francis Philip Meuret, a tailor, whom he married on 17 October 1883, became insane and died towards the end of 1895, and grief on this account contributed to his own death from senile weakness and cardiac arrest. He died at 13 The Avenue, Upper Norwood, London, on 10 February 1896, and was buried in Harlington churchyard. RONALD BAYNE, *rev.* H. C. G. MATTHEW

Sources *Men of the time* (1875) • *The Dial* (7 Jan 1860) • *The Dial* (4 Oct 1861) • *The Dial* (17 April 1862) • private information (1901) • Boase, *Mod. Eng. biog.* • *CGPLA Eng. & Wales* (1896)

Archives NL Scot., letters to Blackwoods

Likenesses portrait, repro. in *ILN*, 108 (1896), 230

Wealth at death £5888 1s. 11d.: probate, 16 March 1896, *CGPLA Eng. & Wales*

Bayne, Robert Turnill (1837–1915). *See under* Heaton, Clement (1824–1882).

Bayne, William (*d.* 1782), naval officer is of unknown parentage and upbringing. He became a lieutenant on 5 April 1749; in 1755 he served in that rank on board the *Torbay*, in North American waters, with Admiral Edward Boscawen, and in November 1756 was advanced to the command of a sloop of war. On 1 July 1760 he was posted into the *Woolwich* (44 guns), and served in that ship at the reduction of Martinique in 1762, and continued there in the frigate *Stag*, under the command of Vice-Admiral George Bridges Rodney. After this he had no command until 1778, when he was appointed to the *Alfred*, a new ship of seventy-four guns, and served in the Channel Fleet through the inglorious summers of 1779 and 1780.

Bayne afterwards went to the West Indies as part of the squadron with Sir Samuel Hood, and was present in the action off Fort Royal in Martinique on 29 April 1781, and in the action off the Chesapeake on 5 September; the *Alfred* had no active share in either of these battles. On returning to the West Indies the *Alfred* was with Sir Samuel Hood at St Kitts, and by the unfortunate accident of fouling the frigate *Nymphe*, cutting her down to the water, and losing her own bowsprit, delayed the fleet at the very critical moment when Hood had proposed an unexpected attack on the French at anchor. No blame was attached to Bayne for this mischance, which was mainly due to the darkness of the night. In fact the quickness with which he refitted his ship and resumed his station in the line won for him as much credit as his distinguished conduct in the action of 26 January 1782. When the fleet was reunited under the flag of Sir George Rodney, the *Alfred* continued under the immediate orders of Sir Samuel Hood, and with other ships of Hood's division was engaged in the partial action with the French off Dominica on 9 April 1782. It was little more than a distant interchange of fire between the respective vans; but one shot took off Bayne's leg about mid-thigh and he died before a tourniquet could be applied. To his memory, jointly with that of captains William Blair and Robert Manners, who fell in the great battle of the Saints three days later, a monument was placed in Westminster Abbey.

J. K. LAUGHTON, rev. RUDDOCK MACKAY

Sources PRO, ADM MSS · W. L. Clowes, *The Royal Navy: a history from the earliest times to the present*, 7 vols. (1897–1903); repr. (1996–7), vol. 3 · D. Syrett and R. L. DiNardo, *The commissioned sea officers of the Royal Navy, 1660–1815*, rev. edn, Occasional Publications of the Navy RS, 1 (1994) · D. Spinney, *Rodney* (1969) · J. Charnock, ed., *Biographia navalis*, 6 (1798)
Archives NL Scot., corresp. with Sir John Halket and financial papers · PRO, ADM MSS

Baynes, Adam (*bap.* 1622, *d.* 1671), parliamentarian army officer, was baptized on 22 December 1622 in Leeds, the first son of Robert Baynes (*d.* 1626) of Knostrop Hall, Leeds, and his wife, Joan Brown. His family had been associated with the Leeds area for many generations, settling just outside the town, at Knostrop, by the mid-sixteenth century. Baynes came from relatively humble origins. His father was a yeoman, and the grant of arms that Baynes received in 1650 was not confirmed after the Restoration. Nothing is known about his education, though the fact that he was later referred to as a merchant suggests that he may have been apprenticed to a local cloth trader. About July 1650 he married Martha (*d.* 1713), daughter of Richard Dawson of Heworth, with whom he had sixteen children.

At the outbreak of civil war Baynes had joined the northern parliamentarian army under Ferdinando, Lord Fairfax. By June 1643 he was a captain of foot in Fairfax's own regiment, and that autumn he raised a troop of horse at his own expense. He fought at numerous engagements against the northern royalists, including Adwalton Moor and Marston Moor, and by about 1646 was an officer in the regiment of Colonel John Lambert (appointed commander of the northern brigade in August 1647). By the winter of 1648–9 Lambert had installed him as the brigade's financial agent in London, where he acted as its attorney in the purchase by debenture of crown and church lands. Baynes bought up many hundreds of soldiers' debentures at a fraction of their face value, contracted for numerous estates on behalf of his fellow officers, and supervised the purchase of Wimbledon House and other substantial properties for Lambert. He also acquired a number of estates and fee farm rents for himself using the profits he made buying and selling debentures and from land speculation. Most of these properties he sold again, but he retained possession of his most spectacular purchase—the royal manor of Holdenby in Northamptonshire, which he bought in 1650 for £22,299. The profits he made from his position aroused resentment among his fellow

officers, and prompted some of his civilian business associates to accuse him of having 'an unconscionable desire of lucre and gayne' (PRO, C6/153/49).

Although Baynes's surviving correspondence is voluminous it contains few of his own letters, making his political views difficult to ascertain. He seems to have favoured the trial and execution of the king—endorsing the northern brigade's declaration of December 1648 demanding justice against capital offenders, and receiving several letters in February 1649 referring approvingly to Charles's demise. There are also signs that he was well disposed towards the Leveller leader John Lilburne, and it may be significant that one of his friends felt it necessary to caution him against accepting the *Agreement of the People* without fuller consideration. On the other hand he had misgivings about taking the engagement, particularly in pledging to maintain the government 'as it is now established' (BL, Add. MS 21426, fol. 341), and several of his correspondents were under the impression that he regarded the Rump as self-interested, tyrannical, and hostile to the interests of the army and the 'saints'.

As a protégé of Lambert, the author of the 'Instrument of government', Baynes was well placed to profit from the establishment of the protectorate. By the spring of 1654 he had been appointed to the army committee and to the commission for regulating customs and excise, at a salary of £300 a year. It may well have been Lambert who was responsible for the enfranchisement of Leeds in 1654, thereby laying the foundation for Baynes's parliamentary career. Baynes already had a number of friends among the town's leading inhabitants, having acted as their attorney under the Rump, and was said to have possessed a considerable estate in the borough. His interest at Leeds owed less to his local connections, however, than to his 'present power in the court' (BL, Add. MS 21426, fol. 97). 'You are always neare the stern of affaires of the comanwealth', one of his correspondents remarked, '& much accquainted with the pasadges & transactions thereof, and much interesed in those that have the cheefe agitation therein' (BL, Add. MS 21423, fol. 117). Above all Baynes enjoyed the patronage of Lambert, 'and hee strikes with great hammer' (Whitaker, 90).

Nevertheless Baynes's election for Leeds in July 1654 did not go unopposed. A powerful faction in the corporation feared (rightly) that he would support the area's clothiers in trying to break the mercantile elite's stranglehold on local political and commercial affairs. There was also a religious dimension to this quarrel, for most of Baynes's opponents were staunch presbyterians, who equated his lack of sympathy for 'high-kirk' presbyterianism with 'disaffection to [godly] religion' in general (BL, Add. MS 21422, fol. 419). The elections to the second protectorate parliament in the summer of 1656 led to further confrontation between Baynes and the 'high-kirk gang' (ibid., fol. 453). Baynes's election for Leeds was again opposed by the senior office-holders, but their efforts to return one of their own number were thwarted at Westminster. They would doubtless have been scandalized in December, when Baynes urged leniency towards the Quaker leader

James Nayler. Indeed Baynes was sympathetic to the Quakers in general, and repeatedly spoke in their defence at Westminster. Several of his correspondents were Quakers, and evidently regarded him as receptive to 'Truth' and 'loving' to Friends. He certainly seems to have shared the Quakers' disdain for the professional, tithe-maintained ministry. None of his children was baptized in church, and he angered his brother-in-law by advising him that if he intended 'to live of the sweate of other men's browes' then he should become a physician rather than a minister (BL, Add. MS 21418, fols. 327–327v). It was probably Baynes's low opinion of the ministry and 'formal' religion that inspired the accusations against him of atheism, i.e. ungodliness. Yet he seems to have shared many of the traditional concerns of the godly, such as the suppression of alehouses and the abolition of Christmas.

Like the majority of Lambert's army friends, Baynes was opposed to 'The humble petition and advice', and in particular the offer of the crown to Cromwell. It was reportedly Baynes's 'first stiffe motion in Parliament' (BL, Add. MS 21424, fol. 239) that ensured that the title of protector was retained. Following Lambert's dismissal by Cromwell in July 1657 for disaffection to the new constitution, Baynes was either cashiered or resigned his commission, and was subsequently removed from the army committee and the West Riding bench. Leeds lost its parliamentary seat in the 1659 elections, and Baynes was returned instead for Appleby in Westmorland. He was elected as a friend and kinsman of Richard Clapham—steward of Appleby Castle's owner, the countess dowager of Pembroke. At Westminster Baynes worked with Lambert and other Commonwealthsmen to impede the passage of the bill recognizing Richard Cromwell as protector. He was outspoken in his condemnation of the Cromwellian 'other house', which he criticized as the tool of government by a single person. He was keen to deny Cromwell any negative voice in the legislative process, declaring that he was not prepared to trust him with control of the militia or public revenue. He also questioned whether he should be acknowledged a hereditary ruler.

Following the downfall of the protectorate in April 1659, Baynes was restored to his captaincy in Lambert's regiment and to his office as a customs and excise commissioner. His own downfall followed closely upon the readmission of the secluded members in February 1660, and in April he was imprisoned on suspicion of harbouring Lambert. Yet there were many who fared worse at the Restoration, for though he was required to relinquish the crown and church lands he had purchased he managed to retain, on leasehold, a substantial amount of land at Holdenby. In addition, he was appointed crown receiver for the manor of Leeds, at a yearly profit of £185. He was apparently in financial difficulty during the mid-1660s, and his fortunes took a further turn for the worse in the autumn of 1666, when he was imprisoned in the Tower on suspicion of 'treasonable practices' (CSP dom., 1666–7, 531). He died on or about 5 January 1671; his place of burial is not known. In his will he bequeathed houses, coalpits, and a 'considerable colliery' in Leeds parish to his wife and ten surviving children. According to one of his trustees, he died 'seized of diverse lands and tenements of a good yearly value, and possessed of diverse leases, goods and chattells of a great value' (PRO, C10/175/113).

DAVID SCOTT

Sources 'Baynes, Adam', HoP, Commons, 1690–1715 [draft] · BL, Baynes corresp., Add. MSS 21417–21427 · D. Hirst, 'The fracturing of the Cromwellian alliance: Leeds and Adam Baynes', EngHR, 108 (1993), 868–94 · Diary of Thomas Burton, ed. J. T. Rutt, 4 vols. (1828) · JHC, 7 (1651–9) · CSP dom., 1654–67 · I. Gentles, 'The debentures market and military purchases of crown land, 1649–1660', PhD diss., U. Lond., 1969 · G. Isham, 'Adam Baynes of Leeds and Holdenby', Northamptonshire Past and Present, 2 (1954–9), 138–46 · W. Yorks. AS, Leeds, Baynes papers, B13, B15, B16, B22 · will, PRO, PROB 11/336, fol. 158 · J. A. Jones, 'The war in the north: the northern parliamentarian army in the English civil war, 1642–1645', PhD diss., York University, Toronto, 1991 · T. D. Whitaker, Loidis and Elmete (1816) · pleadings in chancery in suits involving Baynes, PRO, C6/206/50, C6/125/10, C5/444/70, C6/153/49, C7/241/91, C5/437/7, C10/175/113 · exchequer, king's remembrancer: bills and answers against defaulting accountants, Yorkshire, c.1662, PRO, E113/7, pt 2 · surveyor-general of land revenues: constat books, volume A, 1660, PRO, CRES 6/1, 205 · privy council register, 1666–7, PRO, PC2/59, 610 · commonwealth exchequer papers: fee farm rents, PRO, SP28/288–9 · G. D. Lumb, ed., The registers of the parish church of Leeds, from 1612 to 1639, Thoresby Society, 3 (1895), 111

Archives BL, corresp., Add. MSS 21417–21427 · W. Yorks. AS, Leeds, MSS

Baynes, Alfred Henry (1838–1914), missionary society administrator, was born on 11 April 1838 at Wellington, Somerset, ninth son of Joseph Baynes, Baptist minister at Wellington, and Anna Day Ash, of Broadmead Baptist Chapel, Bristol. He was the younger brother of Thomas Spencer *Baynes (1823–1887), philosopher and man of letters. Educated at Devonshire College, Bath, he originally intended to enter the medical profession. However, he was prevented by ill health from pursuing the necessary training, and at the age of twenty he joined instead the London firm of Messrs Peto, Brassey, and Betts, where he became private secretary to Sir Samuel Morton Peto (1809–1889), the civil-engineering contractor. In 1860 Peto, who was honorary treasurer of the Baptist Missionary Society (BMS), seconded Baynes to the society to attend to its accounts. Baynes never returned to his original employers, and from this relatively humble beginning as the society's accountant he rose to become finance and minute secretary (1870), co-secretary (1876), and from December 1878 to 1906 general secretary. On his retirement in 1906 he was made honorary secretary of the society.

Baynes presided over a considerable increase in the size and range of operations of the BMS, and thus holds an important place in the story of late-Victorian protestant missionary expansion. Between 1876 and 1906 the missionary force of the society grew from 109 to 170. Baynes encouraged the growth of the society's China mission from a minor enterprise into one of the most significant protestant missionary bodies in China. He was the moving spirit behind the BMS Congo mission, which first became firmly established in 1879 and remained his chief enthusiasm. In association with his two leading missionaries, William Holman Bentley (1855–1905) and George Grenfell

(1849–1906), Baynes directed Baptist expansion on the Congo River. He was frequently required to represent the society's interests through contacts with the Foreign Office, Bismarck's German government (in relation to the Cameroons in 1885–7), and King Leopold II of the Belgians. Until 1905, following Grenfell's advice, Baynes was a firm supporter of Leopold's Congo Free State as a guarantee against Portuguese (and hence Roman Catholic) ambitions in central Africa, and he sought to defend Leopold against the mounting volume of criticism directed at the 'rubber atrocities'.

Although Baynes disliked 'platform work', he was an effective communicator of missionary enthusiasm to the religious public, especially in relation to central Africa. As a missionary secretary he combined a certain tendency to autocracy with an aversion to rigid regulations, and exuded an infectious optimism.

During his years at the BMS Baynes resided at Putney, London, then at Wandsworth Common, and finally at Eastbourne, Sussex. On 2 September 1874 he married Emma Katherine (d. 1935), daughter of John Bigwood, minister of Onslow Baptist Church, Brompton, London, where Baynes served as a deacon and Sunday school superintendent. They had one son, Norman Hepburn *Baynes (1877–1961), Byzantine historian, and one daughter. After his retirement Baynes moved to Fitzwalters, Eastbury Road, Ruislip, Northwood, Middlesex, where he was appointed justice of the peace. He died at his home on 16 October 1914, and was buried at Northwood.

BRIAN STANLEY

Sources B. R. Wheeler, *Alfred Henry Baynes, J.P.* (1951) · *Missionary Herald*, new ser., 36 (1914), 345–70 · B. Stanley, *The history of the Baptist Missionary Society, 1792–1992* (1992) · A. L. Humphreys, *Materials for the history of the town and parish of Wellington in the county of Somerset*, 4 (1914), 522–4 · *DNB* · m. cert. · d. cert.
Archives Regent's Park College, Oxford, Angus Library, corresp. with missionaries · W. Yorks. AS, Leeds, corresp. with the Arthington Trust
Likenesses J. H. Bacon, portrait, 1906, Baptist House, Didcot, Oxfordshire
Wealth at death £145,479 5s. 2d.: probate, 9 Dec 1914, *CGPLA Eng. & Wales*

Baynes, James (1766–1837), watercolour painter and drawing-master, was born at Kirkby Lonsdale, Westmorland, in April 1766. According to Samuel Redgrave, his education was paid for by a friend, but this assistance apparently ceased on his marriage. A pupil of George Romney, he entered the Royal Academy Schools only in November 1793, when he was already twenty-seven. He was employed by a firm which proposed to print copies in oil of old masters, but the company failed. However, he established a successful practice as a drawing-master, despite a scandal in the award of premiums by the Society of Arts, which was exposed by Francis Nicholson and John Varley about 1800. As a matter of course Baynes and many of his fellow drawing-masters on the committee of the fine arts had submitted enhanced or redrawn entries under their pupils' names. On this occasion Varley, who had toured Wales with Baynes a year or two before, described him as 'a poor nervous creature' and easily wrung an admission from him. '"How could I avoid it?" answered Baynes; "they were my pupils. Besides, it is well known to be the practice of the masters"' (Roget, 1.164).

Baynes exhibited at the Royal Academy from 1796, was a member of the short-lived Associated Artists in Watercolours from 1808 to 1812, and also showed with the Oil and Watercolour Society until 1820. For most of his professional life he lived in Soho, and latterly in Castle Street, later Berners Street, north of Oxford Street. His son was Thomas Mann Baynes (1794–1854), the lithographer and occasional watercolour painter; his grandson Frederick Thomas Baynes (1824–1874), a painter of fruit and flower subjects in watercolour. As well as Wales and his native Lake District, Baynes also found subjects in Norfolk and Kent. I. O. Williams notes his fondness for 'timbered farmhouses—sometimes drawn slightly in the manner of Girtin' (Williams, 225). There are examples of his work in the British Museum and Victoria and Albert Museum, London; the Ashmolean, Oxford; York City Art Gallery; and the Whitworth Institute, Manchester. Baynes died in early 1837.

HUON MALLALIEU

Sources J. L. Roget, *A history of the 'Old Water-Colour' Society*, 2 vols. (1891); repr. (1972) · I. O. Williams, *Early English watercolours and some cognate drawings by artists born not later than 1785* (1952) · Redgrave, *Artists* · *DNB* · Mallalieu, *Watercolour artists* · Graves, *RA exhibitors* · S. C. Hutchison, 'The Royal Academy Schools, 1768–1830', *Walpole Society*, 38 (1960–62), 123–91, esp. 154

Baynes, John (1758–1787), lawyer and political reformer, was born in April 1758 (probably on the 6th) at Middleham in Yorkshire, the son of William Baynes of Middleham, who later moved to Embsay Kirk in Craven. After attending school at Bradford under Mr Butler, and Richmond grammar school under Anthony Temple, Baynes was admitted as a pensioner to Trinity College, Cambridge, in April 1773, around the time of his fifteenth birthday. His university career was distinguished: he was awarded the Smith prize for philosophy and the chancellor's medal for classics. In 1779 he was elected to a Trinity fellowship, which he retained until his death. His university connections were with John Jebb, fellow of Peterhouse, and a prominent reformer. From April 1777 Baynes studied under Alan Chambré at Gray's Inn, London, where Samuel Romilly, to whom Baynes left his books, was a colleague. Another acquaintance was William Mason, poet and clergyman of Yorkshire, who may have brought Baynes into the reform movement. In December 1779, with his father, Baynes attended the meeting at York which launched Christopher Wyvill's Yorkshire Association, and was placed on the sixty-one member committee of correspondence. He joined the Society for Constitutional Information of London on its foundation in the spring of 1780. Mason seems to have made use of Baynes in 1782 to facilitate the secret publication of *An Archaeological Epistle to Dr Milles, Dean of Exeter*, on the Rowley poems, and in May 1782 wrote to Horace Walpole that Baynes was 'an ingenious young Yorkshire man … he has been very useful to me and may be more so' (Walpole, 42.10, n. 2). Baynes acquired some reputation as a special pleader, operating from chambers at 11 Coney Court, Gray's Inn; he also had literary interests, publishing in the *London Courant* and writing verses reproduced in the *European Magazine* (1787, 12.240). Andrew Kippis acknowledged contributions to his *Biographia Britannica* and Baynes began collecting material on Yorkshire history, which T. D. Whitaker used in his *History of the Deanery of Craven* (1805).

Baynes's religious views were unitarian and many of his friends were reformers; when the reform movement split after Rockingham's death in 1782 Baynes attended the Westminster Committee in November and urged members to have faith in Lord Shelburne's assurances of goodwill. On 25 March 1784 he supported a Yorkshire address attacking the Fox–North coalition and took a leading part in proposing Wilberforce's successful candidacy for the county, which followed. He continued to support Wyvill's collaboration with William Pitt and in January 1785 published a *Third Address for the Society*, urging renewed efforts. At the end of his life he was involved in a protest, with other junior fellows of Trinity, alleging irregularities in the election of fellows by the master and senior fellows. When the master formally admonished the protesters they appealed to the lord chancellor, as visitor of the college, whose advice was that the matter should be settled internally and the admonition expunged. Baynes died at Gray's Inn, of a fever, on 4 August 1787, unmarried; he was buried on 9 August in Bunhill Fields, near the grave of Dr Jebb. An epitaph by Samuel Parr was printed by John Nichols in his *Literary Anecdotes* (8.115) and Wyvill, when he published his *Political Papers* seven years after Baynes's death, acknowledged the loss of 'an able, eloquent and virtuous advocate … a friend whom he highly esteemed' (Wyvill, 4.455n.). JOHN CANNON

Sources *GM*, 1st ser., 57 (1787), 742, 1017–18 · Nichols, *Lit. anecdotes* · Venn, *Alum. Cant.* · Walpole, *Corr.* · C. Wyvill, ed., *Political papers*, 6 vols. [1794–1804] · S. Halkett and J. Laing, *A dictionary of the anonymous and pseudonymous literature of Great Britain*, 1 (1882), 134 · S. Wilberforce, *Life of Wilberforce* (1872) · 'Creech', *Biographica Britannia, or, The lives of the most eminent persons who have flourished in Great Britain and Ireland*, ed. A. Kippis and others, 2nd edn, 5 (1793) · I. R. Christie, *Wilkes, Wyvill and reform: the parliamentary reform movement in British politics, 1760–1785* (1962) · E. C. Black, *The Association* (1963) · *European Magazine and London Review*, 12 (1787), 240 · *The works, theological, medical, political and miscellaneous of John Jebb*, ed. J. Disney, 3 vols. (1787) · T. D. Whitaker, *The history and antiquities of the deanery of Craven, in the county of York* (1805), 320–22

Baynes, Norman Hepburn (1877–1961), historian, was born at Putney, London, on 29 May 1877, the elder child and only son of Alfred Henry *Baynes (1838–1914), general secretary of the Baptist Missionary Society, and his wife, Emma Katherine Bigwood (d. 1935). He lived in London, then in Eastbourne, moving to Northwood in Middlesex on his father's retirement in 1906. He never married and after his father's death in 1914 he continued to live in Northwood with his mother until she died in 1935, when he eventually settled in London. Brought up in a close-knit and devoted family circle, he enjoyed a sheltered and happy childhood and at the same time had instilled into him a strong sense of public duty and Christian purpose. He went to Eastbourne College for which, despite his

intense dislike of organized games, he retained throughout his life a strong affection, though his surviving papers and later personal recollections indicated that the formative influence in his life was his family circle.

Baynes's diaries contain a wealth of factual detail on family holidays and later, as a young man, travel abroad, particularly a visit to Constantinople where he and his father met Sir Edwin Pears. He spent some months in Tübingen gaining considerable mastery of the German language. At New College, Oxford, he took a first class in classical honour moderations (1898), but a second in *literae humaniores* (1900). He was bitterly disappointed at not getting a first, though the more mature judgement of later years admitted that this had been a fair assessment, for he recognized that he was no philosopher. His powers as a historian were, however, shown by his success in winning the Lothian prize (1901) and the Arnold essay prize (1903). In both cases the subject (Heraclius, and then the military reforms of Diocletian and Constantine), as well as entries in his diaries, indicated his growing interest in East Rome. But he first chose as his profession the bar, studying in the chambers of R. J. Parker (later Lord Parker of Waddington); he was called to the bar by Lincoln's Inn in 1903; and until 1916 he was a tutor under the Law Society.

During the First World War, Baynes worked on intelligence matters at Watergate House. It was at this time that he finally decided to abandon the law and turn to the teaching of history. He had already refused an invitation to stand for a Liberal seat in the London area, and in 1913 he had forged his first link with University College, London, when he was appointed assistant in the department of history. After the war he refused an invitation to return as a don to his Oxford college. Indeed he always prided himself on being a cockney and a member of the University of London. In 1919 he became a reader in the history of the Roman empire in the University of London and from 1931 he held a personal chair of Byzantine history; in 1936 he was elected a fellow of University College; from 1937 he gave up all duties in ancient history and was reappointed to an honorary professorship of Byzantine history and institutions. On his retirement in 1942 he was given the title of emeritus professor by the university and was presented by his friends with an *Address and Bibliography* of his writings (privately printed).

During the last years of his academic career Baynes worked in Oxford in the foreign research and press service, for he found it impossible to concentrate on academic work during a time of world crisis. Therefore from 1939 to 1945 he used his historical training in the field of modern German history and produced two large, fully annotated volumes of Hitler's pre-war speeches (1942). The depth of his involvement in the national struggle was demonstrated by his choice of subject for his Romanes lecture in Oxford in June 1942: 'Intellectual liberty and totalitarian claims'; its delivery was said to have been a brilliant caricature of the oratory of the Führer on whose speeches he had been working. In 1945 he returned to London and to Byzantine studies. On his seventieth birthday the *Journal of Roman Studies* (vol. 37, 1947, with a bibliography of his writings) was dedicated to him. He spent much time editing in his own impeccable way a volume of essays on Byzantium (1948), planned more than twenty years earlier, and he collaborated with E. A. S. Dawes to translate the lives of three early Byzantine saints (1948). But he did little of the major work planned, notably a social history of East Rome, because of increasing illness, finally culminating in several years of complete helplessness.

Baynes's interests as a scholar covered a wide range from biblical history to the early middle ages, but he came increasingly to concentrate on the late Roman and early Byzantine periods and is perhaps best known for his work on Constantine I (Raleigh lecture, 1929) and the *Historia Augusta* (1926). He contributed chapters on the sixth- and seventh-century Byzantine emperors to the *Cambridge Medieval History* (vols. 1 and 2) and was one of the editors of the *Cambridge Ancient History* (vol. 12), as well as a contributor on Constantine. Much of his work took the form of reviews or bibliographical notes (many for the *Byzantinische Zeitschrift*), often subjected to ruthless editorial pruning. He was never afraid to combine his exact scholarship with imaginative reconstruction, unlike J. B. Bury, whom he knew and admired, although he realized Bury's inadequacies, as he showed in the perceptive appraisal in his memoir of him (*Dictionary of National Biography*, 1929). In contrast to Bury, Baynes had the power of vivid reconstruction, bringing Byzantium to life for the uninitiated, as his masterly short study of the *Byzantine Empire* (1925) well illustrates. His published work in the academic field was often controversial, but always stimulating and marked by intellectual integrity. The full extent of his activities can best be realized from his continuous stream of correspondence with contemporary scholars, including names such as Delehaye, Ensslin, Stein, Bidez, Grégoire, and Dölger. He was almost over-fastidious in his approach and often put as much work into his letters, or his reviews and biographical notes, as others put into an article or chapter of a book. But in all he did or said he remained essentially a Victorian individualist to whom the elimination of 'alternatives' was unthinkable.

Baynes's influence can never be fully assessed. Above all he valued friendship and he had a genius for making contacts in every walk of life. He had an extensive circle of friends ranging from his non-graduate evening students and his Ancient History Circle to the more severely academic dons invited to the weekend meetings of his Near East Group. Surviving correspondence and press cuttings illustrate the range of lectures, social evenings, discussions, and play-readings which flourished in the stimulating atmosphere he created. From an early age he had been a gifted performer as a comedian and he was always ready to improvise his unrivalled comic turns, whether in his family circle, or in aid of charities, or to amuse soldiers in wartime hospitals. He had a magnificent presence and was a master of Victorian oratory as well as of exact scholarship. In later years he rarely left England, but on his infrequent visits to congresses abroad he created such an impression that he was long remembered not only as a scholar but as a splendid critic and fierce opponent in debate who could yet remain 'an English gentleman'.

Baynes was elected FBA in 1930, an honorary fellow of Westfield College, London (1937), and of New College, Oxford (1947), a corresponding member of the Bavarian Academy of Sciences (1937), and later of the Belgian (1952) and Serbian (1959) academies. He was doctor *honoris causa* of the universities of St Andrews (1934), Oxford (1942), Durham (1946), Cambridge (1949), and London (1951). He died at his home, 4B Abercorn Place, St John's Wood, London, on 12 February 1961. J. M. HUSSEY, *rev.*

Sources An address presented to Norman Hepburn Baynes (privately printed, 1942) [with bibliography] · J. M. Hussey, 'Norman Hepburn Baynes, 1877–1961', PBA, 49 (1963), 365–73 · Bulletin of Dr Williams Library, 72 (1967) · bibliography, Journal of Roman Studies, 37 (1947), 1–9 · personal knowledge (1981) · private information (1981) · CGPLA Eng. & Wales (1961)
Archives BL, corresp. with Sir Idris Bell, Add. MS 59506 · CUL, Gwatkin MSS | SOUND BL NSA, recorded talks
Likenesses photographs, priv. coll.; repro. in Journal of Roman Studies, 37 (1947); also preps. in An address (1942)
Wealth at death £76,083 3s. 4d.: probate, 19 April 1961, CGPLA Eng. & Wales

Baynes, Paul (*c.*1573–1617), godly divine, was born in London but went to school at Wethersfield, Essex, where he was taught by one Cosens. He matriculated pensioner of Christ's College, Cambridge, in 1590/91, graduated BA in 1594 (when he was probably about twenty-one), and proceeded MA in 1597; before Lady day 1600 he was elected fellow. As a young man he incurred his father's disapproval for unspecified failings, to the extent that a legacy of £40 was entrusted to one Wilson of Birchin Lane, London, to be passed on only if Paul forsook his 'evil courses' (Clarke, 22). Evidently he had done so by the time of his fellowship election, whereupon he was transformed into one whose 'sharpnesse of wit, variety of reading, depth of judgment, aptnesse to teache, holy and pleasant language, wise carriage, heavenly conversation' and other virtues were second to none (ibid., 23). He also married Wilson's widow; her forename is unknown. He became a disciple of William Perkins, whom in 1602 he succeeded as lecturer at St Andrew's Church. He recognized the special place of Cambridge in the English Reformation, having been from the first blessed with 'exemplary plain and spirituall preachers' (Salter, 37), and he resolved to follow in that tradition. In time he achieved a high reputation, and after his death was said to be 'reverenced, and beloved of all the children of God, which ever knew him' (Baynes, *Christians Garment*, 1618, sig. A2).

Baynes's formal career was soon terminated. When Archbishop Richard Bancroft's metropolitical visitation of 1608 reached Cambridge, Baynes was summoned to preach. He was anxious about this 'great businesse' (*Christian Letters*, 1628, sig. F6), and not without cause, for he was being entrapped. He duly spoke in Great St Mary's at nine o'clock on 20 September at the start of proceedings for the three deaneries centred on Cambridge, and managed to deliver 'wholesome doctrine ... in such warie manner, that no specious occasion could be taken ... of questioning his libertie' (Baynes, *Diocesans Tryall*, sig. A3). According to his admirers, he then left the church exhausted; and being thus absent when summoned to the visitors, was immediately sequestrated for contempt. The prosaic record of the visitation tells a different story: it was two days later, in Chesterton parish church, that Baynes was cited to appear; it was objected that 'he hathe erected and begun an exercise', and he was required to produce a licence for his regular preaching at St Andrew's. This he was unable to do, and he was consequently banned from the pulpits of the diocese of Ely until he should be properly accredited (CUL, EDR D/2/29, fol. 7v). At this point the formal record ends; only the posthumous recollection of his friends is testimony for what follows. According to this he was persuaded to appeal to the archbishop; an audience with Bancroft was achieved, but began badly when Baynes was taken to task for arriving with dirty cuffs, and went no further. At some later stage he was brought before the privy council, but gave such a good impression that he emerged still at liberty. For the rest of his life Baynes was without preferment or permanent home; but he continued to preach as occasion and his indifferent health allowed. In the summer he moved around the houses of supportive gentry.

His wife died before him, and for a time Baynes lodged with her sister, Mrs Sheafe, at the puritan stronghold of Cranbrook, Kent. One of his published sermons, *A Counterbane Against Earthly Carefulnes*, was delivered there, and dedicated to Alderman Sir William Craven (1618). He played a little chess, but otherwise filled his days with writing; all its publication was posthumous. For the most part his was the familiar reformist message, critical of the materialism of the episcopate, and the arrogance of those who stood on their own dignity in the presence of God. Yet his prescription for family prayers (no more than a quarter of an hour) shows he was no puritan stereotype. He was hot against papists, of course, but his mockery was gentle—'they faile in the thing to put on, and in putting it on' (Baynes, *Christians Garment*, 6). He wrote passionately about the ministry, which for him was 'no supernaturall vertue or qualitie inherent in the soule: but a relative respect founded on this, that I am called by God to this or that actuall administration in his church'. Ordinarily this power was not given to anyone singularly; but he was prepared to concede a modicum of hierarchy: 'one ministeriall power may bee in degree of dignitie above another' (Baynes, *Diocesans Tryall*, 75, 76).

Despite his frustrations with the established church, Baynes remained convinced that separatism was the wrong answer, disapproving of the Brownists 'and other Novelists' who discommuned themselves from the city of God; he has been described as one of the so-called 'non-separatist congregationalists'. His most considerable work was a commentary on the first and second chapters of Colossians, setting him in an exegetical tradition embracing Chrysostom, Aquinas, Erasmus, and Calvin. His 378 pages of solid theology mixed with homely metaphor can still be appreciated for 'practical admonition, insight into the human heart, therapy for the griefs of life, and hortatory appeal for mental control and emotional discipline' (Leland Carson, in Bayne, *Commentary*, 1972, vii). Baynes died in Cambridge in 1617; administration of his goods was granted to his sister Dorothy Cordell on 16 August. At St Andrew's Church, recently reinvigorated as a centre of evangelism, his memory is particularly cherished.

C. S. KNIGHTON

Sources Venn, *Alum. Cant.*, 1/1.8 · J. Peile, *Biographical register of Christ's College, 1505–1905, and of the earlier foundation, God's House, 1448–1505*, ed. [J. A. Venn], 1 (1910), 199–200 · S. Clarke, 'The life of Master Paul Baines, who dyed Anno Christi 1617', *The lives of thirty two English divines*, in *A general martyrologie*, 3rd edn (1677), 22–24, esp. 22–3 · S. Salter, *Moral and religious aphorisms* (1753), appx, 'Eight letters', 37 · W. M. Lamont, *Godly rule* (1969), 45, 63 · M. M. Knappen, *Tudor puritanism* (1939), 413–14 · K. Fincham, *Prelate as pastor: the episcopate of James I* (1990), 21, 122, 218 · C. Hill, *Society and puritanism in pre-revolutionary England*, pbk edn (1969), 226, 276, 455, 461 · B. Brook, *The lives of the puritans*, 2 (1813), 261–4 · CUL, EDR, B/2/29, fols. 5, 14, 19v; D/2/29, fols. 7v–8 · P. Baynes, *The diocesans tryall* (1621); repr. (1971) · P. Baynes, *A commentary upon the first and second chapters of Saint Paul to the Colossians* (1635); repr. (1972) [incl. introduction by L. H. Carlson] · administration, PRO, PROB 6/9, fol. 131 · P. Collinson, 'Towards a broader understanding of the early dissenting tradition', *Godly people: essays on English protestantism and puritanism* (1983), 527–62

Wealth at death see administration, PRO, PROB 6/9, fol. 131

Baynes, Ralph (*d.* 1559), bishop of Coventry and Lichfield, was born in Yorkshire. Nothing certain is known of his parentage, though his father's name may have been Adam. He attended St John's College, Cambridge, graduating BA in 1518 and proceeding MA in 1521, when he also became a fellow. He proceeded BTh in 1532 and DTh in 1555. His clerical career began when he was ordained priest at Ely on 23 April 1519. He was a university preacher in 1527, and at some point became rector of Hardwick, Cambridgeshire, resigning the living in 1545. A traditionalist who became dissatisfied with the religious climate in England, Baynes spent time abroad, including a period as professor of Hebrew at Paris, and was probably the Dr Baines who in 1550 wrote from there to Edmund Bonner, bishop of London, urging him to resign himself to his fate as one of those persecuted by Edward VI's government. He returned home after the accession of Mary, and on 25 October 1554 was nominated bishop of Coventry and Lichfield. He was consecrated on 18 November.

Under Henry VIII, Baynes had been an outspoken critic of the reformist preaching of Hugh Latimer, and during Mary's reign he was involved in the examination of protestants, including John Hooper, Robert Glover, John Philpot, and Joan Waste, all of whom suffered at the stake. Following the accession of Elizabeth he voted consistently against the new religious legislation and took part, as part of the Roman Catholic contingent, in the abortive Westminster conference of 1559. He was adamant that there was no real hope of settling the theological controversies dividing Catholics from protestants, not least because of their differing views on the relative authority of scripture and tradition. He was deprived on 26 June that year and died at Islington, reportedly of the stone, on 18 November. He was buried in St Dunstan-in-the-West, London. Thomas Bentham, his successor as bishop, when trying to improve his own financial position, claimed that Baynes had made an invalid lease of the valuable rectory of 'Hanberry'.

Setting aside the confessional strife of the Reformation, Baynes's principal importance lay in promoting the study of Hebrew in England. All his books were published at Paris. His *Prima rudimenta in linguam Hebraem* (1550) was the first Hebrew grammar published by an Englishman, his *Compendium Michlol* (1554) an influential edition of the medieval exposition of Hebrew grammar by David Kimchi. His commentary on the Hebrew text of the book of Proverbs, *In Proverbia Salomonis tres libri* (1555), was later included in the 1660 collection *Critici sacri*, edited by John Pearson and others.   JONATHAN WRIGHT

Sources L. Jones, *The discovery of Hebrew in Tudor England* (1983) · J. H. Pollen, ed., 'Dr Nicholas Sander's report to Cardinal Moroni', *Miscellanea, I*, Catholic RS, 1 (1905), 1–47 [from a transcript of Archivio segreto vaticano, Armaria 64:28, fols. 252r–274r] · A. Chester, *Hugh Latimer, apostle to the English* (1978) · Venn, *Alum. Cant.*, 1/1.113 · *The examinations and writings of John Philpot*, ed. R. Eden, Parker Society, 5 (1842) · *The acts and monuments of John Foxe*, ed. J. Pratt, [new edn], 8 vols. in 16 (1853–70) · *Sermons and remains of Hugh Latimer*, ed. G. E. Corrie, Parker Society, 20 (1845) · *CSP dom.*, 1547–80 · F. Heal, *Of prelates and princes: a study of the economic and social position of the Tudor episcopate* (1980) · L. B. Smith, *Tudor prelates and politics* (1953) · Cooper, *Ath. Cantab.*, 1.202–3 · *APC*, 1542–70

Baynes, Roger (1546–1623), author and administrator, was the son of Hugh Baynes of Shrewsbury. In his will he mentions a brother who married in Spain and two brothers living in England. He was admitted to the Middle Temple on 24 November 1565. There is no record of his call but after becoming a Roman Catholic he left England and arrived in Rheims on 4 July 1579, and on 27 August he accompanied William Allen to Rome. In a letter of January 1584 to the rector of the English College, Rome, Allen refers to Baynes as a layman capable of assisting college affairs.

In September 1585 Baynes, fearful lest the pension he had received from Pope Gregory XIII should be discontinued, carried a letter of recommendation to the newly elected Sixtus V from King Stephen Bathory of Poland, making use of the fact that he had visited Poland in the company of Cardinal Andrew Bathory, the young nephew of the king. When Allen became a cardinal in 1587 he made Baynes his secretary and he administered the property of the colleges both at Rheims and Rome. About this time Anthony Copley wrote:

> Cardinal Allen hath about him divers English gentlemen; as Mr Banes, who hath been long out of England and sometime in Poland with the young cardinal of that country; a gentleman of some forty years of age, or rather upward, well languaged, and otherwise very well qualified, discreet, secret, and inclined to high matters. He is a cardinal's secretary of outlandish languages.   (Strype, 4.386, no. 204)

His skills in the English language are shown in two publications. One is *The Praise of Solitarinesse*, a philosophical dialogue concerning the extent to which virtue can be practised and preserved in a predominantly vicious society, dedicated to Sir Edward Dyer and published in London in 1577 presumably before he had left for France. Much later, in 1617, there was published in Germany *The Baynes of Aquisgrane*, another writing in the form of a philosophical

and religious dialogue in which a Catholic exile figures. Later writers cite as a source 'Baynes's diary' but nothing is known of this work.

After Allen's death Baynes continued to live in Rome and was in contact with Joseph Creswell and Sir Francis Englefield with a view to serving Philip II. He died in Rome on 9 October 1623 and was buried in the church of the English College there; a memorial tablet was placed on the wall. He designated as the heir to his property the English Jesuit college at Louvain. There were also instructions that the Louvain college (later to be transferred to Liège) was to maintain an alumnus at the college in Rome on part of the income from the bequest. This alumnus was to be a relative, or failing that, to take the name Baynes. It was hoped that the publication and sale of Baynes's writings in ten volumes would help finance the burse. This was never realized, but there are lists of Baynes scholars up to the year 1683. When Cardinal Howard became protector of the college the custom was discontinued.

MICHAEL E. WILLIAMS

Sources J. Strype, *Annals of the Reformation and establishment of religion … during Queen Elizabeth's happy reign*, new edn, 4 (1824), 386 · J. Hutchinson, ed., *A catalogue of notable Middle Templars: with brief biographical notices* (1902) · A. C. Southern, *Elizabethan recusant prose, 1559–1582* (1950), 322–30 · *N&Q*, 3rd ser., 7 (1865), 443 · T. F. Knox and others, eds., *The first and second diaries of the English College, Douay* (1878), 154–5 · *The letters and memorials of William, Cardinal Allen (1532–1594)*, ed. T. F. Knox (1882), vol. 2 of *Records of the English Catholics under the penal laws* (1878–82), 137, 221, 371, 375 · M. E. Williams, *The Venerable English College, Rome* (1979), 37–8 · *DNB* · memorial tablet, church of the English College, Rome

Archives English College at Rome, MSS, incl. last will and testament

Baynes, Thomas Spencer (1823–1887), editor of the *Encyclopaedia Britannica*, was born on 24 March 1823 at Wellington, Somerset, the son of Joseph Baynes (for fifty years minister of Wellington's Baptist congregation) and his wife, Anna Day Ash, a descendant of the lexicographer Dr John Ash. Baynes's boyhood and early youth were spent in Somerset, whose dialect and folklore would mean much to him in later life. Baynes felt close to a sister with whom he grew up and who died in 1851; his brother Joseph Ash Baynes became a Baptist minister in Nottingham. Another brother, Alfred Henry *Baynes, became general secretary of the Baptist Missionary Society. As a boy he spent a good deal of time at Rumhill House (near Taunton), the neighbouring country seat of Mr and Mrs Cadbury.

Schooled briefly at Bath, Baynes rejected the commercial career advised by his parents; they yielded to his desire to study for the ministry at the Baptist college in Bristol. A nonconformist, Baynes matriculated at London University, although he pursued his studies at the University of Edinburgh, matriculating annually for arts classes there between 1845 and 1849. At Edinburgh he came under the influence of the professor of logic and metaphysics, Sir William Hamilton, whose intellectual scope and pedagogical flair inspired him greatly. In 1846 he gained the prize for an essay on logic in Hamilton's class, and he soon acquired the reputation of being Hamilton's

Thomas Spencer Baynes (1823–1887), by Thomas Rodger

leading expositor of the Hamiltonian philosophy and, admiring Hamilton's sense of literature and of topography, he also took an active interest in English literature, reacting with some enthusiasm to the publication of W. E. Aytoun's mock-Spasmodic tragedy *Firmilian* (1854).

In 1854, however, Baynes suffered a partial breakdown in health which was followed by two years spent largely in retirement and comparative leisure at Rumhill House. There he wrote two papers for the Archaeological Society of Somersetshire, entitled 'The Somerset dialect: its pronunciation', which were published in the *Taunton Courier*, then later (in 1861) printed in a limited edition of 250 copies. In 1855 Baynes wrote from Rumhill House in a letter dated 26 February that he wished to pursue 'the critical study of Early English history, language, and literature' (Skelton, 47). In the mid-1850s he also wrote his admired memoir of Sir William Hamilton, published in the volume of *Edinburgh Essays* dated 1856 (published in 1857). This gives a fine sense of Edinburgh student life and of Hamilton as teacher, rather than a full explication of his philosophy. Baynes clearly admired his former professor's emphasis on self-education and heightened self-reflection, in which 'all within the sphere of knowledge— poetry, history, nature, life,—furnished materials for the use of the newly-awakened powers' (*Edinburgh Essays*). This accent on 'all within the sphere of knowledge' links the Hamiltonian Baynes to James Frederick Ferrier, the St Andrews professor of moral philosophy, whose ideas were honed against those of Hamilton, who became a much admired friend of Baynes, and who in 1854 had coined the term 'epistemology'.

In 1856 Baynes resumed a more active journalistic career, moving to London to write for *The Leader*, which had passed into the hands of his lifelong friend Edward F. S. Pigott, afterwards examiner of plays. Shortly after this move he was appointed examiner in philosophy for the University of London. On 22 December 1857 Baynes married Annabella Gale and settled in the neighbourhood of Regent's Park; the marriage was lifelong and childless. Baynes became a regular contributor to the *Daily News*, taking up the post of assistant editor in 1858. For six years he wrote for this paper, advocating liberal causes and writing leaders with an emphasis on foreign questions; a supporter of the federal cause, he is said to have written about 200 articles on the American Civil War. Other interests in this period included educational work in Bedford College, and a continuing interest in English dialects and etymology. In 1860 he published a version of the Song of Solomon written in the Somerset dialect, to form one of a series of versions in dialect of the same book by William Barnes and others.

Baynes continued to keep indifferent health, and to exhaust himself with overwork; his enduring friend from Edinburgh student days, Sir John Skelton, recalled Baynes's having 'a weak heart and only half a lung; he knew that he might die at any moment' (Skelton, 39). In 1864 Baynes suffered a serious breakdown and, having partially recovered, he began to look for an alternative career. In that year the death of his friend, co-examiner,

favourite student. Baynes's wish to be a preacher was supplanted by scholarly and literary ambitions. Though an Edinburgh student, he graduated BA at London University in 1850 and LLB there in 1852, remaining in Edinburgh to teach at the Philosophical Institution, and to assist in conducting Hamilton's class after the latter suffered a paralytic stroke.

In 1850 Baynes began to edit the *Edinburgh Guardian*, a literary, artistic, and political paper, whose contributors included the Spasmodic poets Sydney Dobell and Alexander Smith as well as Baynes's close friend, the critic Eneas S. Dallas. Baynes contributed to the paper under the pseudonym Juniper Agate. Also in 1850 he published with Sutherland and Knox of Edinburgh his prize essay examining Hamilton's philosophy under the title *An Essay on the New Analytic of Logical Forms*. In 1851 he published as *Port Royal Logic* his translation of Arnauld's work with a learned introduction. In Edinburgh, Baynes became friendly with such figures as the technologist George Wilson, John Skelton, and George Henry Lewes. He had met Lewes when the latter came to lecture at the Philosophical Institution. In 1852 when Baynes was visiting London, Lewes took him to meet Thomas Carlyle; in *The Athenaeum* of 2 April 1887 Baynes published a vivid memoir of this encounter, recalling discussing with Carlyle such topics as Dickens's histrionic style, Goethe's *Faust*, and Carlyle's impressions of Sir William Hamilton. Baynes became the and fellow Shakespearian, Professor Ferrier, and the move of Professor John Veitch to Glasgow left vacancies in both the chairs of philosophy at St Andrews. On 2 November 1864 Baynes succeeded Veitch to the chair of logic, metaphysics, and English literature, a post he held until his death. The term 'English literature' had entered the St Andrews curriculum as a result of the 1858 Universities Act, but the subject continued to be taught by the professors of logic who had taught English literary texts as 'Rhetoric and belles lettres' since the mid-eighteenth century. Although Baynes delivered the philosophical teaching adequately, it was the teaching of English literature which fascinated him; in the 1860s and 1870s a significant number of mature students took Baynes's English literature as their only class. American literature was probably taught at St Andrews by William Spalding in the mid-nineteenth century, but in Baynes's time the appearance of an 1874 MA examination question on that topic ('Give some account of American literature') appears to be the first instance of American literature featuring as an examinable subject on a British university course (Crawford, 59). Baynes had some interest in American literature, admiring Hawthorne, for example.

Baynes's concern with etymology and the development of language found focus in the context of reference works 'fitted for general usefulness' in his July 1868 *Edinburgh Review* essay entitled 'English dictionaries' (Campbell, 'Biographical preface'). In July 1869 he wrote for the same periodical 'Shakespearian glossaries'. As a literary critic he was wide-ranging, writing essays on such topics as the text of Chaucer (*Edinburgh Review*, July 1870) and William Michael Rossetti's edition of Shelley (*Edinburgh Review*, April 1871). Though such essays address editorial difficulties, they also contain both enthusiastic paeans (Shelley's 'slight but vigorous frame' is 'swept to music by every breath of material beauty') and moments of close reading which develop the earlier Scottish rhetorical tradition in the direction of modern literary criticism; Baynes is alert to the significance of Shelley's epithets, for instance, and to that poet's use of images such as that of parted lips. In the early 1870s Baynes wrote for the *Edinburgh Review* essays on such diverse topics as Cox's *Aryan Mythology* (October 1870), Tylor's *Primitive Culture* (January 1872), an edition of Berkeley (July 1872), 'New Shakespearian interpretations' (October 1872), and Darwin on the expression of emotions (April 1873).

Emerging from his experience as skilled journalist, editor, and writer, Baynes had established himself as a polymathic educator with special interests in philosophy, language, and literature. Such a combination of skills stood him in good stead when in 1873 he accepted the general editorship of the impressive ninth edition of the *Encyclopaedia Britannica* (24 vols., 1875–89). Having been awarded the honorary degree of LLD from Edinburgh in 1874, Baynes worked intensively on the *Britannica*. His 'Prefatory notice' to this massive editorial project is dated 'St Andrews, 1st January 1875' and set out his vision for a work which can function as 'to some extent at least, an instrument as well as a register of scientific progress'. He was particularly alert to recent scientific advances which had altered the classification of knowledge, and made it clear that he had taken advice from professors T. H. Huxley and Clerk Maxwell about how best to cope with this situation. Alert to 'the comparative method' and to 'the comparatively modern science of Anthropology', Baynes also attempted a scientific treatment of the arts, history, philosophy, geography, and mythology. He hoped to steer clear of heated religious controversy, since an encyclopaedia such as his had 'to do with knowledge rather than opinion'. Aiming to present 'an impartial summary of results in every department of inquiry and research', he marshalled an international team of about 1100 contributors. For the first time a small minority of these were female; most were British, some American, a significant number were Scottish, and those included a good selection of Baynes's fellow St Andrews professors. Authors of articles included such notable figures as R. M. Ballantyne, J. G. Frazer, Patrick Geddes, Edmund Gosse, Andrew Lang, Max Muller, the lexicographer J. A. H. Murray, George Saintsbury, Robert Louis Stevenson, and A. C. Swinburne, among many others. Although his work with the *Britannica* generally led to his setting aside his own authorial projects, Baynes was a thorough and discriminating, but also a pragmatic editor. He liaised carefully with his publishers, Adam and Charles Black in Edinburgh, and sometimes bowed to their judgement.

Over the next few years Baynes's health was unsteady, and he suffered at times serious illness, necessitating his applying for a period of leave from his teaching duties. Accompanied by his wife, he spent some time in Germany recuperating. As the editing of the *Britannica* continued, Baynes found it necessary to devolve part of the work to others; in 1880 Professor William Robertson Smith, who had already relieved him to a degree, was appointed co-editor. Throughout his professorship Baynes and his wife lived at 19 Queen Street (later Queens Gardens), St Andrews, but, despite his ill health, Baynes travelled considerably in Britain. Elected a member of the Athenaeum in 1877, he became a familiar figure there, his talk being regarded as 'quick-witted', in keeping with his 'cheery presence' (Campbell, 'Biographical preface', xv). In 1879–80 he published three essays in *Fraser's Magazine*, 'What Shakespeare learnt at school', and it is significant that in the nineteenth century Baynes was most admired for his article on Shakespeare in the *Encyclopaedia Britannica* (the only article there that he authored). Bishop Charles Wordsworth described it as 'the most wonderfully massive and complete piece of work in the way of literary criticism I have ever seen'; Professor William Minto regarded it as 'far and away the most suggestive biography of Shakespeare yet written' (Campbell, 'Biographical preface', xiii–xiv). In researching the article, Baynes visited Stratford, and the article was admired for its placing of Shakespeare 'in his actual environment' (ibid., xiii). It was reprinted in book form along with some shorter pieces and a biographical preface by Lewis Campbell in 1894 as Baynes's *Shakespeare Studies*. Nevertheless, in the twentieth century it was Baynes's study 'What Shakespeare learnt at school' which made the greatest impact. One of the monuments of twentieth-century Shakespeare scholarship, T. W. Baldwin's *William Shakspere's 'Small Latine & Lesse Greeke'* (1944), is presented as an 'attempt to carry on from where Baynes left off'.

In 1881, as one of several St Andrews professors who wrote testimonials supporting Robert Louis Stevenson's unsuccessful application for the chair of constitutional law and history at Edinburgh University, Baynes wrote perceptively about Stevenson's historical insight. At the end of his life he co-edited with Lewis Campbell a small anthology *Speculum universitatis, or, Alma Mater's Mirror* (1887), which included memoirs of St Andrews figures, and new poems and prose pieces by authors such as R. L. Stevenson, Andrew Lang, Louisa Lumsden, W. A. Craigie, and Edmund Gosse. Baynes died suddenly at 31 Gloucester Crescent, London, on 30 May 1887; he was survived by his wife. Lewis Campbell recalled him in a prefatory note to *Speculum universitatis* as 'the idol of the students' at St Andrews, and paid tribute to his 'Urbanity, *bonhomie*, human kindness, unfailing cheerfulness, faithful comradeship, inalienable affection'. Having known him well for nearly forty years, Sir John Skelton remembered Baynes as '*saintly*' and 'the Galahad of our society'. He was:

> very keen, satirical, intellectually incisive; quite a man of affairs, and accustomed to meet with all sorts and conditions of men—newspaper editors, literary ladies, stolid farmers, college dons … He was not rich … but he was vigilantly honest and exact, and never owed any man a penny. (Skelton, 38–9)

A catalogue of Baynes's impressive private library is in St Andrews University archives. A photograph of him (bearded, resolute) is published in *Launch-Site for English Studies*. An unsigned oil portrait of Baynes (possibly that by Lowes Dickinson, presented to his widow in 1888) is owned by the University of St Andrews, which also possesses several photographs of Baynes.

ROBERT CRAWFORD

Sources L. Campbell, 'Biographical preface', in T. S. Baynes, *Shakespeare studies* (1894), v–xvi · J. Skelton, *The table-talk of Shirley*, 3rd edn (1895), 38–59 · R. Crawford, ed., *Launch-site for English studies: three centuries of literary studies at the University of St Andrews* (1997), 42–79 · *DNB* · *The letters of Robert Louis Stevenson*, ed. B. A. Booth and E. Mehew, 2 (1994), 175–6 · L. Campbell, 'T. S. B.', *Speculum universitatis, or, Alma mater's mirror*, ed. T. S. Baynes and L. Campbell (1887) [prefatory note] · senate minutes, U. St Andr. · testimonials in favour of Robert Louis Stevenson, advocate, U. Edin. L., Dh.5.157 · matriculation records, U. Edin. L., special collections division, university archives · *Wellesley index* · d. cert.

Archives Bodl. Oxf., notes taken from his lectures on English literature, Greek mythology, and philosophy · U. St Andr., letters, MSS | King's AC Cam., letters to Oscar Browning · NL Scot., corresp. with A. and C. Black · U. Edin. L., letters to James Halliwell-Phillipps

Likenesses L. Dickinson?, oils, U. St Andr. · T. Rodger, photograph, U. St Andr. L. [*see illus.*]

Wealth at death £3983 0s. 2d.: confirmation, 1887, *CCI*

Bayning. For this title name *see* Townshend, Charles, first Baron Bayning (1728–1810).

Baynton family (*per.* **1508–1716**), gentry, claimed direct descent from a courtier of Henry II. The quintessential county family, their local significance is still given visible expression in the Baynton chapel in Bromham church, with its tombs and memorials. In the early modern period the head of the family almost always played a leading part in the government of the county—during Elizabeth's reign one of the administrative divisions was known as 'Sir Edward Baynton's division'. Their ascent to eminence was launched as much by luck as by merit, however, when John Baynton (*d.* 1526) inherited Bromham from his cousin Richard Beauchamp, seventh Baron St Amand (*d.* 1508), and was thereby raised to great riches. Bromham, between Calne and Devizes, thenceforward formed the basis of the wealth and influence which eventually made the Bayntons probably the most prominent gentry family in north central Wiltshire. Court connections under Henry VIII helped them to augment their estates after the dissolution of the monasteries. Some prudent marriages, too, brought more lands. The women of the family are generally little recorded, however, apart from bare details of marriages and passing mention in a few deeds.

John's eldest son, **Sir Edward Baynton** (*c.*1495–1544), inherited all his father's estates. Probably knighted in 1522 he was an astute courtier who served in the royal household (he was vice-chamberlain to all save the first of Henry VIII's wives) and on military expeditions to the Scottish borders and France, as well as in local affairs. He sat in the parliaments of 1529 and 1539 as a knight of the shire for Wiltshire, and in that of 1542 as a burgess for Wilton. Probably during his association with Thomas Cromwell he began the family tradition of strong protestantism, and at the dissolution he gained much former monastic land in and near Wiltshire, especially the site of Stanley Abbey and sixteen of its manors. He built an imposing manor house at Bromham, which was said to be almost as large as the king's new court at Whitehall, and which remained the family's chief residence until demolished during the civil war. Edward married, first, Elizabeth Sulyard, and they had four daughters and three sons, Andrew, Edward, and Henry. The second and third sons had the same mother, a fact emphasized in the wills made both by Sir Edward before his death on 27 November 1544 and by his son Edward in 1592. There has been confusion over this, as Sir Edward's second marriage to Isabel Leigh, whom he had married by 1531, produced two sons, one named Henry.

Sir Edward's heir, **Andrew Baynton** (*c.*1516–1564), was a scholar who threatened to cut short the family's rise by losing all its land, and left his heirs difficulties and lawsuits which lasted for four decades. Brought up at court he was educated there by the distinguished linguist John Palsgrave. After travels on the continent he entered the service of Thomas Cromwell, while in the early 1540s he served the crown on missions to France and the empire. Between 1545 and 1559 he was five times returned to parliament as MP for Wiltshire or Sussex boroughs, but his later career was dogged by financial anxieties. His father's legacies from the estate, his own debts, and perhaps hopes of further court favour, may explain why he made an extraordinary exchange in 1545, whereby Sir Thomas Seymour was to hold all the Baynton properties, and vice versa, but without security for Baynton heirs. Worse, when Seymour was executed for treason in 1549 both men's property went to the crown. The family's ruin was temporary, as Queen Mary returned his former lands to Baynton. But the latter also negotiated sales of manors to other Wiltshire gentry, including Nicholas Snell and the notorious Gabriel Pleydell. Pleydell and the corrupt Sir William Sharington appear in his will as executors, with his lands assigned to them, probably as a result of deceit or forgery. Further complications surround Andrew's marriage to Phillipa Brulet; debts to her father are mentioned in his successful suit for annulment in 1562 on the grounds of her pre-contract; his brother Edward encouraged his suit. Andrew then married Frances Lee, and they had one daughter, Anne. She did not inherit, for to keep the property in the name of the Bayntons, in 1560 he had entailed the remaining estates on his brother **Sir Edward Baynton** (c.1520–1593).

This Edward was much embroiled in lawsuits over land. His first wife, Agnes, daughter of Sir Griffith Rhys, whom he married about 1553, had been left an interest in lands belonging to William, Lord Stourton, whose mistress she had been. Stourton's heir tried, but eventually failed, to counter Agnes's claim to Stourton lands, and she and Edward held them from 1557. It is somewhat surprising that Baynton married her: there were rumours that she and Lord Stourton had actually married, and although unfounded they worried the Bayntons. So a memorial brass to Edward Baynton's two wives insisted that Agnes, who died in 1574, was 'his first trew wife' (Kite, 63). Their eldest son, William, died in 1564, allegedly the victim of witchcraft. Their surviving children, out of thirteen, were one son and two daughters. Baynton's second wife was Anne (d. 1578), daughter of Humphrey Packington. Further lawsuits stemmed from his brother Andrew's presumably forged assignment and sales of property to Pleydell, Sharington, and Snell, which conflicted with the previous entail to Edward. Eventually Baynton gained possession by law, and by numerous deeds secured his holdings in Stanley Abbey, Bremhill, his parcels in Chippenham, and other property. He continued to increase his estates by purchase, and became a vital member of the county administration. Knighted in 1574 he represented Wiltshire in the 1563 parliament, and sat twice more for boroughs. He was one of the county's most active JPs, attending quarter sessions very regularly in the 1570s and 1580s, even sending in material until a few months before his death in 1593, and he held other posts from time to time.

Sir Edward's eldest surviving son, **Sir Henry Baynton** (1571–1616), purchased further lands worth perhaps £3000 from Sir William Throckmorton and Sir Thomas Tracy. He was appointed a deputy lieutenant, and became a JP briefly in 1592 and continuously from 1594. He followed his father's example of hard work in running the county, attending several quarter sessions each year, or sending in recognizances, until eighteen months before his death on 14 October 1616. He was four times a member of parliament, sitting as knight of the shire in 1597. A survey begun in 1612 listed a large tenantry on his manors: he exercised great influence around Bromham, Stanley, Chippenham, and also Bremhill, where he had another substantial house. Bromham was an important weaving centre, but the weavers suffered severely during depressions in the cloth trade. Baynton was a man of conscience: he founded a hospital or almshouse in 1614, probably intended for impoverished weavers, and in his will in 1616 he left significant sums to the vicars and the churches where he held property, as well as £5 to the preacher at Steeple Aston, and money for the poor in several parishes. His executors were other Wiltshire gentry. He had married Lucy, daughter of his father's very good friend Sir John Danvers, another fortunate alliance, for she inherited property through her grandfather. They had two children. Lucy's will left money and rings to her daughter Elizabeth, who married John *Dutton [see under Dutton family], and to her Danvers relations, including an 'ashcolour' velvet gown and satin waistcoat and petticoat, and also money for a minister to say the service in Foxham Chapel, in Bremhill parish; she died in 1621 and was buried in Westminster Abbey.

Their son **Sir Edward Baynton** (1593–1657) matriculated at Christ Church, Oxford, on 27 April 1610, but is not recorded as taking a degree. He was knighted in 1613, before his father died. Sir Edward played a major role in the county's politics, but was a more quarrelsome man than his ancestors and made many enemies. He married, first, Elizabeth Maynard (d. 1635), with whom he had a son, Edward, and second, Mary Bowell, with whom there were sons, Henry and Nicholas, and a daughter, Mary. His executors were his wife and son Robert. But he was not a faithful husband, and in 1629 he was charged in the court of high commission with neglecting a woman with whom he had had two illegitimate children; King Charles pardoned him for these adulteries and any others.

Office also brought trouble: Baynton was a deputy lieutenant, but in 1632 the sheriff complained that he neglected his duties. As sheriff himself in 1637–8 he clashed with other leading gentry over his harsh tactics in collecting ship money, yet he was also in trouble with the privy council over his accounts in 1639. He had not immediately followed his father as a JP, but was appointed in 1619. He was very active in that capacity, usually attending at least three sessions a year. Like his forebears he dealt with the tiresome between sessions work as well, such as orders for bridge repairs when Calne inhabitants would not pay as requested, and disputes between Bromham cloth workers. He was listed at the head of the Wiltshire JPs in October 1640, though it is not clear whether he was present at quarter sessions in January 1641 when they made a resolution that ship money was contrary to the laws and statutes of the realm.

Baynton sat in every parliament but one up to 1653, having been first elected for Devizes in 1614. He was MP for Chippenham throughout the Short and Long parliaments. By 1640 he supported the parliamentary side, and although wounded in a duel with another MP he commanded Wiltshire parliamentary troops when the civil war began in 1642: ironically his experience as a deputy lieutenant in the king's militia was to help in the fight against the king. In 1643 he had a violent quarrel with his fellow Wiltshire parliamentary commander Sir Edward Hungerford, and this possibly led to Baynton's temporary move towards the king in 1643. His return to the parliamentary cause came at a high cost for his family: in 1645 royalist soldiers destroyed the great house at Bromham. Sir Edward adhered to the more radical group in the Commons, and as an independent retained his seat after Pride's Purge in 1648, sitting to the end of the Rump in 1653; he had been named as one of the king's judges. One of his sons was a royalist.

Like his forebears Baynton sought to add to his family's wealth, making purchases in Wiltshire, so that along with lands inherited from his mother he passed on an increased estate worth nearly £2000 p.a. to his eldest son. Following the destruction of Bromham House he built another house nearby, at Spye Park (described disparagingly by Evelyn in 1654). His will, made in 1657 shortly before his death, has a long religious preface, expressing fervent hopes for redemption—perhaps he regretted his tumultuous personal life.

The eldest son, yet another **Sir Edward Baynton** (1618–1679), shared his father's commitment to the parliamentary and puritan cause. Like his father he went to Oxford, this time to St John's College, where he matriculated on 15 January 1636, but again like his father cannot be shown to have graduated. He became MP for Devizes in 1640, so that he sat in parliament along with his father up until Pride's Purge in 1648, and assisted his father on committees and in the parliamentary army; captain of horse in 1642 he was a major by 1644. He sat in five further parliaments; defeated in the 1661 election he was returned again in 1675. Although made a knight of the Bath in 1661 he was deeply critical of Charles II and his government; in 1677 he was dismissed as a JP. Bayntun, as he spelt his name, kept a commonplace book between 1657 and 1679 into which he copied political lampoons. The commonplace book also records his activities in local government and his dealings concerning the Baynton lands. He did not marry until 1661, when he married Stuarta, sister of Sir Thomas Thynne of Longleat: they had two sons, Henry and Thomas, and two daughters, Ann and Lucy. But he fell out with his wife, and left her nothing in his will made in 1670, directing that she and her relations were to have no part in his children's education, nor to meddle with their estate.

Sir Edward had a great estate to pass on. He recorded his rents in his commonplace book, which shows that in the 1660s, as in the past, the family's wealth was based upon land. The annual rents from Stanley manor and its dependencies alone amounted to around £730, while those from Bromham, Bremhill, and the smaller estate of Rodbourne added much more, bringing the total of rents and renders (for items like loads of hay) to a little over £2000 per annum for most years in this decade. Income

fell slightly in the 1670s, but still amounted to a very substantial yearly revenue. Moreover there are very many tenants named in the lists, a pointer to the influence the Bayntons could normally expect to exert among the surrounding population. They were to encounter unforeseen problems after Sir Edward's death, however. His elder son and heir, **Henry Baynton** (1664–1691) maintained the family tradition of firm protestantism, and also that of representing Wiltshire boroughs (Calne and Chippenham) in parliament, but times had changed—a tory, in contrast to his father and grandfather, he nevertheless feared the threat posed by James II's Catholicism. He would not agree to the repeal of the Test Act, and was dismissed from the Wiltshire commission of the peace and deputy lieutenancy in 1688, remaining excluded until the end of James's rule.

In 1685 Henry Baynton had married an heiress, Lady Anne Wilmot, daughter of John, second earl of Rochester, an alliance which promised further increase of the family's estate. Henry was eager to continue the Baynton family name and made hopeful provision for sons and their male heirs for 500 years to come. But his careful plans were doomed; for on 11 July 1691 he died aged only twenty-seven. His son John apparently had problems and had no children, dying in his twenties in 1716; his memorial in Bromham church sadly proclaims that he was the nineteenth in lineal descent from Sir Henry Baynton. But he was the last in direct line. John's will of January 1716 bequeathed the major estates to his sister Anne Rolt's second son, his nephew Edward Rolt, the will specifying that Edward and his heirs take the name of Baynton Rolt. Heads of the Baynton family had struggled for centuries to ensure an unbroken father-to-son hold on Bromham, and the influence this conferred in Wiltshire, but they had been foiled by demographic fate.   ALISON WALL

Sources Baynton deeds, indentures, rentals, court books, sales, and other documents, Wilts. & Swindon RO, see esp. MSS 473, *passim*, esp. 473/242/33 and 473/220; 122/1; 2684/7; 776/1032 (includes copy of John Baynton will, 1716); quarter sessions: minute books series, 1572–1642, and great rolls, 1601–1630; 1553/22, commonplace book of Sir Edward Baynton [incl. texts of the lampoons and a nineteenth-century pedigree omitted from the published edition] · PRO, PROB 11/30/28 [Sir Edward Baynton] · PRO, PROB 11/47/8 [Andrew Baynton] · PRO, PROB 11/82/76 [Sir Edward Baynton] · PRO, PROB 11/127/116 [Sir Henry Baynton] · PRO, PROB 11/139/4 [Lucy Baynton] · PRO, PROB 11/272/19 [Sir Edward Baynton] · A. Wall, 'The Wiltshire commission of the peace, 1590–1620', MA diss., University of Melbourne, 1967 · C. Talbot, 'Notes on Spye Park and Bromham', *Wiltshire Archaeological Magazine*, 15 (1875), 321–4 [with 1684 drawing of Spye Park] · W. Clark-Maxwell, 'Sir William Sharington's work at Lacock, Sudely and Dudley', *Wiltshire Archaeological Magazine*, 38 (1913–14), 426–34 · HoP, *Commons*, 1509–58, 1.399–403 · HoP, *Commons*, 1558–1603, 1.409–11 · HoP, *Commons*, 1660–90, 1.607–11 · E. Kite, *Monumental brasses of Wiltshire* (1860), 63 · *The commonplace book of Sir Edward Bayntun of Bromham*, ed. J. Freeman, Wilts RS, 43 (1988) · *VCH Wiltshire*, 7.179–80 · Keeler, *Long Parliament*, 101–2 · G. Yule, *The independents in the English civil war* (1958) · T. Phillipps, *Monumental inscriptions of Wiltshire* (1822) [facsimile edn, ed. P. Sherlock, Wiltshire Record Society 53 (1997), 181, 200, 231, 364] · Foster, *Alum. Oxon.*, 1500–1714, 1.93–4 · G. D. Squibb, ed., *Wiltshire visitation pedigrees, 1623*, Harleian Society, 105–6 (1954) · chancery, inquisitions post mortem, PRO, series II, C 142/234/59

Baynton, Andrew (*c.*1516–1564). *See under* Baynton family (*per.* 1508–1716).

Baynton, Sir Edward (*c.*1495–1544). *See under* Baynton family (*per.* 1508–1716).

Baynton, Sir Edward (*c.*1520–1593). *See under* Baynton family (*per.* 1508–1716).

Baynton, Sir Edward (1593–1657). *See under* Baynton family (*per.* 1508–1716).

Baynton, Sir Edward (1618–1679). *See under* Baynton family (*per.* 1508–1716).

Baynton, Sir Henry (1571–1616). *See under* Baynton family (*per.* 1508–1716).

Baynton, Henry (1664–1691). *See under* Baynton family (*per.* 1508–1716).

Baynton, Thomas (1761–1820), surgeon, was born on 5 October 1761 at Clifton Down, near Bristol. Following his father's death in 1775 he was apprenticed to Thomas Elmes, a Bristol apothecary, after which he established his own practice as a surgeon at Bristol, in 1782. He attempted unsuccessfully to obtain the post of surgeon to the Bristol Infirmary in 1783, and thereafter was hostile to the institution. In 1784 he received a medal from the Humane Society for restoring a person apparently dead by drowning. In the same year, on 22 May, he married Annie Swayne of Hereford.

Baynton established a high reputation among contemporaries for his practical contributions to medicine, particularly in the cure of ulcers and wounds, following the publication in 1797 of his *Descriptive Account of a New Method of Treating Old Ulcers of the Legs*. His simple and effective remedy of applying moist plasters to the wound was very influential and was extensively adopted by the army and navy. In 1813, in his *Account of a Successful Method of Treating Diseases of the Spine*, he put forward a theory on the treatment of spinal injuries by complete rest which was similarly widely acclaimed, though it also aroused much controversy.

As a surgeon Baynton's great success was helped by his charm and verbal facility. He was, according to Richard Smith, one of the surgeons of the Bristol Infirmary, 'rather handsome, being well grown, ruddy, and of a fair complexion … he had an oily smoothness and volubility of tongue which (with strangers especially) was particularly captivating' (Nixon, 100). Baynton died at Clifton Down on 31 August 1820.   PATRICK WALLIS

Sources J. A. Nixon, 'Thomas Baynton, 1761–1820', *Proceedings of the Royal Society of Medicine*, 8 (1914–15), 95–102 [section of the history of medicine] • *GM*, 1st ser., 90/1 (1820), 284 • [J. Watkins and F. Shoberl], *A biographical dictionary of the living authors of Great Britain and Ireland* (1816) • P. J. Wallis and R. V. Wallis, *Eighteenth century medics*, 2nd edn (1988) • *DNB*
Wealth at death £33,000: Nixon, 'Thomas Baynton'

Bayntun, Sir Henry William (1766–1840), naval officer, son of the consul-general at Algiers, entered the navy at an early age, and was made a lieutenant on 15 April 1783. He served at the capture of Martinique in March 1794, and was promoted by Sir John Jervis to the command of the sloop *Avenger*. After the capture of Guadeloupe he was appointed captain of the frigate *Undaunted* on 4 May 1794. With only one brief intermission, in 1796, he continued in the West Indies during the next ten years of active war and the short peace. On his return to England he was appointed to command the *Leviathan* (74 guns), and was sent to the Mediterranean to join Nelson, then blockading Toulon. He took part in the pursuit of the French fleet to the West Indies and back, and at Trafalgar, where the *Leviathan* was closely engaged with, among others, the French flagship *Bucentaur*, the *Santissima Trinidad*, and the *St Augustin* (74 guns). At Nelson's funeral in January 1806 Bayntun bore the guidon in the water procession from the Royal Naval Hospital, Greenwich. In June 1807 he was present with the squadron under Rear-Admiral Murray which was sent to Buenos Aires to co-operate with the army, until compelled to re-embark. On 23 August 1809 he married Sophia Mayhew at Stoke Damerel, Devon. In the same year he commanded the *Milford* (74 guns), and in 1811 was appointed to the command of the yacht *Royal Sovereign*. He had no further active service, and became rear-admiral on 12 August 1812, vice-admiral on 19 July 1821, and admiral on 10 January 1837. On 2 January 1815 he was made KCB and on 25 October 1839 GCB. He died on 17 December 1840. Bayntun was a protégé of St Vincent and a companion of Nelson; there could be no higher commendation.

J. K. LAUGHTON, *rev.* ANDREW LAMBERT

Sources J. S. Corbett, *The campaign of Trafalgar* (1910) • M. Duffy, *Soldiers, sugar, and sea power: the British expeditions to the West Indies and the war against revolutionary France* (1987) • *Letters of … the earl of St Vincent, whilst the first lord of the admiralty, 1801–1804*, ed. D. B. Smith, 2 vols., Navy RS, 55, 61 (1922–7) • J. Marshall, *Royal naval biography*, 1 (1823), 543–5
Archives Beds. & Luton ARS • NMM | Som. ARS, Hippisley MSS
Likenesses oils, *c.*1835, NMM • W. Beechey, oils, Louisiana State University, Baton Rouge

Bazalgette, Sir Joseph William (1819–1891), civil engineer, was born on 28 March 1819 at Enfield, Middlesex, the fourth child and only son of Joseph Bazalgette (1783–1849), naval officer, and his wife, Theresa Pilton (1796–1850). The family were of French origin: Bazalgette's grandfather Jean Louis (1750–1830), born at Ispagnac in southern France, arrived in England in 1784. Bazalgette was educated privately. He began his engineering career in 1836 when he became an articled pupil of John Benjamin Macneill, the eminent Irish civil engineer, acting as resident engineer for him on land reclamation works at lochs Foyle and Swilley in Londonderry. In 1842 he set up in private practice as a consulting engineer with an office in Great George Street, Westminster. In 1845 Bazalgette married Maria, daughter of Edward Keogh. The couple had six sons and four daughters.

During the railway mania years, overwork caused a serious breakdown in Bazalgette's health and during 1847–8 he left London to recuperate. Having recovered, he

Sir Joseph William Bazalgette (1819–1891), by Lock & Whitfield, pubd 1877

returned to London in 1849 and on 16 August was appointed assistant surveyor to the second metropolitan commission of sewers for London. Thus began his career in public health engineering. By 1851 the metropolitan commissioners, under their engineer Frank Forster (1800–1852), had clearly established the broad outline scheme of interceptor sewers to divert sewage from the Thames, with separate systems north and south of the river and with remote outfalls to the east of London. When Forster died in 1852 Bazalgette was appointed engineer, and remained so until the commissioners were replaced by the Metropolitan Board of Works (MBW), established under an act of 1855, which acquired its powers on 1 January 1856. Bazalgette continued to act in a temporary capacity as engineer until his formal appointment as engineer to the MBW on 25 January 1856.

Bazalgette held the post of engineer until the board was replaced by the London county council (LCC) in 1889 and his greatest works were undertaken during this period. He took with him three assistant engineers, John Grant, Thomas Lovick, and Edmund Cooper, who had each worked with him at the metropolitan commission of sewers. The first work of the new authority was to complete the design and implement the sewage commission's plans for the main drainage of London. In 1858 the MBW obtained its enabling act and work began on the northern sewer system on 31 January 1859. Work proceeded more rapidly south of the river and that section was completed in 1865. The northern system was delayed by the complexities of integrating the low-level sewer, the Victoria

Embankment, and the Metropolitan District Railway. The whole system comprised 1300 miles of sewers, 82 miles of the main west–east intercepting sewers, and four magnificent pumping stations, Deptford (1865), Crossness (1865), Abbey Mills (1868), and Western (1875). The northern system was running in 1868 and the whole completed with the opening of the Western pumping station.

As part of the main drainage scheme Bazalgette fulfilled the long-cherished plan of the embanking of the Thames in central London. Three major works were entailed—the Albert (1868), Victoria (1870), and Chelsea (1874) embankments—a total length of 3½ miles for which 52 acres of riverside land was reclaimed. The Thames River, Prevention of Floods Act of 1879 imposed on the board the duty of implementing its requirements which Bazalgette regarded as 'one of the most difficult and intricate things the Board have had to do' ('Royal commission'); 40 miles of river frontage and every wharf had to be inspected and plans prepared after careful study of the nature of business at each site. In 1865 Bazalgette was joined by his son Edward who began four years as an articled pupil; in July 1870 Edward became assistant engineer, eventually with responsibility for metropolitan bridges.

An act of 1877 empowered the MBW to purchase the Thames bridges from the private companies and free them from tolls. To implement this Bazalgette had to survey and value twelve bridges. As a result, much maintenance work was undertaken and Bazalgette decided to replace three of the bridges with new structures to his own design. They were the present masonry arch bridge at Putney (1886), the steel-link suspension bridge at Hammersmith (1887), and the iron arch structure at Battersea (1890). The removal of tolls from the central bridges led to demands for new river crossings below London Bridge and Bazalgette was involved in three major design schemes, for Tower Bridge, Blackwall Tunnel, and Woolwich free ferry. Only the latter was built to his design. Although he submitted three designs for the Tower crossing in 1878, his preferred scheme being an innovative high-level single-span steel arch of 850 feet, the City eventually chose its own architect's scheme. The MBW was about to issue the contract for Bazalgette's Blackwall Tunnel design when it was replaced by the LCC. In addition to the Thames river crossings Bazalgette was concerned to ease the horse-drawn traffic congestion in the capital and initiated a programme of design and construction of new thoroughfares. The principal examples include Southwark Street (1864), Queen Victoria Street (1871), Northumberland Avenue (1876), Shaftesbury Avenue (1886), and Charing Cross Road (1887).

Another important aspect of Bazalgette's work as engineer to the board was to monitor the progress of private bills passing through parliament of works which would have an impact on the public amenities of London. These would include railways, tramways, docks, water supply, and the energy utilities—gas, electricity, and hydraulic power. He produced a detailed annual report to the board on these schemes and he was a well-known and influential figure in the committee rooms of the houses of parliament. Bazalgette described his role in reply to a select committee in June 1874 saying: 'private individuals are apt to look after their own interests first, and to forget the general effect upon the public, and it is necessary that there should be somebody to watch the public interests' ('Select committee on the Metropolitan Buildings and Management Bill', 1874, 10.535).

While acting as a salaried engineer to the MBW, Bazalgette was allowed to take fee-paying pupils and to develop an extensive private practice as a consulting engineer. He was frequently asked to give his professional opinion on drainage schemes produced by other engineers, and to produce designs and estimates of his own for towns in Britain and abroad. Some thirty-two such reports survive from 1858 to 1875, including Epsom (1858), Oxford (1866), Windsor Castle (1868), Northampton (1871), and Margate (1874). In 1863 he was involved in advising on the drainage and street paving of Odessa and he produced a major report on the drainage of the city of Pest in Hungary in 1869. He also designed the masonry bridge over the Medway at Maidstone which was opened in 1879. Unlike many civil engineers, Bazalgette assumed a continuing responsibility for the works he designed and constructed and was responsible for maintenance, staff changes, development of operational techniques, and renewable contracts for the supply of materials.

Bazalgette's career, and the profession of municipal engineering, grew out of the public health problems which were first seriously tackled in the mid-nineteenth century. An engineering career in local government, involving huge capital expenditure of public money, provides many opportunities for alienating politicians, lay committee members, and ratepayers. Bazalgette's career with the MBW, spanning thirty-three years, reveals him as an able administrator of human and financial resources with a gift for selecting competent and loyal engineering colleagues. His career brought him into professional contact with the greatest engineers of his day.

He was elected a member of the Institution of Civil Engineers in 1846, was made a companion of the Bath in 1871, and knighted at Windsor Castle in 1874. Sir Joseph was elected president of the Institution of Civil Engineers in 1884, where appropriately his presidential address discussed 'those engineering works which promote the health and comfort of the inhabitants of large cities, and by which human life may be preserved and prolonged' (Bazalgette). In his office at the MBW he trained several influential public health engineers of the next generation, and to him we owe the standards of municipal engineering now taken for granted in many parts of the world. He retired, as he said, 'after forty years of arduous and responsible work in the public service' (LMA, MBW minutes, 1889, 326), to his Wimbledon house in 1889. Within his 20 acres of land Bazalgette said 'I ride a good deal—usually two or three hours a day. I find it splendid exercise for counteracting the effects of a sedentary life' (Cassell's Saturday Journal, 30 Aug 1890, 1160–61).

Sir Joseph Bazalgette died at his home, St Mary's, Arthur Road, Wimbledon, aged seventy-one, on 15 March 1891. He was buried in a splendid neoclassical tomb at St Mary's Church, Arthur Road, where he was churchwarden for many years. Bazalgette was described as 'very slight and spare, and considerably under the average height; but his face, with its prominent acquiline [sic] nose, its keen grey eyes, and its grey whiskers and black eyebrows, gives you the impression of a man of exceptional power' (Cassell's Saturday Journal, 30 Aug 1890). Sir John Coode, the president of the Institution of Civil Engineers, paid tribute to his career, which was devoted to the 'public health and welfare in all the large cities of the world, and his works … will ever remain as monuments to his skill and professional ability' (PICE, 105/3, 1890–91, 106).

DENIS SMITH

Sources PICE, 105 (1890–91), 302–8 · D. Owen and others, The government of Victorian London, 1855–1889, ed. R. MacLeod (1982) · The Times (16 March 1891) · Boase, Mod. Eng. biog. · CGPLA Eng. & Wales (1891) · DNB · 'Royal commission to inquire into the … metropolitan board of works', Parl. papers (1889), 39.319, C. 5705 · 'Select committee on the Metropolitan Buildings and Management Bill', Parl. papers (1874), 10.535, no. 285 · J. W. Bazalgette, presidential address, PICE, 76 (1883–4), 2–25 · minutes, metropolitan board of works, 8 Feb 1889, LMA, 326 · 'Representative men at home — Sir Joseph Bazalgette, CB, at Wimbledon', Cassell's Saturday Journal (30 Aug 1890), 1160–61
Archives Inst. CE, papers and drawings | LMA, metropolitan board of works minutes
Likenesses Lock & Whitfield, woodburytype photograph, pubd 1877, NPG [see illus.] · A. Ossani, oils, 1878, Inst. CE · G. Simmonds, bronze bust on mural monument, 1901, Victoria embankment
Wealth at death £155,747 1s.: resworn probate, March 1892, CGPLA Eng. & Wales (1891)

Bazalgette [née Seville], **Louise** (1845/6–1918), motorist, was born in Essex, one of the two daughters of John Seville, farmer. Little is known of her education and early life. She was resident in Marylebone, London, when she married, on 9 April 1870, George Bazalgette (1829–1885), of Plymouth, a captain (later major) in the Royal Marines and more than fifteen years her senior; there were no children. George Bazalgette died at their home at 52 Upper Gloucester Place, Dorset Square, London, on 24 August 1885, and Louise moved to nearby 26 Dorset Square, where she kept a successful boarding-house. She later moved again, to 5 Bryanstone Street, Portman Square. Her new home was near the London Benz showroom of Henry Hewetson, one of the pioneer motor enthusiasts in Britain, and Bazalgette became a keen motorist. She later owned several Benz models, which Hewetson supplied. In due course she made headlines as the first woman to drive distances and she was also active in publicity for the movement.

Bazalgette was present at the start of the famous 'emancipation run' on 14 November 1896, when over thirty automobiles set out from London to Brighton to celebrate the passage of the act of parliament which raised the speed limit to 14 m.p.h. and abolished the requirement for an automobile to be preceded by a man on foot. Bazalgette was photographed at this symbolic event on an Arnold motor car, with her friend Hewetson near by. By 1899 she owned and drove her own 3 hp Benz. In the first three months of ownership she had driven about 2000 miles; in August 1899 she was reported to have made the longest run so far by an English lady, by driving from her house in Portman Square to Southampton.

On 20 October 1899 Bazalgette gave a paper at a meeting at the home of Florence Pomeroy, Viscountess Harberton, the promoter of rational dress for women, which was convened to consider the foundation of an automobile club open to ladies as well as gentlemen (ladies were then excluded from the Automobile Club of Great Britain and Ireland). Bazalgette was confident that a boom in 'automobilism' was imminent, but she also believed that, 'like the boom in connection with cycling, it will not come until ladies take up the pastime' (Bennett, 242). She supported the proposed new automobile club in the hope that it would attract more women to motoring. And she spoke at some length on this occasion about the ease with which she drove her own Benz Ideal, giving the results of her practical experience and recommending that ladies drive both for business and for pleasure.

Bazalgette was the only female private entrant in the Thousand Mile Trial in 1900. The purpose of the trial, which was organized by the Automobile Club of Great Britain and Ireland, with the backing of the Harmsworth press, was to introduce the motor car to the people of Britain, many of whom had never seen a car before. Those who were already aware of them often viewed automobiles as a 'rich man's play thing'. The trial was run in stages from London to Edinburgh and back, from 23 April to 12 May 1900, passing through major towns and cities *en route*, with various categories of competition. Women were not then expected to take on technically difficult tasks such as driving cars, but Bazalgette successfully completed the course in her Benz, thus demonstrating to contemporaries the ease with which the car could be managed by a woman.

Bazalgette shared the driving during the Thousand Mile Trial with her mechanic: they drove 562 miles and 530 miles respectively. It was a cold and wet spring, and the conditions were arduous in the extreme. The unsealed roads were either wet and slippery with horse manure, or else dry and dusty, and the car afforded no protection from the elements. Driving through Leeds, she had a minor accident when avoiding a horse and cart. As the correspondent of *Motor-Car Journal* noted: 'She slowed, and did her best to clear, but failed, and jostled a lamp-post. Several standing by at once came to the rescue, and giving a turn of the head of the little car sent it on its way again' (Bennett, 247). Her average speed on five of the timed stages was below 12 m.p.h., but otherwise she had few difficulties. She was awarded the only silver medal for section two (private entries) in class A (cars selling at £200 or less), a remarkable demonstration by any standards.

In 1903 Bazalgette was again at the wheel, at the Bexhill speed trials. But when the Ladies' Automobile Club was founded on 30 April of that year she was not among the founder members, in spite of her early canvassing for such a body. She continued to drive, however, and in 1904 her car was a 4½ hp Benz. Her hobbies included riding as well as motoring, and she belonged to two London clubs, the Empress in Dover Street and the Imperial Institute. She died on 9 March 1918 at her home, 3 Old Quebec Street, Marylebone, London.

ELIZABETH ELLEN BENNETT

Sources E. Bennett, *Thousand mile trial* (2000) · *Daily Mail* (Aug 1899) · *Motor-Car Journal* (3 Nov 1899) · census returns, 1891 · *Hart's*

Louise Bazalgette (1845/6–1918), by Argent Archer, 1900 [with her mechanic Clarkson in her 3 hp Benz Ideal in the Thousand Mile Trial]

Army List (1870) • *Butterfly* (Sept 1898) • 'Veteran Car Club of Great Britain', www.vccofgb.co.uk • m. cert. • d. cert.

Archives National Motor Museum, Beaulieu, Hampshire • Veteran Car Club of Great Britain, Ashwell, Hertfordshire **Likenesses** A. Archer, photograph, 1900, priv. coll. [*see illus.*] • photographs, priv. coll.

Wealth at death £583 8s. 10d.: probate, 11 June 1918, *CGPLA Eng. & Wales*

Bazley, Sir Thomas, first baronet (1797–1885), cotton spinner and politician, was born on 27 May 1797 at Gilnow, near Bolton, Lancashire, the son of Thomas Bazley (1773–1845), sometime cotton manufacturer, mathematician, and journalist, and his wife, Anne, the daughter of Charles Hilton of Horwich, near Bolton. Educated at Bolton grammar school, Bazley was apprenticed in 1812 to Ainsworth & Co. of Bolton before starting his own business as a yarn agent in 1818. In 1826 he moved to Manchester, having formed a partnership with Robert Gardner to control the New Bridge Mills, Manchester, and the Dean Mills, Halliwell, Bolton. Their fine-spinning and linen-thread concern became the most extensive in this branch of Lancashire's textile industry, employing some 1400 hands in 1861. Gardner and Bazley, both Anglicans sharing a keen evangelical sense of responsibility for their workers, created at Dean Mills, Barrow Bridge, Halliwell, a model community comprising a factory canteen, steam kitchens, showers, housing, a sick and burial society, and a co-operative store. Its centrepiece was a widely admired educational institute providing an unusual model of non-denominational education, for Gardner and Bazley deliberately set out to create a community free from the sectarian conflict which had so obstructed educational progress in Lancashire in the 1840s. The institute included a lecture room seating 2000, with a library, newspaper room, and reading society. Dean Mills became a much visited attraction, drawing Prince Albert in 1851, and reputedly providing in part the inspiration for Disraeli's *Coningsby*. This cotton works, of which Bazley became the leading partner on Gardner's withdrawal in 1847, continued under his direction until 1862, when it was sold to W. R. Callender junior.

Bazley, like many cotton masters, was not only a successful entrepreneur, but was also deeply involved in local society and politics. Resident in Salford, he held several local offices between 1835 and 1840, including that of boroughreeve and churchwarden at Christ Church, Salford. He helped to promote the establishment of the magistrates' court and the charter of incorporation granted in 1844. He was also prominent in the Manchester chamber of commerce (he remained a director until 1880) and soon joined Richard Cobden, Henry Ashworth, and other cotton masters in the campaign for free trade, becoming an important second-string figure in the Anti-Corn Law League. When the chamber split over the politics of free trade in 1845, Bazley became its president until it was reunited with the breakaway, more Conservative, Commercial Association in 1858. By this time he had also become a major advocate in the search for new sources of

Sir Thomas Bazley, first baronet (1797–1885), by John & Charles Watkins

raw cotton, urging a 'cotton league', and playing a leading part in both the Cotton Supply Association and the Manchester Cotton Company. As a representative Manchester man, he sat on the royal commissions for the Great Exhibition in 1851 and for amalgamating commercial laws in 1855. He also served on the commissions for the Paris exhibitions of 1855 and 1867 and was admitted to the Légion d'honneur.

By the late 1840s, with Cobden, Bazley played an important part in the National (Lancashire) Public Schools Association, which campaigned for non-sectarian education along the lines Bazley already practised at Dean Mills. He took an active part in Manchester's bitter educational politics, supporting its model secular school while acting as an important proponent of a national system of education, ultimately realized in the Education Act of 1870. He also did much to build up the structures of adult education in Lancashire, serving as president of the Manchester School of Art and of the Lancashire and Cheshire Union of Mechanics' Institutes. He consistently held out to the working classes and their employers the desirability of literacy, not simply as a means of improving human capital, but as a means of individual fulfilment and of social harmony. This was clear not only at Dean Mills but also in Bazley's numerous writings and addresses to working-class audiences. Bazley played a leading role in organizing the Manchester Art Treasures Exhibition in 1857, believing that art should form an important part in the moral discipline of the industrial town. He was later a prominent advocate of higher education in Manchester; he strongly supported the transformation of Owens College into the Victoria University of Manchester, of which he was a founder governor and trustee.

Bazley's energy and ubiquity in Manchester opened up the path to parliament, and in 1858 his return at a by-election helped to restore Liberalism in the city in the wake of the exaggerated 'defeat of the Manchester school' in the election of 1857. Parliament, as well as the cotton famine, also provided the necessary stimulus for Bazley to disengage from his business interests and, following many Victorian businessmen, to invest heavily in landed society. He acquired from the early 1860s various estates in Hertfordshire and Oxfordshire before settling down in Gloucestershire in 1870. Here he enjoyed country life at Eyford Park, while setting up his son at Hatherop Castle, near Fairford; the whole estate comprised some 5000 acres. Such possessions, as well as his interest in working-class welfare, recommended Bazley for a baronetcy in 1869, but the appeal of country life sometimes left his radical Lancashire visitors bemused.

However, gentrification did not imply severance from Manchester and its entrepreneurial interests, of which Bazley was to remain a conspicuous exemplar for the remainder of his life. Besides playing his part in political associations, such as the National Reform Union, he remained one of Manchester's members of parliament until 1880. Within parliament he was an effective, if occasional, speaker, supporting the leading causes of the Gladstonian and radical businessmen, parliamentary reform, public works in India, and decimalization, and displaying suspicion of further factory legislation but strong support for temperance, especially through the United Kingdom Alliance's Permissive Bill, which he seconded in 1869. He also became closely involved in employers' attempts, organized by the National Federation of the Associated Employers of Labour, to resist the Nine Hours Bill, and to prevent legislative sanction of the power of trade unions. To some extent, therefore, Bazley remained bound by his own experience of the 1840s rather than acquiring a readiness to follow the 'new model employers' of the 1870s.

Bazley married, on 2 June 1828, Mary Maria Sarah (c.1804–1897), the daughter of Sebastian Nash, a calico printer, of Clayton Mills. Their only child, Thomas Sebastian (1829–1919), was educated at Cambridge, entered the family firm, and in 1855 married the daughter of his father's partner, Elizabeth Gardner, before becoming a gentleman of leisure in Gloucestershire, and passing his declining years at Bournemouth and Torquay.

Bazley died at his summer residence, Riversleigh, Lytham, in Lancashire, on 18 March 1885, and was buried on 23 March next to his father in St John's Church, Deansgate, Manchester. This was a suitable testimony to Bazley's underlying loyalties, but, in the light of his Anglicanism, cultural interests, and landed possessions, it was ironic that in 1869 he was singled out by Matthew Arnold as a typical 'philistine', an unpolished, narrow, middle-class dissenter—an influential misunderstanding of the Victorian industrialist yet to be wholly dispelled.

A. C. HOWE

Sources　Manchester Guardian (20 March 1885) · Manchester Guardian (24 March 1885) · Manchester Guardian (8 May 1885) · DNB · A. Howe, The cotton masters, 1830–1860 (1984) · ILN (18 Oct 1851) · ILN (25 Oct 1851) · A. W. Silver, Manchester men and Indian cotton, 1847–1872 (1966) · J. Garnett and A. C. Howe, 'Churchmen and cotton masters in Victorian England', Business and religion in Britain, ed. D. J. Jeremy (1988), 72–94 · D. O'Connor, Barrow Bridge, Bolton, Dean Mills estate: a Victorian model achievement (1972) · The Times (March 1885)
Archives　Man. CL, Gardner Trust MSS | BL, letters to W. E. Gladstone and others · Bodl. Oxf., letters to J. E. Thorold Rogers · JRL, Unitarian MSS; Beard MSS · W. Sussex RO, corresp. with Richard Cobden
Likenesses　S. Bellin, group portrait, mixed engraving, pubd 1850 (The Anti-Corn Law League; after J. Herbert), BM, NPG · Ape [C. Pellegrini], watercolour cartoon, NPG; repro. in VF (21 Aug 1875) · Eastham, group portrait, wood-engraving (The treaty of commerce, 1862), NPG; repro. in ILN (1862) · J. & C. Watkins, photograph, NPG [see illus.] · engraving, repro. in ILN, 508 · wood-engraving (after photograph by Kilburn), NPG; repro. in ILN (1851) · wood-engraving (after photograph by J. & C. Watkins), NPG; repro. in ILN (1863)
Wealth at death　£91,977 14s. 6d.: probate, 27 April 1885, CGPLA Eng. & Wales

Bazna, Elyesa [alias Cicero] (b. 1903), spy, was born at Pristina near Belgrade, the son of Albanian parents. He later said that his father, Hafiz Yazan Bazna, was a mullah, and that both his grandfather and one of his uncles were among Atatürk's Young Turks. It is believed that he attended the Fatih military academy in Turkey, and that a cousin and fellow pupil later became mayor of Ankara (1960–62). Bazna was removed from the academy, and under the British occupation of Constantinople in 1919 began a life of petty crime. He served time in a penal camp at Marseilles for stealing British army property and later learned the locksmith's trade at the Berliet motor works. He returned to Turkey in 1925 to work in Constantinople's public transport department, later becoming chief of the fire brigade at Yozgat. In the mid-1930s he drove a taxi and then became a valet (kavass), first to the Yugoslav ambassador (who encouraged his talents for music and photography), then to Douglas Busk, a British diplomat, then to Colonel Class, an American military attaché, and finally to the British ambassador, Sir Hughe Knatchbull-*Hugessen.

Hugessen hired Bazna in 1943, at a crucial time in Turco-British relations. Churchill was determined to pressurize Turkey to join the allies, despite the indifference of both the USA and the USSR, and his main tool to effect the switch in Turkish loyalties was his somewhat maligned ambassador, whom Churchill regarded as being too verbose and insufficiently fierce in dealing with Turkish leaders. By 1943 the Adana conference had come and gone, but its effects were still resonating in the chancelleries of most neutral countries, and formed the substance of the Foreign Office communications which flooded into the British residence at Ankara. Hugessen took the most important of these to his residence, and locked them in a safe, to which Bazna acquired a key. Bazna, who had already stolen and photographed some of Busk's material and was by now proficient with a camera, filched up to 150 top-secret Foreign Office documents from the safe between September 1943 and March 1944. They were, of course, in English, a language Hugessen thought his valet was unable to read. But Bazna, by his own account, was fully aware of the import of the documents, which he sold to the *abwehr* chief at the German embassy, Ludwig Moyzisch. The ambassador there, Fritz von Papen, who had been a senior diplomatist in Berlin in the 1930s and was regarded as a serious candidate to replace Joachim von Ribbentrop as German foreign minister, had no doubt that Bazna's material was of crucial importance to the ending of the war; he devoted a full chapter of his autobiography to describing what became known as the Cicero affair. In Berlin, the photographed documents were variously assessed by Walter Schellenberg, Joseph Goebbels, Ernst von Kaltenbrunner, and Ribbentrop himself. The time and place of the forthcoming D-day landings were said to be revealed therein, as well as the minutes of the Cairo and Tehran conferences, Churchill's determination to bring Turkey into the war, and the allies' commitment to unconditional surrender. Schellenberg also hoped the British diplomatic codes revealed in Cicero's documents might aid the German *Forschungsamt* in their attempt to read the diplomatic messages of their opponents.

Bazna was paid several hundred thousand pounds in forged notes prepared by Balkan prisoners in Romanian prisons. In Ankara, Hugessen learnt that his security arrangements had been penetrated, but a British security visitation in February 1944 failed to identify the source of the leaks. Bazna left the ambassador's employment of his own free will in the summer of 1944, at a time when Hugessen was censured by his Foreign Office masters for failures in his security procedures. Hugessen described the whole episode in his memoirs as 'a period of some difficulty'. It was not until 1950, with the appearance of *Operation Cicero* by Ludwig Moyzisch (which was subsequently made into a film, *Five Fingers*, starring James Mason), that the world heard of the details of an international espionage coup, which the Foreign Office and British secret service were to place on a par with the defection of Guy Burgess and Donald Maclean in 1951.

Bazna himself did not prosper thereafter. He invested in a hotel in Ankara, lost most of his money, came under suspicion of trading with forged notes, sold motor cars, lived a busy sex life, and later, with Hans Nogly, published his memoirs, *I was Cicero* (1962). Nogly validated Bazna's claim to have been Cicero by organizing a meeting between Bazna and Moyzisch, who confirmed that Elyesa Bazna was indeed the man he knew as Cicero. His eventual fate is unknown. ROBIN DENNISTON

Sources E. Bazna and H. Nogly, *I was Cicero*, trans. E. Mosbacher (1962) · L. C. Moyzisch, *Operation Cicero* (1950) · W. Schellenberg, *The Schellenberg memoirs* (1959) · F. von Papen, *Memoirs* (1952) · N. West, *Unreliable witness: espionage myths of the Second World War* (1984) · D. Kahn, *Hitler's spies: German military intelligence in World War Two* (1975) · D. Kahn, *The codebreakers* (1966) · A. C. Brown, *The secret servant: the life of Sir Stewart Menzies, Churchill's spymaster* (1986) · A. C. Brown, *Bodyguard of lies* (1975); pbk edn (1977) · H. M. Knatchbull-Hugessen, *Diplomat in peace and war* (1949) · F. H. Hinsley and others, *British intelligence in the Second World War*, 3 (1984–8) · F. H. Hinsley and C. A. G. Simkins, *British intelligence in the Second World War*, 4: *Security and counter-intelligence* (1990) · M. Howard, *British intelligence in the Second World War*, 5: *Strategic deception* (1990)

Beach, Charles. See Reid, (Thomas) Mayne (1818–1883).

Beach, John. See Marshall, Thomas (d. 1539).

Beach, Michael Edward Hicks, first Earl St Aldwyn (1837–1916), politician, was born on 23 October 1837, in Portugal Street, Grosvenor Square, London. He was the elder son of Sir Michael Hicks Beach, eighth baronet (d. 1854), and his wife, Harriett Vittoria, second daughter of John Stratton of Farthinghoe Lodge, Northamptonshire. The baronetcy had been granted in 1619 by James I to Sir William Hicks; the family adopted the additional surname in 1790 when Michael Hicks, great-grandfather of Earl St Aldwyn, married Henrietta Maria, the heir of William Beach of Netheravon, Wiltshire.

Education, early career, and marriage After attending Eton College, Hicks Beach went in 1855 to Christ Church, Oxford, where he obtained first-class honours in law and modern history in 1858. Tall and lean, with candid grey-blue eyes and a mop of curly brown hair, Hicks Beach presented a striking figure; his daughter, Lady Victoria, described his 'almost statuesque severity of feature' (Hicks Beach, 1.13). But to his contemporaries this severity seemed to be too well reflected in his personality. In fact, throughout his life Hicks Beach remained shy, diffident, and somewhat nervous in temperament. As a result he appeared aloof and unapproachable, was never one to suffer fools gladly, and indulged in sharp verbal attacks on colleagues and opponents; in parliament he was known privately as Black Michael. Thus, despite his political prominence he remained a lonely figure, and owed his early rise to the patronage of Disraeli and to his own administrative ability, not to popularity. His friendship with Lord Randolph Churchill, no doubt an attraction of opposites, was the one important personal relationship in his public life.

After Oxford, Hicks Beach spent some time touring the Middle East before settling down to the life of a country squire and JP in Gloucestershire. The death of his father in 1854 effectively created this role for him. As yet he showed no political ambitions—indeed he refused invitations to stand for parliament—and, in any case, lacked confidence as a public speaker. However, in 1864 he agreed to contest a by-election in East Gloucestershire, the seat once briefly represented by his father. It was also in 1864 that he married Caroline Susan, daughter of John Henry Elwes of Colesbourne Park, Gloucestershire. Following her death (while pregnant) on 14 August 1865, Hicks Beach immersed himself in public work to forget his sorrow. Not until 1874 did he remarry; his second wife was Lady Lucy Catherine (d. 17 March 1940), the third daughter of Hugh

Michael Edward Hicks Beach, first Earl St Aldwyn (1837–1916), by Sir Arthur Stockdale Cope, 1906

*Fortescue, third Earl Fortescue, with whom he had one son and three daughters.

Conservative politician From the outset of his career Hicks Beach was an uncompromising tory squire and high-churchman. He disapproved of compulsory education as an infringement of civil liberties, opposed Derby's and Disraeli's 1867 Reform Bill, though not publicly, and was among a small minority of critics of the secret ballot in 1869. However, before he had time to develop into the role of the independent back-bench rebel for which he seemed suited, he was diverted by the offer of a parliamentary secretaryship at the poor-law board in 1868, followed quickly by an under-secretaryship at the Home Office. His excellent memory and his capacity for mastering dull and intricate detail marked him out as a useful governmental figure in a party not well endowed with administrative talent. As a result, when Disraeli took office in 1874 he made Hicks Beach chief secretary for Ireland, a major post though outside the cabinet. It was in 1876, when a change of viceroy took the duke of Marlborough to Dublin, that Hicks Beach's friendship with Lord Randolph Churchill developed.

In January 1878 Hicks Beach moved further into the limelight when Disraeli appointed him colonial secretary. But in this role the young minister found himself caught between a prime minister anxious to avoid costly imperial adventures and the ambitions of British representatives abroad. In particular he inherited a dangerous situation in

South Africa where Sir Bartle Frere, the high commissioner at the Cape, was keen to extend British control at the expense of both the Zulu and the Boers with a view to creating a federation of the various South African territories. For some months Hicks Beach endeavoured to restrain Frere in his boundary dispute with the Zulu by indicating the government's reluctance to send him any extra troops. 'But', he warned Disraeli, 'I cannot really control [Frere] without a telegraph—and I don't know that I could with one' (Hicks Beach to Disraeli, 3 Nov 1878; Hicks Beach, 1.103). Eventually the British commander, Lord Chelmsford, blundered into Zululand in January 1879, only to suffer a humiliating defeat at Isandlwana. The government curtailed Frere's authority by restricting him to Cape Colony and dispatched Sir Garnet Wolseley as high commissioner for Natal, the Transvaal, and Zululand. None the less, Wolseley's victory over the Zulu at Ulundi meant, in effect, the temporary triumph of Frere's annexationist policy.

The surprise defeat of Disraeli at the 1880 election did nothing to slow Hicks Beach's inexorable rise. While the official party leadership under Sir Stafford Northcote attracted growing criticism from Conservatives, he made several acclaimed speeches attacking the Gladstone government; it was his amendment to the budget on 8 June 1885 that led to Gladstone's resignation. Hicks Beach also acted as a go-between in the controversy between the parties over parliamentary reform in 1884, when he negotiated with Lord Hartington the compromise whereby the Liberals' Franchise Bill would be allowed through the House of Lords on condition that a redistribution bill followed. At the same time he benefited from the internal Conservative disputes between the followers of Lord Randolph Churchill, who wished to strengthen the role of the National Union of Conservative Associations, and the parliamentary leadership. When the two sides reached a compromise in July 1884 they agreed to make Hicks Beach the new chairman of the National Union's council; he was reassuring to the traditional parliamentarians but also friendly enough with Churchill to be acceptable to the rebels.

The result of these developments was to bring the Conservatives under Lord Salisbury back into office in June 1885 and, in the process, to bring Hicks Beach's career to a climax as chancellor of the exchequer and leader of the House of Commons. Yet 1885–6 proved to be a turning-point in more ways than one; Hicks Beach's political weaknesses were exposed and eventually imposed a decisive check on what might otherwise have been an advance on the premiership.

In the first place the electoral reforms of 1884 and 1885 had undermined the comfortable political base which Hicks Beach had hitherto enjoyed. At the election of November 1885 he was rejected by the new voters of East Gloucestershire and forced to withdraw to a wealthy urban seat at Bristol West. This was part of a broader retreat on his part, and his role as the traditional tory squire became increasingly hollow. As the owner of around 4000 acres at Williamstrip in Coln St Aldwyn,

Gloucestershire, and 8000 acres at Netheravon in Wiltshire he suffered a good deal from falling agricultural prices. In 1881 he told the royal commission on agriculture that his rents had fallen from 20–26s. per acre to 14s. The impression created by his daughter, Lady Victoria, of her father as a man dedicated to the improvement and personal running of his estates is misleading. In fact he simply cut his losses by selling the bulk of his land in Wiltshire and compensated by seeking a large number of directorships in banking and other financial institutions. He also let his country home for a time and gave up his London house.

Leader of the house The second major development of the mid-1880s involved Hicks Beach's prominent role as chancellor and leader of the house. He helped to force Salisbury's hand by making it clear that, along with Churchill, he would refuse to join the new Conservative government in June 1885 unless Northcote were sent to the House of Lords. However, the minority administration headed by Salisbury proved unable to win the election in November and was overtaken by the home-rule crisis in January 1886. No doubt Gladstone's failure with the first Home Rule Bill and heavy defeat at the subsequent election put the Conservatives back into office by August 1886. Hicks Beach did not return as either chancellor or leader of the house. The received view is that he modestly made way for Churchill to take over these roles, but this is scarcely credible, though he had indeed been somewhat overshadowed by the flamboyant figure of Churchill. In fact Hicks Beach had not proved a very successful leader of the house. He was too remote and even aggressive towards the backbenchers. Moreover, he had in 1885 handled ineptly the question of the Maamstrasna murders. The Irish leader, Parnell, had demanded a review of the decision to execute three Irishmen convicted of the murders. The cabinet decided to reject his call, but Hicks Beach changed his mind and offered a judicial review, thereby provoking wide dismay in the Conservative Party.

As a result it seemed politic for Salisbury to put Churchill in Hicks Beach's place. The latter found himself in effect demoted as chief secretary for Ireland once more. He now faced the task of suppressing the Plan of Campaign by tenants who were withholding rents from landlords and paying it to trustees until their terms were accepted. In spite of his experience Hicks Beach found the Irish post uncomfortable. He had never really been in agreement with either Churchill or Salisbury on Irish questions, partly because he took a critical view of the behaviour of the landlords there. He also became unhappy about the government's attempts to introduce elective county councils in England, which he saw as a threat to the landed class. Thus, when Churchill suddenly resigned from the cabinet in December 1886, Hicks Beach was no longer in alliance with him. This proved fortunate for Salisbury as Hicks Beach could have brought down the government by joining Churchill. In the event, the prime minister resolved the crisis by bringing George Goschen and W. H. Smith into key posts, leaving Hicks Beach as Irish secretary.

By March 1887 Hicks Beach had decided to resign. The received explanation for this decision was his deteriorating eyesight—he suffered from cataracts in both eyes. Yet after treatment in Germany his sight improved remarkably quickly. This posed a problem for Salisbury who feared that if left on the back benches Hicks Beach would inevitably drift back into co-operation with Churchill. Thus in early 1888 he offered the first vacancy that arose, the Board of Trade, and although this was a lowly cabinet post Hicks Beach accepted it. He found administrative work satisfying and, conversely, had little taste for the party in-fighting that an active association with Churchill would have entailed. He remained at the Board of Trade until the Conservatives lost office in 1892. During this period he was again overtaken by a rival, this time A. J. Balfour, who succeeded him as Irish secretary and who, in 1891, became leader of the house.

Chancellor of the exchequer By 1895, when Salisbury again became prime minister, Hicks Beach no longer appeared to be a threat; as a result he was restored to the exchequer where he remained for the rest of his cabinet career. These years proved to be a crucial period for Conservative financial policy. The new government became subject to acute pressure to strengthen the Royal Navy, to relieve taxation on the party's traditional supporters, and to spend more on social reforms, much favoured by the Liberal Unionist and former radical Joseph Chamberlain. In this situation Hicks Beach pursued a policy of Gladstonianism tempered by electoral expediency. His penchant for retrenchment coincided with the prevailing attitude in the Treasury, but created friction with colleagues, including the prime minister. 'It is rare to get a letter from Hicks Beach without a "No, I will not" on the first page,' complained Salisbury (G. Cecil, *Life of Robert, Marquis of Salisbury*, 1921, 2.177–8). Arthur Balfour, now rising inexorably towards the premiership, described him 'dropping little grains of sand into the wheels of every department' (Balfour to Salisbury, 20 Oct 1900, Salisbury MSS).

For several years, however, this conflict simmered but did not boil. This was partly because trade revived, thereby boosting revenue in the second half of the decade. Moreover, the graduated death duties, introduced by the previous Liberal administration and opposed by Hicks Beach, yielded more than expected and therefore the chancellor usually enjoyed a surplus. He managed to reduce the national debt, relieve half the burden of rates on agricultural land, and keep income tax at 8d. in the pound.

But in time the pressure to expand the navy and finance costly colonial exploits such as the war in the Sudan complicated his retrenchment strategy, and by 1898–9 Hicks Beach was facing a deficit of £4 million. Reluctant to suspend the sinking fund, he preferred to meet this by extra taxation, but found his colleagues most unwilling to take such risks with their supporters. The outbreak of the Second South African War in the autumn of 1899 brought matters to a head by exposing the underlying Conservative dilemma over national taxation. Initially Hicks Beach simply reduced the fixed debt charges and borrowed £8 million for the war. But the early disasters suffered by the British forces in South Africa put the parsimonious Treasury policy firmly in the firing line and, as the war dragged on, the costs were soon out of control; the budget for 1899/1900 involved £111 million of expenditure, and that for 1900/01 £154 million, which threatened a £60 million deficit. Consequently a number of unwelcome expedients were adopted. Hicks Beach increased income tax from 8*d*. to 1*s*. in the pound, imposed extra duties on beer, spirits, tea, and tobacco, suspended the sinking fund, and raised short-term loans. In 1901 a 1*s*. per ton duty on coal was introduced and income tax rose a further 2*d*. The 1902 budget brought another penny on income tax and the revival of the 1*s*. duty on corn which had been abolished in 1869. Although this last measure raised only £2.6 million it proved to be of considerable political importance in that it was immediately welcomed by tory protectionists and condemned by free-traders in both parties.

Resignation and final years These developments rapidly exposed Hicks Beach's isolation in cabinet. After the general election in 1900 Balfour had urged Salisbury to remove him from the exchequer, but the prime minister refused despite his own impatience with Hicks Beach's negative attitude. Meanwhile, the strains of war forced fundamental disagreements to the surface. When Hicks Beach made it clear that he intended to resume the sinking fund, Joseph Chamberlain argued that this was simply not feasible; indeed he challenged the whole assumption that after the war Britain would be able to return to retrenchment and previous levels of taxation. By contrast Hicks Beach continued to believe that low taxation and free trade were the basis of British prosperity. His views were not without some support in cabinet, but his truculence and the sheer pressure of external events weakened his position. He got into the habit of threatening to resign unless his colleagues reduced their demands for expenditure. As a result, when Salisbury resigned as prime minister in August 1902, Hicks Beach took the opportunity to do the same. He could now defend his principles publicly, and when in 1903 Chamberlain launched his campaign for tariff reform, Hicks Beach became, in effect, the leader of some sixty free-trade tory MPs. He believed that protectionism would lead to tariff wars and he accused Chamberlain of splitting the party. In 1904 he decided to give up his seat in the Commons and was given a viscountcy in 1906. In the upper house he opposed many of the social reforms of the new Liberal government, though he considered the rejection of the 1909 budget by the protectionist peers to be unwise. He was now very much an elder statesman in a small minority within his own party.

The outbreak of war in August 1914 gave a brief fillip to Hicks Beach's career. He represented the bankers in negotiations with Lloyd George on the financial adjustments to be made on entry into the war. He served as chairman of the committee on clearing banks and of the Treasury committee on new issues. His work was recognized by his elevation as Earl St Aldwyn in 1915. But his eyesight had deteriorated by this time and he succumbed to bronchial

colds. In the spring of 1916 he suffered heart failure and died at 81 Eaton Place, London, on 30 April of that year; he was buried at Coln St Aldwyn. His son, Viscount Quenington, had been killed just one week earlier, and so the title passed to his grandson, Michael John Hicks Beach.

MARTIN PUGH

Sources *The Times* (1 May 1916) · *The Times* (5 May 1916) · V. Hicks Beach, *The life of Sir Michael Hicks Beach (Earl St Aldwyn)*, 2 vols. (1932) · P. Marsh, *The discipline of popular government: Lord Salisbury's domestic statecraft, 1881–1902* (1978) · R. F. Foster, *Lord Randolph Churchill: a political life* (1981) · *DNB* · Hatfield House, Hertfordshire, Salisbury MSS

Archives Glos. RO, corresp. and papers · LUL, letters | BL, corresp. with Arthur James Balfour, Add. MS 49695 · BL, corresp. with Lord Carnarvon, Add. MS 60774 · BL, corresp. with Sir Edward Walter Hamilton, Add. MS 48614 · BL, corresp. with Sir Stafford Northcote, Add. MS 50021 · Bodl. Oxf., corresp. with Benjamin Disraeli · Bodl. Oxf., corresp. with Sir William Harcourt · Bodl. Oxf., corresp. with Lord Kimberley · Bodl. Oxf., letters to Lord Milner · Bodl. Oxf., Phillipps MSS · CAC Cam., corresp. with Lord Randolph Churchill · CKS, letters to Aretas Akers-Douglas · CKS, letters to Edward Stanhope · CUL, letters to duke of Marlborough · HLRO, letters to David Lloyd George · HLRO, corresp. with fourteenth earl of Pembroke · LPL, corresp. with A. C. Tait · NA Scot., corresp. with A. J. Balfour · National Library of South Africa, Cape Town, corresp. with Sir Bartle Frere · PRO NIre., letters to Lord Abercorn · PRO NIre., corresp. with Lord Dufferin · U. Birm. L., corresp. with Joseph Chamberlain

Likenesses B. Stone, photographs, 1897–8, NPG · A. S. Cope, oils, 1906, NPG [*see illus.*] · Ape [C. Pellegrini], chromolithograph caricature, NPG; repro. in *VF* (22 Aug 1874) · Barraud, photograph, NPG; repro. in *Men and Women of the Day*, 4 (1891) · Bassano, cabinet photograph, NPG · W. & D. Downey, woodburytype photograph, NPG; repro. in W. Downey and D. Downey, *The cabinet portrait gallery*, 3 (1892) · F. C. Gould, caricature, NPG · S. P. Hall, pencil sketches, NPG · Lock & Whitfield, woodburytype photograph, NPG; repro. in *Men of mark* (1876) · B. Partridge, pen-and-ink caricatures, NPG · Russell & Sons, photograph, NPG; repro. in R. J. Albery, *Our conservative statesmen*, 1 (1893) · lithograph, BM; repro. in *Civil Service Review* (1877)

Wealth at death £34,309 9*s*. 4*d*.: probate, 19 July 1916, *CGPLA Eng. & Wales*

Beach, Michael John Hicks-, second Earl St Aldwyn (1912–1992), politician, was born on 9 October 1912 at Sudeley Castle, Gloucestershire, the younger child and only son of Michael Hugh Hicks-Beach (1877–1916), politician, and his wife, Marjorie (*d*. 1916), daughter of Henry Dent-Brocklehurst, of Sudeley Castle. His father was Conservative MP for Tewkesbury, continuing a family tradition of public service which stretched back to the sixteenth century when Sir Michael Hicks had been Lord Burghley's secretary. His paternal grandfather, Sir Michael Edward Hicks *Beach, was a Conservative MP for more than forty years; he served twice as chief secretary for Ireland, and was twice chancellor of the exchequer. On his grandfather's creation as first Earl St Aldwyn in 1915 (he had already been made Viscount St Aldwyn on retiring from the Commons in 1906), Hicks-Beach's father became Viscount Quenington.

Tragedy struck Hicks-Beach and his sister, Delia, in 1916. Their mother died on 4 March. On 23 April their father, a captain in the 4th battalion of the Gloucester regiment, was killed in action in Egypt (thus making Hicks-Beach

Viscount Quenington). Exactly a week later their grandfather died (thus making the three-year-old the second Earl St Aldwyn). Brought up by relatives and governesses, the young earl followed in the footsteps of his father and grandfather by attending Eton College and Christ Church, Oxford, but he left the latter after only a year. With no chance of emulating his forebears in the House of Commons, he applied himself to the substantial farm he had inherited, breeding pedigree cattle and sheep. During the Second World War he served in the Royal Gloucestershire Hussars Yeomanry, ending with the rank of major. On 26 June 1948 he married Diana Mary Christian Smyly (*d.* 1992), only daughter of Henry Christian George Mills, and former wife of Major Richard Patrick Pilkington Smyly. They had three sons: Michael (*b.* 1950), Peter (1952–1990), and David (*b.* 1955).

Although St Aldwyn had been a regular attender in the House of Lords his career in government did not begin until October 1954, when he became a junior minister at agriculture. It was a congenial post for an enthusiastic farmer; he stayed in the ministry for four years.

In June 1958, on the death of Earl Fortescue, Harold Macmillan appointed St Aldwyn government chief whip in the Lords. He served as the Conservative Party's chief whip in the upper house for two decades. It was a transitional period for the house; his appointment coincided with the passage of the Life Peerages Act. There was no overnight transformation; hereditary peers comfortably outnumbered the newcomers until Labour's reforms of 1999, and the overwhelming majority were Conservatives. Even so, St Aldwyn reformed the whips' office in the expectation that the house would need more professional management. His measures were resented in some quarters; members of the Association of Independent Unionist Peers tended to resent telephone calls urging their attendance.

St Aldwyn looked like an old-fashioned disciplinarian, whose attitudes belonged to the pre-war era. In fact his outlook was pragmatic and he could be an engaging companion. But he was hardly the ideal man to help in the choice of a prime minister for the 1960s—a role that was thrust upon him in 1963. He consulted peers on the succession to the ailing Harold Macmillan, and reported a clear majority in favour of Alec Home. Since Home was a colleague in the Lords, and shared St Aldwyn's love of country pursuits, the chief Whip was scarcely an impartial witness. But while others within the so-called 'magic circle' were later accused of fiddling the figures, St Aldwyn was incapable of sharp practice. In fact he recorded a protest against the impending loss of Home from the Lords.

St Aldwyn never won (or sought) a high public profile; his task, rather, was to keep the House of Lords out of the news. For more than half of his period in office Labour was in power, and he was called upon to restrain his troops in case they defeated the government too often. For St Aldwyn, the House of Lords played a valuable role and it was necessary to preserve as much as possible of its traditional ethos against a government which could easily be provoked into radical reforms. Piecemeal change,

though, was acceptable. When R.H.S. Crossman's moderate proposals were rejected in 1969 it was cross-party opposition in the Commons, rather than a Lords revolt, which scuppered the measure. Working closely with Lord Carrington, the Conservative leader in the Lords during both periods of opposition, St Aldwyn was generally successful in restricting the number of rebellions against Labour legislation. His most notable failure came in June 1968, when the Rhodesian sanctions order was defeated. Yet even on this divisive issue the margin was less than ten, and the vote was overturned in the following month. During the minority Labour governments of the 1970s St Aldwyn and Carrington pursued the same objectives with similar results.

St Aldwyn kept up his regular attendance in the Lords after his retirement in December 1977. From 1978 to 1987 he was chancellor of the order of St John, and between 1981 and 1987 he also served as vice lord lieutenant of his beloved Gloucestershire. He was made KBE in 1964 and GBE in 1980. He died on 29 January 1992 at his home, Williamstrip Park, Coln St Aldwyns, near Cirencester, Gloucestershire, of heart disease and cancer of the colon. He was survived by his wife (who died on 10 July 1992) and two of their sons, the elder of whom succeeded him as third Earl St Aldwyn. A memorial service was held at St Margaret's Church, Westminster, on 10 June 1992.

MARK GARNETT

Sources *The Times* (31 Jan 1992) · *The Independent* (31 Jan 1992) · WWW · Burke, *Peerage* · b. cert. · d. cert.
Likenesses photograph, repro. in *The Times* · photograph, repro. in *The Independent*
Wealth at death £1,495,536: probate, 1992, *CGPLA Eng. & Wales*

Beach, Sir Richard (*d.* 1692), naval officer, first appears as captain of the royalist *St Michael* in 1651. By 1654 he was 'admiral' of a squadron of three frigates operating out of Brest, whose capture was a priority for the parliamentary admirals Blake and Penn. At the end of February, Beach was reported about Land's End but by 18 March he had been taken, off the Scillies, by the *Constant Warwick* under Captain Potter. Beach surrendered after losing 20 of his 200 men and with 5 feet of water in the hold; he and his ship, the *Royal James*, were taken into Plymouth. He was freed in an exchange of prisoners on 29 April, resumed his privateering, and was being sought by the state's navy until the eve of the Restoration. On the king's return Beach petitioned for restitution of one of two ships he had built for the royalist fleet, now again in the crown's hands; he received £100 in compensation. He would, in the later 1660s, seek the award of a prize ship as a reward for his 1650s services, and he recalled, perhaps fancifully, that after being five times in prison and once condemned to death, he had declined offers of high commands from Admiral Blake and others.

One of the relatively few cavaliers who secured captains' commissions in the navy in 1660–61, much of Beach's subsequent service was to be in the Mediterranean. From 1661–3 he captained the *Crown*; in April 1662 he was at Tangier, to which he brought engineers for the mole. On 14 December 1663 he was commissioned to the

Leopard, loaned to the East India Company for Mediterranean convoy duties. In September 1664 he joined Thomas Allin, commander in the Mediterranean, at Gibraltar. He was still in command of the *Leopard*, under Allin, at the start of the Second Anglo-Dutch War. His ship was detached from the fleet to search for the French, allies of the Dutch, in the channel and consequently only saw action on the last day of the Four Days' Fight, 1–4 June 1666. On 6 July he was given command of the *Fairfax* and in 1667 he captained the *Greenwich*. In May 1669, as he was in the Thames preparing to sail for the straits in the *Hampshire*, there were complaints of his excessive use of the press and of over-zealous sentries. Men were literally jumping ship (and some drowning) to avoid serving with him. He blamed the desertion of 130 of his original volunteers on the higher pay for merchantmen. He sailed on 17 July, took a prize in the straits on 8 September, and on the 18th was dispatched back to England with a cargo described as 54 'low-grade' black slaves. He left Plymouth in April 1670 and rejoined Allin at Fomentera in May. On 14–18 August he took part in a combined operation with the Dutch under Willem van Ghent in which six Algerine corsairs were destroyed. The temporary allies disputed their respective roles in the chase, but Beach's ships were in at the kill and helped to rescue 250 Christian hostages. On both his voyages with Allin, Beach was frequently sent ashore to negotiate with local rulers. He also tended to detach himself from the fleet on other less purposeful occasions. He returned to England with Allin in February 1671. Following the death of Edward Montagu, earl of Sandwich, at Sole Bay in May 1672, Beach was made rear-admiral of the Red squadron. He hoisted his flag aboard the *Monmouth* and returned to the straits under Admiral Sir Edward Spragge.

Beach became resident commissioner at Chatham from 26 December 1672 and had received a knighthood by 1 February 1676. He found fault with many officers in his yard, particularly the master shipwright Phineas Pett. He judged it was the 'intemperate use of brandy in the king's ships' that had caused the *Anne* to blow up in 1673 (Pepys to Beach, 8 December; Tanner, 2.157). He tried to dismiss two gunners on spurious charges of Catholicism under cover of the Popish Plot scare of 1678–9, having earlier sought to remove at least one of them for idleness. Pepys defeated this ploy, yet Beach defended Pepys against accusations of introducing papists into the navy. In October 1679 he was moved to the commissionership at Portsmouth. During the last years of Charles II's reign he was frustrated by lack of funds, urging the need for speedy repairs lest the king have 'but a rotten navy' (Pool, 20). On 19 April 1686 he was appointed, with a salary of £500, to the special commission which (thanks to a sympathetic parliament) had money to put in hand the repair programme for which he had argued. On the dissolution of the commission in 1688 he continued to serve at Portsmouth. His house there was attacked by disaffected, possibly Jacobite, seamen in 1689. On 3 May 1690 he was appointed commissioner for victualling accounts, which he remained until his death. He

was buried on 13 May 1692 at St Olave, Hart Street, London.

Sir William Coventry had said in 1663 that Beach was one of only three old royalists fit to command in the navy. Pepys thought him 'able and serious' but was more impressed by his Dutch wife ('ingenious woman') for her mastery of English (Pepys, *Diary*, 4.432).

C. S. KNIGHTON

Sources Pepys, *Diary* • *Samuel Pepys and the Second Dutch War: Pepys's navy white book and Brooke House papers*, ed. R. Latham, Navy RS, 133 (1995), 215–16 [transcribed by W. Matthews and C. Knighton] • J. R. Tanner, ed., *A descriptive catalogue of the naval manuscripts in the Pepysian Library at Magdalene College, Cambridge*, 1, Navy RS, 26 (1903), 16 (n. 5), 60 (n. 5), 85, 89, 322; 2, Navy RS, 27 (1904), 157–8; 3, Navy RS, 36 (1909), 165 (n. 1); 4, Navy RS, 57 (1923), 292–3, 583–4, 615, 630, 653 • *CSP dom.*, 1654, pp. 38, 460, 525; 1660–61, p. 123; 1666–71, p. 395; 1668–9, pp. 343, 345, 632; 1670, pp. 141, 242, 250, 386, 394–5, 421 • *The letters of Robert Blake*, ed. J. R. Powell, Navy RS, 76 (1937), 133, 253, 256, 263 • S. R. Gardiner and C. T. Atkinson, eds., *Letters and papers relating to the First Dutch War, 1652–1654*, 6 vols., Navy RS, 13, 17, 30, 37, 41, 66 (1898–1930), vol. 1, pp. 23, 25; vol. 6, pp. 227–8, 235–6, 243–4 • *The journals of Sir Thomas Allin, 1660–1678*, ed. R. C. Anderson, 2 vols., Navy RS, 79–80 (1939–40) • *The journal of Edward Mountagu, first earl of Sandwich, admiral and general at sea, 1659–1665*, ed. R. C. Anderson, Navy RS, 64 (1929), 136 • J. R. Powell and E. K. Timings, eds., *The Rupert and Monck letter book, 1666*, Navy RS, 112 (1969), 17, 24, 180 • B. Pool, *Navy board contracts, 1660–1832* (1966), 20 • *Further correspondence of Samuel Pepys, 1662–1679*, ed. J. R. Tanner (1929), 330 • J. D. Davies, 'Pepys and the admiralty commission of 1679–84', *Historical Research*, 62 (1989), 35–53, esp. 48 • J. D. Davies, *Gentlemen and tarpaulins: the officers and men of the Restoration navy* (1991), 116, 225 • R. Ollard, *Man of war: Sir Robert Holmes and the Restoration navy* (1969), 182 • J. M. Collinge, *Navy Board officials, 1660–1832* (1978), 85 • Magd. Cam., Pepys Library, MS 1490, pp. 175–82, 195–7, 211–13, 215–16, 347–9 • will, PRO, PROB 11/410, fols. 226–7 • W. B. Bannerman, ed., *The registers of St Olave, Hart Street, London, 1563–1700*, Harleian Society, register section, 46 (1916), 236
Wealth at death left £2500 to granddaughter; £240 p.a. to grandson from rents of property in Westminster and Middlesex: will, PRO, PROB 11/410, fols. 226–7

Beach, Thomas (d. 1737), poet, was a wine merchant in Wrexham, Denbighshire. Besides other poems, he published in April 1737 *Eugenio, or, Virtuous and Happy Life*. It was inscribed to Pope, and was submitted by the author to Swift, partly to receive his criticisms and partly to be brought before the notice of Sir William Fownes, who was specially referred to in *Eugenio*. Swift in his reply suggested many verbal emendations, which were adopted by the author, and informed him that Fownes was dead. Beach committed suicide on 17 May 1737.

ALFRED GOODWIN, rev. FREYA JOHNSTON

Sources *The correspondence of Jonathan Swift*, ed. H. Williams, 4 (1965) • *GM*, 1st ser., 7 (1737) • Nichols, *Lit. anecdotes*, vol. 5

Beach, Thomas (bap. 1737, d. 1806), portrait painter, was baptized at Abbey Milton, Dorset, on 4 April 1737, the second son of Thomas Beach and his wife, Ursula, *née* Bryer. He was educated at the grammar school in Abbey Milton, where he had shown such distinct artistic promise that Lord Milton sent him to London to study with Sir Joshua Reynolds from 1760 to 1762, when he was also enrolled at the St Martin's Lane Academy. By 1770 he had settled at 2 Westgate Buildings, Bath, where he soon acquired a profitable reputation among fashionable visitors and residents.

In 1772 he joined the Incorporated Society of Artists, contributing to its annual exhibitions until 1783, when, like so many of his contemporaries, he changed his allegiance to the Royal Academy, where he showed from 1785 to 1790 and in 1797, when he exhibited a portrait of the prince of Wales (Royal Collection). During that time he was partly resident in London living at 3 Charles Street, St James's Square, and later at 54/55 Wigmore Street; like other artists, he followed the *bon ton* in its seasonal ebb and flow between the capital and Bath. The date of his marriage to Maria, *née* Vaughan, of whom he made a portrait (ex Sothebys, 23 March 1977), is unknown. It appears that she died before 1797, for from that year his sister, Frances, kept house for him. The couple were childless.

Like most provincial portrait painters of the time, Beach was dependent on the local patronage of the landowners. At Bath and London he also established a cosmopolitan clientele, including actors and critics whom he met through his interest in the theatre. One of his early portraits is of the actor John Henderson (1773; Garrick Club, London), with whom he was linked in a contemporary couplet:

> Happy life's duties with its joys to blend
> Reynolds his master, Henderson his friend.
> (*Notes and Queries for Somerset and Dorset*, 9, 1905, 67)

In 1782 he made two portraits of Sarah Siddons, who was performing that year in Bath. One, a formal portrait (Auckland Art Gallery, New Zealand), shows her looking up from an open book, as though she was learning a part, and may have been painted that summer in Dorset (Beach, 15). The second, inspired by Milton's *Il Penseroso*, portrayed her as *Melancholy* (ex Sothebys, 10 November 1992). Other theatrical portraits included those of Giusto Tenducci, an Italian castrato and noted opera singer (1782; priv. coll.), John Philip Kemble and Sarah Siddons in the dagger scene from *Macbeth* (1786; Garrick Club, London), and George Steevens, the Shakespearian commentator (*c.*1773–4; Dunedin Art Gallery, New Zealand), on the publication of his edition of Shakespeare's plays.

Beach was an assured figure painter and natural colourist, and was noted for his ability to capture a good likeness. Often in a feigned oval, his portraits were frequently signed and dated. Where appropriate he added an air of spontaneity by showing the sitter's head tilted and the mouth slightly open, to give an impression of the sitter speaking, an impression that was heightened by placing the sitter close to the front plane of the composition. His group portraits display a pleasing and provincial informality of arrangement, for example, *The Stapleton Family* (1789; Holburne Museum of Art, Bath). In 1798 he kept a diary, which, according to Elise Beach, great-great-grandniece and his biographer, was so prosaic that it recorded both the completion of thirty-one portraits and the time he went to bed each night. It was probably towards the end of that year that he decided to retire to Dorchester in Dorset. He continued to paint until at least 1802, the date of his *Self-Portrait* (National Portrait Gallery, London). Beach died in Dorchester, on 17 December 1806. In her biography Elise Beach listed 308 portraits by Beach.

R. E. GRAVES, *rev.* PETER TOMORY

Sources E. Beach, *Thomas Beach: a Dorset portrait painter* (1934) · A. M. Broadley, 'Thomas Beach, portrait painter of Milton Abbas, Dorsetshire', *Notes and Queries for Somerset and Dorset*, 9 (1904–5), 66–8 · Dorset RO · E. Waterhouse, *Painting in Britain, 1530–1790*, 5th edn (1994) · archive material, Courtauld Inst., Witt Library · Waterhouse, *18c painters* · I. Bignamini, 'George Vertue, art historian, and art institutions in London, 1689–1768', *Walpole Society*, 54 (1988), 1–148, esp. 114

Archives Westcountry Studies Library, Exeter, MS diary [transcript]

Likenesses T. Beach, self-portrait, oils, 1802, NPG

Beach, Thomas Billis [*alias* Henri Le Caron] (**1841–1894**), spy, was born on 26 September 1841 at Colchester, Essex, the second son of the family of thirteen children of John Joseph Billis Beach (*d.* 1888/9), a Methodist cooper, and his wife, Maria Beach, *née* Passmore. After an unsuccessful apprenticeship with a local draper Beach left Colchester in May 1857, moving to London where he worked briefly as a clerk, and from there journeying across the south of England before illness drove him back to Colchester. He left for Paris in 1859, where he became a choir member of the English church in the rue D'aguesseau and a clerk in the banking house of Arthur & Co.

At the outset of the American Civil War (1861–5), the nineteen-year-old Beach sailed on the SS *Great Eastern*'s first voyage to New York with several American associates to enlist in the Union army. Beach (who abstained from alcohol throughout his life) enlisted in the 8th Pennsylvanian reserves as a private for three months on 7 August 1861. Posing as a Frenchman, he chose the name of Henri Le Caron although, according to the Fenian John Devoy, Beach's grasp of French was decidedly poor. Transferring to the Anderson cavalry, Le Caron took part in the army of the Potomac campaigns for the next twenty-two months. His regiment was transferred to the western army in October 1862 and he rose to the rank of a non-commissioned officer. Commissioned a second lieutenant in July 1864, he was promoted to the rank of first lieutenant by the end of the year. Throughout the latter part of the war he commanded a reconnaissance company of cavalry in the army of the Cumberland, later serving in various administrative roles, including regimental adjutant. Demobilized in February 1866 after the war's end, Le Caron joined the veterans' organizations of the army of the Cumberland and the Grand Army of the Republic, serving in the latter as vice-commander and post-surgeon, with the rank of major. In April 1864 he had renewed his acquaintance with Nannie Melville, daughter of an Irish Virginian planter and his German wife; Nannie had saved the lives of Le Caron and several of his troopers when they were captured by Confederate irregulars near Nashville, Tennessee, on Christmas eve 1862. He married her shortly afterwards; they were to have six children.

While living in Nashville with his wife, Le Caron's regular letters to his father contained information about Irish-American plots against the British empire, including the abortive Fenian attempt to invade Canada in June 1866 led by 'General' John O'Neill, a former companion in arms of Le Caron. The Fenian strategy was to capture Canada as a

Thomas Billis Beach [Henri Le Caron] (1841–1894), by Sydney Prior Hall, pubd 1889 [giving evidence before the Parnell commission]

base for attacks on England or possibly as ransom for Irish independence. Colonel O'Neill, a leader of the senate wing of the Fenian Brotherhood and the current United States claims agent in Nashville, was Le Caron's most important source. Sensing the potential importance of such intelligence, the elder Beach, now a rate collector, took the letters to Colchester's Liberal member for parliament, John Gurdon Rebow, who in turn showed them to the home secretary, Sir George Grey.

On returning to England in the autumn of 1867, Le Caron was recruited by the Home Office as a secret agent. Paid very modestly over the following years from secret service funds, Le Caron's arrangement with the Home Office included the extraordinary stipulation that his letters should remain his property and subsequently they would be returned to him. Implicit in that deal was Le Caron's perceptiveness that a spy's memoirs would sell well, should he survive to write them. In 1892 he recalled: 'My adventurous nature prompted me to sympathy with the idea; my British instincts made me a willing worker from a sense of right, and my past success promised good things for the future' (Le Caron, 38). The bombing of the Middlesex House of Detention at Clerkenwell on Friday 13 December 1867, part of a failed attempt to release Fenian prisoners, created widespread panic and hysteria; the threat of Irish attacks was henceforth taken with the utmost seriousness. Le Caron now communicated with Robert Anderson, the new Home Office adviser on political crime, a euphemism for terrorism. Le Caron also

reported directly to the Canadian chief commissioner of police, Judge J. G. McMicken, in Ottawa. Thus Henri Le Caron, a small, lean, dark-haired, and moustachioed man, began a career marked out twenty-five years later by *The Times* as one of 'astonishing courage, perseverance, and success'.

On returning to the United States from London, Le Caron moved his young family to Chicago, Illinois, where he studied medicine at the Chicago Medical College for about a year, subsequently joining the Illinois State Penitentiary at Joliet as its resident medical officer. He organized a Fenian circle in Lockport, Illinois, of which he was elected the 'centre', while renewing his friendship with the recently elected (31 December 1867) president of the Irish Republican Brotherhood (IRB), John O'Neill. That summer Le Caron reluctantly resigned his medical post when on 5 August 1868 he was appointed major and military organizer in the service of the Irish republic. In November of the following year he was promoted lieutenant-colonel and acting adjutant-general of the Irish Republican Army. The next invasion of Canada, partly organized and wholly betrayed by Le Caron, began on 23 May 1870 and failed miserably. Any hope for future Fenian attempts against Canada vanished when Gladstone's first government settled the Confederate ship *Alabama* claims for £3.5 million; the United States government no longer needed Fenianism as a lever in negotiations.

Le Caron next moved to Detroit, where he completed his MD degree at the Detroit College of Medicine. Removing to Wilmington, Illinois, he established a pharmacy and a medical practice in nearby Braidwood, a mining town. Retaining his connections with the IRB, Le Caron spent the next four or five years focused on his profession and local politics. However, by 1876 he accepted the necessity of joining the Clan na Gael, founded nine years before and potentially the most dangerous of the Irish-American organizations. Claiming that his mother was Irish to qualify for membership, he subsequently founded a camp at Braidwood (D 463), known as the Emmet Literary Association. As its senior guardian, he was assured access to all of the Clan documents, copies of which soon found their way to London.

Charles Stewart Parnell, leader of the Irish party in the House of Commons, and a colleague, John Dillon, made a fund-raising tour of the United States at the beginning of 1880 on behalf of the Land League, a new organization largely controlled by the radical Clan na Gael. Le Caron subsequently reported to Anderson that Parnell was aware of the league's real purpose and thus actually supported violence in Ireland, rather than the constitutional means that he publicly espoused. Le Caron travelled to Europe in the spring of 1881 charged with infiltrating Fenian groups operating from Paris. Le Caron also met with Parnell in the House of Commons on 23 May 1881, reporting to Anderson that night. Parnell's views, according to Le Caron, were 'a veritable bombshell': '[Parnell] had long since ceased to believe that anything but the force of arms would accomplish the final redemption of Ireland' (Le Caron, 175).

After he returned to New York on 12 June, Le Caron continued his work for the Clan na Gael or United Brotherhood, which involved so much travelling that he had to hire another doctor to care for his patients in Braidwood. Over the next six years Le Caron's reports provided important insights into the bewildering complexity of Irish-American politics. Dynamite attacks within Great Britain, however, were now the dominant strategy of the Clan na Gael and Jeremiah O'Donovan Rossa's Skirmishers. Between 1880 and 1887 Liverpool, Glasgow, and London were the sites of attacks. In London itself Irish-American bombs targeted the City of London, the streets of Westminster, the Tower of London, the House of Commons, London Bridge, railway stations, and the underground. Le Caron, however, was of no help when it came to such highly secret terrorism. Once again on holiday in England (April–October 1887), Le Caron found his secret material was the basis for three anonymous articles in *The Times* (beginning on 13 May 1887) written by Robert Anderson under the heading 'Behind the scenes in America'. Le Caron returned to London again at the end of 1887 in connection with a 'business speculation' which later failed to materialize. The master spy's final trip took place in December 1888, sailing for England to be with his father, who died on the day of his arrival.

Le Caron had written twice to Anderson offering to testify at the government's special commission into the charges by *The Times* of a connection between 'Parnellism and crime'. Le Caron was convinced that only a full disclosure of the 'foul conspiracy' existing in the United States would alert the nation and the world to the dangers. Now Anderson came forward with the news that *The Times* had approached him for a witness on the American side against Parnell. Le Caron agreed to testify on the condition that his family be brought to the comparative safety of England. Anderson returned Le Caron's reports and documents, excluding those made 'official' by being forwarded to the home secretary. On Tuesday morning, 5 February 1889, Le Caron took the stand. Although his six days of testimony withstood the highly critical cross-examination of Sir Charles Russell, counsel for the Irish members, in the end the newspaper failed to prove its allegations of complicity at the cost to itself of over £200,000.

Why did this spy 'come in from the cold', to use John Le Carré's phrase? Le Caron's patriotism, compounded by his strong belief in Parnell's complicity, must have been a major factor. Le Caron had maintained his cover (at times only barely) for more than twenty years. Unable to maintain his double life, at the age of forty-eight and apparently in good health he could have retired from Irish-American politics and British spying to pursue his medical practice. It is hard to imagine that he would have been prepared to expose his family to Fenian revenge for the anticipated proceeds of his spying chronicles. *The Times* reportedly paid for the transport and maintenance of his family, as well as the ongoing, round-the-clock Scotland Yard protection. Le Caron's 1889 will provided for dispensing more

than £5000 to his wife and siblings. By the time of his death he, inexplicably, had only some £500 left.

Le Caron, his wife (who shared his secret), and four of their children (two had remained in America) moved to 11 Tregunter Road, South Kensington. Le Caron turned to writing his memoirs, while continuing to smoke some sixteen cigars a day and nurturing his carefully waxed dark moustache. Published in 1892 by William Heinemann in London as *Twenty-Five Years in the Secret Service: the Recollections of a Spy*, the book contained several portraits, including the author's, and facsimiles of documents. The book's considerable success, even at 14*s*., took it to six editions. In it Le Caron praised Sir Robert Anderson (currently head of the Metropolitan Police's criminal investigation division), criticized the 'miserable pittance' spent on secret service work, and took pride in the fact that he was never an *agent provocateur*.

Le Caron died at his London home of appendicitis and peritonitis on Sunday 1 April 1894, aged fifty-two, and was buried six days later in Norwood cemetery. Remarkably, Dr Thomas Billis Beach MD, dubbed the Prince of Spies and the 'champion spy of the century' by John Devoy, had died in bed, the victim of Victorian medicine rather than an assassin. His family subsequently relocated to his wife's home in Tennessee.   K. R. M. SHORT

Sources H. Le Caron, *Twenty-five years in the secret service: the recollections of a spy* (1892) · J. A. Cole, *Prince of spies* (1984) · K. R. M. Short, *The dynamite war: Irish-American bombers in Victorian Britain* (1979) · J. Sweeney, *At Scotland Yard: experiences during twenty-seven years' service*, ed. F. Richards (1905) · C. Curran, 'The spy behind the speaker's chair', *History Today*, 18 (1968), 745–59 · *Report of the Parnell Commission* (1890), 103–5

Archives PRO, CO 42/686

Likenesses photograph, *c.*1888, repro. in Cole, *Prince of spies* · S. P. Hall, pencil sketches, NPG; repro. in *The Graphic* (16 Feb 1889) [*see illus.*] · portrait, repro. in Le Caron, *Twenty-five years in the secret service*

Wealth at death £523 7*s*. 6*d*.: probate, 3 Aug 1894, *CGPLA Eng. & Wales*

Beachcomber. *See* Morton, John Cameron Andrieu Bingham Michael (1893–1979).

Beaconsfield. For this title name *see* Disraeli, Mary Anne, Viscountess Beaconsfield (1792–1872); Disraeli, Benjamin, earl of Beaconsfield (1804–1881).

Beadle, Sir (Thomas) Hugh William (1905–1980), judge in Southern Rhodesia, was born in Salisbury on 6 February 1905, the only son and eldest of three children of Arthur William Beadle, later secretary to the Southern Rhodesian treasury, and his wife, Christiana Maria Fischer. Educated at Salisbury Boys' School and Milton high school, Diocesan College, Rondebosch, and Cape Town University, Beadle, after his BA and LLB degrees, proceeded in 1928 as a Rhodes scholar to Queen's College, Oxford. He played rugby and tennis for his college, boxed for the university, flew in its air squadron, and graduated with a second-class BCL (1930). He later became an honorary fellow of Queen's College, although in 1968 there was an attempt to strip him of his fellowship.

After practising at the Bulawayo bar from 1930, Beadle was elected in 1939 as MP for Bulawayo North, a seat he held until 1950 for the United Party led by Godfrey Huggins. After a period of military service from 1939 to 1940 as temporary captain in west Africa, Beadle's limitless energies were harnessed by Huggins, whom Beadle served from 1940 to 1946 as parliamentary private secretary, acting also as deputy judge advocate-general. Beadle was appointed minister of internal affairs and justice in 1946, the year he took silk, and was appointed OBE. In 1948 he also took on the education and health ministry. In 1950 Beadle became resident high court judge in Bulawayo. He was created CMG in 1957.

Beadle was a learned, fair but also adventurous judge, restrictively interpreting the scope of the criminal law. Conservative politically, he yet rejected racialism, taking the opportunity in *Mehta* v. *City of Salisbury* (1961), a case involving exclusion from public swimming-baths on racial grounds, to reject South African case law, because of that country's racial policy. Africans, however, viewed Beadle more as the chairman of a tribunal which upheld the detention of nationalist politicians during the 1959 emergency.

In 1961 Beadle became chief justice of Southern Rhodesia and therefore legal adviser to the governor. Knighted in the same year, and privy councillor from 1964, Beadle presided from 1964 over the Southern Rhodesian appellate division, giving judgments generously interpreting the recently introduced Rhodesian declaration of rights. Particularly notable was his invalidation of an act of the legislative assembly seeking to avoid the necessity of declaring a new emergency by extending the period of preventive detention. Had a unilateral declaration of independence (UDI) not occurred Beadle would have been remembered as a Commonwealth chief justice who upheld individual liberty.

Determined to avert UDI, Beadle incessantly initiated procedures for compromise. On UDI in 1965 he moved into the residence of the governor, Sir Humphrey Gibbs, advising him and British ministers, *inter alia*, on the crucial gubernatorial instruction that all those responsible for law and order should carry on with their normal tasks, an injunction assuring the regime of obedience by state servants and effectively giving it legitimating institutions without the embarrassment of replacing the judges. Beadle accompanied the governor to the talks held in November 1966 on HMS *Tiger*. He incurred the disapproval of Harold Wilson who thought him 'spineless' for failing to help pressurize Ian Smith, the Rhodesian leader, into adhering to his undertaking that he would advise his cabinet to support the *Tiger* solution.

The judges had avoided pronouncing on the regime's validity until September 1966, when two of them upheld its detention of Daniel Madzimbamuto, a nationalist politician, on grounds of necessity. On appeal, in January 1968, Beadle temporized, holding the detention invalid on a technicality, asserting that the judges still sat under the 1961 constitution, denying the regime *de jure* status, and

yet simultaneously holding that the regime was a *de facto* government which the Rhodesian courts must recognize.

In February and March 1968, in litigation about Africans sentenced to death before UDI for terrorist offences on facts that would have grounded murder charges, Beadle upheld the regime's power to carry out executions on the basis that a lawful government could have taken such action. Because Ian Smith's minister of law and order had told the court that he would not observe any judgment by the judicial committee of the privy council, Beadle refused leave to appeal to the judicial committee and declined to stay the execution. When the queen, acting on the Commonwealth secretary's advice, commuted the death sentences to life imprisonment, Beadle, arguing that Rhodesia was self-governing, refused to recognize her exercise of the prerogative of mercy. On Beadle's return to Government House, the governor asked him to pack his bags, and the regime began hanging Africans convicted before and after UDI. Two judges resigned, Beadle's reasoning having made it clear that the courts only sat and their decisions were only enforceable with the acquiescence of the regime.

Beadle unequivocally recognized UDI in September 1968, when he held that the Smith regime had attained *de jure* status as the lawful government of an independent state by reason of a successful revolution. He asserted it his duty to declare this the law, and to choose whether to continue in office under the 1965 UDI constitution, stating he was remaining as chief justice because the existing judges would best preserve the rights of citizens. Subsequently Beadle accepted office under Smith's 1969 constitution, which contained arrangements designed indefinitely to postpone African majority rule. After retirement in 1977, Beadle sat for three years as acting judge in trials under the special criminal procedure for serious 'terrorist' cases, carrying the death penalty.

A short, stocky man of ruddy complexion with a toothbrush moustache, Beadle had a blunt manner, looking hard at all whom he encountered. His drive and enthusiasm were overwhelming, whether at work, in charitable activities, or as a courageous hunter and fisherman. He had a warm family life and many friends. In 1934 Beadle married Leonie, daughter of Cecil John Barry, farmer, of Barrydale, Cape Province; they had two daughters. His first wife died in 1953 and the following year he married Olive, daughter of Major Staley Jackson OBE, chief native commissioner, of Salisbury. After her death in a car accident in 1974 he married in 1976 Pleasance Johnson.

Assessment of Beadle depends on the evaluator's predilections. 'Devious' to Harold Wilson, vicar of Bray to British officials, 'white supremacist' to African nationalists, Beadle's own view was that he did his best for his country in a time of difficult choices. His self-confidence, optimism, and drive to get a solution led him to act as go-between, to ever new formulas for compromise, and to entanglement with the regime. Identifying his country's interests with preservation of the kind of Rhodesia he had spent his political career building, rather than with any need for transition to African majority rule, Beadle ultimately saw loyalty to the usurping regime as necessary to avoid radical political reconstruction. Beadle died in Johannesburg on 14 December 1980.

CLAIRE PALLEY, *rev.*

Sources *The Times* (18 Dec 1980) · L. H. Gann and M. Gelfand, *Huggins of Rhodesia: the man and his country* (1964) · H. Wilson, *The labour government, 1964–1970: a personal record* (1971) · R. Blake, *A history of Rhodesia* (1977) · private information (1986) · personal knowledge (1986) · *CGPLA Eng. & Wales* (1981)
Wealth at death £11,598—in England and Wales: Rhodesian probate sealed in England, 1981, *CGPLA Eng. & Wales*

Beadle, John (1595–1667), clergyman and ejected minister, was born at Bramford, Suffolk, on 29 September 1595. He matriculated from Pembroke College, Cambridge, in 1613 and graduated BA in 1617. Ordained deacon in London on 31 May 1618, he proceeded MA in 1620. He became rector of Little Leighs, Essex, in December 1623, serving as a chaplain to a parishioner, Robert Rich, earl of Warwick, one of the major patrons of puritanism in East Anglia. He also came under the tutelage of the celebrated minister Thomas Hooker once the latter became lecturer at Chelmsford in the mid-1620s. Beadle was one of the signatories of a petition defending Hooker addressed to the ecclesiastical authorities in 1629.

During his ministry at Little Leighs, Beadle was not troubled by episcopal discipline, despite his inclusion by William Laud, when bishop of London, in a list of Essex ministers 'who are not conformable in preaching nor practice' (Smith, 41). However, in early 1632 his kinsman Samuel Collins, vicar of Braintree, declined the offer of the rectory of Barnston, Essex, encouraging Bishop Laud to offer it to Beadle. Beadle duly accepted and was instituted on 31 May, but here, where he was not under the aegis of Warwick, Bishop Laud formally presented him for charges relating to a long list of nonconformist practices and some rather intemperate preaching. He submitted and promised conformity, being dismissed with a canonical admonition, the lowest censure available. His submission, however, proved to be illusory. He was later indicted for his refusal to read the anti-sabbatarian Book of Sports to his congregation in 1633 and remained recalcitrant to embrace liturgical conformity. Under the Laudian regime he was last noted as a popular visiting preacher near Canterbury in 1638, delivering a divisive sermon to popular acclaim but taking flight before he could be disciplined.

During the 1640s Beadle embraced the more moderate reforms with enthusiasm, serving on the presbyterian classis for his county. He was, however, no radical, as is shown by his signature on the *Testimony of the Ministers in the Province of Essex to the Truth of Jesus Christ* (1648), a petition supporting their brethren in London against what they saw as the heresies and blasphemies of the extreme sects of the capital. He remained a reliable moderate puritan minister in his parish, accepted as an able preacher in the survey of 1650. In or before 1644 he married Rose, whose other name is unknown.

Beadle is best-known for his tract *Journal or Diary of a*

Thankful Christian, published in 1656 and dedicated to Warwick. It developed out of a series of lectures on Numbers 33: 2 that were first delivered in the 1630s and provided an encouragement to keep a spiritual journal on the grounds that this practice provides an aid to the maintenance of Christian values and an appreciation of one's contribution to the improvement of society and one's failings and inadequacies. The temptations of the world are laid out and the church is lauded as a source of support for weak Christians with the discipline and rigour of the presbyterian system being particularly acclaimed. By December 1662 Beadle had been ejected from the rectory of Barnston. However, following his death on 5 May 1667, he was buried on 11 May in the parish church. In her will dated 13 October 1672 and proved on 20 July 1676, his widow referred to their surviving daughters and two sons, including Joseph (1644/5–1692), who became a Church of England clergyman in Essex.

TOM WEBSTER

Sources J. Beadle, *Journal or diary of a thankful Christian* (1656) · T. W. Davids, *Annals of evangelical nonconformity in Essex* (1863) · *Calamy rev.*, 41 · T. Webster, *Godly clergy in early Stuart England: the Caroline puritan movement, c.1620–1643* (1997) · F. Peck, ed., *Desiderata curiosa*, 2 vols. (1732–5), bk 12 · H. Smith, *Ecclesiastical history of Essex* (1932) · Venn, *Alum. Cant.*

Beadon, Sir Cecil (1816–1880), administrator in India, born on 22 December 1816, was the youngest son of Richard Beadon (son of Richard *Beadon, bishop of Bath and Wells) and his wife, Annabella A'Court. Educated at Eton College and Shrewsbury School, Beadon joined the Bengal civil service through the patronage of his mother's brother the first Lord Heytesbury. Reaching India in 1836, he spent the initial years of his service in the usual district offices held by junior civil servants until 1843, when he was appointed under-secretary to the government of Bengal. From then onwards Beadon's rise was rapid. In 1850 Lord Dalhousie, the governor-general, selected him to represent the Bengal presidency on a commission of inquiry into the Indian postal system. This resulted in the introduction of a uniform rate of postage in the subcontinent, analogous to the English penny postage. Subsequently, and in rapid succession, Beadon served as secretary to the government of Bengal, home then foreign secretary to the government of India, member of the governor-general's council, and, finally, as lieutenant-governor of Bengal. He won high appreciation for his administrative expertise and quality of judgement from three consecutive governors-general: lords Hardinge, Dalhousie, and Canning.

During the greater part of the 1857 mutiny—the first pan-Indian challenge to British authority in India— Beadon was the home secretary, and with his governor-general, Canning, faced criticisms from sections of Calcutta's British community over their handling of the revolt. Beadon was singled out for underestimating the gravity of the crisis, but the government of India's confidence in him remained unshaken and he was appointed lieutenant-governor of Bengal in 1862. He retained this post until 1866. Shortly before his assumption of this

Sir Cecil Beadon (1816–1880), by unknown photographer

office an article in a Calcutta newspaper—otherwise critical of the Indian Civil Service—praised Beadon's honesty and resolution, but foretold a difficult period ahead. The prophecy proved to be true.

Consolidation of British rule in India and preservation of imperial interests were uppermost in Beadon's mind. In the context of the early constitutional reform, in the shape of the 1861 Councils Act, he emphasized the need to strengthen the governor-general's hand, and proposed a 'cabinet of secretaries' to be appointed by and exclusively responsible to the governor-general himself. Beadon established courts of small cases in Bengal, enacted the Calcutta Municipal Act of 1863, exercised careful supervision over revenue administration, and helped in framing the new Calcutta Police Act. He also proposed overhauling the Bengal prison system by removing the central gaol from Calcutta and building a string of prisons in different parts of the province: this latter scheme was rejected by the governor-general on grounds of cost. Beadon's minute on the Settlement of Cuttack (6 November 1866) demonstrated his determination not to deal with the ryots (peasant cultivators) 'lightly'. He even opposed the move to set free a labourer who had served two terms of imprisonment on charges of desertion. Nor were reports of maltreatment of plantation workers in Assam given any credence by Beadon. But two measures which won him popular acclaim were the imposition of checks on ghat murders and Kulin polygamy, and the prohibition, on

health grounds, of the disposal of corpses and carcasses into rivers or *nullahs* (watercourses) within the limits of Calcutta.

Riding on the crest of a conservative reaction in the aftermath of the mutiny, Beadon preferred a 'hard line' in any settlement with 'native powers', including those which had remained loyal during the 1857 tumult. As a member of the governor-general's council, he disapproved of Colonel Davidson's move to reward the nizam of Hyderabad's services during the mutiny by writing off his debts to the raj and concluding a new territorial settlement. He also dealt firmly with the north-eastern tribes and 'agitators' thought to be inciting resentment among the Santal tribal people.

However, Beadon's professional life was marked in other areas by misfortune and failures. An unprecedented depression in the tea industry came in the wake of the visit to Assam that he had undertaken to acquaint himself with the condition of the plantation industry. A staunch advocate of a strong frontier policy, he sought to suppress the recalcitrant Bhutias, but the unsuccessful diplomatic mission to Bhutan in 1864, which resulted in a gross insult to the British envoy, and the initial British reverses in the war which followed, were embarrassing for Beadon.

More significantly, the Orissa famine of 1866–7, which also affected a number of districts in Bengal, and the heavy toll of human lives it extracted, struck a blow to Beadon's administrative reputation from which he never recovered. His absence on medical grounds in the hill station of Darjeeling during the famine provoked widespread criticism, though his apologists rightly argued that his presence could not have averted the calamity; failures in the previous administration had rendered the disaster inevitable. But Beadon erred in trying to play down the impact of the famine. Dismissing the mortality estimates of the Orissa commissioner as 'exaggerated', he informed the viceroy on 22 May 1866: 'There is no actual famine, there is food enough every where but the price being high it is beyond the reach of the poor'. He disapproved of the idea of raising a general subscription for the relief and rehabilitation of famine victims; he was deeply disturbed by the Calcutta relief committee's appeal for help from England. He refused any increase in government contributions to relief operations, and certified efficient management of pauper camps and hospitals for vagrants. Unfortunately, these measures came at a time when newspapers were replete with reports of starvation deaths, the influx of destitutes into Calcutta, and grain robberies in the countryside. A commission of inquiry, subsequently appointed by the secretary of state for India, indicted Beadon's handling of the Orissa famine. The verdict was ratified by the governor-general's council in language which many of Beadon's contemporaries considered unduly severe, especially in view of the supreme government's previous concurrence with his policy. A few months after this criticism Beadon left India, his reputation as an administrator eclipsed and his health severely impaired by the stresses of his final years in office. In May

1866 he was none the less appointed a Knight Commander in the Order of the Star of India.

Beadon was married twice, first in 1837 to Harriet, daughter of Major R. H. Sneyd of the Bengal cavalry, and second, in 1860, to Agnes, daughter of W. H. Sterndale, and had several children. To most of his colleagues Beadon was gracious, conciliatory, and accessible. Lady Canning is said to have remarked that the two most perfect mannered men she knew were Sidney Herbert and Cecil Beadon. Sir Cecil died on 18 July 1880 at his home, The Corner, Latton, Wiltshire, survived by his second wife. SURANJAN DAS

Sources Boase, *Mod. Eng. biog.*, vol. 1 · *Calcutta Review*, 45 (1867), 451–69 · *Calcutta Review*, 46 (1867), 118–36 · *The Quarterly Civil List for Bengal* · C. E. Buckland, *Bengal under the lieutenant-governors*, 2nd edn, 1 (1902); repr. (1976), 272–397 · *CGPLA Eng. & Wales* (1880) **Archives** BL, letters to H. Bruce, Add. MSS 43990, 43999 · BL OIOC, corresp. with Cuthbert Davidson, MS Eur. D 728 · BL OIOC, letters to Lord Elgin, MS Eur. F 83 · BL OIOC, letters to J. C. Haughton, MSS Eur. B 135–136, D 529–530 · BL OIOC, corresp. with John Lawrence, MS Eur. F 90 · BL OIOC, Charles Wood MSS **Likenesses** photograph, BL OIOC [*see illus.*] **Wealth at death** under £16,000: probate, 13 Aug 1880, *CGPLA Eng. & Wales*

Beadon, Frederick (1777–1879), Church of England clergyman and centenarian, third son of the Revd Edward Beadon, rector of North Stoneham, Hampshire, was born in London on 6 December 1777. He was educated at Charterhouse School and at Trinity College, Oxford. He took orders in 1801, and was shortly afterwards presented by his uncle, Richard *Beadon, bishop of Bath and Wells, to the living of Weston-super-Mare. He exchanged this benefice for the vicarage of Titley, and, in 1811, was presented to the rectory of North Stoneham in succession to his father. He held the prebend of Compton Bishop from 26 May 1809 until his death seventy years later. In 1812 he was made a canon residentiary of Wells, and kept residence there each year, without interruption, until 1875. He was also chancellor of Wells Cathedral from 1825 until his death. In 1803 he married Marianne, daughter of the Revd Dr Wilder, of Purley Hall, with whom he had one son and two daughters.

Beadon came from a family distinguished for its longevity. He was of middle stature, a strongly built frame, and great muscular power, which he retained even in extreme old age. There was nothing particular in his diet or habits, except that he ate pastry and fruit more freely than meat. He drank wine in moderation. His temper was equable and cheerful. Shooting, fishing, and gardening were his favourite pursuits. He took out a shooting licence as late as 1872, and when engaged in sport seemed almost incapable of fatigue. At the same time he was never unmindful of his calling, and fulfilled its duties diligently, taking some part in the public service of the church up to his ninety-sixth year. During his residences at Wells he was an active chancellor, especially in promoting the repair of the cathedral church and the efficiency of its services. He took no part in ecclesiastical conflicts, and adhered to the practices and opinions prevalent among the clergy in his early years. He enthusiastically took part in church patronage, including

patronage for his family. He was the last of the non-resident freemen of Southampton whose privileges were reserved by the Reform Bill. In political as well as in ecclesiastical matters he was a strict conservative. Once only, in 1828, does it seem that he travelled on the continent, and he was never thoroughly reconciled to the innovation of railways.

When Beadon attained his 100th year, Queen Victoria sent him her congratulations and her photograph, which she had signed herself. To most of the letters which he received on this occasion Beadon sent immediate replies in his own hand. In the autumn of 1878 he had a severe attack of bronchitis, and from that time was confined to his room. He continued, however, to take a lively interest in the management of his farm. During the early part of 1879 he gradually lost strength, and died on 10 June 1879 at North Stoneham.

WILLIAM HUNT, rev. H. C. G. MATTHEW

Sources *The Times* (12 June 1879) · G. W. Norman, *Memoir on the life of the Rev. Frederick Beadon* (1879) · private information (1885) **Wealth at death** under £16,000: probate, 25 July 1879, *CGPLA Eng. & Wales*

Beadon, Richard (1737–1824), bishop of Bath and Wells, was born and baptized on 15 April 1737, at Pinkworthy, Devon, in the parish of Oakford, the second son of Robert Beadon (*d.* 1759), freeholder, and his wife, Mary (*b.* 1704), eldest child of the Revd Edward Squire, rector of Oakford. Beadon was thus related to Samuel Squire, bishop of St David's, Wales, and to Mrs Newcome, wife of John Newcome (*d.* 1765), master of St John's College, Cambridge.

Beadon was educated in Devon, first at Mr Wood's school, Bampton, then at Blundell's School, Tiverton. He was admitted a pensioner at St John's College, Cambridge, on 30 April 1754, matriculating in the subsequent Michaelmas term. At St John's he was a foundation scholar and Hare exhibitioner and he graduated BA (eighth wrangler) in 1758. Beadon was twice a members' prizeman—junior bachelor in 1759 and senior bachelor in 1760—and he received the chancellor's medal for classics. He proceeded MA in 1761, BD in 1769, and DD in 1780. Beadon was elected to a college fellowship on 25 March 1760 (relinquished 1773), acted as junior dean of the college in 1768–70, and was appointed public orator of the university in 1768, a post he held until resignation on 13 November 1778.

Beadon also made an impact outside Cambridge University after his ordination as deacon on 21 December 1760 and priest on 31 May 1761. He was preacher at Whitehall in 1763 and acted as chaplain to Bishop Terrick of London. The bishop gave him the rectory of Little Burstead, Essex, in 1771, which Beadon exchanged for the rectory of Orsett, Essex, in September 1775; the same year, Lord Hyde, chancellor of the duchy of Lancaster, nominated Beadon to the living of Stanford Rivers, also in Essex. Beadon received the prebend of Reculversland in St Paul's Cathedral in 1771 (collated 12 October) and held it until 1775 when he was named archdeacon of London (instituted 25 February) and awarded the prebend of Mapesbury. He failed to secure election as master of St John's College on the death of Dr Powell in 1775 by one vote—although, as William Cole noted, he 'would have filled that post with dignity' (BL, Add. MS 5864, fol. 50). On 19 August 1778 at Ditton, Beadon married Rachel, daughter of Dr John Gooch, prebend of Ely. In June 1781 Beadon was appointed to the mastership of Jesus College, Cambridge, by the expiring bishop of Ely, Edmund Keene, from a sense of past obligations to the Gooch family. According to William Cole the college was pleased to be sent Beadon rather than either Dr Watson or Dr Hallifax. Beadon had educational charge of Prince William Frederick, subsequently duke of Gloucester, during his residence at the university. Beadon acted, unusually, as vice-chancellor of the university for the consecutive years of 1781 and 1782, a sign of his exceptional administrative competence.

Royal favour made him an obvious choice for the bishopric of Gloucester in 1789 (consecrated 7 June), when he resigned as master of Jesus and archdeacon of London. Beadon was subsequently translated to Bath and Wells in 1802 (enthroned 7 June) and only then did he resign the livings of Orsett and Stanford Rivers and the prebend of Mapesbury. He was kindly and hospitable to his clergy and neighbours, but infirmity made it impossible for him to discharge his episcopal duties towards the end of his life. In politics he was a moderate whig and a correspondent of Robert Robinson, noted Cambridge dissenting minister, who thought Beadon 'a person of amiable manners and of liberal sentiments' (Dyer, 132).

Beadon and his wife had one son, Richard, who was the principal beneficiary, among several Beadon relatives, of Beadon's tenure of the Bath and Wells diocese; he received the rich episcopal manor of Wiveliscombe on a lease for three lives. Bishop Beadon published two sermons, one preached before the House of Lords on 19 April 1798, a fast day, and the other before the Society for the Promotion of the Gospel. He died at Bath on 21 April 1824 aged eighty-seven, and was buried in Wells Cathedral. Mrs Beadon survived him and resided in Charles Street, off Berkeley Square, London.   NIGEL ASTON

Sources Venn, *Alum. Cant.*, 2/1.199 · *Annual Biography and Obituary*, 9 (1825), 395 · *Annual Biography and Obituary*, 10 (1826), 222 · Nichols, *Lit. anecdotes*, 1.578–9 · Nichols, *Illustrations*, 6.650 · E. W. Bentley, *Oakford: the history of a Devon parish* (1982) · M. L. Banks, *Blundell's worthies* (1904), 84–7 · T. Baker, *History of the college of St John the Evangelist, Cambridge*, ed. J. E. B. Mayor, 1 (1869) · R. F. Scott, ed., *Admissions to the College of St John the Evangelist in the University of Cambridge*, 3: *July 1715 – November 1767* (1903), 142, 627–8, 729–31 · *Fasti Angl., 1541–1857*, [St Paul's, London], 8, 42, 55 · *Fasti Angl., 1541–1857*, [Bath and Wells], 4 · *Fasti Angl., 1541–1857*, [Bristol], 43–4 · S. H. Cassan, *The lives of the bishops of Bath and Wells*, 2 (1829), 179–80 · D. M. Greenhalgh, 'The nineteenth century and after', *Wells Cathedral: a history*, ed. L. S. Colchester (1982), 179–203 · G. Dyer, *Memoirs of the life and writings of Robert Robinson* (1796), 89, 132 · parish registers, Oakford, Devon RO · [William Cole], 'Alphabetical collections for an Athenae Cantab', BL, Add. MS 5864, fol. 50 · Som. ARS, DD/DP Box 120 C/1358; DD/CN 15/13C/173; D/D/Ba4

Archives GL, MS 9531/21

Likenesses L. F. Abbott, oils, 1789–1803, Jesus College, Cambridge; copy, bishop's palace, Wells, Somerset · possibly by L. Gahagan, plaster statuette, 25 June 1823, NPG · G. S. Facius, stipple (after L. F. Abbott), BM, NPG

Beadwulf [Baldwulf] (*fl.* **791–795**), bishop of Whithorn (known in Latin as Candida Casa), was consecrated on 17 July 791 by Archbishop Eanbald (I) of York and Bishop Æthelberht of Hexham, the last Anglian bishop of that see. He assisted at the coronation of the Northumbrian king Eardwulf in 795. The date of his death is not known. His see may have come under the nominal charge of the bishop of Lindisfarne, Heathored, but there is no evidence for an Anglian presence at Whithorn thereafter.

T. F. TOUT, *rev.* MARIOS COSTAMBEYS

Sources *ASC*, s.a. 791, 795 (texts E, F) · Symeon of Durham, *Opera*, vol. 1 · John of Worcester, *Chron.*, s.a. 791

Beaglehole, John Cawte (1901–1971), historian, was born in Wellington, New Zealand, on 13 June 1901, the second of four sons (there were no daughters) of David Ernest Beaglehole, a clerk, and his wife, Jane Butler. He grew up in a crowded quarter of the youthful city. Like most of his contemporaries, he enjoyed the benefits of a state education, first at Mount Cook School, then at nearby Wellington College. But the chief formative influence of his boyhood was the modest family home. Both his parents were discriminating readers and to his English-born mother he owed a lifelong interest in music. A brief apprenticeship to the book trade preceded his entry to Victoria University College, the institution to which he was happily affiliated for most of his career. He was active in student affairs, wrote poetry, edited the annual magazine, and assiduously read history. Graduating MA in 1924, he won a postgraduate scholarship for his thesis on William Hobson, first governor of New Zealand, served briefly as assistant lecturer, and left for England in 1926.

To a colonial, as Beaglehole boldly proclaimed himself, London was both fulfilment and challenge. He gloried in the libraries and bookshops, he revelled in the music, and gradually he responded to the shabby elegance of Bloomsbury where he lodged. On the debit side social inequalities troubled him, he was irked by the airs of some academic superiors, and he found difficulty in choosing a subject. At last, with help from Harold J. Laski, whom Beaglehole thought friendly enough to rank as a colonial, he joined University College to undertake research in colonial history. His thesis, completed in 1929, gained him a PhD, but he could not find a publisher and there seemed no prospect of employment. The only course, he reluctantly concluded, was to return home. He had been cheered by the appearance, under an American imprint, of *Captain Hobson and the New Zealand Company* (1928), a version of his MA thesis. Now he was encouraged by a commission to write a book on Pacific exploration.

For some years after his return Beaglehole led an unsettled existence, moving from one temporary job to another, often in the unlikely role of Workers' Educational Association lecturer. His liberal views earned him a reputation for radicalism and lost him a university post in Auckland. More bitter still, in 1935 he failed in his bid for the chair of history at Victoria. In these adversities he had the unfailing support of his wife, Elsie Mary, daughter of Robert Arthur Holmes, a banker; they had married in 1930 and were to have three sons. And no set-back stemmed the flow of publications—poems, articles, and notably, in 1934, *The Exploration of the Pacific*. This book led to his later research and, belatedly, to academic preferment: in 1936 he was appointed lecturer at Victoria University College.

Back in his native city (also the nation's capital), Beaglehole was drawn into many activities and enlarged his already wide acquaintance. The casually dressed scholar, somewhat resembling E. M. Forster, became a well-known figure not only in libraries and lecture halls but in government departments and more exalted centres of power. As a semi-official adviser on cultural matters he was in constant demand and took an active part in producing publications to mark the country's centennial. His contribution was *The Discovery of New Zealand* (1939) but of greater moment was his close association with J. W. A. Heenan, the imaginative public servant behind the enterprise. It was Heenan who after the war ensured state backing for Beaglehole's edition of the *Journals* of Captain James Cook, published by the Hakluyt Society. The first volume, dedicated to Heenan's memory, appeared in 1955 and the last in 1967. A bulky appendix was *The Endeavour Journal* of Sir Joseph Banks (1962). When he died at his Wellington home, on 10 October 1971, he was revising his biography of Cook. Edited by the historian T. H. Beaglehole, his second son, it came out in 1974.

In his last decade Beaglehole received many honours, academic and civic, culminating in the Order of Merit conferred in 1970. He was appointed CMG in 1958 and fellow of the Royal Society of New Zealand in 1967. Victoria (now an independent university) appointed him to the chair of British Commonwealth history in 1963, made him an honorary LittD five years later, and following his death opened in his memory the superbly situated research room, fit setting for the fine portrait by W. A. Sutton. In 1966 he received an honorary DLitt from Oxford. His reputation rests firmly on the Cook journals, surely one of the classic works of historical scholarship. His personal qualities included generosity, a passion for justice, and a sometimes waspish humour. E. H. McCORMICK, *rev.*

Sources *Landfall* (Dec 1971) · *Turnbull Library Record* (Aug 1970) · *Turnbull Library Record* (Oct 1981) · M. Wilson, *John Cawte Beaglehole: a bibliography* (1972) · personal knowledge (1986) · private information (1986)
Archives NHM, corresp. with W. R. Dawson
Likenesses W. A. Sutton, portrait, Victoria University, New Zealand

Beake, Robert (*d.* 1708), local politician and army officer, is of obscure origins. Having served his apprenticeship, by 1642 he had established himself as a member of the Coventry Drapers' Company. On the outbreak of civil war he raised a regiment for parliament in northern Warwickshire and he subsequently fought for parliament throughout the war. He remained under arms during the later 1640s, and in 1650 achieved the rank of major. His motivation to fight was almost certainly religious. A staunch puritan, he was a prominent member of an Independent congregation in Coventry, but also remained on good terms with his presbyterian neighbours.

Following the parliamentary victory in the civil war, Beake played an increasing part in the civil and military administration of Coventry and Warwickshire, acting as governor of Coventry in 1650, as sheriff of Warwickshire from 1650 to 1651, and as an assessment commissioner for the county from 1650 to 1652. He also served as an ejector for Warwickshire from 1654, as a commissioner for securing the peace of the Commonwealth in 1656, and as a justice of the peace for the county from 1656 to 1660. A common councillor in Coventry from 1652 to 1655 and an alderman from 1655 to 1662, he also served as mayor of the city during 1655 and 1656. He represented Coventry in all three protectorate parliaments, was master of the Coventry Drapers' Company from 1656 to 1657, and from 1656 to 1659 held national office as a commissioner for the admiralty.

Throughout the interregnum Beake displayed a conspicuous godly approach to the administering of all these posts. A moderate Independent and conservative Cromwellian in outlook, he proceeded with equal vigour against all those who appeared to threaten the survival of the new godly state in England. When the notorious Ranters Abiezer Coppe and Joseph Salmon appeared at Coventry in 1650, he moved quickly to deal with the threat they posed to public order. He helped to organize their arrest and, according to Salmon, was involved in the discussions in prison which led to their subsequent recantation. Beake's godly zeal is most evident, however, in the diary he kept during his year as mayor of Coventry in 1655 and 1656. This reveals that he was tireless in his prosecution of those who offended his godly values by drinking in unlicensed alehouses, swearing, engaging in illicit sexual activity, or profaning Sunday by working, travelling, or frequenting alehouses.

Beake's year as mayor coincided with the period of Edward Whalley's administration of Warwickshire as major-general. At the outset, the relationship between the two men was strained by disagreements over their respective ranks. To avoid giving the impression that Whalley exercised a superior authority, Beake absented himself from the official delegation which welcomed him to Coventry in late November 1655, and a few days later he protested when the major-general 'upon a mistake' occupied a more prominent position than him in church. Thereafter, however, the two worked together closely to implement the government's policies. Whalley regarded Beake as one of the regime's strongest supporters in the west midlands, and on one occasion commented of him: 'there is none here I am confident will be more faithful to his highness, none I am sure so able to serve him in these parts, having a great interest with the godly' (MS Rawl. A. 33, fols. 39–40). As a member of the 1656 parliament Beake supported both the offer of the crown to Cromwell and the restoration of the House of Lords.

Beake's prominence in local politics was brought to an abrupt end by the restoration of the monarchy in 1660. In July of that year his election the previous March to the

Convention Parliament was declared void, and he was forced to withdraw from the house. Eighteen months later, in February 1662, he resigned his position as alderman of Coventry to avoid being purged under the Corporation Act of that year. While he remained a prominent member of the Coventry dissenting community which met at Leather Hall in the city, he did not hold public office again until the late 1670s. In 1679 he was returned to the first Exclusion Parliament, once again as member for Coventry. He sat on seven of the house's committees and voted in favour of the bill to exclude James, duke of York, from the succession. He failed, however, to secure election for the second Exclusion Parliament. He was clearly regarded as a strong supporter of the whigs, for in the wake of the Rye House plot against Charles II his home was searched for arms. Following the deposition of James II in 1688, Beake served as a local commissioner for inquiring into recusant fines, and in 1701 he once again acted as master of the Coventry Drapers' Company. He remained, however, a contentious figure, and in 1701 he was apparently pelted with stones and vegetables as he went to vote in the election of that year. He died in Coventry in September 1708 and was buried in St Michael's Church, Coventry, on the 22nd of that month. At the time of his death he owned an estate of 80 acres at Stoke Golding in Leicestershire. His wife, Elizabeth, had died in 1689 and was buried on 24 September of that year. Their one child, a daughter, married into a local Warwickshire gentry family.

CHRISTOPHER DURSTON

Sources 'The diary of Robert Beake, mayor of Coventry 1655–6', ed. L. Fox, in *Miscellany I*, ed. L. Fox, Dugdale Society, 31 (1977), 111–37 · A. M. Mimardière, 'Beake, Robert', HoP, *Commons, 1660–90*, 1.611–12 · A. Hughes, 'Politics, society and civil war in Warwickshire', PhD diss., U. Lpool, 1980 · A. Hughes, *Politics, society and civil war in Warwickshire, 1620–1660* (1987) · *Diary of Thomas Burton*, ed. J. T. Rutt, 4 vols. (1828) · E. Whalley, letters to John Thurloe, Bodl. Oxf., MS Rawl. A. 33

Beal, Samuel (1825–1889), Sinologist, was born at Devonport on 27 November 1825, the son of William Beal (1785–1872), a Wesleyan minister, and his wife, Mary Anne. He was the younger brother of William *Beal (1815–1870), a religious writer. He was educated at Kingswood School (1834–40) and the Devonport classical school, before matriculating on 13 November 1843 as a sizar at Trinity College, Cambridge, where he graduated BA in 1847. He was headmaster of Bramham College, Yorkshire, from 1848 to 1850 and was ordained deacon on 18 November 1850 and priest on 23 November 1851.

After serving as curate at Brooke in Norfolk and Sopley in Hampshire, Beal applied for the office of naval chaplain, and was appointed as such to HMS *Queen* on 8 December 1852, and as naval instructor on 14 July 1853. On 18 August 1853 he was appointed to HMS *Sybille* which was sent to China. During his service in China, he devoted his spare time to the study of the Chinese language. He became so proficient in the colloquial as well as the literary dialect that he was able to act as naval interpreter in 1857 during the hostilities in the Canton River. His services were commended by the commodore and gazetted.

But Beal's main object in studying the language was to gain a greater understanding of Chinese Buddhism, of which he was among the first European scholars.

After his return to England in 1857 Beal was appointed chaplain to the marine artillery (1863–7), and then to the Pembroke (1867–72) and Devonport (1873–7) dockyards. He was chaplain of St George's, Portsea (1872–3), and in 1877 he was appointed rector of Falstone in Northumberland. In 1880 he became rector of Wark-on-Tyne, and in 1888 rector of Greens Norton in Northamptonshire. He continued with his Chinese studies and in 1877 he was appointed professor of Chinese at University College, London, and in 1885 the degree of DCL (Durham) was conferred on him in recognition of the value of his researches into Chinese Buddhism, on which he wrote and translated a number of texts. He died, unmarried, at the rectory, Greens Norton, Northampton, on 20 August 1889.

R. K. DOUGLAS, *rev.* JANETTE RYAN

Sources Venn, *Alum. Cant.* · O'Byrne, *Naval biog. dict.* · *The Times* (24 Aug 1889) · Crockford (1885) · Register of Kingswood School, 1910 · Allibone, *Dict.*
Wealth at death £1191 12*s.*: administration, 14 Sept 1889, *CGPLA Eng. & Wales*

Beal, William (1815–1870), religious writer, was born on 9 December 1815 in Sheffield, the eldest son of William Beal (1785–1872), a Wesleyan minister, and his wife, Mary Anne. Samuel *Beal was his brother. Educated at King's College, London, in 1834, and from 1835 to 1842 at Trinity College, Cambridge, he took the degree of BA in 1841. In the same year he was ordained deacon, and was made vicar of Brooke, near Norwich, in 1847, a post he held until his death. He was also curate of Sampford Spiney, Devon, 1841–2, and occasional curate of Bray, 1834–7. He was married; his wife's name was Mary Ann. The degrees of MA and LLD were conferred on him by the University of Aberdeen in 1845. At Brooke he originated the parochial harvest home, and was corresponding member of the Working Men's Congregational Union and vice-president of the YMCA. His interest in promoting the education of the working classes led to his becoming headmaster of Tavistock grammar school, vice-president of the Norwich People's College, and, from 1855 until his death, diocesan inspector of schools. He died on 20 April 1870 at Aigle, Canton de Vaud, Switzerland. His written works include books on Gaelic settlement, church unions, and the people's colleges. He edited a volume of *Certaine Godly Praiers for Sunday Times* (1846) and the *West of England Magazine* from 1840 to 1847.

ALFRED GOODWIN, *rev.* SARAH BROLLY

Sources Boase, *Mod. Eng. biog.* · Allibone, *Dict.* · *Men of the time* (1868) · Crockford (1860) · *CGPLA Eng. & Wales* (1870)
Archives W. H. Smith Ltd Archive, genealogical notebooks
Wealth at death under £3000: probate, 6 July 1870, *CGPLA Eng. & Wales*

Beale family (*per. c.*1836–1912), lawyers, businessmen, and politicians, were already a well-established merchant family in Birmingham by the late eighteenth century.

William John Beale (1807–1883), the founder of Beale & Co., solicitors, of Birmingham and London, was the younger son of William Beale (1770–1843), a leading figure in Birmingham. William's eldest son, **Samuel Beale** (1803–1874), had adopted a commercial career and was engaged in several successful ventures—banking, railways, and ironworks. He was instrumental in founding the Birmingham and Midland Bank in 1836 (later the Midland Bank), of which he later became a director. He was also closely associated with the Midland Railway, being a director and chairman from 1844 to 1864. As well as taking an active role in the public life of Birmingham (he was mayor in 1841), he also sat as member of parliament for Derby (1857–65), a town with strong links with the Midland Railway Company. He died on 11 September 1874.

William John Beale, choosing law as a profession, qualified as a solicitor in 1837, the same year in which he married Martha Phipson. He entered into partnership with Thomas Colmore, a relative of his father's third wife, Ann. The subsequent success of the firm illustrates the significance of family connections as a source of business and the contribution of prominent solicitors in public life.

In addition to managing the Colmore estates, Beale became legal adviser to the Midland Railway. From the mid-1840s this part of the firm became extensive and the large amount of parliamentary work associated with railway promotion led to the establishment of a separate London office. The success brought by railway work attracted large commercial and financial concerns as clients. Though a staunch Liberal and, like the rest of the family a prominent member of the Unitarian denomination, W. J. Beale did not take a large, visible role in local affairs. The exception to this was his philanthropic activities in connection with the general hospital and the organization of the triennial music festivals. He purchased a small estate at Dolgellau in north Wales, building a residence there in 1867: it was here that he died on 21 May 1883.

Three of William John's four sons entered the legal profession. The eldest, **Sir William Phipson Beale**, baronet (1839–1922), born on 29 October 1839 in Birmingham, was called to the bar in 1869 after a scientific education and a brief spell at the Sheffield ironworks, of which Samuel Beale was a director. He married Mary, daughter of William Thompson, on 5 August 1869. William Phipson was elected member of parliament for South Ayrshire (1906–18), having earlier bought an estate in the county. He was created a baronet in 1912, and died in Dorking on 13 April 1922.

The other two sons succeeded to their father's firm; one remained in Birmingham, while the other took over the running of the London office. **James Samuel Beale** (1840–1912), born on 5 December 1840 in Birmingham, became head of the London office and was intimately involved in the affairs of the Midland Railway as its solicitor from 1867 until his retirement in 1905. His knowledge of railway law, and his skill in negotiations and the conduct of parliamentary procedure were widely recognized. This expertise was frequently called on by royal commissions, departmental committees, and the Railway Companies Association, of which he was solicitor for some time. In later years he was a director of the Midland Railway and president of the Law Society (1908) and built Standen in Sussex (acquired by the National Trust in 1972). He married Margaret, daughter of Algernon Sydney Field, another solicitor, on 19 April 1870. He died at Standen on 28 August 1912.

The professional career of the third son, **Charles Gabriel Beale** (1843–1912), though based in Birmingham, had many similarities with that of his elder brother. Born on 10 May 1843 at Courtlands, Harborne Road, Birmingham, and educated at Trinity College, Cambridge, he became solicitor to the Birmingham and Midland Bank and a legal adviser to the Midland Railway. His attributes as a negotiator were also acknowledged and after retirement he was appointed a member of the royal commission on the working of the railway conciliation scheme in 1911. The business experience and legal expertise gained in professional life were also valued in Beale's later years when he became heavily involved in the conduct of municipal affairs in Birmingham in the post-Chamberlain period. He served on many of the corporation's important committees and was thrice mayor in consecutive years between 1897 and 1900. He was active in many areas of public life. On the founding of the University of Birmingham he became vice-chancellor, and, like his father, he was a principal organizer of the music festivals. Beale moved within the influential Unitarian circle and on 7 August 1868 married Alice, daughter of Timothy Kenrick, a local manufacturer, whose sisters married Joseph Chamberlain and Thomas Martineau. He died in Birmingham on 1 September 1912.

By the end of the nineteenth century the Beales were firmly placed in the professional middle class, having built a dynasty based on the practice of law. However, their professional activities demonstrate how the worlds of law and business could overlap.

The firm of Beale & Co. was carried on by the two sons of Charles Gabriel: Hubert (1869–1954) and Edmund (1872–1952). The brothers also introduced their sons into the firm during the inter-war years. James's eldest son, John Beale (1874–1935), though qualified as a solicitor, pursued a successful career in the iron and steel industry. The last member of the family connected with the firm was Charles Beale (1913–1989) of Birmingham, a grandson of Charles Gabriel Beale. The London office remained, but with no family representative.   ANDREW ROWLEY

Sources notes, letters, newspaper cuttings, copies of inscriptions, heraldic and other illustrations, and a pedigree relating to the Beale family of Birmingham and elsewhere, 1865–1958, Birm. CL · *Edgbastonia*, 14 (1894), 145–50 · *Birmingham Magazine*, 2 (1899), 32 · newspaper cuttings by Osborne, Birm. CL, 1.227 · *WWW*, 1941–50 · *Birmingham biography*, newspaper cuttings, Birm. CL, 45, 72, 80, 92 · *Railway Gazette*, 17 (1912), 251, 275, 279 · W. J. Pike, ed., *Birmingham at the opening of the twentieth century: contemporary biographies* (1901), 51 · *WWBMP*, vol. 1 · Boase, *Mod. Eng. biog.* · private information (1996) · *CGPLA Eng. & Wales* (1874) [Samuel Beale] · *CGPLA Eng. & Wales* (1883) [William John Beale] · *CGPLA Eng. & Wales* (1912) [James Samuel Beale and Charles Gabriel Beale] · *CGPLA Eng. & Wales* (1922) [William Phipson Beale] · m. certs. [William Phipson Beale, James Samuel Beale, Charles Gabriel Beale] · Burke, *Peerage* (1916)
Archives Birm. CA

Wealth at death under £350,000—Samuel Beale: probate, 6 Nov 1874, CGPLA Eng. & Wales • £115,748 16s. 11d.—William John Beale: probate, 12 July 1883, CGPLA Eng. & Wales • £150,000—James Samuel Beale: probate, 2 Oct 1912, CGPLA Eng. & Wales • £135,637 12s. 6d.—Charles Gabriel Beale: probate, 18 Oct 1912, CGPLA Eng. & Wales • £95,378 0s. 9d.—William Phipson Beale: probate, 24 May 1922, CGPLA Eng. & Wales

Beale, Bartholomew (bap. 1656, d. 1709). See under Beale, Mary (bap. 1633, d. 1699).

Beale, Charles (bap. 1660, d. 1726?). See under Beale, Mary (bap. 1633, d. 1699).

Beale, Charles Gabriel (1843–1912). See under Beale family (per. c.1836–1912).

Beale, Dame Doris Winifred (1889–1971), nurse, was born on 9 August 1889 at 42 London Road, Sydenham, London, the daughter of George Beale, master draper, and his wife, Annie Maria, formerly King. Doris was educated at Prendergast School, Lewisham, and on leaving school she worked as a clerk before eventually embarking on nurse training at the Royal London Hospital. She was appointed a probationer at the London Hospital on 11 October 1912, and attended the usual six-week preliminary training course at Tradegar House, Bow. Her training certificate was awarded on 16 December 1916 and she passed with honours. The training record proclaimed that 'she gave the impression that she had the latent capacity for ward management and for taking more responsibilities' (Royal London Hospital, archives LH/N/4/4). Doris was promoted to holiday sister on 26 November 1914, and, in the register of sisters and nurses held at the Royal London archives, she is described as one who 'fully justified her promotion as holiday sister' (ibid.). Clearly the London Hospital wished to retain the services of Doris Beale, and the matron, Eva Luckes, offered her an appointment as sister of a children's ward. However, for some time Doris had harboured ambitions to join the Queen Alexandra's Royal Naval Nursing Service. Eva Luckes, recognizing that these ambitions were dearly held, gave Doris her full support.

Thus on 7 February 1917 Doris left the London Hospital to join the Queen Alexandra's Royal Naval Nursing Service. As a nursing sister she worked in the following locations: Royal Naval Hospital (RNH) Plymouth (1917), RNH Haslar (1918), RNH Gibraltar (1919), RNH Chatham (1923), RNH Malta (1925), and RNH Chatham (1927). As sister-in-charge Doris worked at the Royal Naval College, Dartmouth, from 1930 until 1933, when she became the superintending sister at RNH Chatham. On 10 March 1937 she was promoted to the rank of matron, and served first at RNH Haslar and later at RNH Plymouth.

On 14 July 1941 Doris became matron-in-chief, and was based at RNH Haslar until 19 September 1941, when she was moved to RNH Chatham. Here she remained for just over a year. She moved to the medical department of the Admiralty on 10 November 1942, and finally retired from naval service on 13 July 1944. Her main contribution to nursing lay in her commitment to the training of nurses and in her leadership skills. During her years of naval service Doris was awarded the Royal Red Cross second class (ARRC) in 1937, and the Royal Red Cross (RRC) and bar in 1944; she was made a dame of the British empire on 6 June 1944.

After retiring from naval service Doris became a prominent member of the joint war organization of the British Red Cross and the order of St John. Between August 1944 and September 1946 she worked as deputy matron-in-chief of their trained nurses department. Her untiring efforts on behalf of the British Red Cross were recognized in 1951, when she was awarded the Florence Nightingale medal by the international committee of the Red Cross.

Doris Beale's energy was also valued by the governing body of Prendergast School, Lewisham. She displayed a keen interest in the fortunes of her old school, and acted as governor from 1945 to 1964. She was also a member of the United Nursing Services Club, and her recreations included gardening and travel. Throughout her life Doris demonstrated tireless compassion for the sick and wounded, and invaluable leadership skills for her junior nurses. A slim, elegant, and attractive woman, Doris was greatly respected by her friends and colleagues. She died suddenly and peacefully at her home, 84 London Road, Forest Hill, London, on 14 January 1971. Her body was cremated following a service at St Paul's, Forest Hill, two days later. She was unmarried.   PENNY STARNS

Sources private information (2004) [J. Evans, archivist of the Royal London Hospital; Capt. Hambling, director of naval nursing services] • training record; nurses' registers, Royal London Hospital, LH/N/4/4 • b. cert. • d. cert. • WWW • The Times (16 Jan 1971) **Archives** British Red Cross Archives, Surrey • Royal London Archives • Royal Naval Nursing Service Archives, Portsmouth **Wealth at death** £24,541: probate, 13 July 1971, CGPLA Eng. & Wales

Beale, Dorothea (1831–1906), headmistress, was born in London on 21 March 1831 at 41 Bishopsgate Street Within, the fourth child and third daughter of the eleven children of Miles Beale (d. 1862) and Dorothea Margaret Complin (d. 1881).

Family and education Miles Beale came from a Gloucestershire family but spent most of his life as a doctor in London. His high-church views made a deep and lasting impression on Dorothea as did his love of English literature, particularly of Shakespeare, a subject on which he delivered lectures at Crosby Hall, Chelsea, which she attended. He was also probably responsible for the business competence which was so noticeable in her later career. Miles was concerned that his daughters receive the best education then available for women and was an interested and enthusiastic supporter both of his daughter's later aspirations and of the improvement in women's education in general. Four of his daughters became teachers.

Dorothea Beale's mother, who was descended from a French Huguenot family, was a cousin of the feminist Caroline Cornwallis, whose views were influential in the Beale family. Consequently, when Dorothea showed an early interest in books and study she was encouraged to develop it. Mrs Beale took pains to find a competent governess, no easy task at that time, and subsequently a school with a reputation above the average, even though

Dorothea Beale (1831–1906), by G. H. Martyn & Sons

in later years her daughter remembered chiefly its limited syllabus and the rote learning. She left the school at thirteen and for the next three years educated herself at home, drawing on the libraries of the London Institute and Crosby Hall, and what she learned from her mother's sister. Inspired by reading the life of Pascal she set herself to reading Euclid in the original Greek, an experience which she later claimed made her realize the value of original research and of systematic teaching. In 1847 Dorothea and her two elder sisters were sent to Mrs Bray's school for English girls in Paris. She felt that the quality of her study at home was much superior and she hated the rigid routine. The experience was short-lived as the girls were brought home on the outbreak of the 1848 revolution. In the same year, the Governesses' Benevolent Institution extended its activities by opening Queen's College, Harley Street, London. Dorothea and her sisters were among the first to attend lectures there. Over the next few years she received diplomas certifying her ability to teach most of the subjects learned by girls at that time. Within a year she was herself teaching mathematics there. She also continued her study of Greek, a language which she loved for its association with both the New Testament and the philosophy of Plato.

In 1854 Dorothea Beale was asked to teach Latin to the junior class at Queen's College and accepted the post of head teacher of the preparatory school. She was only twenty-three, so the appointment is both a measure of her talents and of the lack of well-trained, experienced teachers. During this period she visited schools in Germany and Switzerland, adopting methods of teaching mathematics which she observed there. She also published an account of the activities of the deaconesses at Kaiserwerth. At the end of 1856 she resigned from Queen's, unhappy with the management of the school, which was in the hands of the dean, Charles Grenfell Nicolay, of whose educational policies she did not approve. Immediately she accepted the post of head teacher in the Clergy Daughters' School at Casterton, Westmorland, the model for Charlotte Brontë's Lowood. This was a mistake and she left after barely a year, being out of sympathy with the strict Calvinistic regime and unable to bear the strain of teaching a wide syllabus to her usual high standard. In the first half of 1858 she wrote *The Student's Text-Book of English and General History* (6th edn, 1862), intended for the use of teachers. It was written in response to an outcry over the alleged Romanizing tendencies in the new edition of Henry Ince's standard school textbook and to meet the need for something other than the catechisms and abridgements so common in girls' schools. Together with her subsequent *The Student's Chronological Maps* (1863) it enjoyed great popularity until superseded by more up-to-date works. It set a new standard in the teaching of the subject by placing the important facts of English history in a coherent order and in the context of European history. It extended the notion of history to cover events up to the mid-nineteenth century, although subsequent editions were not updated. While considering her future, Dorothea Beale was also teaching at a school in Barnes run by her sister Eliza and Miss Elwall. Although careers in social work were suggested to her, there was no doubt in her mind that her life should be devoted to teaching girls and she applied for several headships.

Cheltenham Ladies' College In June 1858 Dorothea Beale was elected principal of Cheltenham Ladies' College, a post which she held until her death. The college had been founded in 1854 by a group of Cheltenham residents wishing to provide, at a reasonable price, an education that did not sacrifice learning to accomplishments and would fit its pupils for their later domestic roles. Founded on the same proprietary system as Cheltenham College it was, and remained for some years, primarily a day school, socially exclusive, taking children from the age of five, initially including small boys. From the start it was envisaged that there would be some form of external examination annually and strict discipline in the classroom, reinforced by a rule of silence. When Dorothea Beale took up her post the school was on the verge of collapse, with a falling roll, little money, and leasehold premises available only for the next two years. The school survived only by the exercise of the strictest economy and reorganization of its finances in 1860. It was hard to find properly qualified staff, a problem which persisted until pupils trained in the school were available for employment.

Parental prejudices had to be taken into account and Miss Beale, always moderate and diplomatic in her approach to changes, initially accepted that mathematics should not be part of the syllabus because parents objected to their girls learning boys' subjects. Much scientific knowledge had to be smuggled into the syllabus through physical geography and more emphasis was placed on 'accomplishments' than she would have liked. Latin was replaced by German, which Miss Beale considered to be equal in value as a mental training, quite apart from her conviction that Latin literature was unsuitable for young girls. For many years she did much of the teaching herself, her particular strengths being history, English, and, when it was finally introduced in 1868, mathematics. History and English literature were taught with what has been described as a puritan regard for the moral lessons to be learned from the deeds of particular role models. Her *Great Englishmen: Short Lives* published in 1881 is a series of such moral portraits. Many of her lectures on Dante, a particular love of hers, Chaucer, Spenser, and other writers were essays concentrating on the moral and spiritual virtues of Beatrice, Britomart, or Griselda, who were held up as examples to the girls. When she reduced her teaching duties, giving way to younger teachers educated with different priorities, she continued to express her views through religious instruction, which she never gave up and which replaced the sermons of boys' schools' headmasters, and through a steady stream of papers and articles, mainly published in the college magazine, which she edited for many years.

Whatever the initial limitations of the syllabus, Dorothea Beale's methods ensured that her pupils were successful. She insisted on regular testing to ensure that information had been properly learned and understood. All work had to be marked and initialled by teachers, the pupils then correcting their errors on a fresh page. Although she was not in favour of competitive examinations for girls on the pattern of those then taken by boys, she ensured from the first that there were annual examinations on their work by external examiners, many of them Oxford dons, to ensure that high standards were maintained and, incidentally, that the school's successful programme was broadcast throughout the educational world. Her strong personality, sense of purpose, and deeply held faith impressed both girls and parents. Numbers rose steadily, and within ten years of her appointment the school was well launched.

The education of girls Beale's success commanded attention and on 19 April 1866 she gave evidence before the schools inquiry commission (the Taunton commission) as one of a few leading women educationists, mobilized by Emily Davies, to appear as witnesses before the commissioners. The publication of the commission's report (December 1867) was a turning point both for the education of girls and for Dorothea Beale. For the first time the gross inadequacies of most girls' schools were exposed in reports written by men, who included Liberal young dons, such as James Bryce and T. H. Green, committed to the extension of high quality education for both sexes. The climate of opinion engendered by the commission encouraged Dorothea Beale to publish articles expounding her own views on the education of middle-class girls.

In 1865 she read a paper at the Bristol Social Science Congress explaining the proprietary school arrangements of the college. This was followed by an article in *Fraser's Magazine* (October 1866) in which she tackled the question of the medical fitness of girls to study and sit exams in the same way as their brothers. She also arranged for the sections on women's education in the Taunton commission report to be published separately (1869), at her own expense, prefaced by her analysis of the problems and their solutions. Here she argued for the release of middle-class girls from 'the tyranny of custom' which forced them to enter either 'a daily round of unceasing visiting and frivolous busy-ness' or to 'cast off the yoke, not of these alone, but of wholesome custom, of lawful authority'. Women had been freed from the drudgery of household tasks by the progress of modern science and technology, so they should be properly taught, using modern textbooks, to use and cultivate their minds in order to become civilized and spiritually enriched. She countered the arguments used by parents and doctors that such study was in any way morally or physically harmful and then outlined in some detail a programme of study based upon her own experiences and achievements at Cheltenham.

In the next fifteen years the college expanded and prospered. During this period Miss Beale provided new, permanent accommodation for the school with proper boarding facilities, and improved both staffing and syllabus. By 1880 Cheltenham Ladies' College was teaching a full syllabus including mathematics and classics. It was to continue growing in size and in functions throughout the decade. Miss Beale had long recognized the need for properly trained teachers. Her solution was to encourage capable pupils to enter the teaching profession and to found in 1876 a small boarding-house for pupil teachers who could not afford the Cheltenham fees. In 1885 this was reconstituted as St Hilda's College, Cheltenham. She had hoped that the guild of old girls would fund this project, but it chose instead to start a settlement in the East End of London, a scheme in which she took little interest. St Hilda's College, Cheltenham, provided many of the teachers for the college, who were encouraged, when it became possible, to study for London University degrees. She also revived the preparatory section, which had not long survived the original foundation of the college. Organized on the principles of Pestalozzi and Froebel, it was instituted in 1883, one of the first of its kind in the country. By the end of the century it was possible to spend one's entire life at Cheltenham from the age of five through to retirement from the staff. The school had become a community of over 1000, linked to many other schools at home and abroad, and teaching children from preparatory level right through to university degrees. Her methods were encapsulated in *Work and Play in Girls' Schools* (1898), to which Miss Soulsby and Miss Dove, headmistresses who had taught at Cheltenham, contributed sections on the moral aspects of education and on sport respectively. Dorothea never took much interest in sport, while recognizing the need for 'rational' exercise of some kind. But, always open to well-argued proposals and aware that in some respects her own views were increasingly regarded as conservative, even out of date, she made provision for it in the 1890s.

The basic principles and aims of Miss Beale's educational system remained, at the end of her life, much the same as they had been at the beginning. For her education was a means to personal fulfilment without the object of earning a living. It had a deeply religious content and motivation; it was the way towards a fuller understanding of God and his works, in itself justification enough for its pursuit. She believed that everybody had talents which it was their duty to develop as far as they were able and then to use to their best ability. In most cases this would be within the context of family life, but for the exceptionally able or for those who had to earn their living it would be in the teaching profession and other fields which were opening up to women as the century progressed. The fully developed syllabus catered for the middle-class girl destined for marriage and motherhood, but also for the talented scholar. The main point was that all should be able to do their duty to the best of their ability and not waste time on frivolous, unprofitable pursuits, summed up in the one dismissive word 'accomplishments'. But, unlike some of her contemporaries, Miss Beale always assumed that most of her girls would not have to earn a living and she was therefore never in favour of placing girls on the same footing as boys. Consequently, she was always opposed to competitive examinations but she did not stop able girls from sitting them. She encouraged her girls to pursue higher education through the college, in preference to Oxford and Cambridge, where women were fighting for equal treatment with men. But she did not discourage the ablest women from going to Oxford and Cambridge. She was always ready to recognize and nurture exceptional talent; her ground rules were designed for the majority who were not so gifted.

Despite her preference for St Hilda's College, Cheltenham, Dorothea Beale already had plans for a college in Oxford in the 1880s. Her intention was that it should be for Cheltenham girls and staff who wished to spend a year pursuing leisurely research and reading without necessarily taking any examinations. The scheme was vigorously resisted by the heads of the other women's colleges, who felt it would devalue their efforts to establish the right of women to take degrees. But in 1893 St Hilda's Hall was opened. Miss Beale's original intentions were soon forgotten, most of the students taking examinations. After the first few years she took little part in the academic affairs of the college but maintained strict financial control, for she had personally provided the funds for its establishment in much the same way as she had for many of the Ladies' College boarding-houses. She never fully understood or sympathized with the aspirations of the heads of the other women's colleges. St Hilda's College, Oxford, never had for her the same importance as Cheltenham Ladies' College. On her death she left it only its furnishings, paid for by herself, and £500, leaving the bulk of her estate, £55,000, to the Ladies' College.

Influence and reputation As the reputation of the Ladies' College spread Miss Beale became involved in the development of women's education more generally. She was one of the founder members of the Association of Head Mistresses, which began with a membership of eight in 1874 but had over 230 members by the end of her life. She took an increasingly active part in educational conferences in England, Europe, and the United States, developing contacts throughout the world. She was approached for help and advice in setting up and staffing girls' schools elsewhere. Although she confined her energies largely to educational matters she had contacts in the women's movement. She was a member of the Kensington Society and she supported both women's suffrage and Josephine Butler's campaign against child prostitution. Her achievements were recognized by a request to give evidence to the royal commission on secondary education (the Bryce commission) in 1894, by numerous invitations to attend conferences and public functions, and, in 1902, by the award of an LLD at Edinburgh University.

Dorothea Beale had, as a headmistress, the same status and role in girls' education as Arnold of Rugby or Thring of Uppingham had in that of boys. At the start of her career, as she often said, education for girls was superficial and inadequate. Middle-class girls were more ignorant than working-class girls who attended state-funded elementary schools. Her generation had to fight for the right to study 'boys' subjects' and to sit examinations. They also had to establish the governess as a respected, professional teacher. In both these endeavours she played a leading and distinctive role. In the development of the Ladies' College as an institution she demonstrated an exceptional capacity for financial management and control which enabled her to weather bad times and to extend the college buildings from one modest house to a large Gothic pile architecturally much influenced by Ruskin, whom she admired and who approved her aspirations. But her administrative skills were accompanied by a personality expressing ideals and aspirations which deeply impressed her pupils. She liked her pupils to talk of her 'marriage' to the college, as if she were a nun, and at one time contemplated setting up a secular religious teaching order. Her faith was central to her life even when, in middle age, she suffered from doubts. Her scripture lessons, conducted amid absolute silence, were remembered with awe as much for the beauty of her speaking voice as for the emotional charge she imparted to her teaching. Though in later years her teaching role decreased, she never permitted anything to diminish her pastoral role. She had the knack of knowing what was going on and a presence in the classroom which was felt even if she was not there. Her manner of dealing with the lawbreaker was quiet but devastating. 'You must never let a child have the satisfaction of holding out against you', she advised young teachers. She sometimes spoke her mind with a frankness bordering on brutality. Personally reserved, austere, small in stature, and dignified, she was in later life often likened to Queen Victoria. But despite her shyness, she developed some strong friendships with former pupils and in times of trouble could always be relied on for practical or spiritual help and much kindness.

Dorothea Beale died on 9 November 1906 in a nursing home at 5 Royal Parade, Cheltenham, following an operation for cancer. After cremation in Birmingham, her ashes were interred on 16 November in Gloucester Cathedral at a ceremony attended by virtually the whole college.   JACQUELINE BEAUMONT

Sources E. Raikes, *Dorothea Beale of Cheltenham* (1908) · M. P. G. Kerr, 'The work and influence of Dorothea Beale in the light of developments in the education of girls and women since 1850', MA diss., U. Lond., 1951 · E. Kaye, *A history of Queen's College, London, 1848–1972* (1972) · N. Glenday and M. Price, *Reluctant revolutionaries: a century of headmistresses, 1874–1974* (1974) · F. C. Steadman, *In the days of Miss Beale: a study of her work and influence* (1931) · A. H. Jackson, *A Victorian childhood* (1936) · J. E. Courtney, *Recollected in tranquillity* (1926) · E. Oswald, *Reminiscences of a busy life* (1911) · *Cheltenham Ladies' College Magazine* (1931) [Dorothea Beale centenary volume] · J. Kamm, *How different from us: a biography of Miss Buss and Miss Beale* [1958]

Archives Cheltenham Ladies' College · St Hilda's College, Oxford

Likenesses photograph, 1859, repro. in Raikes, *Dorothea Beale*, facing p. 108 · B. R. Norton, oils, 1874, Cheltenham Ladies' College · G. H. Martyn & Sons, photograph, *c.*1902, repro. in Raikes, *Dorothea Beale*, facing p. 340 · J. J. Shannon, oils, 1904, Cheltenham Ladies' College · bronze medallion, 1904, NPG · A. Drury, medallion, *c.*1908, Gloucester Cathedral · J. E. Hyett, marble bust, Cheltenham Ladies' College · G. H. Martyn & Sons, photogravure, NPG [*see illus.*] · F. Meyer, miniature, Cheltenham Ladies' College · E. Stirling, plaster bust, St Hilda's College, Oxford · photograph, NPG

Wealth at death £74,106 10s. 8d.: probate, 22 Dec 1906

Beale, Francis (*bap.* 1621?, *d.* in or before **1666**), writer on chess, may plausibly be identified with Francis Beale of Axe Yard, Westminster, who was baptized on 30 November 1621 at St Margaret's, Westminster. If this is correct, he was the first of the four children of Francis Beale (*d.* 1662), gentleman, and his wife, Alice Whittney, who were married at St Margaret's on 1 May 1620. After attending Charterhouse School for three years, he was admitted to St John's College, Cambridge, on 27 May 1640 and matriculated in 1641. He graduated BA at Magdalene College, Cambridge, in 1644, and served Charles I in the civil war. However, his parents were on the parliamentary side and his mother caused him to be prayed for in St Martin-in-the-Fields Church, that he might return and be converted. He probably knew Samuel Pepys, the diarist, who from 1658 to 1660 lived in the same house in Axe Yard as Beale's father, whom Pepys described as 'old Beale' when he paid him rent (S. Pepys, *Diary*, 15 March 1660).

Beale was the author of the *Royall game of chesse play, sometimes the recreation of the late king with many of the nobility, illustrated with almost an hundred gambetts, being the study of Biochimo, the famous Italian* (1656). This contained a translation of one of Gioachino Greco's works, previously circulated in manuscript. According to Murray 'the verb "castle" first occurs in Beale' (*History of Chess*, 832). The book also contained a frontispiece portrait of Charles

I. The daring inclusion of this portrait during the Commonwealth period indicates that the author was a royalist. One edition of the book contains a poem, 'To his Honoured Friend on his Game of Chesse-Play', signed R. Lovelace (Richard Lovelace, 1618–1658, cavalier and poet). Lovelace's poems were republished posthumously in 1659, when this poem was described as being addressed to 'Dr. F. B.'; no other evidence has emerged, however, to confirm Beale's doctorate. Lovelace was also friendly with the poet Charles Cotton (1630–1687), to whom is attributed *The Compleat Gamester* (1674), which includes a chapter on how to play chess. The game was commonly played for stakes in gaming houses (of the kind portrayed vividly by Cotton), and perhaps Beale, Lovelace, and Cotton used to meet in one of them.

Beale was still alive when his father made his will on 4 March 1662. He may or may not be the Francis Beale, citizen of Westminster, who died intestate a year later, administration being granted to his widow, Mercey, on 25 March 1663. He was probably dead, however, by April 1666, when his mother's death resulted in administration being granted to her creditor with no mention of Beale.   C. G. LEWIN

Sources H. J. R. Murray, *A history of chess* (1913) · H. Foulis, *The history of the wicked plots and conspiracies of our pretended saints* (1663), 181 · W. C. Hazlitt, *Lucasta: the poems of Richard Lovelace esq.* (1864) · J. E. B. Mayor, ed., *Admissions to the College of St John the Evangelist in the University of Cambridge*, 1: *Jan 1629/30 – July 1665* (1882), xxiin. · Venn, *Alum. Cant.* · B. Marsh and F. A. Crisp, eds., *Alumni Carthusiani: a record of the foundation scholars of Charterhouse, 1614–1872* (1913), 13 · A. M. Burke, ed., *Memorials of St Margaret's Church, Westminster* (1914) · Westminster rate book, 1659, City Westm. AC, E173, p. 7 (Axe Yard) · administrations [Aliciae Beale 4/1666; Francis Beale, 1663, Bond 10/185; Mercey Beale and others, 1663] · will, 4 March 1662, City Westm. AC [Francis Beale sen.], 163 · BL, Sloane MS 1708, fol. 107 [brief notes on 'Mr Beale a Physitian']

Beale, James Samuel (1840–1912). *See under* Beale family (*per. c.*1836–1912).

Beale, Jerome (*d.* **1631**), college head, was born in Worcestershire. He graduated BA from Christ's College, Cambridge, in 1596 and became a fellow of Pembroke in 1598. He proceeded MA in 1599 and BD in 1607. As a chaplain and protégé of Lancelot Andrewes, master of Pembroke until first consecrated bishop in 1605, Beale received successive appointments in Andrewes's dioceses. In 1608 he was made a prebendary of Chichester and in 1609 he became vicar of Cowfold in that diocese, and of West Wittering. He was also rector of Nuthurst (Chichester) from 1609 to 1613. Following Andrewes's translation to Ely, Beale was granted the rectory of Hardwicke from 1613 and in 1615 he became rector of Willingham: his surviving correspondence suggests that he was actively engaged in that parish, defending his parishioners' interests against Sir Miles Sandys in a land dispute (1622–3).

On 16 March 1617 Beale was collated to the third prebendal stall at Ely. John Whitgift, who had himself been master of Pembroke for three months in 1567, had held the same stall from 1568 to 1577. Supported by Bishop Andrewes in a contested election, Beale became master of Pembroke on 21 February 1619 and received his DD the same year. He served as vice-chancellor (1622–3), when George Herbert first became university orator. Like his younger brother William *Beale (d. 1651), Jerome emerged as an anti-Calvinist, for which he was much criticized at this time by Ralph Brownrigg and others.

As vice-chancellor Beale entertained the Spanish ambassador, Don Carlos de Colonna, and the envoy of the archduchess, Ferdinand de Boisschot, baron of Saventhem, during their joint visit to Cambridge in February 1623. This followed the Brussels conference of the previous summer and was intended to resume the English initiative in the diplomatic negotiations surrounding the proposed Spanish match in which his Pembroke colleague Matthew Wren was much involved. As Beale later assured the king, on 19 March, the university suitably honoured 'the Mercurie of Brabant, and the Mars of Spaine' although the Spanish match later failed (Beale, sig. E2r). He also edited the Cambridge paean *Gratulatio de principis reditu ex Hispaniis* (1623).

As head of a Cambridge college, and while he was vice-chancellor, Beale used the good offices of William Boswell, secretary to the lord keeper, Bishop John Williams, to keep the bishop informed of decisions and developments. That relationship began to sour a little when in January 1623 Beale was unable to secure for him the university living of Ditton, Herefordshire. Nor was it helped when that September he failed to have Boswell's brother Thomas made joint proctor. By the year end there was a distinct cooling, and although Boswell rearranged his family Christmas to accommodate Beale he was telling friends that he thought that no friend of his would entertain Beale if they knew as much of him as he did.

Beale's seeming irascibility made for his downfall; on 8 November 1624 he proceeded, against the college statutes, to pre-elect three fellows when there were no vacancies and no quorum. When, five years later, this was complained against him, Thomas Boswell was one of the petitioners. The resulting case was heard by Samuel Harsnett, archbishop of York, who eight years earlier had himself been forced by his colleagues to resign as master of Pembroke. In February 1630 Harsnett and Earl Holland, the chancellor, found against Beale and suspended him; the draft order for the suspension was written at Whitehall by William Boswell. However, the college heads petitioned for Beale to be allowed to sue for mercy, and the vice-chancellor, Dr Butts, master of Corpus Christi, intervened successfully at court on his behalf: the commission was never enacted. It perhaps helped that Beale had been among those in Cambridge who in 1628 had contested Samuel Ward's Calvinist teachings.

Beale died, probably unmarried, early in 1631; administration of his estate was granted to his brother William on 6 May. The portrait of Gondomar, the former Spanish ambassador, that he had obtained during the negotiations of 1623, passed to his brother, who left it to St John's College, Cambridge.　　　　　　　NICHOLAS W. S. CRANFIELD

Sources Venn, *Alum. Cant.* · J. Beale, *True copies of all the Latine orations made and pronounced* (1623) · PRO, SP 14/132/15; 133/1; 133/15; 133/50; 134/18; 137/8; 137/49; 143/88; 152/14; 154/33; 155/74; 175/93; SP 16/141/20; 144/40; 159/16; 159/29; 160/14–160/44; 161/79; 160/55–160/63; 16/161/2–3; 163/78 · will, PRO, PROB 6/14A, fol. 29r · CUL, Mm 1.39, p. 136 · A. L. Attwater, *Pembroke College, Cambridge: a short history*, ed. S. C. Roberts (1973) · Bodl. Oxf., MS Tanner 71, fols. 10–11, 15; 72, fol. 314; 80, fol. 143 · N. Tyacke, *Anti-Calvinists: the rise of English Arminianism, c.1590–1640* (1987) · W. Sussex RO, Ep 1/1/8, fols. 40r, 42v, 44v · K. Fincham, *Prelate as pastor: the episcopate of James I* (1990), 54, 144 · CUL, department of manuscripts and university archives, VC Prob Inv. 1631

Wealth at death see will, PRO, PROB 6/14A, fol. 29r

Beale, John (*bap.* 1608, *d.* 1683), Church of England clergyman and writer on agriculture and natural philosophy, was baptized at Yarkhill, Herefordshire, on 17 April 1608, the sixth and youngest son of Thomas Beale (1575–1620), a lawyer and prominent gentleman farmer, and his wife, Joanna, *née* Pye (1576–1660). His father was an early exponent of cider orchards, cultivating the famous redstreak apple on his Yarkhill estate, while the Pyes, one of the wealthiest families in Herefordshire, were related to the Scudamores of Holme Lacy, who also helped to establish the county's cider-making reputation. Between 1618 and 1622 Beale attended Worcester Cathedral school, where the headmaster, Henry Bright, inspired his lifelong admiration for Erasmus. From this early age Beale carefully cultivated 'a promptness of knitting all my reading and studies on an everlasting string', learning by heart such works as Ovid's *Metamorphoses*, Melanchthon's *Logicks*, Magirus's *Physica*, and Ursinus's *Theologica* (*Works of … Boyle*, 5.426). He displayed considerable interest in mechanics and physics and experimented with insects and animals. In 1622 Beale entered Eton College, coming under the equally seminal influence of the prominent humanist scholar John Hales. The provost, Sir Henry Wotton, also introduced Beale to Francis Bacon's utilitarian philosophy and stimulated his interest in astronomical optics. At the same time Beale studied many agricultural and horticultural works, and developed a lifelong belief in prophetic dreams. Meanwhile, through his maternal uncles Sir William Pye and Sir Robert Pye, respectively attorney-general of the court of wards and auditor of the exchequer, he had early access to court, and considered himself a favourite of Buckingham before the latter's assassination in 1628. He claimed to have received offers of employment from Archbishop Laud and Charles I, which he rejected because of a growing disaffection with their policies.

On 20 July 1629 Beale matriculated from King's College, Cambridge; he became a fellow in 1632, graduated BA in 1633, and proceeded MA in 1636. His prodigious art of memory stood him in good stead with the usual undergraduate texts:

> I could at last learn them by heart faster than I could read them—I mean, by the swiftest glance of the eye, without the tediousness of pronouncing or articulating what I read. Thus I oft-times saved my purse by looking over books in stationers' shops.

He was subsequently able to lecture without notes to King's College students, 'which I did for two years together, in all sorts of the current philosophy' (*Works of … Boyle*, 5.426). Beale's continuing private study included hermetic and mechanical philosophy, experiments with telescopes, thermometers and sundials, and an examination of the university's recently acquired eastern manuscripts.

Between 1636 and 1638 Beale travelled in Europe, acting as tutor and guardian to his cousin Robert Pye and the latter's future brother-in-law, George Speke, whose Somerset background overlapped with Beale's maternal connections there. In Paris they visited their mutual kinsman John, first Viscount Scudamore, who was then English ambassador. Beale also carefully acquired rare books and manuscripts at Orléans, Lyons, and Geneva. On their return Edward Phelips, another distant relative, presented Beale, on 24 February 1638, to the living of Sock Dennis, Somerset, in succession to the late Philip Edmunds. This was already little more than a sinecure, the church being described in the next century as having been long desolate and the once populous village near Ilchester as reduced to a single dwelling owned by the Phelips family (Collinson, 3.307–8).

Beale now entered what he retrospectively regarded as the most distressing years of his life. Finding his scientific views unpopular at Cambridge, he resigned his fellowship at King's College in late 1640. With the advent of civil war he became an early victim of sequestration, being extruded from Sock Dennis and forced to return to Herefordshire, living for a time at Cobwall, where he had inherited a tenancy. About this time he married Jane Mackworth of Shropshire, perhaps Jane (*bap.* 1621, *d.* in or after 1675), daughter of Thomas Mackworth, MP for Ludlow in 1644; they had at least two sons and three daughters. When Hereford was besieged in the summer of 1645 they were forced to flee to the parliamentary camp at Shrewsbury commanded by Jane's kinsman Humphrey Mackworth, who may have been responsible for Beale's temporary intrusion to the parsonage of Westbury in 1646. When Mackworth shortly afterwards became governor of Shrewsbury, Beale served as his chaplain. Beale was now walking a tightrope: his earlier family connections led to accusations of royalist sympathies, but he was equally castigated for alleged Independent zeal. In reality he was a moderate who happily removed to Stretton Grandison, close to his birthplace, in 1647. In 1649 he became master of St Catherine's Hospital, Ledbury, but was shortly afterwards removed by Major-General Thomas Harrison in favour of the Baptist John Tombes, a dispossession that Beale was unable to overturn at the Restoration. Some time in the early 1650s the patronage of Sir Richard Hopton's wife, Elizabeth, secured Beale's intrusion as vicar of Stretton Grandison, a situation which saw him threatened with a lawsuit in 1658. In August 1654 Beale became a member of the Herefordshire committee for ejecting scandalous ministers and in 1657 and 1658 he took a leading role in establishing the Herefordshire Association of Ministers.

Despite the considerable turbulence of these years Beale continued his practical pursuits. In 1652 he purchased the manor of Cobwall and its associated lands. He actively promoted use of the redstreak and genet moyle apple varieties in the area, where his knowledge of cider production earned him considerable praise. In 1653 he published *A Treatise on Fruit Trees*, containing valuable sections on cider, perry, and English vineyards, which was reissued in 1657. Beale began a weekly correspondence with Samuel Hartlib in 1656, two of his early letters being published as *Herefordshire Orchards, a Pattern for All England* (1657). This work, which reputedly gained his native county some £100,000 within a few years, brought Beale to Oliver Cromwell's favourable notice, but he declined the latter's offer of employment. The pamphlet was reprinted with Richard Bradley's *New Improvement of Planting and Gardening* in 1724 and 1739, but by the early nineteenth century was considered 'scarce and valuable' (Nichols, *Lit. anecdotes*, 1.447). Beale also composed *Observations on some parts of Bacon's natural history, as it concerns fruit trees, fruits and flowers* (1658).

Beale now became an active provincial member of the Hartlib circle, corresponding with John Evelyn, Henry Oldenburg, and Robert Boyle. Hartlib wrote to Boyle on 27 April 1658:

> There is not the like man in the whole island, nor in the continent beyond the seas, so far as I know it … that could be made more universally use of to do good to all, as I in some measure know and could direct. (*Works of … Boyle*, 6.105)

The circle saw him as an important theological commentator on baptism and the eucharist, and empathized with his developing millenarianism, belief in prophetic revelation, and evangelic piety. As a Christian humanist he also espoused a tolerant latitudinarian religious settlement. Between 1657 and 1661 Beale similarly corresponded in Latin with the Revd John Oliver, minister of Montacute, Somerset, concerning various prophetic visions reported at Amsterdam. He also wrote to his Somerset contacts about the attitudes of various Christian denominations to the sacramental nature of matrimony. Such interests were tempered by a utilitarian approach to a wide variety of scientific, horticultural, and agricultural topics. Beale had continued his astronomical and optical investigations with the assistance of his brother Richard (1599–1656), and in December 1658 argued that education in the use of mathematical instruments, optical glasses, and thermometers provided 'more … valuable truth in one houre than a carte loade of monckish philosophy' (Hartlib MSS). Praising the stimulating mutual exchange of information in the search for scientific truth, Beale also communicated details concerning herbal remedies, mnemonic systems, and military ciphers.

Beale's improving fortunes were now confirmed by four key appointments that he held until his death: the rectorships of Yeovil, Somerset (1660), and again of nearby Sock Dennis (April 1661); fellowship of the Royal Society (21 January 1663); and chaplain-extraordinary to Charles II (3 March 1665). This last position, apparently on the recommendation of the Hopton family, granted prestigious status, but was far less onerous than that of either chaplain-in-waiting or chaplain-in-ordinary. It is unclear whether Beale ever actually attended at court in this capacity.

Oldenburg read Beale's paper 'Aphorisms concerning cider' before the Royal Society in 1662. This impressive account of the successful transformation of poor Herefordshire rye land into prosperous cider orchards prompted the society to appoint a committee to investigate ways of promoting such undertakings elsewhere in England. The newly elected Beale was encouraged to collaborate with Evelyn in the preparation of *Pomona* (1664), which incorporated the 'Aphorisms'. Beale subsequently bore the cost of distributing 20,000 grafts of Herefordshire redstreak and genet moyle apples and barland pears to Somerset, Devon, and Dorset. Grafts were also circulated among the society's members, who were encouraged to propagate them for further distribution. In 1677 Beale wrote *Nurseries, Orchards, Profitable Gardens and Vineyards Encouraged*, advocating the greater availability of timber and fruit trees. Beale's passionate encouragement provided a crucial catalyst to the expansion of orchard cultivation well into the eighteenth century.

Beale's campaigning embraced many other subjects, much of it centred on his active membership of the Royal Society's georgical committee. He also gave willing assistance to Oldenburg, editor of the *Philosophical Transactions* between 1665 and 1677, compiling at least one, if not all, of the indexes and contributing numerous articles and reviews, many of them anonymously. Beale's recurrent themes were improvement, expansion, and reform via the dissemination of knowledge and encouragement of ingenuity. Agriculture, horticulture, forestry, botany, diet, technology, trade, and education were all tackled with relish in a visionary desire to transform England into a prosperous, highly industrious, and fully employed island utopia. Beale naturally continued to report experiments on sensory aids, optical instruments, thermometers, and barometers, but he saw labour intensive agriculture as the key. Enclosure, irrigation, and fertilizers were discussed alongside the diversification from grain and wool into root vegetables, kitchen and market gardening, nuts, and silk. The immigration of skilled foreign artisans was also deemed desirable. Beale even planned a history of agriculture and gardening and drew up a questionnaire into current provincial practices, but his ambitious idealism foundered on the rocks of scarce administrative resources and rural resistance to reform.

Beale's submissions to the *Philosophical Transactions* reveal his continuing fascination with local accounts of unusual natural phenomena. In 1666 he provided the 'narrative of a stone taken out of the womb of a woman near Trent in Somerset' and 'some promiscuous observations' including 'oak as black as ebony found in the moors about Bridgwater', 'a vitriolate water at Socke to which pigeons resort, but cattle will not drink', and 'eels in frosty weather found in heaps' between Langport and Bridgwater. In 1669 and 1670 Beale offered several discussions of salt, mineral, and medical springs in the Yeovil district and of a coalmine near Wincanton, while in 1672 he reported on 'a strange frost which hath lately done much hurt about Bristol'. Beale was also responsible for drawing up the rules and orders for a Yeovil almshouse 'extracted out of the translated copy of one of the tripartite indentures' (Collinson, 3.212). When his eldest son, John (d. 1684), a

physician, prepared to set out from Somerset for Jamaica in 1675 Beale witnessed his will.

After Oldenburg's death brought the *Philosophical Transactions* to an end in 1677 Beale sought a new medium for his views, making anonymous contributions to John Houghton's weekly *Collection of Letters for the Improvement of Husbandry and Trade* following its launch in September 1681. However, Beale saw Houghton's subsequent defence of Charles II's courtly extravagance as both atheistic and Hobbesian. He planned a riposte in a lengthy pamphlet 'From Utopia', but this was overtaken by illness. In his last known letter to Boyle, dated 8 July 1682, Beale indicated that he was suffering from infirmities that required him to dictate extempore and that he lacked a regular amanuensis. The thrust of the incomplete manuscript of 'From Utopia' was mercantilist, Beale arguing that England had much to learn from its dangerous Dutch enemy, not least their lowering of interest rates, establishment of a national bank, and adoption of agricultural improvements. Above all, he praised the superiority of their Calvinistic thrift, sobriety, industry, and humility over the debauched excesses and luxuries of French popery. Beale was buried at Yeovil on 16 April 1683.

PATRICK WOODLAND

Sources Sheffield University, Sheffield, Hartlib papers · RS, Boyle papers · RS, early letters · Christ Church Oxf., John Evelyn MSS · letters from Beale to Hartlib and Evelyn, BL, Add. MS 15948 · J. Beale, letters to Christopher Wase, Bodl. Oxf., MS Corpus Christi College C. 332 (CW), fols. 18–29 · *The correspondence of Henry Oldenburg*, ed. and trans. A. R. Hall and M. B. Hall, 1–11 (1965–77) · *The diary and correspondence of Dr John Worthington*, ed. J. Crossley and R. C. Christie, 2 vols. in 3, Chetham Society, 13, 36, 114 (1847–86) · *The works of the Honourable Robert Boyle*, ed. T. Birch, new edn, 6 vols. (1772) · M. Stubbs, 'John Beale, philosophical gardener of Herefordshire: pt I, prelude to the Royal Society (1608–1663)', *Annals of Science*, 39 (1982), 463–89 · M. Stubbs, 'John Beale, philosophical gardener of Herefordshire: part II, the improvement of agriculture and trade in the Royal Society (1663–1683)', *Annals of Science*, 46 (1989), 323–63 · C. Webster, *The great instauration: science, medicine and reform, 1626–1660* (1975), esp. 478–82 · C. Webster, 'The origins of the Royal Society', *History of Science*, 6 (1967), 106–28 · J. Thirsk, ed., *The agrarian history of England and Wales*, 5/2 (1985) · R. K. French, *The history and virtues of cyder* (1982) · parish register, Yarkhill, 17 April 1608, Herefs. RO, AD 56/1 [baptism] · W. Sterry, ed., *The Eton College register, 1441–1698* (1943) · PRO, lord chamberlain's records, LC 3/26, fol. 127v · J. Collinson, *The history and antiquities of the county of Somerset*, 3 (1791), 212, 221, 307–8 · Venn, *Alum. Cant.* · parish register, Yeovil, Som. ARS, 16 April 1683 [burial] · copy presentation to the living of Sock Dennis; corresp. from John Beale to John Oliver, c.1657–61, Som. ARS, DD/PH225/24; DD/PH205 · Nichols, *Lit. anecdotes*, 1.447 · F. W. Weaver, ed., *Somerset incumbents* (privately printed, Bristol, 1889) · C. J. Robinson, *A history of the mansions and manors of Herefordshire* (1872) · F. W. Weaver, ed., *The visitation of Herefordshire … 1569* (1886) · visitation of Hereford, BL, Harley MS 1422, fol. 106 · N. M. Sutherland, 'Pye, Walter', HoP, *Commons, 1558–1603*, 3.265 · E. Rowlands, 'Hopton, Sir Edward', HoP, *Commons, 1660–90*, 2.581–2 · Watt, *Bibl. Brit.* · J. Britten and G. S. Boulger, eds., *A biographical index of British and Irish botanists* (1893) · E. Green, *Bibliotheca Somersetiensis* (1902) · will, PRO, PROB 11/377, sig. 122 [John Beale, son] · G. F. T. Beale, 'Revd. John Beale, D.D., rector of Yeovil', *Notes and Queries for Somerset and Dorset*, 13 (1912–13), 178

Archives BL, letters to Hartlib and Evelyn, Add. MS 15948 · BL, corresp. with Henry Oldenburg, Add. MS 4294 · Bodl. Oxf., letters to Christopher Wase, MS Corpus Christi College C. 332 (CW), fols. 18–29 · Christ Church Oxf., John Evelyn MSS · RS, letters to Royal

Society and Boyle papers · Som. ARS, corresp. with John Oliver · University of Sheffield Library, Hartlib papers, corresp., and papers

Wealth at death est. held approx. 120 acres in Herefordshire in mid-1650s: Stubbs, '*John Beale*', part I, 478

Beale, Lionel Smith (1828–1906), physician and microscopist, was born on 5 February 1828 at Bedford Street, Covent Garden, London, the only son of Lionel John Beale (1796–1871), surgeon and first medical officer of health for St Martin-in-the-Fields, and Frances Smith Beale (1800–1849), the third daughter of James Frost Sheppard. Of his three sisters, one was the artist Sarah Sophia *Beale, and another, Ellen Brooker (1831–1900), was married to the Shakespearian scholar William Watkiss Lloyd. After attending a private school in Highgate, Beale entered King's College School, London, at the age of nine, and began an association that lasted for almost the whole of his career. Apprenticed to an apothecary and surgeon in Islington at thirteen, Beale matriculated at the University of London with honours in chemistry and zoology in 1847; he then worked for two years as assistant to Henry Wentworth Acland in the Anatomical Museum at Oxford. He obtained his licence of the Society of Apothecaries in 1849 and in the same year was an inspector for the Board of Health, monitoring the cholera epidemic in Windsor. In 1850–51 he was resident physician at King's College Hospital, and he graduated MB (London) in 1851. In 1859 he married Frances (*d.* 1892), only daughter of the Revd Peyton Blakiston MD FRS of St Leonards.

In 1852 Beale established a private laboratory in Carey Street and taught medical students physiological chemistry and normal and morbid anatomy, with special emphasis on the use of the microscope. In 1853, at the age of twenty-five, he succeeded Robert Bentley Todd as professor of physiology at King's College, being preferred to Thomas Henry Huxley among other candidates. For the first two years Beale shared the post with William Bowman (1816–1892), who had been Todd's assistant, but he was subsequently sole professor until he resigned the post in 1869. He was then made physician to King's College Hospital and promoted to professor of medicine in 1876. He held both positions until ill health prompted his retirement in 1896, though he retained his links with King's, being nominated emeritus professor and honorary consulting physician. His lectures did not prepare students for passing examinations, but were valued for their scientific merit, and he was also highly regarded as a clinician, especially for speed and intuition in diagnosis. This skill was no doubt honed in the many examinations he made as medical adviser to the Clerical and Medical Assurance Company. He also acted from 1891 to 1904 as physician to the pensions commutation board and as government medical referee for England.

Beale's name became well known in medicine from the 1850s as a result of the popularity of his books on the clinical uses of microscopy. In 1854 he published *The Microscope and its Application to Clinical Medicine*, which set out the procedures of microscopy and showed clinicians how to use the instrument in diagnosis through the examination

Lionel Smith Beale (1828–1906), by Henry Tanworth Wells, 1876

of urine, blood, tumours, and parasites. This manual went through four editions, the last of which was published in 1878. A companion volume, *How to Work with the Microscope*, was first published in 1857 and appeared in its fifth and final edition in 1880. Beale was ahead of his time as a pioneer of clinical pathology, as this medical specialism was not formally established in Britain until the 1920s.

Beale was a tireless researcher and a prolific writer on microscopy, histology, and chemical pathology. Initially he worked with William Bowman on the histology of renal structures and muscle fibres, but his range of interests soon grew, as is evident from his publications: *On some Points of the Anatomy of the Liver of Man and Vertebrate Animals* (1856), *On Urine, Urinary Deposits and Calculi, their Microscopical and Chemical Examination* (1861, and later editions with amended titles in 1863, 1869, and 1885). He edited the journal *Archives of Medicine* from 1857 to 1870. His last major work on clinical medicine appeared in 1880, entitled *On Slight Ailments, their Nature and Treatment*. In this volume, first delivered as a lecture series at King's College, Beale demonstrated his diagnostic acumen and therapeutic knowledge, including many of the wrinkles he had learnt from the previous generation of great clinicians.

To facilitate the differentiation of the component parts of cells and tissues, Beale developed various techniques of staining and fixing, most notably with his carmine solution. He also pioneered the practice of fixing tissues by injections to prevent alterations after death, and the use of high-power, oil-immersion magnification. Notable among his many novel observations was his identification of the pyriform nerve ganglion cells, now called 'Beale's cells'. Beale never shied away from controversy in any field, as was evident in his long dispute with the German histologists Wilhelm Kühne and Rudolf von Kölliker over how nerve endings terminated in voluntary muscle. He illustrated all of his publications with his own excellent drawings, many of which were coloured. In the early 1860s his work on differential staining led him to distinguish two fundamentally different types of protoplasm—'germinal' and 'formed' matter—and his ideas were first published as *On the Structure of the Simple Tissues of the Human Body*, in 1861. The German translation published in the following year caused controversy because of Beale's apparent departure from the dogma of cell theory. Much of the material was then reworked, though with more philosophical reflections, in a series of lectures at King's College in 1865, and published as *On the Structure and Growth of the Tissues, and on Life* (1865).

Beale undoubtedly did more than any other medical scientist of his generation to diffuse the new techniques and approaches of laboratory medicine, especially microscopy, to English-speaking audiences on both sides of the Atlantic. Indeed, this aspect of his work was more influential than his original research and hypotheses on germ theories of disease, the nature of life, and the relations between science and religion.

In 1866 Beale's standing as a researcher led to an invitation from the royal commission on the cattle plague to make investigations of the histology of the epizootic disease that was decimating British livestock. In his report he claimed to have found the 'germs' of the disease. However, he was unable to convince his peers of the truth of his observations, or of the explanation of the disease he proposed. Beale developed a germ theory of disease, in which the causative agents of disease were elements of degraded protoplasm not independent micro-organisms. His 'disease-germs' were composed of what he called 'bioplasm', which he saw as elements of protoplasm that were more like fundamental units of life than cells. He argued that disease-germs arose within the human body, and he opposed the germ theories of Pasteur and others who implicated ferments, fungi, bacteria, parasites, and other 'external' agents. His ideas on disease and germs were set out in his Radcliffe lectures at Oxford in 1868–9, and published in two volumes in 1870: *Disease Germs, their Supposed Nature* and *Disease Germs, their Real Nature, an Original Investigation*. Both works were reissued in 1872 in a single volume, *Disease Germs, their Nature and Origin*. In the same year he published *Bioplasm, an Introduction to the Study of Physiology and Medicine*. Although soon regarded as misguided, Beale's objections to the eventually all-conquering bacterial germ theory were well grounded and in the early 1870s were widely cited by those who were opposed to Pasteur, Lister, Tyndall, and their followers.

Concurrent with his writing on germs Beale produced a cluster of linked publications, both biological and philosophical, on the nature of life. In 1870 he published *Protoplasm, or, Life Force and Matter*, and *The Mystery of Life*, in which he replied to the attack on vitalism mounted by Sir William Gull (1815–1890) in the Harveian oration of that

year. The religious influences on Beale's ideas and work were revealed in *Life Theories: their Influence on Religious Thought* (1871). All these publications advanced the claims of vitalism against what Beale saw as the growing influence of mechanistic materialism in biology, in medicine, and in culture more generally. Polemics against those who sought to reduce biology to physics and chemistry, and to deny that there was an absolute difference between living and non-living matter, became the major theme of Beale's writing. The boldness of his views stemmed from his conviction that modern biological knowledge supported the existence of a vital force in living organisms. Beale's standing in medical science and his prolific output should have made him a major figure in the nineteenth-century debate on science and religion, but he largely failed to engage his peers, despite the production of pamphlets with provocative titles such as *The New Materialism: Dictatorial Scientific Utterances and the Decline of Thought* (1885). In large part this was because the issue of materialism versus vitalism was seen to be largely metaphysical, it not having the same immediacy as, for example, the question of evolution had for relations between humankind and animals. Beale was convinced that there was no necessary conflict between science and faith, and set out the basis of his views in 1887 in a long essay, *Our Morality, and the Moral Question, Chiefly from the Medical Aspect*. After retirement Beale's convictions and penchant for polemics remained as strong as ever and he continued to rail against atheism, materialism agnosticism, monism, and free thought. His series of essays entitled *Vitality* (1898, 1899, and 1900) had more recognition and impact than his earlier writings.

Beale had two sons, the elder of whom died while the family was visiting Beale's lifelong friend Edward Thring (1821–1887), headmaster of Uppingham School. This death deepened Beale's already close friendship with Thring, whose ideas were a major influence on Beale. The second son, Peyton Todd Bowman Beale MRCS, shared his father's interests in microscopy and publishing. An indefatigable worker, Beale took no real holiday after 1858. He eschewed alcohol and ate little meat. He was of moderate height and of sturdy build, with remarkable, abundant hair that remained brown until he was seventy. An enthusiastic gardener, he made his country home in Surrey at Weybridge, where he grew palms and Japanese plants, while in a small greenhouse at 61 Grosvenor Street, where he lived for forty-five years, he successfully grew orchids and other hothouse plants. In 1904 he left Weybridge, where he had taken a cottage in 1885 because of his wife's ill health, and moved to the house of his surviving son, 6 Bentinck Street, London. He died there on 28 March 1906 and was buried at Weybridge cemetery three days later.

Beale was elected a member of the Royal College of Physicians in 1856 and became a fellow in 1859; he was a frequent examiner, a member of its council in 1877 and 1878, censor in 1881 and 1882, and curator of the museum from 1876 to 1888. In 1871 he was awarded the Baly gold medal for his physiological work and in 1875 he delivered the Lumleian lectures. Elected a fellow of the Royal Society in 1857, Beale was Croonian lecturer in 1865; his address was entitled, 'The ultimate nerve fibres distributed to the muscles and some other tissues'. He joined the Royal Microscopical Society in 1852, and was president in 1879 and 1880 and treasurer from 1881 to 1890.

Beale was a key figure in the development and diffusion of medical laboratory techniques in Britain from the 1850s and was a leading London physician for half a century. In the last quarter of the nineteenth century his ideas and commitments, especially his robust defence of vitalism, distanced him from his scientific peers and made him a focus of Christian opposition to scientific materialism. MICHAEL WORBOYS

Sources *Nature*, 73 (1905-6), 540 · *The Lancet* (7 April 1906) · *BMJ* (7 April 1906), 836-7 · *The Times* (29 March 1906) · P. H. P. S., *PRS*, 79B (1907), lvii–lxiii · G. Geison, 'Beale, Lionel Smith', *DSB* · W. D. Foster, 'Lionel Smith Beale and the beginnings of clinical pathology', *Medical History*, 2 (1958), 269-73 · G. H. Brown, ed., *Lives of fellows of the Royal College of Physicians of London, 1826-1925* (1955), 100 · *WWW*
Archives Bodl. Oxf., letters to Sir Henry Wentworth Acland · UCL, Sanderson MSS
Likenesses H. T. Wells, oils, 1876, RCP Lond. [*see illus.*] · Beynon & Co., lithograph (after H. Hale), Wellcome L. · Maull & Polyblank, photograph, Wellcome L.
Wealth at death £14,880 16s. 11d.: probate, 19 April 1906, *CGPLA Eng. & Wales*

Beale [*née* Cradock], **Mary** (*bap.* 1633, *d.* 1699), portrait painter, was born at Barrow rectory, Suffolk, and baptized on 26 March 1633, the elder of two children of the Revd John Cradock (*c.*1595-1652), the puritan rector of Barrow, and his wife, Dorothy Brunton or Brinton (*d.* 1643). Evidence suggests that she received a good education from her father who, as an amateur artist, probably also provided her with tuition in painting.

On 8 March 1652 Mary Cradock married Charles Beale (*bap.* 1631, *d.* 1705), member of a puritan family at Walton Manor, Buckinghamshire. The couple took up residence at Covent Garden, London, later moving to Hind Court, Fleet Street, when Charles succeeded to his father's post of deputy clerk of the patents office about 1660. By this date Mary Beale had not only given birth to two sons, Bartholomew and Charles [*see below*], but had already gained some reputation as an artist: she was mentioned together with three other female painters in Sir William Sanderson's *Graphice … or, The most Excellent Art of Painting* (1658). One of her earliest extant works is the *Self Portrait with Husband and Son* (*c.*1663; Geffrye Museum, London). Her early influences seem to have included Robert Walker, the Commonwealth portraitist, and the miniaturist Thomas Flatman.

By 1664 Charles Beale's job had become insecure, and, with the plague threatening, the family departed for Albrook, Otterbourne, Hampshire. While there, Mary wrote the 'Essay on friendship' (BL, Harleian MS 6828, fols. 510-23) in which she propounds the somewhat radical notion (for the period) of equality between men and women, both in friendship and marriage. Her philosophy was put into practice when, upon their return to the city in 1670, it was decided that she would establish herself as

Mary Beale (*bap.* 1633, *d.* 1699), self-portrait, *c.*1665

a professional artist; accordingly, she set up a studio in their rented house in Pall Mall. Few women were employed as artists in this period, and her career could only have been undertaken with her husband's encouragement. She soon attracted a wide clientele from among the gentry and aristocracy, and from their own distinguished circle of friends, who included fellows of the Royal Society and puritan clergy, notably the future bishops Stillingfleet and Tillotson. Her prices were competitive: £10 for a three-quarter-length and £5 for a half-length portrait. Typical canvases feature warm brown colour tones and a feigned stone cartouche, both of which are apparent in the portrait of Jane, Lady Twisden (1677; Manor House Museum, Bury St Edmunds). Mary Beale's sons assisted her with the painting of draperies and later she was able to train and employ female studio assistants.

While his 'Dearest & Most Indefatigable Heart' (Beale notebook, 7 Aug 1677) was industriously employed, Charles Beale assumed responsibility for organizing the commissions and payments and preparing artists' colours. He recorded these details and much other incidental information in a series of notebooks, which provide an exceptional amount of documentation for an artist of this period; two survive, one for 1677 in the Bodleian Library, Oxford, and the other for 1681 in the National Portrait Gallery. In 1671 Mary Beale's income totalled £118 5s., rising to £429 by 1677; the latter was perhaps her most prosperous year. Additional information about the Beales is provided by their close friend Samuel Woodforde, whose diaries are held in the Bodleian Library. He describes Mary as a sympathetic and hospitable friend, while the attractive, puritan nature of their household is indicated by the family's practice of regularly setting aside 10 per cent of their annual income for the poor, and by Woodforde's comment, following a convivial occasion at their home: 'We were very cheerful, and I hope, without sin' (Woodforde, 2 Dec 1664). Mary's pensive but pleasant countenance is depicted in the numerous self-portraits, such as the *Self Portrait (with Artist's Palette)* (c.1666, NPG).

Of great assistance to Mary Beale's career was the friendship and support of Sir Peter Lely who, as the court painter, already exerted a prevailing influence on her mature style before their acquaintance. By 1672 the notebooks record that he had visited her in her studio and 'commended [her] extraordinarily' (Vertue, *Note books*, 4.168). Later he allowed her to study his own painting techniques, and she was able to build up a lucrative trade from making replicas of his portraits. Obviously ill at ease with his erotically charged depictions of court beauties, she toned down this influence in her own derivative portraits, such as *Jane Fox, Lady Leigh as a Shepherdess* (c.1676; Manor House Museum, Bury St Edmunds).

By 1681 Mary Beale's commissions were beginning to diminish but she busied herself with producing pictures for 'study and improvement' (Beale notebook, 1681, 300), experimenting with informal poses, as in *A Young Girl in Profile* (c.1681; Tate collection), and using alternatives to artists' canvas; her portrait of her son Charles looking up was painted on coarse twill-weave fabric (c.1681; Manor House Museum, Bury St Edmunds). These informal studies are among her finest works, showing that, when not dependent on laborious commissions and the influence of Lely, she was an artist of individuality, sensitivity, and charm. Her current reputation has grown following the retrospective exhibition held at the Geffrye Museum in 1975. Mary Beale died in 1699 at her home next to the Golden Ball, Pall Mall, and she was buried at St James's, Piccadilly, on 8 October. A large number of her portraits survive, but the best and most representative collection is at the Manor House Museum, Bury St Edmunds.

Beale's son **Bartholomew Beale** (bap. 1656, d. 1709) was baptized on 12 February 1656 at St Paul's, Covent Garden, London, and trained in her studio but, having gained an MB at Clare College, Cambridge (1682), thereafter practised as a physician in Coventry. He married Ann Naylor (d. 1725/6), and was buried on 17 May 1709 at St Michael's, Coventry.

Charles Beale (bap. 1660, d. 1726?) was baptized on 23 June 1660 at St Dunstan-in-the-West, Fleet Street, London. He also trained in his mother's studio and studied miniature painting with Thomas Flatman; fine examples of his work are in the Victoria and Albert Museum, London. Between about 1679 and about 1681 he was producing red-chalk sketches of family and friends which, for their informal and direct approach, are unique in British drawing for this period (British Museum and Pierpont Library, New York). By 1688 he had abandoned miniatures for full-scale portraiture, such as the portrait of Jane Bohun (c.1698;

Charlecote Park). The date and place of his death are uncertain but it seems likely that he was buried at St Martin-in-the-Fields, London, on 26 December 1726.

CHRISTOPHER REEVE

Sources E. Walsh, R. Jeffree, and R. Sword, *The excellent Mrs Mary Beale* (1975) [exhibition catalogue, Geffrye Museum, London, and Towner Art Gallery, Eastbourne, 13 Oct 1975 – 21 Feb 1976] · C. Reeve, *Mrs Mary Beale, paintress, 1633–1699* (1994) [exhibition catalogue, Manor House Museum, Bury St Edmunds, Suffolk] · E. Walsh, 'Mrs Mary Beale, paintress', *The Connoisseur*, 131 (1953), 3–8 · E. Walsh, 'Charles Beale 3d book, 1680', *The Connoisseur*, 149 (1962), 248–52 · C. Beale, notebook, 1677, Bodl. Oxf., MS Rawl. 8°572 · C. Beale, notebook, 1681, NPG, Heinz Archive and Library · S. Woodforde, diaries, 1663–5, Bodl. Oxf., MS Eng. misc. f. 381 · Vertue, *Note books*, vols. 1–5 · E. Croft-Murray and P. H. Hulton, eds., *Catalogue of British drawings*, 1 (1960), 148–98 · D. Foskett, *British portrait miniatures* (1963), 108–19 · M. K. Talley, *Portrait painting in England: studies in the technical literature before 1700* (1981), 270–305 · C. H. C. Baker, *Lely and the Stuart portrait painters: a study of English portraiture before and after van Dyck*, 2 vols. (1912) · H. Walpole, *Anecdotes of painting in England … collected by the late George Vertue, and now digested and published*, 4th edn, 5 vols. (1786) · parish register, Covent Garden, St Paul's, 12 Feb 1656 [B. Beale, baptism] · parish register, Coventry, St Michael's Church, 17 May 1709 [B. Beale, burial] · parish register, Barrow, All Saints, 26 March 1633 [baptism] · NPG, Heinz Archive and Library, Richard Jeffree archives · parish register, Fleet Street, London, St Dunstan's, 23 June 1660 [C. Beale, baptism] · parish register, Piccadilly, St James's, 8 Oct 1699 [burial] · T. Barber, *Mary Beale: portrait of a seventeenth-century painter, her family and her studio* (1999) [exhibition catalogue, Geffrye Museum, London, 21 Sept 1999 – 30 Jan 2000]

Archives BL, essay on friendship, Harley MS 6828, fols. 510–23 | Bodl. Oxf., C. Beale, notebook, 1677, MS Rawl. 8°572 · NPG, Heinz Archive and Library, C. Beale, notebook, 1681 · NPG, Richard Jeffree collection, transcripts of source material relating to Mary Beale and chapters of an unpublished monograph

Likenesses M. Beale, self-portrait, c.1660, Geffrye Museum, London · M. Beale, self-portrait, oils, c.1665, NPG [see illus.] · M. Beale, self-portraits, oils, c.1670–1675, Manor House Museum, Bury St Edmunds · M. Beale, self-portrait, c.1681, repro. in Walsh, Jeffree, and Sword, *The excellent Mrs Mary Beale*, 31 · C. Beale, chalk drawing, BM, sketch book · M. Beale, self-portrait, watercolour miniature, repro. in Walsh, Jeffree, and Sword, *The excellent Mrs Mary Beale*, 45 · T. Chambers, line engraving (with son Charles; after M. Beale), BM, NPG; repro. in Walpole, *Anecdotes* · portraits, Witt

Wealth at death studio paintings, furniture, and personal effects shared with husband; their dwelling-house was a rented property

Beale, Robert (1541–1601), administrator and diplomat, was the first son of Robert Beale (d. in or before 1548), mercer, of London, and his wife, Amy, probably the daughter of Sir Richard *Morison (c.1510–1556), humanist and diplomat. Although he made his career in royal service, Beale retained close ties with the London commercial élite, and in fact it may be appropriate to distinguish him as the governmental expert on its affairs. He served repeatedly on commissions sponsored by the privy council to resolve foreign and domestic mercantile problems, and was described as a man of 'speciall experience and exercyse in those causes' (APC, 28.175). When the government considered a forced loan in 1598, Beale was on the commission to evaluate the amounts to be levied against merchant strangers, presumably because of his familiarity with London's more substantial foreigners. He was himself an entrepreneur of sorts, serving as deputy to Sir Francis *Walsingham's governorship of the Company of Mines Royal, owning a quarter share in the Company of Mineral and Battery Works, and holding a patent for either importing or producing steel.

Early years and education, 1541–1572 Beale was educated at Coventry, probably at the school housed by John Hales (1516–1572), administrator and MP, in the choir of the former priory there. Hales had a decided influence on his charge. He imparted to Beale his views on religious and social reform, as well as his interest in classical learning. Beale may also have attended Cambridge University. He began to study civil law before he was twenty and although he never took a degree, he was noted as a person of decided legal training and skill. Gray's Inn admitted him as an honorary member in 1587. He was a Marian exile when he was first a student in Strasbourg, living at Morison's house there. After Morison's death in 1556, Beale was described as a scholar of John Aylmer at Zürich, where he studied logic, rhetoric, and Greek. The connection with Aylmer is particularly ironic because Beale later despised him for his anti-puritan stance. Personal animosity from their time in Zürich was a factor, Beale subsequently writing that Aylmer kept him as a servant without wages and ignored him after Elizabeth I's accession.

On his return to England, Beale had a sufficiently scholarly reputation for Lord John Grey to employ him to travel abroad to solicit the opinions of continental authorities on the validity of the marriage of Edward Seymour, first earl of Hertford, to Grey's niece, Lady Katherine Grey. Hales's association with the Seymour family reinforced Beale's support for Katherine. Beale's tract on its legitimacy, 'A large discourse concerning the marriage between the earl of Hertford and the Lady Katherine Grey' (CUL, MS Ii.5.3, art. 4), could not have pleased either the queen or her privy councillors, but history has vindicated its essential correctness. He turned against the marriage, despite his own writings, presumably because Hertford reportedly reneged on a promised annuity of £40. When an ecclesiastical high commission found the marriage void on 12 May 1562, it was perhaps royal displeasure that prompted him to return to the continent to temporary exile, for he is found at Paris in the early 1560s, during Sir Henry Norris's embassy. He became part of that ambassadorial retinue, serving as a conveyor of messages, an intelligencer, and as Norris's secretary. Subsequently, he was the formal secretary to Walsingham, Norris's successor, and thus began one of the closer personal and working relationships in the Elizabethan bureaucracy. Beale eventually married Edith, daughter of Henry St Barbe of Somerset and the sister of Walsingham's wife. The couple had two sons and nine daughters (all but four of their children died young). While in Paris, Beale was an observer of the St Bartholomew's day massacre (24 August 1572), which led to his account in a 'Discourse after the massacre in France' (BL, Cotton MS Titus F.iii). Beale was highly active during the embassy, with repeated trips between Paris and London as a special messenger, with his independent negotiations for Walsingham in the Low Countries, and with his semi-autonomous role in the marriage discussions between Henri, duc d'Anjou, and Elizabeth of 1571. For this last role he earned the commendations of Sir Thomas Smith, who praised him as a 'rare man of excellent gifts' (PRO, SP 70/73, fol. 567r). Walsingham was certainly instrumental in advancing Beale's career in England, to the extent that at one point Beale was considered as a temporary replacement for him as English ambassador in France at the key Paris post. Beale demurred, however, on the basis of poverty, and another of the entourage, Henry Killigrew, became ambassador instead.

Clerk of the privy council and diplomat, 1572–1601 Smith's encomium must have been substantially accurate, for even before Walsingham returned from France, the queen made Beale one of the clerks of her privy council in July 1572. He held this office until his death, and for the majority of his tenure was the pre-eminent clerk. Frequently, when Walsingham was absent, Beale assumed his duties as well. From these experiences emerged his most famous pamphlet, 'A treatise of the office of a councellor and principall secretarie to her majestie' (BL, Add. MS 48161), which described the duties of the principal secretary. It was also while clerk of the council that Beale became significantly involved in dealing with the problem of what to do with Mary, queen of Scots. He negotiated with her at the direction of the privy council to try to resolve diplomatic questions between Scotland and England, and to encourage her to conform to English expectations of her. He may even have had authorization to offer her freedom in return for certain guarantees about her conduct. Despite his grave reservations about Mary's role in Elizabethan England, and despite what must have been substantial religious hostility, he reportedly treated the captive queen with unusual civility. She in turn felt sufficiently kindly toward him to bestow upon him a gold chain worth £65, and one can only speculate upon his feelings as he delivered her sentence of death in the hall at Fotheringhay Castle, Northamptonshire, on 19 November 1586. As one of the principals in the process leading to the Scottish queen's execution, he did share in William Davison's disgrace, although, unlike his colleague, he returned reasonably quickly to royal favour. However, the exact nature of his role and the extent to which Davison acted willingly as the privy council's scapegoat is unclear.

Beale's clerkship, his involvement with the principal secretaryship, and his prior experience overseas made him an unusually good candidate for a variety of diplomatic activities. Between 16 April and 26 July 1576 he went to the Low Countries as special ambassador on £2 per day to protest at Dutch seizures of English shipping. He had an audience with William of Orange about 1 May and carried with him a scarcely veiled warning: if Dutch piracies did not cease, Elizabeth would consider joining Philip II in suppressing the rebellion there. The queen emphasized her displeasure by sending Sir William Winter to join with Beale, the former arriving with new threats and demands that the Dutch repay outstanding English loans.

The failure of the two men to gain Dutch co-operation led for a time to something not far removed from war between England and the Low Countries.

The next year Beale went abroad again, this time pursuing religious ends, in which he had a particularly keen personal interest. Between 15 August 1577 and 6 February 1578 he moved between German courts as special ambassador, trying to effect a reconciliation among German protestant factions so that they might offer a united opposition to the presumed international Catholic conspiracy ranged against protestant interests. His diet was £2 per day. He had an audience with the elector palatine at Heidelberg on 27 September 1577, another with Duke Casimer-Neustadt on 1 October, and probably another with the duke of Saxony in mid-September. Neither he nor Daniel Rogers, who later joined him, was successful in persuading the German princes to bury confessional differences and to be more tolerant of those with Calvinistic leanings. Beale was embittered by his diplomatic failures, and his frustration was magnified by personal loss. Spoiled by pirates on his voyage across the channel, he never forgot what he claimed were his financial sacrifices on this mission. Other records suggest that his claims were much exaggerated, and it is a fact that few made such a practice as he of complaining so vociferously, or so unjustifiably, about their ill usage at the queen's hands.

Beale served diplomatically only twice more, once for a short period as an English representative on the Dutch council of state between 26 June and about 28 September 1587, along with his old diplomatic partner Killigrew, and again as a senior adviser to the Anglo-Spanish negotiations between 20 April and 8 August 1600. His fellow commissioners in 1600 were Dr John Herbert, Sir Henry Neville, and Thomas Edmondes. Beale was paid £3 per day. The commissioners met at Boulogne with Spanish representatives, including the regent of the Spanish Netherlands, to discuss peace between England and Spain. There was some talk of using Beale as one of the commissioners in the fruitless peace talks that preceded the Armada campaign in 1588, but Robert Dudley, earl of Leicester, encouraged Walsingham to appoint someone of greater ability—an interesting commentary that may have stemmed from disagreements while Beale was on the Dutch council. Even at home, however, Beale remained involved in diplomatic affairs, both by right of his duties as clerk of the privy council, and as a propagandist of considerable ability for the English position in international affairs.

Parliament and puritanism, 1572–1593 Perhaps his greatest contemporary notoriety in Elizabethan England stems from his advocacy of puritan causes. In this he was unusually forward among the queen's servants. He strongly challenged John Whitgift, archbishop of Canterbury, in his administration of the *ex officio* oath to nonconforming clergy, he authored several tracts attacking the episcopacy and supporting a puritan position, and he earned heavy royal displeasure with his religious leanings in parliament, where he was a significant figure. During Walsingham's absence in 1583 Beale sat on the privy council as acting principal secretary (as he had in 1578 and 1581) and

responded favourably to puritan petitions from Kent and Suffolk. Whitgift was furious about this and the two men argued over it when they met on 9 February. Beale responded in 1584 with his 'A book respecting ceremonies, the habits, the Book of Common Prayer, and the power of the ecclesiastical courts'. In this he argued that the Book of Common Prayer (1559) could not be enforced by the Act of Uniformity because it deviated from the sanctioned Book of Common Prayer (1552) in three respects. Beale represented Totnes, Devon, in 1572 and Dorchester, Oxfordshire, in the parliaments of 1584, 1586, and 1589. His rhetoric, often expressed in pamphlets, foreshadowed the arguments of the seventeenth century when references to Magna Carta and policies that confounded common law were the grist of puritanical propaganda efforts. He specifically declared that he only wished to have the settlement of 1559 enforced—'I protest that I am not either donatist, novatian, anabaptist, puritan, nor yet a wayward or misconceited person … It is not her Majesty's authority or the [prayer] book that are misliked, but sundry abused yet remaining in the church' (HoP, *Commons, 1558–1603*, 1.413). His eclipse from court life between 1593 and 1597 may well have been due to his performance in the parliament of 1593, when he represented Lostwithiel in Cornwall, and during which he was a spokesman for the puritan point of view, and an opponent of the royal subsidy. He sat on many committees over the years, including those concerning benefit of clergy (7 March 1576), on seditious practices, the Family of Love, and for the preservation of the queen's safety (1 February, 16 February, and 14 March 1581), on Mary (4 November 1586) and on parliamentary privileges and returns (26 February 1593). Beale spoke out on privilege during the parliament of 1593. He did not sit in the parliament of 1597. His own letters to William Cecil, Lord Burghley, from this period indicate that he certainly saw his exile from court hinging upon his parliamentary performance, although not unexpectedly he made strongly justificatory remonstrations for his actions. It should be also noted that it was during this time that he produced two works urging religious toleration, although it may be surmised that he extolled such a position primarily as a mechanism to ease the pressure on those with whom he was religiously in sympathy.

During his absence from court Beale turned his attentions to his office as secretary of the queen's council of the north, worth £300 per annum (he claimed it only to be worth £33), and to academic enterprises. Besides his substantially documented pamphlets, there are other indications that he was a man of considerable literary talent. This included being conversant in Latin, Dutch, and French. He belonged to the Society of Antiquaries, and his formidable library, as well as his personal papers, passed virtually intact into the Yelverton collection, now at the British Library. Beale was a man of clear intellectual ability, whose liabilities were those of an inflexible conscience, debilitating enough to his career, surely, but ones that did not preclude his making substantial administrative and diplomatic contributions to Elizabeth's reign. He died at his house at Barn Elms, Surrey, on 27 May 1601, only partially restored to royal favour. He was buried in All Hallows, London Wall. GARY M. BELL

Sources HoP, *Commons, 1558–1603*, 1.411–15 · P. Collinson, *The Elizabethan puritan movement* (1967) · M. Dewar, *Sir Thomas Smith: a Tudor intellectual in office* (1964) · S. T. Bindoff, J. Hurstfield, and C. H. Williams, eds., *Elizabethan government and society: essays presented to Sir John Neale* (1961) · M. B. Donald, *Elizabethan monopolies: the history of the Company of Mineral and Battery Works from 1565–1604* (1961) · J. Hurstfield, *The queen's wards: wardship and marriage under Elizabeth I* (1958) · Baron Kervyn de Lettenhove [J. M. B. C. Kervyn de Lettenhove] and L. Gilliodts-van Severen, eds., *Relations politiques des Pays-Bas et de l'Angleterre sous le règne de Philippe II*, 11 vols. (Brussels, 1882–1900) · S. Lehmberg, *Sir Walter Mildmay and Tudor government* (Austin, TX, 1964) · G. Mattingly, *The defeat of the Spanish Armada* (1959) · J. E. Neale, *Elizabeth I and her parliaments, 1559–1601*, 2 vols. (1965) · C. Read, *Mr Secretary Cecil and Queen Elizabeth* (1962) · C. Read, *Lord Burghley and Queen Elizabeth* (1960); pbk edn (1965) · C. Read, *Mr Secretary Walsingham and the policy of Queen Elizabeth*, 3 vols. (1925) · R. R. Reid, *The king's council in the north* (1921) · S. D'Ewes, *The journals of all the parliaments during the reign of Queen Elizabeth both of the House of Lords and the House of Commons* (1682) · *CSP dom., 1547–1603* · *CSP for., 1562–1603* · *CSP Scot., 1581–8* · *APC, 1571–5, 1597–9* · BL, Lansdowne MSS 51, fols. 53r–54r; 52, fol. 145r; 72, fols. 197r–198r; 73, fols. 4r–13r; 79, fol. 192r; 84, fol. 4r; 105, fol. 104r; 107, fol. 41r · *DNB*

Archives BL, corresp. and papers, incl. historical notes and collections, Add. MSS 5935, 14028–14029, 48000–48196; Egerton MSS 1693–1694; Cotton MSS | BL, 'Observations upon the instructions of the states-general to the council of state, Juni 1588', Cotton MS, Galba D.iii.215 · BL, 'A consideration of certain points in the treaty to be enlarged or altered in case her majesty make a new treaty with the states, April 1589', Cotton MS, Galba D.iv.163 · BL, 'Opposition against instructions to negotiate with the states-general, 1590', Cotton MS, Galba D.vii.19 · BL, 'Collection of the king of Spain's injuries offered to the queen of England', dated 30 May 1591. With a 'Vindication of the queen against the objections of the Spaniards', Harley MS, 253, art. 33 · BL, 'A deliberation of Henry Killigrew and Robert Beale concerning requisition for restitution from the states. London, August 1595', Cotton MS, Galba D.xi.125 · BL, 'Discourse after the massacre in France', Cotton MS, Titus F.iii.299 · BL, 'Opinions concerning the earl of Leicester's placard to the United Provinces', Cotton MS, Galba C.xi.107 · CUL, 'Argument touching the validity of the marriage of Charles Brandon, duke of Suffolk, with Mary, queen-dowager of France (sister to King Henry VIII), and the legitimacy of the Lady Frances, their daughter', in Latin, Dd.3, 85, art. 18 · CUL, 'A large discourse concerning the marriage between the earl of Hertford and the Lady Katherine Grey', in Latin, Cambr. Ii.5.3, art. 4

Beale, Samuel (1803–1874). *See under* Beale family (*per. c.*1836–1912).

Beale, Sir Samuel Richard (1881–1964), engineer and industrialist, was born in Birmingham on 7 February 1881, one of two sons of James Samuel *Beale (1840–1912) [*see under* Beale family], solicitor and company director, and his wife, Margaret Field. He was educated at Marlborough College, and Trinity College, Cambridge, where he achieved an engineering degree and a rowing blue. In 1908 he married Sylvia Constance Bell (*d.* 1953); they had three sons.

Beale's father had been chairman of L. Sterne & Co. Ltd, a Glasgow-based engineering firm, since 1882; and in 1903 Beale took up an apprenticeship with the company. His father had built up its traditional products of railway springs, emery wheels, and grinding machines, and he

had also diversified into refrigerating equipment so that, when his son joined the company, refrigeration was the largest single element in the firm's turnover.

Beale began his training in the pattern shop at the company's headquarters—the Crown ironworks in North Woodside Road, Glasgow. He soon saw that the works were in need of reorganization and that the management had become very conservative. Profits were, consequently, less than they had been in earlier years. His opportunity to improve matters came very quickly, in 1905, only two years after he had joined the firm, when John Guthrie, the commercial manager, became ill and Beale was asked to take over the role. His authority, however, seems to have extended beyond the normal tasks associated with his job title. Despite resistance from his father, and in the face of complaints from Guthrie, he had a new machine shop built for the manufacturing of emery wheels, and new machinery, including radial drills, installed, all of which added greatly to the cost competitiveness of the firm. Improvements in the manufacture of springs met with modest success, but Beale was particularly interested in the refrigeration side of the business. Accordingly, Louis Sterne, the founder of the company, and chairman from 1912, brought back some small refrigerators from one of his frequent trips to the United States. One of the machines which found its way to the Crown ironworks was a Remington refrigerator, which Beale set about improving.

It was not just domestic refrigeration in which Beale was interested, however, for in the early years of the twentieth century the iron industry was involved in a dry-blasting process for pig-iron manufacture which necessitated refrigeration installations of 200–300 tons capacity. Beale senior, encouraged by his son, obtained a contract from Guest, Keen, and Nettlefolds (GKN), in which he had an interest, to build the necessary equipment in south Wales. The Commercial Bank of Scotland lent £10,000 to L. Sterne & Co. for the purpose, but GKN eventually decided that the method was not economical and abandoned it. Experiences such as this doubtless confirmed the company in its rather cautious policy.

When Beale's father died in 1912, Sterne became chairman and Beale joined the board as general manager. Under his direction large projects were not neglected, despite the earlier experience with the iron industry. In 1915 the firm obtained a contract, for sizeable cold stores, from the Port of London Authority and several years later similar work was undertaken for the Clyde Cold Storage Company. Other large land-based products included a very large number of ice rinks, including those at Earls Court and Wembley, London. It was not until the First World War that Beale decided to enter the marine refrigeration business.

In the inter-war years Beale pursued a policy of rationalization. Many firms did likewise in these difficult years and achieved only a contraction in their business; but Beale was more successful and his well-judged policies resulted in an expansion of the company. He was the first

Englishman to become president of the Glasgow chamber of commerce (1929) and several years later he served as president of the Association of British Chambers of Commerce. In politics he was an active Unionist and served for a time as president of the St Rollox Unionist Association.

In 1924 Sterne died and Beale's brother, Sir John F. Beale (1874–1935), was brought in as chairman, leaving Samuel as managing director. The death of Sir John in 1935 led to Samuel replacing him as chairman of L. Sterne & Co., though in a non-executive capacity. At the same time he succeeded his brother as chairman of GKN. Apart from his interests in L. Sterne & Co. and its associated and subsidiary companies, he was also a director of other leading engineering firms such as Glenfield and Kennedy Ltd and Mavor and Coulson Ltd. None of these firms specialized in GKN's main lines of business, but with extensive managerial experience and also being 'Ambitious and able, Beale was an obvious candidate for the chairmanship' (Jones, 2.283).

Just before going to England, Beale sent his nephew Peter Brown to North America to identify a firm that produced a small automatic type of refrigerator. Brown found what he was looking for in Ontario, where the Universal Cooler Company had developed just such a machine. L. Sterne & Co. acquired the patent rights, and the Sternette, perhaps the firm's most famous product, came into being with the minimum of development costs. Variants of this machine were produced for domestic use to meet the growing consumer demand for household refrigerators.

The Second World War broke out before Beale could make much of a contribution to GKN, and the firm was then turned over to war production. In 1940 he became a member of the Export Council, which worked to promote exports to help fund the war effort and to allocate scarce industrial materials sensibly, and for a time he served as chairman of this committee. In addition he also served on the consultative council appointed to advise the Treasury on financial problems arising from war conditions. In 1942 he was made a KBE.

Beale retired as chairman of GKN in 1947 but remained a director until 1951. Retirement allowed him to join the boards of Thomas Cook & Son and the Scottish Amicable Life Assurance Society. He also continued to sit on the board of the Union Bank of Scotland—a connection which was maintained after that bank's merger with the Bank of Scotland in 1955. In 1950 he was a director of some nineteen companies. He retired in 1960 and was succeeded as chairman of L. Sterne & Co. by his nephew, Peter Brown.

'A man with a sense of humour, Beale adopted an uncomplicated lifestyle and had the ability to make quick decisions' (Jones, 2.283). During his retirement his interests included shooting, and he divided his time between his London residence at Campden Hill and his Scottish country home, Drumlamford, at Barrhill, Ayrshire. He died at Drumlamford on 10 October 1964.

CHARLES W. MUNN

Sources S. R. Beale, *The Crown Ironworks: the history of L. Sterne & Co. Ltd., 1874–1949* (1951) · *WWW* · C. W. Munn, 'Beale, Sir Samuel Richard', *DSBB* · *Glasgow Herald* (12 Oct 1964) · *CGPLA Eng. & Wales* (1965) · *The Times* (13 Oct 1964) · *The Times* (16 Oct 1964) · d. cert. · E. Jones, *A history of GKN*, 2 vols. (1987–90)
Likenesses photograph, repro. in *Glasgow Chamber of Commerce Journal*, 17/5 (May 1934), 97
Wealth at death £123,648: probate, 8 Jan 1965, *CGPLA Eng. & Wales*

Beale, (Sarah) Sophia (*b.* 1837, *d.* in or after 1912), writer on art and painter, was born on 5 November 1837 in the parish of St Martin-in-the-Fields, London, the daughter of Lionel John Beale (1796–1871), surgeon, and Frances Smith, *née* Sheppard (1800–1849). She was the sister of Lionel Smith *Beale (1828–1906), physician and microscopist, and of Ellen Brooker Beale (later Lloyd) (1831–1900), a landscape painter. Sophia and Ellen Beale attended Queen's College, London, and James Matthew Leigh's private art school, and copied works in the National Gallery and the British Museum. In her *Recollections of a Spinster Aunt* (1908) Sophia records their considerably free lifestyle during the later 1850s and early 1860s; they walked unchaperoned around London, moving between their home and West End museums and galleries. One daringly unconventional activity was eating hot potatoes from a night stall on Charing Cross Road. At the time she wondered 'shall we not be able to move mountains, ie. force open the doors of the R.A. for women students and women Academicians?' (Cherry, *Beyond the Frame*, 19). With her sister she had a studio at 107 Long Acre, in Covent Garden, from 1860 to 1867.

Beale's *Recollections* describe her adventures travelling alone to Paris between 1869 and 1872. There she studied in Charles Chaplin's studio, and financed this by acting as a supervisor at M. Bertin's studio three days a week. Back in London she augmented her income by writing and teaching, and opened an art school at 35 Albany Street (near Regent's Park), advertising herself as a pupil of Charles-Alphonse-Paul Bellay and James-Elie Delauny at a time when French technique was at a premium. Her small watercolour of an outdoor scene including women and children with umbrellas in the foreground (1892) is in the Fine Art Museums of San Francisco collection.

Beale published extensively on art and architecture in periodicals and guide books including *The Louvre, a complete and concise handbook to all the collections of the museum; being an abridgement of the French official catalogues* (1883), *The Amateur's Guide to Architecture* (1887), and *The Churches of Paris from Clovis to Charles X* (1893). She emphasized the educational nature of her *Amateur's Guide to Architecture*, intended for young female students:

> I have no desire to turn every girl into an architect … The utmost I hope or wish to do is to give them some love of Art, which will enable them to take an interest in the subject when they travel, or walk about London, or turn over the pages of a magazine or a review. (Beale, preface)

She held advanced views concerning the opening of the Royal Academy and universities to women, as well as on women's suffrage. She argued in a letter of 1888 to Millicent Garrett Fawcett that taxation and social responsibility were adequate reasons for enfranchisement:

> I pay rent & taxes £130—I have nothing but what I earn painting, teaching and writing—& naturally have to work exceedingly hard … My lodger, a young man 26–30 doing absolutely nothing but moon about the town and amuse(!) himself … *has a vote*. (Cherry, *Beyond the Frame*, 142)

In the following year a fierce debate over suffrage erupted in the periodical press, and Fawcett used Beale's case to contest voting restrictions. Beale was among the 2000 signatories of the ensuing declaration in favour of women's suffrage, and her signature on the women householder's declaration in 1889 highlighted her status as a property owner.

The date of Sophia Beale's death is unknown; her brother's article in the *Dictionary of National Biography* (1912) states: 'Miss Sophia Beale is a painter and author'.

MEAGHAN E. CLARKE

Sources S. S. Beale, *Recollections of a spinster aunt* (1908) • D. Cherry, *Painting women: Victorian women artists* (1993) • D. Cherry, *Beyond the frame: feminism and visual culture, Britain, 1850–1900* (2000) • RG6 series, Bedfordshire and Hertfordshire Quaker Quarterly Meeting, Bedford, PRO

Beale, Thomas Willert (1828–1894), impresario and composer, was born in London, the eldest of the four children of Frederick Beale (1804–1863), of the music publishing firm of Cramer, Beale, and Addison of Regent Street, and his wife, Margaret, *née* Betts, of Charles Street, Grosvenor Square, an accomplished pianist. He was surrounded by music from childhood and came to know many important musicians in the family home. He was taught piano by Edouard Roeckel, harmony and counterpoint by George French Flowers, and melody and rhythm in the Italian style by the ballet composer Cesare Pugni. He received a classical as well as a general education with private tutors and spoke German, French, and Italian fluently. Beale began his professional career organizing touring operatic performances on behalf of his father's firm and later managed opera in London and the provinces. On 18 April 1860 he was admitted as a student at Lincoln's Inn, and in 1863 he was called to the bar and took over responsibility for his father's business interests. In later life he married a widow, Mrs Robinson, a gifted musician and singer. Under the pseudonym Walter Maynard he wrote extensively on music and related topics and was a familiar figure in literary and musical circles, known for his energy, wide sympathies, and warm-heartedness. His book *The Enterprising Impresario* (1867) uses his experiences to give an account of the management of touring opera (especially Italian opera) in the provinces and Ireland in the mid-century, and his autobiography *The Light of other Days* (2 vols., 1890) further illuminates these and many other facets of English musical life in the period 1840 to 1890. He addressed himself to and promoted important musical issues of the day. With his father he helped form the New Philharmonic Society and invited Berlioz to conduct in its first season, 1852. His National Music Meetings (held at the Crystal Palace from 1872 to 1875) pioneered competitive vocal and instrumental performance for young professionals. His *Music Copy Books* (1871) sought to replace traditional rote learning of performance by sensitive musical observation involving written notation. He planned a new university of the fine arts to bring together the study of visual arts, music, literature, and drama. His works as Walter Maynard included many songs (often with Italian influence), piano pieces, and operettas, as well as comedies, plays (including a three-act drama, *A Shadow on the Hearth*), and a novel, *True to her Art*. His *Instructions in the Art of Singing after the Models of the Best Italian Masters* appeared in 1853 (reissued 1872). He died at his home, Pasqua, at 35 Victoria Road, Upper Norwood, on the evening of 3 October 1894, having suffered from throat cancer for two years, and was buried at Norwood cemetery.

MICHAEL MUSGRAVE

Sources T. W. Beale, *The light of other days*, 2 vols. (1890) • *Musical News* (13 Oct 1894), 297 • *The Times* (5 Oct 1894) • 'Walter Maynard', *The catalogue of printed music in the British Library to 1980*, ed. R. Balchin, 38 (1985), 316–19 • *MT*, 35 (1894), 768 • T. W. Beale, *The enterprising impresario* (1867) • Brown & Stratton, *Brit. mus.*, 36 • *DNB* • d. cert.

Beale, William (d. 1651), college head, was born near Thame in Oxfordshire. At Easter 1606 he was elected to a scholarship at Trinity College, Cambridge, from Westminster School. He graduated BA in spring 1610; from 1611 to 1625 he was a fellow of Jesus College, where he proceeded MA in 1613. He was ordained deacon on 25 February 1616. He graduated BD in 1620 as of St John's College, and seven years later he was created DD. He had resigned his fellowship at Jesus College to be made rector of Cottingham in Northamptonshire on 4 February 1625 but returned to the college as master on 14 July 1632.

Following the death of Owen Gwyn, master of St John's College, in June 1633 the senior fellows put forward as his successor Robert Lane, whom the king accepted and nominated at Berwick during the royal progress (11 June 1633). This authority was countermanded by the junior men at the college, who put in the puritan Ralph Holdsworth. The college accepted that it had two masters until, in a move to break the deadlock between the two contenders, Charles I appointed the recent head of Jesus as nineteenth master of the much larger foundation, on Ash Wednesday, 19 February 1634, 'per majorem partem sociorum ex mandato regio'. Beale's position only became workable with the sudden death of Lane in June 1634 and the increasing workload of Holdsworth as Gwyn's successor as archdeacon of Huntingdon. His brother Jerome *Beale had become master of Pembroke College in 1619.

Beale was a generous donor to the college's chapel, providing at the east end a decent wainscot, sixteen tapestries depicting the story of our saviour, and a new ceiling painting. The painting and pictures cost no less than £100. A new communion table was provided, with rails and tapers, and new communion silver, some of it the gift of Bishop Francis Dee, and an organ. This was thought unexceptional but Beale then added a representation of the Holy Spirit as a dove, furnishing William Prynne with the grounds for his objections. He was also generous to his college library, donating fourteen volumes, including a copy

In 1642 Beale was one of the heads of college active in raising funds for the king's cause and he sent £150 and 2065½ ounces of plate to the king at Nottingham (8 August 1642). Although Cromwell failed to intercept this Beale was arrested, in his college chapel during divine service, and with the masters of Queens' and Jesus was taken into custody in London. He was deprived of his college headship by the earl of Manchester on 13 March 1644 and was threatened with deportation 'to Algiers or the American islands' (BL, Add. MS 5808, fol. 152) but was released by exchange after three years in custody and reached Oxford on 14 June 1645 to become one of the chaplains serving Charles I. He was nominated to the deanery of Ely, in succession to William Fuller. As Fuller never became dean of Durham it would appear that Beale was never instituted as his successor. In 1647 Charles asked him to attend him at Holmby. He later went into exile, first in Paris with Lord Cottington and Sir Edward Hyde as a chaplain and then with them to Spain. He died in Madrid on 1 October 1651 and was hastily buried beneath the floorboards of the house, apparently from a concern 'lest his body should fall into the hands of the inquisitors' (Baker).   NICHOLAS W. S. CRANFIELD

Sources Venn, *Alum. Cant.* • H. I. Longden, *Northamptonshire and Rutland clergy from 1500*, ed. P. I. King and others, 16 vols. in 6, Northamptonshire RS (1938–52) • T. Baker, *History of the college of St John the Evangelist, Cambridge*, ed. J. E. B. Mayor, 2 vols. (1869) • M. R. James, *A descriptive catalogue of the manuscripts in the library of St John's College, Cambridge* (1913) • W. Prynne, *Canterburies doome, or, The first part of a compleat history of the commitment, charge, tryall, condemnation, execution of William Laud, late arch-bishop of Canterbury* (1646) • Wood, *Ath. Oxon.: Fasti* (1815), 377 • Wood, *Ath. Oxon.: Fasti* (1820), 80–81 • PRO, SP 16/450/94; 16/452/20; 16/452/114; 16/260/63; 16/381/47; 16/383/49; 16/461/29; 16/461/52; 16/461/28; 16/463/16; 16/473/23 • PRO, LC 5/134, LC 3/1 • J. Nalson, *An impartial collection of the great affairs of state*, 2 vols. (1682–3) • *JHL*, 4 (1628–42) • *The life, diary, and correspondence of Sir William Dugdale*, ed. W. Hamper (1827)
Likenesses oils, St John Cam. [*see illus.*]

William Beale (*d.* 1651), by unknown artist

of the 1604 canons ecclesiastical, John Davenant's 1634 *Determinationes quaestionum quarundam theologicarum* when it was published, and Henry Isaacson's classic defence of episcopacy, *Saturni ephemerides, sive, Tabula historia-chronologia*, as well as a handful of manuscripts.

Beale served as vice-chancellor of Cambridge University in 1634–5 and became rector of Paulerspury on 31 October 1637, at William Laud's behest, and of the sinecure Welsh living of Aberdaron on 28 March 1640. Beale was one of the chaplains in ordinary to the king by 1635 (PRO, LC 5/134, fol. 6) and in 1638 preached one of the Lent sermons at court (PRO, SP 16/381/47). On 18 May 1640 he was denounced in the Short Parliament 'for words spoken in this public and in sermons tending to the disturbance of the State of this Realm' (Nalson, 1.367). This centred on a 1635 sermon that Laud promised that he would investigate. The resulting fuss 'half foiled me in the government of my College, which was the orderliest body for so great a one in the University', as Beale complained to his friend John Cosin (Beale to Cosin, 27 July 1640, PRO, SP 16/461/29). In the Long Parliament he was first attacked by Nathaniel Fiennes (14 December 1640) for his purported role in making the canons and for advancing the claims of the king 'in whom soly he placeth the power of making Laws, and that it is but of grace that he assumeth either the Lords, or Commons for the making of Laws with him' (Nalson, 1.673). With Cosin and Roger Manwaring, Beale was later denounced by Francis Rous (16 March 1641) as a royalist and appointee of the archbishop. He was forced to resign Paulerspury when the Lords reinstated Ezekiel Johnson, the minister deprived by high commission in 1637.

Beale, William (1784–1854), organist and singer, was born at Landrake, Cornwall, on 1 January 1784. He was a chorister at Westminster Abbey under Samuel Arnold and Robert Cooke until his voice broke, after which he served as a midshipman on board the *Révolutionnaire*, a 44-gun frigate which had been captured from the French. During this period it is reported that he was nearly drowned by falling overboard in Cork harbour. When his voice had settled into a pure baritone, he left the sea and devoted himself to the musical profession. He became a member of the Royal Society of Musicians on 1 December 1811, and on 12 January 1813 he won the prize cup of the Madrigal Society for his madrigal 'Awake, sweet muse'. On 30 January 1816, following the death of Robert Hudson, he obtained an appointment as one of the gentlemen of the Chapel Royal. At this time he was living at 13 North Street, Westminster. On 1 November 1820 Beale became organist of Trinity College, Cambridge, and on 13 December the same year he resigned his place at the Chapel Royal. In December 1821 he resigned his appointment at Cambridge and returned to London, where, with the assistance of Thomas Attwood, he became successively organist of Wandsworth parish church and St John's, Clapham Rise. He continued to sing in public occasionally until late in life, and in 1840 he won a prize at the Adelphi Glee Club for a glee for four voices, 'Harmony'. His voice was a light baritone, and he is said to have imitated James Bartleman in his vocalization. An extremely finished singer, he was apparently somewhat wanting in power. His compositions, which consist principally of glees and madrigals, though relatively few in number, were very accomplished. Collections of his vocal works were published in 1815, 1820, and c.1875. The madrigals 'Come let us join the roundelay' and 'This pleasant month of May' were particularly popular and were arranged for various combinations of voices. Beale was twice married, first to Charlotte Elkins, a daughter of the groom of the stole to George IV, and then to Georgiana Grove, of Clapham. He died at his home in Paradise Row, Stockwell, London, on 3 May 1854.

W. B. SQUIRE, rev. DAVID J. GOLBY

Sources W. H. Husk and W. B. Squire, 'Beale, William', *New Grove* · private information (1885)

Beale, William John (1807–1883). *See under* Beale family (*per. c.*1836–1912).

Beale, Sir William Phipson, baronet (1839–1922). *See under* Beale family (*per. c.*1836–1912).

Beales, Edmond (1803–1881), radical, was born at Newnham, Cambridge, on 3 July 1803, the son of Samuel Pickering Beales, a merchant who acquired local celebrity as a political reformer, and his wife, Martha, daughter of John Curtis. He was educated at Bury St Edmunds grammar school, Eton College, and Trinity College, Cambridge, where he was elected to a scholarship; he graduated BA in 1825 and proceeded MA in 1828. Called to the bar at the Middle Temple in 1830, he practised as an equity draftsman and conveyancer. He married Eliza, daughter of James Marshall, manager of the Provincial Bank of Ireland. They had a daughter, Anna Lisa.

For several years he was closely connected with radical groups active in the campaign for American and European democracy. He promoted the earliest demonstration on behalf of the Polish refugees, was a member of the Polish Exiles' Friends Society, and of the Literary Association of the Friends of Poland; was president of the Polish National League, and chairman of the Circassian Committee; a member of the Emancipation Society during the American Civil War, of the Jamaica committee under John Stuart Mill, and of the Garibaldi welcome committee. It was in connection with Garibaldi's visit to Britain in 1864 that Beales first became known to the general public. He defended the right of people to meet on Primrose Hill, in support of Garibaldi, and a conflict with the police occurred. This experience led him to publish a pamphlet on the right of public meeting, but it was in connection with the domestic democratic movement that Beales became best-known. Following the Garibaldi demonstrations, plans were laid for a national political organization of radical working-class groups. On 17 May 1864 Beales

Edmond Beales (1803–1881), by unknown engraver

chaired a meeting to organize for the widening of the franchise. On 22 June a great metropolitan reform meeting took place at the Freemasons' Hall, again with Beales in the chair, but the drive for national organization lapsed until 1865. On 27 February that year Beales convened a meeting at St Martin's Hall, which resolved to establish the Reform League, dedicated to securing universal manhood suffrage and the ballot. In March the rules of the league were formally adopted and Beales became president.

The Reform Bill introduced by Earl Russell's government in 1866 was strongly supported by the league, and after its rejection by the House of Commons the league renewed its agitation. Gigantic meetings were held in Trafalgar Square, which the Conservative government tried vainly to suppress. Sir Richard Mayne, the first commissioner of police, issued a notice to the effect that the meeting announced for 2 July 1866 would not be permitted. Beales, however, stated his determination to attend the meeting, and to hold the government responsible for all breaches of the peace. This step led Mayne to withdraw his ban, and the meeting of 69,000 people was held without incident. Yet on 23 July, an immense gathering near the gates of Hyde Park generated a serious confrontation. While Beales and the other leaders were returning from Marble Arch to Trafalgar Square, the mob pushed down the iron railings surrounding the park, and entered in large numbers, only to be driven out eventually by the combined efforts of the military and the police. The following day Beales had an interview with Spencer Walpole, the home secretary, and afterwards went to the park and intimated that no further attempt would be made to hold a meeting there 'except only on next Monday afternoon (30 July) at six o'clock, by arrangement with the government'. The mission of the league was virtually at an end when Disraeli's Reform Bill was passed in 1867. Beales resigned the presidency on 10 March 1869, and three days later the league was formally dissolved.

Beales was a revising barrister for Middlesex from 1862 to 1866, when, in consequence of the active part he had taken in political agitation, the lord chief justice, Sir Alexander Cockburn, declined to reappoint him. Beales was an unsuccessful candidate for the Tower Hamlets constituency in 1868. In September 1870 Lord Chancellor Hatherley appointed him judge of the county court circuit no. 35, comprising Cambridgeshire and Huntingdonshire. Beales died at his residence, Osborne House, Bolton Gardens, London, on 26 June 1881.

THOMPSON COOPER, *rev.* MATTHEW LEE

Sources *Men of the time* (1875) • Boase, *Mod. Eng. biog.* • Venn, *Alum. Cant.* • *Debrett's Illustrated House of Commons and the Judicial Bench* (1875), 396–7 • H. L. Malchow, *Agitators and promoters in the age of Gladstone and Disraeli: a biographical dictionary* (1983) • *CGPLA Eng. & Wales* (1881)
Archives BLPES, letters • Man. CL, Manchester Archives and Local Studies, letters | Bishopsgate Institute, London, letters to George Howell • BL, letters to W. E. Gladstone, Add. MSS 44407, 44415, 44428, 44433
Likenesses engraving, AM Oxf. [*see illus.*]
Wealth at death £12,191 4*s.*: administration, 29 July 1881, *CGPLA Eng. & Wales*

Beales, Hugh Lancelot (1889–1988), economist and social historian, born at Sedbergh, Yorkshire, on 18 February 1889, was the son of William Beales, a Wesleyan Methodist minister, and his wife, Zaida Mary Ann Elizabeth Scantlebury Green. He grew up in a radical political household. He was sent to the Kingswood School, Bath, a Methodist school, and won a scholarship to Manchester University, where he read medieval history under T. F. Tout. He served in the ranks throughout the First World War, refusing any promotion. Like many others, he would not speak of his wartime experiences either to friends or family; but they seemed to give him a lasting sympathy with 'the common soldier', 'the underdog', 'the common man'—oft-repeated phrases. From army days onwards he was universally known as Lance Beales.

In 1919 Beales became a lecturer in economic history at Sheffield University, with duties that included extramural teaching—which remained a lifelong commitment. A strong supporter of the Workers' Educational Association (WEA), he always believed that mature working people were far better able to understand the social effects of industrialization than were the young straight-from-schools. In 1922 he married Gladys Prydderch (1895–1982), with whom he had two sons and a daughter. He was called to the London School of Economics (LSE) in 1926, and became reader in economic history in 1931; but he maintained a northerner's perspective of 'north–south' as well as 'the two nations' all his life. Three or four important scholarly articles in the *Economic History Review* followed, but that was all at that level. But in 1929 came his *The Industrial Revolution*, a short account written for WEA classes which became almost a bible for the whole adult education movement, and was still in circulation in the 1950s. Some of the Labour Party and trade union leaders emerging from such classes said that it had an influence as great as R. H. Tawney's *Equality* and his *Acquisitive Society*.

The great book on the social preconditions and consequences of the British industrial revolution, long expected, ever promised, from his encyclopaedic knowledge of nineteenth-century economic and social history, never came; but Beales had an extraordinary impact as a lecturer, teacher, and talker. His memory was, like that of Webb, Laski, and Kingsley Martin, almost photographic. So he would lecture without notes, thinking out loud fiercely with his hand on a pile of 'old books' taken (sometimes at random, it seemed) from his vast private collection that seemed to hold up a rambling mid-Victorian house in Finchley. His intellectual strength was to see unexpected connections, but, as he thought as he talked, he would often move back and forth through time and space, and appear to end on a quite different subject matter in a different century from that on which he had begun. To the best students, this was an everlasting stimulus; but to the average student, the pyrotechnic display of historical free association could appear a perplexing muddle. None the less, when the LSE was evacuated to Cambridge in wartime, his lectures drew many auditors from quite different faculties. He and his wife (known as Taff to all) kept open house to LSE students in the evening, but others came too for limited cocoa and biscuits and endless argument.

What was good in lecturing and discussion, however, was fatal in writing. Beales suffered a social historian's version of Acton's disease: knowing so much, it was difficult to construct a narrative when one thing always reminded him of another. A whiff of Marxism, which he scorned, might have helped; he was untheoretical but not simply an empiricist, because he was forever reminding his listeners of the different perspectives and different interpretations that past writers, whether pamphleteers, factory inspectors, or academics, had put on the same events. However, during the thirty years he taught at LSE it is known that he supervised over 300 PhDs, and when his friend and disciple Oliver McGregor helped in his promotion for an honorary degree at Sheffield in 1971, he counted 160 scholarly works that were either dedicated to Beales or gave him the main thanks.

Beales's commitment to adult education made him an early broadcaster from Savoy Hill and he wrote a notable series of articles in the 1930s in the *Political Quarterly* about the policies of the BBC. He shared Reith's educational mission, but had a very different idea of education, which was social, even socialist. He knew Allen Lane and with Krisnan Menon and Tom Williams appeared as joint editor of the early Pelican non-fiction titles. Most of the imagination and input in choosing authors and titles was his. He saw cheap books, drawing on the precedent of Brougham's Society for the Diffusion of Useful Knowledge of the 1830s and 1840s, as the great instrument of social betterment. Apart from some aspects of LSE, he had a hostile view of the neglect by the universities of popular education.

In 1949 Beales was passed over for the chair at LSE when Tawney retired. One reason could obviously have been his lack of that one major publication, but he had also strained the Christian tolerance of Tawney to the point of anger by his militant and sarcastically provocative atheism, and had angered Lionel Robbins too with his contempt for classical theoretical economics—only historical explanations of the economy mattered. When the chair next became vacant, it was only a year before compulsory retirement and again, more understandably, he was passed over. Personal chairs were then rare. He left in bitterness. He refused to set foot in LSE again until a great party for his eightieth birthday arranged by former students. But in the meantime he had conducted a come-all-ye seminar each week across the road in a room in the White Horse on Saturday mornings, only later moving on to the slightly more formal auspices of the university's extramural department in Senate House.

However, Columbia, Harvard, and Washington, Seattle, all honoured Beales with visiting professorships. His mental powers held until a year or two before his end. He would say that 'you can all dance on my grave if I don't finish the book before I go'. Many said they would, so perhaps fortunately he chose cremation. Sadly in his last years he developed an irrational fear of dying in poverty, like so many of his nineteenth-century working-class leaders or writers. So he sold secretively and in small lots his library, dispersing probably the biggest private collection ever gathered of nineteenth-century social history. After his wife's death in 1982, Elizabeth Monkhouse, an extramural lecturer, lived with him and cared for him. He died in his hundredth year, at his home, 16 Denman Drive, Hampstead, London, on 19 April 1988.   BERNARD CRICK

Sources *LSE Magazine*, 76 (Nov 1988) · *The Times* (22 April 1988) · *The Independent* (23 April 1988) · *The Guardian* (26 April 1988) · b. cert. · *WWW* · personal knowledge (2004)
Archives BLPES, letters relating to academic committees and appointments
Wealth at death £167,266: probate, 22 Aug 1988, *CGPLA Eng. & Wales*

Bealknap, Sir Robert (*d.* 1401), justice, was a son of John Bealknap and his wife, Alice. John Bealknap may have been a counsel in 1348 and more probably a commissioner on piracy in Shoreham by Sea, Sussex, in 1354.

Robert Bealknap is recorded on a commission in Berkshire in September 1359, and then on numerous others, chiefly in Kent and Sussex; two early ones, in 1360–61, resemble his father's in being concerned with maritime crime, but thereafter most are the conventional commissions of array, of sewers, and of the peace. He was appointed JP in Kent on 18 May 1362, and repeatedly thereafter. From about that year he also appears in legal records as a counsel. In July 1362 he served with William Wykeham in a commission on lands granted to Wykeham's bishopric of Winchester. After several years of local duties he was appointed in 1365 to commissions to deal with complaints by Richard (II) Fitzalan, earl of Arundel. In 1366 he first appeared as a justice of gaol delivery at Battle in Sussex, and acquired Kingsnorth manor from Battle Abbey. On 14 February 1370 Bealknap's local activities culminated in his appointment as steward of the king's properties in Kent. On 24 October 1373 he received a grant of the manor of Wyltynge in Sussex with his wife Juliana. From 1374 he began to be associated in Kent with John, third Lord Cobham; in the same year he was named as one of the justices for an eyre in Kent, though none was held.

Meanwhile Bealknap's career as a lawyer in the central

courts had clearly prospered. From 1371 he was retained by Westminster Abbey, from 1374 by John of Gaunt, duke of Lancaster. In July 1374 he was sent with John Wyclif on an embassy led by John Gilbert, bishop of Bangor, for negotiations at Bruges over papal provisions. He returned in September and on 10 October he was appointed chief justice of the common bench; by 28 December, on the evidence of a licence to alienate lands to Rochester Cathedral priory for prayers for his parents, he had been knighted. From 1375 until 1388 he served regularly as a trier of petitions in parliament. In 1376 he served on commissions in Essex and Sussex on complaints against the disgraced financier Richard Lyons. Other local business continued to link him with the earl of Arundel (now Richard (III) Fitzalan) in Sussex, with Lord Cobham in Kent, and with Edward III's son Thomas of Woodstock in Essex.

On 26 June 1377, following the death of Edward III, Bealknap was reappointed chief justice of common pleas for Richard II. According to Walsingham, he made himself obnoxious to the Londoners by advising that their claim to exercise the office of butler at the young king's coronation should be rejected. In revenge, the citizens set a likeness of his head on a water conduit in the market place, so that its mouth should spew wine when the king passed by. Nor was this the only time Bealknap found himself unpopular. The Anonimalle chronicle (whose account is in some respects at odds with that of the judicial records) reports that during the peasants' revolt in June 1381 Bealknap was conducting a court of trailbaston in Essex, when the rebels made him swear that he would not hold such sessions again. He returned to London, and was in the Tower with King Richard on 11 June 1381, when the rebels demanded the heads of fifteen people, including Bealknap. Many of those named were killed, but Sir Robert survived. After the revolt Bealknap served on commissions to punish the rebels in Kent, Sussex, and elsewhere. In the next few years he served on many local commissions, as well as on one in 1385 to try John Northampton, the controversial former mayor of London.

Bealknap's downfall began with his advising on the creation of the commission appointed in parliament on 19 November 1386 to reform the government. The king and his advisers saw this commission as an affront to royal authority, and on 25 August 1387 Bealknap and other justices were summoned to Nottingham and presented with the so-called 'questions to the judges' (probably drafted by Sir Robert Tresilian, chief justice of king's bench), asking whether the commission was lawful and, if not, how its creators should be punished. They answered it was unlawful, and its creators should be punished as traitors. Knighton says Bealknap many times refused to seal the answers, which were finally sealed under threat of death from Robert de Vere, duke of Ireland, and Michael de la Pole, earl of Suffolk, and then said: 'Alas, now I need only a hurdle, a horse and a rope to bear me to the death I deserve' (*Knighton's Chronicle*, 395). On 17 November the duke of Gloucester and the earls of Arundel, Warwick, Nottingham, and Derby appealed de Vere, de la Pole, Tresilian, and their allies Nicholas Brembre and Archbishop Neville of York of treason; de Vere's attempts at armed resistance were defeated, and the lords appellant seized power.

Just as the ensuing Merciless Parliament began, on 30 January 1388, Robert Cherlton was appointed to replace Bealknap as chief justice of the bench, and the earl of Nottingham arrested Bealknap and his fellow justices. The justices were brought to trial on 27 February for their answers to the 'questions'. Bealknap and his colleagues pleaded coercion, but were sentenced to death. The archbishop of Canterbury, the bishop of Winchester, and many clerics came 'with heavy heart and light foot' to intercede for them (McKisack, 20). Knighton adds Queen Anne to the intercessors. The justices were pardoned execution, but sentenced to forfeiture and to exile in Ireland. Bealknap was granted a generous £40 a year and sent on 18 July to Drogheda. The exile was revoked in the January parliament of 1397, and the forfeiture of his property by that year's September parliament. Bealknap regained his lands until the 1388 judgment was revived by Henry IV's first parliament, in October 1399.

Sir Robert Bealknap died on 19 January 1401, and was probably buried in Rochester Cathedral. In the days of his prosperity he had become a considerable landowner, with a house in Queenhithe, London, and estates in Hertfordshire, Sussex, and above all Kent, where his influence was such that Bilsington Priory later claimed that it had not dared to sue him for arrears of rent, 'because in those days he was a royal justice and most powerful in the county of Kent' (Tout, *Admin. hist.*, 3.423, n. 1). He had married twice. His first wife, named Amy, whom he had married before 2 December 1365, was dead by 23 October 1373, when he is recorded as married to a woman named Juliana, through whom he acquired his Hertfordshire properties. The latter was the mother of his sons Thomas, John, and Hamo, and of his daughter Juliana, who married Robert Avenell. Following Bealknap's death his widow sued to regain lands forfeited by Sir Robert. Juliana died on 22 July 1414, and in 1425 their surviving son, Hamo, who had served at Agincourt, petitioned parliament for the restitution of estates. No response is recorded, and at his death in 1429 Hamo held only two manors in Kent and one apiece in Essex and Sussex, suggesting that most of his father's gains had proved irrecoverable.

Sir Robert Bealknap was a veteran justice trapped between the claims of Richard's royal prerogative and the appellant opposition. Reluctantly endorsing one, condemned by the other, Bealknap was spared death as being part of the 'fount, marrow and wisdom of English laws' (McKisack, 20).   JOHN L. LELAND

Sources V. H. Galbraith, ed., *The Anonimalle chronicle, 1333 to 1381* (1927); repr. with corrections (1970) · *RotP*, vols. 3–4 · *Chancery records* · *Calendar of inquisitions miscellaneous (chancery)*, PRO, 6 (1963) · *CIPM*, 15 · *Knighton's chronicle, 1337–1396*, ed. and trans. G. H. Martin, OMT (1995) [Lat. orig., *Chronica de eventibus Angliae a tempore regis Edgari usque mortem regis Ricardi Secundi*, with parallel Eng. text] · M. McKisack, ed., 'Historia, sive, Narracio de modo et forma Mirabilis Parliamenti apud Westmonasterium', *Camden miscellany, XIV*, CS, 3rd ser., 37 (1926) · Foss, *Judges* · J. Froissart, *Chronicles of England, France, Spain, and the adjoining countries*, trans. T. Johnes, 2 vols. (1874) · E. Hasted, *The history and topographical survey of the county of Kent*, 2 (1782) · J. Rastell and others, eds., *Le livre des assises et pleas del' corone* (1679) · N. Saul, *Richard II* (1997) · *Johannis de Trokelowe et Henrici de Blaneforde … chronica et annales*, ed. H. T. Riley, pt 3 of *Chronica monasterii S. Albani*, Rolls Series, 28 (1866) · *Thomae Walsingham, quondam monachi S. Albani, historia Anglicana*, ed. H. T. Riley, 2 vols., pt 1 of *Chronica monasterii S. Albani*, Rolls Series, 28 (1863–4) · L. C. Hector and B. F. Harvey, eds. and trans., *The Westminster chronicle, 1381–1394*, OMT (1982) · Tout, *Admin. hist.*, vol. 3 · Medway Archives and Local Studies Centre, Rochester, Kent, Rochester dean and chapter archives, T 87/1–3, T 89, T 94/1 · [T. Walsingham], *Chronicon Angliae, ab anno Domini 1328 usque ad annum 1388*, ed. E. M. Thompson, Rolls Series, 64 (1874) · J. Caley and J. Bayley, eds., *Calendarium inquisitionum post mortem sive escaetarum*, 4, RC (1828) · S. Walker, *The Lancastrian affinity, 1361–1399* (1990)
Archives Medway Archives and Local Studies Centre, Rochester, Kent, Rochester dean and chapter archives, T 87/1–3, T 89, T 94/1
Wealth at death property confiscated in 1399

Beamish, North Ludlow (1797–1872), army officer, writer, and antiquary, was the third son of William Beamish of Beaumont House, co. Cork, and his wife, Anne Jane Margaret, daughter of Robert De-la-Cour of Short Castle, co. Cork. The family claimed descent from one of the followers of William the Conqueror, from Edward I, and from Charlemagne. North Beamish was born at Beaumont House on 31 December 1797. He was educated at the Royal Military College, Sandhurst, and in November 1816 obtained a commission in the 4th Royal Irish dragoon guards, in which he purchased a troop in 1823. In 1825 he published an English translation of a small cavalry manual written by Count F. A. von Bismarck, a distinguished officer then engaged in the reorganization of the Würtemberg cavalry. Beamish's professional abilities brought him to notice, and he received a half-pay majority in the following year. While attached to the viceregal suite in Hanover he published *Lectures on … Cavalry* (1827), a translation of another work by Count von Bismarck, with original notes, in which he suggested various changes soon after adopted in the British cavalry. He also published *History of the King's German Legion* (2 vols., 1832–7), which was highly regarded.

After leaving Hanover, Beamish devoted much attention to Norse antiquities. His publications included *The Discovery of America by the Northmen in the Tenth Century* (1841), a summary of the researches of Professor Rafn of Copenhagen, thus popularizing knowledge of the vikings as explorers. In Stockholm on 27 May 1841 he married Aline Marie, daughter of the Revd John Eric Forsström. They had one son and two daughters; his wife survived him. Beamish, like his younger brother, Richard, at one time in the Grenadier Guards, was a fellow of the Royal Society. He received the KH from King Ernest of Hanover in 1837, after the separation of Hanover and England— one of the few British subjects to be honoured in this way. He was a JP for co. Cork and in 1855 high sheriff of the city of Cork. Beamish died at Ann Mount, near Glanmire, co. Cork, on 27 April 1872.

H. M. CHICHESTER, rev. JAMES LUNT

Sources Burke, *Gen. GB* · *Hart's Army List* · Publications of the Prince Society, Albany, N. Y. · Walford, *County families* · Boase, *Mod. Eng. biog.*

Wealth at death under £450 in England: Irish administration with will sealed in England, 10 June 1872, *CGPLA Eng. & Wales*

Beamish, Tufton Victor Hamilton, Baron Chelwood (1917–1989), army officer and politician, was born on 27 January 1917, one of two sons of Tufton Percy Hamilton Beamish (1874–1951), who retired from the Royal Navy with the rank of rear-admiral in 1925 and sat as Conservative MP for Lewes in 1924–32 and 1936–45, and his wife, Margaret, daughter of Henry Simon. His brother was killed in Burma in the closing stages of the Second World War.

Beamish's early upbringing provided two of the most dominant influences on his life, the one military, the other political, though he was such a multifarious character that they could not be said to be anything like the whole summation of his nature. He was educated at Stowe School, where he was a pupil of no particular distinction, and the Royal Military College, Sandhurst, from which he was, in 1937, commissioned into the Royal Northumberland Fusiliers. He was immediately posted to the British military mission in Cairo. This was the beginning of an extraordinary military odyssey, which saw him serve in every significant theatre of war between 1939 and 1945. Between 1938 and 1939 he served in British-mandated Palestine and, like many other British officers, acquired a lifelong sympathy for the aspirations of the Arab people. (Other officers, most notably Orde Wingate, found themselves much more in sympathy with the Jewish ambition for an independent homeland.)

At the outbreak of war in September 1939 Beamish was sent, as a company commander, with the British expeditionary force to France. The following year, on the retreat to Dunkirk, he was wounded and, after evacuation, awarded the Military Cross. After recovering from his wounds he was sent, in 1941, with the 18th division, to Singapore. The Japanese armies advanced rapidly down the Far Eastern littoral. With the fall of Singapore imminent, Beamish, accompanied by one junior officer and six enlisted men, escaped by rowing boat. They reached Sumatra after eight days at sea, only to find that the Japanese were in occupation there too. Beamish turned the boat round and made for Ceylon, where he finally reached safety. The rest of the year he spent in the comparative tranquillity of the Indian intelligence service.

But Beamish still hungered for action. In 1943 he secured his transfer to the Eighth Army in north Africa, where he served as commander of a machine-gun company. He took part in the allied invasion of Italy, was wounded again, and was twice mentioned in dispatches. He was ever a fearless and intelligent commander of men.

In 1945 his father decided to retire as Conservative MP for Lewes. Beamish was chosen in his place, and in July 1945 entered the House of Commons, where he served for thirty years until his retirement in February 1974. His energy was still ceaseless. But, although he served as an opposition spokesman on defence for two years from 1965, he never sought ministerial office and indeed turned it down more than once. Instead, he devoted himself to many causes (as well as working as a director of a number of companies). His four principal causes were: the advancement of European unity through what was then the European Economic Community; resistance to the threat posed by the Soviet Union through its penetration of eastern Europe (about which, in 1950, he published a book, *Must Night Fall?*); the dangers of the rise of the left in the Labour Party (about which he published another book, *Half Marx*, in 1970); and nature conservancy, which was to secure him a notable parliamentary triumph.

In the course of his bustling life Beamish served, in 1946, as a member of a parliamentary delegation to Poland, and in 1947 and 1948 he served on similar delegations to Germany, Austria, Bulgaria, Romania, and Hungary. He was a member of the Monnet action committee for a United States of Europe between 1971 and 1976 and joint deputy leader of the British delegation to the European assembly (now the European parliament) from 1973 to 1974. Like many of his generation, he had an abiding fear of another European war, and thought that developing the EEC was the best way to avert such a catastrophe.

With all this activity Beamish none the less found time to serve, from 1947 to 1953, on the executive of the 1922 committee—the gathering of all Conservative backbenchers—and from 1960 to 1964 as chairman of the Conservative foreign affairs committee. In 1965, moreover—having spent his spare time on research—he published yet another book, *Battle Royal*, a scholarly account of the battle of Lewes in 1264 between King Henry III and Simon de Montfort. This battle marked the beginning of the advance of parliamentary democracy in England: Beamish until the end of his life drew on its lessons for parliament in his own time.

In 1954 Beamish began a legislative process which became his enduring monument. He was passionate about birds, a long-serving and enthusiastic member of the Royal Society for the Protection of Birds, and from 1978 a member of the Nature Conservancy Council. In 1954 he secured, through diligent and inexorable negotiation with fellow politicians and vested interests, the passage of what was then the longest private member's bill ever to go before the house, the Protection of Birds Act. His ceaseless vigilance, however, led him to detect flaws in the act, so he procured its amendment in a new act in 1967. Nor did he stop there. In 1980 and 1981 in the House of Lords he fought successfully—and against often fierce government opposition—for the Wild Life and Countryside Act. As one of his obituarists noted, 'he was decades ahead of his time in campaigning for "green" issues' (Prestt).

Beamish married on 15 December 1950 Janet McMillan Stevenson (1921/2–1975), daughter of Andrew Stevenson, an engineer; she was a New Yorker and did not much care for his political life in Britain. Though they had two daughters, the marriage was dissolved in 1973. On 2 May 1975 Beamish married again, in delightfully romantic and improbable circumstances, this time a lady he had first courted during his frenetic career in the Second World

War. His second wife, (Maria) Pia McHenry (*b.* 1922/3), daughter of Ernest Von Roretz, a landowner, had also, between times, been married and divorced, and she survived him.

In 1961 Beamish was knighted, and in May 1974 he was created a life peer as Baron Chelwood of Lewes. As a man he was immensely gregarious, and his jovial and bouncy presentation of himself in company often led people to the entirely erroneous conclusion that he was merely an amiable old military buffer of a particularly tory type. He was, in fact, an extremely industrious and highly intelligent man who served his country exceptionally well, and who will be remembered with honour. He died on 6 April 1989. PATRICK COSGRAVE

Sources *WW* (1985) · *The Times* (8 April 1989) · I. Prestt, *The Independent* (13 April 1989) · m. certs · b. cert.
Archives CAC Cam., political diary, corresp., and notes · E. Sussex RO, political, military, and personal papers
Likenesses photograph, repro. in *The Times* · photograph, repro. in *The Independent*
Wealth at death £2,262,870: probate, 10 May 1989, *CGPLA Eng. & Wales*

Beamont, William John (1828–1868), Church of England clergyman and author, was born at Warrington, Lancashire, on 16 January 1828, the only son of William Beamont, solicitor, of that town, and author of *Annals of the Lords of Warrington* and other works. After attending Warrington grammar school for five years he was, in 1842, sent to Eton College, where he remained until 1846; there he won the Prince Albert prize for modern languages, the Newcastle medal, and other prizes. He entered Trinity College, Cambridge, in 1846, took high honours in 1850, gained the chancellor's medal, and was awarded a fellowship in 1852. He graduated BA in 1850, and MA in 1853. After his election as fellow of Trinity he made a tour of Egypt and Palestine, and following his ordination in 1854 he spent some time at Jerusalem, where he helped in the education of intending missionaries to Abyssinia—in Sunday school work and in preaching not only to the English residents but to the Arabs in their own tongue. He afterwards acted as chaplain in the camp hospitals of the British army in the Crimea.

Beamont returned home in 1855 and became curate of St John's, Broad Street, Drury Lane, London, in which parish he worked with great zeal until 1858, when he accepted the vicarage of St Michael's, Cambridge. Beamont was an energetic priest in his parish and in his pioneer efforts for church extension in Barnwell and Chesterton. He was also chiefly responsible for founding the Cambridge School of Art (1858) and the Church Defence Association (1859). Additionally he was the originator of the church congress (1861), in the foundation of which he was aided by his friend, R. Reynolds Rowe FSA. Beamont published several works, including *Catherine, the Egyptian Slave* (1852), *Concise Grammar of the Arabic Language* (1861), and *Cairo to Sinai and Sinai to Cairo* (1861). With Canon W. M. Campion he wrote the learned yet popular *Prayer-Book Interleaved* (1868).

Beamont died, apparently unmarried, at Cambridge, on 6 August 1868; his death was hastened by a fever caught in the East. He was buried in Trinity College chapel.
C. W. SUTTON, *rev.* H. C. G. MATTHEW

Sources *Warrington Guardian* (15 Aug 1868) · *Cambridge Chronicle and University Journal* (15 Aug 1868), 8 · G. W. Weldon, 'Seven years' personal recollections of parochial work in Cambridge', *The Churchman*, 8 (1883), 326 · private information (1885)
Archives Warrington Library, Lancashire, corresp. and diary of visits to the Seven Churches of Asia
Wealth at death under £2000: probate, 31 Aug 1868, *CGPLA Eng. & Wales*

Bean. *See* Beoán (*supp. fl.* 1012×24).

Bean, Charles Edwin Woodrow (1879–1968), historian, was born on 18 November 1879 at All Saints' College in rural Bathurst, New South Wales, Australia. His father, Edwin Bean (1851–1922), was the school's Arnoldian headmaster. His mother, Lucy Madeline Butler (1852–1942), was a gentle daughter of a solicitor. Ginger-haired 'Charlie' entered All Saints' preparatory school in 1886 but three years later sailed to Europe with his family. While Bathurst boys were playing ball in the dry summer heat, Charlie was on the field of Waterloo playing at collecting relics.

After his father became headmaster at Brentwood grammar school in Essex in 1891, Bean was a pupil there until he entered Clifton College near Bristol three years later. He grew to love literature, classics, and cricket, and became head of his house. In 1898 he won a classics scholarship to Hertford College, Oxford. In 1902 he graduated BA with second-class honours, proceeding to MA in 1905. He wanted to join in building up the British empire, but middling exam results and lack of social connections ruled out the military or civil posts he had in mind. There was always the law, a career his father favoured. In 1904 he graduated BCL, was called to the bars of the Inner Temple and New South Wales, and returned to Australia.

Bean set up as a barrister in Sydney, failed to attract briefs, and became a judges' associate. By writing up his impressions of Australia after fifteen years' absence he found a way out of the law when the *Sydney Morning Herald* printed some of them in 1907 and the following year engaged him as a reporter. He had a good ear, a quick pen, stout boots, and keen ambition, and was soon a feature writer. From 1910 to 1912 he was the paper's London correspondent. His journalism, and the books he adapted from it, proclaimed an admiration for ordinary men and an orthodox colonial nationalism. *On the Wool Track* (1910) and *The Dreadnought of the Darling* (1911) insisted that rural Australians would one day infuse the British race with rude vigour. *With the Flagship in the South* (1909) and *Flagships Three* (1913) supported the creation of an Australian navy and urged British support for Australian opposition to Asian immigration.

Many Australians sensed a national awakening when the first division of the Australian Imperial Force was raised in August 1914 to fight alongside the British army. Eager and likeable, Bean was nominated by the journalists' union to be the force's official war correspondent, and the defence minister asked him to write an official history of Australia's part in the war when peace came. Military staff found in Bean a reporter they could trust to be discreet. Ordinary soldiers had their doubts when the 6-foot-tall, frail-looking, bespectacled 35-year-old with a toff's accent reported approvingly on the sending home of some rowdies among them.

Bean landed on Gallipoli on 25 April 1915 soon after the first Australian troops, sharing their dangers and winning their respect. He saw that simple endurance was heroic in modern war and tried to document it fully, which made his reports seem flat beside those of other correspondents. Still, he delivered the verdict his audience expected—that men of a distinctively Australian character, democratic and semi-rural, had rushed the ridges at Gallipoli and held on there. He stayed until the campaign's futile, wintry end, and gathered some of the soldiers' writings and drawings into The Anzac Book (1916), which helped to build the popular image of the laconic Australian. Bean then accompanied most of the Australian Imperial Force to the western front to chart its descent into muddy hell and final, bone-weary victory. His ginger head was often seen in the forward trenches, bent over a notebook. It was sometimes seen at headquarters too, where he joined an intrigue against John Monash's succession to corps command. By the end of the war he had filled 296 notebooks and diaries, and dashed off In your Hands, Australians (1918), a tract urging his people to build a nation worthy of their 60,000 war dead.

In May 1919 Bean was back in Australia, where the government accepted his ambitious plan for a great official history that, like his reportage, would narrate the plain truth as seen from the Australian trenches. He moved to Tuggeranong homestead near Canberra, the new capital city, and began what would be his life's work. His life found meaning in another way at Tuggeranong. He had seemed a confirmed bachelor until he met Ethel Clara Young (1893–1991), a nursing sister, and married her on 24 January 1921 at St Andrew's Cathedral in Sydney. 'Effie' tolerated his devotion to his writing, and cared for him in his worsening health. In 1924 he had a kidney removed, and the following year the couple moved to Sydney to avoid Canberra's grey winters, taking a house in a leafy northern suburb and calling it Clifton. In 1929 they adopted a daughter, Joyce, in the same spirit in which they aided war orphans.

The first volume of Bean's Official History of Australia in the War of 1914–18, published in 1921, differed from its British counterpart. The vastly detailed account of the early days on Gallipoli reported the actions, even the words, of many Australian soldiers in their first great battle, and concluded that their 'mettle' had 'purchased a tradition' (Bean, The Story of Anzac, 1.605, 607). Bean wrote five more massive volumes (1924–42) that followed the Australian Imperial Force from Gallipoli to the Hindenburg line, edited another nine by other authors to complete an Australian vision of the war, and tried to summarize the entire work in Anzac to Amiens (1946). At nearly 4 million words it was by far the largest official history of the war

produced by a British dominion. Deferred to reverently, though rarely read through, it encouraged a new seriousness in Australia's self-image and probably shaped official histories of the Second World War. It earned Bean a Chesney gold medal (1930), a DLitt from the University of Melbourne (1931), and an LLD from the Australian National University (1959). It would also have earned him a knighthood had he not refused it.

Bean's other great monument to the Australian Imperial Force was the Australian War Memorial. Determined that it should combine a library and museum with a secular shrine to the dead, he was its first acting director in 1919 and helped to manage it until 1963. As board chairman from 1951 to 1959 he hastened the completion of its commemorative area and tried to introduce system into its sprawling collection of documents and artefacts. He also helped to systematize government record-keeping generally when in 1942 he chaired a war archives committee that evolved into a national archive. From 1947 to 1958 he chaired the promotions appeals board of the Australian Broadcasting Commission.

Bean's politics were as gentle and high-minded as his character. Between the world wars he hoped that decentralization would abolish slums, town planning would abolish poverty, physical training and recreation grounds would abolish disease and immorality, and the League of Nations would abolish war, and he was active in supporting these causes. For twenty years he held to the trench wisdom of 1918 that another war must be avoided. The depression brought out in him a radical streak, blinding him to the crimes of Soviet Russia, and seeing him cut his pay voluntarily when others had theirs cut. When another war came he shared popular hopes for social reconstruction afterwards, though on old-fashioned terms that his father would have understood. 'May we all play the game with larger wisdom than in 1918', he lectured in his tract War Aims of a Plain Australian (1943, vii) that urged education for all. Not that he wanted the closure of privileged schools like those he had attended, and he celebrated Australia's élite schools in Here, my Son (1950). But he accepted that another institution once dear to him, a white Australia, must eventually be abandoned.

By now his mind and body were fading. In 1956 he and Effie moved to the Sydney seaside suburb of Collaroy, but in 1964 he was admitted at government expense to Concord Repatriation General Hospital for war veterans. He died there on 30 August 1968 and three days later was cremated at the Northern Suburbs crematorium, Sydney, after a memorial service at St Andrew's Cathedral, at which was sung his verse of 1915 'Non nobis'. It was understood that a great and good man had passed away. In the following year the historian K. S. Inglis lectured on his life and work, admitting the latter into the canon of influential Australian writing. In 1982 the poet Les Murray judged that Bean's rank-and-file military history probably fixed Australia's view of the First World War and of all wars to follow.

CRAIG WILCOX

Sources Australian War Memorial, Canberra, C. E. W. Bean papers, AWM38 · Australian War Memorial, Canberra, E. C. Bean papers, PR00283 · K. S. Inglis, *C. E. W. Bean, Australian historian* (1970) · A. W. Bazley, 'C. E. W. Bean', *Historical Studies*, 14 (1969–71), 147–54 · D. McCarthy, *Gallipoli to the Somme: the story of C. E. W. Bean* (1983) · M. Piggott, *A guide to the personal, family and official papers of C. E. W. Bean* (Canberra, 1983) [Australian War Memorial guide] · K. S. Inglis, 'Bean, Charles Edwin Woodrow', *AusDB*, vol. 7 · K. Frewster, ed., *Gallipoli correspondent: the frontline diary of C. E. W. Bean* (1983) · D. A. Kent, 'The Anzac book and the Anzac legend: C. E. W. Bean as editor and image maker', *Historical Studies*, 21 (1984–5), 376–90 · S. Ellis, 'The censorship of the official naval history of Australia in the Great War', *Historical Studies*, 20 (1982–3), 367–82 · J. Barrett, 'No straw man: C. E. W. Bean and some critics', *Australian Historical Studies*, 23 (1988–9), 102–14 · M. McKernan, *Here is their spirit: a history of the Australian War Memorial, 1917–1990* (1991) · E. L. French, 'Bean, Edwin', *AusDB*, vol. 3 · L. Murray, 'Eric Rolls and the golden disobedience', *Quadrant* (1982) [repr. in L. Murray, *A working forest* (1997), 148–66]

Archives Australian War Memorial, Canberra, AWM38 | Australian War Memorial, Canberra, E. C. Bean papers, PR00283 · King's Lond., Liddell Hart C., corresp. with Major J. North and reviews

Likenesses photograph, 1915, Australian War Memorial, Canberra, AWM A5394; repro. in McKernan, *Here is their spirit* · G. Lambert, oils, 1924, Australian War Memorial, Canberra, ART07545; repro. in McCarthy, *Gallipoli*, frontispiece · photograph, Australian War Memorial, Canberra, AWM A5389; repro. in McKernan, *Here is their spirit*, 136

Beane, Sawney (*fl.* 15th–16th cent.), legendary murderer and cannibal, is first mentioned in print in broadsheets about 1700. Various versions of his life appeared: in some he is said to have been active during the reign of James I of Scotland (1424–36), while other accounts date his crimes to the reign of James VI, who ruled Scotland from 1567 before succeeding to the English throne as James I in 1603. The story of Sawney Beane was collected in *A Compleat History of the Lives and Robberies* (5th edn, 1719) and in *A General and True History of the Lives and Actions* (1734) before the legend became enshrined in the *Newgate Calendars*.

According to legend Beane was the son of a hedger and ditcher. He had an unnamed wife with whom he had eight sons and six daughters, who incestuously produced a further thirty-two children. The Beane family lived in a cave by the sea in Galloway. They lived by robbing passing travellers, murdering them, and then consuming the bodies (uncooked but apparently smoked or pickled). This went on for at least twenty-five years, during which many of the local innkeepers were executed for murder as the last people to see the travellers alive, with the result that 'not a few innkeepers … left off their business, for fear of being made examples of' (*History*, 2). This in turn discouraged visitors to the area. Over a thousand people disappeared before a man and his wife returning from a local fair were attacked. The man defended himself while the female Beanes slashed his wife's throat and drank her blood before disembowelling her. A party of thirty people arrived while this was happening and the Beanes made their escape. The crime was reported to the provost in Glasgow, who sent for the king. The king brought 400 soldiers and a pack of bloodhounds which led them into a deep cave whose entrance was covered at high tide. There they found the limbs of men, women, and children 'hung up in rows, like dried beef' and 'lying in pickle' while

heaps of loot lay on the floor (*Life*, 3). The soldiers buried the human remains and took the Beanes and the loot off to Edinburgh (Leith in some versions). The whole clan was executed, the men being dismembered and left to bleed to death while the women and children, having watched this, were burnt alive.

There is no contemporary record of any of this and all versions of the story contain internal discrepancies. The dates suggested for Beane's activities, as well as the appearance of printed accounts in eighteenth-century pamphlets, strongly suggest that the story had most appeal at times when anxieties about the union with Scotland and the barbarous image of the highlander were particularly contentious. Accusations of cannibalism are almost invariably levelled at those whose difference from the accuser is felt to be threatening. This, the constant emphasis in the early texts on the sufferings of 'the King's subjects' and the dismay of 'the whole Kingdom' (*Life*, 3, 4), and the heavily stressed intervention of the king himself, all indicate that this is a fable about the final omnipotence of the head of state over the furthest and most rebellious reaches of the country.   SARAH MOSS

Sources *The history of Sawney Beane* (c.1770) · *The life of Sawney Beane the man eater* (c.1814) · J. Nicholson, ed., *Historical and traditional tales in prose and verse* (1843) · R. Holmes, *The legend of Sawney Bean* (1975)

Bearblock, John. *See* Bereblock, John (*fl.* 1557–1572).

Bearcroft, Philip (1695–1761), antiquary and Church of England clergyman, was born at Worcester on 21 February 1695 and baptized at St Swithin's in the city on 1 March, the son of Philip Bearcroft. Descended from an ancient Worcestershire family, he was educated at the Charterhouse, London, of which he was elected a scholar on the nomination of Lord Somers in July 1710. On 17 December 1712 he matriculated from Magdalen Hall, Oxford, and graduated BA in 1716. In 1717 he became probationary, and in 1719 actual, fellow of Merton College, taking his MA degree in the same year. He was ordained deacon in 1718 at Bristol, and priest in 1719 at Gloucester. He accumulated the degrees of BD and DD in 1730. According to the brief memoir of him by his granddaughter, he acted as tutor to the three sons and niece of John Perceval, first earl of Egmont. He was appointed preacher to the Charterhouse in 1724, chaplain to the king in 1738, and secretary to the Society for the Propagation of the Gospel in Foreign Parts in 1739. He was presented to the Merton living at Elham, Kent, in 1731 and became rector of Stourmouth, Kent, in 1743. He was twice married, first to Elizabeth Lovegrove with whom he had three sons, Philip, Edward, who became an MP, and William. He later married Mary Coventry, first cousin to the earl of Coventry.

In 1737 Bearcroft published *An Historical Account of Thomas Sutton, Esquire, and of his Foundation in Charter-House*, which provided most of the material for Robert Smythe's 1808 history of the foundation. He also intended to publish a collection of the rules and orders of the Charterhouse, but was prevented by the governors, and only a few extracts were printed in a quarto pamphlet and distributed among the officers of the house. On 18 December

1753 he was elected master of the Charterhouse, and in 1755 he was collated to a prebendal stall in Wells Cathedral. He died on 17 October 1761 before he was 'raised to a promised Bishopric' (*Relics*, preface, ix). He was survived by his widow. Some of his sermons were published both before and after his death, and thirteen discourses on moral and religious subjects were published as *Relics of the Sacred Ministry* in 1835.

ALFRED GOODWIN, *rev.* S. J. SKEDD

Sources *Relics of the sacred ministry of the late Rev Philip Bearcroft*, ed. [S. Bearcroft] (1835) · Foster, *Alum. Oxon.* · *GM*, 1st ser., 31 (1761), 538 · Nichols, *Lit. anecdotes*, 1.650 · J. Brooke, 'Bearcroft, Edward', HoP, *Commons, 1754–90* · Venn, *Alum. Cant.* · administration, PRO, PROB 6/137, fol. 273r · IGI
Archives LPL, corresp.

Beard, Charles (1827–1888), Unitarian minister, scholar, and journal editor, was born at Higher Broughton, Manchester, on 27 July 1827, the eldest son of John Relly *Beard (1800–1876), Unitarian minister at Salford, and his wife, Mary Barnes (1802–1887). Educated at his father's school, he studied at Manchester New College (then at Manchester) from 1843 to 1848, graduating BA from the University of London in 1847. He aided his father in compiling the Latin dictionary published by Cassell. In 1848–9 he continued his studies at Berlin. In February 1888, the University of St Andrews conferred on him an LLD.

On 17 February 1850 Beard became assistant to James Brooks (1806–1854) at Hyde Chapel, Gee Cross, Cheshire, a magnificent, newly built Gothic church, becoming sole pastor in 1854. On 4 June 1850 he married Mary Ellen (1823–1910), daughter of Michael Shipman of Liverpool, formerly of Hinckley; there were six daughters and a son, Lewis Beard (1858–1933), who graduated from Trinity College, Cambridge, became a barrister and later solicitor, served as town clerk of Coventry and Blackburn, and was knighted in 1919.

On 3 March 1867 Beard succeeded John Hamilton Thom (1808–1894) at Renshaw Street Chapel, Liverpool. To a busy congregational, denominational, and scholarly life he added an extensive journalistic career. During the cotton famine of 1862–4 he served as special correspondent for the *Daily News* and was for many years a leader writer on the *Liverpool Daily Post*, but his lack of sympathy with Irish home rule led him to give up political journalism. He was a major force in the founding and management of University College, Liverpool, serving as vice-chairman of its council.

A committed Liberal, Beard was active in Liverpool politics and in demand as a political speaker, evoking no little hostility among his Conservative opponents. Imposingly handsome, with a splendid voice, he was equally at home before a popular audience and with congregations over a wide range of sophistication. He was asked to preach the opening sermons at no fewer than twenty-five new Unitarian chapels.

Unitarians, like their Presbyterian forebears, had prided themselves on a learned ministry, but by the middle of the nineteenth century that ideal was giving way to a majority preoccupied with pastoral demands and a small minority of genuine scholars who nevertheless remained active (like Beard) in congregational and public life. In contrast to his father, an indefatigable and miscellaneous publicist, Charles Beard made a deep scholarly impression. His two-volume study *Port Royal: a Contribution to the History of Religion and Literature in France* (1861) achieved classic status, as did his Hibbert lectures of 1883, 'The Reformation … in its relation to modern thought'. These impressive syntheses also show the development of Beard's call (by no means his alone) for a new Reformation that, in his understanding, would reject all forms of infallibility (institutional or textual), reconcile religion and science, and unite Christians and non-Christians alike in understanding the religious impulse as a proper subject for scientific study.

Beard's most important contribution to this end was undoubtedly his editorship of the *Theological Review* from 1864 to 1879, in which he tried to bring together, not always successfully, the conservative and advanced schools of thought within Unitarianism. His own theological sympathies lay with the latter, and, like its acknowledged leader James Martineau (1805–1900) and unlike many younger ministers in the latter part of the century, he rejected most state intervention to remedy social problems, seeing the solution in individual regeneration. In his memorial sermon at Renshaw Street, the Revd James Edwin Odgers (1843–1925) recalled that when, standing before Luke Fildes's famous painting of casual paupers, he remarked 'That makes me want to cry', Beard answered, 'It makes me want to preach.'

The extraordinary demands of Beard's multiple careers challenged even his robust constitution. Suffering from heart disease, he spent six months in Italy in 1886, and his congregation gave him a further year's leave in 1887. He died on 9 April 1888 at 13 South Hill Road, Liverpool, and was buried in the graveyard of the Ancient Chapel, Toxteth Park, on 12 April.

ALEXANDER GORDON, *rev.* R. K. WEBB

Sources *The Inquirer* (14 April 1888) · *The Inquirer* (21 April 1888) · *Christian Life* (14 April 1888) · H. McLachlan, *Records of a family, 1800–1933: pioneers in education, social service and liberal religion* (1935) · A. C. Bradley, 'In memoriam Charles Beard', *Liverpool University College Magazine*, 3 (1888), 94–9 · [E. R. Houghton], 'The *Theological Review*: a Quarterly Journal of Religious Thought and Life, 1864–1879', Wellesley index, 3.505–11 · [Achates], '"As ithers see us": to the Rev. Charles Beard, BA', *The Porcupine*, 19 (1877), 42 · d. cert.
Archives priv. coll., corresp. | JRL, letters to John Gordon
Likenesses J. E. Boehm, marble relief bust, Unitarian church, Ullet Road, Liverpool
Wealth at death £7284 15s. 8d.: probate, 17 May 1888, CGPLA Eng. & Wales

Beard, John (1716/17–1791), actor and singer, of unknown parentage and place of birth, is first recorded as one of the children of the Chapel Royal. He was well educated in music under Bernard Gates, master of the children of the Chapel Royal from 1727 to 1757, and was also taught Latin, mathematics, rhetoric, and history. Beard's singing and acting career started while he was still a boy, when Gates presented a private performance of Handel's *Esther* to the composer on 23 February 1732; Beard sang the part of the

Priest of the Israelites. When his voice changed, he received an honourable dismissal from the king's service in 1734 and a present of clothing worth £10. He was promptly engaged by Handel to perform in his Covent Garden company as a tenor, and was an immediate success as Silvius in *Il pastor fido* (9 November 1734), justifying the favourable advance press report that 'Mr Handell had got an extreme fine English Voice … who never sang on any stage' (Dean). He must have impressed Handel too, for Lady Elizabeth Compton, who was present at this performance, remarked that 'Mr Hendell is so full of [Beard's] praises that he says he will surprise the Town with his performances before the Winter is over' (Highfill, Burnim & Langhans, *BDA*).

During the three years before the failure of Handel's opera company in 1738, Beard sang more Handel parts under the composer than any other singer, performing in ten operas, some church music, and all but one of Handel's oratorios, masques, and odes. He sang for other composers and theatres, notably, in January 1736, in John Ernest Galliard's *The Royal Chase* at Covent Garden, after which the hunting song 'The Early Horn' from this pantomime became his signature tune. From this point on Beard was in constant demand to sing in ballad operas, pantomimes, and burlesques, as well as more serious pieces. In the 1737 season he became a member of the Drury Lane company, where he remained for six years before migrating to Covent Garden. Away from Drury Lane or Covent Garden, he performed at the King's Theatre, Hickford's Room, the Crown and Anchor tavern, Ranelagh Gardens, and the Oxford Music Room. Beard's popularity with audiences was such that many of the entertainments in which he featured enjoyed greater success and longer runs than others of comparable quality.

Although Beard's roles in the major operas and oratorios at the time made him the darling of the critics, it was his English songs which earned him a place in the hearts of the music-loving audiences. After his success with Galliard's 'The Early Horn' Beard was chosen by many of the leading English composers as a vehicle for many traditional songs, such as ballads, soldier songs, love songs, pastorals, and hunting songs. He was also able to perform in character—as a sailor, a west countryman, or a Scot, and he sang many patriotic songs. From 1737 he was a popular Macheath in John Gay's *The Beggar's Opera*.

In addition to his talent as a singer and actor, Beard was reputed to be a charming, cheerful, and polite man with excellent social qualities and a handsome appearance. The combination of his personal and vocal attributes led to a rapid rise up the social and professional ladder. On 8 January 1739, fewer than five years after his first professional vocal performance, Beard married into the upper reaches of British society. His wife was Lady Henrietta (Harriet) Herbert, *née* Waldegrave (*c*.1717–1753), the daughter of James *Waldegrave, first Earl Waldegrave, a granddaughter of James II, and the widow of Lord Edward Herbert, the son of William, second marquess of Powis. Although the marriage was thought to have been happy, it caused considerable scandal in the town. Cruel gossip

about the couple was spread among the lady's acquaintances. John Perceval, first earl of Egmont, entered in his diary five days after the wedding that Lady Henrietta's brother James told her that:

> her lover had the pox, and that she would be disappointed of the only thing she married him for, which was her lust; for that he would continue to lie every night with the player that brought them together, and give her no solace. But there is no prudence below the girdle. (Highfill, Burnim & Langhans, *BDA*)

Egmont also wrote that Lady Harriet had a jointure of £600 per annum, £200 of which was encumbered by debt, and £200 more of which had been sold to pay Beard's debts. Lord Waldegrave ceased to acknowledge his daughter, despite her pleas for forgiveness. Without his support the Beards struggled financially. Early in 1740 they were living in a house in New North Street, just off Red Lion Square, Holborn, and they moved abroad for a brief time, staying in Lille during summer 1740. On their return in 1741–2 they lodged in Red Lion Street, near Lamb's Conduit. They were back in the house in New North Street the following season, and remained until 1751, but by May 1752 they had made a further downward step by moving to the poorer area of Great Russell Street, Covent Garden.

During this period Beard remained a successful singer. In 1743 he began a five-season period at Covent Garden and was elected to the Sublime Society of Beefsteaks. In 1748 he was brought back to Drury Lane by David Garrick. Although his salary from the theatres was very good he remained keen to seek supplementary income. On 31 May 1753 Lady Harriet died, possibly assisted to her grave by the financial worry and rejection from her family. She was buried in the churchyard at St Pancras. Beard moved to Mrs Coleman's in East Street, near his old area of Red Lion Square. His benefit bill of 29 March 1755 places his residence 'next door to Old Slaughter's Coffee house' (Highfill, Burnim & Langhans, *BDA*) in St Martin's Lane, where he probably lived until 1763.

In 1759 Beard married Charlotte Rich (1726–1818), one of four daughters of John *Rich, manager of the theatre in Covent Garden, and he switched his employ to the Covent Garden company at the beginning of the 1759–60 season. He continued to acquire distinctions: in 1759 he received a DMus at Oxford, and in 1760 he became a governor of the Foundling Hospital, where he had performed in Handel's *Messiah* annually since 1750. He was also a member of the Royal Society of Musicians. Upon the death of John Rich in 1761, Beard became jointly responsible for Covent Garden theatre with Rich's widow, Priscilla, effectively taking over active management. This career was successful, marred only by a serious riot in February 1763. After rioters forced Garrick at Drury Lane to grant half-price admission to the theatre at the close of the third act, Beard announced that, for his theatre's next production, 'Nothing under Full Price can be taken' (Fiske, 256). The ensuing disorder resulted in the entire auditorium being wrecked and £2000 worth of damage being done. Covent Garden was shut for a week, and Beard had to publish an apology in the press.

Beard retired from the stage prematurely in 1767, owing to deafness, when he sold the Covent Garden patent for £60,000. He and his wife retired to Hampton, Middlesex, where they lived quietly, and as comfortably as Beard's failing health allowed. Beard died at Hampton on 4 February 1791, in his seventy-fifth year, and was buried in the church there. His second wife died much later, in 1818. His estate totalled around £3000 plus the value of his house in Hampton, and his will included legacies to his widow, his sister Catherine Beard, and a Mrs Mary Morice of Long Acre, as well as £100 to the theatrical fund.

VICTORIA HALLIWELL

Sources Highfill, Burnim & Langhans, *BDA* · T. Gilliland, *The dramatic mirror, containing the history of the stage from the earliest period, to the present time*, 2 vols. (1808) · [J. S. Sainsbury], ed., *A dictionary of musicians*, 2 vols. (1825) · *DNB* · A. H. Scouten, ed., *The London stage, 1660–1800*, pt 3: *1729–1747* (1961) · G. W. Stone, ed., *The London stage, 1660–1800*, pt 4: *1747–1776* (1962) · W. Dean, 'Beard, John', *New Grove*, 2nd edn · R. Fiske, *English theatre music in the eighteenth century*, 2nd edn (1986) · *GM*, 1st ser., 61 (1791), 187–8
Likenesses J. Anlayson, group portrait, mezzotint, pubd 1768 (after J. Zoffany), BM, NPG · portrait, pubd 1769, Harvard TC · engraving, pubd 1787 (after portrait at Hampton) · mezzotint, pubd 1787, BM, NPG · J. Faber junior, mezzotint (after J. M. Williams), BM, NPG · J. Macardell, mezzotint (after T. Hudson), BM, NPG · J. M. Williams, portrait, Royal Opera House, Covent Garden · Zoffany, portrait (as Hawthorn) · prints, BM, NPG
Wealth at death £3000; plus value of property in Hampton

Beard, John Relly (1800–1876), Unitarian minister and educationist, was born on 4 August 1800 at 24 Charlotte Row, Landport, Portsmouth, the eldest of the nine children of John Beard (1775–1831) and his wife, Ann Paine (1777/8–1864). His father was a small tradesman and the family lived in comparative poverty. This, combined with his father's religious evolution out of a rigid Calvinism, helped to make Beard a radical and militant proponent of mid-Victorian Unitarianism.

While a pupil at a local grammar school John Beard started to attend the Unitarian chapel in Portsmouth with his father. A leading member, Sir James Carter, later sent him to a boarding-school in France in 1817. He returned in 1818 to prepare for entry to the ministry at Manchester College, York, in 1820. On leaving college in 1825 he became minister of the newly formed congregation at Greengate, Salford, which migrated to Bridge Street, Strangeways, in 1842, where Beard remained until 1864. A declining stipend, combined with an increasing family, forced him, like many other Unitarian ministers, to keep a school until 1849, which proved a successful and innovative venture. One of his pupils, W. H. Herford, writing in 1876 stated: 'The introduction to literature, the rational geometry and natural science which you provided for us, were all openings-up of rich feasts, after starvation' (McLachlan, *Records*, 1).

Beard wrote controversial books in the 1830s attacking the provision of education in Lancashire, including *The Abuses of the Manchester Free Grammar School* (1837). Unremitting pressure supported by influential friends helped produce significant reforms. He argued increasingly that most of the ills of society flowed from a lack of education, and published a number of popular educational journals

and dictionaries which made his name widely known: *Latin Made Easy* (1848), *Dictionary of the Bible* (1847), and the *People's Biographical Dictionary* are among the leading examples. Beard 'interpreted for the inarticulate masses their intellectual needs and aspirations' (McLachlan, *Records*, 10). The University of Giessen awarded him an honorary DD in 1841 for services to literature.

Beard was a crusading propagandist for Unitarianism; he wrote extensively and preached widely. He was a compiler, popularizer, and translator rather than an advanced thinker. He wrote and translated thirty-eight religious works, and his pen was never still in putting into simple terms religious and doctrinal developments in England, France, and Germany. His translations of French and German theologians in the 1860s had a significant effect on British theological thinking. By the 1860s he was so well known that foreign correspondents needed to address their letters simply to 'John R. Beard DD, Manchester, England' for them to reach him.

In 1862 Beard helped to mobilize the wealthy Unitarians of Manchester to build the memorial hall in Albert Square to mark the bicentenary of the Great Ejection; it was the first non-denominational public hall in the city devoted to religious purposes. He founded the *Christian Teacher* in 1835, and in 1861 was a joint founder, and sometime joint editor, of the *Unitarian Herald*. The latter was considered by many as one of the best religious newspapers of its time. But his most enduring achievement was the creation, in association with William Gaskell, of the Unitarian Home Missionary Board in 1854 for the training of young men for home missions. He became principal and remained in office until 1874. In 1926 the board was renamed the Unitarian College, and later became an integral part of the University of Manchester.

Beard had married Mary (1802–1887), daughter of Charles and Mary Barnes, at the parish church, Portsea, on 28 June 1826, the couple handing the clergyman a signed protest against such parts of the service 'as imply our credence in the unscriptural doctrine of the Trinity'. They had ten children; their eldest son, Charles *Beard, was one of the leading Unitarian ministers and writers of his day, who also collaborated with his father on several publications.

By the late 1860s Beard's energy was waning, though he had moved to a new ministry at Sale Chapel, Cheshire, in 1865. His power of speech declined in the early 1870s and he retired in 1874. He died at The Meadows, Ashton upon Mersey, on 22 November 1876, and was buried in the nearby Brooklands cemetery on 27 November.

ALAN RUSTON

Sources H. McLachlan, *Records of a family, 1800–1933: pioneers in education, social service and liberal religion* (1935), 1–35 · H. McLachlan, *Unitarian Home Missionary College, 1854–1914* (1915) · C. S. Grundy, *Reminiscences of Strangeways Unitarian chapel, 1838–1888* (1888) · G. E. Evans, *Record of the provincial assembly of Lancashire and Cheshire* (1896), 117, 126, 167 · *Manchester Guardian* (24 Nov 1876) · *The Inquirer* (25 Nov 1876) · *The Inquirer* (2 Dec 1876) · *The Inquirer* (9 Dec 1876) · *Christian Life* (25 Nov 1876) · *Christian Life* (2 Dec 1876) · *Christian Life* (9 Dec 1876) · *Unitarian Herald* (1 Dec 1876) · *Unitarian Herald* (4 May 1877)

Archives JRL, corresp. · priv. coll.
Likenesses oils, 1851, Cross Street Unitarian chapel, Manchester · photograph (after painting, c.1840–1859), repro. in McLachlan, *Records of a family*, facing p. 1
Wealth at death under £3000: probate, 22 Dec 1876, *CGPLA Eng. & Wales*

Beard, Thomas (*c*.1568–1632), Church of England clergyman and author, is said to have been a native of Huntingdon, but details of his parents and early life are unknown. He matriculated sizar at Jesus College, Cambridge, in 1584, graduated BA in 1588, and proceeded MA in 1591. Ordained deacon and priest in April 1595, he was collated to the rectory of St Andrew's Kimbolton. This was a wealthy parish, which he supplied with a curate and held in plurality for twelve years after he was presented in 1598 to the livings of Hengrave, Suffolk, and Aythorp Roothing, Essex.

Beard is best known as the author of *The Theatre of Gods Judgements* (1597), an anthology of colourful anecdotes of the divine vengeance visited upon flagrant sinners arranged in accordance with the ten commandments. Containing stories compiled from classical writers, the church fathers, and medieval *exempla* collections, the book was a translation of a French work by the Reformed minister Jean Chassanion, 'augmented by more than three hundred examples'. This in turn borrowed heavily from a German Lutheran source. New editions appeared in 1612 and 1631 enriched with further material, much of it gleaned from contemporary sermons, tracts, chronicles, and news pamphlets. The *Theatre* was posthumously republished in folio in 1648, when it was said to have been jointly authored by Beard and Thomas Taylor, preacher of St Mary Aldermanbury in London, though there is no firm evidence of direct collaboration between the two. The book was also abridged by Edmund Rudierd as *The Thunderbolt of Gods Wrath Against Hard-Hearted and Stiffe-Necked Sinners* in 1618.

In 1604 Beard was instituted warden of the hospital of St John and master of the free grammar school in Huntingdon, where his most famous pupil was to be Oliver Cromwell. Beard is reputed to have written and produced Latin plays for his scholars to enact, and he left in manuscript 'An evangelical tragaedie, or, A harmonie of the passion of our Lord Jesus Christe paraphrastically expounded according to the fower evangelists' (BL, Royal MS 17. D. xvii), an English dramatization of the gospel story in five acts, which he dedicated to James I. He was also vicar of All Saints, in Huntingdon, and in 1611 secured a second parish in the town, that of St John the Baptist. He acquired a prebend's stall in Lincoln Cathedral in 1612, which he held until his death, and was appointed a royal chaplain at some point during the reign of James I. In 1614, the year he proceeded DD, Beard wrote to Sir Robert Cotton declaring that he was 'tyred with my paynfull occupation of teaching and would gladly now be sett free', and asking for preferment to the parsonage of Conington, Cambridgeshire (Cotton MS Julius c.III, fol. 21r). This did not, however, effect his release, and in the event he remained in charge of the school until 1625, by which time he was also rector of Wistow, Huntingdonshire.

Meanwhile, following the suppression of a combination lectureship at Huntingdon in 1614, the corporation financed a fixed lecture on Wednesday and Sunday mornings in All Saints' Church and appointed Beard to the post. It appears from an indenture made between him and the bailiffs and burgesses of the town in 1625 that he was greatly respected and had given 'great comfort' to the inhabitants by means of his learned and 'painefull' preaching (BL, Add. MS 15665, fols. 126r–127r). Three years later he was 'exceedingly rated' by his diocesan, Richard Neile, bishop of Lincoln, for a sermon delivered at the Spittle, in which he had taken the opportunity to expose the 'flat popery' recently expounded at Paul's Cross by William Alabaster, a religious waverer who had reverted from Rome in 1610. Oliver Cromwell referred to the incident in parliament in 1628 in the course of an inquiry into the spread of Arminianism and its sponsorship by high-ranking churchmen including Bishop Neile (Abbott, 1.61–2).

Beard's virulent anti-Catholicism is well attested: in 1616 he published *A Retractive from the Romish Religion: Contayning Thirteene Forcible Motives*, designed 'to confirme and strengthen those that stagger, and are weake in the truth' and dedicated to Cromwell's grandfather, who had 'long time' been one of 'the principall auditors of my unworthy ministery' (sigs. A3r, A2v). In 1625 two further treatises appeared under the title *Antichrist the Pope of Rome, or, The Pope of Rome's Antichrist*, a topic which the changing theological climate was making increasingly contentious, and which Beard remarked revealingly was 'a point undecided in our Church'. Evidently composed at the height of government restrictions on aggressive anti-popery imposed during the negotiations for the Spanish match, the preface reveals that Beard originally intended to conceal his identity, no doubt through fear of official censure. By the time the book was published, however, the marriage talks had collapsed and the political mood was more conducive to his apocalyptic theme: accordingly the title page and dedication now bore the author's name (sigs. A2v, *3r).

Beard's outlook has long marked him out as a 'puritan', but it should be noted that he was never in trouble with the ecclesiastical authorities for liturgical nonconformity. Furthermore, although Beard clearly had close connections with the Cromwells and witnessed Oliver's father's will, his formative influence upon, and intimate friendship with, the future lord protector should not be overstated. In 1630, the year in which Beard, who had already served as a common councillor, was made a justice of the peace for Huntingdonshire, he and Cromwell appear to have been on opposing sides in a factional dispute over the foundation of a new endowed lectureship in Huntingdon, to which Beard was eventually appointed, following a personal intervention on his behalf by Charles I. In the preface to the 1631 edition of his *Theatre* he thanked the mayor and burgesses for standing by him in 'the late busines of the Lecture' in the face of 'the opposition of some malignant spirits' (sig. A3r). Shortly thereafter he swore an affidavit against Cromwell in a further altercation within the civil oligarchy over a new charter for the town, as a result of which Cromwell was politically marginalized.

Beard married, probably twice. With his first wife he had a number of daughters, several of whom died in their infancy or youth. He subsequently married Mary Heriman of Peterborough on 9 August 1627. Beard died on 8 January 1632 at Huntingdon and was buried two days later in All Saints' Church according to instructions left in his will, which was composed only a few days before his death. His wife, who survived him, was buried on 9 December 1642.

ALEXANDRA WALSHAM

Sources letter from Thomas Beard to Sir Robert Cotton, 25 March 1614, BL, Cotton MS Julius c.III, fol. 21r · BL, Add. MS 15665 [official transcripts and translations of various charters and documents relating to local history], fols. 126r–127r · Hunter's Chorus Vatum, vol. 5, BL, Add. MS 24491, fol. 36r · Venn, *Alum. Cant.* · PRO, SP 14/12/77 · *The writings and speeches of Oliver Cromwell*, ed. W. C. Abbott and C. D. Crane, 1 (1937), 22–31, 61–2 · J. Morrill, 'The making of Oliver Cromwell', *Oliver Cromwell and the English revolution*, ed. J. Morrill (1990), 19–48 · will, proved in the archdeaconry of Huntingdon, 1632, Cambs. AS, Huntingdon, bundle 9 · parish register, All Saints, Huntingdon, Cambs. AS, Huntingdon, ref. 3870/2 · J. Britton, E. W. Brayley, and others, *The beauties of England and Wales, or, Delineations topographical, historical, and descriptive, of each county*, [18 vols.] (1801–16), vol. 7, p. 354
Archives BL, 'Evangelical tragaedie', Royal MS D xvii [not autograph]
Likenesses line engraving, pubd 1801 (of Beard?; after print repro. in *Pedantius*, 1631), BM, NPG

Beard, William (1772–1868), tourist guide and collector of bones, was born on 24 April 1772 at Woolvershill, Banwell, Somerset, the eldest of the eight children of John Beard (1738–1801), a farmer, and his second wife, Ann Poole (1760–1833). He was educated by John Tuckey, the village schoolmaster and parish clerk. He worked as a farmer and purchased a small farm at Wints Hill, Banwell, after his marriage to Ruth (1779–1853), daughter of a farmer at Long Ashton.

In 1824 Francis Randolph, vicar of Banwell, sought to rediscover the cave supposed by legend to lie under Banwell Hill. His intention was to raise money for the village school from tourists visiting the burgeoning resort of Weston-super-Mare. In September, during the work on the Deep or Stalactite cave, a smaller cave was found, which contained bones of the bear, buffalo, reindeer, and wolf. Beard, once wrongly supposed to be the discoverer of the caves, began guiding visitors round the site, and took donations for the school on behalf of the bishop of Bath and Wells. By 1826, however, the donations were being expended on exploring and improving the caves. Beard collected together all the bones and geological specimens he could find from the caves and renamed his house Bone Cottage. He let his land and spent all his time guiding visitors and collecting relics from caves at Hutton, Bleadon, and Sandford. He assisted David Williams in excavating Uphill cave. Bishop Law dubbed Beard 'Deputy

William Beard (1772–1868), by Samuel Griffiths Tovey, c.1828–9

Professor of Geology', and the nickname the Professor remained with him for the rest of his life.

Beard died at Bone Cottage on 9 January 1868, and was buried in Banwell churchyard. His monument was surmounted by a portrait bust, which he had commissioned in 1854. His local celebrity was due to his close identification with the caves, and the story that he was the discoverer circulated from early on. He was evidently fairly well off. He was described as a very small and slight man: he was 'highly thought of in his immediate neighbourhood and he thought not a little of himself' (*Weston-super-Mare Gazette*, 6 Feb 1886).

A. P. WOOLRICH

Sources M. Clarke, 'West Mendip worthies', *Bristol Exploration Club: Belfry Bulletin*, 33 (April–May 1979), 8–13 · J. W. Hunt, 'Foreword to Edginton's "Sketch of the life of the late William Beard", 1886', *Axbridge Caving Group and Archaeological Society Journal* (1967–8), 69–75 [incl. full transcript of Edginton's paper] · M. Bertrand-Geslin, 'Note sur la caverne à ossements de Banwell (Somersetshire)', *Bulletin de la Société Philomathique de Paris* (1825), 118–20 · A. N. Hume, 'The professor of Banwell caves', *Country Life*, 115 (1954), 1991 · J. W. Hunt, 'The bust of "Professor" William Beard, set over his burial place in Banwell churchyard with some notes on his life and work', *Axbridge Caving Group and Archaeological Society Journal* (1967–8), 59–68 · D. Powell, 'Sexy and the Victorians', *Search 22: Journal of the Banwell Society of Archaeology* (1986) [incl. family tree] · M. Cousins, 'The caves at Banwell, Avon', *Follies* (spring 1991), 7–11
Archives Som. ARS
Likenesses S. G. Tovey, oils, c.1828–1829, FM Cam. [*see illus.*] · S. G. Tovey?, oils, 1831, priv. coll.; copy Woodspring Museum, Weston-super-Mare · S. G. Tovey, lithograph, Somerset Archaeological and Natural History Society Library, Taunton, Tite collection [copy] · T. Wilcox, bust · lithograph, NPG; repro. in J. Rutter, *Delineations … of the county of Somerset, and of its antedeluvian bone caverns* (1829)

Wealth at death under £1000: probate, 3 Feb 1868, *CGPLA Eng. & Wales*

Beardmore, Nathaniel (1816–1872),

civil engineer, was born at Nottingham on 19 March 1816, the second son of Joshua and Marianne Dorothea Beardmore. The family, having independent means, moved to London and then Devon, where his childhood was largely spent, and he was educated at Chudleigh day school and Devonport grammar school. He began his professional education in 1831 under George Wightwick, a Plymouth architect, and was then articled in the same town for five years to the well-known engineer James Meadows Rendel. He surveyed railways and roads, as well as making drawings for proposed bridges and harbour works. In 1838 he took an office in London and worked on similar surveys, sometimes for Rendel, who subsequently took him into partnership in Plymouth. In 1841 Beardmore married Mary, eldest daughter of J. F. Bernard. His principal works at that time were for Devonport Water Company and the local docks.

In 1843 Beardmore joined Rendel in the London office to which the latter had moved, but the partnership ended by agreement in 1848. He had in that period laid plans for an abortive Glasgow water supply and conducted the survey of the route of a major railway in Spain, as well as being involved in the promotion of (and opposition to) several English railways. Rendel and Beardmore had a major achievement in enabling the Edinburgh Waterworks Company to secure an act for building six reservoirs in the Pentlands; however, with construction spanning 1847–52 it was to James Leslie, the Edinburgh engineer, that ultimate credit went for their successful construction. Extensive experience had been gained by Beardmore's consultancy on northern England water supplies and East Anglian land drainage. He secured a patent in 1848 for a mixed wrought iron and concrete form of lightweight construction, intended for use as a caisson that need not be recovered.

Beardmore became sole engineer in 1850 to the Lea Trustees for works for the drainage and navigation of the River Lee (to which Rendel first introduced him about 1847). His involvement in river gauging from 1849 lends substance to the claim that he was the father of hydrology as a profession in Britain. In 1850 his first book appeared, *Hydraulic Tables*, which in its expanded 1851 second edition enhanced his reputation for hydraulic and river engineering, wherein he was to spend the bulk of his remaining life. However, he did maintain some railway work. Supervising River Lee improvements justified moving to Broxbourne in 1855. His enduring memorial is the 1862 third edition of his book, retitled *Manual of Hydrology*, which remained in print unchanged until about 1910. Its value lies in its wide geographic coverage, British, European and beyond, covering climate, flow, tides, and hydraulics, largely in tables of statistics. Beardmore had been able to draw on knowledge gained by his work on Lyons and Turin waterworks in 1852/3. Much later, in 1865, he visited Russia to work with M. Dessemond on improved water supplies for Moscow and Odessa. He was also a talented artist, making many sketches on his travels. Advice on Essex

drainage strengthened links with the civil engineer James Walker such that in September 1862 a partnership deed was signed, only to be broken by the untimely death of Walker in the following month.

On the night of 11 March 1864 the Dale Dyke Dam was washed out and the flood wave killed nearly 250 in Sheffield; Beardmore was called in to assist Robert Rawlinson, the government inspector. He gave evidence to royal commissions on pollution and water supply (1866–7), often acted as arbitrator in engineering contract disputes, and was a regular and welcome contributor to many discussions of papers at the Institution of Civil Engineers. The sixth president of the British Meteorological Society in 1861–2 and 1862–3, he was also a fellow of the Geological, Royal Geographical, and Royal Astronomical societies, as well as belonging to the Smeatonian Society. With Sopwith, Tripe, Glaisher, and Perigal he was behind a plan for a new paper to be devoted to the weather. In 1861 a share prospectus was published for a 'Daily Weather Map' of Britain and Ireland, because of Beardmore's admiration of Le Verrier's success at the Paris Imperial Observatory in publishing from 1856 a daily bulletin of the weather over the French empire. More profoundly, his presidential address forms the first eight pages of the first volume (1861–3) of the *Proceedings of the British Meteorological Society*. Its forward thinking is seen in its attention to the development of recording instruments, and the contributions of climate data to human welfare as well as science. From 1867 he was consulting engineer to the Thames Conservancy Board and the work occupying him before his death concerned the Teddington/Richmond reach. By then his partners were John Hickman Barnes, and his eldest son, Nathaniel St Bernard Beardmore, both of whom he had trained. This son, who died aged thirty-seven while working in India, inherited Beardmore's business, along with his books and equipment, but their subsequent survival is unknown. A descendant, Austin Bernard Beardmore (1911–1958), was engineer to Bedford corporation's water department in 1953.

Beardmore senior died of congestion of the lungs after a relatively healthy life on 24 August 1872, at Broxbourne. There were ten children from his marriage, eight of whom survived him. The remainder of his estate was to go to his daughter Frances Mary after her mother's death; Frances had married in 1868 Henry Austin Dobson, the poet, author, and Board of Trade clerk. (Dobson's brief coverage of his father-in-law's life for the *Dictionary of National Biography* in 1885 served to reveal only talent as a clerk.) McConnell notes that the obituary in the monthly notices of the Royal Astronomical Society remembered Beardmore 'as a man of rare uprightness and genuine goodness; his ready humour and originality rendered him popular everywhere he went and his courteous hospitality would be long remembered. In private life he was of simple habits, reserved and retiring almost to the point of shyness, but ever ready to proffer advice in a kind and generous manner.'   FRANK M. LAW

Sources PICE, 36 (1872–3), 256–64 · DNB · d. cert. · *CGPLA Eng. & Wales* (1872) · *Proceedings of the British Meteorological Society*, 1 (1861–

3), 1–8 · A. McConnell, 'Beardmore', *Weather*, 55 (2000), 325–7 · M. R. Lane, *The Rendel connection: a dynasty of engineers* (1989) · G. M. Binnie, *Early Victorian water engineers* (1981) · *Journal of the Institution of Water Engineers*, 12 (1958), 384 · *PICE*, 82 (1884–5), 378–80 · *IGI*
Likenesses photograph, repro. in *Weather*, 55 (2000), 326
Wealth at death under £12,000: probate, 7 Oct 1872, *CGPLA Eng. & Wales*

Beardmore, William, Baron Invernairn (1856–1936), engineer and shipbuilder, was born on 16 October 1856 at Deptford, the eldest son of William Beardmore and his wife, Sophia Louisa Halkman. His father was assistant manager of the Deptford works of the General Steam Navigation Company, but subsequently moved to Glasgow in 1861 as a partner in the Parkhead forge. William junior was educated at Glasgow high school and Ayr Academy and when he was fifteen he was apprenticed at the forge, attending evening classes at Anderson's University. At the end of his time, in 1877, he enrolled at the Royal School of Mines in South Kensington, taking courses in metallurgy and chemistry.

Although Beardmore's father died in 1877 leaving him his share in the business, he completed his education and returned to Glasgow in 1879 to be his uncle Isaac's junior partner. He immediately persuaded his uncle to begin making open-hearth steel and to install a steel foundry; and following his uncle's retirement in 1886, William became sole partner. Two years later he diversified into armour plate production and in 1889 began making plates for high pressure Scotch boilers. Other investments quickly followed, including a 12,000 ton press in 1895 to make American Harveyized armour plate. At the turn of the century Beardmore embarked on a massive extension to the works: these included a new office block, a gun factory, and additional armour plate capacity. By late 1899 he was also contemplating building a large naval shipyard at Dalmuir on the lower Clyde, and he managed to acquire the goodwill of the insolvent shipbuilding business of Robert Napier & Sons. Work began on the new yard in 1900. At the same time he joined a syndicate that bought J. I. Thornycroft & Co. of Chiswick, the torpedo boat builders; and Beardmore was subsequently appointed chairman.

This concentrated activity drained Beardmore of credit. He was forced to form the business into a limited liability company early in 1902, exchanging almost 60 per cent of the capital with Vickers, Son, and Maxim for an equivalent stake in that company and a seat on the board. During 1902 Beardmore also became the major shareholder in the motor car building business of Arrol Johnston. In the same year he married Elspeth, daughter of John Tullis, owner of the St Ann's leatherworks in Bridgeton, Glasgow. They had no children. Shortly after his marriage Beardmore purchased Flichity House with a 3000 acre sporting estate in Inverness-shire.

Vickers encouraged Beardmore, who was appointed chairman of the new company, to continue his expansion plans. Although Vickers had told Armstrong Whitworth that it would prevent Beardmore from making gun mountings, the company installed a gun plant in 1902 and

William Beardmore, Baron Invernairn (1856–1936), by Elliott & Fry

joined the 'gun pool', in effect, a cartel of all manufacturers. The additions and extensions to Parkhead were completed in 1904; and the Dalmuir naval construction works, the most modern and best-equipped shipyard on the Clyde, was inaugurated during 1906. During 1905 William Beardmore & Co. purchased the Mossend steel works from the Summerlee and Mossend Iron and Steel Company to secure supplies of ship plates and angles. Work began at once on the reconstruction of the plant, with the installation of a new three-high plate mill. During 1903/4 Beardmore, in co-operation with Vickers, established the Glasgow Electric Crane and Hoist Company, which was sold in 1906. The relationship with J. I. Thornycroft & Co. did not prove to be a happy one for Beardmore, and he resigned as chairman in 1907.

During 1907 Vickers became openly dissatisfied with its investment in William Beardmore & Co., which was becoming illiquid and in need of financial support. Vickers took stiff measures to control Beardmore's activities, appointing a nominee as joint managing director. Although the company's financial strength improved, Vickers unsuccessfully tried to offload part of its investment to Armstrong Whitworth. During 1910 the company's financial health recovered, following the order for the dreadnought HMS *Conqueror*, and Vickers again encouraged Beardmore to invest in new armour plate rolling plant. By 1913 Vickers' nominees had resigned and Beardmore had regained full executive control of the firm. He immediately took the opportunity to diversify into aircraft manufacture. In 1914 he was created a baronet.

On the outbreak of war, Beardmore was immediately called on to supply huge quantities of war material, from field guns to ships and aeroplanes. During the war the company turned out 3500 field guns, 69 vessels totalling 118,089 tons, including the battleship HMS *Ramilles* and the first through-deck aircraft-carrier, HMS *Argus*, 650 planes, two airships, and all the steel helmets for the British army. Beardmore also co-operated in the development of the tank, and his company made all the pedrail shoes for the tracks of every tank built. The firm's plant was greatly extended, with new buildings at Dalmuir to manufacture aeroplanes, field guns, and airship parts. The Mossend steel works were completely rebuilt and factories for munitions work purchased in Paisley and Coatbridge.

In the early part of the war the company's plants were the focus of labour unrest on the Clyde over the issues of rent increases, dilution, and restrictive practices. This resulted in a massive confrontation between Sir William and his workforce led by David Kirkwood. In March 1916, however, after government intervention and Kirkwood's arrest, the strife subsided. Beardmore extended the company's interests during the war, buying Alley and MacLellan Ltd, owners of the Sentinel works at Polmadie, Glasgow, and a steam-wagon factory at Shrewsbury. On his own account he purchased a majority holding in the Sheffield steelmakers, Dunford and Elliott Ltd.

With the coming of peace, Beardmore was convinced that trade would expand. He planned to manufacture passenger vessels, tankers, and steam locomotives at Dalmuir, marine steam and oil engines at the Coatbridge works, buses and lorries on part of the Parkhead site, and taxis at Paisley. He opened a civil aviation department, developing a series of unsuccessful aeroplanes. The company continued to manage the wartime airship works at Renfrew, completing the R34 in 1919 and the R36 in 1921, when the plant closed. He won control of Dunford and Elliott, encouraging the firm to diversify away from steel into the manufacture of motor cycles and cars. He directed Arrol Johnston to tool up its works for the production of heavy motor cars. In 1921 he was created Baron Invernairn of Strathnairn, taking his title from his Inverness-shire home.

Unfortunately, Invernairn's strategy for peacetime trading miscarried, for after 1920 nearly all the departments and subsidiaries of his firm began to lose money. By now in his late sixties, Invernairn was incapable of meeting the crisis. His recipe was to borrow more and instruct his heads of department to exercise economy. During 1926 Vickers sold him its shareholding. Later in the year the accountant Sir William McLintock scrutinized the company's affairs, producing a devastating indictment of Invernairn's lack of management. The following year under the supervision of Montagu Norman of the Bank of England a committee of investigation was appointed. In 1928 Invernairn, whom Norman had unkindly dubbed Beardless, was ousted and over the next two years much of his extensive empire was closed down. In enforced retirement, Invernairn witnessed the collapse of many of his other interests, including Arrol Johnston. He died on 9 April 1936 at his home, Flichity House, Strathnairn, Inverness-shire, where he was buried. He was survived by his wife.

Invernairn's style of doing business was totally autocratic. In many of his investment decisions, he lacked judgement and refused to listen to advice. Despite the scale of his enterprises, which during the First World War employed over 50,000 people, none of them can be said to have been a success. He helped to promote the Industrial Welfare Society in 1918 and was its first chairman.

MICHAEL S. MOSS

Sources J. R. Hume and M. S. Moss, *Beardmore: the history of a Scottish industrial giant* (1979) · G. E. Todd, *Who's who in Glasgow in 1909* (1909) · M. S. Moss, 'Beardmore, William jnr, Lord Invernairn', *DSBB* · d. cert.
Archives U. Glas., Archives and Business Records Centre | CUL, Vickers MSS · NMM, Thornycroft MSS
Likenesses Elliott & Fry, photograph, U. Glas., Archives and Business Records Centre [see illus.]
Wealth at death £842,037 4s. 11d.: confirmation, 10 July 1936, CCI

Beardsley, Aubrey Vincent (1872–1898), illustrator, was born on 21 August 1872 at 12 Buckingham Road, Brighton, Sussex, the son of Vincent Paul Beardsley (c.1840–1909), and his wife, Ellen Agnus (1846–1932), the daughter of Surgeon-Major William Pitt and his wife, Susan.

Childhood Beardsley's childhood was full of social instability and emotional intensity. His father was listed on the birth certificate as 'gentleman' because he had inherited a fortune, but soon after Aubrey was born he lost it. He found a job in London but was unconvincing as a breadwinner, and the Beardsleys lived in lodgings for the next twenty years, fending off poverty. His mother never forgave this fall from grace. She hugged her two children to her, cultivated their genteel talents in music and literature, and presented herself as the victim of a *mésalliance*. Perhaps the best love which Beardsley received as a child was from his older sister, Mabel.

At the age of seven Beardsley was found to have tuberculosis. This was not necessarily life-threatening, but he was a frail boy, 'like a delicate little piece of Dresden China' his mother said (Walker, 75), and there was always concern about his health. From twelve to sixteen he attended Brighton grammar school, where his fees were paid for by a great-aunt and where he made a place for himself as a pale and bookish outsider.

Beardsley left school in December 1888 and obtained a job as a clerk in London. It was a narrow existence: office work during the day, browsing in bookshops in his lunch hour, and browsing again on the way home to the family's lodgings in Pimlico. On Sundays the Beardsleys worshipped at St Barnabas, Pimlico, and sometimes the high-Anglican ritual there was the only note of colour in his week. He read modern French novels, particularly Balzac,

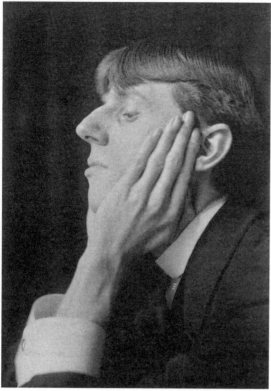

Aubrey Vincent Beardsley (1872–1898), by Frederick Henry Evans, 1893

and hoped to become a writer. Late in 1889 his tuberculosis erupted, and he bled from the mouth for the first time. About a year later he discovered the work of the painter and poet Dante Gabriel Rossetti, and started to draw seriously, hoping to become an artist.

Early career Beardsley spent the year 1891 learning about art, going to galleries and exhibitions, and seeking advancement. In June he went to Frederick Leyland's London house, 49 Prince's Gate, with its superb Pre-Raphaelite and old master paintings, and its Peacock Room decorated by J. McNeill Whistler. The Pre-Raphaelites were Beardsley's favourites at this stage, but he was alert to other current tastes: the New English Art Club, the French *décadents*, Oscar Wilde. And he was certainly ready to learn from Whistler about Japan, and the cult of personality. In July he went to see his then particular hero, Edward Burne-Jones, who praised his work and said he ought to go to art school. As a result, he attended Westminster School of Art in the evenings for about a year.

In January 1892 Beardsley had a visit from (W. H.) Aymer Vallance, a former high-Anglican clergyman who was now talent spotting as an art journalist. Vallance admired Beardsley's work and began to promote him—which was not difficult, because Beardsley had begun to create a public persona for himself, carefully posed, hollow-eyed, and literate. He attracted attention. By the spring of 1892 he had begun to draw in the linear style which would make

him famous, though nothing was published at this stage. He would sketch a design in pencil and then work over it in black ink, producing images of the strongest contrast: black, white, and no greys. He seems to have grasped the potential of the new process blocks, which were replacing wood-engravings at this time as a medium for reproducing images alongside letterpress. Process blocks were made, not of wood, but of metal, on to which the image was transferred photographically. Being stronger than woodblocks, they could sustain finer lines without breaking down in the printing press. The thin, isolated black lines which sweep so voluptuously across the white in some of Beardsley's most famous drawings are a tribute to the process block, which no other illustrator of the 1890s exploited quite so tellingly. In May the young man went to Paris and boldly showed his work to Puvis de Chavannes. The president of the Salon du Champ de Mars was impressed, and introduced him to another artist as 'un jeune artiste anglais qui fait des choses étonnantes' (Sturgis, 103).

In the autumn the publisher J. M. Dent asked Beardsley to illustrate Malory's *Morte d'Arthur* in the style of the books beginning to come from William Morris's Kelmscott Press, with their scrolling borders and wood-engraved illustrations by Burne-Jones. The book was a favourite with the Pre-Raphaelites, there were plenty of illustrations, and the pay was good. Beardsley resigned from his job and began to draw, working at first in something like the Kelmscott style. Dent also commissioned him to draw ornaments for a series of eighteenth-century anthologies, to be titled *Bon mots*. Among the eighty or so calligraphic doodles he produced were pierrots, hermaphrodites, ballet dancers, prostitutes, satyrs, and foetuses with old men's heads and angry eyes. In his imagination, sex was often mingled with sadness and deformity. In his personal life we hardly know what part it played. There are stories of mistresses he may have had, but none of any close or lasting relationship.

Salome At about the same time, through Vallance, Beardsley's work was chosen as the subject of an article in the first number of *The Studio*, a new periodical of fine and decorative art. He was beginning to be known, and wrote to his old housemaster at Brighton grammar school: 'There is quite an excitement in the art world here about my "new method"' (*Letters*, 38). In February 1893 Oscar Wilde's play *Salome* was published in London, and the *Pall Mall Budget* asked Beardsley for a drawing. He wove an ornate, macabre, and, in places, sickening graphic fantasy around the horrific climax of the play, Salome embracing the severed head of John the Baptist. The *Budget* rejected it, but in April it appeared in the first number of *The Studio*. Wilde liked the drawing, and his publishers suggested that Beardsley do an illustrated edition of the play. He was not yet twenty-one, but he had reached the shores of notoriety.

And of respectability. In June 1893 the Beardsleys took a lease on a four-storey house at 114 Cambridge Street, Pimlico, from which you could just see through the trees into Warwick Square. After years of shifting from one set of lodgings to another, they could hold up their heads and entertain their friends, thanks to Aubrey's earnings as an illustrator and a small inheritance. The two connecting rooms on the first floor were turned into a drawing-room-cum-studio, and here the Beardsleys were at home on Thursday afternoons. Ellen sent out the invitations, but Mabel and Aubrey were in reality the hosts. (Vincent Beardsley was no longer in evidence. Aubrey's friends thought he might be dead, or locked in the basement.) Mabel, who had beautiful red hair, greeted the visitors and Aubrey handed round the cakes. Max Beerbohm thought Beardsley was at his best on these occasions, his natural kindliness and good manners shining through the veneer of affectation.

By September Beardsley had completed only half the *Morte d'Arthur* illustrations and was bored stiff with the Holy Grail. He wanted *Salome* and wickedness. In the end he completed them with a bad grace, putting more of Beardsley than of Malory into the later ones. His linear style and sensuality show through the pastiche neo-medievalism. But then Beardsley did not think it was his job to illustrate a writer's words. Though he had a literary imagination, and most of his drawings illustrate texts, he usually drew as if artist and writer were independent. He complained that the illustrator trailed servant-like behind the author in modern English magazines. At the turn of 1893–4 Beardsley and an American friend, the writer Henry Harland, proposed a new, avant-garde magazine in which writers and artists would have equal standing. John Lane, who was publishing *Salome* at the Bodley Head, agreed to publish it as a quarterly, called the *Yellow Book*, with Harland as editor for literature and Beardsley for art.

In February 1894 the illustrated *Salome* appeared and created a *succès de scandale*. (Beardsley perhaps began to feel that that was the only kind of success he needed.) The seventeen illustrations were in his classic, Japanese-influenced style of flat, decorative, asymmetrical images, with intricate detail, large areas of black, and fine lines curving over areas of white. Reviewers acknowledged Beardsley's technical skill but were disturbed, both by the threatening sexuality, rendered with such graphic elegance, and by the fact that many of the drawings were irrelevant to Wilde's text. For the *Art Journal* the effect was 'terrible in its weirdness and suggestions of horror and wickedness' (*Art Journal*, 14, 1894, 139). Some reviewers thought it was all a bitchy joke, Beardsley parodying Wilde in the spaces of his own text.

The *Yellow Book* Two months later the first number of the *Yellow Book* appeared, with a Beardsley cover and four Beardsley drawings. There was much else in it: writing by Henry James, George Saintbury, and Richard Garnett, pictures by Sir Frederic Leighton, president of the Royal Academy, and Robert Anning Bell—serious, irreproachable names. But Beardsley's drawings were all disturbing in one way or another, and *The Times*'s reviewer, pointing to the cover, wrote of 'repulsiveness and insolence' (20 April 1894, 3). The magazine became a talking point because of his work, and the first edition of 5000 copies

sold out in five days. This was notoriety. Beardsley had discovered, long before Andy Warhol or Damien Hirst, that there is a kind of art which consists in shocking the public.

In a sense, Beardsley's public persona was as much a work of art as his drawings. He cultivated a dandified appearance before the world, and liked to appear wicked, witty, and decadent like the French. He let his reddish hair fall in a fringe so that he looked half like a boy, and dressed his poor thin body immaculately, as if he expected not to be touched by life—a grey suit, grey gloves, a golden tie, a tasselled cane. Artificiality became him. He worked ferociously hard, but the painter William Rothenstein remembered that 'His work done, Aubrey loved to get into evening clothes and drive into the town' (Rothenstein, 186). He could be found with his friends, Rothenstein, the caricaturist Max Beerbohm, and the writers Ernest Dowson and Arthur Symons, in the Domino Room of the Café Royal in Regent Street, or among the prostitutes and their gentlemen friends in the St James's Restaurant in Piccadilly Circus, dipping into low life. With the appearance of *Salome* and the *Yellow Book* Beardsley became notorious in a way that his friends were not. He was caricatured in the press and was sung about in music-halls. He almost ranked in the public eye with Oscar Wilde who, though a friend, was older, a hero, and a rival. But notoriety did not change him, perhaps because it was what his so-careful dressing, his shocking drawings, and his mask of wit had been asking for all along.

On 5 April 1895 Wilde was arrested at the Cadogan Hotel in Knightsbridge on twenty charges of gross indecency with young men. As he left the hotel under a police escort, he picked up a book with a yellow cover. The press mistook it for the *Yellow Book*. Thus Beardsley was caught up in the débâcle of Wilde's trials and disgrace. A crowd threw stones through the windows of the Bodley Head office in Vigo Street. On 8 May a group of contributors asked that Beardsley be dismissed as editor for art. John Lane, then in America, felt pressured to agree. Beardsley was unaware of developments for some days. Yet Wilde had nothing to do with the *Yellow Book*: Beardsley and Lane had kept him out, fearing that he would sail the ship. And Beardsley was not homosexual, though he enjoyed camp conversation. But, by sacking him, Lane virtually admitted his complicity with Wilde. With the editorship, Beardsley lost his main source of income, and the house at 114 Cambridge Street, which had given him security for barely two years, had to be given up. In June he and Mabel took a short lease on a house at 57 Chester Terrace (now Chester Row), on the Pimlico side of Belgravia.

The *Savoy* At this point Beardsley acquired two guardian angels. One, André Raffalovich, was an angel of light: a rich, homosexual, thirty-year-old aesthete who became Beardsley's friend and mentor and helped him with money. The other, Leonard Smithers, was an angel of darkness: a pasty-faced, thirty-four-year-old ex-solicitor who sold old books, prints, and pornography from a shop in Arundel Street, off the Strand. Smithers was setting up as a publisher and proposed to start a rival to the *Yellow*

Book, with Arthur Symons dealing with literature and Beardsley with art. They named it *The Savoy*. Beardsley set to work eagerly. He wanted more of the dangerous publishing he had just experienced, not less. A streak of self-destructiveness emerged. In October he took rooms in Geneux's private hotel in St James's Place. They were not cheap, and Wilde had used them two years before for assignations. Raffishness at the Café Royal and St James's Restaurant now gave way to dissipation in low dives round Leicester Square and at a supper club called the Thalia, favoured by Smithers.

The Wilde débâcle was not such a disaster that Beardsley could not have survived it. But, coming when it did, it broke the magic of his short career. He could no longer step from one shocking little triumph to the next, outwitting his physical condition and his spiritual unease with dandyism and hard work. It caused an unravelling. He still drew, and the drawings were as new in style and as remarkable as his earlier work. But his life had become a river of dissolution, and the drawings floated on it like light craft.

The first number of *The Savoy* appeared in January 1896. It was like the *Yellow Book* in style and content, and the press greeted it accordingly, but with less excitement. After the party to launch it, Smithers and a few friends went back to his flat, where Beardsley had a slight haemorrhage. W. B. Yeats recalled Smithers, sweat pouring from his face, turning the handle of a hurdy-gurdy piano while Beardsley, propped up on a chair in the middle of the room and grey from loss of blood, urged him on, exclaiming 'The tone is so beautiful' (Yeats, 329). It lacked only a Roman Catholic priest, blessing it all, for the decadent scene to be complete.

Sex and death And yet Beardsley could work. He wanted to write as well as draw, and had been working on a version of the *Tannhäuserlied*. Its story of sex, sin, and forgiveness touched him. He made some drawings for it, but the more he wrote the more pornographic it became, and in the end Smithers could publish it in *The Savoy* only in unfinished and expurgated form. Late in 1895 Beardsley took up Edmund Gosse's suggestion that he illustrate Pope's *The Rape of the Lock*, for he had not illustrated a complete book since *Salome*. For some time he had admired Watteau and the frippery world of French rococo engravers, so Pope appeared dressed very tellingly in that style rather than in Japanese asymmetry and sweeping lines. When the book was published in May 1896 the press were taken with its ladies in billowing lace and its mincing courtiers. Here were parody and excess quite different from the bourgeois-domestic image of the eighteenth century then popular with illustrators; but there was none of the evil they had felt before. Actually, Beardsley was learning to divide his life with skill. While he was illustrating Pope he was also, at Smithers's suggestion, illustrating *Lysistrata*, Aristophanes' tale of a sex strike among Athenian women, with gross, buttocky Athenians in rococo frills and monstrous, comic penises. Smithers published these privately in 1896.

In February 1896 Beardsley went to Paris with Smithers and a girl from the Thalia. When Smithers went back to London, Beardsley stayed on in Paris, working. Smithers then returned, *en route* for Brussels. Beardsley took him to the station and then got on the train himself, on an impulse. When he arrived in Brussels he collapsed. He was there for about three months. When he returned to London the doctors looked grave. For much of his adult life Beardsley had been fighting a battle with his body. The dandyism, the wicked drawings, the eager baiting of the British philistine, had all been sand thrown in the face of this enemy. It began to seem less possible.

Beardsley and his mother returned to their old ways of shifting from one address to another, from lodgings to hotels, from hotels to guest houses. (Mabel now had a career in the theatre.) The doctors always said that another place would be better for his health. In June it was Epsom; in August it was Boscombe in Hampshire, for the sea air. In December he suffered a violent haemorrhage near the cliff-top, and a trail of blood followed him and his mother down the hill. He was moved to nearby Bournemouth for the mild climate and the smell of pines. And there, on 31 March 1897, he was received into the Catholic church. Mabel had recently become a Catholic and so had Raffalovich. Now Beardsley needed its certainties. Serious, asexual men in black came to his bedside and ministered to his soul.

In April Beardsley was in Paris; in May in St Germain-en-Laye on the outskirts of Paris; in June in Dieppe; in September in Paris again. It was becoming a way of life. In each place there would be a new hotel, the view, the local priest, old friends coming to visit. He would find somewhere to sit outside in the morning under the trees, charming the other guests and the local children, reading Catholic devotional literature and erotica by turns, writing a little, drawing a little. Then there would be another doctor and another move.

Finally, late in 1897, it was Menton on the French riviera, and the Hotel Cosmopolitan. Beardsley's mother made the room look nice with his Mantegna prints on the wall and photographs on the bookshelf: Mabel, Raffalovich, Wagner. He was drawing ornaments for Ben Jonson's *Volpone* and working excitedly in half-tone instead of line. But as he got weaker he could not draw any more. Early in March he wrote a short letter to Smithers:

> Jesus is our Lord and Judge.
> Dear Friend,
> I implore you to destroy *all* copies of Lysistrata and bad drawings ... By all that is holy, *all* obscene drawings.
> Aubrey Beardsley
> In my death agony.
> (*Letters*, 439)

It was his last letter. Smithers, of course, paid no attention to it, knowing what the drawings would soon be worth. Aubrey Beardsley died on 16 March 1898, aged twenty-five, and was buried in the public cemetery at Menton.

Reputation Beardsley's reputation since his death has had little of the scandalous excitement it had during his life. For many years it was maintained in a quiet, cultish way, chiefly by collectors and bibliophiles. Dent and John Lane went on republishing his work. There were studies and memoirs, often coloured by literary nostalgia for the avant-garde culture of the 1890s. Beardsley influenced artists and designers in Europe and America, and there were important exhibitions of his work in Budapest (1907), in Chicago and Buffalo (1911–12), and at the Tate Gallery in London (1923). In the United States the painter and art historian A. E. Gallatin formed the pre-eminent collection of Beardsley's work, which he gave to Princeton University Library in 1948. (The other two major collections are at the Fogg Art Museum, Harvard University, and the Victoria and Albert Museum in London.) In England a book dealer and collector called R. A. Walker did the same for Beardsley memorabilia. His *A Beardsley Miscellany* (1949) underpins parts of all subsequent biography.

Then, for a moment in the 1960s, Beardsley became part of popular culture, in art posters and advertisements, in Haight-Ashbury and swinging London, on T-shirts and record sleeves (the Beatles' *Revolver*, 1966). Both his graphic style and his indecencies were of the time. The year 1966 also saw a major exhibition of Beardsley's work at the Victoria and Albert Museum, which introduced him to a larger, less cultish audience. And since then there has been an important shift in his reputation, which is now in the hands of academics as well as of collectors and bibliophiles. But he is not necessarily better or more widely understood. There has been no outstanding work of scholarship or criticism, no substantial and accessible reassessment. Instead, Beardsley has been parcelled out among different intellectual allegiances—biography, connoisseurship, cultural theory, bibliography, race and gender studies, reception studies. He has been fragmented. No one would have said so during his short and painful life, but now, a hundred years later, it is actually hard to see who Aubrey Beardsley was. ALAN CRAWFORD

Sources M. Sturgis, *Aubrey Beardsley: a biography* (1998) • B. Reade, *Beardsley* (1967) • *The letters of Aubrey Beardsley*, ed. H. Maas, J. L. Duncan, and W. G. Good (1970) • S. Calloway, *Aubrey Beardsley* (1998) • R. A. Walker, ed., *A Beardsley miscellany* (1949) • M. S. Lasner, *A selective checklist of the published work of Aubrey Beardsley* (1995) • N. A. Salerno, 'An annotated secondary bibliography', in R. Langenfeld, *Reconsidering Aubrey Beardsley* (1989), 267–493 • W. Rothenstein, *Men and memories: recollections of William Rothenstein, 1872–1900* (1934) • W. B. Yeats, *Autobiographies* (1956) • K. Keserü, 'Art contacts between Great Britain and Hungary at the turn of the century', *Hungarian Studies*, 6/2 (1990), 141–54 • L. Zatlin, *Aubrey Beardsley and Victorian sexual politics* (1990) • C. Snodgrass, *Aubrey Beardsley: dandy of the grotesque* (1995) • L. Zatlin, *Beardsley, Japonisme and the perversion of the Victorian ideal* (1997) • J. H. Desmarais, *The Beardsley industry: the critical reception in England and France* (1998) • b. cert. • *CGPLA Eng. & Wales* (1898) • will, Probate Department of the Principal Registry of the Family Division, London

Archives Harvard U., Houghton L., writings and drawings • Princeton University Library, drawings, posters, photographs, MSS, sketchbook, and corresp. • Ransom HRC, corresp. with André Raffalovich • U. Reading L., corresp. and papers of and relating to him, incl. letters to John Gray • Yale U., Beinecke L., recollections and related papers | Bodl. Oxf., corresp. with John Lane and André Raffalovich • E. Sussex RO, archives of Brighton grammar school • Harvard U., Houghton L., corresp. with William Rothenstein and Henry James • Hunt. L., corresp. with Leonard Smithers • U. Cal., Los Angeles, William Andrews Clark Memorial Library, corresp. with Florence Farr and Maurice Baring

Likenesses J. Russell & Sons, photograph, c.1890, NPG • D. S. MacColl, drawing, 1893, Princeton University Library, Gallatin collection • F. H. Evans, two photographs, 1893–4, NPG [*see illus.*] • M. Beerbohm, caricature, c.1894, V&A • F. Hollyer, photograph, c.1894, V&A • W. Sickert, oils, 1894, Tate collection • M. Beerbohm, caricature, c.1895, AM Oxf. • J. E. Blanche, oils, 1895, NPG • Grip [A. Brice], caricature, Indian ink and wash, 1896, V&A; repro. in *The Sketch* (13 May 1896) • W. Rothenstein, lithograph, 1897, NPG • photograph, 1897, NPG • A. Beardsley, self-portrait, pen and ink, BM • M. Beerbohm, caricature, repro. in *The Savoy*, 2 • W. Sickert, drawing, NPG

Wealth at death £1015 17s. 10d.: probate, 13 May 1898, *CGPLA Eng. & Wales*

Beare, George (*d.* 1749), painter, of whose parents nothing is known, trained possibly at St Martin's Lane Academy, London, but the earliest reference to his work is at Salisbury in 1745, when he painted portraits of William and Susannah Elderton on the occasion of their wedding. It is possible that he married Elizabeth Sparrow on 1 February 1721 (or 1722) in Monxton, Hampshire.

Window tax returns suggest that Beare's connection with Salisbury may have begun in 1738, when a 'Mr Beer' was assessed at 10s. on a house in New Street ward. Several portraits of local figures other than the Eldertons were made in 1746, notably of John Powell and his son, later Sir Alexander Powell, a future deputy recorder of Salisbury (priv. coll.). A letter from Beare to Sir Alexander Powell in 1746 seeks permission

> to have the red wastcoat which you are to be represented in your picture to paint it from you and your choise of the coullor for the coat and when you come this way if you would take the trouble to step up and see it to give me your approbation on what is allwreaddy done that I may proseed to finnish it at your pleasure. (Baker, 573)

(Powell decided on a stone-grey coat, which sets off the red waistcoat in the picture to advantage.) A visitor to Salisbury in 1754 remarked on 'the great number of gentlemen's houses in the town, especially about the close' (Surry, 4). It was the patronage of these residents, together with the merchants, clergy, and a number of other professional men, which provided Beare with a livelihood. His identified portraits include those of Miss Fort of Alderbury House (Salisbury and South Wiltshire Museum), Francis Price, architect and surveyor of Salisbury Cathedral, and the Revd Thomas Chubb, philosopher and theologian (both National Portrait Gallery, London)—all signed and dated 1747. The last portrait to be associated with the city is the delightful study of the young Jane Coles (1749, priv. coll.).

Other works by Beare point to links with London—more specifically to members of court society and government—such as Sir Frederick Evelyn as a boy (1744, Salisbury and South Wiltshire Museum), whose father was a groom of the bedchamber to Frederick, prince of Wales; Judge Charles Clarke (1745, priv. coll.); and his son John Clarke (1743, priv. coll.), Beare's earliest known portrait. The most intriguing of this group is a relatively unknown painting of the king's messenger (1748, Woburn Abbey, Bedfordshire), which portrays a messenger bearing an envelope addressed to the fourth duke of Bedford, in the same year as his appointment as secretary of state for the southern department. A few sitters, mostly from Hampshire, also had London connections: Judge Clarke was elected MP for Whitchurch, Hampshire, in 1743, on the interest of John Wallop, first earl of Portsmouth. In 1745 Beare painted Lady Anne Wallop (priv. coll.), one of the earl's daughters, possibly on Clarke's recommendation.

At its finest George Beare's work conveys much of Hogarth's directness and the same grasp of character and psychological insight—above all in *Elderly Lady and Young Girl* (1747, Yale U. CBA) and also in the portrait of the Revd Thomas Chubb (1747, National Portrait Gallery, London) which compares very favourably with Hogarth's *Simon, Lord Lovat* (1746, British Museum, London). The semi-formal treatment of Sir Frederick Evelyn as a boy suggests an awareness of Philip Mercier's work, while the vivacious portrait of Miss Fort owes something to that of van Loo for its theatrical qualities. Beare's work is more sympathetic to women and children than to men. At times there is a certain woodenness in the painting of the figures, and the treatment of hands is often clumsy, the gestures stiff and awkward. Beare's palette has an earthy quality, apparent in his draperies and flesh half-tints, though it includes strong reds and dark blue. The paint is usually thinly applied, producing a tempera-like surface. Among his forty-three known works, on the majority of each his signature appears as 'Geo Beare Pinxt' or 'Pinxit' followed by the year in which it was painted. His evident proficiency and professionalism places him in the first rank of portrait painters at that time. George Beare's death was reported in the *Salisbury Journal* of 22 May 1749: 'Last Week died near Andover, Hants, Mr Beare, lately an eminent Face Painter in this City'.   NIGEL SURRY

Sources C. H. C. Baker, 'A portrait painter re-discovered', *Country Life*, 123 (1958), 572–3 · Waterhouse, *18c painters* · N. Surry, *George Beare* (1989) [exhibition catalogue, Pallant House Gallery, Chichester] · D. Robinson, 'George Beare: a new masterpiece', *British art*, ed. F. Trapp (Amherst, MA, 1986), 16–19 · IGI · *Salisbury Journal*, 593 (22 May 1749)
Archives NPG, Heinz Archive and Library, C. H. C. Baker MS, list of portraits by George Beare · Salisbury and South Wiltshire Museum, Salisbury, Blackmore MS · Wilts. & Swindon RO, window tax returns, New Street Ward, Salisbury, 1705–52, WRO G23/1/189–190 · Wiltshire CRO, window tax returns, Mead Ward, Salisbury, WRO G23/1/190

Bearehaven. For this title name *see* O'Sullivan Beare, Donnell Cam, count of Bearehaven in the Spanish nobility (1560–1618).

Bearsted. For this title name *see* Samuel, Marcus, first Viscount Bearsted (1853–1927); Samuel, Walter Horace, second Viscount Bearsted (1882–1948).

Beart, Robert (1801–1873), brick and tile manufacturer, was baptized on 6 September 1801 at Welney, on the Isle of Ely, the son of William Beart, a farmer, and his wife, Susanna. Little is known of his upbringing, except that he first followed his father's occupation, but by the 1820s he had moved to Godmanchester in Huntingdonshire where he lived until his death. By 1830 he was in partnership with Samuel Bates in a milling business, but in 1833 he registered the first of his patents, for a machine for making drainage tiles. This simple device used a piston to raise a column of clay, which was cut with a wire to produce a tile of the correct thickness, and it enabled tile makers or farmers to make large quantities of tiles with unskilled labour. The machine was a considerable success and was praised in the farming press, winning a medal at the royal agricultural show at Cambridge in 1840; at a price of 12 guineas it helped to reduce the price of local drainage tiles from 35s. per 1000 to 20s.

By 1840 Beart was still involved in the milling business but was also established as a tile manufacturer. Other patents followed for a brick mould (1834); a filter for liquids, with a particular application for coffee pots (1838, 1840); and a drill for boring in earth or stone with the use of water to remove debris (1844), a technique which later found application in the oil industry. On 21 December 1841 Beart married Fanny, daughter of Thomas Ekin, farmer, at All Souls Church, Marylebone, Middlesex. The couple had four children. In 1846 Beart ended his partnership with Bates and became mayor of Godmanchester for the first of six times.

In 1845 Beart had patented a process for producing perforated bricks with seventeen holes which used an extruded length of clay forced through a plate and cut by wires. In 1850 he registered a second patent for a perforated brick, this time with twenty-four holes and using an improved moulding plate. The patent also incorporated a means of speeding up the drying process, by using a shed with underfloor heating, through which the bricks travelled on gravity-fed roller conveyors. The advantages of Beart's brick were that it was lighter than a solid brick, without compromising strength; it dried and fired more evenly because of the passage of air through the brick; and in the absence of 'frogs', or indentations, in the brick, it bonded better than other wire-cut bricks.

By 1851 Beart owned a brickworks in Godmanchester which employed fifteen men, and in the following year Beart's Patent Brick Company Ltd built a sizeable works at Arlesey in Bedfordshire, beside the Great Northern Railway (GNR), working a seam of Gault clay which produced a very pale brick. The works were highly mechanized, using steam power both to guide the clay (and force it through the moulding machines) and to dry the green bricks. The company, which licensed Beart's patent to other brickmakers, opened an office in 1853 at the York Road goods depot near Kings Cross, and it sold bricks at Arlesey, London, and other GNR stations. By 1858 the output of the Arlesey works was 8 million bricks and 1 million drainage tiles. Some of the bricks were used for decorative effect rather than as common building bricks; they were included in buildings on the Peabody estate in Farringdon Lane and specified by architects for fashionable parts of South Kensington.

Beart lived at West Street, Godmanchester, and was heavily involved in local affairs, his last term as mayor occurring in 1870–71. He enjoyed a good income from his patents. His death occurred at Godmanchester on 19 September 1873. The business was continued by his sons, William F. Beart and Frederick R. Beart, and merged with other Arlesey brickyards to form the Arlesey Brick Company (Beart's) Ltd in 1898. It became part of the London Brick Company in 1928.

Although Beart's brickyard did not achieve a large output, his patent brick was among the first bricks to be sold under a brand name and one of the first to be distributed by railway into the London market.

PETER HOUNSELL

Sources A. Cox, *Brickmaking: a history and gazetteer* (1979) · R. Beart, 'On the economical manufacture of draining tiles and soles', *Journal of the Royal Agricultural Society of England*, 2 (1841), 99–100 · *Huntingdonshire Guardian* (27 Sept 1873) · Beart's Patent Brick Company Ltd, account books, Beds. & Luton ARS · *CGPLA Eng. & Wales* (1874) · m. cert. · d. cert. · parish register, Welney, Cambs. AS, P163/1/2 [baptism]
Archives Beds. & Luton ARS, account books, Beart's Patent Brick Company Ltd
Wealth at death under £18,000: probate, 14 May 1874, *CGPLA Eng. & Wales*

Beatniffe, Richard (*bap.* 1739, *d.* 1818), bookseller and printer, was born at Louth, Lincolnshire, and baptized at Holton-le-Clay on 13 September 1739, probably the son of Davenport Beatniffe and Jane Hardy. He was adopted and brought up by his uncle the Revd Samuel Beatniffe (1702–1781), rector of the parishes of Gaywood and Bawsey, near King's Lynn, in Norfolk. In 1755 he was apprenticed to the King's Lynn bookseller and bookbinder Thomas Hollingworth; Beatniffe later claimed to have been the only one of Hollingworth's many apprentices, during a forty-year career, to have completed his term. About 1762 he was offered Hollingworth's daughter's hand in marriage, together with the promise of a partnership in the bookselling business, but he chose to move to Norwich, where he worked as a journeyman bookbinder.

In December 1762 the Norwich bookseller Jonathan Gleed was declared bankrupt, and in May 1763 Beatniffe borrowed £500 from his former master to take over Gleed's shop at 6 Cockey Lane (later renamed London Lane). There he remained in business for fifty-five years. In 1764 he purchased the freedom of Norwich as a bookbinder, and in 1766 his name begins to appear as bookseller on the imprints of local publications. In the same year, 'having engaged proper assistance from London and purchased a large quantity of Mr Caslon's excellent type', Beatniffe opened a printing office in St Peter Permountergate (*Norwich Mercury*, 21 June 1766). Beatniffe is named as the printer of a large number of local publications between 1767 and 1795, although it is likely that the printing office was entrusted to journeymen and apprentices. In the latter year Beatniffe took John Payne as a partner in his printing business, and after 1798 Payne was left to continue it on his own.

Richard Beatniffe's considerable fortune was made, however, from his secondhand and antiquarian bookselling business, which developed steadily over fifty-five years. His stock was renowned for being as great as that of any provincial bookseller, and the publication of his catalogues always attracted the attention of the London trade. The first of these appeared in 1779, and another was published in May 1787, by which time it ran to 20,000 titles and included the libraries of several local collectors. His last catalogue was issued in 1803, with an appendix in 1808. Among the notable collections of manuscripts and early printed books handled by him was that of Cox Macro of Bury St Edmunds, which had lain largely unregarded in the forty years since his death in 1767. This collection was bought by Beatniffe for about £150 or £160, approximately one tenth of its resale value. He also imported books from France, Italy, and Spain, when hostilities allowed.

Beatniffe is noteworthy too as the author of the *Norfolk Tour, or, Travellers Pocket Companion*, in which he 'endeavoured to compress into as small a compass as possible, to be useful to a Gentleman Traveller, an epitome of what to me seemed worthy of particular notice in the county' (preface). To this end he made a digest of various historical works relating to the county, supplemented from manuscripts that had passed through his hands. Later editions of this work incorporate the author's own valuable observations about the contemporary state of the county. The *Norfolk Tour* enjoyed sustained popularity and went through six editions between 1772 and 1808, each one larger than its predecessor. Beatniffe was an active supporter of the tory political faction in Norwich, serving on the common council for many years, but when in 1790 he was elected sheriff he chose to pay a fine of £80 to be excused from this duty for ever.

Beatniffe married Martha Dinah Hart (1747–1816), the daughter of a writing-master and alderman of Bury St Edmunds. The couple had a son, who died in infancy, and a daughter, Catherine, who in turn had two sons and two daughters from her second marriage, to Austin Palgrave Manclark of Great Yarmouth. Beatniffe retired from business and died shortly afterwards on 9 July 1818. He was buried, with his wife, in the nave of St Peter Mancroft Church, Norwich. His stock was subsequently dispersed by public auction.

William Beloe describes Beatniffe as 'a shrewd, cold, inflexible fellow' with a 'suspicion of strangers, and a constant apprehension lest he should dispose of any of his *libri rarisimi* to some cunning wight or professed collector' (Beloe, 2.244). Similar anecdotes concerning Beatniffe's occasionally abrasive character and knowledge of early books are related by James Ford and in two obituaries in the *Gentleman's Magazine*.

DAVID STOKER

Sources J. Ford, 'Richard Beatniffe, the author of the "Norfolk tour"', Nichols, *Illustrations*, 6.522–8 · *GM*, 1st ser., 88/2 (1818), 93, 286 · D. Stoker, 'The Norwich book trades before 1800', *Transactions of the Cambridge Bibliographical Society*, 8 (1981–5), 79–125, esp. 82–3 · W. Beloe, *The sexagenarian, or, The recollections of a literary life*, ed. [T. Rennell], 2 (1817), 244 · *IGI* · H. R. Plomer and others, *A dictionary of the printers and booksellers who were at work in England, Scotland, and Ireland from 1726 to 1775* (1932); repr. (1968) · Nichols, *Lit. anecdotes*, 3.672; 8.467; 9.365 · [J. Chambers], *A general history of the county of Norfolk*, 2 vols. (1829), 1183 · *DNB*

Beato, Felice (*c.*1825–*c.*1907), photographer, was, according to most biographies, born in Venice in 1830 and later became a naturalized British subject. However, little is known of his early life. Although he was undoubtedly of Italian ancestry, it is likely that he and his brother Antonio were born in Corfu about 1825. In the early part of the nineteenth century Corfu was a Venetian colony, but in 1814 it came under British rule; children born there could be registered as British subjects.

Beato is acknowledged to be the first photographer to specialize in war photography. He learned photography from his brother-in-law, James Robertson, who married Beato's sister in 1855. Robertson, a native of Britain who was appointed chief engraver of the mint in Constantinople in the 1840s, took up photography professionally in the early 1850s, travelling to the Crimea in 1855 to photograph the war between Britain and Russia. It is not clear whether Beato accompanied him at this time; however, a year later he was sent there by Robertson to photograph the aftermath of the war. At a time when most professional photographers employed the cumbersome wet-plate negative process, Robertson and Beato utilized a secret (and much simpler) dry-plate process which made battlefield photography practical.

In 1856 and 1857 Robertson and Beato travelled around the Mediterranean, photographing the sights at Constantinople, Malta, Egypt, and the Holy Land. In 1857 they established a formal partnership in Malta selling photographs to tourists. However, the partnership was short-lived for, when news of the Indian mutiny reached Malta, Beato set off for Calcutta. British policy had forbidden the photographing of dead bodies in the Crimea, but the prohibition did not apply to India. When Beato arrived in Lucknow in the summer of 1858, he was disappointed to discover that he had arrived too late to photograph the actual massacre of the rebels; undeterred, he had the skeletons of the rebels exhumed and scattered around the courtyard of the *sikandarabagh* to create one of his most dramatic photographs. Beato stayed in India, acting as a semi-official photographer for the army for the next two years, but a new war was in the wind.

In 1858 China took steps to end the British importation of Indian opium into their country; the British retaliated by occupying Canton (Guangzhou) and sinking a major part of the Chinese navy. Following their initial success, the British navy next attacked the Taku (Dagu) Fort complex guarding the river access to Peking (Beijing); here they were beaten off with heavy losses. The British response was to assemble an expeditionary force to invade China. Beato travelled with this army to Kowloon and Canton in the spring of 1860 and remained with it throughout the campaign. In August the army successfully stormed the Taku forts: in the heat of battle Beato followed the troops through the breach in the walls, imploring them not to touch the bodies until he had taken his pictures. He travelled with the army to Peking, where he was able to photograph the Summer Palace complex before it was looted and burned by British troops in retaliation for the torture and killing of allied prisoners. His approximately one hundred large-format photographs

constitute the first and only major surviving images of China before the 1870s.

After a brief trip to London, Beato returned to the Far East and settled in Yokohama for the next twenty years. This was the most prolific period of his career: he produced several hundred images in Japan encompassing landscape, architecture, and ethnography. He is considered the father of Japanese photography, his work the only comprehensive view remaining of the country's life and culture during the 1860s. In 1864 he joined the British forces for the Shimonoseki military expedition in Japan; in 1871 he was appointed the official photographer for the United States Navy during the attack on Korea. He also claimed to have photographed the Mahdist rebellion against the British in the Sudan in 1884, but so far no surviving images of this work have been found. In the 1870s Beato turned away from photography to become a merchant, but in the 1880s he lost all his money speculating in the Yokohama silver exchange. His friends raised the money for his passage to London. In 1889 he settled in Mandalay, Burma, and opened up a photographic studio; he appears to have operated a mail-order export business, dealing in local arts and crafts on the side. He died in Burma about 1907. The most comprehensive collections of his photographs in Britain are in the Victoria and Albert Museum, London, and the National Museum of Photography, Film and Television, Bradford (including the collection of the Royal Photographic Society).

MICHAEL G. WILSON

Sources J. Clark, J. Fraser, and C. Osman, *Japanese–British exchange in art: 1850s–1930s* (privately printed, 1989), appx 5 · I. Crombie, 'China, 1860: a photographic album by Felice Beato', *History of Photography*, 11 (1987), 25–36 · C. Osman, 'The later years of James Robertson', *History of Photography*, 16 (1992), 72–3 · B. A. Henisch and H. K. Henisch, 'James Robertson of Constantinople', *History of Photography*, 8 (1984), 299–313 · M. Harker, 'Robertson and Beato in Malta', *History of Photography*, 17 (1993), 217

Beaton, Sir Cecil Walter Hardy (1904–1980), photographer and designer for screen and theatre, was born at 21 Langland Gardens, Hampstead, London, on 14 January 1904, the eldest of the two sons and two daughters of Ernest Walter Hardy Beaton (1867–1936), timber merchant, and his wife, Esther (Etty; 1872–1962), the daughter of Joseph Sisson, a blacksmith from Temple Sowerby, Cumberland. His first love was the theatre and a strong theatrical strain was evident in all his work. But early success came through photography, the love of which was inspired by a postcard of Lily Elsie (whose notice he contributed to the *Dictionary of National Biography*), which he found on his mother's bed. He cajoled his sisters, Nancy and Baba, into becoming his first photographic models, designing their costumes and entering them into fancy dress competitions.

Beaton was educated at Heath Mount School, Hampstead, St Cyprian's School, Eastbourne, and at Harrow School. From there he went on to St John's College, Cambridge, ostensibly to read history and architecture. He did not graduate, however, and his main contribution was to the theatrical life of the university. He acted in and

Sir Cecil Walter Hardy Beaton (1904–1980), by Dorothy Wilding, 1937

designed sets for the Amateur Dramatic Company (ADC) and Marlowe Society. In 1925 he came down without a degree, and, after spending six months 'doing very little apart from smoking Pera cigarettes and taking long hot baths' (Beaton, *Photobiography*, 38), spent some unhappy months working in the Holborn office of a friend of his father's. He knew that he had to escape from this life, which the author Truman Capote called 'a cocoon of middle-class' respectability ('Beaton by Bailey', television documentary).

Beaton achieved this by his industry and imagination and the judicious use of publicity. He made a name for himself taking glamorous photographic portraits of the 'bright young things' of the day, who soon thirsted for his talents. His use of soft focus was in emulation of an existing technique; it was the unusual props and painted (or reflective) backgrounds, which he executed himself, that were the distinguishing feature of his portrait photographs. His backdrops made creative use of new materials such as cellophane, as well as mirrors—a good example of the latter was his portrait of Mountbatten. Later he would urge aspirant photographers to 'break every photographic rule … a technical "failure" which shows some attempt at aesthetic expression is of infinitely more value than an uninspired success' (Beaton, *Photobiography*, 183). He became a friend of the aesthete Stephen Tennant and others, notably Osbert and Edith Sitwell, and his rise to fame was meteoric. His ingenious photographic portraits of the Sitwells led to his employment with *Vogue* as photographer, caricaturist, and illustrator, first in London and later in New York. In 1927 and 1930 he held one-man exhibitions at the Cooling Gallery, Bond Street, for both of which Osbert Sitwell wrote the introduction. He produced his first book, *The Book of Beauty* (1930). By the end of the 1920s—a decade which Beaton may be said to personify—he had been granted sittings by all whom he had aspired to photograph, except Queen Mary and Virginia Woolf.

In the 1930s Beaton was exposed to influences such as Jean Cocteau and Christian Bérard, and his work became

accordingly more baroque. He branched into the world of ballet and opera, designing revues for Charles Cochran—*Streamline* (1934) and *Follow the Sun* (1936)—while continuing to photograph in London, New York, and Hollywood. But he noted: 'Throughout my photographic career I have always felt that in five years' time I should no longer be a photographer' (Beaton, *Photobiography*, 184). In 1930 he forged a lifelong love of Wiltshire, renting Ashcombe, a derelict house in a glorious, Arcadian setting near Win Green. He converted Ashcombe into a jewel of a house, where he entertained friends such as Rex Whistler, Augustus John, and Edith Olivier, staged a *fête-champêtre*, and made films. He was desolate when the landlord refused to renew his lease in 1945.

In the 1930s Beaton had photographed some members of the royal family, notably the duchess of Gloucester, and in 1937 Mrs Wallis Simpson invited him to take the formal wedding photographs of her marriage to the duke of Windsor in France. Beaton's career was progressing well until he introduced some offensive antisemitic doodles into an illustration for American *Vogue* in February 1938. He denied being anti-Jewish, and declared himself to be 'violently hostile to Hitler' (Vickers, 1993 edn, 208). But Condé Nast promptly dismissed him, and he did no work in the United States for a year and a half. The incident rose to haunt him periodically in later life.

Beaton's career was saved by two events. First, Queen Elizabeth invited him to photograph her at Buckingham Palace in July 1939. Beaton created glorious portrait photographs of her, playing an important role in the creation of her image as queen. Some of these pictures were released during the war as a morale-boosting contrast to the sinister images of Nazi Germany. Second, the war itself came to his aid, because he was able to make an important contribution as a war photographer. He depicted Churchill behind his desk in Downing Street, but more famous was his study of a bombed-out child in hospital, *Eileen Dunne in the Hospital for Sick Children* (1940). This picture was on the front cover of *Life* magazine in September 1940 and was said to have influenced American feeling concerning the war more than any other picture. Beaton travelled throughout England for the Ministry of Information and later to the Middle East, north Africa, and the Far East. By his courage and dedicated approach he earned the respect of the three services. Six books emerged from these years.

After the war, stage, film, ballet, and opera work gave Beaton more opportunities. In 1945 he designed the set for *Lady Windermere's Fan*, with an opulence of style that was a tonic for post-war Britain. The following year he took the part of Cecil Graham in the American production of the play. In 1948 he was responsible for the costumes for the films *An Ideal Husband* and *Anna Karenina* for Sir Alexander Korda. Other noted productions on which he worked were *The School for Scandal* (1949), *Quadrille*, for Noël Coward (London, 1952; New York, 1954), *Turandot* (New York, 1961; London, 1963), and *La traviata* (New York, 1966). His greatest stage success was to design costumes for *My Fair Lady* in

1956; its memorable black and white Ascot scene invariably drew a gasp of delight when the curtain rose. He repeated this success when he spent a year in Hollywood in 1963 working on the film adaptation. For his costume design and art direction he won two Oscars. (He had been awarded his first Oscar in 1958 for the film *Gigi*, arguably a more stunning screen production.) His own play, *The Gainsborough Girls*, was staged at Brighton in 1951 and in a revised version in 1959. Unfortunately it floundered on both occasions.

Beaton also made a considerable contribution to the world of fashion. Perhaps his best book is his personal survey of fifty years of changing fashion, *The Glass of Fashion* (1954). He gave a collection of the dresses he most admired to the Victoria and Albert Museum, and many of them were exhibited there in 1971. He was a dedicated and perceptive diarist from 1922 to 1980; six volumes of his diary were published in his lifetime, along with a *Photobiography* (1951).

Beaton continued to photograph throughout his later years. He photographed all the queen's children as babies, and he was the official photographer at the coronation and at several royal weddings. He also explored what the artist Michael Wishart called 'the Peacock Revolution', photographing rising figures of the 1960s such as the Rolling Stones, Twiggy, Jean Shrimpton, and the cast of the satirical revue *Beyond the Fringe*. Shortly before his death he photographed Little Bo Bitch, one of the lesser lights of the punk rock scene.

In 1968 Beaton's career was crowned with an important exhibition of his photographs at the National Portrait Gallery, where many remain on deposit or on show. In 1950 he was awarded the Légion d'honneur. He was created CBE in 1957 and knighted in 1972. Two years later he suffered a bad stroke, but he gradually learned to paint, write, and take photographs with his left hand. He died at his second Wiltshire home, Reddish House, Broadchalke, on 18 January 1980, and was buried on 23 January in the churchyard of All Saints, Broadchalke.

Beaton was a man of immense style and sartorial elegance, forever fascinated by new ideas and attitudes. He possessed an extraordinary visual sense and an eye which, in a flash, took in every minor detail around him; Capote once ventured that 'The camera will never be invented that could capture or encompass all that he actually sees' (Beaton, *The Best of Beaton*, 11). Beaton's conversation was witty and penetrating, and, while he enjoyed the company of glittering society, above all he valued and sought out talent and individuality. He suffered from the intermittent accusation that much of his work was light or trivial, but the wide range of his achievements and the pleasure that he gave the world makes this an unfair assessment.

Beaton was not granted much happiness in his personal relationships. During his younger years he was miserably and unrequitedly in love with the art connoisseur (Victor William) Peter Watson (1908–1956). He was essentially homosexual but pursued a tormented relationship for several decades with the screen actress Greta Garbo; he proposed to her, but was refused, and he remained unmarried.

The many facets of Beaton's character and career are perhaps best caught in the *bon mots* of his friends. Capote once noted that he was 'a total self-creation' (*Bailey on Beaton*, television documentary); revealingly, Beaton himself once wrote in his diary (9 October 1923): 'I don't want people to know me as I really am but as I'm trying and pretending to be' (Vickers, 1993 edn, xvii). In this aim he appears largely to have succeeded. The critic Kenneth Tynan recorded that he managed to give the impression, on arriving at a society party, of 'an actor who has just made a superb exit; you would think that he had just come from some garish and exhausting rout on the floor above' (ibid., xxvi); more tersely, Cyril Connolly called him 'Rip-Van-With-It' (*Sunday Times*, 13 March 1966). The playwright Alan Jay Lerner (1918–1996) said, of his work in the theatre: 'He was the only designer whose sketches were stunningly beautiful and outrageously funny at the same time' (Vickers, 1993 edn, xxv). Capote rated him as 'one of the three or four best photographers in this century' (ibid., xxvii) and an abiding influence on the succeeding generation. Beaton himself was apt to consider his work ephemeral, but it is certain that his considerable output, both visual and written, amounts to a unique and enduring portrait of the age in which he lived.

HUGO VICKERS

Sources H. Vickers, *Cecil Beaton* (1985); 2nd edn (1993); 3rd edn (2003) · C. Beaton, *The wandering years* (1961) · C. Beaton, *The years between* (1965) · C. Beaton, *The happy years* (1972) · C. Beaton, *The strenuous years* (1973) · C. Beaton, *The restless years* (1976) · C. Beaton, *The parting years* (1978) · C. Beaton, *Photobiography* (1951) · C. Beaton, *Self-portrait with friends*, ed. R. Buckle (1979) · P. Garner and D. A. Mellor, *Cecil Beaton* (1994) · C. Spencer, *Cecil Beaton, stage and film designs* (1975) · R. Misselbeck, 'Beaton, Cecil', *The dictionary of art*, ed. J. Turner (1996) · C. Beaton, *The best of Beaton*, ed. T. Capote (1968) · *The Times* (19 Jan 1980)

Archives NPG, photograph collection · St John Cam., diaries, office papers · V&A, scrapbooks | FILM 'Beaton by Bailey', documentary footage

Likenesses C. Berard, *c*.1935, NPG · D. Wilding, bromide print, 1937, NPG [*see illus.*] · C. Beaton, self-portrait, photograph, repro. in Beaton, *Photobiography*, frontispiece · Tchelitchew, sketches

Wealth at death £597,757: probate, 1 April 1980, CGPLA Eng. & Wales

Beaton [Betoun], **David** (1494?–1546), cardinal and archbishop of St Andrews, was a younger son of John Beaton (*d.* 1532), of Balfour, Fife, and Elizabeth Monypenny (*d.* 1541), daughter of the laird of Pitmilly, Fife.

Early career and appointments Beaton entered St Andrews University in 1508, transferred to that of Glasgow in 1511, and in 1519 was admitted to the University of Orleans. By then he had held first a canonry and then the chancellorship of Glasgow Cathedral through the influence of his uncle, James *Beaton (1524–1603), archbishop of Glasgow. At the French court he gained the patronage of the French-born John Stewart, fourth duke of Albany, governor of Scotland between 1515 and 1524. Albany brought him to Scotland in 1521 and presented him to the young James V. In 1522 Beaton was sent to England on diplomatic business, but he returned to France with Albany in 1524 to negotiate a Franco-Scottish royal marriage, an alliance envisaged in the treaty of Rouen (1517). The same year he received his first major ecclesiastical appointment, the abbacy of Arbroath, resigned to him by his uncle on the latter's translation to the archbishopric of St Andrews. David Beaton, whose papal provision was dated 26 June 1524, was strictly speaking commendator of Arbroath. He never took monastic vows and as late as 1534 he petitioned the pope to be allowed to postpone taking holy orders.

From his return to Scotland at Christmas 1524 until his next embassy to France in 1533 Beaton made a place for himself in the central administration. He became a member of the council, which dealt with both public affairs and legal causes. As abbot of Arbroath he sat in parliament. He was chosen one of the young king's guardians, and on 3 January 1529 he was made keeper of the privy seal. His public career during the minority of James V was not without difficulties. During the ascendancy of the Anglophile earl of Angus (second husband of the queen mother Margaret Tudor) and his Douglas kinsmen, the influence of the Francophile Beaton prelates declined, with long periods when David Beaton was absent from the council. The early 1530s saw a contest of wills between king and clergy over James's taxation of the church for the endowment of a college of justice. The danger of resistance was that it risked provoking the king into following Henry VIII's example and laying hands on monastic property. David Beaton tempered his resistance sufficiently to be able to retain the king's favour, even while his uncle the archbishop was politically under a cloud. The experiences of the 1520s and early 1530s created in him a strong attachment to the Franco-Scottish alliance, a resistance to English influence in Scottish affairs, and an antipathy to the Douglases, who acted as a channel of that influence.

Ambassador and prince of the church Beaton's knowledge of the French court was to his advantage when in 1533 James V renewed negotiations for a French marriage. Of the next ten years he spent the equivalent of four and a half in France, on seven separate occasions: from late April to late July 1533 and in the spring of 1534; from early September 1536 to mid-May 1537, when he accompanied James V on his visit to France during which the king married Princess Madeleine; in the autumn and winter of 1537 and spring of 1538, when he negotiated James V's marriage to Mary of Guise; in the autumn of 1538 and the summer of 1539, mainly on his own ecclesiastical affairs; and from late July 1541 to early August 1542, his longest diplomatic mission. European observers were impressed by his grasp of international affairs; he was referred to during James V's state visit to France as 'one of his *prelati* who conducts everything and is a man of a good wit' (*LP Henry VIII*, 11, no. 1173).

Beaton's diplomatic efforts on Scotland's behalf turned to his own advantage. In 1537 Francis I nominated him to the French bishopric of Mirepoix, to which he received papal provision on 5 December. He crossed to France in the autumn of 1538, probably for his consecration and, as often happened with career-clerics, to receive holy orders on the same occasion. On 20 December 1538, by now also

acting as coadjutor (administrator with prospect of succeeding) of St Andrews for his ageing uncle, he was one of five new cardinals created by the pope, European opinion regarding him as one of the French appointees. When concelebrating at the empress's requiem mass in June 1539, he was referred to as 'the cardinal of Mirepoix' (Lestocquoy, 1.443–4). On his uncle's death on 14 February 1539 he became archbishop of St Andrews. Five years later, in the spring of 1544, he received intimation of his appointment as *legate a latere*, with delegated papal powers over the Scottish church.

Later relations with James V Having passed the zenith of his diplomatic usefulness there developed a tension in Beaton's relations with the king. This partly arose out of the cardinal's initiatives in tackling the problem of heresy among those whose royal service protected them, and partly from fear of the king's designs on the wealth of the church. In 1538, while coadjutor of St Andrews, he ordered a crackdown on religious suspects in Dundee. At the start of his primacy in 1539 a number of heretics were brought to trial, seven of whom were put to death. This forceful beginning was not followed up, largely because Beaton was unable to lay hands on the leading dissidents, a group of nobles, lairds, and lawyers, some of them his own vassals in Fife and Angus (Forfarshire), who wished closer friendship with England: 'the contagion of English impiety', as he called it (*LP Henry VIII*, 18/1, no. 494). Early in 1540 the prelates, led by Beaton, presented the king with a list of those who they asserted might be forfeited for heresy. James threw the list back at them, telling them not to come between him and his servants. Beaton's reaction to this rebuff was to summon for trial a trusted royal servant, Sir John Borthwick, who had outlined a recognizably Cromwellian programme for the reform of the church. Having been warned, Borthwick escaped to England and was condemned *in absentia*. In March 1541 the cardinal put his stamp on a group of anti-heresy statutes whose provisions reflect the extent to which religious dissent had grown since Patrick Hamilton's case in 1528; he targeted criticism of the papacy and of the church's central doctrines and practice, iconoclastic protest, and group discussion of protestant teaching.

The bid for control Anglo-Scottish relations deteriorated in the autumn of 1542, not least because of James V's failure in 1541 to keep an appointment with Henry VIII at York, a meeting which Beaton had been instrumental in preventing. Border hostilities turned into a campaign for the invasion of England, encouraged by Beaton who in his letters to the pope gave it the character of a holy war against the apostate king of England. The campaign ended with the rout of the Scottish army at Solway Moss on 24 November, followed by the death of the king on 14 December, a few days after the birth of his daughter Mary. The power struggle that followed the king's death arose partly from uncertainty about his last wishes for the government during his daughter's minority. On 19 December Beaton was proclaimed head of a council consisting of the earls of Arran (heir-presumptive), Moray, Argyll, and Huntly, but towards the end of the month Arran confided to an English agent that the cardinal had told lies to the council about the king's wishes. On 3 January 1543 Beaton had to acquiesce in the result of a coup which made Arran sole governor. Yet in spite of their antagonism Arran conferred the office of chancellor on Beaton on 10 January, depriving the archbishop of Glasgow, Gavin Dunbar. It has been suggested that in order to gain the coveted chancellorship Beaton may have brought pressure to bear on Arran, who in the church's eyes was of doubtful legitimacy, the annulment of his father's first marriage being of questionable validity. Besides, Arran's name headed the clergy's list of heretics. But although Arran was putting it about in April that the cardinal had first made the king sign a blank paper and then forged his will, Beaton was never charged with forgery.

By mid-January 1543 it was reported that 'the Cardinal is everything in Scotland' (*LP Henry VIII*, 18/1, no. 44), but opposition was mobilizing. The earl of Angus and his brother Sir George Douglas, who had been in England since 1528, crossed the border, and a number of the Solway Moss prisoners came home on parole, having promised in return for English pensions to further Henry VIII's plans for the dynastic union of the two kingdoms. On 27 January the cardinal was arrested in council, on a charge of having invited the French to Scotland, and was removed from the court. Three months' detention ended in house arrest in his own castle at St Andrews, where he worked to break the English intervention in Scottish affairs, playing on the vested interests of all parties. He sent for French military help to withstand England and brought home from France two people whose presence he hoped might unnerve the governor and wean him away from the Anglophile reformist party: Matthew Stewart, thirteenth earl of Lennox, who if Arran's illegitimacy were proved was heir-presumptive, and John Hamilton, abbot of Paisley, the governor's half-brother. Meantime, the parliament which met in March confirmed Arran's governorship, passed an act permitting the reading of the New Testament in English, and instructed commissioners to negotiate a treaty for the marriage of Prince Edward and Queen Mary, the terms of which were finalized in London on 1 July. The governor also appointed protestant preachers at court.

On 20 July the cardinal's party signed a band to protect the queen from Henry VIII's plans and to have her and her mother removed from Linlithgow to Stirling Castle. After a conference with Arran's party the royal removal was accomplished. Beaton stayed away from the ratification of the English treaty at Edinburgh on 25 August. His anti-English attitude gained credibility when the English seized some Scottish merchant ships, provoking a riot in Edinburgh in which the house of the English envoy, Sir Ralph Sadler, was attacked. Losing his nerve, the governor left Edinburgh on 4 September, met the cardinal at Callendar (near Falkirk), home of Lord Livingston, and at Stirling publicly recanted his heresy, receiving absolution from the cardinal's hands. Mary was crowned at Stirling on 9 September. At a meeting of the council in the cardinal's Edinburgh lodging, in the presence of the queen dowager, Mary of Guise, and the governor, Beaton told Sadler that the marriage treaty could not stand as the majority of the nobility had not agreed to it. Henry VIII, who saw the cardinal behind all his problems in Scotland, planned revenge.

Beaton in charge of policy The governor's reconciliation with Beaton shattered the Anglo-Scottish agreements and caused an upheaval in internal Scottish politics. Lennox deserted the cardinal for Angus's party, which became a broadly based opposition, drawing part of its support from the west and including some who had never been compromised by Henry VIII as well as its natural adherents, the Anglophile reformists, who deplored the prospect of war with England and the setback to the 1543 measures for religious reform. Some who had supported Beaton out of enmity to Arran deserted him now that the governor was associated with him. The situation provoked the cardinal into taking punitive action against opponents. In the autumn of 1543 he launched an inquisition which resulted in the arrests not only of some Dundee iconoclasts and a number of priests and laymen in Angus, the Mearns, and Aberdeenshire, but also of lords Maxwell and Somerville (caught on their way to England as Angus's envoys), and the earl of Rothes, Lord Gray, and Henry Balnaves. Beaton had to give up his prominent victims, being warned that the detention of these lords and barons without trial would have serious consequences. Parliament, meeting in December, annulled the English treaty, confirmed the French alliance, and re-enacted the anti-heresy legislation. The chancellorship was restored to the cardinal.

In January 1544 Beaton and Arran descended on Perth, where a group of heretics was put to death, and the cardinal engineered a change of provost in order to demonstrate his authority in the burgh, whose craftsmen had sent a contingent to support Lennox at the end of 1543. After the failure of an attempt at reconciliation between the parties early in 1544, Beaton found it increasingly difficult to hold the unstable political situation together. The Lennox–Angus forces took to the field in the west, but were defeated near Glasgow. Lennox departed for England, not before he had soured Franco-Scottish relations by failing to give an account of the money handed over to him by the French ambassadors towards the end of 1543. Acting in his own interests, Lennox's behaviour lowered the cardinal's credit with France at this juncture. Beaton also watched uneasily throughout the year as Mary of Guise tried to form a party which attracted support from the Douglases and even some of the bishops who wished for peace, and which, before it fell apart, held a convention in June at which Arran was formally suspended from the governorship. On Christmas eve 1544 the cardinal wrote asking for the papacy's moral support against England, considering 'our continual obedience to the Holy See, and their disobedience' (*LP Henry VIII*, 19/2, no. 774).

The English invasions, conspiracy, and murder In 1544 and 1545 the cardinal paid the price of having broken the marriage treaty, in several devastating English invasions, in which the borders and south-east suffered especially. The initial attack from the sea in May 1544 reached Edinburgh. So instinctive was the Scottish reaction to the assaults of the 'auld enemy' that for a time the Douglases fought on the government's side. However, apart from the battle of Ancrum Moor on 27 February 1545, when Angus led the Scots to victory and the English leaders Eure and Layton were killed, the campaign to withstand the English incursions was a failure. French help, when it came, proved a humiliation for the cardinal. François I, waging a war on two fronts, could not afford an army of the size needed to defeat Henry VIII's invading forces. The French military commander, Jacques de Montgomery, seigneur de Lorges, who arrived in May 1545, regarded himself as answerable only to the French king. He and the cardinal almost came to blows over the Frenchman's role in the campaign, while the Scots leaders refused seriously to invade England under his command. English propaganda pilloried the cardinal as the cause of the war.

Meantime a more personal threat was maturing, born out of growing political, religious, and personal antagonism. Henry VIII eventually agreed to a plot to kill Beaton, his conditions being conveyed through Scottish agents to those who promised him to take out of the way 'the worker of all your mischief' (Sanderson, 202). By the winter of 1545–6 Beaton was financially exhausted, his credit with France was at a low ebb, and dislike of his policies had turned into a personal vendetta. Early in 1546 he seized the protestant preacher George Wishart, whose public preaching in defiance of an episcopal ban and the support he received from prominent adherents of reform had recently been making a mockery of the anti-heresy laws. Beaton's show of authority in the trial and execution of Wishart at St Andrews on 1 March 1546 recoiled brutally on himself. On 29 May he was murdered in his castle in St Andrews by a small group of Fife lairds whose motives combined personal quarrels, political frustration, and religious outrage at the death of Wishart, on whom they had counted to advance publicly the cause of reform. Beaton's body, preserved in salt, was handed over for burial when his killers surrendered the castle at the end of July 1547. It is not known where his remains were interred. Some European reports of the assassination remarked how well the cardinal's removal from the political scene suited the king of England.

Assessment Cardinal Beaton has always been prominent in accounts of early sixteenth-century Scotland. Nineteenth- and early twentieth-century biographers, who were largely ultra-protestant and constitutional historians, saw him as an apocalyptic figure whose policies, in the words of Peter Hume Brown, 'ran counter to the development of the country' (Brown, 2.19). He was depicted as the champion of the fading Franco-Scottish alliance and the personification of an ecclesiastical tyranny doomed to destruction. He has sometimes also been seen as a patriot, resisting the aggressions of Henry VIII,

and as having a personal interest in the proposals for internal reform of church standards voiced during his primacy. His reputation for profligacy, so much a part of the earlier folk history surrounding him, still gets a mention.

The result of modern research into the voluminous documentation of Beaton's public career has been to strike a balance in assessing his character and impact. Possibly the most notable revision has been to emphasize the difficulties he experienced in trying to control both the political situation and the rise of religious dissent, thereby helping to modify the earlier stereotype of the dreaded tyrant. His resistance to England has to be set against his concern for his own vested interests in France, noted by contemporaries. His ability to control policy may owe something to the fact that latterly he had the malleable Governor Arran to handle in place of James V, and that he was able to play off one party against another. His own private life would appear to negate any supposed support on his part for the reform of clerical standards, and still leaves him as an example of one of the greatest weaknesses in the structure of the unreformed church, demonstrating the ease with which secularly minded career-clerics might aspire to ecclesiastical leadership. In this connection, however, it should be mentioned that research has identified all his eight recorded children as the sons and daughters of Marion *Ogilvy (d. 1575), the daughter of the first Lord Ogilvy, whom he treated virtually as a wife for more than twenty years until his death. Beaton lived in the style of a Renaissance magnate, with a large household, French personal servants, and six residences, including the castle of St Andrews, the abbot's house at Arbroath, a substantial Edinburgh lodging, and the private residence of Melgund in Angus, on land which he purchased from the crown for his mistress and their family in 1543. He was an international figure, at home in France where, it was claimed, he might have been taken for a Frenchman.

In Beaton's favour as a statesman it may be said that his approach was more truly international than that of most Scottish contemporaries with whom he had to work, and that he was the last Scottish statesman to keep his country within the arena of European politics, wringing all he could for Scotland out of shifting diplomatic situations. On the other hand, his conservatism, which was largely motivated by his need to preserve the political and ecclesiastical systems that had made him what he was, robbed him of the chance of success, which his wider vision might have won. He failed to see that when he needed the French alliance most, in 1544–5, the French king was unable or unwilling to assist him to the extent that he required, and he underestimated the irreversible commitment of many leading Scots to closer relations with England. At the same time his apparent unwillingness to implement any serious internal reform of the church, which was demanded most in those areas upon which the livings and authority enjoyed by himself and his fellow prelates principally depended, only added fuel to the frustration and resentment of those who wanted radical reform. In the end his temperament and personal priorities betrayed his abilities as a politician and churchman in an era in which Scotland's traditional alignments in those fields were increasingly threatened.

MARGARET H. B. SANDERSON

Sources M. H. B. Sanderson, *Cardinal of Scotland: David Beaton, c.1494–1546* (1986) [has full bibliography and list of archival sources] · J. Herkless and R. K. Hannay, *The archbishops of St Andrews*, 5 vols. (1907–15), vol. 4 · acts of the lords of council and session, NA Scot., CS 5; CS 6 · *LP Henry VIII*, 11, no. 1173; 18/1, no. 494; 18/1, no. 44; 19/2, no. 774 · *The state papers and letters of Sir Ralph Sadler*, ed. A. Clifford, 2 vols. (1809) · *The Scottish correspondence of Mary of Lorraine*, ed. A. I. Cameron, Scottish History Society, 3rd ser., 10 (1927) · J. Lestocquoy, ed., *Correspondance des nonces en France*, 3 vols. (Rome, 1961) · J. B. A. T. Teulet, ed., *Papiers d'état, pièces et documents inédits ou peu connus relatifs à l'histoire de l'Écosse au XVIème siècle*, 3 vols., Bannatyne Club, 107 (Paris, 1852–60) · register of supplications, Vatican Archives · [C. Innes], ed., *Liber sancte Marie de Melros*, 2 vols., Bannatyne Club, 56 (1837), vol. 2 · R. K. Hannay, ed., *Rentale Sancti Andree, 1538–1546*, Scottish History Society, 2nd ser., 4 (1913) · *John Knox's History of the Reformation in Scotland*, ed. W. C. Dickinson, 1 (1949) · A. Hay, *Ad illustrissimum tituli s. Stephani in monte Coelio cardinalem, d. Davidem Betoun, primatem Scotiae … de foelici accessione dignitatis cardinalitiae gratulatorius panegyricus Archibaldi Hayi* (Paris, 1540) · P. H. Brown, *History of Scotland to the present time*, 3 vols. (1911) · Charles, eleventh marquis of Huntly, earl of Aboyne, ed., *The records of Aboyne MCCXXX–MDCLXXXI*, New Spalding Club, 13 (1894)
Archives BL, letters, Royal MS Lat. 18 6 · NA Scot. · U. St Andr. L. | U. Glas., department of history, Ross fund microfilm of Scottish material in the Vatican archives
Likenesses oils, *c.*1538, Blairs College, Aberdeenshire; colour transparency, Scot. NPG

Beaton, James (*c.*1473–1539), administrator and archbishop of St Andrews, was the sixth son of John Beaton of Balfour in the parish of Markinch, and Marjory, daughter of Sir David Boswell of Balmouto in the parish of Kinghorn. For one who was later to hold the highest offices in church and state and to exercise immense power, it is noteworthy that he was not connected by blood to any of the noble houses of Scotland. He entered the University of St Andrews as a student in the session of 1487–8, matriculated on 29 February 1488, when he was probably aged about fourteen, determined in 1492, and received his licence in 1493. Of his subsequent academic career nothing has come to light.

Early services to church and state It is highly likely that soon after graduating Beaton was brought into the service of the state by his brother Sir David Beaton of Creich, who in 1501 became treasurer of Scotland. Between 1497 and 1503 he held for short periods a number of benefices, in all probability secured for him by his brother as a source of income, and as a recompense for work he had undertaken for the treasury. In 1504 James IV presented him to the abbacy of Dunfermline, which he was to hold *in commendam* for two years by papal dispensation. This prestigious benefice, which brought with it wealth and political status, indicated that Beaton had begun to make a name for himself. This was confirmed by the fact that on the death of his brother in January 1505 he succeeded him as treasurer. At this stage in his career Beaton had given no indication that he craved a wide field for spiritual labour, but rather that he desired episcopal status and a career as a statesman.

With the support of the king Beaton entered into negotiations with Cardinal Grimani of Venice, the protector of Scottish interests at Rome, in the hope of securing succession to the bishopric of Dunblane, but before these transactions had gone far Beaton was nominated by the crown to the bishopric of Galloway with papal provision on 12 May 1508. His tenure of this benefice was brief, for before he could be consecrated he was nominated by the king, and elected on 9 November, to the archbishopric of Glasgow. He was translated on 19 January 1509 and consecrated at Stirling on 15 April.

On his elevation to the episcopate Beaton demitted the office of treasurer, and as part of the price of his promotion had to surrender Dunfermline Abbey in favour of the king's illegitimate son Alexander Stewart. Moreover, he was not exempt, as his predecessor had been, from the primatial and legatine authority of the archbishop of St Andrews. Beaton's 'spectacular rise to power', as these concessions required of him demonstrate, had been 'followed by a marked diminution of royal favour' (Mackie, xxxvii).

Beaton was an active administrator of his large diocese, and wherever possible sought to uphold the honour of the church and the rights and privileges of the dean and chapter of his cathedral church. He was energetic in promoting the material splendour of his archdiocese. He spent money on strengthening the episcopal castle, on repairing the bridge over the Clyde, on altarages in the cathedral, and on repairs to the fabric of its choir. He also invited principals of quality to the struggling university. By trafficking in benefices he acquired considerable wealth.

Beaton's entry into the political life of the nation was one of the consequences of the disaster at Flodden on 9 September 1513, which deprived the country of both its king and its ecclesiastical primate, Alexander Stewart, archbishop of St Andrews. To Beaton, who was now the senior churchman, was assigned the honour of crowning the infant king, James V, on 21 September at Stirling. He was also made a member of the council to assist the king's mother, Margaret Tudor, in the government of the country. The way to high office in the state and to great power was opening up before him. By 29 September 1513, Beaton had become chancellor of the realm.

Chancellor of Scotland In the exercise of this high office, which he held until 1524, Beaton was guided by one fundamental tenet, the maintenance of Scotland's political independence. In the years immediately following Flodden he pursued this objective by turning to France in order to secure the return to Scotland of the lawful regent, John Stewart, duke of Albany, and by keeping peace with England. The widowed queen married the earl of Angus on 6 August 1514 and, determined to be the ruler of the country during her son's minority, turned against the chancellor, who intensified his desire to secure help from France. Albany returned to Scotland in May 1515 and survived the queen's attempts to crush him with English help in the civil strife that ensued, and Beaton's faithful adherence to the duke was rewarded with the abbacy of Arbroath.

In the troubled years that followed in the faction-ridden country, Beaton continued to pursue his twin objectives—peace with England and support for Albany. The internal situation was complicated by events abroad and was aggravated by a protracted vacancy in the primatial see of St Andrews. Albany was absent in France between 1517 and 1521, and the leading figure in government was James Hamilton, second earl of Arran. He enjoyed the support of Beaton, whose niece he married in November 1516. When Albany returned late in 1521 he nominated Beaton to the archbishopric of St Andrews, thereby assuring himself of Beaton's continued support, which was by now indispensable to anyone who wished to rule in Scotland. On 28 December 1522 Beaton received the pallium, but his translation was not effected until 5 June of the following year.

With the return of Albany to France in May 1524, Beaton's dominant political role was soon to be challenged. Nevertheless as 'the possessor of great wealth and the most experienced diplomatist and the ablest statesman in the land' (Herkless and Hannay, 108), whoever wished to exert influence would have to reckon with him. He distrusted the attempts of Henry VIII to influence events in England's favour, and took no part in the action of Queen Margaret in having her twelve-year-old son proclaimed king in July 1524. Beaton's continuing support for Albany resulted in his being briefly deprived of the chancellorship and imprisoned, but attempts to have him removed from his ecclesiastical office and his wealth failed, and eventually Margaret had to release him and attempt to win him to her side, even offering to try to obtain for him a cardinal's hat. In the meantime Beaton was furthering the political career of his nephew David *Beaton (1494?–1546), the future cardinal, to whom in 1524 he resigned the commendatorship of Arbroath Abbey.

With Albany's failure to return to Scotland, Beaton realized that a lasting peace with England had to be arranged, but he was determined that it must not be at the expense of his country's liberty. In February 1525 he was appointed to the king's council by the estates and was reconciled with Margaret, events which led to his restoration to the chancellorship. It was not for long, however. Beaton was fully immersed in the manoeuvring of the rival political factions which were seeking to gain control over the young king and to determine the country's foreign relations. In June 1526 parliament declared that James V, having reached his majority, was to exercise his full authority. Angus, Margaret's now estranged husband and a leading advocate of peace with England, had the king within his power and was behind Beaton's being immediately deprived of the great seal. This turn of events brought together Beaton and Margaret, who wished to see the king freed from Angus's controlling hand. But their attempt to capture the king failed and Beaton was forced into hiding, until by skilful use of his wealth he came to terms with Angus.

Relations with James V In 1528 the king succeeded in freeing himself from Angus's control. In this action Beaton may possibly have had some part, for almost immediately thereafter he was received into the king's favour. But he was not restored to the chancellorship. The king's determination that Scotland should remain independent of both England and France was in line with Beaton's longstanding desire. A treaty of peace with England was ratified and Beaton effected the divorce of Margaret and Angus. Nevertheless, relations between king and primate were rarely to run smoothly. Beaton's ecclesiastical authority was restrained, so that the legatine powers which he sought were limited to his own archdiocese. Although he was given a place in the newly established college of justice, he attended meetings only rarely, and not at all in 1529 and 1530. When the king sought to raise a large annual levy from ecclesiastical benefices in 1532, Beaton led the opposition so successfully that the king had to be satisfied with less than he wanted.

The issue of taxation must have contributed to the breakdown in relations between James and Beaton, which had begun by March 1532 and which became total in the following year. But of equal importance was the king's foreign policy, which was in danger of leading the country into war with England. For the country's most experienced statesman, who had long regarded peace with England as essential for its independence, such developments could only cause alarm. In April 1533, when military preparations were put in train, Beaton was arrested allegedly for conspiring, as the king stated in a letter to the cardinal of Ravenna, 'against our commonweal' (Herkless and Hannay, 225). The king set out a long list of charges amounting to treason, with the intention of transmitting it to the pope. These accusations demonstrate that the king's anger against Beaton was long-standing, but he secured his freedom, and having promised good conduct was readmitted to favour. Tension over taxes persisted, however. In 1536 the king ordered that a general provincial council be held; after some persuasion Beaton duly summoned it, while at the same time protesting that the matter pertained to him as archbishop and primate. The council agreed to contribute towards the cost of the college of justice, but in fact little was raised, and Beaton appears to have paid nothing. In 1536–7 Beaton was one of the vice-regents appointed to govern Scotland during James V's absence in France. But his days as a statesman were now effectively over, at least partly as a result of old age—in 1537 his nephew David was appointed his coadjutor in the diocese of St Andrews.

Religion and learning During the difficult years of the late 1520s and early 1530s politics had diverted Beaton's attention from the spiritual needs of his people and the problems of St Andrews University of which he was now chancellor. Nevertheless, the material interests of his archdiocese were protected. He supported the Dominicans in their plans for the extension of their friary in St Andrews, concerned himself with a dispute involving an Observant Franciscan, and used some of his riches to increase the income of chaplains at Holy Trinity parish church. Of much greater significance was Beaton's awareness of the impact of Lutheran heresy on Scotland and his action to halt its spreading. He was behind the act of parliament in July 1525 which sought to prevent the importing of Lutheran writings. His determination to crush the advance of heresy launched a period of persecution, which was initially expressed in the action taken against Patrick Hamilton; first summoned in 1527, Hamilton was tried and condemned at St Andrews in the archbishop's presence at the end of February 1528 and subsequently burnt at the stake. Beaton's action against other suspected Lutherans resulted for some in their flight to England and the continent, and for others in execution. Such persecution, backed by the estates in 1532 and 1534, did not have the desired effect.

Archbishop Beaton was not unheedful of the need of the church and the country for a supply of learned men, as he showed by his plans to transform the university's oldest academic centre, the pedagogy, into a college primarily intended for the education of the clergy. In this he may have aimed to emulate the earlier efforts of Bishop Elphinstone at Aberdeen, and even the contemporary plans of Cardinal Wolsey for Oxford. In 1525 a supplication to found the new college was granted by the pope, but Beaton failed to implement it. Ten years later, urged on by his young relatives at Paris, negotiations with Rome were reopened. The papal licence was renewed on 12 February 1538. In the following year and only seven days before Beaton's death at St Andrews Castle on 14 February 1539, the foundation charter was signed and the new college of St Mary of the Assumption formally inaugurated. It was Beaton's last notable action.

It has been stated that Beaton's career afforded 'a vivid illustration of the secularisation of clerical offices, which was counted in the reckoning of the Reformation' (Herkless and Hannay, 245). His statesmanship, it may be argued, saved his country's independence in the aftermath of Flodden, and his 'steadfast purpose and incorruptible devotion' throughout his tenure of high office protected Scotland from those who from without sought to control the country (ibid., 247).

James K. Cameron

Sources J. Herkless and R. K. Hannay, *The archbishops of St Andrews*, 5 vols. (1907–15), vol. 3 · J. M. Anderson, ed., *Early records of the University of St Andrews*, Scottish History Society, 3rd ser., 8 (1926) · A. I. Dunlop, ed., *Acta facultatis artium universitatis Sanctiandree, 1413–1588*, 2, Scottish History Society, 3rd ser., 55 (1964) · D. E. R. Watt, ed., *Fasti ecclesiae Scoticanae medii aevi ad annum 1638*, [2nd edn], Scottish RS, new ser., 1 (1969) · N. Macdougall, *James IV* (1989) · *The letters of James the fourth, 1505–13*, ed. R. K. Hannay and R. L. Mackie, Scottish History Society, 3rd ser., 45 (1953) · J. Lauder, G. Donaldson, and C. Macrae, eds., *St Andrews formulare, 1514–1546*, 2 vols., Stair Society, 7, 9 (1942–4) · G. Donaldson, *Scotland: James V to James VII* (1965), vol. 3 of *The Edinburgh history of Scotland* (1965–75) · W. Macfarlane, *Genealogical collections concerning families in Scotland*, ed. J. T. Clark, 1, Scottish History Society, 33 (1900) · J. Cameron, *James V: the personal rule, 1528–1542*, ed. N. Macdougall (1998) · M. H. B. Sanderson, *Cardinal of Scotland: David Beaton, c.1494–1546* (1986)

Beaton, James (1524–1603), diplomat and archbishop of Glasgow, born in the spring or early summer of 1524, was the son of James Beaton, laird of Balfarg (Fife), and his wife, Helen Melville. He belonged to the third generation of the Beaton hegemony in the church: lesser prelates apart, Archbishop James *Beaton of St Andrews (*d.* 1539) was his great-uncle, and Cardinal David *Beaton (1494?–1546) his uncle. When aged fourteen or fifteen, James was sent by the cardinal to study in France, first at Paris and then in Poitou. When he was almost twenty he was entrusted by the French king with a mission to the Scottish queen mother, Mary of Guise. Having graduated and returned to Scotland, Beaton received the clerical tonsure and minor orders and in March 1546 was provided as abbot of Arbroath, which the cardinal had resigned in his favour. After the conflict following the cardinal's murder two months later, he was in undisputed possession of Arbroath by April 1549 and, having received the abbatial blessing, retained the abbacy until his provision as archbishop. In April 1550 he was in France again on a mission for the queen mother.

At this time there was strife over the vacant archbishopric of Glasgow. Beaton, nominated by the crown as archbishop in February 1550, was eventually provided by Rome on 4 September 1551 with a dispensation for defect of age, as he was not yet thirty. Being then still abroad, he travelled to Rome to be ordained priest in July 1552 and bishop in August. By January 1553 he was back in Scotland, where he served as a privy councillor. As Scotland became increasingly polarized, Beaton remained Roman Catholic and pro-French, and strongly supported the regent, Mary of Guise. He was also close to Queen Mary, and one of her 'four Maries' was his cousin Mary Beaton. In 1558 he was in France again as commissioner of parliament for her marriage with the dauphin.

In 1559 Beaton convoked a diocesan synod to put the enactments of the provincial church council, aimed at reform from within, into effect. Warring military forces were now moving round Scotland, putting church property particularly at risk. Beaton therefore left Glasgow with the queen regent in the early summer, taking the treasures and muniments of Glasgow Cathedral with him. In winter 1559–60 he settled in Leith with the French forces and was a mainstay of their resistance during the siege which followed. When this ended in July 1560 he accepted safe conduct and sailed to France, taking the Glasgow treasures with him. He arrived in Paris in early August, the month of the Reformation Parliament.

When Queen Mary returned to Scotland in August 1561, Beaton remained in Paris as her ambassador, a post for which he was eminently fitted, being well acquainted with France and its court and language. For more than forty years he was ambassador, for Mary during her reign in Scotland and long captivity in England, and then after her death for her son, James VI. Beaton's fortunes in France and Scotland fluctuated with the civil and religious vicissitudes in both countries. In France he naturally sided with the Guise faction, and with the Catholic league formed by it in 1576. When the Guises fell from power and the league collapsed, he was out of favour but was treated sympathetically by Henri IV. His finances also fluctuated, particularly after Queen Mary's death.

While Mary reigned in Scotland, Beaton remained undisputed archbishop of Glasgow and continued to administer the diocese from abroad. But after her fall he was outlawed, in 1568, and he was convicted of treason in 1570, a protestant archbishop was appointed in 1571, and another installed in 1573. In 1587, however, after Mary's death, Beaton was rehabilitated in principle, in that he had title to the benefice, and in 1598 he was restored to all his honours and benefices. However, this hardly benefited him in practice, and he had no ecclesiastical function in Scotland.

Beaton was not only Mary's ambassador but also her agent and administrator, playing a key role in her hopes and plans. As the senior Scots Catholic churchman, too, he provided a focal point for Counter-Reformation plans for Scotland, in touch with all the interested parties. But efforts to preserve Roman Catholicism in Scotland itself were meagre and localized. When James VI went south in 1603 as successor to Queen Elizabeth, and Beaton himself died, the last of the Catholic bishops, Catholicism in Scotland was at a low ebb. Diplomatic efforts on its behalf had achieved very little.

Beaton did, however, leave two important legacies. A fourteenth-century foundation had assisted those Scots studying at Paris University and Beaton, too, assisted Scots students, employing Mary's revenues (due to her as the widow of François II) as well as his own. Before he died he bequeathed a house and his library and estate for the same purpose. In 1639 his benefaction was joined to the earlier foundation to form the Scots College in Paris, which educated Scots Roman Catholics until the French Revolution.

Beaton, having restored its mace to Glasgow University in 1590, left the other precious objects from Glasgow for safe keeping in the Paris Charterhouse, where they remained until they disappeared in the French Revolution. The Glasgow muniments, together with his own diplomatic papers, were housed in the Scots College. Much was destroyed at the revolution, but Glasgow cartularies and other valuable documents were brought to Scotland and housed in Edinburgh. Having settled his affairs, Beaton died in Paris during the night of 24–25 April 1603, faithful to his principles and his religion to the end; he was buried in the church of St Jean de Latran. Remarkably, friends and adversaries alike, in both France and Scotland, praised his personal qualities and cast no slur on his character. MARK DILWORTH

Sources M. Dilworth, 'Archbishop James Beaton II: a career in Scotland and France', *Records of the Scottish Church History Society*, 23 (1987–9), 301–16 · W. J. Anderson, 'On the early career of James Beaton II, archbishop of Glasgow', *Innes Review*, 16 (1965), 221–4 · D. McRoberts, 'The Scottish Catholic Archives, 1560–1978', *Innes Review*, 28 (1977), 59–128 · M. Dilworth, 'Archbishop James Beaton's papers in the Scottish Catholic Archives', *Innes Review*, 34 (1983), 3–8
Archives Scottish Catholic Archives, Edinburgh, corresp. and papers incl. letters of Mary, queen of Scots, 16e · Scottish Catholic Archives, Edinburgh, medieval Glasgow cartularies and later transcripts
Likenesses portrait, Scots College, Paris; repro. in McRoberts, 'The Scottish Catholic Archives', facing p. 61
Wealth at death 10,000 crowns · 80,000 livres: Dilworth, 'Archbishop James Beaton II', 311

Beaton, John (1831–1930), banker, was born at Hampstead, Middlesex, the second son of John Beaton, a Bank of England clerk, and his wife, Margaret. On 23 July 1863 Beaton married Jane Ann, daughter of Samuel Chard of the stock exchange; they had two daughters.

Beaton entered the City and trained as a banker. In 1862 he became secretary of the Anglo-Portuguese Bank at its foundation. In the following year this bank was absorbed by the London and Brazilian Bank, also set up in 1862. Beaton was appointed manager of the Oporto branch but did not take up the post. Instead, he stayed in London as acting secretary, becoming secretary in 1870 and secretary and manager in 1872.

During these years the bank was critically tested, both by the Overend, Gurney collapse and by the mismanagement of its own staff in Brazil. For some five years, from August 1866, Beaton plied between London and Rio de Janeiro to assess the damage and reorganize activities on a more professional basis. The eventual solution was to reconstruct the company totally, writing off considerable capital, to the noisy dismay of certain shareholders.

The New London and Brazilian Bank, created in 1872, was firmly under Beaton's control. He beavered away to rescue something from the illiquid securities of the old company, and in the branches he instilled good banking practice, backed up by firm guidance and control from London. Above all, he strove to improve staff morale. Bonus payments, votes of thanks, a pensions and benevolent fund, and a career path for the ablest men leading from South America to London, instituted loyalty. In 1893, when the Rio branch was made so dangerous from shelling that staff attendance was declared voluntary, not a man stayed away.

Beaton steered the bank into Montevideo, and then into Buenos Aires by 1890. It was not, however, until 1902 that an agency was established at Manáos on the Amazon. By then a net profit of £12,000 in 1872 had risen nearly eightfold. Beaton had become managing director in 1885, the year before the bank reverted to its old title by the omission of 'New'. When the chairman, the Hon. Pascoe Charles Glyn, was ill in 1904, Beaton presided at the annual general meeting; the following year, after Glyn's death, Beaton took the chair in his own right at the age of seventy-four. He was now publicly accountable for the bank he had been effectively running for forty years.

Beaton increased the capital base in 1907 and 1912 and the bank became strong. Return on equity was relatively high (although a little weaker after 1913), while paid-up capital was matched or outpaced by published reserves. In 1912, the bank's jubilee year, Beaton was voted £10,000 from shareholders and praised for his 'highest and best traditions of commercial morality' (AGM report, 1912). For the next nine years, until his ninetieth year, Beaton ran the bank by the same principles of paternalism and sound practice which had won such general respect. He became, as one shareholder put it, their 'grand old man' (AGM report, 1921), a patriarch whose knowledge and experience of South America were matchless and authoritative. He was of sufficient stature to be able to disagree publicly with Sir Edward Holden, eminent head of the Midland Bank, as to the diminishing world role of specialist overseas banks. He criticized over-banking in cities like Rio and Buenos Aires, where branches could 'be played off on each other by astute gentlemen of very small means' (AGM report, 1914). He maintained his conservative values. He saw strikes, particularly in Brazil, as organized by 'anarchic visitors' (AGM report, 1920) and thought the labour movement in Argentina had 'dictatorial pretensions' (AGM report, 1921). When Beaton resigned as chairman in 1921, in a crescendo of adulation, he was voted another £10,000. He was impossible to replace and his bank merged with the London and River Plate Bank in 1923, to form the Bank of London and South America.

Beaton retired to Tunbridge Wells, and later to Folkestone, where he died at his home, The Lawn, 7 Godwyn Road, on 23 October 1930, in his one hundredth year. He was buried in Brompton cemetery, London.

JOHN BOOKER

Sources Kelly, *Handbk* (1921) · *The Times* (29 Oct 1930) · letter books etc., UCL, BOLSA archive, London and Brazilian Bank · Lloyds Bank, TSB Group Archives, records of London and Brazilian Bank · D. Joslin, *A century of banking in Latin America* (1963) · D. C. M. Platt, ed., *Business imperialism, 1840–1930: an inquiry based on British experience in Latin America* (1977) · London and Brazilian Bank, AGM reports, 1912, 1914, 1920, 1921
Likenesses C. G. Anderson, portrait, repro. in Joslin, *A century of banking*, facing p. 164
Wealth at death £26,422 2s. 1d.—value of effects

Beaton, (Donald) Leonard (1929–1971), journalist and strategic analyst, was born on 20 June 1929 in Montreal, the son of John W. Beaton. He was educated in Montreal, at Westmount high school, and at McGill University, where he took an honours degree in economics and in political science. In 1950 he entered St Catharine's College, Cambridge, as an affiliated student where he read part two of the history tripos and then of the English tripos, achieving second class honours in each of these.

Eschewing the chance of employment in the Canadian diplomatic service, Beaton chose to become a journalist, beginning with the Montreal *Gazette*. In the spring of 1954 he joined the London-based staff of Reuters to work on the European and central news desks. Early in 1956 he joined *The Times* as naval correspondent and general reporter. The post of naval correspondent had for long been held by a retired naval officer. It now passed to someone whose maritime experience hitherto consisted of his first transatlantic crossing from Montreal. Beaton soon justified the judgement of the editor, Sir William Haley, that any competent journalist could do the job if intelligent and energetic enough.

In May 1957 Beaton moved to the *Manchester Guardian* as defence and air correspondent. He soon developed a widely recognized expertise on aeronautics and nuclear strategy generally. *The Guardian* also assigned Beaton the task of reporting the 1962 negotiations in Brussels on Britain's application to join the European Common Market. His sceptical attitude regarding the value of these negotiations for Britain and his disinclination to accept the official version of events at face value earned him the displeasure of Britain's chief negotiator, Edward Heath.

While still defence correspondent of *The Guardian* Beaton wrote, with John Maddox, the first serious book-length study of nuclear proliferation, entitled *The Spread of Nuclear Weapons*, published under the imprimatur of the Institute of Strategic Studies in 1962. Beaton left *The Guardian* in 1963 to be the first designated director of studies at the London-based Institute of Strategic Studies (ISS), then in its fifth year since being launched, though he had been closely in touch with the institute from its start. He felt by then that he ought to free himself somewhat from the grind of daily journalism and turn to longer-range analysis and advocacy. Though a generous and encouraging adviser, he was too much of an individualist and too naturally a polemicist to be entirely at ease in this role, and after two years he gave up the post to become a senior research associate at ISS, freer to concentrate on his own work. Throughout the 1960s he continued to be a prolific writer, broadcaster, and lecturer. It was in a television interview with President Eisenhower that he brought out publicly for the first time the extent to which Eisenhower as president had been ready in 1953 to threaten and contemplate the use of nuclear weapons both in Korea and against China.

Beaton was editor of the *Round Table* between 1966 and 1969 and was a principal influence in ending that quarterly journal's practice of anonymous contributions in favour of signed articles. More important, Beaton masterminded the reorientation of the journal away from its strongly flavoured imperialist tradition to the realities of the expanding multi-racial Commonwealth of the late 1960s. Even when not formally a staff member he frequently contributed pieces to *The Times*, before returning as a special writer on strategic affairs at the beginning of 1971. He wrote a more popular and updated version of *The Spread of Nuclear Weapons* under the title *Must the Bomb Spread?* (1966). Soon afterwards he prepared and wrote the script for a major television series on strategy and disarmament, *The Struggle for Peace*. He was twice visiting professor at the University of Toronto. He was once described by a leading American strategist, Bernard Brodie, as 'the most lucid and accurate commentator on defence questions in the press of the English-speaking world' (private information).

Beaton was about 6 feet in height, and had a round face; his eyes often seemed to be twinkling with good humour behind his spectacles. In 1967 he married Katherine Bougarel, daughter of Dr and Mme François Bougarel, of Châteauroux, France, and they had a daughter. Beaton was strongly opinionated on many subjects and liked argument and controversy. For about ten years before his death he rented a cottage near Wells in Somerset, where friends liked to visit. After lengthy walks in the Mendips and during long, reasonably bibulous, evenings by his fire-place they shared with him his keen enjoyment of discussion: his wide-ranging affection for English poets; his reading in devotional and controversial Christian literature; and his spirited challenges to then currently fashionable ideas such as the anachronism of the Commonwealth, the reformability of the Roman Catholic church, and the need for some form of pan-European, or at least pan-west European political organization.

Beaton died from a heart attack on 9 June 1971 while visiting Venice. He had intended to resume a regular commentary on the Common Market, of which he was critical, for *The Spectator* from July 1971. Instead, that weekly journal printed his last article posthumously on 19 June 1971. Entitled 'Speaking for the nation' it endorsed some aspects of Enoch Powell's views on immigration and English nationality.

A memorial service was held for Beaton on 28 June at St Bartholomew-the-Great, Smithfield, London. William Rees-Mogg and Alastair Hetherington, the editors of *The Times* and *The Guardian*, the two newspapers which had most nurtured and displayed his talents, read lessons, and the large, diverse congregation was a testimony to what *The Times* in its sensitive obituary had characterized as his 'huge capacity for friendship'.   PETER LYON

Sources *The Times* (10 June 1971) · *Round Table* (Oct 1971) · A. Buchan, *Survival*, 13 (July 1971) · personal knowledge (2004) · private information (2004)
Archives SOUND BL NSA, performance recording

Beaton, Mary (*c*.1543–1597). *See under* Queen's Maries (*act.* 1548–1567).

Beaton, Norman Lugard (1934–1994), actor, was born on 31 October 1934 in Georgetown, British Guiana, the son of William Solomon Beaton (*d*. 1983), civil servant, and his wife, Ada, *née* Mackintosh (*d*. 1962). He was educated at St Stephen's School and Queen's College, Georgetown, and the Government Teachers' Training College, where he later became a deputy headmaster. In 1958, at the height of the calypso craze, he became calypso champion of British Guiana. He released twenty-four singles with the Four Bees, a close vocal harmony group he formed in Georgetown, and had several hits. One of the singers with the group was Gloria Moshette, a former darkroom technician; they married in 1958 and had a son, Jayme (*b*. 1958), and a daughter, Kim (*b*. 1960), both born in British Guiana.

Beaton left British Guiana for Britain in 1960. He was soon joined by his wife, Gloria, and later by their two children; a third child, Jeremy (*b*. 1962), was born in England. After postgraduate studies at London University's Institute of Education, Beaton became a teacher in Liverpool. The success of *Jack of Spades*, his first stage production at Liverpool's Everyman Theatre, for which he composed the music, encouraged him to give up teaching and become a full-time actor. His reputation grew steadily. He progressed from regional theatre to leading roles at the Old Vic, the National Theatre (where he played Angelo in a black cast version of Shakespeare's *Measure for Measure* in

Norman Lugard Beaton (1934–1994), by unknown photographer, 1977

1981), and the Royal Court Theatre. Apart from Shakespeare, his stage roles also encompassed Pinter, Beckett, Gilbert and Sullivan, Brecht, Molière, and pantomime. In 1974 he started the Black Theatre of Brixton, which was instrumental in developing contemporary black theatre in Britain. For years he acted in plays by a range of black dramatists, including Michael Abbensetts, C. L. R. James, Mustapha Matura, Derek Walcott, and Edgar White.

Beaton also became one of Britain's leading film and television actors. For his performance in *Black Joy* (1977) he was named best film actor by the Variety Club of Great Britain, the first black British actor to be honoured with a film award. Nine years later he starred in *Playing Away*, with a screenplay by the black writer Caryl Phillips. He gave an outstanding performance as the quiet but determined captain of an all-black cricket team invited to a challenge match against a rural Suffolk side. Among his most memorable television successes were *The Fosters* (1976–7), *Black Christmas* (1977), *Empire Road* (1978–9), *Nice* (1984), *Big George is Dead* (1987), and *Little Napoleons* (1993), but his most memorable role was as the manic barber's shop owner in the long-running situation comedy series *Desmond's*. With sharply observed scripts by a young black writer called Trix Worrell, *Desmond's* ran from 1989 to 1994 on Channel 4. This show was described as an African-Caribbean equivalent of America's *Cosby Show* and, as a result of its popularity in America, in 1991 African-American television star Bill Cosby invited Beaton to make a couple of guest appearances in the *Cosby Show*. Beaton readily accepted a role as a cricket-loving doctor, and Cosby was so taken by the actor that he wore Beaton's gift of a *Desmond's* baseball cap in the show.

Beaton's first marriage ended in divorce, and in 1969 he had a third son, William, with Jane Atto, with whom he briefly ran a restaurant in London. In 1976 he married Leah Garady, who adopted the children of his first marriage; but this marriage too broke up, and in 1978 he formed a more lasting relationship with Jane Cash. His autobiography, *Beaton but Unbowed* (1986), detailed several other, shorter-lived, relationships.

Towards the end of his life, Beaton reflected on the roles available to black actors and actresses:

> My own view is that what you've seen me in are the only roles that are available for black men in this country, and they don't really reflect our views, our understanding of life, our intelligence, or where we are coming from. In that respect I would say that Caryl Phillips' scenario for *Playing Away* did get around that particular hurdle. It lived up to nearly all the expectations that black people ought to be living up to. … But what I find difficult to come to terms with is the absence of a heroic figure like Paul Robeson in all the work I've done. There is no writer on that scale, or in those grand, magnificent terms for film and television about a black figure who we all admire or aspire to be like. And I don't know when our people are going to actually start saying 'We are terrific!' and start writing something wonderful about just being us. (Pines, 118–19)

Beaton died on 13 December 1994 in Georgetown, in the land of his birth, Guyana, when he collapsed in a friend's arms hours after going home to die. Carmen Munroe, who played Beaton's wife in *Desmond's*, told *The Voice*:

> He put his whole life and soul into any part he was asked to play and never spared himself. He worked at his craft and produced brilliance. His particular blend of comic energy and professional application will be missed most keenly in the future when excellence is sought. (*The Voice*, 20 Dec 1994)

Shortly after his death Channel 4 screened *Shooting Stars* in its *Black Christmas* season, with a memorable appearance by Beaton, reading a sonnet by Shakespeare.

STEPHEN BOURNE

Sources N. Beaton, *Beaton but unbowed* (1986) · J. Pines, ed., *Black and white in colour: black people in British television since 1936* (1992) · S. Bourne, *Black in the British frame: black people in British film and television, 1896–1996* (1998) · *CGPLA Eng. & Wales* (1995)
Likenesses photograph, 1977, repro. in Bourne, *Black in the British frame*, facing p. 116 · photograph, 1977, Rex Features, London [*see illus.*] · photographs, repro. in Beaton, *Beaton but unbowed*, following p. 128
Wealth at death £203,086: administration, 31 Aug 1995, *CGPLA Eng. & Wales*

Beatrice, Princess [*married name* Princess Henry of Battenberg] (**1857–1944**), the fifth daughter and youngest child of Queen *Victoria and Prince *Albert, was born Beatrice Mary Victoria Feodore at Buckingham Palace on 14 April 1857. Unlike her elder brothers and sisters, she was treated with indulgence by her parents and in her infancy was a lively child. After Albert's death, Queen Victoria

Princess Beatrice (1857–1944), by Heinrich von Angeli, 1875

found solace in her daughter, being over-protective of her 'Baby' until she was well into adult life. The princess was never the play-friend or confidante of any of her brothers or sisters, for the poor health of *Leopold, the closest to her in age, ruled out normal childish play and, deprived of the companionship of other children, she grew up shy and reserved. She was, at maturity, an attractive and well-educated young woman of some musical ability. It appeared, however, that her role was to be 'the prop, comfort and companion of her widowed mother to old age' (Rose, 30). Such was the queen's reliance on her daughter that it seemed unlikely that she would ever marry. Queen Victoria was, however, sympathetic to Beatrice's fondness for the prince imperial (killed in the Anglo-Zulu War in 1879) and promoted the idea of marriage to the grand duke of Hesse and by Rhine, the widower of Beatrice's sister, *Alice. In 1884 Princess Beatrice attended the wedding of her niece, Victoria Alice of Hesse, to Prince Louis of Battenberg (later Mountbatten) and, on her return, told the queen that she wished to marry Prince Louis's brother.

Prince Henry Maurice of Battenberg (1858–1896), born at Milan on 5 October 1858, was the third son of the morganatic marriage between Prince Alexander of Hesse (1823–1888) and Countess Julie von Haucke (1825–1895), who was granted, in 1858, the title of princess of Battenberg. Queen Victoria at first declared that the match 'would never do', but her main concern was to keep her daughter by her side and she did not share the general horror of continental royalty for a pedigree impaired by a morganatic marriage. She gave her consent on condition that Prince Henry ('Liko') resigned his commission in the Prussian army and that the couple made their home with her. The marriage took place at Whippingham church, near Osborne, on the Isle of Wight, on 23 July 1885.

Queen Victoria was fond of Prince Henry and made him governor of the Isle of Wight but he grew restless in the quiet world of Osborne House. When he slipped away for a jaunt to Corsica with his brother Louis Alexander, the queen sent a warship to bring him back. In 1895 he volunteered for service in the Asante expedition and contracted fever from which he died, on the way home, on 20 January 1896. Princess Henry was given her husband's governorship and continued to be the queen's close companion and unofficial private secretary.

After Victoria's death, the princess lived in Osborne Cottage until 1912 when she moved into the governor's house at Carisbrooke Castle. The marriage of her daughter, Princess Ena (1887–1969), to King Alfonso XIII of Spain in 1906 caused some controversy as it entailed her conversion to Catholicism, a step of which *Edward VII disapproved. This marriage was to transmit the haemophilia (of which Beatrice was a carrier and from which her second son, Leopold Henry (1889–1922), suffered) to the Spanish dynasty. Prince Maurice (b. 1891), Beatrice's youngest son, was killed in action in 1914. In 1917, in accordance with George V's policy of divesting the royal family of its German associations, the family name of Battenberg was changed to Mountbatten, the princess resuming her former style of Princess Beatrice, and her eldest son, Alexander (1886–1960), becoming marquess of Carisbrooke.

Princess Beatrice was bequeathed all the queen's private journals, with instructions to modify or destroy any passages which appeared unsuitable for posterity. Although she survived her mother by forty-three years, she continued to be her loyal assistant and fulfilled her instructions all too faithfully. She also translated extracts from the diary of Queen Victoria's maternal grandmother, Augusta, duchess of Saxe-Coburg-Saalfeld, published in 1941 as *In Napoleonic Days*.

Her life was saddened by untimely deaths but she lived, a stout and kindly person, until she was eighty-seven, dying at her last home, Brantridge Park, Balcombe, Sussex, on 26 October 1944. Her funeral was at St George's Chapel, Windsor, and she was buried beside her husband at Whippingham. A. W. PURDUE

Sources M. E. Sara, *The life and times of Princess Beatrice* (1943) · D. Duff, *The shy princess* (1958) · J. Van der Kiste, *Queen Victoria's children* (1986) · A. McNaughton, *The book of kings: a royal genealogy*, 3 vols. (1973) · S. Weintraub, *Victoria: biography of a queen* (1987) · K. Rose, *Kings, queens and courtiers* (1985)
Archives Royal Arch. · U. Southampton L., corresp. and papers | NA Scot., letters to sixth duchess of Buccleuch · Nuffield Oxf., corresp. with Lord Mottistone · PRO NIre., letters to Lady Antrim · Staffs. RO, letters to duchess of Sutherland
Likenesses P. Lauchert, oils, 1850–75, Osborne House, Isle of Wight · L. Caldesi, group portrait, photograph, 1857, NPG · Mrs H. Ward, oils, 1857, Osborne House, Isle of Wight · M. Thornycroft, marble, 1858, Osborne House, Isle of Wight · M. Thornycroft, plaster, 1858, Osborne House, Isle of Wight · W. & D. Downey, carte-de-visite, 1860–69, NPG · N. Paton, drawing, 1863, Royal Collection · Princess Louise, marble bust, 1864, Royal Collection · E. Tayler, miniature, 1864, Royal Collection · oils, 1865–75, NPG · W. & D. Downey, carte-de-visite, 1868, NPG · Wilson, Whitlock & Downey, photograph, 1868, NPG · H. von Angeli, portrait, 1875, Royal Collection [*see illus.*] · E. de Moira, miniature, exh. RA 1883, Royal Collection · C. Sohn junior, oils, 1883, Osborne House, Isle of Wight · W. & D. Downey, photograph, c.1890 (with her son, the marquess of Carisbrooke), NPG · G. O. Reid, group portrait, oils, 1891 (*The baptism of Prince Maurice of Battenberg*), Scot. NPG; study, Royal Collection · G. O. Reid, oils, 1891, Royal Scot. Acad. · J. Sorolla, portrait, 1904, NPG · W. & D. Downey, group portrait, photograph, 1907, NPG · W. Llewellyn, oils, c.1909, Burghley House, Northamptonshire · P. A. de Laszlo, portrait, 1912, repro. in *ILN* (11 June 1927) · W. Bambridge, photograph (*Royal mourning group*, 1862), NPG · G. Middleton, oils (as a young woman; after J. Sant), Osborne House, Isle of Wight · R. C. Woodville, group portrait, oils (*The marriage of Prince Henry of Battenberg to HRH Princess Beatrice at Whippingham, Isle of Wight, 1885*), Royal Collection · photographs, NPG · prints, BM, NPG

Beatson, Alexander (1759–1830), army officer in the East India Company and colonial governor, was born on 24 October 1759 at Dundee. He was the second son of the three sons and one daughter of Robert Beatson (b. 1730), of Kilrie, Fife, and his wife, Jean, daughter of Alexander Read of Torbeg, Forfarshire. Beatson obtained a cadetship in the East India Company's army in 1775, and was appointed to an ensigncy in the Madras infantry on 21 November 1776. In late 1778, following a voyage to the Cape of Good Hope, he was appointed acting lieutenant of engineers, and proceeded to Masulipatam. There he remained as superintending engineer until the end of 1782, when he went to Madras to serve as aide-de-camp to the commander-in-chief, Major-General James Stuart, during the Second Anglo-Mysore War. In 1787 he was appointed captain of the guides, a corps of the company's army, and spent the following three years making a military–topographic survey of the Baramahal hills and passes. This work was praised by the court of directors and proved instrumental in the prosecution of the Third Anglo-Mysore War (1790–92). In 1793 he was appointed chief engineer to an expeditionary force against the Île de France (Mauritius). Whether he actually sailed with these blockading ships is uncertain, but he did compile from contemporary sources an important 'Description of Mauritius and Bourbon (Réunion)' (1794), which remains unpublished. In 1795 he suffered from ill health and took leave in England. After he arrived back at Madras on 5 February 1798, he was appointed aide-de-camp to Richard Wellesley, Lord Mornington, who largely adopted his plan for military operations against Tipu Sultan, resulting in the capture of Seringapatam in 1799, in which Beatson played a significant part. These events were the subject of his book *A View of the Origin and Conduct of the War Against Tippoo Sultaun* (1800). Suffering from sunstroke, Beatson then returned to England, where he purchased four contiguous farms near Frant, Sussex: Knowle Farm (where he lived), Henley, Little Henley, and Delvidiere. He attained the rank of colonel on 1 January 1801. On 9 January 1806 he married Davidson, youngest daughter of David Reid, a

Scottish commissioner of customs. They had six sons and seven daughters.

In October 1807 Beatson was appointed to the governorship of St Helena, which he held from 1808 to 1813. The island, which then belonged to the East India Company, was in a very impoverished condition. The scanty population had been badly affected by an epidemic of measles a short time previously, and was in a wretched state. The acts of the home authorities in suppressing the arrack trade and other matters gave rise to great discontent, resulting in a garrison mutiny in December 1811, which was put down firmly by Beatson, who also introduced a better system of cultivation and many other 'improving' measures. These activities, related in his widely read *Tracts Relative to the Island of St. Helena* (1816), and several other shorter works, have been described as a major contribution to the 'beginnings of global environmentalism' (Grove, 356–60). In recognition of his services on the island he was promoted major-general from 3 August 1813. After his return to England in November 1813 he devoted much attention to experimental agriculture on his farms, his major work in this respect being his influential *A new system of cultivation without lime or dung, or summer fallows, as practised at Knowle-Farm, in … Sussex* (1820), with a supplement (1821). This work ran through three editions in German (1828, 1829, 1830). Beatson died at Henley, Frant, Sussex, on 15 October 1830. He was buried in the churchyard of the parish of Frant.   ANDREW GROUT

Sources A. J. Beatson, *Genealogical account of the families of Beatson* (1860) • M. Archer, *India and British portraiture, 1770–1825* (1979) • W. Anderson, *The Scottish nation*, 9 vols. (1865–7), suppl., pp. 682–3 • R. H. Grove, *Green imperialism: colonial expansion, tropical island Edens, and the origins of environmentalism, 1600–1860* (1995) • H. M. Vibart, *The military history of the Madras engineers and pioneers*, 2 vols. (1881–3) • Dodwell [E. Dodwell] and Miles [J. S. Miles], eds., *Alphabetical list of the officers of the Indian army: with the dates of their respective promotion, retirement, resignation, or death … from the year 1760 to the year … 1837* (1838) • Burke, *Gen. GB* (1858)
Archives BL, descriptions of Mauritius and Bourbon, Add. MS 13670 • BL OIOC, description of India, MSS Eur. D 46–48 • Cambs. AS, MSS map | BL, letters to Lord Wellesley, Add. MS 13868
Likenesses A. W. Devis, oils, 1790–99, repro. in sale catalogue, 66 [Sothebys, London, 10 July 1996] • T. Hickey, charcoal and chalk drawing, 1799, Stratfield Saye, Hampshire; repro. in Archer, *India and British portraiture*, pl. 141

Beatson, Benjamin Wrigglesworth (1803–1874), classical scholar, was born in London on 24 January 1803, the son of Anby Beatson, a merchant of Cheapside, and his wife, Joanna Wrigglesworth. He was educated at Mill Hill and Merchant Taylors' schools, and was admitted at Pembroke College, Cambridge, in 1821, where he graduated BA in 1825 (sixteenth wrangler and sixth classic) and MA in 1828. He was elected a fellow of his college in 1827, was ordained in 1828, and, remaining unmarried, was senior fellow at the time of his death, which took place on 20 July 1874 at 14 Charles Street, Old Street, London. He compiled the *Index Graecitatis Aeschyleae*, which was published at Cambridge in 1830 in the first volume of the *Index in tragicos Graecos*. An edition of Robert Ainsworth's *Thesaurus linguae Latinae*, revised by Beatson, was issued in

1829, and republished in 1830 and in 1860. Beatson produced a popular school book, *Progressive exercises on the composition of Greek iambic verse … for the use of King's School Canterbury* (1836; 10th edn, 1871).   M. C. CURTHOYS

Sources *The Athenaeum* (1 Aug 1874), 147 • Venn, *Alum. Cant.* • Boase, *Mod. Eng. biog.* • *CGPLA Eng. & Wales* (1874)
Wealth at death under £16,000: probate, 7 Aug 1874, *CGPLA Eng. & Wales*

Beatson, George Steward (1814–1874), army medical officer, third son of Duncan Beatson of Campbeltown, Argyllshire, was born at Greenock in May 1814. He graduated in arts and medicine at Glasgow (MD 1836) and became LCS (Edinburgh) in 1836. In 1838 he joined the army medical department as assistant surgeon and served on the staff in Ceylon from 1839 to 1851. He married the daughter of Colonel Cochrane of the Ceylon rifle regiment; she predeceased him. He was surgeon to the 51st regiment in the Second Anglo-Burmese War in 1852–3 and served in Turkey during the Crimean War, where he rendered valuable service in the organization of the hospitals at Smyrna. After serving as deputy inspector-general in the Ionian Islands and in Madras, he became surgeon-general in 1863, and was appointed principal medical officer of European troops in India, an appointment which he held with distinction for the customary five years. For the next three years he was in medical charge of the Royal Victoria Hospital, Netley. In March 1866 he was appointed honorary physician to the queen, and was in 1871 principal medical officer in India for the second time, in which capacity he implemented useful reforms. He was appointed a CB on 2 June 1869. Beatson died suddenly at Knollswood, Simla, India, on 7 June 1874, survived by his second wife, Elizabeth Adams Beatson, eldest daughter of Alexander Hoyes of Bitterne Grove, Southampton, and by four sons and three daughters. He was considered one of the ablest officers in the Army Medical Service and highly regarded throughout his profession.

H. M. CHICHESTER, rev. JAMES FALKNER

Sources *Army List* • *The Lancet* (July 1874) • *Hart's Army List* • Boase, *Mod. Eng. biog.* • *ILN* (5 Sept 1874) • *CGPLA Eng. & Wales* (1875)
Likenesses portrait, repro. in *ILN*, 65 (1874), 229
Wealth at death under £4000: probate, 21 Jan 1875, *CGPLA Eng. & Wales*

Beatson, Robert (1741–1818), writer and army officer, was born at Vicarsgrange, Dysart, Fife, on 25 June 1741, the eldest son of David Beatson (d. 1785) of Vicarsgrange and his wife and cousin, Jean, daughter of Robert Beatson of Kilrie, the descendant of a local laird. His father enjoyed the patronage of the St Clair family, and at fourteen, after being educated at home, Beatson became an ensign in General St Clair's regiment, transferring in the autumn of 1756 to the 2nd battalion, 3rd foot, raised in Staffordshire. In 1757 he participated in the raid on Rochefort; in 1758, as lieutenant in the 61st regiment, he served in the attack on Martinique and at the capture of Guadeloupe. He purchased the captain-lieutenancy of this regiment in 1764. While in service he was befriended by Major-General

Barlow, the regiment's lieutenant-colonel. He retired on lieutenant's half pay in 1766. At the start of the American War of Independence, Beatson took a commission in the Royal Engineers as a 2nd lieutenant (17 January 1776). He became lieutenant on 1 October 1784. He failed to obtain active duty and resigned his commission on 4 April 1789. He later became barrack master at Aberdeen, from whose university he obtained the degree of LLD.

Giving up his military career Beatson turned to literature, which he had always enjoyed. When his father died in 1785 Beatson came into an inheritance and on 18 September married Helen Patton, daughter of the customs collector at Kirkcaldy. Her brothers were officers in the Royal Navy and in the East India Company service; this explained Beatson's interest in recent British naval history. He was befriended by Adam Smith, and benefited for several years from Smith's conversation and library. Smith encouraged Beatson to write; Beatson dedicated his *Political index* to Smith, who advised on its contents. Beatson's literary work obtained for him honorary membership of the board of agriculture, membership of the Royal Highland Society, the London Society for the Encouragement of Arts, and in 1797, fellowship of the Royal Society of Edinburgh.

In *A general view of the agriculture of the county of Fife … drawn up for the consideration of the board of agriculture* (1794), based on personal observations, Beatson suggested improvements in livestock, enclosures, farm tenures, and taxes, and advocated the creation of local agricultural improvement societies to implement reforms. His *Essay on the Comparative Advantages of Vertical and Horizontal Wind-Mills* (1798) recounted research in theory and practical experiments to present a detailed engineering case for horizontal windmills. Beatson patented his wheel (no. 2200 of 1797), and a model was exhibited in London. He also contributed practical papers on farm buildings from his agricultural tour of England to the fifth volume of A. Hunter's *Georgical Essays* (1804).

In 1786 Beatson published the *Political index to the histories of Great Britain and Ireland, or, A complete register of the hereditary honours, public offices, and persons in office, from the earliest period to the present time*. The result of many years' research, correcting previous briefer lists, financed by subscription, it is a laborious and useful compilation. The corrected and enlarged 1788 edition, doubled in size, claimed that it had received public praise and good sales. Beatson had not intended it for publication, merely to satisfy his curiosity upon subjects he considered interesting to society. A third edition (1806) aimed to include more material on the peerage; it was another subscription project. Beatson's *Political index* presented for the first time modern listings of the chief office holders in the state's history. Its accuracy produced a rapid sale of thousands of copies. The third edition, however, although found in most libraries in Beatson's era and the widest in coverage, contained many errors because Beatson had problems in superintending its publication.

In 1790 Beatson published his *Naval and military memoirs of Great Britain, from the year 1727 to the present time*. Continuing Campbell's pre-1727 coverage, Beatson's book contained detailed accounts of naval engagements, with considerable use of official reports, particularly in the appendices. It was well received by critics. The second edition (1804) was dedicated to Beatson's friend Major-General George, marquess of Huntly. Beatson also published a pamphlet on the indecisive naval battle off Ushant between Admiral Keppel and the Count d'Orvilliers, *A new and distinct view of the memorable action of the 27th July 1778, in which the aspersions cast on the flag officers are shown to be totally unfounded* (1791).

A chronological register of both houses of the British parliament from the union in 1708 [to] 1807 (1807), a useful parliamentary compilation, listed peers qualified to sit in each parliament. Counties and boroughs were arranged alphabetically in chronological order with the name of their members. Notes chronicled changes and their causes in each constituency's representation. Election petitions were given, with statements of the electoral franchise in each seat. Beatson left unpublished research in the advocates' manuscripts, National Library of Scotland, Edinburgh. His collections contain genealogical working papers on the British peerage; he compiled in 1802–3 detailed genealogies of the English peerage. Several peers sent him material on their families in 1785 and in 1801–4. Beatson also compiled genealogical tables (*c*.1800) for various Scottish aristocratic families. He left manuscript accounts of the parish of Dysart, his birthplace, and a description of his (undated) tour of Scotland. Beatson died at Edinburgh on 24 January 1818.

FRANCIS ESPINASSE, *rev.* PHILIP A. HUNT

Sources Anderson, *Scot. nat.* · M. F. Conolly, *Biographical dictionary of eminent men of Fife* (1866) · *A new catalogue of living English authors: with complete lists of their publications, and biographical and critical memoirs* (1799) · J. Watkins, *The universal biographical dictionary*, new edn (1821) · [J. Watkins and F. Shoberl], *A biographical dictionary of the living authors of Great Britain and Ireland* (1816) · Irving, *Scots.* · H. J. Rose, *A new general biographical dictionary*, ed. H. J. Rose and T. Wright, 12 vols. (1853) · Chambers, *Scots.* (1855) · R. F. Edwards, ed., *Roll of officers of the corps of royal engineers from 1660 to 1898* (1898) · Allibone, *Dict.* · J. F. Waller, ed., *The imperial dictionary of universal biography*, 3 vols. (1857–63) · parish register (marriage), 18/9/1785, Kirkcaldy, Fife

Archives NL Scot., corresp. and papers, Adv. MSS 34.3.21; 33.5.9–10; 81.1.17

Wealth at death £714 3*s.* 11½*d.*: 1819, recording

Beatson, William Fergusson (1804–1872), army officer, was born on 25 June 1804 at Rossend Castle, Fife, fourth and youngest son of Robert Beatson of Kilrie and Margaret Taylor, his wife and the heiress of Carbiston. He entered the East India Company's service in 1820 and joined the 2nd battalion 25th Bengal native infantry as an ensign. He served in several different regiments of the Bengal native army and was promoted lieutenant (1823), captain (1837), major (1848), lieutenant-colonel (1853), colonel (1864), and major-general (1865). He distinguished himself as a soldier and was a particularly fine horseman, unusually so for an infantry officer. While on furlough from India in 1832–7, he served with permission in the British Legion, raised and commanded by Colonel De Lacy Evans, to fight for Queen Isabella of Spain against Don Carlos in the first Carlist War (1835–6). Beatson commanded the 10th infantry regiment, or Munster light infantry, at the head of which he was severely wounded. He was awarded the cross of the Order of San Fernando for actions on 28 May and 6 July 1836, which he was subsequently permitted to wear.

On his return to India in 1837 Beatson was promoted captain and employed in Bundelkhand, central India, then in a very disturbed state. He raised a local force, the Bundelkhand Legion, with which he captured many forts and subdued recalcitrant rajas and bands of dacoits, receiving for his services the thanks of government. In 1844 he volunteered the Bundelkhand Legion for service in Sind under Napier, and was commended by the latter for the legion's successful operations in the Bugti hills. In 1847 he was appointed to command the nizam's cavalry in Hyderabad, where he remained until 1851 in the local rank of brigadier.

Beatson's reputation as a leader of irregular cavalry was such that on the outbreak of the Crimean War it was suggested that he should raise a force of irregular Turkish cavalry. This was rejected by Lord Raglan whose experience of irregulars during the Peninsular War had powerfully influenced him against them. Beatson, who was on furlough at the time, offered to waive his rank in order to serve on the staff of the Hon. James Scarlett who was commanding the heavy cavalry brigade. He thus took part in the charge of the heavy brigade at Balaklava on 25 October 1854. 'Colonel Beatson … gave me all the assistance which his experience and well-known gallantry enabled him to do throughout the day,' reported Scarlett to the military secretary at the Horse Guards in London (Kinglake, 4.143). He recommended Beatson for recognition to Lord Lucan, commanding the cavalry division, but this was refused by Lucan.

Beatson then offered his services to Omar Pasha, who commanded the Turkish forces in the Crimea. He gave Beatson the rank of major-general in the Turkish army, and he was later to be awarded the gold medal of the imperial order, Nishan Iftikhar, by the sultan of Turkey. Beatson was deputed to raise a force of Turkish irregular cavalry, Bashi-Bazoukhs, about 4000 strong. They were mostly Albanians with a profound distaste for any form of military discipline. Dubbed 'Beatson's horse', they wore their own native dress and were notorious for their brutality. Their unruly behaviour soon brought them into conflict with the Turkish authorities, one of the chief complainants being J. H. Skene, a British vice-consul. As a consequence Beatson was placed under Major-General Robert Vivian, a British officer serving with the Turks. Skene accused Beatson of inciting his Bashi-Bazoukhs to mutiny after Vivian had replaced him in September 1855 with Major-General Smith, on the grounds that Beatson had been dilatory in carrying out Vivian's orders. This Beatson denied and took himself back to England. He later brought an action against Skene to clear his name of the charge. The trial took place in January 1860 and cost Beatson £3000. Although the jury found for Skene on purely legal grounds, they went on to censure him for failing to withdraw his statements after he had discovered that they were unfounded. Beatson might therefore claim a moral victory, albeit at considerable expense.

Beatson had been promoted lieutenant-colonel in November 1853 and returned again to India in 1856 to command the nizam's cavalry. He was serving in Hyderabad when the mutiny broke out in 1857. His services in the mutiny were confined to central India where he raised two regiments of irregular cavalry—the 1st and 2nd Beatson's Horse. He dressed them in green with red turbans and cummerbunds, mounting the 1st regiment on stallions, and the 2nd on mares and a few geldings. They took part in the pursuit of the rebel commanders, Tantia Topi and the rani of Jhansi. One of their officers, Lieutenant Evelyn Wood, won the VC when commanding the 1st Beatson's Horse on 28 December 1859 (Beatson, by then a local brigadier-general, having relinquished command in September 1859). On 16 April 1860 his regiment was joined with Mayne's Horse to form the Central India Horse (CIH).

Beatson was promoted major-general on 8 January 1865 to command the Allahabad division. 'Handsome in appearance, and dignified in bearing, he was a soldier of the austere and earnest type,' records the history of the CIH (Watson, 46). 'He lived camp fashion, and very uncomfortably too. He was on horse back every morning before day-break, and, in order to be prepared for emergencies, he rode invariably with a supply of biscuits and sultanas in his wallets' (ibid.). He commanded in Allahabad from 1866 to 1869, and the Ambala division from 1869 until he returned home on leave in 1872. He died suddenly at the vicarage, New Swindon, Wiltshire, on 4 February 1872, aged sixty-eight.

Beatson married on 12 February 1840 Margaret Marian Humfrays (or Humphreys), daughter of Lieutenant-Colonel Richard Humfrays of the Bengal Engineers. She died on 22 December 1866, at Allahabad, soon after Beatson took command there. They had four daughters, only one of whom, Mrs McMullen, survived him.

JAMES LUNT

Sources W. B. F. Laurie, *Sketches of some distinguished Anglo-Indians* (1875) · W. A. Watson, *King George's own central India horse* (1930) · Boase, *Mod. Eng. biog.* · Burke, *Gen. GB* (1862–3) · A. W. Kinglake, *The invasion of the Crimea*, [new edn], 4 (1877) · Marquess of Anglesey [G. C. H. V. Paget], *A history of the British cavalry, 1816 to 1919*, 2 (1975) · Fortescue, *Brit. army*, vol. 12 · C. Hibbert, *The destruction of Lord Raglan* [1961] · P. Mason, *A matter of honour: an account of the Indian army, its officers and men* (1974) · Major-General Vivian [R. J. H. Vivian], *Narrative of circumstances which led to Major-General Beatson being relieved of command of the Turkish irregular cavalry* (1856) · W. F. Beatson, *The war department and the Bashi Bazouks* (1856) · R. A. Burton, *A history of the Hyderabad contingent* (1905)
Archives NAM, corresp. with Lord Raglan
Likenesses D. J. Pound, engraving, repro. in Watson, *King George's own central India horse*
Wealth at death under £5000: probate, 23 March 1872, *CGPLA Eng. & Wales*

Beattie, David Wilson (1938–1991), venture capitalist, was born on 30 September 1938 at Tir-na-Nog, Carleton Road, Carlisle, Cumberland, the elder son and second child in the family of two sons and two daughters of Ronald Joseph Edward Beattie and his wife, Margaret Knott, *née* Christie. His father was a stonemason, working for the family business making tombstones and monuments. He was educated at Carlisle grammar school, and graduated from Manchester University in 1960 with an upper second class degree in mathematics, statistics, and aerodynamics. His first job was as a statistical assistant with Cadbury Brothers, the chocolate manufacturers, and at the same time he qualified as a cost and management accountant. On 8 June 1963 he married Pauline Holloway, a secretary, daughter of William Ralph Holloway, a civil engineer; they had two daughters, one of whom died in childhood. After a year with Johnson and Johnson, Beattie was invited back to Cadbury in 1964 to be development director of McVitie Cadbury Cakes, and was then appointed financial planning manager for Cadbury Schweppes (Overseas), and finally managing director of the speciality foods division.

In 1974 Beattie left Cadbury to join the National Enterprise Board (NEB), set up in 1974 by the Labour government. One of its roles was to encourage industry by investing government money into smaller companies that were finding it difficult to attract capital, and Beattie was appointed director of the smaller companies division, defined as companies with fewer than 1000 employees. By 1978 the public accounts committee was reporting that of the nineteen companies in which the NEB had invested, only ten had made a profit, but the NEB argued that a few more years were needed before these companies could show a substantial return on government capital. Beattie was then appointed director of the business development division of the NEB, responsible for investment in advanced technology, and he concentrated his efforts on the electronics industry, committing public money to such companies as INMOS, which made silicon chips, INSAC, exporter of British software technology, and ICL, the computer systems manufacturer. But after the election in 1979 of a Conservative government headed by Margaret Thatcher, and the beginning of a wave of privatizations, the government encouraged the NEB to dispose of its companies. Beattie was aware that the smallest NEB investments would be difficult to sell, and in 1981 he persuaded the NEB to set up a new company, Grosvenor Development Capital (so called because the headquarters of the NEB was in Grosvenor Gardens, Victoria, London), as a holding company for the eight smallest NEB companies. In effect this amounted to the privatization of these NEB venture capital investments. Beattie was appointed managing director in 1982, and in February 1982, at a time when the venture capital industry was just beginning to increase in size and scale, Beattie raised £6.9 million from three City institutions, including the British Rail Pension Fund, for Grosvenor Development Capital, reducing the government's stake to 30 per cent. In 1985

Beattie and his team formed their own management company, Grosvenor Venture Managers, based in Slough, to help in the management of several companies, and they were given the contract to manage Grosvenor Development Capital. Beattie was chairman and managing director. Grosvenor Venture Managers launched a new fund, Grosvenor Technology Fund, which attracted £9.5 million in 1985, and two more funds in 1988 and 1989. By 1990 he had raised £60 million for these companies, and he floated Grosvenor Development Capital on the stock market as an investment trust. A profitable and well-run company, Grosvenor Venture Managers was sold to Mercury Asset Management in 1994 for over £4 million.

From a Christian background, Beattie was involved from his university days in stimulating missionary interest, and Christianity remained at the centre of his life. He was an elder of Maidenhead Baptist Church, and from 1983 he was on the council of the Scripture Gift Mission, a mission to distribute free Bible resources in their own languages to people all over the world. Most of his spare time was devoted to church activities, but he was also an enthusiast for steam trains and aeroplanes, keeping a list of every plane he had flown on.

In 1989 Beattie resigned as managing director of Grosvenor Venture Managers but carried on as an active chairman. He died of a heart attack on 13 August 1991, at his home, Caldbeck, Nursery Walk, Marlow, Buckinghamshire.   ANNE PIMLOTT BAKER

Sources M. Grylls and J. Redwood, *The national enterprise board* (1980) · A. Masey, *The adventurers* (1993) · *The Times* (19 Aug 1991) · private information (2004) [Pauline Beattie, widow] · b. cert. · m. cert. · d. cert. · *CGPLA Eng. & Wales* (1991)
Likenesses photograph, repro. in *The Times*
Wealth at death £638,277: probate, 27 Nov 1991, *CGPLA Eng. & Wales*

Beattie, George (1786–1823), poet, was born at Whitehills, near St Cyrus, Kincardineshire, the eldest son of William Beattie, a crofter and salmon fisher, and his wife, Elizabeth, *née* Scott. He received a good education at the parish school where he was notorious both for his love of practical jokes and for his melancholy spells. When he was about thirteen years old his father obtained a position with the excise at Montrose, and George 'walked all the way to his new home with a tame *kae* [jackdaw] on his shoulder' (Cyrus, 15). He obtained a clerkship in Aberdeen, but six weeks later his employer died, bequeathing him a legacy of £50. After returning to Montrose, Beattie entered the office of the procurator-fiscal, and on the completion of his legal education in Edinburgh he established himself in Montrose in 1807 as a notary, where his conversational and his business talents contributed to his speedy professional success.

In 1815 Beattie contributed to the *Montrose Review* a mock-heroic poem, 'John o' Arnha', very much in the style of 'Tam o' Shanter', which he afterwards revised and expanded. In 1818 he published in the *Review* a simple and delicate poem in the old Scottish dialect, written when he was a mere boy, and entitled the 'Murderit Mynstrell'. In 1819 he published, also in the *Review*, the 'Bark', and in

1820 a wild and eerie rhapsody, entitled the 'Dream'. He also wrote several shorter lyrics.

In 1821 Beattie made the acquaintance of a Miss Gibson with whom he was soon engaged. Before, however, the marriage took place, she inherited a small fortune, and rejected Beattie for William Smart, a successful corn merchant. After completing a narrative of his relations with the lady, published by Alexander Silver in 1863 as a 'Statement of fact', and 'The last', a long suicide note, Beattie went back to St Cyrus and shot himself by the side of his sister's grave on 29 September 1823.

T. F. HENDERSON, rev. S. R. J. BAUDRY

Sources A. S. M. Cyrus [A. Smith], *George Beattie, of Montrose: a poet, a humourist, and a man of genius* (1863) · Anderson, *Scot. nat.*

Beattie, James (1735–1803), poet and philosopher, was baptized at Laurencekirk, Kincardineshire, on 25 October 1735, the youngest of six children of James Beattie (*d. c.*1742), tenant farmer and village shopkeeper, and Jean Watson (*c.*1692–1772). His father, who died when Beattie was about seven years old, is said to have written some verse, and was a friend of the Scottish poet Alexander Ross. Beattie went to Laurencekirk parish school, which had a high reputation for classics. He was recognized as an outstanding scholar and was known as 'the poet'. At fourteen he won a bursary to Marischal College, Aberdeen, to take the four-year arts course. He studied Greek under Thomas Blackwell, winning the prize for his year, and moral philosophy under Alexander Gerard. In 1753, after graduating MA, he became village schoolmaster and parish clerk at Fordoun, about 6 miles from Laurencekirk. He probably intended at this time to enter the church, and attended divinity classes at King's College, Aberdeen, for part of the next two years. In his five years at Fordoun, he developed a love of hills, nature, and solitary places. He began to submit poetry for publication, which from 1756 appeared in the *Scots Magazine* and the *Edinburgh Magazine*.

Although Fordoun was isolated, Beattie had intellectual friends in Aberdeen and Montrose, including the poet John Ogilvie, and he drew the notice of important patrons—Francis Garden and James Burnett (later Lord Gardenstone and Lord Monboddo). In November 1757 he was an unsuccessful candidate in the examination for the post of under-master at Aberdeen grammar school, but he sufficiently impressed the examiners to be invited to a new vacancy there in June 1758. In October 1760 he was appointed professor of moral philosophy and logic at Marischal College. Influential friends—particularly Robert Arbuthnot, who had recognized his exceptional talents, and the earl of Erroll—helped to secure this remarkable promotion. One sequel to his appointment was his election to the Aberdeen Philosophical Society, where he was able to sharpen his ideas by discussion with men of intellectual distinction, such as Thomas Reid, George Campbell, John Gregory, and Gerard. Much of Beattie's prose work, on philosophy and literature, was first presented there. Beattie held the chair until his death despite tempting and lucrative offers in the 1770s of a chair at Edinburgh and of two rich livings in the Church of England. He was a gifted and conscientious teacher, as shown by the surviving notes taken in his lectures by his students, by a journal he kept of exactly what he had taught in each session over a thirty-two-year period, and by testimonials from those whom he had taught, such as Alexander Chalmers. Beattie gave about 300 lectures annually to the arts class, in the final year of their four-year course, when the students were aged about seventeen. These discourses ranged

James Beattie (1735–1803), by Sir Joshua Reynolds, 1773 [*The Triumph of Truth, with the Portrait of a Gentleman*]

widely over psychology, ethics, literary criticism, and natural religion. *Elements of Moral Science* (2 vols., 1790–93) is an abstract of his lecture course.

Beattie was a keen musician, playing the cello, composing tunes, and writing several of his short poems as songs. His early poetry was collected in *Original Poems and Translations* (1760), which included translations in heroic couplets of all Virgil's eclogues as well as two Pindaric odes modelled on those of Thomas Gray and some attractive short poems. In 1765 he met Gray, of whose poems he produced a fine edition in 1768. In the late 1760s Beattie wrote the two works on which his fame rested: *Essay on the Nature and Immutability of Truth, in Opposition to Sophistry and Scepticism*, published in 1770, and the greater part of his most influential poem, *The Minstrel*, published in two books in 1771 and 1774. The *Essay on Truth*, written between 1766 and 1769, is a bitterly polemical attack on 'sceptical philosophy', in particular on David Hume, whose writings Beattie believed were undermining religion and morals. It presented a popularized version of the philosophy of Thomas Reid, to show that philosophical scepticism was contrary to 'common sense'. It quickly brought Beattie celebrity, especially among those who saw it as a defence of religion: he was awarded an LLD degree from King's College, Aberdeen, in 1770. It was also a controversial and contentious work, and Beattie became obsessed with the belief that he was the subject of malicious attacks by supporters of Hume.

The Minstrel, a poem in Spenserian stanza, was begun in 1766, probably as a lighthearted, satirical work. In the spring of 1768 Beattie was inspired to continue it as his own poetic autobiography. It describes the childhood of Edwin, a shepherd boy brought up in solitary mountainous country, and his imaginative response to nature. In less than three months Beattie wrote most of the first book of *The Minstrel*, and began the second. The completion of the second book, however, took more than five years; an intended third book was never written. The poetic growth of Edwin was an inspiration to several generations of poets, most particularly to the Romantics, and this work had an important formative influence on William Wordsworth, who greatly admired it.

Beattie was warmly received on a visit to London in 1771, where he met distinguished people in literature, the arts, and the church, including Samuel Johnson, David Garrick, Sir Joshua Reynolds, and Elizabeth Montagu of the bluestocking circle, who was to become a lifelong friend, correspondent, and support. He visited London again in May 1773, hoping to obtain financial benefit in the form of a post or pension, which his well-placed friends had told him he had a good chance of securing because his *Essay on Truth* had provided such an important service to religion. After delays which caused him great anxiety he was granted a royal pension of £200 per year, in August 1773. During this second visit he also received an honorary degree at Oxford, and met George III. Reynolds painted an allegorical portrait of him, *The Triumph of Truth*.

From now, however, Beattie's life was overshadowed by illness and domestic troubles. On 28 June 1767 he had married Mary (Mally) Dun (*bap.* 1744, *d.* 1807), the daughter of the rector of Aberdeen grammar school. Three children were born: James Hay *Beattie in 1768; a son who lived for only an hour in 1772; and Montagu Beattie in 1778. Within a few years of the marriage Mrs Beattie developed signs of mental illness, and Beattie's own health, always poor, became much worse. Throughout life he suffered from headaches and vertigo, and he frequently wrote of being unable to work because of illness. He usually spent his summer vacations taking the waters at Peterhead for his health. The Reynolds portrait of 1773 shows an attractive, alert, eager face, but from the age of fifty he was fat and prematurely aged. Recurrent depression was a feature of his illnesses and may have been the primary disorder. The nature of Mary Beattie's mental illness remains unclear, though both her brothers also had disabling mental disorders. For the first decade of their marriage Beattie was unwilling to believe or to admit that his wife was mentally ill, but by 1780 he found it impossible to continue living with her because of her bizarre behaviour and paranoid delusions. He never saw her after 1784; she outlived him, and died in 1807.

Increasing illness and domestic tragedy limited Beattie's creativity. He wrote little new poetry after 1770, revising or rejecting much of his earlier verse: the final collection which he was prepared to acknowledge comprised *The Minstrel* and eight short poems, of which 'The Hermit', written in 1766, became the best-known. Much of the prose he published after 1770 was a revision or reworking of material written earlier, as lectures for the Aberdeen Philosophical Society or for his students. Nevertheless, his essays are all clear, interesting, and readable: Joseph Addison was Beattie's model for prose style. Three essays, including 'On poetry and music as they affect the mind', were published with a new edition of the *Essay on Truth* in a financially successful subscription quarto volume in 1776. Beattie's best prose work, *Dissertations Moral and Critical* (1783), covers various philosophical and literary topics, and has an extended treatise entitled 'The theory of language'. *Evidences of the Christian Religion* (1786), written with the encouragement of his friend Beilby Porteus, bishop of Chester, became a highly popular guide for young people. Beattie based his philosophy and religion on the 'Argument from design', and on Christian revelation. He believed that nature had been made to provide a benign environment for humankind, and that human nature was fundamentally good. 'Nature' is referred to frequently in his poems and prose: it includes external nature, as celebrated in *The Minstrel*, and the natural moral order, to which conscience is the guide. Beattie believed the duty of universal benevolence included sexual and racial equality: from the early 1760s he had attacked the slave trade in his lectures. In old age his political views were very conservative, but his views on society and human relations remained liberal and humane.

Beattie's only published poem in Scots dialect, 'To Mr Alexander Ross at Lochlee', was written in 1768 to promote Ross's poem 'The Fortunate Shepherdess' (though

Beattie never publicly acknowledged it). At that time Beattie showed an ambiguous attitude to the Scots vernacular: 'I ... am not at all insensible to the expressiveness of some of our phrases, nor to that singular turn of humour to which our vulgar tongue is peculiarly adapted' (Beattie to Thomas Blacklock, 24 May 1768, Fettercairn box 91). However, he also wrote: 'The Scotch tongue is really barren in itself, and ... is now become incapable of expressing any thing but low humour' (Beattie to John Gregory, 1 July 1768, Aberdeen UL, MS 30/1/15). He compiled a list of 'Scoticisms ... designed to correct improprieties of speech and writing', and printed it privately for his students in 1778; it was published in 1787, but in this exercise Beattie was only following other contemporaries, including David Hume. Later in life Beattie turned wholly against the Scots dialect, even for songs. Advising George Thomson in January 1793 on his forthcoming song collection, he wrote 'I can by no means reconcile myself to Broad Scotch words, which the longer I live, I dislike the more' (Robinson, 'Critical edition', 299).

Beattie continued to visit friends in London every few years until 1791, and he had a close circle of friends in north-east Scotland, including Sir William Forbes (later his biographer), Robert Arbuthnot, and James Mercer. He was closely attached to Jane Maxwell, duchess of Gordon, and his flattering letters to her did some harm to his reputation when they were published in Forbes's biography. Though he continued to be a member of the Church of Scotland, he felt more at home in the Scottish Episcopal church, which he attended in Peterhead. He admired the Church of England, into which his son Montagu was confirmed in 1791.

Beattie was deeply attached to his two sons and he suffered further devastating blows when they both died in early adulthood: James Hay after a prolonged consumptive illness in 1790, three years after being appointed Beattie's assistant and successor in the chair of moral philosophy, and Montagu suddenly in 1796. After Montagu's death Beattie went into a final mental and physical decline; he stopped teaching in 1797. He was cared for by his great-niece, Margaret Valentine, and her husband, John Glennie, who was appointed Beattie's successor in 1796. He had a series of strokes from 1799 and was totally helpless before he died in Aberdeen on 18 August 1803. He was buried in St Nicholas's churchyard, Aberdeen, next to the graves of his sons.   ROGER J. ROBINSON

Sources W. Forbes, *An account of the life and writings of James Beattie*, 2 vols. (1806) • M. Forbes, *Beattie and his friends*, ed. M. Knight and M. Forbes (1904) • Aberdeen UL, MS 30 • NL Scot., Acc. 4796, Fettercairn boxes, 37, 41, 83, 91–100 • R. J. Robinson, 'The poetry of James Beattie: a critical edition', PhD diss., U. Aberdeen, 1997 [incl. transcripts of all Beattie's letters concerning the poetry] • *James Beattie's London diary, 1773*, ed. R. S. Walker (1946) • *James Beattie's day-book, 1773–1798*, ed. R. S. Walker (1948) • *Collected works of James Beattie*, ed. R. J. Robinson, 10 vols. (1996) • A. Bower, *An account of the life of James Beattie* (1804) [esp. copy with MS annotations by W. Robertson, U. Aberdeen, special libraries and archives] • R. Robinson, 'The madness of Mrs Beattie's family: the strange case of the "assassin" of John Wilkes', *British Journal for Eighteenth-Century Studies*, 19 (1996), 183–97 • A. Chalmers, 'Memoirs of the life of Dr. James Beattie', *James Beattie, the minstrel, or, The progress of genius:*

with some other poems (1805), vii–xlviii • A. Dyce, 'Memoir of Beattie', in *The poetical works of James Beattie*, ed. A. Dyce (1831), [i]–lxviii • *Fasti academiae Mariscallanae Aberdonensis: selections from the records of the Marischal College and University, MDXCIII–MDCCCLX*, 2, ed. P. J. Anderson, New Spalding Club, 18 (1898) • M. Moorman, *William Wordsworth, a biography*, 1: *The early years, 1770–1803* (1957) • E. H. King, *James Beattie's 'The minstrel' and the origins of Romantic autobiography* (1992) • W. R. Fraser, *History of the parish and burgh of Laurencekirk* (1880) • P. J. Anderson, ed., *Officers and graduates of University and King's College, Aberdeen, MVD–MDCCCLX*, New Spalding Club, 11 (1893) • A. Mackie, ed., *James Beattie, 'The minstrel': some unpublished letters* (1908) • R. Robinson, 'The origins and composition of James Beattie's *Minstrel*', *Romanticism*, 4 (1998), 224–40 • H. L. Ulman, ed., *The minutes of the Aberdeen Philosophical Society, 1758–1773* (1990) • H. F. Morland Simpson, ed., *Bon record: records and reminiscences of Aberdeen grammar school* (1906) • parish register, Laurencekirk, Kincardineshire, 25 Oct 1735 [baptism] • parish register, Aberdeen, 3 Oct 1744 [baptism: Mary Dun, wife] • tombstone, St Nicholas's churchyard, Aberdeen

Archives Hunt. L., letters • NL Scot., corresp. and papers • U. Aberdeen, corresp. and papers • U. Edin. L., lectures, sermons, and papers | NA Scot., William Creech letter-books • NL Scot., letters to Aaron Lithgow

Likenesses engraving, 1770–73, repro. in Walker, ed., *James Beattie's London diary, 1773*, 49 • J. Reynolds, oils, 1773 (*The triumph of Truth*), U. Aberdeen [*see illus.*] • J. Wales?, miniature, c.1781, repro. in Walker, ed., *James Beattie's London diary, 1773*, 81 • J. Tassie, paste medallion, 1789, Scot. NPG • Freeman, engraving, repro. in *The minstrel* (1803) • T. Gaugain, engraving (after J. Reynolds), repro. in Forbes, *Account of the life*, frontispiece • J. Heath, engraving (after J. Reynolds), repro. in A. Chalmers, ed., *Poems* (1806), frontispiece • W. Ridley, stipple, BM, NPG; repro. in *European Magazine* (1801)

Wealth at death approx. £1022: NL Scot., MS Acc. 4796, Fettercairn boxes 41, 95; Forbes, *Account*, vol. 2, p. 348

Beattie, James Hay (1768–1790), writer and university teacher, was born on 6 November 1768 in Aberdeen, the first of two surviving children of James *Beattie (1735–1803), poet and moral philosopher, and his wife, Mary, or Mally (*bap.* 1744, *d.* 1807), daughter of James Dun, rector of Aberdeen grammar school. Named after James Hay, fifteenth earl of Erroll, his father's early patron, he was educated at Aberdeen grammar school from 1774 or 1775 until 1781. His mother's mental illness and her exile into private mental care (even her letters to her children were suppressed), brought the elder Beattie, who was a deeply involved parent, into a very close relationship with James Hay and his brother Montagu. A portrait of James Hay aged eleven shows him as an intelligent, serious, anxious boy, and he became a learned but painfully shy adolescent. In 1781, on the first of three visits to London with his father, he met many of his father's distinguished friends, including Samuel Johnson. He entered Marischal College, Aberdeen, where his father was professor of moral philosophy, in 1781. He studied the arts course for five years instead of the usual four, since at his father's request he repeated the first-year Greek class, and graduated MA in April 1786. He considered entering the church and briefly studied divinity. However, his father had for some years hoped that he would become his assistant and successor in the chair of moral philosophy. From November 1786 the elder Beattie intensively canvassed his Aberdeen colleagues and his influential friends in Scotland and London to secure this appointment. It was approved by the king in

June 1787, and James Hay Beattie was admitted as professor of moral philosophy, and assistant and successor to his father, on 28 September 1787. Moral philosophy was taught in the final year at Marischal College, so the students to whom he lectured from 1787 to 1789, on occasions when his father was ill, were little younger than himself. He worked hard on preparing a lecture course and gave an impressive farewell address to the class that graduated in April 1789. However, from the time of his appointment he was frequently ill, and in November 1789 he went into a final decline from tuberculosis, though he survived a further year of increasing weakness and wasting. He died at his father's house in Aberdeen on 19 November 1790, and was buried in the churchyard of St Nicholas, Aberdeen.

James Beattie's perhaps idealized memoir of James Hay Beattie, written within a few weeks of his son's death, depicts a young man of exceptional piety and remarkable literary and academic talents. James Hay's own letters written in 1787–90 suggest a humorous, confident, and intelligent young man. He became more widely known after his death through the substantial collection of his essays and poems which his father compiled and prefixed with the memoir. James Beattie circulated 200 copies of the book privately in 1794 and published an edition in 1799. The tragedy of James Hay's early death and his father's reputation added to the interest of this work, and it was admired by Hannah More and William Wilberforce. None of the pieces had an enduring reputation, though taken together they show a lively intelligence and some literary talent, more successful in the serious than the comic pieces. This judgement is, however, complicated by the possibility that the elder Beattie was part author of some of the pieces. For example, a Latin translation of Pope's 'Elegy on an Unfortunate Lady' was said by the elder Beattie to have been made by James Hay in November 1786, but the original manuscript shows that it was written by James Beattie himself in 1782, and the most that James Hay can have done was to have made some small revisions. ROGER J. ROBINSON

Sources J. H. Beattie, *Essays and fragments in prose and verse, to which is prefixed an account of the author's life and character* (1794) · J. Beattie, letters, U. Aberdeen, MSS 30/1, 30/2, 30/25 · J. H. Beattie, letters, NL Scot., Acc. 4796, Fettercairn boxes 41, 83, 91–94, 98, 99 · J. H. Beattie, letters, U. Aberdeen, MS 30/26 · R. J. Robinson, 'The poetry of James Beattie: a critical edition', PhD diss., U. Aberdeen, 1997 · R. Robinson, 'The madness of Mrs Beattie's family: the strange case of the "assassin" of John Wilkes', *British Journal for Eighteenth-Century Studies*, 19 (1996), 183–97 · W. Forbes, *An account of the life and writings of James Beattie*, 2 vols. (1806) · J. H. Beattie, letter to Dr James Dun, 7 July 1887, priv. coll. · J. Beattie, *The minstrel, in two books, with some other poems, to which are now added miscellanies, by James Hay Beattie, A.M. with an account of his life and character*, 2 vols. (1799) · *Fasti academiae Mariscallanae Aberdonensis: selections from the records of the Marischal College and University, MDXCIII–MDCCCLX*, 2, ed. P. J. Anderson, New Spalding Club, 18 (1898) · J. Beattie, 'Journal of sessions', U. Aberdeen, MS 30/16 · *Collected works of James Beattie*, ed. R. J. Robinson, 10 vols. (1996) · R. J. Robinson, introduction, in *Collected works of James Beattie*, ed. R. J. Robinson, 10: *Miscellaneous writings* (1996) · M. Forbes, *Beattie and his friends*, ed. M. Knight and M. Forbes (1904) · *James Beattie's day-book, 1773–1798*, ed. R. S. Walker (1948) · *DNB* · bap. reg. Scot.

Archives NL Scot., letters · NL Scot., letters to his father · U. Aberdeen L., letters · U. Aberdeen L., MSS and list of books
Likenesses J. Heath, stipple (after H. Room), BM, NPG; repro. in Beattie, *Minstrel*, vol. 2

Beattie, John [Jack] (1888/9–1960), politician, was born in Belfast into a Presbyterian family. No other verifiable information about his parents or possible siblings has come to light. Jack Beattie was educated until the age of twelve at the Saunders Street and Dee Street national schools in east Belfast. On leaving the latter he found work first in a textile company, then in the Belfast ropeworks. At the age of fourteen he commenced an apprenticeship as a blacksmith in the Harland and Wolff shipyard. Beattie became interested in trade unionism and was appointed assistant secretary to the Associated Blacksmiths' and Ironworkers' Society. By 1918 he had become a full-time organizer for the union throughout the whole of Ireland, a post he held until 1925. In 1919 he was prominent as a strikers' representative in the 'forty-hour week' general strike in the Belfast shipyards.

Beattie involved himself in Belfast labour politics from his early twenties. He was a supporter of Irish home rule, and when Winston Churchill came to Belfast in 1912 to speak to a pro-home rule rally, Beattie helped to protect him from the attacks of loyalist mobs. Beattie continued to be active in Labour and trade union politics after the war and into the early 1920s, when the state of Northern Ireland came into being amid much communal unrest. By this time he was also married with a son and a daughter.

Beattie, standing for the Northern Ireland Labour Party (NILP), was elected to the Northern Ireland House of Commons for East Belfast in 1925 at the top of the poll in an election conducted under proportional representation. This was the first in a series of electoral successes. When the 'first past the post' electoral system was introduced in 1929 only Beattie, for the new constituency of Pottinger, carried Labour's cause to the new parliament. He was to hold the seat until 1949, representing it under a variety of Labour designations. Unusually in the context of Northern Ireland politics, Beattie drew significant support from across the religious divide: his advocacy of Irish unity appealed to Catholic voters, and he seems to have had a personal protestant following based on his local standing and trade unionism. In the 1930s Beattie featured in notable public protests over unemployment and poverty, calling for working-class unity.

Nevertheless, Beattie was central to internal rows over the 'national question' within the NILP, and he cultivated assiduously both the anti-partitionist elements of the party and the nationalist community in general. In 1934 he took up a position with the Dublin-based trade union the Irish National Teachers' Organization, resigning in 1952. He was expelled from the NILP in 1934, readmitted and elected leader in 1942 (occasioning the departure of his pro-Unionist rival Harry Midgley), and expelled again in 1944. From 1943 to 1950 and from 1951 to 1955 (in this period as a member of the Irish Labour Party) Beattie represented West Belfast at Westminster, where he was a constant irritant to the Ulster Unionist Party over questions surrounding the treatment of the Catholic minority in Northern Ireland. Defeat in 1955, on account of the intervention of a Sinn Féin candidate, ended his parliamentary career.

Beattie found more time in his later years for interests such as bowling and golf. He also remarried, his first wife having died in 1943; his second wife, Violet Jane McMaster, survived him. He died suddenly, from cancer, at the Musgrave and Clark Clinic, Belfast, on 9 March 1960, and was buried in Belfast two days later. Beattie's political career stands as one of the most remarkable in Northern Ireland's history. He was a shrewd and dogged survivor in a treacherous political climate for those bearing any kind of Labour label, and especially for one perceived by many as betraying his background and community.

GRAHAM WALKER

Sources T. Cradden, *Trade unionism, socialism and partition* (1993) · G. S. Walker, *The politics of frustration: Harry Midgley and the failure of labour in Northern Ireland* (1985) · PRO NIre., Beattie MSS · d. cert. · *CGPLA NIre.* (1960) · *The Times* (10 March 1960)
Archives PRO NIre., corresp. and papers
Wealth at death £2987 0s. 5d.: administration, 10 June 1960, *CGPLA NIre.*

Beattie, John Hugh Marshall (1915–1990), social anthropologist, was born on 8 May 1915 at 14 Harthill Avenue, Allerton, Liverpool, the only son and first of the two children of John Crawford Beattie (d. 1916), a civil servant and surveyor of taxes, and Maria Jean Jones (1886–1958), a nurse. His parents, who married in 1912, were both born in Ireland: his father came from the north and his mother from a farming family in co. Wicklow. John Crawford Beattie was given civil service postings in Liverpool, and then in Carlisle, near where John Hugh Marshall Beattie was baptized at Stanwick on 31 October 1915. Beattie senior died in an accident at sea on 3 November 1916, while returning on the *Connemara* from a visit to Ireland before planning to enlist; the boat was struck by a collier, and sank with the loss of nearly all on board. His widow returned to Ireland with the children, and settled in Monkstown on the outskirts of Dublin. John Beattie attended Dublin high school (1927–33), and then Trinity College, Dublin, where he took a BA degree in mental and moral science in 1937 (and was awarded first place, gold medal, and moderatorship research prize). He then held the position there of assistant lecturer in logic and ethics (1938–9).

Unusually for a philosopher, Beattie decided to apply for a post in the home or colonial service, and was accepted for the latter. The first stage was a training course in Oxford (1939–40) which introduced him to the study of Africa and to anthropology. He was posted to Tanganyika in 1940, and served in Lake Province. On home leave after the war he married Honor Mary Davy (1917–1978) on 27 December 1946. She was an accomplished cellist, who continued to teach and perform throughout her adult life. They returned together to Tanganyika. John was initially posted to Tunduru in the Southern Province, and then transferred to the secretariat in Dar es Salaam, where he served in the department of African affairs and government and became clerk to the legislative and executive councils. A distinguished career in colonial administration no doubt lay ahead.

However, Beattie's interest had been captivated rather by the people and cultural complexities of Africa itself. During a period of accumulated leave in 1949–50 he opted to take the diploma course in general and social anthropology at Oxford, and subsequently decided to leave the colonial service to return to academia. Having gained the BLitt in 1951 with a thesis about checks on political power in African societies, he left for field research in the kingdom of Bunyoro-Kitara in Uganda, before returning to become a university lecturer (later senior lecturer) in social anthropology at Oxford in 1953. After a further period in Uganda in 1955, during which he was acting director of the East African Institute of Social Research, he completed his DPhil in 1956 with a thesis on Bunyoro. In the same year John and Honor acquired the lovely old residence known as The Cottage, Headington Hill, a warm and welcoming family home where their children, Hugh and Frances, were now growing up.

Already a member of Lincoln College, Beattie became a fellow of Linacre House (later Linacre College) in 1964. This appointment recognized his strengths both in teaching and in research in a discipline which was then finding its feet. He was playing a key role in defining the character of post-war British social anthropology, and also becoming well known in the United States (where he was a fellow at the Center for Advanced Study in the Behavioral Sciences at Stanford in 1959–60 and again in 1966–7). A devoted colleague and disciple of Professor E. E. Evans-Pritchard, Beattie endorsed the shift he advocated from a 'natural science' approach in anthropology to a style informed rather by historical, literary, and culturally sensitive insights. Although Beattie was personally agnostic, his writings evidence deep respect for religion in general and for the moral views of others, which he saw as an essential part of social life and action. He excelled as a sympathetic teacher. His introductory book *Other Cultures: Aims, Methods and Achievements in Social Anthropology* (1964) became a standard teaching text, well known internationally in English (and translated into Japanese, French, Italian, Portuguese, Spanish, and Malay). In addition to his reflective writings on topics such as ritual, sacrifice, aspects of the self, and objectivity in anthropology, he published two short but influential ethnographic books (*Bunyoro: an African Kingdom*, 1960, and *Understanding Bunyoro*, 1965, illuminating his own field methods). He later made an innovative contribution to historical anthropology with *The Nyoro State* (1971). Beattie was greatly distressed at news reports of strife in Uganda during his later years. Although he was not able to follow through his research into this later period, his writings remain a testimony to the cultural riches of the country, and now constitute an important historical source in themselves.

Beattie is remembered for his courteous, if firm, defence of the integrity of 'the native point of view' and the importance of ethnographic evidence in the face of ambitious theoretical claims of the kind then being put forward by proponents of French structuralism. On Evans-Pritchard's retirement, Beattie accepted an invitation from the University of Leiden to take up a chair of African studies (cultural anthropology), which he held from 1971 to his own retirement in 1975 and return to Oxford. Here he continued to write and to participate in academic activities, but the loss of his wife, Honor, in 1978 led him to withdraw more into private life. He eventually developed Parkinson's disease and died of that condition, aggravated by bronchopneumonia, on 13 April 1990 at Guysfield Residential Home, Willian, Letchworth. He was cremated at Luton on 24 April 1990. A memorial service was organized by Linacre College and held for him at St Cross Church in Oxford on 7 July 1990.

WENDY R. JAMES

Sources annual reports, 1949–71, U. Oxf., Institute of Social and Cultural Anthropology [incl. list of publications] · Association of Social Anthropologists of the Commonwealth, register of members, 1969 · T. V. Sathyamurthy, 'John Hugh Marshall Beattie 1915–1990: memorial address', *Journal of the Anthropological Society of Oxford*, 22/1 (1991), 65–73 · *The Guardian* (28 April 1990) · *The Times* (26 April 1990) · *The Independent* (1 May 1990), 15 · J. H. M. Beattie, *Understanding Bunyoro* (New York, 1965) · b. cert. · private information (2004) · Archival papers, Linacre College, Oxford

Archives U. Oxf., Institute of Social and Cultural Anthropology, corresp. and papers

Likenesses photograph, repro. in *The Times* · photograph, repro. in *The Independent*

Beattie, William (1793–1875), physician and poet, was born at Dalton, Annandale, and baptized there on 23 February 1793, the son of James Beattie (d. 1809), architect, surveyor, and builder, and his wife, Janet. The family had been settled in Dumfriesshire for several generations and, aged fourteen, Beattie went to school at Clarencefield Academy in that county; he remained there for six years, under Thomas Fergusson, attaining a competent knowledge of Latin, Greek, and French. He entered Edinburgh University in 1813 and graduated MD in 1818. He helped to maintain himself at the university by teaching, for a time, as master of the parish school at Cleish, Kinross-shire.

Beattie stayed in Edinburgh for two years after taking his degree, living chiefly 'out of his inkhorn'—teaching, lecturing, translating, and conducting a small private practice. During this period he published several of his early poems, 'The Lay of a Graduate', 'Rosalie', and 'The Swiss Relic'. In 1820 he moved to Cumberland, and in 1822 he went to London to prepare to settle in Russia. He abandoned the idea on becoming engaged to Elizabeth Limner (d. 1845), a wealthy young lady of 'no inconsiderable attractions'. He accordingly continued his medical education and spent three months in the Paris hospitals. He returned to London and was married in the autumn of 1822.

Beattie was about to begin a practice at Dover when he received a summons from the duke of Clarence (afterwards William IV), to whom he had been introduced by Admiral Child, a connection of Mrs Beattie's, to attend the duke's family on a visit to the courts of Germany. At the close of the winter he therefore resumed his studies in Paris, after which he spent two years travelling and studying in Italy, Switzerland, and on the Rhine. At the end of 1824 he entered medical practice at Worthing in Sussex, but he left the following March, once more to accompany the duke and duchess of Clarence to Germany. On this occasion, at Göttingen, he made the acquaintance of J. F. Blumenbach, and also busied himself in investigating the medicinal properties of the most renowned German spas.

On his return to London, Beattie published further works, notably 'The Heliotrope' and 'The Courts of Germany'. Early in 1826, for the third time he formed one of the suite of the duke of Clarence on a German visit, during which he was favourably noticed by the queen of Würtemberg, princess royal of Great Britain. When she later visited England Beattie was sent for to attend her at Hampton Court and at Windsor. He repaid her majesty's good opinion with a flattering memoir of her in 1829. The only reward Beattie ever received for all his services to the duke of Clarence, which extended over some fourteen years, including three years as private secretary, was a service of silver plate and a letter certifying him to be 'a perfect gentleman'. Beattie, however, appears to have been grateful. The duchess added 'a pair of bracelets for Mrs. Beattie, knit by her own hands', and, after her coronation, a gold medallion, as a mark of her majesty's esteem and regard. The king of Prussia, whom Beattie had also attended professionally, likewise sent him a gold medallion, accompanied by 'a complimentary autograph letter'.

In 1827 Beattie was admitted a licentiate of the Royal College of Physicians and established himself in London at Hampstead, where for eighteen years he enjoyed an extensive practice. In 1835 and 1836 he travelled in Switzerland and the land of the Waldenses, and he was in Paris at the time of Fieschi's attempt upon the life of Louis-Philippe, in the immediate vicinity of the explosion. Beattie was a frequent contributor to the periodicals, and he published during this period several poems and descriptive and historical works, some being illustrated by his friend W. H. Bartlett. He also edited the *Scenic Annual*, for which the poet Thomas Campbell (1777–1844) was supposed to be responsible, *Beckett's Dramatic Works*, and *Lives of Eminent Conservative Statesmen*. His work was much to contemporary taste, the *Scenic Annual* earning £200 for Campbell, though it was largely Beattie's work.

In 1833 Beattie was introduced to Marguerite, countess of Blessington, and soon became a very useful friend to her. She frequently called on him as a poetical contributor to her *Book of Beauty* and other annuals, bestowing upon him in return for his verses a large amount of fluent flattery, and a general invitation to Seymour Place in central London for any evening, a privilege of which Beattie could unfortunately not avail himself in consequence of the state of his eyes. When Lady Blessington was deserted by many because of her financial difficulties, Beattie remained firmly loyal; he was also a confidant of Lady Byron who, according to an acquaintance of Beattie's, 'had imparted to him the true reason of her separation from her husband, and that it was not the one given by

Mrs. Stowe' (*Dumfriesshire and Galloway Herald*, 24 March 1875).

Beattie was long a close friend of Thomas Campbell and was selected by the poet to be his biographer, an obligation Beattie fulfilled in 1849 with the publication of *The Life and Letters of Thomas Campbell*, in three volumes. In 1833 Beattie speaks of Campbell as coming to stay at Rose Villa, Beattie's cottage at Hampstead, and adds:

> These visits in after life were frequently repeated, and whenever he found himself relapsing into a depressed state of health and spirits, 'Well', he would say, 'I must come into hospital', and he would repair for another week to 'Campbell's Ward', a room so named by the poet in the doctor's house. (Beattie, *Life*, 3.147)

In 1842 Campbell dedicated his *Pilgrim of Glencoe* to Beattie. Both as physician and friend Beattie seems to have been the great stay of the poet's declining years, and he attended him at his death in 1844, at Boulogne. Campbell's wish to be buried in Westminster Abbey would probably never have been realized but for Beattie, nor would a statue have been placed in Poets' Corner to his memory had not Beattie collected contributions to it and made good a considerable deficit out of his own pocket. Beattie was also a friend and physician of the poet Samuel Rogers.

In 1845 Beattie's wife died, and soon afterwards Beattie himself gave up regular practice as a physician; however, he continued to the end of his life to give medical advice to clergymen, men of letters, and others, without accepting professional fees, and he otherwise occupied his time in works of charity. For instance, in 1846 he published a memoir of his friend Bartlett for the benefit of the artist's family, which realized £400, and through his influence with the prime minister he obtained a pension of £75 a year for Bartlett's widow. The memoir was the last of Beattie's major literary works, but he continued to contribute papers to the Archaeological Society, and to write articles for the reviews.

Beattie published nothing on medicine beyond a pamphlet entitled *Home Climates and Worthing* (1858) and a Latin treatise on pulmonary consumption, the subject of his MD thesis. Some of his works were translated into German and French. He was foreign secretary to the British Archaeological Society, fellow of the Ethnological Society, and a member of the Historical Institute and of the Institut d'Afrique, Paris.

Beattie lost £7000 through the failure of the Albert Assurance office, a great shock which probably accelerated his death; but he bore the loss with fortitude, though forced to give up his charitable donations of £300 a year.

Beattie died on 17 March 1875 at 13 Upper Berkeley Street, Portman Square, London, at the age of eighty-two, and was buried beside his wife at Brighton. He had no children. P. B. AUSTIN, rev. PATRICK WALLIS

Sources Munk, *Roll* · *Nomina eorum, qui gradum medicinae doctoris in academia Jacobi sexti Scotorum regis, quae Edinburgi est, adepti sunt, ab anno 1705 ad annum 1845*, University of Edinburgh (1846) · C. Rogers, *The Scottish minstrel*, 2nd edn (1870) · R. R. Madden, *The literary life and correspondence of the countess of Blessington*, 3 vols. (1855) · *Men of the time* (1875) · *Life and letters of Thomas Campbell*, ed. W. Beattie, 3 vols. (1849) · W. Beattie, *Journal of a residence in Germany* (1837) · *The Scotsman* (26 March 1875) · *Dumfriesshire and Galloway Herald* (24 March 1875) · *Medical Times and Gazette* (3 April 1875), 380

Archives Holborn Library, London, Camden Local Studies and Archive Centre, diaries, letters, and notebook · Mitchell L., Glas., corresp. and papers relating to his life of Thomas Campbell · Sci. Mus., letters · Yale U., Beinecke L., letters to T. J. Pettigrew
Likenesses J. Rogers, stipple (after H. Room), BM, Wellcome L.
Wealth at death under £12,000: resworn probate, June 1875, *CGPLA Eng. & Wales*

Beatty, Sir (Alfred) Chester (1875–1968), mining engineer and art collector, was born on 7 February 1875 in New York city, the youngest of the three sons of John Cuming Beatty, banker, of New York city, and his wife, Hetty, daughter of William Gedney Bull. He was educated at Westminster School, Dobbs Ferry, New York, at Princeton University, and then at Columbia University (school of mines), where he came top in every subject except geology, in which he came second. He went to Denver, Colorado, in search of work, and rose rapidly from labourer to manager of a small gold mine. He then established himself as a reputable consultant, and in 1903 he became consulting engineer and assistant general manager of the Guggenheim Exploration Company, working alongside the renowned engineer John Hays Hammond. Together they acquired and developed many of Guggenheim's best mines, including silver mines in Mexico, and copper mines in the western states of the USA, as well as various prospecting concessions in the Belgian Congo (later Zaire).

On 18 April 1900 Beatty married Grace Madeline (*d.* 1911), known as Ninette, daughter of Alfred Rickard, a mining engineer of Denver, with whom he worked. They raised a daughter, Ninette (1901–1958), and a son, Alfred Chester Beatty (1907–1983), in New York. Ninette Beatty was taken ill in 1910, and though she recovered from an operation she died of typhoid fever on 28 March 1911. Beatty himself suffered from lung problems at this time, and afterwards sought winter sunshine. Within two weeks of the funeral, he sailed for England with his children, his brother (William) Gedney Beatty, an architect, and his servants.

On 21 June 1913 Beatty married the divorcee Edith Stone (*c.*1886–1952), daughter of John Dunn of New York. He acquired as his London home Baroda House, Kensington Palace Gardens, which he turned over to the government for use as a military hospital during the war. In 1914 the Beattys made the first of many visits to Egypt, where he subsequently spent many winters and built himself a house, on the outskirts of Cairo.

Also in 1913 Beatty founded Selection Trust Ltd. This remained a small company until after the First World War, when Beatty embarked on the development, finance, and administration of mining businesses throughout the world. In this way he developed zinc and lead mines at Tetiuhe in Siberia, diamond mines on the west coast of Africa, and lead and zinc mines in Serbia. His greatest achievement, however, was the part he played in the development of the copperbelt in Northern Rhodesia (later Zambia), where he formed the great mines of Roan Antelope and Mufulira.

The extraordinary feature of Beatty's work in these territories is that, as far as is known, apart from Trepca, in Serbia, he never visited any of these countries. He assembled a team of expert geologists and mining engineers whom he sent to these places with very specific instructions about where they should explore. Based on his own experience and backed by his unerring flair for potential mining areas, his judgement was seldom proved wrong, and in these four territories great and successful mining enterprises were established. In the subsequent fifty years one by one these were nationalized, first in Siberia and then in Yugoslavia. The last of the nationalizations was in Zambia in 1970. In the meantime, however, Selection Trust had acquired valuable interests in other mines around the world, including in Australia, Canada, South Africa, and South-West Africa (Namibia), as well as interests in the North Sea and the UK.

In 1933 Beatty became a British subject and during the Second World War he gave valuable service to government departments active in his own field. During the war he became estranged from his wife. They lived apart for some ten years, until her death at Baroda House in 1952. By this time Beatty had retired, and, disliking what he considered to be the over-regulation of life in post-war England, he had moved in 1950 to Ireland, the land of his Beatty ancestors, settling at 10 Ailesbury Road, Dublin.

Between the time that he retired from Guggenheim and his arrival in Britain, Beatty spent much time in the Middle and Near East exploring the art treasures of that part of the world. He built up a unique collection of Indian and Persian miniatures and manuscripts and early bibles, including parts of a New Testament which was two centuries older than the *Codex Sinaiticus*; he also acquired the earliest known copy of the *Rubaiyat* of ʿUmar Khayyam. Later he turned his attention to Impressionist art, in which he built up one of the most valuable private collections in the world. He also collected French and Russian gold snuff-boxes, watches from the eighteenth century, clocks, stamps, and a library of rare books which were said to number 9000 and which weighed 35 tons. On retiring to Ireland he gave more than eighty of his Impressionist pictures to the national gallery in Dublin and in 1955 he handed over to the Irish nation a thirteenth-century book of hours which had previously been on loan to the British Museum.

In the philanthropic field he is best known for his interest in cancer research. In the 1930s he purchased the old Freemasons' Hospital in the Fulham Road and converted it into the Chester Beatty Research Institute (later the Institute of Cancer Research: Royal Cancer Hospital).

Beatty was a man of great and bountiful disposition, generous to a fault, not only in his national benefactions but to individuals as well. Cast in a heroic mould, he had a Churchillian sweep and a supreme contempt of every kind of socialist bureaucracy. His endearing mannerisms included a total dislike of smoking in any room in which he was present, and a horror of draughts and cold, which

was obvious from the impressive cloak which he wore, often on the warmest days.

In his professional life Beatty received many honours, including the gold medal of the Institution of Mining and Metallurgy, which he was awarded in 1935, and the Serbian *grand cordon* of the order of St Sava, which he received on the occasion of the opening of the Trepca mines. He was knighted in 1954, and he later became the first honorary citizen of the Irish republic under the Irish Nationality and Citizenship Act of 1956.

Beatty died in hospital in Monte Carlo, Monaco, on 19 January 1968, and was buried in Ireland, being given a state funeral at St Patrick's Anglican Cathedral. His estate in Ireland was valued at over £7 million, his English estate being relatively insignificant. Alfred Chester Beatty junior succeeded his father as chairman of Selection Trust in 1950 and remained in office until 1978, two years before BP paid £412 million for the Selection Trust shares, the most expensive takeover the City had known.

RONALD LINDSAY PRAIN, *rev.* ANITA MCCONNELL

Sources *The Times* (22 Jan 1968) · *New York Times* (21 Jan 1968) · A. J. Wilson, *The life and times of Sir Alfred Chester Beatty* (1985) · CGPLA *Eng. & Wales* (1968) · *Who was who in America* · DNB

Archives BLPES, papers · Chester Beatty Library, Dublin, corresp. relating to establishment of Chester Beatty Library · U. Oxf., Griffith Institute, Egyptological notebooks | Nuffield Oxf., corresp. with Lord Cherwell · TCD, letters to Thomas McGreevy

Likenesses E. Newling, pencil sketch, 1934 · C. Colahan, oils, 1940 · photographs, repro. in Wilson, *Life and times*

Wealth at death £105,468—in England: probate, 15 Feb 1968, CGPLA *Eng. & Wales* · over £7,000,000—in Éire: probate, 1968

Beatty, David, first Earl Beatty (1871–1936), naval officer, was born on 17 January 1871 at Howbeck Lodge, Stapeley, Nantwich, Cheshire, the second of four sons of Captain David Longfield Beatty (1841–1904), of the 4th hussars, and his first wife, Katherine Edith (*d*. 1896), daughter of Nicholas Sadleir of Dunboyne Castle, co. Meath, Ireland.

Early life and career David's brothers all served in the army, and his one sister, Kathleen, known as Trot, married Colonel Miles Courage, of the brewing family, who became master of the Hampshire hunt. David inherited his family's love of hunting, horsemanship, and all country sports, but as a young boy showed such interest in ships and the sea that his parents had him prepared for the navy. In January 1884, at thirteen, the normal age for officer entry, he passed into the Royal Naval College, Dartmouth, tenth out of ninety-nine candidates. He passed out in January 1886, eighteenth of his term of thirty-three. He was not amenable to the punitive discipline and rigid routine of *Britannia*, the training ship, and so was never chosen as a cadet captain. He described himself as 'essentially Irish', and perhaps his high spirits and generally attractive personality were seen as redeeming features. On the other hand he had 'interest', that established factor in furthering a successful naval career. His mother, relying on their shared Irishness, personally appealed to Admiral Lord Charles Beresford and had his original appointment to the China station changed to one on *Alexandra*, the flagship of the Mediterranean Fleet, where the commander-in-chief, Queen Victoria's second son, the duke of Edinburgh, gained a sound professional reputation.

Such a ship attracted an unusual number of officers who subsequently achieved high rank, among them Colin Keppel and Stanley Colville, who could provide valuable role models for the cadets and midshipmen. Beatty's companions in the gun room included Walter Cowan, Richard Phillimore, and Reginald Tyrwhitt, who later served under him as flag officers in the North Sea. Others of his seniors became influential in court circles during the reigns of Queen Victoria's successors. In the meantime his manners, cheerfulness, and good looks made him popular with the royal and other highly placed visitors to the flagship, while his skills as a horseman gained him additional friends and admirers. *Alexandra* was typical of the capital ships of the day: fully rigged for sail, but equipped for steam propulsion and strongly armoured, it mounted heavy, muzzle loading guns and carried Whitehead torpedoes.

Beatty was rated midshipman on 15 May 1886, was promoted sub-lieutenant on 14 May 1890, and began scientific and technical courses at the Royal Naval College, Greenwich, and specialist establishments in Portsmouth in September. In contrast to these he had three periods of sea service under sail in the corvette *Ruby*. The last of these followed his promotion to lieutenant on 25 August 1892; he had not been attracted by the six months' accelerated advancement gained by high performance in the courses and achieved a first-class pass only in torpedoes.

More directly relevant to the newer navy was Beatty's appointment to the battleship *Camperdown* in October 1893, when he entered the world of steam tactics. In 1895 he joined the battleship *Trafalgar*, whose executive officer Stanley Colville had formed a high opinion of his potential during their time in *Alexandra*. This led to promotion and distinction, which enabled Beatty to out-distance his contemporaries for the rest of his career. When Colville was appointed to command the gunboats supporting General Sir Herbert Kitchener's Sudan expedition of 1896 he selected his protégé to command one of his craft.

Beatty did not disappoint him. When Colville was wounded by shore fire, he assumed command of the whole flotilla in its hazardous passage through the cataracts of the Nile, showing exemplary initiative, leadership, and courage under fire. On 22 September 1896 the British forces reached Dongola, and Kitchener halted his advance. At Kitchener's personal request he rejoined for the 1897 completion of the campaign.

The new flotilla under the command of Colin Keppel, another former *Alexandra* man, also performed well. Beatty's exploits gained him wider recognition, including the DSO, while Kitchener in his dispatch of 1898 substantially contributed to his special promotion to commander on 15 November. Aged twenty-seven, and with only six years' service as lieutenant rather than the normal eleven or twelve, he was now well ahead of his contemporaries on the ladder of promotion. He had shown exceptional boldness and also became known to Winston Churchill, another participant in the Sudan expedition.

Beatty was appointed executive officer of the battleship *Barfleur*, flagship of the second in command of the China

David Beatty, first Earl Beatty (1871–1936), by Sir John Lavery, 1917

station, in April 1899. Her captain, Stanley Colville, had again asked for him. Initially he concentrated on the internal working of the ship to ensure the smartness in appearance and drills on which a commander's promotion traditionally depended. But wider events gave him opportunity for more exciting activity and professional advancement. China was in the grip of an uprising by the Boxer nationalist movement, which was opposed to external influence and threatened foreign nationals in Beijing. In subsequent land operations around Tientsin (Tianjin), Beatty played a prominent part, but he was seriously wounded in his left arm. Also wounded was Captain John Jellicoe, Admiral Seymour's flag captain. Beatty's gallantry and leadership were duly noted, and on 9 November 1900 he received one of four special promotions to captain. He was now twenty-nine, compared with the normal age for that promotion of forty-two, and thus further ahead than ever in the race to qualifying for flag rank. It was not however until 2 June 1902 and after prolonged medical treatment that Beatty assumed his first captain's command.

On home leave in 1899 Beatty met his future wife, Ethel (d. 1932), daughter of Marshall Field, the Chicago millionaire and chain-store proprietor. They met in the hunting field, where her hard, almost reckless, riding gave them common ground. A strong mutual attraction developed. On his return from China with an enhanced reputation, her interest increased, and he remained entranced by her complex personality. He was well aware of the advantages of her great wealth, but she was a married woman, although separated from her American husband, Arthur M. Tree. Beatty's career could have suffered as a result of an illicit relationship, and they had to assume complete discretion in their conduct and correspondence. However, Tree obtained a divorce in America on the grounds of his wife's desertion, and despite objections from both families they married at Hanover Square register office in London on 22 May 1901, only ten days after Ethel's divorce was publicized.

Prelude to high command Beatty's appointment as captain of the cruiser *Juno* (launched 1895, 5600 tons) on 2 June 1902 inaugurated a critical period in his career. His qualities of leadership were well established, but his ability to master the problems arising from changing propulsion, weaponry, and communications systems had yet to be tested. The Mediterranean Fleet, in which he was to serve, had been trained by Sir John (Jacky) Fisher, its commander-in-chief from 1899 to 1902, to a high pitch of readiness for war, based on speedy manoeuvring and offensive action. Captains and admirals were tested in regular fleet manoeuvres in which the advent of wireless telegraphy introduced new complications. Beatty's command of *Juno* began with a short attachment to the Channel Fleet under the command of Admiral Sir Arthur Wilson, renowned for his skills in the tactical handling of fleets and squadrons and for the heavy demands he made on his subordinates. In his letters to his wife Beatty admitted to losing his temper with his own officers, who did not

match up to the standards he required in the highly competitive rivalry between ships to meet his admiral's requirements. He also reacted more positively, not only by entertaining his officers in the traditional way but also by trying to lead them into discussions designed to bring out the lessons to be learned from exercises and manoeuvres. Also, and very characteristically, in his letters to his wife he strongly criticized his superiors for not following suit. He was particularly critical of his last commander-in-chief, Lord Charles Beresford, for imposing too much detailed control over his subordinates, while skilful in avoiding involvement in Beresford's quarrel with Fisher, which was splitting the higher ranks of the navy. He became increasingly critical of the repetitive nature of fleet exercises, and especially of the favourite one of blockading the 'enemy' fleet in its own harbour without recognizing that the development of effective torpedoes had made this a risky operation. That his overall performance satisfied his superiors was demonstrated when he was given command of the new cruiser *Suffolk* (9800 tons) on 25 October 1904 for his last eleven months in the Mediterranean.

Long periods of separation had always been resented by naval wives, and Ethel was no exception. She became jealous of David's deep involvement in his professional and social life in Malta, and he, in turn, became critical of the frivolity of her life in London society and of the carping tone of her letters. Their relationship was never easy, but it never lacked vitality and affection. Eventually she joined him in Malta, where they lived in great style; on 22 February 1905 she gave birth to their first son, David Field (later second Earl Beatty). Their second son, Peter, was born on 2 April 1910.

The couple returned to England towards the end of 1905, and after a period on half pay Beatty became naval adviser to the Army Council on 21 December 1906. He was involved in planning the movement of the expeditionary force to France. Owing to Fisher's refusal to disclose his war plans, joint operations were not formally discussed with the military.

Beatty fulfilled the remaining requirement for flag rank by his successful command of the battleship *Queen* (completed 1904, 15,000 tons), serving in the Atlantic Fleet under Prince Louis of Battenberg as part of Fisher's concentration against the German high seas fleet. He exempted his new commander-in-chief from his condemnation of British admirals for their lack of imagination on the nature of future warfare, and the consequent unrealism of their training exercises. In general he approved of Fisher's wholesale reforms but disliked his devious methods of introducing them. His own captaincy of *Queen* was highly commended by Battenberg, and his promotion was promulgated on 1 January 1910. Save for attendance at the war college in spring 1911, he was not employed until January 1912, largely owing to his refusing the Admiralty's offer of an appointment as second in command of the Atlantic Fleet instead of the Home Fleet, which he preferred, judging it to be most important in a future German war. In view of his comparative youth for flag rank, this was perceived as arrogance; along with his wealth, this provoked criticism and jealousy.

Beatty was rescued from this impasse by Winston Churchill's becoming first lord of the Admiralty in 1911. Advised by Fisher to exercise particular care in his choice of naval secretary, Churchill selected Beatty after an interview in which he demonstrated 'the profound sagacity of his comments expressed in language free from technical jargon' (R. Churchill, 550).

In the absence of an organized naval staff, an able and determined naval secretary could exercise considerable influence over his political master. Beatty used the opportunity to the full, and despite his earlier suspicion began to appreciate Churchill's genuine enthusiasm for the navy and his ability in cabinet to further its interests. A paper that he addressed to Churchill in April 1912 on naval dispositions in a German war shows the maturity and perceptiveness of Beatty's contributions to their discussions (*Beatty Papers*, 1.36–45).

The practical result of Churchill's approbation led to Beatty's taking temporary command of an armoured cruiser squadron, with his flag in *Aboukir* for the fleet manoeuvres of July 1912. His success in bringing his command to fighting efficiency must have reminded his critics of his high leadership qualities. It certainly justified Churchill's decision to award him command of the battlecruiser squadron.

As always, difficulties in his marriage accentuated the problems of Beatty's naval career. Ethel seemed to take his successes for granted and did not offer the constant emotional support he expected. Her wealth opened the doors of London society and great country houses, but her divorced status prevented formal presentation at court and led to unrealistic arguments about his seeking another profession.

Ethel was determined to maintain her standard of living, and in July 1905 she had negotiated with her father a permanent financial settlement on which—as she triumphantly told her husband—they could live happily without getting into debt or needing to worry any more about money matters (*Beatty Papers*, 1.15–16). They certainly spent lavishly, with outgoings on houses bought or rented in London and the country, Ethel's extravagant holidays on the continent, horses, gambling, and eventually a steam yacht, *Sheelah*, which seemed to offer relief from her frenetic restlessness.

The battlecruiser squadron, 1913–1916 Beatty's appointment to the battlecruiser squadron did arouse some doubts. He was fourteen years younger than his predecessor and without fleet command experience, but he had the backing of Fisher, Churchill, and influential sections of the press. His temperament seemed ideally matched with the unique speed and hitting power of the force designed to locate the German fleet and prevent it from evading the stronger Grand Fleet.

In the months following his appointment Beatty defined the squadron's role: it should be the essential element in scouting sweeps through enemy waters in a

strength that could be countered only by equivalent capital ships, and thus precipitating the desired fleet action. As the contact developed it would directly support the Grand Fleet by defending its scouting forces and then forming the leading division of the whole line of battle. For such complex tasks the battlecruisers' crews had to display specific qualities of leadership, discipline, and fighting spirit. Captains had to be ready to take the initiative and not wait for detailed orders from Beatty when the circumstances of battle limited his knowledge of a rapidly changing situation, as long as they acted in accordance with his central aim, the annihilation of the enemy. He expected his officers to train their crews accordingly. Throughout the war Beatty consciously designed his visits to ships to inspire his men with his own offensive spirit and his confidence in victory.

At the beginning of war Beatty was confident of the readiness of his command and of the competence of his new commander-in-chief, Jellicoe, and of the Admiralty's ability to exercise overall control. The first months of hostilities soon made him realize that the navy's aim of early victory through a decisive fleet action would be far more difficult to achieve than he and the nation at large had foreseen. The enemy's realistic decision not to risk such an action, together with his own increasing awareness of the inhibition cast by mines and torpedoes on freedom of strategic and tactical mobility, along with the vagaries of weather and visibility in the North Sea, combined to obstruct the fleet's hopes. The Admiralty soon found it difficult to assess enemy intentions correctly and to convey clear information to the fleet, with a consequent growth of distrust among the sea commanders. Beatty faced the prospect of a future characterized by fruitless searches for an elusive enemy, each one followed by a return to base, the exhausting labour of coaling, and a wait for the next alarm, all leading to an increase in frustration throughout the squadron.

The action in the Heligoland Bight on 28 August 1914 was a positive relief. It established Beatty's force's readiness for combat and his own capacity to take responsibility in risking offensive action. His sweep into enemy waters in support of light forces resulted in the destruction of three enemy light cruisers and one destroyer; this was set against one British light cruiser seriously damaged and correspondingly fewer human casualties. Beatty's decision to withdraw his whole force without encountering enemy capital ships demonstrated his grasp of strategic priorities. But investigations after the event revealed omens for the future, prominent among them a weakness in reporting enemy movements, and inaccurate gunnery owing to the battlecruisers' speed and frequent changes of course. The most significant result of the battle was Beatty's disgust at the Admiralty's failure to co-ordinate the elements it had added to his command. This loss of trust in the Admiralty's competence was reinforced by the defeat of Admiral Christopher Craddock at Coronel, and, directly related to Beatty's own responsibilities, the enemy battlecruisers' success in evading interception after mining and bombardment raids on England's north-east coast in November and December 1914. The latter provided opportunity for fleet action, as the high seas fleet sailed in support of the battlecruisers. The Admiralty's intelligence organization directed the battlecruisers' movements, and Beatty—supported by a battleship squadron—was directed towards a good position for interception. But the sailing of the enemy battle fleet was not detected, and Jellicoe did not realize the urgency of approaching the combat area. Beatty's force never engaged his rival Franz von Hipper, largely because of repeated failures in reporting by his scouting cruisers—a situation made worse by Beatty and his signals staff, who caused the cruisers to lose contact with the enemy in the appalling weather which dominated the whole action. In turn, the German fleet commander, von Ingenohl, missed the opportunity to destroy Beatty's battlecruisers with his overwhelming force. On learning of the desultory encounter with light cruisers he decided that the Grand Fleet was approaching and returned to base.

Dogger Bank, 23 January 1915 After the failure to intercept the raid of December 1914 the Admiralty reshaped the Grand Fleet's organization and command structure. The battlecruiser base was moved from Cromarty to Rosyth. Jellicoe remained in overall fleet command, but on the first report of German fleet activity the Admiralty would take control of Beatty's squadron and the submarine, cruiser, and destroyer forces at Harwich and order them to an appropriate rendezvous. Once Jellicoe was at sea and in communication, he would assume operational control of the whole fleet. The battlecruisers were at sea on Christmas day 1914 in support of a seaplane raid against Cuxhaven and again on 18–19 January 1915 in support of a sweep by Commodore Tyrwhitt's Harwich force. No battlecruiser contacts were made, and the German commander-in-chief became confident that further sweeps could be repulsed by battlecruisers without support from the high seas fleet. The Admiralty, warned by the activity of Hipper's battlecruisers on 23 January, planned to cut them off from their base. Beatty was ordered to rendezvous with Tyrwhitt 30 miles off Dogger Bank. A battleship squadron and an armoured cruiser were ordered to positions 40 miles north-west to prevent any German breakaway, and the Grand Fleet was to move south from Scapa to confront any move by the high seas fleet. This plan succeeded when contact was made at 8 a.m. on 24 January, and Beatty, with superior force, stood between Hipper and his base. *Lion*, *Tiger*, *Princess Royal*, *New Zealand*, and *Indomitable* should have overwhelmed *Seydlitz*, *Moltke*, *Derfflinger*, and the armoured cruiser *Blucher*. Hipper turned for home as soon as he identified his enemy's battlecruisers, and Beatty followed in pursuit. *Blucher* and *Seydlitz* (the flagship) were both severely damaged, but events then turned against Beatty. His fire distribution orders were misinterpreted; *Moltke*, being free from attack by a British battlecruiser, concentrated its fire on *Lion*, which was hit repeatedly. Her speed was reduced, and at 10.50 a.m. she lost all electrical power, leaving only flag signals for communicating Beatty's orders. *Princess Royal*, *Tiger*, and *New Zealand* overhauled *Lion*, but their

close pursuit was delayed by Beatty's ordering a change of course; he claimed that he had seen an enemy submarine, but the claim was never confirmed. Rear-Admiral Archibald Moore in *New Zealand*, wrongly influenced by an ambiguous signal from Beatty, concentrated his fire to sink the crippled *Blucher*, thus allowing the battlecruisers to escape. When Beatty transferred to *Princess Royal* and resumed command he decided that it was too late to steam further into German waters and at 12.54 p.m. turned for home.

Modern research has stressed the poor performance of the British battlecruisers' gunnery; aside from the original shooting against *Blucher*, they achieved only six hits but received twenty in return. The bad shooting was due to smoke and the absence of effective director control (or range-finding apparatus) from all but *Tiger*, whose equipment failed during the action. Beatty's signalling difficulties ultimately led him to have the traditional signal 'engage the enemy more closely' reintroduced, and although he reluctantly admitted that the incompetence of his flag lieutenant had been partly responsible for his communication failures, he did not replace him.

The failure to crush his enemy counterparts was Beatty's responsibility. The Admiralty's plan was sound, the weather was neutral, and it was inevitable that after the event his inquiries and actions should be thorough. His most important practical conclusion was that the most favourable range for future engagements was 12,000–14,000 yards. Hitting could be effective at this distance; and it would be outside the reach of enemy secondary armament and surface-launched torpedoes. He was satisfied by the battlecruisers' ability to maintain their top speed, their chief defence against enemy attack, especially as their armour protection was inadequate against German armour-piercing shells. In any future battle, main and secondary armament firing should be as heavy as possible, and supplemented by cruiser and destroyer gunnery and torpedo attacks in a concentrated offensive, which itself was the best form of defence.

Beatty placed the responsibility for failure mainly on Rear-Admiral Archibald Moore, commanding the 2nd battlecruiser squadron in *New Zealand*, for not showing attacking initiative when his superior had to give up command, and on Captain Henry Pelly of *Tiger* for concentrating his fire on *Blucher* instead of *Moltke*. Both had failed to grasp that the objective was 'the complete destruction of the enemy … My signals and Standing Orders are intended for guidance as I have often stated, and not for rigid obedience if they tend to hinder the destruction of the enemy' (*Beatty Papers*, 1.247).

In a revision of his standing orders on 18 February 1915 Beatty developed his thought on the battlecruisers' role when working in close support of the battle fleet. They should avoid obstructing the vision or manoeuvring freedom of the heavier ships, and 'they should not come within range of enemy *Dreadnoughts* until our own Battle Fleet is engaged' (*Beatty Papers*, 1.254). They should then open fire immediately.

After Dogger Bank, Beatty's frustration increased with

his inability to achieve a fleet action and with the navy's failure to find a solution to the enemy's submarine campaign. Moreover his relations with Jellicoe became increasingly delicate, although he continued to hold him in genuine respect and agreed with him on major strategic issues, particularly in thinking that the Grand Fleet's prime task was the negation of its German rival and that no risks must be taken with its precarious superiority. Beatty particularly feared the enemy's increasing strength in torpedo craft, submarines, and the unique reconnaissance capability of Zeppelins; he thought that Jellicoe was not strong enough in his complaints to the Admiralty on these and other shortcomings. He admitted that the whole naval situation left him strained in temper and prone to minor ailments.

The Dogger Bank failure did not break Churchill's or Fisher's confidence in Beatty. In February 1915 Beatty's command was retitled the Battle-Cruiser Fleet and divided into three squadrons, each of three battlecruisers, with *Lion* as fleet flagship in addition. They were to be supported by three light cruiser squadrons, totalling thirteen ships and sixteen modern destroyers, all based at Rosyth. Beatty still agreed with Jellicoe that Scapa was the safer base for the Grand Fleet. What he did press for was greater community of thought with the Admiralty and for opportunities for discussion. His meeting with Jellicoe on 3 February 1916 was the first for five months, and he followed it up with increasing pressures on his commander-in-chief by passing on to him recommendations by two of his squadron commanders, Osmond de Brock and William Pakenham, that the Battle-Cruiser Fleet should be strengthened to balance the new more powerful vessels that were about to join the enemy fleet.

Beatty embodied these views in his own submission to the Admiralty, suggesting that the appropriate answer was to add the fast 5th battleship squadron to his force at Rosyth. Jellicoe argued that the battleships lacked the speed that Beatty claimed, but perhaps his main fear was that Beatty, so strengthened, would be tempted to fight a prolonged action with the high seas fleet rather than concentrate on his primary duty to lead it towards the superior Grand Fleet. This suspicion was probably unjustified, but it reflected the growing gulf between the two men and Jellicoe's resentment at his subordinate's direct correspondence with the Admiralty.

Alongside his professional burdens, Beatty's marriage brought additional strains. Ethel had persuaded the Admiralty to take up her yacht *Sheelah* as a hospital ship. Her genuine interest in the ship gave her grounds to rent Aberdour House, which was near enough to Rosyth for her husband to pay brief visits when the naval situation permitted. These were marked by mutual lack of sympathy and understanding.

Jutland: a marred victory Beatty's command on 31 May 1916 included six battlecruisers, with *Lion* as flagship; the 5th battle squadron of four fast ships under Rear-Admiral Hugh Evan-Thomas in *Barham*; twelve light cruisers; twenty-seven destroyers, plus three light cruisers as flotilla leaders; and the seaplane carrier *Engadine*. The battleships were there as a temporary replacement for three *Invincible* class battlecruisers detached to Scapa Flow for gunnery practice.

The battle of Jutland originated in a plan by the new German fleet commander, Rheinhard Scheer, to cut off Beatty's force without engaging the Grand Fleet. The Admiralty were alerted by enemy radio activity on 30 May and ordered Jellicoe and Beatty to sea. The benefits of this early warning were reduced by a lack of co-operation between the uniformed naval staff and the largely 'amateur' analysts of Room 40 in naval intelligence. Jellicoe was given an overestimate of German battleship strength and, more importantly, was told that it was still in port after it had sailed. This resulted in his moving south slowly and in Beatty's being unaware, when he intercepted the enemy, that he was soon to face not only the five battlecruisers but also the main German battle fleet. His confidence in the naval staff was permanently undermined.

When Beatty's battlecruisers opened fire at 3.48 p.m. on 31 May he failed to co-ordinate his attack with Evan-Thomas's battleships, which did not engage until twenty minutes later. He was totally unaware of the presence of the high seas fleet, but soon realized the destructive power of the German battlecruisers' gunnery; *Lion* was hit on her midship's turret. Worse was to come when *Indefatigable* and *Queen Mary* exploded before his eyes, with the loss of 1283 officers and men. This was the occasion of Beatty's often quoted remark to Chatfield, 'There seems to be something wrong with our bloody ships today' (Roskill, 160). His battleships were now in effective action; he ordered a destroyer attack against what he saw as a fleeing enemy, and seemed on the point of achieving his decisive victory despite his heavy losses. But the arrival of the high seas fleet reversed the situation, and he turned to lead the enemy into the jaws of Jellicoe's Grand Fleet, which unknown to the Germans was approaching the battle area. Beatty was later criticized for the inadequacy of his reporting of the situation, which caused Jellicoe to signal to him twice, 'Where is the enemy's Battle Fleet?' (ibid., 169), and for having to make his fundamental decision on deploying his own fleet to block the enemy retreat to its home ports without knowing its exact location and course. At 6.07 p.m. Beatty took up his allotted position ahead of the Grand Fleet. From then on he had to conform to the fleet's movements. But at 7.47 p.m., apprehensive that Jellicoe's pursuit was lagging, he signalled to him, 'Submit that van of battleships follows battle-cruisers. We can then cut off the whole of the enemy's battle fleet' (ibid., 177). Surprisingly, in view of his distaste for any independent movement by divisions of his fleet, Jellicoe agreed. However, Vice-Admiral Sir Martyn Jerram, commanding the leading division, claimed that he was unable to gain close contact with the battlecruisers, much to Beatty's suspicion and anger. This was an opportunity missed. Beatty did sight and engage the already seriously damaged *Seydlitz* and *Derfflinger* and a squadron of old battleships which, with Jerram's support, could well have been overcome. Beatty played no distinctive part in the confused night action, which ended in Sheer's escape. On 2 June he returned to Rosyth to join the gloom and controversy that followed.

Beatty's early correspondence with Jellicoe was free from rancour and full of sorrow for the heavy losses of ships and men, as well as frustration at the enemy's escape. He did share, however, in the fleet's general anger with the Admiralty's unduly alarmist releases to the press. He also reacted angrily at an Admiralty meeting with Jellicoe when the first sea lord, Sir Henry Jackson, criticized his failure to keep the 5th battle squadron in line with Jellicoe at the opening of the action. Beatty responded that if his earlier request for the battleships to be put under his command had been approved, Rear-Admiral Evan-Thomas and his ships would have absorbed the battlecruisers' combat procedures, and the delay in coming into action would never have occurred. This was a warning of future disputes, as was his wife's contribution to London gossip on Jellicoe's conduct of the battle. Despite its losses, the Grand Fleet was ready for action almost immediately, in numbers superior to those of a high seas fleet so seriously damaged in the battle that it never sought fleet action until October 1918 when, in desperation at Germany's plunge into defeat, the high command ordered it to do so and its crews mutinied.

Commander-in-chief of the Grand Fleet, 1916–1919 When Jellicoe was appointed first sea lord in November 1916 to revitalize the anti-submarine campaign, there was no realistic alternative to Beatty to succeed to the command of the Grand Fleet. He hoisted his flag on board *Iron duke* on 28 November, having been promoted acting admiral on the previous day. Some doubted his ability to handle and administer so huge a force; it had twenty-four battleships, three battlecruisers, nineteen cruisers, and fifty destroyers under direct command at Scapa Flow, in addition to the battlecruiser force at Rosyth now under his friend William Pakenham. The Grand Fleet itself comprised some 35,000 officers and men afloat, including three vice-admirals and six rear-admirals.

Beatty had prepared himself for this gigantic responsibility under the shadow of Jutland, determined that the failures of that day should not be repeated. The technical problems he left to his senior subordinates and his personal staff, but for tactical and strategic doctrine and above all for leadership he drew on his own resources. First was his confidence that victory could be gained, and second was his ability to convey this confidence to his subordinates, from flag officers to stokers. He cultivated decisiveness of speech, eccentricities of uniform, and as much personal contact as possible. 'The first thing that strikes you about him are his penetrating eyes. He has a phenomenally quick brain and he can take in all he wants to know in one glance … and decisions are given without a moment's hesitation' (Roskill, 148).

Beatty's experience since 1914 had increased his awareness of the uncertainties of sea warfare and hardened his insistence that decisive victory could come only from commitment to the offensive and to personal initiative at all levels of command. His display of self-confidence won over the most critical of his senior subordinates, sustained the loyalty of his personal staff, and maintained the fighting spirit of his men throughout the years of frustration that lay ahead. Hence his Nelsonic reputation. His grasp of strategic realities and the need to avoid unnecessary risks has been less clearly appreciated. Despite his hopes for a second Jutland, he accepted that a superior Grand Fleet, vigilant and informed by an efficient Admiralty intelligence system, would provide the essential basis of both a devastating economic blockade and the eventual defeat of the enemy's submarine campaign. He would not agree to any weakening of the fleet to deal with the unlikely danger of invasion. Sufficient deterrence could be provided by the light and submarine forces at Harwich, supported by a squadron of older battleships in the Thames estuary. Connected with this was his conviction, shared with the Admiralty and Jellicoe, of the dangers of any section of the fleet being deployed for battle in the southern North Sea; there German strength in submarines and mines and her Zeppelin reconnaissance might enable her to weaken his force so that it could no longer discharge its fundamental strategic roles.

Although his analysis of grand strategy was realistic, Beatty's hopes always focused on the achievements of the decisive battle which would compensate for the shortcoming of Jutland. His 'Grand fleet battle instructions', promulgated in 1916–18 (*Beatty Papers*, 1.456–506), replaced Jellicoe's 'Battle orders' and embodied his basic demands on his subordinates. They should always concentrate on annihilating the enemy without waiting for detailed orders. To achieve this they should attack with every available means: guns, underwater weapons, and aircraft. The last were to be used both in reconnaissance and in attack with bombs, torpedoes, and machine-guns. A retreating enemy must be hotly pursued by day and night. To avoid torpedo attack, ships should turn towards the enemy rather than away (as had happened at Jutland). The spirit of these instructions was instilled in all ranks by training and exercises. Beatty produced a visible demonstration of this commitment when in February 1917 he transferred his flag from *Iron duke* to *Queen Elizabeth*, which had a design speed of 25 instead of 21 knots. Even more significant were the removal of the Grand Fleet's base from Scapa Flow to the Firth of Forth in July 1917 and Beatty's pressure on the Admiralty to authorize aircraft-carrier strikes on the enemy fleet in harbour.

Events showed that even an imaginative combat doctrine and greater fighting resources could not overcome the uncertainties of sea warfare or individual failures of judgement. In October and December 1917 two lightly defended Scandinavian merchant convoys sustained heavy losses, and on 17 November an unsuccessful sweep by Pakenham's battlecruisers had missed an opportunity to inflict heavy losses.

The likelihood of Beatty's second Jutland receded, and 23 April 1918 was the last time on which he took his entire fleet to sea. In the following months the morale of the high seas fleet, already shaken by protests against poor conditions and harsh repression in August 1917, was hastened by signs of the breakdown of the imperial government and general social discontent caused by the economic blockade. Although Hipper, now commander-in-chief, repeated his readiness to seek action, his ability to do so declined, and with it Beatty's opportunity for battle.

This drawn-out disappointment at failure to secure his objective added to Beatty's exasperation with what he saw as the Admiralty's failure to counter the dangers to the alliance's war effort from the submarine campaign against merchant shipping. Although long aware of the threat of submerged weapons, he had never expected the type of unrestricted operations implemented by Germany in 1917. He never fully appreciated the technical and scientific difficulties of submarine detection and destruction, and denounced the Admiralty for not organizing offensive hunting operations. He was prevented from extreme denunciation of the lack of success only by the apprehension that he might be ordered to the Admiralty to give this leadership himself. He afterwards claimed to be an early advocate of the convoy system, which proved to be a solution to the problems, but he supported it only after deciding that all else had failed. And later he actually released some of his Grand Fleet destroyers for merchant convoy duties.

Perhaps Beatty's most important contribution was to use a meeting with Lloyd George to tackle the Admiralty on its opposition to convoy. In addition, however, he used his position as the allies' leading naval commander to intervene in political and diplomatic issues. He approached these with supreme self-confidence in correspondence and personal interviews with ministers, other influential politicians, and the king.

After the United States entered the war in April 1917 she put six battleships under Rear-Admiral Hugh Rodman at Beatty's disposal. A close professional accord developed between the two, and Beatty was soon reporting that the new ally was enthusiastically accepting his tactical doctrine and command style. But he never allowed himself to be overawed by America's wealth and power. He remained sceptical of her great technical contribution, the North Sea mine barrage. He also persuaded the minister for blockade, Robert Cecil, to modify his strong pressures on Norway, which he thought incompatible with the allies' claim to fight for the freedom of small nations.

Beatty's most significant political impact was made on the armistice of 1918. He insisted that the German fleet should surrender unconditionally to the Royal Navy, while the entire U-boat force should also be handed over. He personally staged the arrival in the Firth of Forth of the German fleet on 21 November so that they moved as prisoners between the lines of the Grand Fleet to receive his unauthorized signal: 'The German flag will be hauled down at sunset today, Thursday, and will not be hoisted again without permission' (Roskill, 279). The symbolism of the surrender was completed on 24 November when the enemy ships moved out of the Firth of Forth to be interned at Scapa Flow, escorted by the 1st battlecruiser squadron, his former command.

Two of Beatty's political objectives were not achieved. First, despite his arguments before the war cabinet, his case for depriving Germany of Heligoland was not pursued. Second, his claim that in the final peace terms the bulk of Germany's most modern capital ships should be allotted to Britain, rather than to her allies, foundered on 21 June 1919 when the ships were scuttled by their crews at Scapa Flow. By then Beatty, having been promoted admiral of the fleet (the youngest ever) on 3 April, had hauled down his flag on 7 April, avoiding responsibility for this ironic achievement of his victory over the high seas fleet.

The period from the immediate aftermath of Jutland to the end of the war was the most testing time of Beatty's career. It also coincided with occasional meetings with his wife that were full of mutual misunderstanding. However, he wrote to her almost daily: sometimes apologizing for his fits of bad temper; more often taking her into his confidence over his professional difficulties and his uninhibited criticisms of his naval and political colleagues. He was to find consolation in his increasingly close relationship with Eugénie Godfrey-Faussett, the wife of Captain Bryan Godfrey-Faussett, an equerry and friend of George V. She was a beautiful woman well known in London society for her wit and gaiety. Beatty at first reacted cautiously to her letters of admiration for the hero of Jutland, but soon responded with increasing warmth. Public scandal had to be avoided, but they probably became lovers during his visit to London in April 1917 and met again during her visits to Scotland. When he became first sea lord more opportunities arose, but the need to maintain secrecy and Beatty's continuing loyalty to Ethel, as her mental instability became more apparent, meant that the relationship with Eugénie was never free from strain.

First sea lord, 1919–1927 Beatty's failure to invite Fisher and Jellicoe to witness the German surrender was typical of the arrogance that characterized the end of his sea service and delayed his appointment as first sea lord until September 1919. He took his succession for granted, argued that his views on future policy were being ignored, and proposed a change in his title, substituting 'commander of his majesty's fleet' for 'chief of the naval staff'. He also quarrelled with the current first sea lord, Sir Rosslyn Wemyss, who had always treated him with consideration. The Northcliffe press strongly argued for Beatty's immediate appointment. In contrast, Churchill, now secretary for war and air in Lloyd George's coalition government, warned that it was necessary to wait for the present Admiralty board to accept deep cuts in naval expenditure before Beatty arrived to provide effective opposition. When the position was formally offered, Beatty accepted it on the traditional terms and soon enjoyed excellent relations with the first lord, Walter Long, who had been exasperated by his previous cantankerous attitude.

As professional head of the navy, Beatty considered that his primary duty was to ensure that Britain maintained the predominance at sea essential to her security, imperial power, and maritime trade. This depended on his ability to secure adequate funding from governments under strong pressures for economic and social reform and conscious of a widespread public abhorrence of preparations for war after the horrors and waste of 1914–18. This entailed working closely with politicians of all parties, fostering support from the press and organizations influential with public opinion. His impact on policy depended on the ability of his political superior, the first lord, to overcome the opposition of the Treasury, headed by the chancellor of the exchequer. Four of the five first lords under whom he served, Walter Long (who suffered from chronic ill health), Leopold Amery, Viscount Chelmsford, and William Bridgeman, respected his professional judgement and his genuine attempts to increase efficiency. They were equally impressed by his powers of argument in presenting the naval case in committee, relying on him to lead in all meetings except those of the cabinet. Occasionally the smooth relationship worked in reverse. During the struggle by the Admiralty in 1922–3 to regain control of naval aviation, Amery supported Beatty's arguments in cabinet, but persuaded him not to lead a resignation of all the naval members of the Admiralty board when the final decision went against him.

The one exception to Beatty's successful partnerships with his first lords was his relationship with Lord Lee of Fareham, who led the British delegation to the Washington conference. Beatty appealed to Arthur Balfour, the foreign secretary and a former first lord. Balfour agreed with Beatty that the American policy for an immediate 'holiday' for capital ship construction harmed Britain, but accepted his cabinet colleagues' decision that close political agreement with the Americans was the greater priority.

Beatty also showed considerable skill throughout his long term in office at cultivating political support for his naval policies: notably from Winston Churchill before he became chancellor of the exchequer; from Lord Curzon, foreign secretary; and from Lord Birkenhead, successively lord chancellor and secretary for India. He even found allies in the Labour government of 1924: J. H. Thomas, colonial secretary, Stephen Walsh, war secretary, and the lord chancellor, Haldane. He was pleasantly surprised by the active support given by the politically neutral Viscount Chelmsford, who accepted office as first lord only on the understanding that he would support Beatty's construction programme and the development of the Singapore base.

Convinced that his major role was to be on the political stage, Beatty ensured that he was freed from detailed administrative labours by a trusted naval staff. These included Osmond de Brock, his former chief of staff, who had been deputy chief of naval staff since August 1919; Chatfield, his flag captain throughout the war, became assistant chief of naval staff in 1920 and controller in 1925. Roger Keyes, a close friend and admirer, succeeded de Brock in 1921, and he himself was succeeded by Frederick

Field, whose professionalism Beatty highly respected. Personally close was the fleet paymaster Frank Spickernell, his secretary since his command of the battlecruiser squadron. These men supplied him with the technical information and draft policy papers which he needed to persuade cabinets, imperial conferences, and other influential bodies and occasions. He accepted that America's demand for naval parity could not be denied, but insisted that Britain's dependence on sea use necessitated superiority in cruisers.

It was inevitable that Beatty's most prominent political opponents were the successive chancellors of the exchequer, who were all equally convinced that drastic reductions in government expenditure were required to redress the vast expenditure and destruction of the war. The preparation of the annual naval estimates and the interdepartmental negotiations, and the ensuing parliamentary debates and final discussion with ministers to reach acceptable compromises, were at the centre of Beatty's attention.

Even before Beatty's arrival at the Admiralty, the board had warned the government that without immediately replacing battleships Britain would become the second naval power, with the battle cruiser *Hood* the only unit equal to the USA's capital ships after 1914. By 1920 the government was demanding a reduction of the 1920/21 naval estimates from £75 to £60 million, and set up a cabinet committee in December under Bonar Law, the leading Conservative in Lloyd George's coalition. Owing to Long's ill health, Beatty acted as a full member of the committee. This enabled him not only to present the Admiralty's case but also to select witnesses and cross-examine those hostile to his arguments. These included some senior officers, Herbert Richmond among them, who alleged that the advent of submarine and air weapons could threaten the supremacy of the battleship. The committee agreed that their case had not been established, but split on the need for immediate construction. Beatty correctly stressed that the expertise of the British battleship-building industry would be dissipated, and this proved a major impediment to naval rearmament in the 1930s. Further deliberations were superseded by the Washington conference of 1921, and it was within its limitation of numbers and size of capital ships that the Royal Navy had to develop for the remainder of Beatty's term of office.

Feeling that he could play no decisive part in the closing stages at Washington, Beatty had no hesitation in returning to London to counter a more serious threat to the navy's future. This was the 'Geddes Axe': *The Interim Report on National Expenditure* (1922), which recommended cuts in all elements of public expenditure. The naval estimates of 1922/3 were to be reduced from £81 million to £60 million, involving cuts in the numbers of officers and men. In his determination to limit the damage, Beatty received strong support from Churchill and Lord Birkenhead. The former was favourably impressed by the economies Beatty had already made, but the heavy reductions still remained, causing anger and bitterness in the service. The final result was a compromise, with estimates of just under £65 million being presented to parliament. The breakup of the coalition government and the Conservative administrations from October 1922 to January 1924 brought no respite. Disagreement over the estimates for 1924/5 was particularly fierce. Beatty decided to introduce a long-term building programme for cruisers, destroyers, aircraft-carriers, and submarines, estimated to cost £32.5 million over five years. This was opposed by Neville Chamberlain, the chancellor, but Leopold Amery, as first lord, secured estimates of £62 million, enabling the cruiser programme to begin. However, the fall of Baldwin and the succession of Ramsay MacDonald with a Labour minority government in January 1924 presented Beatty with an ideologically hostile cabinet, while Chancellor Philip Snowden was a particularly strong advocate of national economy. Beatty confronted them with a building programme of £260 million over nineteen years which would give Britain a 25 per cent superiority over Japan in cruisers and destroyers, as well as providing eighty submarines and four aircraft-carriers. A cabinet committee under J. R. Clynes (lord privy seal) considered Snowden's rejection of the expenditure involved. Beatty's performance in committee was highly impressive, and he gained parliamentary approval for his cruiser construction programme.

With the succession of Baldwin's second administration (December 1924–June 1929) Beatty might well have expected a more peaceful existence, but Winston Churchill, having rejoined the Conservatives, was determined to show himself a strong defender of the national purse against the spending departments. He used all his knowledge of the Admiralty's workings in the prolonged discussions of the 1925/6 estimates. He gradually shifted his attacks away from technical and financial matters to challenge Beatty's anticipation of Japan's likely hostility and naval capabilities over the next ten years. He proposed estimates of £60.5 million in reply to Beatty's proposed amounts, £65 million plus an additional sum for construction. A cabinet committee, this time under Lord Birkenhead, approved a programme of £58 million but extended it over seven years rather than the five favoured by Beatty.

Equally prominent in the continuous struggle for financial resources was Beatty's view of how to maintain Britain's position in the post-war world. He accepted that war with America was inconceivable. In Europe, after the defeat of Germany and the immersion of Russia in post-revolutionary chaos, a major war was improbable. The Far East was much more threatening. Japan was tending towards militaristic expansionism, and the likelihood that China would disintegrate, added to the spread of anti-colonialism throughout the area, would threaten the white dominions and India as well as Britain's vast commercial interests. America was unlikely to give active support, and the only possible defence should be provided by the presence of a British fleet to match Japan's naval potential. Such a fleet would require a base at Singapore to supply and maintain a force sent from European waters. This added greatly to the expense, and Beatty sought to persuade the overseas possessions to contribute to their own defence by joining an imperial navy under the Admiralty's strategic direction. This last requirement aroused strong suspicion from the increasingly independent dominions.

The control of naval aviation In 1917 Beatty had welcomed the new Air Ministry and Royal Air Force as institutions likely to produce more effective maritime air power than the contemporary Admiralty could. He was therefore willing to accept the proposal of the first chief of the air staff, Sir Hugh Trenchard, that the army and navy should refrain from controversy until the RAF had completed its organization. His own commitment to air power was fully illustrated during his command of the Grand Fleet and was shared by his predecessor as first sea lord, Rosslyn Wemyss. As soon as he entered the Admiralty, however, he decided that the existing arrangements with the Air Ministry were unsatisfactory and must be ended. Maurice Hankey, secretary of the committee of imperial defence, advised that this inter-service dispute demanded a high-level inquiry. This was established in 1923 under Balfour. Beatty skilfully narrowed his presentation to the committee to the demand that the navy should have its own small air arm, in the interests of both efficiency and economy. The existing arrangements produced a shortage of naval officers among aircrew, which would increase as more aircraft-carriers appeared. He argued that a sea commander must have confidence in air officers, whom he had himself trained, manning the planes, which were as much a part of the fleet as the guns of the ships. Despite the force of his advocacy, Beatty failed to convince the committee, who suspected that his ultimate aim was to weaken the Air Ministry. However, discussion in 1924 between Trenchard and Keyes, as deputy chief of naval staff, under the guidance of Haldane, decided that all future observers and ratings on the new carriers should be navally entered and trained. It was not until 1937 that full Admiralty control was established. The validity of Beatty's aim was demonstrated during the Second World War, when the Japanese and American navies, which had retained their own air forces, made such decisive use of air power in the war at sea.

As the construction of the Singapore base proceeded, the question of its defence raised a new dispute between the navy and the air force. Beatty's argument was that the base must be available by 1931, when navies would be free from the Washington limitations. He was sure that Japan would take advantage of this, and that only the completion and security of the naval base could provide a deterrent or actual defence. By 1924 the Admiralty planned to send a powerful fleet from home waters through the Mediterranean to Singapore. The most likely enemy attack would be by naval gunfire from Japan's fleet. Beatty argued that this should be provided in the time available by the mounting of heavy guns, which would keep Japan's fleet out of bombarding range. When the fleet had arrived and replenished itself and the base depots, it would move out to destroy the Imperial Japanese Navy. However, Trenchard and his supporters maintained that, given the government's belief in the unlikelihood of major war within ten years, the RAF should be equipped with torpedo bombers and fighter escorts capable of winning any naval action. This was 'substitution' in its starkest form, and Beatty fiercely resisted, particularly in the new forum of the chiefs of staff committee inaugurated in 1923. He was appointed chairman and was strongly supported by two successive chiefs of the imperial general staff, Lord Cavan and Sir George Milne, on this and other disputes with Trenchard.

Despite the continuing dispute over air power, Beatty's conduct of the business of the chiefs of staff committee showed a broadening of his views on inter-service relationships. In 1925 he initiated the chiefs' production of an annual review of defence policy. This was supplemented by increased attention to the quality of joint staff training and the preparation of war plans. He also took the lead in the organization and syllabus of the new imperial defence college, which studied problems forwarded by the chiefs. He was even willing to consider the creation of a Ministry of Defence, provided that the three single service ministers disappeared and the chiefs of staff were made directly responsible only to a secretary of state for defence.

The Jutland controversy, 1916–1927 The post-war analysis of Jutland proved controversial. The technological novelty of the battle, the impact on the guns' effectiveness of frequent changes in visibility, and the difficulties of keeping accurate records all combined to produce widely differing views on what had actually happened. The controversy in Britain was bound to be particularly bitter because her numerically superior fleet, positioned between the enemy and his base, failed to bring about the decisive action expected by the nation and the navy. Was it due to errors in command judgement, gunnery skill, or defective ammunition? The popular press took sides in the disputes which broke out in the service.

Jellicoe led the way with *The Grand Fleet* (1919), which tended to under-represent the achievement of the battle-cruiser force. Beatty's response was more bitter and prolonged. Year by year he became increasingly convinced that a decisive victory could have been won but for Jellicoe's lack of offensive spirit and willingness to take risks. This was a valid criticism. Less acceptable was the use of his personal authority to draw a contrast in all Admiralty publications between the battlecruisers' success in achieving their mission of leading the enemy into Jellicoe's grasp and the battle fleet's failure to seize the opportunity offered it. He never admitted any failures on his own part. Above all, he never produced a convincing answer to Jellicoe's complaint at his failure to report the enemy's exact position and course; the commander-in-chief needed this to guide his crucial decision on how to deploy the Grand Fleet in such a way as to cut off the enemy from its home ports. On the contrary, he ordered Captain J. E. T. Harper, the principal author of the *Official Record of the Battle of Jutland*, to alter diagrams and text to reinforce his interpretations. Although Harper's work was completed in 1920, it was not published in full until 1927 because of irreconcilable disagreements with Jellicoe and his supporters. Beatty also backed 'The naval staff

appreciation of Jutland', written by Commander A. C. Dewar and Captain K. G. B. Dewar as a confidential book; completed in 1922, it was never authorized for issue in full because of its partisan interpretations and criticism of Jellicoe. It was never officially issued, and Beatty's immediate successor, Charles Madden, ordered it to be destroyed in an attempt to end the harmful effects of the dispute. Beatty's copy survives in his papers in the National Maritime Museum. The material was sent to Sir Julian Corbett, author of *The History of the Great War: Naval Operations*, but this did not protect him from the Admiralty's insertion of disclaimers of his judgements in general and from its rejection in volume 3, dealing with Jutland specifically, of his tendency to dilute the operational primacy of the decisive battle. The bitter denunciations between contemporary supporters of Beatty and Jellicoe inevitably died away, but the controversy about what happened at Jutland, and why, retains its inexhaustible fascination for naval historians.

The 1926 review of defence policy, reiterated in Beatty's address to the imperial conference and supported by Sir George Milne (chief of imperial general staff), pointed to a basic degree of tri-service thinking. Politicians agreed that British interests demanded global military capability, and that this depended on freedom of sea passage, without which any system of imperial defence would collapse. This could be provided only by a fleet built to Washington standards, including battleships and aircraft-carriers, and, because aircraft would be used in the security of sea passage, air developments should be carefully watched.

At Beatty's death ten years later the international scene had changed for the worse. But Britain's relative weakness was due more to lack of political will and inadequate provision for defence than to naval conservatism. In his farewell letter Hankey described him as the only first sea lord of the twentieth century

> who could really talk on even terms to the highest cabinet ministers, and stand up to them in argument. Fisher is an exception, but Fisher was a crank, and even he didn't really state a case clearly … you have tremendous achievements to your name but your successful piloting of the COS Committee through its early days … will be one of your great contributions to the Empire's welfare. (*Beatty Papers*, 2.349)

Retirement and last years Retiring in his fifty-seventh year, Beatty could well have expected many years with adequate time and money for the country pursuits which meant so much to him. He could also look back with satisfaction on the outstanding marks of distinction awarded to him in 1919: the earldom, with its well-chosen courtesy title, baron of the North Sea, the parliamentary grant of £100,000, and the Order of Merit. Wider recognition had come from the universities, with their honorary doctorates, and from the acclamation of the press. Similar recognition was given to other war leaders, including Jellicoe, but none shared Beatty's popularity on the lower deck.

On his retirement on 29 July 1927 Beatty was sworn of the privy council, which facilitated his continuing membership of the committee of imperial defence, and in the following years he used his membership of the House of

Lords to speak on naval matters. He spoke from the cross-benches to mark his freedom from party allegiance, and his major speeches were praised for their conciseness and clarity. He was rightly famous for his bravery and spirit; his capacity for mature thought and judgement should equally be recognized.

Despite these official opportunities to further the navy's interests, extended as they were by supporting many voluntary organizations such as the Navy League, there were clouds over the future. Beatty's personal bitterness about Jutland, and the continuing dispute between his and Jellicoe's more extreme partisans, did no credit to the service. The flames of controversy were fanned among his supporters by political memoirs such as Churchill's *The World Crisis* (1923–31) and Lloyd George's *War Memoirs* (1933–6).

At a personal level, Beatty's peace of mind was constantly disturbed by his wife's mental instability. From 1919 she resumed the continental excursions which had relieved her chronic restlessness, now more significantly seeking a 'cure'. Once back in Britain she became increasingly subject to varying periods of eccentric behaviour and depression. Despite her frequent charges of lack of sympathy, her husband was remarkably tolerant for one who had long admitted to a bad temper. He refused to seek separation or divorce, and persuaded his close friends, including Eugénie, to give her companionship and diversion, and himself gave her constant support in the deepening melancholia in which she died at home on 17 July 1932.

By this time Beatty's own physical weakness was becoming apparent. A motoring accident in 1922 had fractured his breastbone, and this led to recurrent problems. In the 1930s a series of riding accidents resulted in a broken arm and a shattered jaw, which required immobility for three months. Recovery was followed by a further fall, resulting in more broken ribs. By 1935 this catalogue of accidents resulted in breathing difficulties and heart strain. He was the last man to accept medical advice for complete rest when it conflicted with his sense of duty. He insisted on acting as a pallbearer at Jellicoe's funeral in November 1935 and on attending George V's funeral in January 1936. After this he did rest, but it was too late, and he died of heart failure at his London home, 17 Grosvenor Square, on 12 March 1936. At his own funeral procession four days later his coffin was draped with the union flag, which he had so proudly flown as admiral of the fleet on *Queen Elizabeth* in April 1919. He was buried on 16 March in the crypt of St Paul's, close to Nelson and to Jellicoe. On 5 May 1936 Baldwin's motion for a memorial was carried in the Commons. However, it was not until 21 October 1948 that memorial busts to Jellicoe and himself were unveiled in Trafalgar Square.

Although best known as the gallant battlecruiser commander of 1914–16, Beatty proved himself as a highly effective fleet commander-in-chief, first sea lord, and chief of defence staff. The ability to meet new challenges demanded deep professional commitment and mental toughness, and he demonstrated possession of these qualities heroically throughout an exceptionally long career of high responsibility.   BRYAN RANFT

Sources S. Roskill, *Admiral of the Fleet Earl Beatty, the last naval hero* (1981) · *The Beatty papers: selections from the private and official correspondence, 1902–1927*, ed. B. Ranft, 2 vols. (1993) [1989] · W. S. Chalmers, *The life and letters of David, Earl Beatty* (1951) · A. J. Marder, *From the Dreadnought to Scapa Flow: the Royal Navy in the Fisher era, 1904–1919*, 5 vols. (1961–70) · J. S. Corbett and H. Newbolt, *Naval operations*, 5 vols. (1920–31) · D. M. Schurman, *Julian S. Corbett, 1854–1922: historian of British maritime policy from Drake to Jellicoe*, Royal Historical Society Studies in History, 26 (1981) · W. S. Churchill, *The world crisis*, 5 vols. (1923–9) · D. Lloyd George, *War memoirs*, 6 vols. (1933–6) · N. J. M. Campbell, *Jutland: analysis of the fighting* (1986) · A. Gordon, *The rules of the game: Jutland and British naval command* (1996) · A. J. P. Taylor, *English history, 1914–1945* (1965) · Burke, *Peerage* (2000) · R. S. Churchill, *Winston S. Churchill*, 1: *Youth, 1874–1900* (1966) · *CGPLA Eng. & Wales* (1936)

Archives NMM, corresp. and papers · NMM, log books | BL, corresp. with A. J. Balfour, Add. MS 49714 · BL, Rear-Admiral Sir Hugh Evan-Thomas, Add. MSS · BL, Vice-Admiral J. E. T. Harper, Add. MSS · BL, corresp. with Lord Jellicoe, Add. MS 49008 · BL, corresp. with Lord Keyes · BL, first Viscount Long, Add. MSS · CAC Cam., Viscount Bridgeman papers · CAC Cam., Admiral Sir Reginald E. E. Drax papers · CAC Cam., material for Sir Shane Leslie's biography and letters to Eugénie Godfrey-Faussett · CAC Cam., S. W. Roskill MSS · CUL, S. Baldwin papers · HLRO, A. Bonar Law papers · HLRO, letters to David Lloyd George · IWM, H. A. Gwynne papers · IWM, Admiral Sir Richard Phillimore papers · NA Scot., corresp. with A. J. Balfour · NMM, corresp. with Lord Chatfield · NMM, corresp. with Sir Julian S. Corbett · NMM, Vice-Admiral K. G. B. Dewar · NMM, Sir Eustace Tennyson d'Eyncourt papers · NMM, Admiral Frederick Hamilton papers · NMM, Admiral Sir John Kelly papers · NMM, letters to D. A. H. Larking · NMM, Captain Dennis Larking papers · Nuffield Oxf., corresp. with Lord Cherwell · priv. coll., L. S. Amery MSS · Royal Arch., King George V papers · Shrops. RRC, letters to first Viscount Bridgeman | FILM BFI NFTVA, 'Irish personalities', 1928 [footage of Beatty at the inauguration of the first Irish Free State parliament] · BFI NFTVA, current affairs footage · BFI NFTVA, documentary footage · BFI NFTVA, news footage · BFI NFTVA, record footage · IWM FVA, actuality footage · IWM FVA, documentary footage · IWM FVA, news footage | SOUND IWM SA, oral history interview

Likenesses F. Dodd, charcoal and watercolour drawing, 1914?, IWM · J. Lavery, oils, 1917, NPG [*see illus.*] · J. Lavery, oils, *c.*1918–1919, IWM · R. S. Sherriffs, ink and charcoal caricature, 1919, NPG · W. Stoneman, photograph, 1919, NPG · A. S. Cope, drawing, *c.*1921, NMM · A. S. Cope, group portrait, oils, 1921 (*Naval Officers of World War I, 1914–18*), NPG; related sketch, NPG · J. Lavery, group portrait, oils, 1924 (*The End*), IWM · W. Orpen, oils, *c.*1926, Scot. NPG · C. Dobson, oils, 1936; formerly, United Services Club, London · W. McMillan, bust, 1948, Trafalgar Square, London · H. Lund, lithograph, IWM

Wealth at death £174,902 18*s.* 2*d.*: probate, 26 May 1936, *CGPLA Eng. & Wales*

Beatty, Sir Edward Wentworth (1877–1943), railway entrepreneur in Canada, was born at Thorold, Ontario, on 16 October 1877, the third son and fourth child of Henry Beatty, shipowner, and his wife, Harriett M. Powell. He was educated at Upper Canada College and at the Harbord Collegiate and Parkdale Collegiate Institute (now the University of Toronto).

After studying at Osgoode Hall law school, Beatty was called to the bar of Ontario in 1901, when he joined the legal department of the Canadian Pacific Railway (CPR),

Sir Edward Wentworth Beatty (1877–1943), by Howard Coster, 1939

almost twenty years after his father had sold his Great Lakes shipping company to the railway, and where he remained as general shipping manager afterwards. Beatty moved rapidly through the ranks becoming general counsel for the railway in 1913, vice-president in 1914, and a director in 1916. Two years later the outgoing CPR president, Sir Thomas Shaughnessy, chose Beatty as his successor in preference to older and more experienced officials. Beatty's youth, as well as his lack of practical railway experience, made this one of the most controversial decisions of the day, and throughout the inter-war years the CPR's profitability fell in the face of vigorous competition from the newly nationalized Canadian National Railway (CNR) and the emerging highway trucking systems. Beatty was blamed by many for CPR's problems, and he was little helped by unsympathetic comparisons to his chief rival, Henry Thornton, the charismatic and outgoing president of the CNR.

Beatty always resented what he viewed as wasteful and unfair competition from the state-backed CNR. He laboured to end it through a merger of the two systems, free from direct state control, and it was a bitter blow to him when a royal commission permanently blocked his attempt at a Canadian railway monopoly in 1932. On the more positive side, Beatty tried to improve CPR's profitability by cutting railway expenses, expanding its more remunerative shipping operations, and moving into passenger airline services. The CPR was in fact beginning to recover when Beatty suffered a massive stroke in 1941, forcing him to retire from the presidency a year later.

A life-long bachelor, Beatty volunteered much of his time, abilities, and money to various causes. He served as chancellor of Queen's University (1919–23). As chancellor of McGill University (1921–43), he did not hesitate to use his position to remove prominent leftist academics from the faculty as part of his ongoing battle against socialism and state ownership. He was also chairman of the Rhodes scholarship committee for the province of Quebec, trustee and president of the Royal Victoria Hospital in Montreal, president of the Boy Scout Association of Canada, and president and chief financial mainstay of the Boys' Farm and Training School at Shawbridge, Quebec. In 1935 he was appointed GBE and made an honorary bencher of the Middle Temple. He became a Dominion KC in 1915 and received honorary degrees from twelve universities.

Beatty died at the Royal Victoria Hospital in Montreal on 23 March 1943.   GREGORY P. MARCHILDON

Sources W. K. Lamb, *History of the Canadian Pacific Railway* (1977) · D. H. Miller-Barstow, *Beatty of the CPR: a biography* (1951) · D. Cruise and A. Griffiths, *Lords of the line: the men who built the CPR* (1988) · *The Canadian Encyclopedia*, 2nd edn, 1 (1988) · M. Bliss, *Northern enterprise: five centuries of Canadian business* (1987) · G. D. Taylor and P. A. Baskerville, *A concise history of business in Canada* (1994) · G. R. Stevens, *History of the Canadian National railways* (1973) · R. F. Legget, *Railways of Canada* (1973)
Archives CPR Archives, Montreal, letter-books · NA Canada, Canadian Pacific Railway (CPR) MSS
Likenesses H. Coster, photograph, 1939, NPG [*see illus.*] · photograph, repro. in Lamb, *History of the Canadian Pacific Railway*, 303 · photographs, repro. in Cruise and Griffiths, *Lords of the line*, pp. 294, 302, 339, 348, 352, 358
Wealth at death over C$1,000,000: *Lords of the line*, 304 · £902 18s. 2d.: administration with will, 24 Jan 1944, *CGPLA Eng. & Wales*

Beatty, Sir William (*d.* 1842), naval surgeon, joined the navy at an early age, and saw much service in it in various parts of the world. In 1806 he was appointed physician to the Royal Naval Hospital, Greenwich, an office which he retained until 1840. He attended Nelson after he received his fatal wound, performed the autopsy, and published *An Authentic Narrative of the Death of Lord Nelson* (1807), which included a representation of the ball which killed Nelson, with the pieces of the coat, gold lace, and silk pad which remained fixed in it. The ball Beatty retained in his possession in a crystal case mounted in gold; he bequeathed this to the queen. Beatty obtained an MD from the University of St Andrews on 14 October 1817, was made LRCP on 22 December of the same year, and was elected FRS on 30 April 1818. On 25 May 1831 he was knighted by William IV. He died at his house in York Street, Portman Square, London, on 25 March 1842.

T. F. HENDERSON, *rev.* ANDREW LAMBERT

Sources T. Pocock, *Horatio Nelson* (1987) · C. Beresford and H. W. Wilson, *Nelson and his times* [n.d.] · C. White, ed., *The Nelson companion* (1995) · *GM*, 2nd ser., 18 (1842), 209
Archives Wellcome L.
Likenesses A. W. Devis, oils, 1805–7, NMM · A. W. Devis, group portrait, oils, 1806 (*The death of Nelson*), NMM

Beauchamp. For this title name *see* individual entries under Beauchamp; *see also* Seymour, Edward, Viscount Beauchamp (1561–1612) [*see under* Seymour, Edward, first earl of Hertford (1539?–1621)]; Lygon, William, first Earl Beauchamp (1747–1816) [*see under* Lygon, Frederick, sixth Earl Beauchamp (1830–1891)]; Lygon, Frederick, sixth Earl Beauchamp (1830–1891); Lygon, William, seventh Earl Beauchamp (1872–1938).

Beauchamp, de, family (*per. c.*1080–*c.*1265), gentry, held a modest barony of about forty-five knights' fees, predominantly in Bedfordshire, with some land in Buckinghamshire, Hertfordshire, Cambridgeshire, Essex, and Huntingdonshire. The family exercised a local dominance in Bedfordshire, but was only occasionally prominent on the national stage. No connection has been found to the Beauchamps of Worcester. The family was first represented by **Hugh de Beauchamp** (*fl.* 1080–*c.*1118), presumably of Norman origin, who acquired his lands and position through marriage to Matilda, apparently the daughter and heir of Ralf Tallebosc, post-conquest castellan of Bedford and sheriff of Bedfordshire, and Azelina, who held lands in Bedfordshire and Cambridgeshire in her own right. Information for the early twelfth century is scarce, but Hugh seems to have had at least two sons, Simon and Robert. **Simon [i] de Beauchamp** (*d.* 1136/7), who witnessed King Stephen's charter of liberties as royal steward in 1136, was probably the eldest son and heir to the barony. His daughter married Hugh Poer, who was granted the honour and castle of Bedford and created earl by King Stephen, to the anger of Robert's sons, who believed they were being deprived of their rightful inheritance. The elder son, **Miles de Beauchamp** (*d.* 1142×53), tried unsuccessfully to turn Stephen's problems to his advantage, promising to support Stephen if he did not try to remove him from Bedford Castle, but he was forced out after a siege at Christmas 1137. In 1141 Miles and his followers recovered the castle, 'as triumphant and fierce as they had once been humble and downcast' (*Gesta Stephani*, 33), only to lose it once again before both barony and castle were returned to the Beauchamps by Henry II.

Miles's brother and heir, **Payn de Beauchamp** (*d.* in or before 1155), was both outlived and overshadowed by his wife, **Rohese** [Rose] **de Beauchamp** (*d.* 1166). The daughter of Aubrey (II) de *Vere (*d.* 1141), she had previously been married to the powerful Geoffrey de *Mandeville, first earl of Essex (*d.* 1144). The connection between the two families remained close for some time, with the Beauchamps adopting a variation of the Mandeville arms. In common with most of their contemporaries the earlier Beauchamps had already made grants to religious houses, including St Albans and Bermondsey, but the Beauchamps' patronage of the church now moved onto a new plane with the foundation of a priory for Gilbertine nuns at Chicksands, Bedfordshire, *c.*1150. Although her husband, Payn, was associated with her in early charters, Rohese was always spoken of as the founder. Her support for the priory and her forceful personality were vividly illustrated by her response to the death of her son from her first marriage, Geoffrey de Mandeville. After his death his men tried to take his body to Walden, Essex, for burial at the abbey founded by his father. On hearing this Rohese gathered a band of armed retainers and caught up with the cortège, ordering it to go instead to Chicksands. However, early the next morning her son's servants turned the bier around and took it to Walden Abbey before Rohese could prevent it. Thwarted in her efforts to have her son's body in her own chosen burial place, Rohese retaliated by taking all the furnishings of Geoffrey's private chapel for Chicksands. Rohese was also closely involved in the early stages of the foundation (*c.*1166) of Newnham Priory by her son **Simon [ii] de Beauchamp** (*c.*1145–1206/7). This conversion of the college of secular canons at St Paul's, Bedford, into a community of regular Augustinian canons was part of the widespread contemporary movement towards the regular monastic orders. It has traditionally been linked with the case of Philip de Broy, a canon of Bedford accused of homicide. The failure of the church courts to deal adequately with his case was one of the grievances of Henry II against Thomas Becket, and this notorious incident may have acted as a catalyst by attracting attention to Bedford. Simon was a generous patron of the church; he made several additions to Newnham's original endowment, and also made grants to Warden Abbey, Chicksands Priory, and the hospital of St John at Bedford.

Simon [ii] de Beauchamp held the Bedford barony for over fifty years, including a nine-year minority. The Beauchamp family clearly had a claim to be hereditary constables of Bedford Castle, but it was not acknowledged as a formality: in 1189/90 Simon had to pay £100 for custody of the castle. From 1194 to 1197 he served as sheriff of Bedfordshire and Buckinghamshire, but only after paying 200 marks for the privilege. Simon was succeeded by his son, William de *Beauchamp (*c.*1185–1260), who served in the royal army in Ireland in 1210 and Poitou in 1214, but who joined the rebels in 1215 and was excommunicated by Pope Innocent III. Captured at the battle of Lincoln, he was soon restored to favour. Bedford Castle, however, had been taken by Falkes de Bréauté in December 1215. Following his fall from power, Bréauté was forced out after a siege in 1224, and the castle partially demolished. It was returned to William on condition that he maintain only an unfortified residence there. In his later years, William served as a baron of the exchequer, as sheriff of Bedfordshire and Buckinghamshire, and as hereditary almoner at the coronation of Henry and Eleanor in 1236. He married first Gunnora de Lanvaley (*d.* before 1220), and second, Ida (*d.* 1266×9), daughter of William *Longespée, earl of Salisbury. William was praised in the *Flores historiarum* as a benefactor of the church, but with Ida he became involved in disputes with Newnham Priory and Warden Abbey. His younger brother Geoffrey was also to be found in the king's service; he fought in both Wales and Gascony, and served as provost of Bayonne in 1253–4.

Clearly another forceful woman, after her husband's death Ida raided Simon of Pattishall's manor of Little Crawley, Buckinghamshire. Marriage to Ida brought William the manor of Newport Pagnell and patronage of the priory there, which she held as dower from her first marriage to Ralph de Somery. The temporary nature of this acquisition is typical of the Beauchamp family, whose land holdings remained virtually constant throughout the twelfth and thirteenth centuries. In 1257 William surrendered his barony to his third son **William de Beauchamp** (d. 1262), his elder sons John and Simon [iii] having predeceased him. He died at an advanced age in 1260. The younger William held the barony for only five years until his death, reputedly by poison, after which the Beauchamp lands were in wardship while his brother and heir **John de Beauchamp** (b. after 1241, d. 1265) was a minor. John was killed fighting for Simon de Montfort at the battle of Evesham on 4 August 1265. His niece and heir Joan, Simon [iii]'s daughter, died soon after. Of John's three sisters, Matilda (d. by 1275) married first Roger de Mowbray and second Roger *Lestrange (d. 1311), Ela married Baldwin de Wake, and Beatrice married first Thomas fitz Otto and second William de Munchensi, of Edwardstone, Suffolk. The barony was broken up by division between the sisters and their heirs. The Beauchamp family arms were quarterly or and gules, a bend gules.

KATHRYN FAULKNER

Sources C. Gore Chambers and G. H. Fowler, *The Beauchamps, barons of Bedford*, Bedfordshire Historical RS, 1 (1913), 1–24 • J. Godber, ed., *The cartulary of Newnham Priory*, 1 vol. in 2 pts, Bedfordshire Historical RS, 43 (1963–4) • G. H. Fowler, *Early charters of the priory of Chicksand*, Bedfordshire Historical RS, 1 (1913), 101–23 • *VCH Bedfordshire* • J. Godber, *History of Bedfordshire, 1066–1888* (1969) • *Chancery records* • *Pipe rolls* • *Ann. mon.*, vol. 3 • *Paris, Chron.* • K. R. Potter and R. H. C. Davis, eds., *Gesta Stephani*, OMT (1976) • H. R. Luard, ed., *Flores historiarum*, 3 vols., Rolls Series, 95 (1890) • *CIPM*, 1, no. 516 • *Calendar of inquisitions miscellaneous (chancery)*, PRO, 1 (1916), 612–13, 629, 936

Beauchamp, Guy de, tenth earl of Warwick (c.1272–1315), magnate, was the son of William (IV) de *Beauchamp, ninth earl of Warwick (c.1238–1298), and his wife, Matilda (or Maud) (d. 1301), daughter of John fitz Geoffrey; he succeeded his father as earl on the latter's death in 1298. During the reign of Edward I he distinguished himself by service in Scotland and elsewhere. Soon after the battle of Falkirk (22 July 1298), he received Scottish lands valued at 1000 marks per annum. In May of the following year he was given protection on going overseas on the king's business, and received a respite of his father's debt of £180 to the Riccardi of Lucca. Present at the wedding of Edward I to Margaret of France at Canterbury on 10 September 1299, in the following year he participated in the siege of Caerlaverock. At Easter 1301 he was among the English negotiators who met with French envoys at Canterbury seeking the release of King John Balliol. He was also one of seven earls who sealed the letter of 12 February 1301 to the pope, rejecting his authority on the Scottish question. In recognition of his service, in 1301 Beauchamp was granted an extension on the payment of his own and his ancestors' debts to the crown. He campaigned in Scotland in 1303–4, being present at Perth and at the siege of Stirling in the company of the prince of Wales. In 1305 he received a grant of murage and pavage for the town of Warwick for a term of seven years. He was ordered to join

Prince Edward in London in March 1307, as a member of the party preparing to travel to France, but this journey was not undertaken. Later in 1307 Edward I rewarded Warwick's service one last time by granting him John Balliol's lordship of Barnard Castle in co. Durham.

Earl Guy was present at the death of Edward I at Burgh-on-Sands on 7 July 1307. He may on that occasion, as the author of the *Brut* chronicle relates, have been one of those charged to look after Edward of Caernarfon, and particularly to prevent the return from exile of Piers Gaveston. He alone among the leading earls did not seal Gaveston's charter of enfeoffment as earl of Cornwall dated 6 August 1307. Indeed, from the outset of the reign of Edward II, Guy de Beauchamp is consistently named by chroniclers and informed correspondents as being among the leaders of the opposition to the crown. In part this may have resulted from the new king's Scottish policy, which jeopardized the earl's own holdings. At the coronation of Edward II, along with the earls of Lancaster and Lincoln, he carried a ceremonial sword. He was certainly among those who called for Gaveston's return to exile following the coronation, and even after this was achieved he remained in opposition. Although he attended the Northampton parliament in August 1308, and appears occasionally in the witness lists of the charter rolls between August and November, Warwick refused to be reconciled with the king, despite such gifts as the grant of four templar manors in Warwickshire in December 1308. As the author of the *Vita Edwardi secundi* remarks, 'The Earl of Warwick alone could not be prevailed upon. He said that he could not with a clean conscience go back upon what had been decided' (*Vita Edwardi secundi*, 7).

After Gaveston's return to England following his second exile in June 1309, tensions again surfaced between the king and his magnates. The Black Dog of Arden, as the favourite nicknamed him, was a driving force behind the commissioning and the drafting of the ordinances of 1311. In October 1309 he joined the earls of Lancaster, Lincoln, Oxford, and Arundel in refusing to attend a council at York because of the favourite's presence. In February of the following year he was forbidden to come armed to parliament, but that very parliament forced the king on 16 March 1310 to agree to the appointment of the *lords ordainer to reform his household and realm. The earl of Warwick was particularly active in the drafting of the ordinances. The author of the *Vita* describes him as the leader of the genuine reformers, and he consistently attended meetings, generally along with the earls of Lancaster, Hereford, and Pembroke, at which the actual drafting of the ordinances took place. He was present at their publication on 27 September 1311 at St Paul's.

Warwick is perhaps best known for his role in the death of Gaveston. After the favourite had surrendered at Scarborough on 19 May 1312, he was conducted south by Aymer de Valence, earl of Pembroke. At Deddington, Oxfordshire, on 10 June, Warwick seized the prisoner and conveyed him back to Warwick Castle, where he was tried after a fashion and sentenced to death. Although Warwick is depicted standing over the beheaded Gaveston in the late fifteenth-century Rous roll, the execution actually took place on the lands of the earl of Lancaster, and according to the *Annales Londonienses* the earl of Warwick refused to accept the corpse when presented with it by four shoemakers, ordering them to return it to the site of the beheading. Needless to say, relations with the king were strained by this violent confrontation. England came close to civil war, and protracted negotiations were entered into which finally resulted in the pardon of Warwick and others only in October 1313. Nevertheless, the earl refused to serve with the king in Scotland in the 1314 campaign that culminated in the disaster at Bannockburn. Despite this military setback, or perhaps because of it, by early 1315 Warwick, according to the *Annales Londonienses*, was 'the principal member of the king's council' (Stubbs, 1.232). Within months, however, the earl was dead.

Warwick died, aged forty-three, on 12 August 1315. He was buried at Bordesley Abbey in Worcestershire, a Cistercian house patronized by the Beauchamps and to which Earl Guy had previously given his library, which included a large number of romances and saints' lives. Walsingham's chronicle reports a rumour that the earl was poisoned by unnamed members of the king's inner circle. Warwick is described in the chronicles as a man of 'wisdom and probity' (*Chronicon de Lanercost*, 216), and 'a discriminating and highly literate man, the wisdom of whom shone forth through the whole kingdom' (Stubbs, 1.236). 'In wisdom and council', the *Vita* says, 'he had no peer' (*Vita Edwardi secundi*, 63). One of the great magnates of England, the earl of Warwick held lands in nineteen counties, the march of Wales, and Scotland, with the greatest concentration of his holdings being in Warwickshire and Worcestershire. Plans for his marriage to Isabel de Clare, daughter of the earl of Gloucester, seem to have fallen through, and he married Alice, widow of Thomas of Leyburn and sister of Robert Tosny, early in 1309. Their son Thomas *Beauchamp, probably born on 14 February 1314 and named after the earl of Lancaster, was his heir.

J. S. HAMILTON

Sources CIPM, 5 · J. R. Maddicott, *Thomas of Lancaster, 1307–1322: a study in the reign of Edward II* (1970) · J. R. S. Phillips, *Aymer de Valence, earl of Pembroke, 1307–1324: baronial politics in the reign of Edward II* (1972) · J. S. Hamilton, *Piers Gaveston, earl of Cornwall, 1307–1312: politics and patronage in the reign of Edward II* (1988) · Chancery records · PRO, Chancery, charter rolls, C53 · N. Denholm-Young, ed. and trans., *Vita Edwardi secundi* (1957) · W. Stubbs, ed., 'Annales Londonienses', *Chronicles of the reigns of Edward I and Edward II*, 1, Rolls Series, 76 (1882), 1–251 · V. B. Richmond, *The legend of Guy of Warwick*, Garland Studies in Medieval Literature, 14 (1996) · GEC, *Peerage*, new edn, 12/2.368–72 · *Thomae Walsingham, quondam monachi S. Albani, historia Anglicana*, ed. H. T. Riley, 2 vols., pt 1 of *Chronica monasterii S. Albani*, Rolls Series, 28 (1863–4) · J. Stevenson, ed., *Chronicon de Lanercost, 1201–1346*, Bannatyne Club, 65 (1839) · M. Blaess, 'L'abbaye de Bordesley et les livres de Guy de Beauchamp', *Romania*, 78 (1957), 511–18
Likenesses seal, 1301, BL; Birch, *Seals*, 5658 · portrait, Bodl. Oxf., Rous roll, Dugdale 14

Wealth at death wealthy; in excess of 100 knight's fees: CIPM, Edward II, vol. 5, 397–413

Beauchamp, Henry, duke of Warwick (1425–1446), magnate, was the only son, and heir, of Richard *Beauchamp, earl of Warwick (d. 1439), with his second wife, Isabella, sister and heir of Richard, Lord Despenser, and widow of Richard Beauchamp, heir of Bergavenny and earl of Worcester. Henry, who had three older sisters from his father's first marriage, to the Berkeley heiress, was born at the Despenser property of Hanley Castle in Worcestershire on 22 March 1425. His godparents were Cardinal Beaufort, the earl of Stafford, Joan Beauchamp, Lady Bergavenny, and Philip Morgan, bishop of Worcester. As a child he accompanied his father overseas at least once. In 1434 he married Cecily Neville (d. 1450), the second daughter of Richard Neville, earl of Salisbury. At the same time Henry's only full sister, Anne, was married to Salisbury's eldest son and heir, also called Richard.

Both of Beauchamp's parents died while he was still a minor, his father in France in April 1439 and his mother the following December. He thus became heir to a large estate, most of it in the west midlands and south Wales, centred on the Beauchamp political capitals of Warwick and Elmley (Worcestershire) and the Despenser one of Tewkesbury (Gloucestershire), although there were outliers in, for example, Cornwall, Staffordshire, the east midlands, Durham, and East Anglia. With the lands went the hereditary offices of chamberlain of the exchequer and sheriff of Worcestershire. He also inherited the Hastings lands, including the lordship of Bergavenny, together with the Warwick estates which had been granted to William Beauchamp, Lord Bergavenny, both of which had come to his father under entail in 1435, although most of the Warwick estates in the entail had been placed in the Beauchamp trust. During his minority, custody of much of his land was held by a group comprising mainly close servants of his father, including William Mountford of Warwickshire, John Throgmorton of Warwickshire and Worcestershire, and John Vampage of Worcestershire, but led by two rising figures at court, Lord Sudeley and Lord Beauchamp of Powick, the latter of whom had a long-standing connection with the boy, as he had presented him at his confirmation.

As early as 1442 Henry Beauchamp was already benefiting from the generosity with grants characteristic of Henry VI's majority. While it is now clear that it would be unwise to divide the nobles in the 1440s into a small number of privileged courtier nobility and a larger body of disgruntled outsiders, Beauchamp seems to have been regarded as a promising recruit by the group around the duke of Suffolk who were managing the kingdom. Indeed part of his father's following, notably Mountford, was moving in the same direction. It may well be that Henry was seen by Sudeley and Beauchamp of Powick as the focus for a possible alternative power base within the household. He continued to be the recipient of grants to the end of his life, including, in 1444, the reversion of the manor and forest of Feckenham, Worcestershire, held by

Humphrey, duke of Gloucester, and the marriage of the heir of the earl of Arundel in 1445. He was a royal counsellor as early as 1441. In 1444 he was given the reversion of a number of offices in the duchy of Lancaster honours of Tutbury and of the High Peak in Staffordshire and Derbyshire, most notably the stewardship of Tutbury, with inheritance in tail male. The Tutbury offices had been granted, eventually for life, to Humphrey, earl of Stafford, in 1435 and 1437, and the prospect of their eventual alienation to someone who was then so young, whose interests in the north midlands were nothing like as strong as his own, and the eventual exclusion of any other grantees, including the Staffords, must have seemed profoundly insulting to Humphrey. That this was much more a matter of indiscriminate gift-giving, and possibly of internal division within the royal household, than a sign that Stafford was no longer *persona grata* at court can be seen from the leap-frogging in titles of the two men in 1444–5: Warwick was made premier earl in April 1444, Stafford created duke of Buckingham in September, Warwick made a duke in April 1445 and given precedence over all other dukes except for Norfolk but, rather farcically, was later made to alternate precedence with Buckingham. Although there is no formal record of grant of livery of Henry Beauchamp's lands (many were in any case in the hands of feoffees), a royal signet letter of July 1445 instructed that he be placed on appropriate commissions of the peace, and in February 1446, just before he was officially of age, he was appointed to the Warwickshire commission.

In Warwickshire Henry Beauchamp inherited a situation in which the power of his father's affinity, which had once embraced the whole county and much of its periphery, had been seriously diluted during his minority. However, no one else had been able to replace Richard Beauchamp's hegemony. The problem was that this was a county whose geography and tenurial structures deprived it of any natural unity, and strong noble leadership, preferably backed by authoritative kingship, would always be essential if it was to function cohesively as a political and administrative entity. Consequently, the coincidence of a minority in the obvious ruling family and failure of kingship had led to a period of incoherence in local governance. Buckingham himself had made an unsuccessful attempt to master the county from his power base in the north midlands and north Warwickshire, and the west Warwickshire/east Worcestershire heartland of Warwick power was being taken over by Beauchamp of Powick and Sudeley. Henry Beauchamp needed to reconstitute his father's affinity and rebuild the family authority in Warwickshire and the west midlands. From 1444 the appointments to Warwickshire offices and other evidence suggest that Beauchamp was succeeding in re-establishing the family position. The fact that he could look forward to possession of the duchy authority in the counties to the north, which his father had never had, should have made his task relatively easier.

However, Henry Beauchamp's efforts foundered on three interlinked difficulties. First there were the divisions within the Warwick affinity which he was never able to heal properly; most damagingly, he was particularly unsuccessful in reabsorbing those at the geographical core who had drifted towards Sudeley and Beauchamp of Powick. Then he came up against Buckingham in local as well as national politics and, here again, he found himself at odds with some of his father's former supporters among the local gentry. Finally, and most seriously, deep rifts began to appear within his own immediate following, notably with the Verneys, a rising family from Compton Murdack (Compton Verney) in south Warwickshire. They had done well out of service to Beauchamp's father and now seem to have been trying to exploit the youth and inexperience of Henry Beauchamp himself and his bad relationship with Buckingham. In 1445–6 there was a period of considerable confusion in Warwickshire politics, caused principally by the personal failure of Duke Henry, the man with much the greatest power within the county, in which none of the local magnates appear to have been able to manage either local governance or their own affinities. It was only the sudden death of Beauchamp at Hanley on 11 June 1446 that made it possible for a measure of local equilibrium to be restored. His commendation in the Rous roll for piety and justice seems somewhat out of keeping with what is known of his career (Rous, ed. Ross, no. 54). He was buried, with the rest of the Despenser line, in Tewkesbury Abbey.

Henry Beauchamp was succeeded by his daughter Anne, then two years old, who was placed in the custody of Suffolk, but who died in 1449 at Suffolk's residence of Ewelme, Oxfordshire. The title and much of the estate descended to Richard Neville, the Kingmaker, as husband of Beauchamp's only full sister. In 1449 Henry Beauchamp's widow married John Tiptoft, later earl of Worcester.

CHRISTINE CARPENTER

Sources Chancery records · PRO, C 139/123; E 368/220, m 107d · W. Dugdale, *The baronage of England*, 2 vols. (1675–6) · Dugdale, *Monasticon*, 2.63–4 · J. Watts, *Henry VI and the politics of kingship* (1996) · C. Carpenter, *Locality and polity: a study of Warwickshire landed society, 1401–1499* (1992) · *Thys rol was laburd and finished by Master John Rows of Warrewyk*, ed. W. Courthope (1859); repr. as *The Rous roll* (1980) [with historical introduction by C. Ross] · R. Somerville, *History of the duchy of Lancaster, 1265–1603* (1953) [appx of officers] · N. H. Nicolas, ed., *Proceedings and ordinances of the privy council of England*, 7 vols., RC, 26 (1834–7) · *Pageant of the birth, life and death of Richard Beauchamp, earl of Warwick*, ed. Viscount Dillon and W. H. St John Hope (1914), 100 · A. F. J. Sinclair, 'The Beauchamp earls of Warwick in the later middle ages', PhD diss., U. Lond., 1987 · M. A. Hicks, 'The Beauchamp trust, 1439–87', *BIHR*, 54 (1981), 135–49 · H. Castor, 'New evidence on the grant of duchy of Lancaster office to Henry Beauchamp, earl of Warwick in 1444', *Historical Research*, 68 (1995), 225–8 · Shakespeare Birthplace Trust RO, Stratford upon Avon, Archer MSS · Worcs. RO, Holland and Martin MSS · Oxon. RO, Dillon MSS · Birm. CL, Birmingham MSS

Archives PRO, account of keepers of his lands, E 368/220 m 107d

Likenesses drawing, repro. in Courthope, ed., *Rous roll* · drawing (as a child), repro. in Dillon and St John Hope, *Pageant of the birth, life and death* · figure on monument, St Mary's Church, Warwick

Wealth at death see PRO, C 139/123

Beauchamp, Hugh de (*fl.* 1080–*c.*1118). *See under* Beauchamp, de, family (*per. c.*1080–*c.*1265).

Beauchamp, Joan (1375–1435). *See under* Beauchamp, William (V), first Baron Bergavenny (*c.*1343–1411).

Beauchamp, John de (*b.* after 1241, *d.* 1265). *See under* Beauchamp, de, family (*per. c.*1080–*c.*1265).

Beauchamp, John, first Baron Beauchamp of Kidderminster (*d.* 1388), administrator and landowner, came from Holt in Worcestershire, and belonged to a cadet branch of the great family of Beauchamp, whose head was the earl of Warwick. He was the son of another John (*b.* 1319), whom he succeeded in the 1360s. His marriage about 1370 to Joan, daughter and heir of Robert Fitzwith, brought him the manors of Bubbenhall, Barnacle, and Shotteswell in Warwickshire, and Wigginton, Ardley, and Weston in Oxfordshire, which with Holt gave him some £80 a year. He had earlier joined his father, John, in the household of Edward III, and in 1365, as an esquire of the chamber, he was granted a life annuity of 10 marks, later increased to £20. A favourite of the ailing king, in the years 1370 to 1375 he received several grants of offices, including the constableship of Bridgnorth Castle. He was elected for Worcestershire to Edward III's last parliament (January 1377) and Richard II's first (October 1377), in the latter testifying against Alice Perrers, the old king's mistress, and he subsequently sat in both the parliaments summoned in 1380. Richard II regarded him warmly, and acted as godfather to his son.

Retained in the household, Beauchamp soon received substantial further patronage, and by November 1384 he had been made receiver of the chamber and keeper of the king's jewels. He took the order of knighthood on Richard II's entry into Scotland in 1385, then being granted £100 a year from Welsh revenues since he had led 'a fine company' in the royal army. That December he was granted for life the office of justiciar of north Wales, to which was added in August 1386 a charter of liberties within his recently purchased estate at Kidderminster. Even though the Commons demanded in October that a new steward of the household be appointed only in parliament, Richard II refused to comply, and in January 1387 he promoted Beauchamp to the stewardship. More provocative still was Sir John's creation on 10 October following as 'Lord of Beauchamp and Baron of Kidderminster', a new dignity to be maintained from the estates of Deerhurst Priory. This, the first creation of a peerage by letters patent, was made in consideration not only of Beauchamp's services and noble birth, but also for his great 'sense and circumspection' (*CPR, 1385–9,* 363).

Beauchamp's rapid rise from esquire to baron could not be borne by the *lords appellant, who included his kinsman and feudal lord, Thomas Beauchamp, earl of Warwick. Although he was summoned to parliament by personal writ on 17 December 1387, he never took his seat, for the defeat of the royalist army at Radcot Bridge precipitated a purge of the household. Arrested and imprisoned along with three other household knights, Beauchamp

was impeached in the Merciless Parliament on 12 March 1388, with written articles against them being delivered by the Commons on the 17th, and on 12 May he was condemned by the lords for treason according to the first article: that he had given false counsel to the youthful, innocent king, causing him to hate his loyal lords and subjects. He was beheaded on Tower Hill the same day and buried in Worcester Cathedral. With the exception of the earls of Suffolk and Oxford, Beauchamp was the wealthiest of those proscribed. Fortunately for his heir, John, then aged eleven, he had entailed certain of his manors, so these were exempt from forfeiture, but other valuable estates which he had purchased were sold for 1200 marks to a syndicate headed by the earl of Warwick. LINDA CLARK

Sources *Chancery records* · *RotP,* 3.14, 241–3 · L. C. Hector and B. F. Harvey, eds. and trans., *The Westminster chronicle, 1381–1394,* OMT (1982), 178, 268–79, 288, 293, 333 · *VCH Worcestershire,* 3.403–4 · HoP, *Commons, 1386–1421,* 2.153–4 · *Calendar of inquisitions miscellaneous (chancery),* PRO, 5 (1962), 151–62 · *Reports … touching the dignity of a peer of the realm,* House of Lords, 1 (1820), 345
Wealth at death £107 p.a. from land: *Calendar of inquisitions miscellaneous*

Beauchamp, John, first Baron Beauchamp of Powick (*c.*1400–1475), nobleman and administrator, was the son and eventually the heir of Sir William Beauchamp of Powick in Worcestershire (*c.*1370–*c.*1421) and his wife, Katherine Usflete (*d.* after 1436). Sir William had been a royal retainer under Richard II, Henry IV, and Henry V, and, on his death, John followed him into the king's service, receiving an annuity of £40 and the designation 'king's servant and esquire' from Henry V on 18 December 1421. The family's handful of manors in the south-west midlands seem to have been shared between his mother and an elder brother, Walter.

During the 1420s Beauchamp served under the duke of Bedford in France: he was captain of Pont de l'Arche in 1422–9, lieutenant of Rouen Castle in 1429, a participant in the Maine–Anjou campaigns, and a counsellor to the duke and member of his household. About the time of Henry VI's visit to France for his coronation, in 1430–32, however, he seems to have taken up a permanent post within the king's domestic establishment. Some time before October 1432 he became one of four king's carvers, receiving an annual wage of £40. Before 1434 he married Margaret Ferrers (who made her will in January 1487 or 1488). On 28 October 1434, and presumably in recognition of his landlessness, he was granted the custody of a manor in his home county of Worcestershire. When the king began to make grants on his own authority, in 1436–7, Beauchamp joined other household men in reaping the benefits: his royal pensions reached a total of £140 plus two tuns of Gascon wine per annum.

The death of his distant relative Richard Beauchamp, earl of Warwick, seems to have been the first major turning point in John Beauchamp's career. In May 1439 he was appointed to the panel controlling the Warwick estates, and in the following November he became a feoffee for the dowager countess. It seems likely that his position in the royal household lay behind his inclusion in these grants, though his close links with Sir Ralph Boteler—another grantee, another household man, and Beauchamp's own cousin—must also have been a factor. Together, these two set about filling the regional vacuum left by Warwick's death, drawing large parts of the earl's retinue into a new connection, focused on their interests in Worcestershire and Gloucestershire and Boteler's offices at Kenilworth. Beauchamp was probably landless until the mid-1440s, but his power was underwritten by a series of royal offices given him in 1439: the constableship of Rhuddlan in north Wales, joint custody (with Boteler) of the Forest of Dean, and a place on the Gloucestershire bench.

During the following decade Beauchamp's importance grew. In 1439 or 1440 he rose up the household ladder to become master of the king's horse. Three years later, he joined the feoffees for the king's colleges at Cambridge and Eton, and in 1445 he became a knight of the Garter. At about the same time he seems to have inherited his father's estates, with their centres at Powick and at Alcester in Warwickshire (he bought the other half of the latter manor in 1444), and, by about the middle of the decade, the Boteler–Beauchamp connection had become the major power in the west midlands. On the death of the short-lived Henry Beauchamp, successively earl and duke of Warwick, in June 1446, Sir John felt sufficiently confident to launch a claim for the earldom of Warwick itself. While the powerful interests clustered around Henry's female heirs assured the failure of the initiative, Beauchamp was able to exact a handsome price for his acquiescence (finally secured in November). Amid a series of grants made in 1446–7, including his father's old office of constable of Gloucester and the post of justice of south Wales, he was on 2 May 1447 elevated to the peerage as Lord Beauchamp of Powick, with annuities worth a further £55 to help maintain his estate.

Beauchamp had done well out of the royal service in the 1440s, but he emerged unscathed—even enhanced—from the crisis of 1449–50 which brought nemesis to so many of his colleagues. In the wake of the Act of Resumption of 1450, from which he was exempted, he picked up a clutch of valuable custodies: the New Forest, the Isle of Wight, and the earldom of Pembroke. On 22 June 1450 he succeeded the hated Lord Saye and Sele as treasurer of England. How Beauchamp escaped the critical backlash of these years is hard to know: the evidence suggests that he was one of those most continuously about the king in the previous decade, and he remained in this position during the years that followed. One possible reason is that he was little involved in the controversial diplomacy of the 1440s; another, that his standing at the centre was matched by real power in the west midlands (even if this power had been composed with central help). In any event, it need not be assumed that he owed his appointment as treasurer to any association with the critics of the regime: as Cade and others protested, the post-Suffolk establishment was made up mainly of the same people as before.

Beauchamp's tenure at the treasury lasted two years, during which policy was probably determined less by the treasurer than by the conflicting designs of parliament and the recipients of royal patronage. Beauchamp himself seems to have done well out of his office: although one chronicle describes him as having been expelled from the treasury (on 15 April 1452), he departed with a reward of £400, for his service during this 'moost troublouseust season' (PRO, E404/68/103), and secured repayment of some £528 owed to him with little difficulty. Between 1450 and 1453 he remained a central figure in the household, under the duke of Somerset, but avoided implication in the duke's more partisan activities, being chosen as a plausible mediator between the government and York's renegade agent Sir William Oldhall, for example. Beauchamp maintained a low profile during the crisis of 1453–4: he stayed at Henry VI's side during the latter's madness, and was allotted a place as one of two 'barons' of the household in the Yorkist ordinances of November 1454.

If his appointment as a councillor on 21 February 1455 was intended to enlist Beauchamp as an ally of Somerset, it did not succeed: he attended the council sporadically (as he had done before) but he played no part in the fighting at St Albans a few months later. A poem of 1458 identified Beauchamp as a member of the royalist party, but this is almost certainly to be explained by his long-standing place in the household (where he became steward at some point in the second half of 1457). There is no evidence that he ever fought for Lancaster, and he attended both a council meeting and a chapter of the Garter during the winter of 1460–61, when the king was under Yorkist control. At the end of 1460 he lost his stewardship, but he was reinstated as a feoffee for the royal colleges, so there is little to suggest that the new regime was hostile towards him. What he did in the difficult early months of 1461 is unknown, but it is unlikely that he gave much serious consideration to the armed struggle on behalf of his former master: Edward IV clearly anticipated loyalty when he placed Beauchamp on a Worcestershire commission of array in August, and a few months later approved his petition for exemption from the Act of Resumption of 1461. In February 1462 Beauchamp received a pardon, and in October of that year an exemption from the obligations of office and attendance, on the grounds of his great age.

So it was that, with the downfall of Henry VI, Beauchamp went into retirement rather than opposition. In the midlands he and Boteler lost their former influence, and if the latter risked participation in the rebellions of 1469–71, the former apparently went to ground, failing to help either king against his enemies. Beauchamp had yielded up his place in politics to his son Richard long before his death between 9 and 19 April 1475. He was buried a few miles from Powick, in the Dominican friary, Worcester.   JOHN WATTS

Sources C. Carpenter, *Locality and polity: a study of Warwickshire landed society, 1401–1499* (1992) · *Chancery records* · R. A. Griffiths, *The reign of King Henry VI: the exercise of royal authority, 1422–1461* (1981) · HoP, *Commons, 1386–1421*, 2.158–63 · J. L. Watts, *Henry VI and the politics of kingship* (1996) · GEC, *Peerage*, new edn, 2.46–7 · D. A. L. Morgan, 'The house of policy: the political role of the late Plantagenet household, 1422–85', *The English court: from the Wars of the Roses to the civil war*, ed. D. R. Starkey and others (1987), 25–70 · N. H. Nicolas, ed., *Proceedings and ordinances of the privy council of England*, 7 vols., RC, 26 (1834–7), vols. 4–6 · J. Anstis, ed., *The register of the most noble order of the Garter*, 2 vols. (1724) · J. Stevenson, ed., *Letters and papers illustrative of the wars of the English in France during the reign of Henry VI, king of England*, 2 vols. in 3 pts, Rolls Series, 22 (1861–4) · A. G. Little, 'The black friars, Worcester', *VCH Worcestershire*, 2.167–8 · exchequer, exchequer of receipt, warrants for issues, PRO, E404 · *Itineraries [of] William Worcestre*, ed. J. H. Harvey, OMT (1969) · N. H. Nicolas, ed., *Testamenta vetusta: being illustrations from wills*, 2 vols. (1826)

Wealth at death probably over £500 p.a.; incl. property in Gloucestershire, Alcester, Warwickshire, and elsewhere: HoP, *Commons, 1386–1421*; Chancery records

Beauchamp, Miles de (*d.* 1142×53). *See under* Beauchamp, de, family (*per. c.*1080–*c.*1265).

Beauchamp, Payn de (*d.* in or before 1155). *See under* Beauchamp, de, family (*per. c.*1080–*c.*1265).

Beauchamp, Richard, thirteenth earl of Warwick (1382–1439), magnate, was the eldest son of Thomas *Beauchamp, twelfth earl of Warwick (1337×9–1401), and of Margaret (*d.* 1407), daughter of William, third Lord Ferrers of Groby.

Background and early career Richard Beauchamp was born at Salwarp, Worcestershire, on 25 or 28 January 1382 and the godparents at his baptism were two other Richards, the king and Richard Scrope, later archbishop of York. Despite this strong 'Ricardian' background, Beauchamp identified himself closely with the Lancastrian kings throughout his career, and this is hardly surprising given that the family was almost destroyed by Richard II in 1397–9 and saved only by the accession of Henry IV. During these years Richard Beauchamp was placed in the custody of Thomas Holland, duke of Surrey. He was knighted at Henry IV's coronation in October 1399, and in 1402 was serving the king in Wales against Owain Glyn Dŵr even before he received livery of his lands in February 1403. His father had died in April 1401, leaving him heir to a large estate. It was concentrated principally in the west midland counties of Warwickshire and Worcestershire—the Beauchamps were hereditary sheriffs in this county—with residences at Elmley, Worcestershire, and Warwick, but it spread across much of the midlands, with outliers in the south-west, East Anglia, the home counties, and the north, and the office of hereditary chamberlain of the exchequer. However, it was not until 1407 that Warwick inherited his mother's dower lands, which had included several of the west midland properties, Elmley among them. Even so, he was placed on the commission of the peace in Warwickshire and Worcestershire soon after his father's death, before he had livery from either parent. He fought on campaigns in Wales until 1404, and again in 1407, participating in the battle of Shrewsbury in 1403, after which, according to the *Pageant of the Birth, Life and Death of Richard Beauchamp, Earl of Warwick*, he was made a knight of the Garter. His spiritual relationship to Scrope did not prevent him assisting in the archbishop's arrest and trial in 1405. From 1408 to 1410 he travelled abroad, visiting Rome and the Holy Land and returning via eastern Europe, 'And in this Jurney Erle Richard gate hym greet

Richard Beauchamp, thirteenth earl of Warwick (1382–1439), by William Austen and others, 1449–54 [tomb effigy]

worship at many turnamentes and other faites of warre' (Dillon and Hope, 44): he was indeed a renowned jouster in his youth. On his return he was retained by the prince of Wales with an annuity of 250 marks, the culmination of a relationship initiated during their Welsh campaigns. In May 1410 he was named a royal councillor, his appointment coinciding with the prince's achievement of ascendancy on the royal council. In May 1411 he was a commissioner to treat with the Scots and in September he was on the expedition against the French sponsored by the prince against his father's wishes. But by the time this returned, in late 1411, the king had recovered his power, and Warwick was among those removed from the council in December.

Under Henry IV, Warwick served the house of Lancaster hard and loyally. He was rewarded well, if not spectacularly, notably at the expense of the Mowbrays, with whom the earls of Warwick had a long-standing dispute over the Welsh lordship of Gower, which Richard II had resolved in the Mowbrays' favour in 1397. In 1404 Warwick was given precedence over Thomas (II) Mowbray, earl of Nottingham, and in 1405, after Mowbray's execution for treason, a life grant of Gower. It seems that Henry IV never mistrusted Warwick, even when the earl's friendship with the prince of Wales might have turned the king against him. Henry was, however, characteristically unwilling to allow Warwick's power to expand beyond the west midlands into northern and eastern Warwickshire, which came within the purview of the royal duke of Lancaster, and where the king expected to be locally supreme. Within this relatively restricted region, by the end of the reign Warwick had successfully dealt with the local division and disorder that followed his father's confiscation and Richard II's deposition, and had managed to rebuild the Warwick affinity after the traumas of 1397–9.

Foreign service and local power under Henry V The accession of Warwick's master, Henry V, in 1413 immediately gave him a new pre-eminence. Among other things, he was steward at Henry's coronation in April, made captain of

Calais in February 1414, took part in the repression of Old-castle's rising in 1414, and was frequently employed on diplomatic missions throughout the reign: for example, he treated with Burgundy and France in July 1413, and was ambassador to the Council of Constance and the German emperor in October 1414. He was at the siege of Harfleur in 1415 but, having been sent to Calais with prisoners, missed the battle of Agincourt. After further military and diplomatic service in 1415–16, he was part of the invasion force for Normandy in 1417 and remained in France with the king until 1421. During this time he was present at several successful sieges, including those of Caen in 1417 and Rouen in 1418–19, where he was chief commissioner for the town's surrender, and he commanded when Dom-front and Caudebec were taken in 1418. In February 1419 he was made captain of Beauvais. He was extensively involved in the negotiations leading up to the treaty of Troyes of May 1420. He returned to England with the king and his new queen in early 1421 and was deputy steward at Queen Catherine's coronation in February 1421. In May 1421 he was back in France and victorious with the king at the siege of Meaux in 1421–2, and as independent com-mander at the sieges of Gamaches and St Valéry-sur-Somme in respectively June and September 1422. He was present at Henry's death at Vincennes on 31 August and named an executor of his will, and accompanied the body of the king back to England at the end of October 1422.

Under Henry V, a king with whom he had almost grown up, and who, through both natural instinct and ambition abroad, was readier to delegate than his father, Warwick flourished. If his only substantial grant was the county of Aumale in Normandy in 1419, and he had indeed to surren-der Gower when John (V) Mowbray was restored in 1413, his local sphere of influence widened considerably in these years. It was at this time that he added by purchase to his existing lands in south Staffordshire, that he began to forge closer ties with the gentry in north Warwickshire and Staffordshire, and that, in 1413, he was appointed for the first time to the Staffordshire commission of the peace. It was also during this reign that his links with gen-try in east Warwickshire and Leicestershire developed. By the end of the reign, he was becoming a powerful figure over much of the midlands and already demonstrating his capacity for keeping local order, even when abroad, not-ably with respect to the Montfort inheritance and to the various adventures of the Burdets of Warwickshire and Worcestershire and of his aunt by marriage, Joan *Beau-champ, Lady Bergavenny [see under Beauchamp, Wil-liam (V), first Baron Bergavenny]. His first wife's inherit-ance, had he been able to secure it in its entirety, would have made him an even more formidable force through-out the west midlands. Warwick had married Elizabeth *Berkeley (c.1386–1422), only daughter and heir of Thomas, fifth Lord Berkeley, before 5 October 1397. On her father's death in 1417 he hoped to obtain the parts of the estate that were entailed on her cousin, James Berkeley, most of them in Gloucestershire, including the castle of Berkeley itself. At first it seemed that James's claims would be denied. However, perhaps partly because of

Warwick's extended absence in these years, leaving his wife to mount the defence of the lands, partly because Berkeley was able to secure the help of the duke of Gloucester, keeper of the realm for some of this time, but probably chiefly because the king himself was unwilling to accept the local upheaval occasioned by the dispute, a series of compromise settlements was arranged. The pro-cess was incomplete at Henry's death and somewhat dis-rupted by it.

Service and politics during Henry VI's minority   In December 1422 Warwick became a member of Henry VI's minority council. The records suggest that until about mid-1425 he was frequently in England and much about the young king, but, at the same time, he was captain of Rouen by early 1423 and of Calais not long after. He may have gone on the Verneuil expedition in 1424 but it seems that it was only from the second half of 1425 that he spent much time in France, where he was made custodian of Normandy by the duke of Bedford, the regent in France, at Christmas 1425. There Warwick remained a fairly constant presence until his replacement by Bedford as captain of Calais in 1427—an appointment to which the earl reacted with some fury. During this time, in early 1427, he captured Pontorson in Brittany, but was defeated at Montargis the following September. He returned to England in March 1428 and in June he was made personal governor and tutor of Henry VI; in this role in November 1429 he famously bore the young king in his arms to his coronation. There ensued a period of almost continuous residence in Eng-land until 1436, broken only, it seems, by service on the coronation expedition and subsequent campaign in 1430–32, in which he won a notable victory near Beauvais in 1431. Remaining in England may have been quite an attractive prospect to Warwick because, in the absence of an adult king, political division, locally and nationally, was emerging in ways that were not to his advantage. Des-pite the contretemps over the Calais captaincy, in the 1420s Warwick was firmly in the camp led by Cardinal Beaufort and the duke of Bedford, with regard to both internal politics and foreign affairs. Thus, when Hum-phrey, duke of Gloucester, looking for allies in his increas-ingly acrimonious dispute with Beaufort, again took up the cause of Lord Berkeley in 1425 and coupled this with espousing the claim for precedence over Warwick of the Mowbrays, Lord Berkeley's in-laws, the situation was fraught with danger for the earl. In that year he was forced to accept both an arbitration over the Berkeley lands which left him with much less than he had originally hoped and the elevation of Mowbray to the dukedom of Norfolk, by which the precedence issue was settled firmly in the latter's favour.

Meanwhile, Warwick was running into difficulties locally. In a sense they were a function of his enormously increased authority. The royal duke of Lancaster was a minor; the Stafford dowager still held much of the War-wickshire and Staffordshire lands of the young earl of Stafford, the only other rival force in north and east War-wickshire and the abutting county of Staffordshire; and

Warwick had acquired at least part of the Berkeley estate. All this gave him an unrivalled hegemony over much of the midlands. This became all the stronger on his marriage to Isabella (1400–1439), the Despenser heir, widow of Warwick's cousin and Joan's son, Richard Beauchamp, earl of Worcester, which took place on 26 November 1423, Warwick's first wife, Elizabeth, having died on 28 December 1422. With Isabella came still more west midland manors, notably Hanley, Worcestershire, and Tewkesbury, Gloucestershire, and, to complete his dominance in this region, the large lordship of Glamorgan in south Wales, as well as substantial other property in the marches, which restored the earls to the position of great marcher lords that they had lost with Gower in 1397. It was during the minority of Henry VI that the Warwick affinity completed its evolution into a large and cohesive following dominating the whole of Warwickshire, probably the whole of Worcestershire, and a large part of the midlands as a whole. Warwick's men monopolized most of the local offices in Warwickshire and Worcestershire and he himself was appointed JP in virtually every county where he held lands. In Warwickshire especially, however, Warwick's hegemony was built on a series of alliances with nobles who had lands outside his principal areas of landed power, west Warwickshire and east Worcestershire, the most important being Lady Bergavenny and Edmund, Lord Ferrers of Chartley, and he began to have difficulties in holding his coalition together. In particular there was the problem of Joan Beauchamp. Her husband, the first Lord Bergavenny, had been a loyal associate to both his brother, Earl Thomas, and his nephew, Earl Richard, and Joan too in her widowhood had been an ally, if at times an unstable one. But in the 1420s she began to challenge Warwick's power, both directly and by acting against Lord Ferrers; within and outside the Warwick affinity there was a growing amount of local disorder involving substantial local landowners. The situation for Warwick was especially difficult in 1425, when he was also being worsted on the national scene, and by 1427 he was in danger of losing control of eastern Warwickshire. It is thus possible that he decided to accept the appointment as Henry VI's governor so that he could be at home for a longer period. Certainly, from 1428 there was less local division and Warwick's hold tightened again on the local officers. If the earl's absence with the king in 1430–32 allowed the stand-off between Joan and Ferrers to develop into open confrontation in 1431, his return ensured that Joan was persuaded to modify her ambitions and that the region was generally peaceful thereafter. In 1435 Joan's death restored the entailed part of the Bergavenny lands, much of it in the midlands, to the main line of the Beauchamps, and also brought a large part of the Hastings lands, including the marcher lordship of Abergavenny. From 1430 the young Humphrey Stafford, earl of Stafford, was being drawn into Warwick's coalition, which became even more dominant in the midlands. Until Warwick's final departure for France in 1437 his sphere of influence was large, assured, and essentially peaceful.

Return to France, death, and legacy Apart from participation on Gloucester's expedition to Calais and Flanders in August 1436, Warwick remained in England until 1437. Politically he was still aligned with Beaufort and Bedford and when, in November 1432, he protested that his powers as the king's governor no longer sufficed, it seems that he was primarily lending his weight to prevent Gloucester's further attempts, by acting in the king's name, to subvert the authority of the minority council. In 1434 the marriage of Warwick's children from his second marriage, Henry and Anne, to Cecily and Richard Neville, children of the earl of Salisbury, endorsed his commitment to the Beaufort camp. In May 1436 he was released from his duties about the king and seems to have spent much of the ensuing period on his estates. In July 1437 he was appointed lieutenant-general and governor of France and Normandy, after protracted negotiations over terms and over payments owed for past services. He left in August and died at Rouen on 30 April 1439: he had managed to hold the fort in northern France against the Burgundians but little more, partly because his strength was undermined by the diversion of resources to the Beaufort expedition to Maine in 1438.

Warwick's widow died on 27 December 1439. His heirs were Henry *Beauchamp, still a minor in 1439, who inherited the Warwick and Despenser lands, and the three daughters from his first marriage who shared what Warwick had managed to obtain of the Berkeley inheritance. These were Margaret, second wife of John Talbot, first earl of Shrewsbury; Eleanor, who married Thomas, Baron Ros (d. 1430), and then Edmund Beaufort, later duke of Somerset; and Elizabeth, married to George Neville, Baron Latimer. Henry's full sister, Anne, was eventually to bring the earldom to Richard Neville. Warwick left a large number of lands in trust, which were used to add to the endowment of the family's collegiate church of St Mary, Warwick, and to rebuild its chapel. There Warwick was buried on 4 October 1439 and commemorated in a magnificent tomb, the effigy on which is probably the most lifelike representation of him. He also made gifts to the chantry at Guy's Cliffe near Warwick, which he had founded, to Elmley Castle chantry, and to the Despenser religious centre of Tewkesbury Abbey.

Although Warwick spent much of his time abroad and, when in England as minority councillor and later royal governor, he was often with the king, he had a core of loyal councillors and servants who looked after his estates and local political interests. At the Warwickshire and Worcestershire heart of the estate, these included John Throgmorton, Thomas Crewe, William Wollashill, William Mountford, the Hugfords, and the Harewells. Among his trusted associates further afield were Robert Andrewe in Wiltshire and John Nanfan in Cornwall. Apart from a crisis of management resulting from an official's dereliction during Warwick's prolonged absence under Henry V, the estate was well run: it is estimated that by the 1430s the earl was the third wealthiest noble in England, after York and Stafford. He was able to invest considerable sums in rebuilding his house in London and he also built at

Hanley, Elmley, Warwick, and elsewhere. The management of both the estates and the affinity, often at a distance, reflect the fact that this was an extremely able nobleman, who demonstrated competence in almost all the spheres to which a noble might aspire: war, diplomacy, administration at home and abroad, local politics, and the care of his own estates. He seems also to have been a most conscientious servant of the crown, who received relatively little reward for it but did not complain, except when he was being asked to serve abroad again, in advanced middle age and before the money owed from his previous service had been repaid. He was at his best under Henry V, whom, in his conventionality combined with great ability, he in some ways resembles. When national direction was less firm under the young Henry VI, Warwick seems to have found the less straightforward, and arguably more tawdry, political world at the centre of affairs harder to handle. Even so, despite the lack of royal leadership and the burdens of war and central government, he coped magisterially with the enormous local responsibilities of this period. Curiously, for such an apparently prosaic man, a conventional poem in praise of his second wife is said to be his work, although it could have been written by his secretary, the poet John Shirley.

CHRISTINE CARPENTER

Sources A. F. J. Sinclair, 'The Beauchamp earls of Warwick in the later middle ages', PhD diss., U. Lond., 1987 · GEC, *Peerage* · C. Carpenter, *Locality and polity: a study of Warwickshire landed society, 1401–1499* (1992) · *Pageant of the birth, life and death of Richard Beauchamp, earl of Warwick*, ed. Viscount Dillon and W. H. St John Hope (1914) · *Chancery records* · W. Dugdale, *The baronage of England*, 2 vols. (1675–6) · G. L. Harriss, *Cardinal Beaufort: a study of Lancastrian ascendancy and decline* (1988) · N. H. Nicolas, ed., *Proceedings and ordinances of the privy council of England*, 7 vols., RC, 26 (1834–7) · K. B. McFarlane, *The nobility of later medieval England* (1973) · C. D. Ross, *The estates and finances of Richard Beauchamp, earl of Warwick*, Dugdale Society, 12 (1956) · BL, Add. MS 16165, fols. 245v–246 [poem on Isabel, countess of Warwick, Z315 is photocopy in Warwick RO] · *CPR, 1396–9*, 245 · E. Stokes, ed., *Abstracts of Gloucestershire inquisitions post mortem*, 6: *33 Edward III to 14 Henry IV, 1389–1413*, British RS, 47 (1914)
Archives Birm. CL, estate records · BL, Egerton rolls · BL, Cotton MS Julius E.iv · BL, Add. MS 16165, fols. 245v–246 · Essex RO, Chelmsford, estate records · Glos. RO, estate records · Gwent RO, Cwmbrân, estate records · U. Nott. L., estate records · Warks. CRO, estate records · Warks. CRO, household accounts | Devon RO, Exeter diocesan records, charter 722 · Longleat House, Wiltshire, marquess of Bath MSS · Oxon. RO, Dillon MSS · Shakespeare Birthplace Trust RO, Stratford upon Avon, Archer collection · Warks. CRO, Warwick Castle MSS; Warwick corporation records · Worcs. RO, Holland and Martin collection
Likenesses W. Austen and others, gilt-bronze tomb effigy, 1449–54, St Mary's Church, Warwick [*see illus.*] · J. Ross of Warwick, manuscript (*The history of the life and acts of Richard Beauchamp, E. of Warwick*), BL, Cotton MS Julius EIV · manuscript portrait (with infant Henry VI), BL, English version of Rous Roll, MS 48976 · portraits, repro. in Dillon and St John Hope, eds., *Pageant of the birth, life and death*
Wealth at death approx. £4900 p.a.: McFarlane, *The nobility*, 197–9

Beauchamp, Richard (d. 1481), bishop of Salisbury, was probably born in Wiltshire, the younger son of Sir Walter *Beauchamp (d. 1430) of Bromham, Wiltshire, speaker of the Commons in March 1416, and his wife, Elizabeth (d.

1447), daughter of Sir John Roches. His eldest brother, William, was created Lord St Amand in 1449. The family's kinship was acknowledged by Richard Beauchamp, earl of Warwick, who was tutor to the child Henry VI; hence the bishop's later claim that 'I grew up almost from the cradle under [Henry VI]' (*CSP Milan*, 64), although he must have been some years older than the king.

Beauchamp studied at Oxford University, possibly being resident in Exeter College in 1440, and was DCnL by 18 August 1442, when he was recommended by the university to the pope. He was on the committee that planned the building of the divinity school c.1447, and retained an affection for the university all his life. Preferment had never been a problem for someone with his connections. The crown presented him to the rectory of Barking, Suffolk, on 8 November 1436, he obtained two more benefices in the following year, and then prebends (briefly) in Exeter Castle and Glasney, Cornwall. When he was elevated to episcopacy, he was archdeacon of Suffolk and a royal chaplain.

Beauchamp seems to have been promoted directly from university life to the episcopate. He was papally provided to Hereford on 4 December 1448, received the temporalities on 31 January following (backdated to 13 December), was consecrated at Lambeth on 9 February 1449, and installed on 3 April. This was a promotion based essentially on birth and personal royal favour, but clearly Beauchamp had academic and intellectual qualities to justify it, and intended to make a diocesan, not political, career. On 2 May 1449 he appealed to Archbishop John Stafford and the pope against machinations he suspected against the rights of himself and the cathedral in the diocese. On 27 April 1450 he effected the first (and only) successful claim to make a visitation of the cathedral before the Reformation, and set about inspecting the whole diocese likewise.

Even as Beauchamp was thus engaged in establishing himself at Hereford, Bishop William Aiscough of Salisbury was murdered on 29 June and his episcopal manors looted. Beauchamp was swiftly translated to fill the vacant see on 14 August, and secured the temporalities on 1 October. By then he had already entered this, his native diocese, and started to tour it; if nothing else, he had courage. He was only formally installed on 5 May 1451, but had already been seen in all parts of his diocese. Subsequently, the Oxford commentator Thomas Gascoigne (who always resented the fact that his own academic talents were overlooked for high office in the church, and no doubt found the easy rise of Beauchamp especially painful), criticized him and Dean Gilbert Kymer for blaming upon preachers the popular unrest in the diocese that had led to Aiscough's death. Gascoigne pointed the finger for discontent at their own poor example in residence, preaching, and hospitality. With respect to residence, it was an unfair charge, for Beauchamp's record is good. What perhaps allowed Gascoigne to cavil was that Beauchamp found himself often called to Windsor by the king. 'Forasmuch as your being about our person is to us full agreeable and your service at such times as you are with us full good and notable', ran one such open-ended summons to join Henry, issued on 15 August 1452 (PRO, E 28/82). Ceremonial duties as chaplain of the Order of the Garter likewise took Beauchamp to Windsor each year. Meantime, the bishop was vigorous around his cathedral city, promoting the canonization cause of St Osmund, and sustaining a protracted dispute with the civic authorities.

Beauchamp's personal ties with the king forced him into political life in the late 1450s, and this was just when Gascoigne wrote. On 14 May 1457 he was appointed as a conservator of the truce with Burgundy. A much more sensitive issue was the fact that he was out of his diocese from 10 April until late July 1458 negotiating secretly, apparently as Queen Margaret's agent, with a representative of the grand seneschal of France (Pierre de Brézé), through whom the queen hoped to make confidential contact with the French crown. (Beauchamp's vicar-general unwittingly or sensitively always described it as 'an embassy on behalf of the king and realm' (Reg. Beauchamp 1, fols. 61v–64).) From 3 October 1458 to June 1460 he lived almost entirely in Chelsea or his Fleet Street house in London, managing only brief visits to Salisbury in May and December 1459. When Henry VI and his army confronted the forces of Richard of York and his allies outside Ludlow on 12 October 1459, Beauchamp was sent to offer an amnesty to all York's followers save those involved in the battle of Bloreheath three weeks before.

Beauchamp's personal position was difficult as civil war became a reality. Clearly Henry VI and the queen regarded him as an intimate supporter. On the other hand, the bishop was a kinsman of Anne Beauchamp, wife of Richard Neville, earl of Warwick, and had known her when they were young. Thus on 10 May 1460 he was the only bishop in the delegation from the crown to the southern convocation in search of funds. On 19 May he presided there over the trial of the heretic John Bredhill. However, as soon as the rebel earls of Warwick, Salisbury, and March entered London in the following month he joined them. As the rival armies faced each other outside Northampton on 10 July 1460, he was sent with other bishops to the royal camp to offer mediation, only to be rebuffed as partisan, and therefore disqualified from any spiritual authority, by the constable, the duke of Buckingham. Perhaps significantly, Beauchamp took himself back to his diocese despite the Yorkist victory.

Beauchamp's defection from the court was doubtless especially bitter to Lancastrians, and for good reason he fled from London on 24 February 1461 as the victorious Queen Margaret approached, but he found no difficulty making the change. He wrote on 4 April:

> I have found such grace and favour that he [Edward IV] has chosen me to be the chief of the three to whose judgements all the most secret matters of the council are referred. From the king, his predecessor … I could not presume such favour. (CSP Milan, 64)

Such eminence lasted only days. There is scant evidence that he played much part in the Yorkist regime. Instead, he returned at once to the full-time diocesan work from which he had been involuntarily diverted. On 21 August 1461 he conducted a visitation of the cathedral chapter. Thenceforth, he spent twenty years as he had always meant to spend his life, as a resident bishop. He attended parliaments regularly, but only once was he persuaded to leave his diocese to serve the crown. On 5 January 1467 he was appointed to head the embassy to arrange the marriage of Margaret of York to Charles, duke of Burgundy. On 3 July 1468 he performed the marriage at Damme. This was personal honour for him, not politics. He kept a low profile during the readeption of Henry VI in 1470–71.

Edward IV had one major project for Beauchamp. On 19 February 1473 he was appointed master and surveyor of St George's Chapel, Windsor, and became much involved in construction of the great new chapel. His role was extended to deal with its constitution too; he was instituted to the deanship of the chapel on 4 March 1478, to hold with his bishopric, and on 6 December 1479 secured incorporation for himself and the canons. The king was evidently increasingly satisfied with the bishop's work at Windsor; Beauchamp had been appointed to the new office of chancellor of the Order of the Garter on 10 October 1475.

As a royal peculiar, Windsor Castle and its chapel were not legally in the Salisbury diocese, but, as the bishop's register indicates, Beauchamp never found his long stays there any obstacle to keeping full personal control of his see. He remained active to the end, working mainly from Salisbury or Windsor. In the first half of 1481 he scarcely stopped in his commuting between the two. In July and August he inspected monastic houses across the breadth of his diocese. Then, on 7 September he came to a halt in his Salisbury palace. There he died on 18 October 1481. In an emotional will made two days before, he traced the stages of a man's life and declared that he had come to the extremity of old age. He left his 'most singular' lord, Edward IV, a 'great and sumptuous bible', and all his estates for a chantry of four priests in whichever of his two new chapels in the cathedral (in the event, the one on the south side of the lady chapel) his executors selected for his burial (PRO, PROB 11/7, fol. 31r–v). All his servants were given six months' salary and a month's expense-free lodging. His nephew, Sir Richard Beauchamp, received a handsome bequest and headed the executors with Bishop John Morton. Beauchamp had been born to privilege, but he devoted his life to deserving it. Like several others advanced by Henry VI, he owed too much to personal favour, was no political helpmate, but made an excellent diocesan. R. G. DAVIES

Sources Emden, *Oxf.*, 1.137–8 · A. T. Bannister and others, eds., *Registrum Ricardi Beauchamp, episcopi Herefordensis*, 1, CYS, 25 (1919) · register of Richard Beauchamp, Wilts. & Swindon RO, 2 vols. · PRO, PROB 11/7, fol. 31r–v · T. Gascoigne, *Loci e libro veritatum*, ed. J. E. Thorold Rogers (1881), 42–3 · CSP Milan, 63–4 · J. S. Davies, ed., *An English chronicle of the reigns of Richard II, Henry IV, Henry V, and Henry VI*, CS, 64 (1856), 95 · J. S. Roskell, 'Sir Walter Beauchamp', *Parliament and politics in late medieval England*, 3 (1983), 237–54 · J. S. Roskell, 'Beauchamp, Sir Walter', HoP, *Commons* · exchequer, treasury of receipt, council and privy seal records, PRO, E 28/82

Archives Hereford diocesan registry, Hereford, Hereford register · Wilts. & Swindon RO, register

Beauchamp, Robert de (*c*.1190–1251/2), justice and baron, was the son of Simon de Vautort and of the daughter and heir of Robert de Beauchamp (*d*. 1195), lord of Hatch Beauchamp in Somerset, whose surname he took. Since he was a minor at his father's death, in 1206 his wardship was granted to Hubert de *Burgh (*d*. 1243), who subsequently sent him overseas as a hostage. He came of age *c*.1212. The lord of seventeen knights' fees in Somerset, Dorset, and Devon, he founded the Augustinian priory of Frithelstock in Devon *c*.1220. In 1223 he was licensed to take scutage from his men in Somerset for that year's Welsh campaign, but in 1230 paid 40 marks for exemption from Henry III's expedition to Brittany. In the same year he was appointed to oversee the assize of arms in Middlesex. His appointment as a justice of the bench in June 1234 can be attributed to his association with Hubert de Burgh, whose supporters helped to bring about that year's political revolution, rather than to any extensive legal experience. He rarely sat at Westminster (although his name appears on several fines from Hilary term 1242), but he served as a justice itinerant in East Anglia and in south and southwest England between 1234 and 1238, and again in Devon and Dorset in 1244. He was also appointed at least twice to be a justice of assize and gaol delivery in Somerset and Dorset in the 1240s. Before 1232 he had married Juliana, widow of Thomas of Barrow, with whom he had a son, Robert. On 7 April 1251 he confirmed the customs of his manor of Stoke under Hamdon in Somerset, perhaps in a valedictory frame of mind, since he swore that 'those customs I will inviolably preserve, and this same form I charge to my beloved son, Robert, my heir, with my blessing, unchangeably to observe' (Maxwell-Lyte, 2–3). He was dead by 1 February 1252.   HENRY SUMMERSON

Sources *Chancery records* (RC) · *Chancery records* · *Pipe rolls* · *Curia regis rolls preserved in the Public Record Office* (1922–) · H. C. M. Lyte and others, eds., *Liber feodorum: the book of fees*, 3 vols. (1920–31) · H. C. Maxwell-Lyte, *Two registers formerly belonging to the family of Beauchamp of Hatch*, Somerset RS, 35 (1920) · I. J. Sanders, *English baronies: a study of their origin and descent, 1086–1327* (1960), 51 · D. Crook, *Records of the general eyre*, Public Record Office Handbooks, 20 (1982)

Beauchamp, Rohese de (*d*. 1166). *See under* Beauchamp, de, family (*per. c*.1080–*c*.1265).

Beauchamp, Simon de (*d*. 1136/7). *See under* Beauchamp, de, family (*per. c*.1080–*c*.1265).

Beauchamp, Simon de (*c*.1145–1206/7). *See under* Beauchamp, de, family (*per. c*.1080–*c*.1265).

Beauchamp, Thomas, eleventh earl of Warwick (1313/14–1369), soldier and magnate, was the son and heir of Guy de *Beauchamp, tenth earl of Warwick (*c*.1272–1315), and his wife, Alice Tosny, widow of Thomas Leyburn.

Childhood and early career Beauchamp was probably born some time between August 1313 and 14 February 1314, most likely the latter date. He was no more than two years

old when his father died on 12 August 1315, and the earldom thus underwent a long minority at a time of political instability. The custody of the lands of the earldom was granted on 21 June 1317 to Edward II's favourite Hugh Despenser the elder, but in July of the following year the young earl's marriage was granted to Roger (V) *Mortimer of Wigmore (1287–1330), and he was placed in Mortimer's guardianship. Before Guy Beauchamp died the two families had apparently arranged that Thomas should marry Mortimer's daughter Katherine, so as to end a feud between the two families over the lordship of Elfael in the Welsh marches. Mortimer's imprisonment and subsequent escape into exile between 1322 and 1326 temporarily frustrated these plans, and Thomas's marriage may have been granted to Edmund Fitzalan, earl of Arundel, who stood high in favour at Edward's court in these years. In 1325 Arundel obtained a papal dispensation to marry the young earl to one of his daughters, but after Edward II's deposition Mortimer was granted the custody of the earldom's lands and he regained Warwick's marriage, for about this time Thomas and Katherine were married.

The return of political stability in the 1330s allowed Warwick, like many other young noblemen of his generation, to earn a reputation for military prowess on campaigns in France and Scotland. He was knighted and given livery of his lands on 20 February 1329, even though he was still well under age: perhaps this reflects the re-establishment of close links with Roger Mortimer. After Mortimer's fall Warwick served Edward III on campaign in Scotland in 1333, in 1334–5, and again in 1337 when he was appointed commander of the army in the north. After 1337, however, Edward's principal concern was the war with France, and Warwick played a leading part in most of the major campaigns of the first phase of the war. He was present at the stand-off at Buironfosse in the autumn of 1339, when both sides were prepared for battle but withdrew. In 1340 he accompanied the king at the siege of Tournai and in the negotiations that led to the truce of Esplechin on 25 September 1340. These campaigns precipitated a financial crisis for the king, however, and Warwick was one of a group of nobles close to the king who were imprisoned in Malines from September 1340 until May 1341 as sureties for the king's debts to the bankers of Malines and Louvain.

'The devil Warwick' When the war resumed in 1342, Warwick served in Brittany and was present with a large retinue at the siege of Vannes. He now began to gain a great reputation for courage and prowess. In 1346 he took part in Edward III's expedition to Normandy and Thomas Walsingham relates how, as the first to land at La Hogue, he and a small band of soldiers repulsed a much larger force of Frenchmen seeking to oppose the English landing, and thus enabled the English to disembark without resistance. At the battle of Crécy, according to Froissart, he was placed in the first battalion alongside Edward, the Black Prince, and fought with him in the fierce encounter late in the battle in which the prince 'won his spurs' (*Chroniques*, 3.183). After the victory at Crécy he accompanied the king to the siege of Calais, and in 1348 Edward granted him an annuity of 1000 marks on condition that he serve the king in war whenever he was required. He had been at the forefront of Edward's campaigns and had become one of the king's most important and distinguished companions-in-arms: well might the abbot and convent of Abingdon salute him in 1344 as 'the magnificent and powerful man and most energetic warrior' (BL, Beauchamp cartulary, fol. 49r).

Warwick's appetite for war seems in no way to have diminished as he grew older. Although he was by now more than forty, he left with the Black Prince for Bordeaux in 1355 and took part in the prince's raid across southern France later that year. At the battle of Poitiers (19 September 1356) he and John de Vere, earl of Oxford, commanded the vanguard, and Geoffrey Baker describes how, at the height of the battle, he and William Montagu, earl of Salisbury, struggled 'like lions' to see which of them could spill most French blood on the soil of Poitou (*Chronicon Galfridi le Baker*, 148). He took part with Edward III in the Rheims campaign of 1359, and in the following year was a witness to the treaty of Brétigny which brought a temporary end to the war.

Other theatres of war, however, still provided opportunities for the pursuit of a military career. In 1364, when Warwick was serving with the Black Prince in Gascony, he made arrangements to join the crusade led by Pierre de Lusignan, king of Cyprus, which culminated in the sack of Alexandria. Late in the year, however, he changed his mind and received authority from the pope to crusade with the Teutonic knights in Prussia instead. According to the *Beauchamp Pageant*, a much later source, which may none the less preserve earlier family traditions, Warwick captured the 'Kynges son of Lettowe [Lithuania] and brought hym into Englond And cristened hym at London namyng hym after hym self Thomas' (*Beauchamp Pageant*, 44). After his return to England Warwick served the king in an administrative rather than a military capacity, going on a mission to Flanders in 1366 and serving as a keeper of the truce on the Scottish border in the following year.

No sooner had the war with France resumed in 1369, however, than he joined John of Gaunt, duke of Lancaster, in the expedition that raided from Calais to the Pays de Caux: according to the Anonimalle chronicle, news of the arrival of 'the devil Warwick' (*Anonimalle Chronicle*, 61) at Calais in support of Gaunt's force was enough to make the duke of Burgundy and his army, encamped near Calais, withdraw under cover of darkness to avoid risk of an encounter with the English. Walsingham, who seems particularly to have admired him, describes him as a 'spirited warrior' (*Historia Anglicana*, 1.282), and, like the Anonimalle chronicle, records that the French army was astonished to hear of his arrival and fled even before he had landed. Warwick's enthusiasm for campaigning not only alarmed the French, but also led to a dispute with Gaunt, who had hitherto confined his military activity to raids in the area around Calais. Burgundy's withdrawal, however, laid the way open for Gaunt, with Warwick, to invade Normandy, but the English army failed to take Harfleur, its main objective, and returned to Calais by the end

of October. There Warwick succumbed to the plague and died on 13 November 1369 at the age of fifty-five.

Wealth and expenditure Warwick's distinction as a soldier brought him both honours and material benefits. In 1344 Edward III appointed him sheriff of Warwickshire and Leicestershire for life, and marshal of England during his pleasure. Some four years later he was one of the founder members of the Order of the Garter, taking precedence after the prince of Wales and the duke of Lancaster. In December 1347 the king made him a gift of £1366 11s. 8d. 'for good service in the war beyond the seas' (*CPR, 1345–8*, 440), and seven months later he was retained by the king for life at a fee of 1000 marks p.a. In 1353 the king ensured Warwick's victory in a lawsuit to recover the lordship of Gower from John (II) Mowbray, although Richard II was to reverse the judgment in 1397. Warwick also acquired, partly by gift and partly perhaps by purchase, a substantial collection of jewels, plate, and reliquaries, most of which he bequeathed to his children. At his baptism, for example, Thomas, earl of Lancaster, had given him a gold box containing a piece of bone of St George, and the Black Prince gave him an eagle brooch, which he left to his daughter Philippa.

Beauchamp spent some of his wealth on building work at Warwick. He began the construction of the new chancel at St Mary's Church, Warwick, but little more than an extension to the crypt and the foundations of the chancel had been built by the time of his death, and he ordered his executors to complete the work. He was responsible for the construction of Caesar's Tower, the Clock Tower, and part of the north-east curtain wall at Warwick Castle. Some of this work may have been financed out of the ransoms of prisoners he took at Poitiers: the archbishop of Sens, for example, was ransomed for £8000. In the early 1340s he bought land and property, mainly in Warwickshire, though he acquired some manors elsewhere. However, the Beauchamp cartulary records few purchases of lands after c.1348, and one of the purposes of his earlier purchases may have been to make provision for his younger sons. In 1344 Edward III granted him permission to carry through a major re-enfeoffment of the lands of the earldom to ensure their descent in tail male, but his younger sons were given a life interest in some of the lands. However, not only Guy, his eldest son, but also his third son, Reinbrun, and fifth son, Roger, died during their father's lifetime, a private sorrow that cast a shadow over his public fame and prestige.

Children and connections by marriage Beauchamp was buried in the chancel of St Mary's Church, Warwick, next to his wife who had predeceased him by no more than three months. Somewhat later, perhaps when the chancel was complete, the present tomb with alabaster effigies of the earl and countess was constructed. He had five sons: Guy, who died on 28 April 1360, leaving two daughters as his coheirs, Elizabeth (d. c.1369) and Katherine, who became a nun (under the 1344 entail they were barred from inheriting the earldom); Thomas *Beauchamp (1337×9–1401) who succeeded to the earldom and, under the entail of 1344, to most of its lands; Reinbrun, who died in 1361; William *Beauchamp (c.1343–1411), who inherited the castle and honour of Abergavenny; Roger, who died in 1361 while still a child; and at least six daughters, most of whom made distinguished marriages that reflected their father's prestige and extended the family's influence widely through the nobility. Maud (d. 1403) married Roger, Lord Clifford; Philippa married Hugh Stafford, earl of Stafford; Alice (d. 1383) married first John Beauchamp of Hatch and afterwards Sir Matthew Gournay; Joan married Ralph, Lord Basset of Drayton, and may have died in her father's lifetime, for she is not mentioned in his will; Isabell (d. 1416) married first John, Lord Strange of Blakemere, and later William Ufford, earl of Suffolk; after his death she became a nun. Margaret married Guy de Montfort and when he died she too became a nun. Dugdale followed John Rous in suggesting that Warwick had three further daughters—Agnes, Juliana, and Katherine—but none of them is mentioned in his will.   ANTHONY TUCK

Sources Beauchamp Cartulary, BL, Add. MS 28024 · Register of Archbishop William Whittlesey, LPL [microfilm in CUL] · *Chancery records* · *CPR, 1345–8* · *CEPR letters*, vol. 2 · *Chronicon Galfridi le Baker de Swynebroke*, ed. E. M. Thompson (1889) · *Thomae Walsingham, quondam monachi S. Albani, historia Anglicana*, ed. H. T. Riley, 2 vols., pt 1 of *Chronica monasterii S. Albani*, Rolls Series, 28 (1863–4), vol. 1 · *Ypodigma Neustriae, a Thoma Walsingham*, ed. H. T. Riley, pt 7 of *Chronica monasterii S. Albani*, Rolls Series, 28 (1876) · Chandos herald, *Life of the Black Prince by the herald of Sir John Chandos*, ed. M. K. Pope and E. C. Lodge (1910) · V. H. Galbraith, ed., *The Anonimalle chronicle, 1333 to 1381* (1927) · *Chroniques de J. Froissart*, ed. S. Luce and others, 3–4 (Paris, 1872–3) · *Pageant of the birth, life and death of Richard Beauchamp, earl of Warwick*, ed. Viscount Dillon and W. H. St John Hope (1914) · *VCH Warwickshire*, vol. 8 · G. A. Holmes, *The estates of the higher nobility in fourteenth-century England* (1957) · A. F. J. Sinclair, 'The Beauchamp earls of Warwick in the later middle ages', PhD diss., U. Lond., 1987 · W. Dugdale, *The antiquities of Warwickshire illustrated*, rev. W. Thomas, 2nd edn, 1 (1730); facs. edn [1973] · W. M. Ormrod, *The reign of Edward III* (1990) · K. Fowler, *The king's lieutenant: Henry of Grosmont, first duke of Lancaster, 1310–1361* (1969) · A. Luttrell, 'English Levantine crusaders, 1363–1367', *Renaissance Studies*, 2 (1988), 143–53 · GEC, *Peerage*
Archives BL, Add. MS 28024
Likenesses alabaster effigy on tomb-chest, c.1370–1400, St Mary's Church, Warwick

Beauchamp, Thomas, twelfth earl of Warwick (1337×9–1401)

Beauchamp, Thomas, twelfth earl of Warwick (1337×9–1401), magnate, was the second but eldest surviving son of Thomas *Beauchamp, eleventh earl of Warwick (1313/14–1369), and his wife, Katherine Mortimer, both of whom died in 1369. He was born some time between 1337 and 16 March 1339, and became earl of Warwick at his father's death on 13 November 1369. His father had been one of Edward III's most celebrated companions-in-arms. He had played a leading part in the successful campaigns of the opening phase of the Hundred Years' War, and he had been a founder member of the Order of the Garter. Thomas's fate, however, was to come to manhood at a time when the war began to go badly for England, and in mature adult life his political career was played out in the reign of a king who enjoyed much less of a rapport with the nobility than Edward III in his heyday.

Early career Little is known of Beauchamp's early life. He became heir to the earldom in 1360, when his elder

brother, Guy, died, and as a younger son it is perhaps not surprising that he attracted little attention, though he figured in his father's plans for the re-enfeoffment of his inheritance in order to ensure that his younger sons received some endowment. In July 1355 he and his elder brother were knighted shortly before taking part in Edward III's campaign in northern France in 1355. At the conclusion of the campaign the king retained both young men, at a fee of £100 for Guy and 100 marks for Thomas. Thomas's links with the court remained close in the 1360s: he was described as one of the king's bachelors in 1366, and he was a knight of the chamber from 1366 until at least 1369.

Both Guy and Thomas accompanied Edward III on the Rheims expedition of 1359, but the conclusion of the treaty of Brétigny in the following year put an end to large-scale campaigning in France for the time being. Thomas was not content to remain inactive, however, and in 1367 he and his younger brother William went on crusade in Prussia with the Teutonic knights, as their father had done two years earlier, though without repeating their father's spectacular success in returning home with a captive member of the Lithuanian royal house.

When the war with France resumed in 1369, Beauchamp soon became involved in campaigning. In that year he took a small retinue to Calais with John of Gaunt, duke of Lancaster, at the start of the expedition that was to culminate in his father's raid into Normandy. In 1372, now earl of Warwick, he took part with a retinue of 100 men-at-arms and 160 archers in Edward III's abortive expedition to relieve La Rochelle, and in the following year he brought a much larger retinue to serve with John of Gaunt on the futile long march from Calais to Bordeaux. In 1375 he joined the expedition to Brittany led by Edmund of Langley, earl of Cambridge, and the duke of Brittany, and was accompanied by Hugh Stafford, earl of Stafford, and Edmund Mortimer, earl of March, with both of whom Warwick seems to have formed a close association. His relationship with the court now seems to have been more distant than it had been in the previous decade.

Loyalty and detachment, 1376–1386 None of these expeditions brought Warwick, or his companions-in-arms, any great fame, and he does not seem to have been as close to the king, nearly thirty years his senior, as his father had been. Indeed, his experiences on the unsuccessful Breton campaign may have inclined him to support the critique of the court that was offered by the Commons, with the support of some nobles, notably the earl of March, in the Good Parliament of April 1376. The Commons saw Warwick as a sympathizer, and he was one of the lay members of the committee of lords appointed to discuss with the Commons how best to resolve their grievances.

Warwick was not appointed to any of the continual councils that held office during Richard II's minority, but the Commons evidently regarded him as a trustworthy noble of independent mind. In the parliament of April 1379 he was appointed, along with March and Stafford, to the committee set up to scrutinize royal finances, and he was reappointed to another, similar, commission in the January parliament of the following year. According to Thomas Walsingham, the Commons in that parliament asked for Warwick to be appointed as governor of the young king, but there is no other evidence that the appointment was ever made. Indeed, in April 1380 he was sufficiently free of other commitments to contemplate joining the earl of March in the expedition to Ireland that culminated in March's accidental death the following year. If he went to Ireland, he had returned by the end of the summer, for in September he joined Gaunt on an expedition to the Scottish border to enforce the truce.

According to the Anonimalle chronicle Warwick was with the king in the Tower of London in June 1381 when the rebellious peasants of Kent and Essex marched on London, but none of the chroniclers reveal what advice, if any, he gave the young king at this moment of crisis. He may have supported the policy of confronting the rebels, for he rode with Richard to Mile End in the courageous action by which the king persuaded the Essex rebels to return home. In the November parliament of 1381 he was appointed to the committee set up to reform the royal household.

Although relations between the king and some of the nobility, particularly Richard (III) Fitzalan, earl of Arundel, deteriorated in the years after 1381, as Richard came to rely more and more upon a small group of friends at court, there was no sign yet that Warwick shared the developing hostility to the king and his favourites. The two close associates of his earlier career in politics and war, the earls of March and Stafford, were dead by 1386, but he does not seem to have formed any close links with Thomas of Woodstock, duke of Gloucester, and the earl of Arundel, whose hostility to the king was increasingly apparent in these years. His role remained that of a loyal, if rather detached, noble. His participation in the king's expedition to Scotland in 1385 was natural in view of his rank and experience, but he played no part in the disputes that punctuated and followed that expedition. According to the *Eulogium*, Warwick, together with Gloucester and Arundel, argued that the Wonderful Parliament of 1386 should concentrate on dealing with enemies within (especially the chancellor, Michael de la Pole) rather than abroad. However, the *Eulogium*'s account of the parliament is inaccurate in a number of respects, and no other contemporary source attributes an active part in the parliament to the earl. He was not appointed as a member of the commission established in that parliament to supervise Richard's government for a year from 20 November 1386. He still probably maintained his position of detachment, if not remoteness, from political controversy.

Lord appellant, 1387–1388 Just over a year later, however, Warwick changed his stance and threw in his lot with the king's opponents. In November 1387 he joined Gloucester and Arundel in accusing five of the king's friends of treason, and by the end of December the three *lords appellant, now joined by Henry, earl of Derby, and Thomas (I) Mowbray, earl of Nottingham, had compelled the king to submit to their demands and agree to have his favourites

brought to trial in parliament. The rest of Warwick's career was to be decisively influenced by his actions in these two months, yet the reasons for them remain obscure. The events of the summer of 1387, in particular the answers given by the judges to Richard's questions about the lawfulness of the proceedings in the Wonderful Parliament, threatened those who had instigated the proceedings—notably Gloucester and Arundel—with the penalties of treason. Yet Warwick had probably not taken a leading part in the proceedings, and was not one of those who were liable to be punished 'as traitors' (*RotP*, 2.233). Nor, unlike Arundel, had he a history of overt hostility to those around the king, and the king's policy towards France. If he had disapproved, he had done so silently. On the other hand, the steward of the royal household, John Beauchamp of Holt, a member of a cadet branch of Warwick's family, had risen by royal favour and patronage to a position of influence in Worcestershire, culminating in the grant to him of the title of Baron Kidderminster on 10 October 1387. The office of sheriff of Worcestershire was hereditary in Warwick's family, and he had extensive estates both there and in Warwickshire. The rise of a potential rival for the loyalty and service of the gentry of the west midland counties may have been decisive in inclining Warwick to join the king's opponents. For their part Gloucester and Arundel no doubt welcomed Warwick's support. His brother William was captain of Calais, and the Beauchamp family more generally had significant social influence both in the midlands and, through marriage, in other parts of England.

The Westminster chronicler suggests that Warwick played a prominent role in the political crisis of November and December 1387. The modern editors of the chronicle, however, have argued that this part of the text may be based on a tract 'written by a member of the earl's household' (*Westminster Chronicle*, liv), and other chronicles, notably that of Henry Knighton, give Warwick a lesser role. According to Westminster, Michael de la Pole believed that Warwick was the instigator of the movement against the king and his friends, though there is no evidence that this is true. More credible is Westminster's suggestion that Warwick's political stance was more moderate than that of his colleagues. In particular he is said to have opposed a suggestion made about 12 December, that Richard should be deposed, and, according to Westminster, to have declared:

> Heaven forfend that I should see a prince so glorious, ... a prince to whom at his coronation in common with other lords of this realm I did homage and swore my corporal oath of fealty, now deposed and brought low! For ourselves, such a proceeding could win little honour or glory—on the contrary, it would be discredit for us and undying reproach for our descendants. (*Westminster Chronicle*, 219)

In the light of his own earlier career, and that of his father, this speech has the ring of truth, and Warwick went on to advise his fellow appellants to concentrate on the most urgent matter facing them, the defeat of the army that Robert de Vere, duke of Ireland, was bringing against them from Cheshire.

The other appellants followed Warwick's advice, and de Vere's defeat at Radcot Bridge, Oxfordshire, on 20 December was probably decisive in persuading Richard to accept the appellants' demands to have the five accused and others (including Beauchamp of Holt) brought to trial. There is no evidence that Warwick dissented from the judgments of exile, death, and forfeiture handed down in the parliament: indeed, he subsequently purchased some of the lands in Worcestershire forfeited by the executed Beauchamp of Holt. Even when some nobles pleaded for the life of the king's former tutor, Simon Burley, to be spared, Warwick held out for the sentence of death to be confirmed. At the end of the parliament he was one of three lay lords appointed to the council established to supervise the king until the opening of the next parliament in September 1388.

Arrest, trial, and imprisonment, 1389–1399 Warwick's political career must now have seemed near its end: he was at least fifty in 1389, and he played no part in the diplomatic negotiations that, under Gaunt's leadership, brought England and France close to a final peace by 1394. His loss of the lordship of Gower to Thomas (I) Mowbray, earl of Nottingham, as the result of a lawsuit in June 1397 which reversed the judgment given in his father's favour in 1353, perhaps made him realize that he no longer enjoyed much influence at court. Not only did he have to restore the lordship to Mowbray, but he also had to compensate him by paying him the issues of the lordship from 1361. At Warwick, however, he seems in these years to have completed the construction of the chancel of St Mary's Church, and at the castle he probably completed his father's work on Guy's Tower and began work on the Watergate Tower.

In July 1397 Richard II arrested Warwick, along with Gloucester and Arundel. According to Walsingham, Richard prepared a banquet, rivalling that of Herod in its infamy, to which the three lords would be invited and then detained. Only Warwick accepted the invitation, however, and realized too late that he had walked into a trap. After Richard had commiserated with him over the loss of Gower, he was taken into custody to await trial in the forthcoming parliament. Richard's action in arresting the former appellants received different interpretations at the time: the story in the *Traïson et mort de Richart Deux*, that Warwick and the others had been involved in a plot against the king, is almost certainly baseless, though Richard may well have thought they were plotting against him and resolved to make a pre-emptive strike. Walsingham saw the arrests as coming out of a clear blue sky, and motivated by malice on the king's part, while the Kirkstall chronicler believed it was an act of revenge by the king for the events of 1387–8. This may well be true: when Warwick and the other appellants were brought to trial in parliament in September, they were charged with treason for their part in the events of those months, and it was evident that their responsibility for the execution of Burley still rankled with Richard.

Warwick's trial marks the nadir of his political career, for though he did not lose his life he forfeited not just his lands and titles but also his self-respect. Both the monk of Evesham and Adam Usk, perhaps using a common source, give a vivid account of the trial. According to Usk he behaved 'like a wretched old woman … wailing and weeping and whining that he had done all, traitor that he was' (*Chronicon Adae de Usk*, 161). He threw himself on the king's mercy, 'bewailing that he had ever been an ally of the appellees' (ibid.). Richard was pleased by his confession: according to Walsingham he said it was dearer to him than the value of all the lands of Gloucester and Arundel. The king spared his life, but he was sentenced to the loss of all his lands and his title, and was ordered to be imprisoned on the Isle of Man. It is not known whereabouts he was held: there is no evidence to link him with the so-called Warwick Tower at Peel Castle. His lands were granted to Richard II's supporters: Thomas Holland, duke of Surrey, received Warwick itself, and was appointed guardian of Warwick's heir, Richard, and his wife.

Final years and death With the overthrow of Richard II in 1399 Warwick was recalled and restored to his lands and honours, though he did not regain Gower. His son was knighted on the eve of Henry IV's coronation, but he himself played little part in politics over the next two years. Both the inventories of his goods, made at the time of his forfeiture in 1397, and his will, drawn up at Warwick in April 1400, suggest that he may have been in financial difficulties as a result of his loss of Gower and the forfeiture of his estates. In his will he ordered his executors to sell his goods and chattels, apart from those that were the subject of specific legacies, and his bequest of gold and silver objects to St Mary's Church, Warwick, was subject to the redemption of the mortgage on them. He died on 8 April 1401, and was buried in the collegiate church of St Mary in Warwick. His tomb was surmounted with modest brass effigies of himself and his wife, compared with the large alabaster effigies of his father and mother on their tomb: perhaps this is another indication of financial difficulties. The tomb was destroyed in a fire in 1694, but the brasses were saved and are now in the south transept of the church.

Some time before 1378 Beauchamp married Margaret, daughter of William, Lord Ferrers of Groby: the exact date is unknown. His son and heir Richard *Beauchamp was born on 25 or 28 January 1382, and Richard II stood as godfather at the child's baptism. Apart from Richard their only offspring was a daughter, Catherine, who was alive in 1400 when her father bequeathed her a brooch in his will, but who died before reaching adulthood. His wife died on 22 January 1407 and was buried beside him in the church of St Mary at Warwick.   ANTHONY TUCK

Sources Beauchamp cartulary, BL, Add. MS 28024 · Exchequer accounts, PRO · Register of Archbishop Arundel, LPL [microfilm in CUL] · L. C. Hector and B. F. Harvey, eds. and trans., *The Westminster chronicle, 1381–1394*, OMT (1982) · *Chronicon Adae de Usk*, ed. and trans. E. M. Thompson, 2nd edn (1904) · *Chronicon Henrici Knighton, vel Cnitthon, monachi Leycestrensis*, ed. J. R. Lumby, 2 vols., Rolls Series, 92 (1889–95) · *Thomae Walsingham, quondam monachi S. Albani, historia Anglicana*, ed. H. T. Riley, 2 vols., pt 1 of *Chronica monasterii S. Albani*, Rolls Series, 28 (1863–4) · *Johannis de Trokelowe et Henrici de*

Blaneforde … chronica et annales, ed. H. T. Riley, pt 3 of *Chronica monasterii S. Albani*, Rolls Series, 28 (1866) · G. B. Stow, ed., *Historia vitae et regni Ricardi Secundi* (1977) · *CIPM* · *Calendar of inquisitions miscellaneous (chancery)*, 7 vols., PRO (1916–68) · *CCIR* · B. Williams, ed., *Chronicque de la traïson et mort de Richart Deux, roy Dengleterre*, EHS, 9 (1846) · *RotP*, vols. 2–3 · W. Dugdale, *The antiquities of Warwickshire illustrated*, rev. W. Thomas, 2nd edn, 1 (1730); facs. edn [1973] · A. Goodman, *John of Gaunt: the exercise of princely power in fourteenth-century Europe* (1992) · G. Holmes, *The Good Parliament* (1975) · A. Tuck, *Richard II and the English nobility* (1973) · J. Sherborne, *War, politics and culture in fourteenth-century England*, ed. A. Tuck (1994) · C. Given-Wilson, ed. and trans., *Chronicles of the revolution, 1397–1400: the reign of Richard II* (1993) · A. F. J. Sinclair, 'The Beauchamp earls of Warwick in the later middle ages', PhD diss., U. Lond., 1987 · D. Craine, *Peel Castle, Isle of Man* (1958) · W. M. Ormrod, *The reign of Edward III* (1990) · C. Given-Wilson, *The royal household and the king's affinity: service, politics and finance in England, 1360–1413* (1986) · *VCH Warwickshire*, vol. 8 · N. Saul, *Richard II* (1997)
Archives BL, Add. MS 28024
Likenesses alabaster tomb effigy, St Mary's Church, Warwick · brass on monument, St Mary's Church, Warwick
Wealth at death estates: *CIPM*

Beauchamp, Walter (I) de (*c*.1065–1130/31), administrator, was a royal official for most of the reign of Henry I. His antecedents are unknown. Initially he was perhaps a tenant in Worcestershire of Urse d'Abetot, whose daughter, probably called Emmeline, he married. Their son William de *Beauchamp was born no later than 1110. Following the death of d'Abetot in 1108, and the forfeiture incurred by his son Roger, *c*.1110, Beauchamp soon succeeded to the dominant position held by Urse in Worcestershire. This was evidently due to his usefulness in the royal administration, and he attested royal charters from about 1111 and perhaps earlier.

Between *c*.1110 and 1115, Beauchamp obtained three royal grants of hunting rights in the shire, and he was granted the lands of Roger d'Abetot between 1114 and 1116. These estates included all the lands formerly held by Urse, and about half of those held by Urse's brother, Robert Dispenser, another royal official, who had died about 1097. While the bulk of these lands lay in Worcestershire, there were outlying estates in several other shires. Between 1123 and 1129, moreover, Henry I conceded to Beauchamp the dower land of Urse's widow, Alice, which she had earlier granted to him.

Beauchamp was granted the shrievalty of Worcester between December 1113 and April 1116. He was also keeper of the forests in Worcestershire, and at some uncertain date he was appointed to the office of royal dispenser, earlier held by Robert Dispenser. As a curial official, he remained sheriff of Worcester for life, contrary to the general royal policy of ending hereditary shrievalties. He received a fourth royal grant of hunting rights between 1129 and his death, which occurred in 1130 or 1131, when he was succeeded in his lands, and his office of dispenser, by his son William. Stephen de Beauchamp, a close friend of Robert, earl of Gloucester, and a tenant of the Beauchamp fief, was probably a younger son of Walter.

EMMA MASON

Sources E. Mason, ed., *The Beauchamp cartulary: charters, 1100–1268*, PRSoc., new ser., 43 (1980) · R. R. Darlington, ed., *The cartulary of Worcester Cathedral Priory (register I)*, PRSoc., 76, new ser., 38 (1968) ·

J. H. Round, *Feudal England: historical studies on the eleventh and twelfth centuries* (1895), 141–8 · *Pipe rolls, 31 Henry I* · *Reg. RAN*, vol. 2 · W. Map, *De nugis curialium / Courtiers' trifles*, ed. and trans. M. R. James, rev. C. N. L. Brooke and R. A. B. Mynors, OMT (1983), 426–9 · E. Mason, 'Magnates, curiales and the wheel of fortune', *Anglo-Norman Studies*, 2 (1979), 118–40
Archives BL, Add. MS 28024

Beauchamp, Walter (II) de (1192/3–1236), justice, was the second son and eventual heir of William (II) de Beauchamp, who was lord of Elmley Castle in Worcestershire, and hereditary castellan of Worcester and sheriff of the county. At William's death in 1197, his heir was his eldest son William, a minor who died before Michaelmas 1211, when Walter was in the custody of Roger Mortimer (*d.* 1214) and his wife, Isabel. Walter married their daughter Johanna in 1212 (she died in 1225), and was in possession of his barony by 1214 (and possibly in 1213). He obtained his shrievalty on 19 August 1215, but lost it when, with nineteen of his knights, he deserted to the rebels in May 1216. He returned to his allegiance to King John in August 1216, however, when he was reinstated in his lands.

Beauchamp witnessed the reissue of Magna Carta on 11 November 1216, and in March 1217 he was restored to his shrievalty and castellanship, and became keeper of the royal forests in Worcestershire. He also witnessed the further reissue of Magna Carta on 11 February 1225. In 1227 he was appointed an itinerant justice for the Gloucestershire eyre of January to February, and for the Oxfordshire eyre of March to April. But he had withheld the profits of his shire continuously from 1224, and consequently he lost his shrievalty early in 1229, though he was reinstated by 20 November in that year. He continued his family's patronage of the priory of Great Malvern. In 1225 or later, he married his second wife, Angaret, who died between 1280 and 1283.

At the coronation of Queen Eleanor in January 1236 Beauchamp performed the ceremonial duties of the dispensership (an office descended from his eleventh-century forebear Robert Dispenser). He died on 11 April 1236. His first wife, Johanna, was the mother of his heir, William (III) de Beauchamp, who married the eventual heiress of the earls of Warwick, and was grandfather of Guy de Beauchamp, tenth earl of Warwick.

EMMA MASON

Sources E. Mason, ed., *The Beauchamp cartulary: charters, 1100–1268*, PRSoc., new ser., 43 (1980) · T. D. Hardy, ed., *Rotuli litterarum patentium*, RC (1835) · T. D. Hardy, ed., *Rotuli litterarum clausarum*, RC, 1 (1833) · *CPR, 1216–25* · *Curia regis rolls preserved in the Public Record Office* (1922–), vol. 13
Archives BL, Add. MS 28024

Beauchamp, Sir Walter (*d.* 1430), soldier and administrator, was probably the second son of Sir John Beauchamp of Powick, Worcestershire, and his wife, Elizabeth. First recorded in 1392 as retained by Thomas of Woodstock, duke of Gloucester (*d.* 1397), he later passed into the service of Henry IV, from whom he received a grant of £40 yearly in 1399, and became an esquire in the royal household. It is likely that he fought for the king at Shrewsbury in 1403, and campaigned in the north against Archbishop Scrope and the earl of Northumberland in 1405, and he was still described as a 'king's esquire' in April 1412. In 1415, now a 'king's knight', he served in the royal army in France, as part of the retinue of Humphrey, duke of Gloucester (d. 1447). In the following year he was elected to parliament as a knight of the shire for Wiltshire, and was promptly chosen to be speaker of the Commons. In 1417 he contracted to serve in France again, and became the first *bailli* of Rouen after its capture in 1419. He remained in Normandy for two years, also becoming treasurer of the royal household and treasurer at war, positions of trust that help to explain his nomination as one of the executors of Henry V's will in June 1421. Shortly afterwards he passed into the service of Queen Catherine, as steward of her household. On Henry V's death Beauchamp was one of the commoners appointed to the council created to assist the protectors of the infant Henry VI, though he seldom attended its sessions. In spite of his earlier connections with Humphrey of Gloucester, he had probably by now joined the duke's opponents, among whom was his distant kinsman Richard Beauchamp, earl of Warwick (d. 1439)—during the parliament of 1425 Sir Walter had taken a prominent part on Warwick's behalf in his dispute over precedence with John (V) Mowbray, earl marshal (d. 1432). As governor of the young king, Warwick would have been responsible for Beauchamp's being named in May 1428 as one of four knights who were to attend continually on the king's person. In April 1429 Beauchamp was made master of the king's horse, but his career was cut short soon afterwards, by his death on 1 January 1430. He was buried at Steeple Lavington church. Walter Beauchamp had before 1400 married Elizabeth (d. 1447), daughter and coheir of Sir John Roches of Bromham, Wiltshire, a union that brought him the manor of Steeple Lavington and other lands in Wiltshire and Hertfordshire. They had two sons, William and Richard *Beauchamp (d. 1481); the latter became successively bishop of Hereford and of Salisbury. HENRY SUMMERSON

Sources J. S. Roskell and L. S. Woodger, 'Beauchamp, Sir Walter', HoP, *Commons*
Wealth at death £4 13s. 4d. in bequests: will, 21 Dec 1429, Roskell and Woodger, 'Sir Walter Beauchamp'

Beauchamp, William (I) de (1100x10–1170), sheriff and baron, was the eldest son of Walter (I) de *Beauchamp (d. 1130/31) of Elmley Castle, sheriff of Worcestershire, and his wife, reputedly named Emmeline, the daughter and eventual heir of Urse d'*Abetot, sheriff of Worcester, and eventual heir of about half the land of her paternal uncle, Robert Despenser. William succeeded his father in late 1130 or early 1131 (being by then of full age). He married Berta, a daughter of the marcher lord William de Briouze, receiving with her lands in three villages in south Gloucestershire. His sons were William (II), his heir, John, Peter, Robert, and Walter; his daughters were Emma and Matilda.

Beauchamp was not confirmed in his father's office when he succeeded to Walter's lands. He was sheriff of Worcester about 1139, but there is no evidence that he ever attended King Stephen's court. Allegedly Stephen granted him a constableship on about 30 November 1139,

at Worcester, after the defection of Miles of Gloucester. Late in July 1141 the Empress Matilda confirmed Beauchamp in the office of sheriff, with the keepership of the royal forests in Worcestershire, and the constableship and dispensership which Urse d'Abetot and Walter (I) de Beauchamp had held from Henry I. It is not known whether Beauchamp was earlier confirmed in these offices by Henry I and by Stephen. Between the summer of 1141 and 1144 he was occasionally in the entourage of the empress, and in April 1149 he was a supporter of Henry of Anjou. About this time Beauchamp and his men attacked Evesham Abbey, but were driven off.

During the 1140s Waleran, count of Meulan, was also earl of Worcester, and in that capacity asserted authority over Beauchamp, addressing him as his *filius* (son). The latter, as sheriff and constable, controlled Worcester Castle. It seems that they reached a compromise by which the earl held the city while Beauchamp held the castle. In 1150 or 1151 King Stephen captured the city. Waleran's men, apparently, headed by Ralph de Mandeville, seized the castle, imprisoned Beauchamp, and kept him in close confinement. Roger, earl of Hereford, persuaded Stephen to besiege Worcester and then to hand the castle over to him. The siege failed, however.

In Henry II's reign Beauchamp was sheriff of Worcestershire between 1155 and 1170. He deputized as sheriff of Gloucestershire in 1156–7, and was sheriff between 1157 and 1163. He was sheriff of Herefordshire from 1160 to 1167, and sheriff of Warwickshire in 1158–9. The inquest of sheriffs, held in 1170, brought to light his abuse of the office of sheriff of Worcestershire, which was taken from him, and regained by his heir only in 1190. The castle and honour of Tamworth, held by Robert Despenser, was granted to Beauchamp by the empress in 1141, despite the fact that successive members of the Marmion family had been in possession for several decades, and subsequently remained so. It was alleged that the Beauchamp claim to Tamworth was finally relinquished when Beauchamp's daughter Matilda married Robert Marmion. In his *carta* of 1166 Beauchamp listed tenants, all holding under terms established by 1135, who owed him a total service of sixteen knights, but he declared that neither he nor his predecessors owed or rendered the crown the service of more than seven knights. He and his descendants persistently rendered this reduced service.

Beauchamp died in 1170, not long after losing control of the shrievalty. He had earlier confirmed his father's grant of land and tithes to Worcester Cathedral priory, and was buried at the entrance to its chapter house. The Beauchamps of Elmley should not be confused with the Beauchamps of Bedford (1066–1265), several of whose members were also called William. EMMA MASON

Sources E. Mason, ed., *The Beauchamp cartulary: charters, 1100–1268*, PRSoc., new ser., 43 (1980) · *Ann. mon.*, vol. 4 · *Calendar of inquisitions miscellaneous (chancery)*, PRO, 1 (1916), 1971 · Pipe rolls, 2–4 Henry II–15 Henry II · K. R. Potter and R. H. C. Davis, eds., *Gesta Stephani*, OMT (1976) · *Reg. RAN*, vol. 3
Archives BL, Add. MS 28024

Beauchamp, William de [William (I) de Beauchamp of Bedford] (c.1185–1260), judge and sheriff, was the son of Simon de *Beauchamp (c.1145–1206/7) [see under Beauchamp, de, family] and his wife, Isabella, whose antecedents are unknown. William's first wife, Gunnora (d. before 1220), was the daughter of William de Lanvaley of Walkern, Hertfordshire. His second wife, Ida (d. 1266x9), was the daughter of William *Longespée, earl of Salisbury (d. 1226), and hence a granddaughter of Henry II. William succeeded his father in 1207 and was charged a relief of 600 marks and six palfreys for the barony, a part of which was to be paid by the mother and brother of his first wife. He was assessed for scutage on forty-five knights' fees, plus a fifth and a twelfth, although he acknowledged service due on only thirty-six fees. Apparently he served in the Irish expedition of 1210 and the Poitevin expedition of 1214, since he was exempted from the scutage levied for each.

In 1215 Beauchamp joined the baronial opposition at Stamford, entertained its leaders in Bedford Castle, and was among the rebels excommunicated by Innocent III. On 20 May 1217 he was captured at the battle of Lincoln, but made his peace with the regency government in the autumn. Falkes de Bréauté captured Bedford Castle in December 1215, and was granted custody of it, although Beauchamp controlled the barony. When Bréauté fell from power, his garrison was besieged and the castle set alight. It was partially demolished on royal orders, but Beauchamp was granted licence to build a residence in its bailey. In 1233 he was with a royal expedition against Richard Marshal which was ambushed near Grosmont and forced to flee. In July 1234 Beauchamp was appointed a baron of the exchequer and held this post again in 1237. Between those years he was also sheriff of Bedfordshire and Buckinghamshire. In 1236 he acted as almoner at the coronation of the queen.

Beauchamp and his second wife waged a violent dispute with Wardon Abbey over conflicting claims of rights of warren. In 1247 Newnham Priory fell vacant and his bailiff attempted to take seisin of its granges; Ida and her seneschal then laid waste to its lands when a new prior was elected without the consent of her husband, who was overseas. Beauchamp claimed that he, 'and the other barons, his peers', had rights of wardship over religious houses which they held in custody during a vacancy. The Dunstable annalist related that in 1254 Beauchamp and Ida used threats to force the prior to come outside the priory gate and request installation from them, whereupon Beauchamp took him by the hand, led him to the choir, and personally installed him. In contrast, the *Flores historiarum* commemorated Beauchamp as a generous patron of monks, nuns, and canons.

Beauchamp's eldest son, Simon, died in Gascony in 1256 and in 1257 he obtained royal licence to grant the barony to William de *Beauchamp [see under Beauchamp, de, family], his eldest surviving son. He died at an advanced age in 1260. William de Beauchamp (d. 1260) should on no account be confused with William (I) de Beauchamp (d.

1170), of Elmley, Worcestershire, nor with the latter's son William (II) (d. 1197) or great-grandson William (III) (d. 1269).   EMMA MASON

Sources C. G. Chambers and G. H. Fowler, 'The Beauchamps, barons of Bedford', *Publications of the Bedfordshire Record Society*, 1 (1913), 1–25 • Paris, *Chron.*, vols. 2, 3, 5 • H. R. Luard, ed., *Flores historiarum*, 3 vols., Rolls Series, 95 (1890), vol. 2 • *Ann. mon.*, vol. 3 • T. Madox, *The history and antiquities of the exchequer of the kings of England* (1711) • I. J. Sanders, *English baronies: a study of their origin and descent, 1086–1327* (1960)

Beauchamp, William de (d. 1262). See under Beauchamp, de, family (*per. c.*1080–*c.*1265).

Beauchamp, William (IV) de, ninth earl of Warwick (c.1238–1298), magnate, was the eldest of eight children of William (III) de Beauchamp of Elmley, Worcestershire, and his wife Isabel, sister of William Mauduit, earl of Warwick.

Inheritance and early career Beauchamp inherited the earldom from his uncle, William *Mauduit, who died on 8 January 1268. He did homage for his uncle's lands on 9 February. According to the inquisitions on the latter's death, William de Beauchamp was then over thirty. He was thus a young man during the period of baronial reform. His father had been a royalist, and according to John Leland's *Itinerary*, the 'old lorde Beauchamp of Helmely' sent his sons to the battle of Evesham to help the king, 'and these Brether and their Band did a greate feate in vanquishing the Host of Montefort'. Whatever the truth of this, it is probable that the young William participated on the royalist side. He married Matilda, daughter of *John fitz Geoffrey, some time between late 1261 (when her first husband, the minor Yorkshire baron, Gerard de Furnival, died) and his own accession to the earldom in January 1268. It cannot have been a particularly propitious marriage, for with two married brothers Matilda had little prospect of inheriting her father's estates. In the event she was to be one of her father's coheirs, bringing a quarter of his property to the Beauchamps in 1297. William (III) de Beauchamp and Peter de Montfort had made an arrangement to marry their respective eldest sons and daughters, which in August 1248 the king promised not to disturb should the parents die before the children came of age. The scheme must have fallen through, quite possibly for political reasons given their radically different stances during the reforms and the civil war that followed. William's father kept a tight rein on his resources so that William the younger was not particularly well endowed. The father had first bestowed upon the couple land to the value of £9 in Sheriffs Lench, Worcestershire, and then later gave them the manor of Letcombe Basset, Berkshire, in exchange. Before 1265 William (IV) de Beauchamp had acquired manors at Beoley and Yardley, partly from an indebted tenant.

His inheritance of the Warwick earldom must have greatly altered William (IV) de Beauchamp's horizons. In 1271 or 1272 he named his infant heir Guy de *Beauchamp, after the legendary Guy of Warwick. Meanwhile, his father had died leaving him the Beauchamp estates, for which his homage was taken on 27 April 1269. From the

Mauduits he inherited the office of chamberlain of the exchequer, while through his father he became hereditary sheriff of Worcestershire and hereditary pantler at royal coronations. He was probably quite high in royal favour, perhaps on account of his own actions during the period of civil war as well as his father's. For his 'laudable service' he was not only allowed to continue his father's arrangement of paying off the latter's debts to the exchequer at the rate of £10 per annum but also to pay off his relief at the same rate. Although he was pardoned of debts to the exchequer at various times during his life, he seems to have remained in permanent debt to the crown.

The resources directly deployed by the earls of Warwick were much depleted, in fact, during the thirteenth century, largely because of the longevity of their widows. It was a situation that continued into the time of William (IV) de Beauchamp, even if less severely than earlier in the century. Ela, daughter of William (I) de Longespée, and widow of Thomas, earl of Warwick (d. 1242), lived until 1298. She held as dower one-third of the property that had come to Earl Thomas on his father's death. Admittedly William (IV) had brought the Beauchamp resources to the earldom in 1268. However, these too were encumbered by dower. Angaret, his grandfather's second wife, held her dower until her death about 1280. It is not perhaps too surprising that William (IV) had to be coerced into assigning her full dower to his aunt, the widowed Countess Alice Mauduit in 1268, and although he was eventually able to negotiate with Ela Longespée for the recovery of some of her dower lands, it is none the less probably true to say that resource problems cast a shadow over the earl's involvement in national affairs.

Warwick did, however, participate in affairs of state. He was present at the council at Westminster on 12 November 1276, when the legal process against Llywelyn ap Gruffudd was recited and the decision was made to go to war, and he was present in parliament when Alexander III, king of Scots, did homage to Edward I at Michaelmas 1278.

Military service Warwick was much employed by the crown in matters concerning Wales and the Welsh marches. He was appointed on a commission to inquire into the trespasses committed by Gilbert de Clare against Llywelyn, for example, on 16 October 1270. On 14 April 1274 he was empowered, with others, to hear and do justice with respect to 'mutual trespasses and raids' between the king and Llywelyn ap Gruffudd, and on 24 April to bring about a truce between Llywelyn and Humphrey (IV) de Bohun. He earned some distinction in his military career, not only in Wales but also on Edward I's early campaigns in Scotland. As part of the preparations for the first Welsh campaign he was made captain of Chester and Lancaster in November 1276. The main muster of the feudal host was ordered to take place at Worcester on 1 July 1277. In the meantime it was necessary to arrange for the protection of the marches, and the earl of Warwick's appointment should be seen in this light. As Edward was able to march forward to Flint during the next summer without fear of any flank attack, it is to be presumed that Warwick

did his job well. He took part in the siege and capture of Dryslwyn, Carmarthenshire, during August and September 1287. In Scotland he was one of the leaders of the force which, under the earl of Surrey, defeated the Scots at Dunbar on 27 April 1296.

It was during the Welsh rising of 1294–5, however, that the earl of Warwick fought his most important engagement. While the king's forces assembled at Chester, Warwick's troops mustered at Montgomery and a third army under William de Valence was at Carmarthen. With the king effectively trapped at Conwy, Warwick was responsible for a major victory when on 5 March 1295 at Maes Moydog he crippled the forces of the Welsh leader Madog ap Llywelyn. Having moved his own troops from Montgomery to Oswestry, Warwick heard from his spies of the whereabouts of the Welsh leader, who had descended with his forces from Snowdonia. Warwick then took his troops on a night march to engage the Welsh on the following day. Madog's forces advanced to fight the English and suffered severe losses, over 600 according to chroniclers. Moreover, another 100 or so died in a secondary action which struck Madog's baggage train and effectively barred his retreat. Others were drowned. Apparently the English had both surprised the enemy and successfully carried through a pincer movement. The army that effected this victory was a small one, comprising about 119 horse and 2500 foot. However, the English losses appear to have been derisory, namely one squire and six infantrymen according to the Hagnaby chronicle. This might be thought to lend some support to the chronicler Nicholas Trivet's assertion that the English victory was due to the novel tactic of interspersing cavalry and archers, foreshadowing later tactics; but doubt has been cast on this version of the battle, given that the payroll for Warwick's army lists only thirteen crossbowmen and archers *per se*. Whatever the precise tactics employed, it looks as though Warwick possessed some skill as a commander. Three months later he achieved a further coup when he escorted the rebel Morgan ap Maredudd and his men to the king.

The payroll for Warwick's subsidiary army of 1294–5 survives in full, but the name of the earl does not appear on the roll. The earls clearly regarded it as beneath their dignity, and probably against their chivalric code, to serve for pay. For the 1282–3 campaign, and again in 1287, Warwick accepted prests or advances of cash but these seem to have been either the wages of the infantry or loans to assist in the general preparations for war. But pay was taken for the expedition that set out for Scotland late in 1297, possibly because it was a winter campaign. The king contracted with six magnates to serve for three months with a total of 500 horse in return for £7691 16s. 8d. The smallest retinue, with only 30 horse, was that of Warwick.

Warwick was only once in serious opposition to the crown. This was during what has been described as the 'near civil war' of 1297. As one of a mere handful of earls present in England during the crisis he was virtually obliged to take part. About 130 magnates were asked by the king to muster at London on 7 July. Before this gathering, however, many of the magnates, including Warwick, held a meeting at Montgomery. They decided that they could not serve the king overseas because they had spent so much already on his wars in Wales and Scotland, and because they were impoverished by the frequent taxes. According to the Evesham chronicle, the earl of Warwick was bribed into submission. He came to the king complaining of poverty. He was given 'a certain sum of money' and was promised more. His opposition to the king promptly ceased. In fact on 14 July he participated in the swearing of fealty to the king's son, Edward of Caernarfon. That the king was able to divide the opposition was due in some measure to Warwick's action. In fact, when mediation finally took place at Stratford, at the meeting at which the Remonstrances were drawn up, Warwick was among those acting for the king.

In the end, however, Warwick did not accompany the king to Flanders, possibly because of illness. When the king summoned him on 17 September 1297 he expressed his pleasure that Warwick's condition had improved. He remained in England during the Flanders campaign as part of Prince Edward's council. Warwick seems to have remained active almost to the end of his life, and on 30 March 1298 he was ordered to be with the king at York at Whitsun to set out against the rebels in Scotland.

Religious affairs, death, and burial In terms of his local power Warwick experienced some difficulty with Godfrey Giffard, bishop of Worcester, chiefly over their respective rights within the hundred of Oswaldslow. In religious matters Warwick favoured the friars. He was a benefactor of the Augustinian friary of Thelsford and he was buried with the Franciscans at Worcester. Like his father and grandfather before him he had been in contention with Worcester Cathedral priory. In the year 1276, according to the Worcester chronicle, he heard a rumour that his father's tomb had been opened and the body thrown out, and he therefore ordered the tomb to be opened so that he could check. The rumour was found to be false and Warwick was excommunicated. Two months later a dispute between Warwick and the prior was settled on payment of £100 to the earl. The prior agreed at this time to find one monk to say a daily mass for Warwick and his family in perpetuity at the altars of saints Philip and James.

Warwick became gravely ill at Elmley in early June 1298. According to the Worcester chronicle he made his will 'in the absence of all his friends' (*Ann. mon.*, 4.537) and on the advice of Brother John of Olney, who caused him to change his mind so that instead of being buried in the cathedral church of Worcester he was buried with the friars. It is hard to believe the implication that this was a last-minute conversion to support the friars. He seems to have made his will the previous year, in fact, and the stipulations of the will show every sign of having been well considered. His body was to be buried in the choir of the Worcester Franciscans. If he died abroad he was to be buried in the nearest Franciscan house. His heart was to be buried wherever his wife chose to be buried. He set aside £200 for the funeral celebrations. The two horses that were to carry his armour in the funeral procession were to be given to the friars. Indeed, as the Worcester chronicle relates, the brethren

> processed through the streets and squares of the city and made a show to the citizens, bearing the body as if carrying the spoils of war and so they buried him in a place which had not previously been used and where in winter time he could be said to be drowned rather than buried. (*Ann. mon.*, 4.537)

Warwick gave £100 to maintain two soldiers in the Holy Land. His bequests to individuals included a gold ring with a ruby in it to his son, Guy. His countess was to have all his silver vessels with his cross, which contained part of the True Cross, the vestments belonging to his chapel to make use of during her life, and the cup given to him by the bishop of Worcester. She was also to have all his horses and moveable goods in his manor of Sheffield. Horses were of vital importance to a military figure like Warwick, but it may be that Warwick had a particular interest in horses. On campaign in 1297 and 1298 the Beauchamps possessed a larger number of highly priced horses than any other family, one at 100 marks, three at 80, and two at 70, besides equally valuable remounts. All his other cups, jewels, and rings the countess was to distribute for the health of his soul as she saw fit. He gave 50 marks to his two daughters, nuns at the Gilbertine priory of Shouldham, and made bequests of the vestments, after his wife's death, to his private chapels; the best suit was to be passed on to Guy. There was, however, no bequest to the cathedral priory, despite the fact that the Beauchamps were its patrons. Warwick died on either 5 or 9 June 1298. His wife died three years later, on 16 or 18 April 1301. She was buried with him on 7 May. Again, according to the—no doubt jaundiced—Worcester chronicler this was done against her wishes, in that she had indicated during her lifetime that she wished to be buried elsewhere. Their son, Guy de Beauchamp, succeeded as earl of Warwick. According to Dugdale two other sons, Robert and John, had predeceased their father, the former dying in infancy, and there were at least three married daughters (Isabel, Maud, and Margaret) and possibly a fourth (Wenthlea), in addition to the two nuns.

PETER COSS

Sources *Ann. mon.*, 4.471–2, 520–21, 527, 537, 549 • E. Mason, ed., *The Beauchamp cartulary: charters, 1100–1268*, PRSoc., new ser., 43 (1980), xii–xiii, xxxi, nos. 41–2, 97–8, 100 • J. W. W. Bund, ed., *Register of Bishop Godfrey Giffard, September 23rd, 1268, to August 15th, 1301*, 2 vols., Worcestershire Historical Society, 15 (1898–1902), vol. 1, pp. xxxii–xxxiii; vol. 2, pp. 7–9, 75, 77, 498 • *CIPM*, 2, nos. 679, 695; 3, no. 477; 4, no. 24 • B. Golding, 'Burials and benefactions: an aspect of monastic patronage in thirteenth-century England', *England in the thirteenth century* [Harlaxton 1984], ed. W. M. Ormrod (1985), 65–6 • E. Mason, 'The resources of the earldom of Warwick in the thirteenth century', *Midland History*, 3 (1975–6), 67–75 • W. Dugdale, *The baronage of England*, 2 vols. (1675–6) • J. H. Denton, 'The crisis of 1297 from the Evesham Chronicle', *EngHR*, 93 (1978), 560–79 • M. Prestwich, *Edward I* (1988), 176, 196, 221–3, 413, 419, 421, 433, 478 • chronicle of Hailes Abbey, BL, Cotton MS Cleopatra D.iii, fols. 59–72 • *The itinerary of John Leland in or about the years 1535–1543*, ed. L. Toulmin Smith, 11 pts in 5 vols. (1906–10) • M. Prestwich, 'A new account of the Welsh campaign of 1294–5', *Welsh History Review / Cylchgrawn Hanes Cymru*, 6 (1973–4), 89–94 • R. F. Walker, 'The Hagnaby Chronicle and the battle of Maes Moydog', *Welsh History Review / Cylchgrawn Hanes Cymru*, 8 (1976–7), 125–38 • GEC, *Peerage*, new edn • M. Prestwich, *War, politics, and finance under Edward I* (1972), 64, 73 • C. Roberts, ed., *Excerpta è rotulis finium in Turri Londinensi asservatis, Henrico Tertio rege*, AD 1216–1272, 2, RC, 32 (1836), 466, 487 • J. E. Morris, *The Welsh wars of Edward I* (1901); repr. (1968), 82 • CPR, 1247–58; 1266–92 • CClR, 1264–8, 1272–88, 1296–302 • W. Dugdale, *The antiquities of Warwickshire illustrated*, rev. W. Thomas, 2nd edn, 2 (1730), 389–91

Wealth at death see *CIPM* 3, no. 477

Beauchamp, William (V), first Baron Bergavenny (*c*.1343–1411), soldier and landowner, was the fourth son of Thomas *Beauchamp, eleventh earl of Warwick (1313/14–1369), and of Katherine (*d*. 1369), daughter of Roger Mortimer, first earl of March.

Early military service As a younger son Beauchamp was destined for the church and attended Oxford University from 1358 until 1361, receiving his first benefice, by papal dispensation, in 1358. It was probably in 1361, following the deaths in quick succession of two of his older brothers, that he re-entered the lay world. He was a knight by 1367 and in 1375 was made a knight of the Garter. In 1367 he fought at Nájera, on the Castilian campaign led by Edward, the Black Prince, and later that year he and his brother Thomas *Beauchamp (*d*. 1401), now heir to the earldom, went on crusade to Prussia. In 1370 he fought in Gascony, in 1373 he participated in John of Gaunt's *chevauchée* in France, and in 1381–2 in Edmund, earl of Cambridge's expedition to Portugal, but, allegedly because of failure to pay him in full, he backed out of Despenser's 'crusade' of 1383. In 1375 Edward III gave him a life annuity of 100 marks for his good service. He was also feed by his brother, who became earl of Warwick in 1369, but almost all this early service was performed in the retinue of John of Gaunt, from whom he received a fee of 100 marks in 1373. During the 1370s he was one of Gaunt's bannerets, but it seems Froissart is incorrect in stating that he went on Gaunt's Castilian expedition of 1386 (Froissart, 11.326).

Landed interests In 1369 Beauchamp was elevated far above the level of a younger son by the grant under his father's will of land to the value of 400 marks, mostly in the midlands. In 1372 his prospects were further enhanced: John Hastings, the last Hastings earl of Pembroke, then childless and at odds with his cousin and heir, Reynold, Lord Grey of Ruthin (*d*. 1440), willed almost all his lands in England and Wales to his cousin William Beauchamp. The exception was Pembroke, which was left to the king. Beauchamp in return was to bear Hastings's arms and try to obtain the recreation of the earldom. Hastings died in 1375 but he left an under-age son who survived until 1389. However, in 1378 Beauchamp was given custody of Pembroke itself during the heir's minority. He also had dealings in Somerset arising out of his sister's marriage to John, Lord Beauchamp of Hatch. All the same, his main commitment in England was to the interests of himself and his family in the west midlands. These had been enhanced in 1376 by the grant for life from his brother of the former Montfort of Beaudesert lands in Warwickshire. In 1386, moreover, he exchanged two Wiltshire properties left him by his father for Snitterfield, also in

Warwickshire. In 1377 he was made keeper of the king's forest and park of Feckenham, Worcestershire, for life, and from 1380 he was on a number of commissions concerned with Feckenham. In 1383 he and his brother helped found the Gild of the Holy Trinity and St Mary at Warwick. Many of his associates were from west midland families linked to the earldom, and during the 1380s he assisted his brother in dealing with the extended conflict over Ladbroke Manor, Warwickshire.

Royal service and Lollard associates Beauchamp's history in the first part of Richard II's reign is interesting for a number of reasons. He was one of Richard's earliest chamber knights, appointed in 1377, probably because he had been councillor to the Black Prince (he was executor to the prince's widow in 1385), and was chamberlain of Richard's household from 1378 to 1380. During the early 1380s he received various grants, including a life grant of 200 marks a year in 1380/81 and the alien priory of Pembroke in 1383. It is through the royal household that he is to be found in the company of some of the 'Lollard knights', and he himself may well have had Lollard sympathies. He was certainly involved with several of these men and with other suspect associates like Sir Philip de la Vache. He had an appropriate background: Oxford cleric during Wyclif's time at the university, member of the royal household under Richard II, and service to Wyclif's protector, Gaunt. Among the more notable transactions involving Beauchamp and others from this group is a release of all actions by the wife of a London citizen against Geoffrey Chaucer for rape. However, the deed is a reminder that these men may have been not so much heretics as a close-knit group in Richard's household, some of them part of the highly educated literary coterie to which Chaucer belonged, where Beauchamp would not have been out of place.

Relations with Richard II and enhancement of status Where Beauchamp stood in the turbulent politics of Richard II's reign is not entirely clear. As the brother of one of the leading lords appellant, he might be expected to have been an antagonist of the king, but he was also a member of Richard II's household, the object of hostility of both parliament and appellants in 1386–8, albeit one of those not singled out for attack. If, apart from the Feckenham commissions, he was hardly used on government business in England, this was surely because he was on campaign for much of the time, and, from 1383 until 1389, captain of Calais. There he performed with some distinction both on land and at sea and was several times on diplomatic missions. As late as February 1387 Beauchamp and his brother were among the group given custody of the lands of the infant earl of Stafford. However, a hostile inquiry into alleged neglect and asset-stripping in Pembroke in 1386–7 suggests that he had enemies at court. Although he was pardoned, the episode led to an informal arrangement by which he relinquished the lands to the heir. In 1387, as the political crisis deepened, Richard commanded Beauchamp to surrender the Calais captaincy. He not only refused but, according to Knighton (Knighton,

406–7), confiscated secret letters from Richard, carried by John Golafre, another chamber knight, requesting help from the king of France, and sent them to Richard's enemy, Thomas of Woodstock, duke of Gloucester. Later that year, Beauchamp refused to admit the disgraced favourite, Michael de la Pole, earl of Suffolk (d. 1389), who had fled to Calais in disguise, and returned him to England. He may well have remained in Calais as the crisis unfolded in 1387–8 but he was awarded a three-year grant of land formerly belonging to Nicholas Brembre, one of the Merciless Parliament's victims.

Beauchamp's relations with the king in the 1390s are, if anything, more opaque, although this may simply reflect the complexity and unpredictability of high politics in these years. He lost the Pembroke custody in 1390, to the same John Golafre whose letters he had opened, and in 1389 he was again being pursued for waste, this time as farmer of the alien priory of Monks Kirby, Warwickshire. He was also involved in a number of recognizances in the early to mid-1390s, some on his own behalf, some on behalf of others, whose purposes are obscure but which risked the loss of massive sums. Some could relate to the alleged temporary imprisonment he suffered, for his disobedience in 1387, on returning to England. In 1394 he and his brother were among those who mainperned for the future good behaviour of Richard's great enemy, Warwick's fellow appellant, Richard (III) Fitzalan, earl of Arundel, on his release from the Tower of London. It was probably about this time, and certainly before 20 February 1396, that he married Arundel's daughter, Joan. While this might seem a rash political act for the brother of a former appellant, given Arundel's worsening relations with the king, it may have had more to do with safeguarding Beauchamp's interests in the Hastings inheritance; Arundel's second wife, married in 1390, was widow of the last Hastings and had a third of the family lands in dower. Indeed, Beauchamp continued to serve on royal commissions until 1395, he acted on several occasions for the courts of chivalry and, above all, between 1390 and 1392 he was able to secure a large part of the Hastings inheritance. Despite the claims of other Hastings heirs, which even Beauchamp's lawyers allegedly told him were hard to gainsay, he was able to divide the lands with Reynold, Lord Grey of Ruthin, the heir-general, to whom he paid 1000 marks for Abergavenny, while the king's acquiescence was secured by the bequest of Pembroke. As well as obtaining extensive lands over much of England, Beauchamp became Baron Bergavenny, and from 1392 he received a personal summons to parliament. He was now a nobleman of considerable means.

Service for Henry IV and death In 1397–9, when Warwick, and others considered enemies by the king, became victims of Richard II's vengeance, Beauchamp again managed to avoid complete identification with his brother. He seems to have escaped almost entirely unscathed and he was even given some of the earl of Arundel's moveables in 1398. But he was present when Richard resigned the crown and close enough to Henry IV to gain access for Adam Usk to the imprisoned Richard II. Only a month after Henry's accession, Beauchamp was made justiciar of south Wales. As lord of Abergavenny, Beauchamp did not replicate the neglect he had shown in Pembroke. Indeed, he was twice besieged in Abergavenny during the Glyn Dŵr revolt. The rebellion may have made the justiciarship too much for a man of his age and he was relieved of the office in 1401, although he was lieutenant in south Wales for six months in 1405 and apparently on active service. He and his wife obtained a number of grants from Henry IV, including the custody of the lands of his nephew, Richard Beauchamp, earl of Warwick (d. 1439), after his brother's death in 1401. From 1401 to 1409, to safeguard his own part in the Hastings lands, he assisted Grey's successful challenge to the use of the Hastings arms by Edward Hastings of Elsing.

Under Henry IV, Beauchamp acted for the first time as JP: in Hereford, as befitted the lord of Abergavenny, but also in Warwickshire and Worcestershire, where he remained an active force. As in the previous reign, his associates in these counties overlapped with those of the Warwick earldom and he seems to have had an amicable relationship with his nephew. However, when he made his will his decision to be buried in the Black Friars, Hereford, the Hastings mausoleum, shows how far he now identified himself with that inheritance, even though in 1385 he had granted advowsons to St Mary's, Warwick, the religious centre of the Warwick earldom. He died on 8 May 1411. His executors were his wife, her uncle, Thomas Arundel, archbishop of Canterbury (d. 1414), and her brother, Thomas Fitzalan, earl of Arundel (d. 1415). His will, made in 1408, is one of the earliest in English, perhaps another indication of 'Lollard' tendencies, although it ordains a large number of masses.

Joan Beauchamp's inheritance Beauchamp's wife, **Joan Beauchamp**, Lady Bergavenny (1375–1435), was daughter of the appellant Richard (III) *Fitzalan, earl of Arundel (d. 1397), and his first wife, Elizabeth, daughter of William de *Bohun, earl of Northampton (d. 1360). At Beauchamp's death both his principal estates—the lands from his father and the Hastings–Bergavenny lands—were held in tail male but, remarkably, both were left in entirety to Joan for her life. She enlarged her property further in 1420 with the primarily midland estate of the lords Botetourt, acquired from Hugh, Lord Burnell, husband of the Botetourt heiress. At her death Joan held lands over much of the midlands, East Anglia, and the south-east. Moreover, she and her two sisters were found heirs to part of the Arundel inheritance when their brother Thomas Fitzalan died in 1415, and in 1421 a council judgment authorized her to take £80 a year from it. Joan contrived to remain unmarried and, with her unusually large widow's portion, became perhaps the most formidable woman in England over the next twenty years. As a woman her influence was local rather than national—although she did appear before the council in 1421, as witness in the Berkeley inheritance dispute—but it was exercised on a wide scale. She had already made sufficient impression in Abergavenny for Adam Usk to refer to her as a 'second Jezebel'

(*Chronicon Adae de Usk*, 63). However, she seems to have spent most of her time after William's death in the west midlands, in Leicestershire, where the Botetourt lands had given her a major centre at Ashby-de-la-Zouch, and in Hertfordshire and Essex, where, on the basis of the Hastings lands, and perhaps of her own ancestry, she seems to have taken over much of the Bohun following. Her closer associates came mostly from these regions. Remarkably, she held local office, as commissioner for loans in Warwickshire, Worcestershire, Gloucestershire, and Leicestershire, between 1426 and 1431.

Conflicts with Warwick It was in the west midlands that Joan Beauchamp had the greatest impact. Some of her energies were directed towards the defence of the Botetourt lands, a burden carried by her descendants for much of the rest of the century, caused by the number of claimants by heredity excluded by Joan's deal with Burnell. About 1418 she was at odds with the west midland esquire, Nicholas Burdet, a case of the meeting of two irresistible forces. But for much of the 1420s Joan's efforts were concentrated on her nephew, Richard Beauchamp, earl of Warwick (*d.* 1439). The reasons for this falling-out within a hitherto harmonious family seem to be these: Joan's growing pretensions in the midlands, Warwick's new alliance with Edmund, Lord Ferrers of Chartley, a power in the Birmingham region where the Botetourt lands were making Joan a major figure, and the conflict in Ireland between Lord Talbot and the earl of Ormond, respectively sons-in-law of Warwick and Joan. Although Joan stood godmother to Warwick's son in 1424, in 1425 her men were involved in an affray with the earl's men in which Talbot's brother was killed. Doubtless to Warwick's embarrassment, it took place at one of Joan's properties in the heart of his Warwickshire lands west of Warwick. In 1427, although the evidence is difficult to evaluate, she seems to have been stirring up opposition to both Ferrers and Warwick in eastern Warwickshire, where the earl's tenurial power was weak, but where she could exert influence from Leicestershire, perhaps in conjunction with other local nobles. Then in 1429 there was a minor confrontation with Ferrers, and in 1431, at Birmingham, a major one, involving sizeable forces led by Joan and Ferrers themselves. Warwick had been in France during much of this local turmoil and would have found it especially awkward because the Bergavenny clientage in Warwickshire and Worcestershire was still closely entwined with his own, but his return in 1428 enabled him eventually to get the better of Joan. Her own suits against Ferrers got nowhere, while she forfeited £1000 pledged in an earlier recognizance to keep the peace. Thereafter she had to accept Warwick's rule in the west midlands, although she seems to have remained a force in Leicestershire.

Death and legacy Like that of her husband, Joan's will, made in January 1435, was in English and it has some 'Lollard' characteristics. She died on 14 November 1435 and requested burial beside her husband in the Black Friars at Hereford, where, Lollard or not, she endowed a chantry.

Their only son, Richard, earl of Worcester, had predeceased her in 1422, leaving a daughter as heir. Their daughter Elizabeth may have died unmarried but their other daughter, Joan (*d.* 1430), had married James Butler, fourth earl of Ormond (*d.* 1452), and it was this family that inherited the Botetourt lands, together with both the clientage and the litigation that went with them. The lands from the Warwick earldom and the Hastings–Bergavenny lands passed by entail to Joan's nephew, the earl of Warwick. When the Warwick male line died out in 1446 they became causes of dispute, between Richard Neville, earl of Warwick, and his uncle, Edward, who had married Worcester's daughter (the Hastings–Bergavenny lands), and among the Beauchamp of Warwick heirs (the Warwick lands).

CHRISTINE CARPENTER

Sources *Chancery records* · PRO [esp. KB9, KB27, CI, and C (inquisitions post mortem)] · Emden, *Oxf.* · W. Dugdale, *The baronage of England*, 2 vols. (1675–6) · K. B. McFarlane, *Lancastrian kings and Lollard knights* (1972) · C. Carpenter, *Locality and polity: a study of Warwickshire landed society, 1401–1499* (1992) · C. Carpenter, ed., *The Armburgh papers* (1998) · *Chronicon Adae de Usk*, ed. and trans. E. M. Thompson, 2nd edn (1904) · R. I. Jack, 'Entail and descent: the Hastings inheritance, 1370–1436', *BIHR*, 38 (1965), 1–19 · S. Walker, *The Lancastrian affinity, 1361–1399* (1990) · *Chronicon Henrici Knighton, vel Cnitthon, monachi Leycestrensis*, ed. J. R. Lumby, 2 vols., Rolls Series, 92 (1889–95) · Rymer, *Foedera* · K. B. McFarlane, *The nobility of later medieval England* (1973), 289–339 · J. B. Post, 'Courts, councils, and arbitrators in the Ladbroke Manor dispute, 1382–1400', *Medieval legal records edited in memory of C. A. F. Meekings*, ed. R. F. Hunnisett and J. B. Post (1978), 289–339 · V. J. Scattergood and J. W. Sherborne, eds., *English court culture in the later middle ages* (1983) · E. F. Jacob, ed., *The register of Henry Chichele, archbishop of Canterbury, 1414–1443*, 4 vols., CYS, 42, 45–7 (1937–47) [wills] · C. Given-Wilson, *The royal household and the king's affinity: service, politics and finance in England, 1360–1413* (1986) · *Thomae Walsingham, quondam monachi S. Albani, historia Anglicana*, ed. H. T. Riley, 2 vols., pt 1 of *Chronica monasterii S. Albani*, Rolls Series, 28 (1863–4) · N. H. Nicolas, ed., *Proceedings and ordinances of the privy council of England*, 7 vols., RC, 26 (1834–7) · J. H. Wylie, *History of England under Henry the Fourth*, 4 vols. (1884–98) · C. Given-Wilson, *The English nobility in the late middle ages* (1987), 147 · GEC, *Peerage* · *Œuvres de Froissart: chroniques*, ed. K. de Lettenhove, 25 vols. (Brussels, 1867–77) · M. D. Harris and G. Templeman, eds., *The register of the Guild of the Holy Trinity … Coventry*, 2 vols., Dugdale Society, 13, 19 (1935–44) · J. Catto, 'Sir William Beauchamp between chivalry and Lollardy', *The ideals and practice of knighthood III* [Strawberry Hill 1988], ed. C. Harper-Bill and R. Harvey (1990), 39–48 · J. Gairdner, ed., *The historical collections of a citizen of London in the fifteenth century*, CS, new ser., 17 (1876)

Archives PRO, valors, estate account, SC 11/12, SC 6. E 101

Likenesses double portrait (William and Joan Beauchamp), repro. in Harris, ed., *Register of the guild*, facing p. 744

Wealth at death £1510 p.a. from lands: Given-Wilson, *The English nobility*

Beauclerk, Lord Amelius (1771–1846), naval officer, was the third son of Aubrey Beauclerk, fifth duke of St Albans (1740–1802), and his wife, Lady Catherine Ponsonby (1742–1789), daughter of William *Ponsonby, second earl of Bessborough. He was entered on the books of the cutter *Jackal* in 1782, and in 1783 was appointed to the *Salisbury*, bearing the flag of Vice-Admiral John Campbell on the Newfoundland station. Afterwards he served in the West Indies under Commodore Gardner, and returned to England in 1789 as acting lieutenant of the *Europa*, in which rank, however, he was not confirmed until 21 September

1790, when the Spanish armament was mobilized. In 1792 he went to the Mediterranean in the frigate *Druid*, and on 16 September 1793 was made captain by Lord Hood and appointed to the command of the *Nemesis* (28 guns). In March 1794 he was transferred to the *Juno* (32 guns), and attached to the squadron, under Admiral Hotham, blockading Toulon. The *Juno* was also in the action of 14 March 1795, which resulted in the capture of the *Ça Ira* and *Censeur*, and was one of the squadron, under Commodore Taylor, which convoyed the homeward trade in the following autumn, when the *Censeur* was recaptured by the French off Cape St Vincent (7 October). On his return to England, Lord Amelius was appointed to the frigate *Dryad*, of 44 guns and 251 men, and on the coast of Ireland, on 13 June 1796, captured the *Proserpine*, of 42 guns and 348 men, after a brilliant and well-managed action, in which the *Dryad* lost only two killed and seven wounded, while the *Proserpine* lost thirty killed and forty-five wounded. He also captured several privateers, and in 1800 was appointed to the *Fortunée* (40 guns), employed in the channel and in attendance on the king at Weymouth. Over the next ten years he commanded different ships—the *Majestic*, *Saturn*, and *Royal Oak*, all 74 guns—in the channel, and in 1809 had charge of the amphibious landing of Lord Chatham's army at Walcheren, and continued, during the operations on that coast, as second in command under Sir Richard Strachan. On 1 August 1811 he became rear-admiral, but during that and the two following years he continued in the North Sea, stretching in 1813 as far as the North Cape in command of a small squadron on the look-out for the American Commodore Rogers. In 1814 he commanded in the Basque roads, and conducted the negotiations for the local suspension of hostilities. On 12 August 1819 he advanced to vice-admiral, and from 1824 to 1827 commanded in chief at Lisbon and on the coast of Portugal. He became a full admiral on 22 July 1830, and was commander-in-chief at Plymouth, 1836–9.

Beauclerk was a fellow of the Royal Society, was made KCB on 2 January 1815, GCH on 29 March 1831, GCB on 4 August 1835, and principal naval aide-de-camp on 4 August 1839. He died, unmarried, at his seat, Winchfield House, near Farnborough, Hampshire, on 10 December 1846. Beauclerk was a fine professional officer who benefited from his family connections to secure early promotion.   J. K. LAUGHTON, *rev.* ANDREW LAMBERT

Sources O'Byrne, *Naval biog. dict.* · *GM*, 2nd ser., 27 (1847), 201–2 · J. Marshall, *Royal naval biography*, 1 (1823), 484–7 · Burke, *Peerage* (1959) · GEC, *Peerage*
Likenesses J. Jackson, oils, 1831 (completed by A. Fusell), NMM · A. Morton, oils, NMM · W. H. Simmons, stipple (after W. Watson), NPG · S. Watts, line engraving (after C. J. Robertson), BM, NPG

Beauclerk, Lord Aubrey (1710?–1741), naval officer, was the eighth son of Charles *Beauclerk, first duke of St Albans (1670–1726), and Lady Diana de Vere (d. 1742), daughter of Aubrey de Vere, earl of Oxford, and a younger brother of Lord Vere *Beauclerk and James *Beauclerk. He married Catherine Alexander (d. 1755), daughter of Sir Henry *Newton, envoy to Tuscany, and widow of Colonel Francis Alexander; they had no children.

After three-and-a-half years' service as a lieutenant on the *Berwick*, *Portland*, and *Monument*, Beauclerk was made post captain on 1 April 1731, and commanded the *Ludlow Castle* (40 guns) on the Leeward Islands station for about eighteen months. Between 1734 and 1735 he commanded the *Garland* frigate in the Mediterranean, and, from February 1736, the *Dolphin* frigate on the same station. He returned home in January 1740, and within a month was appointed to the *Weymouth* (60 guns), from which, in September, he was transferred to the *Prince Frederick* (70 guns), one of the fleet which sailed for the West Indies with Sir Chaloner Ogle on 26 October 1740.

One afternoon early in January 1741, as the fleet was off the west end of Hispaniola, four large ships were sighted. The admiral signalled the *Prince Frederick* and five other ships of the line to chase. Towards dusk the strangers hoisted French colours, but did not shorten sail, and they were not overtaken until nearly ten o'clock. The *Prince Frederick* was the headmost ship, and Beauclerk hailed the ship he came up with, desiring her to heave to. As she neither did so nor answered his hail, he fired a shot across her bows; she replied with a broadside, and as the other ships came up a smart interchange of firing took place, after which they lay by until daylight. Their nationality was then apparent; they were really French ships, and the two squadrons parted with mutual apologies. The affair passed as a mistake, but demonstrated the strained relationship between Britain and France, at that time not officially at war with each other.

The fleet, under Sir Chaloner Ogle, arrived at Jamaica on 7 January and joined Vice-Admiral Vernon, under whose command it proceeded to Cartagena on the Spanish main. There, on 24 March 1741, in the attack on the Boca Chica, Beauclerk was killed in action. He was survived by his wife, who received an annual pension of £200 until her death on 30 October 1755.
     J. K. LAUGHTON, *rev.* RANDOLPH COCK

Sources register of commissions and warrants, PRO, ADM 6/14, 15 · J. Charnock, ed., *Biographia navalis*, 6 vols. (1794–8) · R. Beatson, *Naval and military memoirs of Great Britain*, 3 vols. (1790) · W. L. Clowes, *The Royal Navy: a history from the earliest times to the present*, 7 vols. (1897–1903) · *GM*, 1st ser., 11 (1741), 277
Likenesses G. Vertue, line engraving, 1746, BM, NPG · monument, Westminster Abbey

Beauclerk, Charles, first duke of St Albans (1670–1726), army officer, the illegitimate son of *Charles II and Nell *Gwyn, was born at his mother's house in Lincoln's Inn Fields, London, on 8 May 1670. It is said that one day when the king was with Nell Gwyn she called to the child, 'Come hither, you little bastard', for which the king reproved her. 'Your majesty', she was said to have answered, 'has given me no other name by which I may call him'. The king then gave him the name of Beauclerk and created him earl of Burford (Granger, 2.147). The story is probably accurately told, for the child was created by his father Baron Heddington and earl of Burford, both in Oxfordshire, on 27 December 1676, six years after his birth. On 10 January 1684 he was created duke of St Albans, and on Easter day of that year accompanied his father and two other natural sons of the king, the dukes of Northumberland and Richmond, when Charles II made his offering at the altar at Whitehall, the three boys entering before the king within the rails. He was at that time described by the diarist John Evelyn as 'a very pretty boy' (*Memoirs ... of John Evelyn*, 2.199). During the last illness of his mother in 1687 it was said that the duke was about to go to Hungary, and return a good Catholic, but in fact he was to be a supporter of William and Mary and the protestant succession.

On his mother's death on 14 November 1687 St Albans received a considerable estate, and the following year he served in the imperial army against the Turks and was present at the taking of Belgrade on 20 August. Meanwhile, Princess Anne of Denmark's regiment of horse (the 8th), which he commanded in England, was placed under Lieutenant-Colonel Langston, who in November 1688 brought it to join the prince of Orange. The regiment was disbanded after Steenkerke (1692), where it was almost wiped out. The duke took his place in the House of Lords on 9 November 1691. On 17 May 1693 he left for Flanders, and served under William III in the campaign of Landen. A false report was brought to London that he had fallen in that battle. The duke was a gallant soldier, and was highly esteemed by the king, who gave him many tokens of his regard. On his return from Flanders, William made him captain of the band of pensioners. He attempted to reform the corps, but on a complaint made by certain of the members the council decided that it was to be kept on the same footing as it had been under Lord Lovelace, the last captain. On 17 April 1694 St Albans married Lady Diana de Vere (d. 1742), the second daughter and eventually sole heir of Aubrey de Vere, twentieth and last earl of Oxford. The duchess of St Albans, a celebrated beauty, was first lady of the bedchamber and lady of the stole to Caroline, princess of Wales, though she resigned her places in December 1717 during the quarrel between the king and the prince of Wales. The duke and duchess had eight sons, among them Vere *Beauclerk, naval officer and politician, James *Beauclerk, bishop of Hereford, and Aubrey *Beauclerk, naval officer.

St Albans served in Flanders as a volunteer in July 1695, and in August he received a pension of £2000 a year from the crown, half of which was paid out of the ecclesiastical first-fruits. The hereditary office of master falconer and the reversion of the office of register of the high court of chancery had been granted him by his father. The reversion came to him in 1697, and was worth £1500 a year. In the summer of that year he was again with the king in Flanders. On his return after the conclusion of the peace of Ryswick, William gave him 'a sett of coach horses finely spotted like leopards' (Luttrell, 6.196). In December he was sent to Paris as ambassador-extraordinary to offer the king's congratulations on the marriage of the duke of Burgundy with Mary Adelaide, the daughter of Victor Amadeus II of Savoy. He had the good fortune the following year to escape from three highwaymen, who, on the night of 18 June, plundered between thirty and forty persons on Hounslow Heath, the duke of Northumberland being among those attacked. In 1703 he received a further grant of £800 a year voted by the parliament of Ireland. St Albans voted for the condemnation of Henry Sacheverell. On the triumph of the tory ministry in January 1712 he was dismissed from his office of captain of the pensioners; a whig in politics he was, however, reinstated by George I, and in 1718 was made a knight of the Garter. He died on 10 May 1726 at Bath and was buried at Westminster Abbey on 20 May. His brother James, styled Lord Beauclaire, had died at Paris in 1680, and the duke was succeeded by his eldest son, Charles.

WILLIAM HUNT, *rev.* JONATHAN SPAIN

Sources GEC, *Peerage* · J. Granger, *A biographical history of England, from Egbert the Great to the revolution*, 2 vols. (1769); suppl. (1774) · *Memoirs illustrative of the life and writings of John Evelyn ... comprising his diary, from the year 1641 to 1705-6*, ed. W. Bray, 2 vols. (1818) · N. Luttrell, *A brief historical relation of state affairs from September 1678 to April 1714*, 6 vols. (1857) · PRO, PROB 11/610, sig. 157

Likenesses miniature, *c*.1680, Royal Collection · R. White, line engraving (with Lord James Beauclerk), BM, NPG; repro. in J. Guillim, *A display of heraldrie* (1679) · oils, Berkeley Castle, Gloucestershire

Beauclerk [*née* Spencer; *other married name* St John], **Lady Diana** (1734–1808), artist, was born on 24 March 1734, the eldest daughter of Charles *Spencer, third duke of Marlborough (1706–1758), politician and military commander, and his wife, the Honourable Elizabeth Trevor (d. 1761). Lady Di, as she was familiarly known, grew up at Langley Park, Buckinghamshire, a house much preferred by her father. There she enjoyed a happy upbringing, her taste for drawing developing early under the influence of Sir Joshua Reynolds. His portrait of her holding a sketchbook represents a woman of pleasing aspect with large, wide-set eyes and an aquiline nose in a long, oval-shaped face. This was painted when she was the wife of Frederick St John, second Viscount Bolingbroke (1734-1787), whom she married on 8 September 1757 at Harbledown, Kent. They lived partly at his house, Lydiard Park, Wiltshire, and partly in London. The marriage was not a happy one, although there were two surviving sons. Handsome Lord Bolingbroke, owner of the celebrated racehorse Gimcrack, led a drunken, dissipated life and was notoriously unfaithful to his wife.

From 1762–1768 Lady Bolingbroke was lady of the bedchamber to Queen Charlotte. On 22 January 1768 Bolingbroke petitioned to dissolve the marriage, for which an act of parliament was needed, on the grounds that his wife was carrying on an adulterous association. The bill was read for the first time on 11 February. On the second reading (26 February) a footman in Lady Bolingbroke's house, Clarges Street, Mayfair, gave evidence that since November 1765 Lord Bolingbroke had never been seen there, but Mr Topham *Beauclerk often came and stayed the night. Once when the footman entered the room she was on a sofa with signs of shoes on one end and a great deal of powder at the other. The nature of Lady Bolingbroke's relationship with Beauclerk was further illuminated by the footman's additional evidence that, on 19 August 1766, Lady Bolingbroke had gone into labour; two doctors had arrived incognito, and a daughter was born (she died the following year). The third reading of the bill

Lady Diana Beauclerk (1734–1808), by Sir Joshua Reynolds, 1763–5

blue damask and illustrating Horace Walpole's tragedy *The Mysterious Mother*. Apt to overrate her skills, Walpole placed these at Strawberry Hill in a specially designed hexagonal room named the Beauclerc closet. At the same time he opined absurdly that 'Salvator Rosa and Guido could not surpass their expression and beauty' (*Anecdotes of Painting*, 24.524). Lady Diana also enjoyed the patronage of Josiah Wedgwood, probably from 1785, when her designs, mostly those of laughing bacchanalian boys, were translated as bas-reliefs onto jasper ornaments, plates, and jugs; they proved to be enormously popular. In 1796 she illustrated the English translation of G. A. Burger's ballad *Leonora* and in 1797 *The Fables of John Dryden*; in both cases her illustrations were engraved mostly by Francesco Bartolozzi.

After her husband's death in 1780, Lady Diana Beauclerk moved to Spencer Grove, a 'sweet little box' at Twickenham, better known as Little Marble Hill, where she decorated whole rooms with festoons of flowers. Mounting financial worries later forced her to move to Devonshire Cottage, Petersham Meadows. She had kept a stout heart through all adversities, but her eyes were failing and she was losing the use of her hands. Old age brought her life to a close on 1 August 1808. She was buried in a 'notable grave' on 4 August at the parish church, Richmond, but this has now gone or is unidentifiable.

VIRGINIA SURTEES

Sources B. C. Erskine, *Lady Diana Beauclerk: her life and work* (1903) · A. H. Church, *Josiah Wedgwood* (1908) · *Diary and letters of Madame D'Arblay* (1778–1840), ed. C. Barrett and A. Dobson, 6 vols. (1904–5) · J. Boswell, *The life of Samuel Johnson*, [new edn], ed. R. Ingpen, 1 (1907) · B. Fothergill, *The Strawberry Hill set* (1983), 230–34 · *Anecdotes of painting in England, 1760–1795 … collected by Horace Walpole*, ed. F. W. Hilles and P. B. Daghlian (1937), vol. 5 · S. Buchan, *Lady Louisa Stuart: her memories and portraits* (1932) · HLRO, Main papers collection, HL, Jan to March 1768 · GEC, *Peerage* · Walpole, *Corr.*
Archives HLRO, main papers
Likenesses T. Hudson, group portrait, oils, *c.*1754 (the family of the third duke of Marlborough), Blenheim Palace, Oxfordshire · J. Reynolds, oils, 1763–5, Iveagh Bequest, Kenwood, London [*see illus.*] · A. Kauffman, oils

was agreed without amendment (8 March) and passed with royal assent on 10 March 1768.

Two days later Lady Diana married Topham Beauclerk (1739–1780) at St George's, Hanover Square. He was the great-grandson of Nell Gwyn and Charles II, to the latter of whom it was said he bore a strong resemblance. His brilliance in conversation is recorded, as too is his ill humour, the filth of his person, and the quantity of vermin in his wig. He is remembered chiefly for his close friendship with Dr Johnson, who was slow to subscribe to Lady Diana's attractions, despite Boswell's endeavour to portray her as a woman ill-used by her former husband. 'My dear Sir', rejoined Johnson, 'never accustom your mind to mingle virtue and vice. The woman's a whore and there's an end on't' (Boswell, 1.452). Nevertheless, by degrees he accepted her, and she was much esteemed by many of her husband's circle, including Edward Gibbon, David Garrick, Charles Fox, Edmund Burke, and others. Three children were born of her second inharmonious marriage, which led to a peripatetic life spent at Adelphi Terrace, Hertford Street, Mayfair, a villa at Muswell Hill, and then Thanet House, Great Russell Street.

During those years Lady Diana's artistic talents became particularly evident: she practised portraiture, and her enormous output of small drawings of fat cupids entangled in branches of grapes and little girls wearing mob caps gave place to larger and more ambitious groups of peasantry introduced into landscaped backgrounds. She worked chiefly in pen and ink, pastel, and watercolour. Essentially a designer, she successfully executed seven large panels in 'soot ink' (black wash), mounted on Indian

Beauclerk, Lord Frederick de Vere (1773–1850), cricketer, was born on 8 May 1773 in the parish of St George, Hanover Square, London. He was the fourth child and youngest son of the seven children of Aubrey Beauclerk, fifth duke of St Albans (1740–1802), and Lady Catherine Ponsonby (1749–1789), daughter of William *Ponsonby, second earl of Bessborough (1704–1793), and he was a direct descendant of Charles II and Nell Gwyn. After being privately tutored, in 1790 he went to Trinity College, Cambridge, where he obtained his MA in 1792 and his DD in 1824. He was ordained deacon in 1795 and priest in 1797, and he was vicar of Kimpton, Hertfordshire, from 1797 to 1827 and then vicar of both Redbourn, Hertfordshire, and of St Michael's, St Albans from 1827 to 1850. Like many youngest sons, though, he entered the church reluctantly, and often forsook his clerical duties in favour of sport: 'he ne'er preaches once a twelvemonth' was one biting judgement. He was married on 3 July 1813 to Charlotte (d. 1866), the third daughter of Charles Dillon, twelfth Viscount

Dillon, and of Henrietta Maria, only daughter of the first Baron Mulgrave. The couple had two sons and two daughters. Lord Frederick also later became lord of the manor of Winchfield, Hampshire, which he inherited from his brother, Lord Amelius *Beauclerk, in 1846.

Lord Frederick devoted much of his life to cricket, which was then becoming fashionable and achieving metropolitan recognition, partly because it served the Regency taste, avidly shared by Lord Frederick, for excessive gambling. He claimed to earn 600 guineas a year in this way, roughly the same as from his two clerical livings. As a player he was a quick, bustling figure, usually clad in striped trousers, scarlet sash and white beaver hat, 5 feet 9 inches tall and weighing 12 stone. He was described as a very fast runner, an excellent slip fielder, and a 'wonderfully accurate' underarm bowler; as a batsman he was slow to begin but, once set, capable of attacking offside hitting. He succeeded Silver Billy Beldham as England's finest batsman, and was for several years the most effective 'amateur' single-wicket player in the land. Lord Frederick's career stretched over thirty-five years. In the ninety-nine important matches in which he played, he scored 4555 runs (averaging 27), including four centuries, and took 251 wickets—exceptional figures for the time. In all forms of cricket, his highest score was 170 for Homerton against Montpelier in 1806.

Lord Frederick was the protégé of Thomas Lord's patron, the earl of Winchilsea, and took part in the first recorded match on the present Lord's ground in 1814; he often played for the Gentlemen against the Players between 1806 and 1824. He became a frequent visitor to the ground (accompanied by his dog), and was president of the MCC in 1826. He was not popular, however, being widely regarded into his disgruntled old age as the autocratic arbiter of the game. He had a petulant and unbridled temper, and stories about his fierce disposition abound: David Dawson, an infamous horse poisoner, once refused him entry to his coach because of his 'fluent and expressive language'. Lord Frederick died at his London home, 68 Grosvenor Street, on 22 April 1850, just before his seventy-seventh birthday, and was buried at Winchfield Manor, his country residence. He left properties at Winchfield and Odiham to his son Charles.

ERIC MIDWINTER

Sources Burke, *Peerage* · A. Haygarth, *Arthur Haygarth's cricket scores and biographies*, 15 vols. (1862–1925), vols. 1–4 · P. Bailey, P. Thorn, and P. Wynne-Thomas, *Who's who of cricketers* (1984) · Lord Harris, ed., *The history of Kent county cricket* (1907) · Venn, *Alum. Cant.* · G. D. Martineau, *Journal of the Cricket Society*, 53 (1959)
Likenesses G. Shepheard, watercolour drawing, c.1795, Lord's, London, MCC collection; *see illus. in* Hambledon cricket club (*act. c.*1750–*c.*1796) · W. Beechey, oils (as a boy), Marylebone cricket club
Wealth at death properties in Winchfield and Odiham to son; approx. 600 guineas p.a. from clerical livings, and claimed same again from gambling

Beauclerk [*née* Mellon; *other married name* Coutts], **Harriot**, duchess of St Albans (1777?–1837), actress and banker, was probably born on 11 November 1777, probably the illegitimate daughter of Sarah Mellon, an Irish wardrobe-keeper in Kena's company of strolling players, the lowest level of the theatrical world and regarded in law as rogues and vagabonds. Sarah Mellon claimed to have been married to and deserted by Harriot's father, Lieutenant Mathew Mellon of the Madras infantry, but the ceremony cannot be verified. On 14 July 1782 Sarah married Thomas Entwisle, a musician in Kena's company. Harriot received some education in Lancashire, where the Entwisles worked in Bibby's company. She began to work as a child actor, and on 16 October 1787, in a barn doing duty for a theatre in Ulverstone, she appeared as Little Pickle in the farce *The Spoiled Child* and became an instant success. The family later joined Stanton's company in the midlands, where Harriot earned a guinea a week. She was seen there by the playwright Richard Brinsley Sheridan, who eventually engaged her for Drury Lane Theatre, where she appeared as Lydia Languish in *The Rivals* on 31 January 1795.

From then until 1815 Harriot Mellon played an extensive range of parts in both London and the provincial theatre. Her most successful role was Volante in John Tobin's *The Honey Moon* (1805). She never reached the first rank of actresses—Dorothy Jordan and Sarah Siddons were not challenged by her—but she was praised for her good-natured readiness to take over parts in cases of illness, afterwards returning with good humour to the secondary roles she was accustomed to play. In her published memoirs, fellow actress Anne Mathews described her as 'a young, glowing beauty, endued with great natural powers of mind, talents and vivacity, but … an insuperable rusticity of air and manners'. On 7 February 1815, as Audrey in *As You Like It*, she made her last appearance on the stage, at Drury Lane. She was then earning £12 a week, far more than she could have earned, as a woman without education or patronage, in any other respectable occupation.

During Mellon's early years in the theatre, there was never a whisper of impropriety about her behaviour, but for ten years (1805–15) she was intimate with the banker Thomas *Coutts (1735–1822), one of the richest men in London, who assisted her living in great style. In February 1815, after the death of his first wife, they were married at St Pancras Church, but the marriage was declared invalid, and they went through a second ceremony on 12 April 1815. Coutts was seventy-nine, Harriot thirty-seven. The pre-marriage contract specified that Harriot should retain control of her own estates and properties through trustees. Coutts's three daughters, who had previously been friendly with Harriot, were furious about the marriage and treated their stepmother very badly thereafter. Each had married into the aristocracy and received a large dowry, but their father's marriage damaged their longer-term prospects of inheriting from him. Lady Guilford and Sir Francis Burdett were particularly hostile. This grieved Coutts, who constantly said how happy his wife made him, and when he died, in 1822, he left Harriot the whole of his vast fortune and his partnership in Coutts Bank, without mentioning any other person or leaving a single legacy. He thus left his widow to decide whether she wished to share his estate with his children to any degree whatever.

Harriot Coutts proved to be an excellent business-woman and banker, taking an active role in investment and management decisions. She was also extremely generous to Coutts's daughters, giving them each £10,000 per annum. In return they expressed nothing but ingratitude and hostility. Regarded as an adventuress who had preyed on an old man, Harriot was lampooned, caricatured, and mocked for her extravagant lifestyle and her generous giving to the poor. Sir Walter Scott, however, found her 'a kind, friendly woman, without either affectation or insolence in the display of her wealth' (Lockhart, 8.72). Portraits of Harriot were painted by Romney, Beechey, and Masquerier, among others.

Harriot's weakness was her desire to be *haut ton*, the height of every social climber's ambition, but she was never fully admitted to the inner circles of the aristocracy, even after she married on 16 June 1827 William Aubrey de Vere Beauclerk, ninth duke of St Albans (1801–1849). The duke was twenty-six, Harriot forty-nine. Many considered the duke to be simple-minded, but others found him kind and gentle; the marriage was broadly successful. Harriot thus proved twice over that marriages could be happy even though the world considered the partners mismatched. Observers regarded their union as an exchange of wealth for a title, but that was no uncommon practice among the aristocracy.

The duchess of St Albans died on 6 August 1837 at her home, 80 Piccadilly, London, and was buried in the parish church at Redbourne, Lincolnshire, the St Albans family seat, on 19 August. She left her husband £10,000 a year for his lifetime, and two large houses in London and one in Highgate, with their contents. She continued to direct his life from beyond the grave: a condition of her will was that neither of his brothers, lords Frederick and Charles Beauclerk, or their families, were to reside with him for as much as one week in a year. If they did, all her bequests to him would cease. The Beauclerks had greatly offended her some years earlier. She left £20,000 in trust for the benefit of Sophia Burdett, Coutts's daughter, 'the sum being over and above the sums that I have already given to her amounting to £118,602 15s 0d', for her 'sole and separate use and benefit, exclusively of any husband' and not 'subject to the debts, control, power, inter-meddling, or engagements of any such husband'. Lady Bute, another of Coutts's daughters, was dead, but there was no mention of her children, or of the third daughter, Lady Guilford, or her children.

Harriot left lump sums and small annuities to a long list of friends and servants, but the residue of the estate, some £1.8 million, she left in trust for the youngest granddaughter of Thomas Coutts, Angela Georgina Burdett [see Coutts, Angela Burdett-]. The trustees of the estate were Harriot's partners at the bank, her solicitor, and the accountant-general of the high court of chancery. Harriot did not leave Angela the partnership in the bank, nor could she, her parents, or any future husband touch the capital. Angela was given complete control over the income of the estate, whether or not she married. The will also laid down that, if Angela should marry an alien, the fortune would go to the next person in remainder. Extraordinarily, Angela fell foul of this clause when she was sixty-seven and married her 26-year-old American-born secretary, William Ashmead Bartlett. The will also required that she take the surname Coutts, and it was under this name that Harriot's heir became known as the greatest of Victorian philanthropists. Harriot never explained her choice of heir, but Angela had been a favourite from childhood, and, unlike her siblings and cousins, had not offended Harriot with aristocratic pretensions.

For her great fortune, Angela Burdett-Coutts was indebted solely to her step-grandmother, though she herself always maintained that the money came directly from her grandfather. Thus it was Harriot Mellon, the darling of the frivolous Georgian stage, who became, against all the odds, fairy godmother to the Victorian poor.

JOAN PERKIN

Sources Coutts Bank archives, Strand, London · Theatre Museum, London · M. C. Baron-Wilson, *Memoirs of Harriot, duchess of St. Albans* (1839) · C. E. Pearce, *The jolly duchess* (1915) · E. H. Coleridge, *The life of Thomas Coutts, banker*, 2 vols. (1920) · E. Healey, *Coutts & Co., 1692–1992: the portrait of a private bank* (1992) · *GM*, 2nd ser., 8 (1837), 419–21 · A. Mathews, *Memoirs of Charles Mathews*, 4 vols. (1838–9) · J. G. Lockhart, *Memoirs of the life of Sir Walter Scott*, [2nd edn], 8 (1839) · GEC, *Peerage*
Archives Sandon Hall, Staffordshire, Harrowby Manuscript Trust, letters to Lord Dudley Coutts Stuart and the marchioness of Bute
Likenesses W. Ridley, stipple, 1803 (after C. Allingham), BM; repro. in *Monthly Mirror* (1803) · W. Say, mezzotint, pubd 1804 (after J. Masquerier), BM · C. Turner, portrait, 1805 (as Volante; after W. Beechey), Theatre Museum, London, H. R. Beard collection · W. Beechey, oils, NPG · J. Hopwood, stipples (after S. J. Stump), BM, NPG
Wealth at death £1,800,000: *Morning Herald*, 1837 · under £600,000 personalty: will, 1837

Beauclerk, James (1709–1787), bishop of Hereford, was born at Windsor, the seventh surviving son of Charles *Beauclerk, first duke of St Albans (1670–1726), illegitimate offspring of *Charles II and Nell *Gwyn. Some say his facial characteristics resembled those of his royal grandfather. His mother, Lady Diana de Vere (d. 1742), being the only surviving child of the last earl of Oxford was heraldic heir of England's oldest noble family. Three brothers were at court and others included Vere *Beauclerk, admiral of the blue, and Aubrey *Beauclerk, a courageous naval commander, who was killed in action in 1741. Thus well connected, James Beauclerk's ecclesiastical ascent was predictably rapid.

Beauclerk was educated at Oxford, not at Christ Church, by then more popular with the aristocracy, but at Queen's College, which he entered in 1727. From there he graduated BA (1730), MA (1733), and BD and DD (1744). Nothing is known of his early career, except that in 1743/4–1746 he was canon of Windsor. In 1746 he was consecrated bishop of Hereford at the early age of thirty-six. He remained bishop of Hereford until his death there forty-one years later. With a royal and aristocratic lineage such as his, historians might characterize Beauclerk as the archetypal absentee, lacklustre prelate, neglectful of his distant diocese and living at ease in London. This was not the case. Certainly he tried to use his connections to gain more preferment, but without success. Twice, in 1747 and 1752, he schemed for the clerkship of the closet, a valued court post, and then in 1763 for the deanery of Windsor, an aristocratic perquisite which he hoped to hold *in commendam* with his Hereford bishopric. In 1764, without his overt connivance, his brother Admiral Lord Vere sought to have him preferred to the senior diocese of London. All these approaches met with rebuff.

Despite all these manoeuvrings Beauclerk's activities as bishop suggest that he was clearly no political crony. His House of Lords attendance record, which averaged eight sittings per year, was scant compared with most of his Hereford predecessors. Philip Bisse, for instance, achieved an annual average of thirty-six, and the aristocratic Henry Egerton almost forty-eight. Nor was Beauclerk careless of his flock; throughout his long episcopate records reveal his outstanding conscientiousness and persistent determination to raise diocesan standards. Until a year before his death, at the age of seventy-eight, he personally conducted almost every diocesan ordination, not in London but in his cathedral, and usually as often as four times a year, the greatest frequency in the Hereford diocese since before the civil war. He demanded the highest standards from his ordinands. Candidates for the diaconate found him an unusual stickler over the required canonical age for ordination while non-graduates learned to fear the tests that he demanded. Even his officials had to meet his exacting standards. For instance he insisted that the required ordination documents were presented to him at least three weeks before the ceremony, because 'his lordship requires them in proper time' (ordination papers, 1757). He was also prepared to break with custom, for instance by signing schoolmasters' licences personally and by taking his chancellor's place in court proceedings over an incumbent's neglect of duty. Undoubtedly he was one of three Hereford bishops, with Herbert Croft and Bisse, to make the most conspicuous impact on diocesan life between 1660 and 1800.

Beauclerk never married but kept contact with his family. On 23 December 1752 he performed the marriage, at St George's, Hanover Square, London, of his nephew George Beauclerk, third duke of St Albans; in 1760 he temporarily took St Albans's place as registrar of the court of chancery during the duke's absence abroad. But at his death he left most of his possessions not to his family but to his secretary, Richard Jones. He died in Hereford on 20 October 1787 and was buried in Hereford Cathedral. His only extant publication is one sermon, preached to parliament on 30 January 1752, the anniversary of Charles I's execution. Despite his royal and aristocratic background here was a prelate devoted to his diocese.

WILLIAM MARSHALL

Sources W. M. Marshall, 'The administration of the dioceses of Hereford and Oxford, 1660–1760', PhD diss., University of Bristol, 1979 · bishops' registers, Hereford, 1723–71, Herefs. RO · visitation books, Herefs. RO, HD 5/17 · ordination papers, Herefs. RO, HD 6/12–17 · A. L. Moir, *The bishops of Hereford* (1964) · *Fasti Angl.* (Hardy), 1.473, 3.408 · Foster, *Alum. Oxon.* · D. Adamson, *The house of Nell Gwyn, … 1670–1974*, ed. P. D. Dewar (1974) · Burke, *Peerage* (1970) · *DNB* · *JHL*, 26–29 (1741–60) · GEC, *Peerage*, new edn, vol. 11 · J. Beauclerk, letter to Newcastle, 22 June 1752, BL, Add. MS 32728, fol. 79 · *IGI* · S. L. Ollard, *Fasti Wyndesorienses: the deans and canons of Windsor* (privately printed, Windsor, 1950) · will, PRO, PROB 11/1157, sig. 440

Likenesses oils, *c*.1770; Christies, 1979, formerly in the collection of the duke of St Albans · oils, *c*.1780, Queen's College, Oxford · oils, bishop's palace, Hereford

Beauclerk [*née* Lovelace], **Martha** [Lady Henry Beauclerk] (*bap.* **1710**, *d.* **1788**), courtier, was baptized on 14 January 1710 in St James's, Westminster, the only daughter and the fifth of the five children of John *Lovelace, fourth Baron Lovelace (*d.* 1709) [*see under* Lovelace, John, third Baron Lovelace], governor of New York at the time of his death, and his wife, Charlotte (*d.* 1749), daughter of Sir John Clayton of Richmond. As the sister and heir to Nevill, sixth and last Baron Lovelace (*d.* 1736), she inherited family pride, not wealth. Courtesy of her second cousin, Martha Johnson, Baroness Wentworth *suo jure*, and another Wentworth connection, Mrs Cresswell, respectively, she inherited the manors of Leckhampstead and Heyborne Fields in Buckinghamshire. This gave her both some local political influence and the right to appoint to the rectory of Leckhampstead.

Martha Lovelace's determined and eventually successful quest for patronage for herself and her family throws light on politically astute eighteenth-century women's involvement in patronage. She was an early recipient of patronage, being appointed maid of honour to Queen Caroline in 1732, an appointment probably secured by Lady Wentworth or another Lovelace relative. Once a member of the court, she was expected to use her position to seek patronage for family members—and make a brilliant marriage. Her role in the appointment of her brother, Lord Lovelace, as gentleman of the bedchamber in 1735 remains obscure, but her assertiveness and tenacity in seeking patronage later points to her involvement as a broker. While at court she built networks of powerful friends and acquaintances. Horace Walpole, for instance, was genuinely fond of her. He wrote verses to her on her brother's death in 1736 and was eager in later life to do favours for his 'old and great friend Lady Harry Beauclerk'.

On 25 June 1739 Martha married happily, but not lucratively, Lord Henry Beauclerk (1701–1761) as his second wife. The fourth of the eight sons of Charles *Beauclerk, first duke of St Albans, and his wife, Diana de Vere, brother of Vere *Beauclerk, first Baron Vere, and Lord Aubrey *Beauclerk, and a grandson of Charles II, Lord Henry's rank far outstripped his fortune. Like many younger sons he had made the army his career. His early prospects had been excellent. His actions as a volunteer at the siege of Gibraltar in 1727 had brought him to George II's notice and resulted in patronage appointments and promotions. By 1745 he was an established whig MP (for

Thetford) and colonel of the 31st regiment of foot guards; in 1752 he was appointed ranger of New Lodge Walk. In the meantime his wife had also obtained patronage to help support their family of seven children: one son, Henry (1745–1817), and six plain and portionless daughters: Diana (b. 1741); Henrietta (b. 1742); Mary (b. 1743); Charlotte (b. 1746); Martha (b. 1747); and Anne (1749–1809). Lady Henry had been awarded the reversion of her mother's pension of £200 p.a. in 1749; then, in 1756, she had secured the place of housekeeper of Windsor Castle. This gradual improvement in family circumstances came to an abrupt end when Lord Henry rashly quit his regiment when it was posted to Minorca for three years, claiming that he had not been given enough time to settle his affairs. This incurred the king's lasting displeasure. Lord Henry was consequently stripped of his military rank and the king refused thereafter to consider any of his subsequent requests for military reappointment or other forms of patronage.

To secure adequate provision for her family's—especially her daughters'—future, Lady Henry began her own campaign for patronage in 1759. She first approached Thomas Pelham-Holles, duke of Newcastle, then first lord of the Treasury, for an addition to her own pension. Reminding Newcastle of 'the many pretentions I have to the Royal Favour', she ended her request by listing them: 'Lord Lovelaces daughter, a Servant of the late Queen's; and the Wife of Lord Henry Beauclerk' (BL, Add. MS 32887, fols. 442–3). When the king refused on the grounds that it would set a precedent, she immediately submitted another request. This time she asked for a pension for her children, or a place for her husband. Drawing upon a rhetoric of responsible motherhood, she claimed that she could not rest until her daughters were provided for. Between March 1759 and June 1760 she applied repeatedly to Newcastle: once to have Lord Henry made lieutenant of the Tower of London, twice to have her eldest daughter appointed orchard-keeper, and once again to have her pension increased. She sent a personal memorial to the king. She even threatened to embarrass Newcastle into action by making her claim in person at his levee (traditionally a male event). This prompted an immediate response from a clearly concerned Newcastle: he promised to wait upon her at her own home instead. She reminded him yet again of her family's service to the crown: 'you can find no other person so Slenderly provided whose family has been So great Sufferers for The Crown' (BL, Add. MS 32907, fol. 133). She also made the pension a political point, explaining pointedly to the king that a larger pension would 'enable us to bring up a Family by Nature attach't to your Majesty and by example most faithfull Subjects' (BL, Add. MS 32992, fols. 154–5).

By November 1760 George III was on the throne and the political climate had changed. Furthermore, a royal wedding was in the offing and a new queen's household was being formed. Lady Henry persuaded a relative, Augustus Henry Fitzroy, third duke of Grafton, to approach Newcastle to have her eldest daughter, Diana (who died unmarried in 1809), appointed a maid of honour. However, Newcastle's unpopularity with the new king, his mother, and the king's mentor, John Stuart, third earl of Bute, made this impossible. Lady Henry recognized this and promptly changed patrons. Lord Bute was an old acquaintance and a previous patron of her husband's. He was also at the height of his power. Thus, she finally achieved her goals in 1761. Not only was her eldest daughter appointed maid of honour but, more importantly, she secured her other daughters' futures with a pension of £400 p.a. on the Irish establishment. Only towards the end of her life, in 1783–4, did she briefly become re-engaged in patronage. She then turned to another old patronage contact, Hester Pitt, countess of Chatham, widow of William Pitt the elder, to obtain additional ecclesiastical preferment for her son, Henry, whom she had already made rector of Leckhampstead. Lady Henry died in London on 5 March 1788 and was buried at Stanmore in Middlesex. Her daughters' financial circumstances concerned her to the very last. Since the manor of Leckhampstead went to her son, she left her assets (old South Sea Company annuities worth £1050) to be divided equally among her unmarried daughters.

E. H. CHALUS

Sources corresp. with the duke of Newcastle, BL, Add. MSS 32887–32889, 32904, 32906, 32907, 32992 · Walpole, *Corr.*, vols. 9, 12, 20–22 · GEC, *Peerage*, new edn, 8.235; 11.288 · *Collins peerage of England: genealogical, biographical and historical*, ed. E. Brydges, 9 vols. (1812), vol. 1, pp. 246, 248 · *VCH Buckinghamshire*, 4.183 · PRO, PROB 11/1163, sig. 118 · *Magna Britannia* (1806) · D. Adamson, *The house of Nell Gwyn, … 1670–1974*, ed. P. D. Dewar (1974) · *Correspondence of Thomas Gray*, ed. P. Toynbee and L. Whibley, 3 vols. (1935), 2.721–2 · *Daily Advertiser* [London] (26 Jan 1756) · *VCH Hertfordshire*, 2.41 · *GM*, 1st ser., 9 (1739), 272 · 'Lovelace, John, third Baron Lovelace', *DNB* · Burke, *Peerage* (1999) · *IGI*

Archives BL, corresp. with the duke of Newcastle, Add. MSS 32887, fols. 442–3, 468, 489; 32888, fols. 200, 208; 32889, fol. 167; 32904, fols. 135, 157, 396; 32906, fols. 54, 68; 32907, fol. 133 · BL, petitions to George II, Add. MSS 32904, fol. 137; 32992, fols. 154–5

Wealth at death £1050 in old South Sea stocks: PRO, PROB 11/1163, sig. 118

Beauclerk, Topham (1739–1780), book collector, was born on 21 December 1739, the only son of Lord Sidney Beauclerk (1703–1744), member of parliament, privy councillor, and vice-chamberlain of the royal household, and his wife, Mary (d. 1766), daughter of Thomas Norris of Speke Hall, Lancashire. Lord Sidney, notorious in his day as a fortune-hunter, had persuaded Richard Topham, MP for Windsor, to make him his heir, and his son was named after his benefactor.

Topham Beauclerk was educated at Eton College (1753–7) and Trinity College, Oxford, where he matriculated on 11 November 1757, but left without taking a degree. At Trinity he met Bennet Langton and formed what was to prove a lifelong friendship. Through Langton he met Johnson at Oxford, probably in the summer of 1759, and thereby gained his niche in literary history. When Johnson and Reynolds formed The Club in 1764 Beauclerk became one of the original members and an important contributor to its proceedings. He took an early liking to Boswell, playing a prominent role in his election to The Club, and supplying him with Johnsonian anecdotes. A

On 12 March 1768 Beauclerk married Diana St John, Viscountess Bolingbroke, formerly Lady Diana Spencer [*see* Beauclerk, Lady Diana (1734–1808)], eldest daughter of the third duke of Marlborough, an accomplished artist, two days after her divorce from Frederick St John, second Viscount Bolingbroke. Diana had left her husband in November 1766 but it seems the action for divorce was precipitated by the birth of a son in September 1767, Bolingbroke fearing that Beauclerk's son might inherit his estate and title. The son died a month later, but two daughters were born before the divorce and one son after. The marriage was not happy. Lady Louisa Stuart, describing Beauclerk as 'what the French call *cynique* in his personal habits beyond what one would have thought possible in anyone but a beggar or a gypsey', tells a story of his infesting the company at Blenheim with lice, and of his wife having her sheets changed every day (*Notes*, 22–3). Recurrent illness (possibly the consequence of venereal disease), for which he took up to 400 drops of laudanum a day, destroyed Beauclerk's temper, and at the end of his life Major Floyd described him as living to be 'a torment to himself and all about him' (*Henry, Elizabeth and George*, 351). Beauclerk died on 11 March 1780. In his will he surprised Johnson with a note of tenderness by asking to be buried beside his mother at Speke. JAMES MCLAVERTY

Sources Boswell, *Life* • *The letters of Samuel Johnson*, ed. B. Redford, 5 vols. (1992–4) • Walpole, *Corr.* • *Notes by Lady Louisa Stuart on George Selwyn and his contemporaries*, ed. W. S. Lewis (1928) • A. M. Montague, '"That insuperable idleness": an account of Topham Beauclerk', *South Atlantic Quarterly*, 72 (1973), 587–605 • *Henry, Elizabeth and George, 1734–1780: letters and diaries of Henry, tenth earl of Pembroke and his circle*, ed. S. Herbert (1939) • D. Adamson, *The house of Nell Gwyn, ... 1670–1974*, ed. P. D. Dewar (1974) • B. Erskine, *Lady Diana Beauclerk* (1903) • F. Hardy, *Memoirs of the political and private life of James Caulfeild, earl of Charlemont*, 2nd edn, 2 vols. (1812) • *The letters and journals of Lady Mary Coke*, ed. J. A. Home, 4 vols. (1889–96) • *The correspondence of James Boswell with certain members of the Club*, ed. C. N. Fifer (1976), vol. 3 of *The Yale editions of the private papers of James Boswell*, research edn (1966–) • *The Yale editions of the private papers of James Boswell*, trade edn, ed. F. A. Pottle and others, 14 vols. (1950–89) • *GM*, 1st ser., 9 (1739), 660 • *DNB*

Archives Royal Irish Acad., MSS and corresp. of James, first earl of Charlemont [Caulfeild] • Yale U., Beinecke L., letters to Bennet Langton

Likenesses F. Cotes, pastel, 1756, repro. in Adamson and Dewar, *The house of Nell Gwyn*, facing p. 62 • R. Brompton, group portrait, oils, 1764 (with HRH duke of York and friends), Fonmon Castle, Glamorgan, Wales • S. Bellin, line engraving (after G. P. Harding?), BM, NPG [*see illus.*] • G. P. Harding, watercolour drawing, BM

Topham Beauclerk (1739–1780), by Samuel Bellin (after George Perfect Harding?)

great-grandson of Charles II and Nell Gwyn, Beauclerk was aristocratic, idle, and accomplished. Johnson regarded Beauclerk as The Club's expert on polite literature, but when he toyed with setting up a college at St Andrews, he chose Beauclerk, a fellow of the Royal Society and a keen amateur chemist with his own laboratory, as professor of natural philosophy. Beauclerk was also a collector of books of all kinds, amassing over 30,000 volumes. To store them, he employed Robert Adam to design a library for his house in Great Russell Street, Bloomsbury. According to Walpole it reached 'halfway to Highgate. Everybody goes to see it; it has put the [British] Museum's nose quite out of joint' (Walpole, *Corr.*, 33.136). On Beauclerk's death the library, which had been mortgaged to the duke of Marlborough, was sold over a period of fifty days, beginning on Monday, 9 April 1781, for £5011.

Johnson valued Beauclerk as a man who had 'lived so much in the world' and was 'always ready to talk' (Boswell, *Life*, 3.390). He was prepared to join Beauclerk and Langton on a night-time 'frisk' round London or accept the former as a worthy antagonist in debate, but Boswell notes that Beauclerk was careful to avoid offending Johnson with sallies of infidelity (he held sceptical views) or licentiousness. Although Johnson disliked Beauclerk's predominance over his company and his inclination to inflict pain, he accepted his friend's paradoxical nature, as his comments on Beauclerk's death show: 'His wit and his folly, his acuteness and maliciousness, his merriment and reasoning, are now over. Such another will not often be found among mankind' (*Letters of Samuel Johnson*, 3.231).

Beauclerk, Vere, Baron Vere of Hanworth (1699–1781), naval officer and politician, was born on 14 July 1699, the third son of Charles *Beauclerk, first duke of St Albans (1670–1726), the illegitimate son of Charles II and Nell Gwyn. His mother was Lady Diana de Vere (d. 1742), first daughter and eventually sole heir of Aubrey de Vere, twentieth and last earl of Oxford. James *Beauclerk and Aubrey *Beauclerk were among his brothers. About 1713 Beauclerk entered the navy, was commissioned lieutenant on 23 August 1717, and made post captain on 30 May 1721. In command of the frigate *Lyme* (20 guns), he served on the Mediterranean station from 1722 to 1727, joining Admiral Sir John Jennings's squadron off Cadiz in 1726–7, one of three naval efforts (the other two being in the Baltic and the Mediterranean) to dissuade Spain and Austria from attacks on British possessions. From 1728 to 1731 he served on the Newfoundland station as commodore of the British fishery, where the lawlessness that prevailed, especially in the winter, together with the interference by Samuel Gledhill, lieutenant-governor of Placentia, resulted in Beauclerk's recommendation to place someone 'skilled in the laws' in charge of local justice. In 1729 the cabinet consulted the Board of Trade which, though preferring to remove the inhabitants to Nova Scotia, proposed commissioning the commodore as governor, with civil powers and the authority to create a local magistracy during the nine months when fishing ships were not there. Had Beauclerk not been elected MP for the family seat of New Windsor, Berkshire, in May 1726, the cabinet would have chosen him as the first royal governor of Newfoundland. However, on 22 May 1729 an order in council approved a new form of administration, appointing Captain Henry Osborn of the *Squirrel* to the governorship and leaving Beauclerk—prevented as an MP from holding civil office—as commander-in-chief.

In 1731 Beauclerk took command of the *Hampton Court* (70 guns) and sailed in Admiral Sir Charles Wager's squadron to the Mediterranean. On 24 May 1732 he took office as a commissioner of the navy in the Navy Board; he moved to the Board of Admiralty in 13 March 1738, serving there until 19 March 1742, when the earl of Winchilsea replaced Sir Charles Wager as first lord. Beauclerk returned to the Admiralty on 27 December 1744 when the duke of Bedford became first lord; on 3 July 1745, with Bedford and the earl of Sandwich, he persuaded the duke of Newcastle to select Admiral Edward Vernon to command the fleet in the Downs during Charles Edward Stuart's invasion of England, a measure that was instrumental in cutting off French support for the Jacobite rising. He was promoted rear-admiral of the red on 23 April 1745, and on 14 February 1746 vice-admiral of the blue, when he became senior lord. He received two further promotions, to vice-admiral of the red on 15 July 1747 and admiral of the blue on 12 May 1748. On 21 July 1749 he resigned his rank in the navy and left the Board of Admiralty.

Beauclerk had continued to sit as a member of parliament throughout this period, first for New Windsor and then, at the general election of 1741, for Plymouth. On 13 April 1736 he had married Mary (*d*. 1783) the eldest daughter and coheir (said to be worth £45,000) of Thomas Chambers of Haworth, Middlesex. He was created Baron Vere of Hanworth on 28 March 1750, took his seat in the House of Lords, and in 1761 became lord lieutenant of Berkshire. Beauclerk died on 2 October 1781 at his house on St James's Square, Westminster, and was buried in the vault under St James's Church, Westminster, on 6 October. He was survived by his wife, who died on 21 January 1783.

W. A. B. DOUGLAS

Sources GEC, *Peerage*, new edn, vol. 12/2 · R. S. Lea, 'Beaumont, Lord Vere', HoP, *Commons, 1715–54*, 1.450 · R. G. Lounsbury, *The British fishery at Newfoundland, 1634–1763* (1934) · J. Charnock, ed., *Biographia navalis*, 4 (1796), 89–92 · D. Syrett and R. L. DiNardo, *The commissioned sea officers of the Royal Navy, 1660–1815*, rev. edn, Occasional Publications of the Navy RS, 1 (1994) · D. A. Baugh, *British naval administration in the age of Walpole* (1965) · D. A. Baugh, ed., *Naval administration, 1715–1750*, Navy RS, 120 (1977) · *The Vernon papers*, ed. B. McL. Ranft, Navy RS, 99 (1958) · N. A. M. Rodger, *The admiralty* (1979) · F. F. Thomson, 'Osborn, Henry', *DCB*, vol. 4 · will, PRO, PROB 11 1083 scs. 504

Archives BL, corresp. with duke of Newcastle, Add. MSS 32707–32734, *passim* · NA Canada, copies of the colonial office papers [microfilm] · PRO, captains' letters, ADM 1 · PRO, commissions and warrants, ADM 6/3 · PRO, passing certificates, ADM 107/3 · PRO, CO 194/7, 194/8, 195/7

Wealth at death wealthy: will, PRO, PROB 11/1083

Beaufeu, Robert de [Robert de Bello Fago] (*d*. in or before 1219), poet and cleric, was a canon of Salisbury Cathedral, a prebendary of Horton, and a very minor Latin poet. His usual surname, de Bello Fago (rarely de Bello Foco), is shared with a few people in Salisbury and around Norwich; it has been interpreted as Beaufeu, though no such place is known. John Bale's account, partly repeated in the *Dictionary of National Biography*, depends on Gerald of Wales's self-serving story reporting the praise that Robert gave to Gerald's *Topographia Hiberniae* (dating from c.1188); there is no suggestion—even in Gerald—of a written encomium. Robert engaged in a light-hearted verse debate with Peter of Blois, taking the side of beer against wine; this suggests, according to stereotypes established by Alcuin, Reginald of Canterbury, and Henry of Avranches, that he was English. Robert must have died before 11 April 1219, when the prebend of Horton was transferred to the bishop of Salisbury.

A. G. RIGG

Sources *Gir. Camb. opera*, 1.409–419; 3.92, 335 · *Fasti Angl., 1066–1300*, [Salisbury], 77 · W. H. Rich Jones and W. Dunn Macray, eds., *Charters and documents illustrating the history of the cathedral, city, and diocese of Salisbury, in the twelfth and thirteenth centuries*, Rolls Series, 97 (1891), 86 · A. G. Rigg, *A history of Anglo-Latin literature, 1066–1422* (1992), 86 · A. Wilmart, 'Une suite au poème de Robert de Beaufeu pour l'éloge de la cervoise', *Revue Bénédictine*, 50 (1938), 136–40 · Bale, *Cat.*, 233 · Bale, *Index*, 336–7

Beaufort. For this title name see Somerset, Henry, first duke of Beaufort (1629–1700); Somerset, Mary, duchess of Beaufort (*bap*. 1630, *d*. 1715); Somerset, Henry, second duke of Beaufort (1684–1714); Somerset, Charles Noel, fourth duke of Beaufort (1709–1756) [*see under* Somerset, Henry, second duke of Beaufort (1684–1714)]; Somerset, Henry, seventh duke of Beaufort (1792–1853) [*see under* Somerset, Lord Granville Charles Henry (1792–1848)]; Somerset, Henry Hugh Arthur Fitzroy, tenth duke of Beaufort (1900–1984).

Beaufort, Daniel Augustus (1739–1821), Church of Ireland clergyman and cartographer, was the eldest son of the Revd **Daniel Cornelius de Beaufort** (1700–1788) and his wife, Esther Gougeon. The elder Beaufort was born at Wesel in Westphalia, the seventh child of Count Francis de Beaufort and his wife, Louise Mary Brazy. The family, of Huguenot origin, fled from France to the United Provinces after 1685. Count de Beaufort served in the Dutch army and in 1710 became court chancellor to the prince of Lippe-Detmold. Daniel Cornelius de Beaufort was destined originally to be a soldier but changed track and studied theology at the University of Utrecht. Having been

Daniel Augustus Beaufort (1739–1821), by unknown artist, c.1800–05

ordained, he moved to England, where he ministered to the refugee community in Spitalfields and at the Église de l'Artillerie. After ordination into the Church of England in 1731 he was appointed to the living of St Martin Orgar and officiated at the Savoy chapel. He married on 11 June 1738 in London. In 1739 he moved to the incumbency of East Barnet, which from 1741 he combined with the pastorate of the Little Savoy. Having come to the notice of the influential at court, in 1746 he accompanied the lord lieutenant, the first earl of Harrington, to Ireland as a chaplain. There, in the following year, he received the benefice of Navan in co. Meath. In 1753 he was advanced to be provost of Tuam, a dignity which he relinquished on being appointed to the rectory of Clonenagh in Queen's county. In the year of his death, 1788, he published *A Short Account of the Doctrines and Practices of the Church of Rome*; its appearance attested to the revival of confessional controversy in Ireland.

The younger Daniel, who was born in East Barnet, Hertfordshire, on 1 October 1739 and baptized in St James's Palace, London, was educated first at Preston's endowed school in Navan and then in two Dublin schools, one run by A. McCullen and the other by a Mr Ball. He entered Trinity College, Dublin, in 1754, was elected to a scholarship in 1757, and graduated BA in 1759. He was ordained in 1763 but almost immediately went to the Low Countries, where he visited various relatives. Already he manifested an interest in observation and topographical description that would continue throughout his life. In 1765 he succeeded his father in the living of Navan, which he retained until 1818. The conformist protestant population was small and Beaufort henceforward divided his time

between that neighbourhood, where he rented a succession of houses, and Dublin, Wales, and England. Uncertain finances and disappointment in the quest for further preferment forced him into sundry projects. Thanks to his travels and his continuing intimacy with contemporaries from university, such as Henry Ussher, Richard Lovell Edgeworth, and Henry Dabzac, he was stimulated into a variety of scholarly activities. In recognition of these he was elected an honorary member of the recently established Royal Irish Academy in 1785, became its librarian in 1787, and was awarded the degree of LLD by his old college in the same year. In 1767 he married Mary, the daughter and coheir of William Waller of Allenstown, co. Meath; their elder son, William Louis Beaufort (1771–1849), became rector of Glanmire and prebendary of Rathcooney, co. Cork, from 1814 until his death. Their younger son was Sir Francis *Beaufort (1774–1857), naval officer.

Beaufort's translation of a history of the Roman republic by his uncle Louis Beaufort was greeted with little enthusiasm and was never published. However, in 1786 a pilot scheme to delineate the parishes in the Church of Ireland diocese of Meath was well enough received by the ecclesiastical authorities to encourage him to map the entire island. It also led to his being made an honorary member of the Dublin Society in 1789. For the national map he intended at first to add diocesan and parochial boundaries to an existing one. However, he quickly found that the extant surveys were inaccurate and that few counties had been expertly delineated. Assiduously he sought out unpublished surveys in government offices and private houses. Above all he set about surveying the terrain anew. He conceived his efforts as complementary to those of Charles Vallancey with his military map but the latter regarded them as competitive. In the course of its preparation Beaufort's *A New Map of Ireland, Civil and Ecclesiastical* expanded from a simple delineation of Church of Ireland bishoprics and parishes. Belatedly roads were inserted. Published in 1792 the map used a scale of 6 Irish miles to 1 inch. It included longitudes and latitudes, supplied by acquaintances and correspondents across the kingdom; those for Athlone were provided by his fifteen-year-old son, Francis, at the time a pupil of the astronomer Henry Ussher. The *New Map*, engraved to a high quality and printed in London, sold well. It was reprinted in 1797 and 1813, and went through at least eight impressions between 1821 and 1862. Despite its success the work cost its author at least £1000, and so aggravated his chronic financial problems. Beaufort accompanied it with his *Memoir of a New Map of Ireland*; this described his methods as cartographer. Additionally it estimated acreages and populations of counties, provinces, and dioceses. A few of the observations recorded as he toured the island were incorporated but much more remained in his unpublished diaries and itineraries. In 1792 he also published the first thematic map of the whole island, on which mountains, rivers, and bogs were shown. His detailed map of co. Meath eventually appeared in 1797.

Beaufort had hoped that the patronage of the speaker of the Irish House of Commons, John Foster, would ease his precarious financial position. In 1789 Foster did indeed present Beaufort to the living of Collon, at the heart of his co. Louth estate. Worth £200 p.a., when combined with other preferments valued at an annual £330, it promised but failed to deliver him from indebtedness. He continued to visit London and other parts of England and Wales regularly between 1792 and 1797. These trips were partly motivated by protracted litigation, through which he hoped to secure a share of a legacy. They also enabled him to note new agricultural and manufacturing techniques, a few of which were introduced into his own houses and parishes back in Ireland. His virtuosity and versatility were further demonstrated in architectural designs. Many were for glebe houses to accommodate the clergy, others for churches. The rebuilding of the church at Collon according to a design derived from the chapel of Trinity College, Cambridge, cost more than £6500; it included innovative heating, probably devised by Beaufort's son-in-law William Edgeworth. Another scheme for the church at Navan proved equally costly. For the bishop of Meath, Beaufort remodelled and enlarged the mansion at Ardbraccan after drawings by James Wyatt. He also designed additions at Beauparc in co. Meath. For the Dublin Society he compiled a description of the human and physical geography of co. Louth but it was never published during his life. As his health declined and his finances failed to improve, he removed to co. Cork, where his son was an incumbent. There, at Upton, near Inishannon, he died on 17 May 1821.

Beaufort belonged to a long tradition of improvers, particularly numerous among the clergy of the Church of Ireland. Many of his ideas proved wildly impractical or overambitious. However, the *New Map* of 1792, in both conception and execution, advanced and diffused knowledge of and in Ireland, and immediately proved its usefulness.

TOBY BARNARD

Sources C. C. Ellison, *The hopeful traveller: life and times of D. A. Beaufort* (1987) · J. H. Andrews, *Shapes of Ireland: maps and map-makers* (1997), chap. 8 · C. C. Ellison, ed., 'Materials for the Dublin Society survey of co. Louth by Beaufort', *Journal of the co. Louth Archaeological and Historical Society*, 18 (1974–6) · BL, Add. MS 53711 A and B [corrected copies of *Map* and *Memoir*] · TCD, Beaufort MSS, MSS 4023–4042, 5118, 7096–7097, 7384, 7941 · Beaufort diaries and account books, Hunt. L. [microfilm at TCD] · *North-west Ulster: the counties of Londonderry, Donegal, Fermanagh and Tyrone*, Pevsner (1979) · Burtchaell & Sadleir, *Alum. Dubl.* · D. A. Beaufort, *Memoir of a new map of Ireland* (1792) · *DNB*
Archives BL, MS map of Ireland and notes, Add. MS 53711 · Hunt. L., MSS · NL Ire., MSS · Representative Church Body Library, Dublin, topographical and statistical papers · TCD, diaries, sketches, and family papers | Bodl. Oxf., corresp. with Francis Edgeworth and others · Hunt. L., letters to Sir Francis Beaufort
Likenesses pencil drawing, c.1800–1805, NPG [see illus.] · P. Danloux, miniatures, repro. in Ellison, *The hopeful traveller*

Beaufort, Daniel Cornelius de (1700–1788). *See under* Beaufort, Daniel Augustus (1739–1821).

Beaufort, Edmund, first duke of Somerset (c.1406–1455), magnate and soldier, was the younger brother of John *Beaufort, duke of Somerset (1404–1444); John and

Edmund were the second and third sons of John *Beaufort, marquess of Dorset and of Somerset (c.1371–1410), who was the eldest son of *John of Gaunt and Katherine Swynford [see Katherine, duchess of Lancaster], and his wife, Margaret Holland (d. 1439). Henry, their elder brother, died aged seventeen and unmarried in 1418.

Early life and the affair with Queen Catherine To some degree, possibly to a large degree, Edmund and John were chivalric competitors in the English wars in France until the dismal failure of John's expedition to Maine and Anjou in 1443, which was followed soon after by his death, apparently by suicide, in 1444. The brothers, between whom there was no more than a year or two in age, were not yet eighteen when they were captured at the battle of Baugé in 1421. John remained a prisoner of war until 1438, Edmund only until 1427 or 1428. John's lengthy imprisonment gave Edmund the advantage in their competition. He was an ambassador to the general council at Basel in 1434, and a member of the English embassy at the Congress of Arras in 1435, and for his successful defence of Calais in 1436 he was made a knight of the Garter, three years before his brother was so honoured. By then Edmund had taken the leading part in the last important English military achievements in France: the bold relief of Avranches in 1439, and the well-executed recovery of Harfleur in 1440. For these exploits he was created earl of Dorset in August 1442. A year later he was made marquess of Dorset and in the following year he succeeded his brother as earl of Somerset. He had been count of Mortain in Normandy since 1427.

1427 was also the year of the only blot upon a hitherto copybook career: Edmund's affair with the widow of Henry V, *Catherine of Valois (1401–1437). Almost everything is obscure about a liaison that resulted in a parliamentary statute regulating the remarriage of queens of England, but it is just possible that another of its consequences was Edmund *Tudor. It is all a question of when Catherine, to avoid the penalties of breaking the statute of 1427–8, secretly married Owen Tudor, and of when the association with Edmund Beaufort came to an end. Neither of these dates, as might be expected, is known; nor is the date of birth of Edmund Tudor. As Gerald Harriss has written:

> By its very nature the evidence for Edmund 'Tudor's' parentage is less than conclusive, but such facts as can be assembled permit the agreeable possibility that Edmund 'Tudor' and Margaret Beaufort were first cousins and that the royal house of 'Tudor' sprang in fact from Beauforts on both sides. (Harriss, 178 n.34)

It seems unlikely that Edmund Beaufort would have taken so great a political risk as getting the queen dowager with child, but he was a dashing young man (recently released from prison) as well as a Beaufort, and Catherine, who had fulfilled the only role open to her by immediately producing a son for the Lancastrian dynasty, was a lonely Frenchwoman in England, and at thirty or thereabouts was, the rumour ran, oversexed. Many stranger things have happened, and the idea of renaming sixteenth-century England is an appealing one.

A matter of honour: the quarrel with York After Catherine's early death in 1437, it was Owen Tudor who was imprisoned for having married her without the council's permission, while Edmund Beaufort, who had only had an affair with her, was taking off on his meteoric career. This appeared to culminate in December 1447, when Edmund was appointed lieutenant and governor-general of France and the duchies of Normandy and Guyenne. He succeeded Richard, duke of York, in that position. It used to be assumed that the intense and bitter rivalry between the two dukes—Edmund was created duke of Somerset on 31 March 1448—had its origin in York's resentment at being replaced in France by Edmund Beaufort. Such an assumption does justice neither to Richard of York nor to the extent of the predicament both men found themselves in during the next eight years. The speed with which the English were removed from Normandy in 1449–50, after an occupation of thirty years, followed by the equally dramatic extinction of four centuries of English rule in Gascony, had a traumatic impact. Who was responsible for so great a disaster? The answer late twentieth-century historians wholeheartedly agree upon was not available to mid-fifteenth-century politicians, or at any rate was not pronounceable by them. To stand up in parliament and say it was all the fault of Henry VI was not only impossible because political courtesy forbade it; because political rhetoric did not include it, it was not even contemplated. Politicians had been thinking that the king was an ass ever since Henry had first demonstrated his asininity over a decade previously, but the current vocabulary of politics did not enable them to give such a thought expression.

Someone else had to take the blame. Richard of York blamed Edmund Beaufort. Historians believe he had a case: Somerset's conduct in office, indeed with regard to the county of Maine, his conduct before he at last agreed in December 1447 to take up office, was downright irresponsible and thoroughly reprehensible. The English government had promised to cede Maine to the king of France in 1445; it was a sacrifice it was willing to make in order to hold on to Normandy. Edmund Beaufort had been made captain-general and governor of Maine in 1438; he had received the land rights to the county in 1442. If Maine was to be given up he wanted compensation, and for a year he bargained with the government until he obtained the compensation he wanted—10,000 livres tournois a year from taxation in Normandy, which was fully paid until the outbreak of war in 1449. Only when Beaufort had secured this could the cession of Maine go ahead and only then would he agree to undertake to be lieutenant-general in France, and governor of Normandy. It was scarcely public-spirited to take such an enormous sum from a government that had no money to spare, and Richard of York in his articles of 1452 said so. York was also later critical of Beaufort's administration of Normandy; however, his chief complaint against Somerset concerned the inadequacy of his defence of the duchy when the French invaded in 1449. The entire duchy was overrun in barely a year, with many towns offering no resistance.

Somerset himself surrendered Rouen, the capital of Normandy, and several nearby fortresses with it, on 29 October 1449, and agreed to pay a large ransom for himself, his family and his retinue, and to leave a number of hostages for its payment. He then withdrew to Caen, which he surrendered on 1 July following, handing over eighteen hostages as pledges for his and the garrison's departure.

It was this conduct that caused the breach between the two men, after the disgrace and death of the duke of Suffolk in 1450 the two most prominent politicians of the day; it was a breach that was never closed because it turned upon that touchiest of matters, honour. The impossibility of its closure was what led to the first battle of St Albans in 1455; it may fairly be said, therefore, that the Wars of the Roses, as well as the end of the house of Lancaster, were due to Edmund Beaufort's dishonourable conduct in the last stages of the Hundred Years' War. The duke's failure of nerve (or want of chivalry) undid him, and it discredited him, his family, his dynasty, and his country.

Defeat and near recovery York was not critical, as are historians, of Somerset's involvement in the plan to attack the Breton town of Fougères—the town's capture on 23 March 1449 led to a French declaration of war on 17 July 1449—because Somerset was not solely responsible for the mindless adventurism of the Fougères plan. What enraged him was Beaufort's feeble response to the French invasion of Normandy. York regarded the terms under which Somerset surrendered Rouen and other Norman towns not as misjudged, but as shameful and treasonable. The loss of Normandy, in other words, was due to the self-serving cowardice of his successor as lieutenant-general. As if that was not bad enough, York's own honour was impugned by Somerset's impeachable behaviour, for York himself was captain of the town of Rouen and it was his officers who were at their posts when Somerset's abject composition with Charles VII was made. It is clear that York's return from Ireland in September 1450 was precipitated by Somerset's own return in August, following the English defeat at Formigny and his surrender of Caen. They clashed in the parliament of November 1450, Somerset's castle of Corfe was ransacked by York's tenants, and he himself was attacked by men of York's retinue and ended up in the Tower of London, probably under compulsion, since the king had to intervene to secure his release in December. Ever afterwards, the burden of York's complaints against Somerset was his misconduct in Normandy; he appears to have deemed him unforgivable on that score, imprisoning him in the Tower, when as protector he had the power to do so, in December 1453, and eventually seeing that he was killed at St Albans in May 1455.

It is inaccurate, therefore, to talk only of a personal quarrel between the two dukes. If York was vindictive it was with reason. Neither king nor parliament was willing to try, let alone punish, the man who had given up Henry V's hard-won conquests in France without a fight. Although Somerset came back to England under something of a cloud, and was deprived of his principal estates in the west of England under the Acts of Resumption of 1449–50 (they were later entrusted to the duke of Exeter), he soon recovered his position. As soon as he returned to England he began to attend council meetings, and was shortly afterwards, on 8 September, given responsibility for putting an end to the remnants of disaffection in the south-east, while three days later he was made constable, the supreme military post in the realm. To reinforce what had become his position as effective head of the government, in April 1451 he was appointed captain of Calais. It is not easy to understand Henry VI's trust in Somerset, in the light of the duke's recent failures in Normandy, though the king's dynastic feelings, his natural tendency to put his trust in his Beaufort cousin, cannot be discounted, especially as they would have been bolstered by the queen's support for Somerset, to whom she was paying an annuity of 100 marks from 1451. None the less, it would appear that the duke was moderately, if superficially, successful in restoring the fortunes and reputation of the king's government in the early 1450s. An executive council was established to bring order to the royal finances and oversee daily administration; a series of judicial circuits, headed by King Henry in person, was organized as a means of restoring order; and an expedition to Gascony won back Bordeaux in October 1452. Richard of York was unable to command sufficient influential support to topple his ducal rival. Although the weaknesses of Somerset's government were exposed by its failure to control the increasingly militant rivalry of the Nevilles and the Percys in the north, the acquiescence of king, nobility, and civil service enabled it to keep going. When Margaret of Anjou became miraculously pregnant at Epiphany 1453, it looked as if they might all survive.

Disaster at St Albans No doubt they would have done had the battle of Castillon on 17 July 1453 not been so comprehensive an English defeat, and had Henry VI not had a mental breakdown, ultimately precipitated, apparently, by this news. The king's illness was Richard of York's opportunity. At a meeting of the great council in November 1453 Somerset was charged (by the duke of Norfolk) with treason; the charges related mainly to his mismanagement of the war against the French; two days later he was arrested and put once again into the Tower. There he remained without trial for over a year. But on the king's recovery at or soon after Christmas 1454 he was released and at council meetings in February and March 1455 he was officially exonerated and rehabilitated, and once again assumed his pre-eminent place in government. York and his new allies, the earls of Salisbury and Warwick, could not stomach such a reversal of fortune. Fearing that moves might be made against them at a great council summoned to assemble at Leicester on 21 May, they took to arms and advanced on London. The confrontation with the hastily raised government army took place at St Albans; negotiations failed, principally it seems because Henry VI would not surrender Somerset to the man who had been his implacable enemy for more than five years.

In the resulting engagement on 22 May Somerset, defending himself valiantly, was cut down in the street, and subsequently buried in St Albans Abbey. It was an ignominious but not unfitting conclusion to what had been a very mixed life. He was married before 1436 to the wealthy widow of Thomas, Lord Ros, Eleanor Beauchamp (d. 1467), with whom he had five daughters and three sons, including Edmund *Beaufort, styled third duke of Somerset (c.1438–1471), and Henry *Beaufort, who was badly wounded beside his father at St Albans. Edmund Beaufort's personality is irrecoverable. T. B. Pugh has called him 'unscrupulous and resourceful' (Pugh, 129). In the end he was neither unscrupulous nor resourceful enough. Like his fellow protagonist, Richard of York, he failed to inspire affection, respect, or dread; he had only high birth to recommend him and that was insufficient.

COLIN RICHMOND

Sources R. A. Griffiths, *The reign of King Henry VI: the exercise of royal authority, 1422–1461* (1981) • M. K. Jones, 'Somerset, York and the Wars of the Roses', *EngHR*, 104 (1989), 285–307 • G. L. Harriss, *Cardinal Beaufort: a study of Lancastrian ascendancy and decline* (1988) • M. K. Jones, 'The relief of Avranches (1439): an English feat of arms at the end of the Hundred Years' War', *England in the fifteenth century* [Harlaxton 1992], ed. N. Rogers (1994), 42–55 • T. B. Pugh, 'Richard Plantagenet (1411–60), duke of York, as the king's lieutenant in France and Ireland', *Aspects of late medieval government and society: essays presented to J. R. Lander*, ed. J. G. Rowe (1986), 107–41 • GEC, *Peerage*, new edn, 12/1.49–53 • J. Watts, *Henry VI and the politics of kingship* (1996)

Beaufort, Edmund, styled third duke of Somerset (c.1438–1471), magnate, was the second of the three sons of Edmund *Beaufort, first duke of Somerset (d. 1455), and his wife, Eleanor, daughter of Richard *Beauchamp, earl of Warwick (d. 1439), and widow of Thomas, Baron Ros of Helmsley. He took little part in the early battles of the Wars of the Roses. Left in command of the Isle of Wight in 1460 by his elder brother, Henry *Beaufort, second duke of Somerset, he was soon captured by Geoffrey Gate, one of the retainers of Richard Neville, earl of Warwick, and spent the next two years of his life in captivity, first in Carisbrooke Castle and then in the Tower of London. He was released in the early summer of 1463 as part of Edward IV's ill-judged policy of conciliation towards the Beaufort family, but quickly joined Margaret of Anjou and the Lancastrian exiles in Scotland. After the disastrous defeat at Hexham in May 1464, which saw Henry Beaufort's capture and execution, he escaped to France, reaching Paris in October and the Lancastrian court in exile at Koeur near St Mihiel-en-Bar at the end of the year. He now styled himself duke of Somerset, disregarding the posthumous attainder passed against his brother in the parliament of 1465.

In the following years Somerset struck up a close relationship with Charles, count of Charolais, who succeeded to the dukedom of Burgundy in 1467. He fought with him for the League of the Public Weal at Montlhéry in 1465, and during the Liège campaign two years later. By this time he was in receipt of a regular monthly pension and was frequently to be found at the Burgundian court. His presence attracted many exiled Lancastrian noblemen, including Henry Holland, duke of Exeter, James Butler, earl of Ormond, and John Courtenay, earl of Devon: a highly partisan band (Ormond's correspondence shows him still using the regnal years of Henry VI) that continued to worry the Yorkist regime. Edward IV had hoped that Charles's marriage to his youngest sister, Margaret, in the summer of 1468 would end Burgundian support for these Lancastrian exiles. On 8 July, John Paston wrote from Bruges that Somerset had rejoined Margaret of Anjou at Koeur, 'and shal no more come her ayen, nor be holpyn by the Duk' (Gairdner, 4.299). Such optimism proved to be groundless. Charles had instructed Somerset to leave court at the time of the wedding, but had made generous provision for his expenses. By September 1468 Somerset was once more to be found in Duke Charles's army, alongside a number of other Lancastrians, in the campaign that led to the treaty of Péronne, and soon resumed his prominent position at court.

Somerset's status at the Burgundian court was exceptional for a political exile. Charles the Bold gave him numerous personal gifts, including expensive war-horses, and allowed him to attend council meetings and receptions for foreign dignitaries. On 8 January 1469 Somerset was listed as being present, in the company of senior Burgundian noblemen, at the decision to revoke the commercial privileges of Ghent. On 10 August he was recorded in the company of Charles when the duke formally received ambassadors at The Hague. The chronicler Chastellain felt that Charles the Bold's friendship for the Beaufort family was derived from his sense of kinship, through his own maternal descent from John of Gaunt, from the marriage of Gaunt's daughter Philippa to João I of Portugal. Charles was certainly interested in his Lancastrian lineage. His mother, Isabel of Portugal, Philippa's only surviving daughter, was later to pass over to him, in November 1471, any claim she might have to the English crown. But he was also worried that Edward IV was losing effective political power to Warwick, and that a strongly pro-French foreign policy would emerge to threaten Burgundy's very survival. In December 1469 Somerset was allowed to prepare an invasion force that might effect a Lancastrian restoration should Warwick regain control. The Danzig seaman Paul Beneke began to assemble warships at Berschug, the harbour or roads of Veere on the island of Walcheren. In January 1470 one of Somerset's servants was in the town carrying letters from his master to Beneke. In March 1470 Somerset and his retinue were stationed in Veere. But the danger passed and it was Warwick and Clarence who were forced to flee England.

The political weathervane was soon to turn again. Somerset took no part in the agreement at Angers that was concluded early in August 1470 between Warwick, Clarence, and Margaret of Anjou. The compromise offered little to him beyond the return of his lands, and these were insufficient to support a ducal title. The terms of the accommodation undermined the Beaufort family dynastically and politically: Clarence became residual heir to Henry VI and his son, and Warwick was appointed king's lieutenant. After the restoration of the Lancastrian king

on 13 October 1470 Somerset was, however, prepared to offer the readeption government cautious support, and left the Burgundian court in early November with a generous parting gift from Charles the Bold. He was not willing to accept an alliance with Louis XI that would lead to attacking the duchy of Burgundy. He and Exeter argued as much in an embassy to Charles the Bold at St Pol on 7 January 1471 and in a personal audience with Henry VI on 14 February. Warwick's declaration of war on Burgundy a day later alienated Somerset: its consequences were to be seen when Edward IV landed in Yorkshire. Somerset had been issued with commissions of array and was recruiting men in the south-eastern counties in late March. He and John Courtenay, earl of Devon, had the strength to hold London against Edward and trap him between two armies. Instead he disobeyed Warwick's instructions and moved his forces to Salisbury to await the arrival of Margaret of Anjou. Contemporaries rightly regarded it as a decisive moment in the campaign. Gerhard von Wesel, a Hanseatic merchant living in London, described how Somerset and Devon rode westwards from the capital on 8 April, 'not having taken the field against Edward at that time' (Adair, 67).

After Warwick's defeat at Barnet on 14 April, Somerset encouraged Margaret of Anjou to fight the weakened army of Edward IV as soon as possible. His military reputation ensured his counsel was adopted, and a vigorous policy of recruitment brought in much support from the west country. Somerset was at the head of Margaret's troops as they entered Bristol (1 May) and, commanding the van, decided on the battle plan at Tewkesbury (4 May) that committed the Lancastrians to taking the offensive against Edward's forces. The failure of his assault was attributed, in the official Yorkist account, to the king's superior generalship; later Tudor sources suggest a damaging division between the Lancastrian captains, and that Somerset was not properly supported by the remainder of the army. The result was a débâcle. His younger brother John Beaufort was killed in the fighting. Somerset took sanctuary in Tewkesbury Abbey, but Edward IV was not prepared to allow such a dangerous opponent to survive and broke into the abbey by force. Somerset was executed in the town's market place on 6 May and buried in Tewkesbury Abbey. Edward's ruthlessness clearly showed the threat he had represented to the Yorkist regime, both politically and dynastically, and brought an end to the male line of the Beaufort family.   MICHAEL K. JONES

Sources Archives départementales du Nord, B2064–2079 · J. H. Smit, *Bronnen tot de geschiedenis van de handel net Engeland, Schotland en Ierland*, 2 vols. in 4 pts (The Hague, 1928–50) · L. P. Gachard, *Collection de documents inédits concernant l'histoire de la Belgique*, 3 vols. (1833–5) · Chambre des comptes, 1925, National State Archives, Brussels · PRO, E 404/72 · Wilts. & Swindon RO, G 23/1/2 · *The Paston letters, AD 1422–1509*, ed. J. Gairdner, new edn, 6 vols. (1904) · J. Adair, 'Gerhard von Wesel: the newsletter of 17 April 1471', *Journal of the Society for Army Historical Research*, 46 (1968), 67 · Muniments, Westminster Abbey, 12183, 12190 · G. Chastellain, *Œuvres*, ed. K. de Lettenhove, 8 vols. (Brussels, 1863–6) · 'Hearne's Fragment', *Chronicles of the white rose of York*, ed. J. A. Giles (1845) · *Memoirs of Phillipe de Commynes: the reign of Louis XI, 1461–83*, trans. M. Jones, pbk edn (1972) · C. L. Kingsford, ed., *Chronicles of London* (1905) · J. Bruce, ed.,

Historie of the arrivall of Edward IV in England, and the finall recoverye of his kingdomes from Henry VI, CS, 1 (1838) · *Three books of Polydore Vergil's 'English history'*, ed. H. Ellis, CS, 29 (1844) · *Hall's chronicle*, ed. H. Ellis (1809)

Beaufort, Sir Francis (1774–1857), naval officer and hydrographer, was born on 27 May 1774 at Flower Hill, Navan, co. Meath, the second son of the Revd Daniel Augustus *Beaufort (1739–1821), rector of Navan, a topographer and architect of some distinction, and his wife, Mary Waller of Allenstown, co. Meath. His sister Frances was the fourth wife of Richard Lovell Edgeworth, and thus the stepmother of Maria Edgeworth, the novelist. Having been rejected by a school in Cheltenham on the ground that his Irish accent would corrupt the speech of the other boys, he entered, soon after 1784, Bates's Military and Marine Academy in Dublin. In 1788 he studied for five months under Dr Henry Ussher, professor of astronomy at Trinity College, Dublin. From early boyhood he had determined to go to sea, and in March 1789 he sailed in the East Indiaman *Vansittart*, commanded by the experienced surveyor Captain Lestock Wilson. While surveying the Gaspar Strait the *Vansittart* was wrecked, but Beaufort with most of the crew survived. He returned in time for the 1790 mobilization, when his father's friend Lord Courtown got him aboard the frigate *Latona* (Captain Albemarle Bertie). From her he moved next year into the *Aquilon*, commanded by Courtown's son Captain the Hon. Robert Stopford, which was one of the repeating frigates in Lord Howe's action of 1 June 1794. He followed Captain Stopford to the *Phaeton* (38 guns), and in her he saw much active service, including Cornwallis's retreat, on 17 June 1795, and the capture of the *Flore* on 8 September 1798. Beaufort was made a lieutenant on 10 May 1796. On 28 October 1800, when first lieutenant of the *Phaeton*, under Captain James Nicoll Morris, he commanded her boats when they captured the Spanish ship *San Josef* from under the guns of Fuengirola Castle, near Malaga; in this service he received nineteen wounds in the head, arms, and body, three sword cuts and sixteen musket shots, and dearly won his promotion to the rank of commander, which was dated 13 November, as well as a wound pension of £45. For some years after this he was unemployed at sea, and in 1803–4 assisted his brother-in-law Richard Edgeworth in establishing a telegraph line from Dublin to Galway. In June 1805 he was appointed to the command of the armed store-ship *Woolwich*, in which he made a voyage to Bombay, and helped to evacuate the defeated British troops from Buenos Aires in 1807. In May 1809 he was appointed to the sloop *Blossom*, employed in convoy duty on the coast of Spain.

By now Beaufort's gallant record and his scientific talents had made him well known throughout the navy. Lord Elgin said he had never met one 'who had read more, or to better purpose' (Friendly, 96), while his surveys, notably of the Rio de la Plata, were highly praised by Dalrymple, the hydrographer of the navy. He had to wait for the change of administration in 1810, however, for his merits to be recognized. At the same time he became engaged to Alicia Magdalena Wilson (1782–1834), daughter of his first

Sir Francis Beaufort (1774–1857), by Samuel Pearce, 1855–6

captain. On 30 May 1810 he was advanced to post rank, and appointed to the frigate *Frederiksteen*. During the two following years he was employed in surveying the south coast of Turkey and exploring the spectacular classical ruins, then quite unknown to Europeans. His work was brought to an untimely end by an attack by some Turks on his boat's crew on 20 June 1812. Beaufort was badly wounded in the hip, and after months of danger and suffering at Malta was obliged to return to England, and the *Frederiksteen* was paid off on 29 October. Two months later, on 3 December, he married Alicia Magdalena Wilson; their youngest daughter was Emily Anne *Smythe, Viscountess Strangford.

Beaufort later published his account of his survey and exploration of the southern Turkish coast as *Karamania, or, A brief description of the south coast of Asia minor, and of the remains of antiquity* (1817). For many years after his return to England he was engaged in constructing the charts of his survey, with his own hand, and the charts were engraved directly from his drawings. The book was an instant success both with the learned and with the ordinary reading public, while Beaufort's extraordinarily accurate and thorough charts aroused the admiration of sailors and geographers. He was offered several surveying tasks of importance, but he declined them all for various reasons. His marriage was deeply happy and his scientific interests absorbing, but he had always been easily embittered by supposed neglect, and unemployment did not bring out the best in him. When Captain Hurd, the hydrographer of the navy, died in May 1823 Beaufort was rejected as his successor, probably because J. W. Croker, the first secretary of the Admiralty, an enemy to hydrography as a consumer of public money, did not choose to appoint a candidate whose public and professional standing was so high. When the post next fell vacant in 1829 Beaufort's claims were irresistible.

Beaufort was the ideal candidate for the great and urgent task that presented itself: that of making the seas of the world, most of them (including almost the entire coastline of Britain and Ireland) uncharted or badly charted, safe for the rapidly increasing quantity of British and foreign shipping. For twenty-six years he presided over the hydrographic office with unwearied care, planning and directing surveys, guiding and encouraging the surveyors, correcting and publishing their charts. Although the public connects his name only with his wind scale, among seamen and especially hydrographers Beaufort's achievement is remembered with awe. More than one thousand charts were issued during his time; from 1835 to his retirement in 1855 the average was sixty-eight new charts a year. He had many other duties besides. He served on the Parliamentary Boundary Commission delineating the new constituencies of the 1832 Reform Act; he belonged to commissions dealing with pilotage, life-saving, and harbour construction; he was deeply involved in the affairs of the Royal Society, the Royal Astronomical Society, and the Royal Geographical Society, which he helped found; he had a share, usually an important one, in almost every important project of scientific research of his day, and he effectively directed the 'sacred cause' of discovering Sir John Franklin or his fate. In April 1835 he was a member of a commission on the employment of pilots, and in January 1845 of one on United Kingdom harbours, shores, and rivers. On 1 October 1846 he was made a rear-admiral on the retired list, and on 29 April 1848 a KCB for his civil services as hydrographer. He retired in 1855, and died at Brighton on 17 December 1857. He was buried at Hackney church.

Beaufort was completely fulfilled in his work, and fortunate that it continued into his eighty-first year. His private happiness never recovered from the death of his beloved wife in 1834. For some years his unmarried sister Harriet kept house for him; for a while before he remarried their relationship became incestuous. His second wife was Honora Edgeworth (1792 – February 1858), his step-niece, whom he married on 8 November 1838. The marriage was contented, if not passionate, but she became increasingly disabled, and was paralysed and demented by the time of his death. Beaufort's son **Francis Lestock Beaufort** (1815–1879) served in the Bengal civil service from 1837 to 1876, was a Calcutta judge, and wrote *Digest of the Criminal Law Procedure in Bengal* (1850).

J. K. LAUGHTON, rev. N. A. M. RODGER

Sources A. Friendly, *Beaufort of the Admiralty* (1977) · C. Lloyd, *Mr Barrow of the admiralty* (1970) · A. Day, *The admiralty hydrographic service, 1795–1919* (1967)
Archives CUL, papers relating to testimonial · Duke U., Perkins L., account book · Hunt. L., corresp., journals, and papers · Hydrographic Office, Taunton · RGS, corresp. and papers | Bodl. Oxf., corresp. with Maria Edgeworth and family · CUL, corresp. with Sir George Airy · CUL, letters to Sir William Whewell · Meteorological Office, Bracknell, Berkshire, National Meteorological Archive, weather logs · NL Ire. · NMM, letters to Sir Richard Collinson · priv. coll., Edgeworth MSS · PRO, letters to Sir John Ross, BJ2 · RBG Kew, letters to Sir William Hooker · RGS, letters to Sir George Back · RS, letters to Sir John Hershel · RS, letters to Sir John Lubbock · UCL, letters to Society for the Diffusion of Useful Knowledge
Likenesses W. Brockedon, black and red chalk, 1838, NPG · daguerreotype, 1848, repro. in Friendly, *Beaufort of the admiralty* · S. Pearce, oil on millboard, 1850, NPG · S. Pearce, group portrait, oils, 1851 (*The Arctic Council planning a search for Sir John Franklin*), NPG · S. Pearce, oils, 1855–6, NMM [*see illus.*]

Beaufort, Francis Lestock (1815–1879). *See under* Beaufort, Sir Francis (1774–1857).

Beaufort, Henry [*called* the Cardinal of England] (1375?–1447), bishop of Winchester and cardinal, was the second of four illegitimate children of *John of Gaunt, duke of Lancaster (1340–1399), and Katherine Swynford (1350?–1403), daughter of the Hainaulter Sir Payn Roelt, who was governess to the duke's children [*see* Katherine, duchess of Lancaster]. His siblings were John *Beaufort, Thomas *Beaufort, and Joan *Beaufort.

Early advancement, c.1375–1403 Henry Beaufort was brought up with his brothers and sister in the ducal household. From the first he seems to have been marked out for a clerical career, residing at Peterhouse, Cambridge, in 1388–9 and at Queen's College, Oxford, in 1390–c.1393. Having completed the arts course and commenced the study of theology he was ordained deacon on 7 April 1397. He had been supported in his studies by prebends in the Lincoln diocese, at Thame (1389) and Sutton (1391), and in York diocese at Riccall (1390). He was also made warden of the free chapel of Tickhill in the gift of his father. In 1396 he was provided by papal bull to the deanery of Wells, while the University of Oxford made him its chancellor in April 1397. John of Gaunt, now at the height of his influence with Richard II, married Katherine in February 1396 and their issue, the Beauforts, were legitimized by papal bull and royal charter in 1396–7. On 27 February 1398 Pope Boniface IX was persuaded to remove the aged John Buckingham (against his wish) from the see of Lincoln and to provide Henry Beaufort in his place. He was installed in March 1399, before accompanying Richard II to Ireland. Bishop Beaufort played no part in the deposition of Richard II by his half-brother Henry Bolingbroke, who became Henry IV; indeed during the first years of the new regime he was infrequently at court, and lived mainly within his extensive diocese. About this time a liaison with Alice Fitzalan (*b.* 1383x5), widow of John Charlton of Powys, brought him his only known child, a daughter named Jane or Joan, who later married Sir Edward *Stradling (1389–1453) [*see under* Stradling family]. In 1401–2 Beaufort spent a large part of the year at Oxford. But in the autumn of 1402 he moved decisively into the political centre. He was appointed to the king's council, and in the October parliament was named as one of the lords to intercommune with the Commons and urge convocation to grant a tax. In November he was sent to Brittany to conduct the new queen, Joan of Navarre, to England where, on her arrival, he officiated at the royal marriage. Finally, on 28 February

Henry Beaufort (1375?–1447), stone effigy

1403, he was appointed chancellor of England, a position he was to hold for almost exactly two years.

Political career under Henry IV, 1403–1413 These were years of danger for Henry IV, who faced the revolt of Henry Percy (Hotspur) in July 1403 and that of Archbishop Richard Scrope in May 1405, along with a continuing French threat to Calais. For Beaufort the defence of Calais, under his brother John's command, held high priority as part of a general policy to protect mercantile interests through good relations with the duke of Burgundy and the so-called Four Members of Flanders (Bruges, Ghent, Ypres, and the marc of Bruges) and by reaching a new agreement with the Hanseatic League. As chancellor he opened the two parliaments of January and October 1404, successfully defending the crown's interests against a critical House of Commons, and eventually securing a substantial grant of taxation. His continuous attendance at council in these years left him little time for diocesan duties, and his elevation to the rich see of Winchester in November 1404, in succession to William Wykeham who died in that year, was the reward for his political service to the crown. He resigned the chancellorship on 2 March 1405, though remaining an active member of the council for another year. His influence on appointments within the English church was increasing but he showed little interest in the wider problems of Christendom, and while Robert Hallum led the English embassy to the Council of Pisa in 1408–9, Beaufort was engaged in negotiating a renewal of the truce with France.

In August 1409 Pope Gregory XII (r. 1406–15), declared deposed by the Council of Pisa, named Beaufort as legate in England to combat the council's choice of Alexander V (r. 1409–10), but it was an office that Beaufort neither sought nor exercised. Nevertheless it did not commend him to Archbishop Thomas Arundel on whom Henry IV increasingly relied. When, in January 1410, Henry, prince of Wales, displaced Arundel as head of the council, Bishop Beaufort and his brother Thomas headed the administration. Thomas became chancellor while Bishop Henry opened parliament, of which his cousin Thomas Chaucer (d. 1434) was speaker, and strove to secure the support of the Commons with promises of 'good governance'. For the two years of the prince's administration, until November 1411, Beaufort followed a policy of fiscal solvency, the safeguard of Calais and the sea, and friendship with Burgundy which served to strengthen the bond between crown and subjects. It was Prince Henry's French policy, his military support for John the Fearless, duke of Burgundy, against the Armagnacs in November 1411, contrary to his father's wishes, that precipitated his dismissal at the end of that month. At this juncture there is some evidence that Beaufort urged the prince to demand the king's abdication, but wisely Henry withdrew to await his own succession to the throne and Beaufort had perforce to follow, spending the next eighteen months in his diocese. In March 1410 his elder brother John died, leaving his widow, Margaret, with three young children. Five months later the pope gave a dispensation for her marriage to Thomas of Lancaster (d. 1421), the king's second son. Thomas would thereby enjoy the lands that formed the greater part of the young Beauforts' inheritance. As his brother's executor Bishop Henry tried to impede the marriage, and refused to surrender to Thomas his brother's treasure which he held. In this, as in other future instances, the interests of the Beauforts succumbed to those of the royal family. Yet on the whole the careers of the bishop and his brothers had been furthered by their loyal and arduous service to the house of Lancaster which, by the time of Henry IV's death, they had helped to establish.

Bishop Beaufort and Henry V, 1413–1417 With Henry V's accession Bishop Beaufort again became chancellor (21 March 1413), pledged to implement the royal policy of 'good governance' followed in 1410–11. His opening sermons to the parliaments of 1413 and 1414 extolled the king's concern for enforcement of the law, security on the sea, economical government, and the eradication of heresy, on all of which positive action was taken. In return he appealed to the generosity of the Commons to support the king in claiming his just rights in France. Although the November parliament of 1414 granted the king two subsidies, the Commons still favoured negotiation rather than war. Beaufort himself was not on the embassy that travelled to Paris early in 1415, but he must have helped to frame the competitive offers to the Burgundians and Orleanists in the course of 1414–15 while advancing military preparations. In the summer of 1415 he was raising loans on the security of the taxes and crown jewels, and his palace at Wolvesey became the king's headquarters in the weeks preceding the Agincourt expedition. There, in July, he received and rejected, in the king's name, the final French offers made by the archbishop of Bourges. Before he sailed Henry named Beaufort as the principal executor of his will.

On 29 October Bishop Beaufort announced the news of Agincourt at St Paul's Cathedral and in his letter congratulating the king he expounded the myth of English invincibility. Henry was extolled as a great conqueror, comparable to the heroes of biblical antiquity, but the victory was not to be ascribed to him alone but to God, who had shown the justice of the English cause by giving victory against all odds to a chosen few. Henry was urged to show humility and gratitude but also to prosecute his quarrel in the confidence that God was on the English side. Beaufort's speech as chancellor to the parliament of 1415 followed similar lines and the Commons were led to grant the wool subsidy for Henry V's life, an act of generosity paralleled only by that made under compulsion to Richard II in 1398.

In the subsequent twenty months Beaufort was again at the centre of the political, diplomatic, and financial preparations for the next expedition. As prelate of the Order of the Garter he had a prominent role in the ceremonies for the admission of the emperor Sigismund on 22 May 1416, and for the celebration of the feast of St George, which had been elevated in the previous year to the status of a 'greater double', making it one of the principal feasts in the church's calendar. Sigismund was pressed to enter a formal alliance with Henry V, embodied in the treaty of Canterbury of 15 August. This opened the way for a meeting with Duke John the Fearless at Calais in September, designed to complete the diplomatic isolation of the French. Beaufort attended the negotiations though he may never have known the precise terms of John's undertakings to Henry V. His first task on return was to secure sufficient taxation from parliament to launch the expedition for the conquest of Normandy in 1417. Addressing parliament for the last time as Henry V's chancellor, he reviewed the king's achievements, comparing his labours over six parliaments to the creation of the world in six days and declaring the king's intention to consummate the establishment of justice and peace with a final victory over the French, for which he now asked the Commons to supply the money. But, as the costs of the large army assembled in the summer of 1417 mounted, the taxes proved insufficient; crown jewels had to be pledged and further loans secured. Immeasurably the greatest of these was that on 12 June from Beaufort himself, amounting to £14,000. With this he emerged as a major lender to the crown.

The cardinal's hat, 1417–1422 Six weeks later, on the eve of Henry's departure for France at the end of July, Beaufort resigned the chancellorship to go on pilgrimage. His intentions at this point have been variously interpreted and were intentionally obscure. The immediate purpose of his 'pilgrimage' was undoubtedly to break the deadlock at the Council of Constance where Sigismund was insisting that measures for the reform of the papacy should be adopted before the election of a new pope. The English had hitherto supported this position, but at this moment Henry V was less interested in reform than in securing a pope sympathetic to the English cause in the struggle with France. Beaufort's mission was to swing the English delegation behind the choice of such a candidate. At one point he himself was proposed, but ultimately the choice fell on Odo Colonna who was elected as Martin V (r. 1417–31) with English support. He at once, on 18 December 1417, rewarded Beaufort by naming him a cardinal and appointing him legate *a latere*, while allowing him to retain the see of Winchester *in commendam* and to be exempt from the jurisdiction of Canterbury.

It remains unclear to what extent this matched Beaufort's own aspirations. Though it is understandable that he should covet the superior dignity while wanting to retain his wealthy see, it is difficult to believe that Beaufort would have sought legatine powers, which English kings had always viewed with misgivings. As it became clearer that Martin V's intention was to recover the papacy's powers over taxation and provision in the English church lost during the fourteenth century, Henry V became convinced that Beaufort and the pope had connived to outwit him, and he forbade the acceptance of the dignities on pain of Beaufort forfeiting his see and his wealth. It is unclear at what point Beaufort heard of Henry's reaction, for he had proceeded from Constance to Venice, where in March 1418 he embarked for Jerusalem. Possibly only on his return in September did he fully grasp his predicament, for, making a winter crossing of the Alps, he reached the king at Rouen on 3 March 1419. Martin had not published any of the bulls of promotion of which Beaufort had copies, but if he hoped to mollify the king he failed; Henry remained adamant and Beaufort's resignation was discussed. Finally he returned to England in August 1419, cowed by the threat of *praemunire* if he attempted to publish his bulls, and under surveillance by Thomas Chaucer on the king's instructions.

At this point, having forfeited Henry's trust and favour, confined to his diocese and excluded from politics, Beaufort more than once contemplated resigning his see and making his way to Rome. In the end he reined in his resentment and remained in England. On Henry V's return in February 1421 for the queen's coronation Beaufort received a measure of reinstatement. It was the king's need for money to finance a new army that finally procured his restoration. With parliament reluctant to make a grant Henry turned to the bishop for a loan of £17,666. With £5693 of his previous loan only repaid, it meant that some £26,000 of his wealth was now in the king's hands. Although the repayment of the whole loan was secured on the customs of Southampton and he had the gold crown in pledge, it could take ten years to discharge the loan in full. Henry had squeezed Beaufort hard, but on his departure the bishop again took his place in council and began cautiously to repair his standing with the Holy See. Yet in contrast to the power and influence he had wielded from 1413 to 1417, his position in the closing years of the reign represented a striking reversal of fortune.

The minority regime, 1422–1424 Hitherto Beaufort's career had been determined by the service he had rendered and the favour he had received from two able and active kings. But now, following the death of Henry V on 31 August 1422, with the new king an infant, Lancastrian rule in France and England rested on Henry V's two brothers, John, duke of Bedford (d. 1435), and Humphrey, duke of Gloucester (d. 1447). Already an elder statesman with twenty years' experience in high office, Beaufort was not prepared to render to them the subservience exacted from him by Henry V. Henry had left no written instructions about the government during his son's minority, and the duke of Bedford assumed the regency in France by prescriptive right. In a codicil to his last will Henry had conferred the *tutelam et defensionem* of his heir on Duke Humphrey who, on this basis, claimed an equivalent regency in England. But the lords of the council declined to invest Gloucester with either the title or the power to govern in this way. They would only agree to his becoming principal counsellor with the title of protector. It seems probable that the opposition to Gloucester had been orchestrated if not led by Bishop Beaufort; it was certainly against him that Gloucester came to harbour deep animosity.

The council, now acting *in loco regis*, acquired a new importance, and over the next ten years a permanent core of bishops, lords, and knights became Beaufort's close associates. These included the three officers of state, Bishop John Kemp (d. 1454), who succeeded Beaufort as chancellor in 1426, Bishop John Stafford (d. 1452), and Walter, Lord Hungerford (d. 1449), successively treasurers, and Bishop William Alnwick (d. 1449), keeper of the privy seal, along with Sir John Tiptoft (d. 1443), the steward of the household, and Ralph, Lord Cromwell (d. 1456). The council drew up its own working procedures which emphasised corporate responsibility and allowed Gloucester only a nominal headship. Bedford looked to it to raise and pay for reinforcements for each summer's campaign, but following the treaty of Troyes of 1420 parliament was reluctant to grant direct taxation for war. With indirect taxes (the customs) already pledged for the repayment of Beaufort's loans to Henry V, the council could only meet Bedford's demands by contracting further loans with the bishop. Though still owed some £8000, Beaufort provided a loan of £9333 in March 1424 to send an army which helped Bedford win the crucial victory at Verneuil in August. The partnership thus cemented was to provide a safeguard for Beaufort as Gloucester's own interests diverged from those of the council and led him to an alternative strategy.

Disputes with Duke Humphrey, 1424–1427 For Gloucester was now intent on helping Jacqueline of Hainault, whom he had married in April 1423, to recover her inheritance from her estranged husband, John of Brabant. John had the support of Philip the Good, duke of Burgundy, and since the Anglo-Burgundian alliance was the cornerstone of Lancastrian France, Bedford dared not alienate Philip, and called on Gloucester to desist. But neither he nor the council in England was able to deflect Gloucester from entering Hainault with an army in October 1424. Before he left, Gloucester had invested Beaufort with the chancellorship for a third time, and when, after a fruitless campaign, he returned in April 1425, a confrontation between them rapidly developed. Gloucester played on anti-Burgundian feeling in London to secure further assistance for Jacqueline, while the council strove to provide Bedford with reinforcements for a summer offensive in Anjou. Still failing to extract taxation from parliament, Beaufort agreed to lend almost £9000 to aid Bedford, extending his lien on the customs for repayment. Fearing that Gloucester was planning a coup, he debarred him from the Tower of London, which Gloucester saw as a challenge to his authority as protector.

At the very end of October the armed retinues of Gloucester and Beaufort confronted each other on London Bridge, as Gloucester attempted to remove the infant Henry VI from Eltham into his custody. A withdrawal was arranged to diffuse the situation, and Beaufort appealed to Bedford to return to England. He arrived in January 1426, and at a parliament held at Leicester on 18 February forced the contending parties to accept a settlement. Beaufort was allowed to disclaim any intention of affronting Gloucester's status and authority, but was compelled to surrender the chancellorship and withdraw from the council. For the second time his career had been broken and he himself humiliated. Bedford endeavoured to sweeten the pill by procuring from Pope Martin V the cardinalate that Beaufort had been forced to waive in 1419; this he conferred on Beaufort at Calais when they both returned to France in March 1427, and Beaufort thus became cardinal-priest of St Eusebius. Beaufort had secured repayment of all he had loaned the crown, and his withdrawal from English politics once again foreshadowed a new area of activity. For Martin V had designated him leader of the crusade against the Hussites of Bohemia and given him legatine power in Germany to mobilize an effective army.

The Hussite crusade, 1427–1430 Beaufort parted company from Bedford at Calais. He visited Duke Philip in Flanders, and then, by July, arrived in Nuremberg in time to witness the rout of the German forces by the Hussites at the battle of Tachov (4 August 1427). That strengthened his resolve to organize an effective army, and he spent the winter in negotiations with the princes at Frankfurt, at length persuading them to levy a tax on clergy and laity for the defence of the empire. But by the spring of 1428 the difficulties of assembling a coherent military force from the towns and principalities persuaded him to look to the military resources of England, France, and Burgundy. All were, of course, engaged in wars of their own, but during the summer Beaufort secured support in principle from Bedford and Philip should the war permit. The crusade now became part of a wider Lancastrian strategy. If the fall of Orléans undermined the dauphin's resistance, and a successful campaign could be waged against the Hussites, the pope would be persuaded to recognize Henry VI as legitimate king of France and leader of Christendom.

By the autumn of 1428 Beaufort had moved to England

where he hoped to raise a substantial force of archers and levy a crusading tax. However the response of the council was lukewarm; it permitted him to recruit a force of only half the size he had envisaged and forbade the levy of a tax. Its priority remained the war in France where, with Salisbury's death, the siege of Orléans began to look problematic. The council also induced Beaufort to journey to Scotland in the winter of 1428–9 to renew the truce with James I (r. 1406–37), his own brother-in-law, in order to safeguard the northern frontier. By the time he had returned to London in March the situation in France was becoming critical. Bedford was demanding reinforcements and proposing that Henry VI should come to France for his coronation.

At this point Gloucester chose to renew his challenge to Beaufort by questioning the legality of his retention of Winchester, as a cardinal, and his liability to the penalties of *praemunire* for accepting papal bulls without royal licence. The council ordered Beaufort to absent himself from the Garter ceremony at Windsor, though he protested strongly. But with the retreat from Orléans and the defeat at Patay on 18 June 1429 the council brought overwhelming pressure to bear on Beaufort to send his crusading army to Bedford's assistance. On 1 July the council agreed to take over the payment of this force which Beaufort now led to France. For this flagrant betrayal of his commission Martin V never forgave Beaufort, who lost papal favour and any hope of a career in papal service. Gloucester's renewed hostility likewise excluded him from English politics. But by his action he won Bedford's undying gratitude and protection. At the end of July he engaged to remain in Bedford's service for the rest of the year, and in the months following the repulse of Jeanne d'Arc's assault on Paris he worked with Bedford to strengthen Duke Philip's attachment to the English cause.

The defence of Lancastrian France, 1430–1431 For the next two years Beaufort devoted himself to planning and financing Henry VI's journey to Paris for coronation. He had returned to London for the king's coronation on 6 November, which formally terminated Gloucester's protectorship, and to attend the parliament at which the Commons were finally persuaded to grant taxation for the royal expedition. Despite some resistance from Gloucester, he was permitted to resume his seat in council in recognition of the essential services he would render in the coming months, though the matter of his see was left unresolved. To finance the army of more than 7000 men loans were again raised from Beaufort and from the duchy of Lancaster feoffees whom he headed, his own contribution of £8333 being the largest. Furnished with a large army and secure finance, Henry VI left England for Rouen on 23 April 1430, while Beaufort hastened to Ghent to strengthen the alliance with Duke Philip (recently married to Beaufort's niece Isabella of Portugal), whom the French were trying to detach with offers of peace. However the Anglo-Burgundian offensive in Picardy during

the summer failed to capture Compiègne, ending any prospect of the recapture of Rheims, and necessitating a further campaign in 1431 to secure Henry VI's coronation in Paris.

At the end of the year Beaufort returned once more to England to persuade parliament to grant further taxation for another army of 2600 men. Once more he loaned money on the security of the tax for the wages of the expedition. On his return to Rouen in May 1431 he presided at the trial and burning of Jeanne d'Arc. In a summer of heavy fighting Louviers finally fell to the English (28 October), opening the way to Paris, and Beaufort had the satisfaction of crowning Henry VI in Notre-Dame on 16 December. Throughout the twenty-one months of the king's stay in France Bedford's regency had been suspended, and Beaufort as president of the *grand conseil* had effectively headed the civil administration. Not only had he worked tirelessly to raise money and troops but he had made numerous loans for current expenses and emergencies, so that he could justly feel entitled to recognition and reward.

Disputes at home, crisis in France, 1432–1435 Yet all at once Beaufort found his whole career in jeopardy. The king's impending return to England raised the question of Bedford's continuing authority in France, which Beaufort insisted should henceforth be held under royal commission and not prescriptively. Bedford took this ill and the two quarrelled. In England, too, Gloucester was preparing to renew his assault on Beaufort's position, persuading the council to lend its backing to a charge of *praemunire*. Beaufort thus faced the enmity of both royal dukes, at a time when a large proportion of his wealth was in the crown's hands. On hearing of Gloucester's moves he decided not to return to England with the king but to seek the hospitality of Duke Philip in Ghent, where he stood godfather to Isabella's child. He had ordered his treasure to be shipped in secret from England, and may once again have contemplated going to Rome or taking part in the peace negotiations promoted by Pope Eugenius IV (r. 1431–47). But on 6 February 1432 Gloucester seized and impounded his treasure as it was being loaded at Sandwich, and in the following days writs of *praemunire* were issued against Beaufort and his supporters were removed from the council.

Gloucester's attempt to deprive him of his see, confiscate his wealth, and destroy his political influence before it could be rebuilt in England compelled Beaufort to return and defend himself. This he did in a parliament that met from May to July 1432, aided by the support of the Commons and the reluctance of the Lords to provoke dissension. The *praemunire* charges were dropped, his treasure was restored under bond of £6000, and he purged himself of any charge of treason. Helped by his ability to make a further loan of £6000 Beaufort had survived the attempt to ruin him, though he was forced to retire to his diocese. But for as long as the war with France continued the council could not easily dispense with his wealth and abilities, and by 1433 his financial support was again urgently required by Bedford to send further reinforcements to France. Indeed in May 1433 Bedford decided he must return to England, displace Gloucester as vicegerent, reorganize English finances, and revive support for the war.

Under Bedford's protection Beaufort therefore returned to the council and to his role as financier of the English crown. Armies were sent to France in 1433 and to accompany Bedford's return in 1434, enabling the English to recover much ground in France. But by the end of 1434 the pressure from both the papacy and the Council of Basel to bring the Anglo-French conflict to an end, coupled with Duke Philip's own inclination towards a settlement with France, produced a proposal for a peace congress at Arras in the summer of 1435. English, French, and Burgundian delegations met there along with papal mediators from July to September. Since the French and English could not agree on terms for peace, the real issue was whether the French could detach Philip from his commitment to the treaty of Troyes. As Philip's defection from the English side became certain, Beaufort made a last impassioned plea to him on grounds of their historic alliance and personal friendship. It was in vain, and he left Arras knowing that Henry V's vision of a dual monarchy lay finally in ruins. At the same moment Bedford lay dying at Rouen. The future both for the Lancastrian conquests and for Beaufort himself looked bleak.

The search for peace, 1435–1440 In France crises loomed on many fronts. The French seizure of Dieppe in September triggered risings in the Pays de Caux which threatened to spread throughout Normandy. The English prepared to abandon Paris and Duke Philip to besiege Calais. These events stiffened English resolve and renewed the council's dependence on Beaufort, who in February 1436 loaned £12,666, together with a further £4000 from the duchy of Lancaster, for a large army to be sent to Normandy. By March Philip's preparations to besiege Calais were confirmed, and an impressive army under Gloucester was mobilized for its defence. For this Beaufort loaned a further £6000 in August. For the moment Gloucester was inhibited from any attack on the cardinal; further, by the autumn of 1436 the young Henry VI was beginning to exercise some measure of royal authority, and this afforded Beaufort a degree of security. He was now convinced of the necessity for a settlement with France that could guarantee the retention of Normandy. He still hoped to achieve this through the mediation of Burgundy, with whom commercial and diplomatic relations were gradually re-established in 1437–8. By the beginning of 1439 Beaufort and Duchess Isabella had agreed to summon a conference at Gravelines near Calais for negotiations with the French.

Abandoning any attempt to reconcile the opposing claims of the protagonists, the negotiations concentrated on the proposal for a long truce of twenty years on the basis of the *status quo*, during which Henry VI's title would be held in suspense. Beaufort himself conducted the talks

with Isabella and remained at Calais while their joint proposals were sent to the council in England. After discussion the council found them unacceptable and Beaufort returned from what proved to be his last diplomatic mission. His career had now reached its climax. Over the past two years he had dominated English policy, had loaned almost £26,000, and had received favours from the pliant king, notably the grant of Canford and Poole in Dorset for life, and the sale to him of Chirk and Chirklands in north Wales, which Gloucester bitterly opposed. The duke had likewise led the opposition to the terms for a truce and when Beaufort returned discredited he took the opportunity systematically to denounce his rival.

Retirement, 1440–1447 During the parliament of 1439–40 Gloucester presented to the king a long and detailed indictment of Beaufort, reaching back over the length of his career and designed to destroy his reputation as a statesman and diplomat, and to convict him of corruption and fraud. The reaction of the king and the council, indeed of Beaufort himself, is unknown, for no answer was made and no action taken. Though ineffectual, Gloucester's attack revealed the weakness of Beaufort's position, which was underlined when in this and the following parliament he was forced to surrender the duchy of Lancaster lands that he held as a feoffee of Henry V. It was further underlined by his failure to secure the post of lieutenant in Normandy for his nephew John Beaufort, earl of Somerset (d. 1444), whose career in France, with that of his more successful brother Edmund, he had been promoting with his loans. The post went to Gloucester's candidate, Richard, duke of York (d. 1460).

Beaufort was now aged about sixty-five, and was perhaps unwell. He attended council less frequently after 1440, as the rising power of William de la Pole, earl of Suffolk (d. 1450), gradually displaced his own. It is doubtful whether he had any hand in the prosecution of Eleanor Cobham, Gloucester's wife, on charges of treasonable necromancy in June 1441, though he took a formal part in the proceedings. Likewise he ceased to make major loans to the crown. It was only with the prospect of enabling his nephew John to fill a major command in France that he moved back into the political centre for the last time in 1443. Faced with the threat of major French offensives against Normandy and Gascony, the council decided in the winter of 1442–3 to send a large army to France in the summer. Cardinal Beaufort was ready to supply the cash for this if Somerset was given command.

Though this expedition was to be independent of the duke of York as lieutenant-general, and in the area outside his control, it intentionally diverted resources from the defence of Normandy to an aggressive strategy designed to bring Charles VII to battle in Anjou. In all Beaufort advanced £22,666 for Somerset's army, which was the largest since 1436. In the event Somerset failed to bring the French to battle and, having achieved nothing of military significance, returned in disgrace. It was an ignominious conclusion to the cardinal's political career and he now retired to his episcopal residences in Hampshire. From 1445 to 1446 he resided in a house called Meister

Omers, in the precincts of Christ Church, Canterbury, which he renovated at his own expense. Finally in the autumn of 1446 he returned to Wolvesey. By then the cardinal was nearing his end. He drew up his will on 20 January 1447 and added codicils on 7 and 9 April. He died at Wolvesey on 11 April.

Aspects of Beaufort's career: plutocrat and prelate Henry Beaufort's wealth was notorious—indeed he was the wealthiest English prelate of the late middle ages. He was known as the Rich Cardinal. At the height of his career his fortune was probably not less than £50,000, and was at least half this at the time of his first major loans to Henry V. The source of his wealth remains as unclear as it was to his contemporaries, but the revenues of his see, the perquisites of office and influence, the export of wool, and his elder brother's legacy are all possible sources. His loans to the crown were not technically usurious, the exact sum being repaid from national taxation through the exchequer, but he often held important crown jewels as security, and his right to some retained by the crown's default in 1424 troubled him in his final hours. Beaufort used his loans to protect his political position, to influence policy, to advance the careers of his brothers and nephews, and to maintain the dignity and lifestyle of a prince of the church.

In several respects Beaufort was notable as a prelate. He held episcopal office for almost fifty years, longer than any other English bishop, and he was the first of a new breed of national cardinals to retain his see and reside in England; indeed he employed the title cardinal of England with some pride. Unlike the last of these, Thomas Wolsey (d. 1530), Beaufort did not use his dignity or his legatine power either to overshadow the archbishop of Canterbury or to intervene in the government of the church. Nor did he contribute to its spiritual life. He had no interest in reform, was indifferent to the new devotional movements, and regarded heresy as merely subversive. He adhered to the religious observances of his age. By his will he provided for 10,000 masses to be said for his soul, he made bequests to the principal churches and monasteries with which he was connected, and to the poor by way of charity. He instructed that his tomb and chantry should be sited next to the shrine of St Swithun in Winchester Cathedral.

The man and his reputation Beaufort possessed a keen intelligence and could speak with eloquence, but he showed little appreciation of the intellectual outlook of the humanists with whom he came into contact in Italy. Poggio Bracciolini, one of the most illustrious of these, was his secretary from 1418 to 1422, at a time when Beaufort's career was in crisis, and perhaps on this account found little to satisfy his literary and philosophical interests in his service. Yet Beaufort was a good patron and master to those who served him faithfully. Many were rewarded in his will, and in his last years he refounded the hospital of St Cross at Winchester, as an 'almshouse of noble poverty' for his old servants and retainers, building a gatehouse, kitchen range, and rooms to form an impressive quadrangle. Major additions to the palaces at Wolvesey and Bishops Waltham, as well as the house at Canterbury, marked his later years, but as a builder he did not match the scale of Wykeham or William Waynflete, nor did he have any interest in educational foundations.

Beaufort saw himself first and foremost as a prince of the blood and his life was spent in service to a dynasty in whose destiny he steadfastly believed. He subscribed to Henry V's vision of a dual monarchy which should unite Christendom under the hegemony of the Lancastrian crown. He consistently supported Bedford in attempting to fulfil this ambitious legacy and, as it faltered and collapsed after 1429, he used all his financial and diplomatic resources to sustain the French title and finally to safeguard Normandy by peace. He also fought to advance the fortunes of his family and to defend his position in the council. In each of these spheres he experienced severe and seemingly disastrous set-backs, from which his political acumen and the indispensability of his services enabled him to recover. These vicissitudes bred in him a stoicism tempered by optimism and wry humour, qualities that are manifest in the fine portrait of a cardinal by Jan Van Eyck which has been plausibly identified as that of Beaufort, making it the earliest realistic portrait of any Englishman. Other representations of him occur in a sculptured stone head at Bishop's Waltham and on a roof boss in Fromond's chantry at Winchester College.

Beaufort's reputation as a mainstay of the house of Lancaster was not challenged until the sixteenth century, when Edward Hall (d. 1547), the protestant chronicler of the Wars of the Roses, depicted Beaufort as the precursor of the infamous Cardinal Wolsey. Shakespeare followed Hall in the first two plays in his *Henry VI* trilogy, presenting Beaufort as a haughty, avaricious, and worldly prelate, whose scheming brought retribution on the dynasty. William Stubbs, in the 1870s, still censured him as 'ambitious, secular ... and greedy of honour' (W. Stubbs, *Constitutional History of England*, 3 vols., 1873–8, 3.139), but acknowledged his qualities as a statesman, an approach elaborated in the principal modern biography by Harriss (1989).

G. L. HARRISS

Sources G. L. Harriss, *Cardinal Beaufort: a study of Lancastrian ascendancy and decline* (1989) · Emden, *Oxf.*, 1.139–42 · K. B. McFarlane, *England in the fifteenth century: collected essays* (1981), 79–138 · C. M. D. Crowder, 'Henry V, Sigismund and the Council of Constance', *Historical Studies: Papers Read Before the Irish Conference of Historians*, 4 (1963), 93–110 · R. G. Davies, 'Martin V and the English episcopate', *EngHR*, 92 (1977), 309–44 · M. Harvey, *England, Rome, and the papacy, 1417–1464* (1993) · G. A. Holmes, 'Cardinal Beaufort and the crusade against the Hussites', *EngHR*, 88 (1973), 721–50 · J. C. Dickinson, *The Congress of Arras, 1435* (1955) · M. G. A. Vale, 'Cardinal Henry Beaufort and the Albergati portrait', *EngHR*, 105 (1990), 337–54 · R. Vaughan, *Philip the Good: the apogee of Burgundy* (1970) · *Chancery records* · *RotP*, vol. 4 · N. H. Nicolas, ed., *Proceedings and ordinances of the privy council of England*, 7 vols., RC, 26 (1834–7) · Rymer, *Foedera*, 2nd edn, vols. 8–10 · [J. Nichols], ed., *A collection of ... wills ... of ... every branch of the blood royal* (1780) · *The Council of Constance*, ed. J. Moody and K. Woody, trans. L. R. Loomis (1967) · C. T. Allmand, ed., 'Documents relating to the Anglo-French negotiations of 1439', *Camden miscellany, XXIV*, CS, 4th ser., 9 (1972) · *Letters of Queen Margaret of Anjou and Bishop Beckington and others written* *in the reigns of Henry V and Henry VI*, ed. C. Monro, CS, 86 (1863) · J. Stevenson, ed., *Letters and papers illustrative of the wars of the English in France during the reign of Henry VI, king of England*, 2 vols. in 3 pts, Rolls Series, 22 (1861–4) · M. R. Thielemans, *Bourgogne et Angleterre: relations politiques et économiques entre les Pays-Bas bourguignons et l'Angleterre, 1435–1467* (Brussels, 1966) · J. H. Wylie and W. T. Waugh, eds., *The reign of Henry the Fifth*, 3 vols. (1914–29) · A. N. E. D. Schofield, 'England and the Council of Basel', *Annuarium Historiae Conciliorum*, 5 (1973), 1–117 · G. L. Harriss, 'Cardinal Beaufort, patriot or usurer?', *TRHS*, 5th ser., 20 (1970), 129–48 · F. M. Bartos, 'An English cardinal and the Hussite revolution', *Communio Viatorum*, 4 (1963), 47–54

Archives Bibliothèque Nationale, Paris · BL, Cotton MSS · BL · Hants. RO, episcopal registers · Lincs. Arch., episcopal registers | PRO · PRO, letters and ancient corresp., S.C. I

Likenesses J. Van Eyck, oils, *c*.1430–1435 (after drawing in Kupferstichkabinett, Dresden), Kunsthistorisches Museum, Vienna · effigy, Winchester Cathedral · roof boss, Winchester College, Fromond's chantry · stone effigy, Bishop's Waltham Palace, Hampshire [*see illus.*] · stone effigy, St Cross Hospital, Winchester

Wealth at death over £50,000

Beaufort, Henry, second duke of Somerset (1436–1464), magnate, was born early in 1436, the eldest son of Edmund *Beaufort, first duke of Somerset (*d*. 1455), and his wife, Eleanor, daughter of Richard *Beauchamp, earl of Warwick (*d*. 1439), and widow of Thomas, Baron Ros of Helmsley. The strong links between Henry Beaufort's family and the Lancastrian ruling house were emphasized when Henry VI stood as his godfather. Beaufort, styled earl of Dorset from 1448 to 1455, made occasional appearances at court in the early 1450s. He was present, with his father, at the celebration in Westminster Abbey of the Feast of the Assumption on 15 August 1450 and in May 1455 he was a member of the royal army that left London for a proposed meeting of the great council at Leicester. He succeeded to the dukedom of Somerset on 22 May 1455, after the death of his father at the first battle of St Albans. He had fought by his side and had been so badly wounded that he had to be carried away in a cart. The chronicler Waurin believed his later career was dominated by the desire to avenge his father, the leader of the court faction and chief enemy of the duke of York. Certainly after St Albans he was the only heir of those nobles killed in the battle considered irreconcilable. He was kept in Warwick's custody before the parliament that commenced on 9 July 1455, and on 18 July a bill was passed that blamed the late duke of Somerset for the conflict but removed all mention of Percy and Clifford, providing clear evidence of the reluctance of Somerset's heir to co-operate. The latter was soon to take his father's place as the most prominent Lancastrian nobleman.

Somerset's animosity quickly became apparent. At the great council summoned at Coventry on 10 October 1456 he had to be restrained from attacking York and in November in London nearly came to blows with first Warwick and then his younger brother, Sir John Neville. According to Gregory's chronicle an accommodation had been arranged between Somerset and the Neville family at Coventry in March 1457, when the young duke formally took possession of his estates. However this 'pacification' is not mentioned in any other source, and the attendance of lords recorded in the Coventry leet book reveals that the

Nevilles had wisely decided to stay away. On 14 October 1457 Somerset received his first military command, the constableship of Carisbrooke and the lieutenancy of the Isle of Wight, in the aftermath of the French attack on Sandwich. The measures to defend the south coast saw all the key posts shared among the queen's confidants and aroused considerable suspicion among the Yorkists. The only real attempt at arbitration occurred early in 1458 when the rival lords gathered in London. Somerset and his retinue were billeted outside the city but this did not prevent him from attempting another attack on Warwick on 9 March. The 'loveday' agreement of 25 March, by which Richard, duke of York, settled 5000 marks of debts owed to him by the crown on Somerset and his widowed mother by way of compensation for St Albans, soon proved to be ineffective. In May, Somerset and Rivers jousted with members of the queen's household at the Tower of London and Greenwich. These were not jousts of peace but partisan gatherings that presaged further violence. Waurin believed that Somerset was behind the attack on Warwick in London in late October 1458 and by the summer of 1459 it was clear that both sides were drifting towards war. On 21 September 1459 Warwick and his retinue narrowly escaped an armed clash with Somerset at Coleshill, Warwickshire. The decision to appoint Somerset to the captaincy of Calais, already held by Warwick, on 9 October made further conflict between the two men inevitable, and the rout at Ludford, which followed on 13 October, marked a permanent breach between the court party and the Yorkists.

If Somerset's early career had been dominated by the violence of his vendetta against York and the Nevilles, his valiant efforts to wrest Calais from Warwick were to show his worth as a commander, and established his reputation internationally. On 10 November 1459 he indented with the crown for an army of 1000 men, and crossed the channel with the first part of this force shortly afterwards. Although denied access to Calais itself, Somerset was able to establish himself within the pale at Guînes and launched a series of vigorous raids that impressed contemporaries by their boldness and enterprise. Gregory's chronicle described how he 'fulle manly made sautys [assaults]' to win over Hammes and encourage desertions from Rysbank. Somerset was assisted by the experienced war captain Andrew Trollope, whom he had won over to the Lancastrian cause at Ludford Bridge: together the two men represented a formidable military partnership. But in January 1460 the remainder of Somerset's force, gathering at Sandwich, was dispersed by Warwick, and its commander, Lord Rivers, captured. The Calais staple gave Warwick substantial support and Somerset's own financial situation became increasingly desperate. He chose to engage the enemy on St George's day (23 April 1460) but was repulsed at Newenham Bridge. The news of the destruction of further reinforcements under Osbert Mundeford (25 June) and Lancastrian defeat at Northampton (10 July) made Somerset's position hopeless. He came to terms with Warwick, surrendered Guînes, and took shelter in France. Charles VII, who had been struck by the courage of Somerset's resistance, granted him safe conduct on 16 July 1460, lodged him at Montivilliers, and met the expenses of his retinue. Somerset had also won the admiration of Charles, count of Charolais, the son and heir of Philip the Good, duke of Burgundy. The two met at Ardres on 12 August. Charolais entertained his guest with a lavish dinner and a firm friendship was forged.

In October 1460 Somerset returned to England. He sailed from Dieppe in ships provided by Charles VII, landed in Dorset, and quickly made his way to his regional power base at Corfe. His intention was to join with the Courtenay earl of Devon and raise the west country for Margaret of Anjou. On 10 November, Somerset and the earl of Devon were in Exeter gathering troops. They then moved on to Bridgwater. The anxious citizens of Exeter sent on a gift of £5 to Somerset as a sign of their goodwill, while secretly dispatching a messenger to London to warn York of his activities. Faced with another Lancastrian army growing in the north, York made a disastrous miscalculation. He assumed there would be an attempt on Bristol, and warned the mayor and council of the city to defend the castle against a likely attack by the duke of Somerset. He then divided his strength, leaving Warwick in London and marching north with the earl of Salisbury. Somerset seized his opportunity. After consulting with Trollope, he and Devon secretly took a picked mounted force and rode northwards, through Bath, Cirencester, Evesham, and Coventry. On 21 December they caught up with the unsuspecting scouts of York's army at Worksop, and soon afterwards made contact with Margaret of Anjou. Somerset had totally outmanoeuvred York, who, vastly outnumbered, was overwhelmed at Wakefield on 30 December.

The Wakefield campaign showed a new style of leadership among the Lancastrians, aggressive and imaginative, that owed much to the skill of Somerset and Trollope. Somerset now took command of their forces. He was in overall charge at the second battle of St Albans on 17 February 1461, a victory that opened up the road to London and secured the person of the king, who had been captured by the Yorkists at the battle of Northampton. The capital was in a state of panic at the approach of an army perceived to be full of rampaging northerners, and anxious citizens painted the Beaufort badge, the portcullis, on their doors in an effort to stave off looting. Somerset's advance riders were already nearing London when Margaret of Anjou made her fateful decision to retreat northwards. The initiative had been lost. Henry VI's forces were faced with fresh financial difficulties and, on 6 March, Somerset headed a commission that 'extorted' a forced loan from Boston. The young Edward, earl of March, entered London, was proclaimed king and led a revitalized Yorkist army north to meet them. The two sides clashed at Towton on 29 March, a battle fought in a blinding snowstorm. According to Waurin, Somerset and Trollope set up the possibility of a Lancastrian victory with a daring cavalry attack, but the earl of Northumberland failed to support them in time and the opportunity was lost. Eventually the Yorkists triumphed. Andrew Trollope,

Somerset's able lieutenant, was killed in the fighting; the duke fled into Scotland with the remnants of the Lancastrian party.

Margaret of Anjou now turned to diplomacy. On 20 July 1461 the queen empowered Somerset to negotiate on her behalf with Charles VII, to raise a major loan and recruit a new army, which was to be sent to Wales. Somerset's embassy sailed from Edinburgh into a fresh political crisis. On his arrival in France the duke learnt that Charles had died. The new king, Louis XI, had sent an armed contingent to support the Yorkists at Towton and now moved swiftly, ordering Somerset's arrest on 3 August. He was imprisoned in the castle of Arques. All his letters and papers were confiscated and he was repeatedly interrogated. Louis kept Somerset in custody for over two months and he was only saved through the intercession of the count of Charolais. The duke was escorted to Tours, where he was granted a brief royal audience on 22 October, and given safe conduct to travel to Flanders. Charolais ensured that Somerset was properly received at the Burgundian court and by 11 March 1462 he had set up household in Bruges, where he was to stay throughout the spring and summer. Somerset's isolation from other Lancastrians led to a period of disenchantment. As early as September 1462 he had opened negotiations with Warwick. Although in October he joined the small army recruited by Margaret of Anjou and Pierre de Brézé that occupied the Northumbrian castles, he showed little stomach for the fight; he surrendered Bamburgh on 24 December and came to terms with Edward IV.

The Yorkist king restored Somerset to favour with a speed that shocked contemporaries. In January 1463 he was allowed to join Warwick's forces at the siege of Alnwick, and Edward granted him money to cover his expenses. On 10 March he was granted a full pardon and the Westminster parliament, which sat from 29 April to 17 June 1463, reversed the attainder passed against him in 1461, allowing him to recover his landed estate. On 22 June an annuity of £222 was returned to him and shortly afterwards his younger brother Edmund *Beaufort was released from the Tower. This dramatic reconciliation was followed with considerable interest on the continent; a letter to Louis XI of 1 July 1463 reported how Somerset was in close attendance on the king. Edward had made extraordinary efforts to win the duke's trust and allegiance: he hunted with him, arranged a tournament in his honour, and even shared a bed with him. It was all too much for some of the king's subjects. When the royal entourage passed through Northampton in late July the townspeople rioted and Somerset had to be sent to his Welsh lordship of Chirk for his own safety. He was soon engaged in plotting with other Lancastrians, and in late November rejoined Henry VI in Northumberland leaving a trail of rebellion in his wake. Foreign observers believed that by March 1464 Somerset had been able to establish a small, independent principality in the far north of England. But his act of defiance was quickly brought to heel. An attempt by the Lancastrians to waylay John Neville, Lord Montagu, was repulsed at Hedgeley Moor on 25 April 1464, and a further defeat at Hexham on 15 May saw the complete destruction of their small army. Somerset was executed immediately after the battle and buried in Hexham Abbey. He had died unmarried, but, with a mistress, Joan Hill, had a bastard son, Charles, who was created earl of Worcester in Henry VII's reign.

Somerset's martial exploits won him international renown. But the depth of his vendetta against the Yorkists led to breaches of oaths and promises. Waurin claimed that the terms of his agreement with Warwick at Newenham Bridge in July 1460 included a vow never again to take up arms against the Nevilles; and many contemporaries believed that the battle of Wakefield was the result of Somerset's deliberately breaking a local truce. Given his reputation for untrustworthiness, Somerset's acceptance by Edward IV was remarkable, and his subsequent defection made any further reconciliation extremely unlikely.

MICHAEL K. JONES

Sources Bibliothèque nationale, MS Fr 6967, 6970, 20430 · PRO, C 1/73/69 · PRO, E 404/71 · PRO, E 28 · Archives communales, Bruges, CC 32514 · Exeter receiver's accounts, 1460–61, Devon RO · E. W. W. Veale, ed., *The Great Red Book of Bristol*, [pt 1], Bristol RS, 4 (1933) · G. Chastellain, *Œuvres*, ed. K. de Lettenhove, 8 vols. (Brussels, 1863–6) · *Recueil des croniques … par Jehan de Waurin*, ed. W. Hardy and E. L. C. P. Hardy, 5 vols., Rolls Series, 39 (1864–91) · William of Worcester, 'Annales rerum Anglicarum, 1324–1491', *Letters and papers illustrative of the wars of the English in France during the reign of Henry VI, king of England*, ed. J. Stevenson, Rolls Series, 2/2 (1864) · J. Gairdner, ed., *The historical collections of a citizen of London in the fifteenth century*, CS, new ser., 17 (1876) · *The Paston letters, AD 1422–1509*, ed. J. Gairdner, new edn, 6 vols. (1904) · R. Flenley, ed., *Six town chronicles of England* (1911) · *Mémoires de Jacques Du Clercq: sieur de Beauvoir en Ternois*, ed. C. B. Petitot (Paris, 1826), ser. 1, vol. 11 of *Collection complète des mémoires relatifs à l'histoire de France* (1820–29) · M. D. Harris, ed., *The Coventry leet book*, 2, EETS, 135 (1908) · 'John Benet's chronicle for the years 1400 to 1462', ed. G. L. Harriss, *Camden miscellany, XXIV*, CS, 4th ser., 9 (1972) · J. S. Davies, ed., *An English chronicle of the reigns of Richard II, Henry IV, Henry V, and Henry VI*, CS, 64 (1856) · R. A. Griffiths, *The reign of King Henry VI: the exercise of royal authority, 1422–1461* (1981) · C. L. Scofield, *The life and reign of Edward the Fourth*, 2 vols. (1923) · C. A. J. Armstrong, 'Politics and the battle of St Albans, 1455', *BIHR*, 33 (1960), 1–72 · G. L. Harriss, 'The struggle for Calais: an aspect of the rivalry between Lancaster and York', *EngHR*, 75 (1960), 30–53 · M. A. Hicks, 'Edward IV, the duke of Somerset and Lancastrian loyalism in the north', *Northern History*, 20 (1984), 23–37 · *CPR, 1485–1509*
Wealth at death approx. £700 p.a. from landed estate; £222 p.a., annuity from the crown: CIPM, valors, minister's accounts, warrants for issue · in practical terms Somerset's estate was valueless at the time of his death as a result of his rebellion: PRO C 1/73/69

Beaufort [*married names* Ferrers, Neville], **Joan**, **countess of Westmorland** (1379?–1440), magnate, was the youngest of the four children of *John of Gaunt, duke of Lancaster (1340–1399), and his mistress, Katherine Swynford (1350?–1403) [*see* Katherine, duchess of Lancaster].

Beaufort status and first marriage The dates of birth of all four children are uncertain, though there may be some significance in the pattern of gifts from Gaunt and also from the mayor of Leicester to Katherine. By this criterion, Joan was probably born in 1379: since she seems to have borne her first child in 1393, a later date is unlikely. She was given the same surname as her three elder brothers, John *Beaufort (d. 1410), Henry *Beaufort (d. 1447), and Thomas *Beaufort (d. 1426). The reason for the adoption of this surname for Gaunt's illegitimate offspring is not clear, though it may have been a compliment to Roger Beaufort, brother of Pope Gregory XI, with whom Gaunt had had diplomatic contact and whom he held as an honourable captive in the 1370s. Her mother's sister, Philippa Roelt, was the wife of Geoffrey *Chaucer.

Although they were illegitimate, the Beaufort children played a full part in the family life of Gaunt and his other, legitimate, offspring. They were openly acknowledged as Gaunt's children, and he evidently intended that they should assume a place in society that befitted their paternity. In 1386, therefore, when she was probably only six or seven years old, Joan was betrothed to Sir Robert Ferrers of Oversley, Warwickshire, one of Gaunt's retainers who had been in service with him since at least 1378. Through his mother he was heir to the estates of the Botelers of Wem in Shropshire. Joan and Robert were married in 1392, and in the years immediately after their wedding they both spent some time residing in the ducal household. Her half-brother Henry, earl of Derby (later *Henry IV), regularly made gifts to her during the 1390s, notably a pair of paternosters of gold and coral in 1391. Joan had two children with Ferrers in quick succession: Elizabeth, who was probably born in 1393, and Mary, probably born some time in the following year. At some point between May 1395 and November 1396, however, her husband died and the Ferrers family lands remained under the control of her mother-in-law, Elizabeth Boteler, until her death in 1411.

Legitimacy and second marriage In February 1396 Joan's father and mother had been married in Lincoln Cathedral, and her mother thus became duchess of Lancaster. This opened the way to the legitimation of all four Beaufort children by papal bull in the following September. The papal bull was confirmed by royal charter read in parliament in February 1397. These events, and the unconnected death on 9 June 1396 of Margaret, wife of Ralph *Neville, then sixth Baron Neville of Raby and later first earl of Westmorland (c.1364–1425), were to transform Joan's prospects, and she now advanced to the forefront of English society. Some time in the autumn of 1396 she was married to Ralph Neville. The exact date of the marriage is unknown: it had taken place by 29 November, and was unlikely to have occurred before the bull of legitimation, which was issued on 1 September, had been received in England. Although Neville, like Robert Ferrers, was one of Gaunt's retainers and had a long record of service to the house of Lancaster, he was also an important magnate in his own right, with extensive estates in Durham and north Yorkshire, and was created earl of Westmorland on 29 September 1397. He was a much more substantial and influential person than Robert Ferrers, and his marriage to Joan was intended to tie the Neville family even more firmly to the Lancastrian interest.

Political influence In the course of their marriage Joan had with Neville nine sons and five daughters (details of whom are given in the article on her husband). Among these children were William *Neville, earl of Kent, Edward *Neville, first Baron Bergavenny, and Katherine *Neville, duchess of Norfolk. The marriages that Joan's children made in the reigns of Henry IV and Henry V served to link the family to many of the leading noble dynasties and strengthen the position of the Beauforts at the centre of English society. Joan also enjoyed influence at court in her own right. After the deposition of Richard II in 1399 she remained on good terms with her half-brother Henry who had now become king. Members of Henry IV's household believed she had influence with him: in 1407, for example, she wrote to Henry on behalf of one of his esquires, Christopher Standith, who had served him in Wales but was destitute after being dismissed from his father's service because he and his wife had married each other 'purely for love'. She asked Henry to give his wife, Margaret, a place in the queen's household, and the letter is signed in what is probably her own handwriting: 'Voster tres humble et obaisant servnt si vous plest J de W' (BL, Cotton MS Vespasian F.xiii). When her husband died in 1425 he bequeathed the wardship of *Richard, duke of York (b. 1411), to her, and in the years following her husband's death she resided at court with her young ward, who had been married to her daughter *Cecily in 1424.

Spiritual and literary interests It is also possible to discern in these years the development in Joan of significant spiritual and literary interests and a continuing concern for the children of her first marriage. Thomas Hoccleve dedicated a volume of his poems to her (now Durham University Library, Cosin MS V.iii.9) and sent it to her probably c.1422, saying (perhaps in the hope that she might relieve his poverty):

> Go, smal book to the noble excellence
> Of my lady of Westmerland and seye,
> Her humble seruant with al reuerence
> Him recommandith vn-to hir nobleye.
> (Hoccleve's Works, 1.242)

Among the books which she is known to have possessed was a volume containing the Cronikels of Jerusalem and Le viage de Godfrey Boylion, which she lent to Henry V; in 1424 she had to petition Humphrey, duke of Gloucester, as protector of the realm after Henry's death, to secure the return of the book. Le viage de Godfrey Boylion was probably a French translation of William of Tyre's Historia rerum in partibus transmarinis gestarum. She also received bequests of books from friends and family. John Morton, esquire of York, who died in 1430 left her 'a book in English called Gower' (possibly a manuscript of his Confessio amantis), and her brother Thomas Beaufort, who died in 1426, left her 'a book called Tristram': if this too was in English, it may have been a text of Thomas of Erceldoune's Sir Tristrem. Unfortunately none of these books is mentioned in her will, so there is no evidence for the subsequent destination of any of the books she is known to have possessed.

It has sometimes been suggested that Joan owned, and indeed possibly even commissioned, the unfinished manuscript of Chaucer's Troilus and Criseyde (now Cambridge, Corpus Christi College, MS 61). This manuscript is known to have belonged to an Anne Neville, who has been identified as either Joan's daughter, who married Humphrey *Stafford, first duke of Buckingham, or the wife of her grandson, Richard *Neville, earl of Warwick (the Kingmaker). The manuscript dates from the first quarter of the fifteenth century, but there is no specific evidence that Joan ever owned it.

Joan was visited by Margery Kempe, probably some time in 1413, and according to Margery's account of the visit she told Joan a 'good tale' of a lady who was damned because she would not love her enemies and a bailiff who was saved because he loved his enemies, even though he was regarded during his lifetime as an evil man. Joan was apparently well pleased with Margery's moral lesson. Later, however, Margery was accused of encouraging Joan's daughter Elizabeth to leave her husband John *Greystoke, fourth Baron Greystoke [see under Greystoke family], though Margery denied the accusation and offered to ask Joan to bear witness that Margery had made no such suggestion. The hint that Joan's daughter's marriage was in difficulties is not borne out by other evidence, and the marriage remained intact. Joan's interest in Margery, whose mystical utterances and writings led to charges of heresy and her examination before the archbishops of Canterbury and York, and her obvious approval of what she had to say, are perhaps evidence of a certain independence of mind as well as of spiritual interests that were not uncommon among women of her social rank in the early fifteenth century (Kempe, 133–4).

Joan has also been associated with two other devotional manuscripts. A volume containing various private prayers and devotions together with a text of Richard Rolle of Hampole's Meditations on the Passion (now CUL, Additional MS 3042) has the signature 'Joan countess of Westmorland' on folio 89r. It is, however, in a later hand and although the manuscript dates from the early fifteenth century, and contains material that would have interested her, definite proof of her ownership is lacking. The same is true of Bodl. Oxf., MS e Museo 35, a text of Nicholas Love's Myrrour of the Blessed Lyf of Jesu Christ which has on folio 16 the arms of Neville (erased) and Beaufort, but this may have belonged not to Joan but to her sister-in-law Margaret, wife of Thomas Beaufort, duke of Exeter. Joan's literary and spiritual interests were shared by other aristocratic women of her generation, and it remains uncertain whether these manuscripts which have been associated with her in the past actually belonged to her.

The Neville inheritance secured Joan's strength of character and determination to defend the interests of both her families, but especially her second family, came sharply to the fore after her husband's death in 1425. The grant to Ralph, the earl's second son from his first marriage, of the barony of Bywell and Styford under the terms of his will may be evidence of Joan's concern for the children of her first marriage, for Ralph was married to Mary, her daughter with Sir Robert Ferrers. Of much greater significance, however, was the virtual disinheritance of the senior line of the Nevilles. The heir to the title of earl of Westmorland was her husband's grandson from his first marriage, Ralph *Neville (d. 1484), but even before her husband's death he and Joan had made sure that most of the Neville estates passed to their children rather than to the second earl. After his death Joan showed herself more than capable of realizing this joint ambition on her own.

Joan's dower consisted of Raby and Staindrop in co. Durham together with Middleham and Sheriff Hutton in Yorkshire and a one-third share in Neville lands elsewhere in northern England. With a substantial part of the Neville inheritance in her own hands, Joan set herself to resist the attempts of her husband's grandson and heir, the second earl of Westmorland, to undo the series of transactions that had effectively disinherited the senior branch of the Neville family. In doing so she mobilized in her support the extensive influence of her own family, especially her brother Henry Beaufort, bishop of Winchester (Cardinal Beaufort), and also Thomas Langley, bishop of Durham until 1437. Langley identified himself with the Beaufort interest in the north, and ensured that the second earl never held judicial office in the palatinate of Durham. He also put pressure on the prior of Durham, John Wessington, to hand over to Joan a box of muniments relating to the Neville inheritance which the first earl had deposited in Durham Priory in 1400. Among other documents, this box apparently contained her husband's will of 1400 which was probably more favourable than his final will to the children of his first marriage [see Neville, Ralph, first earl of Westmorland (c.1364–1425)]. This will was, of course, effectively nullified by the transactions in subsequent years which entailed most of the inheritance on his children with Joan, and was effectively revoked by his final will in 1424, but it is not surprising that Joan and her family were anxious to get their hands on it. Wessington eventually handed the muniments over to Joan's attorneys: no copy of the 1400 will now survives.

The principal beneficiary of the second earl's effective disinheritance was Joan's eldest son with Ralph Neville, Richard *Neville, earl of Salisbury (d. 1460), but Joan showed herself just as keen to advance the career in the church of her fourth son, Robert *Neville (d. 1457), who was born in 1404. When he was only twelve he was appointed to one of the prebends of the church of Howden, which belonged to Durham, and in 1425 Joan and her brother Cardinal Beaufort procured his appointment as rector of Hemingbrough, which also belonged to Durham; but the appointment never took effect because the expected vacancy had not yet occurred. Two years later, however, Robert was appointed bishop of Salisbury, no doubt as a result of Beaufort influence, and in 1437 he succeeded Langley as bishop of Durham. He promptly retained his brother the earl of Salisbury for life at an annual fee of £100. The domination of both church and lay society in Durham by Joan's family was now almost total, and it is not surprising that the second earl of Westmorland began to weary of the struggle to reverse his disinheritance. After Joan's death he quickly reached a settlement with Richard, earl of Salisbury.

Death, burial, and monuments Joan died on 13 November 1440 at Howden, probably in the manor house there which belonged to the bishops of Durham. In her will she expressed the wish to be buried beside her mother in Lincoln Cathedral, and asked that her mother's burial place be enlarged and enclosed, if the dean and chapter were agreeable. Three years before her death, on 28 November 1437, Joan had received a licence from Henry VI to found a chantry with two chaplains to celebrate mass daily at the altar in front of her mother's tomb. She was also licensed to appropriate for the support of the chantry the advowson of the church of Welton in Howdenshire which had belonged to the priory of Durham but which had been granted to the Nevilles in the 1380s. This foundation evidently superseded the chantry that John of Gaunt had founded in Lincoln Cathedral in 1398 'for the good estate of himself and Katherine his wife', but which may not have taken effect (Harvey, x). It is uncertain whether the surviving tomb and the wrought iron work surrounding it date from the time of Katherine's death in 1403 or that of Joan in 1440: in view of Joan's request in her will that her mother's burial place be enclosed, it is likely that the wrought iron screen dates from c.1440. Joan's tomb, like that of her mother, originally had a brass effigy upon it under a canopy, with an epitaph which extols her noble birth and marriage, and her offspring. It concludes by saying that the whole nation grieved at her death; the second earl of Westmorland, however, may not have shared in the universal grief. Her effigy appears beside that of her second husband and his first wife on his tomb in Staindrop church, co. Durham, making a statement about the Neville family in death that the reality of their lives belied.

ANTHONY TUCK

Sources BL, Cotton MS Vespasian F.xiii · PRO, inquisitions post mortem, c.139 · PRO, Durham 3/2 · register of wills of Archbishop John Kempe, Borth. Inst. · CClR · CPR · CIPM · RotP, vol. 4 · N. H. Nicolas, ed., *Proceedings and ordinances of the privy council of England*, 7 vols., RC, 26 (1834–7), vols. 3–4 · Rymer, *Foedera*, 2nd edn · [J. Raine], ed., *Testamenta Eboracensia*, 2, SurtS, 30 (1855) · *Historiae Dunelmensis scriptores tres: Gaufridus de Coldingham, Robertus de Graystanes, et Willielmus de Chambre*, ed. J. Raine, SurtS, 9 (1839) · E. F. Jacob, ed., *The register of Henry Chichele, archbishop of Canterbury, 1414–1443*, 2, CYS, 42 (1937) · *The book of Margery Kempe*, ed. S. B. Meech and H. E. Allen, EETS, 212 (1940) · *Hoccleve's works*, ed. F. J. Furnivall, 1: *The minor poems*, EETS, extra ser. 61 (1892) · G. Chaucer, *'Troilus and Criseyde': a facsimile of Corpus Christi College Cambridge MS 61* (1978) · *VCH Warwickshire*, vol. 3 · S. Armitage-Smith, *John of Gaunt* (1904) · A. Goodman, *John of Gaunt: the exercise of princely power in fourteenth-century Europe* (1992) · A. Goodman, *Katherine Swynford*, Lincoln Cathedral Publications (1994) · S. Walker, *The Lancastrian affinity, 1361–1399* (1990) · G. L. Harriss, *Cardinal Beaufort: a study of Lancastrian ascendancy and decline* (1988) · J. Hughes, *Pastors and visionaries: religion and secular life in late medieval Yorkshire* (1988) · C. M. Meale, ed., *Women and literature in Britain, 1150–1500* (1993) · A. Tuck, correspondence with C. M. Meale [J. Beaufort's books] · P. A. Johnson, *Duke Richard of York, 1411–1460* (1988) · R. A. Griffiths, *The reign of King Henry VI: the exercise of royal authority, 1422–1461* (1981) · J. H. Harvey, *Catherine Swynford's chantry*, Lincoln Minster Pamphlets, 2nd ser., 6 (1976) · J. A. Petre, 'The Nevilles of Brancepeth and Raby, 1425–1499 [pt 1]', *The Ricardian*, 5 (1979–81), 418–35 · tomb, Lincoln Cathedral

Archives BL, Cotton MS Vespasian F.xiii | PRO, government records

Likenesses tomb effigy, Staindrop church, co. Durham

Beaufort, Joan. *See* Joan (d. 1445).

Beaufort, John, marquess of Dorset and marquess of Somerset (*c*.1371–1410), soldier and administrator, was the first offspring of the liaison between *John of Gaunt, duke of Lancaster (*d*. 1399), and Katherine Swynford (1350?–1403) [*see* Katherine, duchess of Lancaster]. He became a staunch supporter of Henry IV and helped to establish the Lancastrian dynasty. Katherine, widow of Sir Hugh Swynford and daughter and coheir (with Philippa, wife of Geoffrey Chaucer) of the Hainault knight Sir Payn Roelt, became governess to Gaunt's children after the death of the Duchess Blanche in 1369 and his mistress during his marriage to Constanza of Castile. Between 1371 and 1379 Katherine and Gaunt had three sons and a daughter who were given the name Beaufort: John, Henry *Beaufort, Thomas *Beaufort, and Joan *Beaufort. Following the death of Constanza in 1394 Katherine became his third wife in February 1396, their children being legitimated by papal bull and royal charter in 1396–7.

By that date John Beaufort had acquired a reputation for chivalric valour. Knighted before 6 December 1391, he had jousted at St Ingelvert in 1390 and joined the duke of Bourbon's crusade to Mahdiyya, in north Africa, that year; in 1394 he went crusading in Lithuania, perhaps fighting at the battle of Lettow, and in 1396 may have participated in the battle of Nicopolis. Already a king's knight with an annuity of 100 marks in June 1392, he was created earl of Somerset on 10 February 1397, immediately following his legitimation, and a knight of the Garter. Later in that year he was one of the group of young nobles who, at Richard II's instigation, appealed the duke of Gloucester and the earls of Arundel and Warwick of treason in parliament. He was rewarded with some of Warwick's forfeited lands and elevation to the rank of marquess on 29 September. Richard further showed his confidence in Somerset's loyalty and military capacity by appointing him constable of Wallingford Castle (20 November 1397), constable of Dover Castle and warden of the Cinque Ports (5 February 1398), admiral of the north and west (9 May 1398), and king's lieutenant in Aquitaine (23 August 1398). He was still in England raising a force to go overseas when his half-brother Henry of Lancaster (the future *Henry IV) landed in Yorkshire early in July 1399 to claim his inheritance. Although Somerset joined the duke of York in raising troops for the king, both surrendered to Henry at Bristol without a fight on 27 July. Following Richard II's deposition Somerset was degraded from his marquessate but was pardoned his part in the appeal and quickly demonstrated his commitment to the new Lancastrian regime.

Faced with a depleted and partly disaffected nobility, and dependent in his first years on the untrustworthy Percys, Henry IV relied greatly on Somerset's loyalty and abilities. As chamberlain of England from 7 November 1399 he became the leading figure at court, the channel for royal favour and for contacts between the king and the council. He was intimately involved in royal policy, and was entrusted with a series of missions involving the king's family and honour: the return of Richard II's child bride, Isabella, to France in 1401; the conduct of Henry IV's daughter Blanche to her marriage with Ludwig, duke of Bavaria, in June 1402; the escort of Henry's own queen, Joan of Navarre, from Brittany in 1402–3. He took part in the military expedition to Scotland in 1400 and was briefly lieutenant in south Wales in 1403, but his principal sphere of activity was in Calais, of which he was captain from 1401 until his death. Calais was under constant threat from the French and Burgundian armies and more than once Somerset took personal charge of its defence, notably in routing the attack of the count of St Pol in April 1405. His responsibility was made more onerous by the crown's endemic insolvency resulting in mounting arrears in the pay of the garrison; following a mutiny in March 1407 Somerset persuaded the council to allocate revenue for its defence on a continuing basis. For his safeguard of Calais and the sea and cultivation of good relations with Flanders, Somerset and his brother Henry (*d*. 1447) won support among the Commons in parliament. He was nominated to 'intercommune' with them in 1402, and to membership of the council in 1404 and 1406, when he was specially commended by their speaker. In the period 1404–5 he assiduously attended council alongside his brother Henry as chancellor. In February 1407 he petitioned for an exemplification of Richard II's patent of legitimation, which was reissued with a clause excluding the Beauforts from the royal succession.

By 1407 these strenuous military and political tasks had begun to undermine Somerset's health, but he continued to attend council and is said to have distinguished himself in jousts against knights from Hainault at which the king presided in 1409. Although his reputation for valour, loyalty, and service stood high, his landed estate remained small. To the group of manors in the midlands and Somerset with which his father had endowed him he added those of his wife, Margaret Holland (*d*. 1439), sister and coheir of Edmund Holland, earl of Kent (*d*. 1408), whom he had married before 28 September 1397. The Warwick lands granted to him by Richard II had to be surrendered in 1399 and later grants by Henry IV added little apart from Corfe Castle to his permanent estate, although he had an annuity of £1000 from the crown. He received the forfeited lands of Owain Glyn Dŵr and other rebels, and the custody of the lands of Ivo Fitzwarine and Lord Fitzwalter which were in the king's hands. These enlarged his income but his own lands may have yielded no more than £1000 p.a. They gave him little local influence and his retinue was mainly composed of soldiers. His political influence rested on his membership of the Lancastrian family group and his military commands.

Somerset was taken ill during the parliament of 1410 and died on 16 March at the hospital of St Katharine by the Tower. By a nuncupative will of that date he made his brother Henry sole executor. Within four months his widow had contracted to marry the king's second son, Thomas, duke of Clarence (*d*. 1421), who claimed the custody of Somerset's heirs and estate and half his effects, supposedly including a sum of £20,000 in cash. This was contested by Henry Beaufort, however, with partial success. Three of Somerset's sons, Henry Beaufort (*d*. 1418), John *Beaufort (*d*. 1444), and Edmund *Beaufort (*d*. 1455), succeeded to his title, one daughter, Joan, later married *James I, king of Scotland, and the other, Margaret, married Thomas Courtenay, earl of Devon. Somerset was first buried either in the abbey church on Tower Hill (*English Chronicle*, 37) or in St Thomas's Chapel in Canterbury Cathedral (Van Lennep and others, 26), but his remains were later interred in the tomb constructed by his widow for her two husbands in St Michael's Chapel in the cathedral, where his effigy remains.   G. L. HARRISS

Sources GEC, *Peerage*, new edn, 12.39–45 · G. L. Harriss, *Cardinal Beaufort: a study of Lancastrian ascendancy and decline* (1988) · J. H. Wylie, *History of England under Henry the Fourth*, 4 vols. (1884–98) · J. L. Kirby, *Henry IV of England* (1970) · A. Goodman, *John of Gaunt: the exercise of princely power in fourteenth-century Europe* (1992) · *RotP*, vol. 3 · J. A. Giles, ed., *Incerti scriptoris chronicon Angliae de regnis trium regum Lancastrensium* (1848) · *Chancery records* · J. S. Davies, ed., *An English chronicle of the reigns of Richard II, Henry IV, Henry V, and Henry VI*, CS, 64 (1856) · W. G. Searle, ed., *Christ Church, Canterbury*, 1: *The chronicle of John Stone, monk of Christ Church*, Cambridge Antiquarian RS, 34 (1902) · F. S. Haydon, ed., *Eulogium historiarum sive temporis*, 3 vols., Rolls Series, 9 (1858–63), vol. 3 · [J. Nichols], ed., *A collection of … wills … of … every branch of the blood royal* (1780) · N. H. Nicolas, ed., *Proceedings and ordinances of the privy council of England*, 7 vols., RC, 26 (1834–7), vol. 1
Archives Westminster Abbey, muniments | E. Sussex RO, Glynde Place archives · PRO, E 404
Likenesses alabaster effigy, Canterbury Cathedral, St Michael's Chapel · manuscript illumination, BL, Royal MS 2.A.XVIII, fol. 23*v*
Wealth at death approx. £1000 p.a. in lands; approx. £20,000 effects: *Incerti scriptoris*, 62; Nichols, *Royal wills*, 208–14; PRO C 137/80; Harriss, *Cardinal Beaufort*, 406–9

Beaufort, John, duke of Somerset (1404–1444), magnate and soldier, was the second son of John *Beaufort, marquess of Dorset and of Somerset (*d.* 1410), and Margaret Holland, daughter of Thomas *Holland, earl of Kent. He succeeded to the earldom of Somerset on the death of his elder brother, Henry, in 1418 and in November 1419 he and his younger brothers, Thomas and Edmund *Beaufort, joined their stepfather, Thomas, duke of Clarence, in Normandy. Knighted by Henry V at Rouen, he was at the siege of Melun from July to November 1420. In March 1421 Clarence, as Henry V's lieutenant-general, led a *chevauchée* into Maine and Anjou only to be trapped and killed at the battle of Baugé where John and Thomas were both made prisoner. Negotiations for Somerset's release in exchange for the duke of Bourbon between 1428 and 1430 came to nothing, though Thomas was liberated. Further proposals put forward between 1430 and 1434 for an exchange with the count of Angoulême, held as surety since 1412 for the duke of Orléans's debt to Clarence, proved equally negative. Not until 1438 was agreement reached for his ransom to be offset by the release of the count of Eu (whom he had purchased from the crown) and the payment due from Angoulême. Somerset claimed that his release cost him £24,000 and left him impoverished. Only on his mother's death in 1439 did he secure the Beaufort and Holland lands which raised his income to some £2250 p.a.

Somerset arrived in England late in 1438, but next spring returned to Normandy to join his brother Edmund, earl of Dorset, whose military success had brought him the renown and reward of which John had been deprived by his years in captivity. He now became captain of Cherbourg, Avranches, Falaise, and other fortresses, and on the death of the earl of Warwick in April he assumed direction of the war, as the senior in rank. In November 1439 Somerset returned to England where his claim to succeed Warwick as lieutenant-general was being pressed by his uncle, Henry, Cardinal Beaufort (*d.* 1447), against the claim of Humphrey, duke of Gloucester. Somerset's supreme military command in France was temporarily renewed and early in 1440 he led a substantial force of 2100 men to Normandy, financed by loans from the cardinal. With Dorset and Lord Talbot they relieved Avranches, recaptured Harfleur and Montivilliers, raided Picardy, and finally imposed a truce on the duke of Brittany in July 1440. Despite these successes the duke of York was appointed lieutenant-general, possibly thanks to Gloucester's influence, and John and Edmund Beaufort, their further prospects in Normandy frustrated, returned to England.

Somerset married about 1442 Margaret, widow of Sir Oliver St John and daughter of John Beauchamp of Bletsoe; their daughter, Margaret, was born in May 1443. Despite his uncertain health he welcomed the opportunity to lead an expedition to Guyenne to counter the invasion of Charles VII in the autumn of 1442, but the danger receded and it never took effect. Over the winter the council debated whether to send an army to Guyenne or to Normandy, but by March 1443, when Somerset was negotiating the terms of his command, the objective was northern France. Somerset proposed a major army of over 4000 men which should conduct a devastating *chevauchée* into Maine and Anjou, if necessary crossing the Loire in order to force Charles VII to battle. This both marked a departure from the piecemeal defence which had eroded the English hold on Normandy in recent years and offered Somerset the opportunity to gain for himself any lands and towns he captured. However, the project raised the difficult question of how his command related to that of the duke of York. Somerset was elevated to the rank of duke to afford him parity of esteem while York was assured that the new duke of Somerset would exercise his authority outside areas under York's control and provide a military shield for Normandy; but the effect was none the less to deprive York of the reinforcements he needed and to withdraw an area from his jurisdiction. Undoubtedly he felt slighted.

Somerset's ability effectually to dictate his terms rested on Cardinal Beaufort's unwillingness to lend money for any other form of expedition. He had, moreover, won favour from Henry VI who saw him as a surrogate leader of a 'royal' army, and awarded him the barony of Kendal with lands to the value of £400 per annum. Somerset's force was well provided with arms and equipment but from the first the grand scheme went awry. He failed to attract captains and men-at-arms of the quality and number he had indented for, there were delays in assembling shipping and mustering, and the force assembled at Cherbourg only in August. The campaign proved an anticlimax to the high expectations it had aroused. The army marched down western Normandy and ravaged the area of Angers, but instead of crossing the Loire it turned north to capture towns in the marches of Brittany. In November it moved into Maine and took Beaumont-le-Vicomte but the French army stayed out of reach and, by January, Somerset had paid off his troops and himself returned to England. The campaign may have deflected Charles VII's intended attack, but its positive gains had been small in relation to its cost. Somerset was ignominiously debarred the court, though he was probably not (as a later chronicle alleged) charged with treason. A sick man, he remained at Corfe and Wimborne where he died on 27 May 1444, possibly by his own hand. His widow married again and died on 3 June 1482. His fine tomb in Wimborne Minster carries the effigies of Somerset and his wife, each clasping the other's right hand.

Somerset's only surviving legitimate child, Margaret *Beaufort (1443–1509), was entrusted to her mother, but the custody of her lands and marriage were awarded to William de la Pole, duke of Suffolk, who by 1450 had married her to his son John. In 1453 the marriage was dissolved and in 1455 she became the wife of Edmund Tudor and mother of *Henry VII. The earldom and Corfe Castle descended to Beaufort's brother Edmund but the dukedom was extinguished and Somerset's barony of Kendal and French fiefs reverted to the crown.

G. L. HARRISS

Sources GEC, *Peerage* · G. L. Harriss, *Cardinal Beaufort: a study of Lancastrian ascendancy and decline* (1988) · M. Jones, 'John Beaufort duke of Somerset and the French expedition of 1443', *Patronage, the crown and the provinces*, ed. R. A. Griffiths (1981) · M. Jones, 'Henry VII, Lady Margaret Beaufort, and the Orleans ransom', *Kings and nobles in the later middle ages*, ed. R. A. Griffiths and J. Sherborne (1986) · N. H. Nicolas, ed., *Proceedings and ordinances of the privy council of England*, 7 vols., RC, 26 (1834–7), vol. 5 · *Ingulph's Chronicle of the abbey of Croyland*, ed. and trans. H. T. Riley (1854), 399 · T. Basin, *Histoire de Charles VII*, ed. C. Samaran, 1 (Paris, 1933) · 'John Benet's chronicle for the years 1400 to 1462', ed. G. L. Harriss, *Camden miscellany, XXIV*, CS, 4th ser., 9 (1972) · J. A. Giles, ed., *Incerti scriptoris chronicon Angliae de regnis trium regum Lancastrensium* (1848) · *Chancery records*

Archives Archives Nationales, Paris

Likenesses alabaster effigy, Wimborne Minster, Dorset · engraving, repro. in J. Hutchins, *The history and antiquities of the county of Dorset*, 3 (1868), facing p. 212

Wealth at death approx. £2666 p.a.: Harriss, *Cardinal Beaufort*, 354, Appendix 2

Beaufort, Margaret [*known as* Lady Margaret Beaufort], **countess of Richmond and Derby** (1443–1509), royal matriarch, was born on 31 May 1443, the daughter and heir of John *Beaufort, duke of Somerset (1404–1444), from his marriage to Margaret (*d.* 1482), widow of Oliver St John and daughter and heir of Sir John Beauchamp of Bletsoe, Bedfordshire.

Family background and first marriages Margaret's paternal great-grandfather was John of Gaunt, duke of Lancaster, the fourth son of Edward III, a pedigree that was to determine her subsequent political importance. The marriage of her grandfather, John *Beaufort, earl of Somerset (*d.* 1410), to Margaret Holland gave an additional link to the blood royal, and a right to the Holland estates that

Margaret Beaufort, countess of Richmond and Derby (1443–1509), by Pietro Torrigiano, 1513 [tomb effigy]

would ultimately make her a great landowner. It was a troubled legacy. The Beauforts were the bastard offspring of Gaunt's liaison with Katherine Swynford [*see* Katherine, duchess of Lancaster], and their later legitimization never entirely removed the stigma of their origins. Margaret's own father, who died when she was hardly a year old, was a disgraced war commander and possibly also a suicide. In these difficult circumstances Margaret reserved her personal affection for her family of the half-blood (from her mother's marriage to Oliver St John), which in a very real sense she looked upon as her own, finding them placement within her household, protecting their estates, and securing them advantageous marriages. Fittingly John St John, the inheritor of the estate at Bletsoe, became Margaret's chamberlain after her widowhood in 1504, and served as an executor of her will.

Margaret was forced to enter the political arena at an early age. On the death of her father in 1444 she was made the ward of William de la Pole, marquess of Suffolk, steward of the king's household. Suffolk had sought early in 1450, when threatened with impeachment by the House of Commons, to secure the position of his own son John by marrying him to Margaret. The marriage contract instituted what would now be regarded as a solemn betrothal, for canon law permitted its dissolution while the bride was below the age of twelve, and Margaret herself never subsequently recognized John de la *Pole (1442–1492) as her first husband. Early in 1453 the contract was dissolved on the initiative of Henry VI, who summoned Margaret to appear before him, making generous provision for her 'apparel' (new clothes in honour of her introduction at court) and regranting her wardship to his half-brothers Edmund and Jasper Tudor. The king's intervention on behalf of his family of the half-blood was designed to enable Edmund *Tudor (c.1430–1456) to marry her in 1455, probably in May. Margaret's own memory of these events, passed on many years later to her confessor John Fisher, was recalled in his month's mind sermon after her death: she had experienced a vision of St Nicholas, who had commended the choice of Tudor rather than John de la Pole as her husband. The authenticity of this remarkable story is substantiated by Margaret's later close association with the Guild of St Nicholas for poor parish clerks in London.

The newly married couple took up residence at Lamphey in Pembrokeshire and here Margaret conceived at a dangerously early age, even for a youthful medieval bride. In making her pregnant Tudor had brutally secured, according to the custom known as 'courtesy of England', his own life interest in her estates (worth about £1000 per annum) with little regard for the safety of his wife. Margaret may have suffered permanent damage, and certainly never bore any more children. Her marriage to Edmund Tudor was to end abruptly and traumatically. His sudden death from the plague on 1 November 1456 at Carmarthen left Margaret six months pregnant, isolated and vulnerable in a lawless region of Wales. This terrifying moment may have left a permanent scar. Margaret's fear that the plague might kill her unborn son was vividly remembered by Fisher in his Cambridge oration; her subsequent unease is evidenced by the series of medical tracts and remedies for the pestilence, decorated with her arms and badges, that were later compiled for her use.

Political survivor From such troubling experiences Margaret was to emerge as a resilient survivor. Her life now became deeply embroiled in the bitter struggle between the houses of York and Lancaster. She initially sought the protection of Edmund's brother, Jasper *Tudor, and gave birth to her son, the future *Henry VII, on 28 January 1457 at Pembroke Castle. In March she and Jasper travelled through Wales to Newport in Gwent, to arrange her third marriage, which took place in January the following year, to Henry Stafford (d. 1471), second son of Humphrey *Stafford, duke of Buckingham. Margaret was now taking an active role in planning her own future: her chief aim was to gain Buckingham's protection and avoid another husband being forced upon her. Her marriage with Stafford led to what seems to have been a genuinely affectionate relationship. But the aftermath of the change of dynasty in 1461 meant a fresh price had to be paid, the separation of Margaret from her son, for the new king, Edward IV, chose to reward his staunch supporter William, Lord Herbert, with the grant of the wardship of Henry Tudor on 12 February 1462.

Margaret and Stafford showed themselves ready to acknowledge the facts of political life during the Yorkist ascendancy. Their guiding principle was to secure Margaret's inheritance and safeguard the interests of Henry Tudor. They kept in regular contact with her son, and in September 1467 paid him a visit at Raglan. In December 1468 the couple entertained the king at Brookwood, near their manor of Woking (which Margaret had inherited from her grandmother Margaret Holland, duchess of Clarence), seeking royal support for her title to far-flung lands in Kendal, which were facing encroachment from the Parr family. Political prudence was shown in March 1470, when Stafford was willing to join a royal army to quell the Lincolnshire rising, even though the rebels included Richard, Lord Welles, and his heir, both members of Margaret's family of the half-blood. Nevertheless in October, during the short period of Henry VI's return to power, Margaret, who had briefly been reunited with her son, arranged for a personal audience with the Lancastrian monarch at Westminster. Margaret's love for the king and her confidence in his sanctity (later recalled in the charter for the establishment of Christ's College, Cambridge) may have stemmed from her impressions of this visit; a possible dynastic significance, based on the tradition that Henry VI miraculously forecast the future accession of her son, is derived solely from early Tudor sources.

Lord Stanley and the opposition to Richard III Margaret's renewal of allegiance to the Lancastrians carried considerable political risk, and Edward IV's resumption of the throne after the battle of Tewkesbury on 4 May 1471 confronted her with fresh difficulties. The death of Edward, prince of Wales, in the battle, and Henry VI's murder in the Tower of London on 21 May, left her son as a possible Lancastrian claimant to the throne. In September, on his mother's advice, Henry Tudor set sail for France from the port of Tenby, but was diverted by storms to Brittany. Stafford died on 4 October, leaving his widow to protect her interests and those of her absent son as best she could. On 2 June 1472 she placed her paternal estates in Devon and Somerset in trust, with the intention of providing for Henry Tudor should he return from exile. Her wish to regain the favour of Edward IV was seen a few days later, in her marriage, by 12 June, to Thomas *Stanley, second Baron Stanley (c.1433–1504), steward of the king's household. Having prudently placed Henry beyond Edward's reach she now sought with equal wisdom to cultivate him and his court. Stanley wielded great local power in Cheshire, Lancashire, and north Wales. Margaret's alliance brought him a life interest in her estates; in return she was granted an annual income from Stanley's own lands. She travelled with her husband to his residences at Lathom and Knowsley, and was a party both in 1473 and 1474 to the settlement of disputes around Liverpool, in one case heading an arbitration panel. She also maintained a presence at court, and in 1476 attended the queen and her daughters on the occasion of the reburial of Richard, duke of York, at Fotheringhay.

Henry Tudor was never far from Margaret's concerns. On 3 June 1482, a month after the death of her mother, the duchess of Somerset, she made an agreement with her husband in Edward IV's presence which endorsed Henry's title to the lands held in trust since 1472, and allowed him a share of the duchess's estates, provided that Henry return from exile 'to be in the grace and favour of the king's highness' (Jones and Underwood, 60). Edward's death in 1483, and the usurpation of Richard III, did not at first deter Margaret from seeking an arrangement with Richard whereby Henry's return and possible marriage within the royal family might take place. She was, however, soon to abandon her allegiance to the new king. Either realizing or sharing in the depth of public suspicion that surrounded Richard's detention of Edward V and his brother, the duke of York, in the Tower, she may have participated in an unsuccessful plot to rescue them as early as July 1483. By September, when it was widely rumoured that they were dead, Margaret committed herself thoroughly to rebellion and to the return of her son, negotiating with the Woodvilles for his marriage with *Elizabeth of York.

While never openly advancing Henry's claim to the throne, Margaret's pragmatic co-operation with the duke of Buckingham showed her as a consummate plotter. But the revolt collapsed, and its failure placed her in the most dangerous position of her life. Her marriage to Stanley, who had remained loyal to Richard, saved her person. She was not attainted in the parliament of 1484, but all her property was made over to her husband, and provisions for Henry Tudor's inheritance cancelled. Stanley was also made responsible for her secure custody, without household servants to wait upon her. In the event, his role as his wife's gaoler was not too exacting. Margaret was able to communicate afresh with her son on his landing in Wales in August 1485, and at the battle of Bosworth the critical intervention of the Stanley family helped the first Tudor king to the throne.

The king's mother Henry's victory brought about a complete reversal of his mother's position. So sensitive was Margaret to the turn of fortune's wheel that she wept at the sudden overwhelming success, for fear that it would bring sorrow in its train. This awareness of the fragility of power and prosperity, nourished originally perhaps by tales of her father's disgrace and death, never left her: she would weep once more at the coronation of her grandson. Yet for the present she assisted in the consolidation of her son's power, and never ceased throughout the reign to act as his lieutenant. The first parliament of the reign, which was summoned on 7 November 1485, established her future legal and landed position. She was declared *femme sole*, responsible for her actions at law independent of her husband, and her inherited properties were redistributed between them. In 1486 the most politically important wardship in the kingdom, that of Edward Stafford, duke of Buckingham, was formally granted to her. A year later the king made over to her a substantial body of lands for her sole possession: in effect a great landed trust for the monarchy, since she had no other children. It consisted of much of the property formerly belonging to Henry Holland, duke of Exeter, and additional honour of Richmond lands in Lincolnshire, Cambridgeshire, and Kendal. Margaret substantially renovated the Holland mansion of Coldharbour, on the Thames, which became her chief London residence. Her special position at court was recognized outwardly at Christmas 1487, when she wore robes and a coronet matching those of the queen. Later in the reign, when Katherine of Aragon was received in England, Elizabeth of York and Margaret jointly drew up the names of Katherine's attendants, requesting that she learn French before her arrival to facilitate conversation.

While Margaret's unique position within the Tudor regime worked to the crown's benefit it did not preclude her own efforts, sometimes to the hurt of others, to advantage herself and her kin. Her property transactions showed her at times to be ruthless and acquisitive. As a result of a detailed but specious legal suit in 1492, by which she acquired properties in Wiltshire and Somerset as heir of her great-uncle, Cardinal Henry *Beaufort, she deprived Edward Plantagenet of his inheritance of them as earl of Warwick and Salisbury. The properties had in fact been bought by the cardinal to endow the hospital of St Cross in Winchester, but his pious design was blatantly set aside by Margaret and her lawyers in her desire to augment her estates. But such actions were balanced by examples of a genuine sense of responsibility to the communities where her lands were concentrated. In the Lincolnshire fens she was notable as an improving landlord: her personal initiative prompted the convening of a royal commission to improve the navigation of the River Witham, and the construction of a great tidal sluice at the port of Boston.

Role in government Margaret wielded a conciliar authority in the east midlands reminiscent of other Tudor regional councils. She made her manor of Collyweston, Northamptonshire, her main place of residence between 1499 and 1506, and transformed it into a palace. From here in 1503 Henry VII, in the presence of the entire royal court, took leave of his daughter *Margaret Tudor, on her way north to marry *James IV of Scotland. She also installed her own court of equity, equipped with a council house and prison. This arrangement formalized Margaret's authority in the region, and when on one occasion she wrote to the civic authorities of Coventry on behalf of an aggrieved citizen, she did so in the king's name. The scope of her activities was considerable, including investigation of treasonable intent, and on certain occasions suits specifically delegated from the royal council. The force of her moral standing was such that her council was prepared to intervene in matters that would have normally been heard before an ecclesiastical court. One case concerned a future bishop of London, John Stokesley, who was accused among other charges of baptizing a cat, with the object of finding treasure by magical means. In another instance the Holy Maid of Leominster, alleged to be nourished solely upon the eucharist, was exposed as a fraud while being held in Margaret's custody.

The first decade of the sixteenth century saw Margaret at the plenitude of her power. A rich, high-quality book of hours (commissioned from the Vérard Paris workshops c.1500) displayed Margaret's badge of the royal arms with the differencing taken off the shield, emphasizing through heraldry the image of her viceregal position. Her adoption of the signature 'Margaret R' (found in her letters from 1499) similarly cultivated a royal style. She enjoyed a presiding influence within the realm, closely co-operating with her son and drawing on the expertise of his French secretary to revive her family's opportunist claim to the Orléans ransom, now the legal responsibility of Louis XII. She maintained a watchful interest in foreign affairs, having a *libellus* ('book', 'pamphlet') drawn up for her, detailing the arrival of King Philip of Castile in 1506. The income from her properties (which by 1504 amounted to over £3000 p.a.) funded a lifestyle of appropriate magnificence, displayed in the quality of her purchased jewels and embroideries and the size of her household, the largest in the realm after the king's. In all this Margaret never relaxed an unceasing vigilance over the conduct of her affairs, whether scrutinizing the receipts of her estate officials or guarding against possible threats to the new Tudor dynasty.

Founder of colleges and literary patron Yet this extraordinary pre-eminence allowed Margaret the opportunity, in the last phase of her life, to balance power with spiritual obligation, and aggression with compassion. A significant example of this is found in the detailed composition made between the town and university of Cambridge in 1503, over a variety of economic differences. The resort of the parties from Cambridge to Collyweston in the course of the dispute reflected not only Margaret's authority as king's lieutenant, but also her emergence as the leading patron and benefactor of the university, where she used both her wealth and political influence astutely to secure endowments for her collegiate foundations. Characteristically she employed her own household men strategically within the town. John Fisher (a proctor when he first met Margaret, on unnamed university business in 1494–5) held the office of chancellor of Cambridge when he was made visitor of Margaret's new foundation of Christ's College in 1506, and was thus able to oversee the affairs of the college on her behalf. Henry Hornby, her dean of chapel, served as master of Peterhouse, the base from which he was to superintend the progress of St John's College after her death. Many others of Margaret's council were involved in the financing of both foundations. Her purchase of estates, including the manors of Malton and Roydon, Cambridgeshire, which transformed the poverty-stricken God's House into a wealthier Christ's College, was meticulous and thorough, and can be traced in her accounts, as can her substantial expenditure of £1625 on building work between 1505 and 1509. Her legacy to St John's was drawn from the profits of her movable goods and the revenue of her paternal estates, which, as a reflection of her last pious wishes, helped establish the college between 1511 and 1516.

Margaret was also to make significant contributions to the religious and literary culture of her day, both as patron and translator. The first work that she is known to have commissioned from William Caxton, in 1489, was a thirteenth-century French romance, *Blanchardin and Eglantine*, whose tale of a hero's feats for his beloved, besieged by enemies, may have recalled her own courage in negotiating the marriage of Elizabeth of York and Henry Tudor

in 1483. In 1494 Wynkyn de Worde dedicated to her his edition of Walter Hilton's devotional work the *Scale of Perfection*, in a text established by the work of the Carthusian and Bridgettine orders. The same year Margaret was recognized by the pope as chief promoter in England of the feast of the Name of Jesus. Her chapel, under the direction of Henry Hornby, was furnished with printed books for that office. By the end of the reign it had become an important centre for the composition of polyphonic music and with a total staff of thirty-four rivalled that of the royal household chapel. Margaret's own devotional productions, her translation from the French, *The Mirror of Gold for the Sinful Soul*, and her translation of the fourth book of Thomas à Kempis's *The Imitation of Christ* were printed for her by Richard Pynson in 1506 and 1504, and large quantities bought for her household. *The Imitation*, her translation with William Atkinson, fellow of Jesus College, Cambridge, was not superseded until a fresh translation of the whole work from Latin appeared in 1531.

Death and reputation Margaret survived her son by just over two months, witnessing the coronation of *Henry VIII and *Katherine of Aragon on 24 June 1509. The festivities and fare of the occasion may well have been too much for her, but her elaborate will of January 1509, and the signature of her accounts by her appointed executors after that date, indicate that her health had become increasingly frail. She died at Cheyneygates, the abbot's lodging at Westminster, on 29 June. The contract for her tomb in Henry VII's chapel (where she had founded a chantry in 1506, to be served by two monk–chaplains), which brought the Florentine sculptor Pietro Torrigiano his first major work in England, introduced Renaissance features into an otherwise Gothic monument, providing through the quality of its craftsmanship a suitable monument to the achievements of her life. John Fisher, whose position as Margaret's friend and confessor allowed him a special personal knowledge of her character, preached at her month's mind in July 1509. He celebrated her as a scriptural Martha, a woman not only of strong devotion, regular in observing the rites of penitence and communion, but also of active good works. These extended to the moral force of her lordship, so that with considerable authority she was able to sort out personal differences within her household.

Henry Parker, Lord Morley, writing his reflections on exemplary lives for Margaret's great-granddaughter Queen *Mary, recalled both her magnificence and her generosity, citing how she upheld before her servants the loyalty of Ralph Bigod, who had publicly defended his former master, Richard III. Margaret was never needlessly vindictive, and her prudence and ability to harmonize faction was rightly seen as the key to her political success. Her last years had balanced worldly activity with the regimen of a widow dedicated to God, which meant a regular routine of prayer and liturgical observance for part of the day. She had taken a vow to lead such a life before the death of her husband Lord Stanley in 1504, and afterwards renewed the pledge to John Fisher. It is clear, however, that she by no means withdrew from the affairs of the world. A formidable survivor, she combined her spiritual perspective with the vigorous supervision of the fortunes of her family, dependants, and collegiate foundations. Margaret's lifelong struggle to protect the interests of her son had a heroic quality, rightly perceived by the poet Bernard André: it culminated in her most notable triumph, the safeguarding of the Tudor dynasty.

MICHAEL K. JONES and MALCOLM G. UNDERWOOD

Sources M. K. Jones and M. G. Underwood, *The king's mother: Lady Margaret Beaufort, countess of Richmond and Derby* (1992) • C. H. Cooper, *The Lady Margaret* (1874) • P. Lindley, *Gothic to Renaissance* (1995), 47–54 • F. Hepburn, 'The portraiture of Lady Margaret Beaufort', *The Antiquaries Journal*, 72 (1992), 118–40 • P. H. Coulstock, *The collegiate church of Wimborne Minster* (1993) • F. L. Kisby, 'The royal household chapel in early Tudor London, 1485–1547', PhD diss., U. Lond., 1996 • J. Backhouse, 'Illuminated manuscripts associated with Henry VII and members of his immediate family', *The reign of Henry VII* [Harlaxton 1993], ed. B. Thompson (1995), 175–87 • L. Gill, 'William Caxton and the rebellion of 1483', *EngHR*, 112 (1997), 105–18 • W. D. Macray, *A register of the members of St Mary Magdalen College, Oxford*, 1 (1894), 47–51 • T. More, *Dialogue concerning heresies* (1981), 87 • St John Cam., Archives, D91/2, 3, 6/10, 15; D56/158, 195, 200 • muniments, Westminster Abbey, MS 19606 • BL, Add. MS 12060 • *RotP*, 5.177 • *CEPR letters*, 10.472–3

Archives St John Cam. • Westminster Abbey Muniments, MSS

Likenesses Maynard?, oils, c.1511–1512, Christ's College, Cambridge; version, NPG • P. Torrigiano, tomb effigy, gilt-bronze, 1513, Westminster Abbey [*see illus.*] • L. Hornbolte, miniature, c.1530 • portrait, c.1530 (after M. Wewyck), Christ's College, Cambridge • oils, c.1580–1590 (after portrait by M. Wewyck), Christ's College, Cambridge • R. Lockey, oils, c.1597, St John Cam. • tomb effigy, electrotype, NPG

Wealth at death approx. £15,000 in moveable goods; approx. £3000 p.a. in landed wealth: archives, St John Cam., D91/2, 3, 6/10, 15

Beaufort, Thomas, duke of Exeter (1377?–1426), magnate and soldier, was the youngest of the three illegitimate sons of *John of Gaunt, duke of Lancaster, and Katherine Swynford [*see* Katherine, duchess of Lancaster]. His brothers were John *Beaufort and Henry *Beaufort; he also had a sister, Joan *Beaufort. He was one of the most resolute and trusted of Henry V's commanders and the governor of the infant Henry VI. Raised in the household of John of Gaunt, from whom he received an annuity but no lands, he was married by 1397, while still a minor, to Margaret (*b.* before 1385), granddaughter and heir of Gaunt's retainer, Sir Robert Neville of Hornby. He joined Richard II's retinue in July 1397 and in September 1398 was rewarded with the grant of Castle Rising forfeited on the exile of the duke of Norfolk. Next year he transferred his loyalty to his half-brother *Henry IV and strenuously defended the Lancastrian regime throughout his reign.

As captain of Ludlow (21 August 1402) Thomas Beaufort probably fought alongside Prince Henry at the battle of Shrewsbury in 1403, and from 1404 to 1407 served among the group of the prince's retainers in the hardest phase of the war against Glyn Dŵr, himself commanding garrisons at Carmarthen, Cardigan, Newcastle Emlyn, and Wigmore. His other contribution was to guard the sea. Appointed admiral of the north in November 1403 he

patrolled the Dover Strait for thirteen weeks in the summer of 1404, preventing the count of St Pol's fleet at Gravelines from blockading Calais. In 1408 he was again appointed admiral of the northern and western fleets, and in 1410 and 1411 checked the privateering of John Prendergast and William Longe which threatened the maritime truce with Flanders. In these operations he identified himself with the pro-Burgundian policy of his brothers and Prince Henry. When the prince became head of the council in 1410 Thomas Beaufort was appointed chancellor (31 January 1410), almost certainly as surrogate for his brother Henry (*d.* 1447), who was unacceptable to the king. It was an office ill-suited to his military temperament and which he combined with maritime operations from his base at Bishop's Lynn. Created earl of Dorset on 5 July 1411, he retained the king's favour when the prince of Wales's council was dismissed in December: on 3 March 1412 he was appointed admiral of England for life. By then he was already involved in the expedition led by the prince's brother and rival, Thomas, duke of Clarence, to support the Armagnac lords in Aquitaine.

At Henry V's accession in March 1413 Dorset was appointed lieutenant in Aquitaine which he defended at his own cost against Burgundian forces. In July 1414 he was recalled, to play a leading part in the preparations for the war in France. He was a member of the embassy which early in 1415 presented the English demands in Paris, and on its return in April to report the French rejection he pledged the support of the Lords for war. As admiral he was responsible for gathering and commanding the fleet which sailed from Southampton on 12 August 1415. On arrival at Harfleur he took up position near Graville and when the garrison capitulated to the English assault on 22 September the king delivered the town into his custody. Although Dorset remained at Harfleur during Henry's march to Agincourt, his defence of the town over the next year as it came under siege by the French became an epic of endurance.

With reinforcements brought from England early in 1416 Dorset first made forays into Normandy, on one of which he was ambushed at Valmont (11 March) and fought his way back to Harfleur with heavy losses. The French intensified the siege and the English relief expedition was dangerously delayed by the prolonged peace negotiations at Beauvais; Dorset was temporarily sustained by supplies brought in by ships of the earl of Huntingdon in May, but by the time that Bedford scattered the French fleet at the battle of the Seine on 15 August the town was on the edge of starvation. Dorset's tenacity and firm discipline were rewarded by his elevation as duke of Exeter on 8 November 1416 with an annuity of £1000.

Established as one of Henry V's most trusted commanders and advisers, Exeter attended the king's crucial meeting with John the Fearless, duke of Burgundy, at Calais in October 1416 but remained in England with Bedford when the second invasion of France was launched in July 1417. Together they repulsed the 'foul raid' by the Scots in September, thereby securing the northern frontier. Early in 1418 Exeter was summoned to France, and he indented on 3 March 1418 to take a force of 2000 men. On arrival he played an active part in the second phase of the conquest; he captured Évreux and was positioned at the Beauvoisine gate when Rouen was besieged on 1 August. After its surrender on 13 January 1419 the city was placed in his custody. He then proceeded to reduce the strongholds to the west and north up to Dieppe and afterwards to invest Château Gaillard to the south, which surrendered to him on 23 September.

Exeter's participation in the fruitless negotiations with the duke of Burgundy at Meulan in May and June 1419, and in those of 1420 that led to the treaty of Troyes, brought little interruption to his military activity. He was entrusted with the captaincy of Conches on 26 March 1420, and of Melun when it surrendered to him on 18 November. On Henry V's return to England in January 1421 the king left Exeter as military governor of Paris with the guard of Charles VI. The defeat of Clarence at Baugé in March shook English authority: in Paris, Exeter's arrest of the Burgundian captain Lisle Adam provoked an uprising, forcing him to withdraw to the Bastille. He was later replaced by a Frenchman. He was engaged in the long winter siege of Meaux which surrendered in May 1422 and in Henry's final expedition to the relief of Cosne.

Exeter was present at the king's deathbed in Vincennes on 31 August. His return to England with the cortège effectively closed his military career. He excelled as a leader who commanded his men's loyalty and the king's confidence. Henry entrusted him with the safeguard of his greatest conquests: Harfleur, Rouen, and Paris. He was well, though not lavishly, rewarded. The grant of the *comté* of Harcourt and lordship of Lillebonne in tail male in June 1418 was followed by that of Croisy in June 1419. In England he held the important lordship of Wormegay in Norfolk forfeited by Lord Bardolf in 1405, and at different times was granted the custody of valuable estates during the minorities of Lord Ros, the earl of Oxford, and the earl of March. Although Exeter was only intermittently in Norfolk, his estates there and his office of admiral made him the effective head of the Lancastrian affinity reconstituted under the leadership of Sir Thomas Erpingham (*d.* 1428), and many of his retinue were drawn from the region.

Henry V's confidence in Exeter led not merely to his inclusion among the king's executors and feoffees, but to his nomination in the codicil of the king's last will as governor of the person of his infant heir. At the same time Henry had accorded Gloucester the 'tutelam et defensionem principales' ('principal tutelage and protection') of Henry VI, which the duke interpreted as entitling him to the regency. Thomas and Henry Beaufort, who were both appointed to the council in December 1422, were among those who opposed Gloucester's claim. Despite these responsibilities Exeter still saw his contribution primarily in the military sphere and in March 1423 he indented once more for service in France. Serious illness prevented him from mustering until July, but it is unclear where or for how long he served; he is not recorded at

council until 1425. Failing health may have limited his activity, and he died on the last day of 1426 at his manor of Greenwich where his will was dated two days earlier. This prescribed conventional if restrained obsequies, performed as the cortège conveyed the body to the chapel of St Mary in the abbey of Bury St Edmunds where his wife, who predeceased him, was interred. As he had no children his honours were extinguished, and his lands held in tail male reverted to the crown. The sale of other lands and effects by his executors realized the sum of £6787 from which numerous bequests were made to Carthusian monasteries, colleges, hospitals, recluses, paupers, prisoners, and other charitable purposes. Individual benefactions went to forty-three members of his *familia*. The will echoes William Worcester's later account of his household: the thirteen poor men fed daily at his table and three hundred others given potage; his washing the feet of the poor on Maundy Thursday; his expulsion of swearers, liars, and tale bearers, and care of his soldiers in old age. Exeter exemplified chivalric *noblesse* in his service and fidelity to the king, *courteoisie* to his knights, and *largesse* to his dependants. He furthered the interests and aims of the Lancastrian crown but contributed little to the endowment of the Beaufort family.

G. L. HARRISS

Sources GEC, *Peerage* · G. L. Harriss, *Cardinal Beaufort: a study of Lancastrian ascendancy and decline* (1988) · J. H. Wylie and W. T. Waugh, eds., *The reign of Henry the Fifth*, 3 vols. (1914–29) · R. A. Newhall, *The English conquest of Normandy, 1416–1424: a study in fifteenth-century warfare* (1924) · P. Strong and F. Strong, 'The last will and codicils of Henry V', *EngHR*, 96 (1981), 79–102 · E. F. Jacob, ed., *The register of Henry Chichele, archbishop of Canterbury, 1414–1443*, 2, CYS, 42 (1937), 355–64 · *Itineraries [of] William Worcestre*, ed. J. H. Harvey, OMT (1969), 354–9 · N. H. Nicolas, ed., *Proceedings and ordinances of the privy council of England*, 7 vols., RC, 26 (1834–7) · B. Williams, ed., 'Chronique de Normandie', *Henrici quinti, Angliae regis, gesta, cum chronica Neustriae, Gallice*, EHS, 12 (1850) · T. Walsingham, *The St Albans chronicle, 1406–1420*, ed. V. H. Galbraith (1937) · F. W. D. Brie, ed., *The Brut, or, The chronicles of England*, 2 vols., EETS, 131, 136 (1906–8), vol. 2 · Chancery rolls · H. Castor, 'The duchy of Lancaster and the rule of East Anglia, 1399–1440: a prologue to the Paston letters', *Crown, government, and people in the fifteenth century*, ed. R. E. Archer (1995), 53–78
Wealth at death over £6787: PRO, E 101/514/22

Beaufou [Beaufeu], **Roger** [Roger de Bello Fago] (*d.* 1309), justice, was probably a younger son of Richard de Beaufou of Waterperry in Oxfordshire. He is first mentioned acting as an attorney in a case of 1278. Law reports show that he was a serjeant in the 1293 Kent and 1299 Cambridgeshire eyres, though there is no evidence of his ever being a serjeant in the Westminster bench. Annuity litigation brought by him in the 1285 Oxfordshire eyre suggests that he may have been in practice as a serjeant in local courts in Oxfordshire as early as 1280. Beaufou's first appointment to a judicial commission was in 1302. Between June 1304 and October 1307 he acted as assize justice for a circuit of ten midland counties with William Mortimer. In the Lent parliament of 1305 he was one of the triers of petitions from Ireland and Guernsey. In 1305, 1306, and 1307 he travelled the large western circuit of that day, which stretched from Cornwall to Hampshire and extended north to Staffordshire and Shropshire, as a trailbaston justice. The popular odium which he excited, and of which memory is preserved by a line, 'Spigurnel e Belflour sunt gens de cruelte', in a ballad of the time celebrating the doings of the commission (Aspin, 73–6), proves him to have displayed vigour in the performance of his duty. Between November 1307 and July 1309 he was an assize justice with John Batesford (and later also John Foxley) in an eight-county circuit covering the south and south-west.

In 1293, with Nicholas of Blewbury, Beaufou acquired the manor of Barford St John in Oxfordshire for 500 marks, and by 1297 he had also acquired a substantial holding at Little Barford in the same county. By 1294 he also owned a house in London close to St Paul's. He died between January and July 1309, and was survived by a widow named Joan and two sons, Thomas (of Hartwell) and Roger, and a daughter Katherine, who had been married to John of Monmouth, a royal tenant-in-chief who had died before coming of age. A third son, Fulk, mentioned with Roger in litigation of 1293 relating to a holding at Denton in Oxfordshire which they had acquired jointly, had probably predeceased him.　　PAUL BRAND

Sources Chancery records · PRO, common bench plea rolls, CP 40 · PRO, eyre and assize rolls, JUST 1 · court of common pleas, feet of fines, PRO, CP 25/1 · patent rolls, PRO, C 66 · VCH Oxfordshire, 5.297 · R. R. Sharpe, ed., Calendar of wills proved and enrolled in the court of husting, London, AD 1258 – AD 1688, 1 (1889), 208 · I. S. T. Aspin, ed., Anglo-Norman political songs, Anglo-Norman Texts, 11 (1953), 73–6 · unpublished law reports of the reign of Edward I, including BL MSS

Beaufou, William de. See William (fl. 1085–1091).

Beaufoy, Henry Hanbury (1750–1795), politician, was born in November 1750 at Cuper's Bridge, Lambeth, Surrey, the second child and eldest son of Mark Beaufoy (1718–1782), a distiller and vinegar brewer, and his wife, Elizabeth (c.1720–1772), the daughter of Capel Hanbury of Bristol. He had three sisters, two of whom died in infancy, and two brothers, both of whom outlived him. One was the astronomer Mark *Beaufoy. His father ran a family brewing business, with premises at Lambeth and a residence at Clifton, near Bristol. His family were Quakers, and their strong identification with protestant dissent coloured his whole career. Accordingly, he was educated at the dissenting academy at Hoxton (1765–7), where one of his tutors was the celebrated dissenting minister and author Andrew Kippis. His progress at school indicated an intelligent and perhaps precocious mind, if not the brilliance claimed by the family biographer. Beaufoy was afterwards a student at Warrington Academy (1767–70) and at Edinburgh University (1772–3). Such was his commitment to dissenting education that, in 1786, he joined the committee for the establishment of a new dissenting academy at Hackney and contributed £100 to its funds.

In 1770 Beaufoy eloped with and subsequently married Elizabeth, the daughter and coheir of William Jenks, of Shifnal, Shropshire. The religious differences between their families, for the Jenkses were Anglicans, had prevented the couple from obtaining consent to their marriage, but Beaufoy conformed to the Church of England, at least nominally, immediately afterwards. In 1775 he became a partner in his father's business of Beaufoy, Biddle, and James, yet he never became involved in the detailed work of the firm and set out instead to achieve a parliamentary career. Such was his eagerness to find a seat in the House of Commons that he made repeated solicitations to the earl of Shelburne at the time of the general election of 1780 and was willing to provide funds for this purpose. In the event no suitable vacancy occurred in 1780, and he did not become an MP until March 1783, when, through Shelburne's help, he was elected, at the cost of £3000, in a by-election at Minehead. He subsequently composed an interesting memorandum about his efforts to secure a parliamentary seat.

In parliament, Beaufoy quickly became a frequent speaker. He showed his political sympathies by voting against the India Bill of the Fox–North coalition in November 1783. When the ministry of William Pitt the younger was formed in the following month, Beaufoy became one of its regular supporters. According to the shrewd parliamentary observer Sir Nathaniel Wraxall, however, 'he nevertheless preserved his independence of character, and might be esteemed rather a friend than a follower of the Minister' (Historical and Posthumous Memoirs, 4.139). At the general election of 1784 he was returned for Great Yarmouth, a popular constituency, where he benefited both from public feeling against the coalition and from the support of a group of dissenters in the constituency. His particular interests in the House of Commons were public finance, the East India Company, the fishing industry, and the civil liberties of dissenters. He became director of the Society for British Fisheries in 1786, and received a presentation and address from the Highland Society. His breadth of knowledge on commercial subjects was praised by Wraxall, and he compiled six folio volumes on 'Navigation, commerce and revenue of Great Britain, 1771–1783'.

It was his advocacy of the repeal of the Test and Corporation Acts in 1787–90, however, which brought Beaufoy most public attention. On 28 March 1787 he accepted an invitation from the protestant dissenting deputies to move a parliamentary motion for repeal, and his speech was not only widely reported but published in pamphlet form. His motion was defeated, but on 8 May 1789 he moved a similar motion which failed by only twenty votes. Again his speech was published. The following year, while having yielded the honour of moving the motion for repeal to Charles James Fox, he remained committed to the cause, and pledged himself to the endorsement of 'a proposal that is obviously supported by every principle of justice and of genuine wisdom' (Davis, 45). He spoke on the subject in the debate of 2 March 1790, and, despite the overwhelming defeat of the motion for repeal, received the warm thanks of dissenters.

Although Pitt had opposed the motions on the Test Act

he did not take Beaufoy's advocacy amiss, and in 1791 recognized the latter's expertise on Indian affairs by appointing him secretary to the Board of Control, an office which he held until 1793. Beaufoy, for his part, joined Pitt in supporting the efforts to secure abolition of the British slave trade, voting for abolition in 1791 and speaking in favour of gradual abolition in 1792. He contributed to the publication of the proceedings of the Association for Promoting the Discovery of the Interior Parts of Africa (1788 and 1790). The tendency for voting lists of oppositional, rather than ministerial, MPs to survive in this period explains why only ten votes for him are recorded by Donald E. Ginter in *Voting Records of the British House of Commons, 1761–1820* (2. 102); in fact his parliamentary activity was far more extensive.

In November 1794 Beaufoy was summoned as a witness by John Horne Tooke at his trial for treason at the Old Bailey. Tooke exposed Beaufoy's faulty memory when taxing him with an earlier connection with the Constitutional Club. The experience was an uncomfortable one for Beaufoy, who had to submit to Tooke's taunts, as well as to claims by Tooke that he had only advocated that which Beaufoy himself had previously supported. Whatever the harm to his reputation, however, there is no evidence that the trial damaged his health, as was claimed in some contemporary quarters, for instance, in *The Sun*, on 26 May 1795. Its most significant aspect was probably his reaffirmation of his support for dissenters' causes, although he modestly disclaimed any suggestion that he was their leader.

Beaufoy died at Clifton on 17 May 1795. He was buried shortly thereafter at Ealing, where he had possessed a freehold estate and where there is a memorial to him in the parish church. He was also commemorated at Ealing by a group of almshouses. He had no children, and bequeathed his property, including his house in Great George Street, Westminster, to his wife, his two brothers, and his nephew, while leaving small legacies to his servants. In July 1797 his widow married Joseph Pycroft, a banker from Burton upon Trent. The impression remaining of Beaufoy's political career is that his early advantages—an independent income, speaking ability, and an association with a powerful minister—did not lead to the kind of success which he sought and which might reasonably have been expected. He remained, however, a figure of considerable admiration among dissenters, especially those of a more radical persuasion.

G. M. DITCHFIELD

Sources G. Beaufoy, *Leaves from a beech tree* (1930) · M. M. Drummond, 'Beaufoy, Henry', HoP, *Commons* · R. G. Thorne, 'Beaufoy, Henry', HoP, *Commons* · R. B. Barlow, *Citizenship and conscience: a study in the theory and practice of religious toleration in England during the eighteenth century* (1962) · T. W. Davis, ed., *Committees for the repeal of the Test and Corporation Acts: minutes, 1786–90 and 1827–8*, London RS, 14 (1978) · D. E. Ginter, ed., *Voting records of the British House of Commons, 1761–1820*, 2 (1995), 102 · *The historical and the posthumous memoirs of Sir Nathaniel William Wraxall, 1772–1784*, ed. H. B. Wheatley, 5 vols. (1884), vol. 4, pp. 139–41, 436; vol. 5, p. 141 · B. L. Manning, *The protestant dissenting deputies* (1952), 217–18 · H. McLachlan, *Warrington Academy: its history and influence*, Chetham Society, 107,

new ser. (1943) · A. Lincoln, *Some political and social ideas of English dissent, 1763–1800* (1938) · A. Goodwin, *The friends of liberty: the English democratic movement in the age of the French Revolution* (1979) · J. Ehrman, *The younger Pitt*, 2: *The reluctant transition* (1983) · *GM*, 1st ser., 65 (1795), 445 · *GM*, 1st ser., 67 (1797), 614 · *State trials*, 25.414–18 · *Monthly Repository*, 9 (1809), 268, 290

Archives BL, 'Report by Mr Beaufoy on the [East India] Company's assumption of the revenues of Tanjore in 1790', Add. MS 13691 · Hants. RO, memorandum · NMM, papers relating to fisheries | JRL, Theophilus Lindsey corresp. · PRO, Chatham MSS, 30/8/164

Likenesses T. Gainsborough, oils, c.1785, repro. in J. Hayes, *Thomas Gainsborough* (1980); priv. coll. · W. Ward, mezzotint, pubd c.1797 (after T. Gainsborough), BM, NPG

Wealth at death c.£5000 to brothers, nephew, and servants; leasehold properties at Great George Street and Lambeth, London; freehold estate and house at Castle Bear Hill, Ealing, Middlesex; will, PRO, PROB 11/1260, fols. 190r–192r · also family property at Evesham, Worcestershire

Beaufoy, Mark (1764–1827), astronomer and physicist, was born in the house attached to his father's vinegar brewery at Cuper's Bridge, Lambeth, Surrey, on 4 March 1764, the third and youngest son of Mark Beaufoy (1718–1782), and his wife, Elizabeth (c.1720–1772). Mark Beaufoy sen., of a Bristol Quaker family, had moved his enterprise to Lambeth, on the south bank of the Thames, where it stood until demolished for the construction of the Strand, now Waterloo, bridge.

Beaufoy was taught by William Bayly, who had been astronomer on Cook's third voyage, and probably instilled in his pupil a lifelong interest in mathematics and astronomy. At twenty years of age he eloped with his cousin Margaretta (d. 1800), daughter of Benjamin Beaufoy, who as a Quaker objected strongly to this liaison between two minors. The couple married at Gretna Green on 12 August 1784, and Mark Beaufoy was later deemed to have left the Quaker community by virtue of this marriage. In December that year the Beaufoys crossed the channel and lived in Neuchâtel, Switzerland, where their two eldest children were born. In the summer of 1787 Beaufoy, his wife, and infants went to Chamonix where he hoped to climb Mont Blanc, which had been scaled for the first time the previous year, and by Horace-Bénédict de Saussure a few days before Beaufoy arrived. With ten guides and three days' provisions, Beaufoy set out, unwisely clad only in loose fitting white trousers and white jacket, to throw off the sun's rays. He also rejected the guides' advice to shield his face and eyes, and consequently suffered from sunburn and snow blindness. Despite mountain sickness and bitter cold, the party reached the summit, making Beaufoy the first Englishman to climb Europe's highest peak. On return to England the family lived in Beaufoy's brother Henry *Beaufoy's house in Great George Street, Westminster, where five more children were born, not all surviving infancy. They moved to Hackney Wick about 1795, where two more children were born. Beaufoy was elected to the Royal Society in February 1790.

Beaufoy made his first experiments on the resistance of solids moving through water before he was fifteen. Hearing a mathematician say that a cone met less resistance when drawn base first he procured a wooden cone and, testing it in the cooler of his father's brewhouse, discovered the fallacy of this statement. He was a founder member, in 1791, of the Society for the Improvement of Naval Architecture, set up in recognition of the British inferiority to France in shipbuilding. One of its first acts was to offer £100 or a gold medal to anyone ascertaining the laws of resistance of water, a challenge accepted by Beaufoy. He was allowed free use of Greenland Dock in 1793 and, during the winter months over the next five or six years, he timed the speed of towed wooden models of different shapes. Beaufoy gleaned his rather hazy theory of fluid motion from William Emerson's *Principles of Mechanics* (2nd edn, 1758). He was a patient observer and collector of data, rather than an original or able theoretician; nevertheless he was the first Englishman experimentally to investigate Bouguer's theory of metacentric stability. With the aid of the mathematician Charles Hutton, also a member of the society, techniques were devised to analyse the data from the 1671 runs that were deemed successful. Margaretta Beaufoy was an excellent mathematician and greatly assisted Beaufoy in his calculations. A definitive report was submitted in 1800, with summaries later in other publications. Beaufoy's work was known and consulted by the steamship pioneer Samuel Fulton, but wider recognition followed only when Beaufoy's son Henry published the experiments in 1834 at a time when steam propulsion was becoming practicable. Eventually Beaufoy's name became established as the person who had demonstrated the friction component of a ship's resistance.

The Beaufoys, notwithstanding their Quaker origins, had a taste for military life. Mark Beaufoy's brother was a major, his own two sons were officers in guards regiments. Beaufoy himself was in 1799 gazetted colonel in the 1st Royal Tower Hamlets militia, but was later brought before a court martial which was unusual because the charges comprised breaches of the whole system of military economy. They apparently arose from Beaufoy's disciplining in 1811 of a Lieutenant Scott, an action condemned as vexatious and frivolous; it was Scott who laid charges against Beaufoy which led to the court martial. Beaufoy stood trial at Whitehall on 26 October 1813. The process lasted a month and produced a sensation in military circles. The charges included enlisting unfit men and foreigners, poaching recruits from outside his area, allowing illegal deductions from militiamen's allowances, showing prejudice, and generally mismanaging the economy of his militia. In January 1814 both Scott and Beaufoy were relieved of their commands.

Beaufoy was one of several scientists associated with the Royal Society who were closely monitoring changes in the earth's magnetic field, from which cycles of diurnal and seasonal variation were identified. He published observations showing that the epoch of maximum westerly deviation in England was in March 1819, when the magnetic needle pointed 24° 42′ west of true north. In 1815 Beaufoy moved to Bushey Heath, Hertfordshire, where between 1818 and 1826 he observed some 180 immersions

and emersions of Jupiter's satellites, a series which was the more valuable because all the observations were undertaken by one person using the same instrument, a 5 foot Dollond refractor. The Astronomical Society published his results and on 11 April 1827 awarded him its silver medal. Illness prevented him from accepting it in person; he died at Bushey on 4 May 1827, and was buried at Great Stanmore.   ANITA McCONNELL

Sources G. Beaufoy, *Leaves from a beech tree* (1930) · *Silliman's American Journal*, 28 (1835), 340–7 · *GM*, 1st ser., 97/1 (1827), 476 · R. J. Goulden, 'The court-martial of Colonel Mark Beaufoy in 1813', *Guildhall Miscellany*, 4 (1971–3), 36–43 · *The Times* (2 Feb 1814), 4a–b · B. Ken, *The dispossessed* (1974) · will of Mark Beaufoy sen., 1782, PRO, PROB 4/1091 · will of Mark Beaufoy, 1827, PRO, PROB 2/1728 · M. Beaufoy, *Nautical and hydraulic experiments* (1834) · T. Wright, 'Mark Beaufoy's nautical and hydraulic experiments', *Mariner's Mirror*, 75 (1989), 313, 327 · M. Beaufoy, 'Narrative of a journey from the village of Chamouni, in Switzerland, to the summit of Mount Blanc, undertaken on Aug. 8, 1787', *Annals of Philosophy*, 9 (1817), 97–103 · H. D. Howse, 'The Royal Astronomical Society instrument collection, 1827–1985', *Quarterly Journal of the Royal Astronomical Society*, 27 (1986), 212–36
Likenesses H. Brett, silhouette, stipple, pubd 1834, NPG
Wealth at death under £18,000: PRO, death duty registers, IR 26/1115, 726; will, 1827, PRO, PROB 2/1728

Beaulieu, Henrietta de. *See* Johnston, Henrietta (*c*.1674–1729).

Beaulieu, Luke de (1644/5–1723), Church of England clergyman and religious writer, was a native of France, and was educated at the University of Saumur. Obliged to leave his country on account of his religion he sought refuge in England about 1667 and was naturalized English in June 1682. He rapidly gained a reputation as a cleric, and in November 1670 he received the vicarage of Upton-cum-Chalvey, Buckinghamshire, which he kept until 1681. About 1670 he was also elected divinity reader in the chapel of St George at Windsor. In 1683 he was appointed chaplain to the infamous Judge George Jeffreys, an office which he continued to hold until the revolution of 1688 brought his patron's career to a close. Meanwhile he had become a student at Oxford in 1680; he took the degree of BD on 7 July 1685 at Christ Church, and in October 1686 he was presented by Jeffreys to the rectory of Whitchurch, near Reading. He was made prebendary of St Paul's on 17 January 1687 and, on the following 21 May, prebendary of Gloucester, promotions which he again owed to Jeffreys, now lord chancellor.

Beaulieu published various pieces against Roman Catholicism as well as some sermons on public occasions. His principal work was a manual of devotion, *Claustrum animae, the Reformed Monastery, or, The Love of Jesus* (1677), which was reprinted in 1678 and again in 1865. It is dedicated in gratitude to Dr John Fell, bishop of Oxford and dean of Christ Church, to whom Beaulieu later became chaplain.

Beaulieu died on 26 May 1723, aged seventy-eight, at Whitchurch, where he was buried on 30 May and where his wife, Priscilla, was buried on 5 December 1728. Their son, George de Beaulieu, matriculated at his father's college, Christ Church, on 29 April 1703, aged eighteen, took his BA degree in 1708, and entered into holy orders. He was buried with his parents on 17 May 1736.

GORDON GOODWIN, rev. EMMA MAJOR

Sources Foster, *Alum. Oxon.*, 1500–1714 [Luke Beaulieu] · *ESTC* · private information (1885) · Wood, *Ath. Oxon.*, new edn, 4.668 · G. Lipscomb, *The history and antiquities of the county of Buckingham*, 4 vols. (1831–47), vol. 4, p. 573 · *Fasti Angl.* (Hardy), 1.450; 2.443 · D. C. A. Agnew, *Protestant exiles from France in the reign of Louis XIV, or, The Huguenot refugees and their descendants in Great Britain and Ireland*, 2nd edn, 1 (1871), 30, 42; 3 (1874), 19 · *N&Q*, 2nd ser., 10 (1860), 307 · *N&Q*, 3rd ser., 7 (1865), 37–8

Beauman, (Archibald) Bentley (1888–1977), army officer, was born on 30 November 1888 in Paddington, London, the eldest son of Bentley Martin Beauman, a stockbroker. He was educated at Malvern College and Sandhurst and was commissioned into the South Staffordshire regiment in 1908. He joined the 2nd battalion in South Africa in the same year. After serving in South Africa and England he landed in France with the 2nd battalion South Staffordshire in 1914 with the original expeditionary force, but was wounded in the first battle of Ypres in November 1914 and invalided home.

After recovering from his wounds Beauman returned to France in January 1915 and became adjutant of the 1st battalion. When his commanding officer became ill during the battle of Neuve Chapelle in 1915, Beauman commanded the battalion, and though only a captain at the time held the temporary rank of acting lieutenant-colonel. He was wounded again near Hooge later in the year and then served on the staff as deputy assistant adjutant and quartermaster-general (a major) before returning to command the 1st battalion during the battle of the Somme in 1916.

In May 1918 he was promoted to command 69th infantry brigade in Italy, and thus achieved the temporary rank of brigadier-general at the age of twenty-nine. He was awarded a DSO during the battle of the Somme and earned a bar to it during the third battle of Ypres (Passchendaele) the following year. He was also mentioned six times in dispatches and received the Italian silver medal for valour and the Italian cross of war.

In 1919 Beauman commanded the 20th Durham light infantry, in 1920 he took the course at the Staff College, Camberley, and from 1921 to 1925 he served on the staff in Baluchistan district, India. In 1926 he became chief instructor in tactics and military history at the Royal Military Academy, Woolwich, and he then commanded the 1st battalion York and Lancaster regiment in Northern Ireland from 1928 to 1932.

From 1932 to 1936 he was assistant commandant and chief instructor at the Netheravon wing of the Small Arms School, and from 1934 to 1938 he commanded 15 infantry brigade in Palestine. This last appointment involved active service during the Arab revolt and earned him a CBE and a further mention in dispatches. In 1938 he was aide-de-camp to the king. In that year he married Eva

Pullar (*d.* 1949). They had a son (who predeceased him) and a daughter.

Although he retired from active service in 1938, Beauman was recalled in September 1939 and appointed commander, Cherbourg area. In 1940 he was promoted major-general to command northern district, lines of communication (including the defence of airfields), British expeditionary force. During and after the Dunkirk evacuation he commanded an improvised formation made up of miscellaneous troops gathered from the rear areas and named Beauforce, which later became Beauman division. Despite the circumstances Beauforce fought a creditable and gallant rearguard action. Beauman was mentioned in dispatches twice more at this time. After returning from France he commanded Sheffield sub-area and from 1942 to 1944 North Riding district.

After the war Beauman, who had always been a keen horseman, acted for a time as a racing correspondent. He was an excellent cricketer and a keen fisherman. A popular and much respected commander, he was particularly good as a trainer of troops. In 1919 he wrote a booklet, *With the 38th in France and Italy*—38 being the original number of the 1st Staffordshire regiment—which gave a vivid account of his regiment's First World War experiences, and a book of reminiscences entitled *Then a Soldier* (1960). In 1939 he published *Common Mistakes in the Solution of Tactical Problems*.

On 24 June 1952 Beauman married Barbara Gwendoline Arnold (*b.* 1907/8), who survived him. He died at his home, Orwell, Nursery Road, Walton on the Hill, Tadworth, Surrey, on 22 March 1977 at the age of eighty-eight.

PHILIP WARNER

Sources private information (2004) [material supplied by the Staffordshire regiment (now Prince of Wales's)] · *WW* · L. F. Ellis, *The war in France and Flanders, 1939–1940* (1953) · A. B. Beauman, *Then a soldier* (1960) · m. cert. [Barbara Gwendoline Arnold] · d. cert. · B. Karslake, *1940: the last act: the story of the British forces in France after Dunkirk* (1979)
Archives SOUND IWM SA, Military operations, 1914–19, 1973, 40

Beaumanoir, Philippe de. *See* Rémi, Philippe de (1250–1296), *under* Rémi (1205x10–1265).

Beaumont, Agnes (*bap.* 1652, *d.* 1720), religious autobiographer, was born in Edworth, Bedfordshire, where she was baptized Ann on 1 September 1652, the youngest of seven children (of whom three died in infancy) of John Beaumont, yeoman farmer of Edworth, and his wife, Mary Pakes of Pirton, Hertfordshire. Agnes was the author of a brief but vividly written autobiographical account describing events leading up to and following the death in 1674 of her father, whom she was accused of having poisoned with the help of the separatist minister John Bunyan, a crime for which, had she been convicted, she could have been burnt at the stake.

Her family was strongly nonconformist, and in 1672, having come under the spell of Bunyan's preaching, Agnes joined a congregation of his at Gamlingay. Her father had turned against Bunyan, however, and when he heard that she had ridden behind him to a meeting, he locked her out of the house for two days. When she promised not to attend any more meetings without his permission, they were reconciled, but he died the same night, probably of a heart attack, with only Agnes in the house. A former suitor, Mr Feery, the family lawyer, maliciously suggested that she had murdered him, and her brother had to summon from a neighbouring village a coroner and jury, which cleared her of any guilt. Rumours that she was carrying on an illicit relationship with Bunyan persisted for some time, and in the following year Feery also accused her of having set fire to a house in Edworth. Again these allegations were dismissed, but Bunyan was deeply disturbed by the continuing rumours of sexual misconduct, and added a section to a later edition of his own autobiography, *Grace Abounding to the Chief of Sinners* (1666), vehemently denying them.

In her middle life Beaumont was married twice: first, in 1702, to Thomas Warren of Cheshunt, a landowning gentleman who died in 1707 leaving her half his estate; then, in 1708, to Samuel Storey, a prosperous London fishmonger, who survived her. She died on 28 November 1720 and was buried at her own request near the minister John Wilson, in the yard of the Tilehouse Street Baptist meeting in Hitchin. She had contributed towards the cost of erecting the church building in 1692, and may have been a member before her marriage. Her autobiography remained in manuscript but copies began to circulate, and in 1760 it was published in a frequently reprinted collection of nonconformist conversion narratives. It is a rare example of the genre at this social level in the seventeenth century, and illustrates the power of radical religious belief to inspire resistance to patriarchal authority.

W. R. OWENS

Sources BL, Egerton MSS 2414 and 2128 · S. James, *An abstract of the gracious dealings of God with several eminent Christians* (1760); 9th edn, ed. I. James (1824) · *The narrative of the persecution of Agnes Beaumont in the year 1674*, ed. G. B. Harrison (1929) · *The narrative of the persecutions of Agnes Beaumont*, ed. V. J. Camden (1992)

Beaumont, Basil (1669–1703), naval officer, was the fifth son, among the twenty-one children, of Sir Henry Beaumont, second baronet (1638–1689), of Stoughton Grange and Cole Orton, Leicestershire, a distant cousin of the duke of Buckingham, and his wife, Elizabeth (d. 1727), daughter of George Farmer of Holbeach. Beaumont served as a king's letter boy from 1684 until 1687, and on 28 October 1688 he was appointed lieutenant of the *Portsmouth*. On 21 April 1689 he was promoted captain of the *Centurion*, which was lost in Plymouth Sound in a violent storm on 25 December of the same year. Although Beaumont was a young captain, no blame was attached to him. Because of this, and the patronage of Arthur Herbert, earl of Torrington, he was appointed some weeks later to the *Foresight*, in December 1690 to the *Dreadnought*, and early in 1692 to the *Rupert*, in which he took part in the battle of Barfleur in May 1692. He continued in the *Rupert* during the following year, and in 1694 commanded the *Canterbury* in the Mediterranean.

In 1696 Beaumont commanded the *Mountagu*, in the fleet cruising in the channel and off Ushant, and while detached for a short time as commodore of an inshore squadron, he destroyed some small craft in Camaret Bay. He was afterwards transferred, at short intervals, to the *Plymouth*, *Neptune*, and *Duke*, while in command of the squadron off Dunkirk, during the remainder of 1696 and until the peace of Ryswick (1697). In November 1698 he was appointed to the *Resolution*, and in 1699 he was senior officer at Spithead, until the ship was paid off at the end of August. He commissioned her again some months later and continued in her for the next two years, commanding in the Downs for much of the time and canvassing unsuccessfully for promotion to flag rank. In June 1702 he moved to the *Tilbury*; thereafter he continued to command the squadron in the Downs, at the Nore, and off Dunkirk until, on 1 March 1703, he was promoted rear-admiral, and hoisted his flag on board the *Mary*, then fitting out at Woolwich. Only his rank, not his service, was altered. During the summer he cruised in the North Sea and off Dunkirk, and convoyed the Baltic trade; on the approach of winter he returned to the Downs, where he anchored on 19 October. He was still there on 27 November when the great storm of 1703 hurled the ship on to the Goodwin Sands with the loss of every man, Beaumont included.

The dramatic circumstances of Beaumont's death have given him a posthumous fame which his previous, relatively undistinguished, career had done little to justify. Although he attained flag rank comparatively rapidly, and at the relatively early age of thirty-four, such progress was not uncommon in an age when advancement depended to a considerable extent on the workings of patronage. His death was also devastating for his family, or so his mother claimed when she petitioned Queen Anne for a pension in 1704: he had allegedly been the sole support for his two younger brothers and six sisters, three other brothers having already died in public service, two of them in the navy (William, who died of a fever in the West Indies in 1697, and Charles, blown up in the *Carlisle* in 1700). The six daughters were each granted £50 a year as a result of her request.

J. K. LAUGHTON, *rev.* J. D. DAVIES

Sources J. Charnock, ed., *Biographia navalis*, 2 (1795), 217–20 · NMM, Sergison MSS, SER/136 · *CSP dom.*, 1703–4, 611 · W. L. Clowes, *The Royal Navy: a history from the earliest times to the present*, 7 vols. (1897–1903); repr. (1996–7), vol. 2, pp. 487, 504 · J. Ehrman, *The navy in the war of William III, 1689–1697* (1953) · list of services, PRO, ADM/6/424 · list of recommendations, 1692, PRO, ADM/8/2 · Bodl. Oxf., MS Rawl. 186, fol. 78 · GEC, *Baronetage*

Archives NMM · PRO

Likenesses M. Dahl, oils, NMM

Beaumont, Charles-Louis Leopold Alfred de [*formerly* Alfred Leopold Charles de Beaumont Klein] (1902–1972), fencer, was born at 26 Alexandra Drive, Toxteth Park, Liverpool, on 5 May 1902, the son of Louis Leopold Martial Baynard de Beaumont Klein (1849–1934) and his wife, Kathleen Mary O'Hagan (1876–1974), the daughter of Thomas O'Hagan, first Baron O'Hagan. Klein, a French academic and formerly a Jesuit priest, had been employed by the O'Hagan family to tutor their daughter. In 1913, fearing anti-German prejudice, he changed his name by deed poll to de Beaumont, his mother's maiden name.

Charles de Beaumont and his two elder sisters, Elizabeth and Marguerite, accompanied their parents on regular trips to France and Italy. The family settled in Norfolk and until his tenth year Charles was tutored at home. Eventually he attended the Perse School and entered Trinity College, Cambridge, in 1920, where he took a third in the natural sciences tripos in 1923. He was a keen boxer, huntsman, dancer, banjo player, and boy scout (his mother helped found the Girl Guides), but gravitated to fencing, for which he won his blue.

After university de Beaumont spent a year in Milan. Here he studied under some of the best fencing masters of the day. On his return to Britain he married a family friend and fellow scout, Guinevere Madi Grove-Crofts (d. 1969), daughter of Lieutenant-Colonel James Grove-Crofts. Although the couple had a son, Robin, by 1926 they had separated. Charles moved to Glasgow, and in 1927 won both the Scottish sabre and épée championships. In 1930 he won the leading 'open' épée event in Britain, the Miller-Hallett cup, and was chosen to fence at the European championships (forerunner of the world championships) at Liège. He was also elected to the main committee of the Amateur Fencing Association (AFA), the organization that ran the sport in Britain. In the following year a complete set of rules for fencing appeared in French, and he translated them into English for use throughout the Commonwealth. At the height of his powers as a competitor, he won the Miller-Hallett three years running (1930, 1931, 1932) and again in 1934–5 and 1938; he also came second in 1929 and 1936.

In 1933, aged thirty-one, de Beaumont was made captain of the British team, a post he retained until his death thirty-nine years later. At the world championships in that year, in Budapest, he gained a sabre team bronze medal and missed the final of the individual épée by a single hit, probably as the result of a fight fixed between two of his opponents. His captaincy was also an immediate success: a member of the British team (Gwen Nelligan) won the women's foil title. In 1936 he captained the team at the Berlin Olympics; he himself competed at these controversial games and at those of 1948, 1952, and 1956.

Outside fencing de Beaumont's chosen career was in antiques. His main shop was Gloria Antica, at 170 Brompton Road, London, two minutes' walk from his home in the heart of Knightsbridge. He would travel to fencing competitions in his trademark Bentley, stopping off at shops along the way and piling his purchases into the back seat.

During the war, plagued by poor eyesight, de Beaumont worked on barrage balloons and for combined operations, ending as a wing commander. While stationed in Whitehall he met Paula Holdsworth, a young Wren. She soon joined him in his antiques business, and moved into his Knightsbridge home. They had a daughter, Caroline, and were married a couple of years before his death.

De Beaumont served two terms as president of the British Antiques Federation, and in 1972 was elected president of the World Antique Federation. He was a man of boundless energy, and found time to deal in property, found a wine company, write treatises on his family's history—which with some justice he believed could be traced back to the French crown—and even dabble in politics: he actively supported Sir Oswald Mosley, a fellow international épéeist, when Mosley founded the New Party in the 1930s.

De Beaumont's career as an active fencer was long. He won the national épée title four times, in 1936, 1937, 1938, and again in 1953, on the last occasion when aged over fifty. He also captained the English team in many Commonwealth games; in 1950, at forty-eight, he won the épée gold medal at the first British Commonwealth championships, in New Zealand. It was, however, as an administrator that he contributed most. He was secretary of the AFA from 1933 until he became president in 1956, and effectively ran the sport as a one-man band. Under his care a British fencer won the world épée title in 1958, and the following year the foil title. In Melbourne in 1956 the entire British Olympic team won only two gold medals—but one was at fencing, the women's individual title (won by Gillian Sheen). By 1960 the British team was judged third strongest in the world.

De Beaumont organized a national training scheme, and oversaw the building of a national headquarters for fencing, at the back of the Queen's Club in West Kensington, inevitably christened the De Beaumont Centre. In 1964 he was commandant of the entire British team at the Tokyo Olympics; he later became deputy chairman of the British Olympic Association, as well as serving on other key sports committees that stretched far beyond fencing. He wrote eight books on his chosen sport, and was equally at home on an international committee discussing the finer points of sporting politics or clearing away garbage at the end of a local fencing competition. He died, at home, 44 Montpelier Street, London, on 7 July 1972 from cancer, just before taking a British fencing team to another Olympics, which would have been his eighth as captain. He was buried at Bewerly, near Pateley Bridge, Yorkshire, and was survived by his second wife.

For nearly forty years Charles de Beaumont was the most important figure in British fencing and, in the words of Mary Glen Haig, his immediate successor as AFA president, 'did more for fencing than any one individual will ever be able to do again' (Gray, foreword). Sartorially elegant, always with a red rose in his buttonhole, his fencing socks topped in rings of red, white, and blue, his upper lip sporting a fine moustache, de Beaumont symbolized the fair-minded Englishman abroad for several generations of fencers worldwide.   RICHARD COHEN

Sources E. Gray, *Modern British fencing: a history of the Amateur Fencing Association, 1964–81* (1981) [memorial volume to Charles de Beaumont, including a short biography by R. Cohen] · *The Sword* (1947–72) · personal records and scrapbooks, esp. privately published memoir by Katherine de Beaumont, priv. coll. · *The Times* (1972) · private information (2004) [Paula de Beaumont, widow] · Burke, *Peerage* [O'Hagan] · b. cert. · d. cert.

Wealth at death £226,875: probate, 6 Nov 1972, *CGPLA Eng. & Wales*

Beaumont, Cyril William (1891–1976), dance historian and critic, was born on 1 November 1891 at 37 Stockwell Park Crescent, Lambeth, the eldest of three children of Frederick John Beaumont and his wife, Mary Henrietta Balchin. His father was an engineer and the son of an inventor, and was involved with the entertainment business as a prestidigitator and cinematographer. His mother's family had links with northern France, as her father was a racehorse trainer at Chantilly.

Having failed in his matriculation examination, which prevented him from becoming a research chemist as he had hoped, Beaumont began his career as a bookseller. In 1910 his father bought him a run-down bookshop—75 Charing Cross Road, London—where he worked for fifty-five years. Here he met Alice Mari Beha, already working in the book trade, whom he kept on as his assistant and whom he married on 10 December 1914. He soon specialized in first editions, association copies, and de luxe and private-press volumes. He also sold lithographs, art postcards, and magazines, and helped to popularize post-impressionist art. In 1917 he established the Beaumont Press when he published *Tides*, a volume of poems by John Drinkwater. Among other prestigious authors whose work he published, often in volumes illustrated by notable artists, were D. H. Lawrence and Arthur Symons. He also wrote children's stories, including *The Mysterious Toyshop* (1924) and *The Wonderful Journey* (1927).

Beaumont, who had a general interest in theatre, developed a passion for classical ballet when Alice took him to see Anna Pavlova and Michel Mordkin at the Palace Theatre, London, in April 1911. In the following year, in June, he saw Serge Diaghilev's innovative Ballets Russes, a company he did much to promote. Before the First World War he published portfolios of lithographs of Diaghilev's great star, Vaslav Nijinsky, by Robert Montenegro and Georges Barbier, and the first of a series of wooden cut-out figures of dancers. He also introduced to Britain souvenir programmes for the Ballets Russes based on those published by *Comoedia Illustré* in Paris. Subsequently he published Impressions of the Russian Ballet, a series of booklets, each devoted to an individual work, for which he repeatedly viewed the ballets to ensure accurate descriptions and had his illustrators look closely at the actual sets and costumes to ensure correct documentation.

It is in respect of this very precise documentation that Beaumont's writing has proved so valuable. He noted how productions changed over a number of seasons and gave a much richer impression of colour in productions than other commentators. Among his most important books were the *Complete Book of Ballet* (London, 1937; revised 1951) and its supplements, the first comprehensive detailed record of ballets world wide from 1786. He also laid the foundations for the study of the history of dance in English, translating from the French and publishing key dance texts by Noverre, Rameau, and Gautier.

Beaumont was ballet critic of *Dancing World* from 1921 to 1924 and of the *Sunday Times* from 1950 to 1959; editor of *Dance Journal* from 1924; and a regular contributor to Richard Buckle's *Ballet* and to *Ballet Annual* among many other journals. As a critic he was frustrated by word limits and wrote to formula. This involved giving a detailed description of the ballet and its narrative and appearance, discussing its merits and defects, then considering the contribution of individuals. This worked efficiently for narrative productions, but the method was ridiculed by other writers when used to describe pure dance works. In 1957 Beaumont became the first dance critic to achieve the presidency of the Critics' Circle.

Beaumont, nicknamed Rizhka for his auburn hair, was a regular distinctive, even dandyish visitor backstage during Diaghilev's London seasons, dressing in autumn-coloured velvet jackets and hand-made silk shirts. Apart from his involvement with the Ballets Russes, however, he was remarkably unprejudiced in his writing and aloof from intrigue of the theatre world. He encouraged other critics to be equally unbiased in their work. Impartial in his public utterances, he gave advice that was valued by novice dancers and established choreographers. His shop was a mecca for dancers and lovers of dancing until it closed in 1965.

Although he never trained as a dancer, Beaumont was determined to understand all aspects of the art. Assisted by the virtuoso dancer Stanislav Idzikovsky and supported by the great ballet teacher Enrico Cecchetti, he codified the latter's teaching practice in *A Manual of the Theory and Practice of Classical Theatrical Dancing* (1922). Beaumont was also responsible for founding the Cecchetti Society, which brought him into close contact with professional dancers and teachers. Other books he published focused on design for dance, most notably Vladimir Polunin's *The Continental Method of Scene Painting* (1927).

Having studied the theoretical basis of ballet, Beaumont decided to put his knowledge of ballet into practice and, he hoped, to boost the position of British ballet by attempting to create new works. In 1926 he established the Cremorne Ballet with Flora Fairburn. The project was short-lived, but it involved several emerging talents (Frederick Ashton was among the dancers) and gave Beaumont the insight into production that he desired. Later he remained in the background while providing invaluable advice on productions.

Beaumont collected dance ephemera, and lived among his treasures, many of which he bequeathed to the Theatre Museum at the Victoria and Albert Museum. He was also an authority on military history, period weapons, and uniforms. He was admitted to the Légion d'honneur (1950), and received among other awards the Queen Elizabeth II coronation award of the Royal Academy of Dancing (1962) and the OBE (1962). He died on 24 May 1976 in University College Hospital, London, after a short illness, and was buried at St Pancras cemetery. He was survived by his wife.   JANE PRITCHARD

Sources K. S. Walker, 'Cyril W. Beaumont: bookseller, publisher, and writer on dance', *Dance Chronicle*, 25 (2002), 51–94, 265–302; 447–76 • C. W. Beaumont, *Dancers under my lens: essays in ballet criticism* (1949) • C. Beaumont, *Bookseller at the ballet: memoirs 1891–1929* (1975) • N. Bowden, 'Cyril Beaumont—a birthday tribute', *Dancing Times* (Nov 1972), 79–81 • M. Clarke, *Dancing Times* (July 1976), 533 •

P. Williams, 'Between heaven and Charing Cross', *Dance and Dancers* (July 1951), 8 · *CGPLA Eng. & Wales* (1976)

Archives Theatre Museum, London | V&A, corresp. with A. W. Payne | SOUND Archive of Art and Design

Wealth at death £173,794: probate, 27 July 1976, *CGPLA Eng. & Wales*

Beaumont, Ermengarde de. *See* Ermengarde (*d.* 1233).

Beaumont, Francis (*d.* 1598), judge, was the eldest son of John *Beaumont (*d.* in or after 1556) and his second wife, Elizabeth (*d.* 1588), daughter and coheir of Sir William Hastings of Leicester. John Beaumont, a bencher of the Inner Temple and master of the rolls, was removed from office in 1552 and died in some obscurity, though his two sons, Francis and Henry, were to become benchers of the same inn in their turn. John Beaumont's disgrace had resulted in the confiscation of the family estate at Grace Dieu, in the parish of Belton, Leicestershire, but it had been recovered by Francis's mother and in due course passed to him. At an unknown date Francis married Anne, daughter of Sir George Pierrepoint of Holme Pierrepont, Nottinghamshire, and widow of Thomas Thorold of Marston, Leicestershire.

Francis Beaumont is mentioned as a fellow-commoner of Peterhouse, Cambridge, at the time of the queen's visit in 1564; but he was admitted to the Inner Temple in 1559 or 1560 and called to the bar in 1568. Ten years after call he was elected to the bench of his inn, and delivered a reading in 1571; his brother, Henry, became a bencher in 1580. In 1572 Francis was elected to parliament as member for Aldeburgh, the only occasion on which he served. Nevertheless, although his mother was suspected of harbouring Edmund Campion, whose accomplice Lord Vaux was a relative, and he was thought by reason of his non-attendance at church to have recusant sympathies himself, he continued to rise in the world. In 1589 he was raised to the degree of serjeant-at-law, apparently as a late addition to the general call after no agreement could be reached on a second member from Gray's Inn, his patrons being the earls of Essex, Huntingdon, and Shrewsbury. He joined Serjeants' Inn in Chancery Lane. Then, on 25 January 1593, he was appointed a justice of the common pleas in place of William Peryam. William Burton, the Leicestershire historian and a member of the Inner Temple, described him in his 1622 *Description of Leicestershire* as a 'grave, reverend and learned judge'.

Beaumont remained in office for five years until he died, at Grace Dieu, on 22 April 1598. Although his death occurred at home, it was attributed to gaol fever contracted at Lancaster on the Lent circuit. His fellow commissioner, Serjeant Drew, died at about the same time. Beaumont was buried in Belton church. His wife, Anne, had predeceased him, leaving four children. The eldest son, Henry (1581–1605), was knighted in 1603 but died at the age of twenty-four. The second son was John *Beaumont (*c.*1584–1627) the poet, who succeeded to Grace Dieu and was created a baronet in 1626; and the third son was Francis *Beaumont (1584/5–1616) the renowned dramatist. The baronetcy descended to John's sons but became extinct in 1686. In the judge's brief will, made the day before he died, with a codicil on the day of his death, there is mention of property in Derbyshire as well as Leicestershire, including the manor house of Normanton. His chief legacy was £700 to his only daughter, Elizabeth, who later married Thomas Seyliard of Kent.

J. H. BAKER

Sources HoP, *Commons, 1558–1603*, 1.414–15 · Baker, *Serjeants*, 63, 174, 435, 499 · Sainty, *Judges*, 74 · will, PRO, PROB 11/91, sig. 41 · Cooper, *Ath. Cantab.*, 2.246 · F. Moore, *Cases collect et report per Sir Francis Moore* (1675), 502 · *The letters of John Chamberlain*, ed. N. E. McClure, 1 (1939), 136 · E. Coke, *Le neufme part des reports de Sr. Edw. Coke* (1613), 138 · R. D. Sell, 'Notes on the religious and family background of Francis and Sir John Beaumont', *Neuphilologische Mitteilungen*, 76 (1975), 299–307

Wealth at death £700 legacy to his daughter; plus property in Derbyshire and Leicestershire: will, PRO, PROB 11/91, sig. 41

Beaumont, Francis (1584/5–1616), playwright, was the third son of Francis *Beaumont (*d.* 1598), a judge of the court of common pleas, and younger brother of the poet Sir John *Beaumont (*c.*1584–1627). His mother, Anne Pierrepoint (*d.* in or before 1598), came from a prominent recusant family of Holme Pierrepont, Nottinghamshire. Francis was born at the family seat in Grace Dieu, Leicestershire, where the Beaumonts had long been among the leading county families. Many on both sides of the Beaumont family were recusants and suffered for it, and this suggests that the lack of baptismal records for any of Judge Beaumont's four children resulted from secret baptisms by a Catholic priest.

Oxford and the inns of court Beaumont was admitted to Broadgates Hall (afterwards Pembroke College), Oxford, on 4 February 1597 at the age of twelve. Apparently he left there after the death of his father in 1598. On 3 November 1600 he entered the Inner Temple where, in succession to his grandfather and father, both of his brothers were already resident. Like many inns of court students at this time Beaumont did not study the law seriously, but his satiric 'Grammar Lecture' at the Inner Temple's revels (*c.*1606) indicates that he had been an active and observant participant in the intramural life of the inn; and his selection to write the Inner Temple and Gray's Inn masque for Princess Elizabeth's wedding in 1613 suggests some kind of tie to the Inner Temple throughout his career.

Early in his residence at the inns of court, Beaumont published (anonymously, as was the wont of many gentry writers) the poem *Salmacis and Hermaphroditus* (1602). (The attribution in the unreliable 1640 edition of his poems is confirmed by P. J. Finkelpearl, *N&Q*, 16, 1969, 367–8.) The sophisticated humour and technical proficiency in this tenfold expansion of Ovid's hundred lines by a seventeen-year-old is remarkable. Beaumont wrote a small number of other poems over the next decade, mostly occasional, among them his nostalgic tribute to the brilliant wits at the Mermaid tavern and to his mentor Ben Jonson. Beaumont also praised Jonson in prefatory poems to *Sejanus* (1605) and *Catiline* (1611), and Jonson responded in kind:

> even there, where most thou praysest mee,
> For writing better, I must envie thee.
> (*Ben Jonson*, ed. C. H. Herford, P. Simpson, and E. Simpson, 1947, vol. 8, p. 44, epigram 55)

Jonson's private characterization of Beaumont to

Francis Beaumont (1584/5–1616), by unknown artist

Drummond of Hawthornden reflects another side to their relationship: 'Beaumont loved too much himself and his own verses' (W. Drummond, *Notes of Conversations with Ben Jonson, 1619*, ed. G. B. Harrison, 1923, 8). Beaumont had some reason for his self-regard because very quickly he became one of the most prominent figures in the London theatre world.

Knight of the Burning Pestle But first Beaumont began his theatrical career with a play which its audience 'utterly rejected', ironically the play by which he is best-known today, *The Knight of the Burning Pestle* (1606–7). Written in eight days by a 22 year-old, it is formally the most innovative play in Jacobean drama. It portrays a battle for possession of the stage between the child players, who had ostensibly been planning a satire on the current vogue of bourgeois success plays, and a grocer and his wife who jumped out of the audience to demand that the children stage a chivalric romance with their apprentice as hero. (A connection to *Don Quixote* is evident, but the precise details of how Beaumont knew the novel are murky.) Somehow both 'plays' are presented along with much hilarious contention between the conflicting forces. Sadly, the allegedly sophisticated audience at the private theatre failed to catch the 'privy marke of Ironie', as can be learned from the publisher's preface. Beaumont never again wrote anything so aggressively avant-garde.

A few years after Beaumont's failure, John *Fletcher had a similar experience. His effort at an Italianate pastoral tragicomedy, *The Faithful Shepherdess* (1608–10), was 'before / … [the audience] saw it halfe, damd' (as Jonson said in a

prefatory poem). Both young men had overestimated the aesthetic sophistication of their audiences. Now, perhaps out of economic necessity, they joined forces and together concocted a product that seemed 'new' without being aggressively original. The process of their collaboration, all agree, was made in heaven:

> How Angels …
> Maintaine their parley, Beaumont-Fletcher tels;
> Whose strange unimitable Intercourse
> Transcends all Rules.
> (John Pettus, prefatory poem, *Comedies and Tragedies*, 1647 folio)

The secret of their great success, according to Dryden, was that (unlike Shakespeare) 'they understood and imitated the conversation of gentlemen better; whose wild debaucheries, and quickness of wit in repartee, no poet before them could paint as they have done' (*Essays of John Dryden*, 1.81).

Collaboration with Fletcher At first Beaumont and Fletcher wrote for the 'private' children's acting companies, then *c*.1608–1610 they began their connection with the King's Men at the Globe Theatre. John Aubrey must have been referring to the latter period at the Globe when he said that the friends 'lived together on the Banke side, not far from the Play-house, both batchelors; lay together; had one wench in the house between them, which they did so admire; the same cloathes and cloake, &c. betweene them' (*Brief Lives*, 21).

Even in the seventeenth century the notion of what 'Beaumont and Fletcher' denoted was quite hazy. Their first folio of 1647, *Comedies and Tragedies written by Francis Beaumont and John Fletcher, Gentlemen*, clearly designed to rival the impressive folios of Shakespeare and Jonson, contained thirty-four plays and a masque; eighteen more plays were added in the second folio (1679). The implication that all these plays are collaborations by Beaumont and Fletcher is vastly misleading. Of the folio plays, Fletcher wrote at least sixteen alone; two or three were done with Shakespeare; probably eleven with Philip Massinger; ten or so with the involvement of as many as eight other writers. Beaumont wrote alone just *The Knight* and a masque. Thus only about nine plays of the vast canon were products of the famous collaboration. (Much on this topic is guesswork. The best job of untangling the probably insoluble problems of the canon is a series of articles by Cyrus Hoy, 'The shares of Fletcher and his collaborators in the Beaumont and Fletcher canon', *Studies in Bibliography*, 1956–62. See also the definitive edition edited by Fredson Bowers, *Beaumont and Fletcher, Dramatic Works*, 10.751–2, for a tentative list of ascriptions.)

Regarding the division of labour within a play, much on the topic is based on gossip or guesswork. One contemporary maintained that Beaumont's 'maine businesse was to correct the overflowings of Mr. Fletcher's luxuriant Fancy and flowing witt' (John Earle, quoted in *Brief Lives*, 21); Robert Herrick stated that Fletcher designed the plots (see Herrick's commendatory verses in the 1647 folio); and Dryden thought that Beaumont was such a master of plotting that even Ben Jonson 'submitted all his writings to his [Beaumont's] censure and 'tis thought, used his judgment in correcting, if not contriving, his plots' (*Essays of John Dryden*, 1.68). The problem, as John Aubrey said, is that there was such a 'wonderfull consimility of phansey' (*Brief Lives*, 21) between the collaborators that even an acute critic like Coleridge admitted that he could not distinguish Beaumont's writing from Fletcher's. As George Lisle said in the 1647 folio:

> For still your fancies are so wov'n and knit,
> 'Twas FRANCIS FLETCHER, or JOHN BEAUMONT writ.

Plays for the children's companies Of the nine plays written in collaboration, five were written for children's companies: one for the Children of Paul's, four for the Queen's Revels company. Like many of the children's plays they tend to be set at courts inhabited by perverse characters in bizarre situations: in *The Woman Hater* (c.1606) the main characters are a psychotic misogynist and a comical glutton-epicure; in *The Coxcomb* (1608–10), a fool who virtually forces his best friend to cuckold him; in *The Noble Gentleman* (c.1611–15) the absurd eponymous hero is obsessed with obtaining a title while in the sub-plot a madman suffers from love melancholy. The one tragedy, *Cupid's Revenge* (1610–12), is perhaps the most perverse: a stepmother tries to seduce a stepson to commit incest, the stepson is so honour-bound that he's willing to be executed rather than reveal her misconduct to his father the king, and his princess sister dies of love for a misshapen dwarf.

None of these early plays had much impact except for the immensely popular *The Scornful Lady* (1608–10) for which ten quartos were printed in the seventeenth century. Dryden admired its plot as 'almost exactly formed' and Waller praised it highly, but its success must have come from a nearly total identification of values between the authors and a significant portion of the Blackfriars audience. It is a play about and for young gallants, imitating and sanctioning without much criticism their very tones and manners, their crass vulgarity as well as their liveliness and wit. The plays of Beaumont and Fletcher, according to James Shirley's preface to the first folio, displayed 'the Authentick witt that made Blackfriers an Academy, where the three howers spectacle … were usually of more advantage to the hopefull young Heire, then a costly, dangerous, forraigne Travell'. Beyond the pleasures of recognition and celebration which *The Scornful Lady* so obviously possessed, its deeper fascination must have sprung from its operation as an exemplum: a stripped, bare depiction of how a hopeful young heir should talk and act in order to win a fortune or subdue a scornful lady.

Plays for the King's Men About 1610 the children's theatres were in shaky financial shape, and this may account for the move by Beaumont and Fletcher to the affluent King's Men at the Globe for the rest of their collaborative plays. The first of these, *The Captain* (1609–12), a wild bit of slapstick mixed with a shocking incest seduction scene, may have originally been intended for the free-talking children. But it was *Philaster* (1608–10) that, according to Dryden, brought the playwrights 'in esteem' in the London

theatre (*Essays of John Dryden*, 1.81). It represents a new level of artistic achievement, and it was soon followed by *The Maid's Tragedy* (1610) and *A King and No King* (1610–11).

It is easy to see why *Philaster* made Beaumont and Fletcher the fresh new voices of the London theatre. The plot is filled with surprising twists and turns, the language is probably more readily accessible than in any previous Jacobean play, and the hero Philaster is a fascinating mixture of Hamlet's vices and virtues. This prince, who was deprived of the throne of his recently deceased father by a usurper, is admired by the people, beloved by two perfect maidens, but often acts as if he were half-mad. He responds to crises by ineffectual ranting, is indecisive, credulous, jealous, and inept at princely skills like swordsmanship. A country bumpkin bests him in a swordfight, he stabs in rapid succession his two helpless loved ones (hence the full title, *Philaster, or Love Lies a Bleeding*), but by good fortune and the help of the adoring people rather than by any of his own efforts he ultimately gains the throne and the hand of his wounded loved one. The play explicitly criticizes the doctrine of regal divine right, of which King James was a strong advocate, and insists that princes—there are three imperfect ones in the play—are not gods and should conduct themselves accordingly. Nevertheless the play was twice staged at court.

If *Philaster* portrays an intemperate, dispossessed prince whom Fortune restores to his birthright, *A King and No King* (1611), another collaboration, might be described as the story of an intemperate king whom Fortune deposes from a throne to which he has no natural right. Although King Arbaces is a brave warrior, he is an unbearable braggart totally lacking in self-control. When he meets for the first time his young sister whom he has not seen in years, he instantly falls in love with her and plans to use all his status and power to win her, even, if necessary, to rape her. Only at the last minute is he saved from damnation by the revelation that he and his sister are not really kin. The solution to this exciting romance is an extreme example of what critics of Beaumont and Fletcher damn them for: 'good theatre' at the expense of morality and credibility. Defenders of the play argue that the critics have missed the tone, that Arbaces is a heavily criticized figure whose actions show that absolute power tends to corrupt absolutely.

The Maid's Tragedy (1610–11), also by Beaumont and Fletcher, was the outstanding work of the 'trilogy'. It too depicts an intemperate king who misuses his prerogative. He forces a courtier Amintor to break his engagement to Aspatia, the 'maid' of the title, and marry his own mistress Evadne. On the wedding night Evadne refuses to sleep with Amintor and reveals to the naïve young believer in absolute monarchy that he must abstain from her bed and maintain this ugly secret. Throughout the play there are memorable scenes, some comic, some pitiable (particularly those involving the 'maid'), and some grisly as with the murder of the tyrant king by Evadne.

Beaumont and Fletcher took greater artistic risks in this play than anywhere in their collaboration. These included the presentation of a full 200-line marriage masque subtly linked to the themes of the play and an intricate plot exhibiting a spectrum of responses to regal tyranny. However, it was in the characterizations that they most departed from their normal practice. Only the king might be described as 'flat', a simple tyrant lacking any sense of guilt for what he does and convinced that his absolute power is a God-given right. But the presentation of his victims is richly nuanced. Amintor is a weak, pitiable victim, but he is also a priggish obedient adherent to the doctrine of divine right and the code of honour. Aspatia is helpless and pathetic, but there are neurotic and perverted dimensions in her responses to her plight. As for Evadne, one critic has said, 'As a study in radical perversity, Evadne is more compelling than Lady Macbeth, and more subtle' (J. L. Danby, *Poets on Fortune's Hill*, 1952, 193), while Robert Herrick admired her ardent vitality when she 'swells with brave rage' that makes her 'comely everywhere' (*Comedies and Tragedies*, 1647 folio). Nowhere do the collaborators combine more impressively their theatrical powers with their political commitments.

Final years Beaumont composed one last work by himself, the masque done by the Inner Temple and Gray's Inn to celebrate the marriage of the Princess Elizabeth to Frederick V, elector palatine, in February 1613. Partly subsidized by Francis Bacon and utilizing 150 members of the Inner Temple and Gray's Inn along with some professional actors, it consisted of two antimasques and a main masque. On the surface the masque seems to be merely the lavish celebration of a marriage, but this was a marriage of great political importance. According to Roy Strong, Prince Henry and the anti-Spanish, anti-Catholic protestants he gathered around him hoped that it would cement 'a militant pan-Protestant European alliance to curb Habsburg power' (R. Strong, *Henry, Prince of Wales*, 1986, 177). The project never fully materialized because the prince suddenly died in November 1612, just a month after Frederick had arrived in England for the wedding. Although dimmed down, some remnants of Prince Henry's political agenda can be detected in Beaumont's masque. What was particularly successful was the second antimasque which Beaumont described as 'a confusion, or commixture of all such persons as are naturall and proper for Countrey sports' and signified the approval of the 'Common People' for the marriage (Bowers, 1.127; 2.27-9). It is stated that 'the Musicke was extremely well fitted, having such a spirit of Countrey jolitie, as can hardly be imagined, but the perpetuall laughter and applause was above the Musicke' (ibid., 2.205-7). This dance must have been unusually pleasing because the king demanded that it be repeated at the end of the masque, and it was given further life by insertion into *The Two Noble Kinsmen* (1613) by Fletcher and Shakespeare.

In 1613 Beaumont married Ursula, daughter of Henry Isley of Sundridge, Kent, said to have been an heiress, with whom he had two daughters. It is frequently asserted that this marriage freed him from the need to make a living and hence he stopped writing. Another reason is more

likely. A poem by Thomas Pestell reveals that in the very year of his marriage, 1613, 'Death … hire[d] an apoplexe to shend his brain', that is, that Beaumont suffered a seriously debilitating stroke. (The stroke can be dated precisely in 1613 because Pestell mentions that Beaumont wrote his last poem, the elegy to Lady Penelope Clifton (*d.* 1613) after he suffered the stroke.) He lived on in a melancholic state with 'frequent wishes' for death for three years and died on 6 March 1616 in Westminster. (See the 'Elegie' on Beaumont in *The Poems of Thomas Pestell*, ed. Hannah Buchan, 1940, 71-4. In this same poem Pestell (ll. 35-40) seems to be saying that unlike many in his family Francis Beaumont was not an ardent Catholic.)

Beaumont was interred in Westminster Abbey on 9 March 1616 near to Chaucer and Spenser. It is clear from contemporary references that this placement in what has come to be known as the 'Poets' Corner' was a tribute to his high standing as a writer. (Ben Jonson's first folio poem to Shakespeare and William Basse's 'Elegy' to Shakespeare make this point clear. However it must be mentioned that contrary to what is frequently asserted and unlike his two brothers, Beaumont was never knighted.) It is puzzling that very little is known aside from his publications about the life of someone as important socially and artistically as Beaumont. What G. E. Bentley says about Fletcher is true of both of them:

> Considering his social position and his flourishing reputation from about 1620 to the end of the century, the paucity of information about the career of John Fletcher is very curious, much more unaccountable than the obscurity of Shakespeare which the anti-Stratfordians find so satisfactorily mystifying.   (G. E. Bentley, *The Jacobean and Caroline Stage*, 7 vols., 1941-68, 3.306)

The history of the reputation of Beaumont and Fletcher is one of the most remarkable in English literature. According to Shirley in the first folio preface, their work was 'the greatest Monument of the Scene that Time and Humanity have produced'. As late as the Restoration, according to Dryden, two 'Beaumont and Fletcher' plays were performed for every one by Jonson and Shakespeare. Every age has its inflated reputations, but what is most striking in this case is the quality of the critics—to cite only the greatest, Jonson and Dryden—who took it for granted that the plays were permanent classics. Their decline in the eighteenth century may be attributed to the reformation and sentimentalization of the stage. But in the nineteenth century, despite Lamb's rediscovery of the lesser Elizabethans, he could only rank them as 'an inferior sort of Shakespeares and Sidneys'. For most of the twentieth century the critical consensus has been that Beaumont and Fletcher were the chief contributors to the post-Shakespearian 'decadence' of the English stage. In T. S. Eliot's influential, devastating phrase, 'the blossoms of Beaumont and Fletcher's imagination draw no sustenance from the soil, but are cut and withered flowers stuck in the sand' (*Selected Essays, 1917-1932*, 1932, 135). At the end of the century there have been some earnest efforts by academic critics to refute such views, but aside from some productions of *The Knight of the Burning Pestle* the few attempts to present to live audiences the legendary successes of the seventeenth century have been ineffectual.

P. J. FINKELPEARL

Sources *Aubrey's Brief lives*, 2nd edn, ed. O. L. Dick (1950) · *Comedies and tragedies written by Francis Beaumont and John Fletcher, gentlemen*, first folio (1647) · *Essays of John Dryden*, ed. W. P. Ker, 2 vols. (1900) · M. Eccles, 'A biographical dictionary of Elizabethan authors', *Huntington Library Quarterly*, 5 (1941–2), 281–302, esp. 294 · *The poems of Thomas Pestell*, ed. H. Buchan (1940) · C. Hoy, 'The shares of Fletcher and his collaborators in the Beaumont and Fletcher canon', *Studies in Bibliography*, 8 (1956), 129–46; 9 (1957), 143–62; 11 (1958), 85–106; 12 (1959), 91–116; 13 (1960), 77–108; 14 (1961), 45–67; 15 (1962), 71–90 · *The dramatic works in the Beaumont and Fletcher canon*, ed. F. Bowers, 10 vols. (1966–96) · C. Gayley, *Beaumont the dramatist* (1969) · T. Rymer, *Critical works* (1956) · A. Dyce, ed., *The works of Beaumont & Fletcher* (1843–6) · *DNB* · P. J. Finkelpearl, *Court and country politics in the plays of Beaumont and Fletcher* (Princeton, 1990)

Likenesses G. Vertue, line engraving, 1729 (after oil painting), BM, NPG · mezzotint (after unknown artist), BM, NPG · oils, Knole, Kent [*see illus.*]

Beaumont, Sir George Howland, seventh baronet (1753–1827), art patron and landscape painter, was born on 6 November 1753, at Dunmow, Essex, the only surviving son of Sir George Beaumont, sixth baronet (1726–1762), landowner, and his wife, Rachel (1717/18–1814), daughter of Michael Howland of Stonehall, Dunmow. He succeeded his father, as seventh baronet, in 1762. Beaumont was educated at Eton College, where Alexander Cozens taught him drawing. This became his passion after a sketching holiday spent with his tutor, the Revd Charles Davy, the engraver William Woollett, and the apprentice Thomas Hearne. While at New College, Oxford (*c*.1772–*c*.1776), Beaumont joined the drawing master John Baptist Malchair on sketching expeditions. From 1772 to 1778 he played in Oldfield Bowles's amateur theatre at North Aston, developing into a talented amateur actor, with David Garrick as his model. Through Oxford connections he met the painters who were to be his lifelong heroes, the landscapist Richard Wilson and the portraitist Sir Joshua Reynolds. Both nurtured his interest in the old masters: Wilson introduced him to the work of Claude Lorrain, and in 1792 Reynolds would bequeath him Sébastien Bourdon's *Return of the Ark*, now held by the National Gallery in London.

A grand tour in 1782–3—made with his wife, Margaret (1756–1829), daughter of John Willes of Astrop, whom he had married on 6 May 1778—developed Beaumont's essentially classical taste: some of his finest drawings were executed in Rome, where he worked alongside John Robert Cozens and took painting lessons from Jacob More. On his return, despite modest means, he was able to buy three Claudes including his favourite, *Hagar and the Angel*, and Nicolas Poussin's *Man Washing his Feet at a Fountain*. Lady Beaumont's inheritance of the lease of 34 Grosvenor Square in 1785 rescued the Beaumonts from the anticlimax of home life at Dunmow and enabled them to entertain friends from unusually diverse backgrounds. In 1792 a picture gallery was added to the house for their growing collection of art works. A flirtation with politics as tory MP

Sir George Howland Beaumont, seventh baronet (1753–1827), by John Hoppner, 1803–8

for Beer Alston, Devon (1790–96), widened Beaumont's social circle, but, hating the contention of political life, he continued to concentrate on his artistic interests. An early work, the *View of Keswick* (exh. RA, 1779; Gov. Art Coll.), was much criticized, but his Royal Academy exhibits from 1794 to 1825 earned him recognition as the leading amateur painter of his day.

Often suffering a recurrent fever dating from his 1782 journey, Beaumont with his wife made repeated sketching tours, in some early years with Hearne, to their favourite Lake District and north Wales, where they rented Benarth, near Conwy, from 1799 to 1802. Visitors there included John Sell Cotman, Joseph Farington, and Uvedale Price, to whose voluminous correspondence (now in the Pierpont Morgan Library, New York) Beaumont was a predictably enthusiastic contributor, as he was too to William Gilpin's debates. Price advised on the landscaping of Beaumont's long neglected estate, Coleorton Hall, in north-west Leicestershire. After receiving some £15,000 compensation for coal revenues embezzled by a dishonest agent, Beaumont felt duty bound to live there and another friend, the architect George Dance, rebuilt the house in Gothic style in 1804–8. William Wordsworth and his family, briefly joined by Samuel Taylor Coleridge, were lent the hall farm for the winter of 1806, Wordsworth writing some of his finest short poems there and designing a winter garden. Following a meeting with Coleridge at Greta Hall, Keswick, in 1803, a close friendship, fanned by Lady Beaumont's intensely emotional character, had developed with the lake poets; the Beaumonts introduced Coleridge and Wordsworth into London society in 1804 and

1806 respectively. While Coleridge would prove a disappointment, Beaumont was deeply touched when Wordsworth responded to his *Peele Castle in a Storm* (exh. RA, 1806; Leicester Museum and Art Gallery) with a poem, and each counted the friendship among the blessings of his life. Beaumont's letters (now in the Wordsworth Museum in Grasmere) confess to suffering periods of 'morbid dejection' in the country that only kindred spirits could alleviate. Wordsworth, who preferred penury to patronage, allowed him to contribute engravings from his own paintings to the *Miscellaneous Poems* and *The White Doe* in 1815, and wrote several verses in tribute to Beaumont.

Beaumont's openness to new Romantic trends in poetry was not always matched in his relations with younger artists. His appointment in 1802 to the committee of taste charged with the selection of monuments for St Paul's Cathedral, and in 1806 as a founder member of the British Institution, gave him considerable influence as an arbiter of taste that he exercised in a broadly conservative direction. As the disciple of Reynolds, he took perhaps too seriously the role of disseminating the master's teaching: sympathetic artists were welcomed at Grosvenor Square, where his collection now included the Reynolds portraits of the baronet (exh. RA, 1788; Frick Museum, New York) and his wife (exh. RA, 1776: Frick Museum, New York), two fine Wilson landscapes, and Thomas Gainsborough's *Cottage Door* (Huntington Art Gallery, San Marino). Of the old masters, by far the most expensive was Rubens's *Château de Steen* (now in the National Gallery, London) on which Lady Beaumont spent £1500 from a legacy in 1803. The young John Constable and Samuel William Reynolds were among those to benefit from copying the pictures, though not always from Beaumont's restrictive guidance. He never recognized Constable as the great landscape painter he sought, but he grew to love his fellow East Anglian with whom he painted during five happy weeks at Coleorton in 1823. Beaumont shared several protégés with his friend the collector Lord Mulgrave: for example, he proved a staunch and generous patron to David Wilkie, acquiring his *Blind Fiddler* (exh. RA, 1806; Tate collection) and entertaining him at Dunmow and Coleorton. There in 1809 his latest enthusiasm, the prickly history painter Benjamin Haydon, also a guest, reported that 'they did nothing, morning, noon or night, but think of painting, talk of painting and wake to paint again' (Haydon, 1.96). Beaumont's commission of *Macbeth* was rewarded by tantrums from Haydon that reverberated to their mutual disadvantage.

Unquestionably selective, Beaumont appeared capricious, and artists resented his influence in fashionable circles: his old friend Hearne sourly described him as 'supreme Dictator on Works of Art' (Farington, *Diary*, 10.3508), while James Northcote compared being taken up by Beaumont to a ride on a flying coach. Most conspicuous and contentious was his aggressive hostility to J. M. W. Turner, whose work he constantly criticized for its high colour and liberal interpretation of his beloved old masters. Moreover, Turner was a contributor to the new vogue for elaborate exhibition watercolours which Beaumont,

despite his admiration for early practitioners such as Thomas Girtin, condemned as 'papier-mache' productions. Anonymous *catalogues raisonnés* of old master exhibitions at the British Institution in 1815 and 1816, containing savage satires on Beaumont and his choice of exhibits, were attributed to disaffected artists.

Much chastened, Beaumont withdrew to Coleorton where most of his pictures had hung since 1808. There, in 1812, he had erected a monument to Reynolds, with an inscription by Wordsworth, flanked by busts of Raphael and Michelangelo, as painted in Constable's *The Cenotaph* (exh. RA, 1828; National Gallery, London). Apart from acquiring modest works from newcomers such as Edwin Landseer, Beaumont's later collecting focused on sculpture; he was encouraged by Antonio Canova, a great friend who aided his acquisition of Michelangelo's tondo of *The Virgin and Child with St John*, which Lady Beaumont later gave to the Royal Academy. From Canova's follower John Gibson he commissioned a marble *Psyche and the Zephyrs*. With his wife and rather lacklustre heir, George Howland Willoughby Beaumont, a second cousin, Beaumont had ventured nervously to Italy in 1821; a winter in Rome restored his morale and convinced him that British taste would only improve if the public had access to great works of art. On his return he utilized old political friends to campaign for a national gallery; his offer of sixteen pictures, the cream of his collection, as a foundation gift, on condition that the earl of Liverpool's government purchased the John Julius Angerstein collection, proved crucial to its establishment in 1824.

Beaumont, now a trustee of the British Museum and on the committee of superintendence of the National Gallery, released his paintings in April 1825 to the temporary gallery in Angerstein's former Pall Mall house. He died on 7 February 1827 at Coleorton Hall, after a brief illness, and never saw the Trafalgar Square building plans. He was buried in Coleorton church. John Hoppner's portrait (exh. RA, 1809; National Gallery, London) shows a good-looking man whose Old World charm was admired by friends such as Sir Walter Scott, who considered that Beaumont's 'mild manners' alleviated 'the causticity of the general London tone of persiflage and personal satire' (Whitley, 2.125). His services to the arts were commended even by Haydon, his most difficult protégé: 'his ambition was to connect himself with the art of the country, and he has done it for ever' (Haydon, 1.405–6). Beaumont's wash drawings and oils are held in the family collection and at Leicester Art Gallery and Museum.

FELICITY OWEN and DAVID BLAYNEY BROWN

Sources F. Owen and D. Blayney Brown, *Collector of genius: a life of Sir George Beaumont* (1988) · D. Davies and L. Trench, eds., *Noble and patriotic: the Beaumont gift* (1988) [exhibition catalogue, National Gallery, London] · F. Owen and L. Herrmann, *Sir George Beaumont* [n.d.] [Leicester Museum Catalogue] · B. R. Haydon, *Autobiography and memoirs of B. R. Haydon*, ed. T. Taylor, rev. A. Huxley, 2 vols. (1926) · *DNB* · W. Knight, *Memorials of Coleorton* (1887) · Farington, *Diary* · *The letters of William and Dorothy Wordsworth*, ed. E. de Selincourt, 2nd edn, 2–3, rev. M. Moorman and A. G. Hill (1969–70), vols. 2, 3 · W. Whitley, *Art in England, 1700–1799*, 2 vols. (1968) · C. R. Leslie, *Memoirs of the life of John Constable*, ed. J. Mayne (1951) · *Collected* *letters of Samuel Taylor Coleridge*, ed. E. L. Griggs, 6 vols. (1956–71), vols. 2, 3 · *John Constable's correspondence*, ed. R. B. Beckett, 2–6, Suffolk RS, 6, 8, 10–12 (1964–8) · *John Constable: further documents and correspondence*, ed. L. Parris, C. Shields, and I. Fleming-Williams, Suffolk RS, 18 (1975)

Archives Hunt. L., corresp. · Morgan L., corresp. and papers | Beds. & Luton ARS, letters to Samuel Whitbread · NL Scot., corresp. with Sir David Wilkie · priv. coll., letters to Lord Mulgrave · RA, corresp. with Thomas Lawrence · Wordsworth Trust, Dove Cottage, Grasmere, letters to W. Wordsworth

Likenesses J. Reynolds, oils, 1788, Frick Museum, New York · T. Lawrence, oils, 1793?, Louvre Museum, Paris · J. Hoppner, oils, 1803–8, National Gallery, London [*see illus.*] · G. Dance, pencil, 1807, NPG · B. R. Haydon, two pencil sketches, *c*.1815, Tate collection · J. G. Murray, group portrait, stipple, pubd 1823 (*The trial of Queen Caroline*; after J. Stephanoff), BM · W. J. Ward, group portrait, mezzotint (after J. Jackson), BM, NPG · J. Wright, watercolour drawing (after Hoppner), NPG · mezzotint (after J. Reynolds), BM, NPG

Wealth at death most of estate was entailed (Coleorton, Dunmow, and small properties); best paintings given to National Gallery, London; the Tondo remained for Lady Beaumont to leave to Royal Academy

Beaumont [Newburgh], **Henry de**, first earl of Warwick (*d.* **1119**), magnate, was the younger son of Roger, lord of Beaumont-le-Roger and Pont Audemer, and Adeline, daughter of Waleran, count of Meulan. His first appearance was at the ducal court just before 1066 when he must have been already a young adult. Before 1100 he married Margaret, daughter of Geoffroy, count of Perche.

There is no firm evidence that Henry participated in the conquest of England, though it is known that his brother, Robert de *Beaumont, was at Hastings. According to Orderic Vitalis (writing over fifty years later), Henry was in William the Conqueror's army in England in 1068 and was entrusted with the castle that the king had constructed during his stay in Warwick. It is, however, impossible to verify Orderic's assertion: he might well have been writing retrospectively, with Henry's later earldom of Warwick in mind. If Henry was given Warwick in 1068, he was certainly not holding it in 1086 at the time of the Domesday survey. It is most likely that he spent his young adulthood largely in France in various courts and military households. He appears at the Conqueror's court in the 1070s (though whether in England or in Normandy it is hard to say); in or about 1079 he was with the then count of Meulan, his uncle Hugues, at the abbey of St Pierre-des-Préaux in Normandy. It was doubtless at court in the early 1080s that he made the friendship that guaranteed his future prosperity—his alliance with the Conqueror's second son, William Rufus, who became king in 1087.

Henry de Beaumont is said to have been one of the new king's chief supporters on his accession. He acted as the king's agent in the prosecution of the dissident bishop of Durham, William of St Calais. At some time in 1088, probably before the summer, Henry had his reward and was made the first earl of Warwick. The royal estates suffered heavily from the king's generosity to his friend. Much of Rutland was diverted to Earl Henry; a sizeable part of the estate of the late earl of Hereford, William fitz Osbern (which had come into royal hands in 1075), was made over to him. But it was of Warwick that he was made earl. The king alienated the majority royal holding in the borough of Warwick to Henry, with other royal estates. The bulk of the earldom was provided by the curious expedient of getting Earl Henry's elder brother to give up much of his English patrimony (lands centred in Warwickshire and south Leicestershire). Their father was still alive in 1088, and it is possible that he acted as arbiter in the process of division. Certainly it must have been through his father that Henry obtained a share of the family's estates in Normandy: principally the honour and forest of Le Neubourg (from which genealogists obtained the name Newburgh, by which Henry and his family were on occasion known). Another piece of originality in the creation of the earldom of Warwick (much copied in later creations) was the subordination of several existing barons within the shire to the new earl. There is a good indication of Earl Henry's mettle in reports of his first actions in Warwickshire, chronicled in the records of the abbey of Abingdon. These report that he wasted no time in investigating and asserting his rights over estates to which he might make the barest claim. The abbey paid gold to gain the earl's goodwill and to prevent him swallowing its estates (at Chesterton and Hill in Warwickshire).

According to William of Malmesbury, Earl Henry played an important part in the accession of Henry I in 1100. His power brought further rewards. Around 1107 the earl was granted the marcher lordship of Gower when the client kingdom of the southern Welsh leader, Hywel ap Gronw, broke up. Henry continued to attend on his friend the king until at least 1115. After that date he cannot be proved to have been at court. He was in Warwickshire on one occasion after 1115, but by then his health may have been declining. In, or just before, 1118, the earl left England for good. He entered his family's ancestral abbey at St Pierre-des-Préaux, was received as a monk (the abbey commemorated him in 1122 as *comes et monachus*), and died there on 20 June 1119. He was buried in the chapter house of the abbey. His wife survived him by many years, dying after 1156, and long enjoying a substantial dower settlement, which may have included the lordship of Gower. Earl Henry passed his English lands on to his eldest son, *Roger, who became the second earl of Warwick. He passed his Norman estates on to his second son, Robert de Neubourg. The probability is that this division had been executed at the time of his retirement to Normandy about 1118. Henry left three other sons: Rotrou, later archbishop of Rouen, Geoffrey, and Henry of Gower.

Henry patronized a number of Norman abbeys, but only the Augustinian priory of the Holy Sepulchre, Warwick, had a claim to consider him founder. There is evidence that he was interested in patronizing secular colleges, such as those of the minsters of Warwick and Wellesbourne. The verdict of his contemporaries on Earl Henry was a positive one. William of Malmesbury regarded him as 'a man of honesty and great virtue', and was willing to believe that he had secured the succession for Henry I, following the death of William Rufus in the New Forest in 1100. He also seems to have regarded the earl as mingling the less positive virtue of hedonism with an affable disposition. As far as William was concerned, Earl Henry was less subtle and shrewd than his even more influential elder brother, Robert, count of Meulan and earl of Leicester. However, the affection of the brothers is attested by a Durham source. When Count Robert visited the cathedral monastery in the 1090s, he paid handsomely to have not only his own soul, but also that of his brother, commemorated in the *liber vitae*.   DAVID CROUCH

Sources Ordericus Vitalis, *Eccl. hist.* · William of Malmesbury, *Gesta regum Anglorum / The history of the English kings*, ed. and trans. R. A. B. Mynors, R. M. Thomson, and M. Winterbottom, 2 vols., OMT (1998–9) · Symeon of Durham, *Opera* · T. Jones, ed. and trans., *Brut y tywysogyon, or, The chronicle of the princes: Red Book of Hergest* (1955) · J. Stevenson, ed., *Chronicon monasterii de Abingdon*, 2 vols., Rolls Series, 2 (1858) · [A. H. Thompson], ed., *Liber vitae ecclesiae Dunelmensis*, SurtS, 136 (1923) · L. Delisle, ed., *Rouleaux des morts du IXe au XVe siècle* (1866) · M. Fauroux, ed., *Recueil des actes des ducs de Normandie de 911 à 1066* (Caen, 1961) · J. Mabillon and others, eds., *Annales ordinis sancti Benedicti*, 6 vols. (1703–39) · D. Crouch, 'Oddities in the early history of the marcher lordship of Gower', *BBCS*, 31 (1984), 133–41

Beaumont, Sir Henry de (c.1280–1340), baron, was the younger son of Louis de Brienne, in right of his wife vicomte of Beaumont in Maine, and Agnès, daughter of Raoul, vicomte de Beaumont. Through his great-grandfather, Alfonso IX, king of León, he was distantly related to Edward I's first wife, *Eleanor of Castile: a connection that may have promoted both the marriage of Beaumont's sister, Isabella, to Edward's supporter, John de *Vescy (d. 1289), in 1279 or 1280, and Beaumont's own entrée into English affairs in 1297, when he was made a knight of the royal household. He quickly came to be on close terms both with Edward himself, in whose Scottish wars he regularly served, and with his heir.

After the young Edward's accession in 1307 Beaumont rose rapidly. Joint warden of Scotland in 1308, he was summoned to parliament in 1309, and went on to receive extensive lands in Lincolnshire (augmented by his sister's lands in that county after her death in 1334) and the more contentious grant of the Isle of Man. The king's favour made him the special target of the reforming lords ordainer, who in 1311 called for the exclusion from court of both Beaumont and Isabella, the resumption of his grants from the king, and the transference of the custody of Man to 'a good Englishman' (a phrase that reveals one reason for his unpopularity). These demands, however, were never implemented and Beaumont remained prominent at Edward's court until 1323. Regularly employed on missions abroad, he was also closely involved with the king's attempt to secure the bishopric of Durham for Henry's brother Louis de *Beaumont, which led to the capture and ransoming of both the Beaumonts by Thomas, earl of Lancaster, the court's leading opponent, in 1317. He had his revenge in March 1322, when he was among the royalist army that defeated Lancaster at Boroughbridge. It may have been shortly after this that he served (so John Capgrave (d. 1464) says) in the Italian crusades launched against the enemies of Pope John XXII.

About 1310 Beaumont married Alice or Alicia Comyn (d.

1349), niece of John *Comyn, seventh earl of Buchan, and heir to the Comyn earldom. This claim to a Scottish title and lands did as much as royal favour to determine the course of his career. The status that it gave him as a disinherited lord led him to oppose the Anglo-Scottish truce of 1323 and helped to persuade him to change his allegiance shortly afterwards. Although he was still sufficiently trusted to be appointed one of the young Edward's guardians when the prince was sent abroad to do homage for his father's French lands in September 1325, a year later he had become one of the leading supporters of Queen Isabella in her invasion of England.

After Edward II's deposition Beaumont was well rewarded for his altered loyalties by a large grant of lands in Leicestershire, but the Anglo-Scottish treaty of Northampton of 1328 led him once more into opposition. The treaty had promised the restoration of their Scottish inheritances to Beaumont and the other disinherited; but these promises were not kept. Beaumont became implicated first in the rebellion of Henry, earl of Lancaster, against the regime of Roger (V) Mortimer and Isabella in 1328–9, fleeing to France after its collapse, and then in the inept conspiracy of Edmund of Woodstock, earl of Kent.

The coup of 1330, which finally overthrew the regime and established Edward III as king, opened a second successful phase in Beaumont's career. He returned to England and became the leading supporter of Edward Balliol in Balliol's attempt to secure the Scottish throne for himself and the restoration of their lands for the disinherited. In 1332 he shared Balliol's triumph at the battle of Dupplin Moor and in 1333 he was in the victorious army that defeated the Scots at Halidon Hill and restored Balliol to his throne after a brief Scottish rebellion. In the aftermath of the battle Beaumont was apparently made both earl of Moray and constable of Scotland by the new king. In 1334 he was captured and ransomed by the Scots, gaining his freedom in time to fight in Edward III's major Scottish campaign of 1335; but thereafter he shared in the general decline of English fortunes and interest in Scotland and never obtained recognition of his titles there. In July 1338 he went abroad to the Low Countries with Edward, and died there on 10 March 1340. According to Capgrave he was buried at Vaudey Abbey, a Cistercian house in Lincolnshire. He left a son and heir, John, aged twenty-two, a daughter, Katherine, who had married David Strathbogie, eleventh earl of Atholl, and his widow, who died in 1349. He was essentially an adventurer, who owed his rise to his service to three kings, his military vigour, his fortunate marriage, and his ability to press home the advantages that opportunity offered him.

J. R. MADDICOTT

Sources *Chancery records* · N. Denholm-Young, ed. and trans., *Vita Edwardi secundi* (1957) · W. Stubbs, ed., *Chronicles of the reigns of Edward I and Edward II*, 2 vols., Rolls Series, 76 (1882–3) · *Johannis Capgrave Liber de illustribus Henricis*, ed. F. C. Hingeston, Rolls Series, 7 (1858) · J. C. Davies, *The baronial opposition to Edward II* (1918) · R. Nicholson, *Edward III and the Scots: the formative years of a military career, 1327–1335* (1965) · M. Prestwich, 'Isabella de Vescy and the custody of Bamburgh Castle', *BIHR*, 44 (1971), 148–52 · GEC, *Peerage*

Beaumont [*alias* Harcourt], **Henry** (*c*.1611–1673), Jesuit, was the third son of Sir Henry Beaumont, of Stoughton, Leicestershire, and his wife, Elizabeth, daughter of Sir William Turpen, of Knoptoft in that county. He entered the Society of Jesus at Watten in 1630 and after studies at the English College at Liège was ordained about 1639. He returned in 1641 to Watten, where he was made spiritual coadjutor on 24 May 1643. He returned to England that year and appears in the house of probation of St Ignatius. He is recorded as present in the College of the Blessed Aloysius in 1644–5, the College of the Holy Apostles in 1646–7, and at the Residence of St Thomas in 1649. He appears to have remained in England for the remainder of his life. He translated selections from Bede, published as *England's Old Religion Faithfully Gathered out of the History of the Church of England* at Antwerp in 1658 under the initials H. B. In the preface to the work he sought to demonstrate how the present established church in England had departed from the practices of Bede's time. He died in the Suffolk district on 11 May 1673.

THOMPSON COOPER, rev. RUTH JORDAN

Sources T. M. McCoog, *English and Welsh Jesuits, 1555–1650*, 2, Catholic RS, 75 (1995), 200 · Gillow, *Lit. biog. hist.*, 3.121–2 · D. A. Bellenger, ed., *English and Welsh priests, 1558–1800* (1984) · T. H. Clancy, *A literary history of the English Jesuits: a century of books, 1615–1714* (1996)

Beaumont, Hughes Griffiths [Hugh; *called* Binkie] (1908–1973), theatre manager, was born at 97 West End Lane, Hampstead, London, on 27 March 1908, the younger son of Morgan Morgan (*d.* 1935), a barrister, and his wife, Mary Frances, *née* Brewer. His parents separated when he was two, and were divorced, his mother marrying a timber merchant, William Sugden Beaumont (*d.* 1920). 'Binkie', as he became widely known (he was more formally known as Hugh), grew up believing that Beaumont was his true father.

Throughout his life Hugh Beaumont preserved a passion for anonymity, and was given to disseminating fanciful accounts of his origins. He was brought up in Cardiff and attended Penarth grammar school. He formed an early friendship with Ivor Novello (a close neighbour) and secured a precocious appointment, at the age of sixteen, as assistant manager of the Prince of Wales Theatre, Cardiff. Still in his adolescence, he moved on to a series of other minor managerial jobs before joining the firm of Moss Empires as assistant to H. M. (Harry) Tennent, administrator of Drury Lane, with whom, in 1936, he founded the producing management of H. M. Tennent Ltd. Neither at that time, nor after Tennent's death in 1941, was anything done to publicize the name of Beaumont, but it was at his persuasion that the firm came into existence and through his gifts that it sustained its long supremacy in the West End.

Beaumont and Tennent went into business with a £10,000 float from a stockbroking member of the Cripps family. That was a reasonable sum in the days when a West End play could be presented at the average cost of £1000. However, the partners lost much of their starting capital on a series of flops before they struck lucky with the 1937 production of Gerald Savory's *George and Margaret* which ran for 799 performances at Wyndham's. This was followed by Dodie Smith's *Dear Octopus* and other long-running shows which established Tennents as a highly profitable concern that magnetized backers like a triple-crown Derby winner.

It was during these first years that Beaumont struck up a lifelong and professionally fertile friendship with John Gielgud. All Beaumont's early experience had been on the business side. He was, Gielgud said, 'a modern man with no pretensions to education at all and no knowledge except what he had learned as he became successful'. Throughout his career, his main objective was to have as many productions as possible playing in London. What those productions were, however, reflected a taste acquired partly from Gielgud, with whom he broke into classical territory with a 1939 *Hamlet*, and continued with the famous wartime seasons at the Phoenix and the Haymarket, and again at the Phoenix and the Lyric, Hammersmith, during the 1950s. He also developed a love for superbly dressed, resplendently cast high comedy for which the name of Tennents became a byword.

What won Beaumont such allies as Gielgud and Noël Coward in the first place was an array of personal and managerial skills which he put unreservedly at their disposal. He saw it as his mission to produce the best artists under the best possible conditions; and, having decided who the best were, he looked faithfully after their interests with an invincible blend of paternal care, business acumen, and courteously absolute authority. 'The iron fist', Tyrone Guthrie said of him, 'was wrapped in fifteen pastel-shaded velvet gloves' (Guthrie, 143). Those who worked with him, actors and playwrights alike, had total faith in his artistic judgement. His theatre followed the West End star system, but whereas the usual practice was for a star to appear with a supporting company, stars appeared in constellations on the Tennents stage, persuaded by Beaumont to exchange solitary glory for the satisfaction of working with their equals.

Tennents never owned theatres. They had a long-standing tenancy at the Queen's and the Globe, and periodically occupied the Haymarket and theatres of the Albery group. During the war their profits were subject to the 40 per cent entertainments tax from which Beaumont sought exemption by forming a non-profit-making subsidiary—Tennent Productions—for the presentation of classical work. By the end of the war he had thus amassed a surplus of £70,000 with which, in 1946, he also took over the Lyric, Hammersmith, for classical seasons and West End try-outs by the newly created Company of Four.

The immediate post-war years marked the zenith of Tennents' prestige: a gathering of major stars and new names (including Christopher Fry and Peter Brook) mobilized in a lavish firework display exactly matching the anti-austerity mood of the time. However, there were also growing murmurs against Tennents' non-profit-making status, which reached a head with the officially 'educational' première of *A Streetcar Named Desire* (1949), at which the Arts Council withdrew its support and the Inland Revenue promptly converted the charitable surplus into unpaid tax, and put in a large demand which Beaumont unsuccessfully contested in the House of Lords.

This defeat did nothing to shake the firm's theatrical fortunes or diminish Beaumont's power (in Guthrie's words) as the man, more than any other, who could 'make or break the career of almost any worker in the British professional theatre' (Guthrie, 142).

What did bring the firm into decline was the explosion of new writing that began from the Royal Court theatre in 1956, and the growth of subsidized theatre at the expense of the commercial sector. Beaumont's West End flourished like a traditional grocery shop, selling reliable brands to regular customers. The fashions of 1956 consigned these brands to the dustbin although Beaumont struggled to replace them with such newcomers as Robert Bolt and Peter Shaffer. Nor was there any effective way of fighting subsidized competition by a manager who believed that the theatre should stand on its own feet.

During his twenty years of supremacy Beaumont did more to raise the standard of the London theatre than any other manager, past or present. The new stage that overwhelmed him was one that he had done much to create. A homosexual, he had no family; the theatre was his business, his pleasure, and his life. He died at his home, 14 Lord North Street, London on 22 March 1973.

IRVING WARDLE, rev.

Sources The Times (23 March 1973) · The Times (28–9 March 1973) · The Spectator (31 March 1973) · private information (1986) · T. Guthrie, A life in the theatre (1960) · CGPLA Eng. & Wales (1974) · R. Huggett, Binkie Beaumont: éminence grise of the West End theatre, 1933–1973 (1989) · b. cert. · d. cert.
Likenesses Sasha, photograph, 1933, repro. in R. Huggett, Binkie Beaumont (1989) · C. Beaton, photograph, c.1946, repro. in R. Huggett, Binkie Beaumont (1989) · O. Karminski, photograph, repro. in R. Huggett, Binkie Beaumont (1989) · A. McBean, photograph, repro. in R. Huggett, Binkie Beaumont (1989)
Wealth at death £439,716: probate, 6 March 1974, CGPLA Eng. & Wales

Beaumont, Huntingdon (1561–1624), coal owner, was born probably at Coleorton, Leicestershire, the fourth and youngest son of Nicholas Beaumont (d. 1585), and Anne (d. 1581), daughter of William Saunders, of Wilsford, Northamptonshire. He had three brothers, the second of whom died in infancy, and two sisters. His father owned the Coleorton estate, and by exploiting its extensive coal reserves had become the largest colliery owner in the county. Described as unmarried in 1616, Beaumont must have wed shortly afterwards since he was survived by a wife, Joan, and three small children. Nothing is known of his early education, though he received a thorough training in the management of the family business: he was described in 1622 as 'a man reputed to be very skyllful in Coalworkes, having spent a great part of his life and tyme in suchlyke works' (Smith, Early Coal-Mining, 66). It has also been suggested that he obtained his knowledge of advanced mining technology from a visit to Germany in his youth; but it is more likely that this was acquired through a familiarity both with Agricola's renowned mining text, De re metallica, and with English metal-mining practices, which had been introduced into the midland coalmines from Cornwall and Derbyshire.

The landed gentry played a key role in the rapid development of the coal industry in the sixteenth and early seventeenth centuries. Sufficient profits could be made to attract investment, but it was one of the most risky of industries. Management of profitable family mines at Coleorton and at Bedworth in Warwickshire encouraged Beaumont to seek a personal fortune, first in the larger Nottinghamshire coalfield and ultimately in the northeast, the heart of the industry. Beaumont was an ambitious gentry businessman who attempted to overcome the formidable challenges of the coal industry with boldness and flair—to the point of recklessness, according to his critics.

For an individual colliery owner one of the chief obstacles to business advancement in the late 1500s was that the market for coal suffered both from severe economic fluctuations and from a longer-term tendency to overproduction and excessive competition. Beaumont attempted to overcome this obstacle by a variety of techniques. In the east midlands he created a local monopoly, and when this failed he attempted to tap a national market. In the north-east, however, he introduced new technology which he hoped would give the business a cost advantage over its rivals, in the short term at least. He also tried to eliminate competition and create a monopoly either by paying rivals to cease production or by buying them out. In 1599 Sir Percy Willoughby was paid £100 a year to close Foleshill colliery, which was competing with Bedworth (mined by Beaumont jointly with his brother Thomas [see below]). As a result Bedworth dominated the Warwickshire coal market with an annual output of about 20,000 tons a year. In 1601 Beaumont took over control of Wollaton colliery in Nottinghamshire. He paid the same gentry rival 2s. a rook on sales and two years later gained control of the neighbouring and competing Strelley mines by leasing them from Sir John Byron. In 1604, in an attempt to maintain prices and profitability in the face of trade depression, Wollaton colliery was closed and production became concentrated at Strelley. Consideration was then given to the possibility of purchasing and 'laying down' four other competing mines. However, the plan to 'ingrosse or overthrowe most of the best coalmines in the countree' (Smith, Early Coal-Mining, 68) was not implemented, probably because of insufficient capital, and was soon superseded by an attempt to break through the ceiling on regional sales by entering the largest single market, that of the metropolis, which was dominated by its coastal trade with the north-east. Coal was to be shipped down the River Trent to Hull and thence, like Newcastle coal, down the coast to London. In July 1604 Beaumont entered into partnership with Sir Percival Willoughby, London merchant John Bate, and Hugh Lenton, a Newark merchant, to deliver 7000 loads each year to Nottingham Bridges for transportation down the Trent to London. A number of boats were purchased for the purpose, but the scheme was defeated by the cost of trans-shipment from the land-locked Strelley colliery; coal from Strelley could not profitably be sold for less than £1 a ton in London, which compared unfavourably with Newcastle coal at 15s. Even after the construction of Britain's first wagon way, for 2 miles of the journey to the Trent (from Strelley through Wollaton to Wollaton Lane, Lenton), the price differential remained.

Following the failure of these marketing strategies in Nottinghamshire, Beaumont determined in 1605 to exploit the London market by the alternative method of becoming one of the foremost colliery owners in the north-east. As William Gray in his *Chorographia* of 1649 put it:

> Master Beaumont, a gentleman of great ingenuity and rare parts, adventured into our mines with his twenty thousand pounds; who brought with him many rare engines, not known then in these parts, as the art to boore with iron rods to try the deepnes and thickness of the cole, rare engines to draw water out of the pits; waggons with one horse to carry down water from the pits to the staithes to the river etc. (*History of Northumberland*, p. 228)

Beaumont acquired the leases of mines at Bedlington and also of mines and salt pans at Cowpen and Bebside, in partnership with three London merchants, Robert and William Angell, and Robert Bowyer, and he took up residence at Bebside Hall. By 1609 the partnership had expanded to include Edward Rotherham, a London draper, and John Bate. The partners invested £1000 each, but Beaumont, despite his expertise and talent for technological innovation, 'could not bring the workes to any perfection' (Smith, *Early Coal-Mining*, 70). In 1612 Beaumont and his nephew-in-law, Sir John Ashburnham (d. 1620), purchased the partnership by agreeing to pay the others £1050 a year for the remaining term of the leases. They defaulted on the first payment and the enterprise was abandoned altogether in 1614 as a total loss.

Beaumont the innovator now sought to overcome the limitations of the market by the use of economies of scale to increase production at the Strelley mine. He determined to capture as large a slice of the Nottinghamshire, east Leicestershire, and Trent valley markets as possible by introducing round-the-clock working; double shifts and double corfs replaced the twelve-hour single-shift, single-corf system, which had been the traditional practice at the coalfield. This new system meant that four times as much coal per day could be produced, and an unprecedented annual output of over 20,000 tons was achieved. Despite its competitive price, depressed trading conditions prevented all the coal from being sold, and profits were insufficient to keep Beaumont's creditors at bay indefinitely. In the spring of 1618, the partners in the northern venture took action against Beaumont and Ashburnham for failing to pay their instalments, and they seized control of Strelley to work the mine for their own profit. In October 1618 Beaumont was committed to Nottingham prison until his debts should be paid, and he died from an unknown illness, without gaining his freedom from captivity, on 17 March 1624. He died a bankrupt, and was buried at the expense of his former business partner, Sir Percy Willoughby, at Bilborough, Nottingham, where he had been latterly residing.

Huntingdon Beaumont has been characterized, perhaps unjustly, as a reckless adventurer who squandered the family fortune on desperate business gambles. Yet he should be seen rather as an ambitious younger son of a gentry family who, since he would not inherit the estate, acted entrepreneurially. He deployed impressive technical and managerial skills, which were used to the utmost in a hazardous industry that was subject to the twin dangers of the physical exhaustion of the product and of market instability. These ultimately defeated Beaumont's expertise and drive, particularly in the north-eastern venture in which he and Sir John Ashburnham 'were utterly overthrown and in a manner whooly buried the estate in the said coalmynes' (Smith, *Early Coal-Mining*, 80).

Huntingdon's brother, **Sir Thomas Beaumont** (c.1555–1614), who was his associate in a number of business ventures, was equally entrepreneurial. Thomas was the third born but second surviving son of Nicholas, and was also probably born at Coleorton. About 1575 he married Catherine Farnham (d. 1621) and thereby succeeded to the lordship of the manor of Stoughton in Leicestershire. He also inherited the estate of Henry Beaumont of Giltsham, Devon, on the latter's death without issue. Thomas was knighted in 1603. He and Catherine had three sons and seven daughters. His daughter Elizabeth married Sir John Ashburnham, who died in 1620 in the Fleet debtors' prison in London.

The brothers' joint business activity commenced in 1597 when coal was leased from the crown at Bedworth and Griff, Warwickshire, at which time a large mine was opened at Bedworth. To guarantee the profitability of their heavy investment the brothers began purchasing coal reserves in adjoining estates, and by 1602 they had 'engrossed all the mynes neere thereunto adjoyning, six myles compas on everye side' (Nef, 1.15). With a virtual monopoly of the north Warwickshire market, the mine made a profit of at least £3000 a year, but it was abandoned following extensive flooding in 1610. By then, £10,000 had been invested in the mine, much of it borrowed from other members of the family, including the third brother, Francis. None the less, Sir Thomas continued to support Huntingdon's mining activities. In 1610 he took over the lease of the coal at Strelley, to work it for his own profit until the £2000 which he had lent Huntingdon (probably for his Bedlington enterprise) had been repaid. Sir Thomas made strenuous efforts to increase output and profits by expanding the market in the Trent valley, but the loan had still not been repaid in full by the time of his death on 27 November 1614. He was succeeded by his eldest son and heir, Sir Henry Beaumont, who was never able to recover the debt. Sir Thomas had found, like his brother, that investment in coalmining ultimately meant that 'Instead of dreining the water, ther pockets are dreined' (Stone, 340).   COLIN GRIFFIN

Sources R. S. Smith, *Early coal-mining around Nottingham, 1500–1650* (1989) · R. S. Smith, 'Huntingdon Beaumont: adventurer in coalmines', *Renaissance and Modern Studies*, 1 (1957), 129–53 · J. U. Nef, *The rise of the British coal industry*, 1 (1932), 12 · J. Hatcher, *Before 1700:*

towards the age of coal (1993), vol. 1 of *The history of the British coal industry* (1984–93) · J. Nichols, *The history and antiquities of the county of Leicester*, 3 (1800–04) · *A history of Northumberland*, Northumberland County History Committee, 15 vols. (1893–1940), vol. 9 · W. Camden, *Britannia, or, A chorographical description of the flourishing kingdoms of England, Scotland, and Ireland*, ed. and trans. R. Gough, 2nd edn, 2 (1806) · *VCH Leicestershire*, vol. 3 · L. Stone, *The crisis of the aristocracy, 1558–1641* (1965) · *Report on the manuscripts of Lord Middleton*, HMC, 69 (1911) · C. P. Griffin, 'The economic and social development of the Leicestershire and south Derbyshire coalfield, 1557–1914', PhD diss., U. Nott., 1969 · A. R. Griffin, *Mining in the east midlands, 1550–1947* (1971)

Archives U. Nott., Middleton MSS

Beaumont, Jean François Albanis (1755–1812), engraver and landscape painter, may have been a son of, or related to, the Piedmontese artist Claudio Francesco Beaumont (1694–1766). He was born at Chambéry, entered the engineering school at Mezières, and in 1775 joined the Sardinian army as an engineer. At this time Sardinian territory extended into what is now Provence, and Beaumont was working as a hydraulic engineer at Nice, where he met the duke of Gloucester. In 1780 the duke engaged him as a teacher of mathematics and fortifications to his children; Beaumont then accompanied the duke on his travels in the Alps. Beaumont himself made several crossings of the region, and on one occasion travelled westwards along the Mediterranean coast into French territory. A few years later he travelled through the maritime Alps from Cuneo in Italy to Nice by the newly constructed road across the pass of Lanslebourg. In the 1790s he went through the Lepontine Alps, from Lyons to Turin.

Beaumont's accounts of these journeys show a lively interest in the classical history of the area. He comments on benefits he has received from the works of other scientists active in the region, such as de Saussure, de Luc, and Pictet; he also remarks on the structural geology and mineralogy of the alpine regions and reports altitudes measured with his barometer. Published in large format, these accounts are embellished with maps drawn by himself (which he signed 'A. Beaumont, engineer') and by drawings in simple and sepia-washed versions, the latter coloured by Bernard Lory the elder.

In the early 1790s the duke of Gloucester took Beaumont to London, where he remained during the French Revolution. There he went into partnership with Thomas Gowland and employed Cornelius Apostool as engraver, publishing views of Switzerland, Mediterranean France, and Piedmont. He afterwards took to landscape painting, and in 1806 exhibited *A Storm at Sea* in which the waves were considered very realistic. Under the empire he retired to La Vernaz, in the Haute Savoie, where he reared sheep. In 1808 he was rewarded by the emperor for having acclimatized black merino sheep in that region. He died in 1812.   TIMOTHY CLAYTON and ANITA MCCONNELL

Sources 'Beaumont, Sir Albanis', *Neues allgemeines Künstler-Lexikon*, ed. G. K. Nagler, 1 (Munich, 1835), 349–50 · A. Griseri, 'Beaumont, Claudio Francesco', in A. M. Ghisalberti, *Dizionario biografico degli Italiani*, 7 (Rome, 1965) · *Neues Museum für Künstler und Kunstliebhaber*, ed. J. G. Meusel, 14 (1791), 36–7 · J. F. Albanis Beaumont, introduction, *Travels from France to Italy, through the Lepontine Alps* (1800) · J. F. Albanis Beaumont, introduction, *Travels through the Maritime Alps, from Italy to Lyons* (1795) · J. Philippe, *Les gloires de la Savoie* (1863), 238

Beaumont, John, first Viscount Beaumont (1409?–1460), magnate and courtier, was the elder son and heir of Henry, fifth Baron Beaumont of Folkingham, Lincolnshire (1379/80–1413) and Elizabeth (d. 1427), daughter of William, fifth Baron Willoughby of Eresby. He was one of the most powerful lords in eastern England during the reign of Henry VI, and a firm supporter of the Lancastrian royal family in the troubles of the 1450s.

Four years old at the death of his father, Beaumont became a ward of *Henry V, who granted custody of the boy and his substantial estates, which were concentrated in Lincolnshire and Leicestershire, to Henry *Beaufort (d. 1447), bishop of Winchester. In 1425 Beaumont's marriage was granted to Sir John Radcliffe, and, possibly as early as 1428 (but certainly by July 1436), he wed Elizabeth Phelip, the daughter and sole heir of William *Phelip, Lord Bardolf (d. 1441), a leading figure in the duchy of Lancaster connection in East Anglia. This was to be a valuable association. Not only did Beaumont inherit (in 1441) Bardolf's extensive and conveniently situated holdings in Norfolk, Suffolk, and Lincolnshire, but also his father-in-law's powerful position as chamberlain of the royal household (from 1432) and his close links with William de la Pole, earl of Suffolk (d. 1450), must have helped to secure for him a place in the establishment of the emerging king. Certainly, as the 1430s wore on, the young Beaumont's political standing increased rapidly, and he became one of the most extensively rewarded and important figures in the government. In the summer of 1436 he agreed to accompany the duke of Gloucester on his expedition to protect Calais and (even though this was his first and last involvement in the war in France) he was rewarded with a grant of the county of Boulogne. Two days after Queen Catherine's death on 3 January 1437 he succeeded to the stewardship of the duchy of Lancaster honour of Leicester, which had been part of her dower and which (together with the stewardship of Castle Donington, which he obtained from Henry V's feoffees at the same time) complemented his own holdings in the county superbly. On 12 February 1440 he was made a viscount, the first ever in England, and during the ensuing few years he acquired a life interest in a string of royal lands in Norfolk and Lincolnshire together with the stewardship of the duchy honour of Bolingbroke, Lincolnshire, and (fittingly) a grant of the *vicomté* of Beaumont, Maine. In 1441 or 1442, he was elected to the Garter, and on 29 November 1443 he became a feoffee for the royal foundations at Eton and Cambridge. By 12 November 1445 he had been appointed constable of England.

Beyond his links with Bardolf and the presence of a younger brother, Henry, among the king's esquires, it is difficult to know why Beaumont attracted such an extraordinary heap of honours and perquisites from the crown in these years. Clearly he was not being rewarded for military service overseas. Part of the reason for the favour shown to him must be that, although he does not seem himself to have held any official post in the royal household, he had been part of the royal coterie since Henry VI's childhood. He may actually have been living at court in the later 1420s, since an act of the council in 1425 provided that wards of baronial rank should be permanently about the king. On 12 November 1428, when he was still a minor, he was described as being in the king's service and when, in April 1430, Henry crossed to France for his coronation at Paris, Beaumont was among those accompanying him. It is possible that during these years he established some kind of friendship with the king, and, after Henry began to exercise his powers of patronage from the summer of 1436 onwards, simply petitioned for much, if not all, of what he got. It seems likely, however, that his requests for favour would have had to earn the approval of leading figures of the ruling group as well as that of Henry himself. It may be that Beaumont's partly Lancastrian descent (from Eleanor, daughter of Henry, third earl of Lancaster, his paternal great-great-grandmother) was a factor in obtaining this approval: it was sufficiently widely known for Lord Hungerford to bequeath him a cup of John of Gaunt's in his will. But one of the most important factors in his advancement must surely have been his territorial standing, and this appears to have grown alongside the mound of favours acquired at court. When he came of age, in 1430, he entered into the entire Beaumont patrimony, the widows of the last two lords having died in 1427. From 1441 he controlled the lands of his wife's inheritance and, by royal grant made shortly before her death (before 30 October 1441), the wardship of anything his children might inherit from her. By 25 August 1443 he had acquired an even richer prize by marrying, as her third husband, Katherine Strangways (c.1400–1483) [see Neville, Katherine], the dowager duchess of Norfolk. The daughter of Ralph *Neville, first earl of Westmorland, and Joan *Beaufort, she was the holder of a life interest in the Mowbray estates in Yorkshire, Lincolnshire (Isle of Axholme), Sussex, and the marches of Wales as well as an enormous dowry which included most of the Mowbray manors in Norfolk and Leicestershire. It was this privately held estate in the eastern counties that the grants of royal lands and custodies must have been meant to supplement: the government doubtless intended that the young viscount take his place in the extensive connection of magnates through whom Henry VI's advisers attempted to govern the country.

When the time of reckoning came for Suffolk and his associates in 1450, Beaumont—rather surprisingly—escaped unscathed. He had been involved in some of the regime's most unpopular activities, including the arrest of the duke of Gloucester, the surrender of Maine (for which he was one of only two English lords known to have received the promised compensation), and the maintenance of the notorious William Tailboys (d. 1464). Some local men attacked his manor at Boston, Lincolnshire, in July 1449—no doubt partly in reaction to the extraordinary franchisal powers he had acquired from the king in the previous year—but none the less, to one of the doggerel writers of 1450, he was 'that gentill rache [hound]'

(Robbins, 186): vindicated perhaps by his noble status and his role, as constable, in the arrest of Suffolk. Within days of Suffolk's death Beaumont succeeded him as chamberlain of England, and yielded up his office of constable to the earl of Northumberland a few weeks later.

Although he had been quite closely associated with Richard, duke of York, during the 1430s and 1440s, acting as feoffee for the duke on a number of occasions and probably serving on his council, Beaumont was a consistent supporter of king and court during the 1450s. Initially he may have sought to avoid an open breach with York and his supporters. While he was reluctant to participate in the duke's protectorate of 1454, for example, he came to be on reasonable terms with York's regime: he retained his place in the household in the 'abridgement' of that year and secured a patent protecting his interests in the Bardolf lands; in 1455 he does not seem to have been in the royal army at the battle of St Albans. Even so, there were early signs that he might prove hostile to the Yorkists: he had taken part in the judicial commissions which harried Duke Richard's men in 1452–3 and he had joined the group opposed to York and the Nevilles in the tense winter of 1453–4. As the 1450s wore on, and the lines of division became sharper, his Lancastrian commitment became more overt. One of the most important factors in this was probably his close association with Queen Margaret. As a major Leicestershire landowner and leading courtier Beaumont was an obvious ally and agent for the queen, whose dower centred on the honours of Leicester, Kenilworth, and Tutbury. He had been the chief steward of her lands from as early as 1446 and, as Margaret assumed the leadership of the Lancastrian cause after the death of Edmund Beaufort in 1455, he was one of her principal lieutenants; he became chief steward of Prince Edward's lands on 20 January 1457 and of the northern parts of the duchy of Lancaster on 6 December 1459. It was Beaumont's prominence in the regime of the late 1450s that provoked the Yorkist lords to identify him as one of their three 'mortalle and extreme enemyes' (English Chronicle, 88) in 1460 and, allegedly, to secure his excommunication at the hands of the papal legate at about the same time. Together with other leading associates of the queen (notably the duke of Buckingham, whose daughter had married William, Beaumont's eldest surviving son, in 1452), Beaumont was killed in the Yorkist victory at Northampton on 10 July 1460, possibly by the men of Kent. He was not attainted, and in November 1460 his son was allowed to succeed to his lands without suit, but the new government's conciliatory efforts were unavailing. By the time of the battle of Towton, in March 1461, William, second Viscount Beaumont (d. 1507), had followed his father into the Lancastrian camp.

John Beaumont's appearance is unknown and there is little evidence of his character. It is possible that he was a man of somewhat extreme, though conventional, piety, as he is known to have pressed for action to be taken against the controversial Bishop Pecock in 1457. In this display of orthodoxy, as in his detachment from the war in France and his close association with the royal court, he was perhaps a typical member of the later Lancastrian nobility.   JOHN WATTS

Sources Chancery records · PRO · R. A. Griffiths, *The reign of King Henry VI: the exercise of royal authority, 1422–1461* (1981) · R. L. Storey, 'Lincolnshire and the Wars of the Roses', *Nottingham Mediaeval Studies*, 14 (1970), 64–83 · R. Somerville, *History of the duchy of Lancaster, 1265–1603* (1953) · A. R. Myers, 'The household of Queen Margaret of Anjou, 1452–3', *Bulletin of the John Rylands University Library*, 40 (1957–8), 79–113, 391–431 · C. Carpenter, *Locality and polity: a study of Warwickshire landed society, 1401–1499* (1992) · E. Acheson, *A gentry community: Leicestershire in the fifteenth century, c.1422–c.1485* (1992) · R. E. Archer, 'Rich old ladies: the problem of late medieval dowagers', *Property and politics: essays in later medieval English history*, ed. T. Pollard (1984), 15–35 · J. C. Wedgwood and A. D. Holt, *History of parliament*, 1: *Biographies of the members of the Commons house, 1439–1509* (1936) · C. Richmond, *The Paston family in the fifteenth century: the first phase* (1990) · M. K. Jones, 'Somerset, York and the Wars of the Roses', *EngHR*, 104 (1989), 285–307 · H. L. Gray, 'Incomes from land in England in 1436', *EngHR*, 49 (1934), 607–39 · T. B. Pugh and C. D. Ross, 'The English baronage and the income tax of 1436', *BIHR*, 26 (1953), 1–28 · BL, Add. Ch. 74926 · GEC, *Peerage* · R. H. Robbins, ed., *Historical poems of the XIVth and XVth centuries* (1959) · J. S. Davies, ed., *An English chronicle of the reigns of Richard II, Henry IV, Henry V, and Henry VI*, CS, 64 (1856) · I. M. W. Harvey, *Jack Cade's rebellion of 1450* (1991) · J. L. Watts, *Henry VI and the politics of kingship* (1996)

Wealth at death over £1962—lands and annuities, p.a.: will, BL Add. Ch. 74926; Gray, 'Incomes from land'; Pugh and Ross, 'The English baronage'; PRO; Chancery records

Beaumont, John (*d.* in or after **1556**), lawyer and administrator, was the elder son of Thomas Beaumont of Thringstone, Leicestershire (who was cousin to John Beaumont, first Viscount Beaumont), and his wife, Mary, daughter of Robert Moton of Peckleton, Leicestershire. A member of the Inner Temple by 1529, in that year he was retained as counsel by the borough of Leicester, and in 1530 was appointed reader of Clement's Inn by the Inner Temple. At an unknown date he married Isabel, daughter of Lawrence Dutton of Dutton, Cheshire; they had two daughters. She died some time before 1540. Between August 1534 and June 1536 Beaumont was appointed to commissions to take ecclesiastical surveys of Leicestershire, and in November 1535 became escheator of Warwickshire and Leicestershire, a position he held until December 1536. In 1537 he became recorder of Leicester, retaining the post until 1542, while in 1536 he became a bencher of the Inner Temple, and in November 1537 was elected reader of the inn for Lent 1538.

As a commissioner for the suppression of Leicestershire monasteries, Beaumont answered interrogatories touching alleged irregularities, but when the priory of Grace Dieu, near Belton, Leicestershire, was surrendered in October 1538 he was put in possession. The priory's lands were granted to Sir Humphrey Foster, who conveyed them to Beaumont and his second wife, Elizabeth (*d.* 1588), in special tail. Elizabeth, whom he had married by 1540, was the daughter of William Hastings, younger son of William Hastings, first Baron Hastings, and uncle of George Hastings, first earl of Huntingdon and steward of the honour of Leicester. They had two sons and two daughters. The elder son, Francis *Beaumont (*d.* 1598), became a justice of the court of common pleas, and the younger son, Henry

(*d.* 1585), was a member of the Middle Temple. Beaumont's connection with the Hastings family was not entirely happy. In January 1538 he had written to Thomas Cromwell with legal advice about a land purchase from the earl of Huntingdon, and he wrote again in December 1538, complaining that Huntingdon intended to evict him from Gracedieu, saying that he feared for his life, and asking to purchase the priory lands.

From 1531 until at least 1544 Beaumont was frequently a justice of the peace for Leicestershire and Derbyshire, and served also as a commissioner of oyer and terminer on the midland circuit, and of gaol delivery in Leicester. Lent reader of the Inner Temple in 1543, on 30 January 1545 he was appointed receiver-general of the court of wards and liveries, an office of profit and power for a man of ability. In 1536 Beaumont had been granted the stewardship of Whitwick, Leicestershire, by Margaret Grey, marchioness of Dorset, to whom he was of counsel, but in 1546 came a confrontation with her husband, Henry Grey, marquess of Dorset, at the sessions for the contribution at Leicester. Upon hearing both sides the privy council found Beaumont's charge of ill treatment against Dorset unjustified, warning him 'to know in better sort his superiors' (*LP Henry VIII*, 21/1, no. 599), a set-back that had no lasting effect upon Beaumont's career. In 1547 he became treasurer of the Inner Temple. In 1548 he bought the newly dissolved college of the New Work in Leicester, and in 1550 briefly resumed office as the town's recorder.

Beaumont became master of the rolls on 13 December 1550. Although he was not a civilian, as his predecessors had frequently been, his career at the bar appears to have centred upon the courts of chancery and Star Chamber. The mastership of the rolls was to prove Beaumont's undoing, though the seeds of downfall had been sown in the court of wards. While receiver-general he had, as Edward VI noted in 1552, 'bought land with my money, had lent it, and kept it from me to the [value of] £9000 and above … and £11,000 in obligations' (*Chronicle*, 128). Beaumont had speculated with the court's revenues, and had taken payments from crown debtors while failing to enter them in the record. This was not all: as master of the rolls he had during litigation between Anne, Lady Grey of Powis, and Henry Grey, now duke of Suffolk, forged the signature of Charles Brandon, late duke of Suffolk, to a deed in favour of Lady Grey whose supposed title he then purchased, and had concealed the felony of a servant. In February 1552 Beaumont was imprisoned, and an investigation pressed by John Dudley, duke of Northumberland, revealed his defalcations. Financial charges were brought at this time against several members of Protector Somerset's following, but Beaumont's guilt seems unquestionable. On 28 May 1552 he surrendered the mastership of the rolls, acknowledged a debt to the king of over £20,000, and surrendered his lands to satisfy it. He soon began to deny his guilt, but in June 1552 confessed again before the privy council and in the Star Chamber. In the same year, perhaps seeing its chance, the town of Leicester sent a deputation to London to attempt to recover charity land granted away by Beaumont about 1540.

Beaumont is said to have received a writ for creation as serjeant-at-law in 1552, but was not created. His surrendered lands, including Grace Dieu, were granted in 1553 to Francis Hastings, earl of Huntingdon, although his wife, Elizabeth, recovered them from her relative after Beaumont's death. The dealings with Beaumont's lands gave rise to litigation in the court of wards in *Beaumont's case* (1612). Beaumont continued to attend parliament in the Inner Temple until 1556, and may have died soon thereafter.   N. G. JONES

Sources J. Nichols, *The history and antiquities of the county of Leicester*, 1/2 (1815) · J. Nichols, *The history and antiquities of the county of Leicester*, 3/2 (1804) · *LP Henry VIII* · F. A. Inderwick and R. A. Roberts, eds., *A calendar of the Inner Temple records*, 1 (1896) · *CSP dom.*, 1547–53 · M. Bateson and others, eds., *Records of the borough of Leicester*, 3: 1509–1603 (1905) · W. Camden, *The visitation of the county of Leicester in the year 1619*, ed. J. Fetherston, Harleian Society, 2 (1870) · J. Hurstfield, *The queen's wards: wardship and marriage under Elizabeth I* (1958) · *The chronicle and political papers of King Edward VI*, ed. W. K. Jordan (1966) · W. K. Jordan, *Edward VI, 2: The threshold of power* (1970) · W. Dugdale, *Origines juridiciales, or, Historical memorials of the English laws*, 2nd edn (1671) · E. Foss, *Biographia juridica: a biographical dictionary of the judges of England … 1066–1870* (1870) · Baker, *Serjeants* · Dugdale, *Monasticon*, new edn, vol. 6/1

Beaumont, Sir John, first baronet (c.1584–1627), poet, was the second of the four children of Francis *Beaumont (d. 1598), queen's justice in the court of common pleas, and his wife, Anne Pierrepoint. He was said to be fourteen or thereabouts at his father's death in 1598. More obviously than his younger brother, Francis *Beaumont, the dramatist, John was marked by the family's somewhat paradoxical tradition, with its strong religious and secular currents.

Beaumont grew up in the company of a mother and a paternal grandmother who were both staunch recusants, and he doubtless heard talk of his uncle Gervase Pierrepoint's imprisonment for assisting Campion. The Leicestershire Beaumonts belonged to a whole chain of Catholic families which, with its own secret priesthood, extended from the Manners family of the earls of Rutland at Belvoir down through all the ranks of nearby aristocracy and gentry. Grace Dieu (in the parish of Belton), the family home, had itself been, until the dissolution, a priory for Augustinian nuns, standing 'low in a Valley upon a little Brooke, in a solitary place, compassed around with an high and strong stone wall, within which the Nunnes had made a Garden, in resemblance of that upon *Olivet Gethsemane*' (Burton, 122), a resemblance which Beaumont doubtless came to cherish.

Beaumont always felt that high rank and illustrious pedigrees should be underwritten by a purity of soul, preferably as cultivated under the old religion. When, in 'The Crowne of Thornes', his still unpublished *magnum opus*, he claims descent from John de Brienne, king of Jerusalem, the reason for his satisfaction is that de Brienne, as a result of 'heavenly visions', had come to embrace the rule of St Francis (Wallerstein, 410). On the other hand, both Beaumont's grandfather and father were very much men of the world, the latter becoming particularly well known for his severity towards recusants, even if as a younger

man he had probably joined his womenfolk in their support. John, though he concluded 'The Crowne of Thornes' with a fervent hope that Charles I's marriage to 'our second Marie' would usher in a restoration of the religion once symbolized by Mary, queen of Scots, sometimes saw his own best chance of furthering that end in what can easily seem a cringing deference to powers temporal.

Together with Francis and his elder brother, Henry, Beaumont matriculated at Oxford University (Broadgates Hall) in February 1597, and in November of the same year they went on, like their grandfather and father before them, to the Inner Temple. In London, Beaumont must have consorted not only with several relatives but with established and aspiring men of letters. His friendship with Drayton was established by 1603, and during these early years Beaumont probably wrote his anti-Petrarchan satirical verse, partly under the influence of the Jesuit poetics of Southwell. His own link with the capital's recusant circles is confirmed by his marriage, at some time before August 1607, to Elizabeth, daughter of John Fortescue, officer of the queen's wardrobe, who frequently sheltered Catholic priests in his home in the gatehouse of the old Blackfriars priory. In October 1605, a mere three months after Beaumont had inherited the family estates on the death of Henry, the profits of his own impending conviction for recusancy had been assigned to Sir James Sempill. When on 22 September 1607 the crown commissioners duly seized two thirds of sixteen Leicestershire properties, the law allowed him to keep Grace Dieu as his residence but confined his movements to within 5 miles of it.

In 1610 Beaumont was granted permission to revisit London, probably in connection with a claim on the family estates unsuccessfully lodged on behalf of Henry's posthumous daughter. For the most part his years of rural retirement must have been devoted to his fast-growing family—there were to be seven sons and four daughters in all—and to the consolations of philosophy, religion, and literature. His translations of classical poems on urban vices and the simple virtues of the countryside, together with a number of funeral elegies and didactic poems expressing a Christian-stoical *contemptus mundi*, sufficiently hint at his frame of mind.

Beaumont's career as a court poet began at the instigation of his enterprising kinswoman Maria, countess of Buckingham and mother to George Villiers, marquess (later duke) of Buckingham, the royal favourite. Among other pieces Beaumont wrote an epithalamium for Buckingham's marriage in 1620 to Lady Katherine Manners, daughter of the earl of Rutland. In 1621 Buckingham gave Beaumont a chance to present verses to James I, which during his remaining years he followed up with a sequence of panegyrics and occasional poems for the king, Prince Charles, and Buckingham himself. Even 'Bosworth Field', his most famous work, rather fulsomely endorses James's claim to legitimacy as a descendant of the victorious Henry Tudor.

Yet 'Bosworth Field' is by no means exclusively sycophantic, and is no less Beaumontian in being rather Janus-faced. Its elegantly energetic pentameter couplets are a foretaste of Dryden, and its rationalistic use of figurative language anticipates Hobbes's preference of judgement over fancy. At the same time the account of Richard III's wickedness is almost medieval in its grim horror, and the portrayal of noblemen and gentry on both sides of the battle breathes a nostalgia for what Beaumont sees as pristine virtues. This same ethically motivated interest in history also led him to champion Edmund Bolton's proposal for an academy of honour, of which he himself would have been one of the 'essentials'; a coherent *ars poetica* for celebratory or epic didacticism is developed in two impressive companion poems addressed to James I and Prince Charles. His own funeral elegies on James I, on the earl of Southampton (patron of 'The Crowne of Thornes'), and on other prominent supporters of the old religion are substantial memorials, often rising to considerable eloquence and intensity of feeling. 'The Crowne of Thornes' itself (BL, Add. MS 33392), which probably occupied Beaumont from 1620 to May 1625, meditates on Christ's passion, universal lordship, and earthly representatives with an emotionality of devout wit which makes it one of the most striking expressions of Counter-Reformation sensibility in English. Similar qualities are to be found in a series of shorter devotional poems, whose artistic organization is a good bit tighter. One of the finest is 'Upon the two great feasts of the annunciation and resurrection falling on the same day, March 25 1627'.

On 31 January 1627 Beaumont had been made a baronet. On 19 April he was buried in Westminster Abbey. His old friend Drayton, in a tribute which fiercely decries the baseness of the age, states—perhaps in reference to Beaumont's career at court—that:

[his] care for that which was not worth … [his] breath
Brought on too soon … [his] much lamented death.
(Beaumont, 64)

Both before and after his death Beaumont's poems circulated in manuscript. But in 1629 his eldest son, John, saw 'Bosworth Field' and a selection of other shorter poems through the press, with a dedication to Charles I. Prefatory poems by Jonson, Thomas Hawkins, Thomas Nevill, George Fortescue, Philip Kynder, Ia. Cl. (James Clayton?), John Beaumont junior, and Francis, Beaumont's second son, offer clear testimony to the esteem in which he was held for both his artistry and the holiness of his vocation. Less than a century later Wood's assertion that Beaumont wrote poems only in the early part of his life had been widely accepted, and he was mainly remembered for the couplets of 'Bosworth Field'. His Victorian editor did admire the shorter religious poems yet described him as a puritan. More recently scholars have rediscovered 'The Crowne of Thornes', have illuminated its recusant background, and have emphasized that during Beaumont's last seven years the serious spiritual concerns and the time-serving to some extent went hand in hand. ROGER D. SELL

Sources [J. Beaumont], *The shorter poems of Sir John Beaumont*, ed. R. D. Sell, 49 (1974) • M. Eccles, 'A biographical dictionary of Elizabethan authors', *Huntington Library Quarterly*, 5 (1941–2), 281–302 • R. D. Sell, 'Notes on the religious and family background of Francis and Sir John Beaumont', *Neuphilologische Mitteilungen*, 76 (1975), 299–307 • R. Wallerstein, 'Sir John Beaumont's *Crowne of thornes*: a report', *Journal of English and Germanic Studies*, 53 (1954), 410–34 • W. Burton, *The description of Leicester Shire* (1622) • GEC, *Baronetage*, 2.5–6

Beaumont, John (*c.*1636–1701), army officer, was the second son of Sapcote Beaumont, second Viscount Beaumont of Swords (1614–1658), of Burton, Lincolnshire, and his first wife, Bridget Monson (*d.* 1640), daughter of Sir Thomas *Monson, first baronet, of Carlton, Lincolnshire. He was educated at Market Bosworth grammar school and in 1653 he matriculated at Christ's College, Cambridge. Support for Charles I during the civil war cost Viscount Beaumont his house and a fortune estimated at £10,000. With neither means nor prospects, the young John Beaumont joined Charles II in exile and became a royal favourite: Charles actively assisted his suit of Lady Felicia Compton, *née* Pigott (*d.* 1687), whom he married on 10 September 1663. He began his military career in 1666 as captain of an independent troop of horse, but this command was disbanded after the treaty of Breda in the following year. Probably Beaumont then sold his services to the Dutch army, returning to England in 1674 with a captain's commission in the Holland regiment, transferring into the Irish foot guards in 1676. In 1678 he recrossed the North Sea, and entered the Anglo-Dutch brigade as a captain, in which post he was still serving in 1684.

Following the accession of James II in 1685, Beaumont, who was well known to James, having demonstrated tory sympathies during the exclusion crisis, returned to England to become a royal equerry and lieutenant-colonel of Princess Anne of Denmark's regiment of foot. In addition, he entered national politics as MP for Nottingham in 1685 and was appointed lieutenant-governor of Dover Castle in 1686. His loyalty to James, though, was illusory: his extensive connections in the Dutch army and staunch protestantism made him an ideal member of the growing military conspiracy against the king on behalf of William of Orange. In February 1688 Beaumont's colonel, James, duke of Berwick, was ordered to take between forty and fifty supernumerary Catholic Irish soldiers into his regiment then in garrison at Portsmouth. The 'Portsmouth Captains'—Beaumont, supported by Thomas Paston, Simon Pack, Thomas Orme, William Cooke, and John Port—refused and were subsequently court-martialled in Windsor Castle and cashiered. John Churchill, later duke of Marlborough, was particularly hostile towards Beaumont, presumably because his ill-considered protest might have compromised the pro-Dutch army conspiracy. Beaumont joined William of Orange ten days after his landing and attained the colonelcy of Princess Anne's Foot, the restoration of his lieutenant-governorship of Dover Castle, and election as MP for Hastings in the general elections of 1689 and 1690. After 1689 he settled to his military duties, serving with his regiment at the battle of the Boyne in 1690 and the siege of Namur in 1692. In 1693 he married Philippa Carew, daughter of Sir Nicholas Carew of Bedington, Surrey, his first wife having died in

1687. In May 1695 he fought a duel with Sir William Forrester 'occasioned by some words between them in the parliament house' (Luttrell, 3.564). Beaumont resigned his military commissions in December 1695 and died, childless, on 3 July 1701. He was survived by his second wife.

T. F. HENDERSON, rev. JOHN CHILDS

Sources N. Luttrell, *A brief historical relation of state affairs from September 1678 to April 1714*, 6 vols. (1857) · *The manuscripts of the marquis of Ormonde*, [old ser.], 3 vols., HMC, 36 (1895–1909), vol. 2, p. 212 · C. Dalton, ed., *Irish army lists, 1661–1685* (privately printed, London, 1907) · C. Dalton, ed., *English army lists and commission registers, 1661–1714*, 6 vols. (1892–1904) · *CSP dom.* · J. Nichols, *The history and antiquities of the county of Leicester*, 3 (1800–04) · J. Fitzjames [Duke of Berwick], *Memoirs of the marshal duke of Berwick*, 2 vols. (1779) · J. Childs, *The army, James II, and the Glorious Revolution* (1980) · GEC, *Peerage*

Likenesses R. White, group portrait, line engraving, 1688 (*The Portsmouth captains*), BM, NPG; repro. in T. B. Macaulay, *The history of England from the accession of James the Second*, ed. C. H. Firth (1913–15), vol 3, p. 1073

Beaumont, John (*c*.1640–1731), natural philosopher and collector of geological specimens, spent most of his life at Ston Easton, Somerset, where he practised medicine. He befriended the miners working in the nearby Mendip hills, with whom he explored newly discovered caverns and rock formations. Stimulated by Martin Lister's descriptions of fossils, he sent two letters 'concerning Rock-Plants and their growth' to the secretary of the Royal Society, Henry Oldenburg, who published them in the society's *Philosophical Transactions* in 1676. Beaumont described finds of 'trochites' (which would now be called crinoids) in the Mendips, and supported Lister's hypothesis that these were plants which had grown in the rock. He maintained that all fossils were natural products of the earth's seminal principles, which he described as 'Salts, Sulphurs, and Mercuries', and that their characters derived from those of the locations where they grew. He later supported these ideas by references to the neoplatonic philosophy of Joan Baptista van Helmont.

For a decade Beaumont continued to send material to the Royal Society, and became a fellow in May 1685. His contributions included an account of the use of gunpowder to blast rocks (1685) and observations of the effects of hazardous gases in mines (1679). In 1681 the second number of Robert Hooke's *Philosophical Collections* included Beaumont's account of Wookey Hole, and of the first descent of Lamb Leer—Somerset caves into which Beaumont had first been lowered before 1676, and where he had collected fossils. He was encouraged by Robert Plot to write a natural history of Somerset, and sent proposals for this design to the Oxford Philosophical Society in 1685; however, his plans to win the support of the Somerset gentry were frustrated by the upheavals which followed Monmouth's rebellion, and, to the disappointment of his acquaintances, he abandoned the project.

By 1689 Beaumont was at work on *Considerations on a Book Entitled The Theory of the Earth* (1693), which criticized the writings of Thomas Burnet. John Ray considered this to be the most effective of a number of books attacking Burnet, in particular praising Beaumont's calculations concerning the volume of water needed to cover the earth during the biblical flood. However, both Ray and Hooke worried that parts of Beaumont's book, especially its account of the mythology of the ancients, might be considered to be tainted by religious 'enthusiasm'. Beaumont had argued that it was impossible to give a complete philosophical account of all the events described by the Bible, claiming that some things were simply miraculous. Nevertheless, in a postscript which he published in 1694, Beaumont sought to rebut accusations that his *Considerations* were too credulous.

During the 1680s and 1690s Beaumont was a frequent visitor to London, and took part in philosophical discussions with Hooke and others at Jonathan's Coffee House, in Exchange Alley, Cornhill. But his interests moved away from natural history, and, in October 1694, he offered unsuccessfully to sell his collection of geological and fossil specimens to Oxford University for £20. Edward Lhwyd had visited Beaumont's collection in 1691, but felt that this was too high a price for material which he had judged 'did not seem very considerable'. However, he later praised 'Mr. Beaumont's curious Collection of minerals' (Gunther, 14.254).

Beaumont also proved unlucky as a buyer of specimens. In 1702 he acted without success as an intermediary for Hans Sloane in negotiations to purchase the collection of William Cole of Bristol for the Royal Society's repository. Beaumont had been a friend of Cole, and maintained links with other west-country natural philosophers, notably Andrew Paschall and John Aubrey. He also found a congenial acquaintance in Edward Fowler, bishop of Gloucester, who sent him information for the new project on which he was working, *An Historical, Physiological and Theological Treatise of Spirits* (1705), which discussed accounts of genii, familiar spirits, oracles, and second sight. This was Beaumont's most substantial work, and demonstrated his considerable knowledge of English and continental scholarship. In particular he defended the existence of spirits, and their ability to communicate with human beings, against the criticisms of Balthasar Bekker. His efforts were praised by Fowler, and by William Nicolson, bishop of Carlisle, and were said to have converted his old adversary, Thomas Burnet. The *Treatise* reached a European audience, being translated into German by Theodor Arnold, and published at Halle in 1721, with a generous preface by Christian Thomasius (1655-1728). Beaumont's familiarity with the world of continental scholarship may have been acquired through travel overseas. He was a friend of the Abbé Bignon, secretary of the Parisian Académie Royale des Sciences, who later stated that Beaumont had been a Roman Catholic (BL, Sloane MS 4069, fol. 95v). Beaumont did have links with the Catholic gentry in Somerset, dedicating *The Present State of the Universe* (1694) to the Hon. Charles Cottington. Beaumont's *Treatise*, and *Gleanings of Antiquities* (1724), demonstrated his faith in the miraculous, and sympathy for authors such as Richard Simon or John Toland, who criticised orthodox protestant biblical scholarship. They also revealed his claims to have had personal experience of the spirit world, through voices which he had heard at key moments in the later part of his life. Bignon claimed that fairies had instructed Beaumont to marry Dorothy, daughter of John Speccot, of Penheale, Egloskerry, Cornwall, who did indeed become his wife. Pursuit of her claims to the property of her brother, John, following his death without issue, led Beaumont into a long and expensive lawsuit which ended unsuccessfully in 1714. Beaumont believed that he had heard spirit voices on at least two occasions when he was troubled by this dispute. However, despite his self-confessed melancholy, he lived to be over ninety. He died in 1731, and was buried at Ston Easton on 23 March 1731.   SCOTT MANDELBROTE

Sources R. T. Gunther, *Early science in Oxford*, 4 (1925), 122, 130; 10 (1935), 114, 195; 12 (1939); 14 (1945), 138–9, 254 · BL, Sloane MS, Abbé Bignon to Hans Sloane, 1740, 4069 [fols. 60; 94–103] · J. Jekyll and J. Pratt, *William Darbison, ... plaintiff: the defendants' case* [1714] · P. King and J. Fortescue, *William Darbison, (on the demise of Thomas Long), plaintiff, and John Beaumont and Dorothy his wife, defendants* (1714) · *Further correspondence of John Ray*, ed. R. W. T. Gunther, Ray Society, 114 (1928), 242, 245 · *The diary of Ralph Thoresby*, ed. J. Hunter, 2 (1830), 103, 124 · *The diary of Robert Hooke ... 1672–1680*, ed. H. W. Robinson and W. Adams (1935), 422–30 · R. G. [R. Gough], *British topography*, [new edn], 2 (1780), 189 · BL, Sloane MS, Beaumont to Hans Sloane, 2.5.1702, 4038 [fol. 336] · W. Camden, *Britannia, or, A chorographical description of Great Britain and Ireland*, ed. E. Gibson, 3rd edn (1753), 827 · *The London diaries of William Nicolson, bishop of Carlisle, 1702–1718*, ed. C. Jones and G. Holmes (1985), 335, 352 · T. R. Shaw, 'Lamb Leer in the seventeenth century', *Proceedings of the University of Bristol Spelaeological Society*, 9 (1961–2), 183–7 · DNB

Archives RS, MS B2

Beaumont, John Thomas Barber (1774–1841), artist and founder of insurance offices, was born on 21 December 1774 in Marylebone, Middlesex. His family surname was Barber, but about 1812 he added Beaumont, and thenceforth was usually known as Barber Beaumont. In 1796 he married Sophia Sarah Schabner, and they had ten children. Barber's early career was devoted to painting. Admitted a student of the Royal Academy in 1791, he exhibited regularly there between 1794 and 1806, and was appointed miniature painter to Prince Edward and the dukes of Kent and York. His first publication was a fashionable, illustrated *Tour through South Wales* in 1803. Thereafter he wrote on a range of topical issues, including papers on *Life Insurance* (1814), *Provident and Parish Banks* (1816), *Public House Licensing* (1816–18), *Criminal Jurisprudence* (1821), and *Parliamentary Reform* (1830). During the Napoleonic Wars he advocated national defence, publishing several essays and *The Weekly Register* (1809–11) to propagate his views. In 1803 he raised a rifle corps, known as 'the Duke of Cumberland's sharpshooters', which became renowned for their marksmanship.

In 1806 Barber successfully launched the Provident Life Office, and in the following year the County Fire Office. With the support of landed gentry and West End bankers, the County grew within twenty years to become the fifth largest fire insurer in Britain. As managing director he demonstrated an energy and attention to the details of risk assessment and marketing, as well as to the broad brush of strategy, which quickly made him an important figure in the insurance world. In 1820 Barber Beaumont

was appointed magistrate for Middlesex and Westminster. Always a champion of causes, he was labelled a radical by his critics for his public support of George IV's estranged wife, Queen Caroline. He acquired extensive property in Mile End, and in 1840 founded the Philosophical Institution there for 'the mental and moral improvement' of the residents, to which he bequeathed £13,000. This institution later became Queen Mary College, London University. He died at the County Fire Office in Regent Street on 15 May 1841; he was buried in his private cemetery at Stepney, but was later reinterred in Kensal Green cemetery.   ROBIN PEARSON

Sources A. Noakes, *The County Fire Office, 1807–1957* (1957) · *GM*, 2nd ser., 16 (1841) · *The Times* (17 May 1841) · *The Times* (22 June 1841) · D. A. Beaumont, *Barber Beaumont* (1999) · J. T. Barber, *A tour through south Wales and Monmouthshire* (1803) · IGI · BL cat. · Graves, *RA exhibitors*, vol. 1 (1970) · C. A. G. C. Keeson, 'Barber Beaumont', *East London Papers*, 3 (1960), 13–21 · d. cert.

Archives Royal Sun Alliance plc, 77 Shaftesbury Avenue, London, county fire office MSS

Likenesses J. T. Barber, self-portrait, 1794, Royal Sun Alliance plc, 77 Shaftesbury Avenue, London · J. T. Barber, self-portrait, 1803, Royal Sun Alliance plc, 77 Shaftesbury Avenue, London · H. W. Pickersgill, portrait, 1822, Royal Sun Alliance plc, 77 Shaftesbury Avenue, London · J. Thomson, stipple, 1822 (after J. T. B. Beaumont), BM, NPG · J. H. Lynch, lithograph (after E. H. Baily), BM, NPG

Wealth at death £48,000: will, PRO; Beaumont, *Barber Beaumont*, 186

Beaumont, Joseph (1616–1699), poet and college head, was born at Hadleigh, Suffolk, on 13 March 1616, the second of the four sons of John Beaumont (1584–1653), clothier, and his wife, Sarah Clarke (d. 1646). He was educated at the local grammar school under William Hawkins, in whose masque *Apollo Shroving* (1627) he played two roles. On 26 April 1631 he entered Peterhouse, Cambridge, with the rank of pensioner; he graduated BA in 1635. His academic abilities were recognized by his election to a fellowship on 20 November 1636, simultaneously with the poet Richard Crashaw, with whom he took the MA in 1638.

Besides contributing together to university collections of congratulatory verse Beaumont and Crashaw read widely in religious and secular literature. In a public lecture delivered in 1638 Beaumont revealed a wide acquaintance with foreign poetry and extolled the writings of St Teresa of Avila. Peterhouse under its successive masters Matthew Wren and John Cosin had become a centre of Laudianism, and the two young men played an enthusiastic part in the ritual of the new chapel there. On 29 May 1640 Wren, by then bishop of Ely, granted them dimissory letters for ordination. Their ministrations were described early in the following year in a puritan report on innovations in religion at Cambridge that charged Beaumont with 'commending Legendary Stories & fabulous tales of the vertue of the Crosse to fellow Commoners & others of the Colledge' and with delivering doctrinally unsound sermons (BL, Harley MS 7019, fol. 73). On 8 April 1644, having seen their chapel desecrated by parliamentary warrant, they were among five Peterhouse fellows ejected by the earl of Manchester.

Beaumont retired to his father's house, where for a

while he kept in touch with Crashaw. Even from the Tower, Wren remained a staunch patron, presenting him between 1644 and 1648 to the rectories of Kelshall in Hertfordshire and of Elm with Emneth in Cambridgeshire and to a stall at Ely. Much of Beaumont's side of the correspondence carried on in Latin between 1642 and 1666 survives in a later transcript (BL, Harley MS 7049, fols. 38–57v). Although the composition of his 30,000-verse religious epic *Psyche, or, Love's Mystery* is said to have been completed over eleven months from April 1647, he had already in March 1646 confessed himself 'Tire'd with my PSYCHE' after a year's work on it (*Minor Poems*, 280). In *Psyche* twenty cantos of six-line heroic stanzas trace the course of 'a *Soule* led by divine *Grace*, and her *Guardian Angel* ... through the difficult Temptations and Assaults [of life] to heavenly *Felicitie*' (*Psyche*, 'The Author to the Reader'). The format of this mystical allegory follows Spenser and the Fletchers and the style owes much to Marino, while the author laments the lack of Crashaw's 'kinde-censuring hand' (canto IV, stanza 95, in 1648). The poem was published early in 1648 and reissued in 1651.

On 7 May 1650 at Putney church Beaumont had married Elizabeth (1623–1662), daughter of Robert Brownrigg of Sproughton and stepdaughter of Wren. Deprived of his cures under the Commonwealth, he lived for the next ten years on his wife's estate at Tattingstone, near Ipswich, which was worth more than £500 a year. Here, where his four sons and two daughters were born, he devoted himself to religious study, and in addition to commentaries on Ecclesiastes and the Pentateuch wrote some lost exercises in Latin verse entitled 'Cathemerina'. Beaumont's 177 English poems surviving in manuscript (*Minor Poems*) are apparently disposed in order of composition between March 1644 and June 1652. They consist largely of religious meditations, on saints, church festivals, and private anniversaries, with hymns set to music by 'R. C.' and 'T. T.' Though seldom straying in inspiration or technique from the twin models of Herbert and Crashaw, at their best they transcend mere imitation.

At the Restoration, Beaumont was granted a mandate for the DD, and as a royal chaplain waited his turn each January at Whitehall until past his sixtieth birthday. His sermon on the anniversary of Charles I's execution in 1667 was too well attended to afford John Evelyn admittance. Early in 1661 Beaumont answered Wren's request to reside as domestic chaplain at Ely, where he had recently been installed as canon. There his wife died of fen fever on 29 May 1662, and was buried in the cathedral two days later; a fine tribute was incorporated in the revised version of *Psyche* (canto XVIII, stanzas 1–56, in 1702). Within a month he had moved to Cambridge as master of Jesus College, but on 24 April 1663 transferred to Peterhouse—both apparently through the influence of Wren, who soon afterwards collated him to three further rectories. At Peterhouse, Beaumont showed himself an able administrator and a strict disciplinarian, although he could be high-handed and fractious on occasion.

High-churchmanship now prevailed in the university, and one observer noted that Beaumont and other heads 'carried things so high that I saw latitude and moderation were odious to the greater part' (*Burnet's History*, 464). After some reservations expressed privately to the author of *An Explanation of the Grand Mystery of Godliness* (1660) were made public in *A Modest Enquiry* (1663) Beaumont replied with *Some Observations on the Apologie of Dr. Henry More* (1665). From 1674 he served conscientiously as regius professor of divinity, leaving behind seventeen lectures on Romans and Colossians, series of determinations on questions disputed for degrees, and some sermons. His theological works were praised and a few specimens printed by his first biographer (Gee, 107–39), though Grosart, writing from a radically different religious viewpoint, disputed any claim to true scholarship (*Complete Poems*, 1.xiii, xiv). The failure of the commission for religious comprehension to which he was appointed in the autumn of 1689 spared him any liturgical conflict.

At eighty-three, after preaching the university's annual Gunpowder Plot sermon, Beaumont was attacked by gout in the stomach ('ventriculi arthritis') and died on 23 November 1699. He is commemorated by an inscribed stone and Latin mural epitaph in Peterhouse chapel, from which two scriptural scenes that he had executed in chalk and charcoal beside the altar are now lost (Carter, 30). His youngest son, Charles, 'wrote but never spoke' a Latin panegyric (CUL, MS Mm.I.44, pp. 111–25); there he recalled his father carrying everywhere with him a small edition of Terence, for the style. Charles inherited his father's books and papers now preserved at Peterhouse, being expressly prohibited from publishing any writings 'unless it be the Copy of Psyche revised and augmented to 24 Cantos' that duly appeared in 1702 (will, CUL, 383–6). The frontispiece was engraved by Robert White from the quarter-length portrait in skull cap and gown that is preserved in the college.

W. H. KELLIHER

Sources *Original poems in English and Latin ... by Joseph Beaumont, D.D., to which is prefixed an account of his life and writings*, ed. J. Gee (1749) • *Complete poems of Joseph Beaumont*, ed. A. B. Grosart, 2 vols. (1880) • *Minor poems of Joseph Beaumont*, ed. E. Robinson (Boston and New York, 1914) [MS in Wellesley College, Mass.] • T. A. Walker, *A Peterhouse bibliography* (1924), 12–13 • T. A. Walker, *Peterhouse* (1935) • [J. Gee (?)], *Memoirs of Joseph Beaumont*, ed. T. A. Walker (1934) • H. Pigot, *Hadleigh* (1860), 157–66 • J. J. Muskett, *Suffolk manorial families*, 3 vols. (1900–14) [1894] • A. Warren, *Richard Crashaw: a study in baroque sensibility* (1939) • A. Pritchard, 'Puritan charges against Crashaw and Beaumont', *TLS* (2 July 1964), 578 • E. E. Duncan-Jones, 'Who was the recipient of Crashaw's Leyden letter?', *New perspectives on the life and art of Richard Crashaw*, ed. J. R. Roberts (Columbia, MS, 1990), 174–9 • Evelyn, *Diary* • *A supplement to Burnet's History of my own time*, ed. H. C. Foxcroft (1902) • E. Carter, *The history of the University of Cambridge* (1753) • J. Twigg, *The University of Cambridge and the English Revolution, 1625–1688* (1990) • *Walker rev.* • BL, Add. MSS 5861, 5863 [from Cole MSS] • BL, Harley MSS 7043, 7049 [from Baker MSS] • CUL, Baker MS Mm.I.44 • BL, Add. MSS 19105, 19117 [from Davy MSS] • BL, Harley MS 7019 • CUL, MS Mm.VI.54 • will, CUL, department of manuscripts and university archives, wills IV, 383–6 • parish register, Hadleigh, 21 March 1616, Suffolk RO, Ipswich [baptism]

Archives CUL, question books, Add. MSS 697–699 • Peterhouse, Cambridge, MSS | CUL, Peterhouse MSS, transcripts of lectures, Kk.III.1–17

Likenesses R. White, line engraving (after portrait at Peterhouse), BM, NPG; repro. in J. Beaumont, *Psyche*, 2nd edn (1702) · oils, Peterhouse, Cambridge · portrait on panel, Peterhouse, Cambridge
Wealth at death see will, CUL, wills IV, 383–6

Beaumont, Joseph (1794–1855), Wesleyan Methodist minister, was born at Castle Donington, in Leicestershire, on 19 March 1794. His father was John Beaumont, an itinerant preacher among the Wesleyan Methodists, and his mother was a daughter of Colonel Home of Gibraltar. From them he inherited a keen taste for music and the fine arts. He was educated at Kingswood School, near Bristol, founded by Wesley for training the sons of his preachers. At school he was afflicted with a serious speech impediment which, with great determination, he so completely mastered as to become a fluent and impassioned speaker. Contrary to the wishes of his mother's family, who wanted him to be a clergyman in the Church of England, he chose to become a Methodist minister, like his father. After working for a short time in the shop of a dispensing chemist in Macclesfield, he commenced the itinerant ministry in 1813, and soon became widely known as an eloquent and popular preacher. Beaumont was in great request as the preacher of sermons on special occasions, and vast crowds assembled to hear him whenever he appeared in the pulpit or on the platform. He pleaded effectively for many benevolent objects and public institutions outside the limits of his own church.

Beaumont had a deep-rooted antipathy to hierarchical assumptions, and in the controversies which agitated the Methodist community he always took the liberal side, in opposition to the party of Jabez Bunting. His strong sympathy with the weak and the oppressed occasionally led him into trouble. He clashed with Bunting at the conferences of 1832 and 1834, and in 1841 they came into unusually sharp collision. He was in London at the height of the connexional agitations of the late 1840s. Beaumont was of course subject to the discipline of Methodism which required its ministers to change their pastoral charge every two or three years. In two instances, however, at the request of the people, he was reappointed, after some years, to Edinburgh and Hull, in each of which he had previously served. It was during his residence in Edinburgh in 1836 that he obtained from the university the degree of doctor in medicine. He exercised his ministry for six years in Liverpool, eight years in London, and three years each in Nottingham and Bristol.

In the year 1821 Beaumont married Susan Morton, daughter of Mr Morton of Hardshaw Hall, near Prescot, Lancashire, and sister of the wife of Robert Morrison, the pioneer of missions in China. They had a large family. He was elected by the conference of 1846 as a member of the legal hundred. On Sunday morning, 21 January 1855, he entered the pulpit of Waltham Street Chapel, Hull, and opened the service by announcing the lines

Thee while the first Archangel sings
He hides his face behind his wings

and as the congregation was singing the second of these lines he sank down on the spot and silently died. He was survived by his wife. A posthumous volume of his *Select Sermons* was published in 1859.

W. B. LOWTHER, *rev.* TIM MACQUIBAN

Sources J. Beaumont, *The life of the Rev. Joseph Beaumont* (1856) · *Minutes of the Methodist conferences, from the first, held in London by the late Rev. John Wesley …*, 20 vols. (1812–79) [1855 conference] · W. Hill, *An alphabetical arrangement of all the Wesleyan-Methodist ministers, missionaries, and preachers*, rev. J. P. Haswell (1853) · B. Gregory, *Side lights on the conflicts of Methodism during the second quarter of the nineteenth century, 1827–1852*, popular edn (1899) · W. J. Townsend, H. B. Workman, and G. Eayrs, *A new history of Methodism*, 2 vols. (1909)
Likenesses portrait, repro. in Beaumont, *Life of the Rev. Joseph Beaumont*

Beaumont, Louis de (d. 1333), bishop of Durham, came of a distinguished French noble family. He was the third son of Louis de Brienne and Agnès, heir to the hereditary *vicomté* of Beaumont (Maine), and grandson of Jean de Brienne, king of Jerusalem (d. 1237) and Berengeria, daughter of Alfonso IX, king of León (d. 1230). Consequently he was a cousin of both Eleanor of Castile (d. 1290), wife of Edward I, and of Isabella of France (d. 1358), wife of Edward II. Born in France, he may have come to England by 1285, when he was a canon of York, while by 1291 he was treasurer of Salisbury Cathedral. By 1308 he also held canonries at Le Mans in France, and also at Wells, and at Auckland and Norton in the diocese of Durham. These last are noted in a papal dispensation granted at the request of his kinswoman Queen Isabella. His elder brother was Henry de *Beaumont (d. 1340), whose marriage made him titular earl of Buchan, and his sister was Isabella, wife of John de Vescy, lord of Alnwick, and herself later castellan of the royal castle of Bamburgh. Both Henry and Isabella were prominent in royal circles, so much so that the ordinances of 1311 demanded their removal from court.

Following the death of Bishop Richard Kellawe, on 9 October 1316, there was a disputed election to the see of Durham. The cathedral priory monks put forward the prior of Finchale, Henry Stamford, while the king proposed Thomas Carleton, one of his clerks. The earl of Lancaster (who was trying to extend his influence in northeast England at this time) and the earl of Hereford supported John Kynardsey and John Walwayn respectively, while Queen Isabella had her own candidate in her kinsman Louis de Beaumont. Edward might have been prepared to accept the convent's choice, but he yielded to the queen's entreaties, and referred the matter to the decision of Pope John XXII (r. 1316–34), who agreed to quash the monks' election, and provided Beaumont to the see on 9 February 1317. The temporalities were restored on 4 May, and dies for the Durham mint were sent on 1 June, but Beaumont's consecration was delayed in dramatic circumstances.

In the summer of 1317 Beaumont proposed to take advantage of the presence of two cardinal legates, come to negotiate peace between England and Scotland, by having them consecrate him as bishop at Durham on the feast of the translation of St Cuthbert (4 September). As the party, which included his brother Henry de Beaumont, who was then a warden of the Scottish marches and had previously been keeper of the Durham temporalities, entered the diocese it was attacked at Rushyford, north of Darlington, by a company led by Gilbert Middleton, a former squire of the king's household. The Beaumont brothers were hustled into captivity, one at Morpeth and the other at Mitford, until they were ransomed, but the cardinals were allowed to proceed to Durham. Middleton continued to ravage the countryside, laying siege to Alnwick Castle and Tynemouth Priory, until his capture by a ruse at Mitford. He was subsequently brought to trial for treason in London, where he was executed in the presence of the two cardinals. Beaumont was eventually consecrated at Westminster on 26 March 1318. The Durham chronicler Robert Graystanes, who was hostile to Beaumont, describes him as floundering through the Latin of the service, even though he had had several days' coaching beforehand. As he stumbled over the polysyllables, he was heard to murmur 'By St Louis, he was no gentleman who wrote that word' (*Historiae Dunelmensis*, 118). Graystanes may have exaggerated the bishop's lack of learning, but another contemporary, Adam Murimuth, refers to Beaumont as *mediocriter literatus*, adding that he was club-footed, like most Frenchmen.

Beaumont became bishop at a time of crisis in northern England, as it came under heavy and persistent Scottish attack. The bishopric itself was rarely devastated (though Hartlepool was sacked in 1315, and Beaumont lost his growing crops in 1317), but between 1311 and 1327 it bought off the Scots on eight separate occasions, paying a total of between £4266 and £5333. (Until his death in 1318, a principal agent in organizing these payments was Sir Richard Marmaduke, the steward of the bishopric.) His position as diocesan gave Beaumont a potentially important role in the defence of the north. On 30 July 1317 he was ordered to assist Edmund Fitzalan, earl of Arundel (d. 1326), keeper of the marches of Scotland, with horse and foot and all the power of the bishopric, in the protection of those parts against the Scots. Subsequent orders to defend northern parts were sent on a routine basis, but they culminated in the tart command to repair to Durham for its defence against the Scots. In this mandate of 10 February 1323 Edward II accused the bishop of negligence and laziness, which had contributed to the suffering undergone by the local inhabitants, and rebuked the bishop for his failure, with his friends and relations, to aid the king despite their promises.

With the defeat of Thomas of Lancaster in February 1322, and the consequent forfeiture of land by his supporters, Beaumont attempted to exercise the regalian right of the bishops of Durham to confiscate such land within the palatinate. He was unsuccessful in respect of Silksworth, which passed to Richard Embleton, but the grant of Felling to Thomas Surtees was eventually confirmed by Edward III. With the accession of Edward III, whose coronation he attended, Beaumont made some attempt to re-establish this and other prerogatives of the bishop, jeopardized by the loss by Bishop Antony Bek (d.

1311) of the forfeited lands of John Balliol at Barnard Castle and of Robert I, king of Scots, at Hartlepool, and in 1327 he obtained a formal grant of lands that had been forfeited for treason, with reference to his 'royal rights between the rivers Tyne and Tees' (*CClR, 1327–1330*, 55). But he quickly fell out of favour with the government of Mortimer and Isabella, and was unable to capitalize upon this new privilege. In the same year Beaumont also failed to obtain a licence to issue judicial writs similar to those provided by the royal chancery. And when he attempted to recover the liberty of north Tynedale, acquired by Bek but subsequently seized by Edward I as property illegally alienated by Balliol, Edward III agreed that the bishop's claims be heard, but reserved final judgment to himself.

As diocesan, Beaumont entered into a series of acrimonious disputes with his monastic chapter. He first required the prior to stand surety for a loan of £3000. He then tried to replace the prior, Geoffrey Burdon, who had begun his career as one of the proctors of Prior Richard Hoton (d. 1308). Burdon resigned on 25 January 1323, following a formal visitation in 1322 when various accusations were laid against him. The monks proceeded to elect William Gisburn, who after a week of consideration declined the office. The monks next chose William Couton, who was installed by Beaumont on 3 May 1323. Meanwhile a quarrel had erupted in 1319 between Prior Burdon and the archdeacon of Durham, Thomas Goldsborough, regarding the prior's peculiar jurisdiction within the diocese, in which the bishop supported the archdeacon. Beaumont was alleged to have written to the pope, insinuating that wealth had made the monks mad, so that they would obey neither bishop nor archdeacon; and he sequestered their appropriated churches, threatening to bestow them on secular clerks. Beaumont subsequently relented, and in 1325 confirmed the Durham chapter in their rights.

A similar dispute over peculiar jurisdiction had by 1328 arisen between the bishop and William Melton (d. 1340), archbishop of York, concerning churches in Allertonshire, where Beaumont claimed full episcopal powers. The matter was settled after some degree of violence, and the church at Leake in the North Riding was appropriated to the bishop, but pensions from it were assigned to the archbishop and chapter at York. The nature of the prior's peculiar jurisdiction in the archdeaconry of Northumberland was settled in 1331. Proceeding according to the papal ordinance *Debent* of 1302, Beaumont made a second formal visitation of Durham Priory in 1328, when he tried to secure the dismissal of the almoner, terrar, and feretrar. Prior Couton demurred, but the three obedientiaries agreed to resign, although no serious charges had been brought against them. The bishop then demanded procurations on visiting the priory's appropriated churches, but was finally willing to take 100 marks in settlement of his claim. Beaumont died at Brantingham, in the East Riding of Yorkshire, on 24 September 1333, and on 6 October was buried before the high altar in Durham Cathedral. Graystanes regarded Beaumont as semi-literate, avaricious, and fitfully prodigal, and it is probably true that he owed his clerical advancement primarily to family connections.   C. M. FRASER

Sources 'Chronicle of Robert Graystanes', in *Historiae Dunelmensis scriptores tres: Gaufridus de Coldingham, Robertus de Graystanes, et Willielmus de Chambre*, ed. J. Raine, SurtS, 9 (1839), 36–123, esp. 97–119 · *Chancery records* · *CEPR letters*, 2.49, 54, 136, 414 · M. Prestwich, 'Isabella de Vescy and the custody of Bamburgh Castle', *BIHR*, 44 (1971), 148–52 · C. M. Fraser, ed., *Ancient petitions relating to Northumberland*, SurtS, 176 (1966), 135–56 · C. M. Fraser, ed., *Northern petitions*, SurtS, 194 (1981), 229–39, 251–2, 255–6, 261–2 · J. Scammell, 'The origin and limitations of the liberty of Durham', *EngHR*, 81 (1966), 449–73 · J. Scammell, 'Robert I and the north of England', *EngHR*, 73 (1958), 385–403 · *Adae Murimuth continuatio chronicarum. Robertus de Avesbury de gestis mirabilibus regis Edwardi tertii*, ed. E. M. Thompson, Rolls Series, 93 (1889) · G. O. Sayles, *The functions of the medieval parliament of England* (1988), 381 · [J. Raine], ed., *Wills and inventories*, 1, SurtS, 2 (1835)
Likenesses seals, U. Durham, archives and special collections, Durham Cathedral dean and chapter muniments; repro. in *Archaeologia Aeliana*, 3rd ser., 14 (1917), pl. 50
Wealth at death see Raine, ed., *Wills and inventories*

Beaumont, Robert de, count of Meulan and first earl of Leicester (*d.* 1118), magnate, was the son of Roger, lord of Beaumont-le-Roger and Pont Audemer, and Adeline, daughter of Waleran, count of Meulan. He attested ducal acts before the conquest of England, one as early as 1055, which encourages the belief that he was already of age well before 1066. His participation in the Hastings campaign confirms that assumption. He appears in the witness lists of a small number of royal acts in England and France datable from before he inherited the county of Meulan from his uncle, Count Hugues, late in 1080. One of these is an act of Robert Curthose, which hints that he was associated with the household of William I's heir at one point. Beaumont did not join in Curthose's rebellion against his father in 1078, however, but is mentioned as one of the courtiers who worked to persuade the Conqueror to come to a settlement with his son. In 1086 Count Robert appears as a major landholder in England, with estates concentrated in Warwickshire and Leicestershire. Since there is evidence that his father (still alive and prominent in affairs) had held some of the Warwickshire estates before 1086, it seems that Beaumont's English lands had come to him in a family arrangement. It may be that he held them in 1086 as his father's lieutenant (by the same arrangement as he held Brionne in Normandy from his father); this caretaker role would explain how, in 1088, his brother Henry obtained the bulk (although not all) of Robert's Domesday estate, which became the core of the earldom of Warwick. This explanation would also make it unnecessary to postulate Roger de Beaumont's retirement to Préaux Abbey *c.*1088 to facilitate the exchange, which is a theory in any case contradicted by the fact that Orderic Vitalis and the cartulary of Préaux depict Roger as still active about public affairs in 1090.

Following the death of the Conqueror, Count Robert seems to have decided to pay court to Robert, the new duke of Normandy, and attested several of the acts of the earlier part of the duke's career. However, in 1090 there was a major dispute between count and duke over the castle of Ivry. The count had claimed it as an appurtenance of the castle of Brionne, which his father had earlier had by grant of the duke. Duke Robert, under the influence of a hostile court faction, imprisoned the count and seized Brionne. Roger de Beaumont was able to extract his son from prison, and secured the return of Brionne with some difficulty. Long before Duke Robert mortgaged the duchy to his brother in 1096, Count Robert had transferred his allegiance to William II. Eadmer pictures him in 1093 at Rochester as being then a principal adviser of the king. He appeared at Gloucester with the court in December 1093 with his brother Earl Henry. At Winchester in October 1097 Eadmer describes him as the leader of baronial opinion against Archbishop Anselm. In the same year Count Robert supported William Rufus's campaign in the Vexin, and the next year Orderic portrays him as chief of the king's counsellors, advising the king not to take the exiled Helias, count of Maine, into his court. His ability to influence the king was the excuse for his neighbours to waste his lands when Rufus died. In 1099 he was with the king in England, and attended the celebration held in the new hall of Westminster Palace, while in August 1100 he was in the fatal hunting party in the New Forest when Rufus was accidentally killed. Robert is named as the companion of Count Henry, the king's brother, when he hastened to claim the throne, and he was one of the few magnates (with Henry de *Beaumont, earl of Warwick, his brother) to support the new king in his successful campaign to hold the throne against Robert Curthose. Orderic says that it was by his advice that King Henry used generous promises and gifts to secure even those he suspected to his side, until the danger was past and he could safely deal with them. The count is consistently depicted by all sources as the chief counsellor of the new king.

Rufus had augmented Beaumont's small English estate with some isolated grants of manors, but in 1101 Henry I began the process of raising Count Robert to the status of a great magnate in England. The king obliged Ivo de Grandmesnil, lord of Leicester, who had been disloyal the previous year, to mortgage his lands to the count and to go on crusade. Ivo was to resign his lands to the count for 500 marks and betroth his son to a daughter of Henry of Warwick. In the event, Ivo did not return from the East, and his great midlands honour was never restored to his heir. In 1103 Count Robert was in Normandy acting as mouthpiece of the king's interest in the problems concerning the succession to the honour of Breteuil, and he became embroiled in difficulties with Ascelin Goel, lord of Ivry, who kidnapped one of his commercial agents. The end result, however, was that the count skilfully created a network of local support for King Henry in central Normandy, and was able to secure the succession to Breteuil of Eustace de Breteuil, the king's son-in-law. In 1105 the count was excommunicated by Pope Paschal II for his continuing resistance at court to Archbishop Anselm's demand that the king dispense with investiture. Later in the year the archbishop was still unsatisfied with the count's conduct, and blamed him for delaying the implementation of an agreement he had reached with the king at L'Aigle. It was not until 1108 that the count adopted an outlook more pleasing to Anselm, and became 'a changed character' as he called him in a letter to the pope. In the meantime Henry I had invaded Normandy late in 1104, and Count Robert played the part of leader of the Norman nobility begging the king to restore order to the duchy. Beaumont was next after the king to have his hair cut to satisfy accusations of luxury made against the court by the bishop of Sées. The count commanded the second column at the battle of Tinchebrai on 28 September 1106, when he must have been in his late fifties, at the least.

In 1107 Count Robert accompanied the king back to England and received a grant of the earldom of Leicester. There has been some doubt raised as to whether Robert took the title 'earl of Leicester' as he does not use it in his genuine charters, but in fact he used the titles of Meulan and Leicester on either face of the one surviving impression of his double-sided seal (now in Keele University Library). His earldom was augmented with numerous royal manors and by the subordination of several Domesday honours, such as those of Cahaignes, Guizenboded, and Aubrey de Couci. It was at this point that he had a testament drawn up laying down how his lands were to be divided between his twin sons (born 1104) after his death. His position after the conquest of Normandy was one of unassailable power, and it seems that his connection with the king was so close that he was charged by that politic monarch with the duty of speaking the king's mind and views, particularly in any circumstance where opposition was likely. In 1109, for instance, it was the count who challenged the bishops as to why they had accepted Anselm's prohibition of the consecration of Thomas, elect of York. Although Eadmer assumes that the count was troublemaking, this is a courtly evasion; both he and the bishops knew that the count was speaking the king's mind, hence their fear of the consequences. Attestations reveal that his attendance at the royal court was constant, although we find that in 1110 he was in Meulan, where he supervised the building of a new castle above the town from which he took his title. The count's last datable appearance at the court of Henry I was in February 1116. Henry of Huntingdon describes a gloomy end to his life, plagued by age and depressed by the adultery of his wife with another earl, whom he suggests was working to overthrow Count Robert's influence. This cannot be confirmed, and the gossip about Countess Isabel may simply have arisen from the fact that on the count's death the king promptly married her to William (II) de Warenne, earl of Surrey. Henry of Huntingdon also describes him as dying without absolution because he refused to restore what he had taken from the church, so as to preserve his inheritance intact for his sons. He died on 5 June 1118, in his late sixties, at least. A source stemming from the abbey of La Croix-St Leuffroy indicates that he died in England, conventionally absolved and making restorations; Jumièges Abbey sources note one such in its favour in the county of Meulan. But the fact (recorded by Orderic) that he was buried at Préaux, alongside his father and brother, raises the possibility that he died in Normandy.

His widow was Isabel (d. 1147), daughter of Hugues, count of Vermandois, whom he had married in or about 1101. They had twin sons, *Waleran, count of Meulan, and *Robert, earl of Leicester, born in 1104, and another son Hugh Poer (that is, the Young), born after 1107 and briefly earl of Bedford after 1138. His eldest child was a daughter Adelina, betrothed to Amaury de Montfort in 1103, but ultimately married to Hugues de Montfort in 1123. He had other daughters: Alberada, married in 1123 to Hugues de Châteauneuf; Matilda, married the same year to Guillaume Louvel of Ivry; and Isabel, or Elizabeth, mistress of King Henry, who married Gilbert de Clare, earl of Pembroke.

Robert de Beaumont was a figure of great political importance in his day: Henry of Huntingdon says that at his whim the kings of France and England were at war one year and at peace the next. William of Malmesbury portrays him as setting the social tone of his age for courtly behaviour and abstinence. Eadmer tells us that he could read Latin, and in this too he may have set the tone for his day: he took care to have his heirs educated to a high standard, and other aristocrats may have copied him in this, as much as the king. He was responsible for the setting-up of an exchequer to monitor his fiscal affairs in England, which must have been the first private financial bureau in northern Europe since the fall of Rome. All contemporary writers agree that he was the greatest and richest man of his day, and this may be no exaggeration. All also state that he was politic and cunning above all his contemporaries, and liable to forget the law and justice in pursuit of his aims. As a patron of the church he was not unmindful of his obligations to his family's foundations. His major patronage went to the abbey of Bec-Hellouin, whose advocacy he struggled to have recognized as his by right of his possession of the castle of Brionne. This was the cause of the first major clash between the count and Anselm, then abbot of Bec, who resisted his attempt. But on Anselm's departure the abbey seems to have capitulated, electing the count's cousin William as the new abbot in 1093. Among many grants, the count transferred to Bec the major collegiate church of St Nicaise of Meulan as a priory in the later 1090s. He set up two collegiate churches, one at St Mary-de-Castro, Leicester, another at St Nicholas in Meulan Castle, and also patronized the minster at Wareham.

DAVID CROUCH

Sources Ordericus Vitalis, *Eccl. hist.* · *Eadmeri Historia novorum in Anglia*, ed. M. Rule, Rolls Series, 81 (1884) · Henry, archdeacon of Huntingdon, *Historia Anglorum*, ed. D. E. Greenway, OMT (1996) · William of Malmesbury, *Gesta regum Anglorum / The history of the English kings*, ed. and trans. R. A. B. Mynors, R. M. Thomson, and M. Winterbottom, 2 vols., OMT (1998–9) · D. Crouch, *The Beaumont twins: the roots and branches of power in the twelfth century*, Cambridge Studies in Medieval Life and Thought, 4th ser., 1 (1986) · S. N. Vaughn, *Anselm of Bec and Robert of Meulan: the innocence of the dove and the wisdom of the serpent* (1987) · Cartulary of Préaux, archives départementales de l'Eure, H 711 · B. N. Paris, *Collection du Vexin* · M. Fauroux, ed., *Recueil des actes des ducs de Normandie de 911 à 1066* (Caen, 1961) · *Reg. RAN*, vol. 1 · 'De libertate Beccensis monasterii', *Annales ordinis sancti Benedicti*, ed. J. Mabillon and others, 5, ed. R. Massuet (1713) · GEC, *Peerage*

Beaumont, Robert de. *See* Robert, second earl of Leicester (1104–1168).

Beaumont, Robert de. *See* Breteuil, Robert de, third earl of Leicester (c.1130–1190).

Beaumont, Robert (d. 1567), college head, was probably from a prominent Leicestershire family. After studying at Westminster School he was admitted to Gray's Inn, London, in 1541, and there he befriended Nicholas Bacon. A year later Beaumont was a Bible clerk. After graduating BA from Peterhouse, Cambridge, in 1543–4, he taught 'abroad' before proceeding MA in 1550. He was elected a fellow of Peterhouse the same year, and from 1550 to 1552 he served as bursar of his college. According to Heinrich Bullinger, Beaumont was among the Marian exiles who had arrived in Zürich by 5 April 1554; among those with Beaumont were Laurence Humphrey, James Pilkington, and Robert Horne. In April 1556 Beaumont and Pilkington took up residence in Geneva, where they joined the English congregation of Christopher Goodman and Anthony Gilby. Beaumont may have attempted to heal the breach between the exile churches in Geneva and Frankfurt am Main, for a list of his theology books survives on the back of an unsigned, two-part letter on this theme dated 6 March 1557 (Bodl. Oxf., MS Rawl. D 857, fol. 222; D923, fol. 189). On 14 October 1557 he was formally recognized as a resident of Geneva.

Following Elizabeth's accession Beaumont returned to England, accepting appointments in 1559 as Lady Margaret professor of divinity at Cambridge, succeeding George Bullock, and minister of Little St Mary's. Ordained priest at Ely on 7 July 1560, he proceeded BTh the same year, and on 28 September 1560 was presented to the archdeaconry of Huntingdon by the earl of Rutland. Following the death of William Bill, Beaumont was named master of Trinity College on 25 August 1561. He resigned his professorship the same year and was succeeded by Matthew Hutton in December. Dismayed by the lack of discipline at Cambridge, Beaumont complained to Sir William Cecil on 24 September 1561, proposing the appointment of four new masters: Leonard Pilkington at St John's, William Day at King's, Francis Newton at Jesus, and Hutton or John Robinson at Pembroke. As master of Trinity, Beaumont expelled John Sanderson for teaching 'superstitious' doctrine and denied a fellowship to Walter Travers, ostensibly because of his 'intolerable stomach' according to John Whitgift (Hooker, 1.30). For three years (1562–5) during Beaumont's mastership, Thomas Cartwright was a fellow at Trinity.

In the convocation of 1563 Beaumont was among the thirty-three signatories of a proposal to abolish 'curious' singing and organ playing, baptizing by the laity, the sign of the cross in baptism, saints' days, and copes, surplices, and distinctive clerical garb. He also subscribed a shorter proposal, similar to the first but retaining surplices, but the reform efforts failed. Beaumont additionally supported a petition to ban lay baptism, require communicants to denounce the mass as idolatrous, deface all images of the Trinity and the Holy Spirit, remove roods, and require subscription to the Thirty-Nine Articles before admission to a living in the Church of England. He himself subscribed the articles. In the following year he received the degree of DTh, was one of four senior doctors who carried the canopy over the queen when she arrived at King's College chapel in August, and participated in a theological disputation moderated by the bishop of Ely in Elizabeth's presence. On 15 November 1564 he was collated to a canonry at Ely. Twice—in 1564–5 and 1566–7—he served as vice-chancellor of Cambridge.

A reform-minded Calvinist, Beaumont became embroiled in the vestments controversy. Most members of Cambridge colleges, he informed Archbishop Matthew Parker in February 1565, were wearing the prescribed apparel, and when William Fulke, an opponent of the surplice and cap, preached in Great St Mary's against 'popish trumpery', Beaumont ordered him to provide a summary of the sermon for the chancellor's review. Although Beaumont disliked vestments and was dubious about enforcing vestiarian uniformity, he accepted the prescribed dress if ordered by the supreme governor, preferring this to banishment from the pulpit. On 1 November, preaching in Great St Mary's, Beaumont deplored 'the rash and unlawful attempts of them, which being private men, would by making public reformation thrust themselves into the office of the magistrate' (Porter, 123). On 26 November he joined in an appeal to Sir William Cecil, chancellor of the university, asking him not to enforce the vestments, but when this angered Cecil, Beaumont explained that he had previously urged dissidents to wear the prescribed dress, adding that he himself wore a surplice to avoid 'a greater inconvenience' (BL, Lansdowne MS 8, fol. 129r). Six days later he informed Cecil that he hoped to impose uniformity at Trinity following Cartwright's departure for Ireland. Meanwhile students impatient with Beaumont's moderation clipped the hair from his horse in order to make him a 'popish' crown and strewed what was left in his path as he proceeded from his lodgings to church.

In the midst of the vestments controversy Beaumont found time to complain to Cecil on 22 May 1565 about the impact of high grain prices at Cambridge on poor students, and on 18 June about the amount of grain that was being exported from the region. Another of his interests was sending preachers to Ireland, but on 6 December 1565 he reported to Cecil that his efforts had failed. Beaumont preached at Paul's Cross, London, on Easter Monday, 1566.

Beaumont died on 6 June 1567 and was succeeded as master by Whitgift. His will, which was witnessed by Whitgift and proved on 26 June following, instructed that 'no vayne Jangelynge of belles nor anye other popishe ceremonyes or mystrustfull prayers' be used at his funeral, 'as though my happye state with god were doubtefull' (CUL, 1567, vol. 2, fol. 45v). To Trinity he bequeathed the full-length portrait of Henry VIII that dominates the hall, £40 for the new library, his divinity books (if wanted by the college), and £10 for the college's poor students. He also made bequests of money to his mother, two sisters, and other relatives.

RICHARD L. GREAVES

Sources J. Strype, *Annals of the Reformation and establishment of religion … during Queen Elizabeth's happy reign*, new edn, 1/1 (1824), 489, 501–12 · C. H. Garrett, *The Marian exiles: a study in the origins of Elizabethan puritanism* (1938) · H. C. Porter, *Reform and reaction in Tudor Cambridge* (1958) · P. Collinson, *Godly people: essays on English protestantism and puritanism* (1983) · *CSP dom.*, 1547–80, 186, 252–3, 262, 267, 282 · Cooper, *Ath. Cantab.*, 1.245–6, 555; 3.70 · BL, Lansdowne MS 8, fol. 129r (153r) · J. Nichols, *The progresses and public processions of Queen Elizabeth*, new edn, 1 (1823), 157, 184–7 · *Fasti Angl.* (Hardy) · P. Collinson, *The Elizabethan puritan movement* (1967) · R. Tittler, *Nicholas Bacon: the making of a Tudor statesman* (1976) · *Correspondence of Matthew Parker*, ed. J. Bruce and T. T. Perowne, Parker Society, 42 (1853) · will, 1567, CUL, vol. 2, fols. 45r–46v · *The works of … Richard Hooker*, ed. J. Keble, 3rd edn, 3 vols. (1845) · Venn, *Alum. Cant.*, 1/1.119

Archives BL, Lansdowne MSS 8, fol. 129r (153r); 841, fol. 52 · BL, Harley MS 7030 (Baker MS 3) · CCC Cam., MSS, vol. 106, fol. 627 · CUL, MS Mml. 43 (Baker MS 32) · PRO, state papers, 12/19/54; 12/36/56, 67; 12/38/10, 10.1; 12/39/14; 12/41/19

Wealth at death £50—plus his library: will

Beaumont, Robert (*fl.* 1660), writer, is unknown, except as the author of *Loves Missives to Virtue, with Essaies*, which was published in 1660. He was a man of a retired life and solitary disposition, if his testimony of his own character, which he gives in the preface to his book, is to be believed. The *Missives*, or letters, seem, from one part of Beaumont's epistle to the reader, to be his own composition, and from another part to be the composition of others. But the former intimation has the stronger support. It is evident they were written upon hypothetical occasions. 'Letters', he writes in the preface, 'should be like a wel-furnished Table, where every *Guest* may eat of what *Dish* he pleases' (R. Beaumont, *Loves Missives*, 1660, sig. A4r–v); despite this, all the letters are on the same subject, love. The essays are fifteen in number, and are on the various parts of the body—the head, eye, nose, ear, tongue, and so forth. They are full of trope and figure, frequently with much force of application, quaint and sententious.

JAMES MEW, *rev.* JOANNA MOODY

Sources E. Brydges, *Restituta, or, Titles, extracts, and characters of old books in English literature*, 4 vols. (1814–16), vol. 3, pp. 278–81 · W. T. Lowndes, *The bibliographer's manual of English literature*, ed. H. G. Bohn, [new edn], 1 (1864), 138 · Watt, *Bibl. Brit.*

Beaumont, Sir Thomas (*c.*1555–1614). *See under* Beaumont, Huntingdon (1561–1624).

Beaumont, Thomas Wentworth (1792–1848), politician, was born on 5 November 1792 in Old Burlington Street, London, the first son of Colonel Thomas Richard Beaumont (1758–1829) of Darton, Yorkshire, and his wife, Diana (*d.* 1831), the illegitimate daughter and heir of Sir Thomas Wentworth Blackett, fifth baronet, of Hexham Abbey, Northumberland, and Bretton Hall, near Wakefield, Yorkshire. Colonel Beaumont, who was tory member of parliament for Northumberland from 1795 to 1818, inherited a modest patrimony in Yorkshire; but on the death of her father in 1792 his wife succeeded to extensive estates there and in Northumberland. As the former contained lucrative lead mines, the family's fortunes were dramatically enhanced, to the tune of about £100,000 a year.

Beaumont was educated at Eton College and at St John's College, Cambridge (1809–13). At the general election of 1818 he came forward to replace his father as county member, obtained the blessing of the Liverpool ministry, and was returned unopposed. His conduct in his first parliament, however, was markedly independent, and by opposing the repressive legislation of late 1819 (the so-called Six Acts) he forfeited any claim to government support. After his unopposed return for Northumberland at the general election of 1820 he announced his adhesion to the whigs. He subsequently acted generally with them, supporting Catholic emancipation and parliamentary reform, although he still struck independent attitudes, and his relations with the party hierarchy were strained. Lord Grey, with whom he was at daggers drawn in the county, claimed to detect 'full proofs of insanity' in him in 1823 (Gore, 190). At the contested Northumberland election of 1826 he gave the lie to Grey's son-in-law John George Lambton, whom he accused of prompting Grey's son Lord Howick, one of the other candidates, on the hustings at Alnwick on 30 June. Beaumont and Lambton fought a bloodless duel on Bamburgh Sands the next day. Beaumont lost his seat by forty-seven votes, but in December 1826 he used blatant bribery to secure his return for Stafford at a by-election (Hardcastle, 1.436). On 22 November 1827 he married Henrietta Jane Emma Hawks, daughter of John Atkinson of Maple Hayes, Staffordshire; they had four sons and two daughters. By the deaths of his father in 1829 and his mother in 1831, Beaumont came into full possession of the Blackett estates, which made him an extremely wealthy man. He was returned unopposed for Northumberland at the general elections of 1830 and 1831, and at that of 1832 topped the poll for the southern division, where he was unchallenged in 1835. In July that year Beaumont, president of the Literary Association of the Friends of Poland since 1832, founded the *British and Foreign Review* as an organ for the cause of Polish independence and related political issues. He held the purse strings and contributed a few articles. At a meeting in Edinburgh in December 1835 he denounced Daniel O'Connell as 'the greatest enemy to liberty', but nine months later he publicly subscribed £100 to O'Connell's fighting fund, the 'Catholic rent', and commended his current line (*The Times*, 17, 23 Dec 1835, 26 Sept 1836). After a tour of Ireland in the autumn of 1836 he moved but did not press an amendment to the address on 31 January 1837, calling for payment of the Irish Catholic priesthood (*Hansard 3*, 36, 1837, 41–2). An occasional and 'respectable' speaker, with a fund of ideas and a forceful style, he retired from parliament at the dissolution of 1837 (Grant, 2.67–8).

Beaumont, who spent most of the next six years in continental Europe, died at Bournemouth on 20 December

1848. He was buried on 27 December in Bretton. He was described in an unsympathetic obituary as 'a man of little stability of character' (*GM*, 95–6).   D. R. FISHER

Sources D. R. Fisher, 'Beaumont, Thomas Wentworth', HoP, *Commons, 1790–1820* · *GM*, 2nd ser., 32 (1849), 94–6 · [J. Grant], *Random recollections of the Lords and Commons: second series*, 2 (1838), 66–70 · J. M. Collinge, 'Beaumont, Thomas Richard', HoP, *Commons* · *Wellesley index*, 3.62–76 · *Creevey's life and times: a further selection from the correspondence of Thomas Creevey*, ed. J. Gore, another edn (1937), 190 · S. J. Reid, *Life and letters of the first earl of Durham, 1792–1840*, 1 (1906), 170–72 · Mrs Hardcastle, ed., *Life of Lord Campbell*, 2 vols. (1881), 1.436 · *The Times* (17 Dec 1835) · *The Times* (23 Dec 1835) · *The Times* (26 Sept 1836) · Hansard 3 (1837), 36.41–2 · chronicle, *Annual Register* (1849), 213

Archives Bodl. Oxf., letters to Benjamin Disraeli · Lambton Park, Chester-le-Street, Co. Durham, corresp. with earl of Durham and others · Sandon Hall, Staffordshire, Harrowby Manuscript Trust, letters to Lord Dudley Coutts Stuart · UCL, Brougham MSS

Likenesses T. Lawrence, oils, *c*.1809, Eton · caricatures, repro. in M. D. George, *Catalogue of political and personal satires … in the British Museum*, 11 vols. (1870–1954), vols. 10, 11

Wealth at death £350,000—£40,000 in prerogative court of Canterbury; £250,000 at York; £45,000 in Ireland: PRO, death duty registers, IR26/1826/337

Beaumont, Waleran de. *See* Waleran, count of Meulan and earl of Worcester (1104–1166).

Beauregard. For this title name *see* Haryett, Elizabeth Ann, countess of Beauregard in the French nobility (*bap.* 1823?, *d.* 1865).

Beauvale. For this title name *see* Lamb, Frederick James, Baron Beauvale and third Viscount Melbourne (1782–1853).

Beauvoir, Richard (1730–1780). *See under* Lambert, George (1699/1700–1765).

Beavan, John Cowburn, Baron Ardwick (1910–1994), journalist, was born on 29 April 1910 in Ardwick, Manchester, the district from which he was later to take his title. He was the elder of the two children of Silas Morgan Beavan and his wife, Emily Esther, *née* Hussey (*d.* 1972). His father was a Welsh miner who had emigrated from Merthyr Tudful to Manchester to become a greengrocer. His mother, an exceptionally strong character, was invariably described as formidable as she became successively a leading member of Manchester city council, a JP, and an alderman. Only her husband's ill health forced her to refuse nomination as lord mayor.

Beavan inherited his politics from his mother and his Welshness from his father. From both came his love of words, which provided him with a journalistic career stretching over more than sixty years. He was educated at Manchester grammar school but instead of going on to university, like many of his contemporaries, his family circumstances meant that he went instead to the *Blackpool Times* as a junior reporter. He moved to the *Manchester Evening Chronicle* and then to its rival the *Manchester Evening News*. His transfer was prompted by a conversation he had, during a cricket match between the two papers, with the editor of the *Evening News*, William Haley (later director-general of the BBC and editor of *The Times*). They discussed George Bernard Shaw and Haley, impressed by Beavan's

precocity, hired him on the spot. Beavan at first worked in the paper's London office, but was soon brought back as news editor. Nevertheless he had experienced the attractions of metropolitan life and in 1940 he was persuaded to join the staff of the London *Evening Standard*, where he wrote leaders and helped to edit the diary page. Lord Beaverbrook, like Haley before him, saw Beavan's promise and hinted at great things. But, unlike many other young men, he resisted these blandishments and went instead to *The Observer*, where he was both news editor and chief sub-editor. He seemed settled in London but Haley, about to join the BBC in 1943, suggested that Beavan should succeed him as editor of the *Evening News*. The post offered the added attraction of a seat on the board of the Manchester Guardian and Evening News Ltd.

In 1946 Beavan at last joined the *Manchester Guardian*, the paper he had always loved. He was appointed its London editor, a post of some importance in those days as the *Guardian* was still edited and printed in the north. He spent nine years in charge of the London office—happy at first but gradually frustrated as he realized that office politics would prevent his ever becoming editor of the *Guardian*. It nevertheless came as a surprise when he left journalism in 1955 to become assistant director of the Nuffield Foundation. The foundation's work, ranging from medical research to research into the causes of crime, appealed to Beavan's sense of social justice. But his heart never left journalism and when he was offered the editorship of the *Daily Herald* in 1960 he answered the call with great relish.

The *Herald* was a unique paper, owned partly by Odhams Press and partly by the Trades Union Congress, a body whose policies it was committed to follow. It tended to be crisis-prone but it was steadfastly Labour and for Beavan the editorship seemed a perfect career move. The *Herald*'s politics were his politics and he joined it at a good time, when attempts were being made to turn its fortunes round. He continued this process, recruiting some superior journalists, giving more space to the arts, and brightening it up generally. But he was given little time to succeed. Soon after his appointment the *Herald* was sold to the International Publishing Corporation, owners of the *Mirror* group. Beavan was replaced by a *Mirror* executive, Sydney Jacobson, but recompensed with the post of political editor of the *Mirror* group, whose papers were just as committed to Labour as the *Herald* but much more influential. He spent thirteen productive years as political overlord of the *Mirror* group, interviewing prime ministers, writing leading articles and commentaries, and contributing to the major speeches of both Hugh Gaitskell and Harold Wilson.

Beavan had always been an avid spectator of politics. Now he had a front-row seat and before long he actually entered the arena himself. First he was created a life peer by Wilson, in November 1970, with the remit to speak for journalism in the upper house. Wilson's view was that there were enough peers to represent the proprietors and the publishers, but no practical newspaperman to speak for the press. Lord Ardwick, as he became, spoke on behalf of journalism in the Lords for more than twenty years. Next he became a member of the European parliament, again on Wilson's recommendation. He had survived a serious illness and when he reached the *Mirror*'s retirement age it was thought that he would retire gracefully to the House of Lords. Instead, he started commuting between London, Strasbourg, Brussels, and Luxembourg with the stamina of a much younger man. As a long-term Europhile he created a rapport with European socialists, who had become justifiably suspicious about the Labour government's attitude to European union. He was closest to the French, partly because he knew and loved France and had a deep knowledge of French literature and culture. When he was sixty-nine, however, MEPs were elected directly for the first time and Ardwick decided that it was too late in life to start electioneering.

After his retirement from Strasbourg, Ardwick concentrated on the Lords and until his final years he continued to make authoritative and telling contributions to the debate on media ownership and standards in the press. Though he took an objective view of his profession he remained a good party man, always willing to help his whips and rejecting overtures to defect to the Social Democrats. Meanwhile he served also as chairman of the press freedom committee of the Commonwealth Press Union and was a member of the UK delegation to the North Atlantic Assembly. He married on 6 October 1934 Gladys, *née* Jones (*b.* 1906), a legal secretary. They had an adopted daughter, Jennifer, and he also had a son with Anne Symonds, a BBC radio producer. Beavan died of cancer at Parkside Hospital, Wimbledon, London, on 18 August 1994 and was cremated six days later, after a funeral service at St Mary's, Barnes. He was survived by his wife and both children.   TERENCE LANCASTER

Sources personal knowledge (2004) · private information (2004) [Hon. Mrs Jennifer Fellows] · *The Times* (19 Aug 1994) · *The Independent* (19 Aug 1994) · *WWW* · Burke, *Peerage*
Archives JRL, *Manchester Guardian* archives, letters to the *Manchester Guardian* | SOUND BL NSA, current affairs recording
Likenesses photograph, repro. in *The Times* · photograph, repro. in *The Independent*
Wealth at death £209,680: probate, 12 Oct 1994, *CGPLA Eng. & Wales*

Beavan, Margaret (1875–1931), welfare worker and local politician, was born at 28 Bowring Street, Toxteth Park, Liverpool, Lancashire, on 1 August 1875, the eldest daughter of Jeffrey Beavan, bookkeeper and later fire insurance manager, and his wife, Ellen Catherine Williams. The Beavan children enjoyed a close family childhood in comfortable circumstances. Most of their time was spent at the family home in Liverpool, aside from an unsuccessful attempt to emigrate to the United States which failed when the climate proved unsuitable for the younger children. Margaret herself suffered from frequent bronchial attacks which appear to have kept her close to home, though she keenly involved herself in religious activities and was a regular attender at Sefton Park Presbyterian Church. The Beavans strongly believed in educating their

daughters, and both Margaret and her younger sister Jessie attended Liverpool's progressive Belvedere School as day pupils. This school was a popular choice among the more progressively-minded local middle classes, and fellow pupils included Maude Royden.

Although Margaret Beavan was never particularly academic she was a diligent and popular pupil, and ended her school career as head girl. She went on to Royal Holloway College at Egham, Surrey, where she studied mathematics, French, and English for three years (1894–7) but opted to sit no formal degree. She returned to the family home and took over responsibility for most of its running, caring for her recently widowed mother. However, despite her lack of formal qualifications she found that her college experience made her profoundly dissatisfied with a wholly domestic role and she began to look for something outside the family home. Religious work appealed, and she began voluntary teaching for the Earle Road Mission, a working-class Sunday school overseen by Sefton Park church. Here she discovered an aptitude for the work, and especially for coping with the more difficult adolescent boys.

Through Belvedere Old Girls' Association, Margaret Beavan renewed an acquaintance with Edith Eskrigge who was now working at the Liverpool Victoria settlement. The settlement was looking for a teacher to run small classes for disabled children who had no formal educational provision in the city, and Margaret was persuaded to undertake this work. The move from Earle Road Mission to the Victoria settlement was a significant one, as it took her out of the realm of Christian voluntary work into secular philanthropy. There were many philanthropic networks in Liverpool before the First World War, and she quickly established herself at the centre of them as a worker with a special interest in invalid children, often referred to as the Little Mother of Liverpool. As well as the Victoria settlement school she became a visitor for the Kyrle Society, the favourite charity of Liverpool society, working with its invalid children's branch. In 1908 she took over as secretary to the newly founded Invalid Children's Association, a separate charity which united all her earlier work. This new group was tremendously successful in promoting child welfare. Its most famous success was the establishment of the Leasowe Open-Air Hospital for Children, on the Wirral peninsula, which pioneered treatment of paediatric tubercular cases. Equally remarkable was Margaret's attitude to philanthropy. There was little of the distant, middle-class visitor about her. Before Leasowe was completed most TB children were in non-specialized adult hospitals in Liverpool. They would attend Leasowe for short stays, and Margaret Beavan often transported them herself, treating them to café teas which formed a vital part of her holistic approach to patient care. She believed in helping mothers as well as children, and organized several holidays for 'tired mothers', which she always extended to unmarried women.

Her dedication to children kept Margaret Beavan away from broader political concerns before the First World

War. She was a passive advocate of constitutional suffrage campaigns, but never very involved in this work, although she occasionally appeared in support of her sister Jessie who held office in the local branch of the National Union of Women's Suffrage Societies. After the war she was quick to take advantage of the new political climate, seeing this as a way to advance her deep concern for children. In 1920 she became Liverpool's first woman magistrate, selected for her record of work with disadvantaged youngsters. Despite her privileged background she was sympathetic to many of the cases she encountered. She used her position on the probation committee and her philanthropic contacts to establish a working boys' home aimed at giving first offenders a new start in life.

Increasingly Margaret Beavan felt that she needed a more official platform for effective public work. As a result she stood as a council candidate and was elected in 1923 as a Coalition Liberal, although she quickly switched to the Conservatives. Her high public profile and attachment to children's causes made her a popular figure in the council chamber, and in 1927 she was selected as Liverpool's first woman lord mayor. However, despite her personal following and her flair for philanthropy she made a poor politician. She had rejected the option taken by Eleanor Rathbone, Liverpool's first female councillor, to stand as an independent, but in council she continued to fight for single issues with little regard for party lines or her new position as a Conservative representative. Her lack of political astuteness was painfully obvious when she undertook a civic visit to Italy in May 1928. She was greatly impressed by what she perceived as advances in child welfare under Mussolini, and greeted him warmly in Rome.

Such ill-considered actions undermined public confidence. In the May 1929 general election, Beavan stood as a Conservative parliamentary candidate for Everton but was defeated by her Labour opponent. This was the first time she had lost a campaign, and she took it very much to heart. More painfully, she found that her political errors were thrown up against her volunteer workers, damaging the reputation of her children's charities. Although opposition came from all quarters she increasingly blamed local socialists and this, combined with her actions in Italy, made her particularly unpopular among the very classes for whom she had worked so diligently. She died, unmarried, after an attack of influenza, with chest complications, on 22 February 1931 at the Hospital for Children at Leasowe, which she had helped to found, and was buried at Childwall parish church, Liverpool. Her death allowed for some rehabilitation of her reputation at a large civic memorial service. However, the achievements of her public life have never been fully separated from the mistakes of her final years, and she remains an obscure historical figure despite her prominence in Liverpool life.   KRISTA COWMAN

Sources I. A. Ireland, *Margaret Beavan of Liverpool* (1938) · P. J. Waller, *Democracy and sectarianism: a political and social history of Liverpool, 1868–1939* (1981) · memorial pamphlet, 1931?, Merseyside RO, Child Welfare Association archives [repr. from *Child Welfare News*] · b. cert. · d. cert. · *CGPLA Eng. & Wales* (1931) · NUWSS reports

Archives Merseyside RO, papers and photographs | Lpool RO, Legge MSS · Merseyside RO, Child Welfare Association MSS
Likenesses photograph, repro. in Ireland, *Margaret Beavan*, frontispiece
Wealth at death £18,519 12s.: administration, 14 May 1931, *CGPLA Eng. & Wales*

Beaver, Sir Hugh Eyre Campbell (1890–1967), brewer and civil engineer, was born in Johannesburg on 4 May 1890, the eldest of three sons of Hugh Edward Campbell Beaver, landowner of Montgomeryshire, and his wife, Cerise, daughter of John Eyre, who was of Anglo-Irish extraction. Beaver's father died when he was two years old and the family returned to England to settle in Penn Street, Buckinghamshire. In 1904 he won a scholarship to Wellington College, Berkshire. During his final year in 1910 he was head boy and was awarded the king's medal. Beaver tried unsuccessfully for an open scholarship to Oxford, but took first place in the examination for entry to the Indian police. From 1910 to 1922 he served with the Indian police, where he was engaged mainly in administrative and intelligence work.

Beaver returned to England in 1922, where he met his mother's neighbour, Sir Alexander Gibb, a well-known contractor and engineer then in the process of setting up a new type of consulting engineering practice to cater for the needs of modern factory production. Beaver joined the firm as Gibb's personal assistant, rapidly gaining experience in a wide range of industrial projects. In 1931 he undertook a national survey of Canadian ports and, in addition, the rebuilding in five months of the port of Saint John, New Brunswick, following its destruction by fire. Beaver's report on the Canadian ports was published in 1932 and subsequently implemented. He became company secretary in 1931 and, a year later, a partner of Sir Alexander Gibb & Partners. During the 1930s, two further commissions were of particular note. First, Beaver was responsible for the design and construction of the new Guinness brewery at Park Royal, London, between 1932 and 1936. He impressed the company with his far-sighted decision to acquire additional land for future development and was invited by the managing director, C. J. Newbold, to join the Guinness board. On this occasion the offer was refused. Second, he produced a series of reports for the special areas commission, which provided the basis of the government's relief programme for the distressed areas of the north-east and south Wales. Beaver married in 1925 his second cousin, Jean Atwood, daughter of Major Robert Atwood Beaver MD; they had two daughters before her early death in 1933.

With the approach of war, Beaver was asked by the government to design and commission three ordnance factories. In 1940 he was appointed director-general of the Ministry of Works, where he remained for the duration of the war. In this key position, Beaver was responsible for the planning and execution of the entire wartime programme of construction, and for the supply of building materials. In 1940 he was elected a member of the Institution of Civil Engineers under an 'eminence clause', and in 1943 was knighted for his services.

Immediately after the war, Beaver was invited by Lord Iveagh to join Guinness as assistant managing director. He took over as managing director in 1946 after the sudden death of Newbold. His specific task was to modernize the company, and over the next five years he introduced modern management methods and a policy of diversification, inspired more effective research, saw through a notable growth of exports, and encouraged the development of young managers. Beaver remained at Guinness until his retirement in 1960, during this time demonstrating his outstanding ability as an administrator and manager. He was responsible for its major reorganization into two separate trading companies, Guinness Ireland and Guinness UK. He introduced Harp lager into Ireland, and subsequently into Britain: it rapidly became the leading brand of lager. He also initiated the *Guinness Book of Records*. Beaver took a central role in the brewers' post-war campaign to prevent state purchase of the licensed trade and was prospective chairman of the Brewers' Society in 1959, when ill health forced him to withdraw. He became a vice-president of the society the following year.

After the war Beaver resumed his public service with his appointment to the new towns committee chaired by Lord Reith, and to Stafford Cripps's working party on the building industry. In 1951 he became chairman of the British Institute of Management and deputy chairman of the Colonial Development Corporation. The following year he was chairman of the committee on power stations and in 1953 chaired the committee on air pollution (known as the Beaver committee), whose recommendations were embodied in the 1956 Clean Air Act. In 1954–6 Beaver was also chairman of the advisory council of the Department of Scientific and Industrial Research. He was made a KBE in 1956 for his services to the nation.

Beaver had an unflagging capacity for work. He was an extremely effective chairman and had a great ability to absorb and understand new problems. This was particularly evident during his presidency of the Federation of British Industries between 1957 and 1959. He conducted with great skill the critical council meetings at which the position of British industry to the treaty of Rome was determined. The same was true of the talks in Paris, Stockholm, and London which preceded the formation of the European Free Trade Association (EFTA). He was also chairman of the Industrial Fund for the Advancement of Scientific Education in Schools and of Ashridge College, president of the Institution of Chemical Engineers and of the Royal Statistical Society. In 1956 he joined the council of the Tavistock Institute of Human Relations and served as chairman from 1957 until 1966. A governor of the Lister Institute of Preventive Medicine, he continued as its honorary treasurer until 1966. He received honorary degrees from Cambridge University, Trinity College, Dublin, and the National University of Ireland.

Although poor health caused him to retire from full-time work in 1960, Beaver remained a keen amateur archaeologist and a fine shot. He was also able to devote more time to his garden and his picture collection. He continued his public work, however, often in an unofficial

capacity. He undertook the treasurership of the University of Sussex and the chairmanship of the British Council for the Rehabilitation of the Disabled. His active role at the Federation of British Industries continued long after his presidency, and in the early 1960s he played a leading part in the formation of the National Economic Development Council. Beaver died at his home, Luxford, Crowborough, Sussex, on 16 January 1967.

NORMAN KIPPING, *rev.* CHRISTINE CLARK

Sources private information (1981) · T. Corran, 'Beaver, Sir Hugh Eyre Campbell', *DBB*

Archives BLPES, corresp., diaries, and press cuttings | U. Warwick Mod. RC, papers as president of the Confederation of British Industry

Likenesses W. Stoneman, photograph, 1947, NPG · J. Gunn, pencil drawing, c.1959, Confederation of British Industry · J. Gilroy, portrait, Guinness brewery, Park Royal, London · M. Todd, portrait, priv. coll.

Wealth at death £16,456: probate, 2 May 1967, *CGPLA Eng. & Wales*

Beaver, Philip (1766–1813), naval officer, son of the Revd James Beaver, curate of Lewknor in Oxfordshire, was born in Lewknor on 28 February 1766. His father died when he was eleven; his mother, left poor, accepted the offer of Captain Joshua Rowley, then commanding the *Monarch*, to take the boy with him to sea. His naval service began in October 1777; and during 1778, as midshipman of the *Monarch*, he witnessed the action off Ushant (27 July). In December he followed Rowley to the *Suffolk*, and went in her to the West Indies. He continued with Rowley, by then rear-admiral, in the *Suffolk*, *Conqueror*, *Terrible*, and *Princess Royal*, in the fleet under admirals the Hon. John Byron, Hyde Parker, and Sir George Rodney, during the eventful years 1779–80, and afterwards under Sir Peter Parker at Jamaica. Beaver continued at Jamaica during the rest of the war. On 2 June 1783 his patron, Admiral Rowley, promoted him lieutenant. The next ten years he resided mostly with his mother at Boulogne, and his naval service was limited to a few months in 1790 and in 1791, during the mobilizations of the Spanish and the Russian armaments.

At the end of 1791 Beaver participated in a scheme for colonizing the island of Bulama, near Sierra Leone. He left England for Bulama on 14 April 1792, but the whole affair seems from the beginning to have been conducted without forethought or knowledge. The would-be settlers were, for the most part, idle and dissipated. Beaver found himself at sea in command of a vessel of 260 tons, with sixty-five men, twenty-four women, and thirty-one children, mostly seasick and all useless. When they landed, anything like discipline was unattainable. The party, assembled on shore, had no conception of law, hard work, or discipline. The directors lost heart and returned to England. The command devolved on Beaver, and for eighteen months he attempted to maintain the settlement, but most of the colonists died. The miserable survivors left in November 1793, and went to Sierra Leone, from where Beaver obtained a passage to England, and arrived at Plymouth on 17 May 1794. He published an account of his Bulama experiences, *African Memoranda*, in 1805.

War with France had meantime been declared, and within two months of his return he was appointed first lieutenant of the 64-gun *Stately* (Captain Billy Douglas). She sailed for the East Indies in March 1795, but near the Cape of Good Hope fell in with Sir George Elphinstone, afterwards Lord Keith, and was retained by him to take part in the conquest of that settlement. Subsequently, in the East Indies, the *Stately* was engaged in the capture of Ceylon, and on the homeward voyage again met with Sir George Elphinstone off Cape Agulhas. Beaver's seamanship caught the admiral's attention, and he moved Beaver into his own ship. Elphinstone returned to England in the spring of 1797, and, as first lieutenant of the flagship, Beaver should, in the ordinary course of events, have been promoted. In this, however, he was disappointed; he was still a lieutenant when, in the next year, Lord Keith was appointed to the command of the Mediterranean station, and went out with Keith as first lieutenant of the *Foudroyant* and afterwards of the *Barfleur*. The juniors were appointed, as it seemed to Beaver, for promotion rather than for duty. He was thus driven to bring Lord Cochrane, the junior lieutenant, to a court martial for disrespect. Cochrane, though admonished to avoid flippancy, was acquitted of the charge, which Beaver was told ought not to have been pressed. The circumstance did not, however, interfere with the admiral's goodwill. On 19 June 1799 Beaver was made a commander, and a few months later he was appointed by Keith to the flagship as acting assistant captain of the fleet. During April and May 1800 Beaver was specially employed in command of the repeated bombardments of Genoa, and on the surrender of Masséna was sent home with the dispatches. Unfortunately for him, Marengo had been fought before he arrived; news reached England that Genoa was lost again before reports arrived of how it had first been won; and Beaver went back to Keith without his expected promotion. On his way out he was detained for a fortnight at Gibraltar, where he took the opportunity to marry his young fiancée, Miss Elliott. Shortly after rejoining the admiral, he was promoted captain, on 10 February 1801, and appointed to command the flagship, in which he had an important share in the operations on the coast of Egypt (1800–01); but in June 1801, weary of the monotony of the blockade, he obtained permission to exchange into the frigate *Déterminée* and in her was sent up to Constantinople with dispatches. The sultan wanted to acknowledge this with a large sum of money, which Beaver refused, although he afterwards accepted a diamond box for himself and a gold box for each of the lieutenants. He also received for his services in Egypt the Turkish order of the Crescent.

On the conclusion of the peace of Amiens the *Déterminée* was ordered home, and was paid off at Portsmouth on 19 May 1802. Beaver, now settled down on shore, was placed in charge of the sea fencibles of Essex in July 1803, a duty he discharged with great success. Three years later he was appointed to the 40-gun frigate *Acasta* and in her went to the West Indies, where he remained until after the capture of Martinique in February 1809. He was then sent home in charge of convoy and with many French prisoners. Some months later he was appointed to the *Nisus* (38 guns), a new frigate, and on 22 June 1810 sailed in her for the East Indies. He arrived on the station in time to take a very distinguished part, under Vice-Admiral Albemarle Bertie, in the capture of Mauritius (November 1810), and, under Rear-Admiral the Hon. Robert Stopford, in the conquest of Java (August and September 1811). After nearly a year in Mozambique and on the coast of Madagascar, towards the end of 1812 the *Nisus* received her orders for England, and towards the end of March 1813 put into Table Bay on her homeward voyage. Here Beaver, who had complained of a slight indisposition, was seized with a violent inflammation of the bowels, and, after a few days of the most excruciating pain, died on 5 April.

Beaver's career was built on high standards of professional conduct that attracted the patronage of senior officers. He was a man of remarkable energy and ability, and in the exceptional posts that he held, both in the Mediterranean and in the East Indies, he performed his duty not only effectively, but without arousing the jealousy of his seniors whom he temporarily superseded. He was an almost omnivorous reader: during one cruise he read the entire *Encyclopaedia Britannica*. He was a strict disciplinarian, but at a time when strictness not infrequently degenerated into cruelty, no charge of tyranny was ever made against him, though according to his biographer he might have been more forgiving.

Beaver's early death, and the previous bankruptcy of his agent, left his widow, with six children, poorly provided for; she became matron of Greenwich Hospital school.

J. K. LAUGHTON, *rev.* ANDREW LAMBERT

Sources *The Keith papers*, 2–3, ed. C. Lloyd, Navy RS, 90, 96 (1950–55) · D. Syrett and R. L. DiNardo, *The commissioned sea officers of the Royal Navy, 1660–1815*, rev. edn, Occasional Publications of the Navy RS, 1 (1994) · W. H. Smyth, *The life and services of Captain Philip Beaver* (1828) · G. S. Ritchie, *The Admiralty chart: British naval hydrography in the nineteenth century* (1967)
Archives Hydrographic Office, Taunton, admiralty library, log and memoranda · NMM, journals

Beaver, Stanley Henry (1907–1984), geographer, was born on 11 August 1907 at 69 Clifford Gardens, Willesden, London, the second son and fifth child in the family of two sons and three daughters of William Henry Beaver, Post Office letter sorter, and his wife, Hypatia Florence Hobbs. He was educated at Kilburn grammar school (1919–25), and at University College, London (1925–8) where he gained a first-class honours degree in geography (1928) and the Morris prize in geology. After a course of teacher training he was appointed in 1929 to the staff of the London School of Economics and Political Science (LSE). He quickly earned a high reputation as an economic geographer and collaborated with L. Dudley Stamp in writing the successful *The British Isles* (1933). Beaver's studies concentrated on the mineral, manufacturing, and transport industries. He contributed *Yorkshire, West Riding* (1941) and *Northamptonshire* (1943) to Stamp's *Land Utilization Survey of Britain*. On 5 August 1933 at Battersea parish church he married Elsie Barbara (1908/9–1992), daughter of William

Wallace Rogers, chief traveller for the Jaeger Company. They had a son and three daughters.

After the outbreak of war Beaver's knowledge proved valuable to the geographical section of the naval intelligence division of the Admiralty: he worked at Cambridge, 1941–3, especially on western and south-eastern Europe, on railway matters, and afterwards occasionally contributed to the Geographical Handbooks. In 1943 he joined the Ministry of Town and Country Planning in the research division working on mineral problems and derelict land, and developed the collection of air photographs. He continued to advise the ministry after his return to academic life as Sir Ernest Cassel reader in economic geography at the LSE in 1946. As exemplified by his *Derelict Land in the Black Country* (1946), based on field survey, and by his work on minerals (notably ironstone) and planning, Beaver made contributions of lasting policy significance. His studies of sand and gravel resources were particularly influential at a time of strong demand for wartime construction purposes (such as airfields) and for post-war urban reconstruction and new town development. He contributed pioneer studies of the reclamation of industrial waste land. He was a member of the Waters advisory committee on sand and gravel from 1946. In 1950 Beaver was appointed to a foundation chair in the University College of North Staffordshire at Keele and threw his energies wholeheartedly into the development of the University of Keele (1962). He was chairman of the grounds committee. He founded a climatological station and produced (with E. M. Shaw) *The Climate of Keele* (1971). He wrote vividly on the evolution of the industrial landscape of the Potteries. Through his efforts the library of Air Ministry wartime air photographs, mainly of Europe, was placed on permanent loan at Keele in 1963 and opened in 1966. He also secured for Keele the Le Play House Library and the archive of the Institute of Sociology.

Fieldwork which threw light on the relationships between environment, economy, technical skills, and social conditions lay at the heart of Beaver's work as a geographer. He had been early attracted to the work of the Le Play Society and took part in field surveys, for example in Bulgaria, Albania, and Norway. He joined societies to serve them, not for recognition. His work for the North Staffordshire Field Club was recognized by his election to its presidency, 1961–2. A founder member of the Institute of British Geographers, he was president in 1964. The Geographical Association elected him to its presidency in 1967 and he was twice president of section E of the British Association for the Advancement of Science (1961, 1981). He served on the council of the Royal Geographical Society (1943–7) and received its Murchison award in 1962. He was chairman for many years of the Dudley Stamp Memorial Trust. He was elected an honorary fellow of the LSE in 1982. He was elected also to honorary membership of the Geographical Society of Poland. He maintained strong international links and gained pleasure from translating into English a number of salient works by French geographers. Nearer home, chairmanship of the Staffordshire Community Council occupied time and energy.

Beaver was short, spare, and energetic. His mind was quick: he did not enjoy long committee discussions. He loved railways and knew his Bradshaw. He was a kind man, though when principles were at stake he could speak sharply. He had what was described as a 'pungent humour'. He enjoyed teaching and students responded to his enthusiasm. A central theme was the environmental consequences of technical change. He linked a grasp of geological conditions, detailed knowledge of places, reading in economic history, and an understanding of industrial technologies to analyse the revolution in the British landscape that had resulted from industrial change. Technical development, he argued, did not lead to mastery over nature but rather to increasingly interdependent relationships between societies and environments. Beaver died on 10 November 1984 at his home, The Mount, Stafford Road, Eccleshall, Staffordshire. His work on industrial land reclamation was a starting point of a process which is still in train and much recent work in economic geography, though it deals with knowledge-based rather than manufacturing industry, has similar objectives to his.   M. J. WISE, *rev.* ELIZABETH BAIGENT

Sources *The Times* (14 Nov 1984) · 'Stanley Henry Beaver, 1907–1984', *GJ*, 151 (1985), 305–6 · R. Frankenberg, 'Stanley Beaver', *Sociological Review*, 33/3 (Aug 1985) · 'Professor Stanley H. Beaver', *L.S.E. Magazine*, 69 (1985), 16–17 · A. D. M. Phillips and B. J. Turton, eds., *Environment, man and economic change: essays presented to S. H. Beaver* (1975) · [T. W. Freeman], 'Stanley Henry Beaver, 1907–1984', *Transactions of the Institute of British Geographers*, new ser., 10 (1985), 504–6 · personal knowledge (2004) · private information (2004) [E. Beaver] · b. cert. · m. cert. · d. cert.
Archives RGS, papers
Wealth at death £180,829: probate, 13 March 1985, *CGPLA Eng. & Wales*

Beaverbrook. For this title name *see* Aitken, William Maxwell, first Baron Beaverbrook (1879–1964); Aitken, Marcia Anastasia, Lady Beaverbrook (1909–1994) [*see under* Aitken, William Maxwell, first Baron Beaverbrook (1879–1964)].

Beavor, Edmund (1701?–1745), naval officer, after many years at sea as an able seaman, midshipman, master's mate, and latterly as acting third lieutenant of the *Ludlow Castle*, passed his examination to become a lieutenant on 13 February 1734, at the age of thirty-two. Commissioned as third lieutenant of the *Falkland* on 2 March 1734, he served in several vessels over the next nine years.

In the summer of 1743 he was master and commander of the fireship *Strombolo* which was engaged in convoying home from the West Indies thirty merchant ships; several were lost in bad weather, and the *Strombolo*, dismasted and almost sinking, just reached Kinsale harbour.

From 18 April 1744 Beavor was captain of the frigate *Fox*, and in 1745 he cruised, with some success, against Dunkirk privateers in the North Sea. In September 1745 he was in Leith Roads, assisting the transport of the army and disrupting the communications of the rebels. After the defeat of Sir John Cope's army at Prestonpans on 21 September the *Fox* sheltered some of his soldiers.

A few weeks later Beavor put to sea and on 14 November 1745, in a violent storm, the *Fox* went down with all hands off Dunbar.   J. K. LAUGHTON, *rev.* RANDOLPH COCK

Sources register of commissions and warrants, PRO, ADM 6/14, 15, 16 · lieutenants' passing certificates, 1713–45, PRO, ADM 107/3 · J. Charnock, ed., *Biographia navalis*, 6 vols. (1794–8)

Beazley, Sir John Davidson (1885–1970), classical archaeologist, was born in Glasgow on 13 September 1885, the elder son of Mark John Murray Beazley (*d.* 1940), interior decorator, of London, and his wife, Mary Catherine (*d.* 1918), daughter of John Davidson, of Glasgow. He went to King Edward VI School, Southampton, and as a scholar to Christ's Hospital and to Balliol College, Oxford, where he took firsts in both classical moderations (1905) and *literae humaniores* (1907), and was Ireland scholar and Craven scholar (1904), Hereford scholar (1905), and Derby scholar in 1907. His entry for the Gaisford prize for Greek prose (1907), 'Herodotus at the Zoo', an enchanting work, was reprinted in 1911 and in a collection of classical parodies produced in Switzerland in 1968. He became a close friend of James Elroy Flecker, who addressed his poem 'Invitation' to Beazley ('a young but learned friend to abandon archaeology for the moment, and play once more with his neglected Muse'). It warned Beazley that his 'broken vases widowed of their wine' might 'brand you pedant while you stand divine'. Beazley himself at this time wrote poetry, but abandoned it with the growth into his total dedication to scholarship. T. E. Lawrence was to comment to Sydney Cockerell, 'If it hadn't been for that accursed Greek art, he'd [sc. Beazley] have been a very fine poet' (Ashmole, 'Beazley', 445). His exact contemporary at Balliol was William Compton, who as sixth marquess of Northampton was later to invite Beazley to publish his collection of Greek vases at Castle Ashby, which appeared in the *Papers of the British School at Rome* (1929).

After a year at the British School at Athens, where the director was Richard McGillivray Dawkins, Beazley returned to Oxford and in 1908 he was made student of Christ Church and tutor in classics. This position was held, except for a period of war service as a lieutenant in the Royal Naval Volunteer Reserve at Room 40 of naval intelligence at the Admiralty in London, until 1925. In 1919 Beazley married Marie, daughter of Bernard Bloomfield and widow of David Ezra (with whom she had a daughter who married Louis MacNeice). In the early years of their marriage they kept a goose at Christ Church which Marie used to exercise in Tom quad. Marie devoted her powerful personality entirely to serving Beazley and his work. She learned to photograph vases, took over the practical side of his life completely, and was his guardian dragon. Russell Meiggs was to recall about their later home, 'At 100 Holywell a knock at the door was followed by the opening of a shutter. One faced a glittering eye, before entry was allowed; and the door was not always opened' (Meiggs, 10). Beazley could not have done without her, and he adored her, never recovering from her death in 1967. They had no children.

In 1925 Beazley succeeded Percy Gardner as Lincoln professor of classical archaeology. Gardner himself is

Sir John Davidson Beazley (1885–1970), by Lafayette, 1926

thought to have distrusted Beazley's 'scientific' approach to Greek pottery. Long before this, however, although a fine classical scholar and an able and conscientious tutor, he had established his life's work as devoted to Greek art and in particular to Attic vase-painting. Greek vase-painting, by virtue of its quality and in the all but total loss of other painting from Greece, is of peculiar importance in the history of art. Its study is now on an entirely different footing from what it was at the beginning of the twentieth century; and that is Beazley's work. Among Beazley's first students for the study of vase-painting were Joan Evans, stepsister of Sir Arthur Evans, and Gordon Childe. The former was to recall her first tutorial with Beazley: 'an essay in appreciation of a delightful little red-figured unguent pot, with a peroration on the folly of the English-woman in not using more make-up' (Evans, 74).

Beazley's first article, published in the year of his appointment to Christ Church, is on vases, but is untypical, being concerned mainly with iconography and hardly at all with style. He was already beginning, however, the minute stylistic study of individual vases in all the museums he could visit, the first-fruits of which were the seminal articles which appeared from 1910 in the *Journal of Hellenic Studies* and elsewhere, on individual painters of Attic red-figure. Essays in this direction had already been made by the great German scholars whom Beazley always revered as his masters, Hartwig, Hauser, and Furt-wängler; but their work had two serious limitations. They tended to start from signatures, haphazard in application and still more so in survival; and they only concerned themselves with good work. Beazley never underesti-mated the master and the masterpiece, but he saw that for the study to be properly based he must survey the whole field. He loved and knew well painting of many times and places, and he took his method from Morelli's studies of the Italian masters: minute observation of individual mannerisms of drawing, controlled by a deep sensitivity to style. The Berlin Painter, to whom he devoted the first of many studies in 1911, is a great draughtsman whose style is now as familiar as Dürer's or Utamaro's. Most of the vases first grouped under the name had long been known, but their relation had not been observed and the artistic personality was lost. By recognizing a whole range of such personalities, from the best to the worst, col-leagues or rivals, masters and pupils over many gener-ations, Beazley left the subject, which he had found more or less chaotic, an organized field of study comparable to a school of painting in a documented age.

He began by concentrating on red-figure (and the related white-ground) in the first hundred years or so of its existence, from the later sixth century. Afterwards he pushed forwards to the fourth century and backwards to black-figure. The first phase of his work is summed up in *Attic Red-Figure Vases in American Museums* (1918), where a history of the art is given through an account of artists and their relations, lists of their works being interspersed in the text. *Attische Vasemaler des rotfigurigen Stils* (1925) is lists alone, greatly expanded in number and length. He continued to build up these lists throughout his life: in *Attic Red-Figure Vase-Painters* (1942) and its second (three-volume) edition (1963), the parallel *Attic Black-Figure Vase-Painters* (1956), and *Paralipomena* which supplements and corrects these and was posthumously published (1971). These are the backbone of his work; but it is fleshed out in innumerable articles and many books, wide-ranging and beautifully written: *Greek Vases in Poland* (1928); *Der Berliner Maler* (1930), *Der Panmaler* (1931), and *Der Kleophradesmaler* (1933; the English texts of these three monographs were published in 1974); *Attic Vase-Paintings in Boston* (with L. D. Caskey, 1931–63); *Campana Fragments in Florence* (1933; the most spectacular display of Beazley's astounding visual memory, a gift basic to his work); *Attic White Lekythoi* (1938); *La Raccolta Guglielmi* (with F. Magi, 1939); *Potter and Painter in Ancient Athens* (1945); *The Development of Attic Black-Figure* (1951; lectures given as Sather professor at the University of California, 1949); *The Berlin Painter* (1964); as well as two Oxford fascicles for the *Corpus vasorum antiquorum* (1927 and 1931, the second with E. R. Price and Humfry Payne, his best pupil). *Greek Sculpture and Painting* (with B. Ash-mole, 1932) was for many years considered the best short introduction to the subject, and he did important work in other fields: *The Lewes House Collection of Ancient Gems* (1920) and *Etruscan Vase-Painting* (1947); but it is his work on Attic

vase-painters which is, in the historiography of Greek art, strictly epoch-making.

Beazley was elected FBA in 1927, knighted in 1949, appointed CH in 1959, and held honorary degrees from Oxford, Cambridge, Glasgow, Durham, Reading, Paris, Lyons, Marburg, and Salonika. He was an honorary fellow of Balliol and Lincoln, and honorary student of Christ Church and the British School at Athens. He was honorary vice-president of the Greek Archaeological Society, hon-orary fellow of the Metropolitan Museum, New York, and a foreign member of many learned societies. He was awarded the Petrie medal in 1937, the British Academy's Kenyon medal in 1957 (the first award), and the Antonio Feltrinelli Foundation prize in 1965. He retired from his Oxford chair in 1956 and was succeeded by his former pupil Bernard Ashmole. In 1964 the University of Oxford purchased Beazley's collection of photographs, drawings, and notes which now forms the Beazley Archive. After his wife's death in 1967, Beazley moved into the Holywell Hotel, and he died in Oxford on 6 May 1970.

Beazley was a person of wide culture, interested in and knowledgeable about the arts (and several of the litera-tures) of Europe, though he did not care to look much beyond those bounds. He had great charm, and could be an amusing and delightful companion; but as he grew older his total deafness and his increasing absorption in his work combined to cut him off to some degree from other people. He was modest, and took immense trouble with the guidance of his pupils, treating them as equals and winning their devoted affection. He was completely generous in communicating his knowledge, not only to these but to all who consulted him, as in increasing num-bers scholars, collectors, and dealers constantly did. In appearance he was somewhat under medium height, slight but well made, with striking blue eyes and fair hair (white in age), and fine rather ascetic features which sug-gested to many a fifteenth-century Flemish portrait, a Van Eyck or a Van der Weyden. He was never professionally painted, but his wife, a talented untaught artist, drew sev-eral heads of him in coloured chalks which are preserved in Oxford, at Balliol, Christ Church, and Lincoln.

MARTIN ROBERTSON, rev. DAVID GILL

Sources *The Times* (7 May 1970) · B. Ashmole, 'Sir John Beazley (1885–1970)', *PBA*, 56 (1970), 443–61 · R. Meiggs, 'Sir John Beazley', *Balliol College Annual Record* (1970) · D. von Bothmer, *Oxford Magazine* (12 June 1970) · M. Robertson, 'John Davidson Beazley', *Gnomon*, 43 (1971), 429–32 · C. M. Bowra, *Christ Church Annual Report* (1970), 5–6 [abridged version of address at memorial service] · D. C. Kurtz, ed., *Beazley and Oxford* (1985) · *Greek vases: lectures by J. D. Beazley*, ed. D. C. Kurtz (1989) · C. M. Bowra, *Memories, 1898–1939* (1966) · J. Evans, *Prel-ude and fugue: an autobiography* (1964) · *The collected poems of James Elroy Flecker*, ed. J. C. Squire (1916) · *Bernard Ashmole, 1894–1988: an autobiography*, ed. D. C. Kurtz (1994) · personal knowledge (1981) · P. Rouet, *Approaches to the study of Attic vases: Beazley and Pottier* (2001) · A. L. Rowse, 'A buried love: Flecker and Beazley', *The Specta-tor* (21–8 Dec 1985), 58–60 · D. von Bothmer, 'J. D. Beazley', *Classical scholarship: a biographical encyclopedia*, ed. W. W. Briggs and W. M. Calder III (1990), 1–6

Archives AM Oxf., working notes and papers · AM Oxf., collec-tion of artefacts | BL, corresp. with Sir Sidney Cockerell, Add. MS 52704 · Bodl. Oxf., corresp. with Gilbert Murray

Likenesses Lafayette, photograph, 1926, NPG [*see illus.*] · M. Beazley, coloured chalk and applied silver paper, 1952, Balliol Oxf. · M. Beazley, coloured chalk, Christ Church Oxf. · M. Beazley, coloured chalk, Lincoln College, Oxford · photograph, repro. in Ashmole, 'Sir John Beazley (1885–1970)', pl. xxvii · photograph, repro. in Kurtz, ed., *Greek vases*
Wealth at death £54,371: probate, 4 Dec 1970, *CGPLA Eng. & Wales*

Beazley, Samuel (1786–1851), architect and playwright, was born in Parliament Street, Westminster, the son of an army accoutrement maker. He trained in the office of his uncle Charles Beazley (*c.*1760–1829) and went on to become the leading theatre architect of his time and the first notable English expert in this field. His life was not, however, that of a single-minded specialist. Beazley was a precocious child who showed an early interest in the drama and wrote his first farce at the age of twelve when at school in Acton, where he also 'put together' the theatre in which the play was acted. As a young man he seems to have had an appetite for the dramatic in his own life. He served in the Peninsular War, during which at one point he was assumed dead, and woke to find himself laid out for burial. He is said to have led the daring escape to Spain of the duchesse d'Angoulême, fleeing from the Napoleonic forces in 1815.

After returning to London, Beazley was immediately active as an architect and dramatist. In 1816 he built the New Theatre Royal English Opera House, replacing James Paine's Lyceum. It was for this theatre that he wrote his first performed works, *The Boarding House, or, Five Hours at Brighton*, *Is he Jealous?*, and *Fire and Water*. He went on to write prolifically for the stage, mostly comedies, farces, comic operas, and operettas. In 1829 he wrote an 'Indian spectacle' solely for the purpose of introducing a 'sagacious female elephant', showing off the tricks she could perform. The elephant, rather than the author, took a curtain call. Beazley also translated librettos and is said to have sat by the bed of Madame Malibran in order to adapt the English words of *La sonnambula* to her pronunciation.

Beazley designed or substantially redesigned seven London theatres, including the total rebuilding of his first, which reopened in 1834 as the Royal Lyceum and English Opera House (later known simply as the Lyceum). In 1821 he remodelled the auditorium of Benjamin Dean Wyatt's Theatre Royal, Drury Lane, and in 1831 added a fine Ionic colonnade to the Russell Street front of the same theatre. In 1834 he designed the Royal Soho (later the Royalty Theatre) for Fanny Kelly, the City of London Theatre in Norton Folgate, and, a year later, the St James's Theatre for John Braham. In 1841 he created a lively new Strand façade for the Adelphi Theatre, 'an essay in narrow-shouldered assertiveness' (*Parish of St Paul*, 36.246).

In 1820 Beazley was responsible for the rebuilding after a fire of the Theatre Royal in New Street, Birmingham, and about the same time he provided a design for the Theatre Royal in Hawkins Street, Dublin. It is likely that he also gave advice to William Parsons on the design of the Leicester Theatre of 1836. He also designed theatres for Belgium, India, and South America. Non-theatre work included Leamington Spa New Assembly Rooms, Leamington county library and reading-rooms (1821), Studley Castle, Warwickshire (1834), the Parthenon Club's library in Regent Street (1844), the Pilot House and Lord Warden Hotel in Dover (1848–53), mansions in England, Scotland, and Ireland, and works for the South Eastern Railway Company, including the London Bridge terminus (1851), a number of stations on the north Kent line, and a housing estate.

Beazley adopted a variety of historical styles in his work, but his theatre designs were invariably neo-classical and not strikingly innovative; he drew on European architectural precedents but adapted them skilfully to the uncompromisingly commercial climate of the London and provincial stage. His experience as a playwright and his intimate knowledge of the physical demands of dramatic presentation gave him a significant advantage over his rivals. There is no doubt that his radical amendments at Drury Lane in 1821 produced striking improvements to Wyatt's unsatisfactory auditorium. The range of his theatre-related designs is illustrated, at one extreme, by the Royal Soho (Miss Kelly's), an elegant little room behind a dwelling house, no more ambitious in scale than a simple country playhouse and, at the other, his unexecuted Leicester Square Casino and Promenade Concert Room 'à la Musard' of 1840, with its grand classical front and huge assembly room with two tiers of balconies.

Apart from his plays and two novels, *The Roué* (1828) and *The Oxonians* (1840), Beazley's literary output consisted of one or two architectural papers and a slim book published in 1812 on the enclosure of waste lands. One modern writer has described Beazley as having had the career of 'a Victorian Vanbrugh' and, certainly, both were soldiers, adventurers, playwrights, and architects. Beazley was known as an amusing companion with witty conversation and the mode of life of a man of pleasure. He was married three times: first in 1809 to Eliza Richardson, second in 1824 to Frances Conway, and third in the late 1840s to Marianne Joseph. His first two marriages ended in divorce and his third wife survived him. He died of an apoplexy at his house, Tonbridge Castle in Kent, on 12 October 1851 and was buried at Bermondsey Old Church, London.

JOHN EARL

Sources *GM*, 2nd ser., 36 (1851), 559 · *GM*, 2nd ser., 37 (1852), 2 · *The Builder*, 9 (1851), 694–5 · D. Harbron, 'Samuel Beazley: a Victorian Vanbrugh', *ArchR*, 79 (1936), 131–4 · [W. Papworth], ed., *The dictionary of architecture*, 11 vols. (1853–92) · Colvin, *Archs.* · *The parish of St James, Westminster: south of Piccadilly*, Survey of London, 29 (1960), 300–01 · *The parish of St Anne, Soho*, 2 vols., Survey of London, 33–4 (1966), 215–21, 492 · F. H. W. Sheppard, ed., *The Theatre Royal, Drury Lane, and the Royal Opera House, Covent Garden*, Survey of London, 35 (1970), 24, 64–66 · *The parish of St Paul, Covent Garden*, Survey of London, 36 (1970), 227, 246 · J. Britton and A. C. Pugin, *Illustrations of the public buildings of London* (1825) · Redgrave, *Artists* · R. Leacroft, 'The Theatre Royal, Leicester', *Theatre Notebook*, 40 (1986), 100–01 · d. cert. · *DNB* · G. Garlick, 'Samuel Beazley and the Drury Lane alterations of 1822', *Theatre Notebook*, 50 (1996), 39–50 · G. Garlick, 'Samuel Beazley', *Society for Theatre Research* (2003)
Archives NL Scot., corresp. and papers relating to Leys Castle, Inverness-shire | Som. ARS, corresp. with John Braham and his wife

Beccles, Alan of (*d.* 1240), ecclesiastical administrator, doubtless took his name from Beccles in Suffolk—he was closely associated with East Anglia throughout his career. Styled *magister* by 1201 (of which university is unknown), he appears to have attracted the attention of the papal legate Guala Bicchieri, who wrote to the pope on his behalf in 1216 or 1217, and through whom he entered the service of Pandulf, Guala's successor as legate. Pandulf became bishop of Norwich in 1222, and Beccles is recorded as official of Norwich in the same year, and as archdeacon of Sudbury in Suffolk by 1225. He was clearly an active administrator, collecting the proceeds of the clerical carucage of 1224, issuing instructions to rural deans in Suffolk, and holding pleas in court christian. His rewards included the churches of Haughley and Shelland in Suffolk, and Bunwell and Garboldisham in Norfolk. At one point, probably shortly after the death of Bishop Pandulf in 1226, he left England to teach at the University of Paris—according to Matthew Paris, he was one of the notable English masters who left that city following the dispersal of the university in 1229. He returned to England and continued to act as archdeacon, becoming an ecclesiastically influential figure. In 1239 he was one of three men chosen to arbitrate between Bishop Robert Grosseteste and the dean and chapter of Lincoln. And in the following year, when the papal legate Otto was trying to extract a grant of taxation from the English church, it was the defection of Beccles from previously solid opposition that led to the legate obtaining most of what he wanted. Shortly afterwards, according to Matthew Paris, Beccles died suddenly while dining with some Londoners—a fitting end, the chronicler thought, for a persecutor of the church.   HENRY SUMMERSON

Sources Paris, *Chron.*, 3, 4 · Emden, *Oxf.* · *Curia regis rolls preserved in the Public Record Office* (1922–), vols. 10–11, 14–15 · *CPR, 1216–32* · H. C. M. Lyte, ed., *Liber feodorum: the book of fees*, 1 (1920), 282, 403 · *Roberti Grosseteste episcopi quondam Lincolniensis epistolae*, ed. H. R. Luard, Rolls Series, 25 (1861) · *Matthaei Parisiensis, monachi Sancti Albani, Historia Anglorum, sive ... Historia minor*, ed. F. Madden, 3 vols., Rolls Series, 44 (1886–9), 2.432 · J. H. Bullock, ed., *The Norfolk portion of the chartulary of the priory of St Pancras of Lewes*, Norfolk RS, 12 (1939) · *The letters and charters of Cardinal Guala Bicchieri, papal legate in England, 1216–1218*, ed. N. Vincent, CYS, 83 (1996)

Wealth at death Haughley church valued at £20 p.a. in 1235

Beche, Sir Henry Thomas De la (1796–1855), geologist, was born on 10 February 1796 at Welbeck Street, Cavendish Square, London, the only son of Thomas De la Beche (1755–1801), a brevet major (later lieutenant-colonel) in the Norfolk fencible cavalry regiment, and his wife, Elizabeth. The family name was originally Beach, but his father changed it to create a fictional connection with the medieval Barons De la Beche of Aldworth, Berkshire. In 1800 the family travelled to Jamaica, having inherited a slave plantation. However, his father died there in the following year, and De la Beche and his mother (after being shipwrecked to the north of San Domingo) returned to England.

De la Beche was educated at Mr Taylor's school in Hammersmith, then from 1805 at Keynsham, Somerset, and for a year from 1808 at Mr Holditch's school at Ottery St

Sir Henry Thomas De la Beche (1796–1855), by William Walker, pubd 1848 (after Henry Pierce Bone)

Mary in Devon. Planning to follow a military career, he entered the Royal Military College at Marlow in 1809, but was sent down two years later in disgrace after encouraging a 'dangerous spirit of Jacobinism' (McCartney, 4) among the cadets. He spent the next few years in towns along the south coast, settling at Lyme Regis in 1812. There he associated with Thomas Coulson Carpenter and George Holland, professional men interested in meteorology and geology. De la Beche travelled with them in Scotland and the north of England in 1816, and joined the Geological Society of London a year later. At Lyme, De la Beche also became acquainted with the Annings, an artisan family who were establishing a business selling fossils, and with the daughter Mary he searched the Lias cliffs for remains of extinct reptiles.

Gentleman geologist After coming of age De la Beche began to receive the income from the Jamaican estate. He married Letitia Whyte in the same year, and they set off on a year-long tour of the continent in 1819. De la Beche established contacts with Georges Cuvier, Étienne Geoffroy Saint-Hilaire, and leading naturalists in Paris, Geneva, and other important centres. The tour, and others which followed, laid the foundations for De la Beche's lifelong admiration for French scientific institutions and ideas, and he later published a volume of translations from the *Annales des mines* (1829). While in Europe and after returning to Lyme in 1820, he published his findings, especially on alpine geology. In the following year a joint paper with William Daniel Conybeare described some fragmentary fossil remains (the most important found by Mary

Anning) as a new kind of marine reptile, the pleisi-osaurus, or 'near-lizard'. De la Beche was elected to the Royal Society of London in 1823.

De la Beche, concerned by declining revenue from his inheritance and growing instability in Jamaica, spent a year on his estate in 1823–4. He supported paternalistic reforms of slavery, but opposed abolition. His pamphlet, *Notes on the Present Condition of the Negroes* (1825), idealized the situation and stressed his own good practice, attempting to view the issue simply as one of 'facts'. Privately, however, he recognized that he was likely to lose his property. It also became clear that his marriage was a disaster, as he became suspicious of adultery by his wife while he had been abroad. After an acrimonious public controversy, he obtained a legal separation in 1826. Letitia moved in with her lover, Major-General Henry Wyndham, son of the earl of Egremont, and De la Beche obtained custody of their two daughters. 'Misfortune has followed me from my cradle', he lamented, 'and it will follow me to my grave' (McCartney, 26).

His health breaking under the strain, De la Beche spent several months in 1827–8 and 1828–9 in France, Switzerland, and Italy, gathering material for papers on the geology of the Mediterranean coast. Already known as an expert on the geology of Jamaica, he consolidated his position as a leading man of science, writing several books, notably a *Manual of Geology* (1831) which went through two further English editions, as well as French, German, and American ones. De la Beche believed in the transforming power of science, both for the character of the individual and the nation. He opposed all forms of aristocratic privilege, and was aligned with the philosophic radicals. He read his friend Edwin Chadwick's *Report on the Sanitary Condition of the Labouring Population of Great Britain* (1842) in proof, participated on the royal commission on the health of towns, and issued several books with the 'useful knowledge' publisher Charles Knight. Fiercely anticlerical and denouncing all forms of religious enthusiasm as 'humbug', he placed his faith in common sense, utility, and science.

A skilled draughtsman, De la Beche was noted for his role in pioneering the visual dimensions of geology. His ability is evident throughout his published works, and is displayed to best effect in the forty plates of his innovative *Sections and Views Illustrative of Geological Phenomena* (1830). He was also a keen caricaturist, throwing off amusing sketches in letters and in privately distributed prints. His celebrated lithograph *Duria antiquior* (1830), sold in aid of Mary Anning, was the first time that the extraordinary discoveries of the new science of geology had been recast into an actual scene of the flora and fauna of a 'lost world'.

Into the civil service In the early 1830s the income from Jamaica failed entirely. For some years De la Beche had been colouring geologically the Ordnance Survey's topographical maps of Devon, a project similar to that undertaken by many other gentlemanly geologists at this time. His fortunes having changed so dramatically, he applied to the government in 1832 for £300 to complete his survey.

With support from influential friends in Lord Grey's whig administration, De la Beche was appointed geologist to the ordnance trigonometrical survey of Great Britain under Colonel Thomas Colby. Further funds were granted in 1835 for a survey of Cornwall, and a tiny Museum of Economic Geology was opened in Craig's Court, Charing Cross. From these small beginnings, De la Beche looked to a transformation of British science. Distrusting private initiatives, and following French models, he wanted geology to become part of the state administrative apparatus.

These plans, however, were nearly cut short by a major controversy about the quality of the work in Devon. In 1834 De la Beche had found fossil plants, identical to those of the Coal formation, but apparently in a much lower part of the geological sequence. This led to a bitter controversy involving not only fundamental principles of geological classification, but also De la Beche's competence. As Roderick Murchison said, 'De la Beche is a dirty dog. ... I knew him to be a thorough jobber & a great intriguer & *we* have proved him to be thoroughly incompetent to carry on the survey' (Rudwick, 194). The dispute was resolved in the early 1840s by the widespread adoption of the Devonian as a distinctive period in geological history, and although De la Beche accepted the term he remained wary about its global application.

Expansion and development Despite the Devonian fiasco, De la Beche began to engineer the expansion of his survey, with increasing responsibilities and new posts. In 1839 he published an official *Report on the Geology of Cornwall, Devon and West Somerset*, which summed up his findings and included substantial discussions of mining and economic geology. In the same year John Phillips was appointed palaeontologist, Richard Phillips became curator–chemist, and Trenham Reeks was assistant curator; other positions were gradually obtained, and a Mining Record Office was established to collect statistics relating to British mines. A crucial step came in 1845, when parliament moved the Geological Survey from the Ordnance to an independent position within the Office of Woods and Forests.

De la Beche aimed to create a detailed national geological map, a census of the strata which would accomplish for geology what Chadwick was attempting for sanitary reform. His efforts thus had an important political association with Benthamite reform programmes, as he pressed for recognition of the utility of geological expertise in projects ranging from assessing the quality of coals used in the imperial navy, to searching for an appropriate stone for rebuilding the houses of parliament. The methods and organizational structure De la Beche had established in the survey were copied around the world, not least as men trained under him took up posts in India and elsewhere in the colonies.

By undertaking a census of the strata De la Beche also hoped to transform the basis of geological philosophy. His *Researches in Theoretical Geology* (1834) had agreed with Charles Lyell's *Principles of Geology* (1830–33) in advocating close study of processes in action, but it went on to argue, against Lyell, that this would often point up differences between the present and the past. De la Beche accepted, as did most contemporaries, evidence that the earth was gradually cooling, and that its history had been marked by large-scale catastrophes. Not willing to limit government geology to mapping and collecting, he encouraged his men to use minutely detailed studies of individual localities to reconstruct specific ancient environments. Fossils were not merely to be used for international correlation, but as keys for reconstructing the characteristics of unique places in the past. De la Beche applied this approach in his own account of the formation of the rocks of south-west England and Wales in 1846, and in his hefty *Geological Observer* of 1851, which became known as the survey 'Bible'. Among the senior staff (notably Edward Forbes, T. H. Huxley, Joseph Beete Jukes, John Phillips, and Andrew Ramsay) the approach proved extremely influential.

Recognition and honours De la Beche was an exceptional administrator with good contacts in parliament and Whitehall. He fostered camaraderie and 'jollification' among the young bachelors on his staff, but discouraged them from marrying. From the mid-1840s he became dedicated almost entirely to official work. Many of the men complained that he relied too much on bureaucratic regulations, so that the 'red tape worm' infected everything that went on in the survey. In contrast, the diarist Caroline Fox had described De la Beche in 1836 as 'a regular fun-engine' (C. Fox, *Memories of Old Friends*, ed. H. N. Pym, 2nd edn., 1882, 1.5), full of stories about military school pranks and alligator-hunting. He had 'a handsome but care-worn face, brown eyes and hair, and gold spectacles' (ibid., 1.27). She did not suspect him of being happy.

De la Beche was widely honoured, being elected president of the Geological Society in 1847 and awarded its Wollaston medal in 1855. He was knighted in 1842 and made a companion of the Bath six years later. His greatest triumph came in 1851 when Prince Albert opened the Museum of Practical Geology on Jermyn Street. This became one of the wonders of imperial London, with a vast array of fossils, rocks, and economically useful building stones. It also housed another of De la Beche's great schemes, a government-funded School of Mines and of Science applied to the Arts, modeled on the École des Mines in Paris. The school offered students (especially from the mining districts) training in all the sciences deemed necessary for understanding geology. It attracted few recruits (and particularly few miners) during De la Beche's lifetime, although lectures to working men by Huxley, Lyon Playfair, Ramsay, and others were highly successful. Later in the century the Royal School of Mines did emerge as a leading centre, especially in training geologists for work in the colonies. In 1907 the school was separated from the survey and museum to become part of Imperial College, where the student geology society was subsequently called the De la Beche Club. Although other parts of the institutional empire De la Beche created were dismantled in the twentieth century, the British Geological Survey and the earth galleries at the Natural History Museum bear witness to the legacy of his belief in state support for the earth sciences.

Just as his ambitious plans came to fruition in 1851 De la Beche began to suffer symptoms of a progressive paralysis. He conducted survey business almost up until his death in London on 13 April 1855; he was buried in Kensal Green cemetery on 19 April. J. A. SECORD

Sources P. J. McCartney, *Henry De la Beche: observations on an observer* (1977) · J. A. Secord, 'The geological survey of Great Britain as a research school', *History of Science*, 24 (1986), 223–75 · J. E. Portlock, *Quarterly Journal of the Geological Society*, 12 (1856), xxxiv–xxxviii · *Literary Gazette* (21 April 1855) · M. J. S. Rudwick, *The great Devonian controversy: the shaping of scientific knowledge among gentlemanly specialists* (1985) · H. S. Torrens, 'Mary Anning (1799–1847) of Lyme: "the greatest fossilist the world ever knew"', *British Journal for the History of Science*, 28 (1995), 257–84 · A. Geikie, *Memoir of Sir Andrew Crombie Ramsay* (1895) · L. J. Chubb, 'Sir Henry Thomas De la Beche', *Geonotes: the quarterly journal of the Jamaica group of the Geologists' Association* (1958), 3–28
Archives BGS, corresp. and papers · Glamorgan RO, Cardiff, notebook · NHM, collection of specimens · NMG Wales, corresp., diaries, and papers | GS Lond., Murchison MSS · ICL, letters to Sir Andrew Ramsay · Oxf. U. Mus. NH, letters to John Phillips
Likenesses cameo, *c*.1800, repro. in McCartney, *Henry De la Beche* · W. Brockedon, chalk drawing, 1842, NPG · H. P. Bone, enamel miniature, exh. RA 1847, Geological Museum, London · W. Walker, engraving, pubd 1848 (after miniature by H. P. Bone), NPG [*see illus.*] · E. G. Papworth, bust, Geological Museum, London · engraving (after photograph by Claudet), NPG; repro. in *ILN*, 18 (1851)

Becher, Henry (*fl.* 1559–1568), translator and Church of England clergyman, was admitted vicar of Mayfield, Sussex, in the diocese of Chichester, on 19 July 1559. The parish formed part of the peculiar jurisdiction of South Malling, and provided four of Sussex's protestant martyrs during Mary's reign. Becher may perhaps have been related to the Hampshire man of the same name who matriculated, aged fifteen, at Brasenose College, Oxford, in 1589. During the reign of Mary, and possibly earlier, he attended clandestine meetings of protestants, there encountering groups of 'free-willers' from Kent, Essex, and London, led by Henry Hart. As he explained in less dangerous times: 'we divers and sundry tymes did meet, but had communication with one another, but could not agree'. With the accession of Elizabeth, it became possible to defend a new orthodoxy, and in 1561 Becher, now a 'Minister in the Church of God', issued his translation *Of the Vocation of and Callyng of All Nations*, from the work of St Ambrose, a labour directed, as he explained in the preface, against 'the late strong secte of the Pelagians' whose company he had once kept. He had resigned his living by 20 February 1568, when his successor was admitted, and nothing further is known of him. STEPHEN WRIGHT

Sources St Ambrose, *Twoo bookes of Saint Ambrose bysshoppe of Mylleyne entytuled 'Of the vocation and callyng of all Nations'*, trans. H. Becher (1561) [Latin orig.] · M. J. Kitch, ed., *Studies in Sussex church history* (1981) · E. H. W. Dunkin, 'Contributions towards the ecclesiastical history of the deanery of South Malling', *Sussex Archaeological Collections*, 26 (1875), 9–96, 69

Becher, John Thomas (1770–1848), Church of England clergyman and poor-law reformer, was born in Cork, the son of Michael Becher. Educated at Westminster School, he proceeded to Christ Church, Oxford, where he was elected to a Westminster studentship in 1788. He graduated BA in 1792 and MA in 1795. He married on 6 January 1802 Mary, daughter of the Revd William Becher (d. 1821), prebendary of Southwell, and relinquished his studentship in the same year. In 1799 he was presented to the perpetual curacies of Thurgarton and Hoveringham, Nottinghamshire, in the gift of Trinity College, Cambridge. From 1801 to 1804 he was vicar of Rampton, in the same county. He held the Christ Church living of Midsomer Norton from 1802 to 1827, when he was instituted to the vicarage of Farnsfield, Nottinghamshire. In 1818 he became a prebendary of the collegiate church of Southwell (Southwell Minster), and was later its vicar-general. The chapter of the collegiate church presented him to the rectory of Barnburgh, Yorkshire, in 1830 which, along with his prebend and his livings at Thurgarton, Hoveringham, and Farnsfield, he held until his death.

In 1806, on the arrival at Southwell of the future Lord Byron and his mother, Becher became a regular member of the Byron social circle and respected literary adviser of the apprentice poet himself. It was on Becher's (rhymed) advice that Byron withdrew his first volume of verses from circulation for containing material 'too warmly drawn'. Byron seems to have borne no grudge, as he relied on Becher to see his next volume, *Hours of Idleness* (1807), through the press and nominated Becher co-executor of the will he made before leaving England in 1811.

From 1802 Becher had been establishing himself as an active figure in county administration. His *Report Concerning the House of Correction at Southwell* (1806), together with the *Rules, Orders and Regulations* of that institution (1808), identify him as a reformer in the John Howard mould, aiming to reclaim inmates by a regime of segregation and work discipline. His *Observations on the Punishment of Offenders* (1812) was less reclamatory in focus: dedicated to the duke of Newcastle, lord lieutenant of Nottinghamshire, it urged magistrates not to negotiate with local Luddite leaders over industrial grievances until all outrages had ceased and, even then, to refrain from attempting to regulate manufacturers' use of new technology. The realization that economic change was transforming work relations was, none the less, one which Becher took much to heart, and his social policy experiments which followed were to receive wide publicity as sincere and apparently effective attempts to modernize the delivery of social relief without compromising its paternalist credentials. Becher's plan, most elaborately set out in *The Anti-Pauper System* (1828), related his reform experiments as visiting magistrate at the Southwell workhouse from 1808 and at the Thurgarton hundred incorporated workhouse from 1823. These model workhouses were designed, by systematic application of principles of 'inspection, classification, and seclusion', to deter the able-bodied from entry or reliance on out-relief, but were complemented by the establishment of parish-based voluntary associations for worker self-help under guidance of the propertied. Much of Becher's reputation for his scheme was derived from

the actuarial and book-keeping aids which he devised for the use of the gentleman sponsors of the savings banks and friendly societies that formed key parts of the scheme.

Unlike more extreme reformers Becher opposed the outright abolition of the poor law, arguing that a system of benevolent magisterial oversight administered on behalf of infirm and infant poor served the 'security of the rich' as much as the 'preservation and happiness of the poor'. Becher's system of reform, while impressing the House of Lords select committee on the poor laws in 1831, did not, however, impress assistant commissioner J. W. Cowell of the 1832 poor-law royal commission, who inspected it in operation and found it amateurish and over-indulgent to inmates. Becher's administrative credentials were further weakened by the fact that a key adviser to the 1832 commissioners, and foundation commissioner under the 1834 Poor Law Amendment Act, George Nicholls, had been a rival and critic of Becher ever since acting as overseer of the poor at Southwell in 1821–3. Becher fought on to preserve the rights of magistrates against central officialdom as attempts were made to establish the new district unions under the 1834 act. The poor-law commissioners, realizing the strength of his local support base and, perhaps, fearing to undermine his health, moved cautiously against him, but with the help of the duke of Newcastle succeeded in dislodging him in 1836. He also resigned in that year as chairman of quarter sessions of the Newark division of Nottinghamshire, a position he had held since 1816. He died at Hill House, Southwell, on 3 January 1848, aged seventy-eight.

M. J. D. ROBERTS

Sources GM, 1st ser., 72 (1802), 83 · GM, 2nd ser., 29 (1848), 445 · Foster, *Alum. Oxon.* · W. W. Pratt, *Byron at Southwell* (1948) · J. D. Marshall, 'The Nottinghamshire reformers and their contribution to the new poor law', *Economic History Review*, 2nd ser., 13 (1960–61), 382–96 · A. Brundage, *The making of the new poor law* (1978) · G. Nicholls and T. Mackay, *A history of the English poor law*, 3 vols. (1898–9)

Archives U. Nott. L., letters to fourth duke of Newcastle

Becher, Martin William [*known as* Captain Becher] (1797–1864), jockey, born on 18 May 1797, possibly at Hillington, near King's Lynn, was the son of William Becher (d. 1816), an army man turned Norfolk farmer and horse-dealer. He secured a position in the storekeeper-general's department at Brussels, supplying Wellington's troops. His own later rank of captain was an honorary one in the Buckinghamshire yeomanry cavalry. On his return to Britain he worked initially as a horse-coper but later as first jockey for Thomas Coleman. Proprietor of the Turf Hotel at St Albans, Coleman is generally credited with pioneering the commercial development of steeplechasing when he promoted the St Albans steeplechase in 1830. He encouraged Becher to take up riding over fences; not that the gallant captain required much persuasion, for he had been taught to ride all manner of horses as a child and was a skilled horseman. Although accepted as qualified to ride in races restricted to gentlemen, Becher made a living from riding and from schooling horses over fences for their owners.

Martin William Becher [Captain Becher] (**1797–1864**), by Bryan Edward Duppa, c.1840s

On 14 August 1825 he had married Susan, only daughter of John Dobree.

Becher's name is associated in the national memory with the Grand National steeplechase. In 1836, riding The Duke, he won William Lynn's inaugural chase at Aintree and two years later he came third on the same horse. However, it was in the 1839 race, usually recognized as the first Grand National (even though the title was not formally adopted until 1847), that Becher gained racing immortality. When running second in a field of seventeen, his mount, Conrad, fell at a specially constructed jump in which a brook had been dammed to make it 8 feet wide and a 3½ foot wooden fence set back about a yard in front of the water. The hazard was increased by the landing area being a yard or so lower than the take-off side. Becher landed in the water and sensibly crouched in safety in the deepest part of the brook until the rest of the horses had passed by. Less sensibly, perhaps, he remounted only to take another soaking at the next water jump. Although he never rode again in a Grand National, such was his celebrity that the fence at which he fell became known as Becher's brook.

Becher's last public ride was at Doncaster's Cantley Common course on 19 March 1847. His horse fell. After giving up racing he was appointed inspector of sacks for the Great Northern Railway at Boston, Lincolnshire. A boisterous character, he would drink and sing late into the night at post-race celebrations. His favourite party trick was to run around a room on the wainscoting without touching

the floor. In later life he was described as being thickset, with bushy hair and a kindly, rugged face enlivened by small but penetrating eyes. Becher died on 11 October 1864 at 21 Maida Hill, St John's Wood, London, and was buried at Willesden cemetery. At an auction to dispose of his estate, his seven silk riding jerseys brought 5s. Becher's brook was filled in 1990 but remains a challenging fence on the Aintree circuit, a fitting memorial to a tough and intrepid rider. WRAY VAMPLEW

Sources M. Seth-Smith and others, *The history of steeplechasing* (1966) · R. Munting, *Hedges and hurdles* (1987) · J. Tyrrell, *Chasing around Britain* (1990) · A. Holland, *Grand National* (1991) · J. Hislop, *Steeplechasing* (1951) · R. Longrigg, *The history of horse racing* (1972) · R. Green, *The history of the Grand National* (1993) · M. Ayres and G. Newbon, *Over the sticks* (1971) · D. H. Munroe, *The Grand National, 1839–1931* (1931) · Lord Willoughby de Broke, ed., *Steeplechasing* (1954) · Boase, *Mod. Eng. biog.* · d. cert. · *GM*, 1st ser., 95 (1825), 176

Likenesses J. A. Mitchell, portrait, 1835 · B. E. Duppa, drawing, c.1840–1849, BM [*see illus.*] · C. Rosenberg, portrait, repro. in T. H. Bird, 'Centenary of the Grand National', *Country Life* (1937)

Becher, Sir William (*bap.* 1580, *d.* 1651), diplomat and government official, was the grandson of a London alderman and the eldest son of William Becher, a London merchant tailor, and Judith Quarles, daughter of another merchant tailor. He was baptized at St Lawrence Jewry, London, on 4 May 1580. Educated at Westminster School as befitted the son of a prosperous city family, Becher matriculated from Corpus Christi College, Oxford, on 10 October 1594 and graduated BA in 1597. He entered the Inner Temple the following year.

Becher remained close to Westminster's schoolmaster William Camden. He wrote news letters to Camden and often served as a middleman in Camden's contacts with continental intellectuals. Becher had a substantial reputation as a news writer and intelligencer among a wide circle of contemporaries, including the news writers John Chamberlain and George Garrard.

Becher's first diplomatic post was as a messenger in Sir George Carew's embassy to Paris between 1606 and 1608. Becher had been recommended to Carew by Sir Michael Hicks, a client of Robert Cecil, first earl of Salisbury, secretary of state, and lord treasurer. Becher supervised Salisbury's son and heir in Paris and during travels on the continent while also writing news to the father. Left in Paris as agent when Carew was recalled, Becher was not employed by the new ambassador, Sir Thomas Edmondes. Desperate for a position, two years later he was back in Paris as tutor to Henry, Lord Clifford, only son of the fourth earl of Cumberland and son-in-law of Salisbury. Henri IV's assassination during this time inspired Becher to write a romance about the king's life and loves. In 1614 Becher was a candidate for a duchy of Lancaster seat at Knaresborough, Yorkshire, in the Addled Parliament, likely through the influence of the Slingsby family, local duchy officials, whom he had met in Paris. That same year Becher was sent by Secretary Winwood with Sir John Merricke's embassy to Muscovy, where he was miserably unhappy for the next two years. But in 1617 he was back in London, in touch with the rapidly rising new royal favourite George Villiers, who may also have met Becher in Paris, and through Villiers's good offices secured the post of English agent in France on the departure of Edmondes. Becher was soon recalled, however, as relations between England and France deteriorated.

Becher sat in the parliament of 1621, having been nominated for two seats, one in the gift of Thomas Howard, earl of Arundel, the patron of Camden as Garter king at arms, and the other in the gift of Villiers. Becher chose to accept Villiers's continued patronage, deepening a relationship that endured until the favourite's assassination. Becher was selected on Villiers patronage to every parliament of the 1620s and was one of the duke's most active and vocal defenders in the house and out, to the extent that his fellow MPs considered him little more than the duke's mouthpiece. In 1622 Becher was knighted and accompanied Lord Chichester's embassy to the Palatinate and early in 1623, once again through Buckingham's favour, obtained the post of clerk to the privy council to replace Sir Albertus Morton. But Becher had apparently not completely abandoned his intellectual aspirations since, on the heels of this appointment, he was rumoured to be in hot contention with many of the leading intellectuals of the day for the provostship of Eton College. He had Buckingham's strong support for this position too, but Buckingham, beset by suitors and mired in numerous complicated patronage deals not to mention a trip to Spain, changed his mind, preferring Sir Henry Wotton instead. Becher was compensated with a £2500 payment, reversions to other offices, and continuance in the post of council clerk and Buckingham's good graces.

As a council clerk, Becher was considered to have financial and organizational acumen, and perhaps even a genetic predisposition to these talents as he came from a family of merchants who had also been defence contractors and speculators. Becher was involved in the planning and preparations for all of Buckingham's military expeditions in the 1620s. He was chosen secretary to the council of war in 1624 and, as such, treasurer for Mansfeld's expedition to the Palatinate, which he accompanied in person to report on the mission. Subsequently he seems to have been involved in Charles I's marriage negotiations in France with another old Paris acquaintance, Sir Henry Rich, now earl of Holland, and in June 1625 it was Becher who publicly read the declaration of the king's marriage at Whitehall. In December 1626 Becher sailed with the Rhé fleet as Buckingham's personal secretary and was at the centre of the negotiations with the Rochellois. It was Becher whom Buckingham sent back to England the following summer to obtain further funding and reinforcements for this mission, a task frustrated by lack of funds and bureaucracy, both of which Becher worked furiously to overcome. He returned with little money, few provisions, and few men, and, when the mission ended, was then assigned to disband what was left of Buckingham's army when it returned to England. Becher expected to sail with the duke's planned 1628 expedition as well, despite a severe attack of kidney stones during the final preparations.

After Buckingham's assassination in 1628, Becher

retained the favour of the king, who kept him on as a council clerk and master of requests in extraordinary, and honoured the grants and reversions issued to Becher by the deceased favourite as much as a decade later. In the council office, he served a number of commissions concerned with financial matters including the treasury commission of 1635–6. Becher was also clerk to the Irish committee of the council which brought him into contact with Robert Boyle, first earl of Cork, one of the wealthiest men in the three kingdoms. Cork paid Becher £40 a year to look after his business in the committee and to report to him on other business there. This relationship grew to include private investments and other business deals that benefited Becher's fortunes.

In 1640 Becher had a brush with the investigations undertaken by the Long Parliament and, after a few days in the Fleet, decided to confess he had been in error and divest himself of his clerk's position. While the king, short of money himself, opposed Becher's attempts to sell the office for personal profit, he was apparently not sorry to see Becher go. There is no indication, as Gerald Aylmer asserted, that Becher was forced out because he was suspected of being a Catholic; his greatest sin seems to have been that he was an ageing royalist. Becher's clerkship was sold to Sir Richard Browne, the royal agent in Paris, and Becher himself spent the war years in and out of England and France. Despite comments about his advancing age and declining health, he apparently suffered no impediment in offering to sell guns to the earl of Cork in 1643 or when smuggling guns to the king's forces between 1643 and 1645 from his perch in Rouen. Becher's estate and activities were investigated by the committee for the advancement of money in 1649, although the outcome of their proceedings is unknown. Becher died in 1651 at his home in Putney where he was buried before the high altar in Putney church. Becher never married, but named one natural son, also William Becher, a lawyer, in his will. Taxes of £1000 had been assessed on his estate in 1646 and 1647, indicating that it was substantial. The will left legacies of more than £1250 to his sisters and their children, £300 for poor clergy, and the rest to his son.

S. A. BARON

Sources BL, Add. MS 20774, fol. 19 · *The letters of John Chamberlain*, ed. N. E. McClure, 2 vols. (1939) · J. W. Stoye, *English travellers abroad, 1604–1667*, rev. edn (1989) · *CSP dom., 1640* · R. Lockyer, *Buckingham: the life and political career of George Villiers, first duke of Buckingham, 1592–1628* (1981) · G. E. Aylmer, *The king's servants: the civil service of Charles I, 1625–1642*, rev. edn (1974) · *The Lismore papers*, ed. A. B. Grosart, 10 vols. in 2 series (privately printed, London, 1886–8) · Foster, *Alum. Oxon.* · A. W. Hughes Clarke, ed., *The register of St Lawrence Jewry, London*, 1, Harleian Society, registers, 70 (1940)

Wealth at death over £2000: Stoye, *English travellers abroad*, 54

Beck, Adolf (1841–1909), businessman and victim of two miscarriages of justice, was born in Christiansund, Norway, on 14 June 1841, the son of a trader and ship's captain. Leaving school at sixteen, he led a restless, wandering, and varied life. He was a clerk in merchants' offices, studied industrial chemistry privately, and went to sea, before reaching Britain in 1865 or 1866, where he worked in shipping offices in six ports between Cardiff and Aberdeen. Beck also attempted to become a professional singer. In 1868 he went to South America, where he stayed until 1884, spending time in almost every country of the subcontinent, and making enough money to buy an unprofitable Norwegian copper mine. He arrived in London in 1885, but did not prosper, falling into debt, borrowing money from, and courting—but not marrying—several women. In his later years he was often seen in the company of prostitutes (which may explain the number of women later claiming to identify him in court).

In 1896, and again in 1904, Beck was convicted—wrongly as it subsequently appeared—at the Old Bailey of defrauding numerous women of doubtful character of their jewellery. Seventeen women—eleven in 1896 and six in 1904—mistakenly identified him as the man who, masquerading as Lord Willoughby or Lord Wilton, had deceived them. This was, however, fewer than half the total number of complainants, none of whose property was traced to him. The swindler was in fact an Austrian or German Jew known at different times in England and Australia (where for several years he practised medicine successfully) by a variety of names, both German and English, who had first been convicted (as Thomas Smith) of seventeen very similar frauds in 1877, and sentenced to five years' penal servitude.

The frauds resumed in 1895 and Beck was arrested, tried, convicted, and sentenced to seven years' penal servitude, after the women's identifications had been confirmed by the police constable, now retired, who had arrested 'Smith' in 1877. These mistakes were compounded by the judge, Sir Forrest Fulton, the common serjeant, wrongly refusing to admit the evidence of a handwriting expert, which would have established that the 1877 and the 1895 swindler was, as indeed the prosecution believed, the same person. This would have exonerated Beck, since he could have proved that in 1877 he was in Peru. In addition, the prison authorities soon became aware that Beck, being uncircumcised, and having blue, not brown eyes, was not 'Smith', and accordingly allotted him a new prison number. But the Home Office officials who reported this discovery to Fulton did not recognize its crucial significance, and nor did he.

Released in 1901 after serving five years, Beck was re-arrested in 1904 on similar charges and was again convicted. As the law in 1896 stood, Beck could not himself have given evidence; in 1904 he could have given it but, with the 1896 conviction still standing, was advised not to. This time the judge, Sir William Grantham, doubted the jury's verdict, and while further inquiries were being made 'Smith' was arrested for trying to pawn a stolen ring and confessed to all the frauds. Beck was at once pardoned for the crimes he had not committed and received £2000 (later increased to £5000) compensation. The subsequent inquiry (chaired by Sir Richard Henn Collins, master of the rolls) placed, absurdly, all the blame on the absence of legally trained civil servants in the Home Office, and did not recommend the establishment of a criminal appeal court. But the case for it was overwhelming. Had it existed

in 1896, Fulton's erroneous ruling at Beck's first trial might have been successfully challenged.

The egregious injustice to Beck made irresistible the sixty-year long, and thirty-parliamentary bill, campaign for a court of criminal appeal empowered to quash convictions for errors of fact as of law, which the judiciary and successive home secretaries had persistently opposed. The Court of Criminal Appeal Act of 1907 followed. The new court's judges adopted, however, an exceedingly narrow view of its powers, and devoted most of their attention to reducing scandalous disparities in sentencing. Responsibility for investigating and referring claimed miscarriages of justice to the court of appeal criminal division (as the court of criminal appeal became in 1968) was transferred from the Home Office to the Criminal Cases Review Commission in 1996. Not until then did England begin to have anything approaching a satisfactory system for remedying them. Beck, who soon spent the compensation money, died of pleurisy and bronchitis on 7 December 1909 in the Middlesex Hospital, London.

P. R. GLAZEBROOK

Sources 'Committee of inquiry into the case of Mr Adolf Beck', *Parl. papers* (1905), 62.465, Cd 2315 · E. R. Watson, ed., *Trial of Adolf Beck* (1924) · R. Pattenden, *English criminal appeals* (1996) · *Daily Telegraph* (8 Dec 1909)

Likenesses photograph, July 1904 (in prison), repro. in Watson, ed., *Trial* · photograph, repro. in Watson, ed., *Trial*, frontispiece

Beck, Cave (*bap.* 1622, *d.* 1706), writer on universal language and Church of England clergyman, second son of John Beck, 'pandoxator' or brewer, and Anne Flecher (probably *née* Cave, and widow of Adam Flecher), was born in the parish of St James's, Clerkenwell, and baptized at St Mary, Whitechapel, Stepney, Middlesex, on 6 October 1622. For five years Cave attended William Braithwayte's private school in Leadenhall, London, where his master's work on musical notation, published in 1639, is likely to have provided an early inspiration to Beck for his language ideas. In June 1638 he matriculated from St John's College, Cambridge, where his tutor was John Cleveland, the poet whose witty verses later supported the king's cause. Graduating BA in 1642, Beck enrolled at Gray's Inn that August, but either did not take to the law, or the outbreak of the civil war that autumn distracted him, for he took the study no further.

On the evidence of his name occurring among those on whom Charles I conferred MAs on 17 October 1643 Beck probably then followed Cleveland to join the king at Christ Church, Oxford. Knowing of Beck's later achievements, the likely inference is that he was engaged in undercover cipher work. Certainly there were at Oxford in the 1640s several others interested in universal language, the most eminent being John Wilkins, warden of Wadham from 1648; it was from him that Beck later received harsh criticism of his manuscript.

Beck was 'of Brentwood' (Suffolk RO, Ipswich, C/2/2/2/2), probably usher there, when in September 1650 he was appointed master of Ipswich grammar school. His predecessor at Ipswich was a staunch puritan, and Beck must have smothered his royalist past to obtain the acceptance of the borough corporation, and of the brothers Nathaniel and Francis Bacon, both active on the parliamentary side and influential throughout the region; at least all three had Gray's Inn in common. As master he was also responsible for the town preachers' library. To facilitate the checking and ordering of several hundred volumes of theology he devised a unique system of shelf marks, lines painted obliquely across the fore-edges of sets of books, with the same distinguishing astronomical or alchemical symbol on each book in a set. Basil Breame was paid 3s. on 12 April 1651 'for making the lines on the bookes'.

In 1657 Beck resigned from the school and published his *Universal Character* in English and French editions. The dedication was to the Bacon brothers, 'patronis suis colendissimis' (A4), and four friends, two certainly puritan ministers, added verses in praise of this early attempt at universal language. One of them, Joseph Waite of Sproughton, addressing his 'intimate and ingenious friend', wrote, 'let me be dead before this see the shop' (A6), but in gentle jest. Beck's language used the Arabic numbers 0 to 9, to be pronounced 'aun, too, tray, for, fai, sic, sen, at, nin and o'. About 4000 words in general use are listed in alphabetical order. For example, 'a floor' is 652, written thus and pronounced 'sicfaitoo'. Prefixed letters indicate parts of speech derived from the same word. The title-page claim that 'the practise whereof may be attained in two hours space' is optimistic if that involved learning the dictionary by heart.

There is no record of Beck's ordination but he became perpetual curate at St Margaret's, Ipswich, on leaving the school, signing the registers annually for the next twenty years as 'curate' or 'minister'. He became resident tutor to the children of Leicester Devereux, Viscount Hereford, at neighbouring Christchurch. He was later chaplain there, and, with others, guardian to the children when their parents died. In 1660 Hereford was one of the six peers who was sent to Holland to bring back the king, and Beck was one of his attendant gentlemen. While there, Beck was sent to see Dr John Earle, translator of *Eikon basilike* into Latin. When Richard Hollingsworth published his case for the work having been written by the king himself, Beck gave assurances he had received at Ipswich from the officer who read the manuscript after Naseby, and his opinion that, 'for my part, I am apt to believe no person was able to frame that book, but a suffering King, and no suffering King, but King Charles the Martyr' (Hollingsworth, 27–8).

The living of St Helen's, Ipswich, whose church had been used by Independents during the interregnum, reverted to the crown at the Restoration, and was given to Beck. When the former town preacher refused to conform, Beck was one of three ministers who shared the duty for a time. He then held the two Ipswich livings, and from 1674 also Monk Soham (15 miles north) and another in Worcestershire.

Beck had two wives called Sarah: the first, who gave him a son, John, at the school in 1666 but dead by 1701, died in the plague year 1665 and was buried on 30 November; the second outlived him, dying in 1708. He kept charge of the

town library, forcing successor masters to establish a separate school collection. Very few religious works were now added; donors were encouraged to give mathematics, history, law, topography, and science including a good set of Boyle's works and the earliest publications of the Royal Society. Nathaniel Fairfax, an ejected minister then practising medicine in Woodbridge, advised Secretary Oldenburg to accept Beck as Suffolk correspondent on scientific matters, describing him as 'a divine of steddy reasonings, shrewd fetches, narrow serchings, mathematically given' (*Correspondence of Henry Oldenburg*, 4.125–6). In a reminder Fairfax added 'of a genius made for new works' (Hollingsworth, 337). Once appointed, Beck bombarded Oldenburg with such things as his 'art of memory' and his account of witches (in fact monsters) in Suffolk. How much Beck coveted fellowship of the new society comes through his enthusiasm for the task.

Beck's last surviving achievement is an elaborate display of fifty painted panels between the rafters of the medieval double hammerbeam roof at his church of St Margaret's. This he planned with Devereux Edgar, the wealthy tory Ipswich magistrate who paid for it. The two central panels are an unusual form of the royal arms of William and Mary. Put up between November 1694 and March 1695, the whole celebrates the satisfactory settlement of the religious troubles of the century and of the balanced constitution. Five years later a series of heraldic shields were fixed to the ends of the hammers where much earlier wooden angels had spread their wings. The local worthies honoured in this way were an eclectic group crossing all religious and political divides. Beck himself is unlikely to have been entitled to the arms of the medieval bishop he adopted.

Beck was still chaplain (and had been tutor) to the eighth Viscount Hereford when the latter died in 1700 leaving Beck £10. In August 1706 Beck made his own short will leaving his wife, Sarah, three houses in St Nicholas's parish. The will was not proved until July 1707, but successors at St Helen's and Monk Soham were inducted in December 1706. Sarah was buried at St Margaret's on 4 October 1708, but the register is deficient at the time he must have preceded her.   J. M. BLATCHLY

Sources C. Beck, *The universal character* (1657) • C. Beck, *Le charactere universel* (1657) • V. Salmon, 'Cave Beck: a seventeenth-century Ipswich schoolmaster and his "universal character"', *Proceedings of the Suffolk Institute of Archaeology*, 33 (1973–5), 285–98 • J. Blatchly, *The town library of Ipswich provided for the use of the town preachers in 1599: a history and catalogue* (1989) • R. Hollingsworth, *The character of Charles I* (1692), 27–8, 337 • G. C. Moore Smith, *The family of Withypoll*, rev. P. H. Reaney (1936) • Beck's will, PRO, PROB 6 Alexander (1706) • bill for 'lines on the bookes', Suffolk RO, Ipswich, HD88/3/5 • J. E. B. Mayor, ed., *Admissions to the College of St John the Evangelist in the University of Cambridge*, 1: Jan 1629/30 – July 1665 (1882), 42, xvi • *The correspondence of Henry Oldenburg*, ed. and trans. A. R. Hall and M. B. Hall, 4 (1967), 125–6, 337 • register, St Margaret's, Ipswich • IGI

Likenesses W. Faithorne, group portrait, line engraving (including Beck?), BM; repro. in Beck, *The universal character*, frontispiece

Wealth at death three houses in St Nicholas's parish, Ipswich left to wife: will, PRO [Alexander, 1706]

Beck, David Hendrikszoon (1621–1656), painter, was born in Delft, Holland, on 25 May 1621, the eldest son of the schoolmaster and occasional poet Hendrik Beck, who was born in Cologne before 1593 and died in Rotterdam in 1659, and Eva Aelbertsdochter Schoonharen, who died in Rotterdam between 21 and 27 January 1640. Their marriage took place in Delft on 12 July 1620; they named their son after his uncle, the Hague schoolmaster David Beck. Beck was an apprentice first, in Delft, of Michiel van Miereveldt and then, in London, of Anthony Van Dyck. His style followed that of the Flemish master, but remained extremely varied.

Houbraken states that 'Beck became a favourite of Charles I, whose son Charles II, the dukes of York and Gloucester, even as prince Robbert, he instructed in the art of drawing during their young years' (Houbraken, 2.83). After having been in the service of the kings of France and Denmark, Beck became court painter and *valet de chambre* of Kristina of Sweden from 1647, and received regular payments for this until 1653. In her service he visited the courts of Europe to deliver the queen's portrait and to portray foreign sovereigns. During these travels he acted as Kristina's agent in buying works of art and also formed his own remarkable collection. These missions were commemorated by a number of laudatory poems by Dutch poets (especially by Joost van den Vondel) and Beck received numerous rewards. These and his court service earned him the nickname Golden Sceptre among the 'schildersbent' group of Dutch painters in Rome when he went there with Queen Kristina in 1653.

From Rome, Beck accompanied Kristina on her tour to Paris, where he was granted leave to go to Holland. There he died, unmarried, in The Hague on 20 December 1656 and was buried on 22 or 26 December in Rotterdam. The suspicion that he was poisoned is contradicted by the fact that he changed his testament as a sick man only a fortnight before his death (codicil dated 6 December 1656 to his last will, dated 18 June 1653). The heirs to his rich art collection and considerable fortune were his (half) brothers and sisters and their children.

Beck painted numerous portraits of Kristina and of her civil and military court which remain mostly in Swedish collections (many are in the National Portraitmuseum at Skokloster) and of European princes and intellectuals, for example, Grotius and Salamasius. Many of his works were engraved by the court engraver Jeremias Falck. Beck became godfather to Falck's daughter in Stockholm on 2 August 1652.

A self-portrait of Beck, now lost, was auctioned in Amsterdam on 31 October 1871; an engraved self-portrait with Queen Kristina's portrait on the easel, signed 'Ant.Cognet sc.—Joan. Meyssens exc.', is reproduced in Meyssens, De Bie, and Houbraken (see sources).

JOCHEN BECKER

Sources A. Bredius, *Künstler-Inventare*, 4; Quellenschriften zur neiderländischen Kunstgeschichte, 10 (The Hague, 1917), 1267–83 · J. Meyssens, *Image de divers hommes desprit sublime* (Antwerp, 1649) · C. de Bie, *Het gulden cabinet vande edel ury schilder Const[antyn]* (Antwerp, 1661), 160–61 · D. van Bleyswijck, *Beschrijvinge der stadt Delft* (Delft, 1667), 854–5 · A. Houbraken, *De groote schouburgh der Nederlantsche konstschilders en schilderessen*, 2nd edn, 3 vols. (The Hague, 1753), 2.83–7 · E. Larsen, ed., *La vie, les ouvrages et les élèves de Van Dyck: manuscrit inédit des archives du Louvre par un auteur anonyme* (Brussels, 1975), 80, 122 · *Nieuw Nederlands biografisch woordenboek*, 2 (Leiden, 1912) [H. Ruys] · W. J. L. Poelmans, 'Hendrik en David Beck', *Rotterdamsch Jaarboekje*, 2nd ser., 5 (1917), 74–80 · *Svenskt biografiskt lexikon*, 2 (Stockholm, 1920), 789–91 [A. Hahr] · K. E. Steneberg, 'Kristinatidens maleri', PhD diss., Lund University, Malmö, Sweden, 1955, 127–57 · D. Beck, *Spiegel van mijn leven: een Haags dagboek uit 1624*, ed. S. E. Veldhuijzen (Hilversum, 1993), 233–5 · G. Meissner, ed., *Allgemeines Künstlerlexikon: die bildenden Künstler aller Zeiten und Völker*, [new edn, 34 vols.] (Leipzig and Munich, 1983–)

Likenesses D. H. Beck, self-portrait, engraving; auctioned Amsterdam, 31 Oct 1871

Wealth at death 5100 guilders; jewels; rich art collection: Bredius, *Künstler-Inventare*

Beck, Diana Jean Kinloch (1900–1956), neurosurgeon, was born on 29 June 1900 at Hoole, Chester, the only girl of the three children of James Beck, a master draper of Scottish descent, and his wife, Margaret Helena Kinloch. From the Queen's School at Chester she went to study medicine at the London School of Medicine for Women at the Royal Free Hospital, where she graduated MB BS in 1925, gaining the Gwendolin Lynn prize, the Grant medal in surgery, and the Julia Cock scholarship. After working as house surgeon at the Royal Free Hospital she was made FRCS of Edinburgh in 1930 and FRCS of England in 1931. From 1932 to 1936 she was surgical registrar at the Royal Free Hospital, where she also took an active and enthusiastic part in undergraduate teaching. In 1939 she was awarded the William Gibson research scholarship of the Royal Society of Medicine. Beck decided to specialize in neurosurgery, and trained in this field under Sir Hugh Cairns at the Radcliffe Infirmary in Oxford. The war prolonged her stay in Oxford with the need to provide general surgical treatment to injured soldiers, as well as having to carry out research and teaching. In 1943 she was appointed consultant neurosurgeon to the Royal Free Hospital, but in 1944 the continuing demands of the war took her first to Chase Farm, Enfield, and then to Bristol, where she worked as consultant adviser in neurosurgery to the Emergency Medical Service for the south-west region of England.

In 1947 Beck was elected consultant neurosurgeon at the Middlesex Hospital, London, the first woman to be appointed to a senior clinical position at any of those London teaching hospitals which at that time admitted only male students, and she was for some time the only female neurosurgeon in western Europe or America. Beck was fully active in the life of the hospital, not only as a neurosurgeon but also administratively and socially. She was popular as a teacher, students appreciating her lucid manner and sympathetic approach to patients. Colleagues remembered her for her sound clinical judgement. One of her earliest patients at the Middlesex was A. A. Milne.

Beck published a number of papers of importance on neurosurgery in *Brain*, the *British Journal of Surgery*, and the *Journal of Neurosurgery*, notably on the neurosurgical treatment of cerebral haemorrhage. She lectured in Europe,

Canada, and the USA. She was an active member of the Society of British Neurological Surgeons, and for two years was president of the London Association of the Medical Women's Federation. She was consulting neurological surgeon to the Elizabeth Garrett Anderson, Marie Curie, and New Sussex hospitals.

Beck never married, but was close to her two brothers, Dudley and George, and their families. She was short in stature, elegant in appearance, and strong-minded. Her recreations were embroidery, painting, music, and travel. Beck died suddenly in the Middlesex Hospital on 3 March 1956 when she appeared to be recovering well after a thymectomy operation. Although in her lifetime Beck gained most public recognition for her 'remarkable feat of surgery' (The Times, 6 March 1956) which saved the life of A. A. Milne, in retrospect she is notable as the first woman to have been appointed consultant in a teaching hospital which admitted only male students. HUGH SERIES

Sources The Times (6 March 1956) · WWW · BMJ (17 March 1956), 634–5 · The Lancet (10 March 1956), 323 · CGPLA Eng. & Wales (1956) · b. cert.
Likenesses photograph, repro. in BMJ
Wealth at death £6285 6s. 11d.: probate, 26 June 1956, CGPLA Eng. & Wales

Beck, Gabriel (d. 1662?), lawyer and politician, was the son of Job Beck (b. 1564/5, d. in or before 1619) of Woodstanway, Gloucestershire. He was admitted to Lincoln's Inn on 5 May 1632, with the help of Richard Barnard and Hugh Wyndham. It was probably through Barnard that Beck was introduced to Viscount Saye and other members of the Fiennes family. By June 1643 he was acting as a man of business for Saye's son, Nathaniel, then governor of Bristol, and, following the fall of the city to the royalists, in September he was acting as solicitor to parliament's committee for the advance of money. Beck invested in land in Ireland as early as 1642, and Barnard bequeathed him some Irish land in 1644, and this probably accounts for his role during 1644–5 in keeping the records of the assessment in Ireland. In June 1645 Beck became a clerk to the court of wards. He was named a commissioner to visit of Oxford University on 1 May 1647. He was probably the 'Mr Beck' called to the bar of Lincoln's Inn on 12 February 1648, an honour bestowed because of his importance in official circles, and specifically because of his appointment as counsel for John Lilburne in his trial for libel and scandalum magnatum before the House of Lords. In October 1648 Beck was referred to as 'auditor of the committee for affairs of Ireland' (CSP dom., 1648–9, 305). In April 1649 Beck was named a commissioner of assessment for Oxfordshire, and on 16 August 1650 he was added to the militia commissioners for that county. He may well have owed his appointment to the local influence of the Fiennes family in Oxfordshire. His local appointments continued during the Commonwealth.

Beck's legal talent was next employed by the protectorate regime. On 8 May 1656 Beck was appointed by the council of state to 'solicit the despatch of such public business as he shall receive direction from the Council or Mr. Secretary [Thurloe]' (CSP dom., 1655–6, 312). It was in this

guise that in June, together with William Sheppard, Beck was given the remit to consider all renewals of corporate charters, work which continued into 1658. By July 1656 Beck had married Anne (b. after 1617), daughter of Samuel Dunch of North Baddesley, Hampshire, a member of a well-connected parliamentarian family from Berkshire, which included Dunch's son, John, and his nephew Edmund. On 15 July 1656 it was reported that Samuel Dunch was promoting the candidature of his son-in-law Beck at Abingdon. Although unsuccessful on this occasion, Beck was named on 9 June 1657 to the assessment commission for Berkshire, and also for Westminster, Gloucestershire, and Hampshire. On 23 November 1658 Beck marched in the funeral procession of Oliver Cromwell by virtue of his post of 'solicitor to the Council of State' (Matthews, 65). The Hampshire and Berkshire influence of the Dunches may well have helped Beck into parliament, for on 4 January 1659 he was returned for Andover, although he made little impact on proceedings in the house.

Beck's final local appointment was as a militia commissioner for Westminster in March 1660. His attitude to the Restoration is unknown, but in February 1661 he was ordered by Lord Treasurer Southampton to deliver his records relating to Irish revenue collection into the exchequer. Beck probably died in April 1662, as in that month there is a reference to several plots of land in Westminster, 'the inheritance of Gabriel Beck' (CSP dom., 1661–2, 353), and in Warwickshire administration was granted for his will. STUART HANDLEY

Sources G. E. Aylmer, The state's servants: the civil service of the English republic, 1649–1660 (1973), 276, 418–19 · J. T. Peacey, 'Led by the hand: manucaptors and patronage at Lincoln's Inn in the seventeenth century', Legal History, 18 (1997), 26–44 · HoP, Commons, 1640–60 [draft] · W. P. Baildon, ed., The records of the Honorable Society of Lincoln's Inn: admissions, 1 (1896), 218 · W. P. Baildon, ed., The records of the Honorable Society of Lincoln's Inn: the black books, 2 (1898), 377 · C. H. Firth and R. S. Rait, eds., Acts and ordinances of the interregnum, 1642–1660, 3 vols. (1911) · CSP dom., 1644–50; 1655–62 · E. Ashmole, The visitation of Berkshire, 1664–6, ed. W. C. Metcalfe (1882), 29 · Thurloe, State papers, 5.215 · N. L. Matthews, William Sheppard, Cromwell's law reformer (1984), 35, 52–3, 62, 65 · W. A. Shaw, ed., Calendar of treasury books, 1, PRO (1904), 1.202 · PROB 12.39, fol. 7r [admon. index]

Beck, George Andrew (1904–1978), Roman Catholic archbishop of Liverpool, was born on 28 May 1904 in Streatham, London, the second son of Fleet Street journalist Patrick Beck and his Irish wife, Louisa O'Keefe. He was educated at Clapham College and later at the Assumptionist College of St Michael at Hitchin in Hertfordshire. After completing a two-year noviciate in the Society of St Edmund he transferred in 1924 to the Augustinians of the Assumption and went to their house of studies at Louvain in Belgium. Ordained priest on 24 July 1927 he returned to St Michael's, teaching mathematics and history until he became headmaster in 1940, having obtained an external degree in history from London University. From 1944 to 1948 he was headmaster at the Assumptionist Becket School in Nottingham. He was the leading Roman Catholic clerical expert on educational issues both before and

George Andrew Beck (1904–1978), by Elliott & Fry, 1955

after the Education Act of 1944. He had a very clear mind which enabled him to get quickly to the heart of an argument, and to distinguish certainties from probabilities in a way which was much appreciated by the politicians and civil servants with whom he had to negotiate.

On 21 September 1948 Beck was consecrated titular bishop of Tigia and coadjutor with right of succession to the ageing bishop of Brentwood, Arthur Doubleday. For the next two years he acted as parish priest of Sts Peter and Paul in Ilford which gave him practical parochial experience. During this period he edited a substantial volume of scholarly historical essays, The English Catholics, 1850–1950 (1950), at the request of the bishops to mark the centenary of the restoration of the Catholic hierarchy in England and Wales. When Doubleday died on 23 January 1951 Beck automatically succeeded him as bishop of Brentwood. There were 80,000 Catholics in the diocese, and much work to be done in providing schools and churches for Harlow new town and the proliferating housing estates. Changes in educational theory and government policy led to a vast programme of school building nationwide. The Catholic bishops were unwilling to accept controlled status for their schools, whereby the local education authorities would appoint school managers and governors. Neither could they realistically face the alternative of aided status, where they retained control over Catholic schools but at the cost of finding 50 per cent of any capital expenditure over and above the general

taxes which Catholics were already paying towards the national schooling system.

The national Catholic Education Council was much reorganized in September 1949 with Beck as its first episcopal chairman. It was from this platform that he orchestrated the complex political negotiations of the bishops, and the mass campaigns of the Catholic community. Ten years of negotiation culminated in the Education Act of 1959 which provided 75 per cent building grants for new aided secondary schools needed wholly or mainly to match voluntary aided primary schools of the same denomination. Meanwhile on 28 November 1955 Beck had been appointed seventh bishop of Salford, with a Catholic population of 357,000 and commensurate problems of school provision. During his spell there he had an early hip replacement operation.

When Cardinal Godfrey died in 1963 many thought that Beck would succeed to Westminster. Perhaps because of the doubtful outcome of his operation that did not happen and Heenan of Liverpool was appointed. On 29 January 1964 Beck was appointed to succeed Heenan in the archdiocese of Liverpool with over half a million Catholics, many of whom had been uprooted from the large, long-established parishes of Liverpool inner city to move to new housing estates. He also inherited an unfinished cathedral heavily burdened with debt. Although self-evidently a southerner he won the affection of the people of south-west Lancashire by his unaffected naturalness and his ability to talk about serious subjects with a lightness of touch.

Here began a new phase in Beck's life as he sought to implement the thinking of the Second Vatican Council which involved a deep reorientation in his own attitudes. He was the first bishop in England and Wales to establish a council of clergy (1966), and a pastoral council composed of representative priests, religious, and lay people who could act as a two-way channel of communication between himself and the diocese (1968). He had been suspicious of the ecumenical Sword of the Spirit movement during the war years, and in 1949 wrote a notorious letter to The Times asserting the impossibility of Catholics joining with other Christians in the Lord's prayer. However, in Liverpool, with its long history of sectarian strife, he took a lead in the ecumenical movement: he was the first archbishop of Liverpool to preach in the Anglican cathedral, and an active leader of Call to the North.

In October 1975 Archbishop Beck tendered his resignation to the pope on grounds of ill health (mainly Parkinson's disease). At the installation of Derek Worlock as his successor on 19 March 1976 he retired to live at Upholland College at the Theological Institute which he had founded in 1974. He died in Lourdes Hospital, Liverpool, on 13 September 1978 and was buried in the crypt of the Metropolitan Cathedral. MICHAEL GAINE

Sources B. Plumb, Arundel to Zabi: a biographical dictionary of the Catholic bishops of England and Wales (deceased), 1623–1987 (privately printed, Warrington, [1987]) · Catholic Directory (1948–78) · The Tablet (23 Sept 1978) · personal knowledge (2004) · M. Cruikshank, Church and state in English education, 1870 to the present day (1965) ·

A. Hastings, *A history of English Christianity, 1920–1990*, 3rd edn (1991), 394, 479, 488–9 · Liverpool Roman Catholic Archdiocesan Archives, Liverpool · private information (2004)
Archives Upholland Northern Institute, Liverpool Roman Catholic diocesan archives, papers
Likenesses Elliott & Fry, photograph, 1955, NPG [*see illus.*] · G. Thompson, oils, Upholland Northern Institute · photographs, priv. coll.
Wealth at death £16,225: probate, 27 Oct 1978, *CGPLA Eng. & Wales*

Beck, Henry Charles [Harry] (1902–1974), graphic artist and map designer, was born on 4 June 1902 at 14 Wesley Road, Leyton, West Ham, Essex, the second child and only son of Joshua Try Beck, variously described as a commercial traveller, and an artist and monumental mason, and Eleanor Louisa Crouch. He had an elder sister, Winifred, and two younger sisters, Dorothy and Millicent. The Becks were a close-knit family. They moved to Highgate village, Middlesex, about 1910 and Harry was educated at Grove House School, a boys' private school in Highgate. After having left school he was sent to Italy to study marble, presumably with a view to his following in his father's footsteps as a monumental mason. He also went to art classes in Highgate. There he met Nora (1906/7–1993), daughter of Bryan Millington, of independent means, and they married on 16 September 1933 at St Michael and All Angels' parish church, Mill Hill, Middlesex. They had no children.

Beck found it difficult to find work as a graphic artist but in 1925 was taken on as a temporary junior draughtsman with London Underground in the signal engineers' office. He was made redundant twice during the next five years and remained a temporary staff member until 1937; but he maintained contact with London Underground in and out of employment and began to develop his ideas for what became the definitive map of the underground. London Underground showed no interest in his map when Beck first showed it to the management in 1931 but he continued to develop it and the following year the management agreed to give it a trial. The public, who were asked for their views, responded favourably.

Various maps of the underground railways had already been printed but all were unsatisfactory. Most tried to preserve both angle and area and thus were difficult to follow, particularly in the central area where the rail lines were densest. It was in just this area where most passengers travelled and therefore where the need for clear information was greatest. Most maps also showed the rail lines in relation to surface features, notably roads. Beck's map was topologically correct but topographically distorted— that is, neither angle nor area was preserved but the stations and interchanges stood in correct relation one to another. This enabled Beck to show on one map central areas at far larger scales than peripheral ones, and to route his lines both to give an aesthetically pleasing result and to allow all station names to be legibly displayed. The aesthetic unity of the map was enhanced by his use only of vertical and horizontal lines and those at 45°. Beck's map, or diagram as it is sometimes called, quickly established itself as the definitive map.

Beck continued to maintain, update, and improve his map in his own time, responding also to demands from the underground railways management for alterations, of many of which he rightly disapproved. In November 1937 he agreed to transfer copyright of the design to the management of the railways. He claimed that at the time a gentleman's understanding was reached that all alterations were to be made or edited by Beck himself, Beck to be paid a fee and to be considered a freelance artist for this work. The first alleged violation of this agreement came in 1938 when Zero (Hans Schleger) designed a variant which was printed and circulated. Beck protested, and subsequent changes were made by him as he claimed the agreement stipulated. Further dispute occurred in 1946, and in 1960 the agreement broke down when London Underground published an amateurish variant of his map designed by Harold F. Hutchinson. A bitter correspondence ensued between Beck and the railways management but it was clear that London Transport did not want to use his work further. Colleagues have suggested that his obsession with the map perhaps led him to be rather intransigent over its maintenance and this was perhaps behind the decision of the management; but it seems clear that Beck was shabbily treated by the management, which ended up with markedly poorer maps at a greater cost to itself as a result of having broken off dealings with Beck.

During the Second World War Beck was seconded to the War Office on secret work and afterwards returned to what was then London Transport. In 1947 he resigned to become a lecturer at the London School of Printing and Kindred Trades (later the London School of Printing and Graphic Arts). When Beck retired he and his wife moved to High Barnet and later to The Eyrie, Frogham, Fordingbridge, Hampshire. He died on 18 September 1974 at the Royal South Hampshire Hospital, Southampton, having suffered from bladder cancer. He was survived by his wife, who continued to live at Frogham until her death in 1993.

Beck is remembered as a gentle pleasant man with a great sense of humour, though disputes over copyright left him bitter and his map was clearly an obsession with him, dominating both his professional and private life. In appearance Beck was thick set and round-shouldered, as befits a draughtsman. In his youth he was a keen swimmer and oarsman and he retained his interest in singing (he had a fine baritone voice) and in photography.

Beck's map has remained the basis for London's underground railway map and has shown itself extremely flexible and able to accommodate additional lines and additional information. Its success in London, which has one of the most complex underground railway systems in the world, has ensured the adoption of his concept of the topologically correct map in many other cities of the world.   ELIZABETH BAIGENT

Sources K. Garland, *Mr Beck's underground map* (1998) · b. cert. · m. cert. · d. cert. · D. Leboff, *No need to ask! Early maps of London's underground railways* (1999) · D. F. Croome and A. A. Jackson, *Rails through the clay: a history of London's tube railways*, 2nd edn (1993) · private

information (2004) [Joan Baker] · www.ltmuseum.co.uk/exhibitions, 23 Jan 2002
Wealth at death £24,994: probate, 14 Oct 1974, *CGPLA Eng. & Wales*

Beck, Simon Adams (1803–1883), gas industrialist and lawyer, was baptized at Condover, Shropshire, on 25 July 1803, the son of James Beck of Allesley Park, Warwickshire, and his wife, Sarah Coker. He trained as a lawyer and in 1829 married Sarah Ann, second daughter of Ralph Price (1780–1860) of Sydenham. Beck was elected clerk and solicitor of the Ironmongers' Company in 1834, the same year that Price became master. Beck brought capable management skills to bear on the affairs of the company, dealing with its charitable work, watching over its property holdings, which were increasing greatly in value, and also dealing with the various commissions, boards, and departments interested in the affairs of the old London livery companies.

In 1848 Beck added to his duties those of a director of the Gas Light and Coke Company, which served parts of the cities of London and Westminster. It seems probable that Beck owed his election to the desire of the company to disarm criticism by appointing a respected City figure to the board; just as later, when parliament made difficulties with private bills put forward by Gas Light and Coke, two MPs were elected to the board. At that time gas companies were very unpopular. They were seen as exploiting their position by providing inadequate supplies of poor-quality gas at excessive prices and creating a nuisance with their gasworks. In 1848 the frustration of the corporation of the City of London was such that it considered seeking compulsory powers to municipalize gas supply. Beck was closely involved in negotiations with other London gas companies to present a common front in opposition to this threat. Rather than proceeding with municipalization, the corporation settled for encouraging the formation of a competing company, the Great Central, the effect of whose inauguration was to bring prices down from 7s. per 1000 cubic feet to 4s. within a few years.

Beck became deputy governor of the Gas Light and Coke Company in 1852 and governor in 1860. He gave considerable impetus to rationalizing both its commercial and its engineering activities. Its three small works, two in the City and a third at Westminster, were without access to cheap, water-borne coal supplies, and Beck inspired the drive to concentrate production on a riverside site at which colliers could unload directly. After considering various options, including that of the old Millbank prison (where the Tate Gallery was subsequently erected) the company settled on a 150 acre site owned by the Ironmongers' Company on the Thames at Barking, Essex. The huge new Beckton works, which began production there in 1870, not only resolved Gas Light and Coke's production difficulties, but also enabled the company to offer bulk supplies to other operations with similar problems.

The offer of a secure gas supply proved an irresistible lure when Gas Light and Coke offered full amalgamation to neighbouring companies. In 1869 the company provided only a seventh of London's gas, but this increased to two-thirds after a series of takeovers, including that of the Imperial company, which in 1869 was twice as large as Gas Light and Coke itself. The takeover of Imperial in 1876 provided the occasion for Beck's retirement. His leadership was sorely missed, however, as his successors mishandled a proposed amalgamation with the south London gas companies. These opted to merge instead with the South Metropolitan Gas Company, under the leadership of its formidable chief engineer, George Livesey. This engendered a rivalry between the two large London gas-producing companies that persisted until nationalization in 1949.

Beck had the reputation of being a benevolent and fair employer, but only among compliant workers. Following a strike in 1859 he refused to take back any union members. After another strike in 1872, the protest leaders were convicted of conspiracy and sentenced to twelve months' imprisonment; none of the strikers was re-employed. In organizational matters Beck achieved results through patient negotiation, and the short obituary notice in the *Journal of Gas Lighting* (6 March 1883) that described his governorship as 'a period of inaction' was wide of the mark. His métier was that of a manager rather than an entrepreneur.

After his retirement from Gas Light and Coke Beck remained clerk to the Ironmongers' Company until shortly before his death on 26 February 1883, at Cheam in Surrey; this position passed to his son, Ralph Coker Adams Beck, and thereafter to two further generations of Becks. His wife survived him. FRANCIS GOODALL

Sources S. Everard, *The history of the Gas Light and Coke Company, 1812–1949* (1949) · *Journal of Gas Lighting* (6 March 1883) · E. Glover, *A history of the Ironmongers' Company* (1991) · J. Nicholl, *Some account of the Worshipful Company of Ironmongers*, 2nd edn (1866) · J. W. Field, *Field's analysis* (1869–76) · court books, GL, Ironmongers' Company MSS, 16967, 17045 · d. cert. · IGI
Likenesses T. Hall, portrait, 1879–80, Ironmongers' Hall, London · H. T. Wells, portrait, repro. in Everard, *History of the Gas Light and Coke Company*
Wealth at death £36,727 5s. 4d.: resworn probate, Aug 1884, *CGPLA Eng. & Wales* (1883)

Beck, Thomas Alcock (1795–1846), antiquary, was born at Newcastle upon Tyne on 31 May 1795, and was baptized at St John's Church, Newcastle, on 26 September 1797. He was the son of James Beck (1752/3–1812) of The Grove, Hawkshead, Lancashire, and his wife, Jane Alcock (1767/8–1849), a native of Northumberland. Beck was educated in Hawkshead at Archbishop Sandys's Grammar School and later by a private tutor. He never adopted any profession, since he had become unable to walk quite early in life, owing to a spinal complaint. Around 1819 he commenced building Esthwaite Lodge, a regency mansion near Hawkshead; he had the grounds laid out with easy gradients for his invalid chair. Here he mitigated the tedium of confinement by the composition of *Annales Furnesienses*, published in 1844 in a splendid quarto volume. This pioneering work was sumptuously produced, and contained fine engravings and full transcripts of many significant documents. Although now dated, it remains by far the most comprehensive account of the history of the abbey of St Mary of

Furness, and is of prime importance for antiquarian research throughout the whole district. The book appeared in a limited issue of 250 copies, priced at 7 guineas, and the loss on the edition must have been considerable.

Beck also collected material for histories of North Lonsdale, the parish of Cartmel, and the priory of Conishead, but these were never published. He additionally worked on William Close's incomplete notes of 'An itinerary of Furness', which he edited into a continuous narrative. He was also active as a governor of Hawkshead grammar school. In 1835 he was elected to membership of the new Kendal Natural History Society. He was recalled as 'an agreeable companion' on account of his 'social, cheerful and communicative disposition' (*Soulby's Ulverston Advertiser*, 30 Dec 1880).

On 25 April 1838 Beck was married in his own home, by special licence, to Elizabeth (1799–1880), the daughter of William Fell of Ulverston. There were no children. When Beck died, on 24 April 1846, following a short illness, his property passed to a kinsman, William Towers. He was buried on 30 April in Hawkshead churchyard under an altar tombstone, and a beautiful mural tablet was afterwards erected inside the church. His property included a library of two thousand books. By his will, he stipulated that his heirs should assume the name of Alcock-Beck and they were also granted the arms of the family.

AIDAN C. J. JONES

Sources H. S. Cowper, *Hawkshead: its history, archaeology, industries, folklore, dialect* (1899), 379–80 [biography] · R. S. Boumphrey, C. R. Hudleston, and J. Hughes, *An armorial for Westmorland and Lonsdale* (1975) · H. S. Cowper, *Monumental inscriptions of Hawkshead, Lancashire* (1892) · G. M. Tweddell, *Furness past and present: its history and antiquities*, 1 (1880), 80 [mural tablet inscription] · A. C. Gibson, 'The lakeland of Lancashire: Hawkshead town, church and school', *Transactions of the Historic Society of Lancashire and Cheshire*, new ser., 5 (1864–5), 139–60, esp. 154 [mural tablet inscription] · E. Twycross, *The mansions of England and Wales illustrated in a series of views of the principal seats: the county palatine of Lancaster* (1847), vol. 2 · *Lancaster Gazette* (2 May 1846) · will, proved, 8 Aug 1842, Lancs. RO [and codicil, 19 April 1846] · parish registers, Newcastle upon Tyne, St John · parish registers, Hawkshead, Cumbria AS · d. cert. · *DNB*

Archives Armitt Library, Ambleside, corresp. and papers · Bodl. Oxf., printer's copy of parts of his published works with MS notes and additions | Cumbria AS, Barrow, Furness collection

Wealth at death under £4000: will, Lancs. RO

Becke, Edmund (*fl.* 1549–1551), theological writer, whose origins are obscure, was ordained deacon by Bishop Ridley in 1551. A staunch protestant, Becke played an important role in the Reformation book trade. He is remembered for his supervision of the publication of popular English translations of the Bible. His involvement in the book trade at both London and Canterbury suggests that he divided his time between those two centres.

Although Becke speaks of his 1549 first folio edition of the Bible as 'the fruits of my industry', it represents a revision of the version attributed to Thomas Matthew, which actually contains John Rogers's compilation of the work of William Tyndale and Miles Coverdale. This edition, published by John Day and William Seres, is preceded by a long dedication addressed by Becke to Edward VI. The text contains numerous ancillary materials, including Tyndale's preface to the New Testament as well as Becke's only original contribution, 'a perfect supputation of the years and time from Adam to Christ, proved by the Scriptures, after the collection of diverse Authors'. In 1551 Becke published a second folio Bible, simultaneously printed by John Day and Nicolas Hill. Advertised as a faithful reprint of the 'Matthew' translation, it republished the 1539 version of Richard Taverner. It duplicated the prefatory material and editorial apparatus of the previous version and added prologues and annotations for 'the better understanding of many hard places throughout the whole Bible'.

Becke's bibles demonstrate special concern for the common reader. Publisher and editor collaborated in producing an inexpensive version in order to bolster sales that had stagnated due to 'the price of late time'. In 1549–50 John Day marketed Becke's revision of the Taverner version, with the New Testament in Tyndale's translation, in six octavo volumes. Small format publication enabled individuals to spread the purchase of the volumes over several years. Drawing on current apologies for poetry, Becke viewed the 1551 folio Bible in Erasmian terms as a collection of sacred literature, comparable to 'Chronicles and Canterbury Tales', which may teach while delighting the reader. Becke's concordance aimed to enhance the enjoyment of the novice reader by explaining 'certain Hebrew tropes, translations, similitudes, and manners of speaking'. This Bible also participated in the tradition of using the Bible as a royal emblem. Its richly iconographic woodcut title-page, specially commissioned for this volume, symbolizes divine revelation and resurrection through the agency of the crown. In such a manner, this Bible insisted that obedience to royal authority complements divine worship.

Becke's other works include a popular rhyming pamphlet entitled *A brief confutation of this most detestable and Anabaptistical opinion that Christ did not take his flesh of the blessed Virgin Mary nor any corporeal substance of her body*. This tract, printed by Day in 1550, is a moralistic attack on Anabaptism on the occasion of the martyrdom of Joan Bocher, and is reprinted in the second volume of Collier's *Illustrations of Early English Popular Literature* (1864). Becke's only other extant work is a translation of two Erasmian colloquies, printed in Canterbury at the press of John Mychell. Although the exact date of this dialogue is uncertain, it may have been printed as early as 1538 and no later than 1557, when the chartering of the Stationers' Company centralized the printing trade in London. Nothing is known of Becke's death.

JOHN N. KING

Sources *DNB* · *STC, 1475–1640* · A. G. Dickens, *The English Reformation*, 2nd edn (1991) · J. N. King, *English Reformation literature: the Tudor origins of the protestant tradition* (1982)

Becker, Lydia Ernestine (1827–1890), suffragist leader, daughter of Hannibal Leigh Becker (1803–1877), a chemical manufacturer, and Mary Becker (1807–1855), daughter of James Duncuft, a Hollinwood mill owner, was born in Cooper Street, Manchester, on 24 February 1827. She was the eldest of fifteen children. Her grandfather, Ernest

Hannibal Becker, was a German, naturalized in England, who settled in business in Manchester. Her father joined the family-owned chemical works at Altham, near Accrington, Lancashire, moved with Mary and the children to Reddish, Stockport, where he began a calico-printing firm, and returned to Altham in 1850. Except for a short stay at a boarding-school in Everton, Liverpool, and a visit to relatives in Germany in 1844–5, Lydia lived with her family and was educated at home. During her residence in the country she developed a great love of botany and astronomy: in 1862 she was awarded a gold medal by the Horticultural Society of South Kensington, and in 1864 she published a small volume entitled *Botany for Novices*. She gave lectures in girls' schools, corresponded with Charles Darwin, and read a paper before the British Association in 1869, 'On alternation in the structure of Lychnis diurna, observed in connection with the development of a parasitic fungus'. She also wrote an elementary treatise on astronomy, which was circulated in manuscript only. On moving to Manchester in 1865 she started a Ladies' Literary Society for the study of science, providing free lectures; however, it had only modest success. Although her life subsequently became centred on public work, chiefly women's suffrage and education, she always retained an informed interest in science, and frequently attended the annual meetings of the British Association. She used the occasion of the 1884 meeting held in Canada to write a series of descriptive letters which were published in the *Manchester Examiner and Times*.

Lydia Becker's interest in women's suffrage was aroused by the petition presented by John Stuart Mill to the House of Commons in June 1866, and by a paper given by Barbara Bodichon at the meeting of the Social Science Association at Manchester in October of the same year. Although Lydia's parents were tories, she attributed her own political sympathies to the influence of her paternal grandfather, who had been a staunch Liberal. She was thus drawn away from her family towards a circle of radicals and reformers which included Jacob and Ursula Bright, Dr Richard Pankhurst, and Elizabeth Wolstenholme. Lydia's enthusiasm coincided with the setting up of a Manchester committee in January 1867. Part of a widening network of suffrage organizations, the Manchester National Society for Women's Suffrage, with Becker as its secretary, embarked upon a vigorous local campaign in 1867 to register women ratepayers on the electoral roll, thus exploiting a loophole in existing legislation. Although this strategy failed, the suffrage movement was duly launched, and the co-ordinating National Society for Women's Suffrage, which had been formed at Lydia's instigation in 1867, began its long march towards electoral reform. While its efforts to obtain the parliamentary vote provoked strong opposition, it succeeded in gaining an opening for women in local government. Acknowledging the crucial support of John Bright and John Hibbert in the House of Commons, Becker welcomed the passing of the Municipal Franchise Act of 1869 which restored the electoral rights of female householders. As she noted in her pamphlet *The*

Rights and Duties of Women in Local Government (1874): 'Political freedom begins for women as it began for men, with freedom in local government'.

Lydia Becker became active in other issues: she expressed concern at the conditions of work for women in industry and supported the idea of women-only trade unions; she was national treasurer of both the Vigilance Association for the Defence of Personal Rights and the Manchester-led Married Women's Property Committee, formed in 1868, the members of which included reformers working for suffrage and for women's access to higher education. In common with other suffragists, especially those with radical sympathies, Becker fully understood that the disabilities resulting from coverture were closely bound up with other disabilities based upon sex; the domestic and political subordination of women were intertwined. After a keenly fought and well-publicized campaign, the Married Women's Property Act of 1870 thus proved a disappointment: in guarding only that property which formed a married woman's separate estate, it failed to extend the rights and freedom which were accorded a feme sole, and the principle of coverture remained intact. Moreover, Lydia and her colleagues on the Married Women's Property Committee were soon to disagree over strategy, particularly on the question of support for a suffrage bill presented by William Forsyth in 1874 which expressly excluded married women. Her subsequent attempts to assert the primacy of the suffrage question over that of married women's property reform, in the tactical (and mistaken) belief that a restricted franchise bill would more likely meet with success, met with strong resistance. The disagreement resulted in much ill-feeling and in her departure from the committee in 1875: it denoted the opening up of serious divisions within the ranks of suffragists which the passing of the Married Women's Property Act of 1882 did nothing to assuage.

For Lydia it also marked a turning point. The suffrage movement became her life's work: it propelled her into a political world that was unaccustomed to the formal participation of women, and brought her esteem and notoriety in equal measure. Her published articles included 'Female suffrage' in the *Contemporary Review* (March 1867), the 'Political disabilities of women' in the *Westminster Review* (January 1872), and a pamphlet entitled *Liberty, Equality, Fraternity: a Reply to Mr Fitzjames Stephen's Strictures on Mr J. S. Mill's Subjection of Women* in 1873. She founded the Manchester-based *Women's Suffrage Journal* (1870–90), an influential and indispensable record of the movement, and served as its editor and chief contributor. As a public speaker she lacked oratorical flair, but was noted for persuasiveness and clarity of thought; she undertook onerous lecture tours at a time when it was thought unseemly for a lady to appear on a public platform. Physically stout from early womanhood, her broad, flat face, wire-rimmed spectacles, and plaited crown of hair were a cartoonist's delight, and she was much lampooned in the popular press. However, she quickly gained recognition as the movement's key strategist, directing national policy and tactics with a statesmanlike mind: the women-only great demonstrations held throughout the country in 1880 attracted capacity crowds and enormous publicity for the cause. As a later biographer was to write, 'Lydia Becker was the indefatigable centre around which the majority of the activities circled. Organising, speaking, writing innumerable letters and articles, keeping her finger on the pulse of Parliament and public opinion, she was a notable tower of strength to the movement' (Holmes, 18).

Becker's initial correspondence in 1866 with Emily Davies, a key member of the Langham Place circle, had been the prelude to a deepening organizational involvement with the work of the suffrage campaign in London. While continuing to work with the Manchester Society, she established a base in the capital, becoming secretary of the central committee of the National Society for Women's Suffrage in 1881, and subsequently its parliamentary agent, demonstrating a formidable knowledge of parliamentary procedure. The failure to include women's suffrage in the Reform Bill of 1884, on which many had pinned their hopes, led to a period of retrenchment and reorganization in the suffrage movement as campaigners rethought both policy and tactics. The movement was to divide over two contentious issues in the ensuing decade: the right of newly emergent women's political associations to affiliate to the National Society for Women's Suffrage (which Lydia believed would compromise their neutrality), and continuing disagreement over whether they should fight for a limited franchise which excluded married women, on the grounds that this might be more acceptable to opponents—an issue which caused intense debate and much friction.

Lydia Becker's other main concern was education: a paper entitled 'Some supposed differences in the minds of men and women with regard to educational necessities', read at the proceedings of the British Association in Norwich in 1868, had been much discussed. Like many suffragists she was keenly aware of the importance of education, and the role that could be played by women in shaping the curriculum, caring for the welfare of children, and promoting the occupational interests of female teachers. Having campaigned for the inclusion of a clause in the Elementary Education Act of 1870 which allowed women to serve as members of school boards, she was elected to the Manchester board in 1870 and served consecutive terms until her death. A very able and effective board member, although initially independent of any party or faction, she worked particularly for the provision of educational facilities for girls, for the welfare of children in ragged schools, and for the improvement of the position of women teachers.

Immersed in a public life of meetings, deadlines, and lecture tours, Becker endured financial worries and unhappiness caused by the initial disapproval of her family. She never married, but found much comfort in the friendship of the Brights and others who worked for the cause. The unremitting work eventually told on her health. A journey to the continent to 'take the waters' brought on a rapid decline, and she died of diphtheria on 18 July 1890 at Geneva, where she was buried on 21 July in the cemetery of St George. The news of her death was widely reported: the obituaries paid tribute to her remarkable powers of organization and her great dedication. She was duly acknowledged as the leader of the movement for women's suffrage. LINDA WALKER

Sources H. Blackburn, *Women's suffrage: a record of the women's suffrage movement in the British Isles* (1902) · M. Holmes, *Lydia Becker*, 2nd edn (1913) · A. Kelly, *Lydia Becker and the cause* (1992) · J. Parker, 'Lydia Becker: pioneer orator of the women's movement', *Manchester Region History Review*, 5/2 (1991–2), 13–20 · M. L. Shanley, *Feminism, marriage and the law in Victorian England* (1989) · L. Holcombe, *Wives and property: reform of married women's property law in nineteenth-century England* (1983) · F. Shepherd, 'Lydia Becker: some biographical notes' (typescript), Man. CL, Manchester Archives and Local Studies · S. S. Holton, *Suffrage days: stories from the women's suffrage movement* (1996) · scrapbook of newspaper cuttings of letters and lectures, 1871–9, Man. CL, Manchester Archives and Local Studies · *Women's Suffrage Journal* [memorial number] (Aug 1890) · *CGPLA Eng. & Wales* (1890)

Archives Women's Library, London, corresp. and papers | Man. CL, Manchester Archives and Local Studies, corresp. as secretary of Manchester National Society for Women's Suffrage

Likenesses S. I. Dacre, oils, 1886, Man. City Gall. · portrait, repro. in Parker, 'Lydia Becker'

Wealth at death £2064 2s. 1d.: probate, 6 Sept 1890, *CGPLA Eng. & Wales*

Becket, Thomas [St Thomas of Canterbury, Thomas of London] (1120?–1170), archbishop of Canterbury, was a London merchant's son who rose to be royal chancellor then archbishop, only to be murdered in his cathedral church. His posthumous reputation as a saint and martyr, with enduring thaumaturgical powers, was considerable throughout western Christendom, and in England unrivalled.

Youth and schooling Born in Cheapside, London, on St Thomas the Apostle's day (21 December), in 1120 according to the liturgical tradition, and baptized that evening in the tiny neighbouring church of St Mary Colechurch, Thomas was, apparently, the only surviving son of Gilbert Beket and his wife Matilda. Four daughters of the marriage also survived into adulthood, of whom Agnes was eventually Gilbert's heir; and descent continued through Theobald de Helles (of Hills-Court, Kent), her son or nephew. Both Thomas's parents were Normans. Gilbert's father was a farmer or rural knight from Thierville (Eure), in the lordship of Brionne, close to the abbey of Bec; and he was a neighbour and perhaps kinsman of Theobald, abbot of Bec and archbishop of Canterbury (d. 1161). Gilbert seems to have become a trader, perhaps in textiles; and his wife, who may have had the pet name of Roheise, is said to have come from Caen. By 1120, however, Gilbert was a property owner in London, living on rents. He had bought for himself a fine house on the north side of Cheapside, in the block between Ironmonger Lane and Old Jewry, an area inhabited by important citizens. At the height of his prosperity he served a term as sheriff of the City (the office of mayor had yet to be created). But later, perhaps after Thomas had grown up, he suffered heavy losses when his properties were destroyed by fire.

Becket's cradle tongue must have been French, and this

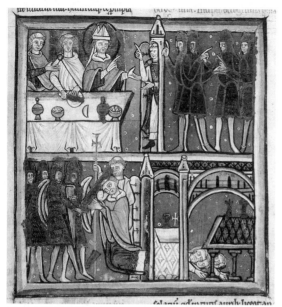

Thomas Becket [St Thomas of Canterbury] (1120?–1170), manuscript illumination

was, with Latin for official, ceremonial purposes, the language of all the societies in which he spent his life. But it may be assumed, and the early biographers possibly took it for granted, that as a Londoner he could understand and speak English. What the biographers, however, make clear is that his Latin was never first-rate, and that this was so because of the general insufficiency of his education. Moreover, in his youth he never progressed beyond the trivium and quadrivium, the basic curriculum. Law and theology he had to work up later. His schools were not to blame: they were the best that money could buy. At the age of ten he was sent to board at the Augustinian priory at Merton in Surrey, which had a good scholastic reputation. Later he was put into one of the London grammar schools, perhaps St Paul's. And finally, when he was twenty, he spent about a year in Paris.

Becket's schooling may, however, have been intermittent. Even the hagiographers thought that in his youth he was more interested in rural sports than in his books and that his way of life was frivolous. It must have been when living at home after Merton that he became attached to an important Norman baron, Richer de l'Aigle, who, possibly because of some former territorial connection, used to lodge with the Bekets when in the city. Richer, a greatgrandson of a knight killed at the battle of Hastings, and himself a soldier of considerable experience, was lord of Hastings in Sussex, an honour granted to his father by Henry I. His mother was the sister of Rotrou (II), count of Perche and Mortagne, and two of his younger brothers had served in Henry I's military household, but were lost when the *White Ship* went down in 1120. Richer, an older man, used to take Becket on holidays into the country, presumably Sussex, where they hunted and hawked. On one of these expeditions Becket fell into a millstream, either because his horse slipped off a narrow bridge or because he plunged in to rescue his hawk; and he almost drowned. One of his biographers, Edward *Grim, thought that the citizen's son learned much from the baron. Indeed, courtly manners helped him greatly in his career. He retained for life an interest in horses and hawks; and he took up soldiering when the opportunity arose. How long his intimacy with Richer lasted is not known. They would meet again at Henry II's court, and Becket may have helped him to recover the lordship of Hastings which he had lost in Stephen's reign. Richer was one of those barons who in 1164 declared the ancient customs in the royal court at Clarendon, an event that launched Becket on the road to martyrdom.

Although as a scholar Becket would have been tonsured, there is no reason to think that his parents intended their only son for a career in the church or that he had a vocation for the priesthood and the cure of souls. While the family was rich, it was expected, no doubt, that Becket would consolidate its position in the urban aristocracy. When his father lost his money the son had to become a practising clerk. So Gilbert got him first into the banking house of his richer kinsman, Osbert Huitdeniers, one of the greatest London merchants, and then into the household of Theobald, archbishop of Canterbury.

Appearance and character Becket was endowed with, or acquired, most of the qualities that make for worldly success. He is described in the Icelandic sagas, which drew on Robert of *Cricklade's lost work, as tall and slender, with a fair skin and dark hair. His features were regular, though his nose was rather long and aquiline. His forehead was wide, his eyes were bright, and his expression was calm and happy. His elegance was enhanced by vivacity. Goodlooking in youth, he was handsome when older. He had excellent manners and was a good talker. Clearly he had the ability and the will to please: he was a charmer. John of *Salisbury says that he had very acute senses of smell and hearing and a good memory. Such endowments make a little education go a very long way. He was undoubtedly intelligent, alert, responsive. Once he realized that he had to make his own way he became extremely ambitious. But he could placate rivals as well as ingratiate himself with his masters. Until he became soured by his misfortunes as archbishop he was a very attractive man. But even his friends and champions were aware of some faults. John of Salisbury considered him something of a time-server, a rather harsh judgement on one who served a succession of very different masters with equal zeal. But all the early biographers thought that until he became archbishop (or a little later) he was guilty of frivolity, ostentation in dress, and pursuit of all the follies of the fashionable world.

Nevertheless, they all state unequivocally that Becket always lived a celibate life. This may simply be a feature of the hagiographical legend; but it cannot be disproved. It is clear from his physical activities and achievements that his constitution was basically robust. That he had strong passions can hardly be doubted. According to *William fitz Stephen, he accepted penitential discipline of scourging on his bare back even when royal chancellor. But contemporaries thought that he had a congenitally 'cold', that is to say delicate, stomach, and this seems to have made him particularly liable to stress. There is good tradition that he had a slight stammer. After 1145 he was always an outsider, making his way by his wits; and his struggle to succeed could undoubtedly exert intolerable pressure on him. Enough bouts of what seem to have been psychosomatic illnesses are recorded to suggest that stress and repression were features of his life. It may be that among the emotions he repressed was the sexual. It does not seem, however, that he was attracted to women. He was brought up among them and was close to his mother. But, although he was free to marry until ordained deacon in 1154, there is no evidence at any time of women lovers, friends, or even disciples and confidantes. On the other hand, although some men, for instance Archbishop Theobald and Henry II, found him very attractive, there is no compelling evidence that he was homosexually inclined. It could be that he lacked warmth and disliked physical intimacy.

Clerkships and royal chancellorship, 1145–1162 From early 1143 until some time in 1145 Becket kept the accounts of the London banker, Osbert Huitdeniers. He then managed to secure a place in the household of Theobald, archbishop of Canterbury—a considerable move up into the purlieus of power. At first derided and intimidated by his much better educated and ecclesiastically orientated fellow clerks, he soon made friends and also gained the archbishop's favour. He was sent for a year to study law at Bologna and Auxerre and was even employed on missions to the papal curia. Thus he not only entered into the fellowship of men who were to be of importance in the English church but also was groomed to join them. In 1154, when Theobald secured the archbishopric of York for his archdeacon, Roger de Pont l'Évêque (d. 1181), he gave the vacant archdeaconry to Becket. This formed the nucleus for a collection of benefices, including Bramfield in Hertfordshire, St Mary-le-Strand in London, Otford in Kent, prebends in London and Lincoln cathedrals, and the provostship of Beverley in Yorkshire—mostly the gifts of promoted Canterbury clerks. Becket was becoming rich, and at the age of thirty-four was ready for greater things.

Within a year, although he retained the archdeaconry and benefices, Becket changed his master again. He had probably been involved in the negotiations, led by Theobald, which secured the succession of the Angevin, Henry FitzEmpress, to the English throne after Stephen's death; and shortly after Henry's coronation in his twenty-second year on 19 December 1154, Becket was witnessing royal charters as chancellor. It seems that the archbishop and bishops pushed him on Henry as their agent in the royal court and as one who might restrain a youthful ruler widely suspected of being headstrong and anti-clerical. The royal chancellorship was basically only another, even if more prestigious, clerkship. But Becket, by becoming Henry II's intimate friend, was to transform it into an important office. He soon became Henry's boon companion on the *iter* round the Angevin 'empire', mostly on the continent, sharing all his master's pastimes except, as sources affirm, the sexual. He certainly shared in the royal

wealth, receiving valuable custodies and other bounties from his master. In 1164, when Henry, by then an enemy, called in his debts, he asked him to account for £30,000. His identification with royal policies, consequent on his complete dependence on royal favour, inevitably disappointed his clerical backers. With hindsight, some of the memorialists considered that this was an aberrant interlude in the martyr's career, in which he dissimulated and did his best for the church. But to all appearances Becket revelled in this period of worldly grandeur, although once again he had to overcome the contempt and envy of established servants and courtiers. The high points in his career as a royal favourite were his magnificent legation to the French king in 1158, and his participation the next year in Henry's campaign to 'recover' the county of Toulouse. In the latter he had 700 knights under his command and took an active part in the fighting. Although the archdeacon's grandeur and military exploits were not necessarily abhorrent to the English church, the 'scutage of Toulouse', the tax to pay for the war which fell heavily on the church, and for which Becket was held responsible, was never forgotten, even by his friends and apologists, such as John of Salisbury.

Archbishop of Canterbury: the early years, 1162–1163 On 18 April 1161 Archbishop Theobald died, his last months saddened by the refusal of the king and Becket, both busy on the continent, to visit him. The archdeacon was still on campaign, this time in the Vexin, commanding troops in a border war against Henry's overlord, the French king Louis VII (r. 1137–80), and, apparently, displaying outstanding courage and gallantry. Theobald, who, despite some disillusion, wanted Becket to succeed him at Canterbury, accused his protégé of ingratitude. At this juncture Becket too fell ill, and, in contrast, was visited by both kings, who had made a truce. Henry took his time over Theobald's replacement. He had quickly given Becket custody of the temporalities of the archbishopric; but secrecy and procrastination had been drilled into him by his mother, he had many other things on his mind, and to get Becket elected to the see would not be plain sailing in view of his obvious unfitness for the office. All archbishops of Canterbury since the conquest, but one, had been monks; and the monks of the cathedral see, Christ Church, claimed sole right of election. They had no reason to love Becket, for he had no love for them and had abetted Theobald's repression of the convent. Also, monastic bishops were available, primarily Gilbert Foliot, bishop of Hereford (d. 1187), who was later bishop of London, a pious theologian, who could be thought ideally suited. But Becket's promotion from archdeacon to archbishop would support some of Henry's ambitions. He wanted to secure his dynasty by having his eldest son, Henry, crowned king of England. He aimed at safeguarding his vast French fiefs, and even, perhaps, uniting England and France, by marrying the young Henry to Louis VII's heir, Margaret. And he would obtain Pope Alexander III's assistance for his schemes by supporting him against imperial antipopes. A capable and amenable archbishop of Canterbury could have an important role. He could crown the young Henry, act as his guardian, direct a subordinate government in England, and also put through some administrative reforms. Moreover, to have a chancellor archbishop would put Henry on a par with the great German emperor, Frederick Barbarossa (r. 1152–90).

By the time the king had come to a decision, Becket himself had misgivings. He had enjoyed to the full his life at the royal court, the archbishopric would confer few worldly advantages, and he must have been conscious of some unsuitability for the office. But the papal legate overcame his reluctance; Becket conducted the young Henry to England; the royal will smothered all opposition among the electors and associated bishops; and on 23 May 1162 a royal council of bishops and notables at Westminster confirmed the election by the monks, and the young Henry, empowered by his father, duly gave the royal consent. Becket must have done homage and fealty to Henry II, presumably in April when taking leave of him in Normandy. A novelty, apparently demanded by Henry de Blois, bishop of Winchester (d. 1171), at the Westminster council, was that Becket was given by those acting for the king some form of acquittance from all secular obligations, an attempt on the part of the uneasy church to get the slate wiped clean. On 2 June he was ordained priest at Canterbury and on the following day, in the presence of the young Henry, consecrated archbishop by Henry of Winchester, *vice* London, and the other fourteen suffragan bishops. A mission to the pope secured the pallium, and on 10 August the archbishop received this token of his papal vicariate barefooted and prostrate in the cathedral. The one part of the grand scheme left uncompleted was the coronation of the Young King, perhaps because of the rivalry between Canterbury and York, in the person of Roger de Pont l'Évêque. It had to wait eight years.

In 1162 Becket was archbishop, archdeacon, royal chancellor, and the holder of a large number of ecclesiastical benefices and royal custodies—an arch-pluralist of transient offices and properties. He was also separated from the king, who lingered on the continent. It is clear that the tyro priest had decided to play a completely new role, which he had to learn. It was not entirely unfamiliar; but his life for some eight years had been to all appearances that of a royal courtier and knight. It took him a little time to adjust. He retained, perhaps until after the Council of Clarendon (January 1164), his light-coloured clothes, which affronted the Christ Church monks, whose respect he never obtained before his death; and he recruited a staff of secular clerks on the model of Theobald's. He took over three or four clerks, including John of Salisbury (d. 1180), from his predecessor, and from the Chapel Royal went with him five or six, among whom were Herbert of *Bosham and William fitz Stephen. These three wrote lives after his death. Some of the rest were recruited from the households of other bishops. He is said to have had fifty-two clerks as chancellor and to have attended the Council of Northampton in October 1164 with almost forty. Although they included those whom Herbert of Bosham called the *eruditi* (scholars), most were chosen for their legal and administrative competence. This large clerical contingent was paralleled in his household by the secular component of knights, noble boys, and servants; and the size of his *familia* was a feature of his grandeur. Indeed, as archbishop Becket improved on the magnificence he had displayed as chancellor. His hospitality was lavish, his alms-giving extravagant. He also, under the tuition of his chaplains and Herbert of Bosham, carried out his duties meticulously, spent time in private devotions, and studied theology. The new purpose in his life was not only to be a great archbishop but also to recover and, no doubt, extend the rights of the archbishops of Canterbury. His taking his predecessor, Anselm (1093–1109), as his model, portended a stormy tenure of his see. His receipt of the pallium seems to have triggered his renunciation of his other offices, the royal chancellorship and the archdeaconry—the former presumably because it was now beneath his dignity. Henry was offended; and it may be that it was he who forced Becket to surrender the archdeaconry to Geoffrey Ridel (d. 1189), keeper of the king's privy seal and hitherto Becket's deputy and workhorse at the chancery, who continued to perform as acting chancellor.

Becket's arrival at Canterbury after a thirteen months' vacancy upset many vested interests. He was thought to have obtained a royal writ authorizing him to recover lands wrongfully alienated by his predecessors or usurped by laymen. Consequently he revoked all existing leases of archiepiscopal demesne and reactivated claims to several estates and services presently in the hands of some important barons. One of those he disturbed was an important royal servant, John Marshal, and this affair was to play an important part in his downfall in 1164. The king returned to England in January 1163, but, although distressed by Becket's behaviour, concealed his feelings. At the end of April Becket left, with most of the English hierarchy, for Alexander III's general council at Tours, and seems to have repeated the glory of his embassy to Louis VII in the ecclesiastical sphere. He took the opportunity to petition for Anselm's canonization; but the process was crowded out, and subsequent events prevented its completion.

The quarrel with the king, 1163–1164 Becket returned from Tours apparently inspired to defend the liberties of the English church, especially those of Canterbury, against lay tyrants. And almost immediately, at the beginning of July, he clashed with Henry at Woodstock over the king's proposal that sheriff's aid, a traditional surcharge to the general land tax (geld), should be diverted from the sheriffs to the royal treasury. A measure which, as chancellor, he would probably have supported, he now vehemently opposed; and Henry, for the moment isolated, had to drop it. This was the point when a growing estrangement became an unbridgeable rift. Henry could not forgive the man he had raised from the dust and heaped with honours and riches for repaying him in this fashion. He aimed at Becket's humiliation and destruction. And the archbishop, a proud man and serving under a new banner, would not willingly back down. Principles were at stake.

The battlefield turned out to be the 'evil' royal customs

in the English church, particularly those concerning criminous clerks. Since the eleventh century ecclesiastical reformers in western Christendom had been attempting to free the church from improper lay control and those practices that were repugnant to canon law. In England, Archbishop Anselm had been active in the cause against William II and Henry I; and during Stephen's relatively weak reign the church had made gains that Henry II wanted to reverse. He thought that the laity was being harassed by archidiaconal and rural decanal courts, intent on punishing sins as a source of revenue. He was enraged at the church's protection of criminals in holy orders from the appropriate penalties under secular law (benefit of clergy). And he disliked the growing practice of litigants appealing from English church courts to the papal curia. None of these particular matters had caused much, if any, trouble in the past since all authorities had joined forces in the struggle against criminals and other dissidents. However, the increasing disentanglement of church and state (often symbolized as the two swords) and the renewed interest in jurisprudence sharpened the distinction between the several jurisdictions, especially royal and ecclesiastical, and made rivalry and collisions inevitable. Yet the basic common interest remained and usually prevented serious conflict.

Several cases where the archbishop had prevented a clerk, convicted in a lay court of a felony, from suffering the appropriate lay penalty of mutilation or death, were brought to Henry's notice. On 13 October 1163 he assembled an old-fashioned national church council at Westminster to honour the translation of the body of Edward the Confessor to a new tomb in the abbey, consequent on his canonization by Alexander III on 7 February 1161 as an appropriate reward to Henry for his allegiance. After the ceremony Henry, fortified by contact with his saintly predecessor, aired some of his grievances in the assembly. And when he elicited no support, he asked the bishops if they would observe the ancient customs of the realm. This was reminiscent of demands made by William II and Henry I on Anselm; and at Westminster Becket and his colleagues echoed Anselm's reply: they could only do so 'saving their order', that is to say, excepting anything that was contrary to canon law. Next morning Henry disgraced Becket by removing the young Henry from his tutorship and depriving him of all the custodies and honours he had granted him as chancellor. Although Becket still had the nominal support of the episcopate for his attitude towards 'evil' royal customs, there was nowhere any stomach for a battle with the crown. Alexander III was of the same mind. He relied on Henry's assistance and regarded the conflict as unnecessary and inopportune. This view he was to hold until the end, yet would stand up for ecclesiastical rights when he could and never throw a principled archbishop to the wolves. As for Becket, he was to have ample time in which to produce a theological objection to the double punishment he perceived in the custom that Henry wished to confirm or revive, by which a man in holy orders, convicted in a lay court of a serious crime, was released to an ecclesiastical court to be stripped of his

orders and then returned as a layman to the secular authorities to receive his punishment under secular law.

After Westminster both king and archbishop appealed to the pope, the one to get English customs allowed, the other to get them condemned. Henry also wanted privileges for the archbishop of York which would allow his use as an alternative primate in England. Alexander prevaricated, but in November sent Philip, abbot of Aumône in Blois, to urge moderation, even dissimulation, on Becket. In the end, the archbishop, assured that Henry required only a verbal assent to the customs (like Anselm in similar circumstances in May 1095), promised Henry at Woodstock, without making any verbal reservations, that he would observe the customs of the realm. Whereupon Henry summoned a great council to meet at Woodstock towards the end of January 1164 in order to confirm and publicize his victory. Using the support of his barons and officials and taking advantage of divisions among the bishops, Henry browbeat Becket into declaring in the hearing of all that he would observe the laws and customs of the kingdom in good faith; and the rest of the bishops followed suit. The king then ordered that these customs be discovered and declared; and by the following morning a schedule of sixteen miscellaneous clauses was produced as a chirograph dated 29 January. But, although Becket and the bishops evaded sealing this document, it was accepted even by the hagiographers that Becket, and at his command all the bishops, had agreed unconditionally to observe the constitutions of Clarendon, including a clause that defined the customary method of treating criminous clerks. Becket also accepted that in so doing he had sinned. He suspended himself from priestly duties, imposed penance on himself and sent a report to the pope. But he agreed to write to Alexander asking him to confirm the English customs. The pope, typically, simply took no notice.

Disgrace and exile, 1164–1165 Once Becket had incurred royal disgrace, his servants and friends began to abandon him and, fearing the worst, he began to negotiate with Louis VII of France for asylum, a correspondence which the royalists would have considered treasonable. After an unsuccessful attempt in the late summer to escape to France in order to consult the pope, then at Sens, he was summoned by the king to attend a council of the magnates to be held in Northampton Castle on 6 October, where he was to answer a charge made by John Marshal that he had denied him justice in his feudal court. When this charge fizzled out, Henry accused him of the embezzlement of royal revenues while serving as chancellor. And Becket knew, when the king refused an offer of 2000 marks, which Henry, bishop of Winchester, offered to find, in settlement of all claims, that he was in great peril, perhaps, he thought, of imprisonment or even death, although he probably mistook rumoured threats for serious intentions.

On Tuesday 13 October, before the bishops could declare the court's judgment on him, Becket made a preventative appeal to the pope. Whereupon Henry decided that they should make a counter-appeal and do their best to get

Alexander to depose him. Judgment would be pronounced by the barons. It was also decided to add Becket's appeal, deemed to be in breach of the constitutions of Clarendon, which he had sworn to observe, to the list of his crimes. But when the chief justiciar approached, Becket refused to hear the judgment: he had been cited only in the case of John Marshal; besides, barons were incompetent to judge an archbishop. He marched out of the room, slipped out of the castle, and the next day, before dawn, in a downpour, found a way out of the walled town and with three companions rode hard for Lincoln. Then, in disguise, he made a slow and devious way to Eastry, a Canterbury manor near Sandwich. Finally, on 2 November, he crossed the channel in a small boat, landing that afternoon near Dunkirk in the county of Flanders.

Becket's first aim was to seek the protection of the king of France, who welcomed him at Soissons, and then secure the support of the pope, a fellow exile at Sens, despite Henry's efforts to keep these princes at least neutral. But Louis realized that he could use Becket against Henry and the pope started as he was to continue throughout Becket's exile, by avoiding the trap of having to pronounce a definitive sentence on any of the matters at issue. When Becket produced his copy of the constitutions of Clarendon and took Alexander through them clause by clause, his weary auditor eventually declared that none of the laws was good and some were directly contrary to canon law; but some others were tolerable. Since he seems not to have indicated which were which, and never put his views into writing, the matter remained satisfactorily in suspense. If Becket offered to resign his see because of his transgressions, it was refused. And it was decided that he should retire to the Cistercian abbey at Pontigny in the duchy of Burgundy, outside the French royal demesne, not too distant from Sens and the courier routes, but situated in a wilderness, out of sight.

Dependent on charity—mainly Louis VII's, for Henry had confiscated all his possessions and taken the archbishopric into custody—Becket could afford to assemble no more than a basic household at Pontigny from the large pool of his family, servants, and supporters whom the king had banished from England. Robert, canon of Merton, remained his chaplain. William de Capes, his marshal, was in charge of the lay servants, including Becket's valet, Brown, and all secular matters. Herbert of Bosham seems to have been at the head of the chancery and to have had the archbishop's ear. Other important clerks were Alexander-Llywelyn, Becket's Welsh cross-bearer, Lombardo di Piacenza, John Cantor (Planeta), Henry of Houghton, and Gunter of Winchester. John of Salisbury distanced himself by living at Rheims with his old friend, Pierre de Celle, abbot of St Rémi, but could always be called on for help. These clerks served Becket in three main ways. They produced the letters needed for the constant collection of intelligence and diplomacy on behalf of the archbishop's cause. They served as bearers of the letters and as diplomats, operating usually in pairs. And they formed an academy in which Becket improved

his education, especially—to John of Salisbury's regret—in the field of law.

Once again Becket's life had taken a sharp turn. His disgrace and reclusion were a great shock to one so outgoing and in many ways so worldly. He gave himself to private devotions and despair and had to be coaxed back to some normality by Herbert. But, although living among devout monks, he never became a monk, even, it seems, *in petto*. He blamed his fall on the 'traitor' bishops, particularly Gilbert Foliot of London, and other evil courtiers rather than directly on the king. And some vestiges of his love for Henry persisted until the end. The exile was a souring experience. Although dependent on Louis and Alexander, he could not completely trust either; and there was dissension in his household as in all émigré societies. Becket had become a pawn in two intertwined power struggles, the rivalry of Henry and Louis and the contest between Alexander and the imperial antipope. And the great web of diplomacy he spun does not seem to have had much influence on what happened. He had to wait on events. *Expectavi* (I have been waiting) is a word which occurs often in the 'Becket correspondence'; and the event most awaited was a death. Yet he was not passive. And his endurance, persistence and courage are remarkable. He stood at times *contra mundum*, and, after the first shock, could not be moved.

Attempts at reconciliation, 1165–1169 In August 1165, when Alexander was about to venture back into Italy, he imposed a truce on Becket to last at least until Easter 1166. He would not have Henry provoked at such a time. And while the king celebrated Easter at Angers he received some of the archbishop's clerks, including John of Salisbury and Herbert of Bosham, who wished to explore the possibility of returning to England, possibly because they feared what might happen when the truce expired. Neither was offered acceptable terms. And the worst was to happen. Alexander, back in Rome, at Becket's urgent entreaty, began to arm him against his enemies. Among a portfolio of privileges and measures dated April–May was the grant of a papal legation in England, excluding only the diocese of York but not the person of the king. In anticipation of its receipt, Becket started to go on pilgrimages. In June he travelled south from Soissons to the Cluniac abbey of Vézelay, with the secret intention, hidden even from his clerks, who he feared might try to stop him, of using his legatine powers to strike against his enemies. On Whitsunday (12 June), at the invitation of the abbot, he celebrated the public mass, preached to the congregation on his wrongs and sufferings, and then launched his anathemas. He condemned the constitutions of Clarendon and those who supported and enforced them, quashed explicitly about half the clauses, and finally passed sentences of anathema and excommunication on all the royal servants who had been involved in the various measures against him, some of them by name, but not the king. In November the pope, rather grudgingly, confirmed his legate's actions.

Henry replied to these sentences by getting both the Norman and the English bishops to appeal to the pope against them and by pressing the Cistercian order to expel Becket from Pontigny. The archbishop's clerks, if not their master, had tired of their seclusion; and in November 1166 the exiles, at the invitation of Louis, moved to the ancient Benedictine abbey of St Columba outside the north wall of the royal and archiepiscopal city of Sens. There Becket remained for four years. Edward Grim, on the authority of Becket's chaplain, Robert of Merton, and Guernes, on the testimony of the servant Brown, describe the archbishop's secret austerities behind a façade of normality. Their master participated in the monastic horarium and celebrated mass each day. He drank the best wine that money could buy, but always diluted with water, and only so as to warm his congenitally cold stomach. He ate handfuls of ginger and cloves for the same purpose. His bedchamber was furnished with a leather-bound wooden bed covered with costly sheets of the finest and whitest linen and an embroidered quilt strewn with a little straw. But his shirt and breeches were of the roughest goat's-hair; engaged in private prayer, he was hardly ever in his bed; and at least three times a day he was scourged by his chaplain on his bare back until the blood flowed. With these and other mortifications he destroyed all carnal desires.

Papal attempts at a settlement, 1167–1170 While Becket was at Sens it was the pope, always under threat from a rival, who was most anxious for a settlement of the quarrel, and he dispatched legates *a latere* to this end in 1167, 1168–9, and 1170. But, since neither Henry nor Becket shifted substantially from their entrenched positions, and Alexander would not until 1170 authorize his legates to impose a solution on the parties, there was stalemate. Becket merely clarified his terms. He required the abrogation of all 'evil' customs affecting the church in England, the restoration of himself and all his fellow sufferers in the cause to all their former offices and possessions, compensation for all their losses during their exile, and the punishment of all those who had injured them in any way. Henry, however, although he was determined to keep the rights he claimed to have inherited from his ancestor Henry I, did in 1169 offer a series of important concessions: he would abandon any bad customs introduced since 1154, or 1135, and would even have them all scrutinized by learned churchmen. Also, when negotiations for a settlement began seriously in that year, he abated some of the financial claims he had made against Becket at Northampton. In fact, many of Becket's less fanatical supporters believed that the king was offering terms on which the archbishop could honourably return to Canterbury and, with Henry's co-operation, settle outstanding details.

Becket, however, so distrusted the king that he regarded all these concessions as no more than baits to lure him into Henry's dominions where he would be arrested and the projected reforms abandoned. His fears were expressed in his reiterated demand for a kiss of peace from Henry as a pledge of his good faith. His attitude began to be regarded by many of his well-wishers as paranoid, and throughout 1169 there was growing irritation and despair at the wanton prolongation of this scandalous situation. It can be thought that the end shows how right Becket was. But his protraction of the dispute and its untidy resolution at Fréteval in July 1170 contributed to the dreadful result. Between 1167 and 1170 Alexander kept Becket on a fairly tight rein. In 1167 the legates, impatient with his intransigence, allowed all those excommunicated at Vézelay to be absolved, if penitent; and many were. Becket regarded these absolutions as invalid. In the winter of 1167–8 Alexander in effect suspended Becket's legation until he and the king were reconciled or, at the latest, 5 March 1169. When the deadline expired, Becket, at Clairvaux on Palm Sunday (13 April), excommunicated ten persons, including the bishops of London (Gilbert Foliot) and Salisbury (Jocelin de Bohun, *d.* 1184), whose offences he considered notorious, and announced that he would extend the list on Ascension day (29 May). All these sentences, at the pope's request suspended until Michaelmas (29 September), Becket reactivated on that day.

Negotiating a return to England, 1169–1170 What the principal intermediaries—the legates *a latere* and Louis of France—worked to achieve was a personal reconciliation of the parties on general terms, in the hope that shelved problems and disputes would disappear in time. Once Becket had recovered Canterbury, Henry and Louis could themselves make a permanent peace treaty and together set out on a crusade to the Holy Land. Becket and Henry did meet at Montmirail on 7 January 1169, only for the archbishop, to the dismay of all except Herbert of Bosham, to add a saving clause to the agreed words of his submission to the king. They then came very close to an agreement at Montmartre in Paris on 18 November, when Becket backed out because of Henry's prevarication over a kiss of peace. After this failure Becket reactivated all sentences imposed on his enemies, threatened that unless peace was made by 2 February 1170 he would impose a general interdict on England, and sent for a new portfolio of papal bulls against his opponents in the kingdom.

Alexander, too, had run out of patience. In letters dated 19 January 1170 he rehearsed what he believed to be an agreed 'form of peace'. This was essentially the terms laid down by Becket, but slightly modified to make them less offensive to the king. And the pope commissioned Rotrou, archbishop of Rouen, and Bernard, bishop of Nevers, to get them formally accepted by the contestants. Moreover, if Henry would not complete the major requirements within forty days of being ordered so to do, the commissioners were to subject all his continental lands to an interdict, without hindrance of appeals. But before the ultimatum, delayed by the usual expedients, expired, the conflict ended unexpectedly and fortuitously. Henry wanted, for various reasons, to have his eldest son, the young Henry, immediately crowned king; and he still had some papal bulls, obtained in 1161 when Canterbury was vacant, which allowed the archbishop of York to perform the ceremony. Becket, alerted by rumours, secured papal prohibitions of such a grave breach of Canterbury's privileges; but it is doubtful whether, in view of Henry's security measures, these were published in England. The coronation was performed on 14 June in Westminster Abbey by

Roger de Pont l'Évêque assisted by some ten English and Norman bishops; and then Henry returned to Normandy to face the music.

When Becket recovered from the shock, his anger was directed more at the bishops who had taken part in the ceremony than at the king. He also believed, erroneously, that the order of service had been revised, so that the young Henry, instead of swearing to protect the holy church of God, its liberties, and servants, was made to swear to observe the ancient customs of the kingdom (that is, the constitutions of Clarendon). He therefore sent to Alexander for bulls against all the guilty bishops and supporters of the constitutions and prepared to complete the peace negotiations with the king, so that he could wreak vengeance on his treacherous suffragans. The preliminaries were easily achieved. Henry, when presented on his arrival in Normandy about 24 June with Alexander's ultimatum, accepted from the commissioners the 'form of peace', with the only reservation of the kiss of peace, since he had sworn at Montmartre never to give it. The commissioners then persuaded Becket to attend a conference between Henry and Louis planned for 21 July near Fréteval in Touraine.

An insubstantial reconciliation and its breakdown, 1170 The business went through with hardly a hitch. The one obstacle, the kiss of peace, was negotiated by Henry's oath, warranted by the archbishop of Sens, that by refusing it he was not laying a trap for the archbishop, and he also gave some assurance about giving the kiss freely at some later date. This was the only concession Becket made except for a temporary postponement of the receipt of damages. On 22 July, in a long private meeting, with both men on horseback, Becket rehearsed his grievances, and Henry gave soft answers and assurances which, inevitably, were recollected differently by the parties in the following months. But at the time Becket was satisfied. Both men were deeply moved by the meeting, and there was an emotional reconciliation. It was not, however, without reservation. Henry granted his peace and their possessions to all Becket's clerks and companions. But when Becket was asked to reciprocate in respect of the king's supporters, particularly Geoffrey Ridel, he refused. His useful excuse, to be repeated on later occasions, was that the sentences of excommunication were Alexander's and only he could remove them.

Becket, Henry of Bosham informed the pope, had won a glorious victory. But the archbishop, despite plenty of advice and warning from Alexander and many others, had not the mind to win the peace. From Fréteval to the end, however much he disguised his motives by an appeal to principles, he was intent on revenge. Although Henry at Fréteval urged him to rejoin the court and travel with him at the royal expense, the exile insisted on returning immediately to France and Sens to give thanks to all those who had helped him. He then refused to go to England until he was sure that the terms of the agreement, especially the return of his and the others' estates, were being implemented. He also needed money to pay off his creditors.

Moreover, he was waiting for the arrival of papal sentences against the English bishops. Hence, after his one-day meeting with Henry in July, he did not see him again until the end of September in the Loire valley, when he complained about the slowness of the restoration of his estates, provoked a quarrel, and then made it up. He left Sens for England on 1 November.

The recovery of properties after six years' alienation was no easy matter, and the senior king's absence from England did not help. So Becket and his party, still short of money, lingered in France. Further delay was caused by the unsuitability of the papal letters that arrived towards the end of October in answer to Becket's complaints about the coronation. Alexander suspended all those bishops who had taken part in the ceremony and sworn to observe the constitutions of Clarendon, and he also decreed that the bishops of London and Salisbury had lapsed into excommunication. There were also references to the improper coronation service and to Henry's crimes against the church. Even Becket could see that in the postwar period these letters were needlessly provocative, and he sent immediately to the pope for a new set with the same penalties but without the offensive passages. These could not be expected much before February 1171. However, a confirmation of Becket's legatine powers, which reached him towards the end of November in a batch of letters dated 8–13 October, after Alexander had heard of the peace, gave him the power to act, although, typically, the pope counselled mercy and magnanimity. And, about the same time, he was given cause to act, for he heard that the English bishops, together with the electors to all the sees that had fallen vacant during the exile, were preparing to cross the channel to join the king and not only take defence measures against the archbishop's threats but also, probably, elect some of those royal clerks who had been Henry's agents against their spiritual lord. Naturally Becket regarded all this as an intolerable injury to the church of Canterbury. He decided to return to England and act. He and a small party travelled to Wissant in the county of Boulogne. He sent ahead a servant in disguise to serve sentences against Roger of York, Gilbert of London, and Jocelin of Salisbury, and, probably on 30 November, crossed at night to Sandwich.

Becket knew that his return would be perilous. But he was a brave man, a fatalist who put his trust in God, and, despite the views of some of the hagiographers, it is clear that he did not seek martyrdom: his aim was to defeat his enemies. He dealt successfully with the royal officials who met his arrival; his reception by the Christ Church monks on 2 December was at least decorous, and he gave each of them a kiss of peace. To all who asked him to remit the sentences on the bishops, he gave his standard reply, that they were the pope's—although his legation was not completely consistent with that. While Roger of York, Gilbert of London, and Jocelin of Salisbury went to Normandy to complain to the king, Becket started a visitation of his diocese, which alarmed many, and hoped to spend Christmas with the young king at Winchester. But since it was believed that the archbishop held his coronation invalid, and rumoured that he intended to dethrone the youth, the king's guardians and advisers refused the visit and ordered him to return to Canterbury and stay there. Becket, who had a warm regard for young Henry, probably intended only to insist on his recrowning in order to remove any possible defect, and he was disappointed by his failure. The enthusiastic welcome, however, that he received from the people wherever he went, although it alarmed the regency government, buoyed him up.

On his return to Canterbury, Becket began to discipline his monks, refusing to ordain all those, save one, who had been admitted since his departure in 1164—a penalty he later revoked; and he was blockaded in the city by Ranulf de Broc, a royal servant who had had custody of the temporalities during the exile and had been stripping them before handing them back. On Christmas day Becket preached to the people in the cathedral and then from the pulpit excommunicated all violators of the rights of his church and the fomenters of discord in general, and named just a few. Next he announced the sentences which had been awarded to all those prelates involved in the illegal coronation. On the following day he dispatched some of his most trusted clerks, including Herbert of Bosham and Alexander of Wales, on missions to the pope, Louis of France, and other French notables to report that the terms of the peace promised by Henry at Fréteval had not been carried out, and, presumably, to ask the pope to lay an interdict on the king's continental lands.

Murder in the cathedral, 29 December 1170 At Henry II's Christmas court at Bur-le-Roi, near Bayeux, the events were regarded very differently. The three visiting prelates probably voiced the general view that it was Becket who had violated the peace, particularly by suspending nearly the whole bench of bishops. It seems to have been decided that a party under William de Mandeville, earl of Essex, and the constable, Richard de Humet, should go to England, confront the archbishop with the various complaints and demands, and, in case of his defiance, arrest him. But, probably on Christmas day, Henry II in his exasperation uttered the fateful words, 'What miserable drones and traitors have I nurtured and promoted in my household who let their lord be treated with such shameful contempt by a low-born clerk!' (Robertson and Sheppard, 2.429). Four of his knights, William de *Tracy, Reginald *Fitzurse, Hugh de *Morville, and Richard Brito (or le Bret)—the first three barons of middling rank—were stung to action and acted secretly within, or on the fringe of, the official mission. Bad weather in the channel, which dispersed the unit, also confused the operation. William de Mandeville did not reach Canterbury until after Becket was dead. The constable, on arrival in England, ordered the Young King's guardians to send, without informing their lord, a squadron of knights to Canterbury to arrest the archbishop. The four conspirators, however, reached by different routes their rendezvous at Saltwood Castle, held by Ranulf de Broc, at about the same time, the evening of 28 December. With Ranulf they planned to beset the cathedral complex on the following day, put direct pressure on Becket to absolve the bishops and give

pledges of good behaviour, and perhaps arrest him. Local garrison troops were mobilized, and next morning the operation was mounted. Ranulf seized the gatehouse to the courtyard while the four barons, led by Reginald Fitzurse, with about a dozen knights and some other helpers, went on to corner their quarry.

Becket, after dining in the hall of his palace at two o'clock, had retired with some of his inner circle to his chamber when the arrival of messengers from the king overseas was announced. When the visitors were ushered in, although Becket knew at least the three seniors well, for they had been his vassals when chancellor, he did not break off his conversation with a monk or eventually rise to greet them. The apparently rambling and hostile interchanges that followed, with the stock charges and countercharges, ended when others of the archbishop's household crowded in and the barons retreated to summon reinforcements. Once the clerks realized how great the danger to Becket was, they hustled him, very much against his will, by an internal route to asylum in the church, which they entered from the south cloister. When Fitzurse rushed in, after Becket had ordered that the door should not be barred, the archbishop turned and stood by a pillar in the centre of the opening to the north transept. By this time he had been deserted by all his clerks, including John of Salisbury, and had in close attendance only his chaplain, Robert of Merton, a monk, William, who left after the first blow was struck, and a visitor, Edward Grim, who was to write one of the first lives. The monks, who had been celebrating vespers in the choir, and the others watched from a safe distance. Daylight was fading, and only the main outline of the subsequent events can be trusted.

Although Becket knew that he could hide from his assailants, he chose deliberately to face them. He trusted in God, the sanctity of the place, and his priestly order. Also he would not be browbeaten by social inferiors. When the four barons demanded that he release the bishops from their sentences, he refused. When Fitzurse tried to arrest him and hoist him onto William de Tracy's shoulders, he fought back fiercely. Insults also were traded. Finally, while Hugh de Morville kept the watchers at bay, Fitzurse and the others struck in turn. The first blow, partly deflected by Grim's protective arm, sliced off the top of the archbishop's head. Becket fell face downwards, with his head to the north and the altar of St Benedict to his right. Richard Brito delivered the *coup de grâce* and Hugh de Horsea, a subdeacon who had accompanied the soldiers, scattered his brains on the floor. Becket, as he collapsed, had commended his soul to God, the Blessed Mary, St Denis, and the patron saints of his church.

After the soldiers had retreated to Saltwood Castle, the terrified monks began to pay some attention to the corpse. In the morning a kinsman of Ranulf de Broc returned and ordered it to be buried immediately in some obscure place; and a marble sarcophagus, already prepared for another burial and sunk into the floor of the Trinity Chapel at the eastern end of the crypt, was chosen.

The body was not washed or embalmed, as was the custom, nor was there, because of the pollution of the church, any religious service. It was probably just after Becket's fiftieth birthday, and at the time many men thought that a traitor to the king had met an end he well deserved.

Canonization Both English kings expressed their sorrow at Becket's death and protested their innocence. But they could do little against a great surge of popular horror at the murder and the demands for vengeance made by Becket's clerks to sympathizers in France and the papal court. On 25 January 1171 the archbishop of Sens, despite the objection of his fellow commissioner, the archbishop of Rouen, laid an interdict on all Henry's French fiefs. News of the death reached Alexander at Frascati in March, and on Maundy Thursday (25 March) he excommunicated generally the killers and all their supporters. Shortly afterwards he confirmed the interdict and all Becket's sentences against the English bishops, and placed a personal interdict on Henry II. But a process of reconciliation was soon in motion; and by 19 May 1172, when Henry submitted at Avranches to the papal legates Albert and Theodwin on agreed terms, almost all involved in the quarrels and murder had expressed penitence and been absolved.

Meanwhile a cult, associated with the belief in the curative power of Becket's blood, had started spontaneously at Canterbury, and soon spread widely. The first recorded miraculous cure was in the city on 4 January 1171, and by Whitsun the miracles were proliferating. The timorous monks, cowed by royal officials, were at first hostile, and fastidious theologians looked askance at the drinking of blood other than Christ's and despised these vulgar signs of sanctity. As St Augustine had remarked, in relation to the Donatists, it is not the penalty that makes true martyrs, but the cause. But the martyrdom had a cathartic effect and the cause was largely abandoned by adherents and opponents alike. Attention was concentrated on the cult. The cathedral was reopened to the public in Easter week 1171 and on Becket's secular birthday, 21 December, it was reconciled by papal permission by bishops Bartholomew of Exeter and Richard of Chester. The crowds of pilgrims and the cures created a great stir. John of Salisbury asked members of his circle, to whom he sent a letter describing the passion, whether it would be proper to honour the martyr as a saint before a formal canonization. And Pierre de Celle, abbot of St Rémi at Rheims, who had sheltered John during his exile, answered that it would. But both kept their heads. Celle reminded his old friend of how in the past they had often joked together about Becket and groaned at the impossibility of ever being able to find a shrine big enough to contain him. But now God had made a laughing-stock of them. For now everyone in both England and France was flocking to his shrine—and he himself was intending to go. But he never did. Sceptics were simply amazed. At an assembly of the English magnates, Henry of Houghton, formerly one of Becket's clerks in exile, was approached by one of the grandees and asked a shrewd question. How was it that Becket, who, as chancellor, had been the most severe of them all against the church, now surpassed all the saints they knew in the number and magnitude of his miracles? The clerk answered that the archbishop had suffered exile and many injuries culminating in his cruel death. If St Peter and the thief on the cross could obtain God's pardon for their sins, surely Becket had more than atoned for his much less serious transgressions.

After Becket's enemies had been reconciled to the church in 1171-2, there was, except among a few zealots, a general desire to regularize the situation. A basic measure would be the martyr's canonization. The pressure for this came from the French church and royal court, activated by Herbert of Bosham and John of Salisbury. And when the pope discovered that the chastened Henry had no strong objection and that the English hierarchy would at least acquiesce, he canonized Becket on Ash Wednesday (21 February) 1173 at Segni. On 12 July 1174 Henry II, beset by rebellions, made a pilgrimage to the tomb, humiliated himself and was scourged. In August 1179 Louis VII of France, Philippe, count of Flanders, Baudouin, count of Guînes, and Henri, duke of Louvain, crossed from Wissant to visit the shrine. Henry met them at Dover and conducted them to and from Canterbury. He was demonstrating that the saint was now his and that he had deprived Louis of this valuable asset.

Becket's shrine remained popular with pilgrims throughout the middle ages. It provided the monks of Christ Church with a considerable, and corrupting, revenue. Guardians of the shrine were soon appointed and records of the cures kept. A method of distributing the 'blood' to pilgrims in phials cast from tin or lead was devised; and these were sold for a farthing and filled with 'the water of St Thomas' from a jug. The recipients wore the phials suspended from the neck as a recognizable badge. The monks had quickly protected the sarcophagus with a stone box, pierced by four oval portholes through which pilgrims could peer and touch. When canonizing Becket, Alexander had, as was customary, ordered the monks to translate the body to a more honourable tomb. But because of various obstacles this was not done until 7 July 1220 by Archbishop Stephen Langton (d. 1228) to celebrate the martyr's jubilee.

Some of the immediate sources of the cult, such as admiration for a man who had withstood the mighty oppressors of the poor, anger at his treatment, and eagerness to participate in the gifts he bestowed after his death, soon dried up. What probably perpetuated the cult was the general acceptance of Thomas as the kingdom's patron saint. Louis VII and France had St Denis with his popular shrine outside Paris. England's St Edmund at Bury and St Edward the Confessor at Westminster were not in the same class, and St George had not yet caught on. The shrine at Canterbury met the needs of popular piety. Geoffrey Chaucer's *Canterbury Tales* illustrates the pilgrims' way in the fourteenth century. And there is no reason to think that the destruction of the shrine in September 1538 by order of Thomas Cromwell, acting as Henry VIII's vicar-general, and the proscription of the cult, were popular. Yet, with the growth of secularism, the popularity of St

Thomas has waned. The play *Becket*, written by Alfred, Lord Tennyson, which in 1884 he dedicated to the subject's successor as lord chancellor, the earl of Selborne, opens dramatically with 'Henry and Becket at chess', but found no place on the English stage. T. S. Eliot's *Murder in the Cathedral* (1935), which has had a considerable success, is a somewhat enigmatic pageant of the archbishop's last days at Canterbury, by no means entirely sympathetic to the martyr.

Assessment Although Thomas of Canterbury was revered for some four centuries in England and his tomb for a time rivalled that of St James of Compostela as a pilgrim shrine in western Christendom, in his lifetime and again after the Reformation he was a controversial figure. Most observers have considered that he was not a born saint. It would also seem that his brilliant, if chequered, career had a mostly harmful effect on all those connected with it. And in whatever way the causes for which he fought are regarded, the zeal with which he advanced them would appear excessive. But he must also be credited with important achievements. On the matter of the 'evil' royal customs in the church, his murder forced Henry to make important concessions to the pope in 1172–6. As regards the 'double punishment' of clerical criminals, he almost single-handedly conquered both traditional practices and the hostility of the best legal opinion. His martyrdom converted the Bolognese masters, and eventually Alexander, to his views and created a wide and irrational 'benefit of clergy' to the detriment of both church and state. Becket also reanimated the subversive element in Christianity which his predecessor and hero, Anselm, had exemplified. Stephen Langton, who displayed the martyrdom on his counterseal, Edmund Rich (*d.* 1240), and John Pecham (*d.* 1292) were archbishops of Canterbury in the thirteenth century who were not unmindful of the example of their awkward and determined predecessor. By defending the rights of the church against the lay powers they sometimes helped to protect the rights of those less protected against tyrannical rulers.

Becket's contemporaries provide the best spectrum of opinions on his life and work. For Gilbert Foliot, bishop of London, a pious, learned, and conservative Benedictine monk, he was an unsuitable and untrustworthy leader who brought the English church to ruin, only to flee in disguise at night, although no one went in pursuit. For his candid clerk, John of Salisbury, he was a flawed instrument of God, spoilt by his follies in the royal court when chancellor, who, although fighting for a just cause, failed because he had given too many hostages to fortune. For Herbert of Bosham he was in all things mighty—great in the palace, great in hall, great in the church, great in exile, great in his return, and especially great at journey's end. Herbert, who was one of Becket's longest serving clerks and probably his closest friend, was conscious of an innate and constant grandeur.   FRANK BARLOW

Sources F. Barlow, *Thomas Becket*, [2nd edn] (1997) · J. W. Alexander, 'The Becket controversy in recent historiography', *Journal of British Studies*, 9/2 (1969–70), 1–26 · J. C. Robertson and J. B. Sheppard, eds., *Materials for the history of Thomas Becket, archbishop of Canterbury*, 7 vols., Rolls Series, 67 (1875–85) · G. de Pont-Sainte-Maxence, *La vie de Saint Thomas le martyr*, ed. E. Walberg (Lund, 1922) · E. Magnússon, ed. and trans., *Thómas saga Erkibyskups*, 2 vols., Rolls Series, 65 (1875–83) · *The historical works of Gervase of Canterbury*, ed. W. Stubbs, 2 vols., Rolls Series, 73 (1879–80) · *English historical documents*, 2nd edn, 2, ed. D. C. Douglas and G. W. Greenaway (1981) · A. Duggan, *Thomas Becket: a textual history of his letters* (1980) · J. C. Robertson, *Becket: a biography* (1859) · W. H. Hutton, *Thomas Becket* (1910) · R. Foreville, *L'église et la royauté en Angleterre sous Henri II Plantagenet, 1154–1189* (Paris, 1943)
Likenesses manuscript illumination, BL, Cotton MS Claudius B.ii, fol. 341 [*see illus.*]

Becket, William (1684–1738), surgeon and antiquary, was born at Abingdon, Berkshire. In the early years of the eighteenth century he was well known in London as a surgeon and an enthusiastic antiquary. He was elected a fellow of the Royal Society on 11 December 1718 and read three papers on 'The antiquity of the venereal disease' at its meetings during the same year (*Philosophical Transactions*, 6, 1718, 368, 467, and 492), and one on another subject in 1724 (ibid., 7, 1724, 25). Becket was an original member of the Society of Antiquaries, which was virtually established in 1717, and was friendly with William Stukeley, William Bowyer, Browne Willis, and other antiquaries. He lived in Hatton Garden and may have been surgeon to St Thomas's Hospital, Southwark, but some time before 1736 he retired to Abingdon, where he died on 25 November 1738. Stukeley adds in his commonplace book to his note of the death of 'my old friend William Becket, surgeon', that his papers were bought 'by the infamous Curl,' (*Family Memoirs*, 97), and purchased from Curll for 30 guineas by Edward Milward.

Becket wrote *New Discoveries Relating to the Cure of Cancers* (1711 and 1712), *An enquiry into the antiquity and efficacy of touching for the king's evil, with a collection of records* (1722; John Anstis the elder gave Becket some assistance in this work), *Practical surgery, illustrated and improved, with remarks on the most remarkable cases, cures, and discussions in St. Thomas's Hospital* (1740), and *A Collection of Chirurgical Tracts* (1740). Richard Gough in his *British Topography* (1780) remarks, on Stukeley's authority, that Becket examined the wills in the prerogative office referring to Lincolnshire and other counties (Gough, 1.519).

SIDNEY LEE, *rev.* MICHAEL BEVAN

Sources *The family memoirs of the Rev. William Stukeley*, ed. W. C. Lukis, 1, SurtS, 73 (1882) · Nichols, *Lit. anecdotes*, 2.88, 495, 796; 5.278 · R. G. [R. Gough], *British topography*, [new edn], 2 vols. (1780) · Watt, *Bibl. Brit.* · T. Thomson, *History of the Royal Society from its institution to the end of the eighteenth century* (1812), appx 34 · introduction, *Archaeologia*, 1 (1770), i–xxxix, esp. xxxv
Likenesses R. Pan, line engraving, Wellcome L.

Beckett, Sir Edmund [*known as* Edmund Denison], **fourth baronet** (1787–1874), railway promoter and politician, was born at Gledhow Hall, Leeds, on 29 January 1787, the sixth son of the banker Sir John Beckett, first baronet (1743–1826), and his wife, Mary, daughter of Christopher Wilson, bishop of Bristol. On 14 December 1814 he married Maria, daughter of William Beverley of Beverley. Among their children were Edmund *Beckett (1816–1905) and William *Beckett (1826–1890) [see under Beckett, Rupert Evelyn]. Through his wife Beckett inherited the estate of Sir Thomas Denison (d. 1765) on condition of taking on the surname Denison. On 17 November 1872 he inherited the baronetcy of Beckett, on condition that he resume the surname Beckett. He did so, after obtaining counsel's opinion that he did not thereby forfeit the Denison inheritance. Throughout his active career, however, he was known as Edmund Denison.

In 1818 Denison settled in Doncaster, whose richest citizen he became. His wealth may have arisen from his share in the Beckett family bank, although he was never active in it, or from the Denison inheritance (or both). He became active in municipal and county politics, and in the 1841 general election was elected tory MP for the West Riding. Having expected an unopposed return in 1847, he withdrew when the Liberals nominated Richard Cobden, but was returned again at a by-election in 1848 and sat until 1859. He was close to Sir Robert Peel (indeed he supplied Peel with the horse that threw and fatally injured him); although he voted against the repeal of the corn laws in 1846, by 1848 he opposed a return to protection and by 1857 described himself in *Dod* as a Liberal.

Denison is best-known, however, for his role in the development of the railway. In 1844 there were two railway routes north from London: one (later the Midland Railway) controlled by George Hudson, and the other (later the London and North Western Railway) under Mark Huish. The direct but thinly populated route from London to York was not served. Denison became chairman of the Great Northern Railway (GNR), which proposed a direct line from London to York via Peterborough and Doncaster, with a loop to serve Lincolnshire. Bitterly fought by both Hudson and Huish, because it would draw away their traffic, the GNR prospectus was opposed by the railway department of the Board of Trade, and faced a petition alleging that its list of subscribers was inflated. However, the petition was rejected, and the GNR's private bill was approved in 1846. At over £600,000, this was the most expensive parliamentary contest in British railway history. Perhaps as a consequence, the line's terminus at King's Cross was to be built 'for less than the cost of the ornamental archway at Euston Square', according to Denison's engineer. Denison became famous for calling Hudson a blackguard on Derby Station platform in 1845, and featured in a *Punch* cartoon of the incident. The opening of the GNR defeated Hudson, but not Huish, who built an alliance of lines to try to undercut the GNR. This dispute went to arbitration under W. E. Gladstone, whose rulings mostly favoured Denison, by awarding the GNR at least as high a proportion of the revenue as it claimed from most of the routes it contested with Huish's confederation. When Denison retired in 1864 the GNR constituted, as it subsequently remained, the southern end of the fastest route from London to north-east England and Scotland.

On all the surviving evidence Denison was tough and uncompromising. An 1856 photograph shows him clean-shaven and grimly determined. At his death even the local tory paper, in its long effusive obituary, described him as 'brusque in his manner, impatient to a degree of human vanity in all its ugly shapes, and with little trace of sentiment or poetry of any description' (*Doncaster Chronicle*, 29 May 1874, 4–5). Denison died at Doncaster on 24 May 1874, his wife having died on 27 March that year. A funeral service was held at Christ Church, Doncaster, on 29 May, after which he was buried in a family vault there. He was succeeded by his eldest son, Edmund Beckett, first Baron Grimthorpe.

IAIN MCLEAN

Sources *Doncaster Chronicle* (3 April 1874) · *Doncaster Chronicle* (29 May 1874) · *Doncaster, Nottingham and Lincoln Gazette* (3 April 1874) · *Doncaster, Nottingham and Lincoln Gazette* (29 May 1874) · C. H. Grinling, H. V. Borley, and C. H. Ellis, *History of the Great Northern Railway, 1845–1922*, new edn (1966) · J. Wrottesley, *The Great Northern Railway*, 1 (1979) · Doncaster Metropolitan Borough Council, Records of Baxter & Somerville, solicitors · W. M. Acworth, *The railways of England*, 4th edn (1890) · R. S. Lambert, *The railway king ... a study of George Hudson and the business morals of his time* (1934) · T. R. Gourvish, *Mark Huish and the London–North Western Railway* (1972) · 'Report of the railway department ... on schemes for extending railway communication between London and York', *Parl. papers* (1845), 39.261, no. 153

Archives PRO, records of Great Northern Railway

Likenesses R. A. Pickersgill, portrait, c.1845, repro. in Grinling, *History of the Great Northern Railway*, frontispiece · cartoon, 1845, repro. in Lambert, *The railway king*, 139 · Maull & Fox, photograph, 1856, repro. in Wrottesley, *The Great Northern Railway*, 1, following p. 128

Wealth at death under £300,000: resworn probate, Aug 1875, *CGPLA Eng. & Wales* (1874)

Beckett, Edmund [*formerly* Edmund Beckett Denison], **first Baron Grimthorpe** (1816–1905), ecclesiastical controversialist, architect, and horologist, was born at Carlton Hall, near Newark, on 12 May 1816, the eldest son of Sir Edmund *Beckett, fourth baronet (1787–1874), later MP for the West Riding, and his wife, Maria (d. 27 March 1874), daughter of William Beverley and great-niece and heir of Anne Denison, widow of Sir Thomas Denison. His father had assumed the additional surname of Denison in 1816 but reverted to his original surname on succeeding to the baronetcy in 1872. His brothers included the banker William *Beckett [see under Beckett, Rupert Evelyn].

Beckett Denison was educated at Doncaster grammar school, Eton College, and Trinity College, Cambridge, where he matriculated in 1834 and graduated BA in 1838 (MA 1841, LLD 1863). He was called to the bar at Lincoln's Inn in 1841, became a QC in 1854, a bencher of his inn in the same year, and its treasurer in 1876. On 7 October 1845 he married Fanny Catherine Lonsdale (d. 1901), daughter of John *Lonsdale, bishop of Lichfield, of whom he wrote a biography (1868). He soon acquired a large practice chiefly in connection with railway bills. Advancing rapidly in his profession, by 1860 he was recognized as the leader of the parliamentary bar, as a result more of his assertive manner than of his knowledge of law. He accumulated a large fortune and ceased to practise regularly after 1880. On his father's death on 24 May 1874, he succeeded to the baronetcy and followed his father's example in discarding the second surname. As Sir Edmund Beckett he was appointed chancellor and vicar-general of the province of York in 1877, an office which he held until

Edmund Beckett, first Baron Grimthorpe (1816–1905), by unknown photographer

1900. In recognition of his activity in ecclesiastical matters, as well as his architectural and mechanical contributions, Beckett was created a peer by the title of Baron Grimthorpe of Grimthorpe, Yorkshire, on 17 February 1886.

Beckett had many interests outside the law and was a vigorous and acrimonious controversialist on ecclesiastical, architectural, scientific, and other topics. Among his earliest causes was a measure of relaxation in the law surrounding marriage with a deceased wife's sister. He was a strong advocate of reform in church discipline, giving evidence before the royal commission on ecclesiastical courts of 1883 and drafting a disciplinary bill of his own with racy notes which he sent to the commissioners. He took exception to the revised version of the New Testament, publishing in 1882 *Should the Revised New Testament be Authorized?* Alarmed by the spread of ritualism in the Church of England, he became president of the Protestant Churchmen's Alliance, which held its inaugural meeting in Exeter Hall in 1889. Archbishop Benson's judgment in 1890 in the trial of the bishop of Lincoln for ritual offences stirred him to write what Benson called a 'furious letter', entitled 'A review of the Lambeth judgment in Read v. Bishop of Lincoln'. On occasions his involvement in ecclesiastical affairs was helpful: his assistance with the Church Patronages Bill of 1893, for example, was welcomed. But at other times he was spiteful and vituperative: he made a startling attack on the archbishop of York in 1895 while opposing in the Lords a divorce bill amending the act by which the clergy were compelled to lend their churches for the remarriage of those guiltily divorced. His standpoint through all his disputes was strongly Erastian and orthodox, as he understood orthodoxy. In 1883, for the Society for the Promotion of Christian Knowledge, he published *A Review of Hume and Huxley on Miracles*, which Bishop Harold Browne considered one of the best books in defence of Christianity.

Architecture, especially on its ecclesiastical side, was another of Beckett's interests, and he published widely on this subject between 1855 and 1876. One of the projects with which he was involved, the rebuilding of St George's Church at Doncaster, led the architect Sir George Gilbert Scott to acknowledge Beckett's generosity but also to remark upon his 'unpleasant way of doing things' (G. G. Scott, *Personal and Professional Recollections*, 1877, 173). Beckett claimed to have 'substantially designed' many buildings, including the church of St James, Doncaster; St Chad's Church, Headingley; Cliffe parish church in the East Riding; St Paul's, Burton upon Trent; the tower top of Worcester Cathedral; Doncaster grammar school; and the extension of Lincoln's Inn Library. His influence is also to be traced in the poorly received restoration of Lincoln's Inn chapel in 1882, but his contemplated demolition of Sir Thomas Lovell's gatehouse in Chancery Lane was happily frustrated.

Living in a house at Batch Wood, St Albans, Hertfordshire, designed by himself ('the only architect with whom I have never quarrelled'), he was interested in the unsound condition of St Albans Abbey, and the attempts of the St Albans reparation committee to fit it for cathedral and parochial service. He subscribed generously to the funds, contributing, from first to last, some £30,000, and interfered freely with Scott, the architect. 'The leader among those who wish me to do what I ought not to do is Sir Edmund Beckett', Scott wrote in 1877 (G. G. Scott, *Personal and Professional Recollections*, 1877, 357). In 1880 various parts of the building were in danger of falling down, and the committee was £3000 in debt. Beckett obtained permission to restore the church at his own expense. He set to work with characteristic zeal, and by 1885 the nave was finished. But his arbitrary architectural decisions excited fierce criticism, and he entered into arguments with both George Edmund Street, architect, and Henry Hucks Gibbs who had obtained concurrent permission to restore the high altar screen. This conflict of authority came before Sir Francis Jeune, chancellor of the diocese, in 1889, Beckett conducting his own case. Neither side was completely successful. Beckett described his part in the St Albans controversies in *St Albans Cathedral and its Restoration* (1885), which, though purporting to be a guidebook, is also a somewhat vehement review of the old arguments.

Through his long life Beckett worked on mechanical inventions and was a keen horologist. In 1850 he published *A Rudimentary Treatise on Clock and Watchmaking* which passed through eight editions, in the preface to the last of which he claimed to have designed over forty clocks, in churches, cathedrals, railway stations, and town halls, including some in the colonies. He contributed articles on clocks, watches, and bells to the *Encyclopaedia Britannica*. He designed the great clock for the International Exhibition of 1851, made by Edward John Dent, which was later installed at King's Cross railway station. In the same year he undertook, in conjunction with George Biddell Airy and Dent, the construction of the great clock for the clock tower in the Houses of Parliament, Westminster. The design was Beckett's, as an inscription records, and it included a new gravity escapement designed by him. Beckett also prepared the specifications for the bell commonly called Big Ben, after Sir Benjamin Hall, commissioner of public works. The clock and Big Ben, like most of Beckett's undertakings, involved him in fierce controversies. He antagonized the respected horologist B. L. Vulliamy by ridiculing his design for the clock. Vulliamy was effectively ousted by Beckett from involvement in the project. Airy, too, felt forced to withdraw. And Barry suffered sixteen years of disputes. Beckett was elected president of the Horological Institute in 1868, on condition that he should not attend dinners, and was annually re-elected, though not always without opposition.

Although a man of arrogance and bile, Beckett was capable of generosity, strong friendships, and kindness towards people in need of help. He was tall and stern looking and remained faithful to early Victorian dress. He died at Batch Wood, St Albans, on 29 April 1905, after a short illness, aggravated by a fall, and was buried by his wife's side in the burial-ground of St Albans Cathedral. His personal estate was valued at £1,562,500, and he left a complicated will with many codicils which was the cause of prolonged litigation. Having no children, he was succeeded in his titles by a nephew, Ernest William Beckett.

L. C. SANDERS, rev. CATHERINE PEASE-WATKIN

Sources P. Ferriday, *Lord Grimthorpe, 1816–1905* (1957) · Venn, *Alum. Cant.* · *The Times* (1 May 1905) · *The Guardian* (3 May 1905) · *Law Times* (6 May 1905) · F. J. Britten, *Horological Journal*, 47 (1904–5), 142–50 · F. J. Britten, *Old clocks and watches and their makers*, 3rd edn (1911); repr. with corrections (1977)
Archives East Riding of Yorkshire Archives Service, Beverley, notebook | BL, corresp. with Daniel Biddle, Add. MSS 48717–48718 · BL, corresp. with S. Butler, Add. MSS 44036–44040 · W. Yorks. AS, Leeds, letters to William Potts
Likenesses Spy [L. Ward], chromolithograph caricature, NPG; repro. in *VF* (2 Feb 1889) · photograph, British Horological Institute [*see illus.*] · photographs, repro. in Ferriday, *Lord Grimthorpe*, facing pp. 90 and 130
Wealth at death £1,562,500: administration, 17 Oct 1905, *CGPLA Eng. & Wales*

Beckett, Sir (William) Eric (1896–1966), lawyer and Foreign Office official, was born on 20 October 1896 at Warren Bank, Broughton, Hawarden, Chester, the son of Thomas Abel Beckett, land agent, and his wife, Jessie Smith. He was educated at Sherborne School and Wadham College, Oxford, of which he was a scholar. He obtained a first class in the honour school of jurisprudence and won the Eldon scholarship. His career at Oxford was preceded by war service. He served in the 3rd battalion of the Cheshire regiment in France, Salonika, and the Caucasus, becoming a captain.

After his undergraduate days Beckett was elected a prize fellow at All Souls in 1921 and was called to the bar by the Inner Temple in 1922. On 16 December 1925 Beckett married Katharine Mary, younger daughter of Sir Henry Erle Richards; they had two sons and one daughter. Also in 1925 he entered the Foreign Office as assistant legal adviser, becoming second legal adviser in 1929 and legal adviser in 1945. When Beckett joined 'the office' in 1925 it numbered only four staff, and was run on a shoe-string. Much of the work fell disproportionately on Beckett, and it was not until after the war that the legal staff started to increase; but the legal advisers were still (as always) overburdened. 'As chief legal adviser from 1945 to 1953', Sir Gerald Fitzmaurice recalled, 'it fell to him to originate and carry through the changes necessary for putting the legal service of the foreign office on a modern footing' (*The Times*, 14 Sept 1966). He achieved this by the quality of his work, and by the impressive example he set his staff. Illness caused his retirement in 1953.

Beckett made a key behind-the-scene contribution at The Hague codification conference (League of Nations) of 1930, and also in connection with the legal drafting of the arrangements for the final termination of the capitulatory regime in Egypt in 1934. In 1944 he advised the government at the Bretton Woods conference, which created the post-war financial system. According to Fitzmaurice, Beckett also played an outstanding part in the arrangements made during the first three assemblies of the United Nations.

Beckett's final years at the Foreign Office coincided with a season of heavy litigation, involving the United Kingdom, in the International Court of Justice, and 'to him equally fell the entire organization of, and a major share in, the substantive legal and forensic work connected with the series of cases' (*The Times*, 14 Sept 1966). Beckett led the British team of counsel in the *Corfu Channel case* (1947–9), the *Anglo-Norwegian Fisheries case* (1951), and the *Anglo-Iranian Oil Company case* (1952), and had a role in several other cases.

Beckett's workload and his capacity to cope with his extensive responsibilities are legendary among British international lawyers. His public service absorbed most of his energies, but he contributed regular pieces to the *British Year Book of International Law*. These contributions included a classical exposition of the problem of classification in private international law (in 1934), still cited in the principal sources. He became a king's counsel in 1946, and was knighted in 1948. Sir Eric died on 27 August 1966 at the Priory Hospital, Wells, Somerset. He was survived by his wife.

IAN BROWNLIE

Sources G. Fitzmaurice, *The Times* (14 Sept 1966) · *The Times* (29 Aug 1966) · personal knowledge (2004) · *WWW* · b. cert. · m. cert. · d. cert. · G. Robertson, *Crimes against humanity: the struggle for global justice* (1999) · *CGPLA Eng. & Wales* (1966) · A. W. B. Simpson, 'Rights talk, rights acts', *TLS* (27 Aug 1999), 9 · G. Fitzmaurice, *A British* *digest of international law: compiled principally from the archives of the foreign office* (1965)

Archives Bodl. Oxf., corresp. with Lord Monckton

Wealth at death £16,885: probate, 2 Dec 1966, *CGPLA Eng. & Wales*

Beckett [*née* Bousfield; *other married name* Thomas], **Frances Sarah** [Fanny] (*bap.* **1821**, *d.* **1902**), philanthropist and a founder of Scottish Home Industries, was baptized on 27 June 1821, at Frimley, Surrey, the only child of George Thomas Frederick Bousfield, solicitor, and his wife, Elizabeth Dingley. Frances Bousfield married Lieutenant Frederick William Leopold Thomas RN on 2 December 1841 at the parish church of St Paul, Deptford, London.

In 1857 Mrs Thomas accompanied her husband, by that time a captain, to Harris in the Outer Hebrides, where he was working on the Scottish hydrographical survey. While living on Harris, her attention was drawn to the extreme poverty of the islanders. Following a tour of investigation she formulated a means of developing a local economy through the home industries of the women islanders. Having been presented with a pair of hand-knitted stockings, she resolved to teach the women to knit and shape well. On returning to Edinburgh she promoted the knitted work and developed markets for Harris stockings and socks through an agency which she opened in Edinburgh in 1859. Together with Catherine Murray, Lady Dunmore, she was a principal force behind the cultivation of the Harris tweed industry through the marketing and sale of Harris tweed. The success of these home industries was such that at the Edinburgh Exhibition of 1886 Harris stockings were awarded first prize, and the tweeds gained the medal for excellence of make. It was the belief of a Harris minister that more families would have been destitute, had it not been for the efforts of Mrs Thomas. Several hundred women were employed in the home industries, and the textiles proved to be more remunerative than the land and fishing during the early 1880s.

Mrs Thomas moved to London in 1888 and opened a depot in Berners Street. This was a seminal step in the development of the Scottish Home Industries, which became a limited company in 1896. She became one of seven directors of the Scottish Home Industries Association Ltd, with the duchess of Sutherland as president.

Not long after moving to London, and by now a widow, Fanny Thomas married a widower, James Flowers Beckett, retired naval officer, at All Saints' Church, Paddington, on 2 July 1890; they lived at his house, Avondel, Hollington Park, St Leonards, Sussex. Besides her involvement in the tweed industry she undertook a number of other philanthropic projects on Harris, including the education of children of the poorer ministers, and the building of the Free Church and manse at Tarbert in 1860. She is thought to have helped over 800 people to emigrate from Harris to Queensland and Canada. In 1897 she built and endowed a cottage at Manish to provide a village nurse.

In his evidence given to the Napier commission of 1883, the Reverend Roderick Mackenzie of Tarbert stated, 'Harris, perhaps, owes more to her than to anybody else' ('Royal commission of inquiry'). Appreciation of Frances Beckett's services in promoting the interests of the Harris and Lewis crofters was formally recorded at a meeting of directors of the Scottish Home Industries Association following her death. Frances Sarah Beckett died on 7 September 1902, at Morningside Drive, Craighouse, Edinburgh, from cerebral thrombosis. She was survived by her second husband.   CHRISTINE LODGE

Sources *Englishwoman's Review*, 34 (1903), 63–5 · *The Scotsman* (18 Oct 1902) · *Inverness Courier* (12 Sept 1902) · W. R. Scott, *Report to the board of agriculture for Scotland on home industries in the highlands and islands* (1914), 15 · 'Royal commission of inquiry into the condition of crofters and cottars in … Scotland', *Parl. papers* (1884), 34.1183–90, C. 3980-II [Harris evidence] · will of Frances Sarah Beckett · m. certs. · d. cert. · *Programme of second exhibition of the Scottish Home Industries Association Ltd* (4 July 1898) · J. Gifford, *The buildings of Scotland: highlands and islands* (1992) · parish register (baptism), Surrey, Frimley, 1821 · *CGPLA Eng. & Wales* (1902)

Wealth at death £1608 13s. 2d.: resworn probate, 1902, *CGPLA Eng. & Wales*

Beckett, Isaac (1652/3–1688), engraver, is said by George Vertue to have been born in Kent, and to have been thirty years old in 1683. The only source for his early career is Vertue's record of information from Edward Luttrell, another early mezzotint engraver:

> Isaac Beckett then a prentice to a callicoe printer & tillet [a kind of cloth] painter then in Morefields … being acquainted with Mr Luttrel, usd to come to see him often at his chambers & see his method then of proceeding in mezzotint, of which, haveing a little drawing, gave him an itch to be doing something that way. It chancd he got a maid with child, for which he absented himself sometime till it was made up, during which time, knowing not what to do, Floyd [John Lloyd] imployed him in scraping of plates for him and showd him the secret of laying grounds with the chisel upon certain conditions … At length Beckett marrys a woman with a round sum of money (about 500 pounds), then he sate up for himself. (Vertue, 1.42–3)

The evidence of Beckett's prints, of which 103 are catalogued by Chaloner Smith, supports this account. The earliest that bear his name are datable to about 1681. Twelve were published by Edward Cooper and five by Alexander Browne, but almost all the rest Beckett published himself, often using the address at the Golden Head in the Old Bailey. He married Grace Compton on 9 September 1684, and had set up on his own account before 13 December 1686, when he placed an advertisement in the *London Gazette* for two portraits of James II and Mary of Modena after Largillierre. He was buried on 29 May 1688 and on 8 July 1688 his widow announced in the *London Gazette* that she was continuing his business at the Golden Head, but on her remarriage on 4 October she sold the shop and stock to John Savage.

Beckett was the first great mezzotint engraver of the English school. His signed mezzotints are for the most part portraits, in particular after paintings by Willem Wissing and Godfrey Kneller. The plates after Wissing were mostly made for Edward Cooper, with whom Wissing had come to some arrangement. Beckett made a similar deal with Kneller; a quarter of his plates are after Kneller's paintings. He also published portrait mezzotints by others, as well as numerous smaller mezzotints of landscape and other genre subjects. He made himself four etchings as illustrations. Beckett's premature death left the field open for his pupil John Smith, who took over his relationship with Kneller, and eventually much of his stock.

ANTONY GRIFFITHS

Sources Vertue, *Note books*, 1.42–3 · J. C. Smith, *British mezzotinto portraits*, 4 vols. in 5 (1878–84) · A. Griffiths and R. A. Gerard, *The print in Stuart Britain, 1603–1689* (1998), 243–9 [exhibition catalogue, BM, 8 May – 20 Sept 1998] · *LondG* (8 July 1688) · private information (2004) [J. A. Ganz]
Likenesses J. Smith, mezzotint, 1689, BM; repro. in J. C. Smith, *British mezzotinto portraits*, 1 (1833), 17 · W. H. Watt, line engraving (after J. Smith), BM, NPG; repro. in Walpole, *Anecdotes* (1849)

Beckett, John William (1894–1964), political activist and journalist, was born at 165 King Street, Hammersmith, London, on 11 October 1894, the only son of William Beckett, master draper, and Eva Dorothy (*née* Salmon). He was educated at the local elementary school and Latymer Upper School, but left at fourteen to become a shop assistant. Later he became a part-time student at the polytechnic, and studied journalism and advertising by correspondence course. At the outbreak of the First World War he immediately volunteered for the army. He was wounded and discharged in March 1917 as unfit for further service. On 2 April 1918 he married Helen, *née* Shaw (*b.* 1892), daughter of a commercial traveller.

Beckett's experiences as a 'temporary soldier' (*WW*) wrought a profound change in his thinking. In Sheffield, where he was seeking work, he was converted to socialism, joining the Independent Labour Party (ILP) in September 1917. When his employers dismissed him for publicly advocating socialism, he returned to the south of England, settled in Hackney, and joined the local branch of the ILP. He became co-founder and chairman of the National Union of ex-Servicemen. The union was soon dissolved for, unlike similar associations, it refused to amalgamate into the British Legion.

Beckett swiftly established a reputation as an effective public speaker. Elected to Hackney council, his angry words once again caused offence to his employers and he was dismissed. Unabashed he pursued his political activities with even greater purpose. In 1920 he was elected to the divisional council of the ILP. Later that same year he was appointed Clement Attlee's full-time political agent. Next, he became secretary both to the ILP's divisional council and the No More War Movement. At Clifford Allen's invitation Beckett, with other enthusiasts, helped to draft the ILP programme for the 1922 national conference. When Attlee entered parliament in 1922, Beckett became his private secretary. In 1923 came Beckett's own first, unsuccessful, attempt to enter parliament, for North Newcastle, but the following year he was adopted for Gateshead and was returned in a three-cornered contest with a majority of more than 9000. In 1929, for personal as much as for political reasons, Beckett abandoned Gateshead for Peckham, serving as their ILP MP until 1931.

Though comparatively short, Beckett's parliamentary career was packed with tumult and incident. He was twice suspended from the Commons: in 1929 for calling the prime minister a liar, and in 1930 for seizing and making off with the mace. He had little respect for the traditions of parliament, believing them to be outdated. His relations with most of his colleagues were not easy. Many thought him vulgar and untrustworthy. He was certainly indiscreet, both in his extramarital relations and in his eagerness to tackle issues that others as eagerly avoided. His impatient, passionate, incautious nature was offended by what he supposed was the Labour Party's reluctance to implement its supporters' wishes. His disillusion was compounded by the death of the left-wing Labour MP John Wheatley in 1930, and made complete when MacDonald's government introduced the Unemployment Insurance Anomalies Bill. This measure, Beckett openly avowed, discriminated unfairly against the most vulnerable groups of workers. In the subsequent general election he stood against the official Labour candidate to no avail: the National Government candidate was elected.

Beckett's first marriage ended in divorce in 1929. The following year, on 5 July, he married Violet Kyrle (1892/3–1948), daughter of Louis Hance Falck, solicitor, and widow of Arthur Bourchier, actor and theatre manager. She was herself better known as the actress Kyrle Bellew. From 1921 to 1923 Beckett successfully edited a monthly magazine he had founded, the *East London Pioneer*. When his other duties allowed, he contributed occasional articles to the small Labour press. His journalistic skills enjoyed more scope when, like some other disillusioned Labour supporters, he joined the British Union of Fascists in March 1934. This inversion of political loyalties followed an unsuccessful period as business manager of his wife's theatre, the Strand, which ended in bankruptcy. Oswald Mosley's New Party provided Beckett with unrivalled opportunities to indulge his pugnacity in street-corner confrontations. His histrionic skills made him a rousing public orator, and he was appointed the New Party's director of publicity. For all his anti-Jewish ranting, Beckett was never a doctrinaire antisemite: Jews were a convenient focus for his anger and aggression. He edited *Fascist Weekly*, supposedly the more highbrow of the party's two weekly papers. It was renamed *Action* in 1936, the reincarnation of the equally pitiful little paper that Harold Nicolson had edited until its closure in 1931. Beckett's diatribes attracted a series of sensational lawsuits. In March 1937 Mosley told his senior staff there was insufficient money to continue paying them. Beckett, together with William *Joyce, did not wait for their dismissal, but left to form the National Socialist League. This hopelessly ineffectual organization at least afforded Joyce and Beckett a platform from which to censure Mosley, the leader to whom they had previously shown sycophantic loyalty.

Beckett admired Joyce, but in 1939 they parted, for Beckett, the old soldier, could not bring himself to support Hitler. Beckett acquired new, more aristocratic political associates in Viscount Lymington and the duke of Bedford. They formed the British People's Party (BPP), another hopelessly impotent political grouping that espoused a bizarre hotchpotch of contradictory ideas on pacifism, fascism, and social credit. At the outbreak of war, they renamed themselves the British Council for Settlement in Europe. In May 1940 Beckett, then secretary of the BPP and an enthusiastic member of the Local Defence Volunteers, was arrested under regulation 18B of the Emergency Powers (Defence) Act of 1939, which allowed the government to imprison without trial and without term anyone thought to endanger national security. This was because of his former association with Mosley. Though his imprisonment was clearly politically motivated, his *ex parte* application for a writ of habeas corpus failed, and Beckett was one of the last of those imprisoned under the regulation to be released in October 1943. It was a neat, though cruel, irony that the man responsible for Beckett's tardy release was home secretary Herbert Morrison: in the early 1920s, when Morrison was appointed mayor of Hackney, Beckett had accused him of political jobbery.

Ill, and under a restrictive order, Beckett re-established contact with the BPP. In the public's mind, whatever was claimed to the contrary, the BPP was tarred with anti-semitism and pro-Nazi sentiments. BPP meetings invariably prompted public protest. When the duke of Bedford, who had been effectively Beckett's patron since his release from prison, died in 1953, Beckett's career as a political activist was ended. In the years that remained, he supported himself and his family (he had two sons and two daughters) by publishing a fortnightly stock market tip sheet, *Advice and Information*. An interest in Roman Catholicism prompted by his painful experiences in both world wars culminated in Beckett's reception into that church in 1952. He died at his home in London, 187 Queen's Gate, on 28 December 1964, leaving a third wife as his widow. A. J. A. MORRIS

Sources C. Holmes, 'Beckett, John William Warburton', *DLB*, vol. 6 • A. W. B. Simpson, *In the highest degree odious* (1992) • b. cert. • m. cert. • d. cert. • *WW* (1930) • *WWW* • *WWBMP* • *Dod's Parliamentary Companion* • F. Beckett, *The rebel who lost his cause: the tragedy of John Beckett MP* (1999)
Archives Labour History Archive and Study Centre, Manchester, MS autobiography • University of Sheffield, papers

Beckett, Ronald Brymer (1891–1970), administrator in India and art historian, was born on 17 January 1891 in Micklefield Terrace, Rawdon, Yorkshire, the son of James Robertson Beckett (1855–1923), manager in a firm of silk and woollen merchants, and his wife, Annie Bertha Murray (1864–1952), a schoolteacher, the daughter of a Scottish land surveyor. When Beckett was four the family moved to Pocklington, where Beckett helped at a local farm. For the sake of his health, after an attack of measles he was sent at the age of six to the Talbot Heath School for Girls at Bournemouth, before attending the Highbury House School at St Leonards and then Woodbridge School. After achieving the highest grades in England in his higher certificate in 1907, he proceeded to Lincoln College, Oxford, where he cultivated a wide range of interests, learning Basque and Erse, joining the Gaelic League, studying the Elizabethan poets, and taking up morris dancing. He also developed a deep love of art, learning to paint himself, visiting Florence and Venice, and reading Vasari.

Beckett's preoccupation with extracurricular interests was such that he attained only a third-class degree in classics, a result which shocked him as he had previously won several scholarships during his school career. On his father's advice he decided to enter the Indian Civil Service. After a probationary year at University College, London, he sailed for India, arriving at Bombay shortly after the outbreak of the First World War. He was assistant commissioner at Jullundur, where he was desperately lonely, before becoming tutor to the nawab of Mamdot, where he became a highly proficient polo player. Attempts to return to England and join the war were blocked by his superiors; when he did return in 1917 he was passed not fit for the army. He joined the Middle Temple and read for the bar, although he was not called until November 1936. On 12 November 1918 he married his second cousin Norah Ford Anderson (1891–1972), daughter of John Ford Anderson, a doctor, and his wife, Gabrielle Coudron; she was secretary of the prisoners of war in Turkey committee set up after the disaster in Kut in Mesopotamia, with which he had assisted during his leave.

After recovering from a bout of the worldwide influenza epidemic, Beckett returned to India in January 1918, and was posted to Amritsar as city magistrate. There Beckett and his wife were involved in containing the demonstrations which preceded the events in Amritsar in mid-April 1919: Beckett, unarmed, with only three men, held back a large crowd from the Hall Bridge; he was later put in charge of escorting British and Indian women (including his wife) to the shelter of the fort. Both of the Becketts subsequently defended the actions of General Dyer, which they believed had saved their own and many other lives. Beckett was later transferred to Rawalpindi and then to Lahore, where he served as under-secretary to the Punjab government; further legal appointments followed. The family finances were tight, and Beckett attempted to supplement his pay by writing two novels and dealing in stamps and postmarks, becoming a philatelic expert. He also collected Indian art and sculpture; his collection of Mughal miniatures was sold to the Metropolitan Museum in New York in the 1960s.

Norah Beckett twice returned to England in the 1920s, to give birth to the couple's two daughters, Antoinette and Elisabeth. Both were subsequently educated in England, visited by their parents during the long vacations which Beckett's legal career ensured him. In the early 1930s he held a variety of senior judicial positions in Lahore and Delhi; in 1932 he was chosen to deal with the serious problem of the maharaja of Alwar, who was removed from his position and replaced by his son. From February 1936 to February 1937 he was seconded to the India Office to draft the part of the India Act of 1935 which dealt with Burma; his efforts were praised on the BBC Third Programme. Beckett returned to Lahore in 1937 and was appointed puisne judge in 1941; in 1946 he retired despite pleas to continue, declaring that he had given enough of his life to India. He attracted friendship among Indians and loyalty from his Indian servants, one of whom remained with him for twenty-nine years.

On his return to England Beckett rejoined University College, London, studying psychology and philosophy, and also pursued his interest in art. He put on an exhibition of the work of Blake and Hogarth at the Tate Gallery, London, and published pioneering catalogues of the paintings of Hogarth (1949) and Lely (1951). His art historical research culminated in a magisterial edition of John Constable's correspondence (1962–8), in which he combined an immaculate transcription of the letters with a comprehensive chronological and explanatory narrative: it was described by Kenneth Clark as a masterpiece of editing. An additional volume, devoted to Constable's more public utterances, followed in 1970. He carried out much of his research by commuting his pension and buying drawings and paintings by English artists, including forgeries so he could learn to spot the differences between genuine and fake. His work on Blake was not published but is held by the Victoria and Albert Museum. He also published *Constable and the Fishers* (1952), containing the correspondence between the artist and his close friend John Fisher.

The Becketts lived first in Eldon Road, Kensington, where Beckett built up his art collection and received a constant stream of visitors. When this proved too much for them, they moved to 7 Farncombe Road, Worthing. In 1969 they moved to a bungalow, The Chanonry, in the orchard of their daughter Elisabeth, at Northmoor in Oxfordshire. There Beckett died on 1 December 1970, with his daughter beside him, calling on his wife's name. She survived him for just over a year. His remains were cremated and the ashes interred at Northmoor. Fair-skinned with red hair, Beckett stood 6 feet tall, and was always an elegant figure with a quietly charming manner.

ELISABETH BECKETT

Sources family MSS and correspondence, including unpublished autobiography (1944–5), priv. coll. • b. cert. • m. cert. • d. cert. • correspondence between R. B. Beckett and Norman Scarfe, Tate collection • *WWW*, 1961–70 • personal knowledge (2004) • private information (2004) • *The Times* (3 Dec 1970)
Archives NRA, priv. coll., family corresp. and MSS • Tate collection, letters to Norman Scarfe relating to edition of Constable's corresp. • V&A, MSS
Wealth at death £12,762: probate, 6 Sept 1971, *CGPLA Eng. & Wales*

Beckett [*formerly* Beckett Denison], **Rupert Evelyn** (1870–1955), banker, was born on 2 November 1870 at Meanwood Park, Chapel Allerton, near Leeds, the third son of **William Beckett** (1826–1890), banker and politician, and his wife, Helen, *née* Duncombe, third daughter of the second Baron Feversham. Rupert was the grandson of Sir Edmund *Beckett, fourth baronet (1787–1874). When, in 1814, Edmund married the great-great-niece and heir of Sir Thomas Denison (1699–1765), a judge in the king's bench, he added Denison to his surname, but he resumed his patronymic when he succeeded to the baronetcy in 1872. His third son, William Beckett Denison, followed his example only in 1886 (when he chose to be called William Beckett).

By the 1860s the Becketts of Leeds were prominent north-country bankers of a century's standing. In this and the following decade they acquired a number of well-established banks elsewhere in Yorkshire and Nottinghamshire to extend their business beyond the wool textile region. Two of these were in the rich agricultural area around Malton (Bower, Hall & Co., acquired in 1875) and York (Swann, Clough & Co., in 1879). In 1879 they were formed into Beckett & Co., the York and East Riding Bank. William Beckett Denison became the bank's managing partner, grandly renting Nun Appleton Hall near York for his residence. He later became president of the Country Banker's Association. He was MP for East Retford, 1876–80, and for Bassetlaw, 1885–90.

His marriage, in 1855, allowed him to straddle the world of the Yorkshire aristocracy and that of his own plutocratic banking and railway-promoting circle. William Beckett was killed by a passing train while walking along the track at Wimborne, Dorset, on 23 November 1890. He was survived by his wife. His sons all achieved eminence in Yorkshire affairs. The eldest, Ernest William (1856–1917), MP for the Whitby division of the county from 1885 to 1905, succeeded his uncle Edmund *Beckett (1816–1905) as second Baron Grimthorpe in 1905; the second, Sir Gervase Beckett (1866–1937), was MP for several Yorkshire constituencies between 1906 and 1929.

Rupert, the third and youngest, was educated at Eton College and at Trinity College, Cambridge. He was destined to carry on the family's great banking tradition, becoming a partner on leaving Cambridge. Having completed his apprenticeship in Leeds, he became resident managing partner of the Doncaster branch (formerly Cooke, Yarborough & Co., acquired in 1868). An officer in the Yorkshire hussars, he built up for himself a first-rate reputation as a businessman in the West Riding of Yorkshire. He became a director of two important companies, the Great Northern Railway (of which his grandfather had been a principal promoter, ensuring that the route from London to York did not bypass Doncaster) and the Aire and Calder Navigation Company. On 21 December 1896 Beckett married Muriel Helen Florence (d. 1941), daughter of Lord Berkeley Paget, and the couple had four daughters.

Around 1910 Beckett moved to Leeds and became deeply involved in its affairs. He was nominated a director of the Yorkshire Penny Bank on its reconstruction by Sir Edward Holden and of the Yorkshire Conservative Newspaper Company in 1911, holding both appointments for forty-four years. During the First World War he was an active member of the directing board of a munitions factory in Leeds, and in 1918 sat on the Treasury committee on bank amalgamations. Three years later, and by this time senior partner, he carefully steered Becketts, with its thirty-seven branches, assets of over £12 million, and status as one of the last two private note-issuing banks in England, into a merger with one of the 'big five' banks—the Westminster. Becketts brought to the new bank, which as a result of earlier amalgamations already possessed good bases in London, the west country, the east midlands and the north-west, a strong presence east of the Pennines. Rupert and his brother Gervase became main board directors.

A decade later, reversing usual practice, Rupert Beckett, the representative of an acquired subsidiary, became chairman of the Westminster Bank in 1931—not a propitious year in which to assume a senior banking post. As chairman for twenty years, he guided the bank's affairs 'with complete reliability and with sturdy Yorkshire good sense' (*The Times*, 29 April 1955). Another *Times* correspondent (3 May 1955) thought him 'a giant amongst bankers', while the 'Men and Matters' column in the *Financial Times* (quoted in the *Yorkshire Post*, 27 April 1955) maintained that he 'was outstandingly the best British Banker of this century'. Certainly, during his chairmanship the bank's assets grew from £300 million to over £800 million and its branch network was sensibly extended. In 1947 he became chairman of the Committee of London Clearing Bankers and of the British Bankers' Association. Aged eighty, he retired as chairman of the Westminster Bank in 1950, though he continued as a board member until 1955, attending a meeting only a few days before his death.

Rupert Beckett was a big man, with a high-pitched laugh; he was modest, generous, and well liked. He hid a decisive financial brain behind a genial exterior. Reckoned to be a good judge of character, he enjoyed a game of bridge and golf and the smart house parties of the interwar years; he liked to entertain his friends at York and Doncaster races. Above all, however, he possessed a great sense of duty. Operating easily in metropolitan social and banking circles, he was nevertheless most at home in Leeds. He was a great fosterer of Yorkshire industry; he held a formidable string of offices in Leeds, of which he was a freeman from 1931. He was treasurer of the university for more than thirty years, of the chamber of commerce and of the Leeds Club.

Beckett's chief interest after banking was newspapers. Associated with the company which produced the *Yorkshire Post*—the Conservative voice of the county—Beckett served as its chairman for more than thirty years, and guided its finances wisely, while preserving its editorial freedom. A true Conservative in the long tradition of the Becketts, he was a JP and a deputy lieutenant of the West Riding. But with a father, an uncle, and two brothers in the House of Commons, he himself declined entering parliament, preferring to concentrate upon his banking and business interests.

Beckett died on 25 April 1955 at his apartment in the Park Lane Hotel, Piccadilly, London. His wife had predeceased him in 1941. He was cremated at Golders Green on 28 April and his ashes interred at Acaster Selby, Yorkshire, on 1 May.   R. G. WILSON

Sources *Yorkshire Post* (26 April 1955) · *Yorkshire Post* (27 April 1955) · *Yorkshire Post* (3 May 1955) · *The Times* (29 April 1955) · *The Times* (3 May 1955) · GEC, *Peerage* [see Grimthorpe] · Burke, *Peerage* (1970) · R. Reed, 'Beckett, Rupert Evelyn', *DBB* · T. E. Gregory and A. Henderson, *The Westminster Bank through a century*, 2 vols. (privately printed, London, 1936) · b. cert. · d. cert. [48805, William Beckett]
Archives National Westminster Bank, London, archives
Likenesses W. Rothenstein, chalk drawing, repro. in Gregory, *The Westminster Bank* · photograph, Leeds Central Library, Leeds, print collection

Wealth at death £1,202,344 12s. 8d.: probate, 10 May 1955, *CGPLA Eng. & Wales* · £460,425 14s. 5d.—William Beckett: probate, 1891

Beckett, Samuel Barclay (1906–1989), author, was born on 13 April 1906 at Cooldrinagh, Kerrymount Avenue, Foxrock, co. Dublin, the second of two children of William Frank Beckett (1871–1933), a quantity surveyor, and his wife, Maria, known as May (1871–1950), daughter of Samuel Roe, a miller of Newbridge in co. Kildare, and his wife, Annie. He was descended from middle-class, solidly protestant, Anglo-Irish stock. William Beckett was an affectionate father and a charming, clubbable, 'absolutely non-intellectual' man, as his son described him (Knowlson, 10), who left his case of Dickens and encyclopaedias unopened. The fiercely independent, strong-willed Beckett had a much more difficult relationship with his protective, equally strong-willed mother, whose 'savage loving' at times overwhelmed him. On the whole he grew up happily in prosperous Foxrock, a village close enough to Dublin for businessmen to commute by train, but rural enough for Beckett to take himself off into the countryside to wander or read alone. He was a fearless, adventurous boy, later an intrepid motorcyclist and an excellent sportsman.

Early years and education   After attending a small kindergarten school run by Miss Ida and Miss Pauline Elsner in nearby Stillorgan, Beckett went to private schools, first Earlsfort House in Dublin, then Portora Royal School in Enniskillen, co. Fermanagh, where his elder brother, Frank, was already a boarder. He entered Trinity College, Dublin, in 1923 and read French and Italian in the modern European literature course. It is often forgotten that he also studied English literature for two years with the Shakespeare scholar Professor Wilbraham Fitzjohn Trench. In 1927 he obtained a first-class degree with a gold medal, doing outstandingly well in French, under his true mentor at Trinity College, Professor Thomas Brown Rudmose-Brown, who inspired Beckett's love of Ronsard, Scève, Petrarch, and Racine, as well as introducing him to a wide range of modern French poets. Beckett also took Italian classes from a private tutor, Bianca Esposito, who took him through Dante's *Divina commedia*. Dante's great poem was a constant source of fascination and a great inspiration to him. While he was at Trinity College, he had his first experience of love in the person of a scintillating, brilliant young woman, Ethna MacCarthy, also a pupil of Rudmose-Brown. Although he adored her and she inspired two of his most beautiful poems, 'Alba' and 'Yoke of liberty', she did not reciprocate his love—though they remained friends for the rest of her life. After graduating he taught French for two terms at Campbell College, Belfast, an experience which he disliked intensely. To his parents' horror he then had a serious love affair with his first cousin, Ruth Margaret (Peggy) Sinclair.

In November 1928 Beckett took up a post as *lecteur d'anglais* (teaching assistant in English) in Paris at the distinguished École Normale Supérieure in the rue d'Ulm. He became friendly in the capital with the self-exiled Irish writer James Joyce. Beckett was strongly influenced by the force of Joyce's personality, by the range of his culture, and by his total dedication to his art. Joyce's example inspired him to write. But, although aware from an early stage that he needed to discover his own distinctive voice, he found it extremely difficult at first to escape from Joyce's stylistic influence: 'I vow I will get over J. J. ere I die. Yessir', he wrote in 1931 to Samuel Putnam.

Early writings While living in Paris Beckett wrote (and saw published) a prize-winning poem about Descartes called *Whoroscope* (1930). He also published his first two critical essays, one (guided in his reading by Joyce) on early sections of what was to become *Finnegans Wake*, entitled 'Dante … Bruno. Vico … Joyce' (*transition*, 1929), the other a brilliant, precocious study of Proust, published in 1931. He returned to Dublin in autumn 1930 to take up a lecture-ship in French at Trinity College, where he lectured on Racine, Molière, the Romantic poets, Balzac, Stendhal, Flaubert, Proust, Gide, and Bergson. He was, however, pathologically shy and detested the self-exposure that lecturing involved. Always a stern auto-critic, he also regarded this activity as 'teaching others what he did not know himself'. So he resigned his appointment after only four terms and set out instead to become a writer, translator, and literary journalist.

After a short stay with Peggy Sinclair's family in Kassel early in 1932, Beckett returned to live in Paris, where, installed for six months in the Trianon Palace Hotel, he wrote the major part of a novel entitled *Dream of Fair to Middling Women*, begun in Dublin a year earlier. He failed to get the book published at the time, however, and it appeared posthumously in 1992. It is a clever, probably much too clever, linguistic extravaganza, full of reworked literary quotations. But it overturns most of the conventions of traditional fiction and is a remarkable bravura performance for so young a man. Because of a clamp-down on foreigners, Beckett found that he had to leave Paris and, desperately short of money, he returned home via London to a family situation where he found himself in constant conflict with his concerned but dominant mother.

Just two months after the death of Peggy Sinclair from tuberculosis, Beckett's father died on 26 June 1933, leaving him feeling guilty and depressed—primarily at having let down his father by resigning from his academic post. He was suffering from panic and a racing heart, which had disturbed him in a milder form ever since his student days; his troubles were diagnosed as likely to be mental in origin, and he was forced to go to England to seek psychological help in London (psychoanalysis was not permitted in Dublin at the time). He underwent psychotherapy for almost two years with Wilfred Rupert Bion at the Tavistock Clinic. During this period, Beckett also read books on psychology and psychoanalysis by Freud, Stekel, Adler, Jones, and Rank. He several times visited the Bethlem Royal Hospital, where an old Portora schoolfriend worked as a doctor. Beckett's own experience of psychotherapy and his enduring interest in schizophrenia, obsessional neuroses, and other forms of mental disturbance had a deep impact on his later prose fiction and plays. Although he had turned his back earlier on an academic career, he remained a scholar at heart, reading widely in the mid-1930s on philosophy, literature, and science; most of his philosophy notes have been preserved. From this date on, his writings had a strong philosophical infrastructure.

In 1934 Beckett published *More Pricks than Kicks*, a collection of ten witty and satirical short stories about an Irish intellectual called Belacqua Shuah, borrowing the name of Belacqua from Dante's indolent figure in the *Purgatorio*. He had also used the name in *Dream of Fair to Middling Women* and recycled some of the abandoned *Dream* material in *More Pricks than Kicks*. In 1935 he assembled the best of

Samuel Barclay Beckett
(1906–1989), by Henri Cartier-Bresson, 1964

his erudite but highly personal poems into a slim volume entitled *Echo's Bones and other Precipitates*. He also tried to create a name for himself in literary circles by contributing poems and book reviews to *The Spectator*, *The Bookman*, and *The Criterion*. But both the poems and the reviews tended to be learned and obscure, and he had scant success.

During his stay in London for psychotherapy Beckett began a novel, set in London and Dublin, called *Murphy*. Completed by June 1936, this was turned down by dozens of publishers and was not published until 1938. An intellectual, comic novel of ideas, *Murphy* is probably one of Beckett's least experimental works. Yet it still deals with some of his most persistent themes: the uneasy relationship of mind and body and the desire to escape from the 'big blooming buzzing confusion' (Beckett, *Murphy*, 245) of a world of ambition, aspiration, and will, to seek out instead a state of quietistic peace.

In 1936–7, dogged by ill health, Beckett toured Nazi Germany, indulging his passionate interest in painting and sculpture. On returning home he became involved in a celebrated court case when he acted as chief witness for his uncle, Harry Sinclair, who had been libelled by Oliver St John Gogarty. While standing up for his uncle's good name, he was publicly humiliated as the 'bawd and blasphemer from Paris'. After a blazing row with his mother he left Ireland to settle down finally in Paris, where on 5 January 1938 he was stabbed by a pimp. When his assailant met Beckett in court, he told him that he did not know why he had done it. Beckett had been in a coma for a few hours and, although the knife had narrowly missed his heart, he was seriously ill for some time.

Before and after the stabbing Beckett had a number of affairs. One was with the American art collector and heiress Peggy Guggenheim, who admitted that she was 'entirely obsessed for over a year by the strange creature, Samuel Beckett' (P. Guggenheim, *Out of this Century*, 1980, 167); they had a turbulent sexual relationship which evolved into a strange friendship. Another was with the Frenchwoman Suzanne Georgette Anna Deschevaux-Dumesnil (1901–1989), an accomplished pianist. He had met Suzanne some ten years before, and when she learned of his stabbing from a newspaper she visited him several times in hospital. They were soon living together at 6 rue des Favorites but did not marry until 1961.

Although Beckett described the period just before the outbreak of the Second World War as a 'period of lostness, drifting around, seeing a few friends—a period of apathy and lethargy' (Knowlson, 295), he was evolving specifically as a French writer. In 1938–9 he wrote some poems in French and translated *Murphy* with the help of a friend, Alfred Péron, who had been the French *lecteur* during Beckett's final year as a student.

After the fall of France in June 1940 Péron introduced Beckett, supposedly neutral as an Irishman, to a British-controlled Special Operations Executive (SOE) resistance cell, Gloria SMH. Beckett worked as a liaison officer and translator, receiving and passing on messages from various agents, first to a photographer for microfilming, then to a courier to be taken over the line into the unoccupied zone. But the cell was infiltrated, and in August 1942 its members were betrayed by a French priest, Robert Alesch, who was working for the German Abwehr. Many members of the group were arrested and deported to concentration camps but, forewarned by Péron's wife, Beckett and Suzanne managed to escape with hours to spare. After spending several weeks on the run, they lived out the rest of the war in the little village of Roussillon in the Vaucluse, where Beckett wrote his extraordinary novel *Watt*, partly as a stylistic exercise and partly in order to stay sane in a place where he was cut off from most intellectual pursuits. Written in English, it was a daring linguistic experiment and, because of its strange subject matter as well as its manner, was not published until 1953. After the war he was decorated with the medals of the Croix de Guerre and the médaille de la Reconnaissance Française. Characteristically, he told nobody about these decorations—not even his closest friends.

'A frenzy of writing' After the war Beckett returned to Ireland to see his mother, but in order to obtain permission to return to France to join Suzanne he volunteered to work as an interpreter and storekeeper at the Irish Red Cross hospital in the Normandy town of St-Lô, which had been devastated by allied bombing and shelling after the D-day landings. He returned to Paris to endure the most poverty-stricken years of his life. At this time he engaged in a remarkable 'frenzy of writing' in French, while Suzanne worked at dressmaking and gave music lessons in an attempt to make ends meet.

The war had a lasting effect on Beckett's personal philosophy and his writing. Many aspects of his later works were born out of his experiences of uncertainty, disorientation, danger, deprivation, and exile. While visiting his mother in Foxrock he also had a 'revelation' which marked something of a turning point in how he approached his writing: '*Molloy* and the others came to me the day I became aware of my own folly. Only then did I begin to write the things I feel' (Graver and Federman, 217). He recognized earlier that he had to divorce himself from Joyce's stylistic influence. Now he realized that he had to follow a radically different path from Joyce, who believed that knowledge was a creative way of understanding and controlling the world. Beckett's 'own way was in impoverishment, in lack of knowledge and in taking away, in subtracting rather than adding' (Knowlson, 352). Light, knowledge, understanding, and success were replaced by darkness, impotence, ignorance, and failure. Beckett also realized that he needed to draw on the turmoil and uncertainty of his own inner consciousness rather than on the external, 'real' world; contradictions would be allowed greater freedom; the imagination would be given the scope to construct alternative worlds. To express this vision Beckett rejected some of the techniques that he had followed earlier. Writing in French allowed him to achieve a greater simplicity and objectivity. His prose was no longer full of the densely layered quotations and erudite allusions of his English prose of the 1930s.

Beckett's first novel in French, *Mercier et Camier* was finished in 1946. He regarded it later as an apprentice work and was unwilling to have it published until 1970. It was, however, something of a sourcebook for his later writing and allowed him to experiment with dialogue, preparing him for his excursions into drama. At the beginning of 1947 he wrote his first full-length play in French, *Eleutheria*—the title being a Greek word for freedom. He was very insistent throughout his life that this should be neither published nor performed, perhaps because it contained certain autobiographical features or had some flaws in its construction. As a result the play was published only after his death.

Beckett's financial situation and his health were precarious immediately after the war. But he wrote frenetically and in French. He completed the novel trilogy *Molloy* (1951), *Malone meurt* (*Malone Dies*) (1951), and *L'innommable* (*The Unnamable*) (1953), on which, with his play *En attendant Godot* (*Waiting for Godot*), so much of his reputation as an innovator and a master stylist in French and English rests. For, unusually, Beckett himself translated most of his prose texts and his plays from one language into the other, working in both directions and re-creating the work each time in the other language. The novels and novellas of the post-war years showed how much the revelation in his mother's house had affected his writing. Characters blend into each other; clues followed, as if in a detective novel, lead nowhere; radical uncertainties about the world and the self predominate; philosophical, psychological, literary, or artistic motifs are no longer used allusively but are integrated into the structure of the work. Suzanne carried the original French manuscripts of the novels around a variety of publishers and, after dozens of refusals, a young publisher, Jérôme Lindon, at the Éditions de Minuit finally accepted them.

Waiting for Godot was first written in French between October 1948 and January 1949. Beckett's theatrical imagery for this play is stark and minimalist. Two tramp-clowns, Estragon and Vladimir, wait for someone called Godot to come. They hope that his visit will 'save' them. In the meantime they fill in 'the terrible silence that is waiting to flood into this play like water into a sinking ship' (Beckett) with banter and repeated actions. Two other passers-by (Pozzo and Lucky) arrive to provide a distraction (and display a view of life as a series of purposeless movements). After the visitors have left, a boy messenger comes to inform them that Mr Godot will not come today, but will certainly come tomorrow. The same pattern is repeated with significant variations in the second act: Lucky has become mute; Pozzo has gone blind. But a boy messenger returns to convey the same message about Mr Godot. Such apparent simplicity disguises some profound themes: life's brevity and its pain; the human need for something to confer meaning on a mysterious existence; in its absence, a compensatory need for friendship to protect and sustain, yet fail to satisfy; a Cartesian concern with the uneasy interplay of mind and body; and, above all, a radical uncertainty which characterizes every aspect of the two friends' lives. Man is seen, in Beckett's own words, as a 'non-know-er, a non-can-er'. The French actor–director Roger Blin, again contacted by Suzanne, then by Lindon, eventually managed to raise enough money to put on *En attendant Godot* at the tiny Théâtre de Babylone in Paris in January 1953. The extraordinary success of this first production in French was responsible for Beckett's rise to worldwide fame, as the play rapidly became an object of intense international interest and controversy. The first production of Beckett's own English translation, directed by Peter Hall, was staged at the Arts Theatre Club in London in August 1955. Kenneth Tynan's and Harold Hobson's reviews made it into an intellectual hit which has since been regarded as having transformed the British stage.

Later work With money left to him by his mother Beckett had a small country house built near Ussy-sur-Marne outside Paris. For the first time in his adult life he also found himself comfortably off owing to the success of *Waiting for Godot*. In 1954 he lost his brother to cancer. He was with Frank until the end in what was one of the most devastating experiences of his life. Soon after this, however, he felt the return of his creative energy and wrote a first draft of *Fin de partie* (*Endgame*), a play profoundly marked by his brother's death. It was premiered in French in London on 3 April 1957.

In 1956, at the request of the BBC, Beckett wrote a radio play, *All that Fall*. It drew on memories of his protestant childhood and his later abandoned faith. While writing the play Beckett was plunged into a state of depression, but the play itself is full of wit and vitality. He was further shattered by news that Ethna MacCarthy, married by then to one of his closest friends, A. J. Leventhal, was dying of cancer. But memories of her, combined with a number of related themes—a gnostic contrast of light and dark; the relationship with one's former self; an exploration of similarity and difference in human life—inspired his short play *Krapp's Last Tape*. At about this time he began a long-term relationship with Barbara Bray, a script editor at the BBC, with whom he remained on very close terms for the rest of his life, while never leaving his wife, Suzanne. He received an honorary degree of DLitt from Trinity College, Dublin, in 1959.

Beckett started writing the play *Happy Days* (1961) in October 1960 and it opened on 1 November 1962. As in all Beckett's plays, philosophical concerns take the form of striking theatrical images. In this play a woman is buried up to her waist in act I and up to her neck in act II: 'a new stage metaphor for the old human condition—burial in a dying earth, exposure under a ruthless sun' (Cohn, *The Comic Gamut*), as the sands of time literally engulf her. *Krapp's Last Tape* and *Play* tend to 'destabilize and disperse' (Lawley) individual identity in plays which are built on a clever use of monologue. Yet we respond first at a human level to the physical, the concrete, and the visual. Only then do we move to the philosophical significance of the images, actions, or words.

Beckett felt that, because of its very physical, corporeal nature, theatre inevitably involved compromise. In his post-war prose fiction he was less restricted in exploring his deepest concerns. He was freer to explore and attempt to express being, which for him was chaotic, formless, enigmatic, and mysterious. Language is form and form represents an obstacle to capturing being. Form is a sign of strength, whereas Beckett was seeking what he once referred to as a 'syntax of weakness'. So breaking down the traditional forms of fictional and theatrical structure and language became an essential element in a bold attempt to express such formless being. The novel trilogy, and *Comment c'est* (*How It Is*) (1961) in particular, deal with issues of consciousness and the self. For to talk of the self one must objectify that self, hence create a self which is different from the one doing the observing or the describing. This results in a constantly receding series of observers or storytellers, voices or listeners.

On 25 March 1961 Beckett secretly married Suzanne Deschevaux-Dumesnil in Folkestone. He wanted Suzanne to inherit the rights to works whose publication she had tirelessly arranged. But he continued to see Barbara Bray, who had moved to live in Paris. His next play, *Play* (1964), parodied the conventional responses of a man and two women involved in an emotional triangle.

In the mid-1960s Beckett's theatre commitments became very taxing. From that time on he directed his own plays both for the stage and for television. Chiefly he directed at the Schiller-Theater in Berlin and in the studios of Süddeutscher Rundfunk in Stuttgart, but also in Paris and London. In his own productions he refined his plays in the light of theatrical practicalities, introducing many small cuts and changes to his texts. Beckett's own theatrical notebooks prove that he was an excellent choreographer, with a talent for what he described as 'form in movement'. He also worked in New York on a film, entitled *Film* (1965), starring Buster Keaton and directed by his American director friend Alan Schneider; and on a play for television, *Eh Joe* (1967). While receiving treatment for what turned out to be a benign tumour in the roof of his mouth, he wrote a short play in English, *Come and Go* (1967), in which three women comment on their illnesses or imminent deaths.

During this same period Beckett wrote a number of spare, minimalist prose texts in French. *Imagination morte imaginez* (*Imagination Dead Imagine*) (1965) is set in a white rotunda in which two figures exist like embryos waiting for birth or extinction. In *Le dépeupleur* (*The Lost Ones*) (1971) a larger cylinder is inhabited by 200 people who live out a strictly regulated Dantesque existence. *Bing* (*Ping* in English) (1966) features a single figure in a small white cube. These works come very close to being formalist constructs, creating alternative worlds. Yet the texts are powerful as well as enigmatic and, in spite of all appearances, they do draw from and reflect on the 'real' world. What remains of consciousness in a world where all is reduced? How can the imagination persist when it seems already to have died? Such 'residua' are attempts to continue expressing in a world of receding possibilities where one of the major restrictions is an acute awareness of the inadequacy of language to express.

Beckett's plays of the 1970s come much closer to basic human concerns: in *Not I* (1973), a Mouth high in the darkness spews out words in an unstoppable stream—the theatrical equivalent of a Munch-like scream of despair; in *Footfalls* (1976) we are confronted by an image of distress and loss in the person of May, literally 'revolving it all in her poor mind', as she paces across the stage; in *That Time* (1976) the discontinuity of self, yet persistence of a basic consciousness, is revealed in a verbal kaleidoscope of images from different periods of the narrator's life. The central visual image, often inspired by particular paintings of the old masters (Giorgione, Rembrandt, Antonello, Dürer), is crucial to the dramatic effect. Yet Beckett combines words and visual images in a highly innovative way, as he explores what is essential to theatre for it still to remain theatre.

In the early 1980s Beckett produced for a Beckett conference in Ohio a play called *Ohio Impromptu* (1981), which, with its two almost identical, gowned figures sitting at a table, resembles a Rembrandt or a Terborch painting. He also wrote the beautiful short play *Rockaby* (1981), in which a woman dressed in black is rocked backwards and forwards in a chair to the rhythm of her recorded voice. Her recorded words take the form of a poem. From time to time the live figure repeats the line 'Time she stopped' in synchronicity with the recording. Billie Whitelaw, one of Beckett's favourite actresses, played the woman in its first production.

Last years In 1980 *Company*, a highly original prose text, first written in English, was published. Although there are autobiographical reminiscences, especially from Beckett's childhood, it is in no sense a conventional autobiography, for the text revolves around some of his most basic themes: solitude, loneliness, the unreliability of memory, uncertainties to do with both the self and the other. Another woman in black is recalled by the narrator of the prose piece *Mal vu mal dit* (*Ill Seen Ill Said*), written in French and published in 1981. Surrounded by twelve shadowy figures, the woman is drawn to a stone that resembles a white tombstone. Then, this time in English, and partly inspired by Edgar's speech in *King Lear*, 'The worst is not so long as one can say, This is the worst', he wrote another quite extraordinary prose piece, *Worstward Ho* (1983), about the will to 'fail better'. Though concerned with the failure of language, it achieves a chilling vibrancy in its stark prose. *Stirrings Still* (1988) was Beckett's last prose text, although his final piece of writing was a poem, *Comment dire* (*What is the Word*) (1989), written after he had regained consciousness in a hospital following a fall.

As a young man Beckett was shy, taciturn, and self-absorbed. In later life he became far more genial and was noted for his kindness and his generosity towards others. Although witty, warm, and friendly with close friends, he was never gregarious and hated invasions of his privacy. He refused to be interviewed or to have any part in promoting his books. His physical appearance was very striking: he was 6 feet tall, with a face like an Aztec eagle, piercing blue eyes, large ears, and spiky hair.

Beckett's interests were highly intellectual. He read widely in English, French, Italian, and German literature.

In his late twenties and early thirties he read a lot of philosophy: the pre-Socratics, Plato, Descartes, and the occasionalists, Spinoza, Leibniz, and Kant. His interest in the painting of the old masters and in sculpture remained with him throughout his life and he was a friend of many modern painters, in particular Bram and Geer van Velde, Henri Hayden, and Avigdor Arikha. He owned paintings by all these artists. He was a good pianist, who loved Haydn, Schubert, Beethoven, Chopin, and Mozart and attended concerts and recitals with his wife, who was also an excellent pianist. He did not generally like opera, but he did go to see several ballets in the 1930s. Music and painting were probably among the most important influences on Beckett's own writing, and his late work for the stage appears sometimes closer to painting or sculpture than it does to traditional theatre.

In his political views Beckett was broadly left-wing and anti-establishment, although not a communist. He felt a natural sympathy for the underdog, the victim, the down-and-out, and the prisoner. He never allowed his art, however, to become part of any political agenda, although he wrote one play, *Catastrophe*, in 1982 for the Czech dissident writer Václav Havel, then under house arrest, who later became president of Czechoslovakia. He was a firm supporter of human rights movements throughout the world and a fierce opponent of all forms of censorship and repression.

Beckett's health, which had so often been precarious, began to decline seriously in 1986 with the onset of respiratory troubles soon diagnosed as emphysema. In the following year, being deprived of oxygen, he had several falls, and in the summer of 1988, after falling badly, he went to live in a modest nursing home, called Le Tiers Temps (the Third Age). He was taken ill again on 6 December and died in the Hôpital St Anne in Paris of respiratory failure on 22 December 1989. After a small private funeral he was buried with his wife, who had died fewer than six months before, in the cemetery of Montparnasse, Paris, on 26 December.

Beckett changed the entire face of post-war theatre and also inspired many modern painters and video or installation artists. His prose, too, was immensely influential. He is often described as a pessimist or nihilist, and it would be wrong to understate the sombre nature of his dark vision. Yet such categorizations are wholly inadequate. They ignore the persistent need of the characters in his fiction and his drama to go resolutely, stoically on. They also ignore the humour which is a major feature of what might be called his early and middle periods. Beckett was awarded the Nobel prize for literature in 1969: 'For his writing which—in new forms for the novel and drama—in the destitution of modern man acquires its elevation' (citation). And it is easy to ignore a positive, almost cathartic effect that may be gained from laughing at the worst that life can throw at you or from merely enduring it in a brave, perhaps even an uplifting way.

JAMES KNOWLSON

Sources personal knowledge (2004) • private information (2004) [heirs, family, and friends] • L. Harvey, notes of interviews, 1960x69, Dartmouth College, Baker Library • J. Knowlson, *Damned to fame: the life of Samuel Beckett* (1996) • S. Beckett, *More pricks than kicks* (1934) • S. Beckett, *Murphy* (1938) • S. Beckett, *Molloy, Malone dies, The unnamable* (1959) • S. Beckett, *Collected shorter plays* (1984) • S. Beckett, *Collected shorter prose, 1945–1980* (1988) • citation for the Nobel prize for literature, 1969, Nobel Foundation • R. Federman and J. Fletcher, *Samuel Beckett: his works and his critics* (1970) • L. Graver and R. Federman, *Samuel Beckett: the critical heritage* (1979) • J. Knowlson and J. Pilling, *Frescoes of the skull: the recent prose and drama of Samuel Beckett* (1979) • R. Cohn, *The comic gamut* (1962) • R. Cohn, *Just play: Beckett's theater* (1980) • P. Chabert, ed., *Revue d'Esthétique* (1986) [special Beckett issue] • L. E. Harvey, *Samuel Beckett: poet and critic* (1970) • H. Kenner, *Samuel Beckett: a critical study* (1968) • C. Lake, ed., *No symbols where none intended* (1984) • P. Lawley, 'From *Krapp's last tape* to *Play*', *The Cambridge companion to Beckett*, ed. J. Pilling (1994) • C. Locatelli, *Unwording the world: Samuel Beckett's prose texts after the Nobel prize* (1990) • J. Pilling, *Beckett before 'Godot': the formative years, 1929–1946* (1997) • P. J. Murphy, *Reconstructing Beckett: language for being in Samuel Beckett's fiction* (1990) • E. Brater, *Beyond minimalism: Beckett's late style in the theater* (1987) • S. E. Gontarski, *The intent of undoing in Samuel Beckett's dramatic texts* (1985)

Archives BBC WAC • Boston College, Massachusetts, John J. Burns Library • Harvard U., Houghton L., corresp., literary MSS, and papers • Indiana University, Bloomington, Lilly Library • Institut des Mémoires de l'Édition Contemporaine, Paris • Princeton University Library, New Jersey • Syracuse University, New York • TCD, ephemeral material • U. Reading L., letters and literary MSS; further papers • Washington University, St Louis, Missouri, letters, literary MSS and papers | Harvard U., Houghton L., letters to Miss Willard • TCD, letters to Bettina Jonic • TCD, letters to Thomas MacGreevy • TCD, corresp. with Alan Simpson relating to the Pike Theatre productions of his plays • TCD, corresp. with Percy Arland Ussher • TCD, letters to Herbert Martin Oliver White • University of British Columbia, corresp. with Laure Riese | SOUND BL NSA

Likenesses P. Joyce, photograph, 1949, NPG • photographs, c.1950–c.1986, Hult. Arch. • H. Hayden, pen-and-ink drawing, 1957 (*Samuel Beckett*), priv. coll. • H. Cartier-Bresson, photograph, 1964, NPG [*see illus.*] • A. Arikha, brush and India ink on paper, 1967 (*Samuel Beckett leaning*), priv. coll. • pen-and-ink drawing, 1967, priv. coll. • portrait, 1969, priv. coll. • brush and sumi ink drawing, 1970, Centre Pompidou, Paris • etching, 1971, priv. coll. • graphite drawing, 1971, NPG • portrait, 1971, priv. coll. • silverpoint drawing, 1971, priv. coll. • silverpoint drawing, 1975, priv. coll. • J. Brown, photograph, 1976, NPG • graphite drawing, 1976, priv. coll. • J. Baner, photograph, 1978, NPG • L. le Brocquy, oils, 1979 • T. Philips, lithograph, 1984, priv. coll. • T. Philips, lithograph, 1984, NPG • B. O'Toole, pastel drawing, 1989, U. Reading L., department of archives and manuscripts • L. le Brocquy, oils, 1992 • M. Abbott, pastel drawing, 2000, U. Reading L., department of archives and manuscripts • S. O'Sullivan, charcoal drawing (*Portrait of Samuel Beckett*), priv. coll.

Beckett, William (1826–1890). *See under* Beckett, Rupert Evelyn (1870–1955).

Beckford, Peter (*bap.* **1643**, *d.* **1710**), planter in Jamaica and politician, was baptized on 19 November 1643 at St James, Clerkenwell, Middlesex, the son of Peter Beckford, 'a shadowy and humble figure' whose dates of birth and death are unknown (Alexander, 29), and his wife Phillis. He was a descendant of the Beckfords of the parish of Beckford in Gloucestershire, one of the oldest families in England.

Samuel Pepys recorded in his diary on 5 January 1661 that Thomas Fuller, the English divine and historian, had come to his home to desire a kindness for a friend of his. The friend was Beckford, who 'hath a mind to go to

Jamaica with these two ships that are going, which I promised to do' (Diary, 2.6). Few records of Beckford's early years in Jamaica have survived. One contemporary historian, who described him as being very active, honest, and sober, said he was bred a seaman, then became a merchant, and, having some knowledge of gunnery, was appointed captain of the forts at Port Royal. In 1675 he was described as a merchant at Port Royal, and six years later was the owner of land, a dwelling house, a storehouse, and a wharf in that town. Port Royal was a place of clamorous, murderous, drunken, brutal men, and reputedly the wickedest city in the West Indies in the lifetimes of Beckford and the buccaneer Sir Henry Morgan. Frank Cundall wrote that Beckford 'was at the capture of St Jago de Cuba', and suggests that he was present at 'the taking of Panama' by Morgan and his buccaneers in 1671 (Cundall, 1937, 13).

Beckford was elected to the house of assembly of Jamaica from the parish of St Catherine in 1675; in later years he represented the parishes of Clarendon, St Dorothy, and St John. In 1691 he was elevated to the island's council and later became its president. He was an active member of the militia, moving up from captain to colonel; in 1683 he was made commander of the forts at Port Royal. Moreover, he was receiver-general of Jamaica in 1691, and in the following year became commander and custos of Port Royal. After the earthquake of 1692 destroyed the greater part of Port Royal, he became the first custos or principal justice of the peace of the port town of Kingston.

On the death of the governor, Major-General William Selwyn, Beckford was elevated to the post of lieutenant-governor of Jamaica on 5 April 1702 and authorized to act by the same powers and instructions as did the late governor. In his inaugural speech to the assembly he said, 'I have gone through most of the offices of the island, though with no great applause, yet without complaint'. He promised to protect the liberties of the white citizens, observing that he had 'some small interest in this island, which, had I no other consideration, would induce me as far as it lies in my power, to support each particular in its just right' (Journals of the Assembly of Jamaica, 1.236). Beckford's short tenure of eight months came in the early part of the War of the Spanish Succession, leading him to urge the strengthening of the military posture of the island against the Spanish and French enemies.

The goal of merchants, government officials, and professional and military men who went from England to Jamaica and other Caribbean islands without capital was to use their surplus income to acquire land, indentured servants, African slaves, and milling equipment to establish sugar plantations and other income-producing properties. Beckford was pre-eminent among the Jamaicans who competed fiercely for wealth and power. By 1670 he had acquired 2238 acres in Clarendon parish, and he added to his holdings during his lifetime, notably several large properties he purchased from the London alderman Richard Beckford. Besides the large tracts of land he

acquired by patent and deed, he purchased nearly a hundred small properties which were consolidated into sugar plantations of several hundred acres, each equipped with mills, boiling and curing houses, and rum distilleries, and manned by a labour force of upwards of a hundred African slaves. At his death in 1710 he was reputed to have owned twenty estates, 1200 slaves, and £1,500,000 in bank stock. Cundall claimed that Beckford possessed the largest property, real and personal, of any subject in Europe and the overseas colonies.

Beckford's first wife was Bridget (d. 1671), the daughter of Sir William Beeston, a planter and governor of Jamaica from 1692 to 1702. His second wife, Anne, was a relative of Colonel Thomas Ballard, a leading planter. She had three sons, Peter *Beckford (1672/3–1735), who became speaker of the assembly, Charles, who died in infancy, and Thomas, who was killed in 1731 by a man he had offended; and two daughters, Priscilla (b. 1675) and Elizabeth (b. 1678).

The circumstances of Beckford's death illustrate the quarrelling and violence of the planter élite. It occurred on 3 April 1710 at Government House in Spanish Town. The discussion in the assembly chamber waxed so furious that Speaker Peter Beckford the younger sought in vain to adjourn the house. Some of the members barred the door, while others drew their swords and forced the speaker to reoccupy the chair. Peter Beckford senior, who was in the council chamber, heard his son's cry for help and ran with the guards to batter down the door to rescue him. In the excitement the elder Beckford either fell accidentally or suffered a stroke and died suddenly. Boyd Alexander, the biographer and historian of the Beckford family, claims that the elder Beckford himself was 'ruthless, unscrupulous and violent', and that the Beckfords were men of violent temper that led them even to murder (Alexander, 30–31). In the cathedral at Spanish Town, where he was buried, is a white marble slab in his memory, inscribed:

> Here lyes Interr'd the body of the Honble. Coll. Peter Beckford, late Presidt. of the Councill, sometime Lieut. Govr. and Commander in Chief of this Island, who departed this life the 3rd Apr. 1710 in the 67th year of his age. (Cundall, 1937, 25)

In his will of 7 September 1705, Beckford bequeathed £100 to the poor of St Catherine's parish, £500 to his son Thomas, £250 to each of Thomas's two daughters, and £100 to his friend Thomas Nicholls. Furthermore, he set free his slaves Francis and Phillip, and devised to each an annuity of £10 annually. All of the remainder of his estate in Jamaica and England he bequeathed to his son Peter and his heirs. On the basis of the fortune acquired by Peter Beckford, the family was distinguished by William *Beckford (bap. 1709, d. 1770), a grandson who became lord mayor of London and member of parliament, three brothers of the lord mayor who were members of parliament, and the lord mayor's son, William Thomas *Beckford (1760–1844), a later Romantic author and prominent art collector.   RICHARD B. SHERIDAN

Sources B. Alexander, *England's wealthiest son: a study of William Beckford* (1962) · F. Cundall, *The governors of Jamaica in the seventeenth*

century (1936) · *The diary of Samuel Pepys*, ed. H. B. Wheatley and others, 10 vols. (1893–9) · W. A. Feurtado, *Official and other personages of Jamaica from 1655 to 1790* (1896) · R. Pares, *Merchants and planters* (1960) [Economic History Review, suppl. 4] · *Journals of the Assembly of Jamaica*, ed. Assembly of Jamaica, 14 vols. (1811–29), vols. 1–2 · C. Bridenbaugh and R. Bridenbaugh, *No peace beyond the line: the English in the Caribbean, 1624–1690* (1972) · R. S. Dunn, *Sugar and slaves: the rise of the planter class in the English West Indies, 1624–1713* (1972) · C. V. Black, *History of Jamaica* (1958) · R. B. Sheridan, *Sugar and slavery: an economic history of the British West Indies, 1623–1775* (1974) · F. Cundall, *The governors of Jamaica in the first half of the eighteenth century* (1937) · W. J. Gardner, *A history of Jamaica*, new edn (1909)

Archives Jamaica Public RO, Spanish Town, deeds, patents, wills **Likenesses** Murphy, mezzotint, repro. in Cundall, *Governors of Jamaica in the first half of the eighteenth century*, following p. 24 · portrait, repro. in Cundall, *Governors of Jamaica in the first half of the eighteenth century*, following p. 24

Wealth at death est. twenty estates, 1200 slaves, and £1,500,000: N. Deerr, *The history of sugar* (1949), vol. 1, p. 175; C. and R. Bridenbaugh, *No peace*, 369 · £478,000; also extensive real estate: Cundall, *Governors of Jamaica in the first half of the eighteenth century*

Beckford, Peter (1672/3–1735), planter and politician in Jamaica, was the son of Peter *Beckford (*bap.* 1643, *d.* 1710) and his second wife, Anne Ballard. Beckford was elected to the assembly (like his father, who was a member of the house of assembly before he was elevated to Jamaica's privy council and appointed lieutenant-governor) in most of the years from 1701 to 1731, and was speaker from 1707 to 1713 and again in 1716. He was also comptroller of the customs in Jamaica. Like his father, young Beckford possessed a violent temper, and, according to Boyd Alexander, he 'shamefully murdered the Deputy Judge-Advocate in Jamaica who was more than twice his age' (Alexander, 31).

Few details are known of Beckford's career, but at his death he was the wealthiest planter in Jamaica and reputedly 'in possession of the largest property real and personal of any subject in Europe' (Leslie, 267). His great wealth is revealed, in part, by the inventories of his personal property. They show that Beckford was sole owner of nine sugar plantations and part owner of seven more, of which his personal property equity amounted to £69,486 Jamaica currency. Nine cattle pens, together with a provision farm and storehouse, amounted to another £13,098. In Spanish Town, the seat of government, his personal property was valued at £5686. Much of his personal property took the form of black slaves, of whom he was sole owner of 1737 and half owner of 577 others.

Moreover, Peter Beckford was a financier of great magnitude, for his inventories list 128 individuals and firms that owed him a total of £135,044 on the security of mortgages, bonds, and open accounts. Altogether, Beckford's personal property amounted to £223,314. But this does not include the value of buildings and planted canes, which probably amounted to another £100,000 or more. Thus Beckford's personalty and realty amounted to nearly £325,000 Jamaica currency or £222,000 sterling. Another £20,000 sterling was said to consist of personal property in England, 'besides diverse large Quantities of Sugar and other Merchandise' (Pares, 25) consigned to Thomas Beckford, his cousin and London commission agent. Historian

Richard Pares has estimated that Beckford's 'whole fortune must have amounted to £300,000 or so' (ibid., 70).

Peter Beckford married Bathshua Hering; they had nine children: six sons, Peter, William *Beckford (*bap.* 1709, *d.* 1770), Richard, Nathaniel, Julines, and Francis, and three daughters, Ellis, Bathshua, and Elizabeth (1725–1791). By his will proved on 6 October 1735 Beckford gave and bequeathed to his wife £1000 sterling per annum and her choice of Dirty Pitt Pen or Dry Sugar Works. To his eldest son Peter he added to what he had already given him all of his property in Great Britain. He gave and bequeathed to his 'five sons now in England, vizt. William, Richard, Nathaniel, Julines & Francis all my Estates in Jamaica both real & personal to hold to them their Heirs & Assigns for ever' (will). He gave and bequeathed to his daughter Ellis £2000 Jamaica money and £500 to each of her two children. To his two youngest daughters, Bathshua and Elizabeth, he bequeathed £5000 Jamaica money. Elizabeth Beckford later married Thomas Howard, second earl of Effingham, and was the mother of Thomas Howard, third earl, who was governor of Jamaica in 1791 before his untimely death. Furthermore, Speaker Beckford gave and bequeathed to the poor of Jamaica £2000 Jamaica money, of which £1000 was to be given to the poor of St Catherine, and the other thousand to be applied towards the building of a free school or hospital for the poor. Other clauses in his will provided an annual salary for his white bookkeeper, and instructions to set free his 'Negro man Slave Named Diego' (ibid.) and allow him £10 per annum and the use of 10 acres of land.

Peter Beckford died, aged sixty-two, in Spanish Town, Jamaica, on 3 April 1735. He was succeeded in the bulk of his estate by his eldest son, Peter, but the latter's premature death in 1737 meant that most of the Beckford lands passed to his second son, Alderman William Beckford. In 1754 William possessed 22,021 acres of land, whereas Richard had 9241, Julines 8197 and Francis 2616. Beckford's greatest legacy was that he had accumulated an estate great enough to support his sons in their British ambitions; three, William, Richard, and Julines, became members of parliament. RICHARD B. SHERIDAN

Sources B. Alexander, *England's wealthiest son: a study of William Beckford* (1962) · W. A. Feurtado, *Official and other personages of Jamaica from 1655 to 1790* (1896) · C. Leslie, *A new history of Jamaica* (1740) · inventories, Jamaica Public RO, Spanish Town, Jamaica, vols. 18–21 · will, Jamaica Public RO, Spanish Town, Jamaica [proved 6 Oct 1735] · will, PRO, PROB 11/677, fols. 47r–49r · R. Pares, *Merchants and planters* (1960) [Economic History Review, suppl. 4] · list of landholders in Jamaica, 1754, PRO, CO 142/31 · J. Brooke, 'Introductory survey', HoP, *Commons, 1754–90*, 1.1–204 · G. Metcalf, *Royal government and political conflict in Jamaica, 1729–1783* (1965) · R. B. Sheridan, *Sugar and slavery: an economic history of the British West Indies, 1623–1775* (1974)

Wealth at death approx. £300,000: will, Jamaica Public RO, Spanish Town; Pares, *Merchants and planters*, 25, 70

Beckford, Peter (1739/40–1811), dog breeder and writer on hunting, was the son of Julines Beckford (1717?–1764) of Steepleton Iwerne, Dorset, and Elizabeth, daughter of Solomon Ashley or Ashby, of Northamptonshire. His

Peter Beckford (1739/40–1811), by Pompeo Batoni, 1766

grandfather was Peter *Beckford (*bap.* 1643, *d.* 1710), sugar planter and lieutenant-governor of Jamaica, and William Beckford (*d.* 1770), lord mayor of London, was his uncle. He was educated at Westminster School, which he left in 1752. After a year's private tuition he entered New College, Oxford, matriculating on 12 April 1757 and leaving later that year without a degree. On 22 March 1773 he married Louisa (1755/6–1791), daughter of the politician George Pitt (later Lord Rivers); they had four children, two of whom died in infancy. Of the two surviving children, William Horace, who was to succeed his father, was born on 2 December 1777, and Harriet, the daughter whom he idolized, in 1779. The marriage was beset by problems, particularly when the couple were living in England. They spent a good deal of time in Italy, where their relationship improved, but whatever benefits their emotional life gained from the change of climate were more than counterbalanced by its debilitating effect on Louisa's health, which had been poor since 1784. She contracted a fever and on 30 April 1791 died in Florence, aged thirty-five.

Beckford's reputation rests largely on the two works he issued in 1781, *Thoughts upon Hare and Fox Hunting in a Series of Letters* and *Essays on Hunting: Containing a Philosophical Enquiry into the Nature of Scent*. The former was a particularly popular work, and in 1798 Beckford successfully sued a publisher for issuing a pirated edition of it two years earlier. Beckford's works were remarkable because they detailed the grubby nitty-gritty of animal husbandry in a light, eloquent prose. Clearly an expert in every aspect of managing hunting animals, Beckford offered detailed advice on all aspects of animal welfare, specializing at various periods in the breeding of harriers, foxhounds, and buck-hounds. Almost a hundred years later his tips on various practical topics were quoted in D. P. Blaine's authoritative *An Encyclopaedia of Rural Sports* (1870). For all his eloquence, however, his works were already proved to be somewhat out of date, on account of their discussion of an older, slower, form of hunting using harriers not foxhounds. In *Thoughts upon Hare and Fox Hunting* he wrote:

> the morning is the part of the day which generally affords the best scent; and the fox himself is, in such a case, then less able to run away from you … the whole aim of fox hunting being to keep the hounds well in blood, sport is but a secondary consideration. (p. 173)

By contrast, adherents to a new system, introduced by Hugo Meynell and well established by the 1770s, started hunting at midday and pursued the fox for many hours, often at great speed. Ironically, it appears that many of the hounds from Meynell's famous Quorn pack were originally bred by Beckford, who sold them when he went on one of his extended foreign excursions.

These foreign tours, which began in 1765, reveal Beckford to have been a man of considerable culture, fluent in a number of languages. During several long stays on the continent he visited such intellectual celebrities as Voltaire, Rousseau, and Lawrence Sterne. Beckford had an eye for detail and recorded his observations of foreign life in a large number of entertaining letters, collected and published as *Familiar Letters from Italy to a Friend in England* (1805). His foreign travels appear to have continued into the 1790s, when Napoleon's advance in Italy forced Beckford to make a rapid exit to Sardinia. After this his appetite for the continent seems to have palled somewhat.

Despite his significant social and matrimonial connections, apart from becoming MP for Morpeth in 1768 Beckford exerted comparatively little political influence. His last years were spent back in England where in 1802 a special patent granted that his son, William Horace, could succeed to Lord Rivers's barony. Neither Beckford nor his son appears to have been wise with money and the family estate was heavily mortgaged, prompting a number of letters from Beckford to his son urging retrenchment. Beckford died at Steepleton Iwerne on 18 February 1811, aged seventy-one, leaving a voluminous will in which he expressed immense affection for his daughter. He was buried at Steepleton Iwerne church with a piece of doggerel,

> We die and are forgotten; 'tis Heaven's decree:
> Thus the fate of others will be the fate of me,

inscribed above his grave (Higginson, 25).

ADRIAN N. HARVEY

Sources A. H. Higginson, *Peter Beckford, Esquire* (1937) · Watt, *Bibl. Brit.* · N. Elias and E. Dunning, *The quest for excitement* (1986) · J. Brooke, 'Beckford, Peter', HoP, *Commons*

Likenesses P. Batoni, oils, 1766, Statens Museum for Kunst, Copenhagen [*see illus.*]

Wealth at death see will, Higginson, *Peter Beckford*, 290–301

Beckford, William (*bap.* 1709, *d.* 1770), planter and politician, was baptized on 19 December 1709, in Jamaica, the son of Peter *Beckford (*d.* 1735), sugar planter, speaker of the Jamaica house of assembly, and comptroller of customs, and Bathshua, daughter and coheir of Julines Hering, also of Jamaica. His grandfather, Peter *Beckford (*bap.* 1643, *d.* 1710), went to Jamaica as a young man, was the founder of the greatest sugar fortune in the West Indies, and served as lieutenant-governor of the island. The Jamaican Beckfords were descended from a cadet branch of a family long established in Gloucestershire. One ancestor was Sir William Beckford, who was among the principal adherents of Richard III.

Education in England At the age of fourteen, in 1723, Beckford arrived in England. He was placed under the care of the Revd Robert Freind, then the able headmaster of Westminster School, who in later years spoke of Beckford as one of the best scholars the school ever had. At Westminster Beckford secured the lasting friendship of William Murray, later first Lord Mansfield, the chief justice. From Westminster he went to Balliol College, Oxford, in 1721–5. In 1731 he was admitted to the University of Leiden as a medical student and studied under Albinus and Boerhaave. From there he went to Paris and studied at the Hôpital des Invalides (Alexander, *England's Wealthiest Son*, 31–5; Smith, 18).

Managing the Jamaican estates The sudden death of his father on 3 April 1735 forced Beckford to abandon his medical studies and return to Jamaica to help manage the family estates. Two years later, on the death of his elder brother Peter who was principal heir of Peter Beckford II, William inherited the greater part of the family's vast estates in Jamaica. The remainder went to the younger sons—Richard, Nathaniel, Julines, and Francis. Inventories of Peter Beckford II in 1739 show that he was sole owner of eleven sugar plantations and part owner of five more, and that he was sole owner of 1737 slaves and half owner of 577 others (Pares, *Merchants and Planters*, 25; Jamaica Public Record Office, wills series). That William Beckford in the course of three decades inherited and added to his Jamaica sugar properties until they probably exceeded the total bequeathed by his father to his six sons is shown by inventories taken after his death in 1770. William Beckford's estate in Jamaica consisted of thirteen sugar plantations in sole ownership, together with numerous smaller establishments such as provision plantations, cattle pens, and stores, and approximately 3000 slaves (Jamaica Public Record Office, inventories series). Lands held by the Beckford brothers in Jamaica in 1754 totalled 42,075 acres, of which William held 22,021, Richard 9241, Julines 8197, and Francis 2616 (PRO, CO 142/31).

Jamaican politics Beckford lived in Jamaica during an eventful period in the island's history. He saw the end of a

William Beckford (*bap.* 1709, *d.* 1770), by unknown engraver, *c.*1769

long period of armed conflict between the highly organized frontier communities of maroons, or runaway slaves and their descendants, and local militia units and British regiments. He was present at the centre of the trade conflict between Spain and Britain which erupted into international war from 1739 to 1748. Beckford befriended Cudjoe, the maroon leader, whom he took sailing and got thoroughly seasick. He also became an enthusiastic member of his local militia unit. In 1737 he was elected to a vacancy in the Jamaica house of assembly from his home parish of Clarendon. There he took an active part in legislative matters, serving on committees that were concerned with strengthening the island's fortifications, suppressing clandestine trade, laying duties on wines and spirituous liquors, encouraging white immigrants from Scotland, inspecting the courts of justice, and preventing frauds and breaches of trust by attorneys or agents of absentee proprietors. William was not the only Beckford to serve in the Assembly; indeed, he was joined by brothers Richard, Julines, and Nathaniel, by cousin Ballard Beckford, and by cousins who had married Beckford women. During the nearly ten years that William Beckford lived in Jamaica he was primarily occupied with the management of his numerous properties; that is, purchasing lands, slaves, equipment, and supplies; lending money to impecunious planters; and engaging in trade and shipping (Feurtado, 8–10; Metcalf, 17, 21–2, 64, 78).

Return to Britain and involvement in British politics An item in the *Journals of the Assembly of Jamaica* for 20 December 1744 says, 'Resolved, That Mr. W. Beckford and Mr. Baldwin, having departed this island without leave, be and stand expelled the house' (*J.A.J.*, 3.672). Settling in London, where he was described as a West India merchant, Beckford's trading interests seem to have been restricted to supervising the sale of the produce of his own estates and the purchase of equipment and supplies to send to Jamaica. He also became involved in the metropolis in high finance. Richard Pares observed that 'the Beckford family had made its huge fortunes by a judicious combination of money-lending with planting' (Pares, *War and Trade in the West Indies*, 514).

Within three years of his arrival in England Beckford had entered parliament. On the interest of the fourth earl of Shaftesbury, with whom he was closely associated in politics, he was elected member of parliament for Shaftesbury, where he served from 1747 to 1754. From 1754 until his death in 1770 he served as MP for London. Absentee planters from the West Indies were widely criticized for their identification with slavery, penchant for conspicuous consumption, purchase of rotten borough seats in parliament, and manipulation of the sugar market. The Beckford brothers were singled out for criticism in a pamphlet of 1754, asserting that 'No less than three brothers from one of our Sugar-islands having offered themselves, one for London, one for Bristol, and one for Salisbury; and a fourth brother, according to what has been published in the publick papers, intended for a Wiltshire Borough' (*A Short Account of the Interest and Conduct of the Jamaica Planters*, 1754, 3).

On 25 June 1752, with the support of tory allies in the House of Commons and the City of London, Beckford took up the freedom of the Ironmongers' Company and shortly after was elected alderman of Billingsgate ward. Two years later he was elected simultaneously member of parliament for the City of London and the borough of Petersfield, and chose to sit for London. In 1755 he was installed in the office of sheriff of London. He was again elected MP for the City of London on 4 April 1761, and before the close of the following year he became lord mayor. He served another term as lord mayor in 1769 and 1770, prior to his death in June of the latter year. Beckford's mayoralty was memorable for its luxurious character. While extremely moderate in his own diet, his public banquets were most sumptuous, attended by dukes, marquesses, earls, viscounts, barons, and members of the Commons and the livery companies (Beaven, *Aldermen of London*, 1.81, 280, 348).

Estates and marriage Compared with the knowledge of his public life, little is known of Beckford's private life. About 1736 he purchased the 4000 or 5000 acre estate of Fonthill in Wiltshire. Here he built one of the most splendid mansions in England and furnished it on a lavish scale. In 1756, at the age of forty-seven, he married Maria, daughter of

the Hon. George Hamilton, second son of James, sixth earl of Abercorn, and widow of Francis Marsh, another City man. Beckford's only legitimate son was William Thomas *Beckford (1760–1844), the eccentric dilettante, author of the Gothic novel *Vathek*, and builder of Fonthill Abbey. He was the sole heir of his father's estates in Jamaica and England, which were reputed to yield about £40,000 a year and to be equal to those of Robert Clive, the nabob. Alderman Beckford fathered six illegitimate sons and two daughters, who were recognized in his will. During his lifetime it was a commonplace for public figures to keep mistresses and walk out in public with them. A nephew of some prominence was William Beckford of Somerley (1744–1799), the illegitimate son of Richard Beckford. He was the historian of Jamaica who had spent several years as a debtor in the Fleet prison (Alexander, *England's Wealthiest Son*, 31–58, 151; HoP, *Commons*; Sheridan, 1964, 36–58).

Beckford and the West Indian interest Beckford was the leader of an influential group of MPs who were absentee proprietors from the West Indies. They were concerned with resolving political debates in their favour regarding such matters as military defence of the colonies, trade and shipping, and public and private finance. According to Dame Lillian M. Penson, 'At the time when the greatest successes were won for the West India interest, the agents were aided by the assistance of a powerful body of men, including Beckford, the intimate associate of the Elder Pitt, and a vast number of others whose wealth could command influence in British politics' (L. M. Penson, *Colonial Agents*, 25).

It may seem incongruous for a colonial slave owner of great wealth to also be a radical middle-class reformer of the British government, but that was the role Beckford played in his devoted support of William Pitt, the 'great commoner'. He used his power in the City of London to further the cause of Pitt's government in national politics. These reforms included annual parliaments, equal representation, extension of the franchise, invalidation of general warrants, and championing the rights of the American colonies. Beckford's speech in the House of Commons on 13 November 1761 defined

> the middling people of England as the manufacturer, the yeoman, the merchant, the country gentleman, they who bear all the heat of the day. … They have a right, Sir, to interfere in the condition and conduct of the nation. … [They] are a good natured, well-intentioned and very sensible people who know better perhaps than any other nation under the sun whether they are well governed or not. (BL, Add. MSS, 38, 334, fols. 29ff)

The Beckfords were newcomers to the British ruling class, which was beginning to include not only the old aristocracy and county families, but also those who had acquired wealth and gained influence through commerce, slave-plantation agriculture, eminence in the professions, or adventure and speculation. As with the *nouveaux riches* at other times and places, the leaders of these new families were targets of criticism for their bad manners and ostentatious lifestyles. William Beckford, the rich colonial, occupied a difficult position in English society because of his ugly Jamaican accent, lack of charm, and ostentatious display of immense wealth. He was reputed to have had a violent temper and a streak of vulgarity. Horace Walpole described Beckford as a 'noisy good humoured flatterer', vulgar and absurd, pompous in his expense, and vainglorious (Walpole, *Memoirs of the Reign of George II*, 1849, 3.177).

Beckford, Wilkes, and death The most controversial event in Beckford's political career came in 1770, in connection with the Middlesex parliamentary election. John Wilkes, the political agitator and reformer and an alderman of London, had been elected to the House of Commons by a large majority, but was expelled by the government and his opponent returned in his place. Attended by the aldermen and common councilmen of London, Beckford marched from Guildhall to St James's Palace on 14 March 1770, and presented to George III a strongly worded address, remonstrance, and petition complaining that by supporting the government's action in the Middlesex election, he was tampering with the constitution and pursuing a course similar to that which lost James II his crown. The king's answer to the remonstrance was couched in words of strong reproof.

On 23 May of the same year Beckford, accompanied by the aldermen and livery, presented a second remonstrance to the crown from the City of London. When the king again expressed his dissatisfaction with the remonstrance, Beckford, either in an impromptu manner or by reading a prepared statement, had the temerity to respond to the king's reply. 'We do therefore, with the greatest humility and submission', he said, 'more earnestly supplicate your Majesty that you will not dismiss us from your presence without expressing a more favourable opinion of your faithful citizens, and without some comfort, some prospect, at least, of redress' (Besant, 23–4). The king made no reply. Beckford was widely criticized for violating all custom and precedent by delivering a speech which had not been previously submitted to the king. On the other hand, his supporters in the City and elsewhere regarded his speech as an honourable and dignified assertion of the privileges of the City and the rights of the people. William Pitt, now Lord Chatham, declared that he was rejoiced 'to hear that my lord mayor asserted the City with weight and spirit', and that 'the spirit of old England spoke, that never to be forgotten day' (*Chatham Correspondence*, 3.459–60, 462–3).

Beckford died on 21 June 1770 while travelling from Fonthill to London, four weeks after his altercation with the king, from the effects of a violent fever, caused, as was supposed, by political excitement. He was buried on 30 June at Fonthill Gifford. His supporters showed their respect by voting a statue in his memory to be placed in the Guildhall; it represented him in his robes of office, delivering his speech to the king, which was inscribed on the pedestal in letters of gold. RICHARD B. SHERIDAN

Sources B. Alexander, *England's wealthiest son: a study of William Beckford* (1962) · W. A. Feurtado, *Official and other personages of Jamaica from 1655 to 1790* (1896) · R. W. Innes Smith, *English-speaking students of medicine at the University of Leyden* (1932) · L. B. Namier, *England in the age of the American revolution*, 2nd edn (1961) · R. Pares, *War and trade in the West Indies, 1739–1763* (1936) · R. Pares, *Merchants and planters* (1960) [Economic History Review, suppl. 4] · F. W. Pitman, *The development of the British West Indies, 1700–1763* (1917) · J. Adolphus, *The history of England from the accession to the decease of King George the third*, 1 (1840) · R. B. Sheridan, *Sugar and slavery: an economic history of the British West Indies, 1623–1775* (1974) · G. Metcalf, *Royal government and political conflict in Jamaica, 1729–1783* (1965) · K. Hotblack, *Chatham's colonial policy* (1917) · *GM*, 1st ser., 40 (1770) · *Annual Register* (1770) · B. Alexander, 'Fonthill and portraits of William Beckford (1760–1844)', *The Register of the Museum of Art, University of Kansas*, 3/8–9 (1967) · R. B. Sheridan, 'William Beckford (1744–1799), patron of painters of Jamaica', *The Register of the Museum of Art, University of Kansas*, 3/8–9 (1967) · R. B. Sheridan, 'Planter and historian: the career of William Beckford of Jamaica and England, 1744–1799', *The Jamaican Historical Review*, 4 (1964) · G. Rudé, *Wilkes and liberty: a social study of 1763 to 1774* (1962) · L. B. Namier, *The structure of politics at the accession of George III*, 2nd edn (1957); repr. (1961) · R. Porter, *English society in the eighteenth century* (1982) · W. Besant, *London in the eighteenth century* (1903), 23–7 · HoP, *Commons* · DNB · will, PRO, PROB 11/595, sig. 256

Archives BL, corresp. relating to Porto Bello, Add. MS 12431 | PRO, letters to first earl of Chatham, PRO 30/8

Likenesses attrib. T. Kettle, oils, 1760–70, Palace of Westminster, London · J. F. Moore, marble statue, 1767, Ironmonger's Hall, London · J. Dixon, mezzotint, pubd 1769, BM, NPG · R. Houston, group portrait, mezzotint, pubd 1769, BM, NPG · engraving, c.1769, NPG [see illus.] · J. Kirk, bronze medal, 1770, priv. coll. · N. Smith, terracotta model, 1770, V&A · J. F. Moore, statue, 1772, Guildhall, London · attrib. J. Reynolds, oils, Upton House, Warwickshire · mezzotint, BM · portrait, repro. in Besant, *London in the eighteenth century*, 25 · print, NPG

Beckford, William (1744–1799), sugar planter and historian, was born in Jamaica in 1744, the son and heir of Richard Beckford (d. 1756) and his common-law wife, Elizabeth Hay. His uncle was William Beckford, lord mayor of London, and his first cousin was William Thomas Beckford of Fonthill Abbey, the author of *Vathek*. In 1762 he matriculated from Balliol College, Oxford, and three years later was designated a master of arts. In 1767 or 1768 he went abroad with two companions under the travelling preceptorship of the traveller and author Patrick Brydone and made an extensive tour of the continent.

At the death of his father in 1756 Beckford inherited the greater of part of his estate in Great Britain and Jamaica. It consisted chiefly of four sugar estates and 910 slaves in Jamaica. The total value of the estate was approximately £120,000 sterling. Beckford and his wife (about whom nothing is known) went to Jamaica in February 1774 and remained there for thirteen years. Beckford was primarily concerned to restore his estates to their former productive levels and to pay off accumulated debts, but he was thwarted by trade dislocations during the American War of Independence, the negligence of his plantation attorneys, and destructive hurricanes. During his stay in Jamaica he was a patron of painters, whom he invited to his home on the island. One of these was Philip Wickstead, who was chiefly a portrait painter; another was George Robertson, who was mainly a landscape painter. Among the latter's paintings are six *Views in Jamaica*, which include Beckford's sugar plantations. Beckford was the exceptional planter whose education, travel, and love

William Beckford (1744–1799), by unknown engraver, pubd 1799 (after John? Miers)

From a Shade by Miers

of art placed him in a unique position to describe the island's scenic splendours in his writings and to patronize painters he had befriended in England.

Beckford returned to England in 1786. Within a few days of his landing he was intercepted by a bailiff and incarcerated in the Fleet prison as a debtor. He later wrote that his onerous situation was the consequence of 'imprudences which I might have prevented, and of misfortunes which I could not foresee' (Beckford, *Descriptive Account*, 1.v). His imprudence was to become a security for a friend, and his misfortunes stemmed from destruction to his properties from the great hurricane of 1780. In the confines of the Fleet prison he took up his pen, partly to gain the attention of men of influence who might intervene on his behalf, partly to relieve his pecuniary embarrassment, and partly to defend the institution of slavery at the same time that he urged a course of amelioration upon his planter friends in the West Indies. His published works were *Remarks upon the situation of the negroes in Jamaica, impartially made from a local experience of nearly thirteen years in that island* (1788), *A descriptive account of the island of Jamaica: with remarks upon the cultivation of the sugar-cane throughout the different seasons of the year, and chiefly considered in a picturesque point of view* (1790), and *History of France from the most Early Records to the Death of Louis XVI* (1794); the early part of this last is by Beckford, and the more modern by an anonymous Englishman who had been sometime resident in Paris.

Beckford died on 5 February 1799, of an apoplectic fit, at the home of his cousin by marriage, the earl of Effingham, in Wimpole Street, London. He is said to have prided himself on his friendships with Sir Joseph Banks, Sir Joshua Reynolds, and the duke of Dorset.

RICHARD B. SHERIDAN

Sources GM, 1st ser., 69 (1799), 172 • V. L. Oliver, ed., *Caribbeana*, 1 (1909–10), 95–6 • W. Beckford, *Remarks upon the situation of the negroes in Jamaica, impartially made from a local experience of nearly thirteen years in that island* (1788) • W. Beckford, *A descriptive account of the island of Jamaica: with remarks upon the cultivation of the sugar-cane throughout the different seasons of the year, and chiefly considered in a picturesque point of view*, 2 vols. (1790) • *An unpublished letter of William

Beckford of Hertford, ed. T. B. Brumbaugh, Jamaica Monograph, no. 17 • F. Cundall, 'Jamaica worthies, William Beckford, historian', *Journal of the Institute of Jamaica*, 1/8 (1893); 2/2 (1895) • F. Cundall, *Historic Jamaica* (1915) • B. Alexander, *England's wealthiest son: a study of William Beckford* (1962) • inventories, Jamaica Public RO, vols. 18, 19 • wills, Jamaica Public RO, vol. 30 • R. Pares, *Merchants and planters* (1960) [*Economic History Review*, suppl. 4] • R. B. Sheridan, 'Planter and historian: the career of William Beckford of Jamaica and England, 1744–1799', *The Jamaican Historical Review*, 4 (1964), 36–58 • B. Alexander, 'Fonthill and portraits of William Beckford (1760–1844)', *The Register of the Museum of Art, University of Kansas*, 3/8–9 (1967), 14–23

Likenesses stipple, silhouette, pubd 1799 (after J.? Miers), BM, NPG; repro. in *Monthly Mirror* (1799) [*see illus.*]

Wealth at death probably bankrupt: Alexander, *England's wealthiest son*

Beckford, William Thomas (1760–1844), writer and art collector, was born at one of his father's houses, in Westminster or Fonthill, Wiltshire, and baptized soon afterwards at Fonthill on 6 January 1761, the only legitimate son of William *Beckford (bap. 1709, d. 1770), sugar planter and politician in Jamaica and London, and his wife, Maria, *née* Hamilton, granddaughter of the sixth earl of Abercorn. Maria was the widow of Francis Marsh, another Jamaican planter and City man, with whom she had a daughter, Elizabeth. Beckford's grandfather Peter *Beckford (bap. 1643, d. 1710) founded the greatest sugar fortune in the West Indies; the family owned twenty estates. Peter and his son were important figures in Jamaican political life, but in 1744 William Beckford senior returned to London, whence he managed his overseas interests. About 1756 he purchased a 4000–5000 acre estate in Wiltshire. He replaced the earlier house in 1768 with a Palladian mansion, Fonthill, so lavishly furnished that it was named by Colt Hoare, and afterwards generally known, as Splendens. He entered parliament, sitting as MP for Shaftesbury from 1747 to 1754, then for London, until his death in 1770. He was alderman for Billingsgate, served as sheriff, and held office as lord mayor in 1762–3 and again in 1769–70.

Education and travels His father's death left the young Beckford in the nominal charge of three guardians, but under the day-to-day control of his possessive and tyrannical mother and her Hamilton relatives. She had him educated at Fonthill, first under the dour Scot Robert Drysdale, then under the Revd John Lettice. He found more sympathetic tutors in Alexander Cozens, his drawing master, and Sir William Chambers, who also taught him drawing and the rudiments of architecture. Cozens had spent his early life in Russia and introduced Beckford to the Arabic and Persian languages. He taught at Eton College and had numerous pupils besides Beckford. Chambers had also spent many years in India and China, and, no doubt encouraged by their stories, William acquired a familiarity with the characters and background of oriental tales, to the extent that thereafter he referred to his mother as the Begum, wielding power over her empire. This eastern influence shows up in his earliest writings. At Fonthill he was surrounded by his father's books and works of art, and from the duty of taking visitors round Splendens he began to compile the witty parodies of

William Thomas Beckford (1760–1844), by George Romney, 1781–2

imaginary artists later published as *Biographical Memoirs of Extraordinary Painters* (1780), although the artist and diarist Joseph Farington was dismissive: 'The book on painters foolish' (Farington, *Diary*, 3.756).

To complete his education, Beckford was sent in 1777, along with his tutor Lettice, to live in Geneva with his uncle, Colonel Hamilton, a former soldier of the East India Company army. In Switzerland he was emotionally moved by the dramatic landscapes and skies, and in his writing he often described his inner feelings in terms of landscape. His lively letters to his step-sister Elizabeth Hervey contained passages moving towards story form. In a letter to Cozens in 1777–8 he described a building with a Gothic tower and baronial hall with stained glass and brightly coloured interior—a vision reinforced by his visit to the Grande Chartreuse, where he was welcomed as the custodian of Witham Priory, the earliest Carthusian house in England, inherited from his father; this vision remained to inspire his own later building of Fonthill Abbey. Some of Beckford's writing from this time has only recently been published; it includes *A Vision* (1930), and some at least of the tales published as *Suites de contes arabes* (1991). He befriended artists of the Swiss landscapes, maintaining a friendship with Jean Huber and his son over many years. By the time that he returned to England

in December 1778 Beckford had managed to meet the aged Voltaire at Ferney and various other notables.

In the last year of his minority Beckford and Lettice went on the grand tour, arriving in Venice in 1780. Familiar with its history, he explored the monuments and churches, recalling their ancient past. Here he moved in the circle of Madame d'Orsini-Rosenberg and enjoyed a romantic attachment to a young man of the distinguished Cornaro family. Music was a major theme of his residence. He became an acquaintance of the influential castrato Gasparo Pacchierotti, who later performed at Beckford's twenty-first birthday party. This musical environment may have inspired his only published score, for an overture to the ballet *Phaeton*, engraved in Paris in 1781–2, but he left various other scores for songs and small orchestral pieces, written between 1780 and 1839. His commentary on the Venetian-born artist and architect G. B. Piranesi (1720–1778) began a fashion for 'Gothic' depictions of the artist that were later pursued by, among others, Samuel Taylor Coleridge and Thomas De Quincey. Beckford next moved on to Lucca, revelled in the Medici collections at Florence, called at Pisa, and was completely overcome by the vast delights of Rome. His arrival there excited the artists, but their hopes that he might commission some works seem on this occasion to have been misplaced. He arrived in Naples in November as the guest of his kinsman Sir William Hamilton and to be cared for by his wife Lady Catherine, with whom Beckford shared a passion for music. She became a good friend and confidante.

Beckford came into his inheritance in 1782, an event celebrated at a cost of £40,000 by lavish entertainments at Splendens. At the Christmas party that year he hired the theatrical designer Philip de Loutherbourg to convert Splendens into a scene of hedonistic richness, full of light and colour. None the less, the delights of Italy proved more attractive than those of Wiltshire, and he departed for Naples in the following year. Besides Lettice and John Robert Cozens, the artist son of Alexander, he was accompanied by Projectus Errhardt, his physician, John Burton the harpsichordist, and many servants. So grand was his retinue that in Augsburg he was taken for the emperor of Austria. They passed through Venice, Padua, and Rome, reaching Naples in July, where he lived in Sir William Hamilton's villa at Portici. Most of the party caught malaria; Burton died in Naples, and Cozens was ill for a long time and rejoined Beckford only later, at Geneva. Lady Hamilton also succumbed, and after her death on 25 August Beckford returned to England. A collection of Beckford's travel writings was published in 1783 under the title *Dreams, Waking Thoughts and Incidents, in a Series of Letters from Various Parts of Europe.* Part 1 chronicled his European tour of 1780 as far as Naples; part 2 the second journey to Naples in 1782; part 3 his visit to Switzerland in 1778, including the Grande Chartreuse. This time Farington enthused about a publication 'written with genius— full of reflections on individuals and on nations—malevolent and expressive of a bad heart. The descriptions of landscapes &c were admirable, throughout the whole there was a spirit like Champaigne prevailing, sparkling everywhere' (Farington, *Diary*, 4.755). But Beckford was persuaded to suppress its distribution by his family, who were concerned that its contents might prove damaging to his reputation.

Plans were now ongoing to secure Beckford the social position his birth deserved. His family decided that he should find a wife, and in May 1783 he married Lady Margaret Gordon, aged twenty-one and daughter of the impoverished earl of Aboyne; their first child, Maria Margaret Elizabeth, was born in 1784. At his coming of age Lord Shelburne had endeavoured to interest Beckford in politics, but without much success. However on 2 April 1784 he wrote to his guardian, Lord Thurlow, that he was willing to sit in parliament and he was duly elected MP for Wells, a seat once held by his maternal grandfather. A letter to his cousin Louisa Beckford implies that William had taken his seat in the Commons, but that he was already pressing Lord Thurlow to procure him a peerage. A title was approved, and his name was included in published lists of forthcoming creations, but it was then his world collapsed about him in consequence of his infamous relationship with William Courtenay.

The Beckford scandal and the writing of *Vathek* In autumn 1784 Beckford was entangled in a romantic affair with Louisa, daughter of George Pitt MP and wife of his cousin Peter Beckford, and at the same time enamoured of Viscount William Courtenay (1768–1835), 'one of the most beautiful boys in England and the spoilt child of doting parents and thirteen sisters' (Gray, 23). They had first met at Splendens during his coming-of-age party. All three were at Powderham Castle, seat of Courtenay's father, the earl of Devon, when, according to Farington, who heard it later from Benjamin West, the affair with Louisa

> was discovered by a letter carelessly dropped by *young Mr Courtenay*. Beckford, on discovering it, went to his [Courtenay's] room, and horsewhipped him, which created a noise, and the door being opened, Courtenay was discovered in his shirt, and Beckford in some posture or other—Strange story. (Farington, *Diary*, 4.1175)

Courtenay's uncle, Lord Loughborough, who was Beckford's political enemy, took advantage of the episode to wage a press campaign against Beckford. While the accusations hinted at a homosexual act, at a time when sodomy was punishable by death, no charges were ever laid against Beckford and it remains unclear whether the relationship had exceeded the bounds of youthful sentimentality. But his reputation was destroyed, and henceforth he was a social outcast among English communities at home and overseas.

Obliged to go abroad, the Beckfords travelled to Switzerland and took up residence in a secure house at La Tour de Peilta, near Vevey. It was here that he composed, in French, his oriental novel *Vathek*, which remains his best-known literary work. The novel relates the story of the Caliph Vathek and his journey to Eblis, or hell, together with the conjoined tales, or Episodes, being stories recounted to Vathek by those he meets in Eblis. Beckford faced more personal anguish when on 26 May 1786, soon after the birth of a second daughter, Susan Euphemia, his wife, Margaret, died. Beckford was devastated, and further wounded by accusations in the press that she had died in consequence of his ill-treatment. In August he received another set-back when an English version of *Vathek* was published, translated and annotated by the literary scholar Revd Samuel Henley, who had been his editorial collaborator on his earlier publication, *Dreams, Waking Thoughts and Incidents*. In his 'Introduction' to the English text, Henley claimed that the tale had been composed by 'a man of letters' who had gathered this and other stories while in the East; he signed the pirated copy, now at the Bibliothèque Nationale, 'From the author Revd S Henley' (May, 387). Henley had been translating the work under Beckford's supervision, but the 'Episodes' were still in progress, and Beckford had made it clear that he wished the French edition of *Vathek* to appear first. This, minus the 'Episodes', was finally published in Lausanne in 1787, but the numerous Anglicisms, untypical of a linguist of Beckford's ability, were, according to May, proof that Beckford had passed his only manuscript to Henley and had hastily recreated a French text by translating Henley's printed English version (ibid., 408). Though angered by the piracy, Beckford appreciated Henley's expertise as an orientalist and retained his notes to *Vathek* in this and in later editions. Of these, it was the 1834 English edition (part of Bentley's Standard Novels series) which secured *Vathek*'s success and celebrity as a classic of British Gothic fiction, alongside Horace Walpole's *The Castle of Otranto*, Ann Radcliffe's *Mysteries of Udolpho*, and Matthew Gregory Lewis's *The Monk*. Though less imitated than these other novels (not least because of its exotic setting and provocative sexual allusions), Beckford's story has inspired later works, including a symphonic poem, *Vathek* (1913), by the Portuguese composer Luís de Freitas Branco.

The 'Episodes', which Beckford had originally planned to be published with *Vathek*, comprised three stories. 'The Tale of Prince Alasi', a lightly disguised autobiography, charts the self-destructive qualities of an obsessional homosexual; 'The Tale of Prince Barkiarokh' is one of bawdy lust, while 'The Tale of Princess Zulkaïs and Prince Kalilah' explores an incestuous love between brother and sister. By their nature they could not be published independently of *Vathek* without risking further scandal and, having intended to include them in the corrected edition of *Vathek* published in Paris in 1815, Beckford withdrew them. The potential for controversy also prompted their exclusion from Bentley's edition of 1834. None the less Beckford retained an interest in their development, and throughout his life he revised the tales. As late as 1837 he provided another version of the first story, now entitled 'The Tale of Prince Alasi and the Princess Firouzka', in which the boy Firouz of the original essay is revealed as a princess in disguise. The 'Episodes' vanished after Beckford's death but were discovered by Louis Melville when he was researching the *Life and Letters*, and were translated by Sir Frank Marzials and published as W. B., *The Episodes of Vathek* (1912; repr. 1994).

Sojourns in Portugal Beckford returned to England from Switzerland in January 1787, a grieving widower whose two small children were put in the care of his mother. The whiff of scandal remained, and the family decided to send him to Jamaica, a most inappropriate setting for such a man. He sailed on 15 March, but decided to disembark at Lisbon, the first port of call. Robert Walpole, the English ambassador, was well aware of his reputation and refused to introduce him to Queen Maria, an action which automatically excluded him from official functions and the English community. Instead Beckford installed himself in the Ramalhão Palace at Sintra and soon found a warm welcome in the circle of Dom Diogo, fifth marquess of Marialva, and his family. He also met Gregorio *Franchi (1769/70–1828), the son of a Neapolitan singer in the Portuguese royal service. They became fast friends, and in 1788 Franchi's father, seeing Beckford's wealth as likely to benefit his son, sent him to join William, who was then in Madrid. When Franchi married in 1795 Beckford settled an annuity of £400 on the couple, but Franchi tired of married life and, leaving his wife and daughter in Lisbon, went to England where he collaborated with Beckford on the building and furnishing of Fonthill Abbey. He parted from Beckford about 1822 and lived in London until his death in August 1828.

Life in the upper strata of Portuguese society suited Beckford's temperament, even while he was amused by the comical gravity of the court, the protocol, the orientalizing dress of the women, and the eccentricity of the nobles. He had joked about the religious life while in Italy, but he was nevertheless sympathetic to the ritual of Roman Catholicism and claimed a special devotion to St Anthony of Padua. In Portugal he attended mass—behaving, as he tells us, with great piety. This apparent conversion naturally alarmed his family, to whom he wrote in 1795 to reassure them that he had not changed his religion.

Beckford was in Paris during the early part of the revolution in 1791, when he acquired certain possessions of fleeing aristocrats which were being sold by the state. He returned to Portugal later that year, living for a further twelve months at Monserrate, near Sintra, an estate rented from the English merchant Gerard Devisme. He practically rebuilt the houses he lived in, planning their gardens and importing exotic flowers. During his third visit, in 1793–6, he resided mostly at Sintra, inhabiting luxurious apartments near the convent of Our Lady of the Necessities and a more picturesque villa at the mouth of the Tagus. Resuming his friendship with Marialva, he was drawn again into a lively cosmopolitan circle, far from the revolutionary troubles in Europe and his own domestic difficulties. Youthful companions were always at hand; on his travels, as he tells us, his cavalcade resembled a caravan on its way to Mecca. He ran into trouble in 1793, when he got into a fight with a beggar and was injured, and again towards the end of 1794, when certain garments were stolen from his house. This third residence in Portugal was undoubtedly the most important, as in June 1794 he visited the monastery churches of Alcobaça and Batalha, both north of Lisbon in the province of Estremadura. These two sites differed considerably. Alcobaça had

been built by the Cistercians in the twelfth century in a style intermediate between Roman and Gothic. Batalha, built by the Dominicans in the late fourteenth century, was more massive and theatrical, reached, as Beckford's journey took him, across the plain of Aljubarrota, the field of a bloody battle in the fourteenth century. These two monuments strongly influenced his plans at Fonthill, where he was already engaged with a new building to replace Splendens.

In October 1795 Beckford embarked with the aim of sailing to Naples, but the ship was approached by pirates and took refuge at Alicante. From there he made several local excursions before travelling overland to England, where he arrived in June 1796. A sale of his goods was held in Lisbon after his departure. Little is known of his activities beyond some notes published long after the event. It seems, however, that Dom João commissioned him to send diplomatic intelligence, and that from time to time he reported back on British attitudes, probably through Marialva. In 1796–7 he bought Edward Gibbon's entire library, auctioned after his death for £950, 'to have something to read when I passed through Lausanne … I shut myself up for six weeks from early in the morning until night … The people thought me mad. I read myself nearly blind' (Redding, 2.332). Beckford travelled to Portugal for the last time in 1798–9, a pass being issued to him in October 1798. In March of the following year he received a permit to load on board the *Prince of Wales* packet six cases of goods, containing respectively wine, hams, books, prints, cotton fabric for hangings, and wardrobe fittings. Another permit was issued for goods shipped on *Harriot* in April.

The building of Fonthill Abbey About 1790 Beckford had approached the architect James Wyatt, who was already building in the Gothic style at Lee Priory, Kent. His intention was to make improvements and additions to Splendens, with a hill-top tower and a chapel on Stop's Beacon. While in Portugal he corresponded with Wyatt about projects in Lisbon and at Fonthill and, following Beckford's return to England in 1796, they at last proceeded with a scheme for a mock convent on the ridge of Hinkley Hill. This structure began as an octagonal chapel, and when Wyatt exhibited plans at the Royal Academy exhibition of 1797 it had acquired a squat tower and 145 foot spire, with apartments and galleries extending to the west and south. It owed much to Batalha, a church with which Wyatt was also familiar, and was also influenced by Monserrate.

In 1797 Joseph Farington, whose social circle included most of the architects and artists then active, confided to his diary that Beckford's income in this year was £155,000; that he had just received news of seven of his ships arriving uninsured, by which he had saved a further £12,000; and that he paid £75,000 duties on his sugar to the government. Backed by this reassuringly comfortable flow of money, Beckford had determined to pull down Splendens and to surround his tower with a complete building, which became Fonthill Abbey. Wyatt's designs, exhibited at the Academy exhibition of 1798, presented a spire of 300 feet and an extensive northern wing. In the following year plans showed the spire exceeding that of St Peter's in

Rome by 17 feet. By this time Beckford had decided that the abbey should house his mausoleum. The exact form taken by the original structure at any one time remains uncertain; the young J. M. W. Turner was commissioned to paint watercolours of the abbey against its landscape during construction, but in May 1800 the tower—hastily erected at Beckford's urging, and made of wood faced with Wyatt's 'compo-cement'—fell. It was repaired just in time for the most important visit in December 1800 of Horatio Nelson, Sir William Hamilton, and his second wife (and Nelson's mistress), Lady Emma. The party was accommodated at Splendens and taken to the abbey for an evening of theatrical display—the only recorded social event at Fonthill—to which Beckford invited all the artists who had collaborated on the abbey's construction and embellishment. Parts of Splendens were demolished in 1801–2, Beckford lodging in the remainder until 1806, when the site was cleared. Farington noted on 26 May 1801 that £242,000 had already been spent on Fonthill Abbey: 'It will cost him near as much more to complete it' (Farington, *Diary*, 4.1554). Few, however, doubted his ability to finish the work, as Beckford's (in truth fluctuating) fortune was by now legendary. Writing in 1809 Byron, who greatly admired Beckford's writing, included a reference to him in his *Childe Harold's Pilgrimage*—addressing him 'There thou too, Vathek! England's wealthiest son' (canto 1, stanza 22) in stanzas later published as 'To Dives' (1833).

Wyatt hired more men and the project speeded up in 1805, but much effort was expended in taking down other structures on the site clad in the compo-cement. By summer 1807 Beckford was able to move in, though scaffolding remained until 1809. Fonthill borrowed from Alcobaça the ogival vaults and the delicate tracery; from Batalha the overall effect, majestic and somewhat troubling. The Octagon, the main room at Fonthill, echoed the main room at Batalha, its star-shaped vault reflecting the light filtering through the glass. The price of sugar, which had fallen during the first decade of the nineteenth century, rose sharply again from 1812 and Beckford felt able to begin the eastern transept. Much of this was to his own design, and did not accord with the scale and proportions of the older work. Following Wyatt's death in September 1813, Beckford's megalomania was unrestricted. He devised a baronial hall on the second floor celebrating the signatories of Magna Carta, from all of whom he claimed descent, but it was never built. In addition to the structure itself Beckford built a wall 12 feet high surrounding the most elevated part of his 500 acres to exclude sightseers, and planted numerous pines and firs, hoping to recreate a romantic alpine landscape. Hares and game animals roamed free. Few visitors were invited, but he surrounded himself with youthful servants, causing a certain amount of jealousy between himself and Franchi. Poor parents were eager to place their sons in his service in the hope of being able to blackmail him; he was spied on and his letters opened, but Beckford was now too wary in his behaviour to give cause for such accusations, and it was Franchi who was preached against in the neighbouring Fonthill parish church.

Notwithstanding its magnificence the abbey continued to be a source of frustration for the gentleman architect. Beckford complained that there were no convenient living rooms, and although by 1818 there were eighteen bedrooms, with services, kitchen, and laundry, he had certainly given more thought to accommodating himself when dead than to his comforts while alive. By February of the following year the south-west tower, with his living quarters, was showing signs of fatigue and had to be rebuilt. It was again a period of declining sugar prices, which left him heavily in debt. With his Jamaican estates mortgaged, Beckford faced reality and held his first sale. In 1821 the *Gentleman's Magazine* reported that 'the tower is acknowledged to be a weak and dangerous structure and so tottering are the eight surmounting pinnacles that they are held on to their bases by strong iron bars' (*GM*, 1821, 2.495). In 1825 the tower collapsed for the final time, demolishing most of the western hall. As Wilton-Ely remarks: Beckford had planned a ruined convent—he now had a ruined abbey.

The collector Beckford inherited Splendens and its contents, a motley assemblage of ancient and modern art of many kinds, including a large organ. Three sales—held in 1801, 1802, and 1807—disposed of unwanted items (the organ, sold in 1807, is now in the Victoria and Albert Museum). Beckford began collecting before he had even conceived the abbey, buying on his visits to Europe and storing his purchases of art and books in a rented house in Paris which was looked after by Auguste Chardin, his book dealer during the difficult years of the revolution, until 1797, when Beckford's agent collected the contents and the products of further purchases. Beckford regularly attended sales, and profited hugely during the revolution, when much of the nobility hastily sold, or was forcibly deprived of, its possessions. From 1802 Franchi acted as Beckford's agent, buying from dealers and at auction, as well as working with Beckford in the design of metalwork and mountings for hardstone pieces.

The design of Fonthill Abbey, laid out as a cross, permitted long vistas past the lofty octagon. Each gallery was conceived as part of an elaborate scene of heraldic and genealogical decoration. The King Edward gallery centred on a portrait of Edward III, copied from the original at Windsor. Beckford's false claim for his daughter's descent from this monarch was shown by the arms and symbols of Edward as founder of the Order of the Garter, together with the knightly ancestors of his daughter. To his father's art collection Beckford added fine paintings from all periods. Two landscapes by Claude, *The Landing of Aeneas* and *The Sacrifice of Apollo*, were bought in Paris in 1799 for 6500 guineas and were sold in 1808 for 10,000 guineas (now in Anglesey Abbey, Cambridgeshire). Other works by Claude, Poussin, Murillo, Rembrandt, and Hogarth were also bought and sold during his lifetime, usually at a good profit. His Italian primitives included *The Crucifixion* in the style of Orcagna, Giovanni Bellini's *Doge Leonardo Loredan*, and Perugino's *Virgin and child with St John* (all National Gallery, London).

The galleries were lit by stained glass designed by Benjamin West and painted by Francis Eginton and his son, Francis the younger, and by James Pearson. According to Clive Wainwright, the Fonthill windows comprised the most extensive stained-glass commission ever carried out in Gothic revival buildings before the 1820s (Wainwright, 117). There were also examples of antique glass, including Renaissance roundels from the Château d'Écouen, which is among the finest and most important to survive from this period. Beckford did not disclose exactly how he had acquired it, and it may have passed through several hands before it entered his possession. Some of the *pietre dure* tables and other works, originally from Italy, may have been brought to Paris by Napoleon and obtained there by Beckford. A great *pietre dure* table-top of sixteenth-century Roman manufacture stood in the King Edward III gallery and is now at Charlecote Park, Warwickshire. The wooden tables in Tudor style may have been designed by Jeffry Wyatville. Beckford relied largely on the London cabinet-making firms of Foxall and Fryer, and of the two Robert Humes, father and son, carvers and gilders; Edward Foxall and Robert Hume also bought on his behalf. One of Beckford's earliest passions was for lacquer. The Japanese coffer (now at the Victoria and Albert Museum), possessed by Cardinal Mazarin about 1638 and subsequently acquired from the duc de Bouillon, was a great treasure. He also owned eighteenth-century French furniture incorporating Japanese panels. His collection of metalwork spanned the centuries, from Limoges enamels and medieval vessels to his own commissions, fabricated using his collection of agate, jade, rock crystal, and other semi-precious hardstones. His ceramics and statuary similarly ranged over time, including Greek and Roman marbles and bronzes to modern works. Among other major pieces in the collection was the Fonthill Ewer, probably created in a Prague workshop during the 1680s, and provided with enamelled gold mounts and diamonds in France, 1814–17; the fourth-century Rubens vase with a French gold mount, 1809–19 (Walters Art Gallery, Baltimore); and the Bureau du Roi Stanislas (Wallace Collection, London).

Throughout his later years Beckford was in almost daily communication with his booksellers, dealing in London with William Clarke and then with his son George, from whom he ordered numerous books for examination and kept only those few that pleased him. In his description of Beckford's library the elder Clarke noted a long series of Spanish and Portuguese chronicles, Elzevier classics, Gibbon's library, voyages, and travels, and remarked on the fine bindings, both from private libraries and commissioned by Beckford. The library also held cabinets of folio prints of old masters, all choice impressions. It was notable for the absence of Greek and Latin classics (W. Clarke, *Repertorium bibliographicum*, 2 vols., 1819, 203–330). Beckford presented some 6000–7000 books to his physician, Frederic Schöll, and was still able to bequeath 10,000 books and 80 manuscripts to his daughter Susan.

Last years and reputation By the 1820s Beckford's income from Jamaica had fallen catastrophically and was continuing to diminish. He was in huge debt to his West India merchants; mortgages on Fonthill were £70,000, with interest mounting relentlessly on all these debts. Some of his Jamaican estates were sold, but with falling sugar prices their value was now small. Beckford's son-in-law, the tenth duke of Hamilton, though eager to be master of Fonthill, nevertheless declined to advance £80,000 to deal with his most pressing debts. Eventually there was no option but to sell Fonthill. Arrangements were made for the auctioneers Christies to sell the abbey and its contents. But after they had spent many months listing the valuables and publicizing the forthcoming event, the sale was withdrawn. Beckford then negotiated a private sale of the abbey through the auctioneers Phillips; it was bought by John Farquhar, a gunpowder millionaire, for £300,000—more than Beckford had dared to hope for. Later sales in 1823 attracted many visitors to this previously inaccessible building and disposed of much of his art. Two years later Farquhar saw his own investment collapse into ruins.

On leaving Fonthill Beckford retired with a choice selection of his art to a pair of houses in Lansdown Crescent, Bath, which he linked by a gallery room to span the intervening mews. He later sold the smaller house. He bought several small farms in order to own the fields between his house and Lansdown Hill, driving a linear track to its summit, landscaped by the gardener who accompanied him from Fonthill. He built a tower 120 feet tall, based on the Choragic monument of Lysicrates and surrounded by a two-storey block with rooms and a kitchen. Each morning he walked up the approach road, through a Norman gateway and flanked by such attractions as a Moorish kiosk, a Tuscan-style farmhouse, and an alpine garden. From the tower belvedere he could look out over five counties before rearranging his various treasures within the rooms.

Beckford was not on good terms with his daughter Maria Margaret Elizabeth, who had married Colonel James Orde without his consent. Susan's marriage to Alexander Douglas, from 1819 tenth duke of Hamilton (1767–1852), was more to his liking. Father and son-in-law corresponded, the duke receiving advice on his own collecting for the embellishment of Hamilton Palace, Lanarkshire. However Beckford, now in his seventies, seems to have grown dissatisfied and had a reputation for bad temper. Late in 1834 he commissioned Goodrich to devise a tomb of pink granite in the upper corridor of the tower; the project was abandoned, then revived in 1843 for a mausoleum elsewhere. He brought out his notebooks and diaries, editing them for publication as *Italy, with Sketches of Spain and Portugal* (1834) and *Recollections of an Excursion to the Monasteries of Alcobaça and Batalha* (1835). When Henry Venn called on Beckford in 1838 he met a small, slender, agile man of seventy-eight who, with his teeth gone, gave the impression that his nose nearly met his chin. Beckford died at Bath on 2 May 1844, having refused both protestant and Catholic rites; he was buried in the granite sarcophagus at nearby Lyncombe cemetery. His daughter Susan then presented a plot of his land to Walcot parish and his body, after the land was consecrated, was reinterred there. Susan inherited the major part of his estate, valued at under £80,000.

During the twentieth century editions of *Vathek* and *Dreams* have been published in English and in translation; Beckford's correspondence with Gregorio Franchi and with his book dealer have also been published. His manuscript diaries and journals, formerly with the Hamilton family, are now in the Bodleian Library, Oxford, where they are accessible to art historians studying his collecting practices. In 1995 the Beckford Society was founded to promote an interest in the man and his circle. It publishes the *Beckford Journal* and supports the preservation of Beckford's tower in Bath. The art itself has been widely dispersed, some items remaining at Brodick Castle, others passing into museums or private hands. In *The Rule of Taste* (1936) John Steegman described Beckford as an actor playing the leading role in his own theatre, but noted that the socialites of his day were not impressed by such drama: 'Men marvelled at Fonthill but did not imitate it; they stared at it, invented wild tales of what went on inside it, and when it fell down, forgot it' (p. 83). The late twentieth century saw a revival and broadening of interest in the man, not just for his literary work and personal conduct, but increasingly for his collecting and for what little remains of his building works. Following an exhibition at Yale in 1960, 'A viagem de uma paixão—William Beckford in Portugal' was held at the Palácio de Queluz in Lisbon in 1987, and 'William Beckford—an Eye for the Magnificent' celebrated his collecting in an exhibition held at the Bard Graduate Centre, Yale, in 2001–2 and at the Dulwich Picture Gallery in London in 2002. ANITA McCONNELL

Sources D. E. Ostergard, *William Beckford, 1760–1844: an eye for the magnificent* (2001) · J. Pinto de Carvalho, *Lisboa de Outrora*, 3 vols. (1938), vol. 1, pp. 99–112 · B. Alexander, ed., *The journal of William Beckford in Portugal and Spain, 1787–1788* (1954) · B. Alexander, *Life at Fonthill, 1807–1822, with interludes in Paris and London* (1957) · B. Alexander, *From Lisbon to Baker Street: the story of the Chevalier Franchi, Beckford's friend* (1977) · C. Wainwright, *The romantic interior: the British collector at home, 1750–1850* (1996) · T. Tuohy, 'Beckford at Dulwich', *British Art Journal*, 3/2 (2002), 81–2 · M. H. Port, 'Beckford, William (1760–1844)', HoP, *Commons, 1754–90* · Farington, *Diary* · J. Ingamells, ed., *A dictionary of British and Irish travellers in Italy, 1701–1800* (1997) · W. Beckford, '*Vathek*', with the '*Episodes of Vathek*', ed. G. Chapman (1929) · J. Whitton-Ely, 'The genesis and evolution of Fonthill Abbey', *Architectural History*, 23 (1980), 40–51 · R. G. Gemmett, ed., *The consummate collector: William Beckford's letters to his bookseller* (2001) · L. Melville, *The life and letters of William Beckford of Fonthill* (1910) · M. May, *La jeunesse de William Beckford et la genèse de son 'Vathek'* (1928) · C. Redding, *Memoirs of William Beckford of Fonthill*, 2 vols. (1859) · parish register, Fonthill Gifford, 6 Jan 1761, Wilts. & Swindon RO [baptism] · will, PRO, PROB 11/2005, fols. 314–5

Archives Bath Central Library, letters; sales catalogues · Bodl. Oxf., corresp. and papers; literary notes and Jamaican estate letter-books; commonplace books · Harvard U., Houghton L., papers, recollections · NRA, priv. coll., papers · Yale U., Farmington, Lewis Walpole Library, letters · Yale U., Beinecke L., letters and adversaria | V&A NAL, Forster MSS, letters, mainly to Henry Bohn

Likenesses G. Romney, oils, 1781–2, Upton House, Warwickshire [*see illus.*] · J. Reynolds, oils, 1782, NPG · J. Hoppner, oils, 1790–99, Salford City Art Gallery · caricature, etching, pubd 1826, NPG · W. Maddox, oils, 1844, Brodick Castle, Isle of Arran · F. Bromley, mezzotint, pubd 1862 (after J. Reynolds), BM, NPG · J. Doyle, lithograph, BM, NPG; repro. in *Equestrian sketches*, pl. 42 · A. de St Aubin, line engraving (after P. Sauvage), BM

Beckingham, Charles (1699–1731), poet and playwright, was born in London on 25 July 1699, the son of a linen draper in Fleet Street. Beckingham was educated at Merchant Taylors' School, London. He 'very early discovered an uncommon Genius in Poetry' (Whincop); Baker says 'he made a very great proficiency in all his studies, and gave the strongest testimonials of extraordinary abilities' (Baker). He did not however proceed to university.

On 18 February 1718 Beckingham's first play, *Scipio Africanus*, a five-act blank-verse tragedy, was performed at the theatre in Lincoln's Inn Fields. Dr Matthew Smith, assistant usher at Merchant Taylors', gave the boys a 'Holiday on the Afternoon of the Author's third Day, that those who pleased might pay their Compliments to their Schoolfellow at his Benefit' (Whincop). Despite this boost, and the presence of James Quin in the lead role, the play was performed only four times; unusually two of the nights were benefit nights. The play was printed the same year. It is founded on a story told by Livy (xxvi, 49–50), and by Polybius and Valerius Maximus: Scipio, having conquered Carthage but fallen in love with Almeyda, a captive woman, restores her to her Spanish lover Allucius; Scipio's invincible military prowess is contrasted with the greater struggle to master his own passions. The play was considerably puffed for its diction, its dramatic unity, and its characterization, by Giles Jacob in *The Poetical Register* (1723), but it was never revived.

A second tragedy by Beckingham, *Henry IV of France*, again turns on a contrast between political strength and amatory weakness in its depiction of the king's love for the prince de Condé's wife. But this play is more ambitious in its political and historical scope; it ends with a greater sense of catastrophe, in the assassination of the king by Ravaillac at the instigation of the villainous papal nuncio. The play was again performed four times at Lincoln's Inn Fields, with Quin in the title role, and an epilogue by George Sewell, from 7 November 1719, with two benefit nights. It was published by Edmund Curll with a dedication to the prominent whig politician Charles, earl of Sunderland, on 21 November. Curll paid 50 guineas for it, along with *Christus patiens, or, The Sufferings of Christ, an Heroic Poem*, a translation from the Latin of Rapin dedicated to Sir William Dawes, archbishop of York, and a fellow alumnus of Merchant Taylors'. For Curll, Beckingham edited a selection of *Maxims* from *The Guardian* (1719) and *Musarum lachrymae, or, Poems to the Memory of Mr. Rowe, Esq* (1719). His own 'Poem to the Memory of Nicholas Rowe, Esq' appeared in Rowe's *Poetical Works* of 1720. Beckingham followed this with *Verses on the Death of Mr. Prior*, dedicated to Lady Henrietta Cavendish (1721) and a dedicatory poem to Allan Ramsay in the latter's *Works* of 1721. Beckingham was praised by his brother-in-law Thomas Cooke in *The Battle of the Poets* (1725). Later he produced *An Ode to the Right Honourable Sir Robert Walpole* (1726), *The Lyre* (1726), and *A Poem on His Most Sacred Majesty King George the IId, his Accession to the Throne* (1727). Dr Johnson thought he was the main author of *The Life of Mr. Richard Savage* (1727). Two humorous poems on sexual scandals are also ascribed to him: *Sarah the Quaker* (Bodl. Oxf., MS) and *An Epistle from Calista to Altamont* (both 1729). He did not merit a place in Pope's *Dunciad*, though James Thomson mentions him in a list of obvious dunces. He died on 18 February 1731.

PAUL BAINES

Sources T. Whincop, *Scanderbeg, or, Love and liberty: a tragedy* (1747) · C. J. Robinson, ed., *A register of the scholars admitted into Merchant Taylors' School, from AD 1562 to 1874*, 2 (1883) · D. E. Baker, *Biographia dramatica, or, A companion to the playhouse*, rev. I. Reed, new edn, rev. S. Jones, 3 vols. in 4 (1812) · [G. Jacob], *The poetical register, or, The lives and characters of all the English poets*, 2 vols. (1723) · E. L. Avery, ed., *The London stage, 1660–1800*, pt 2: *1700–1729* (1960), 482–4, 554–5 · C. Tracy, *The artificial bastard: a biography of Richard Savage* (1953) · S. Johnson, *Life of Savage*, ed. C. Tracy (1971) · J. Sambrook, *James Thomson, 1700–1748: a life* (1991), 50 · Genest, *Eng. stage* · A. Nicoll, *A history of English drama, 1660–1900*, 2 (1952) · *DNB*
Archives BL, MS receipt for copyright of *Henry IV*

Beckingham, Elias [Ellis] (*d.* 1307?), justice, came from Beckingham in Lincolnshire. He is first mentioned as a court clerk in 1258. He was probably already then a relatively senior clerk in the service of the senior royal justice, Gilbert of Preston. Beckingham was Preston's chief clerk in his final eyre circuit of 1268–72. He was a senior clerk of the Westminster bench between 1273 and 1278 and keeper of the writs and rolls there between 1278 and 1285. He was also a regular assize justice from 1273 onwards. In 1285 he became a justice of the Westminster bench. He was the only justice of that court not to be dismissed from office and punished for misconduct in 1289–90. He probably owed his survival to his good fortune in being absent from the court for a single term in 1288 while acting as a justice of the Dorset eyre, for at least one of his colleagues, Roger of Leicester, was dismissed and punished simply for failure to prevent wrongdoing by chief justice Weyland in litigation heard that term. He remained a justice of the Westminster bench until 1307, when he either died or retired from the court. Surviving law reports do not suggest that he made a major contribution to the court's work and there is some evidence to suggest that much of his time was spent on the more routine procedural business of the court.

Beckingham's major property acquisitions were at Bottisham in Cambridgeshire, and these were settled jointly on himself and his nephew John or niece Alice, the children of his sister Isolda and her husband Adam de Sancto Licio. As an ordained cleric, Beckingham held a succession of livings in Northamptonshire, Lincolnshire, and Rutland, and in Devon and Cornwall. He was presented to three of these livings by the abbey of Peterborough. He in turn assisted the abbey by acting as an intermediary in its acquisition of property at Polebrook and Southorpe in Northamptonshire pending the granting of a mortmain licence by the crown, and by acting as an arbitrator in the abbey's disputes with the bishop of Lincoln and the abbots of Barlings and Thorney. He seems also to have been a regular visitor to the abbey. He was buried in the church of Bottisham, where there is a monument dedicated to his memory. He may also have had the nave of Bottisham church rebuilt.

PAUL BRAND

Sources court of common pleas, feet of fines, PRO, CP 25/1 · Curia regis rolls, PRO, KB 26 · Common bench plea rolls, PRO, CP 40 · *Chancery records* · P. Brand, *The making of the common law* (1992) · P. A. Brand, *The earliest English law reports*, 1, SeldS, 111 (1995) · E. King, *Peterborough Abbey, 1086–1310: a study in the land market* (1973)
Likenesses memorial on brass matrix, Bottisham church, Cambridgeshire

Beckington [Bekynton], **Thomas** (1390?–1465), administrator and bishop of Bath and Wells, was the son of a weaver from Beckington, Somerset. He was admitted as a scholar to Winchester College in 1403, nominated a scholar of New College, Oxford, in 1406, and held a fellowship at New College between June 1408 and November 1420. He was sub-warden of the college in 1419. He was admitted BCL in 1414–15 and incorporated DCL in 1418. His college gave him his first living, the rectory of St Leonard's Chapel near Hastings, Sussex, in 1418, and his will shows that after Humphrey, duke of Gloucester, he regarded William Wykeham (*d.* 1404) and John Elmer, the head of Wykeham's diocesan administration, as his benefactors. He was made subdeacon in 1421 and ordained priest in 1423.

Probably on the resignation of his fellowship in 1420, and certainly by January 1423, Beckington came into the service of Duke Humphrey as his chancellor. However, by July 1422 and perhaps as early as 1419, he had acquired a still more important patron when he became a leading member of the provincial legal staff of Henry Chichele, archbishop of Canterbury; he was in office by February 1423 as dean of the court of arches, and by 1431 occupied the more senior post of official of the court of Canterbury, which he still held in April 1438. In spite of Humphrey's eminence, and the esteem that his will shows Beckington felt for the duke, it seems clear that the basis of Beckington's career was to be his work in the government of the English church. It was his ecclesiastical connections that brought him the lucrative rectory of Sutton Courtenay, Berkshire, in 1420, and a prebend in the church of Gnosall, Staffordshire, in 1423, while he was still only in minor orders, and also in just the two years 1423–4 canonries and prebends in York, Salisbury, and Penkridge, a parish in Ely diocese held only briefly, and the archdeaconry of Buckingham, the last 'by advice of the [king's] council' during a vacancy in the bishopric of Lincoln (*CPR, 1422–9*, 232).

Beckington was probably still Gloucester's chancellor when in 1427 he was granted a papal indult to visit his archdeaconry by deputy in response to a request from John, duke of Bedford, who wrote of the 'arduous public and private occupations' of his 'beloved clerk' both at home and abroad (Beckington, *Correspondence*, 2.255). Beckington may have remained in Gloucester's service until Bedford returned to head Henry VI's government in 1433. For eleven years he received no further ecclesiastical

Thomas Beckington (1390?–1465), tomb effigy

preferment, but he remained an influential figure in provincial affairs: in 1428 he was one of the collectors of a clerical subsidy, and in 1433–4 and 1438 he was prolocutor of the lower clergy in the Canterbury convocation. Early in 1432, moreover, he was a member of an embassy appointed to negotiate a peace or truce with France and was abroad during the autumn and winter of that year.

The beginning of Henry VI's personal rule brought Beckington into prominence. Probably in 1437, and certainly by February 1438, he was the king's secretary. In 1439 he was appointed to serve under Cardinal Beaufort to negotiate with the French at Calais and kept a journal of its progress. On 28 May 1442 he was appointed to what was to be his final embassy, to treat for a marriage between the king and a daughter of Jean (IV), count of Armagnac. On his return, without a match, in February 1443 he met the king at Maidenhead and in the next few days visited the duke of Gloucester, the lord mayor of London, and Ralph, Lord Cromwell, the treasurer, before rejoining the king at Sheen. Five months later, on 18 July, he was moved to the keepership of the privy seal.

Beckington's intimacy with Henry VI inevitably led to his involvement with the king's foundation of Eton College as an overseeing commissioner in 1440. He was also involved in conveying land to both Wykeham's foundations. There had, of course, been ecclesiastical preferment since 1435: richer stalls at York and Salisbury, additional ones at Lichfield, London, and Wells, the mastership of St Katharine by the Tower, which gave him a London base, and a prebend in the chapel of Exeter Castle. On 12 April 1443 Beckington's patron Archbishop Chichele died, to be succeeded by John Stafford (d. 1452), bishop of Bath and Wells. It had been intended that William Aiscough, bishop of Salisbury, would move to Wells, but Aiscough refused to move, whereupon Beckington was nominated to succeed Stafford as bishop of Bath and Wells. He received papal provision on 24 July, the temporalities were restored on 24 September, and he was consecrated on 13 October 1443 in the old collegiate church at Eton. He celebrated his first mass as bishop in the partly built new church beside the college buildings. He resigned the privy seal on 11 February 1444, and although he occasionally attended the king's council up to 1454, he

was excused future attendance at both parliaments and councils on 18 June 1452, on account of age and infirmity.

The excuse was to be rather belied by Beckington's vigour as bishop, and his leaving the government in 1444 would appear to require explaining. It is true that he had been lobbying the papacy for a see in the early 1440s, but that does not mean that he intended his ecclesiastical promotion to be accompanied by political relegation. The likeliest explanation is that his standing at court had been seriously undermined first by the failure of the Armagnac marriage scheme, with which he had been closely associated, and then by the death of Archbishop Chichele. In such a scenario, his becoming keeper of the privy seal could be construed as involving a demotion within the administration, with his subsequent residence in his diocese stemming primarily from his inability to maintain his position at court.

Beckington was indeed an assiduous diocesan, visiting monasteries, ordaining regularly in person, and dealing firmly with Lollards. He also showed firmness in his dealings with successive dukes of Somerset, whom he rebuked in 1444 and 1455 for the protection they were said to be giving to evil-doers among their tenants. In his concern to raise educational standards among the clergy he required some ordinands and newly appointed clergy to undertake further study. He gathered around him a group of distinguished Oxford scholars, several of them Wykehamists, who served in his administration and were members of the Wells chapter. Among them were Thomas Chaundler, Robert Stillington, Thomas Gascoigne, and Gilbert Kymer. Kymer and one of the four Wykehamists in the group, Andrew Holes, had, like Beckington, been closely associated with Humphrey, duke of Gloucester. Holes, a diplomat and scholar of repute, reflected Beckington's humanistic sympathies. Beckington's concern for learning was also expressed both in his ordinances for the Wells choir school, and in his bequests of money to support students at Oxford.

Beckington was remembered by William Worcester as a builder, most notably in Wells where his rebus, a flaming barrel on a pole (beacon tun), is frequently to be found. Among the buildings are four embattled gates, the water supply that still runs through the city streets, and two ranges of houses, which form the north side of the market place. He also built at the monasteries of Bath and Witham and at his manor house at Banwell.

Beckington died at Wells on 14 January 1465 and was buried in a tomb within a chantry chapel, both constructed and consecrated by himself in 1452, on the south side of the cathedral presbytery. The tomb comprises an effigy in Derbyshire alabaster of the bishop in eucharistic vestments, lying on the table of Drundry stone that forms a canopy over a tonsured cadaver in an open shroud. The body, apparently without vestments but wearing an episcopal ring, rested on a wooden tray in a small vault beneath.

In his will, dated 12 November 1464 and proved on 23 January 1465, Beckington made munificent bequests to the parish church of Beckington, to Winchester College and New College, Oxford, to the churches he had formerly held at Sutton Courtenay and Bedwyn, Wiltshire (of which he had been prebendary in Salisbury Cathedral), to St Katharine's Hospital, London, and to his cathedrals of Wells and Bath. The canons of Wells, given £400 to make a full and matching set of vestments for all the cathedral clergy, were warned that should they make any financial claims on his estate or disturb arrangements made for his burial, the legacy would pass to New College. His executors paid for work on the college of the vicars-choral at Wells and for building at Lincoln College, Oxford, and conveyed land to Merton College, Oxford.

During his career as a diplomat Beckington made a collection of documents supporting the right of the English king to the throne of France. Letters written during his long career as diplomat, government official, and bishop reveal 'incredible diligence and industry' (Beckington, *Correspondence*, 1.xi), while the clear and elegant Latin in which they are composed places the writer in an important position in the introduction of Italian humanist learning into government administration in England. Thomas Chaundler appreciated the bishop's interest in classical scholarship and dedicated a book to him; and Beckington was also given at least three Latin works by others working in the humanist field, Vincent Clement, John Tiptoft, earl of Worcester, and the papal chaplain Flavio Biondo.

ROBERT W. DUNNING

Sources Emden, *Oxf.* · *Memorials of the reign of Henry VI: official correspondence of Thomas Bekynton, secretary to King Henry VI and bishop of Bath and Wells*, ed. G. Williams, 2 vols., Rolls Series, 56 (1872) · H. C. Maxwell-Lyte and M. C. B. Dawes, eds., *The register of Thomas Bekynton, bishop of Bath and Wells, 1443–1465*, 2 vols., Somerset RS, 49–50 (1934–5) · A. F. Judd, *The life of Thomas Bekynton* (1961) · A. H. Thompson, *The English clergy and their organization in the later middle ages* (1947) · R. Weiss, *Humanism in England during the fifteenth century*, 3rd edn (1967) · *Itineraries [of] William Worcestre*, ed. J. H. Harvey, OMT (1969) · R. A. Griffiths, *The reign of King Henry VI: the exercise of royal authority, 1422–1461* (1981) · *CPR, 1422–9*, 232 · *Letters of Queen Margaret of Anjou and Bishop Beckington and others written in the reigns of Henry V and Henry VI*, ed. C. Monro, CS, 86 (1863) · E. F. Jacob, ed., *The register of Henry Chichele, archbishop of Canterbury, 1414–1443*, 4 vols., CYS, 42, 45–7 (1937–47) · I. J. Churchill, *Canterbury administration: the administrative machinery of the archbishopric of Canterbury*, 2 vols. (1933) · P. Heath, *Church and realm, 1272–1461* (1988) · M. Deanesly, *The Lollard Bible* (1920) · F. W. Weaver, ed., *Somerset medieval wills*, 1, Somerset RS, 16 (1901)

Likenesses alabaster tomb effigy, Wells Cathedral, Wells, Somerset [*see illus.*]

Wealth at death a man of means: Weaver, ed., *Somerset medieval wills*, 202–7

Beckley, William (d. 1438), prior of Sandwich and theologian, joined the Carmelite order at Sandwich, in Kent. He was studying at the Carmelite house in Maldon, Essex, when he was ordained deacon on 17 December 1401 in London. He continued his studies at Cambridge where, in 1411, he was appointed prior, an office he held until 1414. In 1420–21 he incepted as a doctor of theology, and was teaching in his first year as regent master when, as one of his required duties, he was appointed to give the sermon at a university convocation. However, when the day came, he did not appear, and the procession and ceremony of

convocation had to go ahead without the customary homily. When he was summoned before the congregation of the university, Beckley was unable to provide a reasonable excuse, and consequently was declared to have broken his obligation as a master and suspended from teaching. He appealed to a letter containing instructions from the king, Henry V, but when questioned about its contents, he asked for an adjournment. In the interval, he left the university without informing anyone. On 5th July 1421 the chancellor and congregation wrote a formal letter of complaint to the Carmelites, then meeting in their annual provincial chapter at Northampton, complaining of his conduct. Thomas Netter (d. 1430), the Carmelite provincial, replied on behalf of the chapter, saying that Beckley had given a reasonable explanation and asking the congregation to treat the matter leniently. The two letters still survive and although the issue is not completely clear, it would appear that Beckley was pleading urgent royal business as his excuse for being absent. At this time Netter was himself confessor to Henry V, and a number of other Carmelites were involved at court. However, in his reply to the university, Netter did not feel justified in exonerating Beckley completely and clearly judged that he had been imprudent.

John Bale notes that Beckley was a celebrated preacher, giving sermons before important gatherings throughout England and also in Calais. In later years, he returned to his own convent of Sandwich as prior, where he died in 1438 and was buried. Weever records his epitaph, a commonplace reflection on mortality. Beckley wrote a number of works, but none of them has survived; one was a defence against the Carmelites' liability to pay tithes, and another a set of *quodlibeta* (disputations), and there were also the usual *quaestiones* and sermons. Thomas Dempster claims that Beckley was a Scot who, after joining the Carmelites, went to study in France and then returned to work in England. However, his account is based on the lost *Annales* of the Italian Carmelite Pietro-Tommaso Saraceno (1566–1643) and of one Gilbert Brown (d. 1605). There are no grounds for believing that this account is true.

RICHARD COPSEY

Sources J. Bale, Bodl. Oxf., MS Bodley 73 (SC 27635), fols. 2–2v, 39, 79, 99v–100v, 120 · K. Alban, 'The letters of Thomas Netter of Walden', *Carmel in Britain*, ed. P. Fitzgerald-Lombard, 2 (1992), 362–6 · T. Dempster, *Historia ecclesiastica gentis Scotorum* (Bologna, 1627), 104 · C. de S. E. de Villiers, ed., *Bibliotheca Carmelitana*, 2 vols. (Orléans, 1752), vol. 2, pp. 616–18 [details of Pietro-Tommaso Saraceno and his lost *Annales*] · J. Bale, BL, Harley MS 3838, fols. 97, 205 · Bale, *Cat.*, 1.579 · Emden, *Cam.* · J. Bale, *Illustrium Maioris Britannie scriptorum … summarium* (1548), fol. 251v · *Commentarii de scriptoribus Britannicis, auctore Joanne Lelando*, ed. A. Hall, 2 (1709), 437 · J. Weever, *Ancient funerall monuments* (1631), 62

Beckman, Sir Martin (1634/5–1702), pyrotechnist and military engineer, was born in Stockholm, Sweden, the son of Melcher Beckman and his wife, Christiana van Benningen. Their names and his profession suggest a Dutch origin.

Career to 1664 By his own account Beckman left his native Sweden about 1645 in order to serve the English crown. His brother served as a royalist captain in the civil war and was royal engineer to the exiled Charles II, but died before the Restoration. Beckman took an early interest in fireworks and was injured in an explosion while preparing a display to celebrate Charles's coronation in April 1661. The king awarded him £100 compensation. In June 1661 he was the firemaster to the fleet in the earl of Sandwich's expedition to Tangier. He left Tangier in early 1662 having prepared a map of the defences, but returned that August as chief engineer, a position he lost through his 'ill usage as he calls it by the means of my lord Peterborough', the governor (Chappell, 114).

After leaving Tangier, Beckman made charts of Ceuta, Tétouan, and Cadiz by disguising himself as a servant and wearing 'a cloak as a Spaniard' under which he concealed a compass (Chappell, 114). While in Cadiz in October 1663 he offered to help the Spanish take Tangier and even accepted payment from the duke of Medinaceli, whom he then betrayed by copying the duke's correspondence with the king of Spain and handing it over to the English consul. Beckman returned to London to report to Lord Arlington, who had been warned that 'Beckman the Intelligencer is to be feared' and made the mistake of visiting the Dutch ambassador (Marshall, 180). He was arrested and until early 1664 was held in the Tower, from where he complained 'I have been near a half year a close prisoner only from one persons malicious and false tongue' (PRO, SP 29/89, fol. 6). He was released and sent back to Tangier where with the Dutch engineer Bernard de Gomme he laid plans for the new defences.

Engineer to the ordnance Beckman returned to Europe before the work was complete and joined the Swedish army as a captain of artillery. He was posted to Stade in Germany where in June 1667 he heard of the Dutch raid on Chatham. Within days he wrote to Charles II claiming that he had 'brought to perfection a mode of firing ships' and had a series of propositions for defending harbours, making petards, and destroying sails by musket fire. His methods would do infinite service against the Dutch 'to ruin who he would risk his life for the wrongs they had done him' (CSP dom., 1667, 228). His letter was well timed and Beckman was again set to work under Gomme. His position was regularized on 19 October 1670 when he was appointed engineer to the ordnance. He was housed in the Tower of London, where he lived for the rest of his life. At an unknown date he married Elizabeth (d. 1677), daughter of Talbot Edwards, the deputy keeper of the regalia. They had several children, none of whom lived to adulthood.

Beckman was resident in the Tower on 9 May 1671 when Thomas Blood attempted to steal the crown jewels. Beckman overpowered him and recovered the crown, receiving £100 'for resisting that late villainous attempt' (Calendar of Treasury Books, 3.937). In 1673 he accompanied Prince Rupert's naval expedition against the Dutch as an engineer on the ordnance train, and on 27 August he was commissioned as a major in Rupert's dragoon regiment, which was disbanded later that year.

In March 1677 Beckman was appointed 'chief engineer of all His Majesty's castles forts, blockhouses and other fortifications in England, Wales and Berwick', in reversion

to Gomme. In 1678 he was sent to prepare a report on the poor state of the defences of the Channel Islands where Sir Thomas Morgan found him to be 'a diligent, knowing man' (CSP dom., 1677–8, 584). He returned to Jersey in 1679 to work on Orgeuil Castle. In June 1680 he was again posted to Tangier as chief engineer. He arrived to find the garrison in great danger, with most of the surrounding forts overrun by the Moors. 'We have not above six cannons about town to fire, three are broken, no gunners worth bread, no garrison so neglected' (Dartmouth MSS, 1.52). On 21 September his expertise was instrumental in securing the outlying Pole Fort, which was recaptured in a sally. 'Immediately, Major Beckman, who is a brave man, in four hours pallisadoed the fort round and the same night 500 men lodged in the fort' (ibid.). The lieutenant governor described Beckman as 'an able man in his profession and a valiant steady man' (Routh, 189).

In 1681 orders were given that Hull's defences were to be built to Beckman's plans. Over the next two years he supervised the work, often in hard conditions, having to travel the 4 miles each day 'in the clay up to the ankles, and stand all day in the wet' (Tomlinson, 62). He last travelled to Tangier in August 1683 with the expedition led by Lord Dartmouth. Beckman was given the task of destroying the fortifications and stayed there until the final evacuation in April 1684.

Chief engineer In April 1685 Beckman prepared the lavish fireworks display, again on the Thames, by Westminster, for the coronation of James II. In anticipation of Argyll's uprising he was sent to Scotland to direct work on the defences of Stirling. On his return in May he toured the north and east of England to prepare a report on the defences of the main towns. On the outbreak of Monmouth's rebellion he was given a captaincy in the Royal Regiment of Fusiliers, then an ordnance regiment. More significant promotion came on the death of Gomme in November 1685, when Beckman succeeded as chief engineer at a stipend of £300 a year and £1 a day for expenses. He was knighted on 20 March 1686.

As chief engineer Beckman initially concentrated on the new fort at Tilbury, but by 1687 he was working on the defences of Berwick and in September he was again directing work at Hull, where he complained that he could not get the soldiers to work for the mere 6d. a day on offer. Nevertheless, by June 1688 Lord Langdale was reporting on the great progress being made on the new water bastion.

Beckman organized the fireworks display on the Thames on 17 July 1688 to celebrate the birth of the prince of Wales. John Evelyn noted that the fireworks 'were very fine, and had cost some thousands of pounds about the pyramids and statues etc: but were spent too soon, for so long a preparation' (Evelyn, 4.591). Nevertheless, the display 'concluded with the continued shouts and huzzas of the people' (Englands Triumphs, 2), and so pleased the king that he granted Beckman the sole rights 'of prints in mezzo tinto' depicting the event. On 11 August he was made the first 'comptroller of fireworks' at an annual salary of £200. His duties included managing the royal laboratory, where he developed a 'much better and quicker fire for your majesty's fireships than was ever before practised' (*CSP dom.*, 1691-2, 244).

When William of Orange entered London in December 1688 Beckman, fearing that he would be mistaken for 'a heretic of Rome' (*Dartmouth MSS*, 3.136), took to frequenting Church of England services to prove himself 'as good a protestant as any in the parish and has received the sacrament' (ibid., 1.236), thereby losing a 10 guinea bet with Dartmouth that he would never convert from the Lutheran church. According to a document entitled 'The reason why I have been accounted a papist', dated 10 December, he faced pressure from Father Petre from about mid-1687 to convert to Roman Catholicism. He subsequently decided to take the sacrament according to the rites of the Church of England and the oaths and tests, and had duly done so at St Peter's, Cornhill, in London. Beckman organized the fireworks display for the coronation of William and Mary in April 1689. He then returned to Hull. Despite being twice requested by the duke of Schomberg, his work on the home defences prevented his taking part in the war in Ireland until May 1691 where as chief engineer to the army he was present in the campaign that ended with the treaty of Limerick on 3 October. He was naturalized by act of parliament on 7 November following. On 31 May 1692 he was appointed the chief engineer and colonel of a train of brass ordnance for sea service which he paid off in Ghent on 1 November 1692.

At war with the French Beckman spent the spring of 1693 inspecting the defences of Plymouth and Portsmouth and was again appointed colonel of a train of ordnance for sea service. On 28 August 1693, aged fifty-eight, he was licensed to marry Ruth Mudd (*b.* 1631/2), a widow from Stepney, the wedding taking place on 31 August at St Dunstan's, Stepney. In June 1694 he sailed with the Brest expedition, with instructions to attack French coastal towns with his bomb-ketches and his specially designed 'machines' or fire ships, which were intended to explode when close to other ships or against harbour defences. These machines were not a success and were paid off in September 1695.

In July 1695 Beckman took part in the attacks on Dieppe and Le Havre. In September an attack on the mole at Dunkirk by two of his machines was frustrated by bad weather, and later that month, much against his advice, he was ordered to attack Calais with eleven bomb-vessels and tenders. The brisk weather and low tide kept him a mile and three-quarters from the forts, and although he passed the town three times, he could only 'cast fifty bombs to little purpose' (*CSP dom.*, 1691-2, 311). On 4 and 12 October he directed the attack on the French-held town of Palamós in Catalonia, using bombships towed behind galleys. The citadel was bombarded and left on fire in three places, and 'where the town was not burnt, it was shattered' (*CSP dom.*, 1695, 354). He returned to London to prepare another 'famous and very chargeable fireworks' display to welcome the

king back from the continent on 13 November 1695 (Evelyn, 5.223).

In June 1696 Beckman set out to raid the French coast with a convoy of warships commanded by Captain George Mees. On 5 July he hoisted French colours to get his ten bomb-vessels close into the shore and bombarded St Martin on the Île de Ré day and night until the morning of the 7th 'which burnt and destroyed the most considerable part of it' (BL, Add. MS 38701, fol. 86). That night he sailed along the coast to Olonne, which he bombarded for twenty-four hours 'setting the town on fire fifteen times, three of which continued burning when we left off ... In the two actions 4,200 bombs and carcasses were thrown to good purpose' (ibid.).

Last years In 1697 Beckman was given a fresh warrant as comptroller of the fireworks and was allocated £5000 to prepare a fireworks display in St James's Square to celebrate the peace of Ryswick. It was, Evelyn noted, 'of great expence as would have erected a Triumphal Arch of Marble and the fireworks in nothing answering expectation, but were the destruction of some spectators' (Evelyn, 5.277).

In February 1699 Beckman presented a House of Lords select committee with the accounts of the state of the fortifications at Plymouth, Chatham, and Portsmouth: 'Portsmouth is in that ill condition that if not timely taken care of, it will demolish itself' (*House of Lords MSS*, new ser., 3.305) as the stone fortifications were sinking into the moat. He estimated that £87,700 was needed to protect the country's fleet, rivers, and ports.

Beckman died on 24 June 1702 at the Tower of London, his will ordering his burial in the Lutheran church in London. A Swedish aunt and her daughter received the interest of 2000 'rix dollars' paid into the bank of Sweden. His nephews John and Frederick Conradi, both in the service of Hesse, received 200 rix dollars. Most of his estate passed to a third nephew, George Conradi, 'engineer to Queen Anne'. His wife survived him, as do his plans of Tangier (BL and British Museum) and his design for a howitzer (Armouries Library, in the Tower). PIERS WAUCHOPE

Sources A. Marshall, *Intelligence and espionage in the reign of Charles II* (1994) • *N&Q*, 170 (1936), 200–01 • PRO, PROB 11/465, fols. 161-2 • PRO, SP 29/89; SP 29/206 • BL, Add. MS 38701 • H. C. Tomlinson, *Guns and government: the ordnance office under the later Stuarts* (1979) • E. Chappell, ed., *The Tangier papers of Samuel Pepys*, Navy RS, 73 (1935) • C. Dalton, ed., *English army lists and commission registers, 1661-1714*, 6 vols. (1892–1904) • W. A. Shaw, ed., *Letters of denization and acts of naturalization for aliens in England and Ireland, 1603-1700*, Huguenot Society of London, 18 (1911) • J. L. Chester and J. Foster, eds., *London marriage licences, 1521–1869* (1887) • N. Luttrell, *A brief historical relation of state affairs from September 1678 to April 1714*, 6 vols. (1857) • *CSP dom.*, 1667–95 • *Englands triumphs for the prince of Wales* (1688) • *IGI* • *The manuscripts of the earl of Dartmouth*, 3 vols., HMC, 20 (1887–96), vols. 1, 3 • *The manuscripts of the House of Lords*, new ser., 12 vols. (1900–77), vol. 3 • Evelyn, *Diary* • E. M. G. Routh, *Tangier, England's lost Atlantic outpost* (1912) • W. A. Shaw, ed., *Calendar of treasury books*, 3, PRO (1908) • A. St H. Brock, *A history of fireworks* (1949) • J. Bailey, *The history of the antiquities of the Tower of London* (1830) • A. D. Saunders, *Tilbury fort* (1980) • *DNB* • F. Duncan, *History of the royal regiment of artillery* (1874) • G. Story, *Continuation of the impartial history of the wars of Ireland* (1693)

Beckwith, Sir George (1752/3–1823), army officer and colonial governor, was the second son of John Beckwith (*fl.* 1733–1772) and his wife, probably the Janet Wishart who married Captain John Beckwith in Edinburgh on 10 June 1750. The elder Beckwith was an officer in the 20th regiment of foot who became lieutenant-colonel in 1758 and commanded the regiment at Minden. All four sons became officers; one was Sir Thomas Sydney *Beckwith.

George Beckwith entered the 37th (North Hampshire) regiment of foot as an ensign on 20 July 1771. He obtained his lieutenancy on 7 July 1775 and in October embarked with his regiment for America where it was attached to the 3rd brigade under Major-General Jones. He was promoted to captain on 4 December 1778. During the American War of Independence he took part in several actions including the capture of Elizabeth Town and Brunswick in New Jersey. On 30 November 1781 he was granted the brevet (non-regimental) rank of major, 'for his spirited assistance in the assault on fort Griswold' (*American MSS*, 2.356). During 1781 he was made an aide-de-camp with the general staff with responsibility for secret service expenditure for intelligence gathering in the colonies. This work brought him to the attention of Sir Guy Carleton, later first Baron Dorchester. After the end of hostilities the 37th foot were stationed in Nova Scotia. When they returned to England in 1789 Beckwith remained in Canada, as aide-de-camp to Lord Dorchester, now governor of Canada, who also entrusted him with a confidential diplomatic mission to the United States between 1787 and 1791. On 10 November 1790 he obtained the brevet rank of lieutenant-colonel and that of colonel on 21 August 1795.

In April 1797 Beckwith was appointed governor of Bermuda. On 18 June 1798 he was promoted to the rank of major-general and in the following July was made military commander on Bermuda. In October 1804 he became governor of St Vincent and was made lieutenant-general on 2 November 1805. On 8 October 1808 he was transferred to the governorship of Barbados, with the command of the forces in the Windward and Leeward islands. In 1809 he led the successful expedition against the French colony of Martinique. With a force of 11,000 men he sailed from Carlisle Bay on 28 January 1809, arrived off Martinique on the 29th, and completed the conquest of the island by 24 February. The captured French eagles were sent home to great public acclaim—they were the first to be seen in Britain, and a broken eagle was incorporated into Beckwith's coat of arms. Having received the thanks of the Commons and the Lords, on 1 May 1809 he was created KB. On 22 January 1810 he led an equally successful expedition against Guadeloupe, the last of the French possessions in the area, completing the conquest of the island by 6 February.

Beckwith returned to Barbados on 29 July 1810 and remained there until June 1814, when with health failing he returned home and was made a full general. After his departure the Barbados legislature voted him a service of plate valued at £2500 in recognition of his services. His health somewhat restored, in October 1816 he was appointed to command the forces in Ireland. He held this office

until March 1820. He died after an illness of several months at his home in Half Moon Street, London, on 20 March 1823, aged seventy. He was buried without public ceremony in the vaults of Marylebone cemetery, alongside other members of his family. A biographical sketch in manuscript is in the War Office papers in the Public Record Office. JONATHAN SPAIN

Sources GM, 1st ser., 93/1 (1823), 372 · C. T. Atkinson, *Regimental history: the royal Hampshire regiment*, 1: *To 1914* (1950) · C. T. Atkinson, 'The highlanders in Westphalia, 1760–62', *Journal of the Society for Army Historical Research*, 20 (1941), 208–23 · W. Y. Carmen, 'The capture of Martinique', *Journal of the Society for Army Historical Research*, 20 (1941), 1–4 · B. Smyth, *History of the XXth regiment, 1688–1888* (1889) · R. H. Schomburgk, *The history of Barbados* (1848) · *Report on American manuscripts in the Royal Institution of Great Britain*, 4 vols., HMC, 59 (1904–9), vol. 2 · C. Dalton, *George the First's army, 1714–1727*, 2 vols. (1910–12) · *Army List* (1740) · *Army List* (1757) · *Army List* (1760–61) · *Army List* (1763) · *Army List* (1765) · *Army List* (1769) · *Army List* (1771–2) · A. C. Burns, *History of the British West Indies* (1954)

Archives PRO, extracts from corresp., FO 95/1/1 | BL, letters to Sir Robert Peel, Add. MSS 40260–40262, 40269–40273 · NL Scot., corresp. with Sir A. F. I. Cochrane

Likenesses S. W. Reynolds, mezzotint (after portrait by J. Eckstein), BM, NPG

Beckwith, John [*called* Christmas Beckwith] (1750–1809), organist and composer, was born at Norwich on 25 December 1750, the son of Edward Beckwith. Though widely called Christmas Beckwith on account of his date of birth, he did not use the sobriquet. He came from a musical family, his father and his uncle serving as lay clerks at Norwich Cathedral under the organist Thomas Garland, and he showed early talent. He was apprenticed in 1775 to William Hayes, professor of music at Oxford, and later became his assistant and also his son's. He took both the bachelor's and the doctor's degree in music at Oxford in 1803. He had married his wife, Mary Elizabeth, by 1787, when their daughter Elizabeth Charlotte was baptized in Norwich Cathedral on 7 March. They had two more daughters and three sons.

Renowned in Norfolk as an organist, Beckwith played an important part in the 'musical meetings', generally held in St Peter Mancroft in Norwich, that supported charities (with many of which he was associated as a founder or through other administrative involvement) with miscellaneous programmes; he also played the organ for annual charity services in the cathedral. At the inauguration of the Longman and Broderip organ at Wymondham Abbey on 14 August 1793 Beckwith opened with an anonymous voluntary, probably of his own composition, and then presided at the keyboard for a vocal and instrumental programme dominated by excerpts from Handel's oratorios. On 16 January 1794 he was appointed organist at St Peter Mancroft.

Though not prolific or markedly original as a composer, Beckwith published works in various forms, including a few glees. His *Six Voluntaries for Organ or Harpsichord* (1780) are short and under-developed, providing no opportunity for superior performing skills. The subscription list shows a high proportion of Oxford addresses. His *Six Anthems* show some variety within the verse anthem pattern, yet remain conventional. Perfunctory in the musical treatment of the texts, they demand little of the soloists, except occasionally the bass. The vivid word-painting in 'The Lord is very great' was, however, admired until late into the Victorian era. Beckwith's most considerable work was *The First Verse of every Psalm of David with an Ancient or Modern Chant* (1808). A list of 200 subscribers testifies to contemporary interest in psalmody. Beckwith did not write all the chants; he selected the remainder from a wide range of composers from as early as Tudor times to his own age. A pretentious but sketchy account of the history of religious music prefaces a defence of congregational participation in psalm singing. Adopting a suggestion by John Marsh of Chichester, Beckwith urges that choirs should meet regularly under the organist throughout a month in order to 'point' the psalms, indicating 'with a conspicuous *red* mark' exactly where reciting should end in both parts of the chant. Intended originally for local use, but now offered to the Church of England generally, the compilation, 'first conceived full fifteen years since', had been begun 'about ten years ago, during a week's visit to Cromer for sea bathing'. Its completion had been delayed by 'an almost daily occupation of thirteen or fourteen hours in the most slavish part of my profession'.

Among Beckwith's many pupils were the singer Thomas Vaughan and the writer on music Edward Taylor. Beckwith succeeded Garland as organist at Norwich Cathedral on Garland's death in 1808, but himself died of a paralytic stroke on 3 June 1809, in Norwich, and was buried in St Peter Mancroft. He was survived by his wife. His eldest son, John Charles Beckwith (*bap.* 20 July 1788), succeeded him as organist of Norwich Cathedral. Beckwith enjoyed a considerable reputation in his native city and, had he lived longer, might have made larger contributions to its musical development. CHRISTOPHER SMITH

Sources H. W. Shaw, *The succession of organists of the Chapel Royal and the cathedrals of England and Wales from c.1538* (1991) • F. Newman, *Two centuries of Mancroft music* (1932) • N. Boston, *Musical history of Norwich Cathedral* (1963) • M. Betts, *A jewel or ornament: the illustrated story of the historic organ in the abbey church of St Mary and St Thomas of Canterbury, Wymondham* (1973) • J. Beckwith, *The first verse of every psalm of David with an ancient or modern chant* (1808), preface • tombstone, Norwich, St Peter Mancroft • parish register, Norwich, St Peter Mancroft [appointment as organist; burial] • *GM*, 1st ser., 79 (1809), 589

Likenesses C. Turner, mezzotint, pubd 1812 (after J. Clover), BM

Beckwith, John Charles (1789–1862), army officer and missionary, was born at Halifax, Nova Scotia, on 2 October 1789. He was the grandson of Major-General John Beckwith, and nephew of the generals Sir George and Sir Thomas Sydney Beckwith. His father, like his four brothers, had held a commission in the army, but had soon resigned it on his marriage with Miss Haliburton (a sister of Judge Haliburton) of Halifax in Nova Scotia, where he settled. John Beckwith obtained an ensigncy through his uncle's influence in the 50th regiment in 1803. In 1804 he exchanged into the 95th (Rifle brigade), of which his uncle, Sydney Beckwith, was lieutenant-colonel. He became lieutenant in 1805, and accompanied

his regiment to Hanover, to Denmark, where he was present at Kjöge, and to Portugal.

Beckwith was with the 95th on Moore's retreat to Corunna, and became captain in 1808. He was with the 2nd battalion in the Walcheren expedition, and accompanied it to Portugal in the winter of 1810, when he found Wellington's army in the lines of Torres Vedras and Sydney Beckwith in command of a brigade. He was with the light division in all the engagements which took place with Masséna's retreating army in the spring of 1811, at Pombal, Redinha, Condeixa, Foz d'Aronce, and Sabugal. In 1812, after his uncle had gone to England for his health, he was appointed by Brigadier-General Andrew Barnard, his successor, brigade-major to the 1st brigade of the light division, and was present at the storming of Ciudad Rodrigo and Badajoz, and at the battles of Salamanca, Vitoria, the Pyrenees, the Nivelle, the Nive, and Orthez. His distinguished services brought him to the repeated notice of Wellington and of General Alten, who had succeeded Craufurd in the command of the light division, and he was appointed deputy assistant quartermaster-general to the division. He was present at the battle of Toulouse, and in 1814, at the conclusion of the war, was made major by brevet.

In 1815 Beckwith was appointed in the same capacity to Picton's division in the Netherlands, and was present at Waterloo, where he had four horses killed under him, lost his left leg, and after which he was promoted lieutenant-colonel and made a CB. His injury made it impossible for him to expect active employment, and in 1820 he went on half pay. Beckwith was only twenty-six years old when he lost his leg, and still a young man when he retired; he hardly knew to what occupation he could turn. He was on friendly terms with Wellington, and one day in 1827, when visiting the duke in Apsley House, he took down a book from the library shelf to pass the time as he waited. It happened to be Dr Gilly's book on the Waldenses, the protestant sect in northern Italy which was persecuted by the Roman Catholic church and the Piedmontese government. Gilly's account of the Waldenses' sufferings inspired Beckwith, and in the same year he visited Piedmont. The history of the people and their squalor and ignorance so influenced him that he decided to settle among them and, taking a house (La Torre in Rémont), lived among them during the last thirty-five years of his life.

Beckwith's aims were to educate the people and to revive in them the old evangelical faith which had first attracted him. He established no fewer than 120 schools, all of which he regularly inspected, and the one-legged English general was well known and much loved throughout the Italian valleys. His services were recognized by King Charles Albert of Sardinia, who made him a knight of the order of St Maurice and St Lazarus in 1848. He married a Waldensian, Caroline Valle, on 20 June 1850. He maintained his links with England, corresponding with Gilly and others interested in the Waldenses. He had been promoted colonel in 1837 and major-general in 1846, but continued to live at La Torre until his death there on 19 July

1862. He was buried at the cemetery of Tour Pellice, his funeral attended by thousands of the peasants whose lives he had ameliorated. Of all the former officers of the light division, few did such a great and self-denying work.

H. M. STEPHENS, *rev.* JAMES LUNT

Sources J. P. Meille, *General Beckwith: his life and labours among the Waldenses of Piedmont*, trans. W. Arnot (1873) [Fr. orig. (1872)] • J. P. Meille, *Il generale Beckwith: sua vita e sue opere in mezzo ai Valdesi del Piemonte*, ed. and trans. A. Meille, condensed edn (Rome, 1879) [Fr. orig. (1872)] • *The Times* (5 Aug 1862) • *The Times* (14 Aug 1862) • *GM*, 3rd ser., 13 (1862), 362 • Boase, *Mod. Eng. biog.*
Wealth at death under £25,000: probate, 17 Sept 1862, *CGPLA Eng. & Wales*

Beckwith, Josiah (1734–1788×1800), lawyer and antiquary, was born on 24 August 1734 at Rothwell, near Leeds, where his father, Thomas Beckwith, practised as an attorney. He also became an attorney and settled at Masbrough, near Rotherham. He married on 14 August 1763 at St Peter's, Sheffield, Mary (*bap.* 1739, *d.* 1788), the eldest daughter and only surviving child of George D'Oxon, of Woodhead, in Cheshire; they had two sons and four daughters.

Beckwith enjoyed antiquarian pursuits and was elected a fellow of the Society of Antiquaries. He is known for his enlarged and improved edition of Thomas Blount's *Fragmenta antiquitatis, or, Ancient Tenures of Land, and Jocular Customs of some Manuors*, which he published in 1784; the first edition of this work had appeared in 1679. In its review of Beckwith's edition the *Monthly Review* remarked: 'Few persons were better qualified for this business, and Mr. Beckwith has enriched this edition with many valuable improvements. He has subjoined many notes and observations, which have been communicated by some of the most respectable antiquaries of the present day' (*Monthly Review*, 73, 1785, 459). Beckwith left materials for a still further enlarged edition, which was published after his death by his son Hercules Malcbysse Beckwith, who had an appointment in the Royal Mint. His wife predeceased him in 1788 and Beckwith had died by May 1800, when an obituary of his nephew Ray Beckwith was printed in the *Gentleman's Magazine*.

T. F. T. DYER, *rev.* J. A. MARCHAND

Sources *GM*, 1st ser., 56 (1786), 265 • *GM*, 1st ser., 70 (1800), 485 • Nichols, *Lit. anecdotes*, 8.329–30 • *IGI*
Archives Bodl. Oxf., letters to J. C. Brooke

Beckwith, Julia Catherine. *See* Hart, Julia Catherine Beckwith (1796–1867).

Beckwith, Sir Thomas Sydney (1772–1831), army officer, was the third son of Major-General John Beckwith, who commanded the 20th regiment at Minden, and four of whose sons became distinguished general officers. Beckwith was appointed lieutenant in the 71st regiment in 1791, and at once went to join it in India. He found Lieutenant-Colonel Baird in command of the regiment, and under him learned both how to lead and how to organize a regiment. With the 71st he was present at the siege of Seringapatam in 1792, at the capture of Pondicherry by Colonel Baird in 1793, and during the operations in Ceylon in 1795. He was promoted captain in 1794, and

returned to England with the headquarters of his regiment in 1798.

Beckwith had established his reputation as a good officer in India, and when in 1800 he volunteered for a company in Manningham's new rifle corps his services were accepted. Colonel Manningham had proposed to the Horse Guards to be allowed to raise a regiment of light troops for outpost duties, like the French *voltigeurs*. His offer was accepted, and volunteers were called for from every regiment. Beckwith had in the 71st made the acquaintance of William Stewart, the lieutenant-colonel of the new rifle corps, and obtained a captaincy under his friend. He soon got his company into such good order that it was assigned in 1801 to accompany the expedition to Copenhagen, where its adjutant was killed. Beckwith was promoted major in Manningham's Rifles (later called the 95th) in 1802, and was one of the officers whom Sir John Moore trained at Shorncliffe. He became lieutenant-colonel in 1803, and under Moore's supervision got his regiment into model order. He was admired by his officers and by his men, whose welfare was always his first concern. In 1806 he served in Lord Cathcart's abortive expedition to Hanover, and in 1807 his regiment formed part of the division which, under Sir Arthur Wellesley, won the battle of Kjöge in Denmark. In July 1808 he accompanied General Acland to Portugal, and was present at the battle of Vimeiro. After Moore's arrival, and on his taking the command of the troops in Portugal, the 95th was brigaded with the 43rd and 52nd under General Anstruther, and formed part of the reserve under General Edward Paget. The conduct of this brigade, and more especially of the 95th regiment under Beckwith, has been described by Napier; it closed the retreat and was daily engaged with the French, but although it suffered the most terrible privations it never broke line or in any way relaxed its discipline. The regiment particularly distinguished itself at Cacabelos, where it faced round and with the help of the 10th hussars fought successfully the entire French advanced guard. The 95th and Beckwith crowned their services at Corunna, when they were the last troops to leave the city and managed to take with them seven French officers and 156 men whom they had taken prisoner on the previous day. In 1809 the 95th was again brigaded with the 43rd and 52nd, and sent to the Peninsula. Craufurd was leading them up to the main army when he heard that a great battle had been fought, and that General Wellesley had been killed. Nothing daunted he pressed forward, and after a forced march of twenty-five hours reached Talavera on the evening of the battle. When Wellington retired from Spain, and cantoned his army on the Coa, the light brigade was stationed far in front to watch the French movements. There were frequent conflicts, in which the 95th and Beckwith proved their efficiency. At the skirmish of Barba del Puerco and the battle of Busaco the light brigade won the special praise of Wellington; when, in 1811, it was increased by three Portuguese regiments to a division Beckwith received the command of one of the brigades. The division led the pursuit of Masséna, was warmly engaged at

Pombal, Redinha, and Foz d'Aronce, and defeated a whole army corps, though with great loss, at Sabugal. There Beckwith particularly distinguished himself, was wounded in the forehead, and had his horse shot under him. The discipline and valour of his men were again proved, and the disgraceful blunders of Sir William Erskine (1769–1813), who had temporarily succeeded Craufurd, were remedied by the men's bravery. Shortly after the battle of Fuentes d'Oñoro, Beckwith was obliged by ill health to return to England, and to hand over his regiment and brigade to Colonel Barnard. He had inspired his men with such confidence 'that they would follow him through fire and water when the day of trial came' (Cope, 53). He recovered his health, and in 1812 was knighted as proxy for his brother George *Beckwith, and appointed assistant quartermaster-general in Canada. He was made a knight of the Tower and Sword of Portugal in 1813.

Beckwith commanded an expedition to the coast of the United States which took Littlehampton and Ocrakoke, and had Charles Napier under him as brigadier. Colonel from 1811, in 1814 he was promoted major-general, and was (January 1815) among the first KCBs. He saw no more active service, but in 1827 was made colonel commandant of the rifle brigade, which he had done so much to organize. In 1829 he was appointed commander-in-chief at Bombay, and in 1830 became lieutenant-general. He died of fever on 15 January 1831 at Mahabaleshwar, India. His only son, also Thomas Sydney, was a captain in the rifle brigade and died at Gibraltar on 21 March 1828. The light division was the greatest creation of Sir John Moore; and Beckwith was the practical creator of one of its most distinguished regiments. 'He was', according to Kincaid, 'one of the ablest outpost generals, and few officers knew so well how to make the most of a small force'.

H. M. STEPHENS, *rev.* ROGER T. STEARN

Sources W. Cope, *The history of the rifle brigade* (1877) · W. Surtees, *Twenty-five years in the rifle brigade* (1833) · J. Leach, *Sketch of the field services of the rifle brigade from its formation to the battle of Waterloo* (1838) · J. Kincaid, *Adventures in the rifle brigade in the Peninsula, France, and the Netherlands, from 1809 to 1815* (1830) · Mrs F. M. Fitzmaurice, *Recollections of a rifleman's wife at home and abroad* (1851) · E. Costello, *The adventures of a soldier*, 2nd edn (1852) · D. Gates, *The Spanish ulcer: a history of the Peninsular War* (1986) · R. Muir, *Britain and the defeat of Napoleon, 1807–1815* (1996) · *GM*, 1st ser., 101/1 (1831)

Archives NL Scot., letters to Sir George Brown

Becon, John (d. 1587), ecclesiastical lawyer and reformer, was born in Suffolk of unknown parentage. Educated at St John's College, Cambridge, he was admitted as a scholar in 1559, graduated BA in 1561, was admitted a fellow on 21 March 1561, and proceeded MA in 1564. His degrees were incorporated at Oxford in 1566. He became principal lecturer of St John's in 1564, and in July 1571 he was elected public orator of the university; he served as proctor in 1571–2. It was during this period that Becon's penchant for contentiousness first became apparent. He led the senate's opposition to new university statutes, approved in 1570, and with others toured the colleges soliciting signatures to a petition against them. The disorder that ensued led the heads of colleges to issue articles against him and his followers. The archbishops and the bishops of London

and Ely stepped in to endorse the new statutes and to censure Becon and his adherents for their audacity. Becon resigned the position of public orator in 1573. Late in 1574 he was presented by the crown to a prebend at Norwich and in the following year he became chancellor of that diocese under Bishop John Parkhurst. He proceeded DCL in 1576.

At Norwich Becon gained a reputation as a reforming chancellor. He joined with the bishop in criticizing the conduct of the diocesan registrars in matters of probate and that of apparitors throughout the system. In 1578 he turned his attention to answering the complaints of those of puritan sympathies by associating prominent preaching clergy with the bishop. An antiquary himself, he recommended the revival of the once-significant role of rural dean in diocesan administration and pastoral care. Becon intended that this official should become a superintendent in each deanery, summoning ministers to a monthly prophesying, exercising disciplinary powers in minor cases and reporting severe offences to the bishop, undertaking probate jurisdiction, and reporting on recusants. The rural dean would preside with the bishop and his chancellor during their synods, at ordinations, and at the admission of ministers to benefices. JPs would also be associated with the bishop, suggesting a partnership between ministry and magistracy that has been described as 'a real alternative to clericalism on the one hand and naked Erastianism on the other' (Collinson, *Godly People*, 187). Becon clashed with his bishop at Norwich but, fortunately for himself, was in good esteem with the privy council, which looked favourably upon attempts to curb the bishops' powers. About this time Bishop Richard Curteys of Chichester narrowly avoided deprivation by agreeing with the council to delegate the spiritual administration of his diocese to John Becon, chancellor of Norwich. As he informed Sir Francis Walsingham on 30 March 1579: 'By order of the counsaill I was contented to my great charge to referr ouer all the dealings in iurisdiction to Mr doctor Becon a man verie well liked of mee, so speciallie named and commended by your honor' (PRO, SP 12/130/22).

On 16 February 1580 Becon was collated to the precentorship of Chichester Cathedral, but Curteys forced a compromise with the council whereby Becon shared the chancellorship with Henry Worley, who had been in post since 1573. It was several months before Becon could disentangle himself from quarrels at Norwich to attend to matters in Chichester, but once there he was befriended by William Overton, who promised Becon preferment once he himself was translated to the bench. Overton was true to his word, and when he became bishop of Coventry and Lichfield in 1580 Becon was appointed his first chancellor and vicar-general. It was not long, however, before the two men quarrelled. It is possible that Becon combined his duties at Lichfield with those at Chichester (Curteys died in 1582) but he seems to have played little part in the courts at Lichfield, and by October 1583 Zachary Babington had been appointed chancellor and was frequently appearing as judge in consistory. Overton had granted the office to both men and to the longer lived of them. Such sharing arrangements were common enough, but Becon would have none of it and a major quarrel ensued. Following a great riot and disturbance in the cathedral, the case came before the Star Chamber, the privy council, and the archbishop of Canterbury. Four visitors appointed by the archbishop finally achieved a compromise.

While at Lichfield Becon nevertheless made his mark by again espousing the cause of reform. He and Overton partially implemented a plan, embodied in his 'Certain advertisements' of 1584, similar to the one he had brought forward in Norwich. Unfortunately some parts of it attracted privy council disapproval—especially when the bishop, on the strength of congregational reservations, questioned a crown presentation to Church Eaton that year. None the less, there are signs that there were genuine attempts to broaden the involvement of preaching clergy in diocesan discipline and pastoral responsibility. Becon (whose name was often also spelt Beacon) appeared occasionally as vicar-general in cases brought against errant clergymen in 1584, but there is little other mention of him in the diocesan archives before his death. He was buried at St Giles Cripplegate, London, on 4 September 1587.   ROSEMARY O'DAY

Sources *The letter book of John Parkhurst, bishop of Norwich*, ed. R. A. Houlbrooke, Norfolk RS, 43 (1974–5) · R. B. Manning, *Religion and society in Elizabethan Sussex* (1969) · P. Collinson, *The Elizabethan puritan movement* (1967) · P. Collinson, *Godly people: essays on English protestantism and puritanism* (1983) · *CSP dom.*, 1547–90, with *addenda, 1547–65; 1566–79* · registers, St John Cam. · Lichfield diocesan records · Venn, *Alum. Cant.*, 1/1.114 · state papers domestic, Elizabeth I, PRO, SP 12/130/22 · parish register, London, St Giles Cripplegate, 4 Sept 1587, GL [burial] · Cooper, *Ath. Cantab.*, 2.16–17, 542
Archives Lichfield diocesan records

Becon, Richard (*fl.* 1567–1611), author and administrator, is of unknown parents but is said to have descended from a Suffolk family. If this is so, then he and his family would appear to have eluded the heralds in 1561—unless, that is, they failed to attract their attention. He entered St John's College, Cambridge, on 12 November 1567, graduated BA in 1571, and proceeded MA in 1575. His close contemporary at the college was Theodore Becon, son of the noted theologian and chaplain to Archbishop Cranmer, Thomas Becon of Norfolk, to whom Richard was himself possibly related. Leaving Cambridge, he then entered Gray's Inn. At his admission on 19 June 1577 he was described as 'of Barnard's Inn', which may indicate an interim internship in preparation for the legal career on which he was now clearly embarked. He was called to the bar on 27 January 1585 and appointed the queen's attorney for the province of Munster on 17 December 1586 at an annual salary of little more than £17. He held the post only until 1591 or 1592. An undertaker for the plantation of the province under the scheme first established in 1586, as of 1592 Becon held 6000 Irish acres at Cork and Waterford for an annual rent, payable to the crown, which was doubled at Michaelmas 1594 to £33 6s. 8d.

Becon was the author of a political pamphlet on Ireland entitled *Solon his follie, or, A politique discourse touching the reformation of common weales conquered, declined, or corrupted*, which was published at Oxford in 1594. It takes the form of a conversation between Solon, Epimenides, and Pisistratus as to the policy that Athens (England) should adopt towards its colony Salamina (Ireland). Dedicated to Queen Elizabeth, exhorted by the author to the emulation of the works of Brutus, the conqueror of tyranny and the reformer of the Roman commonwealth, it partakes very much of the protestant New English attitude to the reformation of a colony whose administration had been corrupted profoundly by governors who shared with the governed many aspects of their culture, and worst of all their devotion to heretical religious beliefs. Conventionally overshadowed by Edmund Spenser's far more famous *A View of the Present State of Ireland*, it has been claimed that the true significance of Becon's text lies far beyond the narrow Irish context. For the author 'was perhaps the first Englishman to make thorough and positive use of Machiavelli's republicanism of the *Discorsi* … [and] perhaps the most important as well as the most radical exponent of classical humanist political discourse in England before the 1650s' (Peltonen, 76). Perhaps *Solon his Follie* might also be said to demonstrate the difficulty in sustaining a meaningful distinction between republican ideas and any number of basic concepts of law, social hierarchy, economy, and morality commonplace to early modern English culture.

The great burden of Becon's argument was to demonstrate the priority of reforming colonial government and society by carrot and stick. Undeniably, however, Becon laid greater emphasis on the latter, urging the adoption of strong coercive measures in order to eradicate Irish national feeling, and assuming that success would depend on building from entirely new foundations laid in the wake of a total military conquest. Ironically, some years earlier he and Sir William Herbert had been heavily criticized by Herbert's rival in the affairs of Kerry, Sir Edward Denny, for establishing a regime ostensibly intended to civilize the native population (principally by enforcing the adoption of English dress codes) which was effectively exploited to no other end than the enrichment of the two settlers—one of the abuses which Becon subsequently diagnosed as a source of Ireland's 'declination'. It is worth noting that Becon's discussion of the causes of corruption in a society also included passing reference to the dangers of 'faction' and 'bitter adversities' among colonists.

For all the intellectualism characteristic of an elevated and highly bookish Renaissance humanism, it would be surprising if Becon's text were not firmly rooted in its author's experiences as one of those responsible for restoring order in Munster in the aftermath of the Desmond rebellion. In 1611 Becon was described as the owner of land in the province, although he was no longer in Ireland. His date of death is unknown.   SEAN KELSEY

Sources R. Becon, *Solon his follie, or, A politique discourse touching the reformation of common weales conquered, declined, or corrupted*, ed. C. Carroll and V. Cary (1996) · *DNB* · R. Lascelles, ed., *Liber munerum publicorum Hiberniae … or, The establishments of Ireland*, 2 vols. [1824–30], vol. 2, p. 186 · *CSP Ire.*, 1586–92; 1611 · J. S. Brewer and W. Bullen, eds., *Calendar of the Carew manuscripts*, 6 vols., PRO (1867–73) • S. Anglo, 'A Machiavellian solution to the Irish problem: Richard Beacon's *Solon his follie* (1594)', *England and the continental Renaissance*, ed. E. Chaney and P. Mack (1990), 153–64 • M. Peltonen, *Classical humanism and republicanism in English political thought, 1570–1640* (1995) • Venn, *Alum. Cant.* • J. Foster, *Register of admissions to Gray's Inn, 1521–1881* (privately printed, London, 1887)

Becon, Thomas (1512/13–1567), theologian and Church of England clergyman, was born in Norfolk, near Thetford, in 1512 or 1513 to unknown parents.

Early evangelicalism Becon entered Cambridge in 1527, when the university was home to such future reformers as Hugh Latimer and Thomas Bilney. He long remembered hearing Latimer preach, especially his famous 'card' sermons of 1529, which he recalled hearing at the age of sixteen, and traced his own enthusiasm for an English version of the scriptures to his awakening by Latimer. After graduating in 1531 Becon began his lifelong career as a teacher at St John's College, Rushworth (now Rushford), Norfolk, in July 1532, declaring himself 'artium baccalaurius, acolitus, praeceptor puerorum' ('bachelor of arts, acolyte, instructor of children'; Bailey, *Becon and the Reformation*, 11). On 12 April following he was ordained priest. Becon's name does not appear on the list of collegians who subscribed to the royal supremacy in August 1534, so it is presumed that by then he had taken up residence as a tutor in a private household. By 1538 he had attracted the notice of Thomas, first Baron Wentworth, known for his patronage of reformed preachers, and was recommended (unsuccessfully) to Cromwell for preferment. At some point he became a chantrist in the parish of St Lawrence, Ipswich.

Nothing further is known about Becon until he attracted the attention of Bishop Edmund Bonner's commission on the six articles in February 1541. The commission examined Becon over sermons he had preached in Norwich diocese, and forced him to recant. Becon appears to have spoken against the third article (celibacy of priests), and perhaps against the first (the real presence in the eucharist) in addition to criticizing prayers for the dead, the cult of saints, and the sacraments of confirmation and extreme unction. Upon his release he retired to Kent, where he disguised himself as a layman, adopted the pseudonym of Theodore Basil, and in his own words 'changed the form of teaching the people from preaching to writing' (Bailey, *Becon and the Reformation*, 18).

During the next two years Becon wrote more than a dozen works, some of considerable length, which appeared in over twenty editions under his pen-name of Theodore Basil. His printer, John Mayler, took advantage of Becon's popularity when he printed Miles Coverdale's translation of Bullinger's treatise on marriage. This work, Becon states, was 'for the more ready sale, set forth in my name by the hungry printer with my preface, to make it the more plausible to the readers' (Becon, 1.29). His prolific output, published by one of the more notoriously protestant printer–publisher teams of John Mayler and

Thomas Becon (1512/13–1567), by unknown engraver, pubd 1564

John Gough, eventually drew the attention of the authorities. Mayler himself had been investigated as a sacramentary during the aftermath of the Act of Six Articles, and although Becon had taken precautions to conceal his identity, his alliance with a printer suspected of heresy could not go unnoticed. After the publication of the King's Book, which curtailed further reform, he was forced into a second recantation, on 8 July 1543. From the pulpit at Paul's Cross Becon was forced into the humiliating confession that he had feigned knowledge of Greek in his works in order to appear more learned, and had publicly to cut to pieces eleven of his own offending books.

First writings In these works Becon had avoided defending any explicit heresies, but he did espouse a strong Lutheran emphasis on the depravity of man, on 'sola scriptura', and on the frauds of the ecclesiastical hierarchy. He had avoided any discussion of the mass, thus steering clear of the six articles, and had been ambiguous on ceremonies and auricular confession. His association with Mayler seems to have led the privy council to examine his works, which they could not help but find too radical in the main without being heretical in their particulars. Most of his works of this period were hortatory rather than polemical, providing the lay reader with a catechetical exploration of scripture which aimed at increasing biblical literacy, and a vigorous protestant spirituality. Among his most popular writings was a series of dialogues based on his experiences as a tutor in sympathetic gentry house-holds in Kent. Beginning with *A Christmas Bankette* (1542), Becon wrote four such dialogues before falling foul of the authorities. Outwardly modelled on a genre highly popu-lar in the early modern period, these dialogues are akin to sermons in print, with his own literary persona, Phile-mon, setting out the reformed 'sola scriptura' agenda. Eschewing the rhetorical refinement of their Erasmian models, Becon's dialogues relied on copious catenae of biblical passages to support his theological assertions. Doubtless the abundance of scriptural material he pre-sented accounts for much of their popularity, especially as they appeared at a time when increasing restrictions were being placed on the reading of the English Bible.

Following this second recantation Becon again sought internal exile, this time among sympathetic gentry in rural Derbyshire, Staffordshire, and finally Warwickshire. In Staffordshire he linked up again with Robert Wisdom, who had shared the pulpit at his 1543 abjuration. Becon supported himself by tutoring and teaching, met Latimer briefly in Baxterley Hall, Warwickshire, and wrote. By 1546 his works had fallen under the royal ban on protest-ant literature.

Spokesman for reform After the accession of Edward VI in 1547, Becon's efforts on behalf of protestant reform began to attract more favourable attention than hitherto. His *Jewel of Joy* (written c.1547–8) addressed the pressing need to consolidate the progress of reform by suggesting that itinerant preachers be commissioned to tour the provin-ces whose efforts 'should help very much unto an uni-formity in religion' (Becon, 2.422). The idea went unreal-ized, but both Protector Somerset and Archbishop Cran-mer included him among their personal chaplains. Becon's links with the former were evidently close. Two of his prayers published in 1550 were recorded as having been 'a humble petition to the lord in the common prayer of the whole family at Shene, during the trouble of their lord and master the duke of Somerset his grace; gathered and set forth by Thomas Becon, minister there' (ibid., 3.34n.), and he dedicated books to the protector's wife and to his daughter Jane. Cranmer appointed Becon one of the six preachers at Canterbury, and his own *Catech-ism* (1548) and *Defence* (1550) show signs of Becon's influ-ence, as does the most significant instrument for achiev-ing uniformity—the prayer book of 1549. His influence has been seen, for instance, in the prayer of thanksgiving following the administration of communion.

Becon himself produced a *Catechism* during Edward's reign, but it remained unprinted until his collected works appeared under Elizabeth. It is of considerable interest in recording his humanistic views on education, recom-mending the study of the classics as well as of the scrip-tures, not least for the promotion of civility—'to interlace godliness in the lessons of profane writers maketh greatly unto the advancement of virtue; and heathen authors so read profit very much', he declared, and offered the opin-ion that 'learning without manners is as a gold ring in a swine's snout' (Becon, 2.383). He urged those who

instructed the young to treat their charges with consider-ation, arguing that a schoolmaster should be like a good father, who 'rather so useth his correction that the child-ren are more amended than hindered' (ibid., 2.385), and also advocated schooling for girls, declaring that:

> in my judgment, they do no less deserve well of the christian commonweal, that found and establish schools with honest stipends for the education of the women-children in godliness and virtue, than they which erect and set up schools for the institution of the men-children in good letters and godly manners. (ibid., 2.377)

In addition to his chaplaincies Becon received the lucra-tive London rectory of St Stephen Walbrook in 1548. The *de facto* lifting of the ban on clerical marriage enabled him to marry Elizabeth Godfrey of Winchester about this time. They had several children: Theodore, Basil, and Christophile died in infancy, but Becon was survived by Rachel, another Theodore, and a second Basil.

As always, Becon continued to publish new works, this time largely under his own name. His writings begin to show a drift toward Zwinglian theology, while retaining the strong pastoral interest for which he had become fam-ous. His concern with current social and economic prob-lems, seen most clearly in his *The Fortresse of the Faythfull*, (1550), drove him to express guarded sympathy for the oppressed, even for those who rebelled in Devon and Nor-folk in 1549. His talent for penning inspiring prayers led to the inclusion of more than three dozen of his, drawn largely from *The Pomander of Prayer* (published in 1558 but written in 1553) and *The Flower of Godlye Prayers* (c.1550), in the primer of 1553.

Some time before the end of Edward's reign, Becon wrote the last of his series of seven dialogues: *The Sycke Man's Salve*. It was to prove his most enduring work, appearing in eleven editions before 1600. Although not published until about 1560, it features the same interlocu-tors familiar to readers of his earlier dialogues. In essence the dialogue presents a protestant version of the late medieval genre of the *ars moriendi*, coupling a Calvinist emphasis on man's depravity with a rich scripturalism designed to demonstrate the need for faith in Christ's redemptive promises and to help effect the conversion that accompanies such faith. Becon's characters gather at the deathbed of a friend to instruct and comfort him as he faces death, seen here in traditional terms as the final moral battle of a man's life.

As in all his works Becon eschews traditional exegetical techniques, preferring to rely upon the plain sense of scripture. His lengthy catenae of biblical passages, which he provides in overwhelming abundance, give the reader an abridged and topically arranged digest of scripture. Despite the overtly pastoral orientation of the work, its polemical purpose is never far from the surface: even the prayers exhibit this trait, one common to mid-Tudor devo-tional literature.

Exile and return In August 1553, shortly after Mary's acces-sion, Becon was stripped of his offices and imprisoned in the Tower as a seditious preacher, along with Ridley, Sandys, Cox, and others. Released in March 1554, he joined a large group of English exiles in Strasbourg, where he lived intermittently until his return to England after Mary's death. He moved to Frankfurt in late 1554, and was one of the exiles who followed the leadership of Richard Cox in favouring a form of worship based on the 1552 Book of Common Prayer, rather than the more radical form urged by John Knox. Although he now wrote for a Latin-speaking readership, he also continued to address English works to his countrymen at home.

By the summer of 1556 Becon had moved to Marburg, where his wife was living, and he lectured at Marburg University, establishing himself under the patronage of Philip, landgrave of Hesse, whose son he tutored. At least two children were born to the Becons in exile: the second Theodore in 1556 and Rachel in 1558. Another son, Basil, was born in 1559 and was baptized in Becon's old cure of St Stephen Walbrook in January.

By now Elizabeth was on the throne, and Becon returned to a series of clerical preferments as one of England's leading protestant writers. He was one of the most active and exacting reformers on Elizabeth's first royal visitation of the clergy in 1559, heading the circuit made up of the dioceses of Canterbury, Rochester, Chichester, and Winchester. He was considered for a bishopric, but either declined episcopal office or was not eventually offered it. But he was presented to the canonry and prebendary of the fourth stall at Canterbury Cathedral on 17 September that year; he became rector of Buckland, Hertfordshire, on 21 October 1560; vicar of Christ Church, Newgate, on 3 March 1561; vicar of Sturry, near Canterbury, in April 1562; and rector of St Dionis Backchurch, in London, in August 1563. He was also briefly rector of his old living of St Stephen Walbrook in 1563. Despite being an outspoken critic of pluralism and non-residence throughout his life, Becon held these livings until his death.

Owing to his years in exile among such articulate reformers as John Foxe and John Bale, and to the uneven pace of reform after 1558, Becon's writings became more stridently anti-Catholic as time passed. As he himself wrote, he 'somewhat more sharpened my pen in some place against antichrist and his Babylonical brood' (Becon, 1.29). He began collecting and revising his works in preparation for a massive three-volume edition (*The Worckes of Thomas Becon*, 1564) which contained not only his earliest publications as Theodore Basil but also the polemics he wrote in exile and shortly after his return. In addition to his writing, Becon maintained an active preaching schedule and filled in for Archbishop Parker in routine diocesan visitations. He died on 30 June 1567 and was probably buried in Canterbury, perhaps in the cathedral itself.

Typical of the popular works of the Tudor Reformation, Becon's writings show a marked transformation in his views over time. His earliest works espouse a modified Lutheran theology while his last are decidedly Zwinglian, particularly regarding the sacraments. His homely and colloquial style, to which he undoubtedly owed his wide readership, attests the truth of his own estimate of his powers: 'Let others entreat of high mysteries, and climb up to the highest heavens: I shall be content to write of things according to my knowledge ... and to creep upon the ground' (Becon, 2.481).   SEYMOUR BAKER HOUSE

Sources D. S. Bailey, *Thomas Becon and the reformation of the church in England* (1952) · D. Bailey, 'Thomas Becon: some additional biographical notes', *N&Q*, 227 (1982), 402–4 · T. Becon, *Works*, ed. J. Ayre, 3 vols., Parker Society, 10–12 (1843–4) · *ESTC* · Bale, *Cat.* · Bale, *Index* · N. Beaty, *The craft of dying* (1970), 108–56 · S. House, 'Thomas Becon', *Sixteenth-century British nondramatic writers: second series*, ed. D. A. Richardson, DLitB, 136 (1994) · R. Pineas, 'Polemical technique in works of Thomas Becon', *Moreana*, 5 (1980), 49–55 · S. House, 'Reforming the Tudor dialogue', *Renaissance and Reformation*, 23 (1999), 4–23 · D. MacCulloch, *Thomas Cranmer: a life* (1996) · J. F. Davis, *Heresy and reformation in the south-east of England, 1520–1559*, Royal Historical Society Studies in History, 34 (1983) · W. P. Hangaard, *Elizabeth and the English Reformation* (1968)
Archives CCC Cam., autograph letter to Archbishop Parker, MS 114
Likenesses woodcut (aged forty-nine), BM, NPG; repro. in T. Becon, *The worckes of Thomas Becon ... with diverse other newe bookes*, 3 vols. [1564] [*see illus.*] · woodcut (aged forty-one), BM, NPG; repro. in T. Becon, *Principles of Christian religion* (1976) · woodcuts, repro. in J. Ayre, ed., *Early works*

Beconsall, Thomas (1663/4–1709), philosopher and Church of England clergyman, was the son of John Beconsall of Lemster, Cheshire. He matriculated, aged sixteen, on 30 March 1680, at Brasenose College, Oxford. He graduated BA in 1683, MA in 1686 (in which year he became a fellow), and BD in 1697. He was vicar of Steeple Aston in Oxfordshire from 1706 until his death.

Beconsall is significant as a critic of the philosopher John Locke, against whom he published a sermon and a treatise. *The Doctrine of a General Resurrection*, preached in the university church, Oxford, on Easter Monday 1697, assailed the theory of personal identity in Locke's *Essay Concerning Human Understanding*. In Locke's location of personal identity 'purely in consciousness' he found a kind of Platonism that denied that the body is integral to the self. Beconsall quickly equated this with a Socinian rejection of the Christian doctrine of bodily resurrection. He concluded that heresy lurked in Locke.

Much more important is Beconsall's *The Grounds and Foundations of Natural Religion* (1698) which contains, in its eleventh chapter, the first published critique, indeed one of the earliest mentions, of Locke's *Two Treatises of Government* (1689). Interestingly Beconsall analysed the *Treatises* and the *Essay* together, subsuming Locke's politics under his moral philosophy. Beconsall was conventional in his ethical sentiments and tory in his politics, but he provided a perceptive account of Locke. Thomas Hearne rightly described the book as 'a discourse about the law of nature' (*Remarks*, 1.231). It defended natural law and innate moral knowledge against 'the modern scepticks and latitudinarians' (Beconsall, title-page). Beconsall charged Locke with destroying natural law by his attack on innatism; with reducing moral knowledge to opinion, fashion, and custom; with making 'consciousness and conscience the same' (ibid., 249), thereby destroying conscience properly understood; and with undermining revealed religion as being mere priestcraft.

Beconsall next urged that parental and filial duties were

cardinal branches of natural law. No moral obligations more certainly 'carry the appearance of being innate' (Beconsall, 126). Yet Locke destroyed these duties. Beconsall takes the *Two Treatises* to be pre-eminently a critique of patriarchalism, and he correspondingly defends the 'empire' and 'dominion' which men have as fathers, husbands, and originally as kings and priests. He thinks Locke an incipient feminist for elevating 'the mother as an equal sharer in that power which accrues to the father as a parent' (ibid., 143). All this sounds like Sir Robert Filmer's divine right theory of monarchy, which had shored up the house of Stuart. But Beconsall flatly denied any 'disloyalty towards our present sovereign' (ibid., 181), and this seems ingenuous, for the Jacobite Hearne irritably called him 'an admirer of King William' (*Remains*, 1.231). Beconsall shows the beginnings of the repositioning of post-revolution toryism, which made possible the persistence of patriarchal moral and political theory for another century, but by then no longer encumbered with the special claims of the Stuart cause.

What is strikingly original in Beconsall's critique of Locke is that he identifies the Lockean state of nature and original contract not as a mythic history about primeval origins but as a juridical fact about present-day societies. On Beconsall's reading, for Locke political legitimacy is constantly re-created by every generation of citizens as it comes of age. Hence the crux of Locke's theory is taken to be the repudiation of filial obligation at the age of majority. He explores Locke's well-known paragraphs about what constitutes express and tacit consent, and shows how precarious Lockean political obligation is, since oaths of allegiance and inheritance of property apply to only a fraction of the population. It is a theory that quickly leads to the 'total dissolution' of government. Beconsall also dwells on Locke's passage about a person's right of withdrawal to other commonwealths or to empty places, '*vacuis locis*' (Beconsall, 171). Here he takes Locke seriously as a proponent of untrammelled emigration. Hence the Lockean dissolution of government is seen less as a theory of rebellion than as a theory about the right of withdrawal. This construal would be fundamental to American readings of the *vacuis locis* passage in the 1760s, but Beconsall deprecates it in the light of mercantilist concerns about the nation's demographic, and hence economic and military, strength. By Locke's dangerous principle, 'a nation may be dispeopled at pleasure, and consequently drained of her riches and treasure' (ibid., 178), and exposed to her enemies. Beconsall rounds off with a personal attack on Locke, by then a member of the Board of Trade, as a hypocritical salaried functionary of a mercantilist state bureaucracy.

On 23 June 1709 Hearne reported that Beconsall died 'last week at his parsonage suddenly, having been for a great while in a melancholy, hippish condition'; he had earlier described him as 'a strange hypochondriacal person' (*Remarks*, 1.231, 2.213–14). By his will dated 2 May 1709 Beconsall left money to his wife, Anne, and his two sisters; there is no mention of children. An inventory valued his

chattels and moneys at £297 11s., the largest items of value being glebe corn, books in the study, and moneys owed by Brasenose. MARK GOLDIE

Sources T. Beconsall, *The grounds and foundations of natural religion* (1698) · *Remarks and collections of Thomas Hearne*, ed. C. E. Doble and others, 11 vols., OHS, 2, 7, 13, 34, 42–3, 48, 50, 65, 67, 72 (1885–1921) · Foster, *Alum. Oxon.* · J. W. Yolton, *John Locke and the way of ideas* (1968)
Wealth at death £297 11s.: inventory of goods and chattels, Oxon. RO, B/3/44

Beconsawe, Alice. *See* Lisle, Lady Alice (*c*.1614–1685).

Beddingfield [née Rowe, Row], **Margery** (*bap.* 1742, *d.* 1763), murderer, was the daughter of John Rowe or Row (*c*.1702–1778), a substantial Suffolk farmer, and his wife, Margery (*c*.1710–1756). The couple had two sons while living at Kelsale and moved to Red House Farm, Blaxhall, in time to baptize Margery at the local church on 29 June 1742. On 3 July 1759, aged seventeen, she married a yeoman farmer, John Beddingfield (1738?–1762) of Hill Farm, Sternfield. They had two children, a daughter, Pleasance, who was baptized on 6 June 1760, and a son, John, who died in infancy in November 1761.

At Michaelmas 1761 John Beddingfield took on Richard Ringe (*bap.* 1740, *d.* 1763) as his husbandman. He was the only surviving son in a family of six of Samuel Ringe and Mary (*née* Cacamole), tenants of Moat Farm, Bredfield, near Woodbridge. Six months after Ringe joined the Beddingfield household he was noticed engaging in open displays of affection with Margery. Ringe was reckless, naïve, and lacking in discretion. Emboldened by Margery Beddingfield's offer of marriage Ringe began planning his master's murder. On one occasion he tried unsuccessfully to persuade another servant, Elizabeth Riches, to poison Beddingfield. A later attempt to lace his master's water with arsenic failed when Beddingfield noticed the sediment in his cup and refused to drink.

On 27 July 1762 John Beddingfield shared 3 pints of punch before bedtime with James Scarlett, a Saxmundham butcher, to seal the sale of a beast. He asked his wife to sleep with him in the parlour chamber, but she, determined to share a bed with her nurserymaid, Elizabeth Cleobald, refused. At 10 o'clock they wished each other goodnight without ill humour, and the house was soon quiet, with only Ringe lying awake. Half an hour later he entered Beddingfield's room and there strangled his master. Margery ignored her husband's muffled cries, and waited for Ringe to report success on his way through her room to the backhouse chamber. When eventually the servants were roused they were told that their master had died by falling out of bed head first. The Saxmundham surgeon, Sparham, made such a cursory examination that he failed to notice the obvious signs of foul play. Beddingfield was buried in Sternfield churchyard on 30 July.

It was some time before Elizabeth Cleobald, having left Margery Beddingfield's employment, gave evidence which led to a more thorough investigation. In the following March a trial was ordered at Bury St Edmunds assizes before Sir Richard Adams, a baron of the court of exchequer. Margery and Richard Ringe were tried for murder and petty treason, the justification for the latter charge being that the deceased was the master of one and husband of the other. The prosecution had the upper hand throughout, for the defence case was weak, and first Richard and then Margery were found guilty and sentenced to death, she by burning and he by hanging, his body to be dissected.

Ringe was the first to make a full confession, stating (probably truthfully) that he and Margery only became 'criminally acquainted' after her husband's death, and that in the course of the next few weeks her affection turned to dislike and then to hatred. Margery's confession came very late, only triggered by his, which she resented. She declared that 'she was guilty, and deserved to die, for having been too much privy to the murder of her husband, having held conversation with Ringe for that purpose for three months' (*Genuine Trial*, 40–44).

On 8 April 1763 the condemned pair were drawn on a sledge to Rushmere St Andrew, near Ipswich; both appeared penitent. Richard was hanged. Margery, as had become customary, was strangled before her body was burnt, in one of the last instances of this practice before its repeal in 1789. Ringe was then twenty-two and Margery Beddingfield not quite twenty-one. The *Ipswich Journal* reported the trial and executions briefly and unsensationally. However, there was no shortage of sightseers. The blue coat boys of the charity school Christ's Hospital were given 'half a day's liberty … to see Mrs Beddingfield executed'. Soon afterwards a London publisher produced *The Genuine Trial*, a verbatim report, including the pair's confessions, and in June the *Gentleman's Magazine* carried almost as full an account. Nowhere in print was Margery's maiden name disclosed, nor was it stated that her father still farmed at Blaxhall, and Ringe's at Bredfield. John Rowe held the Beddingfield assets in trust for his orphaned granddaughter, Pleasance. These she inherited, with £1000 from him, at his death in 1778.   J. M. BLATCHLY

Sources *The genuine trial of Margery Beddingfield and Richard Ringe* (1763) · *Ipswich Journal* (26 March 1763) · *Ipswich Journal* (2 April 1763) · *Ipswich Journal* (9 April 1763) · Suffolk RO, Ipswich, C/5/1/2/4/9 · *GM*, 1st ser., 33 (1763), 295–300 · G. R. Clarke, *History of Ipswich* (1830) · parish register, 29 June 1742, Blaxhall, Suffolk [baptism] · parish register, 3 July 1759, Sternfield, Suffolk [marriage]

Beddington, John Louis [Jack] (1893–1959), publicity manager, was born on 30 January 1893, at Barkston Gardens, South Kensington, London, one of three sons of Charles Lindsay Beddington (*b*. 1866), barrister, and his wife, Stella Goldschmidt de Libantia. His family were Jewish and came originally from Alsace, but they made a great deal of money out of the 'rag trade' in London. Their surname was Moses, but in the mid-1850s Jack's grandfather changed it to Beddington. The family firm of H. E. and M. Moses was wound up in the 1880s, and later generations of the family had no connection with the clothing industry.

Jack Beddington was educated at Wellington College and at Balliol College, Oxford, where he did no work but was 'ecstatically happy' (Ullstein, 15–17) and was ploughed

in Greats. He enlisted in the King's Own Yorkshire light infantry at the outbreak of the First World War and served until 1919, though severely wounded at Ypres. On 31 January 1918, at Holy Trinity, Brompton, Beddington married Olivia Margaret, daughter of Arthur Newton Streatfeild, and they had a son and a daughter.

After the war Beddington worked for the Asiatic Petroleum Company (the Far Eastern arm of Royal Dutch–Shell) in Shanghai, until he was invalided home in 1928. In London, on his complaining of the poor standard of advertising, he was promptly given the job of publicity manager under the general manager, F. L. Halford, taking on the same role in Shell-Mex and BP Ltd when that joint company was set up in 1932 to market petrol and other oil products for Shell and BP (though the BP advertising was never as successful as that produced for Shell). Continuing in the pioneering tradition of Frank Pick at London Transport, Beddington became famous for the posters and press campaigns created under his aegis.

Advertising posters had from the early 1920s been fixed onto Shell lorries, and Beddington made this 'lorrybill' series his own, creating for Shell a strong identity both with art and with the countryside. Fine artists as well as graphic designers were used, unknown as well as established. In 1932 Beddington gave Graham Sutherland his first commission. Other artists included Paul Nash and Ben Nicholson. His experimental approach traded uniformity for the spontaneous individuality of numerous artists. An exhibition catalogue later described the Shell and London Transport posters as 'glittering islands in a becalmed sea of unrelieved banality' (Guyatt, foreword). Beddington was also responsible for the injection of wit and humour into the company's press campaigns, using artists such as Rex Whistler and Edward Bawden. He was receptive to new ideas and, as a result of an approach by John Betjeman, the Shell County Guides were published, the first of which appeared in 1934.

The advertising could be self-indulgent, Beddington himself even appearing in one press advertisement—one of a series advertising the advertising. However, his judgement though shrewd was not condescending, and it was perhaps in this ability to combine quality with popular appeal that his supreme talent lay. His policies gained for Shell-Mex and BP a reputation for enlightened patronage and sophisticated advertising, the lorrybills idea in particular provoking much praise for not cluttering the countryside with hoardings, a contemporary obsession. Beddington was influential in breathing vitality and vision into the British advertising and design world, where art and commerce were seldom seen to mix.

Flamboyant, dapper, and with a keen wit, Beddington was businesslike and brusque. However, he appreciated talent, and his kindness and encouragement to young painters and writers were well known. In 1936 he was appointed assistant general manager of Shell-Mex and BP Ltd, keeping his position as publicity manager but taking on some responsibility for staff matters, and when the Second World War began he was appointed joint manager of the staff department of the Petroleum Board. In April

1940 he was appointed director of the films division at the Ministry of Information, where he remained until 1946. Among the documentaries produced in his time there were *Desert Victory* (1943) and *The True Glory* (1945). Beddington also coined the anti-gossip slogan, 'Be like Dad: keep Mum'. He was made a CBE in 1943.

After the war Beddington joined Colman Prentis and Varley Ltd, an advertising agency, and became deputy chairman, a post he held until his death. An honorary fellow of the Society of Industrial Artists and of the Royal Society of Arts, and a governor of the Foundation for Visual Education, he was also a member of the National Advisory Council on Art Education, and of the council of the Royal College of Art.

Jack Beddington died suddenly of a heart attack on 13 April 1959, aged sixty-six, at 22 Knightsbridge Court, London. He was survived by his wife.   V. JOHNSON

Sources W. S. Mitchell, 'Obituary for Jack Beddington', May 1959, BP Archive, University of Warwick · *Shell-BP News*, 141 (May 1959) · *The Times* (15 April 1959) · V. Nye, 'Recollections of Shell and BP advertising', BP Archive, University of Warwick · M. Haworth-Booth, *E. McKnight Kauffer: a designer and his public* (1979) · G. Ullstein, 'Jack Beddington', *Design*, 31 (1951), 15–17 · J. Beddington, 'Patronage in art to-day', *Art in England*, ed. R. S. Lambert (1938), 82–7 · '50 years of Shell advertising', *Shellman* (June 1969), supplement · D. Bernstein, 'Personal view', *That's Shell — that is! An exhibition of Shell advertising art*, ed. T. Sheppard and J. Hoole (1983) [exhibition catalogue, Barbican Art Gallery, London, 5 July – 4 Sept 1983] · R. Guyatt, foreword, *Fifty years of Shell advertising* (1969) [exhibition catalogue, London, 1969] · W. Mitchell, *A brush with industry*, Shell UK Ltd, c.1983, BP Archive, University of Warwick [interview on video] · Shell-Mex and BP Ltd, *The first 25 years—history as mirrored in advertising of Shell-Mex and BP Ltd, 1932–1957* (1957) · J. Hewitt, 'The "nature" and "art" of Shell advertising in the early 1930s', *Journal of Design History*, 5 (1992), 121–39 · I. McLaine, *Ministry of morale—home front morale and the ministry of information in World War II* (1979) · Shell UK Ltd, 'The fine art of motoring', *The Shell art collection at the National Motor Museum, Beaulieu* (May 1993) · W. Gaunt, introduction, in *Art in British advertising*, Advertising Creative Circle (1955) [exhibition catalogue, RBA Galleries, 22 Nov –7 Dec 1955] · *CGPLA Eng. & Wales* (1959) · d. cert.
Archives University of Warwick, BP Archive, incl. posters and press material produced under Beddington and some artwork | FILM University of Warwick, BP Archive, *A brush with industry*, Shell UK Ltd [video; concerns Beddington's work]
Likenesses R. Whistler, portrait, 1930–39 (*A plain publicity manager*), priv. coll. · portrait in advertisement, April 1933, University of Warwick, BP Archive, 23/01293 · J. Armstrong, poster, 1939 ('These men use Shell—farmers'), University of Warwick, BP Archive, 538 · photograph, repro. in Ullstein, 'Jack Beddington', p. 15 · portrait, repro. in Bernstein, 'Personal view'
Wealth at death £28,408 19s. 5d.: probate, 23 June 1959, *CGPLA Eng. & Wales*

Beddoe, John (1826–1911), physician and anthropologist, was born in Bewdley, Worcestershire, on 21 September 1826, the son of John Beddoe JP, a merchant, and Emma, daughter of Henry Barrer Child of Bewdley. Educated at Bridgnorth School, he studied medicine at University College, London, graduating in 1851. He then studied at Edinburgh University where he received an MD in 1853 and became house physician at the Edinburgh Royal Infirmary. In 1846 Beddoe began observations on hair and eye colours in the west of England, and continued these in Orkney (1852). During the Crimean War he was assistant physician at a civil hospital at Renkioi. After completing his medical training at Vienna, Beddoe made an extended continental tour. In 1857 he began practising as a physician at Clifton in Bristol. On 15 September 1858 in Foulden, Berwickshire, he married Agnes Montgomerie (*b.* 1828/9), daughter of the Revd Alexander Christison and his wife, Helen, and niece of Sir Robert Christison. They had one son and one daughter. Beddoe was physician to the Bristol Royal Infirmary (1862–73) and consulting physician to the children's hospital there (1866–1911).

Beddoe began active research in ethnology during his early travels in Europe scanning bodies 'ready to hand in streets and market places' (Beddoe, *Races*, 2), and became an authority on the physical characteristics of living European races. He was to have an important influence on the development of anthropology in both Britain and continental Europe, leaving an inheritance of great taxonomic subtlety as he strove to compile, county by county, a detailed physical anthropological account of the races of Britain before the railway confused older patterns of distribution. Beddoe devised three categories for eye colour: the first consisted of blue and light grey, the second of dark grey and very light hazel or yellow, the third of brown, hazel, and black. In England he found the 'British Bronze race' (ibid., 270), a 'richly endowed' breed, was preserved in its greatest purity in those with blue eyes and light hair, while the artisan class was 'generally darker' and increasing disproportionately through 'rapid multiplication' (ibid.). His empirical observations were influenced by racialist ideas which emerged through his choice of language, with terms such as 'purity' and 'rapid multiplication' betraying his prejudices and alignments. Beddoe's observations on colour and race hierarchy had already been endorsed by the renowned ethnologist James Cowles Prichard, who argued that the lighter varieties of the human race were analogous to 'the finer, and more delicate specimens in other kinds' which are often endowed with 'a more beautiful appearance' (ibid., 169); these ideas were soon taken up and developed by Francis Galton, founder of eugenics. Beddoe and Galton corresponded and exchanged research: for example, in 1887 Beddoe sent Galton his 'promised paper on the stature of the older races of England, as deduced from their long bones' (Beddoe to Galton, 26 April 1887, UCL, Galton MS, 199). Evidently, the class and race based statistics Beddoe had accumulated were useful for Galton's own researches into heredity and population.

The cluster of ideas informing Beddoe's researches directly influenced the work of the late nineteenth-century sexologist Havelock Ellis. Ellis took up the pattern of sexual difference at work in Beddoe's observations on colour, observing in *Man and Woman: a Study of Human Sexual Secondary Characters* (1894): 'women have darker hair than men, and decidedly darker eyes' (pp. 314–15). He noted that the question of the proportion of brown eyes among women in a given population 'was fully studied in the first place by the late Dr. Beddoe' (ibid., 309) and declared himself 'indebted to Dr. Beddoe for a series of figures showing the sexual differences in various parts of Great Britain' (ibid.). Charles Darwin drew on Beddoe's work in *The Descent of Man, and Selection in Relation to Sex* (1871), arguing:

> Dr Beddoe has lately proved that, with the inhabitants of Britain, residence in towns and certain occupations have a deteriorating influence on height; and he infers that the result is to a certain extent inherited, as is likewise the case in the United States. Dr Beddoe further believes that wherever a 'race attains its maximum of physical development, it rises highest in energy and moral vigour'. (Darwin, 115)

Beddoe emphasized 'the theory of a hereditary and progressive physical degeneration in certain classes of the inhabitants of towns', selecting Cornwall as one of the few places in Britain 'which produce the finest and largest men'. These men 'yield more than their share of ability and energy for the national benefit' (Beddoe, 'Stature', 566–7). His research was underpinned by ideas of social and racial hierarchy and national worth, ideas which reached full fruition in Galton's theories of 'civic worth' in the late nineteenth century. Beddoe's interest in the relationships among physical appearance, moral qualities, and social position was part of the enthusiasm for a biological basis for hierarchy which came to birth in the nineteenth century.

In 1853 Beddoe published 'Contributions to Scottish ethnology' and in 1908, in 'A last contribution to Scottish ethnology', he surveyed intervening developments in the field. In 1867 he received from the Welsh national eisteddfod a prize of 100 guineas for the best essay on the origin of the English nation; this became part of *The Races of Britain: a Contribution to the Anthropology of Western Europe* (1885). Beddoe's racial data 'On the stature and bulk of man in the British Isles' appeared in 1870 in *Memoirs Read before the Anthropological Society of London*. In 1903 he published a paper in *L'Anthropologie*, 'De l'évaluation et de la signification de la capacité crânienne', which was received with hostility by Karl Pearson, professor of applied mathematics and mechanics at University College, London, from 1884, and founder of biometrics, and M. A. Lewenz, in a joint paper in *Biometrica* in 1904. They accused him of showing 'a complete ignorance of the nature of modern statistical theory', namely correlation—the mathematical process of finding the best linear relation between the known value of one character and the most probable value of a second—and the regression curve; it was, they emphasized, only with such methods that 'we can hope to render anthropometry in all its branches a real science. The day for the old methods is once and for ever gone' (Lewenz and Pearson, 367–8). Conceding that Beddoe had 'done good service in widening the field of anthropometric interest in this country', they stressed that

> statistical enquiry is not a field for guesswork and elementary arithmetic; there is a mathematical science of statistics which must be learnt, and papers dealing numerically with anthropometric and craniometric data which do not now apply this theory are simply outside the field of science.

They also emphasized that in addition to method in statistical reduction a craniologist should distinguish between 'what holds for a local race of man, and what may be applied to mankind as a whole', and criticized Beddoe for drawing no distinction here, or between the sexes.

> Dr Beddoe makes no attempt to deduce intra-racial formulae from fairly homogeneous racial series by recognised statistical methods; he does not then compare these among themselves and see whether an inter-racial one can be deduced from them. He simply makes a guess, tries it on a most heterogeneous series, and if it does not fit makes another guess … This is not science; it is the dilettantism which in the past has made anthropometry and craniometry impossible subjects for academic study. (ibid., 396–7)

Beddoe replied in the *Journal of the Royal Anthropological Institute* (34, 1904).

Beddoe was a founding member of the Ethnological Society, president of the Anthropological Society (1869–70) and of the Anthropological Institute (1889–91). In 1905 he delivered the Huxley lecture of the Anthropological Institute, 'Colour and race', and received the Huxley memorial medal. He served on the council of the British Association, 1870–75, and co-authored its 'Anthropological instructions for travellers'. In 1890 he was made Officier (première classe) de l'Instruction Publique, France; he was a member of a number of European anthropological societies. He was elected FRCP in 1873 and after retiring from practice in Bristol in 1891 he moved to Bradford-on-Avon, Wiltshire. In the same year the University of Edinburgh conferred on him the honorary degree of LLD and in 1908 the University of Bristol elected him honorary professor of anthropology. A founder member of the Bristol and Gloucestershire Archaeological Society (established in 1875), Beddoe became its president in 1890, and in 1909 was president of the Wiltshire Archaeological and Natural History Society. At the time of his death he was president of the British Kyrle Society. Beddoe died on 19 July 1911 at his home, The Chantry, Bradford-on-Avon, as a result of a prostatic haemorrhage.

ANGELIQUE RICHARDSON

Sources DNB · WWW · J. Beddoe, *The races of Britain: a contribution to the anthropology of western Europe* (1885) · J. Beddoe, 'On the stature and bulk of man in the British Isles', *Memoirs read before the Anthropological Society of London*, 3 (1870) · C. Darwin, *The descent of man, and selection in relation to sex*, 2 vols. (1871); repr. in 1 vol. (1981) · J. Beddoe, letter to F. Galton, 26 April 1887, UCL, Galton MS 199 · J. C. Prichard, *Researches into the physical history of man* (1813); repr. ed. by G. W. Stocking (1973) · A. Richardson, '"Some science underlies all art": the dramatization of sexual selection and racial biology in Thomas Hardy's *A pair of blue eyes* and *The well-beloved*', *Journal of Victorian Culture*, 3 (1998), 302–38 · M. D. Biddiss, ed., *Images of race* (1979) · IGI · m. cert. · d. cert. · M. A. Lewenz and K. Pearson, 'On the measurement of internal capacity from cranial circumference', *Biometrica* (1904), 366–97

Archives University of Bristol, corresp. and papers | Salisbury and South Wiltshire Museum, letters to A. H. L. F. Pitt-Rivers · UCL, letters to Sir Francis Galton · UCL, letters to Karl Pearson

Likenesses E. B. Warne, portrait, 1907, Municipal Art Gallery, Bristol

Wealth at death £1534 10s. 11d.: probate, 10 Nov 1911, CGPLA Eng. & Wales

Beddoes, Thomas (1760–1808), chemist and physician, was born at Shifnal in Shropshire on 13 April 1760, the son of Ann Beddoes (*née* Whitehall), and her husband, Richard Beddoes (*d.* 1803), a tanner who was part of a prosperous

Thomas Beddoes (1760–1808), by Charles Turner Warren, pubd 1810 (after Edward Bird)

and politically liberal commercial circle. Thomas Beddoes was educated at Bridgnorth grammar school, and tutored (1773) by the Revd Samuel Dickenson at Plymhill, Staffordshire. He was at Pembroke College, Oxford, from 1776 (after one year, when he was mistakenly enrolled at St John's). While at Oxford, he attended chemical demonstrations at the Ashmolean Museum, as well as teaching himself French, Italian, and German. He graduated BA in 1779 and moved to London to work under John Sheldon, a former pupil of William Hunter, at the Great Windmill Street school of anatomy. Beddoes also attended the chemical laboratory of Bryan Higgins in Greek Street. In 1784 he translated the work of the Italian naturalist and physiologist Lazzaro Spallanzani and then proceeded to Edinburgh to study medicine.

At Edinburgh Beddoes was impressed less by the teaching of the ageing William Cullen than by the chemical lectures of Joseph Black and their medical implications. In December 1786 he returned to Oxford to take his MB and MD, with plans to advance his knowledge of chemistry. He continued his translations of continental chemical works, and the following summer visited France, especially the academy at Dijon, where Guyton de Morveau was working on the purification of air. During that visit, which included a meeting with Antoine Lavoisier in Paris, Beddoes became aware of political developments in France and of the varying feelings among scientists about their implications. His own support for the democratic aspirations of French political activists was established at this time. Back in Oxford by the end of 1787, he was appointed reader in chemistry in the spring of 1788. No full lecture notes survive, but he lectured on both chemistry and geology, taking a firm stance in the latter against geologists who emphasized the power of water—as against heat—as a geological agent.

Beddoes spent the early years of the French Revolution in various states of political distress as the early hopes of the democratic revolution were lost in bloodshed and betrayal. He was constantly in dispute with the Bodleian Library in Oxford, judging the library and its purchasing policies to be obstacles to advanced scientific learning in Oxford, especially in chemistry. In the political world Beddoes came to see the French Jacobins as agents of sabotage against a vital political advance. In 1793 Beddoes left Oxford for Bristol, tainted with a reputation for sedition, but still relatively optimistic about the hopes for a chemically based medical agenda, at least in Britain. He had come to feel that social change, involving a renewed social asceticism, had to be the foundation for the reformation of medicine. The irony was that these hopes had to be nourished at the very time that the French experience was generating intense counter-reaction in his native land.

This longed-for conjunction between a reformed (chemical) medicine and a reformed social order was the fruit of Beddoes's education in medicine and science and his liberal and anti-imperialist politics. Around this joint project he conceived an Enlightenment idea of social medicine that developed in two parts. First, chemistry had shown a new way of describing human physiology and human health, and had then generated agents to influence those for the better: Beddoes advanced this ideal in practical ways by collaborating with the inventor James Watt, who in the mid-1790s designed apparatus for Beddoes's experiments. Second, this scientific insight had been the work of doctors and scientists opposed to the old regime of political corruption, social disease, and medical deception. Social disorder and social consumption, the world of snobbery, fashionable illness, drunkenness, bad education, all were cited as agents of disease. Beddoes exempted neither the apparently ill society ladies of Bath nor the irresponsible and family-destroying male agricultural labourers whose drinking of cider wrecked their employment and their children's future hopes. The years in Bristol from 1793 to his death saw Beddoes trying to provide medical care that endorsed his social explanation for most illness while also seeing him writing long and often ironical accounts of the likely failure of both his projects. His medical therapeutics relied on gases and their curative powers. His medical anthropology suggested that no real community of understanding, either within medicine or without, especially in a period of political reaction, would come to realize the possibilities of chemical (or 'pneumatic') medicine at all.

In April 1794 Beddoes married Anna (1773–1824), a daughter of Richard Lovell *Edgeworth, and sister of the novelist Maria Edgeworth. The marriage represented both the extent of Beddoes's closeness to the midlands world he had geographically left, especially the Lunar Society of Birmingham (Edgeworth was a member), and the personal strains in his private life (the marriage was not a success). Political pressures increased in the mid-1790s, with counter-revolution in France and increasing repression at home. For a time in Bristol Beddoes was part of a group of active opponents of government policy, a group that included the publisher Joseph Cottle, and the poets Robert Southey and Samuel Taylor Coleridge. He was thereby a central player, even a kind of actor–manager, in the early political history and fortunes of English Romanticism. Medically, he began to establish a venue for the use of gases in the treatment of illness, and the Pneumatic Institute was opened in Dowry Square in Hotwells, Bristol, in 1799. A strong encouragement to that opening was provided by the arrival the previous October of the young Cornishman Humphry Davy; in his brief time in Bristol as Beddoes's assistant Davy became famous for his work on the properties of nitrous oxide, and in 1801 he took up an appointment at the Royal Institution in London. Political opponents of Beddoes and his circle made extensive use of the satirical possibilities of the pneumatic medical project, with images of pompous English friends of Britain's enemies talking dangerous nonsense under the influence of gas.

By 1802 the Pneumatic Institute had changed its name and its aspirations, becoming the Preventive Medical Institution for the Sick and Drooping Poor. The aim was early treatment, especially in tubercular cases, but many of the rules and practices indicated Beddoes's ambivalent feelings towards the poor. Quacks might prey on them, but many of the poor brought misery on themselves through negligence, laziness, and ignorance. Beddoes never altered his view that the medicine of the future, which he had hoped would be advanced by the use of gases, would always be governed by a new and strengthened medical élite of the right kind. Political commitment to democracy accompanied by a progressive and dominant medical leadership, providing therapies on terms that it set for the people, was the motive force of Beddoes's career and his writings, with their contradictions. Many of the extended writings he composed on the culture of medicine and sickness were written after he felt that the tide had turned against the chemical medicine and social reforms he proposed; the most systematic of these were *Hygeia*, which appeared in eleven monthly instalments between 1802 and 1803, and *The Manual of Health* (1806). These have a bitterness and a diagnostic edge that suggest a romantic image of the writer as political exile, a disillusioned critic of the vanities of commercial society and its fashions, as well as of the idiocies of the poor. For his opponents, both scientific and political, Beddoes's attacks on everything—from book-based education to medicine as a trade and a breeding ground for quacks—express the sarcastic and élitist disappointments of a patrician revolutionary whose misconceived project had failed. Those close to Beddoes in his last years testified to his deep sense that failure and isolation were his fate in times that had forced him into pessimism and marginality. He entrusted his financial affairs, the guardianship of his children, and (as was widely known) the companionship of his wife to his friend the Cornish landowner Davies Gilbert, formerly Giddy (1767–1839), who later became a Conservative MP.

Beddoes died at his home, 3 Rodney Place, Clifton, Bristol, on 23 December 1808, of a 'dropsy in his chest', although one account states: 'He died of experiments tried upon himself' (*GM*, 79, 1809, 88, 120). His wife survived him. Speculation abounds as to why his papers were almost entirely destroyed. Some of the gloomy feelings buried with those papers, ruminations no doubt on the failure of a medical version of Enlightenment absolutism, may have been handed on to his son, the medical man, poet, and eventual suicide, Thomas Lovell *Beddoes.

MICHAEL NEVE

Sources J. E. Stock, *Memoirs of the life of Thomas Beddoes* (1811) · Davies Gilbert correspondence, Cornwall RO · R. Porter, *Doctor of society: Thomas Beddoes and the sick trade in late Enlightenment England* (1992) · D. A. Stansfield, *Thomas Beddoes, MD, 1760–1808: chemist, physician, democrat* (1984) · M. R. Neve, 'Natural philosophy, medicine and the culture of science in provincial England', PhD diss., U. Lond., 1984 · *GM*, 1st ser., 79 (1809), 88, 120, 157

Archives Bodl. Oxf., corresp. and papers | Birm. CA, letters to Boulton family; letters to James Watt · Cornwall RO, letters to Davies Gilbert · Glos. RO, letters to T. E. B. Estcourt · Keele University, Thomas Wedgwood corresp. · U. Edin., Joseph Black's corresp.

Likenesses S. T. Roche, miniature on ivory, 1794, NPG · T. West?, colour etching, 1803, Wellcome L. · C. T. Warren, line engraving, pubd 1810 (after E. Bird), BM, NPG [*see illus.*] · J. Sharples, pastel drawing, Bristol City Art Gallery · pencil drawing (after E. Bird), Wellcome L.

Beddoes, Thomas Lovell (1803–1849), poet, was born on 30 June 1803 at 3 Rodney Place, Clifton, the second of the four children of Dr Thomas *Beddoes (1760–1808), physician and author, and his wife, Anna (1773–1824), daughter of Richard Lovell *Edgeworth (1744–1817) of Edgeworthtown and his first wife, Anna Maria. At Dr Beddoes's death his children were left in the guardianship of their mother and Davies Giddy, later known as Sir Davies Gilbert, president of the Royal Society. The family moved to Great Malvern in 1811 and in 1814 to Bath, where Beddoes attended the grammar school. He went on to Charterhouse School in 1817. He achieved academic distinction, winning the Latin prize essay in 1818, and began to show his impatience with authority and convention. He read widely in Elizabethan and Jacobean drama during this period and wrote *Scaroni, or, The Mysterious Cave: a Romantic Fiction*, but his first publication was a poem, 'The Comet' (*Morning Post*, 5 July 1819).

Beddoes entered Pembroke College, Oxford, on 1 May 1820 and published *The Improvisatore, in Three Fyttes, with other Poems* in March 1821. He regretted the publication, destroying many copies. In November 1822 Rivington published *The Brides' Tragedy* which was praised by Bryan Waller Procter (Barry Cornwall) and George Darley and represents Beddoes's most finished attempt to write a drama modelled on the Jacobean. Between 1823 and 1825 he worked on several plays: four acts of *The Second Brother* survive, act I only of *Torrismond*, and fragments of *Love's Arrow Poisoned* and *The Last Man*. T. F. Kelsall wrote of 'the great vigour & fertility of his mind' at this time:

> He would write a scene in one of his many contemplated dramas, & being dissatisfied with it, the next day produce another—identical in design but replete with different imagery—yet both of the noblest & most impressive

character—& the first composition would be tost aside or destroyed with the utmost nonchalence. (Kelsall, xvi)

In 1824 Beddoes stood guarantor with Procter, Kelsall, and Nicholas Waller for the publication of the *Posthumous Poems* of P. B. Shelley, whom he admired above all his near contemporaries. Illness in February 1824 caused temporary loss of Beddoes's hair; the close-cropped head in Nathan C. Branwhite's 1824 portrait appears broad-browed and somewhat square, the eyes wide-set. He spent May to July 1824 recuperating and travelling in Italy, arriving too late to visit his dying mother in Florence. His examination for the BA degree was delayed until 5 May 1825, by which time he was again planning to leave England.

Beddoes's interests turned towards medicine and amid the often startling imagery of his later poetry there are recurrent references to scientific ideas; he argued that anatomy and related sciences were necessary to the 'correct and masterly delineations of the passions: ... it still remains for some one to exhibit the sum of his experience in mental pathology & therapeutics ... developed for the purpose of ascertaining some important psychical principle—i.e. a tragedy' (Beddoes, 609). He told Kelsall he was searching for 'every shadow of a proof or probability of an after-existence, both in the material & immaterial nature of man' (ibid., 629): he distrusted metaphysics but associated his scientific and literary work with a spiritual quest which encompassed alchemical, Kabbalistic, rabbinical, and Islamic texts. On 27 July 1825 he matriculated at Göttingen University where he studied physiology (under Blumenbach), surgery, and chemistry. He remained at Göttingen until 1829 and there wrote the first version of the five-act play which was his major work, *Death's Jest-Book, or, The Fool's Tragedy*. The play shows his mastery of blank verse, as well as the influence of contemporary German literature, particularly the work of Ludwig Tieck and his theory of 'romantic irony'. The plot turns on the raising of a body from the grave and was intended to depict a triumph over death but even in this first version the triumph is Death's, as Beddoes later acknowledged by changing the subtitle to *The Day will Come*. The text is an interplay of alchemical and anatomical themes, of the Gothic and burlesque, its revolutionary politics underwritten by evolutionary ideas which compound the theories of Erasmus Darwin with Blumenbach's studies in craniology and comparative anatomy. *Death's Jest-Book* also includes most of the lyrics for which Beddoes is chiefly remembered. He planned to publish the play in 1829 but was discouraged by Procter, Kelsall, and J. G. H. Bourne; he revised and added to it through the 1830s and 1840s but never prepared a final version.

After receiving his friends' criticism Beddoes became depressed and suicidal, and was expelled from university for riotous drinking bouts on 12 and 17 August 1829. Beddoes called himself 'a non-conductor of friendship' (Beddoes, 610); his letters reveal no intimacy with women and his most intense relationships appear to have been with Bernard Reich in Göttingen from 1826 to 1829 and

later with Konrad Degen in Frankfurt. Blumenbach's testimonial that his 'amount of talent exceeded that of every student who had received instruction [at Göttingen] during his professorship' (Donner, *Beddoes*, 270) enabled Beddoes to continue his studies under Professor J. L. Schönlein at Würzburg, where he received the degree of doctor of medicine on 10 September 1831. The lyrics he wrote at this time, including the much anthologized 'Dream Pedlary', are among his finest but again Beddoes's interests were straying from poetry: always a radical he became involved in the *Burschenschaft* movement for a united Germany. He was soon a popular speaker and contributed articles on reform to the *Volksblatt*. Following a speech made at Gaibach supporting the campaign for Polish freedom and attacking the aristocracy, Beddoes was made a member of the *Freie Reichstadt* but also received a government order to leave Würzburg on 10 July 1832. After a short period in Strasbourg he followed Schönlein to Zürich, matriculating in the university on 25 April 1833 and contributing German political poems to *Der Republikaner*.

In 1837 Beddoes was again revising and expanding *Death's Jest-Book*; he proposed to include the play in a volume called *The Ivory Gate*, the title of a sequence of poems and prose stories which survive only in fragments. Beddoes prepared a title-page (his name aptly anagrammed as Theobald Vesselldoom) but soon abandoned the project. In 1839 he became notorious in Zürich as the author of *Antistraussianischer Gruss*, a satirical poem concerning the dismissal of the radical Dr Strauss from the theological chair. His reputation as a satirist perhaps obliged him to leave Zürich in April 1840, seven months after the fall of the radical regime. During the 1840s he lived for short periods in Berlin, Baden in Aargau, and Frankfurt. *Lines Written in Switzerland* is a powerful statement of his alienation from English cultural life and the work of his contemporaries. He visited England in 1846–7, unnerving his cousins at Cheney Longville by arriving on a donkey. He was suffering from neuralgia and spent long periods alone. 'Scientific researches, far and wide in the fields of natural philosophy, and psychological speculations, ... appeared alone to fill up the measure of his thoughts' (Kelsall, cx–cxi). He appears neatly bearded in the 1847 portrait by Tobler, the long nose fleshier than Branwhite had shown; neither portrait suggests the 'eccentric' or 'grotesque' appearance mentioned in some accounts.

On his return to Frankfurt Beddoes resumed scientific work but blood poisoning caused by an accident while dissecting led to a six-month illness. He left Frankfurt on 3 July 1848; a fortnight later in the Cigogne Hotel in Basel he opened an artery in his leg. His life was saved but Beddoes is reported to have torn the bandage from his wound. Gangrene developed; in October the leg was amputated below the knee. The hospital record states that Beddoes died of 'apoplexy' on 26 January 1849. His suicide (probably by curare) was kept secret by his family and friends for many years but is implicit in his deathbed letter: 'I ought to have been among other things a good poet; Life was too great a bore on one peg & that a bad one' (Beddoes, 683). He was buried in Basel Hospital cemetery on 29 January. He left the small estate at Hopesay, Shropshire, which had provided his main income, to his brother Charles and his work in manuscript to T. F. Kelsall with the instruction to 'print or not as *he* thinks fit' (ibid.). Kelsall carried out this request with loyalty and conviction, publishing *Death's Jest-Book* in 1850 and the *Poems Posthumous and Collected* in 1851. *The Works* edited by H. W. Donner (1935) is the definitive edition, including a variorum of *Death's Jest-Book* and seventy letters. Beddoes's work has been unavailable for long periods and despite the admiration of poets such as Robert Browning—'the power of the man is immense & irresistible' he wrote to Kelsall in 1868 (Donner, *Browning*, 105)—and Ezra Pound, and critics including Northrop Frye and Christopher Ricks, he has never been widely read; the extraction of lyrics from *Death's Jest-Book* has perhaps paradoxically diverted attention from the one work by which his achievement may be judged.

ALAN HALSEY

Sources T. F. Kelsall, 'Memoir', in T. L. Beddoes, *The poems posthumous and collected* (1851) • T. L. Beddoes, *The works*, ed. H. W. Donner (1935) [incl. letters and bibliography] • H. W. Donner, *Thomas Lovell Beddoes: the making of a poet* (1935) • H. W. Donner, ed., *The Browning box* (1935) • *DNB* • J. W. Lundin, 'T. L. Beddoes at Göttingen', *Studia Neophilologica*, 48 (1971), 484–99 • T. L. Beddoes, *Selected poetry*, ed. J. Higgens and M. Bradshaw, rev. edn (1999) [with 'Introduction' by J. Higgens and M. Bradshaw] • N. Frye, *A study of English Romanticism* (1968) • J. R. Thompson, *Thomas Lovell Beddoes* (1985)

Archives Bodl. Oxf., corresp. and papers | Charterhouse School, Scaroni MS

Likenesses N. C. Branwhite, portrait, 1824 (after portrait, Pembroke College, Oxford), repro. in Donner, *Thomas Lovell Beddoes* • L. Tobler, portrait, 1847 (after photograph), repro. in Donner, ed., *The works*; portrait was in Tobler's collection

Wealth at death £1850 5*s.*; also books, scientific instruments, and remaining property, incl. small estate at Hopesay, Shropshire: will, Donner, ed., *Works*, 687–8

Beddome, Benjamin (1717–1795), Particular Baptist minister and hymn writer, the son of John Beddome (*d.* 1757), Baptist minister, and Rachel Brandon, was born at Henley in Arden, Warwickshire, on 23 January 1717. He was baptized in 1739 at the Baptist church at Prescott Street, Goodman's Fields, London, by Samuel Wilson. He studied under Bernard Foskett at Bristol Academy, where he established a close friendship with Caleb Evans and John Ash, and later at the Independent academy at Mile End in Middlesex. In 1740 he became pastor at the Baptist church in Bourton on the Water, Gloucestershire, where he remained for fifty-five years. He was ordained in 1743, when Joseph Stennett preached the sermon and Bernard Foskett gave the charge. On 11 December 1749 he married Elizabeth Boswell (1732–1784), daughter of Richard Boswell, Baptist deacon of Bourton, at Gloucester; they had three sons, John, Benjamin, and Foskett, all of whom predeceased him.

Beddome is best-known as a writer of hymns, of which he composed more than 800, published as *Hymns Adopted to Public Worship or Family Devotion* in 1818. His hymns were intended to be sung after his sermons, as they illustrated the truths on which he had been preaching. He was a

noted preacher, whose labours were 'unremitted and evangelical', and, 'though his voice was low, his delivery was forcible and demanded attention' (Rippon, 320–21). He was a leader in the Midland Baptist Association and wrote an association letter in 1765. He also wrote an *Exposition on the Baptist Catechism* (1752; repr. 1776). Three posthumous volumes of his sermons were also printed. In 1770 he was awarded an MA degree by Providence College in Rhode Island in recognition of his literary gifts.

Beddome died at Bourton, the scene of his lifelong labours, on 3 September 1795, aged seventy-eight years, and was buried in the Baptist meeting-house graveyard there. According to the *Cambridge Intelligencer* (12 September 1795), which noticed his death, he was a BD.

W. B. LOWTHER, *rev.* KAREN E. SMITH

Sources 'Memoir', B. Beddome, *Sermons* (1835) • J. Ivimey, *A history of the English Baptists*, 4 vols. (1811–30), vol. 4, pp. 461–9 • J. Rippon, ed., *The Baptist Annual Register*, 2 [1797], 314–28 • S. A. Swaine, *Faithful men, or, Memorials of Bristol Baptist College* (1884), 41–6 • J. Julian, ed., *A dictionary of hymnology*, rev. edn (1907), 121–4 • D. M. Lewis, ed., *The Blackwell dictionary of evangelical biography, 1730–1860*, 2 vols. (1995) • *IGI* • *Cambridge Intelligencer* (12 Sept 1795), 2

Archives Bourton on the Water Baptist church, manuscript records and copies of letters • Bristol Baptist College • Regent's Park College, Oxford, Angus Library, hymns and his library

Bede [St Bede, Bæda, *known as* the Venerable Bede] (673/4–735), monk, historian, and theologian, in his *Historia ecclesiastica* (731) outlines his own life. Born in northern Northumbria, his relations put him in the monastery of Wearmouth at the age of seven. He transferred to the nearby sister house of Jarrow, where he remained. He was in his fifty-ninth year at the time of writing and had been ordained deacon in his nineteenth year, priest in his thirtieth. Bede says nothing of his social origins. A coincidence of names in a list (*c.*800) of the kings of Lindsey strengthens the considerable likelihood that he was of high birth: a Beda there appears in succession to a king called Biscop, the name of the noble founder and first abbot of Bede's monastery. Bede says of himself that his life had been devoted to prayer, learning, teaching, and writing. The truth of this is illustrated by his disciple Cuthbert in his account of Bede's death on 26 May 735. Bede spent his last hours in working on the *De natura rerum* of Isidore of Seville (570–636)—probably to correct, possibly to excerpt or translate it—and in dictating an English translation of St John's gospel, which he completed in his final moments.

In his autobiographical account Bede lists over thirty of his written works. It is not quite complete, omitting in particular the important *Epistola ad Ecgbertum*, not written until 734, his book on the holy places, and his English translations of the gospel of St John, the Lord's prayer, and the creed. (He mentions the two last in the letter to Ecgberht.) Nearly all his works survive, though his collections of hymns and epigrams do so only as fragments. His revision of a Latin translation of a Greek life of St Anastasius, generally regarded as lost, has recently been identified with considerable certainty. The most important loss is that of the St John's gospel translation. Had it survived it would have been the earliest substantial piece of English prose.

Works on the use of language and on computation and chronology Important among Bede's works are those which were intended to play a part, as textbooks or works of reference, in the teaching of 'grammar' in the monastic school, to supplement the work of, in particular, the fourth-century Latin grammarian Aelius Donatus. 'Grammar', as then understood, comprised the use of language in a fairly wide sense, and included some of what in earlier times would have been termed rhetoric. Bede wrote three books in this area: *De metrica ratione* (a collection of examples of different types of verse, with commentary), *De schematibus et tropis sacrae scripturae* (an explanation of the rhetorical figures of the Bible), and *De orthographia* (a kind of glossary of difficult words, alphabetically arranged, with some account of meanings and of Greek equivalents). A major concern of Bede's was the relationship between Christian and pagan learning. The problems were not new; for the roots of language and means of Christian learning lay deep in the pagan past. Bede regarded pagan literature as highly suspect, though he thought it could have its uses and seems to have known Virgil well. His grammatical manuals have a firmly Christian basis. All the examples in that on metre come from Christian poetry. *De schematibus …*, in discussing the rhetorical figures of the Bible, seeks to demonstrate its supremacy over profane literature.

Among the most important and influential of Bede's works were those on chronology and computation. *De temporibus* (written probably about 703) is a brief treatise on divisions of time, largely based on the relevant parts of Isidore's *Etymologiae*: appended is a world chronicle based on that of Eusebius of Caesarea (*d.* 340) and chronologically revised mainly by reference to Jerome's biblical translation. *De temporum ratione* was written some twenty years later and is a much longer account of most aspects of chronology and computation with a longer chronicle. The study of time was of fundamental importance to Christians. For them the world had begun at a definite time. Its history could be considered as divided into six ages, the sixth beginning with the birth of Christ. It was commonly assumed, following Isidore, that the first five ages had occupied more than five thousand years. Bede recalculated the chronology and arrived at 3952 years. It was this which led in 708 to his being accused (to his fury) of heresy because his revision could be misunderstood as putting the birth of Christ in the fifth age. Even more important was the calculation of the date of Easter, the hinge of the Christian year. It was a complicated matter, requiring the correlation of solar and lunar measurements; and a peculiar requirement was that of keeping Easter separate from the Jewish passover from which, however, it derived. Easter had a special edge for Bede because of the divergence between the calculation of Easter which he saw as correct and that used by many Celtic churches, which could, in certain circumstances, diverge from the Roman Easter by up to twenty-eight days. The simultaneous activity of Roman and Irish missionaries in England had highlighted the problem. In 664 the Roman Easter was ordained for all the Northumbrian churches. By the time Bede wrote the *Historia ecclesiastica* the great Irish monastery of Iona and the Picts had accepted it; only the Britons held out. The Easter question has central significance in Bede's *Historia ecclesiastica*. His writings (and a letter attributed to Abbot Ceolfrith, but which may really be Bede's) explain why it meant so much. Easter had to come just after the equinox, for lengthening days represent Christ's triumph over the powers of darkness. It had to be in the first month of the lunar year, for this was that in which the world had been created and should be newly created. It had to be as the moon was about to wane, for then the moon moves from facing the earth to facing the sun, just as we should turn from earthly to heavenly things. Bede's treatment of Easter brings together the study (one might almost say, the scientific study) of computation with analogical theology, historical learning, and the homiletic use of history. This well illustrates the integrated nature of his superficially diverse works.

Biblical commentaries The larger part of Bede's work consists of biblical commentaries: in all he wrote over twenty works on books or parts of the Old and New Testaments. They are not generally easy to date; and in any case the texts may sometimes represent cumulative activity extending over many years. Perhaps the earliest of his commentaries (and certainly among the earliest) is that on the Apocalypse, dated to some time between 703 and 709. A considerable number of his commentaries seem to have been written or to have reached their final form in the last few years of his life. Perhaps the most important of these is his second commentary on the Acts of the Apostles, called the *Retractatio* by reference to an earlier work, completed not long after 709, which it corrects and supplements. *Inter alia* it reveals a better knowledge of Greek than its predecessor. Interestingly, it can be shown that a Greek manuscript of Acts probably used by Bede survives in the Bodleian Library, Oxford (Bodl. Oxf., MS Laud græc. 35). An example of his careful attention to linguistic detail in this work is his explanation that while in the earlier book he had written that in Greek 'Stephen' means 'crowned', he now knows that it means 'crown'. A characteristic of his work here, and generally, is his careful attention to textual detail. He not infrequently compares the texts of the different translations of the Bible to which he had access. In the main Bede's system of commentary and interpretation follows the analogical, or Alexandrian, rather than the literal, or Antiochene, system, in this presenting an important contrast to the work of Theodore of Tarsus, archbishop of Canterbury (*d.* 690). He does not, however, neglect the literal meaning of his texts; and in some of his works, such as the (early) commentary on the Catholic epistles (those of James, Peter, John, and Jude), lays more stress on literal and historical interpretations than he does in others. The same is partly true of the *Retractatio* and of the commentary on Mark's gospel. His dominant interests, however, are in typological, analogical, and moral approaches, such that the literal meaning was seen as an outer husk to the real food. Typological interpretation of the Old Testament was chiefly concerned to show how its actors and events anticipated those of the New Testament. The deduction of general moral guidance from incidents of scripture generally presented no great difficulty. It was the use of analogy and anagogy which presented the widest necessity for learning and opportunities for its display. Parts of holy writ could be brought into complicated relationships with one another. (In this process Bede shows a most intimate knowledge of the Bible.) Parallels and symbolisms of many kinds could be discovered on the most extensive scale. Various kinds of special knowledge were necessary. Numerology was important among these. For example, the addition of Matthias to make up the number of the apostles to twelve was exceedingly significant; it took them away from the bad number eleven, associated with sin because it involves going beyond the ten commandments. Seven could stand for the incarnation because it combines the four elements of the world with the number of the Trinity. Other kinds of learning were valuable. Thus in his commentary on the Apocalypse Bede displays a wide knowledge of the qualities associated with precious stones. Allegorical exegesis can seem strained to the point of being bizarre. But it approaches the habits of mind of those who composed some of the scriptures (at an extreme the Revelation). And to many generations, indeed for centuries, it was the means by which learned men revealed, in all their complex integrity and wonderful depth, the inexhaustible treasures of holy writ. It has to be borne in mind that analogical interpretation had to deploy a good deal of fact. Thus in his (strictly analogical) commentary on the Song of Solomon Bede supplies information on the qualities of such woods as cedar and cypress.

In his commentaries Bede was following close in the footsteps of the western fathers: Ambrose (c.339–97), Augustine (354–430), Jerome (c.342–420), and Gregory (c.540–604)—above all Augustine and Gregory. His style of interpretation is theirs. To take but one example, Augustine had been very interested in numerology. Bede's very words are often theirs, for his commentaries can be to a significant extent a mosaic of quotations from his predecessors. In his commentaries on Mark and Luke, Bede (remarkably) indicates his use of the four fathers by marginal abbreviations which he beseeches copyists to retain. There is, of course, a distinction to be drawn between those of his commentaries which had substantial predecessors, and those which did not. In the former he is largely concerned to assemble, to clarify, and to abbreviate what already existed, though he does so with thoughtful care and sometimes with more originality than at first appears. In the introduction to his work on the Apocalypse Bede says that he has compressed the substance to allow for the laziness of the English. (Although he necessarily implies that those whom he indicates must have learned Latin fairly well.) For some of his commentaries he had no, or hardly any, predecessors. This was true of his works on Ezra and Nehemiah and on the Catholic epistles. His commentaries were supplemented by factual manuals relating to the Bible. Thus he wrote a separate treatise on the holy places and produced a tract on places mentioned by Jerome and Josephus, which he put as an appendix to a commentary on the book of Samuel. Another such tract on areas and places mentioned in the Acts of the Apostles is probably his.

Hagiography, biography, and homilies Bede's learning extended to almost all subjects of ecclesiastical importance; commonly he could both operate very skilfully in existing genres and introduce modifications, generally in the interests of comprehensiveness and intellectual efficiency. A leading example is his hagiographical work. Bede produced lives of three saints, Anastasius, Felix, and Cuthbert. What is plausibly argued to be his translation of a Greek life of Anastasius is an improved version of an earlier translation which may well have been by Archbishop Theodore. Bede's life of the third-century saint, Felix, was based on poems written by Paulinus of Nola (353–431). His avowed purpose was to take rather difficult hexameters and to transmute them into 'common and suitable' prose for the benefit of 'simple readers' (*Patrologia Latina*, 94.789b). In short it was a popularized version for people who knew Latin, but not exceedingly well: ordinary monks, it may be. His treatment of Cuthbert (*d*. 687) was different. A prose life, written at Lindisfarne, was already in existence. Bede rewrote and reordered the text, augmented it by collecting information from Lindisfarne, and emphasized the spiritual and moral lessons to be drawn, completing it in 721. Although his work lacks some of the simple charm of the anonymous life, it is a more sophisticated production for an audience which required a thoroughly professional job. This is even more true of the poem on the life of Cuthbert which Bede wrote at some time between 705 and 716. His operation here is the converse of that which he had performed for St Felix. With high technical competence he produces nearly 1000 hexameters drawing on Virgil and a considerable number of late antique authors. This is high-style writing for a well-educated audience and marks a point where piety meets sophisticated literary appreciation.

The most original of Bede's contributions to hagiography was that of a new kind of martyrology. He went beyond simply recording martyrs and places of execution in a calendar (which is all existing work of this kind did) but rather sought briefly 'to record' as he put it, 'all I could discover, not only the day of martyrdom but by what kind of combat and under whom as judge they overcame the world' (Bede, *Hist. eccl.*, 5.24). Thus he gives short accounts of 116 saints. The work reflects extensive research. In 716 or later Bede completed a history of the foundation of his monastery and of its abbots. It is largely non-hagiographical in style. Though concerned to edify, it contains much solid information and nothing of the miraculous, and has been claimed to be the most 'modern' of Bede's works in its treatment of motive. It has a predecessor in an anonymous life of Abbot Ceolfrith. It is possible that this work is in fact by Bede; if it is not, it is a further demonstration how far Bede's Latin style was that of other monks at Wearmouth–Jarrow.

Important elements in Bede's work were intended to

have direct liturgical or pastoral usefulness. Prose lives could be intended for reading out to a monastic community in church or elsewhere. Bede also composed two books each containing twenty-five homilies. They were intended for use at key points in the Christian year, clustering largely round Christmas and Easter. Three were for specific Wearmouth–Jarrow occasions: the anniveraries of the dedications of their churches and of the death of Benedict Biscop. While his homilies were in Latin, Bede's translations of the Lord's prayer, the creed, and the gospel of St John speak for a willingness to serve a wider, non-monastic audience. Here should be mentioned five lines of Anglo-Saxon verse which Cuthbert says Bede spoke as he was dying, 'Bede's Death-Song'. It says that no one can be too careful in facing the enforced journey if he considers what, for good or ill, may happen to his spirit after his death. The poem is probably not (as has sometimes been supposed) Bede's; but its survival, with Bede's account of Cædmon, and Cuthbert's statement that Bede was fond of English verse is a reminder that Bede may have had more involvement with vernacular learning than can be proved. It has to be remembered that the manuscript tradition for works produced in England in this period, not least those of Bede, is very largely continental; and vernacular work naturally stood less chance of survival abroad.

Historia ecclesiastica gentis Anglorum The work for which Bede is best known and most admired is *Historia ecclesiastica gentis Anglorum*, completed in 731. He himself seems to have regarded it as the culmination of his achievement, for he concludes it with an almost elegiac sketch of his own life and list of his works. The *Historia ecclesiastica* seeks to relate the history of English Christianity in some 85,000 words. After a short geographical and historical introduction, Bede gives some account of Christianity in Roman Britain, but devotes much of the first book and the whole of the remaining four to its progress in England between St Augustine's arrival, in 597, and 731.

Bede to a considerable extent used late antique models. His introduction was imitated from (and largely drew on) the work of Orosius (*fl.* 414–17). As an ecclesiastical historian, his principal model was Eusebius of Caesarea, whom he followed, for example, in including many original documents. (They comprise about a fifth of the whole book.) The works of earlier writers provided Bede not only with models, but also with much of the information for his first book. His account of Roman Britain came largely from Orosius and Eutropius (*fl.* 363–4). He had a *passio* (account of martyrdom) of St Alban and drew on Constantius (*fl.* 480) for his account of the fifth-century visits to Britain by Germanus. A major contribution came from the sixth-century British historian Gildas. For the period after 597 he had a handful of narrative (essentially hagiographical) sources. A major source of information was papal letters which were obtained for Bede from Rome, by a priest called Nothhelm (later archbishop of Canterbury, 735–9). Virtually all that he knew about the mission of St Augustine came from the correspondence of Gregory the Great. But for most of his knowledge of the history of the English

churches in the seventh century Bede was dependent on information from his contemporaries. In his preface he lists some of his informants: Albinus, abbot of St Peter's and St Paul's (later St Augustine's), Canterbury; Daniel, bishop of the West Saxons; monks of Lastingham; an Abbot Esi; Bishop Cyneberht of Lindsey; and many Northumbrians. It is possible, occasionally, to identify a passage in the *Historia ecclesiastica* probably copied verbatim from a letter. For example, a famous passage in book 1, chapter 15, giving the origins of the German invaders of England, calls the South Saxons *Meridiani* and the West Saxons *Occidui*. Elsewhere Bede invariably uses *Australes* and *Occidentales*. The aberrant usage suggests that the language is not his own. He may have learned a lot from direct personal contact. One of his former pupils was Ecgberht, bishop and archbishop of York from about 732 to 766, and brother of Eadberht, later king of Northumbria (*r.* 737–58); Bede visited him at York at least once. Bede's own monastery cannot have been without important and informed visitors. The grandeur of its, and his, contacts can be seen from the fact that a draft of the *Historia ecclesiastica*, was sent for correction to Ceolwulf, king of Northumbria.

There were serious lacunae in Bede's information. For example, he does not give the date of the death of St Augustine; and he is less adequately informed about such an area as the west midlands than he is about others. All the same, the amount of information Bede gathered from numerous kingdoms and dioceses was most remarkable. It was variously dated, if at all. Bede's achievement in co-ordination was outstanding. He gave dates in as many forms as possible; and linked them by the frequent use of *anno Domini* dating. In this he was original. This form of dating seems to have been first used by Dionysius Exiguus (*d. c.*527); but Bede's employment of it in his chronicles and *Historia ecclesiastica* led to its coming into general use. In this and other regards Bede marks himself out as the outstanding historian of the early middle ages. By far the larger part of present knowledge of the church and rulers of early England comes from him.

Bede can indeed seem almost like a modern historian, for example in his inclusion of original documents, his concern to state and to cite his sources, his exact chronology. But his work was dominated by purposes which, if they sometimes resemble those of a modern historian, more generally do not. As an ecclesiastical historian working considerably on the lines of Eusebius, he had as a primary concern the requirement to record episcopal successions and the appearance and fate of heresy. The wrong (as he saw it) calculation of Easter was the nearest seventh-century England came to heresy and Bede gave it full treatment accordingly. He was not concerned to record political and secular events except in so far as they related to the history of the church or displayed God's judgment at work in history. Thus to the extent that he deals with kings it is largely with a view to setting examples. He says in his preface that he is concerned that the pious reader or listener should be affected in such a way as to seek to follow the good and shun the bad.

The *Historia ecclesiastica* is in part an attempt to demonstrate the role of the Christian king, what he ought to do for the church and what the church could do for him. A characteristic episode is one relating to Oswiu, king of Northumbria in the mid-seventh century. When he was hard-pressed by his enemy Penda, he sought to buy him off; rejected, he made a corresponding offer to God and so won a great victory. Oswald was somewhere in sight of a Bedan ideal of kingship. Bede says that he was not only most Christian, but also most victorious; not only did he learn to hope for heavenly kingdoms unknown to any of his ancestors, he also gained earthly kingdoms wider than any of theirs. Oswald patronized Áedán, the Irish missionary who converted much of Northumbria, and himself acted as the saint's interpreter. He brought peace by unifying Northumbria. Yet in the end he did not succeed in this world, for he died in battle. Bede presents him as a saint, one who had died in battle against the pagan Mercians, and relates some of his posthumous miracles. Such canonization of a warrior king was not normal. The original impulse to glorify Oswald was not Bede's; but he follows it with enthusiasm. It is important to observe that Bede (who is seldom so simple as he may sometimes seem on the surface) has more than one type of ideal king. Beside the Christian warrior can be set admired kings who abandoned the world for a monastery or for Rome.

Bede is still more concerned to set models for the church. A most important indication of the extent to which the *Historia ecclesiastica* is dominated by exemplary and homiletic purpose is provided by the letter which he wrote to Ecgberht, bishop of York, in 734. In it he criticizes much in the church of his own day. There are bishops who do not perambulate their dioceses as they should and who are too avaricious. Some are too much given to parties and to laughter. Set against this the account Bede gives of bishops such as John of Beverley, bishop of Hexham, and above all of Áedán. If bishops in Bede's day levied immense tribute, Áedán and his immediate successors at Lindisfarne had no money but, rather, cattle. Áedán gave great men nothing but food when they came to see him. The money they gave him he gave to the poor or to ransom captives. There was, Bede thought, all too much ecclesiastical entertaining and drinking in his own day. But in the past all attention was paid to hearts, not bellies. If contemporary bishops failed to visit remote settlements it was to just such places that Cuthbert had been particularly concerned to go. It is interesting that Bede stresses aspects of Áedán's conduct which contravened the mores of Anglo-Saxon life in relation, for example, to hospitality and to gift exchange.

A more general message is preached by the stories of miracles and visions which abound in the *Historia ecclesiastica*. Such stories played there something of the role which accounts of the passions of the martyrs played for Eusebius. Although Bede was a devout believer in miracles, it seems certain that he was highly selective. A high proportion of those he includes are susceptible of a natural explanation, particularly miracles of healing; plainly he does not seek to explain miracles away but he does

seem to have preferred to avoid the more flabbergasting. Even more unusual is the near avoidance of the miraculous in his accounts of his own monastery. He makes no attempt at all to suggest that its lands and interests were defended by God and the saints. A notable feature of Bede's pious stories is that they are not infrequently told to exemplify some piece of moral teaching which he treated in a more abstract way elsewhere. Thus in his commentaries he says that there are two kinds of compunction with the same manifestations: one derives from the fear of hell, the other from the hope of heaven. In the *Historia ecclesiastica* he tells of one Adamnan who was led by accident and scruple long to continue a regime of mortification originally intended to last a shorter time. Thus, Bede says, having formerly been *conpunctus* (made remorseful) by the fear of God, he now continued for the rewards of divine love. The most striking of the moral educative episodes included in the *Historia ecclesiastica* are visions of the next world. There are four of these and they are principally concerned with the reality and horrors of hell. A high proportion of Bede's poem on judgment day is devoted to the pains of hell.

A surprising feature of the *Historia ecclesiastica* is that Bede devotes proportionately less space to the decades immediately before writing than he does to an earlier period. Furthermore, a high proportion of the last book is devoted to visions and other wonders. The more he must have known about the course of events, the less does he seem to have to say. One explanation for this is that he disapproved of much that happened in his own day. The letter to Ecgberht proves that he thought that much was wrong with the church, particularly with the conduct of bishops. He is explicit in his commentaries that it is wrong publicly to denounce even wicked prelates. In the whole of the *Historia ecclesiastica* there is but one remark which is damaging to a bishop, a single sentence to say that Wini bought the see of London from Wulfhere, king of the Mercians. It could well be that he had relatively little to say about the church in his own day because there was too little to say about it that could edify.

A particularly interesting difficulty arises here in relation to the great northern bishop, Wilfrid (d. 709). Wilfrid was a powerful figure. Familiar with Gaul and Italy, a great monastic founder, he established Christianity in Sussex and sought to do so in Frisia. His career was stormy; for he was at odds with Archbishop Theodore of Canterbury, other bishops, and kings of Northumbria. A contemporary biography by Stephen of Ripon (Eddius Stephanus) reveals major aspects of his power and grandeur: the secular nobles in his service, his possession of a treasure. Some of the considerable amount Bede has to say about Wilfrid may well derive from Stephen or a related source; but his emphasis is very different. He says more about Wilfrid's missionary activities and defence of orthodoxy but virtually nothing about his conflict with Theodore; and he says nothing to indicate the aristocratic elements in Wilfrid's style of life. It has often been suggested that Bede was hostile to Wilfrid, at a feast in whose presence he had been accused of heresy. It has been argued that the Northumbrian church in Bede's day was riven by faction and that the cults of Cuthbert and of Wilfrid were in a rivalry representative of such dissension; and the suggestion has been made that Bede gave deliberate preference to Cuthbert and his cult. It is true that the politics of Northumbria and its church were fraught; that must be why Bede's diocesan and friend, Acca, bishop of Hexham, was deposed in 731. Moreover, Bede wrote lives of Cuthbert but not of Wilfrid and says nothing about the latter to match his statement in the verse life of Cuthbert that that saint was the saint for Britain just as Peter and Paul were for Rome. But Bede writes at length about Wilfrid and in a way that is consistently favourable. What is more, Acca was not only Bede's friend and correspondent, but was also closely associated with Wilfrid, succeeded him at Hexham, and commissioned his biography. What Bede's treatment of Wilfrid shows is not demonstrable *parti pris* in Northumbrian ecclesiastical politics, but rather extreme discretion so that, were there not another source, there would be but a limited apprehension of the nature and significance of Wilfrid's career.

A similar reticence appears in the *Historia ecclesiastica*'s account of monasticism. In general (and rather remarkably) it directs less attention to monastic affairs than to episcopal; but nevertheless supplies considerable information. Book 5, chapter 23, contains a notable passage in this regard. In these times of peace, it says, many of the Northumbrian people, noble and non-noble, have laid aside their weapons; and, laying aside their weapons, have, with their children, taken monastic vows. The reference to children is curious. Perhaps there is an implied reference to familial monasteries or quasi-monasteries of a kind denounced in Bede's letter to Ecgberht. The reference to the laying aside of arms in this chapter can gain an added dimension from the statement in the letter that the endowment of monasteries or pseudo-monasteries had led to the neglect of Northumbrian defences. These resonances give a cryptic, possibly ominous, implication to the conclusion of the passage in the *Historia ecclesiastica*: what the result of this will be, says Bede, the next age shall see.

There can be a veiled quality in the *Historia ecclesiastica* which reflects Bede's extreme discretion. Such discretion, and a reluctance to have too much to say about the contemporary, may in some way account for the most extraordinary omission in the work: that of any mention of Boniface. By 731 Boniface, with a notable career as an evangelist, had for nine years been a bishop and was about to become an archbishop. Bede concerns himself with other English missionaries in Germany. It is most unlikely that Bede did not know about Boniface. Just possibly Boniface was omitted by oversight. It seems more probable that the omission reflects some unexplained disquiet about Boniface. Bede's treatment (or non-treatment) of Boniface is suggestive of a degree of depth and complexity which is not plain in its immediately simple effect. Straightforward prose can contain complexity of view. There is an implicit tension in some of Bede's writing, partly connected, it may be, with the contrast between the apparent success of Christianity in England on the one hand, and on the other oppressive kings and false monasteries at home, Saracens advancing abroad.

Bede's intellectual milieu Bede's mind and work were the product of and response to an intellectual milieu of a remarkable kind. The accurate power of his Latin speaks for the effectiveness of elementary education in the first generation of monastic life at Wearmouth–Jarrow. The monk Cuthbert, in his account of Bede's death, employs a style indistinguishable from that of his master. Most important elements in Bede's *œuvre* are the elementary manuals concerned with education in the use of Latin in prose and verse. Bede may very well have been the community's schoolmaster. It is an important question as to how far knowledge of Latin extended outside the clerical world. One king of Northumbria (Aldfrith) was almost certainly literate; there are indications that other laymen may have been so. The *Historia ecclesiastica* was intended for the laity as well as the clergy; and it is not impossible that when Bede sent Ceolwulf a draft for correction that king could actually read it.

The essential background to Bede's learning was access to an extensive library. Some sixty years ago M. L. W. Laistner worked out that Bede had access to approximately 150 works by seventy-five authors. This list could undoubtedly be corrected and extended. A high proportion (perhaps all) the works he used were of Wearmouth–Jarrow: some had been brought from Italy and elsewhere by Benedict Biscop; Bede says that the library had been doubled in size by Ceolfrith. Books could be very expensive; their abundance at Wearmouth–Jarrow was an indication of the lavish scale on which it had been founded.

At the same time Wearmouth–Jarrow was by no means the only major centre of intellectual life in England. The most important one was that established at Canterbury by Theodore. Bede speaks of it with warm praise; Abbot Ceolfrith, who must have taught him, had studied there. The most eminent English writer of the day, other than Bede, was Aldhelm of Malmesbury; Bede knew at least some of Aldhelm's work. Aldhelm had not only been educated at Canterbury, but had earlier come under Irish influence. Some of the most important centres of learning in Europe were Irish, and Bede emphasizes the importance of Irish learning for Englishmen. It is not easy to assess his own debt to it; but Wearmouth–Jarrow had quite close links with Irish-founded Lindisfarne and at least one of Bede's fellow monks had formerly been a member of another such community at Lastingham and the only one of his teachers whom he mentions, Trumbert, was educated there. Bede certainly had access to a number of works originating in or transmitted via Irish centres. Adomnán of Iona's work on the holy places is a case in point. Bede's letters, and his account of his sources, show that he was in communication with ecclesiastics over much of England.

The context into which Bede's life, intellectual activity, and contacts must be put is one of numerous monasteries and widely distributed learning. That there were far more monasteries than are explicitly mentioned in the sources is plain for more reasons than one. When, most unusually, as at Worcester, a fairly full local archive survives, the number of eighth-century monasteries recorded is very high. An important number of monasteries are known from single references in a relatively meagre group of sources. Some are known only by archaeological means. The letters of Boniface and Lull provide the most widespread (but by no means only) evidence for learning and manuscript production in at least a considerable number of these institutions. A major difference between Bede's age and all that followed is the prominence of women. Some important monasteries were 'double': communities of nuns, with ancillary monks, presided over by important royal ladies. What is more, there is conclusive evidence for important learned activity in such establishments. Bede was in correspondence with at least one nun and admired the achievements of others. Any attempt to establish the full context of Bede's achievement runs into the difficulty that he was part of a monastic and intellectual world whose dimensions and nature can be understood only imperfectly and episodically. Much of the evidence for its nature and productions was destroyed by the viking invasions and by internal English changes. Questions such as that of the reasons for the difference between the largely Antiochene emphasis of Theodore's biblical work and the Alexandrian of Bede's remain for investigation: it may well be inconclusive. So too with Bede's debt to Irish learning; and on such a crucial question as that of by what route he obtained access to the work of Gildas. What is certain is that he belonged to a quite extensive world of information, the connections of which extended beyond the shores of Britain. Not only did he have access to letters of Gregory the Great, but also to the *Liber pontificalis* (the collection of papal biographies kept, and kept up, at Rome). Information in his second commentary on Acts had been supplied by Pope Gregory II (or Gregory III) via an unnamed friend. In the range of his sources and contacts Bede was a key figure in an Indian summer of the late antique world.

Bede's reputation and legacy Bede died at Jarrow on Ascension day, 26 May, 735 and was buried there. His reputation, legacy, and lasting authority were outstanding. From his own times his works were in great demand. The survival of manuscripts of his works is in itself evidence of his long popularity and wide influence. In the case of the *Historia ecclesiastica* some 150 medieval manuscripts survive. A developed version was probably already being circulated before Bede's death; for this is the most plausible explanation for there being two manuscript traditions—the principal difference between them being that one version (the M-type) contains a chapter relating to Oswald (obviously Bedan) not contained in the other (the C-type). Two manuscripts were written close to Bede's lifetime: the Leningrad Bede (St Petersburg, public library, MS Q.v.I, 8) and the Moore Bede (Cambridge University Library, MS Kk. 5.16). The latter's fluent script has been suggested to be of a type developed at Wearmouth–Jarrow to assist in meeting the demand for Bede's works. This demand extended far beyond his *Historia ecclesiastica*. Others of his works, especially those on chronology, remained standard textbooks long into the middle ages. His scriptural commentaries long remained in wide demand. The power and success of his *Historia ecclesiastica* has for numerous observers overshadowed the importance of others of his works as mainstays of monastic education for many centuries.

A notable feature of the manuscript tradition of Bede's works is the extent to which it appears largely to have been transmitted through manuscripts which had been on the continent from an early date. This appears to be an indication of how far the monastic culture of Bede's England was destroyed in ensuing generations. At the same time, Bede's works, and in particular the *Historia ecclesiastica*, had a long influence in England which was more than merely intellectual. An English translation of the *Historia ecclesiastica* was among those made in association with King Alfred's educational campaign. It omits most documents and poems and matter not concerned with England. The manuscript tradition suggests the translated version was that best known to tenth-century Englishmen. It is an interesting question how far the *Historia ecclesiastica* was instrumental in creating English self-consciousness. Bede regarded the *gens Anglorum* as in some sense united, though he was perfectly aware of how politically divided they were. He was anxious to emphasize how far the saints of individual *provinciae* were the common property of all the *Anglii* (among whom for generalizing purposes he included the *Saxones*). He seems to have seen the *Anglii* as having a common destiny before God. By his own account the Anglo-Saxon sense of unity was connected to the use of a common language; migration and marriage must also have done much to integrated dynasties and kingdoms. At the same time his sense of English unity in a providential context could have had a deep, if unquantifiable, effect. A narrower, more distinct effect from Bede may have been that curious phenomenon, the monastic cathedral; that is to say, a cathedral which was also a Benedictine monastery, served by monks rather than canons. The first such clearly identifiable arrangements appear in the tenth century, and they were extended to further sees after the Norman conquest. In Bede's letter to Ecgberht he recommends the endowment of needed additional sees by locating their *sedes* in monasteries. He was probably drawing on knowledge of, for example, early Lindisfarne where Áedán seems to have been both abbot and bishop. The letter to Ecgberht survives in only three manuscripts. But, that the institution of the monastic cathedral was (virtually) unique to England makes the Bedan influence on it plausible. More broadly, Bede provided for over a thousand years, and to a large extent still provides, nearly all the knowledge available of the early history of England. His *Historia* is the only work, other than parts of the Bible, which has been read by every English generation from his own day to the present. It has the power to move and to convey something of the personality of its author, to a degree which has called forth not only admiration but a kind of affection.

Recognition of Bede's qualities has flourished since his

own day. Boniface wrote that he shone like a candle of the church by his knowledge of the scriptures (Monumenta Germaniae Historica, Epistolae Selectae, 1, 1916, no. 76). Soon after his death he came to be regarded as a saint. In his poem on the bishops, kings, and saints of York, Alcuin attributes a miracle to his relics. Boniface gave Abbot Cuthbert silk in which to wrap them. In due course both Fulda and Glastonbury claimed to have such relics. At the Council of Aachen in 836, he was characterized as an 'honourable and admirable teacher' (Monumenta Germaniae Historica, Concilia, 2/2, 1908, 359) and put on an equal level with the fathers. From the ninth century he was sometimes or commonly called *Venerabilis* (but this sobriquet was commonly given to priests). His reputation extended as far as Ireland. In a later century he was commemorated by Dante who put him beside Isidore in paradise. The extent of his fame can be judged partly by the extent to which works by others were falsely attributed to him.

Bede's *Historia ecclesiastica* was first printed at Strasbourg, probably at some time between 1474 and 1482. A number of sixteenth- and seventeenth-century printings followed. All previous editions were superseded by that of John Smith, completed by his son George and published in 1722. The first English translation was that of Thomas Stapleton (1565). As a major Roman Catholic controversialist Stapleton was clearly determined to demonstrate the close and subordinate relationship between the early English church and the papacy. The modern study of the *Historia ecclesiastica* is largely based on Charles Plummer's edition of 1896 with its full and most learned commentary.

The papacy pronounced Bede *doctor ecclesiae* in 1899 and *sanctus* in 1935. Although he was buried at Jarrow, his remains were claimed to have been removed in the early eleventh century to Durham. His tomb there was desecrated in 1541 but its contents are believed to be interred in the Galilee chapel of Durham Cathedral.

J. CAMPBELL

Sources G. H. Brown, *Bede the Venerable* (1987) · B. Ward, *The Venerable Bede* (1990) · B. Colgrave and others, *Bede and his world: the Jarrow lectures, 1958–1993*, 2 vols. (1994) · W. D. McCready, *Miracles and the Venerable Bede* (1994) · Bede, *Hist. eccl.* · *Venerabilis Baedae opera historica*, ed. C. Plummer, 2 vols. (1896) · G. Bonner, ed., *Famulus Christi: essays in commemoration of the thirteenth centenary of the birth of the Venerable Bede* (1976) · W. Goffart, *The narrators of barbarian history* (1988) · J. Campbell, *Essays in Anglo-Saxon history* (1986) · G. H. Brown, *Bede the educator* (1996)
Likenesses drawing, Bodl. Oxf., MS Digby 20, fol. 194

Bedel, Henry (*b.* 1536/7, *d.* in or after 1576), Church of England clergyman, was born in Oxfordshire and attended Corpus Christi College, Oxford, from 1552. He graduated BA there on 13 February 1556 and proceeded MA on 5 July 1566. He was ordained in 1561, aged twenty-four, and was collated by Archbishop Matthew Parker to the rectory of St Pancras, Soper Lane, one of his peculiars in the city of London, on 4 October that year, but he resigned in 1567. On 28 January 1568 he acquired the vicarage of Christ Church Greyfriars with a fixed stipend of £26 13s. 4d. from the lord mayor and commonalty of London. Bedel argued vehemently against the surplice and also opposed the use of wafer bread in the eucharist. By 12 April 1566, however, Parker reported that Bedel had convinced himself that it was lawful to conform to the latter practice. In June 1567 he was openly accused of 'false doctrine'—presumably on the subject of conformity—by one of the separatists arrested at Plumbers' Hall and examined by Edmund Grindal, bishop of London.

Bedel's conformity was rewarded with further preferment. On 9 June 1570, at the petition of Alexander Nowell, dean of St Paul's, he was presented to the prebendal rectory of Timberscombe, in the diocese of Bath and Wells, though he appears not to have taken it up. He was certainly at Christ Church on 15 November 1571, for a sermon he preached there was published in the following year as *A Sermon Exhorting to Pitie the Poore*, to which is appended a prayer for Queen Elizabeth and against 'satan his religion'. In 1576, however, he was forced to resign this living after repeated complaints by parishioners to the mayor and corporation about his non-residence. Nothing is known of his activities after this date.

STEPHEN WRIGHT

Sources H. G. Owen, 'The London parish clergy in the reign of Elizabeth I', PhD diss., U. Lond., 1957 · *Reg. Oxf.*, 1.228 · R. Newcourt, *Repertorium ecclesiasticum parochiale Londinense*, 1 (1708) · G. Hennessy, *Novum repertorium ecclesiasticum parochiale Londinense, or, London diocesan clergy succession from the earliest time to the year 1898* (1898) · Foster, *Alum. Oxon.* · Wood, *Ath. Oxon.: Fasti* (1815), 146, 172 · H. Bedel, *A sermon exhorting to pitie the poore* (1572) · *Correspondence of Matthew Parker*, ed. J. Bruce and T. T. Perowne, Parker Society, 42 (1853) · *Fasti Angl., 1541–1857*, [Bath and Wells] · BL, Lansdowne MS 443, fol. 184v · W. Nicholson, ed., *The remains of Edmund Grindal*, Parker Society, 9 (1843), 204

Bedell, William (*bap.* 1572, *d.* 1642), Church of Ireland bishop of Kilmore, was baptized on 14 January 1572 at Black Notley, Essex, where he was born, the second of three sons among six children of John Bedell (*d.* 1600), yeoman, and Elizabeth Aliston or Elliston (*d.* 1624). Although partly deaf, he went to school in Braintree, where he was an apt pupil.

Cambridge and Bury St Edmunds, 1584–1607 On 1 November 1584 Bedell was admitted pensioner at the newly founded and puritan-inclined Emmanuel College, Cambridge, where he was elected a scholar on 12 March 1585. He graduated BA early in 1589, proceeded MA in 1592, and was elected a fellow of the college in 1593. Ordained priest at Colchester on 10 January 1597, he proceeded BD in 1599.

Knowledge of Bedell's life relies heavily on two admiring contemporary biographies: one by his elder son, also William; the other by his son-in-law, Alexander *Clogie (1614–1698). The major influences on Bedell's life at Cambridge were reportedly Laurence Chaderton, master of Emmanuel from its foundation in 1584 until his resignation in 1602, and William Perkins, fellow of Christ's College. Such mentors suggest an early orientation towards protestant activism and Calvinist theology, but among his friends at Emmanuel were not only the future bishop Joseph Hall, but also James Wadsworth, who in 1605 went to Spain as chaplain to the English ambassador and infamously apostatized to Rome. Bedell's own theology, like his career, defies simple classification.

In 1602 Bedell left Emmanuel to join the ministry of the substantial church of St Mary in Bury St Edmunds, Suffolk, where he enjoyed the patronage of Sir Edmund Bacon. Little is known of his early career, but his son claimed that he 'had not long been' in Bury before 'he had gained a great reverence, as well from all that savoured of the power of Godliness as from the Gallants, Knights and Gentlemen, who reverenced him for his impartial, grave, and holy preaching and conversation' (Jones, 7). According to his eulogists, he had qualities of learning and intellect far above those needed by a godly puritan minister. Proficient in Latin and Greek, 'he attained also no mean skill in the Syriack, Arabick, and Hebrew tongues; although in these (as in the Chaldee tongue) he bettered himself much after his travels' (ibid., 3). In 1607 his extraordinary learning and his useful Cambridge connections gained him the invitation to go to Venice as chaplain to Bacon's friend Sir Henry Wotton, English ambassador there since the previous year.

Venice and its influence, 1607–1627 Bedell arrived in Venice that summer and, judging from his few surviving letters of this period, embarked on a rich and formative interlude in his life. Writing to his friend Adam Newton, tutor to Prince Henry and dean of Durham, he deplored the idolatry he saw all around him, but came to appreciate the positive effects on the people of the beautification of churches and spectacular ecclesiastical ceremony. The serene republic had only just emerged from under the cloud of an interdict pronounced against it by Pope Paul V in April 1606 and revoked a year later. The dispute between the pontiff and the republic raised the hopes of many protestants, including the English ambassador, that a rich and powerful Italian state might be wooed away from papal allegiance, and these outlived the end of the interdict. Wotton and Bedell found numerous men of spirit and learning with whom they could discuss the pressing ecclesiastical and theological questions of the day. In addition to improving his Hebrew by taking lessons from the storied figure of the Venetian ghetto Rabbi Leon da Modena, Bedell added Italian to his repertory of European languages. For the benefit of friends he translated the prayer book and other pious works into Italian; a posthumous edition of *Il libro delle preghiere publiche ed administrazione de sacramenti … secundo l'uso della chiesa Anglicana* appeared in London in 1685. He was the confidant of those who were already protestants or disposed to convert, cultivating the friendship of Marco Antonio De Dominis, archbishop of Spalato, with whose work he is said to have assisted, and becoming an intimate of the Servite father Paolo Sarpi. Venice had a cosmopolitanizing effect on Bedell, and the memory of sympathetic Venetians always qualified his subsequent animated criticism of Rome.

In late 1610 or early 1611 Bedell returned to England and to Bury. He was accompanied by a Venetian physician, Jasper Despotine, who successfully settled in the town,

where he married and had a family. On 29 January 1612 Bedell himself married Leah L'Estrange or Bowles (c.1581–1638), widow of the town recorder Robert Mawe (d. 1609). Leah already had two sons and a daughter; with Bedell she had four further children, William (14 February 1613), Grace (29 May 1614), John (9 August 1616), and Ambrose (21 March 1618). In 1616 Bedell was instituted as rector of the nearby and more prosperous parish of Horningsheath, which was in the gift of Sir Thomas Jermyn. An early quarrel with the bishop of Norwich, John Jegon, over the exactions demanded of the new rector by the diocese, anticipated Bedell's later impatience with the preference of the institutionalized Church of Ireland for the customary and worldly over the ideal.

Bedell had not abandoned his earlier interests and perspectives. In 1620 he published *Petri Suavis Polani historiae Concilii Tridentini*, his rendering in Latin of part of his friend Sarpi's history of the Council of Trent, thus making it available for a wider English audience. The apostacy of his schoolfellow James Wadsworth was examined in *The copies of certaine letters which have passed betweene Spaine and England in matter of religion* (1624), while the next year he translated another of Sarpi's works, on the question of the legality of military service to a prince of another religion, as *The Free Schoole of Warre* (1625). As he explained in an epistle to the reader,

> it will serve to open the understandings of sober and dispassionate men, that they may detest the Practises of Factious Papalines, and discerne with what impious cunning they adulterate Religion, and force her to play a part on the Stage of their State-reasons, and Temporall interests. (sig. Aiii)

A Latin version of Sarpi's history of the interdict imposed on Venice by the papacy appeared as *Interdicti Venetia historia* (1626), dedicated to Charles I.

Dublin, 1627–1629 Bedell had apparently hoped for preferment as a result of his work in Venice, and his publications seem to have arisen partly from an aspiration to return there and do 'some good' (Stoye, 339). He might thus have received some encouragement when about 1627, as Clogie recounted, by chance Bedell re-encountered in Cheapside one of his Venetian intimates, Giovanni Diodati, who was on a visit to London. Astonished that Bedell was not better known for his scholarship, Diodati, the protestant translator of the Bible into Italian, introduced him to Thomas Morton, bishop of Coventry and Lichfield. When it finally came, however, promotion was in an unexpected direction. In March 1627 Bedell was informed by James Ussher, archbishop of Armagh and vice-chancellor of Trinity College, Dublin, that he was a candidate for the provostship of Trinity College. Following the death of the previous incumbent, Sir William Temple, a succession struggle had erupted, and not only Ussher but also the archbishop of Canterbury, George Abbot, and the king had become involved in its resolution. Both Ussher and Bedell were in regular correspondence with Samuel Ward, master of Sidney Sussex College, Cambridge, and Bedell wrote to Ward of his surprise at being considered. He had no prior connection with Ireland and knew little of Trinity; the provostship offered him little financial advantage, for its emoluments were roughly the same as those of his Suffolk rectory; neither he nor his wife wished to leave 'a good seate in an wholesome aire, with a little parrish within the compasse of my weake voice'. 'Yet', continued Bedell, 'if I should see clearely that it was the will of God I should goe, I esteemed I was to close mine eyes against mine owne inconveniencyes, and follow his call' (Shuckburgh, 266).

Bedell duly went to Dublin, where he was admitted provost on 16 August 1627, but he remained anxious and even reluctant. He returned to England in the late autumn of 1627 and spring of 1628 to gather up his family and household, but clung to his living at Horningsheath until forced to surrender it on grounds of pluralism. He had another work of anti-Catholic controversy in the press to distract him: *An Examination of Certaine Motives to Recusansie* appeared in 1628 with a dedication to his friend Sir Thomas Barker. In any case, it was not an easy time in which to give up the relative comfort and security of an English benefice for the uncertainties and asperities of an Irish mission. Bedell's short, two-year, career as provost of Trinity was less than triumphant. Turmoil within the college had continued unabated. Bedell's son recounts his father's run-in with Joshua Hoyle, professor of divinity and later master of University College, Oxford. 'Mr Bedell in his catechisings and sermons and at other discourses used still rather to contract the differences between protestants and papists than to widen them' (Shuckburgh, 26). Professor Hoyle thought otherwise. Ussher supported Bedell and welcomed his reforms, particularly the frequent lectures in the Irish language which he instituted. There was division over the wisdom of this course, some administrators and churchmen believing that religious reform needed to await the extirpation of the Irish language and culture, which they viewed as pernicious impediments in themselves. From his arrival in Ireland, Bedell strove to bring the reformed faith to the Irish in their language. Always a gifted linguist, he sedulously began the study of Irish and energetically advocated its use among Gaelic speakers.

Bishop By a patent of 20 May 1629 Charles I appointed Bedell to the combined Irish bishoprics of Kilmore, co. Cavan, and Ardagh, co. Longford, in which he was consecrated by Archbishop Ussher on 13 September. Kilmore was the more important and lucrative, and on 28 February 1632 Bedell resigned Ardagh in favour of John Richardson, alleging the pernicious effects of pluralism, and the diocese's need for its own resident bishop. Whether his elevation to the hierarchy of the Church of Ireland was a cloaked ejection from the provostship, a reward for work well done, or the rescue operation of an embattled administrator by powerful friends, it is difficult to say. But once again a posting set Bedell, now fifty-eight, on a different track that he pursued with zeal, this time until his death. Bedell's considerable fame from the late seventeenth century onwards was wholly a consequence of his career as a prelate in the Church of Ireland.

That church was in turmoil. Long impoverished, by the early seventeenth century it had lost the allegiance of the bulk of the Old English and Gaelic Irish population, many of whom were being openly served by Counter-Reformation clergy. The New English plantocracy was increasingly its exiguous mainstay. The challenge in Kilmore, as at the more sheltered Trinity College, was to preserve and extend the protestant Reformation against the vigorous encroachments of Rome. Bedell had clear and somewhat inflexible opinions about how this could best be accomplished, and they brought him into conflict with William Laud, the archbishop of Canterbury from 1633; the lord deputy, Thomas Wentworth; many of his peers (especially, from 1633, John Bramhall, bishop of Londonderry); and even his friend and patron, Ussher.

Bedell did not share the prevailing Church of Ireland sentiment that the Irish were either irredeemably lost or predestined to damnation. Perhaps it was his newness to the island, perhaps his experience of Venice, that allowed him to believe that his Gaelic Irish parishioners (more numerous in his diocese than the Old English) would embrace reformed religion if it was propagated among them in their language, and if the church and its clergy were truly exemplary. It was the former assumption that prompted his catechism with parallel English and Irish texts, *The A. B. C., or, The Institution of a Christian* (1631); perhaps it was the latter that led him to import from Essex some of the practices of clerical mentoring and support that had assisted him in his own early career. Both of these views were unpopular with many prelates: the first, because practical considerations usually dictated that native Irish clergy be employed, and there was deep doubt as to their sincerity and fidelity to the cause; the second, because idealism conflicted with the institutional arrangements by which the church was trying to secure its crumbling foundations.

The latter dilemma is exemplified in Bedell's longrunning, ultimately unsuccessful, feud with Dr Alan Cooke, who had been granted a patent to be chancellor of Kilmore by Bedell's predecessor, Bishop Thomas Moigne. The Catholics of the diocese complained of Cooke's exactions, and Bedell, taking their part, struggled to force the chancellor from his office, arguing that souls would be won by persuasion rather than harassment. To Bedell's exasperation, the church courts found for Cooke, who had legally acquired the right as chancellor and could not be ejected by his high-minded bishop. Bedell's idealism in this and other matters reveals him to have been in the pastoral tradition which flourished in the reign of James I, rather than the prelatical tradition of bishop as executive, or administrator, which found favour under Archbishop Laud in the 1630s. The evidence is strong that Bedell was a 'people's bishop', to the distress of Laud and Bramhall; yet his enemies could regard him as an Arminian on the grounds of his comparatively liberal attitude towards Roman Catholicism. This contradiction has rendered Bedell something of an enigma, though one with enduring appeal.

It was Bedell's death, as much as his scholarship or ecclesiastical career, which secured his memory. When the Irish rising of 1641 broke out, the plantation of Ulster came down about the bishop's ears. His wife had died on 26 March 1638, but his son William and son-in-law, Alexander Clogie, were with him, both having cures within his diocese, and their accounts strive to show how exceptional was the treatment accorded Bedell by the rebels of the area, led by the O'Reillys:

> And though the daily report of cruelties acted about in the country came so thick that the business they were in hand with could not be hidden any longer; yet these O'Reillys still gave comfortable words to the Bishop; and for a week or fortnight's space did not so much as take away of his cattle. (Jones, 65)

As a result of this leniency, and Bedell's generosity, the modest episcopal palace soon became crowded with protestant refugees, and was allowed to continue as a sanctuary until nearly Christmas, when it was taken by the rebels, the refugees driven out, the bishop, his son, and son-in-law arrested, and the Roman Catholic bishop of Kilmore, Eugene Sweeny, installed. The bishop and his party were then confined for several weeks in Clough Oughter, a disused and derelict O'Reilly island fortress which afforded poor shelter in an unusually severe winter. They were released in early January in an exchange of prisoners, but the bishop's health was broken. Having been taken in at Drumcor by Dennis Sheridan, one of Bedell's devoted native Irish clergy, Bedell lingered until 7 February 1642, when he died. His sons William and Ambrose survived him.

Reputation and legacy Bedell's remarkable funeral at Kilmore on 9 February is described in both memoirs. Despite the high tension and hostility of the moment, the rebels, from respect for the bishop, allowed his family to give him a decent burial, though they prudently forbore to use protestant rites. The rebels, for their part, gave the cortège a military escort, and fired a volley of shot over the grave, with the (ambiguous) words: 'requiescat in pace ultimus Anglorum!' ('rest in peace ultimate/best of/last of the English'; Shuckburgh, 205–6). By the end of the seventeenth century this vignette of the pastor–bishop who could not hate even the parishioners who turned against his church and countrymen, and who was accorded a measure of grudging respect in return, had been given currency by a popular biography written by Bishop Gilbert Burnet. Based on the two memoirs of Clogie and William the younger, and other materials furnished by Clogie, Burnet's *Life* was first published in 1685, translated into French, and issued at Amsterdam two years later. It provided the basis of the admiring article in Pierre Bayle's influential *Dictionnaire historique et critique* (1697–), which gave a universal stamp to the image of Bedell as a pioneer of toleration. Modern interpretations have gone little beyond the Clogie/Burnet/Bayle version, which is substantially corroborated by the scant surviving literary material. According to Clogie, the bishop's library and effects were burnt by the rebels after his ejection from Kilmore.

Bedell remains a hero of liberal, cosmopolitan protestantism, and of that variant of missionary Christianity which accepts and adapts to the culture of the population to which it ministers. The monument of his literary heritage is the Irish translation of the Old Testament, the bulk of which was prepared under his direction and with his assistance, even though it was not completed and published until 1685, long after his death. It is this great work of missionary linguistics which distinguishes Bedell's memory in a twenty-first century in which the Irish language has survived—and been revived—as the classic language of a sovereign Irish state.

Bedell's protestant champions have contended that more clergy like him would have advanced the stalled course of the Irish Reformation, but this is not easily proved. His Catholic admirers stress the humanity and generosity of his evangelical approach.

KARL S. BOTTIGHEIMER and VIVIENNE LARMINIE

Sources E. S. Shuckburgh, ed., *Two biographies of William Bedell* (1902) • T. W. Jones, ed., *The life and death of William Bedell* (1872) • C. McNeill, ed., *The Tanner letters*, IMC (1943) • A. Clarke, 'Bishop William Bedell (1571–1642) and the Irish Reformation', *Worsted in the game: losers in Irish history*, ed. C. Brady (1989) • K. S. Bottigheimer, 'The hagiography of William Bedell', *'A miracle of learning': studies in manuscripts and Irish learning*, ed. T. Barnard and others (1998) • A. Ford, *The protestant Reformation in Ireland, 1590–1641* (1997) • R. B. Knox, *James Ussher, archbishop of Armagh* (1967) • A. Milton, *Catholic and Reformed: the Roman and protestant churches in English protestant thought, 1600–1640* (1995) • *DNB* • G. Rupp, *William Bedell, 1571–1642* (1972) • Venn, *Alum. Cant.* • J. Stoye, *English travellers abroad, 1604–1667*, 2nd edn (1989) • T. Webster, *Godly clergy in early Stuart England: the Caroline puritan movement, c.1620–1643* (1997)

Archives Bodl. Oxf., letters to Robert Ussher • Bodl. Oxf., Tanner MSS, corresp. • University of Sheffield Library, letters to John Durie

Likenesses engraving, 19th cent. (after a seventeenth-century portrait?); in possession of a descendant of Bedell, 1931 • Heaton, Butler, and Bayne, stained-glass window, 1884 (after seventeenth-century portrait?), Emmanuel College, Cambridge • line engraving, TCD

Wealth at death medieval Hebrew bible acquired in Venice was willed (and conveyed) to the library of Emmanuel College, Cambridge: will, repr. in Jones, ed. *Life and death of William Bedell*, 192–5

Bedeman, Laurence. *See* Stephen, Laurence (d. in or before 1423).

Bederic [Bury, Teesdale], **Henry** (b. before 1350, d. c.1395), prior of Clare and theologian, was probably born at Bury St Edmunds, Suffolk, shortly before 1350. He became an Augustinian friar at the order's convent at Clare, Suffolk, its premier community with a distinguished reputation for learning. He probably studied at Oxford at some point in the 1360s and 1370s, and may, as Bale suggests, have incepted as a doctor of theology in the University of Paris. He was appointed prior provincial of the order in England probably before 1387, and later served as prior at Clare. He was a distinguished theologian and preacher. Several works are attributed to him by Bale, including lectures on *The Sentences* of Peter Lombard, theological *quaestiones*, and a collection of sermons on the Blessed Virgin Mary, though none survives. Some of his work seems to have been controversial, and, like a number of Augustinian friars in this period, he may have been suspected of heresy. In his sequence of sermons on the Virgin he is said to have upheld the doctrine of her conception in original sin, but there is no further proof. Bederic remained at Clare for the rest of his career and he died in the last years of the fourteenth century.

Henry Bederic can probably be identified with the Augustinian friar Henry Teesdale. Teesdale was prior provincial of the order by July 1377, was re-elected to the office in 1385, and had resigned it by 1388. These dates coincide exactly with Bederic's term of office. Teesdale left books to the convent of Augustinian friars at York, which were recorded in the library catalogue of 1372, suggesting he had once been a member.   JAMES G. CLARK

Sources Emden, *Oxf.* · Bale, *Cat.*, 1.481 · Tanner, *Bibl. Brit.-Hib.*, 92 · M. R. James, ed., 'The catalogue of the library of the Augustinian friars at York', *Fasciculus Joanni Willis Clark dicatus* (1909), 2–96 · A. Gwynn, *The English Austin friars in the time of Wyclif* (1940)

Bedford. For this title name *see* Isabella, countess of Bedford (1332–1379); Coucy, Enguerrand (VII) de, earl of Bedford (*c.*1340–1397); John, duke of Bedford (1389–1435); Tudor, Jasper, duke of Bedford (*c.*1431–1495); Russell, John, first earl of Bedford (*c.*1485–1555); Russell, Francis, second earl of Bedford (1526/7–1585); Russell, Lucy, countess of Bedford (*bap.* 1581, *d.* 1627); Russell, Francis, fourth earl of Bedford (*bap.* 1587, *d.* 1641); Russell, William, first duke of Bedford (1616–1700); Russell, John, fourth duke of Bedford (1710–1771); Russell, Francis, fifth duke of Bedford (1765–1802); Russell, John, sixth duke of Bedford (1766–1839); Russell, Francis Charles Hastings, ninth duke of Bedford (1819–1891) [*see under* Russell, Lord George William (1790–1846)]; Russell, Adeline Mary, duchess of Bedford (1852–1920); Russell, Herbrand Arthur, eleventh duke of Bedford (1858–1940); Russell, Dame Mary Du Caurroy, duchess of Bedford (1865–1937) [*see under* Russell, Herbrand Arthur, eleventh duke of Bedford (1858–1940)]; Russell, Hastings William Sackville, twelfth duke of Bedford (1888–1953).

Bedford, Arthur (*bap.* 1668, *d.* 1745), Church of England clergyman and moral reformer, was baptized on 8 September 1668 at Tiddenham, Gloucestershire, the son of Richard Bedford, who was himself a Church of England clergyman. He was educated in 'grammar learning' (Bodl. Oxf., MS Rawl. J, fol. 2, fol. 160r) at Tiddenham and matriculated from Brasenose College, Oxford, where he was Claymond scholar, on 13 May 1684; he graduated BA on 23 February 1688 and took his MA on 9 July 1691. He was ordained deacon on 23 September 1688 and in due course took priest's orders. From September 1688 he served as curate to Dr John Read at St Nicholas, Bristol. On 6 April 1693 the corporation of Bristol presented him to the living of Holy Cross, or Temple Church, and on 12 June he married Christian, daughter of John Read. From November 1699 Bedford was a corresponding member of the Society for Promoting Christian Knowledge (SPCK). He attempted unsuccessfully to promote a monthly meeting of the Bristol clergy, and by April 1700 had joined a local society for the reformation of manners.

Acutely aware of his 'Duty ... to reprove the Vices of the Age' (Bedford, *Serious Reflections*, sig. A3v), Bedford published a succession of attacks on the theatre from 1705.

These drew particular attention to the blasphemous language and apparent idolatry that he identified in contemporary plays. They eventually culminated in *A Serious Remonstrance in Behalf of the Christian Religion* (1719), in which Bedford amassed a catalogue of 1400 texts of scripture supposedly ridiculed in drama. A strong sense of the likelihood that divine judgement and punishment would fall rapidly on a nation that tolerated immorality dominated Bedford's approach to the stage. The success of players at Bristol and Bath and the perception that the theatre encouraged drunkenness and lewd behaviour in the local community also motivated his campaign. Bedford argued that contemporary drama was helping to promote hell on earth. His awareness of the activity of the devil in the world was heightened by counselling several individuals who claimed to have conjured up evil spirits. After one such incident, in 1703, Bedford wrote to Edward Fowler, bishop of Gloucester, recounting the experiences of the mathematician, astrologer, and blacksmith Thomas Perks. This letter circulated widely in manuscript and was printed anonymously in 1704. The success of the campaign for moral reformation that Bedford undertook depended substantially on the patronage that he was able to obtain. He took a close interest in the hospital founded by the wealthy merchant and politician Edward Colston, who helped him to set up a charity school in Temple parish in 1709. At the election in 1710, however, Bedford chose not to support his tory patron in Bristol, preferring to use a right, conveyed by the freehold that he had held at Tiddenham since 1701, to cast his vote for the whigs at the Gloucestershire county poll. His target seems to have been Joseph Earle, Colston's fellow tory candidate, who had expressed sympathy for the playhouse. Bedford's action cost him Colston's favour and led to accusations that he was 'an Enemy of the Church' (Bristol RO, MS AC/JS/33(4)b).

In 1713 Bedford was rescued by a landowner and former MP for Bath, Joseph Langton, who placed him in the rectory at Newton St Loe, Somerset. In 1721, however, he again voted with his conscience in the whig interest, thus losing the support of George Hooper, bishop of Bath and Wells. Along with his parishioners he supported the government in order to win a pardon for a local soldier who had been condemned to death for deserting. Quarrels over the administration of Langton's estate, of which Bedford was an executor, led to an adverse decision in chancery, and he was lucky to escape in 1724 to become chaplain to the Haberdashers' Company hospital at Hoxton, Middlesex. He also served for a time as lecturer at St Botolph, Aldgate, where, in 1730 he preached against the newly erected playhouse in Goodman's Fields. Despite suffering setbacks Bedford was not unsuccessful in the quest for patrons for his ideas. He acted as chaplain to Wriothesley Russell, second duke of Bedford, from 1702 and tutored his son, Lord John Russell, later fourth duke of Bedford. From the late 1730s he styled himself chaplain to Frederick, prince of Wales.

At Hoxton, Bedford supervised the school and singing classes, perhaps drawing on ideas about music that he developed from the start of his career in Bristol. As vicar of Temple he had set up an organ in his church and campaigned for the proper learning and singing of psalms. In 1706 he published *The Temple Musick*, in which he argued that the style of singing preserved in English cathedral worship was a close imitation of the liturgy of the temple in Jerusalem, and preserved traces of the religion of the patriarchs. He extended this argument in *The Great Abuse of Musick* (1711), where he sketched out a great tradition in English church music running from the Elizabethan composers, through Orlando Gibbons, to Benjamin Rogers. For Bedford the restoration of church music had a providential purpose and would play a role in the conversion of the Jews to Christianity. He tried unsuccessfully to interest the SPCK in this aspect of his work. The society did express interest, however, in Bedford's parallel campaign for the improvement of oriental learning. Throughout his career Bedford insisted on the importance for clergymen of a good knowledge of Hebrew. He also argued in favour of learning Arabic as an aid to the comprehension of the language of the Old Testament. His high standards, especially with regard to the punctuation of the text, proved exasperating to others during the early 1720s, when he acted as a corrector for an Arabic psalter and New Testament that the SPCK was preparing. Bedford's concern with the missionary dimension of moral reformation was also reflected in his involvement with the Trustees of Thomas Bray and, later, with the Georgia Society.

Bedford argued that ancient music 'had a greater latitude, & was applicable not only to one particular Science, but ... indeed to all the Mathematical Sciences' (BL, Add. MS 4917, fol. 3v), and he developed a wide interest in astronomy, calendrical calculation, and chronology. During the early 1720s he began in earnest his *Scripture Chronology Demonstrated by Astronomical Calculations*, a vast work 'recommended by Archbishop Usher in his Annals, but never attempted 'til then; the Consequence of which was the Establishing the Authority of the Hebrew Chronology' (Wilts. & Swindon RO, MS 1178/631). It was published by subscription in 1730. Bedford was highly critical of Sir Isaac Newton's *The Chronology of Ancient Kingdoms Amended*, printing extensive objections to it in *Animadversions* (1728). He correctly noticed the heretical implications of some of Newton's alterations to traditional biblical chronology and associated them with the revival of anti-Trinitarian theology. Despite this Bedford was quick to criticize the ideas of the Bristol anti-Newtonian Alexander Stopford Catcott, with whom he became embroiled in an extensive pamphlet controversy between 1736 and 1741. In Bedford's opinion Catcott and his Hutchinsonian allies were also guilty of misrepresenting scripture through their peculiar interpretation of the Old Testament and their denial of the usefulness of Arabic for Hebrew scholarship. Bedford's attack on both Newton and John Hutchinson culminated in the eight lectures on the foundation of Lady Moyer that he preached at St Paul's Cathedral between November 1739 and July 1740. They were published in 1741.

Although Thomas Hearne reported that Bedford was 'looked upon as a crazed man' (*Remarks*, 10.7) his chronological work was presented to the royal family and was widely circulated by the SPCK. Throughout his career Bedford opposed all forms of dissent from the Church of England. His views on the providential role of that church and the necessity of loyalty and uniformity were set out in three sermons that he published in 1717. They later informed his criticism of the theology of George Whitefield in a sermon on the doctrine of assurance preached in 1738. Bedford's last years were marred by sciatica, which eventually deprived him of the use of his limbs. Although he published *Horae mathematicae vacuae* (1743), a treatise on golden and ecliptic numbers, much of his time was spent on administration of the estate of William Stretton, the nephew of his second wife, Martha (d. 1743/4). Bedford died at Hoxton on 13 August 1745, at the Haberdashers' hospital, in which he had served, and was buried in its graveyard.   SCOTT MANDELBROTE

Sources Bodl. Oxf., MS Rawl. J, fol. 2, fols. 160–67 · Bristol RO, MS AC/JS/33(4)b · Wilts. & Swindon RO, MSS 1178/622–1178/632 · *Remarks and collections of Thomas Hearne*, ed. C. E. Doble and others, 10, OHS, 67 (1915), 7, 305 · A. Bedford, *Serious reflections on the scandalous abuse and effects of the stage* (1705) · A. Bedford, 'Observations concerning musick', c.1705/6, BL, Add. MS 4917 · J. Barry, 'Hell upon earth, or, The language of the playhouse', *Languages of witchcraft*, ed. S. Clark (2001), 139–58 · W. Weber, *The rise of musical classics in eighteenth-century England* (1992), 47–56 · J. Barry, ed., 'The Society for the Reformation of Manners, 1700–5', *Bristol Record Society's Publications*, 44 (1994), 1–62 · E. Ralph, ed., *Marriage bonds for the diocese of Bristol, 1637–1700* (1952), 243

Archives BL, observations on music, Add. MS 4917 · CUL, Society for Promoting Christian Knowledge archives, corresp. · McGill University, Montreal, McLennon Library, collection of devotions · Wilts. & Swindon RO, letters and papers | Bristol Central Library, corresp. and minutes of the Bristol Society for the Reformation of Manners · Bristol RO, archives of Temple parish

Wealth at death £175—small estate in Gloucestershire: will, 16 Feb 1744, Wilts. & Swindon RO, MS 1178/632

Bedford, Francis (1799–1883), bookbinder, was born at Paddington, Middlesex, on 18 June 1799. His father is believed to have been a courier attached to the establishment of George III. At an early age he was sent to a school in Yorkshire, and on his return to London his guardian, Henry Bower, of 38 Great Marlborough Street, apprenticed him in 1817 to a bookbinder named Haigh, in Poland Street, Oxford Street. Only a part of his apprenticeship was served with Haigh, and in 1822 he was transferred to a binder named Finlay, also of Poland Street, with whom his indentures were completed. At the end of his apprenticeship he entered the workshop of one of the best bookbinders of the day, Charles Lewis, of 35 Duke Street, St James's. He was Lewis's foreman for many years and, when Lewis died in 1836, managed the business for Lewis's widow, Maria. It was during this period that Bedford's talent was noticed by the duke of Portland, who became not only a patron but a friend. In 1841 Bedford entered into partnership with John Clarke of 61 Frith Street, Soho, who was known for binding books in tree-marbled calf. Clarke and Bedford carried on their business in Frith Street until 1850, when the partnership was dissolved. In 1851, prompted by ill health, Bedford went to the Cape of Good Hope where he remained for several years, the expenses of his stay being met by the duke of Portland, and on his return to England he established himself in Blue Anchor Yard, York Street, Westminster. He afterwards added 91 York Street to his premises.

Bedford was considered the leading English bookbinder of his time, surpassed only by the best French binders. He was a craftsman rather than a designer and his work, though well executed, is not innovative. The number of volumes bound by him is large, and according to his obituary in *The Bookbinder*, 'year after year a constant stream of beautifully bound books went forth from his hands'. Many of his best bindings are imitations of the work of the French bookbinders of the sixteenth, seventeenth, and eighteenth centuries, and the bindings of Samuel Rogers's *Poems* and *Italy*, of which he bound several copies in morocco inlaid with coloured leathers and covered with delicate gold tooling in the style of Padeloup, are fine examples of his skill.

Bedford himself considered that an edition of Dante, which he bound in brown morocco and tooled with a Grolier pattern, was his *chef d'œuvre*, and wished it placed in his coffin; but his request was not complied with, and it was sold at the sale of his books for £49. He obtained prize medals at several of the great English and French exhibitions. His books were sold by Sotheby, Wilkinson, and Hodge, in March 1884, and realized £4876 16s. 6d. Many of the best examples of his work were among them.

Bedford was married twice but had no children. He died at his home, 12 Connigham Road, Shepherd's Bush, London, on 12 July 1883. A few months after his death the business was bought from Bedford's nieces by Joseph Shepherd. Shepherd ran the business and continued to use the Bedford name until 1893.

W. Y. FLETCHER, rev. AMANDA GIRLING-BUDD

Sources *The Athenaeum* (16 June 1883), 765 · *The Bookbinder* (1887), 55 · C. Ramsden, *London bookbinders, 1780–1840* (1956) · E. Howe and J. Child, *The Society of London Bookbinders, 1780–1951* (1952) · H. M. Nixon, *Five centuries of English bookbinding* (1978) · Boase, *Mod. Eng. biog.* · *Men of the time* (1885) · G. Meissner, ed., *Allgemeines Künstlerlexikon: die bildenden Künstler aller Zeiten und Völker*, [new edn, 34 vols.] (Leipzig and Munich, 1983–) · M. Packer, *Bookbinders of Victorian London* (1991) · J. R. Abbey, *English bindings, 1490–1940, in the library of J. R. Abbey*, ed. G. D. Hobson (privately printed, London, 1940) · *CGPLA Eng. & Wales* (1883)

Wealth at death £5245: administration with will, 12 July 1883, *CGPLA Eng. & Wales*

Bedford, Francis (1816–1894), lithographer and photographer, was born probably at 8 Southampton Street, Bloomsbury, London, the son of Francis Octavius Bedford (1784–1858) and his wife, Sophie Curtis. His father studied under Sir John Soane to become a well-respected architect responsible for a number of London churches. Nothing is known of Bedford's early education, but the implication that he trained formally as an artist and draughtsman is confirmed by his regular submission of architectural studies to the annual exhibitions of the Royal Academy between 1833 and 1849.

During this same period Bedford illustrated several publications concerned with the ecclesiastical architecture of London and York. It is thought that these brought him to the attention of the celebrated publishers and lithographers Day & Sons, whose innovative and costly production techniques placed them at the forefront of printing technology. Bedford's role at Day & Sons was to transfer the drawings and designs of artists intended as illustrations directly on to the lithographic stone in preparation for printing, a procedure that was both exacting and highly regarded. In this role he was responsible for the complex lithographs in colour and gold for both Digby Wyatt's *Industrial Arts of the Nineteenth Century* of 1851 and J. B. Waring's *The Art Treasures of the United Kingdom* of 1857. Working with a team of four assistants Bedford completed the hundred plates for Owen Jones's *Grammar of Ornament* (1856) in less than a year, and was credited by Jones for having taken personal responsibility for their perfection.

Given his training as an artist and his meticulous attention to detail, it is not surprising that Bedford turned to photography about 1853, just at the time when the medium was emerging more fully into the public domain following the introduction of the collodion process. This process offered a delicacy and tonal balance that must have appealed to Bedford's acutely sensitive eye, for throughout his long career as a photographer it remained his preferred medium. He first came to public notice in 1854 when Queen Victoria and Prince Albert bought examples of his work from the first annual exhibition of the Photographic Society, of which they had recently become patrons. Later in the year they commissioned him to photograph the works of art from the Royal Collection on public exhibition at Marlborough House. As a further mark of her regard the queen commissioned Bedford to travel to Germany incognito in order to photograph scenes associated with her husband's childhood in Coburg. The album she gave the prince as a surprise birthday present in August 1857 was warmly received and as a consequence Bedford was sent to photograph the adjoining principality of Gotha in 1858. When the prince of Wales undertook an educational voyage of the Mediterranean, Egypt, the Holy Land, and Syria in spring 1862, Bedford was chosen to accompany the royal party and document the tour. Despite the many discomforts of heat, dust, and insects Bedford made over 200 negatives. A comprehensive selection was shown in London at the German Gallery, Bond Street, and published as a series of portfolios by Day & Sons, the most expensive of which cost 43 guineas, a price placing it well beyond the reach of all but the most wealthy. Doubtless royal patronage helped to establish Bedford's status among the growing band of artist–photographers who were starting to define the professional future of the medium during this period. Bedford became an active member of the Photographic Society shortly after its formation in 1853; he was elected to its council in 1858 and twice became vice-president, first in 1861 and then again in 1878.

Even before his trip to the Middle East, Bedford was well established as a leading photographer and publisher of topographic and architectural views for the burgeoning middle-class market. Francis Frith, George Washington Wilson, and James Valentine dominated this market in England and Scotland respectively, leaving Bedford to range freely in Wales, which he effectively colonized as his own photographic territory. Initially he specialized in publishing stereoscopic views when they were the height of fashion. In the latter half of the 1860s he published a series of portfolios of *Photographic Views* of Wales, Devon, and Warwickshire and consolidated the repertoire of his catalogue by travelling widely in his specially built carriage which functioned both as darkroom and living quarters. His surviving prints are characterized by their rich tonalities and deep purple-brown colour. Throughout his career as a photographer Bedford exhibited widely both in Britain and abroad, winning numerous medals and awards for the excellence of his landscapes and topographic studies. Examples of his work are preserved at the Victoria and Albert Museum, London; the National Museum of Photography, Film and Television, Bradford; in the Royal Archives at Windsor; and at George Eastman House, Rochester, New York, among other repositories.

On 1 November 1840 Bedford married Mary (*b.* 1807/8), daughter of William Graham, upholsterer. According to the 1881 census their only son William, born in 1846, was living at the same address with his own wife and son. By this date William was shouldering the day-to-day responsibilities of his father's business, and he went on to become an eminent photographer in his own right. Francis Bedford died at his home at 326 Camden Road, Islington, on 15 May 1894, and was buried on 26 May in Highgate cemetery.   ROGER TAYLOR

Sources B. Jay, 'Francis Bedford', diss., University of New Mexico, 1974 · F. Dimond, 'A present from Coburg', in F. Dimond and R. Taylor, *Crown and camera: the royal family and photography, 1842–1910* (1987), 50 · Boase, *Mod. Eng. biog.* · *British Journal of Photography* (1860–94) [reviews of work pubd and exhibited] · *Photographic News* (1858–94) [reviews of work pubd and exhibited] · *The Bookseller* (6 June 1894), 475 · census return for 326 Camden Road, Islington, London, 1881 · m. cert.
Archives Royal Arch.
Likenesses photograph, National Museum of Photography, Film and Television, Bradford, Royal Photographic Society collection · photograph, repro. in *British Journal of Photography* (25 May 1895) · photograph, repro. in G. Seiberling and C. Bloore, *Amateurs, photography, and the mid-Victorian imagination* (1986) [exhibition catalogue, Rochester, NY, London, and Bradford, Sept 1984–June 1985]
Wealth at death £17,902 6s. 5d.: resworn probate, Sept 1894, *CGPLA Eng. & Wales*

Bedford, Hilkiah (1663–1724), bishop of the nonjuring Church of England, was born on 23 July 1663 in Hosier Lane, near West Smithfield, London, where his father, also Hilkiah (*b.* 1632), was a mathematical instrument maker. The family originally came from Sibsey, near Boston, in Lincolnshire, whence Hilkiah's grandfather, who later became a Quaker, moved to London and established himself as a stationer in the early part of the seventeenth century. The younger Hilkiah Bedford was educated at Bradley, in Suffolk, and in 1679 proceeded to St John's College, Cambridge, where he was elected as the first scholar on

the foundation of his maternal grandfather, William Plat. In 1685 he was elected fellow of St John's, and having received holy orders was instituted to the rectory of Wittering, Northamptonshire, in 1687.

Following the revolution of 1688–9 Bedford refused to take the oaths, and was consequently ejected from his preferment in 1690. Like many other nonjurors he had recourse to tuition, and spent a couple of years in France and Italy as a travelling tutor. He finally settled in London, probably after his marriage to Alice Cooper (1667–1728) about 1693. Employing himself with theological writings and religious polemics, he translated and edited several books from Latin to English, most notably Peter Barwick's *The Life of John Barwick* (1724). Two answers to the writings of the deist Anthony Collins, and several other pamphlets dating from about 1710, show him defending both the nonjuring principles and the leading figure of the sect, George Hickes.

Oddly enough, the book for which Hilkiah Bedford is most famous and which brought him most trouble was not written by him. This volume was published anonymously in 1713, entitled *The Hereditary Right of the Crown of England Asserted*. Bedford had taken part in the collaborative effort of several nonjurors to print and distribute the book, which was a learned study with an obviously Jacobite argument. He was arrested in February 1714 and, having been tried at the court of king's bench, was found guilty of writing, printing, and publishing it. He was condemned to appear before the court with a paper on his hat confessing the crime, but, probably because of an intervention by Queen Anne herself, this part of the sentence was remitted. He was fined 1000 marks and imprisoned until May 1718 in the queen's bench prison, when he finally succeeded in gaining a royal pardon. The real author of *Hereditary Right* was George Harbin, the chaplain to Lord Weymouth, who was sent by his patron to Bedford with £100 to alleviate his sufferings. Bedford certainly knew the real author's identity, but apparently preferred to suffer than betray a fellow nonjuror.

After his release Bedford became chaplain to Heneage Finch, earl of Winchilsea, in January 1719, who had already provided patronage to Bedford in the 1680s. He also opened a boarding-house at Westminster for the scholars of Westminster School. Being a well-known tutor and scholar held in high regard by the high-church aristocracy, the venture turned out to be extremely successful, and he made a considerable fortune by it. The last years of his life saw him involved in the usages controversy within the nonjuring community, siding with the nonusager party, and he was consecrated as a nonjuring bishop in January 1721. He died at his house in Millbank, Westminster on 26 November 1724, leaving an estate of several thousand pounds to his wife, their six children, and other nonjurors. The burial took place at St Margaret's churchyard three days later. Among his manuscripts, now in the Bodleian Library, Oxford, was a biography of his friend George Hickes, who had been buried at the same churchyard.   CHRISTOPH V. EHRENSTEIN

Sources Bodl. Oxf., MSS Rawl. letter 42; D. 835 • Venn, *Alum. Cant.*, 1/1 • PRO, PROB 11/601, fols. 5–8 • Nichols, *Lit. anecdotes* • BL, Eg. charter 7591 • J. H. Overton, *The nonjurors: their lives, principles, and writings* (1902) • *Remarks and collections of Thomas Hearne*, ed. C. E. Doble and others, 11 vols., OHS, 2, 7, 13, 34, 42–3, 48, 50, 65, 67, 72 (1885–1921) • *A chorus of grammars: the correspondence of George Hickes and his collaborators on the 'Thesaurus linguarum septentrionalium'*, ed. R. L. Harris (1992) • J. B. Mullinger, *St John's College* (1901) • J. C. Findon, 'The nonjurors and the Church of England, 1689–1716', DPhil diss., U. Oxf., 1978 • T. Lathbury, *A history of the nonjurors* (1845) • H. Bedford, letters to Thomas Brett, Bodl. Oxf., MS Eng. th. c. 26, fols. 138, 249, 289 • Bedford's commonplace book, Bodl. Oxf., MS Eng. th. c. 45 • H. Bedford, biography of George Hickes, Bodl. Oxf., MS Eng. misc. e. 4 • continuation of biography 15, Bodl. Oxf., MS Eng. hist. b. 2 • P. Simpson, *Proof-reading in the sixteenth, seventeenth and eighteenth centuries* (1935) • J. Smith, ed., *A descriptive catalogue of Friends' books*, 2 vols. (1867); suppl. (1893) • IGI

Archives Bodl. Oxf., commonplace books

Wealth at death 'died worth 6,000 libs. or more'; £2650 bequeathed; also house in London and estate in Kent: *Remarks and collections of Thomas Hearne*, ed. Doble, 131; PRO, PROB 11/601, fols. 5–8

Bedford, Jessie [*pseud.* Elizabeth Godfrey] (1852/3–1918), novelist and historian, was born in Twyford, Hampshire. She was probably the daughter of the Revd Charles Bedford (1817/18–1878) and his wife, Emma (*b.* 1818/19). She contributed short pieces to *Temple Bar* (January 1890) and *Macmillan's Magazine* (September 1893) before publishing her first book, *Cornish Diamonds* (1895), a novel about a talented violinist who rejects an independent career in favour of a conventional marriage. (For this and all her subsequent work she used the pseudonym Elizabeth Godfrey.) She followed it with *A Stolen Idea* (1899), a novel about a female writer who steals the idea for a successful book from the man whom she eventually marries, and *Poor Human Nature* (1898). *The Winding Road* (1903) is the tragic tale of a woman from a farming community who marries a wandering fiddle player; as in *Cornish Diamonds*, the influence of Hardy's Wessex novels was apparent. Still very readable, if often sensationalist, Bedford's novels showed a deep concern with the problems and conflicts of marriage and careers for contemporary women.

After the turn of the century Bedford began to publish works dealing mainly with seventeenth-century history. *Home Life under the Stuarts, 1603–49* was published in 1903 and was closely followed by *Social Life under the Stuarts* (1904). Favourably if condescendingly, reviewed in *The Athenaeum*, *Home Life* was described as 'excellent, delicate in flavour, vibrating with humanity, and refreshing and delightful from cover to cover' (*Athenaeum*, 58). *English Children in the Olden Time*, published in 1907, was a genuinely pioneering study of the history of infancy. These three works were largely based on diaries and family papers, such as those of the Verney family, published by Parthenope and Margaret Maria Verney. *Heidelberg: its Princes and its Palaces* (1906) revealed Bedford's interest in German history, and was succeeded by *A Sister of Prince Rupert*, a biography of Elizabeth, Princess Palatine and abbess of Herford (1909). The choice of this seventeenth-century spinster and scholar, the friend of Descartes, may reflect Bedford's preoccupation with contemporary debates about women's political and educational rights.

Little is known of Bedford's life, although her works suggest that she spent most of her life in southern England. In 1881 she was living in Winchester with her widowed mother. Her last years were spent at Moor Cottage, Setley, Brockenhurst, Hampshire; her interest in the New Forest is reflected in the publication of *The New Forest* (1912). She died unmarried at Grosvenor House Nursing Home, Southampton, on 22 May 1918, leaving the bulk of her property to her sister Lucy Palmer, wife of John Cecil Palmer.

ROSEMARY MITCHELL

Sources Blain, Clements & Grundy, *Feminist comp.*, 434 • *Wellesley index* • *The Athenaeum* (11 July 1903), 58 • will, proved London, 17 June 1919 • CGPLA Eng. & Wales (1919) • census returns, 1881 • Foster, *Alum. Oxon.*

Wealth at death £11,443 17s. 5d.: probate, 17 June 1919, CGPLA Eng. & Wales • £10,639 4s. 6d.: further grant, 30 Sept 1919, CGPLA Eng. & Wales

Bedford, John (1810–1879), Wesleyan Methodist minister, son of John and Elizabeth Bedford, was born on 27 July 1810 at Rothwell, near Wakefield. His father died when he was about five years old. John was educated in the town and studied for several years in a solicitor's office, but, resolving to become a Wesleyan minister, he was appointed by the conference in 1831 to the Glasgow circuit. There he was an effective fundraiser for chapels heavily encumbered by debt. In 1835 he married Maria Gledhill of Brighouse. They had two sons.

Although Bedford chiefly ministered in Manchester and adjacent Lancastrian towns, he also served with conspicuous success for a period of three years in Derby, West Bromwich, and Birmingham, before returning to Stockport and Manchester in 1852. While at Bolton in 1842 he had correspondence with William Sutcliffe, curate of Farnworth, subsequently published, in which he vigorously defended the doctrines and ministry of the Wesleyan Methodists then under attack from Anglicans.

In 1860 Bedford was appointed general secretary to the general chapel committee. His early legal training and orderly habits were invaluable in administering the chapel affairs of the connection. He spared no pains to place the trust property of the Methodist church on a secure basis. At the same time he kept abreast of the thought and theology of the day. His sermons were logical and impressive, and he especially excelled as a debater at conference.

At the conference of 1858 he was elected into the legal hundred to take the place vacated by the death of Jabez Bunting. From that time on Bedford was one of the foremost men in his own denomination, and his breadth of sympathy enabled him to exert a powerful influence upon the religious world in general. After being one of the assistant secretaries and letter writers of the conference for several years, he was in 1867 unanimously elected president. A partial failure of health in 1872 led him to retire from the more onerous duties of his secretaryship, but he continued as secretary of the board of trustees for chapel purposes until his death. He died at Carlton Villas, his home at Chorlton-cum-Hardy, near Manchester, on 20 November 1879, survived by his wife and two sons.

W. B. LOWTHER, rev. TIM MACQUIBAN

Sources *Minutes of the Methodist conference* (1880) · W. Hill, *An alphabetical arrangement of all the Wesleyan-Methodist ministers and preachers*, rev. M. C. Osborn, 12th edn (1874) · W. Sutcliffe, *A correspondence between the Rev. William Sutcliffe … and the Rev. John Bedford* (1842) · *CGPLA Eng. & Wales* (1879)
Archives Bolton Central Library, private minute book of centenary conference · JRL, Methodist Archives and Research Centre, corresp. and journals of conferences
Likenesses J. H. Baker, stipple (after G. P. Green), NPG · T. W. Hunt, stipple (after portrait), NPG
Wealth at death under £8000: probate, 19 Dec 1879, *CGPLA Eng. & Wales*

Bedford, John (1903–1980), department store manager, was born on 16 January 1903 at 26 Court 6 New John Street, west Birmingham, the only son of John Bedford and his wife, Rosalind Nicholls. His father was a journeyman brass-caster who established his own small brass foundry, money from which was to be used to enable his son to enter the legal profession. Unfortunately, the business failed and his son was required to start work. He did so in a Birmingham department store, first as an assistant and later as a buyer. It was this experience that was to set his future career in the retail trade.

At the age of twenty-nine Bedford became manager of the department store of J. C. Smiths in Stratford upon Avon after it had been taken over by Debenhams. Three years later he was put in charge of a newly acquired Debenhams store in Great Yarmouth. His management skills were to be fully tested three years after that, however, when he was appointed to run the Plymouth outlet, Spooners.

Managing the store during the difficulties of the war years, Bedford established a reputation as a dynamic business teacher. Spooners was one of the earliest buildings to be destroyed by German bombing, but Bedford quickly reopened in makeshift premises. He also played an active role in the Home Guard, firewatching, and in the eventual planning of the new store. In recognition of his wartime role Bedford was appointed a military MBE, as well as an OBE.

Bedford was to become a rapidly rising star in the Debenhams organization under the chairmanship of G. M. Wright. His useful experience of provincial store management was recognized in 1949, when he was sent to London to examine the difficulties of using Debenhams' fragmented buying power. Appointed a director, Bedford nevertheless continued for a time to run the Plymouth store as well as representing the board in Scotland.

The key problem facing Debenhams was its lack of co-ordination: the Debenhams group had grown through the haphazard acquisition of stores throughout the country, each of which retained its own name, purchasing policy, and distinctive identity. Bedford realized that Debenhams needed a more concerted strategy to respond to changes in consumer taste and spending power, and he managed to persuade the various factions in its organization to support some element of centralization in purchasing, stock control, and planning. One positive step towards integration was the decision that each department store should carry notices declaring that it was 'A Debenhams Store'.

In 1954 Bedford was appointed deputy chairman, and then chairman and managing director two years later. He proved to be a tireless managing director who made regular visits to all the stores. Bedford was responsible for introducing a contributory pensions scheme for employees in 1957. When he reorganized the main Debenhams board of directors in the following year, Bedford secured the appointment of a number of younger figures (each of whom was to direct a group of stores, and also serve as chief executive of the principal store in that division).

Bedford undertook a strong expansionist policy that saw many new stores added to the group. One consequence was the much publicized and unsuccessful attempt to take over the Harrods group of department stores in 1959. Bedford later confessed that 'I do not like take-over bids, and I do not like the people who make them' (*The Times*, 28 Aug 1959). He had only begun merger talks with Harrods after Sir Hugh Fraser had begun buying up its shares; nevertheless, he was bitterly disappointed when Fraser won over a majority of Harrods shareholders.

By nature a shy man who disliked personal publicity, Bedford was also a complex character who had strong personal beliefs. On 22 August 1927 he married Florence Mary, daughter of Aaron Illingworth Oddy; they had one daughter. A keen and active Methodist, Bedford for many years served as a lay preacher. In this role he occupied the pulpits of many of the small chapels in the Greater London area, and he was for some years a member of the Hinde Street Church in the West End of London. His greatest passion away from work, community service, and the church, however, was sport. As a young man he was keen on cricket and football, and in later years he moved to snooker, badminton, and golf.

In addition to his role at Debenhams, Bedford served as a director of the Commercial Union Insurance Company from 1952 to 1973, as well as serving on the executive council of the Association of British Chambers of Commerce. In 1962 he served on the Banwell committee for the Ministry of Public Building and Works. He was also a director of London Transport.

Bedford gave up active managerial responsibilities in 1970, and stepped down as chairman early in 1971. He made a positive contribution to the reorganization of Debenhams, but its underlying problems were hard to resolve; and the positive effect of central buying and the closure of loss-making outlets only began to be felt after Bedford's departure. He died of prostate cancer on 11 November 1980 at his home, 23 Kepplestone, Staveley Road, Eastbourne, Sussex. He was survived by his wife.

GARETH SHAW

Sources M. Corina, *Fine silks and oak counters: Debenhams, 1778–1978* (1978) · *The Times* (28 Aug 1959) · *The Times* (28 May 1970) · *The Times*

(8 Jan 1971) • *The Times* (20 Nov 1980) • C. Shaw, 'Bedford, John', *DBB* • *WWW* • *CGPLA Eng. & Wales* (1981) • b. cert. • m. cert. • d. cert.
Likenesses photograph, repro. in Corina, *Fine silks and oak counters*
Wealth at death £201,014: probate, 24 Feb 1981, *CGPLA Eng. & Wales*

Bedford, Paul John (1794?–1871), actor, was born in Bath, probably in 1794, and entered the acting profession through the customary route of amateur theatricals. His first appearance was at Swansea. After playing at Southampton, Portsmouth, and other towns in the south of England, he obtained an engagement in Bath, probably in 1815, as he is known to have appeared with Edmund Kean in *Richard III*, which was staged there in that year. He remained with the company until 1819, and on 19 May played Don Guzman in *Govanni in London* for his own benefit. He then proceeded to Dublin as one of a company engaged by Henry Harris of Covent Garden to play in the new theatre in that city. Among the company was the actress Elizabeth Green (1801–1833), whom Bedford married in 1822. Two successive tours in Scotland with Madame Catalani followed, without breaking the Dublin engagement, which ended only when Bedford accepted an offer from Sir Henry Bishop for Drury Lane. His first appearance at this theatre was as Hawthorn in Isaac Bickerstaff's *Love in a Village* (2 November 1824), his wife playing Rosetta. He then took the role of Bernhard, head ranger of the forest, in Soane's version of *Der Freischütz*, the fifth adaptation of Weber's great opera staged in 1824. Soon afterwards he was promoted to Caspar in the same work. Bedford was retained through the successive managements of R. W. Elliston, Stephen Price, Polhill and Lee, and lastly Bunn, chiefly on account of his vocal capacity. In 1833, still as a singer, he joined the company at Covent Garden under W. C. Macready, and appeared in Auber's *Fra Diavolo*, *Gustave III*, and other operas. In April 1833 Elizabeth Bedford died at the age of thirty-two.

With his engagement at the Adelphi from 1838 under the management of Frederick Yates, the later and better-known phase of Bedford's popularity commenced. Blueskin in J. B. Buckstone's *Jack Sheppard* (1839) and Tom Codlin in Edward Stirling's *The Old Curiosity Shop* (1840) added to his reputation, which reached a climax with his performances of Jack Gong in Buckstone's *The Green Bushes* (1845), and the Kinchin Cove in *The Flowers of the Forest* (1847). For many years he played secondary low-comedy parts at the Adelphi, initially with Edward Wright, and after his death with John Lawrence Toole. His Peter Pantile in Watts Phillips's *Paper Wings* (1860), Calchas in Burnand's *Helen* (1866), and Jack Longbones in Phillips's *Lost in London* (1867) were perhaps his most successful roles, while his performances in *Guy Mannering* (1859) and *Rip Van Winkle* (1865) were also very popular. In 1864 Bedford published a volume of gossipy memoirs, *Recollections and Wanderings*.

Memories of Bedford's portly figure and his deep and portentous voice uttering his favourite sentence, 'I believe you, my boy', persisted long after his death. He was a sound and trustworthy actor of the rollicking sort whose figure and voice formed a conspicuous portion of his stock in art. Recalling his singing in Adelphi farces, in a whole series of which he took part, it was easy to forget that he had much success in Lablache's great character of Don Pasquale. He appeared for a short time at Weston's Music Hall and at Hall by the Sea, Margate. A farewell benefit was given for him at the Queen's Theatre on 18 May 1868, when he played the Kinchin Cove in a selection from *The Flowers of the Forest* for the last time. He had then been on the stage for more than fifty years. He died of a dropsical complication on 11 January 1871, at his residence, 6 Lindsey Place, Chelsea, and was buried on 19 January in Norwood cemetery.

JOSEPH KNIGHT, *rev.* NILANJANA BANERJI

Sources P. Bedford, *Recollections and wanderings* (1864) • *The Era* (15 Jan 1871) • Adams, *Drama* • *The life and reminiscences of E. L. Blanchard, with notes from the diary of Wm. Blanchard*, ed. C. W. Scott and C. Howard, 2 vols. (1891) • P. Hartnoll, ed., *The Oxford companion to the theatre*, 3rd edn (1967) • Hall, *Dramatic ports.* • Genest, *Eng. stage* • *Drama, or, Theatrical Pocket Magazine*, 3 (1822), 206 • *Drama, or, Theatrical Pocket Magazine*, 3 (1822), 251 • *Drama, or, Theatrical Pocket Magazine*, 7 (1824–5), 101, 103–4 • d. cert.
Archives U. Birm. L., letters and agreements with Ben Webster
Likenesses R. J. Lane, lithograph, pubd 1839, NPG • C. Baugniet, lithograph, pubd 1847, BM • Cent, 1890, Harvard TC • Whyte, 1898 (with J. L. Toole), Harvard TC • A. Bryan, watercolour, NPG • F. R. Window, photograph, NPG • portrait, repro. in *ILN* (13 May 1843) • prints, BM, NPG

Bedford, Richard Perry (1883–1967), sculptor and curator, was born on 15 November 1883 at 4 Chatsworth Terrace, Berner's Hill, Torquay, Devon, the second son of the four children of George Bedford (*d.* 1920) and his wife, Maria, *née* Harris. George Bedford was the principal of Torquay School of Art, and encouraged his four children in artistic ways, giving Richard lessons in wood-carving. Bedford went to Dean Close School in Cheltenham. In 1903 he qualified as a technical assistant in the department of woodwork in the Victoria and Albert Museum, London, and a few years later he was transferred to the department of architecture and sculpture there; thus began his study of the history and materials of sculpture. As a boy he had learned to carve wood, and in the Victoria and Albert Museum he learned from one of the masons in his own department how to carve stone. In his evenings he studied sculpture at the Central School of Arts and Crafts and at Chelsea School of Art. In 1911 he was promoted assistant keeper in architecture and sculpture, and during the First World War he took charge of the department. In 1924 he became keeper, and around the same time he got to know Henry Moore, with whom he shared an interest in African sculpture. Bedford transferred in 1938 to the circulation department, which was responsible for interesting touring exhibitions from the museum's collections, and he remained there until his retirement in 1946. In the time left over from his museum career he worked as a sculptor, choosing to carve semi-abstract shapes in stone and wood. He liked to base his sculptures on plant, animal, and insect forms, and he loved to carve in marble, of which he had an encyclopaedic knowledge, particularly the marbles found around Torquay, his home town. He also used

Connemara, Belgian, and Sienese marbles, admiring their colour ranges.

In 1947, anxious to keep working in a museum context, Bedford found employment for two years as curator of pictures for the Ministry of Works. He then moved from London to West Mersea in Essex, where he cultivated his garden, in which he placed many of his stone carvings. He sent his sculpture to group exhibitions, including the Royal Academy Summer Exhibition, the London Group, the civil service exhibitions, the National Society, the Royal West of England Academy, and elsewhere in the regions. He had a solo exhibition at the Lefevre Gallery, London, in 1936, one at the Minories Galleries, Colchester, in 1961, and a posthumous one at the latter venue in 1968. He was described as 'a smiling gnome of a man [who] endeared himself to all who knew him', but 'what he really thought one had to guess behind a protective covering of badinage' (Reade and Bensusan-Butt, 15). He was elected a member of the Royal West of England Academy in 1947.

Bedford died on 3 October 1967 at his home, Daisybank, Firs Chase, West Mersea, Essex, leaving a widow, Benjie, and two sons, Dick and John. His large carving of a cat is in the collection of the Leicestershire education committee; other works are in the collections of the Royal West of England Academy, the Victoria and Albert Museum, Mersea Island Museum Trust, Colchester Art Society, and Bristol City Art Gallery.   JUDITH COLLINS

Sources B. Reade and J. Bensusan-Butt, *The world of Richard Bedford* (1968) [exhibition catalogue, The Minories, Colchester, March 1968] · b. cert. · d. cert. · *CGPLA Eng. & Wales* (1968)
Wealth at death £9011: administration, 9 July 1968, *CGPLA Eng. & Wales*

Bedford, Thomas (*d.* 1653), Church of England clergyman and author, was probably born in Northamptonshire, but his parents are unknown. Having matriculated from Queens' College, Cambridge, in the Easter term of 1606 he graduated BA in 1609, was ordained at Peterborough deacon on 23 December 1610 and priest on 7 June 1612, and proceeded MA in 1616.

At Cambridge, Bedford sat at the feet of John Davenant, fellow of Queens' and master from 1614, and Lady Margaret professor of divinity from 1609, and of Samuel Ward, then at Sidney Sussex College. Bedford said that his theology was mainly derived from these two men, and it was to Davenant, who with Ward had been a delegate at the Synod of Dort, that he dedicated his *The Sinne unto Death* (1621), a sermon which defended the Synod of Dort for distinguishing between 'temporisers and true beleevers' and which emphasized the doctrine of perseverance while attacking 'Arminius's brood'. It closely followed William Perkins. Bedford addressed two kinds of hearers: those who presumed upon God's grace and ought to fear committing the unpardonable sin, and those 'poore soules who are vehemently troubled with this feare, lest they have thus fallen'. Such fear was a sign that no such sin had been committed, he said. Those without fear ought to fear, because apostates usually fall by 'steps and degrees', which ultimately lead to determined impenitency and

rebellion with no hope of pardon from God (pp. 18, 23, 51, 65–72).

The Calvinist theology of Bedford's sermons was, however, accompanied by a more complex churchmanship. Having proceeded BD from Cambridge in 1633 he became, in the mid-1630s, lecturer at St Andrew's, Plymouth, where his position was complicated by religious politics. Thomas Ford had previously been nominated to the post, but when he preached against the conversion of the communion table into an altar his election had been forbidden by Archbishop Laud by means of a royal order. The corporation of St Andrew's then nominated another puritan, Alexander Gross. Charles I and Laud blocked this second nomination and named Bedford to the post instead. In 1638 Bedford published *The Ready Way to True Freedom*, a sermon originally preached at Paul's Cross, to defend the king, but later claimed that it had been tampered with at the press.

Bedford's theological writings are marked by a temperance unusual for his time. They also reveal his extensive reading both in the ancient church fathers and in the continental theology of the period. Most of Bedford's published work deals with the sacraments. His major work, *A Treatise of the Sacraments According to the Doctrin of the Church of England* (1639), contains three parts: first, the nature, elements, and number of the sacraments (against Roman Catholicism); second, why sacraments were ordained and how believers benefit from them (against sacramentarians and Anabaptists); third, the qualifications of those who receive the sacraments: repentance, faith, and, for the Lord's supper, thanksgiving. Like most seventeenth-century Anglicans, Bedford espoused a Calvinistic view of the Lord's supper, holding that the sacrament is not only an appropriation of the saving benefits of Christ's death but also a true receiving of the person of Christ, which furthers the believer's sense of union with Christ. Further development of these ideas came in his subsequent works on the subject, *A Moderate Answer to Two Questions* (1645), *Some Sacramentall Instructions* (1649), and *Vindiciae gratiae sacramentalis* (1650).

Bedford likewise held a predominantly Calvinistic view of baptism. When, in the context of the late 1640s and 1650s debates on paedobaptism, Richard Baxter published a criticism of Bedford's view, Bedford responded with a letter in which he said he had been convinced of 'the efficacy of the sacrament [of baptism] to the elect' by reading Cornelius Burgess's *Baptismal Regeneration of Elect Infants* (1629). He sought to show that his view was fundamentally in harmony with Baxter's. Baxter conceded the point in his reply, *A Friendly Accommodation with Mr. Bedford*, included in the 1656 edition of his *Plain Scripture Proof of Infants Church-Membership and Baptism*.

In 1643 Bedford was imprisoned in London by parliament for refusing to take the oath of the solemn league and covenant and for refusing to declare where his allegiance lay. 'We know not to which to wish or pray for the entire victory over the other,' Bedford said (*Walker rev.*, 108). He was also charged with favouring ceremonies and having Arminian tendencies. The corporation of St Andrew's, on 21 October 1643, elected George Hughes, a leading Presbyterian, to replace Bedford in the Plymouth lectureship, and he was instituted early in 1644. After nine months in prison Bedford wrote an apology, took the oath of the solemn league and covenant, and afterwards faithfully adhered to parliament. He still had sufficient standing among the godly in the mid-1640s to be appointed lecturer at St Antholin's, London. In 1647 he published *An Examination of the Chief Points of Antinomianism*, taken from lectures given at St Antholin's, and *The Compassionate Samaritan*, in which he upheld the right and duty of the civil power to punish heresy. That same year he was appointed rector of St Martin Outwich, in London. In 1649 he dedicated his *Sacramental Instructions* to his people at St Martin's. He also participated in the London provincial assembly until his death in 1653.

Bedford was survived by his wife, Testance; two sons, John and James; and two daughters. In his will he was careful to renounce Arminianism and other errors. He left £10 to the new church of Charles, Plymouth, and 40s. to the poor of St Martin and Aderstone.   JOEL R. BEEKE

Sources *Walker rev.*, 108 · Venn, *Alum. Cant.* · P. S. Seaver, *The puritan lectureships: the politics of religious dissent, 1560–1662* (1970), 107–8, 338 · B. Tipson, 'A dark side of seventeenth-century English protestantism: the sin against the Holy Ghost', *Harvard Theological Review*, 77/3–4 (1984), 301–30 · N. Tyacke, *Anti-Calvinists: the rise of English Arminianism, c.1590–1640* (1987), 87ff., 150, 259–60 · Tai Liu, *Puritan London: a study of religion and society in the City parishes* (1986), 84–5, 100 · J. Davenant, *Baptismal regeneration and the final perseverance of the saints, a letter … to Dr. Samuel Ward*, trans. J. Allport (1864) · R. Baxter, *Plain scripture proof of infants church-membership and baptism: being the arguments prepared for … the publike dispute with Mr. Tombes … hereto is added an appendix against … a tractate of Mr. Th. Bedford's* (1651) · R. Baxter, *Plain scripture proof … and a friendly accommodation with Mr. Bedford*, 3rd edn (1653) · J. Walker, *An attempt towards recovering an account of the numbers and sufferings of the clergy of the Church of England*, 2 pts in 1 (1714), pt 1, p. 3; pt 2, p. 193 · C. J. Cocksworth, *Evangelical eucharistic thought in the Church of England* (1993) · Tai Liu, *Discord in Zion: the puritan divines and the puritan revolution, 1640–1660* (1973), 163 · J. Davies, *The Caroline captivity of the church: Charles I and the remoulding of Anglicanism, 1625–1641* (1992), 168

Wealth at death bequests of £10 to new church of Charles, Plymouth, and 40s. to poor of St Martin and Aderstone: *Walker rev.*

Bedford, Thomas (1707–1773), nonjuring Church of England clergyman and historian, was the second son of Hilkiah *Bedford (1663–1724), nonjuring Church of England clergyman, and his wife, Alice (1667–1728), daughter of William Cooper. He was born in Westminster, where his father kept a boarding-house for the scholars of Westminster School. From Westminster, where he had been admitted in July 1718, Bedford followed his father (who had been a fellow) to St John's College, Cambridge, the most important nonjuring centre in either of the English universities. Here he was admitted on 5 May 1724, aged seventeen, matriculating as sizar to the master, Dr Robert Jenkin, but he scrupled to take any degree on account of his nonjuring principles. By 1731 he was at Burn Hall, near Durham, where his elder sister, Christian, had married their cousin George Smith (1693–1756), one of their father's former pupils, who had been consecrated as a

nonjuring bishop in 1728. Another of Bedford's sisters, Elizabeth, married Robert Gordon (d. 1779), who in 1741 became the last English nonjuring bishop of the regular succession. While at Burn Hall, with Smith's encouragement, Bedford prepared an edition of Symeon of Durham's *De exordio atque procursu Dunhelmensis ecclesiae libellus*, which was published by subscription in 1732.

On 27 December 1731 Bedford entered the nonjuring ministry, being ordained priest by bishop Henry Gandy in order to serve as chaplain to Sir Robert Cotton and his son John, Jacobite exiles living at Angers. He was accompanied to Angers by Nicholas, son of the nonjuring bishop Thomas Brett, with whom Bedford maintained an important correspondence on liturgical and theological matters from 1729 until the latter's death in 1743. On returning to England in 1736 Bedford lived once more in Durham, until he assumed pastoral care of the nonjuring congregation around Compton and Ashbourne in Derbyshire in December 1741, following the death of the Revd Henry Burdyn. Here he continued to pursue his literary interests, publishing an adaptation of the Abbé Fleury's *Catéchisme historique* in 1742 and translating the same author's *Les moeurs des Israélites* (as *A Short History of the Israelites*) in 1756 for the benefit of Ellis Farneworth, a neighbouring conforming clergyman. However, with the rapidly declining fortunes of the nonjuring cause, Bedford was required to minister more widely, and it was observed that he was accustomed 'to traverse the North-West parts from Chester to York. When at home he has a congregation only of seven or eight, and at several of his halting places only two or three' (Robert Lyon to Bishop John Alexander, 27 Aug 1757, Broxap, 238).

Bedford died, unmarried, at Compton, and was buried in the parish churchyard at Ashbourne on 25 February 1773, where the register recorded his character as 'a Non-Juring Preacher'. Having inherited 'some original fortune, and being withal a very frugal man … he died rich' (Nichols, *Lit. anecdotes*, 1.169). By his will, dated 11 March 1771, he distributed legacies to surviving members of the nonjuring community, including several to his own relations and £20 in trust for the children of Dr Thomas Deacon in Manchester.   RICHARD SHARP

Sources H. Broxap, *The later nonjurors* (1924) · J. H. Overton, *The nonjurors: their lives, principles, and writings* (1902) · *Remarks and collections of Thomas Hearne*, ed. C. E. Doble and others, 11 vols., OHS, 2, 7, 13, 34, 42–3, 48, 50, 65, 67, 72 (1885–1921), vols. 10–11 · Nichols, *Lit. anecdotes*, 1.169, 2.392 · *DNB* · Venn, *Alum. Cant.* · *Old Westminsters*, 1.68

Archives Bodl. Oxf., Brett MSS, corresp. with T. Brett, MS Eng. th. c.30–31, 33–35, 37, *passim*

Wealth at death substantial: Broxap, *Later nonjurors*, 233n.; Nichols, *Lit. anecdotes*, 1.169

Bedford, William (1764?–1827), naval officer, was made a lieutenant in the navy on 12 September 1781. He served during the Russian armament of 1791 on the *Edgar*. He was afterwards in the *Formidable*, and in May 1794 was first lieutenant of the *Queen*, flagship of Rear-Admiral Gardner. In the action of 29 May the *Queen*'s captain was severely wounded, so Bedford commanded her on 1 June, and for this service was, on the captain's death some weeks afterwards, promoted into the vacancy, first as commander on 5 July and then captain on 15 August 1794. He continued in the *Queen* with Sir Alan Gardner, and was present in Lord Bridport's action off Lorient on 23 June 1795. Afterwards he moved with Sir Alan to the *Royal Sovereign*, and continued with him until he struck his flag in August 1800. Bedford was then appointed to the *Leyden* (68 guns), in the North Sea, and was present at the attack on the invasion flotilla on 15 August 1801, when he offered to serve as a volunteer under the junior officer in command of the boats. The offer, however, was declined by Nelson. In 1803 he was captain of the *Thunderer* (74 guns), and in 1805 in the *Hibernia*, flagship of his old chief, now Lord Gardner, commanding the blockade of Brest.

In 1808 Bedford married Susan, one of the nine daughters of Captain Robert Fanshawe, commissioner of the navy at Portsmouth, and was thus a brother-in-law of Sir Thomas Byam Martin, comptroller of the navy, and of Admiral Sir Robert Stopford. In 1809, he was flag captain in the *Caledonia* with Lord Gambier, in the expedition to the Basque roads, from which, though he escaped blameless, it was impossible to derive any credit. He attained flag rank on 12 August 1812, and served in the North Sea under Sir William Young as captain of the fleet. He had no further service, though on 19 July 1821 he was promoted to the rank of vice-admiral. He died at his house, Stone Hall, Stonehouse, near Plymouth, Devon, in October 1827, and was buried at St George's, Stonehouse, on 20 October. Bedford had a solid career, built on competence, patronage, and service politics. His lack of personal distinction was indicated by the absence of any award.

J. K. LAUGHTON, rev. ANDREW LAMBERT

Sources D. Syrett and R. L. DiNardo, *The commissioned sea officers of the Royal Navy, 1660–1815*, rev. edn, Occasional Publications of the Navy RS, 1 (1994) · J. Marshall, *Royal naval biography*, 1 (1823), 574–6 · parish register, Stonehouse, Devon, St George's, Plymouth and West Devon Record Office, Plymouth [burial], 20/10/1827 · *GM*, 1st ser., 97/2 (1827), 465–6
Archives NMM, letters to Lord Nelson

Bedford, William Kirkpatrick Riland (1826–1905), antiquary and genealogist, born at Sutton Coldfield rectory on 12 July 1826, was the eldest of five sons of William Riland Bedford (1794/5–1843), rector of Sutton Coldfield, Warwickshire, and his wife, Grace Campbell, daughter of Charles Sharpe of Hoddam, Dumfriesshire. Charles Kirkpatrick Sharpe, a Scottish antiquarian, was his maternal uncle. After education at Sutton Coldfield grammar school, Bedford won a Queen's scholarship at Westminster School in 1840, and qualified for a studentship at Christ Church, Oxford. An attack of scarlet fever prevented him from taking up the studentship, and on 5 June 1844 he matriculated as a commoner at Brasenose College. In 1847 he was secretary of the Oxford Union. He graduated BA in 1848 and proceeded MA in 1852. In 1849 he became curate of Southwell, Nottinghamshire, and in 1850 he was ordained priest and succeeded an uncle, Dr Williamson, as rector of Sutton Coldfield. He held the post for forty-two years, and was rural dean for twenty-five. He

was also chaplain of the grand lodge of freemasons in 1861.

On 18 September 1851 Bedford married Maria Amy, the youngest daughter of Joseph Houson (d. 1890) of Southwell, Nottinghamshire. They had seven sons and three daughters. His second marriage was to Margaret (b. 1871/2), daughter of Denis Browne, and took place on 27 November 1900.

Bedford was an acknowledged authority on the antiquities of Sutton Coldfield, which he described in *Three Hundred Years of a Family Living, being a History of the Rilands of Sutton Coldfield* (1889) and *The Manor of Sutton, Feudal and Municipal* (1901). He was well versed in heraldry and genealogies, and was a frequent contributor to *Notes and Queries*. From 1878 to 1902 he was chaplain of the order of St John of Jerusalem and in his capacity of official genealogist, he compiled many works dealing with the history and regulations of the knights hospitallers, including *Malta and the Knights* (1870; 2nd edn, 1894), *Notes on the Old Hospitals of the Order of St John of Jerusalem* (1881), and a history of the English hospitallers (1902), in collaboration with R. Holbeche.

Bedford was a keen cricketer in the early days of the game. On 20 July 1856 he founded the Free Foresters, an amateur wandering club with headquarters at Sutton Coldfield, and he recorded the fortunes of the club in his *Annals of the Free Foresters from 1856* (1895). He was also an expert archer and in 1849 joined the Woodmen of Arden at Meriden, Warwickshire, where he frequently attended meetings, and won the Arden medal on 16 July 1857. In 1885 he published *Records of the Woodmen of Arden from 1785*, and he later contributed to the volume on *Archery* in the Badminton Library series (1894). In addition to the works already mentioned, his chief publications were a *Memoir of C. K. Sharpe*, his uncle, written from family papers (1888), *The Blazon of Episcopacy*, his first work, published in 1858, and *Outcomes of Old Oxford* (1899).

Bedford died at his home, 209 Fordwych Road, Cricklewood, on 23 January 1905; his ashes were buried after cremation at Golders Green.

G. S. WOODS, rev. JOANNE POTIER

Sources *The Times* (25 Jan 1905) · *WWW, 1897–1915* · Allibone, *Dict.* · G. F. R. Barker and A. H. Stenning, eds., *The Westminster School register from 1764 to 1883* (1892), 19 · [C. B. Heberden], ed., *Brasenose College register, 1509–1909*, 1, OHS, 55 (1909), 532 · Foster, *Alum. Oxon.* · *N&Q*, 10th ser., 3 (1905), 120 · *Wisden* (1906) · S. Reynolds Hole, *The memories of Dean Hole* (1892) · *Crockford* (1902)
Archives S. Antiquaries, Lond., corresp., illustrations, and notes relating to second edition of *Blazon of episcopacy* | Bodl. Oxf., corresp. with Sir Thomas Phillipps · NL Scot., corresp. with Blackwoods
Likenesses C. Silvy, carte-de-visite, 1861, NPG · Meisenbach?, portrait, repro. in W. K. R. Bedford, *Annals of the Free Foresters from 1856* (1895)
Wealth at death £22,001 3s. 6d.: probate, 15 March 1905, CGPLA Eng. & Wales

Bedi, Sir Khem Singh [Khem Singh Bedi Baba] (1832–1905), religious leader and social reformer, was born on 21 February 1832 in the village of Kallar, the Punjab, India, the second son of Baba Atar Singh Bedi (d. 1839), holy man and landowner. The family was descended from Guru Nanak (1469–1539), the founder of the Sikh faith, as a result of which the male members of the lineage received the title Baba ('holy man'). The family had a large religious following among Sikhs and Hindus in north-western Punjab. Baba Khem Singh inherited large landed estates in the Punjab granted to his forebears by Maharaja Ranjit Singh (*reigned* 1799–1839) of Lahore and other Sikh rulers and notables, some of which were resumed by the new British administration of the Punjab after the annexation of 1849. He married and had six sons and four daughters.

Baba Khem Singh's material fortunes began to rise after his personal military support of the British during the mutiny of 1857. In addition to raising contingents of troops, he personally participated in many campaigns. Khem Singh was honoured after the end of the mutiny, and in 1886 he received a land grant consisting of 10 per cent of the area of the new Sohag Para canal colony in Montgomery district. His stalwart support of the British Indian government led to a number of further honours throughout his life. He was appointed a magistrate in 1877 and an honorary district judge in the following year. From 1878 to 1879, Baba Khem Singh assisted in the recruitment of 1500 Sikh soldiers for the Punjab frontier force. He was made a companion of the Order of the Indian Empire in 1879 and a knight commander of the order in 1898. He was nominated to the viceroy's legislative council in 1893 and to the Punjab legislature, then entirely appointed, in 1897.

Baba Khem Singh played an important role in efforts to reform nineteenth-century Punjabi society. In 1865 he was a founding member of the Anjuman-I Punjab, or Society for the Diffusion of Useful Knowledge. The group held public meetings to promote social reform causes and founded public institutions such as the Punjab's first public library. The Anjuman also mobilized support for the Oriental College in Lahore, which grew to become part of the new Punjab University founded in 1869. Khem Singh was a charter member of the university's senate. His efforts and financial contributions led to the foundation of a number of schools, including girls' schools, throughout western Punjab and a college in the town of Rawalpindi. Khem Singh's campaigning led to the widespread acceptance of vaccination initiatives in the regions inhabited by his followers. He also furthered the cause of agriculture in the Punjab, purchasing wasteland in the Montgomery district and inducing peasants to settle and cultivate it.

Baba Khem Singh was deeply involved in Sikh reform movements in the 1880s and 1890s. He was a founder member of the Sri Guru Singh Sabha (or Singh Sabha) reform association founded at Amritsar in 1873, which spurred the foundation of similar Sabhas throughout the Punjab. He was made president of the Khalsa diwan founded at Amritsar in 1882 to knit together the hitherto loosely bound local Sabhas and represent the views of the community to the government on social and religious issues. Splits in the diwan after 1885 and disputes among the Singh Sabhas led to a decline in Khem Singh's influence in the reform movement after this date, although he continued to lead the Amritsar-based branches of both organizations.

During an extended tour to visit his followers, Baba Khem Singh died in the town of Montgomery, the Punjab, India, on 10 April 1905.　　Jeevan Singh Deol

Sources C. F. Massy and L. Griffin, *The Panjab chiefs* (1890) · C. F. Massy and L. Griffin, *Chiefs and families of note in the Punjab*, rev. W. L. Conran and H. D. Craik, 2 (1910) · H. Oberoi, *The construction of religious boundaries* (1994) · I. Ali, *The Punjab under imperialism, 1885–1947* (1988) · H. Singh, ed., *The encyclopaedia of Sikhism*, 2nd edn, 2 (Patiala, 1997) · H. Singh, *The heritage of the Sikhs* (1983)
Likenesses J. Lafayette, photograph, V&A

Bedingfeild [*née* Draper], **Anne** (1560–1641), theatre landlord and benefactor, was born in August 1560, the daughter of John Draper (*d.* 1576) and his wife, Margery, *née* Wilkes (*d.* 1600/01), of the parish of St Dunstan-in-the-West, London. Her father was a rich city brewer who owned various freehold properties in the Blackfriars precinct, the Barbican, and in Middlesex. When he died in 1576 he left his brewery, which was in Whitefriars, to his wife and children, according to the custom of the city of London. Among other properties in Clerkenwell he left some leasehold land to Anne that was on 'the Seckford Estate'. This was a piece of charitable property that was left in the will of Thomas Seckford, a Tudor master of requests, to fund an almshouse for the poor in his home town of Woodbridge, Suffolk.

Soon after her father's death Anne's single, propertied status attracted attention. John Draper's clerk, Thomas Hobson, took Margery Draper to court after she had dismissed him; in her defence she claimed that he had 'most shamefully, wickedly and horribly' tried to marry her daughter (PRO, REQ2, 78/56). Two years later, by licence dated 4 June 1579, Anne married Eustace Bedingfeld (*d.* 1599), a member of a famous recusant family, the Bedingfelds of Oxburgh Hall, in Norfolk. His father, Anthony Bedingfeld, was of Holme Hale, near Oxborough, and his uncle Sir Henry Bedingfeld was recorded in Foxe's *Actes and Monuments* as the gaoler of Princess Elizabeth before she became queen. Eustace and Anne had several children, including a daughter called Anne who was buried in 1581 at the expense of her grandmother Margery. When Margery Draper drew up her will she forgave her son-in-law a large debt of £400, although she outlived him and died in late December 1600 or early January 1601. Eustace paid poor rates at the parish of St Clement Danes from 1591 until his death on 19 May 1599 and Anne continued to pay this money intermittently until 1614.

By 1605 Anne had sublet part of her Seckford estate property to Aaron Holland, a tailor and innkeeper, and to Martin Slater, an actor associated with the acting company the Servants of Queen Anne. On this land Holland built the Red Bull theatre and thus Anne became one of many widows associated with the history of the stage in the early modern period. The theatre housed the repertoire of the Queen's Servants, who had been the Earl of Worcester's Men before the accession of King James.

These players, whose main playwright was Thomas Heywood, were known for their citizen drama but also for their overtly protestant and nationalist plays. It is therefore ironic that their repertoire includes the two-part drama by Heywood *If You Know Not Me You Know Nobody*. Part 1 tells the story of Princess Elizabeth before she acceded to the throne and includes the character of Sir Henry Bedingfeld, who is made a considerable figure of fun.

Anne Bedingfeild ended her days not in London or its environs but in the village of Darsham, in Suffolk; she died on 29 March 1641, probably at Darsham, aged eighty years and seven months, according to her memorial brass in the chancel floor, before the altar, of the parish church of All Saints (Suckling, 2.224). Above the inscription is an illustration of the widow wearing a distinctive, wimple-like headdress and a 'watchman's great-coat' (ibid., 2.225). It would seem that she involved herself, like many widows, in charitable giving, as her involvement on the Seckford estate bears witness. In her will of 1636 she instructed her daughter, also called Anne, to continue to benefit seven poor men of the parish of St James, Clerkenwell, with proceeds from her property there. The members of her family were no strangers to charity; her maternal aunt Alice Wilkes, later Dame Alice *Owen (1547–1613), was a famous Middlesex almsgiver.

EVA GRIFFITH

Sources E. Griffith, 'New material for a Jacobean playhouse: the Red Bull Theatre on the Seckford estate', *Theatre Notebook*, 55 (2001), 5–23 · J. M. Bennett, *Ale, beer and brewsters in England: women's work in a changing world, 1300–1600* (1996) · J. Golland, 'Anne Bedingfeld: the brasses in Pinner church', *Pinner Local History Society Newsletter: Silver Jubilee, 1972–1997*, 25–8 · A. Suckling, *The history and antiquities of the county of Suffolk*, 2 (1848) · will, PRO, PROB 11/58 [John Draper] · will, PRO, PROB 11/97 [Margery Draper] · will, PRO, PROB 11/187 · J. L. Chester and G. J. Armytage, eds., *Allegations for marriage licences issued by the bishop of London*, 2 vols., Harleian Society, 25–6 (1887) · *Hobson v. Draper*, PRO, REQ2, 78/56 · parish records, St Clement Danes; surveyors' accounts, 1581–1621, City Westm. AC, B1 · inquisitions post mortem, PRO, C142/261/51; 269/56 · memorial inscription, chancel, All Saints, Darsham, Suffolk

Archives Suffolk RO, Ipswich, Seckford Foundation papers, HB10/427/214

Likenesses memorial brass, 1641, All Saints, Darsham, Suffolk; repro. in Suckling, *History and antiquities*

Wealth at death Seckford estate property in Clerkenwell: will, PRO, PROB 11/187

Bedingfeld [Bedingfield], **Sir Henry** (1509x11–1583), administrator, was the eldest son of Sir Edmund *Bedingfield (1479/80–1553) [*see under* Bedingfield family] and his wife, Grace (*d*. in or after 1553), the daughter of Henry, first Baron Marney. There is some confusion about his birth date: his father's inquisition post mortem, held in June 1553, states that he was then forty-three years old, but the family missal gives his birth as 8 September 1511 (PRO, C142/98/51; BL, Harleian MS 3866, fol. 7). He was admitted to Lincoln's Inn in 1528. His marriage to Katherine (*d*. 1581), the daughter of Sir Roger Townshend of Raynham, Norfolk, had occurred before 1535, when the first of his ten children was born. The second of their five sons was Thomas *Bedingfield, translator. The Bedingfeld family,

Sir Henry Bedingfeld (1509x11–1583), by unknown artist, 1573

long established in Norfolk and Suffolk, belonged to the circle of prominent gentry who were clients of the Howards, dukes of Norfolk. Both Henry's grandfather and father had also served the crown: his grandfather Sir Edmund *Bedingfeld (1443–1496) [*see under* Bedingfield family], the builder of the much admired Oxburgh Hall, Oxborough, Norfolk, had been knight of the body to Henry VII, and his father had been one of Katherine of Aragon's keepers at Kimbolton. Henry Bedingfeld followed this family tradition. He spent his early adult years in his father's shadow, serving on local commissions from 1534 onwards, while in 1544 he led his tenants in the vanguard of the army sent to France. After the political struggle of 1546 between the Howards and Seymours over control of the future Edward VI, he sat on the jury for the treason trial of Henry Howard, earl of Surrey, chosen, it may be surmised, as a test of his loyalty to the victorious Seymour faction. Although Surrey was condemned, Bedingfeld's family connection with the Howards probably inhibited him from taking local or royal office during the early years of Edward VI's reign, but his help at the time of Ket's rebellion and his capture when defending Norwich recommended him to John Dudley, earl of Warwick.

Bedingfeld's political fortunes began to change as soon as Warwick asserted his control of the government in the autumn of 1549. He was appointed to county commissions again, and had been knighted before May 1551, while in 1552 the council recommended him to the Suffolk county electors as a man of 'wisdom and experience'; he sat in Edward's last parliament (BL, Lansdowne MS 3, fol. 36). The presence of Bedingfeld's name on William Cecil's list of 'men thought favourable to Lady Jane' (BL, Lansdowne MS 103, fol. 2) makes his prompt adherence to Mary's cause in the critical days of July 1553 all the more significant. He was the 'first gentleman to be mindful of his fealty and hasten to aid the queen' at Kenninghall (MacCulloch, 253–4). Mary included him on her 'consell' and made him knight marshal, or third in command of her growing forces. While he remained a privy councillor after Mary's accession to the throne, and served as knight of the shire for Norfolk in her first parliament, his primary duties seem to have centred on Norfolk. He was there during Wyatt's rebellion at the beginning of 1554, but shortly afterwards Mary made him constable of the Tower and committed her sister Elizabeth to his charge. Bedingfeld's reputation has suffered over the centuries because, according to protestant mythology as transmitted by John Foxe, he was a stern and even cruel gaoler. The job was politically hazardous; it was a time of unrest, the rebels had used Elizabeth's name, and some councillors wanted to have her executed; yet she was the legitimate heir to the throne, a protestant, and not particularly co-operative. Sir Henry's letters to the council are very similar to those his father wrote as steward of Katherine of Aragon's household. Neither man wished to exceed instruction, both worried about treating a popular prisoner correctly, both had to deal with the prisoner's problems of health as well as the possibility of charges of poisoning, and both expressed concern about visitors, messages, and a shortage of money. Bedingfeld may have seemed rigid and he showed little initiative, but there is no evidence of the cruelty Foxe alleged.

After this assignment, which lasted from May 1554 to the following April, Mary rewarded Bedingfeld in October 1555 by appointing him lieutenant of the Tower and captain of the guard. In this capacity he was in charge of the prisoners accused of complicity in the Dudley conspiracy of 1556. He was relatively sympathetic to pleas for leniency, better conditions, and familial visits. He relinquished this post at the end of 1556 to return to Norfolk, where he was soon actively engaged in preparations for the war with France. At the end of 1557 he was recalled to court, when Mary appointed him vice-chamberlain of her household in place of his closest friend on the council, Sir Henry Jerningham. Shortly afterwards, on 30 March 1558, Bedingfeld witnessed Mary's will. He had now reached a position of political prominence, but his hopes of further promotion were dashed when Mary died on 17 November, and his government career died with her. There is no evidence that Elizabeth held her sojourn at Woodstock against him, but as a Catholic he had no place in her household or government. His portrait painted some time after his retirement reveals a sombre individual, which perhaps reflects his experience after Mary's reign. Neither he nor his wife accepted the Elizabethan settlement: she helped arrange Catholic baptisms for the family servants, and after the outbreak of the northern rising in 1569 he refused to sign the government statement of loyalty. He was placed under bond for his good behaviour, and in 1578 the continuation of Catholic activity at Oxburgh brought a renewed effort to induce him to conform. The council increased his bond to £500, ordered him to appear before it, and instructed him to dismiss all his servants who did not attend church. Illness prevented his council appearance, but in 1581 he was in trouble again because of suspect persons at his house. This time his son-in-law, Henry Seckford, a groom of the privy chamber, was able to intercede by citing Bedingfeld's distress over his wife's recent death. Bedingfeld was licensed to remain at his daughter Alice Seckford's house while he recovered from his bereavement. He died on 22 August 1583, was buried on the 23rd or 24th in the parish church of Oxborough, and his descendants remained Catholic.   ANN WEIKEL

Sources D. MacCulloch, 'The *Vita Mariae Angliae Reginae* of Robert Wingfield of Brantham', *Camden miscellany, XXVIII*, CS, 4th ser., 29 (1984), 181–301 · A. Weikel, 'The rise and fall of a Marian privy councillor: Sir Henry Bedingfeld, 1509/11–1585', *Norfolk Archaeology*, 40 (1987–9), 73–83 · K. Bedingfeld, *The Bedingfelds of Oxburgh* (1912) · D. MacCulloch, 'Kett's rebellion in context', *Past and Present*, 84 (1979), 36–59 · W. R. Trimble, *The Catholic laity in Elizabethan England, 1558–1603* (1964), 15, 53, 93, 95 · BL, Add. MS 34563 [repr. in C. R. Manning, 'State papers relating to the custody of the Princess Elizabeth at Woodstock, in 1554', *Norfolk Archaeology*, 4 (1855), 133–226] · APC, 1552–1554, 430; 1577–1578, 310, 313, 315; 1579–80, 15; 1581–1582, 6, 25, 142, 295 · LP Henry VIII, 19/1.273–4; 21/2.366 · state papers domestic, Elizabeth I, PRO, SP12/60/62 [repr. in *CSP domestic*, 1547–80, 357] · *The acts and monuments of John Foxe*, ed. S. R. Cattley, 8 vols. (1837–41), vol. 8, pp. 613–18 · HoP, *Commons, 1509–58*, 1.408–9 · CPR, 1547–58 · chancery, inquisitions post mortem series II, PRO, C142/98/51; C142/200/61 · will, PRO, PROB 11/36, sig. 19 [Johan Watson] · will, PRO, PROB 11/66, sig. 16 · W. P. Baildon, ed., *The records of the Honorable Society of Lincoln's Inn: admissions*, 1 (1896) · *Third report*, HMC, 2 (1872) · BL, Harleian MS 3866

Archives HLRO, papers · Oxburgh Hall, Norfolk, MSS | BL, papers relating to custody of Princess Elizabeth, Add. MS 34563

Likenesses oils, 1573, Oxburgh Hall, Norfolk [*see illus.*] · J. Swaine, line engraving, NPG

Wealth at death see PRO, C 142/200/61

Bedingfeld, Thomas (1760–1789), poet, was born at York on 18 February 1760, the second son of Edward Bedingfeld (b. 1730) of York, and Mary, daughter of Sir John Swinburne, of Capheaton, Northumberland. He was educated at the University of Liège, and in 1780 was placed in the office of John Davidson, of Newcastle upon Tyne, with a view to the study of conveyancing. There he became acquainted with George Pickering (1758–1826) and James Ellis, who, together with Davidson's sons, formed a literary fraternity not very common in a lawyer's office. In 1784 Bedingfeld moved to Lincoln's Inn, and continued his legal studies under Matthew Duane, the eminent conveyancer. In 1787 he began practice as a chamber counsel—being, as a Roman Catholic, incapable of being called to the bar—and he was rising rapidly in his profession when he suddenly died in London on 5 November 1789. In person he is said to have resembled William Pitt, so much as sometimes to have been mistaken for him by the London populace.

Bedingfeld's poems were surreptitiously published in London as *Poems by T. B.—g—d, esq., of the Inner Temple* (1800). Afterwards they were collected by James Ellis and published under the title of *Poetry, fugitive and original; by the late Thomas Bedingfeld, esq., and Mr George Pickering. With notes and some additional pieces by a friend* (1815). The most laboured of his poems is 'The Triumph of Beauty', addressed to the duchess of Devonshire on her successful canvass for Charles James Fox in 1784, but his best-known piece was the 'Instructions to a Porter'.

THOMPSON COOPER, *rev.* M. CLARE LOUGHLIN-CHOW

Sources J. Ellis, 'Introductory memoir', in *Poetry, fugitive and original, by the late Thomas Bedingfeld, esq., and Mr George Pickering* (1815) • M. A. Richardson, ed., *The local historian's table book … historical division*, 5 vols. (1841–6), vol. 2, pp. 327–8; vol. 3, pp. 331–2 • *GM*, 1st ser., 59 (1789), 1058, 1127 • R. Welford, *Men of mark 'twixt Tyne and Tweed*, 3 vols. (1895) • Burke, *Peerage* (1857)

Bedingfield [Bedingfeld] **family** (*per.* 1476–1760), gentry, originated from the parish of that name in Suffolk, where a branch of the family continued to reside into the seventeenth century. Their move to Norfolk resulted from the marriage of Margaret Tuddenham (*d.* 1476) to Edmund Bedingfield of Bedingfield (*d.* 1451); she inherited her brother Thomas's estate, which comprised twenty-three manors in Norfolk and Suffolk, following his execution in 1462. On Margaret's death in 1476 the estate, which included the Norfolk manor of Oxburgh, passed to her grandson **Edmund Bedingfield** (1443–1496), who was the son of Thomas Bedingfield (*d.* 1453) and Anne Waldegrave (*d.* 1453). It was Edmund who decided to move the family's main residence to Oxburgh, erecting a fine brick-built moated house there about 1482. Oxburgh thereafter became the home of the main branch of the family with cadet branches residing at Quidenham in Norfolk, Redlingfield and Bedingfield in Suffolk, and elsewhere. Edmund, a Yorkist supporter, was knighted by Richard III about 1483, but the family soon accommodated itself to the Tudor regime, entertaining Henry VII and the court at Oxburgh in 1487. Sir Edmund was married twice, first to Alice Shelton and then to Margaret Scot (*d.* 1514).

On Edmund's death at Oxburgh in 1496, his eldest son, Thomas (*d.* 1539), succeeded to the estate. Thomas was knighted at the coronation of Henry VIII, but it was Edmund and Margaret's youngest son and eventual heir, **Sir Edmund Bedingfield** (1479/80–1553), who served the dynasty most successfully, being knighted for his bravery in the French wars by Charles Brandon, duke of Suffolk, in 1523. He was later entrusted with the custody of Katherine of Aragon at Kimbolton Castle in Huntingdonshire after the royal divorce and was responsible for the arrangements for her funeral procession from there to Peterborough in 1536. In 1539, aged fifty-nine, he inherited Oxburgh from his brother Robert. He married Grace Marney (*d.* in or after 1553), the daughter of Henry, first Baron Marney, and had died by June 1553, when he was succeeded by his son Sir Henry *Bedingfeld (1509x11–1583). Henry was a privy councillor to Mary Tudor but remained a staunch Roman Catholic under Elizabeth, which led to the family's withdrawal from active participation in national and county politics by the time of his death. His recusancy occasionally brought him into conflict with diocesan authorities, and members of the family (especially his son John) were often cited before the courts; however, the relative isolation of their main estates around Oxburgh and their detachment from more politically active forms of Catholicism afforded some protection to the family. Henry was succeeded in turn by his son Edmund (*d.* 1585) and grandson Thomas (*d.* 1590).

Sir Henry Bedingfield (1581/2–1657), the son of Thomas Bedingfield and Frances Jernegan, was still a child at his father's death and the ensuing minority compounded the effect of the family's recusancy, increasing its financial difficulties and further excluding its members from engagement in local politics. By this time the family had withdrawn socially into the recusant community, forging marriage alliances with such other well-known East Anglian Catholic families as the Southwells and the Jerninghams. In 1604 Henry, then aged twenty-two, reinforced the alliance by marrying Mary (*d.* by 1611), daughter of Lord William Howard of Naworth (Cumberland) and granddaughter of the duke of Norfolk, who had been executed for treason in 1572. Like many other Roman Catholic gentry, Henry was a loyal supporter of Charles I and was restored to the county bench in the 1620s. During the civil wars he raised troops for the king and three of his sons took up arms; one of them, John, was killed at the battle of Worcester. Henry was knighted for his services to the crown about 1645, but after the defeat of Charles he was imprisoned in the Tower from 1647 to 1649. There he composed a meditation on the passion which he dedicated to his second wife, Elizabeth Hoghton (*d.* 1662), of the well-known Lancashire Catholic family, whom he had married in 1611. As an active royalist Henry's estates were sequestered by parliament in 1652 and the house suffered extensive damage from fire at this time. He was succeeded at his death on 22 November 1657 by his eldest son Thomas (*d.* 1665), who had been a colonel in the royalist army and was wounded during the siege of Lincoln, and on Thomas's death by Henry's second son, **Sir Henry Bedingfield** (*d.* 1685), who had been living abroad with the royal court since the end of the civil wars. Another son, Edmund, had been educated abroad at St Omer and was ordained priest at Seville about 1644; he later returned to Flanders as chaplain to the Carmelite nuns at Antwerp, where two of his cousins had been sisters, and he moved with that community to its new home at Lierre in Brabant in 1648, remaining there as a canon of the cathedral until his death on 2 September 1680. During the 1650s two other cousins of the Suffolk branch of the family resident at Bedingfield were also working in Flanders as Jesuit priests, one of them, Henry (*d.* 1659), as provincial of the order there.

At the restoration of Charles II the royalist Henry Bedingfield returned to England but not to Oxburgh, where the damage done to the house and the losses incurred on the estate during the wars, estimated by him at more than £45,000, proved too daunting. In recognition of his service to the Stuarts he was made a baronet by Charles II in 1661, but no financial recompense was forthcoming. Henry made safe the buildings at Oxburgh when he finally regained possession of it and the family's other Norfolk properties in 1665, but chose to reside at Beck Hall near Billingford from 1660 until his death on 24 February 1685. He retained the family's strong attachment to

Roman Catholicism, having married a member of another Norfolk recusant family, Margaret Paston (d. 1703) of Appleton, in 1634. Two of their daughters joined the Carmelite nuns at Lierre, where their uncle Edmund was chaplain; another, Frances, married Richard Caryll of West Grinstead, the younger son of a recusant family which produced many priests and religious figures during the eighteenth century; and a fourth, Mary, married Thomas Eyre of Hassop in Derbyshire, with whom she had ten children, two sons entering the priesthood and two daughters becoming nuns. In the house at Oxburgh there is an attractive votive painting showing the family of Sir Henry under the protection of Our Lady's mantle: Sir Henry is depicted in his armour and two of his daughters are in their nun's habits, while in the background there are two scenes depicting his escape from the battle at Marston Moor and his subsequent departure overseas. It is true to say that, notwithstanding its connections among the recusant families of East Anglia and further afield, the immediate circle of the Bedingfields at this time was as likely to be found on the continent as in England.

The continental connection was most pronounced through the branch of the family which resided at Redlingfield and which was descended from John, the third son of Sir Henry Bedingfeld (1509x11–1583). John was a known harbourer of priests and was reputed always to have kept a priest in his house. This was a tradition maintained by his son Francis (d. 1644), who also educated his children on the continent, where they were to make a substantial contribution to English Catholic life. Francis and his wife, Katherine Fortescue, had eleven daughters who all became nuns, and it is worth recording some of their careers. Helena (1603–1661), the eldest, went to St Omer when she was eight to live with her grandmother, who was resident there. She was professed in 1622 at the Augustinian house at Louvain where her aunt, Mary Fortescue, was also a nun. In 1629 she was sent with others to establish a house at Bruges; eventually she became prioress of the community, and she retained the position until her death in 1661, when she was succeeded by her niece Mary Bedingfield, who continued as prioress until her own death in 1693. The community at Bruges also included Grace Bedingfield, a sister of Helena, who had been professed at Louvain in 1635, and Elizabeth, the widow of Sir Alexander Hamilton and the mother of Mary, who was prioress in 1661. Margaret, the second daughter of Francis, joined the Poor Clares at Gravelines in 1624, and moved in 1645 to the community of Rouen where she too became the superior. A younger sister, Anne (1623–1697), also joined the Poor Clares at Gravelines; she was professed in 1639 and elected as abbess in 1667, a post which she held for thirty years until her death. The third daughter, Philippa (d. 1636), entered the Benedictine community at Ghent, being professed as Sister Thecla in 1630; she died there on 14 December 1636, having filled the office of infirmarer. Catherine, the sixth daughter (1614–1650), entered the Carmelite convent at Antwerp in 1632, taking the name Lucy. She was subsequently sent to the convent at Dusseldorf as sub-prioress, but was recalled to Antwerp, where she died in 1650 as prioress. Another sister, Magdalen (1621–1684), also joined the Antwerp Carmelites and subsequently moved to Dusseldorf, where she became sub-prioress and then prioress. She was then chosen to head a new community, established by Philip, elector palatine of the Rhine, at Newburg, and remained there until her death in 1684. Her reputation for sanctity was enhanced in 1727, when her body was found to be entire and 'the habit she was buried in whole and not the least rotted' (Coleridge, 54). Three other sisters joined the Institute of the Blessed Virgin Mary, the order recently founded by Mary Ward. Winifred (1610–1666) had been entrusted to the care of Mary Ward as a young woman and later joined the institute; she became head of the Munich house in 1631, when the community there faced financial ruin. Despite her youth she was an effective administrator and leader, freeing the house from debt before her death in 1666.

Another sister, Mary, also joined the institute, but the most celebrated member of this impressive sisterhood was **Frances Bedingfield** (1616–1704). Frances went to Rome in 1632 to join Mary Ward, who was regrouping the remnants of her suppressed order there, and was professed on 8 September 1633 in the church of Santa Maria Maggiore. Frances remained a close companion of the founder, returning to England with her and remaining with her until her death at Heworth near York in 1645. At some date after 1650 Frances went to Paris and then to Rome to assist the superior of the institute; later she was superior of the mother house of the order at Munich. She returned to England, probably in 1667, as superior of the newly established house in Hammersmith in Middlesex. Operating from there she travelled between London and Yorkshire during the 1670s looking for a suitable site on which to establish a community and a school for Catholic girls, with money which her friend Sir Thomas Gascoigne had provided. We have a vivid picture of her in these years, learned in Latin, Greek, and Hebrew but busying herself with practical affairs, both legal and domestic, and with a 'majestical presence' which awed those magistrates required to administer the recusancy laws against her (Kirkus, 43). Frances eventually moved to York in 1685, and on 5 November 1686, with Gascoigne's money, she purchased a house and garden in York on a site just beyond the city walls at Micklegate Bar where she established a community which still exists today, and a school which continued until 1985. The deeds were signed using an alias, Frances Long, which she continued to use during her time at York, and the convent possesses a portrait of their founder revealing a matronly but steely figure. During its early years Frances provided effective leadership to the fledgeling community of nine or ten nuns and to the school, adding a school for poor girls to the establishment in 1699. Her reputation for holiness gained her admirers among the protestant leaders in the city, though this did not protect her from brief periods of imprisonment and the community from harassment during the 1690s—until in 1696 or 1697 she placed the York convent in the care of her great-niece, Dorothy Paston Bedingfield. In 1699, aged eighty-four, she was recalled to the mother house in Munich, where she died on 4 May 1704, the last surviving sister to have had direct contact with the institute's founder.

The lives of all these sisters, in both senses of the word, reveal a history often lost in national accounts: they provided spiritual leadership to religious communities spread across five European states and stretching from York to Munich, as well as an enduring network of contacts for English Catholics abroad which could be replicated in other families, though perhaps not quite so extensively. At least two of the sisters were succeeded in office by other family members, and the importance of these women in sustaining English Catholicism by providing education for gentry children and hospitality to travellers cannot be overestimated. Moreover, the influence of this cousinage endured well into the eighteenth century, as the case of the Caryll family of West Grinstead demonstrates. Frances Bedingfield of Oxburgh, the daughter of the first baronet, married into that family which, in subsequent generations, produced eight Benedictine nuns, two Augustinian canonesses, two nuns of the Holy Sepulchre, two Benedictine monks, and three Jesuits, who served their co-religionists at home and abroad. The Redlingfield branch provided a base for a Jesuit mission in the later seventeenth century and, as recusants, registered their lands at the annual value of £275 11s. 1/2d. in 1715. The cost of their recusancy, and the succession of children into the clergy and religious life, resulted in the family line having no direct heirs, and the Redlingfield property was sold some time before 1747, when it was owned by the Willis family.

The century following the accession of Elizabeth I had taken its toll on the fortunes of the family, whose commitment to Catholicism had cost it much in financial terms, so that the estate was somewhat diminished and decayed by the Restoration. The family then regained its chief properties and returned to reside at Oxburgh in 1666 following the marriage of the first baronet's son, **Henry Bedingfield** (d. 1704), to Lady Anne Howard (d. 1682). The newlyweds lived at Oxburgh and, following the death of his father in 1685, the second baronet set about restoring the house and estate, making it the centre of a Jesuit mission and becoming well known for the hospitality he provided there. Despite the financial and legal penalties which continued to inconvenience Roman Catholics, from this period the Bedingfields could now settle to the life of country landowners, entering into the social if not the political life of the county and acting as supportive landlords to the tenantry on their estates. A period of renewed prosperity meant that outwardly the lifestyle of the family did not differ greatly from that of their protestant neighbours, though domestically it continued to be marked by their Catholic piety and their children were still educated abroad. Following the death of Anne in 1682, the second baronet married Elizabeth Arundell (d. 1690), and in 1699 their son, **Henry Arundell Bedingfield** (d. 1760), travelled to Lierre, where his three sisters were staying at the convent with their aunt Margaret and two of their Eyre cousins who were nuns there, probably

to attend the celebrations on the fiftieth anniversary of the convent. Henry and his sisters then moved on to Brussels with Henry's tutor, Thomas Marwood, whose diary records their stay there and provides details of the extensive networks of English Catholics in the Low Countries at this time and the social and religious milieu in which they lived. The Bedingfield daughters returned to Lierre to continue their education before they moved on to the Benedictine convent at Dunkirk, where one of their Caryll aunts was abbess. Henry Arundell and Marwood remained behind in Brussels, where Henry's education was continued by his tutor and the Jesuits, who had a school there. They left Brussels later in 1700 and, travelling under the alias of Nelson, Henry Arundell moved around the Low Countries with his tutor, often staying with family members at various convents until, in January 1701, they arrived in Paris on their way to the Jesuit college at La Flèche. This college, which had English Jesuits on its staff, educated a number of English Catholic gentlemen; among them Henry Arundell found a friend from another Norfolk family, James Waldegrave, with whom he spent one holiday travelling to Mont-St Michel, as well as sons of other well-known recusant families: Brudenell, Scrope, Browne, and Widdrington. Henry Arundell remained at the school until 1705 when, following the death of his father a few months earlier on 14 September 1704, he returned briefly to Oxburgh before setting out on the grand tour in 1710. He returned again to Oxburgh in 1713 and set about improving the estate and remodelling the house, rebuilding the south-east wing. Henry Arundell continued as a Roman Catholic, registering his Norfolk estates at the annual value of £1551 in 1715, though he later married a protestant, Lady Elizabeth Boyle (d. 1755), daughter of the earl of Burlington. Their son, Richard, was educated abroad by the Jesuits at St Omer, but despite having Jacobite sympathies the family accommodated itself to the Hanoverian regime. It continued to produce priests, and a cousin of Henry Arundell, Anthony, of the Redlingfield branch, joined the Jesuits and was ordained priest at Ghent in 1723. Anthony worked at Flixton in Suffolk during the 1730s and later in Liverpool before eventually returning to Flanders, where he died at Liège on 2 June 1752. Henry Arundell Bedingfield died at Oxburgh on 15 July 1760.

The family's adherence to Catholicism throughout the period cost it dearly both in political power and financially throughout the later sixteenth and the seventeenth centuries, though some recovery was seen after 1700. Its close association with the Stuarts led to two members of the family, from cadet branches, achieving public positions in the law, albeit briefly: Sir Thomas *Bedingfield (1591/2–1661) was appointed a serjeant-at-law by Charles II at the Restoration, and Sir Henry *Bedingfield (bap. 1632, d. 1687) acted as chief justice of the common pleas under James II. To that degree the story of the Bedingfields is representative of the history of post-Reformation English Catholicism, but unexceptionally so, as there was no martyr and the family kept aloof from plots. What marks it out as exceptional in these years, however, is the number of members, especially among the women, who entered the religious life, and the influence which they exercised on the English Catholic community abroad, as leaders of religious communities, educators of the sons and daughters of the Catholic gentry, and providers of hospitality to their co-religionists. In this respect their experience testifies to the close contact between English and continental Catholicism during this period, contact often overlooked in the traditional accounts of the social isolation of Catholic gentry families within English society at the time.

Under the terms of her will of 1513, Margaret, widow of Sir Edmund Bedingfield, established a chantry chapel dedicated to the Holy Trinity in Oxburgh parish church, which became the burial place for succeeding generations of the family and the location of a number of monuments and memorials to its members.

WILLIAM JOSEPH SHEILS

Sources K. Bedingfeld, *The Bedingfelds of Oxburgh* (privately printed, 1912) · J. H. Pollen, ed., *The Bedingfeld papers*, Catholic RS, 7 (1909) · *Oxburgh Hall* (2000) · H. Foley, ed., *Records of the English province of the Society of Jesus*, 5 (1879) · T. M. McCoog, *English and Welsh Jesuits, 1555–1650*, 2 vols., Catholic RS, 74–5 (1994–5) · G. Holt, *The English Jesuits, 1650–1829: a biographical dictionary*, Catholic RS, 70 (1984) · A. H. Smith, *County and court: government and politics in Norfolk, 1558–1603* (1974) · R. W. Ketton-Cremer, *Norfolk in the civil war: a portrait of a society in conflict* (1969) · H. J. Coleridge, *St Mary's Convent, Micklegate Bar, York* (1887) · P. Guilday, *The English Catholic refugees on the continent, 1558–1795* (1914) · G. Kirkus, *An IBVM biographical dictionary of English members and major benefactors (1667–2000)*, Catholic RS, 78 (2001) · F. Blomefield and C. Parkin, *An essay towards a topographical history of the county of Norfolk*, [2nd edn], 11 vols. (1805–10)
Archives Oxburgh Hall, Norfolk
Likenesses portrait (Frances Bedingfield), Bar Convent, York · portraits, Oxburgh Hall, Norfolk; repro. in Bedingfeld, *The Bedingfelds of Oxburgh*

Bedingfield, Sir Edmund (1443–1496). *See under* Bedingfield family (*per.* 1476–1760).

Bedingfield, Sir Edmund (1479/80–1553). *See under* Bedingfield family (*per.* 1476–1760).

Bedingfield, Frances (1616–1704). *See under* Bedingfield family (*per.* 1476–1760).

Bedingfield, Sir Henry. *See* Bedingfeld, Sir Henry (1509x11–1583).

Bedingfield, Sir Henry (1581/2–1657). *See under* Bedingfield family (*per.* 1476–1760).

Bedingfield, Sir Henry, first baronet (*d.* 1685). *See under* Bedingfield family (*per.* 1476–1760).

Bedingfield, Sir Henry (*bap.* 1632, *d.* 1687), judge, was the fourth son of John Bedingfield (*bap.* 1595, *d.* 1680) of Halesworth in Suffolk and Joyce (*d.* 1666), daughter and coheir of Edmund Morgan of Lambeth, and was a nephew of Sir Thomas *Bedingfield. He was baptized on 9 December 1632 at Darsham in Suffolk. After attending Norwich grammar school Bedingfield was admitted to Gonville and Caius College, Cambridge, in November 1650, but his main education took place at Lincoln's Inn, where his father was a bencher. He was admitted in May 1650 and was called to the bar seven years later.

In 1658 Bedingfield was elected a freeman of Dunwich, which placed him in a prime position to secure a seat in the Convention of 1660. Bedingfield supported the restoration of Charles II, but he was an inactive MP, and when a new election was called he stepped down in order to concentrate on his legal practice. On 20 September 1671 he married his cousin, Dorothy (*d.* 1725), the daughter of Robert Bedingfield, rector of Newton, Cambridgeshire. At least seven children were baptized at Halesworth, but only two daughters survived infancy. Nothing further has been ascertained of his career until in 1683 he presented a loyal address from Dunwich abhorring the Rye House plot. However, Bedingfield soon benefited from the 'tory reaction'. On 17 November 1683 he became a bencher of Lincoln's Inn, and in January 1684 he was made a serjeant-at-law. Other honours followed, such as his appointment as deputy steward of Great Yarmouth under the new borough charter. In July 1684 he was being pushed by Lord Keeper Guilford as a replacement for the recently deceased judge Sir Hugh Wyndham. As Roger North described it, 'there was one serjeant Bedingfield, a grave but rather heavy lawyer, but a good churchman, and loyal by principle' (North, 1.323), whom Guilford (North's brother) had intended to nominate to the king to succeed Wyndham. However, when Lord Chief Justice Jeffreys heard of this he put pressure on Bedingfield's younger brother, Robert, a prominent London wool merchant and future lord mayor, to ensure that Bedingfield would accept only the patronage of Jeffreys. As Bedingfield's 'spirits were not formed for heroics' (ibid.), he let the opportunity pass.

On 3 November 1684 Bedingfield became a king's serjeant, and on the 14th he was knighted. He was returned to parliament for the borough of Aldeburgh in the election following the accession of James II. However, he gave up the seat upon his appointment on 6 February 1686 as a justice of common pleas, and on 21 April he was raised up to be the chief justice of that court on both occasions—no doubt with the approbation of Jeffreys, now lord chancellor. There seemed little doubt among contemporaries that Bedingfield had replaced Sir Thomas Jones because of the latter's opinion as to the dispensing power.

Bedingfield does not seem to have left any mark on the legal or general history of his time during the nine months that he presided in the common pleas, although he did assist Jeffreys in some chancery cases. Bedingfield died suddenly, probably at Serjeants' Inn, on 6 February 1687, 'having received the Sacrament in both kinds, (was observed to deliver the chalice, with some trembling, into the hands of the minister that officiated,) never spake more, but fell into a fit of apoplexy, and died quickly after' (Bramston, 268). He was buried in Halesworth church on 12 February, where his widow erected a mural in his memory. She died on 24 April 1725.

STUART HANDLEY

Sources HoP, *Commons, 1660–90* · A. L. Bedingfield, *Pedigrees of the Bedingfields* (1957), 36–7, 101, 104 · Baker, *Serjeants*, 199, 448, 499 · Sainty, *Judges*, 50, 78 · R. North, *The lives of … Francis North … Dudley North … and … John North*, ed. A. Jessopp, 1 (1890), 323 · *The autobiography of Sir John Bramston*, ed. [Lord Braybrooke], CS, 32 (1845), 268 ·

G. W. Keeton, *Lord Chancellor Jeffreys and the Stuart cause* (1965), 245–6, 355–6 • A. I. Suckling, *The history and antiquities of the county of Suffolk*, 2 (1848), 337, 342 • will, PRO, PROB 11/386, sig. 17 • *Memoirs of Sir John Reresby*, ed. A. Browning, 2nd edn, ed. M. K. Geiter and W. A. Speck (1991), 420–21 • *Le Neve's Pedigrees of the knights*, ed. G. W. Marshall, Harleian Society, 8 (1873), 467 • Foss, *Judges*, 7.213–4 • IGI

Likenesses R. White, line engraving, 1685 (after R. White), BM; version, Oxburgh Hall, Norfolk • R. White, oils, Lincoln's Inn, London

Bedingfield, Sir Henry, second baronet (*d.* 1704). *See under* Bedingfield family (*per.* 1476–1760).

Bedingfield, Sir Henry Arundell, third baronet (*d.* 1760). *See under* Bedingfield family (*per.* 1476–1760).

Bedingfield, Thomas (early 1540s?–1613), translator, was born probably in the early 1540s at Oxburgh Hall, Oxburgh, Norfolk, the second of the five sons of Sir Henry *Bedingfeld (1509×11–1583), administrator, and his wife, Katherine (*d.* 1581), daughter of Sir Roger Townshend of Raynham, Norfolk, and his wife, Amy, daughter of Sir Thomas Brewse of Wenham. Thomas Bedingfield is often confused with his nephew who died in 1595. The Bedingfields figure prominently in the recusant rolls of Norfolk and Suffolk; however the absence of Thomas and his brother Nicholas from any recusant roll suggests they conformed quite early, which may explain why Catherine Bedingfield states that Sir Henry had only three sons.

On going to London, probably in the late 1560s, Bedingfield came under the notice of Edward de Vere, the earl of Oxford, to whom he dedicated *Cardanus Comforte, Translated into English* (1573), his translation of the social and spiritual handbook by Girolamo Cardano, the Italian mathematician. According to the dedication (dated 1572) de Vere commissioned the translation despite Bedingfield's doubts over 'my long discontinuance of study' (Cardano, sig. A2r). In a printed reply to this dedication de Vere was pleased that the book showed how 'it ornifyeth a gentleman to be furnished in mynde wyth glittering virtues' (ibid., sig. A3v). It may have been about this time that Queen Elizabeth made Bedingfield a gentleman pensioner, as this is how he was addressed by de Vere. Joseph Gillow claims she was recognizing his literary achievements: certainly his translations form part of the courtesy literature translated from Italian. But she may have been repaying a debt of gratitude to his father for easing her imprisonment under Queen Mary. As the cordial tone of a letter Elizabeth wrote to Sir Henry early in her reign shows, they were still on good terms.

Bedingfield's translation *The art of riding containing diverse necessary instructions … appertaining to horsemanship* by Claudio Corte, a manual of manners as well as horsemanship, was published in 1584. 'To enterteine myself' (Machiavelli, sig. A2r), in 1588 he translated as *The Florentine Historie* the work by Machiavelli, but he did not publish it until 1595. 'The translation thereof was diverse yeares past desired by an honourable personage, not now living', Bedingfield wrote (ibid., sig. A4r), almost certainly referring to Sir Christopher Hatton to whom the book is dedicated. Bedingfield's 'To the reader' introduced the 'observations of the Author … wherein be discovered the

causes of forraine and domesticall discords, the commodities and discommodities of treaties, and the secret humours of Princes' (ibid., sig. A2r). He had scant enthusiasm for aristocracy as a form of government, little respect for 'the State Populer' (democracy), and argued that 'the Monarke is alone in soveraigntie … as God onely ruleth the whole world' (ibid., sig. A4v, A5r). Prudence may have caused Bedingfield to delay publishing his *Histories*; although 'the end of all Histories is to moove men unto vertue' (ibid., sig. A2r), Machiavelli's reputation for underhand dealings, chicanery, and atheism made it difficult to sell him to the Tudor public as a trustworthy guide to political ethics. One of the anonymous manuscript translations of *Il principe*, which were suppressed by royal command, has been ascribed to him on rather slim evidence.

By new year 1600 Bedingfield had long been a member of the parish of St James's, Clerkenwell, Middlesex, when his house was burgled and £100 stolen. In May 1603 James I appointed him to the office of master of tents, pavilions, and hale.

Bedingfield died at Clerkenwell some time between 26 May 1613, when he dated his will, and 2 August 1613, when the will was proved. He left his house in Clerkenwell to 'Mrs Precilla Skillicorne my daughter in lawe' (PRO, PROB 11/122, fol. 91r). A reference to 'my wives sonne in lawe Mr John Skillicorne' indicates Bedingfield had been married, but as there is no further mention of a wife, he was presumably a widower at the time of his death (ibid., fol. 91v). He is known to have had a son, but none is mentioned in the will. The rest of his bequests were to friends, the poor of the parish, and his brother Nicholas, who received 'all my bookes printed and written' (ibid., fol. 91r). Bedingfield was buried in the chapel of St James's Church, Clerkenwell. L. G. KELLY

Sources P. Ryan, ed., 'Diocesan returns of recusants for England and Wales, 1577', *Miscellanea, XII*, Catholic RS, 22 (1921), 1–114, esp. 54–5 • J. Stow, *A survey of the cities of London and Westminster and the borough of Southwark*, ed. J. Strype, new edn, 2 vols. (1720) • E. Gasquet, *Le courant machiavellien dans la pensée anglaise* (1974) • Gillow, *Lit. biog. hist.* • J. C. Jeaffreson, ed., *Middlesex county records*, 4 vols. (1886–92), vol. 1 • H. Craig, ed., *Machiavelli's 'The prince': an Elizabethan translation* (1944) • C. Bedingfield, *The Bedingfields of Oxburgh* (1912) • will, PRO, PROB 11/122, fol. 91r–91v • G. Cardano, *Cardanus comforte*, trans. T. Bedingfield (1573) • N. Machiavelli, *The Florentine historie*, trans. T. Bedingfield (1595)

Bedingfield, Sir Thomas (1591/2–1661), judge, was born at Redlingfield, Suffolk, the second son of Sir Thomas Bedingfield (1555–1636), a barrister from an old Suffolk recusant family, who in 1595 bought an estate at Darsham, and his wife, Dorothy, daughter of John Southwell of Barham, Suffolk. After schooling at Southwold, on 24 June 1608, aged sixteen, he was admitted as a pensioner to Gonville and Caius College, Cambridge, but on 1 November that year he was admitted to Gray's Inn, and he was called to the bar in 1616. Bedingfield was MP for Dunwich in the parliaments of 1621—where he spoke little—and 1626, and by at least 1628 he had married Elizabeth (*c.*1604–1699), daughter of Charles Hoskins of Oxted, Surrey, formerly a citizen of London. They had a son, Thomas (1627/8–1684?), who was born in London (he attended school at Hadleigh, Suffolk, before being admitted to Christ's College, Cambridge, in November 1644, aged sixteen), and three daughters: Elizabeth, who died aged nine, Mary, and Dorothy.

In 1636 Bedingfield was Lent reader at Gray's Inn, and on 17 March he gained his son, Thomas, a special admittance. In 1638, having been appointed attorney-general of the duchy of Lancaster, he was knighted. Assigned by the House of Lords in 1642 as one of the counsel for the defence for the attorney-general, Sir Edward Herbert, in his impeachment trial, Bedingfield, among others, stalled for time, according to Clarendon because they had been warned by the Commons not to meddle in Commons business (Clarendon, *Hist. rebellion*, 3.25). The Lords then committed Bedingfield to the Tower for contempt, but he was released after three days. He was proposed as a commissioner for the great seal several times in 1646 and 1647, but this was never ratified. However, in 1647 he was a commissioner for assessment in Norfolk and Suffolk. In October 1648 he was made a serjeant-at-law, and on 22 November he was appointed a judge of common pleas. After declining, on 8 February 1649, reappointment after the death of Charles I, Bedingfield retired to the estate at Darsham, which he had bought from his elder brother, Philip. He was reappointed as a serjeant-at-law at the Restoration, but died at Darsham on 24 March 1661, and was buried in the church there. He was survived by his wife, who erected a memorial to him in 1662, and who herself died at the age of about ninety-five on 19 July 1699.

VIVIENNE LARMINIE

Sources A. I. Suckling, *The history and antiquities of the county of Suffolk*, 2 (1848), 222, 226–7 • W. R. Prest, *The rise of the barristers: a social history of the English bar, 1590–1640* (1986), 344 • Venn, *Alum. Cant.* • J. Foster, *The register of admissions to Gray's Inn, 1521–1889, together with the register of marriages in Gray's Inn chapel, 1695–1754* (privately printed, London, 1889) • Clarendon, *Hist. rebellion*, 3.25 • B. Whitelocke, *Memorials of English affairs*, new edn, 4 vols. (1853) • Sainty, *Judges* • E. Foss, *Biographia juridica: a biographical dictionary of the judges of England … 1066–1870* (1870) • D. MacCulloch, *Suffolk and the Tudors: politics and religion in an English county, 1500–1600* (1986) • W. Notestein, F. H. Relf, and H. Simpson, eds., *Commons debates, 1621*, 7 vols. (1935) • *DNB*

Bedlay. For this title name *see* Roberton, James, Lord Bedlay (*c*.1590–1664).

Bedloe, William (1650–1680), informer and adventurer, was the second son of Isaac Bedloe (*d.* 1656). William Bedloe was born in Chepstow on 20 May 1650 and spent his early life both there and in Bristol. Much of his early life was deliberately clouded in obscurity. His own published account of his parentage and ancestry remains dubious. He claimed that his father had been a gentleman soldier who had served the king in the civil wars and whose own father was Major George Bedloe, who came from Ireland in 1633. In December 1679 William Bedloe married Anna Purifoy, the daughter of an Irishman, Colonel Purifoy of Bristol, and the couple lived afterwards in an expensive rented house in the city until William's death in August 1680.

William Bedloe (1650–1680), by Robert White, pubd 1681

Bedloe had skirted close to the Roman Catholic community in his youth and had been thought a promising enough youth for Father David Lewis (later executed in the course of the Popish Plot) to attempt his conversion. Ultimately he had little religion and even fewer morals. While there is little doubt that Bedloe possessed a shrewd and cunning mind and could, as an adult, have a charming manner, he was, like Titus Oates, foul-mouthed and mainly seems to have seen the Catholic church as a source of funds when in trouble.

In 1670 William Bedloe fell out with his stepfather (his mother having remarried and moved to Bristol some years earlier) and he made his way to London. While in the metropolis he fell into a life of crime. Although many of Bedloe's early biographers related his adventures in London in detail most of these tales were bawdy fictions, cobbled together from the readily available rogue literature of the time. At the height of his fame Bedloe was always ready to exaggerate greatly his adventures to any listener. It is clear that he had been on the wrong side of the law in his youth and that for at least part of the 1670s he spent some time in gaol for fraud. In the course of these crimes Bedloe invariably passed himself off as a person of quality under an assumed title and name. With his imposing personality Bedloe took to working his way through the fringes of London life. While most of the tales about Bedloe at this time are somewhat implausible, it does seem that he used his previous Catholic connections to obtain service in a Catholic household, possibly that of Lord Bellasis. It is also possible that Bedloe's claim that other Catholics in London had used him as a courier in this period was also true. Bedloe was later to state that knowledge of the incipient Popish Plot had come to him by this route, and some of the queen's servants at Somerset House were aware of Bedloe's activities in this period. It is also clear that it was during the course of this service that Bedloe first came across Titus Oates, for at this point in his career Oates was a member of the household of the Catholic earl of Norwich.

In 1677 Bedloe's criminal activities finally led him to flee the country with his brother James, and together the brothers undertook a number of obscure European adventures, including awarding themselves military titles and indulging in horse stealing. At Salamanca in 1677, having engineered one fraud too many, the Bedloes, disguised as an English aristocrat and his servant, were conveyed under arrest to Valladolid. Once they had disentangled themselves from the law the pair were destitute and, learning of the presence there of Titus Oates, at that point idling away his time at the local college, they sought his assistance. William Frankland, a London merchant, later claimed that the pair were at Valladolid for some eight days and that 'Oates was many times … in their company' (*CSP dom.*, 1680–81, 602). Oates and Bedloe were later alleged to have concocted a scheme at this time in which William and his brother would play witnesses to Oates's information, but in fact the Bedloes and Oates parted with some bad feeling. William and James robbed Oates of some money and disappeared while Titus was generously obtaining them some dinner. The Bedloes then returned to England where William Bedloe continued his fraudulent lifestyle and spent the summer of 1678 in gaol, where the local Jesuits gave him some financial support.

With the mysterious death of the London magistrate Sir Edmund Godfrey, Bedloe finally emerged into the public eye by claiming he knew how Godfrey had died. On 2 November 1678 Secretary of State Henry Coventry received a letter from Bedloe in which he claimed that he knew the magistrate's murderers and was prepared to make other revelations about the affair. In reality Bedloe had only just been released from prison and had never even met Godfrey. Nevertheless, Bedloe was swiftly brought up to London and examined by an anxious privy council. Bedloe's tale subsequently varied with each telling, but the essentials were that he claimed to have been four years among the Jesuits and he had also been in Spain and other parts of the continent acting as a messenger for them. He also revealed that he knew the papists had murdered Godfrey because he himself had been asked to help shift the body from Somerset House, the residence of the queen, by the killers. The authors of the murder were, Bedloe claimed, two Jesuits of his acquaintance by the names of Le Fevre, or Phaire, and Walsh, who were attached to the queen's entourage in Somerset House. They had revealed their plot to Bedloe and invited him to join in it, but Bedloe on learning more of the scheme, and having seen the body of the dead magistrate hidden in a room in Somerset House, had fled the town and returned to Bristol.

While Bedloe's initial tale was deliberately vague, by the next day he appeared in a rather more confident light before parliament and gave a more elaborate story to a somewhat gullible audience. Indeed, so confident in his tale did Bedloe now appear that the king was certain someone had further instructed him overnight. Whoever his new sponsors were William Bedloe's rise was now rapid, in spite of the fact that when faced with the unfortunate, and innocent, Samuel Atkins (whom he had accused of being a party to the murder), Bedloe had not been able to recognize him. Despite this set-back Captain Bedloe, as he now called himself, became, alongside a rather jealous Titus Oates, the darling of the nation. Further revelations flowed from his mouth and pen as he grew ever more confident in his accusations. Bedloe now revealed that he had also been an agent of the Jesuits on other business and was well aware of their dealings. As the poor unfortunates whom he had caused to be arrested began to reach the courts Bedloe also joined Oates as a witness for the prosecution. Although he was to perform poorly in court, of far more importance was the fact that Bedloe, after some prompting, managed to implicate Miles Prance, a Roman Catholic silversmith, in the death of Sir Edmund Godfrey. Bedloe subsequently appeared at a number of the trials that followed in the wake of the revelations of the plot and with his version of events now cautiously set, he established himself as the man of action who had tried to infiltrate Jesuit designs for the good of the protestant nation.

As a witness Bedloe subsequently attracted many rivals and was also to claim that a number of attempts had been made to tamper with his evidence or even to poison him. In spite of his history Bedloe was given an allowance from the royal Treasury, and with this and other sums of money and rewards coming his way he was finally able to live the life of a real gentleman. For a time he became a national hero and was the subject of an 'infinite number of … pictures' and bad verse (*Life and Death*, 108). It was even claimed that he wrote a dramatic work in 1679 entitled *The Excommunicated Prince, or, The False Relique: a Tragedy*. In reality the author was Thomas Walter, an Oxford scholar of Jesus College, and Bedloe's name was merely added to boost its sales. In November 1679 he returned to Bristol for his marriage there in December. This affair was satirically celebrated by a mock heroic poem composed by Richard Duke. Bedloe visited London in July 1680 to act as a witness in further trials, but made a poor showing. In August 1680 he fell ill of vomiting and 'extreme looseness' (*Righteous Evidence*, 1). Hearing also of his wife's illness in Bristol, Bedloe made strenuous efforts to return to her bedside. As a consequence, and despite the efforts of the doctors, he fell mortally ill in Bristol that same month. On his death-bed Bedloe gave an interview to Lord Chief Justice North, who was visiting the city for the local assizes. Bedloe insisted on the truth of his Popish Plot revelations and asked for money from the king. On 20 August 1680, how-ever, Bedloe's powers of speech finally failed and he died at two o'clock that afternoon. His death was the subject of further poetry, mostly of a satirical nature. Although he had died in poverty his body was respectfully treated, lying in state in Merchant Taylors' Hall in Bristol and being subsequently buried in the mayor's chapel there, attended by the mayor and a numerous company. In the aftermath of the collapse of the Popish Plot schemes Bed-loe's tombstone, situated in the entrance to the chapel, was lost in rebuilding work.

William Bedloe was an opportunistic rogue, fraud, and criminal. His rambling evidence led to the deaths of a number of innocent people. Although he was less odious, except to his victims, than Titus Oates, Bedloe's imposing personality and opportunism seem to have led his dupes not to see through his elaborate and, to a neutral eye, improbable lies until it was too late. Although he claimed the reward Bedloe apparently knew little enough of the death of Edmund Godfrey (he himself is a highly unlikely candidate for the killing) and even less of any popish schemes. Ultimately Bedloe was rather more typical of the type of criminal that the hysteria over the Popish Plot in London allowed to come to the fore in the politics of the day, being able to exploit the situation for his own greedy ends. Fortunately for himself, his death in 1680 meant that he was also spared the punishments meted out to his fellow informers, Oates, Dangerfield, Prance, and Dugdale.   ALAN MARSHALL

Sources The life and death of Captain William Bedloe, one of the chief discoverers of the horrid Popish Plot (1681) • The righteous evidence wit-nessing the truth being an account of the sickness and deathbed expressions of Mr William Bedlow (1680) • W. Bedloe, A narrative and impartial dis-covery of the horrid Popish Plot (1679) • A succinct narrative of the murder of Sir E. G[odfrey] (1683) • The tryal and conviction of Thomas Knox and John Lane (1680) • An elegy upon the unfortunate death of Captain William Bedloe (1680) • The examination of Captain William Bedlow deceased (1680) • T. Walter and W. Bedloe, The excommunicated prince, or, The false relique (1679) • M. Petherick, Restoration rogues (1951) • A. Mar-shall, The strange death of Edmund Godfrey: plots and politics in Restor-ation London (1999) • J. Kenyon, The Popish Plot, pbk edn (1974) • PRO, state papers, Charles II, SP 29 • PRO, privy council registers, PC 2/66
Archives HLRO, material relating to career as informer • PRO, privy council registers, PC 2/66
Likenesses R. White, line engraving, BM, NPG; repro. in Life and death of Captain William Bedloe (1681) [see illus.] • engraving, repro. in Life and death of Captain William Bedloe • engraving, repro. in Bedloe, A narrative and impartial discovery of the horrid Popish Plot
Wealth at death was renting expensive house in Bristol; received £500 with thanks of parliament 1679; £10 per week from secret service funds; allegedly lived at £2000 p.a., 1679–80; died in poverty

Bedo Brwynllys (fl. 1469), poet, among those known as *Cywyddwyr, took his name from Brwynllys, now Bron-llys, in the lordship of Brecon. He may be identical with Bedo Phylip Bach, who likewise came from the Brecon dis-trict. His extant work comprises much love poetry charac-teristic of the followers of Dafydd ap Gwilym. Also extant are a few religious and eulogistic poems, including an elegy on Sir Richard Herbert written in 1469, and his poetic flytings with Ieuan Deulwyn and Hywel Dafi.

ARTHUR MILLER, rev. MARIOS COSTAMBEYS

Sources DNB • DWB • Cywyddau serch y tri Bedo, ed. P. J. Donovan (1982)
Archives NL Wales

Bedoyere, Michael Anthony Maurice Huchet de la, **Count de la Bedoyere in the French nobility** (1900–1973), author and journalist, was born on 16 May 1900 in St Servan, Brittany, France, the only child of Vicomte Yvon Huchet de la Bedoyere and his wife, Sybil Emily, daughter of Anthony Wilson *Thorold, bishop of Rochester and then bishop of Winchester, and sister of Algar Thorold, biographer and journalist. The de la Bedoyeres were an old Breton family of whom the vicomte was the first to gain acceptance in London, in the 1890s. Michael de la Bedoyere came under the influence of the Jesuits early, first at a school in Jersey, and then at Stonyhurst College where, being exceptionally gifted, he enjoyed the intellec-tual stimulus of work. A creature of routine, at school he avoided organized sports; so far as he dared, he accepted them passively. Like quicksilver in tackling demanding problems, he gave such promise that soon the Jesuits were earmarking him as a likely candidate for the society. He made few friendships; only once did he display a flash of indignation by taking part in a protest march against the school authorities during the First World War. Having made his point, there was no comeback.

De la Bedoyere's decision to enter the society, as a nov-ice, seemed ill-advised. In his nineteenth year and still unformed, he was possibly under the influence of over-zealous spiritual directors. After the rigorous training of noviciate he enjoyed his Oxford interlude at Campion Hall, obtaining first-class honours in 1928 in the newly founded school of philosophy, politics, and economics. He was the only man in his year who took his finals in hos-pital, after recovering from peritonitis. Then he slowly realized that he was not only wasting his time but could no longer believe in Catholicism. The long crisis left him both bewildered and uncertain. He wandered through Europe and scarcely knew where to turn. It was a tempor-ary lapse. His relatives advised him to wait and rest, and gradually pull himself together. One person above all who imparted strength, love, and a new reason for living was Catherine Thorold (d. 1959), his cousin, then living in Flor-ence. Eventually they became engaged and in 1930 they married. She was the daughter of Algar Labouchere Thorold.

Because of de la Bedoyere's grounding as a scholastic and philosopher, in 1930 he was invited to lecture in the University of Minnesota. His wife accompanied him, although neither of them wished to settle down in Amer-ica. They returned in 1931 when their first child was expected. De la Bedoyere was helped to break into active journalism by his father-in-law, Algar Thorold, the editor of the *Dublin Review* and the biographer and former kinsman of Henry Labouchere of *Truth*. Thorold made room for him in the advisory role of assistant editor. By now his first two books, both biographies, had appeared; *Lafayette* (1933) and *George Washington* (1935) were somewhat affected by his recent American experience and his Anglo-French inspiration.

Then came a touch of providence when the proprietor of the *Catholic Herald*, Charles Diamond, advertised for a young Catholic, possessing some journalistic experience and flair, who would learn the business and might eventually take over the paper on Diamond's death. De la Bedoyere responded at once and got the job. In 1934 the paper's circulation was meagre, its outlook was narrow, and its Irish influence still predominated. With the support of new members of his small staff, de la Bedoyere transformed the *Catholic Herald* in both content and readability. In five years circulation tripled, for the paper became at once lively and radical, yet intellectual. At the height of the war its circulation had slowly risen to nearly six figures. De la Bedoyere had been influenced by his uncle, Algar Thorold, once a devoted disciple of Baron von Hügel. It was said of the new editor that he was 'ecumenical long before his time'. He also used forceful language, which was hardly designed for a weekly previously as traditional as this. There were strong critics of the paper, notably among the clergy. A number of bishops and priests tended to be hurt, even scandalized, by some of his articles and cavalier opinions, which were often controversial and disrespectful. Thus de la Bedoyere created difficulties for himself by being occasionally 'banned', for the *Catholic Herald* in the 1940s and 1950s still depended on church door sales. He retired as its editor in 1962.

De la Bedoyere also wrote numerous books. Apart from the essay he wrote in Edward Eyre's *European Civilization* (vol. 5, 1936), he produced in the earlier part of the Second World War *Christian Crisis* (1940), *Christianity in the Market Place* (1943), and *No Dreamers Weak* (1944). The combination of writing and editing made his thoughts flow. Being independent-minded, he attacked political critics, including MPs and some members of Winston Churchill's wartime government. He was never at a loss for pithy answers, particularly when false morality and dubious values were involved. He was the first, for example, to point out the destructive and totally disproportionate effects of area bombing; he was equally forthright in questioning the proposal for unconditional surrender by the allies, as well as the betrayal of Poland by the Soviet Union at the end of the war.

De la Bedoyere finally decided to retire after twenty-eight years as editor without too much regret. By then he had completed most of the serious work that he wanted to do. His best books, in both Britain and America, belonged to the closing period of his work. They included *Catherine, Saint of Siena* (1947), *Francis: a Biography of the Saint of Assisi* (1962), and *The Meddlesome Friar: the Story of the Conflict between Savonarola and Alexander VI* (1958); and studies of von Hügel (1951) and Fénelon's correspondence with Madame Guyon, entitled *The Archbishop and the Lady* (1956).

He also wrote memoirs of Cardinal Griffin (1955) and Canon Cardijn (1958).

Great credit was due to de la Bedoyere for his exceptional work as an editor, for he had, despite the claims of his worst critics, the power of seeing things in perspective. In 1962 he founded, and until 1968 edited, *Search Newsletter*, a monthly, which won respect and had a sympathetic response. In a sense the second Vatican council of the mid-1960s cut ground from under his feet, even before his premature retirement. He both contributed to and edited *Objections to Roman Catholicism* (1964), which attracted much attention and reflected the unchanged spirit of questioning authority which he had long embodied.

De la Bedoyere's first wife died in 1959, and in 1961 he married Charlotte, daughter of Julian Halbik, merchant. The first marriage produced four sons and one daughter; the second two sons. He died on 13 July 1973 at The Priory, Roehampton Lane, London. ANDREW BOYLE, *rev.*

Sources personal knowledge (1986) · private information (1986) · *The Times* (16 July 1973)

Wealth at death £26,094: probate, 1 May 1975, *CGPLA Eng. & Wales*

Bedson, Sir Samuel Phillips (1886–1969), bacteriologist, was born on 1 December 1886 at Newcastle upon Tyne, the second son of Peter Phillips Bedson, professor of chemistry in the Durham College of Science, and his wife, Annie, daughter of Samuel Hodgkinson, cotton spinner, of Marple, Cheshire. He was educated at Abbotsholme School, Derbyshire. Before he left school he had decided on a medical career, but he was persuaded by his father to take a degree in science first. He graduated BSc with distinction in 1907. From 1907 to 1912 he studied medicine at Durham University and graduated with honours in 1912. Influenced by the teaching of H. J. Hutchens, he decided to specialize in bacteriology and went to the Pasteur Institute in Paris, where he studied under brilliant French microbiologists, among them P. P. E. Roux, A. Borrel, C. L. A. Laveran, A. Besredka, and I. Mechnikov. The research work which he carried out in M. Weinberg's laboratory at this time on the toxic substances obtained from parasitic worms was embodied in a thesis which gained him the MD (1914) and gold medal of Durham University.

In 1913 Bedson returned to England where he worked as British medical scholar at the Lister Institute in London under John Ledingham. Their experimental work on blood platelets and purpura was interrupted by the outbreak of war in 1914. Refused a commission in the Royal Army Medical Corps, which had no vacancies for doctors trained in research, Bedson joined the Northumberland Fusiliers as a combatant officer and went with the 8th battalion to Gallipoli in 1915. In August of that year he suffered a severe chest wound and was evacuated to England. He was later sent to France, where in 1916 he was transferred to the Royal Army Medical Corps. From then until his demobilization in 1919 he served as a pathologist in various laboratories in France and became adviser in pathology to the Fifth Army (France). For two years after the war he was lecturer in bacteriology at the medical school in Durham. He returned in 1921 to the Lister Institute, where he continued his work on the origin and disposal of blood platelets and their role in the production of purpura. The conclusions he reached on the basis of his experimental studies were confirmed by the subsequent work of others.

In 1924 Bedson was seconded to work on foot-and-mouth disease at the Lister Institute under the supervision of Joseph Arkwright, and thus began his research on virus disease, then largely an unexplored field. The work by Bedson and his colleagues both on the causal virus of foot-and-mouth disease and on immunity to it provided a sound basis for subsequent advances in the knowledge of virus diseases.

In 1926 Bedson married Dorothea Annie Hoffert, a research assistant at the Lister Institute, and elder daughter of Henry Herman Hoffert, senior inspector of schools. There were three sons, the second of whom, Henry Samuel Bedson, became reader in virology at Birmingham University. In the same year as his marriage Bedson was appointed to a Freedom research fellowship at the London Hospital, where his eight years as fellow were to prove the most productive of his scientific career. He published several important papers on the nature of viruses, using the viruses of vaccinia and herpes simplex in his experiments. In 1929 there occurred the pandemic of human psittacosis infection. Bedson discovered and described the causal agent of the disease and much of his subsequent work was devoted to the study of this and related micro-organisms. This group of infective agents became commonly referred to as the bedsoniae. While Bedson was a pioneer investigator in virology, his international reputation was associated mainly with his work on the micro-organisms of the psittacosis-lymphogranuloma group, which was summarized in his Harben lectures (1959). He was elected FRS in 1935.

In 1934 Bedson succeeded William Bulloch as professor of bacteriology at the London Hospital medical college. Although his teaching and administrative duties lessened the time he could spend in the laboratory he enjoyed contact with the students. He was a good lecturer and took a keen interest in the welfare and subsequent careers of his pupils. From 1939 to 1944 he was pathologist to metropolitan region 5 of the Emergency Medical Service, with his headquarters at Billericay in Essex. He returned to the London Hospital in 1944 and in 1946 succeeded Philip Panton as director of the division of pathology, thus adding to his responsibilities in the medical college. In 1949 he followed Panton as consultant adviser in pathology to the Ministry of Health, an office which he held until 1960. When he retired from the chair at the London Hospital in 1952 he took charge of the British Empire Campaign virus unit in the Middlesex Hospital, where he continued his research for the next ten years.

Bedson was a member of the governing body of the Foot-and-Mouth Disease Research Institute at Pirbright (1950–55), the council of the Imperial Cancer Research Fund (1942–55), the army pathological advisory committee (1937–62), the governing body of the Lister Institute (1944–54), the Public Health Laboratory Service Board (1950–57), the Medical Research Council (1941–5), and the council of the Royal Society (1937–8 and 1941–2). He was awarded the Conway Evans prize in 1952. The honorary degree of DSc was conferred on him by the Queen's University of Belfast in 1937 and by the University of Durham in 1946. He was elected FRCP in 1945 and knighted in 1956.

Bedson was slim and of less than average height. He almost invariably wore a bow-tie. He was neat and orderly in all he did. He was a very skilful technician and preferred to do all his own experiments which were devised with care and precision. His opinions were tenaciously held and would be abandoned only if convincing evidence were forthcoming. He was regarded with great affection and respect by his colleagues and pupils, and in private life he was a delightful companion and host. His favourite hobby was trout-fishing. Bedson died in Hove, Sussex, on 11 May 1969, and his widow died later in the same year.

A. W. DOWNIE, rev.

Sources A. W. Downie, *Memoirs FRS*, 16 (1970), 15–35 · personal knowledge (1981)
Likenesses photograph, repro. in *Memoirs FRS*
Wealth at death £56,900: probate, 4 Aug 1969, *CGPLA Eng. & Wales*

Bedwell, Thomas (c.1547–1595), engineer and practical mathematician, was the youngest son of William Bedwell (d. 1556) of Braughing, Hertfordshire, yeoman, and his wife, Joan, daughter of John Wall. Bedwell was educated at Trinity College, Cambridge, where he matriculated as a sizar in 1562, graduated BA in 1566–7, and proceeded MA in 1570. He had become a fellow of the college in 1569 and remained so until at least 1574.

Neither Bedwell's early interests nor career are documented; the claim that he became a minister in London is probably based on a misunderstanding. At an unknown date he entered the service of Thomas Radcliffe, third earl of Sussex—he was referred to in 1582 as 'my Lord Chamberlain's man' (PRO, SP 12/155/14)—and was subsequently rewarded with the manor of Shering in Essex.

The evidence for Bedwell's engineering career begins in 1582 when he became a technical consultant and supervisor at Dover harbour, one of the largest of Elizabethan building projects. He was still offering suggestions and estimates there in March 1583. After Sussex's death in 1583 Bedwell transferred to the service of the earl of Leicester, and had particular responsibility for works at Wanstead House in 1585. At the end of that year he followed Leicester to the Netherlands as colonel of the pioneers, directing the construction of ramparts, earthworks, and trenches. After Leicester's death in 1588, Bedwell was still owed £200 from the estate.

In 1587, after his return from the Netherlands, Bedwell's views on the fortification of Portsmouth were sought and during the Armada crisis of 1588 he co-operated with the Italian engineer Federico Genebelli on strengthening the defences of the River Thames. He then successfully petitioned for a permanent position and in 1589 became keeper of the ordnance store at the Tower of London, an office which he held until his death in 1595.

The key to Bedwell's unusual transition from outwardly unremarkable academic studies to engineering was his interest in practical mathematics. Presenting his credentials for employment at Dover in 1582 he announced a water clock that could be used to find longitude at sea and an instrument for measuring timber, and he held out the prospect of a solution to the problem of determining ballistic trajectories.

Bedwell's timber rule was a development of the standard carpenter's rule, with the advantage that it needed no accompanying numerical tables. His manuscript on the use of the rule remained unpublished but the instrument continued to circulate after his death: the carpenter and author Richard More knew of it in 1602 and the Gresham professor of geometry Henry Briggs wrote a letter explaining its use in 1606. Bedwell's nephew William *Bedwell (bap. 1563, d. 1632) subsequently publicized the instrument in several texts, most fully in *Mesolabium architectonicum* (1631).

Bedwell's preoccupation with artillery and ballistics resulted in another instrument, whose use was again described in a manuscript text. This gunner's rule, which was similar in appearance to the earlier carpenter's rule, could be used to set up and elevate ordnance and was meant to provide a more sophisticated alternative to the simple devices used by gunners. Bedwell also harboured higher intellectual ambitions and to this practical text he added 'an Apendix of Certaine Questions, touching greate Artillary etc Philosophically examined' (Bodl. Oxf., MS Laud misc. 618) which tackled issues raised in the work of authors such as Niccolò Tartaglia and Girolamo Cardano. Bedwell evidently hoped that his position at the Tower would provide access to the resources necessary for further experimentation in the field of ballistics.

Bedwell was an early example of the academically trained engineer, securing patronage through mathematical skills and the invention of instruments. He successfully carved out a role for himself as a technical consultant and an intermediary between privy councillors and artisans. Mirroring this career success, Bedwell's upward social mobility is suggested by his receipt of a grant of arms. He married Elizabeth Drywood (d. 1609) and, from her family, apparently received the manor of Overhall in Little Yeldham, Essex, shortly before his death. Bedwell was buried in St Peter ad Vincula, the Tower of London on 30 April 1595, survived by his wife and an infant daughter. STEPHEN JOHNSTON

Sources S. Johnston, 'Mathematical proceedings and instruments in Elizabethan England', *Annals of Science*, 48 (1991), 319–44 • S. Adams, ed., *Household accounts and disbursement books of Robert Dudley, earl of Leicester, 1558–1561, 1584–1586* (1995) • A. Hamilton, *William Bedwell, the Arabist, 1563–1632* (1985) • *Calendar of the proceedings in chancery in the reign of Queen Elizabeth*, 1 (1827), 109 • Cooper, *Ath. Cantab.*, 2.539–40 • H. M. Innes, *Fellows of Trinity College, Cambridge* (1941), 25 • P. Morant, *The history and antiquities of the county of Essex*, 1 (1763), 304 • administration, PRO, PROB 6/5, fol. 132v
Archives Bodl. Oxf., MS Laud 618 (misc.) • Bodl. Oxf., MS Tanner 298 (4) • PRO, State Papers Elizabeth I
Wealth at death see administration, PRO, PROB 6/5, fol. 132v

Bedwell, William (*bap.* 1563, *d.* 1632), Arabist and mathematician, was born in Great Hallingbury in Essex, where he was baptized on 2 October 1563, one of at least four children of John Bedwell, a small landowner, and his wife, Anne. After an early interest in mathematics had been encouraged by his father's youngest brother, Thomas *Bedwell (*c.*1547–1595), a military engineer and fellow of Trinity College, Cambridge, he matriculated as a sizar at the college in Lent 1578, becoming a scholar in 1584 and proceeding MA in 1588. At Cambridge, Bedwell encountered other mathematicians—Thomas Hood, Henry Briggs, and Edward Wright—and, like them, was interested in the application to mathematics of the anti-Aristotelian method devised by Peter Ramus. He also fell in with a circle of scholars at Pembroke College concerned with biblical studies and Semitic languages—above all Lancelot Andrewes, the future bishop of Chichester, Ely, and Winchester. With their encouragement Bedwell progressed in the study of Hebrew (both ancient and rabbinic), Aramaic, and Syriac, and began to concentrate on Arabic, a language still little known in the west.

By 1595 Bedwell had completed a specimen (some 800 pages) of his Arabic–Latin dictionary which, he then hoped, would be the first of its kind to be published in Europe. The most promising Arabist in England, he was occasionally employed as a translator of official documents and as an interpreter, and met the Moroccan ambassadors to Queen Elizabeth who arrived in August 1600. On 8 December 1601 Bedwell was made rector of St Ethelburga, Bishopsgate, in London. In the same year he produced his first publication, a Latin translation of the biblical book of Obadaiah, the Aramaic paraphrase, and three rabbinic commentaries. In July 1603 he entered into correspondence with a Huguenot scholar then in Paris, Isaac Casaubon, with whom he was to develop a close friendship, especially after Casaubon settled in England in 1610. Still in search of patronage, he planned an edition of the Arabic New Testament as part of a polyglot Bible and dedicated his manuscript transcription of the epistle to the Colossians to Richard Bancroft, bishop of London, and of the epistles of John to James I. His true patron, however, was to be Lancelot Andrewes, who appointed him in 1604 to the first Westminster company of translators preparing the new version of the English Bible.

In October 1607 Andrewes presented Bedwell with the vicarage of Tottenham High Cross in Middlesex, where he took up residence with his wife, Marsie (Mary) Chipperfield, whom he had married in the 1590s, and their four daughters, and officiated at the church of All Hallows. Bedwell's reputation was at its height. Renowned as one of the few Arabists in northern Europe, he had become an object of pilgrimage for an international group of scholars. Towards the end of 1608 he was approached by a young Dutch friend of Casaubon, Thomas Erpenius, who had just graduated at the University of Leiden and, encouraged by the chronologist Joseph Justus Scaliger, had decided to study Arabic. Bedwell gave him his first lessons. Erpenius was to be the finest Arabist of his generation and the first professor of Arabic at Leiden.

In 1612 Bedwell travelled to Holland, his only recorded journey abroad. He did so on the advice of Casaubon and Erpenius and with the financial backing of Lancelot Andrewes. He wished to consult the Arabic manuscripts left to the Leiden University Library by Scaliger, to arrange for the publication of his Arabic version of the Johannine epistles by the Officina Plantiniana, the best printers of Arabic in northern Europe, and to purchase the firm's Arabic types in order to print his own Arabic dictionary in England. He may also have hoped to gather information about the Dutch Arminians who had an ally in Andrewes.

After arriving in Leiden in August, Bedwell lodged at the house of the English-born printer Thomas Basson (in the 1990s Rapenburg 56) opposite the university. He was welcomed by the most illustrious scholars. He saw the Scaliger manuscripts, met Hugo Grotius in The Hague, and, on his way back to England in October, stopped in Middelburg to call on another prominent Arminian, Johan Boreel, Grotius's fellow ambassador to James I in 1613. The Officina Plantiniana published his Johannine epistles, and the managers, the sons of the Arabist Franciscus Raphelengius, undertook to sell him their Arabic types. Yet Leiden also provided Bedwell with a disappointment from which, as Casaubon predicted (*Epistolae*, 485), he would never recover. He heard that the Officina Plantiniana was about to publish posthumously the Arabic–Latin dictionary compiled by Franciscus Raphelengius with emendations by Erpenius and that his own dictionary would no longer be the first in Europe.

After his return to Tottenham High Cross, Bedwell still gave tuition in Arabic, his most famous pupil being Edward Pococke, the future professor of Arabic at Oxford, whom Bedwell brought to the attention of his first patron, William Laud, then bishop of London. He published, too, his *Mohammedis imposturae*, the English translation of an anti-Islamic dialogue, accompanied by *The Arabian Trudgman*, an explanation of Islamic terms (1615). As an Arabist, however, Bedwell had been surpassed by Erpenius, and later, after Erpenius's death in 1624, was to be so also by his successor to the Leiden chair, Jacobus Golius.

Meanwhile Bedwell also brought out some of the works connected with mathematics which he had prepared soon after leaving Cambridge. In 1612 at his own expense he issued in *Wilhelmi Bedwelli trigonum architectonicum* the diagrams of the carpenter's rule, for the 'measuring of Boord, Glasse, Stone, and such like', devised by his uncle Thomas. There followed, published by Richard Field, his English adaptation of *De numeris geometricis* (1614), a treatise by the German Ramist mathematician Lazarus Schoner, which Bedwell transformed into an introduction to his uncle's instrument, and *The Principles of Arithmeticke* (1616), the translation of a work by the French Ramist Bernard Salignac. Then, finally, came his translation of Ramus's *Via regia ad geometriam*, published posthumously in 1636. Bedwell's main contribution to the subject was the popularization of the work of others. He took part in the widespread contemporary endeavour to make the latest works on arithmetic, geometry, and mensuration accessible to craftsmen—carpenters, surveyors, and ship-builders—who had no university education and were unable to read Latin. Like his friends Hood, Briggs, and Wright, he helped to advance techniques of calculation in the seventeenth century, but the *Carpentars Rule*, reprinted twice in his lifetime and once more after his death, seems to have been thoroughly outdated by the time Pepys was faced with the problem of measuring timber in the 1660s.

Until his death Bedwell's main scholarly concern was his Arabic dictionary, but he never published it. The types he had bought in Leiden were too worn to be used and the work itself was unpublishable. In contrast with his aim to provide practical assistance to the uneducated, the specimens of the 1590s gradually swelled into an immensely learned work of seven folio volumes which, despite its later use by Edmund Castell for his own archaic polyglot lexicon, served little practical purpose. Bedwell emphasized the affinities between Arabic and Hebrew, but hardly drew on the monolingual Arabic dictionaries, so essential for western lexicographers, and ignored the Persian and Turkish sources used by the younger Leiden Arabists.

Although they display the breadth of Bedwell's knowledge—sharing the antiquarian interests of his circle, he even brought out a description of Tottenham and the early English burlesque poem, *The Turnament of Tottenham* (1631), the manuscript of which had been lent him by George Wither—none of Bedwell's publications did justice to his high reputation as a scholar. Dilatory by nature, he was easily discouraged and, as is suggested by his apparent reluctance ever to apply for an academic post, retiring and self-effacing—'humble, void of pride', wrote John Clarke, the husband of his youngest daughter Margaret, but 'ever ready to impart his knowledge to others … loving and affecting those that affected learning' (Bedwell, sig. A1r). At his happiest in the society of his family, Bedwell was known for his kindliness and generosity. He was, according to Casaubon, the only educated Englishman who was 'neither the slave of envy, nor of his own fancy, and was not given to detracting from other people's studies' (*Epistolae*, 485).

Bedwell died at Tottenham High Cross on 5 May 1632 and was buried five days later in the church of All Hallows; his wife died in 1635. He left his Arabic dictionary, types, punches, and matrices to Cambridge University.

ALASTAIR HAMILTON

Sources A. Hamilton, *William Bedwell the Arabist, 1563–1632* (1985) · *Isaaci Casauboni epistolae*, ed. T. Janson ab Almeloveen, 2 vols. in 1 (Rotterdam, 1709) · A. Hamilton, 'The victims of progress: the Raphelengius Arabic type and Bedwell's Arabic lexicon', *Liber amicorum Léon Voet*, ed. F. de Nave (1985) · G. J. Toomer, *Eastern wisedome and learning: the study of Arabic in seventeenth-century England* (1996) · A. Hamilton, 'An Englishman in Leiden: William Bedwell's album amicorum', *Niet alleen kijken: over het gebruik van handschriften en handschriftencollecties: vijf lezingen bij het afscheid van prof. dr. P. F. J.*

Obbema als conservator westerse handschriften van de Universiteitsbiblio-theek Leiden, ed. A. T. Bouwman (1996), 71–92 • W. M. C. Juynboll, *Zeventiende-eeuwsche beoefenaars van het Arabisch in Nederland* (1911) • *DNB* • W. Bedwell, *Via regia ad geometriam* (1636)

Archives BL, MS Sloane 1796 • Bodl. Oxf., MS Bodl. Or. 819; MS Laud Or. 819; MS Laud Or. 58; MS Selden supra 50 • Bodl. Oxf., 'Description of Tottenham High Cross', with MS notes and additions • U. Cam., transcriptions of Arabic versions of the Scriptures, MS Dd.15.4 • University of Leiden, *Album amicorum*, MS BPL 2753

Bedyll, Thomas (*c*.1486–1537), administrator and canon lawyer, was born at Winchester, where his father was a college tenant. In 1498 he was admitted a scholar at Winchester College and two years later proceeded to New College, Oxford. Elected a fellow of New College in March 1502, Bedyll was admitted to the degree of BCnL in November 1508. Soon afterwards he entered the household of William Warham, archbishop of Canterbury, where he joined a circle of Wykehamists that included his relative Ingram Bedyll, as well as Warham himself. As secretary to the archbishop, Bedyll corresponded regularly with Erasmus, who addressed him as his 'dearest Pylades' (loyal companion to the fugitive Orestes). Bedyll's services to the archbishop brought rich rewards, for Warham collated him to a string of rectories, including Offord Cluny, Huntingdonshire (1511), Halton, Buckinghamshire (1512), East Peckham, Kent (1517), Bocking, Essex (1522), Bishopsborne, Kent (1524), St Dionis Backchurch, London (1528), and Wrotham, Kent (1532). Bedyll also secured canonries at Lincoln (1518) and Chichester (1528).

Upon Warham's death on 22 August 1532, Bedyll swiftly transferred his services to Thomas Cromwell, who employed him both on private business and as a clerk of the king's council. Within a month he was revising a memorandum on the king's 'Great Matter'; during the winter of 1532 he joined a committee of canon lawyers assembled to advise Archbishop Cranmer, and later witnessed the primate's oath to the papacy (and accompanying protestation). In May 1533 he served as one of the king's counsel, and as Cromwell's personal observer, at the court convened by Cranmer to judge the validity of Henry's first marriage, where he helped to draft the sentence of annulment. Bedyll's labours as a Cromwellian agent were many: for example, he helped to investigate the affair of the Nun of Kent in late 1533, and reported to his master on rumours of sedition in the household of Katherine of Aragon. By May 1534 he and Rowland Lee were visiting religious communities around London to administer the oath to the succession imposed by statute that year. On this occasion they succeeded, but when they demanded explicit repudiations of the papal supremacy in the following year, the visitors ran into difficulties. While Syon and Sheen proved generally tractable, at the Charterhouse there was determined resistance. Months of mixing threats and blandishments accomplished little, nor were the Carthusians converted by the books supporting the royal supremacy which Bedyll later brought them.

Bedyll assisted Cromwell in the day-to-day administration of his vicegerency, the control of the English church which the minister exercised in the king's name; indeed he had originally been included in the abortive vicegerential commission proposed in December 1534. As a royal councillor and trusted servant of Cromwell, Bedyll participated in the interrogations of Sir Thomas More and Bishop John Fisher conducted in the Tower during May and June 1535. Here his argument, that since the king was the head of the people and the people constituted the church it followed that the king was head of the church, unsurprisingly failed to convince Fisher. Later that summer Bedyll turned his attention to revising a printed defence of the supremacy for unlearned priests to read to their congregations. By January 1536 he was busy visiting monasteries in the East Anglian fens, gathering acknowledgements of the supremacy. While at Ramsey he searched through the house's Anglo-Saxon charters for evidence supporting the king's ecclesiastical title, which he forwarded gleefully to Cromwell. In August of the same year Bedyll was given added responsibilities for implementing the supremacy, when he joined two other canon lawyers (William Petre and John London) on a commission appointed to examine all papal bulls and faculties, issuing replacements as necessary, under the king's great seal.

Already a wealthy pluralist by 1532, Bedyll's forwardness in pursuing promotion continued to bear fruit under Cromwell. Having briefly been archdeacon of Cleveland (1533), and then London (1533–4), in June 1534 he was installed as archdeacon of Cornwall. He also added canonries at Wells (1533) and York (1536) to his clutch of benefices, together with the rectory of All Hallows-the-Great (London). Despite his many ecclesiastical livings, Bedyll never became a priest, and in 1535 and 1537 received dispensations from the archbishop of Canterbury from doing so.

Although suffering a bout of fever in early 1537 Bedyll continued to harry opponents of the royal supremacy. Three of the Charterhouse monks had been executed in 1535 and the others were subsequently put under severe pressure. Finally in mid-May 1537 a number of them appeared before Bedyll to acknowledge the royal title, and the following month he received the surrender of their house. The fate of the remaining Carthusian prisoners, who starved to death in Newgate, elicited no sympathy from Bedyll, weary of their open resistance to the supremacy. He spent the summer of 1537 at his residence at Otford in Kent, and it was probably there that he died in early September.

Bedyll's energetic support for Cromwell's merciless persecution of opponents of reform, and his insatiable appetite for benefices, have earned him a reputation for cruelty and avarice among historians, as 'one of the least attractive of Cromwell's minions … [with] coarse texture of mind and snuffling accents' (Knowles, 3.274). This harsh judgement is not entirely just, however, for Bedyll's loyalty and industry earned him the gratitude of two very different masters (Warham and Cromwell), and he himself was no mean scholar. Although his victims deserve sympathy, it must be acknowledged that Bedyll was an indefatigable agent of the royal supremacy, whose labours were richly rewarded by those whom he served.

P. R. N. CARTER

Sources *LP Henry VIII*, vols. 1–12 · D. Knowles [M. C. Knowles], *The religious orders in England*, 3 (1959) · G. R. Elton, *Policy and police: the enforcement of the Reformation in the age of Thomas Cromwell* (1972) · H. A. Kelly, *The matrimonial trials of Henry VIII* (1976) · Emden, *Oxf.*, 1.148–9 · *The correspondence of Erasmus*, ed. and trans. R. A. B. Mynors and others, 22 vols. (1974–94), vols. 3, 4 · *The correspondence of Erasmus*, ed. and trans. R. A. B. Mynors and others, 22 vols. (1974–94), vols. 5–8 · G. R. Elton, *Reform and renewal* (1973) · J. S. Block, *Factional politics and the English Reformation, 1520–1540* (1993) · F. D. Logan, 'Thomas Cromwell and the vicegerency in spirituals: a revisitation', *EngHR*, 103 (1988), 658–67 · W. H. Dunham and S. Pargellis, eds., *Complaint and reform in England* (1938) · D. S. Chambers, ed., *Faculty office registers, 1534–1549* (1966)

Bedyngham, John (*d.* 1459/60), composer, is of unknown parentage and birth, though his name suggests a family of Norfolk origins. A hypothesis that he is identical with John Bodenham (1422–1458), scholar and fellow of New College, Oxford, has not won general acceptance. Bedyngham left a small but distinguished body of secular and sacred music. Apart from three mathematically intricate proportional puzzle motets, his works are known almost entirely from manuscripts compiled on the continent of Europe. This may suggest that he travelled, as does his composing a chanson mass, but the presence of texts in foreign languages among his songs is by no means conclusive evidence for this, since in many cases it can be shown that the words are not original; and the marked propensity of foreign copyists to ascribe his works to more famous masters suggests that he was not personally known to them.

Bedyngham's music, especially his secular songs, survives in a surprising number of different manuscripts. He probably composed the famous setting of Giustinian's 'O rosa bella' commonly ascribed to John Dunstaple (Paris, Bibliothèque Nationale, 'Chansonnier de Jean de Montchenu', MS Rothschild 2973 (I.5.13), fols. 8v–10r, item 7). The song does not observe the niceties of the ballata form. The eight songs attributable to Bedyngham are between them supplied with no fewer than twenty different texts in four languages; three remain doubtful as to their form, but two are ballades and three rondeaux, types well known and widely practised in England at the time.

Expertise in the medium of song may have led Bedyngham to become one of the first composers, along with Walter Frye and Guillaume Dufay, to experiment with the technique of building a mass cycle not on plainchant, but on a model taken from secular music. There is a remarkable cycle on Gilles Binchois's ballade 'Deuil angoisseux', in which material from all voices of the song informs other parts than the tenor alone (Trento, Castello del Buonconsiglio, Monumenti e Collezioni Provinciali, MS 1375, fols. 27v–31r and 17v–21r). Two other masses (one of doubtful attribution) are hardly less distinguished. In turn, Bedyngham's own songs served as models on which other composers based mass cycles, including three on 'O rosa bella'.

Bedyngham appears to have spent the last seven years of his life in Westminster. By Michaelmas 1453 he was in the employ of the lady chapel of Westminster Abbey, while by May 1456 he had become verger to the collegiate church of St Stephen, Westminster, a post he still held in 1457–8, when he made over all his property to others by letters patent. The membership list of the Confraternity of St Nicholas, the London guild of parish clerks, of which he was already a member in 1449, reveals that Bedyngham died between 3 May 1459 and 22 May 1460.

BRIAN TROWELL

Sources D. Fallows, 'Bedyngham, Johannes', *New Grove* · D. Fallows, 'Dunstable, Bedyngham and *O rosa bella*', *Journal of Musicology*, 12 (1994), 287–305 · R. Bowers [unpubd article] · A. Wathey [unpubd article] · D. Fallows, 'Words and music in two English songs of the mid-15th century: Charles d'Orléans and John Lydgate', *Early Music*, 5 (1977), 38–43 · D. Fallows, *A catalogue of polyphonic songs, 1415–1480* (1999) · Emden, *Oxf.* · PRO, C 81/1478/25 · PRO, C 54/308 · lady chapel radia and stipendia, Westminster Abbey muniments · bursars' receipt rolls MS 2124; bursars' expense rolls MS 7413; *Registrum protocollorum 1453–1495*, fols. 2, 4; 'White Book', MS 9754, fol. 149, New College Archives, Oxford · GL, MS 4889/PC · H. Baillie, 'A London gild of musicians, 1460–1530', *Proceedings of the Royal Musical Association*, 83, 15–28 · Chancery records

Beeard [Berde], **Richard** (*fl.* 1553–1574), poet and Church of England clergyman, is of unknown origins. He was admitted to the rectory of St Mary-at-Hill, near Billingsgate, London, on 31 May 1560, after the death of its incumbent Alan Percy.

Beeard's commitment to the protestant faith is apparent from his writing. In 1553, on the accession of Mary I, the printer John Kingston published the ill-judged *Godly Psalm of Mary Queen*, written by Beeard and set to music in four parts, along with *A Godly Psalme in Meetre* by Thomas Bownell. In this poem Beeard celebrates the potential 'vnytie' offered by Mary as 'the true enheritoure' of the English crown 'as hathe her brother beene'—presumably in reaction against the disruptiveness caused by the short reign of Lady Jane Grey (July 1553)—and calls for continued reformation of the English church along protestant lines, hoping that Mary

> wil strongly build vpon
> Her brothers good fondacaion […]
> To buyld the house, and fortresse vp
> Of trew religion

Beeard's strong affiliations to the protestant religion are also indicated by his authorship of an undated manuscript treatise 'concerning the doctrine of justification', dedicated to Elizabeth I, the prefatory matter of which (relating the various erudite sources consulted by Beeard, who is dubbed a 'learned divine') is printed at length by John Strype in his *Annals of the Reformation*.

In 1560 Beeard became involved in a literary spat between the authors Thomas Churchyard and Thomas Camell, which arose after the latter's criticism (in verse) of Churchyard's satirical poem *Davey Dicers Dreme*, a piece of alliterative verse calling for an ideal world, which placed itself in the *Piers Plowman* tradition, being 'brought vp in Pierces scole', and may well draw its title from a poem of

Thomas More's, 'Davey the Dicer', published in 1557. Beeard entered the quarrel, which spawned a considerable amount of printed matter, on the side of Churchyard with two broadsides attacking Camell for the unnecessary fractiousness of his critique: *Alphabetum primum Beeardi, or, Camels Crosse Rowe* (republished by Owen Rogers in 1560 as part of *The Contention Betwyxte Churcheyard and Camell, vpon Dauid Dycers Dreame*, a 'compilation' of publications resulting from this literary furore) and *M. Harry Whobals Man to M. Camel Greetes*, both published as single folio sheets in 1560. The latter poem is notable for its author's phonetic attempts to recreate a thick rural accent, and for its conclusion with an obscure twelve-line acrostic, from which the reader is invited to deduce the poet's name.

Beeard's protestantism may well have developed into puritanism. He was 'legitimately deprived' (bishop's register, fol. 176r) of his living in 1574, a revealing date in the light of the anti-puritan backlash in 1573. That he was one of the hotter sorts of protestants is indicated by the fact that, unusually, the inauguration of his successor, Thomas Staller, is noted twice in the bishop's register (on 9 May and 4 June 1574), between which entries Staller testifies to his 'prompt and ready adherence to the articles of religion published in the year of our lord 1562', presumably the Thirty-Nine Articles of 1563, the *'raison d'être* of Anglicanism' and 'the doctrinal statement to which, after 1571, clergy were required to subscribe as the standard of the church's public teaching' (Guy, 303). Nothing more is known of Beeard after 1574. CATHY SHRANK

Sources R. Newcourt, *Repertorium ecclesiasticum parochiale Londinense*, 2 (1710) · R. Lemon, ed., *Catalogue of a collection of broadsides in possession of the Society of Antiquaries of London* (1866) · W. C. Hazlitt, *Hand-book to the popular, poetical and dramatic literature of Great Britain* (1867) · J. Ritson, *Bibliographia poetica* (1802) · W. T. Lowndes, *The bibliographer's manual of English literature*, ed. H. G. Bohn, [new edn], 6 vols. (1864) · J. Strype, *Annals of the Reformation and establishment of religion ... during Queen Elizabeth's happy reign*, new edn, 4 (1824), 512–16 · *STC, 1475–1640* · GL, MS 9535A, fol. 176r [bishop's register] · P. Collinson, *The Elizabethan puritan movement*, pbk edn (1990) · J. Guy, *Tudor England* (1988)

Beecham, (Helen) Audrey (1915–1989), poet and eccentric, was born at Weaverham, Cheshire, on 21 July 1915, the eldest of five children and only daughter of Henry (Harry) Beecham (1888–1947) and his wife, Ethel Anne Baxter (d. 1951). Her great-grandfather, Thomas Beecham, founded the family fortune with his celebrated pills; Sir Thomas Beecham, the conductor, was her uncle. Harry Beecham liked to style himself 'landed proprietor, Lympne Castle', but he soon ran through his share of the family fortune, and Audrey and her brothers were educated at various schools up and down the country. Finally she attended Wycombe Abbey School, from where in 1934 she won a scholarship in politics, philosophy, and economics to Somerville College, Oxford. She took a second-class degree in 1937. Having been brought up in comparative luxury, when she went to Oxford she was already used to riding horseback, driving cars, indulging her passion for dogs, and also to getting her own way. She was inevitably a rebellious and adventurous undergraduate, taking

off in the long vacation of 1936 to run guns for the anarchists in the Spanish Civil War. Her experience there confirmed her in anarchism and anti-communism for the rest of her life. When she left Oxford in 1937 she lived briefly in Paris as one of the group surrounding Henry Miller, Anaïs Nin, and Lawrence Durrell. She quickly lost touch with Miller, but continued to admire Anaïs Nin for her beauty and sophistication, and corresponded with Durrell for many years.

Audrey Beecham returned to Oxford and divided her time between Oxford's and London's bohemians. In Oxford she was a friend of 'Colonel' Kolkhorst and of Maurice Bowra, to whom she was briefly engaged. Though this engagement inevitably came to nothing they remained close friends, and Bowra left her his excellent cellar in his will. She was also one of the circle surrounding Enid Starkie and Dan Davin. Meanwhile, although from 1940 she was working somewhat desultorily as a senior research assistant at the Agricultural Economics Research Institute, she was often in London. There she began to cultivate a serious reputation for her poetry, encouraged by her uncle, Sir Thomas Beecham, and by M. J. T. Tambimuttu, the editor and patron of aspiring poets. Through him she met Antonia White, who became a close friend, Dylan Thomas, and Jo Ackerley. Her own published poetry, *The Coast of Barbary* (1957) and *Different Weather* (1979), was well received, and though traditional in form was praised by critics as various as John Wain, Edwin Muir, Kathleen Raine, and Al Alvarez for its authenticity and strength.

Beecham became restless in her job in Oxford, and to the astonishment of many friends she applied in 1950 for the post of warden of Nightingale Hall, the women's residence at the University of Nottingham. She was appointed there in December 1950, also taking the post of lecturer in economic history. She had been received into the Church of England and remained a convinced high-Anglican for the rest of her life, although she never lost her fascination with witchcraft and folklore. She treasured her great-grandfather's shepherd's crook, elaborately carved with a lengthy rebus, and she believed herself capable of casting spells and affecting friends and enemies by them. She shocked several audiences by suggesting in lectures on her family history that old Thomas Beecham had murdered his first wife, and was astonished by their horrified reaction. When challenged by friends for supporting her application to Nottingham, Lord David Cecil remarked 'There's no martinet like a reformed rake'. But she was never a martinet, and she was much loved by her students and colleagues there until her retirement in 1980. She retained, however, many of her obsessions and eccentricities. Chief among these was her addiction to conspiracy theory. She was convinced that some of her Nottingham colleagues—many of them well-known academics—were 'moles'. Some of her suspicions were entirely unfounded, but others were justified, one at least dramatically.

In 1980 Audrey Beecham returned to Oxford, to her house at 26 Park Town. Her last years were darkened by the chronic asthma which eventually killed her: unable to drive or cycle, she hated walking, and this curtailment of her activities depressed her. But she kept up her interest in her neighbours and friends. On one occasion she asked a friend to drive her to the shops, and on their return instructed her to drive slowly round the crescent of Park Town and look cautiously at the last house on the north side. 'What do you see?' she asked. The friend said it looked very much as if there were sandbags and a plastic curtain on the first-floor window. When they returned to her house, Audrey said that the inhabitants were Libyan trainee pilots and that she believed they were preparing for an attack on the house. She insisted on ringing the police, who took down details noncommittally. Three days later the local paper reported that the Libyan pilots had been expelled from the country, accused of sabotage at the Oxford airfield training centre. They had departed overnight from their Park Town hideout, an outcome that gave her much satisfaction. In spite of all this, she remained completely loyal to friends who had been at one time or another connected with the Communist Party, for loyalty and friendship were among her priorities, and in her last years, when she could seldom go out alone, she cherished their company and conversation. An earlier strain of pugnacity in her temper (she prided herself on her mastery of martial arts and on her claim to have knocked out Dylan Thomas cold when he made unwelcome advances to her) grew less as she aged, and though she remained easily irritated her humour and curiosity about life and people increased. She died at the Churchill Hospital in Oxford on 31 January 1989.

Audrey Beecham was mischievous, but entirely without malice. Generous and affectionate, she retained a quality of innocence that was entirely disarming. She was devoted to horses and dogs (especially a generation of dachshunds who shared her house) and to children, with whose view of life she was always entirely in sympathy. Her many friends, colleagues, and students not only remembered her for her eccentricities but loved her for her charm and her warmly sympathetic spirit.

RACHEL TRICKETT

Sources private information (2004) · personal knowledge (2004) · Somerville College, Oxford, Somerville College records · Burke, *Peerage* (1967) · P. Adams, *Somerville for women: an Oxford college, 1879–1993* (1996) · b. cert. · d. cert.
Archives Bodl. Oxf., MSS
Wealth at death £343,806: probate, 16 May 1989, *CGPLA Eng. & Wales*

Beecham, John (1787–1856), Wesleyan Methodist minister, was born at Barnoldby-le-Beck, near Grimsby. His father died at Waltham while he was a child. He was educated privately under a clergyman, the incumbent of the neighbouring parish of Irby. His friends hoped he would become a clergyman in the Church of England. Young Beecham, however, preferred to join the Methodists. After a short period of preparation he became, in 1815, an itinerant preacher with the Wesleyan Methodists, and soon reached a position of influence. He showed a thorough mastery of the principles of Wesleyan Methodism in his *Essay on the Constitution of Wesleyan Methodism* (1829) and in

his writings and speeches on the work of missions. He was appointed in 1831 to the office of general secretary of the Wesleyan Missionary Society, a post he held for twenty-four years. He displayed great ability in administering its affairs at the mission house, in counselling its agents all over the world, and in advocating its cause. He wrote in 1841 a historical study of the Asante kingdom and the Gold Coast, and in 1842 an important paper, *The claims of the missionary work in western Africa and the importance of training a native ministry*. In 1850 he was elected president of the Wesleyan Methodist conference. Beecham's later years were chiefly spent forming new Methodist conferences in France, in British North America, which he visited in 1856, and in Australasia. His wife died in 1853. Their family consisted of one son and two daughters. Beecham died in London on 22 April 1856.

W. B. LOWTHER, *rev.* TIM MACQUIBAN

Sources *Minutes of conference of Wesleyan Methodists* (1856) · W. Hill, *An alphabetical arrangement of all the Wesleyan-Methodist ministers, missionaries, and preachers*, rev. J. P. Haswell (1853)
Archives JRL, Methodist Archives and Research Centre, corresp. and papers · Wesley's Chapel, London, letters
Likenesses T. A. Dean, stipple and line engraving (after M. Claxton), NPG

Beecham, Sir Joseph, first baronet (1848–1916), manufacturer of patent medicines, was born at Wigan on 8 June 1848. He was the eldest of the family of two sons and two daughters of Thomas *Beecham (1820–1907), founder of Beecham's pills, and his first wife, Jane Evans (1811/12–1872). Educated from 1859 onwards at Moorflat Church of England school, St Helens, in 1863 he entered his father's business, which produced digestive and cough pills. Until the late 1870s, they ran it jointly with only a few employees; he later claimed to have worked daily from 5.30 a.m. until midnight, occasionally escaping to Liverpool for an evening in the gods at a concert or opera.

In 1873 Beecham married Josephine (c.1850–1934), daughter of William Burnett, a silk dealer of St Helens. Of their ten children, two sons and six daughters survived childhood. With a narrow provincial outlook, she failed to unlock his deeply introverted nature, caused by an overbearing father and domestic tension in early life. Then, in 1882, he met the eighteen-year-old Helen McKey Taylor (1864–1920), a Scottish girl who had been brought up in New York. In 1889 he installed her in a London suburb. Their relationship lasted until his death, and although childless provided the emotional and domestic support he sought as he pursued his entrepreneurial activities.

Having appointed the publicity-minded Charles Rowed (1855–1933) as his general manager, Beecham increased the firm's advertising outlay to £109,856 in 1890. Light-hearted advertisements, such as 'What are the wild waves saying (Try Beecham's pills)', printed on boats' sails and billboards stretched over beauty spots, offended the fastidious but sold his pills—no fewer than 250 million, or a quarter of all factory-made pills in Britain, in 1890, and 366 million in 1915. Exports over that period rose from 14 to 28 per cent of turnover. In 1890 he established a manufacturing subsidiary in New York. By then he had become

Sir Joseph Beecham, first baronet (1848–1916), by unknown photographer

a cosmopolitan, claiming to have bought his tie in Cairo, his coat in Australia, and his boots in San Francisco.

In 1899 Beecham had Josephine secretly committed to an asylum in Northampton. Later discovered by two of their children and released, she obtained a judicial separation and an allowance. The elder son, Thomas *Beecham (1879–1961), the conductor, broke with his father over this cold-hearted act. By the new century Joseph was concentrating on his outside interests. He was mayor of St Helens three times between 1889 and 1911 and a very active chairman of the town's electricity committee. He also acquired a large collection of British landscape and other paintings. Having in 1909 become reconciled with Thomas, between 1910 and 1914 Beecham subsidized, at a reported cost of £300,000, a sequence of brilliant grand opera and ballet seasons at top London theatres. For these and philanthropic services (he gave £30,000 to Bedford College, London), Beecham was knighted in 1912 and in 1914 made a baronet; he was also created a knight of the Russian order of St Stanislaus.

In 1914 Beecham was induced to underwrite the purchase for £2 million of the Covent Garden estate and market in London. The deal went awry when the outbreak of the First World War prevented the flotation of a company to sell off the properties. After two years of increasing anxiety, he died of an undiagnosed heart complaint; he was found dead in his bed at his Hampstead home, West Brow, 9 Arkwright Road, on 23 October 1916. He was buried on the 27th at Denton Green cemetery, St Helens. His estate had to be put in Chancery, and was finally wound up in 1924 with a valuation of £1,479,447.

Unimpressive in appearance, with a reddish moustache and grey eyes, Joseph Beecham combined shyness and inarticulacy with a hankering after the grand gesture. By inspired publicity he made his firm one of the best-known in Britain, but he did almost nothing to modernize its products or organization; it was not even a limited company until 1924. He was at ease only with a few close associates; an unselfish love for his son, Thomas, was repaid with condescension. Helen Taylor was loyal to him until the end but few such men of achievement can have enjoyed so little affection in their lives.

T. A. B. CORLEY

Sources T. A. B. Corley, 'Beecham, Sir Joseph', DBB · A. Francis, A guinea a box (1968) · A. Jefferson, Sir Thomas Beecham: a centenary tribute (1979) · C. Reid, Thomas Beecham: an independent biography (1962) · T. Beecham, A mingled chime (1944) · Daily News and Leader (24 Oct 1916) · Liverpool Courier and Times (24 Oct 1916) · Chemist and Druggist (28 Oct 1916) · C. R. Grundy, 'Sir Joseph Beecham's collection at Hampstead [pt 1]', The Connoisseur, 35 (1913), 69–78 · C. R. Grundy, 'Sir Joseph Beecham's collection at Hampstead [pts 3–4]', The Connoisseur, 38 (1914), 223–34; 39 (1914), 75–84 · 'Patent Medicines', BPP, 9 (1914), 414 [HC] · The parish of St Paul, Covent Garden, Survey of London, 36 (1970) · Burke, Peerage · d. cert.

Archives PRO, chancery records, J4 8853–9621 (1917–24), J15 3417–3691 (1917–24) · St Helens Central Library, St Helens Local History and Archives Library, Beecham Group archives

Likenesses photograph, St Helens Central Library, St Helens Local History and Archives Library [see illus.] · photographs, St Helens Central Library

Wealth at death £1,479,447: PRO, chancery records, J4 8853–9621 (1917–24), J15 3417–3691 (1917–24)

Beecham, Thomas (1820–1907), manufacturer of patent medicines, was born at Curbridge, Oxfordshire, on 3 December 1820, the eldest of three sons and four daughters of Joseph Beecham, an agricultural labourer, and his wife, Sarah, daughter of James Hunt. He received a year's schooling before becoming a shepherd's boy at the age of eight. For the next twelve years as a shepherd, he educated himself and acquired herbal lore. From 1840 onwards he undertook casual work at Kidlington, where for a time he acted as village postman and sold in nearby markets some pills of his own invention, whose main constituents were powdered aloes and powdered ginger and which acted as a mild purgative.

In 1847 Beecham migrated to Liverpool, where, on 26 May of that year, he married Jane Evans (1811/12–1872) from Bangor, north Wales, who was eight years his senior. They had two sons and two daughters. Shortly after the marriage they settled in Wigan, where he made and marketed his pills. After his chemist's shop failed, the family moved to St Helens in 1859. In time, a combination of pertinacity and persuasiveness brought Beecham success. Using the slogan 'Worth a guinea a box', he began to advertise his pills in the local press, and gradually created a network of wholesale agents, mainly in London and towns in Lancashire and Yorkshire. In 1865, having set up a small workshop, and with the help of his elder son, Joseph, he achieved an annual turnover of £2500. Within fifteen years he had multiplied this to £23,000 and was completing his first purpose-built factory.

In contrast to his single-mindedness in business, in his private life Beecham was a persistent philanderer; he callously inscribed the name of an illegitimate daughter (*b.* 1862) in the family Bible. After not a few publicly aired rows and scandals, his wife left him; she died of drink in 1872. In January of the following year he married Sarah, daughter of Henry Pemberton, a London labourer; although she was thirty years younger than Beecham, she died in 1877. In September 1879 Beecham married 28-year-old Mary Sawell, daughter of James Putt, contractor, and already three times widowed. Having been brought up in Canterbury, she detested St Helens, and coerced Beecham into moving in 1881 to Mursley Hall, Buckinghamshire. There at first he relished the novelty of country-house life, but discord soon erupted, and relations collapsed after his wife accused him of having tried to poison her. An acrimonious separation followed, and in 1884 he returned to St Helens.

By this time, Beecham's son, Joseph *Beecham, was very much in control of the firm, and in 1886 opened a grand new factory. Thomas occupied himself in writing letters to the press which yielded valuable free publicity. In 1893, having visited the world fair in Chicago, he retired to a newly built villa at Southport. Living alone with a Welsh housekeeper, Jane Roberts, in 1895 he was presented by her with a daughter. That year he handed over the whole business to Joseph. He died at his home, Wychwood, 2 Norwood Avenue, Southport, of pulmonary congestion, on 6 April 1907; he was buried at Dent Green cemetery, St Helens. His estate was valued at £86,680 gross.

Short, squat, and with a shock of white hair, unkempt beard, and piercing blue eyes, Beecham customarily wore an antique frock coat, paper collar, and hard round hat. His grandson, Sir Thomas *Beecham, remembered with awe his voluminous trousers hitched well up to the chest, many-hued, and of rough, thick material. Beecham's manners were as off-putting as his rustic appearance. Seldom if ever going into society and entirely unselfconscious, he scandalized his genteel daughter-in-law with his coarse eating habits, yet few women could resist his powerful sexual magnetism. He gave idiosyncratically to good causes. In later life he became a Congregationalist. As a founding entrepreneur, he lacked the largeness of vision to create a giant business: this task he left to his son Joseph.   T. A. B. CORLEY

Sources A. Francis, *A guinea a box* (1968) • T. A. B. Corley, 'Beecham, Thomas', *DBB* • T. Beecham, *A mingled chime* (1944) • St Helens Central Library, St Helens Local History and Archives Library, Beecham Group archives • private information (2004) • *The Times* (8 April 1907) • *St Helens Newspaper and Advertiser* (9 April 1907) • *Chemist and Druggist* (15 April 1907) • T. C. Barker and J. R. Harris, *A Merseyside town in the industrial revolution: St Helens, 1750–1900* (1954) • parish register (baptism), 17 Dec 1820, St Mary the Virgin, Witney • d. cert.
Archives St Helens Central Library, St Helens Local History and Archives Library, Beecham Group archives

Likenesses bust • photographs, priv. coll.
Wealth at death £86,680 0s. 11d.: probate, 25 May 1907, *CGPLA Eng. & Wales*

Beecham, Sir Thomas, second baronet (1879–1961), conductor, was born on 29 April 1879 in Westfield Street, St Helens, Lancashire, the elder son and second child of Sir Joseph *Beecham, first baronet (1848–1916), manufacturing chemist, and his wife, Josephine Burnett (*c.*1850–1934). The family's prosperity began with Thomas Beecham's grandfather, the first Thomas *Beecham (1820–1907), who invented, advertised, and sold huge quantities of the digestive pills bearing his name. The young Thomas Beecham had a better relationship with his grandfather than with his father—from whom, nevertheless, he inherited a deep love of music. From the boy's first piano lesson it was all-consuming, while his pungent use of words, and the ease with which he memorized huge chunks of prose, was another extraordinary gift.

Beecham attended Rossall School, Fleetwood, Lancashire (1892–7), where he cultivated a passion for cricket and football, and then went up to Wadham College, Oxford. His truancies in Dresden and Berlin to hear opera had been noticed, so he opted to leave in 1898 to avoid being sent down. Half a century later he received Oxford's honorary degree of DMus. Beecham had already practised conducting with the amateur St Helens Musical Society but, in 1899 and at short notice, when Dr Hans Richter cancelled, he successfully took over a local concert with the Hallé Orchestra.

Joseph Beecham had split his family by committing his wife to an asylum. This incensed Thomas, who went to London and eventually obtained his mother's release through the High Court. While there he studied composition with Charles Wood and Frederic Austin, lodging in South Kensington with Charles Stuart Welles, the American embassy's doctor. On 27 July 1903 Beecham married Welles's daughter Utica Celestina (1881–1977). Her 'dowry' was a loan of £50,000 repayable in full at the groom's death. An injury to his wrist in 1904 destroyed Beecham's chances of being a concert pianist.

The newly-weds spent their honeymoon in Europe, where Beecham bought large quantities of French operatic scores and Utica fascinated Giacomo Puccini. This was an unhappy marriage: their two sons went to live with Utica in Boreham Wood and later in St John's Wood, but their father was seldom there. He formed a chamber orchestra which he first conducted in 1906, then brought up to strength as the New Symphony Orchestra. It was engaged by Frederick Delius in 1907 for a concert of his music that marked the beginning of Beecham's lifelong devotion to the composer and his works. In 1908 Beecham presented several works by his new friend, with whom he went on holiday. In 1909 Beecham formed the Beecham Symphony Orchestra (also known as the 'Fireworks Orchestra' because of the members' pranks on tour), and he made it the most talked-of band in Britain; it included such young players as Albert Sammons, Lionel Tertis, and Eric Coates. After only three months he had trained it to

Sir Thomas Beecham, second baronet (1879–1961), by Stephen Glass

give the first performance of Delius's *A Mass of Life* at the Queen's Hall.

A preliminary excursion into opera with Ethel Smyth's *The Wreckers* brought about a complete reconciliation between father and son, and Joseph was now prepared to underwrite his son's operatic plans for three London seasons in 1910. They included two at Covent Garden, including Richard Strauss's advanced operas *Elektra* and *Salome*, as well as a summer season of little-known Mozart and French operas. In 1911, coronation year, Thomas Beecham sponsored Serge Diaghilev with Vaslav Nijinsky and Tamara Karsavina in the sensational Imperial Russian Ballet's first visit to Covent Garden. The Russian Ballet returned in 1912 when Beecham conducted two ballets new to London, and Beecham's orchestra was booked by Diaghilev for his Berlin tour, becoming the first English orchestra to go there. These lavish seasons continued in 1913 at Drury Lane when Beecham brought over Fyodor Chalyapin (as well as giving the first London performance of Richard Strauss's *Der Rosenkavalier*). Beecham put on Russian operas and finally gave Sir Joseph Beecham's Drury Lane season of 1914 (his father had recently been created a baronet). Meanwhile, he incorporated the ailing Denhof Grand Opera Company into his enterprise so as to form the Beecham Opera Company.

In 1909 or early 1910 Beecham began a love affair with Lady Maud Alice (known as Emerald) Cunard (d. 1948). Although they never lived together, it continued—despite other relationships on his part—until his remarriage in

1943. During the 1920s and 1930s he also had an affair with Dora Strang (Labbette; 1898–1994), a soprano known as Lisa Perli, with whom he had a son.

With the outbreak of war in 1914 Covent Garden was closed, but Beecham set himself the task of keeping music going in England. He declared to the Hallé Orchestra, 'Command me! I place myself unreservedly at your disposal', and in October conducted the first of many wartime concerts with it. He also supported the Royal Philharmonic Society at the Queen's Hall and was created knight in January 1916. Sir Joseph, meanwhile, had bought the Covent Garden estate from the duke of Bedford for £250,000, intending to sell it at a profit but to keep Covent Garden and Drury Lane theatres for his son, who was taking the Beecham Opera Company up and down the country giving performances at cinema prices, then conducting London seasons at the Shaftesbury and Aldwych theatres and at Drury Lane in 1917 during the Zeppelin raids. The sudden death of Sir Joseph in October 1916, one day before his will was proved, coupled with inevitable wartime restrictions, started the reversal of the family fortune. Until 1920 Beecham battled on with opera seasons, financially helped by Lady Emerald Cunard. He was made bankrupt, the opera company and its orchestra collapsed, and Beecham was forced to retire from the musical scene for three years while he became a businessman, showing great commercial ability by gradually selling off the millstone of his father's Covent Garden estate.

Beecham first reappeared on the rostrum with the Hallé at Manchester in March 1923, then in London with the combined Royal Albert Hall Orchestra (the renamed New Symphony Orchestra) and London Symphony Orchestra (LSO) with Clara Butt in April 1924. Elements of the Beecham Opera Company, renamed the British National Opera Company, had been reconstituted as a self-governing body in 1922 and were playing at His Majesty's Theatre in 1924 when in came Sir Thomas Beecham, bt, to give a single, rousing, and packed performance of Wagner's *The Mastersingers* to remind them of the past. A single concert with the LSO in the following year convinced him that without his own orchestra he might as well leave England, so he went to the USA and, despite few personal funds, he characteristically stayed at the New York Ritz. Soon he quietly returned home and began flirtations with English orchestras. The need for an independent and first-class London orchestra was in the air, and Beecham's sights were on the LSO between March and December 1928. His overtures to the BBC were met with 'Keep Beecham out!' Concentrating on the 1929 Delius festival in London at the end of 1929 with the composer present, and twice using the BBC Symphony Orchestra for broadcasts, he continued to puzzle the musical world as to his real intentions.

In 1931 Beecham conducted Borodin's *Prince Igor* and his own Handelian score *The Gods Go a-Begging* in a special season of Russian dancers and singers at the Lyceum Theatre. He had been quietly vetting individual members of the orchestra whom he had raised for this season and effectively concealed the real reason for his recent return to Covent Garden, in partnership with Colonel Eustace Blois, managing director of the syndicate.

On 7 October 1932 another new Beecham orchestra, the London Philharmonic (LPO), was born in the Queen's Hall and immediately showed itself to be the finest in Britain, if not in Europe. Despite outstanding debts to former players of the Fireworks Orchestra, the members were only too glad to come back and play for 'Tommy' Beecham because he could guarantee them work from concerts, recordings, and every summer season in the Covent Garden pit until 1939. Beecham was himself again. Sometimes he conducted the Hallé, but neither the LSO nor the BBC enjoyed such successes as he had with the LPO. In 1934 he gave his services to the Royal College of Music with three enchanting student performances of Delius's *A Village Romeo and Juliet*. Delius had died only a few days before, and was buried in a small Surrey churchyard where Beecham, an equivocal believer in Delius's atheism, delivered a passionate oration. In 1936 Beecham took his orchestra to Nazi Germany. His secretary, Berta Geissmar, documented the evening when Beecham refused to precede Adolf Hitler into the concert hall, thus avoiding having to salute the arrival of the Führer.

Britain was at war again in September 1939, and Beecham put all his vigour into keeping music going in England. During the war his reputation as a wit and a raconteur grew as rapidly as his stature as a conductor. When the Queen's Hall was gutted by incendiary bombs in May 1941 most of the LPO's instruments were destroyed, but the players begged and borrowed others and gave their concert, undefeated, at the Royal Albert Hall. With call-up and a complete change in orchestral life, Beecham again felt himself redundant and returned to the USA. He gave typical concerts there and conducted the Metropolitan Opera in New York. Between 1941 and 1943 he took over the Seattle Orchestra.

Beecham had seen nothing of the first Lady Beecham since the First World War, and he wished to marry again. He did not even refer to her as Lady Beecham but as Dame Beecham or Mrs Beecham, because she had played no part in his life after his knighthood and baronetcy. She would not consent to a divorce, however, remained faithful to him from their marriage in 1903 onwards, and outlived him. To overcome this impasse Beecham filed a suit for divorce in Idaho City, USA, on 4 October 1942. After arrival from England of a deposition from Mrs Beecham that carried no weight in the USA, the divorce was granted by the district judge of Idaho City. Beecham married (Margaret) Betty Humby (1908–1958) on 23 February 1943. A pianist, Betty was the daughter of Daniel Morgan Humby, a London surgeon. She had previously secured a divorce in Idaho from her first husband, an English clergyman, but on 7 September 1944 she and Beecham went through a second marriage ceremony in New York, 'to assure compliance with technicalities of the English law'.

Beecham returned home to a utilitarian, post-war England but, in spite of the fact that a new recording orchestra called the Philharmonia was being formed, he prepared to raise yet another. 'You'll never do it!' went up the cry; 'I always get the best players!' he retorted, and he was right. On 15 September 1946 his last orchestra, the Royal Philharmonic (RPO), lifted the roof of the Davis Theatre, Croydon. He proudly paraded it round the country, and a month later its London début at the Royal Albert Hall began another Delius festival. Then came a celebration at Drury Lane to help the rehabilitation of his 83-year-old friend Richard Strauss. Strenuous RPO tours followed through the USA and South Africa.

Beecham never got over the indignity of being denied a role at Covent Garden in 1946. For the first time it had a government subsidy, but his known profligacy was at odds with Labour Britain. Nor was he invited to conduct in the opening series of concerts at the Royal Festival Hall in 1951 ('that biscuit box'); in spite of swearing never to set foot in it, however, he became used to taking the RPO there. He was likewise persuaded to return and conduct opera at Covent Garden. A short run of Michael Balfe's Victorian opera *The Bohemian Girl* (with tongue in cheek) was followed by an uncut *Die Meistersinger* in German.

In 1953 at Oxford, Beecham presented the world première of Delius's first opera, *Irmelin*, and his own last, staged performances were in 1955 at Bath, with A.-E.-M. Grétry's *Zémire et Azor*. He was made a Companion of Honour in 1957, an event which was clouded for him by the death of his second wife, Betty, on 2 September 1958. Nevertheless, he married his secretary, Jean (known as Shirley) Hudson (b. 1932), in Zürich on 10 March 1959.

Indulging his fondness for Berlioz at concerts with the larger choral works, Beecham was set to achieve a long ambition to conduct *Les Troyens* at Covent Garden, as well as making his Glyndebourne début in opera with *Die Zauberflöte*, but his declining health prevented both. At the Portsmouth Guildhall, after a very short morning rehearsal of the RPO, Beecham and the RPO sat and watched the 1960 cup final on television. The concert that night was his last. Nursed by the third Lady Beecham (who survived him), he struggled against the odds of all those years and died of a thrombosis at his home, 21 Harley House, Marylebone Road, London, on 8 March 1961; he was buried two days later in Brookwood cemetery, Surrey. His sense of humour might well have been tickled by the fact that, owing to changes at Brookwood, he could not stay there. His mortal remains were taken in 1991 to lie in peace beside those of Frederick Delius in St Peter's churchyard, Limpsfield, Surrey. He was succeeded in the baronetcy by his elder son, Adrian Welles Beecham.

Thomas Beecham is best remembered as a portly figure with short legs, an imposingly jutting beard, and penetrating eyes, the key to a personal hypnotism which his players acknowledged; while his verbal drawl, with a Lancastrian tinge, was couched in impeccable Edwardian English. His musical abilities and achievements were unsurpassed by any Englishman in the twentieth century, but to foreigners he remained an enigma: by flouting convention, he was often making innocent fun of them.

ALAN JEFFERSON

Sources private information (2004) · T. Beecham, *A mingled chime* (1944) · T. Beecham, *Delius* (1959) · E. Smyth, *Beecham and Pharaoh*

(1935) • A. Jefferson, *Sir Thomas Beecham—a centenary tribute* (1979) •
C. Reid, *Thomas Beecham* (1962) • A. Francis, *A guinea a box* (1968) •
H. Proctor-Gregg, *Beecham remembered* (1976) • N. Cardus, *Sir Thomas
Beecham* (1961) • J. D. Gilmour, ed., *Sir Thomas Beecham — 50 years in
the New York Times* (1988) • *CGPLA Eng. & Wales* (1961)

Archives BL, corresp. with R. Broughton and corresp., Add. MSS
52364, 52549 • St Helens Central Library, Beecham Group archives
|FILM BFI NFTVA, performance footage • BFI NFTVA, 'Beecham',
Yorkshire Television, 1 July 1990 |SOUND BBC WAC • BL NSA,
'Beecham and opera', 1 May 1979 • BL NSA, 'Beecham: legend – true
or false', T21 88W C1 • BL NSA, 'Conversation with Wynford
Vaughan-Thomas', MS403W C1 • BL NSA, *In tune*, 1996, H6996/1 • BL
NSA, 'Sir Thomas Beecham', B8433/05 • BL NSA, 'Sir Thomas
Beecham', 7T7926/01 TR2 • BL NSA, 'Sir Thomas Beecham', 17
March 1969, T532R P874R C1 • BL NSA, 'Sir Thomas Beecham – a
tribute', M4763WBD1 • BL NSA, 'Why he took up music and a story
of Shalyapin', BBC, 1 April 1959, 1LP005889551 BD6 BBC

Likenesses I. Mestrovic, bronze bust, 1915, Man. City Gall. •
E. Kapp, ink, chalk, and charcoal drawings, 1919–58, U. Birm. •
E. Dulac, caricature, *c.*1925, Museum of London • E. Procter, pencil
drawing, 1929, NPG • W. R. Sickert, oils, 1930, Museum of Modern
Art, New York • H. B. Wiener, pencil drawing, 1935, V&A • F. Man,
photograph, 1936, NPG • G. T. Stuart, oils, 1953–4, NPG • D. Wynne,
bronze sculpture, 1957, NPG • D. Wynne, bronze statuette, *c.*1957,
St Helens Museum and Art Gallery • M. Liddle, bust, *c.*1961, Royal
Philharmonic Orchestra, London • H. W. Barnett, two photographs, V&A • S. Glass, photograph, NPG [*see illus.*] • D. Wynne,
bronze sculpture, Royal Philharmonic Society; on loan to Royal
Festival Hall

Wealth at death £10,801 14s.: probate, 26 June 1961, *CGPLA Eng. &
Wales*

Beechey, Anne Phyllis, Lady Beechey (1764–1833). *See
under* Beechey, Sir William (1753–1839).

Beechey, Frederick William (1796–1856), naval officer
and hydrographer, son of Sir William *Beechey, RA (1753–
1839), and his second wife, Anne Phyllis *Beechey, *née*
Jessop (1764–1833) [*see under* Beechey, Sir William], the
miniature painter, was born on 17 February 1796. His
brother was George Duncan *Beechey and his half-
brother Henry William *Beechey. He entered the navy in
July 1806 under the patronage of Lord St Vincent, and
afterwards of Sir Sidney Smith. He served in the channel,
on the coast of Portugal, and on the East India station. The
only occasion on which he engaged with the enemy was
when, as midshipman of the *Astraea* under Captain
Schomberg, he was present at the capture of the *Clorinde*
and *Néréide* on the coast of Madagascar, 20–25 May 1811. In
1814 he was appointed to the *Tonnant* (80 guns), the flagship of Sir Alexander Cochrane, commander-in-chief in
North America, and on 8 January 1815 took part in the boat
operations on the lower Mississippi. For this he was promoted lieutenant on 10 March, and he remained on the
North American station. On 14 January 1818 he was
appointed to the hired brig *Trent*, commanded by Lieutenant John Franklin, and that year served on the Arctic
expedition of which he later published an account, *Voyage
of discovery towards the North Pole, performed in his majesty's
ships Dorothea and Trent, under the command of Captain David
Buchan* (1843). Franklin held a very high opinion of
Beechey. In 1819 Beechey returned to the Arctic, on board
the *Hecla*, under Lieutenant William Edward *Parry, during a remarkable voyage, of which Parry wrote an account
(1821).

Frederick William Beechey (1796–1856), by Stephen Pearce,
1850

In January 1821 Beechey was appointed to the sloop
Adventure, under Captain William Henry Smyth, and during the next two years was employed on the survey of the
north coast of Africa, an account of which he afterwards
published (with his brother Henry William Beechey), as
*Proceedings of the expedition to explore the northern coast of
Africa from Tripoli eastward, in 1821 and 1822* (1828). On 25
January 1822 he was promoted commander, and in January 1825 he was appointed to command the *Blossom*, which
was engaged for the next four years in the Pacific, and in
endeavouring by passing through the Bering Strait to
meet the polar expeditions from the Atlantic. His narrative of this voyage was published by authority of the
Admiralty in 1831. On his return from this expedition he
married, in December 1828, Charlotte, daughter of
Lieutenant-Colonel Stapleton, of Thorpe Lee, near
Egham, Surrey, and having been, while still in the Pacific,
advanced to the rank of captain (8 May 1827), he now
remained for some years on shore. In September 1835 he
was appointed to the *Sulphur*, for the survey of part of the
coast of South America; but his health failing, he was compelled to come home in the autumn of 1836. In the following year he was appointed to the survey of the coast of Ireland, and, in various steam vessels, continued on that duty
until 1847. His unique expertise was used to improve
steamship links to Ireland. He also surveyed the River Severn to Worcester. From 1850 until his death he was superintendent of the marine department of the Board of
Trade; he was consulted on all Arctic issues and occasionally contributed papers to the Royal and other societies of
which he was a fellow. In 1853 he represented the hydrographer at the Brussels conference, where Beaufort's wind

scale was universally adopted. In 1855 he was elected president of the Royal Geographical Society, an office which he still held at his death, on 29 November 1856.

Besides the works already named, Beechey was the author of two reports of observations on the tides in the Irish Sea and English Channel (*PTRS*, 1848, 1851), which made a critical contribution to the modern understanding of tides, and of the presidential address to the Royal Geographical Society in 1856. Beechey was an outstanding professional hydrographer who served in the last years of heroic endeavour, and lived to publish the results of his scientific observations on tides.

J. K. LAUGHTON, rev. ANDREW LAMBERT

Sources G. S. Ritchie, *The Admiralty chart: British naval hydrography in the nineteenth century* (1967) · A. Friendly, *Beaufort of the Admiralty* (1977) · H. R. Mill, *The record of the Royal Geographical Society, 1830–1930* (1930) · A. Day, *The admiralty hydrographic service, 1795–1919* (1967) · Waterhouse, *18c painters*
Archives NL Aus., autobiography | RS, letters to Sir John Herschel
Likenesses G. Beechey, oils, exh. RA 1828, NMM · S. Pearce, oils, 1850, NPG [*see illus.*] · S. Pearce, group portrait, oils, 1851 (*The Arctic Council planning a search for Sir John Franklin*), NPG

Beechey, George Duncan (1797–1852), portrait painter, son of Sir William *Beechey (1753–1839), portrait painter to Queen Charlotte, and his second wife, Anne Phyllis *Beechey, née Jessop (1764–1833) [*see under* Beechey, Sir William], miniature painter, was born at Great George Street, Hanover Square, London, on 20 October 1797. His godfather was George III. Nothing is known about Beechey's education except that he was taught by his father, a number of whose paintings he copied and whose profession he followed. He exhibited portraits at the Royal Academy from 1817, for example *Captain Frederick Beechey* (exh. RA, 1828; NMM), but as his father's success began to wane so George Beechey's commissions declined. Encouraged by his friends to visit India, he obtained the necessary permission from the East India Company on 18 June 1828, arriving in Calcutta a year later. He quickly established himself as a portrait painter with a half length of Dr John Adam, secretary to the medical board (1829; Asiatic Society of Bengal, Calcutta), a full length of Lord Combermere (1830), for the Bengal Club, and a number of family portraits painted for his patron Prosunno Kumar Tagore. He exhibited portraits at the Calcutta Brush Club in 1831 and 1832. The last painting Beechey sent to the Royal Academy, for the exhibition of 1832, was a portrait, *A Hindoo Lady* (engraved as *Hinda* by G. H. Phillips, 1835), which received much favourable comment.

Six years after the retirement in 1828 of Robert Home from the service of the king of Oudh, Beechey succeeded him as court painter and controller of the household in continuation of the long-established enthusiasm of the nawabs for British culture. His uncompromising integrity enabled him to put a rein on the excesses of the palace until he withdrew from the court on the death of Muhammad Ali Shah in 1842. He remained in Lucknow until his death, painting both Englishmen—Lord Auckland (1837)—and Indians, including Wajid Ali Khan, the last of the kings of Oudh, and was remarkably given access to the

royal zenana to portray Wajid Ali's favourite wife and other court beauties, one in the guise of *The Death of Cleopatra*. Few of Beechey's paintings appear to have been identified, and a number must have perished during the Indian mutiny of 1857, but those that are known reflect his father's style, the pose clearly outlined, the eyes sparkling and direct, the finish smooth, as seen in *Two Children, Herbert and Rose, on a Terrace at Poona* (1844; ex Sothebys, 16 July 1986) and a portrait of the young Duleep Singh (1851; ex Sothebys, 22 May 1990) seated in solemn majesty, commissioned by his protector, the govenor-general of India, James Ramsay, tenth earl of Dalhousie.

Embracing the customs of his adopted land, Beechey married Hussaini Begam, daughter of Muhammad Ali Shah, king of Oudh, and set up his own house, Dar ol Sarf in the Mariaon cantonment of Lucknow, where their only son, Stephen Richard, was born in 1835. With another woman, named Laddoo, he had a daughter, Charlotte (b. 1837), who was removed from her mother and adopted by Hussaini Begam to be brought up with their son. His wife and the two children were the sole beneficiaries under his will apart from a small bequest to Pecari Sahib, a third consort. In his duties as controller, having married the daughter of the king, Beechey wore Indian dress. A group portrait of a tall European wearing the costume of a nawab standing with his Indian wife and young son (Asiatic Society of Bengal, Calcutta), has been identified as a portrait of the Beechey family. According to his obituarist (*Delhi Gazette*, 26 October 1852), in addition to his accomplishments as an artist, George Beechey was an amusing companion, a warm and generous friend, liberal and kind-hearted, and of the most incorruptible integrity.

Beechey's fortune was very moderate, and his death on 17 October 1852 was said to have been hastened by grief at hearing of the total loss of the ship in which he had sent to England a large number of his best portraits for exhibition, but his spirit was reported to have lived on to haunt the house in the Mariaon cantonment in which he died.

MARY WEBSTER

Sources G. D. S. Beechey, *The eighth child, George Duncan Beechey 1797–1852, royal portrait painter to the last four kings of Oudh* (1994) · W. Foster, 'George Duncan Beechey', *Bengal Past and Present*, 41 (1931), 101–4 · W. Roberts, *Sir William Beechey, R.A.* (1907), 187, 193, 288–9 · J. J. Cotton, 'George Beechey and his Indian wife', *Bengal Past and Present*, 24 (1922), 49–52 · will, BL OIOC, L/AG/34/29/88, fols. 103–6 · E. Roberts, *Scenes and characteristics of Hindustan*, 2 (1835), 144–5 · F. S. Aijazuddin, *Sikh portraits by European artists* (1979), 74–6 · M. Archer and W. G. Archer, *Indian painting for the British, 1770–1880* (1955), 58, 119 · baptism of children at Futtehghur, BL OIOC, N/1/60, fol. 94 · E. Eden, *Up the country* (1930), 387
Archives BL OIOC, baptisms of his children at Futtehghur, N/1/60, fol. 94
Likenesses W. Khan, pencil drawing, repro. in Beechey, *Eighth child*, facing p. 10 · group portrait (with his wife and son), Asiatic Society of Bengal, Calcutta
Wealth at death more than Rs7000, East India Company; more than Rs7000 in Agra Bank: will, BL OIOC, L/AG/34/29/88, fols. 103–6

Beechey, Henry William (1788/9–1862), painter and explorer, was born probably at 37 Hill Street, Berkeley Square, London, the eldest son of the portrait painter Sir

William *Beechey (1753–1839) and his first wife. Nothing is known of his education. In August 1815 he became secretary to Henry Salt, the newly appointed British consul-general in Egypt, who commented that he drew well and understood both French and Italian. In 1817 he was sent by Salt to oversee the excavations of Giovanni Belzoni at Thebes and to make drawings of the monuments, including the interior of the newly discovered tomb of Seti I. He joined Belzoni and captains Charles Leonard Irby and James Mangles in digging out the buried temple of Abu Simbel, and some of his drawings illustrate this section of the captains' account of their travels. In 1818–19 he accompanied Salt and William John Bankes to Abu Simbel and, with Bankes, made an unsuccessful attempt to reach Meroe in upper Nubia. Recalled to England by his father, he left Egypt in October 1819.

During 1821–2, having been appointed by Earl Bathurst for the Colonial Office, Beechey and his half-brother, Lieutenant Frederick William *Beechey RN (1796–1856), surveyed the coastline of north Africa from Tripoli to Darnah. Henry's part was to examine and report on the antiquities of Cyrenaica, and he illustrated the chronicle of the expedition published by the brothers in 1828. He became an FSA in 1825. At the Royal Academy in 1829 he exhibited a seascape, and in 1838 a portrait of Mrs Worthington; another seascape was shown at the British Institution in 1838. He wrote a painstaking and thoughtful memoir of Sir Joshua Reynolds to preface the 1835 edition of Reynolds's *Literary Works*.

On 14 November 1824 Beechey married Maria Frost. His wife died, and on 23 August 1834 he married Harriet Eyres (1809/10–1864); there were children of both marriages. Apparently beset by vicissitudes in England, at the age of sixty-one and accompanied by Harriet, four of his children, and a daughter-in-law, he emigrated to New Zealand in the *Castle Eden*, arriving there on 7 February 1851. He took up land and farmed it at Governors Bay, Lyttleton, near Christchurch, where he died of pulmonary congestion on 4 August 1862. He was buried in the cemetery at Lyttleton on 7 August.

Beechey's half-brother, **Richard Brydges Beechey** (1808–1895), marine painter and naval officer, was born on 17 May 1808, probably at 13 Harley Street, Cavendish Square, London, the youngest son of Sir William Beechey and his second wife, Anne Phyllis *Beechey, *née* Jessop (1764–1833) [*see under* Beechey, Sir William], who was herself a painter of miniatures. He entered the Royal Naval College, Portsmouth, on 1 March 1821. From March 1825 to September 1828, as a midshipman in HMS *Blossom* commanded by his brother, Captain Frederick William Beechey, he was on a voyage of discovery in the south seas and north to the Bering Strait in an attempt to re-provision Captain John Franklin's polar expedition. Richard provided two illustrations to Frederick's account of the voyage.

Promoted lieutenant on 15 September 1828, Richard Beechey was from then, as he wrote in 1844, 'except for three years when ill health prevented me … constantly in active service of some shape or other' (BL, Add. MS

38039/446). In 1835 he was appointed to the survey service in Ireland, in which he remained until put on half pay in 1857. He was promoted commander on 31 March 1846 and captain on 1 January 1857. Although he retired on 2 July 1864, he became an admiral, on seniority, on 31 March 1885. He married Frideswaide, daughter of Robert Smyth of Portlich Castle, co. Westmeath, Ireland.

From 1832 to 1877 Richard Beechey exhibited seascapes nearly every year at the Royal Academy, the British Institution, or the Suffolk Street Gallery, London. His retirement enabled him to concentrate on his art, and during that time he often worked up sketches made during his naval service. Brook-Hart says of him that he was of 'quite considerable talent and competence' (Brook-Hart, 339); according to Archibald, 'the best painter the navy ever produced' (Archibald, 65). Richard Beechey died at his home, 9 Portland Terrace, Southsea, Hampshire, on 8 March 1895.   PETA RÉE

Sources W. Roberts, *Sir William Beechey, RA* (1907) · Graves, *RA exhibitors* · Graves, *Artists* · F. W. Beechey and H. W. Beechey, *Proceedings of the expedition to explore the northern coast of Africa from Tripoli eastward in 1821 and 1822* (1828) · J. J. Halls, *The life and correspondence of Henry Salt*, 2nd edn, 2 vols. (1834) · G. B. Belzoni, *Narrative of the operations and recent discoveries within the pyramids, temples, tombs and excavations in Egypt and Nubia* (1820) · C. L. Irby and J. Mangles, *Travels in Egypt and Nubia, Syria, and Asia Minor, during the years 1817–18* (privately printed, London, 1823) · G. Finati, *Narrative of the life and adventures of Giovanni Finati*, ed. and trans. W. J. Bankes, 2 (1830) · *Navy List* · D. Brook-Hart, *British 19th century marine painting* (1974) · E. H. H. Archibald, *Dictionary of sea painters* (1980) · F. W. Beechey, *Narrative of a voyage to the Pacific and Beering's strait, to co-operate with the polar expeditions* (1831) · BM, Add. MS 38039/446 · CGPLA Eng. & Wales (1895) [Richard Brydges Beechey] · IGI · 'Beechey, Sir William', *DNB* · registrar general's list, New Zealand · burial register, 1862, Lyttleton, New Zealand
Likenesses W. Beechey, portrait, repro. in Roberts, *Sir William Beechey*; priv. coll.
Wealth at death £526 0s. 6d.—Richard Brydges Beechey: probate, 1895, *CGPLA Eng. & Wales*

Beechey, Richard Brydges (1808–1895). *See under* Beechey, Henry William (1788/9–1862).

Beechey, Sir William (1753–1839), portrait painter, was born on 12 December 1753 in Burford, Oxfordshire, the first of five children of William Beechey (*d.* 1789) and Hannah Read.

Early years and education Beechey's parents were both apparently from Dublin. For unknown reasons they passed the care of their children to William Beechey's brother Samuel, a lawyer, who had settled in Chipping Norton. From family tradition, as published by William Roberts in 1907, it appears that Beechey had a natural aptitude for drawing but Samuel Beechey intended his nephew to become a lawyer. Accounts published during the artist's life testify to his being articled to solicitors in Stow-on-the-Wold and London. By chance Beechey met students from the Royal Academy Schools; he was attracted to their work, arranged for his release from his work with the solicitor, and entered the schools in 1772. Contemporary accounts suggest that Beechey married for the first time shortly after he entered the Royal Academy

Sir William Beechey (1753–1839), self-portrait, 1799

Schools. Nothing is known of the first Mrs Beechey apart from the facts that she was the mother of several of his children, including the painter and explorer Henry William *Beechey, and must have died before 27 February 1793. Little is known of his studies at the academy; he is known to have painted panel decorations for coaches while living in London. Beechey exhibited for the first time at the Royal Academy in 1776 and continued exhibiting annually until he moved to Norwich after the 1782 exhibition. His early work consisted of 'small portraits' (as they were described in the academy catalogues), bust-length and full-length, on a scale much smaller than life. They have been described as being similar to conversation pieces such as were painted by William Hogarth and Johann Zoffany; one critic wrote that he had received training from Zoffany; precisely when this training occurred is unclear since Zoffany left for six years in Italy in July 1772.

It is likewise unclear what prompted Beechey's move to Norwich; one account related that 'an opening' at Norwich led to the change while his biographer quotes a source that 'he was "invited to spend a month" in that city, where he "found himself in the immediate receipt of so many commissions in that town and neighbourhood that he was induced to take up his abode there altogether"' (Roberts, 18). He may in addition have lived for several months in Yarmouth. In Norwich city directories he is listed as a medallion and portrait painter and a limner. His work in Norwich continued both in small scale and life-size (from the evidence of works submitted to the Royal Academy), and the few works that survive are precisely

painted and pleasant. Among them is Beechey's first life-size full-length portrait, of Robert Patterson (St Andrew's Hall, Norwich), probably painted to celebrate his election as mayor in 1784. Beechey submitted three paintings to the Society of Artists exhibition in London in 1785 (two life-size and one family group of 'small whole lengths') and a similar division of small and life-size work to the Royal Academy in 1785 and 1786, in addition to some subject pictures. His work received little notice until 1787, when two frames containing fifteen small portraits (one of the miniature painter Edward Miles) were rejected by the academy council because the rules stated that all paintings must be framed separately. The pictures were taken up by the artist–dealer Benjamin Vandergucht, who in a brilliant example of public relations exhibited them in his own gallery, acquiring for himself and Beechey much free publicity as the newspapers covered their rejection by the academy while ignoring the reasons behind it.

After the exhibition in 1787 Beechey settled at 20 Lower Brook Street, near Grosvenor Square, London, moving to 37 Hill Street, Berkeley Square, before the exhibition in 1789. By autumn 1789 Thomas Gainsborough was dead and Sir Joshua Reynolds had ceased painting. Gilbert Stuart had moved to Ireland in 1787 and only John Hoppner was a serious rival among younger artists. From his account books for 1789–91 it appears that Beechey had stopped making small portraits by the middle of 1789, but not before completing his most ambitious work of the type, a large group portraying ten members of the family of Archdeacon John Strachey. On a large horizontal canvas and set in an outdoor loggia with views to surrounding woodland, Beechey arranged Strachey, his wife, Anne, and eight of their children engaged in conversation and reading, with one son posed in a variation of the celebrated *Cleopatra* (Vatican, Rome), reclining and resting on his left elbow, his right arm bent over his head, and looking at a portfolio of drawings. Strachey and the artist may have shared a Norwich connection, but the *Monthly Mirror* of May 1798 said that the cleric noticed a work of Beechey's by accident, and was so pleased 'that he immediately employed the artist to paint himself and his family' (p. 282). Beechey was paid £105 for the painting, considerably more than for any work recorded in his surviving account books for 1789–91. The painting is attractive, with particular attention paid to the white costumes of the female figures and small still lifes of flowers resting on a table and in a basket on the floor.

The Strachey portrait was not exhibited, and from 1789 Beechey exhibited only life-size portraits. His clientele consisted of clergy, gentry, and military officers, complemented by his brother artists. One of his exhibited portraits in 1789 depicted Charles Herbert, brother of Lord Carnarvon, to whom he had been introduced by the artist Paul Sandby. Herbert's portrait was well received and proved extremely profitable for Beechey; he painted nine portraits of the Herbert family in 1789–90, and this prompted a commission from the duke of Montagu that opened doors for further portraits of nobility, seven of which he exhibited in 1790.

Beechey's portraits from his early maturity are unadventurous, unpretentious, well-coloured, straightforward images. When the young Thomas Lawrence exhibited his sensational full-length portraits of Queen Charlotte and the actress Miss Farren in 1790, Beechey's clientele was not much affected since Lawrence's style was much more flamboyant and the younger artist's reputation impinged more upon Hoppner's clients.

Royal patronage and maturity, 1793–1810 On 27 February 1793 the widowed Beechey married at St George's, Hanover Square, Anne Phyllis Jessop [**Anne Phyllis Beechey**, Lady Beechey (1764–1833)], a miniature painter. She was born on 3 August 1764 at Thorpe near Norwich, the daughter of William Jessop of Bishopsgate, Norwich, and his wife, whose maiden name was Hart. She had a successful career as a miniature painter in Norwich, where she probably met Beechey during his residence there from 1782 to 1787. She exhibited five drawings at the Royal Academy in 1787 under her maiden name, given in the catalogue as Miss A. P. Jessup; she exhibited in 1795 and 1798 as Mrs Beechey, and in 1799, 1804, and 1805 as Lady Beechey. All her exhibits were portraits, including, in 1793, a self-portrait and a portrait of Mrs Wheatley (Clara Maria Pope (1767–1838)). Farington recorded that Lady Beechey 'taught Mrs. Opie to draw' (Farington, *Diary*, 3.1108). Lady Beechey died in Harley Street on 14 December 1833. The turning point in Beechey's life and career was his patronage by the royal family from about 1793. Spanning the decades when Hoppner and Lawrence were enjoying critical and commercial success, each painting portraits of socialites, aristocracy, and whig and tory politicians, Beechey's straightforward and superficially decorative style appealed to the unadventurous taste of George III and his queen. Beechey came to royal attention when a portrait of a nobleman who cannot now be identified was rejected by the Royal Academy exhibition hanging committee. The incensed sitter sent the portrait to be inspected by the king, and while the work was not reinstated to the exhibition, the royal family became in consequence attracted to the artist's work and began a generation of patronage. Some sources attest to Beechey's painting a portrait of the queen in 1793, but because it was not exhibited at the academy until 1797 others have suggested that the portrait was made in 1796. Beechey was appointed portrait painter to the queen in 1793 and in November of that year he was elected an associate of the Royal Academy at the same time as his rival John Hoppner. In that year Beechey painted a full-length portrait of Sarah Siddons portrayed with the emblems of tragedy (NPG) for exhibition in 1794. The picture was not well received; unlike Reynolds's portrait *Sarah Siddons as the Tragic Muse* (1784), Beechey's is neither conventional portrait nor wholly allegory. Pasquin wrote of it that 'it conveys the semblance of a gypsey in sattin, disporting at a masquerade, rather than the murder-loving Melpomene' (Roberts, 45). Beechey exhibited prodigiously over the next few years but despite his

title as portrait painter to the queen he did not exhibit portraits of the royal family until 1797. A reviewer in the *Monthly Mirror* (May 1796) surveyed Beechey's reputation, and accurately described his work:

> Beechey has fewer eccentricities than his competitors—for he never distorts his figures for the sake of extravagant attitude—he is less fantastic in his design and less exuberant in manner, in short, he has more nature than [Hoppner and Lawrence]. … Beechey, who is more fixed and determinate, both in his colouring and outline, studies only to be *chaste*.

At the same time Pasquin used the term 'delicate' to describe Beechey's work, and it is precisely this lack of extravagance, and his delicacy and chastity in colour, composition, and finishing (even in his portraits of military officers) that give Beechey his distinct style and that caused him to appeal to a slice of British society for which the flamboyance of Hoppner and Lawrence was considered 'eccentricity'. It was this 'nature' in Beechey's work that made him attractive to the king, who in 1795 opined that Beechey was 'first' in the Royal Academy exhibition that year (Farington, *Diary*, 2.339) and expressed favourable opinions on Beechey's works into the nineteenth century. The king's opinion of Beechey's work was such that Joseph Farington recorded gossip in 1796 'that a Mandate will come from the King requiring the Academy to make Beechy an Academician' (ibid., 2.552) and in 1797 that 'the King says Beechy was not elected an Academician *because he is the best painter*' (Farington's emphasis; ibid., 3.884). Beechey was eventually elected Royal Academician in February 1798, and received his diploma in November. At the exhibition that year Beechey had been commanded by the king to exhibit what many regard as his masterpiece, the 14 feet by 17 *His Majesty Reviewing the Third Dragoon Guards and the Tenth Light Dragoons* (destroyed during the fire at Windsor Castle in 1992). The commission came after Beechey showed the king a sketch of a scene he had drawn in Hyde Park of the king reviewing the household troops. Beechey worked feverishly to finish the painting in time for the exhibition, even receiving an extension to the deadline for submission. It was given a place of honour over the fireplace in the Great Room at Somerset House, and resulted in a knighthood for the artist on 9 May 1798, 'at the express intimation of the Queen' (*Monthly Mirror*, May 1798, 282), the first knighthood given to an artist since Reynolds and the cause of some astonishment among Beechey's fellow artists.

Beechey was a conscientious courtier. However, the state of the mind of the monarch for whom he worked, combined with his own public pride at his unusual honours, made him the object of much attention from royalty and fellow artists alike. While the king's appreciation of Beechey's work is evident, it is unclear whether he was knowingly perplexing the artist with his art criticism or whether the royal comments were the result of his affliction. At one point the king remarked on Beechey's 'red and yellow trees' (Roberts, 63), a criticism he also levelled at John Hoppner. In 1806, when Beechey was supporting an unpopular but pro-royalist faction in Royal Academy politics, the king decided that the artist did not understand colouring and wanted no further pictures from him. In June that year the king discovered that Beechey had painted—for half price—a copy of his portrait for the impoverished bishop of Chester, and in a passionate outburst and advancing towards him said, 'West is an American, and Copley is an American, and you are an Englishman, and were you all at the Devil I should not care' (Farington, *Diary*, 17 June 1806; 7.2786). Beechey was so mortified at the episode that he fled from the royal presence into the nearest open room—a maid of honour's apartment—and fainted. These stories were repeated gleefully at the Royal Academy and recorded by Joseph Farington in his diary.

There are, however, more occasions of royal pleasure at Beechey's work; at one point the king even contemplated a separate room for the artist's many royal portraits. Beechey's familiarity with the king and the royal family, combined with his honours and his own idiosyncratic personality, made him an obvious target. In 1800 Farington had noted that Beechey gossiped about the royal family's opinions about art and artists, and in 1817 the elderly John Fisher, bishop of Salisbury (known particularly for his fine manners), related to John Constable how Beechey 'took freedoms' with the royal family, 'which were laughed at [at] the time, but were remembered with disgust' (Farington, *Diary*, 5 July 1817; 14.5047).

Beechey's obituary in *The Times* stated that the 'leading features in [his] character were a genuine simplicity in mind and manner, united with a frankness and cheerful urbanity' (Roberts, 14). This frankness may have led Lord Lyttelton to remark to Farington that he hesitated to invite Beechey to social events because he heard that he swore.

> [H]e was of the old school, who did not abstain from the thoughtless use of unmeaning oaths. Calling on Constable, the landscape painter, he addressed him, 'Why, d—n it, Constable, what a d—d fine picture you are making; but you look d—d ill, and have got a d—d bad cold'. (Redgrave and Redgrave, 341)

It is said that in his later years he complained of the increasing sobriety and decreasing conviviality of both artists and patrons of art:

> At one of the annual dinners of the Academy he remarked that it was confoundedly slow to what was the wont in his younger days, when the company did not separate until a duke and a painter were both put under the table from the effects of the bottle. (ibid.)

Despite his 'somewhat warm' temperament, his obituarist related that 'his disposition was very cheerful all through life' (*GM*, 433). That cheerfulness manifested itself on one occasion when Beechey was painting the portrait of Princess Augusta. She told the artist Henry Edridge 'that while Beechey was painting Her portrait when He thought He had succeeded He would dance about the room' (Farington, *Diary*, 6 July 1809; 10.3508). His personality was distinct enough for Farington to record that the actor Charles Bannister entertained others with a Beechey imitation. Beechey was a liberal entertainer of colleagues

and a mentor to a variety of younger artists, most notably John Constable.

Later career and death Beechey exhibited at the Royal Academy annually from 1785 to 1805 and from 1807 to 1838 (and again, posthumously, in 1839). That he did not exhibit at the academy in 1806 was possibly the result of rancorous politics there (a number of other artists, including the president, Benjamin West, did not exhibit) and the establishment of the British Institution, at which Beechey exhibited landscapes and subject pictures from 1806 to 1808, and with some regularity from 1810 to 1831. Beechey's portrait style changed little as the nineteenth century progressed. From the mid-1790s and well into the first decade of the 1800s he was consistently regarded as highly as Hoppner and Lawrence, depending on who was making the comparison (although Lawrence's personal problems affected his work during those years). However, the opinion of Beechey that has dogged the artist's reputation for generations is, paradoxically, most apt for explaining precisely why he was so popular. In 1795 John Opie believed that Beechey's

> pictures were of that mediocre quality as to taste & fashion, that they seemed only fit for sea Captains & merchants: whereas Lawrence & Hoppner had each of them a portion as it were of gentility in their manners of painting. (Farington, *Diary*, 1.289–90)

This quality, mediocre or otherwise, was precisely what the vast number of sea captains, merchants, and their wives wanted, and led to countless commissions. His work at the turn of the century is perhaps his most successful, with inventive poses and cheerful interaction in group portraits. As his career progressed after 1810 his portraits became more formulaic although no less popular. He painted the occasional royal portrait, by 1814 was named portrait painter to the duke and duchess of Gloucester, and during the reign of William IV was described as principal portrait painter to the king. That he was extremely successful is reflected not only by the number of portraits he exhibited, but is also documented in his account books from 1807 to 1826, now in the Royal Academy library. On leaving his home in Harley Street in 1836 Beechey sent unsold works for auction on 9 and 10 June at Christies and Mansons together with his collection of old-master paintings, books, and prints. He died on 28 January 1839.

Posthumous reputation Beechey's unparalleled royal patronage is the basis for his posthumous reputation. The seeming paradox of that patronage combined with Opie's opinion that his work was mediocre and fit only for merchants and sea captains has influenced most subsequent writers on his work. In the late nineteenth and early twentieth centuries Beechey's work was frequently misattributed to other more marketable artists, and later in the twentieth century his name was attached to countless works of serviceable quality by unknown artists. Ironically, perhaps the most attention he received after his death was the result of the fire at Windsor Castle in 1992 which destroyed his monumental painting *His Majesty*

Reviewing the Third Dragoon Guards and the Tenth Light Dragoons. This even prompted a mention (although not by name) in *Private Eye*.   JOHN WILSON

Sources W. Roberts, *Sir William Beechey R.A.* (1907) · R. Redgrave and S. Redgrave, *A century of British painters* (1866), new edn (1947) · D. Turner, *Sepulchral reminiscences of a market town* (1848) · *GM*, 2nd ser., 11 (1839), 432–3 · O. Millar, *The later Georgian pictures in the collection of her majesty the queen*, 2 vols. (1969) · Farington, *Diary* · R. Asleson, ed., *A passion for performance: Sarah Siddons and her portraitists* (Los Angeles, 1999) · Redgrave, *Artists* · *IGI* · B. Ormsby and M. Kempski, 'The commission and restoration of six portraits of the daughters of George III, by Sir William Beechey', *Hamilton Kerr Institute Bulletin*, 3 (2000), 107–18

Archives RA, account book

Likenesses G. Dance, chalk drawing, 1795, RA · W. Beechey, self-portrait, miniature, exh. RA 1799 · W. Beechey, self-portrait, oils, 1799, Detroit Institute of Arts [*see illus.*] · W. Evans, pencil drawing, 1799 (after W. Beechey), NPG · attrib. J. Saunders, miniature, c.1800, V&A · W. Beechey, self-portrait, oils, c.1805 (finished by J. Wood, c.1836), NPG · W. Beechey, self-portrait, oils, c.1814, RA · E. H. Baily, marble bust, 1826, NPG · Miss Turner, lithograph, 1830 (after W. Beechey), BM, NPG · attrib. R. Rothwell, oils, 1835, Boston Museum of Fine Arts · W. Skelton, lithograph, 1837 (after T. Phillips?), BM, NPG · E. Scriven, stipple (after W. J. Newton), BM; repro. in *Library of the Fine Arts*, 3 (1832) · H. Singleton, group portrait, oils (*Royal Academicians, 1793*), RA · W. Ward, mezzotint (after W. Beechey), BM

Beeching, Henry Charles (1859–1919), dean of Norwich and author, was born on 15 May 1859 at 16 Dorset Street, London. He was the second son of James Plumer George Beeching, and came from a Sussex family of shipowners and bankers who had long held land at Bexhill. His mother was Harriet, daughter of William Skaife, of Knaresborough, whose family had lived for many generations near Pateley Bridge, Yorkshire. In 1875 he went to the City of London School, where he came under the influence of Dr Edwin A. Abbott, who became his mentor. In October 1878 he went up to Balliol College, Oxford, as an open exhibitioner, and soon became one of a circle which included J. W. Mackail, J. St Loe Strachey, Clinton Dawkins, Rennell Rodd, and Sidney Lee. His enthusiasm for English literature, and more especially for English poetry, was stimulated by his Balliol friendships, and his own gift for writing verse was soon apparent. He contributed to an undergraduate periodical, *Waifs and Strays*, and in 1879 published, with J. W. Mackail and J. B. B. Nichols, a small volume of poems entitled *Mensae secundae*; this was followed by *Love in Idleness* (1883) and *Love's Looking-Glass* (1891), both written with the same collaborators. He graduated BA in 1883.

In 1882 Beeching was ordained deacon, and became curate of St Matthew's, Mossley Hill, Liverpool, where he remained until 1885, when he moved to the living of Yattendon, Berkshire. In 1890 he married Mary, daughter of the Revd A. J. Plow and niece of Robert Bridges, the poet. They had three daughters. In his country parish, Beeching devoted himself to literary work, particularly the study of the English poets. In 1895 he published his best-known volume of verse, *Love in a Garden and other Poems*. In 1896 he began to contribute anonymously to the *Cornhill Magazine*, of which his friend St Loe Strachey was then editor. These

contributions were published in book form, also anonymously, in 1898, as *Pages from a Private Diary*; the second edition (1903) bore the pseudonym Urbanus Sylvan. In 1900 his edition of Milton was published by the Clarendon Press, Oxford.

In 1900 Beeching gave up his work as a country clergyman, and became chaplain of Lincoln's Inn and professor of pastoral theology at King's College, London. In 1902 he was appointed canon of Westminster, a most congenial post for a man of his tastes. He was select preacher at Oxford in 1896–7 and again in 1912–13; at Cambridge in 1903, 1909, and 1912; and at Dublin in 1905. In 1906 he published *Provincial Letters and other Papers*, and in 1909 a life of Francis Atterbury. During this London period he also produced several volumes of sermons and lectures, including *Religio laici* (1902), *The Bible Doctrine of Atonement* (1907), and *William Shakespeare … a Reply to Mr George Greenwood, MP* (1908). He also edited two volumes of sermons and lectures by his friend Alfred Ainger.

In 1911 Beeching was appointed dean of Norwich. He became keenly interested in the history and services of his cathedral, and took an active part in the life of the city. His health began to fail in 1918, and on 25 February 1919 he died at the deanery, Norwich, from heart failure. His ashes were buried in Norwich Cathedral on 3 March. His wife survived him.

Beeching was eminent both as churchman and man of letters. A man of wide sympathies and varied interests, he was beloved and successful alike as country rector, canon of Westminster, and dean of Norwich. As a preacher he showed learning and eloquence. He was a liberal churchman, but no controversialist, and he had a deep love for the ritual and liturgy of the Church of England. He was an essayist and critic who was 'sound rather than brilliant' (A. Ralli, *History of Shakespeare Criticism*, 3, 1932, 269, 371–3). His own poetry, though slender in volume, is marked by technical skill, polished wit, and the verbal dexterity which made his epigrams famous.

F. P. SPRENT, *rev.* H. C. G. MATTHEW

Sources *The Times* (26 Feb 1919) · *Church Times* (28 Feb 1919) · *Eastern Daily Press* (26 Feb 1919) · *Eastern Daily Press* (3 March 1919) · S. Lee, 'Memoir', *Norwich Public Library Readers' Guide*, 7/6 (April 1919) · G. A. Stephen, 'Bibliography', *Norwich Public Library Readers' Guide*, 7/6 (April 1919) · L. Huxley, *Cornhill Magazine*, [3rd] ser., 46 (1919), 444–8 · *Oxford Magazine* (7 March 1919) · *CGPLA Eng. & Wales* (1919)

Archives Norfolk RO, draft journal, historical papers, autobiographical MS of his first seven years as dean, press cuttings, and sermon and lecture notes | Westminster Abbey, letters to Dean Robinson

Likenesses W. Strang, coloured drawing, 1908, priv. coll. · A. Batchelor, pastel drawing, priv. coll. · B. Nichols, drawing, priv. coll.

Wealth at death £5213 5s. 5d.: probate, 2 July 1919, *CGPLA Eng. & Wales*

Beeching, James (1788–1858), lifeboat designer, was born at Bexhill, Sussex, and was subsequently apprenticed to a boat builder at Hastings. Some little time after his apprenticeship he went to Flushing, and there, in 1819, built the famous smuggling cutter known as the *Big Jane*. On leaving Flushing he settled at Great Yarmouth, where he introduced a handsome type of fishing vessel which remained in use at that port until the development of steam. In 1851 attempts were made under the auspices of the prince consort to revive the activity of the Royal National Lifeboat Institution, which was at a very low ebb. A prize of £100 for the best model of a lifeboat, and another £100 towards the cost of building, were offered by the president, the duke of Northumberland. Out of 280 models from various countries, many of which were displayed at the Great Exhibition of 1851, Beeching's design, based on a 'self-righting' principle, was awarded the prize; with a few slight modifications suggested by Mr Peake, master shipwright of Woolwich Dockyard and one of the judges, it served as the model for the fleet of rowing lifeboats built for the Royal National Lifeboat Institution during the remaining years of the nineteenth century. So confident was Beeching about his invention that he built a boat before the prize was awarded, which became the property of the trustees of Ramsgate harbour, and helped save several hundreds of lives on the Goodwin Sands.

Beeching was married with two sons, James and Samuel, both of whom were shipbuilders, at Great Yarmouth and Ramsgate respectively. Beeching died on 7 June 1858 at Norwich.

H. M. Chichester, *rev.* Andrew Lambert

Sources personal information (1885) · O. Warner, *A history of the Royal National Lifeboat Institution* (1974) · Boase, *Mod. Eng. biog.* · *Reports of the Royal National Lifeboat Institution* · J. Gilmore, *Storm warriors, or, Life-boat work on the Goodwin Sands* (1874) · *CGPLA Eng. & Wales* (1858)
Wealth at death under £1500: probate, 15 Sept 1858, *CGPLA Eng. & Wales*

Beeching, Richard, Baron Beeching (1913–1985), businessman, was born on 21 April 1913 in Sheerness, Kent, the second of the four sons of Hubert Josiah Beeching, journalist, and his wife, Annie Twigg, schoolteacher. He was educated at Maidstone grammar school and at Imperial College of Science and Technology, London, where he was awarded a first-class degree in physics in 1934 and a PhD in 1937 for his research into electrons. He published *Electron Diffraction* (1936). In 1938 he married Ella Margaret, daughter of William John Tiley, engineer, of Maidstone. They had no children.

After a year's work at the fuel research station in Greenwich in 1936, Beeching was recruited by William Griffiths (1895–1952) to work at the new research laboratory set up by the Mond Nickel Company Ltd in Birmingham, and in 1943 was seconded to the Ministry of Supply to work in the armaments design department, which dealt with the design and development of weapons and ammunition for all three services. He continued working there after the war as deputy chief engineer of armaments design from 1946 until he joined the technical department of Imperial Chemical Industries Ltd (ICI) in London at the invitation of Sir Ewart Smith (1897–1995), technical director of ICI, who had headed the armaments design department during the war. At ICI he worked on the development of man-made

Richard Beeching, Baron Beeching (1913–1985), by Elliott & Fry, 1961

fibres as a member of the Terylene Council, which became the board of the ICI fibres division. As a vice-president of ICI of Canada Ltd from 1953, Beeching spent two years in charge of building a fibres plant at Millhaven, Ontario, and was appointed chairman of the metals division of ICI in 1955. He became technical director of ICI in 1957, with a seat on the board.

But it was as chairman of the British Railways board that Beeching became a national figure. He had been a member of the special advisory group on the British Transport Commission set up in 1960 by the minister of transport, Ernest Marples, under the chairmanship of Sir Ivan Stedeford, chairman of Tube Investments Ltd, which advised the government that the railways should be run as a business. Helped by the advice of the Stedeford group, the government published a white paper, *The Reorganization of the Nationalized Transport Undertakings*, in December 1960, proposing to break up the British Transport Commission, which presided over not only British Railways but also British Road Services, London Transport, British Transport Hotels, and Thomas Cook, and to put the railways under a British Railways board appointed by the minister of transport. General Sir Brian Robertson, chairman of the British Transport Commission since 1953, who saw the railways as a public service, was retired two years early, and Beeching was appointed in his place as chairman of the British Transport Commission and chairman-designate of the proposed British Railways board for a five-year period, with a salary of £24,000 p.a. (equal to his existing ICI salary), far higher than that of any other head of a nationalized industry.

Beeching's brief was to modernize British Railways and turn it into a profitable business. By the time he was appointed, the modernization plan of 1955 was being implemented, including investment in diesel locomotives, and the House of Commons select committee on the nationalized industries had published its report in July 1960 concluding that the losses sustained by British Railways—a £42 million deficit in 1959—were mainly due to the uneconomic passenger services. At the British Transport Commission's headquarters, Stanley Raymond, who was to be Beeching's successor as chairman of British Railways, had commissioned regional studies of the rail system to find out which lines were making a loss and which parts of the system were commercially viable. Beeching spent most of his first two years drafting the report *The Reshaping of British Railways* (1963), always known as the 'Beeching report'. Although what he proposed was not new, he came to be identified in the public mind with the argument that British Railways should concentrate on those tasks for which the railways were best qualified. In his report he revealed that half of the 7000 railway stations generated only 2 per cent of the total rail traffic, one-third of the track carried only 1 per cent of the traffic, and only one-third of the stock of railway carriages was used all the year round. In the appendix he listed 2000 stations and 250 lines which he thought should be closed on economic grounds, with a reduction of 70,000 staff, and the term 'Beeching axe' was coined by the press. Bitterly criticized at the time by the railway unions and large sections of the public, especially in communities which lost their branch lines, Beeching continued to be branded as the man who destroyed the railway system. Less publicity was given to the more positive aspects of the report, the development of those parts of the system which were economically viable, including liner trains, the forerunner of the Freightliner service. Beeching followed this with *The Development of the Major Trunk Routes* (1965), a survey of how rail traffic could be concentrated on the 3000 miles of main lines. He also completely reorganized the management structure of British Railways, bringing in businessmen to middle and senior management posts.

With the Labour victory in October 1964, Beeching's unpopularity led him to resign at the end of May 1965, one year earlier than intended. Appointed minister of transport in December 1965, Barbara Castle began to take a fresh look at transport policy, and although she admired Beeching's intellect, and agreed with much that he had done, especially in light of the expansion in the use of road transport, she found that he approached transport policy 'with an arrogance that comes, I suspect, from a clear mind that sees a logical answer to a situation and cannot tolerate any modification of it to meet human frailty' (*Castle Diaries, 1964–70*, 122). Although not all his recommendations were implemented, by 1969 the track had been reduced from 18,214 miles in 1961 to 12,098, and the number of railway stations from 7025 in 1961 to 3002. Critics later pointed out that he should have been more aware of the interdependence of the parts of the railway system: for example, many passengers used main-line services only because they connected with local branch lines. British Railways continued to run at a deficit (£134 million in 1963, £147 million in 1969), but Beeching's four years at British Railways succeeded in bringing public attention to bear on the question of how to run the railway system and make it pay. Even before his resignation, Beeching allowed himself to be drawn into political arguments. Tony Benn, after a lunch in January 1965 at which Beeching had launched an attack on 'overblown democracy', observed: 'I think Beeching imagined himself as a new de Gaulle, emerging from industry to save the nation' (Benn, 205). Unwisely, he continued to rise to the bait, as when he found himself arguing in a Cambridge Union debate in 1968 that managerial efficiency was the ultimate goal.

Beeching received a life peerage in 1965. He returned to ICI as deputy chairman, but, disappointed at having been passed over as chairman, he left in 1970 to serve as chairman of Redland Ltd, the building materials group, until 1977. He remained as a director until 1984 and continued to advise on research and development. He was also a director of Furness Withy & Co. Ltd, the shipowners, from 1972 to 1975, and chairman from 1973 to 1975. He served on several public bodies, including the National Economic Development Council from 1962 to 1964 and the Top Salaries Review Body from 1971 to 1975. He was also chairman of the royal commission on assizes and quarter sessions in 1966: his report was implemented in the Courts Act of 1971. Beeching was awarded an honorary LLD by the University of London in 1966. He died on 23 March 1985 in the Queen Victoria Hospital, East Grinstead, Sussex.

ANNE PIMLOTT BAKER

Sources T. R. Gourvish, *British Railways, 1948–73: a business history* (1986) [research by N. Blake and others] · M. Bonavia, *British Rail: the first 25 years* (1981), 112–23 · S. Joy, *The train that ran away: a business history of British Railways, 1948–1968* (1973), 69–87 · *The Times* (25 March 1985) · *WW* · R. H. N. Hardy, *Beeching: champion of the railway?* (1989) · *The Castle diaries, 1964–1970* (1984) · T. Benn, *Out of the wilderness: diaries, 1963–67* (1987) · *CGPLA Eng. & Wales* (1985)
Archives FILM BFI NFTVA, documentary footage · BFI NFTVA, propaganda film footage (British Railways) |SOUND BL NSA, 'Frankly speaking', NP775W BD1 · BL NSA, 'Hindsight (1)', NP4959W BD1 · BL NSA, current affairs recordings · BL NSA, oral history interviews
Likenesses Elliott & Fry, photograph, 1961, NPG [*see illus.*] · photograph, c.1961, Hult. Arch. · A. Jones, photograph, 1962, Hult. Arch. · Moore, photograph, 1963, Hult. Arch. · G. Davien, ceramic sculpton, 1964, NPG · D. N. Smith, two photographs, 1965–c.1966, Hult. Arch. · D. N. Smith, double portrait, photograph, c.1966 (with Tony Benn), Hult. Arch. · S. Franklin, pen-and-ink, NPG · W. Papas, pen-and-ink, NPG · photograph, repro. in Bonavia, *British Rail* · terracotta sculptoon, NPG
Wealth at death £839,403: probate, 12 April 1985, *CGPLA Eng. & Wales*

Beecroft [*née* Skirrow], **Elizabeth** [Betty] (1748–1812), iron manufacturer and butter seller, was born Elizabeth Skirrow, and had at least one brother. She married George Beecroft (1739–1820), a respected tenant farmer, and together they lived at Bramley in Yorkshire, close to Leeds, with

Betty producing butter for sale at local markets. They had a son and a daughter.

A woman of remarkable business enterprise and spiritual strength, Betty recorded in her diary how one evening in October 1778 she first discussed with her husband the possibility of leasing Kirkstall forge. On the banks of the River Aire, 4½ miles to the west of Leeds, the forge had manufactured iron since the early thirteenth century. However, in 1778 the business and its attached farm, owned by the earl of Cardigan, were once again to let.

Betty relentlessly overcame her husband's reluctance to proceed. George Beecroft protested that 'It would take too much money!', but she replied, 'Never mind *that*. We shall do for that, I warrant thee' (Butler, 23). Nevertheless, after discussions with the earl of Cardigan's agent it became clear that the forge was in a ruinous condition and that new tenants would have to spend at least £1000 on it. Despite her husband's 'Dither & Shak' and at least one attempt by him to withdraw from the venture, Betty persuaded George and his family to proceed. A passionate follower of John Wesley, she recalled that 'I began by talking about God's kind providence in so clearly opening our way in this matter and if we gave it up we should never have another chance again' (ibid., 24–6).

A number of possible partners in the venture were considered—and rejected—by Betty Beecroft. The Dixon family were 'very sharp people and if they see a good penny-worth come their way may be they will not be generous enough with my husband, and may try to throw him out and take the whole to themselves' (Butler, 24). In the event Betty found better partners in two members of the Butler family, long established in the wool trade: John Butler (1738–1826), who was also married to her husband's sister Jane; and Thomas Butler, a man of substance in Lichfield and sheriff there in 1770. The Butlers each invested £500, and with some difficulty George and Betty managed to raise £800.

'And, now with much diligence, and I believe upright-ness', Betty wrote, 'we proceeded on our way with our new business' (Butler, 27). The articles of agreement were signed, and the Beecrofts took possession of the dwelling house at the forge on 3 May 1779. While her husband looked after the farm, Betty was in sole charge of the forge. 'I undertook the care of the trade and the books: also the buying and selling and all the engagements of the men up to March 31st 1780' (ibid., 27). However, it became clear that John Butler, who came over once a week and paid the wages, was to be the key figure once he had wound up his other business; and from 1780 everything was 'generally ordered and decided' by him (ibid., 28).

Kirkstall forge was transformed by its new management. The existing water-wheels were replaced, and the old races leading to them from the abbey mill were enlarged. The screw mill was rebuilt, a plate mill was added, and in 1797 a puddling furnace was commissioned to exploit Henry Cort's new process. Iron was imported from the Netherlands, Russia, and Sweden; and from the mid-1790s, in addition to rods, bars, screws, and plates of

iron, the forge was manufacturing more lucrative finished products. Initially these were spades, shovels, and patten rings, but in 1798 the first cart-arms were produced, and these and other axles later became the firm's speciality. Betty Beecroft's son George and John Butler's son Thomas both became partners at about this time, ensuring a future for 'Butlers and Beecrofts'.

After 1785, when John Butler built himself a house at the forge, Betty's role steadily declined, but she continued to help in the counting-house until 1805. A curious advertisement that she placed in the *Leeds Mercury* on 4 May 1793 indicates that Betty continued selling farm produce: this condemned the 'vile and malicious' reports that she had exported butter and bacon to revolutionary France and offered a reward of 10 guineas for the discovery of the propagator of the rumour (Butler, 22).

Local tradition records that John Wesley was attacked by a mob in the area, and took refuge in a chamber in Kirkstall forge. Whether Betty met Wesley then is not recorded, but she certainly did so in London shortly before he died in 1791. As she wrote to her mother, 'I hope I shall be ever thankful that he gave his blessing upon one so unworthy of his notice' (Butler, 29).

A much-loved figure in both the Butler and Beecroft families, Betty died in 1812. A tribute from a Wesleyan minister accurately noted that, though 'neither free from defects nor destitute of eccentricities', Betty was legendary for her 'industry, economy, integrity, firmness of mind and inviolable attachment to the Scriptures' (Butler, 110). Guided by a sure sense of providence, Betty Beecroft was also a remarkably astute businesswoman.

ROBERT BROWN

Sources [R. Butler], *The history of Kirkstall forge*, 2nd edn (1954) · **Archives** Kirkstall Forge Engineering Co. Ltd, Kirkstall, West Yorkshire · **Likenesses** portrait, repro. in Butler, *The history of Kirkstall forge*, 27

Beecroft, John (1790–1854), west African explorer and consul, was born near Whitby. Little is known about his early years beyond the fact that in 1805, while serving aboard a coasting vessel, he was captured by a French privateer and held prisoner until the peace of 1814. He subsequently joined the merchant service, rising in due course to become commander of a transport vessel, in which capacity he accompanied one of the expeditions to Greenland led by Sir William Parry.

The significant part of Beecroft's career began in 1829 with his appointment as superintendent of works at Fernando Po, an island in the Gulf of Guinea nominally under Spanish control but where Britain was establishing a base for combating the slave trade. Beecroft pressed ahead with building docks and shore installations. Very quickly, however, his superiors recognized his talent for understanding and winning the goodwill of Africans, as when he successfully resolved a dispute with the rulers of Old Calabar, upon which the settlement was largely dependent for provisions. In 1830, when the governor, Edward Nicholls, returned to England on sick leave, Beecroft took over as acting governor, a post conferred on him by the Spanish government with the rank of lieutenant in the Spanish navy, and which he held with distinction for the next two years. Finding that Spain was unwilling to part with Fernando Po, Britain gave up its settlement in 1833. Beecroft, however, stayed on as a partner in the firm of Dillon, Tennant & Co., which controlled the shore establishments from 1833 to 1837. Strictly speaking he was simply a private citizen, but effectively he continued to govern the island, maintaining a court of justice, and generally overseeing its affairs. In 1843 he was made governor of Fernando Po and two other Spanish islands.

Beecroft's other principal concern was using steam power to open up the interior of Africa to trade. The great difficulty was that, although steamers could ascend the Niger and other rivers, the effectiveness of quinine as a prophylactic against malaria had not yet been fully grasped, with the result that the death-rate among Europeans was appallingly high. However, Beecroft's attempts, little noted at the time because they were mounted from Fernando Po, proved much more successful than the highly publicized expeditions that set out from England. Employing crews composed largely of Africans he systematically explored the rivers flowing into the Gulf of Guinea, ascending the Niger as far as Raba, 400 miles from the coast, on more than one occasion. As a result he became the most knowledgeable and influential European in that part of Africa and was continually being called on by traders, missionaries, and humanitarians for advice or to sort out local disputes.

Beecroft was thus already something of an institution when, in 1849, the third Viscount Palmerston appointed him consul to the bights of Benin and Biafra. (This post was not incompatible with his governorship of Fernando Po which he continued to hold until his death.) Although Britain had long had trading connections with these areas, hitherto she had had no territorial ambitions there. Under Beecroft that changed. As the senior resident British official on the coast he was largely responsible for the British occupation of Lagos in 1851 and the deposition of King Pepple of Bonny in 1854. If the years 1829–49 show Beecroft's genius for winning the friendship and respect of Africans, the period 1849–54 reveals him as a forceful interventionist, determined to establish British paramountcy over what was eventually destined to become the colony of Nigeria.

With the support of the British government and of the Royal Geographical Society, to which he had been elected on the recommendation of its president, Sir Roderick Murchison, Beecroft was appointed leader of the Niger expedition in 1854, but before it was fully under way he died, on 10 June 1854 at Fernando Po, where he was buried; his place as leader of the expedition was taken by William Baikie. HOWARD TEMPERLEY, *rev.* ELIZABETH BAIGENT

Sources K. O. Dike, 'John Beecroft', *Journal of the Historical Society of Nigeria*, 1/1 (1956), 5–14 · K. O. Dike, *Trade and politics in the Niger delta, 1830–1885* (1956) · J. F. A. Ajayi, *Christian missions in Nigeria, 1841–1891* (1965) · *Journal of the Royal Geographical Society*, 25 (1855), lxxxiv · R. A. Stafford, *Scientist of empire: Sir Roderick Murchison, scientific exploration and Victorian imperialism* (1989) · J. B. King, 'Details of

explorations of the Old Calabar River in 1841 and 1842', *Journal of the Royal Geographical Society*, 14 (1844), 260–83

Beedome, Thomas (*d.* in or before 1641), poet, was the author of *Poems Divine and Humane*, published posthumously in 1641. The collection was edited by Henry Glapthorne, the dramatist and occasional poet, whose brief prose address 'to the reader' commends the text as a living monument to Beedome's worth. This is followed by a series of complimentary verses composed by Glapthorne (in English and Latin), the dramatist and masque writer Thomas Nabbes, and the poet's brother, Francis Beedome, among others. The chief poem in the sequence 'The Jealous Lover, or, The Constant Maid' uses six-line stanzas to relate a classical romantic tale. The main part of the volume consists of songs, epistles, epigrams, elegies, and devotional poems. Some of the verses are acknowledged to have been influenced by Ben Jonson, and others are addressed 'to Sir Henry Wotten, Knight', George Wither, William Harrington, and William Pearle. The poet John Donne, 'an Eversary', is celebrated in an epigram, as are the geographical discoveries of Thomas Janes, and the achievements of the late king of Sweden.

A number of phrases in the commendatory verses suggest that Beedome died at an early age, and little is known of his life. He did, however, contribute a sixteen-line commendatory verse to Robert Farley's *Lychnocansia … Lights Morall Emblems*, printed in 1638. In 1657 the poet Henry Bold produced *Wit a Sporting in a Pleasant Grove of New Fancies*. The first thirty-two pages borrow heavily from Beedome's earlier work.

A. H. BULLEN, *rev.* ELIZABETH HARESNAPE

Sources T. Beedome, *Poems divine and humane* (1641) · T. Corser, *Collectanea Anglo-poetica, or, A … catalogue of a … collection of early English poetry*, 2, Chetham Society, 55 (1861)

Beeke, Henry (1751–1837), writer on taxation and finance, was born at Kingsteignton, Devon, on 6 January 1751, the son of Christopher Beeke, a Church of England clergyman. He was elected a scholar of Corpus Christi College, Oxford, on May 1769 and was awarded the degrees of BA (1773), MA (1776), BD (1785), and DD (1800). At Oxford he was also made a fellow of Oriel College in 1775 and junior proctor in 1784, and he was regius professor of modern history between 1801 and 1813. His church career simultaneously progressed through the posts of vicar of St Mary the Virgin, Oxford (1762), rector of Ufton Norcot, Berkshire (1789), dean of Bristol (1813), and vicar of Weare (1819).

Beeke acquired a sound reputation as a fiscal authority with his *Observations on the produce of the income tax, and on its proportion to the whole income of Great Britain* (1799), which was reprinted in an expanded form in 1800. This book was written amid debate on the consequences of the introduction of an income tax. Taxes had risen notably throughout the eighteenth century, mainly in order to finance military expansion and to service the growing national debt. Unprecedented demands upon the national purse, stemming from the war with revolutionary France, led William Pitt in 1799 to seek further sources of revenue in the form of a new and untested tax upon incomes above £50. Many interests opposed the new tax and predicted chaos in its wake. State statistical compilations were in their infancy and a large margin of error was a constant feature of debates. Even such elementary totals as the population and the surface area of the country were subject to guesswork. It was here that Beeke's work shone and established his reputation for accurate estimates amid a bewildering array of competing calculations. Arthur Young, the secretary to the board of agriculture and a respected public commentator, for instance, had estimated the total surface area of England and Wales to be 47 million acres with some 40 million of these under cultivation. This was a serious overestimate on both counts, as Beeke was able to demonstrate. Pitt himself had assumed that the new tax would bring to the exchequer £7 million. Again, Beeke revised this figure down to £6.2 million. From these calculations Beeke argued that, even if the income tax did produce less revenue than projected, this was not as a result of economic weakness. 'On the contrary', he argued, 'we are more powerful, have resources more permanent, a population more numerous, and an income more considerable than the most enlarged computations which have been hitherto published' (Beeke, 2nd edn, 2). It should be noted, however, that Beeke too was fallible: he overestimated the population of England and Wales by about 2 million.

Evidence of Beeke's wider interests in economics can be found in his unpublished manuscripts and correspondence. A memorandum on corn prepared for Viscount Sidmouth has sometimes been seen (for example by Salim Rashid) as the first clear statement of the economic theory of the 'Giffen good', the idea that some commodities (bread in Beeke's case) experience increasing demand as their price rises. Nicholas Vansittart, chancellor of the exchequer between 1812 and 1823, valued his correspondence. Lecturing at Oxford in the early nineteenth century, Beeke may have been the first person to teach political economy at that university. His interest in the subject predated this appointment, as demonstrated by a story told of his days as a fellow at Oriel. Arriving early at the Angel Inn for a meeting of his club, Beeke fell into conversation with a travelling merchant. The discussion ranged over the subject of commerce and Beeke impressed his new acquaintance with his informed views upon trade. So much so that upon parting the merchant, unaware of his academic status, thanked him for his information and inquired 'pray, sir, may I ask if you are not in the carpet line?' (Felix Farley's Bristol Journal, 25 March 1837). He died at Torquay on 9 March 1837.   R. D. SHELDON

Sources H. Beeke, *Observations on the produce of the income tax, and on its proportion to the whole income of Great Britain* (1799) · H. Beeke, *Observations on the produce of the income tax, and on its proportion to the whole income of Great Britain*, 2nd edn (1800) · S. Rashid, 'The Beeke good: a note on the origin of the "Giffen good"', *History of Political Economy*, 11 (1979), 606–7 · *Felix Farley's Bristol Journal* (18 March 1837) · *Felix Farley's Bristol Journal* (25 March 1837)
Archives BL, corresp. with N. Vansittart, Add. MS 31229, fols. 7–20, 67, 69, 75, 84; Add. MS 31230, fols. 117, 121, 124, 126, 372; Add. MS 31231, fols. 228, 232, 260; Add. MS 31231, *passim* · Devon RO, corresp. with Viscount Sidmouth, 152M/C1800/OG4

Beekman, Yolande Elsa Maria (1911–1944). *See under* Women agents on active service in France (*act.* 1942–1945).

Beer, Esmond Samuel de (1895–1990), historian and benefactor, was born on 15 September 1895 in Dunedin, South Island, New Zealand, the second son and fourth and youngest child of Isidore Samuel de Beer (1860–1934), merchant, and his wife, Emily (1864–1930), daughter of Bendix Hallenstein. His family on both sides was Jewish (though his maternal grandmother came of Lincolnshire farming stock) and had reached New Zealand from Germany, by way of Australia, during the 1860s, in his grandfather's generation. The continuing success of Hallensteins, the family clothing chain, gave him ample means for a life of private research in England, where he lived from his schooldays onward; it was never necessary for him to hold a salaried post. After early schooling in Dunedin he attended Mill Hill School, London, from 1910 to 1914, in which year he went up to New College, Oxford, to read history. After army service, first in the ranks of the Oxfordshire and Buckinghamshire light infantry and then as a lieutenant in the 2nd battalion 35th Sikh regiment of the Indian army (1916–19), he returned to Oxford, taking a special wartime BA in 1920 (MA 1925). He then studied at University College, London, and in 1923 received a London MA for a thesis on political parties during the ministry of Thomas Osborne, first earl of Danby (1631–1712).

The later seventeenth century remained de Beer's lifelong intellectual centre. As he wrote of his mentor, Sir Charles Firth, whose assistant he became, he was at home there and almost on terms of friendship with its men and women. He built up a large private library, most of which was dispersed by gift, chiefly to the University of Otago in Dunedin, in the 1980s, when he could himself no longer use it. An omnivorous reader, he retained so well what he read that, in his last bedridden years when his sight had failed, he could pass time by recalling it verbatim. Together with his sisters, Mary (1890–1981) and Dora (1891–1982), his companions in a succession of London houses, he acquired a small but well-chosen art collection, which he gave to the Dunedin Public Art Gallery in 1982. He and his sisters had already given Iolo A. Williams's library of eighteenth-century English literature to the university and made a succession of other substantial gifts to the Dunedin Public Art Gallery and the Otago Museum.

De Beer's scholarly reputation derived from his editions of the diary of John Evelyn and the correspondence of John Locke. They were carried through virtually singlehanded, despite the impression given by the punctilio of his acknowledgements. Taken together, they provide a remarkable overview of the cultural and intellectual milieu of their time, being marked by an easy mastery of bibliographical, biographical, literary, and historical skills as well as of the circumstances of living in and out of seventeenth-century England. Their editor's curiosity and his conviction that the treatment of any topic should be complete, as far as its carefully weighed merits allowed, exactly balance his feeling for conciseness and his passion for eliminating the otiose. He began work on Evelyn in the late 1920s by revising an existing transcript. Early in the 1930s he was formally invited by the Clarendon Press to prepare their edition. As published in 1955 the six volumes are the first satisfactory rendering of the diary and its author: a full and scrupulous text, sustained by an introduction and appendices and by some 12,000 footnotes, the whole made accessible by a large and exemplary index. Separately published by-products were magisterial essays on the origin and diffusion of the term 'Gothic', the development of the European guidebook, and the early history of London street lighting.

In 1956, after the task had been refused by another scholar, de Beer began the second great instalment of his life's work, his Clarendon Press edition of Locke's correspondence. He himself brought together much of the material. When its first two volumes appeared in 1976 he was already past eighty, but he followed them punctually with five more before his health began seriously to decline in 1982. The eighth, completing the record of some 3650 items, came out in 1989.

De Beer's direct services to scholarship were supplemented by unstinting generosity to institutions, societies, and individuals, for preference through intermediaries, in his lifetime and by bequest. He gave generous and judicious support to the Bodleian, British, and London libraries, where he was a regular reader; his subsidies ensured the publication of John Cawte Beaglehole's edition of the journals of Captain James Cook and the Anglo-Australian edition of Cook's charts and views. He was both benefactor and practical helper of the Royal Historical Society, the Historical Association, the Bibliographical Society, and the London Topographical Society. Two London University institutes engaged his special loyalty: he was honorary librarian at the Institute of Historical Research (1940–45), and he and his sisters established at the Warburg Institute a fund in memory of Fritz Saxl. He was an honorary fellow of New College, Oxford (1959), and the Warburg (1978), and a fellow of the Royal Historical Society (1927), the Society of Antiquaries (1942), the Royal Society of Literature (1958), and University College, London (1967), as well as being vice-president (1966) and president (1972–8) of the Hakluyt Society and vice-president of the Cromwell Association (1980). He held honorary doctorates from the universities of Durham (1956), Oxford (1957), and Otago (1963), and he was a trustee of the National Portrait Gallery (1959–67) and a member of the Reviewing Committee on the Export of Works of Art (1965–70). In 1965 he was elected a fellow of the British Academy and in 1969 was appointed CBE.

De Beer valued such recognitions. He prized more highly, however, the private, individual state which allowed him freedom personally and vicariously to advance learning. By disposition bookish, shy, and a little stiff, mildly pedantic, and deliberate and precise in manner and speech, he was also courteous, friendly, and humorous. He had a knowledgeable love of comfort, food, wine, and travel, especially in Italy. His physical stamina matched his scholarly tenacity. A tireless walker and a climber, he took special pleasure in the far south of the South Island of New Zealand and the island of Raasay near Skye in Scotland, where he spent summer holidays in company with his sisters and others. He had a wide acquaintance with literature, particularly drama, Shakespeare and Ibsen being two of his heroes, and with music, principally opera. In adult life he neither practised the Jewish religion nor adopted another. De Beer's aspect was dapper and benevolent: he had a small moustache and wore spectacles. Of middle height, he was broadshouldered but thinnish in build, with a large and powerful head. A confirmed and lifelong bachelor, he died on 3 October 1990 in Stoke House, a residential home for the aged in Stoke Hammond, near Milton Keynes, north Buckinghamshire. J. B. Trapp, *rev.*

Sources M. Strachan, *Esmond de Beer (1895–1990), scholar and benefactor: a personal memoir, with a bibliography by J. S. G. Simmons* (1995) • J. Simmons, 'Esmond Samuel de Beer, 1895–1990', *PBA*, 94 (1997), 415–25 • C. Brasch, *Indirections: a memoir, 1909–1947* (1980) • J. S. G. Simmons, *Esmond Samuel de Beer (1895–1990): obituary notices and a bibliography* (1990) • R. Notman, 'Esmond de Beer, patron of the arts', *Bulletin of New Zealand Art History*, 15 (1994), 33–54 • addresses given at a memorial meeting at the Warburg Institute, London, 6 Dec 1990

Archives Bodl. Oxf., MSS • Oxford University Press • University of Otago, MSS

Likenesses photograph, 1965, NPG; repro. in Strachan, *Esmond de Beer* • A. Stones, bronze sculpture, 1983, University of Otago Library, Dunedin; repro. in Strachan, *Esmond de Beer* • photographs, repro. in Strachan, *Esmond de Beer* • photographs, Bodl. Oxf., De Beer MSS • photographs, repro. in Simmons, 'Esmond Samuel de Beer, 1895–1990' • photographs, repro. in Simmons, *Esmond Samuel de Beer: obituary notices*

Wealth at death £899,072: probate, 28 Jan 1991, *CGPLA Eng. & Wales*

Beer, Sir Gavin Rylands de (1899–1972), zoologist and historian, was born on 1 November 1899 at Malden, Surrey, the only son and elder child of Herbert Chaplin de Beer, journalist, and his wife, Mabel. Herbert was the son of Arnold de Beer and Irene Chaplin and his wife was the daughter of John Rylands and Anne Chaplin (sister of Irene).

The nature of his father's job meant the young de Beer was widely travelled. He was educated by tutor and governesses, and attended the École Pascal in Paris for three years (1909–12). He also attended Harrow School, from which he won a leaving scholarship, and in 1917 he went with a demyship to Magdalen College, Oxford. After one term de Beer became a second lieutenant in the Grenadier Guards and was posted to France, but saw no fighting, and served in the army education scheme in the army of occupation.

Returning to Oxford in 1919 de Beer took first-class honours in zoology in 1921. He taught in the zoology department at Oxford until 1938, as demonstrator and, from 1926, Jenkinson memorial lecturer in embryology. He also became a prize fellow of Merton College (1923) and subwarden. In 1925 he married Cicely Glyn, daughter of the

Sir Gavin Rylands de Beer (1899–1972), by Elliott & Fry, 1950

Revd Sir Hubert James Medlycott, sixth baronet, and Julia Ann Glyn. They had no children.

In 1938 de Beer became reader in embryology, and in 1945 professor, at University College, London. During the Second World War he served on the general staff, dealing with military intelligence and propaganda, and later in the Supreme Headquarters Allied Expeditionary Force (SHAEF), as lieutenant-colonel in charge of psychological warfare in the field. After the Normandy landings in 1944 he was concerned with supervising amplifier and leaflet units. In 1950 de Beer was appointed director of the British Museum (Natural History), and in 1958 president of the Fifteenth International Congress of Zoology. After his retirement in 1960 he became director of a publishing firm. He lived at Bex in Switzerland from 1965 to 1971.

De Beer was an international scholar, both as a scientist and a humanist. As a boy he had visited many countries and was fluent in French, German, and Italian; he read widely and had a good memory. His major scientific work was on the structure of the skull. His treatise *The Development of the Vertebrate Skull* (1937) contained many anatomical facts but hardly mentioned function, and revealed no new principles of morphology. He was interested in the early experiments on the development of embryos and his books *Growth* (1924) and *An Introduction to Experimental Embryology* (1926) were successful pioneer summaries. His most influential scientific writing was his analysis of the relationship between the development of the embryo and evolutionary change. In his book *Embryology and Evolution* (1930) he demolished the theory of recapitulation.

De Beer was also interested in evolution. As director of the British Museum, he organized the exhibits on evolution in the main hall and arranged for the publication of an authoritative *Atlas of Evolution* (1964), which was translated into German, Dutch, and Spanish. He was an expert on the life and works of Charles Darwin and devised a card index from which he could tell what Darwin was studying at any time. This led to an edition of *Darwin's Notebooks on the Transmutation of Species* (1960), and *Charles Darwin* (1963).

De Beer also wrote on humanism, covering subjects as diverse as Gibbon, Voltaire, Byron, Shelley, and Madame de Staël. His *Jean-Jacques Rousseau and his World* (1972) was published posthumously. He was fascinated by Switzerland and its people. He wrote many books and papers on tourism, climbing, and the history in that country, including *Alps and Elephants: Hannibal's March* (1955).

De Beer was of small stature, but assertive in character. With his pleasure in using his knowledge of languages and of historical matters he was a vivacious and interesting companion.

De Beer was elected to fellowship of the Royal Society in 1940 and from 1946 to 1949 was president of the Linnean Society. He was a chevalier of the Légion d'honneur, held honorary doctorates at the universities of Bordeaux, Lausanne, and Cambridge, and received the Darwin medal of the Royal Society (1958) and also the gold medal of the Linnean Society (1958). He was knighted in 1954 and was FSA. He died at The Star inn, Alfriston, Polegate, Sussex, on 21 June 1972.   JOHN YOUNG, *rev.*

Sources E. J. W. Barrington, *Memoirs FRS*, 19 (1973), 65–93 · W. T. Stearn, *The Natural History Museum at South Kensington: a history of the British Museum (Natural History), 1753–1980* (1981) · personal knowledge (1986)

Archives King's Lond., notebooks and papers · King's Lond., Liddell Hart C. · NHM, TS atlas of evolution · U. Oxf., department of zoology, zoological corresp. and papers · UCL, corresp. and papers | Bodl. Oxf., corresp. with C. D. Darlington · NHM, corresp. with W. R. Dawson · Rice University, Houston, Texas, Woodson Research Center, corresp. with Sir Julian Huxley · Wolfson College, Oxford, corresp. with H. B. D. Kettlewell

Likenesses Elliott & Fry, photograph, 1950, NPG [*see illus.*] · W. Stoneman, photograph, 1955, NPG · photograph, repro. in *Memoirs FRS*, 65

Wealth at death £53,921: administration with will, 19 Dec 1972, *CGPLA Eng. & Wales*

Beer, Patricia (1919–1999), poet, was born in Exmouth, Devon, on 4 November 1919, the younger daughter of Andrew William Beer, a railway clerk at Exeter station, and his wife, Harriet Jeffery (d. 1935), a schoolteacher. She grew up in the nearby village of Withycombe Raleigh. One of her grandfathers was a mason specializing in tombstones; the other made coffins. She referred in her writing, with mournful humour, to her early acquaintance with the language of death and memorials. She was brought up in the stern religion of the Plymouth Brethren, to which her parents belonged; the inculcation of its inward-looking Christianity, especially by her mother, affected her deeply. She described it compellingly in her memoir of childhood, *Mrs Beer's House* (1968). Though she left the faith behind her, religious metaphors and the cadences of hymns and prayers returned in her poetry.

After a local primary education Patricia Beer won a scholarship to Exmouth grammar school (where she continued after the death of her dominant mother), and took a first-class degree in English at Exeter University. Her family expected her to train as a teacher, but instead in 1941 she went to St Hugh's College, Oxford, to take a BLitt. This marked a break with her family and with the religion in which she grew up. She then went to Italy, where she lived for several years, teaching English literature at the University of Padua (1947–9), the British Institute in Rome (1949–51), and the Ministero della Aeronautica, Rome (1951–3). She returned to England in 1953 to a series of temporary jobs which supported her as she began writing poetry. She published her first book, *The Loss of the Magyar*, in 1953; she later regarded with candid embarrassment the 'lush and loose' poems from this and her second book, *The Survivors* (1963). Few works from these volumes were included in her *Collected Poems* (1988). She returned to academia in 1962, becoming lecturer in English at Goldsmiths' College, London. She taught there until 1968, when she became a full-time writer. *Reader, I married him* (1974) was a product of her work at Goldsmiths': a study of the lives of Victorian women novelists and their fictional creations, it enjoyed considerable success.

After a short-lived marriage to the literary scholar Philip Nicholas Furbank, Beer in 1964 married (John) Damien Parsons, an architect, with whom she refurbished a Tudor farmhouse at Up Ottery, near Honiton, in Devon. They lived there for the rest of her life. Every few years she published a small collection of poetry: *The Resurrection* (1967), *The Estuary* (1971), *Driving West* (1975), *Poems* (1979), and *The Lie of the Land* (1983); the last received particular critical praise. Her poetry, always informed by a strong sense of place, came increasingly to re-imagine her own local history. An admirer of Wordsworth and Hardy, she drew a good deal on her personal topography in the collections published in the 1970s and 1980s. Her verse was characterized by wry melancholy and astringent irony; the poet Carol Rumens called her 'a religious poet stripped of the blurring consolations of religion' (*The Times*). Her last collections of poetry were *Friend of Heraclitus* (1993) and *Autumn* (1997), the latter dwelling on illness, age, and mortality, but more often droll than sad, and returning to the careful but simple stanza patterns and unobtrusive but controlling rhyme schemes of her earlier work.

Beer also published a historical novel, *Moon's Ottery* (1978), set in Elizabethan Devon, and reviewed for *The Listener* in the 1960s and latterly for the *Daily Telegraph*, the *Times Literary Supplement*, and the *London Review of Books*. A collection of her longer reviews entitled *As I was Saying* was published posthumously in 2002, edited by Sarah Rigby. Patricia Beer died at Up Ottery on 15 August 1999, survived by her husband.   JOHN MULLAN

Sources T. Chevalier, *Contemporary poets*, 5th edn (1991) · P. Beer, *Mrs Beer's house* (1968) · P. Beer, *Collected poems* (1988) · *The Times* (18 Aug 1999) · *The Guardian* (19 Aug 1999) · *The Independent* (26 Aug 1999) · *Daily Telegraph* (17 Aug 1999) · *The Scotsman* (25 Aug 1999)

Archives NRA, corresp. and literary papers | SOUND BL NSA, performance recordings
Likenesses photograph, repro. in *The Times* · photograph, repro. in *The Guardian* · photograph, repro. in *The Independent* · photograph, repro. in *Daily Telegraph*

Beer [*née* Sassoon], **Rachel** (1858–1927), newspaper proprietor and editor, was born in Bombay, India, the middle child and only daughter of Sassoon David Sassoon (1832–1867), a Jewish merchant, and his wife, Farha, *née* Reuben (*b.* 1828). Rachel's father arrived in England towards the end of 1858 to manage the London branch of the family business, followed a few months later by his wife and their two children. They chose Ashley Park estate in Surrey to be their family home.

The merchant dynasty of the Sassoons originated in Iraq. The family was often described as 'the Rothschilds of the East' (Jackson, 1); their wealth was derived from trading in cotton, opium, and other goods in China and the Far East. Rachel's mother became absorbed in 'romantic pretensions to culture and gentility' after her husband's death (ibid., 73). A determined matriarch, she had a temper and wit to match, though she was not unknown for her generous, somewhat indulgent gestures. Farha ostracized her younger son Alfred for marrying a non-Jew, the first member of the family to do so. His name was never again mentioned in her presence.

Rachel Sassoon was small in build, with 'an ivory skin envied by her sallower kinswomen' (Jackson, 74). Gentle and compassionate, she had no time for the hearty young men who sought her company at social gatherings. Instead, she took up unpaid hospital nursing. Despite her mother's threats she continued to visit Alfred and his wife, Theresa Thornycroft, and their growing family. Their younger son, and Rachel's favourite nephew, was the future poet Siegfried *Sassoon (1886–1967).

Approaching thirty, with perhaps a fear of spinsterhood, in 1887 Rachel announced her engagement to the gentile Frederick Arthur Beer (*d.* 1903). Frederick was 'small and dapper', with a gentle smile and 'a brownish beard curling silkily over his cravat' (Jackson, 79). He was the son of Julius Beer who, like the Rothschilds, had come from Frankfurt. Through dealings on the stock exchange in London, Julius had become very wealthy: his son inherited an income of £20,000 a year, as well as ownership of *The Observer* (which his father had acquired as an outlet for his views on international relations, rather than as a profitable business). The couple married on 4 August 1887 at Chelsea parish church. W. E. Gladstone and his wife were present, and signed the marriage register as witnesses. The Beers settled at 7 Chesterfield Gardens, Mayfair, a house with a fine Adam staircase. Unfortunately, it soon became clear that Frederick Beer was ill: he suffered from 'strange "headaches" which suddenly made this mild man … irritable or, at times, feverishly gay' (Jackson, 80). Although not then diagnosed, his illness was probably caused by syphilis, his symptoms being those common to the early stages of general paralysis of the insane. Despite Frederick's illness, the splendours of visits to Chesterfield Gardens were much enjoyed by Rachel's nephews, and memorably described by Siegfried Sassoon in *The Old Century and Seven More Years* (1938).

Despite her husband's illness, Rachel Beer began to write articles for *The Observer* and eventually took over as editor. In October 1893 she ambitiously purchased the *Sunday Times*, then an eight-page penny newspaper, for £11,000 and also edited this. Though not considered a brilliant editor, Rachel Beer came to be known in Fleet Street for her 'occasional flair and business-like decisions' (Jackson, 95). She insisted on the need for an objective political approach by the *Sunday Times* and orchestrated one of the major journalistic scoops of 1898: Major Esterhazy's confession of forgery against Dreyfus. A known Jewish newspaper owner, Rachel Beer bravely endured vilification for her pro-Dreyfus stance.

Frederick Beer's mental and physical state was still bad, if not deteriorating: he insisted, for example, on having the Beer family crest clipped out on his black poodle's back. Rachel herself was writing book reviews, occasional features, and leaders. The latter she would write in an indecipherable hand and have delivered at the eleventh hour by a footman, to the annoyance of her sub-editors.

Frederick Beer's death in 1903 left Rachel distraught for months, and eventually led to her own breakdown. Strange leading articles began to appear in *The Observer* and the *Sunday Times* on subjects such as the advantages of cannibalism, and her ability to cope apparently collapsed halfway through an editorial for *The Observer* with a 'continued in the next' (Jackson, 115). In 1904 Rachel Beer was certified and committed to the care of the commissioners of lunacy. Both newspapers were sold by her trustees in the course of 1904.

Although Rachel Beer gradually recovered her mental health, she continued to need nursing care until the end of her days. She was allowed to buy Chancellor House, an imposing residence in Tunbridge Wells, and lived there with a butler and servants, in addition to her nurses. Although often too ill to receive visitors, she allowed local charities to make use of the house and grounds when needed. She acquired a fine organ and occasionally gave performances for a few friends in her drawing-room.

Rachel Beer died at Chancellor House, Tunbridge Wells, on 29 April 1927. Her favourite nephew, Siegfried Sassoon, received a legacy of £30,000 from her estate, and in his library at Heytesbury House in Wiltshire later kept a splendid oil painting of her over the fireplace.

VANESSA CURNEY

Sources S. Jackson, *The Sassoons: portrait of a dynasty*, 2nd edn (1989) · S. Sassoon, *The old century and seven more years* (1986) · H. Hobson, P. Knightley, and L. Russell, *The pearl of days: an intimate memoir of the Sunday Times, 1822–1972* (1972) · private information (2004) · m. cert. · d. cert. · *CGPLA Eng. & Wales* (1927)
Likenesses H. T. Jones, portrait
Wealth at death £318,283 12s. 4d.: administration, 9 July 1927, *CGPLA Eng. & Wales*

Beerbohm, Sir Henry Maximilian [Max] (1872–1956), caricaturist and writer, was born at 57 Palace Gardens Terrace, London, on 24 August 1872 and was baptized on 16 October at the church of All Saints, Kensington. His

Sir Henry Maximilian [Max] **Beerbohm (1872–1956)**, by Sir William Nicholson, 1905

father, Julius Ewald Edward Beerbohm (1810–1892), of Dutch, Lithuanian, and German origin, had come to England about 1830 and set up as a prosperous corn merchant. He married an Englishwoman, Constantia Draper, and the couple had four children. When Constantia died, Beerbohm married her sister, Eliza (d. 1918), with whom he had five children, three of whom survived. Max was their youngest child.

Education and early years From 1881 to 1885 Max—he was always called simply Max and it is thus that he signed his drawings—attended the day school of a Mr Wilkinson in Orme Square. Mr Wilkinson, Max said, 'gave me my love of Latin and thereby enabled me to write English' (Rothenstein, 370–71). Mrs Wilkinson taught drawing to the students, the only lessons Max ever had in the subject. In 1885 he entered Charterhouse School, where, in spite of his aversion to athletics, he seems to have been reasonably happy, even though he later wrote: 'My delight in having been at Charterhouse was far greater than my delight in being there ... I always longed to be grown-up!' (Beerbohm, *Mainly on the Air*, 151, 154). At Charterhouse he found pleasure and escape in reading, especially Thackeray (who had himself gone to Charterhouse and was also an illustrator). And he took to drawing caricatures, of other boys, of the schoolmasters, and of public figures, especially the prince of Wales, later Edward VII.

In 1890 Max went up to Merton College, Oxford, to study classics. He loved Oxford. 'Undergraduates,' he wrote, 'owe their happiness chiefly to the consciousness that they are no longer at school. The nonsense which was knocked out of them at school is all put gently back at Oxford or Cambridge' (Beerbohm, *More*, 156). Max found 'this little city of learning and laughter' the perfect place for the development of his dandyism, his aestheticism, his distinctive spectator persona. At Merton, Max came to know the man who was to be his dearest friend, the novelist Reggie Turner. Through Turner, Max became friends with Oscar Wilde and his inner circle, which comprised art critic Robert Ross, Lord Alfred Douglas, and Turner. In Max's third year at university, the artist William Rothenstein arrived from Paris to draw portraits of Oxford 'characters' (eventually including Max among them). Rothenstein became another close and life-long friend.

Max's career as a professional caricaturist began when he was twenty: in 1892 the *Strand* magazine published a series of his drawings of 'club types'—thirty-six in all. Their publication dealt, Max said, 'a great, an almost mortal blow to my modesty' (M. Beerbohm, 'When 9 was nineteen', *Strand Magazine*, October 1946, 51). In 1893 Rothenstein introduced him to the publisher John Lane, who was about to launch *The Yellow Book*. Max contributed essays to its first and later volumes. He also wrote for other publications, and he drew caricatures for *The Yellow Book*, *Pick-Me-Up*, *Sketch*, and the *Pall Mall Budget*. Then in 1896 he published, under the imprint of John Lane, a collection of essays, disarmingly named *The Works of Max Beerbohm*, and, under the imprint of Leonard Smithers, a collection of drawings, *Caricatures of Twenty-Five Gentlemen*. He was famous at twenty-four.

Max never made much money. A freelance writer and artist, he held only one regular job in his lifetime: from 1898 to 1910 he was drama critic for the *Saturday Review*, on the recommendation of his predecessor, George Bernard Shaw. Max's first column explained with nice irony how unfit he was for the position: although from his very cradle he had been at the fringe of the theatre world because of his elder half-brother, Herbert Beerbohm *Tree, one of London's foremost actor–managers, he himself had no great love for drama. He consoled himself with the thought that other callings, such as that of porter in the underground railway, were more uncomfortable and dispiriting than that of theatre critic: 'Whenever I feel myself sinking under the stress of my labours, I shall say to myself, I am not a porter on the Underground Railway' (Beerbohm, *Around Theatres*, 4). But in time he grew into an able, discerning, and demanding critic of the London theatre.

Max's personal life was peculiar. For a time in 1893 he had a sentimental crush on a happily unobtainable fifteen-year-old music-hall star, Cissie Loftus. In 1895 he became vaguely attached to Grace Connover, an actress in his brother's theatre company (Max nicknamed her Kilseen, for killing scenes on stage). The 'engagement' lingered for eight years before dying out. Next, in 1903, he became briefly engaged to another actress, Constance Collier, a successful, glamorous leading lady, again from his brother's theatre company; she broke off the engagement after a few months. In 1904 he met and became much taken with an American actress, Florence Kahn (*d.* 1951),

the only daughter of a Jewish family from Memphis, Tennessee. By 1908 they were engaged. On 4 May 1910 Max and Florence were married at the Paddington register office; he quit his post at the *Saturday Review*, and went to live the rest of his life in the Villino Chiaro, a small house on the coast road overlooking the Mediterranean at Rapallo, Italy. Max and his wife seem to have had a thoroughly happy life together. There has been speculation that he was a non-active homosexual, that his marriage was never consummated, that he was a 'natural celibate' (Hall, *Max Beerbohm: a Kind of Life*, 120–21). The fact is, not much is known of Max's private life.

The writer By the time Max had married, retired from London, and settled in Italy, his position as one of England's foremost essayists was firmly in place. As early as 1898 Shaw had, famously, pronounced Max 'incomparable' (G. B. Shaw, *Our Theatres in the Nineties*, 1931, 25.407). As a writer he had progressed towards a relaxed natural style. The early influence of Oscar Wilde on his prose, the constant paradoxes, the showiness, the over-cleverness had for the most part disappeared. By the turn of the century Max had found a surer, more distinctive voice, a prose distinguished by clarity and grace. The essays collected as *Yet Again* (1909) exemplified this style. But Max's writing attained even greater success with his next four books: in 1911 he published to great critical acclaim his only novel, *Zuleika Dobson*. This fantasy about the beautiful young woman whose visit to Oxford occasions the suicide of all the undergraduates has proved his most popular prose work; it has been the most continuously in print of all his books. An expanded edition, *The Illustrated Zuleika Dobson*, appeared in 1985. *Zuleika Dobson* was included in the 1998 controversial Modern Library list of '100 best novels' of the twentieth century, ranking fifty-ninth (*New York Times*, 20 July 1998). In 1912 Max published a collection of seventeen parodies of contemporary writers, *A Christmas Garland* (new edn 1993), and again the critical reception was impressive: Filson Young, for example, writing in the *Saturday Review*, said: 'He has not only parodied the style of his Authors, but their minds also' (9 Nov 1912, 578–9); and the *New York Times* proclaimed: 'Max has reached the Olympian heights of great satire' (25 Jan 1913, 32). In 1919 he published *Seven Men*, his collection of short stories or 'memories', including 'Enoch Soames'. (The title character, a decadent 'Catholic Diabolist' poet of the 1890s, sells his soul to the Devil in exchange for the privilege of visiting the British Museum reading room 100 years later, at which time he hoped to find that posterity had been kind to his reputation. His eagerly awaited 'appearance' on 3 June 1997 caused a stir in the London press.) In 1920 Max's last book of collected familiar essays, *And even now*, crowned his work in his favourite genre; it included such frequently anthologized titles as 'No. 2 The Pines' (on visiting Swinburne in the poet's old age), 'Hosts and Guests', 'A Clergyman' (on a minor figure in Boswell's *Life* of Samuel Johnson), and 'Laughter'. Among the encomiums heaped upon him as essayist, Virginia Woolf's is representative: Max is the 'prince of his profession', someone who brought 'personality' into that genre for the first time since Montaigne and Charles Lamb (V. Woolf, *The Common Reader*, 1925, 216). Privately, she wrote to Max: 'If you knew how I had pored over your essays—how they fill me with marvel—how I can't conceive what it would be like to write as you do!' (*Letters*, 29 Jan 1928, 167).

The caricaturist Max's reputation as a caricaturist was if anything higher than that as an essayist. In the late 1890s his drawing had also developed: it became more subtle, more intricate, more understated, the general softening of tone owing much to the addition of light colour washes, something Will Rothenstein had urged on him. Max himself remarked that as he got older (on into his late twenties) he found that his two arts—his 'two dissimilar sisters'—were growing more like each other: his drawing had become 'more delicate and artful ... losing something of its pristine boldness and savagery', while his writing, 'though it never will be bold or savage, is easier in style, less ornate, than it used to be' (typescript, Merton College, Oxford). Max's was one of those rare talents equally distinguished in two arts. His sister arts sometimes come together in those of his drawings with more or less lengthy captions. A drawing, for example, of a clowning and self-satisfied G. B. Shaw bears the legend: 'Magnetic, he has the power to infect almost everyone with the delight he takes in himself.' Another, *London in November and Mr Henry James in London*, shows James, enveloped in a London fog, holding his hand up in front of his face; the legend, an adroit parody of the Master's style, reads:

It was, therefore, not without something of a shock that he, in this to him so very congenial atmosphere, now perceived that a vision of the hand which he had, at a venture, held up within an inch or so of his eyes was, with an almost awful clarity being adumbrated ...

Max once described caricature as 'the delicious art of exaggerating, without fear or favour, the peculiarities of this or that human body, for the mere sake of exaggeration' (Beerbohm, *A Variety*, 119). He admitted privately that he hoped also to get at the 'soul' of a man, but through the body:

When I draw a man, I am concerned simply and solely with the physical aspect of him ... [But] I see him in a peculiar way: I see all his salient points exaggerated (points of face, figure, port, gesture and vesture), and all his insignificant points proportionately diminished ... In the salient points a man's soul does reveal itself, more or less faintly ... It is ... when (and only when) my caricatures hit exactly the exteriors of their subjects that they open the interiors, too. (*Letters*, 35–6)

The perfect caricature, Max explained, must be

the exaggeration of the whole creature, from top to toe. ... The whole man must be melted down, as in a crucible, and then, as from the solution, be fashioned anew. He must emerge with not one particle of himself lost, yet with not a particle of himself as it was before. (Beerbohm, *A Variety*, 127–8)

Moreover, the caricaturist does not exaggerate this or that salient point deliberately: he 'exaggerates instinctively, unconsciously' (ibid., 124). Accordingly, Max believed that the caricaturist should never draw from the life because he would be 'bound by the realities of it' (ibid., 128). His own manner of operation was to stare at a person for a few moments and draw him later—that evening, or many evenings, or even years, later.

Max's first public showing had been at the Fine Art Society's exhibition in 1896, 'A century and a half of English humorous art, from Hogarth to the present day', to which he contributed six caricatures. His first one-man show was at the Carfax Gallery in 1901. By 1904, the year of his second published book of caricatures, *The Poets' Corner*, and of his second one-man exhibition at the Carfax Gallery, the *Athenaeum* was calling him 'our one and only caricaturist' (28 May 1904, 695). After two more Carfax exhibitions, in 1907 and 1908, Max contributed to four group shows at the New English Art Club, 1909–11. Thereafter, he exhibited his work exclusively at the Leicester Galleries, first in 1911. By the time of the second such show, in 1913, *The Times* confidently acclaimed Max 'the greatest of English comic artists' (12 April 1913, 6). Six more Leicester Galleries exhibitions followed during his lifetime, in 1921, 1923, 1925, 1928, 1945, and 1952. Almost the only complaint heard among the reviewers was the occasional one that he was not a draughtsman, but the objection was almost always followed by a retreat. One reviewer in 1913 said:

There is, of course, a negligible sense in which [Max] is no draughtsman. He does not, perhaps cannot, and probably does not care to make his figures stand on their feet, or sit in their chairs; yet he is a master of expressive line. (Edward Marsh, *Blue Review*, June 1913, 145)

In 1926 another reviewer wrote:

In terms of aesthetics Mr Beerbohm is not a draughtsman at all; he has a delicate sense of color, decorative felicity ... but he has never learned to draw ... For his own purposes, however, his drawing is consummate ... He has a genius for likenesses; better than anyone else he understands how to convey the attitudes of his subjects ... Add to these humor without venom and refined imagination and you have lifted caricature into the realm of art. (*New York Herald Tribune*, 'Books', 7 Feb 1926, 2)

In 1954 Edmund Wilson judged Max 'the greatest caricaturist of the kind—that is, portrayer of personalities—in the history of art' (Behrman, 262). This assertion, in regard to quantity, certainly, was to find support in the figures set forth in the 1972 Hart-Davis *Catalogue of the Caricatures of Max Beerbohm*: in more than 2000 formal caricatures the artist drew almost 800 'real people'.

Many of the people Max drew he knew personally, and, with a few exceptions—Kipling for one—those he knew he liked, and they liked him. His subjects, or 'targets', included many well-known figures: Oscar Wilde, Thomas Hardy, Henry James, G. B. Shaw, W. B. Yeats, Joseph Conrad, Lytton Strachey, J. A. M. Whistler, Aubrey Beardsley, John Singer Sargent, Augustus John. A few of his subjects he never met: W. E. Gladstone, Benjamin Disraeli, Theodore Roosevelt, Woodrow Wilson, and royalty, including Queen Victoria (Max seldom caricatured women, though he drew the queen at least nine times), Edward VII, George V, Edward VIII. Max also drew innumerable lawyers, musicians, financiers, professors, restaurateurs, sportsmen, newspaper magnates, dandies, tailors, industrialists, landowners. Hundreds of these individuals would be utterly forgotten today, had not Max 'got' them. It is note-worthy, too, that Max often caricatured himself. The Hart-Davis *Catalogue* lists ninety-seven self-caricatures, more entries than for any other subject, Edward VII and George Bernard Shaw being the closest, with seventy-two and sixty-two entries, respectively.

None the less, although most of Max's caricatures are of his contemporaries, he made two major ventures into the past, working from old portraits, drawings, and photographs. The result was some of his most enduring work, and the two most popular of his ten published books of caricatures, *The Poets' Corner* (1904) with subjects ranging from Dante and Shakespeare to Wordsworth and Coleridge and Tennyson and Browning; and *Rossetti and his Circle* (1922, new edn 1987), which offers such notables as A. C. Swinburne, John Ruskin, George Meredith, and William Morris in the company of Max's favourite nineteenth-century personality, the painter/poet Dante Gabriel Rossetti.

Major collections of Max Beerbohm's caricatures are to be found in the Ashmolean Museum, Oxford; the Tate collection; the Victoria and Albert Museum; Charterhouse, Godalming; the Clark Library, University of California; and the Lilly Library, University of Indiana, Bloomington; depositories of both caricatures and archival material include Merton College Library, Oxford; the Harry Ransom Humanities Research Center, University of Texas at Austin; the Robert H. Taylor collection, Princeton University Library; the Houghton Library, Harvard University; and the privately owned Mark Samuels Lasner collection.

Italian years After 1910 Max lived contentedly in Rapallo, as a reclusive English gentleman (he never took the trouble to learn Italian). He returned to England only during the two world wars, and occasionally on personal business, chiefly to arrange exhibitions with the Leicester Galleries. Around 1930 he gave up caricaturing: 'I found that my caricatures were becoming likenesses. I seem to have mislaid my gift for dispraise. Pity crept in. So I gave up caricaturing, except privately' (Behrman, 140).

In 1935 Max began broadcasting for the BBC, reading essays, always as 'an interesting link with the past' (Beerbohm, *Mainly on the Air*, 34). He continued to make fourteen broadcasts in all, right through to the year of his death. Rebecca West said, 'I felt ... that I was listening to the voice of the last civilized man on earth. Max's broadcasts justify the entire invention of broadcasting' (Behrman, 265). But Max wanted no part of television. In 1955 the National Broadcasting Company in New York offered him considerable money to do a series of television talks. A representative of the company visited him in Rapallo:

> You see, Sir Max, it will all be very simple. Our people will come and arrange everything. You will sit, if you like, where you are sitting now. You will simply say, 'My dear friends, I am very happy to be here addressing you.' Max replied, 'Do you wish me to start with a lie?'   (Cecil, 491)

In 1939 George VI offered him a knighthood, and Max, who had so satirized the royal family, gratefully accepted.

The irony of it pleased him. Always the dandy, he took special care with his dress. After the ceremony, he wrote to a friend,

> My costume yesterday was quite all right ... Indeed, I was (or so I thought, as I looked around me) the best-dressed of the Knights, and quite on a level with the Grooms of the Chamber and other palace officials. I'm not sure that I wasn't as presentable as the King himself—*very* charming though he looked.   (typescript, Merton College, Oxford)

In 1942 Max received an honorary degree from his alma mater, Oxford, and in 1945 his old college, Merton, made him an honorary fellow.

In many ways Max, in the latter part of his life, was out of step with the times; he remained a voice from the past. The works of D. H. Lawrence, for example, gave him little pleasure. Although willing to admit Lawrence's 'unquestionable genius', Max thought his prose style 'slovenly' and the man himself 'afflicted with Messiahdom' (Cecil, 483). When shown a copy of Joyce's *Finnegans Wake* shortly before being made Sir Max Beerbohm, he leafed through it and remarked, 'I don't think he will get a knighthood for that!' (ibid., 443). When Edward Marsh wrote to Max to ask if he would allow the Contemporary Art Society to commission Graham Sutherland to paint his portrait, Max declined, telling Marsh that although he had in his time been 'a ruthless monstrifier of men', he was, like the proverbial bully, a coward (*Letters*, 219). Privately, he told Samuel Behrman that in Sutherland's portrait of Somerset Maugham—which Marsh in his letter had held up as a masterpiece—'Maugham looks ... as if he had died of torture' (Behrman, 148–9). Max would have nothing to do with modern psychology or the theories of Freud: 'I adored my father and mother and I adored my brothers and sisters. What kind of complex would they find me the victim of? ... They were a tense and peculiar family, the Oedipuses, weren't they?' (Bacigalupo, 29).

After the death of Max's wife, Florence, in 1951, Elisabeth Jungmann, formerly the personal secretary of the German writer Gerhart Hauptmann, became Max's secretary and companion. On 20 April 1956 Max, from what was to be his deathbed, married her, to ensure that under Italian law she would inherit all his possessions. Max Beerbohm died at Rapallo on 20 May 1956. His body was cremated at Genoa, and the ashes taken to London, where they were interred in St Paul's Cathedral on 29 June.

N. JOHN HALL

Sources N. J. Hall, *Max Beerbohm: a kind of life* (2002) · D. Cecil, *Max: a biography* (1964) · S. N. Behrman, *Portrait of Max: an intimate memoir of Sir Max Beerbohm* (1960) · *Letters of Max Beerbohm, 1892–1956*, ed. R. Hart-Davis (1988) · *Max Beerbohm's letters to Reggie Turner*, ed. R. Hart-Davis (1965) · *Max and Will: Max Beerbohm and William Rothenstein, their friendship and letters, 1893 to 1945*, ed. M. Lago and K. Beckson (1975) · R. Hart-Davis, ed., *A catalogue of the caricatures of Max Beerbohm* (1997) · *The works of Max Beerbohm* (1896) · M. Beerbohm, *More* (1899) · M. Beerbohm, *Yet again* (1909) · M. Beerbohm, *And even now* (1920) · M. Beerbohm, *Mainly on the air* (1957) · M. Beerbohm, *Around theatres*, new edn (1954) · M. Beerbohm, *A variety of things* (1928) · *Siegfried Sassoon letters to Max Beerbohm: with a few answers*, ed. R. Hart-Davis (1986) ·

W. Rothenstein, *Men and memories: recollections of William Rothenstein, 1900–1922* (1932) · G. Bacigalupo, *Ieri a Rapallo* [1992], 29

Archives AM Oxf. · Harvard U., Houghton L., corresp. and papers · Indiana University, Bloomington, Lilly Library, corresp. and drawings · Merton Oxf., corresp. and papers incl. literary MSS and drawings · NRA, priv. coll., corresp. and literary papers · Tate collection · U. Cal., Los Angeles, corresp. and literary papers · V&A · Yale U., Beinecke L., corresp. and literary MSS | BL, corresp. with William Archer, Add. MS 45290 · BL, letters to Lydia and Walter Russell, RP2565 [copies] · BL, letters to George Bernard Shaw, Add. MS 50529 · Bodl. Oxf., corresp. with Sibyl Colefax · Bodl. Oxf., corresp. with Geoffrey Dawson · Bodl. Oxf., letters to the Lewis family and papers · CAC Cam., letters to Cecil Roberts · CUL, letters to Kathleen Bruce · CUL, letters to Lady Kennet · Harvard U., Houghton L., letters to Sir William Rothenstein · priv. coll., corresp. · PRO, letters to J. Ramsay Macdonald, 030/69 · Ransom HRC, corresp. with John Lane · U. Edin. L., letters, mainly to Alfred Wareing · U. Glas. L., letters to D. S. MacColl · U. Leeds, Brotherton L., letters to Edmund Gosse | FILM Ransom HRC | SOUND BL NSA, documentary recordings; performance recordings incl. the BBC broadcasts 'Music halls of my youth', 'Nat Goodwin—and another', 'George Moore', and 'Hethway speaking' · L. Cong., 'First meetings with W. B. Yeats', 'London revisited' · *Sir Max Beerbohm reading his own works*, Angel recording, no. 35206 ['The crime' and 'London revisited']

Likenesses H. M. Beerbohm, caricature drawing, *c*.1893, Merton Oxf. · W. Rothenstein, lithograph, 1898, NPG · H. M. Beerbohm, caricature drawing, *c*.1900, AM Oxf. · J. E. Blanche, oils, 1903, AM Oxf. · W. Nicholson, oils, 1905, NPG [*see illus.*] · A. L. Coburn, photogravure, 1908, NPG · A. Rutherston, portrait, 1909, U. Texas · W. Rothenstein, pencil drawing, 1915, Man. City Gall. · F. Young, photograph, 1916, NPG · H. M. Beerbohm, watercolour caricature, 1923, NPG · E. Kapp, ink, charcoal, and wash drawing, 1923, Barber Institute of Fine Arts, Birmingham · W. Rothenstein, pencil drawing, 1928, NPG · R. G. Eves, oils, 1936, Tate collection · R. G. Eves, pencil drawing, 1936, NPG · K. Bell Reynall, bromide photographs, 1955, NPG · C. Beaton, photograph, NPG · H. M. Beerbohm, pen and wash caricature, U. Texas · K. Kennet, statuette, Merton Oxf. · W. Nicholson, drawing, NPG · W. Rothenstein, drawing, Merton Oxf. · C. H. Shannon, lithograph, NPG

Wealth at death £9222 5s. 2d. in England: administration, 3 July 1957, *CGPLA Eng. & Wales*

Beesley, Alfred (1799/1800–1847), antiquary, was born into a Quaker family, but subsequently left the Society of Friends. He was apprenticed to a watchmaker in Deddington, Oxford, but only served part of his time. Subsequently he devoted himself to literary and scientific pursuits. He was a keen astronomer and botanist, and collected scientific instruments. In 1834 Longman published a collection of his poems, entitled *Japheth: Contemplation and other Pieces*. This was followed in 1841 by his well-researched *History of Banbury*, which gained a favourable review in the *Gentleman's Magazine*; his own copy was grangerized. Beesley was a member of the Cambridge Camden Society, founded in 1838 to promote interest in medieval ecclesiastical architecture, and of the Shakespeare Society. He was a supporter of the 1832 Reform Act, but later became a Conservative, before losing interest in political activities. He died at Cornhill, Banbury, on 10 April 1847, and was buried in Banbury churchyard.

JOANNE POTIER

Sources *GM*, 2nd ser., 28 (1847), 99 · *GM*, 2nd ser., 15 (1841), 65–6 [review] · C. Dellheim, *The face of the past: the preservation of the medieval inheritance in Victorian England* (1982) · P. Levine, *The amateur and the professional: antiquarians, historians and archaeologists in Victorian England* (1986), 2 · d. cert.

Archives Bodl. Oxf., corresp. relating to history of Banbury | BL, letters to Philip Bliss, Add. MSS 34571–34574

Beesley, George (1562–1591), Roman Catholic priest and martyr, was born at The Hill in Goosnargh, Lancashire. He was the son of George and Ellen Beesley, and the brother of Richard, who also became a seminary priest. His family was from the gentry and noted for its recusancy. He trained as a priest at the English College, then at Rheims, received the first tonsure in 1583, was ordained on 14 March 1587, and departed to go to England as a missionary priest on 2 November 1588, landing probably on the coast of Norfolk. He used the alias Passelaw, and was reported at first to be staying with Margaret Middleton, widow, of Leighton Hall, Lancashire. About April 1590 he performed the marriage of Richard Webster, a Catholic schoolmaster who was prisoner in the Marshalsea in London, although this does not mean he was necessarily himself imprisoned at that point.

Beesley was probably arrested while staying at St John's Street, Clerkenwell, with John and Margaret Gage, who were sentenced to death for harbouring him but subsequently reprieved. On 21 December 1590 he was committed to solitary confinement in the Tower of London. On the orders of the privy council he was placed in Little Ease, a cell too small to stretch out in, and was further tortured by Richard Topcliffe, the official government inquisitor, who wanted information about Catholics who had harboured him. He was mistreated to such an extent that, to quote Bishop Challoner, 'he was reduced to a mere skeleton, insomuch that they who before were acquainted with him could scarce know him to be the same man when they saw him drawn to execution' (Challoner, 167). While in the Martin Tower he scratched an inscription on the wall which survives to this day. He was convicted under the statute which made being a Catholic missionary priest treason. On 1 July 1591 he was hanged, drawn, and quartered in Fleet Street with another priest, Montford Scott. The government reported that when he was questioned he had said that he would support an invasion of England and the assassination of the queen.

PETER HOLMES

Sources *DNB* · G. Anstruther, *The seminary priests*, 4 vols. (1969–77) · R. Challoner, *Memoirs of missionary priests*, ed. J. H. Pollen, rev. edn (1924), 166–8 · *APC*, 1590–91, 148, 204 · *VCH Lancashire*, 7.195, 205 · T. F. Knox and others, eds., *The first and second diaries of the English College, Douay* (1878), 14, 30, 198, 212–14, 220–21, 238, 240, 263 · C. Talbot, ed., *Miscellanea: recusant records*, Catholic RS, 53 (1961), 350 · H. Bowler, ed., *Recusant roll no. 3 (1594–1595) and recusant roll no. 4 (1595–1596)*, Catholic RS, 61 (1970), 164 · H. Bowler, *Recusant roll no. 2 (1593–1594)*, Catholic RS, 57 (1965), 74 · C. Dodd [H. Tootell], *The church history of England, from the year 1500, to the year 1688*, 2 (1739), 90 · *The letters and despatches of Richard Verstegan, c. 1550–1640*, ed. A. G. Petti, Catholic RS, 52 (1959), 2–3, 9, 19, 28 · A. G. Petti, ed., *Recusant documents from the Ellesmere manuscripts, 1577–1715*, Catholic RS, 60 (1968), 68 · J. Strype, *Annals of the Reformation and establishment of religion … during Queen Elizabeth's happy reign*, new edn, 4 (1824), 90 · *An inventory of the historical monuments in London*, RCHM, 5 (1930), pl. 35, p. 83 · *Miscellanea, V*, Catholic RS, 6 (1909), 163–4, 241–2 · J. H. Pollen, ed., *Unpublished documents relating to the English martyrs*, 1, Catholic RS, 5 (1908), 12, 200–03, 214–15, 291 · H. Foley, ed., *Records* *of the English province of the Society of Jesus*, 4 (1878), 208 • E. H. Burton and T. L. Williams, eds., *The Douay College diaries, third, fourth and fifth, 1598-1654*, 2, Catholic RS, 11 (1911), 571 • J. H. Pollen and W. MacMahon, eds., *The Ven. Philip Howard, earl of Arundel, 1557-1595: English martyrs*, Catholic RS, 21 (1919), 346-7

Beesley, Michael Edwin (1924-1999), economist, was born on 3 July 1924 at 127 Sandon Road, Edgbaston, Birmingham, the second son of Edwin Sherman Beesley (1889-1969), clerk, later a broker at Stewart and Lloyds, and his wife, Kathleen Daisy Peacey (1891-1975), who ran her own tailoring business. After King Edward's Grammar School, Birmingham, he went to the University of Birmingham and gained a first-class bachelor of commerce degree. He was of medium height and stocky, with a square, cheerful face. Childhood diphtheria left him with deafness which his sociable nature overcame. At the age of thirteen, just after being offered a place in the Warwickshire schoolboys' cricket eleven, he was run over by a bus. His parents, who were Christian Scientists, refused to have his left leg amputated, and instead he had forty-nine skin grafts. The leg remained painful, and he limped for the rest of his life. He remained a cricket enthusiast, playing with a runner at the crease whenever he could. He was a table tennis demon and a golfer as well. On 1 April 1947 he married (Eileen) Eleanor Yard (b. 1925), a professional singer and cellist. Beesley, who was himself an accomplished classical and light-music pianist, often accompanied her. The couple had two daughters and three sons.

After graduating, Beesley and his father set up a small metals firm in the city's jewellery quarter. It lasted only a year, but this experience lastingly influenced his ideas, since it showed him the powerful and frequently devious instincts of collusion which often drove businessmen, through interlocking directorships and by other means, to avoid competition when they could. This experience gave him one of his lifetime interests: the question of how the state can provide the mixture of incentive, regulation, and freedom which businesses require to perform well. Immediately it inspired him to return to Birmingham University to work for a PhD on these issues in the jewellery

quarter. In 1950 he stood as the Liberal candidate for the Birmingham constituency of King's Norton and came third in the poll. In 1951, on completing his PhD which he had interrupted with a spell in the local regional planning authority, he was appointed a university lecturer in commerce at Birmingham. There he became one of a talented group of economists—also including Alan Walters, Frank Hahn, Ezra Bennathan, Frank McManus, and Terence Gorman—around Gilbert Walker, who was to give several of them, including Beesley, another enduring interest, transport economics.

Beesley carried out one of the earliest cost-benefit studies, on the M1 motorway after it had already been decided to build it. In 1961 he moved to a fellowship in transport economics at the London School of Economics, where he became a reader in 1964. In 1962 he combined with Christopher Foster to work on the cost-benefit analysis of the Victoria Line of the London underground, and in 1964 he was on the Smeed committee, which carried out the first investigation into road pricing. Among his most innovative articles was one on the valuation of time, an extraordinary example of his ability to think through novel complex issues which were normally expected to require a mathematical ability that he did not possess. He was part-time chief economic adviser until 1969 to the Ministry of Transport, where he helped build its economics team. His subsequent papers on transport economics included studies of the evaluation of transport investment, cost-benefit analysis, congestion, problems connected with subsidies, the economics of the taxi trade and the perils and pitfalls of a land-use planning approach to decision making. His earlier papers were collected in his book *Urban Transport: Studies in Economic Policy* (1973).

In 1965 Beesley became one of the two founding professors at the new London Business School, where he stayed for the rest of his life and where he broadened his interests from transport to other industries, still writing frequent articles (he was never one for books). He started the small business unit at the London Business School, and later (1985-90) ran its PhD programme. He moved towards

Michael Edwin Beesley (1924–1999), by Kelvin Brodie, 1973

the school of Austrian economics, which stressed the importance of entrepreneurship and innovation and of the political and economic conditions which would permit economic dynamism. He developed his ideas on competition, mergers, and economic regulation, and an economic theory of the state; he became one of the driving forces behind the programme of privatization and new regulatory initiatives of the 1980s through his influence on the Conservative cabinet minister Sir Keith Joseph. His report *Liberalisation of the use of the British telecommunications network: an independent economic inquiry* (1981), commissioned by Joseph, was seminal. In 1983, with Stephen Littlechild, he wrote a fundamental paper on the principles of RPI-X regulation. Many of his papers on these topics were collected in *Privatisation, Regulation and Deregulation* (1990). He advised governments at home and abroad extensively, and was an influential member of the Monopolies and Mergers Commission from 1988 to 1994. He became a CBE in 1985.

Beesley was a fine teacher of research students, because of the fertility of his outpouring of research ideas. When he first came up with a complicated new idea he could be incomprehensible, but he soon showed that he was developing an original perspective on an old problem. His very struggles to work out his ideas, which he then wrote up in plain English, stimulated students. After becoming emeritus professor in 1990, he went on teaching and writing until his death on 24 September 1999 in University College Hospital, London. His funeral and burial took place at St Lawrence's, Whitchurch, Edgware, on 15 October. He was survived by his wife.   CHRISTOPHER FOSTER

Sources *The Guardian* (8 Oct 1999) · *The Times* (30 Sept 1999) · *The Independent* (6 Oct 1999) · *The Scotsman* (6 Oct 1999) · C. D. Foster, 'Michael Beesley and cost-benefit analysis', *Journal of Transport Economics*, 35 (Jan 2001) · personal knowledge (2004) · private information (2004) [Jacqueline Henderson, daughter] · b. cert. · m. cert. · d. cert.
Archives U. Birm., Birmingham Business School
Likenesses K. Brodie, photograph, 1973, News International Syndication, London [*see illus.*] · photograph, repro. in *The Guardian* · photograph, repro. in *The Independent*

Beesly, Edward Spencer (1831–1915), positivist and historian, was born on 23 January 1831 in Feckenham, Worcestershire, the eldest son of the Revd James Beesly and his wife, Emily Fitzgerald, of Queen's county, Ireland. After reading Latin and Greek with his father, in the autumn of 1846 he was sent to King William's College on the Isle of Man, an evangelical establishment whose inadequate instruction and low moral tone were later depicted in *Eric, or, Little by Little*, by his school friend F. W. Farrar.

In 1849 Beesly entered Wadham College, Oxford, another evangelical stronghold. He held two exhibitions and a Bible clerkship. His flair for quoting scripture yielded to radical rhetoric under the influence of his tutor Richard Congreve, a covert disciple of Auguste Comte's positivism. Along with his Wadham friends Frederic Harrison and John Henry Bridges, Beesly actively engaged in the debates of the Oxford Union and became recognized

Edward Spencer Beesly (1831–1915), by Barraud

as a Comtist, though his adhesion to the French philosophy was still tenuous.

Beesly received his BA in 1854 and proceeded MA in 1857. After failing to secure a first class (he obtained seconds in classical moderations and *literae humaniores*) or a fellowship, he became an assistant master at Marlborough College. His brother Augustus Henry, a historian and classical scholar, also taught at the school. Beesly left for London in 1859 to serve as principal of University Hall, a student residence in Gordon Square serving University College. The next year he was appointed professor of history there and professor of Latin at Bedford College for women, with a combined salary of £300. He also had a private income. His tall, willowy figure became a familiar sight in the Reform Club and London drawing-rooms, including that of George Eliot and George Henry Lewes, whose *Fortnightly Review* welcomed Beesly's articles.

Beesly joined Congreve and Harrison, both now in London, in supporting the struggle of the workers in the building trades for shorter hours. He also attacked the economic theories used by critics of the 'new model' trade unions of the 1860s. The notoriety he gained culminated in 1867, when he declared in the aftermath of the 'Sheffield outrages' that a trade union murder was no worse than any other: he almost lost his post at University Hall and *Punch* dubbed him Dr Beastly. His radical agenda included promoting international solidarity among working-class leaders. He helped organize the most important pro-Union demonstration in England during the American Civil War, and he chaired the historic meeting (28 September 1864) advocating co-operation between English and French workers in support of Polish nationalism, which led to the formation of the International Working Men's Association (the First International), soon dominated by his friend Karl Marx.

Foreign affairs were always a passion of Beesly's. For *International Policy*, a positivist volume published in 1866, he wrote on British sea power, asserting a connection between protestantism and commercial immorality. A critic of imperialism, he was a member of the committee founded in 1866 to prosecute Edward Eyre, governor of Jamaica. Beesly and other positivists incurred hostility for advocating intervention on the side of France in the Franco-Prussian War, and for defending the Paris commune. Their republican views found expression not only in the press but also at the positivist centre in Chapel Street (now Rugby Street) that they opened in 1870 under Congreve's direction. There they introduced sacraments of the Religion of Humanity and published a co-operative translation of Comte's *Positive Polity*. When Congreve repudiated their Paris co-religionists in 1878, Beesly, Harrison, Bridges, and others formed their own positivist society, with Beesly as president, and opened a rival centre, Newton Hall, in a courtyard off Fleet Street. Beesly headed its political discussion group, which produced occasional papers. Retirement from University College in 1893 (he had left Bedford College in 1889) enabled him to found and edit the *Positivist Review*.

In 1869 Beesly married Emily, youngest daughter of Sir Charles John *Crompton, justice of the queen's bench, and his wife, Caroline. The Beeslys lived in University Hall until 1882, when they moved to Finsbury Park. Mrs Beesly was not a positivist—as were her brothers Albert and Henry Crompton—but she shared some of her husband's political and historical interests. He unsuccessfully stood for parliament as a Liberal at Westminster in November 1885 and at Marylebone in July 1886. Emily Beesly became president of the women's liberal association of Paddington after their move to Warrington Crescent in 1886. Both advocated Irish home rule, he in hard-hitting articles, she in new lyrics for 'The Wearing of the Green'. In 1878 he published *Catiline, Clodius, and Tiberius*, and she brought out her *Stories from the History of Rome*, written for their four sons. She died in 1889, aged forty-nine.

Beesly's later publications included seventy-four biographical entries on military and political figures for the positivists' *New Calendar of Great Men*, and *Queen Elizabeth*, both of which appeared in 1892. In 1901 he retired to 21 West Hill, St Leonards, Sussex, where he published translations of Comte and continued to write for the *Positivist Review*. He died at home on 7 July 1915 and was buried in Paddington cemetery. He left a name still honoured by labour historians.   MARTHA S. VOGELER

Sources *The Times* (9 July 1915), 11d · *Positivist Review*, 23 (1915) [with bibliography] · C. L. Davies, *The Spectator* (17 July 1915), 77–8 · *Sociological Review*, 8 (July 1915), 187–8 · Foster, *Alum. Oxon.* · C. Kent, 'Beesly, Edward Spencer', *BDMBR*, vol. 2 · R. Harrison, 'Professor Beesly and the working-class movement', *Essays in labour history in memory of G. D. H. Cole, 25 September 1889 – 14 January 1959*, ed. A. Briggs and J. Saville (1960), 205–41; repr. (1967) · M. S. Vogeler, *Frederic Harrison: the vocations of a positivist* (1984) · J. E. McGee, *A crusade for humanity: the history of organized positivism in England* (1931) · R. Harrison, 'E. S. Beesly and Karl Marx', *International Review of Social History*, 4 (1959), 22–59, 208–38 · R. Harrison, *Before the socialists: studies in labour and politics, 1861–1881* (1965) · R. Harrison, 'E. S. Beesly', in R. Harrison, *The English defence of the Commune, 1871* (1971), 37–106

Archives UCL, corresp., lecture notes, and papers mainly relating to historical interests | Bishopsgate Institute, London, letters to George Howell · BL, corresp. with Richard Congreve, Add. MS 45227 · BL, Positivist MSS · BLPES, corresp. with Frederic Harrison · BLPES, London Positivist Society MSS · Internationaal Instituut voor Sociale Geschiedenis, Amsterdam, letters to Karl Marx · Maison d'Auguste Comte, Paris, letters to Constant Hillemand and others · Yale U., Beinecke L., letters to George Eliot

Likenesses E. Armitage, sketch, NPG · Barraud, photograph, NPG [*see illus.*] · photograph, BLPES, London Positivist Society MSS · photograph, repro. in Vogeler, *Frederic Harrison*

Wealth at death £21,055 2s. 0d.: probate, 17 Aug 1915, CGPLA Eng. & Wales

Beeston, Alfred Felix Landon (1911–1995), orientalist, was born at 12 Glebe Road, Barnes, south London, on 23 February 1911, the second child and only son of Herbert Arthur Beeston (1872–1941), an engineer and draughtsman, and Edith Mary Landon (1873–1965). In his undergraduate days he came to be called Freddie, a name by which he was universally known to friends, colleagues, and students for the rest of his life, though he was called Rogo by his close family.

At fourteen Beeston was elected a king's scholar at Westminster School. From at least the age of ten he had had 'a passionate interest in foreign languages' (Beeston, 'The Making of an Orientalist', 4) and he spent much of his spare time exploring them. While he 'avidly scanned any language manuals I could lay my hands on, from ancient Egyptian hieroglyphs to Spanish and Welsh, etc.—the more exotic the better' (ibid.), his principal 'interest was in theoretical linguistics, in the structure of a language and its strategies for expressing ideas' (ibid.). He had 'always had an inclination for specializing in something unusual and exotic' (Beeston, *Autobiography*, xv) and toyed with the idea of studying Sanskrit or Chinese, but was unable to find suitable books. However, when he picked up an Arabic grammar in a second-hand bookshop he began to teach himself as much Arabic as he could, helped by an Arabic dictionary and a copy of the Koran which he had asked for as school prizes. Thus it was almost by chance that he concentrated his considerable energies on Arabic, though in later life he also acquired a knowledge of Chinese and a sophisticated understanding of its structures with which he sometimes startled Sinologists.

In 1929 Beeston won a scholarship to Christ Church, Oxford, where he read classics for honour moderations and then Arabic and Persian for the final honours school under the Laudian professor, D. S. Margoliouth. To his delight he discovered that Margoliouth had placed on the Arabic syllabus an optional paper on South Arabian epigraphy. Beeston was the first student to take this and, after he had graduated with a first in 1933, he decided to make Sabaean inscriptions the subject of his DPhil thesis.

In 1935, while he was still working on his DPhil, Beeston was appointed a senior assistant in the department of oriental books of the Bodleian Library, where he remained for twenty years (not counting five and a half years of war service from 1940 to 1946). There he threw himself into several cataloguing and catalogue revision projects, the most important of which resulted in his completion in 1954 of the *Catalogue of the Persian, Turkish, Hindustani, and Pushtu manuscripts in the Bodleian Library, part III: additional Persian manuscripts*. During this period he also produced a number of articles on the Bodleian's oriental holdings (Arabic, Persian, Chinese), and a booklet on Mughal miniatures, as well as numerous papers on South Arabian epigraphy. However, he regarded his principal service to the library to have been 'the acquisition of several particularly fine manuscripts at pretty reasonable prices' (Beeston, 'The Making of an Orientalist', 5). After he left the library he continued to make generous donations from his own resources to enable the Bodleian to acquire important oriental manuscripts.

During the Second World War, Beeston served in Palestine as lieutenant, and then captain, in the intelligence corps. There he improved his spoken Arabic, though he later recalled that, when caught off guard, he was still capable of answering the shouts of boys in the street with literary expressions which elicited gales of laughter. On his return to the Bodleian in 1946 he was promoted to the post of keeper of the oriental department and sub-librarian. He remained there until 1955, when Sir Hamilton Gibb, who had succeeded Margoliouth as Laudian professor of Arabic, resigned to take up a post at Harvard. Sir Godfrey Driver immediately 'instructed' Beeston 'in the most positive terms' to apply for the chair (Beeston, 'The Making of an Orientalist', 5). At this point Beeston had reached the summit of his career in the Bodleian and had completed all but one of the major projects on which he had embarked. Thus a change of direction offered exciting, if slightly alarming, prospects. The chair carried with it a professorial fellowship at St John's College. There he quickly found himself entirely at home.

Beeston brought to the chair a profound knowledge and understanding of all periods of the Arabic language and the literature expressed in it. In 1955, when he was appointed, the Arabic syllabus did not go beyond AD 1400 and one of his major achievements was to rewrite it so that students were required to read works from all periods, from the pre-Islamic poetry to twentieth-century plays and novels—and this at a time when the English literature syllabus at Oxford stopped at 1900.

Beeston had an intense love of his subject and his enthusiasm inspired generations of students. He was a modest, courteous, and patient teacher with a deep interest in awakening in others an understanding and appreciation of the Arabic language and its literature. Unlike most Oxford professors of his day he undertook a great deal of undergraduate teaching, in lectures, classes, and tutorials, and both during his tenure and after his retirement

he was in great demand as an examiner of doctoral theses. His lecturing style was ponderous, full of long pauses, and punctuated by appalling fits of coughing (he was a very heavy smoker), but the content and his enthusiasm held his audience fascinated. Many of the books he wrote were intended for students, though they had a far wider readership; they included *Written Arabic* (1968), *Arabic Historical Phraseology* (1969), *Samples of Arabic Prose in its Historical Development* (1977), *Baidāwī's Commentary on Sūrah 12 of the Qurʾān* (1963), and *The Epistle on Singing-Girls of Jāḥiz* (1980). He was interested in languages not simply as abstract systems but in how they could be used to express complex thoughts. This came out in his numerous articles on points of grammar, in his classes on the translation of poetry and difficult passages in al-Tanukhi and Ibn Khaldun's *Muqaddimah*, and above all in his book *The Arabic Language Today* (1970).

Beeston was, without doubt, one of the foremost Arabists of the twentieth century, but by the time he retired in 1978 he was also the doyen of experts in Ancient South Arabian. He produced two grammars of Sabaic (1962 and 1984), led the project which produced the *Sabaic Dictionary* (1982), and wrote innumerable articles and contributions to books on every aspect of life in pre-Islamic Arabia. Here again his passion for teaching was engaged, and he was the driving force in the multi-author Arabic *Chrestomathy of Ancient Yemeni Inscriptions* (1985), designed to introduce Arab students to the subject. Between his retirement in 1978 and his death in 1995 he produced an astonishing number of books and articles on the Arabic language, Arabic literature, and pre-Islamic Arabia which have made major contributions to all three fields.

Beeston could be a devastating reviewer, but he was never vicious or personal in his criticism. He simply and calmly pointed out faults when necessary and gave praise where it was due. He believed that 'error must be corrected' (personal knowledge) and was himself happy to be corrected by others. His interest was in the progress of knowledge and there was no shred of personal vanity in him. He received two Festschriften. One, *Ṣayhadica: recherches sur les inscriptions de l'Arabie préislamique* (1987), is devoted to pre-Islamic Arabia and the other, *Arabicus Felix: luminosus Britannicus*, which was presented on his eightieth birthday in 1991, mainly contains works on Arabic language and literature.

Until 1963 Beeston's appearance was relatively conventional, largely out of respect for the views of the president of St John's College, Austin Lane Poole. However, after the latter's death, Beeston developed the flowing locks and informal garb which made him instantly recognizable in Oxford and elsewhere. He loved good food and drink and good company. His appearance and somewhat 'monumental' manner were reminiscent of Dr Johnson and could be a little daunting on first meeting. However, his modesty, humour, and total lack of pretension quickly put people at their ease. He was as comfortable playing darts with the college servants in the pub as he was dining at high table, and frequently did both in the same evening.

Indeed there were many in Oxford who knew him simply as 'Freddie' and had no idea that he was a professor.

He was a very popular participant in conferences and was a co-founder and one of the most faithful members of the annual international Seminar for Arabian Studies. He served on the councils of many learned societies and was elected fellow of the British Academy in 1965. Throughout his life he was a devout Anglo-Catholic and regularly attended mass at the church of St Mary Magdalen in Oxford.

On his retirement Beeston bought a small house in Iffley, but still spent much of his day in college since St John's had made him an emeritus fellow. He never married and though he was a much-loved uncle, great-uncle, and godfather the college was in many ways his home and close family. In 1993 he developed cancer and moved back into college to be closer to the hospitals for treatment. His death, when it came, was swift and merciful. He collapsed and died on 29 September 1995 at the gates of St John's College.   M. C. A. MACDONALD

Sources Bodl. Oxf., Department of Oriental Collections, A. F. L. Beeston papers · A. F. L. Beeston, 'Alfred Felix Landon Beeston, an autobiography', *Sayhadica: recherches sur les inscriptions de l'Arabie préislamique offertes par ses collègues au Professeur A. F. L. Beeston*, ed. C. Robin and M. A. Bāfaqīh (Paris, 1987), xv–xx · A. F. L. Beeston, 'The making of an orientalist', *Oxford Magazine*, 122 (1995), 4–5 [repr. in *Union of European Arabists and Islamicists newsletter*, 1995, 3–8] · M. Gilsenan, 'A personal introduction', *Arabicus Felix: luminosus Britannicus. Essays in honour of A. F. L. Beeston on his eightieth birthday*, ed. A. Jones, Oxford Oriental Institute Monographs, 11 (1991), ii–vi · A. D. S. Roberts, 'Alfred Felix Landon ('Freddie') Beeston', *The Bodleian Library Record*, 15/4 (1996), 231–3 · A. Jones, *The Times* (6 Oct 1995) · W. W. Müller, 'In memoriam A. F. L. Beeston (1911–1995): personal reminiscences of a friend and scholar', *Proceedings of the Seminar for Arabian Studies*, 27 (1977), 7–20 · M. C. A. Macdonald, 'A bibliography of Professor A. F. L. Beeston', *Proceedings of the Seminar for Arabian Studies*, 27 (1997), 21–48 · E. Ullendorff, 'Alfred Felix Landon Beeston, 1911–1995', *PBA*, 94 (1997), 295–316 · personal knowledge (2004)

Archives Bodl. Oxf., Department of Oriental Collections

Likenesses pencil drawing, St John's College, Oxford · photograph, Oriental Institute, Oxford; repro. in Jones, 'Professor Alfred Beeston'

Wealth at death £612,322—large bequest to St John's College, Oxford: probate, 1 March 1996, *CGPLA Eng. & Wales*

Beeston [Hutchinson], Christopher (1579/80–1638), actor and theatre impresario, gave his age as forty-three in a court case in October 1623. Though Beeston became probably the most potent and influential theatre entrepreneur through the first forty years of the seventeenth century, he came into the new world of London theatre from no known origin. Christopher's name appears in Jacobean sessions records for Middlesex as Beeston alias Hutchinson or Hutchinson alias Beeston, and he signed his will as Christopher Hutchinson. A company of players called 'Bedston and his felows', was paid for performing a play at Barnstaple in Devon in 1561–2, but it is not known whether Christopher came from a family of players (Wasson, 43). Thomas Nashe in *Strange Newes* (1592) refers to a generous friend he addresses as 'Gentle M. William' and 'Apis Lapis' (that is, Bee-Stone), his 'pottle-pot Patron',

but this William Beeston cannot be linked with Christopher (Chambers, 2.302). Robert Beeston, who acted with Christopher in Queen Anne's Men and was probably his brother, identified his mother, Alice, as of St Botolph without Bishopsgate, where she was buried in 1604 at the age of fifty-four. St Botolph's was a parish familiar to players who worked in Shoreditch, as Christopher did in the 1590s.

Beeston married Jane Sands, a Roman Catholic, on 10 September 1602. Four children, all of whom died young, were registered at St Leonard, Shoreditch, between 1604 and 1610, when the family moved to Clerkenwell. There Beeston was threatened with outlawry in 1617 unless he appeared to answer charges against him—perhaps for recusancy, probably over the responsibilities of his theatre for the upkeep of highways. His wife was certainly indicted several times for recusancy between 1615 and 1618. Robert Beeston underwent the same charges and it seems likely that the whole family was Roman Catholic. Jane was on occasion described in the records as 'wife of Christofer Beeston gentleman', although there is no evidence as to how he qualified for the title 'gentleman', and he also appears in the same records as yeoman and 'stageplayer' (Bentley, 2.365; Le Hardy, 4.91, 4.143). After Jane's death Beeston married again; his second wife, Elizabeth, whom he had married by December 1634, survived him.

Beeston began as a player in the Shakespeare company, the Lord Chamberlain's Men. The 1616 Jonson Folio records him as a player in *Every Man in his Humour*. Augustine Phillips, a senior player and 'sharer' in the Lord Chamberlain's, left in his will in 1605, along with similar bequests to his fellow players Condell and Shakespeare, 30s. to Beeston, naming him as a former 'servant': this indicates that Beeston started work as a boy player under Phillips's control in the Lord Chamberlain's. (In turn, Beeston named his son born in 1604 Augustine.) Beeston acted in *Every Man in his Humour* between its first staging in 1598 and some time before 1602, when he was working for Worcester's Men, a company recently formed from two other groups as the third licensed company in London alongside the Lord Chamberlain's and the Lord Admiral's. He stayed with this company, which became Queen Anne's Men at the end of 1603, for the next fifteen years.

Beeston was capable with people and with money. Thomas Heywood, a major figure as supplier of plays to the Queen's Men and other playing groups under Beeston's control, was a constant friend. Beeston wrote a complimentary verse for the publication of *An Apology for Actors* in 1612, and gave money for a picture in Heywood's *The Hierarchie of the Blessed Angels* in 1634. Almost all the twenty or more extant Heywood plays were written for the Beeston companies, a mark of the two men's steady friendship. Heywood wrote the prologue and epilogue for Beeston's revival of Marlowe's *Jew of Malta* in 1633, when it was presented at court.

Where money was at stake Beeston's constancy was more to his own interests. From 1612, when the senior player in Queen Anne's Men, the clown Thomas Greene, died, he took over its financial affairs at considerable profit to himself, and moved on in good time. A lawsuit brought against the company in 1623 by Greene's widow suggests that he used the company's profits to turn himself from player to theatre owner and impresario. His business concern as a theatre impresario really started in August 1616, when he took out a thirty-one year lease on a set of buildings called 'the cockpits' in Drury Lane, and converted them into a hall theatre. The plan was to add to his amphitheatre, the Red Bull, a new hall theatre imitating the King's Men's Blackfriars theatre. It was not an easy ride. He soon got into trouble with both the Red Bull in Clerkenwell and with the new property near Lincoln's Inn. In September his housebuilders were stopped by an order in council seeking to enforce the recent order that no new buildings be erected in that part of London. A letter from the privy council to the Middlesex high sheriff named Beeston as one 'fittest to be made an example' (Bentley, 2.366). He pleaded that it was his dwelling-house in Clerkenwell which was being extended. The Drury Lane theatre was also described as 'the dwellinge house of Christopher Beeston' in March 1617 when fifty apprentices were charged with 'riotous assalte and spoyle' on it (ibid.). That was part of a Shrove Tuesday holiday attack on the new Cockpit by a mob of apprentices who liked Red Bull plays but lost them when Beeston transferred the company and its plays to the more expensive new venue. The king himself joined the wrangles in September 1617. As the privy council noted, there was:

> a base tenement erected by one Christopher Beeston in Clerkenwell, neere unto his Majesties passage, pulled downe and demolished by vertue of the late order, which since is buylt up agayne, and his Majesty passing that way of late hath taken speciall notice thereof, being highly offended with the presumption. (ibid., 2.367)

These concerns faded with time. Beeston repaired the damaged Cockpit, aptly renaming it the Phoenix, and from then on ran two companies in his two different venues, not now as a player or company manager but as an impresario. One of his playhouses was a roofed and all-seated space, close to the inns of court and their avid students; the other was an amphitheatre in the northern suburbs for poorer customers. Into them he put two companies, allowing each to run for about three years before replacing them. The view that he financed the building of the Cockpit and took control of the Red Bull out of his profits from running Queen Anne's Men, while the players themselves and Greene's widow, Susan Baskervile, made little from it, seems inescapable.

In 1616 when he opened his new hall playhouse Beeston moved his old company, the Queen's Men, into the new venue and gave their former playhouse, the Red Bull, to Prince Charles's, a company until then playing at the Curtain, the oldest playhouse in London. As Edward Alleyn of the Fortune moved away from his theatre management and impresario roles to create his College of God's Gift at Dulwich, Beeston became the strongest impresario in London. The Red Bull continued to rival the Fortune as the town's theatre for citizens, while the Cockpit rivalled the King's Men's Blackfriars as the favourite resort for the gentry and aristocracy. Under his control one Cockpit company came close to matching the King's Men's in supplying entertainment at court for each lengthy Christmas season. Beeston ran companies at his two playhouses until his death. Normally he allowed each company to run for three years before bringing in a new group. The only exception to this pattern was the company he formed in 1626, under the patronage of the new queen, Henrietta Maria; with Richard Perkins as its leader it ran at the Cockpit for ten years and during that time it rivalled the King's Men's at Blackfriars as London's premier playhouse for the gentry. In 1636, however, another long close-down for plague made Beeston evict it and install a new company at the Cockpit chiefly made up of 'youths', a group known as Beeston's Boys.

Between 1626 and his death in 1638, Beeston's Cockpit theatre staged more new plays than even the Blackfriars. For writers he took John Ford and James Shirley from the Blackfriars, and even when the young courtiers William Davenant and Thomas Carew started a fresh kind of competition by writing plays for the queen's faction at Blackfriars, he maintained a strong repertory of plays and strong companies of players. He died in October 1638, and was buried in St Giles-in-the-Fields on 15 October. Christopher left to his son William *Beeston one half-share and to his widow, Elizabeth, one and a half shares (out of six shares in all); William took over the role of 'governor' of Beeston's Boys, and the management of Christopher's Cockpit/Phoenix.

ANDREW GURR

Sources E. A. J. Honigmann and S. Brock, eds., *Playhouse wills, 1558–1642: an edition of wills by Shakespeare and his contemporaries in the London theatre* (1993), 73, 191–4 · G. E. Bentley, *The Jacobean and Caroline stage*, 7 vols. (1941–68), vol. 2, pp. 363–70 · E. K. Chambers, *The Elizabethan stage*, 4 vols. (1923), vol. 2, pp. 302–3 · M. Eccles, 'Elizabethan actors, I: A–D', *N&Q*, 236 (1991), 38–49, esp. 39–40 · J. M. Wasson, ed., *Records of early English drama: Devon* (1986) · W. Le Hardy, ed., *Calendar to the sessions records, county of Middlesex*, 4 vols. (1935–41) · J. J. LaRocca, ed., *Jacobean recusant rolls for Middlesex: an abstract in English*, Catholic RS, 76 (1997)

Beeston [Hutchinson], **William** (1610/11?–1682), theatre impresario and actor, was the son of the leading theatre manager Christopher *Beeston (1579/80–1638) and his first wife, Jane Sands. Like his father, William sometimes appears in the records with the alternative surname of Hutchinson, and he seems to have inherited his family's Catholicism. William was presumably Jane's and Christopher's oldest surviving son, although he was not one of the three born in St Leonard, Shoreditch, between 1604 and 1610, when the family moved to Clerkenwell. It seems likely therefore that he was born in 1610 or 1611. In a lawsuit he described himself as 'bred up in the art of stage playing' (Bentley, 2.370), but nothing is known of his career before 1632, when he is noted in management with Richard Gunnell and William Blagrave at the Salisbury Court Theatre.

William Beeston joined his highly successful father in running the Cockpit Theatre in Drury Lane in 1636–7, during a long closure because of the plague when companies, theatres, and loyalties all changed radically. During this period the two Beestons threw out the company that had run there for ten years and replaced them with a new company of mainly young players, who became known as Beeston's Boys. The older Beeston had been planning the change for some time. A privy council order of 12 May 1637 keeping the theatres closed names the responsible individuals at the Cockpit as 'Christopher and William Biston Theophilus Bird Ezech: Fenn & Michael Moone', the latter three senior 'boy' players (*Malone Society Collections*, 1/5.392). Altogether there were at least twelve 'boys' beside the adults in the company. When Christopher died in October 1638 William inherited a thriving and well-supported business. By his father's will he received half a share (out of six) in the company, and in April 1639 he was duly sworn in as 'Governour & Instructer of the Kings and Queens young Company of Actors'. Richard Brome, once a 'servant' to Ben Jonson, wrote a note for the published text of *The Antipodes* in 1640, which he had offered to the Cockpit Theatre before contractual obligations forced him to have it staged at the Salisbury Court, giving a plug for 'my most deserving friend Mr William Beeston, unto whom it properly appertained' (Brome, 120).

The new company's plays included almost half of the cream of the time, rivalling those of the former Shakespeare company, the King's Men. They are known because of an order which forbade other companies to perform them issued by the lord chamberlain on the same day as his warrant for the players, 10 August 1639. It was prompted by William Beeston as 'governor' of the company and appears to be the list of the best playbooks he had inherited from his father. Some of them date back to the beginning of the century. The forty-five titles, almost all extant, exemplify the tradition of writing for the stage that followed Shakespeare, Beaumont's *The Knight of the Burning Pestle*, Beaumont's and Fletcher's *Cupid's Revenge*, Massinger's *The Bondman* and *A New Way to Pay Old Debts*, Shirley's *The Young Admiral* and *Hyde Park*, Middleton's and Rowley's *The Changeling*, and Ford's *'Tis Pity she's a Whore*.

The younger Beeston proved rather less adroit than his father in managing company affairs in the four years before parliament in September 1642 banned the public staging of all plays. In May 1640 Beeston and two of his adult helpers were put in the Marshalsea for acting an unlicensed play. The master of the revels, official censor of plays, noted that:

> the play I calde for, and, forbiddinge the playeinge of it, keepe the booke, because it had relation to the passages of the K.s journey into the Northe, and was complayned of by his Majestye to mee, with commande to punishe the offenders. (Bawcutt, 208)

It was the king who in 1639 ordered the lord chamberlain to name the plays belonging to Beeston, but his interest in playgoing made him alert to hostile allusions. This offence appears to have cost Beeston his managerial role, and in his place the master of the revels made William Davenant the company's new 'governor'. Impresario control was still far from absolute, and government orders still largely directed what happened to the acting companies. An order dated 27 June 1640 told the Cockpit company that the lord chamberlain was giving control of the Beeston company to Davenant. Selling playgoing to the general public was not yet an entirely private enterprise: the government took over when the management stepped out of line.

Davenant had been in the job less than a year when his entanglement in the army plot put him in prison. Beeston once again became 'Governor of the Cockpitt Players' (Bentley, 2.373), but by then there was barely a year before the closure of the theatres. On 15 July 1642 Beeston married Alice Bowen (*d.* 1686) at St Giles-in-the-Fields (she was possibly not his first wife). A daughter was baptized in 1644 and they had at least two sons, George (who became an actor and died before his father) and Sackville. Through the years of closure Beeston remained in business of various kinds, evidently hoping that he could return to theatre work. He may have staged some of the surreptitious performances at Gibbons's Tennis Court and other places. In 1649 he tried to buy the empty Salisbury Court Theatre, a deal completed in 1652 for a lower price after it was damaged by a mob of soldiers and apprentices. In winter 1650 he started training a new boy company to play at the Cockpit, which he also tried to secure, unsuccessfully. There were various projects to revive theatre in the 1650s, but Beeston's name does not recur in them, apart from a recommendation by Richard Flecknoe, published at the end of *Love's Dominion* in 1654, that he would be the most suitable man to manage 'the REFORMED Stage', 'his long Practice and Experience in this way, as also for having brought up most of the Actors extant' (Bentley, 2.373–4). But once again William Davenant intervened, and the first new stagings at the Cockpit in 1659 and 1660 were under his control, not Beeston's. Beeston did start a new company in 1660 at his other property, the Salisbury Court, and ran plays there until it burnt down in 1666. Subsequently he became an actor with the King's Company. Pepys saw him in 1668 in a comedy by Flecknoe, and the following year in *The Heiress*, a play part-authored by the duke of Newcastle. Beeston, standing in, had to read his part, 'and thereby spoils the part and almost the play, it being one of the best parts in it', though Pepys was amused by the sight of Beeston reading by candle-light in a scene meant to be in darkness (Pepys, 9.436).

By then Beeston had other interests as property owner and property manager, and his name does not appear in further records of Restoration theatre management. In his later years, according to John Aubrey, 'he was not a company keeper; lived in Shoreditch; would not be debauched, and if invited to court, was in paine' (*Brief Lives*, 1.97). Beeston's long career and long memory led Dryden to call him 'the chronicle of the stage', while he provided Aubrey with tales of Jonson and Shakespeare. He was charged with recusancy in 1680, like his mother before him. He died in 1682, about 24 August. He was then living in Bishopsgate Street in the parish of St Leonard, Shoreditch, and his will indicates that his estate consisted chiefly of properties including a 'house called the blacke

'Swanne' and tenements in King's Head Yard. His widow, Alice, and son Sackville survived him, while his son George had left a 'reputed sonne' Benaniah, whom William left to the care of his widow and who was to inherit the property in Shoreditch after her death (Honigmann and Brock, 219).

ANDREW GURR

Sources E. A. J. Honigmann and S. Brock, eds., *Playhouse wills, 1558–1642: an edition of wills by Shakespeare and his contemporaries in the London theatre* (1993), 219–21 [William Beeston] · *The control and censorship of Caroline drama: the records of Sir Henry Herbert, master of the revels, 1623–73*, ed. N. W. Bawcutt (1996), 66, 208, 326 · G. E. Bentley, *The Jacobean and Caroline stage*, 7 vols. (1941–68), vol. 2, pp. 370–74 · *Malone Society Collections*, 1 (1907–11), 392 · *Brief lives, chiefly of contemporaries, set down by John Aubrey, between the years 1669 and 1696*, ed. A. Clark, 1 (1898), 96–7 · Highfill, Burnim & Langhans, *BDA*, 1.414–19 · R. Brome, *The Antipodes*, ed. D. S. Kastan and R. Proudfoot (2000) · Pepys, *Diary*, 9.307, 436

Beeston, Sir William (1636–1702), merchant and colonial governor, was born on 19 November 1636 at Posbrook, Titchfield, Hampshire, the second son of William Beeston of Posbrook and Elizabeth, daughter of Arthur Bromfield. His elder brother, Henry, was master of Winchester School and warden of New College, Oxford.

Early career Nothing is known of Beeston's life until, in common with many younger sons of gentry families, he decided to try his luck overseas. He set sail for Jamaica, where he arrived in April 1660, a month before the final defeat of the Spaniards, from whom the English had seized the island in 1655. At the Restoration, Charles II was widely expected to return Cromwell's prize but, in fact, the king retained Jamaica, disbanded the army, and in 1662 appointed Thomas, seventh Baron Windsor, as governor with orders to frame civil government. Beeston lived in Jamaica for almost thirty of his remaining forty years of life and played a major role in shaping the political and economic development of the island.

In 1662 Beeston was elected member for Port Royal in Jamaica's first assembly, which embarked with enthusiasm on legislating to regulate life in the infant colony. Beeston reported the good fellowship of the new house until the arrival of Thomas Modyford, a successful Barbados planter, as governor in 1664. His pursuit of profit soon caused clashes with the pioneer settlers and fomented a lasting factionalism in the island. Beeston played a leading part in the assembly's efforts to curb the governor's ambitions and suffered brief imprisonment. Squabbles culminated in the murder of one member and, apart from a three-day session in 1665, Modyford did not call another assembly during his seven years in government. The governor further tightened his personal grip on island affairs by turning out office-holders and substituting his friends. Many disgruntled islanders (including Beeston's friend Thomas Lynch, who lost his place as provost marshal) returned home, but Beeston remained, and prospered as the island economy was put on a sound footing.

At Beeston's arrival in Jamaica the economy was based largely on trade in prize goods brought in by privateers exploiting the island's location in the heart of the Spanish Indies. Plunder continued to be important after 1660 and the decade was renowned for the exploits of Henry Morgan and others, but, as the future became more certain, privateering was supplemented, and ultimately surpassed, by a smuggling trade with the Spanish colonies and the planting of cash crops. Beeston, based in Port Royal, seized all opportunities. He purchased shares in prize vessels, traded in prize goods and island commodities (both on commission and on his own account), and from 1662 onwards began to patent land in the interior. By 1670 he had 878 acres in St Andrews and had accumulated sufficient resources to begin the expensive work of setting up a sugar plantation.

In 1670 England and Spain signed the treaty of Madrid promising mutual peace and friendship in America, and Modyford's pro-privateering policy became an embarrassment. Thomas Lynch was sent back to Jamaica to take over the reins of government, and, with help from old friends, made an immediate effort to use the peace to extend trade with the Spanish colonies. Beeston was sent to Cartagena with the Madrid treaty, and in December Lynch placed Beeston in command of HMS *Assistance* with orders to cruise around Cuba and Hispaniola in pursuit of pirates. These activities provided openings for underhand commerce, and there is evidence that trade was put on a regular footing. The governor and his associates, including Beeston, were able to secure an advantage, which was broadly maintained for decades, but the engrossing of the trade (especially the slave trade) into few hands caused resentment among others grouped around Morgan.

After the outbreak of war with the Dutch in 1672 Beeston was ordered to convoy a fleet of merchantmen back to England, where he stayed a year, marrying Anne Hopegood, a merchant's daughter, on 11 December. The couple returned to Jamaica in 1673, and Beeston resumed business in Port Royal using surplus funds to improve his plantations in the country. He also picked up his active role in island politics. He served as member for Port Royal in the assembly of 1673, and each succeeding house, until he left the island in 1680. In 1675 he was appointed a commissioner of the Admiralty court. In 1677 Charles Howard, first earl of Carlisle, arrived as governor with orders to pass a permanent revenue bill, on the model of an Irish act, which, by depriving the assembly of its revenue raising role, would have undermined its power. Beeston, who became speaker in that year, and Samuel Long led the house's opposition on the grounds that it was contrary to the government of England 'of which country we [are]' and therefore 'desired to live under those laws' (BL, Add. MS 12430, fol. 71). Beeston and his friends further resented Carlisle as he allied with Henry Morgan's faction to the detriment of their business, and in 1680 Beeston returned to England with his wife and young daughters (a son had died at the age of fourteen months in 1677), taking a fund of about £300 subscribed by supporters to help him and Long present the assembly's case to the lords of trade and plantations and to lobby for the return of Lynch as governor. Lynch was reappointed governor in 1682.

Meanwhile, Beeston, having accumulated capital and contacts during his years in the Caribbean, resolved to resettle in England. In 1686 he was among London's sixty leading West Indies traders with imports from Jamaica valued at £2762. His enemies, Morgan and Bindloss, tried to cause trouble by informing the lords of trade and plantations of his involvement in the *Hawk*, a slaver trading contrary to the Africa Company's monopoly. But he retained his good name, reflecting the widespread animosity to monopolies, and was regularly called before the lords of trade to provide information and advice about Jamaica. However, he and his associates did suffer severe damage to their interests in 1688, when, after the death of Lynch and his successor, Hender Molesworth, Christopher Monck, second duke of Albemarle, was appointed governor of Jamaica and, on arrival in the island, allied himself with Morgan. Matters improved little after Albemarle's death, and Beeston's circle did all they could to discredit the regime and return the government to one of their own number. Beeston was appointed lieutenant-governor in September 1692, knighted by William III on 30 October, and set sail for Jamaica in December, arriving on 9 March and presiding over his first council meeting the next day.

Lieutenant-governor of Jamaica Beeston reported that he found Jamaica in a 'mean condition' (Beeston to lords of trade, 23 March 1693, *CSP col.*, 14, no. 209). After three decades of growth the outbreak of war in 1689 seriously disrupted trade. Shipping was in short supply, although Beeston claimed that it was impossible to enforce the Navigation Acts during the war and it is plain he allowed the Dutch to step into the breach. Wartime dislocation was exacerbated by a devastating earthquake in 1692. Beeston reckoned that the damage to his own property had cost him £300 a year. Half of the densely built town of Port Royal, perched at the end of a sand spit, was plunged into the sea, and the king's house was under water and past recovery. Beeston moved into the government residence at Spanish Town, which he complained was cramped and inconvenient, and he made various improvements during his government.

In the aftermath of earthquake severe sickness swept away hundreds of lives. Newcomers proved especially vulnerable, and Beeston's own eighteen-year-old daughter, Elizabeth, and a number of his servants died during his first summer back in Jamaica. Hardship drove many more to desert the island, as did the threat of impressment by naval captains stationed at the island: a repeated source of complaints from Beeston. By 1696 he estimated that the island had as few as 1300 white men (over 1000 fewer than a year earlier) and it was intensely vulnerable, not only to French depredations, but to an internal uprising among the 40,000 or so slaves.

Privateers based in Hispaniola plundered Jamaica's coastal settlements throughout the war to the detriment of planting interests, and in June 1695 du Casse, the governor of San Domingo, led a major assault on the island. Beeston had some weeks' warning and took steps to improve fortifications and prepare a defence strategy. He ordered the island's small numbers to concentrate in St Andrews, allowing critics to point to self-interest as his

own most valuable property was in that parish. The strategy left other parts of the island undefended, and when the French landed in the eastern quarters they laid the land waste. After a month there was a fierce battle in which the English, led by Colonel Lloyd rather than the governor, held their own, and the French finally withdrew at the end of July. Beeston reported that 'they have done themselves no great good but they have done this people and country a spoil that cannot soon be estimated' (Narrative by Sir William Beeston on the descent on Jamaica by the French, BL, Add. MS 12430, fol. 3). The French had killed over 100 people, burned 200 or so houses, destroyed fifty sugar plantations, and carried away over 1200 slaves. Beeston estimated that the destruction had cost the island £30,000.

Beeston's report of the invasion did not reach England until August, after the French had withdrawn, underlining the difficulties of defending distant empires in the seventeenth century and the heavy reliance on the courage and competence of those on the spot. The king declared himself very sensible of the 'infinite importance of the safety of Jamaica to England and her allies the Spaniards' (Blathwayt to Trenchard, 2 Sept 1695, *CSP col.*, 14.1277). The fleet departed the following spring and reached Jamaica in summer 1696 after an ineffectual campaign in Hispaniola. With some justification Beeston complained loudly about their conduct. The expedition displayed the same weaknesses as others in the West Indies: poor and divided leadership; ill-defined strategy; and extremely heavy mortality through sickness. Fortunately for the English their French enemy proved as ineffectual, and stalemate prevailed.

Problems of the governorship and lieutenant-governorship Beeston reported financial hardship throughout his period of office. Having been appointed as lieutenant-governor he was allowed £1000 a year (half the governor's salary). He claimed that this did not cover his expenses, especially as the cost of living was high in Jamaica. Furthermore, his salary was always in arrears. He had great difficulty persuading the assembly to vote any taxes, even when under threat of invasion, and the treasury was always in debt. However, in 1698 the assembly voted him a gift of £1500 towards his wartime expenses, and in 1700 his friend Gilbert Heathcote persuaded the Board of Trade to have him made governor, with a salary of £2000 per year.

Despite complaining of hardship, Beeston found abundant opportunities for profit. He participated in the Spanish slave trade and drew criticism for his use of naval vessels to convoy the traders. However, supply difficulties damaged this trade in 1696, and it recovered less well than expected after the peace in 1697 owing to Spanish hostility, which he blamed on the Scottish attempt to settle at Darien in 1698. Although the English government disowned the scheme, and Beeston issued a proclamation forbidding any correspondence with the settlers, the Spaniards were not convinced of English innocence. In 1699 Beeston reported the collapse of the Darien project with some relief. He had compensated for wartime difficulties by engaging in the profitable business of provisioning troops (a much more secure business than competitive peacetime trade). Gilbert Heathcote organized the trade in London using his brother Josiah and Beeston as agents and bankers in Jamaica. After war ended in late 1697 the island's trade and shipping boomed and Beeston shared in the general prosperity.

Despite his own claims to the contrary, Beeston does not appear to have been popular with his peers in Jamaica in these years, perhaps because he could use his position to gain a competitive edge in the ferocious pursuit of profit which characterized life in the high-mortality and high-risk environment of the Caribbean. He was at loggerheads with every naval commander stationed at the island as each was jealous of his own interests. By 1697 the council of Jamaica was half empty with six members only. Beeston admitted that there were sufficient rich men to fill the places, but claimed that they wanted other qualifications, suggesting his trouble lay in finding men he could count on for support. In 1700 he appointed Sir Thomas Modyford, the young grandson of the former governor, who had married his only remaining child, Jane, the previous year, although his wife later claimed he opposed the marriage. Ironically, the governor tried throughout his term of office to persuade the assembly to pass a permanent revenue bill on the model he had resisted in the 1670s but failed, as the island élite remained stubborn in its refusal to surrender power to the crown (which would, in practice, have been vested in the governor), rehearsing similar arguments to those used by Beeston himself in the 1670s. The Admiralty and a number of islanders (including Richard Lloyd, who had led the defence against the French in 1695) complained to the home authorities about the governor's conduct, specially at the time of the French invasion. Beeston dismissed all as 'malicious' and 'unfounded', and on every occasion his business associate Gilbert Heathcote, the agent for the island, defended him with some success before the Board of Trade. Distance made it hard to distinguish between contradictory testimonies, and time makes it more difficult still, especially as much surviving evidence was written by Beeston himself.

Beeston became increasingly sickly and repeatedly asked to be recalled. In 1702 his request was granted and he made his final departure from the island where he had spent most of his adult life and built a substantial fortune. He died soon after his return, on 3 November, and was buried in St Peter's, Titchfield, where he had been baptized. Beeston's will left all his property in England and an estate in Jamaica (which his widow claimed was worth £30,000) to his widow, Anne (and after her death his nephews), apart from a bequest of £3000 to his daughter, Jane, Lady Modyford (who had already received a dowry of £10,000). Lady Beeston, who married Sir Charles Orby in 1707, claimed that Lady Modyford was disinherited after marrying without her parents' consent. Lady Modyford (herself widowed in 1702 and remarried, to Charles Long, in 1703) denied the story and, in the absence of her mother, took possession of her father's Jamaican estate. Despite a long court case, and a judgment in Lady Beeston's favour, the decision proved impossible to enforce in Jamaica.

P. B. AUSTIN, *rev.* NUALA ZAHEDIEH

Sources Beeston's journal, BL, Add. MSS 12424, 12430 · entry books, Jamaica, PRO, CO 138/1–9 · *CSP col.*, vols. 1, 5, 7, 9–18 · F. Cundall, *The governors of Jamaica in the seventeenth century* (1936) · BL, Sloane MS 2282, fols. 6v–7 · Carlisle's papers relating to Jamaica, BL, Sloane MS 2724 · complaint of Sir Charles Orby and Dame Anne Hopegood Orby against Sir Charles and Anne Long, PRO, C 10/306/50 · answer of Charles Long and Dame Jane Modyford, PRO, C 10/307/58 · summary of case between Jane Long and Anne Orby, BL, Hargrave MS 391, fols. 91v–95 · will, PRO, PROB 11/467, sig. 172 **Archives** BL, journals, Add. MSS 12424, 12430 | PRO, entry books, Jamaica, CO 138/1–9 **Wealth at death** approx. £30,000 in Jamaica; also property in England: widow's evidence in court case against daughter, PRO, C 10/306/50

Beeth [Beith, Bethus], **William** (*supp. fl.* 1498), supposed Dominican author. The name first appears in the *Bibliotheca* of the Dominican order of Antonio of Siena, published in 1585; Beeth is said there to have been alive in 1498 and to have been the Dominican provincial of England, and he is credited with several writings. From Siena he was taken up by Anthony Wood (*d.* 1695), who claims him as an Oxford divine and fills out his life in eulogistic terms. This secured his place in Dominican and British repertoria, including the *Dictionary of National Biography*. In 1878 Raymund Palmer adduced evidence from the master general's registers to show that Beeth was provincial in 1500 (but the provincial actually named there is William Richford). The whole edifice rests on Siena, who gives *Epitome bibliothecae Conradi Gesneri* as his authority; but there is no mention of Bethus in Gesner. Siena has simply taken over and misreported what the *Epitome* says about Guilhelmus Hothun [*see* Hotham, William of]—namely, that he was alive in 1298—for some reason changing 'Hothun' to 'Bethus' and '1298' to '1498'. There is thus no evidence that Beeth ever existed.

SIMON TUGWELL

Sources C. Lycosthenes, *Epitome bibliothecae Conradi Gesneri*, ed. J. Simmler (Zürich, 1555), fol. 67r · A. Senensis, *Bibliotheca ordinis Fr. Praed.* (1585), 97–8 · Wood, *Ath. Oxon.* · C. F. R. Palmer, 'Fasti ordinis fratrum praedicatorum: the provincials of the friar-preachers, or Black friars, of England', *Archaeological Journal*, 35 (1878), 134–65 · Emden, *Oxf.* · W. Gumbley, 'Fasti ord. praed. in Anglia', typescript, *c.*1936, Istituto Storico Domenicano, Rome, p. 35 · S. Tugwell, 'William Beeth, the Dominican provincial who never was', *EngHR*, 113 (1998), 663–6

Beeton [*née* Mayson], **Isabella Mary** (1836–1865), writer on household management and journalist, was born on 12 or 14 March 1836 at Milk Street, off Cheapside in the City of London, the eldest in the family of three daughters and a son of Benjamin Mayson, linen factor of Milk Street, London, and his wife, Elizabeth Jerram. Isabella's father died when she was four, and in 1843 her mother married Henry Dorling of Epsom, who had two sons and two daughters from a previous marriage. To these eight, a further thirteen children were added over the next twenty years. They were housed for most of the year with their 'Granny Jerram' in the Epsom grandstand, which was let to Henry

Isabella Mary Beeton (1836–1865), by Maull & Polyblank, *c.*1860–65

Dorling in his capacity as clerk of the course. As the eldest girl among the twenty-one children, Isabella was her grandmother's chief assistant, and in this unusual establishment her informal education began. Her formal education, after a brief period in Islington, was in a school in Heidelberg where, as well as developing her musical talents, she acquired a facility in languages which was to be useful in her later career. She also took to pastry making, which she continued to practise at a local confectioners when she returned to Epsom in 1854, though her family thought this to be 'ultra modern and not quite nice'.

On 10 July 1856 Isabella married Samuel Orchart *Beeton (1831–1877), the son of Samuel Powell Beeton, an innkeeper at Milk Street, London. They had four sons, the first of whom died in infancy (1857) and the second aged three (1864). Samuel Beeton had already begun to make a name for himself as a publisher and editor. His early involvement in the English edition of Harriet Beecher Stowe's *Uncle Tom's Cabin* had helped to finance a series of innovatory publications. The most important of these for Mrs Beeton was the *English Woman's Domestic Magazine*, a twopenny monthly launched in 1852, which pioneered the middle-class woman's magazine.

For the eight and a half years of their marriage the Beetons developed a partnership in which the personal and professional were intertwined. Mrs Beeton entered almost immediately into her husband's publishing business, and within a year was writing on domestic matters for the *English Woman's Domestic Magazine* and had begun

the 'four years' incessant labour' which she claimed *Beeton's Book of Household Management* cost her. Her role in the production of the various Beeton journals is not self-evident in their pages, since a public persona was not part of her style. However, she was 'editress' of the *Domestic Magazine* and was involved in the upmarket weekly *The Queen* which was launched in 1861. A visit to Paris in 1860 established a French connection for the firm, and a new series of the *English Woman's Domestic Magazine* included monthly accounts of the latest Paris styles, a high-quality colour fashion-plate, and the offer of a pattern service for readers, a combination which was to become a staple of twentieth-century women's magazines. Whether she was visiting Paris, writing articles, dealing with layout, even demonstrating how to cut out a pattern for a perplexed reader, Mrs Beeton's energy and organizational skills were crucial to the management of the publishing house. It is not for this, however, that she is remembered, but for her writing on domestic matters and especially for *Beeton's Book of Household Management* (1859–61), which in its various editions made 'Mrs Beeton' a household name in a double sense.

Part of the extraordinary success of this book may be attributed to skilful marketing—as a part-work between 1859 and 1861, the illustrated edition in 1861, and the cheap reissues begun by Samuel Beeton and continued by Ward, Lock, and Tyler, to whom he sold his titles after Isabella's death. Its success, however, also rested on its quality, especially the combination of clear structure and precise detail. Recipes, for example, were arranged alphabetically in sections, with ingredients, prices, weights, and cooking times all precisely stated. The book's style moved easily between detailed instructions and neat aphorisms.

For Mrs Beeton, a people's 'way of taking their meals, as well as their way of treating women' were marks of civilization. Dining well 'implies both the will and the skill to reduce to order, and surround with idealisms and grace, the more material conditions of human existence'. That will and skill she showed in large measure. The popular image of Mrs Beeton as a middle-aged housewife given to the confection of extravagant recipes is doubly mistaken. First, her book is notable for its attempt to combine good living with economy. Second, she never lived to middle age; she died aged twenty-eight at her home, Mount Pleasant, Swanscombe, Kent, of peritonitis and puerperal fever on 6 February 1865, eight days after the birth of her son Mayson, who later had a distinguished career in journalism and government. MARGARET BEETHAM, *rev.*

Sources S. Freeman, *Isabella and Sam: the story of Mrs Beeton* (1977) · H. M. Hyde, *Mr. and Mrs. Beeton* (1951) · N. Spain, *The Beeton story* (1956) · G. Nown, *Mrs Beeton: 150 years of cookery and household management* (1986) · d. cert. · m. cert. · *Beeton's book of household management* (1861) · *The Times* (3 Feb 1932) · *English Woman's Domestic Magazine*

Likenesses attrib. H. Dorling, watercolour, 1848, NPG · Maull & Polyblank, photograph, *c.*1860–1865, NPG [*see illus.*]

Beeton, Samuel Orchart (1831–1877), publisher and journalist, was born on 2 March 1831 at 39 Milk Street in

Cheapside, London, the only son of Samuel Powell Beeton (1804–1854), warehouseman and publican, and his first wife, Helen (d. 1831), daughter of Thomas Orchart, a baker. Because his mother died soon after his birth, Samuel was brought up by his Beeton grandmother. His only formal education was at Pilgrim's Hall Academy, a small private school in Brentwood, Essex, which he attended aged twelve to fourteen. He was then apprenticed to a paper merchant in the City for seven years during which apparently he had 'quite a gay time' but must also have laid the foundations for his subsequent career (Spain, 42).

At twenty-one, with some money from his father, Beeton set up as a publisher in partnership with Charles H. Clarke. Through a series of accidents they immediately had the opportunity to publish *Uncle Tom's Cabin* by an unknown American, Harriet Beecher Stowe. Beeton saw the novel's potential for the British market and its message chimed with his politics. He seized the chance to publish, showing that combination of energy, financial shrewdness, and faith in popular print as a medium for social improvement which was to characterize his career. The immense sales of this book helped underpin his innovative publishing ventures. In April 1852, the same month as *Uncle Tom's Cabin* appeared, Beeton launched the first magazine for middle-class women, a twopenny monthly, the *English Woman's Domestic Magazine*. He followed it in January 1855 with another pioneering journal, the *Boy's Own Magazine*.

In the following year (10 July 1856) in Epsom parish church, Beeton married Isabella Mary Mayson (1836–1865) [see Beeton, Isabella Mary], the eldest daughter of Benjamin Mayson, a linen merchant, and his wife, Elizabeth, whose second husband was Henry Dorling, clerk of the Epsom racecourse. The marriage of Sam and Bella proved a happy partnership in both personal and business terms. He encouraged her to write the work for which the name Beeton is still remembered, *Beeton's Book of Household Management*, which was first issued in parts between 1859 and 1861. She played an increasingly active role in the business, from which Clarke now departed, and with her support, Beeton entered the happiest stage of his career, producing a series of Beeton titles including dictionaries, guides, and All About It books, as well as a *Christmas Annual*. Together they built on his earlier successes with women's and boys' magazines, launching new titles and expanding existing ones.

Beeton's private life was more clouded, despite his happy marriage. Neither of the couple's first two children—both sons called Samuel Orchart—survived, the first dying immediately, the second aged three. However, they had another son, called simply Orchart, born on new year's eve 1863 in Greenhithe, Kent, to which they had just moved from Pinner, Middlesex. He survived, as did their fourth son, Mayson, born on 29 January 1865. However, as a result of this last confinement Isabella developed puerperal fever and died on 6 February, aged twenty-eight.

This was a professional as well as a personal tragedy. Beeton's publishing and writing continued but his financial position was undermined by the collapse in May 1866

of the house of Overend and Gurney in which he had substantial investments. He was forced to sell his titles and his name to his rivals, Ward, Lock, and Tyler, for whom he undertook to work exclusively in future. He continued to produce Beeton titles with enormous energy, publishing nearly thirty in the next five years. However, from 1867 the *English Woman's Domestic Magazine* was caught up in controversy over a correspondence on tight-lacing and on beating. More seriously, in 1872 Beeton's relationship with Ward and Lock (as it now was) deteriorated sharply over his use of the *Beeton Christmas Annual* to satirize the royal family. The legal tangle over the name Beeton led to two court cases in 1874 and 1875, which left him free but without possession of his earlier titles. His return to independent publishing was hampered by ill health and he died at Sudbrook Park, Petersham, Richmond, Surrey, on 6 June 1877 of pulmonary consumption, which had affected him for years.

Physically slight, but attractive, and prodigiously energetic, Beeton was a republican, a supporter of women's suffrage, and anti-establishment in religion and politics, as well as an innovative publisher, editor, and journalist. His achievement is difficult to assess; firstly, because these roles tended to overlap in his work and, secondly, because of the sale of his name and titles. Nevertheless he stands as one of the pioneers of popular print—particularly for women and boys.   MARGARET BEETHAM

Sources S. Freeman, *Isabella and Sam: the story of Mrs Beeton* (1977) · H. M. Hyde, *Mr. and Mrs. Beeton* (1951) · N. Spain, *Mrs. Beeton and her husband* (1948) · *The Athenaeum* (9 June 1877), 739 · J. Shattock, ed., *The Cambridge bibliography of English literature*, 3rd edn, 4 (1999) · m. cert. · d. cert. · *CGPLA Eng. & Wales* (1877)
Likenesses drawing, repro. in Hyde, *Mr. and Mrs. Beeton*, 26
Wealth at death £3000: resworn administration with will, Dec 1879, *CGPLA Eng. & Wales* (1877)

Beever, Mary (1802–1883). *See under* Women artists in Ruskin's circle (*act.* 1850s–1900s).

Beever, Susanna (1805–1893). *See under* Women artists in Ruskin's circle (*act.* 1850s–1900s).

Beevor, Charles Edward (1854–1908), neurologist, born in London on 12 June 1854, was the eldest son of Charles Beevor FRCS, and Elizabeth, daughter of Thomas Burrell. He received his early education at Blackheath proprietary school and afterwards studied medicine at University College, London. He became MRCS in 1878, and graduated MB in 1879, and MD in 1881. He became MRCP in 1882 and FRCP in 1888. On 7 February 1882 he married Blanche Adine, daughter of Dr Thomas Robinson Leadam. After holding the appointments of house physician at University College Hospital, and resident medical officer at the National Hospital for the Paralysed and Epileptic, Queen Square, he went abroad in 1882–3, and studied under Heinrich Obersteiner, Carl Weigert, Julius Cohnheim, and Wilhelm Heinrich Erb, at Vienna, Leipzig, Berlin, and Paris. On his return in 1883 he was appointed assistant physician to the National Hospital, Queen Square, and to the Great Northern Central Hospital (later the Royal Northern Central Hospital) in 1885. In the course of time he became full physician to both institutions, offices which he held until his death.

From 1883 to 1887 Beevor was engaged with Victor Horsley in experimental research on the localization of cerebral functions, especially with regard to the course and origin of the motor tracts. This work confirmed results obtained by previous investigators and established the reputation of the authors (*PTRS*, 181B, 1890; also 1887–9). In 1903 Beevor delivered the Croonian lectures before the Royal College of Physicians, on muscular movements and their representation in the central nervous system (published in 1904), and in 1907 he delivered the Lettsomian lectures entitled 'The diagnosis and localization of cerebral tumours' before the Medical Society of London. He contributed many papers on subjects connected with neurology to *Brain* and other medical journals, and his *Handbook on Diseases of the Nervous System* (1898) became a leading textbook. His most important work was 'On the distribution of the different arteries supplying the brain', which was published in the *Philosophical Transactions of the Royal Society* (200B, 1909, 1–56) and was the first published work to contain an accurate description of the cerebral arterial circulation. Beevor succeeded in injecting simultaneously the five arteries of the brain with different coloured substances held in solution in gelatin and by this means he determined exactly the blood supply to different parts of the brain. The importance of Beevor's discovery was not only from the anatomical side but also from the pathological, for it enabled the physician to know the exact portions of the brain which are liable to undergo softening when any particular artery is blocked by a clot of blood.

In May 1908 Beevor went to America, where his lectures were received with enthusiasm by the members of the American Neurological Society, and by the American Medical Association at its fifty-ninth annual session. In 1907–8 he was president of the Neurological Society of London, and on its amalgamation with the Royal Society of Medicine he became the first president of the society's corresponding section, and died in office. For ten years he was honorary secretary to the Association for the Advancement of Medicine by Research.

Beevor ranks among the great authorities on the anatomy and diseases of the nervous system. He possessed great intellectual power, energy, and industry, and was unsurpassed in his accuracy of observation and recording of facts. He was however cautious in publishing his own observations when they seemed at variance with tradition and accepted teaching. Beevor died from sudden cardiac failure on 5 December 1908 at his residence, 135 Harley Street, and was buried at Hampstead cemetery on 9 December. He was survived by his wife and a son and daughter.   LEONARD GUTHRIE, rev. CAROLINE OVERY

Sources E. Clarke, 'Beevor, Charles Edward', *DSB* · *The Lancet* (19 Dec 1908) · *BMJ* (12 Dec 1908), 1785–6 · presidential address, Royal College of Physicians, 1909 · *CGPLA Eng. & Wales* (1909)
Likenesses photograph, National Hospital, Queen Square, London
Wealth at death £41,349 16s. 2d.: probate, 9 Feb 1909, *CGPLA Eng. & Wales*

Beevor, Edward. *See* Lombe, Edward (d. 1852).

Beffin, Sarah. *See* Biffin, Sarah (1784–1850).

Bega [St Bega] (*supp. fl.* late 7th cent.), abbess of Hartlepool, was a legendary Irish saint, supposedly active in northern England in the seventh century. Her life and miracles are described in an anonymous account, probably written at the priory of St Bees in Cumbria c.1200, in which she is presented as the daughter of an Irish king who vowed to preserve her virginity and who was confirmed in this intention by a visionary figure who gave her an arm-ring as a token of her espousal to Christ. She fled to England to avoid a proposed marriage and at first lived a solitary life in Copeland (Cumbria), before moving to Northumbria, leaving behind her arm-ring. She was consecrated the first nun in Northumbria by Áedán, during the reign of King Oswald (r. 634–42), and ruled over a community at Hartlepool which she handed over to St Hild before retiring to Tadcaster. Bega saw Hild's death in a vision while at the monastery of Hackness, and shortly afterwards she herself died and was buried there. Her feast was celebrated on 31 October. The anonymous author, after relating how Bega's bones had been translated from Hackness to Whitby in the twelfth century, narrates a series of miracles centred on her holy arm-ring, preserved at St Bees, which was employed especially for swearing judicial oaths.

One source of the legend is a chapter in Bede's *Historia ecclesiastica* (4.23) that describes how a nun of Hackness, called Begu, saw St Hild's death in a vision. Bede also mentions another nun, called Heiu, the first nun in Northumbria, who was consecrated by Áedán, founded the monastery of Hartlepool, and retired to Tadcaster. Clearly Bega's Northumbrian career as reported in the twelfth century is a conflation of Bede's Begu and Bede's Heiu. Since Bega's bracelet was the focus of the Cumbrian cult and the Old English word for ring or bracelet is *beag*, the suspicion naturally arises that originally St Bega *was* a bracelet and that the Cumbrian cult started from a holy armband that only gradually metamorphosed into the person, St Bega. The Irish section of her life is probably pure literary invention.   ROBERT BARTLETT

Sources 'Vita et miracula sancte Bege virginis', *The register of the priory of St Bees*, ed. [J. Wilson], SurtS, 126 (1915), 497–520 · J. M. Todd, 'St Bega: cult, fact and legend', *Transactions of the Cumberland and Westmorland Antiquarian and Archaeological Society*, [new ser.] 80 (1980), 23–35 · R. Bartlett, 'Cults of Irish, Scottish and Welsh saints in twelfth-century England', *Britain and Ireland, 900–1300*, ed. B. Smith (1999), 67–86

Begbie, James (1798–1869), physician, was born in Edinburgh, the son of James Farquhar Gordon (d. 1797/8), writer to the signet, and Margaret Begbie, formerly Gordon (née Skeid). He was educated at Edinburgh high school and at the University of Edinburgh, where he took the degree of MD in 1821. His inaugural dissertation was on delirium tremens. Begbie became a fellow of the Royal College of Surgeons of Edinburgh in 1822. A pupil, and then the assistant, of the talented Edinburgh physician, pathologist, and teacher John Abercrombie (1780–1844),

Begbie worked for Abercrombie during the final years of the apprenticeship system when Abercrombie was using his large medical practice as a kind of private medical school. As Abercrombie's trusted friend and assistant he taught some of Abercrombie's many apprentices and he conducted post-mortem examinations and pathological investigations.

After this excellent training Begbie entered Edinburgh's competitive medical market place by starting his own general practice—which soon became extensive. By November 1826 he had married Elizabeth Speirs (or Spears), with whom he had two sons, the younger of whom was James Warburton *Begbie (1826–1876). In 1847 Begbie became a fellow of the Royal College of Physicians of Edinburgh and from then on he devoted himself to consulting practice and increased both his reputation and his popularity.

Begbie acted as medical adviser to the Scottish Widows' Fund and Life Assurance Society for thirty-five years and described the result of his experiences in his essay 'Mortality of the Scottish Widows' Fund'. This paper opened up a new field in vital statistics and made its author's name known far beyond the limits of his own profession. Begbie also wrote a series of other medical essays which were published in book form in 1862 as *Contributions to Practical Medicine*. The most important is 'Anaemia and its consequences', which gives an account of exophthalmic goitre—commonly known as Graves' disease. This was first read before the Medico-Chirurgical Society of Edinburgh on 3 January 1849. Begbie was president of the Medico-Chirurgical Society from 1850 to 1852. He was president of the Royal College of Physicians of Edinburgh from 1854 to 1856 and for several years he was physician-in-ordinary to Queen Victoria.

Begbie died from heart disease at his home, 10 Charlotte Square, Edinburgh, on 26 August 1869 after a few months' illness. His *Lancet* obituarist wrote: 'throughout his entire life he exhibited an irreproachable Christian character—a character which during his trying illness and at death shone forth with peculiar brilliancy'. IAIN MILNE

Sources *Edinburgh Medical Journal*, 15 (1869–70), 380–83 · *The Lancet* (4 Sept 1869), 356 · R. Thin, *College portraits* (1927), 14–15 · b. cert. [J. W. Begbie] · d. cert. · W. S. Craig, *History of the Royal College of Physicians of Edinburgh* (1976) · *DNB*
Likenesses oils, Royal College of Physicians of Edinburgh · photograph, Royal College of Physicians of Edinburgh
Wealth at death £11,712 16s. 0½d.: confirmation, 15 Oct 1869, NA Scot., SC70/1/145/151

Begbie, James Warburton (1826–1876), physician, was born in Edinburgh on 19 November 1826, the second son of James *Begbie (1798–1869), physician, and his wife, Elizabeth Speirs. Apart from a short spell at an English school he was educated at the Edinburgh Academy. In 1843 he became a medical student at the University of Edinburgh. He was successful there and was twice elected president of Edinburgh University's prestigious student society, the Royal Medical Society. In 1847 he proceeded MD and his dissertation, 'On some of the pathological conditions of the urine', received a special commendation.

Begbie then visited Paris, where he continued his medical studies. In 1849 he stayed for some months with the family of the earl of Aberdeen at Haddo House, Aberdeenshire, before embarking on a European tour with the only son of John Hope, lord justice clerk of Scotland.

1852 was an eventful year for Begbie: he settled in Edinburgh, where he worked as a family practitioner and became one of the medical officers attached to the New Town Dispensary; he was also made a fellow of the Royal College of Physicians of Edinburgh (at the early age of twenty-six), and on 13 December married Anna Maria Churchill Reid, daughter of the late Nevile Reid of Runnymede, Windsor, Berkshire. In 1854 he was appointed physician to the (temporary) cholera hospital in Edinburgh, and in 1855 he became physician to the Edinburgh Royal Infirmary, a post which he held for the statutory period of ten years. During this time he gave clinical lectures in the infirmary and on the practice of physic at the extramural school. Contemporaries suggest that (like his father) he was better suited to bedside teaching than to delivering more formal lectures. In a biographical notice in the *Edinburgh Medical Journal* the then editor Joseph Bell wrote:

> it must in fairness be owned he was no orator … Begbie as a teacher was greatest at the bedside. His clinical visits were masterpieces both in precept and example…he was great both in diagnosis and prognosis; and with a rarer power still had the patience to use and profit by the use of remedies— not merely drugs but diet. (*Edinburgh Medical Journal*, 21, 1876)

Begbie also gave a short annual course of lectures on the history of medicine which made full use of his knowledge of both ancient and modern languages.

After 1865 Begbie ceased to teach or hold hospital appointments, and in 1869, on the death of his father, he decided to limit himself to consulting practice. He also 'inherited' the post of physician to the Scottish Widows' Fund and Life Assurance Society. Begbie's report entitled 'The causes of death among the assured, 1857–1863', published in the *Edinburgh Medical Journal*, is a valuable contribution to the statistics of life assurance. His other writings are mainly commentaries on cases, though he did write *A Handy Book of Medical Information and Advice by a Physician*, published anonymously in 1860, and thirteen articles in J. R. Reynolds's *System of Medicine*. The best of his journal articles were edited by Dyce Duckworth and reprinted in 1882 by the New Sydenham Society as *Selections from the Works of the Late J. Warburton Begbie*.

By the 1860s Begbie had become one of the most popular and highly esteemed physicians in Scotland, and he made full use of the railway system to build up the largest consulting practice in the country. In 1875, at the meeting of the British Medical Association in Edinburgh, he delivered the address on medicine, and at the same time Edinburgh University conferred upon him the honorary degree of LLD. Immediately after this event the effects of heart disease forced Begbie to stop work, and he died at his home at 16 Great Stuart Street, Edinburgh, on 25 February 1876, just six years after his father's death from a similar condition. He was buried in Dean cemetery, Edinburgh.

Begbie was well fitted for the work of his profession, and he was remarkably successful, not only in relieving the bodily ills of his patients, but in winning their confidence and affection. He predeceased his wife and his three sons and four daughters, one of whom, Florence Anne, was the mother of the politician Alan Tindal Lennox-*Boyd (1904–1983).   IAIN MILNE

Sources *Edinburgh Medical Journal*, 21 (1875–6), 950–59 · 'Memoir', D. Duckworth, *Selections from the works of the late J. Warburton Begbie* (1882) · *BMJ* (11 March 1876), 337–8 · W. T. Gairdner, *BMJ* (11 March 1876), 311 · J. D. Comrie, *History of Scottish medicine*, 2nd edn, 2 vols. (1932) · W. S. Craig, *History of the Royal College of Physicians of Edinburgh* (1976) · *DNB* · bap. reg. Scot. · parish register (marriage), Edinburgh, St George's, 13 Dec 1852

Likenesses J. Steell, bust, 1877, Royal College of Physicians of Edinburgh · photograph, Royal College of Physicians of Edinburgh · photograph, repro. in Duckworth, *Selections from the works*

Wealth at death £20,926 16s. 8d.: confirmation, 8 May 1876, NA Scot., SC 70/1/178/221

Begg, James (1808–1883), Free Church of Scotland minister, was born in the manse at New Monkland, Lanarkshire, on 31 October 1808. He was the second surviving son of James Begg (1762–1845), Church of Scotland minister of New Monkland, and his wife, Mary (1777–1831), daughter of John Matthie, a merchant in Greenock. Begg received his early education at New Monkland parish school, which left him a lifelong enthusiast for the Scottish parochial school system. He entered the University of Glasgow in 1820, taking his MA degree in arts in 1824, and then following the theology course. The major formative influences on him were his father, a popular evangelical preacher who mediated an austere covenanting inheritance, and Stevenson McGill, professor of divinity at Glasgow, who instilled into his pupils a socially concerned and politically engaged Christian zeal.

In 1828 Begg went to Edinburgh to study under Thomas Chalmers, thus completing his preparation for the ministry of the Church of Scotland. Following his licensing by the presbytery of Hamilton on 10 June 1829, he became assistant to James Buchanan at North Leith. He was ordained by the presbytery of Dumfries on 18 May 1830 and took charge of the newly erected chapel of ease in the suburb of Maxwelltown. In December 1830 he returned to Edinburgh to be assistant minister at Lady Glenorchy's Chapel, an evangelical stronghold. Begg moved again in November 1831, becoming minister of the Middle Church at Paisley, where he remained until January 1835, when he again returned to Edinburgh, this time as minister of the parish of Liberton. He held this office until the Disruption. On 23 September 1835 Begg married Margaret (d. 1845), daughter of Alexander Campbell, sheriff substitute of Renfrewshire. They had five children, of whom two sons and a daughter survived infancy.

Begg quickly established himself as one of the leaders of the evangelical and non-intrusionist party in the Church of Scotland. He was a fluent extemporaneous preacher

James Begg (1808–1883), by David Octavius Hill and Robert Adamson

who drew large congregations. Meanwhile he became actively involved in ecclesiastical politics, arguing for the rights of ministers of proprietary chapels, advocating church extension and opposing voluntaryism. His ideal was 'an Established Church so good that dissent would be unnecessary' (T. Smith, 1.227). Nevertheless, despite Begg's commitment to church establishment in principle, the escalation of patronage disputes inexorably drove him, like many others, towards secession. In 1840 he was among those who preached in Strathbogie in defiance of the interdict of the court of session. By 1843 he saw the Church of Scotland as locked in a struggle for the headship of Christ over the church, and the conviction that 'there is no aristocracy in the Church of God' (J. Begg, *Reply to Sir James Graham's Letter*, 1843, 3).

When the Disruption came in May 1843 Begg was resolute and prominent in his adherence to the Free Church. He rallied support for its cause in England, and went on preaching tours of the highlands and of North America. He preached before the United States congress and in 1847 was awarded the degree of DD by Lafayette College, Pennsylvania. Meanwhile he became the first minister of Newington Free Church, where he was to remain for the rest of his life. Begg's authoritarian style of ministry was criticized as inconsistent with the democratic principles he professed, but he attracted a large congregation from many parts of Edinburgh. He energetically promoted efforts to evangelize the urban poor, both in a mission staffed by his own congregation, and as convenor of the

Free Church Home Mission and Church Extension Committee from 1847 to 1857. Begg's first wife having died in 1845, he married, on 25 November 1846, Maria (*d.* 1892), daughter of Ferdinand Faithfull, rector of Headley, Surrey. They had six sons, one of whom died young, and one daughter.

In 1850 Begg took a leading role in the formation of the Scottish Reformation Society, which sought to mobilize public opinion against the Roman Catholic church, to resist political concessions to Rome, and to heighten an awareness of Scottish protestant identity and tradition. Begg was editor of the society's journal, *The Bulwark*, for over twenty years from its establishment in 1851. He published *A Handbook of Popery* (1852) which sold 150,000 copies in his lifetime and became regarded as a standard work of protestant polemic. He was also a key supporter of the Protestant Institute of Scotland, which was set up in the early 1860s.

At this period of his life, Begg threw himself with equal zeal into endeavours to improve the living conditions of the Scottish people, believing that poor material conditions had inevitable moral and spiritual consequences. He was a founder in 1850 of the Scottish Social Reform Association, and in 1851 delivered a lecture under its auspices entitled 'How every man may become his own landlord'. He took a strong ongoing interest in the provision of better working-class housing. At his instigation the Free Church in 1858 appointed a committee to investigate the matter, which subsequently operated energetically under his own leadership. Begg was a trenchant critic of the bothy system of barrack-style labourers' lodgings in the Scottish countryside, and pressed rural landowners to build decent houses for them. In the towns he facilitated support for workers who wished to purchase their own homes, notably through his involvement in the Edinburgh Co-operative Building Company, founded in 1861. He was also a strenuous advocate of a national system of education.

Begg's progressive social concerns were linked to his conservative theology by an underlying conviction that Scottish society and values needed to be rooted in the Reformation heritage of the nation. The Reformation and its Calvinist legacy were in his view not only the fountainhead of spiritual truth and salvation, but also the essential inspiration for effective education and social justice. A firm Scottish patriot, who advocated an extension of the franchise and a measure of home rule, he saw himself as a latter-day John Knox crusading for the spiritual regeneration and national liberation of a 'politically dead and socially degraded people' (J. Begg, *Scotland's Demand for Electoral Justice*, 1857, 33).

Begg's career reached its formal culmination in 1865 when he was moderator of the general assembly of the Free Church of Scotland, but by this time there was already a waning of support within the denomination for his conservative theological position and his adherence to the principle of a national church. Begg, however, rose to the challenge. In his opening address as moderator he vigorously advocated his own principles as representing the

essential tradition of the Disruption, and in subsequent years he strenuously opposed proposals for union with the United Presbyterian church, frustrating them by the threat of legal action. His ire was also directed against liturgical innovation and theological liberalism. In the 1870s he denounced the recent introduction of hymns and organs into Presbyterian worship as 'sensuous and sensational' and liable to lead to 'frivolity, apostacy and Rome' (J. Begg, *Anarchy in Worship*, 1875, 27). He led attacks on the biblical critic William Robertson Smith, and in 1881 secured Smith's dismissal from his professorial chair at Aberdeen.

In his later years Begg suffered from diabetes and from the effects of a serious accident in 1865, but, although his health was noticeably in decline by 1879, he remained in harness to the end. He died at home in Newington, Edinburgh, on 29 September 1883. Two thousand people reportedly attended his funeral, and he was buried in Newington cemetery on 3 October (*The Scotsman*, 4 Oct 1883).

Begg was an imposing man of pronounced and inflexible views, with a keen intellect of a polemical rather than a subtle cast. He had a rugged honesty and integrity, a 'rough bonhomie' and a deep-rooted concern for the welfare of his fellow countrymen. Nevertheless he was too combative to inspire affection as opposed to respect, and he was unable to generate widespread and sustained enthusiasm for the causes he advocated. 'There was', as an obituarist put it, 'no principle held more firmly by him than that of the duty of the State to uphold the Church, but it must be his Church' (*The Scotsman*, 1 Oct 1883). It is ironic, given his lowland origins, that in his last years his support in the Free Church was largely limited to conservative highlanders. Begg's legacy is therefore to be found not, as he had hoped, in the mainstream of Scottish religious and political life, but in the Free Presbyterian church and the continuing Free Church of Scotland, which have stood out against the processes of reunification and theological modernization.　　　　JOHN WOLFFE

Sources *The Scotsman* (1 Oct 1883) · T. Smith, *Memoirs of James Begg*, 2 vols. (1885–8) · *Fasti Scot.*, new edn · kirk session minutes, Newington Free Church, NA Scot., CH3/1195/23 · 'Disruption in Mr Begg's Free Church', 26 Sept 1844, NL Scot., Broadsheet APS d. 44 [Edinburgh] · J. Wolffe, *The protestant crusade in Great Britain, 1829–1860* (1991) · S. Bruce, *No pope of Rome: anti-Catholicism in modern Scotland* (1985) · S. Mechie, *The church and Scottish social development, 1780–1870* (1960) · D. C. Smith, *Passive obedience and prophetic protest: social criticism in the Scottish church, 1830–1945* (1987) · H. J. Hanham, *Scottish nationalism* (1969) · W. R. Nicoll, *Princes of the church* (1921) · *The Scotsman* (4 Oct 1883)

Archives NA Scot., Church of Scotland and Free Church of Scotland records · U. Edin., New Coll. L., letters to Thomas Chalmers

Likenesses N. Macbeth, oils, 1864, Scottish Reformation Society, Edinburgh · D. O. Hill, oils, 1866 (after photograph by R. Adamson) · D. Macnee, oils, 1869, Scot. NPG · D. O. Hill and R. Adamson, calotype (for group; first general assembly of the Free Church), NPG · D. O. Hill and R. Adamson, calotypes, Scot. NPG; negative, U. Glas. Lib. [*see illus.*] · D. O. Hill and R. Adamson, group portrait, oils, Free Church College, Edinburgh · bust, Free Church College, Edinburgh, Senate Hall

Wealth at death £15,269 16s. 5d.: confirmation, 14 Nov 1883, *CCI*

Begg, Sir Varyl Cargill (1908–1995), naval officer, was born in Kensington, London, on 1 October 1908, the son of Francis Cargill Begg, of Henley-on-Thames, and his wife, Muriel Clare, *née* Robinson. He was educated at St Andrews School, Eastbourne, and Malvern College, before joining the navy as a special entry cadet in September 1926. After service in *Delhi*, *Durban*, *Marlborough*, and *Shropshire*, he went to HMS *Excellent*, the gunnery school at Whale Island, and in 1934 qualified as a gunnery specialist. He was second gunnery officer of the battleship *Nelson*, flagship of the Home Fleet, before returning to Whale Island on the experimental staff in 1936. He was appointed flotilla gunnery officer in the destroyer *Cossack* in 1937, and two years later was gunnery officer of the 6-inch-gun cruiser *Glasgow*, which participated in north Atlantic convoys, the Norwegian campaign, and the occupation of Iceland, before being badly damaged in a torpedo attack by Italian aircraft in Suda Bay, Crete.

In 1940 Begg was appointed gunnery officer of the battleship *Warspite* in the Mediterranean when it was flagship of the commander-in-chief, Admiral Sir Andrew Cunningham. Begg was in charge of *Warspite*'s main 15 inch armament off Cape Matapan on the night of 28 March 1941, when *Warspite*, *Barham*, and *Valiant* caught the Italian heavy cruisers *Fiume* and *Zara* by surprise, with their guns still trained fore and aft, and sank them both in a brutally short action of less than two minutes. A third heavy cruiser, *Pola*, and two Italian destroyers were also sunk that night. Begg was awarded the DSC for his part in the action. He was promoted commander in December 1942 and then went to the gunnery division in the Admiralty, where he was involved in the development of gun design and tactics for the post-war period. On 7 August 1943 he married Rosemary Cowan, daughter of Francis Edward Patrick Porter Cowan, of Craigavad, co. Down. They had two sons, Timothy (*b.* 1944) and Peter (*b.* 1948).

After tactical and staff courses Begg was promoted captain in 1947 and was staff officer (operations) to the rear-admiral (destroyers) in the Mediterranean. From 1948 to 1950 he was captain in charge of the gunnery school at Chatham. In the latter year he joined the destroyer *Cossack* again, this time in command and as captain (D) of the 8th destroyer flotilla. The *Cossack* served in the first two years of the Korean War, and with other Commonwealth ships carried out blockading patrols of the west coast of Korea as far north as the Yalu River; it was also in the bombarding force of cruisers and destroyers for the crucial Inchon landings in September 1950, which turned the tide of the war in the United Nations' favour, and went on to make many bombardments in support of UN forces ashore. Like all the destroyers, the *Cossack* was worked hard, and it was not unusual for it to steam 8000 miles in a month. For his service in Korea, Begg was mentioned in dispatches in 1951 and appointed DSO the next year. From 1952 to 1955 he was captain of HMS *Excellent*. He commanded the light fleet carrier *Triumph* from 1954 to 1956, when it was a cadet training ship. Promoted rear-admiral in 1957, he was chief of staff to the commander-in-chief, Portsmouth, from 1957 to 1958, and then flag officer, second in command,

Far East Fleet, from 1958 to 1960. He was appointed CB in 1959.

Begg was promoted vice-admiral in 1960 and went to the Admiralty in 1961 as a lord commissioner of the Admiralty and vice-chief of naval staff. The first sea lord was Caspar John, the first naval aviator to hold the office. The two men liked and respected each other. It was a time of great financial and political turmoil for the navy, and John soon came to value Begg's experience and good sense, as well as the influential contacts he had through the gunnery world. Begg and John reluctantly decided that the navy could no longer afford three fleets. Together they implemented the difficult—and, in some quarters, bitterly resented—decision to disband the fleet in the Mediterranean, a historic station where the navy had won so many battle honours. In 1963 Begg went out to the Far East again as a full admiral, commander-in-chief of British forces in the Far East, and British military adviser to the South-East Asia Treaty Organization, at a time of undeclared war between Malaysia, a newly independent state, and Indonesia. As the overall commander on the spot Begg had to wage a maritime war of convoy, blockade, and air strike, and support the army over distances of thousands of miles. The war was played down in the media by both sides, and very few of those who did not take part were aware of its extent or duration. Begg was promoted KCB in 1962 and GCB in 1965, and in 1966 was appointed to the Panglima Mangku Negara, a Malaysian order.

Begg returned to Britain in 1965 as commander-in-chief, Portsmouth, and became first sea lord and chief of the naval staff the next year, the first special entry officer to do so. He had the difficult task of restoring the navy's morale after the Labour government's rejection in the defence review of February 1966 of the giant aircraft-carrier CVA01. A whole generation of naval officers, many of them with service in the Second World War, had taken it as an article of faith that the Royal Navy would always have its own air power. The sudden cancellation of the CVA01 project led to the resignations of Begg's predecessor as first sea lord, Admiral Sir David Luce, and the minister of defence (Royal Navy), Christopher Mayhew. Begg had to do his best to repair the situation against a background of sustained lobbying by the Royal Air Force personnel to take over all aircraft movements at sea. For some years it seemed that the Fleet Air Arm might become not much more than a helicopter search-and-rescue service, with some anti-submarine capabilities. Begg wasted no time repining over the loss of the CVA01 but at once set up a future fleet working party, which was specifically forbidden to consider the resurrection of aircraft-carriers. When the working party's chairman included in the final report a project for a large helicopter and vertical take-off aircraft-carrier, Begg ended that officer's career. Ironically, just such a ship, in the form of the Invincible class, eventually arrived in the fleet.

Begg was promoted admiral of the fleet in 1968, only the second special entry officer, after the duke of Edinburgh, to achieve that rank. The following year he went to Gibraltar, as governor and commander-in-chief, thus breaking a

250-year tradition of military governors. A tense political situation, when Spain was making life as difficult as possible for the Gibraltarians, was exacerbated when the Spanish government protested at the presence in Gibraltar of the prince of Wales, who had arrived to join his ship *Norfolk*. Begg dealt with that and subsequent potential embarrassments with such skill and tact that when he retired in 1973, Julian Amery, minister of state at the Foreign Office, compared him to General Sir George Elliott, who successfully held off the Spaniards during the great siege of 1779–83, saying that Begg had 'conducted the present siege with as much skill as Elliott and far fewer casualties' (*The Independent*, 15 July 1995).

With his craggy features and aquiline nose Begg was a man of striking appearance, who looked the part of a distinguished admiral and sailor. David Owen, who became minister for the navy in 1968, recalled Begg as 'an Admiral with salt both in his ears and his tongue', who 'did not suffer fools gladly' (*The Independent*, 15 July 1995). A keen sportsman Begg was president of the Combined Services Winter Sports Association and of Royal Navy Cricket. In retirement he took an active interest in village life at Chilbolton, near Andover, Hampshire; he fished and gardened, and was a keen shot. In his last years he suffered from Alzheimer's disease. He died at the Dower House Nursing Home, Headbourne Worthy, Hampshire, on 13 July 1995. He was survived by his wife and two sons. A memorial service was held at St Martin-in-the-Fields on 18 October 1995.   JOHN WINTON

Sources *Daily Telegraph* (15 July 1995) · *The Times* (15 July 1995) · *The Independent* (15 July 1995) · E. J. Grove, *Vanguard to Trident: British naval policy since World War II* (1987) · *Navy List* · *WWW* · Burke, *Peerage*
Archives NRA, priv. coll.
Likenesses photograph, repro. in *Daily Telegraph* · photograph, repro. in *The Times* · photograph, repro. in *The Independent*
Wealth at death under £145,000: probate, 26 Sept 1995, *CGPLA Eng. & Wales*

Bégin, Louis-Nazaire (1840–1925), cardinal and archbishop of Quebec, born at La Pointe-Lévis in French Canada on 10 January 1840, was the son of Charles Bégin, farmer, and his wife, Luce Paradis. His parents came of farming stock of French descent. He began his education at the Lévis model school, whence he proceeded to the commercial college, St Michel, and entered the archdiocesan seminary at Quebec in 1857. After graduating BA from Laval University, Quebec, he was sent to Rome in 1863 in order to complete his theological studies at the French College and at the Gregorian University. He was ordained priest at Rome in 1865, and received the degree of DD from the University of Innsbruck two years later. On returning to Canada in 1868 Bégin was appointed professor of theology and church history at Laval University, and he held the chair until 1884 when he was appointed principal of the Laval normal school.

Bégin was raised to the episcopate as bishop of Chicoutimi, one of the suffragan sees of the province of Quebec, in 1888, and three years later he returned to the city of Quebec as coadjutor to Cardinal Taschereau and titular

archbishop of Cyrene. Owing to the state of the cardinal's health Bégin was appointed administrator of the archdiocese in 1894, and he succeeded Taschereau as archbishop of Quebec in 1898. While teaching at Laval, Bégin had published papers on the primacy and infallibility of the sovereign pontiffs and on scripture and the rule of faith. During his episcopate he published *La chronologie de l'histoire des États Unis d'Amérique* (1895) and a *Catéchisme de controverse* (1902). His tenure of the see of Quebec was marked by the formation of many new parishes, the introduction of fresh religious communities, and, above all, by a campaign of social action. As bishop of Chicoutimi he had joined the other members of the Canadian hierarchy in their protests against the Manitoba school law of 1890. In 1907 he founded the organization known as L'Action Sociale Catholique, with its publication *L'Action Sociale*. He was greatly assisted in this work by Monseigneur Paul Eugène Roy who, at Bégin's request, was appointed titular bishop of Eleutheropolis in 1908. During the archbishop's later years much of the administrative work of the archdiocese of Quebec was undertaken by Monseigneur Roy, who became titular archbishop of Seleucia in 1914 and coadjutor with right of succession in 1920. Meanwhile, in May 1914, Archbishop Bégin had been created cardinal priest by Pope Pius X, with the titular church of San Vitale. He lived to the age of eighty-five, and was survived by only a few months by his coadjutor, who was already suffering from an incurable disease at his succession. Cardinal Bégin died at Quebec on 18 July 1925 and was buried in the crypt of his cathedral.

D. MATHEW, *rev.* H. C. G. MATTHEW

Sources A. Robert, 'Le cardinal Bégin', *Le Canada français* (1925) · J. B. A. Allaire, *Dictionnaire biographique du clergé canadien-français*, 6 vols. (1908–34)

Behan, (Francis) Brendan (1923–1964), writer, was born on 9 February 1923 at Holles Street Hospital, Dublin, the first of the four sons of Stephen Behan (d. 1968), house painter, and his wife, Kathleen, daughter of John Kearney, grocer. Stephen was doing time for IRA activities and Kathleen held the baby up high so that from a prison cell the father might see his first-born. He was Kathleen's second husband. From her first marriage she had brought two sons, Rory and Sean Furlong, one of them to become a socialist, both book lovers. Peadar Kearney, her brother, had written the 'Soldier's Song' which became the Irish national anthem.

Brendan, a precocious child, could read before he went to school, which in his case was the William Street Convent, where the French Sisters of Mercy adored him. The Christian Brothers of St Canice's, Brunswick Street, to whom he was sent at eleven, were less keen on the tenement kid, themselves being of peasant stock.

Growing up in the classic Dublin of Sean O'Casey with the songs of Ireland and the stories of her martyrs, Behan lived for Ireland to be 'Free from the centre to the sea'. He lived at 14 Russell Street, in a house owned by Granny English, his paternal grandmother, widow of Patrick English, her second husband. Granny English adored the boy, spoiled him, and gave him the taste for strong drink,

(Francis) Brendan Behan (1923–1964), by Daniel Farson, 1952?

while his maternal grandmother, Granny Furlong, would sound off about the splendid work the communists were doing upsetting the English. His family being so well read, Behan was soon familiar with Swift, Sheridan, Wilde, and Shaw as well as the English classics. P. J. Bourke, whose company played at the Queen's Theatre, was married to his aunt and as a boy Behan delighted in the shows there.

At fourteen when he left school Behan was apprenticed to his father's trade at the Bolton Street Technical School and became 'Peintre comme Picasso? Non! Peintre des bâtiments'. He read widely not only in the English language but also in Irish, carried a banner for the IRA, and thought up heroic speeches to be made from the dock in the style of Wolfe Tone and Robert Emmet. A member of Fianna Éireann, the junior branch of the IRA, Behan at an early age began contributing to the republican newspapers, anxiously waiting for the time when he could join the IRA. He had been rejected as too young also by the International Brigades. Some say that the IRA made use of the boy Behan in their bombing campaign in England, but others insist that he went to Liverpool on his own initiative, taking his home-made explosives, or 'conjuring tricks' as he called them. In any event, he was followed and arrested. He made a patriotic speech at his trial in February 1940, got sentenced to three years in borstal (he served only two), and was, for a while, denied the solace of his religion.

The borstal he was detained in at Hollesley Bay, Suffolk, had an unexpected effect on Behan. Very quickly the writer in him had to recognize the wit of the English boys around him. Their accents and speech rhythms had to be learned. C. A. Joyce, the governor, was an enlightened man who favoured dialogue and a sense of fair play. He encouraged Behan in his reading and writing. The debating and swimming which Behan enjoyed were just part of the curriculum. He could go to mass but not holy communion. In this liberal atmosphere Behan flourished and his blind hatred of the English began to dissolve. However, he would not forswear his IRA activities. In April 1942, six months after his release, Behan was sentenced to fourteen years' penal servitude for the attempted murder of an Irish policeman. In prison he noted all the Dublin characters he had known, tried writing a play, read anything he could get his hands on, and improved his Irish, 'Largely so

that the screws couldn't understand what we were saying'. He found the IRA men in with him were an uninteresting lot and he looked for intellectual companionship. While he was in Mountjoy prison (his sentence was not served in just the one place) two prisoners were hanged. This had a profound effect on him, which found expression in *The Quare Fellow*, the name given in Irish prisons to the condemned man. Behan was released under general amnesty in 1946, having also served his time at Arbor Hill barracks and Curragh camp.

Dublin had changed. The young ones had created their own Bohemia. Tired of Yeats, Lady Gregory, George Russell (Æ), and George Moore, they met in pubs or the smoke-filled cellars of the club known as The Catacombs. Parties went on all night, Behan holding court with his stories and songs, being entertainer, clown, satirist. In ordinary conversation he stammered, but once in full flow he left his impediment behind. No one was safe from his wicked tongue. He would do Hugh MacDiarmid, the Scots nationalist poet, reciting endlessly in gibberish. MacDiarmid replied that you could hear Behan's language in any boozer.

Soon Behan took refuge among the Irish-speaking people of Kerry, where he found refreshment for his soul, thinking and writing in the language he loved as dearly as he loved English. When he saw Marlowe's *Edward II* at the Theatre Royal, Stratford-le-Bow, he said that he had thought so highly of Gaveston's first speech that he had translated it into Irish 'And claimed it as me own'.

In March 1947 Behan was again in an English prison, for visiting England, which was forbidden to him, and spent four lonely months in Strangeways gaol. Back in Dublin, he served a month inside for starting a punch-up in a pub: he had been provoked by an antisemitic boozer.

Tired of it all, Behan made for Paris, where he lived on his wits, the occasional cheque, and the hospitality of anybody who cared to offer it. Desperately hungry, he tried his hand at pornography but even with the vision of half a pound of steak and a jug of wine floating before his eyes, he could not manage it until inspiration seized him. He made his chosen heroine an undercover agent for the IRA. Then it went swimmingly. Finally, he turned to house painting again, bars mainly. One found itself graced with 'This is the finest fucking bar in Paris' beautifully painted on the white wall.

In 1950 Behan was in Dublin again and made a serious attack on *Borstal Boy*, the account of his experience at Hollesley Bay. It was a short spurt, but from it came the first chapter. Stories and articles were accepted and in 1952 he was still working on his autobiography. In 1953 the *Irish Times* announced the first instalment of a serial about the Dublin underworld, *The Scarperer*, by Emmet Street. The story ran for thirty days but nothing further was heard from Mr Street. Behan published *The Confirmation Suit* under his own name. By now he was presenting a regular ballad programme, writing sketches for Radio Éireann and three columns a week for the *Irish Press*. These columns were later published as a book, *Hold your Hour and have Another* (1963).

It was in this year, 1953, that diabetes attacked Behan, but it was not diagnosed until 1956. From then on drinking became much more dangerous while the effects of the disease could be mistaken for drunkenness. As a teenager Behan had been slim, fit, and good-looking with black hair, clear skin, and even teeth. A few short years of boozing and brawling had put an end to most of that. His face and body had run to fat. Only his tiny hands and feet gave a clue to the shape he should have been. In 1954 he sent his version of *The Quare Fellow*, which he had first called *Another Twist of the Rope*, to the Abbey Theatre. He had already sent a play, *The Landlady*, to them in 1946. Both were turned down. He also tried The Gate, run by Hilton Edwards and Micheál MacLiammóir. They too turned it down but The Pike, a pocket theatre with fifty seats run by Alan Simpson and Carolyn Swift, were delighted with it and agreed to stage the play if Behan consented to work on it. In November 1954, on its first night, *The Quare Fellow* was acclaimed in Dublin. Brendan Behan made £25 and found a lifelong love, Beatrice ffrench-Salkeld (1925–1993), a botanist, the daughter of Cecil ffrench-Salkeld, a painter. They met at a performance and were married in February 1955. In January 1956 Behan sent his play to Theatre Workshop, where the style was exactly suited to his. It opened on 24 May and was a phenomenal hit, the first Irish play to succeed in London. Two months later it transferred to the Comedy Theatre in the West End.

Meanwhile Behan was selling extracts from *Borstal Boy* to the *Sunday Dispatch* and *The People* without letting the one know about the other. With Beatrice watching over him, early rising, regular hours, and tea instead of booze, Behan managed to complete the book that was to be *Borstal Boy*.

When the first English hostage was taken in Cyprus, Theatre Workshop proposed a play on the subject. Behan offered to go away and write it if Theatre Workshop could pay him. They did, and bits of script began to arrive from Kerry, the hostage in Behan's work being Irish. In fact, as with the *Dispatch* and *The People*, he was selling the play twice over, first in Irish in Dublin as *An Giall* then in English, fragments only, to Theatre Workshop as *The Hostage*.

The subject was exciting and the company cared deeply for Behan but the play had to be finished from its memories of his stories. Luckily it had among it good memories. The drink was already taking hold of Behan. The writer was already submerged in the entertainer. He would join in *The Hostage* every night during the Stratford East production. Some nights he would be anti-British, other nights anti-Irish, and his participation then and later became a great draw. The show opened on 14 October 1958 and in 1959 was selected for the international festival of theatre at the Sarah Bernhardt Theatre in Paris, where Behan joyously joined in. Later it was voted play of the year there. In Germany it was panned. Perhaps Behan did not realize that his plays would not take the conventional nineteenth-century style still affected by the commercial theatres.

Four days after the first night of *The Hostage*, *Borstal Boy* was published to universal acclaim. In autumn 1960 *The Hostage* was presented on Broadway at the Cort Theater. Behan went over for the first night. *Borstal Boy* had just been published in America, so New York was ready for him. In turn he was ready for it. Interviews and TV appearances, not to mention interruptions of his own play, ensured that he scored a great personal hit. The entertainer in Behan had triumphed. But he found it increasingly difficult to write, so his publishers encouraged him to record his stories and fragments of experience on tape. It was a way of appearing to be still at work but it was no substitute for writing and Behan knew it. He made an attempt at a new play, *Richard's Cork Leg*, but it was stillborn. Drink exacerbated by diabetes had damaged his health. Lack of discipline combined with the fatal ability to entertain by talking had weakened the writing muscle. Beatrice at his Dublin home, 5 Anglesea Road, had been ready to provide the right conditions for work but Behan's violent rages were now making her keep her distance. In any case, he was spending most of his time roaming from pub to pub, stopping out at night and talking, endlessly talking. In 1963 Beatrice bore a daughter, Blanaid. Behan, although delighted, was unable to pull out of the nosedive. Three months into the following year he was taken to Meath Hospital, where he died, Beatrice by his side, on 20 March 1964. A glorious talent, a humane and gracious but very angry man died young. His coffin was draped in the tricolour and accompanied by an IRA guard of honour. A fourteen-year-old bugler from Fianna Éireann sounded the 'Last Post'. The funeral was said to have been the biggest since those of Michael Collins and C. S. Parnell as Brendan Behan was buried on 22 March 1964 at Glasnevin cemetery, Dublin.

Various memoirs recalling Behan were published in the years following his death, including those by his wife and his brother. *Brendan Behan's New York* (1964), *Confessions of an Irish Rebel* (1965), and *The Scarperer* (1966), put together from his various tape recordings and sketches, were also published posthumously. Ulick O'Connor's *Brendan Behan* (1970) remains the standard biography. *Richard's Cork Leg* was staged in 1972 at the Peacock Theatre by Alan Simpson, who later assembled the *Collected Poems* in 1978. The *Collected Letters* appeared in 1992. JOAN LITTLEWOOD

Sources personal knowledge (2004) · U. O'Connor, *Brendan Behan* (1970) · H. Goorney, *The Theatre Workshop story* (1981) · B. Behan, *My life with Brendan* (1973) · b. cert.
Archives priv. coll. | FILM BBC WAC | SOUND BBC WAC
Likenesses D. Farson, photograph, 1952?, NPG [*see illus.*] · photographs, Hult. Arch.

Behn, Aphra [Aphara] (1640?–1689), writer, kept her early life obscure. The only person who claims to have known her as a child was the cavalier Colonel Thomas Colepeper who declared in his manuscript 'Adversaria' (BL, Harley MSS 7587–7605) that her mother had been his wet-nurse, that she was born 'at Sturry or Canterbury', that her father's name was Johnson, that she had a 'fayer' sister, Frances, and that she herself was 'a most beautifull woman, & a most Excellent Poet'. Another contemporary testimony is that of Anne Finch, countess of Winchilsea, who in 'The Circuit of Apollo' gives 'the desolate Wye' as

Aphra Behn (1640?–1689), by Robert White, pubd 1716 (after John Riley)

the place of her birth, and in marginalia on the poem (Finch MS Collection, Folger Shakespeare Library, Washington) states that she was reputed to be 'Daughter to a Barber, who liv'd formerly at Wye a little market town (now much decay'd) in Kent'.

The two accounts fit an Eaffrey Johnson, sister of Frances and daughter of Bartholomew Johnson from Bishopsbourne, who was, among other functions, a barber in Canterbury. His wife, Eaffrey's mother, was Elizabeth Denham from a trading family in Smeeth; Elizabeth's brother was a doctor educated at Oxford. The Johnson–Denham marriage took place at St Paul's, Canterbury, on 25 August 1638. Frances was baptized in Smeeth on 6 December. Eaffrey was born on 14 December 1640 at Harbledown near Canterbury. At least two other births followed, of George, buried at St Margaret's in 1656, and of an unnamed boy alive in the 1660s. In 1654 Bartholomew was appointed an overseer of the poor for St Margaret's in central Canterbury. When she wrote her fiction *Oroonoko*, Behn created a more elevated identity for herself as narrator, and her first biographer, author of the 'Memoir' (published with the 1698 edition of her histories and novels), accepted it as fact; thus she is often described as the daughter of a gentleman who became the 'lieutenant-

general of six and thirty islands, besides the continent of Surinam'. No contemporaries gave her this high status, however, and John Dryden after her death implied she was lowly born. The lack of clarity has allowed much interesting speculation from readers wanting her to be more ethnically or aristocratically connected.

Surinam and Antwerp During the final years of the interregnum Behn may have acted as a royalist spy or agent, since she was later trusted with an important mission and somewhere got to know Charles II's courtier Thomas Killigrew, himself involved in espionage. Or, since she wrote a good hand, she may have acted as a copyist for Killigrew and others. By 1664 her father was probably dead, since the hearth tax returns for his parish do not list him. Late in 1663 she apparently arrived with her mother and siblings, but not her father, in Surinam, the new English colony in the proprietorship of Lord Willoughby but administered by a deputy governor, William Byam. She stayed on a plantation owned by Sir Robert Harley and became involved in the political squabbles of the colony. It is possible that Behn was acting in some intelligence capacity in the colony, since Byam probably denoted Behn in his letters under the pseudonym Astrea and described with distaste her intimacy both professionally and personally with the dangerous dissident William Scot, whom he named Celadon, son of the executed regicide and former secret service chief Thomas. Behn later used the pseudonym Astrea in her documented mission to Antwerp and adopted it for her literary career.

In Surinam, if *Oroonoko* can be credited, Behn also became friendly with John Trefry, Lord Willoughby's agent, and with George Marten, brother of the famous republican Henry; she used George's name for the hero of *The Younger Brother* (1696). Behn claimed that her virgin muse was American and implied that it was in Surinam that she wrote her first play, *The Young King*, partly based on the romance *Cléopâtre* by La Calprenède. When Behn and her family left Surinam early in 1664, Scot followed shortly and was soon collaborating with the Dutch in the Netherlands. Back in London, Behn apparently married a merchant of German extraction resident there, possibly Johann Behn, the man who served on the *King David* in the Caribbean in the 1650s; she immediately lost him through death or separation. A reference to a 'Widow Behn' in connection with a dead husband's involvement in a ship called the *Abraham's Sacrifice* in 1669 occurs in a letter in the Huntington Library from William Blathwayt; this may refer to Behn, although she never called herself a widow. In 1666, probably through the influence of Killigrew, Behn was sent to Antwerp as a government agent under the name Astrea by the secretary of state, Lord Arlington, to liaise with Scot to see if he would turn double agent and betray his Dutch masters. From letters in The Hague archives there is evidence that he double-crossed her while giving her snippets of useful information; at the same time letters from a fellow spy, William Corney, tended to undermine her in London. As weeks passed she became desperate for money in expensive Antwerp and appealed both to Arlington and to Killigrew. Neither sent sufficient funds and in the end she had to borrow in order to return to England. She could not repay the loan and was threatened with the debtors' prison. It is unclear whether or not she was incarcerated, but it is possible that she bought her freedom with another espionage mission.

Career as a playwright By 1670 Behn had turned to the stage. During the 1660s she had probably written poems and some comic fiction but, with *The Forc'd Marriage*, which opened the season of the Duke's Company on 20 September 1670, she began a career as a professional writer working for the Duke's Company, primarily under the actor–manager Thomas Betterton; her sex and past were alluded to in her first prologue ('The Poetess too, they say, has Spies abroad'), and possibly in the character of Falatius, who with his patches may have represented Arlington who had abandoned her in Antwerp. In writing for the stage Behn was a remarkable phenomenon. Katherine Philips, Frances Boothby, and possibly Elizabeth Polwhele preceded her as Restoration dramatists, but they each wrote only one or two plays or translations. Over the next years Behn had at least nineteen plays staged and probably contributed to many more. Her first plays—the tragicomedies of sex and power struggles *The Forc'd Marriage* and *The Amorous Prince* (staged 1671), and *The Young King* (not staged until 1679 when it was adapted for the political situation of the Exclusion crisis)—were probably all written at about the same time, since they draw on the common 1660s theme of royal restoration and, like Caroline plays, use masques and depend on costume and disguise. At the same time they already reveal Behn's remarkable command of the new theatrical medium and suggest an early interest in state politics and the interaction of power and sex. *The Forc'd Marriage* suggests the power of legitimacy over brute force and the appropriateness of marrying for love; *The Amorous Prince* openly alludes to fornication and homosexuality, and shows the abuse of power when a prince is ruled by sex. Both plays were mocked in Buckingham's *The Rehearsal*.

In 1671 Edward Howard's *The Six Days Adventure* failed, and Behn wrote a commendatory pindaric poem for its publication, urging Howard to ignore critics and continue writing. She was possibly the editor of *The Covent Garden Drolery* (1672), a theatrical anthology of verse mainly from the King's Company, possibly supplied by Killigrew; it included four of her poems, one of which was the versatile and popular description of pastoral lovemaking, 'I led my *Silvia* to a grove'. By now Behn seems to have known many theatrical people including the young Elizabeth Barry, possibly 'Amoret' in her poem 'Our Cabal', Thomas Otway, and Edward Ravenscroft to whom she addressed her 'Letter to a Brother of the Pen in Tribulation' when he undertook a cure for syphilis. Possibly at this time she began a liaison with John Hoyle, a bisexual lawyer with a reputation for violence, republicanism, and freethinking. It seems to have continued for some years since her name was coupled with his throughout her professional life; Roger Morrice in a manuscript record in Dr Williams's Library, London, wrote in 1687 that it was 'publickly known that Mr Hoyle 10. or 12. yeares since kept *Mrs. Beane*'. Her

depictions of libertines may have drawn on Hoyle, as may her portrayals of Amyntas and Lycidus, to whom some of her most complex love poems are addressed. It was possibly to Hoyle that she wrote a series of cajoling letters complaining of neglect; they were posthumously published as the short story 'Love Letters to a Gentleman'. Behn seems to have responded emotionally to many people in her life, and her works, which may or may not have an autobiographical component, address both men and women amorously.

Behn's *The Dutch Lover* was performed in 1673 on the new stage at Dorset Garden; it tried to exploit the anti-Dutch feeling of the Third Anglo-Dutch War and cleverly amalgamated several short stories of Francisco de Quintana from *The History of Don Fenise*. Although another tragicomedy of sexual intrigue, cruelty, and apparently incestuous love, it was for Behn a new departure in its depiction of the rake—a 'brisk young Lover'—and a pert heroine, a minor character in the earlier plays, but one she would thoroughly exploit in later ones. The play was unsuccessful and she published it with a burlesque epistle to the reader mocking male pretensions to dominate playwriting and the notion of dramatic rules which she had been criticized for flouting. Plays were not the highest human endeavour, she argued, but 'among the middle if not the better sort of Books'. In 1676 her only tragedy, *Abdelazer*, was performed. An adaptation of an old play, *Lust's Dominion*, which followed the mode for horror and vicious women, it opened with her powerful song 'Love in fantastique triumph satt', later much anthologized. Her play was similar to a group of curious horror plays by Nathaniel Lee and Elkanah Settle, depicting motiveless and exotic evil and vicious women who preyed on rivals and children; Behn changed the story in her source to avoid any repentance in the evil queen. The play was moderately successful and was revived with Purcell's music in 1695.

Behn was probably by now associated with the circle of the earl of Rochester who, she claimed, helped her with her poetry, and whose elegy she wrote in 1680. It was probably within the Rochester circle that she wrote some of her most risqué poems, including 'The Disappointment', a translation from the French which, by stopping before the original, stressed the woman's rather than the man's amorous irritation, and 'On a Juniper-Tree, Cut Down to Make Busks', which presented a voyeuristic and leering tree watching the copulation of mortals. These and other poems were more explicitly sexual than those published by any other woman of her time; in print they were first attributed to Rochester. The most significant poem probably from this period is 'The Golden Age', an adaptation via an untraced French intermediary of a famous passage from Tasso's *Aminta*, in which she pleaded for a love untrammelled with economy and for sex as pleasure not power. By 1680 she had a reputation as a competent poet, and contributed a paraphrase of Oenone's complaint to the Dryden–Tonson collection of *Ovid's Epistles*, although she knew no Latin.

In the theatre Behn followed *Abdelazer* with her first London comedy, *The Town-Fopp* (performed 1676), adapted from George Wilkins's *Miseries of Inforst Marriage*; it displayed an unpleasant and foppish rake, and at moments came close to tragicomedy. Probably other adaptations and collaborations followed, including *The Debauchee* (staged 1677), a shortened version of a Richard Brome comedy, published anonymously. These works form a transition to her first light comedy of intrigue and her most enduringly popular play, *The Rover*, based on Killigrew's *Thomaso*. The play, featuring a comic drunken rake, a sprightly heroine, and an impassioned whore, was set in the interregnum and called on cavalier nostalgia for a poorer but politically simpler moment. Elizabeth Barry, who seems to have become a friend of Behn's, played Helena and William Smith Willmore. *The Rover* was twice performed at court and was admired by James, duke of York. Anonymously published in 1677, it appeared with a postscript defending the playwright against the charge of plagiarism—a charge which, together with that of bawdiness, would plague Behn throughout her career; the next issue declared her name.

In the late 1670s the Exclusion crisis and Popish Plot politicized dramatists, and Behn became a propagandist for the king and the emerging tory faction. She took many opportunities to attack the duke of Monmouth, whom she saw as a danger to legitimacy and national stability, and she lambasted City dissenters regarded as the heirs of the 1640s rebels. *Sir Patient Fancy* (staged 1678), taking some plot elements from several Molière plays, was another sex comedy like *The Rover*; the most cynical of her dramas, it allows adultery to go unpunished and hypocrisy to be rewarded. It mocked old dissenting merchants and country bumpkins; its assertive epilogue defended a woman's right to compose plays. When published, *Sir Patient Fancy* included a defence of Behn against both plagiarism and bawdiness: she was writing 'for Bread and not ashamed to owne it'. In 1679 she published her next play, *The Feign'd Curtizans*. Up to this point she had not dedicated her plays to great personages, but this one was addressed to the king's mistress Nell Gwyn. Subsequently she dedicated her works to many elevated men and one more royal mistress, the duchess of Mazarine, whose style she greatly admired. *The Feign'd Curtizans* was set in Catholic Rome and follows *The Rover* in presenting a troupe of intermeshed young people trying to form themselves into suitable couples; there is the usual libertine contempt for moral reputation but all end married. The topical comedy derives from a Titus Oates figure, a travelling chaplain called Tickletext. Probably early in 1680 there followed an anonymously published, partly revised and partly adapted version of Marston's *The Dutch Courtezan* called *The Revenge*, in which Marston's moral was changed so as to explain wrongdoing and forgive the whore; the play was ascribed to Behn by the collector Narcissus Luttrell.

Politics now dominated the theatre, and to take financial advantage Behn speedily wrote four plays, two adapting and two using earlier plays; all were performed within months of each other from 1681 to 1682. The first was a sequel to *The Rover*, again based on *Thomaso* and dedicated to the duke of York; it was more farcical than the earlier play and depicted the hero choosing the whore over the virgin and avoiding the 'formal foppery of marriage'. *The False Count* was performed with a prologue ferociously but ironically attacking the whigs and praising Behn as a royal propagandist; it delivered a mixed message, that instruction could make a gallant but that a shoemaker and his daughter would never be 'quality': property was not, as whigs supposed, the basis of civic worth. *The Roundheads*, deriving from Tatham's *The Rump* about the final parliament before the Restoration, was an energetic farce which crudely attacked the whigs as old republicans; it was Behn's most openly propagandist play, even using conventional fear of petticoat rule to make its point that any destabilizing of royal government was to be resisted. *The City-Heiress*, an innovative play based on Middleton's *A Mad World, my Masters* and Massinger's *The Guardian*, again mocked hypocritical whig dissenters, but its main interest was its treatment of Behn's usual trio, especially the relationship between the poxed rake hero Wilding and a rich passionate widow, Lady Galliard, whom he rejects for the rich young virgin. A less politically committed play now lost, *Like Father, Like Son*, was also performed during this time.

The success of both *The City-Heiress* and *The Roundheads* prompted attacks on Behn as a propagandist and bawdy writer from the whig Thomas Shadwell and the satirist Robert Gould, and, more affectionately, from William Wycherley, who compared the crowded theatre for *The City-Heiress* to a sweating tub for pox. In 1682 Behn provided a prologue and epilogue for the anonymous *Romulus and Hersilia* in which, with a glance at Monmouth, she declared that rebelling against a king and father was unforgivable. Charles II was displeased and she and the actress Lady Slingsby were briefly taken into custody. Possibly her dislike of Monmouth endeared her to one of his enemies, the earl of Mulgrave, who had improperly courted the Princess Anne. Apparently Behn provided a poem in apology using the story of Ovid and Julia. By now Behn was associated with libertinism and freethinking, as is suggested in a commendatory poem she wrote at the beginning of 1683 to praise a translation of Lucretius's *De rerum natura* by Thomas Creech. Creech was eager to neutralize his dangerously unchristian subject matter but Behn saw the poem as a triumphant assertion of rationalism and materialism, a victory of reason over faith. She published this uncompromising view of Lucretius in her own *Poems upon Several Occasions* (1684) but Creech used a different version of her poem for his volume, in which faith became 'the secure Retreat of Routed Argument'. In the same poem Behn praised Creech for rescuing women from the 'ignorance of the female sex'.

Prose fiction and poetry At this point in her life Behn may have visited Paris—her competence at French seems suddenly to have improved and she became familiar with the latest French writing. Back in England she lodged near one of her publishers, Jacob Tonson, in New Street. The

King's Company had long been declining and in November 1682 it had merged with her own Duke's Company into the United Company. Without competition, and with the whole repertory of past drama to choose from, the new company needed few new plays, and playwrights including Behn looked to other genres for income. The need coincided with a major shift in Behn's thinking. After Willmore, her rake figures tended to darken and her passionate women grow more complex; these figures appear in more rounded form in her first published prose fiction, part 1 of *Love-Letters between a Nobleman and his Sister* (1684), an epistolary novel loosely based on a scandal involving Ford, Lord Grey and Lady Henrietta Berkeley. Grey, who was also a central figure in the Rye House plot and later in the Monmouth rising, had fled to the continent with his sister-in-law Henrietta Berkeley after a sensational public trial before the king's bench in 1682. Behn's novel is a series of letters between the lovers which charts both the political and passionate trajectories of their lives up to their escape from England in 1683.

Shortly after the Monmouth rising Behn published *Love-Letters*, part 2, which followed the lovers through their exile in Cleve and the breakdown of their relationship. Here, however, letters were framed by a third-person narrative which carried much of the action of the novel, and the heated prose of part 1 became farcical as the partners entered new amours and the servant to whom Silvia had been married for the convenience of his lord woke up to his manhood and desired his wife. In part 3, *The Amours of Philander and Silvia* (1687), Behn concluded the story of the now debased lovers and dealt with the actual events leading up to the Monmouth rising, again employing the combination of letters and third-person narrative. In its complete form *Love-Letters* stands at over 1000 pages; it was a popular work which ran to seven editions by 1765, a serialization in the *Oxford Journal* in 1736, and a verse edition. It is an important landmark in the development of the epistolary novel and the *roman à clef*, an extraordinary analysis of erotic arousal. The work appeared anonymously and it remains unclear who commissioned it, but, since part 3 was dedicated to the disreputable son of the current secretary of state, the earl of Sunderland, Sunderland seems a possible instigator of the project.

Behn was in London for the harsh winter of 1683–4 when the Thames froze; she commemorated the occasion in a comic poem to Creech following the celebration of twelfth night. This may have been the occasion of her meeting Thomas Brown, who was later remarkably free with her works and reputation. The short story attributed to her, 'Memoirs of the Court of the King of Bantam', may have dated from this period since it concerned twelfth night and was said to be her contribution to a story-writing competition. At this time she also expended much effort on a poem based on Abbé Paul Tallemant's *Voyage de l'isle d'amour*, a 2196-line seduction poem in which the sex act becomes a strenuous journey through Honour, Respect, and Jealousy to Opportunity. All this literary activity did not compensate for lost theatrical revenue, however, and a rare letter to her publisher Tonson reveals

Behn trying to get an extra £5 for her 'Island of Love', which Tonson was publishing together with some of her earlier works as *Poems upon Several Occasions*. The volume included a verse letter to Rochester's half-niece Anne Wharton, in which Behn defended herself from the now common charge of bawdiness, this time levelled at her by the whig clergyman Gilbert Burnet. Probably at Wharton's instigation Behn provided a prologue to Rochester's posthumously performed play, *Valentinian*, staged in 1684.

Poems upon Several Occasions appeared in 1684 with commendatory poems by Creech and others, one apparently by Dryden but probably written by Tonson himself. In the dedication to the young earl of Salisbury Behn made the point that aristocracy should support monarchy and art: the patron of the poet was the patron of England. She enlarged on the theme in the following year when she published another collection, *Miscellany* (1685), using her own and other people's poems and including a rather careless translation of La Rochefoucauld's maxims and a curious paraphrase on the Lord's prayer in which she moaned that authors could not earn their 'daily Bread' and 'Trespasses' were not to be resisted. It is likely that *The Younger Brother*, published and performed posthumously as her last play, was composed at this time, since its subject of sexual adventuring and unrepentant libertine women fits with the theme of some of the poems as well as with the prose *Love-Letters*. It is unclear why she did not stage the play now, but, having missed the moment, it may have seemed unsuitable for other theatrical seasons when libertine investigations and mockery of elderly cuckolds were less in vogue. The play was altered and staged by Charles Gildon in 1696 following the success of Southerne's adaptation of Behn's short story *Oroonoko*; it was a failure. Behn now began a sequel to her popular 'Island of Love' in which she switched from the sincere lover Lysander to his cynical friend Lycidus and from romance to intrigue, rather in the manner of her switch from part 1 to parts 2 and 3 of *Love-Letters*. The work mixed prose and poetry and was closer to Tallemant than the earlier paraphrase.

Behn was interrupted in her projects by the sudden death of Charles II in February 1685. For this event she wrote her first major public poem, *A Pindarick on the Death of our Late Sovereign*, much concerned with the transfer of legitimate power from one king to another. She followed it with a poem to the widowed Catherine of Braganza and with her longest and most elaborate political poem, *A Pindarick Poem on the Happy Coronation of His Most Sacred Majesty James II*, nearly 800 lines of baroque extravaganza in praise of her 'Godlike Patron' and his wife, Mary of Modena. She eulogized the loyalty of many in James's entourage who would betray him three years later. Her ode was politically correct in its insistence that the coronation only confirmed and did not make a king. In the same year she provided a graceful 'Pastoral Pindarick' for the marriage of the earl of Dorset and a commendatory poem for Thomas Tryon's book on health (1685). Behn's attraction to free-thinking as well as to the trappings of Catholicism make

her an unlikely author of the anti-Catholic satire on Dryden written about this time, 'On Dryden Renegade',
although her name is added to more than one manuscript
copy. In 1687 she provided further commendatory poems
for Henry Higden's translation of a Juvenal satire and for
Sir Francis Fane's play *The Sacrifice*; she also wrote a pindaric to the second duke of Albemarle on his departure to
become governor of Jamaica. In the same year Francis
Barlow reissued his engravings of Aesop's Fables, for
which Behn provided four-line stanzas summarizing the
fable and two lines to convey the moral commentary. As
with her translations from Tallemant she set the material
in the present and provided touches of Restoration London as well as making frequent allusions to the recently
defeated Monmouth.

Despite the arrival of a welcome new order and her considerable activity in prose and poetry, Behn remained
impecunious and an IOU dated August 1685 (Folger Shakespeare Library) recorded a loan of £6 to be repaid from the
proceeds of her next play. She may also have done some
copying for money, since a manuscript book of lampoons
in the Bodleian Library (Firth c. 16), entitled 'Astrea's
Booke for Songs & Satyr's', includes a hand which Mary
Ann O'Donnell believes to be similar to Behn's; there are
also some marginalia supporting her known opinions.
The mortgaged play was probably *The Luckey Chance*, now
considered one of Behn's best. It was the final play in her
series of intrigue comedies beginning with *The Rover* and
of city plays beginning with *The Town-Fopp*, and it was
probably performed in late spring 1686; it was the last
mainly original drama she would stage and it revisits her
old theme of an elderly rich man demanding exclusive
possession of a young wife. Despite some ambiguity in the
depiction of the married heroine, it was more morally
respectable than *Sir Patient Fancy*, which it resembles in
plot. There is some pity for the losing old men, and the
heroine thoroughly rejects her old husband only when
she learns he has gambled her away; the young men are
less daring and libertine than her earlier rakes, but love
appears a fantasy in both young and old.

Unhappily taste had moved against Behn's kind of sex
comedies and for all her care some attacked the play as
bawdy and inappropriate for a woman's pen. When she
published it in 1687 she provided a spirited preface in
defence of her right to write and of her kind of drama. She
wrote as men wrote, she claimed, and was no more or less
bawdy than they:

> All I ask, is the Priviledge for my Masculine Part the Poet in
> me ... to tread in those successful Paths my Predecessors
> have so long thriv'd in ... I value Fame as much as if I had
> been born a *Hero*; and if you rob me of that, I can retire from
> the ungrateful World, and scorn its fickle Favours.

In contrast to her earlier defences, she no longer insisted
that playwriting was trivial. Before Charles II's death she
had sought to please the king by beginning a version of
the stylized *commedia dell'arte* based on a published French
scenario. She now returned to it, entitling it *The Emperor of
the Moon*. It attacked pedantic male scholarship, one of

Behn's butts throughout her career, and mocked gullibil-
ity, as *Love-Letters* had done in its presentation of the credulous Monmouth. The play, concerning theatre, transformation, and pageantry and featuring Harlequin and Scara-
mouch, was a spectacular demanding blacked actors,
descending chariots, embodied signs of the zodiac, and a
symphony of music; it was a fitting end to a theatrical career of seventeen years.

Final years Behn was often in poor health; towards the
end of 1686 her health worsened. She had trouble walking
and writing, and may have had a form of arthritis. Gould
insinuated that it was gout; another satirist asserted pox
and poverty. With an elegy to Edmund Waller (1687) she
sent a covering note to the poet's daughter-in-law in
which she declared that she was 'very ill and [had] been
dying this twelve month'. None the less she continued to
write furiously. She continued her French adaptations
with a prose allegory of Balthasar de Bonnecorse called *La
montre* (1686); it was a lengthy work—too long according
to Matthew Prior—which combined prose and poetry. It
was more static and playful than the erotic 'Island of Love'
and Behn added to its instructions for a day in love her
own descriptions of hypocritical and seductive men. She
also finished her continuation *Lycidus*, again combining
prose and poetry. In this she changed the sincere hero of
'The Island of Love' into the more worldly and sophisticated Lycidus, and replaced romance with coquetry and
flirtation; the atmosphere became more theatrical than
pastoral. The ending of the work accepting the death of
love and bidding farewell to the genre of escapist and
enriching pastoral poetry sounds like Behn's farewell to
the genre in which she had had such success.

Affixed to *Lycidus* were other poems, including the
ambiguous 'To the Fair Clarinda, who Made Love to me,
Imagin'd More than Woman' addressed to a transvestite,
hermaphrodite, or lesbian lover. Other poems suggest a
more everyday reality than in her earlier poems: for
example they mention a visit to Tunbridge Wells and
gratitude for a bottle of orange flower water. She also produced translations from two French works that popularized the new Copernican science, *Discovery of New Worlds*
(1688), from Bernard de Fontenelle's controversial original, and *The History of Oracles*, also from an original by
him. The first, concerning planetary systems, was prefaced by her own 'Essay on translated prose' which treated
the idiosyncrasies of particular languages and parodied
and exemplified the scholastic method of dispute used by
biblical scholars; the second was a comparative history of
pagan religions, which by implication mocked the early
church fathers. The topics were dangerous since both
books implied some doubts about the revealed Christian
religion.

Most significant for Behn's future reputation was her
publication of five short fictions, *The Fair Jilt*, *Oroonoko*,
Agnes de Castro, *The History of the Nun*, and *The Lucky Mistake*.
The first two, her most famous stories, both make use of
Behn's past life in Surinam and Flanders and both, like the
last two parts of *Love-Letters*, use an allegedly autobiographical narrator as a character in the story, gauging and

responding to public opinion and rumour. *The Fair Jilt* depicts the career of a ruthless woman who uses sex to gain power in society and over men; in many ways she is another version of Silvia from *Love-Letters*. The hero, a naïve prince fooled by others, may be a glancing reference to James II, to whom Behn remained extraordinarily loyal but whose political mismanagement was by now taxing the nation. James may also be alluded to in *Oroonoko*, the hero of which is similarly heroic, exaggerated, and gullible. *Oroonoko* is Behn's most famous work and it allowed her name to have some currency throughout the nineteenth and early twentieth centuries when her plays were denigrated as unladylike and bawdy. Despite its hero's slave owning and his opinion that some men deserved slavery, the work was often taken as an abolitionist tract, and many sentimental versions of the story appeared in England and France. In more recent times it has given Behn fame as a commentator on imperialism, race, and ethnicity.

Another startling short story is Behn's *History of the Nun*, in which a young girl is led into real crime by being confined too young to a nunnery; its message appears to be that people change and should be allowed to do so, but the moral is supposedly the danger of vow breaking, a useful one for the wavering subjects of James II in 1688. The last of the fictions that can be securely attributed to Behn, *The Lucky Mistake*, was published posthumously in 1689; it is a slighter, more folkloric tale but with an interesting depiction of a young and vulnerable intellectual girl. Nine further short stories were published posthumously; they may be by Behn or partly by her, or they may be partly or entirely forgeries, possibly by Thomas Brown and Charles Gildon working with the publisher Samuel Briscoe.

Behn hymned James II to the end of his reign. Although the nation was racked with plots and was much aware of William of Orange waiting over the water, Behn provided *A Congratulatory Poem … on the Universal Hopes of All Loyal Persons for a Prince of Wales* when she learned of the queen's pregnancy; robustly she assumed a live boy child and inadvertently helped to fan the rumour that the king was going to have a male heir by nature or fraud. In June the boy was born, and Behn was ready with *A Congratulatory Poem … on the Happy Birth* addressed to James; both poems stressed the royal need to reward poets for their loyal efforts and expressed the hope that 'POETS shall by *Patron* PRINCES live'. For her zeal Behn was mocked by another court poet, John Baber, to whom in retaliation she addressed 'To Poet Bavius' reducing him to a toady and amateur. Her loyalty to James II was further demonstrated by a eulogy to the chief government propagandist Roger L'Estrange for his part in the Popish Plot and his propagandist history, and by her translation of book 6 of Abraham Cowley's Latin original for Nahum Tate's English edition, *Of Plants*. Into this latter she made her famous insertion 'in her own Person':

> Let me with *Sappho* and *Orinda* be
> Oh ever sacred Nymph, adorn'd by thee;
> And give my Verses Immortality.

Her sense of impending doom can be caught in what was probably her final play, *The Widdow Ranter*, set in the chaotic colony of Virginia and featuring a political rebellion and a doomed hero much in the manner of Oroonoko. The possible accession of William of Orange filled Behn with alarm, but when it occurred she had to make a partial peace if she was to survive as a public writer. From her *Pindaric Poem to the Reverend Doctor Burnet* it seems that she resisted the idea of writing for William III, while ironically praising Burnet's flexible loyalty and ability to control meaning and the reader's response with his 'fine ideas' and 'nobler pen'; she who could not so easily change notions and principles remains an 'excluded Prophet' on '*Brittains* Faithless Shore'. She did, however, supply a *Congratulatory Poem to … Queen Mary* for Mary II, in which she declared she saw 'the Lines of your great Father's face' and asked James, 'Great Lord, of all my Vows', to accept her tribute to his usurping daughter. Behn died on 16 April 1689, five days after the coronation of William and Mary. She was buried in the cloisters of Westminster Abbey.

Reputation In her own period Behn was held to be a considerable author, famous as a playwright, propagandist poet and panegyrist, novelist, and translator. Soon after her death a group of women playwrights, including Delariver Manley and Catherine Trotter, entered the theatre, acknowledging their debt to Behn, and for the first half of the eighteenth century *The Rover* and *The Emperor of the Moon* continued to be performed. Yet even before her death Behn's personal reputation frequently rested on the binary opposition of modesty and lewdness, and she was contrasted with the chaste Katherine Philips. The eighteenth-century emphasis on femininity brought a demand that the many women writers now entering the market place should write in a feminine style and confine themselves to modest subject matter. Although she was occasionally assessed dispassionately—especially as a playwright, in encyclopaedias such as the English edition of Bayle's *Dictionnaire* (1734–41)—Behn was most often damned for monstrously writing like men; she was castigated as personally unfeminine by major authors such as Pope, Johnson, and Richardson. As the century progressed, *The Rover* had to be modernized for 'decency' and her poems decreased in number in the anthologies of women authors until by 1800 she was hardly represented at all. Apart from *Oroonoko*, sentimentalized into an antislavery tale in Britain and France, her novels fell from public view.

In the nineteenth century Behn was either ignored or vilified, both as a representative of the culturally disreputable Restoration and as a lewd woman whose works, excepting the redeeming *Oroonoko*, should not even be opened. Edmund Gosse in *English Poets* (1880) declared that, although Behn's poems had moments of fire and audacity, they caused later generations to blush for the author; Julia Kavanagh in *English Women of Letters* (1863) condemned her 'inveterate coarseness' of mind: Behn's plays were 'so coarse as to offend even a coarse age'.

With the twentieth century came a change. The Victorian disapproval gave Behn new champions among the moderns and her supposed role in the development of the novel allowed her to be studied by scholars presumed immune to her grossness. In 1915 Montague Summers produced a six-volume edition of her work, attempting to rescue Behn as a woman and an author by displaying her as a generous, energetic figure who could command the lyrical and personal mode and take a first rank among dramatists. Vita Sackville-West in *Aphra Behn: the Incomparable Astrea* (1927) portrayed Behn as a writer of fiction and stressed that her importance was less literary than sociological: she was the first professional woman writer, significant for being there rather than for any literary merit in what she wrote. Virginia Woolf in *A Room of One's Own* (1929) agreed, declaring that Behn had earned women 'the right to speak their minds'. Despite this limited acclaim, Behn and her works remained largely unknown to a wider public until the women's movement in the 1970s, when she began to be assessed in the tradition of female authors. Even then, however, she did not quite suit a criticism that sought victims or resisters of patriarchal oppression.

Only in the last two decades of the twentieth century was Behn finally thrust into prominence when *Oroonoko* became part of the new literary canon, with numerous paperback editions appearing, usually with extracts setting it within later discussions of slavery. Now critical taste demanded the fragmentary and playful, and this, coupled with fashionable concern for race and gender, made Behn one of the most frequently taught Restoration writers in colleges and schools on both sides of the Atlantic. At the same time, especially in Britain, Behn was discussed by scholars within a historical context: she was seen as woman of letters, a huge influence on the Restoration theatre, from whose history she had largely been omitted by earlier critics, as well as a major force in the development of the early British novel. She also emerged as a political writer of stature, whose work revealed a growing sense of the power of art to influence politics and national culture.

JANET TODD

Sources J. Todd, *The secret life of Aphra Behn* (1996) · *The works of Aphra Behn*, ed. J. Todd, 7 vols. (1992–6) · M. Duffy, *The passionate shepherdess* (1977) · A. Goreau, *Reconstructing Aphra* (1980) · P. A. Hopkins, 'Aphra Behn and John Hoyle', *N&Q*, 239 (1994), 176–85 · J. Jones, 'New light on the background … of Aphra Behn', *N&Q*; repr. in *Aphra Behn studies* (1996) · S. H. Mendelson, 'Stuart women's diaries …', *Women in English society, 1500–1800* (1985) · M. A. O'Donnell, *Aphra Behn: an annotated bibliography* (1986) · M. A. O'Donnell, 'A verse miscellany of Aphra Behn', *English Manuscript Studies, 1100–1700*, 2 (1990) · *The works of Aphra Behn*, ed. M. Summers (1915) · G. Woodcock, *The incomparable Aphra* (1948) · W. J. Cameron, *New light on Aphra Behn* (1961) · *CSP dom., 1660–70* · *CSP col., 1660–70* · 'Life and memoirs', *All the histories and novels* (1698) · 'Aphara Behn', *A general dictionary, historical and critical*, 3 (1735)

Likenesses attrib. Lely, portrait, *c.*1670–1679, priv. coll. · J. Fittler, line engraving, pubd 1822 (after T. Uwins), NPG · G. Scharf, drawing, 1873, NPG · attrib. M. Beale, portrait (of Behn?), St Hilda's College, Oxford · R. White, line engraving (after J. Riley), BM, NPG; repro. in A. Behn, *Plays*, 2 vols. (1716) [*see illus.*]

Behnes [*later* Burlowe], **Henry** (1801/2–1837), sculptor, was the younger brother of William *Behnes the sculptor. Henry was probably born in London, the second of three sons of a Hanoverian piano maker who married an Englishwoman. The family lived in Dublin for several years before returning to settle in London, where the brothers are said to have assisted their father in his trade. According to the *Art Journal*, it was after seeing the work of 'a French sculptor' (probably P. F. Chenu), who was a fellow lodger in the family's house in Charles Street, that 'Henry Behnes first, then William, formed the resolution of settling definitively to sculpture as their profession' (*Art Journal*, 1864, 83). In 1821, at the age of nineteen, Henry entered the Royal Academy Schools where two years later he won a silver medal.

In the late 1820s Behnes began to establish a successful practice as a sculptor of portrait busts: his sitters included the poet John Clare (plaster, 1828; Northamptonshire Central Library, Northampton), the editor Samuel Carter Hall (marble, exh. RA, 1833; V&A), the engraver John Pye (plaster, 1831; NPG), and Henry Bathurst, bishop of Norwich (exh. RA, 1833). Behnes exhibited at the Royal Academy in 1831 and 1833 and at the Society of British Artists, Suffolk Street, in 1831. He signed a monument to Katherine Noel (*d.* 1832) in All Saints, Kirkby Mallory, Leicestershire.

About 1834 Behnes went to Rome where he received many commissions from English visitors to the city. E. V. Rippingille noted that his work was executed 'in a style directly opposed to that which was prevalent among the artists of Rome generally, being much broader and bolder' ('Personal Recollections', 202). His busts, like those of his brother, are characterized by a lively naturalism, and a varied treatment of facial contour—informed by his study of phrenology—which would have been in marked contrast with the neo-classical style of Anglo-Roman sculptors such as John Gibson and Lawrence Macdonald.

In 1837, during the cholera epidemic in Rome, most of the English residents fled the city. Behnes, however, chose to remain, maintaining that as 'he had so many busts in progress … he could not afford to leave them' (*Art Union*). He contracted cholera and was discovered on his deathbed by the artist Charles Lambert. He died, presumably unmarried, on 4 September 1837 and was buried in the protestant cemetery at Monte Testaccio, Rome, where his tomb remains.

Behnes adopted the name Burlowe probably to avoid confusion with the elder Behnes, though it has also been suggested that he did this to dissociate himself from his brother, whose irregular life was well known. The *Art Journal* observed that Henry was 'in every way superior to his brother as a man', although he was 'his inferior as an artist' (*Art Journal*, 1864, 83). To S. C. Hall he was 'in all ways steady, upright, conscientious, just; and he would certainly have attained distinction' had his career not been suddenly terminated (Hall, 2.238). Rippingille described him as: 'tall, well-built, fresh-looking, cheerful, open, amiable … the very man that, meeting in the street and catching his pleasant eye, you would like to speak to, and be acquainted with' ('Personal Recollections', 202).

MARTIN GREENWOOD

Sources 'Personal recollections of artists by the late E. V. Rippingille, no. 3: Burlowe the sculptor', *Art Journal*, 21 (1859), 201–2 · *Art*

Union, 2 (1840), 193 • *Art Journal*, 26 (1864), 83–4 • R. Gunnis, *Dictionary of British sculptors, 1660–1851* (1953); new edn (1968) • Redgrave, *Artists* • *DNB* • Graves, *RA exhibitors* • J. Johnson, ed., *Works exhibited at the Royal Society of British Artists, 1824–1893, and the New English Art Club, 1888–1917*, 2 vols. (1975), 67 • S. C. Hall, *Retrospect of a long life: from 1815 to 1883*, 2 (1883), 238 • R. Ormond, *Early Victorian portraits*, 2 vols. (1973) • S. C. Hutchison, 'The Royal Academy Schools, 1768–1830', *Walpole Society*, 38 (1960–62), 123–91, esp. 174
Archives BL, letters to John Clare, Egerton MSS 2247–2249 • JRL, Fairfax Murray collection, William Behnes MSS

Behnes, William (1791×7–1864), sculptor, was born in London, the eldest of the three sons of a piano maker, of Hanover, Germany, and his English wife. He may have been the 'William Bennes' who was born in Portman Square, Middlesex, on 13 December 1791 and baptized at St Mary's, Marylebone Road, on 2 September 1792, the son of William and Elizabeth Bennes. He was brought up in Dublin, where he attended a public drawing-school. He returned with his family to London and enrolled at the Royal Academy Schools on 23 March 1813, when his age was recorded as eighteen, initially planning to be a painter. After he and his brother Henry received lessons in modelling from Peter Francis Chenu, they both turned to sculpture. After winning silver medals at the academy in 1816, 1817, and 1819, Behnes was awarded a gold medal by the Society of Arts in 1819 for inventing 'an instrument for transferring points to marble' (Gunnis, 45).

From the 1820s to the 1840s Behnes was second only to Francis Chantrey as England's most prolific and successful portrait sculptor. Henry Weekes, who worked for both men, believed that Behnes possessed greater natural talent, considering him 'the best manipulator of surface of the two … His heads … have greater freedom of handling, less mannerism, more variety and greater difference of character' (Weekes, 303). Chantrey's greater reputation was due to his consistency and social skills, whereas Behnes exasperated even his friends who, Weekes claimed, 'felt they had been made unfair use of' (ibid., 302–3). Behnes suffered, moreover, from 'evil habits', darkly alluded to by his biographers. S. C. Hall offered a partial explanation, describing Behnes as 'another victim to the pest of drink' (Hall, 2.238). This was probably triggered by his decision to move in 1823 to larger London premises at 91 Dean Street, Soho, which proved impracticable to convert to a studio. He was left financially crippled and a prey to moneylenders. His waywardness probably led to his exclusion from Royal Academy membership, though he exhibited there between 1815 and 1863. His brother, the sculptor Henry *Behnes (1801/2–1837), changed his surname to Burlowe about 1830 because, claimed Hall, of the 'tarnish on the name' (ibid.).

Behnes nevertheless won the affection and admiration of the young sculptor Thomas Woolner, who worked in his studio between about 1838 and 1844. Woolner later stated that he had received his necessary artistic education from Behnes, and little in comparison from the Royal Academy Schools. George Frederic Watts was another

famous pupil, while Behnes's studio assistants included several major Victorian sculptors such as Weekes, John Henry Foley, Musgrave Lewthwaite Watson, and Timothy Butler.

Behnes's work has received little art historical attention, probably because he belongs to a still underrated era in English sculpture. Yet his works vindicate his contemporaries' praise. He excelled in conveying the character of his sitters, as seen for example in his busts of Robert Vernon (Tate collection) and Richard Porson (1845, Eton College Library, Berkshire). The marble bust of Princess Victoria at the age of ten (1829, Royal Collection) radiates a baroque sense of animation. On her accession in 1837 Behnes was appointed sculptor-in-ordinary to Queen Victoria, but he received no further commissions. His church monuments are relatively few but impressive. Francis Turner Palgrave called the statue of William Babington (1837, St Paul's Cathedral, London) 'at once grand and delicate' (Palgrave, 223), and its crisply rendered drapery influenced Woolner. The high-relief monument to Charlotte Botfield (1825, All Saints' Church, Norton, Northamptonshire), which portrays her grieving widower, convincingly fuses Romantic pensiveness with early Victorian naturalism. Behnes's motif of guardian angels pointing heavenward in the monuments to Esther North (1825, Old Alresford, Hampshire) and John Bourne (1833, St Peter's Church, Stoke-on-Trent) influenced later funerary sculpture. His outdoor statuary is generally less successful. Behnes's best-known public monument, to Sir Henry Havelock (1861, Trafalgar Square, London, and Mowbray Park, Sunderland), is a stolidly competent example of realism. The statue of Sir Robert Peel (1852, Woodhouse Moor, Leeds) was the earliest monument erected to him and the first large-scale bronze cast in one piece in Britain.

Behnes was declared bankrupt in 1861 and moved to lodgings at 72 Charlotte Street. According to Hall, he was found one night 'literally in the gutter, with threepence in his pocket' (Hall, 2.238) and was taken to the Middlesex Hospital near by, where he died, unmarried, on 3 January 1864. He was buried on the 12th in Kensal Green cemetery, London. Although the Royal Academy registers and cemetery records support a birth date of 1795, and his death certificate gives his age at death as sixty-seven, which would place his year of birth in either 1796 or 1797, if Behnes was the son of William and Elizabeth Bennes his age at death would have been seventy-three. Attempts by a committee, headed by George Cruikshank, to erect a memorial sculpture over his grave foundered for want of sufficient subscriptions.   MARK STOCKER

Sources *Art Journal*, 26 (1864), 83–4 • R. Gunnis, *Dictionary of British sculptors, 1660–1851* (1953); new edn (1968), 45–8 • H. Weekes, *Lectures on art* (1880), 294–317 • S. C. Hall, *Retrospect of a long life: from 1815 to 1883*, 2 (1883), 238–9 • M. Greenwood, 'Behnes, William', *The dictionary of art*, ed. J. Turner (1996) • F. T. Palgrave, *Essays on art* (1866), 42–4, 217–25 • B. Read, *Victorian sculpture* (1982) • N. Penny, *Church monuments in Romantic England* (1977) • J. Darke, *The monument guide to England and Wales* (1991) • *DNB* • B. Read and J. Barnes, eds., *Pre-Raphaelite sculpture: nature and imagination in British sculpture, 1848–1914* (1991) · J. Blackwood, *London's immortals: the complete outdoor commemorative statues* (1989) · S. C. Hutchison, 'The Royal Academy Schools, 1768–1830', *Walpole Society*, 38 (1960–62), 123–91, esp. 167 · H. Meller, *London cemeteries: an illustrated guide and gazetteer*, 3rd edn (1994) · d. cert. · Graves, *RA exhibitors*, 1 (1905), 166–9 · baptismal register of St Mary's, Marylebone Road, London, City Westm. AC · census returns, 1861

Archives JRL · RSA, reference to 1819 prize

Wealth at death bankrupt, 1861: R. Gunnis, *Dictionary of British sculptors, 1660–1851* (1968); S. C. Hall, *Retrospect of a long life: from 1815 to 1883* (1883), etc.

Behrens, (Catherine) Betty Abigail (1904–1989), historian, was born on 24 April 1904 in London, the elder of two children of Noel Edward Behrens (1879–1967), a civil servant until his retirement in 1921 and banker, and his wife, Vivien (1880–1961), daughter of Sir Cecil Allen *Coward (1845–1938). It is characteristic of her complex identity that she had three forenames: to the family she was Kate or Jane, to her undergraduate friends Abi, and to colleagues and the public Betty. She had a double identity from birth, half-Jewish, half-Christian. In her unpublished 'Notes for an autobiography' written in her eighties, she explains that her Behrens grandfather, Edward (d. 1905), already a millionaire, bequeathed a large capital sum to her father. Betty attributed her brains to her father and her ambivalent Jewishness. Her mother, Vivien, had in Betty's eyes a 'disadvantage' worse than her father's Jewishness; she was 'stupid'. Her mother once warned her that intellectual interests might make her 'clever and want to go to college and be like a man' ('Notes for an autobiography', Behrens MSS).

Betty Behrens grew up with governesses, private tutors, and holidays abroad. She could not remember a time when she had not spoken French and in due course her German became as fluent. She often said that her first proper school was Lady Margaret Hall, Oxford, to which she was admitted to read modern history in 1923; she went down with a first (1926) and the award of a Commonwealth fellowship to Radcliffe College in the United States. On her return she began research in English history at Bedford College, London. In 1935 she was elected a fellow of Newnham College, Cambridge, and in 1938 took up a university assistant lectureship in the faculty of history. She published four articles in the mid-1930s which dealt with Henry VIII and his divorce, and the evolution of resident diplomats in that reign. After her appointment in Cambridge her interests changed to a later period of English history and in 1941 'The whig theory of the constitution in the reign of Charles II' appeared in the *Cambridge Historical Journal*.

The war took Betty Behrens away from academic history and helped her to understand the workings of the Ministry of War Transport, of which she became in time the official historian. As she wrote to a former pupil, 'you could see the machine from the inside, every historian should do that once' (letter to Mrs M. Cox, 1944, in private possession). Her *Merchant Shipping and the Demands of War*, published by HMSO in 1955, cost a decade of her life and,

though it is a brilliant analysis, scarcely got a notice in the press. Later she said bitterly, 'I should never have accepted it if I had known before hand what I was in for' ('Notes for an autobiography', Behrens MSS).

Gradually, even while working on her history of merchant shipping, Betty Behrens began to ponder the theme which was to occupy the rest of her intellectual life and which made her for a decade famous throughout the literary world: the nature of the French *ancien régime* and the causes of the French Revolution. In her fifties and early sixties she began to write powerful, incisive, and increasingly influential attacks on the Marxist view of that revolution, and in 1967 she published *The Ancien Régime*, an illustrated and handsomely produced short history of France in the eighteenth century. In the preface she thanked Cambridge University and Newnham College, 'whose ways of proceeding have made certain aspects of the Ancien Régime intelligible which otherwise might not have been so'. The university did not mind, but the governing body of Newnham was not amused and refused to renew her fellowship. She moved to Clare Hall, where she remained as fellow and then fellow *emerita* until her death. During this period she began to review regularly in the *New York Review of Books* and for a while belonged to the Anglo-American intellectual élite. As quickly as fame came, it went. Her last book and undoubtedly her greatest, *Society, government and the Enlightenment: the experiences of eighteenth-century France and Prussia*, was published by Thames and Hudson in 1985 when she was eighty-one. It received good reviews but nobody bought it. She was shattered.

In 1966 Betty Behrens married the historian, diplomatist, and journalist Edward Hallett *Carr (1892–1982) and for a time tried to live the role of married woman. Deep incompatibilities drove them apart, and by the time E. H. Carr died Betty and 'Ted' lived separately in some bitterness of spirit.

Betty Behrens was a formidable figure, a slender, elegant woman with her hair always immaculately coiffed and her clothes and possessions in perfect taste. She inspired awe as well as affection. She had a sharp, rather penetrating voice, a loud explosive laugh, and an ability to deal out crushing judgements. Her vocabulary contained too many 'absurds' and 'nonsenses' for easy popularity. Throughout her life Betty read fiction voraciously in three languages and kept vivid notes on her reactions. She was an acute critic.

There was, on the other hand, a curious unworldliness. Betty Behrens had no idea how to promote herself. She assumed that one wrote brilliant books showing how everybody else had been wrong and the world said 'Amen'. It refused to do so and she never received the conventional rewards of academic achievement which lesser intellects collect as a matter of course. She loved beautiful things and spent her last years in an apartment in Swallowfield Park, near Reading, once Lord Clarendon's country home, where she died on 3 January 1989.

JONATHAN STEINBERG

Sources J. Steinberg, *Based on fact but told like a novel: the historical legacy of C. B. A. Behrens* (1989) [memorial lecture, Newnham College] · CAC Cam., Behrens MSS · *The Times* (17 Jan 1989) · *Daily Telegraph* (18 Jan 1989) · *The Independent* (17 Jan 1989) · priv. coll. · private information (2004) · *WW* · *Times index*
Archives CAC Cam., corresp., lecture notes, and research papers
Likenesses photograph, repro. in Steinberg, *Based on fact but told like a novel*
Wealth at death £526,345: probate, 18 May 1989, *CGPLA Eng. & Wales*

Behrens, Sir Jacob (1806–1889), textile merchant, was born on 20 November 1806, one of the sons of Nathan Behrens (*d.* 1842), a Jewish merchant, and Clara Hahn, daughter of a Hamburg silk merchant, at Pyrmont, in the small German principality of Waldeck between Hanover and Westphalia. The Behrens family had for generations traded as textile merchants. At the end of the Napoleonic wars the family moved to Hamburg. Jacob was educated by a family tutor, a theological student of the Reformed church, aided by an émigré Jesuit abbé who provided instruction in the French language, and by a shipwrecked Scottish sailor who taught English. A competent teacher of mathematics was also employed. It is recorded that Jacob was fluent in several languages.

Jacob joined his father's firm in Hamburg, assisting with the merchanting activity of the family, and taking control of the declining business in 1826. He travelled widely. His first crossing to England was in 1832, on board a paddle steamer from Hamburg to Hull. He returned in 1833 in order to attempt to persuade Thomas Clapham, a Leeds merchant with whom he traded, to adopt a different finish to the goods being supplied, and to pack them in small bales. He failed, and a visit the following year showed little more success. In 1834 he settled in Leeds, renting a small warehouse, and thus establishing his own firm of Jacob Behrens. This enabled him to finish cloth himself according to the requirements of his German market. In due course Behrens began to sell directly to Germany on his own account and not via the Hamburg business. The Leeds firm expanded rapidly, and two younger brothers, Louis and Rudolf, joined him in 1837, Louis acting as the business's traveller in Germany.

Jacob Behrens helped to pioneer the transition of merchanting from Leeds to Bradford, which was to become the dominant mercantile centre for the wool textile industry. The move brought him closer to his main suppliers and set him further on the path to a major position in the textile merchanting field. In 1840 Louis set up a branch of the business in Manchester to trade in cotton goods. He was soon joined by another brother, Edward. Their father, Nathan, died in 1842, shaken by a disastrous fire at his Hamburg premises, though the firm's stocks escaped its ravages. Subsequently, the firm set up branches in Manchester, London, Glasgow, Calcutta, and Shanghai.

In 1844 Jacob Behrens married Dorothea Hohenemser (*d.* 1884), daughter of a wealthy Jewish family from the south-west of Germany. They had five daughters, Wilhelmina, Clara, Julia, Louisa, and Rosa Emily, and four sons, Gustav (1846–1936), Charles (1848–1925), Fred (1849–1933),

Sir Jacob Behrens (1806–1889), by Ernest Leopold Sichel

and Harry (1854–1921). His brother Rudolf retired from the business in 1864, and Edward died in 1866. In 1870 Louis and his four sons started their own business. The following year Gustav entered into partnership with Jacob, followed in due course by the other three sons. Gustav remained a partner for sixty-five years, becoming a director of the Midland Railway for forty-five years and helping to establish the Hallé Concert Society in Manchester.

By the time of his marriage Jacob Behrens was firmly established in the Bradford trade and making his mark as an important member of the large local merchant community. He gained a reputation as a hardworking but cautious businessman, researching the trade and becoming extremely knowledgeable about its operation. That knowledge developed through the rest of his life, and he was often called upon for advice and information. He represented Bradford in negotiations about commercial conditions and foreign tariffs, and he provided regular commercial advice to the government. He helped to form the very influential Bradford chamber of commerce, serving as its vice-president for seven years, and its president for six. He was chairman of its important tariff committee for nearly forty years. In 1860 he advised the government about the commercial treaty with France, and became involved in negotiations for its creation. At various times in the later nineteenth century he helped to provide statistical information on the industry. He was reputed to be an avid reader of the government blue books. He was one of the founders of the Association of Chambers of Commerce, and it was pressure from him that helped in the formation of the commercial department of the Foreign Office in 1872. In 1882 he was knighted for his services to commerce.

Behrens's business specialized in the export of textiles to Germany. He traded with Belgium, the Netherlands, and Italy, and took the opportunity to trade with Japan when that market began to open up from the 1850s. His goods also found their way into China. He was a strong believer in the virtues of free trade. It was said that, initially, he found it difficult to be accepted in Bradford society. But it is clear that he gradually gained a great deal of respect. He gave much time to local issues and was a strong supporter of local charities. He campaigned for the improvement of postal services. He took a particular interest in the Bradford Eye and Ear Hospital.

Sir Jacob Behrens died at the Imperial Hotel, Torquay, on 22 April 1889, five years after his wife, and following a long period of failing health; he was buried at Undercliff cemetery, Bradford, on 26 April. The tribute to him from Bradford chamber of commerce remarked: 'He seemed to exist only to be of service to his fellow man.' The local newspaper, the *Bradford Observer* (23 April 1889), recognized him as a 'warm-hearted philanthropist' with 'an unreserved devotion to the commercial interests of the town' and 'an unswerving fidelity in the principles of free trade'. D. T. JENKINS

Sources *The first one hundred and fifty years: Sir Jacob Behrens & Sons, Ltd* (1984) · *Bradford Observer* (23 April 1889) · D. T. Jenkins, 'Behrens, Sir Jacob', *DBB* · *Sir Jacob Behrens, 1806–1889*, trans. H. Behrens (privately printed, London, 1925) [based on the unpubd memoirs of Sir J. Behrens] · W. R. Millmore, 'A chronicle of initiative and progress', *Wool Record*, 81 (1952), 17–18 · A. R. Rollin, 'The Jewish contribution to the British textile industry: "Builders of Bradford"', *Transactions of the Jewish Historical Society of England*, 17 (1951–2), 45–51 · *Bradford Daily Telegraph* (23 April 1889) · *Bradford Daily Telegraph* (27 April 1889) · d. cert.

Likenesses daguerreotype, 1844, repro. in *Sir Jacob Behrens & Sons, Ltd* · E. L. Sichel, portrait, Bradford City Art Gallery, Cartwright Hall, Bradford [*see illus.*]

Wealth at death £83,112 15s. 5d.: probate, 3 Sept 1889, CGPLA Eng. & Wales

Beighton, Henry (1686/7–1743), surveyor, was born between September 1686 and August 1687 at Griff, in the parish of Chilvers Coton, Nuneaton, Warwickshire, and baptized there on 20 August 1687. He was one of three children of Henry Beighton (1661–1710?), constable of Chilvers Coton, and his wife, Ann Payne (1658–1710?). He came from a family of yeoman surveyors and engineers, a branch of which had settled in Griff by the early seventeenth century. Charles, Samuel, Benjamin, James, and John Beighton, all surveyors active in Derbyshire in the eighteenth century, were his second cousins. Nothing is known of his education, but he evidently had good training as well as considerable talent in surveying, cartography, draughtsmanship, engineering, meteorology, and mathematics.

The first of Beighton's surveying and cartographic activities were a draft survey of Bedworth, Warwickshire, in 1707, and a copy of Robert Hewitt's 1690 survey of the lord

of Coventry's land at Griff and Arbury, both in Warwickshire, in 1708; but the work for which he is best-known was his map of Warwickshire. He first proposed such a map in 1711 and confirmed his plans in 1720 and 1722–3. County mapping at a large scale and based on original field survey was widely recognized to be at a low ebb in Britain at this time and the inadequacies of existing, by then outdated, maps were commonly noted. Beighton's proposal for an accurate and up-to-date county map, though not unprecedented, was undoubtedly ambitious and, unlike many such proposals, actually bore fruit. Between 1722 and 1725 he undertook the required field surveying of the county, during which he constructed and used a 'way-wiser' based on the preliminary designs of Thomas Eyre of Kettering. The first printing of his map (1727–8) at 1 inch to the mile in four sheets, which showed ten types of minerals but no hundred boundaries, was quickly followed by a revised version (1728–9) at the same scale and in four sheets, with hundreds marked. The map was incorporated at a reduced size and a smaller scale in the second edition of Sir William Dugdale's *Antiquities of Warwickshire* (2 vols., 1730), which also included four other maps by him of individual hundreds. The county map was reprinted in 1750 after his death on the initiative of his widow, Elizabeth (c.1690–1759), whom he had married about 1720 and with whom he had a son, Marcellus (1724–1743), and a daughter whose name may have been Celia. He continued as an active land surveyor in Warwickshire producing surveys, accounts, and terriers of small areas in the county such as Thurlaston, Hampton in Arden, and Caldecote. Between 1731 and 1733 he was enclosure commissioner for Attleborough, Nuneaton, Chilvers Coton, Arbury, and Griff in Warwickshire and Chipping Warden in Northamptonshire and he surveyed and mapped those areas to effect the settlements there. He also left several drawings, notably those of St Michael's Church, Coventry, and Coventry Cross, both of which were among his drawings engraved for Dugdale's *Antiquities* (1730).

While an active surveyor Beighton was also closely involved in engineering, particularly to solve problems encountered in mining, in which he also had a commercial interest. His interest was perhaps sparked by the existence of a coal mine at Griff where a Newcomen engine was installed in 1714. In 1711 he studied the Newcomen-Savery steam engine with J. T. Desaguliers and he soon thereafter invented a new puppet clack or safety valve on which he became an authority. He published articles on steam power and in 1718 installed a steam engine at Washington, co. Durham, and was asked to comment on the designs of others. He designed and erected a multiplying bucket engine in 1725 at Chicheley, Buckinghamshire. He seems to have been involved in the lead trade and owned shares in Heaton colliery, Newcastle upon Tyne, though the losses he sustained in the later part of his life through his involvement in the uneconomic pumping engines of Stonier Parrott and George Sparrow followed him to his grave.

Beighton maintained a regular correspondence with the Royal Society from 1707 and was elected fellow in 1720, not least through the influence of the coal baron and entrepreneur Sir Richard Newdigate of Arbury, for whom he had done survey work. To the society's *Philosophical Transactions* and other publications he contributed articles on engineering, scientific instruments, and meteorological observations. Underlying Beighton's surveying and engineering work was a deep interest in mathematics. He edited the *Ladies' Diary* between 1714 and 1743 and used the journal as a vehicle to encourage women to study mathematics, as well as to publish his own meteorological records. He was helped in his editorial work by his wife, and a relative, probably his daughter, contributed to the journal. He also corresponded with notable mathematicians such as Thomas Simpson.

From the age of twenty Beighton kept comprehensive meteorological records, many of which were published from 1716 to his death. His report on the 1712 Nuneaton hurricane to the Royal Society and calculations for lunar and solar eclipses are fine examples of his work. He was an acute observer and had a detailed understanding of the instruments he used. Beighton died on 9 October 1743 at Griff House, Chilvers Coton, Warwickshire, and two days later was buried in the parish church at Chilvers Coton, where a small tablet was erected to his memory.

ALAN F. COOK

Sources W. Dugdale, *The antiquities of Warwickshire illustrated*, rev. W. Thomas, 2nd edn, 2 vols. (1730) · J. T. Desaguliers, *A course of experimental philosophy*, 2nd edn, 2 vols. (1744–5) · L. R. Stewart, *The rise of public science: rhetoric, technology, and natural philosophy in Newtonian Britain, 1660–1750* (1992) · R. Jenkins, 'Savery, Newcomen and the early history of the steam engine, pt II', *Transactions* [Newcomen Society], 4 (1923–4), 113–31 · R. Jenkins, 'Supplementary note on Beighton's drawing of Newcomen's engine, 1717', *Transactions* [Newcomen Society], 4 (1923–4), 132–3 · R. Jenkins, *Links in the history of engineering and technology from Tudor times: the collected papers of Rhys Jenkins* (1936) · R. V. Wallis and P. J. Wallis, eds., *Biobibliography of British mathematics and its applications*, 2 (1986) · L. T. C. Rolt and J. S. Allen, *The steam engines of Thomas Newcomen* (1963) · R. L. Galloway, *Annals of coal mining and the coal trade*, 1st ser. (1898) · F. W. Steer and others, *Dictionary of land surveyors and local map-makers of Great Britain and Ireland, 1530–1850*, ed. P. Eden, 2nd edn, ed. S. Bendall, 2 vols. (1997) · D. Smith, *Antique maps of the British Isles* (1982) · D. Smith, *Maps and plans for the local historian and collector* (1988) · F. L. Colvile, *The worthies of Warwickshire who lived between 1500 and 1800* [1870] · census, parish of Griff and Chilvers Coton, Dec 1684, Warks. CRO, CR136/V 12 · parish registers, Chilvers Coton, Warks. CRO

Archives BL, essays and plotting table, Add. MS 4432 · BL, hurricane report, plotting table, and corresp., Add. MS 4433 · BL, south-east side of Fairford church, Add. MS K.13.67 (1) · BL, Warwickshire map surveyed, Add. MS K.42.74.8 · Durham RO, William Cotesworth MSS, steam engine details, and agreements for Durham coalfield · GL, London Bridge water works data · Northumbd RO, Newcastle upon Tyne, articles and agreements · Northumbd RO, Newcastle upon Tyne, Beighton willing to buy and sell lead · RS, barometer and weather data · RS, register book for London Bridge water works 1730 · RS, weather data, journal book · RS, council minutes · Warks. CRO, erecting bucket wheel at Chicheley and engraving · Warks. CRO, personal MSS and enclosures · Warks. CRO, renewing foundations for Griff colliery engine · Warks. CRO, surveys, wages book, enclosures | Col. U., letters to Thomas Simpson FRS

Wealth at death old est. £100, challenged: Stewart, *Rise of public science* · in arrears with RS, 1736; adversely financially affected by Stonier Parrott's and George Sparrow's steam engine ventures: T. Pennant, *The journey from Chester to London* (1811); RS correspondence to Desaguliers, BL, Add. MS 4433, fol. 276 (1736); A. W. A. White, *Men and mining in Warwickshire* (1970)

Beighton, Thomas (1790–1844), missionary, was born at Ednaston, Derbyshire, on 25 December 1790. He was educated by the liberality of a Unitarian minister, but he adopted evangelical principles and was sent by the London Missionary Society as a missionary to Malacca, which he reached in September 1818. Together with the other junior missionaries (John Ince and Samuel Milton), he dissented from the dictatorial rule of William *Milne, the head of the Malacca mission. Beighton and Ince were sent by Milne in 1819 to open a permanent mission in Penang. Milne's death in 1822 eased matters.

Besides teaching in schools and holding religious services, Beighton set up a printing press, from which he published works in the Malay language, including a translation of parts of *The Pilgrim's Progress*, the Anglican liturgy, a catechism, and in 1825 a book on arithmetic. On a rumour that the mission was to be removed, fifty-six Malayan merchants and others petitioned against Beighton's removal. Beighton died at Penang on 14 April 1844.

H. C. G. MATTHEW

Sources 'A sketch of the life and labours of the Rev. T. Beighton', *Evangelical Magazine and Missionary Chronicle*, new ser., 23 (1845), 113–22, 169–75 · *Sunday at Home* (Dec 1881) · private information (1885) · B. Harrison, *Waiting for China: the Anglo-Chinese college at Malacca, 1818–1843, and early nineteenth-century missions* (1979)

Archives SOAS, corresp. from Malacca and Penang [transcripts and photocopies]

Beilby family (*per. c.*1755–1819), glass enamellers and engravers, originated with **William Beilby** (1740–1819), glass enameller, born on 9 July 1740 in Durham, the fourth of the seven children of William Beilby (1706–1765), a silversmith, and his wife, Mary Bainbridge (d. 1778). The elder William Beilby established himself as a silversmith in Durham after his marriage in 1733; in 1759, after years of financial problems, he gave up his business and moved to Gateshead. The younger William was admitted in 1751 as king's scholar at Durham grammar school, where he was noted for his interest in the classics. However, owing to the family's persistent financial misfortune he was sent to Birmingham in the same year to begin an apprenticeship as an enameller. There he appears to have lived with his elder brother Richard and was indentured in 1755 to a John Hezeldine. His acquaintance with glass is likely to have begun at this period, in what was then a centre of the British glass industry.

William moved to Gateshead in 1760 to join his family, in particular his brother Ralph Beilby [*see below*], who had set up a workshop at Amen Corner, near Newcastle Cathedral. The following years were crucial in William's technical experiments with firing enamels onto glass goblets. These were carried out at the nearby Closegate flint glass-houses and yielded the first results in rather weak white enamels but, from 1761, also in colour.

The delicately hand-painted glassware of the 1760s shows the development of the artist's skills. In co-operation with Ralph, who had established himself as an expert in heraldry, William produced the masterpieces of his 'heraldic phase', in particular the royal goblets (*c*.1764; Fitzwilliam Museum, Cambridge, and Philadelphia Museum of Art). While commissions poured in from aristocratic patrons, he must still have experienced a degree of financial hardship, as he advertised as a drawing-master in 1767; his drawing school continued until 1778. At the time the family was resident at the Forth Gardens, Newcastle upon Tyne.

The young artist Thomas Bewick (1753–1828) joined the Beilby workshop as an apprentice in 1767, and his influence may first be discerned in the pastoral scene on the reverse of the flask for Thomas Brown (1769; Ashmolean Museum, Oxford). The introduction of landscapes, birds, exotic flora, and so on may be regarded as characteristic of William's later style. However, this flask is also the last-known authenticated and dated work by William Beilby. He continued to produce enamelled glassware throughout the 1770s, yet his output appears to have slowed, partly on account of the devastation caused by the 1771 Tyne flood, and partly as a result of his sister's illness. His departure from Newcastle at the end of the 1770s seems to have been motivated both by the break-up of his family after his mother's death in 1778 and by Bewick's being taken into full partnership at the family firm in 1777. There is sufficient evidence of William Beilby in Battersea over the next few years to substantiate the common view of his having set up as a drawing-master. On 12 October 1785 he married Ellen Purton (*b*. 1765), twenty-five years his junior, the niece of John Falconer, a wealthy City merchant of Scottish descent. About 1788 the couple moved to Fife to live on an estate which Falconer had bought for his niece; nothing is known about their life there.

William Beilby's subsequent move to Hull is equally obscure, especially given his wife's significant inheritance from her uncle's fortune. In 1814 he is recorded as living in English Street. The question of his artistic activities in the years after Newcastle has been contentious, in particular the possibility of glass made in Scotland. Some watercolours survive in private collections in the Hull area, alongside earlier views of Battersea. The Beilbys appear to have had two sons and a daughter, of whom only William Turton Beilby is recorded in Hull in 1822. William Beilby died at home on 8 October 1819; no tombstone or memorial of him survives in Hull.

Ralph Beilby (*bap.* 1743, *d*. 1817), engraver and businessman, was baptized on 12 August 1743 at St Margaret's, Durham, the third son of William and Mary Beilby. He was educated at Durham grammar school and was then apprenticed to his father. While he started to engrave in silver, he moved on to copper-engraving and seal-cutting upon the return of his brother Richard from Birmingham. Ralph was the driving force behind the family's move to Gateshead after his father's business folded. He set up Beilby & Co. and moved the business to Amen Corner in Newcastle upon Tyne after the trial for forgery of the well-known engraver Jameson had created a vacancy in the city. In addition to acting as the family's business brain, Ralph Beilby acquired considerable expertise in the fields

of heraldry and chivalry, which made him the preferred engraver of the northern aristocracy.

Ralph's own artistic work flourished through his collaboration with the historian John Brand, which produced the engraving of Thornton's monument plate for Brand's history of Newcastle and a plan of Newcastle in 1788. Yet he is mostly remembered as Thomas Bewick's master after the latter's entry into the Beilby workshop. Their collaboration produced, among other works, *A General History of Quadrupeds*; however, disagreement over the fourth edition of this work led to the dissolution of the enterprise in January 1798.

Ralph Beilby's artistic output became less prolific after his marriage on 3 December 1780 to Ellen Hawthorne (*d*. 1833). He set up a new business with James Hawthorne, his brother-in-law, which dealt in the production of watchglasses and clockwork. Their premises were destroyed by fire in 1806 and subsequently rebuilt, and shortly afterwards Ralph Beilby took early retirement. He remained active as a patron of the arts and was a founder member of the Literary and Philosophical Society of Newcastle upon Tyne. He died on 4 January 1817 and was buried at St Andrew's, Newcastle.

Mary Beilby (*bap.* 1750, *d*. 1797), glass artist, was baptized on 12 February 1750 at St Nicholas's Church, Durham, the last of the seven children of William and Mary Beilby. She was educated privately at Durham and appears to have joined the family workshop at a very young age. Her contribution is associated principally with William Beilby's work in the 1760s. A considerable number of items have been attributed to her, yet disentangling the Beilby hands is problematic. Many attributions to Mary Beilby seem to be a result of our lack of knowledge about other artists active at the time. Mary's romance with Thomas Bewick after the young artist's entry into the family workshop is related in Bewick's *Memoir*. Yet nothing came of it, and in 1774 Mary suffered a paralytic stroke from which she does not appear to have recovered. It is unclear whether she followed her brother to Battersea. At any rate, she joined William and his wife at their estate in Fife, where she died in 1797.   ALEXANDER KOLLER

Sources J. Rush, *The ingenious Beilbys* (1973) · S. Cottle, 'The other Beilbys: British enamelled glass of the 18th century', *Apollo*, 124 (1986), 315–27 · *A memoir of Thomas Bewick written by himself*, ed. I. Bain (1975) · W. A. Thorpe, *A history of English and Irish glass* (1929) · parish register, Durham, St Margaret, Durham RO [baptism, Ralph Beilby] · parish register, Durham, St Nicholas, Durham RO [baptism, Mary Beilby] · parish register, Newcastle upon Tyne, St John, Northumbd RO [marriage, Mary Beilby] · parish register, Newcastle upon Tyne, St Andrew, Northumbd RO [burial, Ralph Beilby]

Archives Tyne and Wear Archives Service, Newcastle upon Tyne, business records [Ralph Beilby] | V&A NAL, corresp. with Thomas Bewick [Ralph Beilby]

Beilby, Sir George Thomas (1850–1924), industrial chemist, was born in Edinburgh on 17 November 1850, the youngest son of George Thomas Beilby MD and his wife, Rachel, daughter of the Revd Jonathan Watson, minister of Dublin Street Baptist Church, Edinburgh. He was educated at private schools and at Edinburgh University. In

1869 he joined the Oakbank Oil Company as a chemist and began his association with the Scottish paraffin shale industry. With William Young he improved the process of distillation of shale and greatly increased the recovery of ammonia (in great demand for agricultural purposes as guano reserves became exhausted); the process using continuous retorts, introduced by Beilby and Young in 1881, brought about a large increase in the yield of paraffin and ammonia.

In 1890 Beilby turned his attention to the production of cyanides, to meet the new demand prompted by the invention of the McArthur–Forrest process for the treatment of gold ores. He devised a process which involved the action of ammonia on a mixture of potassium carbonate and carbon, sufficient cyanide always being present to keep the mass fluid. The Cassel Gold Extracting Company, later called the Cassel Cyanide Company (of which Beilby became a director), used this process until 1906, when Beilby introduced a new process invented by Hamilton Castner, in which metallic sodium was employed. Beilby's association with Castner led him to become a director of the Castner-Kellner Alkali Company, which manufactured sodium at Runcorn and now set up new works for the production of sodium at Newcastle upon Tyne. Beilby remained closely connected with these branches of the chemical industry for the rest of his life.

Beilby observed the rapid destruction of metals by ammonia at high temperature during the course of his manufacturing operations. He began a detailed series of private investigations into the flow of solids. As a result of elegant experiments with the microscope, carried out with simple laboratory equipment, he concluded that when a metal is caused to flow, for example during polishing, the normal crystalline structure is partly broken down, and a vitreous layer is formed. This theory seemed to explain the hardening of metals by cold working, with the vitreous layer forming on crystal slip-planes, thus resisting further flow along these planes and hardening the metal. Beilby's theory, expressed in his only book, *Aggregation and Flow of Solids* (1921), enjoyed support from British and American chemists but was less popular with continental scientists. Subsequent X-ray analysis suggested the formation of a vitreous layer to be much rarer than Beilby first thought.

Beilby's manufacturing experience led him to take great interest in the economical use of fuel, and in his presidential address to the Society of Chemical Industry in 1899 he reviewed the subject and gave a detailed breakdown of national coal consumption. He made a report to the royal commission on coal supplies (1902–4), and he was a member of the royal commission on fuel oil engines for the navy (1912–13). In 1906 he made a series of important experiments in the low-temperature carbonization of coal, and later he carried out microscope studies on the cell structure and properties of coke. He was actively involved in directing scientific research during the First World War, and in 1917 he became the first chairman and director of the Fuel Research Board. It was under his direction that the fuel research station at East Greenwich was designed and erected, and in the six years that he was director of the research board attention was directed mainly to the production of oil from coal by carbonization and to a survey of British coal reserves. Beilby also introduced the term 'therm' as a unit for measuring gas consumption in towns.

Beilby was a modest man of high character. In 1877 he married Emma Clarke, daughter of the Revd Samuel Newman; they had one son and one daughter. He was keenly interested in educational matters, and from 1907 until 1923 he was chairman of the governing body of the Royal Technical College, Glasgow, to which he was also a generous benefactor. He was president of the Institute of Chemistry from 1909 to 1912 and of the Institute of Metals from 1916 to 1918. He received honorary degrees from the universities of Glasgow and Birmingham, and he was president of the chemical section of the British Association at its meeting in South Africa in 1905. He was elected a fellow of the Royal Society in 1906 and knighted in 1916.

Beilby died at his home, 29 Kidderpore Avenue, Hampstead, London, on 1 August 1924. He was survived by Lady Beilby.   C. H. DESCH, rev. JOHN BOSNELL

Sources H. C. H. C., *PRS*, 109A (1925), i–xvii • private information (1937) • G. T. Beilby, *Chemistry and practical life: being an address delivered to the Andersonian Chemical Society of the Royal Technical College, Glasgow, on October 23rd 1914* (1914) [19 pp.] • *CGPLA Eng. & Wales* (1924)

Likenesses W. Stoneman, photograph, 1918, NPG • photograph, repro. in *Obits. FRS*

Wealth at death £163,689 19s. 1d.: probate, 16 Sept 1924, *CGPLA Eng. & Wales*

Beilby, Mary (*bap.* 1750, *d.* 1797). *See under* Beilby family (*per.* c.1755–1819).

Beilby, Ralph (*bap.* 1743, *d.* 1817). *See under* Beilby family (*per.* c.1755–1819).

Beilby, William (1740–1819). *See under* Beilby family (*per.* c.1755–1819).

Beilby, William (1783–1849), obstetric physician, was born at Sheffield on 13 April 1783, the son of Thomas Beilby and his wife, Isabella. In 1807 he entered into a partnership in the linen trade with some relatives in Dublin, but in 1813 he moved to Edinburgh to study medicine. After graduating MD in 1816, he settled in Edinburgh to practise midwifery. He soon achieved a wide reputation in his profession, and was appointed physician accoucheur to the New Town Dispensary. On 2 November 1824 he became FRCP (Edinburgh) and in 1844 he was elected president of the Royal College of Physicians of Edinburgh, delivering the inaugural address (published in 1847) when the college's new hall in Queen Street was opened on 27 November 1846. Beilby took a prominent interest in benevolent and religious matters, including the schemes of the Evangelical Alliance. He was a member of the Elder Street (later Canonmills) Baptist Church and was a confidant of Dr Innes, the pastor. Beilby was a founder of the Edinburgh Medical Missionary Society in 1841 and was president from 1844 until shortly before his death. He was also one of the founders of the Edinburgh Obstetrical Society, of which he became the first president in 1845, and a governor of the Orphan Hospital. A contemporary of Beilby's described him as a man of integrity who 'possessed amazing vivacity and energy', and commented that:

> Among his acquired excellencies, may be named the self-command he had obtained over the irascible passions; which in an ardent temperament like his, must in early life have been impatient of control; the result, no doubt, of much self-inspection and earnest prayer.   (Watson, 18, 23)

He died at his home, 57 Northumberland Street, Edinburgh, on 30 May 1849, after being ill for over a year.

ORNELLA MOSCUCCI

Sources *DNB* · W. S. Craig, *History of the Royal College of Physicians of Edinburgh* (1976) · D. M. Lewis, ed., *The Blackwell dictionary of evangelical biography, 1730–1860*, 2 vols. (1995) · *IGI* · *The Post Office Edinburgh and Leith directory* (1849) · J. Watson, *Luke, the beloved physician: tribute to … the late William Beilby* (1849)
Likenesses oils, repro. in Craig, *History of the Royal College of Physicians of Edinburgh*

Beirdd y tywysogion. *See* Gogynfeirdd (*act. c.*1080–1285).

Beirne, Dominick (*c.*1843–1915). *See under* Knock, visionaries of (*act.* 1879).

Beirne, Dominick (*c.*1858–1885). *See under* Knock, visionaries of (*act.* 1879).

Beirne, Margaret (*c.*1810–1909). *See under* Knock, visionaries of (*act.* 1879).

Beirne, Margaret (*c.*1858–1880). *See under* Knock, visionaries of (*act.* 1879).

Beirne, Mary (*c.*1850–1936). *See under* Knock, visionaries of (*act.* 1879).

Beirne, Patrick (*c.*1863–1943). *See under* Knock, visionaries of (*act.* 1879).

Beit, Alfred (1853–1906), mining magnate and philanthropist, born at Hamburg on 15 February 1853, was the eldest son of Siegfried and Laura Beit. His father was a merchant belonging to a well-known Hamburg family descended from Portuguese Jews, and Lutheran by religion. Beit was educated privately, and at eighteen entered the Amsterdam office of Messrs Robinow, diamond merchants, after which he joined the Cape Colony branch of D. Lippert & Co., to whom he was related. Early in September 1875 he sailed for Cape Town, and, proceeding to the diamond mining centre of Kimberley by wagon, was one of Lippert's representatives there until 1878, when he revisited Hamburg. His Amsterdam training enabled him to see that Cape diamonds, so far from deserving their reputation of being an inferior product, were generally as good as any in the world, and were being sold in Africa at a price far below their worth in Europe. Accordingly borrowing £2000 from his father by way of capital, he returned to Kimberley in the same year, and set up under his own name as a diamond merchant. Foreseeing the growth of Kimberley, he is said to have invested most of his capital in purchasing ground on which he put up a number of corrugated iron offices. For twelve of these the

Alfred Beit (1853–1906), by Giovanni Boldini, 1904

rent ultimately received by him was estimated at £1800 a month, and later he is believed to have sold the ground for £260,000.

In 1882 Beit became associated in the diamond business at Kimberley with J. Porgès and Julius *Wernher. In 1884 Porgès and Wernher returned to England and constituted the London firm of J. Porgès & Co., dealing in diamonds and diamond shares, and after 1888 in goldmines as well. Beit was sole representative of this firm at Kimberley until 1889, when he made London his headquarters, although his subsequent visits to Africa were frequent. On 1 January 1890 the firm of Wernher, Beit & Co. replaced J. Porgès & Co. in the same line of business.

When settled at Kimberley, Beit made the acquaintance of Cecil John Rhodes, and close business relations followed. Yielding to the force of Rhodes's personality, he became his intimate friend, accepting his ideas and aspirations with enthusiasm. He soon joined Rhodes on the board of the original De Beers Diamond Company (founded in 1880) and played an important part in Rhodes's great scheme for the amalgamation of the chief diamond mines of Kimberley as De Beers Consolidated Mines. The scheme took effect in 1888 after Beit had advanced to Rhodes without security a sum of £250,000.

By this time goldmining activity in the Transvaal republic, which first began at Barberton in 1884, had spread to the conglomerate formation of Witwatersrand, familiarly known as the Rand. The Rand was declared a public gold-field on 20 September 1886. Early in 1888 Beit paid it a visit, and before leaving Kimberley he arranged provisionally that Hermann Eckstein should establish a branch of his firm on the Rand, trading as H. Eckstein—later H. Eckstein & Co. Perceiving the possibilities of the area, Beit acquired a large interest in the best of the outcrop mines, which soon became valuable properties. But his chief stroke was made several years later, when he revisited South Africa and illustrated his characteristic perception of possibilities. Adopting the suggestion, in face of much expert scepticism, that it might be possible not only to work the outcrop but to strike the slanting reef by deep level shafts, at some distance away from the outcrop, he evolved, and devoted capital to testing, the deep levels of the Rand. Beit was the first to recognize the importance of employing first-class mining engineers, and with their aid he proved the scheme to be practicable. In the whole deep level system Beit's firm were forerunners and creators; other firms, including Rhodes's Consolidated Goldfields, followed in their footsteps.

Beit, who had become a naturalized British subject, was deeply interested in Rhodes's scheme of northern expansion. On the formation of the British South Africa Company in 1889 for the conquest of the extensive territory afterwards known as Southern and Northern Rhodesia (and later as Zimbabwe and Zambia), Beit became an original director. He first visited the country in 1891. He later joined the boards of the various Rhodesian railway companies. But when extensive prospecting failed to locate goldfields of any significance between the Limpopo and Zambezi rivers, Beit's interest in the Rand redoubled. Like a number of Randlords, Beit was impatient with the rule of President Kruger. Rhodes and Beit together placed Starr *Jameson with an armed force on the Transvaal border (December 1895). After nebulous intrigue with Johannesburg there followed the raid into the Transvaal. Beit's share in this blunder cost him £200,000. Censured for his part in the affair by the British South Africa committee of the House of Commons in 1897, he resigned his directorship of the chartered company. During the Second South African War of 1899–1902 he spent immense sums on the Imperial light horse and on the equipment of the Imperial yeomanry, and before and after the war he poured money into land settlement, immigration, and kindred schemes for the development of South Africa.

Beit pursued interests other than politics and commerce. With a genuine love of beautiful things he formed from 1888 onwards, under the guidance of Dr Bode, director of the Berlin Museum, a fine collection of pictures and works of art, including Italian Renaissance bronzes. He finally housed these treasures in a mansion in Park Lane, which the architect Eustace Balfour built for him in 1895. He had a thorough knowledge of painting, and among his pictures were the Prodigal Son series of Murillo, six pictures acquired from Lord Dudley's Gallery, and many of the finest examples of the Dutch and English schools.

On Rhodes's death in March 1902 Beit succeeded to much of his friend's position. He became the chief figure on the boards of the De Beers Company and of the chartered company, which he rejoined in that year. Beit was also one of Rhodes's trustees under his will. But his health had long been poor, and in the autumn of 1903, when he visited southern Africa for the purpose of examining the administration of Rhodesia, he suffered a stroke near Salisbury. Attended by Dr Jameson, he rallied but never fully recovered. His interests, however, were unslackened. Beit identified himself with the movements for a better understanding with Germany and for tariff reform. He bore witness to his colonial interests by founding at Oxford in 1905 the Beit professorship of colonial history and the Beit assistant lectureship in colonial history, besides giving a sum of money to the Bodleian Library for additions to its collections of books on colonial history. In the early spring of 1906 he was sent to Wiesbaden on account of heart trouble, but by his own wish he was brought home to England, a dying man, and passed away at his country residence, Tewin Water, Welwyn, Hertfordshire, on 16 July 1906. He was buried in the churchyard there.

Beit, who was unmarried, was survived by his mother, two sisters, and his younger brother Sir Otto *Beit (1865–1930); while providing liberally for various relatives and friends he left the residue of his fortune to his brother. At the same time his public benefactions, amounting in value to £2,000,000, were impressive alike by their generosity to England and Germany, and by their breadth of view. To the Imperial College of Technology, London, he left £50,000 in cash and De Beers shares, valued at the testator's death at £84,843 15s. To Rhodesia, for purposes of education and charity, £200,000 was bequeathed to be administered by trustees. King Edward's Hospital Fund and the trustees of Guy's Hospital were left £20,000 each. Rhodes University at Grahamstown received £25,000, Rhodes Memorial Fund £10,000, and the Union Jack Club, London, £10,000. Funds for benefactions in the Transvaal, in Kimberley, and Cape Colony were also established. Two sums of £20,000 were left to his executors for distribution to the charities of London and Hamburg respectively. Finally £1,200,000 passed to trustees for the extension of railway and telegraph communication in South Africa, with a view to forwarding the enterprise known as the Cape to Cairo railway. Beit made his public bequests elastic. Thus, while bequeathing an estate at Hamburg as a pleasure ground to the people of that city, he provided that twenty years later Hamburg might realize the estate and apply the proceeds to such other public objects as might seem desirable. Two of the bequests—£200,000 for a university at Johannesburg and £50,000 destined for an Institute of Medical Sciences—lapsed into the residuary estate owing to the schemes in question being abandoned, but Otto Beit intimated his intention of devoting the £200,000 to university education in South Africa, and the £50,000 was made by him the nucleus of a fund of £215,000, with which he founded in 1909 thirty Alfred Beit fellowships for medical research in memory of the testator. Beit also left parts of his art collections to the National Gallery in London, to the Kaiserliche Museum in Berlin, and to the Hamburg Museum.

A wealthy financier of abnormal intuition and power of memory, combined with thoroughness of method, Beit was an extraordinarily successful mining magnate. While the full extent of his speculative interests have yet to be established, his investments in the Rand decisively influenced key money markets. Shy and retiring to excess, he was devoid of social ambition, and was little known beyond a small circle of intimates who included men in high positions such as Lord Rosebery and Lord Haldane. An ardent belief in the great causes of his day led him to distribute vast sums of money, but his benefactions were always made privately with rare self-effacement. Because of his close association with Rhodes, he was the target through life for much abuse, some deserved, some not.

C. W. BOYD, *rev.* IAN PHIMISTER

Sources G. S. Fort, *Alfred Beit: a study of the man and his work* (1932) · P. H. Emden, *Randlords* (1935) · J. J. van Helten, 'Beit, Alfred', *DBB* · R. V. Turrell, *Capital and labour on the Kimberley diamond fields, 1871–1890* (1987) · J. J. van Helten, 'British and European economic investment in the Transvaal with specific reference to the Witwatersrand gold field district, 1886–1910', PhD diss., U. Lond., 1981 · F. Harris, ed., 'How I came from poverty to riches: Mr Alfred Beit's own account', *John Bull* (28 July 1906), 184–5 · *CGPLA Eng. & Wales* (1906)
Archives Barlow Rand, Sandton, South Africa, archives | Bodl. RH, papers of Wernher, Beit & Co. · Derbys. RO, Gell MSS
Likenesses G. Boldini, portrait, 1904; Christies, 2 July 1968, lot 27 [*see illus.*] · A. Hayward, portrait, 1913, Africana Museum, Johannesburg, South Africa · E. Mills, portrait, University of Cape Town Medical School, Cape Town, South Africa · P. Montford, relief bust, ICL · W. H. Schroder, cartoon, University of Cape Town Library, Cape Town, South Africa · P. Tennyson-Cole, portrait, Africana Museum, Johannesburg, South Africa · bust, University of Cape Town Library, Cape Town, South Africa
Wealth at death £3,000,000: probate, 28 July 1906, *CGPLA Eng. & Wales*

Beit, Sir Alfred Lane, second baronet (1903–1994). *See under* Beit, Sir Otto John, first baronet (1865–1930).

Beit, Sir Otto John, first baronet (1865–1930), financier, philanthropist, and art connoisseur, was born on 7 December 1865 in Hamburg, Germany, twelve years after his brother Alfred *Beit. He was the third son of Siegfried Beit (1818–1881), silk merchant, and his wife, Laura Caroline Hahn (*b.* 1819). The Beits, who were of Sephardic Jewish descent, had settled in Hamburg in the seventeenth century. After completing his education Otto joined in 1888 the London branch of Jules Porgès & Co., which in 1890 became Wernher, Beit & Co. He was first sent to Kimberley to learn the diamond business and then to Wernher Beit's Johannesburg branch, H. Eckstein & Co. ('the Corner House'), to handle the firm's share business. He was a member of the Johannesburg stock exchange and was elected its deputy chairman in March 1896.

On his return to London the same year, Beit acquired British citizenship and became a partner in the stockbroking firm L. Hirsch & Co. which represented Wernher Beit

Sir Otto John Beit, first baronet (1865–1930), by H. Walter Barnett

on the Paris bourse. Surprisingly, he never became a partner in his brother's company nor a director of its successor, the Central Mining and Investment Corporation Ltd, despite being a major shareholder. In 1897 he married Lilian (*d.* 1946), daughter of the American Thomas Lane Carter, manager of one of the Corner House mines, and niece of Hamilton Smith, a well-known mining engineer on the Witwatersrand. Like his brother Alfred, Beit was a staunch supporter of Cecil John Rhodes and a close friend of Leander Starr Jameson. However, he was not implicated in the Jameson raid which, coincidentally, occurred while he was staying at Groote Schuur with Rhodes, whom he accompanied to England in 1896. He succeeded his brother as a Rhodes trustee as well as director of the British South Africa Company and of Rhodesia Railways Ltd. He succeeded Lord Milner as chairman of the Rhodes Trust.

After Alfred Beit's death on 16 July 1906 Otto Beit retired from active business to administer the Beit Trust and its endowment of £1,200,000; this had doubled by 1927 when the trust, established mainly to promote education, transport, and communication in central and southern Africa, came of age. Alfred had nominated three trustees: his brother Otto, who knew him better than anyone else and possessed all the desirable qualities for the position, his former partner Sir Julius Charles Wernher (1906–1912), and Bourchier Francis Hawksley (1906–1915), legal adviser to the British South Africa Company. But Otto Beit was the dominant spirit and mainly responsible for the bridge building programme, the first being the Beit Memorial Bridge linking Rhodesia and South Africa, which was opened on 31 August 1929. Having completed the bridge building programme, the trustees turned to education, mainly bursaries, scholarships, and training. Alfred Beit's bequest of £200,000 to the University of Johannesburg, which was diverted to Cape Town, was augmented by £250,000 from Sir Julius Wernher and £50,000 from Otto, who in 1920 received the honorary degree of LLD from the universities of Cape Town and Edinburgh. Otto Beit was a benefactor of the Imperial College of Science and Technology in London and in 1909 established the Beit memorial fellowship for medical research and became FRC. His philanthropic work earned him a knighthood in 1920 and a baronetcy in 1924.

Beit was an unassuming and reserved man who lived quietly and unostentatiously in his house full of great treasures at 49 Belgrave Square and at Tewin Water, Welwyn, Hertfordshire, where his brother Alfred's art collection and part of his own collection were housed. He contributed £10,000 to the Johannesburg Art Gallery and presented the Otto Beit Convalescent Home to Johannesburg in March 1914. His health declined rapidly in his fifties and he died of pernicious anaemia at 49 Belgrave Square on 7 December 1930, his sixty-fifth birthday, leaving his wife, two daughters, and a son. Their elder son, Theodore Hamilton, had died on 27 January 1917.

Their younger son, **Sir Alfred Lane Beit**, second baronet (1903–1994), politician, philanthropist, and art collector, was born in London on 19 January 1903. Educated at Eton College and at Christ Church, Oxford, he succeeded to the baronetcy on the death of his father in 1930. As Beit trustee from 1930 to 1994 he ensured that the trust became a major source for the development of Zimbabwe, Zambia, and Malawi. In 1939 he married Clementine, second daughter of Major the Honourable Clement Mitford. He was the Conservative member of parliament for South-East St Pancras from 1931 to 1945, and served as parliamentary private secretary to the secretary of state for the colonies (1944–5), but lost his seat in the 1945 election.

After serving with the RAF as a squadron leader during the Second World War, Beit and his wife settled in Cape Town, South Africa, in 1945. However, in 1952 the Beits, who were opposed to the Nationalist government's racial policies, left South Africa to live at Russborough, co. Wexford, Ireland. The restored Palladian mansion was a suitable setting for one of the world's greatest private art collections and was the headquarters of the Alfred Beit Foundation from 1976. In 1986, after the house was burgled a second time—the first burglary had occurred in 1974—Beit donated seventeen old masterpieces to the National Gallery of Ireland, and the rest of the collection was given to the foundation in 1987. The Irish government awarded Sir Alfred and Lady Beit honorary citizenship on 11 May 1993, and in the same year Beit received an honorary fellowship from the Imperial College for Science, Technology and Medicine.

Tall and fair, Beit was a charming and generous man with wide interests, a lover of art and music, and founder of the Wexford operatic festival. He predeceased his wife, dying at Mount Carmel Hospital, Churchtown, Ireland, on 12 May 1994, aged ninety-one. As he had no children, the baronetcy became extinct. A funeral service was held at Christ Church in Dublin on 16 May 1994.

MARYNA FRASER

Sources DSAB · A. Beit and J. G. Lockhart, *The will and the way* (1957) · T. Gutsche, *No ordinary woman: the life and times of Florence Phillips* (1966) · M. Bryant, *Taking stock: Johannesburg stock exchange* (1987) · L. Weinthal, *The story of the Cape to Cairo and river routes*, 2 vols. (1923) · R. Trevelyan, *Grand dukes and diamonds* (1991) · CGPLA Eng. & Wales (1931) · private information (2004) · *The Times* (14 May 1994) · *Irish Times* (13 May 1994) · *Irish Times* (16 May 1994) · *Irish Times* (20 May 1994) · *Irish Independent* (13 May 1994) · *Deutsche Botschaft Lusaka* (6 June 1994) · WW (1984) · WWBMP, vol. 3
Archives ICL, corresp. and papers relating to Imperial College · Royal Holloway College, Egham, Surrey, corresp. relating to Beit memorial fellowship | BL, letters to Lord Gladstone, Add. MSS 46082–46084 · Derbys. RO, corresp. with P. L. Gell
Likenesses W. Orpen, oils, 1914, Johannesburg Art Gallery, South Africa · O. Ramsden, bronze relief, 1932, ICL · H. W. Barnett, photograph, NPG [*see illus.*]
Wealth at death £3,784,342 16s. 3d.: probate, 26 Jan 1931, CGPLA Eng. & Wales · £2514 7s. 6d. trustee effects only: probate, 15 May 1931, CGPLA Éire

Beith, Alexander (1799–1891), Free Church of Scotland minister and author, was born at Campbeltown, Argyllshire, on 13 January 1799, the son of Gilbert Beith and Helen Elder. Beith's father, a land agent and farmer in the Kintyre district of Argyllshire, was well read, especially in theology and church history. After schooling in Campbeltown Beith entered Glasgow University with the intention of becoming a minister in the Church of Scotland. He was licensed by the presbytery of Kintyre on 7 February 1821. He was appointed to the chapel of ease at Oban the following June, where he remained until he was transferred to Hope Street church in Glasgow. There he ministered to a large congregation for two years. During this period, on 21 February 1825, he married Julia Robson (d. 1866). They had fourteen children, of whom seven—three sons and four daughters—lived to adulthood. In 1826 he moved to Kilbrandon, Argyllshire, and in 1830 to Glenelg, Inverness-shire. In 1839 he was called to the first charge of Stirling.

As the Disruption crisis approached, Beith was one of the seven ministers appointed in 1842 to preach at Strathbogie in spite of the prohibition of the civil courts. He was one of the 474 ministers who in 1843 left the established church and formed the Free Church of Scotland; subsequently he and his congregation moved to the newly erected North Free Church of Stirling. In 1847 Beith gave evidence on the question of sites before a committee of the House of Commons, after the refusal of several landowners to sell land on which Free Church buildings could be erected. He took a prominent part in educational and other matters relating to his new denomination. The degree of DD was conferred upon him in 1850 by the University of Princeton, USA, and in 1858 he was elected moderator of the general assembly of the Free Church. Beith retired from the active ministry of the church in Stirling in 1876, but continued to take part in the general work of the denomination. He was held to be a fluent speaker and able preacher, and his theological position was a liberal one: when the deposition of the controversial theologian William Robertson Smith (1846–1894) was first moved in the general assembly, Beith proposed and carried a motion that the charges be withdrawn and Smith restored to his professorial chair in Aberdeen. Beith argued that critical study of the Bible was not inconsistent with reverence for it and belief in its divine inspiration.

Beith was a prolific writer: besides many pamphlets on public questions, his published works included *A Treatise on the Baptist Controversy* (in Gaelic, 1823), *The Two Witnesses Traced in History* (1846), *Biographical Sketch of the Rev. Alex. Stewart, Cromarty* (1854), *Christ our Life* (1856), *Scottish Reformers and Martyrs* (1860), and *Memoirs of Disruption Times* (1877). Beith died at Edinburgh on 11 May 1891 in his ninety-third year; his wife had predeceased him in 1866. Two of his sons, Gilbert and John Alexander—one an MP and the other a JP—were partners in the well-known firm of Beith, Stevenson & Co., East India merchants of Glasgow and Manchester.

T. B. JOHNSTONE, *rev.* ROSEMARY MITCHELL

Sources *Fasti Scot.*, 4.322 · Boase, *Mod. Eng. biog.* · personal knowledge (1901) · private information (1901)
Likenesses N. Macbeth, portrait; formerly in the possession of his son, Gilbert Beith, 1901
Wealth at death £4037 8*s.* 4*d.*: confirmation, 17 June 1891, *CCI* · £232 3*s.* 11*d.*: additional valuation, 16 Oct 1899, *CCI*

Beith, John Hay [*pseud.* Ian Hay] (1876–1952), writer, was born on 17 April 1876 in Manchester, the third son and sixth child of John Alexander Beith (*d.* 1896), cotton merchant and magistrate, and his wife, Janet, daughter of David Fleming, also a merchant in Manchester. He was the grandson of Alexander *Beith, one of the founders of the Free Church of Scotland in 1843. Educated at Fettes College, Edinburgh, and then at St John's College, Cambridge, Beith obtained in 1898 a second class degree in classics, and distinguished himself at rowing. He showed early interest in the theatre, writing reviews for the popular press.

In 1901 Beith taught at Fettes before returning to Cambridge for a short period to study science. In 1902 as a junior science master he joined Durham School, where he also coached the rugby teams and river crews. A charming companion, with a developed social sense, he was extremely popular. Durham featured in one of his best books, *Housemaster* (1936).

In 1906 Beith returned to Fettes. While sharing largely in school life, he spent most of his leisure time in writing. He was a resourceful if unconventional teacher, knew public-school boys instinctively, and enjoyed schoolmastering. When in 1912 he left Fettes to make writing his career his decision was generally regretted, perhaps even eventually by himself.

John Hay Beith (1876–1952), by Howard Coster, 1930s

Beith's first novel, *Pip* (1907), coloured by early Manchester schooldays, was a best-seller and was followed by other equally light comic novels, among them *The Right Stuff* (1908) and *A Man's Man* (1909). With the publication in 1914 of *A Knight on Wheels* and *The Lighter Side of School Life*, which owes much to Fettes, his career as a writer was assured. His humour, gift for story-telling, shrewd observation, sentimentality, and truly 'English' talent for sympathetically conveying eccentric characters perfectly suited the age.

In the First World War Beith served first with the Argyll and Sutherland Highlanders, then transferred to the machine-gun corps. In 1915 he married Helen Margaret Speirs; they had no children. Also in 1915 he reached the rank of captain and was mentioned in dispatches; he was awarded the MC in 1916. Meanwhile his best-known book, *The First Hundred Thousand*, was published in 1915. Written in billets at home and in France, it 'impressed upon a notoriously unmilitarist public the lighter side of Kitchener's army' (*The Times*). First serialized in *Blackwood's Magazine*, it became one of the most popular books of the period, running to multiple editions in Britain and America, and being translated into French. Beith followed this success with *Carrying on* (1917) and *The Last Million* (1918). Earlier employed in recruiting, Beith spent 1916–18 in America with the information bureau of the British War Mission, where his energy and success were rewarded by a CBE (1918) and promotion to the rank of major.

In 1919 Beith turned to the theatre, living from then on in London, absorbed in its social and theatrical life. He was particularly successful in translating his own novels into plays, among them *A Safety Match* (1921), *Housemaster* (1936), and, perhaps his most successful play, *Tilly of Bloomsbury* (1919, based on his novel *Happy-Go-Lucky*, 1913). *Tilly of Bloomsbury* was adapted for film, as was *The Middle Watch* (1929). Beith's wit, romanticism, decorous mind, and exceptional theatrical sense kept his plays popular. He proved an excellent collaborator with other writers, among them Seymour Hicks (*Good Luck*, 1923); Stephen King-Hall (*The Middle Watch*, 1929, and others); A. E. W. Mason (*A Present from Margate*, 1933); and P. G. Wodehouse (*A Damsel in Distress*, 1928, *Leave it to Psmith*, 1930, and others).

Although Beith's theatrical flair was unfaltering, through some curious change in emphasis his later novels never achieved his pre-war success. He failed to adjust, and his last works were poorly received. *The King's Service* (1938), an informal history of the army, may have helped him to the directorship of War Office public relations (1938–41) and the rank of major-general, but this and the war cut him off from his public. *The Times* described him as 'turning resolutely, perhaps too resolutely, away from the brutal face of the war', and his tribute to Malta, *The Unconquered Isle* (1943), an attempt at a second *Hundred Thousand*, misjudged the mood of a people who with their own experience of bombing resented his cheerful glossing.

On the lapse of his directorship Beith returned to work in America. After 1945 he wrote semi-official histories, which met with little success; his one serious play, *Hattie Stowe* (1947), about Harriet Beecher Stowe, failed, possibly only through an over-large cast.

Beith apparently enjoyed his London years. He travelled, was chairman of the Society of Authors (1921–4, 1935–9), a member of the council of the League of British Dramatists from 1933, and president of the Dramatists Club from 1937. He was an officer of the order of St John of Jerusalem, for long a governor of Guy's Hospital, and gave his services also to St Dunstan's. Skilled at archery, he was a member of the queen's bodyguard for Scotland (Royal Company of Archers), a history of which he wrote in 1951. He was noted for charm, striking personality, equable temperament, after-dinner speeches, and personal austerity. Some observers, however, thought they detected an inner unhappiness; perhaps his essential Calvinism evoked a sense of regret discernible in his own reported remark, bitter though humorously offered, that all his life he had lived on his wits.

Beith died in the Hillbrow Nursing Home, in Liss, Hampshire, on 22 September 1952. There is a portrait at the Garrick Club by T. C. Dugdale.

PATRICK MURRAY, rev. KATHERINE MULLIN

Sources D. C. Browning, ed., *Everyman's dictionary of literary biography*, 3rd edn (1962) · *The Times* (23 Sept 1952) · S. J. Kunitz and H. Haycraft, eds., *Twentieth century authors: a biographical dictionary of modern literature* (1942) · *The picturegoer's who's who and encyclopaedia of the screen today* (1933) · *The Scotsman* (23 Sept 1952) · *The Fettesian* (Dec 1952) · H. R. Pyatt, *Fifty years of Fettes: memories of old Fettesians, 1870–1920* (1931) · *CGPLA Eng. & Wales* (1952)
Archives NL Scot. · NRA, corresp. and literary papers | BL, corresp. with League of Dramatists, Add. MS 63359 · BL, corresp. with Society of Authors, Add. MSS 56664–56667, 63211 · NL Scot., corresp. with Blackwoods and literary papers
Likenesses H. Coster, photographs, 1930–39, NPG [*see illus.*] · W. Stoneman, photograph, 1939, NPG · T. C. Dugdale, oils, *c.*1940, Garr. Club · H. L. Oakley, silhouette, NPG · photograph, repro. in Kunitz and Haycraft, *Twentieth century authors*, 104 · photograph, repro. in *The Times*
Wealth at death £13,527 4s. 2d.: probate, 6 March 1953, *CGPLA Eng. & Wales*

Beith, William. *See* Beeth, William (*supp. fl.* 1498).

Bek family (*per. c.*1150–*c.*1350), gentry, is principally noteworthy for having produced four bishops in two generations in the reigns of Edward I and Edward III. The family owed its estates at Eresby and elsewhere in Lincolnshire to the marriage of Walter Bek to the heiress of the hereditary stewards of the bishops of Durham in the mid-twelfth century, while in the thirteenth century its members served the earls of Lincoln as constables of Lincoln Castle. According to a brief family history, added to the register of the Gilbertine priory at Alvingham in the late thirteenth century (Bodl. Oxf., MS Laud misc. 642), the estates had been divided among four younger sons at the end of the previous century, after the death of the eldest son, Hugh Bek, on crusade. Of the family of Henry Bek of Eresby (*fl. c.*1200), said to be 'not very wise', two grandsons became bishops, Thomas (I) *Bek (d. 1293), bishop of St David's, and Antony (I) *Bek (*c.*1245–1311), bishop of Durham. The eldest of Walter Bek's grandsons, **John Bek**, Lord Bek (d. 1303/4), had a career in royal administration, acting on a variety of commissions, mostly of an economic nature, and as a justice of assize from 1276. In 1255 he secured a grant of a market and fair at Spilsby, founded a chapel there, and was probably responsible for the first of a tradition of great houses in the adjoining manor at Eresby. He took part in Edward I's Scottish campaigns and was summoned to the parliaments of 1295 and 1296. In his will drawn up in 1301, he sought burial at Kirkstead Abbey. With an unknown wife he had a son, Walter, who predeceased his father, and three daughters.

Of the descendants of Henry Bek's brother, Walter Bek of Lusby, two great-grandsons were bishops, Thomas (II) *Bek (1283–1347), bishop of Lincoln, and Antony (II) *Bek (1279–1343), bishop of Norwich. This Antony had also produced a brief family descent (preserved in BL, Harley MS 3720) before his elevation to a bishopric, and the two histories are remarkable in demonstrating the family's close and continuing interest in its own lineages. The eldest grandson, **Sir John Bek of Lusby** (1278–*c.*1324), had been a prominent member of the affinity of Henry de Lacy, earl of Lincoln, but continued in the service of Thomas, earl of Lancaster, on the latter's acquisition of the Lacy earldom, perhaps with the support of Sir Robert Holland. He was a witness to the agreement at Horninglow, Staffordshire, in 1318 which had sought to bring peace between Lancaster and Edward II, in 1319 served under Lancaster in the Berwick campaign, and in 1321 acted as the earl's spokesman in delivering the bill of grievances which was presented to the magnates at Sherburn in Elmet. In the following year he was captured in the earl's service at the battle of Boroughbridge, but was later pardoned and employed in royal service. He died about 1324.   PHILIP MORGAN

Sources Chancery records · Bodl. Oxf., MS Laud misc. 642 · C. T. Beke, 'Observations on the pedigree of the family of Beke or Eresby in the county of Lincoln', Collectanea Topographica et Genealogica, 4 (1837), 331–45 · C. M. Fraser, A history of Antony Bek, bishop of Durham, 1283–1311 (1957) · BL, Harley MS 3720 · J. R. Maddicott, Thomas of Lancaster, 1307–1322: a study in the reign of Edward II (1970) · J. R. Maddicott, 'Thomas of Lancaster, 1307–1322', DPhil diss., U. Oxf., 1967, esp. appx 4, 'Lancaster's retainers: summary biographies' · F. Palgrave, ed., The parliamentary writs and writs of military summons, 2 vols. in 4 (1827–34) · special collections, PRO, ancient petitions, SC1 · Canon of Bridlington, 'Gesta Edwardi de Carnarvon', Chronicles of the reigns of Edward I and Edward II, ed. W. Stubbs, 2, Rolls Series, 76 (1883), 25–151 · GEC, Peerage, 2.89

Archives BL, Harley MS 3720 [register of Antony Bek]

Bek, Antony (I) (c.1245–1311), bishop of Durham, was the third son of Walter Bek, lord of Eresby in Lincolnshire [see also Bek family].

Early years and promotion to Durham Probably born about 1245, Antony Bek had entered the service of Henry III by 1265, when he and the steward of the earl of Lincoln were nominated to inquire into lands forfeited in Lincolnshire by Montfortian rebels, and in 1266 he was designated as a king's clerk. Between 1267 and 1270 he joined his brother Thomas (I) *Bek at Oxford University, where they occupied a house given by Walter of Merton to his newly founded college. He accompanied the Lord Edward on crusade in 1270, and in June 1272 he and Robert Burnell were among the eight executors nominated by Edward prior to a surgical operation at Acre, with full powers of administration should Henry III die while Edward's heir was still a minor. On Edward's return to England in 1274 as king, Bek was temporarily keeper of the wardrobe, but relinquished this in favour of his brother Thomas, and in January 1275 he was appointed constable of the Tower of London, with control of the military stores of the great wardrobe. Thereafter Bek was closely involved both with preparations for war in Wales and with raising loans abroad to pay for troops there. He was also frequently employed in diplomatic negotiations abroad.

Since 1276 Bek had been precentor of York and archdeacon of Durham. He held numerous prebends and livings, contrary to recent decrees against pluralism, and in 1281 was warned by Archbishop Pecham of Canterbury that unless he at least obtained a papal dispensation he would never be considered for a bishopric. That year Archbishop Wickwane of York tried to make a metropolitan visitation of the diocese of Durham. There was no precedent for such a visitation, except during a vacancy, and the Durham monks argued that the bishop of Durham, as their titular abbot, would have to attend. Pope Martin IV sent judges-delegate to hear the appeals; Edward I regarded this intervention as scandalous, and sent Bek to arbitrate. A compromise seemed possible, but in June 1283 Bishop Robert de Insula died and Wickwane attempted another visitation. In this delicate situation Edward recommended that the monks elect Bek as their new

Antony (I) Bek (c.1245–1311), seal [obverse]

bishop, which was done on 9 July 1283. Wickwane confirmed the election on 1 September, and Bek was consecrated bishop at York on 9 January 1284, the occasion being marked by the translation, at Bek's expense and in the king's presence, of the body of St William of York to a more honourable position in the minster. The quarrel over the nature of York's jurisdiction over Durham was not settled until November 1286, by which date Wickwane was dead. The agreement accepted that the archbishop had diocesan authority there, but only during a vacancy.

Service in France and Scotland Bek continued in the royal service, both in England and France, and was one of the negotiators to treat with Scottish and Norwegian envoys over the future governance of Scotland following the unexpected death in 1286 of Alexander III of Scotland without male heirs. With the death of Alexander's heir presumptive, Margaret, the Maid of Norway, in September 1290, the field was open for claims from more distant heirs to the Scottish throne, and Edward I was invited to arbitrate. In May 1291 Edward agreed to undertake this, using Bishop Bek as his spokesman. During the debates over how the decision on succession should be reached Bek recommended that the customs of both Scotland and England should be observed, together with imperial law if appropriate. The succession was finally decided in favour of John Balliol, who swore fealty to Edward I on 19 November 1292 in Norham Castle, within the liberty of Durham. Bek subsequently served as a link between the English and Scottish kings until in July 1295 King John was persuaded by his Scottish counsellors to negotiate an alliance with France.

Relations between Edward I and the king of France had been under strain since May 1293, and in February 1294 Philippe IV had occupied Gascony. Bek was then sent to negotiate the raising of troops from Flanders, the Netherlands, and the German empire, at a cost of £60,000. In April 1295 Bek was with Edward I in Anglesey to suppress a third Welsh uprising, and in August 1295 he was the king's spokesman in parliament, arguing, against papal envoys who were urging peace, that England was bound by a treaty with Adolf of Nassau, king of the Romans (d. 1298), to fight the French. By this date the alliance between French and Scots was known, and Bek was appointed with John de Warenne, earl of Surrey (d. 1304), as keeper of the northern English counties. In March 1296 Bek supplied 500 horsemen and 1000 foot soldiers to the English army which invaded Scotland, and was present during the subsequent campaign, as Edward's representative accepting the submission of King John in July 1296. Attention could now be returned to the continent, and in May 1297 a special summons was sent for a Durham contingent, including thirty bannerets, to be raised to cross to France. Bishop Bek stood surety for a number of Scottish nobles willing to serve Edward in Flanders, and was with the king when he opened negotiations for a truce in October 1297. The truce was sealed in February 1298, to enable the king to stem an invasion of the north of England by the Scots. By July Edward had reached Roxburgh, a division of his army under Bek being responsible for the capture of Dirleton Castle, which commanded the south shore of the Firth of Forth east of Edinburgh. The bishop then rejoined the main force to participate in the English victory at Falkirk on 22 July, which temporarily ended the Scottish revolt.

Bishop of Durham and the dispute with Durham Priory Meanwhile, encouraged by his knowledge of the workings of royal administration Bek sought to copy this model for his liberty of Durham, his degree of success being tested in the *quo warranto* proceedings at Newcastle in the spring of 1293. There he claimed that the sheriff of Northumberland had no jurisdiction 'between Tyne and Tees', or in Norhamshire, Islandshire, and Bedlingtonshire north of the Tyne. A formal inquiry revealed that within the liberty of Durham the bishop appointed his own judicial officers, and exercised the power of gallows, outlawry and pardon, and exchange of felons. He also had a mint and created free warren. All this was confirmed in parliament in October 1293 as his by prescription. To these regalian rights he added in practice the prerogatives of seizure of lands of traitors, wardship, prison, and wreck. Edward I was content to tolerate such special privileges as long as Bek was producing troops and taxes for the Scottish wars, but in 1299 the local gentry refused to co-operate and, using the uproar of an ecclesiastical dispute over the bishop's right to visit his cathedral chapter, called on the king to intervene. In May 1300 Bek had announced his intention of holding a formal visitation. Prior Richard *Hoton objected that the bishop was entitled to make only an

unaccompanied visit, and issued a series of appeals against Bek's proposals, for which he was himself excommunicated, while the priory was first blockaded and then stormed by the bishop's men. Hoton was imprisoned, though he subsequently escaped and appealed to the king and the pope against Bek's conduct. In June 1301 Edward arraigned Bek at Tynemouth to answer for his imprisonment of a messenger bringing royal letters of protection covering Durham Priory, and its land and tenants during Hoton's absence at the curia. Bek admitted his fault, but also faced a summons to appear before Pope Boniface VIII to answer for his depriving Hoton of the priorate. In April 1302 Richard Kellawe, sub-prior of Durham, published the papal letter restoring Hoton, but this was violently resisted by the bishop's officers. In May Bek left for Rome to pursue the case against his chapter. Edward I reacted by ordering the seizure of the temporalities of Durham on 7 July 1302 and bringing to trial Bek's palatine officers for abuse of power. The 'commonalty of Durham', led by Ranulf Neville of Raby and John Marmaduke of Horden, pressed for a charter of liberties to define the temporal powers of the bishop over them. Eventually in May 1303 Bek agreed to various demands restricting his use of forest law and reclamation of waste land, but his right to prerogative wardship was upheld by the king, as was the liability of the 'Haliwerfolk' for military service outside the liberty. In July bishop and commonalty forgave each other for past offences, and temporal administration was restored to Bek.

Instead, however, of consolidating this improved situation, in August 1303 Bek returned to Rome to continue his feud against Hoton, leaving his officers to continue obstructing the judgments brought during the year of confiscation. In return, the royal exchequer sought to collect arrears of taxes and fines, and personal debts of over £6000, and royal customs collectors were appointed for Hartlepool within the liberty. In March 1305 Edward appointed two justices to hear further complaints against Bek within the liberty, and in December the liberty was resumed into the king's hand. This remained the situation until the accession of Edward II, who restored administration to Bek in September 1307. As this period saw Robert Bruce make his bid for the throne of Scotland with the consequent forfeiture of his Durham estates around Hartlepool and their grant by Edward to Robert Clifford, the bishop was unable to exert his prerogative right to seize them; and his successors were unable to obtain more than a nominal recognition of their palatinate authority there. Similarly, the Balliol forfeiture of Barnard Castle, after a brief annexation by Bishop Bek, was granted by Edward I to Guy Beauchamp, earl of Warwick, who with his heirs steadfastly refused to acknowledge any palatine jurisdiction. In other respects the Durham palatinate maintained its distinctive autonomy until legislation under Henry VIII (1536) and William IV (1836).

Last years and death If the first years of Bek's episcopate saw little diocesan activity apart from the creation of collegiate churches at Lanchester (1284) and Chester-le-Street (1286), and re-creation at St Andrew Auckland (1293), to provide prebends for household clerks and chapels of ease for communities established on assarted moor (arable land), the latter years were dominated by the dispute with Durham Cathedral priory over the bishop's right of visitation. After appeal and counter-appeal Pope Boniface decreed in July 1302 that the bishop should be accompanied by two or three honest clerks, one at least being a Benedictine monk, together with a notary. The battle of wills between Prior Hoton and Bishop Bek over control of the priory and its lands continued under Benedict XI and Clement V, who in February 1306 created Bek patriarch of Jerusalem. This gave Bek the rank of senior prelate in England, and explains his nomination in 1308 as principal inquisitor into the affairs of the knights templar in England, Scotland, and Ireland. In February 1309 he visited Durham Priory in accordance with the papal ordinance *Debent* of 1302, and Hoton's successor, Prior Tanfield, formally renounced the convent's right to take any legal actions for past disciplinary measures against the Durham monks.

Bek died at Eltham, Kent, on 3 March 1311, and his body was brought back for burial in Durham Cathedral on 3 May, the first to be buried there since the translation of St Cuthbert in 1104. During his life Bek had been remarkable for a charisma (*magnanimus*) which at various times gained him the friendship of Edward I, a reputation for bravery and exuberant extravagance, and the tentative affirmation by later Durham monks that he was a saint. The Durham chronicler Robert Greystones referred to his chastity, modesty with women, and confident handling of the translated bones of St William of York. The revenues of the bishopric of Durham contributed to his great wealth. On his death his personal effects were valued at 6000 marks (£4000). Edward II reserved for his own use Bek's famous Weardale stud of 240 horses and the pick of his jewels, and later bought from his executors his gold plate for 2075 marks (£1383). He also bought for £500 Bek's campaign tents, consisting of two *aulae*, three *camerae*, a chapel, and ten *stabuli* for destriers, palfreys, sumpters, and other horses.   C. M. FRASER

Sources C. M. Fraser, *A history of Antony Bek* (1957) · BL, Cotton MS Nero C.viii, fols. 54, 60 · QR memoranda rolls (Durham mint), PRO, 73, m 29d · *Records of Antony Bek … 1283–1311*, ed. C. M. Fraser, SurtS, 162 (1953) · *Historiae Dunelmensis scriptores tres: Gaufridus de Coldingham, Robertus de Graystanes, et Willielmus de Chambre*, ed. J. Raine, SurtS, 9 (1839) · *Registrum Roberti Winchelsey, Cantuariensis archiepiscopi, AD 1294–1313*, ed. R. Graham, 2 vols., CYS, 51–2 (1952–6)
Likenesses seal, U. Durham L., Durham Cathedral muniments, 2.13.Pont.6 · seal, U. Durham L., Durham Cathedral muniments, 3a.2e.Pont.15 [*see illus.*]
Wealth at death £1386 13s. 4d.—gold plate, tents, embroidered cloth: *CPR, 1307–13*, 332, 356, 385 · £2554—temporalities of Durham: *Registrum palatinum Dunelmense* 4 (1878), 89–92 · said to have owed the king £1353 6s. 8d.: memoranda rolls, 78, m 82d

Bek, Antony (II) (1279–1343), bishop of Norwich, according to the Bek memorandum book was born on 4 August 1279, the second son of Walter Bek (c.1250–1291) of Lusby, Lincolnshire, constable of Lincoln. The eldest of the three brothers was Sir John Bek, lord of Normanby, the youngest Thomas (II) *Bek, who became bishop of Lincoln (d.

1347). There were also three sisters, Alice, Margaret, and Joan, while Antony (I) Bek, bishop of Durham (d. 1311), and the latter's brother Thomas (I) Bek, bishop of St David's (d. 1293)—whose family home was at nearby Eresby—were kinsmen [see Bek family].

On Bek's admission as rector of Wainfleet St Mary in 1301 John Dalderby, the Lincoln diocesan (d. 1320), granted him a full seven-year licence of absence to study in England or abroad. At Oxford he was one of the proctors of the university in its dispute with the Dominicans in 1314, and in the following year was a member of a panel of doctors of theology—as was Simon Mepham, the future archbishop of Canterbury (d. 1333)—that condemned certain articles as heretical. Bishop Dalderby collated him to the prebend of Thorngate in Lincoln on 10 June 1313, and three years later to that of North Kelsey together with the chancellorship. A licence dated 20 September 1327 permitted a messuage in the suburb of Lincoln to be diverted to a grammar school and a residence for the master, who was to be nominated by the chancellor. He exchanged the chancellor's house for another on the east side of the close and substantially extended it. In January 1328 the dean and chapter granted him the farm of the rectory of Normanby for life at an annual rent of 32 marks.

Meanwhile, on 3 February 1320, he had been elected to the see of Lincoln—following the refusal of Henry Mamesfeld (d. 1328) to accept. Edward II confirmed the election on the 20th but Archbishop Walter Reynolds (d. 1327), apparently aware that the pope had reserved the see, demurred. At the same time Edward advanced the cause of Henry Burghersh (d. 1340) in the papal curia and he was duly provided. On becoming dean of Lincoln in 1329 Bek was involved in a dispute with the chapter about the extent of decanal jurisdiction. He decided to pursue his suit at Avignon in person. The king wrote to John XXII (r. 1316–34) urging the dean's return and stressing the importance of residence. Bek, however, so impressed the pope that he was appointed a papal chaplain and licensed (30 April 1334) to enjoy the fruits of his benefices for three years while at the curia.

In 1337, thanks to papal reservation, Bek was provided to the see of Norwich—to which one of the monks, Thomas Hemenhale, had been elected—and was consecrated at Avignon on 30 March 1337. The temporalities were restored on 9 July. He was a vigorous defender of the rights of his see, secured damages from the executors of his predecessor, William Airmyn (d. 1336), for dilapidations, and carried out an investigation before the prior and senior monks of the cathedral priory with respect to the appointment of major obedientiaries. It was decided that election of these last belonged to the prior and seniors, their appointment to the bishop alone.

Bek appealed against the metropolitan visitation of Archbishop John Stratford (d. 1348), which was launched in September 1343. Stratford had armed himself with a papal indult permitting him to vary canonical practice with respect to the order of metropolitan visitation, but this was impugned on the specious ground that it was obtained under false pretences. Bek replied with armed resistance, whereupon the archbishop excommunicated both bishop and prior and placed Norwich under an interdict. The case in the curia was not decided until May 1344 after the bishop's death, which occurred at his manor of Hevingham, Norfolk, during the night of 18–19 December 1343, allegedly (and improbably) from poison administered by his servants.   ROY MARTIN HAINES

Sources process concerning Dalderby's projected canonization, Lincs. Arch., Di/20/2(B) 1, 3 · fragment of Antony Bek's Norwich register, Lincs. Arch., D/C A/2/12 · Norfolk RO, Reg. 1/3 · Bek memorandum book, BL, Harley MS 3720 · 'Continuatio historiae Bartholomaei Cotton', *Anglia sacra*, ed. [H. Wharton], 1 (1691), 413–17 · W. O. Massingberd, 'An account of the family of Bek, of Lusby', *Associated Architectural Societies' Reports and Papers*, 24/1 (1897), 33–53 · D. M. Smith, *Guide to bishops' registers of England and Wales: a survey from the middle ages to the abolition of the episcopacy in 1646*, Royal Historical Society Guides and Handbooks, 11 (1981) · *The book of John de Schalby, canon of Lincoln, 1299–1333, concerning the bishops of Lincoln and their acts*, trans. J. H. Srawley (1949) · *Fasti Angl., 1300–1541*, [Lincoln] · *Fasti Angl., 1300–1541*, [Monastic cathedrals] · *Fasti Angl., 1300–1541*, [Introduction] · Emden, *Oxf.* · J. R. Wright, *The church and the English crown, 1305–1334: a study based on the register of Archbishop Walter Reynolds* (1980) · R. M. Haines, *Archbishop John Stratford: political revolutionary and champion of the liberties of the English church*, Pontifical Institute of Medieval Studies: Texts and Studies, 76 (1986) · Dugdale, *Monasticon*, new edn, vol. 4
Archives BL, Harley MS 3720 · Lincs. Arch., register, D/C A/2/12 [fragment] · Norfolk RO, register, Reg. 1/3

Bek, John, Lord Bek (d. 1303/4). *See under* Bek family (*per. c.*1150–*c.*1350).

Bek, Sir John, of Lusby (1278–*c.*1324). *See under* Bek family (*per. c.*1150–*c.*1350).

Bek, Thomas (I) (d. 1293), bishop of St David's, was the second son of Walter Bek of Ereseby, Lincolnshire [*see* Bek family], and the older brother of Antony (I) *Bek. His early career is sparsely recorded. He was a graduate of Oxford, a *magister*, and later DCL. He was chancellor of the university between 1269 and 1271; in 1269 he supported the Franciscans in their conflict with the Oxford Dominicans. During this period, by April 1264, Antony had already established links with the royal household. Both brothers acquired livings in Henry III's reign: Thomas was appointed to All Saints, Pontefract, in May 1267, and to Castleford in September 1270. Never as close to Edward I as was Antony, he is not recorded in royal service before his appointment as keeper of the wardrobe on 18 October 1274 and it may be right to see his brother's influence as a decisive factor at that point. Like other wardrobe clerics he was rewarded generously with ecclesiastical preferments, including lucrative canonries and archdeaconries. His relations with Edward I may be seen in his attendance on the king and queen on 19 April 1278, when they visited Glastonbury to view relics of King Arthur, and in the occasional responsibilities given to him. He was present when Alexander III of Scotland did homage to Edward I in 1278, and was temporary custodian of the great seal when the king was abroad between 8 May and 19 June 1279. In the

same year he was identified as lord treasurer, though that may be a loose description of his function at the wardrobe.

Bek was consecrated bishop of St David's at Lincoln on 6 October 1280 by Archbishop Pecham and nine other bishops, including the bishops of Llandaff, Bangor, and St Asaph. The king and queen and a large assembly of notables were then in Lincoln for the translation of the relics of St Hugh of Avalon to a new shrine in the 'angel choir' of the cathedral. Bek bore the cost of the ceremony and the festivities which marked the occasion. He continued in office as keeper of the wardrobe for some six weeks after his consecration. He was in his diocese early in 1281, celebrating his first mass there at Strata Florida, on 2 February, and moving on to the cathedral for his enthronement on 1 March, St David's day. He took no further part in royal administration, but his appointment brought to St David's a trusted royal supporter and an experienced administrator. He raised troops for the war against Llywelyn ap Gruffudd in 1282. In the following year he negotiated papal sanction for the politically sensitive marriage of Rhys ap Maredudd of Ystrad Tywi and Ada de Hastings, which was one element in the royal policy of retaining Rhys's loyalty at a critical juncture.

In 1284 Archbishop Pecham made a metropolitical visitation of the Welsh dioceses. Bek accepted his mandate, and the minor proviso that the visitation of his diocese should begin at Llanbadarn Fawr and not at St David's. The visitation was well advanced when Pecham came to the cathedral, and at that late stage Bek made an unexpected protest, denying the archbishop's metropolitical rights over his diocese. Pecham reacted swiftly, reminding him of his profession of obedience, and of the lack of any protest at earlier stages of the visitation. After a careful and reasoned answer, he threatened excommunication if the protest was maintained, and Bek gave way. The archbishop proposed a special clause in professions made by future bishops of St David's, specifically rejecting any claims to exemption from Canterbury's control, but this show of severity was never put into effect. This trial of strength did not affect the close accord between Edward I and Bek. On 1 June 1284 the king gave Bek the advowsons of thirty-four livings in his diocese, with authority to appropriate them as he wished. Later, on 26 November, the king and queen visited St David's as pilgrims. These were substantial expressions of confidence in the bishop.

Bek increased the bishop's patronage. In the chapter he created the office of chancellor and endowed that of treasurer. In 1283 he founded a collegiate church at Llangadog. In 1287 he transferred this to Abergwili, and founded a second college at Llanddewibrefi. His manor at Llawhaden was much enlarged and he fostered the growth of the borough there. He founded hospitals at Llawhaden and St David's, and secured two weekly markets for St David's. He was responsible for the walled enclosure around the cathedral precincts. The episcopal palace was extensively rebuilt late in the thirteenth century; this may have been initiated by Bek, perhaps in preparation for the royal visit in 1284. In 1287 Edward I committed himself to a new crusade and Bek was among those who took the cross, but the project lapsed. Bek died on 12 May 1293, when he may have been about sixty.   DAVID WALKER

Sources Chancery records · A. W. Haddan and W. Stubbs, eds., Councils and ecclesiastical documents relating to Great Britain and Ireland, 1 (1869) · T. Jones, ed. and trans., Brut y tywysogyon, or, The chronicle of the princes: Peniarth MS 20 (1952) · F. N. Davis and others, eds., Rotuli Ricardi Gravesend, Lincoln RS, 20 (1925) · R. M. T. Hill, ed., The rolls and register of Bishop Oliver Sutton, 1, Lincoln RS, 39 (1948) · The register of William Giffard, lord archbishop of York, 1266–1279, ed. W. Brown, SurtS, 109 (1904) · Gir. Camb. opera, vol. 7 · Calendar of papal letters, 2 · G. Williams, The Welsh church from conquest to Reformation (1962) · D. L. Douie, Archbishop Pecham (1952)

Bek, Thomas (II) (1283–1347), bishop of Lincoln, was born on 22 February 1283, the third son of Walter Bek of Lusby, Lincolnshire, and younger brother of Antony (II) *Bek, bishop of Norwich (d. 1343). A sister, Margaret (wife of Sir William Hiltoft), is mentioned in his will, as are nephews Henry and Antony (III) Bek, and William Hiltoft, his clerk [see also Bek family]. Owing to his father's early death in 1291 he was brought up by his kinsman, Antony (I) Bek, bishop of Durham (d. 1311). Thanks to an expectative grace he was collated on 26 August 1317 to the prebend of Ruscombe Southbury in Salisbury Cathedral, which he was to exchange in 1339 for Brompton rectory in Yorkshire. At the time of his collation he was MA, probably of Oxford. He was rector of St Peter's, Ingoldmells, in 1322, when the Lincoln diocesan, Henry Burghersh (d. 1340), granted him licence to be absent for three years for purposes of study. He occurs in 1327 as a canon of Lincoln, by which time he was a doctor of canon law, and in 1336 he was appointed rector of Clayworth, Nottinghamshire. Archbishop William Melton of York (d. 1340) appointed him his official on 7 May 1329.

In 1334 Bek received a royal licence to assign six messuages, 3 acres of land, and rent to the value of 24s. with appurtenances in Lincoln, Ingoldmells, and Normanby (together with £10 from the manor there) to the dean and chapter of Lincoln to provide two chaplains: one to celebrate mass in Normanby for the soul of Sir John Bek—his eldest brother—and for his own soul, the other to celebrate the divine offices at Ingoldmells in honour of the Virgin Mary.

Licence to elect a successor to Bishop Burghersh was issued on 4 January 1341. Bek was elected, and on 1 March his election received royal assent. Fearing papal reservation he travelled to Avignon, but made little progress, and Benedict XII's death in April 1342 further delayed proceedings. Clement VI (r. 1342–52) confirmed his election on 26 June 1342 and consecrated him on 7 July. His episcopal register survives in three volumes. In response to a royal mandate of 1342, for a grant of taxation in anticipation of a formal tenth, he convoked his clergy to the church of St Mary at Stamford, but they could not be persuaded to consent. In the following year he ordered the officials of the archdeacons to publish the constitutions of the archbishop of Canterbury, John Stratford (d. 1348). The third volume of his register contains a quaternion of Bek's own visitation injunctions, issued between 1343 and 1346. His

episcopate saw the resolution (in 1345) by a compromise favourable to the university of a long-standing jurisdictional dispute between it and the proctors of the archdeacon of Oxford, Cardinal Gaillard de la Mothe. Bek himself had in 1343 objected to the use of the term 'election' with respect to the Oxford chancellor, and only confirmed the appointment 'de gracia speciali'.

Bek drew up his lengthy will on 18 November 1346 at Nettleham, Lincolnshire, added a codicil there on 11 February of the following year, and died on the 15th (Lincs. Arch., Reg. 6, Bek, fol. 26r), rather than on the 2nd, the date regularly given (for instance by Emden and the revised Le Neve). He allotted £200 for the expenses of his funeral, but under threat of a perpetual curse his body was not to remain above ground for more than eight days, and his exequies were not to be elaborate. He directed that after the repayment of substantial debts £100 should be assigned to Sir William St Quintin, husband of Joan (another of Bek's sisters), so that he could secure the alienation in mortmain of the church of Benniworth, Lincolnshire, and of lands there, as well as of tenements in Lincoln, which the bishop had given him. The appropriation was not effected, but some of Bek's property in Lincoln was later sold to William Burton (named as a creditor in Bek's codicil) and used to endow the Burton chantry in the cathedral. There were numerous bequests to his relatives and members of his household and a legacy of £40 to the rector of Ingoldmells, half for the repair of the rectory manse, the choir, nave, and tower of the church, the other half for distribution to poor parishioners. The residue of his goods was to be assigned to chaplains to celebrate mass for the souls of his brother John, of himself, his parents, benefactors, and all the faithful departed. He wished to be buried in Lincoln Cathedral, to the north of the steps leading from the chapter house to the choir, near the high altar.   ROY MARTIN HAINES

Sources Lincs. Arch., Reg. 5 [Burghersh] · Lincs. Arch., Regs. 6, 7, 7B [Bek] · Bek memorandum book, BL, Harley MS 3720 · Borth. Inst., Reg. 10 (Archbishop Zouche), fols. 310v–312r [official copy of Bek's will] · W. O. Massingberd, 'An account of the family of Bek, of Lusby', Associated Architectural Societies' Reports and Papers, 24/1 (1897), 33–53 · [J. Raine], ed., Testamenta Eboracensia, 1, SurtS, 4 (1836) · Adae Murimuth continuatio chronicarum. Robertus de Avesbury de gestis mirabilibus regis Edwardi tertii, ed. E. M. Thompson, Rolls Series, 93 (1889) · Fasti Angl., 1300–1541, [Lincoln] · Fasti Angl., 1300–1541, [Salisbury] · Emden, Oxf.
Archives BL, Harley MS 3720 · Lincs. Arch., regs. 6, 7, 7B
Wealth at death many debts; numerous bequests: will, Borth. Inst., Reg. 10, fols. 310v–312r

Beke, Charles Tilstone (1800–1874), traveller and geographer, was born on 10 October 1800 at Stepney, London, the son of James Beke. The family had ancestral connections to Bekesbourne in Kent, where Beke lived in later life. He was educated at a private school in Hackney and in 1820 took a position in a commercial firm, for which he worked in London, Genoa, and Naples. He later studied law at Lincoln's Inn, but eventually supported himself by commercial activities. His passions were early biblical history and the geography and exploration of north-east Africa. He was a controversialist, and aired his views in

Charles Tilstone Beke (1800–1874), by Maull & Fox

public lectures, in correspondence, and in *The Times* with more energy than judgement.

In 1834 Beke published *Origines biblicae, or, Researches in Primeval History*, a work which set an intellectual framework for much of the rest of his life. He tried to harmonize recent scientific discoveries, especially those in geology, with a belief in the Bible as an inspired work of divine revelation. He was particularly interested in the geography of the Middle East as understood in the light of the Pentateuch and the principles of geological change. On the one hand, he argued that the biblical account of the geography of the Tigris–Euphrates valley could be understood only in the light of several thousand years of sedimentation at the mouth of the Euphrates River; but, on the other, he treated literally biblical accounts such as those of the Israelite crossing of the Red Sea and wanderings in Sinai and sought to trace them on the nineteenth-century landscape of Palestine. His account of human history reduced all languages to families descended from the three sons of Noah—Shem, Ham, and Japheth. An abiding conviction, set forth in *Origines*, was that human history was a story of decline, not progress. Thus, cultural phenomena which many of his contemporaries interpreted as fumbling attempts at progress by non-European peoples were understood by Beke to be residual signs of their earlier participation in a common civilization. The work

set forth in *Origines*, and a number of contemporary articles, won him election to a variety of learned societies, most notably the Oriental Society of Germany, the Asiatic Society, and the geographical societies of London and Paris. The University of Tübingen awarded him the PhD degree. He published vigorously in this vein for the rest of the decade.

After having served for nine months in 1837–8 as acting British consul in Leipzig, and drawn up a report on the Leipzig commercial fair, Beke spent the years 1840 to 1843 travelling in Abyssinia, spending most of his time in the provinces of Shoa and Gojam. His governing concerns were to advance commerce; aid the suppression of the slave trade; and make further geographical discovery, with the elucidation of the sources of the Nile River as his goal. By the time of his death he had neither had much impact on, nor derived much benefit from, the trade of north-east Africa or the Red Sea. On the slave trade, his was but one of many voices contributing to an atmosphere which led the emperor, Téwodros (Theodore), in the late 1850s, to take Abyssinia's first hesitant steps towards its suppression. Yet he proved a careful and diligent observer, and scholars of Abyssinian history and ethnography still read his published papers and his unpublished travel diary with profit. Three notable papers arising from these travels were published in 1843, 1844, and 1847 in the *Journal of the Royal Geographical Society*, which had supported the expedition at a time of considerable financial retrenchment.

Beke's journey resulted in his first making known the true physical structure of Abyssinia and of eastern Africa generally, showing that the principal mountain system of Africa extends north–south on the eastern side of the continent, and that Ptolemy's Mountains of the Moon are a part of that north–south range. He also discovered Lake Assal, a salt lake at 150 m below sea level inland of the Gulf of Tadjowa. He fixed, by astronomical observations, the latitude of more than seventy stations, and mapped more than 70,000 square miles of country. He visited and mapped the watershed between the Nile and the Hawash (or Awash) rivers, along a line of 50 miles northward of Ankober, a town north-east of Addis Ababa, and he discovered the River Gojeb (or Gojeb Wenz), which drains west and eventually south into Lake Rudolf (Urkana). He also constructed a very valuable map of the regions of Gojam and Damot on the western slopes of the mountain range, and determined approximately the course of the Abai. In recognition of his discoveries he received medals from the geographical societies of London (founder's medal, 1845) and Paris (gold medal, 1846).

In the *Proceedings of the Philological Society* for 1845 Beke described fourteen languages and dialects whose vocabularies he had studied, and his paper 'Description of the ruins of the church of Mártula Mártula Mariam, in Abessinia' was published in *Archaeologia* in 1847. Material gathered on the trip informed a stream of letters which he wrote to the Foreign Office and the Board of Trade, letters which he published in pamphlet form in two separate editions in 1852 under the title *Letters on the Commerce of*

Abessinia and other Parts of Eastern Africa. A four-volume diary kept during his travels was printed in 1846 for private use.

During his travels in Abyssinia, Beke crossed paths with W. C. Harris and the embassy which Harris led from the government of India to the court of Shoa, and with the French traveller Antoine d'Abbadie. He later engaged in public controversy with both of them, particularly d'Abbadie. While in Abyssinia, on the basis of information collected at the great market site of Baso, north of the southernmost reach of the Blue Nile, Beke correctly divined that the principal source of the Nile River must lie in the equatorial highlands of east Africa and that the Blue Nile was a tributary to the White. He published this conclusion in a map in 1848 to accompany a paper in the *Edinburgh New Philosophical Journal*. Two years later he attacked d'Abbadie in a widely circulated pamphlet. The latter had received the gold medal of the Paris Geographical Society for papers recounting his travels in southern Abyssinia. Unlike Beke, d'Abbadie had actually crossed the Blue Nile and penetrated much further south than his rival. Beke denounced d'Abbadie's trip as 'pretended' and, when the Paris Geographical Society curtailed the debate, returned the gold medal he had been awarded in 1846; he had no further ties with the society. However, on the important question of how the major river basins of Abyssinia contribute to the larger Nile basin, Beke was right and d'Abbadie wrong.

Meanwhile, in 1848 Beke organized support for an expedition to explore the Nile basin of east Africa from the Mombasa coast, which a German, Friedrich Bialloblotzky, agreed to lead. The expedition collapsed before achieving its objectives, and in 1858 John Hanning Speke took up the search, which was to gain for him the public acclaim which Beke craved. In vain Beke pursued recognition as the 'theoretical' discoverer of the Nile's origins.

In 1853 Beke became a partner in a commercial firm in Mauritius, where he met and, on 25 April 1856 at Port Louis, married his second wife, Emily Alston, the youngest daughter of William Alston, of Leicester, and Elizabeth Wagstaff Hyde Clarke Alston; his first wife, Eliza von Griesbach, the great-niece of Sir John Herschel, had died in 1853. He enjoyed a degree of prosperity and maintained his interest in Abyssinia, although his attempts to expand commerce with the country met mixed success. He issued propaganda on Abyssinian affairs, and angled unsuccessfully for appointment as British consul to Abyssinia.

In the 1860s Beke's lifelong passions again brought him into the public eye. He continued, by lecture and articles, and his *Sources of the Nile* (1860), to debate the geography of the Nile basin. In 1861 and 1862 Beke and his wife travelled in Syria and Palestine, taking up issues of biblical geography first raised almost thirty years before in *Origines*. An account of this trip was published in 1865 by Emily Beke under the title *Jacob's Flight*. Their travels had also taken them to Egypt, which Beke saw as an important channel for trade between Europe and central Africa.

In 1864 Téwodros, emperor of Abyssinia, imprisoned the British consul, Duncan Cameron, and then a number

of other European travellers and missionaries. Most of the missionaries were German-speaking protestants, but they were under British protection, and one of them, Henry Stern, was a British subject. In addition to writing another stream of letters to the newspapers and the Foreign Office and giving public addresses on the subject, Beke accepted a commission from Stern's family to travel to Abyssinia to seek the release of Stern and his colleagues. Beke twice went to Abyssinia, the second time in 1866 accompanied by his wife, but, after apparent initial success, ultimately failed in his objective, and was blamed, probably unfairly, for exacerbating a delicate situation. Beke claimed that the information, maps, and advice with which he provided the British government greatly assisted the military expedition which was launched from India in 1867 to free the captives, and he was incensed that a meagre grant of £500 was all he received in return. The award in 1870 of a civil-list pension of £100 per annum mollified him somewhat, but in 1871 lack of money forced him to abandon his residence at Bekesbourne.

In December 1873 Beke left England on his last trip, designed to vindicate an argument first set forth in *Origines* concerning the geography of Mount Sinai and the Red Sea. He returned to England the following March and died suddenly on 31 July 1874 at Holly Villa, Spring Hill, Bromley, Kent. He was buried at Bekesbourne on 5 August. The results of the Red Sea expedition were posthumously edited and published in 1878 by his widow, Emily, who in 1876 also published a valuable pamphlet account of her husband's published works, 'and of his inadequately requited public services'. The 1878 volume, considered by some contemporaries to be his most important, aroused considerable controversy at the time, but left no lasting mark on biblical research.

Beke's widow deposited the papers arising from his travels in Abyssinia in the 1840s in the British Museum. In addition to both a diary and journal, they contain a variety of notes and observations, some watercolour sketches, and maps. Beke embodied the passion and concern of his age to reconcile evolving natural history with the Bible as divinely inspired; to contribute to geographical discovery; and to promote commerce and suppress the slave trade in Africa. Driven by a restless energy, he made lasting contributions to the study of Abyssinia: in the field of political and social affairs; through his scientific observations on climate, topography, and language; and through his skills as a watercolour painter. DONALD CRUMMEY

Sources *Summary of the late Dr Beke's published works, and of his inadequately requited public services*, by his widow (1876) · H. R. Mill, *The record of the Royal Geographical Society, 1830–1930* (1930) · C. R. Markham, *The fifty years' work of the Royal Geographical Society* (1881) · DNB · CGPLA Eng. & Wales (1874)

Archives BL, travel journals and papers, Add. MSS 30247–30258 · JRL, corresp. and papers · U. Birm. L., theological papers · Wellcome L., corresp. and papers | Lpool RO, letters to Lord Stanley · RGS, letters to Royal Geographical Society · RS, corresp. with Sir J. F. W. Herschel · U. Newcastle, corresp. with Sir Walter Trevelyan · W. Sussex RO, letters to dukes of Richmond

Likenesses Maull & Fox, photograph, NPG [*see illus.*] · photograph, repro. in E. Beke, ed., *The late Dr Charles Beke's discoveries of Sinai in Arabia and of Midian* (1878), preface

Wealth at death under £200: probate, 25 Sept 1874, *CGPLA Eng. & Wales*

Bekinsau [Beckinsau], **John** (1499/1500–1559), scholar, was born at Broad Chalk, Wiltshire, the younger of two sons of John Beckinsau of Hartley Wespell, Hampshire. Whether he belonged to an ancient Lancashire family (Becconsall) or to a native Wiltshire family (from Bekinsettle) is debatable, but they were related to the Bulkeley family and counted Robert Bekensau (president of Queens' College, Cambridge, from 1509 to 1519, and chaplain and almoner to Katherine of Aragon) a kinsman.

Bekinsau was educated at Winchester College, where he was admitted a scholar in 1514, aged fourteen, and proceeded to New College, Oxford, on 6 May 1518. He was elected fellow (8 May 1520), and was admitted BA (31 March 1522) and MA (12 July 1526) and may have supplicated BTh (26 February 1529). Wood called him 'an admirable Grecian' (Wood, *Ath. Oxon.*, 1.129), and he continued his Greek studies at Paris, but probably never lectured. Goodwin's description of him in the *Dictionary of National Biography* as a Greek lecturer at the time of François I's foundation of royal professorships in Greek is misleading and based on an earlier description of Bekinsau as a 'royal scholar' in 1530. Letters from Thomas Winter, John Leland, Miles Coverdale, and others praise his honesty and integrity but refer to him only as 'a young man of good learning' or as 'scholar', never as anything more. The term 'royal scholar' refers to his work on the king's behalf (during the divorce) for which a payment of £5 was made out of the privy purse on 30 April. He may have been involved in the determinations of the Paris faculties of canon law and divinity of the same period, working with Reginald Pole.

Bekinsau funded his further studies by performing minor duties for the Lisles and English officials in Paris. There are at least two dozen letters between him and Lady Lisle, largely concerned with the education of her son, James Bassett. William Knight, Stephen Gardiner, Edmund Bonner, and Thomas Thirlby employed his services, and he also carried letters and aided Reginald Pole and Richard Pate (for which he faced conspiracy charges in 1543). He was under official scrutiny, however, as early as 1538, when he failed to accompany Gardiner back to England. He wrote to Cromwell claiming a lack of sufficient funds, but it was rumoured that Bekinsau had spoken out against dissolving the monasteries and the royal supremacy. He admitted only his opposition to Thomas Starkey (whom he suspected was a sacramentarian—someone who denied the real presence in the eucharist).

In Paris Bekinsau married a French woman named Andrea, which necessitated the vacating of his fellowship by March 1539. Coverdale defended him to Cromwell, telling of his good nature and lack of funds 'in a right lamentable sort' (*Remains*, 496–7). Indeed, Bekinsau's loyalty to the king hindered his work in Paris as the French priests habitually obstructed him, saying he 'smelt of the fire', referring to events in England (*LP Henry VIII*, 13/2, 1422). In August 1539 Lord Lisle offered him the clerkship of the merchants of the staple in Calais, but instead he returned to England in September 1540 as a gentleman usher to Anne of Cleves, for which he received £10. He returned to Paris in October (funded by William Roper), and by 1543 he was employed by Gardiner. Bekinsau may have played a role in the so-called prebendaries' plot, but was granted a royal pardon in April 1544 and in July was reappointed a gentleman usher for the king with a life annuity of £10 (rising to £25 in 1546). He was later granted a lease of property in Somborne, Hampshire, from the president and fellows of Magdalen College (deprived under Edward VI, regained under Mary on 6 May 1555, vacated under Elizabeth in 1558).

Bekinsau wrote *De supremo et absoluto regis imperio* (1546), a minor supremacy tract rehearsing earlier and more famous tracts of Gardiner and Foxe; it was reprinted in 1611 in Melchior Goldast's *Monarchia S Romani imperii*. John Bale praised the work, comparing Bekinsau with Cato. When Bekinsau accepted papal supremacy under Mary, however, Bale accused him of returning to Rome 'like a dog to his vomit' (Bale, 234v). He sat in Mary's first parliament as member for Downton (and later for Hindon), a client of both Gardiner and William Paulet. In April 1556 he exchanged his annuities for a new grant of £35 a year for life (and moneys owed). On the accession of Elizabeth, and in ill health, he retired to Sherborne St John, Hampshire, where he died, and where he was buried on 20 December 1559. His will, proved on 15 or 16 January 1560, provided books worth £20 to a nephew and further properties (valued at approximately £46) to his wife, who received letters of denization in November 1558.   ANDREW A. CHIBI

Sources HoP, *Commons, 1509–58* • M. St C. Byrne, ed., *The Lisle letters*, 6 vols. (1981) • *LP Henry VIII* • *CPR, 1553–8* • *Remains of Myles Coverdale, bishop of Exeter*, ed. G. Pearson, Parker Society (1846) • N. Harpsfield, *The life and death of Sr Thomas Moore, knight*, ed. E. V. Hitchcock, EETS, original ser., 186 (1932) • G. Redworth, *In defence of the church catholic: the life of Stephen Gardiner* (1990) • Wood, *Ath. Oxon.*, new edn • Foster, *Alum. Oxon.* • *Reg. Oxf.* • Ro: Ba:, *The lyfe of Syr Thomas More, sometymes lord chancellor of England*, ed. E. V. Hitchcock and P. E. Hallett, EETS, 222 (1950) • Emden, *Oxf.*, vol. 4 • Hants. RO, wills B. 1558 • PRO, C 219/22/94, C 219/23/151 • J. Bale, *Illustrium Maioris Britannie scriptorum … summarium* (1548) • *DNB*
Wealth at death £66 13s. 10d.: HoP, *Commons, 1509–58*

Bekynton, Thomas. *See* Beckington, Thomas (1390?–1465).

Bel, Jean le (*c*.1290–1370), ecclesiastic and chronicler, was of noble rank, according to the chronicler Jean d'Outremeuse. He was born about 1290 into a patrician Liégeois family with important dynastic links to the more rurally based nobility. His father was the armigerous Gilles le Bel, a money changer who became *échevin* of Liège like his father and grandfather before him. The name of his mother is unknown, but she was descended from the noble Renier de Thys. His great-uncle, Jean de Cange, a canon of St Lambert and provost of St Jean at Liège, and a shrewd political operator, may have been a formative early influence. He had two younger brothers (Henri, who travelled with him to England and was knighted at Harwich in 1327, and Gilles, also a Liégeois cleric), and a sister who married a local knight. In old age he fathered—and handsomely endowed—twin sons, Jean and Gilles, the fruit of his liaison with a woman of noble descent, Marie le Hardy, from the des Pres family.

Le Bel's lifestyle was very much that of the worldly cleric, and the chronicler Jacques de Hemricourt provides a vivid description of his sumptuous, richly jewelled clothing, his hounds, hawks, and horses, comparing his appearance with that of a knight-banneret. His hospitality was legendary, and a retinue rivalling that of the bishop of Liège accompanied him to church on feast days. He saw active service in his youth in both war and tournament, and Hemricourt's description of his joyful, pleasure-seeking character, composing secular verse, is in many ways reminiscent of Chaucer's squire. His good sense and ability to manage men were turned to good account, not only in obtaining substantial pensions and grants of land with his versifying, but in the management of his household and the bringing-up of squires there.

By 1313 le Bel had become a canon of St Lambert, and from 1331 to 1361 he was also provost of St Jean. He became actively involved in local and regional politics, and was evidently an able negotiator: documentary references reflect his close links with the Hainault comital family, as well as the duchy of Brabant, and Jean de Luxembourg, king of Bohemia (r. 1310–46). In 1327 he formed part of the retinue of John of Hainault, the count of Hainault's brother, who was aiding Edward III against the Scots. It is impossible to assess whether and how often he accompanied John of Hainault in the latter's wide-ranging activities in the Low Countries, but the recording of capitular business transacted in the chronicler's house at Liège from time to time after the mid-century may reflect an increased degree of residence there.

Le Bel's narrative, usually known as his *Chronique*, was intended as an accurate relation of the wars and events of 1326–61, focusing predominantly on the great achievements of the kings of England and France. Although his method requires further analysis, the first section, covering 1326–40, is generally believed to have been written between 1352 and 1356; the second (1340–58) in 1358; and the final chapters (1359–61) piecemeal, as he noted events. According to d'Outremeuse, John of Hainault was responsible for initiating the *Chronique*, specifically requiring an accurate and objective account and (with other witnesses) correcting it.

Le Bel's narrative of the campaign of 1327 against the Scots is essentially an eyewitness account, and includes invaluable details—notably of the miseries inflicted by terrain and climate, Scottish military practices, and tensions among the lower ranks. Le Bel is also an important source for dealings between the Low Countries and England in 1338–40, besides detailing the diplomatic activities that resulted in Edward III's accession in 1327 and his marriage to Philippa of Hainault in the following year.

Le Bel himself repeatedly emphasizes both the superior accuracy of his prose account and his endeavours to obtain information, a claim supported by d'Outremeuse. Nevertheless, he should be used with caution, for despite his evident regard for accuracy and his plain style there are occasions where his reliance on oral testimony is misleading, resulting not simply in factual error but reflecting any bias in his source or uncorroborated stories then current and generally accepted as true. The exaggerated notion of Robert d'Artois's influence in England in 1334 is such an area (a misconception shared by another Low Countries chronicler, 'Le Bourgeois de Valenciennes'), and his account of Edward III's supposed rape of the countess of Salisbury may similarly reflect a tale current and accepted in le Bel's milieu. His narrative perspective was inevitably influenced by the defection of Jean of Hainault, Edward III's uncle by marriage and long-standing ally, to Philippe VI of France, as well as by the links of Liège with Philippe's ally, the king of Bohemia. It is no coincidence that his account of the battle of Crécy (1346) focuses on the heroism of the blind Jean de Luxembourg. Much of Froissart's *Chronique* is heavily dependent on le Bel's; however, some later versions depart considerably from le Bel's narrative. Although ultimately overshadowed by his successor, le Bel nevertheless remains a vital source for the early decades of the reign of Edward III.

According to Jacques de Hemricourt, who knew him well, Jean le Bel enjoyed robust good health until the end of his long life, and this is borne out by the wording of his will. He died at Liège on 15 February 1370, and was buried in the cathedral church of St Lambert, where he was commemorated by a chantry and an epitaph until these were destroyed in 1793.   JULIET VALE

Sources *Chronique de Jean le Bel*, ed. J. Viard and E. Déprez, 2 vols. (Paris, 1904–5) • É. Poncelet, ed., *Cartulaire de l'église de Saint-Lambert de Liège*, 6 vols., Académie Royale de Belgique, Commission Royale d'Histoire (1893–1933) • 'Le mirior des nobles de Hesbaye', *Œuvres de Jacques de Hemricourt*, ed. C. de Borman, A. Bayot, and É. Poncelet, 1 (Brussels, 1910) • J. d'Outremeuse, *Ly mireur des histors, chronique de Jean des Preis dit d'Outremeuse*, ed. A. Borgnet and S. Bormans, 6 (Brussels, 1880) • *Œuvres de Froissart*, ed. K. de Lettenhove, 1, pts 2–3 (Brussels, 1873) • *Œuvres de Froissart*, ed. K. de Lettenhove, 22 (Brussels, 1875) • J. G. Schoonbroodt, ed., *Inventaire analytique et chronologique des chartes du chapitre de Saint-Martin à Liège* (Liège, 1871) • L. Lahaye, ed., *Inventaire analytique des chartes de la collégiale de Saint-Jean l'Évangéliste à Liège*, 2 vols. (Brussels, 1921–31) • J. de Theux de Montjardin, *Le chapitre de Saint Lambert à Liège*, 4 vols. (1871–2) • C. Renardy, *Le monde des maîtres universitaires du diocèse de Liège, 1140–1350: recherches sur sa composition et ses activités* (1979) • A. Jorris, 'Note sur la pénétration du droit savant au pays de Liège, XIIᵉ–XVᵉ siècles', *Villes, affaires, mentalités: autour du pays mosan* (Brussels, 1993), 183–205 • P. F. Ainsworth, *Jean Froissart and the fabric of history* (1990) • K. de Lettenhove, ed., *Récits d'un bourgeois de Valenciennes (XIVᵉsiècle)* (1877)
Archives Bibliothèque Municipale, Chalons-sur-Marne, MS 81
Wealth at death see Poncelet, ed., *Cartulaire*, vol. 6, pp. 426–7

Belaney, Archibald Stansfeld [*called* Grey Owl] (1888–1938), impostor and conservationist, was born at 32 St James's Road, Hastings, Sussex, on 18 September 1888, the son of George Furmage Belaney (*b.* 1857). His mother's name appears in various forms on legal documents, as Kittie Morris and Kitty Cox before Archibald's birth, and as Kathleen Verena Scott-Brown at her death at the age of eighty in 1950. Abandoned by his parents, he was raised by his father's sisters, Ada and Carrie Belaney. From an early age Belaney loved animals and kept a menagerie in the

Archibald Stansfeld Belaney [Grey Owl] **(1888–1938)**, by Howard Coster, 1930s

attic of their home. Although his mother visited him occasionally in Hastings, he never saw his father, who was believed to have left for North America. While a student at Hastings grammar school from 1899 to 1904 he began to build for himself a fantasy world centred on the North American Indian. He spent countless hours playing Indian in the neighbouring St Helen's Woods.

Belaney's aunts wanted him to take up a profession after leaving grammar school, but he resisted. Finally, with their consent, he left in 1906 for northern Canada, where, apart from three years in the Canadian army during the First World War, he spent the remainder of his life, as a trapper and guide, and later as a conservationist. Through his first wife, Angel Aquena (Angele Egwuna), an Ojibwa, whom he had married at Lake Temagami on 23 August 1910, he learned about the wilderness. He behaved as his father had and left his wife and child in 1912. Several other relationships followed, the most important emotionally being that with Gertrude Bernard, or Anahareo, whom he was to marry in an Indian ceremony. Before he met the beautiful young Iroquois woman in 1925, he had married Ivy Holmes, an Englishwoman, on 10 February 1917 while on a visit to England. She had subsequently obtained a divorce on 9 August 1922, on the grounds of bigamy when she learned of his previous marriage to Angele Egwuna.

In the late 1920s Anahareo convinced Belaney, now known as Grey Owl, to abandon trapping and to work instead for conservation, encouraging him to write about the necessity of protecting Canada's wildlife and forests. Impressed by his early articles, the Canadian government invited him to join the Canadian parks branch as a 'caretaker of park animals'. He published his first book as Grey Owl in 1931. Entitled *Men of the Last Frontier*, it was a collection of wilderness tales. In his second and perhaps best book, *Pilgrims of the Wild*, which appeared in 1934, he movingly told of his life with Anahareo, and of his conversion from trapper to conservationist. He completed it and his subsequent two books, *The Adventures of Sajo and her Beaver People* (1935) and *Tales of an Empty Cabin* (1936), at Prince Albert National Park in Saskatchewan, where he looked after beaver conservation. Grey Owl lived at Beaver Lodge, a small cabin at best 6 by 7 metres in extent. The beaver had built their lodge outside, and partially inside, his home, appropriating a quarter of his living space.

By the late 1930s Grey Owl's four books on the Canadian north and its animal and human inhabitants had won him a devoted readership throughout the English-speaking world. Audiences throughout the British empire had seen his films on the beaver. At the request of Lovat Dickson, his publisher in England, he made two highly successful lecture tours of the British Isles, the first in 1935. *The Canadian Who's Who* of 1936–7 summarized Grey Owl's story of his origins. The entry reads: 'Born encampment, State of Sonora, Mexico, son of George, a native of Scotland, and Kathrine (Cochise) Belaney; a half-breed Apache Indian … adopted as blood-brother by Ojibway tribe, 1920 … speaks Ojibway but has forgotten Apache.' At least one prominent plains Indian leader at the time disbelieved Grey Owl's story, but John Tootoosis of Saskatchewan said nothing, for he respected the importance of Grey Owl's fight to conserve the beaver, 'and more beavers meant more dams to hold back the water and that in turn meant better conditions for the muskrat and waterfowl population' (Sluman and Goodwill, 169).

Grey Owl's lecture tour and workload put a strain on his relationship with Anahareo, and they parted in 1936. In December of that year he married Yvonne Perrier at St James's Church in Montreal, using the name Archie McNeil, and further elaborating upon the fiction of his past.

On 10 December 1937, on his second British lecture tour, Grey Owl, the modern Hiawatha, gave a command performance at Buckingham Palace attended by Queen Mary, King George VI and Queen Elizabeth, and the two princesses. The tall, hawk-faced man, dressed in buckskins, spoke to the royal family about the Canadian north, about its forests and animals, and about the North American Indians. His royal audience loved the lecture and films. Queen Mary had previously given copies of his books to her granddaughters Elizabeth and Margaret Rose. After the three-hour performance the royal audience spoke to Grey Owl for nearly half an hour. At the time of his royal command performance Grey Owl had already been on the lecture circuit for nearly two months. More appearances awaited him in Britain, the United States, and Canada.

Grey Owl returned to Beaver Lodge in early April 1938, in a state of total exhaustion. Only three days later he had to be rushed to hospital. He died of pneumonia in Prince Albert on 13 April and was buried in the national park over 60 miles north of the city. Then came the bombshell. Swift detective work in the week after his death allowed reporters on both sides of the Atlantic to discover Grey Owl's real identity. Almost overnight Canada's most popular Indian was exposed as English-born Archie Belaney. Disappointment followed, but opinion in Canada turned in the 1970s when a new generation of readers discovered his books. Despite his misrepresentation of himself as an Indian many recognized the English-born Archie Belaney's attainments as a writer and campaigner for the wise use of natural resources and the protection of wildlands and wildlife. A feature film based on his life starring Pierce Brosnan and directed by Richard Attenborough was released in 1999.   DONALD B. SMITH

Sources D. B. Smith, *From the land of shadows: the making of Grey Owl* (1990) · L. Dickson, *Wilderness man: the strange story of Grey Owl* (1973) · L. Dickson, ed., *The green leaf: a tribute to Grey Owl* (1938) · Anahareo, *My life with Grey Owl* (1940) · Anahareo, *Devil in deerskins: my life with Grey Owl* (1972) · N. Sluman and J. Goodwill, *John Tootoosis: biography of a Cree leader* (1982) · A. G. Ruffo, *Grey Owl: the mystery of Archie Belaney* (1996) · b. cert. · m. cert. [mother] · d. cert. [mother] · parish register (baptism), Hastings, Christ Church, 27 Nov 1888

Archives Glenbow Archives, Calgary, Alberta, Grey Owl collection · McMaster University, Hamilton, Ontario, Macmillan collection · NA Canada, Grey Owl collection | FILM NA Canada, Moving Image and Sound Archives, Historical Resources Branch | SOUND NA Canada, Moving Image and Sound Archives, Historical Resources Branch, Grey Owl collection

Likenesses H. Coster, photographs, 1930–38, NPG [*see illus.*] · W. J. Oliver, photographs, 1931–6, Glenbow Archives, Calgary, Alberta, Canada · Y. Karsh, photograph, 1936, NA Canada · J. Lavery, oils, 1936, National Gallery of Canada, Ottawa · photograph, Hult. Arch.

Belasyse, Anthony. *See* Bellasis, Anthony (*d.* 1552).

Belasyse, Sir Henry (1648–1717), army officer, was born in Biddick House, Durham, the son of Sir Richard Belasyse (*b.* 1612, *d.* before 1670) of Potto, Yorkshire, and Ludworth and Owton, co. Durham, and his second wife, Margaret (*d.* after 1670), daughter of Sir William Lambton of Lambton, co. Durham. Initially a pupil at Houghton School, co. Durham, he went up to Christ's College, Cambridge, on 29 March 1666, matriculating in the following year, before attending the Middle Temple between 1667 and 2 April 1668. Belasyse entered the Anglo-Dutch brigade in 1674, probably as a captain. He fought at the siege of Maastricht (1676), and the battles of Mont Cassel (1677) and St Denis (1678), where he was wounded. He was promoted colonel of the first English regiment of the Anglo-Dutch brigade in 1677. He and his battalion went to England in June 1685 as part of the Anglo-Dutch brigade sent by William of Orange to assist in the suppression of Monmouth's rebellion. During 1687 he displeased William of Orange and was forbidden the court but was allowed to retain his regiment until April 1688, when, after sailing to England, he 'lurked long here in Yorkshire for his [William of Orange's] service' (*Memoirs of Sir John Reresby*, 530). Heavily

involved in the earl of Danby's northern conspiracy against James II, he was a principal in the seizure of York on 22 November 1688, but it is unclear whether he was acting independently or as a Dutch agent. He was rewarded by promotion to brigadier-general on 1 April and colonel of a battalion of foot on 28 September 1689.

Although avaricious and unpopular, Belasyse was an accomplished soldier: even William III respected his abilities. While in camp at Dundalk (1689) his new battalion had 'hardly any good officers, and an entire absence of good order; clothing not good, but Brigadier Belasyse expected to work reforms' (Walton, 80). Marlborough commented that he was 'not beloved but he has good sense, and is a good officer' (Snyder, 1.107). Belasyse fought in William's campaigns in Ireland, serving at the Boyne, Limerick, and Aughrim before transferring to Flanders in 1692, where he was promoted major-general on 1 April. With Thomas Tollemache he successfully extricated the defeated confederate infantry from the battlefield of Landen in 1693. Raised to lieutenant-general on 4 October 1694, in the following year he commanded the rearguard along the Bruges Canal covering Vaudémont's retreat through Ghent after the delaying action at Aarsele. Later in 1695 he presided at the court martial of Major-General Johann Ellenburg and Colonel Francis Fergus O'Farrell for failing to defend Dixmuyde.

After the peace of Ryswick (1697) Belasyse supervised the evacuation of the British troops from Flanders. On 28 June 1701 he became colonel of the Queen's regiment (2nd foot). Marlborough considered Belasyse for a command in the West Indies in 1702—he had sought the governorship of Jamaica in 1689—but he went instead as second-in-command to Ormond on the expedition to Cadiz (1702) in the War of the Spanish Succession. Along with Charles O'Hara, Belasyse was held responsible for the sacking of Puerto Santa Maria and, despite protestations of innocence and Marlborough's advice to defuse the incident, both were court martialled in February 1703. O'Hara was acquitted but Belasyse, perhaps because of his widespread unpopularity, was found guilty and cashiered. The episode raised adverse remarks about his professionalism, especially the report by Prince George of Hesse-Darmstadt, but these are contradicted by the greater part of the evidence. Thus ended his active career, although he was quietly reinstated into the army and appointed governor of Berwick upon Tweed (13 June 1713). He had first married Dorothy, daughter of Tobias Jenkins of Grimston and widow of Robert Benson of Wrenthorp, Yorkshire. Their eldest child, Mary, died at the age of seventeen and both Thomas and Elizabeth predeceased their father. His second wife was Fleetwood (1686–1732), daughter of Nicholas Shuttleworth. Belasyse died in London on 16 December 1717 and was buried in Westminster Abbey, as was his second wife after her death in 1732. They had two children: William died on 11 February 1769, but Margaret died an infant.   JOHN CHILDS

Sources *Memoirs of Sir John Reresby*, ed. A. Browning (1936) · C. Dalton, ed., *English army lists and commission registers, 1661–1714*, 6 vols. (1892–1904) · *CSP dom.*, 1664–5; 1702–3 · *The Marlborough–Godolphin*

correspondence, ed. H. L. Snyder, 3 vols. (1975) · BL, Add. MS 61317 · *Calendar of the Clarendon state papers preserved in the Bodleian Library*, 5: 1660–1726, ed. F. J. Routledge (1970) · F. J. G. ten Raa, F. de Bas, and J. W. Wijn, eds., *Het staatsche leger, 1568–1795*, 8 vols. in 10 (Breda, 1911–64) · A. D. Francis, *The First Peninsular War, 1702–1713* (1975) · S. B. Baxter, *William III* (1966) · R. Surtees, *The history and antiquities of the county palatine of Durham*, 4 vols. (1816–40) · C. Walton, *History of the British standing army, A.D. 1660 to 1700* (1894)

Archives BL, letters to Sir William Blathwayt, Add. MSS 9731, 38698

Belasyse [Bellasis], **John, first Baron Belasyse of Worlaby** (*bap.* **1615,** *d.* **1689**), royalist army officer, was born at Newburgh in the North Riding of Yorkshire, and baptized on 24 June 1615 at nearby Coxwold, the second son of Thomas Belasyse, first Viscount Fauconberg of Henknowle (1577–1653), and his wife, Barbara Cholmley (*c.*1580–1619), daughter of Sir Henry Cholmley of Whitby and his wife, Margaret. Educated at home until he was twelve, Belasyse was reared a Roman Catholic, to which faith his father had recently converted. He reportedly attended Peterhouse, Cambridge, in 1628, though the only entry for a John Belasyse in the college's admission register is one that was made ten years later, and seems to be not a clerical error but a reference to a kinsman of his from Durham. Subsequently sent to France for two years with the marquess of Huntly, Belasyse attended court at Fontainebleau, and was educated in the Italian Signor Arnolfen's academy in Paris.

After his return Belasyse was maintained at the English court by his father. He was fined £150 by the court of high commission for his clandestine marriage on 8 March 1636 to Jane Boteler (*bap.* 1621, *d.* 1657), daughter and sole heir of Sir Robert Boteler of Watton Woodhall, Hertfordshire. Belasyse settled at Worlaby, Lincolnshire, served in the king's life guard in the first bishops' war, and later helped arrange for the treaty at Ripon. Despite his closet Roman Catholicism he sat for Thirsk in both parliaments of 1640, and on 16 March 1641 was admitted to Gray's Inn. Later that year he was teller on the royalists' side in divisions, and he was noted as absent from the house on 16 June 1642.

Attending the king at York, Belasyse raised a troop of horse, but he quitted it in August to lead a regiment of foot, maintained by his father, to the king at Nottingham. Having been excluded from parliament on 6 September he commanded a royalist brigade at Edgehill in October. He was shot in the head during the assault on Bristol on 26 July 1643, but recovered within a month, only to have his horse shot from under him at the first battle of Newbury on 20 September. In January 1644 he was appointed governor of York and lieutenant-general of Yorkshire, Nottinghamshire, Lincolnshire, Derbyshire, and Rutland; and having arrived in York by 25 January, he reorganized the county's defences, mustering 5000 foot and 1500 horse. Detachments from his army were, however, defeated by Colonel John Lambert in two engagements at Bradford in March, while on 11 April parliament's northern army commanded by Belasyse's cousin Lord Fairfax destroyed his army at Selby. Wounded and captured, he was conveyed first to Hull and then to London where he was charged with high treason and imprisoned in the Tower.

In January 1645 Belasyse's exchange was negotiated, and on 27 January the king created him Baron Belasyse of Worlaby. He served as a volunteer at Naseby and after the earl of Lichfield's death at Rowton Heath he was appointed general of the king's guards, 'a single troop of 500 horse, many noblemen, all gentlemen and reformado officers' (Moone, 388). On 26 October he witnessed Prince Rupert's confrontation with the king at Newark, and when the governor, Sir Richard Willys, resigned his post in sympathy with Rupert, Belasyse was appointed in his place. When subsequently challenged to a duel by Willys, Belasyse was ordered to desist by the king and was closely guarded. Besieged in Newark by the Scots and parliamentarian forces, Belasyse organized a vigorous defence until 4 May when the king commanded him to make terms. He was escorted back to his plundered home at Worlaby, and he compounded for delinquency on the Newark articles on 20 June; and on 8 September his fine was reduced to one tenth and set at £2073.

Belasyse travelled abroad, entering into the service of the prince of Condé at the siege of Mardyke. Received at Paris by the French queen mother, Anne of Austria, he delivered a letter to her from Charles I. He was subsequently entertained at the court of Savoy, the duchess recommending him to Venice for service against the Turks. He met Pope Innocent X at Rome, who was 'pleased to discourse with my Lord in two or three several audiences of things not fit to be communicated' (Moone, 395). On his return to Paris in 1648 he was appointed general of horse under the marquess of Newcastle, but his plans to land in Yorkshire and serve in the second civil war were thwarted by news of Cromwell's victory at Preston. His father procured a pass for him to visit Yorkshire, but Belasyse was arrested and imprisoned by the council of state, accused of intending to raise royalist forces. After being released on bail for £5000 in 1650 he continued to conspire against the republic. He was the intended general of the northern forces raised to support Charles II's Scottish invasion, but he was imprisoned in the Tower in April 1651. On 9 September he was again released on bail, this time for £6000. He was granted his estate on security of £3000 and after he had paid the fine his pardon was ordered in 1652. Nevertheless he remained an active conspirator and joined the Sealed Knot. In 1659 Edward Hyde remarked that Belasyse would 'heartily engage' in future risings (Newman, *Royalist Officers*, 22). On 24 July 1659, his first wife having died late in 1657, Belasyse married Anne Armyne (*d.* 1662), daughter and coheir of Sir Robert Crane, bt, of Chilton, Suffolk, at St Vedast's, Foster Lane.

In August 1659, shortly before Sir George Booth's uprising, Belasyse was taken prisoner at Worlaby and imprisoned in Hull and subsequently the Tower of London. After his release in November he attended the king in the Netherlands, and at the Restoration he was appointed lord lieutenant of the East Riding, a position he held until 1673. In June 1660 he was appointed captain of gentlemen pensioners (1660–72), and in December governor of Kingston upon Hull (1660–73). His second wife died on 11 August 1662, and his final marriage was to Anne Paulet (d. 1694), daughter of John Paulet, fifth marquess of Winchester. On 4 January 1665 he was appointed governor of Tangier and general of the royal forces in Africa; he served there from April 1665 to April 1666.

Belasyse resigned these posts when he was unable to take the oaths required by the Test Acts (1673); he was accused of high treason during the Popish Plot crisis and imprisoned in the Tower from 25 October 1678. It was alleged that he procured Sir Edmund Berry Godfrey's murder and hid the corpse in his coach, that he plotted to poison the king, and that he was the general of a secretly mustering Catholic army. Impeached by the House of Commons he remained in the Tower, recounting his memoirs to his secretary, Joshua Moone. He was released on 10 February 1684, the duke of York paying £30,000 as bail.

Formally cleared of all charges on 25 May 1685, Belasyse was appointed to James II's privy council on 17 July 1686. As a Catholic, his appointment as first lord commissioner of the Treasury on 4 January 1687 was highly controversial. Sir John Reresby reported that Belasyse later reflected to him on 3 March 1689, 'that he had been very averse (though a papist) to the measures used in that reign for promoteing that religion … but his council was suspected as comming from a man that the hott party informed the King was ould and timerous, and that haveing a good estate was in fear to hazard it' (Memoirs of Sir John Reresby, 561). Belasyse died on 10 September 1689, 'one of the wisest men of that party' (Memoirs of Sir John Reresby, 562), and was buried on 14 September at St Giles-in-the-Fields, Middlesex, a monumental inscription being placed both there and at Worlaby. His only son had been mortally wounded in a drunken quarrel in 1667, so he was succeeded by his grandson, upon whose death in August 1691 the title became extinct.   ANDREW J. HOPPER

Sources J. Moone, 'A brief relation of the life and memoirs of John Lord Belasyse', Calendar of the manuscripts of the marquess of Ormonde, new ser., 2, HMC, 36 (1903), 376–99 · G. Risdill Smith, In well beware: the story of Newburgh priory and the Belasyse family, 1145–1977 (1978) · D. Underdown, Royalist conspiracy in England, 1649–1660 (1960) · GEC, Peerage, new edn · CSP dom., 1651, 1660–87 · M. A. E. Green, ed., Calendar of the proceedings of the committee for compounding … 1643–1660, 2, PRO (1890) · J. Foster, ed., Pedigrees of the county families of Yorkshire, 3 (1874) · Memoirs of Sir John Reresby, ed. A. Browning (1936) · P. R. Newman, 'The defeat of John Belasyse: civil war in Yorkshire, January–April, 1644', Yorkshire Archaeological Journal, 52 (1980), 123–33 · P. R. Newman, Royalist officers in England and Wales, 1642–1660: a biographical dictionary (1981) · P. R. Newman, The old service: royalist regimental colonels and the civil war, 1642–1646 (1993) · 'The Dictionary of National Biography: John Belasyse', BIHR, 4 (1926), 48–9 · H. Aveling, Northern Catholics: the Catholic recusants of the North Riding of Yorkshire, 1558–1790 (1966) · J. T. Cliffe, The Yorkshire gentry from the Reformation to the civil war (1969) · P. Watson, 'Belasyse, Sir Henry', HoP, Commons, 1660–90 · J. Foster, The register of admissions to Gray's Inn, 1521–1889, together with the register of marriages in Gray's Inn chapel, 1695–1754 (privately printed, London, 1889) · R. L. H. Lloyd, ed., The parish registers of Coxwold, Yorkshire Parish Register Society, pt 1 (1955), 120 · J. Gough Nichols, ed., 'Lincolnshire families, temp. Charles II, from the note book of Sir Joseph Williamson', Herald and Genealogist, 2 (1865), 116–26 · will, PRO, PROB 11/401, sig. 165 · Venn, Alum. Cant., 1/1 · Keeler, Long Parliament · T. A. Walker, ed., Admissions to Peterhouse or St Peter's College in the University of Cambridge (1912)

Archives BL, corresp. and papers as governor of Tangier, Sloane MSS 1519, 1952, 1955, 3299, 3496, 3499, 3509, 3513 · N. Yorks. CRO, family papers, Newburgh Priory MSS · NL Ire., life and memoir | BL, Add. MSS 5752, 18981, 34195, 38038, 36273q, 40717, 42154 · BL, Egerton MS 3330 · BL, Harley MSS 991, 7010 · BL, Stowe MS 210

Likenesses S. Cooper, miniature, V&A; repro. in Underdown, Royalist conspiracy · R. White, line engraving (as young man; after A. Van Dyck), BM, NPG · portrait, repro. in Risdill Smith, In well beware

Wealth at death £2300 p.a. in land in Yorkshire and Lincolnshire c.1667: Gough Nicols, ed., 'Lincolnshire families', 118 · lands in Durham, Yorkshire, Lincolnshire, Nottinghamshire, Middlesex; many houses in London and Westminster; £2450 left in gifts; £2800 owed him in pay arrears; portions totalling £8000 provided for daughters upon their marriages: will, 1690, PRO, PROB 11/401, sig. 165

Belasyse [née Cromwell], **Mary**, **Countess Fauconberg** (bap. **1637**, d. **1713**), daughter of Oliver Cromwell, was born in Ely, Cambridgeshire, and baptized at St John's Church, Huntingdon, on 9 February 1637, the eighth of nine children and the third of four daughters of Oliver *Cromwell (1599–1658), the future lord protector, and his wife, Elizabeth *Cromwell, née Bourchier (1598–1665), daughter of Sir James Bourchier. She and her younger sister remained in the parental home long after their surviving siblings married and moved away. These included Henry *Cromwell and Bridget *Fleetwood. Thus she was with her parents when they became protector and protectress, was assigned apartments at Whitehall and Hampton Court, and was often referred to as 'Lady' Mary or 'Princess' Mary. During the 1650s there were rumours of several possible matches until in 1657, with the encouragement of Secretary John Thurloe, almost certainly acting with the explicit approval of Oliver Cromwell, Thomas *Belasyse (1627/8–1700), second Viscount Fauconberg and later (from 1689) first Earl Fauconberg, sought and won Mary's hand as his second wife (his first having died in May 1656). Despite the royalist connections of the Belasyse family, the protectoral couple warmly approved the match, providing a dowry of £15,000, and the civil wedding took place in their presence at Hampton Court on 18 November. The celebrations continued at Whitehall and elsewhere including, the earl of Clarendon alleges, a second marriage conducted privately by an ordained minister in accordance with the prayer book (Clarendon, Hist. rebellion, 4.34).

For a time the Fauconbergs continued to occupy apartments at Hampton Court and Whitehall. In summer 1658 they travelled north to view the viscount's estates in Yorkshire, returning to London in time to be on hand for the deaths of Mary's sister Elizabeth *Claypole and of her father, a particularly severe blow—Fauconberg wrote that 'I know not what in the Earth to do with' his wife, for 'when seemingly quieted, she bursts out again into passion that tears her very heart in pieces' (Waylen, 100).

Although the couple retired to the countryside after the fall of the protectorate, Fauconberg won renewed favour at the Restoration and resumed his career as diplomat, politician, administrator, and courtier. He and Mary divided their time between their estates in Lancashire and Yorkshire, principally Newburgh Priory, near Coxwold, and their properties in and around London, especially Sutton House in Chiswick, Middlesex, and a new house they built in Soho Square. According to a rather implausible tradition, Oliver Cromwell's body lies buried at Newburgh, rescued by his daughter and carried there soon after his death in September 1658; it is one of many stories concerning the removal and secret burial of Oliver's remains, all of them almost certainly spurious. The Fauconbergs' surviving correspondence suggests that the marriage, though childless, was strong and happy. They were both close to Mary's surviving sister, Frances *Russell, and to Fauconberg's nephew Thomas Frankland and his wife, Frances's daughter Elizabeth. Wealthy and contented, they entertained a wide circle of friends and courtiers. Fauconberg died after a long illness in December 1700, and while the title and Newburgh estate passed to his brother's son, his widow retained the bulk of the London properties.

Countess Fauconberg spent her widowhood principally at Sutton House, and was described by one visitor as 'still fresh and gay, though of a great age' (Ramsey, 59). Although in good health, she drew up her will on 27 November 1711, noting that 'the frailty of humane nature, the certainty of death and the uncertainty of the hour thereof' were such that she wished to make her will now so that 'none of the affairs of this present Life may when I come to dye interrupt the peaceable and quiet resignation of my Soul unto the hands of my blessed Saviour and Redeemer'. Her will also emphasizes her wealth, for she left bequests totalling well over £10,000, including £4000 and a share of her plate to her sister Frances and £100 'to my dear brother Richard Cromwell' (PRO, PROB 11/533, sig. 130). In fact, she outlived Richard *Cromwell, proving his will in August 1712. She died, 'a Lady in great Esteem for her exemplary Piety and Charity' (The Political State of Great Britain, 1713, 161), on 14 March 1713, probably in London, and was buried on 24 March in Chiswick church.

PETER GAUNT

Sources The writings and speeches of Oliver Cromwell, ed. W. C. Abbott and C. D. Crane, 4 vols. (1937–47) · J. Waylen, The house of Cromwell and the story of Dunkirk (1897) · M. Noble, Memoirs of the protectoral house of Cromwell, 2 vols. (1787) · R. W. Ramsey, Studies in Cromwell's family circle (1930), chap. 3 · R. Sherwood, Oliver Cromwell: king in all but name, 1653–58 (1997), esp. chap. 9 · Report on the manuscripts of Mrs Frankland-Russell-Astley of Chequers Court, Bucks., HMC, 52 (1900) · Report on manuscripts in various collections, 8 vols., HMC, 55 (1901–14), vol. 2 · CSP dom., 1656–60 · Thurloe, State papers · BL, Add. MS 69377 · will, PRO, PROB 11/533, sig. 130 · will of Thomas, Earl Fauconberg, PRO, PROB 11/460, quire 87 · Clarendon, Hist. rebellion, 4.34
Archives BL, letters, Add. MS 69377 · BL, Henry Cromwell's letters, Lansdowne MSS 821–823 · Bodl. Oxf., MSS Rawl., Thurloe state papers
Likenesses attrib. M. Dahl, oils, c.1653, Cromwell Museum, Huntingdon · miniature or engraving (after miniature), repro. in Sherwood, Oliver Cromwell, 108; priv. coll. · oils, Newburgh Priory, Yorkshire · portrait, repro. in Ramsey, Studies in Cromwell's family circle, facing p. 35 · portrait, BM; repro. in A. J. Shirren, The chronicle of Fleetwood House (1951), pl. 25
Wealth at death property and bequests totalling over £10,000: will, PRO, PROB 11/533, sig. 130

Belasyse, Thomas, **first Earl Fauconberg** (1627/8–1700), nobleman, was born at Newburgh Priory, near Coxwold, North Riding of Yorkshire, the son of Henry Belasyse (1604–1647) and his wife, Grace Barton of Smithells, Lancashire. He may have been educated at Trinity College, Cambridge. The first Viscount Fauconberg, Belasyse's grandfather, fled to Europe after Marston Moor (2 July 1644) and died at Hamburg in 1653 after converting to Catholicism. Belasyse succeeded to the title on 18 April 1653. The committee for compounding fined the family £5012. The second lord was in France in spring 1657, after the death in 1656 of his first wife, Mildred Saunderson (whom he had married on 3 July 1651), daughter of the second Viscount Castleton, when negotiations for a new match began. Fauconberg's second wife was Mary Cromwell (bap. 1637, d. 1713), the third of the protector's four daughters [see Belasyse, Mary]. After assuring himself that Fauconberg was a protestant and that his estate was sufficient—he was said to have about £5000 p.a.—Cromwell gave his blessing. The wedding took place on 18 November 1657 at Hampton Court, and was conducted by John Hewitt, an Anglican divine who in 1658 was executed for treason. The Venetian ambassador, who considered Fauconberg 'an accomplished young man of many talents and undoubted courage' was nevertheless surprised at the match, for he considered Fauconberg a royalist, and had heard that he not only corresponded with the exiled Charles Stuart, but even sent him money (CSP Venice, 1657, 134). Even so, the protector was fond of his new son-in-law. He became colonel of Lambert's regiment of horse in July 1657, and was present whenever Cromwell received foreign ambassadors. Cromwell also named him to his 'other house' and he took his seat in January 1658 as Thomas, Lord Fauconberg.

In May 1658 Fauconberg went to France as ambassador-extraordinary, but after the protector's death in September he took steps to safeguard his interests. In October he agreed to provide the French ambassador with political information in return for jewels for his wife and barbary horses for himself. In late spring 1659 he sent £1000 to the future king and retired to the country to avoid further trouble. In September 1659 the council of state ordered his arrest, but he was free in time to greet George Monck as he marched his army through Yorkshire. The general named him colonel of Heselrigge's regiment, and after the king's return he was taken into favour despite his Cromwellian connections.

On 27 July 1660 Fauconberg became lord lieutenant of Durham and the North Riding of Yorkshire, although he resigned the former post to the bishop of Durham in September 1661. He served the crown loyally as lord lieutenant and actively pursued sectarians and plotters throughout the 1660s. His prominence in Yorkshire led him to clash with rivals there, however. In August 1666 the second duke of Buckingham challenged Fauconberg to a duel, and though the quarrel was composed without violence, in October he fought Buckingham's erstwhile supporter Sir Thomas Osborne, and was seriously wounded. In October 1669 Charles II appointed him ambassador-extraordinary to Venice, and after his return in 1672 he became captain of the band of gentlemen pensioners and a privy councillor. Though a friend of the duke of Monmouth, he worked hard to secure the election of pro-Yorkist MPs to the Exclusion parliaments. He refused, however, to co-operate with James II's policies, and lost his lieutenancy in November 1687. As early as May 1687 he had met Dykveldt, William of Orange's agent in England, and he played a particularly important role in the convention of 1689. At first identified as a supporter of Princess Mary's sole rule, he soon shifted to support a joint monarchy. For this he was rewarded on 9 April 1689 with an earldom. He also chaired the Lords' committee that negotiated the declaration of rights.

Fauconberg continued to be politically active until 1692, after which he gradually withdrew from politics. In July 1697 he wrote to his dying brother-in-law, Sir William Frankland,

> for my own particular, that have seen all the vanities and acted an unhappy part upon all the scenes and stages of human life, it is more than time I should endeavour to get the taste and relish of this world out of my mouth by withdrawing from the noise and bustle of it to a more heavenly conversation. (*Frankland-Russell-Astley MSS*, 89)

He died, leaving no children, at Sutton House, his house in Chiswick, on 31 December 1700, aged seventy-two, and was buried at Coxwold parish church on 30 January 1701. He was succeeded by his nephew Thomas Belasyse, the second earl.   VICTOR STATER

Sources CSP Venice, 1657–9; 1669–71 · CSP dom., 1656–7; 1659–61; 1663–4; 1666–7; 1686–7 · Report on the manuscripts of Mrs Frankland-Russell-Astley of Chequers Court, Bucks., HMC, 52 (1900) · Report on manuscripts in various collections, 8 vols., HMC, 55 (1901–14), vol. 2 · GEC, Peerage · P. Aubrey, Mr Secretary Thurloe: Cromwell's secretary of state, 1652–1660 (1990) · The writings and speeches of Oliver Cromwell, ed. W. C. Abbott and C. D. Crane, 4 vols. (1937–47) · R. Sherwood, The court of Oliver Cromwell (1977) · L. G. Schwoerer, The declaration of rights, 1689 (1981) · A. Browning, Thomas Osborne, earl of Danby and duke of Leeds, 1632–1712, 3 vols. (1944–51) · Memoirs of Sir John Reresby, ed. A. Browning, 2nd edn, ed. M. K. Geiter and W. A. Speck (1991) · J. W. Clay, 'The gentry of Yorkshire at the time of the civil war', Yorkshire Archaeological Journal, 23 (1914–15), 349–94 · Report on the manuscripts of F. W. Leyborne-Popham, HMC, 51 (1899) · Calendar of the manuscripts of the marquess of Ormonde, new ser., 8 vols., HMC, 36 (1902–20), vol. 5
Archives BL, letter-book and notebook, Add. MSS 41254–41255 · N. Yorks. CRO, corresp. and papers | BL, report on the Italian states, Sloane MS 2752 · NL Scot., corresp. with marquess of Tweeddale · NRA, priv. coll., corresp. with Sir William Frankland
Likenesses A. Blooteling, line engraving, 1676 (after M. Beale), BM, NPG · R. White, line engraving, BM, NPG; repro. in J. Guillim, A display of heraldry, 5th edn (1679) · sculpture, funeral monument, Coxwold parish church, Yorkshire

Belcher, Sir Edward (1799–1877), naval officer and hydrographer, second son of Andrew Belcher of Halifax, Nova Scotia, and Roehampton, Surrey, and grandson of William Belcher, governor of Nova Scotia, was born in that colony. He entered the navy in 1812, and after serving in

several ships in the channel and on the Newfoundland station was in 1816 a midshipman of the *Superb* (Captain Ekins), at the bombardment of Algiers. He was made lieutenant on 21 July 1818, and after continuous though unimportant service in 1825 was appointed assistant surveyor to the *Blossom*, then about to sail for the Pacific Ocean and Bering Strait on a voyage of exploration, of more than three years. He was made commander on 16 March 1829, and from May 1830 to September 1833 commanded the *Aetna*, surveying parts of the west and north coasts of Africa. On 11 September 1830 he married Diana, daughter of Captain George Jolliffe HEICS.

Through the winter of 1832 the *Aetna* served on the River Douro, protecting British interests during the Miguelite War. The results of the *Aetna*'s work were afterwards embodied in the Admiralty charts and sailing directions for the rivers Douro and Gambia. On paying off the *Aetna*, Belcher was employed for some time on the home survey, principally in the Irish sea, and in November 1836 was appointed to the *Sulphur*, a surveying ship, then on the west coast of South America, from which Captain Beechey had been obliged to invalid out. During the next three years the *Sulphur* was employed on the west coast of both North and South America, and at the end of 1839 received orders to return to England by the western route. After visiting several of the island groups in the south Pacific and making such observations as time permitted, Belcher arrived at Singapore in October 1840, where he was ordered back to China, because of the war there; during the following year he was actively engaged, especially in operations in the Canton River. The *Sulphur* finally arrived in England in July 1842, after a commission of nearly seven years. Belcher had already been advanced to post rank (6 May 1841) and was made a CB (14 October 1841); in January 1843 he was made a knight, and that year published his *Narrative of a Voyage Round the World Performed in H.M.S. Sulphur during the Years 1836–42* (2 vols.).

In November 1842 Belcher was appointed to the *Samarang* for the survey of the coast of China, which the recent war and treaty had opened to British trade. More pressing necessities, however, changed her field of work to Borneo, the Philippines, and Formosa (Taiwan), and on these and neighbouring coasts Belcher was employed for nearly five years surveying and fighting pirates. He returned to England on the last day of 1847. In 1848 he published *Narrative of the Voyage of H.M.S. Samarang* (2 vols.), and in 1852 was appointed to command an Arctic expedition in search of Sir John Franklin. The appointment was unfortunate; for Belcher, though an able and experienced surveyor, had already demonstrated that he had neither the temper nor the tact necessary for a commanding officer under circumstances of peculiar difficulty. Despite his abilities, Belcher evidently inspired strong personal dislike among his superiors and his subordinates, and the customary exercise of his authority did not make Arctic service less trying. His expedition is distinguished from all other Arctic expeditions as the one in which the commanding officer showed an undue haste to abandon his ships when in difficulties, and in which one of the ships so abandoned rescued herself from the ice, and was picked up floating freely in the open Atlantic. Belcher's account, published in 1855 under the extravagant title of *The Last of the Arctic Voyages* (2 vols.), may be compared with the description of the abandonment of the *Resolute* by Admiral Sherard Osborn in his *Discovery of a North-West Passage* (4th edn, 1865, 262–6). Belcher was never employed again, although in course of seniority he attained his flag on 11 February 1861, became vice-admiral on 2 April 1866, and admiral on 20 October 1872. He was made a KCB on 13 March 1867. He passed his remaining years in literary and scientific activities. His publications included *A Treatise on Nautical Surveying* (1835), long a standard work; *Horatio Howard Brenton, a Naval Novel* (3 vols., 1856), a little regarded work; and in 1867 he edited Sir W. H. Smyth's *Sailors' Word Book* (1867). He died on 18 March 1877 at his home, 6 Melcombe Place, Dorset Square, London. As Admiral Sir William Parker told him in 1843: 'A skilful navigator and a clever seaman you may be, but a great officer you never can be, with that narrow mind' (Phillimore, 2.616). Belcher had great ability in his chosen speciality, but was utterly lacking in the qualities required of a leader, or an obedient subordinate.   J. K. LAUGHTON, rev. ANDREW LAMBERT

Sources G. S. Ritchie, *The Admiralty chart: British naval hydrography in the nineteenth century* (1967) · O'Byrne, *Naval biog. dict.* · *Journal of the Royal Geographical Society*, 47 (1877) · *Dod's Peerage* (1858) · Boase, *Mod. Eng. biog.* · A. Phillimore, *The life of Admiral of the Fleet Sir William Parker*, 2 (1879)
Archives BL, papers relating to Franklin search expedition, Add. MSS 35307–35309 · BLPES, letters and papers · Hydrographic Office, Taunton · NA Canada, documents relating to search for Sir John Franklin · NL NZ, Turnbull L., private journal on HMS *Blossom* · NMM, corresp., letter-books, and order books · PRO, Admiralty records · RGS, letters and papers · University of British Columbia Library, family corresp. and papers, incl. Arctic exploration papers | BLPES, letters to John Philippart · Bodl. Oxf., letters to Sir William Napier · NL Scot., letters to Sir Thomas Cochrane · NMM, letters to John Philippart · PRO, letters to Sir John Ross, Bj2
Likenesses S. Pearce, oils, c.1859, NPG · wood-engraving, 1877, NPG; repro. in *ILN*, 70 (1877), 300 · C. Silvy, photograph, NPG · portrait, repro. in *Army and Navy Magazine* (1882) · portrait (after photograph by Beard), repro. in *ILN* (1852)
Wealth at death under £3000: resworn probate, July 1877, *CGPLA Eng. & Wales*

Belcher, James [Jim, Jem] (**1781–1811**), prize-fighter, was born at his parents' house near St James's churchyard, Bristol, on 15 April 1781. His mother was a daughter of John *Slack (c.1721–1768), the noted pugilist, who defeated John Broughton in April 1750. Jim (or Jem) Belcher worked as a butcher, but early distinguished himself by pugilistic and other feats at Lansdown fair. He was a natural fighter and the family environment favoured the development of his interests. His sister was married to another Bristol fighter, Bill Watson, already well known in London, and when Belcher moved there in 1798 yet another Bristolian, the veteran boxer Bill Warr, was on hand to spar with him at his tavern in Covent Garden and show off the youngster's skills. Belcher was a considerable prospect, personable, handsome, finely proportioned, and elegant in movement. He soon attracted influential support as he disposed, in rapid succession, of Tom (Paddington) Jones

James [Jem] **Belcher** (1781–1811), by unknown artist, c.1800

in April 1800, the 37-year-old Jack Bartholomew a month later, and the Irish champion, Andrew Gamble, in five rounds in December.

With Gentleman John Jackson having announced his retirement and refusing all challenges, the championship was vacant and the twenty-year-old emerged as the strongest rival to Joe Berks (or Bourke), a rough, tough fighter from Wem in Shropshire. The two met in Buckinghamshire in November 1801, although the fight had been forbidden by the lord lieutenant of the county. Belcher won after sixteen desperate rounds, but both men and their seconds were committed to Reading gaol. Belcher's influential friends quickly secured his release by having the case transferred to the king's bench, but Berks languished in prison for some time. They fought again on 20 August 1802, and Berks retired at the end of the fourteenth round, by which time he could scarcely stand and was shockingly cut about the face. In April 1803 Belcher severely punished John Firby, 'the Young Ruffian', in a hastily arranged encounter. Next month he had to appear before Lord Ellenborough in the court of king's bench for rioting and fighting, upon which occasion he was defended by Erskine and Francis Const, and was merely bound over to come up for judgment upon his own recognizance in £400.

In July 1803 Belcher lost an eye when struck by a ball while playing at rackets. His high spirits and general health began to deteriorate. He took over the Jolly Brewers public house in Wardour Street, Soho, but unhappily he was stirred by jealousy of a former pupil, Hen Pearce, 'the Bristol Game-Chicken', once more to try his fortune in the ring. He had a terrible battle with Pearce on Barnby Moor, near Doncaster, on 6 December 1805. He displayed all his old courage but not his old skill or form, and was defeated in eighteen rounds. He fought yet again two heroic but unsuccessful fights with Tom Cribb—the first on 8 April 1807 at Moulsey in forty-one rounds, the second on 1 February 1809, in answer to a challenge for the belt and 200 guineas. Belcher was again defeated after a punishing fight in thirty-one rounds, though the best judges were of the opinion that, at his former best, Belcher would have been the winner. This was Belcher's last fight. He was one of the gamest fighters ever seen in the prizering, and probably the most rapid in his movements: 'you heard his blows, you did not see them.' A truly courageous man, Belcher was in private life good-humoured, modest, and unassuming; but after his last fight he became increasingly taciturn and depressed. He was deserted by most of his old patrons: one of the best of these was Thomas Pitt, the second Lord Camelford, who at his death on 10 March 1804 left Belcher his famous bulldog Trusty. Belcher died on 30 July 1811 at the Coach and Horses, Frith Street, Soho, a property which he left to his widow; he was interred in the Marylebone burial-ground.

A link between the silver and golden ages of the prizering, Belcher was 'as well known to his own generation as Pitt or Wellington'. Like the latter he is commemorated by an article of attire, a 'belcher' or blue and white spotted neckerchief, though the term is also applied loosely to any parti-coloured handkerchief tied round the neck. His character and appearance are highly eulogized in Arthur Conan Doyle's novel *Rodney Stone* (1896, chaps. 10 and 15). In 1805 a very brief but bloodthirsty 'Treatice [*sic*] on boxing by Mr J. Belcher' was appended to Barrington's *New London Spy* for that year.

Jim's younger brother, **Thomas** [Tom] **Belcher** (1783–1854), was also a prize-fighter, and though less effective than Jim, played an important role in the ring for many years. In a carefully protected early career he won fights in succession with Dogherty, Firby, and some fighters of less repute, but he was badly defeated in 1807 by Dutch Sam (Samuel Elias). He was a stylish prize-fighter and sparrer, and always ready to appear at benefits for fellow pugilists at the Fives Court and the Tennis Court. His tavern, the Castle, Holborn, which he kept from 1814 to 1828, became virtually the headquarters of the sport both in his day and subsequently under Tom Spring. He was one of the eighteen pugilists chosen by Gentleman John Jackson to guard the entrance to Westminster Abbey at the coronation of George IV on 19 July 1821. Tom Belcher, who is described as 'gentlemanly and inoffensive', died of apoplexy at 19 Trafalgar Square, Peckham, Surrey, on 9 December 1854, aged seventy-one, universally respected.

THOMAS SECCOMBE, *rev.* DENNIS BRAILSFORD

Sources H. D. Miles, *Pugilistica: the history of British boxing*, 1 (1906), 132–66 · *Pancratia, or, A history of pugilism*, 2nd edn (1815) · P. Egan, *Boxiana, or, Sketches of ancient and modern pugilism*, 5 vols. (1812–29) · P. Egan, *Pierce Egan's book of sports* (1832) · *Sporting Magazine* (July 1803) · *Sporting Magazine* (Aug 1803) · *Sporting Magazine* (Dec 1804) · *Sporting Magazine* (Aug 1807) · *Sporting Magazine* (April 1808) · *Sporting Magazine* (Oct 1808) · *Sporting Magazine* (Feb 1809) · *Sporting Magazine* (April 1811) · *Sporting Magazine* (June 1811) · Boase, *Mod. Eng. biog.*

Likenesses oils, c.1800, NPG [*see illus.*] · T. Rowlandson, watercolour caricature, 1805–10 (Thomas Belcher; after Guest?), Brodick Castle, Garden and Country Park, Isle of Arran · C. Turner, mezzotint, pubd 1811 (Thomas Belcher; after G. Sharples), BM · C. Turner, mezzotint (Thomas Belcher; after D. Guest), BM · portrait, repro. in Miles, *Pugilistica*, vol. 1, facing p. 132 · portrait (Thomas Belcher), repro. in Miles, *Pugilistica*, vol. 1, facing p. 154

Belcher, John (1841–1913), architect, was born on 10 July 1841 at 3 Montague Terrace, Trinity Square, London, the eldest of the ten children of John Belcher (1816/17–1890), architect, and his first wife, Anne Woollett, a descendant of Philip Woollett, father of the engraver William Woollett (1735–1785). The family were members of the Catholic Apostolic church, in which Belcher was a minister throughout his life. He was educated at private schools and at Luxembourg, and after spending a few months in Paris as an architectural student (1862–3) he became a partner in his father's architectural practice in 1865. On 8 June that year he married Florence, daughter of Matthew Parker, a minister, of Dublin. They had no children.

After his father's retirement in 1875 Belcher was joined by James W. James until 1882, and from 1885 to 1897 was in partnership with Arthur Beresford Pite. Together they had a strong influence on the development of the grand manner in late nineteenth-century architecture, not only through their executed work, but also through their unsuccessful competition entry for the Victoria and Albert Museum (1891), which was widely discussed within the profession.

Belcher was also sympathetic to arts and crafts ideas; indeed, he took the chair at the first meeting of the Art Workers' Guild, an organization devoted to raising the status of the decorative arts. He compared the architect to the conductor of an orchestra, 'leading and directing the executants in the interpretation of a work of his own composition' (*RIBA Journal*, 3rd ser., 21, 1913, 77). He was particularly keen that the sculptor should work with the architect from the early days of a commission as 'the most perfect achievement can be attained by their joint action' (*Transactions of the RIBA*, new ser., 8, 1892, 49). But he rejected the insistence on taking vernacular buildings as the source of a new style.

Instead, Genoese baroque—an enthusiasm Belcher developed on a trip to Italy—seemed to offer a model for the incorporation of sculpture and painting in the service of architecture, while allowing a free treatment of the classical tradition. There is evidence of this at the Institute of Chartered Accountants, Moorgate Place, London (1890–93), a building with a complex programme of exterior sculpture by Harry Bates and Hamo Thornycroft, an old family friend. If Belcher claimed that every detail of this building had been worked out by himself, other contemporary sources make it clear that it was jointly designed with Pite. Some recent writers have tended to downplay Belcher's role, seeing him as the business-minded front man to Pite the designer, but it seems more likely to have been a real design partnership. Yet Pite, who wrote

John Belcher (1841–1913), by Sir Frank Dicksee, exh. RA 1908

Belcher's entry in the *Dictionary of National Biography*, mentioned neither himself nor John James Joass, who worked in the office as assistant from 1897 and partner from 1905, and was equally influential on the later work of the firm.

Belcher's Colchester town hall (1898–1902) shows that he was capable of producing good work independently. He cannot have received any help from Pite, who entered the competition separately, and the real impact of Joass in the office had yet to be felt. Indeed, the last building which can be said to be more Belcher than Joass was the Ashton memorial, Williamson Park, Lancaster (designed 1904, built 1907–9), a gargantuan folly paid for by Lord Ashton as a memorial to his family, where English sources were now stronger. In 1901 he had published, with Mervyn Macartney, *Later Renaissance Architecture in England*, a close study that served as a visual textbook for the developing English classical revival.

In later work the hand of Joass became more dominant as illness restricted Belcher's contribution. Mappin House, 158–62 Oxford Street, London (1906–8), the former Royal Insurance building at the corner of St James's and Piccadilly (1907–8), Whiteley's stores, Bayswater (1910–12), and Holy Trinity Church, Kingsway (1910–12), all show the bolder touch of a designer trained to detail for Glasgow masons.

Joass wrote that Belcher 'was endowed with a most receptive and inquiring type of mind', and that 'new ideas appealed to him irresistibly' (*RIBA Journal*, 3rd ser., 22, 1915, 125). This helps to explain the stylistic variety of his work, from red brick Gothic influenced by William Burges in the Mappin and Webb building, Queen Victoria Street,

London (1870–72, dem.), to Norman Shaw 'Queen Anne' in the aptly named Queen Anne Chambers, 1 Poultry, London (1875, dem.), or Stowell Park, Gloucestershire (1886), for the earl of Eldon. It explains also the strong influence of his much younger partners.

Belcher's friends remarked upon his unassuming modesty, which, combined with a 'quiet insistence and determination', made him an ideal president of the Royal Institute of British Architects (1904–6) at a time of division within the profession. He was awarded the 1907 royal gold medal for architecture, and in the same year published *Essentials in Architecture*, a primer aimed at the architectural student. The other great interest in his life was music: he performed publicly as a solo bass singer, and lectured the Royal Institute of British Architects on church organs, and on the musical requirements of church planning. He also published a *History of Ecclesiastical Music* (1872).

Belcher was elected an associate of the Royal Academy in 1900 and Royal Academician in 1909. He died on 8 November 1913 at his home, Redholm, Champion Hill, Surrey, and was buried in Norwood cemetery. He was survived by his wife.   A. B. PITE, *rev.* IAN DUNGAVELL

Sources A. Service, 'Belcher and Joass', *ArchR*, 148 (1970), 282–90 · M. Macartney, 'John Belcher', *RIBA Journal*, 21 (1913–14), 50 · J. W. James, 'The late John Belcher, a biographical notice', *RIBA Journal*, 21 (1913–14), 75–8 · *The Builder*, 105 (1913), 507, 560 · *Building News*, 105 (1913), 688–9, 716 · J. J. Joass, 'The work of the late John Belcher', *RIBA Journal*, 22 (1914–15), 97–106, 121–30 · C. G. Harper, 'The work of John Belcher, architect', *ArchR*, 4 (1898), 130–33, 201–6, 237–42 · T. Wilson, 'John Belcher: building for the millennium', *Victorian Society Annual* (1997), 19–24 · *CGPLA Eng. & Wales* (1913) · A. S. Gray, *Edwardian architecture: a biographical dictionary* (1985)

Archives RIBA, MSS

Likenesses H. Thornycroft, bronze bust, *c*.1882, RA · photograph, 1882, RIBA · H. Thornycroft, sculpture in marble?, *c*.1889, repro. in *Building News*, 58 (1890) · photograph, *c*.1907, repro. in *RIBA Journal*, 3rd ser., 14 (1907), frontispiece · F. Dicksee, oils, exh. RA 1908, RIBA [*see illus.*] · photograph, repro. in *Building News*, 91 (1906)

Wealth at death £23,926 16s. 0d.: probate, 20 Dec 1913, *CGPLA Eng. & Wales*

Belcher, John William (1905–1964), politician and trade unionist, was born on 2 August 1905 at 12 Radington Road, Kensington, London, the first surviving child of John Thomas Belcher, an assurance agent and later a postal sorting worker, and his wife, Lillie Harriett, *née* Garrard. From 1912 onwards the family lived in Hammersmith, west London; John Belcher attended the local Brackenbury Road elementary school and won a scholarship to Latymer Upper School, Hammersmith, in 1916. He left school at sixteen and entered clerical employment, finding a secure job at the Smithfield goods depot of the Great Western Railway in December 1922. Soon afterwards he joined the Railway Clerks' Association (RCA) and became a trade union activist, a decision he regarded as 'the turning point of my life' (Belcher, 'How I ... rose and fell'). He became branch secretary about 1929, served on local and regional bodies of the RCA and the wider labour movement during the 1930s, and founded a Workers' Educational Association study group on economics among the

Smithfield clerks. He took an external London University diploma in economics and social science in 1932 and became a fellow of the Royal Economic Society.

Belcher married Louisa Moody on 5 June 1927, when both were aged twenty-one; she was the daughter of William Moody, an engine man of Chalk Farm. He recalled that 'we took a chance on marrying so young, but our interests and political sentiments were so identical, and we were so much in love, that we never thought about waiting' (Belcher, 'John Belcher's tribute'). They remained in love for the rest of their lives, although their marriage was childless until their daughter Jill was born on 22 June 1940. Shortly afterwards the family moved from Camden Town, north London, to Sydney Road in Enfield, Middlesex. The Belchers had three children.

Belcher suffered from poor health for much of his life. He had surgery in 1931 for intestinal problems including a duodenal ulcer and was classified disabled during the Second World War, during which he worked as a lecturer for the Ministry of Information. He was elected Labour MP for Sowerby, Yorkshire, in July 1945 and was among the first of the 1945 intake to be given a ministerial job—parliamentary secretary at the Board of Trade—on 12 January 1946. A large proportion of his workload lay in dealing with the complex apparatus of controls, permits, and rationing administered by the Board of Trade during the 1940s. While a popular and well-regarded minister, he suffered from severe stress, and by the middle of 1947 'luncheons and dinners which I had to attend in increasing numbers became an ordeal and I only kept going by dosing myself with various powders to relieve the almost constant pain. I knew I was heading for a breakdown' (Belcher, 'What happens'). He turned increasingly to alcohol, which worried the president of the Board of Trade, Harold Wilson, and Belcher's own civil servants. His health did indeed collapse and he spent several weeks in hospital in May 1948.

Belcher tried to meet as many business people as possible directly, operate controls reasonably, and win trust for the Labour government. Unfortunately he formed his closest links with a fraudster, illegal alien, and undischarged bankrupt known as Sidney Stanley. Stanley was a 'contact man' who claimed to be able to arrange favours from government for businessmen on production of a fee. One such was Harry Sherman, an unscrupulous football pools promoter. Stanley showered Belcher with minor gifts, such as a suit, a week in a hotel in Margate, and frequent visits to the dog track. Belcher naïvely accepted these as friendly gestures. He also saw no harm in accepting gifts from other people who had dealings with the Board of Trade, such as a few Max Factor cosmetics and a prodigious amount of sherry from Maurice Bloch distillers. Stanley falsely claimed to clients that Belcher took cash bribes but pocketed the money himself.

Rumours started to circulate about corruption at the Board of Trade in summer 1948; Wilson called in the police on 9 October 1948 and Belcher was suspended from duty on 18 October. On 9 October the prime minister, Clement Attlee, announced the appointment of a tribunal of inquiry under Sir George Lynskey to investigate the allegations. The proceedings were highly publicized. John Belcher appeared before it and was harshly examined by the attorney-general, Sir Hartley Shawcross. Belcher's counsel conceded that the gifts were incompatible with his position as a minister of the crown, but not that his ministerial activities had been influenced. Louisa Belcher also underwent a rigorous public investigation of her finances. John Belcher resigned as a minister on 13 December 1948.

The tribunal's report, which was put before parliament on 22 January 1949, was harsher than the government, or Belcher, expected. It found that he had been influenced by accepting gifts, although Belcher and his ministerial and civil service colleagues continued to believe that he had not. A parallel Metropolitan Police investigation found that it would be possible to charge him and Maurice Bloch over their relationship, but Shawcross advised that if Belcher resigned his seat in parliament it would not be in the interests of justice to proceed.

Belcher resigned his seat in parliament just before the debate on the Lynskey report on 3 February 1949. He made a dignified resignation speech, reaffirming his belief in a business-friendly form of socialism and condemning the antisemitism that had flared up during the scandal, but he was despondent about the consequences of his mistakes, and blamed himself for damaging the labour movement. He returned to his job at the Smithfield depot. His health continued to deteriorate during the 1950s, although he found some consolation in Labour's election victory a few days before he died, on 26 October 1964, at Chase Farm Hospital in Enfield. Belcher was a bright, idealistic, working-class socialist, who was harshly treated for his naïve attempts to forge a good relationship with business and became a martyr to the puritanical standards of conduct in public life in the austere Attlee era.

LEWIS BASTON

Sources J. Belcher, 'How I, John Belcher, rose and fell', *Sunday Express* (6 Feb 1949) · J. Belcher, 'John Belcher's tribute to my wife, a friend in sunshine and sorrow', *Sunday Express* (13 Feb 1949) · J. Belcher, 'What happens when a man becomes a minister of the crown', *Sunday Express* (20 Feb 1949) · J. Belcher, 'I walk into the spider's web', *Sunday Express* (27 Feb 1949) · J. Belcher, 'After the tribunal, hope for the future', *Sunday Express* (6 March 1949) · C. Attlee, corresp. with attorney-general, lord chancellor, and lord president (on the Lynskey tribunal and police investigation), PRO, PREM 8/1035 · C. Attlee, corresp. with president of the Board of Trade (on John Belcher), PRO, CAB 127/153 · Metropolitan Police interviews and investigation (on Board of Trade corruption allegations), PRO, MEPO 3/3055 · private information (2004) [James Cross, Barbara Castle, Jill Mumford] · L. Baston, *Sleaze: the state of Britain* (2000) · H. Rhodes, *The Lynskey tribunal* (1949) · W. March, *The story of the Lynskey tribunal* (1949) · H. Shawcross, *Life sentence* (1995) · S. Wade Baron, *The contact man: the story of Sidney Stanley and the Lynskey tribunal* (1966) · J. Gross, 'The Lynskey tribunal', *Age of austerity*, ed. M. Sissons and P. French (1963), 255–75 · *CGPLA Eng. & Wales* (1965) · b. cert. · m. cert. · d. cert.

Archives FILM BFI NFTVA, news footage · IWM FVA, actuality footage

Wealth at death £813: administration, 5 April 1965, *CGPLA Eng. & Wales*

Belcher, Jonathan (1682–1757), merchant and colonial governor, was born on 8 January 1682 in Cambridge, Massachusetts, the fifth of seven children of Andrew Belcher (1648–1717), merchant and politician, and his wife, Sarah (1651–1689), the daughter of Jonathan Gilbert, Connecticut merchant and politician.

Following his father's example Belcher scrambled towards the top of Massachusetts society. While boasting that his ancestors had come in the great puritan migrations of the 1630s, Belcher could not forget that his father had pulled himself up from innkeeper to merchant prince. So that he might realize his father's ambitions Belcher was enrolled in Harvard College from where he graduated BA in 1699 and MA in 1702. His father arranged his marriage, on 8 January 1706, to Mary Partridge (1685–1736), the daughter of New Hampshire's former lieutenant-governor.

Expected to learn the family business, Belcher was sent to Europe, in 1704 and 1708, to establish connections in the commercial community, to cultivate patrons, to acquire the manners of an English gentleman, and to visit the court at Hanover where he met his future king. Together, father and son turned their political connections into profitable government contracts to supply provincial and British forces during the New England campaigns of the War of the Spanish Succession. On Queen Anne's death the Massachusetts executive fell vacant, rival politicians struggled to control the succession, and Belcher sped to London where he manipulated court connections to obtain the appointment of Samuel Shute to the governorship.

The death of his father in 1717 gave Belcher sole control of the family's business. The next year he was elected to the governor's council. His expectations that with Shute's appointment he would enjoy commanding influence turned to disappointment as the colony's house of representatives mounted an unrelenting opposition to the administration and its principal architect. When Shute left in defeat in 1722, Belcher was struggling, often unsuccessfully, to retain his council seat. In desperation he abandoned old allies and joined former enemies in the legislature. When Governor William Burnet arrived in 1727 with the king's instruction to secure a permanent governor's salary from the legislature, the representatives chose Belcher to represent their objections before the London government. While arguing that a permanent fund freed the executive from legislative scrutiny, Belcher learned that Burnet had died and immediately applied for the vacancy. Aided by patrons at court, business associates, and allies among leading protestant dissenters, he won commissions as governor of both Massachusetts and New Hampshire.

As governor, Belcher struggled to reconcile the tensions between cosmopolitan London and provincial New England. Although he had risen to the pinnacle of Massachusetts society by emulating London fashion, by cultivating his patrons and allies in court and parliament, and finally by holding the king's commissions, he identified with

Jonathan Belcher (1682–1757), by John Faber junior, 1734 (after Richard Philips)

Massachusetts's puritan heritage. He had won his appointment on the promise that, as a native, he could resolve the conflict between royal authority and the legislature. His tenure depended on acquiring a permanent salary, wresting control of Treasury appropriations from the legislature, checking the issuance of paper money, and promoting the welfare of the Church of England. He courted opinion, employed his patronage powers (sometimes ruthlessly), made alliances and then broke them, and deliberately deceived. Simultaneously he manipulated London politics by recruiting patrons and allies to his defence and by deception. After five years he had achieved peace by conceding the salary to the legislature and convincing his superiors that their principles had not been forsaken, by wringing control of Treasury funds from the legislature, by avoiding a currency controversy, and by feigning support for the Church of England interest in New England while maintaining the Congregational establishment.

Belcher's eleven-year tenure testifies to his political skills. Yet he was creating a determined opposition, at first located in New Hampshire. He recklessly antagonized the powerful Wentworth family and its allies, who joined with a small band of disgruntled politicians and placeseekers in Boston. With well-placed allies and patrons in England, Belcher was able to deflect this attack until the decade's end, when London merchants grew impatient with his inability to check Massachusetts's inflation and Sir Robert Walpole's government was collapsing. In 1741 Belcher was replaced by William Shirley.

Alone (his wife had died in 1736 and his three adult children had left home), Belcher yearned for office and in 1743 returned to London, hoping to regain the Massachusetts government. After three frustrating years, however, he settled for appointment as governor of New Jersey.

Belcher came to New Jersey in 1747, homesick for his native Massachusetts and disappointed in his position. In 1748 he married Louisa Teale (1699–1778), a wealthy Quaker widow, whom he had courted in London. He elected to avoid political entanglements whenever possible, and settled on his Burlington estate, World's End (Jonathan Belcher letter-books, 8.207). However, Belcher arrived in New Jersey during difficult times. The proprietor-dominated governor's council was pitted against the elected assembly, fighting especially over credit controls and land. Disagreements over proprietary land rights, which included the issues of land tenure and taxation, resulted in riots in the early years of Belcher's governorship. Deadlock in the legislature resulted in its inability to pass a budget for two years, and Belcher, who was viewed with the suspicion of an outsider, did not receive his salary during this period.

Embittered by his last visit to London and suffering from a 'Paralytic disorder' (Jonathan Belcher letter-books, 9.448), Belcher gave perfunctory attention to the duties of imperial governance. He hoped that by avoiding partisan politics, divisions over the proprietary interest could be reconciled. While tempers seemed to calm, the fundamental issues remained, with the proprietors in the council pressing the assembly for an invigorated militia to quell the riots and their opponents proposing amnesty. Later the two parties disagreed on a tax bill with the assembly refusing to allow lower assessments on proprietors' unimproved lands. The treasury was drained empty, and the governor clashed first with the council and then with the assembly in a desperate, but ineffective, effort to break the deadlock. Eventually New Jersey's leaders came to a compromise on tax policy. Slowly the rioting seemed to diminish. But whatever peace was achieved, it was principally the accomplishment of local politicians and not the governor.

Belcher found fulfilment as champion of evangelical reform. A long-time friend of George Whitefield and Jonathan Edwards, Belcher embraced evangelical proposals to reform the 'wilds' (Jonathan Belcher letter-books, 8.43) of New Jersey, including plans to build a college at Princeton. He granted a charter to the college, named himself to the board of trustees, enlisted crucial financial and political support, and donated his library. In recognition of his patronage the trustees proposed to name the first building Belcher Hall, an honour which he declined.

In 1751 Belcher moved to Elizabethtown, New Jersey, an evangelical Presbyterian enclave. The only public issue that roused his interest was the war with France. He prodded reluctant assemblymen relentlessly to support this crusade to destroy French Catholic Canada. In 1757 he prevailed upon the lawmakers to raise 500 troops but only after the most urgent appeals. He died soon after, on 31 August 1757. He was buried in Cambridge, Massachusetts.

MICHAEL C. BATINSKI

Sources M. C. Batinski, *Jonathan Belcher, colonial governor* (1996) · C. K. Shipton, *Sibley's Harvard graduates: biographical sketches of graduates of Harvard University*, 17 vols. (1873–1975), vol. 4 · J. Belcher, letter-books, Mass. Hist. Soc. · J. Belcher, 'A journal of my intended voyage, and journey to Holland, Hanover, etc.', [1704], Mass. Hist. Soc. · New Hampshire Historical Society, Concord, Jonathan Belcher papers · misc. MSS collections, Princeton University Library, New Jersey · L. Cong., manuscript division, Waldron–Belcher MSS · New Hampshire Historical Society, Concord, Richard Waldron papers · W. H. Whitmore, 'Notes on the Belcher family', *New England Historical and Genealogical Register*, 27 (1873), 239–45 · J. G. Bartlett, 'The Belcher families in New England', *New England Historical and Genealogical Register*, 60 (1906), 125–36, 243–56, 358–64 · G. K. Hall, ed., *Index of obituaries in Boston newspapers, 1704–1800* (1968)

Archives Mass. Hist. Soc., 'A journal of my intended voyage, and journey to Holland, Hanover, etc.'; letter-books · Mass. Hist. Soc., papers · New Hampshire Historical Society, Concord, papers · New Jersey Historical Society, Newark, corresp. and papers · Princeton University, New Jersey, MSS collections, MSS | L. Cong., letters to Richard Waldron · LPL, letters to Edmund Gibson · New Hampshire Historical Society, Concord, Richard Waldron papers · NYPL, George Bancroft transcripts, 'Belcher the apostate'

Likenesses F. Lippold, portrait, 1729, Mass. Hist. Soc.; repro. in Shipton, *Biographical sketches* · J. Faber junior, mezzotint, 1734 (after R. Philips), AM Oxf. [*see illus.*] · N. Emmons, portrait, American Arts Association, New York; repro. in Shipton, *Biographical sketches*

Wealth at death substantial: wills, archives, New Jersey State Library, Lib F, 456–9

Belcher, Mary Anne [Marian] (1849–1898), headmistress, was born at Great Faringdon, Berkshire, on 12 March 1849, the daughter of Thomas Belcher, a grocer, and his wife, Mary Anne, formerly Saunders. The Revd Thomas Hayes Belcher, principal of Brighton College, was her elder brother. She was educated at the school of Eliza Beale, sister to Dorothea Beale, at Barnes, Surrey. Her career as a teacher began in 1871 when, at the age of twenty-one, she went to Cheltenham Ladies' College, where Dorothea Beale had been headmistress since 1854. There began a lifelong professional association which was to develop into an important and deep friendship.

Marian Belcher's move to Cheltenham, where she taught from 1871 to 1883, becoming vice-principal in 1877, enabled her to take the general examination of the University of London (the London BA was not opened to women until 1878). Dorothea Beale sought to train, mould, and discipline her young staff to follow her own model of personal religious life and public duty. She encouraged her assistant mistresses to move to other schools, often as headmistresses (by 1899 Cheltenham had produced forty). Central to her philosophy was the principle of the woman teacher as moral and religious preceptor, and by 1900 there was a recognized Cheltenham 'type' among girls' schools.

Marian Belcher became deeply committed to these principles. Her most abiding characteristic was her religious devotion to duty. She saw her work as an extension of her faith, carrying her religious belief into her teaching in scripture, literature, and history, and her ideas about duty into her school organization and her guidance to pupils about their adult lives and purpose. She was a high-church Anglican, who prepared pupils for confirmation and insisted that public duty came before private affairs.

In 1883 Marian Belcher was appointed headmistress of Bedford high school, the first headmistress, Ada McDowall, having died suddenly a few months after the school opened in May 1882. The high school was one of two girls' schools provided for in the 1873 scheme for the Harpur Trust. During her fifteen years as head, Marian Belcher shaped the school—its ethos, curriculum, and organization—leaving a legacy lasting well into the twentieth century. By 1898 there were more than 600 pupils at the school, in a town well endowed with girls' schools.

During these years Marian Belcher developed for the school a broad philosophy of girls' education, embracing both academic excellence, as represented in examination successes, and a highly developed sense of public duty. These were achieved in a context where perceptions about social distinctions and the eligibility of girls from particular social backgrounds made entry to schools, especially girls' schools, as much dependent upon social class as academic ability or the ability of a parent to pay the school fees.

Like many girls' schools of the day Bedford high school was organized into a long morning, from 9.25 a.m. to 1.15 p.m., and mistresses were available to supervise lesson preparation (according to a timetable) from 2.30 p.m. to 4 p.m. Under the scheme for the Harpur Trust schools the headmistress had full responsibility for academic matters, although the Harpur Trust governors had powers to appoint internal examiners. From its inception Bedford high school included in the curriculum religious knowledge, English subjects, arithmetic, mathematics, French, German, Latin, history, geography, botany, drill, and, by 1886, general science, including elementary science. A cookery room, fitted out by the governors in 1882, was never put to use, and the omission of 'Domestic Economy and the Laws of Health' (which had been included in the 1873 scheme) reflected Marian Belcher's conviction that such matters were best left to home instruction, being inappropriate for school.

By 1886 all the academic subjects were being offered for public examination, most often either the Cambridge or the Oxford local examinations. Marian Belcher's commitment to publicly acknowledged academic standards was shared by most other headmistresses of 'first-grade' schools of the day. It reflected a goal of providing a demonstrably first-class education, but went hand in hand with a determination to use that education for both public and private service.

Marian Belcher's obituarist spoke of her 'rare combination of practical wisdom with a childlike singleness of moral aim' (The Guardian, 28 Dec 1898, 2022), and photographs show her 'beaming kindness and friendliness' (Godber and Hutchins, 410). At Cheltenham she had joined other ladies' college mistresses in daily worship at local churches. In Bedford she was closely associated with St Paul's Church, near the school. She did not marry, but her Bedford household included nieces and nephews, one of whom, Ethel Belcher, attended Bedford high school and subsequently became classics and games mistress there, ending her career as headmistress of James Allen's Girls' School at Dulwich. In 1892 Marian Belcher had been instrumental in helping to found a guild of old girls at Bedford which encouraged former pupils of the school to carry the principles and duties imbued from school life into the wider world. This characterized her own philosophy, which had been nurtured at Cheltenham Ladies' College, alongside Dorothea Beale, developed in her own school at Bedford, and exemplified in her life. Marian Belcher died on 15 December 1898, after a painful illness, at her home, 9 Lansdown Road, Bedford.

FELICITY HUNT

Sources J. Godber and I. Hutchins, eds., A century of challenge: Bedford high school, 1882 to 1982 (privately printed, Bedford, 1982) • K. M. Westaway, ed., A history of Bedford high school (1932) • E. Raikes, Dorothea Beale of Cheltenham (1909) • F. C. Steadman, In the days of Miss Beale: a study of her work and influence (1931) • D. Beale, L. H. M. Soulsby, and J. F. Dove, Work and play in girls' schools (1898) • Bedford High School archives • The Guardian (28 Dec 1898), 2022 • b. cert. • d. cert. • will
Archives Bedford High School, archives, letters, and MS notes
Likenesses photograph, repro. in Godber and Hutchins, eds., A century of challenge
Wealth at death £13,629 9s. 8d.: resworn probate, 18 Feb 1899, CGPLA Eng. & Wales

Belcher, Thomas (1783–1854). *See under* Belcher, James (1781–1811).

Belchiam, Thomas (1505/6–1534?), Observant Franciscan friar and Catholic martyr, is recorded only in the Franciscan martyrology of Thomas Bourchier, first published at Paris in 1582, and in works derived from it. The context for the events Bourchier relates is entirely plausible. Belchiam was an Observant friar at Greenwich, a house founded by Edward IV and subsequently supported by Henry VII and the young Henry VIII, and also by Katherine of Aragon, who may have been married to Henry in its church. As Henry's pursuit of his divorce intensified, the Greenwich friars stood firmly by the queen and traditional religion—when the king's commissioners visited Greenwich on 15 June 1534 they found the inmates resolved 'to live and die in the observance of St Francis' religion' (LP Henry VIII, 7, no. 841). On 17 June two cartloads of friars were reported to have been taken to the Tower, and the Greenwich convent was probably one of the houses whose inmates were expelled about 11 August.

Bourchier (who may himself have been a friar at Greenwich during the house's brief revival under Mary, and so able to tap authentic tradition for his narrative) places Belchiam's death in 1537, but it is more likely to have taken place at the time of the convent's suppression. He tells how Belchiam, whom he describes as a priest and preacher, on 3 August enlisted in the opposition to the king's proceedings, declaring Henry to be a heretic and producing a 'book'—perhaps a written-out sermon—on the text 'Behold, they that wear soft clothing are in kings' houses' (Matthew, 11: 8). In it he attacked the court as a sink of iniquity, rebuked the clergy for avarice, and denounced the bishops as time-servers who failed in their duty to speak the truth to the king. For his own plain-speaking Belchiam was starved to death in Newgate, where he probably died on 30 August 1534, aged twenty-eight. In an account coloured by hagiographical convention, Bourchier tells how as he died, having continued in prayer throughout the previous night, Belchiam was reading Psalm 31 in his breviary—'In thee O Lord have I put my trust, let me never be put to confusion'—while the moment of his passing was marked by an earth tremor. His body was allowed burial, while a copy of his 'book' was taken to the king, who was moved to tears by it, though he had it burnt all the same. Another copy had been left at Greenwich and was carefully preserved thereafter, according to Bourchier, who expressed the hope of publishing it, if his superiors approved. It never appeared, however, and is not known to have survived.

HENRY SUMMERSON

Sources T. Bourchier, *Historia ecclesiastica de martyrio fratrum ordinis divi Francisci* (1582), 17–24 · A. Parkinson, *Collectanea Anglo-Minoritica* (1726), 240–41 · Angelus à Sancto Francisco [R. Mason], *Certamen seraphicum provinciae Angliae pro sancta Dei ecclesia* (1649), 345–6 · A. R. Martin, 'The Grey Friars of Greenwich', *Archaeological Journal*, 80 (1923), 81–114 · *VCH Kent*, 2.194–8 · D. Knowles [M. C. Knowles], *The religious orders in England*, 3 (1959) · *LP Henry VIII*, vol. 7

Belchier, Dabridgcourt (*bap.* 1581, *d.* 1621), playwright, was baptized on 17 September 1581 at Solihull, Warwickshire, the eldest of five sons and three daughters of William Belchier (*c.*1557–1609), landowner and antiquary, of Guilsborough, Northamptonshire, and Christian Dabridgecourt, daughter of Thomas Dabridgecourt of Longdon Hall in the parish of Solihull. Together with his younger brother John he matriculated as a fellow-commoner at Corpus Christi College, Cambridge, on 2 March 1598, to which he later presented a silver cup bearing his coat of arms. After eight terms he migrated to Christ Church, Oxford, where he received his BA on 8 February 1601. He went on to the Middle Temple, where he was admitted on 29 June 1601, to share a chamber with Henry Martyn. Belchier remained in the chamber until 2 May 1605. Belchier married Elizabeth Fisher, daughter and coheir of Richard Fisher of Warwick, at Solihull on 11 March 1599. The baptismal records of their five sons and four daughters, born between 1603 and 1615, show the family dividing their time between Solihull and Guilsborough, the manor of which belonged to Belchier. Other records attest to Belchier's continuing presence at Guilsborough and, in particular, to his role in setting up the free school there.

At some point Belchier moved to Utrecht, from where, on 14 November 1617, he wrote the 'Preface' to his one surviving work, *Hans Beer-Pot, his Invisible Comedy of See me and See me not*. It is dedicated to Sir John Ogle, governor of that town. *Hans Beer-Pot* was printed in 1618. It is 'a plain Dialogue or conference between so many persons' (*Hans Beer-*

Pot, sig. A3r), composed, the reader is told, in sixteen days. The nine characters include Cornelius Hammants, a Dutchman, and his eponymous servant; English soldiers including Sergeant Goodfellow; and Abnidaraes Quixot, a tawny Moor. Together they engage in a series of songs and conversations on subjects such as the worth of poetry, the relative merits of infantry and cavalry, and the importance of getting very drunk. The work used to be thought a translation of an unknown Dutch play, but this seems unlikely, given the Britishness of the references; rather, it seems to be designed for amateur performance in front of an audience of soldiers. Whatever the nature of Belchier's connection with Utrecht it was apparently there that he died in 1621. His son William inherited the family estate at Guilsborough.   MATTHEW STEGGLE

Sources E. L. Renton and E. L. Renton, eds., *Records of Guilsborough, Nortoft and Hallowell, Northamptonshire* (1929) · G. E. Bentley, *The Jacobean and Caroline stage*, 7 vols. (1941–68) · R. Masters, *The history of the College of Corpus Christi and the B. Virgin Mary ... in the University of Cambridge* (1753) · W. G. F. A. Van Sorgen, *De Toneelkunst te Utrecht en de Utrechtse Schouwburg* (1885)
Wealth at death held at least two manors: Renton and Renton, eds., *Records of Guilsborough*

Belchier, John (*bap.* 1706, *d.* 1785), surgeon, the son of James Belchier, innkeeper and bailiff of Kingston, was born at Kingston, Surrey, and was baptized there on 5 March 1706. He entered Eton College as a king's scholar in 1716. On leaving school he was apprenticed to William Cheselden, head surgeon at St Thomas's Hospital, London. By perseverance Belchier became eminent in his profession, and in 1736 he was appointed surgeon to Guy's Hospital. In 1732 he was elected a fellow of the Royal Society, and his name appears on the list of the council from 1769 to 1772. He contributed some papers to the society's *Philosophical Transactions*. On Belchier's retirement as surgeon of Guy's Hospital he was elected one of its governors, and also a governor of St Thomas's Hospital. He had an exaggerated reverence for the name of Guy, saying 'that no other man would have sacrificed £150,000 for the benefit of his fellow-creatures'.

In the *Gentleman's Magazine* for 1743 is the following story:

One Stephen Wright, who, as a patient, came to Mr. Belchier, a surgeon, in Sun Court, being alone with him in the room clapt a pistol to his breast, demanding his money. Mr. Belchier offered him two guineas, which he refused; but, accepting of six guineas and a gold watch, as he was putting them in his pocket Mr. Belchier took the opportunity to seize upon him, and, after a struggle, secured him. (*GM*, 1st ser., 13, 1743, 50)

A stout but active man, Belchier died suddenly in Sun Court, Threadneedle Street, on 6 February 1785. His manservant had attempted to raise his master but was told 'No John—I am dying. Fetch me a pillow; I may as well die here as anywhere else' (Wilks and Bettany, 127). He was buried in the founder's vault in the chapel attached to Guy's Hospital.   P. B. AUSTIN, *rev.* MICHAEL BEVAN

Sources *GM*, 1st ser., 55 (1785), 156 · *GM*, 1st ser., 13 (1743), 50 · 'Roubiliac, Cheselden, and Belchier', *BMJ* (31 Dec 1931), 820 · R. A. Austen-Leigh, ed., *The Eton College register, 1698–1752* (1927) · S. C.

Lawrence, *Charitable knowledge: hospital pupils and practitioners in eighteenth-century London* (1996) • S. Wilks and G. T. Bettany, *A biographical history of Guy's Hospital* (1892)
Likenesses attrib. O. Humphrey, oils, RCS Eng. • attrib. L. F. Roubiliac, terracotta bust, RCS Eng. • A. Walker, engraving (after O. Humphrey), Wellcome L.

Beldam, Asplan (1841–1912), marine engineer, was born in Bluntisham, Huntingdonshire, on 5 October 1841, one of a family of eleven children of William Beldam and his wife, Mary Peat. After serving an apprenticeship with Kitson, Thompson, and Hewitson, locomotive engineers in Leeds, he turned to marine engineering and from 1864 to 1869 gained experience with several shipbuilding firms on the Thames. From 1870 to 1873 he was outside manager at G. Forrester & Co.'s Vauxhall foundry, Liverpool, where he had charge of repairs to vessels and the fitting out of new ships.

By the time Beldam left Liverpool in 1873 he had been appointed consulting and superintending engineer to a number of shipping companies, including the Flower Line, the Castle Line, and the Eastern Telegraph Company. One particularly notable vessel which he designed was the *Stirling Castle*, famed for her speed, for example, when in 1882 she brought home a cargo of 6000 tons of China tea from Hangchow (Hangzhou) in twenty-eight days, beating the previous best time by more than a week.

From 1873 to 1876 Beldam acted as marine superintendent with Hargrove, Fergusson, and Jackson, for whom he constructed both ships and machinery, striving always to achieve greater power, efficiency, and economy. During this time he developed and patented several new types of high-pressure steam boiler as well as making improvements to steam-tight glands, valves for pumps, and anti-clinkering fire bars.

By 1876 the growing interest in his metallic asbestos packing encouraged Beldam to patent it and found the Beldam Packing and Rubber Company, which later became Beldam Crossley. At the same time he set up in practice as a consulting engineer and naval architect in London, where he remained until his death. Beldam took a leading part in the formation of the Institute of Marine Engineers and was elected the first president in 1889. He continued to take a very active interest in its affairs, and he was also a member of the institutions of Mechanical Engineers and Naval Architects and of the London chamber of commerce. His advice and opinion as an arbitrator were frequently sought, his fair and impartial judgement being held in high esteem.

Beldam married Elizabeth Leonie Knowles, with whom he had eleven children; their two sons both went to Cambridge University before entering the family business, of which they later became directors. He died suddenly at his residence, Torrens House, North Common Road, Ealing Common, London, on 16 December 1912.

RONALD M. BIRSE, *rev.*

Sources *Transactions of the Institute of Marine Engineers*, 24 (1912–13), xvii • *Engineering* (20 Dec 1912), 842 • private information (1993) • d. cert.
Wealth at death £96,091 0s. 9d.: probate, 13 Feb 1913, *CGPLA Eng. & Wales*

Belden, Albert David (1883–1964), Congregational minister, was born on 17 February 1883 at 109 Great Dover Street, London, the son of William Belden (*fl.* 1850–1914), boot tree and last manufacturer, and his wife, Hester Evans. He was educated at Wilson's Grammar School, Camberwell, before entering business at the age of fourteen in 1897. In 1902 he entered New College, London, to train for the Congregational ministry and he later gained the BD degree of London University. His first pastorate was at South Bar Congregational Church in Banbury from 1908 until 1912. Belden married Doris Hunter Richman (d. 1961) in 1909, and they had a son. In 1912 he was called to be the first minister of the newly founded Crowstone Congregational Church, Westcliff-on-Sea, which soon became one of the largest and strongest free churches in the country. In 1927 he moved to become superintendent minister of Whitefield's Central Mission in Tottenham Court Road, London, following in the earlier footsteps of Silvester Horne. Here he exercised a great social and preaching ministry which was influential throughout and beyond his own denomination.

Small in stature, Belden was a powerful and uncompromising evangelical preacher who was not afraid to support unpopular causes. He was proud to preach from a pulpit named after George Whitefield, whom he regarded as 'the raging flame' of the evangelical revival. In his book *George Whitefield the Awakener: a Modern Study of the Evangelical Revival* (1930) he used the story of Whitefield to challenge the churches to a new understanding of the relation between politics and the churches. Belden was a socialist, and once wrote that 'voluntary Christian communism is the ultimate economic goal of the Christian Spirit' (*Congregational Quarterly*, 1926, 344). His ecumenical outlook was combined with a strong belief in the importance of the local church. He described the four emphases of his ministry at Whitefield's as an appeal to youth, the preaching of the social gospel, opposition to violence, and the application of psychological insights to pastoral ministry. During this ministry he was awarded an honorary DD by Ursinus College, Pennsylvania.

In March 1939 Belden resigned from Whitefield's to devote his time to writing and political activism. He was a lifelong pacifist, an early member of the Fellowship of Reconciliation, and founder director of the Pax Christi League. Not long before the outbreak of war he had represented the British peace societies in a lecture tour of the United States. In 1942 he published *Pax Christi: a New Policy for Christendom Today*, in which he attempted to formulate a policy for overcoming war altogether. He was an executive member of the Labour Peace Fellowship, and during the war was adopted as prospective parliamentary candidate for Lowestoft, though when the general election came in 1945 he was not elected.

In 1948 Belden accepted the role of honorary superintendent of the Pilgrim Fathers' Memorial Church in south London, whose Sunday school he had attended as a boy. The church had been bombed during the war and was then meeting in temporary premises. Belden was proud to see its new building opened by the American ambassador in 1958.

Belden was a great traveller, especially on preaching tours to the American continent, and was well known in Chicago. He was a prolific and effective writer. For twenty-five years he contributed a regular weekly column to the *Manchester Evening News*, which stimulated more correspondence to that newspaper than the writing of any other contributor. Four volumes of these articles were published. In addition he contributed articles to the journal of the Philosophical Society, of which he was chairman, and to the *Congregational Quarterly*. He wrote a number of religious books for both adults and children, including *Prison Church and Pilgrim Ship* (1958) and *Pilgrims of the Impossible* (1961). He was also concerned about animal welfare, and was elected a vice-president of the National Anti-Vivisection Society.

In 1962 Belden married Cecily Maud Glenister, who survived him. He died at his Putney home, 1 Ulva Road, on 14 December 1964. ELAINE KAYE

Sources *Congregational Year Book* (1965–6) · *British Weekly* (31 Dec 1964) · *WWW, 1961–70* · 'A. D. Belden's farewell to Whitefields', *Christian World* (30 March 1939) · M. Caedel, *Pacifism in Britain, 1914–1945: the defining of a faith* (1980) · J. Walsh, *Valiant for peace* (1991) · Whitefield's Central Mission, manual and report, 1927, BL · CGPLA Eng. & Wales (1965) · b. cert. · d. cert.
Likenesses photograph, repro. in *British Weekly*, 3
Wealth at death £1882: probate, 28 Jan 1965, CGPLA Eng. & Wales

Beldham, William (1766–1862). *See under* Hambledon cricket club (*act. c.*1750–*c.*1796).

Beler, Sir Roger (*d.* 1326), justice, was the son of William and Amice Beler and the grandson of Roger Beler, sheriff of Lincolnshire in 1255–6. His family was of only local importance, but he achieved a significant social rise. Nothing is known about his training and early career. He successfully served Thomas, earl of Lancaster (*d.* 1322), and first came into public view in October 1318 when he acted as the earl's agent at the autumn parliament, securing pardons for his master and his adherents, including himself. In November 1318 he was granted the farm of Framelond hundred in Leicestershire for his services. In the following spring he became the earl's steward for Stapleford, also in Leicestershire, and other estates. However, his service was no longer exclusively given to Thomas of Lancaster. He also began to act for the king, as a justice, from December 1318 and continued in this capacity until the time of his death, mostly in commissions of oyer and terminer, sometimes to investigate the conduct of royal officials, and sometimes as justice of assize. His advance is reflected in private business deals from 1321 onwards, in which he appears as creditor for increasingly large sums, up to £300 in 1324.

Beler's economic prosperity was largely due to the opportunities created by the fall of Thomas of Lancaster. Already in June 1321, when Edward II pardoned him a significant debt, Beler had clearly abandoned the earl's cause (he was later branded traitor by the author of the *Flores historiarum*). For almost two months after Lancaster's death, between March and May 1322, he was in complete control of the earl's possessions in Staffordshire, Derbyshire, and Leicestershire. He also confiscated lands belonging to other rebels, and since he acted at first as auditor for other keepers his actions were hardly controlled. He wielded considerable power until July 1323, being in charge of prisoners suspected of supporting the earl's side, and having access to the revenues of numerous estates, some of which he handed over to Hugh Despenser the younger. His partisanship of the Despensers was rewarded. On 20 July 1322 he was appointed a baron of the exchequer, and on the following day he was named as his attorney by the younger Despenser. Both as baron of the exchequer and in his capacity as justice he favoured the Despensers and acted upon their orders. He soon gained a senior position in the exchequer, being appointed acting treasurer in August 1325. His project to reform the exchequer by creating two separate courts for northern and southern affairs gave him further prominence, but was not adopted on a permanent basis.

Already in 1317 Beler had begun to acquire lands additional to his original estate at Kirby in Leicestershire, but significant acquisitions began only in 1323. At the time of his death he held nine manors and other estates in six counties, the centre of his lands being in Leicestershire. Apart from his legal and administrative career he also made his mark as founder of the chantry chapel of St Peter at Kirby in 1316 (transformed into an Augustinian priory in 1359), which he provided with estates and advowsons and also organized as a religious institution. His murder, at Rearsby in Leicestershire on 19 January 1326, by members of the Zouche and Folville families, may have been the result of a private feud, but also had political overtones as an act of resistance against the Despenser regime. The suspects were vigorously prosecuted and their estates were confiscated, but most of them escaped to Wales or overseas. One of the first measures of the Mortimer government in January and February 1327 was to issue pardons for them. Beler and his wife, Alice, had two sons, Roger and Thomas. JENS RÖHRKASTEN

Sources L. Fox, 'Ministers' accounts of the honour of Leicester (1322 to 1324)', *Transactions of the Leicestershire Archaeological Society*, 19 (1936–7), 200–07 · N. Fryde, *The tyranny and fall of Edward II, 1321–1326* (1979), 80, 101, 152 · J. R. Maddicott, *Thomas of Lancaster, 1307–1322: a study in the reign of Edward II* (1970), 229 · E. L. G. Stones, 'The Folvilles of Ashby-Folville, Leicestershire, and their associates in crime', *TRHS*, 5th ser., 7 (1957), 117–36 · T. F. Tout, 'The Westminster Chronicle attributed to Robert of Reading', *EngHR*, 31 (1916), 450–64 · T. F. Tout, *The place of the reign of Edward II in English history: based upon the Ford lectures delivered in the University of Oxford in 1913*, rev. H. Johnstone, 2nd edn (1936), 200, 330, 333, 343 · *VCH Leicestershire*, 2.25–6 · *CIPM*, 6, no. 708 · Chancery records · *Chronicon Henrici Knighton, vel Cnitthon, monachi Leycestrensis*, ed. J. R. Lumby, 2 vols., Rolls Series, 92 (1889–95), vol. 1, pp. 432–3 · H. R. Luard, ed., *Flores historiarum*, 3 vols., Rolls Series, 95 (1890)
Wealth at death a substantial estate: *CIPM* 6, no. 708

Belet, Michael (*d.* 1201), justice and administrator, was the son of Hervey Belet, a landowner in Northamptonshire and Oxfordshire; the name of his mother is unknown, but he later endowed a lamp over her tomb in East Rudham Priory, Norfolk. In 1166 Robert Foliot's return to the inquest into feudal subtenancies stated that Michael Belet held four fees of him; these probably included Wroxton in Oxfordshire and lands in Lincolnshire. Belet was also hereditary royal butler, holding the manors of Sheen and Bagshot, both in Surrey, and in 1166 is recorded as transporting wine to the court at Woodstock. He is described as butler on the pipe rolls from 1172, and at the accession of Richard I paid £100 for confirmation in his office. But although he was quite frequently in attendance on the king—between 1175 and 1189 he witnessed about twenty of Henry II's charters, at least one of them in Normandy—Belet's principal importance was as a justice.

From 1176 Belet was a justice itinerant nearly every year for the rest of Henry II's reign, and in the 1180s also sat several times in the exchequer. Moreover he was sheriff of Worcestershire from Michaelmas 1175 to Easter 1185, and of Leicestershire and Warwickshire from Easter 1185 to Michaelmas 1189. He witnessed six of Richard I's charters in 1189, went on the Norfolk and Suffolk eyre of 1191, and sat in the bench between 1190 and 1192. An interval of apparent inactivity lasting for five years followed, but Belet resumed his work as a justice itinerant in 1197, and appears to have been on eyre in the south-west when he died, probably in the summer of 1201. His wife, Emma, daughter of John de Chesney, who had brought him the manor of East Rudham, Norfolk, survived him. They had three daughters and seven sons, the second of whom, Master Michael *Belet, followed his father into royal service.   JULIA BOORMAN

Sources Pipe rolls · VCH Oxfordshire, 9.175–6 · VCH Surrey, 3.376–7, 502, 541; 4.410 · J. H. Round, The king's serjeants and officers of state (1911) · J. H. Round, 'The origin of the Stewarts and their Chesney connection', The Genealogist, new ser., 18 (1901–2), 1–16 · D. M. Stenton, ed., Pleas before the king or his justices, 1198–1212, 3, SeldS, 83 (1967), appx 1 · J. C. Holt and R. Mortimer, eds., Acta of Henry II and Richard I (1986) · W. Farrer, Honors and knights' fees … from the eleventh to the fourteenth century, 3 (1925), 320–22 · L. F. Salzman, 'Sussex Domesday tenants, IV: the family of Chesney or Cheyney', Sussex Archaeological Collections, 65 (1924), 20–53 · Dugdale, Monasticon, new edn, 6.485–6 · H. Hall, ed., The Red Book of the Exchequer, 3 vols., Rolls Series, 99 (1896), vol. 1, p. 331 · H. C. M. Lyte and others, eds., Liber feodorum: the book of fees, 3 vols. (1920–31), 66, 70, 184, 1002, 1029, 1031, 1037, 1093–4 · Chancery records · R. V. Turner, 'Richard Barre and Michael Belet: two Angevin civil servants', Medieval Prosopography, 6 (1985), 25–48 · R. V. Turner, The English judiciary in the age of Glanvill and Bracton, c.1176–1239 (1985) · T. D. Hardy, ed., Rotuli de oblatis et finibus, RC (1835), 180 · J. M. Boorman, 'The sheriffs of Henry II and their role in civil litigation, 1154–89', PhD diss., U. Reading, 1989

Belet, Michael (d. in or before **1219**). See under Belet, Michael (d. in or before 1247).

Belet, Michael (d. in or before **1247**), royal servant, was the second son of Michael *Belet (d. 1201), the justice of Henry II's reign, and Emma de Chesney. An Oxfordshire man who was in royal service by 1198, Belet was styled 'master' by 1201, indicating a university training, very possibly at Oxford. In 1200 he was described as a clerk of the king's household, and in 1206 he undertook to pay £100 for the office of assistant royal butler, which went with the serjeanty he held in West Sheen, Surrey. He continued in royal service until 1208, when his promising career was

cut short, presumably as a result of the interdict. In any event, in 1211 he was charged with 500 marks as a fine for the king's benevolence. Despite his absence from the royal circle for at least three years, he was still able to muster an impressive list of the king's curiales in support of his fine. By this year his nephew of the same name had reached his majority, and Michael lost his serjeanty to him.

The younger **Michael Belet** (d. in or before 1219) was a son of Robert Belet (d. c.1205), Michael's younger brother. In November 1215 and July 1216 his lands were confiscated, presumably because he had joined the rebel cause, but on 16 April 1217 he regained some of them, which must have included the serjeanty at West Sheen, and on 2 July 1217 he received letters of safe conduct for his reconciliation with the new administration. By 1219 he was dead, and had been succeeded in his lands by his daughter Matilda (the child of his marriage to Alice), who was a ward of Wimund de Raleigh. As well as the serjeanty in West Sheen, Michael Belet held lands in Bagshot, Windlesham, and Hook, Surrey, and Eastwood, Essex. Confusion between Master Michael and his nephew makes it difficult to establish which of them held particular lands. However it seems clear that Master Michael Belet was a considerable landholder. He was rector of Hintlesham, Suffolk, from September 1200, the advowson of which his father had acquired from King Richard; he was rector of Sebergham, Cumberland, from May 1204; and he was rector of Wroxton, Oxfordshire, from about 1215. He inherited from his brother, John Belet (d. c.1204), land in Thorpe Belet, Northamptonshire, and a knight's fee in each of the vills of Syston, Aunsby, and Scott Willoughby, Lincolnshire, all held from the Ledet barony, and in September 1216 he received the confiscated lands of the rebel Wischard Ledet in Northamptonshire. He also held land in Norfolk, while with Walter de Verdun, the husband of his sister Annora, he owned land in Balscott, Oxfordshire. In Wroxton he held a knight's fee, inherited from John Belet, and here, between 1215 and 1222 (probably 1216 or 1217) he founded an Augustinian house for a prior and twelve canons, which evidently caused dissension within the family, as Walter de Verdun appears to have hoped to succeed to the property. Belet endowed the priory with his lands in Wroxton, in Syston, Lincolnshire, and in Thorpe Belet, Northamptonshire, and also with the chapel of Balscott, and the advowson of Syston and Aunsby.

Master Michael Belet appears again in royal service in January 1224, when he was given custody of the temporalities of the bishopric of Coventry, which he held until the appointment of the new bishop in May of that year. In February 1225 he was appointed a justice in Northamptonshire and in the following January he was appointed to audit the accounts for the fifteenth of 1225. After February 1226 little is known of his activities, and it may be supposed that he went into retirement. His final act in royal service was to officiate as assistant butler at the coronation of Eleanor of Provence in 1236, by right of his serjeanty in West Sheen, which he had clearly been able to reunite with the manor. By February 1247 he was dead. He was succeeded in West Sheen by Emma Oliver and Alice de Vautort, daughters and coheirs of John Belet.

S. D. CHURCH

Sources Dugdale, *Monasticon*, new edn · T. D. Hardy, ed., *Rotuli litterarum clausarum*, 2 vols., RC (1833–4) · T. D. Hardy, ed., *Rotuli litterarum patentium*, RC (1835) · *Calendar of the charter rolls*, 6 vols., PRO (1903–27), vols. 1–2 · T. D. Hardy, ed., *Rotuli chartarum in Turri Londinensi asservati*, RC, 36 (1837) · *Curia regis rolls preserved in the Public Record Office* (1922–), 1198–1232 · F. Palgrave, ed., *Rotuli curiae regis: rolls and records of the court held before the king's justiciars or justices*, 2 vols., RC, 27 (1835) · *Pipe rolls · CPR, 1216–47* · T. D. Hardy, ed., *Rotuli de oblatis et finibus*, RC (1835) · H. C. M. Lyte and others, eds., *Liber feodorum: the book of fees*, 3 vols. (1920–31) · C. W. Foster and K. Major, eds., *The registrum antiquissimum of the cathedral church of Lincoln*, 3, Lincoln RS, 29 (1935) · *VCH Oxfordshire*, vols. 2, 6 · W. P. W. Phillimore and others, eds., *Rotuli Hugonis de Welles, episcopi Lincolniensis*, 3 vols., CYS, 1, 3–4 (1907–9) · F. N. Davis, ed., *Rotuli Roberti Grosseteste, episcopi Lincolniensis*, CYS, 10 (1913) · J. H. Round, *The king's serjeants and officers of state* (1911) · Emden, *Oxf.*

Beleth, Jean (*fl.* 1135–1182), ecclesiastical writer, has sometimes been claimed as English on the strength of his seemingly English surname. Pits, the first to raise the possibility of his Englishness, none the less inclined towards defining him as French. Tanner was firm that his surname was English, but there can be little doubt that he was mistaken, just as Pits was wrong to ascribe to him a floruit in 1328. Beleth is recorded at Tiron in 1135, and is also known to have studied at Chartres under Gilbert de la Porrée, who was chancellor there from 1126 to 1137. He is later said to have taught theology at Paris, a suggestion borne out by his own passing reference to 'our Paris'. By 1182 he was at Amiens. It is not known when or where he died.

Beleth is principally known for his *Summa de ecclesiasticis officiis*, more usually known as *Rationale divinorum officiorum*, a full and detailed account of the liturgical practices of his day. It reports a number of the usages of the church of Chartres, but clearly circulated widely, in England as well as in France, a circumstance called in aid of claims made for its author's English origins. It was several times printed, first by Cornelius Laurimann at Antwerp in 1553; this edition was reprinted by Migne in 1855. A full critical edition was published in 1976. Beleth also wrote a treatise on the seven deadly sins and their opposing virtues, a tract on difficult passages in the Old and New testaments, a commentary on Peter Lombard's *Sentences*, and other theological works; none of these has been published.

HENRY SUMMERSON

Sources *Johannis Beleth Summa de ecclesiasticis officiis*, ed. H. Douteil, 2 vols. (Turnhout, 1976) · P. Calendini, 'Jean Beleth', *Dictionnaire d'histoire et de géographie ecclésiastiques*, ed. A. Baudrillart and others, 7 (Paris, 1934), 517–18 · F. Cabrol, 'Jean Beleth', *Dictionnaire d'archéologie chrétienne et de liturgie*, 2 (1910), cols. 649–50 · J. Pits, *Relationum historicarum de rebus Anglicis*, ed. [W. Bishop] (Paris, 1619), 869 · Tanner, *Bibl. Brit.-Hib.*, 93

Belfast. For this title name *see* Chichester, Frederick Richard, earl of Belfast (1827–1853).

Belford, William (1709–1780), army officer, was born in 1709, possibly the son of William and Mary Belford baptized at St Paul's, Covent Garden, London, on 21 January 1709. He entered the Royal Regiment of Artillery as a cadet matross in a company on 1 February 1726. Apparently showing special aptitude, he was commissioned fireworker on 2 November 1729, second lieutenant on 1 December 1737, first lieutenant on 1 April 1740, and captain lieutenant on 5 February 1741, in which year he served at Cartagena.

Having been promoted captain on 1 February 1742, Belford served in Flanders until 1745 and was present at Dettingen. He was promoted brevet major in the army for his services, and commanded the artillery at Fontenoy. He next commanded the artillery, to great effect, at Culloden in 1746 and in consequence was promoted brevet lieutenant-colonel in the army. He achieved the same rank in the regiment on 16 February 1749, having again commanded the artillery in Flanders from 1746 to 1748. He succeeded Albert Borgard as colonel of the regiment on 8 March 1751 and as commandant of the Woolwich garrison until 1757, the year in which, on the regiment's expansion, he became colonel commandant of the 1st battalion. He was promoted major-general on 25 January 1758, lieutenant-general on 17 December 1760, and general on 29 August 1777, remaining throughout at Woolwich in command of The Warren.

Belford joined the Royal regiment early in its formal existence. He was highly experienced, having served in a bomb vessel in 1738 and in the company of miners in 1740 in addition to his employment as a field gunner. During his time in Flanders in 1746, as a strict disciplinarian, he set about the very necessary work of strengthening the orderliness of his command and introduced small-arms training. His insistence on strict order and on training in the use of infantry weapons continued when he moved to Woolwich as colonel, and the excellent results became obvious. He was very strong in defence of the regiment, insisting on the equality of its officers with those of the army; this was mostly achieved in 1751. The duke of Cumberland, under whom he served in Flanders and Scotland, was probably a powerful ally.

Belford was made assistant and clerk of the Royal Academy (which became the Royal Military Academy in 1764) in 1752 to impose discipline there, but met with only partial success when dealing with high-spirited and wholly undisciplined schoolboys. His time at The Warren at Woolwich (which became the Royal Arsenal in 1805) saw many changes. He retained command of the 1st battalion for the rest of his life. His experience, gained in Flanders, led Muller, in his 1757 edition of his *A Treatise of Artillery*, to include an entry 'Order of Colonel Belford's march of the artillery', as a guide for officers to follow when organizing a train of artillery for movement.

In addition to his administrative achievements, Belford presided over the introduction of screw—as opposed to quoin—elevation for the guns in Flanders in 1747 and designed, in later years, a light 6-pounder which served briefly as the 1st horse artillery equipment in the 1790s. In 1748 he recruited a Hanoverian fifer, Johan Ulrich, to teach the fifers of the regiment, an early step in the creation of the Royal Artillery band. The Gordon riots saw a major threat to The Warren, but Belford established effective defences with some thirty guns, which provided a satisfactory deterrent. It is reported by the *Gentleman's Magazine* that, as a result of his energetic labours on this occasion, Belford fell ill, and he died at his residence at 4 Dial Square, The Warren, on 1 July 1780. He left extensive property to his two sons, Gustavus and William (*b.* 1765), whose commissions in the army he had purchased. He also made generous provision for Mrs Mary Barber, the mother of William. There is no evidence that he was ever married.　　　H. M. STEPHENS, rev. P. G. W. ANNIS

Sources J. Kane, *List of officers of the royal regiment of artillery from the year 1716 to the year 1899*, rev. W. H. Askwith, 4th edn (1900) · F. Duncan, ed., *History of the royal regiment of artillery*, 2nd edn, 1 (1874) · O. F. G. Hogg, *The Royal Arsenal: its background, origin, and subsequent history*, 1 (1963) · H. L. Geary, ed., *The Forbes Macbean correspondence* (1902) · 'Memoirs of the royal regiment of artillery by Colonel Forbes Macbean, 1743–1779', *Minutes of the Proceedings of the Royal Artillery Institution*, 4 (1865), 259–70 · *GM*, 1st ser., 50 (1780), 347 · W. D. Jones, *Records of the Royal Military Academy (1741–1840)* (1851) · will, PRO, PROB 11/1068 · J. Muller, *A treatise of artillery* (1757) · *IGI* · W. T. Vincent, *The records of the Woolwich district*, 2 vols. [1888–90] · J. A. Browne, *England's artillerymen* (1865) · *Army List* (1780–81) · *DNB* · private information (2004) [A. B. Caruana]
Archives Royal Artillery Institution, Woolwich, London, corresp. with Forbes Macbean, MD 910

Belfour, Hugo John [*pseud.* St John Dorset] (**1801/2–1827**), poet, was born in or near London, and baptized at St Marylebone in September 1802, the eldest child of Edward Belfour, of the Navy Office, and Catherine Mary, daughter of John Greenwell, of the India House. By the time he was nineteen, he had produced *The Vampire, a Tragedy in Five Acts* (1821), a work with an Egyptian setting. Its second edition was inscribed 'To To W. C. Macready, Esq.'; the work had been submitted to Macready in manuscript. Belfour also wrote *Montezuma, a Tragedy in Five Acts, and other Poems* (1822). In May 1826 he was ordained, and 'appointed to a curacy in Jamaica, with the best prospects of preferment' (*GM*, 97/2, 570). He died in Jamaica in September 1827, aged twenty-five.　　　ARTHUR H. GRANT, rev. JOHN D. HAIGH

Sources *GM*, 1st ser., 71 (1801), 479 · *GM*, 1st ser., 86/1 (1816), 93 · *GM*, 1st ser., 88/2 (1818), 285 · *GM*, 1st ser., 97/2 (1827), 570 · S. Halkett and J. Laing, *A dictionary of anonymous and pseudonymous publications in the English language*, ed. J. Horden, 3rd edn (1980–)

Belfour, John (**1768–1842**), Hebrew and Coptic scholar and poet, was a member of the Royal Society of Literature and died from 'decay of nature' at 65 Westmorland Place, Hoxton New Town, London, on 8 June 1842, aged seventy-four; he was buried later in June. Little is known of him. His works included various poems and biblical translations, notably the Psalms, translated from Coptic into English in 1831 (a manuscript, BL, 1110 E. 31). Mary Hart, the witness to his death, was illiterate.

THOMPSON COOPER, rev. ROGER T. STEARN

Sources [J. Watkins and F. Shoberl], *A biographical dictionary of the living authors of Great Britain and Ireland* (1816) · *GM*, 2nd ser., 18 (1842), 213 · Watt, *Bibl. Brit.* · *BL cat.* · d. cert.

Belfrage, Henry (**1774–1835**), United Secession minister and writer, was born in Falkirk, Stirlingshire, on 24 March 1774, the fourth son in a family of seven daughters and five sons. His father, John Belfrage (1736–1798), was minister of the Erskine church, where his wife, Jean Whyt (*d.* 1808), had been one of his congregation. His parents' earliest wishes were for Henry to follow his father's calling, and the boy's intelligence and love of learning also inclined him in that direction. After a good grounding at the parish school he went to attend classes at Edinburgh University with his brother Andrew in 1786. In 1789 he began the study of divinity under George Lawson at the Secession Divinity Hall in Selkirk, while continuing his attendance at classes in Edinburgh. He was licensed by the presbytery of Stirling and Falkirk in July 1793. While it was customary at this time for new Secession ministers to receive a number of calls, the claims of congregations at Saltcoats and Lochwinnoch could not compete with those of his father's own church in Falkirk, where he was ordained as his colleague, and eventual successor, on 18 June 1794, still barely twenty years of age.

From the beginning Belfrage distinguished himself as a preacher, a craft he had practised since childhood, and demonstrated great energy and diligence in his pastoral work among a large but scattered congregation. He was one of those responsible for the foundation of Falkirk charity school, which opened in the spring of 1813. In 1817 the increase in the congregation required a comprehensive rebuilding of his church. From 1814 onwards, starting with *Sacramental Addresses and Meditations*, Belfrage began to publish a series of largely devotional works which greatly extended his celebrity and influence. The steady output which he maintained thereafter, on top of his regular ministerial duties, was considered by some to have been detrimental to his health. It included his *Practical Exposition of the Assembly's Shorter Catechism* (1832) as well as works specifically addressed to the young and the old. Most of his publications were produced cheaply in order to give them as large a circulation as possible. He also prepared several memoirs, one of his former professor, George Lawson (1833), and another of his friend Alexander Waugh (1830). His growing reputation was recognized by the award of the degree of DD by St Andrews University in 1824, on the recommendation of a Church of Scotland minister, Sir Henry Moncrieff-Wellwood. This was an unusual honour for a dissenting clergyman, but not so surprising, given his excellent relations with ministers of the established church; while a loyal inheritor of his church's traditions, he was never interested in the more contentious issues of church politics. He was, however, a scrupulous attender of church courts and was presbytery clerk for some years, as well as moderator of synod in 1824.

Belfrage married, in September 1828, Margaret, daughter of Richard Gardner, comptroller of customs in Edinburgh. The couple's first child died at birth, but a son and daughter survived their father. Ill health dogged him for the last two years of his life, and he died on 16 September 1835 at his home, Rose Park, Falkirk, and was buried on 23 September in the cemetery that adjoined his church. Tall, and with dark eyes, Belfrage's likeness suggests the pleasant, straightforward personality that his contemporaries knew; a man as cheerful and lively as his position would allow. A life that was lived largely in one location was not constrained by it but, by virtue of fluency of expression, reached through the printed word to millions in Britain, her colonies, and the United States.

LIONEL ALEXANDER RITCHIE

Sources *Life and correspondence of the late Rev. Henry Belfrage DD of Falkirk*, ed. J. McKerrow and J. Macfarlane (1837) · J. M'Kerrow, *History of the Secession church*, rev. edn (1841), 886–90 · R. Small, *History of the congregations of the United Presbyterian church from 1733 to 1900*, 1 (1904), 658 · W. Mackelvie, *Annals and statistics of the United Presbyterian church*, ed. W. Blair and D. Young (1873), 265 · *DSCHT* · *DNB* **Likenesses** Roffe, stipple (after J. R. Wildman), BM, NPG; repro. in *Evangelical Magazine* · engraving, repro. in McKerrow and Macfarlane, eds., *Life and correspondence*, frontispiece **Wealth at death** £884 13s. 7d.: inventory, 1835, Scotland

Belhaven. For this title name *see* Douglas, Robert, Viscount Belhaven (1573/4–1639).

Belhaven and Stenton. For this title name *see* Hamilton, John, second Lord Belhaven and Stenton (1656–1708).

Belisha, (Isaac) Leslie Hore-, Baron Hore-Belisha (1893–1957), politician, was born in London on 7 September 1893, the only son of Jacob Isaac Belisha (*d.* 1894), an insurance company manager, and his wife, Elizabeth Miriam (*d.* 1936), daughter of John Leslie Miers. His father, who died when Belisha was an infant, came from a family of Sephardic Jews, settled in England for more than a century and a half, and latterly active in the business life of Manchester. His mother married in 1912 Sir (Charles Fraser) Adair Hore, later permanent secretary to the Ministry of Pensions, whose surname Belisha then added to his own.

Education, war service, and election to parliament Hore-Belisha was educated at Clifton College (which had a house for Jewish boys) and was then sent to Heidelberg and the Sorbonne for short periods of study before going up to St John's College, Oxford, in 1913. He had an early intention to make a name for himself in public life and to this end, even at school, was adept at declaiming many of Burke's speeches in preparation for Westminster duty at the dispatch box. That stood him in good stead in the Oxford Union, where he identified himself as a radical. In August 1914 he returned from a holiday in Germany and at once enlisted in the public schools battalion of the Royal Fusiliers. He was commissioned in the Army Service Corps and in November 1914 went to France, where he saw heavy fighting at Neuve Chapelle. A year later, with the rank of captain, he was attached to the Third Army and showed ingenuity in handling supplies. That led to a posting to Salonika in the early months of 1917 and, in turn, visits to Cyprus and Egypt. He was promoted to the rank of major. In March 1918 he was invalided home with malaria.

Hore-Belisha resumed his Oxford career with comprehensive enthusiasm and in 1919 became the first post-war president of the union. His witty epigrams and general flamboyance did not altogether obliterate an underlying radical allegiance. He was called to the bar by the Inner Temple in 1922. The House of Commons beckoned. He won Plymouth Devonport for the Liberals in 1923, having been defeated when he first stood for the constituency in

(Isaac) Leslie Hore-Belisha, Baron Hore-Belisha (1893–1957), by Howard Coster, 1938

the previous year. There were occasions thereafter when he was the sole Liberal MP to sit for a constituency in the south of England. He was taken up by Lord Beaverbrook at this time but his highly profitable journalism was not confined to the *Daily Express*, the *Sunday Express*, and the *Evening Standard*. He also accepted certain directorships in companies which proved not to be very successful. It was clear, however, that these activities only provided means to an end that was political. His allegiance to the Liberal cause did not offer the prospect of swift ministerial advancement. He was certainly a 'name' in the corridors of the Commons and for the newspaper-reading public but that did not guarantee further success. At Westminster his self-publicity did not invariably enthuse. None the less he did give serious attention to a number of issues. Inevitably, in a constituency which contained a royal dockyard, one of these was defence. He looked, unsurprisingly, for increased naval construction, though that was not a cause which galvanized his Liberal colleagues. At the same time he remained in his own eyes a strong social reformer and sympathetic to the unemployed. In 1929 he substantially increased his majority at Devonport, but the national picture offered little prospect of a Liberal government. Indeed, as its leaders of pre-1914 vintage jostled for position, the dissolution of the historic Liberal Party looked imminent. Hore-Belisha, as a Liberal, was a young coming man whose moment might never come.

National Liberal: transport minister The financial crisis of 1931 brought about a fundamental change in Hore-Belisha's prospects. He aligned himself with Sir John Simon and those Liberals who offered general support for the hastily formed and ostensibly temporary National Government under the leadership of Ramsay MacDonald. He retained his Devonport seat with a greatly increased majority. He had let it be known that he would go 'the whole hog' as regards a tariff. His reward came immediately with his appointment as parliamentary secretary to Walter Runciman, fellow Liberal and president of the Board of Trade, quickly followed in 1932 by a promotion to become financial secretary to the Treasury. It was gratifying to the chancellor of the exchequer, Neville Chamberlain, and galling to free trade Liberals, to have Hore-Belisha, now a National Liberal, spending his time expounding new tariff arrangements and the benefits to be derived from the Imperial Economic Conference held in Ottawa that summer.

In 1934 Hore-Belisha became minister of transport and arguably the first politician in the fifteen-year life of the ministry to grasp that the post could advance a career. He began to grapple with the motor car. Pedestrians needed to be able to cross roads in relative safety and he backed illuminated amber globes on black and white posts at appropriate crossing points to allow them to do so. They quickly became known as Belisha beacons. He also thought it appropriate that new motorists should pass a driving test and would benefit from a revised highway code. He believed that trunk roads were too important to be left in the hands of local authorities. In these and other respects his flair for publicity was used to good effect. Sworn of the privy council in 1935 and raised to cabinet rank in October 1936, he put the Ministry of Transport on the political map.

War Office: army reform In May 1937 the new prime minister Neville Chamberlain made Hore-Belisha secretary of state for war. At forty-three he was one of the youngest men to hold this appointment. Even more significant, perhaps, was the fact that, unlike most of the cabinet, he had seen active service in the First World War. It was not an appointment casually made. The prime minister had a view that the War Office was wedded to obsolete methods and needed the invigorating shake-up that Hore-Belisha would be sure to bring. The new minister's priorities soon became clear. An army needed to recruit—in the absence of conscription—and with considerable success he set about making enlistment more attractive. Pay and allowances were increased, barracks modernized, and catering improved—the latter with the advice of the managing director of Joe Lyons as honorary adviser. Battledress was introduced and infantry drill simplified. Irksome restrictions on the freedom of soldiers when off duty were removed. It was thought that the extent of service abroad could be reduced. At another level he pushed through changes in staff training by means of new tactical schools and courses. He also carried through a far-reaching revision of the officer career structure. The retiring age for senior officers was lowered and the period of command

and staff appointments reduced. The half-pay system was abolished. These and other changes were designed to facilitate the promotion of talent. Accompanied by appropriate publicity, they proved that the secretary of state was 'the soldier's friend' who, in his own happy phrase, wanted the army to be 'a part of the nation not apart from the nation'.

Changes of this kind, however desirable, did not directly address the underlying problem: what was an army for? In his early months in office Hore-Belisha shared with the prime minister the view that Britain would never again send an army to the continent on the scale that had been reached in the First World War. He turned to the then defence correspondent of *The Times*, Captain Basil Liddell Hart, for opinions which confirmed a stance which was fundamentally imperialist or isolationist but which was not continental. This relationship was another indication of Hore-Belisha's eagerness to seek advice beyond that of the general staff, but it inevitably provoked in the latter the view that they were really dealing with Liddell Hart, not the secretary of state. That did not make for trust. The debates and differences of opinion that ensued all took place in the context of the general discussion in and beyond the cabinet both about foreign policy as a whole and about the overarching importance, allegedly, of financial and economic stability. Was Britain arming—at whatever speed—to defend itself or to make an effective, if restricted, continental contribution? Could troops be spared from India? Would there be major theatres of war in the Middle East and east Asia? Could the French get by with only a little help from their friends? On these and other issues Hore-Belisha's voice in cabinet was one among many. Eden, for example, in July 1937 successfully poured scorn on Hore-Belisha's apparent willingness to entertain a suggestion from the Italian ambassador that the two countries should hold joint staff discussions. More generally, it did look initially as though he remained convinced that any continental commitment would indeed be limited. A visit to France in September 1937 had convinced him that the Maginot line would hold up a German offensive indefinitely. In November he reported to the prime minister that the army should remain committed to the defence of Britain and the British empire and that it should not be organized with a military prepossession in favour of a continental commitment. He suspected that the chief of the Imperial General Staff, Sir Cyril Deverell, did not agree. Early in December, in a purge of members of the army council, Deverell, whose stance was deemed reactionary and obstructive, was replaced by Lord Gort. It was a bold move and enhanced Hore-Belisha's reputation for decisive action, though still, within the senior ranks of the army, there was suspicion that in policy terms he did little more than echo the views of Liddell Hart.

War Office: towards the continental commitment The debates in which Hore-Belisha participated in the first half of 1938 continued to revolve around the continental commitment. Arguments for limited liability looked for a time as though they envisaged no liability. On the other hand, Hore-Belisha was confronted by some senior soldiers who argued that it was an illusion to suppose that Britain would not be drawn into a major European conflict if one began. They therefore argued that it was vital that troops should be trained for this purpose. However, when Hore-Belisha presented his first army estimates in March 1938—the month in which Austrian independence came to an end—they continued to reflect the view that there should be no continental commitment. Nevertheless events suggested to some that there would be merit in extensive staff talks with France. Hore-Belisha pointed out that, since it would be a matter of telling the French how little Britain could do, the talks could not be extensive. In the event, talks were held between May and November 1938 and did reveal how limited the British presence would be.

The secretary of state for war now had a colleague in Sir Thomas Inskip, briefed to co-ordinate defence. Fears of a German knock-out blow from the air were strong and there was an acceptance of the view that air defence had first priority. Only if that was effective could there be any question of sending a field force overseas. One further concern centred on the supposed need to control a civilian population which might panic under massive aerial attack. Given the contemporary anxiety about air defence and its political sensitivity, it is not altogether surprising that Hore-Belisha reacted heavy-handedly in summer 1938 when Duncan Sandys, a young Conservative MP, made public confidential information which showed shortcomings in anti-aircraft defences. It caused Winston Churchill, the father-in-law of Sandys, to withdraw the support to Hore-Belisha which he had in general previously given.

It is in the aftermath of the Munich crisis of September 1938 that a shift in Hore-Belisha's approach is detectable. During the crisis itself he had continued to accept the well-entrenched view that there was nothing that Britain could have done to prevent Czechoslovakia's being defeated by a German invading force. Czechoslovakia could be restored only at the conclusion of a successful prolonged war against Germany. Britain was not ready for such a conflict. Even so, Hore-Belisha's personal perspective on Germany hardened. How far this reflected his Jewishness is difficult to judge. In their diaries a number of senior generals spoke of him as 'the Jew' and supposed the increasing willingness on his part to be inveigled by France into a military alliance reflected the fact that as a Jew he was necessarily anti-German. Be that as it may, Hore-Belisha came increasingly to the view that, despite all that had been said over the previous eighteen months, Britain would have to support France by sending troops, and there was a severe danger that they would be overwhelmed. In an important memorandum in mid-December he pressed for a substantial increase in military expenditure, though he was careful not to be too explicit about his underlying reason. Even so, both in the cabinet and among the chiefs of staff, disagreement about the role of the army remained.

By February 1939 Hore-Belisha could claim that he had made some headway financially and, consequentially, could begin both to expand and better equip a field force. In his second army estimates of March 1939 his vision of what this would amount to rather ran away with him. In the same month his suggestion that the Territorial Army be doubled was taken up and in April his was the most influential voice in persuading the prime minister to introduce conscription in peacetime—a step fraught with logistical difficulties but symbolically important. The political context for these moves was the German invasion of Bohemia and the British guarantee to Poland. Hore-Belisha was also influential in getting the cabinet in July to establish a Ministry of Supply. In these months his stock was high and, with the advent of war in September 1939, might have been expected to go even higher.

Second World War, marriage, and death Yet Hore-Belisha had a very bad war. His way of conducting himself, summed up by irritated generals as a culpable 'showmanship', had long upset them. Lord Gort had been Hore-Belisha's own choice as commander-in-chief of the expeditionary force. Gort found himself soon vastly upset by critical remarks on the progress of the defences in France made by his minister. Personal relationships deteriorated sharply and others were drawn in. Having tried and failed to smooth matters over, Chamberlain in January 1940 decided that Hore-Belisha had to be moved and told him that he was not blameless in relation to the strong prejudice against him. The presidency of the Board of Trade was offered—his Jewishness was apparently thought to disqualify him from becoming minister of information—but he would not take it. In his reply Hore-Belisha reiterated his anxieties and specifically alluded to the weakness he believed apparent in the gap between the Maginot line and the sea. He also realized that he could not publicly draw attention to this matter in the context of his own resignation. That in turn made it difficult for his admirers to rally round, and his departure was something of a mystery.

Moreover, as things turned out, this was not a temporary blip in his career. He resigned from the chairmanship of the National Liberal parliamentary party. The advent of a Churchillian administration brought no restoration to favour, and he sat on the back benches as a national independent. On 22 June 1944 he married Cynthia, daughter of the late Gilbert Compton Elliot, of Hull Place, Sholden, Kent; she had served with the British women's mobile canteen unit and been held as a prisoner of war by the Germans from 1940 to 1943. In 1944 she was awarded the British Empire Medal. Hore-Belisha briefly returned as a minister—of national insurance—in Churchill's caretaker government, from May to July 1945, but was not in the cabinet. In the ensuing general election he lost his Devonport seat to Labour. He then became a Conservative, but no seat was quickly found for him and in 1950 he unsuccessfully fought Coventry South. In 1954 he accepted a peerage and thereafter made occasional speeches in the Lords. He died on 16 February 1957 in

France at Rheims, where he was leading a British parliamentary delegation.

A brief career In essence, therefore, Hore-Belisha's career in front-line politics was limited to the less than three years during which he was secretary of state for war. Although only forty-six when he resigned, nothing of political significance followed. In that office he had demonstrated drive and determination, and the reforms he initiated brought greater efficiency as well as greater social cohesion. He shared rather than resolved the contemporary ambiguity about the continental commitment, although when events on the continent did lead to both a different mood and different thinking in Britain, he was quicker than many to shift his position. It has frequently been remarked, however, by contemporaries and subsequently, that in large measure he fell victim to those aspects of his personality which had also brought success. He was by common admission a brilliant debater and forceful advocate but with these capacities went self-centredness and conceit. Yet he also irritated by his impatience, by an indifference to the feelings of others—which may only have been apparent—and even by his unpunctuality. Military men with different codes and conventions found him hard to stomach, and they had their revenge. Some have alleged that antisemitism contributed to his downfall but this is difficult to prove, and it could have been only one element among others.

Looked at in a broader perspective, however, Hore-Belisha's career demonstrates how difficult it was to be any kind of Liberal and obtain or retain a position in the front rank of government. It was only the extraordinary circumstance of 1931 which gave him his chance. The position he had held in the National Government and a certain clumsiness in his dealings with the Churchillian family entourage, as it turned out, prevented him from emerging as a wartime Churchillian. After 1945, when he saw himself at last as a Conservative, it was too late to establish himself in its ranks when that party returned to government in 1951. Extraordinary personal qualities and extraordinary circumstances combined to enable Hore-Belisha both to shine brightly and to shine briefly.

KEITH ROBBINS

Sources *The private papers of Hore-Belisha*, ed. R. J. Minney (1960) · *DNB* · B. H. Liddell Hart, *The memoirs of Captain Liddell Hart*, 2 (1965) · *Chief of staff: the diaries of Lieutenant-General Sir Henry Pownall*, ed. B. Bond, 1 (1972) · B. Bond, *British military policy between the two world wars* (1980) · B. Bond, 'Leslie Hore-Belisha at the war office', *Politicians and defence: studies in the formulation of British defence policy, 1845–1970*, ed. I. Beckett and J. Gooch (1981), 110–31 · A. J. Trythall, 'The downfall of Leslie Hore-Belisha', *Journal of Contemporary History*, 16 (1981), 391–411 · J. P. Harris, 'Two war ministers: a reassessment of Duff Cooper and Hore-Belisha', *War and Society*, 6/1 (May 1988), 65–78 · M. Howard, *The continental commitment* (1972) · R. P. Shay, *British rearmament in the thirties: politics and profits* (1977) · G. C. Peden, *British rearmament and the treasury, 1932–1939* (1979) · G. Alderman, *The Jewish community in British politics* (1983) · *CGPLA Eng. & Wales* (1957)

Archives CAC Cam., diaries, corresp. and papers · King's Lond., Liddell Hart C., corresp. and papers | Flintshire RO, Hawarden, letters to Sir J. H. Morris-Jones · HLRO, letters to R. D. Blumenfeld · HLRO, letters to David Lloyd George · JRL, letters to *Manchester Guardian* · NA Scot., corresp. with Lord Lothian

Likenesses W. Stoneman, two photographs, 1930–49, NPG · C. White, oils, 1936, NPG · H. Coster, photograph, 1938, NPG [*see illus.*]

Wealth at death £47,556 10s. 0d.: probate, 15 April 1957, *CGPLA Eng. & Wales*

Belknap, Jeremy (1744–1798), Congregationalist minister in America and historian, was born on 4 June 1744 in Ann Street, Boston, Massachusetts, the eldest son of Joseph Belknap (d. 1797), a moderately prosperous leather dresser and furrier, and Sarah Byles. A fifth-generation New Englander on his father's side, Belknap was baptized by Thomas Prince, the puritan historian and minister of Old South Church, where his family had been members since the seventeenth century. Through his mother he had ties to the influential Mather family, and was especially close to his great-uncle Mather Byles, Boston's unofficial poet laureate. Intended for the pulpit from a young age, Belknap spent seven years at the Boston Latin school (1751–8) and another four at Harvard, where he graduated bachelor of arts in 1762, and master of arts three years later.

Like aspiring protestant clergy throughout Europe and North America, Belknap prepared for the ministry by teaching, moving first to Milton, Massachusetts (1762–4), then to southern New Hampshire, where he held posts at Portsmouth (1764–5) and Greenland (1765–6). As was typical for someone immersed in the 'new light' theology of the great awakening, he struggled with whether he had experienced the religious conversion necessary to preach the gospel to others, a question that he eventually answered in the affirmative. In January 1767, having earlier rejected an offer to teach at Eleazar Wheelock's American Indian charity school in Lebanon, Connecticut, Belknap accepted a position as junior pastor of the First Parish Church of Dover, New Hampshire, where he was ordained on 18 February. Later that same year, on 15 June, he married Ruth Eliot (d. 1809), a Boston bookseller's daughter, with whom he moved to Dover and purchased a two-storey house overlooking the lower falls of the Cocheco River. The couple had six children—two daughters and four sons—the last of whom was born in 1779. Following the death of the senior pastor in 1769, Belknap became the First Church's sole minister.

Dover was a rustic port of some 1500 inhabitants, situated only 10 miles north of Portsmouth but a world removed from Belknap's native Boston. His nearly twenty years there (1767–86) were marked by a series of bitter controversies. Although Belknap eventually became a confirmed moderate in matters of theology, the first of these involved his unsuccessful attempt to have the First Church repudiate the so-called halfway covenant by limiting membership to parishioners who had undergone a conversion experience. Later, as Belknap's family grew—and Dover felt the economic effects of the American revolution—tensions arose from the congregation's refusal to increase his initial salary of $150 or, on several occasions, even to pay him what he was already owed. No doubt Belknap contributed to these difficulties by cultivating a haughty demeanour and delivering sermons so dull that even friends claimed he 'scarcely … appear[ed] … to move his lips' (Tucker, 12). His years in Dover left him with a deep distrust of democracy. Although he supported the American patriot cause he worried as much about the 'tyranny' of patriotic mobs as about the effects of parliamentary taxation (Shipton, 182). Likewise, during the 1780s, he became a staunch federalist, advocating a hard line against Shays's revolt in western Massachusetts (1786) and supporting the strong central government enshrined in the federal constitution of 1787. Indeed, in 1788 he allowed the Massachusetts convention that ratified the constitution to meet at Long Lane Church in Boston, where he had become pastor in January 1787.

Even as Belknap came to despise what he called 'the semi-barbarous region of the North' (Tucker, 18), it was in Dover that he began writing his three-volume *History of New Hampshire* (1784–92). It was there, too, that he started *American Biography*, the two-volume collection of essays that he published in 1794 and 1798. Despite Belknap's insistence on orthodoxy among his flock at Dover, both works reveal a familiarity with—and deep commitment to—Enlightenment historiography, including recognition of the importance of social and environmental contexts, extensive use of primary sources (many gleaned from correspondence with other Congregational ministers), and a conscious rejection of the moral tone characteristic of traditional puritan histories. They also attest to Belknap's keen interest in natural science. Taken together the two works eventually helped establish him as one of America's leading men of letters.

The writing of these works brought Belknap into contact with the sort of intellectual community that Dover so obviously lacked. In 1784 he was elected to the American Philosophical Society; two years later, the American Academy of Arts and Sciences voted him the same honour. He also formed a lasting friendship with Ebenezer Hazard, the Philadelphia printer and bookseller who was instrumental in helping him publish his histories.

Despite Belknap's growing literary reputation, his relations with his Dover congregation remained vexed. In April 1786 he resigned his post to search for another position, eventually moving to Long Lane Church in Boston. Not only did Belknap's new pulpit relieve the worst of his financial problems, it also allowed him to take up residence in one of the leading centres of American cultural and intellectual life. His literary production increased accordingly, with contributions to magazines and newspapers; a popular collection of psalms and hymns; and a book-length political allegory, *The Foresters* (1792), which satirized the American revolution in the manner of John Arbuthnot's *History of John Bull* (1712). Belknap also became an active reformer in education, temperance, and anti-slavery. Most important of all, he showed a growing determination to preserve the manuscript sources that had been so vital to his own historical research; toward that end he took the lead in founding the Massachusetts Historical Society (1791), the first organization of its kind in the United States. In words that clearly reflected his own scholarly philosophy, Belknap wrote: 'We intend to be an *active*, not a *passive*, literary body; not to lie waiting, like a bed of oysters, for the tide (of communication) to flow in upon us, but to *seek* and find, to *preserve* and *communicate* literary intelligence, especially in the historical way' (Kirsch, *Jeremy Belknap*, 137). Over the next seven years he served the society intermittently as corresponding secretary and collector of books and manuscripts; he also helped edit its first published *Collections*.

Although intellectually vital to the end, Belknap was seriously overweight for most of his adult life. His corpulence did not prevent him from making an unsuccessful attempt in 1784 to ascend the Great Mountain (Mount Washington) in New Hampshire's White Mountains; nor did it stand in the way of a strenuous mission to the Oneida Indians in upstate New York, which he undertook in 1796 at the request of the American commissioners for the Edinburgh-based Society for Promoting Christian Knowledge. During the mid-1790s, however, his health began to fail, with recurring bouts of rheumatism and influenza. In March 1798 he suffered two minor strokes, followed by a paralytic stroke early on the morning of 20 June 1798, from which he died shortly before 11 a.m., at his home on Lincoln Street, Boston. As an indication of the prosperity that came during his final years, Belknap left an estate that included the house on Lincoln Street valued at $4441, and cash and stocks worth $3800; in addition he estimated the income from future sales of *The History of New Hampshire* at $1500 and income from his hymnal at $2500 (Kirsch, *Jeremy Belknap*, 203, 214–15, n. 5). According to Belknap's will, each of his five surviving children received $100; the rest of his estate went to his wife, who died in 1809. He was interred in the Belknap family plot at Boston's Granary burying-ground.   ELIGA H. GOULD

Sources L. L. Tucker, *Clio's consort: Jeremy Belknap and the founding of the Massachusetts Historical Society* (1990) · G. B. Kirsch, *Jeremy Belknap: a biography* (1982) · C. K. Shipton, 'Jeremy Belknap', *Sibley's Harvard graduates: biographical sketches of those who attended Harvard College*, 15 (1970), 175–95 · G. B. Kirsch, 'Belknap, Jeremy', *ANB* · R. M. Lawson, *The American Plutarch: Jeremy Belknap and the historian's dialogue with the past* (1998) · J. B. Marcou, *Life of Jeremy Belknap DD, the historian of New Hampshire* (1847)
Archives Mass. Hist. Soc., MSS · New Hampshire Historical Society, Concord, MSS
Likenesses H. Sargent, oils, 1798, Mass. Hist. Soc.; repro. in Tucker, *Clio's consort*
Wealth at death $8241 incl. house in Boston; plus cash and stocks; excl. est. total expected income from his publications valued at $4700: Kirsch, *Jeremy Belknap*

Bell family (*per.* 1814–1968), publishers, came to prominence with **George Bell** (1814–1890), who was born on 12 October 1814, the eldest of thirteen children of Matthew Bell, bookseller, stationer, and bookbinder in Richmond, Yorkshire, and his wife, Mary, *née* Fall. Bell went to the local grammar school run by the Revd James Tate. After leaving school he assisted his father for two years before he moved to London in 1832 and joined the wholesale booksellers Whittaker & Co. in Ave Maria Lane. There he lodged with his maternal uncle, George Fall, who was an accountant in the City. Having had some success with his shilling handbooks on chess, cricket, angling, and other sports, he set up on his own at 1 Bouverie Street towards the end of 1839, financed by his own savings and a loan from relatives. He married Hannah Simpson (*d*. 1875) on 24 February 1840 and two months later issued his first catalogue.

Early in his career Bell became the London representative for the academic publishers Parker, Vincent, and Slatter in Oxford and Deighton, Grant, Hall, Stevenson, and Johnson in Cambridge. Bell and the Macmillan brothers, Alexander and Daniel, started out in publishing at the same time and the three men were great friends. The Macmillans introduced Bell to the Scottish trade, and he commissioned six schoolbooks from Scottish schoolmasters. When the brothers moved to Cambridge in 1843 they co-published a book by William Hugh Miller with Bell, and he also issued Alexander Macmillan's anonymous biography of Percy Bysshe Shelley.

An unfortunate partnership with Henry Wood in 1842 ended with Bell paying Wood's creditors after he went bankrupt. For a while Bell continued by himself. He established the corner-stone of his list about 1845 when he began his series of editions of classics with English notes for use in schools. The scholarship and advice of his former headmaster and his son James Tate gave weight to what became Bell's Grammar School Series. In 1848 Whittaker & Co. bought a half share in the series, enabling Bell to make swifter progress with publication. Such financial assistance contributed in 1849 to a second series, the Bibliotheca Classica, which gained high standing through F. A. Paley's editions of Hesiod, Homer, Aeschylus, and Euripides.

In 1847 Bell began the *Journal of Education* and three years later established, at the instigation of W. J. Thomas, librarian to the House of Lords, *Notes and Queries*. About the same time Bell made an unsuccessful venture into bookselling, installing his brother John as manager of 80 St George Road, Brighton, bookseller to the college. His aim of having a retail outlet was fulfilled in 1854 when Bell purchased the business of J. and J. Deighton of Cambridge.

Bell found another partner in F. R. Daldy in 1855. Daldy had been at Rivingtons and brought with him the custom of devotional publishers of suspending business on the principal feasts in the calendar. The partnership lasted until 1873 under the name Bell and Daldy. Together they published the Elzevier series of standard authors, Pocket Volumes, select works of favourite authors, and Library of English Worthies. On a business trip to America and Canada in 1869 Daldy obtained the English right to publish Mrs Beecher Stowe's *Little Foxes*. While there he became an advocate for the rights of English authors especially in Canada and later became an authority on copyright, becoming an active member of the English Copyright Association founded in 1872 and giving evidence before the royal commission on copyright in 1897. After Daldy's departure the firm became George Bell & Sons.

Bell established a reputation for books on art, architecture, and archaeology. He published the guides to art treasures by Henry Cole (pseudonymously Felix Summerly), including *The National Gallery* (1843). Bell also worked in collaboration with Joseph Cundall, using photographical illustration. Together they produced *Examples of Ornament* (1855) and *The Great Works of Raphael Sanzio of Urbino* (1866). In 1865 Bell travelled to the south of France and Italy, and brought home photographs which were engraved and used to illustrate Robert Burns's *Rome and the Campagna* (1871). Many of his art titles were printed at the Chiswick Press, under Charles Whittingham's management. After Whittingham's death the firm came up for sale and Bell bought it, installing his brother John as manager. About the same time Bell bought the publishing business of his former employer, Whittaker & Co.

Within the profession Bell was called upon to judge trade disputes, and on one occasion at least was authorized by the High Court to do so. He regularly acted as referee on valuation of copyrights. After surveying Hardwick & Co.'s stock he was requested to endorse his valuation of Sowerby's *Botany*. He bought the plates and reprinted the edition, but never revised the work.

Under Bell's guidance the firm published an authoritative edition of Pepys's *Diary* by Henry B. Wheatley. The firm's list also included Elrington Ball's critical edition of Swift's correspondence and Annie Raine Ellis's editions of Fanny Burney's novels and diary. Bell also bought most of Pickering's publications, including Samuel Weller Singer's ten-volume edition of Shakespeare, which he reissued in 1855. He acquired the Aldine series of poets in fifty-two volumes revising many and extending the series to eighty-one volumes. However, his biggest purchase was in 1864, when he bought Henry George Bohn's libraries, more than doubling his stock. He paid £33,000 over a period of five years for 435,072 volumes, copyrights, and plates. The purchase was underwritten by William Clowes, the printers, and Spalding and Hodge, the paper merchants. The success of the libraries under his management was such that he soon added to them, establishing his own series.

The firm published reference works including Ferdinand E. A. Gasc's *French Dictionary* and Byran's *Dictionary of Painters*, and after 1865 became the British publishers of Noah Webster's dictionary. Its list included historical works by Agnes Strickland and Abbot Gasquet and the poetry of C. S. Calverley, Coventry Patmore, Adelaide Proctor, and later Robert Bridges. In the education field, Bell published Pendlebury's famous school arithmetics and the textbooks of Algernon Methuen Marshall Stedman until the author turned publisher in his own right.

In 1860 Bell moved from his address at 28 Belsize Park Gardens to Westcroft, a neighbouring property, where he kept a menagerie of animals on 4 acres of land. In 1882 he moved again, this time to Bramerton, Hampstead Hill Gardens, where, on his uncle's death, his aunt joined him. He inherited much of his uncle's plate, pictures, and furniture. Together with a namesake (but no relation), George William Bell, he supported the Regent's Park Home for Boys, and he took an active role as a churchwarden in the parish. In 1888 he retired from business, dividing the bulk of his property between his six living children, and he died of bronchitis on 27 November 1890. His sons Edward and Ernest *Bell followed him into the business.

George Bell's son **Edward Bell** (1844–1926) was born in Stockwell, London, in October 1844, and educated at St Paul's School and at Trinity College, Cambridge. After taking his degree in 1867 he joined his father's firm. In 1873 Bell married Alice van Rees Hoets (d. 1917). They had one son, Arthur Hugh Bell [see below], and three daughters. A man of scholarly abilities, Bell translated, edited, and wrote works, adding to the firm's list in the field of art and architecture. Under his guidance there was a steady growth of the firm's educational business and he expanded the firm's trade with the empire through Bell's Indian and Colonial Library, a series which sold over 1,433,341 books between 1894 and 1911.

The most important new textbooks published by the firm were Baker's and Bourne's mathematics books; these were followed later by the popular schoolbooks of C. V. Durell and Marc Ceppi's French books. In science Bell published the textbooks of the Nobel laureates Sir William Bragg and his son Professor W. L. Bragg, and he extended the firm's reputation on art and architecture with the works of Walter Crane, G. C. Williamson, and Sir Reginald Blomfield.

Bell contributed to the firm's list of translations of the classics and definitive editions of standard English authors. He edited the poetical works of Thomas Chatterton (1875), and translated Goethe, producing *Wilheim Meister's Travels* (1881) and *Early and Miscellaneous Letters of Goethe* (1884); he also translated the *Nibelungenlied* (1898). He wrote books on the architecture of ancient Egypt and western Asia, and the pre-Hellenic and Hellenic architecture of the Aegean, as well as various papers.

Bell was the president of the Publishers' Association between 1906 and 1909, and took a leading part in the negotiations with the trade known as the book war, an attempt to establish price regulation which led to the net pricing of books, retelling the events in his account *The Net Book Agreement, 1899, and the Book War, 1906–1908*.

Bell's interests included sketching and photography. He was a fellow of the Society of Antiquaries, the Classical Association, and the Society for the Promotion of Hellenic Studies, and was a member of the Wells and Camden Trust. He died on 8 November 1926 of heart failure at his home, The Mount, Hampstead, London.

In 1904 the firm moved to purpose-built offices at York House, in Portugal Street, Kingsway, London. In 1910 George Bell & Sons became a private limited company and Edward and Ernest became directors. Ernest had followed his brother to Trinity College, Cambridge, and into the firm in 1874. He was an advocate of vegetarianism and contributed several books on the subject to the firm's list, including *In a Nutshell: Cons and Pros of the Meatless Diet* (1920). He was a passionate defender of animal rights, writing for the *Animal's Friend* and the Humanitarian League. In 1911 he was joined by another member of the family, Kenneth Bell, grandson of the founder of the firm,

who had returned from Toronto, where he had been a lecturer at the university, to take an active part in the business. In 1913 Kenneth was elected a director of the firm. Though after the First World War he resumed his academic career and became a tutor at Balliol College, Oxford, he continued his editorial interest in the company. After Edward's death Ernest Bell succeeded as chairman of the company and Edward's son, Colonel Arthur Hugh Bell, joined the board.

Arthur Hugh Bell (1878–1968) was born at 4 Fellows Road, Hampstead, London, on 16 April 1878. He was educated at Charterhouse School and the Royal Military Academy, Woolwich. On 10 October 1905 he married Gabrielle (b. 1883/4), daughter of James Kennedy. Bell's early career was in the Royal Engineers, and he served in the Second South African War from 1900 to 1902 and in the First World War from 1915 to 1916, when he was wounded. In 1917 and again in 1919–20 he was in India on the northwest frontier, Waziristan, and he served in the Third Anglo-Afghan War of 1919. He was appointed DSO (1916) and OBE (1919). He was posted to southern Ireland during the Anglo-Irish War (1920–21) and to Turkey in 1922–3, during the Chanak crisis. Bell retired from the army in 1928 to take a more active role in his father's company, becoming chairman in 1936. He continued to develop the firm's educational list, as conditions following the Second World War had created a need for new books and a new approach. Bell was also an expert on dowsing. In addition to a number of articles which he published in a military journal, he translated four French books on the subject and was the editor of *Practical Dowsing* (1965). Arthur Hugh Bell died at his home, the Old Vicarage, Cuckfield, Sussex, on 21 February 1968.

In 1977, on retiring as chairman, Richard Glanville, great-grandson of the founder, sold the list to Robin Hyman. The company, renamed Bell and Hyman Ltd, merged with Allen and Unwin in July 1986 to form Unwin Hyman. The Bell and Hyman imprint thus disappeared and in 1990 Unwin Hyman was sold to HarperCollins.

ALEXIS WEEDON

Sources E. Bell, *George Bell, publisher: a brief memoir* (1924) · *The Times* (29 Nov 1890), 6a · *The Times* (9 Nov 1923), 16b · *The Bookseller* (Dec 1890), 1375–6 · *British Book Binder* (Dec 1896), 6 · *ILN* (6 Dec 1890), 107 · M. Lang, 'George Bell & Sons', *British literary publishing houses, 1820–1880*, ed. P. J. Anderson and J. Rose, DLitB, 106 (1991), 22–31 · *WWW* · U. Reading L. · J. P. C., 'The makers of books, VII: a great series and its rise', *Pall Mall Magazine* (July 1907) · Boase, *Mod. Eng. biog.* · *ArchR*, 15 (1904), 261–8 · I. Norrie, *Mumby's publishing and bookselling in the twentieth century* (1982) · A. Weedon, 'A quantitative survey: George Bell & Sons', *Publishing History*, 33 (1993), 5–35

Archives U. Reading L., business papers and corresp. | CUL, papers of Deighton Bell, booksellers · NL Scot., letters to Blackwoods [George Bell] · Trinity Cam., letters to C. W. King [George Bell]

Likenesses photograph, 1851 (George Bell), repro. in Bell, *George Bell*, following p. 38 · E. Walker, photograph (George Bell), repro. in Bell, *George Bell*, frontispiece

Wealth at death £35,599 15s.—George Bell: probate, 31 Jan 1891, *CGPLA Eng. & Wales* · £95,420 18s. 6d.—Edward Bell: probate, 8 Jan 1927, *CGPLA Eng. & Wales* · £69,218—Arthur Hugh Bell: probate, 13 June 1968, *CGPLA Eng. & Wales*

Bell, Adrian Hanbury (1901–1980), writer, was born on 4 October 1901 at 5 Birch Avenue, Stretford, Lancashire, the son of Robert Bell (1865–1949), news editor of *The Observer*, and his wife, Emily Frances Jane Hanbury (1873–1954), artist. His family moved to London, and he was educated at Glengorse School, Eastbourne, and from 1915 to 1920 at Uppingham School, Rutland.

After working for a very short time at *The Observer* Bell left London for Suffolk in 1920 to be a farm apprentice to Victor Savage at Great Lodge, Hundon, a decision partly influenced by recurrent migraine, which had closed off many careers. In the early 1920s he bought a small farm, Stephenson's in Stradishall, and later added to it Seabrook's Farm. He sold up in 1929 and began to fulfil an ambition to write, calling on his experiences of rural life. His first novel, *Corduroy* (1930), was written at The Gables, Sudbury, recalling his farming apprenticeship, and the second, *Silver Ley* (1931), recreated Stephenson's Farm. *The Cherry Tree* (1932) completed the trilogy. In 1930 he set the first *Times* crossword, and he continued to devise crosswords for the paper for the next fifty years. On 12 January 1931 Bell married Marjorie Hilda Gibson (1908–1991). They had three children: Anthea, Sylvia, and Martin (the international news reporter, and independent MP for Tatton from 1997 to 2001). He followed up his success with *Folly Field* (1933), *The Balcony* (1934), *By-Road* (1937), *The Shepherd's Farm* (1939), *Men and the Fields* (1939), *Apple Acre* (1942), and *Sunrise to Sunset* (1944).

After the war and for the next three decades Bell wrote 'A countryman's notebook' for the *Eastern Daily Press*, for which he was affectionately remembered. From the 1940s he lived at many places in East Anglia including Redisham, Barsham, Gillingham, and Beccles. In Westhall, near Beccles, he bought Brick Kiln Farm with the proceeds from *Apple Acre*. He sold that in 1949 and ceased farming. He continued to write books including *The Budding Morrow* (1946), *The Flower and the Wheel* (1949), *The Path by the Window* (1952), *A Young Man's Fancy* (1955), *A Suffolk Harvest* (1956), *The Mill House* (1958), his autobiography, *My Own Master* (1961), and *The Green Bond* (1976). He published over twenty-five books including two collections of poetry.

Bell's books are often fictionalized autobiography, documenting his agricultural experiences, and he gained a literary reputation that matched those of H. J. Massingham, A. G. Street, or C. Henry Warren. His early writing had as its context the inter-war rural depression in East Anglia. In *By-Road* he discussed 'new' farming methods—modern machinery, motorized transport, factory farming, new marketing and business methods, hedge removals, fruit specialization, and so on—showing options for the future. However, his own sympathies clearly lay with older styles of farming, and he had a great respect for earlier rural artefacts, horse power, hand technologies, and the people skilled in them, even though he knew he was describing the passing of a whole culture. The lantern was giving way to electricity, pantiles to sheet iron. Agriculture, he thought, was 'the basis of all culture', but it was now highly transitional. A persistent theme in his farming work and 'land literature' was an effort to link past, present, and future in village life, to find 'some basis of unity, the germ of a new coherence'.

Bell had an animated and original turn of phrase and an approachable and evocative style. He wanted 'to put into words the way unrelated things came together and formed a relation'. He was a particularly strong interpreter of small episodes and happenings, and he fondly drew out their significance, their vitality, and often their humour, bringing their details into artistic life. He revealed expansive significance in things that were small and immediate to the senses, expressing the beauty of that which is circumscribed, domestic, and locally known. His senses were acutely alive to noise, colour, dust, tools, animals, and people. Whether he was describing Suffolk or Westmorland (in *Sunrise to Sunset*), his atmospheric language conveyed a vivid sense of landscape, of animal life, of the friendliness of people connected in rural work, and of how these fused to create a spirit of place. For Bell the physical experience of work was fundamental to provide meaning in life, to connect means with ends. Family farming—'rich in fundamental relationships', having 'a natural coherence'—was always central to his writing:

> I felt as though I could not bear life to be any the less than the aliveness I felt in me when I was first in love. I am always seeking some recognition of it also in other people … It is only through this that I have been impelled always to try to bring something out of nothing, a poem out of my head, or a potato out of the earth, doing what I wanted to do in my own time and in my own peace, at whatever cost in money and security. (Bell, 83)

Bell had a gift for friendship, and among his friends were Edmund Blunden, F. R. Leavis, H. J. Massingham, Alfred Munnings, John Nash, Henry Warren, and Henry Williamson. He was a member of the inter-war group Kinship in Husbandry. He died on 5 September 1980 at his home, 9 Hemmant Way, Gillingham, Norfolk, and was buried in Barsham churchyard, Suffolk.

K. D. M. SNELL

Sources A. Bell, *My own master* (1961) · private information (2004) [Anthea Bell, Martin Bell, Ronald Blythe, Moya Leighton, Ann Gander] · *Eastern Daily Press* (18 Feb 1974) · *East Anglian Daily Times* (8 Sept 1980) · *The Times* (6 Sept 1980) · *Adrian Bell Society Journal* · CGPLA Eng. & Wales (1980) · b. cert. · Uppingham School register · m. cert. · d. cert. · A. Gander, *Adrian Bell: voice of the countryside* (2001)
Archives priv. coll., family MSS · Suffolk RO, Ipswich, family MSS, HD 1439 | U. Reading, letters to George Bell & Sons
Likenesses photograph, repro. in *Adrian Bell Society Journal*, cover · photograph, repro. in *Eastern Daily Press* · photograph, repro. in *East Anglian Daily Times* · photograph, repro. in A. Bell, *The cherry tree* (1941) · photograph, repro. in Bell, *My own master*, jacket · photograph, repro. in *Book and Magazine Collector*, 60 (March 1989), p. 50 · photographs, priv. coll.
Wealth at death £43,633: probate, 14 Nov 1980, CGPLA Eng. & Wales

Bell, Alexander Graham (1847–1922), teacher of deaf people and inventor of the telephone, was born on 3 March 1847 at 16 South Charlotte Street, Edinburgh, the second of three sons of Alexander Melville Bell (1819–

Alexander Graham Bell (1847–1922), by John Wycliffe Lowes Forster, 1919

1905), speech therapist and elocutionist, and his first wife, Eliza Grace, daughter of Samuel Symonds, surgeon in the Royal Navy, and his wife, Mary. Bell was educated initially at home and then at James Maclaren's Hamilton Place Academy, Edinburgh (1857–8), and at the Royal High School, Calton Hill, Edinburgh, from 1858. In 1862, at the age of fifteen, he left Edinburgh to stay in London with his grandfather, Alexander Bell (1790–1865), who was a well-known elocutionist, and author of *The Practical Elocutionist* and *Stammering, and other Impediments of Speech*.

From 1863 to 1864 Bell was a pupil teacher at Weston House, Elgin, Moray, where he taught both music and elocution and received instruction in Latin and Greek. These disciplines were further studied at the University of Edinburgh from 1864 to 1865. He returned to Weston House as an assistant master in 1865, and in 1866 became a master at Somerset College, Bath. In 1867 he joined, as an assistant, his father, who was continuing his own father's work in London and who was also a notable elocutionist; he had written *A New Elucidation of the Principles of Speech and Elocution* (1849), and *Principles of Speech* (1863).

Bell became adept at teaching deaf people. He matriculated at the University of London in 1868 and attended physiology and anatomy classes from October of that year. In 1870 he and his parents emigrated to Brantford, Ontario, Canada. He continued his work for deaf people in the USA, in Boston and Northampton, Massachusetts, and in Hartford, Connecticut, and he was appointed professor of vocal physiology and elocution at Boston University in 1873. He became a naturalized American citizen in 1874.

Bell's early experimental work was influenced by A. J.

Ellis, a phonetician, who had been converted to A. M. Bell's system of 'visible speech'. In 1866 he introduced Bell to the work of Helmholtz and his electric tuning-fork apparatus, which could produce composite vowel-like sounds. Ellis suggested that Bell should repeat Helmholtz's experiments. Bell soon conceived the notion of a multiple, or harmonic, telegraph, using tuned reeds, which would permit a number of telegraph messages to be sent simultaneously over a single wire by means of interrupted tones of different frequencies. He worked intermittently on such a scheme for several years.

In 1874 Bell saw demonstrations of Koenig's manometric flame apparatus and Scott's phonautograph, which produced visual images of sounds. Both apparatus used membrane diaphragms. P. Reis's 'telephone' of 1861, which was well known by 1874, also employed a membrane diaphragm at the transmitter. Soon afterwards, about October 1874, Bell produced his ear phonautograph, which utilized a human ear (with its eardrum). This had been suggested by Dr C. J. Blake, who became a renowned American otologist. During the autumn and winter of 1874, and subsequently, Bell, with his young assistant, Thomas A. Watson, spent more and more time on his experimental work. Their efforts were rewarded when, on 2 June 1875, Bell's first membrane diaphragm telephone transmitter produced speech sounds. Watson told Bell: 'I could hear your voice plainly. I could almost make out what you said.' In January 1876 Bell set up a workshop at 5 Exeter Place, Boston. On the evening of 10 March Watson, with a tuned reed receiver operated from a liquid transmitter, distinctly heard Bell's voice say: 'Mr Watson, come here. I want you.' Subsequently, on 25 June, using his membrane transmitters and membrane receiver, Bell showed that intelligible speech could be transmitted over wires. His patents of 7 March 1876 and 30 January 1877 became the fundamental telephone patents. Over a period of eighteen years they were tested in around 600 separate actions.

While Bell was working on his telegraph system, T. Sanders, a leather merchant and friend, made Bell a verbal offer of help to finance his endeavours, in return for a share in whatever patent rights might accrue. Soon afterwards, Gardiner G. Hubbard, a Boston attorney and Bell's future father-in-law, made a similar offer. These offers were accepted, and on 27 February 1875 the Bell Patent Association was formed. This organization became, in several stages, the American Telephone and Telegraph Company (incorporated on 3 March 1885). Bell married Mabel Gardiner, daughter of G. G. Hubbard, on 11 July 1877. She had been deaf from early childhood. They had two daughters, Elsie and Marian.

By early 1880, Bell had abandoned business matters relating to the telephone, and was engaged with Charles Sumner Tainter, in developing the photophone. This was an invention which enabled speech signals to be transmitted from one place to another by means of a light beam. The invention utilized a selenium cell, in which the photoconductive property of selenium (discovered in

1873) was used. Bell in 1898 was of the opinion that the photophone was his greatest invention, and in 1921 he stated his view that 'in the implementation of the principles involved' the invention was 'greater than [that of] the telephone'. However, the rapid development of radio and the very limited range of the photophone were not conducive to its general application.

Until his death in 1922, Bell's fertile imagination and interests ranged over many topics. Apart from multiple telegraphy, the telephone, and the photophone, his experimental activities embraced, among others, spectrophones, phonographs, telephonic probes, kites, aeroplanes, hydrofoil boats, and air conditioning, and he took a keen interest in sheep breeding, longevity, eugenics, and the National Geographic Society of America. 'There cannot be mental atrophy', he wrote, 'in any person who continues to observe, to remember what he observes, and to seek answers for his unceasing hows and whys about things' (Bruce, 486–7).

Bell was greatly honoured during his lifetime. He received twelve honorary doctorates, and was the recipient of the Volta prize of the French government (1880), the Hughes medal of the Royal Society (1913), the freedom of the city of Edinburgh (1920), and honorary fellowship of the Institution of Electrical Engineers (1913). He suffered from diabetes and died, on 2 August 1922, at his house, Beinn Bhreagh (beautiful mountain), Baddeck, Cape Breton Island, Nova Scotia, Canada. He was buried at the top of Beinn Bhreagh on the 4th and, at the time of the burial, 6.25 p.m., all the telephone traffic throughout the United States was stopped for one minute.   R. W. BURNS

Sources R. V. Bruce, *Bell: Alexander Graham Bell and the conquest of solitude* (1973) · M. D. Fagen, ed., *A history of engineering and science in the Bell system* (1975) · *Journal of the Institution of Electrical Engineers*, 60 (1922), 949–50 · A. R., 'Dr Alexander Graham Bell', *Nature*, 110 (1922), 225 · *Engineering* (11 Aug 1922), 183 · *The Engineer* (4 Aug 1922), 121 · *The Times* (3 Aug 1922), 13b · *The Times* (3 Aug 1922), 14b · *The Times* (3 Aug 1922), 8c · *The Times* (5 Aug 1922), 7b · *The Times* (7 Aug 1922), 7c
Archives Alexander Graham Bell Association for the Deaf, Washington, DC, Volta Bureau Library · Alexander Graham Bell National Historic Park Archives, Baddeck, Nova Scotia, corresp. and papers · Boston University · L. Cong., corresp. and papers · National Geographic Society, Washington, DC | American Telephone and Telegraph Company, New York, telephone historical collection · NL Scot., letters to Thomas Borthwick · Smithsonian Institution, Washington, DC, Charles Sumner Tainter MSS
Likenesses J. W. L. Forster, portrait, 1919, Smithsonian Institution, Washington, DC, NPG [*see illus.*] · M. W. Dykaar, marble bust, 1922, NPG SI · W. W. Russell, oils, 1930, Inst. EE · photographs, repro. in *The Times* (3–7 Aug 1922) · process block print (after photograph), BM; repro. in *Das Neunzehnte Jahrhundert in Bildnissen*, 5 vols. (Berlin, 1898–1901)

Bell, Alexander Montgomerie (1808–1866), jurist, was born in Paisley on 4 December 1808, the son of John Bell (1775–1835), manufacturer, and his wife, Elliott Montgomerie (1775–1841). He studied at Paisley grammar school before matriculating at the University of Glasgow in 1822. From 1827 to 1831 he studied law at the University of Edinburgh, after which he served an apprenticeship to James Dundas; he was admitted a member of the Society of Writers to the Signet in 1835. On 21 June 1836 he married Margaret Colquhoun (1812–1886), daughter of Hugh Colquhoun, a Glasgow merchant, and Margaret Gourlay. Their son, John Montgomerie Bell, writer to the signet, was born in 1837.

In 1856 Bell was appointed professor of conveyancing at the University of Edinburgh. In this chair he greatly distinguished himself by the thoroughness and clearness of his expositions of the law of conveyancing. In the last years of his life he suffered severely from asthma, and a substitute read his lectures to the class. He had recovered sufficiently, however, to lecture in his final year, but he died of the disease at his home, East Morningside House, on 19 January 1866. At his own suggestion his lectures were afterwards published. For long, they were the standard treatise on the subject, and reached a third edition in 1882. Though superseded, his lectures continue to enjoy a respectable reputation. Bell combined tenure of the chair with a partnership in the firm of Dundas and Wilson, CS, and specialized in the practice of conveyancing. Personally he was of quiet retiring habits and sincerely religious temperament.   W. G. BLAIKIE, *rev.* JOHN W. CAIRNS

Sources *Journal of Jurisprudence*, 10 (1866), 53–4 · W. I. Addison, ed., *The matriculation albums of the University of Glasgow from 1728 to 1858* (1913) · Register of births, marriages and deaths, NA Scot. · *Register of the Society of Writers to Her Majesty's Signet* (1983) · d. cert.
Archives NA Scot., letters to John Hope

Bell, Andrew (1725/6–1809), engraver and publisher, was probably born in Edinburgh, the son of John Bell, a baker. He was apprenticed to Richard Cooper the elder and began his career modestly as an engraver of letters, names, and crests on plates and dog collars. One of his customers was the Scottish Society of Freemasons, which he joined in 1755. Although he was a mediocre engraver who often copied the plates of others, he trained such engravers as Hector Gavin, Francis Legat, Alexander Robertson, and Daniel Lizars and produced book illustrations for such works as William Smellie's translation of Buffon's *Histoire naturelle* (1781–5), Bernhard Siegfried Albinus's *Tables of the Skeleton and Muscles of the Human Body* (1777), and his own *Anatomica Britannica: a System of Anatomy* (1798). He was a fellow of the Society of Antiquaries of Scotland and engraver to the prince of Wales.

Bell made his mark less as an engraver than as co-publisher with the printer Colin Macfarquhar and others of the early editions of the *Encyclopaedia Britannica*. He furnished the plates, and Macfarquhar did some of the printing. Resourceful, industrious, and practical, the two were exceptional businessmen: they kept costs down, knew how to attract a readership not only in Scotland but also in the rest of Great Britain, and gained the support of George III and other political authorities. The *Britannica*, over the course of several editions, became a great storehouse of knowledge. More conservative than the French *Encyclopédie* of Diderot and d'Alembert, the work was typical of the Scottish Enlightenment: it stressed practicality,

Andrew Bell (1725/6–1809), by George Watson

opposed slavery and superstition, and championed natural science, economic expansion, and the value of universal knowledge.

The first edition of the *Britannica* appeared in instalments from 1768 to 1771 and then as a three-volume quarto set in 1771; it contained 160 plates by Bell and was edited by William Smellie, who copied verbatim and abridged so much from earlier works that the edition was pedestrian. Bell, Macfarquhar, and eight others then published an expanded and improved second edition. The new editor, James Tytler, compiled most of the work himself. There were more than 320 of Bell's engravings, an expanded treatment of many branches of knowledge, and a wider coverage by including biographies. The work appeared in instalments from 1777 to 1784 and was issued in ten quarto volumes with imprints from 1778 to 1783. The third edition, published alone by Bell and Macfarquhar (until his death in 1793) was largely, if not entirely, edited by Macfarquhar and George Gleig. Issued in instalments from 1788 to 1797 and then as an eighteen-volume quarto set in 1797, this edition established the *Britannica* as the premier British eighteenth-century general encyclopaedia. It was the first British encyclopaedia to be compiled by more than a handful of contributors and boasted long articles by a noted scientist, John Robison, plus about 540 engravings by Bell. Bell went on to publish the fourth edition himself until his death. Edited by James Millar, it appeared in instalments from about 1801 to 1810 and then in twenty quarto volumes with the imprint 1810; Bell provided nearly 600 engravings. This edition, although not so

innovative as the third edition, did bring many articles up to date and add some notable new ones.

Bell and Macfarquhar made a sizeable fortune from the *Britannica*. It became a best-seller, and the combined printings of the first four editions reached more than 15,000 sets. However, the two publishers' profits should not be overestimated: they sold many copies at a large discount to booksellers such as Charles Elliot.

In appearance, Bell was remarkable for his very short stature, immense nose, and deformed legs; fortunately, he had the capacity to joke about his grotesque looks. Pugnacious in temperament, he quarrelled with the trustees of Macfarquhar's estate, with his own son-in-law Thomson Bonar, who was the publisher of the supplement to the third edition (1801, 1803 revised), and with Millar; Gleig, too, found him to be a difficult employer.

Bell married Anne, the daughter of Joseph Wake, an excise officer, on 20 June 1756; they had two daughters. He died on 10 June 1809 in Edinburgh. His estate included printing works, a linen factory, a home on Lauriston Lane in a fashionable residential suburb of Edinburgh, and perhaps about £25,000.

FRANK A. KAFKER

Sources F. A. Kafker, 'The achievement of Andrew Bell and Colin Macfarquhar as the first publishers of the *Encyclopaedia Britannica*', *British Journal for Eighteenth-Century Studies*, 18 (1995), 139–52 · J. Kay, *A series of original portraits and caricature etchings … with biographical sketches and illustrative anecdotes*, ed. [H. Paton and others], new edn [3rd edn], 1 (1877), 10–13, 206, 210 · T. Constable, *Archibald Constable and his literary correspondents*, 1 (1873), 8, 68–9, 141–3; 2 (1873), 311–17 · R. Kerr, *Memoirs of the life, writings and correspondence of William Smellie*, 2 vols. (1811); repr. (1996), vol. 1, pp. 361–5; vol. 2, pp. 117, 161ff., 214–15 · F. J. Grant, ed., *Register of marriages of the city of Edinburgh, 1751–1800*, Scottish RS, 53 (1922), 52, 68 · C. B. B. Watson, ed., *Roll of Edinburgh burgesses and guild-brethren, 1761–1841*, Scottish RS, 68 (1933), 17 · M. Wood, ed., *Register of Edinburgh apprentices, 1756–1800*, Scottish RS, 92 (1963), 24, 38 · J. C. Guy, 'Edinburgh engravers', *Book of the Old Edinburgh Club*, 9 (1916), 91–5 · W. Cowan, 'The maps of Edinburgh, 1541–1851', *Book of the Old Edinburgh Club*, 12 (1923), 221 · J. Smith, 'Dalry House: its lands and owners', *Book of the Old Edinburgh Club*, 20 (1935), 52–4 · NL Scot., Gleig MS 3869, fols. 7, 9, 11r, 12, 17r, 19v, 35r · Andrew Bell, trusts, wills, and codicils, NA Scot., MS RD3/328, fols. 866–97, 960–63 · *Edinburgh Evening Courant* (22 Feb 1798) · *Edinburgh Evening Courant* (24 March 1798) · A. M. Mackay, 'Andrew Bell, of the *Encyclopaedia Britannica*', *Ars Quatuor Coronatorum*, 24 (1911), 248–50 · G. H. Bushnell, *Scottish engravers* (1949), 4

Archives NA Scot., trusts, wills, and codicils, MS RD3/328, fols. 866–97, 960–63 | NL Scot., Gleig MSS, MS 3869, fols. 7, 9, 11r, 12, 17r, 19v, 35r

Likenesses J. Kay, group portrait, etching, 1784, repro. in Kay, *Series of original portraits and caricature etchings*, vol. 1, facing p.10 · J. Kay, double portrait, etching, 1787 (with William Smellie), BM, NPG; repro. in Kay, *Series of original portraits and caricature etchings*, vol. 1, facing p. 206 · E. Mitchell, engraving (after G. Watson), Scot. NPG · G. Watson, oils, Scot. NPG [*see illus.*]

Wealth at death approx. £25,000: Constable, *Archibald Constable*, vol. 1, pp. 142–3; Andrew Bell, trusts, wills, and codicils, NA Scot., MS RD3/328, fols. 866–97, 960–63

Bell, Andrew (1753–1832), Church of England clergyman and educationist, was born on 27 March 1753 in South Street, St Andrews, the second son of baillie Alexander Bell (*d.* 1789) and his wife, Margaret Robertson. His father, who was talented and well-educated, figured prominently in the community; by trade a wig-maker, he was also discipline, he distinguished himself in mathematics and natural philosophy, and graduated in 1774, aged twenty-one, with prizes and impressive testimonials. According to his first biographer, Robert Southey, Bell became a member of the town's small Episcopalian congregation, which worshipped in the pastor's own house, but according to David Salmon he was a Presbyterian.

Without, it seems, any definite plan for a career, Bell accepted in 1774 the position of private tutor to the sons of Carter Braxton, a wealthy tobacco planter in West Point, Virginia. Other engagements came his way: one American testimonial, quoted by Southey, refers to his 'teaching the learnèd languages, both in a public and a private capacity'. Braxton paid his annual £200 salary partly in tobacco shares and bonds, accompanied by shrewd advice on commodity investment, so that by the time Bell left Virginia he owned assets, as he recorded in his account book, worth nearly £900. Uneasy about remaining in Virginia during the American War of Independence, he embarked for England in March 1781, survived a dramatic shipwreck—stranded, as his journal recorded, on 'an uninhabited sea-girt waste' in frozen snow—and was eventually rescued by a whaler, which, dodging American privateers, sailed to Nova Scotia. From there he secured a passage to London, and finally arrived in June. Most of his papers were lost in the shipwreck; his journal and account book survived.

After a series of short-term tutoring contracts in London and St Andrews, Bell decided, with help from his friend George Berkeley (son of Bishop Berkeley) to enter the Church of England. He was ordained deacon in September 1784 by Shute Barrington, bishop of Salisbury, and priest in August 1785 by Edmund Law, bishop of Carlisle. Plans to return to Virginia as an ordained priest were frustrated by the continuing wars and the precarious position of the American church. Bell's first charge instead was the small Episcopal chapel in Leith, near Edinburgh, which he held for three years until George Dempster, MP for Fife, suggested that he might seek more remunerative employment as a 'philosophical lecturer' in India. Dempster organized for him not only a free passage and letters of introduction but also, in 1787, an honorary degree (in medicine, to Bell's chagrin) from St Andrews University.

India and the Madras system, 1786–1796 Bell embarked for Calcutta in February 1787, busying himself with teaching classes during the voyage. The ship called first at Madras, however, where he stepped ashore—and stayed for ten years. Influential local contacts, together with Bell's powerful contacts in Scotland, procured for him, via Whitehall, no less than eight highly paid chaplaincies and deputy chaplaincies in Fort St George, to the various British regiments and to the 4th regiment of European infantry, plus the position of superintendent to the undertakers' office, which meant officiating at funerals and weddings. These duties nevertheless allowed him time to give his courses of scientific lectures in Madras and Calcutta until the spring of 1793; armed with apparatus and

Andrew Bell (1753–1832), by Charles Turner, pubd 1825 (after William Owen)

assistant at Professor Walker's scientific classes, watch- and clock-maker, and regulator of the St Andrews University library clock. His hobbies included playing chess and inventing print typecasts. Bell's mother came from a well-connected Brechin family of Dutch origin, also with intellectual leanings. She was a niece of Walter Glendie, dean of Cashel and prebendary of St Michael's, Dublin, who left a bursary to support a kinsman at St Andrews University.

Early years and education The family home, which Alexander Bell owned, was a social and intellectual focus for students and academics, and provided a stimulating environment for the precocious young Andrew, who was a keen chess player. One morning, at the age of four, Andrew trailed after his elder brother to the local school; allowed to stay, he proved himself serious and self-motivated. The child's critical powers then asserted themselves: dissatisfied with the arithmetic textbook, he laboriously compiled his own, over many years, to the amusement of his family. Dissatisfaction with the tyrannical rote-learning methods, however, and fear of the corporal punishments that he endured, affected him to the end of his life. His education continued, according to M. F. Conolly, in the grammar school.

In 1769 Bell entered St Andrews University, supported by the Glendie family bursary, which he supplemented by tutoring his (considerably older) classmates. Under the inspired teaching of Robert Watson and William Wilkie he followed the four-year 'regular course' in mathematics, natural philosophy, metaphysics, Greek, and Latin. A diligent student with a reputation for tenacity and self-commanding high fees, Bell demonstrated, *inter alia*, electricity, hot-air balloons, and ice—producing the first balloon and the first ice ever encountered in India. This resulted in his election to membership of the Asiatic Society in 1789. It also inspired Maria Edgeworth's semi-fictional short story 'Lame Jervas' (written 1799, published 1804), in which she features by name Bell and William Smith, Bell's protégé, who was appointed court science tutor by Sultan Tipu. Both Maria and her father, Richard Lovell Edgeworth, advocates of Rousseau's pragmatic educational theory and admirers of Bell's work in India, corresponded with Bell and later sought his advice on introducing the Madras system to Ireland.

In 1789 the East India Company opened its Male Orphan Asylum at Egmore Redoubt, Madras, for the orphaned, illegitimate, and abandoned sons of European officers, and invited Bell to draw up its regulations and to become its superintendent. He accepted, but refused to take a salary. From the outset Bell was determined to remove the stigma of the boys' illegitimacy and to reform the characters, with fairness but kindness, of those who were delinquent. As their father-figure who eventually won their respect, he involved himself in every aspect of their welfare: their diet, clothing, and playtime, as well as their education, both cerebral and moral. Essentially Bell's principles were pragmatist, and equally concerned with the child's character development as with scholastic attainments. All pupils were instructed in the Christian faith, worked from SPCK textbooks, and were trained to leave school literate, numerate, honest, and prepared for apprenticeship to a trade. With potential futures on board ship, learning to swim, under Bell's regime, was obligatory.

A chance encounter with some Malabar schoolchildren who were teaching younger ones the alphabet by drawing in the sand on the seashore gave Bell the inspiration that was to become known as the Madras system and his own lifelong passion. It also solved the asylum's immediate problem of a shortage of teachers in an increasingly popular school. Trays of sand were promptly constructed, and the brighter pupils of each class (the 'tutors') placed in charge of a group of slower ones, with the result that small groups of slower pupils learned more quickly under an eight-year-old than in a large class under an adult teacher. Bell's earliest reference to his experiment is in a letter home dated May 1792: 'Every boy is either a master or a scholar, and generally both. He teaches one boy, while another teaches him. The success has been rapid.' After the alphabet had been mastered this way Bell experimented, successfully, with simple words and basic arithmetic. While never claiming to invent the monitorial system of teaching—which Southey and Barnard anyway trace back to the seventeenth century—Bell developed and refined his own technique of 'mutual tuition', grafting it onto the tradition of using ushers (boys who supervised conduct and order) that was already commonplace in other British schools in India. Thus a school employing only one or two teachers, if supplied with an army of monitors, could educate several hundred pupils.

Bell's experiment evolved purely within the asylum, driven by its own empirical success, by his innate empathy with and observation of children, and perhaps by his conscious rejection of the role models of his own schooldays. He had not at this stage studied any other teaching theories, and it was many years before he was to research the methods of the European reformers Pestalozzi and Fellenberg. His keen financial eye introduced a scheme of small payments to the older monitors, aged between twelve and the leaving age of fourteen, thereby saving the asylum's directors an impressive £1440 per year in teachers' salaries. Using sand trays and suspended pasteboard spelling cards for the beginners' classes was economically advantageous over slates and copybooks. Novel teaching ideas introduced by Bell included a structured hierarchy of monitors, class streaming (grouping children by ability, not by age), and a prohibition on learning by rote and copying the 'abstract lectures' of his own schooldays (Russell, 110n.). Bell's pupils were thus encouraged to learn through understanding and to think for themselves, and to master simultaneously writing, reading, and pronunciation. Priorities included syllabic reading, frequent fifteen-minute lessons (considered a very short timespan) for beginners, explanation in simple terms of difficult concepts, constant engagement of the pupil's mind and hand, and a measured, graded progress that required the perfecting of each step before advancing to the next. Monitors were trained to pre-empt rather than correct mistakes. Hence every child, taught as an individual within a small group, progressed at varying rates, recorded his progress weekly, and moved in and out of different monitorial groups. Every infant who graduated out of the sand was also required to rule his own copybook and even to construct his own pen.

Bell's more radical reforms entailed teaching through encouragement and a generous system of rewards—book prizes and medals—including rewards for attendance. 'Emulation' (his own, reiterated word) of other scholars' achievements, together with a relaxed environment, he believed were spurs to improvement. He forbade corporal punishment; he banned any sort of chastisement for poor work, and gave his own personal protection to any victims of bullying. Punishment of unethical behaviour took the form of detention, extra written work, and loss of playtime, and was decided by a supervised 'jury' of pupils; the miscreant, his crime, and the punishment were duly registered in the asylum's 'Black Book'. Although this approach was criticized by sceptics the academic progress of the scholars and the improvement in their behaviour attracted considerable notice, not least from incredulous visitors from Britain, and the boys themselves held Bell high in their respect and affection. Later visitors and inspectors praised the cheerfulness as well as the orderliness evident in the classrooms.

Bell's physical health, however, became problematic, and he left India in August 1796, never to return. Many former pupils kept in touch with him in later years, reporting successful careers and expressing their gratitude: 'My dear and worthy Benefactor, for such you have truly been to ... hundreds of poor orphans ... you have rescued us from wretchedness and ruin' (Southey and Southey, 2.192–6).

England: church career and marriage, 1796–1806 Now settled in London, Bell printed the report that he had drawn up of his achievements in the asylum and circulated 1000 copies at his own expense. In the autumn of 1797 he published it as *An experiment in education made at the Male Asylum at Madras, suggesting a system by which a family may teach itself under the superintendence of the master or parent*; to garner support he sent copies to some of the most influential people in England. As a result the Madras system made its earliest appearance in England in 1798, first at London's oldest protestant charity school—St Botolph's, Aldgate—a trustee, D. P. Watts, and its master, Samuel Nichols, having been immediately impressed by Bell's report. Next, in 1799, a local vicar, Briggs, introduced it into his two industrial schools in Kendal. From then on until his death Bell was obsessed with spreading his system, and without changing its fundamental principles he constantly modified and worried at its minutiae. His career in the church was, in a way, incidental to his obsession, and his private life was entirely driven by it.

Known to be parsimonious, Bell had accumulated great wealth and had left India with over £25,000, plus an East India Company pension. Much of this financed future publications and travel in connection with his work, and his many magnanimous school treats and book prizes. He was also anxious to be able to support his two sisters financially. While he was in India his elder brother, a merchant in Ostend, died, a penniless victim of fraud; his mother, a depressive who became manic, committed suicide, and then his beloved father died.

Bell's next project, in February 1798, was to buy a 415 acre estate in Kirkcudbrightshire, which provided him with an occasional rural retreat and an annual income of four farm rents; one part of the estate he renamed Egmore. But after briefly studying agriculture, and even designing his own farm buildings, he abandoned all interest in farming and, being too restless to retire, left the running of the estate to his factor. After visiting Liverpool in April 1799, where he toured and admired the prison built to the specifications of the reformer John Howard, Bell was invited to officiate at the Episcopal chapel in Edinburgh's Cowgate. He officiated until March 1800, but though he was evidently liked by his congregation, and was approached for election to the new St George's Chapel, he declined to remain in the capital. In June of that year Bell was elected a member of the Royal Society of Edinburgh, in recognition of his achievements in India, but he was no longer interested in scientific pursuits and was never active in the society's work. His only ambition in Edinburgh seems to have been to plant his Madras system, but the teaching establishment was (and remained for decades) unreceptive to it.

On 3 November 1800, in Edinburgh, Bell married Agnes (1769–1846), daughter of the late Dr George Barclay,

Church of Scotland minister at Haddington and contributor to volume 6 of John Sinclair's *Statistical Account of Scotland*. After an itinerant year Bell accepted the rectorship of Swanage, Dorset. He and Agnes moved there in December 1801 and threw themselves into pastoral work: visiting the sick, supporting the benefit and friendly societies, advising farmers, running the two Sunday schools (where they both taught literacy), and turning the annual Sunday-school examination into a children's party in the rectory garden. Bell's acerbic biographer John Meiklejohn quotes a parishioner who remembered Bell in the pulpit as 'a vigorous revolutionary ... no vague, shadowy statements of abstract doctrines, but attacked Satan wherever he found him' (Meiklejohn, 37).

Not content with the conventional duties of a country parson, Bell decided to vaccinate his flock against smallpox. He travelled to Edinburgh to procure the vaccine and, with Agnes, vaccinated 658 consenting parishioners, including children. All their patients survived both the ordeal and future epidemics. Bell also acted as spokesman for his parishioner Benjamin Jesty, the farmer who claimed to have discovered smallpox vaccination in 1774, before Edward Jenner; Bell sent a printed paper to the Jennerian Society, which, although it had recognized Jesty's discovery, now formally acknowledged it.

Bell then discovered straw-plaiting. He dispatched two parishioners to study the craft, return to Swanage, and open an industrial school for girls in their father's house, where Bell installed thirty little straw-plaiters and a Madras-style infants' department that he supervised every day, wearing a straw hat himself. From this school evolved the Swanage straw hat industry, with ultimately ninety girls manufacturing 5000 hats each year. Bell researched straw-hat patterns in London, negotiated with straw dealers, and attempted exports of hats to the British colonies. When the school's teacher resigned—through overwork—and the health of some of the children suffered Bell replaced straw-plaiting with knitting, and returned to his principal 'mission', his Madras system.

In December 1804 the Bells were visited by Joseph Lancaster, the Quaker, who had independently devised his own monitorial method in his Royal Free School, Borough Road, London. His pamphlet published in 1803 acknowledged the influence of Bell's report, and although Bell declined to be interviewed or to contribute to the cost of Lancaster's publication the visit was cordial; the two educationists were later, however, propelled into hostilities. Bell set to work training monitors in a Swanage school with promising results, and his Madras system was gradually being introduced to a few schools elsewhere. By request he published in 1805 a second, more detailed, edition of his *Experiment in Education* as *An Analysis of an Experiment in Education*, fifty copies of which he sent to Lancaster. He sent 2000 copies to Charles Manners-Sutton, archbishop of Canterbury. In that year Bell, concerned about national illiteracy and haphazard educational opportunity, suggested initiating a state-funded board of education for England and Wales, similar to the board of agriculture but controlled by the Church of England. Then began a correspondence between Bell and the pious Sarah Trimmer, whose spelling and catechism books he recommended but whose ardour was to spark the flames of the celebrated dispute between Bell and Lancaster.

Lancaster's system absorbed Bell's use of sand, suspended cards, and syllabic reading but differed in the techniques of teaching and in the role of monitors. Lancaster employed children in three sets of monitors—to tutor, to maintain order, and to inspect—all of whom were answerable to the monitor-general. These monitors undertook light administrative duties, exposed idlers, awarded and removed merit badges, demoted and promoted pupils within any group, and wrote assessments. They reported rather than checked errors, and demonstrated to beginners rather than explained. Rewards were meted out, but so were punishments, some humiliating, although Lancaster converted some disruptive pupils by turning them into monitors and giving them responsibilities.

At Easter 1806 Bell obtained a two-year leave of absence to visit any parish in need of educational reform. But before that 'unhappy dissensions' in the Bell marriage surfaced, ending in an acrimonious judicial separation in the English courts in April of that year. The reasons are not recorded.

Bell and the National Society for the Education of the Poor
Bell lived for two years in London working as his system's self-appointed evangelist and persuading charitable foundations, the Church of England, and members of parliament, including Samuel Whitbread, to adopt it in all their schools for poor children throughout the country. A catalyst was Whitbread's poor laws motion in the House of Commons on 19 February 1807, in which he advocated a national programme of education, but recommended that of Joseph Lancaster. The ensuing feud between the disciples of the respective systems raged for seven years; the Bell faction was fundamentally Anglican anti-dissenter, the Lancaster faction rejoined that their teaching was religious and welcomed children of all faiths. The newspaper *The Star* unfortunately named Lancaster as the inventor of the Madras system; Bell's response was to publish *The Madras School, or, Elements of Tuition* (1808), which contained his 'Sketch of a national institution for training the children of the poor'. Popular opinion, however, was wary of overeducating the poor, and the government was neither ready nor able to finance a national education scheme. Finally, in October 1811, Robert Southey wrote a long article in the *Quarterly Review* setting out the facts and the history of Bell's system. This was then published in book form as *The Origin, Nature and Object of the New System of Education* (1812).

Through early influential enthusiasts such as the archbishop of Canterbury; Beilby Porteous, bishop of London; Henry Maxwell, bishop of Meath; and lords Kenyon and Radstock schools and Sunday schools based on the Madras (or 'new') system spread throughout the south and west of England, Ireland, and Wales. A crisis of staff shortage was solved by instituting three 'nurseries' for training teachers in the system, all within existing schools, the largest

being the two central schools in London. Impetus was given by the adoption of the system in such institutions as the army's regimental schools and the Clergy Orphan School, which all enjoyed royal patronage; the schoolships of the Marine Society; and the preparatory department of Christ's Hospital. The greatest impact, however, was through the founding in November 1811 of the powerful National Society for the Education of the Poor in the Principles of the Christian Church, which championed the Madras system in all its schools. With the archbishop of Canterbury as president and Edward Vernon Harcourt, archbishop of York, plus several bishops and SPCK members among its vice-presidents and subscribers, the society's teachings were irradicably those of the Church of England. By 1813 its ledgers record the education of c.40,484 poor children in 230 schools. By 1815 every diocese was involved; numbers increased until, by the time of Bell's death, the society and the Madras system were responsible for over 12,000 schools and over 346,000 children in England, Wales, Ireland, and British colonies worldwide. The Madras system was also employed by other independent and charitable foundations such as the Bluecoat schools, Liverpool's Blind Asylum, and the Church Missionary Society abroad. It was exported to Burma, Tasmania, Ceylon, New Zealand, New South Wales, the West Indies, New Brunswick, Russia, South Africa, Sierra Leone, Gibraltar, the Caribbean, and Nova Scotia. The Methodist School Society, undeterred by the system's religious teaching syllabus and compulsory catechism, simply modified it.

Bell became increasingly fanatical. In May 1809 he had been appointed master of Sherburn Hospital, near Durham, which allowed him time for his copious writings and his formidable crusades throughout England and Wales inspecting 'his' schools; in one year alone 'I rode my hobby horse 1,282 miles', he wrote to the bishop of Salisbury in November 1813 (Southey and Southey, 2.462). In June 1813 the society awarded Bell honorary life membership. St Andrews University had conferred on him its highly prestigious honorary degree of LLD in 1811.

By this time Bell was intent on persuading teachers in middle-class schools to convert to his 'Ludus Literarius', a Madras system for teaching the classical languages that he had formulated in 1808 and eventually published, to a lukewarm response, in 1815. In the following summer he toured France, Switzerland, and the Rhineland, as much to hand out his own publications as to survey the schools of Pestalozzi and Fellenberg. Only Fellenberg's gymnastics classes impressed him, but Bell noted in his journal: 'Gymnastics deserve imitation … but what a pity they can't be madrassed'. Bell's system on the other hand attracted some interest in Europe and Russia; it was described in German and Dutch publications, translated into French and Italian, and adopted (for a time) in Prussian charity schools and no less than six schools in Freibourg, Switzerland.

In recognition of Bell's public services he was offered a prebendal stall in Hereford Cathedral in July 1818, but stayed for only eight months. Though unable to travel because of his duties at Hereford he was no less active; he employed assistants, whom he treated with increasing tyranny, delivered a one-and-a-half-hour-long sermon on the history of the Madras system, completely remodelled the Barrington School in Durham, attempted to Anglicize his Scots accent, and published part 1 of his essays on corporal punishment, *The Wrongs of Children*, in 1819. In March of that year he exchanged Hereford for a stall in Westminster Abbey, where he remained until he retired. He officiated at the funeral of the actress Eva Garrick and elegantly barred Queen Caroline's entry to the coronation of George IV. Though a conscientious prebend Bell still devoted himself indefatigably to his school inspecting, public speaking, advising, and to new editions of his published works, optimistically intending the Madras system to spread all over the world. Unfortunately he still had to conquer Scotland. That his native country was largely unwilling to embrace his doctrines (mainly because it had sophisticated educational systems of its own) was a lifelong and bitter disappointment to him.

Final years Bell's farewell sermon in Westminster Abbey was preached in July 1828. It concluded with a tribute to his loyal supporter the archbishop of Canterbury, who had just died. Bell retired to Cheltenham, to the house that he had bought in 1824, where he installed three domestic servants and Thomas Davies, his faithful and long-suffering amanuensis. Between attacks of illness, and even after he had lost the power of speech, Bell pursued his professional correspondence and haranguing; he determinedly prepared a new edition of his *Manual of Instruction* and an abridgement of *The English School, Part II*. The year 1831 Bell devoted to the perpetual rewriting of his will, imperiously summoning potential beneficiaries to Cheltenham and overriding advice from his solicitors and five executors. He left over £120,000 in generous bequests for specified educational purposes in England and Scotland—legatees included the Royal Naval School, Greenwich; the Episcopal Theological Institute, Edinburgh; and St Andrews, which was to receive £50,000 to found a new burgh school to be called Madras College— but with difficult and exacting conditions that resulted in much litigation in the Scottish courts. He died at his home—Lindsay Cottage, Cheltenham—on 27 January 1832, aged seventy-eight, and was buried with great ceremony in Westminster Abbey on 14 February. His grave, under the central aisle of the nave, was originally inscribed, at his own request, simply 'The author of the Madras system' but the gravestone, becoming worn, was subsequently moved. Behnes's white marble monument with sarcophagus was installed in 1838.

The Madras system did not survive Bell for long. It was controllable in small rural parishes and in the two model central schools, and was sustained by the National Society when crucially short of funds and teachers before state aid. Its merits were its cheapness in producing mass literacy up to rudimentary levels, short training (one day), gentle encouragement, and focusing of pupils' concentration. But it was a fragile system dependent upon the vigilance of the individual teacher and upon the abilities and personalities of the monitors. Contemporary sceptics condemned the usurpation of monitors' own time for learning, and the years spent by young pupils in learning without the authority or perspective of an adult. Even before Bell's death reading skills in certain national schools were deteriorating, which their opponents were quick to report. Criticism was also levelled at the use of the word 'national' and at high-church indoctrination of young children.

In character Bell was egotistical and obsessive, impetuous, inflexible, idealistic, and inclined to despotism. He rarely relaxed from his labours, and failed to see why others should either. His friends, with whom he occasionally walked and rode, included Lord Kenyon, William and Dorothy Wordsworth, and the family of Robert Southey, to whose daughter he stood godfather. Children, however, he loved and they him. When Bell's funeral cortège started out in Cheltenham all the pupils of the national school lined the streets—'affected even to tears', as the Revd Allen of Cheltenham recorded in the conclusion of Southey's biography; 'in him they lost a father, and, with great truth, he might emphatically be called *the children's friend*'.

JANE BLACKIE

Sources R. Southey and C. Southey, *The life of the Rev. Andrew Bell*, 3 vols. (1844) · M. Russell, *The abridged works of Andrew Bell and account of his life* (1833) · R. Southey, *The origin … nature, and object, of a new system of education* (1812) · J. Meiklejohn, *An old educational reformer: Dr. Andrew Bell* (1881) · H. J. Burgess and P. A. Welsby, *A short history of the National Society, 1811–1961* (1961) · National Society for the Education of the Poor, annual reports, 1811 ff. (1811) · M. Edgeworth, 'Lame Jervas', *Popular tales* (1804) · H. J. Burgess, *Enterprise in education* (1958) · G. C. Bartley, *Schools for the people* (1871) · H. Barnard, ed., *American Journal of Education*, 10/25 (June 1861) · G. Moody, ed., *English Journal of Education*, 1–3 (1843–5) · J. M. Beale, *A history of the burgh and parochial schools of Fife*, ed. D. J. Withrington (1983) · J. Leitch, *Practical educationists and their systems of teaching* (1876) · W. M. Humes and H. M. Paterson, *Scottish culture and Scottish education, 1800–1980* (1983) · J. Currie, *The principles and practice of common-school education* (1861) · M. F. Conolly, *Biographical dictionary of eminent men of Fife* (1866) · *DNB* · *Fasti Scot.*, new edn, vol. 1, pt 1 · *IGI*

Archives BL, MSS | BL, corresp. with earl of Liverpool, Add. MSS 38253–38273, 38572, *passim* · NA Scot., Leven & Melville muniments · U. St Andr. L., Madras College papers

Likenesses W. Owen, portrait, 1813, probably LPL · C. Turner, mezzotint, pubd 1813 (after W. Owen), BM, NPG · C. Turner, engraving, pubd 1825 (after W. Owen), NPG [*see illus.*] · S. Joseph, alabaster bust, 1832, Madras College, St Andrews · S. W. Reynolds, mezzotint, pubd 1844 (after W. Owen), NPG · W. Behnes, marble relief figure, Westminster Abbey, London · engravings (after W. Owen), NMM, NPG, Scot. NPG; repro. in Southey and Southey, *Life*, vol. 1, frontispiece

Wealth at death £120,000 plus Linday Cottage, Cheltenham: will, repr. in Southey and Southey, *Life*, vol. 3

Bell, Archibald (1755–1854), writer, is said to have been educated in Edinburgh and at Oxford. He travelled in Europe for some years, and was admitted a member of the Faculty of Advocates, Edinburgh, in 1795. He became sheriff-depute of Ayrshire and for more than forty years was sheriff, but his main interests were literary. He was the author of *An inquiry into the policy and practice of the prohibition of the use of grain in the distilleries* (1808; 2nd edn,

1810). *The Cabinet: a Series of Essays, Moral and Literary* (2 vols.), published anonymously in 1835, was in the manner of Addison. *Count Clermont: a Tragedy* and *Caius Toranius: a Tragedy, with other Poems* (1841) made little stir. More notable was *Melodies of Scotland* (1849), an attempt to supply words for the old national airs 'containing nothing which can offend the most scrupulous delicacy' (introduction, xv). The verses are pleasant and sometimes lively but did not supplant the traditional words. Bell died at Edinburgh on 6 October 1854.

T. F. HENDERSON, *rev.* JOHN D. HAIGH

Sources library catalogues, Faculty of Advocates, Edinburgh · [A. Bell], *The cabinet: a series of essays, moral and literary*, 2 vols. (1835) · 'Introduction', A. Bell, *Melodies of Scotland* (1849), iii–xv · Allibone, *Dict.* · Boase, *Mod. Eng. biog.* · R. Inglis, *The dramatic writers of Scotland* (1868)
Likenesses J. H. Robinson, line engraving (after Allen), BM, NPG

Bell, Arthur [*name in religion* Francis] (**1591–1643**), Franciscan friar, was born on 13 January 1591 at Temple Broughton, in the parish of Hanbury near Worcester, one of the nine children of William *Bell (*d.* 1598) of Temple Broughton, and his wife, Dorothy Daniel of Acton Place, near Long Melford in Suffolk. He traced his ancestry on both father and mother's side to the time of Edward I. He was tutored at home and after his father's death in 1598 he was educated for three years in Suffolk with the children of his uncle, Francis Daniel. At the age of twenty-four he entered the English College at St Omer. After a year there he was sent to Spain to the English College of St Alban at Valladolid and was ordained priest at Salamanca on 14 April 1618. On 9 August 1618 he took the habit of St Francis in the convent of Segovia and on 8 September 1619 was admitted to his solemn vows and profession and assumed the name of Francis.

In 1620 Bell was appointed to the English Franciscan College of St Bonaventure in Douai, at that time in the Spanish Netherlands, travelling from Spain by sea. He became confessor to the Poor Clares at Gravelines in 1622 and from 1623 to 1630 was confessor to the nuns of the third order of St Francis, then living at Brussels. At the first general chapter of the restored Franciscan province of England which was held in December 1630 in their convent of St Elizabeth at Brussels, he was officially appointed guardian or superior of St Bonaventure's Convent at Douai and lector in Hebrew. Before this term of office expired he was summoned to Brussels and appointed the first provincial of the restored province of Scotland and in that capacity he was sent to the general chapter of the order held at Toledo in Spain in 1633. He wrote an account in Spanish of his journey (BL, Sloane MS 1572). He travelled with three companions on foot across France and Spain, showing a lively interest in the manners and recent history of the people he met. He visited the Escorial, witnessed an *auto-da-fé* in Toledo, and returned to the Low Countries by sea after spending some time in Lisbon.

Shortly after his return Bell was sent on the mission to England where he arrived on 8 September 1634. Here he laboured with great zeal for nine years, but on 6 November 1643 he was apprehended at Stevenage in Hertfordshire by a party of soldiers belonging to the parliament's army on suspicion of being a spy. The documents found in his possession revealed his true identity and he was sent under strong guard to London where he was examined by three commissioners deputed by the parliament for that purpose, who committed him to Newgate. He had already been designated by the archbishop of Cambrai a member of the commission to enquire into the cause for the beatification of recent English Catholic martyrs and while at Newgate he received letters notifying him of his election for the second time as guardian of the convent at Douai. He was tried on 7 December, found guilty, and executed at Tyburn on 11 December 1643. On the very day of his execution there was published a hostile tract relating 'the confession, obstinacy and ignorance of Father Bell, a Romish Priest'.

As a linguist Bell was distinguished for his knowledge of Hebrew, Greek, Latin, Spanish, French, and Flemish. He was the author of a number of spiritual writings translated into English from the original Spanish. These include a translation of a life of Sister John of the Cross of the third order of St Francis which he dedicated to Margaret and Elizabeth Radcliffe, professed sisters of the English Poor Clares at Gravelines. He also translated the rule of St Francis as approved by Leo X for the third order regular which he dedicated to the English nuns of the third order at Brussels, to whom he was chaplain, and Andrés de Soto's *A Brief Instruction of how we Ought to Hear Mass*, originally dedicated to the infanta, Clara Eugenia, governor of the Netherlands, to whom de Soto was chaplain. The translator appended an additional dedication to Lady Ann, countess of Argyll. Bell was beatified by John Paul II on 22 November 1987.

THOMPSON COOPER, *rev.* MICHAEL E. WILLIAMS

Sources C. A. Newdigate, 'Some hostile "true reports" of the martyrs ... VI. Ven Arthur Bell', *Miscellanea* [XV], Catholic RS, 32 (1932) · 'A genealogical notebook of the Venerable Arthur Bell, OSF, martyr, 1638', *Miscellanea, I*, Catholic RS, 1 (1905), 117–22 · [A. Bell], 'Diary of a traveller written in the year 1633', BL, Sloane MS 1572 · J. M. de Elizondo, 'Paso por tierras vascas del venerable mártir Fray Francisco Bel (1590–1643) Franciscano ingles', *Revista Internacional de Estudos Vascos*, 14 (1923), 1–26 · Gillow, *Lit. biog. hist.*, 1.171–3 · L. Wadding, *Annales minorum*, ed. J. M. Fonseca and others, 2nd edn, 29 (1948), 148–50
Archives BL, 'Diary of a traveller written in the year 1633', Sloane MS 1572
Likenesses print, 1649, BM; repro. in R. Mason, *Certamen seraphicum* (1649) · portrait, 1700?–1740?, St Alban's College, Valladolid, Spain · pen-and-ink drawing (after engraving), NPG

Bell, Arthur (**1825–1900**), wine and spirit merchant, was born on 30 November 1825 at Surrey Square, London, the eldest son of Robert Fitzroy Bell, a general agent, and his wife, Hannah Bruce.

Nothing is known about Bell's upbringing but by the late 1840s he was employed as a traveller by James Roy, who owned a wine and spirit business in Perth. This had been established, probably in 1825, by Thomas Sandeman, an agent for Sandeman & Co. of Oporto. Sandeman died in

1837, leaving a business with annual profits of over £900 to his clerk James Roy. The shop in Kirkside, Perth, sold wines, spirits, malt liquors, tea, black beer, and cider, all dutiable commodities. Trade was mainly local and retail but some wholesale trade was done with publicans and hoteliers. Bell's duties were to extend sales beyond Perth and each spring he toured the highlands seeking orders and collecting payments. He became Roy's partner in 1851, an arrangement which continued until 1862 when Roy retired and Bell formed a new partnership with a nephew, Thomas R. Sandeman. On 16 November 1864 Bell married Isabella Warden (b. 1835/6), daughter of Robert Duff, a merchant; they had two sons.

The partnership between Bell and his nephew was dissolved in 1865 when they quarrelled over expenses which Sandeman had incurred on personal business but charged to the partnership. The dissolution grieved Bell, for Sandeman had been best man at his wedding, but the business was hardly returning sufficient profit (£1925 in 1865) to sustain two partners, let alone the eleven relatives Bell supported, eight of whom were female, whose financial well-being was a constant anxiety. Bell replaced Sandeman's capital of £2597 by bank borrowing, the only time in his career he did this. Although he repaid the bank by 1870 he was determined to be independent and met his future capital requirements by reinvesting a high proportion of profits.

Other misfortunes affected Bell's attitude to business. His early attempts to market whisky in England, following the assimilation of English and Scottish excise duties in 1856, floundered. None of his London agents was successful and it was not until 1886 that Bell again tested the English market; by then Scotch whisky was becoming very popular. This was followed, in 1890, by the appointment of his first overseas agent, in Australia. Both were responses to intense competition in the Scottish spirit trade but another powerful motive was Bell's ambition to pass on a successful enterprise to his sons.

Bell was a cautious businessman. His advice to a nephew in 1890 was: 'I think the best motto in business is "slow and sure", but I see the present generation prefers "fast and insecure" and in most cases they land themselves in the mud' (Arthur Bell & Sons Ltd, letter-book, 26 July 1890, United Distillers Archive). His methods were conservative. He refused to advertise and just 'allowed the qualities of my goods to *speak* for *themselves*' (ibid., 9 Dec 1879). Before he retired he was still arguing that 'the reason I can keep up the quality is that I do *not* advertise' (ibid., 16 Jan 1891). His initial blending technique was extremely crude, for he simply added whisky to a tun which was never emptied. Later he recognized the importance of accumulating mature stocks and became reluctant to alter the constituents of his blends. Independence mattered to Bell. He fell out with the Distillers Company when it refused to include him in a discount scheme and thereafter refused to buy grain whisky from Distillers, an act which denied him access to credit for expansion. He supported the two independent grain distilleries, North British (founded 1885) and Ardgowan (1896). His distrust of agents also impeded expansion and he was forced to reverse the policy between 1886 and 1893 when he finally created a network of agents in England.

Bell was totally absorbed by business and meticulous in his attention to detail. His private journals include the following note for 1897: 'Assets: Cash £16.14.1 plus 9d.— undiscovered error for the first time since 1851!' (Arthur Bell & Sons Ltd, personal journal, 1897). Bell was not a dynamic entrepreneur. Prudence in business was a perpetual refrain in his correspondence. He was an exponent of careful, plodding management and that is his very fascination, for without advertising, overseas sales trips, and brand registration Bell built a business which, by 1895, was selling Scotch whisky in England and exporting to Australia, Tasmania, New Zealand, and Ceylon. He epitomized, more often than business historians recognize, the myriad numbers of small businessmen who formed a majority of the whisky trade before it became increasingly concentrated. The firm provided Bell and his family with a more than adequate income.

Bell began to withdraw from the day-to-day running of the firm as his sons became partners. His elder son, **Arthur Kinmond Bell** (1868–1942), Scotch whisky blender and philanthropist, was born on 4 October 1868 at Moncrieff Terrace, Craigie, Perth. He was educated at Perth Academy and Craigmount School, Edinburgh. After an apprenticeship with a blending firm in Edinburgh, he joined the family wine and spirit business in 1889, at a time when it had considerable unrealized potential for expansion, and his arrival coincided with a rapid growth in demand for Scotch whisky. Profits, a modest £1753 in 1889, rose to £5276 in 1895, when he became a partner with a half-share in the profits. He was joined the following year by his younger brother, Robert Duff Bell, who had established agencies in Australia, Tasmania, and New Zealand during a tour in 1892. Until their father's death the profits were shared equally between all three.

On 8 June 1899 'A. K.' or 'Atty', as Arthur Kinmond Bell was known in the whisky trade, married Camilla Bruce (b. 1871/2), daughter of Robert Bruce, medical practitioner. Arthur Bell died on 16 February 1900 at Craigenvar, Scone, Perthshire, from cardiac disease and hemiplegia. By then annual profits had risen to £11,795, and his sons had begun to change the management of the business. More agents were appointed, a modest amount of advertising began, and, in 1904, the name Bell's first appeared on the firm's labels. A. K. Bell's bench-mark was another Perth blending firm, John Dewar & Sons, and these changes, together with the introduction of Bell's whisky to Canada, yielded impressive growth in profits to £24,573 in 1913. A. K. Bell remained the driving force in Bells' expansion, but profits were so buoyant that his brother Robert withdrew from the firm on the eve of the First World War to pursue the life of a country gentleman.

The partners also reinvested an increasing proportion of profits in mature whisky stocks—by 1915 stocks were valued at £105,000, five times their value in 1900—and this proved crucial in enabling Bells to withstand the shortages following the Immature Spirits Act of 1915.

Indeed, Bells would have been an attractive purchase for the larger blenders but 'A. K.' inherited his father's strong streak of independence. In 1921 the partnership was converted into a private limited liability company, with A. K. Bell as governing director holding all the ordinary shares.

Life for an independent blending house between the wars proved extremely difficult. In the worst year, 1932, Bells lost £10,952 but reserves enabled the firm to survive. In 1933 A. K. Bell expanded by purchasing the Edinburgh whisky firm, P. Mackenzie & Co., which owned two malt distilleries, Blair Atholl and Dufftown–Glenlivet. A third, Inchgower, was purchased in 1936. Some doubted the wisdom of buying distilleries when most were silent and the trade's future highly uncertain but all were acquired extremely cheaply and enabled Bells to benefit from the recovery of exports (then the most profitable part of the industry) by 1938. A. K. Bell is remembered as 'a man who always bought cheap and never let a penny go by' (private information).

A. K. Bell was also a noted local philanthropist. In 1922 he purchased the Gannochy and Muirhall estates and began a model housing scheme to provide cheaply rented homes. The estate, consisting of 150 houses, was completed in 1932. Five years later he founded the Gannochy Trust and in 1941 allocated some of his shareholding in Arthur Bell & Sons to the trust. He also purchased Quarrymill Den, a local beauty spot, and presented it to the town. Other activities that he supported included the allotment garden movement, the Boy Scouts, local bands, and his favourite sport, cricket. Bell also resurrected the local linen industry following the voluntary liquidation in 1936 of John Shields & Co., manufacturers of linen damask, and one of Perth's largest employers. Bell bought the premises, re-equipped them for artificial fibre production, and reconstructed the firm. For this and his philanthropy he was made a freeman of the city of Perth in 1938.

By 1941, with profits of £100,000, Bells' future seemed assured. However, the death of A. K. Bell on 26 April 1942 at Campsie Hill, Perthshire, left an acute problem of succession. He had no children and his finances were intricately connected to the firm's. His younger brother, by then aged seventy, stood in as caretaker for just over a month until W. G. Farquharson, a chartered accountant recruited by A. K. Bell in 1927, was appointed chairman. Robert Bell died later in 1942, the last of the family to be associated with Bells. The firm owed £247,000 to A. K. Bell's estate and family, and in 1949 Bells was converted to a public company to pay off the loan and finance reconstruction.   RONALD B. WEIR

Sources R. B. Weir, 'The distilling industry in Scotland in the nineteenth and early twentieth centuries', PhD diss., 2 vols., Edinburgh, 1974, 2.411–93 · 'Bell's o' Perth: an independent Scotch whisky house', *Wine and Spirit Trade Record*, 87 (1958), 176–82, 186, 188 · J. House, *Pride of Perth* (1976) · private information (2004) · b. cert. · b. cert. [Arthur Kinmond Bell] · m. cert. · m. cert. [Arthur Kinmond Bell] · d. cert. · d. cert. [Arthur Kinmond Bell]
Archives United Distillers and Vintners Archive, Leven, records of Arthur Bell & Sons Ltd
Likenesses portrait, repro. in House, *Pride of Perth*, 26

Wealth at death £22,903 5s. 5d.: confirmation, 12 Oct 1900, *CCI* · £465,198 5s. 6d.—Arthur Kinmond Bell: confirmation, 1 Aug 1942, *CCI*

Bell, Arthur Hugh (1878–1968). *See under* Bell family (*per.* 1814–1968).

Bell, Arthur Kinmond (1868–1942). *See under* Bell, Arthur (1825–1900).

Bell, Aubrey FitzGerald (1881–1950), Portuguese and Spanish scholar, was born on 20 August 1881 at the vicarage of Muncaster, Ravenglass, Cumberland, the son of the Revd Henry Bell (1838–1919), rural dean of Gosforth and subsequently canon of Carlisle Cathedral, and his wife, Katherine, daughter of Sir Peter Fitz-Gerald, knight of Kerry. At the age of five he moved with his mother to St Jean-de-Luz where he was educated privately before going as a classical scholar to Keble College, Oxford, in 1900. He took a second in classical moderations (1902) and graduated with a third in *literae humaniores* (1904).

Between 1905 and 1908 Bell was assistant keeper of printed books at the British Museum. After leaving the British Museum he travelled in Spain and Portugal, settling eventually at Manique de Baixo, near Estoril, in 1911. He may have had his years of travel in mind when he wrote in a letter to Sir Idris Bell: 'I saw many beautiful & interesting things but in hardships, noise & general weariness I paid amply for every one of them' (28 Aug 1925, Idris Bell papers, fol. 69). His first book, a collection of poems entitled *Songs of Rest*, was published in 1911 under the pseudonym of A. F. Gerald. He used this pseudonym on three other occasions and once employed a Hispanicized version, Álvaro Giráldez, though most of his work was published under his own name.

In Portugal Bell became correspondent for the *Morning Post* and wrote regularly for other journals, including *The Athenaeum*, and the *Times Literary Supplement*, which became his principal source of income. Although he lived a retired and almost reclusive life he took a keen interest in contemporary events, as can be seen in works such as *Portugal of the Portuguese* (1915), where his comments on Portuguese politics were direct, incisive, and unflattering. The Avenida da Liberdade in Lisbon had never become popular, he wrote, because 'It seems to be too far from the centres of gossip: before you had walked [from one end to the other] a ministry might have fallen' (*Portugal of the Portuguese*, 41–2). His activities as newspaper correspondent more than once aroused the suspicion of the authorities in Spain as well as in Portugal and he served a term in a military prison in 1912.

While living in Portugal Bell wrote a succession of major scholarly works. *Portuguese Literature* appeared in 1922 and *The Oxford Book of Portuguese Verse* in 1925, both enthusiastically reviewed. In 1933, during a spell in the British Hospital in Lisbon, he met and subsequently married a nurse, Barbara Lindsay Wilkie from Edinburgh. They had two sons who, Aubrey wrote, would have to be brought up as 'illiterate peasants [as] there will be no money to educate either of them' (1 July 1936, Idris Bell papers, fol. 74). In August 1940, shortly after the outbreak of war, the family moved to Toronto. Before he left Portugal, the ministry of education awarded him the order of Santiago. Bell sold his library to the Instituto Español in Lisbon, which eventually disposed of it to the University of Salamanca.

From Toronto the Bells moved to Victoria, British Columbia. There, in 1947, Aubrey completed his last major work, *Cervantes*. He died at Saanich, Victoria, British Columbia on 7 May 1950. His ashes were brought back to Ravenglass. His wife subsequently moved to California and resumed her career as a nurse.

Aubrey Bell never held any academic post, or indeed any salaried position at all, after he left the British Museum, and his scholarship was entirely self-taught and self-generated. He was a prolific writer and in all published thirty-five books on Spanish and Portuguese topics. Some of these were printed privately in very limited editions. He wrote important critical studies of the major classical Spanish and Portuguese authors as well as a number of more general works of travel, history, and bibliography. He was also a regular reviewer for the *Times Literary Supplement*, the *Bulletin of Spanish Studies*, and the *Modern Language Review*. His work is characterized by a highly individual and original style of writing and by meticulous attention to bibliographical scholarship. He was also a translator of note, and included in his writings many of his own translations into English verse.

Aubrey Bell's particular distinction lay in his pioneering study of Portuguese literature. Before he wrote, the English-speaking world knew little about any Portuguese writers except Camões. Bell introduced English readers to Gil Vicente, many of whose plays he translated, to the historians Lopes, Correa, Barros, and Couto, and to the early Portuguese poets. In particular he drew attention to the medieval *Cantigos do amigo* and *Cantigos de amor*. He had a nostalgic admiration for early Portuguese literature and for the purity of language which he believed existed in the early Renaissance: 'The restoration of the Portuguese language to its original purity is an essential condition … since it is vain to hope to gather figs from thistles' (*Portugal of the Portuguese*, 151). His work was always carefully crafted so that even such slight historical works as his *Portuguese Portraits* (1917) can be read with pleasure. Among his other writings were *In Portugal* (1912), *The Magic of Spain* (1912), *Poems from the Portuguese* (1913), *Lyrics of Gil Vicente* (1914), *Portuguese Bibliography* (1922), *Spanish Galicia* (1922), *A Pilgrim in Spain* (1924), *Contemporary Spanish Literature* (1933), and *Castilian Literature* (1938).

Bell was a shy and reclusive person, though well known to the small circle of scholars of Portuguese and Spanish literature. He cultivated a lifestyle that verged on the eccentric—rising regularly in the middle of the night to do his writing. As well as his studies of literature, Bell was a keen gardener, as his father had been, and wrote attractively about the gardens and flowers of Portugal.

MALYN D. D. NEWITT

Sources M. A. Buchanan, 'Aubrey Fitz Gerald Bell', *Portugal and Brazil*, ed. H. Livermore (1953), 15–20 · S. G. Morley and H. Livermore, 'Bibliography of Aubrey Fitz Gerald Bell', *Portugal and Brazil*, ed. H. Livermore (1953), 21–7 · BL, Idris Bell papers, Add. MS 59523 · *TLS* (9 March 1922) · *TLS* (29 Oct 1925) · *TLS* (3 Dec 1931) · *TLS* (31 Aug 1940) · *Carlisle Journal* (20 June 1919) · *Keble College Centenary Register, 1870–1970* · Crockford (1896) · letter from H. Livermore, 13 Nov 2001 · *WW* · b. cert. · *CGPLA Eng. & Wales* (1951)
Archives BL, corresp. with Sir Idris Bell
Wealth at death £814 8s. 2d.: administration with will, 12 Jan 1951, *CGPLA Eng. & Wales*

Bell, Beaupré (1704–1741), antiquary, was the only son of Beaupré Bell (*b. c.*1673) and his wife, Margaret (*d.* 1720), daughter of Sir Anthony Oldfield of Spalding, Lincolnshire. He was descended from the ancient family of Beaupré, which had settled in Upwell and Outwell, Norfolk, early in the fourteenth century. He was educated at Westminster School and entered Trinity College, Cambridge, in 1723, where he took the degree of BA in 1725, proceeding MA in 1729. He devoted himself to the study of antiquities, taking particular pleasure in ancient coins. Although his father squandered a large part of the estate, Bell inherited property at Beaupré Hall worth, even in its reduced state, as much as £1500 p.a., which enabled him to fully satisfy his antiquarian interests. He issued proposals for a work on the coins of the Roman emperors, which, though well advanced long before his death, was never published. He was admitted to the Peterborough Society in 1730 or 1731. He was also an active member of the Spalding Gentlemen's Society, and several papers which he communicated to it are mentioned in the 'Reliquiae Galeanae' in volume 3 of John Nichols's *Bibliotheca Topographica Britannica* (1790). The same volume also contains several letters to and from Bell. Four of his letters on the 'horologia' of the ancients are printed in the *Archaeologia* (6.133–43), two are in Nichols's *Literary Illustrations* (3.572, 582), and several others may be found in the 'Stukeley memoirs' published by the Surtees Society. From these it appears that he retained chambers at Trinity College. He assisted Francis Blomefield in his history of Norfolk and Thomas Hearne in many of his antiquarian works, and he corresponded with Samuel Pegge who recorded receiving 'many favours from him' (Bodl. Oxf., MS Eng. lett. d. 43, fol. 329). C. N. Cole's edition of Dugdale's *Imbanking* (1772) was corrected from a copy formerly in Bell's possession.

That Bell's life was not without its vicissitudes may be inferred from an advertisement placed in the *London Gazette* by Lord Harrington, the secretary of state. This reported that the life of Bell had been threatened, his servant shot, and his house beset several times, and offered a free pardon to any of the criminals who would disclose the identity of his accomplices. As a further inducement Bell offered a reward of £50.

His friend William Stukeley described Bell as 'an ingenious gentleman, of learning and curiosity, [and] great knowledge in medals' (*Family Memoirs*, 3.468). Bell died, unmarried, of consumption, while on a journey to Bath in August 1741; the estate passed to his youngest sister, but he left his personal property of books, medals, and manuscripts to Trinity College, Cambridge. He was buried on 6 September 1741 in the family burying-place in St Mary's Chapel, Outwell church, but there is no entry of the burial in the parish register, nor is there any mention of his name among the members of his family commemorated in the inscriptions on the family tomb in the chapel.

W. P. COURTNEY, *rev.* DAVID BOYD HAYCOCK

Sources Nichols, *Lit. anecdotes*, 5.278–82 · Nichols, *Illustrations*, 3.572, 582 · *The family memoirs of the Rev. William Stukeley*, ed. W. C. Lukis, 3 vols., SurtS, 73, 76, 80 (1882–7) · Venn, *Alum. Cant.* · *IGI* · F. Blomefield and C. Parkin, *An essay towards a topographical history of the county of Norfolk*, [2nd edn], 11 vols. (1805–10), vol. 7, pp. 459–60 · J. Welch, *The list of the queen's scholars of St Peter's College, Westminster*, ed. [C. B. Phillimore], new edn (1852) · Bodl. Oxf., MS Ey lett., d. 43, fol. 329; d. 45, fol. 171

Archives BL, memoranda relating to history of Isle of Ely and extracts relating to his seat and family · Bodl. Oxf., corresp. and papers · Trinity Cam., papers | Norfolk RO, letters to Francis Blomefield

Likenesses H. R. Morland, chalk drawing, 1738, Trinity Cam.

Bell, Benjamin (1749–1806), surgeon and farmer, eldest son of the fifteen children of George Bell (1722–1813), farmer, and Anne, *née* Corrie, of Speddoch, was born at Dumfries in April 1749. He was descended from landed proprietors of long standing in Dumfriesshire. Subsequently the family moved to Woodhouselees, Canonbie, in Eskdale, about a mile from the border with England, where George Bell was considered 'one of the best improvers of the land in the district in which he lived' (Bell, *Essays*, X). Benjamin Bell was educated at Dumfries grammar school, and in 1764 was apprenticed to James Hill, surgeon, of Dumfries. In 1766 he entered the Edinburgh medical school, where Monro primus and secundus, Joseph Black, and John Gregory were among his teachers. House surgeon to the Royal Infirmary, he became fellow of the College of Surgeons of Edinburgh in 1770, and then studied surgery in London and Paris for almost two years, being appointed surgeon to the Royal Infirmary, Edinburgh, in August 1772. About 1776 he married Grizel, daughter of Robert Hamilton DD, with whom he had a numerous family which included George Bell (1777–1832), a well-known surgeon; a grandson, Benjamin Bell (1810–1883), was also a surgeon and wrote a biography of his grandfather. Shortly after his marriage Bell sustained a severe injury in falling from a horse and gave up practice for two years to settle on a farm near Edinburgh, where his family lived from spring to autumn of every year. There he developed a profound interest in agriculture; later he was to occupy another farm, near Melrose Abbey. His earliest writings on agriculture appeared in 1783.

Bell's first book, *A Treatise on the Theory and Management of Ulcers*, published in 1778, attracted considerable attention, achieved a seventh edition in 1801, and was translated into French, Italian, Spanish, Portuguese, and German. His most important work, *A System of Surgery*, illustrated with ninety-nine plates of instruments and equipment, appeared in six volumes between 1783 and 1788; it too reached a seventh edition in 1801, and was translated into Italian, French, Spanish, and German, despite criticisms from John Bell and Benjamin Brodie. In this textbook Bell proposed methods of reducing pain and of conserving

Benjamin Bell (1749–1806), by Sir Henry Raeburn

skin during operations by careful techniques; he discouraged the proliferation of instruments, yet illustrated many new items from Europe and some of his own, which had been refined by extensive experience. James Wardrop wrote: 'He was a successful operator, and during many years, was more employed than any other surgeon in Scotland' (Bell, *Life*, 112).

However, Bell led an arduous life, with many night journeys to visit distant patients in Scotland and northern England. Accumulating money, he purchased extensive estates near Jedburgh and near Melrose, and in Newington, Edinburgh. But his health suffered and periodically he stopped work to recuperate in southern England, where he also took note of local methods of agriculture. These breaks provided the opportunity to write, and in 1793 he published *A Treatise on Gonorrhoea virulenta and Lues venerea* in two volumes, which achieved three editions and was translated into Italian, Spanish, and French. Bell defined these venereal infections as separate diseases at a time when many, including John Hunter, believed that they were related. In 1794 he published *A Treatise on the Hydrocele, on Sarcocele, or Cancer, and other Diseases of the Testis*; no further editions appeared. Bell, who was concerned that agricultural production was not keeping pace with population growth, also wrote essays on taxation, the national debt, the corn laws, and agricultural reform. These were collected and published in 1802 as *Essays on agriculture, with a plan for the speedy and general improvement of the land in Great Britain*. Bell's conclusions were commended by Adam Smith.

Bell was of medium but powerful stature and, according to Wardrop, 'was of a kindly disposition … He had an impressive mode of expressing himself, giving great assurance and confidence to the sick. In all the excitement of surgical operations he displayed the greatest composure' (Bell, *Life*, 112). As his infirmities increased he became too feeble to travel to Cheltenham and Bath for his health, and ultimately developed 'a complete failure of appetite' (ibid., 107). He died at Newington House, Edinburgh, on 5 April 1806; he was survived by his wife.

JOHN KIRKUP

Sources B. Bell, *The life, character and writings of Benjamin Bell, FRCSE, FRSE* (1868) · Chambers, *Scots.* (1835) · J. D. Comrie, *History of Scottish medicine to 1860* (1927), 213–14 · A. Miles, *The Edinburgh school of surgery before Lister* (1918), 48–59 · B. Bell, *Essays on agriculture* (1802) · D. Guthrie, *A history of medicine* (1945), 230 · O. H. Wangensteen and S. D. Wangensteen, *The rise of surgery* (1978), 36, 48 · B. Bell, 'A brief review and estimate of the professional writings of Benjamin Bell', *Edinburgh Medical Journal*, 14 (1868–9), 408–33 · J. D. Comrie, *History of Scottish medicine*, 2nd edn, 1 (1932), 331–2 · P. J. Wallis and R. V. Wallis, *Eighteenth century medics*, 2nd edn (1988) · *DNB* · *IGI*

Likenesses J. Kay, cartoon, 1791, BM, NPG · W. and J. Walker, line engraving, pubd 1791 (after H. Raeburn), BM, NPG; repro. in B. Bell, *A system of surgery* (1801), frontispiece · J. Tassie, paste medallion, 1792, Scot. NPG · plaster medallion, 1792 (after J. Tassie), Scot. NPG · H. Raeburn, painting; Sothebys, 4 July 2001, lot 55 [*see illus.*] · engraving, repro. in Comrie, *History of Scottish medicine* · plaque, repro. in Bell, *The life … of Benjamin Bell*, frontispiece

Bell, Sir Charles (1774–1842), physiologist and surgeon, the youngest of the six children of William Bell (1704–1779), an Episcopal clergyman, and his wife, Margaret Morrice, the daughter of a clergyman, was born in November 1774 at Fountainbridge, at that time a suburb of Edinburgh. The family subsequently moved to George Street. One of his brothers was John *Bell (1763–1820) who also attained fame as a surgeon; another was George Joseph *Bell (1770–1843) who became professor of Scots law at Edinburgh University. Following his father's death Bell received his early education from his mother. It was she who first developed in him a talent for drawing.

Education and early career Bell studied at Edinburgh high school between 1784 and 1788 before attending classes at the university. Among the professors Bell encountered was Dugald Stewart, whose lectures on moral philosophy left a lasting impression on him. Although he showed little active interest in politics, Bell became familiar with members of the whig circle in the city, including Francis Jeffrey and Henry Brougham and the other founders of the *Edinburgh Review*.

By the early 1790s Bell had determined on a career in medicine. Between 1792 and 1799 he attended several of the courses on offer at the university medical school including anatomy, botany, chemistry, and the practice of medicine, as well as following the clinical lectures at the Royal Infirmary. At the same time he began to assist his brother John, who was teaching anatomy and surgery in the Edinburgh extramural school. According to a contemporary skit the brothers arranged between them a 'prudent division of labour': while John lectured on surgical

Sir Charles Bell (1774–1842), by John Stevens, c.1821

practice, Charles taught 'the guts and the brains / The uterine system and all that'.

In addition to strictly professional studies Bell sought to enhance his skills as an artist, seeking assistance from the painter David Allan. Bell made good use of his artistic talents in his later career. While still a student he, in 1798, published a *System of Dissections* illustrated by his own drawings. In this text Bell tried to introduce a new mode of anatomy teaching, maintaining 'that the common books are not fitted to be assistants in dissections' (Bell, *System*, iii). Throughout the work Bell tried to address the needs of the student of practical anatomy. He also emphasized the relevance of anatomy to practice. While assisting his brother Bell developed a talent for making wax models of anatomical and pathological specimens for teaching purposes, some of which survive in the museum of the Royal College of Surgeons of Edinburgh.

In 1799 Bell was admitted as a Fellow of the College of Surgeons of Edinburgh and began to practise at the Edinburgh Royal Infirmary. In 1802 he published *The Anatomy of the Brain, Explained in a Series of Engravings*. He provided his own illustrations to this work, and insisted that in this department of anatomy in particular the task could not be left to an artist who lacked a training in the field. While the artist's task 'no doubt is to copy accurately from the dissected Brain, yet such previous knowledge, and the study of the subject, give to his representations a minuteness of intention which cannot otherwise be attained' (Bell, *Anatomy of the Brain*, vi). Along with John Bell he also published an *Anatomy of the Human Body*. Charles's special contribution on the anatomy of the brain and nerves appeared in 1804. The work passed through numerous editions.

Following the reorganization of the surgical service at the Royal Infirmary—of which John Bell had been a fierce opponent—Charles failed to obtain one of the new posts of surgeon-in-ordinary to the hospital. He found it increasingly difficult to establish himself as a practitioner and teacher in Edinburgh: it may be that his known whig connections militated against his professional advancement.

Move to London In 1804 Bell decided to move to London where opportunities were more extensive and patronage more diffuse although the competition was no less intense. He at first lived at 22 Fluyder Street then in 1805 moved to Leicester Street; he subsequently occupied addresses in Soho Square and Brook Street. Bell's early years in London proved a struggle: he found it difficult to attract both patients and students. He wrote:

> I could see that much could be done—but where to begin? Where to find a resting place? How show my capacity for teaching or illustrating my profession. These days of misery greatly tended to fortify me so that nothing afterwards could come amiss or bring me to a condition of suffering equal to what I then endured. (Crosse, 32)

Bell first circulated, before publishing, in 1806, his *Anatomy of Expression* in an attempt to enhance his reputation in the capital. This work attempted to explain the anatomical basis for the artistic representation of emotion. Despite the favourable attention the book received in polite society, however, professional advancement still proved elusive. Bell's fortunes improved when on 3 June 1811 he married Marion Shaw, the daughter of Charles Shaw, clerk of the county of Ayr, and his wife, Barbara Wright. He used the dowry to buy from James Wilson for £2000, 'all my money to the last penny and eighteen pence more' (Crosse, 33), a share in the Hunterian School of Medicine in Great Windmill Street, London. Bell was in 1814 appointed a surgeon to the Middlesex Hospital. In the same year he became a member of the Royal College of Surgeons of London. In 1824 Bell lectured as the senior professor of anatomy and surgery at the college and subsequently became a member of the council. In 1831 he was knighted by William IV.

After Wilson's death in 1821 Bell taught at Great Windmill Street in conjunction with his brother-in-law, John *Shaw (1792–1827). Bell's lectures had previously been conducted in less prepossessing surroundings at his (allegedly haunted) house in Leicester Street, on the purchase of which he said he did 'not know that at any time I was more distressed than when I found the sort of house I possessed' (Crosse, 32). In his teaching Bell paid special attention to the anatomy of the nerves and brain, and from about 1807 he used his lectures as an opportunity to expound novel notions of the structure and function of these organs. He had by this time developed an ambition to make a grand discovery comparable to William Harvey's demonstration of the circulation of the blood. Bell's Windmill Street School attracted artists eager for anatomical instruction as well as medical students: the painter Benjamin Robert Haydon was among those who followed Bell's classes and required his pupils—including members of the Landseer family—to do likewise. Haydon also supported Bell in his attempts to become professor of anatomy at the Royal Academy; these efforts were, however, unsuccessful.

Bell throughout retained an interest in improving the practice of surgery. Many of his pupils were army and naval surgeons serving during the Napoleonic wars; and Bell devoted particular attention to the problems of military surgery. In 1809 he attended the Haslar Hospital to help treat wounded soldiers evacuated from Corunna, and in 1815 he travelled to Brussels to assist in caring for casualties from the battle of Waterloo. In 1814 Bell published *A Dissertation on Gun-Shot Wounds* in which he attempted to establish principles for the treatment of these injuries which, he maintained, posed special problems for the surgeon. As with all surgical practice, however, Bell insisted on the need for a sound knowledge of the anatomy of the parts before attempting any operation. At the same time he maintained that in many cases surgical intervention was unnecessary and might even do harm, noting that 'it requires address to compose the patient, and to convince the friends that nothing ought to be done' (Bell, *Dissertation*, 26).

Work on the brain and the nervous system In 1811 Bell committed his views on the structure and function of the nervous system to print in *Idea of a New Anatomy of the Brain*. Only a small number of copies was printed, which Bell distributed among his circle of acquaintances: he appears to have had misgivings about presenting his theories immediately to a wider public. Bell set out to refute the commonly held notion that the brain as a whole constituted a common sensorium and that the nerves performed both sensory and motor functions. He maintained instead that different parts of the brain discharged different offices: the cerebrum and the cerebellum were functionally distinct. Bell argued that the anatomical differences between these two structures alone made this probable.

Throughout his career Bell relied on anatomical investigation as his principal method for investigating the functions of the nervous system. Unlike contemporary French physiologists Bell always showed a great reluctance for humanitarian reasons to resort to vivisection as a means of physiological enquiry. Moreover, he doubted the scientific value of many of the investigations that were undertaken by others: 'Experimenters', he argued, 'are ever leading themselves into errors, and making fruitless dissections on living animals from inattention to the lessons of anatomy' (C. Bell, *A Series of Engravings, Explaining the Course of the Nerves*, 1816, xv). When he did make such experiments he took pains to reduce the amount of suffering to the animal. Although his doctrine rested mainly on anatomical evidence, Bell reluctantly recognized that some experiments on living subjects were necessary to corroborate the new understanding of the operations of the brain he propounded.

Bell maintained that there were severe practical difficulties in experimenting directly on the brain. He held that it was, however, possible to trace the fibres proceeding from the cerebrum and cerebellum into respectively the anterior and posterior columns of the spinal cord. Bell therefore hit on the plan of seeking to establish the functions of these parts of the brain by acting on the two roots of the spinal nerves. In his 1811 work Bell reported that he could cut across the posterior root without causing muscular contractions. If, however, he touched the anterior fasciculus with his knife the muscles of the animal's back were thrown into convulsions. This result led Bell to conclude that 'the cerebrum and cerebellum were parts distinct in function' (Bell, *Idea*, 23) because the spinal nerves that arose in them displayed different properties. He maintained that the anterior column derived from the cerebrum possessed both motor and sensory functions. The nerves proceeding through the posterior column from the cerebellum were, on the other hand, involved in the more secret operations of the body: that is, those that were not under the immediate control of the will.

It is important to insist on the detail of what Bell said in his 1811 text because of a priority dispute in which he later became involved with the French physiologist François Magendie. Magendie in 1822 undertook a series of experiments that showed the anterior roots of the nerves to be exclusively motor in function, while the posterior roots conveyed sensory impressions to the brain. Bell subsequently held that this was merely a restatement of the doctrine he had propounded in 1811, overlooking the manifest differences between his and Magendie's results. In an 1824 account of his own experiments, for instance, Bell maintained that on 'finding this confirmation of the opinion, that the anterior column of the spinal marrow and the anterior roots of the spinal nerves were for motion, the conclusion presented itself that the posterior column and the posterior roots were for sensibility' (C. Bell, *An Exposition of the Natural System of the Nerves of the Human Body*, 1824, 33–4). Contemporaries and some historians were persuaded by Bell's disingenuous claims: in Germany the distinction between the function of the anterior and posterior roots became known as the *Lex Belliana*. More recent commentators have, however, awarded Magendie priority in ascertaining the distinct functions of the spinal nerves.

London University and return to Edinburgh Bell was involved in the establishment of the London University. He saw the projected medical school as a means of remedying shortcomings in the existing provision for the teaching of medicine in London. Through his former Edinburgh associates, such as Henry Brougham and Leonard Horner, Bell was able to exercise some influence over plans for the new institution. Along with J. F. Meckel and G. S. Pattison, Bell was in 1827 appointed as a professor of anatomy, surgery, and physiology. When in October 1828 the university medical school formally opened Bell gave the inaugural address.

The early history of the university's medical department was to prove fraught with difficulties. Meckel soon withdrew from his chair leaving Bell and Pattison to divide the teaching between them. Bell agreed to serve as professor of physiology and clinical surgery, and also to lecture on surgery until a professor was appointed. There was much friction between him and Pattison, however, over the organization of the anatomical department. In 1830 Bell threatened to resign unless reforms were made to the medical school. In September of that year he gave up the chairs of surgery and clinical surgery. Later in 1830 the university council relieved him of his responsibilities for physiology teaching.

Bell had conducted his clinical lectures at the Middlesex Hospital. After severing his links with the university he endeavoured together with other members of staff to establish a regular medical school at the hospital. In April 1835 they petitioned the hospital in favour of the measure and met with a favourable reception. When the new school was opened in October of that year Bell was to teach surgery and anatomy. Almost at once, however, he was offered the opportunity to fill the vacant post of professor of surgery at Edinburgh University. He accepted and returned to Edinburgh in August 1836, living in Ainslie Place.

Bell spent the remainder of his career working in Edinburgh. These years were to prove a considerable financial disappointment: he earned only around £400 p.a. from his chair, and his private practice was also poor. As well as publishing his lectures on surgery Bell worked on a new edition of the *Anatomy of Expression*. To this end, in 1840 he travelled to Italy in order to view various works of art.

Bell and natural theology Along with Henry Brougham and others of the whig party Bell became involved with the work of the Society for the Diffusion of Useful Knowledge. Bell was concerned to resist what he saw as the materialist tendencies of some medical writers and to show that science was fully compatible with Christian belief. Between 1827 and 1829 he produced a series of tracts for the society designed to show that the animal body displayed signs of God's wisdom. These were published in 1838 as *Animal Mechanics*. In 1833, also at Brougham's instigation, Bell published a Bridgewater Treatise on the *Hand* illustrated with his own drawings. This was another exercise in natural theology that argued that the structure of the hand provided evidence of divine design and benevolence. In 1836 Bell and Brougham produced an annotated edition of William Paley's *Natural Theology*. Bell's various writings on natural theology proved extremely popular: the work on the *Hand* in particular passed through numerous editions.

Bell enjoyed literature, music and, when he had time, fishing. He loved the countryside and kept a copy of Gilbert White's *Natural History of Selborne* close by. In his later years Bell suffered from angina pectoris, a condition that seriously restricted his activities. He died on 28 April 1842 from heart disease while visiting acquaintances at Hallow Park, near Worcester, and was buried in Hallow churchyard, where a tablet was erected in his memory with an inscription by Lord Jeffrey. He left his widow in straitened financial circumstances; she was, however, awarded a civil-list pension of £1000 by Robert Peel's government.

L. S. JACYNA

Sources G. Gordon-Taylor and E. W. Walls, *Sir Charles Bell: his life and times* (1958) · A. Pichot, *The life and labours of Sir Charles Bell* (1860) · *Letters of Sir Charles Bell*, ed. G. J. Bell · H. H. Bellot, *University College, London, 1826–1926* (1929) · P. F. Cranefield, *The way in and the way out: François Magendie, Charles Bell and the roots of the spinal nerves* (1974) · E. Clarke and L. S. Jacyna, *Nineteenth-century origins of neuroscientific concepts* (1987) · A. Desmond, *The politics of evolution* (1989) · M. Cazort, M. Kornell, and K. B. Roberts, *The ingenious machine of nature: four centuries of art and anatomy* (1996), nos. 72–74.4 [exhibition catalogue, National Gallery of Canada, 31 Oct 1996 – 5 Jan 1997] · V. M. Crosse, ed., *A surgeon in the eighteenth century: the life and times of John Green Crosse* (1968) · m. cert. · administration, PRO, PROB 6/218, fol. 48v

Archives LUL, journal of Italian tour · NL Scot. · Royal College of Surgeons, Edinburgh, papers · U. Edin. L. · UCL · University of Kansas, Medical Center, Kansas City, Clendering History of Medicine Library and Museum, travel journal · Wellcome L., drawings and letters · Wellcome L., MSS relating to anatomy of brain | UCL, letters to Lord Brougham; letters to Society for the Diffusion of Useful Knowledge

Likenesses A. Stewart, portrait, 1804 · J. Stevens, oils, c.1821, NPG [see illus.] · H. Weeks, marble bust, 1856, Royal College of Surgeons of Edinburgh · J. Thompson, stipple (after Ballantyne), BM, NPG; repro. in T. J. Pettigrew, *Medical portrait gallery*, 3 vols. (1839) · coloured mezzotint, Wellcome L. · lithograph, Wellcome L. · lithograph, NPG; repro. in *Lancet gallery of medical portraits* · memorial tablet, Hallow church, Worcester · oils, Scot. NPG

Wealth at death £3000: administration, PRO, PROB 6/218, fol. 48v

Bell, Sir Charles Alfred (1870–1945), administrator in India and Tibetologist, was born in Fort William, Calcutta, on 31 October 1870, the third son of Henry Bell, of the Indian Civil Service, and his wife, Anne, daughter of George Dumbell, of Douglas, Isle of Man. From Winchester Bell passed the Indian Civil Service examinations of 1889 and, after two years at New College, Oxford, went to Bengal in 1891. For nine years he worked in the plains, but in 1900, after a run of bad health, he was transferred to the gentler climate of Darjeeling.

Darjeeling introduced Bell to the culture of Tibet, which fascinated him. In 1904 he was given charge of the Chumbi valley, temporarily ceded by Tibet as a result of Francis Younghusband's controversial mission to Lhasa, and in 1905 he published *A Manual of Colloquial Tibetan*. In 1908 he was appointed political officer in Sikkim, which made him additionally the diplomatic agent for Bhutan and Tibet. He remained in this post until 1919, marrying, on 15 January 1912, Cashie Kerr (1876/7–1935), daughter of David Fernie, shipowner, of Liverpool and Blundellsands, Lancashire.

In Sikkim Bell restored internal autonomy to the local ruler and, wary of the potential for ethnic conflict, attempted to limit the influence of Marwari traders from the plains. Similarly, in Bhutan he negotiated a treaty (1910) whereby the king retained autonomy in internal matters but handed over foreign affairs to the British, in effect establishing Bhutan as a British protectorate. In Tibet, however, Bell was forced to watch Britain reverse Younghusband's forward policy and allow the Chinese to occupy the country, although he in part compensated for Britain's apathy by befriending the thirteenth Dalai Lama, who sought sanctuary in Darjeeling in 1910. Bell was himself a religious man, slightly built, with delicate features and an unassuming demeanour, and the Dalai Lama warmed to him, thereafter treating him as a friend and trusted adviser.

After the revolution of 1911–12 in China, during which the Tibetans repulsed the Chinese, Bell finally convinced his superiors that they should confront the power vacuum in Tibet. In 1913, the Chinese were brought, somewhat truculently, to a tripartite convention at Simla, which Bell attended as adviser to the British plenipotentiary, Sir Henry McMahon. McMahon won initial agreement to an accord which recognized Tibet's symbolic subordination to China while actually subjecting her to British influence, but the Chinese refused to ratify it, justly accusing Bell of telling the Tibetan plenipotentiary what to say in the negotiations. Bell's influence with the Tibetan plenipotentiary, the Lönchen Shatra, went further. He persuaded him that in return for Britain undertaking to shield Tibet from China, Tibet should allow goods from British India to enter duty-free and agree to shift the Indo-Tibetan border from the foothills to the crest of the Himalayas, giving India the fertile territory of Tawang (now Arunachal Pradesh) and establishing a new frontier known as the McMahon line. Bell was created CMG for his work with McMahon, but again he saw Britain squander its potential for influence. Several times during the First World War the Dalai Lama begged him to persuade the Indian government to allow Tibet to purchase modern weaponry and to levy duties on British Indian imports to pay for military expansion. Embarrassed by the tepidity of Britain's performance as an ally, Bell wholeheartedly endorsed these requests but was repeatedly rebuffed by the government.

In 1919 Bell retired, but he stayed on in Darjeeling to research Tibetan culture. He was thus on hand to be recalled in October 1920 to undertake a mission to Lhasa, a move triggered by the news that China had dispatched a new mission there. For Bell it was a wonderful personal opportunity, but the recent Montagu–Chelmsford reforms forced him to modify his previously hawkish stance. He had never liked Indian interference in the region and, now that Britain had signalled its eventual departure from Asia, he began to push for meaningful Tibetan independence rather than the satellite status he had advanced earlier. He knew that independence depended on bureaucratic reform and a bigger army, but Lhasa's three great monasteries opposed any extension of military authority and exhibited a militancy throughout his mission which brought Tibet to the verge of civil war. When posters appeared in Lhasa calling for his death, Bell was moved to tone down his advice to the Dalai Lama, suggesting that he proceed cautiously with reform. As a result of his mission the arms embargo was lifted and Britain agreed to deal directly with Tibet without reference to the Chinese, measures which were sufficient to establish an Anglo-Tibetan cordiality that survived until 1947.

Bell retired permanently in 1921. He had been made CIE in 1919 and in 1922 was promoted to KCIE. He devoted the rest of his life to making Tibet intelligible to the wider world, and in 1924 published *Tibet Past and Present*, followed by *The People of Tibet* (1928) and *The Religion of Tibet* (1931). His final work, *Portrait of the Dalai Lama* (1946), was completed only a few days before his death. In researching it he revisited Tibet in 1934 and travelled on to Mongolia, Siberia, Manchuria, and China. He was accompanied throughout by his wife, but she died of cerebral meningitis in Peking (Beijing) in September 1935, after which he returned home. No longer constrained as an official, he had on this trip advised his Tibetan friends to seek an accommodation with China while their bargaining position was still strong. He saw little hope of lasting independence.

In 1939, with war in Europe imminent, Bell uprooted himself from his Berkshire home and went to British Columbia to finish his book. He died there, at his residence, the Old Charming Inn, Oak Bay, Victoria, on 8 March 1945. He was survived by a son, Major Arthur Fernie Bell (*b.* 1912), and two daughters.   KATHERINE PRIOR

Sources C. J. Christie, 'Sir Charles Bell: a memoir', *Asian Affairs*, 64 (1977) · A. Lamb, *Tibet, China and India, 1914–1950* (1989) · A. K. J. Singh, *Himalayan triangle* (1988) · M. C. Goldstein, *A history of modern Tibet, 1913–1951* (1989) · P. Collister, *Bhutan and the British* (1987) · ecclesiastical records, BL OIOC · *The Times* (12 March 1945), 6 · *The Times* (21 Sept 1935), 12 · *WWW* · H. J. Hardy, ed., *Winchester College, 1867–1920: a register*, 2nd edn (1923) · *DNB*
Archives BL OIOC | CUL, Hardinge MSS
Likenesses photograph, *c.*1920, repro. in C. Bell, *Tibet past and present* (1924) · photograph, 1933, BL OIOC
Wealth at death £16,328 3*s.* 11*d.*—(in England): Canadian probate sealed in England, 22 Oct 1946, *CGPLA Eng. & Wales*

Bell, Charles Frederic Moberly (1847–1911), journalist and newspaper manager, was born on 2 April 1847 in Alexandria, youngest of six children of Thomas Bell (*d.* 1859), merchant, and his first wife, Hester Louisa Dodd, *née* David, widow of a naval chaplain. Following his wife's premature death, Thomas Bell sent his children to England into the care of a relation by marriage; he remarried in 1853. After attending a local day school in south London, Bell was enrolled at a school in Wallasey, Cheshire, kept by the Revd William Clayton Greene, who remembered his pupil 'Charlie Bell' with affection and pride. The offer of a clerkship in his father's old firm, Peel & Co., brought Bell back to Alexandria in 1865. He soon approached *The Times* to propose speedier arrangements for transmitting news. With the lists of materials forwarded (part of the documentation for cargoes shipped to Britain) Bell enclosed reports on events he thought of public interest, showing an instinct for journalism that led to his appointment as Egyptian correspondent in 1867. Bell's work for Peel & Co. was eventually rewarded by a partnership and most departments were placed under his general management. His standing in the local business community was reflected in an appointment to one of the Egyptian mixed courts.

Charles Frederic Moberly Bell (1847–1911), by George Charles Beresford, *c.*1910

In 1874 Bell met Ethel Chataway, a cousin of his brother-in-law, Edmund Carver, and eldest daughter of the Revd James Chataway. They were married, at Rotherwick, Southampton, on 5 August 1875. It was a happy marriage, from which Bell derived much comfort and support. Two sons and four daughters resulted; one daughter predeceased her father. On the eve of the wedding, Bell was informed of his dismissal from Peel & Co. In November 1875 the Bells were back in Egypt. An agency for a Belgian trader was soon supplemented by other employments. From 1876 Bell resumed his connection with *The Times* as an occasional correspondent, being reappointed Egyptian correspondent in 1882. Bell's descriptions of events following from Arabi Pasha's revolt, including the bombardment of Alexandria, were masterpieces of reporting, earning him a reputation as an ideal correspondent. In 1880 Bell, with others, founded the *Egyptian Gazette*, though he severed his connection in 1882 when legislation threatened to suppress independent journalism in Egypt. Bell's exceptional knowledge of Egyptian affairs and personalities was displayed in three books published between 1884 and 1888, and subsequently in letters in *The Times* signed by 'A twenty years resident in Egypt'. In September 1884 Bell sustained a severe ankle injury, which left him permanently lame. A bone had to be removed, and Bell had this mounted in a stick, declaring it should yet help him walk. While convalescing he visited London and met members of the Walter family. Arthur Walter, nominally joint manager of *The Times* alongside John Cameron Mac-Donald, was much impressed by Bell's energy and capabilities. In February 1890, after MacDonald's death, Walter asked Bell to 'come over here for a few months'. He arrived in March, and his appointment was soon made permanent. Since Arthur Walter played little part in the paper's management, Bell was *de facto* in charge.

The Times had lost money and reputation through its publication of the Pigott forgeries of C. S. Parnell's letters in 1887. Bell immediately set out to repair the damage. His prime interest was in the paper's standing as an organ of influence in public life. He strengthened the foreign news service by establishing a foreign department in Printing House Square. Bell also succeeded, by subtle means, in appointing Flora Shaw as *The Times* colonial expert within the hitherto entirely masculine editorial preserve. His political interests—he described himself as a radical with imperialistic leanings—led Bell to maintain direct contact with certain overseas correspondents, while at home he cultivated a personal network of influential contacts, entertaining them at his own expense and gaining a reputation for absolute discretion. Bell was continually seeking ways of increasing circulation, but realized that *The Times* needed a subsidy from other sources. He launched several profitable publishing sideshows. With Messrs Hooper and Jackson, American publishers, Bell negotiated favourable terms for further ventures, culminating in 1905 with The Times Book Club. The club's practice of selling nearly new books at discount prices led to a 'book war' with the publishers, which Bell waged with customary vigour. By 1908 the proprietors of *The Times* were pressing for a financial reconstruction. Bell learned from a news item received for publication that *The Times* was to be reorganized under C. Arthur Pearson's direction. Convinced that this arrangement would be detrimental to the paper, Bell acted independently to find an alternative. Through an intermediary a meeting was set up with Lord Northcliffe, and plans were made to establish The Times Publishing Co. Ltd with leading members of *The Times* staff as directors and Bell as managing director. Bell sought guarantees for the paper's character and editorial independence, but was obliged to agree to carry out Northcliffe's absolute instructions. At first things went well under the new ownership; Bell was credited with having saved *The Times*. Northcliffe respected 'old Bell', but increasingly found him an obstacle in the way of change. Bell saw himself as the sole protector of the *status quo*, and continued to be a restraining influence in spite of failing health.

Bell was a large man, with a strong face and dark complexion, which suggested to some opponents a Jewish ancestry (a family tradition among the Montefiores identified Sir Moses as his father). Able to work long hours at high pressure and full speed, he was often impatient and confrontational, though always ready to admit his mistakes. At home he was a genial family man; his sense of humour emerged in conversation—talking was his sport—and in correspondence. Bell's constant motivation was the well-being of *The Times*, and his disregard for self-

interest earned him great respect. His working methods were old-fashioned, and he never learned to delegate. He particularly enjoyed letter writing, and it was as he ended a paragraph in a typically witty letter on newspaper copyright that he succumbed to a heart attack in his office at Printing House Square on 5 April 1911; he was buried in Brompton cemetery on 8 April.

GEOFFREY HAMILTON

Sources E. H. C. M. Bell, *The life and letters of C. F. Moberly Bell* (1927) · [S. Morison and others], *The history of The Times*, 3 (1947) · *Egyptian Gazette* (6 April 1911) · *The Times* (6 April 1911) · F. H. Kitchin, *Moberly Bell and his times* (1925) · J. C. Woollan, 'The Men of The Times', *Caxton Magazine* (May 1902), 23–8 · O. Woods and J. Bishop, *The story of 'The Times'* (1983) · E. Bell, 'The Times Book Club and the Publishers' Association', in F. Macmillan, *The net book agreement and the book war, 1906–1908* (1924), 33–67 · E. H. C. M. Bell, *Flora Shaw* (1947) · W. S. Blunt, *Mr Blunt and The Times: a memorandum as to the attitude of The Times newspaper in Egyptian affairs* (privately printed, London, 1907) · S. E. Koss, *The rise and fall of the political press in Britain*, 2 (1984) · *The Times* (7 April 1911) · *The Times* (10 April 1911)
Archives Hunt. L., letters · News Int. RO, papers | BL, corresp. with Macmillans, Add. MS 55038 · BL, corresp. with Lord Northcliffe, Add. MS 62258 · Bodl. RH, letters to Ernest Gedge · HLRO, letters to John St Loe Strachey · Mitchell L., NSW, letters to G. E. Morrison · NL Scot., corresp. with Lord Rosebery · PRO, corresp. with Lord Cromer, FO 633
Likenesses G. C. Beresford, two photographs, *c*.1900–1910, NPG [*see illus.*] · sketch, 1902, repro. in *Caxton Magazine* (May 1902) · E. Fuchs, oils, 1904, Times Newspapers Ltd art collection, London · G. C. Beresford, photograph, 1908, repro. in Kitchin, *Moberly Bell*, frontispiece · photograph, 1910, repro. in *History of The Times* · Histed, photograph (aged fifty-five), repro. in Kitchin, *Moberly Bell*, facing p. 70
Wealth at death £13,963 10s. 6d.: resworn probate, 27 April 1911, CGPLA Eng. & Wales

Bell, (Arthur) Clive Heward (1881–1964), art critic and writer, was born on 16 September 1881 at East Shefford, Berkshire, the second son of William Heward Bell (1849–1927), civil engineer, and his wife, Hannah Taylor Cory (1850–1942). In the words of his son Quentin, he came from a 'family that drew its wealth from Welsh mines and expended it upon the destruction of wild animals' (Q. Bell, *Bloomsbury*, 23). Their home, Cleeve House at Seend in Wiltshire, was a Regency villa rebuilt as a mock Jacobean mansion and decorated throughout with sporting trophies: growing up there filled Bell with a lifelong horror of vulgarity and a disdain of philistinism. He was educated at Marlborough College (1895–9), where he professed to have been miserable, and at Trinity College, Cambridge, which he entered in the same term (October 1899) as Thoby Stephen, Lytton Strachey, Saxon Sydney-Turner, and Leonard Woolf. The reading society which these freshmen founded in their first year was always claimed by Bell to have laid the foundations of the so-called Bloomsbury group. Like Thoby Stephen, he combined a love of hunting and the outdoors with intellectual curiosity—and in his case an early interest in visual art. Although thought by his fellow undergraduates too worldly for membership of the select Cambridge Conversazione Society (known as the Apostles), Bell anyway fell under the sway of that secret brotherhood's presiding spirit, the philosopher

(Arthur) Clive Heward Bell (1881–1964), by Roger Fry, c.1924

G. E. Moore, whom he later said was 'the dominant influence in all our lives' (C. Bell, 28). Despite obtaining only a second class in both parts of the historical tripos, he was awarded an Earl of Derby studentship in 1902. He went to Paris in 1904, ostensibly to pursue historical research, but in fact wasted his time profitably acquainting himself with the work of the old masters and of modern French painters, and acquiring a taste for café life and the company of artists.

On his return to London, Bell was prominent in the group of friends who met on Thursday evenings at 46 Gordon Square in Bloomsbury, the house shared by the four children of Sir Leslie *Stephen (1832–1904), the eminent Victorian man of letters and first editor of the *Dictionary of National Biography*. Following the early death of Thoby Stephen, Bell married, on 7 February 1907, Thoby's elder sister Vanessa (1879–1961) [*see* Bell, Vanessa]. Clive and Vanessa Bell had two sons: Julian Heward *Bell (1908–1937), a poet who was killed in the Spanish Civil War, and Quentin *Bell (1910–1996), an artist, teacher, and writer. The marriage ceased to exist in anything but name before the First World War, partly because of Bell's flirtation with his sister-in-law Virginia (1882–1941) [*see* Woolf, (Adeline) Virginia] who in 1912 married Leonard Woolf. Thereafter Bell was free to enjoy a succession of love affairs, while remaining on the best of terms with Vanessa, who from 1915 lived with her artistic collaborator, Duncan Grant. Angelica Bell (*b.* 1918), whose father was Grant and who later married David Garnett, was brought up as Clive Bell's daughter.

A chance meeting in 1910 with Roger Fry, in a railway carriage between Cambridge and London, altered the whole tenor of Bell's life. Fry was considerably older, and was already well known as an authority on the early Italian Renaissance; but his new interest in contemporary French painting coincided with Bell's. Bell was Fry's eager lieutenant in the organization of the first Post-Impressionist Exhibition at the Grafton Galleries in London that autumn; for the second show, in 1912, he selected an 'English Group'. His huge admiration for Cézanne—whom he called 'the Christopher Columbus of a new continent of form' (C. Bell, *Art*, 1914, 207)—was advertised in the book for which he is chiefly remembered, *Art*, published in 1914. Here he put forward his famous theory of 'significant form', the proposition that the quality common to all works of art, from the Byzantines to the cubists, consists of 'relations and combinations of lines and colours' (ibid., 8). The representational elements in a picture were, he believed, irrelevant to aesthetic contemplation: in a much-quoted passage he declared that 'to appreciate a work of art we need bring with us nothing from life, no knowledge of its ideas and affairs, no familiarity with its emotions' (ibid., 25). There is much that is tautologous in Bell's argument, and a good deal that is absurd—see, for instance, his insistence that 'The bulk ... of those who flourished between the High Renaissance and the contemporary movement may be divided into two classes, virtuosi and dunces' (ibid., 40)—and his central thesis has been widely discounted; but it should be allowed that he is much less dogmatic than is usually supposed. *Art* owed much to the writings of Fry, as well as to Moore's *Principia ethica* (1903); it is best read, however, in the context of its time, as a manifesto for post-impressionism. Bell's polemical style was ideally suited to his demolition of canonical aesthetic values, and his book had an enormously liberating effect on a generation of artists and viewers.

Later Bell abandoned theory almost entirely, but he continued to wield considerable influence as a critic, and his exhibition reviews for *The Nation* and later the *New Statesman* between 1913 and 1944 were compulsory reading for a wide audience. If he was rather too prone to denigrate English art in favour of French, and was sometimes guilty of over-praising his friends, he was surely right in 1920 to recognize Picasso and Matisse as the two giants of the modern movement. He also encouraged younger painters such as Ivon Hitchens and Victor Pasmore; but he never came to terms with abstractionism, which his earlier writings had anticipated. His books of criticism, mostly comprising articles for newspapers and periodicals, included *Pot-Boilers* (1918), *Since Cézanne* (1922), *Landmarks in Nineteenth-Century Painting* (1927), *An Account of French Painting* (1931), and *Enjoying Pictures* (1934).

Bell was an unwavering pacifist in both world wars. He spent much of the first at Garsington, the Oxfordshire home of Philip and Lady Ottoline Morrell, where he undertook desultory employment as a farmworker. His pamphlet *Peace at Once* (1915), in which he courageously argued for a negotiated settlement with Germany, was seized by the police, became the subject of a court case, and was destroyed. In a little-known essay entitled *On*

British Freedom (1923) he made a spirited attack on the modern state's interference in matters of censorship, prohibition, and sexuality. He returned to political themes in *Civilization: an Essay* (1928), in which he characteristically upheld the superiority of spiritual values over material needs. However, his belief that these could flourish under the rule of dictators presaged his support for appeasement in the 1930s. 'Civilized' was Bell's highest term of praise, and he maintained that it was best exemplified by the societies of Periclean Athens, fifteenth-century Florence, and France during the *grand siècle*; but Virginia Woolf maliciously remarked of his book that 'in the end it turns out that civilization is a lunch party at No. 50 Gordon Square' (Q. Bell, *Bloomsbury*, 88).

During the 1920s Bell was frequently in Paris, often accompanied by his mistress at that time, the stylish hostess, patron, and writer Mary Hutchinson, née Barnes (1889–1977). He relished his contact there with artists—especially Picasso and André Derain, the leading exponent of fauvism—musicians, and writers, and he was a witness at some of the great set piece occasions of that decade, such as the famous party given to celebrate the première of Diaghilev's production of *Renard* in 1922 at which Stravinsky, Picasso, Proust, and James Joyce were among the guests. Between the wars he was the best-informed English commentator on the Parisian scene, which he brought alive in the pages of a number of journals, including the *New Republic* in America and *Vogue* in Britain. He always preferred the literature of France (particularly of the eighteenth century) to that of his own country; and his sympathetic study *Proust* (1928) was the first book in English on that author. Bell's Francophilia was sometimes a joke to his friends—his speech and his letters were larded with French phrases—and it was reported that he celebrated his appointment as a chevalier of the Légion d'honneur in 1936 by addressing a bemused audience at Oxford in French.

In 1939 Bell gave up his London home at 50 Gordon Square and based himself at Charleston, the Sussex farmhouse which he shared with Vanessa Bell and Duncan Grant. Thereafter he travelled regularly to France, where he renewed his friendships with Picasso and Matisse; and in 1950 he was invited to undertake a lecture tour of America. For the last twenty years of his life his devoted companion was Barbara Bagenal, née Hiles (1891–1984). In 1956 he published a collection of memoirs, *Old Friends*, which celebrated his friendships with the leading figures of his time on both sides of the channel, among them Walter Sickert, Maynard Keynes, T. S. Eliot, and Jean Cocteau. It was Bell's immense enthusiasm and passionate engagement with life that endeared him to his many friends. He was a noted host—to David Garnett he seemed 'an almost perfect example of James Mill's Utilitarian theory that a man cannot become rich without enriching his neighbours' (Garnett, 24)—and a welcome guest at a variety of salons. More sociable than most in his immediate circle, he never allowed his society to become exclusive or dull; his comparative wealth (which meant that he never had to earn a living) also ensured that it never lacked comfort.

His talent for gossip, however, often got him into trouble; so too did his barely concealed snobbery. He was equally at home entertaining in London restaurants as he was tramping through the Sussex countryside in threadbare tweeds with his dog and a gun. But he was not without vanity, and his comic habits included 'the anxious rearrangement of the thick carroty hair that grew on only part of his cranium, and had a way of getting out of place, much to his agitation' (Partridge, 80). The portrait of him painted by Virginia Woolf in her diaries, in which he is often likened to a flamboyant and voluble parakeet, highlights his absurdities: and in the rehabilitation of Bloomsbury which occurred after his death his reputation alone did not flourish. Bell died at Fitzroy House Nursing Home, Fitzroy Square, London, on 17 September 1964, from cancer, and was cremated four days later at the West London crematorium.   JAMES BEECHEY

Sources C. Bell, *Old friends* (1956) · Q. Bell, *Elders and betters* (1995) · J. Beechey, *Clive Bell* (2000) · Q. Bell, *Bloomsbury* (1968) · J. Russell, *Encounter*, 23/6 (1964), 47–9 · D. Garnett, *The flowers of the forest* (1955) · F. Partridge, *Memories* (1981) · D. A. Laing, *Clive Bell: an annotated bibliography of the published writings* (1983) · F. Spalding, *Vanessa Bell* (1983) · *DNB* · b. cert. · m. cert. · d. cert. · *CGPLA Eng. & Wales* (1964) · personal knowledge (2004) · Marlborough College records · records, Trinity Cam. · West London crematorium records

Archives King's Cam., corresp. · Trinity Cam., papers · U. Sussex, corresp. | BL, letters to Lord Carnarvon, Add. MS 60802 · BL, letters to Harold Nicolson, RP 2553 [photocopies] · Charleston Trust, Sussex, collection of pictures, books, etc. · King's Cam., letters to Julian Bell; letters to John Maynard Keynes · Ransom HRC, Mary Hutchinson MSS · Tate collection, corresp. with Vanessa Bell · U. Sussex, corresp. with Leonard Woolf; letters to Virginia Woolf, incl. poems

Likenesses photographs, 1907–69, Tate collection · H. Lamb, pencil, 1908, Charleston Trust, Sussex · M. Beerbohm, pencil cartoon, *c*.1915, priv. coll.; repro. in Bell, *Old friends*, jacket · P. Picasso, group portrait, 1919, Musée Picasso, Paris · V. Bell, group portrait, oils, 1924, City Art Gallery, Leicester · R. Fry, oils, *c*.1924, NPG [*see illus.*] · Ramsey & Muspratt, bromide print, 1932, NPG · B. Anrep, mosaic sculpture, 1933, NPG · photographs, NPG

Wealth at death £43,380: probate, 4 Dec 1964, *CGPLA Eng. & Wales*

Bell, (George) Douglas Hutton (1905–1993), plant scientist, was born at 37 Glanmor Crescent, Swansea, on 18 October 1905, the elder son of George Henry Bell, civil engineer, and his wife, Lilian Mary Matilda, née Hutton. His father worked principally for municipal authorities in the Swansea area. His mother was related by marriage to the Massachusetts philosopher Ralph Waldo Emerson, whose well known aphorism, 'If a man write a better book, preach a better sermon, or make a better mousetrap than his neighbour, though he build his house in the woods, the world will make a beaten path to his door', could well have been applied to Bell in his middle age, at the height of his creativity in plant breeding. Bell was educated at schools in the Swansea area, first at the Brymill primary school from 1913 to 1918 and then at Bishop Gore's Grammar School from 1918 to 1924. The arts side at school appealed to Bell more than the sciences. He particularly liked English usage, which was taught by D. T. Thomas (the father of Dylan). This teaching stayed with

Bell throughout his life as those who subsequently were his students and junior colleagues learned when they split infinitives or commenced lists with 'Firstly'.

After school Bell went up to the University College of North Wales, Bangor, where he graduated with a first in botany and agricultural botany in 1928. He had chosen these subjects because he had experienced the food shortages of the First World War and he had become concerned about famines in other parts of the world. Sir Rowland Biffen, professor of agricultural botany at Cambridge, had been the external examiner of Bell's BSc and had seized his attention, so when Bell was awarded a research studentship by the Ministry of Agriculture he naturally sought to take it up at Cambridge. For his PhD in the Cambridge school of agriculture, Bell chose to study the distinctions between barley varieties, and in this work he was supervised by Sir Frank Engledow. He was greatly assisted by being allowed to spend a year in the USA at the University of Idaho, where he could compare the barley varieties that he had studied on the university farm in Cambridge in the very different environment of Idaho. In Idaho he had the good fortune to work alongside Dr H. V. Harlan, the foremost barley scientist of his day. When he submitted his PhD thesis in 1931 it had not been read by Engledow until it was bound and ready for submission.

Having succeeded in taking the PhD degree Bell stayed in Cambridge as an assistant research officer in the Plant Breeding Institute of the school of agriculture, where he helped Biffen and Engledow with their breeding programmes in wheat and barley. In 1933 he was appointed university demonstrator and his commitment to wheat and barley breeding continued with, in addition, some attention paid to pea breeding. With the security of a demonstrator's salary, he was able to marry, on 3 September 1934, Eileen Gertrude Wright (1905/6–1993), daughter of Alfred Wright, retired jeweller; they had first met on a transatlantic liner when returning from the USA. Their happy union lasted until their deaths within a few days of each other fifty-nine years later. There were two daughters.

Bell was appointed university lecturer in 1944. During the war his attention was concentrated on very practical affairs, including bolting and seed production in sugar beet—sugar being in very short supply in the wartime period. He also researched the use of tuber fragments as seed in potato production. But his continued attention to barley resulted in real progress towards the development of winter varieties.

Often someone's life story can be written in the history of an institution. This is very much the case with Bell and the Plant Breeding Institute, Cambridge. He was its acting director from 1946, and in January 1948 became director with the appointment backdated to October 1947. This appointment was in accord with an agreement among the university, the Ministry of Agriculture, and the Agricultural Research Council that the institute should be separated from the university and become jointly the responsibility of the ministry and the council. This arrangement was to continue until 1955 when responsibility for the

institute would fall to the council alone. Bell was given the responsibility of building an independent institute which, by research, was to improve the agricultural industry of the drier and primarily arable sector of eastern Britain. The mission statement for the institute spoke of the need for pure and applied scientific research on plant breeding for the betterment of agriculture, the production of new varieties, the development of new techniques and the support of appropriate research. From 1947 until 1971 (the time that he directed the institute) and indeed afterwards Bell was the doyen of plant breeding in Britain. From scratch he built a research establishment in which the very practical research needed to serve the industry was carried out alongside underpinning research in plant physiology and pathology, in genetics, cytogenetics, and molecular biology, in entomology, statistics, and chemistry. Starting with a staff of three in 1947 he had recruited a total staff of 231 by 1971, when he retired. Since there was no pre-existing model for such an institution, unusual creativity was needed by Bell in its generation.

The Ministry of Agriculture had bought Anstey Hall Farm, Trumpington, just to the south of Cambridge, at Bell's instigation in March 1950. Here the institute's premises were constructed and eventually all of the farm's 153 hectares were brought into experimental use. It had a friable, free draining, sandy clay loam soil overlying chalk marl, in great contrast to the land on which Bell had worked at the Cambridge University farm, which was unforgiving gault clay, inaccessible after rain. Bell often debated the balance of the institute's programme between pure and applied research, but eventually concluded that there could be no separation because breeding improved varieties must involve the use of the most up-to-date knowledge and methods from pure science. As a result, the programme of the Plant Breeding Institute extended from very practical work aimed at producing varieties to strategic work in relevant scientific disciplines. This structure was aimed at changing plant breeding from being a complex craft which made occasional references to science but relied principally on the eye and the intuition of the breeder into a science-based technology. Despite the reluctance of some of the old hands this objective was successfully achieved.

At its fullest stretch the objectives of the institute were to produce new varieties of barley, wheat, oats, triticale, potato, marrow-stemmed kale, field beans, red clover, maize, oil-seed rape, lucerne, and various species of forage grass. Bell's leadership was based upon the remarkable achievements of his personal large-scale breeding programmes in barley. The pinnacle of his success with barley came with the release of the spring barley variety Proctor in 1953. Because of its high yield, lodging resistant short straw, malting quality, and resistance to *Rhyncosporium*, Proctor was widely accepted by farmers. It transformed British agriculture. When it was introduced in 1953 there were 0.9 million hectares of barley in Britain, but by 1963 there were 2.4 million hectares. In 1956 the area in barley exceeded that in oats for the first time since 1879, while by 1966 barley occupied more than half of the national area under tillage and 70 per cent of this area was sown to Proctor. This variety satisfied the needs of the newly intensified, mechanized agriculture, where barley was replacing oats as the principal feed for livestock.

By the time of his retirement Bell could look back on a life in which he had succeeded in attaining all the practical objectives he had set himself in agriculture and for agricultural research. As would be expected in the light of his contributions to the transformation of British agriculture he received many honours. He was a fellow of Selwyn College over the period 1944–54 and became an honorary fellow in 1965. He was elected to the Royal Society in 1965 and appointed CBE in the same year. Among many other honours he was awarded the Mullard medal of the Royal Society in 1967 and the Massey-Ferguson national award of the Royal Agricultural Society of England in 1973. He died of bronchopneumonia at the Humanitas Foundation, Bottisham, Cambridgeshire, on 27 June 1993; he was survived by his wife and two daughters.

RALPH RILEY

Sources The Times (10 July 1993) · The Independent (23 July 1993) · b. cert. · m. cert. · d. cert. · WWW · RS · private information (2004) · personal knowledge (2004)
Archives John Innes Foundation Historical Collections, corresp., papers, and research notes | CUL, corresp. with J. S. Mitchell
Likenesses photograph, repro. in The Independent

Bell, Edward (1844–1926). See under Bell family (per. 1814–1968).

Bell, Edward Ingress (1837–1914). See under Webb, Sir Aston (1849–1930).

Bell, Ernest (1851–1933), publisher and animal welfare campaigner, was born on 8 March 1851 at West Croft, England's Lane, Hampstead, Middlesex, the second son of the publisher George *Bell (1814–1890) [see under Bell family] and Hannah Simpson (d. 1875). Ernest went to St Paul's School, and was admitted as a pensioner to Trinity College, Cambridge, on 5 June 1869, graduating BA (1873), and MA (1876). He became converted to vegetarianism at Cambridge in 1874 after having read a pamphlet by Thomas Low Nichols entitled How to Live on Sixpence a Day; Bell was known throughout his life for his spartan habits and simple tastes. After Cambridge he went to Dresden to learn German, and in 1893 he married Marie Ann von Taysen. There were apparently no children.

Bell spent most of his adult years in the family publishing business, G. Bell & Sons, in Portugal Street, Kingsway, London, joining as partner in 1888. Ernest became a competent editor for the company, translating Bohn's Standard Library of Classics from German, and editing the popular All England Series of Athletic Sports. It may be due to him that from the 1890s G. Bell & Sons is also found publishing for the Vegetarian Society and the Humanitarian League. Bell was known to be the first English publisher to develop an interest in the works and followers of the American primitivist philosopher Ralph Waldo Emerson. Bell's personal beliefs brought him further publishing successes and a public profile later in his career. He was

described as modest and retiring, with an amiable personality and firm convictions: 'it may be that others were more prominent … but no contemporary leader has equalled him in effective humanitarian work in all its phases. His main purpose was to lighten the load of the suffering man and beast' (Vegetarian Messenger and Health Review, 310). After 1893 he gave much of his time to administration and fund-raising for three main reform causes: vegetarianism, humanitarianism, and animal welfare. Bell's fervency, family wealth, and publishing background made him an effective organizer. He became the honorary secretary of the Hampstead branch of the Society for the Prevention of Cruelty to Animals, and was later chairman of the Anti-Vivisection Society. At various times he was on the governing councils of the Royal Society for the Protection of Birds, the National Canine Defence League, the Cat's Protection League, the Pit-Ponies Protection Society, and the Anti-Bearing-Rein Association. He was in particular a main force behind the Animals' Friend Society (founded 1834). Twenty-two separate societies joined in giving him a lifetime award in 1929 in recognition of his work for animal causes. He was also an early member of the Humanitarian League, which had close connections with the Vegetarian Society; he became vice-president of the Vegetarian Society in 1896, and finally its president in 1914, a long tenure which only ended with his death in 1933.

Throughout his life Bell donated much of his income to his societies, including donating all the profits from the best-selling Bell's Joy Book (1926, a collection of printed games and puzzles) to the Vegetarian Home for Children, of which he was a strong supporter. His first known publication, The Animals' Friend (with 68 illustrations), was published in 1904. This was followed by 'Christmas cruelties', in 1905, published in The Humane Review by the Humanitarian League; and a well-known series of schoolbooks called the Animals Life Readers. The Animals' Friend magazine, which he edited, ran into the 1920s and was revived as an imprint for pamphlets and books after 1926, when he succeeded his brother Edward *Bell [see under Bell family] as chairman of G. Bell & Sons. In 1920 he published In a Nutshell: Cons and Pros of the Meatless Diet. Bell was active into old age—his well-known Fair Treatment for Animals, which first appeared in the Animals' Friend, was still in print, and his final text, the Proper Relationship between Men and the other Animals, was published in 1927. Bell died on 14 September 1933, at his home, Althorpe, Waverley Grove, Hendon, Middlesex. He was survived by his wife.

VIRGINIA SMITH

Sources WWW · Vegetarian Messenger and Health Review, 30/10, 8th ser. (Oct 1933), 301, 310–13 · The Times (15 Sept 1933), 24 · Venn, Alum. Cant. · CGPLA Eng. & Wales (1933)
Likenesses portrait, repro. in Vegetarian Messenger and Health Review, 313
Wealth at death £36,740 0s. 1d.: probate, 13 Nov 1933, CGPLA Eng. & Wales

Bell [née Olliffe], **Florence Eveleen Eleanore**, Lady Bell (1851–1930), author, social investigator, and playwright,

Florence Eveleen Eleanore Bell, Lady Bell (1851–1930), by unknown photographer

Maria (*née* Shield), had died in 1871, leaving him with two children, Gertrude and Maurice. Thus his second wife became stepmother to Gertrude *Bell (1868–1926), the intrepid explorer and scholar of the Middle East. The Bells had three children of their own: Hugh Lowthian (Hugo), (Florence) Elsa, and Mary Katharine (Molly) [*see* Trevelyan, Mary Katharine], who married Sir Charles Trevelyan MP. The Bells lived at Red Barns, a windswept house near Redcar designed by Philip Webb. In 1905 they moved to Rounton Grange, near Northallerton. This became a centre for entertaining family, friends, fellow Liberals, and business and civic colleagues. Here Florence Bell also welcomed literary friends such as the writer Mrs Humphry Ward.

Lady Bell became a prolific writer, publishing over forty works. Some of her books for children, for example *Pauline's First Reading Book* (1912) and *Nora's Little Songbook*, were initially written for her grandchildren. Her French upbringing prompted *French without Tears* (3 pts, 1895–7), while in her best-known novel, a triple-decker, *The Story of Ursula* (1895), the heroine is caught between the competing cultures of England and France. She also wrote many essays, a selection of which was published in 1929, entitled *Landmarks*. She produced several political allegories such as *Down with the Tariff!* (1908) and a number of plays for children and adults. Her most sombre work was a secret. Collaborating with the American-born actress and writer Elizabeth Robins (1862–1952), she co-wrote the play *Alan's Wife* (1893), based on a story by the Swedish writer Elin Ameen. The Bell–Robins play, performed on the London stage and published without the playwrights' identities being revealed, was set, like a number of Lady Bell's plays, in northern England. It dealt with working-class infanticide, provoking strong reactions about the suitability of the subject matter. Elizabeth Robins, famed for her Ibsen roles, took the lead as she had done in Lady Bell's comedietta *A Joint Household* (1892) and her play *Karin* (1892), translated from a Swedish play.

Elizabeth Robins became Florence Bell's closest friend. Although from markedly different backgrounds and not always sharing the same outlook (Lady Bell disapproved of her friend's militant suffragism) they shared a passion for the theatre and commitment to writing. When apart they corresponded weekly and provided constructive criticism of each other's literary efforts from the 1890s onwards. They dedicated books to each other and Lady Bell wrote an appreciation of 'Lisa' for *Time and Tide* in 1920. Henry James's short story *Nona Vincent* (1891) centres on two characters, apparently based on Lady Bell and Elizabeth Robins, while more than half of the latter's book of correspondence with James, *Theatre and Friendship* (1932), is actually about Lady Bell. Florence Bell was also a key figure in promoting the stage career of Dame Sybil Thorndike.

Yet Lady Bell is probably best remembered for *At the Works* (1907), a detailed investigation of Middlesbrough where her husband's workforce lived. Dedicated to Charles Booth, it nevertheless rejects an approach dominated by statistics, and focuses not just on the workplace

was born on 9 September 1851 at 2 rue St Florentin, Paris, the youngest of the four children of Sir Joseph Olliffe (1808–1869), physician to the British embassy in Paris, and his wife, Laura, daughter of Sir William Cubitt MP, a member of the wealthy family of English builders. When she was ten her grandfather became lord mayor of London. She received a private education in Paris. Here she met Charles Dickens, developed a love for the theatre, and enjoyed a cosmopolitan, cultured lifestyle. In 1870, not long after her father's death, the Franco-Prussian War forced the family to flee to England. They settled at 95 Sloane Street, and this Knightsbridge home remained her London base for the rest of her life. Her ambition was to study music at the Royal College but this was considered inappropriate: she retained an appreciation of classical music throughout her life.

On 10 August 1876 Florence Olliffe married (Thomas) Hugh Bell (1844–1931). The son of the ironmaster Sir (Isaac) Lowthian *Bell, first baronet, he became the director of Bell Brothers. In addition to running the ironworks at Port Clarence on the north side of the Tees, opposite Middlesbrough, his business interests encompassed collieries and railways. In 1902 Bell Brothers merged with Dorman Long, major manufacturers of steel girders. He held a number of civic offices, including that of mayor, and was lord lieutenant of the North Riding for twenty-five years. He succeeded to his father's baronetcy in December 1904. When Florence Olliffe first met Hugh Bell (through his sisters), he was widowed. His first wife, but also on the homes of more than one thousand families, emphasizing especially the role of women in household management and containing much unique information on working-class reading habits (expanded in its second edition, 1911). The evidence for this classic study was gathered by Lady Bell, Gertrude Bell, and a few others over a period of nearly thirty years.

Concerned about the lack of recreational facilities locally, Lady Bell started an imaginative pioneering venture in Middlesbrough known as the Winter Gardens, providing an attractive venue for inexpensive recreation. Herbert Samuel MP, under-secretary of state for home affairs, described it as 'one of the most hopeful social experiments now being tried in England'. Her work in the locality extended to presidency of the British Red Cross Society. For acting as commandant of a hospital during the First World War she was made DBE in 1918. Yet close friends understood that this public figure and elegant hostess, almost invariably clad in loose gowns of grey, lavender, or silver, was actually a shy and private person. She could, however, appear daunting, as she was a stickler for etiquette. When her son Hugo's fiancée first met Lady Bell, she found her very much the *grande dame*, expecting her to talk French so that she could judge her accent.

Hugo became a clergyman whose work took him to South Africa. In 1926 on his return voyage he died of typhoid fever. He was forty-eight. His mother wrote a poignant memoir, privately published. Six months later, Gertrude died in Iraq. Meanwhile the Bell financial fortune was beginning to crumble slightly. Rounton Grange was closed, the family settling at the Manor House of Mount Grace Priory at Rounton. Still fascinated by drama, in 1927 Lady Bell organized an ambitious pageant in the grounds of the priory. It lasted for more than three days, had a cast of 118, and was attended by the queen and Princess Mary. It provided a temporary, albeit lavish and costly, diversion from the tragedies of 1926. She also published a selection of Gertrude's letters (1927). Lady Bell lived for only three more years, dying aged seventy-nine at 5 Lennox Gardens, Knightsbridge, London, on 16 May 1930. She was buried in Yorkshire at Rounton.

ANGELA V. JOHN

Sources Lady Bell [F. E. E. Bell], *At the works: a study of a manufacturing town* (1907); repr. (1985) · diaries of Elizabeth Robins; corresp. with Elizabeth Robins, New York University, Fales Library, Elizabeth Robins MSS · E. Robins, *Theatre and friendship* (1932) · M. Trevelyan, diaries, U. Newcastle, Robinson L., Trevelyan MSS · H. V. F. Winstone, *Gertrude Bell* (1978) · A. V. John, *Elizabeth Robins: staging a life, 1862–1952* (1995) · R. I. McKibbin, 'Social class and social observation in Edwardian England', *TRHS*, 5th ser., 28 (1978), 175–99 · J. W. Leonard, 'Lady Bell's survey of Edwardian Middlesbrough', *Bulletin* [Cleveland and Teesside Local History Society], 29 (1975), 1–19 · J. J. Turner, 'The people's Winter Garden, Middlesbrough', *Bulletin* [Cleveland and Teesside Local History Society], 46 (1984), 30–37 · *The Times* (17 May 1930) · Burke, *Peerage* · private information (2004) [K. Wang]
Archives New York University, Fales Library, Elizabeth Robins MSS, letters, etc.
Likenesses photograph, Middlesbrough Public Library [*see illus.*] · photographs, Middlesbrough Public Library · photographs (with family), New York University, Fales Library, Elizabeth Robins MSS

Wealth at death £1680 8s.: probate, 3 Oct 1930, *CGPLA Eng. & Wales*

Bell, Sir Francis Henry Dillon (1851–1936), lawyer and prime minister of New Zealand, was born in Nelson, New Zealand, on 31 March 1851, the eldest of the six sons (he had one sister) of Sir Francis Dillon Bell (1821/2–1898) and his wife, Margaret (d. 1892), who was the daughter of a leading Wellington Jewish merchant, Abraham Hort. Bell senior had been winding up the affairs of the New Zealand Company and was to become a significant politician, administrator, and diplomat. He was descended from the Quaker apologist Robert Barclay of Ury, and was therefore related to Edward Gibbon Wakefield and Elizabeth Fry.

After early years in Lower Hutt, young Harry Bell was educated at the Church of England grammar school in Auckland and between 1864 and 1868 at the High School of Otago (later Otago Boys' High School), where he was dux every year and also became head boy. In 1869 he entered St John's College, Cambridge, where he graduated BA in 1873, bracketed as eighth senior optime in the mathematical tripos. He worked for a solicitor and was then admitted to the chambers of a family friend, John Gorst. He was called to the bar by the Middle Temple in June 1874, after which he went on a court circuit with John Holker. The following year he returned to New Zealand, where his father had arranged that he enter into legal practice in Wellington under the leading lawyer C. B. Izard. The firm was to evolve into one of New Zealand's leading law practices.

On 24 April 1878, in St John's Church in Christchurch, Bell married Caroline (Carrie) Robinson (1853–1935), the third daughter of the wealthy Cheviot Hills run-holder and legislative councillor William (Ready Money) Robinson. Of their four sons and four daughters, three sons died in tragic circumstances. On his father-in-law's death in 1889 Bell became head trustee for the huge Robinson estate. From 1892, 'unexpectedly paving the way for a new era in state land settlement' (*DNZB*), he began negotiating to sell Cheviot Hills to the crown.

Bell's legal impact upon the colony was enormous and varied. In his first year of practice he and others initiated New Zealand law reporting with the *Colonial Law Journal*, and he later worked on systematizing and expanding such reporting. He served as crown solicitor in Wellington from 1877 to 1890 and again from 1902 to 1910. He quickly became 'a leading light in the Wellington bar' (Millen, 68) and was made a senior partner in 1886. He twice declined a judgeship in the 1880s, and on Sir Robert Stout's appointment as chief justice in 1899 he became the acknowledged leader of the New Zealand bar.

Bell's pronouncements were lucid and intelligible, and one of his specialties lay in law relating to Maori resources. His conduct of significant appeals to the privy council won praise from lords Haldane and Macnaghten, and eventually he became 'famous for his winning record' in the council (Millen, 140). A founder of the Wellington District Law Society (and president, 1888–9), he went on to be a prime mover in establishing the New Zealand Law Society and then to dominate it as president from 1902 to

1918. He was frequently involved in law reform and in the drafting of new statutes, for which he was renowned, and he was among the first batch of king's counsellors appointed within the country in 1907.

Throughout a busy life Bell engaged in many disparate activities. He headed a number of sporting organizations, including New Zealand's rowing and amateur athletic associations, the New Zealand Rugby Union, and Wellington boating, rugby, racing, and cricket organizations, the last for forty-three years. He was variously a member of the Victoria University council, the first president of the Wellesley Club (from 1891), and consul for Denmark, and later he headed public institutions such as the League of Nations Union. More than six decades of active freemasonry included a spell as grand master in 1894–5.

Bell's political career began in municipal affairs. As mayor of Wellington in 1891–3 and again in 1896–7 he presided over significant initiatives, especially the securing of proper drainage and refuse services; between these years he was also twice a member of the harbour board. Abortive attempts to enter parliament in 1890 and 1892 had been followed by his election in 1893 as member of the house of representatives for Wellington City.

A virulent campaign by the populist tabloid *Fair Play* to brand Bell as a fake liberal, essentially dedicated to self-interest, led to a libel case that he won only nominally. This was one of several factors which made political life uncongenial, and he stood down in 1896. An enduring legacy of his term was a close friendship with William Massey. When Massey's conservative Reform ministry took office in 1912 Bell was persuaded not only to accept an appointment to the legislative council but also to be its leader—as well as minister for internal affairs and immigration. He was the first New Zealand-born European to sit respectively in both parliamentary chambers.

Bell had agreed to become a legislative councillor in order to help carry out an election promise he had enjoined upon Reform: to make the second chamber elective, in order to prevent any future progressive government 'stacking' it with radicals. Ironically, it took so long to get sufficient nominees to ensure the passage of such a measure through the council that it lapsed amid the negotiations surrounding the formation of the wartime coalition (National) government in 1915. As a long-time councillor, however, he ably guided the chamber in its role as a revising body, frequently detecting anomalies and flaws in legislation sent up by the house of representatives.

Bell's dominating intellect and personality enabled him to exercise great influence within the Reform government of 1912–15 (often referred to as the Massey–Bell regime), the subsequent wartime coalition—which retained him in the immigration portfolio and made him attorney-general in 1918—and the post-war Massey government (1918–25). In the last, in which his attorney-general's portfolio was at various times supplemented by eight other responsibilities, the truism of the times was that Bell was 'in regard to all important matters of legislation or Cabinet action, the real power behind the throne'

(*Otago Daily Times*, 14 March 1936). Massey often sought his advice, and he was acting prime minister in 1921, 1923, and 1925. With the prime minister's decline in health from late 1924 he was virtually the leader of the dominion, and when Massey died he became the first New Zealand-born prime minister—albeit only between 14 and 30 May 1925. He felt that he was too old to hold the office permanently, despite his party's wishes. However, he served in the ministry of his successor, J. G. Coates, until its fall in late 1928.

During the First World War, with the solicitor-general, Sir John Salmond, Bell drafted much intricate special legislation; after the war he oversaw its dismantling. As first commissioner of state forests (1918–22) he was able to indulge his interests in conservation, minimizing native forest destruction and other timber wastage and establishing a regulated system of state forestry, thus becoming known as 'the Father of Forestry' in the country (Stewart, 195). He negotiated the Rotorua Lakes settlement with Te Arawa in 1922, and in the following year he initiated the rationalization of New Zealand land law.

Bell drafted the legislation for New Zealand's assumption of the League of Nations mandate in Western Samoa, and as minister for external affairs (1923–6) he presided over that responsibility. While he was far more enthusiastic over the league than most of his political colleagues, as his country's representative at its third assembly he attacked the right of the (unelected) permanent mandates' commission to criticize New Zealand's actions in Samoa (in this case, on the matter of indentured Chinese labour). His greatest international commitment was to a British empire led firmly by the mother country, and he consistently opposed the drift of the dominions from Britain.

Bell remained an active legislative councillor until his death, but his later years were focused on his legal work and on external affairs—especially on the promotion of imperial unity, but also on global issues such as the creation of the International Court of Justice at The Hague. It was a fittingly statesmanlike ending to a full politico-legal life. Along the way he had been appointed KCMG in 1915, GCMG in 1923, and a privy councillor in 1926. Lady Bell died on 8 September 1935 and Sir Francis himself on 13 March 1936, at their home, Taumaru, in Lowry Bay, Wellington. He was buried in Karori cemetery after a state funeral.

A Labour parliamentarian had in 1921 acknowledged Bell to be 'the uncrowned king of New Zealand' as well as 'one of the ablest men in the southern hemisphere' (*Otago Daily Times*, 14 March 1936). He was undoubtedly one of the ablest conservative leaders of a country where conservative leadership has generally been in the ascendancy. Along with some other such politicians he was not afraid to propound liberal views. Hence he gained support in the 1890s from such disparate forces as land reformers, prohibitionists, and suffragist women, and courted unpopularity in the First World War by introducing into the conscription legislation a clause to exempt religious objectors. Indeed he would even—when expounding, say, on welfare—call himself a socialist, although a 'tory radical' might be a closer description, and *Fair Play* and other commentators would not have gone even that far.

During his long and varied career Bell was highly influential in his country. Politically he was content to remain largely behind the scenes, despite a domineering personality which could veer towards bullying in the face of opposition. 'It is difficult to find a parallel to so many-sided a man in New Zealand public life' concluded the author of his biography in *DNZB*. Although he left his legacy in a number of significant ways, his relative political self-effacement has meant that his name is now little known.   RICHARD S. HILL

Sources W. D. Stewart, *The Right Honourable Sir Francis H. D. Bell, P.C., G.C.M.G., K.C.: his life and times* (1937) · J. Millen, *The story of Bell Gully Buddle Weir, 1840–1990* (1990) · W. J. Gardner, 'Bell, Francis Henry Dillon', *DNZB*, vol. 2 · *Otago Daily Times* (14 March 1936) · G. H. Scholefield, ed., *A dictionary of New Zealand biography*, 2 vols. (1940) · G. H. Scholefield, ed., *Who's who in New Zealand*, 3rd edn · Dictionary of New Zealand Biography database · A. Frame, *Salmond: southern jurist* (1995) · NL NZ, Turnbull L., Bell Gully Buddle Weir MSS · Bell Gully offices, Wellington, Bell Gully Buddle Weir archives · *DNB*

Archives priv. coll., family records | Bell Gully offices, Wellington, New Zealand, Bell Gully Buddle Weir archives · NL NZ, Turnbull L., Bell Gully Buddle Weir archives

Likenesses A. F. Nicoll, oils, National Gallery of New Zealand · A. F. Nicoll, oils, Parliament House, Wellington, New Zealand · A. F. Nicoll, oils, Wellington Club, Wellington, New Zealand · W. Stoneman, photograph, NPG · photograph, repro. in Stewart, *The Right Honourable Sir Francis H. D. Bell*, frontispiece · photograph, repro. in Millen, *The story of Bell Gully Buddle Weir*, p. 9

Bell, Sir Gawain Westray (1909–1995), colonial administrator and diplomatist, was born on 21 January 1909 in Cape Town, the only son of William Westray Bell (*d.* 1946), shipping executive and later a stockbroker, and his wife, Emily Helen, *née* Kisch (1880–1971), daughter of an Anglo-Austrian mining engineer in South Africa. His family originally came from Latterhead in the Cumbrian sheep-farming uplands. Bell spent his childhood in South Africa, where his father was employed by the New Zealand Shipping Company (founded by his grandmother's family, the Westrays of Whitehaven), first in Basrah and then from 1901 in Cape Town. After preparatory school at Wynburg he went to Britain in 1919, entering the Dragon School, Oxford, and then Winchester College in 1922 and Hertford College, Oxford, in 1927. At Oxford he read medieval and modern history (graduating with a second-class degree in 1930), followed the Magdalen and New College beagles, was a member of the Officers' Training Corps, and captained the Oxford shooting eight. Putting aside the thought of the army but seeking a career abroad, Bell applied for both the colonial administrative and the Sudan political service. Accepted for the élite latter, he was at twenty-two too young to be sent to Africa, so he spent an extra year at Oxford attending the tropical African services course for colonial probationers. Part of his training was to witness surgery at the Radcliffe Hospital, 'to accustom ourselves to the sight of blood and severed limbs' (Bell, *An Imperial Twilight*, 16). He promptly fainted.

Bell arrived in Khartoum in 1931. Although he was to spend over twenty years in Sudan, unusually in the political service he was given a number of outside assignments. In 1938 he was seconded to the colonial service administration of the Palestine mandate, serving as deputy district commissioner in Gaza and Beersheba. An accomplished horseman, he reconstituted the camel gendarmerie. He had a colourful war in the Middle East, joining the Cruze cavalry and rising to colonel in the Arab Legion under General Sir John Glubb. He returned to Sudan in 1945 as district commissioner of al-ʿUbayd, and again served outside when he became deputy Sudan agent in Cairo in 1949. Back in Khartoum in 1951, he was promoted deputy civil secretary and then permanent secretary to the new ministry of the interior. He was the last member of the administration to leave Sudan, in December 1954.

At forty-five Bell was too young and his Arabic too fluent for him to wait long among colleagues testing the job market in Britain. Ironically, in view of what was to come, he was offered the job of managing a soda water factory in Northern Nigeria. The Colonial Office had him in mind for the chief secretaryship of Aden, but the Foreign Office got in first and Bell went as political agent to Kuwait. An attempt was made on his life in Kuwait in 1956, as in Palestine in 1938. In 1957 the Colonial Office's turn came, when Bell accepted the patently final governorship of Northern Nigeria. One of the attractions was that he would once again be working with his longtime Sudan colleague Sir James Robertson, now governor-general of the federation of Nigeria. It was a post which called for all Bell's previous experience of the transfer of power and all his skill as a diplomat. Not only was there the challenge of being a colonial governor yet with an elected premier and cabinet, there was also the legendary sensitivity of the premier, Alhaji Ahmadu Bello, to handle. The extremes in gubernatorial style between Bell and his predecessor Sir Bryan Sharwood Smith were widely perceived.

Having retired for the second time in 1962 (the Northern Nigerian cabinet paid him the compliment of asking him to stay on as governor for two years beyond independence), Bell had a short spell as secretary-general of the Council for Middle East Trade before again being approached for government service. With Sir Ralph Hone he helped to devise a new constitution for the federation of south Arabia in 1965. Other Arabian missions followed, to Oman in 1966 (and again in 1974), and to the Trucial States. From 1966 to 1970 he was secretary-general of the South Pacific Commission, based in New Caledonia.

In retirement the Bells occupied the National Trust property at Hidcote Bartrim Manor, Chipping Campden, where they had resided since 1959. On 19 January 1945 he had married Silvia Cornwell-Clyne, a photographic technician, whom he had known since 1937. She was the daughter of Adrian Cornwell-Clyne, a photographic expert, of Esher, Surrey, and the cousin of a colleague in Sudan, Martin Parr, who in turn was the brother of Bell's teacher at Winchester, Jack. She shared her husband's life-long love of riding, and her wedding present to him was a superb grey, Cloud (a whole chapter in his memoirs was given over to horses). For five years Bell sat as part-time chairman of the civil service commission (1972–7). He became vice-president of the charity Lepra, was on the governing body of the School of Oriental and African Studies, and was active in the Anglo-Jordanian Society. He turned to writing his memoirs, publishing *Shadows on the Sand* (1983) and *An Imperial Twilight* (1989). The critic Marghanita Laski praised them for their 'knack of immensely attractive and inviting story-telling' (Kirk-Greene). In 1990 the Bells moved to a smaller house in East Ilsley, Berkshire, anticipating the ill health that was to accompany their later years. Bell continued to research into local Eberington history as well as to co-compile a register of his Sudan colleagues' post-retirement employment. He organized a major conference on Sudan at Durham University, resulting in a valuable expansion of the Sudan archive there.

Of Bell it was said that 'spiritually he never left Winchester, with its legacy of those myriad meaningful ways in which Manners truly maketh Man' (Kirk-Greene). Forty years' experience as an overseas administrator and consummate diplomat, combined with a reputation throughout the Arab world for courtesy and cultural empathy, contributed to Bell's image as a model latter-day proconsul. Intimately involved in overseeing the process of the transfer of power in Sudan, Nigeria, and the south Pacific, he was on each occasion the last British holder of the post. He was appointed MBE (military) in 1942, CBE in 1955, KCMG in 1957, and a knight of St John in 1958. He died of pneumonia at Battle Hospital, Reading, on 26 July 1995. His body was donated for medical research, and his ashes were deposited at Winchester College by the Bell gate (named after his uncle Gawain Murdoch Bell, a housemaster who was killed at Ypres in 1917). He was survived by his wife, who died in 1996, and by three daughters.

A. H. M. KIRK-GREENE

Sources G. Bell, *Shadows on the sand* (1983) · G. Bell, *An imperial twilight* (1989) · *Daily Telegraph* (27 July 1995) · *The Times* (31 July 1995) · *The Independent* (10 Aug 1995) · *West Africa* (4–10 Sept 1995) · A. Kirk-Greene, memorial service address, 2 Dec 1995, Winchester College chapel · personal knowledge (2004) · private information (2004) [A. Buchan] · A. Bello, *My life* (1960) · D. Lavin, ed., *The condominium remembered*, 1 (1991) · m. cert. · d. cert.
Archives Bodl. RH, papers relating to governorship of Nigeria · Bodl. RH, MSS. Afr. S. 2001 [transcript] · NRA, priv. coll., papers · U. Durham L., corresp., diaries, and papers relating to Sudan
Likenesses double portrait, painting (with Glubb Pasha), Amman military museum · photograph, repro. in *The Times* · photograph, repro. in *Daily Telegraph* · photograph, repro. in *The Independent* · photographs, repro. in Bell, *Shadows on the sand* · photographs, repro. in Bell, *Imperial twilight* · photographs, priv. coll.
Wealth at death £145,541: probate, 2 Nov 1995, *CGPLA Eng. & Wales*

Bell, Sir George (1794–1877), army officer, son of George Bell, of Belle Vue, on Lough Erin, co. Fermanagh, and Catherine, daughter of Dominick Nugent MP, was born at Belle Vue on 17 March 1794. The genealogist Henry Nugent *Bell was his elder brother. While still at school in Dublin, George was gazetted an ensign in the 34th foot, on 11 March 1811. Sent to Portugal, he carried the colours of his regiment for the first time in the action of Arroyo dos Molinos; he was present at the second and final siege of Badajoz, and in the majority of the celebrated actions between that and the battle of Toulouse.

On being gazetted to the 45th regiment in 1825 Bell went to India, and was at Ava during the First Anglo-Burmese War. He became a captain in 1828, and in 1836 was in Canada, where he was actively employed during the rebellion of 1837–8. He commanded the fort and garrison of Couteau-du-Lac, an important position on the St Lawrence River, and received the thanks of the commander of the forces and his brevet majority (29 March 1839) for recovering the guns of the fort.

Bell became lieutenant-colonel of the 1st foot, known as the Royal regiment, on 5 December 1843, and served in Gibraltar, Nova Scotia, the West Indies, the Mediterranean, and Turkey, after which he landed with the allied armies in the Crimea, and was present at the Alma and Inkerman, and the siege of Sevastopol, where he was wounded and mentioned in dispatches. Lord Raglan appointed him to the command of a brigade. On his return to England he was made a CB, 5 July 1855, and took up his residence at Liverpool as inspecting field officer until 1859, when he became a major-general in the army. He was in the Royal regiment for thirty years.

From this time onwards Bell never obtained any further employment, the consequence, he believed, of a letter which he wrote to *The Times* (12 December 1854) complaining of the deficiencies of the commissariat in the siege of Sevastopol. On 23 October 1863 he was appointed colonel of the 104th foot; he became colonel of the 32nd foot on 2 February 1867 and colonel of the 1st foot on 3 August 1868. His *Rough Notes by an Old Soldier during Fifty Years' Service* (2 vols., 1867), a gossiping and amusing account of his life and services, was published early in 1867. He was created KCB on 13 March 1867, lieutenant-general on 28 January 1868, and general on 8 March 1873. He was twice married; the first time to Alicia, daughter and heir of James Scott of Ecclesjohn and Commiston, Scotland, and secondly, in 1820, to Margaret Addison, a daughter of Thomas Dougal of Scotland, banker. Bell died at 156 Westbourne Terrace, Hyde Park, London, on 10 July 1877, survived by his wife.

G. C. BOASE, rev. JAMES LUNT

Sources *Dod's Peerage* · *Army List* · G. B. [G. Bell], *Rough notes by an old soldier during fifty years' service*, 2 vols. (1867) · Boase, *Mod. Eng. biog.*
Archives NAM, letters relating to Peninsular War and Crimean War
Likenesses portrait, repro. in Bell, *Rough notes*
Wealth at death £16,000 — in England: probate, 21 Nov 1877, *CGPLA Eng. & Wales*

Bell, George (1814–1890). *See under* Bell family (*per.* 1814–1968).

Bell, George Joseph (1770–1843), jurist and legal writer, was born on 26 March 1770 at Fountainbridge near Edinburgh, the third of the four sons of Revd William Bell (1704–1779), a Scottish Episcopal clergyman, and his wife, Margaret Morrice. His eldest brother, Robert *Bell, was a lawyer of some distinction; his other brothers, John *Bell

George Joseph Bell (1770–1843), by Sir Henry Raeburn, 1816

and Charles *Bell, became distinguished surgeons. On 22 October 1806 he married Barbara, eldest daughter of Charles Shaw, solicitor, of Ayr. The marriage ended with her death on 28 March 1827. They had five sons and five daughters.

Although all Bell's brothers were pupils at Edinburgh high school, George Bell's own formal schooling ended when he was eleven, for financial reasons. His mother then taught him herself. He probably attended the moral philosophy class at Edinburgh University in 1785–6, and rhetoric and *belles-lettres* in 1788–9. He certainly attended David Hume's class in Scottish law in 1787–8. He passed advocate on 22 November 1791, after public examination on 19 November.

Bell, a lifelong friend of Francis Jeffrey, was a whig in politics. In a period of tory ascendancy this did not assist his practice. He turned to writing, and settled in 1797 on reviewing the law of bankruptcy, then a new institution. The renewal of the Bankruptcy (Scotland) Act, 1772, was building bankruptcy into the fabric of Scottish mercantile law. The first volume of Bell's *Treatise on the Laws of Bankruptcy in Scotland* appeared in 1800, and the second followed in 1804. The whole work, which was to make his reputation and was accorded institutional status as a work of authority by the courts, was also published in 1804 as *Commentaries on the Municipal and Mercantile Law of Scotland Considered in Relation to the Subject of Bankruptcy*. A second edition appeared in 1810, entitled *Commentaries on the Law of Scotland and on the Principles of Mercantile Jurisprudence*, a title retained thereafter for the editions which Bell himself prepared. The new title reflected Bell's aim to develop

the principles of Scottish mercantile law—which he regarded as having been neglected since the time of Lord Stair—by drawing extensively on greater English experience in the mercantile field and on English and continental authorities. The first volume of a third edition of Bell's work appeared in 1816, but the second volume was delayed until 1819. From 1816 to 1818 Bell lectured at Edinburgh University for the Society of Writers to the Signet, delivering the lectures on conveyancing which his brother Robert had given until his death in 1816, and passing the fees to his brother's widow. A fourth edition of his *Commentaries* followed in 1821 and in 1822 Bell was nominated as David Hume's successor in the chair of Scots law, proposed by the dean of faculty and seconded by Sir Walter Scott. In 1822 Bell was also elected an honorary member of the Juridical Society and FRSE. A fifth edition of the *Commentaries*, the last by Bell himself, appeared in 1826 but Patrick Shaw, Bell's brother-in-law and literary executor, states that Bell continued to work on the text. Bell also produced short treatises on recent legislation affecting diligence and bankruptcy (1840), and on sale (1844). Shaw issued a further edition of the *Commentaries* in 1858, having made considerable changes; it is not clear how far some of these were authorized by Bell but the 1870 edition, reprinted in 1990, mainly reverts to the 1826 text.

Bell was actively involved on law reform commissions during the tenure of his chair. He sat on the 1823 commission which led to the Court of Session Act 1825 and the 1826 commission which led to the Court of Session Act 1830; he also drafted the first bill to give effect to the report of the former commission. Making no provision for the absorption of the jury court into the court of session as proposed, a proposal which Bell saw as premature, the bill aroused fierce opposition. Bell wrote a valuable *Examination of the Objections Against the Bill* (1825) but was not entrusted with drafting the replacement bill which became the 1825 act, and his attitude on the jury court—reflected also in his opposition to the bill's capacity to give effect to the report of the latter commission—both severely damaged his practice and proved a barrier to a judicial appointment. He was made a principal clerk of session in 1831, which provided him with a salary to supplement his professorial income. From 1833 to 1839 Bell was further involved in law reform as chairman of the royal commission for the amendment of Scottish law; this was first set up in 1833 by the whig government elected after the Reform Acts of 1832. The commission, which finally expired in 1839 when Bell was in failing health, produced three substantial reports which were the foundation of much reforming legislation on bankruptcy, conveyancing, the courts, diligence, and heritable securities.

A product of Bell's teaching was his other main work, *The Principles of the Law of Scotland*, which also came to be accorded institutional status. It first appeared in 1829 and was intended as a guide for his students and a first resort in practice. Student comment on his early lectures suggests that they were not very well arranged or prepared, but his *Principles* has a deserved reputation as a clear and concise exposition of Scottish private law. Bell himself produced new editions in 1830, 1833, and 1839, expanding the text considerably but with some variation in the material covered. Patrick Shaw issued a new edition, with his own changes, in 1860. A later editor, William Guthrie (whose editions were published in 1872, 1876, 1885, 1889, and 1899, reprinted 1989), mainly reverted to the 1839 text, indicating his changes and additions. For the benefit of his students Bell supplemented the *Principles* with three volumes of *Illustrations* from leading cases (1836, 1838).

Bell was described as being 'of a genial disposition and courteous manners' (*DNB*). In his latter years he was in poor health, and an inflammation of the eyes in 1841 led to blindness. He died on 23 September 1843 at his home, 3 Park Place, Edinburgh, and was buried with his wife in St John's Episcopal Church, Edinburgh. He left most of his estate, some £3000 net, to his second daughter, Barbara, in token of the care given to himself and the family since her mother's death.   W. M. GORDON

Sources G. W. Wilton, *George Joseph Bell* (1929) · G. J. Bell, *Principles of the law of Scotland*, rev. W. Guthrie, 10th edn, 2 vols. (1899); facs. edn in 1 vol. with introduction by W. M. Gordon (1989) · G. J. Bell and J. MacLaren, *Commentaries on the law of Scotland and on the principles of mercantile jurisprudence*, 7th edn, 2 vols. (1870); facs. edn with introduction by R. Black (1990) · W. M. Gordon, 'George Joseph Bell—law commissioner', *Obligations in context: essays in honour of Professor D. M. Walker*, ed. A. J. Gamble (1990), 77–99 · W. M. Gordon, 'George Joseph Bell—law commissioner', in D. M. Walker, *Scottish jurists* (1985) · N. Phillipson, *The Scottish whigs and the reform of the court of session, 1785–1830*, Stair Society, 37 (1990) · minutes, NL Scot., Faculty of Advocates MSS FR3, FR5, FR8 · *Edinburgh Annual Register* (1825), 331

Archives U. Edin. | NRA, priv. coll., letters to Lord Moncreiff · U. Edin., New Coll. L., letters to Thomas Chalmers

Likenesses J. Kay, etching, 1811, NPG; repro. in J. Kay, *A series of original portraits and caricature etchings … John Kay*, 2 (1837–8), pl. 156 · H. Raeburn, oils, 1816, Parliament House, Edinburgh; copy, 1856, priv. coll. [*see illus.*] · B. W. Crombie, double portrait, coloured engraving, 1839 (with Professor John Wilson), repro. in W. S. Douglas, *Modern Athenians … original portraits … 1837 to 1847* (1882), pl. 12 · B. W. Crombie, pencil study for engraving, Scot. NPG · J. Tannock, oils, Scot. NPG · photograph (after B. W. Crombie), repro. in Wilton, *George Joseph Bell*

Wealth at death £3000 after payment of debts; £12,000 furniture, arrears of salary, life policies: Wilton, *George Joseph Bell*, 18

Bell, George Kennedy Allen (1883–1958), bishop of Chichester, was born at the vicarage, Hayling Island, within sight of the spire of Chichester Cathedral, on 4 February 1883, the eldest child of James Allen Bell, the vicar of Hayling Island, and his wife, Sarah Georgina Megaw. The Bells were a family of farmers and businessmen; the Megaws were bankers from the north of Ireland. It was the kind of secure, comfortable, middle-class clerical home that produced many of the bishops of the church in the twentieth century. When, in his student days, George Bell was asked why he was a Christian, he replied, 'First, I was born one' (Jasper, 17). The Bells moved by stages northwards, first to Southampton, then to Pershore in Worcestershire, and then to Balsall Heath in Birmingham. In 1903 they moved again to Wimbledon in London. Throughout his boyhood George Bell endured a succession of schools, but in 1896 he was awarded a place at

George Kennedy Allen Bell (1883–1958), by Howard Coster, 1936

Westminster School. This placed him in the heart of the London of power and eminence the school represented.

In 1901 Bell went with a number of peers to study at Christ Church, Oxford. At first his religious beliefs were, in his own words, 'suspended' (Jasper, 17). He was not a man of abstractions and doctrines; he was drawn by the holiness of great souls. The essentially humane quality of his intelligence was confirmed and matured. He secured a first class in classical moderations in 1903, but two years later missed another in Greats. He liked poetry above all, editing five anthologies for the publishing house Routledge (newly acquired by the father of a friend), and winning the Newdigate prize for a poem entitled *Delphi*.

In April 1906 Bell went to Wells Theological College for a year, and here he discovered ecumenism. Soon he led weekly services to pray for the unity of the church. He was ordained deacon in Ripon Cathedral in 1907 and then priest a year later in Leeds parish church. It was in Leeds that he served his curacy, encountering the austerities of urban working-class life and labour and sharing them, even to the cost of his own health. Although he returned to Christ Church, first as a tutor and lecturer, and then as a student, Leeds had left its mark. Every now and then he disappeared with groups of students up to Leeds and Liverpool. His commitment to social justice grew in the company of Albert Mansbridge, Henry Scott Holland (by now also at Christ Church), and a brilliant young fellow of Queen's, William Temple. Bell lectured for the university extension movement and supported a number of socially concerned local bodies. His room, above the junior common room, became a centre for vigorous discussion, 'as living a "cell"', recorded a friend, provocatively, 'as would have contented the reddest communist' (Jasper, 13). Theological disputes, of which there were many in the Oxford of his day, did not much draw him. 'Christianity', he simply responded, 'is a life before it is a system and to lay too much stress on the system destroys the life' (ibid., 17).

By 1914 two of the great commitments of Bell's life had become explicit: the young ecumenical movement and the work of the church in a world of political and social injustice. In that year Archbishop Davidson required a new domestic chaplain, and he chose Bell. With characteristic caution Bell hesitated, sought advice, and accepted. It was a turning point. This new role he made his own, growing in confidence and watching the world of institutional responsibility sensitively and minutely in what became almost at once an age of international conflict. Davidson was not obviously one to inspire the idealist, but Bell's loyalty to him contained an element of devotion and in time he became his respectful biographer. The Davidson of that epic, two-volume work was a Christian statesman who played an active and influential role in the life of the state, both sustaining and condemning government policies in peace and wartime. At Lambeth, Bell's ecumenical concerns also flourished. In 1919 he went to Oud Wassenar in Holland to view the beginning of the new, post-war World Alliance for International Friendship through the Churches. There he met Archbishop Söderblom, its leading light, and was fired by his vision (Söderblom was equally impressed by Bell). At the 1920 Lambeth conference he worked hard on the famous 'Appeal to all Christian people', at once regarded as the defining statement of that gathering.

A Lambeth chaplaincy was often in the twentieth century seen to be a strong foundation for an eminent career in the Church of England, and Bell's abilities were both confirmed and extended by his role there. On 8 January 1918 he married Henrietta Millicent Grace (d. 1968), daughter of Canon R. J. Livingstone and sister of Sir Richard Livingstone. There were no children. In 1924 Ramsay MacDonald offered Bell the deanery of Canterbury and he accepted it. He was now forty-one. His predecessor had been eighty-seven. To Canterbury he brought change, encouraging visitors, writing guides, and abolishing fees. The broadcasting of services was encouraged and became regular. Visiting preachers from different traditions appeared in the pulpit. His sense of Christian worship was reverent, orderly, and beautiful in language. He took advice from choirboys on the length of services and confronted those who resisted change with a quiet tenacity.

Responsible for the life of a great church, Bell also found that he was able to put his love of literature and art to good effect. In 1928 John Masefield's play *The Coming of Christ* was performed in the cathedral; it was widely judged to be the first dramatic performance to take place in an English cathedral since the middle ages. In time he encouraged the contributions of young writers whose work would be

seen to characterize the culture of the period: Charles Williams, Dorothy Sayers, Christopher Hassall, and Christopher Fry. After 1929, when he was consecrated bishop of Chichester, he continued to develop a relationship with the arts, and not always in his new diocese. From T. S. Eliot he commissioned *Murder in the Cathedral* for the Canterbury festival in 1935. He also commissioned the work of artists in the diocese. Bell was a strong and committed diocesan bishop. At Chichester itself he worked successfully and respectfully with two impressive deans, A. S. Duncan-Jones, who shared his commitment to German affairs, and Walter Hussey, who proved a bold partner in the commissioning of new art.

Bell was a member of the 1935 commission on church and state, a body set up in response to the prayer book crisis of 1927–8. Although its report subsequently sank without trace, it confirmed Bell's reputation as a bishop concerned with the outward life of the Church of England and with its relationship with the political society it inhabited. By now his ecumenism was primarily international, and it was increasingly defined by the political dangers of the period. In 1928–30 he fostered three series of theological discussions between leading British and German theologians of the day. These produced a succession of articles which did something to build a bridge between the thinkers of two very different protestant communities. He became a leading light in the new life and work movement, an ecumenical body devoted to the relationship between Christian faith and public life. Between 1932 and 1934 he was chairman of its council and subsequently chaired its administrative committee until 1938.

Murder in the Cathedral was, in part, a response to the stark realities of national socialism in Germany. Bell's participation in the German crisis after Hitler came to power in January 1933 became increasingly intense. He worked as an ally of those he perceived to be withstanding the onslaught of tyranny and also as a friend of those who were the victims of National Socialist policy. His vision of Christian mission and responsibility was marked by a new urgency and breadth. He spent numberless hours reading reports from Germany and discussing the situation with ecumenical contacts. In 1934 he became a close friend of the young German pastor Dietrich Bonhoeffer, then responsible for the German congregation in Sydenham. He devised plans to settle refugees in his diocese and across Great Britain. Advised that those defined as non-Aryan Christians in Germany needed support still more than Jews or Christians he campaigned for them vigorously, organizing a succession of national campaigns. His maiden speech in the House of Lords in 1938 was on their behalf. In these matters he was deftly supported by a sympathetic archbishop, Cosmo Gordon Lang. Meanwhile, Bell's personal diplomacy showed an astute, even creative, ability to draw on the privileges of his status and to place them at the service of those who might seem marginal or powerless. 'What would suit me best of all', he once wrote to Bonhoeffer, 'would be if you could come and have breakfast with me at the Athenaeum at 9 o' clock on Thursday morning. Is that too outrageous?' (Bell MSS, vol. 42, fol. 18, 24 Feb 1934).

Bell was an unlikely campaigner. His was not a striking public presence; his voice was gentle and rather high. He had little feel for the pungent generalizations of rhetoric. More important to him were the intricate facts that lay behind complicated issues. In a world of propaganda and confrontation he perceived that credibility and influence grew above all out of exactitude. Denunciations were rarely, to his mind, influential, though his language became increasingly condemnatory as the decade unfolded and the international situation deteriorated. Like most church leaders, he supported the appeasement policy of Chamberlain because he believed that only peace could bring change while war must bring only destruction. Thereafter, his belief that war would do more to justify and sustain Hitler in power than peace was more unusual.

It was during the war against Germany that Bell acquired a reputation for provocation and controversy. He acted as an emissary for Germans dedicated to the removal of the Hitler regime in June 1942, after meeting for the last time his friend Bonhoeffer in neutral Sweden. The foreign secretary, Anthony Eden, sarcastically referred to him as 'this pestilent priest', and suspected him of pacifism. For its determined refusal to offer explicit encouragement to resistance circles in Germany Bell never forgave the British government, holding it partly responsible for the calamitous failure of the coup attempt of 20 July 1944. That a Christian bishop could effectively work on behalf of a political conspiracy to assassinate the head of a European state remains a striking fact. Meanwhile, in the House of Lords he did all he could to combat the words of Lord Vansittart, who argued that national socialism was the expression of German character and that any distinction between the Nazis and the Germans was simple foolishness. But there was more. The development of British air policy during the war alarmed him. In February 1944 he attacked the government in the House of Lords in a speech which combined military insight (he was advised by the military historian Sir Basil Liddell Hart) with moral force. But he was more and more to be seen in sympathy not with the main body of opinion, but on the fringe. It was not difficult to find Christians who denied the weight of such views—Archbishop William Temple, for one.

That he did not become archbishop of Canterbury on Temple's death in 1944 has occasioned some debate, but the roots of this lay not merely in Bell's political controversialism in wartime, but in his commitment to issues that were not so much institutional as humanitarian. In this sense Geoffrey Fisher's appointment in succession to Temple foreshadowed a growing tendency in the church to concentrate primarily on its own affairs and to organize its structures more efficiently.

After the destruction of national socialism Bell visited Germany and inspired a number of German pastors to write what became known as the Stuttgart declaration of guilt. He protested publicly against the explosion of the first atomic bomb and remained a critic of nuclear weapons in the new cold war. He was elected moderator of the central committee of the new World Council of Churches at its first assembly in Amsterdam in August–September 1948. In 1954 Bell became a president of the organization. His reputation among Christians in many countries grew impressively, and he was a committed friend of the new Church of South India. He remained bishop of Chichester until announcing his retirement on 4 June 1957, and died soon afterwards, at 1 Starrs House, The Precincts, Canterbury, on 3 October 1958. The burdens of the age weighed heavily upon Bell to the end. 'I cannot grieve for his going', his widow told a young friend, 'he felt so much for all that was happening in the world' (Chandler, 459). George Bell's ashes were interred by St Richard's altar in Chichester Cathedral, a week after his death. The location is nicely suggestive: at the very centre of the great church, but unobtrusive, and rarely noticed by the passing eye.

The significance of Bell's contribution to the Church of England, to the ecumenical movement, and to the age he inhabited is inevitably difficult to judge. The conviction that Christianity required a commitment to political affairs, an enduring characteristic of British Christian experience in the twentieth century, was certainly fortified by his vision. His written works retain some power. *Christianity and World Order* (1940) was the first theological book to be written expressly for publication as a paperback and it sold more than 80,000 copies. This and an edition of his wartime speeches, *The Church and Humanity* (1946), bring together the best, the most urgent, of his moral prophecy.

ANDREW CHANDLER

Sources R. Jasper, *George Bell: bishop of Chichester* (1967) · G. Rupp, *I seek my brethren: Bishop George Bell and the German churches* (1975) · K. Slack, *George Bell* (1971) · E. Duffy, *The stripping of the altars: traditional religion in England, c.1400–c.1580* (1992) · LPL, Bell MSS · *CGPLA Eng. & Wales* (1959) · b. cert. · d. cert. · *DNB* · A. Chandler, 'The death of Dietrich Bonhoeffer', *Journal of Ecclesiastical History*, 45 (1994), 448–59

Archives LPL, corresp., diaries, and papers, incl. working papers for biography of Archbishop Davidson; corresp. and papers relating to Community of Holy Cross · W. Sussex RO, addresses, diplomas, and warrants | BL, corresp. with Lord Cecil of Chelwood, Add. MS 51154 · BL, corresp. with Albert Mansbridge, Add. MSS 65254–65256 · Bodl. Oxf., corresp. with William Clark · Bodl. Oxf., letters to Sir J. Marchant · Bodl. Oxf., corresp. with Gilbert Murray · Bodl. Oxf., corresp. with third earl of Selborne · CAC Cam., corresp. with Monty Belson · CAC Cam., corresp. with John Hankey · JRL, letters to *Manchester Guardian* · King's Cam., letters to John Maynard Keynes relating to Sussex churches scheme · King's Lond., Liddell Hart C., Cambridge, corresp. with Liddell Hart · King's School, Canterbury, corresp. with Viscountess Milner relating to King's School, Canterbury · LPL, corresp. with John Douglas · LPL, corresp. with Arthur Cayley Headlam · LPL, letters to Athelstan Riley · RIBA BAL, corresp. with Sir Ninian Comper · U. Southampton L., corresp. with James Parkes · W. Sussex RO, corresp. with Walter Hussey · Wellcome L., letters to Charles Singer

Likenesses P. A. de Laszlo, portrait, c.1930 · H. Coster, photographs, c.1936–1954, NPG [*see illus.*] · E. Kennington, portrait, 1949 · W. Coldstream, oils, 1954, Tate collection · A. R. Middleton Todd, oils, 1955, bishop's palace, Chichester · E. Kennington, oils, c.1958,

Canterbury, deanery · photograph, Hult. Arch. · photographs, NPG

Wealth at death £3914 18s. 9d.: probate, 7 Jan 1959, *CGPLA Eng. & Wales*

Bell, Gertrude Margaret Lowthian (1868–1926), traveller, archaeologist, and diplomatist, was born at Washington Hall, co. Durham, on 14 July 1868, the elder child and only daughter of (Thomas) Hugh Bell (1844–1931), an ironmaster, who succeeded his father as second baronet in 1904, and his first wife, Mary (or Maria; 1844–1871), daughter of John Shield of Newcastle.

Family and education Gertrude Bell is often described as a 'favoured child of fortune' (Graham-Brown, vi), brought up amid the wealth accumulated by her industrialist grandfather, Sir (Isaac) Lowthian *Bell, first baronet. She was also favoured by an enlightened upbringing, at Red Barns, the family home near Redcar. Mary Bell's death in 1871, after giving birth to Gertrude's younger brother, Maurice, brought much pain to young Gertrude, a physically restless and intellectually gifted child. The loss of her mother also increased Gertrude's sense of independence and self-reliance; these early years fashioned her into a strong-willed adolescent, whose determination, however, concealed great sensibility and a certain vulnerability.

The special relationship that developed between Gertrude and her father during these formative years continued during her later life. Hugh Bell's dedication to the children of his first marriage was unaffected by his marriage to Florence Olliffe [see Bell, Florence Eveleen Eleanore, Lady Bell], in 1876. Florence managed to win the hearts of young Gertrude and Maurice, filling the void left by the death of their mother, though the births of her own children—Hugh (Hugo) Lowthian Bell (1878–1926), Florence Elsa (1880–1971), who married Admiral Sir Herbert William Richmond, and Mary (Molly) Katharine [see Trevelyan, Mary Katharine]—inevitably altered the family's dynamic. As the eldest of the five, Gertrude affirmed her leadership by excelling in all sorts of intellectual and athletic activities, displaying an immense drive and great readiness to measure up to challenges.

Brilliant, opinionated, and quick at light repartee, Gertrude projected a sense of inner strength unmatched by other young women in her circle. These qualities, together with her aptitude for work, turned her into an outstanding pupil at Queen's College, Harley Street, London, a leading girls' school, and at Lady Margaret Hall, Oxford, which she entered in April 1886, not yet eighteen, 'half child, half woman, rather untidy' (Courtney, 57). Contemporaries were impressed by her athletic accomplishments—she could swim, fence, row, play tennis and hockey—as well as her breadth of reading and considerable self-confidence. Through solid study, seven hours per day, and after only two years, she gained a first in modern history in 1888. At Oxford she formed long-standing friendships with Janet Hogarth (later Courtney), Edith Langridge, and Mary Talbot (later Burrows).

After completing her studies, Gertrude was sent by her

Gertrude Margaret Lowthian Bell (1868–1926), by unknown photographer, c.1900

family on a European tour, staying in Bucharest during 1888–9 with her stepmother's sister, Mary, and her husband, Sir Frank Lascelles, who was then British minister to Romania. Her encounters there with Valentine Chirol ('Domnul' in her letters), the *Times* correspondent in eastern Europe, familiarized her with developments in great power diplomacy and led to important introductions, notably to Charles Hardinge, later Lord Hardinge of Penhurst who, as India's viceroy, later enabled her to play one of the most influential roles in the post-First World War Middle East. She visited Constantinople early in 1889, returning to England later that year. The following three years were divided between the family home in Redcar and London. In Redcar she tutored her younger sisters and assisted her stepmother in philanthropic work among working people employed in the family's ironworks and collieries at Clarence in the Cleveland Hills and later at Middlesbrough. Summers were spent attending the London social season, where she acquired a lifelong habit of cigarette smoking. Without corresponding to the beauty standards of her time, she had become an attractive young woman in her way. She was slender and erect, with fine features, piercing greenish eyes, and a mass of thick light auburn hair usually assembled on the top of her head. Gertrude's attractiveness drew much from her vivacity, physical fitness, and constant, sometimes excessive, preoccupation with clothes. The round of balls and entertainments failed, however, to culminate in marriage.

Persia and the Alps A visit during 1892 to Persia, where Lascelles had become British minister, led to a formative romantic experience and also to the earliest manifestation of her outstanding literary and linguistic skills. Her stay was abruptly curtailed when her parents refused permission for her intended engagement to the embassy's first secretary, Henry George Gerald Cadogan (1859–1893), grandson of the third Earl Cadogan. Cadogan, who died not long after her departure from Tehran, was known to lack financial means to support a wife and was believed to have contracted gambling debts. His death reinforced Bell's personal impressions of the East as the domain of the emotional and it became for her a constant refuge from hard-hearted, sometimes unfulfilling, personal relations in the West. On her return to England she was persuaded to publish, anonymously, a series of her travel sketches adapted from her letters, *Safar Nameh: Persian Pictures* (1894), notable for their 'vision of Persia as a land with a heroic past' and her depictions of the Persians as 'kindly, hospitable, gifted people' (Arberry, 5). Having studied Persian with the oriental scholar Sandford Arthur Strong during the winter prior to her journey, she embarked on a verse translation of the mystical poet Hafiz (*Poems from the Divan of Hafiz*, 1897), to which she brought an insightful interpretation of the East's cultural depth and of the underlying ambiguities of Hafiz's poems. Her translation received a favourable critical reception on its publication and was long regarded as the best free-verse translation into English (Ross, 29).

During the 1890s Gertrude undertook many travels with family and friends to France, Germany, Italy, and Switzerland. She made a world tour by steamship with her brother, Maurice, in 1897–8, while on a further such voyage with her half-brother, Hugo, during 1902–3, Gertrude, who had become atheistic in her beliefs, attempted without success to undermine his religious faith (he subsequently became a clergyman). In the summers of 1899–1904, with the brothers Ulrich and Heinrich Fuhrer as guides, she undertook a series of expeditions in the Alps, where her determination, bravery, physical strength, and endurance became evident. She tackled the Meije in August 1899 and Mont Blanc in the following summer. During the seasons of 1901 and 1902 she systematically explored the Engelhorner group in the Bernese Oberland, achieving in August–September 1901 ten new routes or first ascents. An attempt in 1902 on the north-east face of Finsteraarhorn ended in failure, but was remarkable for the terrifying ordeal which she and her two guides underwent when the weather broke and they were caught in appalling conditions on the mountainside for two nights, roped together, during lightning storms and blizzards. Her ascent of the Matterhorn in August 1904 marked the end of her alpinism.

Travels and archaeology in the Middle East Gertrude Bell's attraction to the East grew with the frequency of her visits to the area. A visit to Jerusalem early in 1900, at the invitation of Friedrich Rosen, the German consul, was an opportunity to improve her Arabic. Travels on horseback to Petra, Palmyra, and Baalbek were the first of a series of desert journeys, and aroused an interest in Syrian archaeology. She returned to Jerusalem in January 1905 and embarked on a journey through the Syrian desert to Konia in Asia Minor, where she pursued her interest in the Byzantine churches of Anatolia. After meeting the archaeologist Sir William Ramsay, she agreed to revisit the area to make further investigations, in the meantime publishing her preliminary findings in the *Revue Archéologique* (1906, 1907). Her account of the Syrian portion of her journey, *The Desert and the Sown* (1907), became a classic of pre-First World War travel literature. Politically, it described the heavy Ottoman presence in the Arab towns and cities (the 'sown' areas) but practical absence from the desert areas where the Bedouin tribes were the effective rulers; personally, it revealed her perception of travel in the Middle East as an escape from the restrictions of Western domestic life.

In December 1906 Bell set out to resume her architectural and archaeological researches in Anatolia. She joined Ramsay in May 1907 and they explored the Hittite and Byzantine site of Bin-bir-kilisse in Turkey. Her particular contribution was in establishing the chronology of Byzantine churches in the region. More practical than the absent-minded Ramsay, she directed the team of Turkish diggers. Returning to Britain in August 1907 she and Ramsay published their results in *The Thousand and One Churches* (1909), to which she contributed the greater part, writing the chapters on the buildings and ecclesiastical architecture.

Gertrude Bell's next expedition, in 1909, was to survey the Roman and Byzantine fortresses on the banks of the Euphrates in Mesopotamia. This has been regarded as her most important journey of exploration, covering territory previously unfamiliar to westerners. Starting from Aleppo she reached the palace of Ukhaidir in March 1909, returning by way of Baghdad and Mosul to Asia Minor. Her account of her journey, *Amurath to Amurath* (1911), one of her most famous books, was dedicated to Evelyn Baring, first earl of Cromer, British agent and consul-general in Egypt until 1907. She described it as 'the attempt to record the daily life, the speech of those who had inherited the empty ground where empires had risen and expired'. It is most notable for its account of the changes that had taken place in the Arab provinces of the Ottoman empire after the Young Turks' rise to power in 1908 and the dissemination of their ideas in the empire's provinces: among other promising changes, foreign books and papers had become available, and greater freedom of speech and liberty of movement (also for the non-Muslim minorities) had been registered. Describing how she had witnessed 'the confused beginnings [that] were a translation of a generous ideal into the terms of human imperfection' (1924 edn, preface, p. ix), she urged Cromer to help her raise sympathy in England for the Young Turks' movement.

A further expedition to Mesopotamia in 1911 enabled Bell to undertake a fuller survey of the palace of Ukhaidir (the 'little green palace'), completing her initial sketches and drafts while exchanging notes with a German arch-aeological team. Belonging either to the Sasanian (or even Lakhmid) pre-Muhammadan types of construction with vestiges of buildings belonging to later periods, including Abbasid (after AD 750), the palace on the west bank of the Euphrates, some 120 miles south-west of Baghdad, remains one of the finest surviving examples of early Islamic architecture. Ukhaidir had not been scientifically explored until 1908–9 when Louis Massignon published some preliminary notes in the *Bulletin de l'Académie des Inscriptions et Belles Lettres* (March 1909) and in the *Gazette des Beaux-Arts* (April 1909), and later in his *Mission en Mésopotamie* (1910). Her own findings were initially pub-lished in the *Hellenic Journal* (1910, pt 1, p. 69), a preliminary to her most important contribution to archaeology, a scholarly monograph, *The Palace and Mosque of Ukhaidir: a Study in Early Mohammadan Architecture* (1914). Ukhaidir was presented by Bell in her letters as a national symbol repre-senting the historical continuity linking ancient Mesopo-tamia to modern Iraq.

The results of Bell's archaeological excursions in 1909 and 1911 to Turkish Mesopotamia, where she surveyed and photographed the surviving early Christian architecture of Tur ʿAbdin, the 'Mountain of the Servants of God', were also published (in M. van Berchem and J. Strzygowski, eds., *Amida*, 1910), and in *Zeitschrift für Geschichte der Architektur*, 9 (1913). Her work remains valuable, not least because some of the monuments no longer survive (see her *The Churches and Monasteries of Tur ʿAbdin*, ed. M. M. Mango, 1982).

Bell's intervals in England, between expeditions, were partly spent in laying out the garden in her late grand-father's house, now the family's home, Rounton Grange, near Northallerton. In the years before 1914 her most con-spicuous public work in England was as an organizer of the campaign against enfranchising women in parliamen-tary elections. She became a founder member and later president of the northern section of the Women's National Anti-Suffrage League, launched in July 1908 and chaired by Lady Jersey, which was in 1910 subsumed in the National League for Opposing Women's Suffrage under the presidency of Lord Cromer. Her family was divided on the issue: while her father and stepmother, Sir Hugh Bell and Florence Bell, were both anti-suffragists, her half-sister Molly Trevelyan was a constitutional suffragist. Ger-trude was among a number of highly talented, well-to-do, and imperially minded women affiliated to the anti-suffrage cause. Like her friend Violet Markham, she sup-ported Mary Ward's Local Government Advancement Committee, founded in 1912 to promote the idea of women's public service in local government, where their expertise in issues of health, education, and welfare, gained through philanthropy, could be most effectively exercised.

Arabia and the Arab Bureau   The man in Bell's life was Charles Hotham Montagu (Dick) Doughty-*Wylie (1868–1915), a married army officer whom she had first met in 1907 in Konia, where he was serving as British military vice-consul. After he visited Rounton in August 1913 they started to exchange love letters. The next phase of her travelling has often been seen as an escape from the per-sonal confusion, desolation, and uncertainty arising from their physically unconsummated relationship. Her fam-ous expedition (1913–14) to Haʾil in central Arabia, the seat of the Banu Rashid dynasty, should, however, be con-nected to Gertrude's inner need to be part of the historical moment, both as a voluntary agent of Britain's interests in the Middle East and as a woman trying to break one of the most challenging barriers of her time: the physical con-quest of the desert and the decoding of the moral and eth-ical code of its inhabitants.

Bell, who had been elected a fellow of the Royal Geo-graphical Society in June 1913 soon after membership was opened to women, set out from Damascus with her cara-van of camels in December 1913. As with most of her other expeditions, she was the only European among the ret-inue of Arab drivers and guides. Passing through Amman she crossed the Nefud desert, and reached Haʾil in Febru-ary 1914. In the absence of Amir Ibn Rashid, his sheikhs kept her captive there for eleven days. Returning through Baghdad, she arrived back in Damascus in May 1914. Her intention to publish an account of the journey (for which she received the Royal Geographical Society's gold medal in 1918), was thwarted by the outbreak of war, though after her death D. G. Hogarth wrote it up in the *Geograph-ical Journal* (1927). Her day-to-day diary, together with a journal of the Amman to Damascus section written for the benefit of Doughty-Wylie, were published in 2000. Her diaries and letters written during the expedition remain the most colourful descriptions of life in the city-fortress and a fascinating study of the customs and practices in central Arabia on the eve of the First World War. Although her journey covered previously uncharted areas of the desert, it was not principally notable as one of explor-ation; Lady Anne Blunt (whom Bell met in 1906) had trav-elled in the same region a generation earlier. Rather it was of diplomatic importance for the information that Bell, as the first European to reach Haʾil for over a decade, was able to gather about the Rashids, the Ottoman clients in the region.

During the early months of the First World War, Bell served as an officer of the Red Cross, assigned with the search for missing and wounded soldiers. After service in Boulogne she was recalled in February 1915 to reorganize the headquarters in London. Doughty-Wylie's heroic death at Gallipoli in April 1915 was a devastating blow; thereafter her life was mainly dedicated to the politics of the Middle East.

An opportunity to return there arose in autumn 1915 when the military intelligence department in Cairo sought the assistance of British subjects with expert knowledge of pre-war Arabia. At the invitation of the archaeologist D. G. Hogarth (the brother of her Oxford friend Janet), she reached Cairo at the end of November 1915. In the following year the organization formally became known as the Arab Bureau, set up in January 1916 as an adjunct to the intelligence offices of general head-quarters (military) to reassess Britain's policy in the region. At first under Hogarth's directorship, the bureau's officers included Ronald Storrs, Kinahan Cornwallis, G. P. Dawnay, and T. E. Lawrence among other British experts in the area. Their main aim was to hasten the departure of the Turks and to provide Britain with a link to the Arabs that would ensure Britain's hegemony over the Middle East once the war was over.

Early in 1916 Bell was summoned to India and asked by Lord Hardinge to proceed to Basrah on a liaison mission as the viceroy's personal envoy in order to assess the effects of the Arab Bureau's schemes, whose approach differed from the India Office's imperial policy. The Arab Bureau took a more pragmatic, flexible, and—in the view of some—insidious strategy, ready to exploit the advantages to be extracted from a rising Arab nationalism to perpetuate Britain's presence in the area. Annexed to the military intelligence department at the headquarters of the Mesopotamian Expeditionary Force, Bell was charged with gathering information on the movements of Bedouin tribes in central Arabia and in the Sinai peninsula. In Basrah in June 1916 she joined the staff of Sir Percy Cox, chief political officer with the expeditionary force, and was appointed assistant political officer, the only woman to hold formal rank within the force. Among her contributions during these years were informative articles for Hogarth's *Arabian Report* and for the famous *Arab Bulletin*, one of the best sources of information on the events in the Middle East during the war.

Oriental secretary in Iraq After the capture of Baghdad from the Turks by Lieutenant-General Sir Stanley Maude in March 1917, Bell continued to act as Cox's right hand in the civil administration of Mesopotamia, as his oriental secretary in charge of daily contacts with the population. In 1917 she was appointed CBE. On Cox's transfer to Tehran in 1918 to negotiate an Anglo-Persian agreement, Bell served his successor, Lieutenant-Colonel Arnold Wilson, though their relationship was uneasy as she actively promoted her own policies, sometimes conspiring with Wilson's superiors at the India Office, among them Sir Arthur Hirtzel, against the acting civil commissioner.

Bell's conflicts with Wilson represented not just a clash of personalities, but also a profound disagreement over Iraq's future. She had previously been sceptical about the possibility of Arab self-government, preferring the model of British rule in Egypt as that for the post-war administration of captured Ottoman territories. But after attending the Paris peace conference in 1919 she became converted to the idea of Arab governments, though guided by British advisers. A staunch believer in the administrative methods of the India Office (and rejecting the promises of autonomy exposed in the 1918 Anglo-French declaration), Wilson opposed Bell's more liberal approach concerning the establishment of an Arab government as the best and cheapest way to maintain Britain's presence in Iraq, and complained that she intrigued behind his back to gain her ends. In two memoranda, 'Self-determination in Mesopotamia' (1919) and 'Syria in October 1919', Bell argued that

Arab self-government and administration were a viable option. She also completed her acclaimed *Review of the Civil Administration of Mesopotamia*, commissioned by Wilson and published as a white paper in 1920. The review which, among other things, described the social conditions in Iraq's tribal areas, remains a widely used source of information.

In April 1920 the San Remo conference established Britain's League of Nations mandate over Iraq. This was followed in summer 1920 by tribal disturbances fanned by Iraqi nationalists of the ʿAhd. Although the uprising had other causes related to tribal politics and reinforced by discontent with taxation and rural conditions the short-lived alliance between Shiʿi tribal sheikhs and mujtahids and Sunni nationalists became a national myth or landmark with far-reaching consequences—among them, the end of the regime of military occupation and the establishment of an Arab provisional government under the presidency of the naqib of Baghdad. The uprising brought the return of Sir Percy Cox in October 1920 as British high commissioner and with it an enhanced role for Bell as oriental secretary, a position she held under him and his successor until her death. Cox set about creating a council of state under the naqib, with whom Bell maintained close contact.

In the light of Britain's financial difficulties after the war, Winston Churchill, secretary of state for the colonies, initially favoured British withdrawal from Iraq. But at the Cairo conference of British Middle East officials in March 1921, Churchill came to adopt Cox's and Bell's position for maintaining a presence in Iraq by setting up an Arab regime advised by British officers. This system of indirect rule became a heavy burden on the young state's treasury and was later considered by Iraqi nationalists as an obstacle in the country's path to independence. Bell also played a significant role in securing the throne for Feisal ibn Hussein, whose coronation as king of Iraq took place in August 1921. A close adviser to King Feisal, the Khatun ('Lady of the Court', as she became widely known) also stood behind the negotiations for the ratification of the Anglo-Iraqi treaty (October 1922), which formally replaced the mandate.

Bell took part in organizing the elections for the constitutional assembly, and in preparing the electoral law that provided the king and the British high commissioner with the authority to administer the country and create the mechanisms necessary for political representation of all sectors of the population. Together with Kinahan Cornwallis ('Ken' in her letters), adviser to Iraq's ministry of the interior and the king's personal counsellor, Bell continued to intervene in the political arrangements that led to the signing of the protocol of 1923. Among other things the protocol fixed Iraq's frontiers with Jordan and Saudi Arabia and, more importantly, with Turkey. It left unsolved, however, the question of the former Mosul vilayet with its Kurdish population, which was settled only in 1925, after the visit to the area of a commission appointed by the League of Nations. Bell was also involved in the discussions regarding the terms of the subsidiary agreements (financial, judicial, and military), the appointments of officials and qadhis, and the question of establishing Arabic as the country's official vernacular. She played an important part in the debates on the methods and aims of the educational system to be created in Iraq, which mainly involved the adoption of more appropriate educational methods for the rural (that is, Shiʿi and Kurdish) areas, mediating at times between Satiʿ al-Husri (the director of education who favoured the establishment of a uniform educational system for all the segments of the population), the subsequent Shiʿi ministers of education, and her close friend Lionel Smith, the British adviser to the ministry. She tried to help the Muslim women in Baghdad, who were largely confined indoors; she organized tea parties for them and arranged a series of lectures from a woman doctor.

Death and retrospect Gertrude Bell's position in Iraq was eroded after Iraq's new constitution (1924) and administrative structures replaced the old, colonial order. She was often at odds with Cox's successor, Sir Henry Dobbs. Her later letters were a barometer of her feelings at the end of her mission in Iraq. Isolated, grief-stricken, and disappointed by Cornwallis's apparent indifference to her infatuation for him (which grew after his divorce in 1925), Bell found consolation in archaeology, gathering funds for a national museum in Baghdad, which was inaugurated in 1923 and installed in a permanent building in 1926. There was little consolation to be found in England, where economic depression had weakened the family's financial position and forced them to close up Rounton Grange. Having returned to Iraq after a sick leave in England in summer 1925, Gertrude Bell died in her sleep at Baghdad during the night of 11/12 July 1926 and was buried on the evening of the 12th in the British military cemetery there. The cause of her death was an overdose of sleeping tablets, taken on the night of 11 July. Close friends, who were aware of her depression, believed that she had taken her own life, but there was no direct evidence as to whether the fatal dose was intentional. A memorial service was held at St Margaret's, Westminster.

Bell's adult life divided into three phases. In the first, during the 1890s, contemporaries saw her as 'an accomplished young lady of good family and brilliant intellectual gifts' (Arberry, 6). But dissatisfied with the conventional role of domesticity and philanthropy assigned to well-to-do, unmarried women, she turned to independent travel, first in the Alps, then in the Middle East, with the intellectual dimensions of archaeological discovery and political observation. The latter enabled her to assume a public role as the First World War and the end of Ottoman rule in Arab lands created an official outlet for her expertise. At her death she was commemorated as a brilliant public servant, who helped to shape the post-war settlement in the Middle East and in particular the creation of the kingdom of Iraq. H. St J. Philby called her 'the maker of Iraq' and reflected that if Feisal's kingdom survived the vicissitudes of time, 'it will stand forth in history a monument to her genius, to the versatility of her knowledge

and influence, and to the practical idealism tempered with honest opportunism which were the outstanding characteristics of a remarkable Englishwoman' (Arberry, 8). Her vitality and vigour were admired by many of her female European contemporaries. 'With a man's grasp of affairs she united a woman's quick instinct', wrote her friend Janet Courtney (Courtney, 62), who placed her in stature alongside the great imperial proconsuls Cromer, Curzon, and Milner.

Bell's legacy in Iraq proved ambiguous; the regime she helped to create was toppled in 1958. Later generations, however, became familiar with her through publication of her letters, first heavily edited by her stepmother (1927) and subsequently in fuller selections edited by Elizabeth Burgoyne (1958, 1961). Later studies brought to light the emotional trauma of her relationship with Doughty-Wylie. Most of all they reveal her ability as a writer and observer, and the extent of her engagement with a Middle East which is also documented in the large collection of technically impressive photographs taken by her during her journeys in the area. Indeed, it is as one of the greatest chroniclers of Britain's imperial moment in the Middle East that she is best remembered.   LIORA LUKITZ

Sources Gertrude Bell papers, U. Newcastle, Robinson L., special collections · colonial and foreign office files, PRO · BL OIOC · A. T. Wilson papers, BL · Elizabeth Robins papers, New York University, Fales Library · *The letters of Gertrude Bell*, ed. Lady Bell (1927) · *The earlier letters of Gertrude Bell*, ed. E. Richmond (1937) · E. Burgoyne, *Gertrude Bell from her personal papers*, 2 vols. (1958–61) · S. Deardon, 'Gertrude Bell: a journey of the heart', *Cornhill Magazine*, no. 1062 (winter 1969–70), 457–510 · *Gertrude Bell: the Arabian diaries, 1913–1914*, ed. R. O'Brien (2000) · *DNB* · D. Hogarth, *GJ*, 68 (1926) · R. P.-H., *Alpine Journal*, 34 (1926), 29 · *Alpine Journal*, 34 (1926), 296–9 · J. E. Courtney, *Brown Book* (Dec 1926), 57–62 [Lady Margaret Hall, Oxford] · M. R. Ridley, *Gertrude Bell* (1941) · J. Kamm, *Daughter of the desert: the story of Gertrude Bell* (1956) · S. Hill, *Gertrude Bell (1868–1926): a selection from the photographic archive of an archaeologist and traveller* (1976) · H. F. V. Winstone, *Gertrude Bell* (1978); rev. edn (1993) · S. Goodman, *Gertrude Bell* (1985) · L. Gordon, *Gertrude Bell* (1994) · J. Wallach, *Desert queen: the extraordinary life of Gertrude Bell* (1996) · E. D. Ross, preface, *Poems from the Divan of Hafiz*, trans. G. Bell (1928) · K. Cornwallis, introduction, in G. Bell, *The Arab war: dispatches from the 'Arab Bulletin'* (1940) · A. J. Arberry, preface, in G. Bell, *Persian pictures*, 3rd edn (1947) · S. Graham-Brown, introduction, in G. Bell, *The desert and the sown* (1985) · M. Gilbert, *Winston S. Churchill*, 4: *1916–1922* (1975) · P. P. Graves, *The life of Sir Percy Cox* (1941) · B. Harrison, *Separate spheres: the opposition to women's suffrage in Britain* (1978) · L. James, *The golden warrior: the life and legend of Lawrence of Arabia* (1990) · J. Lewis, *Women and social action in Victorian and Edwardian England* (1991) · L. Lukitz, *Iraq: the search for national identity* (1995) · J. Marlowe, *Late Victorian: the life of Sir Arnold Talbot Wilson* (1967) · P. Marr, *The modern history of Iraq* (1985) · B. Melman, *Woman's Orient: English women and the Middle East, 1718–1918* (1992) · E. Monroe, *Britain's moment in the Middle East, 1914–1956* (1963) · P. Sluglett, *Britain in Iraq, 1914–1932* (1976) · ʿAbd al-Razzaq Al-Hasani, *Taʾrikh al-wizarat al-ʿiraqiyya*, 3, 4 (1939–40) ['The history of Iraq's cabinets'] · ʿAbd al-Razzaq Al-Hasani, *Al Thawra al-ʿarabiyya al-kubra sanat 1920*, 3rd edn (1978) ['The 1920 great Iraqi revolution'] · ʿAbd al-Razzaq Al-Hasani, *Al-ʿIraq: qadima wa haditha* (1973) ['Iraq: ancient and modern'] · SatiʿAl-Husri, *Mudhakkirati fi al-ʿiraq*, 2 vols. (1966) ['Memoirs from Iraq'] · *Al-Waqaʾi al-ʿiraqiyya* (1920–) ['Iraqi Gazette', official publication]

Archives BL, travel diaries, Add. MS 45158 · RGS, notebooks · St Ant. Oxf., Middle East Centre, letters to Mr and Mrs Humphrey Bowman; copy of travel diary; corresp. and papers relating to her ·

U. Durham L., intelligence reports on Iraq, Syria, and Ibn Saud · U. Newcastle, Robinson L., corresp. and papers incl. diaries | BL, A. T. Wilson papers · Bodl. Oxf., corresp. with Lord Lovelace and Lady Lovelace · CUL, corresp. with Lord Hardinge and papers · Mitchell L., NSW, letters to G. E. Morrison · NA Scot., letters to Philip Kerr · NL Scot., letters to members of the Campbell family · St Ant. Oxf., Middle East Centre, corresp. with H. St J. B. Philby · U. Durham, Sudan archives

Likenesses F. Russell, watercolour drawing, 1887, NPG · photograph, *c.*1900, Hult. Arch. [*see illus.*] · photograph, 1918, RGS · J. S. Sargent, drawing, 1925, priv. coll. · A. Acheson, bronze bust (after J. S. Sargent; posthumous, 1923), RGS · A. Acheson, bust, Baghdad Museum, Iraq · J. Weston & Sons, photograph, RGS · photographs, U. Newcastle, Gertrude Bell archive

Wealth at death £25,604 9*s.* 11*d.*: probate, 1926

Bell, (Frank) Graham (1910–1943), painter and writer, was born on 21 November 1910 near Brakpan, Johannesburg, Transvaal, the eldest of the three sons of Frank Graham Bell (1874–1948), a British mining engineer, and his wife, Marjorie, *née* Hewitt (1888–1979). The family spent from 1915 to 1922 in England, where Bell attended schools in Berkshire and Dorset, then went back to South Africa and settled in or near Durban. From 1923 Bell, a strong and intelligent boy, was at Michaelhouse School, Balgowan, Natal, leaving in 1926 with unrealistic dreams of being an artist. He intermittently attended art classes at the Natal Technical College and exhibited pictures in Durban; but under family pressure he took work in a bank, then in 1929 undertook to manage a sugar farm in Zululand bought by his father. Within a year, however, he decamped to Durban, where he subsisted precariously, living with friends and devoting himself to painting to such effect that he could exhibit some forty oils at the Durban Art Gallery in March 1931. These post-impressionist essays were thought daringly 'modern'; public attention ensured enough sales to enable Bell, aged twenty, to sail for England that April, accompanied by Eileen (known as Anne) Bilbrough (1909–2001), a designer and gallery assistant, who contributed substantially to their support. They married in London on 23 February 1937, when it was stated that they had been previously married in South Africa on 5 March 1931. Their daughter was born later in 1937; however, increasing discord culminated in a separation in January 1938.

In London, Bell encountered paintings previously known to him only through reproductions, becoming temporarily infatuated with Duncan Grant's work. Hoping to paint and exhibit, he sought friends among fellow painters, many of them former students of the Slade School of Fine Art. But chronic lack of money deflected him: he decorated pottery for Phyllis Keyes, served as an assistant at the Contemporary Arts Society, helped to edit the short-lived journal *London Week*, and, increasingly, reviewed for the *New Statesman and Nation*. Aesthetic speculations shared by his friends Rodrigo Moynihan and Geoffrey Tibble led him in March 1934 to contribute three amorphous canvases to the exhibition 'Objective abstractions' at the Zwemmer Gallery in London; but sensing that this constituted a dead end, he virtually abandoned painting for the next two years.

Discussions with his friend William Coldstream, who was in a similar quandary, eventually rekindled Bell's belief in painting. The two devised 'A Plan for Artists', submitting it early in 1937 to Kenneth Clark, the young (and wealthy) director of the National Gallery. Clark responded by creating a fund offering painters in their situation modest financial support. Artistically, the plan proposed— against the contemporary prevalence of abstraction and surrealism—a return to the exploration and expression, through observation, of the visible world. This approach, corresponding to that of their friends Victor Pasmore and Claude Rogers, led to the opening in October 1937 of a school of drawing and painting. Although Bell was not formally a director of the *Euston Road School (as it was later known), its strength, according to Pasmore, largely stemmed from his conviction and sense of purpose.

(Frank) Graham Bell (1910–1943), by Olivier Bell, 1938 [painting *Dover Front*]

Following this renewal of confidence, Bell's painting prospered during the next years, albeit against a background of the gathering menace of reactionary political and military forces, which concerned him deeply. He was active in anti-fascist initiatives through exhibitions and his writing; his pamphlet *The Artist and his Public* was published in 1939. While effectively homeless (in London he was given house room by Clark, his patron and now his friend), he shared studios with Coldstream and worked frequently with students at the school; he spent weeks at a time painting in Bolton, Lancashire (the seat of the Mass-Observation movement), Dover, Hampshire, Dublin, France, and Suffolk, producing landscapes, portraits, and still lifes. When war came he awaited his call up with undeceived impatience, being finally accepted for aircrew training in September 1940. He passed much of the next year marooned by the RAF on Anglesey with his leg badly broken as a result of playing football. Subsequent training took him back to South Africa, where he was reunited with his parents and gained his commission as an observer. Further intensive training in England was brought to an end on 9 August 1943, when his Wellington bomber crashed on landing at RAF Ossington, near Newark, Nottinghamshire, killing the entire crew. His funeral took place at Golders Green crematorium, London, on 13 August. The one fixed point in these six final itinerant years was his attachment to the art historian (Anne) Olivier Popham (b. 1916)—the subject of a 1938 portrait in the Tate collection—whom, owing to the divorce laws and the disruptions of wartime, he was never free to marry.

The force of Graham Bell's personality and the combative vigour of his writing contrasts with the sensitive restraint and scrupulous tenderness of his painting; yet both uphold realist values with lean, self-critical distinction. In his death British art lost a cohesive and potentially commanding figure.   ANNE OLIVIER BELL

Sources B. Laughton, *The Euston Road School* (1986) · *Paintings of Graham Bell* (1947) [introduction by Sir Kenneth Clark] · G. G. Bell, unpublished family memoir, 1993 · personal knowledge (2004) · *CGPLA Eng. & Wales* (1944) · private information (2004) · m. cert.
Archives Tate collection, sketch/notebooks, containing written material (some diary form, autobiographical accounts, drafts) and drawings from observation; letters; corresp. and papers [photocopies] | Tate collection, corresp. with Lord Clark
Likenesses O. Bell, photograph, 1938, priv. coll. [*see illus.*] · photograph, 1938, repro. in *Paintings of Graham Bell* · F. G. Bell, self-portrait, oils, 1939, priv. coll.
Wealth at death £85 17s. 3d.: administration, 5 June 1944, *CGPLA Eng. & Wales*

Bell, Henry (*bap.* 1647, *d.* 1711), architect and merchant, was baptized on 8 July 1647 in King's Lynn, Norfolk, the son of Henry Bell (*d.* 1686), mercer. He was educated at the local grammar school and then Gonville and Caius College, Cambridge, where he took his BA degree in 1665, before embarking on a grand tour. On 28 February 1678 he married Anne Brumble; they had five sons and one daughter. In 1686 he inherited his father's properties and continued his successful business as a producer of linseed and rape oil. His status in the merchant community is attested by his becoming an alderman in 1690 and, following his father, serving as mayor of King's Lynn in 1692 and 1703.

An educated and cultivated gentleman, Bell's travels played an important part in the formation of his taste, both as a connoisseur of paintings and as an architect. His own collection, bequeathed to his youngest son, William, included works said to be by Hans Holbein, Rembrandt, Egbert van Heemskerk and his father, and Hendrick Goltzius. He practised architecture as a pastime rather than as a full-time profession. In the brief memoir of his life, which prefixes his posthumously published *An Historical Essay on the Original of Painting* (1728), Bell's travels are said to have 'conduced very much to his Improvement' in architecture, the 'Mistress of … (his) Affections'. His style owed a great deal to Dutch architecture, as well as to the work of Sir Christopher Wren. He first came to notice for his role in planning the rebuilding of Northampton after the fire of 1675. He was certainly at least jointly responsible for the rebuilding (1677–80) of the town's All Saints' Church and was perhaps involved also in the designing of the sessions house (1676–88), as well as houses in the market place.

Bell's most important surviving building is the custom house, King's Lynn, built in 1683 as an exchange, at the expense of the wine merchant and member of parliament Sir John Turner, and sold to the customs authorities in 1718. This square building, with an arcaded ground floor, steep roof, and lantern, is articulated by superimposed orders which carry Bell's characteristic garlanded, Ionic capitals. This motif occurs also at his church at North Runcton, Norfolk, rebuilt in 1703–13, which shares with All Saints' in Northampton the plan of a Greek cross within a rectangle, probably derived from Wren's St Mary-at-Hill. Of Bell's other documented works, all in King's Lynn, the domed, octagonal market cross (1707–10; dem. 1831) was the most notable. It is likely that he was responsible also for the surviving Duke's Head inn, in the town's Tuesday Market, built about 1684 for Sir John Turner to accommodate those visiting the exchange. On stylistic grounds we may also attribute to him the church of St Genevieve at Euston, Suffolk (1676), the courtyard of Kimbolton Castle, Huntingdonshire (c.1685), and Stanhoe Hall, Norfolk (1703), built for Thomas Archdale (MP for High Wycombe in 1698–9) and his wife, Jane, the daughter of Charles Turner, Sir John's younger brother.

Bell has a small but significant place in English architectural history, not only for the strength of his designs but also as an occasional architect coming, unusually, from the mercantile community rather than from the court or the gentry. He signed his will in 1706 and died in King's Lynn on 11 April 1711, leaving substantial properties to his wife and family. He was buried in St Margaret's Church, King's Lynn, in which he had been baptized and married.

JOHN BOLD

Sources Colvin, *Archs.* · H. M. Colvin and L. M. Wodehouse, 'Henry Bell of King's Lynn', *Architectural History*, 4 (1961), 41–62 · M. Archdale, 'Henry Bell as a country house architect [pts 1–2]', *Country Life*, 140 (1966), 614–16, 756–8 · A. Oswald, 'King's Lynn, Norfolk: 3', *Country Life*, 110 (1951), 194–8

Wealth at death substantial properties, incl. messuages, tenements, malthouses, granaries, gardens, lands, money, and paintings: will, PRO, PROB 11/521, sig. 99

Bell, Henry (1767–1830), hotelier and developer of steam navigation, was born at Torphichen Mill, Linlithgowshire, on 7 April 1767, the fifth son of Patrick Bell and his wife, Margaret Easton. He was educated at the village school and then in Falkirk. Despite the reputation of Scottish schools, his education served him badly and for the rest of his life he was unable to spell and made many grammatical errors in his extensive correspondence. At the age of thirteen he was apprenticed as a stonemason and then in 1783 as a millwright—two trades much in demand at a time when Scottish industry was growing rapidly. In 1786 he began work in the shipyard of Shaw and Hart at Bo'ness on the Firth of Forth; but he left after a year to become an engineer with James Inglis near Motherwell in Lanarkshire. He went to London in 1788 to gain experience with the distinguished engineer John Rennie, and returned to Glasgow in 1790 to set up as a wright and builder. Over the next twenty years he participated actively in the wave of new building as the city expanded.

On 26 March 1794 Bell married Margaret Young, and three years later he was enrolled as a burgess. In 1806 the Bells purchased ground alongside the road from Dumbarton to Helensburgh, a new resort for the well-to-do promoted by Sir James Colquhoun of Luss. Within a year they had built the Bath's Inn, equipped with hot and cold fresh and sea water therapeutic baths. When the first Helensburgh town council was elected in 1807, Bell was returned as provost. Until he stood down in 1811 he was involved in a number of civic projects, including an abortive initiative to build a town house and a successful venture to provide a public water supply.

Like many others in the west of Scotland, Bell had been interested in the propulsion of ships by steam since William Symington's prototype was abandoned. About 1810 Bell, assisted by a Glasgow engineer John Thomson, began his own practical experiments, which he seems to have financed by mortgaging the hotel for £2000. The following year he placed a contract for the hull with John Wood, a shipbuilder in Port Glasgow. The engines were supplied by John Robertson, a Glasgow engineer, and the boiler and smokestack by David Napier of the Camlachie foundry, also in Glasgow. The vessel, the *Comet*, was launched in July or August 1812 and, despite technical shortcomings, demonstrated the feasibility of paddle steam propulsion.

Typical of many pioneers, Bell was an incompetent man of business and lacked both the capital and credit to exploit his innovation. He quickly had imitators who were better able to develop steamer services on the Clyde. Frustrated, Bell attempted to pioneer services on the Forth, coastwise to London from the Clyde, and north to the western highlands and islands using the *Comet*, which had been lengthened and re-engineered. Chronically in debt and pathologically given to exaggeration and intrigue, he was again thwarted and it was others who executed his bold plans. During 1820 the ownership of the *Comet*,

Henry Bell (1767–1830), by James Tannock

which was then operating a service between the Clyde and Fort William, was about to be transferred to a company whose shareholders included a number of west Highland landowners, when she was wrecked in the Sound of Jura. Bell had no interest in her successor, *Comet II*, but seems to have served as ship's husband (manager).

Apart from his steamship interests, Bell continued to manage the Bath's Inn and to work as an architect and contractor, reconstructing the Dalmonach calico printing works on the River Leven at Dumbarton in 1812. He also put forward visionary but flawed proposals for draining part of Loch Lomond and converting Glasgow harbour into an enormous floating dock. During the 1820s, dogged by poor health and in financial difficulties, Bell persisted in his efforts to promote steamer services on the west coast, inaugurating the Glasgow–Inverness route by way of the Caledonian Canal with the *Stirling* in 1825 and participating in the ownership of the *Highland Chieftain* used on the Skye route. The *Stirling* foundered in Loch Linnhe in 1828 with loss of life.

The success of steamships in the late 1820s fuelled Bell's appetite for vanity and self-deception. His visiting card showed a picture of the *Comet* with the caption 'the first steamboat' and he concocted a story of a trip to America in 1807 to instruct Robert Fulton in the design of his steamer. However, he had his supporters, who petitioned for public recognition of his achievement through the award of modest pensions from organizations that had benefited from the steamship. The Clyde Navigation Trust responded with an annual gratuity of £50, later raised to £100. In 1828 George Canning, shortly before his death, made Bell a Treasury grant of £200 to help him out of his serious financial problems. These and other gifts scarcely covered his debts.

Bell died after a long illness on 14 November 1830 at the Bath's Inn, leaving an estate of £707, mostly made up of the value of the contents of the inn. He was survived by his wife, who died in 1856. They had no children. They were both seceders and members of the Old Light Burghers' church in Helensburgh. Although Henry Bell was acknowledged by his contemporaries as the pioneer of the steamship, he had little of the talent or business acumen of his peers in the engineering profession, James Watt or David Napier. His achievement was marred by his failure to concede that others had contributed to the success of the *Comet*.   MICHAEL S. MOSS

Sources B. Osbourne, *The ingenious Mr Bell* (1995) · D. D. Napier, *David Napier, engineer, 1790–1869: an autobiographical sketch with notes*, ed. D. Bell (1912) · H. Bell, *Observations on the utility of applying steam engines to vessels* (1813)
Archives NL Scot., letters relating to the *Comet* steamboat · U. Glas., Napier collection · U. Glas., Scott collection
Likenesses T. O. Barlow, mixed-method engraving, NPG · J. Tannock, oils, Scot. NPG [*see illus.*] · photograph, repro. in Napier, *David Napier, engineer*, facing p. 80
Wealth at death £707: Osbourne, *Ingenious Mr Bell*

Bell, Henry Glassford (1803–1874), writer and sheriff, was born in Glasgow on 8 November 1803, the eldest son of James Bell, advocate, and brother of Jonathan Anderson *Bell, the architect. He was educated at Glasgow high school and subsequently at the University of Edinburgh after his family moved to that city. While an undergraduate, from 1820 to 1822, he became interested in literature, writing reviews of books and plays in the *Edinburgh Observer*. His articles on the theatre under the pen name Acer won him acclaim and are reputed to have contributed to the improvement of the quality of the Edinburgh stage. In 1824 he published privately a volume of verse in the Byronic style. Three years later he spoke at the dinner of the Edinburgh Theatrical Fund, when Sir Walter Scott acknowledged his authorship of the Waverley novels. In 1828 Bell started the *Edinburgh Literary Journal*, which included among its contributors Thomas Aird, Mrs Hemans, Thomas Campbell, John Wilson (Christopher North), James Hogg (the Ettrick Shepherd), Allan Cunningham, G. P. R. James, and Sheridan Knowles. With Bell as editor the *Journal* won a considerable reputation. Bell left in 1831, and the *Journal* continued as the *Edinburgh News and Literary Chronicle* and merged in 1848 with the *Scottish Pilot* as the *Edinburgh Weekly Chronicle*. Bell published a collection of most of his contributions in two volumes, *Summer and Winter Hours* (1831) and *My Old Portfolio* (1832). The first volume consisted of poetry, including 'Mary Queen of Scots', which became a favourite with teachers of elocution. The second volume, of prose, contained three passages that were soon popularly recited—'The Marvellous History of Mynheer von Wodenblock', later rewritten in doggerel under the title 'Cork Leg' and translated into French and German; 'The Dead Daughter'; and 'The Living Mummy'. In 1828 Bell at the invitation of Archibald Constable published a defence of Mary queen of Scots, which quickly became a best-seller and was pirated in America

and translated into French. During this time he was one of the promoters of the Royal Scotch Academy.

While he had been developing his literary skills, Bell had been studying law; he took classes at the University of Edinburgh in 1831 and became an advocate in the same year. At a time when the Scottish bar was well stocked with glittering talent, Bell found advancement slow. However, he was a junior counsel in the brilliant defence by Duncan McNeill and Patrick Robertson in the notorious Glasgow cotton spinners' trial of 1838, and his skilful performance led to an offer of the post of one of the sheriff-deputes for Lanarkshire in 1839. He quickly became as well known in Glasgow for his interest in literature and the theatre as he had been in Edinburgh, and he was much in demand as a thoughtful and witty speaker in the city's numerous clubs and societies. In the most rapidly growing industrial area in Britain, Bell became an expert in trying complex commercial and mercantile cases, particularly those involving insolvency. His judgments were widely respected and rarely contested in a higher court. A contemporary commented 'he realised the ideal of what a judge ought to be' and another remarked,

> the older members of the legal profession hold the opinion that Sheriff Glassford Bell was the best judge that ever sat in the sheriff court of Glasgow … Approaching every case without a shade of bias, he listened so quietly to the arguments on either side that it was only when his decisions, always remarkable for their clearness, were made that it was seen how carefully he had weighed the matters at issue (*DNB*)

When in 1852 it was believed that the sheriff-principal, Sir Archibald Alison, was to be made a lord of session, the Glasgow Faculty of Procurators petitioned the lord advocate to promote Bell. As it turned out Bell had to wait until Alison's death in 1867 before taking over as sheriff-principal.

Apart from his judicial office, Bell played an active part in a variety of philanthropic and educational associations in the city. He was deeply involved in the Glasgow Athenaeum, which provided evening classes and training in commercial subjects and in music and drama. He was its president in 1851. He gave of his time to help raise money for the new buildings for the University of Glasgow. He lectured, himself, on the history of art, attracting large audiences. The only publications during his time in Glasgow were the introduction to his 1865 edition of *The Dramatic Works of William Shakespeare*, and his *Romances and Minor Poems* (1866). Most of these poems were written while on holiday, as an escape from the restraints of 'legal pursuits'. Bell was also a skilled angler and a chess champion for the west of Scotland.

Bell married in 1831 Sophia Stewart, the only daughter of Captain Charles Stewart of Sheerglass, Glengarry. They had six children before his wife died, in 1847. Bell later married Marian Sandeman, on 14 August 1872. The following year he became ill with an infected hand. He died in Glasgow, still in office, on 7 January 1874. He was so well regarded in the city that he was the first person in the nineteenth century to be buried in the nave of St Mungo's Cathedral. Throughout his life Bell was a staunch tory; but he had many Liberal friends. He was well known for his generosity and kindliness.   MICHAEL S. MOSS

Sources *Journal of Jurisprudence*, 18 (1874), 97–103 · *Glasgow Herald* (8 Jan 1874) · *The rights of labour defended, or, The trial of the Glasgow cotton spinners* (1837) · personal knowledge (1885) [*DNB*] · *DNB* · private information (1885)
Likenesses J. Mossman, marble bust, 1874, Scot. NPG
Wealth at death £5144 5s. 10d.: probate, 10 March 1874, SC 36/48/73/442–5

Bell, Sir Henry Hesketh Joudou (1864–1952), colonial governor and author, was born on 17 December 1864 in the West Indies, the eldest son of Henry A. J. Bell. Little is known of his early life other than that he was said to be of French extraction, and he lived for extended periods with his father in Belgium and France where he received only a limited education. However, he spoke French perfectly. In 1882 he began his career as a third-class clerk working in the office of the governor of Barbados and the Windward Islands. His financial acumen was soon recognized and he was transferred to the treasury department of Grenada where he served successfully for seven years. Given long-standing local sensitivities about revenue collection, Bell must have gained a good grounding in the art of stretching very limited resources a long way.

In 1890 Bell joined the colonial service and was posted to the Gold Coast as supervisor of customs. He served here for four years in both financial and administrative positions, being promoted several times. This was not a happy period as he particularly feared the climate of tropical Africa, and was therefore relieved to return to the Bahamas to take up the post of receiver-general in 1894. Several good appointments followed, including administrator of Dominica and acting governor of the Leeward Islands, between 1895 and 1905. His service during this period impressed the Colonial Office, as well as Joseph Chamberlain, and his career advanced rapidly thereafter. Bell was particularly aided in his dealings with the Colonial Office by his ability to write lucid and interesting accounts of his activities. He was appointed CMG in 1903 and more importantly in 1905 was offered the post of high commissioner to Uganda, his first major appointment. In spite of his reservations about the climate, Bell felt that he could not reject such a promising offer. One of the first major problems that he had to deal with in Uganda were epidemics of sleeping sickness that claimed many lives. Having ascertained that cases of the sickness were generally confined to areas within 2 miles of open water, he sought permission from the Colonial Office to move all communities living by the tsetse-fly infested shores and islands of Lake Victoria to new plots on crown land further away. While the Colonial Office demurred at the political implications of forcibly moving large sections of the population, Bell ordered the moves to be carried out regardless. As a consequence many lives were saved and no unrest was reported. His actions in this matter were recognized with advancement to KCMG in 1908.

During his time in Uganda, Bell continued to develop his ideas on economic development, believing that the region would be best served through nurturing the interests and improving the agricultural methods of the local farmers. He was also determined that the activities of the European planters should be curtailed as far as possible. The role of government, he argued, was to provide leadership, set standards, and bear the cost of agricultural experiments as well as to provide scientific advice, particularly in relation to the development of cash crops. To these ends he introduced the 1908 Uganda cotton ordinance which gave the governor wide powers to control the quality of cotton produced, and wrote his own useful report on the subject in 1909 for the Colonial Office. He worked very

Sir Henry Hesketh Joudou Bell (1864–1952), by unknown photographer

hard to improve the transport infrastructure, steering every available penny into the construction of new roads.

In 1909 Bell was promoted to the post of governor of Northern Nigeria and it was at this point that his career began to falter. The permanent officials at the Colonial Office, particularly Charles Strachey, felt that he had too little knowledge of Nigerian affairs to cope unaided. Charles Temple was appointed chief secretary, with a dormant commission, to shore up Bell's administration. Temple was a ruthlessly determined, ambitious, and very skilful officer who had been in Nigeria since 1901 and had been one of Sir Frederick Lugard's pioneering administrators. Bell arrived in the protectorate already seriously handicapped in his dealings with the tough and independently minded Northern Nigerian political officers. It was hoped that he would have some impact on the economic development of the region, but in practice his influence was so limited that he could do little more than occasionally delay and question the actions of his senior officers who were convinced proponents of the policy of indirect rule. These officers had little time for Bell, decrying his lack of social background, his fear of the climate, and, above all, his apparent lack of credibility when compared to Temple. Events came to a head when a satirical doggerel verse outlining the many faults of Bell was passed around the protectorate until, inevitably, someone could not resist placing it on his desk. Bell unwisely made a great play to find the culprit, even taking the matter up with the Colonial Office. It was thought that this ditty explained his departure from Nigeria in 1912, nearly a year earlier than expected. Lugard was appointed as his successor.

After Nigeria, Bell returned to the Caribbean, serving as the governor of the Leeward Islands from 1912, and was then posted to Mauritius in 1915. Once again he was able to demonstrate his skill in fostering economic development, and he took a frank pleasure in the trappings of his office. He retired in 1925 and was made a GCMG the following year. Immediately after retiring he travelled extensively throughout Java and French Indo-China, and on his return wrote *Foreign Colonial Administration in the Far East* (1928), which won the Royal Empire Society's gold medal. In all he published ten books on various subjects including the occult. His first book, a study of witchcraft, appeared in 1889; his last, *Witches and Fishes*, appeared in 1948. He continued to travel for the rest of his life, sojourning in the Bahamas during the Second World War. Bell did not make a home in England after his retirement but he frequently visited London (where he was a member of the Athenaeum). He died, unmarried, on 1 August 1952, at 92 Redcliffe Gardens, Kensington, London.

C. J. F. ALDERMAN

Sources H. H. J. Bell, *Glimpses of a governor's life* (1946) · H. H. J. Bell, *Foreign colonial administration in the Far East* (1928) · K. Ingham, *The making of modern Uganda* (1958) · K. Ingham, *A history of East Africa* (1962) · C. J. F. Alderman, 'British imperialism and social Darwinism: C. L. Temple and colonial administration in Northern Nigeria, 1901–1916', PhD diss., Kingston University, 1996 · R. Heussler, *The British in Northern Nigeria* (1968) · E. D. Morel, *Nigeria: its people and its problems* (1911) · J. Barber, *Imperial frontier* (1968) · *The Times* (5 Aug 1952) · *WWW* · *CGPLA Eng. & Wales* (1952)

Archives BL, diaries · CUL, Royal Commonwealth Society Library, corresp. and papers · PRO, CO 446/90–105 | Bodl. Oxf., corresp. with Lewis Harcourt · Bodl. RH, Edwardes MSS, Afr. r. 106, 4 · Bodl. RH, Grier MSS, Afr. s. 1379, box 2/1
Likenesses P. A. de Laszlo, portrait; formerly in the collection of governor's portraits, official residence of the governor of Mauritius · photograph, CUL, Royal Commonwealth Society collection [*see illus.*]
Wealth at death £8672 1s. 2d.: probate, 5 Nov 1952, *CGPLA Eng. & Wales*

Bell, Henry Nugent (1792–1822), genealogist, was the eldest son of George Bell, of Belle Vue, co. Fermanagh, and Catherine, daughter of Dominick Nugent MP. He followed the profession of a legal antiquary, and, in order to obtain a recognized status, entered himself at the Inner Temple on 17 November 1818. In the same year he acquired considerable distinction and celebrity by his successful advocacy of the claim of Hans Francis Hastings to the long-dormant earldom of Huntingdon; the estates, however, with the exception, it was said, of a mill in Yorkshire, had passed away from the title, and were legally invested in the earl of Moira's family. Bell published a detailed account of the proceedings in *The Huntingdon Peerage* (1820), which includes a narrative of his various adventures during the investigation. It was designed not only as a genealogical treatise, but also as a general account of the history and restored succession of the house of Hastings, furnished with many curious anecdotes relating to the subject. A new title-page, genealogical table, and portraits were added to the unsold copies in 1821. Bell was also employed by J. L. Crawfurd to further his claim to the titles and estates of Crawfurd and Lindsay, and reportedly received £5,036 for prosecuting the suit. Bell died insolvent before the matter was decided, and the claimant's money was largely lost.

According to Lady Anne Hamilton's *Secret History of the Court of England*, Bell, with other agents, was delegated by Lord Sidmouth in 1819 to incite the starving people of Manchester to demonstrate against the government; by their instigation the meeting of 16 August was said to have been convoked, which led to the massacre of Peterloo. However, the statement has dubious authority as the book is believed to have been produced by Olivia Serres, who made various false claims to be the daughter of the duke of Cumberland, the brother of George III. Curiously, Bell is believed to have reported favourably on her cause. Bell died on 18 October 1822, the same day as he lost an action to recover money advanced to him by an engraver named Cooke. He probably never married, but lived with his younger brother, Sir George *Bell, KCB.

GORDON GOODWIN, *rev.* MYFANWY LLOYD

Sources *GM*, 1st ser., 90/2 (1820), 51–2 · *GM*, 1st ser., 91/1 (1821), 44–7 · *GM*, 1st ser., 92/2 (1822), 474 · H. N. Bell, *The Huntingdon peerage*, 2nd edn (1821) · J. Dobie, *Examination of the claim of John Lindsay Crawfurd* (1831) · *N&Q*, 5th ser., 12 (1879), 475 · *N&Q*, 6th ser., 1 (1880), 66 · A. Hamilton, *Secret history of the court of England*, 2 vols. (1832) · Allibone, *Dict.* · J. S. Crone, *A concise dictionary of Irish biography*, rev. edn (1937) · W. Beckett, *A universal biography*, 3 vols. (1835–6) · J. Gorton, *A general biographical dictionary*, 3 vols. (1841)

Likenesses W. S. Lethbridge, portrait, 1821, repro. in Bell, *Huntingdon peerage* · E. Scriven, stipple, 1821 (after W. S. Lethbridge), BM, NPG; repro. in Bell, *Huntingdon peerage*

Bell, Horace (1839–1903)

Bell, Horace (1839–1903), civil engineer and author, was born at 81 Guilford Street, London, on 17 June 1839, the son of George Bell, a London merchant, and his wife, Frances Dude, of Norfolk. Bell received his early education in France and at Louth, Lincolnshire. He began engineering at fifteen under John Wilson in London but soon sought broader based training as an apprentice to D. Cook & Co. of Glasgow. He next served in the workshops and surveys of the Caledonian Railway before taking employment (1859–62) as an assistant engineer on the London, Chatham, and Dover Railway.

Success in an open competition led to Bell's appointment on 7 July 1862 to the Indian public works department as a probationary assistant engineer. He reached India in December 1862 where he was employed from 1862 to 1870 on the Grand Deccan Road in the Central Provinces during which, in April 1866, he was promoted to executive engineer fourth class (first class, March 1871). Railway work followed and he was among the early appointees to the state railway service initiated in 1870. In 1870 he participated in the Chanda and the Wardha valley railway surveys followed by service on the Indore (1870), the Punjab Northern (1874), Rajputana (1875), Sind (1876), and Neemuch (1878) state railways.

Promoted to superintending engineer third class in January 1880 (first class, March 1886) and chief engineer third class in October 1890 (first class, January 1892), he had charge of the Dacca–Mymensingh railway surveys (1881–4) during which he served, in August 1883, on a committee considering a scheme for the reorganization of the public works department engineering establishment. In the period 1884–90 he held in rapid succession a series of important positions: testimony to his flexibility and competence. He had the engineering and managerial charge of the Tirhut State Railway (1884 and 1887–8) and charge of the Nalhati railway (1884), and served as the acting director of the large North-Western Railway (1887). Stints as the engineer-in-chief of the surveys for the Great Western of India and the Mughal Sarai to Howrah railways followed (1888–9). In August 1890 he went to Calcutta as the consulting engineer to the government of India for state railways. From January to April 1893 he served as officiating director-general of railways and deputy secretary from which he reverted to consulting engineer until his retirement in June 1894.

Bell possessed many friends and was considered to be a person of energy, technical ability, and administrative capacity: witness his promotions to high posts and his commendations by the government of India. He also wrote extensively on engineering and other topics, including unpublished reports and memoranda in his official capacity, and published articles, pamphlets, and a book. The book was the substantial and useful *Railway Policy in India* (1894). He wrote pamphlet length primers on economics (*The Laws of Wealth*, 1883) and government (*The Government of India: a Primer*, 3rd edn, 1893) that were adopted for Indian students in government schools.

After Bell retired he established himself as a private consulting engineer in London in which capacity he maintained a close contact with India. The Southern Punjab Railway and the Nilgiri mountain rack railway were among his clients. In quite a different sphere he provided advice regarding the construction of the Marconi masts at Poldhu in Cornwall, England. Made an associate of the Institution of Civil Engineers on 5 March 1867 and transferred to the status of member on 30 January 1872 he was elected in 1897 to the institution's council, on which he served until his death on 10 April 1903. He died at 114 Lexham Gardens, Brompton, London, from heart disease, and was buried in Brompton cemetery. He was survived by his wife, Marcia Napier Ogilvy, one of their four sons, and three of their five daughters.   IAN J. KERR

Sources *PICE*, 153 (1902–3), 319–21 · *The Times* (13 April 1903) · *The Times* (16 April 1903) · Government of India, *History of services of the officers of the engineering, accounts, and state railway revenue establishments, including the military works department under the military department*, 4th edn (1889) · BL cat. · H. Bell, *Railway policy in India* (1894) · H. Bell, 'Indian railways', *Asiatic Quarterly Review*, 3 (1887), 331–55 · H. Bell, 'The Rajpootana (State) Railway', *PICE*, 50 (1876–7), 148–56 · H. Bell, 'Railways and famine', *Journal of the Society of Arts*, 49 (1900–01), 290–305 · W. J. Weightman, 'The Nilgiri mountain railway', *PICE*, 145 (1900–01), 1–19 [see also discussion, 20–38] · *India Office List* (1895) · b. cert. · d. cert.
Wealth at death £3340 5s. 4d.: resworn probate, Nov 1903, CGPLA Eng. & Wales

Bell, Sir (Harold) Idris (1879–1967)

Bell, Sir (Harold) Idris (1879–1967), papyrologist and scholar of Welsh literature, was born on 2 October 1879 at Epworth, Lincolnshire, the son of Charles Christopher Bell (*b.* 1845), chemist, and his wife, Rachel Hughes (*d.* 1880). His father's family had been yeoman farmers in the north midlands and had marked literary leanings, his father not least; but the Welsh inheritance from his mother meant more to Bell and was a determining factor in his life. He was educated at Nottingham high school and Oriel College, Oxford, which he entered as an Adam de Brome scholar in 1897; he was placed in the first class in classical moderations in 1899 and two years later narrowly missed a first in *literae humaniores*. More significant for his future career was the year he subsequently spent in Hanover, Halle, and Berlin learning German and studying Hellenistic history; classical scholarship in Germany was then in its heyday and among the lecturers he heard were Friedrich Blass, Eduard Meyer, and U. von Wilamowitz-Moellendorf. This experience both deepened his knowledge of the classical world and introduced him to the most rigorous methods of contemporary scholarship, reinforcing a native tendency to painstaking accuracy and objectivity.

If Bell's ancestry and his period of study in Germany were decisive factors in his development, a third was his appointment as an assistant in the department of manuscripts in the British Museum in 1903. Here, more by chance than design, he found himself working before long on Greek papyri with F. G. Kenyon. After he had collaborated with him for the third volume of the museum

Sir (Harold) Idris Bell (1879–1967), by Walter Stoneman, 1955

catalogue on documents of an earlier period, chance again directed him to the department's large holdings of Byzantine papyri. Verbose, complex, and often illiterate and lacking the obvious attractions of many Ptolemaic and Roman texts, documents of this period had been largely ignored both in England and on the continent. Bell's edition of these papyri in volumes 4 and 5 of the catalogue, two massive volumes with an ample commentary (1910 and 1917), which provided a striking picture of the Byzantine empire seen from a provincial standpoint and one to which in an article in the *Journal of Egyptian Archaeology* (vol. 4, 1917) he supplied the title 'The Byzantine servile state', both set a new standard for the museum's publications in accuracy of decipherment and in interpretation, and established him as the leading authority on Byzantine and early Arab Egypt.

While Bell always retained his interest in Byzantine studies, Roman Egypt later became his main field of study. Both his *Jews and Christians in Egypt* (1924), an elaborate edition of some remarkable and important documents, and *Fragments of an Unknown Gospel and other Early Christian Papyri* (1935), jointly edited by him and his colleague T. C. Skeat, long remained indispensable in spite of the numerous re-editions and discussion they occasioned. Bell's achievement was due in part to his technical expertise and capacity for hard work, and in part to the fact that he rightly saw papyrology as a *Hilfsdisziplin* to be pursued in the wider perspective of the historian; he demonstrated

this belief most clearly in the chapters he contributed on Roman Egypt to the *Cambridge Ancient History* (in vols. 10 and 11), which were a definitive statement of their subject. His work as editor, writer, and contributor of numerous articles in learned journals was done against the background of, and largely in the intervals from, steadily increasing departmental duties; in 1927 he was promoted to deputy keeper, and on the death of J. P. Gilson in 1929 he became keeper, a post he held until his retirement in 1944. In these years the much-debated Codex Sinaiticus was acquired, as well as the Luttrell psalter and some of the missing Paston letters; the department also became the centre of international papyrology from which, thanks mainly to Bell's activities, an understanding of Greek papyri extended to an ever wider circle of studies and in which many younger scholars received an invaluable if informal training. In 1935 he was made an honorary reader in papyrology at Oxford where until 1950 he did much to secure the continuity of papyrological studies; in 1936 he became an honorary fellow of Oriel College.

Bell's training and long practice in the school of severely objective scholarship controlled but did not inhibit a mercurial temperament and lively imagination. This found scope in his translations from Welsh poetry in which a lifelong devotion to poetry (especially for that in the tradition of Swinburne) joined with a no less deep and lasting enthusiasm for Welsh language and literature. *Poems from the Welsh*, a work of collaboration between Bell and his father, had appeared in 1913 and was followed in 1925 by *Welsh Poems of the Twentieth Century in English Verse*, again by father and son. The pattern was continued in a more ambitious venture, an edition of fifty poems of the greatest Welsh poet of the later middle ages, Dafydd ap Gwilym, consisting of text, translation, and introduction, in which Bell collaborated with his son David. Here scholarship had its part to play too, as it did in his admirable *The Development of Welsh Poetry* (1936) and in his translation of Thomas Parry's history of Welsh literature down to 1900, to which Bell added an appendix of his own, amounting to a quarter of the whole, on the twentieth century. In this book, which appeared in 1955, and in its predecessors, he was concerned to introduce the English reader to the often unsuspected riches of Welsh literature, just as in much of his papyrological work he was intent on making available to scholars generally the information lurking in the technical publications of papyrologists. For his services to Welsh literature he was awarded the Cymmrodorion medal in 1946 and was president of this society in 1947; he was also admitted to the gorsedd as a druid in 1949.

Bell was appointed OBE in 1920 and CB in 1936, and was knighted in 1946. Elected a fellow of the British Academy in 1932, he served as its president from 1946 to 1950, helping to renew the ties with continental scholarship, a task much after his own heart. He received honorary degrees from the universities of Liverpool, Brussels, Michigan, and Wales, and he was a member of many foreign academies; he was vice-president of several learned societies, and president of the Society for the Promotion of Roman

Studies from 1937 to 1945, of the International Association of Papyrologists from 1947 to 1955, and of the Classical Association in 1955.

Unassuming, courteous, kindly, always accessible, a man of wide sympathies and considerable power of enjoyment, Bell had many friends at all levels. He was a lifelong supporter of the Labour Party and in matters of religion an agnostic for most of his working life. Shortly after the Second World War, however, for reasons he made clear in a volume of essays, *The Crisis of our Time* (1954), he returned to the Christian faith. On leaving the British Museum in 1944 he retired to Wales, where he had always spent his holidays, and in his later years played an active part in the intellectual life of the principality and in that of the Church in Wales, of whose governing body he became a member.

Bell married Mabel Winifred, daughter of Ernest Ayling, in 1911; there were three sons of the marriage, of whom the eldest and the youngest survived him. He died on 22 January 1967 at his home, Brogynin, Iorwerth Avenue, Aberystwyth, a week after his wife's death.

                                                        C. H. ROBERTS, rev.

Sources C. H. Roberts, 'Sir Harold Idris Bell, 1879–1967', *PBA*, 53 (1967), 409–22 • E. G. Turner and T. C. Skeat, *Journal of Egyptian Archaeology*, 53 (1967) • personal knowledge (1981) • *CGPLA Eng. & Wales* (1967)
Archives BL, corresp. and papers, Add. MSS 59506–59534 • NL Wales, papers | BL, letters to Warren Dawson, Add. MS 60347 • BL, notes and corresp. relating to Codex Sinaiticus, Add. MSS 68923–68932 • Egypt Exploration Society, London, corresp. with Egypt Exploration Society • King's AC Cam., corresp. with Geoffrey Keynes • NL Wales, letters and postcards to John Glyn Davies • NL Wales, letters to Raymond Garlick • NL Wales, letters to T. Gwynn Jones • NL Wales, letters in Welsh to Sir Thomas Parry-Williams • U. Oxf., Griffith Institute, notes on the price of slaves in ancient Egypt
Likenesses W. Stoneman, photograph, 1955, NPG [*see illus.*] • Bassano & Vandyck, photograph, repro. in Roberts, 'Sir Harold Idris Bell' • P. Evans, chalk, NMG Wales • pencil drawing; known to be in family possession in 1981
Wealth at death £14,501: probate, 4 April 1967, *CGPLA Eng. & Wales*

Bell, Jacob (1810–1859), pharmacist and politician, was born on 5 March 1810 at 338 Oxford Street, London, the eldest surviving son of John Bell (1774–1849), pharmacist, and his wife, Eliza (d. 1839), daughter of Frederick Smith, pharmacist of the Haymarket, London, and his wife, Sarah; both families were Quakers. Jacob was educated near Darlington, co. Durham, at the school of his mother's brother, Henry Frederick Smith. On leaving school in 1827 he became an indoor apprentice in his father's pharmacy under Thomas Zachary, previously an apprentice and now one of the two partners of John Bell.

A man of many interests Jacob Bell attended lectures on chemistry at the Royal Institution, even setting up a laboratory in the Oxford Street attic. He went to the new King's College for lectures on the practice of physic and studied comparative anatomy, conducting examinations of monkeys, rats, and porcupines in his father's home at Wandsworth. He obtained leave to attend art classes at Henry Sass's academy in Bloomsbury and to have lessons from

H. P. Briggs RA, a distant relation. He made many friends in the art world, particularly Edwin Landseer, with whom he travelled on the continent in 1840 when Landseer was suffering from ill health, and William Frith, helping them in many practical matters such as copyright law. He lent Myles Birket Foster proofs of Landseer's work for him to study and took control of the latter's financial affairs, and he commissioned Frith's famous *Derby Day*.

Bell had considerable artistic ability himself but was aware of his limitations and in the end devoted his energy and powers of organization to the cause of British pharmacy. He and his brother, Frederick John, the younger by four years, were made partners in 1836 with their father on the retirement of Thomas Zachary and John Walduck. Bell remained nevertheless a practical pharmacist all his life as may be seen from the list of his published papers. He experimented with ether and chloroform anaesthesia at the nearby Middlesex Hospital, of which he was both a governor and a member of the medical committee.

John Bell had long been involved in pharmaceutical politics, and his son was to follow him even more effectively. The Hawes Bill, 'To amend the laws relating to the Medical profession' and introduced to the house on 5 February 1841, would have put the chemists and druggists under the control of a body on which they were not even represented. A committee of pharmacists was formed to oppose the bill, and as it did not please many of the medical profession either, even after modification, it was counted out.

For the moment the pharmacists had kept their freedom but the more thoughtful realized it was only a breathing space. What was needed was an organization to protect their interests and also provide a science-based but pharmaceutically orientated education. On 20 March 1841 Bell held the first of his famous 'pharmaceutical tea parties' at 338 Oxford Street, when it was decided that a permanent professional body must be formed. Another general meeting was called for 15 April 1841 at the Crown and Anchor, where William Allen moved and John Bell seconded that in order to protect their interests and also to raise their standards an association was to be formed called the Pharmaceutical Society of Great Britain. Another public meeting on 1 June approved the regulations, objectives, and constitution. To Jacob Bell's great satisfaction the society received its royal charter of incorporation on 18 February 1843.

The first of the society's objectives was 'to elevate the profession of pharmacy by furnishing the proper means of instruction', and the establishment of a school of pharmacy was discussed and agreed at the first council meeting, which was held in the society's recently leased premises of 17 Bloomsbury Square, London, on 6 January 1842. Preliminary lectures began on 16 February 1842 when Dr Anthony Todd Thomson lectured on materia medica. Bell had a great belief in scientific pharmacy and hammered this home in every number of his journal. The School of Pharmacy established a laboratory where practical instruction was to be given from October 1844 to eight students; this was so popular that ten were admitted. The following year an extra eighteen were admitted.

Although well thought of by doctors and civil servants the school was for many years far from popular with many members of the society; it was a constant drain on the society's finances, and even prominent council members suggested it should be closed. It has been argued that 'the Journal and the School of Pharmacy would have been casualties [in the mid-1840s] if they had not had Bell's powerful support' (Morson, 191). The society gave valuable support to the 1851 bill regulating the sale of arsenic, whereupon it decided to try once more to obtain a pharmacy act. It had had little success in the past in interesting any MP, so with this in mind Bell had already decided two years earlier that he must become a member himself.

Bell stood at a by-election for St Albans in the Liberal interest and was elected in November 1850. Unfortunately St Albans was a notoriously corrupt seat and his disappointed opponent, Sir Robert Carden, petitioned for Bell's removal on grounds of bribery. A select committee, unable to find vital witnesses in April 1851, declared Jacob Bell the elected member but wanted a commission to be set up to investigate the 1850 and earlier elections at St Albans. The commission sat from October 1851 to January 1852 and found that Thomas Hyde Hills had advanced £2500 for purposes of bribery, but that bribery by all sides was the norm in St Albans. As a result that borough was disfranchised, though Bell was allowed to keep his seat until parliament was dissolved.

The question of Bell's guilt or innocence has been much debated. Certainly at first he had insisted there should be 'no bribery … no treating … no intimidation', but later he discovered it was occurring. As he wrote to a Quaker friend in Manchester, George Dawson, 'it was too late to retract. … I was like a person who has taken his seat on a train and is unable to stop it' (Bell papers).

Bell had no time to waste and on 12 June 1851 asked leave to introduce 'A Bill for regulating the qualifications of pharmaceutical chemists and other … purposes in connexion with the practice of pharmacy'. The Pharmacy Act 1852, after several amendments and rigorous examination by a select committee, received royal assent on 30 June. Parliament was dissolved the next day and Bell lost his seat. To his great disappointment the act had been so emasculated that it bore little resemblance to his original bill, and further legislation was required. However, although Bell again stood for parliament (Great Marlow later in 1852, and Marylebone in 1854) he was not successful.

Bell's troubles were not confined to these: first he had a long fight with two of the society's council members, William Dickinson and William Bastick, concerning the introduction of certain by-laws to which they took exception—they lost the challenge in the end. Then, in 1851, Bell's friend Jonathan Pereira suffered such blatant plagiarism of his popular lectures on materia medica given at the School of Pharmacy that he refused to continue. Finally Bell became involved in the highly controversial and tortuous Poisons Bill.

It is often thought that Bell's most important and influential action was the production of the *Pharmaceutical Journal*. Bell was both editor and proprietor, and he claimed its emergence was due to the success of the scientific meetings held in London at 338 Oxford Street. The journal also allowed Bell to put forth his strongly held views on education and responsibility. The first issue appeared in July 1841; by September it was fifty pages long and by January 1842 it had become in many respects the journal still known 150 years later. A friend from his apprenticeship days, Theophilus Redwood (1806–1892), became sub-editor and was later helped by 'young Hanbury'—Daniel Hanbury (1825–1875)—and Joseph Ince (1794–1853). In 1856 Bell, having been a member of council of the Pharmaceutical Society since 1841, was induced to become president. He was also an honorary member of many foreign scientific societies and a fellow of the Chemical, Linnean, and Zoological societies of London.

By the late spring of 1859 it was clear to many, including Bell himself, that he was dying. His immediate concern was for the future of his journal, and he finally decided to give the copyright of his brainchild to the Pharmaceutical Society. On opiates since January, almost voiceless, and scarcely able to swallow, he worked for weeks during what he called his 'lucid' periods on the legalities and setting up of an editorial committee after his death. The transfer document of 1 June 1859 was signed by Bell and Thomas N. R. Morson (1799–1874), vice-president and friend of many years, and witnessed by Thomas Hyde Hills (1815–1891), Bell's partner since 1852. The document shows that Bell had never taken an editorial salary and that he had lost between £20 and £60 a year on the production of the journal.

Bell died on 12 June 1859 at Tunbridge Wells and was buried there. He was unmarried. On the day of his funeral pharmacists throughout the country closed their shops. In his will, to the Pharmaceutical Society he bequeathed £2000 and to the nation he gave thirteen paintings from his magnificent art collection valued at £18,000–£20,000; his two-thirds share of his flourishing business, including stock and equipment, passed to T. H. Hills; and £500 each went to his former laboratory superintendent George Baggett Francis, his prescription supervisor Francis Middleton, and his secretary John Barnard. After his death Bell was described as 'the driving force in pharmaceutical politics … a man of powerful personality' who quickly established his authority over his contemporaries (Morson, 174).

JUANITA BURNBY

Sources L. G. Matthews, 'Statesman of pharmacy: Jacob Bell, 1810–59', *Chemist and Druggist* (6 June 1959), 610–13 · 'The life and work of Jacob Bell', *Pharmaceutical Journal*, 128 (1959), 447–52 · D. W. Hudson, 'The last act', *Pharmaceutical Journal*, 128 (1959), 452–4 · monthly meeting records, RS Friends, Lond. · J. Bell and T. Redwood, *Progress of pharmacy* (1880) · T. E. Wallis, *History of the School of Pharmacy* (1964) · '150 years of the *Pharmaceutical Journal*', *Pharmaceutical Journal*, suppl. (6 July 1991), esp. J17–18 · P. H. Thomas, 'Theophilus Redwood (1806–92)', *Medical men of Glamorgan* [n.d.], 89–106 · J. Burnby, 'The family history of Jacob Bell', *Pharmaceutical Journal*, 230 (1983), 582–4 · S. W. F. Holloway, *The Royal Pharmaceutical Society of Great Britain, 1841–1991* (1991) · A. Morson, *The operative*

chymist (1997) · letters, RS Friends, Lond., Bell papers · J. Burnby, C. P. Cloughly, and M. P. Earles, eds., *'My dear Mr. Bell': letters from Dr. Jonathan Pereira to Jacob Bell, 1844–1853* (1987) · private information (2004) · *DNB*
Archives RS Friends, Lond., corresp. and MSS · Wellcome L., letters to Thomas Morson, notes, and sketches
Likenesses J. Landseer, portrait, 1858, Pharmaceutical Society, London · E. Landseer, oils, 1859, Pharmaceutical Society, London · R. J. Lane, lithograph, pubd 1860 (after J. Landseer, 1858), NPG, Wellcome L. · T. Landseer, mezzotint, pubd 1869 (after E. Landseer), BM, NPG, Wellcome L.
Wealth at death under £30,000: probate, 30 July 1859, *CGPLA Eng. & Wales*

Bell, James (1523/4–1584), Roman Catholic priest and martyr, was born at Warrington in Lancashire. He was educated at Oxford, and ordained priest in the reign of Queen Mary. At the beginning of Queen Elizabeth's reign he initially refused to conform to the new religion, but soon took a different course and officiated for twenty years as a Church of England clergyman in different parts of the country. In 1581 he was converted to Roman Catholicism through the persuasions of a Catholic woman in Lancashire, from whom he had sought support in securing a lectureship in the established church which was in the gift of her husband. After a period of penitential exercises, and when he had recovered from a bout of ill health, he undertook the dangerous work of an undercover Catholic priest for two years, working in Lancashire.

Bell was arrested in January 1584 by a pursuivant, and was brought before the earl of Derby, who committed him to gaol in Salford. He was arraigned at the quarter sessions in Manchester and convicted of recusancy and of saying mass in a private house at Golborne, near his native Warrington. He was also committed for trial at the Lancaster assizes, and was taken the 60 miles to Lancaster on horseback with his hands tied behind his back and his feet bound cruelly under the belly of the horse. He was sentenced to death for high treason, admitting that he had become a Roman Catholic. The judge in his questioning elicited from him the admission that, if there were to be an invasion of England sanctioned by the pope, he would support it against the queen. According to Gillow, Bell requested of the judge that his lips and the tops of his fingers be cut off when sentence was imposed, in punishment for having subscribed to heresy. He was executed, aged sixty, at Lancaster on 20 April 1584.

PETER HOLMES

Sources *DNB* · Gillow, *Lit. biog. hist.* · R. Challoner, *Memoirs of missionary priests*, ed. J. H. Pollen, rev. edn (1924), 100–01 · [J. Gibbons and J. Fenn], *Concertatio ecclesiae catholicae in Anglia adversus Calvinopapistas et puritanos*, 2nd edn (1588), 160–63 · C. Dodd [H. Tootell], *The church history of England, from the year 1500, to the year 1688*, 2 (1739), 102–3 · H. Bowler, *Recusants in the exchequer pipe rolls, 1581–1592*, ed. T. J. McCann, Catholic RS, 71 (1986), 19 · L. Hicks, ed., *Letters and memorials of Father Robert Persons*, Catholic RS, 39 (1942), 210, 232, 238 · T. E. Gibson, *Lydiate Hall and its associates*, Roxburghe Club (1876), xxxiv–xxxv · Wood, *Ath. Oxon.: Fasti* (1815), 132, 137 · J. H. Pollen, ed., *Unpublished documents relating to the English martyrs*, 1, Catholic RS, 5 (1908), 8, 70, 74–8, 80, 87, 199 · H. Foley, ed., *Records of the English province of the Society of Jesus*, 2 (1875), 135–6, 138, 143 · P. McGrath, 'The bloody questions reconsidered', *Recusant History*, 20 (1990–91), 305–19, esp. 309

Bell, James (*d.* 1606?), translator, was born in Somerset, in the diocese of Bath. He was admitted as a scholar of Corpus Christi College, Oxford, *c.*1547 and is known to have been at Corpus Christi on 21 April 1548. He was apparently chaplain of Magdalen College in 1548. He supplicated for the BA in 1551 and was elected fellow of Corpus Christi on 20 February 1551. He was elected fellow of Trinity College and appointed rhetoric lecturer on 30 May 1556. In that same year he resigned his fellowship to become—in the words of Philip Bliss—'a zealous partizan of the reformation' (Wood, *Ath. Oxon.*, 1.651).

Bell is remembered chiefly for his narrative of Swedish princess Cecilia Vasa's 1565 visit to England. He probably composed his manuscript shortly after the princess's arrival. It is clear from certain passages that he is giving a secondhand account, from Cecilia's departure in Stockholm to her arrival in London. Ethel Seaton speculates that Bell may have been 'one of the party sent to meet Cecilia on her landing, possibly included as a chaplain', and that he received details of the princess's trip from the Latin journal of the Swedish chaplain (Seaton, 5, 9). Moreover, she suggests that the princess's unpopularity at her departure may explain why the manuscript was not printed in its own day. There have been two modern editions of Bell's narrative, one edited by Margaret Morison in 1898 and the other by Seaton in 1926.

Bell's four remaining works, all translations from Latin, were printed between 1578 and 1581. The first, *A Sermon Preached at the Christening of a Certaine Jew, at London* (1578), is a translation of John Foxe's *De oliva evangelica. Concio, in baptismo Judaei*, of the same year. The second, *A Treatise Touching the Libertie of a Christian* (1579; reprinted in 1636 and 1817), is a translation of a work by Martin Luther; in his dedication to the countess of Warwick, Bell alludes to his familiarity with 'the Court ... by the space of many yeares now passed' (sig. A3r). The third, *The Pope Confuted* (1580), is a translation of John Foxe's *Papa confutatus*, published the same year. In the translator's address, Bell discusses his conversion to protestantism, that is, his 'escape out of that Laterane Laberinth' after having 'wandered long in the selfesame mizmaze' (sig. *2v–r*). The last work, *Against Jerome Osorius Byshopp of Silvane in Portingall* (1581; reprinted in 1812), is a translation of *Contra Hieron. Osorium … responsio apologetica* (1577), a work begun by Walter Haddon and continued by John Foxe. Bell's bitter address to his readers, all 'unlettered Englishmen', reveals that his previous works had been attacked by critics.

Thomas Tanner identifies Bell as the man who held the prebends of Holcombe and Combe, Somerset, in the 1590s. Both Thomas Warton and Anthony Wood's editor Philip Bliss accept this identification. In fact, a James Bill was installed as prebendary of Holcombe on 13 February 1596 and by proxy as prebendary of Combe IV on 11 October 1596. A James Bell was installed by proxy as prebendary of Warminster or Luxville on 31 May 1599; he died before 5 December 1606, when John Still was collated to this living. Joseph Foster raises the possibility that Bell was the same James Bell who was vicar of Stewkley and rector of Cheddington, Buckinghamshire, in 1554.

EDWARD A. MALONE

Sources E. Seaton, ed., *Queen Elizabeth and a Swedish princess: being an account of the visit of Princess Cecilia of Sweden to England in 1565* (1926) · Wood, *Ath. Oxon.*, new edn · *Calendar of the manuscripts of the dean and chapter of Wells*, 2, HMC, 12 (1914) · *Fasti Angl., 1541–1857,* [Bath and Wells] · *Reg. Oxf.*, vol. 1 · *ESTC* · J. R. Bloxam, *A register of the presidents, fellows … of Saint Mary Magdalen College*, 8 vols. (1853–85) · Tanner, *Bibl. Brit.-Hib.* · T. Warton, *The life of Sir Thomas Pope, founder of Trinity College, Oxford* (1772) [incl. 3 pp. biography of Bell] · M. Morison, 'A narrative of the journey of Cecilia, princess of Sweden, to the court of Queen Elizabeth', *TRHS*, new ser., 12 (1898), 181–224 · *British Museum catalogue of printed books* · Foster, *Alum. Oxon.*

Archives BL, narrative of journey of Princess Cecilia from Stockholm to London, Royal M17C xxix

Bell, James (1769–1833), geographer, was born in Jedburgh, the son of Thomas *Bell (1733–1802), Presbyterian minister of the Relief church. Nothing is known of his mother or any siblings. In 1777 he accompanied his father to Glasgow, where the latter was appointed minister of Dovehill Chapel. James was a sickly youth, but grew stronger with age; he read widely, if unsystematically. After serving an apprenticeship as a weaver, he set up in Glasgow in 1790 as a manufacturer of cotton goods, but after the depression of 1793 he gave up his own business to work as a warper for other manufacturers. As his unworldliness made him ill suited to business his father settled on him a small annuity which enabled him to spend his life teaching, studying, and writing. From 1806 he supplemented his annuity by teaching Greek and Latin to university students. At the same time he studied history, theology, and especially geography, and presided enthusiastically over a debating society. He contributed several chapters to the popular *Glasgow Geography* (5 vols., 1815), which was to become the basis of his system of geography. His article about the sources of the River Ganges was published in *Critical Researches in Philology and Geography* (1824), an anonymous work now known to be by James Bell and the (unrelated) philology student John Bell. On the strength of these publications Bell was asked to prepare an edition of Charles Rollin's *Ancient History* (3 vols., 1828), and his notes and life of Rollin were well received. His *System of Geography* (6 vols., 1830), which drew heavily on the work of continental scientific geographers, such as Ritter, to give a comprehensive description of the world, was popular in Scotland, though never widely used elsewhere. His last work, *A … Gazetteer of England and Wales* (4 vols., 1836), published posthumously, contained several maps finely engraved on steel, but also included articles plagiarized from Samuel Lewis's *Topographical Dictionary* (1831). In July 1839 Lewis obtained an injunction preventing further sale of Bell's *Gazetteer*. In 1840–44 Bell's publishers, Archibald Fullerton, issued *The Parliamentary Gazetteer* using both text and maps from Bell's *Gazetteer*. Fullerton dismissed accusations of plagiarism on the grounds that less than a third of the *Parliamentary Gazetteer* material was Bell's.

Because he was prevented from travelling by his poor health and limited means, Bell's geographies were necessarily derivative, though they were assiduously researched and competently, if not always scrupulously, put together. He was a Calvinist and could argue theological points effectively, but remained tolerant of differing religious views. Increasing attacks of asthma, from which he had always suffered, obliged him to retire about ten or twelve years before his death to Campsie, north of Glasgow. He died there on 3 May 1833 and was buried there.

ELIZABETH BAIGENT

Sources D. Smith, *Victorian maps of the British Isles* (1985) · D. Kingsley, *Printed maps of Sussex, 1575–1900*, Sussex RS, 72 (1982) · T. Chubb, *The printed maps and atlases of Great Britain and Ireland: a bibliography, 1579–1870* (1927); repr. (1977) · Chambers, *Scots.* (1835) · *DNB*

Bell, James (1825–1908), chemist, was born in Altnanaghan, Newtownhamilton, co. Armagh, in November 1825. He was educated privately and at University College, London, where he studied mathematics and chemistry, the latter under A. W. Williamson. In 1846 he became an assistant in the Inland Revenue laboratory at Somerset House, which had been established to carry out the provisions of the Tobacco Act of 1842, and was successively deputy principal (1867–74) and principal until his retirement in 1894.

The work of the laboratory was not restricted to the examination of tobacco, but extended to the quality of brewing materials, the denaturing of alcohol for use in manufacture, and other matters affecting the excise. When the Food and Drugs Act of 1872 was amended in 1875, Bell was made chemical referee for all cases of disputed food analyses that appeared before the magistrates. In this capacity he developed methods for the chemical analysis of foods regulated by the act, and published his results in a successful book, *The Analysis and Adulteration of Foods* (2 vols., 1881, 1883). In 1882 he was awarded a PhD from the University of Erlangen in Germany in recognition of this work.

In connection with his official position, Bell was the chemical inspector for the lime and lemon juice supplied to the British merchant navy to prevent scurvy in seamen (1868–94), and he was also consulting chemist to the Indian government, 1869–94. His researches into the grape and malt ferments were published in his revised edition of the *Excise Officers' Manual* (1865) and in the *Journal of the Chemical Society* (1870). His research on tobacco was summarized in a pamphlet, *The Chemistry of Tobacco* (1887).

Bell's scientific contributions were recognized in 1884 by his election as FRS, and by the award of an honorary degree of DSc from the Royal University of Ireland (1886). He was made CB in 1889. He was a member of the Playfair committee on British and foreign spirits, and served as president of the Institute of Chemistry 1888–91.

In 1858 Bell married Ellen (d. 1900), daughter of W. Reece of Chester. They had one son, Sir William James Bell, alderman of the London county council (1903–7). Bell was generally well liked. The bad relations that existed between the Inland Revenue laboratory and the public analysts after the 1875 act did not extend to him, and had largely disappeared at the time of his death, which occurred at his home, 52 Cromwell Road, Hove, on 31 March 1908. He was buried on 4 April at Ewell, Surrey, where he had formerly resided.

ROBERT STEELE, rev. K. D. WATSON

Sources A. T. C. Pratt, ed., *People of the period: being a collection of the biographies of upwards of six thousand living celebrities*, 1 (1897) · *Men and women of the time* (1899) · P. W. Hammond and H. Egan, *Weighed in the balance: a history of the laboratory of the government chemist* (1992) · T. E. T., 'Dr James Bell', *Nature*, 77 (1907–8), 539–40 · T. E. T., *PRS*, 82A (1909), v · B. D., *The Analyst*, 33 (1908), 157–9 · *Proceedings of the Institute of Chemistry*, 3 (1908), 13 · *The Times* (2 April 1908), 12d · WWW

Archives ICL, Armstrong MSS · PRO, collection of the government chemist

Likenesses W. V. Herbert, oils, 1886, priv. coll. · pencil sketch, PRO, Collection of the Government Chemist; repro. in Hammond and Egan, *Weighed in the balance*

Wealth at death £9111 7s. 2d.: probate, 25 April 1908, *CGPLA Eng. & Wales*

Bell, John (d. 1556), bishop of Worcester, came from minor gentry stock in Worcestershire. He studied at Balliol College, Oxford, for at least a short period before the end of the fifteenth century, but then began to read law at Cambridge (admitted BCL, 1503/4). He next attended an unidentified foreign university, where he proceeded to a doctorate in the two laws by 1516, and his degree was incorporated as DCL at Oxford in 1531.

Bell's rising career owed much to the special character of the bishopric of Worcester, which had been conferred upon Italian churchmen since 1497, as recompense for representing English interests in Rome. Worcester provided able English clerics with a ladder for advancement in the Catholic church, leading to diplomatic appointments and papal audience chambers. Many of its livings and offices were used to fund important missions abroad, and in the diocese itself administrators had broad powers to exercise their own initiative in the permanent absence of the bishop. Bell first served under Bishop Silvestro de' Gigli (bishop until 1521), attending him at the Lateran Council. The offices with which Bell was entrusted speak highly of his abilities, and included those of: master of the English College in Rome (1514); dean of the court of arches (c.1517); archdeacon of Gloucester (from 1518); canon and prebendary of the collegiate church of St Stephen in Westminster Palace (until 1539); and royal chaplain, as well as numerous other livings and responsibilities. In 1518 Gigli made him vicar-general and chancellor of the diocese, and warden of the collegiate church of Stratford upon Avon, offices he kept under succeeding bishops. In the 1520s he served as a member of Cardinal Wolsey's legatine court of audience.

Bell's experience made him extremely useful in promoting Henry VIII's divorce from Katherine of Aragon, for which he worked tirelessly, in the beginning with Gigli's successor, Geronimo de' Ghinucci (bishop in 1522–35). He was a proctor for the king in 1527 and again in 1529. In 1530 Bell served as one of the royal commissioners who canvassed Oxford for the university's opinion concerning the validity of the Aragon marriage, in order to secure judgment in Henry's favour. He served as proctor for the king at the trial at Dunstable Abbey in May 1533 which definitively nullified Henry's first marriage in time for the coronation of Anne Boleyn.

In matters of religion, Bell should be placed among those conservative humanists with whom he worked closely in much of his career. In 1526 he and Edmund Bonner investigated heresy in Worcester diocese, and he looked to John Stokesley (Bonner's predecessor as bishop of London) for leadership in the 1530s, at the height of Henry's flirtation with reformed doctrine. It would appear that Bell took part in the preparation of the Bishops' Book, *The Institution of a Christian Man* (1537), a formulary that tempered conservative doctrine with Lutheran positions; the exact extent of his involvement is uncertain, but it was sufficient to justify his inclusion in the list of clergy which prefaces the volume.

Bell bore great antipathy toward the new bishop, the protestant Hugh Latimer, who was elevated when Ghinucci was deprived in 1535 (as the breach from Rome had made it pointless to have an Italian as bishop of Worcester), and broke precedent by being resident in the diocese. Bell viewed Latimer as nothing short of an intrusive menace to true faith, especially as he established heretics among his administrators, chaplains, and licensed preachers, including Robert Barnes (burnt in 1540), Thomas Garrard (burnt in 1540), and Rowland Taylor (burnt in 1555). As archdeacon of Gloucester, Bell banished Latimer's protégés when he could, and along with his influential relatives colluded with Stokesley towards the end of 1536 to bring about Latimer's downfall. Initially they were unsuccessful, for the influence Bishop Stokesley could bring to bear was no match for the protection Latimer enjoyed in the confidence of Thomas Cromwell. Probably as punishment, Bell was forced to resign his wardenship of Stratford upon Avon. But a better opportunity arose in 1539, when Henry promoted passage of a new act through parliament, the six articles, which invested renewed confidence in such traditional tenets as transubstantiation and masses for the dead. Once Latimer proved himself to be a liability by refusing to work for the passage of the act, he was forced to resign, on 1 July 1539.

Bell was immediately raised to the vacant bishopric— licence to elect was granted on 7 July, royal assent on 1 August. The temporalities were restored four days later, and he was consecrated on the 17th. Bell used the new act to attack the men Latimer had promoted by forcing them out of the diocese, or making them submit to the conservative doctrinal positions that the king now favoured. Among the laity, Bell suppressed any signs of sacramentarian heresy, though without resorting to the death penalty in his diocese. He also returned diocesan administration to its veteran officers, and to the familiar routines which Latimer's brief tenure had disturbed.

For reasons that remain obscure, however, Bell resigned his bishopric on 17 November 1543. Certainly the position of any bishop was precarious under Henry's supremacy over the English church, but Bell's retirement appears to have been voluntary and uncontroversial. The remaining years of his life were spent quietly as the incumbent of the wealthy parish of St James's, Clerkenwell, in London. When he made his will on 10 August 1556, he left bequests for poor scholars of Oxford and Cambridge, and for the maintenance of two students from Worcester diocese at Balliol. He also left £2 to the poor of Clerkenwell, and £5 to those of Stratford upon Avon. He had died by 24 October following, when his will was proved, and was buried with episcopal honours in the chancel of the church of St James.   SUSAN WABUDA

Sources S. Wabuda, '"Fruitful preaching" in the diocese of Worcester: Bishop Hugh Latimer and his influence, 1535–1539', *Religion and the English people, 1500–1640*, ed. E. J. Carlson (1998), 49–74 · D. MacCulloch, 'Worcester: a cathedral city in the Reformation', *The Reformation in English towns*, ed. P. Collinson and J. Craig (1998), 94–112 · Emden, *Oxf.*, 4.38–9 · *The institution of a Christian man* (1537) · F. A. Gasquet, *A history of the venerable English College, Rome* (1920), 50 · state papers, general series, Henry VIII, PRO, SP 1/115, fols. 166r–167r · *LP Henry VIII*, 12/1, no. 308 · G. Bedouelle and P. Le Gral, *Le divorce du roi Henry VIII: études et documents*, Travaux d'Humanisme et Renaissance, 221 (1987)
Archives register and visitation book, MSS 6716.093 BA.2648/9 (iii); 802/BA.2764
Wealth at death see will, 24 Oct 1556, PRO, PROB 11/38/18, fols. 118r–119r

Bell, John (1691–1780), diplomatist and traveller, the son of Patrick Bell of Antermony, Stirlingshire, and Anabel Stirling of Craigbarnet, was born on his father's estate at Antermony. No details of his education are extant, but it is stated that, after obtaining the degree of doctor of medicine, he decided to visit foreign countries. He obtained letters of recommendation to Dr Areskine, chief physician and privy counsellor to Tsar Peter I, and left London in July 1714. The tsar was at this time planning a diplomatic mission to the sophy of Persia, and on Dr Areskine's advice Bell was engaged in the tsar's service and included in the mission. He left St Petersburg on 15 July 1715 and proceeded to Moscow, and from there to Kazan and south along the Volga to Astrakhan. The mission then sailed down the Caspian Sea to Derbent and travelled on to Esfahan in Persia, where they arrived on 14 March 1717. They left Esfahan on 1 September and returned to St Petersburg via Saratov on 30 December 1718.

On his return Bell learned of another mission, to China, on which he was included following the recommendation of the British ambassador. Bell's account of his remarkable journey is recorded in his one publication, *Travels from St Petersburg in Russia to Various Parts of Asia* (1763). Despite the tedium of the sixteen-month expedition, Bell's account of the journey to Kazan and through Siberia to China is the most complete and interesting part of his travels. Of particular note are his descriptions of the Dalai Lama and the Chinese wall, and his residence in Peking (Beijing). The embassy left the capital on 2 March 1721 and arrived at Moscow on 5 January 1722. In the same year Bell accompanied an expedition into Persia as far as Derbent, but returned to St Petersburg in December 1722.

Soon afterwards Bell travelled to Scotland. He spent the next decade in Scotland, though he moved back to St

Petersburg in 1734. Three years later he was sent to Constantinople by the Russian chancellor and Claudius Rondeau, the British minister at the Russian court, in what was his last involvement in Russian diplomacy. He afterwards abandoned the public service, and seems to have settled at Constantinople as a merchant. About 1746 he married Mary Peters, a Russian woman, and returned to Scotland. He spent the latter part of his life on his estate at Antermony, where he wrote up the notes of his work as a diplomat. It was these that were published as the *Travels* in 1763 by Robert and Andrew Foulis of Glasgow. The *Quarterly Review* of 1817 (pp. 464–5), says that Bell had initially asked the historian William Robertson to carry out the task. Robertson, being busy, advised Bell to take *Gulliver's Travels* 'for your model, and you cannot go wrong'. The *Gentleman's Magazine* (1st ser., 33, 1763, 392) contains a long extract from the *Travels*. Besides the Glasgow edition, the work was published in Dublin (1764) and Edinburgh (1788 and 1806), and reprinted in the seventh volume of Pinkerton's *Collection of Voyages and Travels*. A French translation of the whole work appeared in Paris in 1766. Bell died at Antermony on 1 July 1780.

ROBERT HARRISON, *rev.* PHILIP CARTER

Sources Chambers, *Scots.* (1856) · D. B. Horn, ed., *British diplomatic representatives, 1689–1789*, CS, 3rd ser., 46 (1932) · Irving, *Scots.* · J. Bell, *Travels from St Petersburg in Russia to various parts of Asia* (1763)

Bell, John (1735–1806), bookseller, was born on 24 November 1735, the middle child of the Revd John Bell (*d.* 1767), minister of the parish of Gordon in Berwickshire, whose father, Robert, and grandfather John were also Church of Scotland ministers, and Elizabeth Ewing (*d.* 1788), daughter of John Ewing of Craigston, writer to the signet. His elder brother Robert (*b.* 1734) followed their father into the Presbyterian ministry but eventually took orders in the Church of England and became a chaplain in the Royal Navy. His younger sister Margaret (1737–1781) married another Scottish clergyman John Bradfute (1725–1793), and one of their sons would later become Bell's partner and successor in the book trade.

Nothing is known about Bell's life until he entered the employ of the Edinburgh bookseller Alexander Kincaid and his partner, Alexander Donaldson, becoming an apprentice on 20 November 1754 and a burgess by right of his masters on 13 January 1762. Writing in 1821, Archibald Constable maintained that Bell had been educated for the church, and the likelihood that he attended a grammar school and a university is increased by a reference to him as 'a man of liberal education' in an obituary in the *Edinburgh Advertiser* and the *Caledonian Mercury*, and by the appearance of a Joannes Bell in George Stuart's humanity (Latin) classes in 1748–9 and 1750–51. In May 1758 Bell succeeded Donaldson as Kincaid's partner, thus establishing one of the leading Scottish bookselling and publishing firms of its day. In association with Andrew Millar and Thomas Cadell of London, Kincaid and Bell published important new books by Adam Smith, Adam Ferguson, Thomas Reid, Lord Kames, and other Scottish authors. Bell's letter-book from this period confirms Charles Dilly's assertion, in correspondence with James Beattie, that it was Bell rather than Kincaid who managed the firm with respect to 'printing and vending articles for the shop' (21 May 1771, Aberdeen University Library, MS 30/2/58). A prolonged dispute with Cadell over the publication and reprinting of Ferguson's *Essay on the History of Civil Society* may have weakened Bell's standing with Kincaid, who was pressured for three years by his old friend William Strahan, Cadell's publishing partner, into replacing Bell with William Creech, and finally did so in May 1771.

During the 1770s and 1780s Bell operated in Edinburgh on his own, in Addison's Head (1771–7) and then in Parliament Square (1778–88). He remained actively involved in publishing and reprinting books by Scottish authors, particularly Lord Kames and Adam Ferguson, and made a speciality of works on the law. In 1785 Bell and the London publisher George Robinson scored a coup by outbidding Strahan and Cadell for the rights to Thomas Reid's *Essays on the Intellectual Powers of Man*, which they purchased for £300, marking the beginning of a productive relationship between Bell and Robinson. From November 1788 Bell operated in partnership with his nephew John Bradfute as Bell and Bradfute, a firm that remained in business until well into the twentieth century. The thick catalogues issued by Bell, and later by Bell and Bradfute, sometimes running to over 200 pages and costing up to 1s. themselves, testify to the large scale of the firm's retail bookselling business, as does the fact that Bell's will left his partner one-half of the firm's stock-in-trade at a value of £4155. After the death of Charles Elliot in 1790 the firm purchased his handsome shop, which is pictured in a collaborative oil painting of Parliament Square that hangs in Huntly House Museum, Edinburgh.

Bell could be abrasive, and the London bookseller John Murray found him 'difficult to work with' on account of 'the peculiar turn of his mind' (Murray to Gilbert Stuart, 4 Oct 1777, Murray MSS). But Archibald Constable, who was Bradfute's close friend, considered Bell:

> the most thorough gentleman of the profession in Edinburgh at this period … a man of excellent talents, kind and benevolent in his intercourse with his brethren, of rather a humorous and facetious turn of mind, particularly when associated of an evening with a few friends. (Constable, 536)

On 11 December 1758 Bell joined the most prestigious lodge of freemasons in Scotland, Canongate Kilwinning no. 2. In February 1776 Bell was among the founders of the Edinburgh Booksellers' Society; when the society was reconstituted on 17 December 1792 he was elected its first praeses, and after his death on 22 September 1806 the members dressed in mourning as a sign of respect. Bell left most of his property to his nephew John Bradfute, and is not known to have married, though his will mentions a natural daughter born of a woman called Margaret Lawrie. A large amount of his business papers have survived, especially from the latter part of his career, including many Bell and Bradfute ledgers that were accidentally discovered in the late 1990s by contractors working in the cellars beneath the Edinburgh city chambers.

RICHARD B. SHER

Sources C. B. Boog-Watson, ed., *Register of Edinburgh apprentices, 1701–1755* (1929) · A. Constable, 'Edinburgh booksellers of the period', in T. Constable, *Archibald Constable and his literary correspondents*, 1 (1873), 533–40 · *Edinburgh Advertiser* (10–12 Oct 1806) · *Caledonian Mercury* (11 Oct 1806) · J. Morris, 'Scottish book trade index', www.nls.uk/catalogues/resources/sbti/ · *Fasti Scot.*, new edn · R. B. Sher, 'Corporatism and consensus in the late eighteenth-century book trade: the Edinburgh Booksellers' Society in comparative perspective', *Book History*, 1 (1998), 32–93 · Bell and Bradfute catalogues, NL Scot., NG.1615.d.15(1–5) · H. Evans and M. Evans, *John Kay of Edinburgh: barber, miniaturist and social commentator, 1742–1826* (1973) · U. Aberdeen, MS 30/2/58 · John Murray, London, archives, Murray MSS · matriculation registers, 1748–9, U. Edin. L., special collections division, university archives · matriculation registers, 1750–51, U. Edin. L., special collections division, university archives

Archives Bodl. Oxf., letter-books · Edinburgh City Archives · NL Scot. | NL Scot., Edinburgh Booksellers' Society MSS

Wealth at death substantial property in real estate and book stock

Bell, John (1745–1831), printer and bookseller, was a major figure in the London printing and book trade for much of the late eighteenth and early nineteenth centuries. Bell succeeded a Mrs Bathoe in 1769 to run the British Library, a bookshop in the Strand which was to be home to his diverse printing and publishing business for the next thirty years. Bell quickly established himself as one of the most successful booksellers of his day, and became bookseller to the prince of Wales in the 1780s.

From the 1770s onwards Bell acted as agent for the Martin brothers, owners of the Edinburgh-based Apollo Press, which Bell eventually purchased in 1806. Between 1777 and 1782 they published *The Poets of Great Britain* in direct competition with the edition produced by a combination of around forty London publishers who had previously claimed a monopoly in this area. Bell's edition ran to 109 volumes in a relatively cheap yet well-produced, pocket format which ensured its success. Similar editions of Shakespeare in 1774, and the 21-volume British Theatre Series published between 1776 and 1778, were also popular and as a whole they earned Bell an impressive reputation.

Bell's publishing interests also extended to newspapers. He was one of the original proprietors of the *Morning Post* in 1772, selling his shares in 1786 only to reinvest the money in a new paper, *The World*, which he launched with Edward Topham in 1787. The partnership dissolved on bad terms in 1789, when Topham bought Bell out. Bell promptly began *The Oracle* in June 1789. Such was his dedication to this new venture that in 1794 he travelled to France in order to report on the war. In 1796 Bell began another new paper, *Bell's Weekly Messenger*, which he ran until 1819. During the same period he also established a magazine aimed at fashionable society entitled *La Belle Assemblée*.

Charles Knight, who called Bell the 'puck of booksellers', described his love of innovation as 'really awful' (Knight, 276–7), for not only was Bell famous for his cheap editions and newspaper activities, but he is also credited with having introduced 'modern' face into English printing and, in particular, with discarding the long 's'. In 1781 he commissioned the Caslon foundry to produce a new modern type for the *Morning Post*, and in 1788 he started the British Letter Foundry. According to Timperley, 'few men have contributed more, by their industry and good taste, to the improvement of the graphic and typographic arts' (Timperley, 916).

Yet despite gaining such a reputation, John Bell was not always successful in his career. In 1792 he was found guilty of a libel on the foot guards, and he was declared bankrupt in 1793 and again in 1797. Leigh Hunt suggested that such failures were due to the expense of entertaining the prince of Wales coupled with 'as great a taste for neat wines and ankles as for pretty books' (Hunt, 277), but Stanley Morison blames Bell's problems on a lack of reserves and a legal battle with his partner, George Cantham. Although Bell lost his shop in the Strand in 1795, he opened another nearby in the following year, moving to Drury Lane in 1813.

Bell appears never to have married and left his estate to his niece, Jane Holt, in trust for his great-nephew. Hunt described Bell as 'a plain man, with a red face, and a nose exaggerated by intemperance; and yet there was something not unpleasing in his countenance, especially when he spoke' (Hunt, 276). After ten years in retirement, Bell died at his house at North End, Fulham, Middlesex, on 26 February 1831.   HANNAH BARKER

Sources S. Morison, *John Bell, 1745–1831* (1930) · I. Maxted, *The London book trades, 1775–1800: a preliminary checklist of members* (1977) · L. Hunt, *The autobiography of Leigh Hunt, with reminiscences of friends and contemporaries*, 3 vols. (1850) · L. Werkmeister, *The London daily press, 1772–1792* (1963) · W. Hindle, *The Morning Post, 1772–1937: portrait of a newspaper* (1937) · C. Knight, *Shadows of the old booksellers* (1865) · C. H. Timperley, *A dictionary of printers and printing* (1839) · K. A. Burnim and P. H. Highfill, *John Bell, patron of British theatrical portraiture: a catalog of the theatrical portraits in his editions of 'Bell's Shakespeare' and 'Bell's British theatre'* (1998) · G. Ashton, *Pictures in the Garrick Club*, ed. K. A. Burnim and A. Wilton (1997)

Likenesses R. Dighton, coloured etching, pubd 1821, BM, NPG, V&A · G. Arnald, polyautography print, BM · G. Clint, oils, V&A · W. Douglas, pencil and watercolour drawing, Scot. NPG · portraits, repro. in Morison, *John Bell*, frontispiece, facing p. 48, facing p. 82

Bell, John (1746/7–1798), army officer and inventor, was born in the parish of St Cuthbert's, Carlisle, the eldest son of William Bell, hatter, of Botchergate, Carlisle. He was baptized at St Cuthbert's Church on 22 February 1747. After working in the family business, Bell enlisted in the Royal Artillery, aged eighteen, in September 1765. Between 1766 and 1772 he served at Gibraltar, and in 1777 he was promoted sergeant. As an eyewitness of the foundering of the *Royal George* at Southsea in 1782, Bell devised a method of destroying the wreck with gunpowder, the same as was ultimately employed by Charles Pasley in 1839. He also, as a proof inspector at Woolwich Warren, invented the 'sunproof' for testing the soundness of gun barrels, as well as Bell's 'gyn' or hoist and a type of petard. The Society of Arts awarded him premiums for his invention of a whale harpoon and of a safe crane for descending mines, and in 1792 it presented him with 50 guineas for demonstrating how a line and grapple fired from a mortar could be used to rescue shipwrecked mariners. His daughter, Mrs Elizabeth Whitfield, was in 1815 voted £500 by parliament in recognition of the same invention. Bell's technical expertise secured him a commission from the duke of Richmond as second lieutenant in the artillery in 1793, and on 1 January 1794 he was promoted full lieutenant in the invalid battalion. He died of apoplexy at Queenborough, Kent, on 1 June 1798, while engaged in fitting out fireships.   [ANON.], *rev.* ALASTAIR W. MASSIE

Sources 'A notice of the late Lieutenant Bell, R.A.', *United Service Journal*, 1 (1840), 526–9 · J. Bell, correspondence with the Society of Arts, 1791–4, RSA, PR/MC/101/10 · 3rd battalion Royal Artillery description book, PRO, WO 54/272, fol. 9 · parish register, St Cuthbert's, Carlisle, 22 Feb 1747, Cumbria AS, Carlisle [baptism] · *Transactions of the Society for the Encouragement of Arts, Manufactures, and Commerce*, 9 (1791), 205–6 · *Transactions of the Society for the Encouragement of Arts, Manufactures, and Commerce*, 10 (1792), 204 · *Transactions of the Society for the Encouragement of Arts, Manufactures, and Commerce*, 11 (1793), 185–92 · *Transactions of the Society for the Encouragement of Arts, Manufactures, and Commerce*, 25 (1807), 135–42 · *GM*, 1st ser., 68 (1798), 725 · J. Kane, *List of officers of the royal regiment of artillery from the year 1716 to the year 1899*, rev. W. H. Askwith, 4th edn (1900) · M. E. S. Laws, ed., *Battery records of the royal artillery, 1716–1859* (1952)

Archives Royal Artillery Institution, Woolwich, London, MD/1080/186, 190, 193 | Royal Society for the Encouragement of Arts, Manufactures, and Commerce, corresp. · RSA, letters to the Society of Arts

Bell, John (1763–1820), surgeon and anatomist, was born on 12 May 1763 in Edinburgh, the second son of the Revd William Bell (1704–1779) and his wife, Margaret Morrice. Despite the impoverishment of the family which was caused by Bell's father's conversion from the Church of Scotland to the Scottish Episcopal church, the Bell children were all well educated. Bell's brothers Robert *Bell and George Joseph *Bell both became advocates and professors of law. His youngest brother, Charles *Bell, followed John into medicine. John and Charles Bell may have learnt their notable artistic skills from their mother. Bell received a comprehensive education in the liberal arts from Edinburgh high school. He retained his interest in general subjects throughout his life but showed an early inclination for medical studies. At the age of seventeen he was apprenticed to Alexander Wood, the leading surgeon at Edinburgh Royal Infirmary, and attended classes and lectures by Joseph Black, William Cullen, and Alexander Monro secundus at the University of Edinburgh.

After completing his apprenticeship, Bell travelled to Russia but was back in Edinburgh by 1786 when he was admitted freeman surgeon apothecary by the Royal College and Corporation of Surgeon Apothecaries of Edinburgh. Bell believed new methods of surgical training were essential and he soon started his own programme of lectures and training for surgeons in addition to running his private practice. In 1790 Bell opened his own lecture theatre in Surgeons' Square, Edinburgh. His methods emphasized practical experience of surgical techniques and his eloquence and zeal won him a large following. His brother Charles became his apprentice and other students included Joseph Lizars and Ephraim McDowell. Bell's popularity and professionalism ensured his success.

He published a series of textbooks on surgical anatomy which complemented his lectures and stressed the need for the firsthand experience of techniques as essential in surgical training. His mission was to make his work easy to understand as well as comprehensive. Bell did his own drawings and engravings for *The Anatomy of the Bones, Muscles, and Joints* (1793–4), and his *Discourses on the Nature and Cure of Wounds* (1793–5) had their origins in Bell's personal experiences of wound observation and treatment. His innovative techniques and readable style added to his reputation.

When the college and the Royal Infirmary discontinued their traditional links in 1800, Bell became involved in an ugly controversy. He was one of the many surgeons who lost their right to practise at the infirmary. The new policy hit at the very core of Bell's beliefs about training for young surgeons who would now be forced to learn from textbooks and traditional lectures without being able to practise techniques. Bell's own success had caused his problems. His main opponent was James Gregory, professor of the practice of physic in the university, who led an anti-Bell faction and began a pamphlet war when he issued a warning to students not to attend Bell's private lectures. Bell's and Gregory's mutual animosity continued for years and culminated in Bell's *Letters on Professional Character and Manners* (1810), a defence of his idea of the surgeon as a dignified and skilled professional who had a respectable place in society. Bell attempted to help his students after his exclusion from the infirmary by publishing the monumental and influential *The Principles of Surgery in Two Volumes* (1801–6) which combined anatomical knowledge with detailed examples of operations. Bell's treatment of arterial surgery was especially original and places him with P. J. Desault and John Hunter as a founder of modern vascular surgery. Further editions of Bell's anatomical textbooks added sections on the heart, arteries, nervous system, abdomen, and the lymphatic system. In these he had the able assistance of his brother Charles.

Bell was a kind, generous, and compassionate man who was concerned about limiting the patients' pain during surgical operations. In appearance he was short but well proportioned, with an intelligent face. He was known for his elegant and fashionable clothing. In 1805 Bell married Rosina Congleton, a talented musician and the daughter of a retired physician. Together they made their Edinburgh home into a showplace of artistic taste and became known for their extravagant musical parties. They had no children. Bell's private practice boomed despite his exclusion from the infirmary, and he was the premier surgeon of Edinburgh for nearly twenty years. Bell was thrown from his horse in 1816 and never fully recovered from his injuries. His illness caused great concern in the medical community and in 1817 the *London Medical and Physical Journal* asked him for details of his ailment in the hope that their readers would be able to offer advice. Bell declined the request. Instead he decided on a recuperative trip to Italy and probably left Britain in May 1817. By June, Bell was in Paris, where he suffered a considerable haemorrhage, but this did not stop him from visiting the Hotel-

Dieu out of medical interest. As he toured through Italy, Bell kept a diary recording not only the places he visited but also his remarks on the art treasures he saw. In 1818 he and his wife settled in the fashionable English quarter in Rome. Despite his invalidity, he continued to follow his profession. Bell was a regular visitor to Canova's studio where he and the artist discussed anatomy in art. Bell disapproved of the over-evident use of anatomy in sculpture and preferred ancient classical sculpture to more modern styles. His observations on art in Italy are lively and fiercely critical, even of the works he loved most. Bell's health, however, did not recover and he died of dropsy in Rome, near the Piazza di Spagna in the English quarter, on 15 April 1820. He was buried in the city's protestant cemetery. Bell's widow published his *Observations on Italy* in 1825.   K. GRUDZIEN BASTON

Sources E. W. Wallis, 'John Bell, 1763–1820', *Medical History*, 8 (1964), 63–9 · Chambers, *Scots.* (1856) · F. H. Garrison, *An introduction to the history of medicine*, 4th edn (1929); repr. (1967) · H. Avery, 'John Bell's last tour', *Medical History*, 8 (1964), 69–77 · J. Bell, *Observations on Italy*, ed. R. A. Bell (1825) · J. Bell, *Letters on professional character and manners* (1810) · C. H. Creswell, *The Royal College of Surgeons of Edinburgh: historical notes from 1505 to 1905* (1926) · Irving, *Scots.* · J. Bell and C. Bell, *The anatomy of the human body*, 4 vols. (1802–4) · *DNB*

Likenesses oils, c.1801, NPG · oils, Wellcome L.; repro. in Garrison, *Introduction*

Bell, John (1764–1836), barrister, son of Matthew Bell, was born at Kendal, Westmorland, on 23 October 1764. He lost both parents at an early age and was brought up by an aunt. He was educated at Kirkby Lonsdale School and the grammar school at Beetham, both in Westmorland, and at Trinity College, Cambridge. There he graduated BA in 1786 as senior wrangler and first Smith's prizeman of his year; in 1789 he was elected to a fellowship at his college. He entered the Middle Temple on 10 November 1787 and Gray's Inn on 8 November 1790, having taken his MA degree in 1789. After reading for some time in the chambers of Samuel Romilly, in 1790 Bell began to practise as a special pleader. He was called to the bar in 1792.

Bell devoted himself to the equity branch of the profession, and gradually acquired an extensive practice in the court of chancery, gaining a reputation as a lawyer second to that of none of his contemporaries. On 5 December 1797 he was admitted to Lincoln's Inn and in 1810 Henry Bickersteth (later Lord Langdale), also a native of Westmorland, became his pupil. In 1813 he became a bencher of Gray's Inn, and he was twice treasurer (1818–19 and 1834–5). In 1816 he became a KC.

In conversation with the prince regent (later George IV), Lord Chancellor Eldon was said to have described Bell as the best lawyer then at the equity bar, though he could 'neither read, write, walk, nor talk': Bell was lame, spoke with a broad Westmorland accent, the effect of which was heightened by a confirmed stammer, and wrote in a hand never more than barely legible. He was accustomed to say that he wrote in three hands—one which he himself could read, one which his clerk could read and one which neither he nor his clerk could read. He was described as being short, stout, and round-shouldered, with a prominent mouth and large teeth.

Nevertheless, Bell's keen intelligence and thorough knowledge of the law secured for him a large and lucrative practice. Between 1816 and 1819, in particular, his name occurs with extraordinary frequency in the reports. He once gave evidence for eight days—before the commission which was appointed in 1824 to inquire into and report upon the procedure of the court of chancery, though his lifelong familiarity with the business of this court appears to have rendered him almost as obstinately opposed to change as Eldon himself. Conservative as a lawyer, in politics Bell was a whig. In 1830 he published a pamphlet entitled *Thoughts on the Proposed Alterations in the Court of Chancery*. Late in life he married Jane (*d.* 1866), daughter of Henry Grove, and they had one son, Matthew Bell, later of Bourne Park, Kent. Bell died at his house in Bedford Square, London, on 6 February 1836. He was buried at Milton, near Canterbury, where he had an estate. His will, proved at Doctors' Commons, left a considerable fortune to his widow and son, then still under age at his decease. Lord Langdale was one of his executors.

J. M. RIGG, rev. BETH F. WOOD

Sources T. D. Hardy, *Memoirs of the Right Honourable Henry Lord Langdale*, 1 (1852) · *GM*, 2nd ser., 5 (1836), 670–71 · H. J. Rose, *A new general biographical dictionary*, ed. H. J. Rose and T. Wright, 12 vols. (1853) · J. F. Waller, ed., *The imperial dictionary of universal biography*, 3 vols. (1857–63) · J. Hutchinson, ed., *A catalogue of notable Middle Templars: with brief biographical notices* (1902) · Venn, *Alum. Cant.* · ER, vols. 35–7 · *The Times* (7 Oct 1826) [chancery report] · T. Cooper, *A new biographical dictionary: containing concise notices of eminent persons of all ages and countries* (1873)
Likenesses S. Cousins, mezzotint, pubd 1832 (after T. Stewardson), BM, NPG

Bell, Sir John (1782–1876), army officer, was born on 1 January 1782, at Bonytoun, Fife, the son of David Bell of Bonytoun. It was not until 1805 that he abandoned the more lucrative prospects of mercantile life open to him by family connections, and followed his own inclination by accepting a commission as ensign in the 52nd foot on 15 August. He joined his regiment in Sicily in 1806. Throughout the Peninsular War he was actively engaged in most of the more celebrated actions, and was wounded at the battle of Vimeiro by a shot through the shoulder. He was appointed permanent assistant quartermaster-general during the later years of the war. He received the gold cross for the battles of the Pyrenees, Nivelle, Orthez, and Toulouse. His last active service was in the Anglo-American War, in Louisiana, from December 1814 to January 1815.

From 1828 to 1841 Bell was chief secretary to the government at the Cape, and from 1848 to 1854 lieutenant-governor of Guernsey. The colonelcy of the 95th foot was awarded to him in 1850, which he exchanged for that of the 4th foot three years later. He was made a CB on 4 June 1815, a KCB on 6 April 1852, and a GCB on 18 May 1860. Immediately afterwards he became a general, and before his death was the senior general in the army. He married, on 14 June 1821, Lady Catharine Harriot, the elder daughter of James *Harris, the first earl of Malmesbury. She was

born at St Petersburg on 29 May 1780, and was named after her godmother, the Empress Catharine. She died in Upper Hyde Park Street, London, on 21 December 1855. Bell died at his home, 55 Cadogan Place, London, on 20 November 1876, and was buried in Kensal Green cemetery.

G. C. BOASE, rev. JAMES LUNT

Sources *Army List* · *ILN* (2 Dec 1876), 541 · *Men of the time* (1875) · Boase, *Mod. Eng. biog.* · *Dod's Peerage* (1858)
Archives Bodl. Oxf. · Chetham's Library, Manchester
Likenesses J. Lucas, oils, exh. RA 1857, Royal Court House, Guernsey · C. Silvy, carte-de-visite, 1860–61, NPG · H. Cousins, mezzotint (after J. Lucas), NPG · engraving, repro. in *ILN*
Wealth at death under £25,000: probate, 11 Dec 1876, CGPLA Eng. & Wales

Bell, John (1783–1864). *See under* Bell, Thomas (1785–1860).

Bell, John (1812–1895), sculptor and designer, was born on 19 August 1812 at Hopton, Suffolk. Of his parents, nothing is known. He was educated at Catfield village school in Norfolk before moving to London, where he spent much of the rest of his life. He entered the Royal Academy Schools in 1829 and exhibited his first work there, a religious group, in 1832. In 1833 he won a large silver medal from the Society of Arts for a model of a bust. He would continue to exhibit at the Royal Academy for nearly fifty years, showing some sixty-six works. He also exhibited six works at the British Institution and seventeen at the Suffolk Street and Sidney Sussex galleries. His works incorporate a variety of subjects, including the religious, such as *John the Baptist* (1833), *David* (1838), *The Women of Bethlehem* (1859), and *The Foot of the Cross* (1866); and the literary and mythological, including a series of works depicting *Psyche* (1834, 1836, 1837), *Heracles* (1837), and figures of *Ariel* (1834) from Shakespeare, *Dorothea* (1839) from Cervantes, and *Clorinda Wounded by her Lover* (1848) from Torquato Tasso. Bell also received many royal and state commissions, including *Queen Victoria* (1841), a bust of Sir Robert Walpole (marble, 1854, Eton College, Berkshire), *The United States Directing the Progress of America* as part of the Albert memorial (marble, 1864–9, Kensington), a Wellington monument (1856), and statues of *Peace and War* (1855–6) and *Armed Science* designed to commemorate the Crimean War. His most popular work was probably *The Eagle-Slayer* (1841), also known as *The Archer*, which he first exhibited at the academy in 1837. It was executed in bronze (London), marble (1844, Wentworth Woodhouse, near Sheffield), and iron (1851, Bethnal Green Museum of Childhood, London). The iron version was cast by the Coalbrookdale Company and shown at the Great Exhibition of 1851. It was the success of this piece which led to subsequent prestigious commissions. 'Stylistically and iconographically, Bell's work achieved a compromise between neo-classical tradition and meticulous contemporary realism' (*Dictionary of Art*).

Bell took a particularly active part in the movement which led to the Great Exhibition of 1851, and afterwards to the foundation of the South Kensington Museum (later the Victoria and Albert Museum). He was also one of the first British sculptors to experiment in the use of polychrome and new materials such as terracotta, which again became popular at the end of the nineteenth century for symbolist and the 'new' sculpture. Many of his imaginary subjects were reproduced in Parian porcelain by W. T. Copeland and by Henry Cole's Art Manufactures, including *Babes in the Wood* (marble, 1842, Victoria and Albert Museum, London) and *Andromeda* (bronze, *c*.1851, Royal Collection, Osborne House, Isle of Wight). In 1851 Bell made a bronze and ormolu statue, *Queen Victoria and her Consort*, and, in 1876–7, terracotta representations of Byron (1877) and *The Woman that Bled for All Mankind*. He was also keen to break down the boundaries between sculpture and the applied arts, designing for the exhibition of British manufacture and decorative art in 1848 a series of bread- and fish-knives and wooden bread-platters which, unlike several of his other exhibits which included a cast-iron doorstop in the shape of Cerberus (1849) and a crusader's altar tomb matchbox (1848), were immensely popular in mid-Victorian Britain; and, in 1858, a series of animal heads to decorate the Metropolitan cattle market in Pentonville, London. In 1845 he designed for the Coalbrookdale Company a desk table supported by four full-sized deerhounds cast in iron covered with emblems of the chase and vine (Ironbridge Museum, Coalbrookdale, Shropshire).

Contemporaries felt that Bell's works of applied art and his later sculpture revealed a decline in power from the immense vigour, imagination, and strength of feeling characteristic of his earlier work, which had provided a refreshing departure from the frigid classicism then prevailing in British neo-classical sculpture. The *Art Journal*, for example, felt that his later works were marred by a sickly sentimentality and 'looked best in a thick fog' (*Dictionary of British Sculptors, 1660–1851*, 48). Bell continued to sculpt and write prolifically, however. In 1852 his *Free-Hand Outline*, a guide to drawing, was published by George Bell, followed by an essay on the sublime and beautiful entitled *The Four Primary Sensations of the Mind* (1852) and *Ivan III, or, A Day and Night in Russia: a Dramatic Sketch* (1855). At the end of the 1850s he also published a famous paper, *On the Application of Entasis to the Obelisk*, for which he received a medal from the Society of Arts. (An obelisk designed by him on this principle was later erected in Bermuda.) This was followed in 1858 by *British Sculpture, in Connection with the Department of Science and Art* and, in 1861, his lecture to the Society of Arts, 'Colour on statues and paintings'.

Bell exhibited for the last time in 1879 and was not an active sculptor in his final years, which he spent peacefully at 15 Douro Place, Victoria Road, Kensington, London, a house in which he had resided for some forty years. He did not retire from public life entirely: shortly before his death at his home, on 14 March 1895, he published *The Lost Venus of Knidos: an Attempt at her Reconstruction* in the *Magazine of Art* (17, 1894, 16–17). In recent years Bell's work has undergone re-evaluation and he has come to be perceived as more innovative as an industrial designer than as a sculptor.

CAMPBELL DODGSON, *rev.* JASON EDWARDS

Sources R. Gunnis, *Dictionary of British sculptors, 1660–1851* (1953), 48–9 • M. H. Grant, *A dictionary of British sculptors from the XIIIth century to the XXth century* (1953) • Boase, *Mod. Eng. biog.* • Graves, *RA exhibitors* • *The Times* (28 March 1895) • *The Athenaeum* (6 April 1895) • *Biograph and Review*, 3 (1880), 178–85 • *Men and women of the time* (1895), 66 • *ILN* (6 April 1895), 406 • *Literary Gazette* (20 July 1844), 466 • G. Meissner, ed., *Allgemeines Künstlerlexikon: die bildenden Künstler aller Zeiten und Völker*, [new edn, 34 vols.] (Leipzig and Munich, 1983–) • M. Stocker, 'Bell, John', *The dictionary of art*, ed. J. Turner (1996) • B. Read, *Victorian sculpture* (1982) • S. C. Hutchison, 'The Royal Academy Schools, 1768–1830', *Walpole Society*, 38 (1960–62), 123–91 • *CGPLA Eng. & Wales* (1895)
Archives V&A NAL, draft for proposed statue of Alfred in Hyde Park | BL, corresp. with Austen Layard, Add. MSS 38992–38997 • U. Leeds, Brotherton L., letters to E. Gosse • V&A NAL, memoranda and letters to R. H. Soden-Smith, mainly relating to Bell's statue of Cromwell
Likenesses portrait, repro. in *Magazine of Art*, 17 (1894), 16 • wood-engraving (after photograph by Chapman and Sons), NPG; repro. in *ILN*
Wealth at death £220 14*s.* 2*d.*: probate, 26 April 1895, *CGPLA Eng. & Wales*

Bell, John Gray (1823–1866), bookseller, was born at Newcastle upon Tyne on 21 September 1823, the sixth son of the fourteen children of Thomas *Bell (1785–1860), surveyor and bibliophile, and his wife, Hannah, *née* Blakey. At sixteen he and an older brother ran his father's bookshop, and in 1848 he set up as a bookseller and publisher in Covent Garden, London. He had married Dorothy, the daughter of Emanuel Taylor, on 27 September 1847, and they had three sons and a daughter. He moved to Manchester in 1854, where he traded until his death. Like his grandfather, father, and uncle, Bell became a distinguished collector of books and ephemera. He compiled, for example, an authoritative overview (1851) of the works of Thomas Bewick, the wood-engraver, and a genealogy of the Bells (1855), affectionately dedicated to his father, showing their descent from John of Gaunt. After 1850 he published a valuable series, Tracts on the Topography, Dialects, &c, which covered some sixteen English counties. His main interests were in the north-east, where vestiges of the Bell collections are of great antiquarian importance, but his specialisms included collections of the records of the British army in North America and during the Napoleonic wars, and of the engravings in Macklin's Bible. Bell died of pneumonia at his home, 11 Wright Street, Greenheys, Manchester, on 16 February 1866, and was buried in the family vault at Jesmond, Newcastle upon Tyne; his wife survived him.

LOUIS STOTT

Sources E. Lockey, 'The Bell family', diss., 1980, City of Newcastle Central Library • J. G. Bell, *A genealogical account of the descendants of John of Gaunt, duke of Lancaster* (1855) • private information (2004) [Manchester department of libraries and theatres] • *DNB* • d. cert. • *CGPLA Eng. & Wales* (1866)
Archives Bodl. Oxf., corresp. with Sir Thomas Phillipps
Wealth at death under £3000: resworn probate, April 1867, *CGPLA Eng. & Wales* (1866)

Bell, John Montgomerie (1804–1862), lawyer and sheriff, was born at Paisley and educated at the Paisley grammar school. He studied at the University of Glasgow and was called to the Edinburgh bar in 1825. A poem which he wrote soon afterwards, 'The Martyr of Liberty', was published posthumously in 1863.

From 1830 to 1846 Bell assisted, with conspicuous ability, in conducting the court of session reports. In 1847 he was appointed an advocate-depute, and in 1851 sheriff of Kincardine. In 1861 he published his comprehensive *Treatise on the Law of Arbitration in Scotland*, which became the standard work on the subject. Bell died from injuries sustained in an accident at Linnhouse, Midcalder, on 16 October 1862.   T. F. HENDERSON, *rev.* ERIC METCALFE

Sources *The Scotsman* (23 Oct 1862) · catalogue, Library of the Faculty of Advocates, Edinburgh · W. I. Addison, *A roll of graduates of the University of Glasgow from 31st December 1727 to 31st December 1897* (1898) · NA Scot., SC 70/1/114, p. 239

Wealth at death £14,248 4s. 2d.: inventory, 20 Nov 1862, NA Scot., SC 70/1/114, p. 239

Bell, John Stewart (1928–1990), theoretical physicist, was born into a protestant working-class family in Belfast on 28 July 1928, the eldest of three sons and second of four children of John Bell. The latter worked as a horse dealer, but his health was poor and after army service he had no real job, and his wife, (Elizabeth Mary) Ann Brownlee, did some casual sewing work. After leaving the Belfast Technical High School at sixteen, John Stewart Bell worked for a year as a laboratory assistant in the physics department of the Queen's University, Belfast (1944–5); his supervisors gave him physics books to read and he was able to skip a year after he entered the university in 1946. He graduated with first-class honours in experimental physics in 1948 and in mathematical physics in 1949.

Bell worked for the Atomic Energy Research Establishment (AERE) at Malvern and Harwell from 1949 to 1953 on the theory of particle accelerators; he applied Hamiltonian dynamics to develop various analytical approaches, and he discovered the 'Courant–Snyder' invariant. He spent 1953 on leave working for a PhD in Birmingham under P. T. Matthews and Rudolf Peierls. After returning to Harwell, he completed his thesis in 1956 and began to work on many body problems and quantum field theory, with particular reference to atomic nuclei. His thesis contains a proof of the profound and fundamental parity-charge conjugation–time reversal (PCT) theorem, though his discovery of this theorem had been anticipated by G. Lüders. In 1954 he married Mary, daughter of Alexander Munro Ross, a shipyard commercial manager in Glasgow; the couple had no children. They had met when both were working for AERE on accelerator theory, and they published a joint report in 1952.

In 1960 Bell moved to the theoretical studies division at the Conseil Européen de Recherches Nucléaires (CERN), the European particle physics laboratory near Geneva, Switzerland, where he remained until his death in 1990, apart from one year's leave in 1963–4 at the Stanford Linear Accelerator Center in California. His wife also joined CERN, as an accelerator physicist. He published a large number of important papers on particle physics, his contributions including articles on CP (charge conjugation–parity) violation; the discovery that, despite having a mean free path of millions of miles in matter, neutrinos are 'shadowed' in nuclei; the observation that the algebra of electroweak charges is strongly suggestive of a gauge theory; and an illuminating explanation of the upper limit on the polarization of particles in storage rings as a manifestation of interaction with the black body radiation experienced by accelerated observers. The best-known of his 'conventional' contributions was his discovery (with R. Jackiw) of the 'Alder–Bell–Jackiw' anomaly, which leads not only to constraints on models of elementary particles but also to surprising and deep connections between physics and geometry.

Bell was best-known for work on what he described as 'his hobby—the problem of quantum mechanics'. His first contribution was to demolish John von Neumann's celebrated theorem that purported to show that 'quantum mechanics would have to be objectively false in order that another description of the elementary process than the statistical one be possible'. He then showed (Bell's theorem) that certain predictions of quantum mechanics cannot be reproduced by any 'local' theory in which the results of a measurement—or experiment, as he preferred to call it—on one system are unaffected by operations on a distant system with which it interacted in the past. The subsequent verifications of these predictions were of fundamental importance.

Bell's masterly expositions of the 'rotten' state of the foundations of quantum mechanics (collected in *Speakable and Unspeakable in Quantum Mechanics*, 1987), in which he stressed that without a definition of a 'measurement' the predictions are in principle ambiguous, did much to shake the 'complacent' views of other physicists. He made the most important contribution to 'quantum philosophy' since the birth of quantum mechanics, though—by exposing its essential non-locality—he only deepened the fundamental mysteries of the subject. He also had a profound knowledge of the foundations of other pillars of theoretical physics, especially classical electromagnetism.

Bell's work was recognized by his election as a fellow of the Royal Society in 1972 and as a foreign honorary member of the American Academy of Arts and Sciences in 1987; the award of the Reality Foundation prize in 1982; the Dirac medal of the British Institute of Physics, an honorary DSc from Queen's University, Belfast, and an honorary ScD from Trinity College, Dublin (all in 1988); and the Dannie Heineman prize of the American Physical Society and the Hughes medal of the Royal Society in 1989.

John Bell had red hair and a beard and spoke with a lilting Ulster accent. He generally dressed informally and was a vegetarian. He and his wife were a rather private couple, but excellent company for those who got to know them. He was a brilliant writer and teacher, both in formal lectures and in private discussions, delighting in teasing out the truth by means of Socratic dialogue and paradox. He was amused by the widespread publicity that his theorem attracted, though perhaps also mildly resentful that it tended to obscure his other contributions. He enjoyed the encounters it generated with people such as the Dalai

Lama, which he described in an amused and sceptical manner.

In the 1980s Bell and his wife published several joint papers on electron cooling in storage rings and quantum beam- and bremsstrahlung. Mary Bell's comments on the drafts of her husband's papers on quantum mechanics helped improve their clarity; he wrote that in them 'I see her everywhere'. John Bell died suddenly and unexpectedly of a cerebral haemorrhage in Geneva on 1 October 1990.   C. H. LLEWELLYN SMITH, rev.

Sources *Europhysics News*, 22/4 (1991) · *Physics Today* (Aug 1991), 82 · J. Bernstein, *Quantum profiles* (1991) · *CGPLA Eng. & Wales* (1991) · private information (1996) · personal knowledge (1996)
Wealth at death £106,993: probate, 20 Sept 1991, *CGPLA Eng. & Wales*

Bell, Jonathan Anderson [John Anderson] (1809–1865), architect, was born in Glasgow, the second son of James Bell, advocate, and brother of sheriff Henry Glassford *Bell. He was educated at Edinburgh University. From 1829 to 1833 he studied art in Rome. On his return he was articled in Birmingham to the Gothic revival architect Thomas Rickman, with whom he became good friends. Bell's education and training gave him a good knowledge of Gothic architecture, of which he made correct and elegant drawings. Thirty of these were engraved by John Le Keux and published in his *Memorials of Cambridge* (1841).

Bell returned about 1838 to Edinburgh, where he continued to practise as an architect. He exhibited a design for New College, Edinburgh, at the Royal Academy in 1845, and also exhibited regularly at the Royal Society of Artists between 1834 and 1861. Two of his designs, for a new corn exchange at Leith, and the Victoria Buildings in Glasgow, were exhibited in collaboration with John Burbridge. A contemporary noted that:

> his larger works were not numerous, but they are of great merit and evince refined taste. The country houses he erected were always justly admired. The extensive range of premises in Glasgow, known by the name of Victoria Buildings, which he designed for Mr. Archibald Orr Ewing, exhibit a very pure specimen of Scotch Gothic, finely adapted to commercial purposes, and form one of the most imposing elevations in the city.

He designed monuments to several eminent Scots, including George Chalmers, Archibald Constable, and the architect Robert Reid; other examples of his work may also be found in the principal cemeteries of Edinburgh and Glasgow. Bell was a member of the Institute of Scottish Architects. In 1839, he was appointed secretary to the Royal Association for the Promotion of the Fine Arts in Scotland, an office he retained until his death.

Bell was also an accomplished watercolour artist: he drew landscapes, sea pieces, Italian churches, and Roman ruins, as well as still lifes, examples of which may be found in the British Museum and the National Gallery of Scotland. Following his death in Edinburgh, aged fifty-six, on 28 February 1865, a volume of his poems was privately printed, to which was prefixed a memoir of his life. He was buried in the Dean cemetery, Edinburgh.

ERNEST RADFORD, rev. ANNETTE PEACH

Sources J. A. Bell, *Poems* (privately published, Edinburgh, 1865) [incl. memoir] · Graves, *RA exhibitors* · Mallalieu, *Watercolour artists* · *Catalogue of the drawings collection of the Royal Institute of British Architects: B* (1972) · *The Scotsman* (2 March 1865) · P. J. M. McEwan, *Dictionary of Scottish art and architecture* (1994)

Bell, Joseph (1837–1911), surgeon, the son of Benjamin Bell, surgeon, and his wife, Cecilia Craigie, was born on 2 December 1837 at St Andrew Square, Edinburgh. He was educated at the Edinburgh Academy and entered the University of Edinburgh at the early age of sixteen; he graduated MD in 1859. He travelled to the continent but was not attracted to stay and study there. Bell returned to become house surgeon to Professor James Syme, and then house physician to William Gairdner.

Bell became a demonstrator in anatomy, and at the early age of twenty-six he set up his own classes of systematic and operative surgery. He was special assistant to Syme for five years and was held in high esteem by his master and mentor. In 1865 he married Edith Katherine (d. 1874), daughter of the Hon. James Erskine Murray of the Elibank family; they had a son and two daughters. In 1872 Bell became a senior surgeon to the Royal Infirmary of Edinburgh. During these years he also served with great distinction in the Edinburgh Eye Infirmary. Having completed the statutory fifteen years' service, he then 'retired' from the Royal Infirmary to become the first surgeon to the Royal Hospital for Sick Children.

Bell's reputation as a brilliant, caring craftsman and surgeon has been extensively recorded, but he was also a dedicated mentor of nurses. He introduced the new Nightingale ward design to the Royal Infirmary and began the clinical teaching of nurses on Sunday morning rounds. He was the founder and vice-president of the Queen Victoria Jubilee Institute of Nurses. Bell was a strong churchman and after seeing two or three patients on a Sunday morning would go without fail to St George's United Free Church, where he was a senior elder.

Bell was not a prolific writer, but his book *Some Notes on Surgery for Nurses* (1887), dedicated to Florence Nightingale, ran to six editions. His other publications included *A Manual of the Operations of Surgery*, which ran to seven editions, and articles on scapulo-humeral dislocation and pulsating tumours of the orbit. He served Edinburgh University from 1895 as the assessor of the university court and was soon elected a curator of patronage, a post he held until he died. He was also committed to and involved in the admission of women to the medical school, which obviously involved much tact and understanding in order to break down prejudice. He was an examiner for the Royal College of Surgeons of Edinburgh for more than forty-two years, treasurer for eleven, and president in 1887–9. He was a fellow of the Royal Society of Edinburgh and deputy lieutenant of the county.

Bell won notoriety as the inspiration for the creation of the character of Sherlock Holmes. Arthur Conan Doyle was a medical student in Edinburgh and had been impressed if not inspired by Bell's professional appearance—'a tall, stately, kindly man, keen eyes and aquiline features contributing to his air of intent investigation. He

Joseph Bell (1837–1911), by James Irvine, exh. Royal Scottish Academy 1889

would study with close interest all the mannerisms, features, expressions and personal traits of a patient' (Liebow). Bell died on 4 October 1911 at his home, Mauricewood, Milton Bridge, Midlothian. He is buried in Dean cemetery, Edinburgh. R. B. Duthie, *rev.*

Sources *BMJ* (14 Oct 1911) · *The Lancet* (14 Oct 1911) · *Edinburgh Medical Journal*, 3rd ser., 7 (1911), 454–9 · *Journal of the Royal College of Surgeons of Edinburgh*, 14 (1969) · *The Scotsman* (23 May 1959) · E. Liebow, *Dr Joe Bell: model for Sherlock Holmes* (1982) · J. M. E. Saxby, *Joseph Bell: an appreciation by an old friend* (1913) · D. Guthrie, 'Sherlock Holmes and medicine', in D. Guthrie, *Janus in the doorway* (1963), 287–97 · B. F. Westmoreland and J. D. Key, 'Sir Arthur Conan Doyle, Joseph Bell, and Sherlock Holmes: a neurologic connection', *Archives of Neurology*, 48/3 (March 1991) · bap. reg. Scot., 16 March 1838, St Andrew's, Edinburgh · *N&Q*, 166 (1934), 458

Archives BL, letters to Florence Nightingale, Add. MSS 45805, 45808, 45814, *passim*

Likenesses J. Irvine, exh. Royal Scottish Academy 1889, Royal College of Surgeons, Edinburgh [*see illus.*] · F. Watt, portrait, 1896, repro. in Saxby, *Joseph Bell: an appreciation by an old friend* · portrait, Royal College of Surgeons, Edinburgh; repro. in Liebow, *Dr Joe Bell*, frontispiece

Wealth at death £62,654 1s. 11d.: confirmation, 29 Dec 1911, *CCI*

Bell, Julia (1879–1979), geneticist, was born on 28 January 1879 at Sherwood, Nottinghamshire. She was tenth of the fourteen children of James Bell, printer, and Katherine Thomas Heap. She was educated at Nottingham Girls' High School and in 1898 entered Girton College, Cambridge, to study mathematics. Illness prevented her from taking the exam and in 1901 she was awarded an aegrotat degree. At that time women were permitted to take

courses at Cambridge but not to graduate. This anomalous situation meant that in 1907 Julia Bell went to Ireland to receive her MA from Trinity College, Dublin, which from 1904 to 1907 offered this facility to Cambridge women.

From 1902 until 1908 Bell was a postgraduate student at the Cambridge observatory where she worked on the solar parallax under A. R. Hincks. During this period she was also doing mathematical calculations for the Revd Osmond Fisher on the physics of the earth's crust. It was Bell's skill as a mathematician which brought her to the attention of Karl Pearson, professor of applied mathematics and director of the Galton Laboratory for National Eugenics at University College, London. In 1908 he appointed her as one of his assistants. Bell did her calculations from home in Nottingham for a while but eventually settled in London. She had a connection with the Galton Laboratory lasting over fifty years.

Her appointment by Pearson was fortunate in a number of ways. Pearson espoused women's rights and in 1885 had been a co-founder, with Olive Schreiner, of the Men and Women's Club which promoted contact between the sexes on the basis of social and intellectual equality. His laboratory employed a number of distinguished women working in science both before and after Julia Bell joined it. Pearson was interested in the application of statistical methods to the study of heredity, and this was to become the dominant scientific interest in Bell's life. However, Pearson was hostile to the Mendelian theory of discrete and particulate inheritance. Instead he held to the theory of small, continuous variations which he believed better accorded with the Darwinian theory. Thus, while statistical techniques at the Galton Laboratory advanced considerably, an increasingly arid dispute with Mendelism prevented the full flowering of heredity studies.

From 1908 until 1914 Bell was involved in a series of mathematical investigations linked to heredity. These helped further the science of statistics but, based as they were on Pearson's biometrical theory of heredity, their value as contributions to the study of inheritance can be questioned. Bell was involved in the Galton Laboratory's most ambitious project, *The Treasury of Human Inheritance*, which collected and recorded pedigrees of human hereditary diseases and anomalies. This project took several decades and ran to five volumes of observations (published 1909–58), each volume containing several distinct monographs. Bell contributed to volumes 2 (1922–33), diseases of the eye; 4 (1934–48), diseases of the nervous system; and 5 (1951–8), digital abnormalities. The *Treasury* proved an invaluable source of information for students of heredity, and contained several pertinent interpretations of the data by Bell.

It was Bell's increasing interest in the more observational side to the study of heredity that led her to train as a doctor. In 1914 she entered the London School of Medicine for Women at the Royal Free Hospital, qualifying MRCS LRCP in 1920. She returned to the Galton Laboratory to continue her studies of heredity, and throughout the 1920s she practised medicine one day a week. She was awarded membership of the Royal College of Physicians in 1926 and elected fellow in 1938. She always retained an interest in the professional status and intellectual concerns of the medical world and at the age of eighty, in 1959, published an article in the *British Medical Journal* on the effects of rubella in pregnancy.

Bell was employed as a full-time research worker by the Medical Research Council (MRC) until 1944. From 1926 to 1944 she was Galton research fellow at University College, London. In 1936 she also joined the MRC neurological unit at the National Hospital, Queen Square. During the 1930s she assembled family pedigrees on, among other conditions, ataxia, Huntington's disease, and haemophilia, travelling considerable distances to track down family pedigrees. The first stage of Bell's professional life during the 1920s was not without its frustrations. She was constrained by the necessity to get her grants renewed and to bargain up her salary with the MRC. Her position reflected the insecurity of many women in science on short-term research contracts.

In 1932 the most significant decade of Bell's scientific career began with her appointment to the genetics committee of the MRC. She accepted the appointment with characteristic diffidence although it was clearly in recognition of both her statistical skill and medical knowledge. Between 1933 and 1944 she became a permanent member of the MRC scientific staff. Serving with the committee gave her the opportunity to work with the foremost geneticists in Britain, including R. A. Fisher who in 1933 replaced Pearson as director of the Galton Laboratory, and J. B. S. Haldane who from 1933 to 1936 was professor of genetics at University College. Fisher was a Mendelian and his appointment to the laboratory signalled the decline of the influence of the biometrical school of heredity there.

Bell was now in a position to bring her unique qualities to overtly Mendelian studies of heredity. Her collaboration with Haldane, whom she regarded as being a great stimulus, was particularly fruitful. While collecting material for *The Treasury of Human Inheritance* in 1936 Bell came across evidence of a linkage between haemophilia and red–green colour blindness in males. A notice of this was sent by Bell and Haldane to *Nature* on 15 October 1936 and a full-length exposition, written jointly, appeared in the *Proceedings of the Royal Society* in 1937. The paper detailed one of the first actual pedigrees confirming a significant male genetic linkage.

Bell continued work on linkage, publishing in the *Journal of Neurology* in 1943, with J. P. Martin, evidence of a link between mental retardation in males and the X chromosome. In 1940 Bell produced another important paper in *Annals of Eugenics* on the rate of consanguinity in England and Wales.

Bell's formal position in academia never matched her achievements, probably because of a combination of gender bias and limited opportunities in genetics. She was, however, in a unique position, with both statistical and medical training, to make a significant contribution to the development of genetic science. She was one of the pioneers who laid the foundations for the mapping of human chromosomes.

In 1941 Bell's career in statistics was rewarded by the presentation of the Weldon memorial prize and medal for biometry by Oxford University. In 1944 she retired from the Galton Laboratory but was appointed honorary research associate and, until 1965, remained on its staff. She continued to be an active researcher, helping prepare the fifth volume of *The Treasury of Human Inheritance* for publication in 1958. Relations with Lionel Penrose, who took over directorship of the Galton Laboratory in 1945, were good and it was on his initiative that her eightieth birthday in 1959 was celebrated by a reception at University College.

Julia Bell never married. She had a large circle of friends and family. Her numerous letters to colleagues reveal a talent for friendship and wide interests outside science which she listed in *Who's Who* as music, plays, and reading. She remained independent until, at the age of ninety-seven, she was obliged to enter St George's Nursing Home, 61 St George's Square, Westminster, where she died on 26 April 1979 aged 100.   GRETA JONES

Sources S. Bundey, 'Julia Bell', *Journal of Medical Biography*, 4 (1996), 8–13 · PRO, Medical Research Council MSS, FD.1./591 · K. T. Butler and H. I. McMorran, eds., *Girton College register, 1869–1946* (1948) · UCL, Pearson MSS · *WW* (1970) · R. Love, 'Alice in eugenics land', *Annals of Science*, 36 (1979), 145–58 · *Nature*, 281 (1979), 163–4 · *BMJ* (2 May 1979), 1289 · *The Times* (19 Nov 1979) · *Daily Telegraph* (2 May 1979) · d. cert. · *CGPLA Eng. & Wales* (1979)
Archives PRO, Medical Research Council archives · UCL, Penrose MSS · UCL, Haldane MSS
Likenesses portrait, repro. in Bundey, 'Julia Bell' · portrait, priv. coll.
Wealth at death £36,413: probate, 14 Nov 1979, *CGPLA Eng. & Wales*

Bell, Julian Heward (1908–1937), poet, was born on 4 February 1908 at 46 Gordon Square, Bloomsbury, London, the son of (Arthur) Clive Heward *Bell (1881–1964), art critic and historian, and his wife, Vanessa *Bell (1879–1961), artist, daughter of Sir Leslie *Stephen, and sister of Virginia *Woolf (1882–1941). Quentin *Bell was his younger brother. The family and its circle included many of the important Bloomsbury figures. He was educated at Leighton Park School, a Quaker institution, and at King's College, Cambridge (1927–34), where he was a contemporary of John Lehmann and William Empson. While at Cambridge, he contributed to *The Venture*, and was a member of the élite society called the Apostles. His first book of poems, *Winter Movement* (1930), sold poorly, but was greeted as one of the most promising of its day, and compared to W. H. Auden's *Poems* (1930).

Winter Movement was dedicated to Richard Jeffries and consists largely of poems about the English countryside. They are extremely finished and controlled performances, with a firmness of diction and an exactness of observation, although their inspiration was Georgian rather than modernist, and they have not gained the status of major works. The book ends with a set of 'Characters in the manner of Pope'; and a modernized version of Pope's style was Bell's aim for the next two years. It was a style that he came to command, although it could hardly be a fruitful one for a twentieth-century poet.

Poems by Bell appeared alongside those of William Empson, W. H. Auden, and Stephen Spender in *New Signatures* (1932), a seminal anthology edited by Michael Roberts, which brought together much of the important new poetry of the 1930s; but Bell did not belong with Auden and Spender, either artistically or politically. In 'A brief view of poetic obscurity' (1930) he had set out his unsympathetic view of modernism; and, as a socialist, Bell felt that Auden and Spender, and his own close friend John Lehmann, were romantic in seeing the salvation of society in communism. His own contribution to *New Signatures*, 'Arms and the Man', was a satire on armament written in Popean couplets.

In 1933 Bell experienced another spurt of creativity, which led to the poems collected in *Works for Winter* (1936). This book had none of the vividness or decided character of *Winter Movement*, although it includes some touching personal poems. While he was critical of Auden and Spender, Bell's political poems show the same divided feeling as theirs did concerning the privileged upper middle-class, Liberal tradition in which he had grown up.

Bell's brief life was one of unfulfilled promise. He is remembered only as a very minor poet; and he could not find a place for himself in the world of Cambridge and Bloomsbury to which he was born. He stayed on at Cambridge, only to have his thesis rejected, even though Roger Fry, a friend of the family, was one of its readers. His Bloomsbury upbringing seemed to have left him with the sense that the intellectual life could be one of effortless achievement; his uncle Leonard Woolf once said of him that 'he never quite grew up' (Woolf, 253). In addition to his thesis he wrote a number of pamphlet-length prose pieces on political and ideological subjects. One of these was 'War and peace: a letter to E. M. Forster'; and Forster described the writing as being 'all over the shop' (Stansky and Abrahams, 179).

In 1935 Bell accepted the position of professor of English at the University of Wuhan in China. He returned in 1937, before his contract was completed, drawn, like many other young intellectuals of his day, to the conflict of the Spanish Civil War and to the ideological position represented by the government side. From an early age Bell was fascinated by war; and the possibility of experiencing it at first hand was one of his reasons for going to Spain. However, the pacifist leanings of his family led him to enrol as an ambulance driver with Spanish Medical Aid. He was wounded at Villanueva de la Cañada in the battle of Brunete, west of Madrid, on 18 July 1937, and taken to the military hospital at El Escorial near Madrid, where he died that day. He had written no poetry in the last two years of his life. His death epitomized a certainty of purpose that his life did not have, and made him a figure of memory.   A. T. TOLLEY

Sources P. Stansky and W. Abrahams, *Journey to the frontier* (1966) · L. Woolf, *Downhill all the way* (1967) · *Julian Bell: essays, poems and letters*, ed. Q. Bell (1938) · A. T. Tolley, *The poetry of the thirties* (1975) · *CGPLA Eng. & Wales* (1937)

Archives King's AC Cam., corresp. and papers | King's AC Cam., letters to Vanessa Bell · King's AC Cam., corresp. with Angelica Garnett · U. Sussex, letters to Virginia Woolf
Likenesses photographs, repro. in Stansky and Abrahams, *Journey to the frontier*
Wealth at death £2602 5s. 5d.: probate, 9 Dec 1937, *CGPLA Eng. & Wales*

Bell, Sir (Isaac) Lowthian, first baronet (1816–1904), iron and steel manufacturer, was born at Newcastle upon Tyne on 15 February 1816, the eldest of four sons (out of seven children) of Thomas Bell (1774–1845), chemical and iron manufacturer, and his wife, Catherine, née Lowthian (d. 1875). Lowthian Bell (as he was usually known) was steeped in the local coal, iron, and shipbuilding industries. His father operated the Walker ironworks for the firm of which he later became a partner, Losh, Wilson, and Bell, and his family had links with Lord Dundonald, who had pioneered the Leblanc soda process in England. A second brother, Thomas, was involved in the iron trade; a third brother, John, became a geologist and an important adviser to the family.

After a nonconformist education at Bruce's academy, Newcastle, Bell visited Germany and Denmark before attending Edinburgh University. He then went to the Sorbonne, and later finished what was an unusually wide (and influential) continental education by undertaking practical work on alkali manufacture at Marseilles. He joined the Walker ironworks in 1835, aged nineteen, and under the influence of the firm's rolling-mill superintendent, John Vaughan, he began studying the operations of blast furnaces and rolling mills. A desire to master thoroughly the technology of any manufacturing process was to be one of the hallmarks of Bell's career. In 1842 he married Margaret (d. 1886), daughter of Hugh Lee *Pattinson, a well-known chemical manufacturer. The couple had two sons and three daughters. Eight years later Bell started his own chemical factory at Washington in Gateshead, where he operated the new French Deville patent, used in the manufacture of aluminium. Bell expanded these chemical interests in the mid-1860s, when he developed with his brother John a large salt working near the ironworks.

In 1844 Lowthian Bell and his brothers Thomas and John formed a new company, Bell Brothers, to operate the Wylam ironworks. These works, based at Port Clarence on the Tees, began pig-iron production with three blast furnaces in 1854 and became one of the leading plants in the north-east iron industry. The firm's output had reached 200,000 tons by 1878 and the firm employed about 6000 men. The company's need for ironstone led to the association of Bell Brothers with Ralph Ward Jackson, who leased the Bells important ironstone beds. Bell and Jackson then built the Cleveland Railway to convey material to the Clarence works, thus freeing the company from the railway monopoly formed by the local Quaker industrialist Joseph Pease. It was part of a strategy which allowed Bell eventually to control his own supplies of coal, ironstone, and limestone—all carried on railways free of freight charges set by his rivals.

Jackson's activities later bankrupted him, and Bell

Sir (Isaac) Lowthian Bell, first baronet (1816–1904), by Elliott & Fry, 1880

bought out certain of his colliery properties. In the aftermath Jackson's railway interests (he had also promoted the West Hartlepool Harbour and Railway Company) were acquired by the North Eastern Railway (NER). The latter also negotiated for the purchase of the Cleveland Railway and in 1865 Bell became an NER director, a post he held until his death. From 1895 until 1904 Bell was deputy chairman of the company. He was not the only industrialist on the NER board, though he was one of the most influential. He ensured that the local ironmasters were well protected by a sliding scale of rates; and the NER also funded attempts at the Bell ironworks to rid Cleveland iron of the phosphorus which prevented its use in the manufacture of rails and other products. Bell also influenced policy making at the NER with a wide-ranging series of policy papers on matters as diverse as operating costs and investment in new technology. These papers are said to have been 'remarkable for the statistical concepts employed, for the lucidity of analysis and above all for their bearing on the question of costs, the most pressing business problem of the organisation at that time' (DBB).

In the face of competition from steel, the demand for iron inevitably weakened after the late 1870s. In 1889 Bell therefore erected open-hearth furnaces at Clarence and began utilizing Cleveland pig iron for the manufacture of steel. The business was competently launched, but competition in the UK steel industry was by now keen, and an ageing Bell and his managers were too old to pioneer steel technology as successfully as they had iron. In 1899, therefore—when Bells became a public company—the more

dynamic neighbouring steel firm of Dorman Long took a half share. In 1902 the latter acquired Bells' remaining ordinary shares in exchange for 225,000 shares in Dormans and the merger was complete. Bells survived as a separate iron and steel firm through the First World War, but the Clarence works was to close in the inter-war depression, when the Dorman empire fell on hard times. Bell's eldest son, (Thomas) Hugh Bell (1844–1931), who succeeded to the baronetcy, was later associated with Dorman Long.

Bell's reputation depended not only on his career as a mostly successful company manager. For over a quarter of a century he was the unchallenged spokesman for the north-eastern iron industry, and was recognized as one of the 'fathers' of the trade. He was also a respected scientist who was recognized as a world authority on blast-furnace technology. The way in which he combined business and science was unusual in Victorian Britain: nevertheless, his abilities as chemist, mineralogist, and metallurgist challenge the view that the economy at that time was run only by empiricists. His principal works, which combined technical knowledge with international comparative surveys, can still be read with profit. They include: *The Principles of the Manufacture of Iron and Steel* (1884); *The Iron Trade of the United Kingdom* (1886); *The Chemical Phenomena of Iron Smelting* (1872); *Notes on a Visit to Coal and Iron Mines and Ironworks in the United States* (1875); *Report on the iron manufacture of the United States of America, and a comparison ... with ... Great Britain* (1877). His writings, when they discussed non-technical matters, espoused a guardedly optimistic view of British industry. He was anti-protectionist, committed to competitive wage rates, and—not surprisingly—a promoter of attempts to improve the scientific base of British industry.

Bell's sensitivity to Britain's declining competitive standing (nurtured by frequent trips abroad, especially to the USA) and his commitment to technology, management, and labour relations led logically to his strong support for more business and technical organizations. He helped to create the British Iron Trade Association in 1875 (and became its first president) and was a key instigator in the formation in 1869 of the Iron and Steel Institute. He was the third president of the latter in 1873, when the institute held its first meeting overseas. Typically, Bell gave his presidential address in French. In the following year, when he was again president, he was the first recipient of the Bessemer gold medal. He was also involved with the Institute of Mining Engineers and was its president in the year of his death. Closer to home, he was an active supporter of Armstrong College at Newcastle.

Besides receiving awards from technical societies (such as the Albert medal of the Society of Arts in 1900), Bell was also elected FRS in 1875 and in the 1880s and 1890s he accepted a string of honorary degrees. He was twice mayor of Newcastle and was deputy lieutenant and high sheriff for the county of Durham. A liberal in politics, he eventually became MP for Hartlepool in 1875, but took little part in Commons life. He was a member of the Légion d'honneur (1878) and, on Gladstone's nomination, he received a baronetcy in 1885. Florence *Bell was his daughter-in-law and Gertrude *Bell was his granddaughter.

In his later years Bell looked every inch the typical Victorian middle-class industrialist: broad-shouldered, heavily bearded, eminently worthy. His passionate belief in the application of science to industry, however, did mark him out as someone unusual among his contemporaries. His moderation and lucidity, and his rigid adherence to the evidence and scientific facts, were recognized as being among his chief qualities. His contemporaries had no doubts about his standing and spoke of him having 'made a name that will live in history with those of Bessemer, Siemens and others ... who devoted so large a portion of their careers to the scientific study of the manufacture of iron and steel' (*North-Eastern Daily Gazette*). Yet Bell lacked the flash of genius or egotism that was apparent in men such as Bessemer and Siemens; and that may explain why his historical profile has always seemed less prominent than that of the other great Victorian engineers. It was perhaps typical of Bell that, despite his massive researches into separating phosphorus from pig iron, the technical problem was eventually solved by Sidney Gilchrist Thomas, who had started his career as a police court clerk. It was typical, too, that such was Bell's generosity of spirit that he was the first to hail Thomas's success in pre-empting him.

Active until the end, Sir Lowthian Bell died at his home, Rounton Grange, Rounton, Northallerton, North Riding of Yorkshire, on 20 December 1904. He was buried at Rounton on 23 December.   GEOFFREY TWEEDALE

Sources C. Wilson, 'Bell, Sir Isaac Lowthian', *DBB* · *The Engineer* (23 Dec 1904) · *Engineering* (23 Dec 1904) · *North-Eastern Daily Gazette* (20 Dec 1904) · D. L. Burn, *The economic history of steelmaking, 1867–1939* (1940) · J. C. Carr and W. Taplin, *History of the British steel industry* (1962) · R. J. Irving, *The North Eastern Railway Company, 1870–1914: an economic history* (1976) · G. Jones, 'A description of Messrs Bell Brothers' blast furnaces from 1844–1908', *Journal of the Iron and Steel Institute*, 77 (1908) · CGPLA Eng. & Wales (1905) · DNB
Archives BLPES, Bell Bros. pay books · British Steel Records Centre northern region, Middlesbrough, Bell Bros. MSS | British Steel Records Centre northern region, Middlesbrough, Dorman Long MSS · Cleveland Archives, Middlesbrough, Dorman Long MSS · U. Durham L., Havard MSS · U. Durham L., letters to Lord Carlisle · U. Durham L., letters to third Earl Grey · U. Newcastle, Robinson L., letters to Sir Walter Trevelyan
Likenesses H. T. Wells, oils, 1865; in possession of Lord Sheffield in 1912 · Elliott & Fry, photograph, 1880, NPG [*see illus.*] · H. T. Wells, oils, 1894, Corporation of Middlesbrough; replica, in possession of Sir Hugh Bell in 1912 · F. Bramley, portrait, North Eastern Railway Company, York · W. Richmond, oils; replica, in possession of Sir Hugh Bell in 1912
Wealth at death £768,676 7s. 2d.: probate, 30 Jan 1905, CGPLA Eng. & Wales

Bell [*née* Hamilton], **Maria**, **Lady Bell** (1755–1825), painter and sculptor, was born on 26 December 1755 in Chelsea, Middlesex, and baptized on 28 December at St Martin-in-the-Fields, Westminster, the daughter of William Hamilton, an architect of Scottish descent, and his wife, Sarah. Maria was the pupil of her brother, William *Hamilton

RA, and received some instruction from Sir Joshua Reynolds, whose pictures she copied. These copies, principally of celebrated ladies, were noted to be 'the more valuable because they retain their fine colouring of which time has deprived the originals' (*GM*). Her copy of Reynolds's portrait of Sheridan is said to be the only one permitted to be taken. She also copied the works of Rubens at Carlton House: her *Holy Family* was highly commended. Between 1807 and 1820 she exhibited first at the British Institution in 1807 and 1809, and at the Royal Academy as Mrs Bell between 1816 and 1820, six portraits, among them, in 1816, one of Sir Matthew Wood, bt, lord mayor of London, and another of her husband, possibly that engraved by William Dickinson. Her self-portrait was reproduced in mezzotint by George Clint. She had married c.1808 Thomas Bell (d. 1824), sheriff of Middlesex, who was knighted in 1816. Of the two busts she exhibited at the Royal Academy in 1819, one was of her husband. He was entered in the poll book (1818) as 'Sir T. Bell, 69 Dean Street, Knight'. Local directories refer to a Sir Thomas Bell, merchant, of 18 St Swithin's Lane, City of London. Sir Thomas Bell of Dean Street died aged seventy-three and was buried according to his wishes, set out in his will, on 18 February 1824 in St Dunstan, Cranford, Middlesex. Lady Bell was entered in Dean Street ratebooks after Sir Thomas's death as owing £100 rates in 1824. In his will, Sir Thomas Bell bequeathed property to his 'dear wife Katherine Bell'. The burial register at St Dunstan, Cranford, records the burial, on 18 March 1825, of Lady Catharine (*sic*) Bell of St Anne, Soho. In the absence of evidence to the contrary, it is assumed that Katherine Bell, named in his will as wife and beneficiary, was identical to Maria Bell. Reference in his will to his son 'Henry Hamilton Martin Bell', would appear to confirm that this Sir Thomas Bell was the spouse of Maria Bell, *née* Hamilton. Lady Bell died in London at her home, 47 Dean Street, Soho, on 9 March 1825.   ANNETTE PEACH

Sources GM, 1st ser., 95/1 (1825), 570 · Waterhouse, *18c painters* · Redgrave, *Artists* · Graves, *RA exhibitors* · Graves, *Brit. Inst.* · R. Gunnis, *Dictionary of British sculptors, 1660–1851* (1953); new edn (1968) · G. Hamilton, *A history of the house of Hamilton* (1933), 933 · N&Q, 156 (1929), 10, 52 · *Royal Kalendar* (1816) · A. Hughes, *List of sheriffs for England and Wales: from the earliest times to AD 1831*, PRO (1898); repr. (New York, 1963) · burial register, St Dunstan, Cranford, Middlesex · will of Sir Thomas Bell, PRO, PROB 11/1682, fols. 282v–283r
Likenesses G. Clint, mezzotint, exh. RA 1806? (after self-portrait by M. Bell), BM · E. Scriven, stipple, pubd 1821 (after miniature by W. S. Lethbridge), NPG · W. S. Lethbridge, miniature

Bell, Patrick (1799–1869), Church of Scotland minister and inventor of agricultural machinery, was born in April 1799 at mid-Leoch, in the parish of Auchterhouse, a few miles north-west of Dundee. He was one of at least two sons of George Bell, a tenant farmer at mid-Leoch, and his wife, Margaret Lunan. He studied at the University of St Andrews with a view to going into the church; while there he turned his attention to the design of a reaping machine, prompted by seeing the heavy toil of workers at harvest on his father's farm. In 1827 he made a working model of a reaping machine, and the following year he built a full-

Patrick Bell (1799–1869), by unknown engraver, pubd 1868 (after E. Strachan)

sized version which was tested successfully on the farm occupied by his brother, George. This machine was exhibited to the Highland and Agricultural Society in 1828–9, and a premium of £50 was awarded.

A number of machines were built to Bell's basic design during the few years following, and they were reported to have achieved some success on farms in lowland Scotland. Some machines also went overseas, to Australia, America, and Poland. By the late 1830s, interest in Bell's machines, and in reaping machines generally, had subsided. Bell never took out a patent for his reaper, because he wished to make it available. As he came to realize later, this policy had the drawback that he was unable to control the standards of manufacture. The indifferent quality of many machines cannot have encouraged people to take up Bell's invention.

The Great Exhibition of 1851 saw the introduction to Britain of reaping machines made in the United States of America, principally those designed by Cyrus Hall McCormick and Obed Hussey. These, especially McCormick's, had many similarities with Bell's and other early reaping machines, notably that made by John Common in 1812. There has been debate ever since about whether the American machines derived their designs from the British ones. The evidence is inconclusive but does not, in any case, diminish the place of Patrick Bell as one of the pioneers in the development of mechanical harvesting.

Bell was ordained in the Church of Scotland in 1843, and became minister of the parish of Carmyllie, Arbroath; he served there until his death. He was married to Jane Lawson. As a recognition of his services to agriculture he was presented by the Highland Society with £1000 and a

piece of plate, subscribed for by the farmers of Scotland and others. He also had conferred on him the honorary degree of LLD by the University of St Andrews. Bell died from kidney disease on 22 April 1869 at the manse, Carmyllie. He was survived by his wife.

JONATHAN BROWN

Sources P. Bell, 'Some account of Bell's reaping machine', *Journal of Agriculture* (Jan 1854), 185–204 · 'On the use and advantages of a reaping machine', *Quarterly Journal of Agriculture*, 1 (1828–9) · 'On the working of Bell's reaping machine', *Quarterly Journal of Agriculture*, 4 (1832–4) · G. E. Fussell, *The farmer's tools* (1952) · *Engineering* (30 April 1869) · d. cert.
Archives U. Aberdeen, Canadian journals
Likenesses wood-engraving, pubd 1868 (after photograph by E. Strachan), NPG; repro. in *ILN* (1868) [*see illus.*]

Bell, Philip (*fl.* 1627–1650), colonial governor, was probably born in England, but nothing is known of the date or place of his birth, his family, his education, or his early career. His first documented appearance is in 1627, when he became governor of the island of Bermuda, on which he owned several plantations. In July 1641 he arrived in Barbados bearing a commission as the island's governor signed by the colony's proprietor, James Hay, third earl of Carlisle. During his tenure as governor Bell carried out a programme of administrative reforms which consolidated and expanded the island's executive and judicial systems, yielding a solid political and economic structure upon which Barbados's later prosperity flourished.

Under Bell's rule the elected assembly gained the power to initiate legislation; previously it had debated local issues, but lacked the legislative authority through which to deal with them. Bell also reorganized the colony's militia and levied a tax on landholdings in order to pay for its upkeep. So effective were these measures that by the late 1640s the visiting commentator Richard Ligon claimed that Barbados's armed forces consisted of '10,000 foot, as good men and as resolute as any in the world and a 1,000 good horse' (Ligon, 100). Bell did not neglect the issue of religion: he set up vestries, encouraged the building of churches, made church attendance mandatory for all residents, and in 1647 gained the assembly's approval of an act forbidding heterodoxy. Perhaps most important, in a small island with limited arable land, Bell settled the issue of land tenure by encouraging the assembly to make legislation on this subject a priority. In 1643 the legislature passed a series of acts which settled outstanding questions regarding estates and titles.

Although his administrative and legal reforms encouraged that Bell 'be styled the Barbadian Justinian' (Poyer, 36), his administration was undermined by the outbreak of the English civil wars. Bell attempted to keep peace in Barbados by adopting a posture of neutrality and discouraging faction among the assemblymen by giving all a stake in local administration, which he facilitated by unilaterally shrugging off imperial control and moving towards complete self-government. Bell attempted to minimize conflict by mandating that 'whoever nam'd the word "Roundhead" or "Cavalier" should give to all those that heard him a shot and a Turkey' (Ligon, 57), but after

1648, when soldiers of both king and parliament migrated to Barbados, he was unable to maintain order in the face of a persistent campaign of plots, banishments, and rebellions which each side carried out against the other. In 1650 the Barbadian royalists defeated the local parliamentarians and banished them from the island, allowing Charles II to annul the earl of Carlisle's patent and assume direct control of Barbados. The king sent Francis, Lord Willoughby, to serve as Barbados's first royal governor, at which time Bell departed the island for Britain. Nothing is known of his later years or of the date or place of his death.   NATALIE ZACEK

Sources R. Tree, *A history of Barbados* (1972) · F. G. Spurdle, *Early West Indian government* [1962] · H. McD. Beckles, *A history of Barbados* (1990) · F. A. Hoyos, *Barbados: a history from the Amerindians to independence* (1978) · P. F. Campbell, *Some early Barbadian history* (1993) · V. T. Harlow, *A history of Barbados, 1625–1685* (1926) · J. Poyer, *The history of Barbados* (1808) · R. S. Dunn, *Sugar and slaves: the rise of the planter class in the English West Indies, 1624–1713* (1972) · J. Kennedy, *Island of devils: Bermuda under the Somers Island Company, 1609–1685* (1972) · R. Ligon, *A true and exact history of the island of Barbados* (1657)

Bell, Quentin Claudian Stephen (1910–1996), art historian and potter, was born into the heart of the Bloomsbury group on 19 August 1910, the younger son of (Arthur) Clive Heward *Bell (1881–1964), art critic, and his wife, Vanessa *Bell (1879–1961), painter, and the daughter of Sir Leslie *Stephen. Brought up at 46 Gordon Square (where he was born) and, during school holidays, at the house his parents leased at Charleston in Sussex, he was educated at Peterborough Lodge in Swiss Cottage, London, and at Leighton Park School, the Quaker boarding-school in Reading. In contrast to his brother Julian Heward *Bell, he left school at the age of seventeen intending to become a painter. Following a tour of central European galleries with Roger Fry, he spent periods of time in both Paris and Rome.

In 1933 Bell contracted chest infections which led to seven months in a sanatorium in Switzerland (leaving him with a lifelong aversion to the Alps) followed by convalescence near Monaco, where he began a history of the principality. In 1935 he was again painting in Rome, and his collages were exhibited at the Mayor Gallery. But later that year he decided to become a potter rather than a painter and enrolled himself at Burslem School of Art. While living in Stoke-on-Trent he was also active in the affairs of the local Labour Party. Two years later he returned to Charleston, installed a kiln, and continued his political activities both in Sussex and with the Artists' International Association. On the outbreak of the Second World War he would have joined up, but was prevented from doing so on account of his medical history. Instead he worked as a labourer on Maynard Keynes's farm at Tilton in Sussex and helped his mother and Duncan Grant with the mural decorations of Berwick church, before being given a job in the political warfare department of the Foreign Office by David Garnett.

In 1947 Bell published his first major book, *On Human Finery*, a pioneering study of the history of fashion, much influenced by the writings of Thorstein Veblen. Following his marriage on 16 February 1952 to (Anne) Olivier

Quentin Claudian Stephen Bell (1910–1996), by Duncan Fraser, 1982 [in his pottery at Cobbe Place]

Popham, art historian, and the daughter of Arthur Ewart *Popham, keeper of prints and drawings at the British Museum, he needed an income and was appointed to a senior lectureship at King's College, Newcastle upon Tyne, by his friend Lawrence Gowing. In 1959 he and his family—including three young children, Julian, Virginia, and Cressida—moved to Leeds, where he was a lecturer in the department of fine art and, from 1962 to 1967, its inaugural professor. In 1963 he published a short study of Ruskin and *The Schools of Design*, a scholarly study of the origins of the national system of art education. In 1964 he was appointed Slade professor of fine art at Oxford University and, in 1965, Ferens professor of fine art at Hull. He was a racy lecturer with a particular interest in Victorian painting.

In 1967 Bell returned south to Sussex to become professor of the history and theory of art at Sussex University and bought a large house under the downs, close to Charleston. The move coincided with an invitation to write the biography of his aunt Virginia Woolf. From this point onwards he was increasingly involved in the revival of public interest in Bloomsbury. He published a succinct analysis of the group in 1968, and his biography of Virginia Woolf was published in two volumes in 1972 to great acclaim.

After retiring from his post at Sussex in 1975, Bell was able to spend more time and energy on his pottery. In 1985 he and his wife, Olivier, moved to a smaller house next door to the park in Firle and each morning he would wake up early and disappear to his kiln, only emerging for gin and ginger beer in the evening. He undertook a mixture of work, some rough, painted plates and mugs, which he saw as belonging to an artisan tradition, but also more ambitious ceramic sculpture. Neither style fitted comfortably within the work of contemporaries, as his pots were too utilitarian to be regarded as art and his ceramic sculpture too conventionally figurative. But this in no way deterred him from turning out a great amount of work which was both vigorous and affordable, a crossover between the Omega workshop and folk art.

By the 1980s Bell had very much inherited the mantle of

Bloomsbury and was a sage-like figure with a white beard and a humorous, slightly quizzical air, dispensing information and advice to the many visiting academics who came to research the lives of his family. He was particularly instrumental in establishing the Charleston Trust, which was responsible for saving his mother's house, but he also found time to write a pseudo-Victorian novella, *The Brandon Papers* (1985), and to collect his essays and lectures in *Bad Art* (1989). In the 1990s he embarked on his autobiography, but discovered that he was much better at writing about others than about himself. In the end it emerged as a series of character sketches, *Elders and Betters* (1995), which revealed his own character only intermittently in a series of dry asides. Gradually weakened by ill health, he died at his home, 81 Heighton Street, Firle, Sussex, on 16 December 1996. He was survived by his wife, Olivier, and their three children.   CHARLES SAUMAREZ SMITH

Sources *The Times* (18 Dec 1996) · *The Independent* (18 Dec 1996) · *Daily Telegraph* (18 Dec 1996) · *The Guardian* (18 Dec 1996) · Q. Bell, 'An autobiographical essay', *Bad art* (1989), 216–31 · Q. Bell, *Elders and betters* (1995) · N. Lynton and others, *Quentin Bell: a man of many arts* (1999) · *WWW* · personal knowledge (2004) · private information (2004) · b. cert. · m. cert. · d. cert.

Archives Henry Moore Institute, Leeds, papers relating to *The Dreamer* · U. Sussex Library, MS of biography of Virginia Woolf with some corresp. | King's AC Cam., corresp. with J. H. Bell · U. Sussex Library, corresp. with L. Woolf | SOUND BL NSA, documentary recordings · BL NSA, performance recordings

Likenesses D. Fraser, photograph, 1982, NPG [*see illus.*] · photograph, repro. in *The Times* · photograph, repro. in *The Independent* · photograph, repro. in *Daily Telegraph* · photograph, repro. in *The Guardian* · photographs, repro. in Bell, *Elders and betters*

Wealth at death under £180,000: probate, 2 April 1997, *CGPLA Eng. & Wales*

Bell, Richard (*b. c.*1410, *d.* in or after 1495), bishop of Carlisle, was almost certainly a native of Durham, where he entered the religious life in 1426 or early 1427. Five years later Bell was sent to Durham College, Oxford, where he held office as one of the two college bursars between Michaelmas 1435 and Michaelmas 1440. Much more surprising was Bell's collation (on 13 February 1441) to the small alien priory of Holy Trinity, York, by Henry VI. This curious episode in Bell's early career would not have been possible without the backing of Henry Percy, second earl of Northumberland (*d.* 1455), and other northern magnates. In the event the Benedictine monks of Holy Trinity, York, fought so vigorous a campaign against Bell's claims to be their prior that he was forced to withdraw and seek readmission to Durham Cathedral priory in December 1443.

Immediately afterwards Bell rapidly rose to influential office within his community. Steward of the prior's hospice from 1443 to 1447, and monastic almoner from 1447 to 1450, he returned to Oxford as warden of Durham College between 1450 and 1453, a period during which he secured a bachelor's degree in theology. Although several manuscripts that once formed part of Richard Bell's personal library still survive, it was his administrative rather than scholastic talents that led to his recall to the Durham cloister in 1453, where he went on to hold the obediences

Richard Bell (*b. c.*1410, *d.* in or after 1495), memorial brass

of hostillar, terrar, and sub-prior before declaring himself a candidate for the prior's office on the resignation of William Ebchester in 1456. On 25 October, after an exceptionally divisive electoral contest, Bell was defeated by John Burnby, who received thirty-eight votes as opposed to his own twenty-five. From 1457 to 1464 Bell accordingly found himself in comparative and no doubt involuntary seclusion as prior of Durham's cell at Finchale. The sudden death of Prior Burnby on 17 October 1464 immediately transformed Bell's future prospects. Five weeks later he was elected prior of Durham, an office he held with considerable success for fourteen years. On the abundant evidence for his priorate, particularly his small register or letter-book, Bell was a highly vigorous superior of his house, and by 1478 seems to have restored his monastery to much greater prosperity than it had enjoyed when he became prior. His most ambitious initiative was to inaugurate a complete reconstruction of the central tower of Durham Cathedral.

As prior of Durham between 1464 and 1478, Richard Bell owed much of his reputation to the skill with which he defended his house amid national political instability and the feuds of many of the northern magnates and gentry. By 1474, if not earlier, the prior had accordingly won the favour of Richard, duke of Gloucester (the future Richard III), with whose powerful support he finally succeeded in securing the bishopric for which he was already intriguing at the curia. On 11 February 1478 Bell's ambitions were at last rewarded by papal provision to the episcopate of Carlisle, although his extraordinary attempt to continue to hold the priorate of Durham *in commendam* with his new and impoverished bishopric was successfully resisted by his former and now outraged community. He was the last member of the medieval community of St Cuthbert to become a bishop. Unfortunately the evidence for Bell's seventeen-year tenure of the see of Carlisle is much less abundant than that for most earlier stages of his career. Already aged about seventy when he was finally enthroned in Carlisle Cathedral in 1480, he played a progressively less significant role in northern political affairs after that date. However, the surviving accounts of his receivers-general give some impression of his severe financial problems, of his concern with diocesan administration, of his extensive building operations at his palace of Rose Castle, and even of his diet. It was no doubt due to extreme old age that Bell resigned his see (the only bishop of Carlisle to do so between 1246 and 1946) on 4 September 1495. The place and the date of his death remain obscure, unrecorded even in the inscription around his magnificent memorial brass on the floor of the cathedral choir at Carlisle.   R. B. DOBSON

Sources Muniments, Dean and Chapter of Durham, Registrum 3, 4 · Muniments, Dean and Chapter of Durham, Registrum parvum 4 · Muniments, Dean and Chapter of Durham, Obedientiary account rolls, 1432–1478 · Episcopal officers' accounts, 1478–94, Cumbria AS, DRC/2, 13–21 · R. B. Dobson, 'Richard Bell, prior of Durham (1464–78) and bishop of Carlisle (1478–95)', *Transactions of the Cumberland and Westmorland Antiquarian and Archaeological Society*, new ser., 65 (1965), 182–221 · R. B. Dobson, *Durham Priory, 1400–1450*, Cambridge Studies in Medieval Life and Thought, 3rd ser., 6 (1973), 59, 61, 76–7, 119, 188, 202, 235, 311 · H. Summerson, *Medieval Carlisle: the city and the borders from the late eleventh to the mid-sixteenth century*, 2, Cumberland and Westmorland Antiquarian and Archaeological Society, extra ser., 25 (1993), 463, 560, 580, 582, 586, 591–4, 602, 608, 616–17, 672, 678 · Emden, *Oxf.* · C. M. L. Bouch, *Prelates and people of the lake counties: a history of the diocese of Carlisle, 1133–1933* (1948), 128–32 · J. Wilson, *Rose Castle* (1912), 75, 86, 125–6, 212–19 · B. Colgrave, 'The St Cuthbert paintings on the Carlisle Cathedral stalls', *Burlington Magazine*, 73 (1938), 16–21

Archives Cumbria AS, episcopal officers' accounts, DRC/2, 13–21 · Muniments, Dean and Chapter of Durham, Obedientiary account rolls; Registrum 3, 4; registrum parvum 4

Likenesses memorial brass, Carlisle Cathedral, Cumbria [*see illus.*]

Richard Bell (1859–1930), by Sir Benjamin Stone, 1903

Bell, Richard (1859–1930), trade union leader and politician, was born at Penderyn, Glamorgan, on 29 November 1859, the son of Charles Bell, a quarryman, and his wife, Ann (*née* Thomas). As a young boy Bell was shocked by the death of his uncle, killed in a quarry accident while working alongside his father, who narrowly escaped injury in an attempt to rescue him. Bell's father moved soon afterwards to Merthyr Tudful, where he became a policeman. Bell learned from his father both the dangers met with in industrial employment and the need for a strict observance of the law. A fluent Welsh speaker, Bell confessed that he had received no more than a perfunctory education up to the age of twelve in church and national schools.

Bell's first job was as an office boy at the Cyfarthfa iron works at Merthyr Tudful, where he graduated to clerk before moving on to become foreman in the boiler department of a steel-rail mill. He switched to the Great Western Railway in 1876, aiming to become an engine driver. Working as shunter, guard, and then as head goods guard at Pontypool Road, he experienced the great dangers associated with railway employment: statistics reveal that, as late as 1899, 1 in every 197 shunters employed in the UK was killed and 1 in 12 injured annually. Bell saw strong trade union organization as the remedy, and joined the Amalgamated Society of Railway Servants (ASRS) in 1881. With his dominant and persuasive personality he quickly recruited many of his fellow workers into the union. The railway company reacted by posting him to Carn Brea in a remote part of Cornwall. To the union this victimization was one of the qualifications for Bell's appointment as organizer in 1892. From this vantage point his influence at head office rapidly increased and when in 1897 the health of Edward Harford, his predecessor in office, broke down he was chosen by the executive to stand in; he was confirmed as general secretary by a vote of the membership in June 1898.

In the next twelve years the organization of the union's head office greatly improved under the industrious and businesslike leadership of Bell. The ASRS gained the reputation of being one of the most efficiently run unions in the country. On the other hand, George Alcock, a trustee of the union who worked under Bell's direction, declared that 'His way was *the* way. He had the touch of the autocrat' (Alcock, 403). As the union's executive became increasingly permeated by socialists in the 1900s, confrontations with the general secretary increased in frequency. On 5 October 1898 the annual general meeting of the union resolved that the ASRS should be directly represented in parliament by the general secretary, who was to be independent of both the Conservative and the Liberal Party. In the general election of October 1900 Bell was elected as junior member of the two-member constituency of Derby. However, both the Derby Trades Council and the ASRS executive insisted on his standing as a Labour candidate, though he would have been happier as a Liberal. He worked harmoniously with Sir Thomas Roe, the Liberal senior member for Derby, and was welcomed on the Liberal benches in the Commons, while Keir Hardie, the only other Labour member elected in October 1900, sat 'below the gangway'.

In his ten years in the Commons, Bell's main concern was to expose the excessive hours worked by railwaymen and to press the president of the Board of Trade to use the powers given to him under the Railways (Prevention of Accidents) Act of 1900. However, following the strong lead given by Samuel Laing MP, chairman of the London, Brighton and South Coast Railway from 1848, railway company directors who were members of parliament argued that recognition of trade unions would impair operational discipline. Unquestioning obedience to superiors' orders was imperative for the safe working of railways. Despite this opposition, Bell fought to improve the working conditions of all railway staff who handled goods traffic. He was also a strong advocate of conciliation and arbitration for the settlement of industrial disputes. Bell's most notable achievement in industrial relations was to persuade his union executive to accept in August 1897 the arbitration award of Lord James of Hereford for the settlement of the dispute on the North Eastern Railway. He also served on the TUC parliamentary committee in 1899 and from 1902 to 1909, and was chairman of the TUC in 1903–4.

During the decade in which Bell was an MP his relationship with his union and with the Labour Representation Committee (LRC), which Thomas Steels and James Holmes, distinguished ASRS members, had helped to set up in February 1900, and which he chaired in 1902–3, became increasingly strained. His habit of sending telegrams in support of Liberal candidates fighting Labour men, as at the Norwich by-election in January 1904; his opposition to the political levy on trade union members; his disagreement with his own union on aspects of the Taff Vale (1901) and Osborne (1909) judgments; and his refusal to sign the constitution of the Labour Party, were indicative of a growing rift. The LRC deselected him from the Derby candidature before the general election of 1906 and he resigned both his parliamentary seat and his post of general secretary of the ASRS in 1909.

During his years in parliament Bell had many contacts with officials of the Board of Trade, and this facilitated his holding a post in that department after he ceased to be an MP. From 1910 until he reached retirement age in 1920 Bell was employed as a senior civil servant in the board's employment exchange branch in London. He was also active locally at Southgate where he had taken up residence, being elected to its urban district council in 1922 and serving as its chairman from 1925 to 1926. Bell was married three times and had three sons and five daughters. He married Annie Halten on 3 August 1878, and then Esther Ann Woozley on 25 September 1895. His third wife, whose name is unknown, outlived him. Bell died of cerebral thrombosis on 1 May 1930 at his home, 19 Derwent Road, Palmers Green, and was buried in Southgate cemetery alongside his successor as general secretary of the ASRS, J. E. Williams.   PHILIP S. BAGWELL

Sources D. E. Martin, 'Bell, Richard', *DLB*, vol. 2 · F. Bealey and H. Pelling, *Labour and politics, 1900–1906: a history of the Labour Representation Committee* (1958) · P. S. Gupta, 'Railway trade unionism in Great Britain, c.1880–1900', *Economic History Review*, 2nd ser., 19 (1966), 124–53 · G. W. Alcock, *Fifty years of railway trade unionism* (1922) · P. S. Bagwell, *The railwaymen: the history of the National Union of Railwaymen*, [1] (1963) · G. Alderman, *The railway interest* (1973) · W. Collison, *The apostle of free labour* (1913) · C. Benn, *Keir Hardie* (1992) · D. Marquand, *Ramsay MacDonald* (1977) · *Railway Review* (1897–1910) [1–15 October annually] · *Railway Review* (14 Jan 1930) · *Palmers Green and Southgate Gazette* (9 May 1930) · 'Royal commission on the railway conciliation scheme of 1907', *Parl. papers* (1912–13), vol. 45, Cd 6014 · decisions of the AGM, Oct 1898, U. Warwick Mod. RC, ASRS MSS, resolution 61, p. 11 · b. cert. · d. cert.

Archives Labour History Archive and Study Centre, Manchester, papers | U. Warwick Mod. RC, corresp. with ITWF; letters and papers relating to Taff Vale case · U. Warwick Mod. RC, Labour Party records and papers of ASRS/NUR

Likenesses B. Stone, photograph, 1903, NPG [see illus.] · photograph, repro. in Bagwell, *The railwaymen*, facing p. 320

Wealth at death £4633 16s. 10d.: probate, 26 June 1930, CGPLA Eng. & Wales

Bell, Sir Robert (d. 1577), judge and speaker of the House of Commons, is of unknown parentage and origins, although he may have come from a Norfolk or Yorkshire family. He was possibly educated at Cambridge and certainly at the Middle Temple, where he was a bencher, autumn reader in 1565, and Lent reader in 1572. He was married three times: first, to Mary, daughter of Anthony Chester; second, following Mary's death, to Elizabeth, widowed daughter-in-law of Sir Edmund Anderson, lord chief justice of common pleas; and on 15 October 1559, after Elizabeth's death, to Dorothy, daughter and coheir of Edward Beaupré. By his third marriage he acquired Beaupré Manor in Upwell and Outwell, Norfolk, and had four sons—Edmund, Robert, Synolphus, and Philip—and three daughters—Dorothy, Mary, and Frances.

Bell was active in both law and local administration. He was appointed counsel to King's Lynn (1560) and its recorder (from 1561). In 1563–4 he became counsel for life and commissioner of the peace for Yarmouth. Between 1564 and his death he was on various commissions in Norfolk: of the peace (from 1564), oyer and terminer, sewers, grain, and musters; he was also appointed to commissions to investigate a range of misdemeanours and controversies, and conduct inquisitions post mortem. He was crown counsel at the Norwich assizes in 1570, in the trial of those charged with instigating an uprising in support of the duke of Norfolk. In April 1577 he was named, with others, for a special visitation of Oxford University. Bell acquired a contemporary reputation, figuring in the reports of James Dyer and Edmund Plowden and being variously described by William Camden as 'a grave man, and famous for his knowledge in the law' (Camden, *Historie*, bk 2.86) and as a lawyer 'of great renowne' (Camden, *Annales*, bk 1.130).

In March 1559 Bell appeared at the bar of the House of Commons as counsel for patentees of the bishop of Winchester's lands who were promoting a bill to protect their patents. Then in 1563, 1571, and 1572 he was regularly returned to the Commons for King's Lynn. Although he does not figure in the recorded Commons' proceedings in 1563, he was busily engaged in the parliamentary search for a settled succession during the second session in 1566. He was active in debate, with lengthy arguments in favour of a bicameral petition to the queen and the need for a royal answer; he was also one of the Commons' spokesmen who put its case to the Lords. He was the target of the queen's anger when she addressed a joint delegation on 5 November. She referred to 'those unbridled persons' in the Commons, in particular 'Mr. Bell with his complices'. William Cecil too regarded him as a leading parliamentary nuisance.

In the parliament of 1571 Bell once again presented the image of a trouble-maker. He made provocative attacks on promoters and royal purveyors and, on the second occasion, sought redress during a debate on supply. Peter Wentworth later recalled that Bell was sent for by the privy council and 'so hardly dealt with that he came into the House with such an amazed countenance that ... for 10, 12 or 16 days there was not one of the House that durst deal in any matter of importance' (Hartley, 1.436). He was cautious thereafter, but still very active, speaking on the usury and resident burgesses bills and being named to fourteen bill committees and four joint conferences.

Despite royal and conciliar censures in 1566 and 1571 Bell was approved by Elizabeth as Commons' speaker in 1572. He had a difficult managerial task in a session dominated by a parliamentary search for the execution of the already condemned duke of Norfolk and the enactment of the harshest possible measures against Mary, queen of Scots. Throughout he was a model of circumspection: in his opening address, a lawyer's piece larded with legal precedent; in his careful transmission of royal messages and his preference that attempts to persuade a reluctant queen should be by written arguments rather than by his spoken word; and in his closing address, when his appeal to her to execute speedily the bill against Mary, passed by both houses, was sustained and accompanied by classical precedents, one of Æsop's fables, and glowing expressions of love and devotion. He was speaker again when the prorogued parliament was recalled in 1576, for the purpose of a subsidy. On 21 or 22 January 1577 he was knighted, and on 24 January was created serjeant-at-law and appointed chief baron of the exchequer. That summer, during the Oxford assizes, he presided at the trial of Rowland Jenke, 'an impudent talker ... for speaking injurious words against the Queen'. Bell 'and about three

hundreth more' were taken ill from 'the stink, whether of the prisoners or the prison' (Camden, *Annales*, bk 2.376). He added a codicil to his will on 26 July 1577, and died shortly afterwards at Leominster, where he was buried.

MICHAEL A. R. GRAVES

Sources T. E. Hartley, ed., *Proceedings in the parliaments of Elizabeth I*, 1 (1981) · *JHC*, 1 (1547–1628) · HoP, *Commons, 1558–1603* · Cooper, *Ath. Cantab.*, vol. 1 · Foss, *Judges* · *CPR, 1563–78* · W. Camden, *Annales: the true and royall history of the famous Empresse Elizabeth*, trans. A. Darcie (1625) · Baker, *Serjeants* · *Calendar of the manuscripts of the most hon. the marquis of Salisbury*, 1, HMC, 9 (1883) · J. Strype, *Annals of the Reformation and establishment of religion ... during Queen Elizabeth's happy reign*, new edn, 1–2 (1824) · *DNB* · will, PRO, PROB 11/59, sig. 35 · W. Camden, *The historie of the most renowned and victorious princesse Elizabeth*, trans. R. N. [R. Norton] (1630)

Likenesses W. C. Edwards, line engraving (after crayon drawing), BM, NPG · portrait; formerly in possession of the Misses Bell of North Runcton, 1885 · portrait; formerly in possession of the Revd H. Creed of Mellis, 1885

Bell, Robert (*c*.1760–1816), lawyer and jurist, was born in Edinburgh, the eldest of the six children of the Revd William Bell (1704–1779), Scottish Episcopal minister in Edinburgh, and Margaret Morrice, his second wife. Little is known of Bell's early life or schooling, though surviving correspondence of relatives indicates that the family lived in straitened circumstances, especially after the death of William Bell. In early manhood, Robert Bell was apprenticed to William Macdonald, writer to the signet, and was admitted a member of the Society of Writers to the Signet on 22 June 1784. In the course of his apprenticeship he would have attended classes in Scots and Roman law in the University of Edinburgh. He married, on 3 April 1790, Mary Hamilton (*d*. 1838), the granddaughter of a country solicitor, and carried on the practice of a writer.

Bell became interested in the education and training of apprentices to the profession, which was almost exclusively based in Edinburgh. In May 1793 he put a paper before the general meeting of the writers to the signet proposing publication of a collection of decisions of the court of session and the institution of an annual series of lectures on the law and practice of conveyancing. Advising on and drafting property deeds was one of the main activities of writers to the signet at this time. This proposal, if not the salary, was enthusiastically approved later in that year, with Bell being appointed lecturer and collector of decisions. At that time, law reporting was disapproved of by the court, and Bell was warned in the strongest terms. The difficulty was smoothed over only when the course of lectures was finally begun in December 1794 and was well received. Although Bell only published two volumes of cases, he was no longer harried by the court and resigned as official collector of decisions to concentrate on his lectures, which he published in a revised form in 1815.

Perhaps disillusioned with continuing difficulties in obtaining the full salary for the post of lecturer and the absence of a permanent location from which to teach, Bell resigned from the Society of Writers to the Signet and took the step—uncommon at the time—of seeking admission to the Faculty of Advocates, the Scottish bar. He passed advocate on 4 July 1812 and practised at the bar until his death. Nothing is known of his practice, but during his time at the bar his lectures and several other works on conveyancing were published. His son William followed him into that branch of the profession on 14 December 1824, and edited and updated several of Bell's texts. Apart from his lectures, his *Dictionary of the Law of Scotland* is perhaps his most important work, which has been described as being 'full of still valuable information on nineteenth century law' (Walker, 385). Two of Bell's brothers, Sir Charles *Bell and John *Bell, were distinguished surgeons, while a third, George Joseph *Bell, became professor of Scots law in the University of Edinburgh and a jurist of pre-eminent rank. Robert Bell died, probably in Edinburgh, on 1 November 1816 and was survived by his wife, who died on 4 January 1838.

K. J. CAMPBELL

Sources D. M. Walker, *The Scottish jurists* (1985) · [F. J. Grant], *A history of the Society of Writers to Her Majesty's Signet* (1890) · *Letters of Sir Charles Bell*, ed. G. J. Bell (1870) · 'Jardine collection', MSS, Signet Library, Edinburgh, vol. 1 · F. J. Grant, ed., *The Faculty of Advocates in Scotland, 1532–1943*, Scottish RS, 145 (1944) · 'Bell, Sir Charles', *DNB* · 'Bell, George Joseph', *DNB* · 'Bell, John', *DNB*

Bell, Robert (1800–1867), journalist and writer, was the son of an Irish magistrate, and was born at Cork on 16 January 1800. He was educated at Trinity College, Dublin, where he founded the Dublin Historical Society to replace the College Historical Society which had been suppressed. After graduating in 1818 he obtained a government appointment in Dublin, and for a time edited the *Patriot*, a government organ. He was also one of the founders of, and contributors to, the *Dublin Inquisitor*, and the author of two dramatic pieces, 'Double Disguises' and 'Comic Lectures'. In 1828 he settled in London, having published a pamphlet on Catholic emancipation at about this time. He was appointed editor of the *Atlas*, then one of the largest London weekly journals, and conducted it creditably and successfully for many years. In 1829, at a time when press prosecutions were rife, he was indicted for a libel on Lord Lyndhurst, a paragraph in the *Atlas* having stated that either he or his wife had trafficked in the ecclesiastical patronage vested in the lord chancellor. The indictment would have been withdrawn if Bell had consented to reveal the name of his authority, but he refused. His skilful defence impressed both the judge, Lord Tenterden, and the attorney-general, and, though the jury found him guilty of publishing a libel, he was virtually acquitted of any malicious intention, and escaped punishment.

To Lardner's Cabinet Cyclopaedia (1830–49), Bell contributed the *History of Russia* (3 vols., 1836–8), the *Lives of the English Poets* (2 vols., 1839), and the concluding volumes of both Southey's *Lives of the British Admirals* (vol. 5, 1840) and the continuation of Sir James Mackintosh's *History of England* (vol. 10, 1840), begun by Wallace. Meanwhile he assisted Bulwer, afterwards the first Lord Lytton, and Dr Lardner in establishing the *Monthly Chronicle* (1838–41), and ultimately became its editor. He also edited *The Story-Teller* (1843) and in 1849 the concluding volumes of the *Correspondence of the Fairfax Family*. Bell's other writings included

three five-act comedies, *Marriage* (1842), *Mothers and Daughters* (1843), and *Temper* (1847). He also wrote two novels, *Ladder of Gold* (1850) and *Hearts and Altars* (1852). But his greatest literary enterprise, unfortunately left unfinished, was his annotated edition of the English poets (29 vols., 1854–7). The earliest poet in the series was Chaucer, and the latest Cowper, and a memoir was prefixed to the works of each poet selected.

During his later years Bell assiduously edited *Home News*, a monthly journal circulating among English residents in India and the East. His last productions were selections from the poets to accompany the pictorial illustrations in *Golden Leaves from the Works of the Poets and Painters* (1863), and *Art and Song* (1867). Latterly he became interested in spiritualism, and among his contributions to periodicals was an 1860 paper on table-rapping in the *Cornhill Magazine*. A very prominent and active member of the committee of the Literary Fund, Bell personally helped many struggling and unsuccessful men of letters, and his death on 12 April 1867 at his home, 14 York Street, Portman Square, London, was widely regretted. He was survived by his wife, Elizabeth. In accordance with his request he was buried near the grave of his friend W. M. Thackeray in Kensal Green cemetery.

FRANCIS ESPINASSE, rev. NILANJANA BANERJI

Sources *Encyclopaedia Britannica*, 11th edn (1910–11), vol. 3, pp. 686–7 · Allibone, *Dict.* · *Home News* (May 1867) · *Atlas* (27 Dec 1829) · *Chambers's encyclopaedia: a dictionary of universal knowledge*, new edn, 2 (1901), 59 · CGPLA Eng. & Wales (1867)

Archives BL, letters as sponsor to the Royal Literary Fund, loan no. 96 · BL, corresp. with Messrs Spottiswoode & Shaw, Add. MS 48903 · NL Scot., letters to William Blackwood & Sons · U. Edin. L., letters to James Halliwell-Phillipps and David Laing

Likenesses Clarkington, carte-de-visite, c.1860, NPG · J. and C. Watkins, carte-de-visite, c.1860, NPG

Wealth at death under £1500: probate, 27 April 1867, CGPLA Eng. & Wales

Bell, Robert Anning (1863–1933), artist and designer, was born at 1 Little Street, Andrew Street, St Giles, London, on 14 April 1863, the son of Robert George Bell, a cheesemonger, and his wife, Mary Charlotte Knight. He received his early education at University College School, but left at the age of fourteen because of straitened family circumstances, and was then articled in the architectural office of his uncle. He thus acquired considerable skills as a draughtsman through detailing architectural drawings. Subsequently he studied under Professor Fred Brown at the Westminster School of Art and at the Royal Academy Schools, following these studies with a year in Paris under the tuition of M. Aimé Morot. On his return he shared a studio at 98A Warner Road, Camberwell, with George Frampton where they experimented with a form of low-relief painted plaster sculpture inspired by the work of the Renaissance artist Luca della Robbia. The influence of Italian art was paramount, particularly the woodblock illustrations from the *Hypnerotomachia Poliphili* by Francesco Colonna, issued in Venice in 1499 as a guide to artists and republished as the *Dream of Poliphilus* (by J. W. Appel) by the Department of Science and Art in 1893. It was further reinforced by extensive travel throughout

Europe, including Italy. These travels were partly financed by a generous gift from the purchaser of one of Bell's half-crown watercolour pot-boilers which he produced in the studio as a means of earning a living.

The newly formed Arts and Crafts Exhibition Society gave Bell an early opportunity to display his talent working in the applied arts. In 1889 and 1890 he exhibited various designs for an altarpiece comprising low-relief sculptural panels and paintings carried out in association with his studio partner Frampton. These were later installed in the Roman Catholic church of St Clare, Liverpool. These designs marked the start of a long association with the Arts and Crafts Exhibition Society. He showed regularly with the group, in exhibitions at home and abroad, notably at Turin in 1902, where he served on the hanging committee with Walter Crane and W. A. S. Benson. The society was itself an offshoot of the Art Workers' Guild to which Bell was elected in 1891, remaining a member throughout his life: he was appointed master in 1921. The *Studio*, an influential monthly art magazine which espoused the arts and crafts movement and progressive contemporary arts generally, began publication in 1893. From its inception it gave Bell favoured treatment: the first issue illustrated four of his ex-libris bookplates, and the second contained a photograph of his plaster relief panel *Harvest* (1890), using it as a frontispiece, together with other illustrations of bas-relief decorations by him. Subsequent issues showed numerous book illustrations, ex-libris designs, and plaster reliefs.

The arrangement of sharing a studio with George Frampton ended in 1895 when Bell at the age of thirty-two was appointed instructor at Liverpool University school of architecture, a position he held until 1899. By this time he had already achieved a considerable reputation particularly in the field of the decorative arts. At the end of 1893 Harold Rathbone had established the Della Robbia pottery in Birkenhead which, as the name suggests, shared its source of inspiration with Bell. From the pottery's inception Bell was associated with it, designing its trade-mark galleon motif and providing designs for ceramic relief panels.

Following the death of his first wife, Amy Caroline, *née* Ditcham, whom he had married on 8 September 1900, Bell married on 15 August 1914 Laure Caroline Richard (formerly Richard-Troncy; 1867–1950), a French-born divorcée. She studied art in Paris and at the Slade School under Legros, and later exhibited at the Royal Academy and the Paris Salon where she was awarded medals in 1913 and 1920.

From the mid-1890s onwards Bell became increasingly successful as a book designer and illustrator. The subjects chosen were usually from literary sources including fairy tales, works by the romantic poets, and the Bible. His illustrations from Shakespeare were particularly distinctive: those for *The Tempest* (1901) are widely regarded as among his finest. His distinctive style, characterized by dreaming maidens in a setting of symbolist swirls, was redolent of the emerging European art nouveau movement. He was greatly admired and secured important commissions in France and Spain where his first biography was written and published in 1910.

Public commissions played an increasingly important role in Bell's work, and to accommodate the necessary practicalities he extended his range of skills to include mosaic and stained glass. Commissions included designs for a mosaic on the façade of the Horniman Museum at Dulwich, the tympanum over the west door of Westminster Cathedral, and also the altarpiece in the lady chapel. He carried out important works over several years at the Palace of Westminster, including two of the four patron saints in the octagon hall; all these works were carried out in mosaic by workmen trained by Bell.

At no stage in his career did Bell neglect painting either in oil or watercolour. He exhibited his first painting at the Royal Academy in 1885; but it was not until 1914, when he was elected an associate member, that he began to exhibit there regularly. From then onwards he showed annually until his death; he was elected royal academician in 1922. From 1888 until 1901 he showed at the New English Art Club, both paintings and coloured plaster reliefs. In 1901 he was invited to become an associate of the Royal Society of Painters in Water Colours (OWS) and he was elected a member three years later; in that time he exhibited twenty-nine works. During that period watercolours became Bell's principal form of expression, and he wrote enthusiastically about the merits of the watercolour medium, which he prized above all others, in the second annual volume of the *Old Water-Colour Society's Club*. The Tate collection has four of his works, three of which are watercolours; several others are in provincial and foreign galleries. Nearly all Bell's work is figurative; *The Battle of Flowers*, his diploma work for the OWS, is a particularly ambitious composition with many figures. It is described by his Spanish biographer, Alejandro Riquier, as 'a poem, a poem of life, of colour and of line' (Erskine, 55).

After his departure from Liverpool, and throughout his life, Bell maintained an interest in his work, giving lectures and writing articles. In 1911 he took up teaching again at Glasgow School of Art where he was appointed chief of the design section. In 1918 he was appointed professor of design at the Royal College of Art, a post he held until 1924. In the year following his death at 28 Holland Park Road, London, on 27 November 1933 a memorial exhibition of Bell's work was held at the Fine Art Society. Bell epitomized the arts and crafts ideal, in which movement he was a central figure. He was master of many skills and excelled in all the diverse fields he undertook. In his own lifetime Bell received a good measure of popular as well as critical appreciation for his prolific and varied work, particularly his many public commissions mainly executed in mosaic and stained glass. These showed a versatility which one obituarist compared to 'the great artists of the Renaissance' (*The Times*, 28 Nov 1833). Writing about his work as a painter, T. Martin Wood also perceived in his work 'the issues of the Italian Renaissance … its ability to revive in art remote experiences which have passed into its veins' (Wood, 256). After the memorial exhibition at the Fine Art Society in 1934, Bell's reputation languished until 1989 when fifteen of his works were included in the exhibition 'The Last Romantics' held at the Barbican Art Gallery, London. The exhibition catalogue refers to Bell's 'mastery of so many art forms [which] brought him numerous duties and honours' (Christian, 155).

PETER ROSE

Sources *The Times* (28 Nov 1933) · Mrs S. Erskine, 'Robert Anning Bell RA', *Old Water-Colour Society's Club*, 12 (1934–5), 51–61 · P. Rose, 'The coloured relief decoration of R. A. Bell', *Journal of the Decorative Arts Society*, 14 (1990), 16–23 · M. Chamot, D. Farr, and M. Butlin, *The modern British paintings, drawings, and sculpture*, 1 (1964), 49–50 [catalogue, Tate Gallery, London] · Graves, *RA exhibitors* · A. Jarman and others, eds., *Royal Academy exhibitors, 1905–1970: a dictionary of artists and their work in the summer exhibitions of the Royal Academy of Arts*, 1 (1973), 118–19 · b. cert. · d. cert. · *WWW, 1897–1915* · *WWW, 1929–40* · T. M. Wood, 'Mr Robert Anning Bell', *The Studio*, 49 (1910), 256 · J. Christian, ed., *The last Romantics: the Romantic tradition in British art* (1989) [exhibition catalogue, Barbican Art Gallery, London, 9 Feb – 9 April 1989]; repr. (1995)
Likenesses R. A. Bell, self-portrait, *c*.1921, Art Workers' Guild, London
Wealth at death £2122 7*s*.: probate, 9 Jan 1934, *CGPLA Eng. & Wales*

Bell, Robert Charles (1806–1872), engraver and draughtsman, was born in Edinburgh on 15 September 1806. At an early age he was articled to John Beugo, a friend of Robert Burns, and while in his studio he also attended the classes at the Trustees' Academy, then under the direction of Sir William Allan. After leaving Beugo he engraved a series of Scottish views, including many for Joseph Swan of Glasgow, and a considerable number of vignette portraits. Bell employed mezzotint for portraits such as that of Alexander Jamieson, after A. Richardson. In 1830 he married Margaret Constable; among their children were Robert Purves Bell ARSA, a figure, portrait, and landscape painter, and his brother Joseph.

Bell was best known for his numerous engravings on copper and steel after some of the most important historical genre painters of the day, including William Mulready, Sir David Wilkie, Charles Robert Leslie, and John and Thomas Faed. A number of these were engraved for the annual publications of the Fine Arts Association of Scotland, among them *The Widow* and *Roger and Jenny*, after Sir William Allan, and *The Quarrel Scene in the Dowie Dens o' Yarrow*, after Sir J. Noël Paton. He exhibited at the Royal Scottish Academy in 1837 and 1838. Several of his best plates appeared in the *Art Journal* between the years 1850 and 1872. They included *The Duet*, after William Etty, *The Bagpiper*, after Sir David Wilkie, and *The Young Brother*, after William Mulready, from the pictures formerly in the Vernon Gallery and published in *The Vernon Gallery of British Art*, ed. S. C. Hall (3 vols., 1854). Bell's engravings of old master paintings included *Teasing the Pet*, after Frans van Mieris, in the Royal Collection. The largest and most important plate he ever undertook was *The Battle of Preston Pans*, after Sir William Allan, upon which he was engaged at intervals for some years, and which he had only just completed at the time of his death. He died at 4 Preston Terrace, Edinburgh, on 5 September 1872. Two examples

of his work are in the Scottish National Portrait Gallery, one being a pencil portrait sketch of John Beugo; others are in the City of Edinburgh collection.

R. E. GRAVES, *rev.* GREG SMITH

Sources *Art Journal*, 34 (1872), 284 · R. K. Engen, *Dictionary of Victorian engravers, print publishers and their works* (1979) · B. Hunnisett, *A dictionary of British steel engravers* (1980) · B. Hunnisett, *An illustrated dictionary of British steel engravers*, new edn (1989) · P. J. M. McEwan, *Dictionary of Scottish art and architecture* (1994) · J. C. Guy, 'Edinburgh engravers', *Book of the Old Edinburgh Club*, 9 (1916), 91–5 · d. cert. · IGI
Archives BM, department of prints and drawings · City of Edinburgh Collection · Scot. NPG

Bell, Ronald Percy (1907–1996), physical chemist, was born on 24 November 1907 at Willowfield, Court House Road, Maidenhead, Berkshire, the eldest child of Edwin Alfred Bell (*d*. 1954) and his wife, Beatrice Annie, *née* Ash (*d*. 1929), elementary school teachers. He had a younger brother and an adopted younger sister. He was educated at Gordon Road School, Maidenhead, where his father was headmaster; Maidenhead County Boys' School, where he was influenced by Frank Sherwood Taylor; and Balliol College, Oxford, where he read chemistry under the tuition of H. B. Hartley. His Balliol open scholarship was won at the precocious age of sixteen. In 1927 he was awarded the Gibbs scholarship (*proxime accessit* 1926), and in 1928 he took a first-class honours degree. At Hartley's suggestion he then went to work with J. N. Brønsted in Copenhagen, and spent four years there, with senior studentships from Oxford University (1928–30) and the Goldsmiths' Company (1930–32).

Association with Brønsted determined the main line of Bell's future research: reaction kinetics in solution, especially acid–base catalysis. During his career he published more than 200 scientific papers and three important monographs: *Acid–Base Catalysis* (1941); *The Proton in Chemistry* (1959); and *The Tunnel Effect in Chemistry* (1980). His main achievement was to sharpen understanding over the whole range of reactions involving proton transfer. An ingenious experimentalist, for example using a tape recorder to follow fast reactions, he was also a perceptive theoretician, introducing the quantum mechanical tunnelling concept into chemistry. Languages came easily to him, and he was proficient in many: he translated three major physical chemistry books from Danish and one from German. On 16 April 1931 he married Margery Mary (1905–1999), only daughter of Cornelius West, retired builder, of Maidenhead, and his wife, Elizabeth Martha, *née* Last; they had one son, born in 1936.

Hartley arranged for Bell to take over the physical chemistry teaching at Balliol in 1932, and in 1933 he was elected to a tutorial fellowship. His teaching methods were anachronistic, following Hartley's in starting with essays on the accurate determination of atomic weights. This drew caustic comment from his students, but did them no harm—at least ten of them were elected later to the Royal Society. When H. C. Longuet-Higgins produced a speculative essay proposing a novel hydrogen-bridged structure for diborane, then a major conundrum, the idea was refined under Bell's guidance, and published jointly while Longuet-Higgins was still a second-year undergraduate.

In the 1930s Bell was involved in helping academic refugees from Hitler. During the war he worked half time on Scandinavian intelligence analysis—mostly involving the study of newspapers, but including the debriefing of escapees, one of whom was Niels Bohr, in 1943. His scientific interests became increasingly theoretical at this time, and he initiated a collaboration with C. A. Coulson, who was then in Dundee. This led to Coulson's migration to Oxford in 1945, and was the seed from which the Oxford school of theoretical chemistry grew.

After the war Bell held many appointments in the university, on government bodies, and in learned societies, most notably the presidency of the Faraday Society (1956). In Balliol he chaired the committee which planned the Balliol–St Anne's Graduate Institution (opened in 1967), the first venture into co-education by any of the traditional Oxford colleges. Historian Christopher Hill was elected master of Balliol in 1965 by a very narrow majority over Bell, who was appointed the first vice-master of the college. Two years later, however, he left to become professor of chemistry at the University of Stirling. The parting with Balliol was amicable: he was elected to an honorary fellowship. Although he enjoyed helping to build up a new university, his later years at Stirling were marred by student unrest, which caused him a lot of worry because he was a member of the disciplinary appeals committee.

Ronnie Bell was a small man, bespectacled, with somewhat prominent ears, trim in figure and in dress; he had a taste for good cigars, a discerning ear for music, and a love of hill-walking, especially in the Lake District, where he and his wife had a second home by Buttermere. He invariably expressed himself with precision, and was a stickler for accuracy in others, but he had an impish sense of humour. Elected a fellow of the Royal Society in 1944, he acquired many distinctions, but was inclined to be self-effacing. He had abandoned plans to submit for a Copenhagen doctorate on election to his Balliol fellowship, and so for the greater part of his career stood out on official lists as a splendid oxymoron: 'Mr R. P. Bell *FRS*'.

On retirement from Stirling in 1975 Bell moved to Leeds, where he was an honorary research professor of the university from 1976 to 1990. He had a disabling stroke on 30 October 1991, and died on 9 January 1996 at the Kingston Nursing Home in Leeds. He was cremated on 22 January at Lawnswood, Leeds.   JOHN JONES

Sources B. G. Cox and J. H. Jones, *Memoirs FRS*, 47 (2001), 19–38 · *The Independent* (18 Jan 1996) · *WWW* · personal knowledge (2004) · private information (2004) · b. cert. · m. cert. · d. cert. · *The Times* (11 Jan 1996) · personal record, RS · *CGPLA Eng. & Wales* (1996)
Archives Balliol Oxf., notebooks and his collection of material, mostly printed, concerning J. N. Brønsted · RS, personal record, list of publications compiled by him etc. | Balliol Oxf., archives, CR's file on the subject, already deposited, MISC 293 · Balliol Oxf., archives, letter concerning his wartime work, MISC 108(a) · Balliol Oxf., archives, corresp. with E. F. Caldin, MISC 294 · Balliol Oxf., college archives, personal file · Balliol Oxf., college archives, sabbatical leave reports, appended to college meeting minutes · Balliol Oxf., letters to H. B. Hartley, Hartley MSS 4, 7 · Bodl. Oxf., corresp. with C. A. Coulson, Coulson MSS A.2.3, B.34.12 · Danish National Archives, corresp. with J. N. Brønsted, Private Archive 5237 · Goldsmiths' Company Archives, MSS concerning the subject's Exhibition and Studentship from the Goldsmiths' Company, T IV/1/64, 85 · personal file, FA9/2/72 · report to the general board, FA1/2/16, 171–4 · files giving details of involvement in refugee matters, especially UR6/PSL/2 | FILM priv. coll. | SOUND Balliol Oxf., archives, recorded lecture, July 1974, MISC 294
Likenesses W. Stoneman, photograph, *c.*1945, RS · ffolkes, group portrait, caricature, 1964, Balliol Oxf. · Ramsey & Muspratt, photograph, *c.*1965, Balliol Oxf. · R. B. Stewart, photograph, *c.*1975, Balliol Oxf.
Wealth at death £156,600: probate, 2 April 1996, *CGPLA Eng. & Wales*

Bell, Sam Hanna (1909–1990), writer and broadcaster, was born in Glasgow on 16 October 1909, the eldest of the three sons of James Hanna Bell (1879–1918), a journalist on, and later manager of, the *Glasgow Herald*, of Ulster descent, and his Ulster-born wife, Jane Ferris McCarey McIlveen (*c.*1880–*c.*1960). When his father died his mother went back to her family at Raffrey, near Strangford lough, co. Down, and Sam lived on the family farm, attending the local national school. This locality and its people, much revisited, dominated his imagination and provided settings for three of his four novels, though in 1921 the family moved to Belfast, to share an uncle's house in India Street. He left school in 1923, was apprenticed to the potato trade, and had a wide variety of jobs in and around Belfast including a spell in a clothing warehouse, reflected in his novel *The Hollow Ball* (1961), and a longer period as a clerk with the Canadian Pacific Steamship and Railway Company. For a time he attended art classes in the evenings at the Belfast Technical College. He was not encouraged to persist, though a strong visual sense informs his writing.

Alienated by the poverty, unemployment, and sectarianism of industrial Belfast in the 1930s Bell became increasingly involved in socialist politics and in the Belfast Left Book Club, and began to write, helping to edit the socialist newspaper *Labour Progress*. Early literary successes included stories for radio sold to *Children's Hour* and the country story 'Summer loanen' submitted with the encouragement of Dennis Ireland to Sean O'Faolain's progressive and controversial Dublin journal *The Bell*, where it was published in 1941. 'Summer loanen' and other Stories was published by a local press in 1943.

When war broke out Bell worked as a fire warden and then as an air raid precautions welfare officer, responsible for emergency food supplies in Belfast. He also made time to found the leftist literary periodical *Lagan* with his friends John Boyd and Bob Davidson in 1943. In August 1945 he joined the Northern Ireland region of the BBC as a features producer and continued to work as a producer and broadcaster, mainly for radio, up to and beyond his official retirement in 1969. On 31 October 1946 he married Mildred Ferguson Reside (*d.* 1989), a teacher; a son, Fergus, was born in 1948. His friend and mentor in the BBC, Louis MacNeice, read and commented on his first radio feature script, *Their Country's Pride: a Script on the Drift from the Land*,

Sam Hanna Bell (1909–1990), by Doris V. Blair

broadcast in 1949, a dramatized story of successive generations of an Ulster country family. Perhaps his most popular and successful radio programme was *This is Northern Ireland*, a complex, nuanced portrait of the region which he wrote and produced in 1949 for the BBC silver jubilee. He wrote and produced *The Orangemen*, a carefully researched history of the Orange order, which was broadcast in July 1967, interviewed local celebrities such as the painter William Conor (1968), and adapted stage plays for broadcasting, including his friend Sam Thompson's *The Evangelist* (1966). Some of his best work was for series such as *Within our Province*, *Country Magazine*, *It's a Brave Step*, and *The Fairy Faith* which reported on traditions and folk ways in different parts of Northern Ireland. As outside broadcasting became technically possible this involved constant travel with the awkward wax discs then used for recording, and close co-operation with local people and with folklorists such as Michael J. Murphy. Enduring memorials to this work are the archive he created of scripts and recordings and the collection of folksongs and traditional music made with the musicologist Sean O'Boyle, now in the Ulster Folk Museum. At times his programmes were controversial: there were obvious hazards in broadcasting about popular culture and folk traditions in a religiously and politically divided region tainted by the prejudices and injustice which were sharply criticized in Bell's fiction. But he adroitly sidestepped sectarian pitfalls and brought humour and even-handedness to his task, celebrating rather than scolding farmers, fishermen, and shipyard workers, nationalists and Orangemen.

Some of the rich variety of Bell's broadcast material is reflected in his sketches of local traditions and customs in *Erin's Orange Lily* (1956) and his miscellany of Ulster writing *Within our Province* (1972). These volumes testify not just to the vitality of his region but to his own liberal tolerance and breadth of outlook. He had long known and worked with most of the leading writers, artists, and actors in Northern Ireland and from these contacts arose the Festival of Britain symposium *The Arts in Ulster* (1951) which he edited with the historian Nesca Robb and the poet John Hewitt, and his authoritative critical survey *The Theatre in Ulster* (1972). His formative years had been spent in the Ulster countryside and this was reflected in his first and best novel, *December Bride* (1951). This bleak, laconic narrative of two farming brothers and the servant woman who bears the child of one of them—but which?—was adapted by the author as a stage play (*That Woman at Rathard*, 1955). The novel was filmed by Thaddeus O'Sullivan in 1990 as *December Bride*. Bell went on to write *The Hollow Ball* (1961), a Belfast novel about unemployment and the ambiguous success of a professional footballer, and two historical novels, *A Man Flourishing* (1973), set in Belfast and co. Down just after the 1798 Irish rising, sardonically reviewing the growth of protestant prosperity, and *Across the Narrow Sea* (1987), set in the early years of the seventeenth-century Scots settlement in co. Down, both of which challenged the comfortable mythopoeia of earlier Ulster protestant historical novelists such as W. F. Marshall. He was an occasional contributor to the *Belfast Telegraph*, and in his retirement literary editor of the *Ulster Tatler*: his sketches from this were published as *Tatler Tales* (1981). Though many of his books were published, and reviewed, usually quite respectfully, in England, his writing and broadcasting attracted mainly local interest.

An enthusiastic rugby player in his younger days, convivial, immensely well informed, Bell was generous and helpful to younger writers, serving for many years on the Northern Ireland Arts Council. He was awarded an honorary MA from the Queen's University of Belfast in 1970 and an MBE in 1977 in recognition of his contribution to the cultural life of Northern Ireland. He died at 160 Knock Road, Belfast, on 9 February 1990, and his remains were buried at Roselawn crematorium, just outside the city.

NORMAN VANCE

Sources S. McMahon, *Sam Hanna Bell: a biography* (1999) • R. Welch, ed., *The Oxford companion to Irish literature* (1996) • 'Sam Hanna Bell', *Fortnight* [special supplement] (Jan 1991) • S. McMahon, *Linen Hall Review*, 7 (summer 1990), 7 • D. Keys, 'Sam Hanna Bell: a study of his contribution toward the cultural development of the region', MA diss., 1982, Queen's University of Belfast • A. de Marco, 'Reality of images: images of Ireland in contemporary films based on literary sources', MPhil diss., TCD, 1994 • private information (2004) [F. Bell and J. Boyd] • d. cert.

Archives priv. coll., scrapbooks of MSS, press-cuttings, and typescripts |SOUND BBC Northern Ireland, archive recordings • BL NSA, performance recording • Ulster Folk and Transport Museum, Cultra, co. Down, archive of folksongs, traditional music, etc.

Likenesses R. Friers, drawing, c.1955, repro. in D. Carson, 'Sam Hanna Bell, 1909–1990', *Honest Ulsterman*, 89 (1990), 47 • L. Stuart, photograph, c.1960, repro. in S. H. Bell, *The hollow ball* (1961), jacket • D. V. Blair, pencil drawing, Ulster Museum [see illus.] • photograph, repro. in S. H. Bell, *December bride* (1974), cover

Bell [*alias* Burton], **Thomas** (*b. c.*1551, *d.* in or after 1610), Roman Catholic priest and protestant polemicist, was born at Raskelf, near Thirsk, in Yorkshire. His parents are unknown, but he had several sisters and brothers, one of whom was later a merchant at York. He matriculated sizar at St John's College, Cambridge, at Easter 1565. Ordained deacon, he served as curate of Thirsk in 1569–70 and may also have acted as the local schoolmaster. In the summer of 1570, after reading several books lent to him by one of his parishioners, Bell fervently embraced Catholicism and abandoned his post. He was arrested and imprisoned in York Castle, where his stubborn adherence to the Church of Rome led to his confinement in stocks in the lowest ward of the Kidcote. A later commentator remarked that he was 'more troublesome to the keepers than all the rest of the prisoners together' (Walsingham, 58).

In 1576 Bell escaped and fled to the Low Countries, studying at Douai College before proceeding to the newly established English College at Rome, which he entered as a student of philosophy in 1579. While there Bell participated in the first stirrings of the acrimonious dispute between the Jesuits and some of the secular clergy which would culminate in the 'archpriest' and 'appellant' controversies, preaching a sermon actively dissuading his companions from joining the Society of Jesus. He took Catholic orders and was sent to England on the mission in May of 1582.

For the next decade Bell (alias Thomas Burton) was one of the most energetic, daring, and influential priests working in the north of England, first in Yorkshire and later in Lancashire, where he played a key role in setting up a network of safe houses and enjoyed the protection of Miles Gerard of Ince. In 1586 he was reported to be 'a dangerous person for sedition, and well learned' (PRO, SP 12/193/13), and two years later, with a somewhat inflated sense of his own self-importance, he can be found styling himself the 'Bishop of Chester' (PRO, SP 12/215/79). In the context of a renewed drive against recusancy in the early 1590s, Bell began to teach that Catholics could attend protestant services provided they made an open confession of their faith and declared that they conformed solely as a gesture of political loyalty. Disseminated in a manuscript tract entitled 'A comfortable advertisement to afflicted Catholics', his opinions were fiercely denounced by a number of his clerical colleagues, notably the superior of the English Jesuits, Henry Garnet, who published two tracts refuting him.

Bell's obstinate refusal to back down and irascible attacks upon his critics precipitated rumours of his excommunication and in December 1592 Cardinal William Allen issued a letter obliquely condemning his teachings. However, by the late summer of that year, at least partly as a result of his increasing marginalization, Bell had already 'voluntarily discovered himself' (APC, 1592–3, 164) to the protestant authorities, promising to reveal details of Catholic plots and conspiracies. Examined by Archbishop John Whitgift in London, he supplied the government with a wealth of information about the organization of the mission before returning to the north to assist in the apprehension of those priests and lay people whom he had betrayed. At the request of the earl of Huntingdon he also engaged in a preaching campaign and in 1600 delivered one of the sermons to which recusants incarcerated in York Castle were forcibly dragged. Perhaps unsurprisingly, he 'seemed doubtful of his credit with the prisoners' (BL, Add. MS 34250, fol. 67r).

In November 1593, with the approval of Lord Burghley and the privy council, Bell published a recantation treatise entitled *Thomas Bels Motives*, the first of a dozen virulently anti-Catholic tracts which streamed from his pen. Notable among these is *The Anatomie of Popish Tyrannie* (1603), a summary of the bitter controversy which had erupted between the Jesuits and the appellants. In each Bell employed the technique of selectively quoting Romanist writers in contradiction of their own religion, a device he claimed (without justification) to have invented himself. Several of his books were answered by the Catholic priests Philip Woodward and Richard Smith. Bell repeatedly challenged his opponents to a public debate and alleged in his last book, *The Catholique Triumph* (1610), that in June 1609 they had sent him a parcel containing poison with the intention of assassinating him. He also wrote a treatise on usury and an earnest defence of the Church of England against the criticisms of the 'proude Brownists, saucie Barrowists, and arrogant puritans' (*The Regiment of the Church*, 1606, 96–7), which he dedicated respectfully to Archbishop Richard Bancroft.

James I continued the government pension of £50 p.a. first granted to Bell by Elizabeth. Bell died some time after the publication of his last book in 1610.

ALEXANDRA WALSHAM

Sources high commission cause papers and act books, Borth. Inst., HC.CP 1570/5; HC.AB 1572–4, 1574–6 • T. F. Knox and others, eds., *The first and second diaries of the English College, Douay* (1878) • W. Kelly, ed., *Liber ruber venerabilis collegii Anglorum de urbe*, 1, Catholic RS, 37 (1940) • T. Bell, *Thomas Bels motives* (1593) [containing MS CUL, Syn. 6.59.30, 159] • A. Kenny, 'A martyr manqué: the early life of Anthony Tyrrell', *Clergy Review*, new ser., 42 (1957) • PRO, SP 12/193, 215, 242, 243 • APC, 1592–3 • I. G., 'An answer to a comfortable advertisement, with an addition written of late to afflicted Catholics, concerning going to church with protestants', St Mary's College, Oscott, MS E. 5. 16 • H. Garnet, *An apology against the defence of schisme* (1593) • P. Renold, ed., *The Wisbech stirs, 1595–1598*, Catholic RS, 51 (1958) • *Letters of William Allen and Richard Barret, 1572–1598*, ed. P. Renold, Catholic RS, 58 (1967) • BL, Lansdowne MS 70, fol. 42r • BL, Lansdowne MS 72, fol. 125r • BL, Lansdowne MS 75, fols. 12r, 40r • BL, Add. MS 34250 • BL, Harleian MS 360 • F. Walsingham, *A search made into matters of religion* (1609)

Archives BL, letters to William Cecil, Lord Burghley, and Richard Young, Lansdowne MS 75, fols. 12r, 40r

Bell, Thomas (*b.* 1713), fraudster, was born on 18 February 1713 in Boston, Massachusetts, the first of three recorded children of Thomas Bell (*d.* 1729), sea captain and shipwright, and his wife, Johanna Adams. The younger Thomas, who became known as Tom Bell (except when he was posing as someone else), was the focus of the aspirations of an upwardly mobile family who had accumulated, besides two slaves, a house and some other Boston real estate. Bell attended Boston Free Latin School from 1723 to 1730. Then, although the death of his father in 1729 increased the family's financial burden, Bell matriculated at Harvard College in 1730. He got into trouble almost immediately, provoking a beating from an older student. Reprimanded for his 'saucy behavior', Bell soon engaged in misdeeds of his own, stealing letters, bottles of wine, and, in early 1733, a cake of chocolate. He also engaged in lies the faculty judged 'notorious'. Along with 'the most notorious complicated lying' and a 'scandalous neglect of his college Exercises', these offences led to expulsion in February 1733 (Shipton, *Harvard Graduates*, 9.380).

Bell's activities over the next several years are obscure. A 1739 newspaper article suggested that he left Boston 'to avoid Prosecution … and has been a Fortune hunting for several Years past' (*Boston Evening Post*). In July 1738 a Virginia constable reported that Bell had escaped from gaol after having posed as someone else. In November of that same year a newspaper reported his conviction for forgery in New York. A bold deception the following year aroused broader interest. In 1739 Bell arrived in Barbados claiming to be Gilbert Burnet, son of the late governor of New York, New Jersey, and Massachusetts, and grandson of the celebrated Gilbert Burnet, bishop of Salisbury. With such an illustrious background Bell was welcomed by Barbadian society. He borrowed £250 and bought several fine suits of clothes. When a Jewish man discovered that he was also stealing, Bell claimed to be outraged. He filed a lawsuit seeking £10,000 damages. He also tried to escape from the island and then, when he was foiled, went into hiding. At first most Barbadians sided with Bell. Angry at the disrespect shown to the grandson of a man who had helped assure the protestant succession, they burned down the Speightstown synagogue and drove local Jews from the town. Soon, however, the discovery of the disguised Bell and reports from the mainland revealed his true identity. Bell was sentenced to be whipped, pilloried, and branded on both cheeks.

Though Bell escaped the pillory and the branding, the incident attracted widespread attention in mainland newspapers. Reports of further crimes ranging from South Carolina to New Hampshire continued for the next ten years. Impersonation of a New Jersey clergyman in 1741 allowed him to steal goods and horses. Pretending to be a merchant outside Boston led to the theft of cloth—as well as a conviction in December 1743, only a couple of months after he had, seemingly, married Esther Bell on 18 October in the Church of England King's Chapel under his own name. As often happened, however, Bell escaped from the gaol and continued his activities. The *Pennsylvania Gazette* (10 February 1743) noted:

> He has it seems, made it his Business for several Years to travel from Colony to Colony, personating different People, forging Bills, Letters of Credit, &c. and frequently pretending Distress … He has been in every Colony on the Continent, and … knows and talks familiarly of all Person[s] of Note.

Despite this continuing reinvention (the press recorded the use of nineteen different names), accounts of Bell's activities and descriptions of a thin, middle-sized man, with a slim face, good teeth, and a lively way of talking soon appeared in almost every colonial newspaper.

Eventually Bell's growing notoriety made it difficult to continue his activities. He wrote a long letter defending himself to a New York city newspaper in 1749 and then seems to have stopped his crimes. He became a schoolmaster in Hanover county, Virginia. In July 1752 Bell visited Williamsburg, Virginia, using his own name and bearing testimonials of his good behaviour. He now sought subscriptions for his memoirs, although (to avoid suspicions) he requested only a voluntary, token payment. In 1754 he made further attempts to arouse interest in the volume in Charles Town, South Carolina, and travelled in the West Indies for his health. Bell's later activities are unclear. A 1790 periodical article reported that he was keeping a school in Edenton, North Carolina, as late as 1782 (*The Christian's, Scholar's and Farmer's Magazine*).

Bell was not the first American to engage in fraud by using a false identity, but he was one of the earliest to pass himself off as a gentleman and the first to gain widespread celebrity for such exploits, marking the start of the long tradition of the American confidence man. Because he (perhaps predictably) failed to fulfil his promises to publish his memoirs, he was forgotten by Americans after the War of Independence. In his time, however, he was perhaps the best known of all native-born Americans, a man widely noted as 'the famous Tom Bell' (*South Carolina Gazette*).

STEVEN C. BULLOCK

Sources S. C. Bullock, 'A mumper among the gentle: Tom Bell, colonial confidence man', *William and Mary Quarterly*, 3rd ser., 55 (1998), 231–58 • C. Bridenbaugh, '"The famous infamous vagrant" Tom Bell', *Early Americans* (1981), 121–49 • C. K. Shipton, *Sibley's Harvard graduates: biographical sketches of those who attended Harvard College*, 9 (1956), 375–86 • B. E. Kleber, 'Notorious Tom Bell', *Pennsylvania Magazine of History and Biography*, 75 (1951), 416–23 • *Boston Evening Post* (10 Sept 1739) • *Pennsylvania Gazette* (10 Feb 1743) • *South Carolina Gazette* (24 July 1752) • 'Story of Thomas Bell, a native of America', *The Christian's, Scholar's, and Farmer's Magazine*, 2 (1790), 364–5 • *A report of the record commisioners of the city of Boston, containing Boston births from A.D. 1700 to A.D. 1800* (Boston, 1893), 24th report, 81 • *A report of the record commisioners of the city of Boston, containing the Boston marriages from 1700 to 1781* (Boston, 1898), 28th report, document 150–1898, 49, 334, 376

Bell, Thomas (1733–1802), minister of the Relief church, was born at Moffat on 24 December 1733, of parentage unknown. After attending the local parish school he went to the University of Edinburgh, where he left the Church of Scotland and joined the Relief church founded by Thomas Gillespie in 1761. The denomination was noted for its commitment to religious liberty, open communion, and non-sectarian attitudes towards other churches. He was licensed in 1767 and settled as minister of the Relief congregation at Jedburgh as successor to the son of Thomas Boston of Ettrick. In 1777 Bell became the minister of a large congregation of the Relief church in Glasgow, a move opposed by the Relief Synod. In the face of this opposition both he and the congregation left the church. In 1780, along with the congregation, Bell applied to be readmitted into the Relief church and, following a two-week period of discipline, Bell was formally inducted into the congregation on 28 April.

Bell was actively involved in various theological controversies during his life. In 1778, when evangelicals within the Church of Scotland united with other dissenting groups in opposing the Roman Catholic Relief Bill, the majority of Relief ministers refused to join the 'no-popery' alliance and declared that 'they heartily detested the doctrine of persecution for conscience sake'. During this period, however, Bell was still not connected to the Relief Synod, and he published a series of sermons against popery in 1780. In 1790 he responded to the writings of William McGill of Ayr, who had been charged with Socinianism, by writing *The Articles of Ayr Contrasted with the Oracles of Truth* as well as translating Peter Allinga's treatise on Socinianism, *The Satisfaction of Christ*. In 1794 Bell opposed the introduction of hymns into the worship of the Relief church, favouring the traditional Scottish Presbyterian practice of using only the psalter in public worship.

Details of Bell's marriage are not known, although he had at least one child, James *Bell (1769–1833), the geographical author. Following a five-year period of illness, during which time the congregation employed an assistant minister, he died at Glasgow on 15 October 1802. A collection of Bell's sermons was published in Glasgow in the following year. KENNETH B. E. ROXBURGH

Sources G. Struther, *The history of the rise, progress and principles of the Relief church* (1843) · W. Mackelvie, *Annals and statistics of the United Presbyterian church*, ed. W. Blair and D. Young (1873) · R. Small, *History of the congregations of the United Presbyterian church from 1733 to 1900*, 2 vols. (1904)

Bell, Thomas (*fl.* 1783–1784), inventor of cylinder printing in the textile industry, was probably born in Scotland. He became a copperplate-engraver and printer, and by the 1780s he was living at Mosney, then at Walton-le-Dale, near Preston, an important region of calico printing. His move to Lancashire may have been prompted by a bid to obtain the patent and rights to license the printing machinery on which he was already at work. He may also have been brought south by his employers, who also recruited journeymen printers from London and Hampshire. As a result of innovations in textile spinning and weaving, allied to the increasing use of steam power, by the late eighteenth century it was possible to mass produce linen and cotton, which led, in turn, to a rapid growth of the finishing trades of printing, dyeing, and bleaching. Printing, by contrast, remained a cumbersome and labour-intensive process carried out by hand, using wooden blocks or copper-engravings mounted on wood. Here Bell evidently saw the potential for mechanization. He would certainly have been familiar with rotary devices already used in the textile industry, and quite possibly with Andrew Meikle's application of rotary motion to the threshing machine in agriculture. Other inventors, both in England and France, had earlier developed printing machines, but these were not commercially successful, a problem Bell managed to overcome.

Bell's machine was first used by Livesey & Co., one of the largest calico printers in Mosney. The first patent he obtained (no. 1378), dated 17 July 1783, was for a machine capable of 'printing with one or various colours at one time, linens, lawns, cambrics, cottons, calicoes, muslins, woollen goods, silks, etc.'. The printing rolls were made of iron and covered with engraved copper plates which could 'be taken off at pleasure and by that means fresh patterns put on as often as required'. Dye was fed from a box fixed above the printing cylinder. Bell claimed his device could print in six colours, but it probably could not do so simultaneously. However, his second patent (no. 1443), dated 9 July 1784, described a refined machine capable of printing 'five colors (more or less) at once'; this machine was driven by steam, which was also used for heating rollers to dry the cloth.

While similar devices using cylinders for machine printing, including that of John Slater, were developed and patented at about the same time, Bell's was most commonly adopted in the main centres of cotton and linen printing. The benefits of cylinder machines for calico printing were considerable. According to Edward Baines's *History of the Cotton Manufacture in Great Britain* (1835), the cylinder machine employing one man and one boy printed and dried one piece of cloth in two minutes, equivalent to the production of 100 hand-block printers and their assistants.

Bell's technology reached the United States in 1809 after Joseph Siddall visited England to recruit workers and obtain equipment. Calico and other textile printing also expanded rapidly in Scotland after Bell's invention. In his *General Report of the Agricultural State and Political Circumstances of Scotland* (1814), Sir John Sinclair reproduced an account by James Boaz of Glasgow which stated that calico printing was 'carried to great extent' in Scotland and that cylinder printing had already made a significant contribution to the industry. Nothing is known about Bell's subsequent career, but his invention had a substantial impact on the productive capacity of textile manufacturing, and contributed significantly to the sector's vital role in early industrialization. IAN DONNACHIE

Sources E. Baines, *History of the cotton manufacture in Great Britain* (1835) · C. Singer and others, eds., *A history of technology*, 4: *The industrial revolution, c. 1750 to c. 1850* (1958) · H. Hamilton, *The industrial revolution in Scotland* (1932); repr. (1966) · A. P. Wadsworth and J. de Lacy Mann, *The cotton trade and industrial Lancashire, 1600–1780* (1931) · D. Hunt, *A history of Walton-le-Dale and Bamber Bridge* (1997) · F. Coupe, *Walton-le-Dale: a history of the village* (1954) · V. Reilly, *The Paisley pattern* (1987) · J. Sinclair, *General report of the agricultural state and political circumstances of Scotland*, 5 vols. (1814), appx II · D. J. Jeremy, *Transatlantic industrial revolution: the diffusion of textile technologies between Britain and America, 1790–1830s* (1981)

Bell, Thomas (1785–1860), land surveyor and book collector, was born on 16 December 1785 in Newcastle upon Tyne, the second son of John Bell (1755–1816), a land surveyor and bookseller, and his wife, Margaret, the daughter of John Gray, of Combfield House, co. Durham. His older brother **John Bell** (1783–1864), bookseller and antiquary, was born in Newcastle, on 7 October 1783. On 22 November 1806 John Bell married Barbara, the daughter of Thomas Pringle, of Newcastle; they had nine children. Thomas Bell married, on 17 February 1810, Hannah, the daughter of William Blakey, of Morton Banks, Yorkshire;

they had fourteen children, among them John Gray *Bell, bookseller.

On leaving school, both the Bells joined their father in his businesses, and Thomas with another brother, James Maddison, eventually succeeded their father. In 1803 John Bell left his father's establishment in Union Street, Newcastle, formerly the premises of the printers and booksellers Solomon and Sarah Hodgson, and set up as a bookseller on the Quayside. There he started his collecting of coins, antiquities, and, most important, ephemera dealing with a great range of topics, which have since proved invaluable sources of information about contemporary life, especially, but not exclusively, the book trade. During his first year in his bookselling business Bell started a numismatic society in Newcastle, which had only a short life; he published two undated charts of British silver coinage.

Shortly after the collapse of the numismatic society Bell issued *Proposals, for publishing, by subscription, reprints of a rare and curious collection of old English tracts*, but nothing came of this, and it was not until 1818 that the Newcastle Typographical Society came into being under the leadership of John Trotter Brockett. In 1812 Bell published his only substantial work, *Rhymes of Northern Bards*, a collection of songs and poems from Newcastle, Northumberland, and Durham. Over the next five years he published some eleven pamphlets of local interest. Although his collecting and antiquarian interests attracted many people to his Quayside shop, Bell was declared bankrupt in December 1817. His assignees, who included his brother Thomas, ordered all his possessions to be sold up, including his burgeoning collections of ephemera, which were widely dispersed, some for almost nothing.

Conscious of the importance of Roman and other antiquities in Northumberland and Durham, John Bell felt that it was desirable to form a society for the study and preservation of relics of the past, and in November 1812 he sent a circular proposing this to the leading gentry of the two counties. The success of the project was assured after it received the support of Hugh, second duke of Northumberland, and, after a preliminary meeting on 23 January, the Society of Antiquaries of Newcastle upon Tyne was formally established on 6 February 1813. John Bell was elected treasurer, an office he held until his bankruptcy; he was the society's librarian until 1849, and published seven papers in its transactions, now *Archaeologia Aeliana*, three of them jointly.

In the last years of their father's life Thomas Bell carried the main burden of the surveying practice, which was always his principal interest. When two of his sons were old enough he entrusted the bookselling and stationery business to them. Thomas became one of the most successful land surveyors in the northern counties, numbering among his clients the duke of Northumberland and the earl of Strathmore. He was closely concerned with many of the enclosures of common land in Northumberland, Durham, Cumberland, and Yorkshire, as he was with railways being developed in the region, notably the Brandling Junction, the Newcastle and Carlisle, and the Stanhope and Tyne railways. Many of his surveys continue to be useful at the beginning of the twenty-first century.

Thomas Bell was an indefatigable book collector, and left a library of 15,000 volumes, which was auctioned in October 1860. His special interest was the history of local families, and he gathered much material, mainly topographical and genealogical, which was later used by local historians. He became a member of the Society of Antiquaries of Newcastle upon Tyne on 2 June 1813, and was a fellow of the Society of Antiquaries of London. He died in Cumberland Row, Newcastle, on 30 April 1860, aged seventy-four, and was buried in the family vault in Jesmond cemetery on 4 May.

John Bell, after his bankruptcy, gave up his shop on the Quayside, and moved to Gateshead to practise as a land surveyor; he occasionally also sold books. He continued his omnivorous collections of ephemera, and was visited by many bibliophiles, including the Revd Dr T. F. Dibdin, who gives his usual purple account of the occasion. Many of his collections of ephemera came into the possession of his brother Thomas, who also made voluminous collections. John Bell died on 31 October 1864, aged eighty-one, and was buried in St John's cemetery, Elswick.

PETER ISAAC

Sources R. Welford, *Men of mark 'twixt Tyne and Tweed*, 1 (1895), 234–9, 244–8 · C. J. Hunt, *The book trade in Northumberland and Durham to 1860: a biographical dictionary* (1975) · P. J. Wallis, *The book trade in Northumberland and Durham to 1860: a supplement to C. J. Hunt's biographical dictionary* (1981) · *GM*, 3rd ser., 9 (1860), 196 · *Records of the Society of Antiquaries of Newcastle upon Tyne*, centenary vol. (1913), 1–3, 40–43, 113–16 · I. Bain, *John Bell's Album de Novo Castro* (1963)
Archives Gateshead Central Library, collection relating to parish of Gateshead Fell · Keep and Blackgate Museum, Newcastle upon Tyne, Northumberland collections · Northumbd RO, Newcastle upon Tyne, Northumberland collections · Tyne and Wear Archives Service, Newcastle upon Tyne, corresp., deeds, and papers · U. Durham L., papers · U. Newcastle, Robinson L., Northumbrian collection | Newcastle Central Library, Welford MSS
Likenesses J. Crawhall, sketch (John Bell), repro. in Bain, *John Bell's Album* · double portrait, line blocks (with John Bell; after pen-and-ink sketches), repro. in Welford, *Men of mark*, 1, 235, 245
Wealth at death under £3000: resworn probate, March 1861, *CGPLA Eng. & Wales* (1860)

Bell, Thomas (1792–1880), dental surgeon and zoologist, was born at Poole, Dorset, on 11 October 1792, the only son of the surgeon Thomas Bell and his wife, Susan Gosse (*d.* 1829), formerly a teacher. After initial training with his father, Bell entered Guy's Hospital, London, as a student in 1813; he also studied at St Thomas's. In 1815 he became a member of the Royal College of Surgeons and was made a fellow in 1844. He succeeded James Fox as the dental surgeon and lecturer at Guy's in 1817, as well as taking over his private dental practice. Bell is regarded as one of the pioneers of dentistry in Britain, through his efforts to establish it as a separate branch of medicine. He was responsible for innovations in the use of various dental instruments and was the first to treat teeth as living structures by applying scientific surgery to dental disease. His lectures included many original observations and were published as a textbook *The Anatomy, Physiology and Diseases of the Teeth* (1827).

Thomas Bell (1792–1880), by Maull & Polyblank, 1855

During his childhood in Dorset, encouraged by his parents, Bell had developed an interest in natural history, especially zoology. When at Guy's, for several years Bell was asked to lecture on comparative anatomy. In 1836 he was appointed professor of zoology at King's College, London, but this was virtually an honorary post for very few lectures were required. On his election as a fellow of the Linnean Society in 1815, Bell's supporters emphasized his interest in botany; but Crustacea, Reptilia, and Amphibia became his main interests and all his publications were on zoological subjects. He began with a succession of popular works written for John Van Voorst: *History of British Quadrupeds* (1837; rev. edn, 1874) was followed by *History of British Reptiles* (1839) and then *History of British Stalk-Eyed Crustacea* (1853). These compilations were open to criticism for their inclusion of domestic animals, and for important omissions, as well as for their lack of any original research. However, Bell's descriptions of Reptilia for the *Zoology of the Voyage of the Beagle* (1843) and of Crustacea in Sir Edward Belcher's *Last of the Arctic Voyages* (1855), together with contributions to the monographs *Fossil Reptilia* (1849), *Fossil Crustacea* (1857, 1862), and his *Catalogue of Crustacea in the British Museum* (1855), enhanced his scientific reputation. The unfinished, exquisitely illustrated *Monograph of the Testudinata* (1836–42) was a considerable achievement, for he was forced to describe newly discovered turtles and tortoises and then ensure that their features were accurately drawn, despite unfavourable conditions in captivity that frequently led to their death. Bell seldom had time for detailed field observation and was dependent upon collectors for all the animals he described. Consequently his understanding of their significant characters or behaviourial traits needed for reliable classification was often inadequate.

Bell became involved with the Linnean Society's zoological club and the short-lived *Zoological Journal* (1832–45), in an effort to promote and improve the professional treatment of zoology, which eventually led to the formation of the Zoological Society in 1826. His excellent administrative qualities were recognized early, for during its formative decade he was made a vice-president of that society. He was elected a fellow of the Royal Society in 1828, and was (surprisingly) appointed one of its secretaries in 1848, holding that office until 1853. When the Ray Society was founded in 1843, Bell became its first president and served until 1859. In an effort to revive the Linnean Society, his fellow members ensured that he was made president in 1853; under his guidance until 1861, the society improved its financial position, increased its membership, revitalized its meetings, and re-established its scientific role. Bell was also largely responsible for ensuring that the major scientific societies were able to occupy Burlington House in 1857, despite strong government opposition.

As president, Bell was in the chair at the Linnean Society meeting on 30 June 1858, when Darwin and Wallace presented their controversial papers on selection and the origin of species. Although a personal friend of Darwin's, he remained hostile to the theory of evolution throughout his life. It has been suggested by some commentators that his unwillingness to permit any discussion that evening was due to his own strong opposition to such theories but it is more likely that his decision was based on procedural difficulties.

Bell was married, though it is not known whether he and his wife, Sarah Jane, had any children. Approaching the age of seventy, Bell retired from practice and all his official positions to reside permanently at The Wakes, in Selborne, Hampshire. He occupied himself in collecting relics of Gilbert White, improving the house, and producing a major edition of the *Natural History of Selborne* with the addition of a new memoir and other material (1877). He died at Selborne on 13 March 1880 and was buried in the local churchyard.

Bell has been described as a short, thick-set man, with a cheery, chubby, hairless face (Wilks and Bettany, 1892). Darwin always regarded him as a delightful, kind-hearted man, and believed that a more good-natured person did not exist but that his overwhelming administrative roles and professional work prevented him from achieving very much (Burkhardt and Smith, 5.168). Huxley echoed that view but qualified it by suggesting that Bell needed the qualities of originality and grasp of mind, though conceding, 'he has the learning and can write intelligibly' (Huxley, 1.94). R. J. CLEEVELY

Sources A. T. Gage, *A history of the Linnean Society of London* (1938) • 'Thomas Bell (1792–1880)', *Curtis's Botanical Magazine: dedications, 1827–1927*, ed. E. Nelmes and W. Cuthbertson [1931], 139–40 • K. C. Davies and J. Hull, eds., *The zoological collections of the Oxford University Museum* (1976) • *Nature*, 21 (1879–80), 473, 499–500 • J. Chatfield,

'Professor Thomas Bell (1792–1880)', *The Selborne Association Newsletter*, 6 (1980), 5–15 · R. J. Cleevely, 'The Sowerbys and their publications in the light of the manuscript material in the British Museum (Natural History)', *Journal of the Society of the Bibliography of Natural History*, 7 (1974–6), 343–68 · S. Wilks and G. T. Bettany, *A biographical history of Guy's Hospital* (1892), 397–400 · E. Bennion, *Antique dental instruments* (1986) · F. Colyer, *Old instruments used for extracting teeth* (1952) · R. J. Cleevely, *World palaeontological collections* (1983) · *The correspondence of Charles Darwin*, ed. F. Burkhardt and S. Smith, 1–5 (1985–9) · L. Huxley, *Life and letters of Thomas Henry Huxley*, 2 vols. (1900) · R. J. Cleevely, 'Picture quiz: Thomas Bell (1792–1880)', *The Linnean*, 12/4 (1997), 6–10 · B. Gardiner, *The Linnean*, 12/4 (1997), 1–2 · B. Gardiner, 'Postscript: Bell's involvement with The Wakes at Selborne', *The Linnean*, 12/4 (1997), 11–12

Archives Gilbert White Museum, Selborne, Hampshire · NHM, corresp. with Richard Owen and William Clift · NHM, letters to members of the Sowerby family · Oxf. U. Mus. NH, corresp., notebooks, and papers | Hants. RO, letters to William Wickham · Hants. RO, Wych Place MSS · Linn. Soc., Swainson MSS with corresp. · Linn. Soc., Zoology Club MSS with corresp. · NHM, Owen MSS · NHM, Ray Society MSS · NHM, Sowerby MSS · North Yorkshire County Library, York, Allis MSS · RBG Kew, Bentham MSS · RBG Kew, Hooker MSS · Royal Institution of Great Britain, London, Grove MSS

Likenesses T. H. Maguire, lithograph, *c.*1851, BM, Linn. Soc., Wellcome L.; repro. in T. H. Maguire, *Portraits of honorary members of the Ipswich Museum* (1852) · Maull & Polyblank, albumen print, 1855, NPG [*see illus.*] · H. W. Pickersgill, oils, 23 May 1857, Linn. Soc. · P. Slater, marble bust, in or before 1862, probably Linn. Soc.; presented by Linnean Club · Benyon & Co., coloured lithograph vignette (after M. Hanhart), Wellcome L.; repro. in F. Hager, *The past surgeons and physicians of Guy's Hospital, Southwark, London* · E. Edwards, photograph, NPG; repro. in L. Reeve, ed., *Men of eminence* (1864), vol. 3 · G. Zobel, mezzotint (after Taples), Wellcome L., Linn. Soc.

Wealth at death under £16,000: resworn probate, Jan 1881, *CGPLA Eng. & Wales* (1880)

Bell, Sir Thomas (1865–1952), engineer and shipbuilder, was born on 21 December 1865 at Sirsawa in India, the son of Imrie Bell, a consultant engineer specializing in the design of lighthouses, and his wife, Jane Walker of Edinburgh. His early education was undertaken at the *Gymnasium* in Celle, Hanover, and then at King's College School, London. In 1880 he entered the Royal Naval Engineering College at Devonport, and graduated in 1886 as a fully qualified engineering officer; he was intent on a naval career, but was denied this path due to deficient eyesight. Fortunately this was no barrier to a commercial career, and he was appointed to the engineering design staff in the large new engine works which J. and G. Thomson had opened at its famous Clydebank yard. Bell was quickly given experience in the engineering shop, the drawing office, and the estimating department. His promotion was rapid: he was appointed assistant to the engineering director in 1895, and was also the 'outside' manager for the engineering work in the yard. When John Brown of Sheffield acquired the yard in 1899 Bell's qualities were quickly recognized. He was appointed engineering manager and by 1903 had become a local director on the board. When the senior Clydebank manager, John Gibb Dunlop, retired in 1909, Bell was appointed director in charge, a position later to be known as managing director.

Bell's experience and breadth of outlook made him alert to the many developments in his professional field,

Sir Thomas Bell (1865–1952), by unknown photographer

and he applied himself with vigour to keeping the Clydebank firm in the forefront of these advances. He undertook his management duties when the steam turbine was appearing in the field of marine propulsion. Under his direction Clydebank acquired a Parsons licence in 1903, and had erected a set of experimental engines by 1904, subsequently installed in the Clyde passenger ferry *Atlanta*. Turbines were then quickly installed in the *Carmania* in 1905, Cunard's first such venture, and in the prototype of the quadruple screw machinery of the *Lusitania*, launched the following year. The performance of this innovative machinery was the subject of a paper presented in 1908 by Bell to the Institution of Naval Architects. This early application to the development of turbine machinery was carried a stage further in the building of the *Aquitania* in 1913. The production of turbine machinery for merchant ships under Bell's guidance reached its climax in the *Queen Mary*, launched in 1934.

Similar progress was also made in the field of naval machinery. In 1908 Bell acquired for Clydebank the UK licence to the American Curtis turbine, this being the beginning of the development of the Brown–Curtis turbine, especially suited to heavy duty naval service. The first Brown–Curtis turbines were fitted in the cruiser *Bristol*. The Brown–Curtis turbine was widely installed and was taken up under sub-licence by most other naval builders in Britain. The Admiralty sought Bell's assistance in 1917 as deputy controller of dockyards and warshipbuilding; his qualities were appreciated and quickly rewarded when in 1918 he was appointed KBE. He served in the Admiralty until the end of 1918, returning to Clydebank in January 1919.

With the armistice the flow of naval orders to Clydebank dried up, and after the signing of the Washington treaty on naval disarmament in 1921, the Clydebank yard received no Admiralty order between 1918 and 1924. Bell consequently had to redirect the work of the yard into the merchant market, where slack demand and over-capacity prevailed. He kept the yard going through skilful negotiation of preferential links with major shipping lines, particularly Cunard, the Orient Steam Navigation Company, the Royal Mail group, and especially the Canadian Pacific Railway, which delivered six of the seventeen contracts obtained by Clydebank between 1925 and 1930. Even with this success the yard was running out of work, and by September 1930 all eight berths were vacant. The yard was only saved from closure by Bell's success in landing the Cunard contract in December 1930, for the construction of their new giant transatlantic express liner, the vessel ultimately to be launched as the *Queen Mary*. The yard number for the contract was 534, worth £4 million. Work on 534 was brought to a halt on 12 December 1932, when Cunard could not continue financial provision in the wake of the disruption of the bill markets, following the financial crisis of 1931. Work was not resumed until 3 April 1934, on the conclusion of the Cunard–White Star merger, which brought government assistance to complete the liner. During this time Bell presided over a yard whose workforce slipped from over 7600 in 1928 to 422 in 1932. The vessel was finally launched on 27 September 1934, and six months later, in March 1935, Sir Thomas Bell retired from his post as managing director, but continued to serve as a director of John Brown & Co. Ltd until 1946.

Bell was tall of stature, grave in demeanour, and his strength of character was evident to all who met him. His initial naval training accustomed him to discipline and authority. He exercised both, and was a strict disciplinarian, not least with himself. While he was autocratic and patriarchal with his workforce, he made immense efforts to minimize the hardship of unemployment for his men and their families in the depression. In 1932 he leased 15 acres of land to provide allotments for 150 of his skilled men, and obtained seeds and implements through an English allotment association run by the Society of Friends. In 1900 Bell married Helen MacDonald, daughter of Malcolm MacDonald, a Scottish coal merchant; they had two daughters, one of whom died in childhood.

In addition to his professional work Bell interested himself in the public life of Clydebank. He was an active member and benefactor of St Columba's Episcopal Church. Together with his wife he had founded the Clydebank Nursing Association, and in 1914 they established for it a residential home in which he and his wife took active interest. After his retirement from executive duties in 1935 he became district commissioner of the Boy Scouts in the Clydebank area, and in 1947 was elected honorary president of the Dunbartonshire Association, to the affairs of which he had given very vigorous support. As a

young man he was a keen gymnast; in later years his recreations were golf and gardening.

Bell finally retired as a director of John Brown & Co. in 1946 due to failing health. He died six years later, on 9 January 1952, at his home, Furzecroft, in Helensburgh, and was buried in the same town. His wife had died in 1926, and he was survived by his remaining daughter. His personal estate was a modest £28,632, nearly £12,000 of which was held in stock of the company he had served for sixty years.   J. BROWN, *rev.* ANTHONY SLAVEN

Sources A. J. Grant, *Steel and ships: the history of John Brown's* (1950) · A. Slaven, 'A shipyard in depression: John Browns of Clydebank', *Business History*, 19 (1977), 192–217 · *DSBB*, vol. 1 · d. cert. · inventory, NA Scot., SC/63/35/88 · will, NA Scot., SC/65/36/54
Archives U. Glas. L., papers of John Brown & Co., Clydebank, UCSI
Likenesses drawing, Mitchell L., Glas.; repro. in *DSBB* · photograph, Mitchell L., Glas. [*see illus.*] · photographs, repro. in *The Engineer* (18 Jan 1952), 102
Wealth at death £28,632 15s. 11d.: confirmation, 28 March 1952, *CCI* · £561 18s. 11d.: additional estate, *CCI* · £1: additional estate, *CCI*

Bell, Valentine Graeme (1839–1908), civil engineer, born in London on 27 June 1839, was the youngest son of William Bell, merchant, of Aldersgate Street, London, who was subsequently official assignee in bankruptcy. Educated at private schools and apprenticed in 1855 to Messrs Wren and Hopkinson, engineers, of Manchester, Bell became, in 1859, a pupil of James Brunlees. For Brunlees he was resident engineer in 1863–5 on the Cleveland Railway in Yorkshire, and in 1866–8 on the Mont Cenis Railway (on the Fell system), for which he directed the construction of special locomotives in Paris in 1869–70. While in charge of the Mont Cenis line he rebuilt for the French government the *route impériale* between St Jean de Maurienne and Lanslebourg after its destruction by flood. In 1864 Bell married Rebecca (d. 1868), daughter of Alexander Bell Filson MD; they had a son and a daughter. Bell was elected a member of the Institution of Civil Engineers on 4 May 1869. In 1871 he set up in private practice in London, and in 1872–5 he carried out waterworks at Cadiz for a company which failed and caused him financial losses. During the same period, with Sir George Barclay Bruce, he constructed a railway for the Compagnie du Chemin de Fer du Vieux Port de Marseille.

From 1880 Bell worked for the Colonial Office in Jamaica where he spent much of his professional life. In 1882 he married Emilie Georgina, daughter of Francis Robertson Lynch, clerk of the legislative council of Jamaica; they had two daughters and a son, Archibald Graeme, who became director of public works in Trinidad. Until 1883 Bell was engaged in reconstructing the government railway in Jamaica between Kingston and Spanish Town, which was in disrepair. He extended the line to Ewarton and Porus, and later to Montego Bay and Port Antonio. The governor, Sir Henry Norman, who recognized Bell's capacity and energy, appointed him in 1886 a member of the legislative council. Despite clear reservations within the Colonial Office concerning Bell's overall suitability, he was appointed director of public works in 1887 and held the office for nearly twenty-one years with admirable results. Under his direction the mileage of improved roads was extended from 800 to near 2000; 110 bridges and many modern public buildings were built, and works for water supply, drainage, and lighting were carried out. Energetic in his opposition, he was unable to prevent the transfer, in 1889, of the government railways to an American syndicate. This controversial move proved a failure, and the government resumed possession in 1900. He was made CMG in 1903 in recognition of his valuable public service. The Jamaican earthquake of 1907 seriously affected his health; Bell resigned his appointment in March 1908, and returned to England. He failed to recover from a serious operation and died at the Home Hospital, 16 Fitzroy Square, London, on 29 May 1908. He was survived by his second wife.

W. F. SPEAR, *rev.* B. P. CRONIN

Sources *PICE*, 172 (1907–8), 311–13 · *The Times* (1 June 1908) · *WWW*, 1897–1915 · d. cert.
Archives RS | PRO, CO 137/495, 525, 527–9
Wealth at death £1657 13s. 2d.: probate, 18 June 1908, *CGPLA Eng. & Wales*

Bell [*née* Stephen], **Vanessa** (1879–1961), painter, was born at 22 Hyde Park Gate, London, on 30 May 1879, the eldest in the family of two sons and two daughters of Sir Leslie *Stephen (1832–1904), the first editor of the *Dictionary of National Biography*, and his second wife, Julia Prinsep Jackson (1846–1895) [*see* Stephen, Julia Prinsep], widow of Herbert Duckworth. Leslie Stephen also had a daughter from his previous marriage, and Julia had two sons and a daughter from her marriage to Herbert Duckworth. From an early age Vanessa and her sister Virginia *Woolf (1882–1941) determined the one to be a painter, the other a writer. They were educated at home; in 1896 Vanessa began to attend Arthur Cope's School of Art in South Kensington, London, and in 1901 she gained admission to the Royal Academy Schools, where she was much influenced by the teaching of John Singer Sargent. By the time she left in 1904 it is clear that she had moved far from the artistic dominion of her mother's family, which had been on familiar terms with the Pre-Raphaelites and which venerated the work of George Frederic Watts.

The domestic and social pressures which fell upon Vanessa Stephen as the eldest daughter of an eminent widower and the protégée of her more socially ambitious relatives were eased on the death of her father in 1904, and later that year she moved with her sister and two brothers from Kensington to Bloomsbury, a respectable but unfashionable district, where they set out to follow their own pursuits without undue regard to the conventionalities and constrictions of formal London society. Increasingly they found themselves in the company of the Cambridge contemporaries of the elder brother, Thoby Stephen. In 1905 Vanessa founded the Friday Club in order to provide a meeting-place for artists and persons interested in art, and this led to a closer friendship with the art critic (Arthur) Clive Heward *Bell (1881–1964), the most visually educated and aware of Thoby's friends, and, following Thoby's untimely death in 1906, to their marriage on 7 February 1907. The Bells' home at 46 Gordon Square was

Vanessa Bell (1879–1961), by Duncan Grant, *c*.1918

thereafter one of the focal points of what has come to be referred to as the Bloomsbury circle, which included such friends as Lytton Strachey, Desmond MacCarthy, and, somewhat later, Maynard Keynes, Leonard Woolf (who married Virginia in 1912), Roger Fry, and Duncan *Grant (1885–1978).

Although Vanessa Bell shared her husband's interest in the developments of contemporary French art, her own painting remained essentially sober and tonal, having much in it of Whistler and of the New English Art Club, with which she sometimes exhibited. However, early in 1910 a close and lasting friendship between the Bells and Roger Fry began; this had a profound influence, both personally and intellectually—and particularly upon Vanessa, with whom Fry was to fall deeply and enduringly in love. In November of that year, with their enthusiastic co-operation, Fry promoted the notorious exhibition 'Manet and the post-impressionists', which was to give the British public virtually its first opportunity to see the work of such painters as Cézanne, Gauguin, and Van Gogh. In its successor of 1912, the 'Second post-impressionist exhibition', four of Vanessa Bell's paintings were hung, with examples by other British and Russian artists, among works by Picasso, Matisse, Derain, and other representatives of the school of Paris. Liberated from the English tradition of direct representation by the intoxicating example of the French and the stimulating theorizing of Bell and Fry, Vanessa's work grew increasingly bold, with a simplification of design and form and a free and joyous use of colour, a progression which was to lead her, before 1916, to paint some of the first totally abstract pictures in Britain. But underlying the audacious innovations of this period, her passion for order, serenity, and harmony was always evident.

In 1913 Roger Fry founded the Omega workshops to enable artists fired by post-impressionism to apply their gifts to the decorative arts. Although it failed in 1919, Vanessa Bell was from the outset a wholehearted collaborator in this venture, from which she derived, besides a number of commissions, a permanent interest in the use of ornament and decoration. Textiles, embroideries, ceramics, painted furniture, and the many book jackets designed for the Hogarth Press are evidence of her remarkable and felicitous talent as a decorator. However, changes of taste and the disasters of war have all but obliterated her larger decorative schemes, which were usually undertaken in conjunction with Duncan Grant. The mural decorations (1940–42) at Berwick church, Sussex, and rooms at nearby Charleston, Firle (which became her country home in 1916 and after her death was preserved by a trust for the public benefit), survive from among the considerable body of work which they carried out together, mainly for private patrons; but she herself seldom lived in a house, studio, or flat without feeling impelled to decorate its walls and furnishings. This partnership with Grant was one of the happiest in the history of art, and from 1913— while remaining always on terms of amity with Clive Bell—they lived virtually as man and wife.

Vanessa Bell had two sons—Julian *Bell (1908–1937) and Quentin Claudian Stephen *Bell (1910–1996)—with her husband, and a daughter, Angelica Vanessa (b. 1918), with Duncan Grant. Julian, who lost his life driving an ambulance for the republican forces during the Spanish Civil War, was a poet; Quentin was a painter, potter, teacher, and writer. Angelica, an artist, became the wife of the writer David Garnett and wrote an account of her upbringing, Deceived with Kindness (1984).

During the First World War Vanessa Bell, as did most of her circle, held pacifist views; she lived in the country with Duncan Grant and her children, and the difficulties of domestic life in wartime left little time for painting. But she appears during this period to have come to feel that in abstraction she approached a dead end, and that, as she put it, 'Nature was more interesting'. She turned to the form of representational art which she felt best suited her. Her method, which allowed her to explore and to celebrate the solidity and brilliance of the natural world, was not radically changed for the rest of her life. Although she had a considerable gift for portraiture and used her friends and family as subjects when she could prevail upon them to sit, she painted few formal portraits and, from necessity as much as choice, applied herself to still life, landscape, interiors with figures and, from time to time, interpretations of the work of the Old Masters.

Vanessa Bell contributed regularly to group exhibitions, particularly the London Group, of which she became a member in 1919, the London Artists' Association, and from the 1950s the Royal West of England Academy. The first exhibition consisting solely of her own work was held at the Independent Gallery in London in 1922, and in the years that followed she had solo shows at the Cooling, Lefevre, Leicester, and Adams galleries. In 1964 a memorial exhibition of her work, organized by the Arts Council, was shown in six English cities. She gave generous encouragement to fellow artists, particularly the young, and was a sponsor of, and taught at, the School of Painting and Drawing (later known as the Euston Road School) when it opened in Fitzroy Street in 1937. From 1949 to 1959 she was an active committee member of the Edwin Austin Abbey memorial trust, which commissioned mural paintings for public buildings.

Between the wars Vanessa Bell lived very privately, mainly in London, devoted to her painting, her family, and her close friends. She travelled in Spain, Germany, and Austria, and made extended stays in Provence, Italy, and Paris. The death of Roger Fry in 1934 was a severe loss to her; but that of her son Julian in 1937 was a shattering blow from which she never fully recovered. The suicide of her sister Virginia Woolf four years later was a further calamity. With the outbreak of the Second World War she again began to live almost wholly in Sussex, with Duncan Grant and Clive Bell, painting industriously to the last. After a brief illness she died at Charleston, Firle, near Lewes, Sussex, on 7 April 1961 and was buried on 12 April, without benefit of clergy, in Firle parish churchyard.

Vanessa Bell was a woman of grave and distinguished beauty, with a low and beautiful speaking voice—characteristics which tended to mask her wit and humour and capacity for laughter. Her affections when given were strong and enduring; she was a powerful centripetal force in the small group of friends whom she thought of as 'old Bloomsbury', and among such often difficult and egotistical people she was a conciliator and a peacemaker. As an artist she may be accounted one of the most gifted of her time in Britain, blessed as she was with an instinctive sense of colour and design. She had the intelligence and self-awareness not to be seduced by the pioneering experimentalism of her brilliant post-impressionist period into a sterile extremism; her integrity and sincerity of purpose, and her workmanlike discipline and total lack of affectation led her, during the last four decades of her life, to produce a body of work which affirmed her belief in the simpler pleasures and beauties of the visible world. Her own humility and her unwavering confidence in the superiority of Duncan Grant's genius may have encouraged critics to regard her as his follower, and thus to undervalue her real originality. Their community of interest was indeed close, but in fact the influences were reciprocal.

ANNE OLIVIER BELL

Sources F. Spalding, *Vanessa Bell* (1983) · *Selected letters of Vanessa Bell*, ed. R. Marler (1993) · Q. Bell, *Virginia Woolf: a biography*, 2 vols. (1972) · V. Bell, *Sketches in pen and ink* (1997) · R. Shone, *Bloomsbury portraits: Vanessa Bell, Duncan Grant and their circle*, 2nd edn (1993) ·

L. Stephen, *Sir Leslie Stephen's mausoleum book*, ed. A. Bell (1977) • N. G. Annan, *Leslie Stephen: the godless Victorian*, rev. edn (1984) • *The diary of Virginia Woolf*, ed. A. O. Bell and A. McNeillie, 5 vols. (1977–84) • F. Spalding, *Duncan Grant* (1997) • *CGPLA Eng. & Wales* (1961) • private information (1981, 2004)

Archives Tate Collection, photograph albums and negatives • U. Sussex, corresp. [copies] | King's AC Cam., letters to Julian Bell and John Maynard Keynes • Morgan L., letters to John Maynard Keynes • NYPL, Berg collection, letters to Virginia Woolf • Tate Collection, letters to Clive Bell, Julian Bell, R. Fry, Angelica Garnett, Portia Holman • U. Sussex, corresp. with Leonard Woolf • V&A NAL, letters to Julian Bell

Likenesses G. C. Beresford, photograph, 1902, NPG • D. Grant, oils, c.1918, NPG [*see illus.*] • M. Gimond, bronze head, c.1920–1921, Charleston Trust, Sussex • M. Gimond, lead cast of bust, 1922–6, NPG • D. Grant, oils, 1942, Tate collection • V. Bell, self-portrait, oils, c.1958, Charleston Trust, Sussex • photographs, NPG, Strachey collection

Wealth at death £19,299 19s. 4d.: probate, 17 July 1961, *CGPLA Eng. & Wales*

Bell, William (*b.* in or before **1538**, *d.* **1598**), lawyer, was born to a family of Worcestershire gentry, the son of John Bell. According to his own account Bell's great-grandfather had been forced to sell his patrimony to support a dissolute wife, the natural daughter of Arthur Plantagenet. Bell was educated at Warwick, and at Balliol College, Oxford, where he obtained his BA in 1562 and was elected to a fellowship. Accused of 'discontention' in religion (Bel, 25), he left the university and entered the employ of Sir John Throckmorton of Feckenham, a prominent Catholic and chief justice of Chester. Through Throckmorton's agency Bell spent some time at Clement's Inn and subsequently acted as deputy clerk of the peace for Worcestershire. He made the oration to Elizabeth I on her visit to Worcester in 1575.

Throckmorton died in 1580, by which time Bell was firmly established within the recusant community in Worcestershire. Through Throckmorton he had acquired a house at Temple Broughton, Worcestershire, and in 1582 he married Dorothy Daniel of Acton Place, near Long Melford, Suffolk, a fellow Catholic. The following year he was among the Worcestershire gentry suspected of assisting Campion and Parsons. By 1587 he had three children and it appears to have been the illness and subsequent death of his elder son in that year that led Bell to write a will, which incorporated a detailed exposition of his faith, an account of his life, and precepts for the guidance of children he feared he would leave 'young and tender' (Bel, 24) at his own death. He died at Temple Broughton on 29 June 1598, having fathered a further six children, and was buried at St Mary's, Handbury, Worcestershire. His heir, Edmund, was brought up by Edward Sheldon of Beoley alongside his own son, while two of his daughters were raised in the household of Sheldon's sister Lady Russell. Three decades after Bell's death his will of 1587 with some later additions was found among the Sheldons' papers and sent to his son Francis [see Bell, Arthur (1591–1643)], who published it with his own commentary as *The Testament of William Bel, Gentleman* (1632).

JAN BROADWAY

Sources F. Bel [F. Bell], *The testament of William Bel, gentleman* (Douai, 1632) • D. Grissell, 'The autobiographical and genealogical notebook of the Ven. Arthur Bell, OSF, 1638', *Catholic Record Society*

Miscellanea, 1 (1905), 117–22 • Foster, *Alum. Oxon.* • Worcs. RO, Buchanan-Dunlop papers, 1529/1 • *VCH Worcestershire*, 2.53; 3.377

Bell, William (**1625–1683**), Church of England clergyman, was born on 4 February 1625 in the London parish of St Dunstan-in-the-West. His parents may have been Thomas Bell, a merchant of London, and his wife, Mary, daughter of William Paule of London. He was educated at Merchant Taylors' School (1638–43) and elected a scholar of St John's College, Oxford, in 1643; he graduated BA in July 1647. Bell was also elected a fellow of St John's and became 'well skilled in the practical part of music', but was ejected by the parliamentary visitors in 1648 (Wood, *Ath. Oxon.*, 4.94). Anthony Wood reports that Bell visited France the following year and that in 1655 he was prevented by the triers from taking up a Norfolk living. It seems, however, that Bell was in fact admitted to the rectory of Blickling, Norfolk, and held it for some time, for he left money to the poor of the parish. It was perhaps during his time in the county that he met Anna (1635/1636–1665), daughter of Thomas Sotherton of Haylesdon and his wife, Cecily, daughter of Sir John Corbet. The couple married, but Anna died on 20 August 1665 aged twenty-nine, and was buried at Haylesdon; if there were children, none survived their father. In 1661 Bell was appointed chaplain to Sir John Robinson, lieutenant of the Tower. On 12 September that year, having been restored to his place at St John's, he was admitted BD, and in 1662 he was presented by his college to the living of St Sepulchre, Holborn, London. On 20 March 1666 he was collated to the prebendal stall of Reculverland in St Paul's Cathedral, and on 23 June 1668 he was awarded his doctorate of divinity. Also in 1668 he was appointed chaplain-in-ordinary to Charles II, 'and was for his eminence in preaching made soon after one of the lecturers of the Temple' (ibid.). On 8 April 1671 he was collated to the archdeaconry of St Albans in the diocese of London. Despite these honours, he was still living at St Sepulchre's on 28 November 1671, when the preface to a sermon, published the following year as *Joshua's Resolution to Serve God with his Family*, reveals that his own house, like others in the parish, had been rebuilt 'out of the ashes of the late dreadful fire' (sig. A2). Bell also announced that from the following spring, on one afternoon a week, he would be taking the children and servants of parishioners for catechizing. He died on 19 July 1683, aged fifty-eight, and was buried on 26 July in the chancel of St Sepulchre's Church. An elegy was published on his death. He left money, and property in London and St Albans to many nephews and nieces, and there were bequests to the library of Sion College and to the poor of several parishes. Bell also provided for the preaching of two anniversary sermons, one on 30 January and the other on 29 May, respectively the dates of the execution of Charles I in 1649 and the arrival in London of Charles II in 1660.

A. R. BUCKLAND, rev. STEPHEN WRIGHT

Sources Wood, *Ath. Oxon.*, new edn, vol. 4 • will, PRO, PROB 11/374, sig.110 • F. Blomefield and C. Parkin, *An essay towards a topographical history of the county of Norfolk*, [2nd edn], 11 vols. (1805–10), vols. 6, 10 • *Fasti Angl., 1541–1857*, [St Paul's, London] • *Walker rev.* •

C. J. Robinson, ed., *A register of the scholars admitted into Merchant Taylors' School, from AD 1562 to 1874*, 2 vols. (1882–3) · W. Bell, *Joshua's resolution to serve God with his family, recommended to the inhabitants of St Sepulchre's parish* (1672) · W. Bell, *City security stated: in a sermon preached at St Pauls August 11th 1661* (1661) · *The visitation of London, anno Domini 1633, 1634, and 1635, made by Sir Henry St George*, 1, ed. J. J. Howard and J. L. Chester, Harleian Society, 15 (1880) · Foster, *Alum. Oxon.*

Wealth at death property in London and St Albans; several bequests: will, PRO, PROB 11/374, sig. 110

Bell, William (1731–1816), Church of England clergyman and benefactor, was born in Greenwich, the son of William Bell. He was educated at Greenwich School, and admitted pensioner at Magdalene College, Cambridge, on 26 May 1749. He graduated BA, as eighth wrangler, in 1753, the year in which he was elected fellow of Magdalene. He was ordained deacon, at Lincoln, on 27 September 1754 and priest on 21 December 1755. Also in that year he secured the senior bachelor's dissertation prize. He graduated MA in 1756, when he also was awarded one of the first dissertation prizes on the subject of trade recently founded by Charles, third Viscount Townshend. His successful essay became his first publication. *A dissertation on the following subject: what causes principally contribute to render a nation populous? And what effect has the populousness of a nation on its trade?* was published by the university press at Cambridge in 1756, and dedicated to Thomas Pelham-Holles, duke of Newcastle, on whose behalf Bell was quickly to prove an able university politician. Bell's was a fairly conventional argument, namely that an increase in population was a sign of vigour and growth, and was therefore to be promoted. Refinement, luxury, and elegance were seen as undermining population growth, while agriculture and the 'necessary arts' were seen as aiding it, and were thus to be encouraged. Luxury promoted an increase in the number of useless servants, who could not afford to marry, and the numbers of children decreased proportionately. Commerce was slighted in favour of agriculture, though Bell concluded, more equivocally, that 'TRADE can no where be brought to so flourishing and permanent a state, as where it has from the first been cultivated by an exceeding numerous people' (p. 36). The essay was not without influence on the debates on population that were so prominent in the mid-eighteenth century, and a German translation of it appeared in 1762.

Bell was a firm believer in the priority of the Bible in deciding doctrinal matters, and he devoted much of his literary labour to developing an Anglican apologia in conformity with this conviction. In 1761 he published *An enquiry into the divine missions of John the Baptist and Jesus Christ; so far as they can be proved from the circumstances of their births, and their connection with each other*, a lengthy explication of biblical texts that sought to establish the nature of the indissoluble bonds that Bell traced between the New Testament narratives concerning Jesus and John the Baptist as constituting a hitherto neglected proof of the divine origin of the Christian revelation. Bell continued in this strain when he published in 1765 *A defence of the revelation in general and the gospel in particular; in answer to the objections advanced in a late book entitled, 'The morality of the New Testament, digested under various heads'*. This book was published anonymously; as Bell noted when sending a copy of it to the duke of Newcastle in May 1766 this would enable him 'to avoid those Disagreeables, which too frequently attend Controversial Writings, even in the best of Causes' (BL, Add. MS 33069, fol. 483). Bell had by this time left Cambridge to be domestic chaplain to Princess Amelia, aunt of George III, through whom he gained a prebend of Westminster in 1765; her influence also helped him to secure his DD, *per literas regias*, in 1767. In 1776 he was presented by the dean and chapter of Westminster to the vicarage of St Bride's, London, which he vacated in 1780 on presentation to the rectory of Christchurch, Newgate Street, London, which he resigned in 1799.

In 1774 Bell published *A sermon preached in Lambeth Chapel, at the consecration of the Right Reverend Father in God, John Thomas, LL.D., lord bishop of Rochester*, in which he defended the principle of a distinct order of clergy that was to be properly funded in order to be set apart for teaching and pastoral duties. The clergy were also to promote the religiously inflected politics of virtue with which Bell had been so concerned in his Townshend prize essay. He concluded the sermon with the observation that 'the Comparative Virtue of such an Order may be conducive to the practical influence of Religion, and add increase and security to the blessings of Social Life' (p. 23). Bell was very concerned with practical charity, and his obituary in the *Gentleman's Magazine* paid particular regard to his annual distributions of alms, which were dedicated to 'succouring the indigent, promoting industry, and contributing to the good of every useful institution'. His acts of beneficence 'were great beyond example' but 'were also without ostentation or vanity … He was always looking out for objects of distress' (*GM*, 1817). In this he was at one with the example of Princess Amelia, whose charitable giving he continued after her death. It was in honour of the princess that he published in 1787 Pierre François Le Courayer's *Déclaration de mes dernier sentimens sur les différens dogmes de la religion*, a tract which she had left him with a view to its eventual publication. The *Déclaration* voiced Le Courayer's central conviction that the protestants were closer to the truth and the word of God than were his fellow Catholics on matters where the two denominations differed. Bell later had the work translated by the Revd Dr John Calder but was otherwise not overkeen on associating himself with a controversial text that only his piety towards Princess Amelia had induced him to publish.

Bell's most important and controversial work was *An attempt to ascertain and illustrate the authority, nature, and design of the institute of Christ commonly called the communion of the Lord's supper* (1780; 2nd edn, 1781). The work was dedicated to Princess Amelia and was designed to reinforce the purely scriptural foundation of the beliefs promoted by the Church of England and 'her Reformation' (p. xvi). Bell argued that the eucharist was a purely commemorative rite instituted by Christ and recommended by the apostles as a memorial of his sacrifice. It had no other significance whatsoever; it was a plain Christian duty to celebrate communion in these terms, and Bell concluded accordingly that 'the Lord's Supper is a rite of the simplest and plainest nature, perfectly intelligible to every capacity' (p. 38). The treatise itself was short (some forty pages) but a great deal of appended matter was included to illustrate his argument, and notes were added to the appendix in which he attacked William Warburton's interpretation of the eucharist and defended that made by Benjamin Hoadly. Bell was a firm latitudinarian, and his work provoked a short-lived controversy in which he was praised by a dissenter and censured by a high-churchman. Peter Emmans, a Presbyterian minister, described Bell as 'a judicious divine' in his review of the treatise (*Monthly Review*, 450), recommending it as 'the most complete, rational, and satisfactory treatise on the subject hitherto published, written with equal learning and judgment, and discovering in the worthy Author the most commendable liberality and candour of sentiment and disposition' (ibid., 457). In *A letter to the Rev. William Bell, D.D. prebendary of St Peter's Westminster, on the subject of his late publication upon the authority, nature and design of the Lord's supper* (1781) Lewis Bagot, dean of Christ Church, Oxford, accused Bell of promoting Socinian doctrines utterly inconsistent with the teachings of the Church of England. Whatever Bell's feelings about this might have been it did not prevent him from adding a supplement to the treatise in 1790 that effectively restated his argument and that he published as *An enquiry whether any doctrine relating to the nature and effects of the Lord's supper can be justly founded on the discourse of Our Lord recorded in the sixth chapter of the gospel of St. John.*

Bell was given the treasurer's stall in St Paul's Cathedral in 1810. In that year he transferred £15,200 in consols to Cambridge University to fund eight new scholarships, two for each year of study, to enable the sons or orphans of Church of England clergy, whose circumstances would otherwise have made it impossible for them to do so, to graduate from the university. The first elections took place in 1810; no scholar was to be elected from either King's College or from Trinity Hall. Bell died on 29 September 1816 in his prebendal house, in Little Dean's Yard, Westminster, and is buried in Westminster Abbey. His interest had been primarily in promoting practical piety, and this informed the two volumes of his sermons that appeared under the editorship of Joseph Allen in 1817. Allen accurately described the sermons as 'a body of practical Christianity' and noted that what Bell taught 'he most conscientiously endeavoured to practise' (W. Bell, *Sermons on Various Subjects*, 1.v, vii–viii).   B. W. YOUNG

Sources GM, 1st ser., 80 (1810), 490; 86/2 (1816), 371; 87/1 (1817), 646 • Venn, *Alum. Cant.* • *Monthly Review*, 63 (1780), 448–58 • J. R. Raven, 'Viscount Townshend and the Cambridge prize for trade theory, 1754-1756', *HJ*, 28 (1985), 535-55 • R. R. Kuczynski, 'British demographers' opinions on fertility, 1660 to 1760', *Political arithmetic*, ed. L. Hodgson (1938), 283-327

Bell, William (1734/5–1806?), portrait and history painter, was born at Newcastle upon Tyne, Northumberland, the son of a bookbinder. On 30 January 1769 aged thirty-four, he enrolled as the first student in the Royal Academy Schools. He tried, unsuccessfully, to win the academy gold medal in 1770, but won it in the following year for his picture of *Venus Entreating Vulcan to Forge Arms for her Son Aeneas.* His models were local people from Newcastle; Welford records that 'William Carr, the strong man of Blyth, figur[ed] as Vulcan' (Welford, 1.249). His patron was Lord Delaval, several members of whose family he painted in full-length portraits for the gallery at Seaton Delaval in Northumberland, the family seat, where they remain. He exhibited at the Royal Academy in 1775 two views of Seaton Delaval, when his address was given as 'At Sir John Delaval's' (Graves, *RA exhibitors*, 1.176), and a history painting *Susanna and the Two Elders* at the Free Society of Artists in 1776. He was noted for the fineness of his draperies, a skill that brought an offer of employment from Sir Joshua Reynolds, which he refused. He maintained himself by portrait painting and running a drawing school, in the Back Row, assisted by a settlement of £50 a year and a cottage from Lord Delaval. Long recorded seeing a miniature of Queen Elizabeth, painted, according to an inscription on the verso by William Bell, in 1800. 'It was rather well ptd in a soft manner' (Long, 26). He died probably in 1806.
    A. NISBET

Sources R. Welford, *Men of mark 'twixt Tyne and Tweed*, 1 (1895), 249 • Redgrave, *Artists* • M. Hall, *The artists of Northumbria* (1973) • Waterhouse, *18c painters* • Graves, *RA exhibitors* • Graves, *Soc. Artists* • W. T. Whitley, *Artists and their friends in England, 1700–1799*, 2 vols. (1928) • B. S. Long, *British miniaturists* (1929) • G. Meissner, ed., *Allgemeines Künstlerlexikon: die bildenden Künstler aller Zeiten und Völker*, [new edn, 34 vols.] (Leipzig and Munich, 1983–) • records, RA

Bell, William Blair- (1871–1936), gynaecologist, was born on 28 September 1871 at Rutland House, New Brighton, Cheshire, the second of eight children of William Bell JP, general practitioner, and his wife, Helen Barbara, daughter of General Butcher. In 1931 he added his second forename to his surname by means of a hyphen; at the height of his career he thought that Blair-Bell would be a more distinguished name by which to be known and remembered. He was educated at Rossall School, Lancashire (1885–90), and at King's College Hospital and medical school, London (1890–96). He won distinction in a number of sports, including hurdling, and showed a precocious bent for research, carrying out interesting anatomical dissections and publishing a paper in the *King's College Hospital Reports* while still a student. After qualifying in 1896 he returned to Cheshire, set up in general practice in Wallasey, and on 7 June 1898 married his cousin Florence Bell (d. 1929), daughter of his uncle John Bell, a solicitor in Surbiton, Surrey.

In 1905 Bell was appointed honorary assistant consulting gynaecologist to the Liverpool Royal Infirmary. While still a general practitioner he published more than a dozen papers on a wide variety of subjects, the beginning of a series of no fewer than 130 major contributions to medical literature made over the next thirty years. His *Principles of Gynaecology* was published in 1910. In 1921 he succeeded Henry Briggs as professor of midwifery and gynaecology at Liverpool University, a post he retained until 1931. In 1916 he published *The Sex Complex*, and in 1919 *The Pituitary*, both of which were recognized as classics and which contained much new material; they described a series of laboratory and animal experiments which he had undertaken himself. At that time knowledge of endocrinology was very elementary and it was the acknowledged belief that the sex of an individual depended solely upon the gonads (ovary and testis). Blair-Bell's original research, both laboratory and clinical, broadened the concept of the interaction of the numerous ductless glands between one and the other, the subject of his Arris and Gale lecture at the Royal College of Surgeons in 1913, which was published in *The Lancet* in the same year.

During the next ten years Bell carried out major research, in collaboration with colleagues at London University, on the causes and nature of cancer; *Cancer and Cancer Research* was published in 1928, and *Some Aspects of the Causes of the Cancer Problem* in 1930. 566 patients were treated with a compound of lead as an adjunct to surgery; this was one of the first uses of a chemotherapeutic agent in the treatment of cancer. Although this particular agent failed the foundation was laid for the development of other, more successful, ones in future years. In 1929 the British (later Royal) College of Obstetricians and Gynaecologists was founded, after several years of planning by Bell and his colleagues. This was a milestone in medical history because it established the principle of giving recognition to a specialism previously included in the wider field of medicine and surgery. Bell became the college's first president; his benefactions to the college after his death included a house in Queen Anne Street, London, which became the first home of the college, as well as funds for lectures and research.

Blair-Bell was an outstanding teacher, clinician, and surgeon. He was universally regarded as the most distinguished gynaecologist of his era, noted not only for his original clinical and scientific researches but also for the administrative abilities and the legalistic knowledge which he displayed in drawing up the final constitution of the new college which he had founded. His achievements were remarkable and were recognized by the many honours and distinctions conferred upon him. He was awarded honorary fellowships of the Royal College of Surgeons and of the American College of Surgeons, as well as of many obstetric and gynaecological societies in Great Britain and overseas. He was awarded the LLD of both Glasgow and Liverpool universities. He became a commander of the royal order of the Star of Romania. Yet in spite of his great distinctions he was a complex character in many ways. He was an outspoken autocrat, who resented criticism and who enjoyed a fight with anyone who opposed his views; this brought him enemies as well as admirers and friends. Although childless himself he was fond of children, and his spaniel, Rogue, was his constant companion when he was at home. Lord Dawson best summarized his character: 'He was a torch bearer who never forgot—or allowed anyone else to forget—that he was carrying a torch'. His portrait, which hangs in the president's room at the Royal College of Obstetricians and Gynaecologists, portrays a man with a dynamic personality, upright stance, and determined features.

Blair-Bell died of a coronary thrombosis, on 25 January 1936, while on a train carrying him from London to Shrewsbury. He was buried at St Chad's parish church, West Felton, Shropshire.   JOHN PEEL

Sources J. Peel, *William Blair-Bell, father and founder* (1986) · J. Peel, *The lives of the fellows of the Royal College of Obstetricians and Gynaecologists, 1929–1969* (1976) · *The Lancet* (1 Feb 1936) · *BMJ* (8 Feb 1936), 287–9 · W. Fletcher-Shaw, *Twenty-five years* (1954) · W. Blair-Bell, diary, Royal College of Obstetricians and Gynaecologists, London, 2 vols. · *WWW* · *CGPLA Eng. & Wales* (1936) · d. cert.

Archives Liverpool Medical Institution · Royal College of Obstetricians and Gynaecologists, London, casebooks and notebooks; corresp. and papers; history of the British College of Obstetricians and Gynaecologists; papers · Royal Society of Medicine, London | Royal College of Obstetricians and Gynaecologists, London, corresp. with Sir W. F. Shaw

Likenesses J. B. Souter, portrait, 1932 (as president of Royal College of Obstetricians and Gynaecologists), Royal College of Obstetricians and Gynaecologists, London · J. Bacon & Sons, photograph, Wellcome L. · Rothenstein, portrait

Wealth at death £91,488 15s. 7d.: probate, 13 March 1936, *CGPLA Eng. & Wales*

Bellamont. For this title name *see* Bard, Henry, first Viscount Bellomont [Bellamont] (1615/16–1656); Coote, Richard, first earl of Bellamont (1636–1701); Kirkhoven, Charles Henry, Baron Wotton and earl of Bellamont (1643–1682/3) [*see under* Stanhope, Katherine, *suo jure* countess of Chesterfield, and Lady Stanhope (*bap.* 1609, *d.* 1667)].

Bellamy, Daniel, the elder (*b.* 1687), lawyer and writer, was born on 25 December 1687 in the parish of St Martin Pomeroy, in Ironmonger Lane, London, the son of John or Daniel Bellamy. He entered Merchant Taylors' School on 12 March 1702 before matriculating from St John's College, Oxford, on 4 March 1706. The following year, on 4 July, he was admitted as a member of Lincoln's Inn. He left Oxford in 1709 without taking a degree and became a conveyancer's clerk to Nicholas Martyn of Lincoln's Inn. Unexpected family misfortunes made him turn to writing for the public as a source of income.

Bellamy's range of publications over the next fifty years show him to have been a gifted, versatile man with a strong religious presence. He translated moral works from Greek, Latin, and French, most typical being *Thoughts on the Trinity … Concerning the Truth of the Christian Religion* (1721), his twenty-seven moral tales and fables adapted from Fénelon (1729), and a Latin edition of the fables of Phaedrus (1734). He could be witty, as in his poems *Taffy's Triumph* (1709), his translation of Holdsworth's *Muscipula* (1708), and *Back-Gammon* (1734).

Above all, Bellamy was keen on the education of the young, writing pastoral plays for the girls at the schools run by his wife, Martha, and his sister Mrs Hannah Ward. Typical is his *Young Ladies' Miscellany* (1723) which includes 'Innocence Betray'd, or, The Royal Imposter' and 'The

Rival Nymphs, or, The Merry Swain' as well as an essay on pronunciation and his views on education: 'Children are like precious Diamonds … the more valuable the Jewel, the more Art and judgment is requisite to make it shine in its full Lustre' (p. 168). The title-page to the first edition gives the address of his wife's school as Old Boswell Court, near Temple Bar. By the second edition of 1726 it had migrated to High Wycombe.

In 1739 and 1740 Bellamy collaborated with his son Daniel *Bellamy the younger in the publication of *Miscellanies in Prose and Verse*. He was probably still alive in early 1768 when his son praised him in *Ethic Amusements* (preface, iv).

F. D. A. BURNS

Sources DNB · Foster, *Alum. Oxon.* · W. P. Baildon, ed., *The records of the Honorable Society of Lincoln's Inn: the black books*, 3 (1899), 332, 334 · C. J. Robinson, ed., *A register of the scholars admitted into Merchant Taylors' School, from AD 1562 to 1874*, 2 (1883), 7 · D. E. Baker, *Biographia dramatica, or, A companion to the playhouse*, rev. I. Reed, new edn, rev. S. Jones, 1 (1812), 31 · D. Bellamy, *Ethic amusements*, rev. D. Bellamy the younger (1768) · D. F. Foxon, *English verse, 1701–1750: a catalogue of separately printed poems with notes on contemporary collected editions*, 1 (1975), 54–5 · IGI · D. Bellamy, *The young ladies' miscellany, or, Youth's innocent and rational amusement* (1723)

Bellamy, Daniel, the younger (*bap.* 1717, *d.* 1788), writer, was baptized on 1 October 1717 at St Andrew's, Holborn, the son of Daniel *Bellamy the elder (*b.* 1687) and Martha. He was educated at St Paul's School before matriculating as a sizar at Trinity College, Cambridge, on 30 April 1736. He gained his MA *per literas regias* in 1759.

Like his father, whose talents he admired, Bellamy became a writer of religious works intended to educate the general public. His first work was *Miscellanies in Prose and Verse* (1739–40) in collaboration with his father. In 1741 he took holy orders and first served at Kingston upon Thames, Surrey. Twelve of the discourses he gave there were published as *The Truth of the Christian Religion*, dated 15 August 1744, with a dedication to the vicar of Kingston. His paraphrase of the book of Job followed in 1748. In 1749 he became vicar of St Stephen's, St Albans, Hertfordshire.

Bellamy attached considerable importance to preaching. On 29 June 1756 he gave a sermon on benevolence in St Paul's to those educated at his former school, and he began gathering material for *The Family Preacher*. From 1758 until 1766 he was assistant minister at Richmond, Surrey, and in 1759 was also appointed rector of Hedgerley, Buckinghamshire. In 1766 he became chaplain of Kew and Petersham, Surrey, a position which he held for the rest of his life. He revised his father's *Ethic Amusements* (1768), but his main publication was *The Family Preacher* (1776) in two volumes, with discourses for every Sunday through the year, some by James Carrington, chancellor of Exeter. In selecting from 'nearly four hundred manuscripts accumulated in the course of thirty-five years ministry' (Bellamy, *Family Preacher*, vi), Bellamy showed not only his biblical knowledge but also his honesty, sincerity, and directness in emphasizing the use of 'the language of the heart' rather than 'studied phrases' (ibid., 2.398). The work was dedicated to Queen Charlotte.

Bellamy's contact with the royal palace at Kew also led to occasional poems, such as the ode to the princess dowager of Wales of 10 May 1768 and the serenetta in 1771 for George, prince of Wales. Bellamy died on 15 February 1788 at Kew and was buried in Kew churchyard. He was survived by his wife, Frances.

F. D. A. BURNS

Sources DNB · IGI · Venn, *Alum. Cant.* · D. Bellamy, jnr, *The truth of the Christian religion demonstrated both from reason and revelation* (1744) · D. Bellamy, jnr, *The family preacher*, 2 vols. (1776) · GM, 1st ser., 26 (1756), 453 · GM, 1st ser., 58 (1788), 272 · N&Q, 2nd ser., 2 (1856), 507 · N&Q, 2nd ser., 10 (1860), 129 · PRO, PROB 11/1163, sig. 120
Likenesses J. K. Baldrey, stipple, pubd 1789 (after Folkestone), BM, NPG
Wealth at death see will, PRO, PROB 11/1163, sig. 120

Bellamy, Ethel Frances Butwell (1881–1960). *See under* Bellamy, Frank Arthur (1863–1936).

Bellamy, Frank Arthur (1863–1936), astronomer and philatelist, was born on 17 October 1863 at St John's Street, Oxford, the youngest of the six children of Montague Bellamy (1830–1882), a college butler and master bookbinder in St Giles', Oxford, and his wife, Zilpah, *née* Butwell (1828–1887). He attended Magdalen College School. In July 1881 Bellamy followed his two brothers who had been junior assistants at the Radcliffe Observatory. He learned to use all the instruments, and had charge of photography and meteorology. His parents' deaths having left him living with two sisters, Bellamy supplemented his income as a tutor in meteorology, astronomy, and botany. As a boy he had played on the building site of the university observatory, and in September 1892 he was engaged as an assistant there. In June 1893 the new Savilian professor of astronomy, H. H. Turner, confirmed him as first assistant. His eldest brother left two daughters—Ethel Frances Butwell [*see below*] and Edith Winifred, an invalid—to live in a house given by their aunt. Frank drew Ethel into astronomy, and lived with his nieces for the rest of his life.

Bellamy devoted forty-six years to the *Astrographic Catalogue*, the first international scheme to use photography to catalogue stars in both hemispheres. The sky was partitioned into zones and shared between eighteen observatories. In ten years Bellamy took 1180 plates for the Oxford zone and was responsible for the laborious measurement and reduction of the star positions. For this in 1905 he was made an honorary MA. In 1913 Turner arranged for Bellamy to reduce the Hyderabad observatory's zone. By 1928 Bellamy and Ethel had catalogued nearly 1 million stars. He was then assigned the Potsdam zone, which he had almost completed by the time of his death.

Bellamy participated in two discoveries in 1903: of Nova Geminorum in March, and of a new star cluster in Cygnus. He took follow-up photographs of other novae, including the one in Perseus (1901). In 1905 he accompanied Turner, Robert T. Gunther, and J. H. Reynolds to Aswan to observe and photograph the total eclipse of the sun. Bellamy published thirty-five astronomical papers between 1899 and 1930, mostly in *Monthly Notices of the Royal Astronomical Society*. He had been elected a fellow of the Royal Astronomical Society in 1896. He was a life member of the British

Association for the Advancement of Science and regularly attended its meetings.

After starting by using the wet collodion process, Bellamy developed a wide interest and expertise in photography. For his own teaching, and for Turner's academic and popular lectures on astronomy, he created both photographic and mechanical lantern slides. In 1889 he was a founder of the Oxford Photographic Society; as its secretary from 1890 to 1892 he organized a collection of glassplate negatives on local history, architecture, and geology. He donated his own collection of negatives and prints to the Oxford City Library. In 1892 he resigned from the Oxford Photographic Society over a matter of principle, and afterwards refused to join its successor, the Oxford Camera Club. Instead he joined the Banbury Photographic Club.

Bellamy was the last non-graduate first assistant at the observatory, but his energy and interests nevertheless enabled him to move within a wide academic circle. He co-operated with G. C. Druce in field botany and compiled 'Notes on flowers in Oxfordshire and Gloucestershire, 1901–03'. He also donated specimens to the Fielding Herbarium in Oxford. Meteorology led him to phenology and the observation of the recurring times of natural phenomena; for fifty-three years, from 1882 to 1935, he reported observations for the Royal Meteorological Society, of which he was a fellow from 1883 to 1901. Bellamy was a member of the Oxfordshire (from 1901 the Ashmolean) Natural History Society. He was president of the meteorology (1896–9) and (from 1899) the photography sections, president of the society (1902–3), and a frequent lecturer; while secretary (1906–9), he detailed the society's history (1908). In addition he catalogued its library and established its lantern slide collection.

Bellamy had a national reputation as a philatelist. He was a founder (1890), life member, secretary, and treasurer of the Oxford Philatelic Society, and he was elected a fellow of the Royal Philatelic Society of London in 1908. The hobby originated in a large box of stamps, given to Bellamy's eldest brother by Bodley's Librarian Bulkeley Bandinel (1781–1861), to which Bellamy had a longstanding sentimental attachment. He actively collected from the age of five, and eventually assembled a collection of over 200,000 items relating to the postal history of the world, including a library of great historic interest, and a unique collection of 2500 Oxford and Cambridge college messenger stamps; it was estimated to be worth over £6000 in 1925. Not least because of its origins, in 1915 he bequeathed, and in 1920 directly offered, the 'Bellamy collection' to the university. In spite of widespread support within the university, in 1926 Bellamy's offer was rejected, to his great chagrin.

Turner's death in 1930 made changes at the observatory inevitable. While acting director until 1932, Bellamy made a spirited public attack on a committee considering the future of the observatory. He was a practical astronomer of the old school, while the new professor, H. H. Plaskett, privately described the Bellamys as having 'never had an original thought' (Plaskett to Douglas Veale, 23 July 1934,

Bodl. Oxf., UR6/Ast/4/3). By 1933 Bellamy was bitterly opposed to Plaskett's adapting the observatory to astrophysics, and sad that the Radcliffe Observatory was closing. He scoured both observatories, listing and labelling the old instruments. When Plaskett was away in March 1934 he spent three days dismantling the famous De La Rue reflector, 'labelling every part, putting back every screw and bolt', and hiding all he could (Museum of the History of Science, Oxford, MS Gunther Archive). His concern to preserve the past, and considerable physical effort when aged over seventy, helped save much historic material.

Bellamy and Plaskett did not speak for the last months of 1935. At the visitors' meeting of 30 January 1936 Bellamy faced the vice-chancellor and listed his complaints against Plaskett, then resigned. He continued his work on the *Astrographic Catalogue* at his home, 2 Winchester Road, Oxford, but died there suddenly on 15 February. Ethel wrote: 'We were such a happy family of three—and we took such care of him … I dread my work without his help and sympathy' (E. F. B. Bellamy to Gunther, 5 March 1936). Bellamy was buried in the family grave at St Sepulchre's cemetery.

Ethel Frances Butwell Bellamy (1881–1960), astronomical computer and seismologist, was born on 17 November 1881 at 36 Kingston Road, Oxford, one of the six children of Montague Edward James Butwell Bellamy (1850–1908), a bookbinder who worked with his father, and his wife, Mary, *née* Castell. Nothing is known of her education, and she never married. In 1899 she started part-time work at home, computing for the *Astrographic Catalogue*. She was expert also in clerical and photographic work, and in 1912 Turner engaged her full-time at £50 per year.

Between 1913 and 1947 Ethel made a remarkable contribution to seismology and to Turner's annual *International Seismological Summary* (*ISS*). In 1918 she became the seismology assistant, paid from small grants. Despite recurrent ill health, and discomfort working in an unheated hut until 1927, she collated, measured, and corrected the readings of eventually 600 seismology stations, and maintained correspondence with them. From 1930 she edited the *ISS*, and during the Second World War she also computed the epicentres. Turner had produced an index catalogue of epicentres for 1918 to 1924. By 'voluntary work at home … as a contribution to earthquake science and as a personal memorial' to Turner, Ethel produced two indices covering 1925 to 1935, and the world map locating them also seems to have been her own work.

Between 1911 and 1928, to relieve her uncle's burden, Ethel reduced the measurements of the Vatican observatory's zone of the *Astrographic Catalogue* and brought them to publication; Frank compiled extensive notes for the last volume. The pair accomplished all this mostly at home and without payment. In 1928 they each received a Vatican silver medal (Turner was awarded a gold), and in 1934 Ethel was made an honorary MA in recognition of her work on the *Astrographic Catalogue* and seismology. From

1935 until the war she was brought onto the British Association for the Advancement of Science's committee for seismological investigations. Through the Second World War she was 'independently a mainstay of seismology' (Plaskett, 122), only to see it discontinued by Plaskett in 1947. A lifelong member of the British Astronomical Association, she was elected a fellow of the Royal Astronomical Society in 1926. Between 1913 and 1939 she published seven papers under her own name and two co-authored with Frank Bellamy. She retired in July 1947, and died in a nursing home at Weymouth, Dorset, on 7 December 1960.

Frank Bellamy never married. By an extraordinary codicil to his will in 1926, in the opinion of a university official 'framed for his own glory without consideration for his nieces' welfare' (Matheson to vice-chancellor, 4 April 1936, Bodl. Oxf., UC/135/2), he bequeathed his postal history collection to Cambridge University. A letter eight days before his death evidenced concern for his nieces' financial position, but paradoxically reaffirmed that the Bellamy collection was not for their benefit. He died believing that Queens' College, Cambridge, was accepting it. But, despite an insurance policy for £500 to benefit 'my girls', Bellamy's estate was insolvent. Oxford University made a £100 grant to Ethel, and Cambridge was persuaded to decline the bequest. Much of the collection passed to a dealer for dispersal.

On the one hand meticulous, dedicated, and generous to enquirers, on the other obsessive and curmudgeonly, what seems to unite Bellamy's diverse fields of activity was a passion for cataloguing. In his collection the university turned down a remarkable gift. Its quality was recognized by John Johnson, who obtained all he could of it and retained Bellamy's name within his own collection, which is now in the Bodleian Library. The Bellamys' work for the observatory was routine, but their efforts typify the affordable assistants upon whom scientific institutions depended.   ROGER HUTCHINS

Sources [H. P. Hollis], *Monthly Notices of the Royal Astronomical Society*, 97 (1936–7), 263–6 · [H. C. Plummer], *The Observatory*, 59 (1936), 135–7 · H. H. Plaskett, *Quarterly Journal of the Royal Astronomical Society*, 2 (1961), 121–3 · private information (2004) [A. V. Simcock] · F. A. Bellamy, will, 28 Oct 1915, codicil, 19 April 1926, proved in Durham probate registry, 26 Aug 1936 · F. A. Bellamy, *A historical account of the Ashmolean Natural History Society of Oxfordshire, 1880–1905* (1908) · F. A. Bellamy to R. T. Gunther, 25 March 1934, MHS Oxf., MS Gunther archive, OA/2/26 · E. F. B. Bellamy to R. T. Gunther, 5 March 1936, MHS Oxf., MS Gunther archive, OA/2/26 · annual reports to the visitors of the university observatory, *Oxford University Gazette* · H. H. Plaskett, letter to Douglas Veale, 23 July 1934, Oxf. UA, university registry files, UR6/Ast/4/3 · census returns for Oxford, 1891, PRO, RG 12/1166, 91–3 · P. S. Matheson to vice-chancellor, 4 April 1936, Oxf. UA, university chest files, UC/135/2 · E. F. B. Bellamy, 'Catalogue of earthquakes', *Report of the British Association for the Advancement of Science* (1935), 230–33 · b. cert. [E. F. B. Bellamy] · b. cert. · will [E. F. B. Bellamy]

Archives Bodl. Oxf., MS catalogue of Philatelic Library, letters · Bodl. Oxf., university registry files, UR6/Ast/4 · MHS Oxf., documents, OA/2/10 · MHS Oxf., letters, OA/2/26 · MHS Oxf., letter, notes, photos, museum 117 | Bodl. Oxf., Radcliffe Science Library, MS Radcliffe 68 [note 12 March 1935 re Radcliffe instruments]

Likenesses photographs, 1896–1902 (with observatory staff), MHS Oxf., box 3 · F. Bellamy, self-portrait?, *c.*1931, MHS Oxf., box 3

Wealth at death £1577 10*s.* 5*d.*: probate, 26 Aug 1936, *CGPLA Eng. & Wales* · £2139 10*s.* 6*d.*—Ethel Bellamy: probate, 16 Feb 1961, *CGPLA Eng. & Wales*

Bellamy, George Anne (1731?–1788), actress, probably born in Fingal, Ireland, was the daughter of a minor actress, Mrs Bellamy, *née* Seal, later Mrs Walter (*d.* 1771), and James *O'Hara, second Baron Tyrawley (1681/2–1773). Her year of birth appears variously as 1733, 1727, 1730, and 1731, though the last of these, supposedly relating to a birth affidavit, is the most probable. Her Christian name—Georgiane—reflecting her birthday, St George's day (23 April), was discovered to have been mistakenly noted in her birth records as George Anne, the name by which the actress later elected to be known.

Although George Anne took the name Bellamy from her mother's first husband, her birth shortly after their marriage resulted in the hasty exit of Captain Bellamy. Her mother had supposedly eloped with her actual father, Lord Tyrawley, when she was only fourteen. Tyrawley, an ambassador in Lisbon at the time of George Anne's birth, accepted his paternity, and when she was about four sent her to be educated in an Ursuline convent in Boulogne, where she remained for some five years and converted to Roman Catholicism. She lived with her father when he returned to London about 1742, but the following year, when Tyrawley moved to Russia as ambassador, she chose to live with her mother, now Mrs Walter. Her decision defied her father's instructions that she should have no associations with the woman, and their relationship thereafter proved to be turbulent and ended in virtual estrangement.

As early as 1741 George Anne appeared at Covent Garden in a benefit performance of *Harlequin Barber*, playing the non-speaking part of the servant to Colombine. On 27 March 1742 she appeared as Miss Prue in William Congreve's *Love for Love* and in 1743 she played Andromache in a private performance of Ambrose Phillips's *The Distrest Mother*, appearing alongside Garrick. Recalling the performance, she wrote that, although it was staged to test the abilities of Polly, sister of the actress Peg Woffington, 'the laurel was bestowed upon me' (*BDA*). An equally opportune event is claimed to have led to her professional début, as Monimia in Thomas Otway's *The Orphan* at Covent Garden on 22 November 1744. George Anne had become friendly with the daughters of the theatre manager John Rich, and the girls amused themselves by performing plays together. During their rehearsal of *Othello* Rich is said to have incidentally witnessed George Anne's rendition of the Moor and been so impressed by it that, after congratulating her, he proceeded to guarantee her an engagement at Covent Garden should she wish to pursue a theatrical career.

As Monimia, George Anne initially suffered acute stage fright, but by the end of the show her 'début' was considered such a success that the venerable actor James Quin

George Anne Bellamy (1731?–1788), by F. Lindo, mid-1750s?

supposedly lifted her up and declared her 'a divine creature'. Throughout his life Quin adopted an avuncular role towards the actress, offering her support, kindness, and advice—one particular piece of which, as her life proved, she would have been wise to follow: 'Do not let the love of finery, or any other inducement, prevail upon you to commit an indiscretion. Men in general are rascals' (Hartmann, 34).

In 1745 the actress, by all accounts beautiful, with fair skin, blue eyes, and dark hair, moved to Dublin to perform at the Smock Alley Theatre, where she remained until 1748. Between 1748 and 1759 she was engaged at both Covent Garden and Drury Lane, then in 1760–61 was back at Smock Alley. She acted in Edinburgh from 1762 to 1764, and made a brief appearance in Glasgow in May 1764. Although she was never considered a truly great actress, George Anne was nevertheless highly esteemed. For the opening of the 1750 season Drury Lane presented *Romeo and Juliet*, with George Anne as Juliet playing opposite Garrick as Romeo, while at Covent Garden Mrs Cibber and Spranger Barry played the same roles. The competition between the two theatres lasted twelve consecutive nights, and Francis Gentleman, comparing the two actresses, wrote that 'One excelled in amorous rapture, the other called every power of distress and despair to her aid' (Gentleman, *The Dramatic Censor*, 1.193). While George Anne could perhaps never truly compete with Mrs Cibber, she nevertheless excelled at playing parts which required displays of love, tenderness, and pathos. Throughout her career she appeared regularly in some ninety-six roles, but was known particularly for her renditions of

Belvidera in Otway's *Venice Preserv'd*, Almeyda in *Don Sebastian*, and Alicia in Nicholas Rowe's *Jane Shore*.

George Anne's strong-willed personality perhaps had as much bearing on her success as her acting abilities. In December 1758, bravely disregarding both the conventions of the time and the opinions of her fellow actors, she scored an immediate theatrical success in the title role of Robert Dodsley's *Cleone* at Covent Garden, which she elected to play simply and quietly—'an effort worth trying; as from its novelty I should, at least, have the merit of its being all my own' (Hartmann, 190). This determination to succeed was often directed at those perceived to stand in her way, and her declaration 'Though I despise revenge, I do not dislike retaliation' (ibid., 164) appears to be borne out by numerous events. When the management of Covent Garden cast Miss Wilford as Cordelia, George Anne made a direct challenge to them by having hand-sheets distributed to the audience, stating that the part had been taken from her the night before. As Miss Wilford had not been well received in the role previously, the sheet closed with the statement that George Anne would be ready to play Cordelia should the audience prefer it. When the curtain rose there were loud calls for Mrs Bellamy, and Miss Wilford's first entrance was greeted with such outcries that she was forced to cede the part. Similarly, in 1755, when her rival and enemy Peg Woffington was cast in the leading part of Jocasta, with Mrs Bellamy playing the minor role of the young Eurydice, the latter claims to have distracted the audience by fainting on the appearance of the ghost—a skill she frequently employed at particularly convenient moments.

Although George Anne was dubbed by William Chetwood as the 'Inchanting Bellamy' (Hartmann, 52), her life, at least as depicted in the autobiographical *An Apology for the Life of George Anne Bellamy* (1785), suggests instead the 'Unfortunate Bellamy'. She never married, although she was the mother of three children—one with Sir George Montgomery Metham (1716–1793) and two with John *Calcraft (*bap.* 1726, *d.* 1772)—and she professed that she was led to believe by both that marriage would be forthcoming. When living in Scotland with the actor West *Digges (1725?–1786) she claimed that she thought they were legally married. She was apparently unaware that both Calcraft and Digges were already married prior to their relationship with her. Between 1767 and 1777 she resided with the actor Henry *Woodward (1714–1777), although she insisted that this relationship remained platonic.

Mrs Bellamy was plagued throughout her life by debts incurred from gambling, living well beyond her means, and entertaining lavishly, as well as, if she is to be believed, her naïvely trusting and generous nature and her propensity for being swindled. The actress's latter years were spent writing begging letters to old friends and acquaintances. Although assistance was generally forthcoming (as indeed it always had been, since even at the height of her career she frequently resorted to borrowing from friends), such money immediately disappeared in the payment of debts. A benefit was held for her on 24 May

1785 at Drury Lane, but by 4 May 1786 George Anne, by now a frequent resident in sponge-houses, was once again destitute. During a life in which she moved repeatedly from fashionable to unfashionable addresses, from Richmond and Parliament Square to Soho and St James, her last residence was in Eliot's Row, St George's Fields, where she lived under the rules of the king's bench prison. She died there on 16 February 1788.   DEIRDRE E. HEDDON

Sources Highfill, Burnim & Langhans, *BDA* · G. A. Bellamy, *An apology for the life of George Anne Bellamy*, ed. [A. Bicknell], 3rd edn, 6 vols. (1785) · C. H. Hartmann, *Enchanting Bellamy* (1956) · Genest, *Eng. stage* · T. Wilkinson, *Memoirs of his own life*, 4 vols. (1790) · T. Wilkinson, *The wandering patentee, or, A history of the Yorkshire theatres from 1770 to the present time*, 4 vols. (1795)
Likenesses F. Lindo, oils, 1753–1757?, Garr. Club [*see illus.*] · Ravenet, engraving, 1765 (after B. Wilson) · engraving, 1781 · S. Harding, engraving, 1784 · R. Sands, stipple, pubd 1805 (after F. Cotes and J. Ramberg), NG Ire. · F. Bartolozzi, stipple (after F. Cotes and J. Ramberg), BM, NPG; repro. in J. Bell, *Bell's British theatre* (1785) · J. Collyer, engraving (as Erixene in *The brothers*; after D. Dodd), repro. in *The new English theatre … containing the most valuable plays which have been acted on the London stage* (1777) · A. van Haecken, mezzotint, Harvard TC · R. Laurie, engraving (as Juliet in *Romeo and Juliet*; after B. Wilson) · Mackenzie, engraving (after F. Cotes and J. Ramberg), repro. in *Eccentric biography, or, Memoirs of remarkable female characters, ancient and modern* (1803) · Maradan, engraving (after Benoist), Harvard TC · Newham, engraving (*Elopement from Covent Garden Theatre*; after Ramberg), repro. in J. Bell, *Bell's British theatre* (1786) · Stayer, engraving (after B. Wilson) · engraving, repro. in *Town and Country Magazine* (1776) · engraving (as Clarinda in *The suspicious husband*) · prints, Harvard TC, BM, NPG
Wealth at death near destitute: Highfill, Burnim & Langhans, *BDA*; Hartmann, *Enchanting Bellamy*

Bellamy, James (1819–1909), college head, born on 31 January 1819 in the school house of Merchant Taylors' School, then in Suffolk Lane, London, was elder son in the family of two sons and three daughters of James William Bellamy BD (1788–1874). The father (of an old Huguenot family settled in Norfolk and Lincolnshire) was headmaster of Merchant Taylors' School from 1819 to 1845. His mother was Mary, daughter of Thomas Cherry BD, headmaster of Merchant Taylors' School, London, from 1795 to 1819. In 1822 the father, while still headmaster, became vicar of Sellinge, Kent, a living which he held until his death in 1874. The son James entered Merchant Taylors' School in June 1826. The *Merchant Taylors' Magazine* (1833–4) contains three poems by him. In 1836 he was elected scholar (leading to a fellowship) at St John's College, Oxford. He graduated BA, with a second class in classics and a first class in mathematics, in 1841. In that year he was librarian of the Oxford Union Society. Although he was not a follower of the Tractarians, he was an admirer of J. H. Newman, whose sermons at St Mary's he attended, and became a friend of Charles Marriott and E. B. Pusey. He proceeded MA in 1845, BD in 1850, and DD in 1872; he was ordained deacon in 1842 and priest in 1843, and settled down to the routine of a college don. He held the college offices in turn, made a very efficient bursar in his year of office, and was a successful tutor; the future Lord Salisbury was among his private pupils. Until 1871 he was precentor, with charge of the college choristers. He was a keen and capable musician, a devoted admirer of Handel, and a

James Bellamy (1819–1909), by Frank Holl, 1886

friend of John Hullah and other musicians. His fine collection of music was given in trust, after his death, by his sister, Eleanor Coates Tylden, to form the nucleus of a historical library of music in Oxford. During the vacations he occasionally visited Germany, where he studied music, but his home was with his father in Kent.

On 7 December 1871 Bellamy was elected president of his college, a position he held for over thirty years. Leader of the Conservative Party in the university at a time when his former pupil and friend Lord Salisbury was university chancellor, he was appointed a member of the statutory commission chaired by Lord Selborne which was established in 1877 to draw up new statutes for the university and colleges. Bellamy, who was closely associated with E. B. Pusey in academic politics, attempted to preserve restrictions limiting college headships and fellowships to clergymen; his college resisted the commission's secularizing policy to the end, making an unsuccessful last-ditch stand before the universities' committee of the privy council in 1883. He was a member of the university's hebdomadal council from 1874 to 1907 and was vice-chancellor from 1886 to 1890 as successor to Benjamin Jowett, whom he had known from childhood but with whom he disagreed trenchantly on almost every subject.

During his presidency of St John's Bellamy embodied the college's conservative traditions, which he strove to uphold. Himself a convivial bachelor, he fortified the resistance to allowing married men to hold fellowships, most controversially in the case of Sidney Ball. Agricultural depression, which reduced estate revenues, threatened to undermine the college, forcing in 1888 a 22 per cent reduction in the emoluments of fellows and scholars:

Bellamy, a wealthy man by inheritance, made good the deficiency to the undergraduate scholars from his own pocket. He did not attempt a 'modern' style of headship, remaining a remote figure to undergraduates and, unlike many of his peers, he never preached in his college chapel. Nor did he publish any scholarly work. His reputation as a common-room raconteur and wit—sometimes caustic—overshadowed his shrewd administrative abilities: under him the college grew rapidly, its fortunes restored by the astute and far-sighted development of its property in north Oxford.

Bellamy maintained a long-standing association with the Merchant Taylors' Company, of which he received the honorary freedom in June 1894. From 1895 to 1907 he held the sinecure rectory of Leckford, Hampshire, paying the income into college funds. Until extreme old age he retained his powers: up to his ninetieth year he sang the service in the college chapel on stated days, in perfect tune and with remarkable power of voice. Failing health led him to resign the presidentship on 24 June 1909. He retired to Ingoldisthorpe Manor, Norfolk, the property which he had inherited from his uncle, and died there on 25 August 1909. He was buried in the churchyard adjoining his garden.　　W. H. HUTTON, rev. M. C. CURTHOYS

Sources The Times (28 Aug 1909) · Oxford Magazine (21 Oct 1909), 22 · W. H. Hutton, St John Baptist College (1898) · court minutes of the Merchant Taylors' Company, 1397–1929, with index, Merchant Taylors' Hall, London [microfilm] · register of St John's College, Oxford · private information (1912) · O. H. Ball, Sidney Ball: memories and impressions of an 'ideal don' (1923) · P. Morgan, 'Bellamy and his fellows', Oxford Magazine (7 Dec 1961), 126–8

Likenesses F. Holl, oils, 1886, St John's College, Oxford [see illus.] · W. Strang, chalk drawing, 1906, St John's College, Oxford

Wealth at death £335,470 2s. 7d.: probate, 11 Nov 1909, CGPLA Eng. & Wales

Bellamy, Peter Franklyn (1944–1991), folk-singer, was born on 8 September 1944 at 23 Knole Road in Bournemouth, the fourth of five children. Shortly afterwards his parents, Richard Reynell Bellamy (1901–1988) and Hilda Maud Bellamy, née Steel (1907–1994), moved to Norfolk, which became Bellamy's spiritual home. His parents had met in Australia in 1925 and married in 1926. They initially grew cotton in Australia, and later coffee in Melanesia, where drought and floods ruined them. In 1931 they resettled in England, where Richard Bellamy drew on their South Seas adventuring in The Real South Seas (1933) and Mixed Bliss in Melanesia (1934). He became a Mosleyite organizer in Manchester and was imprisoned under the 1940 Emergency Powers Act, an episode thereafter referred to only obliquely at home. Peter Bellamy was educated at primary schools in Holkham and Wells next the Sea, and at Fakenham grammar school.

The experience of hearing Bill Haley and Elvis Presley shook Bellamy's musical world-view. It provided the impetus to learn the guitar, which his eldest brother, Richard, already played. Like many of his generation who took up music, Bellamy was shaped by the art college system. At seventeen he began at Norwich Art School, and there was weaned off American folk and blues and collected two folk-songs, 'Yarmouth Town' and 'Fakenham Fair',

from Peter Bullen, which Bellamy recorded on Mainly Norfolk (Xtra Records, 1968). He next went to Maidstone College of Art. By then he was under the sway of Ewan MacColl and Bert Lloyd, but Norfolk traditional singers such as Harry Cox (1885–1971) and Sam Larner (1878–1965) were equally influential. He realized that he 'would be a better singer of English folksong than … the "grandson" of a slave from Mississippi' (Allenby, 9). One critic felicitously described Bellamy's voice as a combination of 'Norfolk vowels and English grammar-school education' (Dallas, 'A celebration of Peter Bellamy', 23); Bellamy later compared himself to a 'curator of a museum' (Anderson and Holland, 12).

Early on, Bellamy unashamedly filched from the repertories of MacColl and Lloyd. After outgrowing the 'revivalist orthodoxy' of these two influences, and galvanized by the realization that however good his Cox impersonation it would bypass most people, Bellamy set about developing his own voice and style of folk-song interpretation. His unmistakable characteristic 'bleating' and tradition-derived vocal mannerisms thereafter polarized opinion. Tickled pink to be anagrammatized as Elmer P. Bleaty in Southern Rag's cartoon strip 'Borfolk', he sought out Lawrence Heath's original artwork. Bellamy, himself a gifted pictorial artist, occasional sculptor, and cartoonist, retained a lifelong passion for art, and his original artwork illustrated several albums: puckishly, for Bill Shute's and Lisa Null's album American Primitive (1980) he took the eye past the musicians and down the garden path to white blossoms atop luxuriant marijuana foliage. The Who, King Oliver, Mississippi Fred McDowell, and Walter Pardon happily co-existed in Bellamy's own huge collection of records.

In Rochester and Maidstone Bellamy became a resident folk-club singer. While at Maidstone he attempted suicide for the first time, and in November 1964 he dropped out of college. Encouraged by the singer Anne Briggs, he resolved to make a career as a professional folk-singer. In 1965 he became a founder member of the Young Tradition, with the (unrelated) singers Royston Wood and Heather Wood. On 16 August 1966 he married Anthea Elizabeth Birch (b. 1947), a student. Sartorially flamboyant, the Young Tradition presented folk seen through a 'swinging sixties' pop prism, folk with image. The group's interwoven harmony lines and its appearances at the Newport folk festival and in Judy Collins's In my Life (Elektra, 1967)—an ill kept secret—won it an American following. In September 1969, however, the Young Tradition broke up.

By then Bellamy had released the first of a stream of solo recordings for what eventually exceeded a dozen record companies internationally. The brightest flashes in the pan were Both Sides Then (Topic Records, 1979)—its title punning on Joni Mitchell's Both Sides, Now—and his magnum opus, the 'ballad opera' The Transports (Free Reed Records, 1977), arranged by Dolly Collins, with its array of folk luminaries. A tale of transportation based on a true story, The Transports took on a life beyond the recording, being staged by the Norwich folk club (1978) and at the Whitby folk week (1992) among others.

Brought up on Rudyard Kipling from boyhood, Bellamy was inspired to set Kipling to music. Wedded to traditional melodies on *Oak, Ash & Thorn* (Xtra Records, 1970) and latterly using original tunes, his 'traditional or original—but essentially *popular*—musical settings' (Webb, 'Peter Bellamy') and multimedia presentations proved a fillip to Kipling's legacy, long associated with tainted imperialism. In 1973 he joined the Kipling Society; in 1981 he was elected vice-president. Bellamy's core repertory balanced traditional folk music with Bob Dylan, Alex Glasgow, Al Stewart, and Kipling. An important strand of his craft was his evangelism for source singers (traditional songcarriers born into a folk tradition) such as the East Anglian singer Walter Pardon (1914–1996) and the Copper family of Rottingdean, Sussex; he nudged Bob Copper into approaching Heinemann to publish his *Song for every Season* (1971) and the Leader label into releasing its historic four-LP boxed set of Copper family recordings (1971). His friendship with Copper's son John neatly brought the folk-song revival back to its roots.

On 31 October 1987 the divorced Bellamy married Jenny Anne (formerly Marjorie Anne) Crow (*b.* 1951), a teacher. He suffered periodically from depression. Wearying of what seemed like an uphill struggle, and feeling he had painted himself stylistically into a corner, he died at his own hand from an overdose of amitriptyline, chloral hydrates, and alcohol. He was found on the bank of the Leeds–Liverpool Canal at Riddlesden, Keighley, Yorkshire, on 24 September 1991, having achieved what he had attempted several times; he was buried at Keighley. Both his wife and his former wife survived him. The English folk revival lost its single most idiosyncratic voice, and the nation one of its most memorable singers. A collection of fifty-seven songs sung by Bellamy was released on CD in 1999 under the title *Wake the Vaulted Echoes* (Free Reed Records).   KEN HUNT

Sources D. Allenby, 'Peter Bellamy', *Swing 51*, 5 (1982), 8–16; 6 (1982), 14–18 • I. Anderson and M. Holland, 'The Bellamy style', *Southern Rag*, 7 (1981), 12–19 • B. Blackman, 'The value of the old songs', *Sing Out!* (spring 1991), 14–23 • K. Dallas and others, *Wake the vaulted echoes* (Free Reed Records, 1999) [disc notes] • G. Webb, 'Peter Bellamy', *Kipling Journal* (Dec 1991), 9 • P. Bellamy and T. Coady, 'Peter Bellamy discography', *Swing 51*, 4 (1981), 8–9 • A. Means, 'Bellamy: museum exhibit', *Melody Maker* (21 Nov 1970), 37 • K. Dallas, 'A celebration of Peter Bellamy', *Living Tradition* (Sept–Oct 1999), 20–23 • K. Dallas, 'Adding more flavour', *Melody Maker* (1 March 1980), 38 • G. Webb, '"That I may sing of crowd or king or road-borne company"', *Kipling Journal* (Dec 1981), 8 • 'South Sea memories', *North Norfolk News* (14 March 1986), 9 • K. Dallas, *The Independent* (25 Sept 1991) • D. Arthur and others, 'Peter Bellamy, 1944–1991', *English Dance and Song*, 53/4 (1991), 2–3 • D. Arthur, 'Bellamy, Peter', *New Grove*, 2nd edn • personal knowledge (2004) • private information (2004) [Helen Walters] • b. cert. • m. certs. • d. cert. • *The Guardian* (26 Sept 1991) • *Daily Telegraph* (26 Sept 1991)
Archives priv. coll.
Likenesses B. Shuel, photographs, 1960–69, Collections (photo-archive), London; repro. in www.collections.btinternet.co.uk • K. R. Hunt, photographs, *Swing 51* archives, Hounslow, Middlesex

Bellamy, Richard (*bap.* 1743?, *d.* 1813), singer, was probably the son of Richard and Susannah Bellamy, baptized at Billinghay, Lincoln, on 12 June 1743. He was appointed a gentleman of the Chapel Royal on 28 March 1771 and a lay vicar of Westminster Abbey on 1 January 1773. He took a MusB at Cambridge University in 1775, and in 1777 became vicar-choral of St Paul's Cathedral. From 1793 to 1800 he was also almoner and master of the choristers there. In 1784 he was one of the principal basses at the Handel commemoration in Westminster Abbey. Bellamy published a volume of music in 1788 which included a set of anthems and a Te Deum for full orchestra, which was performed at the installation of the knights of the Bath in that year. He married Elizabeth, daughter of Thomas Ludford; their son, the singer and stage manager Thomas Ludford *Bellamy (1771–1843), inherited considerable property from his maternal grandfather, who died in 1776. Richard Bellamy retired in 1801 and died on 11 September 1813.

W. B. SQUIRE, *rev.* K. D. REYNOLDS

Sources W. H. Husk, 'Bellamy, Richard', Grove, *Dict. mus.* (1927) • C. Burney, *An account of the musical performances … in commemoration of Handel* (1785) • Venn, *Alum. Cant.* • IGI • GM, 1st ser., 46 (1776), 142

Bellamy, Thomas (1745–1800), writer, was born at Kingston, Surrey, the son of a lawyer and his wife, Anne, daughter of Caleb Lomax, MP for St Albans. Bellamy 'received only the common rudiments of education which are requisite for the purposes of inland commerce' (Baker), and was apprenticed to a Mrs Allen, a hosier in Newgate Street, setting up in business for himself on the conclusion of his training. He began writing verse early on, and some of the pieces in his *Miscellanies* (1794) are dated as early as 1763. After running a successful business as a London tradesman for twenty years, Bellamy became tired of serving at the counter, relinquished his business, and served as a clerk in a bookseller's in Paternoster Row. 'But Bellamy', says his biographer, 'was not calculated for a subordinate position'. A disagreement arose between him and his employer, and Bellamy had to seek a living elsewhere.

In 1787 Bellamy started the *General Magazine and Impartial Review*, which ran for some months. This venture was followed by *Bellamy's Picturesque Magazine and Literary Museum*, which contained engraved portraits of living persons, with some account of their lives; but it failed to attract a large audience. He also wrote *The Benevolent Planters*, a drama performed at the Haymarket in 1789, and some years later published a novel, *Sadaski, or, The Wandering Penitent* (1798). In 1794 he collected into two volumes the moral tales which he had written for the *General Magazine*, adding some verses, unpublished tales, and a life of Parsons, the comedian. These *Miscellanies in Prose and Verse* were dedicated to Charles Dibdin, with whom the author afterwards quarrelled. Later he projected the *Monthly Mirror*, which was chiefly concerned with the stage. When this periodical had run its race, he established a circulating library. On the death of his mother he became possessed of some property, which enabled him to retire from business and devote himself to literary pursuits. But he did not long enjoy his leisure; seized with a sharp and sudden illness he died, after four days' suffering, on 29 August 1800. His final novel, *The Beggar Boy*, was published posthumously in 1801, with a biographical memoir of the author by Mrs Villa-Real Gooch.

A. H. BULLEN, rev. M. CLARE LOUGHLIN-CHOW

Sources Mrs V.-R. Gooch, 'Memoir', in T. Bellamy, *The beggar boy* (1801) · D. E. Baker, *Biographia dramatica, or, A companion to the play-house*, rev. I. Reed, new edn, rev. S. Jones, 3 vols. in 4 (1812) · Watt, *Bibl. Brit.*

Likenesses I. Purden, stipple, pubd 1800 (after S. Drummond), BM, NPG

Bellamy, Thomas Ludford (1771–1843), singer, was born on 15 September 1771 in St John's parish, Westminster, the son of Richard *Bellamy (*bap.* 1743?, *d.* 1813), singer, and his wife, Elizabeth, daughter of Thomas Ludford (*d.* 1776). He learned singing and music from his father and trained under Benjamin Cooke in the choir of Westminster Abbey. In 1784 he sang among the trebles at the Handel commemoration festival in Westminster Abbey. After his voice broke, to a 'tenor bass', he continued his studies with Tasca, and in 1791 he sang in the oratorios at Drury Lane.

In 1794 Bellamy went to Ireland, probably in connection with the Irish property he had inherited from his maternal grandfather in 1776. In 1797 he was stage manager at the Crow Street Theatre, Dublin, and he made his début there on 9 February 1798. In May 1799 he married the actress Mrs Harriet Berry (*b.* 1777?), the daughter of the actor Thomas Grist. They had at least two daughters. In 1800 Bellamy bought shares in the Manchester, Chester, Shrewsbury, and Lichfield theatres; here his singing was applauded, but the management (which he shared with his partner Thomas Ward) of the Manchester theatre was criticized. In 1805 he sold his interest and became sole proprietor of the Belfast, Londonderry, and Newry theatres. This speculation having failed he returned to London, where he was engaged to sing at Covent Garden from 1807 to 1812, making his début as the eponymous hero of *Robin Hood*. In 1812 he was engaged for five years at Drury Lane.

In 1818 Bellamy founded an academy of music based on J. B. Logier's system, which was still operating in 1826. In 1819 he became choirmaster at the chapel of the Spanish embassy, and in 1821 he succeeded James Bartleman as principal bass singer at the Concerts of Ancient Music. He edited a volume of the poetry of glees, madrigals, catches, rounds, canons, and duets (1840), continuing the work begun by Richard Clark in his 1814 publication. Bellamy died on 3 January 1843 at Judd Street, Brunswick Square, London.

W. B. SQUIRE, rev. ANNE PIMLOTT BAKER

Sources *New Grove* · Highfill, Burnim & Langhans, *BDA* · *Grove, Dict. mus.* · D. Baptie, *A handbook of musical biography* (1883) · Brown & Stratton, *Brit. mus.*

Likenesses I. Purden, engraving, 1800 (after portrait published by Earle & Herlet; after S. Drummond) · S. Freeman, stipple, 1808 (after portrait published by Vernor, Hood & Shaft; after Allingham), Harvard TC; repro. in *Monthly mirror*, new ser., 3 (1808), 307 · H. R. Cook, engraving, 1814 (as Dr Pangloss; after stipple vignette by R. Jean)

Wealth at death no value given; left all funds and stocks, furniture and personal estate to wife: Highfill, Burnim & Langhans, *BDA*

Bellasis family (*per. c.*1500–1653), gentry, held lands in the bishopric of Durham from at least the mid-fourteenth century. A Durham priory rental of 1340–41 details the landed holdings of William and John Bellasis in Wolviston, in the south-east of the county. About 1380 John Bellasis exchanged these lands for the manor of Henknowle, near Bishop Auckland, which became the principal residence of the family until the sixteenth century. It was in the 1520s that the family began its climb towards the social and political prominence which by 1627 was to result in its elevation to the peerage. The architects of the family's rise to prominence were Richard and Anthony, the sons of Thomas Bellasis (*d.* 1500) and his wife, Margaret Thirkeld or Thirkell (*d.* in or after 1545).

Richard Bellasis (*c.*1489–1540), Thomas's heir, married Margery (*d.* 1587), the daughter of Richard Errington of Cockle Park Tower in Northumberland and of Morton Grange in the bishopric of Durham. Little is known of his education and early career. However, during the episcopacy of Thomas Wolsey, who held the see of Durham from 1523 to 1529, Bellasis came increasingly to be associated with the local administrative élite and to enjoy the cardinal's patronage. By 1527 he had been appointed constable of Durham Castle and had acquired some valuable grants of property, including a sixty-year lease of the episcopal manor and grange of Morton, near Houghton-le-Spring. This property, formerly held by his father-in-law, became the focal point of the cadet branch of the family's later coalmining enterprises and remained in the family until the late seventeenth century.

Bellasis's political career after Wolsey's fall was relatively quiet, though seemingly not harmed by his connections with the disgraced cardinal. He apparently played no part in the Pilgrimage of Grace in 1536, perhaps because by this time his younger brother Anthony was in the service of the king's chief minister, Thomas Cromwell. This connection probably served to advance Richard's political career, for he was subsequently appointed to the newly reconstituted council of the north. In addition Bellasis was one of the commissioners appointed to oversee the surrenders of the dissolved monasteries in the northern counties. As in his earlier career he sought to profit from his involvement in this enterprise. In 1539 he obtained various grants of lands of former monastic properties, including the lease of the priory of Newburgh, in the North Riding of Yorkshire. This property was later to become the principal seat of the Yorkshire branch of the Bellasis family. Richard Bellasis remained active in the sphere of northern politics and administration until his death on 28 March 1540. His inquisition post mortem, taken at Durham on 5 June 1540, named his sixteen-year-old son William as his heir.

Richard's younger brother Anthony *Bellasis (*d.* 1552) pursued a dual career in the church and the law. Educated at Cambridge and at a foreign university, he was ordained priest in 1533. Having survived the fall of his master Cromwell he became a chaplain to Henry VIII and went on to acquire a succession of profitable benefices. His legal career prospered to the extent that he was appointed a master in chancery in 1544, and became a member in 1550 of the council of the north, which he served until his death in August 1552. In 1540, following his brother's death, Anthony was granted the house and site of Newburgh Priory, with other lands nearby, but this seems to have been superseded in 1545 by a grant in fee of the Newburgh Priory estate, together with a larger number of other properties, made jointly to Anthony, his mother, and his nephew and ward William. The latter had entered his father's estates in 1545, and following his uncle's death the newly acquired Yorkshire properties also passed into his hands.

Under the direction of **Sir William Bellasis** (*c.*1524–1604) the geographical focus of the senior Bellasis line shifted from Durham to the North Riding of Yorkshire. William's marriage to Margaret (*d.* in or after 1577), the daughter of Sir Nicholas Fairfax of Gilling, also in the North Riding, further consolidated his kinship ties within the locality. Ultimately Sir William's predilection for enclosing, improving, and expanding his Yorkshire estates enabled him to pass on to his heir an inheritance which was one of the wealthiest in the North Riding. But initially his political career reflected rather his Durham origins. In 1555 he was appointed a JP for Durham, and in 1558 he was knighted at Newcastle. Increasingly, however, his name appeared in connection with commissions in Yorkshire. He had been appointed to the commission of the peace for the North Riding by 1564 and served as high sheriff for Yorkshire in 1574. While there were hints that he may have been a crypto-Catholic, he was nevertheless by 1577 considered sufficiently reliable in religion to be included on the ecclesiastical high commission for the province of York. He died at Newburgh Priory on 13 April 1604 aged eighty-one, and was buried in his parish church of Coxwold, situated on the estate.

Sir Henry Bellasis, first baronet (1555–1624), was the second-born but eldest surviving son of Sir William, and consequently succeeded to the main Newburgh and Henknowle estates. He was educated at Jesus College, Cambridge, which he entered in 1572. In 1587, during a period of military service on the Anglo-Scottish borders, he acquitted himself with distinction and was mentioned in dispatches. Thereafter he enjoyed a high-profile career in regional and local politics. He served five times as an MP, representing his local borough of Thirsk in 1586, 1589, 1593, and 1601, and that of Aldborough in the West Riding (close to the seat of his father-in-law) in 1597. He was first appointed a JP for the North Riding about 1586–7, though his early career on the bench was somewhat compromised by his uncomfortably close connections with the local Roman Catholic gentry. Nevertheless, by 1601 he had secured his place as a North Riding JP, and thereafter he served regularly until his death. Bellasis was knighted by James I at York on 17 April 1603. He was appointed to the council of the north in the same year and again served until his death. In 1603–4 he also served as high sheriff of

Yorkshire. His social and political ambitions reached their apogee when on 29 June 1611, following the creation of the order of baronets, he was one of the first six Yorkshiremen to purchase the title. Shortly afterwards, clearly conscious of his new-found status, he became a leading figure in the dispute within the council of the north concerning the order of precedence to be set for baronets within that institution. In managing his estates Bellasis continued the policy of enclosure, acquisition, and consolidation begun by his father. His landed estate at his death in August 1624 was worth more than £4000 per annum, while his personal estate was valued at some £8000. Bellasis was buried in the church of St Saviour's in York, on 19 August, and is commemorated by a fine wall monument in York Minster. From his marriage to Ursula (*d.* 1633), daughter of Sir Thomas Fairfax of Denton in the West Riding, he had one son, Thomas, who succeeded him.

The cadet line of the Bellasis family, which was resident in Durham, also rose to local prominence at this time as a result of the career of **Sir William Bellasis** (*c.*1593–1641) of Morton House. Sir William was the son of Sir Henry's younger brother Brian (1559–1608), who had acquired the lease of the family's Morton estate in east Durham, and his wife, Margaret Lee. In 1611 he married Margaret (*d.* 1671), the daughter and coheir of Sir George Selby of Whitehouse, a leading coal owner. He was appointed a JP for Durham in 1614 and went on to become a leading member of the Durham administrative élite, gaining a reputation for reliability and application to duty. Knighted in 1617, he was appointed deputy lieutenant of the Durham ward of Easington in 1621 and served as high sheriff of the bishopric from 1625 until 1640. Bellasis became one of the gentry's leading coal owners and entrepreneurs within the bishopric, playing a leading role in the exploitation of the coal trade within the Wear valley. In 1634 he became the first mayor of Sunderland. Despite his close commercial links with such 'arrant covenanters' as George Lillburne of Sunderland, Bellasis retained his royalist sympathies as the breakdown into civil war approached. He died on 3 December 1641, probably at Morton, during the Scottish occupation of the bishopric. Sir William's sons continued their father's support for the crown during the civil war and subsequently had their estates sequestered for delinquency.

Support for King Charles was a position which Sir William shared with his cousin **Thomas Bellasis** (1577–1653), who became successively Baron Fauconberg of Yarm (1627) and Viscount Fauconberg (1643). Educated at Jesus College, Cambridge, where he was recorded about 1592, Thomas entered political life in 1597 with his election as MP for his father's former seat of Thirsk. He went on to represent the borough in the parliaments of 1614, 1621, and 1624. In 1601 he married Barbara, the daughter of Sir Henry Cholmley of Roxby in Whitby Strand, thus forming an alliance with a family noted for its strong recusant connections. While outwardly conforming in religion, he retained links with Roman Catholicism and had converted to the Catholic faith by the time of his death. He was knighted by James I at York in 1603 and later served as a JP for the North Riding. In the 1620s he became embroiled in the power struggle for political control within Yorkshire between Sir John Savile, the *custos rotulorum* of the West Riding, and Sir Thomas Wentworth. It was probably as a consequence of his support for Savile, a client of the duke of Buckingham, that in 1627 he was raised to the peerage as Lord Fauconberg of Yarm. Animosities between the Bellasis family and Wentworth deepened after the latter's appointment as president of the council of the north in 1628. In 1631 Fauconberg's son Henry was called before the privy council and suffered a brief imprisonment as a result of his insolent behaviour towards the lord president. In 1633 Fauconberg too was forced to make apology to the council at York for behaviour that culminated in his being arrested for contempt of court.

The Bellasis family's enmity towards Wentworth and towards the arbitrary government with which the latter was associated continued until his fall in 1640. Nevertheless, during the civil war Fauconberg and his sons were staunch supporters of the royalist cause. In January 1643, in recognition of his loyalty, he was created Viscount Fauconberg of Henknowle (his second son, John, was made Baron Bellasis of Worlaby in 1645). After taking part in the battle of Marston Moor in 1644 he fled abroad. His estates were subsequently sequestered for delinquency, with his fine for compounding being set at £5012 18s. He returned to the North Riding in 1649 but refused to swear to the oath of abjuration and was convicted of recusancy. He died on 18 April 1653 at Coxwold and was buried in the church there. His eldest son having predeceased him, his title and estates passed to his grandson Thomas, whose political loyalties, unlike those of the other members of his family, had lain with parliament, and who subsequently married Mary, daughter of Oliver Cromwell.

CHRISTINE M. NEWMAN

Sources Venn, *Alum. Cant.*, 1/1 · GEC, *Peerage*, 5.264–5 · GEC, *Baronetage*, vol. 1 · [F. W. Dendy], ed., *Visitations of the north*, 1, SurtS, 122 (1912) · *LP Henry VIII* · R. Surtees, *The history and antiquities of the county palatine of Durham*, 1 (1816) · M. E. James, *Family lineage and civil society: a study of society and mentality in the Durham region, 1500–1640* (1974) · J. T. Cliffe, *The Yorkshire gentry from the Reformation to the civil war* (1969) · R. R. Reid, *The king's council in the north* (1921) · H. Aveling, *Northern Catholics: the Catholic recusants of the North Riding of Yorkshire, 1558–1790* (1966) · W. A. Shaw, *The knights of England*, 2 (1906) · G. Ridsdill Smith, *In well beware: the story of Newburgh Priory and the Belasyse family, 1145–1977* (1978) · *CSP dom.*, 1639–40 · N. Yorks. CRO, ZDV X/L2844 · J. C. Atkinson, ed., *Quarter sessions records*, 2–3, North Riding RS, 2–3 (1884–5) · *Report of the Deputy Keeper of the Public Records*, 36 (1875); 44 (1883) · M. Bateson, ed., 'A collection of original letters from the bishops to the privy council, 1564', *Camden miscellany, IX*, CS, new ser., 53 (1893) · G. E. Aylmer and R. Cant, eds., *A history of York Minster* (1977) · J. W. Clay, ed., *Yorkshire royalist composition papers*, 2, Yorkshire Archaeological Society, 18 (1895) · [H. M. Wood], ed., *Wills and inventories from the registry at Durham*, 4, SurtS, 142 (1929) · HoP, *Commons, 1558–1603*, 1.424
Archives BL, family MSS · Col. U., Butler Library, account book and other papers [Henry Bellasis] · Durham RO, deeds and papers pertaining to the family · Harvard U., Houghton L., estate papers [Henry Bellasis] · N. Yorks. CRO, County Durham deeds, Fauconberg (Belasyse) of Newburgh Priory, ZDV, 1, 70 (MIC 1354) · N. Yorks. CRO, Newburgh District deeds, Fauconberg (Belasyse) of Newburgh Priory, ZDV, 1, 5 (MIC 1352) · N. Yorks. CRO, personal and official papers, Fauconberg (Belasyse) of Newburgh Priory, ZDV X (MIC 1282) | PRO, Durham cursitor's records, class DURH 3 · PRO, Durham inquisitions *post mortem* · PRO, Durham Palatine Chancery enrolments
Likenesses N. Stone, effigies on monument (Henry Bellasis with wife and children), York Minster · effigies on monument (William Bellasis (*c.*1524–1604) with family), Coxwold church, North Riding · effigies on monument (Thomas Bellasis with wife), Coxwold church · portrait (William Bellasis (*c.*1524–1604)), Newburgh Priory; repro. in Ridsdill Smith, *In well beware* · portrait (Henry Bellasis), Newburgh Priory; repro. in Ridsdill Smith, *In well beware*
Wealth at death landed estate est. at £4000; personal estate valued at £8000; Sir Henry Bellasis: Cliffe, *Yorkshire gentry*, 96, 110

Bellasis, Anthony (*d.* 1552), clergyman and civilian, was the second son of Thomas Bellasis of Henknowle, co. Durham, and Margaret, *née* Thirkell. He was thus a member of a prominent border gentry family; his elder brother, Richard *Bellasis [see under Bellasis family], was a member of the council of the north. Anthony graduated BCL from Cambridge in 1520; by November 1532 he had obtained his doctorate, of which the source is unknown. In 1528 he was admitted to the College of Advocates. On 1 August 1530 he was collated to a canonry of Chester-le-Street, co. Durham. On 4 May 1533 he was collated to the rectory of Whickham in the same county, which he had resigned by 8 June 1540. On 7 June 1533 Bishop Tunstall, his early patron, ordained him priest.

From 1533 to 1539 Bellasis was vicar of St Oswald's, Durham. In 1536 he entered Cromwell's service, soon establishing himself as the minister's chief recruitment and patronage agent. By May 1538 he was living in Cromwell's house. On 20 May he was dispensed to hold up to three benefices. On 7 January 1540 he became canon of Exeter, and on 3 March rector of Brancepeth, co. Durham, both posts held until his death. On 29 June he was granted the site and certain lands of Newburgh Priory, Yorkshire, for a consideration of over £1000. On 29 August he was presented by the crown to the rectory of Hartlebury, Worcestershire, in replacement of the attainted Thomas Garrett. He was instituted on 5 October and held the living until his death.

Bellasis's career lost no obvious momentum with Cromwell's fall. On 17 December 1540 he was named to the chapter of the new cathedral of Westminster; he retained this canonry until his death, serving as chapter receiver and in other administrative and legal capacities. On 27 June 1541 he received an annuity from the wardship of his elder brother's heir, William. On 9 November he was collated to a prebend in Auckland College, co. Durham. On 23 March 1543 the king named him archdeacon of Colchester, which he remained until his death. On 27 April he became canon of Ripon. On 2 August, as king's chaplain, he had a further dispensation for plurality. About this time he was among those whom Cranmer was allowed by the king to appoint for investigation of the 'prebendaries' plot' (heresy charges concocted against the archbishop himself by his own cathedral clergy). On 15 January 1544 he was made prebendary of Haydour-cum-Walton in Lincoln Cathedral. Also in 1544 he became a master in chancery and a member of Gray's Inn.

On 17 October 1544 Bellasis and other masters were appointed to deputize for the lord chancellor. A similar commission to which he was appointed on 18 February 1547 prompted complaints from the common lawyers at the growth of equity jurisdiction. By 19 December 1545 he had acquired the prebend of Timberscombe in Wells Cathedral. Also in 1545 he became master of Sherburn Hospital, co. Durham, which he remained until his death, plundering the house by granting beneficial leases. On 11 February 1549 he was licensed to assign properties in Westmorland, late of Byland Abbey, Yorkshire, to his nephew Richard and himself. On 24 June he was appointed a commissary of the dean and chapter of Westminster in their peculiar jurisdiction of St Martin's-le-Grand, London. On 16 December he was collated to the prebend of Knaresborough in York Minster. On 21 February the king presented him to the vicarage of Aycliffe, co. Durham. In March 1551 he was recommended by Sir John Mason as 'grave, learned, languaged' and qualified by local birth for an Anglo-Scottish border commission (*CSP for.*, 1547–53, 81), but it appears he did not serve. He was designated canon of Carlisle on 12 June 1552, at the lord chamberlain's request. On 21 June he was again named a deputy in chancery. At his death he was also rector of Ripley, Yorkshire, master of St Edmund's Hospital, Gateshead, and canon of Hereford.

Bellasis died between 11 and 20 August 1552. He left the bulk of his property to his nephews William (later knighted) and Richard. Dr Nicholas Wotton was to have a choice of his books; specific volumes were bequeathed to Sir Walter Mildmay and Bellasis's cousin Edward Thirkell, fellow of King's College, Cambridge. Other beneficiaries were Archbishop Holgate and the earl of Northumberland. Wotton and Anthony Hussey were overseers.

C. S. KNIGHTON

Sources D. S. Boutflower, ed., *Fasti Dunelmenses: a record of the beneficed clergy of the diocese of Durham*, SurtS, 139 (1926), 12 • *The registers of Cuthbert Tunstall … and James Pilkington*, ed. G. Hinde, SurtS, 161 (1952), 47, 50, 75, 78, 86, 101, 111 (nos. 75–7, 81, 167, 169, 189, 238, 286, 328) • [J. W. Clay], ed., *North country wills*, 1, SurtS, 116 (1908), 220–23 • D. S. Chambers, ed., *Faculty office registers, 1534–1549* (1966), 134, 231 • *Fasti Angl., 1300–1541*, [Exeter], 66 • *Fasti Angl., 1541–1857*, [St Paul's, London], 12 • *Fasti Angl., 1541–1857*, [York], 44 • *Fasti Angl., 1541–1857*, [Bath and Wells], 81 • *Fasti Angl., 1541–1857*, [Ely], 74 • R. E. G. Cole, ed., *Chapter acts of the cathedral church of St Mary of Lincoln*, 2, Lincoln RS, 13 (1917), 86 • C. S. Knighton, ed., *Acts of the dean and chapter of Westminster*, 1 (1997), 8, 12, 14–15, 16–17, 25, 48 • D. Marcombe, ed., *The last principality* (1987), 126 • G. R. Elton, *Reform and renewal* (1973), 24–5 • *LP Henry VIII*, 11, no. 594; 15, nos. 831(84), 1027(46); 16, no. 947(64); 18/1, no. 346(62); 19/2, no. 527(24) • *CPR, 1549–51*, 65, 326; *1550–53*, 184, 276, 310, 409 • *CSP dom., 1547–53*, p. 137, no. 367; p. 242, no. 662 • *CSP for., 1547–53*, 81 • *APC, 1547–50*, 48–54, esp. 51, 53 • T. Nash, *Collections for the history of Worcestershire*, 1 (1781), 573 • Foss, *Judges*, 5.91 • J. Foster, *The register of admissions to Gray's Inn, 1521–1889, together with the register of marriages in Gray's Inn chapel, 1695–1754* (privately printed, London, 1889), 17 • D. MacCulloch, *Thomas Cranmer: a life* (1996), 316

Wealth at death £1069 in goods and properties: Clay, ed., *North country wills*, 220–22

Bellasis, Edward (1800–1873), serjeant-at-law and Roman Catholic convert, the only son of the Revd George Bellasis of Queen's College, Oxford, rector of Yattendon and vicar of Basilden and Ashampstead, Berkshire, and his second wife, Leah Cooper, only surviving child and heir of Emery Viall of Walsingham, Norfolk, was born on 14 October 1800 at his father's vicarage at Basilden. His father died when he was two, and his mother remarried; her new husband was the Revd Joseph Maude. The family lived in the precincts of the ruins of Reading Abbey. Bellasis was educated at Christ's Hospital, 1808–15, where he became known as an idle child. The headmaster, Dr Trollope, told his mother, 'Madam, he is a bad boy' (Bellasis, 4). He then worked in a solicitors' office but on the advice of Sir Alan Chambre, a family friend, he became a student at the Inner Temple on 8 November 1818, being called to the bar on 2 July 1824. He was of evangelical and tory inclinations, and his chief friends included Lewis Hayes Petit, Edmund Lodge, the genealogist, and Daniel Maclise, the artist, who twice painted his portrait. He was interested in science, was acquainted with Michael Faraday, and became one of the managers of the Royal Institution.

On 17 September 1829 Bellasis married Frances, the only surviving child and heir of William Lycett of Stafford; they had one child, Charlotte, who died aged two, soon followed by her mother, who died on 27 December 1832. In 1835 Bellasis married Eliza Jane, the only daughter of William Garnett of Lark Hill, Salford, who in 1843 was high sheriff of Lancashire. They had ten children.

Bellasis was soon launched on a highly successful legal career in chancery and in the county palatine of Lancaster. In 1836 he represented the interests of Mr Wood of Hanger Hill when Brunel was planning the Great Western Railway, and from then until his retirement in 1866 he specialized in legal cases relating to parliamentary matters, and especially the great flood of cases which resulted from the railway boom of the 1840s. He also influenced the reconstruction of the laws on salmon fisheries, and the acts by which water was supplied to major cities, including Manchester, Liverpool, Glasgow, Edinburgh, and London. On 10 July 1844 Bellasis became serjeant-at-law. His rise at the bar was mirrored by a change in religion. Of evangelical upbringing, he, like a number of young professional men in London in the 1830s including his friend James Hope (later Hope-Scott), attended the Margaret Chapel, associated with the Tractarian movement. He dabbled in historical research on Anglican orders and shared J. H. Newman's increasing doubt as to their validity. He was the correspondent of E. B. Pusey, Frederick Oakeley, and other Tractarians, and became a minor participant in the many clerical rows in the 1840s on such subjects, publishing four letters on the orders written in 1847 (republished in 1872 as *Anglican Orders, by an Anglican since Become a Catholic*), as well as several other pamphlets, including *The Judicial Committee of the Privy Council* (1850) and *Convocations and Synods: are they the Remedies for Existing Evils?* (1850). Bellasis and his wife shared religious interests; he noted their conversations, later published as *Philotheus and Eugenia: Dialogues between Two Anglicans on Anglican Difficulties* (1874).

Agitated by the Gorham judgment in December 1850 and by Anglican reaction against the restoration of the

Roman Catholic ecclesiastical hierarchy in the same year, Bellasis became a Roman Catholic, being received by Father Brownhill SJ. He was followed in his conversion by his wife and children. Bellasis also published two pamphlets on the 'papal aggression' of 1850: one as an Anglican (1850), the other as a Roman Catholic (1851).

The Serjeant, as Bellasis was generally known, became a useful legal and financial adviser to the Roman Catholic community. From 1853 to 1856 he and his fellow convert Hope-Scott handled the affairs of the earl of Shrewsbury, and administered the Shrewsburys' estates after the earl's death in 1856 and during the prolonged law suit over it between Lord Talbot and the duke of Norfolk. From 1863 Bellasis was steward to Norfolk's manors in Norfolk and Suffolk. He was treasurer of St Anselm's Society for the Diffusion of Good Books and active in many Catholic philanthropic and educational societies. He was a magistrate of Middlesex and Westminster.

After retiring from the bar in 1866 Bellasis lived part of the year near Hope-Scott at Hyères, France, where he was visited by H. E. Manning and other dignitaries. Bellasis was Lancaster herald, and in 1869 was appointed a commissioner of the earl marshal to examine and report on the working of the College of Arms. After retiring, Bellasis's health declined. In 1872 he moved permanently to Hyères, where he died on 24 January 1873 and was buried in the vault of the Bona Mors Chapel. In 1888 his tomb was moved to the new town cemetery, and later his remains were placed in St Mary Magdalen's, Mortlake. A memorial window was made for him and placed in St Ethelreda's, London. Two of Bellasis's sons, Richard Garnett and Henry Lewis Bellasis, became Oratorian priests, and another, William, helped to found the Roman Catholic Westminster Cathedral; three of his daughters, Mary,

Cecilia, and Monica, joined the Society of the Holy Child Jesus.

His second son, **Edward Bellasis** (1852–1922), genealogist, was educated at the Oratory School, Birmingham, under J. H. Newman, and was called to the bar in 1873 but never practised, since in the same year he was appointed Bluemantle pursuivant of arms at the Herald's College. He was a sound genealogist and was registrar of the college from 1894, having been deputy registrar. From 1882 he was Lancaster herald. He was ill from depression from 1899 and died in London on 17 March 1922.

H. C. G. Matthew

Sources E. Bellasis, *Memorials of Mr Serjeant Bellasis*, 3rd edn (1923) · *The Tablet* (1 Feb 1873), 138 · *Law Times* (1 March 1873) · *DNB* · *CGPLA Eng. & Wales* (1873) · d. cert. [Edward Bellasis, jun.]
Archives CUL, letters to Lord Acton
Likenesses D. Maclise, pencil, 1829 · J. P. Knight, oils, 1846 · D. Maclise, sepia
Wealth at death under £25,000: probate, 19 March 1873, *CGPLA Eng. & Wales*

Bellasis, Edward (1852–1922). *See under* Bellasis, Edward (1800–1873).

Bellasis, Sir Henry, first baronet (1555–1624). *See under* Bellasis family (*per. c.*1500–1653).

Bellasis, Richard (*c.*1489–1540). *See under* Bellasis family (*per. c.*1500–1653).

Bellasis, Thomas, first Viscount Fauconberg (1577–1653). *See under* Bellasis family (*per. c.*1500–1653).

Bellasis, Sir William (*c.*1524–1604). *See under* Bellasis family (*per. c.*1500–1653).

Bellasis, Sir William (*c.*1593–1641). *See under* Bellasis family (*per. c.*1500–1653).

PICTURE CREDITS

Baron, Bartholomew (1610–1696)—
© National Portrait Gallery, London

Barr, Archibald (1855–1931)—
© National Portrait Gallery, London

Barré, Isaac (1726–1802)—private
collection. Photograph: The Paul
Mellon Centre for Studies in
British Art

Barrett, Wilson (1846–1904)—
© National Portrait Gallery, London

Barrie, Sir James Matthew, baronet
(1860–1937)—© National Portrait
Gallery, London

Barrington, Daines (1727/8–1800)—
© National Portrait Gallery, London

Barrington, George (1755–1804)—by
permission of the National Library of
Australia T275

Barrington, Samuel (1729–1800)—
© National Maritime Museum,
London, Greenwich Hospital
Collection

Barrington, Shute (1734–1826)—by
kind permission of the Lord Bishop
of Durham and the Church
Commissioners of England.
Photograph: Photographic Survey,
Courtauld Institute of Art, London

Barrington, William Wildman, second
Viscount Barrington (1717–1793)—
private collection. Photograph:
Photographic Survey, Courtauld
Institute of Art, London

Barriteau, Carl Aldric Stanley (1914–
1998)—photograph by Alan Duncan;
Val Wilmer Collection

Barron, William (1805–1891)—Royal
Horticultural Society, Lindley Library

Barrow, Florence Mary (1876–1964)—
© reserved

Barrow, Isaac (1630–1677)—© National
Portrait Gallery, London

Barrow, Sir John, first baronet (1764–
1848)—© National Portrait Gallery,
London

Barrow, William (c.1609–1679)—
© National Portrait Gallery, London

Barrowby, William (bap. 1682,
d. 1758)—© National Portrait Gallery,
London

Barry, Sir Charles (1795–1860)—
© National Portrait Gallery, London

Barry, Sir Gerald Reid (1898–1968)—
Norman Parkinson Ltd., courtesy
Fiona Cowan

Barry, James, fourth earl of Barrymore
(1667–1748)—private collection.
Photograph: Photographic Survey,
Courtauld Institute of Art, London

Barry, James (1741–1806)—by courtesy
of the National Gallery of Ireland

Barry, James (c.1799–1865)—Trustees of
the Army Medical Services Museum

Barry, Sir Redmond (1813–1880)—La
Trobe Picture Collection, State
Library of Victoria

Barrymore, Lionel (1878–1954)—Getty
Images - Clarence Sinclair Bull

Bartholomaeus Anglicus (b. before
1203, d. 1272)—© The Bodleian
Library, University of Oxford

Bartholomew, Frederick Llewellyn
(1924–1992)—© National Portrait
Gallery, London

Bartlett, Sir Frederic Charles (1886–
1969)—© National Portrait Gallery,
London

Bartlett, Josiah (1729–1795)—New
Hampshire Historical Society

Bartley, Sarah (1783?–1850)—Garrick
Club / the art archive

Bartolozzi, Francesco (1728–1815)—
Saltram, The Morley Collection (The
National Trust). Photograph:
Photographic Survey, Courtauld
Institute of Art, London

Barton, Sir Derek Harold Richard
(1918–1998)—Getty Images - Hulton
Archive

Barton, Sir Edmund (1849–1920)—by
permission of the National Library of
Australia

Barton, Pamela Espeut (1917–1943)—
© Empics

Barttelot, Edmund Musgrave (1859–
1888)—© National Portrait Gallery,
London

Barwell, Richard (1741–1804)—
unknown collection / Christie's;
photograph National Portrait
Gallery, London

Basevi, George (1794–1845)—
reproduced by permission of the
Bishop of Ely and Church
Commissioners; photograph
National Portrait Gallery, London

Baskerville, John (1706–1775)—
Birmingham Museums & Art Gallery

Basnett, David, Baron Basnett (1924–
1989)—© News International
Newspapers Ltd

Bass, Michael Arthur, first Baron
Burton (1837–1909)—© National
Portrait Gallery, London

Bass, Michael Thomas (1799–1884)—
© National Portrait Gallery, London

Basset, Francis, Baron de Dunstanville
and Baron Basset (1757–1835)—in the
collection of the Corcoran Gallery of
Art, William A. Clark

Basset, Fulk (d. 1259)—The British
Library

Bassey, Okon Asuguo (1932–1998)—
© News International
Newspapers Ltd

Bastable, Charles Francis (1855–1945)—
photograph reproduced by courtesy
of The British Academy

Bastwick, John (1595?–1654)—
© National Portrait Gallery, London

Bateman, Henry Mayo (1887–1970)—
© National Portrait Gallery, London

Bateman, Hezekiah Linthicum (1812–
1875)—V&A Images, The Victoria and
Albert Museum

Bates, Henry Walter (1825–1892)—
© National Portrait Gallery, London

Bates, Herbert Ernest (1905–1974)—
© Mark Gerson; collection National
Portrait Gallery, London

Bates, Joshua (1788–1864)—ING Bank,
NV, London Branch

Bates, Sir Percy Elly, fourth baronet
(1879–1946)—© National Portrait
Gallery, London

Bateson, William (1861–1926)—
© National Portrait Gallery, London

Bathurst, Henry (bap. 1744, d. 1837)—
The Bishop of Norwich; photograph:
The Paul Mellon Centre for Studies
in British Art

Bathurst, Lilias Margaret Frances,
Countess Bathurst (1871–1965)—The
de László Foundation; photograph:
Witt Library, Courtauld Institute of
Art, London

Bathurst, Ralph (1619/20–1704)—
© National Portrait Gallery, London

Batoni, Pompeo Girolamo (1708–
1787)—Galleria degli Uffizi, Florence,
Italy / Bridgeman Art Library

Batsford, Bradley Thomas (1821–
1904)—© National Portrait Gallery,
London

Batsford, Henry George (1880–1951)—
© reserved; photograph National
Portrait Gallery, London

Battell, Ralph (1649–1713)—© National
Portrait Gallery, London

Battie, William (bap. 1703, d. 1776)—by
permission of the Royal College of
Physicians, London

Bauer, Franz Andreas (1758–1840)—
© National Portrait Gallery, London

Bawden, Edward (1903–1989)—
© National Portrait Gallery, London

Bax, Sir Arnold Edward Trevor (1883–
1953)—© Jenny Letton, administered
by Composer Prints Ltd.; collection
National Portrait Gallery, London

Baxter, James Keir (1926–1972)—
Alexander Turnbull Library, National
Library of New Zealand, Te Puna
Matauranga o Aotearoa

Baxter, John (1896–1975)—Getty
Images - Kurt Hutton

Baxter, Mary Ann (1801–1884)—
University of Dundee Archive
Services

Baxter, Richard (1615–1691)—by
permission of Dr Williams's Library

Baxter, William Alexander (1877–
1973)—reproduced with permission
of Archives and Special Collections
Department, Glasgow City Libraries,
Information and Learning

Bayfield, Robert (bap. 1629)—
© National Portrait Gallery, London

Bayley, Sir John, first baronet (1763–
1841)—© National Portrait Gallery,
London

Baylis, Lilian Mary (1874–1937)—V&A
Images, The Victoria and Albert
Museum

Bayly, Nathaniel Thomas Haynes
(1797–1839)—© National Portrait
Gallery, London

Baynes, Thomas Spencer (1823–1887)—
courtesy of St Andrews University
Library

Bazalgette, Sir Joseph William (1819–
1891)—© National Portrait Gallery,
London

Bazalgette, Louise (1845/6–1918)—
© Elizabeth Bennett, from
E. Bennett, The Thousand Mile Trial
(2000)

Bazley, Sir Thomas, first baronet (1797–
1885)—© National Portrait Gallery,
London

Beach, Michael Edward Hicks, first Earl
St Aldwyn (1837–1916)—© National
Portrait Gallery, London

Beach, Thomas Billis [Henri Le Caron]
(1841–1894)—© National Portrait
Gallery, London

Beadon, Sir Cecil (1816–1880)—The
British Library

Beale, Dorothea (1831–1906)—
© National Portrait Gallery, London

Beale, Lionel Smith (1828–1906)—by
permission of the Royal College of
Physicians, London; photograph
National Portrait Gallery, London

Beale, Mary (bap. 1633, d. 1699)—
© National Portrait Gallery, London

Beale, William (d. 1651)—by
permission of the Master and
Fellows of St John's College,
Cambridge

Beales, Edmond (1803–1881)—
Ashmolean Museum, Oxford

Beard, William (1772–1868)—
© Fitzwilliam Museum, University of
Cambridge

Beardmore, William, Baron Invernairn
(1856–1936)—courtesy of Glasgow
University Archive Services

Beardsley, Aubrey Vincent (1872–
1898)—© National Portrait Gallery,
London

Beaton, Sir Cecil Walter Hardy (1904–
1980)—© Tom Hustler / National
Portrait Gallery, London

Beaton, Norman Lugard (1934–1994)—
Rex Features

Beatrice, Princess (1857–1944)—The
Royal Collection © 2004 HM Queen
Elizabeth II

Beattie, James (1735–1803)—University
of Aberdeen

Beatty, David, first Earl Beatty (1871–
1936)—by courtesy of Felix
Rosenstiel's Widow & Son Ltd.,
London, on behalf of the Estate of
Sir John Lavery; collection National
Portrait Gallery, London

Beatty, Sir Edward Wentworth (1877–
1943)—© National Portrait Gallery,
London

Beauchamp, Richard, thirteenth earl of
Warwick (1382–1439)—Beauchamp
Chapel, St Mary's Church, Warwick /
Photograph A. F. Kersting

Beauclerk, Lady Diana (1734–1808)—
Kenwood, Iveagh Bequest / © English
Heritage Photo Library

Beauclerk, Topham (1739–1780)—
© National Portrait Gallery, London

Beaufort, Daniel Augustus (1739–
1821)—© National Portrait Gallery,
London

Beaufort, Sir Francis (1774–1857)—
© National Maritime Museum,
London, Greenwich Hospital
Collection

Beaufort, Henry (1375?–1447)—
© English Heritage. NMR

Beaufort, Margaret, countess of
Richmond and Derby (1443–1509)—
© Dean and Chapter of Westminster

Beaumont, Francis (1584/5–1616)—
National Trust Photographic Library;

photograph National Portrait Gallery, London

Beaumont, Sir George Howland, seventh baronet (1753–1827)—© The National Gallery, London

Beazley, Sir John Davidson (1885–1970)—© National Portrait Gallery, London

Beche, Sir Henry Thomas De la (1796–1855)—© National Portrait Gallery, London

Becher, Martin William [Captain Becher] (1797–1864)—© Copyright The British Museum

Beck, George Andrew (1904–1978)—© National Portrait Gallery, London

Becket, Thomas [St Thomas of Canterbury] (1120?–1170)—The British Library

Beckett, Edmund, first Baron Grimthorpe (1816–1905)—by courtesy of the British Horological Institute Limited; original on display at the Upton Hall Time Museum, Upton, Newark, Nottinghamshire; photograph © National Portrait Gallery, London

Beckett, Samuel Barclay (1906–1989)—© Henri Cartier-Bresson / Magnum Photos; collection National Portrait Gallery, London

Beckford, Peter (1739/40–1811)—Statens Museum for Kunst, Copenhagen

Beckford, William (bap. 1709, d. 1770)—© National Portrait Gallery, London

Beckford, William (1744–1799)—© National Portrait Gallery, London

Beckford, William Thomas (1760–1844)—National Trust Photographic Library / John Hammond

Beckington, Thomas (1390?–1465)—Chapter of Wells Cathedral

Becon, Thomas (1512/13–1567)—© National Portrait Gallery, London

Beddoes, Thomas (1760–1808)—© National Portrait Gallery, London

Bedingfeld, Sir Henry (1509x11–1583)—National Trust Photographic Library / John Hammond

Bedloe, William (1650–1680)—© National Portrait Gallery, London

Beecham, Sir Joseph, first baronet (1848–1916)—St Helens Local History & Archives Library

Beecham, Sir Thomas, second baronet (1879–1961)—© reserved; collection National Portrait Gallery, London

Beechey, Frederick William (1796–1856)—© National Portrait Gallery, London

Beechey, Sir William (1753–1839)—Gift of Dr. Hugo and Hortense G. Freund, Photograph © 2004 The Detroit Institute of Arts

Beeching, Richard, Baron Beeching (1913–1985)—© National Portrait Gallery, London

Beer, Sir Gavin Rylands de (1899–1972)—© National Portrait Gallery, London

Beerbohm, Sir Henry Maximilian [Max] (1872–1956)—© Elizabeth Banks; collection National Portrait Gallery, London

Beesley, Michael Edwin (1924–1999)—© News International Newspapers Ltd

Beesly, Edward Spencer (1831–1915)—© National Portrait Gallery, London

Beeton, Isabella Mary (1836–1865)—© National Portrait Gallery, London

Begg, James (1808–1883)—Scottish National Portrait Gallery

Behan, (Francis) Brendan (1923–1964)—© Estate of Daniel Farson; collection National Portrait Gallery, London

Behn, Aphra (1640?–1689)—© National Portrait Gallery, London

Behrens, Sir Jacob (1806–1889)—Bradford Art Galleries and Museums

Beit, Alfred (1853–1906)—Christie's Images Ltd. (2004)

Beit, Sir Otto John, first baronet (1865–1930)—© National Portrait Gallery, London

Beith, John Hay (1876–1952)—© National Portrait Gallery, London

Bek, Antony (I) (c.1245–1311)—Chapter of Durham Cathedral

Beke, Charles Tilstone (1800–1874)—© National Portrait Gallery, London

Belaney, Archibald Stansfeld [Grey Owl] (1888–1938)—© National Portrait Gallery, London

Belcher, James [Jem] (1781–1811)—© National Portrait Gallery, London

Belcher, John (1841–1913)—RIBA Library Photographs Collection

Belcher, Jonathan (1682–1757)—Ashmolean Museum, Oxford

Belisha, (Isaac) Leslie Hore-, Baron Hore-Belisha (1893–1957)—© National Portrait Gallery, London

Bell, Alexander Graham (1847–1922)—National Portrait Gallery, Smithsonian Institution

Bell, Andrew (1725/6–1809)—Scottish National Portrait Gallery

Bell, Andrew (1753–1832)—© National Portrait Gallery, London

Bell, Benjamin (1749–1806)—photograph by courtesy Sotheby's Picture Library, London

Bell, Sir Charles (1774–1842)—© National Portrait Gallery, London

Bell, Charles Frederic Moberly (1847–1911)—© National Portrait Gallery, London

Bell, (Arthur) Clive Heward (1881–1964)—© Estate of Roger Fry; collection National Portrait Gallery, London

Bell, Florence Eveleen Eleanore, Lady Bell (1851–1930)—courtesy of Middlesbrough Libraries & Information

Bell, George Joseph (1770–1843)—in the collection of the Faculty of Advocates; photograph courtesy the Scottish National Portrait Gallery

Bell, George Kennedy Allen (1883–1958)—© National Portrait Gallery, London

Bell, Gertrude Margaret Lowthian (1868–1926)—Getty Images – Hulton Archive

Bell, (Frank) Graham (1910–1943)—private collection

Bell, Henry (1767–1830)—Scottish National Portrait Gallery

Bell, Sir Henry Hesketh Joudou (1864–1952)—by permission of the Syndics of Cambridge University Library

Bell, Sir (Harold) Idris (1879–1967)—© National Portrait Gallery, London

Bell, Joseph (1837–1911)—reproduced with the kind permission of the Royal College of Surgeons of Edinburgh

Bell, Sir (Isaac) Lowthian, first baronet (1816–1904)—© National Portrait Gallery, London

Bell, Patrick (1799–1869)—© National Portrait Gallery, London

Bell, Quentin Claudian Stephen (1910–1996)—© Duncan Fraser; collection National Portrait Gallery, London

Bell, Richard (b. c.1410, d. in or after 1495)—© James Armstrong; by permission of the Chapter of Carlisle Cathedral

Bell, Richard (1859–1930)—© National Portrait Gallery, London

Bell, Sam Hanna (1909–1990)—© Mme Doris Bourguignon. Photograph reproduced with the kind permission of the Trustees of the National Museums & Galleries of Northern Ireland

Bell, Thomas (1792–1880)—© National Portrait Gallery, London

Bell, Sir Thomas (1865–1952)—reproduced with permission of Archives and Special Collections Department, Glasgow City Libraries, Information and Learning

Bell, Vanessa (1879–1961)—© National Portrait Gallery, London

Bellamy, George Anne (1731?–1788)—Garrick Club / the art archive

Bellamy, James (1819–1909)—The President and Fellows of St John's College, Oxford